Constitutional Law and Politics
Volume Two

Eleventh Edition

Other Books by David M. O'Brien

Storm Center:
The Supreme Court in American Politics
12th ed.

The Judicial Process: Law, Courts, and Judicial Politics
2nd
(co-author)

Justice Robert H. Jackson's Unpublished Opinion in Brown v. Board:
Conflict, Compromise, and Constitutional Interpretation

Judges on Judging
5th ed.
(editor)

Congress Shall Make No Law:
The First Amendment, Unprotected Expression,
and the U.S. Supreme Court

Animal Sacrifice and Religious Freedom:
Church of Lukumi Babalu Aye v. City of Hialeah

Privacy, Law, and Public Policy

The Public's Right to Know:
The Supreme Court and the First Amendment

What Process Is Due?:
Courts and Science-Policy Disputes

Judicial Roulette

The Politics of Technology Assessment:
Institutions, Processes and Policy Disputes
(co-editor)

Views from the Bench:
The Judiciary and Constitutional Politics
(co-editor)

Abortion and American Politics
(co-author)

The Politics of American Government
3rd ed.
(co-author)

Supreme Court Watch
(annual, 1991–2015)

To Dream of Dreams:
Religious Freedom and Constitutional Politics in Postwar Japan

The Lanahan Readings on Civil Rights and Civil Liberties
3rd ed.
(editor)

Judicial Independence in the Age of Democracy:
Critical Perspectives from Around the World
(co-editor)

Government by the People
22nd ed.
(co-author)

Courts and Judicial Policymaking
(co-author)

Other Books By Gordon Silverstein

Imbalance of Powers: Constitutional Interpretation
and the Making of American Foreign Policy

Law's Allure: How Law Shapes, Constrains, Saves and Kills Politics

Consequential Courts: Judicial Roles in Global Perspective
(co-editor)

CONSTITUTIONAL LAW AND POLITICS

VOLUME TWO

Civil Rights and Civil Liberties

ELEVENTH EDITION

DAVID M. O'BRIEN
UNIVERSITY OF VIRGINIA

GORDON SILVERSTEIN
YALE UNIVERSITY

W. W. NORTON & COMPANY
Independent Publishers Since 1923

W. W. Norton & Company has been independent since its founding in 1923, when William Warder Norton and Mary D. Herter Norton first published lectures delivered at the People's Institute, the adult education division of New York City's Cooper Union. The firm soon expanded its program beyond the Institute, publishing books by celebrated academics from America and abroad. By midcentury, the two major pillars of Norton's publishing program—trade books and college texts—were firmly established. In the 1950s, the Norton family transferred control of the company to its employees, and today—with a staff of four hundred and a comparable number of trade, college, and professional titles published each year—W. W. Norton & Company stands as the largest and oldest publishing house owned wholly by its employees.

Composition by Westchester Publishing Services
Manufacturing by LSC Communications, Crawfordsville
Book design by Martin Lubin Graphic Design
Production Manager: Elizabeth Marotta
Project Editor: Layne Broadwater
Drawn art by John McAusland

ISBN: 978-0-393-69674-5 (pbk.)

Library of Congress Cataloging-in-Publication Data

Names: O'Brien, David M., author. | Silverstein, Gordon, author.
Title: Constitutional law and politics / David M. O'Brien, Late of University of
    Virginia; Gordon Silverstein, Yale University.
Other titles: Struggles for power and governmental accountability
Description: Eleventh edition. | New York : W. W. Norton & Company, [2020] |
    Includes bibliographical references and index. | Contents: volume 1. Struggles
    for power and governmental accountability—volume 2. Civil rights and civil
    liberties.
Identifiers: LCCN 2020005558 | **ISBN 9780393696721** (v. 1 ; paperback) |
    ISBN 9780393696745 (v. 2 ; paperback)
Subjects: LCSH: Constitutional history—United States. | United States. Supreme
    Court. | Constitutional law—United States. | Political questions and judicial
    power—United States. | Civil rights—United States. | LCGFT: Casebooks (Law)
Classification: LCC KF4541 .O27 2020 | DDC 342.73/00264—dc23
LC record available at https://lccn.loc.gov/2020005558

W. W. Norton & Company, Inc., 500 Fifth Avenue, New York, N.Y. 10110
www.wwnorton.com

W. W. Norton & Company Ltd., Castle House, 75/76 Wells Street,
London W1T 3QT

1 2 3 4 5 6 7 8 9 0

For Claudine, Benjamin, Sara, and Talia
—D. M.

For David O'Brien, his students, and mine
—G. S.

CHAPTER 3 ■ *Economic Rights and American Capitalism*   232

CHAPTER 4 ■ *The Nationalization of the
Bill of Rights* 315

CHAPTER 5 ■ *Freedom of Expression and Association*   416

CHAPTER 7 ■ *The Fourth Amendment Guarantee against Unreasonable Searches and Seizures*   838

CHAPTER 10 ■ *Cruel and Unusual Punishment*   1167

Photos and Illustrations

PREFACE

Because there is no dearth of casebooks, perhaps an explanation is needed of how this one differs from others. What distinguishes this casebook is its treatment and incorporation of material on constitutional history and American politics. Few casebooks pay adequate attention to the forces of history and politics on the course of constitutional law. Yet constitutional law, history, and politics are intimately intertwined.

The Constitution and Bill of Rights, of course, are political documents. Rooted in historic struggles and based on political compromises, their provisions and guarantees continue to invite competing interpretations and political contests over, for example, the separation of powers between Congress and the president, federalism, and civil rights and liberties. Because the Constitution says nothing about *who* should interpret it or about *how* it should be interpreted, constitutional law is animated by the politics of interpretation and the interpretation of politics. Neither do we have a single accepted theory of constitutional interpretation, nor do the justices write on a clean slate. Instead, we face constitutional choices and competing judicial and political philosophies, as well as new issues as a result of social, economic, and technological changes.

The Supreme Court's decisions do not occur in a political vacuum, standing apart from history and the political struggles within the Court and the country. Virtually every major political controversy raises questions of constitutional law, as do technological changes, social movements, and economic forces. The development and direction of constitutional law also shift (more or less quickly) with the Court's changing composition. Members of the Court, just like other citizens, differ in their readings of the Constitution. Moreover, major confrontations in constitutional law and politics, such as those over the powers of the national government, school desegregation, abortion, and the right of privacy, involve continuing struggles that run from one generation to another. In the course of those struggles, constitutional law evolves with changes in the Court and the country. The Constitution and the Bill of Rights bind the Court, other political institutions, and the people in an ongoing dialogue over the exercise of and limitations on governmental power.

By providing the historical context and explaining the political contests among the justices and between the Court and the country, this casebook aims to make constitutional law more accessible for students. History and politics are also important for analysis of particular decisions and their relation to developments and changes in constitutional law and politics. They are crucial as well for critically evaluating competing interpretations and to appreciate the political consequences of alternative interpretations. And they are essential if students are to engage in the dialogue of constitutional law, confront constitutional choices, and come to terms with their and others' views of the Constitution and the Bill of Rights.

The casebook remains different in several ways. First, it comes in two very comprehensive, anthology-like volumes. Volume One, *Struggles for Power and Governmental Accountability*, deals with separation of powers, federalism, and the democratic process. Volume Two, *Civil Rights and Civil Liberties*, is devoted to the enduring struggles to limit governmental power and guarantee civil rights and liberties. As a two-volume set, it not only includes more Court decisions than other casebooks, it also permits more introductory background material. Instructors, therefore, have greater flexibility when assigning cases, and students will find useful the additional cases and guides to other cases and resources.

Second, two chapters dealing with the politics of constitutional interpretation and Supreme Court decision-making contain material not usually found in casebooks. Chapter 1 goes beyond dealing with the establishment of the power of judicial review, and political criticisms of the Court's exercise of that power, to examining rival theories of constitutional interpretation. Students are introduced to differing judicial and political philosophies and referred to cases and opinions found in subsequent chapters that illustrate these different positions on constitutional interpretation. Chapter 2 combines an introduction to jurisdictional matters, such as standing, with a discussion of how the Court operates as an institution and in relation to other political institutions, which may help promote compliance with and implementation of its rulings, or thwart and even reverse them. In short, Chapter 1 prepares students for critically evaluating competing interpretations of constitutional provisions in subsequent chapters. And Chapter 2 prepares them for understanding the political struggles that take place within the Court as well as between the Court and other political institutions over its decisions. While the volumes together are designed for a two-semester course, both of these chapters, as well as the Constitution of the United States, are included in each volume for the convenience of teachers and students who might be involved in only one of the two-semester constitutional law course sequence. In addition, both volumes include in the Appendix discussions of how and why to brief cases, and also include a glossary of legal definitions.

As already noted, each chapter and subsection contains lengthy introductory essays. These essays focus on particular provisions of the Constitution and the Bill of Rights, why they took the form they did, and what controversies surrounded them during the Founding period and later. Most begin with the debates at the Constitutional Convention of 1787 and those between the Federalists and Anti-Federalists during the ratification period, and then review subsequent cases and controversies. Besides providing a historical and political context for the cases in each chapter, the essays highlight the continuity and changes in the debates over constitutional law and politics that run from the Founding period to those rulings of the Roberts Court.

Something should also be said about the case excerpts. Most are preceded by "headnotes," short explanations of the facts and why the case was appealed to the Court. But, unlike the brief (and usually dry) headnotes typically found in casebooks, these reveal something about the personal and political struggles of those who appeal to the Court. Throughout, there is an attempt to help students understand the judicial and political process and appreciate how questions of constitutional law are embedded in everyday life. For this reason, students will also find excerpts from oral arguments before the Court and other materials bearing on the political struggles that they represent. Along with excerpts of the opinion announcing the decision of the Court, there are excerpts from separate concurring and dissenting opinions. These are included to help students appreciate the choices that the Court and they must make when interpreting the Constitution and the Bill of Rights. Related to this is a good suggestion made by a number of adopters of the first edition: the headnotes record the actual Court vote.

In addition, each volume contains four types of boxes, which include materials that further place constitutional interpretation and law in historical and political perspective. One set of boxes, *CONSTITUTIONAL HISTORY*, presents important background material, such as excerpts from John Locke on the connection between property and liberty, explanatory notes on the "Watergate crisis," and civil liberties in wartime. Another set, *THE DEVELOPMENT OF LAW*, shows changes and patterns in constitutional law and refers students to other cases on topics of special interest. The third, *INSIDE THE COURT*, illustrates the internal dynamics of the Court when engaged in the process of constitutional interpretation and deciding cases. Finally, *IN COMPARATIVE PERSPECTIVE* boxes illustrate how courts around the world have dealt with similar constitutional controversies. These boxes are indicated by □ in the contents. Also included at the end of each volume are brief biographies of the current sitting justices.

This eleventh edition updates the introductions, the cases, and the four types of boxes. Along with adding a number of new and updated boxes on *CONSTITUTIONAL HISTORY, INSIDE THE COURT, THE DEVELOPMENT OF LAW,* and *IN COMPARATIVE PERSPECTIVE,* this edition includes a number of other features. RESEARCHING LEGAL MATERIALS provides a guide for students to access and to search for legal materials and law-related sources on the Internet. THE HOW, WHY, and WHAT TO BRIEFING and CITING COURT CASES discusses the "how, why, and what" to briefing and citing court decisions and opinions. In response to requests from adopters of past editions, the chapter titled "Economic Rights and American Capitalism" is included in both volumes; it appears as Chapter 9 in Volume One and as Chapter 3 in Volume Two.

What follows, we hope, will enrich students' understanding of constitutional law, politics, and history, as well as open them to the possibilities in interpreting the Constitution and the Bill of Rights. But the Constitution is where students should begin their study, and it is assuredly where they will return again and again. For that reason, the Declaration of Independence, Constitution, and Bill of Rights appear at the outset of both volumes.

D. M. O.

G. S.

ACKNOWLEDGMENTS

I am indebted to my students and colleagues for the favorable reception given to earlier editions, but I still owe a larger debt to Claudine, my wife, for giving me the freedom to work as I do and to enjoy life's pleasures with Benjamin, Sara, and Talia. I continue to be grateful for the inspiration and support of my teacher, C. Herman Pritchett, University of California, Santa Barbara, and my long-time colleague at the University of Virginia, Henry J. Abraham. Ira Carmen, University of Illinois; Phillip Cooper, University of Vermont; Jerome Hanus, The American University; and Gerald Rosenberg, University of Chicago, read and made very helpful suggestions on the first edition for which I am grateful. Also, I thank Thomas Baker, Florida International University; Sue Davis, University of Delaware; Susan Fino, Wayne State University; Christine Harrington, New York University; and H. N. Hirsch for offering comments that helped shape the casebook early in its development.

I very much appreciate the support and suggestions made by countless undergraduate and graduate students. In particular, several former graduate students deserve special recognition: Christopher Banks, John Blakeman, Stephen Bragaw, Steve Brown, Richard Drew, Scott Gerber, Jeffrey Hockett, Robert Hume, Nathan Jones, Edward Kelly, Charles Kromkowski, William Mandel, Rick Mayes, Stacy Nyikos, Gavin Reddick, James Staab, Jon Talotta, Stephen Tauber, and James Todd. Numerous colleagues around the country offered support and very helpful suggestions for changes and corrections that have improved each edition. Among many other colleagues, I am grateful to the following: John Q. Adams, Maria Antonini, Gordon Baker, Jack Barlow, J. M. Bordelon, John Brigham, Jess Brown, Joseph Callahan, David Carrithers, Richard Claude, George F. Cole, Ronald Collins, Sheila Collins, Akiba Covitz, Michele D. Dearorff, John Domino, S. A. Dwyer-Shick, John Evans, Judy Failer, Cary Federman, Louis Fisher, Jack Fruchtman Jr., Richard A. Glenn, Hal Goldman, Leslie Goldstein, Martha Good, Susan Grogan, Robert Hardgrave Jr., Laura Hatcher, Milton Heumann, Sidney Heyman, Harry N. Hirsch, Michael Horan, Robert Howard, Elizabeth Hull, Carolyn Johnson, Susan Johnson, Robert M. Johnstone, Nancy Kassop, Robert Katzmann, Paul Kens, J. Morgan Kousser, Byron Lander, Drew Noble Lanier, Susan Lawrence, James Lennertz,

Thomas Lewis, Quan Li, Pricilla Macadeo, David Manwarring, Wendy Martinek, David T. Mason, Kevin McGuire, W. McKercher, Eddie L. Meaders, Lucas Morel, Bruce Murphy, Jill Norgren, Karen O'Connor, Jack W. Peltason, David Pogue, Marie Provine, John Robey, Alisa Rosenthal, Stephen Ross, John Scheb, Guy Scoffoni, David Skover, Caleb Smith, Daniel Smith, Rogers Smith, Neil Snortland, Richard Sobel, Donald Songer, Gene Straughan, Harold Sullivan, John Taylor, James Todd, Mary Volcansek, Jerold Waltman, Paul Weber, Teena Wilheim, and John Winkle.

In addition, this eleventh edition incurs even more debt. I am grateful to a number of reviewers, including John W. Aughenbaugh, Philip Benesch, Davis Brown, Matthew Brogdon, Douglas Casson, Jonathan Chausovsky, Whitney Hafer, Bradley Hays, Brendan Horan, Robert Hume, John Koritansky, Julie Lane, Evan McKenzie, William McLauchian, Paul Rasor, John Reynolds, Rob Robinson, Emily Neff-Sharum, Dan Smith, and Martin Zingo.

Finally, the generous support of the American Philosophical Society and the Earhart Foundation contributed to this project as well. Donald Fusting, a patient and wise editor, worked with me on the first two editions, as did Steve Dunn on the third, Sarah Caldwell on the fourth, Ann Marcy on the fifth, Aaron Javsicas on the sixth and eighth, Brian Baker and Matthew Arnold on the seventh, Jake Schindel and Sarah Wolf on the ninth edition, Samantha Held on the tenth edition, and Pete Lesser and Anna Olcott on this edition. Work on these volumes, I should also acknowledge, was indirectly but significantly helped by the U.S. Fulbright Commission. The first edition was largely completed during 1987–1988 while I was a Fulbright Lecturer in Constitutional Studies at Oxford University. The third edition was completed while I was a Fulbright Research Fellow in Japan. And the fourth edition was completed while I held the Fulbright Chair in History and Political Science at the University of Bologna. I worked on the seventh edition while I was a Visiting Professor at the Institut d'Etudes Politique, Universite Lyon-2, Lyon, France. I am thus deeply indebted to the Fulbright Commission and a number of scholars who made my stays so productive. In particular, I am grateful to Byron Shafer, Yasuo Ohkoshi, Vincent Michelot, and Tiziano Bonazzi. This edition benefited from a Fudan University Senior Fellowship in the summers of 2017 and 2018 at Fudan University School of Law in Shanghai, China, and notably from discussions with Professor Tu Yunxin of the Law School, and Professor Hu Xiaolin of the Chinese University of Political Science and Law, in Beijing, China. I am grateful as well for permission to reproduce materials here granted by the following individuals and organizations: Justices William J. Brennan Jr. and Antonin Scalia; the curator of the Supreme Court of the

United States; the Library of Congress; the Supreme Court Historical Society; the National Portrait Gallery/Smithsonian Institution; *New York Times*; the Roosevelt Library; Sygma/*New York Times Magazine*; Paula Okamoto; Wide World Photos; and Getty Images.

—D. M. O.
DECEMBER 2018

I deeply appreciate the trust and faith that David O'Brien's family and W. W. Norton have placed in me. It is an honor as well as an opportunity and a deeply satisfying challenge to carry on his calling: helping students learn to understand constitutional law and the ways in which politics and political ideas interact with law to shape the United States, its citizens, and its institutions.

I am profoundly grateful and excited to have a chance to publish with W. W. Norton—the last truly independent (and employee-owned) publisher in the United States. They are exemplars of what a great publisher can and should be. My particular thanks to Roby Harrington, Pete Lesser, and Anna Olcott at Norton for their confidence, skill, and support.

I also am grateful to my colleagues at Yale Law School and Yale University, particularly to Robert Post, Reva Siegel, and Megan Barnett, who brought me to Yale, and to Heather Gerken, Joe Crosby, and George Levesque, who have made it possible for me to maintain and balance my commitments to teaching, writing, and administration.

—G. S.
OCTOBER 2019

A Note on Authorship

The study of the U.S. Supreme Court and constitutional law sits at the crossroads of political theory, political institutions, history, literature, and sociology. And no one has done a more masterful job of illuminating these intersections than Professor David O'Brien.

I first assigned his work in a course on the Supreme Court and American constitutional law at Dartmouth College in 1992. Though we never met, I have been his student ever since.

I have used Professor O'Brien's books in various courses over many years—not only at Dartmouth but also at the University of Minnesota and the University of California at Berkeley. I learned—as did my students—from *Storm Center*, from *Judges on Judging*, and of course, from his casebooks on constitutional law and civil liberties.

I was deeply honored and quite humbled to be asked to continue Professor O'Brien's work on the W. W. Norton casebooks, which I have every confidence will continue to teach generations to carefully and critically study the work of the U.S. Supreme Court, its unique role as both a political and legal institution and the locus for the greatest debates in American law and politics.

Professor O'Brien's commitment to helping us understand the Court's attention to its institutional, political, and legal roles has always set his work apart for me. Of the many casebooks I have read and taught from over the years, his came closest to my own understanding of the Court, its role, and its impact. I also follow Professor O'Brien in his interest in comparative constitutional law, an area in which I have published work on the rule of law in Singapore, Hong Kong, and the European Union—though my primary work has been in the area of American constitutional law and the separation of powers.

I will work very hard to maintain Professor O'Brien's standards and to build on his tremendous contribution. I regret that I cannot express my debt to Professor O'Brien himself, but I will try to let my work on his casebooks speak for me.

—Gordon Silverstein
October 2019

The Declaration of Independence, United States Constitution, and Amendments

THE DECLARATION OF INDEPENDENCE

In Congress, July 4, 1776

The unanimous Declaration of the thirteen united States of America,

When in the Course of human events, it becomes necessary for one people to dissolve the political bands which have connected them with another, and to assume among the powers of the earth, the separate and equal station to which the Laws of Nature and of Nature's God entitle them, a decent respect to the opinions of mankind requires that they should declare the causes which impel them to the separation.

We hold these truths to be self-evident, that all men are created equal, that they are endowed by their Creator with certain unalienable Rights, that among these are Life, Liberty and the pursuit of Happiness.— That to secure these rights, Governments are instituted among Men, deriving their just powers from the consent of the governed.—That whenever any Form of Government becomes destructive of these ends, it is the Right of the People to alter or to abolish it, and to institute new Government, laying its foundation on such principles and organizing its powers in such form, as to them shall seem most likely to effect their Safety and Happiness. Prudence, indeed, will dictate that Governments long established should not be changed for light and transient causes; and accordingly all experience hath shewn, that mankind are more disposed to suffer, while evils are sufferable, than to right themselves by abolishing the forms to which they are accustomed. But when a long train of abuses and usurpations, pursuing invariably the same Object evinces a design to reduce them under absolute Despotism, it is their right, it is their duty, to throw off such Government, and to provide new Guards for their future security.—Such has been the patient sufferance of these Colonies; and such is now the necessity which constrains them to alter their former Systems of Government. The history of the present King of Great Britain is a history of repeated injuries and usurpations, all having in direct object the establishment of an absolute Tyranny over these States. To prove this, let Facts be submitted to a candid world.

He has refused his Assent to Laws, the most wholesome and necessary for the public good.

He has forbidden his Governors to pass Laws of immediate and pressing importance, unless suspended in their operation till his Assent should be obtained; and when so suspended, he has utterly neglected to attend to them.

He has refused to pass other Laws for the accommodation of large districts of people, unless those people would relinquish the right of Representation in the Legislature, a right inestimable to them and formidable to tyrants only.

He has called together legislative bodies at places unusual, uncomfortable, and distant from the depository of their public Records, for the sole purpose of fatiguing them into compliance with his measures.

He has dissolved Representative Houses repeatedly, for opposing with manly firmness his invasions on the rights of the people.

He has refused for a long time, after such dissolutions, to cause others to be elected; whereby the Legislative powers, incapable of Annihilation, have returned to the People at large for their exercise; the State remaining in the mean time exposed to all the dangers of invasion from without, and convulsions within.

He has endeavoured to prevent the population of these States; for that purpose obstructing the Laws for Naturalization of Foreigners; refusing to pass others to encourage their migrations hither, and raising the conditions of new Appropriations of Lands.

He has obstructed the Administration of Justice, by refusing his Assent to Laws for establishing Judiciary powers.

He has made Judges dependent on his Will alone, for the tenure of their offices, and the amount and payment of their salaries.

He has erected a multitude of New Offices, and sent hither swarms of Officers to harrass our people, and eat out their substance.

He has kept among us, in times of peace, Standing Armies without the Consent of our legislatures.

He has affected to render the Military independent of and superior to the Civil power.

He has combined with others to subject us to a jurisdiction foreign to our constitution, and unacknowledged by our laws; giving his Assent to their Acts of pretended Legislation:

For Quartering large bodies of armed troops among us:

For protecting them, by a mock Trial, from punishment for any Murders which they should commit on the Inhabitants of these States:

For cutting off our Trade with all parts of the world:

For imposing Taxes on us without our Consent:

For depriving us in many cases, of the benefits of Trial by Jury:

For transporting us beyond Seas to be tried for pretended offences:

For abolishing the free System of English Laws in a neighboring Province, establishing therein an Arbitrary government, and enlarging its Boundaries so as to render it at once an example and fit instrument for introducing the same absolute rule into these Colonies:

For taking away our Charters, abolishing our most valuable Laws, and altering fundamentally the Forms of our Governments:

For suspending our own Legislatures, and declaring themselves invested with power to legislate for us in all cases whatsoever.

He has abdicated Government here, by declaring us out of his Protection and waging War against us.

He has plundered our seas, ravaged our Coasts, burnt our towns, and destroyed the lives of our people.

He is at this time transporting large Armies of foreign Mercenaries to compleat the works of death, desolation and tyranny, already begun with circumstances of Cruelty & perfidy scarcely paralleled in the most barbarous ages, and totally unworthy the Head of a civilized nation.

He has constrained our fellow Citizens taken Captive on the high Seas to bear Arms against their Country, to become the executioners of their friends and Brethren, or to fall themselves by their Hands.

He has excited domestic insurrections amongst us, and has endeavoured to bring on the inhabitants of our frontiers, the merciless Indian Savages, whose known rule of warfare, is an undistinguished destruction of all ages, sexes and conditions.

In every stage of these Oppressions We have Petitioned for Redress in the most humble terms: Our repeated Petitions have been answered only by repeated injury. A Prince whose character is thus marked by every act which may define a Tyrant, is unfit to be the ruler of a free people.

Nor have We been wanting in attentions to our Brittish brethren. We have warned them from time to time of attempts by their legislature to extend an unwarrantable jurisdiction over us. We have reminded them of the circumstances of our emigration and settlement here. We have appealed to their native justice and magnanimity, and we have conjured them by the ties of our common kindred to disavow these usurpations, which, would inevitably interrupt our connections and correspondence. They too have been deaf to the voice of justice and of consanguinity. We must, therefore, acquiesce in the necessity, which denounces our Separation, and hold them, as we hold the rest of mankind, Enemies in War, in Peace Friends.

We, Therefore, the Representatives of the United States of America, in General Congress, Assembled, appealing to the Supreme Judge of the world for the rectitude of our intentions, do, in the Name, and by Authority of the good People of these Colonies, solemnly publish and declare, That these United Colonies are, and of Right ought to be Free and Independent States; that they are Absolved from all Allegiance to the British Crown, and that all political connection between them and the State of Great Britain, is and ought to be totally dissolved; and that as Free and Independent States, they have full Power to levy War, conclude Peace, contract Alliances, establish Commerce, and to do all other Acts and Things which Independent States may of right do. And for the support of this Declaration, with a firm reliance on the protection of divine Providence, we mutually pledge to each other our Lives, our Fortunes and our sacred Honor.

The foregoing Declaration was, by order of Congress, engrossed, and signed by the following members:

John Hancock

NEW HAMPSHIRE
Josiah Bartlett
William Whipple
Matthew Thornton

MASSACHUSETTS BAY
Samuel Adams
John Adams
Robert Treat Paine
Elbridge Gerry

RHODE ISLAND
Stephen Hopkins
William Ellery

CONNECTICUT
Roger Sherman
Samuel Huntington

William Williams
Oliver Wolcott

NEW YORK
William Floyd
Philip Livingston
Francis Lewis
Lewis Morris

NEW JERSEY
Richard Stockton
John Witherspoon
Francis Hopkinson
John Hart
Abraham Clark

PENNSYLVANIA
Robert Morris
Benjamin Rush
Benjamin Franklin
John Morton
George Clymer
James Smith
George Taylor
James Wilson
George Ross

DELAWARE
Caesar Rodney
George Read
Thomas M'Kean

MARYLAND
Samuel Chase
William Paca
Thomas Stone
Charles Carroll, of Carrollton

VIRGINIA
George Wythe
Richard Henry Lee
Thomas Jefferson
Benjamin Harrison

Thomas Nelson, Jr.
Francis Lightfoot Lee
Carter Braxton

NORTH CAROLINA
William Hooper
Joseph Hewes
John Penn

SOUTH CAROLINA
Edward Rutledge
Thomas Heyward, Jr.
Thomas Lynch, Jr.
Arthur Middleton

GEORGIA
Button Gwinnett
Lyman Hall
George Walton

Resolved, That copies of the Declaration be sent to the several assemblies, conventions, and committees, or councils of safety, and to the several commanding officers of the continental troops; that it be proclaimed in each of the United States, at the head of the army.

THE UNITED STATES CONSTITUTION AND AMENDMENTS

We the people of the United States, in Order to form a more perfect Union, establish Justice, insure domestic Tranquility, provide for the common defence, promote the general Welfare, and secure the Blessings of Liberty to ourselves and our Posterity, do ordain and establish this Constitution for the United States of America.

ARTICLE I

Section 1. All legislative Powers herein granted shall be vested in a Congress of the United States, which shall consist of a Senate and House of Representatives.

Section 2. The House of Representatives shall be composed of Members chosen every second Year by the People of the several States, and the Electors in each State shall have the Qualifications requisite for Electors of the most numerous Branch of the State Legislature.

No Person shall be a Representative who shall not have attained to the Age of twenty five Years, and been seven Years a Citizen of the United States, and who shall not, when elected, be an Inhabitant of that State in which he shall be chosen.

[Representatives and [direct Taxes] shall be apportioned among the several States [which may be included within this Union,] according to their respective Numbers, which shall be determined by adding to the whole Number of free Persons, including those bound to Service for a Term of Years, and excluding Indians not taxed, three fifths of all other Persons. *(This clause was changed by section 2 of the Fourteenth Amendment.)*] The actual Enumeration shall be made within three Years after the first Meeting of the Congress of the United States, and within every subsequent Term of ten Years, in such Manner as they shall by Law direct. The Number of Representatives shall not exceed one for every thirty Thousand, but each State shall have at Least one Representative; and until such enumeration shall be made, the State of New Hampshire shall be entitled to chuse three, Massachusetts eight, Rhode-Island and Providence Plantations one, Connecticut five, New-York six, New Jersey four, Pennsylvania eight, Delaware one, Maryland six, Virginia ten, North Carolina five, South Carolina five, and Georgia three.

When vacancies happen in the Representation from any State, the Executive Authority thereof shall issue Writs of Election to fill such Vacancies.

The House of Representatives shall chuse their Speaker and other Officers; and shall have the sole Power of Impeachment.

Section 3. The Senate of the United States shall be composed of two Senators from each State, [chosen by the Legislature thereof, *(This provision was changed by section 1 of the Seventeenth Amendment.)*] for six Years; and each Senator shall have one Vote.

Immediately after they shall be assembled in Consequence of the first Election, they shall be divided as equally as may be into three Classes. The Seats of the Senators of the first Class shall be vacated at the Expiration of the second Year, of the second Class at the Expiration of the fourth Year, and of the third Class at the Expiration of the sixth Year, so that one third may be chosen every second Year; [and if Vacancies happen by Resignation, or otherwise, during the Recess of the Legislature of any State, the Executive thereof may make temporary Appointments until the next Meeting of the Legislature, which shall then fill such Vacancies. *(This clause was changed by section 2 of the Seventeenth Amendment.)*]

No Person shall be a Senator who shall not have attained to the Age of thirty Years, and been nine Years a Citizen of the United States, and who shall not, when elected, be an Inhabitant of that State for which he shall be chosen.

The Vice President of the United States shall be President of the Senate, but shall have no Vote, unless they be equally divided.

The Senate shall chuse their other Officers, and also a President pro tempore, in the Absence of the Vice President, or when he shall exercise the Office of President of the United States.

The Senate shall have the sole Power to try all Impeachments. When sitting for that Purpose, they shall be on Oath or Affirmation. When the President of the United States is tried, the Chief Justice shall preside: And no Person shall be convicted without the Concurrence of two thirds of the Members present.

Judgment in Cases of Impeachment shall not extend further than to removal from Office, and disqualification to hold and enjoy any Office of honor, Trust or Profit under the United States: but the Party convicted shall nevertheless be liable and subject to Indictment, Trial, Judgment and Punishment, according to Law.

Section 4. The Times, Places and Manner of holding Elections for Senators and Representatives, shall be prescribed in each State by the Legislature thereof; but the Congress may at any time by Law make or alter such Regulations, except as to the Places of chusing Senators.

The Congress shall assemble at least once in every Year, and such Meeting shall be [on the first Monday in December, *(This provision was changed by section 2 of the Twentieth Amendment.)*] unless they shall by Law appoint a different Day.

Section 5. Each House shall be the Judge of the Elections, Returns and Qualifications of its own Members, and a Majority of each shall constitute a Quorum to do Business; but a smaller Number may adjourn from day to day, and may be authorized to compel the Attendance of absent Members, in such Manner, and under such Penalties as each House may provide.

Each House may determine the Rules of its Proceedings, punish its Members for disorderly Behaviour, and, with the Concurrence of two thirds, expel a Member.

Each House shall keep a Journal of its Proceedings, and from time to time publish the same, excepting such Parts as may in their Judgment require Secrecy; and the Yeas and Nays of the Members of either House on any question shall, at the Desire of one fifth of those Present, be entered on the Journal.

Neither House, during the Session of Congress, shall, without the Consent of the other, adjourn for more than three days, nor to any other Place than that in which the two Houses shall be sitting.

SECTION 6. The Senators and Representatives shall receive a Compensation for their Services, to be ascertained by Law, and paid out of the Treasury of the United States. They shall in all Cases, except Treason, Felony and Breach of the Peace, be privileged from Arrest during their Attendance at the Session of their respective Houses, and in going to and returning from the same; and for any Speech or Debate in either House, they shall not be questioned in any other Place.

No Senator or Representative shall, during the Time for which he was elected, be appointed to any civil Office under the Authority of the United States, which shall have been created, or the Emoluments whereof shall have been encreased during such time; and no Person holding any Office under the United States, shall be a Member of either House during his Continuance in Office.

SECTION 7. All Bills for raising Revenue shall originate in the House of Representatives; but the Senate may propose or concur with Amendments as on other Bills.

Every Bill which shall have passed the House of Representatives and the Senate, shall, before it become a Law, be presented to the President of the United States; If he approve he shall sign it, but if not he shall return it, with his Objections to that House in which it shall have originated, who shall enter the Objections at large on their Journal, and proceed to reconsider it. If after such Reconsideration two thirds of that House shall agree to pass the Bill, it shall be sent, together with the Objections, to the other House, by which it shall likewise be reconsidered, and if approved by two thirds of that House, it shall become a Law. But in all such Cases the Votes of both Houses shall be determined by yeas and Nays, and the Names of the Persons voting for and against the Bill shall be entered on the Journal of each House respectively. If any bill shall not be returned by the President within ten Days (Sundays excepted) after it shall have been presented to him, the Same shall be a Law, in like Manner as if he had signed it, unless the Congress by their Adjournment prevent its Return, in which Case it shall not be a Law.

Every Order, Resolution, or Vote to which the Concurrence of the Senate and House of Representatives may be necessary (except on a question of Adjournment) shall be presented to the President of the United States; and before the Same shall take Effect, shall be approved by him, or being disapproved by him, shall be repassed by two thirds of the Senate and House of Representatives, according to the Rules and Limitations prescribed in the Case of a Bill.

SECTION 8. The Congress shall have Power To lay and collect Taxes, Duties, Imposts and Excises, to pay the Debts and provide for the common Defence and general Welfare of the United States; but all Duties, Imposts and Excises shall be uniform throughout the United States;

To borrow Money on the credit of the United States;

To regulate Commerce with Foreign Nations, and among the several States, and with the Indian tribes;

To establish an uniform Rule of Naturalization, and uniform Laws on the subject of Bankruptcies throughout the United States;

To coin Money, regulate the Value thereof, and of foreign Coin, and fix the Standard of Weights and Measures;

To provide for the Punishment of counterfeiting the Securities and current Coin of the United States;

To establish Post Offices and post Roads;

To promote the Progress of Science and useful Arts, by securing for limited Times to Authors and Inventors the exclusive Right to their respective Writings and Discoveries;

To constitute Tribunals inferior to the supreme Court;

To define and punish Piracies and Felonies committed on the high Seas, and Offences against the Law of Nations;

To declare War, grant Letters of Marque and Reprisal, and make Rules concerning Captures on Land and Water;

To raise and support Armies, but no Appropriation of Money to that Use shall be for a longer Term than two Years;

To provide and maintain a Navy;

To make Rules for the Government and Regulation of the land and naval Forces;

To provide for calling forth the Militia to execute the Laws of the Union, suppress Insurrections and repel Invasions;

To provide for organizing, arming, and disciplining, the Militia, and for governing such Part of them as may be employed in the Service of the United States, reserving to the States respectively, the Appointment of the Officers, and the Authority of training the Militia according to the discipline prescribed by Congress;

To exercise exclusive Legislation in all Cases whatsoever, over such District (not exceeding ten Miles square) as may, by Cession of particular States, and the Acceptance of Congress, become the Seat of the Government of the United States, and to exercise like Authority over all Places purchased by the Consent of the Legislature of the State in which the Same shall be, for the Erection of Forts, Magazines, Arsenals, dock-Yards, and other needful Buildings;—And

To make all Laws which shall be necessary and proper for carrying into Execution the foregoing Powers, and all other Powers vested by this Constitution in the Government of the United States, or in any Department or Officer thereof.

SECTION 9. The Migration or Importation of such Persons as any of the States now existing shall think proper to admit, shall not be prohibited by the Congress prior to the Year one thousand eight hundred and eight, but a Tax or duty may be imposed on such Importation, not exceeding ten dollars for each Person.

The Privilege of the Writ of Habeas Corpus shall not be suspended, unless when in Cases of Rebellion or Invasion the public Safety may require it.

No Bill of Attainder or ex post facto Law shall be passed.

No Capitation, or other direct, Tax shall be laid, unless in Proportion to the Census or Enumeration herein before directed to be taken.

No Tax or Duty shall be laid on Articles exported from any State.

No Preference shall be given by any Regulation of Commerce or Revenue to the Ports of one State over those of another: nor shall Vessels bound to, or from, one State, be obliged to enter, clear, or pay Duties in another.

No Money shall be drawn from the Treasury, but in Consequence of Appropriations made by Law; and a regular Statement and Account of the Receipts and Expenditures of all public Money shall be published from time to time.

No Title of Nobility shall be granted by the United States: And no Person holding any Office of Profit or Trust under them, shall, without the Consent of the Congress, accept of any present, Emolument, Office, or Title, of any kind whatever, from any King, Prince, or foreign State.

SECTION 10. No State shall enter into any Treaty, Alliance, or Confederation; grant Letters of Marque and Reprisal; coin Money; emit Bills of Credit; make any Thing but gold and silver Coin a Tender in Payment of Debts; pass any Bill of Attainder, ex post facto Law, or Law impairing the Obligation of Contracts, or grant any Title of Nobility.

No State shall, without the Consent of the Congress, lay any Imposts or Duties on Imports or Exports, except what may be absolutely necessary for executing it's inspection Laws: and the net Produce of all Duties and Imposts, laid by any State on Imports or Exports, shall be for the Use of the Treasury of the United States; and all such Laws shall be subject to the Revision and Controul of the Congress.

No State shall, without the Consent of Congress, lay any Duty of Tonnage, keep Troops, or Ships of War in time of Peace, enter into any Agreement or Compact with another State, or with a foreign Power, or engage in War, unless actually invaded, or in such imminent Danger as will not admit of delay.

ARTICLE II

SECTION 1. The executive Power shall be vested in a President of the United States of America. He shall hold his Office during the Term of four Years, and, together with the Vice President, chosen for the same Term, be elected, as follows

Each State shall appoint, in such Manner as the Legislature thereof may direct, a Number of Electors, equal to the whole Number of Senators and Representatives to which the State may be entitled in the Congress: but no Senator or Representative, or Person holding an Office of Trust or Profit under the United States, shall be appointed an Elector.

[The Electors shall meet in their respective States, and vote by Ballot for two Persons, of whom one at least shall not be an inhabitant of the same State with themselves. And they shall make a List of all the Persons voted for, and of the Number of Votes for each; which List they shall sign and certify, and transmit sealed to the Seat of the Government of the United States, directed to the President of the Senate. The President of the Senate shall, in the Presence of the Senate and House of Representatives, open all the Certificates, and the Votes shall then be counted. The Person having the greatest Number of Votes shall be the President, if such Number be a Majority of the whole Number of Electors appointed; and if there be more than one who have such Majority, and have an equal Number of Votes, then the House of Representatives shall immediately chuse by Ballot one of them for President; and if no Person have a Majority, then from the five highest on the List the said House shall in like Manner chuse the President. But in chusing the President, the Votes shall be taken by States, the Representation from each State having one Vote; A quorum for this purpose shall consist of a Member or Members from two thirds of the States, and a Majority of all the States shall be necessary to a Choice. In every Case, after the Choice of the President, the Person having the greatest Number of Votes of the Electors shall be the Vice President. But if there should remain two or more who have equal Votes, the Senate shall chuse from them by Ballot the Vice President. *(This clause was superseded by the Twelfth Amendment.)*]

The Congress may determine the Time of chusing the Electors, and the Day on which they shall give their Votes; which Day shall be the same throughout the United States.

No Person except a natural born Citizen, or a Citizen of the United States, at the time of the Adoption of this Constitution, shall be eligible to the Office of President; neither shall any Person be eligible to that Office who shall not have attained to the Age of thirty five Years, and been fourteen Years a Resident within the United States.

[In Case of the Removal of the President from Office, or of his Death, Resignation, or Inability to discharge the Powers and Duties of the said Office, the Same shall devolve on the Vice President, and the Congress may by Law provide for the Case of Removal, Death, Resignation or Inability, both of the President and Vice President, declaring what Officer shall then act as President, and such Officer shall act accordingly, until the Disability be removed, or a President shall be elected. *(This clause was modified by the Twenty-Fifth Amendment.)*]

The President shall, at stated Times, receive for his Services, a Compensation, which shall neither be increased nor diminished during the Period for which he shall have been elected, and he shall not receive within that Period any other Emolument from the United States, or any of them.

Before he enter on the Execution of his Office, he shall take the following Oath or Affirmation:—"I do solemnly swear (or affirm) that I will faithfully execute the Office of President of the United States, and will to the best of my Ability, preserve, protect and defend the Constitution of the United States."

SECTION 2. The President shall be Commander in Chief of the Army and Navy of the United States, and of the Militia of the several States, when called into the actual Service of the United States; he may require the Opinion, in writing, of the principal Officer in each of the executive Departments, upon any Subject relating to the Duties of their respective Offices, and he shall have Power to grant Reprieves and Pardons for Offences against the United States, except in Cases of Impeachment.

He shall have Power, by and with the Advice and Consent of the Senate, to make Treaties, provided two thirds of the Senators present concur; and he shall nominate, and by and with the Advice and Consent of the Senate, shall appoint Ambassadors, other public Ministers and Consuls, Judges of the supreme Court, and all other Officers of the United States, whose Appointments are not herein otherwise provided for, and which shall be established by Law: but the Congress may by Law vest the Appointment of such inferior Officers, as they think proper, in the President alone, in the Courts of Law, or in the Heads of Departments.

The President shall have Power to fill up all Vacancies that may happen during the Recess of the Senate, by granting Commissions which shall expire at the End of their next Session.

Section 3. He shall from time to time give to the Congress Information of the State of the Union, and recommend to their Consideration such Measures as he shall judge necessary and expedient; he may, on extraordinary Occasions, convene both Houses, or either of them, and in Case of Disagreement between them, with Respect to the Time of Adjournment, he may adjourn them to such Time as he shall think proper; he shall receive Ambassadors and other public Ministers; he shall take Care that the Laws be faithfully executed, and shall Commission all the Officers of the United States.

Section 4. The President, Vice President and all civil Officers of the United States, shall be removed from Office on Impeachment for, and Conviction of, Treason, Bribery, or other high Crimes and Misdemeanors.

ARTICLE III

Section 1. The judicial Power of the United States, shall be vested in one supreme Court, and in such inferior Courts as the Congress may from time to time ordain and establish. The Judges, both of the supreme and inferior Courts, shall hold their Offices during good Behaviour, and shall, at stated Times receive for their Services, a Compensation, which shall not be diminished during their Continuance in Office.

Section 2. The judicial Power shall extend to all Cases, in Law and Equity, arising under this Constitution, the Laws of the United States, and Treaties made, or which shall be made, under their Authority;—to all Cases affecting Ambassadors, other public Ministers and Consuls;—to all Cases of admiralty and maritime Jurisdiction;—to Controversies to which the United States shall be a Party;—to Controversies between two or more States;—between a State and Citizens of another State;—between Citizens of different States,—between Citizens of the same State claiming Lands under Grants of different States, and between a State, or the Citizens thereof, and foreign States, Citizens or Subjects.

In all Cases affecting Ambassadors, other public Ministers and Consuls, and those in which a State shall be Party, the supreme Court shall have original Jurisdiction. In all the other Cases before mentioned, the supreme Court shall have appellate Jurisdiction, both as to Law and Fact, with such Exceptions, and under such Regulations as the Congress shall make.

The Trial of all Crimes, except in Cases of Impeachment, shall be by Jury; and such Trial shall be held in the State where the said Crimes shall have been committed; but when not committed within any State, the Trial shall be at such Place or Places as the Congress may by Law have directed.

SECTION 3. Treason against the United States, shall consist only in levying War against them, or in adhering to their Enemies, giving them Aid and Comfort. No Person shall be convicted of Treason unless on the Testimony of two Witnesses to the same overt Act, or on Confession in open Court.

The Congress shall have Power to declare the Punishment of Treason, but no Attainder of Treason shall work Corruption of Blood, or Forfeiture except during the Life of the Person attainted.

[handwritten: MARBURY V MADISON   HOLMES V WATSON   JUDICIAL REVIEW —1780 UNCONSTITUTIONAL —1803   15TH RIGHT TO VOTE .]

ARTICLE IV

[handwritten: 13TH AND — ABOLITION SLAVERY]

SECTION 1. Full Faith and Credit shall be given in each State to the public Acts, Records, and judicial Proceedings of every other State; And the Congress may by general Laws prescribe the Manner in which such Acts, Records and Proceedings shall be proved, and the Effect thereof.

SECTION 2. The Citizens of each State shall be entitled to all Privileges and Immunities of Citizens in the several States.

A Person charged in any State with Treason, Felony, or other Crime, who shall flee from Justice, and be found in another State, shall on Demand of the executive Authority of the State from which he fled, be delivered up, to be removed to the State having Jurisdiction of the Crime.

[No Person held to Service or Labour in one State, under the Laws thereof, escaping into another, shall, in Consequence of any Law or Regulation therein, be discharged from such Service or Labour, but shall be delivered up on Claim of the Party to whom such Service or Labour may be due. *(This clause was superseded by the Thirteenth Amendment.)*]

SECTION 3. New States may be admitted by the Congress into this Union; but no new State shall be formed or erected within the Jurisdiction of any other State; nor any State be formed by the Junction of two or more States, or Parts of States, without the Consent of the Legislatures of the States concerned as well as of the Congress.

The Congress shall have Power to dispose of and make all needful Rules and Regulations respecting the Territory or other Property belonging to the United States; and nothing in this Constitution shall be so construed as to Prejudice any Claims of the United States, or of any particular State.

Section 4. The United States shall guarantee to every State in this Union a Republican Form of Government, and shall protect each of them against Invasion; and on Application of the Legislature, or of the Executive (when the Legislature cannot be convened) against domestic Violence.

ARTICLE V

The Congress, whenever two thirds of both Houses shall deem it necessary, shall propose Amendments to this Constitution, or, on the Application of the Legislatures of two thirds of the several States, shall call a Convention for proposing Amendments, which, in either Case, shall be valid to all Intents and Purposes, as Part of this Constitution, when ratified by the legislatures of three fourths of the several States, or by Conventions in three fourths thereof, as the one or the other Mode of Ratification may be proposed by the Congress; Provided that no Amendment which may be made prior to the Year One thousand eight hundred and eight shall in any Manner affect the first and fourth Clauses in the Ninth Section of the first Article; and that no State, without its Consent, shall be deprived of its equal Suffrage in the Senate.

ARTICLE VI

All Debts contracted and Engagements entered into, before the Adoption of this Constitution, shall be as valid against the United States under this Constitution, as under the Confederation.

This Constitution, and the Laws of the United States which shall be made in Pursuance thereof; and all Treaties made, or which shall be made, under the Authority of the United States, shall be the supreme Law of the Land; and the Judges in every State shall be bound thereby, any Thing in the Constitution or Laws of any State to the Contrary notwithstanding.

The Senators and Representatives before mentioned, and the Members of the several State Legislatures, and all executive and judicial Officers, both of the United States and of the several States, shall be bound by Oath or Affirmation, to support this Constitution; but no religious Test shall ever be required as a Qualification to any Office or public Trust under the United States.

ARTICLE VII

The Ratification of the Conventions of nine States, shall be sufficient for the Establishment of this Constitution between the States so ratifying the Same.

DONE in Convention by the Unanimous Consent of the States present the Seventeenth Day of September in the Year of our Lord one thousand seven hundred and Eighty seven and of the Independence of the United States of America the Twelfth.

IN WITNESS whereof We have hereunto subscribed our Names.

AMENDMENT I

[The first ten amendments (the Bill of Rights) were ratified December 15, 1791.]

Congress shall make no law respecting an establishment of religion, or prohibiting the free exercise thereof; or abridging the freedom of speech, or of the press, or the right of the people peaceably to assemble, and to petition the Government for a redress of grievances.

AMENDMENT II

A well regulated Militia, being necessary to the security of a free State, the right of the people to keep and bear Arms, shall not be infringed.

AMENDMENT III

No Soldier shall, in time of peace be quartered in any house, without the consent of the Owner, nor in time of war, but in a manner to be prescribed by law.

AMENDMENT IV

The right of the people to be secure in their persons, houses, papers, and effects, against unreasonable searches and seizures, shall not be violated, and no Warrants shall issue, but upon probable cause, supported by Oath or affirmation, and particularly describing the place to be searched, and the persons or things to be seized.

AMENDMENT V

No person shall be held to answer for a capital, or otherwise infamous crime, unless on a presentment or indictment of a Grand Jury, except in cases arising in the land or naval forces, or in the Militia, when in actual service in time of War or public danger; nor shall any person be subject for the same offence to be twice put in jeopardy of life or limb, nor shall be compelled in any criminal case to be a witness against himself, nor be deprived of life, liberty, or property, without due process of law; nor shall private property be taken for public use, without just compensation.

AMENDMENT VI

In all criminal prosecutions, the accused shall enjoy the right to a speedy and public trial, by an impartial jury of the State and district wherein the crime shall have been committed; which district shall have been previously ascertained by law, and to be informed of the nature and cause of the accusation; to be confronted with the witnesses against him; to have compulsory process for obtaining Witnesses in his favor, and to have the assistance of counsel for his defence.

AMENDMENT VII

In Suits at common law, where the value in controversy shall exceed twenty dollars, the right of trial by jury shall be preserved, and no fact tried by a jury, shall be otherwise re-examined in any Court of the United States, than according to the rules of the common law.

AMENDMENT VIII

Excessive bail shall not be required, nor excessive fines imposed, nor cruel and unusual punishments inflicted.

AMENDMENT IX

The enumeration in the Constitution, of certain rights, shall not be construed to deny or disparage others retained by the people.

AMENDMENT X

The powers not delegated to the United States by the Constitution, nor prohibited by it to the States, are reserved to the States respectively, or to the people.

AMENDMENT XI

[Ratified February 7, 1795.]

The Judicial power of the United States shall not be construed to extend to any suit in law or equity, commenced or prosecuted against one of the United States by Citizens of another State, or by Citizens or Subjects of any Foreign State.

AMENDMENT XII

[Ratified June 15, 1804.]

The Electors shall meet in their respective states, and vote by ballot for President and Vice-President, one of whom, at least, shall not be an inhabitant of the same state with themselves; they shall name in their ballots the person voted for as President, and in distinct ballots the person voted for as Vice-President, and they shall make distinct lists of all persons voted for as President, and of all persons voted for as Vice-President, and of the number of votes for each, which lists they shall sign and certify, and transmit sealed to the seat of the government of the United States, directed to the President of the Senate;—The President of the Senate shall, in the presence of the Senate and House of Representatives, open all the certificates and the votes shall then be counted;—The person having the greatest number of votes for President, shall be the President, if such number be a majority of the whole number of Electors appointed; and if no person have such majority, then from the persons having the highest numbers not exceeding three on the list of those voted for as President, the House of Representatives shall choose immediately, by ballot, the President. But in choosing the President, the votes shall be taken by states, the representation from each state having one vote; a quorum for this purpose shall consist of a member or members from two-thirds of the states, and a majority of all the states shall be necessary to a choice. [And if the House of Representatives shall not choose a President whenever the right of choice shall devolve upon them, before the fourth day of March next following, then the Vice-President shall act as President, as in the case of the death or other constitutional disability of the President—*(This clause was superseded by section 3 of the Twentieth Amendment.)*] The person having the greatest number of votes as Vice-President, shall be the Vice-President, if such number be a majority of the whole number of Electors appointed, and if no person have a majority, then from the two highest numbers on the list, the Senate shall choose the Vice-President; a quorum for the purpose shall consist of two-thirds of the whole number of Senators, and a majority of the whole number shall be necessary to a choice. But no person constitutionally ineligible to the office of President shall be eligible to that of Vice-President of the United States.

AMENDMENT XIII

[Ratified December 6, 1865.]

SECTION 1. Neither slavery nor involuntary servitude, except as a punishment for crime whereof the party shall have been duly convicted, shall exist within the United States, or any place subject to their jurisdiction.

SECTION 2. Congress shall have power to enforce this article by appropriate legislation.

AMENDMENT XIV

[Ratified July 9, 1868.]

SECTION 1. All persons born or naturalized in the United States, and subject to the jurisdiction thereof, are citizens of the United States and of the State wherein they reside. No State shall make or enforce any law which shall abridge the privileges or immunities of citizens of the United States; nor shall any State deprive any person of life, liberty, or property, without due process of law; nor deny to any person within its jurisdiction the equal protection of the laws.

SECTION 2. Representatives shall be apportioned among the several States according to their respective numbers, counting the whole number of persons in each State, excluding Indians not taxed. But when the right to vote at any election for the choice of electors for President and Vice President of the United States, Representatives in Congress, the Executive and Judicial officers of a State, or the members of the Legislature thereof, is denied to any of the male inhabitants of such State, being twenty-one years of age, and citizens of the United States, or in any way abridged, except for participation in rebellion, or other crime, the basis of representation therein shall be reduced in the proportion which the number of such male citizens shall bear to the whole number of male citizens twenty-one years of age in such State.

SECTION 3. No person shall be a Senator or Representative in Congress, or elector of President and Vice President, or hold any office, civil or military, under the United States, or under any State, who, having previously taken an oath, as a member of Congress, or as an officer of the United States, or as a member of any State legislature, or as an executive or judicial officer of any State, to support the Constitution of the United States, shall have engaged in insurrection or rebellion against the same, or given aid or comfort to the enemies thereof. But Congress may by a vote of two-thirds of each House, remove such disability.

SECTION 4. The validity of the public debt of the United States, authorized by law, including debts incurred for payment of pensions and bounties for services in suppressing insurrection or rebellion, shall not be questioned. But neither the United States nor any State shall assume or pay any debt or obligation incurred in aid of insurrection or rebellion against the United States, or any claim for the loss of emancipation of any slave; but all such debts, obligations and claims shall be held illegal and void.

SECTION 5. The Congress shall have power to enforce, by appropriate legislation, the provisions of this article.

AMENDMENT XV

[Ratified February 3, 1870.]

SECTION 1. The right of citizens of the United States to vote shall not be denied or abridged by the United States or by any State on account of race, color, or previous condition of servitude.

SECTION 2. The Congress shall have power to enforce this article by appropriate legislation.

AMENDMENT XVI

[Ratified February 3, 1913.]

The Congress shall have power to lay and collect taxes on incomes, from whatever source derived, without apportionment among the several States, and without regard to any census or enumeration.

AMENDMENT XVII

[Ratified April 8, 1913.]

The Senate of the United States shall be composed of two Senators from each State, elected by the people thereof, for six years; and each Senator shall have one vote. The electors in each State shall have the qualifications requisite for electors of the most numerous branch of the State legislatures.

When vacancies happen in the representation of any State in the Senate, the executive authority of such State shall issue writs of election to fill such vacancies: *Provided*, That the legislature of any State may empower the executive thereof to make temporary appointments until the people fill the vacancies by election as the legislature may direct.

This amendment shall not be so construed as to affect the election or term of any Senator chosen before it becomes valid as part of the Constitution.

AMENDMENT XVIII

[Ratified January 16, 1919.]

SECTION 1. After one year from the ratification of this article the manufacture, sale, or transportation of intoxicating liquors within, the importation thereof into, or the exportation thereof from the United States and all territory subject to the jurisdiction thereof for beverage purposes is hereby prohibited.

SECTION 2. The Congress and the several States shall have concurrent power to enforce this article by appropriate legislation.

SECTION 3. This article shall be inoperative unless it shall have been ratified as an amendment to the Constitution by the legislatures of the several States, as provided in the Constitution, within seven years from the date of the submission hereof to the States by the Congress.

AMENDMENT XIX

[Ratified August 18, 1920.]

The right of citizens of the United States to vote shall not be denied or abridged by the United States or by any State on account of sex.

Congress shall have power to enforce this article by appropriate legislation.

AMENDMENT XX

[Ratified January 23, 1933.]

SECTION 1. The terms of the President and Vice President shall end at noon on the 20th day of January, and the terms of Senators and Representatives at noon on the 3d day of January, of the years in which such terms would have ended if this article had not been ratified; and the terms of their successors shall then begin.

SECTION 2. The Congress shall assemble at least once in every year, and such meeting shall begin at noon on the 3d day of January, unless they shall by law appoint a different day.

SECTION 3. If, at the time fixed for the beginning of the term of the President, the President elect shall have died, the Vice President elect shall become President. If a President shall not have been chosen before the time fixed for the beginning of his term, or if the President elect shall have failed to qualify, then the Vice President elect shall act as President until a President shall have qualified; and the Congress may by law provide for the case wherein neither a President elect nor a Vice President elect shall have qualified, declaring who shall then act as President, or the manner in which one who is to act shall be selected, and such person shall act accordingly until a President or Vice President shall have qualified.

SECTION 4. The Congress may by law provide for the case of the death of any of the persons from whom the House of Representatives may choose a President whenever the right of choice shall have devolved upon them, and for the case of the death of any of the persons from whom the Senate may choose a Vice President whenever the right of choice shall have devolved upon them.

SECTION 5. Sections 1 and 2 shall take effect on the 15th day of October following the ratification of this article.

Section 6. This article shall be inoperative unless it shall have been ratified as an amendment to the Constitution by the legislatures of three-fourths of the several States within seven years from the date of its submission.

AMENDMENT XXI

[Ratified December 5, 1933.]

Section 1. The eighteenth article of amendment to the Constitution of the United States is hereby repealed.

Section 2. The transportation or importation into any State, Territory, or possession of the United States for delivery or use therein of intoxicating liquors, in violation of the laws thereof, is hereby prohibited.

Section 3. This article shall be inoperative unless it shall have been ratified as an amendment to the Constitution by conventions in the several States, as provided in the Constitution, within seven years from the date of the submission hereof to the States by the Congress.

AMENDMENT XXII

[Ratified February 27, 1951.]

Section 1. No person shall be elected to the office of the President more than twice, and no person who has held the office of President, or acted as President, for more than two years of a term to which some other person was elected President shall be elected to the office of the President more than once. But this Article shall not apply to any person holding the office of President when this Article was proposed by the Congress, and shall not prevent any person who may be holding the office of President, or acting as President, during the term within which this Article becomes operative from holding the office of President or acting as President during the remainder of such term.

Section 2. This article shall be inoperative unless it shall have been ratified as an amendment to the Constitution by the legislatures of three-fourths of the several States within seven years from the date of its submission to the States by the Congress.

AMENDMENT XXIII

[Ratified March 29, 1961.]

SECTION 1. The District constituting the seat of Government of the United States shall appoint in such manner as the Congress may direct:

A number of electors of President and Vice President equal to the whole number of Senators and Representatives in Congress to which the District would be entitled if it were a State, but in no event more than the least populous State; they shall be in addition to those appointed by the States, but they shall be considered, for the purposes of the election of President and Vice President, to be electors appointed by a State; and they shall meet in the District and perform such duties as provided by the twelfth article of amendment.

SECTION 2. The Congress shall have power to enforce this article by appropriate legislation.

AMENDMENT XXIV

[Ratified January 23, 1964.]

SECTION 1. The right of citizens of the United States to vote in any primary or other election for President or Vice President, for electors for President or Vice President, or for Senator or Representatives in Congress, shall not be denied or abridged by the United States or any State by reason of failure to pay any poll tax or other tax.

SECTION 2. The Congress shall have power to enforce this article by appropriate legislation.

AMENDMENT XXV

[Ratified February 10, 1967.]

SECTION 1. In case of the removal of the President from office or of his death or resignation, the Vice President shall become President.

SECTION 2. Whenever there is a vacancy in the office of the Vice President, the President shall nominate a Vice President who shall take office upon confirmation by a majority vote of both Houses of Congress.

SECTION 3. Whenever the President transmits to the President pro tempore of the Senate and the Speaker of the House of Representatives his written declaration that he is unable to discharge the powers and duties of his office, and until he transmits to them a written declaration to the contrary, such powers and duties shall be discharged by the Vice President as Acting President.

SECTION 4. Whenever the Vice President and a majority of either the principal officers of the executive departments or of such other body as Congress may by law provide, transmit to the President pro tempore of the Senate and the Speaker of the House of Representatives their written declaration that the President is unable to discharge the powers and duties of his office, the Vice President shall immediately assume the powers and duties of the office as Acting President.

Thereafter, when the President transmits to the President pro tempore of the Senate and the Speaker of the House of Representatives his written declaration that no inability exists, he shall resume the powers and duties of his office unless the Vice President and a majority of either the principal officers of the executive department or of such other body as Congress may by law provide, transmit within four days to the President pro tempore of the Senate and the Speaker of the House of Representatives their written declaration that the President is unable to discharge the powers and duties of his office. Thereupon Congress shall decide the issue, assembling within forty-eight hours for that purpose if not in session. If the Congress, within twenty-one days after receipt of the latter written declaration, or, if Congress is not in session, within twenty-one days after Congress is required to assemble, determines by two-thirds vote of both Houses that the President is unable to discharge the powers and duties of his office, the Vice President shall continue to discharge the same as Acting President; otherwise, the President shall resume the powers and duties of his office.

AMENDMENT XXVI

[Ratified July 1, 1971.]

SECTION 1. The right of citizens of the United States, who are eighteen years of age or older, to vote shall not be denied or abridged by the United States or by any State on account of age.

SECTION 2. The Congress shall have power to enforce this article by appropriate legislation.

AMENDMENT XXVII

[Ratified May 7, 1992.]

No law varying the compensation for the services of Senators and Representatives shall take effect until an election of Representatives shall have intervened.

1

THE SUPREME COURT, JUDICIAL REVIEW, AND CONSTITUTIONAL POLITICS

Judicial review is one of the greatest and most controversial contributions of the Constitution to the law and politics of government. Article III of the Constitution simply provides that "[t]he judicial Power of the United States, shall be vested in one supreme Court, and in such inferior Courts as the Congress may from time to time ordain and establish." Remarkably, that power is not further defined in the Constitution. But in the course of constitutional politics, *judicial review* has come to be the power of the Supreme Court and the federal judiciary to consider and overturn any congressional and state legislation or other official governmental action deemed inconsistent with the Constitution, Bill of Rights, or federal law.

Like other provisions of the Constitution, the three brief sections in Article III register compromises forged during the Constitutional Convention; the Constitution, as the renowned historian and editor of *The Records of the Federal Convention of 1787*, Max Farrand, observed, is "a bundle of compromises."[1] The first section of Article III makes clear that the Supreme Court is the only federal court constitutionally required. The convention left it for the First Congress to establish a system of lower federal courts, which it did with the Judiciary Act of 1789. Both the convention and the First Congress rejected proposals that would have left the administration of justice entirely in the hands of state courts (with appeals to the Supreme Court). Also rejected was

James Madison's proposal to join justices and executive branch officials in a "council of revision" with a veto power over congressional and state legislation. Agreement on the importance of guaranteeing judicial independence resulted in the first section of Article III also providing that federal judges "hold their Offices during good Behaviour," subject only to impeachment, and forbidding the diminution of their salaries. That guarantee reflects colonial opposition to royalist judges under the English Crown. One of the grievances listed in the Declaration of Independence as a justification for the Revolutionary War was that King George III had "made Judges dependent on his Will alone."[2] The two remaining sections of Article III specify the kinds of cases and controversies that the federal judiciary may hear (that is, jurisdiction) (see Ch. 2) and empower Congress to establish the Court's appellate jurisdiction and punish individuals for treason.

The Framers, it is fair to say, failed to think through the power of judicial review and its ramifications for constitutional politics. "[T]he framers anticipated some sort of judicial review," noted political scientist Edward S. Corwin, but he added that "it is equally without question that the ideas generally current in 1787 were far from presaging the present role of the Court."[3] In a letter to Corwin, Max Farrand also concluded that "[t]he framers of the Constitution did not realize it themselves [how markedly different their conceptions of judicial review were]: they were struggling to express an idea and their experience was as yet insufficient."[4]

The Constitutional Convention left the power of the judiciary (and much else set forth in the Constitution) to be worked out in practice. As John Mercer, a delegate to the Constitutional Convention from Maryland, observed, "It is a great mistake to suppose that the paper we are to propose will govern the United States. It is the men whom it will bring into the government and interest in maintaining it that is to govern them. The paper will only mark out the mode and the form."[5] The Constitution, of course, is not self-interpreting, and crucial principles—such as judicial review, separation of powers, and federalism—are presupposed rather than spelled out. Moreover, in creating separate institutions that share specific and delegated powers, the Constitution amounts to a prescription for political struggle and an invitation for an ongoing debate about enduring constitutional principles.

Almost immediately following the convention in 1787, controversy erupted over the powers granted the national government and in particular to the federal judiciary. Those opposed to the states' ratification of the Constitution, the Anti-Federalists, warned that "[t]here are no well defined limits of the Judiciary Powers, they seem to be left as a boundless ocean."[6] Fears that "the powers of the judiciary may be extended to any degree short of Almighty" were echoed by Thomas Tredwell, among others, during New York's convention.[7] Robert Yates, one of the most articulate Anti-Federalists writing under the name of Brutus, attacked both the independence and the power of federal judges:

> There is no authority that can remove them, and they cannot be controuled [sic] by the laws of the legislature. In short, they are independent of the people, of the legislature, and of every power under heaven. Men placed in this situation will generally soon feel themselves independent of heaven itself. . . .

> And in their decisions they will not confine themselves to any fixed or established rules, but will determine, according to what appears to them, the reason and spirit of the constitution. The opinions of the supreme court, whatever they may be, will have the force of law; because there is no power provided in the constitution, that can correct their errors, or controul their adjudications. From this court there is no appeal.[8]

"This power in the judicial," charged Brutus, "will enable them to mould the government, into almost any shape they please."

Defenders of the Constitution countered that "the powers given the Supreme Court are not only safe, but constitute a wise and valuable part of the system."[9] In North Carolina's convention, Governor Johnston observed that "[i]t is obvious to every one that there ought to be one Supreme Court for national purposes."[10] During the fight for New York's ratification, Alexander Hamilton provided the classic defense of the judiciary as "the least dangerous branch." Responding to Brutus in *The Federalist*, No. 78, Hamilton argued,

> Whoever attentively considers the different departments of power must perceive, that in a government in which they are separated from each other, the judiciary, from the nature of its functions, will always be the least dangerous to the political rights of the constitution; because it will be least in a capacity to annoy or injure them. The executive not only dispenses the honors, but holds the sword of the community. The legislature not only commands the purse, but prescribes the rules by which the duties and rights of every citizen are to be regulated. The judiciary on the contrary has no influence over either the sword or the purse, no direction either of the strength or of the wealth of the society, and can take no active resolution whatever. It may truly be said to have neither Force nor Will, but merely judgment; and must ultimately depend upon the aid of the executive arm even for the efficacy of its judgments.

> If it be said that the legislative body are themselves the constitutional judges of their own powers, and that the construction they put upon them is conclusive upon other departments, it may be answered, that this cannot be the natural presumption, where it is

not to be collected from any particular provisions in the constitution. It is not otherwise to be supposed that the constitution could intend to enable the representatives of the people to substitute their *will* to that of their constituents. It is far more rational to suppose that the courts were designed to be an intermediate body between the people and the legislature, in order, among other things, to keep the latter within the limits assigned to their authority. The interpretation of the laws is the proper and peculiar province of the courts. A constitution is in fact, and must be, regarded by the judges as a fundamental law. It therefore belongs to them as to ascertain its meaning as well as the meaning of any particular act proceeding from the legislative body. If there should happen to be an irreconcilable variance between the two, that which has the superior obligation and validity ought of course to be preferred; or in other words, the constitution ought to be preferred to the statute, the intention of the people to the intention of their agents.

Nor does this conclusion by any means suppose a superiority of the judicial to the legislative power. It only supposes that the power of the people is superior to both; and that where the will of the legislature declared in its statutes, stands in opposition to that of the people declared in the constitution, the judges ought to be governed by the latter, rather than the former. . . .

If then the courts of justice are to be considered as the bulwarks of a limited constitution against legislative encroachments, this consideration will afford a strong argument for the permanent tenure of judicial offices, since nothing will contribute so much as this to that independent spirit in the judges, which must be essential to the faithful performance of so arduous a duty.

The Federalists' interpretation of Article III was advanced by others in the effort to win ratification. In Pennsylvania's convention, James Wilson, who was one of the first justices appointed by President George Washington, argued that

under this Constitution, the legislature may be restrained, and kept within its prescribed bounds, by the interposition of the judicial department. . . . [T]he power of the Constitution [is] paramount to the power of the legislature acting under that Constitution; for it is possible that the legislature, when acting in that capacity, may transgress the bounds assigned to it, and an act may pass, in the usual *mode*, notwithstanding that transgression; but when it comes to be discussed before *the judges*,—when they consider its principles, and find it to be incompatible with the superior power of the Constitution,—it is their duty to pronounce it *void*.[11]

In Connecticut, Oliver Ellsworth, another who was later appointed to the Court, declared, "If the general legislature should at any time overleap their limits, the judicial department is a constitutional check."[12]

Even among the Federalists, however, there were differing views of the judiciary's power. Alexander Hamilton and James Madison agreed that the Court would exercise some checking power over the states. The Court, in Madison's words, was "the surest expositor of . . . the [constitutional] boundaries . . . between the Union and its members."[13] But they were in less agreement on whether the Court had the power to check coequal branches, the Congress and the president. In *The Federalist*, Madison called the judiciary an "auxiliary precaution" against the possible domination of one branch of government over another. Later, during a debate in the First Congress in 1789, he observed that "in the ordinary course of Government, . . . the exposition of the laws and Constitution devolves upon the Judiciary." Still, Madison doubted that the Court's interpretation of the Constitution was superior to that given by Congress. "Nothing has been offered to invalidate the [view]," he argued, "that the meaning of the Constitution may as well be ascertained by the legislative as by the judicial authority."[14] The Court stood as a forum of last resort, Madison explained, but "this resort must necessarily be deemed the last in relation to the authorities of the other departments of the government; not in relation to the rights of the parties to the constitutional compact, from which the judicial, as well as the other departments, hold their delegated trusts."[15]

From the initial debate in the Constitutional Convention in 1787 to those between the Federalists and the Anti-Federalists over state ratification of the Constitution and into the First Congress, the power of judicial review and the meaning of other key provisions and principles of the Constitution have remained a continuing source of controversy in constitutional politics. And the Supreme Court has remained, as Justice Oliver Wendell Holmes observed, a "storm centre" of political controversy.

A | *Establishing and Contesting the Power of Judicial Review*

In its first decade, the Supreme Court had little business, frequent turnover in personnel, no chambers or staff, no fixed customs, and no institutional identity. When the Court initially convened on February 1, 1790, only Chief Justice John Jay and two other justices arrived at the Exchange Building in New York City. They adjourned until the next day when Justice John Blair arrived; the two other justices never arrived. With little to do other than admit attorneys to practice

■ How to Locate Decisions
of the Supreme Court

The decisions of the Supreme Court are published in the *United States Reports* by the U.S. Government Printing Office. Each decision is referred to by the names of the appellant, the person bringing the suit, and the appellee, the respondent: hence, *McCulloch v. Maryland*. After the name of the case is the volume number in which it appears in the *United States Reports* and the page number on which the Court's opinion begins, followed by the year of the decision. *McCulloch v. Maryland*, 17 U.S. 316 (1819), thus may be found in Volume 17 of the *United States Reports* beginning on page 316.

Prior to the publication of the *United States Reports* in 1875, the Court's opinions used to be cited according to the name of the reporter of the Court, who published the Court's opinions at his own expense. Decisions thus would originally be cited as follows:

1789–1800	Dallas	(1–4 Dall., 1–4 U.S.)
1801–1815	Cranch	(1–9 Cr., 5–13 U.S.)
1816–1827	Wheaton	(1–12 Wheat., 14–25 U.S.)
1828–1842	Peters	(1–16 Pet., 26–41 U.S.)
1843–1860	Howard	(1–24 How., 42–65 U.S.)
1861–1862	Black	(1–2 Bl., 66–67 U.S.)
1863–1874	Wallace	(1–23 Wall., 68–90 U.S.)
1875–		(91– , U.S.)

The full citation for *McCulloch v. Maryland* is 4 Wheat. (17 U.S.) 316 (1819). But with Volume 91 in 1875, the reporters' names were dropped, and decisions were then cited only by the volume number and the designation "U.S."

In addition, two companies print editions of the Court's decisions. There is the *Lawyers' Edition*, published by the Lawyer's Cooperative, and *The Supreme Court Reporter*, published by West Publishing Company. The *Lawyers' Edition* is cited as L.Ed. (e.g., 91 L.Ed. 575), and *The Supreme Court Reporter* is cited as S.Ct. (e.g., 104 S.Ct. 3005).

See also "Researching Legal Materials" at the end of the book.

before its bar, the Court concluded its first sessions in less than two weeks.

When the capital moved from New York City to Philadelphia in the winter of 1790, the Court met in Independence Hall and in the Old City Hall, until the capital again moved to Washington, DC, in 1800. Most of the first justices' time was spent riding circuit. That is, each would travel throughout a particular area, or circuit, in the country. Under the Judiciary Act of 1789, they were required twice a year to hold court, in the company of local district judges, in a circuit to hear appeals from the federal district courts. Hence, the justices resided primarily in their circuits, rather than in Washington, and felt a greater allegiance to their circuits than to the Court.

The Court's uncertain status was reflected in the first justices' exercise of their power of judicial review. Although in its initial years the Court had few important cases, *Chisholm v. Georgia*, 2 Dall. (2 U.S.) 419 (1793) precipitated the country's first constitutional crisis. In that case, Justice James Wilson, who had been a delegate to the Constitutional Convention and Pennsylvania's ratifying convention, ruled that citizens of one state could sue another state in federal courts. That provoked an angry dissent from Justice James Iredell, a southerner who had attended North Carolina's ratifying convention and a strong proponent of "states' rights." His dissent invited the adoption by Congress of the Eleventh Amendment in 1795, overturning *Chisholm* and guaranteeing state immunity from lawsuits brought by citizens of other states (see Vol. 1, Ch. 7 for further discussion). The outcry over *Chisholm* convinced Chief Justice John Jay that the Court would remain "the least dangerous branch." He resigned in 1795 to become New York's governor and later declined reappointment as chief justice.

The Court, though, in *Ware v. Hylton*, 3 Dall. (3 U.S.) 199 (1796), upheld the provisions of a federal treaty, the 1783 peace treaty with England, over state law. And *Hylton v. United States*, 3 Dall. (3 U.S.) 171 (1796), affirmed, over objections raised by the states, Congress's power to levy a carriage tax (and thus implicitly asserted the Court's power to nullify acts of Congress).

Still, two years later, *Calder v. Bull*, 3 Dall. (3 U.S.) 386 (1798), illustrates how uncertain and divided the justices were about exercising their power of judicial review. There the Court declined to assert its power when ruling that conflicts between state laws and state constitutions are matters for state, not federal, courts to resolve. But Justice Iredell maintained that a state law might run against principles of "natural justice" and the Court still would have no power to strike it down. By contrast, Justice Samuel Chase contended that the Court had the power to overturn laws that violate fundamental principles, explaining,

> I cannot subscribe to the omnipotence of a State legislature, or
> that it is absolute and without controul; although its authority
> should not be expressly restrained by the Constitution, or funda-
> mental laws of the State. The people of the United States erected
> their Constitution . . . to establish justice, to promote the general
> welfare, to secure the blessings of liberty; and to protect their per-
> sons and property from violence. . . . There are acts which the
> Federal, or State, Legislature cannot do. . . . It is against all reason
> and justice to entrust a Legislature with SUCH [despotic] powers;
> and therefore, it cannot be presumed that they have done it. The
> genius, the nature, and the spirit of our State Governments,
> amount to a prohibition of such [unlimited] acts of legislation; and
> the general principles of law and reason forbid them.

Justice Chase was not alone in claiming that the judiciary had the
power of judicial review. As an ardent Federalist, James Kent (1763–1847)
staunchly defended the power of judicial review in his Introductory Law
Lecture at Columbia University in 1794 (excerpted below). Like Alexander Hamilton, James Wilson, and other Federalists, Kent justified judicial
review in terms of fundamental principles of constitutional government.
But, unlike Hamilton's arguments in *The Federalist*, No. 78, Kent stressed
the uniquely American basis for the doctrine of judicial review.

The uncertainty and controversy over the power of judicial review
was, nevertheless, further underscored in 1798 with the passage of the
Virginia and Kentucky Resolutions (excerpted below), in response to
Congress's enactment of the Alien and Sedition Acts. Drafted by James
Madison and Thomas Jefferson, the Virginia and Kentucky Resolutions
not only contended that Congress had violated the First Amendment but
claimed that state legislatures had the power to judge the constitutionality
of federal laws. Jefferson went so far as to assert that states could nullify
federal laws that they deemed unconstitutional. The "sovereign and independent" states, in his words, "have the unquestionable right to judge . . .
and, that a nullification [by] those sovereignties, of all unauthorized acts
done under the color of that instrument is the rightful remedy."

Jefferson remained opposed to the power of judicial review and the
view that the Supreme Court's interpretation of the Constitution was
binding on the other branches of government. In an 1819 letter to Spencer Roane, a Virginia state judge, Jefferson explained his departmental
theory of constitutional interpretation:

> My construction of the Constitution is . . . that each department is
> truly independent of the others, and has an equal right to decide
> for itself what is the meaning of the Constitution in the cases sub-
> mitted to its action most especially where it is to act ultimately and
> without appeal. . . . Each of the three departments has equally the
> right to decide for itself what is its duty under the Constitution,

without any regard to what the others may have decided for themselves under a similar question.[16]

Although less strident than Jefferson, Madison thought that the "true and safe construction" of the Constitution would emerge with the "uniform sanction of successive legislative bodies; through a period of years and under the varied ascendency of parties."[17]

Chief Justice John Marshall provided the classic justification for the power of judicial review in the landmark ruling in *Marbury v. Madison* (1803) (excerpted below; see also the brief of that decision in "The How, Why, and What to Briefing and Citing Court Cases" at the end of this book). Notice that Marshall's arguments draw on both general principles and the text of the Constitution and are not unassailable. In an otherwise unimportant state case, *Eakin v. Raub* 12 Sargeant & Rawle 330 (Pa., 1825) (excerpted below), for example, Pennsylvania Supreme Court Justice John Gibson expressly refuted Marshall's arguments. It does not inexorably follow from Marshall's claim that the Constitution created a limited government that *only* the judiciary should enforce those limitations. No more persuasive is the argument that judges have the power to authoritatively interpret the Constitution based on their taking an oath to uphold the document, because all federal and state officers take an oath to support the Constitution. Like Madison and Jefferson, Justice Gibson rejected *Marbury*'s implication that the judiciary has a monopoly (or supremacy) over interpreting the Constitution or, as Chief Justice Charles Evans Hughes later put it, "We are under a Constitution but the Constitution is what the judges say it is."[18] In providing a rationale for judicial self-restraint, Gibson embraces a departmental theory of constitutional interpretation—namely, that each branch has the authority to interpret the Constitution and its own powers.

Chief Justice Marshall's arguments based on the text of the Constitution fare better. In specifying that the "judicial Power shall extend to" cases and controversies "arising under this Constitution," Article III implies that constitutional questions may be decided by the judiciary. And, as Marshall points out, the supremacy clause of Article VI makes it clear that the Constitution is "the supreme Law of the Land." Judicial review is thus a logical implication of the Constitution, for as Justice Joseph Story observed,

> The laws and treaties, and even the constitution, of the United States, would become a dead letter without it. Indeed, in a complicated government, like ours, where there is an assemblage of republics, combined under a common head, the necessity of some controlling judicial power, to ascertain and enforce the powers of the Union is, if possible, still more striking. The laws of the whole

would otherwise be in continual danger of being contravened by the laws of the parts. The national government would be reduced to a servile dependence upon the states; and the same scenes would be again acted over in solemn mockery, which began in the neglect, and ended in the ruin, of the confederation.[19]

Still and undeniably, the power of judicial review is not expressly provided for in the Constitution and its exercise remains a continuing source of controversy.

The immediate political controversy over the exercise of judicial review in *Marbury* in striking down a section of the Judiciary Act of 1789 was defused by Chief Justice Marshall's conclusion that the Court had no power to order the delivery of Marbury's commission. Though outraged by Marshall's assertion of judicial review, Madison and Jefferson had not been compelled by the Court to do anything. Jefferson continued to maintain that each branch of government could interpret the Constitution and to deny that the Court's interpretations were binding on the president's exercise of executive powers. In a letter to John Adams's wife, Abigail, in 1804, explaining his decision to pardon those tried and convicted under the Sedition Act of 1798, Jefferson wrote,

> The Judges, believing the law constitutional, had a right to pass a sentence of fine and imprisonment; because that power was placed in their hands by the Constitution. But the Executive, believing the law to be unconstitutional, was bound to remit the execution of it; because that power has been confided to him by the Constitution. The instrument meant that its co-ordinate branches should be checks on each other. But the opinion which gives to the Judges the right to decide what Laws are constitutional, and what not, not only for themselves in their own sphere of action, but for the Legislative and Executive also in their spheres, would make the Judiciary a despotic branch.[20]

Jefferson was not the last president to contest the authority of the Court. An irate President Andrew Jackson, on hearing of the decision in *Worcester v. Georgia*, 31 U.S. 515 (1832), holding that states could not pass laws affecting federally recognized Indian nations, reportedly declared, "John Marshall has made his decision, now let him enforce it."[21] Jackson elaborated his view in his Veto Message of 1832, explaining his vetoing of legislation rechartering the national bank. Besides contending that *McCulloch v. Maryland*, 17 U.S. 316 (1819) (see Vol. 1, Ch. 6) was not binding on his actions, Jackson reiterated the position that

> [t]he Congress, the Executive, and the Court must each for itself be guided by its own opinion of the Constitution. Each public officer who takes an oath to support the Constitution swears that he will support it as he understands it, and not as it is understood by

others. . . . The opinion of the judges has no more authority over Congress than the opinion of Congress has over the judges, and on that point the President is independent of both.[22]

Jackson's Veto Message drew an impassioned response from Senator Daniel Webster, who thundered in the halls of Congress that

> [t]he President is as much bound by the law as any private citizen. . . . He may refuse to obey the law, and so may a private citizen; but both do it at their own peril, and neither of them can settle the question of its validity. The President may say a law is unconstitutional, but he is not the judge. . . . If it were otherwise, there would be no government of laws; but we should all live under the government, the rule, the caprices of individuals. . . .

> [President Jackson's] message . . . converts a constitutional limitation of power into mere matters of opinion, and then strikes the judicial department, as an efficient department, out of our system. . . .

> [The message] denies first principles. It contradicts truths heretofore received as indisputable. It denies to the judiciary the interpretation of law.

Controversy over judicial review continues, but it bears emphasizing that Jefferson, Jackson, and subsequent presidents concede that the Court's rulings are binding for the actual cases decided and handed down. Technically, a decision of the Court is final only for the parties involved in the case. Yet, because the justices in their opinions give general principles for deciding a case and because they generally adhere to precedents (or tend to do so until the composition of the bench markedly changes), the Court's rulings are usually considered controlling for other similar cases and the larger political controversy they represent. But in major confrontations in constitutional politics—like those over the creation of a national bank, slavery, school desegregation, and abortion—the Court alone cannot lay those controversies to rest.

What presidents, Congress, the states, and others occasionally deny is *judicial supremacy* or the finality of the Court's interpretation of broad constitutional principles for resolving major political controversies. In his famous debates with Stephen Douglas, for instance, Abraham Lincoln denounced the Court's ruling in *Dred Scott v. Sandford*, 60 U.S. 393 (1857) (see Ch. 12), that blacks were not citizens of the United States. While Lincoln doubted that "we, as a mob, will decide [Dred Scott] to be free," he exclaimed that

> we nevertheless do oppose that decision as a political rule which shall be binding on the voter, to vote for nobody who thinks it wrong, which shall be binding on the members of Congress or the President

to favor no measure that does not actually concur with the principles of that decision. . . . We propose so resisting it as to have it reversed if we can, and a new judicial rule established upon this subject.[23]

Later, in his first Inaugural Address in 1861, Lincoln elaborated,

> I do not forget the position assumed by some, that constitutional questions are to be decided by the Supreme Court; nor do I deny that such decisions must be binding in any case, upon the parties to a suit, as to the object of that suit, while they are also entitled to a very high respect and consideration, in all parallel cases, by all other departments of government. And while it is obviously possible that such a decision may be erroneous in any given case, still the evil effect following it, being limited to that particular case, with the chance that it may be over-ruled, and never become a precedent for other cases, can better be borne than could the evils of a different practice. At the same time the candid citizen must confess that if the policy of the government, upon vital questions, affecting the whole people, is to be irrevocably fixed by the decisions of the Supreme Court, the instant they are made, in ordinary litigation between parties, in personal actions, the people will have ceased, to be their own rulers, having to that extent, practically resigned their government, into the hands of that eminent tribunal. Nor is there, in this view, any assault upon the court, or the judges. It is a duty, from which they may not shrink, to decide cases properly brought before them; and it is no fault of theirs, if others seek to turn their decisions to political purposes.

In major confrontations with the Court, other presidents have taken similar positions to that of President Lincoln. During the constitutional crisis of 1937, resulting from the Court's invalidation of much of the early New Deal progressive economic legislation, President Franklin D. Roosevelt proposed that Congress expand the size of the Court from nine to fifteen justices, and thereby enable him to secure a majority sympathetic to his programs and policies. And in a "Fireside Chat" in March 1937 (see excerpt below), FDR followed in the footsteps of Jefferson, Jackson, and Lincoln in attacking the Court for becoming a "super-legislature." (See also the INSIDE THE COURT box on FDR's Court packing-plan and the constitutional crisis of 1937, later in this chapter.)

Judicial supremacy over interpreting the Constitution remains controversial. In *Marbury*, however, Chief Justice Marshall did not lay claim to judicial supremacy, only that the Court, no less than the president and Congress, has the authority and duty to interpret the Constitution.[24] By contrast, in the twentieth and twenty-first centuries, justices have more often asserted the supremacy of their decisions. In *United States v. Butler*, 297 U.S. 1 (1936), Justice (and later Chief Justice) Harlan Stone claimed that "[w]hile unconstitutional exercise of power by the executive and legislative branches of government is subject to judicial restraint, the only check upon our own exercise of power is our own sense of self-restraint." In the wake of massive resistance to the Court's watershed ruling on school desegregation, in *Brown v. Board of Education*, 347 U.S. 483 (1954) (see Ch. 12), all nine justices took the unusual step of signing the opinion announcing *Cooper v. Aaron*, 358 U.S. 1 (1958) (see Ch. 12), which ordered the desegregation of schools in Little Rock, Arkansas. And they interpreted *Marbury* to have

> declared the basic principle that the federal judiciary is supreme in the exposition of the law of the Constitution. . . . It follows that the interpretation of the Fourteenth Amendment enunciated by this Court in the *Brown* case is the supreme law of the land, and Article VI of the Constitution makes it have binding effect on the States. . . . Every state legislator and executive and judicial officer is solemnly committed by oath taken pursuant to Article VI, 3 "to support this Constitution."

The Court likewise proclaimed itself the "ultimate interpreter of the Constitution" in *Baker v. Carr*, 369 U.S. 186 (1962) (excerpted in Ch. 2), when holding that courts could decide disputes over the malapportionment of state legislatures. And again citing *Marbury* in *Powell v. McCormack*, 395 U.S. 486 (1969) (excerpted in Vol. 1, Ch. 5), involving a controversy over the House of Representatives' exclusion of a duly elected representative, the Court declared that "it is the responsibility of this Court to act as the ultimate interpreter of the Constitution." The Rehnquist Court underscored its authority, in *City of Boerne v. Flores*, 521 U.S. 507 (1997) (excerpted in Ch. 6 of Vols. 1 and 2), when reasserting that Congress's power under the Fourteenth Amendment is only remedial, not definitive, and thus only the Court, and not Congress, has the power to define constitutional rights. See also *Boumediene v. Bush* 553 U.S. 723 (2008) (excerpted in Vol. 1, Ch. 3), striking down Congress's stripping federal courts' jurisdiction over *habeas* petitions filed by enemy combatants held in Guantánamo Bay.

Despite the Court's occasional claims of judicial supremacy, the president, Congress, and the states may in various ways undercut and thwart compliance with, if not ultimately overturn, the Court's rulings (see Vol. 1, Ch. 2). By deciding only immediate cases, the Court infuses constitutional meaning into the larger surrounding political controversies by bringing them within the language, structure, and spirit of the Constitution. The Court may thus raise a controversial issue, as it did with school desegregation in *Brown* and with the right to abortion in *Roe v. Wade*, 410 U.S. 113 (1973) to the national political agenda. But by itself the Court cannot lay those controversies to rest because its power, in Chief Justice Edward White's words, rests "solely upon the approval of a free people."[25] In areas of major and continuing political

■ CONSTITUTIONAL HISTORY

Decisions of the Supreme Court Overruled, Acts of Congress Held Unconstitutional, and State Laws and Municipal Ordinances Overturned, 1789–2018

Year	Supreme Court Decisions Overruled	Acts of Congress Overturned	State Laws Overturned	Ordinances Overturned
1789–1800, Pre-Marshall				
1801–1835, Marshall Court	3	1	18	
1836–1864, Taney Court	4	1	21	
1865–1873, Chase Court	7	8	33	
1874–1888, Waite Court	11	7	7	
1889–1910, Fuller Court	4	14	73	15
1910–1921, White Court	5	9	107	18
1921–1930, Taft Court	5	12	131	12
1930–1940, Hughes Court	14	14	78	5
1941–1946, Stone Court	12	1	25	7
1947–1952, Vinson Court	12	1	38	7
1953–1969, Warren Court	56	23	150	16
1969–1986, Burger Court	55	30	192	15
1986–2005, Rehnquist Court	42	42	97	21
2005– , Roberts Court	16	15	50	11
Totals	246	178	1,020	127

Note that in *Immigration and Naturalization Service v. Chadha* (1983), the Burger Court struck down a provision for a "one-house" legislative veto in the Immigration and Naturalization Act but effectively declared all one- and two-house legislative vetoes unconstitutional. While 212 statutes containing provisions for legislative vetoes were implicated by the Court's decision, *Chadha* is here counted as a single declaration of the unconstitutionality of congressional legislation. Note also that the Court's ruling in *Texas v. Johnson* (1989), striking down a Texas law making it a crime to desecrate the American flag, invalidated laws in forty-eight states and a federal statute. It is counted here, however, only once. This table is based on Leon Friedman and Fred Israel, eds., *Justices of the United States Supreme Court*, Vol. 4, 4th ed. (New York: Facts on File, 2013), 573–600, and various Congressional Research Studies and Senate Reports, as updated by the authors through the 2018 term, as of July 1, 2019.

controversy, constitutional law is a kind of dialogue between the Court and the country over the meaning of the Constitution, and judicial review may be in historical perspective more provisional than final.

Even more than Chief Justice Marshall's arguments in *Marbury*, the establishment of judicial review turned on public acceptance and the forces of history. That is not to gainsay Marshall's contributions. He had a keen understanding of the malleable nature of the young republic and the important role that the first generation would play in establishing the power of the national government. Marshall's long tenure (1801–1835) and that of others who served with him may have contributed as well. After *Marbury*, moreover, the Court did not again strike down another act of Congress or challenge a coequal branch of government until the 1857 ill-fated ruling in *Dred Scott*, which left the Court at a low ebb for two decades. Instead, the Marshall Court buttressed its own power by defending the interests of the national government against the states and striking down state laws that were barriers to the flow of interstate commerce.

Finally, social forces have shaped the Court's role in the kinds of cases and controversies brought to it for review. As already noted, the Court had little important business during its first decade. Over 40 percent of its business consisted in admiralty and prize cases (disputes over captured property at sea). About 50 percent raised issues of common law, and the remaining 10 percent dealt with matters like equity, including one probate case. By the late nineteenth century, the Court's business gradually changed in response to developments in American society. The number of admiralty cases, for instance, had by 1882 dwindled to less than 4 percent of the total. Almost 40 percent of the Court's decisions still dealt with either disputes of common law or questions of jurisdiction and procedure in federal courts. More than 43 percent of the Court's business, however, involved interpreting congressional statutes. Less than 4 percent of the cases raised issues of constitutional interpretation. The decline in admiralty and common-law litigation and the increase in statutory interpretation reflected the impact of the Industrial Revolution and the growing governmental regulation of social and economic relations. In the latter part of the twentieth century, the trend continued. About 47 percent of the cases decided annually by the Court involved matters of constitutional law. Another 38 percent dealt with the interpretation of congressional legislation. The remaining 15 percent involved issues of practice and procedure, administrative law, taxation, patents, and claims. However, in recent years the Roberts Court (2005–) has tended to give greater attention to questions of jurisdiction, practice, and procedure, along with cases involving statutory interpretation.

The Court is no longer "the least dangerous branch" or primarily concerned with correcting the errors of lower courts. In response to growing and changing litigation, the Court more frequently overturns prior rulings, congressional legislation, and state and local laws. The Court takes only "hard cases," involving major issues of legal policy and "not primarily to preserve the rights of the litigants." In the words of Chief Justice William Howard Taft, "The Supreme Court's function is for the purpose of expounding and stabilizing principles of law for the benefit of the people of the country, passing upon constitutional questions and other important questions of law for the public benefit."[26]

The Court and the country have changed with constitutional politics. From 1789 to the Civil War, the major controversies confronting the Court involved disputes between the national government and the states, and the Court employed its power to preserve the Union (see Vol. 1, Chs. 6 and 7). Between 1865 and 1937, during the Reconstruction Era and the Industrial Revolution, the dominant political controversy revolved around balancing regulatory interests and those of businesses, and the Court defended the interests of American capitalism and private enterprise (see Ch. 3). Only after 1937 did the Court begin to assume the role of "a guardian for civil liberties and civil rights" in defending the rights of minorities (see Chs. 4–12). The Court's role has changed with constitutional politics, as the late Harvard Law School professor Paul Freund nicely expressed by analogy, "As Hamlet is to one generation a play of revenge, to another a conflict between will and conscience, and to another a study in mother-fixation, so the Constitution has been to one generation a means of cementing the Union, to another a protectorate of burgeoning property, and to another a safeguard of basic human rights and equality before the law."[27]

Notes

1. See Max Farrand, *The Framing of the Constitution* (New Haven, CT: Yale University Press, 1913); Max Farrand, ed., *The Records of the Federal Convention of 1787*, 4 vols. (New Haven, CT: Yale University Press, 1911); and John P. Roche, "The Founding Fathers: A Reform Caucus in Action," 55 *American Political Science Review* 799 (1961).

2. The Supreme Court has enforced the tenure and salary provisions in *Ex parte Milligan*, 4 Wall. 2 (1867) (see Ch. 3), holding that civilians cannot be tried before military tribunals; in *O'Donoghue v. United States*, 289 U.S. 516 (1933), holding that judicial salaries cannot be reduced, even during the Great Depression; and *Northern Pipeline Construction Co. v. Marathon Pipe Line Co.*, 458 U.S. 50 (1982), striking down a statute expanding the power of bankruptcy judges.

3. Edward S. Corwin, "The Constitution as Instrument and as Symbol," 30 *American Political Science Review* 1078 (1936).

4. Letter from Max Farrand to Edward Corwin, January 3, 1939, in Edward Samuel Corwin Papers, Box 3, Princeton University Library, Princeton, NJ.

5. Quoted in James Madison, *Notes of Debates in the Federal Convention of 1787* (Athens: Ohio University Press, 1966), 455–456.

6. A Columbia Patriot, in *The Complete Anti-Federalist*, Vol. 4, ed. Herbert J. Storing (Chicago: University of Chicago Press, 1981), 276.

7. Thomas Tredwell, in *The Debates in the Several State Conventions on the Adoption of the Federal Constitution*, Vol. 4, ed., Jonathan Elliot (New York: Burt Franklin, 1974), 401.

8. Brutus, in *The Complete Anti-Federalist*, Vol. 2, ed. Storing, 438–439, 420, 422.

9. James Wilson, in *The Debates*, Vol. 2, ed. Elliot, 494.

10. Governor Johnston, in *The Debates*, Vol. 4, ed. Elliot, 142.

11. James Wilson, in *The Debates*, Vol. 2, ed. Elliot, 445–446.

12. Oliver Ellsworth, in *The Debates*, Vol. 2, ed. Elliot, 196.

13. Letter from James Madison to an unidentified person, August 1834, reprinted in *Letters and Other Writings of James Madison*, Vol. 4 (Philadelphia, 1865), 350.

14. James Madison, in *Annals of Congress*, Vol. 1 (Washington, DC: Gales & Seaton, 1789), 500, 546–547.

15. James Madison, "Report on the Virginia Resolutions," in *The Debates*, Vol. 5, ed. Elliot, 549.

16. Thomas Jefferson, *The Works of Thomas Jefferson*, Vol. 12, ed. Paul Ford (New York: G. P. Putnam's Sons, 1904–1905), 137–138.

17. Quoted in Robert J. Morgan, *James Madison on the Constitution and the Bill of Rights* (Westport, CT: Greenwood Press, 1988), 196. For more on Jefferson's and Madison's views, see the discussion of the controversy over Congress's creating a national bank and *McCulloch v. Maryland*, 17 U.S. 316 (1819) (excerpted in Vol. 1, Ch. 6).

18. Charles Evans Hughes, *Address and Papers of Charles Evans Hughes* (New York: Columbia University Press, 1908), 139.

19. Joseph Story, *Commentaries on the Constitution* (Durham, NC: Carolina Academic Press, 1987), reprint of 1833 ed.

20. Thomas Jefferson, Letter to John Adams, September 11, 1804, as quoted in Charles Warren, *The Supreme Court in United States History*, Vol. 1 (Boston: Little, Brown, 1922), 265.

21. Quoted in Edward Corwin, *The Doctrine of Judicial Review* (Princeton, NJ: Princeton University Press, 1914), 22.

22. President's Veto Message (July 10, 1832), *A Compilation of the Messages and Papers of the Presidents*, Vol. 2, ed. J. Richardson (New York: Bureau of National Literature, 1917), 582.

23. Abraham Lincoln, *The Collected Works of Abraham Lincoln*, Vol. 2, Roy Basler, ed. (New Brunswick, NJ: Rutgers University Press, 1953), 401.

24. See David M. O'Brien, "Judicial Review and Constitutional Politics: Theory and Practice," 48 *University of Chicago Law Review* 1070 (1981).

25. Quoted in David M. O'Brien, *Storm Center: The Supreme Court in American Politics*, 11th ed. (New York: W. W. Norton & Company, 2017).

26. William H. Taft, *Hearings before the House Committee on the Judiciary*, 67th Cong., 2nd sess., 1922, 2.

27. Paul Freund, "My Philosophy of Law," 39 *Connecticut Bar Journal* 220 (1965).

SELECTED BIBLIOGRAPHY

Ellis, Joseph. *Founding Brothers: The Revolutionary Generation.* New York: Knopf, 2000.

Klarman, Michael. *The Founder's Coup: The Making of the United States Constitution.* New York: Oxford University Press, 2016.

Maier, Pauline. *Ratification: The People Debate the Constitution, 1787–1788.* New York: Simon & Schuster, 2011.

Nelson, William. *Marbury v. Madison: The Origins and Legacy of Judicial Review.* Lawrence: University of Kansas Press, 2000.

Van Cleve, William. *We Have Not a Government: The Articles of Confederation and the Road to the Constitution.* Chicago: University of Chicago Press, 2017.

Warren, Charles. *The Supreme Court in United States History,* 3 vols. Boston: Little, Brown, 1922.

James Kent's Introductory Law School Lecture in 1794

James Kent (1763–1847) began a long legal career as a professor at Columbia University Law School in 1794. He later became a master of chancery and, in 1804, the chief justice of New York's supreme court. His Columbia Law Lectures were later expanded into *Commentaries on the American Law* (1826–1830), which Justice Joseph Story called "our first judicial classic." Excerpted here is part of his "Introductory Lecture," which did not remain intact in his *Commentaries* but which uniquely justified judicial review in terms of established principles of republican government in America.

■ ■ ■

The British Constitution and Code of Laws, to the knowledge of which our Lawyers are so early and deeply introduced by the prevailing course of their professional inquiries, abounds, it is true, with invaluable Principles of Equity, of Policy, and of Social Order; Principles which cannot be too generally known, studied and received. It must however be observed at the same time, that many of the fundamental doctrines of their Government, and Axioms of their Jurisprudence, are utterly subversive of an Equality of Rights, and totally incompatible with the liberal spirit of our American Establishments. The Student of our Laws should be carefully taught to distinguish between the Principles of the one Government, and the Genius which presides in the other. He ought to have a correct acquaintance with genuine Republican Maxims, and be thereby induced to cultivate a superior regard for our own, and I trust more perfect systems of Liberty and Justice. . . .

The doctrine I have suggested, is peculiar to the United States. In the European World, no idea has ever been entertained (or at least until lately) of placing constitutional limits to the exercise of the Legislative Power. . . .

No question can be made with us, but that the Acts of the Legislative body, contrary to the true intent and meaning of the Constitution, ought to be absolutely null and void. The only inquiry which can arise on the subject is, whether the Legislature is not of itself the competent Judge of its own constitutional limits, and its acts of course to be presumed always conformable to the commission under which it proceeds; or whether the business of determining in this instance, is not rather the fit and exclusive province of the Courts of Justice. It is easy to see, that if the Legislature was left the ultimate Judge of the nature and extent of the barriers which have been placed against the abuses of its discretion, the efficacy of the check would be totally lost. The Legislature would be inclined to narrow or explain away the Constitution, from the force of the same propensities or considerations of temporary expediency, which would lead it to overturn private rights. Its will would be the supreme law, as much with, as without these constitutional safeguards. Nor is it probable, that the force of public opinion, the only restraint that could in that case exist, would be felt, or if felt, would be greatly regarded. If public opinion was in every case to be presumed correct and competent to be trusted, it is evident, there would have been no need of original and fundamental limitations. But sad experience has sufficiently taught mankind, that opinion is not an infallible standard of safety. When powerful rivalries prevail in the Community, and Parties become highly disciplined and hostile, every measure of the major part of the Legislature is sure to receive the sanction of that Party among their Constituents to which they belong. Every Step of the minor Party, it is equally certain will be approved by their immediate adherents, as well as indiscriminately misrepresented or condemned by the prevailing voice. The Courts of Justice which are organized with peculiar advantages to exempt them from the baneful influence of Faction, and to secure at the same time, a steady, firm and impartial interpretation of the Law, are therefore the most proper power in the Government to keep the Legislature within the limits of its duty, and to maintain the Authority of the Constitution. . . .

This power in the Judicial, of determining the constitutionality of Laws, is necessary to preserve the equilibrium of the government, and prevent usurpations of one part upon another; and of all the parts of government, the Legislative body is by far the most impetuous and powerful. A mere designation on paper, of the limits of the several departments, is altogether insufficient, and for this reason in limited Constitutions, the executive is armed with a negative, either qualified or complete upon the making of Laws. But the Judicial Power is the weakest of all, and as it is equally necessary to be preserved entire, it ought not in sound theory to be left naked without any constitutional means of defence. This is one reason why the Judges in this State are associated with the Governor, to form the Council of Revision, and this association renders some of these observations less applicable to our own particular Constitution, than to any other. The right of expounding the Constitution as well as Laws, will however be found in general to be the most fit, if not only effectual weapon, by which the Courts of Justice are enabled to repel assaults, and to guard against encroachments on their Chartered Authorities.

Nor can any danger be apprehended, lest this principle should exalt the Judicial above the Legislature. They are co-ordinate powers, and equally bound by the instrument under which they act, and if the former should at any time be prevailed upon to substitute arbitrary will, to the exercise of a rational Judgment, as it is possible it may do even in the ordinary course of judicial proceeding, it is not left like the latter, to the mere controul of public opinion. The Judges may be brought before the tribunal of the Legislature, and tried, condemned, and removed from office.

I consider then the Courts of Justice, as the proper and intended Guardians of our limited Constitutions, against the factions and encroachments of the Legislative Body. . . .

The Virginia and Kentucky Resolutions of 1798

In the spring of 1798, President John Adams and his Federalist-dominated Congress enacted the Alien and Sedition Acts, regulating immigration and making criticism of the government a crime of seditious libel. The laws aimed at silencing partisan criticism of the Adams administration's pro-British policies by Jeffersonian-Republicans. Although Jeffersonian-Republicans were prosecuted under the laws, often receiving stiff penalties, no court ruled on the constitutionality of the laws or whether they violated the First Amendment's guarantee for freedom of speech and press. The Kentucky legislature adopted a resolution secretly written by Thomas Jefferson, and Virginia adopted a similar resolution drafted by James Madison. Prosecutions for seditious libel ended in 1801, when the laws expired and Jefferson became president. Over

160 years later, the Supreme Court in a landmark ruling on libel, in *New York Times Company v. Sullivan*, 376 U.S. 254 (1964) (see Ch. 5), declared the Sedition Act and seditious libel unconstitutional and inconsistent with the First Amendment.

■ ■ ■

■ Virginia Resolutions, December 21, 1798

1. *Resolved*, That the General Assembly of Virginia doth unequivocally express a firm resolution to maintain and defend the Constitution of the United States, and the Constitution of this State, against every aggression, either foreign or domestic, and that it will support the government of the United States in all measures warranted by the former. . . .

3. That this Assembly doth explicitly and peremptorily declare that it views the powers of the Federal Government as resulting from the compact to which the States are parties, as limited by the plain sense and intention of the instrument constituting that compact; as no further valid than they are authorized by the grants enumerated in that compact; and that in case of a deliberate, palpable, and dangerous exercise of other powers not granted by the said compact, the States, who are the parties thereto, have the right, and are in duty bound, to interpose for arresting the progress of the evil, and for maintaining within their respective limits, the authorities, rights, and liberties appertaining to them.

4. That the General Assembly doth also express its deep regret that a spirit has in sundry instances been manifested by the Federal Government, to enlarge its powers by forced constructions of the constitutional charter which defines them; and that indications have appeared of a design to expound certain general phrases (which, having been copied from the very limited grant of powers in the former articles of confederation, were the less liable to be misconstrued), so as to destroy the meaning and effect of the particular enumeration, which necessarily explains and limits the general phrases, and so as to consolidate the States by degrees into one sovereignty, the obvious tendency and inevitable result of which would be to transform the present republican system of the United States into an absolute, or at best, a mixed monarchy.

5. That the General Assembly doth particularly protest against the palpable and alarming infractions of the Constitution, in the two late cases of the "alien and sedition acts," passed at the last session of Congress, the first of which exercises a power nowhere delegated to the Federal Government; and which by uniting legislative and judicial powers to those of executive, subverts the general principles of free government, as well as the particular organization and positive provisions of the federal Constitution; and the other of which acts exercises in like manner a power not delegated by the Constitution, but on the contrary expressly and positively forbidden by one of the amendments thereto; a power which more than any other ought to produce universal alarm, because it is levelled against that right of freely examining public characters and measures, and of free communication among the people thereon, which has ever been justly deemed the only effectual guardian of every other right.

6. That this State having by its convention which ratified the federal Constitution, expressly declared, "that among other essential rights, the liberty of conscience and of the press cannot be cancelled, abridged, restrained, or modified by any authority of the United States," and from its extreme anxiety to guard these rights from every possible attack of sophistry or ambition, having with other States recommended an amendment for that purpose, which amendment was in due time annexed to the Constitution, it would mark a reproachful inconsistency and criminal degeneracy, if an indifference were now shown to the most palpable violation of one of the rights thus declared and secured, and to the establishment of a precedent which may be fatal to the other.

■ KENTUCKY RESOLUTIONS, NOVEMBER 10, 1798

1. *Resolved*, That the several states composing the United States of America, are not united on the principle of unlimited submission to their general government; but that by compact, under the style and title of a Constitution for the United States, and of amendments thereto, they constituted a general government for special purposes, delegated to that government certain definite powers, reserving, each state to itself, the residuary mass of right to their own self-government; and that whensoever the general government assumes undelegated powers, its acts are unauthoritative, void, and of no force: That to this compact each state acceded as a state, and is an integral party, its co-states forming as to itself, the other party: That the government created by this compact was not made the exclusive or final *judge* of the extent of the powers delegated to itself; since that would have made its discretion, and not the Constitution, the measure of its powers; but that, as in all other cases of compact among parties having no common judge, each party has an equal right to judge for itself, as well of infractions, as of the mode and measure of redress.

2. *Resolved*, That the Constitution of the United States having delegated to Congress a power to punish treason, counterfeiting the securities and current coin of the United States, piracies and felonies committed on the high seas, and offences against the laws of nations, and no other crimes whatever, . . . all other [of] their acts which assume to create, define, or punish crimes other than those enumerated in the Constitution, are altogether void, and of no force, and that the power to create, define, and punish such other crimes is reserved, and of right appertains, solely and exclusively, to the respective states, each within its own territory.

3. *Resolved*, That it is true as a general principle, and is also expressly declared by one of the amendments to the Constitution, that "the powers not delegated to the United States by the Constitution, nor prohibited by it to the states, are reserved to the states respectively, or to the people"; and that no power over the freedom of religion, freedom of speech, or freedom of the press, being delegated to the United States by the Constitution, nor prohibited by it to the states, all lawful powers respecting the same did of right remain, and were reserved to the states, or to the people; that thus was manifested their determination to retain to themselves the right of judging how far the licentiousness of speech and of the press may be abridged without lessening their useful freedom, and how far those abuses which cannot be

separated from their use, should be tolerated rather than the use be destroyed; and thus also they guarded against all abridgment by the United States of the freedom of religious opinions and exercises, and retained to themselves the right of protecting the same, as this state by a law passed on the general demand of its citizens, had already protected them from all human restraint or interference: and that in addition to this general principle and express declaration, another and more special provision has been made by one of the amendments to the Constitution, which expressly declares, that "Congress shall make no law respecting an establishment of religion, or prohibiting the free exercise thereof, or abridging the freedom of speech, or of the press," thereby guarding in the same sentence, and under the same words, the freedom of religion, of speech, and of the press, insomuch, that whatever violates either, throws down the sanctuary which covers the others, and that libels, falsehoods, and defamations, equally with heresy and false religion, are withheld from the cognizance of federal tribunals: that therefore the act of the Congress of the United States, passed on the 14th day of July, 1798, entitled, "an act in addition to the act for the punishment of certain crimes against the United States," which does abridge the freedom of the press, is not law, but is altogether void and of no effect. . . .

Marbury v. Madison
1 CR. (5 U.S.) 137 (1803)

This case grew out of one of the great early struggles over the course of constitutional politics. Shortly after the ratification of the Constitution, two rival political parties emerged with widely different views of the Constitution and governmental power. The Federalists supported a strong national government, including the power of the federal courts to interpret the Constitution. Their opponents, the Anti-Federalists and later the Jeffersonian-Republicans (who after the 1832 election became known as Democrats), remained distrustful of the national government and continued to favor the states and state courts. The struggle between the Federalists and the Jeffersonian-Republicans finally came to a head with the election of 1800. The Jeffersonians defeated the Federalists, who had held office since the creation of the republic and feared what the Jeffersonian-Republicans might do once in office.

Before leaving office, President John Adams and his Federalist-dominated Congress vindictively created a number of new judgeships and appointed all Federalists in the hope that they would counter the Jeffersonians once in office. But with time running out before the inauguration of Thomas Jefferson as president in 1801, not all of the commissions for the new judgeships were delivered.

John Marshall, whom Adams had just appointed as chief justice, continued to work as secretary of state, delivering the commissions. But he failed to deliver seventeen commissions before Adams's term expired and left them for his successor as secretary of state, James Madison, to deliver. The Federalists' attempt to pack the courts infuriated the Jeffersonian-Republicans. And President Jefferson instructed Madison not to deliver the rest of the commissions.

William Marbury was one whose commission went undelivered. He decided to sue to force Madison to give him his commission. Specifically, he sought a *writ of mandamus*, which is simply a court order directing a government official (Madison) to perform a certain act (hand over the commission). Marbury argued that Section 13 of the Judiciary Act of 1789 had authorized the Supreme Court to issue such writs. He saw this as a way of getting back his commission and for the Marshall Court to take a stand against the Jeffersonians.

Marbury v. Madison was a politically explosive case for the Court and the country over the still-untested power of judicial review. The Court faced a major dilemma. On the one hand, if the Marshall Court ordered Marbury's commission, it was likely that Jefferson would refuse to comply. The Court would then be powerless, perhaps permanently. On the other hand, if the Court refused to issue the writ, it would appear weak and that would confirm the Jeffersonian argument that the courts had no power to intrude on the executive branch. Chief Justice Marshall's opinion, handed down on February 24, 1803, however, shrewdly asserted the power of judicial review and for the first time overturned part of an act of Congress but gave Jefferson no opportunity to retaliate and thus helped to defuse the political controversy surrounding the case. While Jeffersonians fervently disagreed with Marshall's ruling, there was little for them to do because Marshall had not ordered the delivery of Marbury's commission.

The Court's decision was unanimous.

■ ■ ■

☐ *Chief Justice MARSHALL delivers the opinion of the Court.*

At the last term on the affidavits then read and filed with the clerk, a rule was granted in this case, requiring the secretary of state to show cause why a *mandamus* should not issue, directing him to deliver to William Marbury his commission as a justice of the peace for the county of Washington, in the District of Columbia.

No cause has been shown, and the present motion is for a *mandamus*. The peculiar delicacy of this case, the novelty of some of its circumstances, and the real difficulty attending the points which occur in it, require a complete exposition of the principles on which the opinion to be given by the court is founded.

These principles have been, on the side of the applicant very ably argued at the bar. In rendering the opinion of the court, there will be some departure in form, though not in substance, from the points stated in that argument.

In the order in which the court has viewed this subject, the following questions have been considered and decided.

1st. Has the applicant a right to the commission he demands?

2d. If he has a right, and that right has been violated, do the laws of his country afford him a remedy?

3d. If they do afford him a remedy, is it a *mandamus* issuing from this court?

The first object of inquiry is,

1st. Has the applicant a right to the commission he demands?

His right originates in an act of congress passed in February, 1801, concerning the District of Columbia.

After dividing the district into two counties, the 11th section of this law enacts, "that there shall be appointed in and for each of the said counties, such number of discreet persons to be justices of the peace as the president of the United States shall, from time to time, think expedient, to continue in office for five years."

It appears, from the affidavits, that in compliance with this law, a commission for William Marbury, as a justice of the peace for the county of Washington, was signed by John Adams, then President of the United States; after which the seal of the United States was affixed to it; but the commission has never reached the person for whom it was made out.

In order to determine whether he is entitled to this commission, it becomes necessary to inquire whether he has been appointed to the office. For if he has been appointed, the law continues him in office for five years, and he is entitled to the possession of those evidences of office, which, being completed, became his property.

The 2d section of the 2d article of the constitution declares, that "the president shall nominate, and, by and with the advice and consent of the senate, shall appoint, ambassadors, other public ministers and consuls, and all other officers of the United States, whose appointments are not otherwise provided for."

The 3d section declares, that "he shall commission all the officers of the United States."

An act of congress directs the secretary of state to keep the seal of the United States, "to make out and record, and affix the said seal to all civil commissions to officers of the United States, to be appointed by the president, by and with the consent of the senate, or by the president alone; provided, that the said seal shall not be affixed to any commission before the same shall have been signed by the President of the United States."

These are the clauses of the constitution and laws of the United States, which affect this part of the case. They seem to contemplate three distinct operations:

1st. The nomination. This is the sole act of the president, and is completely voluntary.

2d. The appointment. This is also the act of the president, and is also a voluntary act, though it can only be performed by and with the advice and consent of the senate.

3d. The commission. To grant a commission to a person appointed, might, perhaps, be deemed a duty enjoined by the constitution. "He shall," says that instrument, "commission all the officers of the United States." . . .

The last act to be done by the president is the signature of the commission. He has then acted on the advice and consent of the senate to his own nomination. The time for deliberation has then passed. He has decided. His judgment, on the advice and consent of the senate concurring with his nomination, has been made, and the officer is appointed. . . .

It is . . . decidedly the opinion of the court, that when a commission has been signed by the president, the appointment is made; and that the commission is complete when the seal of the United States has been affixed to it by the secretary of state.

Where an officer is removable at the will of the executive, the circumstance which completes his appointment is of no concern; because the act is at any time revocable; and the commission may be arrested, if still in the office. But when the officer is not removable at the will of the executive, the appointment is not revocable, and cannot be annulled. It has conferred legal rights which cannot be resumed. . . .

Mr. Marbury, then, since his commission was signed by the president, and sealed by the secretary of state, was appointed; and as the law creating the office, gave the officer a right to hold for five years, independent of the executive, the appointment was not revocable, but vested in the officer legal rights, which are protected by the laws of his country.

To withhold his commission, therefore, is an act deemed by the court not warranted by law, but violative of a vested legal right.

This brings us to the second inquiry; which is,

2d. If he has a right, and that right has been violated, do the laws of this country afford him a remedy?

The very essence of civil liberty certainly consists in the right of every individual to claim the protection of the laws, whenever he receives an injury. One of the first duties of government is to afford that protection. In Great Britain the king himself is sued in the respectful form of a petition, and he never fails to comply with the judgment of his court. . . .

By the constitution of the United States, the president is invested with certain important political powers, in the exercise of which he is to use his own discretion, and is accountable only to his country in his political character and to his own conscience. To aid him in the performance of these duties, he is authorized to appoint certain officers, who act by his authority, and in conformity with his orders.

In such cases, their acts are his acts; and whatever opinion may be entertained of the manner in which executive discretion may be used, still there exists, and can exist, no power to control that discretion. The subjects are political. They respect the nation, not individual rights, and being intrusted to the executive, the decision of the executive is conclusive. . . .

But when the legislature proceeds to impose on that officer other duties; when he is directed peremptorily to perform certain acts; when the rights of individuals are dependent on the performance of those acts; he is so far the officer of the law; is amenable to the laws for his conduct; and cannot at his discretion sport away the vested rights of others.

The conclusion from this reasoning is, that where the heads of departments are the political or confidential agents of the executive, merely to execute the will of the president, or rather to act in cases in which the executive possesses a constitutional or legal discretion, nothing can be more perfectly clear than that their acts are only politically examinable. But where a specific duty is assigned by law, and individual rights depend upon the performance of that duty, it seems equally clear that the individual who considers himself injured, has a right to resort to the laws of his country for a remedy. . . .

It is, then, the opinion of the Court,

1st. That by signing the commission of Mr. Marbury, the President of the United States appointed him a justice of peace for the county of Washington, in the District of Columbia; and that the seal of the United States, affixed thereto by the secretary of state, is conclusive testimony of the verity of the signature, and of the completion of the appointment; and that the appointment conferred on him a legal right to the office for the space of five years.

2d. That, having this legal title to the office, he has a consequent right to the commission; a refusal to deliver which is a plain violation of that right, for which the laws of his country afford him a remedy.

It remains to be inquired whether,

3d. He is entitled to the remedy for which he applies. This depends on,

1st. The nature of the writ applied for; and,

2d. The power of this court.

1st. The nature of the writ. . . .

[T]o render the *mandamus* a proper remedy, the officer to whom it is to be directed, must be one to whom, on legal principles, such writ may be directed; and the person applying for it must be without any other specific and legal remedy.

1st. With respect to the officer to whom it would be directed. The intimate political relation subsisting between the President of the United States and the heads of departments, necessarily renders any legal investigation of the acts of one of those high officers peculiarly irksome, as well as delicate; and excites some hesitation with respect to the propriety of entering into such investigation. Impressions are often received without much reflection or examination, and it is not wonderful that in such a case as this the assertion, by an individual, of his legal claims in a court of justice, to which claims it is the duty of that court to attend, should at first view be considered by some, as an attempt to intrude into the cabinet, and to intermeddle with the prerogatives of the executive.

It is scarcely necessary for the court to disclaim all pretensions to such jurisdiction. An extravagance, so absurd and excessive, could not have been entertained for a moment. The province of the court is, solely, to decide on the rights of individuals, not to inquire how the executive, or executive officers, perform duties in which they have a discretion. Questions in their nature political, or which are, by the constitution and laws, submitted to the executive, can never be made in this court.

But, if this be not such a question; if, so far from being an intrusion into the secrets of the cabinet, it respects a paper which, according to law, is upon record, and to a copy of which the law gives a right. . . .

If one of the heads of departments commits any illegal act, under colour of his office, by which an individual sustains an injury, it cannot be pretended that his office alone exempts him from being sued in the ordinary mode of proceeding, and being compelled to obey the judgment of the law. How, then, can his office exempt him from this particular mode of deciding on the legality of his conduct if the case be such a case as would, were any other individual the party complained of, authorize the process?

It is not by the office of the person to whom the writ is directed, but the nature of the thing to be done, that the propriety or impropriety of issuing a *mandamus* is to be determined. . . .

This, then, is a plain case for a *mandamus*, either to deliver the commission, or a copy of it from the record; and it only remains to be inquired,

Whether it can issue from this court.

The act to establish the judicial courts of the United States authorizes the Supreme Court "to issue writs of *mandamus* in cases warranted by the principles and usages of law, to any courts appointed, or persons holding office, under the authority of the United States."★

The secretary of state, being a person holding an office under the authority of the United States, is precisely within the letter of the description, and if this court is not authorized to issue a writ of *mandamus* to such an officer, it must be because the law is unconstitutional, and therefore absolutely incapable of conferring the authority, and assigning the duties which its words purport to confer and assign.

The constitution vests the whole judicial power of the United States in one supreme court, and such inferior courts as congress shall, from time to time, ordain and establish. This power is expressly extended to all cases arising under the laws of the United States; and, consequently, in some form, may be exercised over the present case; because the right claimed is given by a law of the United States.

In the distribution of this power it is declared that "the supreme court shall have original jurisdiction in all cases affecting ambassadors, other public ministers and consuls, and those in which a state shall be a party. In all other cases, the supreme court shall have appellate jurisdiction."

It has been insisted, at the bar, that as the original grant of jurisdiction, to the supreme and inferior courts, is general, and the clause, assigning original jurisdiction to the supreme court, contains no negative or restrictive words, the power remains to the legislature, to assign original jurisdiction to that court in other cases than those specified in the article which has been recited; provided those cases belong to the judicial power of the United States.

If it had been intended to leave it in the discretion of the legislature to apportion to the judicial power between the supreme and inferior courts according to the will of that body, it would certainly have been useless to have proceeded further than to have defined the judicial power, and the tribunals in which it should be vested. The subsequent part of the section is

---

★Note that Chief Justice Marshall selectively quotes from Section 13 of the Judiciary Act of 1789, which he construes ostensibly to confer authority on the Court to hear Marbury's case under the Court's original jurisdiction and, in turn, declares unconstitutional. The relevant part of Section 13 reads:

> The Supreme Court shall also have appellate jurisdiction from the circuit courts and courts of the several states, in the cases herein after specifically provided for; and shall have power to issue writs of prohibition to the district courts, when proceeding as courts of admiralty and maritime jurisdiction, and writs of *mandamus*, in cases warranted by the principles and usages of law, to any courts appointed, or persons holding office, under the authority of the United States.

mere surplusage, is entirely without meaning, if such is to be the construction. If congress remains at liberty to give this court appellate jurisdiction, where the constitution has declared their jurisdiction shall be original; and original jurisdiction where the constitution has declared it shall be appellate; the distribution of jurisdiction, made in the constitution, is form without substance.

Affirmative words are often, in their operation, negative of other objects than those affirmed; and in this case, a negative or exclusive sense must be given to them, or they have no operation at all.

It cannot be presumed that any clause in the constitution is intended to be without effect; and, therefore, such a construction is inadmissible, unless the words require it.

If the solicitude of the convention, respecting our peace with foreign powers, induced a provision that the supreme court should take original jurisdiction in cases which might be supposed to affect them; yet the clause would have proceeded no further than to provide for such cases, if no further restriction on the powers of congress had been intended. That they should have appellate jurisdiction in all other cases, with such exceptions as congress might make, is no restriction; unless the words be deemed exclusive of original jurisdiction.

When an instrument organizing fundamentally a judicial system, divides it into one supreme, and so many inferior courts as the legislature may ordain and establish; then enumerates its powers, and proceeds so far to distribute them, as to define the jurisdiction of the supreme court by declaring the cases in which it shall take original jurisdiction, and that in others it shall take appellate jurisdiction; the plain import of the words seems to be, that in one class of cases its jurisdiction is original, and not appellate; in the other it is appellate, and not original. If any other construction would render the clause inoperative, that is an additional reason for rejecting such other construction, and for adhering to their obvious meaning.

To enable this court, then, to issue a *mandamus*, it must be shown to be an exercise of appellate jurisdiction, or to be necessary to enable them to exercise appellate jurisdiction.

It has been stated at the bar that the appellate jurisdiction may be exercised in a variety of forms, and that if it be the will of the legislature that a *mandamus* should be used for that purpose, that will must be obeyed. This is true, yet the jurisdiction must be appellate, not original.

It is the essential criterion of appellate jurisdiction, that it revises and corrects the proceedings in a cause already instituted, and does not create that cause. Although, therefore, a *mandamus* may be directed to courts, yet to issue such a writ to an officer for the delivery of a paper, is in effect the same as to sustain an original action for that paper, and, therefore, seems not to belong to appellate, but to original jurisdiction. Neither is it necessary in such a case as this, to enable the court to exercise its appellate jurisdiction.

The authority, therefore, given to the supreme court, by the act establishing the judicial courts of the United States, to issue writs of *mandamus* to public officers, appears not to be warranted by the constitution; and it becomes necessary to inquire whether a jurisdiction so conferred can be exercised.

The question, whether an act, repugnant to the constitution, can become the law of the land, is a question deeply interesting to the United

States; but, happily, not of an intricacy proportioned to its interest. It seems only necessary to recognize certain principles, supposed to have been long and well established, to decide it.

That the people have an original right to establish, for their future government, such principles, as, in their opinion, shall most conduce to their own happiness is the basis on which the whole American fabric has been erected. The exercise of this original right is a very great exertion; nor can it, nor ought it, to be frequently repeated. The principles, therefore, so established, are deemed fundamental. And as the authority from which they proceed is supreme, and can seldom act, they are designed to be permanent.

This original and supreme will organizes the government, and assigns to different departments their respective powers. It may either stop here, or establish certain limits not to be transcended by those departments.

The government of the United States is of the latter description. The powers of the legislature are defined and limited; and that those limits may not be mistaken, or forgotten, the constitution is written. To what purpose are powers limited, and to what purpose is that limitation committed to writing, if these limits may, at any time, be passed by those intended to be restrained? The distinction between a government with limited and unlimited powers is abolished, if those limits do not confine the persons on whom they are imposed, and if acts prohibited and acts allowed, are of equal obligation. It is a proposition too plain to be contested, that the constitution controls any legislative act repugnant to it; or, that the legislature may alter the constitution by an ordinary act.

Between these alternatives there is no middle ground. The constitution is either a superior paramount law, unchangeable by ordinary means, or it is on a level with ordinary legislative acts, and, like other acts, is alterable when the legislature shall please to alter it.

If the former part of the alternative be true, then a legislative act contrary to the constitution is not law: if the latter part be true, then written constitutions are absurd attempts, on the part of the people, to limit a power in its own nature illimitable.

Certainly all those who have framed written constitutions contemplate them as forming the fundamental and paramount law of the nation, and, consequently, the theory of every such government must be, that an act of the legislature, repugnant to the constitution, is void.

This theory is essentially attached to a written constitution, and, is consequently, to be considered, by this court, as one of the fundamental principles of our society. It is not therefore to be lost sight of in the further consideration of this subject.

If an act of the legislature, repugnant to the constitution, is void, does it, notwithstanding its invalidity, bind the courts, and oblige them to give it effect? Or, in other words, though it be not law, does it constitute a rule as operative as if it was a law? This would be to overthrow in fact what was established in theory; and would seem, at first view, an absurdity too gross to be insisted on. It shall, however, receive a more attentive consideration.

It is emphatically the province and duty of the judicial department to say what the law is. Those who apply the rule to particular cases, must of necessity expound and interpret that rule. If two laws conflict with each other, the courts must decide on the operation of each.

So if a law be in opposition to the constitution; if both the law and the constitution apply to a particular case, so that the court must either decide that case conformably to the law, disregarding the constitution; or conformably to the constitution, disregarding the law; the court must determine which of these conflicting rules governs the case. This is of the very essence of judicial duty.

If, then, the courts are to regard the constitution, and the constitution is superior to any ordinary act of the legislature, the constitution, and not such ordinary act, must govern the case to which they both apply.

Those, then, who controvert the principle that the constitution is to be considered, in court, as a paramount law, are reduced to the necessity of maintaining that courts must close their eyes on the constitution, and see only the law.

This doctrine would subvert the very foundation of all written constitutions. It would declare that an act which, according to the principles and theory of our government, is entirely void, is yet, in practice, completely obligatory. It would declare that if the legislature shall do what is expressly forbidden, such act, notwithstanding the express prohibition, is in reality effectual. It would be given to the legislature a practical and real omnipotence, with the same breath which professes to restrict their powers within narrow limits. It is prescribing limits, and declaring that those limits may be passed at pleasure.

That it thus reduces to nothing what we have deemed the greatest improvement on political institutions, a written constitution, would of itself be sufficient, in America, where written constitutions have been viewed with so much reverence, for rejecting the construction. But the peculiar expressions of the constitution of the United States furnish additional arguments in favour of its rejection.

The judicial power of the United States is extended to all cases arising under the constitution.

Could it be the intention of those who gave this power, to say that in using it the constitution should not be looked into? That a case arising under the constitution should be decided without examining the instrument under which it arises?

This is too extravagant to be maintained.

In some cases, then, the constitution must be looked into by the judges. And if they can open it at all, what part of it are they forbidden to read or to obey?

There are many other parts of the constitution which serve to illustrate this subject.

It is declared that "no tax or duty shall be laid on articles exported from any state." Suppose a duty on the export of cotton, of tobacco, or of flour; and a suit instituted to recover it. Ought judgment to be rendered in such a case? Ought the judges to close their eyes on the constitution, and only see the law?

The constitution declares "that no bill of attainder or *ex post facto* law shall be passed."

If, however, such a bill should be passed, and a person should be prosecuted under it; must the court condemn to death those victims whom the constitution endeavors to preserve?

"No person," says the constitution, "shall be convicted of treason unless on the testimony of two witnesses to the same overt act, or on confession in open court."

Here the language of the constitution is addressed especially to the courts. It prescribes, directly for them, a rule of evidence not to be departed from. If the legislature should change that rule, and declare one witness, or a confession out of court, sufficient for conviction, must the constitutional principle yield to the legislative act?

From these, and many other selections which might be made, it is apparent, that the framers of the constitution contemplated that instrument as a rule for the government of courts, as well as of the legislature.

Why otherwise does it direct the judges to take an oath to support it? This oath certainly applies in an especial manner, to their conduct in their official character. How immoral to impose it on them, if they were to be used as the instruments, and the knowing instruments, for violating what they swear to support!

The oath of office, too, imposed by the legislature, is completely demonstrative of the legislative opinion on this subject. It is in these words: "I do solemnly swear that I will administer justice without respect to persons, and do equal right to the poor and to the rich; and that I will faithfully and impartially discharge all the duties incumbent on me as ————, according to the best of my abilities and understanding agreeably to the constitution and laws of the United States."

Why does a judge swear to discharge his duties agreeably to the constitution of the United States, if that constitution forms no rule for his government? if it is closed upon him, and cannot be inspected by him?

If such be the real state of things, this is worse than solemn mockery. To prescribe, or to take this oath, becomes equally a crime.

It is also not entirely unworthy of observation, that in declaring what shall be the *supreme law* of the land, *the constitution* itself is first mentioned; and not the laws of the United States generally, but those only which shall be made in *pursuance* of the constitution, have that rank.

Thus, the particular phraseology of the constitution of the United States confirms and strengthens the principle, supposed to be essential to all written constitutions, that a law repugnant to the constitution is void; and that *courts*, as well as other departments, are bound by that instrument.

The rule must be discharged.

Eakin v. Raub

12 SARGEANT & RAWLE 330 (PA., 1825)

In this case involving the power of the Pennsylvania Supreme Court to invalidate a state law, Justice John Bannister Gibson wrote a dissenting opinion aimed at refuting Chief Justice John Marshall's arguments for judicial review in *Marbury v. Madison* (1803) (see excerpt above). Note that Justice Gibson's criticism of *Marbury* was limited to the exercise of judicial review over coequal branches of government. While he contended that state courts had no power to overturn state laws deemed to violate the state constitution, he did not deny that state courts could strike down state laws that were inconsistent with federal law or the Constitution. Moreover, twenty years later, Justice Gibson repudiated the position taken in his opinion here. In *Norris v. Clymer*, 2 Pa. 277 (1845), he explained his change in opinion for two reasons. "The late convention (which drafted Pennsylvania's state constitution), by their silence, sanctioned the pretensions of the courts to deal freely with the Acts of the Legislature; and from experience of the necessity of the case."

■ ■ ■

☐ *Justice GIBSON, dissenting.*

I am aware, that a right [in the judiciary] to declare all unconstitutional acts void . . . is generally held as a professional dogma, but, I apprehend, rather as a matter of faith than of reason. I admit that I once embraced the same doctrine, but without examination, and I shall therefore state the arguments that impelled me to abandon it, with great respect for those by whom it is still maintained. But I may premise, that it is not a little remarkable, that although the right in question has all along been claimed by the judiciary, no judge has ventured to discuss it, except Chief Justice MARSHALL, and if the argument of a jurist so distinguished for the strength of his ratiocinative powers be found inconclusive, it may fairly be set down to the weakness of the position which he attempts to defend. . . .

I begin, then, by observing that in this country, the powers of the judiciary are divisible into those that are political and those that are purely civil. Every power by which one organ of the government is enabled to control another, or to exert an influence over its acts, is a political power. . . .

The constitution and the right of the legislature to pass the act, may be in collision. But is that a legitimate subject for judicial determination? If it be, the judiciary must be a peculiar organ, to revise the proceedings of the legislature, and to correct its mistakes; and in what part of the constitution are we to look for this proud pre-eminence? Viewing the matter in the opposite direction, what would be thought of an act of assembly in which it should be declared that the supreme court had, in a particular case, put a wrong construction on the constitution of the United States, and that the judgment should therefore be reversed? It would doubtless be thought a usurpation of judicial power. But it is by no means clear, that to declare a law void which has been enacted according to the forms prescribed in the constitution, is not a usurpation of legislative power. . . .

But it has been said to be emphatically the business of the judiciary, to ascertain and pronounce what the law is; and that this necessarily involves a consideration of the constitution. It does so: but how far? If the judiciary will inquire into anything besides the form of enactment, where shall it stop? . . .

In theory, all the organs of the government are of equal capacity; or, if not equal, each must be supposed to have superior capacity only for those things which peculiarly belong to it; and as legislation peculiarly involves the consideration of those limitations which are put on the law-making power, and the interpretation of the laws when made, involves only the construction of the laws themselves, it follows that the construction of the constitution in this particular belongs to the legislature, which ought therefore to be taken to have superior capacity to judge of the constitutionality of its own acts. But suppose all to be of equal capacity in every respect, why should one exercise a controlling power over the rest? That the judiciary is of superior rank, has never been pretended, although it has been said to be co-ordinate. It is not easy, however, to comprehend how the power which *gives* law to all the rest can be of no more than equal rank with one which receives it, and is answerable to the former for the observance of its statutes. Legislation is essentially an act of sovereign power; but the execution of the laws by instruments that are governed by prescribed rules and exercise no power of volition, is essentially otherwise. . . . It may be said, the power of the legislature, also, is limited by prescribed rules. It is *so*. But it is nevertheless, the power of the people, and sovereignty as far as it extends. It cannot be said, that the judiciary is coordinate merely because it is established by the constitution. If it were sufficient, sheriffs, registers of wills, and recorders of deeds, would be so too. Within the pale of their authority, the acts of these officers will have the power of the people for their support; but no one will pretend, they are of equal dignity with the acts of the legislature. Inequality of rank arises not from the manner in which the organ has been constituted, but from its essence and the nature of its functions; and the legislative organ is superior to every other, inasmuch as the power to will and to command, is essentially superior to the power to act and to obey. . . .

The oath to support the constitution is not peculiar to the judges, but is taken indiscriminately by every officer of the government, and is designed rather as a test of the political principles of the man, than to bind the officer in the discharge of his duty; otherwise it is difficult to determine what operation it is to have in the case of a recorder of deeds, for instance, who, in the execution of his office, has nothing to do with the constitution. But granting it to relate to the official conduct of the judge, as well as every other officer, and not to his political principles, still it must be understood in reference to supporting the constitution, *only as far as that may be involved in his official duty;* and, consequently, if his official duty does not comprehend an inquiry into the authority of the legislature, neither does his oath. . . .

But do not the judges do a positive act in violation of the constitution, when they give effect to an unconstitutional law? Not if the law has been passed according to the forms established in the constitution. The fallacy of the question is, in supposing that the judiciary adopts the acts of the legislature as its own; whereas the enactment of a law and the interpretation of it are not concurrent acts, and as the judiciary is not required to concur in the enactment, neither is it in the breach of the constitution which may be the consequence of the enactment. The fault is imputable to the legislature, and on it the responsibility exclusively rests. . . .

But it has been said, that this construction would deprive the citizen of the advantages which are peculiar to a written constitution, by at once declaring the power of the legislature in practice to be illimitable. . . . But there is no magic or inherent power in parchment and ink, to command respect and protect principles from violation. In the business of government a recurrence to first principles answers the end of an observation at sea with a view to correct the dead reckoning; and for this purpose, a written constitution is an instrument of inestimable value. It is of inestimable value, also, in rendering its first principles familiar to the mass of people; for, after all, there is no effectual guard against legislative usurpation but public opinion, the force of which, in this country is inconceivably great. . . .

For these reasons, I am of [the] opinion that it rests with the people, in whom full and absolute sovereign power resides, to correct abuses in legislation, by instructing their representatives to repeal the obnoxious act. What is wanting to plenary power in the government, is reserved by the people for their own immediate use; and to redress an infringement of their rights in this respect, would seem to be an accessory of the power thus reserved. It might, perhaps, have been better to vest the power in the judiciary; as it might be expected that its habits of deliberation, and the aid derived from the arguments of counsel, would more frequently lead to accurate conclusions. On the other hand, the judiciary is not infallible; and an error by it would admit of no remedy but a more distinct expression of the public will, through the extraordinary medium of a convention; whereas, an error by the legislature admits of a remedy by an exertion of the same will, in the ordinary exercise of the right of suffrage—a mode better calculated to attain the end, without popular excitement. It may be said, the people would probably not notice an error of their representatives. But they would as probably do so, notice an error of the judiciary; and, besides, it is a postulate in the theory of our government, and the very basis of the superstructure, that the people are wise, virtuous, and competent to manage their own affairs; and if they are not so, in fact, still every question of this sort must be determined according to the principles of the constitution, as it came from the hands of the framers, and the existence of a defect which was not foreseen, would not justify those who administer the government, in applying a corrective in practice, which can be provided only by convention. . . .

But in regard to an act of [a state] assembly, which is found to be in collision with the constitution, laws, or treaties of the *United States*, I take the duty of the judiciary to be exactly the reverse. By becoming parties to the federal constitution, the states have agreed to several limitations of their individual sovereignty, to enforce which, it was thought to be absolutely necessary to prevent them from giving effect to laws in violation of those limitations, through the instrumentality of their own judges. Accordingly, it is declared in the sixth article and second section of the federal constitution, that "This constitution, and the laws of the *United States* which shall be made in pursuance thereof, and all treaties made, or which shall be made under the authority of the *United States* shall be the *supreme law* of the land; and the *judges* in every *state* shall be BOUND thereby: anything in the *laws* or *constitution* of any *state* to the contrary notwithstanding."

President Roosevelt's Radio Broadcast, March 9, 1937

During President Franklin D. Roosevelt's first term (1933–1937), the Supreme Court by a vote of 5–4 invalidated much of his New

Deal program and plan for the country's economic recovery from the Great Depression. After his landslide reelection in November 1936, FDR proposed in February 1937 that Congress expand the size of the Court from nine to fifteen justices and thereby give him the chance to secure a majority sympathetic to his policies. On March 9, 1937, the Democratic president made the following radio address in an effort to marshal public support for his "Court-packing plan." But that same month, while the Senate Judiciary Committee was considering his proposal, Justice Owen Roberts, who had previously cast the crucial vote for overturning progressive economic legislation, switched sides and voted to uphold New Deal legislation. The Court's proverbial "switch-in-time-that-saved-nine" then contributed to the Democrat-dominated Senate's defeat of FDR's proposal. The constitutional crisis that loomed over the Court and the country in 1937 is discussed further in Volume 1, Chapter 6; and in this volume, Chapter 3.

■ ■ ■

Tonight, sitting at my desk in the White House, I make my first radio report to the people in my second term of office.★ . . .

In 1933 you and I knew that we must never let our economic system get completely out of joint again—that we could not afford to take the risk of another great depression.

We also became convinced that the only way to avoid a repetition of those dark days was to have a government with power to prevent and to cure the abuses and the inequalities which had thrown that system out of joint.

We then began a program of remedying those abuses and inequalities— to give balance and stability to our economic system—to make it bomb-proof against the causes of 1929.

Today we are only part-way through that program—and recovery is speeding up to a point where the dangers of 1929 are again becoming possible, not this week or month perhaps, but within a year or two.

National laws are needed to complete that program. Individual or local or state effort alone cannot protect us in 1937 any better than ten years ago. . . .

The American people have learned from the depression. For in the last three national elections an overwhelming majority of them voted a mandate that the Congress and the President begin the task of providing that protection—not after long years of debate, but now.

The Courts, however, have cast doubts on the ability of the elected Congress to protect us against catastrophe by meeting squarely our modern social and economic conditions. . . .

I [have] described the American form of Government as a three horse team provided by the Constitution to the American people so that their field might be plowed. The three horses are, of course, the three branches of government—the Congress, the Executive and the Courts. Two of the horses are pulling in unison today; the third is not. Those who have intimated that the President of the United States is trying to drive that team,

★From 1937 *Public Papers and Addresses of Franklin D. Roosevelt* (1941), 122.

overlook the simple fact that the President, as Chief Executive, is himself one of the three horses.

It is the American people themselves who are in the driver's seat.

It is the American people themselves who want the furrow plowed.

It is the American people themselves who expect the third horse to pull in unison with the other two.

I hope that you have re-read the Constitution of the United States. Like the Bible, it ought to be read again and again.

It is an easy document to understand when you remember that it was called into being because the Articles of Confederation under which the original thirteen States tried to operate after the Revolution showed the need of a National Government with power enough to handle national problems. In its Preamble, the Constitution states that it was intended to form a more perfect Union and promote the general welfare; and the powers given to the Congress to carry out those purposes can be best described by saying that they were all the powers needed to meet each and every problem which then had a national character and which could not be met by merely local action.

But the framers went further. Having in mind that in succeeding generations many other problems then undreamed of would become national problems, they gave to the Congress the ample broad powers "to levy taxes . . . and provide for the common defense and general welfare of the United States."

That, my friends, is what I honestly believe to have been the clear and underlying purpose of the patriots who wrote a Federal Constitution to create a National Government with national power, intended as they said, "to form a more perfect union . . . for ourselves and our posterity." . . .

But since the rise of the modern movement for social and economic progress through legislation, the Court has more and more often and more and more boldly asserted a power to veto laws passed by the Congress and State Legislatures in complete disregard of this original limitation.

In the last four years the sound rule of giving statutes the benefit of all reasonable doubt has been cast aside. The Court has been acting not as a judicial body, but as a policy-making body.

When the Congress has sought to stabilize national agriculture, to improve the conditions of labor, to safeguard business against unfair competition, to protect our national resources, and in many other ways, to serve our clearly national needs, the majority of the Court has been assuming the power to pass on the wisdom of these Acts of the Congress—and to approve or disapprove the public policy written into these laws.

That is not only my accusation. It is the accusation of most distinguished Justices of the present Supreme Court. I have not the time to quote to you all the language used by dissenting Justices in many of these cases. But in the case holding the Railroad Retirement Act unconstitutional, for instance, Chief Justice Hughes said in a dissenting opinion that the majority opinion was "a departure from sound principles," and placed "an unwarranted limitation upon the commerce clause." And three other Justices agreed with him. . . .

In the face of these dissenting opinions, there is no basis for the claim made by some members of the Court that something in the Constitution has compelled them regretfully to thwart the will of the people.

In the face of such dissenting opinions, it is perfectly clear, that as Chief Justice Hughes has said: "We are under a Constitution but the Constitution is what the Judges say it is."

The Court in addition to the proper use of its judicial functions has improperly set itself up as a third House of the Congress—a super-legislature, as one of the Justices has called it—reading into the Constitution words and implications which are not there, and which were never intended to be there.

We have, therefore, reached the point as a Nation where we must take action to save the Constitution from the Court and the Court from itself. We must find a way to take an appeal from the Supreme Court to the Constitution itself. We want a Supreme Court which will do justice under the Constitution—not over it. In our Courts we want a government of laws and not of men.

I want—as all Americans want—an independent judiciary as proposed by the framers of the Constitution. That means a Supreme Court that will enforce the Constitution as written—that will refuse to amend the Constitution by the arbitrary exercise of judicial power—amendment by judicial say-so. It does not mean a judiciary so independent that it can deny the existence of facts universally recognized. . . .

What is my proposal? It is simply this: whenever a Judge or Justice of any Federal Court has reached the age of seventy and does not avail himself of the opportunity to retire on a pension, a new member shall be appointed by the President then in office, with the approval, as required by the Constitution, of the Senate of the United States.

That plan has two chief purposes. By bringing into the Judicial system a steady and continuing stream of new and younger blood, I hope, first, to make the administration of all Federal justice speedier and, therefore, less costly; secondly, to bring to the decision of social and economic problems younger men who have had personal experience and contact with modern facts and circumstances under which average men have to live and work. This plan will save our national Constitution from hardening of the judicial arteries.

The number of Judges to be appointed would depend wholly on the decision of present Judges now over seventy, or those who would subsequently reach the age of seventy.

If, for instance, any one of the six Justices of the Supreme Court now over the age of seventy should retire as provided under the plan, no additional place would be created. Consequently, although there never can be more than fifteen, there may be only fourteen, or thirteen, or twelve. And there may be only nine.

There is nothing novel or radical about this idea. It seeks to maintain the Federal bench in full vigor. It has been discussed and approved by many persons of high authority ever since a similar proposal passed the House of Representatives in 1869.

Why was the age fixed at seventy? Because the laws of many States, the practice of the Civil Service, the regulations of the Army and Navy, and the rules of many of our Universities and of almost every great private business enterprise, commonly fix the retirement age at seventy years or less.

The statute would apply to all the Courts in the Federal system. There is general approval so far as the lower Federal courts are concerned. The plan has met opposition only so far as the Supreme Court of the United States itself is concerned. If such a plan is good for the lower courts it certainly ought to be equally good for the highest Court from which there is no appeal.

Those opposing this plan have sought to arouse prejudice and fear by crying that I am seeking to "pack" the Supreme Court and that a baneful precedent will be established.

What do they mean by the words "packing the Court"?

Let me answer this question with a bluntness that will end all *honest* misunderstanding of my purposes.

If by that phrase "packing the Court" it is charged that I wish to place on the bench spineless puppets who would disregard the law and would decide specific cases as I wished them to be decided, I make this answer—that no President fit for his office would appoint, and no Senate of honorable men fit for their office would confirm, that kind of appointees to the Supreme Court.

But if by that phrase the charge is made that I would appoint and the Senate would confirm Justices worthy to sit beside present members of the Court who understand those modern conditions—that I will appoint Justices who will not undertake to override the judgment of the Congress on legislative policy—that I will appoint Justices who will act as Justices and not as legislators—if the appointment of such Justices can be called "packing the Courts," then I say that I and with me the vast majority of the American people favor doing just that thing—now.

Is it a dangerous precedent for the Congress to change the number of the Justices? The Congress has always had, and will have, that power. The number of Justices has been changed several times before—in the Administrations of John Adams and Thomas Jefferson,—both signers of the Declaration of Independence—Andrew Jackson, Abraham Lincoln and Ulysses S. Grant. . . .

It is the clear intention of our public policy to provide for a constant flow of new and younger blood into the Judiciary. Normally every President appoints a large number of District and Circuit Judges and a few members of the Supreme Court. Until my first term practically every President of the United States had appointed at least one member of the Supreme Court. President Taft appointed five members and named a Chief Justice—President Wilson three—President Harding four including a Chief Justice—President Coolidge one—President Hoover three including a Chief Justice.

Such a succession of appointments should have provided a Court well-balanced as to age. But chance and the disinclination of individuals to leave the Supreme bench have now given us a Court in which five Justices will be over seventy-five years of age before next June and one over seventy. Thus a sound public policy has been defeated.

I now propose that we establish by law an assurance against any such ill-balanced Court in the future. I propose that hereafter, when a Judge reaches the age of seventy, a new and younger Judge shall be added to the Court automatically. In this way I propose to enforce a sound public policy by law instead of leaving the composition of our Federal Courts, including the highest, to be determined by chance or the personal decision of individuals.

If such a law as I propose is regarded as establishing a new precedent—is it not a most desirable precedent? . . .

This plan of mine is no attack on the Court; it seeks to restore the Court to its rightful and historic place in our system of Constitutional Government and to have it resume its high task of building anew on the Constitution "a system of living law."

■ Inside the Court

The 1937 "Constitutional Crisis" and the Court's "Switch-in-Time-That-Saved-Nine"

During President Franklin D. Roosevelt's first term, the Court invalidated most of the early New Deal program and other progressive legislation, which in turn impeded the country's recovery from the Great Depression. In 1935 FDR proposed the Social Security Act, along with other major legislation, that appeared likely to be struck down because Justice Owen Roberts (an appointee of President Hoover) had cast his vote with the most conservative justices—Justices George Sutherland, James McReynolds, Pierce Butler, and Willis Van Devanter. They were called the "Four Horsemen" because they voted together, regularly arrived at the Court in the same car, and were portrayed as the allegorical figures of the Apocalypse associated with death and destruction. That bare majority struck down two corner-stones of the New Deal—the National Recovery Act and the Agricultural Adjustment Act. See, for example, *Schechter Poultry Corporation v. United States* (1935) (excerpted in Vol. 1, Ch. 4). Then, in June 1936 by a five-to-four vote, the Court struck down a New York state law establishing minimum wages for women and children in *Morehead v. New York ex rel. Tipaldo*, 298 U.S. 587 (1936). The case had asked the Court to distinguish, but not overrule, *Adkins v. Children's Hospital*, 261 U.S. 525 (1923), in which a bare majority invalidated the District of Columbia's minimum wage law for women and made clear that the *Lochner* era was still alive; see *Lochner v. New York* (1905) (excerpted and discussed in Vol. 1, Ch. 9, and Ch. 3).

Still, in his first term FDR had no opportunities to fill a seat on the high bench. In February 1937 after his landslide reelection in November 1936, Roosevelt proposed judicial reforms allowing him to expand the size of the Court to fifteen by appointing a new member for every justice over seventy years of age. In the spring of 1937, however, when the Senate Judiciary Committee was debating FDR's "Court-packing plan," the Court abruptly upheld major pieces of New Deal legislation. Justice Roberts appeared to have (but in fact had already) changed his mind and in March abandoned the Four Horsemen in *West Coast Hotel v. Parrish* (1937) (excerpted in Vol. 1, Ch. 9, and here in Ch. 3) to uphold Washington state's minimum-wage law. Two weeks later, in *National Labor Relations Board v. Jones & Laughlin Steel Corporation* (1937) (excerpted in Vol. 1, Ch. 6), he again voted to affirm a major piece of New Deal legislation, the National Labor Relations Act.

The Court's "switch-in-time-that-saved nine" was widely speculated to have been due to FDR's Court-packing plan. Yet, even though the rulings did not come down until the spring, Justice Roberts had voted in conference to overturn *Adkins* in December 1936, two months before FDR announced his plan. At that conference the Court split four to four because Justice Stone was absent due to illness and Chief Justice Hughes proposed putting off a final vote until Justice Stone returned in order to obtain a firm five-to-four vote in *West Coast Hotel Co. v. Parrish*. The reversal of the Court's position in *West Coast Hotel*, nonetheless, contributed to the Senate Judiciary Committee's rejection of FDR's proposal in May, as well as popular speculation that the Court had made "a switch in time to save nine."

However, as Justice Frankfurter (1939–1962), an FDR intimate and one of his appointees, explained in a letter to his former clerk and later long-time professor at Harvard Law School:

> Robert[s], J. was no doubt unwise in not being more explicit about his position than the Court's opinion in *Tipaldo* indicated. But is inexcusable . . . to talk about Roberts's joining in *West Coast Hotel Company v. Parrish* as a "crucial switch." The fact is that Roberts did not switch. He was prepared in [*Morehead v.*] *Tipaldo* to make a majority overruling *Adkins*. He was not prepared to distinguish *Adkins*. Since there was no majority for overruling *Adkins* he was in the majority in the *Morehead* case on the basis of which *Morehead* was decided. What was that basis? [Chief Justice] Hughes stated it in *Parrish*:
>
> > That view led to the affirmance by this Court of the judgment in the *Morehead* case, as the Court considered that the only question before it was whether the *Adkins* case was distinguishable and that reconsideration of that decision had not been sought.

Chief Justice Hughes also later recalled in his autobiographical notes: "[A]s to Justice Roberts, I feel that I am able to say with definitiveness that his view in favor of [the 1937] decisions of the Court would have been the same if the President's bill had never been proposed. The Court acted with complete independence."

As it happened, Justice Van Devanter—one of FDR's staunchest opponents—subsequently told the president that he would resign at the end of the term. FDR had the first of eight appointments and the elevation of Justice Stone to chief justice over the next six years. He thereby infused a progressive/liberal philosophy into the Court. Although his

(continues)

■ INSIDE THE COURT
The 1937 "Constitutional Crisis" and the Court's
"Switch-in-Time-that-Saved-Nine" (continued)

---

plan to enlarge the size of the Court failed, FDR succeeded in packing the Court and fundamentally turning around the direction of
constitutional law.

Sources: Justice Felix Frankfurter Papers, Letter to Paul Freund (October 18,
1953), Box 184, Manuscripts Room, Library of Congress; and David Danelski
and Joseph Tulchin, eds., *The Autobiographical Notes of Charles Evans Hughes*
313 (Cambridge: Harvard University Press, 1973). See also Barry Cushman,
Rethinking the New Deal Court: The Structure of a Constitutional Revolution (New
York: Oxford University Press, 1998); Marian McKenna, *Franklin Roosevelt
and the Great Constitutional War: The Court-packing Crisis of 1937* (New York:
Fordham University Press, 2002); James Simon, *FDR and Chief Justice Hughes:
The President, the Supreme Court, and the Epic Battle Over the New Deal* (New
York: Simon & Schuster, 2012); and Edward Carter and Edward Adams, "Jus-
tice Owen J. Roberts on 1937," 15 *Green Bag* 2d 375 (2012).

B | *The Politics of Constitutional Interpretation*

Constitutional interpretation and law, Justice Felix Frankfurter observed,
"is not at all a science, but applied politics."[1] The Constitution, of
course, is a political document and as a written document is not self-
interpreting; its interpretation is political. *How* the Constitution should
be interpreted is thus as controversial as the ongoing debate over *who*
should interpret it.

For much of the nineteenth century, theories of constitutional
interpretation were generally not debated.[2] The Court's interpretation
of the Constitution, of course, remained politically controversial. Yet,
the great debates between Jeffersonian-Republicans and Federalists centered on disagreements over fundamental principles of constitutional
politics (the power and structure of government and guarantees for civil
rights and liberties), rather than competing interpretative theories. Their
struggle was over rival political philosophies and interpretations of the
political system created by the Constitution. That struggle continues
except that contemporary debates, within the Court and the legal com-

munity, tend to be more complex and linked to rival theories of constitutional interpretation that aim to justify or criticize the Court's exercise of judicial review.

In 1833, for example, Justice Joseph Story in his influential *Commentaries on the Constitution of the United States* saw no need to offer a theory of constitutional interpretation, explaining that

> [t]he reader must not expect to find in these pages any novel views and novel constructions of the Constitution. I have not the ambition to be the author of any new plan of interpreting the theory of the Constitution, or of enlarging or narrowing its powers by ingenious subtleties and learned doubts. . . . Upon subjects of government, it has always appeared to me, that metaphysical refinements are out of place. A constitution of government is addressed to the common sense of the people, and never was designed for trials of logical skill or visionary speculation.[3]

Story assumed that "[t]he first and fundamental rule in the interpretation of all instruments is, to construe them according to the sense of the terms and the intention of the parties."[4] This "plain meaning rule" was set forth by Chief Justice John Marshall in *Sturges v. Crowninshield*, 17 U.S. 122 (1819):

> [A]lthough the spirit of an instrument, especially of a constitution, is to be respected not less than its letter, yet the spirit is to be collected chiefly from its words. . . . [I]f, in any case, the plain meaning of a provision, not contradicted by any other provision in the same instrument, is to be disregarded, because we believe the framers of that instrument could not intend what they say, it must be one in which the absurdity and injustice of applying the provision to the case, would be so monstrous that all mankind would, without hesitation, unite in rejecting the application.

While the plain meaning of the Constitution for Story and Marshall was derived from a commonsense, rather than a literal, reading of the Constitution, Jeffersonian-Republicans nevertheless charged them with distorting the plain meaning of the document to advance their nationalistic political vision.

One reason political struggles in the nineteenth century did not invite debates over competing theories of constitutional interpretation is that Federalists and Jeffersonian-Republicans largely professed acceptance of the English *declaratory theory of law*. This theory, or philosophy, of legal positivism holds that judges have no discretion, make no law, but simply discover and "declare" the law.[5] According to one of the most widely read English jurists, Sir William Blackstone, in his

Commentaries on the Laws of England (1765–1768), judges were merely the "depositories of the laws; the living oracles" of law. Hamilton and Marshall considered themselves Blackstonians; judges, Hamilton wrote in *The Federalist*, No. 78, "may truly be said to have neither force nor will, but merely judgment."

By the late nineteenth century, the Blackstonian theory of law was under sharp attack. Oliver Wendell Holmes (1841–1935) was one of the first to debunk the idea that law is "a brooding omnipresence in the sky."[6] In his words, "The life of the law has not been logic; it has been experience. The felt necessities of the time, the prevalent moral and political theories, intuitions of public policy, avowed or unconscious, even the prejudices which judges share with their fellow-men, have had a good deal more to do than the syllogism in determining the rules by which men should be governed."[7] Holmes took it for granted that judges make law and pointed toward the empirical study of law: "The prophecies of what the courts will do in fact, and nothing more pretentious, are what I mean by the law."[8] Nor was Holmes alone in the revolt against legal formalism and the "mechanical jurisprudence" associated with the declaratory theory of judicial decision making.[9] Roscoe Pound (1870–1964), the founder of "sociological jurisprudence" and dean of Harvard Law School, encouraged the use of sociology and the study of law in relation to changing social forces. Unlike Holmes, though, Pound also encouraged judges to creatively mold law to the needs of society; judges should become "social engineers."[10]

One immediate consequence of this revolt against legal formalism was the innovation in legal argumentation that became known as "the Brandeis brief," after its author, a progressive legal reformer and later justice, Louis D. Brandeis. In 1908, in support of Oregon's law limiting working hours for women, Brandeis filed a brief in *Muller v. Oregon*, 208 U.S. 412 (1908), which included only two pages of legal argumentation, followed by ninety-seven pages of statistics and other social science data documenting the health risks for women working long hours. Drawing on social science in legal argumentation was necessary, claimed Brandeis, if law was to keep "pace with the rapid development of our political, economic, and social ideals."[11]

By the 1920s and 1930s a diverse group of law professors, political scientists, economists, and sociologists emerged, calling themselves "American legal realists."[12] They further questioned the determinacy of formal legal rules and the facts of cases for judicial decision-making, thereby underscoring that judges interpret (and manipulate) both legal rules and the facts when deciding cases.[13] Karl Llewellyn, one of the most influential legal realists, brought these insights to bear on constitutional interpretation when calling for a "jurisprudence of a living Constitution":

A "written constitution" is a system of unwritten practices in which the Document in question, by virtue of men's attitudes, has *a little influence. Where it makes no important difference which way the decision goes,* the Text—in the absence of countervailing practice— is an excellent traffic light. . . . The view advanced here *sounds* unorthodox. It sounds unorthodox only because it puts into words the *tacit* doing of the Court, and draws from that doing conclusions not to be avoided by a candid child. . . . Whatever the Court has *said*, it has repeatedly turned to established governmental practice in search of norms. What the Court has *said*, it has shaped the living Constitution to the needs of the day as it felt them. The whole expansion of the due process clause has been an enforcement of the majority's ideal of government-as-it-should-be, running free of the language of the Document.[14]

The Supreme Court was not immune from this change in legal thinking. On the bench sat Holmes (1902–1932), Brandeis (1916–1939), Benjamin Cardozo (1932–1938),[15] Hugo L. Black (1937–1971), Felix Frankfurter (1939–1962), and William O. Douglas (1939–1975), among other legal progressives. Moreover, even judicial conservatives on the Court no longer denied that the process of interpreting the Constitution involves making law. As Chief Justice Harlan F. Stone, a political and judicial conservative, reflected in a letter to Princeton's political scientist Edward Corwin, "I always thought the real villain in the play was Blackstone, who gave to both lawyers and judges artificial notions of the law which, when applied to constitutional interpretation made the Constitution a mechanical and inadequate instrument of government."[16] Justice Frankfurter, a former liberal professor at Harvard Law School who became an advocate of judicial self-restraint on the bench, elaborated his view in a letter to Justice Hugo Black:

> I think one of the evil features, a very evil one, about all this assumption that judges only find the law and don't make it, often becomes the evil of a lack of candor. By covering up the law-making function of judges, we miseducate the people and fail to bring out into the open the real responsibility of judges for what they do. . . .
>
> That phrase "judicial legislation" has become ever since a staple of a term of condemnation. I, too, am opposed to judicial legislation in its invidious sense; but I deem equally mischievous—because founded on an untruth and an impossible aim—the notion that judges merely announce the law which they find and do not themselves inevitably have a share in the law-making. Here, as elsewhere, the difficulty comes from arguing in terms of absolutes when the matter at hand is conditioned by circumstances, is contingent upon the everlasting problem of how far is too far and how much is too much. Judges as you well know, cannot escape the

responsibility of filling in gaps which the finitude of even the most imaginative legislation renders inevitable. . . .

So the problem is not whether judges make the law, but when and how and how much. Holmes put it in his highbrow way, that "they can do so only interstitially; they are confined from molar to molecular motions." I used to say to my students that legislatures make law wholesale, judges retail.[17]

Once constitutional interpretation was candidly conceded to be a lawmaking process, the Court and its commentators squarely faced what has been called the Madisonian dilemma and "the counter-majoritarian difficulty" for judicial review. As former judge and unsuccessful 1987 Supreme Court nominee Robert Bork explains,

The United States was founded as what we now call a Madisonian system, one which allows majorities to rule in wide areas of life simply because they are majorities, but which also holds that individuals have some freedoms that must be exempt from majority control. The dilemma is that neither the majority nor the minority can be trusted to define the proper spheres of democratic authority and individual liberty. The first would court tyranny by the majority; the second tyranny by the minority.[18]

When overturning legislation, the Court exercises a counter-majoritarian power and substitutes its interpretation of the Constitution for that of elected representatives. Theories or rationalizations of the Court's interpretation of the Constitution thus appear necessary to justify the Court's countermajoritarian role in American politics, especially in the last sixty years as the Court increasingly overturned legislation in defense of civil rights and liberties.

In addition, in the aftermath of the American legal realist movement, legal scholarship became more pluralistic and interdisciplinary. Again quoting Judge Bork:

The fact is that the law has little intellectual or structural resistance to outside influences, influences that should properly remain outside. The striking, and peculiar, fact . . . is that the law possesses very little theory about itself. . . . This theoretical emptiness at its center makes law, particularly constitutional law, unstable, a ship with a great deal of sail but a very shallow keel, vulnerable to the winds of intellectual or moral fashion, which it then validates as the commands of our most basic compact.[19]

Since World War II, legal scholars have turned not only toward moral and political philosophy as a guide for constitutional interpretation and the Court's exercise of judicial review, but they have also called for the development of a "political jurisprudence," combining normative theory with empirical studies;[20] proposed an economic approach to law, which would make rights turn on cost-risk-benefit analysis;[21] drawn on theories of literary criticism;[22] and advocated "legal pragmatism."[23] Still others in the feminist, Critical Race Theory, and the Critical Legal Studies movements attack theories of liberal legalism in an effort to deconstruct legal reasoning and law to show its drawbacks for minorities, women, and the poor.[24]

The rest of this section surveys and illustrates various theories of constitutional interpretation in terms of two broad approaches that have come to be known as *interpretivism* and *noninterpretivism*. Broadly speaking, interpretivists hold that constitutional interpretation should be limited solely to the text and historical context of particular provisions of the Constitution and Bill of Rights. By contrast, noninterpretivists maintain that constitutional interpretation frequently requires going beyond the text and historical context of specific provisions to articulate and apply broader principles of constitutional politics. Neither approach is inextricably linked to either a liberal or a conservative political philosophy; for example, a predominantly conservative Court in the late nineteenth century invented and wrote into constitutional law a "liberty of contract" to strike down progressive economic legislation (see Vol. 1, Ch. 9 or Ch. 3), while in the twentieth century a more liberal Court proclaimed and enforced a "right of privacy" to overturn legislation restricting the use of contraceptives and the availability of abortions (see Ch. 11). Moreover, the distinction between interpretivists and noninterpretivists is one of degree, not a difference in kind.

Notes

1. Felix Frankfurter, in *Law and Politics*, ed. E. Prichard Jr., and Archibald Macleish (New York: Harcourt, Brace, 1939), 6.

2. See Robert H. Bork, "Styles in Constitutional Theory," 1984 *Supreme Court Historical Society Yearbook* 53 (1985).

3. Joseph Story, *Commentaries on the Constitution of the United States* (Durham, NC: Carolina Academic Press, 1987), vi, reprint of 1833 ed.

4. Story, *Commentaries on the Constitution of the United States*, 135.

5. See, generally, Lord Lloyd, *Lloyd's Introduction to Jurisprudence*, 5th ed. (London: Stevens & Sons, 1985); H. L. A. Hart, *Essays in Jurisprudence and Philosophy* (Oxford, UK: Clarendon Press, 1983), chs. 1–5, 13; William Nelson, *Americanization of the Common Law* (Cambridge, MA: Harvard University Press, 1975); and Morton Horwitz, *The Transformation of American Law, 1780–1860* (Cambridge, MA: Harvard University Press, 1977).

6. *Southern Pacific Co. v. Jensen*, 244 U.S. 205 (1917).

7. Oliver W. Holmes, *The Common Law* (Boston: Little, Brown, 1881), 1.

8. Oliver W. Holmes, "The Path of Law," 10 *Harvard Law Review* 39 (1897).

9. See, generally, Morton White, *Social Thought in America: The Revolt against Formalism* (New York: Viking Press, 1949); and Benjamin Twiss, *Lawyers and the Constitution* (Princeton, NJ: Princeton University Press, 1942).

10. See Roscoe Pound, *An Introduction to the Philosophy of Law* (New Haven, CT: Yale University Press, 1922).

11. Louis Brandeis, "The Living Law," 10 *Illinois Law Review* 461 (1916).

12. See Wilfred Rumble, *American Legal Realism* (Ithaca, NY: Cornell University Press, 1968).

13. See Jerome Frank, *Law and the Modern Mind* (New York: Coward-McCann, 1930), and *Courts on Trial* (Princeton, NJ: Princeton University Press, 1949).

14. Karl Llewellyn, "The Constitution as an Institution," 34 *Columbia Law Review* 39–40 (1934).

15. See Benjamin Cardozo's highly acclaimed *The Nature of the Judicial Process* (New Haven, CT: Yale University Press, 1921).

16. Letter to E. Corwin, November 5, 1942, in Harlan F. Stone Papers, Box 10, Library of Congress, Washington, DC.

17. Letter to Justice Black, December 15, 1939, in Frankfurter Papers, Box 13, LC.

18. Bork, "Styles in Constitutional Theory," 53.

19. Robert H. Bork, "Tradition and Morality in Constitutional Law," in David M. O'Brien, ed., *Judges on Judging*, 5th ed. (Washington, DC: C. Q. Press, 2017).

20. See Martin Shapiro, "Political Jurisprudence," 52 *Kentucky Law Review* 294 (1964); Harry Stumpf, Martin Shapiro, David Danelski, Austin Sarat, and David O'Brien, "Whither Political Jurisprudence?: A Symposium," 36 *Western Political Quarterly* 533 (1983).

21. See, for example, Richard Posner, *Economic Analysis of Law*, 2nd ed. (Boston: Little, Brown, 1977).

22. See William Bishin and Christopher Stone, *Law, Language and Ethics* (Mineola, NY: Foundation Press, 1972); James White, *The Legal Imagination* (Chicago: University of Chicago Press, 1973); James White, *When Words Lose Their Meaning* (Chicago: University of Chicago Press, 1984); Richard Posner, *Law and Literature: A Misunderstood Relation* (Cambridge, MA: Harvard University Press, 1988); and James White, *Justice as Translation* (Chicago: University of Chicago Press, 1990).

23. See, for example, Richard Posner, *The Problems of Jurisprudence* (Cambridge, MA: Harvard University Press, 1990); Richard Posner, *The Problematics of Moral and Legal Theory* (Cambridge, MA: Harvard University Press, 1999): Stephen Breyer, *Active Liberty: Interpreting Our Democratic Constitution* (New York: Knopf, 2005).

24. See David Kairys, ed., *The Politics of Law*, 3rd ed. (New York: Pantheon, 1998); and Editors of the Harvard Law Review, *Essays on Critical Legal Studies* (Cambridge, MA: Harvard Law Review Association, 1986); Catharine MacKinnon, *Only Words* (Cambridge, MA: Harvard University Press, 1993); Richard Delgado et al., eds., *Critical Race Theory* (Philadelphia: Temple University Press, 1999); and Kimberle Crenshaw, Neil Gotanda, Gary Peller, and Kendell Thomas, eds., *Critical Race Theory: The Key Writings That Formed the Movement* (New York: The New Press, 1995).

■ (1) THE TEXT AND HISTORICAL CONTEXT

The Supreme Court has been criticized by presidents from Thomas Jefferson to Ronald Reagan and George W. Bush for departing from a "strict" or "literal" interpretation of the Constitution. During the 1968 presidential election campaign, for instance, Republican nominee Richard Nixon attacked the "liberal jurisprudence" of the Warren Court (1953–1969) and promised to appoint only strict constructionists to the bench. *Strict constructionists* hold that constitutional interpretation should be confined to the "four corners" of the document, the literal language of the text of the Constitution.

Within the Court, Chief Justice Roger Taney expressed a strong version of strict constructionism in *Dred Scott v. Sandford*, 60 U.S. 393 (1857) (see Ch. 12), when holding that blacks were not citizens of the United States within the meaning of "citizens" in Article III:

> No one, we presume, supposes that any change in public opinion or feeling, in relation to this unfortunate race [of blacks], in the civilized nations of Europe or in this country, should induce the court to give to the words of the Constitution a more liberal construction in their favor than they were intended to bear when the instrument was framed and adopted. . . .

> It [the Constitution] speaks not only in the same words, but with the same meaning and intent with which it spoke when it came from the hands of its framers, and was voted on and adopted by the people of the United States. Any other rule of construction would abrogate the judicial character of this Court and make it the mere reflex of the popular opinion or passion of the day.

This version of strict constructionism unrealistically (or disingenuously) denies the basic choices involved in constitutional interpretation. For example, much turns on whether the Court analyzes church–state controversies from the perspective of the First Amendment's free exercise clause or its establishment clause (see Ch. 6). When applying the Fourth Amendment's guarantee against "unreasonable searches and seizures," the Warren Court chose to enforce strictly the requirements specified in that amendment's warrants and probable cause clauses. By contrast, the Burger Court (1969–1986), Rehnquist Court (1986–2005), and Roberts Court (2005–) tended to give less force to those requirements by relying instead on the justices' reading of what is "reasonable" under the amendment's reasonableness clause. Whether the Fourth Amendment is enforced primarily in terms of its reasonableness clause or its warrants and probable cause clauses represents a basic constitutional choice with important consequences for individual rights and law enforcement interests (see Ch. 7).

Justice Hugo Black claimed to be an "absolutist," a "literalist." In his words:

> My view is, without deviation, without exception, without any if's, but's, or whereas, that freedom of speech means that government shall not do anything to people, or, in the words of the Magna Carta, move against people, either for the views they have or the views they express or the words they speak or write. Some people would have you believe that this is a very radical position, and maybe it is. But all I am doing is following what to me is the clear working of the First Amendment that "Congress shall make no law . . . abridging the freedom of speech or of the press."[1]

However, Justice Black acknowledged that the Constitution presents some interpretive problems and constitutional choices. In the controversy over the Court's application of the Bill of Rights to the states under the Fourteenth Amendment, for instance, Black became convinced that those guarantees were included in the amendment's privileges or immunities clause, whereas other justices contended that they were included in the Fourteenth Amendment's due process clause (see Ch. 4).

Justice Black's absolutism was in response to the Court's *balancing* of First Amendment freedoms against governmental interests in national security in cases like *Dennis v. United States*, 341 U.S. 494 (1951) (see Ch. 5), under the guise of the "clear and present danger" test. He opposed the Court's invention and use of such tests and metaphors. Still, much of constitutional law consists of metaphors created by the Court when explaining and applying constitutional provisions; consider the debates over executive privilege (see Vol. 1, Ch. 4), states' sovereignty (see Vol. 1, Ch. 7), the liberty of contract (see Vol. 1, Ch. 9 or Ch. 3), the high wall of separation between church and state (see Ch. 6), or the controversy over whether the Constitution is color-blind (see Ch. 12).

Interpretivism is usually only the beginning, not the end, of constitutional interpretation. The most frequently contested guarantees of the Constitution are neither unambiguous nor amenable to a literal or strict interpretation. What is the literal meaning of the reasonableness clause of the Fourth Amendment, for example, or of the due process and equal protection clauses of the Fourteenth Amendment? Nor do interpretivists, like Justice Black, deny First Amendment protection for posters and songs on the ground that they are not strictly speaking "speech"; although Black drew a line at extending protection to speech-plus-conduct and "symbolic speech" (see Ch. 5).

Crucial provisions in the Constitution have what philosophers call an "open texture."[2] They are framed in general terms that are nonexhaustive of all future applications and have an essential incompleteness in dictating unforeseeable applications. The commerce clause in Article I, for example, gives Congress the power to regulate interstate commerce but fails to define *interstate commerce*. No one today, though, contends that interstate commerce should include only the methods of transportation available in 1787 or exclude modes of commerce, such as telecommunications and the Internet, that were unforeseen by the Constitutional Convention.

These are only some of the problems with strict constructionism, as federal court of appeals Judge Richard Posner notes in an essay titled, "What Am I? A Potted Plant? The Case against Strict Constructionism." Moreover, Posner underscores that nothing in the Constitution commands the Court to construe either "strictly" or "broadly" the document:

> Even the decision to read the Constitution narrowly, and thereby "restrain" judicial interpretation, is not a decision that can be read directly from the text. The Constitution does not say, "Read me broadly," "Read me narrowly." That decision must be made a matter of political theory, and will depend on such things as one's view of the springs of judicial legitimacy and of the relative competence of courts and legislatures in dealing with particular types of issues.[3]

Strict constructionism is incomplete as a theory of interpretation and inadequately deals with the fact that the Constitution was framed in generalities in order to express general principles. Because this is so, interpretivists often turn to the historical context of the Constitution. Consider, for example, the call for a *jurisprudence of original intent* by Ronald Reagan's attorney general, Edwin Meese III:

> As the "faithful guardians of the Constitution," the judges were expected to resist any political effort to depart from the literal provisions of the Constitution. The text of the document and the original intention of those who framed it would be the judicial standard in giving effect to the Constitution. . . . [But] it seems fair to conclude that far too many of the court's opinions are, on the whole, more policy choices than articulations of constitutional principle. The voting blocs, the arguments, all reveal a greater allegiance to what the court thinks constitutes sound public policy than to a deference to what the Constitution—its text and intention—demands.[4]

Meese was not the first to contend that the text and the Framers' intent should solely guide constitutional interpretation.[5] Nonetheless, he sparked considerable debate and provoked Justice William J. Brennan to respond in a speech, observing,

> In its most doctrinaire incarnation, this view demands that Justices discern exactly what the Framers thought about the question under consideration and simply follow that intention in resolving the case before them. It is a view that feigns self-effacing deference to the specific judgments of those who forged our original social compact. But in truth it is little more than arrogance cloaked as humility. It is arrogant to pretend that from our vantage we can gauge accurately the intent of the Framers on application of principle to specific, contemporary questions. All too often, sources of potential enlightenment such as records of the ratification debates provide sparse or ambiguous evidence of the original intention. Typically, all that can be gleaned is that the Framers themselves did not agree about the application or meaning of particular constitutional provisions, and hid their differences in cloaks of generality. Indeed, it is far from clear whose intention is relevant—that of the drafters, the congressional disputants, or the ratifiers in the states?—or even whether the idea of an original intention is a coherent way of thinking about a jointly drafted document drawing its authority from a general assent of the states. And apart from the problematic nature of the sources, our distance of two centuries cannot but work as a prism refracting all we perceive. . . .
>
> We current Justices read the Constitution in the only way that we can: as [Twenty-first] Century Americans. We look to the history of the time of framing and to the intervening history of interpretation. But the ultimate question must be, what do the words of the text mean in our time. For the genius of the Constitution rests not in any static meaning it might have had in a world that is dead and gone, but in the adaptability of its great principles to cope with current problems and current needs. What the Constitution's fundamentals meant to the wisdom of other times cannot be their measure to the vision of our time. Similarly, what those fundamentals mean for us, our descendants will learn, cannot be the measure to the vision of their time.[6]

As Justice Brennan suggests, there are methodological difficulties with a "jurisprudence of original intent." For one thing, determining "intent" is a subjective enterprise; it proposes to discover what the Framers had in mind when drafting and ratifying the Constitution. But as already noted, the Framers often disagreed and were forced to compromise on the language of the Constitution. At best, this approach considers the intentions of the drafters and ratifiers of the Constitution.

■ In Comparative Perspective

Written and Unwritten Constitutions: The United Kingdom's and Israel's Constitutions

What is a constitution? Does a constitution have to be written? Most of the world's 185 countries have written constitutions. Yet several do not, including Bosnia-Herzegovina, Libya, New Zealand, Oman, Qatar, Saudi Arabia, the United Kingdom, and, at least until 1995, Israel. Furthermore, British legal scholars have long contended that the United Kingdom has a "historic constitution." By contrast, the Supreme Court of Israel declared its Basic Laws to constitute a constitution in 1995.

The British constitution, according to some legal scholars, is best understood not as an "unwritten" constitution but as a "historic constitution," a written and unwritten product of historical development, not of deliberate design; it is a romantic, pre-Enlightenment constitution. Parts of the British constitution are found in historic documents, such as the Magna Carta, the Act of Settlement, and the Parliament Acts, but it is not entrenched, and is therefore flexible, because it may be changed by ordinary legislation. Still, as Vernon Bogdanor emphasizes:

> [T]here is a sense in which the British Constitution can be summed up in eight words: What the Queen in Parliament enacts is law. The essence of the British Constitution is thus better expressed in the statement that it is a historic constitution whose dominating characteristic is the sovereignty of Parliament, than in the statement that Britain has an unwritten constitution.

Because parliamentary sovereignty is at the heart of the British constitution, Bogdanor and others deem it "pointless to rationalise it in an enacted constitution which could forbid nothing, nor could it provide a list of basic freedoms which governments would be unable to infringe."[1] In other words, the British constitution is not based on a particular theory or ideology, but rather a historical constitutionalism, incorporating statutes, common law, European conventions, legal treatises, and laws and customs of Parliament. As Sir William Blackstone, in his *Commentaries on the Laws of England* (bk. 1), put it: "Parliament can do everything that is not naturally possible."

(continues)

■ IN COMPARATIVE PERSPECTIVE
*Written and Unwritten Constitutions: The United
Kingdom and Israel's Constitutions (continued)*

In October 2000, however, the United Kingdom became subject to
the European Convention on Human Rights as a result of the Human
Rights Act of 1998, which incorporated those guarantees into British
law, going into effect. British courts had jurisdiction over human rights
claims, though they still have no power to declare laws unconstitutional.
If they find conflicts with legislation, they issued declarations of incompatibility and the Parliament must decide whether to amend the legislation accordingly.

Moreover, over the last two decades the United Kingdom enacted a
number of important reforms, though not in a "codified" constitution or
single document. Among them are limiting Parliamentary terms to five
years, devolving power to Scotland and Wales, reforming the House of
Lords, and creating a supreme court, though without the power of judicial
review. (English justices only have the power to issue "declarations of
incompatibility" of legislation with, for example, a treaty or other law, and
then Parliament reconsiders the legislation.[2]) However, in 2016 voters
approved a referendum to withdraw from the European Union, the so-
called Brexit vote, and relations with the European Union remain fluid
and unresolved.

In contrast, when Israel was proclaimed a state in 1948, it was
expected to eventually enact a written constitution. But, due to initial
opposition, the Knesset (parliament) in 1950 agreed, as a compromise,
to the Harari Resolution, to build a constitution chapter by chapter
through the enactment of Basic Laws. Accordingly, the Knesset enacted
Basic Laws on The Knesset (1958); Israel Lands (1960); The President of
the State (1964); The Government (1968); The State Economy (1975);
Israel Defense Forces (1976); Jerusalem, The Capital of Israel (1980); The
Judiciary (1984); and The State Comptroller (1988). These Basic Laws
largely codified existing practices. But in 1992 the Knesset enacted two
more, dealing for the first time with human rights: the Basic Laws on
Freedom of Occupation and on Human Dignity and Liberty. Notably,
Section 5 of the Basic Law on Freedom of Occupation also stipulated
that it could not be changed "except by a Basic Law enacted by a majority of the Knesset members."

Until the 1990s, the prevailing view in Israel was that the Knesset's
sovereignty was virtually unlimited and that the Supreme Court would
exercise only limited judicial review, invalidating legislation only when in
conflict with specific provisions of a Basic Law. But, in *United Mizrachi
Bank plc v. Migdal Cooperative Village* (1995),[3] the Supreme Court reversed a

lower court's ruling and proclaimed Israel's Basic Laws a constitution. A district court had struck down, as a violation of the 1992 Basic Law on Human Dignity and Liberty, a Knesset law aimed at providing agricultural relief. It was the first time an Israeli court had asserted "American-style" substantive judicial review of legislation. On appeal, though reversing that court's decision, all but one of the nine justices agreed that the Knesset had the "constituent authority" to frame a constitution, binding on its own powers, and that it had done so when enacting the 1992 Basic Laws on human rights. Furthermore, the Supreme Court held that Israel's constitution authorized the judiciary's exercise of "American-style" judicial review.

In *United Mizrachi Bank*, the Israeli Supreme Court embraced a theory that its President (or chief justice) Aharon Barak had championed following the enactment of the 1992 Basic Laws. According to Chief Justice Barak[4]:

> Under these new Basic Laws, several human rights—among them Dignity, Liberty, Mobility, Privacy, Property—acquired a constitutional force above regular statutes. . . . A regular Knesset (Parliamentary) statute can no longer infringe upon these rights, unless it fulfills the requirements of the Basic Laws (the "limitations clause"), namely, it befits the values of the State of Israel, it was passed for a worthy purpose and the harm caused to the constitutional Human Right is proportional to the purpose. Thus, we became a constitutional democracy. We joined the democratic, enlightened nations in which human rights are awarded a constitutional force above regular statutes. Similar to the United States, Canada, France, Germany, Italy, Japan, and other western countries, we now have a constitutional defense for Human Rights. We too have the central chapter in any written constitution, the subject-matter of which is Human Rights; we too have restrictions on the legislative power of the legislator; we too have judicial review of statutes which unlawfully infringe upon constitutionally protected human rights; we too have a written constitution, to which the Knesset in its capacity as legislator is subject and which it cannot alter. . . .
>
> The Constitutional Revolution has led to a change in the judiciary's status. Great responsibilities have been imposed on it. It must fill the mould created by the "majestic generalities" in the new Basic Laws. The judiciary must be aware of the fundamental values of the people. It must balance them in accordance with the views of the "enlightened general public" in Israel. . . . Constitutional interpretation should not be formalistic or pedantic. It should be purposive. It should be done from a wide perspective and adopt a substantive approach. A constitution is a living organism. . . .

(continues)

■ In Comparative Perspective
*Written and Unwritten Constitutions: The United
Kingdom and Israel's Constitutions (continued)*

1. Vernon Bogdanor, "Britain: The Political Constitution," in Vernon Bogdanor, ed., *Constitutions and Democratic Politics* 53, 55 (Aldershot, England:
Gower, 1988). See also Peter Leyland, *The Constitution of the United Kingdom*, 3rd
ed. (Oxford: Hart Publishing, 2016).

2. See Graham Gee, R. Hazell, K. Malleson, and P. O'Brien, *The Politics of
Judicial Independence in the U.K.'s Changing Constitution* (Cambridge: Cambridge
University of Press, 2015).

3. A translation of and commentary on *United Mizrachi Bank plc v. Migdal
Cooperative Village*, 48 (iv) P.D. 221 (1995), may be found in 31 *Israel Law
Review* 754 (1997).

4. Aharon Barak, "The Constitutionalization of the Israeli Legal System as
a Result of the Basic Laws and Its Effect on Procedural and Substantive
Criminal Law," 31 *Israel Law Review* 3–23 (1997). See also Aharon Barak,
The Judge in a Democracy (Princeton, NJ: Princeton University Press, 2006).

And, who are "the Framers"? Should the views of only the thirty-nine signers of the document be considered, or should those of the other sixteen delegates who left before the Constitutional Convention concluded or refused to sign the document be considered as well? There are also compelling reasons for including the views of delegates to the thirteen-state ratifying conventions, for as a result of those conventions the Bill of Rights was immediately added to the Constitution (see Ch. 4).

Problems with discovering the intentions of the Framers also arise because the proceedings of the Constitutional Convention were conducted in secrecy and records of that convention and those in the states are far from complete and reliable. Moreover, it is debatable that the Framers expected their intentions to limit or guide constitutional interpretation.[7] Not until 1819 were speeches, resolutions, and votes of the delegates to the Constitutional Convention published. Almost another decade passed before Jonathan Elliot began publishing his collection of the debates in the state ratifying conventions. James Madison, who took notes of the debates at the Constitutional Convention and whose notes provide the only full record, refused to allow the publication of his notes until 1840, after his death. Madison insisted that the intent and literal reading of the text would be a "hard rule of construction."

Instead, among the "obvious and just guides applicable to the Constn. of the U.S.," he listed

> 1. [T]he evils & defects for curing which the Constitution was called for & introduced. 2. The comments prevailing at the times it was adopted. 3. The early, deliberate & continued practice under the Constitution as preferable to constructions adopted on the spur of occasions, and subject to the vicissitudes of party or personal considerations.[8]

In addition, it bears noting that in its first fifty years the Supreme Court infrequently cited works such as the *Federalist Papers* in its opinions. Between 1790 and 1839, the *Federalist Papers* were cited in only fifteen decisions; by comparison, since 1950 they have been cited in more than 100 cases.[9]

Because of these difficulties, Justices Antonin Scalia and Clarence Thomas, among others associated with interpretivism and the "originalist" approach to constitutional interpretation, have more modestly contended that the Court should remain faithful to the "original understanding," "original meaning," "original public understanding," "original textualism," or "textual originalism"[10] of the governing principles or political philosophy of the Framers. They do not claim to be uncovering the Framers' subjective intentions but rather limiting the interpretation of constitutional provisions to those principles that the Framers might fairly be said to have embraced when drafting and ratifying the Constitution. Judge Bork explains that

> [a] major problem with the idea of original intention is that the Framers articulated their principles in light of the world they knew, a world very different in important respects from that in which judges must decide cases today. . . . In order to protect the freedoms the Framers envisaged, the judge must discern a principle in the applications the Framers thought of and then apply that principle to circumstances they did not foresee.[11]

Nor do they claim that originalism eliminates the burden of making basic constitutional choices. Rather, they argue that this approach is superior to other noninterpretivist approaches because it ostensibly sharply limits the exercise of judicial review and thus proves more responsive to criticisms of the Court's countermajoritarian power. In Justice Scalia's words,

> The principal theoretical defect of nonoriginalism, in my view, is its incompatibility with the very principle that legitimizes judicial

review of constitutionality. Nothing in the text of the Constitution confers upon the courts the power to inquire into, rather than passively assume, the constitutionality of federal statutes. . . . Quite to the contrary, the legislature would seem a much more appropriate expositor of social values, and *its* determination that a statute is compatible with the Constitution should, as in England, prevail.[12]

Justice Scalia conceded that originalism poses methodological problems in practice but nonetheless claims that it is "the lesser evil" in constitutional interpretation:

[It] *is* true that it is often exceedingly difficult to plumb the original understanding of an ancient text. Properly done, the task requires the consideration of an enormous mass of material—in the case of the Constitution and its Amendments, for example, to mention only one element, the records of the ratifying debates in all the states. Even beyond that, it requires an evaluation of the reliability of that material—many of the reports of the ratifying debates, for example, are thought to be quite unreliable. And further still, it requires immersing oneself in the political and intellectual atmosphere of the time—somehow placing out of mind knowledge that we have which an earlier age did not, and putting on beliefs, attitudes, philosophies, prejudices and loyalties that are not those of our day. It is, in short, a task sometimes better suited to the historian than the lawyer. . . .

I can be much more brief in describing what seems to me the second most serious objection to originalism. In its undiluted form, at least, it is medicine that seems too strong to swallow. Thus, almost every originalist would adulterate it with the doctrine of *stare decisis* [which holds that prior decisions should be respected]. . . . But *stare decisis* alone is not enough to prevent originalism from being what many would consider too bitter a pill. What if some state should enact a new law providing public lashing, or branding of the right hand, as punishment for certain criminal offenses? Even if it could be demonstrated unequivocally that these were not cruel and unusual measures [which are forbidden under the Eighth Amendment] in 1791, and even though no prior Supreme Court decision has specifically disapproved them, I doubt whether any federal judge—even among the many who consider themselves originalists—would sustain them against an Eighth Amendment challenge. It may well be . . . that this cannot legitimately be reconciled with originalist philosophy—that it represents the unrealistic view of the Constitution as a document intended to create a perfect society for all ages to come, whereas in fact it was a political compromise that did not pretend to create a perfect society even for its own age (as its toleration of slavery, which a majority of the founding generation recognized as an evil, well enough demonstrates).

Even so, I am confident that public flogging and hand-branding would not be sustained by our courts, and any espousal of originalism as a practical theory of exegesis must somehow come to terms with that reality.[13]

Justice Scalia's discussion of public flogging and the Eighth Amendment is revealing not only by indicating that he was (in his words) "a faint-hearted originalist," because he would hold public flogging unconstitutional despite the fact that the Framers permitted that practice. (However, he subsequently renounced that position—whatever was acceptable in 1787 was for him permissible today.) Justice Scalia, nonetheless, continued to champion what he termed "textual originalism";[14] that is to say, judges should "look for meaning in the governing text, ascribe to that text the meaning that it has borne from its inception, and reject judicial speculation about the drafters' extra-textually derived purposes and the desirability of the fair reading's anticipated consequences." Still, the original understanding of constitutional guarantees, as Justice Anthony Kennedy observed during his 1987 Senate confirmation hearings, is a "necessary starting point," not an "adequate methodology" or "mechanical process" that "tells us how to decide a case."

What Scalia's discussion also points out is that crucial *concepts* in the Constitution give rise to competing *conceptions* and political philosophies.[15] Scalia did not limit the concept of cruel and unusual punishment in the Eighth Amendment to the Framers' conception of that punishment in 1791. Nor did Scalia go as far as Justice Brennan in interpreting the Eighth Amendment to bar capital punishment based on his "constitutional vision of human dignity" (see Ch. 10). But, why not? What divides justices like Scalia and Thomas from Chief Justice Roberts and Justices Brennan, Kennedy, Souter, Ginsburg, Breyer, Sotomayor, and Kagan is their underlying judicial and political philosophies of the Constitution and the exercise of judicial review. Just as the Federalists and Anti-Federalists had competing political visions of the separation of powers and federalism, for example, even originalists such as Chief Justice Rehnquist and Justices Scalia and Thomas may disagree and have rival conceptions and interpretations of "the original public understanding" of the separation of powers and individual rights; see, for instance, *Zivotofsky v. Kerry*, 576 U.S. 1059 (2015) (excerpted in Vol. 1, Ch. 3); *Morrison v. Olson*, 487 U.S. 654 (1988) (see Vol. 1, Ch. 4); *McIntyre v. Ohio Elections Commission*, 514 U.S. 334 (1995) (excerpted in Vol. 1, Ch. 8); and *Brown v. Entertainment Merchants Association*, 564 U.S. 786 (2011) (excerpted in Ch. 5).

In the last couple of decades, given the criticisms and methodological difficulties of the quest for a jurisprudence of "originalism," in the last decade or so, legal scholars and justices like Scalia and Thomas have increasingly embraced a theory of "the original public understanding" of constitutional provisions, or what Justice Scalia came to term "textual originalism" or "original textualism."[16] In recent years even progressive/liberal scholars have also championed theories of "the original public meaning" of guarantees like the Fourteenth Amendment's equal protection clause.[17] Besides the text, they look to the "original framework" of the Constitution and Bill of Rights. Conservative scholars and jurists gauge "the original public meaning" not from floor statements by members of Congress but rather from the "original public meaning" as determined by dictionaries and grammar books that were widely used at the time a provision was adopted, as well as legal authorities at the time such as Sir William Blackstone. In other words, the focus is on discerning the *likely expectations of how a provision would apply at the time it was adopted.* As Justice Thomas explained, when interpreting a constitutional provision, "the goal is to discern the most likely public understanding of [that] provision at the time it was adopted." *McDonald v. Chicago,* 561 U.S. 742 (2010) (Thomas, J., con. op.) (excerpted in Ch. 4, extending the Second Amendment "right to bear arms" to the states). Because the Constitution is a written document, "its meaning does not alter. . . . That which it meant when adopted, it means now." *McIntyre v. Ohio Elections Commission* (Thomas, J., con. op.).

Yet, as noted, even conservatives and "originalists" like Justices Scalia and Thomas occasionally disagree about "the original public understanding or meaning" and the levels of generality of provisions such as the First Amendment guarantee for freedom of speech or the Fourteenth Amendment's equal protection clause. See and compare, for example, Justice Scalia's opinion for the Court and Justice Thomas's dissenting opinion in *Brown v. Entertainment Merchants Association,* 564 U.S. 786 (excerpted in Ch. 5, holding that California's law on the sale of violent video games to minors runs afoul of the First Amendment). See also their respective opinions in *McIntyre v. Ohio Elections Commission* (1995), and *Obergefell v. Hodges* (2015) (excerpted in Ch. 12).

An underlying problem for interpretivists and noninterpretivists is how broadly or narrowly they conceive and express the concept or principle of a constitutional provision. Consider, for example, the constitutional choices presented in interpreting and applying the Fourth Amendment and the equal protection clause of the Fourteenth Amendment. The Fourth Amendment guarantees the people a right "to be secure in their persons, houses, papers, and effects against unreason-

The Supreme Court, 2019. (*Fred Schilling, Collection of the Supreme Court of the United States*)

able searches and seizures." That guarantee was interpreted in *Olmstead v. United States*, 277 U.S. 438 (1928) (see Ch. 7), not to cover wiretaps because a majority of the Court limited the amendment's application to Framers' conception of "unreasonable searches and seizures," giving the lowest level of generality to the amendment's principle, so as to bar only actual physical trespass by police and the seizure of tangible materials. By contrast, dissenting Justice Louis Brandeis argued for a broader conception of the amendment and a more general principle of privacy in the home that would have extended the guarantees of the amendment to cover electronic surveillance. Almost forty years later, in *Katz v. United States*, 389 U.S. 347 (1967) (see Ch. 7), the Court finally embraced the broader principle of Fourth Amendment–protected privacy.

The Fourteenth Amendment guarantees "the equal protection of the laws." The principle of equality embodied there might be interpreted to bar only discrimination against blacks, because in the historical context of the post–Civil War period the Thirty-ninth Congress was indisputably primarily concerned with ensuring that states did not deny certain rights of newly freed blacks. Indeed, early drafts of the equal protection clause banned only discrimination "on account of race and colour." But, John Bingham, a representative from Ohio and a leading proponent of the amendment, managed to win agreement on broadening the language to prohibit states from denying "the equal protection of the laws" to anyone, on any account. Moreover,

■ IN COMPARATIVE PERSPECTIVE

China's Written Constitution without Constitutionalism?

After the 1949 revolution by the Chinese Communist Party (CCP), the new People's Republic of China (PRC) began developing a new constitutional and legal structure. In doing so, it immediately abandoned the 2,000-year-old tradition of Confucianism's teaching of *li*— "rites" or "propriety"—that had formed the basis of a kind of social constitution, on the one hand, and, on the other hand, rejected "Western rule-of-law constitutionalism" as imperialistic. In the last sixty years, China has had one provisional and four formal constitutions.

Initially, a provisional Common Programme was enacted in 1949. It proclaimed the "people's democratic dictatorship" and laid out, in seven chapters and sixty articles, principles that became the basis for later constitutions. In 1954 the National People's Congress (NPC) adopted the first written constitution, containing 106 articles in four chapters. That constitution, however, was neither seriously implemented nor provided a barrier to the abuse of governmental power and denial of human rights. Subsequently, Mao Zedong initiated a series of political campaigns—from the anti-rightists movement (1957) to the Great Leap Forward (1958) and the Great Proletarian Cultural Revolution (1966–1976)—resulting in a Chinese holocaust and eliminating virtually any basis for constitutionalism.

A second constitution was adopted shortly before the end of the Cultural Revolution. The 1975 constitution was more of a political outline and essentially removed most of the 1954 constitution's provisions for individual rights and institutional powers, with only thirty articles remaining. After Mao's death in 1976, the NPC enacted a third constitution. The 1978 constitution included sixty articles— deleting some of the previous constitution, adding some human rights and institutional provisions, and laying down Four Modernizations as primary objectives in the areas of agriculture, defense, industry, and science and technology. Subsequently, that constitution was revised and amended in 1979 and 1980 and then replaced in 1982.

The 1982 constitution is in some respects a return to the pre– Cultural Revolution period in establishing a dualist judiciary and a tripartite national administrative structure. The judicial power is exercised by a series of people's courts as well as the Supreme People's Court, which reports to the National People's Congress and the Standing

Committee. The tripartite national administrative structure includes (1) the state president (largely symbolic); (2) the State Council, which wields substantial powers in operating as the Central People's Government (CPG); and (3) a separate Central Military Commission (CMC), which overlaps with the CCP. This constitution was subsequently amended in 1988, 1993, 1999, 2004, and 2017. Most of the amendments in various ways primarily promoted a market economy—moving away from communal or collective ownership, particularly in rural areas—and, at least until the 2004 amendments, paid little attention to human rights.

In 2017, the 19th National People's Congress of the Communist Party approved further constitutional amendments that made it possible for President Xi Jinping to hold a third term or more in contrast to prior constitutional limitations to two terms; created a National Supervision Commission, above the judiciary, to combat corruption, along with providing legal reforms, including greater professionalism and transparency within the judiciary; and reaffirming the CCP's domination of the legal system. Moreover, the CCP enshrined "Xi Jinping Thought on Socialism with Chinese Characteristics for a New Era and Basic Policy" into the constitution.

The Chinese judiciary remains weak, when viewed in terms of Western standards. The Communist Party controls all judicial appointments, assignments, and reappointments. There is no power of judicial review akin to that established in *Marbury v. Madison* (1803), the European Court of Justice, and elsewhere. China remains influenced by the civil law tradition, and judges do not exercise "judicial independence" nor are they bound by "precedents," as in common-law countries. Since 1985, the Supreme People's Court (SPC) has published the *Gazette of the Supreme People's Court,* providing transparency and some guidance on its rulings in "typical" cases for the lower courts and the public. Over the last decade, the SPC developed a system of "guiding cases," but they are only de facto binding—binding in the sense that they must be considered but not necessarily binding—by lower courts. Notably, neither the SPC nor lower courts may supersede the law-making authority of the National People's Congress.

In sum, the fusion of constitutional and socialist legal systems bears, as is often said, distinctive "Chinese characteristics." In other words, China's constitutional system stands apart from a more American-style constitutionalism—with judicial independence and review, and the supremacy of the rule of law—and is closer to the "rule by law," as determined by the CCP, associated with the unwritten constitutionalism of tradition and political discourse in the United Kingdom (see the

(continues)

■ IN COMPARATIVE PERSPECTIVE
China's Written Constitution without
Constitutionalism? (continued)

---

box IN COMPARATIVE PERSPECTIVE: Written and Unwritten Constitutions: The United Kingdom's and Israel's Constitutions, in this chapter).

For further reading, see Qianfan Zhang, *The Constitution of China: A Contextual Analysis* (Oxford: Hart Publishing, 2012); Qianfan Zhang, "A Constitution without Constitutionalism? The Paths of Constitutional Development in China," 8 *I*Con* 950–976 (2010); but compare Michael W. Dowdle, "Of Comparative Constitutional Monocropping: A Reply to Qianfan Zhang," 8 *I*Con* 977 (2010). See also "Chinese Common Law? Guiding Cases and Judicial Reform," 129 *Harvard Law Review* 2213–2234 (2016); and compare Tu Yunxin, "Guiding Cases in Chinese Legal System," in Ingo Wolfgang Sarlet and Marco Felix Jobim, eds., *Precedentes Judiciais: Dialogos Transnacionais* (Rio de Janeiro, Brazil: Tirant lo Blanch, 2019). O'Brien is indebted to Professor Tu and to Fundan University, as a Visiting Senior Fellow, summers 2017 and 2018.

---

the Court has given broader application and a higher level of generality so as to bar other kinds of racial discrimination against, for example, Hispanics and Asians. And even more broadly (as further discussed in Ch. 12), the amendment has been construed to forbid forms of nonracial discrimination against women and members of the LGBTQ community. But how and on what basis may this broader application of the equal protection clause be defended and the Court's exercise of judicial review in this way justified?

In sum and in Judge Bork's words, "The question is always the level of generality the judge chooses when he states the idea or object of the Framers."[18] Interpretivists, no less than noninterpretivists, cannot evade making basic constitutional choices in their conceptions and formulations of the underlying principles of constitutional provisions.

NOTES

1. Hugo Black, *A Constitutional Faith* (New York: Knopf, 1968), 45.

2. See H. L. A. Hart, *The Concept of Law* (Oxford, UK: Clarendon Press, 1961), 124–132.

3. Richard Posner, "What Am I? A Potted Plant?" *New Republic*, September 28, 1987, 23.

4. Edwin Meese, "The Attorney General's View of the Supreme Court: Toward a Jurisprudence of Original Intention," in *Special Issue, Law and Public Affairs*, ed. Charles Wise and David O'Brien, 45 *Public Administration Review* 701 (1985).

5. See also Raoul Berger, *Government by Judiciary* (Cambridge, MA: Harvard University Press, 1977); and Walter Berns, *Taking the Constitution Seriously* (New York: Simon & Schuster, 1987).

6. William J. Brennan Jr., "The Constitution of the United States: Contemporary Ratification," Georgetown University, Washington, DC (October 12, 1985); reprinted in David M. O'Brien, ed., *Judges on Judging*, 5th ed. (Washington, DC: C.Q. Press, 2017).

7. See H. Jefferson Powell, "The Original Understanding of Original Intent," 98 *Harvard Law Review* 885 (1985); and James Hutson, "The Creation of the Constitution: The Integrity of the Documentary Record," 65 *Texas Law Review* 1 (1986).

8. Quoted in Robert Morgan, *James Madison on the Constitution and the Bill of Rights* (Westport, CT: Greenwood Press, 1988), 196–197.

9. See James Wilson, "The Most Sacred Text: The Supreme Court's Use of *The Federalist Papers*," 1985 *Brigham Young University Law Review* 65 (1985).

10. See Antonin Scalia, "Originalism: The Lesser Evil," 57 *Cincinnati Law Review* 849 (1989); reprinted in O'Brien, *Judges on Judging*.

11. Robert Bork, "Foreword" to Gary McDowell, *The Constitution and Contemporary Constitutional Theory* (Cumberland, VA: Center for Judicial Studies, 1985), x.

12. Scalia, "Originalism," 854.

13. Scalia, "Originalism," 856–857.

14. See, generally, Antonin Scalia and Bryan A. Garner, *Reading Law: The Interpretation of Legal Texts* (St. Paul, MN: Thomson/West, 2012).

15. On the distinction between concepts and conceptions, see Ronald Dworkin, *Taking Rights Seriously* (Cambridge, MA: Harvard University Press, 1977), 135–137.

16. See Antonin Scalia and Bryan A. Garner, *Reading Law: The Interpretation of Legal Texts* (St. Paul, MN: Thomson/West, 2012).

17. See, for example, Akhil Reed Amar, *America's Constitution* (New York: Random House, 2005); Jack Balkin, *Living Originalism* (Cambridge, MA: Harvard University Press, 2011); and David A. Strauss, *The Living Constitution* (New York: Oxford University Press, 2010).

18. Bork, "Foreword," x.

SELECTED BIBLIOGRAPHY

Amar, Akhil Reed. *America's Constitution: A Biography*. New York: Random House, 2005.

Amsterdam, Anthony, and Jerome Bruner. *Minding the Law: How Courts Rely on Storytelling, and How Their Stories Change the Ways We Understand the Law—and Ourselves*. Cambridge, MA: Harvard University Press, 2000.

Balkin, Jack. *Living Originalism*. Cambridge, MA: Harvard University Press, 2011.

Berger, Raoul. *Government by Judiciary: The Transformation of the Fourteenth Amendment*. Cambridge, MA: Harvard University Press, 1977.

Bickel, Alexander. *The Morality of Consent*. New Haven, CT: Yale University Press, 1975.

Black, Hugo. *A Constitutional Faith*. New York: Knopf, 1968.

Bork, Robert. *The Tempting of America*. New York: Free Press, 1989.

Calabresi, Steven, ed. *Originalism: A Quarter-Century of Debate*. Washington, DC: Regnery, 2007.

Cogan, Neil, ed. *The Complete Bill of Rights: The Drafts, Debates, Sources, & Origins*. New York: Oxford University Press, 1997.

Crapanzano, Vincent. *Serving the Word: Literalism in America from the Pulpit to the Bench*. New York: New Press, 2000.

Cross, Frank. *The Failed Promise of Originalism*. Palo Alto, CA: Stanford University Press, 2013.

Goldford, Dennis. *The American Constitution and the Debate over Originalism*. New York: Cambridge University Press, 2005.

Holton, Woody. *Unruly Americans and the Origins of the Constitution*. New York: Hill & Wang, 2007.

Jaffa, Harry V. *Original Intent and the Framers of the Constitution*. Washington, DC: Regnery Gateway, 1994.

Levy, Leonard. *Original Intent and the Framers' Constitution*. Chicago: Ivan Dee, 2000.

Lynch, Joseph. *Negotiating the Constitution: The Earliest Debates over Original Intent*. Ithaca, NY: Cornell University Press, 1999.

McDowell, Gary. *The Language of the Law and the Foundations of American Constitutionalism*. New York: Cambridge University Press, 2010.

O'Neill, Jonathan. *Originalism in American Law and Politics*. Baltimore, MD: Johns Hopkins University Press, 2005.

Rakove, Jack. *Original Meanings: Politics and Ideas in the Making of the Constitution*. New York: Knopf, 1996.

————, ed. *Interpreting the Constitution: The Debate over Original Intent*. Boston: Northeastern University Press, 1990.

Scalia, Antonin. *A Matter of Interpretation: Federal Courts and the Law*. Princeton, NJ: Princeton University Press, 1997.

Scalia, Antonin, and Bryan Garner. *Reading the Law: The Interpretation of Legal Texts*. St. Paul, MN: Thompson/West, 2012.

Tamanaha, Brian. *On the Rule of Law: History, Politics, Theory*. New York: Cambridge University Press, 2004.

————. *Beyond the Formalist-Realist Divide*. Princeton, NJ: Princeton University Press, 2010.

Thayer, Bradley. *Thayer's Legal Essays*. Boston: Boston Book Company, 1908.

Whittington, Keith. *Constitutional Interpretation: Textual Meaning, Original Intent, and Judicial Review*. Lawrence: University Press of Kansas, 1999.

■ (2) IN AND BEYOND THE TEXT

Noninterpretivism differs from interpretivism in the sources and kinds of argumentation marshaled in support of giving broader scope or higher levels of generality to constitutional principles. Whereas interpretivists confine analysis to the text and historical context of a provision, noninterpretivists tend to formulate more broadly the underlying principle of a constitutional provision. Noninterpretivists may turn to history and social science, for example, or appeal to natural law, natural rights, and moral or political philosophy, or call on process-oriented theories of judicial review and arguments about the structure of the Constitution.

Historical, economic, technological, and political changes are obviously relevant to constitutional interpretation. Yet, when and how should the Court use *history?* The Sixth Amendment, for instance, guarantees criminal defendants the right to a jury trial but does not define *jury.* When confronted with the question of whether juries must consist of twelve members, in *Thompson v. Utah*, 170 U.S. 343 (1898), the Court simply ruled that the Sixth Amendment incorporated the traditional common-law practice of twelve-member juries because that practice was firmly rooted in English history and familiar to the Framers of the Bill of Rights. The Court may also take *judicial notice* of historical events without the benefit of their being adjudicated, such as the fact that there was an economic depression in the 1930s. Chief Justice Morrison Waite drew heavily on history as a guide when upholding under the commerce clause the power of Congress, over that of the states, to regulate interstate telegraph lines, in *Pensacola Telegraph Co. v. Western Union Telegraph, Co.*, 96 U.S. 1 (1877):

> The powers thus granted are not confined to the instrumentalities of commerce . . . known or in use when the Constitution was adopted, but they keep pace with the progress of the country, and adapt themselves to the new developments of time and circumstance. They extend from the horse with its rider to the stage-coach, from the sailing-vessel to the steamboat . . . and from the railroad to the telegraph, as these new agencies are successively brought into use to meet the demands of increasing population and wealth. . . . As they were intrusted to the general government for the good of the nation, it is not only the right, but the duty, of Congress to see to it that intercourse among the States and the transmission of intelligence are not obstructed or unnecessarily encumbered by State legislation.

Justice Holmes took an even more expansive view of the use of history in the famous case dealing with the national government's treaty-making power in *Missouri v. Holland*, 252 U.S. 416 (1920) (see Ch. 3). Note his observation that "[t]he case before us must be considered in light of our whole experience and not merely in that of what was said a hundred years ago."

The Court's reliance on history is not unproblematic, however.[1] Justices are not trained as historians and they may confront problems in evaluating different schools of history and the works of revisionist historians. More fundamentally, Chief Justice William Rehnquist, among others, cautioned against turning to history because it encourages the notion that the "Constitution is a living document" and that the Court ought to keep the Constitution in "tune with the times." In Rehnquist's view, there are three serious flaws with the notion of a living Constitution:

> First, it misconceives the nature of the Constitution, which was designed to enable the popularly elected branches of government, not the judicial branch, to keep the country abreast of the times. Second, [it] ignores the Supreme Court's disastrous experiences when in the past it embraced contemporary, fashionable notions of what a living Constitution should contain. Third, however socially desirable the goals to be advanced, . . . advancing them through a free-wheeling, non-elected judiciary is quite unacceptable in a democratic society.[2]

Social science may prove a no less controversial source of support for the Court's decisions. In the landmark school desegregation ruling in *Brown v. Board of Education*, 347 U.S. 483 (1954) (see Ch. 12), for example, the Court cited in footnote 11 several social science studies in support of overturning the racial doctrine of "separate but equal facilities." Among those studies was Swedish economist and sociologist Gunnar Myrdal's book *An American Dilemma* (1944), the premier work on race relations in America. The Court's mention of *An American Dilemma* intensified the antagonism of powerful southerners, such as the South Carolina governor and former Supreme Court Justice James F. Byrnes and Mississippi Senator James O. Eastland. They and others attacked the Court for citing the work of "foreign sociologists," bad social science research, and, most of all, for drawing on social science in the first place, instead of simply sticking to the text and historical context of the Constitution.

The Court's use of social science materials may raise questions about judicial competence and the legitimacy of basing decisions on social science evidence.[3] Consider *Williams v. Florida*, 399 U.S. 78 (1970) (see Ch. 9), upholding juries composed of fewer than twelve members, despite history and the ruling in *Thompson v. Utah* that the Sixth Amendment jury consisted "as it was at common law, of twelve persons, neither more nor less." *Williams* proved controversial because the Court held on the basis of psychological and sociological studies of small-group behavior that juries of fewer than twelve members were "functionally equivalent" to traditional twelve-member juries.

Natural law and *natural rights*, or what Edward Corwin termed, the "higher law" background of the Constitution, is an older tradition and source of constitutional interpretation.[4] The Framers took seriously natural law and natural rights in maintaining that individuals enjoy certain rights prior to the establishment of government and which may not be denied by government. Federalists, though, contended that the Constitution adequately safeguarded natural rights by creating a government of limited and specifically delegated powers. But the Anti-Federalists pushed for the addition of a bill of rights containing a statement of natural rights (see Ch. 4).

Although the natural rights tradition runs throughout much of constitutional law, controversy has ensnarled appeals to natural law and rights ever since Justices Iredell and Chase debated, in *Calder v. Bull*, 3 Dall. 386 (1798), whether the Court has the power to strike down legislation based on principles of natural justice. Chief Justice John Marshall faced the problem of enforcing his own acceptance of natural rights against the claims of Spanish and Portuguese slave traders in *The Antelope Case*, 23 U.S. 66 (1825). Slaves had been seized by pirates, who were later captured by an American naval ship, and the slave traders and owners sued to recover their "property." Of slavery and the slave trade, Chief Justice Marshall observed "[t]hat it is contrary to the law of nature will scarcely be denied. That every man has a natural right to the fruits of his own labor, is generally admitted, and [that] no other person can rightfully deprive him of those fruits, and appropriate them against his will, seems to be the necessary result of this admission." But Marshall concluded that

> [w]hatever might be the answer of a moralist to this question, a jurist must search for its legal solution, in those principles of action which are sanctioned by the usages, the national acts, and the general assent, of that portion of the world of which he considers himself as a part, and to whose law the appeal is made. If we resort to this standard as the test of international law, the question . . . is decided in favor of the legality of the [slave] trade.

Other members of the Court, though, have sided with Justice Chase's position in *Calder* that with respect to "certain vital principles . . . [a]n act of the Legislature (for I cannot call it a *law*) contrary to the *great first principles* of the social compact, cannot be considered a *rightful exercise* of legislative authority" and, therefore, must be overturned. Consider the debate over fundamental rights and the formulations and standards used by the Court when interpreting the Fourteenth Amendment's due process clause (see Ch. 4). In *Hurtado v. California*, 110 U.S. 516 (1884) (see Ch. 4), for example, Justice Stanley Matthews speaks of the "well-springs of justice." In *Adamson v. California*, 332 U.S. 46 (1947) (see Ch. 4), and *Rochin v. California*, 342 U.S. 165 (1952) (see Ch. 4), Justice Frankfurter invokes "the shocks the conscience test" and "fundamental fairness standard" for determining what process is due under the due process clause. Frankfurter's "shocks the conscience" test was undoubtedly rooted in his view of the role of the Court and often quoted his mentor, Justice Holmes, who said that he would not vote to strike down a law for violating due process unless it "made him puke."[5]

The principal criticisms of "natural law formulations" were levied in opinions by Justice Hugo Black, particularly in his dissent from the Court's recognition of a right of privacy in *Griswold v. Connecticut*, 381 U.S. 479 (1965) (see Ch. 4), where he observes that

> [o]ne of the most effective ways of diluting or expanding a constitutionally guaranteed right is to substitute for the crucial word or words of a constitutional guarantee another word for the word or words, more or less flexible and more or less restricted in meaning. . . . Use of any such broad, unbounded judicial authority would make this Court's members a day-to-day constitutional convention.

Moreover, the natural rights tradition was fundamentally discredited by the Legal Realist movement in the early twentieth century, and progressives' criticisms that the Court under the guise of natural law was simply imposing its own substantive value choices. No member of the Court in almost a hundred years has embraced natural law as a basis for constitutional interpretation, except for Justices George Sutherland and Clarence Thomas. See, especially, Thomas's dissent from the ruling on same-sex marriages in *Obergefell v. Hodges* (2015) (excerpted here in Ch. 12).

This criticism of the Court for imposing its own substantive value choices applies as well to those arguing that the Court should draw on *moral* and *political philosophy*. Yet Professor Ronald Dworkin and other contemporary legal scholars call for "a fusion of constitutional law and moral theory" or political philosophy.[6] Contemporary legal scholarship is indeed marked by a proliferation of expressly normative theories that would rationalize and guide constitutional interpretation according to "abstract beliefs about morality and justice,"[7] the "voice of reason,"[8] "a moral patrimony" implicit in "our common heritage,"[9] "the circumstances and values of the present generation,"[10] "conventional morality,"[11] "public morality,"[12] "constitutional morality,"[13] "fundamental values,"[14] and the "essential principles of justice,"[15] or "the idea of progress."[16] But this movement toward more specialized and abstract theories of constitutional interpretation raises the ante for reaching consensus within the Supreme Court and the country.[17]

Interpretivists counter that the turn to moral and political philosophy only exacerbates the problems of constitutional interpretation and the countermajoritarian difficulty of judicial review. As former Stanford University Law School professor John Hart Ely cleverly put it, "The Constitution may follow the flag, but is it really supposed to keep up with the *New York Review of Books?*"[18] Judge Bork raises other concerns:

> The abstract, universalistic style of legal thought has a number of dangers. For one thing, it teaches disrespect for the actual institutions of the American polity. These institutions are designed to achieve compromise, to slow change, to dilute absolutisms. They embody wholesome inconsistencies. They are designed, in short, to do things that abstract generalizations about the just society tend to bring into contempt.[19]

Interpreting the Constitution, nevertheless, presupposes a judicial and political philosophy and poses inescapable questions of substantive value choices. As Justice Brennan explained,

> Faith in democracy is one thing, blind faith quite another. Those who drafted our Constitution understood the difference. One cannot read the text without admitting that it embodies substantive choices; it places certain values beyond the power of any legislature. . . .
>
> To remain faithful to the content of the Constitution, therefore, an approach to interpreting the text must account for the existence of these substantive value choices, and must accept the ambiguity inherent in the effort to apply them to modern circumstances. The Framers discerned fundamental principles through struggles against particular malefactions of the Crown; the struggle shapes the particular contours of the articulated principles. But our acceptance of the fundamental principles has not and should not bind us to those precise, at times anachronistic, contours. Successive generations of Americans have continued to respect these fundamental choices and adopt them as their own guide to evaluating quite different historical practices. Each generation has the choice to overrule or add to the fundamental principles enunciated by the Framers; the Constitution can be amended or it can be ignored. Yet with respect to its fundamental principles, the text has suffered neither fate. . . .
>
> The Constitution on its face is, in large measure, a structuring text, a blueprint for government. And when the text is not prescribing the form of the government it is limiting the powers of that government. The original document, before addition of any of the amendments, does not speak primarily of the rights of man,

but of the abilities and disabilities of government. When one reflects upon the text's preoccupation with the scope of government as well as its shape, however, one comes to understand that what this text is about is the relationship of the individual and the state. The text marks the metes and bounds of official authority and individual autonomy. When one studies the boundary that the text marks out, one gets a sense of the vision of the individual embodied in the Constitution.

As augmented by the Bill of Rights and the Civil War Amendments, this text is a sparking vision of the supremacy of the human dignity of every individual. This vision is reflected in the very choice of democratic self-governance: the supreme value of a democracy is the presumed worth of each individual. . . . It is a vision that has guided us as a people throughout our history, although the precise rules by which we have protected fundamental human dignity have been transformed over time in response to both transformations of social conditions and evolution of our concepts of human dignity.[20]

Neither do alternative theories and modes of constitutional interpretation elude a dependence on political philosophy. Interpreting the Constitution frequently requires, as former Professor Charles L. Black Jr., argued, "inference from the structure and relationships created by the constitution in all its parts or in some principal part."[21] Chief Justice Marshall's watershed opinion in *McCulloch v. Maryland*, 4 Wheat. (17 U.S.) 316 (1819) (see Vol. 1, Ch. 6), illustrates the role of *structural analysis* of the Constitution. There, Marshall upheld the constitutionality of the national bank as a necessary and proper exercise of Congress's powers based on inferences from the structure of federalism, instead of relying on the necessary and proper clause per se. Still, Jeffersonian-Republicans disagreed with the infusion of Marshall's nationalistic political philosophy into constitutional law. Moreover, differences rooted in rival political philosophies over the structure of federalism persist in the Court and the country (see Vol. 1, Ch. 6).

Nor do attempts to reconcile the exercise of the Court's power with majoritarian democracy in terms of what has become known as *process-oriented theory of judicial review* fare much better.[22] Justice Harlan Stone initially suggested that the Court's role ought to be limited to policing the political process and ensuring that it does not discriminate against "discrete and insular minorities," in footnote 4 of *United States v. Carolene Products Co.*, 304 U.S. 144 (1938) (see Ch. 12). In a book titled *Democracy and Distrust*, Professor John Ely further developed the theory that the Court's role should be limited to policing the democratic process and facilitating the representation of minorities in the electoral process: "[T]he general theory is one that bounds judicial review under the Constitution's open-ended provisions by insisting that it can appropriately concern itself only with questions of participation, and not with the substantive merits of the political choice under attack."[23] In this way, Ely aimed to justify the Court's supervision of the electoral process (see Vol. 1, Ch. 8) and reconcile judicial review with democratic theory. But Ely failed to provide a general theory in saying nothing about how the Court should handle cases involving disputes over presidential power and federalism, for example.[24] Moreover, the process-oriented theory of judicial review has been criticized for too sharply limiting the Court's role in protecting civil liberties and civil rights. As Justice Robert Jackson in *West Virginia State Board of Education v. Barnette*, 319 U.S. 624 (1943) (see Ch. 5), observed, "The very purpose of a Bill of Rights was to withdraw certain subjects from the vicissitudes of political controversy, to place them beyond the reach of majorities and officials and to establish them as legal principles to be applied by the courts" (see also Ch. 4).

The process-oriented theory of judicial review is closely related to an *institutionalist approach* that is less concerned with "textualism" and "originalism" than the Court's role in American law and politics. Chief Justice Roberts champions this view in deferring to precedent and co-equal branches, when possible, as well as in trying to decide cases on the narrowest possible ground (and, if possible, statutory rather than constitutional grounds). His institutionalism also set him apart from other conservatives on the Court, particularly Justices Scalia and Thomas. See, for example, Chief Justice Roberts's opinions for the Court upholding the Affordable Care Act ("Obamacare") in *National Federation of Independent Business v. Sebelius*, 567 U.S. 519 (2012) (excerpted in Vol. 1, Ch. 6), and *King v. Burwell*, 135 S.Ct. 2480 (2015), as well as his dissent in the same-sex marriage ruling in *Obergefell v. Hodges* (2015) (excerpted in Ch. 12). Compare the dissents by Justices Scalia and Thomas in those cases. To be sure, Justice Scalia also at times emphasizes the Court's institutional role in his opinions; see, for instance, *Employment Division, Department of Human Resources of Oregon v. Smith*, 494 U.S. 872 (1990) (excerpted in Ch. 6), and compare Justice Scalia's opinion with Justice Jackson's opinion and very different view of the role of the Court in *West Virginia State Board of Education v. Barnette* (1943) (excerpted here in Ch. 5).

Recently, some justices and scholars have advanced theories of *pragmatism* or *consequentialism*, avoiding "bright-line" rulings in favor of taking "one-case-at-a-time."[25] For a prime example, see Justice Breyer's concurring opinion explaining his pivotal vote in *Van Orden v. Perry* and *McCreary v. American Civil Liberties Union* (2005) (both cases are excerpted in Ch. 6). On the one hand, he agreed to join a majority upholding a 40-year-old, 6-foot granite monument engraved with the

■ CONSTITUTIONAL HISTORY

What Is the Constitution? Could a Constitutional Amendment Violate the Constitution?

What is the Constitution? Could a constitutional amendment violate the Constitution or fundamental principles of a constitution? These questions continue to be debated, especially in countries such as Germany and India that have constitutional provisions forbidding, or their high courts have interpreted their constitutions to forbid, amendments infringing on fundamental principles such as "human dignity." Other countries prohibit constitutional amendments changing official languages, national anthems, or the boundaries of subnational units; Turkey, for instance, forbids any amendment changing its constitutional provisions declaring the state a secular democracy and a republic.

The German Constitutional Court, for instance, struck down a provision of its Constitution in the *Southwest Case*, 1 BverfGE 14 (1951).[1] After World War II, the occupation forces divided two states, Baden and Wurttemberg, into three for the purposes of administration. When the new Constitution of the Federal Republic of Germany went into effect in 1949, these three territories became länder (states) with their own constitutions. Article 118 of Germany's Basic Law, however, provided that these three territories could be reorganized according to their own agreement or, if they failed to reach an agreement, by federal legislation and a referendum of the people. They were unable to reach an agreement and in 1951 the parliament passed two reorganization laws, creating a single länder to be called Baden-Wurttemberg. Baden immediately challenged the constitutionality of these laws on the ground that they diminished Baden's status as a länder and treated it unfairly and unequally by calling for a referendum of the people instead of just its own population. In holding unconstitutional Article 118, the German court observed:

> An individual constitutional provision cannot be considered as an isolated clause and interpreted alone. A constitution has an inner unity, and the meaning of any one part is linked to that of other provisions. Taken as a unit, a constitution reflects certain over-arching principles and fundamental decisions to which individual provisions are subordinate. Article 79, paragraph 3, makes it clear that the Basic Law agrees with the statement of the Bavarian Constitutional Court:

That a constitutional provision itself may be null and void, is not conceptually impossible just because it is part of the constitution. There are constitutional principles that are so fundamental and to such an extent an expression of a law that precedes even the constitution that they also bind the framer of the constitution, and other constitutional provisions that do not rank so high may be null and void because they contravene these principles. . . .

From this rule of interpretation, it follows that any constitutional provision must be interpreted in such a way that it is compatible with those elementary principles and with the basic decisions of the framer of the constitution. This rule applies also to Article 118, sentence 2.

In the United States, some legal scholars also contend that the proposed constitutional amendment to forbid desecration of the American flag would violate the Constitution. Following the Supreme Court's ruling in *Texas v. Johnson* (excerpted in Ch. 5), holding that flag-burning is protected speech under the First Amendment, Congress passed the Federal Flag Protection Act of 1989. That statute was then struck down in *United States v. Eichman* (1990). Following those rulings, an attempt in 1995 to override the Court's decisions by means of a constitutional amendment failed to pass the Senate by three votes. In 1997, the House of Representatives passed another proposed constitutional amendment and the Senate was closely divided on whether to send it to the states for ratification. Moreover, forty-nine state legislatures, far more than the thirty-eight required to amend the Constitution, had indicated that they would ratify a constitutional amendment outlawing flag-burning. The Senate has reconsidered the matter several times but failed to muster the 67 votes needed for passage.

The constitutionality of constitutional amendments was raised previously in challenges to the validity of the Eighteenth and Nineteenth Amendments. The Eighteenth Amendment, ratified in 1919, prohibited the manufacturing, sales, and transportation of intoxicating liquors; it was later repealed by the Twenty-first Amendment in 1933. The Nineteenth Amendment, ratified in 1920, extended federal and state voting rights to women.

Shortly after the ratification of the Eighteenth Amendment, the Court consolidated seven lawsuits challenging the amendment's constitutionality in *The National Prohibition Cases, State of Rhode Island v. Palmer*, 253 U.S. 350 (1920). When arguing for Rhode Island, Herbert Rice contended that "the Amendment is an invasion of the sovereignty of the complaining State and her people . . ." Continuing, he argued:

(continues)

■ CONSTITUTIONAL HISTORY
*What Is the Constitution? Could a Constitutional
Amendment Violate the Constitution? (continued)*

It is "This Constitution" that may be amended. "This Constitution" is not a code of transient laws but a framework of government and an embodiment of fundamental principles. By an
amendment, the identity or purpose of the instrument is not to
be changed; its defects may be cured, but "This Constitution"
must remain. It would be the greatest absurdity to contend that
there was a purpose to create a limited government and at the
same time to confer upon that government a power to do away
with its own limitations. . . .

In the case of this so-called amendment, the representatives of the people of the United States have attempted, not to
amend the Constitution of the United States, but to amend the
constitution of every State in the Union. If the amending function is construed as extensive with absolute sovereignty, then
the basis of our political system is no longer the right of the
people of a State to make and alter their constitution, for their
political institutions are at the mercy of others and may be
changed against their will. . . .

Attorneys Elihu Root and William D. Guthrie also sought to persuade the Court of the amendment's unconstitutionality, arguing:

If, as contended by the defendants, the power of amendment
vested in Congress and three-fourths of the state legislatures be
absolute and unrestricted, then there would be no limitation
whatever upon their legislative authority. They could then by
amendment establish a state religion, or oppress or discriminate
against any denomination, or authorize the taking away of life,
liberty and property, without due process of law, etc., etc. This
would destroy the most essential limitation upon power under
the American system of government, which is that the rights
of the individual citizen shall be protected by withholding
from the legislative function the power to do certain things
inconsistent with individual liberty. This was the reason of the
irresistible demand for the first ten amendments. . . .

By contrast, Solicitor General Alexander King countered, first, that whether the amendment was within the amending power of Article V and whether it in fact had been ratified "are questions committed by the Constitution to the political branch and not to the judicial branch of the Government." Second, "It has always been understood that there is no limitation upon the character of amendments which may be adopted, except such limitations as are imposed by Article V itself. . . . The fact that the Eighteenth Amendment confers upon Congress a power which had previously belonged exclusively to the States does not prevent that Amendment from being within the amending power conferred by Article V of the Constitution." Finally, he concluded: "No State by any provision of its laws or its constitution can make the ratification of an amendment to the Constitution of the United States by its legislature subject to a referendum vote of the people. The only method of ratification mentioned in the Constitution is through representatives assembled either in the legislature or a convention called for that purpose."

The arguments of the solicitor general prevailed and in a brief opinion for the Court Justice Van Devanter stated only "the conclusions of the Court," not its reasoning. Subsequently, the Nineteenth Amendment was challenged on the grounds that it was enacted without Maryland's consent and that state's constitution limited suffrage to men. Writing for the Court in *Leser v. Garnett*, 258 U.S. 130 (1922), Justice Brandeis dismissed that claim as well.[2]

Countries (e.g., Germany, Ireland, and South Africa) have so-called *eternity clauses* that render parts of the Constitution immune to amendments, and still, some scholars continue to maintain that some amendments might run afoul of those underlying constitutional principles. For further discussion, see Yaniv Roznai, *Unconstitutional Constitutional Amendments* (New York: Oxford University Press 2017); and Sanford Levinson, ed., *Responding to Imperfection: The Theory and Practice of Constitutional Amendment* (Princeton, NJ: Princeton University Press, 1995).

1. The *Southwest Case* is translated and excerpted in Walter F. Murphy and Joseph Tanenhaus, eds., *Comparative Constitutional Law: Cases and Commentaries* (New York: St. Martin's Press, 1977). See also *Article 117 Case*, 3 BverfGE 225 (1953); *Privacy in Communications (Klass) Case*, 30 BverfGE 1 (1970); and Donald Kommers, ed., *The Constitutional Jurisprudence of the Federal Republic of Germany*, 2d ed. (Durham, NC: Duke University Press, 1997).

2. See also *Schneiderman v. United States*, 320 U.S. 118 (1943).

Ten Commandments on Texas public grounds, but on the other hand deemed a violation of the First Amendment (dis)establishment clause the more recent posting of the Ten Commandments in Kentucky courthouses, because of their different consequences and public reactions.

Ultimately, what divides the justices, and sometimes the Court and the country, has less to do with interpretivism and noninterpretivism than fundamentally rival political philosophies and views of the role of the Court in American politics. It is not just that constitutional interpretation draws on the text, structure, history, doctrines, practices, and moral and political philosophy that is important, but how these sources and modes of analysis are employed. Admittedly, as Justice Scalia noted, there may be a "sense of dissatisfaction" with finding that we "do not yet have an agreed-upon theory" of constitutional interpretation. "But it should come as no surprise."[26] That conclusion has also led Judge Richard Posner of the Court of Appeals for the Seventh Circuit, a prolific author and advocate of pragmatism, to argue against the need for specialized constitutional theories to justify legal doctrines, and for more empirical research into the socioeconomic complexities underlying legal controversies.[27] To be sure, there is no denying that in constitutional politics there are no simple solutions but instead an invitation for reflection and enduring political struggles.

NOTES

1. See Willard Hurst, "The Role of History," in *Supreme Court and Supreme Law*, ed. Edmond Cahn (New York: Clarion Books, 1971); Charles Miller, *The Supreme Court and the Uses of History* (Cambridge, MA: Harvard University Press, 1969); and G. Edward White, "The Arrival of History in Constitutional Scholarship," 88 *Virginia Law Review* 485 (2002).

2. William Rehnquist, "The Notion of a Living Constitution," in David M. O'Brien, ed., *Judges on Judging*, 5th ed., (Washington, DC: C.Q. Press, 2016).

3. See Paul Rosen, *The Supreme Court and Social Science* (Urbana: University of Illinois Press, 1972); and David O'Brien, "The Seduction of the Judiciary: Social Science and the Courts," 64 *Judicature* 8 (1980).

4. See Edward S. Corwin, *The "Higher Law" Background of American Constitutional Law* (Ithaca, NY: Cornell University Press, 1955); Thomas Grey, "Do We Have an Unwritten Constitution," 27 *Stanford Law Review* 703 (1975); Robert Goldwin and William Schambra, eds., *How Does the Constitution Secure Rights?* (Washington, DC: American Enterprise Institute, 1985).

5. Memo to Justice Harold Burton on No. 142 *Louisiana v. Resweber* (December 13, 1946), observing that "Holmes used to express it by saying that he would not strike down a State action unless the action of the State made him puke." Robert H. Jackson Papers, Box 138, Library of Congress.

6. See Ronald Dworkin, *Taking Rights Seriously* (Cambridge, MA: Harvard University Press, 1977), 149; Ronald Dworkin, *A Matter of Principle* (Cambridge, MA:

Harvard University Press, 1985); and Ronald Dworkin, *Law's Empire* (Cambridge, MA: Harvard University Press, 1986).

7. See David L. Faigman, *Laboratory of Justice* (New York: Times Books, 2004).

8. Henry Hart, "Foreword: The Time Chart of the Justices," 73 *Harvard Law Review* 84 (1959).

9. Charles Black, "Old and New Ways in Judicial Review," address given at Bowdoin College, 1957.

10. Terrance Sandalow, "Constitutional Interpretation," 79 *Michigan Law Review* 1033 (1981).

11. Harry Wellington, "Common Law Rules and Constitutional Double Standards: Some Notes on Adjudication," 83 *Yale Law Journal* 221 (1973). See also Michael Perry, *The Constitution, the Courts, and Human Rights* (New Haven, CT: Yale University Press, 1982); and Michael Perry, *Morality, Politics & Law* (New York: Oxford University Press, 1988).

12. Owen Fiss, "Objectivity and Interpretation," 34 *Stanford Law Review* 739 (1982).

13. Dworkin, *Taking Rights Seriously*, 149.

14. Kenneth Karst, "The Freedom of Intimate Association," 89 *Yale Law Journal* 624 (1980); and Richard Richards, "Human Rights as the Unwritten Constitution: The Problem of Change and Stability in Constitutional Interpretation," 4 *University of Dayton Law Review* 295 (1979).

15. Michael Michelman, "In Pursuit of Constitutional Welfare Rights: One View of Rawls's Theory of Justice," 121 *University of Pennsylvania Law Review* 962 (1979).

16. Alexander Bickel, *The Supreme Court and the Idea of Progress* (New York: Harper & Row, 1970).

17. See David O'Brien, "'The Imperial Judiciary': Of Paper Tigers and Socio-Legal Indicators," 2 *Journal of Law & Politics* 1 (1985).

18. John Ely, *Democracy and Distrust* (Cambridge, MA: Harvard University Press, 1980), 58.

19. Robert Bork, "Tradition and Morality in Constitutional Law," in *Judges on Judging*, ed. O'Brien.

20. William Brennan Jr., "The Constitution of the United States: Contemporary Ratification," speech given at Georgetown University, October 12, 1985, reprinted in *Judges on Judging*, ed. O'Brien.

21. Charles Black Jr., *Structure and Relationship in Constitutional Law* (Baton Rouge: Louisiana University Press, 1969).

22. See Laurence Tribe, "The Puzzling Persistence of Process-Based Constitutional Theories," 89 *Yale Law Journal* 1063 (1980); and Mark Tushnet, "Darkness on the Edge of Town: The Contributions of John Hart Ely," 89 *Yale Law Journal* 1037 (1980).

23. Ely, *Democracy and Distrust*, 181.

24. See David O'Brien, "Judicial Review and Constitutional Politics: Theory and Practice," 48 *University of Chicago Law Review* 1052 (1981).

25. See, for example, Stephen Breyer, *Active Liberty* (New York: Knopf, 2005); Richard Posner, *Law, Pragmatism, and Democracy* (Cambridge, MA: Harvard University Press, 2003); and Cass Sunstein, *One Case at a Time: Judicial Minimalism on the Supreme Court* (Cambridge, MA: Harvard University Press, 1999).

26. Antonin Scalia, "Originalism: The Lesser Evil," 57 *Cincinnati Law Review* 850 (1989), 865, reprinted in *Judges on Judging*, ed. O'Brien.

27. Richard A. Posner, "Against Constitutional Theory," 73 *New York University Law* 1 (1998). See also R. Posner, *The Problematics of Moral and Legal Theory* (Cambridge, MA: Belknap Press, 1999).

Selected Bibliography

Amar, Akhil Reed, *America's Unwritten Constitution*. New York: Basic Books, 2012.

Arkes, Hadley. *Constitutional Illusions and Anchoring Truths: The Touchstone of Natural Law*. New York: Cambridge University Press, 2010.

Balkin, Jack. *Living Originalism*. Cambridge, MA: Harvard University Press, 2011.

Barber, Sotirios, and James Fleming, *Constitutional Interpretation: The Basic Questions*. New York: Oxford University Press, 2007.

Black, Charles, *Structure and Relationship in Constitutional Law*. Baton Rouge: Louisiana State University Press, 1969.

————. *A New Birth of Freedom: Human Rights, Named and Unnamed*. New York: Grosset/Putnam, 1997.

Bloom, Lackland H. *Methods of Interpretation: How the Supreme Court Reads the Constitution*. New York: Oxford University Press, 2009.

Bobbitt, Philip. *Constitutional Fate*. New York: Oxford University Press, 1982.

Breyer, Stephen. *Active Liberty: Interpreting Our Democratic Constitution*. New York: Knopf, 2005.

————. *Making Our Democracy Work: A Judge's View*. New York: Knopf, 2010.

————. *The Court and the World: American Law and The New Global Realities*. New York: Knopf, 2015.

Corwin, Edward. *The "Higher Law" Background of American Constitutional Law*. Ithaca, NY: Cornell University Press, 1955.

Crenshaw, Kimberle, Neil Gotanda, Gary Peller, and Kendall Thomas, eds., *Critical Race Theory: The Key Writings That Formed the Movement*. New York: The New Press, 1995.

Delgado, Richard, and Jean Stefancic. *Critical Race Theory: The Cutting Edge*. Philadelphia: Temple University Press, 1999.

Devins, Neal, and Louis Fisher. *The Democratic Constitution*. New York: Oxford University Press, 2004.

Dworkin, Ronald. *Taking Rights Seriously*. Cambridge, MA: Harvard University Press, 1977.

————. *Law's Empire*. Cambridge, MA: Harvard University Press, 1986.

————. *Justice for Hedgehogs*. Cambridge, MA: Harvard University Press, 2011.

Ely, John. *Democracy and Distrust*. Cambridge, MA: Harvard University Press, 1980.

Farber, Daniel, and Suzanna Sherry. *Beyond All Reason: The Radical Assault on Truth in American Law*. New York: Oxford University Press, 1997.

————. *Desperately Seeking Certainty: The Misguided Quest for Constitutional Foundations*. Chicago: University of Chicago Press, 2003.

————. *Judgment Calls: Principle and Politics in Constitutional Law.* New York: Oxford University Press, 2008.

Fleming, James. *Securing Constitutional Democracy.* Chicago: University of Chicago Press, 2006.

George, Robert P. *In Defense of Natural Law.* New York: Oxford University Press, 1999.

Goldstein, Leslie, ed. *Feminist Jurisprudence.* Lanham, MD: Rowman & Littlefield, 1992.

Hackney, James, Jr. *Legal Intellectuals in Conversation: Reflections on The Construction of Contemporary American Legal Theory.* New York: New York University Press, 2012.

MacKinnon, Catharine, *Toward a Feminist Theory of the State.* Cambridge, MA: Harvard University Press, 1989.

————. *Feminism Unmodified.* Cambridge, MA: Harvard University Press, 1987.

Murphy, Walter, *Constitutional Democracy: Creating and Maintaining a Just Political Order.* Baltimore, MD: Johns Hopkins University Press, 2007.

O'Brien, David M., ed. *Judges on Judging,* 5th ed. Washington, DC: C.Q. Press, 2016.

Peretti, Terri Jennings. *In Defense of a Political Court.* Princeton, NJ: Princeton University Press, 1999.

Posner, Richard. *The Problems of Jurisprudence.* Cambridge, MA: Harvard University Press, 1990.

————. *The Problematics of Moral and Legal Theory.* Cambridge, MA: Belknap Press, 1999.

————. *Law, Pragmatism, and Democracy.* Cambridge, MA: Harvard University, Press, 2003.

Powell, H. Jefferson. *Constitutional Conscience: The Moral Dimension of Judicial Decision.* Chicago: University of Chicago Press, 2008.

Redish, Martin. *The Constitution as Political Structure.* New York: Oxford University Press, 1995.

Schlegel, John. *Legal Realism and Empirical Social Science.* Chapel Hill: University of North Carolina Press, 2011.

Strauss, David A. *The Living Constitution.* New York: Oxford University Press, 2010.

Sullivan, Michael. *Legal Pragmatism.* Bloomington: Indiana University Press, 2007.

Tamanaha, Brian. *Law as a Means to an End: Threat to the Rule of Law.* New York: Cambridge University Press, 2006.

Tribe, Laurence. *The Invisible Constitution.* New York: Oxford University Press, 2008.

Tribe, Laurence, and Michael Dorf. *On Reading the Constitution.* Cambridge, MA: Harvard University Press, 1991.

Tushnet, Mark. *Red, White, and Blue: A Critical Analysis of Constitutional Law.* Cambridge, MA: Harvard University Press, 1988.

Weinreb, Lloyd. *Legal Reason: The Use of Analogy in Legal Argument.* New York: Cambridge University Press, 2005.

White, James. *Justice as Translation.* Chicago: University of Chicago Press, 1990.

————. *When Words Lose Their Meaning.* Chicago: University of Chicago Press, 1984.

2

LAW AND POLITICS IN THE SUPREME COURT: JURISDICTION AND DECISION-MAKING PROCESS

The Supreme Court is the only federal court in the United States to have complete power to decide what to decide—that is, which cases to hear. This power enables the Court to set its own agenda as well as to manage its docket. Like other courts, the Supreme Court, however, must await issues brought by lawsuits; it does not initiate its own. Also, like other social institutions, it is affected by social change. One hundred fifty years ago, the Court's docket did not include issues of personal privacy raised by electronic surveillance and computer data banks, for instance, or controversies over abortion and the patenting of organic life forms. As technology develops and society changes, courts respond. Law evolves more or less quickly in response to social change. Another change occurring over the past several decades has been a substantial increase in the number of cases, the caseload, sent to the Court. Unable to hear them all, the Court was given by Congress the power to pick which issues it will decide outside of those arising under Article III. The Court now functions like a roving commission in responding to social forces.

A | *Jurisdiction and Justiciable Controversies*

Jurisdiction is the authorized power of a court to hear a case and to exercise judicial review. The Court's jurisdiction derives from three sources: (1) Article III of the Constitution, which defines the Court's original jurisdiction; (2) congressional legislation, providing the basis for hearing appeals of lower courts' decisions, or appellate jurisdiction; and (3) the Court's own interpretation of 1 and 2 together with its own rules for accepting cases.

Article III of the Constitution provides that the judicial power extends to all federal questions; that is, "all Cases, in Law and Equity, arising under this Constitution, the Laws of the United States, and Treaties." The Court also has original jurisdiction over specific kinds of "cases or controversies": those affecting ambassadors and other public ministers and consuls; disputes to which the United States is a party; disputes between two or more states, disputes between a state and a citizen of another state, if a state waives its sovereign immunity under the Eleventh Amendment; and disputes between a state (or its citizens) and foreign countries. The Court today has only about ten cases each term (the first Monday in October through June) coming on original jurisdiction. Most involve states suing each other over land and water rights, and they tend to be rather complex and carried over for several terms before they are finally decided.

Congress establishes (and may change) the appellate jurisdiction of the federal judiciary, including the Supreme Court. Most cases used to come as direct appeals, requiring obligatory review. But as the caseload increased, Congress expanded the Court's discretionary jurisdiction by replacing appeals with petitions for *certiorari* (a petition asking a court to inspect the proceedings and decision of a lower court), which the Court may in its discretion grant or deny. Prior to the Judiciary Act of 1925, which broadened the Court's discretionary jurisdiction, appeals amounted to 80 percent of the docket and petitions for *certiorari*, less than 20 percent. Today, well over 99 percent of the docket comes on *certiorari*.

Although most cases now come as *certiorari* petitions, Congress provides that appellate courts may submit a writ of certification to the Court, requesting the justices to clarify or "make more certain" a point of federal law. The Court receives only a handful of such cases each term. Congress also gave the Court the power to issue certain extraordinary writs, or orders. In a few cases, the Court may issue writs of *mandamus* and prohibition, ordering lower courts or public officials to either do something or refrain from some action. In addition, the Court has the power to grant writs of *habeas corpus* ("produce the body"), enabling it to review cases by prisoners who claim that their constitutional rights have been violated and they are unlawfully imprisoned.

Congress also established the practice of giving the poor, or the indigent, the right to file without the payment of fees. When filing an appeal or petition for *certiorari*, indigents may file an affidavit requesting that they be allowed to proceed *in forma pauperis* ("in the manner of a pauper"), without the usual filing fees and forms. The Court sets both the rules governing filing fees and the form that appeals, *certiorari* petitions, and other documents must take. Except for indigents, the Court requires $300 for filing any case and another $100 if a case is granted oral argument. Indigents are exempt as well from the Court's rules specifying particular colors and lengths of paper for various kinds of filings. All *cert.* petitions, for instance, must have a white color, whereas opposing briefs are light orange. Any document filed by the federal government has a gray cover. No petition or appeal may exceed thirty pages, and for those few cases granted oral argument, briefs on the merits of cases are limited to fifty pages.

The Constitution and Congress thus stipulate the kinds of cases and controversies the Court may consider. Yet, as Charles Evans Hughes, who later became chief justice (1930–1941), candidly remarked, "We are under the Constitution, but the Constitution is what the Judges say it is."[1] The Court has developed its own doctrines for denying a large number of cases review and for setting its own agenda. Specifically, the Court considers whether it has jurisdiction over a "case or controversy," and then whether that dispute is justiciable, or capable of judicial resolution. Justices thus may, or may not, deny a case if it (1) lacks adverseness or (2) is brought by parties who lack "standing to sue," or poses issues that either (3) are not "ripe," (4) have become "moot," or (5) involve a "political question." What all this means is discussed next.

■ ADVERSENESS AND ADVISORY OPINIONS

The Court generally maintains that litigants, those involved in a lawsuit, must be real and adverse in seeking a decision that will resolve their dispute and not some hypothetical issue. The requirement of real and adverse parties means that the Court will not decide so-called friendly suits (when the parties do not have adverse interests in the outcome of a case). Nor will the Court give "advisory opinions" on issues not raised

Avenues of Appeal:
The Two Main Routes to the Supreme Court

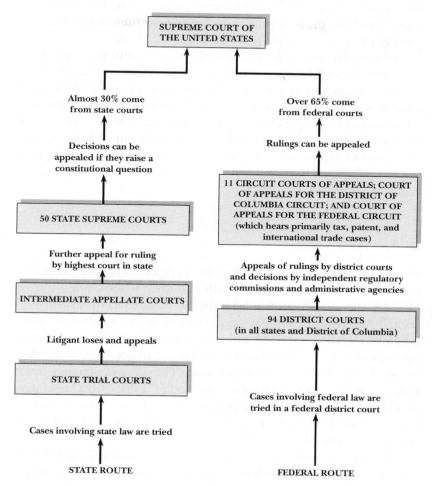

**SUPREME COURT OF
THE UNITED STATES**

**Almost 30% come
from state courts**

**Over 65% come
from federal courts**

**Decisions can be
appealed if they raise a
constitutional question**

Rulings can be appealed

**11 CIRCUIT COURTS OF APPEALS; COURT
OF APPEALS FOR THE DISTRICT OF
COLUMBIA CIRCUIT; AND COURT OF
APPEALS FOR THE FEDERAL CIRCUIT
(which hears primarily tax, patent, and
international trade cases)**

50 STATE SUPREME COURTS

**Further appeal for ruling
by highest court in state**

**Appeals of rulings by district courts
and decisions by independent regulatory
commissions and administrative agencies**

INTERMEDIATE APPELLATE COURTS

**94 DISTRICT COURTS
(in all states and District of Columbia)**

Litigant loses and appeals

STATE TRIAL COURTS

**Cases involving federal law are
tried in a federal district court**

Cases involving state law are tried

STATE ROUTE

FEDERAL ROUTE

Note: In addition, some cases come directly to the Supreme Court from trial courts when they involve reapportionment or civil rights disputes. Appeals from the Court of Military Appeals also go directly to the Supreme Court. A few cases come on "original jurisdiction" and involve disputes between state governments.

in an actual lawsuit. The Jay Court denied two requests for advisory opinions: one in 1790 by Secretary of Treasury Alexander Hamilton on the national government's power to assume state Revolutionary War debts, and the other in 1793 by Secretary of State Thomas Jefferson for an interpretation of certain treaties and international law. Chief Justice John Jay held that it would be improper for the Court to judge such matters, because the president may call on cabinet heads for advice. The Court continues to maintain that it is inappropriate "to give opinions in the nature of advice concerning legislative action, a function never conferred upon it by the Constitution and against the exercise of which this court has steadily set its face from the beginning."[2]

Historically, justices have nevertheless extrajudicially advised attorneys, members of Congress, and presidents. They occasionally even accuse each other of including in opinions *dicta* (statements of personal opinion or philosophy not necessary to the decision handed down) that is tantamount to "giving legal advice."[3] The Court, furthermore, upheld the constitutionality of the Declaratory Judgment Act authorizing federal courts to declare, or make clear, rights and legal relationships even before a legislature has mandated a law to take effect, although only in "cases of actual controversy."[4]

■ STANDING TO SUE

Standing, like adverseness, is a threshold requirement for getting into court. "Generalizations about standing to sue," as Justice William O. Douglas discouragingly, but candidly, put it, "are largely worthless as such."[5] Nonetheless, the basic requirement is that individuals show injury to a legally protected interest or right and demonstrate that other opportunities for defending that claim (before an administrative tribunal or a lower court) have been exhausted. The claim of an injury "must be of a personal and not official nature" and of "some specialized interest of [the individual's] own to vindicate, apart from political concerns which belong to it."[6] The interest must be real as opposed to speculative or hypothetical.

The injuries and legal interests claimed traditionally turned on a showing of personal or proprietary damage. Typically, plaintiffs had suffered some "pocketbook" or monetary injury. But in the last fifty years, individuals have sought standing to represent nonmonetary injuries and "the public interest."

The law of standing is a combination of judge-made law and congressional legislation, as interpreted by the Court. During Earl Warren's tenure as chief justice (1953–1969) the Court substantially lowered the threshold for standing and permitted more litigation of public policy issues. *Frothingham v. Mellon*, 262 U.S. 447 (1923), was the leading case on taxpayer suits until it was overturned in *Flast v. Cohen* (1968) (see excerpt below). In *Frothingham*, the Taft Court had denied taxpayers standing to challenge the constitutionality of federal legislation. Mrs. Frothingham, a taxpayer, had attacked Congress's appropriation of federal funds to the states for a maternal and infant care program. She claimed that Congress exceeded its power and intruded on "the reserved rights of the states" under the Tenth Amendment of the Constitution. Writing for the Court, Justice George Sutherland avoided confronting the merits of her claim by denying standing. He did so on the grounds that an individual taxpayer's interest in the financing of federal programs is "comparatively minute and indeterminable," when viewed in light of all taxpayers. *Frothingham*'s "injury" was neither direct nor immediate and the issue raised was basically "political, not judicial." As Sutherland put it,

> [T]he relation of a taxpayer of the United States to the Federal Government is very different [from that relationship with state and local governments]. His interest in the moneys of the Treasury—partly realized from taxation and partly from other sources—is shared with millions of others; is comparatively minute and indeterminable; and the effect upon future taxation, or any payment out of the funds, so remote, fluctuating and uncertain, that no basis is afforded for an appeal to the preventive powers of a court of equity.

To gain standing, according to Sutherland, a taxpayer "must be able to show not only that the statute is invalid but that he has sustained . . . some direct injury as the result of its enforcement, and not merely that he suffers in some indefinite way in common with people generally."

Frothingham's "direct injury" test was met in *Pierce v. Society of Sisters*, 268 U.S. 510 (1925). There, a religious school won a court order barring the enforcement of Oregon's 1922 constitutional amendment requiring children between the ages of eight and sixteen to attend public schools. The Court affirmed on the grounds that the law directly damaged the business and property interests of the school and because it "unreasonably interferes with the liberty of parents and guardians to direct the upbringing and education of children under their control."

The federal government relied on *Frothingham* to provide an absolute barrier to subsequent federal taxpayer suits until the Warren Court made an exception to that doctrine in *Flast v. Cohen* (1968) (see excerpt below). In his opinion for the Court, Chief Justice Warren created a two-pronged standard for granting standing to federal taxpayers to challenge public expenditures for religious schools: taxpayers must show a logical relationship between their status as taxpayers and the challenged congressional statute as well as a connection between that status and the "precise nature of the constitutional infringement alleged."

The Burger Court (1969–1986) and the Rehnquist Court (1986–2005) tightened the requirements for standing in some cases, but relaxed

Jurisdictional Map of the U.S. Courts of Appeal and
U.S. District Courts

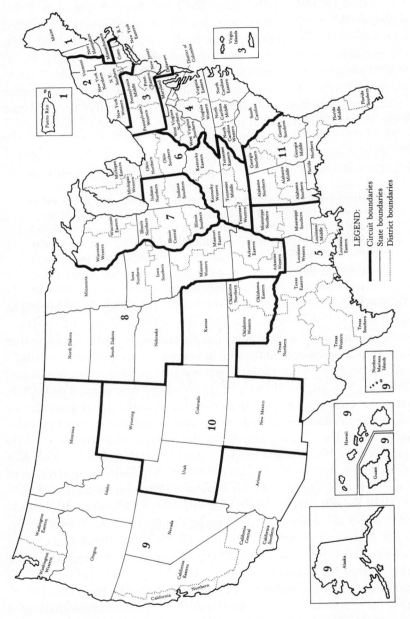

Note: The court of appeals for the federal circuit and the District of Columbia circuit are located in the District of Columbia. (*Administrative Office of the U.S. Courts, Washington, DC.*)

them in others. In 1972, in two sharply divided decisions, the Burger Court denied standing to a group challenging military surveillance of lawful political protests in public places and to the Sierra Club when challenging the construction of a ski resort in Mineral King National Park. In both *Laird v. Tatum*, 408 U.S. 1 (1972), and *Sierra Club v. Morton*, 405 U.S. 727 (1972), a bare majority found that the groups failed to show a "personal stake in the outcome" of the litigation. In *Sierra Club*, Justices Douglas and Blackmun dissented, and with Powell and Rehnquist recused, the majority was not firm. Moreover, Douglas's powerful dissent questioned the majority's premises and reasoning. Citing a recent and highly influential article (later published as a book, 3rd ed., 2007) by Christopher Stone, "Should Trees Have Standing? Toward Legal Rights for Natural Objects," Justice Douglas observed:

> Inanimate objects are sometimes parties in litigation. A ship has a legal personality, a fiction found useful for maritime purposes. . . . The ordinary corporation is a "person" for purposes of the adjudicatory process, whether it represents proprietary, spiritual, aesthetic, or charitable causes.
>
> So it should be as respects valleys, alpine meadows, rivers, lakes, estuaries, beaches, ridges, groves of trees, swampland, or even air that feels the destructive pressures of modern technology and modern life. The river, for example, is the living symbol of all the life it sustains or nourishes—fish, aquatic insects, water ouzels, otter, fisher, deer, elk, bear, and all other animals, including man, who are dependent on it or its life. . . .
>
> Those people who have a meaningful relation to that body of water—whether it be a fisherman, a canoeist, a zoologist, or a logger—must be able to speak for the values which the river represents and which are threatened with destruction.

A year later, though, a majority of the Court embraced Justice Douglas's dissenting position in *Sierra Club* when granting standing to a group of law students challenging a proposed surcharge on railroad recycled freight. The students contended that the surcharge would discourage the recycling of bottles and cans, and thus contribute to environmental pollution. In *United States v. Students Challenging Regulatory Agency Procedure (SCRAP)*, 412 U.S. 669 (1973), in granting standing the Court observed, "Aesthetic and environmental well-being, like economic well-being, are important ingredients of the quality of life in our society, and the fact that particular environmental interests are shared by the many rather than the few does not make them less deserving of legal protection through the judicial process."

Plaintiffs, those bringing suit, must still claim a personal injury, but they could now act as surrogates for special interest groups. The personal injuries claimed thus embrace a public injury. Congress at the same time expanded the principle even more by providing that any individual "adversely affected or aggrieved" may challenge administrative decisions. Health, safety, and environmental legislation passed in the 1970s mandated such "citizen suits" and right to judicial review of regulatory action. Even when legislation does not provide for the citizen suits, individuals may claim personal injuries, or a "private cause of action," to gain access to the courts and to force agency compliance with the law.

The more conservative Burger and Rehnquist Courts restricted standing requirements in several ways. First, they refused to recognize new interests and injuries in granting standing. In *Linda R. S. v. Richard D.*, 410 U.S. 614 (1973), for instance, an unwed mother sought enforcement of child support under the Texas Penal Code because the local prosecutor refused to enforce the statute against fathers of illegitimate children. A majority of the Court ruled that she had no recognizable injury and no standing because she could not prove that payments stopped because that particular statute was unenforced.

In *Paul v. Davis*, 424 U.S. 693 (1976), the Court's majority rejected a claim of injury to personal reputation by an individual who objected to the circulation of a flyer to local merchants that carried his photograph along with that of other alleged "active shoplifters." Rehnquist dismissed the claim out of hand. But Justice William Brennan in dissent responded that "[t]he Court by mere fiat and with no analysis wholly excludes personal interest in reputation from the ambit of 'life, liberty, or property' under the Fifth and Fourteenth Amendments, thus rendering due process concerns *never* applicable to the official stigmatization, however, arbitrary."

The Court went even further with its reinterpretation of the application of *Flast*'s test for taxpayer suits in *Valley Forge Christian College v. Americans United for Separation of Church and State, Inc.* (1982) (see excerpt below). And a bare majority of the Roberts Court (2005–) further limited taxpayers' standing to challenge federal policies under *Flast v. Cohen* in *Hein v. Freedom from Religion Foundation, Inc.* (2007) (excerpted below). Although declining to overrule *Flast*, writing for the majority Justice Alito limited *Flast* to permit taxpayer suits under the First Amendment (dis)establishment clause to challenges to congressional appropriations, but not to general expenditures for policies of the executive branch. Notably, concurring Justice Scalia, joined by Justice Thomas, would have overturned *Flast*. By contrast, Justice Souter, joined by Justices Stevens, Ginsburg, and Breyer, dissented and would have granted standing to challenge President George W. Bush's faith-based initiatives.

A bare majority of the Roberts Court continued its movement toward further limiting taxpayers' standing in *Arizona Christian School Tuition Organization v. Winn*, 563 U.S. 125 (2011) (excerpted below). Sharply limiting *Flast* in writing for the Court, Justice Kennedy drew a bright line between taxpayer challenges to state appropriations for private religious schools and programs that give taxpayers dollar-for-dollar tax credits on their state taxes for contributions to nonprofit groups that provide scholarships to private schools, including religious schools. Justice Kennedy held that while taxpayers under *Flast* had standing to challenge appropriations aiding religious schools under the First Amendment (dis)establishment clause, they did not have standing to challenge tax credit programs that permitted contributions to aid religious schools. He did so on the theory that the subsidy for scholarships was not actually from state tax revenues but from donations of taxpayers who then received tax credits. In a concurring opinion, Justice Scalia, joined by Justice Thomas, once again argued for overturning *Flast*. Justice Kagan filed a dissenting opinion, joined by Justices Ginsburg, Breyer, and Sotomayor.

Almost two decades after the Court liberalized the law of standing so as to allow citizens' suits for environmental damages, a majority of the Rehnquist Court tightened standing requirements by raising new obstacles for citizens bringing environmental lawsuits. Writing for the majority in *Lujan v. Defenders of Wildlife*, 504 U.S. 555 (1992) (see excerpt below), Justice Scalia denied two environmentalists standing because they failed to show "imminent injury," or that they were in immediate danger of suffering a concrete harm that supported their filing a suit under the Endangered Species Act of 1973. Although Justice Stevens concurred, he would have granted standing, as would have the two dissenters, Justices Blackmun and O'Connor.

In another important ruling on standing, in *Northeastern Florida Chapter of the Associated General Contractors of America v. City of Jacksonville, Florida*, 508 U.S. 656 (1993) (see Ch. 12), the Rehnquist Court made it easier for whites to gain standing to challenge affirmative action and minority set-aside programs. With Justices O'Connor and Blackmun dissenting, the Court held that a building association could challenge a city's set-aside program, even though during the course of the litigation the city had repealed its program. Writing for the majority, Justice Thomas held that in asserting standing to sue a building association did not have to show that any of its members, in the absence of the program, would have received building contracts set aside for women and minorities. While the ruling makes it easier to bring suits attacking set-aside and affirmative action programs, the decision more generally invites lawsuits against governments over the administration

■ THE DEVELOPMENT OF LAW

Other Important Rulings on Standing

CASE	VOTE	RULING
Schlesinger v. Reservists Committee to (Stop the War, 418 U.S 208 (1974)	6–3	Held that members of an organization of present and past members of the military reserves opposed to the Vietnam War had no standing to file a class action suit against the secretary of defense, attacking the constitutionality of members of Congress holding commissions in the reserves and voting on appropriations for the war, as an alleged violation of Article I, Section 6, Clause 2, which declares that "no person holding any office under the United States, shall be a Member of either House during his continuance in office."
United States v. Richardson, 418 U.S. 166 (1974)	5–4	Denied taxpayer standing to bring suit against Congress's secret funding for the Central Intelligence Agency, as an alleged violation of Article I, Section 9, Clause 7, which provides that "no Money shall be drawn from the Treasury, but in Consequence of Appropriations made by Law; and a regular Statement of Account of the Receipts and Expenditures of all public money shall be published from time to time."
Warth v. Seldin, 422 U.S. 490 (1975)	5–4	Denied standing to various organizations in Rochester, New York, seeking to sue officials of the suburban town of Penfield, claiming that the latter's zoning ordinance excluded low- and moderate-income persons from living in the town and violated their rights under the Bill of Rights. The Court held that the individuals and organizations failed to show that they had been "personally" injured.
Simon v. Eastern Kentucky Welfare Rights Organization, 426 U.S. 26 (1976)	9–0	Denied standing to indigents seeking to challenge federal tax regulations reducing the amount of free medical care hospitals must provide in order to receive certain tax benefits.

CASE	VOTE	RULING
City of Los Angeles v. Lyons, 461 U.S. 95 (1983)	5–4	Held that an arrestee had standing to sue the city for damages incurred as a result of police subjecting him to a "choke hold," but that he had no

standing to seek an injunction against the police practice of using choke holds, because he failed to show that he might ever be subjected to a choke hold again.

Allen v. Wright, 468 U.S. 737 (1984)	5–3	Denied standing to parents of black children attending public schools in districts around the country that were

in the process of desegregation to sue various government officials and present their contention that the IRS failed to fulfill its obligation under the law to deny tax-exempt status to private schools engaged in racial discrimination.

Renne v. Geary, 501 U.S. 312 (1991)	7–2	Held that a challenge to a section of California's constitution, which prohibits political parties from endorsing

candidates in nonpartisan elections for judgeships and local government offices, was nonjusticiable because members of the San Francisco County Republican and Democratic Central committees did not have standing and failed to present a ripe case in challenging the state's restrictions as a violation of their First Amendment freedoms. Justices Blackmun and Marshall dissented.

Lujan v. Defenders of Wildlife, 504 U.S. 555 (1992)	7–2	Writing for the Court, Justice Scalia denied standing to two environmentalists to bring a suit because they failed to show "imminent injury,"

or that they were in immediate danger of suffering a concrete harm that supported their challenge to federal funding for projects in foreign countries, under the Endangered Species Act of 1973. Although Justice Stevens concurred, he would have granted standing, as would have dissenting Justices Blackmun and O'Connor.

(continues)

■ THE DEVELOPMENT OF LAW
Other Important Rulings on Standing (continued)

CASE	VOTE	RULING

Wyoming v. Oklahoma, 6–3 Expanded standing for states to sue one
502 U.S. 437 (1992) another, under the dormant commerce
clause theory, on the grounds that one
state's regulations diminished the tax revenues of another. Dissenting Chief
Justice Rehnquist and Justices Scalia and Thomas denounced the majority's
expansive interpretation of standing under the commerce clause and
warned that the ruling would invite a flood of litigation from the states.

Northeastern Florida 7–2 Held that a building association had
Chapter of the Associated Gen- standing to challenge an affirmative
eral Contractors of America v. action set-aside program for contrac-
City of tors, even though during the course
Jacksonville, Florida, of the litigation the city had repealed
508 U.S. 656 (1993) its program and the building association did not present any evidence that
its members, in the absence of the program, would have received building contracts set aside for women and minorities. Justices Blackmun and
O'Connor dissented.

Bennett v. Spear, 9–0 Held that property owners, no less
520 U.S. 154 (1997) than environmentalists, may assert
standing to bring "citizen suits" under
the Endangered Species Act, and thereby challenge proposed environmental regulations. Writing for the Court, Justice Scalia ruled that the act's
permitting "any person" to sue should be broadly interpreted because "the
overall subject matter of this legislation is the environment . . . a matter in
which it is common to think all persons have an interest." As a result, landowners have new legal standing to challenge environmental regulations.

Raines v. Byrd, 7–2 Writing for the Court, Chief Justice
521 U.S. 811 (1997) Rehnquist held that several members
of Congress who challenged the con-
stitutionality of the Line Item Veto Act of 1996, delegating to the president the power of line-item vetoes, did not have standing to sue, because
they did not assert any personal injury and "the institutional injury [to
Congress] they allege[d] is wholly abstract and widely dispersed." Dissenting Justices Stevens and Breyer would have granted standing and
reached the merits presented.

CASE	VOTE	RULING

Friends of the Earth, Inc. v. Laidlaw Environmental Services, 528 U.S. 167 (2000)   7–2   Upheld the right of Friends of the Earth, Inc., to sue Laidlaw Environmental Services for failing to comply with the Clean Water Act by impermissibly dumping mercury into a South Carolina river on 489 occasions from 1987 to 1995. Writing for the Court, Justice Ginsburg held that the group had shown sufficient personal injury from their loss of enjoyment of the river to gain standing to sue without also having to prove "direct injury" to the river. The test for standing, in her words, is "not injury to the environment but injury to the plaintiff." Moreover, Justice Ginsburg ruled that the fact that fines won under such citizen suits go to the federal government, not to the individuals bringing the suits, does not diminish the personal injury at stake or deprive plaintiffs of standing. Justices Scalia and Thomas dissented.

Alexander v. Sandoval, 532 U.S. 275 (2001)   5–4   Writing for the Court, Justice Scalia held that individuals do not have standing to sue in order to enforce compliance with Title VI of the Civil Rights Act, which bars state and local governments from spending federal funds in a discriminatory manner, unless they can show that the intent of the institution—a state, school district, hospital, etc.—was to discriminate. Previously, the Department of Justice and federal courts had held that, in most cases, individuals could sue upon showing that the effect of a particular practice or policy—hiring or admissions rules, for example—worked to disadvantage minorities and women. Thus, the threshold for standing for private individuals to enforce state and local government compliance with Title VI was raised and the filing of so-called disparate-impact lawsuits limited. Justices Stevens, Souter, Ginsburg, and Breyer dissented.

Palazzolo v. Rhode Island, 533 U.S. 606 (2001)   5–4   Writing for the Court, Justice Kennedy held that once property owners take title to property that includes land-use restrictions, they have standing to challenge those restrictions, even if the restrictions were imposed years earlier. In Justice Kennedy's words, the government may not be relieved "of its obligation to defend any action restricting land use, no matter how extreme or unreasonable." Although inviting more challenges to environmental regulations, on the merits the Court reaffirmed that to prevail such challenges must demonstrate that the owner was deprived of all economic value of the land. Justice Ginsburg, joined by Justices Souter and Breyer, dissented, contending that the case was not "ripe" for decision.

(continues)

■ THE DEVELOPMENT OF LAW
Other Important Rulings on Standing (continued)

CASE	VOTE	RULING
Massachusetts v. Environmental Protection Agency, 549 U.S. 497 (2007)	6–3	Writing for the Court, Justice Stevens held that Massachusetts had standing to sue the Environmental Protection Agency (EPA) over its failure to regulate green-

house emissions. Justice Stevens reasoned that the state owned a great deal of the territory affected and had the sovereign prerogative to force reductions in the emissions, as well as that the EPA Act granted a procedural right to challenge the EPA's rulemaking as arbitrary and capricious, since the state's risk was both "actual" and "imminent." Chief Justice Roberts and Justices Scalia, Thomas, and Alito dissented.

of benefit programs by individuals who need not show they were actually denied or would have obtained benefits.

In *Wyoming v. Oklahoma*, 502 U.S. 437 (1992), however, a majority of the Rehnquist Court expanded standing for states to challenge the constitutionality of other states' regulations under the commerce clause on the grounds those regulations diminished the state's tax revenues. In order to promote local jobs and to increase tax revenues, in 1986 Oklahoma enacted a law requiring its public utilities to purchase at least 10 percent of the coal they used from mines within the state. As a result, Oklahoma's public utilities purchased less Wyoming-mined coal, and Wyoming lost revenues from severance taxes on coal that would have otherwise been sold to Oklahoma's public utilities. Writing for the Court, Justice White struck down Oklahoma's statute as a violation of the commerce clause, which "prohibits economic protectionism—that is, regulatory measures designed to benefit in-state economic interests by burdening out-of-state competitors." In doing so, he held that states could invoke the Court's original jurisdiction, granted in Article III, and rejected Oklahoma's argument that Wyoming was neither engaged in interstate commerce nor had asserted an injury or interest covered by the commerce clause. "It is beyond peradventure," Justice White claimed, "that Wyoming has raised a claim of 'sufficient seriousness and dignity.'

Oklahoma, acting in its sovereign capacity, passed the act, which directly affects Wyoming's ability to collect severance tax revenues, an action undertaken in its sovereign capacity." Having granted Wyoming standing to sue on the basis of its loss of revenue, Justice White struck down Oklahoma's law, observing that "when a state statute clearly discriminates against interstate commerce, it will be struck down, unless the discrimination is demonstrably justified by a valid factor unrelated to economic protectionism, see, e.g., *Maine v. Taylor*, 477 U.S. 131 (1986)" (Vol. 1, Ch. 7). By contrast, in a dissenting opinion joined by Chief Justice Rehnquist and Justice Thomas, Justice Scalia took strong exception to the majority's exercise of its original jurisdiction, granting of standing to Wyoming, and holding that a state's loss of revenue was within the "zone of interests" covered by the commerce clause. Wyoming, in his view, failed to assert a direct injury or an interest within the "zone-of-interests" embraced by the commerce clause; a state's interest in collecting taxes, as he put it, was "only marginally related to the national market/free trade foundation of our jurisprudence" of applying the commerce clause in the absence of congressional legislation to strike state regulations deemed to burden interstate commerce.

The Rehnquist Court avoided the controversy over whether requiring school children to recite the Pledge of Allegiance violates the First Amendment by denying standing in *Elk Grove Unified School District v. Newdow* (2004) (excerpted below). Writing for the Court, Justice Stevens held that Michael A. Newdow, who challenged the policy on behalf of his daughter, even though he was not her legal custodian, lacked "prudential standing"—a Court-made rule. In other words, when legal claims are based on domestic relations law, a field largely left to states, "the prudent course is for the federal court to stay its hand rather than reach out to resolve a weighty question of federal constitutional law." But in concurring opinions, Chief Justice Rehnquist and Justices O'Connor and Thomas dismissed the ruling on "prudential standing" as "novel" and "like the proverbial excursion ticket—good for this day only." They would have granted standing and rejected Newdow's First Amendment claims. The controversy over the Pledge and the motto "In God We Trust" is nonetheless certain to continue and to return to the Court in another case. The Roberts Court, even more than the Rehnquist Court, invokes standing doctrines and demands for concrete personal injuries in order to avoid or delay deciding major controversies. For example, prior to the ruling in *Obergefell v. Hodges* 133 S.Ct. 2652 (2015) (excerpted in Vol. 2, Ch. 12), two same-sex couples sued state officials claiming that California's Proposition 8, a ballot initiative banning same-sex marriages, violated

■ THE DEVELOPMENT OF LAW

Class-Action Suits

The Federal Rules of Civil Procedure provide for "class-action" suits—suits filed by an individual for himself and for all others who have suffered the same injury. This rule enables individuals who have suffered small monetary damages to bring lawsuits that they might not otherwise have brought because of the prohibitively high cost of litigation. Specifically, Rule 23 provides that

> [o]ne or more members of a class may sue or be sued as representative parties on behalf of all only if (1) the class is so numerous that joinder of all members is impracticable, (2) there are questions of law or fact common to the class, (3) the claims or defenses of the representative parties are typical of the claims or defenses of the class, and (4) the representative parties will fairly and adequately protect the interests of the class. . . .

> In any class action maintained under [this Rule], the court shall direct to the members of the class the best notice practicable under the circumstances, including individual notice to all members who can be identified.

The scope of this rule, however, was limited by *Eisen v. Carlisle & Jacquelin*, 417 U.S. 156 (1974), holding that when a representative of a class-action suit refuses to pay the cost of giving actual notice to all reasonably identifiable class members, federal courts are required to dismiss the suit. Here, representatives had to notify 2,250,000 class members at a cost of $225,000.

In 2005, President George W. Bush signed into law the Class Action Fairness Act, which moved from state to federal courts large, interstate class-action lawsuits brought by consumers against businesses for fraud and faulty products. For over a decade business groups had lobbied for the legislation. They contended that businesses faced too many frivolous lawsuits and excessive punitive damage awards, and that lawyers filed such suits in states known to be favorable to consumers. Consumer advocates, trial lawyers, and the U.S. Judicial Conference opposed the law. They countered that the law would burden the federal judiciary; that federal courts were ill equipped to deal with such suits, which usually involve the application of state consumer protection laws; and that consumers would be discouraged from bringing such suits.

Under the law, class-action suits seeking $5 million or more remain in state courts only if the primary defendant and more than one-third of the plaintiffs are from the same state. If fewer than one-third of the plaintiffs are from the same state as the primary defendant, and more than $5 million is sought, the case goes to a federal court. In addition, the law also limits attorney fees when plaintiffs receive only discount coupons on products instead of financial settlements, by linking the fees to the coupon's redemption rate or the actual hours spent working on the case.

The Roberts Court also limited class-action lawsuits in several cases. In *AT&T Mobility v. Concepcion*, 563 U.S. 333 (2011), a bare majority held that a California law was preempted by the Federal Arbitration Act (FAA). Under California's law, class arbitration was permitted, but the majority struck down that law for running afoul of the federal statute. A bare majority, however, upheld a class-action suit against California prison officials for violating the Eighth Amendment due to prison overcrowding and the conditions of inmates in *Brown v. Plata*, 563 U.S. 493 (2011) (further discussed in Ch. 10). *AT&T*, nonetheless, has prevented class actions from being filed since it encourages businesses and corporations to require employees and consumers of their goods and services (such as those who purchase a cell phone from them) to "agree" not to file a lawsuit or join a class-action suit against the company.

In a widely watched case involving the largest "class action" suit ever, *Wal-Mart Stores, Inc. v. Dukes*, 564 U.S. 388 (2011), the Court overturned the certification of a nationwide class of some 1.5 million female employees of Wal-Mart, who claimed that the company systematically discriminated against them in violation of the Civil Rights Act of 1964. Writing for the Court, Justice Scalia held that such a class was too large and inconsistent with the Federal Rule of Civil Procedure 23(a). Wal-Mart has some 3,400 stores across the country—each with its own managers—and therefore was entitled to individual determinations of discrimination and employees' eligibility for back pay. In other words, Rule 23(a) requires showing a commonality shared by each member of the class and a single indivisible remedy that provides the same relief to each class member. Justice Ginsberg, joined by Justices Breyer, Sotomayor, and Kagan, agreed that the section of Rule 23 that permits class-action requests for injunctions or declaratory judgments does not generally allow claims solely for monetary payments, but otherwise dissented. In their view, the women's lawyers had presented enough evidence "that gender bias suffused Wal-Mart's company culture." The Roberts Court's ruling in *Wal-Mart Stores* effectively tipped the balance in favor of defendants (businesses and corporations) and made class-action suits more difficult to win. A majority of the Roberts Court subsequently made it more difficult to file large class-action suits in *Bristol-Myers Squibb Co. v. Superior Court of California*, 137 S.Ct. 1773 (2018), when ruling that state courts lack jurisdiction over class-action suits that include residents of other states. Bristol-Myers was

(continues)

■ The Development of Law
Class-Action Suits (continued)

sued for injuries associated with a blood-thinning drug that allegedly posed risks of strokes. Only eighty-six members of the suit resided in the state of the pharmaceuticals company, while 593 were non-California residents. In denying California courts' jurisdiction, writing for the Court, Justice Alito observed:

> The mere fact that other plaintiffs were prescribed, obtained, and ingested Plavix in California—and allegedly sustained the same injuries as did the non-residents—does not allow the state to assert specific jurisdiction over the non-residents' claims.

In her dissent, Justice Sotomayor lamented:

> The majority's rule will make it difficult to aggregate the claims of plaintiffs across the country whose claims may be worth little alone. . . . It will make it impossible to bring a nationwide mass action in state court against defendants who are "at home" in different States. And it will result in piecemeal litigation and the bifurcation of claims. None of this is necessary.

The Court underscored its limiting of the forums for class-action suits in *TC Heartland v. Kraft Food Group Brands,* 137 S.Ct. 1514 (2017), a patent dispute over brands of flavored water, in ruling that the "residence" of members of the suit include only those residing in the state of an incorporated U.S. company. And *BNSF Railway Co. v. Tyrrell,* 137 S.Ct. 1549 (2017), over Justice Ginsburg's dissent, held that state courts may not exercise jurisdiction over suits against states involving work-related injuries that occur from work out of the state, once again making it more difficult for non-residents to bring or join class-action suits against businesses.

their due process and equal protection rights. Yet state officials, including the governor, attorney general, and others, refused to enforce Proposition 8. And the original proponents of Proposition 8 sought to intervene and defend the law on behalf of the state. In *Hollingsworth v. Perry,* 133 S.Ct. 2652 (2015), however, the Court denied standing because they merely asserted a "generalized grievance" rather than a "direct stake" in Proposition 8's enforcement. As Chief Justice Roberts explained, "Without a judicially cognizable interest of their own, [the original proponents of Proposition 8] attempt to invoke that of someone else," namely state officials. Hence, they do not have a "sufficiently concrete interest" in the dispute and thus not an "injury in fact."

Likewise, the Roberts Court avoided ruling on extreme partisan gerrymandering by denying standing in *Gill v. Whitford,* 138 S.Ct. 1916 (2018). The Wisconsin Republican legislature and governor in 2011 redrew voting district lines to favor Republicans. In the next election, the GOP took control of the State Senate, and held on to the State House, despite winning just 48.6 percent of the statewide vote. The Republicans were able to do this through a process known as "packing" and "cracking" districts—that is, cramming Democratic voters into a few districts and thinly spreading them across other districts. Writing for the Court, Chief Justice Roberts held that the challengers, claiming an unconstitutional vote dilution, did not have standing to sue because they claimed a personal injury based on outcomes in their individual voting districts. Quoting *Baker v. Carr* (1962), the chief justice ruled that they failed to demonstrate a "personal stake in the outcome," which is distinct from a "generally available grievance about government."

■ RIPENESS AND MOOTNESS

With the doctrines of ripeness and mootness the Court wields a double-edged sword. Appellants, those appealing a lower court ruling, may discover that a case is dismissed because it was brought too early or because the issues are moot and the case was brought too late. Cases are usually rejected as not ripe if the injury claimed has not yet been realized or if other avenues of appeal have not yet been exhausted. Petitioners raising a federal claim when appealing a state court ruling, for example, must exhaust all appeals in the state courts and the Court will not exercise jurisdiction until a "final judgment" has been rendered by the highest court in the state. The Court underscored its adherence to that rule when it dismissed *Johnson v. California,* 541 U.S. 428 (2004), because the petitioner failed to include (as required under the Court's rules) in an appendix to the petition for *certiorari* all opinions and final decisions in the case. Here, the state appellate court published only part of its decision (and, like other state and federal appellate courts in the last thirty years, withheld publication of part of its judgment, due to the mounting number of decisions annually handed down). Johnson included in the appendix only the published opinion and not the

unpublished portion (which, like other unpublished opinions, was nonetheless available on Lexis). When the Court discovered from the
unpublished opinion that the state appellate court's decision was not in
all respects final, it dismissed the case. The Court thereby signaled petitioners to append any published and unpublished opinions of state high
courts in order to establish that the decision appealed is indeed "final."

Alternatively, a case may be dismissed if pertinent facts or laws
change so that there is no longer real adverseness or an actual case or
controversy. The issue becomes moot because "there is no subject matter
on which the judgment of the court can operate," and hence a ruling
would not prove "conclusive" and final.[7] In practice both doctrines
bend to the Court's will, because the requirement of ripeness permits
the Court to avoid or delay deciding certain issues.

A finding of mootness likewise enables the Court to avoid, if not
escape, deciding controversial political issues. *DeFunis v. Odegaard*, 416
U.S. 312 (1974), for example, involved a white student who was denied
admission to the University of Washington Law School. The student
claimed that the school's affirmative action program discriminated
against him by allowing the entrance of minorities with lower LSAT
test scores, and he was admitted into the law school after the trial judge
ruled in his favor. On appeal the state supreme court reversed this decision, but by the time his case reached the Supreme Court he was completing his final year and assured of graduation. Over four dissenters,
the majority held that the case was moot. Yet, as the dissenters predicted, the issue would not go away. Within four years, the Burger
Court reconsidered the issue of reverse discrimination in university
affirmative action programs in *Regents of the University of California v.
Bakke*, 438 U.S. 265 (1978) (see Ch. 12).

The issue of mootness could have presented a problem when the
Burger Court ruled on abortion in *Roe v. Wade*, 410 U.S. 113 (1973)
(see Ch. 11). There the Court struck down Texas's criminal statute
prohibiting abortions, except when necessary to save a mother's life.
When defending the law, the state's attorney general argued that the
plaintiff was a single woman whose pregnancy had already resulted in
birth by the time the case reached the Court, and hence her claim was
moot. However, Justice Harry Blackmun, writing for the Court,
rejected that view out of hand:

> [W]hen, as here, pregnancy is a significant fact in the litigation,
> the normal 266-day human gestation period is so short that the
> pregnancy will come to term before the usual appellate process is
> complete. If that termination makes a case moot, pregnancy litiga-
> tion seldom will survive much beyond the trial stage, and appellate

review will be effectively denied. Our law should not be that rigid. Pregnancy often comes more than once to the same woman, and in the general population, if man is to survive, it will always be with us. Pregnancy provides a classic justification for a conclusion of non-mootness. It truly could be "capable of repetition, yet evading review."

Subsequently, the Roberts Court dismissed as moot *Claiborne v. United States*, 551 U.S. 87 (2007), a case appealing an appellate court's reversal of a district court's sentencing of Mario Claiborne below the recommended mandatory federal sentencing guidelines, which the Court declared unconstitutional in *United States v. Booker*, 543 U.S. 220 (2005), in ruling that they are only advisory. Claiborne, a twenty-one-year-old convicted of selling cocaine, was sentenced to fifteen months in prison instead of the prescribed thirty-seven to forty-six months. But after serving his sentence, while his appeal was pending before the Court, he was shot to death. The Roberts Court thus dismissed his appeal and granted another case raising the issue of federal judges' discretion in sentencing, on which federal circuit courts are divided. In addition, in *Camreta v. Greene*, 563 U.S. 692 (2011), Justice Kagan held that a suit against a social worker and a sheriff who allegedly violated the Fourth Amendment rights of a nine-year-old student by questioning her without a warrant about possible sexual abuse was moot because she was now almost eighteen years old and had moved from California, where the incident occurred, to Florida. Justices Kennedy and Thomas dissented.

Recently, *United States v. Microsoft*, 138 S.Ct. 1186 (2018), in a *per curiam* opinion, declared moot a case against Microsoft because of a newly enacted law—Clarifying Lawful Overseas Use of Data Act (CLOUD Act) of 2018. The government had obtained a warrant directing Microsoft to turn over all e-mails and other records of an account believed to be connected to drug trafficking, but the company refused on because the e-mails were stored in a data center in Dublin, Ireland. While the case was on appeal, the CLOUD Act became law, providing that service providers must comply with orders to turn over the contents of electronic communications regardless of whether stored inside or outside the country. The government obtained another warrant under that act and, on appeal, the Court held there was no longer a live dispute between the parties.

■ INSIDE THE COURT

Standing and the Connecticut Birth Control Cases

Between 1943 and 1965, the Court continually refused standing to individuals attacking the constitutionality of a late nineteenth-century Connecticut statute. The law prohibited virtually all single and married individuals from using contraceptives and physicians from giving advice about their use. In *Tileston v. Ullman*, 318 U.S. 44 (1943), a doctor sued charging that the statute prevented him from giving information to patients. But the Court ruled that he had no real interest or personal injury because he had not been arrested.

More than a decade later in *Poe v. Ullman*, 367 U.S. 497 (1961), a doctor, C. Lee Buxton, and a patient were likewise denied standing on the ground that the law had not been enforced for more than eighty years, even though the state had begun to close birth control clinics. This time the justices split five to four and only Chief Justice Warren and Justices Clark and Whittaker joined Justice Frankfurter's opinion for the Court (Justice Brennan concurred in the decision but not in the opinion). There, Frankfurter observed that

> [t]he Connecticut law prohibiting the use of contraceptives has been on the State's books since 1879. . . . During more than three-quarters of a century since its enactment, a prosecution for its violation seems never to have been initiated, save in [one] case. . . . Neither counsel nor our own researches have discovered any other attempt to enforce the prohibition of distribution or use of contraceptive devices by criminal process. The unreality of these law suits is illuminated by another circumstance. We were advised by counsel for appellants that contraceptives are commonly and notoriously sold in Connecticut drug stores. Yet no prosecutions are recorded. . . .
>
> The various doctrines of "standing," "ripeness," and "mootness," which this Court has evolved with particular, though not exclusive, reference to such cases are but several manifestations—each having its own "varied application"—of the primary conception that federal judicial power is to be exercised to strike down legislation, whether state or federal, only at the instance of one who is himself immediately harmed, or immediately threatened with harm, by the challenged action. . . .

Dissenting Justices Douglas, Harlan, and Stewart disagreed. Notably, Justice Harlan's dissent in *Poe v. Ullman* would have granted standing and reached the merits of the case in a lengthy and influential opinion, observing that

> I consider that this Connecticut legislation, as construed to apply to these appellants, violates the Fourteenth Amendment. I believe that a statute making it a criminal offense for married couples to use contraceptives is an intolerable and unjustifiable invasion of privacy in the conduct of the most intimate concerns of an individual's personal life. . . .

> [I]t is not the particular enumeration of rights in the first eight Amendments which spells out the reach of Fourteenth Amendment due process, but rather, as was suggested in another context long before the adoption of that Amendment, those concepts which are considered to embrace those rights "which are . . . fundamental; which belong . . . to the citizens of all free governments," *Corfield v. Coryell*, for "the purposes [of securing] which men enter into society," *Calder v. Bull*. Again and again this Court has resisted the notion that the Fourteenth Amendment is no more than a shorthand reference to what is explicitly set out elsewhere in the Bill of Rights. . . .

> Due process has not been reduced to any formula; its content cannot be determined by reference to any code. The best that can be said is that through the course of this Court's decisions it has represented the balance which our Nation, built upon postulates of respect for the liberty of the individual, has struck between that liberty and the demands of organized society. If the supplying of content to this Constitutional concept has of necessity been a rational process, it certainly has not been one where judges have felt free to roam where unguided speculation might take them. The balance of which I speak is the balance struck by this country, having regard to what history teaches are the traditions from which it developed as well as the traditions from which it broke. That tradition is a living thing. A decision of this Court which radically departs from it could not long survive, while a decision which builds on what has survived is likely to be sound. No formula could serve as a substitute, in this area, for judgment and restraint . . .

> Precisely what is involved here is this: the State is asserting the right to enforce its moral judgment by intruding upon the most intimate details of the marital relation with the full power of the criminal law. Potentially, this could allow the deployment of all the incidental machinery of the criminal law, arrests, searches and seizures; inevitably, it must mean at the very least

(continues)

■ Inside the Court
Standing and the Connecticut Birth Control Cases (continued)

the lodging of criminal charges, a public trial, and testimony as to the *corpus delicti* [the body of crime]. . . . In sum, the statute allows the State to enquire into, prove and punish married people for the private use of their marital intimacy. . . .

I think the sweep of the Court's decisions, under both the Fourth and Fourteenth Amendments, amply shows that the Constitution protects the privacy of the home against all unreasonable intrusion of whatever character. . . .

Finally, after Dr. Buxton and Estelle Griswold, executive director of Planned Parenthood League of Connecticut, were tried and found guilty of prescribing contraceptives to a married couple, the Court in *Griswold v. Connecticut* (1965) (excerpted in Ch. 4) struck down what Justice Potter Stewart called Connecticut's "uncommonly silly law." In his opinion for the Court, Justice Douglas explained why Buxton and Griswold were now granted standing:

> The appellants were found guilty as accessories and fined $100 each, against the claim that the accessory statute as so applied violated the Fourteenth Amendment. . . . We think that appellants have standing to raise the constitutional rights of married people with whom they had a professional relationship. *Tileston v. Ullman*, is different, for there the plaintiff seeking to represent others asked for a declaratory judgment. In that situation, we thought that the requirements of standing should be strict, lest the standards of "case or controversy" in Article III of the Constitution become blurred. Here those doubts are removed by reason of a criminal conviction for serving married couples in violation of an aiding-and-abetting statute. Certainly the accessory should have standing to assert that the offense which he is charged with assisting is not, or cannot constitutionally be a crime.

Griswold was limited to the privacy and marital decisions of couples. Consequently, in *Eisenstadt v. Baird*, 405 U.S. 438 (1972), to gain standing to claim that single individuals also have a right to acquire and use contraceptives, a doctor arranged to be arrested after delivering a public lecture on contraceptives and handing out samples to single women in the audience. The Court accepted the case and ruled that single women also have the right to acquire and use contraceptives.

■ POLITICAL QUESTIONS

Even when the Court has jurisdiction over a properly framed suit, it may decline to rule because it decides that a case raises a "political question" that should be resolved by other political branches. Like other jurisdictional doctrines, the political question doctrine means what the justices say it means.

The doctrine has its origin in Chief Justice Marshall's observation in *Marbury v. Madison*, 5 U.S. 137 (1803) (see Ch. 1), that "[t]he province of the Court, is, solely, to decide on the rights of individuals. . . . Questions in their nature political, or which are, by the constitution and laws, submitted to the executive can never be made in this Court." Yet as the French commentator Alexis de Tocqueville noted in the 1830s, "Scarcely any political question arises in the United States that is not resolved, sooner or later, into a judicial question."[8] Litigation that reaches the Court is political, and the justices for political reasons decide what and how to decide cases on their docket.

The Taney Court first developed the doctrine in *Luther v. Borden*, 7 How. [48 U.S.] 1 (1849). There, the Court held that whether Rhode Island had a "republican form of government," as guaranteed by Article IV of the Constitution, was a question for Congress, not the Court, to decide. Subsequent rulings elaborated other reasons for the doctrine besides deference to separation of powers. The Court may lack information and resources needed for a ruling. In some areas, as in foreign policy and international relations, the Court lacks both adequate standards for resolving disputes and the means to enforce its decisions.

For many decades the Court relied on the doctrine to avoid entering the "political thicket" of state representation and apportionment; that is, the ways by which a state is divided geographically as a basis for representation in state and federal elections. When declining to rule on the malapportionment of Illinois's congressional districts in *Colegrove v. Green*, 328 U.S. 549 (1946), Justice Felix Frankfurter explained,

> We are of the opinion that the petitioners ask of this Court what is beyond its competence to grant. This is one of those demands on judicial power which cannot be met by verbal fencing about "jurisdiction." It must be resolved by considerations on the basis of which this Court, from time to time, has refused to intervene in controversies. It has refused to do so because due regard for the effective working of our Government revealed this issue to be of a peculiarly political nature and therefore not meet for judicial determination.
>
> This is not an action to recover for damages because of the discriminatory exclusion of a plaintiff from rights enjoyed by other

citizens. The basis for the suit is not a private wrong, but a wrong suffered by Illinois as a polity. . . . In effect this is an appeal to the federal courts to reconstruct the electoral process of Illinois in order that it may be adequately represented in the councils of the Nation. Because the Illinois legislature has failed to revise its Congressional Representative districts in order to reflect great changes, during more than a generation, in the distribution of its population, we are asked to do this, for Illinois. . . .

Of course no court can affirmatively remap the Illinois districts so as to bring them more in conformity with the standards of fairness for a representative system. At best we could only declare the existing electoral system invalid. The result would be to leave Illinois undistricted and to bring into operation, if the Illinois legislature chose not to act, the choice of members for the House of Representatives on a state-wide ticket. The last stage may be worse than the first. . . .

Nothing is clearer than that this controversy concerns matters that bring courts into immediate and active relations with party contests. From the determination of such issues this Court has traditionally held aloof. It is hostile to the democratic system to involve the judiciary in the politics of the people. And it is not less pernicious if such judicial intervention in an essentially political contest be dressed up in the abstract phrases of the law.

The one stark fact that emerges from the study of the history of Congressional apportionment is its enrollment in politics, in the sense of party contests and party interests. The Constitution enjoins upon Congress the duty of apportioning Representatives "among the several States . . . according to their respective Numbers. . . ." Article I, Sec. 2. Yet, Congress has at times been heedless of this command and not apportioned according to the requirements of the Census. It never occurred to anyone that this Court could issue mandamus to compel Congress to perform its mandatory duty to apportion.

Still, whites, blacks, and other minorities in urban and suburban areas were often denied equal representation in Congress and state legislatures until the Court reversed itself in *Baker v. Carr* (1962) (excerpted below).

In *Goldwater v. Carter* (1979) (excerpted below), the Court issued an order vacating (overturning) a lower court decision in a dispute between several congressmen, headed by conservative Senator Barry Goldwater, and Democratic President Jimmy Carter over the termination of a defense treaty with Taiwan. There, Justices Lewis F. Powell and William Rehnquist took quite different views of the application of the "political questions" doctrine in controversies between Congress and the president. *Goldwater v. Carter* also represents the Court's entertaining in the late twentieth century of *congressional standing*—members of the Senate and House of Representatives—challenging the constitutionality of congressional legislation and executive action; see, for example, *Bowsher v. Synar*, 478 U.S. 714 (1986) (excerpted in Vol. 1, Ch. 4). The Court, however, drew the line on congressional standing to challenge the constitutionality of newly enacted legislation in *Raines v. Byrd*, 521 U.S. 811 (1997), denying standing to challenge the Line Item Veto Act of 1996; subsequently the Court struck down that law in another suit brought by public and private parties in *Clinton v. City of New York*, 524 U.S. 417 (1998) (excerpted in Vol. 1, Ch. 4).

The Court also reconsidered the "political question" doctrine in *Nixon v. United States*, 506 U.S. 224 (1993) (see Vol. 1, Ch. 5). There, the Rehnquist Court held that a former federal judge's challenge to the Senate's expedited impeachment procedure was nonjusticiable. While also upholding the constitutionality of the Senate's procedure in his opinion for the Court, Chief Justice Rehnquist appeared to go out of his way to justify the application of the doctrine and ostensible exercise of judicial self-restraint.

The doctrine's logic is admittedly circular. "Political questions are matters not soluble by the judicial process; matters not soluble by the judicial process are political questions. As an early dictionary explained," political scientist John Roche says, "violins are small cellos, and cellos are large violins."[9] Still, Columbia Law School professor Louis Henkin points out, even when denying review because of a political question, "the court does not refuse judicial review; it exercises it. It is not dismissing the case or the issue as nonjusticiable; it adjudicates it. It is not refusing to pass on the power of the political branches; it passes upon it, only to affirm that they had the power which had been challenged and that nothing in the Constitution prohibited the particular exercise of it."[10]

Another illustrative controversy over the "political question" doctrine that continues to dog the Court involves the justiciability of political gerrymandering (redrawing voting district lines by the majority party in a legislature to benefit incumbents and to disadvantage candidates and voters in opposing parties). In *Davis v. Bandemer*, 478 U.S. 109 (1986), a plurality held that political gerrymandering controversies were justiciable, but failed to provide a standard for adjudicating such disputes. Almost twenty years later in *Vieth v. Jubelirer*, 541 U.S. 267 (2004) (excerpted in Ch. 8), a plurality would have overruled *Davis v. Bandemer* and held that such controversies were nonjusticiable. But Justice Kennedy, who cast the deciding vote, would not go along with that and maintained that a standard for adjudicating the matter might still evolve. The four dissenters—Justices Stevens, Souter, Ginsburg, and

Breyer—countered that such disputes were non-justiciable and proposed their own standards, but they could not agree on a standard for determining when political gerrymanders are unconstitutional.

The Roberts Court also initially evaded deciding whether Congress has the authority to dictate how the executive branch issues birth certificates for U.S. citizens born abroad, by holding that lower courts erred in ruling that the controversy presented a "political question," and remanded the case for consideration of the constitutionality of the statute in question. At issue in *M.B.Z. v. Clinton*, 566 U.S. 189 (2012), was the validity of a ten-year-old law in which Congress aimed to acknowledge Jerusalem as the capital of Israel, even though the U.S. government did not recognize it as part of Israel. After State Department officials refused to fill out a report on the foreign birth of Menachem Binyamin Zivotofsky (M.B.Z.), born in a Jerusalem hospital, to show his birthplace as "Israel," his parents sued, seeking to enforce the 2002 law that directed the State Department to do just that. A federal district and appellate court had held that the controversy presented a "political question." On remand, the appellate court held that the congressional statute was unconstitutional and a bare majority of the Roberts court affirmed that Congress had intruded on presidential power in *Zivotofsky v. Kerry*, 576 U.S. 1059 (2015) (excerpted in Vol. 1 Ch. 3).

■ STARE DECISIS AND OTHER POLICIES

The justices occasionally rely on other self-denying policies to avoid reaching issues as well. They, for example, may invoke what has been called the doctrine of *strict necessity*, and thereupon formulate and decide only the narrowest possible issue.

Another doctrine, *stare decisis* ("let the prior decision stand"), is also not a mechanical formula. It is rather a judicial policy that promotes "the certainty, uniformity, and stability of the law." Even conservative Justice George Sutherland recognized that members of the Court "are not infallible, and when convinced that a prior decision was not originally based on, or that conditions have so changed as to render the decision no longer in accordance with, sound reason, [they] should not hesitate to say so."[11] "*Stare decisis* is usually the wise policy," Justice Louis Brandeis remarked, "because in most matters it is more important that the applicable rule of law be settled than that it be settled right."[12] On constitutional matters, however, Justice Douglas among others emphasizes, "*stare decisis*—that is, established law—was really no sure guideline because what did . . . the judges who sat there in 1875 know about, say, electronic surveillance? They didn't know anything about it."[13]

There is, however, an important distinction between prior rulings involving statutory interpretation and those involving constitutional interpretation and, hence, how much deference should be given to those precedents. In general, the Court tends to be more deferential to prior rulings decided on statutory grounds because Congress may override its decision by rewriting a statute, unlike a constitutional ruling that may be reversed only by a constitutional amendment. As the Roberts Court has reaffirmed, *stare decisis* has " 'special force' . . . [with] respect to statutory interpretation [because] Congress remains free to alter what [the Court has] done." (*Halliburton Co. v. Erica P. John Fund*, 573 U.S. 258 [2014], quoting *John R. Sand & Gravel Co. v. United States*, 552 U.S. 130 [2008]).

More recently, when asked to overturn a precedent dealing with patents and royalties for a Spider-Man toy, in *Kimble v. Marvel Entertainment, LLC.*, 135 S.Ct. 2401 (2015), Justice Kagan writing for the Court declined to do so. Her opinion emphasized that *stare decisis* has enhanced force with respect to statutory rulings because (1) Congress could have overridden the prior decision, (2) the precedent's underpinnings had not been eroded, and (3) the precedent had not proven unworkable. Chief Justice Roberts and Justices Thomas and Alito, however, dissented.

The Rehnquist Court's deference to *stare decisis* on constitutional matters was highly controversial both on and off the bench for several years. Indeed, Justice Scalia's sharp attack on a number of prior rulings prompted a response from retired Justice Lewis F. Powell Jr., in his 1989 Leslie H. Arps Lecture, delivered to the Association of the Bar of the City of New York and entitled "*Stare Decisis* and Judicial Restraint." In Justice Powell's words:

> Those who would eliminate *stare decisis* in constitutional cases argue that the doctrine is simply one of convenience. . . . But elimination of constitutional *stare decisis* would represent explicit endorsement of the idea that the Constitution is nothing more than what five Justices say it is. This would undermine the rule of law. . . .
>
> It is evident that I consider *stare decisis* essential to the rule of law. . . . After two centuries of vast change, the original intent of the Founders is difficult to discern or is irrelevant. Indeed, there may be no evidence of intent. The Framers of the Constitution were wise enough to write broadly, using language that must be construed in light of changing conditions that could not be foreseen. Yet the doctrine of *stare decisis* has remained a constant thread in preserving continuity and stability.

But the debate over *stare decisis* continues and was especially sharp when by a 6–3 vote the Rehnquist Court overturned two of its own earlier decisions, in *Payne v. Tennessee*, 501 U.S. 808 (1991) (see Ch. 10), striking down the use of "victim impact statements" in death penalty cases. Note, however, that subsequently Justices O'Connor, Kennedy, and Souter balked at applying *Payne's* analysis of *stare decisis* in *Planned Parenthood of Southeastern Pennsylvania v. Casey*, 505 U.S. 833 (1992) (see Ch. 11). There, they gave the doctrine of *stare decisis* a new twist when justifying their refusal to overrule entirely the landmark abortion ruling in *Roe v. Wade* (1973) (see Ch. 11) and drew sharp criticism from Chief Justice Rehnquist and Justices Scalia, Thomas, and White.

It also bears emphasizing, perhaps, that most precedents are not reversed. In fact, of the thousands of decisions handed down, only a small number of precedents are reversed, as indicated in the box, CONSTITUTIONAL HISTORY: The Supreme Court's Reversal of Precedent, in this chapter. But, of those overruled, empirical studies find that about half did not survive more than twenty years. Moreover, reversals tend to occur when there is a sharp change in the composition of the bench and a shift in direction. Studies, furthermore, support Chief Justice Rehnquist's observation, in *Payne v. Tennessee*, that precedents "decided by the narrowest of margins, over spirited dissents"— that is, decisions handed down by bare majorities or pluralities with multiple concurring or dissenting opinions—are more likely to be overturned than those unanimously decided.[14]

In sum, *stare decisis* and the precedential value of prior rulings, as Justice Jackson quipped, "are accepted only at their current valuation and have a mortality rate as high as their authors."[15] Or, as Justice Alito has observed, "*Stare decisis* is like wine. If it's really new, you don't want to drink it, it has to age for a while. If it's really old, it is very valuable, or it has possibly turned to vinegar. There's this magical period in between. It [is] not difficult for a judge to make the *stare decisis* inquiry come out however the judge wants it [to] come out."[16]

■ FORMAL RULES AND PRACTICES

Except for government attorneys and members of the practicing bar, few people pay any attention to the technical Rules of the Court. Yet, they are an exercise of political power and determine the nation's access to justice. The rules govern the admission and activities of attorneys in filing appeals, petitions, and motions and conducting oral arguments. They stipulate the fees, forms, and length of filings. Most important, they explain the Court's formal grounds for granting and disposing of cases.

To expedite the process of deciding what to decide, the Court periodically revises its rules. For example, even after the Judiciary Act of 1925 expanded the Court's discretionary jurisdiction, the justices still felt burdened by mandatory appeals. Accordingly, in 1928 the Court required the filing of a jurisdictional statement explaining the circumstances of an appeal, the questions presented, and why the Court should grant review. The requirement also allowed the justices to screen appeals just like petitions for *certiorari*.

One of the reasons for granting *certiorari* given in the Court's rules is whether "a federal court of appeals has rendered a decision in conflict with the decision of another federal court of appeals on the same matter." This rule is especially advantageous for the federal government. The Department of Justice has a relitigation policy. If it receives an adverse ruling from a circuit court of appeals, it will relitigate the issue in other circuits to obtain favorable decisions and generate a conflict among the circuits, which then may be brought to the Court. The rule for granting circuit conflicts, however important, does not control the justices' actual practice of granting *certiorari*. The government and individuals often allege circuit conflicts simply in an effort to get their cases accepted. But most circuit conflicts are "tolerable" and need not be immediately decided. The justices often feel that conflicts should percolate in the circuits before they take them. Sometimes, the justices may want to avoid or delay addressing an issue that has created a conflict among the circuits. Most crucial in granting *certiorari* is simply that at least four justices agree on the importance of the issue presented.

NOTES

1. Charles E. Hughes, *Addresses of Charles Evans Hughes* (New York: Putnam's, 1916), 185–186.

2. *Muskrat v. United States*, 219 U.S. 346 (1911).

3. See *Duke Power Co. v. Carolina Environmental Study Group*, 438 U.S. 59 (1978); and *Bellotti v. Baird*, 443 U.S. 622 (1979).

4. *Aetna Life Insurance Co. v. Haworth*, 300 U.S. 277 (1937).

5. *Data Processing Service v. Camp*, 397 U.S. 150, 151 (1970).

6. *Braxton County Court v. West Virginia*, 208 U.S. 192 (1908); and *Coleman v. Miller*, 307 U.S. 433 (1939) (Frankfurter, J., dis. op.).

7. *Ex parte Baez*, 177 U.S. 378 (1900).

8. Alexis de Tocqueville, *Democracy in America*, Vol. 1, ed. P. Bradley (New York: Vintage, 1945), 288.

9. John Roche, "Judicial Self-Restraint," 49 *American Political Science Review* 768 (1955).

10. Louis Henkin, "Is There a 'Political Question' Doctrine?" 85 *Yale Law Journal* 606 (1976).

11. Draft of an opinion, George Sutherland Papers, Manuscript Room, Library of Congress.

12. *Burnet v. Coronado Oil*, 285 U.S. 393 (1932) (Brandeis, J., dis. op.).

13. William O. Douglas, interview on *CBS Reports*, September 6, 1972, CBS News, transcript p. 13.

14. See, for example, and sources cited therein, Michael H. LeRoy, "Death of a Precedent: Should Justices Rethink Their Consensus Norms?" 43 *Hofstra Law Review* 377 (2014).

15. Robert Jackson, "The Task of Maintaining Our Liberties: The Role of the Judiciary," 39 *American Bar Association Journal* 962 (1953).

16. Justice Alito, Speech at the Federalist Society's Texas Chapter's Conference (September 21, 2015), as reported by Josh Blackman, "Justice Alito Reflects on His Tenth Anniversary on SCOTUS," available at joshblackman.com/blog/2015/09 /21/justice-alito-reflects-on-his-tenth-anniversary-on-scotus (accessed September 22, 2015).

SELECTED BIBLIOGRAPHY

Banks, Christopher, and David M. O'Brien. *The Judicial Process*. 2nd ed. St. Paul, MN: West Academic, 2020.

Clayton, Cornell, and Gillman, Howard, eds. *Supreme Court Decision-Making*. Chicago: University of Chicago Press, 1999.

Gerhardt, Michael. *The Power of Precedent*. New York: Oxford University Press, 2008.

Hansford, Thomas, and Spriggs, James. *The Politics of Precedent on the U.S. Supreme Court*. Princeton, NJ: Princeton University Press, 2006.

Kloppenberg, Lisa. *Playing It Safe: How the Supreme Court Sidesteps Hard Cases and Stunts the Development of Law*. New York: New York University Press, 2001.

Mourtada-Sabbah, Nada, and Cain, Bruce. *The Political Question Doctrine and the Supreme Court of the United States*. Lanham, MD: Rowman & Littlefield, 2007.

O'Brien, David. *Storm Center: The Supreme Court in American Politics*, 12th ed. New York: W. W. Norton & Company, 2020.

Posner, Richard. *The Federal Courts*. Cambridge, MA: Harvard University Press, 1996.

Stone, Christopher. *Should Trees Have Standing? Toward Legal Rights for Natural Objects*. 3rd ed. New York: Oxford University Press, 2007.

Urofsky, Melvin, ed. *100 Americans Making Constitutional History*. Washington, DC: C. Q. Press, 2004.

■ CONSTITUTIONAL HISTORY

The Supreme Court's Reversal of Precedent

Precedents are neither fixed in stone and self-enforcing nor provide inflexible, mechanical rules. Most justices, more or less, acknowledge this inescapable fact. "*Stare decisis* is usually the wise policy," Justice Louis D. Brandeis (1916–1939) famously remarked, "because in most matters it is more important that the applicable rule of law be settled than that it be settled right."

Historically, the Court reverses itself on average about once or twice each term. In the nineteenth century, reversals were less frequent because there were fewer decisions to overturn. Notably though, when the Court's composition changes dramatically in a short period of time, or a pivotal justice leaves the bench, the Court tends to overturn prior rulings. That occurred in the late 1930s and early 1940s after Franklin D. Roosevelt's eight appointments and elevation of Justice Harlan F. Stone to chief justice. The Warren Court (1953–1969) was even more "activist" in reversing fifty-six precedents. During Chief Justice Burger's tenure (1969–1986), the Court gradually became more conservative, and, as its composition changed, a total of fifty-five prior rulings were expressly abandoned. Once again, a high number of reversals occurred during the first few terms of the Rehnquist Court (1986–2005), but that abated as more moderate centrists came to command a majority due to Democratic President Bill Clinton's appointees. Under Chief Justice John Roberts (2005–), the Court was initially less inclined to outright overrule prior decisions. Instead, the Roberts Court was more inclined to simply narrow the continued use of precedents. (See, e.g., *Hein v. Freedom from Religion Foundation, Inc.* (2007), and *Arizona Christian School Tuition Organization v. Winn* (2011), both excerpted in this chapter). With the arrival of Justices Gorsuch and Kavanaugh, in 2017 and 2018, a new solid conservative majority appears more likely to reconsider prior holdings.

Besides changes in the Court's composition and direction, precedents may be overturned for a number of reasons. Obviously, precedents may come to be considered so erroneous to render them no longer "good law" or proven unworkable given technological and socioeconomic changes. Two precedents may occasionally come into conflict (real or contrived) and one must be jettisoned.

(continues)

■ CONSTITUTIONAL HISTORY
The Supreme Court's Reversal of Precedent (continued)

The following table places the Court's explicit reversals of precedents in historical perspective.

COURT	NUMBER OF PRECEDENTS OVERTURNED
Marshall Court (1801–1836)	3
Taney Court (1836–1864)	4
Chase Court (1864–1873)	7
Waite Court (1874–1888)	11
Fuller Court (1888–1910)	4
White Court (1910–1921)	5
Taft Court (1921–1930)	5
Hughes Court (1930–1941)	14
Stone Court (1941–1946)	12
Vinson Court (1946–1953)	12
Warren Court (1953–1969)	56
Burger Court (1969–1986)	55
Rehnquist Court (1986–2005)	42
Roberts Court (2005–)	16
Total	246

Based on Leon Friedman and Fred Israel, eds., *Justices of the United States Supreme
Court,* vol. 4, 4th ed. (New York: Facts on File, 2013), 573–600, and as updated
by the authors through the 2018 term, as of July, 1, 2019.

Significantly, precedents may more generally not stand the test of
time; yet, instead of being expressly overturned, they are abandoned
without the Court's saying so and no longer followed or applied. Two
illustrative cases are *Buck v. Bell* (1927) (excerpted in Vol. 2, Ch. 11),
which held that the government may sterilize "feebleminded" men
and women without violating due process of law, and in *Korematsu v.
U.S.* (1944) (excerpted in Vol. 1, Ch. 3), the Court upheld the internment of even loyal Japanese Americans. While not overruled, both
have been discredited and are no longer precedential.

The Court may also decline to overrule watershed precedents
but hold that they no longer apply to particular cases and controversies. The Warren Court did so without overruling the doctrine of
"separate but equal" in holding that it no longer applied to segre-

gated public schools. Rather than a sweeping ruling reversing *Plessy v. Ferguson* (1896) in *Brown v. Board of Education* (1954) (both excerpted in Vol. 2, Ch. 12), the Court merely observed in *Brown* that *Plessy*'s doctrine of "separate but equal" no longer applied to dual public schools systems. Questions about racial segregation in other areas of public accommodations—hotels, restaurants, and so forth—were thus left for another day.

Decisions may remain precedential but so diminished by subsequent exceptions that their rationales are fundamentally undermined. *Mapp v. Ohio* (1961) (excerpted in Vol. 2, Ch. 7), for instance, was highly controversial in holding that evidence must be excluded at trial if obtained in violation of the Fourth Amendment's "exclusionary rule." In the following decades, however, the Court carved out exceptions—such as the "good faith" exception and the "inevitable discovery rule"—that permitted the use of illegally obtained evidence, thereby circumscribing the scope of the exclusionary rule, if not completely eliminating its utility and underlying rationale. Similarly, the "bright line rules" for police interrogations of criminal suspects, laid down in *Miranda v. Arizona* (1965) (excerpted in Vol. 2, Ch. 6) are no longer bright or even clear due to the Court's reinterpretation of *Miranda*. Contrary to *Miranda*, police are no longer required to give the exact warnings of a suspect's rights to remain silent and to have an attorney present during questioning. Moreover, the Court sanctioned the use of "police trickery" and undercover agents' eliciting incriminating confessions that then may be introduced at trial.

In other words, precedents may be *said* to hold up even when in practice they don't, and much of their reasoning has been eroded or rejected outright in subsequent cases. For instance, in the opinion for the Court in *Planned Parenthood of Southeastern Pa. v. Casey* (1992) (excerpted in Vol. 2, Ch. 11), a plurality reaffirmed the "essence of *Roe v. Wade*" (1973). *Roe* had held that restrictions on a woman's right to have an abortion are subject to the "strict scrutiny" test, the highest standard of review, and laid out a "trimester" approach to balancing a woman's interests against those of the government in restricting access to abortion services. In ruling contrariwise, *Casey* discarded the "strict scrutiny" test and "trimester" analysis, despite reaffirming *Roe*, when substituting an "undue burden" test and upholding precisely the kinds of regulations that were struck down under *Roe*.

(continues)

■ CONSTITUTIONAL HISTORY
The Supreme Court's Reversal of Precedent (continued)

It also bears emphasizing that statutory and constitutional precedents are treated differently. Statutory rulings are less likely to be reversed because Congress may override them by modifying or passing new legislation. Whereas constitutional rulings may be overturned only by a constitutional amendment, which is exceedingly difficult. When deciding whether to reconsider statutory rulings, the Court usually considers how long ago a decision was handed down (the longer, the less likely to be discarded), whether it has proven unworkable, and whether its analysis led to problems that other branches had not resolved. For those reasons, the majority in *South Dakota v. Wayfair,* 138 S. Ct. 2080 (2018), overturned a precedent holding that states and localities could not tax out-of-state sales on the Internet, leaving it to Congress to decide that controversy.

Flast v. Cohen

392 U.S. 83, 88 S.CT. 1942 (1968)

Florance Flast and several other taxpayers sought standing to challenge the constitutionality of the Elementary and Secondary Education Act of 1965. The act provided funding for instructional materials and purchase of textbooks for religious schools. Flast contended that the act violated the First Amendment's ban on the establishment of religion by the government and guarantee for the free exercise of religion. In a federal district court in New York, she filed suit against Wilbur Cohen, the secretary of Health, Education, and Welfare (now the Department of Education), to enjoin the spending of funds authorized for religious schools. The district court denied standing and Flast appealed to the Supreme Court.

The Court's decision was 8–1, with the majority's opinion announced by Chief Justice Warren. There were concurrences by Justices Douglas, Stewart, and Fortas. Justice Harlan dissented.

■ ■ ■

☐ *Chief Justice WARREN delivers the opinion of the Court.*

In *Frothingham v. Mellon* [262 U.S. 447] (1923), this Court ruled that a federal taxpayer is without standing to challenge the constitutionality of a federal statute. That ruling has stood for 45 years as an impenetrable barrier to suits against Acts of Congress brought by individuals who can assert only the interest of federal taxpayers. In this case, we must decide whether the *Frothingham* barrier should be lowered when a taxpayer attacks a federal statute on the ground that it violates the Establishment and Free Exercise Clauses of the First Amendment. . . .

This Court first faced squarely the question whether a litigant asserting only his status as a taxpayer has standing to maintain a suit in a federal court in *Frothingham v. Mellon, supra,* and that decision must be the starting point for analysis in this case. The taxpayer in *Frothingham* attacked as unconstitutional the Maternity Act of 1921, which established a federal program of grants to those States which would undertake programs to reduce maternal and infant mortality. . . . The Court noted that a federal taxpayer's "interest in the moneys of the Treasury . . . is comparatively minute and indeterminable" and that "the effect upon future taxation, of any payment out of the [Treasury's] funds, . . . [is] remote, fluctuating and uncertain." As a result, the Court ruled that the taxpayer had failed to allege the type of "direct injury" necessary to confer standing.

Although the barrier *Frothingham* erected against federal taxpayer suits has never been breached, the decision has been the source of some confusion and the object of considerable criticism. The confusion has developed as commentators have tried to determine whether *Frothingham* establishes a constitutional bar to taxpayer suits or whether the Court was simply imposing a rule of self restraint which was not constitutionally compelled. The conflicting viewpoints are reflected in the arguments made to this Court by the parties in this case. The Government has pressed upon us the view that *Frothingham* announced a constitutional rule, compelled by the Article III limitations on federal court jurisdiction and grounded in considerations of the doctrine of separation of powers. Appellants, however, insist that *Frothingham* expressed no more than a policy of judicial self-restraint which can be disregarded when compelling reasons for assuming jurisdiction over a taxpayer's suit exist. The opinion delivered in *Frothingham* can be read to support either position. . . .

To the extent that *Frothingham* has been viewed as resting on policy considerations, it has been criticized as depending on assumptions not consistent with modern conditions. For example, some commentators have pointed out that a number of corporate taxpayers today have a federal tax liability running into hundreds of millions of dollars, and such taxpayers have a far greater monetary stake in the Federal Treasury than they do in any municipal treasury. To some degree, the fear expressed in *Frothingham* that allowing one taxpayer to sue would inundate the federal courts with countless similar suits has been mitigated by the ready availability of the devices of class actions and joinder under the Federal Rules of Civil Procedure, adopted subsequent to the decision in *Frothingham*. . . .

The jurisdiction of federal courts is defined and limited by Article III of the Constitution. In terms relevant to the question for decision in this case, the judicial power of federal courts is constitutionally restricted to "cases" and "controversies." As is so often the situation in constitutional adjudication, those two words have an iceberg quality, containing beneath their surface simplicity submerged complexities which go to the very heart of our constitutional form of government. Embodied in the words "cases" and "controversies" are two complementary but somewhat different limitations. In part those words limit the business of federal courts to questions presented in an adversary context and in a form historically viewed as capable of resolution through the judicial process. And in part those words define the role assigned to the judiciary in a tripartite allocation of power to assure that the federal courts will not intrude into areas committed to the other branches of government. Justiciability is the term of art employed to give expression to this dual limitation placed upon federal courts by the case-and-controversy doctrine.

Justiciability is itself a concept of uncertain meaning and scope. Its reach is illustrated by the various grounds upon which questions sought to be adjudicated in federal courts have been held not to be justiciable. Thus, no justiciable controversy is presented when the parties seek adjudication of only a political question, when the parties are asking for an advisory opinion, when the question sought to be adjudicated has been mooted by subsequent developments, and when there is no standing to maintain the action. Yet it remains true that "[j]usticiability is . . . not a legal concept with a fixed content or susceptible of scientific verification. Its utilization is the resultant of many subtle pressures," *Poe v. Ullman* [367 U.S. 497 (1961)].

Part of the difficulty in giving precise meaning and form to the concept of justiciability stems from the uncertain historical antecedents of the case-and-controversy doctrine. For example, Justice FRANKFURTER twice suggested that historical meaning could be imparted to the concepts of justiciability and case and controversy by reference to the practices of the courts of Westminster when the Constitution was adopted. . . .

However, the power of English judges to deliver advisory opinions was well established at the time the Constitution was drafted. And it is quite clear that "the oldest and most consistent thread in the federal law of justiciability is that the federal courts will not give advisory opinions." Thus, the implicit policies embodied in Article III, and not history alone, impose the rule against advisory opinions on federal courts. When the federal judicial power is invoked to pass upon the validity of actions by the Legislative and Executive Branches of the Government, the rule against advisory opinions implements the separation of powers prescribed by the Constitution and confines federal courts to the role assigned them by Article III. However, the rule against advisory opinions also recognizes that such suits often "are not pressed before the Court with that clear concreteness provided when a question emerges precisely framed and necessary for decision from a clash of adversary argument exploring every aspect of a multifaceted situation embracing conflicting and demanding interests." Consequently, the Article III prohibition against advisory opinions reflects the complementary constitutional considerations expressed by the justiciability doctrine: Federal judicial power is limited to those disputes which confine federal courts to a role consistent with a system of separated powers and which are traditionally thought to be capable of resolution through the judicial process.

Additional uncertainty exists in the doctrine of justiciability because that doctrine has become a blend of constitutional requirements and policy considerations. And a policy limitation is "not always clearly distinguished from the constitutional limitation." . . . The "many subtle pressures" which cause policy considerations to blend into the constitutional limitations of Article III make the justiciability doctrine one of uncertain and shifting contours.

It is in this context that the standing question presented by this case must be viewed and that the Government's argument on that question must be evaluated. As we understand it, the Government's position is that the constitutional scheme of separation of powers, and the deference owed by the federal judiciary to the other two branches of government within that scheme, present an absolute bar to taxpayer suits challenging the validity of federal spending programs. The Government views such suits as involving no more than the mere disagreement by the taxpayer "with the uses to which tax money is put." According to the Government, the resolution of such disagreements is committed to other branches of the Federal Government and not to the judiciary. Consequently, the Government contends that, under no circumstances, should standing be conferred on federal taxpayers to challenge a federal taxing or spending program. An analysis of the function served by standing limitations compels a rejection of the Government's position.

Standing is an aspect of justiciability and, as such, the problem of standing is surrounded by the same complexities and vagaries that inhere in justiciability. . . .

Despite the complexities and uncertainties, some meaningful form can be given to the jurisdictional limitations placed on federal court power by the concept of standing. The fundamental aspect of standing is that it focuses on the party seeking to get his complaint before a federal court and not on the issues he wishes to have adjudicated. The "gist of the question of standing" is whether the party seeking relief has "alleged such a personal stake in the outcome of the controversy as to assure that concrete adverseness which sharpens the presentation of issues upon which the court so largely depends for illumination of difficult constitutional questions," *Baker v. Carr*, [369 U.S. 186] (1962). In other words, when standing is placed in issue in a case, the question is whether the person whose standing is challenged is a proper party to request an adjudication of a particular issue and not whether the issue itself is justiciable. Thus, a party may have standing in a particular case, but the federal court may nevertheless decline to pass on the merits of the case because, for example, it presents a political question. A proper party is demanded so that federal courts will not be asked to decide "ill-defined controversies over constitutional issues," *United Public Workers of America v. Mitchell*, 330 U.S. 75 (1947), or a case which is of "a hypothetical or abstract character," . . . So stated, the standing requirement is closely related to, although more general than, the rule that federal courts will not entertain friendly suits. . . .

When the emphasis in the standing problem is placed on whether the person invoking a federal court's jurisdiction is a proper party to maintain the action, the weakness of the Government's argument in this case becomes apparent. The question whether a particular person is a proper party to maintain the action does not, by its own force, raise separation of powers problems related to improper judicial interference in areas committed to other branches of the Federal Government. Such problems arise, if at all, only from the substantive issues the individual seeks to have adjudicated. Thus, in terms of Article III limitations on federal court jurisdiction, the question of standing is related only to whether the dispute sought to be adjudicated will be presented in an adversary context and in a form historically viewed as capable of judicial resolution. It is for that reason that the emphasis in standing problems is on whether the party invoking federal court jurisdiction has "a personal stake in the outcome of the controversy," *Baker v. Carr*, and whether the dispute touches upon "the legal relations of parties having adverse legal interests." A taxpayer may or may not have the requisite personal stake in the outcome, depending upon the circumstances of the particular case. Therefore, we find no absolute bar in Article III to suits by federal taxpayers challenging allegedly unconstitutional federal taxing and spending programs. There remains, however, the problem of determining the circumstances under which a federal taxpayer will be deemed to have the personal stake and interest that impart the necessary concrete adverseness to such litigation so that standing can be conferred on the taxpayer *qua* taxpayer consistent with the constitutional limitations of Article III. . . .

Whether such individuals have standing to maintain that form of action turns on whether they can demonstrate the necessary stake as taxpayers in the outcome of the litigation to satisfy Article III requirements.

The nexus demanded of federal taxpayers has two aspects to it. First, the taxpayer must establish a logical link between that status and the type of legislative enactment attacked. Thus, a taxpayer will be a proper party to allege the unconstitutionality only of exercises of congressional power under the taxing and spending clause of Art. I, Sec. 8, of the Constitution. It will not be sufficient to allege an incidental expenditure of tax funds in the administration of an essentially regulatory statute. . . . Secondly, the taxpayer must establish a nexus between that status and the precise nature of the constitutional infringement alleged. Under this requirement, the taxpayer must show that the challenged enactment exceeds specific constitutional limitations imposed upon the exercise of the congressional taxing and spending power and not simply that the enactment is generally beyond the powers delegated to Congress by Art. I, Sec. 8. When both nexuses are established, the litigant will have shown a taxpayer's stake in the outcome of the controversy and will be a proper and appropriate party to invoke a federal court's jurisdiction.

The taxpayer-appellants in this case have satisfied both nexuses to support their claim of standing under the test we announce today. Their constitutional challenge is made to an exercise by Congress of its power under Art. I, Sec. 8, to spend for the general welfare, and the challenged program involves a substantial expenditure of federal tax funds. In addition, appellants have alleged that the challenged expenditures violate the Establishment and Free Exercise Clauses of the First Amendment. Our history vividly illustrates that one of the specific evils feared by those who drafted the Establishment Clause and fought for its adoption was that the taxing and spending power would be used to favor one religion over another or to support religion in general. James Madison, who is generally recognized as the leading architect of the religion clauses of the First Amendment, observed in his famous Memorial and Remonstrance Against Religious Assessments that "the same authority which can force a citizen to contribute three pence only of his property for the support of any one establishment, may force him to conform to any other establishment in all cases whatsoever." 2 *Writings of James Madison* 183, 186 (Hunt ed. 1901). The concern of Madison and his supporters was quite clearly that religious liberty ultimately would be the victim if government could employ its taxing and spending powers to aid one religion over another or to aid religion in general. The Establishment Clause was designed as a specific bulwark against such potential abuses of governmental power, and that clause of the First Amendment operates as a specific constitutional limitation upon the exercise by Congress of the taxing and spending power conferred by Art. I, Sec. 8.

The allegations of the taxpayer in *Frothingham v. Mellon, supra*, were quite different from those made in this case, and the result in *Frothingham* is consistent with the test of taxpayer standing announced today. The taxpayer in *Frothingham* attacked a federal spending program and she, therefore, established the first nexus required. However, she lacked standing because her constitutional attack was not based on an allegation that Congress, in enacting the Maternity Act of 1921, had breached a specific limitation upon its taxing and spending power. The taxpayer in *Frothingham* alleged essentially that Congress, by enacting the challenged statute, had exceeded the general powers delegated to it by Art. I, Sec. 8, and that Congress had thereby invaded the legislative province reserved to the States by the Tenth Amendment. To be sure, Mrs. Frothingham made the additional allegation that her tax liability would be increased as a result of the allegedly unconstitutional enactment, and she framed that allegation in terms of a deprivation of property without due process of law. However, the Due Process Clause of the Fifth Amendment does not protect taxpayers against increases in tax liability, and the taxpayer in *Frothingham* failed to make any additional claim that the harm she alleged resulted from a breach by Congress of the specific constitutional limitations imposed upon an exercise of the taxing and spending power. In essence, Mrs. Frothingham was attempting to assert the States' interest in their legislative prerogatives and not a federal taxpayer's interest in being free of taxing and spending in contravention of specific constitutional limitations imposed upon Congress' taxing and spending power.

We have noted that the Establishment Clause of the First Amendment does specifically limit the taxing and spending power conferred by Art. I, Sec. 8. Whether the Constitution contains other specific limitations can be determined only in the context of future cases. However, whenever such specific limitations are found, we believe a taxpayer will have a clear stake as a taxpayer in assuring that they are not breached by Congress. Consequently, we hold that a taxpayer will have standing consistent with Article III to invoke federal judicial power when he alleges that congressional action under the taxing and spending clause is in derogation of those constitutional provisions which operate to restrict the exercise of the taxing and spending power. The taxpayer's allegation in such cases would be that his tax money is being extracted and spent in violation of specific constitutional protections against such abuses of legislative power. Such an injury is appropriate for judicial redress, and the taxpayer has established the necessary nexus between his status and the nature of the allegedly unconstitutional action to support his claim of standing to secure judicial review. Under such circumstances, we feel confident that the questions will be framed with the necessary specificity, that the issues will be contested with the necessary adverseness and that the litigation will be pursued with the necessary vigor to assure that the constitutional challenge will be made in a form traditionally thought to be capable of judicial resolution. We lack that confidence in cases such as *Frothingham* where a taxpayer seeks to employ a federal court as a forum in which to air his generalized grievances about the conduct of government or the allocation of power in the Federal System.

Valley Forge Christian College v. Americans United for Separation of Church and State, Inc.

454 U.S. 464, 102 S.CT. 752 (1982)

Americans United for Separation of Church and State, an organization dedicated to the separation of religion from government, filed a suit in federal district court in Pennsylvania to stop the Department of Health, Education, and Welfare (now the Department of Education) from conveying as "surplus property" a closed and former army hospital to Valley Forge Christian College. Under the Federal Property and Administrative Services Act of 1949, the department has authority to sell surplus government property for educational use to nonprofit, tax-exempt educational institutions. Congress has the power to "dispose of and make all needful Rules and Regulations respecting the . . . Property belonging to the United States," under Article IV, Section 3, Clause 2. But Americans United for Separation of Church and State contended that the department's conveyance here abridged its members' First Amendment rights to religious freedom and "deprived [them] of the fair and constitutional use of [their] tax dollars." The district court dismissed the suit but the Court of Appeals for the Third Circuit reversed. Thereupon, Valley Forge Christian College appealed to the Supreme Court.

The Court's decision was 5–4, with the majority's opinion announced by Justice Rehnquist. Dissents were by Justices Stevens and Brennan, who were joined by Justices Blackmun and Marshall.

■ ■ ■

☐ *Justice REHNQUIST delivers the opinion of the Court.*

We need not mince words when we say that the concept of "Art. III standing" has not been defined with complete consistency in all of the various cases decided by this Court which have discussed it, nor when we say that this very fact is probably proof that the concept cannot be reduced to a one-sentence or one-paragraph definition. But of one thing we may be sure: Those who do not possess Art. III standing may not litigate as suitors in the courts of the United States. Article III, which is every bit as important in its circumscription of the judicial power of the United States as in its granting of that power, is not merely a troublesome hurdle to be overcome if possible so as to reach the "merits" of a lawsuit which a party desires to have adjudicated; it is a part of the basic charter promulgated by the Framers of the Constitution at Philadelphia in 1787, a charter which created a general government, provided for the interaction between that government and the governments of the several States, and was later amended so as to either enhance or limit its authority with respect to both States and individuals. . . .

[I]n *Flast v. Cohen*, [392 U.S. 83 (1968)], [t]he Court developed a two-part test to determine whether the plaintiffs had standing to sue. First, because a taxpayer alleges injury only by virtue of his liability for taxes, the Court held that "a taxpayer will be a proper party to allege the unconstitutionality only of exercises of congressional power under the taxing and spending clause of Art. I, Sec. 8, of the Constitution." Second, the Court required the taxpayer to "show that the challenged enactment exceeds specific constitutional limitations upon the exercise of the taxing and spending power and not simply that the enactment is generally beyond the powers delegated to Congress by Art. I, Sec. 8."

Unlike the plaintiffs in *Flast*, respondents fail the first prong of the test for taxpayer standing. Their claim is deficient in two respects. First, the source of their complaint is not a congressional action, but a decision by HEW to transfer a parcel of federal property. *Flast* limited taxpayer standing to challenges directed "only [at] exercises of congressional power." See *Schlesinger v. Reservists Committee to Stop the War*, [418 U.S. 208 (1974)] (denying standing because the taxpayer plaintiffs "did not challenge an enactment under Art. I, Sec. 8, but rather the action of the Executive Branch").

Second, and perhaps redundantly, the property transfer about which respondents complain was not an exercise of authority conferred by the Taxing and Spending Clause of Art. I, Sec. 8. The authorizing legislation, the Federal Property and Administrative Services Act of 1949, was an evident exercise of Congress' power under the Property Clause, Art. IV, Sec. 3, cl. 2. Respondents do not dispute this conclusion, and it is decisive of any claim of taxpayer standing under the *Flast* precedent.

☐ *Justice BRENNAN, with whom Justice MARSHALL and Justice BLACKMUN join, dissenting.*

The opinion of the Court is a stark example of this unfortunate trend of resolving cases at the "threshold" while obscuring the nature of the underlying rights and interests at stake. The Court waxes eloquent on the blend of prudential and constitutional considerations that combine to create our misguided "standing" jurisprudence. *But not one word is said about the Establishment Clause right that the plaintiff seeks to enforce.* And despite its pat recitation of our standing decisions, the opinion utterly fails, except by the sheerest form of *ipse dixit*, to explain why this case is unlike *Flast v. Cohen* (1968), and is controlled instead by *Frothingham v. Mellon* (1923). . . .

It is at once apparent that the test of standing formulated by the Court in *Flast* sought to reconcile the developing doctrine of taxpayer "standing" with the Court's historical understanding that the Establishment Clause was intended to prohibit the Federal Government from using tax funds for the advancement of religion, and thus the constitutional imperative of taxpayer standing in certain cases brought pursuant to the Establishment Clause. The two-pronged "nexus" test offered by the Court, despite its general language, is best understood as "a determinant of standing of plaintiffs alleging only injury as taxpayers who challenge alleged violations of the Establishment and Free Exercise Clauses of the First Amendment," and not as a general statement of standing principles. The test explains what forms of governmental action may be attacked by someone alleging *only* taxpayer status, and, without ruling out the possibility that history might reveal another similarly founded provision, explains why an Establishment Clause claim is treated differently from any other assertion that the Federal Government has exceeded the bounds of the law in allocating its largesse. . . .

The nexus test that the Court "announced," sought to maintain necessary continuity with prior cases, and set forth principles to guide future cases involving taxpayer standing. But *Flast* did not depart from the principle that no judgment about standing should be made without a fundamental understanding of the rights at issue. The two-part *Flast* test did not supply the rationale for the Court's decision, but rather its exposition: That rationale was supplied by an understanding of the nature of the restrictions on government power imposed by the Constitution, and the intended beneficiaries of those restrictions.

It may be that Congress can tax for *almost* any reason, or for no reason at all. There is, so far as I have been able to discern, but one constitutionally imposed limit on that authority. Congress cannot use tax money to support a church, or to encourage religion. That is "*the* forbidden exaction." *Everson v. Board of Education* [330 U.S. 1 (1947)]. In absolute terms the history of the Establishment Clause of the First Amendment makes this clear. History also makes it clear that the federal taxpayer is a singularly "proper and appropriate party to invoke a federal court's jurisdiction" to challenge a federal bestowal of largesse as a violation of the Establishment Clause. Each, and indeed every, federal taxpayer suffers precisely the injury that the Establishment Clause guards against when the Federal Government directs that funds be taken from the pocketbooks of the citizenry and placed into the coffers of the ministry.

A taxpayer cannot be asked to raise his objection to such use of his funds at the time he pays his tax. Apart from the unlikely circumstance in which the Government announced in advance that a particular levy would be used for religious subsidies, taxpayers could hardly assert that they were being injured until the Government actually lent its support to a religious venture. Nor would it be reasonable to require him to address his claim to those officials charged with the collection of federal taxes. Those officials would be without the means to provide appropriate redress—there is no practical way to segregate the complaining taxpayer's money from that being devoted to the religious purpose. Surely, then, a taxpayer must have standing at the time that he learns of the Government's alleged Establishment Clause violation to seek equitable relief in order to halt the continuing and intolerable burden on his pocketbook, his conscience, and his constitutional rights.

Blind to history, the Court attempts to distinguish this case from *Flast* by wrenching snippets of language from our opinions, and by perfunctorily applying that language under color of the first prong of *Flast's* two-part nexus test. The tortuous distinctions thus produced are specious, at best: at worst, they are pernicious to our constitutional heritage.

First, the Court finds this case different from *Flast* because here the "source of [plaintiffs'] complaint is not a *congressional* action, but a decision by HEW to transfer a parcel of federal property." This attempt at distinction cannot withstand scrutiny. *Flast* involved a challenge to the actions of the Commissioner of Education, and other officials of HEW, in disbursing funds under the Elementary and Secondary Education Act of 1965 to "religious and sectarian" schools. Plaintiffs disclaimed "any intent[ion] to challenge . . . all programs under . . . the Act." Rather, they claimed that defendant-administrators' approval of such expenditures was not authorized by the Act, or alternatively, to the extent the expenditures were authorized, the Act was "unconstitutional and void." In the present case, respondents challenge HEW's grant of property pursuant to the Federal Property and Administrative Services Act of 1949, seeking to enjoin HEW "from making a grant of this and other property to the [defendant] so long as such a grant will violate the Establishment Clause." It may be that the Court is concerned with the adequacy of respondents' pleading; respondents have not, in so many words, asked for a declaration that the "Federal Property and Administrative Services Act is unconstitutional and void to the extent that it authorizes HEW's actions." I would not construe their complaint so narrowly.

More fundamentally, no clear division can be drawn in this context between actions of the Legislative Branch and those of the Executive Branch. To be sure, the First Amendment is phrased as a restriction on Congress' legislative authority; this is only natural since the Constitution assigns the authority to legislate and appropriate only to the Congress. But it is difficult to conceive of an expenditure for which the last governmental actor, either implementing directly the legislative will, or acting within the scope of legislatively delegated authority, is not an Executive Branch official. The First Amendment binds the Government as a whole, regardless of which branch is at work in a particular instance.

The Court's second purported distinction between this case and *Flast* is equally unavailing. The majority finds it "decisive" that the Federal Property and Administrative Services Act of 1949 "was an evident exercise of Congress' power under the Property Clause, Art. IV, Sec. 3, cl. 2," while the Government action in *Flast* was taken under Art. I, Sec. 8. The Court relies on *United States v. Richardson*, 418 U.S. [166] (1974), and *Schlesinger v. Reservists Committee to Stop the War*, 418 U.S. 208 (1974), to support the distinction between the two Clauses, noting that those cases involved alleged deviations from the requirements of Art. I, Sec. 9, cl. 7, and Art. I, Sec. 6, cl. 2, respectively. The standing defect in each case was *not*, however, the failure to allege a violation of the Spending Clause; rather, the taxpayers in those cases had not complained of the distribution of Government largesse, and thus failed to meet the essential requirement of taxpayer standing recognized in *Doremus* [*v. Board of Education*, 342 U.S. 429 (1952)]. . . .

Plainly hostile to the Framers' understanding of the Establishment Clause, and *Flast*'s enforcement of that understanding, the Court vents that hostility under the guise of standing, "to slam the courthouse door against plaintiffs who [as the Framers intended] are entitled to full consideration of their [Establishment Clause] claims on the merits." *Barlow v. Collins*, 397 U.S. 159 (1970) (BRENNAN, J., concurring in result and dissenting). Therefore, I dissent.

Lujan v. Defenders of Wildlife

504 U.S. 555, 112 S.Ct. 2130 (1992)

Under the Endangered Species Act (ESA) of 1973, federal agencies are required to consult with the Department of the Interior (DOI) to make sure that their policies and actions will not jeopardize endangered or threatened species or their habitats. For more than a decade, the DOI interpreted that act to apply to federally funded projects at home and abroad. But in 1986, the Reagan administration reversed course, announcing that the law no longer applied to projects overseas. Immediately, Defenders of Wildlife, other environmental groups, and their members challenged that reinterpretation of the law.

To gain standing to file a lawsuit, members of Defenders of Wildlife—its president, Joyce Kelly, and another member, Amy Skilbred—filed affidavits alleging that they would suffer injuries due to the failure of the Agency for International Development (AID) and other agencies to consult with the DOI about a federally funded irrigation project on the Mahaweli River in Sri Lanka and a redevelopment project on the Nile River in Egypt. Those projects, they claimed, threatened endangered elephants and leopards in Sri Lanka and the crocodile and other species in Egypt. And when asserting their standing to sue and personal injuries, Kelly and Skilbred testified that they were environmentalists and had traveled to each site, although neither indicated specifically when she would again visit those sites. A federal district court dismissed the suit for lacking standing, but the Court of Appeals for the Eighth Circuit reversed.

The George H. W. Bush administration appealed the appellate court's holding that Kelly and Skilbred had standing to sue under the ESA's provision conveying on citizens the right to sue the secretary of the DOI for failure to consult with other federal agencies on projects potentially threatening to endangered species and their habitats, even though they failed to allege concrete injuries. Relying on *dicta* in several recent cases (see Justice Scalia's concurring opinion in *Gwaltney of Smithfield, Ltd. v. Chesapeake Bay Foundation*, 484 U.S. 49 [1987], and *Lujan v. National Wildlife Federation*, 497

U.S. 871 [1989]), the Bush administration asked the Court to sharply limit standing in such citizen suits.

The Court's decision was 7–2; the opinion was announced by Justice Scalia. Concurring opinions were delivered by Justice Kennedy, whom Justice Souter joined, and by Justice Stevens. Justice Blackmun dissented and was joined by Justice O'Connor.

■ ■ ■

☐ *Justice SCALIA delivers the opinion of the Court with respect to Parts I, II, III-A, and IV, and an opinion with respect to Part III-B in which Chief Justice REHNQUIST and Justices WHITE, KENNEDY, SOUTER, and THOMAS join.*

■ II

Over the years, our cases have established that the irreducible constitutional minimum of standing contains three elements: First, the plaintiff must have suffered an "injury in fact"—an invasion of a legally protected interest which is (a) concrete and particularized, *Warth v. Seldin*, 422 U.S. 490 (1975); *Sierra Club v. Morton*, 405 U.S. 727 (1972); and (b) "actual or imminent, not 'conjectural' or 'hypothetical.'" Second, there must be a causal connection between the injury and the conduct complained of—the injury has to be "fairly . . . traceable to the challenged action of the defendant, and not . . . the result [of] the independent action of some third party not before the court." *Simon v. Eastern Kentucky Welfare Rights Org.*, 426 U.S. 26 (1976). Third, it must be "likely," as opposed to merely "speculative," that the injury will be "redressed by a favorable decision."

When the suit is one challenging the legality of government action or inaction, the nature and extent of facts that must be averred (at the summary judgment stage) or proved (at the trial stage) in order to establish standing depends considerably upon whether the plaintiff is himself an object of the action (or foregone action) at issue. If he is, there is ordinarily little question that the action or inaction has caused him injury, and that a judgment preventing or requiring the action will redress it. When, however, as in this case, a plaintiff's asserted injury arises from the government's allegedly unlawful regulation (or lack of regulation) of someone else, much more is needed. In that circumstance, causation and redressability ordinarily hinge on the response of the regulated (or regulable) third party to the government action or inaction—and perhaps on the response of others as well. The existence of one or more of the essential elements of standing "depends on the unfettered choices made by independent actors not before the courts and whose exercise of broad and legitimate discretion the courts cannot presume either to control or to predict," *ASARCO Inc. v. Kadish*, 490 U.S. 605 (1989); and it becomes the burden of the plaintiff to adduce facts showing that those choices have been or will be made in such manner as to produce causation and permit redressability of injury. Thus, when the plaintiff is not himself the object of the government action or inaction he challenges, standing is not precluded, but it is ordinarily "substantially more difficult" to establish.

■ III

We think the Court of Appeals failed to apply the foregoing principles. . . . Respondents had not made the requisite demonstration of (at least) injury and redressability.

■ A

Respondents' claim to injury is that the lack of consultation with respect to certain funded activities abroad "increases the rate of extinction of endangered and threatened species." Of course, the desire to use or observe an animal species, even for purely aesthetic purposes, is undeniably a cognizable interest for purpose of standing. "But the 'injury in fact' test requires more than an injury to a cognizable interest. It requires that the party seeking review be himself among the injured." . . . [R]espondents had to submit affidavits or other evidence showing, through specific facts, not only that listed species were in fact being threatened by funded activities abroad, but also that one or more of respondents' members would thereby be "directly" affected apart from their "'special interest' in the subject." . . .

We shall assume for the sake of argument that these affidavits contain facts showing that certain agency-funded projects threaten listed species— though that is questionable. They plainly contain no facts, however, showing how damage to the species will produce "imminent" injury to Mses. Kelly and Skilbred. That the women "had visited" the areas of the projects before the projects commenced proves nothing. . . .

Besides relying upon the Kelly and Skilbred affidavits, respondents propose a series of novel standing theories. The first, inelegantly styled "ecosystem nexus," proposes that any person who uses any part of a "contiguous ecosystem" adversely affected by a funded activity has standing even if the activity is located a great distance away. . . . [But to] say that the Act protects ecosystems is not to say that the Act creates (if it were possible) rights of action in persons who have not been injured in fact, that is, persons who use portions of an ecosystem not perceptibly affected by the unlawful action in question.

Respondents' other theories are called, alas, the "animal nexus" approach, whereby anyone who has an interest in studying or seeing the endangered animals anywhere on the globe has standing; and the "vocational nexus" approach, under which anyone with a professional interest in such animals can sue. Under these theories, anyone who goes to see Asian elephants in the Bronx Zoo, and anyone who is a keeper of Asian elephants in the Bronx Zoo, has standing to sue because the Director of AID did not consult with the Secretary regarding the AID-funded project in Sri Lanka. This is beyond all reason. . . .

■ B

The most obvious problem in the present case is redressability. Since the agencies funding the projects were not parties to the case, the District Court could accord relief only against the Secretary: He could be ordered to revise his regulation to require consultation for foreign projects. But this would not remedy respondents' alleged injury unless the funding agencies were bound by the Secretary's regulation, which is very much an open question. Whereas in other contexts the ESA is quite explicit as to the Secretary's controlling authority, with respect to consultation the initiative, and hence arguably the initial responsibility for determining statutory necessity, lies with the agencies. When the Secretary promulgated the regulation at issue here, he thought it was binding on the agencies. The Solicitor General, however, has repudiated that position here, and the agencies themselves apparently deny the Secretary's authority. . . .

A further impediment to redressability is the fact that the agencies generally supply only a fraction of the funding for a foreign project. AID, for example, has provided less than 10 percent of the funding for the Mahaweli Project. Respondents have produced nothing to indicate that the projects they have named will either be suspended, or do less harm to listed species, if that fraction is eliminated. . . .

We hold that respondents lack standing to bring this action.

☐ *Justice BLACKMUN, with whom Justice O'CONNOR joins, dissenting.*

I part company with the Court in this case in two respects. First, I believe that respondents have raised genuine issues of fact—sufficient to survive summary judgment—both as to injury and as to redressability. Second, I question the Court's breadth of language in rejecting standing for "procedural" injuries. I fear the Court seeks to impose fresh limitations on the constitutional authority of Congress to allow citizen-suits in the federal courts for injuries deemed "procedural" in nature. I dissent. . . .

To survive petitioner's motion for summary judgment on standing, respondents need not prove that they are actually or imminently harmed. They need show only a "genuine issue" of material fact as to standing. Federal Rules of Civil Procedure 56(c). This is not a heavy burden. A "genuine issue" exists so long as "the evidence is such that a reasonable jury could return a verdict for the nonmoving party respondents." *Anderson v. Liberty Lobby, Inc.*, 477 U.S. 242 (1986). "This Court's function is not itself to weigh the evidence and determine the truth of the matter but to determine whether there is a genuine issue for trial." . . .

I think a reasonable finder of fact could conclude from the information in the affidavits and deposition testimony that either Kelly or Skilbred will soon return to the project sites, thereby satisfying the "actual or imminent" injury standard. . . .

By requiring a "description of concrete plans" or "specification of when the same day [for a return visit] will be," the Court, in my view, demands what is likely an empty formality. No substantial barriers prevent Kelly or Skilbred from simply purchasing plane tickets to return to the Aswan and Mahaweli projects. . . .

In conclusion, I cannot join the Court on what amounts to a slash-and-burn expedition through the law of environmental standing. In my view, "the very essence of civil liberty certainly consists in the right of every individual to claim the protection of the laws, whenever he receives an injury." *Marbury v. Madison*, 1 Cranch 137 (1803).

Hein v. Freedom from Religion Foundation, Inc.

551 U.S. 587, 127 S.Ct. 2553 (2007)

In 2001, President George W. Bush issued an executive order creating the White House Office of Faith-Based and Community Initiatives, with the aim of ensuring that "private and charitable community groups, including religious ones . . . have the fullest opportunity permitted by law to compete on a level playing field, so long as they achieve valid public purposes" and adhere to "the bedrock principles of pluralism, nondiscrimination, evenhandedness, and neutrality." The office was charged with the task of eliminating regulatory barriers that could impede such organizations' ability to compete equally for federal assistance. In separate executive orders, the president also created centers for Faith-Based and Community Initiatives within several federal agencies. They were given the job of ensuring that faith-based community groups would be eligible to compete for federal financial support, by holding conferences and giving assistance on grant applications. No congressional legislation specifically authorized the creation of the centers or appropriated funds for them. Instead, their activities were funded through general executive branch appropriations.

These faith-based initiatives were challenged by Freedom from Religion Foundation, Inc., a group of atheists and agnostics, who argued that these initiatives violated the First Amendment (dis)establishment clause by promoting religious community groups over secular ones. A federal district court dismissed the suit for lack of standing, concluding that under *Flast v. Cohen*, 392 U.S. 83 (1968) federal taxpayer standing is limited to challenges to the constitutionality of "exercises of congressional power under the taxing and spending clause of Art. I, Sec. 8." Subsequently, a divided panel of the Court of Appeals for the Seventh Circuit reversed. That decision was appealed and the Supreme Court granted review.

The appellate court's decision was reversed by a 5–4 vote. Justice Alito delivered the opinion for the Court. Justices Scalia and Kennedy filed concurring opinions. Justice Souter issued a dissenting opinion, which Justices Stevens, Ginsburg, and Breyer joined.

■ ■ ■

☐ *Justice ALITO announced the judgment of the Court and delivered an opinion in which THE CHIEF JUSTICE and Justice KENNEDY join.*

This is a lawsuit in which it was claimed that conferences held as part of the President's Faith-Based and Community Initiatives program violated the Establishment Clause of the First Amendment because, among other things, President Bush and former Secretary of Education

Paige gave speeches that used "religious imagery" and praised the efficacy of faith-based programs in delivering social services. The plaintiffs contend that they meet the standing requirements of Article III of the Constitution because they pay federal taxes.

It has long been established, however, that the payment of taxes is generally not enough to establish standing to challenge an action taken by the Federal Government. In light of the size of the federal budget, it is a complete fiction to argue that an unconstitutional federal expenditure causes an individual federal taxpayer any measurable economic harm. And if every federal taxpayer could sue to challenge any Government expenditure, the federal courts would cease to function as courts of law and would be cast in the role of general complaint bureaus.

In *Flast v. Cohen*, 392 U.S. 83 (1968), we recognized a narrow exception to the general rule against federal taxpayer standing. Under *Flast*, a plaintiff asserting an Establishment Clause claim has standing to challenge a law authorizing the use of federal funds in a way that allegedly violates the Establishment Clause. In the present case, Congress did not specifically authorize the use of federal funds to pay for the conferences or speeches that the plaintiffs challenged. Instead, the conferences and speeches were paid for out of general Executive Branch appropriations. The Court of Appeals, however, held that the plaintiffs have standing as taxpayers because the conferences were paid for with money appropriated by Congress.

The question that is presented here is whether this broad reading of *Flast* is correct. We hold that it is not. We therefore reverse the decision of the Court of Appeals. . . .

The only asserted basis for standing was that the individual respondents are federal taxpayers who are "opposed to the use of Congressional taxpayer appropriations to advance and promote religion." In their capacity as federal taxpayers, respondents sought to challenge Executive Branch expenditures for these conferences, which, they contended, violated the Establishment Clause. . . .

Article III of the Constitution limits the judicial power of the United States to the resolution of "Cases" and "Controversies," and "Article III standing . . . enforces the Constitution's case-or-controversy requirement."

The constitutionally mandated standing inquiry is especially important in a case like this one, in which taxpayers seek "to challenge laws of general application where their own injury is not distinct from that suffered in general by other taxpayers or citizens." This is because "[t]he judicial power of the United States defined by Art. III is not an unconditioned authority to determine the constitutionality of legislative or executive acts." *Valley Forge Christian College v. Americans United for Separation of Church and State, Inc.*, 454 U.S. 464 (1982). The federal courts are not empowered to seek out and strike down any governmental act that they deem to be repugnant to the Constitution. Rather, federal courts sit "solely, to decide on the rights of individuals," *Marbury v. Madison*, 1 Cranch 137 (1803), and must "refrai[n] from passing upon the constitutionality of an act . . . unless obliged to do so in the proper performance of our judicial function, when the question is raised by a party whose interests entitle him to raise it." *Valley Forge*. As we held over 80 years ago, in another case involving the question of taxpayer standing: "We have no power per se to review and annul acts of Congress on the ground that they are unconstitutional. The question may be considered only when the justification for some direct injury suffered or threatened, presenting a justiciable issue, is made to rest upon such an act. . . . The party who invokes the power must be able to show not only that the statute is invalid but that he has sustained or is immediately in danger of sustaining some direct injury as the result of its enforcement, and not merely that he suffers in some indefinite way in common with people generally." *Frothingham v. Mellon*, 262 U.S. 447 (1923). . . .

As a general matter, the interest of a federal taxpayer in seeing that Treasury funds are spent in accordance with the Constitution does not give rise to the kind of redressable "personal injury" required for Article III standing. Of course, a taxpayer has standing to challenge the collection of a specific tax assessment as unconstitutional; being forced to pay such a tax causes a real and immediate economic injury to the individual taxpayer. But that is not the interest on which respondents assert standing here. Rather, their claim is that, having paid lawfully collected taxes into the Federal Treasury at some point, they have a continuing, legally cognizable interest in ensuring that those funds are not used by the Government in a way that violates the Constitution.

We have consistently held that this type of *interest is too generalized and attenuated to support Article III standing*. In *Frothingham*, a federal taxpayer sought to challenge federal appropriations for mothers' and children's health, arguing that federal involvement in this area intruded on the rights reserved to the States under the Tenth Amendment and would "increase the burden of future taxation and thereby take [the plaintiff's] property without due process of law." We concluded that the plaintiff lacked the kind of particularized injury required for Article III standing: "[I]nterest in the moneys of the Treasury . . . is shared with millions of others; is comparatively minute and indeterminable; and the effect upon future taxation, of any payment out of the funds, so remote, fluctuating and uncertain, that no basis is afforded for an appeal to the preventive powers of a court of equity." . . .

Because the interests of the taxpayer are, in essence, the interests of the public-at-large, deciding a constitutional claim based solely on taxpayer standing "would be not to decide a judicial controversy, but to assume a position of authority over the governmental acts of another and co-equal department, an authority which plainly we do not possess." . . .

In *Flast*, the Court carved out a narrow exception to the general constitutional prohibition against taxpayer standing. The taxpayer-plaintiff in that case challenged the distribution of federal funds to religious schools under the Elementary and Secondary Education Act of 1965, alleging that such aid violated the Establishment Clause. The Court set out a two-part test for determining whether a federal taxpayer has standing to challenge an allegedly unconstitutional expenditure: "First, the taxpayer must establish a logical link between that status and the type of legislative enactment attacked. Thus, a taxpayer will be a proper party to allege the unconstitutionality only of exercises of congressional power under the taxing and spending clause of Art. I, Sec. 8, of the Constitution. It will not be sufficient to allege an incidental expenditure of tax funds in the administration of an essentially regulatory statute. . . . Secondly, the taxpayer must establish a nexus between that status and the precise nature of the constitutional infringement alleged. Under this requirement, the taxpayer must show that the challenged enactment exceeds specific constitutional limitations imposed upon the exercise of the congressional taxing and spending power and not simply that the enactment is generally beyond the powers delegated to Congress by Art. I, Sec. 8." . . .

Respondents argue that this case falls within the *Flast* exception, which they read to cover any "expenditure of government funds in violation of the Establishment Clause." But this broad reading fails to observe "the rigor with which the *Flast* exception to the *Frothingham* principle ought to be applied." *Valley Forge.*

The expenditures at issue in *Flast* were made pursuant to an express congressional mandate and a specific congressional appropriation. The plaintiff in that case challenged disbursements made under the Elementary and Secondary Education Act of 1965. That Act expressly appropriated the sum of $100 million for fiscal year 1966, and authorized the disbursement of those funds to local educational agencies for the education of low-income students. . . .

The expenditures challenged in *Flast*, then, were funded by a specific congressional appropriation and were disbursed to private schools (including religiously affiliated schools) pursuant to a direct and unambiguous congressional mandate. Indeed, the *Flast* taxpayer-plaintiff's constitutional claim was premised on the contention that if the Government's actions were "within the authority and intent of the Act, the Act is to that extent unconstitutional and void." . . .

Given that the alleged Establishment Clause violation in *Flast* was funded by a specific congressional appropriation and was undertaken pursuant to an express congressional mandate, the Court concluded that the taxpayer-plaintiffs had established the requisite "logical link between [their taxpayer] status and the type of legislative enactment attacked." In the Court's words, "[t]heir constitutional challenge [was] made to an exercise by Congress of its power under Art. I, Sec. 8, to spend for the general welfare." But as this Court later noted, *Flast* "limited taxpayer standing to challenges directed 'only [at] exercises of congressional power'" under the Taxing and Spending Clause. *Valley Forge.*

The link between congressional action and constitutional violation that supported taxpayer standing in *Flast* is missing here. Respondents do not challenge any specific congressional action or appropriation; nor do they ask the Court to invalidate any congressional enactment or legislatively created program as unconstitutional. That is because the expenditures at issue here were not made pursuant to any Act of Congress. Rather, Congress provided general appropriations to the Executive Branch to fund its day-to-day activities. These appropriations did not expressly authorize, direct, or even mention the expenditures of which respondents complain. Those expenditures resulted from executive discretion, not congressional action. . . .

In short, this case falls outside "the narrow exception" that *Flast* "created to the general rule against taxpayer standing established in *Frothingham.*" Because the expenditures that respondents challenge were not expressly authorized or mandated by any specific congressional enactment, respondents' lawsuit is not directed at an exercise of congressional power, and thus lacks the requisite "logical nexus" between taxpayer status "and the type of legislative enactment attacked." . . .

☐ *Justice SCALIA, with whom Justice THOMAS joins, concurring in the judgment.*

Today's opinion is, in one significant respect, entirely consistent with our previous cases addressing taxpayer standing to raise Establishment Clause challenges to government expenditures. Unfortunately, the consistency lies in the creation of utterly meaningless distinctions which separate the case at hand from the precedents that have come out differently, but which cannot possibly be (in any sane world) the reason it comes out differently. If this Court is to decide cases by rule of law rather than show of hands, we must surrender to logic and choose sides: Either *Flast v. Cohen* (1968), should be applied to (at a minimum) all challenges to the governmental expenditure of general tax revenues in a manner alleged to violate a constitutional provision specifically limiting the taxing and spending power, or *Flast* should be repudiated. For me, the choice is easy. *Flast* is wholly irreconcilable with the Article III restrictions on federal-court jurisdiction that this Court has repeatedly confirmed are embodied in the doctrine of standing. . . .

☐ *Justice SOUTER, with whom Justice STEVENS, Justice GINSBURG, and Justice BREYER join, dissenting.*

Flast v. Cohen (1968) held that plaintiffs with an Establishment Clause claim could "demonstrate the necessary stake as taxpayers in the outcome of the litigation to satisfy Article III requirements." Here, the controlling, plurality opinion declares that *Flast* does not apply, but a search of that opinion for a suggestion that these taxpayers have any less stake in the outcome than the taxpayers in *Flast* will come up empty: the plurality makes no such finding, nor could it. Instead, the controlling opinion closes the door on these taxpayers because the Executive Branch, and not the Legislative Branch, caused their injury. I see no basis for this distinction in either logic or precedent, and respectfully dissent. . . .

The plurality points to the separation of powers to explain its distinction between legislative and executive spending decisions, but there is no difference on that point of view between a Judicial Branch review of an executive decision and a judicial evaluation of a congressional one. We owe respect to each of the other branches, no more to the former than to the latter, and no one has suggested that the Establishment Clause lacks applicability to executive uses of money. It would surely violate the Establishment Clause for the Department of Health and Human Services to draw on a general appropriation to build a chapel for weekly church services (no less than if a statute required it), and for good reason: if the Executive could accomplish through the exercise of discretion exactly what Congress cannot do through legislation, Establishment Clause protection would melt away. . . .

Because the taxpayers in this case have alleged the type of injury this Court has seen as sufficient for standing, I would affirm.

Arizona Christian School Tuition Organization v. Winn

563 U.S. 125, 131 S.Ct. 1436 (2011)

Since 1999 Arizona has provided tax credits for contributions to school tuition organizations (or STOs). Under the program, taxpayers can choose to contribute to secular or religious STOs and receive tax credits. STOs provide scholarships to students attending private schools, primarily Catholic schools. A group of Arizona taxpayers challenged the STO tax credit as violation of the First Amendment's (dis)establishment clause. After the state supreme court rejected a similar suit, the taxpayers filed a suit in federal court. In order to do so, they had to demonstrate their standing to sue based on a direct harm of a violation of the (dis)establishment clause, such as a mandatory prayer in public school classes. On remand, the Arizona Christian School Tuition Organization intervened and the district court once again dismissed the suit, but the Court of Appeals for the Ninth Circuit reversed and held that the taxpayers had standing to bring the suit under *Flast v. Cohen* (1968). That decision was appealed and the Supreme Court granted review.

The appellate court's decision was reversed by a bare majority. Justice Kennedy delivered the opinion for the Court and Justice Scalia filed a concurring opinion, joined by Justice Thomas, contending that *Flast* should be overturned. Justice Kagan filed a dissenting opinion, which Justices Ginsburg, Breyer, and Sotomayor joined.

■ ■ ■

☐ *Justice KENNEDY delivered the opinion of the Court.*

To state a case or controversy under Article III, a plaintiff must establish standing. The minimum constitutional requirements for standing were explained in *Lujan v. Defenders of Wildlife*, 504 U.S. 555 (1992). "First, the plaintiff must have suffered an 'injury in fact'—an invasion of a legally protected interest which is (a) concrete and particularized, and (b) 'actual or imminent, not "conjectural" or "hypothetical." Second, there must be a causal connection between the injury and the conduct complained of—the injury has to be 'fairly . . . trace[able] to the challenged action of the defendant, and not . . . th[e] result [of] the independent action of some third party not before the court.' Third, it must be 'likely,' as opposed to merely 'speculative,' that the injury will be 'redressed by a favorable decision.'" In requiring a particular injury, the Court meant "that the injury must affect the plaintiff in a personal and individual way." The question now before the Court is whether respondents, the plaintiffs in the trial court, satisfy the requisite elements of standing.

Respondents suggest that their status as Arizona taxpayers provides them with standing to challenge the STO [school tuition organizations] tax credit. Absent special circumstances, however, standing cannot be based on a plaintiff's mere status as a taxpayer. This Court has rejected the general proposition that an individual who has paid taxes has a "continuing, legally cognizable interest in ensuring that those funds are not used by the Government in a way that violates the Constitution." *Hein v. Freedom From Religion Foundation, Inc.*, 551 U.S. 587 (2007). This precept has been referred to as the rule against taxpayer standing.

The doctrinal basis for the rule was discussed in *Frothingham v. Mellon*, 262 U.S. 447 (1923). There, a taxpayer-plaintiff had alleged that certain federal expenditures were in excess of congressional authority under the Constitution. The plaintiff argued that she had standing to raise her claim because she had an interest in the Government Treasury and because the allegedly unconstitutional expenditure of Government funds would affect her personal tax liability. The Court rejected those arguments. The "effect upon future taxation, of any payment out of funds," was too "remote, fluctuating and uncertain" to give rise to a case or controversy. And the taxpayer-plaintiff's "interest in the moneys of the Treasury," the Court recognized, was necessarily "shared with millions of others." As a consequence, *Frothingham* held that the taxpayer-plaintiff had not presented a "judicial controversy" appropriate for resolution in federal court but rather a "matter of public . . . concern" that could be pursued only through the political process.

In holdings consistent with *Frothingham* and *Doremus [v. Board of Education of Hawthorne*, 342 U.S. 429 (1952)], more recent decisions have explained that claims of taxpayer standing rest on unjustifiable economic and political speculation. When a government expends resources or declines to impose a tax, its budget does not necessarily suffer. On the contrary, the purpose of many governmental expenditures and tax benefits is "to spur economic activity, which in turn increases government revenues." . . .

These well-established principles apply to the present cases. Respondents may be right that Arizona's STO tax credits have an estimated annual value of over $50 million. The education of its young people is, of course, one of the State's principal missions and responsibilities; and the consequent costs will make up a significant portion of the state budget. That, however, is just the beginning of the analysis.

By helping students obtain scholarships to private schools, both religious and secular, the STO program might relieve the burden placed on Arizona's public schools. The result could be an immediate and permanent cost savings for the State. . . .

The primary contention of respondents, of course, is that, despite the general rule that taxpayers lack standing to object to expenditures alleged to be unconstitutional, their suit falls within the exception established by *Flast v. Cohen*. It must be noted at the outset that, as this Court has explained, *Flast*'s holding provides a "narrow exception" to "the general rule against taxpayer standing." *Bowen v. Kendrick*, 487 U.S. 589 (1988). . . .

Respondents contend that . . . the tax credit is, for *Flast* purposes, best understood as a government expenditure. That is incorrect.

It is easy to see that tax credits and governmental expenditures can have similar economic consequences, at least for beneficiaries whose tax liability is sufficiently large to take full advantage of the credit. Yet tax credits and governmental expenditures do not both implicate individual taxpayers in sectarian activities. A dissenter whose tax dollars are "extracted and spent" knows that he has in some small measure been made to contribute to an establishment in violation of conscience. In that instance the taxpayer's direct and particular connection with the establishment does not depend on economic speculation or political conjecture. The connection would exist even if the conscientious dissenter's tax liability were unaffected or reduced. When the government declines to impose a tax, by contrast, there is no such connection between dissenting taxpayer and alleged establishment. Any financial injury remains speculative. And awarding some citizens a tax credit allows other citizens to retain control over their own funds in accordance with their own consciences.

The distinction between governmental expenditures and tax credits refutes respondents' assertion of standing. When Arizona taxpayers choose to contribute to STOs, they spend their own money, not money the State has collected from respondents or from other taxpayers. . . .

Furthermore, respondents cannot satisfy the requirements of causation and redressability. When the government collects and spends taxpayer money, governmental choices are responsible for the transfer of wealth. In that case a resulting subsidy of religious activity is, for purposes of *Flast*, traceable to the government's expenditures. . . . Here, by contrast, contributions result from the decisions of private taxpayers regarding their own funds. Private citizens create private STOs; STOs choose beneficiary schools; and taxpayers then contribute to STOs. . . .

Few exercises of the judicial power are more likely to undermine public confidence in the neutrality and integrity of the Judiciary than one which casts the Court in the role of a Council of Revision, conferring on itself the power to invalidate laws at the behest of anyone who disagrees with them. In an era of frequent litigation, class actions, sweeping injunctions with prospective effect, and continuing jurisdiction to enforce judicial remedies, courts must be more careful to insist on the formal rules of standing, not less so. Making the Article III standing inquiry all the more necessary are the significant implications of constitutional litigation, which can result in rules of wide applicability that are beyond Congress' power to change. . . .

☐ *Justice KAGAN, with whom Justice GINSBURG, Justice BREYER, and Justice SOTOMAYOR join, dissenting.*

Beginning in *Flast v. Cohen* and continuing in case after case for over four decades, this Court and others have exercised jurisdiction to decide taxpayer-initiated challenges not materially different from this one. Not every suit has succeeded on the merits, or should have. But every taxpayer-plaintiff has had her day in court to contest the government's financing of religious activity.

Today, the Court breaks from this precedent by refusing to hear taxpayers' claims that the government has unconstitutionally subsidized religion through its tax system. These litigants lack standing, the majority holds, because the funding of religion they challenge comes from a tax credit, rather than an appropriation. A tax credit, the Court asserts, does not injure objecting taxpayers, because it "does not extract and spend [their] funds in service of an establishment."

This novel distinction in standing law between appropriations and tax expenditures has as little basis in principle as it has in our precedent. Cash grants and targeted tax breaks are means of accomplishing the same government objective—to provide financial support to select individuals or organizations. Taxpayers who oppose state aid of religion have equal reason to protest whether that aid flows from the one form of subsidy or the other. Either way, the government has financed the religious activity. And so either way, taxpayers should be able to challenge the subsidy.

Still worse, the Court's arbitrary distinction threatens to eliminate all occasions for a taxpayer to contest the government's monetary support of religion. Precisely because appropriations and tax breaks can achieve identical objectives, the government can easily substitute one for the other. Today's opinion thus enables the government to end-run *Flast*'s guarantee of access to the Judiciary. From now on, the government need follow just one simple rule—subsidize through the tax system—to preclude taxpayer challenges to state funding of religion. . . . Because I believe these challenges warrant consideration on the merits, I respectfully dissent from the Court's decision. . . .

Baker v. Carr

369 U.S. 186, 82 S.Ct. 691 (1962)

In 1901, the Tennessee legislature apportioned both houses and provided for subsequent reapportionment every ten years on the basis of the number of people in each of the state's counties as reported in the census. But for more than sixty years proposals to redistribute legislative seats failed to pass, while the state's population shifted from rural to urban areas. Charles Baker and several other citizens and urban residents sued various Tennessee officials. Baker claimed that as an urban resident he was being denied the equal protection of the law under the Fourteenth Amendment. He asked the court to order state officials to hold either an at-large election or an election in which legislators would be selected from constituencies in accordance with the 1960 federal census. The federal district court dismissed the suit, conceding that Baker's civil rights were being denied but holding that the court could offer no remedy. Baker made a further appeal to the Supreme Court.

When the Supreme Court granted review in *Baker v. Carr*, it faced two central issues: first, whether the malapportionment of a state legislature is a "political question" for which courts have no remedy and, second, the merits of Baker's claim that individuals have a right to equal votes and equal representation. With potentially broad political consequences, the case was divisive for the

Court and was carried over and reargued for a term. Allies on judicial self-restraint, Justices Frankfurter and Harlan were committed to their view, expressed in *Colegrove v. Green*, 328 U.S. 549 (1946), that the "Court ought not to enter this political thicket." At conference, Justices Clark and Whittaker supported their view that the case presented a nonjusticiable political question. By contrast, Chief Justice Warren and Justices Black, Douglas, and Brennan thought that the issue was justiciable. They were also prepared to address the merits of the case. The pivotal justice, Potter Stewart, considered the issue justiciable, but he refused to address the merits of the case. He voted to reverse the lower court ruling only if the Court's decision was limited to holding that courts have jurisdiction to decide such disputes. He did not want the Court to take on the merits of reapportionment in this case.

Assigned the task of drafting the opinion, Brennan had to hold on to Stewart's vote and dissuade Black and Douglas from writing opinions on the merits that would threaten the loss of the crucial fifth vote. After circulating his draft and incorporating suggested changes, he optimistically wrote Black, "Potter Stewart was satisfied with all of the changes. The Chief also is agreed. It, therefore, looks as though we have a court agreed upon this as circulated." It appeared that the decision would come down on the original 5–4 vote.

Clark, however, had been pondering the fact that in this case the population ratio for the urban and rural districts in Tennessee was more than nineteen to one. As he put it, "city slickers" had been "too long deprive[d] of a constitutional form of government." Clark concluded that citizens denied equal voting power had no political recourse; their only recourse was to the federal judiciary. Clark thus wrote an opinion abandoning Frankfurter and going beyond the majority to address the merits of the claim.

Brennan faced the dilemma of how to bring in Clark without losing Stewart, and thereby enlarge the consensus. Further negotiations were necessary but limited. Brennan wrote his brethren:

> The changes represent the maximum to which Potter will subscribe. We discussed much more elaborate changes which would have taken over a substantial part of Tom Clark's opinion. Potter felt that if they were made it would be necessary for him to dissent from that much of the revised opinion. I therefore decided it was best not to press for the changes but to hope that Tom will be willing to join the Court opinion but say he would go further as per his separate opinion.

Even though there were five votes for deciding the merits, the final opinion was limited to the jurisdictional question.★

★Sources of quotations are internal Court memos, located in the William J. Brennan Jr. Papers, Library of Congress; and the Tom C. Clark Papers, University of Texas Law School.

The Court's decision was 6–2, with Justice Whittaker not participating and with the majority's opinion delivered by Justice Brennan. There were concurrences by Justices Douglas, Clark, and Stewart. Justice Frankfurter dissented and was joined by Justice Harlan.

■ ■ ■

☐ *Justice BRENNAN delivers the opinion of the Court.*

[W]e hold today only (a) that the court possessed jurisdiction of the subject matter: (b) that a justiciable cause of action is stated upon which appellants would be entitled to appropriate relief; and (c) because appellees raise the issue before this Court, that the appellants have standing to challenge the Tennessee apportionment statutes. Beyond noting that we have no cause at this stage to doubt the District Court will be able to fashion relief if violations of constitutional rights are found, it is improper now to consider what remedy would be most appropriate if appellants prevail at the trial.

■ JURISDICTION OF THE SUBJECT MATTER

The District Court was uncertain whether our cases withholding federal judicial relief rested upon a lack of federal jurisdiction or upon the inappropriateness of the subject matter for judicial consideration—what we have designated "nonjusticiability." The distinction between the two grounds is significant. In the instance of nonjusticiability, consideration of the cause is not wholly and immediately foreclosed: rather, the Court's inquiry necessarily proceeds to the point of deciding whether the duty asserted can be judicially identified and its breach judicially determined, and whether protection for the right asserted can be judicially molded. In the instance of lack of jurisdiction the cause either does not "arise under" the Federal Constitution, laws or treaties (or fall within one of the other enumerated categories of Art. III, Sec. 2), or is not a "case or controversy" within the meaning of that section; or the cause is not one described by any jurisdictional statute. Our conclusion that this cause presents no nonjusticiable "political question" settles the only possible doubt that it is a case or controversy. . . .

The appellees refer to *Colegrove v. Green*, 328 U.S. 549 [(1946)], as authority that the District Court lacked jurisdiction of the subject matter. Appellees misconceive the holding of that case. The holding was precisely contrary to their reading of it. Seven members of the Court participated in the decision. Unlike many other cases in this field which have assumed without discussion that there was jurisdiction, all three opinions filed in *Colegrove* discussed the question. Two of the opinions expressing the views of four of the Justices, a majority, flatly held that there was jurisdiction of that subject matter. Justice BLACK joined by Justice DOUGLAS and Justice MURPHY stated: "It is my judgment that the District Court had jurisdiction. . . ." Justice RUTLEDGE, writing separately, expressed agreement with this conclusion. . . . Indeed, it is even questionable that the opinion of Justice FRANKFURTER, joined by Justices REED and BURTON, doubted jurisdiction of the subject matter. . . .

■ JUSTICIABILITY

In holding that the subject matter of this suit was not justiciable, the District Court relied on *Colegrove v. Green, supra,* and subsequent *per curiam* cases. The court stated: "From a review of these decisions there can be no doubt that the federal rule . . . is that the federal courts . . . will not intervene in cases of this type to compel legislative reapportionment." We understand the District Court to have read the cited cases as compelling the conclusion that since the appellants sought to have a legislative apportionment held unconstitutional, their suit presented a "political question" and was therefore nonjusticiable. We hold that this challenge to an apportionment presents no nonjusticiable "political question." The cited cases do not hold the contrary.

Of course the mere fact that the suit seeks protection of a political right does not mean it presents a political question. Such an objection "is little more than a play upon words." Rather, it is argued that apportionment cases, whatever the actual wording of the complaint, can involve no federal constitutional right except one resting on the guaranty of a republican form of government, and that complaints based on that clause have been held to present political questions which are nonjusticiable.

We hold that the claim pleaded here neither rests upon nor implicates the Guaranty Clause and that its justiciability is therefore not foreclosed by our decisions of cases involving that clause. . . . To show why we reject the argument based on the Guaranty Clause, we must examine the authorities under it. But because there appears to be some uncertainty as to why those cases did present political questions, and specifically as to whether this apportionment case is like those cases, we deem it necessary first to consider the contours of the "political question" doctrine.

Our discussion, even at the price of extending this opinion, requires review of a number of political question cases, in order to expose the attributes of the doctrine—attributes which, in various settings, diverge, combine, appear, and disappear in seeming disorderliness. . . .

We have said that "In determining whether a question falls within [the political question] category, the appropriateness under our system of government of attributing finality to the action of the political departments and also the lack of satisfactory criteria for a judicial determination are dominant considerations." *Coleman v. Miller* [307 U.S. 433 (1939)]. The nonjusticiability of a political question is primarily a function of the separation of powers. Much confusion results from the capacity of the "political question" label to obscure the need for case-by-case inquiry. Deciding whether a matter has in any measure been committed by the Constitution to another branch of government, or whether the action of that branch exceeds whatever authority has been committed, is itself a delicate exercise in constitutional interpretation, and is a responsibility of this Court as ultimate interpreter of the Constitution. To demonstrate this requires no less than to analyze representative cases and to infer from them the analytical threads that make up the political question doctrine. We shall then show that none of those threads catches this case.

Foreign relations: There are sweeping statements to the effect that all questions touching foreign relations are political questions. Not only does resolution of such issues frequently turn on standards that defy judicial application, or involve the exercise of a discretion demonstrably committed to the executive or legislature; but many such questions uniquely demand single-voiced statement of the Government's views. Yet it is error to suppose that every case or controversy which touches foreign relations lies beyond judicial cognizance. Our cases in this field seem invariably to show a discriminating analysis of the particular question posed, in terms of the history of its management by the political branches, of its susceptibility to judicial handling in the light of its nature and posture in the specific case, and of the possible consequences of judicial action. . . .

Dates of duration of hostilities: Though it has been stated broadly that "the power which declared the necessity is the power to declare its cessation, and what the cessation requires," *Commercial Trust Co. v. Miller*, 262 U.S. 51 [1923], here too analysis reveals isolable reasons for the presence of political questions, underlying this Court's refusal to review the political departments' determination of when or whether a war has ended. Dominant is the need for finality in the political determination, for emergency's nature demands "A prompt and unhesitating obedience." *Martin v. Mott*, 12 Wheat. [256 U.S. 19 (1827)] [Calling up of militia.] . . . Further, clearly definable criteria for decision may be available. In such case the political question barrier falls away. . . .

Validity of enactments: In *Coleman v. Miller, supra,* this Court held that the questions of how long a proposed amendment to the Federal Constitution remained open to ratification, and what effect a prior rejection had on a subsequent ratification, were committed to congressional resolution and involved criteria of decision that necessarily escaped the judicial grasp. Similar considerations apply to the enacting process: "The respect due to coequal and independent departments," and the need for finality and certainty about the status of a statute contribute to judicial reluctance to inquire whether, as passed, it complied with all requisite formalities. *Field v. Clark*, 143 U.S. 649 [1892]. . . .

The status of Indian tribes: This Court's deference to the political departments in determining whether Indians are recognized as a tribe, while it reflects familiar attributes of political questions, also has a unique element in that "the relation of the Indians to the United States is marked by peculiar and cardinal distinctions which exist nowhere else. [The Indians are] domestic dependent nations. . . . Their relation to the United States resembles that of a ward to his guardian." *Cherokee Nation v. Georgia*, 5 Pet. 1 [1831]. Yet, here too, there is no blanket rule. . . .

It is apparent that several formulations which vary slightly according to the settings in which the questions arise may describe a political question, although each has one or more elements which identify it as essentially a function of the separation of powers. Prominent on the surface of any case held to involve a political question is found a textually demonstrable constitutional commitment of the issue to a coordinate political department; or a lack of judicially discoverable and manageable standards for resolving it; or the impossibility of deciding without an initial policy determination of a kind clearly for nonjudicial discretion; or the impossibility of a court's undertaking independent resolution without expressing lack of the respect due coordinate branches of government; or an unusual need for unquestioning adherence to a political decision already made; or the potentiality of embarrassment from multifarious pronouncements by various departments on one question.

Unless one of these formulations is inextricable from the case at bar, there should be no dismissal for nonjusticiability on the ground of a political question's presence. The doctrine of which we treat is one of "political questions," not one of "political cases." . . .

Republican form of government: Luther v. Borden, 7 How. 1 [1849], though in form simply an action for damages for trespass was, as Daniel Webster said in opening the argument for the defense, "an unusual case." The defendants, admitting an otherwise tortious breaking and entering, sought to justify their action on the ground that they were agents of the established lawful government of Rhode Island, which State was then under martial law to defend itself from active insurrection; that the plaintiff was engaged in that insurrection; and that they entered under orders to arrest the plaintiff. The case arose "out of the unfortunate political differences which agitated the people of Rhode Island in 1841 and 1842," and which had resulted in a situation wherein two groups laid competing claims to recognition as the lawful government. . . .

Chief Justice TANEY's opinion for the Court reasoned as follows: (1) If a court were to hold the defendants' acts unjustified because the charter government had no legal existence during the period in question, it would follow that all of that government's actions—laws enacted, taxes collected, salaries paid, accounts settled, sentences passed—were of no effect; and that "the officers who carried their decisions into operation [were] answerable as trespassers, if not in some cases as criminals." There was, of course, no room for application of any doctrine of *de facto* status to uphold prior acts of an officer not authorized *de jure*, for such would have defeated the plaintiff's very action. A decision for the plaintiff would inevitably have produced some significant measure of chaos, a consequence to be avoided if it could be done without abnegation of the judicial duty to uphold the Constitution.

(2) No state court had recognized as a judicial responsibility settlement of the issue of the locus of state governmental authority. Indeed, the courts of Rhode Island had in several cases held that "it rested with the political power to decide whether the charter government had been displaced or not," and that that department had acknowledged no change.

(3) Since "[t]he question relates, altogether, to the constitution and laws of [the] . . . State," the courts of the United States had to follow the state courts' decisions unless there was a federal constitutional ground for overturning them.

(4) No provision of the Constitution could be or had been invoked for this purpose except Art. IV, Sec. 4, the Guaranty Clause. Having already noted the absence of standards whereby the choice between governments could be made by a court acting independently, Chief Justice TANEY now found further textual and practical reasons for concluding that, if any department of the United States was empowered by the Guaranty Clause to resolve the issue, it was not the judiciary:

"Under this article of the Constitution it rests with Congress to decide what government is the established one in a State. For as the United States guarantee to each State a republican government, Congress must necessarily decide what government is established in the State before it can determine whether it is a republican or not. And when the senators and representatives of a State are admitted into the councils of the Union, the authority of the government under which they are appointed, as well as its republican character, is recognized by the proper constitutional authority. And its decision is binding on every other department of the government, and could not be questioned in a judicial tribunal. It is true that the contest in this case did not last long enough to bring the matter to this issue; and . . . Congress was not called upon to decide the controversy. Yet the right to decide is placed there, and not in the courts."

"So, too, as relates to the clause in the above-mentioned article of the Constitution, providing for cases of domestic violence. It rested with Congress, too, to determine upon the means proper to be adopted to fulfill this guarantee. . . . [B]y the act of February 28, 1795, [Congress] provided, that, 'in case of an insurrection in any State against the government thereof, it shall be lawful for the President of the United States, on application of the legislature of such State or of the executive (when the legislature cannot be convened) to call forth such number of the militia of any other State or States, as may be applied for, as he may judge sufficient to suppress such insurrection.'

"By this act, the power of deciding whether the exigency had arisen upon which the government of the United States is bound to interfere, is given to the President" [*Luther v. Borden*].

Clearly, several factors were thought by the Court in *Luther* to make the question there "political": the commitment to the other branches of the decision as to which is the lawful state government; the unambiguous action by the President, in recognizing the charter government as the lawful authority; the need for finality in the executive's decision; and the lack of criteria by which a court could determine which form of government was republican. . . .

But the only significance that *Luther* could have for our immediate purposes is in its holding that the Guaranty Clause is not a repository of judicially manageable standards which a court could utilize independently in order to identify a State's lawful government. The Court has since refused to resort to the Guaranty Clause—which alone had been invoked for the purpose—as the source of a constitutional standard for invalidating state action. . . .

We come, finally, to the ultimate inquiry whether our precedents as to what constitutes a nonjusticiable "political question" bring the case before us under the umbrella of that doctrine. A natural beginning is to note whether any of the common characteristics which we have been able to identify and label descriptively are present. We find none: The question here is the consistency of state action with the Federal Constitution. We have no question decided, or to be decided, by a political branch of government coequal with this Court. Nor do we risk embarrassment of our government abroad, or grave disturbance at home if we take issue with Tennessee as to the constitutionality of her action here challenged. Nor need the appellants, in order to succeed in this action, ask the Court to enter upon policy determinations for which judicially manageable standards are lacking. Judicial standards under the Equal Protection Clause are well developed and familiar, and it has been open to courts since the enactment of the Fourteenth Amendment to determine, if on the particular facts they must, that a discrimination reflects *no* policy, but simply arbitrary and capricious action.

This case does, in one sense, involve the allocation of political power within a State, and the appellants might conceivably have added a claim under the Guaranty Clause. Of course, as we have seen, any reliance on that clause would be futile. But because any reliance on the Guaranty Clause could not have succeeded it does not follow that appellants may not be heard on the equal protection claim which in fact they tender. . . .

We conclude that the complaint's allegations of a denial of equal protection present a justiciable constitutional cause of action upon which appellants are entitled to a trial and a decision. The right asserted is within the reach of judicial protection under the Fourteenth Amendment.

The judgment of the District Court is reversed and the cause is remanded for further proceedings consistent with this opinion.

Reversed and remanded.

□ *Justice DOUGLAS, concurring.*

While I join the opinion of the Court and, like the Court, do not reach the merits, a word of explanation is necessary. I put to one side the problems of "political" questions involving the distribution of power between this Court, the Congress, and the Chief Executive. We have here a phase of the recurring problem of the relation of the federal courts to state agencies. More particularly, the question is the extent to which a State may weight one person's vote more heavily than it does another's.

So far as voting rights are concerned, there are large gaps in the Constitution. Yet the right to vote is inherent in the republican form of government envisaged by Article IV, Section 4 of the Constitution. . . .

Race, color, or previous condition of servitude is an impermissible standard by reason of the Fifteenth Amendment, and that alone is sufficient to explain *Gomillion v. Lightfoot*, 364 U.S. 339 [1960].

Sex is another impermissible standard by reason of the Nineteenth Amendment.

There is a third barrier to a State's freedom in prescribing qualifications of voters and that is the Equal Protection Clause of the Fourteenth Amendment, the provision invoked here. And so the question is, may a State weight the vote of one county or one district more heavily than it weights the vote in another?

The traditional test under the Equal Protection Clause has been whether a State has made "an invidious discrimination," as it does when it selects "a particular race or nationality for oppressive treatment." Universal equality is not the test; there is room for weighting. . . .

□ *Justice CLARK, concurring.*

Although I find the Tennessee apportionment statute offends the Equal Protection Clause, I would not consider intervention by this Court into so delicate a field if there were any other relief available to the people of Tennessee. But the majority of the people of Tennessee have no "practical opportunities for exerting their political weight at the polls" to correct the existing "invidious discrimination." Tennessee has no initiative and referendum. I have searched diligently for other "practical opportunities" present under the law. I find none other than through the federal courts. The majority of the voters have been caught up in a legislative strait jacket. Tennessee has an "informed, civically militant electorate" and "an aroused popular conscience," but it does not sear "the conscience of the people's representatives." This is because the legislative policy has riveted the present seats in the Assembly to their respective constituencies, and by the votes of their incumbents a reapportionment of any kind is prevented. The people have been rebuffed at the hands of the Assembly; they have tried the constitutional convention route, but since the call must originate in the Assembly it, too, has been fruitless. They have tried Tennessee courts with the same result, and Governors have fought the tide only to flounder. It is said that there is recourse in Congress and perhaps that may be, but from a practical standpoint this is without substance. To date Congress has never undertaken such a task in any State. We therefore must conclude that the people of Tennessee are stymied and without judicial intervention will be saddled with the present discrimination in the affairs of their state government.

☐ *Justice FRANKFURTER, with whom Justice HARLAN joins, dissenting.*

The Court today reverses a uniform course of decision established by a dozen cases, including one by which the very claim now sustained was unanimously rejected only five years ago. The impressive body of rulings thus cast aside reflected the equally uniform course of our political history regarding the relationship between population and legislative representation—a wholly different matter from denial of the franchise to individuals because of race, color, religion or sex. Such a massive repudiation of the experience of our whole past in asserting destructively novel judicial power demands a detailed analysis of the role of this Court in our constitutional scheme. Disregard of inherent limits in the effective exercise of the Court's "judicial Power" not only presages the futility of judicial intervention in the essentially political conflict of forces by which the relation between population and representation has time out of mind been and now is determined. It may well impair the Court's position as the ultimate organ of "the supreme Law of the Land" in that vast range of legal problems, often strongly entangled in popular feeling, on which this Court must pronounce. The Court's authority—possessed of neither the purse nor the sword—ultimately rests on sustained public confidence in its moral sanction. Such feeling must be nourished by the Court's complete detachment, in fact and in appearance, from political entanglements and by abstention from injecting itself into the clash of political forces in political settlements.

A hypothetical claim resting on abstract assumptions is now for the first time made the basis for affording illusory relief for a particular evil even though it foreshadows deeper and more pervasive difficulties in consequence. The claim is hypothetical and the assumptions are abstract because the Court does not vouchsafe the lower courts—state and federal—guidelines for formulating specific, definite, wholly unprecedented remedies for the inevitable litigations that today's umbrageous disposition is bound to stimulate in connection with politically motivated reapportionments in so many States. In such a setting, to promulgate jurisdiction in the abstract is meaningless. It is as devoid of reality as "a brooding omnipresence in the sky," for it conveys no intimation what relief, if any, a District Court is capable of affording that would not invite legislatures to play ducks and drakes with the judiciary. For this Court to direct the District Court to enforce a claim to which the Court has over the years consistently found itself required to deny legal enforcement and at the same time found it necessary to withhold any guidance to the lower court how to enforce this turnabout, new legal claim, manifests an odd—indeed an esoteric—conception of judicial propriety. One of the Court's supporting opinions, as elucidated by commentary, unwittingly affords a disheartening preview of the mathematical quagmire (apart from divers[e] judicially inappropriate and elusive determinants) into which this Court today catapults the lower courts of the country without so much as adumbrating the basis for a legal calculus as a means of extrication. Even assuming the indispensable intellectual disinterestedness on the part of judges in such matters, they do not have accepted legal standards or criteria or even reliable analogies to draw upon for making judicial judgments. To charge courts with the task of accommodating the incommensurable factors of policy that underlie these mathematical puzzles is to attribute, however flatteringly, omnicompetence to judges. . . .

From its earliest opinions this Court has consistently recognized a class of controversies which do not lend themselves to judicial standards and judicial remedies. To classify the various instances as "political questions" is rather a form of stating this conclusion than revealing of analysis. Some of the cases so labelled have no relevance here. But from others emerge unifying considerations that are compelling.

1. The cases concerning war or foreign affairs, for example, are usually explained by the necessity of the country's speaking with one voice in such matters. While this concern alone undoubtedly accounts for many of the decisions, others do not fit the pattern. It would hardly embarrass the conduct of war were this Court to determine, in connection with private transactions between litigants, the date upon which war is to be deemed terminated. But the Court has refused to do so. A controlling factor in such cases is that, decision respecting these kinds of complex matters of policy being traditionally committed not to courts but to the political agencies of government for determination by criteria of political expediency, there exists no standard ascertainable by settled judicial experience or process by reference to which a political decision affecting the question at issue between the parties can be judged. . . .

2. The Court has been particularly unwilling to intervene in matters concerning the structure and organization of the political institutions of the States. The abstention from judicial entry into such areas has been greater even than that which marks the Court's ordinary approach to issues of state power challenged under broad federal guarantees. . . .

3. The cases involving Negro disfranchisement are no exception to the principle of avoiding federal judicial intervention into matters of state government in the absence of an explicit and clear constitutional imperative. For here the controlling command of Supreme Law is plain and unequivocal. An end of discrimination against the Negro was the compelling motive of the Civil War Amendments. . . .

4. The Court has refused to exercise its jurisdiction to pass on "abstract questions of political power, of sovereignty, of government." *Massachusetts v. Mellon*, 262 U.S. 447 [1923]. The "political question" doctrine, in this aspect, reflects the policies underlying the requirement of "standing": that

the litigant who would challenge official action must claim infringement of an interest particular and personal to himself, as distinguished from a cause of dissatisfaction with the general frame and functioning of government—a complaint that the political institutions are awry. . . . What renders cases of this kind non-justiciable is not necessarily the nature of the parties to them, for the Court has resolved other issues between similar parties; nor is it the nature of the legal question involved, for the same type of question has been adjudicated when presented in other forms of controversy. The crux of the matter is that courts are not fit instruments of decision where what is essentially at stake is the composition of those large contests of policy traditionally fought out in non-judicial forums, by which governments and the actions of governments are made and unmade. . . .

5. The influence of these converging considerations—the caution not to undertake decision where standards meet for judicial judgment are lacking, the reluctance to interfere with matters of state government in the absence of an unquestionable and effectively enforceable mandate, the unwillingness to make courts arbiters of the broad issues of political organization historically committed to other institutions and for whose adjustment the judicial process is ill-adapted—has been decisive of the settled line of cases, reaching back more than a century, which holds that Art. IV, Sec. 4, of the Constitution, guaranteeing to the States "a Republican Form of Government," is not enforceable through the courts. . . .

The present case involves all of the elements that have made the Guarantee Clause cases non-justiciable. It is, in effect, a Guarantee Clause claim masquerading under a different label. But it cannot make the case more fit for judicial action that appellants invoke the Fourteenth Amendment rather than Art. IV, Sec. 4, where, in fact, the gist of their complaint is the same—unless it can be found that the Fourteenth Amendment speaks with greater particularity to their situation. We have been admonished to avoid "the tyranny of labels." Art. IV, Sec. 4, is not committed by express constitutional terms to Congress. It is the nature of the controversies arising under it, nothing else, which has made it judicially unenforceable. Of course, if a controversy falls within judicial power, it depends "on how he [the plaintiff] casts his action," whether he brings himself within a jurisdictional statute. But where judicial competence is wanting, it cannot be created by invoking one clause of the Constitution rather than another. . . .

Appellants invoke the right to vote and to have their votes counted. But they are permitted to vote and their votes are counted. They go to the polls, they cast their ballots, they send their representatives to the state councils. Their complaint is simply that the representatives are not sufficiently numerous or powerful—in short, that Tennessee has adopted a basis of representation with which they are dissatisfied. . . . What is actually asked of the Court in this case is to choose among competing bases of representation—ultimately, really, among competing theories of political philosophy—in order to establish an appropriate frame of government for the State of Tennessee and thereby for all the States of the Union. . . .

To find such a political conception legally enforceable in the broad and unspecific guarantee of equal protection is to rewrite the Constitution. See *Luther v. Borden, supra.* Certainly, "equal protection" is no more secure a foundation for judicial judgment of the permissibility of varying forms of representative government than is "Republican Form." . . .

Goldwater v. Carter

444 U.S. 996, 100 S.Ct. 533 (1979)

In 1979, Senator Barry Goldwater and several other senators filed suit against President James ("Jimmy") Carter, challenging the constitutionality of Carter's termination of a defense treaty with Taiwan without the approval of the Senate. Underlying the case was the enduring support that the nation's conservative leadership extended toward Taiwan. A tiny island, Taiwan housed the Chinese nationalist government after it was forced out of the China mainland by the new communist government. Granting a petition for *certiorari* but without hearing oral arguments, the Court vacated a court of appeals ruling and remanded the case to a federal district court with directions to dismiss the complaint. In separate concurring opinions, Justice Powell rejected the application of the "political question" doctrine here, while Justice Rehnquist contended that it applies here and in other controversies over foreign policy. In his dissenting opinion, Justice Brennan rejected the idea that the question presented here is "political" and further discussed the scope of the judicial power.

The Court by a vote of 6–3 ordered the appellate court's judgment vacated and remanded the case to the district court. There were concurrences by Justices Powell and Rehnquist, who were joined by Chief Justice Burger and Justices Stewart and Stevens. Justice Marshall concurred without filing or joining an opinion. Justice Brennan filed a dissent. Justice Blackmun, joined by Justice White, filed a dissent from the Court's refusal to hear oral arguments in the case.

■ ■ ■

☐ *Justice POWELL, concurring.*

Although I agree with the result reached by the Court, I would dismiss the complaint as not ripe for judicial review.

This Court has recognized that an issue should not be decided if it is not ripe for judicial review. Prudential considerations persuade me that a dispute between Congress and the President is not ready for judicial review unless and until each branch has taken action asserting its constitutional authority. Differences between the President and the Congress are commonplace under our system. The differences should, and almost invariably do, turn on political rather than legal considerations. The Judicial Branch should not decide issues affecting the allocation of power between the President and Congress until the political branches reach a constitutional impasse. Otherwise, we would encourage small groups or even individual Members of Congress to seek judicial resolution of issues before the normal political process has the opportunity to resolve the conflict.

In this case, a few Members of Congress claim that the President's action in terminating the treaty with Taiwan has deprived them of their constitutional role with respect to a change in the supreme law of the land. Congress has taken no official action. In the present posture of this case, we do not know whether there ever will be an actual confrontation between the Legislative and Executive Branches. Although the Senate has considered a resolution declaring that Senate approval is necessary for the termination of any mutual defense treaty, no final vote has been taken on the resolution. Moreover, it is unclear whether the resolution would have retroactive effect. It cannot be said that either the Senate or the House has rejected the President's claim. If the Congress chooses not to confront the President, it is not our task to do so. I therefore concur in the dismissal of this case.

Justice REHNQUIST suggests, however, that the issue presented by this case is a nonjusticiable political question which can never be considered by this Court. I cannot agree. In my view, reliance upon the political-question doctrine is inconsistent with our precedents. As set forth in the seminal case of *Baker v. Carr*, [369 U.S. 186] (1962), the doctrine incorporates three inquiries: (i) Does the issue involve resolution of questions committed by the text of the Constitution to a coordinate branch of Government? (ii) Would resolution of the question demand that a court move beyond areas of judicial expertise? (iii) Do prudential considerations counsel against judicial intervention? In my opinion the answer to each of these inquiries would require us to decide this case if it were ready for review. . . .

In my view, the suggestion that this case presents a political question is incompatible with this Court's willingness on previous occasions to decide whether one branch of our Government has impinged upon the power of another. Under the criteria enunciated in *Baker v. Carr*, we have the responsibility to decide whether both the Executive and Legislative Branches have constitutional roles to play in termination of a treaty. If the Congress, by appropriate formal action, had challenged the President's authority to terminate the treaty with Taiwan, the resulting uncertainty could have serious consequences for our country. In that situation, it would be the duty of this Court to resolve the issue.

☐ *Justice REHNQUIST, with whom THE CHIEF JUSTICE, Justice STEWART, and Justice STEVENS join, concurring.*

I am of the view that the basic question presented by the petitioners in this case is "political" and therefore nonjusticiable because it involves the authority of the President in the conduct of our country's foreign relations and the extent to which the Senate or the Congress is authorized to negate the action of the President. In *Coleman v. Miller*, 307 U.S. 433 (1939), a case in which members of the Kansas Legislature brought an action attacking a vote of the State Senate in favor of the ratification of the Child Labor Amendment, Chief Justice HUGHES wrote in what is referred to as the "Opinion of the Court": . . .

The precise question as now raised is whether, when the legislature of the State, as we have found, has actually ratified the proposed amendment, the Court should restrain the state officers from certifying the ratification to the Secretary of State, because of an earlier rejection, and thus prevent the question from coming before the political departments. We find no basis in either Constitution or statute for such judicial action. Article V, speaking solely of ratification, contains no provision as to rejection.

Thus, Chief Justice HUGHES' opinion concluded that "Congress in controlling the promulgation of the adoption of a constitutional amendment has the final determination of the question whether by lapse of time its proposal of the amendment had lost its vitality prior to the required ratifications." . . .

I believe it follows *a fortiori* from *Coleman* that the controversy in the instant case is a nonjusticiable political dispute that should be left for resolution by the Executive and Legislative Branches of the Government. Here, while the Constitution is express as to the manner in which the Senate shall participate in the ratification of a treaty, it is silent as to that body's participation in the abrogation of a treaty. . . .

I think that the justifications for concluding that the question here is political in nature are even more compelling than in *Coleman* because it involves foreign relations—specifically a treaty commitment to use military force in the defense of a foreign government if attacked. In *United States v. Curtiss-Wright Corp.*, 299 U.S. 304 (1936), this Court said:

> Whether, if the Joint Resolution had related solely to internal affairs it would be open to the challenge that it constituted an unlawful delegation of legislative power to the Executive, we find it unnecessary to determine. The whole aim of the resolution is to affect a situation entirely external to the United States, and falling within the category of foreign affairs.

The present case differs in several important respects from *Youngstown Sheet & Tube Co. v. Sawyer*, 343 U.S. 579 (1952), cited by petitioners as authority both for reaching the merits of this dispute and for reversing the Court of Appeals. In *Youngstown*, private litigants brought a suit contesting the President's authority under his war powers to seize the Nation's steel industry, an action of profound and demonstrable domestic impact. Here, by contrast, we are asked to settle a dispute between coequal branches of our Government, each of which has resources available to protect and assert its interests, resources not available to private litigants outside the judicial forum. Moreover, as in *Curtiss-Wright*, the effect of this action, as far as we can tell, is "entirely external to the United States, and [falls] within the category of foreign affairs." Finally, as already noted, the situation presented here is closely akin to that presented in *Coleman*, where the Constitution spoke only to the procedure for ratification of an amendment, not to its rejection.

Elk Grove Unified School District v. Newdow

542 U.S. 1, 124 S.CT. 2301 (2004)

In 2000, Michael A. Newdow, an atheist, challenged the constitutionality of Elk Grove Unified School District's requirement that teachers lead their classes in reciting the Pledge of Allegiance. Because the Pledge contains the words "under God," he contended that the practice amounted to religious indoctrination and violates the First Amendment. At the time, his daughter was in kindergarten and Newdow was in a custody battle with her mother, Sandra Banning. Banning and Newdow were awarded shared "physical custody," but Banning had "exclusive legal custody." A federal district court dismissed Newdow's complaint, but the Court of Appeals for the Ninth Circuit reversed, holding Newdow had standing as a parent to sue and that the school district's policy violated the (dis)establishment clause. Banning, then, filed a motion to have the case dismissed on the ground that she was the sole legal custodian and that she did not feel that it was in her daughter's interest to be a party to the suit. The Ninth Circuit, nonetheless, reaffirmed Newdow's standing to challenge allegedly unconstitutional governmental practices, and that under California law he retained the right to expose his child to his religious views, even though they contradicted her mother's Christian views. The school district appealed that decision to the Supreme Court, which granted review. Subsequently, Newdow filed a motion requesting Justice Scalia to recuse himself due to his off-the-bench comments criticizing the Ninth Circuit's ruling that the school district's policy violated the First Amendment.

The Ninth Circuit's decision was unanimously reversed, with Justice Scalia not participating. Justice Stevens delivered the opinion for the Court, holding that Newdow lacked "prudential standing" to raise the challenge on behalf of his daughter, and declined to reach the merits of the case. In three separate concurring opinions, Chief Justice Rehnquist and Justices O'Connor and Thomas indicate that Newdow had standing and they would, though each for different reasons, uphold the school district's policy over First Amendment objections.

■ ■ ■

☐ *Justice STEVENS delivered the opinion of the Court.*

As part of the nationwide interest in commemorating the 400th anniversary of Christopher Columbus' discovery of America, a widely circulated national magazine for youth proposed in 1892 that pupils recite the following affirmation: "I pledge allegiance to my Flag and the Republic for which it stands: one Nation indivisible, with Liberty and Justice for all."

In the 1920's, the National Flag Conferences replaced the phrase "my Flag" with "the flag of the United States of America."

In 1942, in the midst of World War II, Congress adopted, and the President signed, a Joint Resolution codifying a detailed set of "rules and customs pertaining to the display and use of the flag of the United States of America." This resolution, which marked the first appearance of the Pledge of Allegiance in positive law, confirmed the importance of the flag as a symbol of our Nation's indivisibility and commitment to the concept of liberty.

Congress revisited the Pledge of Allegiance 12 years later when it amended the text to add the words "under God." The resulting text is the Pledge as we know it today: "I pledge allegiance to the Flag of the United States of America, and to the Republic for which it stands, one Nation under God, indivisible, with liberty and justice for all." . . .

We granted the School District's petition for a writ of *certiorari* to consider two questions: (1) whether Newdow has standing as a noncustodial parent to challenge the School District's policy, and (2) if so, whether the policy offends the First Amendment. . . .

The command to guard jealously and exercise rarely our power to make constitutional pronouncements requires strictest adherence when matters of great national significance are at stake. Even in cases concededly within our jurisdiction under Article III, we abide by "a series of rules under which [we have] avoided passing upon a large part of all the constitutional questions pressed upon [us] for decision." *Ashwander v. TVA*, 297 U.S. 288 (1936) (BRANDEIS, J., concurring).

Consistent with these principles, our standing jurisprudence contains two strands: Article III standing, which enforces the Constitution's case or controversy requirement; and prudential standing, which embodies "judicially self-imposed limits on the exercise of federal jurisdiction," *Allen [v. Wright*, 468 U.S. 737 (1984)]. . . . Although we have not exhaustively defined the prudential dimensions of the standing doctrine, we have explained that prudential standing encompasses "the general prohibition on a litigant's raising another person's legal rights, the rule barring adjudication of generalized grievances more appropriately addressed in the representative branches, and the requirement that a plaintiff's complaint fall within the zone of interests protected by the law invoked." *Allen.*

One of the principal areas in which this Court has customarily declined to intervene is the realm of domestic relations. Long ago we observed that "[t]he whole subject of the domestic relations of husband and wife, parent and child, belongs to the laws of the States and not to the laws of the United States." *In re Burrus*, 136 U.S. 586 (1890). [W]hile rare instances arise in which it is necessary to answer a substantial federal question that transcends or exists apart from the family law issue, in general it is appropriate for the federal courts to leave delicate issues of domestic relations to the state courts. . . .

Newdow's standing derives entirely from his relationship with his daughter, but . . . the interests of this parent and this child are not parallel and, indeed, are potentially in conflict.

Newdow's parental status is defined by California's domestic relations law. Our custom on questions of state law ordinarily is to defer to the interpretation of the Court of Appeals for the Circuit in which the State is located. In this case, the Court of Appeals, which possesses greater familiarity with

California law, concluded that state law vests in Newdow a cognizable right to influence his daughter's religious upbringing. . . . Animated by a conception of "family privacy" that includes "not simply a policy of minimum state intervention but also a presumption of parental autonomy," the state cases create a zone of private authority within which each parent, whether custodial or noncustodial, remains free to impart to the child his or her religious perspective. . . .

In our view, it is improper for the federal courts to entertain a claim by a plaintiff whose standing to sue is founded on family law rights that are in dispute when prosecution of the lawsuit may have an adverse effect on the person who is the source of the plaintiff's claimed standing. When hard questions of domestic relations are sure to affect the outcome, the prudent course is for the federal court to stay its hand rather than reach out to resolve a weighty question of federal constitutional law. There is a vast difference between Newdow's right to communicate with his child—which both California law and the First Amendment recognize—and his claimed right to shield his daughter from influences to which she is exposed in school despite the terms of the custody order. We conclude that, having been deprived under California law of the right to sue as next friend, Newdow lacks prudential standing to bring this suit in federal court.

☐ *Chief Justice REHNQUIST, with whom Justice O'CONNOR joins, and with whom Justice THOMAS joins as to Part I, concurring in the judgment and dissenting in part.*

The Court today erects a novel prudential standing principle in order to avoid reaching the merits of the constitutional claim. I dissent from that ruling. On the merits, I conclude that the Elk Grove Unified School District policy that requires teachers to lead willing students in reciting the Pledge of Allegiance, which includes the words "under God," does not violate the Establishment Clause of the First Amendment.

[T]he Court does not dispute that respondent Newdow satisfies the requisites of Article III standing. But curiously the Court incorporates criticism of the Court of Appeals' Article III standing decision into its justification for its novel prudential standing principle. The Court concludes that respondent lacks prudential standing, under its new standing principle, to bring his suit in federal court.

We have, in the past, judicially self-imposed clear limits on the exercise of federal jurisdiction. In contrast, here is the Court's new prudential standing principle: "[I]t is improper for the federal courts to entertain a claim by a plaintiff whose standing to sue is founded on family law rights that are in dispute when prosecution of the lawsuit may have an adverse effect on the person who is the source of the plaintiff's claimed standing." . . .

First, the Court relies heavily on *Ankenbrandt v. Richards*, 504 U.S. 689 (1992), in which we discussed both the domestic relations exception and the abstention doctrine. . . . We . . . conclude[ed] that the domestic relations exception only applies when a party seeks to have a district court issue a "divorce, alimony, and child custody decree." We further held that abstention was inappropriate because "the status of the domestic relationship ha[d] been determined as a matter of state law, and in any event ha[d] no bearing on the underlying torts alleged."

The Court['s] conclusion does not follow from *Ankenbrandt*'s discussion of the domestic relations exception and abstention; even if it did, it would not be applicable in this case because, on the merits, this case presents a substantial federal question that transcends the family law. . . .

Although the Court may have succeeded in confining this novel principle almost narrowly enough to be, like the proverbial excursion ticket— good for this day only—our doctrine of prudential standing should be governed by general principles, rather than ad hoc improvisations. . . .

The phrase "under God" in the Pledge seems, as a historical matter, to sum up the attitude of the Nation's leaders, and to manifest itself in many of our public observances. Examples of patriotic invocations of God and official acknowledgments of religion's role in our Nation's history abound.

At George Washington's first inauguration on April 30, 1789, . . . "Washington put his right hand on the *Bible*, opened to Psalm 121:1: 'I raise my eyes toward the hills. Whence shall my help come.' The Chancellor proceeded with the oath: 'Do you solemnly swear that you will faithfully execute the office of President of the United States and will to the best of your ability preserve, protect and defend the Constitution of the United States?' The President responded, 'I solemnly swear,' and repeated the oath, adding, 'So help me God.' He then bent forward and kissed the Bible before him."

Later the same year, after encouragement from Congress, Washington issued his first Thanksgiving proclamation, which began: "Whereas it is the duty of all Nations to acknowledge the providence of Almighty God, to obey His will, to be grateful for his benefits, and humbly to implore his protection and favor—and whereas both Houses of Congress have by their joint Committee requested me 'to recommend to the People of the United States a day of public thanksgiving and prayer to be observed by acknowledging with grateful hearts the many signal favors of Almighty God especially by affording them an opportunity peaceably to establish a form of government for their safety and happiness.'"

Almost all succeeding Presidents have issued similar Thanksgiving proclamations. Later Presidents, at critical times in the Nation's history, have likewise invoked the name of God. . . .

The motto "In God We Trust" first appeared on the country's coins during the Civil War. [I]n 1956, Congress declared that the motto of the United States would be "In God We Trust."

Our Court Marshal's opening proclamation concludes with the words "God save the United States and this honorable Court." . . .

I do not believe that the phrase "under God" in the Pledge converts its recital into a "religious exercise" of the sort described in *Lee* [*v. Weisman*, 505 U.S. 577 (1992)]. Instead, it is a declaration of belief in allegiance and loyalty to the United States flag and the Republic that it represents. The phrase "under God" is in no sense a prayer, nor an endorsement of any religion. . . . Reciting the Pledge, or listening to others recite it, is a patriotic exercise, not a religious one; participants promise fidelity to our flag and our Nation, not to any particular God, faith, or church. . . .

When courts extend constitutional prohibitions beyond their previously recognized limit, they may restrict democratic choices made by public bodies. . . . The Constitution only requires that schoolchildren be entitled to abstain from the ceremony if they chose to do so. To give the parent of such a child a sort of "heckler's veto" over a patriotic ceremony willingly participated in by other students, simply because the Pledge of Allegiance contains the descriptive phrase "under God," is an unwarranted extension of the Establishment Clause, an extension which would have the unfortunate effect of prohibiting a commendable patriotic observance.

☐ *Justice THOMAS, concurring in the judgment.*

Because I agree with THE CHIEF JUSTICE that respondent Newdow has standing, I would take this opportunity to begin the process of rethinking the Establishment Clause. I would acknowledge that the Establishment Clause is a federalism provision, which, for this reason, resists incorporation. Moreover, as I will explain, the Pledge policy is not implicated by any sensible incorporation of the Establishment Clause, which would probably cover little more than the Free Exercise Clause.

In *Lee* [v. *Weisman*], the Court held that invocations and benedictions could not, consistent with the Establishment Clause, be given at public secondary school graduations. . . . It brushed aside both the fact that the students were not required to attend the graduation, and the fact that they were not compelled, in any meaningful sense, to participate in the religious component of the graduation ceremony. The Court surmised that the prayer violated the Establishment Clause because a high school student could—in light of the "peer pressure" to attend graduation and "to stand as a group or, at least, maintain respectful silence during the invocation and benediction"—have "a reasonable perception that she is being forced by the State to pray in a manner her conscience will not allow."

Adherence to *Lee* would require us to strike down the Pledge policy, which, in most respects, poses more serious difficulties than the prayer at issue in *Lee*. A prayer at graduation is a one-time event, the graduating students are almost (if not already) adults, and their parents are usually present. By contrast, very young students, removed from the protection of their parents, are exposed to the Pledge each and every day. . . .

I conclude that, as a matter of our precedent, the Pledge policy is unconstitutional. I believe, however, that *Lee* was wrongly decided. *Lee* depended on a notion of "coercion" that . . . has no basis in law or reason. The kind of coercion implicated by the Religion Clauses is that accomplished "by force of law and threat of penalty." Peer pressure, unpleasant as it may be, is not coercion. But rejection of *Lee*-style "coercion" does not suffice to settle this case. Although children are not coerced to pledge their allegiance, they are legally coerced to attend school. Because what is at issue is a state action, the question becomes whether the Pledge policy implicates a religious liberty right protected by the Fourteenth Amendment.

I accept that the Free Exercise Clause, which clearly protects an individual right, applies against the States through the Fourteenth Amendment. But the Establishment Clause is another matter. The text and history of the Establishment Clause strongly suggest that it is a federalism provision intended to prevent Congress from interfering with state establishments. Thus, unlike the Free Exercise Clause, which does protect an individual right, it makes little sense to incorporate the Establishment Clause. In any case, I do not believe that the Pledge policy infringes any religious liberty right that would arise from incorporation of the Clause. Because the Pledge policy also does not infringe any free-exercise rights, I conclude that it is constitutional.

■ CONSTITUTIONAL HISTORY

Rules for Judicial Self-Restraint and Avoiding Constitutional Questions

Justice Louis D. Brandeis, concurring in *Ashwander v. Tennessee Valley Authority*, 297 U.S. 288 (1936), summarized some prudential rules for exercising judicial self-restraint and avoiding ruling on the constitutionality of congressional legislation:

> The Court developed, for its own governance in the cases confessedly within its jurisdiction, a series of rules under which it has avoided passing upon a large part of all the constitutional questions pressed upon it for decision. They are:
>
> 1. The Court will not pass upon the constitutionality of legislation in a friendly, non-adversary, proceeding, declining because to decide such questions "is legitimate only in the last resort, and as a necessity in the determination of real, earnest and vital controversy between individuals."
>
> 2. The Court will not "anticipate a question of constitutional law in advance of the necessity of deciding it." *Liverpool, N. Y. & P. S. S. Co. v. Emigration Commissioners*, 113 U.S. 33 [(1885)]. . . .
>
> 3. The Court will not "formulate a rule of constitutional law broader than is required by the precise facts to which it is to be applied." *Liverpool.*
>
> 4. The Court will not pass upon a constitutional question although properly presented by the record, if there is also present some other ground upon which the case may be disposed of. . . . Appeals from the highest court of a state challenging its decision of a question under the Federal Constitution are frequently dismissed because the judgment can be sustained on an independent state ground.
>
> 5. The Court will not pass upon the validity of a statute upon complaint of one who fails to show that he is injured by its operation. Among the many applications of this rule, none is more striking than the denial of the right of challenge to one who lacks a personal or property right.

(continues)

■ CONSTITUTIONAL HISTORY
*Rules for Judicial Self-Restraint and Avoiding
Constitutional Questions (continued)*

6. The Court will not pass upon the constitutionality of a statute at the instance of one who has availed himself of its benefits.

7. "When the validity of an act of the Congress is drawn in question, and even if a serious doubt of constitutionality is raised, it is a cardinal principle that this Court will first ascertain whether a construction of the statute is fairly possible by which the question may be avoided." *Crowell v. Benson*, 285 U.S. 22 [(1932)].

B | *The Court's Docket and Screening Cases*

The justices' interpretation of their jurisdiction and rules governs access to the Court. But they also need flexible procedures for screening cases and deciding what to decide. This is because the Court's docket has grown phenomenally (see CONSTITUTIONAL HISTORY: Docket and Decisions, 1800–2018, in this chapter).

When any appeal or *cert.* petition arrives at the Court it immediately goes to the clerk's office. Staff look at whether it satisfies requirements as to form, length, and fees, and if the filing is from an indigent, whether there is an affidavit stating that the petitioner is too poor to pay fees. All unpaid cases are assigned a number in the order they arrive, and placed on what is called the Miscellaneous Docket. Paid cases are also assigned a number but placed on the Appellate Docket. The clerk then notifies the other party, or respondent, in each case that he or she must file a brief in response within thirty days. After receiving briefs from respondents, the clerk circulates to the justices' chambers a list of cases ready for consideration and a set of briefs for each case.

For much of the Court's history every justice was responsible for reviewing each case. The justices did not work by panels or delegate responsibility for screening cases to others. That is no longer true. In 1972, the "*cert.* pool" was established. Seven of the justices now share their collective law clerks' memos on all paid and unpaid cases. The memos explain the facts, issues raised, and lower court ruling as well as recommend whether the case should be granted or denied. Those justices not joining the pool—now only Alito and Gorsuch—receive copies of unpaid cases along with other filings. Stevens also had his clerks screen all the cases and write memos only on those they thought were important enough for him to consider.

C | *The Rule of Four and Agenda Setting*

When Congress gave the Court discretionary jurisdiction in the Judiciary Act of 1925, by substituting petitions for *certiorari* for mandatory appeals, the justices developed the informal "rule of four" to decide which petitions they would grant. During conference, at least four justices must agree that a case warrants oral argument and consideration by the full Court.

The rule of four operates in a fraction of cases due to the increasing caseload, which is a result of a number of factors. Most important, institutional norms promote a shared conception of the role of the Court as a tribunal for resolving only issues of national importance. Justices agree that the overwhelming proportion of cases is "frivolous," and that there is a limited number of cases to which they may give full consideration.

The caseload and institutional norms push toward limiting the operation of the rule of four. But the rule remains useful, particularly if there is a bloc of justices who share the same ideological orientation. The rule of four thus enables a bloc of justices to work together in picking cases on which they want the Court to rule.

Denial of *certiorari* is an important technique for managing the Court's caseload. But its meaning in particular cases may be far from clear. The Court has few fixed rules, and even the rule of four is not "an absolutely inflexible rule."[1] Although enabling the Court to manage its business, denials invite confusion and the suspicion, as Justice Jackson once observed, "that this Court no longer respects impersonal rules of law but is guided in these matters by personal impression which from time to time may be shared by a majority of the justices."[2]

■ CONSTITUTIONAL HISTORY

Docket and Decisions, 1800–2018

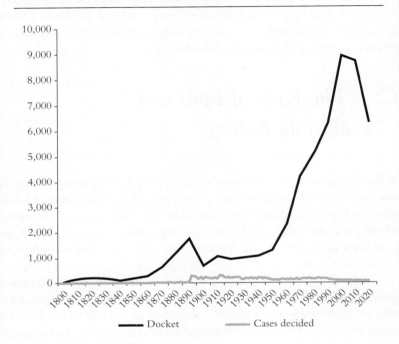

Based on data through the 2017–2018 term.
The docket includes cases filed during the term and cases carried over from the previous term.

Source: David M. O'Brien, *Storm Center: The Supreme Court in American Politics,* 12th ed. (New York: W. W. Norton & Company, 2020); Supreme Court, Year-End Report on the Federal Judiciary.

The Court now decides less than 1 percent of the cases annually arriving on its docket.[3] That is far less than forty years ago, when about 3 percent of a much smaller docket were granted and decided. Then, the docket was just reaching 5,000 cases and the justices decided between 150 and 180 cases a term. The docket now hovers around 9,000, yet the justices decide fewer than 80 cases a year. That is the same number decided by the Court in 1955 when the docket remained under 2,000. Even if the Court in the 1990s and 2000s had continued to grant as many cases as it did in the 1970s and 1980s, the percentage granted would have declined, of course, due to the continued growth in the caseload. Still, the diminished plenary docket is striking and probably reflects a combination of factors internal and external to the Court, which undoubtedly contributed to the inflation of the plenary docket during the Burger Court years (1969–1986) and to its contraction thereafter. Early in his chief justiceship, Burger expanded the size of the oral argument calendar in order to accommodate more cases, because of his concern about the Court's declining supervisory capacity. During Burger's chief justiceship, the discipline imposed by the rule of four was also weakened by the emergence of the practice of casting Join-3 votes and the increased circulation of dissents from denial of review, especially by Justice White, who drew attention to cases raising conflicts among the lower courts that the Court was not resolving. A Join-3 vote is a vote to provide a fourth vote if others vote to grant review, but is otherwise considered as voting to deny. In the 1970s and 1980s, Join-3 votes arguably lowered the threshold for granting cases, thereby weakening the self-discipline imposed by the rule of four and contributing to the inflation of the plenary docket.

As the Court's composition changed from the 1990s through the first decade of the twenty-first century, so did the justices' voting practices when deciding what to decide: both Join-3 votes and dissents from denial became no longer commonplace and the justices became more tolerant of intercircuit conflicts. In addition, the Judicial Improvements and Access to Justice Act of 1988 eliminated virtually all remaining nondiscretionary appellate jurisdiction, thereby increasing the Court's "managerial capacity" for controlling the plenary docket by denying *cert.* to more cases. Finally, the institutionalization of the *cert.* pool over the last forty years undoubtedly contributed to the shrinking plenary docket in several ways: more justices now rely, and rely to a greater degree than before, on their law clerks' *cert.* memos; there is, thus, less independent review of petitions by the justices themselves; and, as Stevens has suggested, the clerks tend to be "risk averse" when recommending that cases be granted.

NOTES

1. Potter Stewart, "Inside the Supreme Court," *New York Times*, October 1, 1979, 17A, col. 2.

2. *Brown v. Allen*, 344 U.S. 443, 535 (1953) (Jackson, J., con. op.).

3. This discussion draws on David O'Brien's analysis in "Join-3 Votes, the Rule of Four, the *Cert.* Pool, and the Supreme Court's Shrinking Plenary Docket," 13 *Journal of Law & Politics* 779 (1997); and in "A Diminished Plenary Docket: A Legacy of the Rehnquist Court," 89 *Judicature* 134 (2005).

SELECTED BIBLIOGRAPHY

Johnson, Timothy, and Jerry Goldman, eds. *A Good Quarrel: America's Top Legal Reporters Share Stories from Inside the Supreme Court.* Ann Arbor: University of Michigan Press, 2008.

■ INSIDE THE COURT

The Rules of the Supreme Court Governing Review of Certiorari Petitions*

RULE 10. CONSIDERATIONS GOVERNING REVIEW ON *CERTIORARI*

Review on a writ of *certiorari* is not a matter of right, but of judicial discretion. A petition for a writ of *certiorari* will be granted only for compelling reasons. The following, although neither controlling nor fully measuring the Court's discretion, indicate the character of the reasons the Court considers:

(a) a United States court of appeals has entered a decision in conflict with the decision of another United States court of appeals on the same important matter; has decided an important federal question in a way that conflicts with a decision by a state court of last resort; or has so far departed from the accepted and usual course of judicial proceedings, or sanctioned such a departure by a lower court, as to call for an exercise of this Court's supervisory power;

(b) a state court of last resort has decided an important federal question in a way that conflicts with the decision of another state court of last resort or of a United States court of appeals;

(c) a state court or a United States court of appeals has decided an important question of federal law that has not been, but should be,

*As of July 1, 2013

Pacelle, Richard L. *The Transformation of the Supreme Court's Agenda: From the New Deal to the Reagan Administration.* Boulder, CO: Westview Press, 1991.

Perry, H. W. *Deciding to Decide: Agenda Setting in the United States Supreme Court.* Cambridge, MA: Harvard University Press, 1991.

Scalia, Antonin, and Bryan Garner. *Making Your Case: The Art of Persuading Judges.* St. Paul, MN: West, 2008.

Wrightsman, Lawrence. *Oral Arguments before the Supreme Court.* New York: Oxford University Press, 2008.

settled by this Court, or has decided an important federal question in a way that conflicts with relevant decisions of this Court.

A petition for a writ of *certiorari* is rarely granted when the asserted error consists of erroneous factual findings or the misapplication of a properly stated rule of law. . . .

RULE 13. REVIEW ON *CERTIORARI*: TIME FOR PETITIONING

1. Unless otherwise provided by law, a petition for a writ of *certiorari* to review a judgment in any case, civil or criminal, entered by a state court of last resort or a United States court of appeals . . . is timely when it is filed with the Clerk of the Court within 90 days after entry of the judgment. . . .

RULE 14. CONTENT OF A PETITION FOR A WRIT OF *CERTIORARI*

1. A petition for a writ of *certiorari* shall contain, in the order indicated:

(a) The questions presented for review, expressed concisely in relation to the circumstances of the case, without unnecessary detail. The questions should be short and should not be argumentative or repetitive. . . . The questions shall be set out on the first page following the cover, and no other information may appear on that page. . . . Only the questions set out in the petition, or fairly included therein, will be considered . . . .

3. A petition for a writ of *certiorari* should be stated briefly and in plain terms and may not exceed the word or page limitations specified in Rule 33 [providing that a petition must be in a 6⅛ by 9¼ inch book format, with a white cover and no more than 9,000 words, and filed electronically along with forty hardbound copies].

■ IN COMPARATIVE PERSPECTIVE

The "European Model" of Constitutional Courts and Judicial Review

In most European states, the institution and power of "American-style" judicial review has been rejected. Instead, institutions called constitutional courts have been established in Austria (1945), Italy (1948), the Federal Republic of Germany (1949), France (1958), Portugal (1976), Spain (1978), and Belgium (1985), as well as in many of the postcommunist countries in Eastern Europe (after 1989), including the Czech Republic, Hungary, Poland, Romania, Russia, and Slovakia.

In contrast to the United States federal judiciary, which has general jurisdiction over issues of constitutional and statutory law, European courts have historically been subordinate to legislatures and denied jurisdiction over constitutional matters. The constitutional courts created in post–World War II Europe thus were an innovation, although their powers of judicial review differed from the American model in several key respects. European constitutional courts are (1) formally detached from the judiciary, (2) given exclusive jurisdiction over constitutional questions, and (3) authorized to exercise review as well as to issue advisory opinions at the request of other governmental institutions.

Unlike the U.S. federal judiciary's jurisdiction over only actual cases or controversies, European constitutional courts may exercise abstract and concrete constitutional review of legislation. *Abstract constitutional review* of legislation is initiated by elected officials or national and regional governmental bodies with respect to legislation that has been recently adopted that either (1) has not yet been put into force (as in France) or (2) has not yet been enforced, or has been suspended, pending review by the constitutional court (as in Germany, Italy, and Spain). In short, before controversial legislation goes into effect the constitutional court must pass on its constitutionality, and thereafter the legislation may be revised. *Concrete constitutional review* arises from litigation in the courts when ordinary judges are uncertain about the constitutionality or the application of a statute or ordinance; in such cases the judges refer the constitutional question or complaint to the constitutional court for resolution.

The principal features of the European model of constitutional courts and judicial review in France, Germany, Italy, and Spain are summarized in the following table.

	FRANCE	GERMANY	ITALY	SPAIN
Court and Date of Creation	Constitutional Council (1958)	Federal Constitutional Court (1949)	Italian Constitutional Court (1956)	Spanish Constitutional Court (1978)

JURISDICTION

	FRANCE	GERMANY	ITALY	SPAIN
Abstract review	Yes	Yes	Yes	Yes
Authority to initiate abstract review of legislation	President, Presidential Assembly, or Senate	Federal and länder (state) governments or one-third of the Bundestag	National government (against regional laws); regional governments (against national laws)	Prime minister, president of the Parliament, 50 deputies or senators, executives of autonomous regions, and ombudsmen
Laws referred	National	Federal and länder legislation	National and regional legislation	National and regional legislation
Laws must be referred	Within 15 days of adoption	Within 30 days of adoption	Within 30 days of adoption	Within 90 days of adoption
Concrete review	Yes (as of 2008)	Yes	Yes	Yes
Authority to initiate concrete review of legislation	Judiciary	Judiciary and individuals (after exhaustion of judicial remedies)	Judiciary	Judiciary, ombudsmen, and individuals (after exhaustion of judicial remedies)

COMPOSITION, RECRUITMENT, TENURE

	FRANCE	GERMANY	ITALY	SPAIN
Number of judges	9	16	15	12
Recruitment	Named by the president (3) and assembly (6)	Elected by the Bundestag (8) and Bundesrat (8)	Named by the president (5), judiciary (5); elected by the Parliament (5)	Named by the federal government (2), judiciary (2); elected by the Congress (4) and Senate (4)

(continues)

■ In Comparative Perspective

The "European Model" of Constitutional Courts and Judicial Review (continued)

	FRANCE	GERMANY	ITALY	SPAIN
Length of term	9 years	12 years	9 years	9 years

For further reading, see Donald P. Kommers, *The Constitutional Jurisprudence of the Federal Republic of Germany* 2d ed. (Durham, NC: Duke University Press, 1997); Alex Stone, *The Birth of Judicial Politics in France* (New York: Oxford University Press, 1992); Michael Livingston et al., *The Italian Legal System* 2d ed. (Stanford: Stanford University Press, 2016); Carlo Guarnieri and Patrizia Pederzoli, *The Comparative Study of Courts and Democracy* (Oxford: Oxford University Press, 2002); and Georg Nolte, ed., *European and U.S. Constitutionalism* (New York: Cambridge University Press, 2005). See also Karen Alter, *The European Court's Political Power* (New York: Oxford University Press, 2009).

D | *Summarily Decided Cases*

Even before the 1988 Act to Improve the Administration of Justice, which eliminated virtually all mandatory appeals, the distinction between mandatory and discretionary review of appeals and *cert.* petitions had largely disappeared in the Court's process of deciding what to decide. Forty years ago, the Court annually received between 300 and 400 appeals, and the overwhelming majority were summarily decided (without hearing oral arguments and full consideration). They simply dismissed them for want of jurisdiction or failure to present a substantial federal question, or they ordered the lower court ruling affirmed or reversed.

Summarily decided cases enabled the Court to cut down on its workload. But they also engendered confusion among the lower courts. Summary decisions take the form of rather cryptic orders or *per curiam* (unsigned) opinions. Like denials of *cert.* petitions, they may invite confusion over how the Court views the merits of a case and the lower court ruling. The problem is one of the Court's own making. The Court holds that summarily decided cases do not have the same precedential weight as plenary decisions, but they are nonetheless binding on lower courts "until such time as the Court informs [them] that [they] are not." *Hicks v. Miranda*, 422 U.S. 322 (1975). The Court now summarily decides only about ten cases per term by *per curiam* opinion. It does so primarily to reverse a state or lower federal court decision deemed not to have applied or followed one of its decisions. Recently, for instance, in *Pavan v. Smith,* 139 S.Ct. 62 (2018), the Roberts Court reversed Arkansas's state supreme court decision that the state could require the name of the biological father on birth certificates, and thereby discriminate against LBGTQ parents with adopted children. In doing so, the Court reaffirmed its holding barring discrimination against same-sex marriages, in *Obergefell v. Hodges* (2015) (excerpted in Chapter 12), and that state laws are unconstitutional "to the extent they treat same-sex couples differently from opposite-sex couples."

E | *The Role of Oral Argument*

The Court grants a full hearing—that is, oral argument—to less than 80 of the approximately 9,000 cases on the docket each term. When cases are granted full consideration, attorneys for each side submit briefs setting forth their arguments and how they think the case should be decided. The clerk of the Court circulates the briefs to each chamber and sets a date for the attorneys to argue their views orally before the justices. After hearing oral arguments, the justices vote in private conference on how to decide the issues presented in a case.

For fourteen weeks each term, from the first Monday in October until the end of April, the Court hears arguments on Monday, Tuesday, and Wednesday about every two weeks. The importance of oral argument, Chief Justice Hughes observed, lies in the fact that often "the impression that a judge has at the close of a full oral argument accords with the conviction which controls his final vote."[1] The justices hold conference and take their initial, often decisive, vote on cases within a day or two after hearing arguments. Oral arguments come at a crucial time. They focus the minds of the justices and present the possibility for fresh perspectives on a case. It is the only opportunity for attorneys to communicate directly with the justices. Two basic factors appear to control the relative importance of oral argument. As Justice Wiley Rutledge observed, "One is brevity. The other is the preparation with which the judge comes to it."[2] When the Court revised its rules in 1980, the justices underscored that "*[t]he Court looks with disfavor on any oral argument that is read from a prepared text.*" Central to preparation and delivery is a bird's-eye view of the case, the issues and facts, and the

Page from Docket Book

Court..CA - 2..................   Voted on......*11/8*......./...., 19.*80*

Argued....*11/28*............ 19.*90*.   Assigned...*11/13 CQ*....., 19.*90*.

Submitted................., 19.....   Announced....*5/23*..., 19.*91*.

No. 89-1391
Vide 89-1392

IRVING RUST, ETC., ET AL., Petitioners

vs.

LOUIS W. SULLIVAN, SECRETARY OF HEALTH AND HUMAN SERVICES

03/01/90 - Cert.

5/29/91 - cert. granted

HOLD FOR		CERT.			JURISDICTIONAL STATEMENT				MERITS		MOTION			
		G	D	G&R	N	POST	DIS	AFF	REV	AFF	G	D		
Rehnquist, Ch. J. *argued*										✓				
Brennan, J.										✓				
White, J.		✓							✓					
Marshall, J.		✓												
Blackmun, J.									✓					
Stevens, J.									✓		*in P.x*			
O'Connor, J.									✓					
Scalia, J.										✓				
Kennedy, J.										✓				

19020-2-88

(Library of Congress, Justice Thurgood Marshall Papers.)

reasoning behind legal developments. Crisp, concise, and conversational presentations are what the justices want. An attorney must never forget, in Chief Justice Rehnquist's words, that "[h]e is not, after all, presenting his case to some abstract, platonic embodiment of appellate judges as a class, but . . . nine flesh and blood men and women." Oral argument is definitely not a "brief with gestures."[3]

Notably, in 2000 the Supreme Court created its own website (at www.supremecourt.gov) that makes available transcripts of oral arguments and the full text of its decisions and opinions, until they are officially published. In 2006, the Roberts Court began posting transcripts on its website on the same day of hearing oral arguments. In addition, for the first time the transcripts indicated the name of the justice asking questions and responding to attorneys. The oral arguments in prior decisions may also be heard at the Oyez Project at www.oyez.org.

NOTES

1. Charles E. Hughes, *The Supreme Court of the United States* (New York: Columbia University Press, 1928), 61.

2. Wiley Rutledge, "The Appellate Brief," 28 *American Bar Association Journal* 251 (1942).

3. William Rehnquist, "Oral Advocacy: A Disappearing Art," Brainerd Currie Lecture, Mercer University School of Law, October 20, 1983, msp. 4. See, generally, Timothy Johnson, *Oral Arguments and Decision Making on the U.S. Supreme Court* (Albany: SUNY Press, 2011).

SELECTED BIBLIOGRAPHY

Johnson, Timothy, *Oral Arguments and Decision Making on the U.S. Supreme Court.* Albany: SUNY Press, 2011.

Wrightsman, Lawrence. *Oral Arguments Before the Supreme Court.* New York: Oxford University Press, 2008.

F | *Conference Deliberations*

The justices meet alone in conference to decide which cases to accept and to discuss the merits of those few cases on which they hear oral arguments. Throughout the term during the weeks in which the Court hears oral arguments, conferences are held on Wednesday afternoons to take up the four cases argued on Monday, and then on Fridays to discuss new filings and the eight cases for which oral argument was heard on Tuesday and Wednesday. In May and June, when the Court

The justices' private conference room. (*Steve Petteway, Collection of the Supreme Court of the United States.*)

does not hear oral arguments, conferences are held on Thursdays, from ten in the morning until four or four-thirty in the afternoon, with the justices breaking for a forty-five-minute lunch around twelve-thirty. A majority may vote to hold a special session during the summer months, when extraordinarily urgent cases arise.

Summoned by a buzzer five minutes before the hour, the justices meet in the conference room, located directly behind the courtroom itself and next to the chief justice's chamber. The oak-paneled room is lined with *United States Reports* (containing the Court's decisions). Over the mantel of an exquisite fireplace at one end hangs a portrait of Chief Justice Marshall. Next to the fireplace stands a large rectangular table where the justices sit. The chief justice sits at one end and the senior associate justice at the other. The other justices take seats in order of seniority, although variations occur due to individual justices' preferences. Two conference lists are traditionally circulated to each chamber by noon on Wednesday prior to the Friday conference. They structure conference discussion and enable the justices to get through their caseload. On the first list—Special List I, or the Discuss List—are jurisdictional statements, petitions for *certiorari*, and motions that are ready and worth discussing. The Discuss List typically includes between forty and fifty cases for each conference. There used to be attached a second list—Special List II, or what was called the Dead List—containing those cases considered unworthy of discussion, but Chief

- INSIDE THE COURT

On the Tentativeness of Votes and the Importance of Opinion Writing

In two controversial cases, involving claims by the press to a First Amendment right of access to visit and interview prisoners, Chief Justice Burger switched his vote after conference. During the conference discussion of *Pell v. Procunier*, 417 U.S. 817 (1974) and *Saxbe v. Washington Post*, 417 U.S. 843 (1974), the vote went five to four for recognizing that the press has a First Amendment right of access. But Burger later changed his mind and explained that the final outcome of the cases depended on how the opinions were written:

> This difficult case has few very clear cut and fixed positions but my further study over the weekend leads me to see my position as closer for those who would sustain the authority of the corrections administrators than those who would not! I would therefore reverse in 73–754, affirm in 73–918 and reverse in 73–1265.

> This is another one of those cases that will depend a good deal on "how it is written." The solution to the problem must be allowed time for experimentation and I fear an "absolute" constitutional holding adverse to administrators will tend to "freeze" progress.

The Court ultimately divided five to four but held that the press does not have a First Amendment right of access to interview inmates of prisons.

For other notable instances of vote-switching that dramatically affected the outcome, see in Volume 1, Chapter 7, the box INSIDE THE COURT and the discussion of *Garcia v. San Antonio Metropolitan Transit Authority*, 469 U.S. 528 (1985) (excerpted there); and in Volume 2, Chapter 6, the box INSIDE THE COURT: Justice Kennedy Switches Positions and the Outcome in *Lee v. Weisman*; and Volume 2, Chapter 11, the box INSIDE THE COURT: Vote-Switching in *Bowers v. Hardwick* and Justice Powell's April 8, 1986, Memorandum. These examples illustrate how important postconference deliberations and communications among the chambers have become for the Court's decision-making.

Source: Library of Congress, Justice William J. Brennan Jr. and Justice Harry A. Blackmun Papers, Manuscripts Room; Justice Lewis F. Powell Papers, Washington & Lee School of Law, Manuscripts Room.

Justice Roberts ended the practice of circulating that list. Still, any justice may request that a case be put on the Discuss List, and only after the chief's conference secretary has heard from all chambers do the lists become final. Over 90 percent of the cases on the conference lists are automatically denied without discussion, and most of those that do make the Discuss List are denied as well. The conference lists are an important technique for saving time and focusing attention on the few cases deemed worthy of consideration.

The significance of conference discussions has changed with the increasing caseload. Conference discussions do not play the role that they once did. When the docket was smaller in the nineteenth century, conferences were integral to the justices' collective deliberations. As the caseload grew, conferences became largely symbolic of past collective deliberations. They now serve only to discover consensus. There is no longer time to reach agreement and compromise on opinions for the Court. "In fact," Justice Antonin Scalia claimed, "to call our discussion of a case a conference is really something of a misnomer. It's much more a statement of the views of each of the nine Justices."[1] More discussion, however, he admitted would probably not contribute much or lead justices to change their minds when voting on cases. This is because the justices confront similar issues year after year and, as Chief Justice Rehnquist observed, "it would be surprising if [justices] voted differently than they had the previous time."[2]

The justices' votes are always tentative until the day the Court hands down its decision and opinion. Before, during, and after conference justices may use their votes in strategic ways to influence the disposition of a case.

NOTES

1. Antonin Scalia, comments at George Washington National Law Center, February 16, 1988, quoted in "Ruling Fixed Opinions," *New York Times*, February 22, 1988, p. 16A.

2. William H. Rehnquist, quoted in David M. O'Brien, *Storm Center: The Supreme Court in American Politics*, 12th ed. (New York: W. W. Norton & Company, 2020).

SELECTED BIBLIOGRAPHY

Dickson, Del. *The Supreme Court in Conference*. New York: Oxford University Press, 2001.

O'Brien, David M. *Storm Center: The Supreme Court in American Politics*, 11th ed. New York: W. W. Norton & Company, 2017.

Schwartz, Bernard. *Decision: How the Supreme Court Decides Cases*. New York: Oxford University Press, 1996.

G | *Postconference Writing and Circulation of Opinions*

Opinions justify or explain votes at conference. The opinion for the Court is the most important and most difficult to write because it represents a collective judgment. Because conference votes are tentative, the assignment, drafting, and circulation of opinions is crucial to the Court's rulings. At each stage justices compete for influence in determining the Court's final decision and opinion.

By tradition, when the chief justice is in the majority, he assigns the Court's opinion. If the chief justice did not vote with the majority, then the senior associate justice who was in the majority either writes the opinion or assigns it to another. Chief justices may keep cases for themselves. This is in the tradition of Chief Justice Marshall, but as modified by the workload and other justices' expectations of equitable opinion assignments. In unanimous decisions and landmark cases the chief justice often self-assigns the Court's opinion.

Parity in opinion assignment now generally prevails. But the practice of immediately assigning opinions after conference as Hughes did, or within a day or two as Stone did, was gradually abandoned by the end of Vinson's tenure as chief justice. Warren and Burger adopted the practice of assigning opinions after each two-week session of oral arguments and conferences. With more assignments to make at any given time, they thus acquired greater flexibility in distributing the workload. They also enhanced their own opportunities for influencing the final outcome of cases through their assignment of opinions.

Writing opinions is the most difficult and time-consuming task of the justices. Justices differ in their styles and approaches to opinion writing. They now more or less delegate responsibility to their clerks for assisting in the preparation of opinions. Chief Justice Rehnquist, for example, usually had one of his clerks do a first draft, without bothering about style, and gave him about ten days to prepare it. Before having the clerk begin work, Rehnquist went over the conference discussion with the clerk and explained how he thought an opinion could be written "supporting the result reached by the majority."

Only after a justice is satisfied with an initial draft does the opinion circulate to the other justices for their reactions. The practice of circulating draft opinions is pivotal in the Court's decision-making process because all votes are tentative until the final opinion is handed down.

Final published opinions for the Court are the residue of conflicts and compromises among the justices. But they also reflect changing institutional norms. In historical perspective, changes in judicial norms have affected trends in opinion writing, the value of judicial opinions, and the Court's contributions to public law.

"The business of the Court," Justice Stewart once observed, "is to give institutional opinions for its decisions." The opinion for the Court serves to communicate an institutional decision. For much of the Court's history, there were few concurring opinions (those in which a justice agrees with the Court's ruling but not the reasons given in its opinion) and dissenting opinions (those in which justices disagree with the Court's ruling and give an alternative interpretation). It was also rare for a justice to write a separate opinion in which he or she concurred and dissented from parts of the opinion for the Court. But in the last forty years there has been a dramatic increase in the total number of opinions issued each term, as depicted in CONSTITUTIONAL HISTORY: Opinion Writing, 1937–2018. However, during the last twenty years, the Court has granted fewer cases plenary consideration and, hence, has annually handed down fewer opinions. From the 1990s through the first decade of the twenty-first century the justices also cut back somewhat on writing separate dissenting opinions, instead joining one another in a single dissenting opinion. But, the early years of the Trump administration saw a rise in the number of dissents filed and their length, except in cases deemed especially important and divisive. The dissenters instead joined one another in a single dissenting opinion more frequently than was the prior practice.

The increase in the number of opinions reflects in part that the justices are now more interested in merely the tally of votes than arriving at an institutional decision and opinion. The number of cases decided by a bare majority has thus grown in the last few decades. In addition, sometimes a bare majority for deciding a case a certain way cannot agree on an opinion for the Court's decision and the author of the opinion announcing the Court's decision must write for only a plurality.

In contrast to the author of an opinion for the Court, a justice writing a separate concurring or dissenting opinion does not carry the burden of amassing other justices. Dissenting opinions are more understandable and defensible. Dissenting opinions in the view of Chief Justice Charles Evans Hughes, who rarely wrote dissents, appeal "to the brooding spirit of the law, to the intelligence of a future day, when a later decision may possibly correct the error into which the dissenting judge believes the Court to have been betrayed."[1] The first Justice John M. Harlan's dissent from the doctrine of "separate but equal" in *Plessy v. Ferguson*, 163 U.S. 537 (1896) (see Ch. 12), was eventually vin-

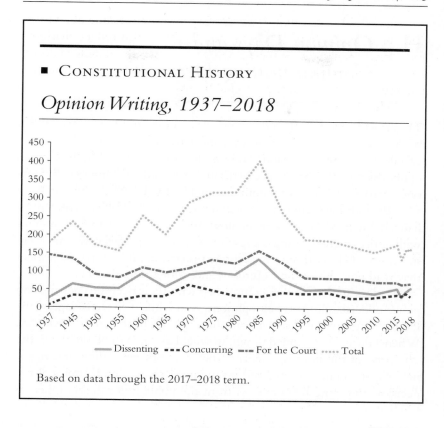

■ CONSTITUTIONAL HISTORY

Opinion Writing, 1937–2018

—— Dissenting ■■■ Concurring ■·■ For the Court ····· Total

Based on data through the 2017–2018 term.

dicated in *Brown v. Board of Education* (1954). Dissents may also appeal for more immediate legislative action: Justice James Iredell's dissent in *Chisholm v. Georgia*, 2 U.S. 419 (1793), invited the adoption of the Eleventh Amendment overturning the Court's decision; and the dissenters' arguments in *Dred Scott v. Sandford*, 60 U.S. 393 (1857) (see Ch. 12), lent support to the passage of the Thirteenth, Fourteenth, and Fifteenth Amendments after the Civil War. A dissenting opinion is a way of undercutting the Court's decision and opinion. The threat of a dissent may thus be useful when trying to persuade the majority to narrow its holding or tone down the language of its opinion.

NOTE

1. Charles Evans Hughes, *The Supreme Court of the United States* (New York: Columbia University Press, 1928).

H | *Opinion Days and Communicating Decisions*

The justices announce their decisions in the courtroom, typically crowded with reporters, anxious attorneys, and curious spectators. When several decisions are to be handed down, the justices delivering the Court's opinions make their announcements in reverse order of seniority. Authors of concurring or dissenting opinions are free to give their views orally as well. By tradition there is no prior announcement as to when cases will be handed down. Most opinions are now announced in two to four minutes with justices merely stating the result in each case. In especially controversial cases, such as those concerning restrictions on abortion, justices may read portions of their opinions and, sometimes, dissents.

Justices appreciate that compliance with their decisions depends on public understanding of their opinions. And while media coverage of the Court has grown, it is still anachronistically traditional in its own way. When a decision is handed down, in what has come to be known as the "running of the interns," interns from network news divisions, major newspapers, radio stations, and online news sources grab copies of the decision and quite literally dash from the public information office to

News media interns run to deliver the Court's ruling in *Obergefell v. Hodges* to their bosses. This tradition is known as the "running of the interns." (*Pete Marovich/UPI/ Alamy Stock Photo*)

the Court's front steps. There, they hand off the freshly printed decisions to waiting journalists who scan the syllabus quickly so they can be the first to broadcast the news. (A short time later, the public information office posts the Court's decisions online.) The Court's information office serves primarily reporters (not members of the general public, whose inquiries are typically handled by the offices of the clerk, marshal, or curator) and provides space for a pressroom with sixteen assigned cubicles. The public information officer makes available all filings and briefs for cases on the docket, the Court's conference lists and final opinions, and speeches made by the justices. The Court also now makes its opinions and transcripts of oral arguments available on its website at www.supremecourt.gov.

SELECTED BIBLIOGRAPHY

Johnson, Timothy, and Goldman, Jerry, eds. *A Good Quarrel: Reporters Share Stories from Inside the Supreme Court.* Ann Arbor: University of Michigan Press, 2009.

O'Brien, David M., ed. *Judges on Judging: Views from the Bench.* 5th ed. Washington, DC: C.Q. Press, 2016.

Slotnick, Elliot E., and Segal, Jennifer A. *Television News and the Supreme Court.* New York: Cambridge University Press, 1998.

I | *The Impact of Supreme Court Decisions: Compliance and Implementation*

"By itself," political scientist Robert Dahl observed, "the Court is almost powerless to affect the course of national policy."[1] This is because the Court's rulings are not self-executing. Enforcement and implementation require the cooperation and coordination of all three branches of government.

Brown v. Board of Education (1954) (see Ch. 12), the public school desegregation case, dramatically altered the course of American life but also reflected the justices' awareness that their decisions are not self-executing. When striking down the "separate but equal" doctrine, which was practiced in segregated public school systems, the Warren Court waited a year after *Brown I* (1954) before issuing in *Brown II* its mandate for "all deliberate speed" in ending racial segregation in public education. The Court knew that there would be substantial public resistance to the social policy announced in *Brown I*. A rigid timetable for desegregation would have only intensified opposition. President Dwight Eisenhower refused to endorse the ruling for some time. Hence, implementation of *Brown* was deliberately slow and uneven. The Department of Justice had little role in ending school segregation before the passage of the Civil Rights Act of 1964 during Lyndon B. Johnson's presidency. For over three decades problems of implementing and achieving compliance with *Brown* persisted. Litigation by civil rights groups forced change, but it was piecemeal, costly, and modest. The judiciary alone could not achieve desegregation.

Public opinion serves to curb the Court when it threatens to go too far or too fast in its rulings. Life in the marble temple is not immune from shifts in public opinion.[2] But justices deny being directly influenced by public opinion. The Court's prestige rests on preserving the public's view that justices base their decisions on interpretations of the law, rather than on their personal policy preferences. Yet complete indifference to public opinion would be the height of judicial arrogance. In the highly controversial 1992 abortion ruling in *Planned Parenthood of Southeastern Pennsylvania v. Casey*, 505 U.S. 833 (1992) (see Ch. 11), the justices engaged in an unusual debate over the influence of public opinion on the Court with the dissenters, Chief Justice Rehnquist and Justices Scalia, Thomas, and White, accusing the plurality (Justices O'Connor, Kennedy, and Souter) of bending to public opinion and following "not a principle of law . . . but the principle of Realpolitik."

Most of the Court's decisions do not attract widespread public attention. Most people find the Court remote and confusing or identify with its institutional symbols. The public perceives the Court as a temple of law rather than of politics—impartial and removed from the pressures of special partisan interests.[3] Issues such as school desegregation, school prayer, and abortion focus public attention and may mobilize public support or opposition for the Court. But those issues are also the most divisive within the country as well. Public opinion, therefore, tends to be diffuse and indirectly expressed by public officials and elected representatives.

Less concerned about public opinion than elected public officials, justices are sensitive to the attitudes of the Court's immediate constituents: the solicitor general, the attorney general and the Department of Justice, counsel for federal agencies, states' attorneys general, and the legal profession. Their responses to the Court's rulings help shape public understanding and determine the extent of compliance.

The solicitor general, attorney general, and agency counsel interpret the Court's decisions and advise the White House and agencies on compliance. Justices may find a favorable or unfavorable reception from the executive branch. The solicitor general decides which and what kinds of cases to take to the Court. In selecting cases he or she tries to offer the Court (or a majority) opportunities for pursuing their policy goals and those of the president.

The attorney general, cabinet heads, and agency counsel may likewise extend or thwart the Court's policies. They do so through their advisory opinions, litigation strategies, and development of agency policy and programs. The reactions of the fifty state attorneys general are no less important. Each has a pivotal role in advising governors, mayors, police chiefs, and others in his or her state. Their responses tend to reflect state and local reactions to the Court's rulings. Regional differences were evident in responses to the 1962 and 1963 school prayer decisions. In upholding separation of church and state, the Court struck down a state-composed prayer in *Engel v. Vitale*, 370 U.S. 421 (1962), and the reciting of the Lord's Prayer in public schools in *Abington School District v. Schempp*, 374 U.S. 203 (1963) (see Ch. 6). Long-standing practices of school prayer in the East and South were not to be easily relinquished. Voluntary school prayer, silent meditation, and "the objective study of the Bible and of religion" were viewed as still permissible. Where school prayer received support in state constitutions or legislation, state and local officials denied the legitimacy of the Court's decrees and refused to obey.

The justices do consider anticipated reactions of the immediate audience of the Court's rulings. One example is that of Chief Justice Warren's opinion in *Miranda v. Arizona*, 384 U.S. 436 (1966) (see Ch. 8), which held that police must read suspects their rights, granted them by the Fifth and Sixth Amendments, to remain silent and to consult and have the presence of an attorney during police questioning. A former attorney general in California, Chief Justice Warren knew full well that not all state attorneys general and police supported the Court's rulings on criminal procedure. He, therefore, strove to outline in *Miranda* a code for police procedures governing the interrogation of criminal suspects that police could not easily evade.

The Court's decisions have traditionally applied retroactively, permitting individuals to have retrials. In *Linkletter v. Walker* (1965) (see excerpt below), however, the Court refused to apply retroactively its controversial ruling in *Mapp v. Ohio*, 367 U.S. 643 (1961) (see Ch. 7), which extended to the states the Fourth Amendment exclusionary rule, forbidding the use at trial of evidence obtained in violation of the requirements for a proper search and seizure. The Court subsequently developed what became known as its *ambulatory-retroactive doctrine*—the doctrine that a new ruling's retroactive application to prior decisions may depend on the ruling and its consequences, such as administrative costs; thus, not all new rulings apply retrospectively but only prospectively to new cases. "That doctrine," Justice Harlan explained, "was the product of the Court's disquietude with the impacts of its fast-moving pace in constitutional innovation in the criminal field." But he also objected that the doctrine merely rationalizes the Court's freedom "to act, in effect, like a legislature, making its new constitutional rules wholly or partially retroactive or only prospective as it deems wise."[4] In *Griffith v. Kentucky*, 479 U.S. 314 (1987), Justice Blackmun held for the Court that a new rule for the conduct of criminal proceedings applies retroactively to all cases pending or not final at the time of the ruling.

Subsequently, the Court established guidelines for when new decisions apply retroactively in *Teague v. Lane*, 489 U.S. 288 (1989). Under *Teague* an old ruling applies both on direct and collateral (an independent challenge to overturn a judgment) review. But a new rule, overturning a precedent, applies only to cases still on direct review and applies retroactively in collateral proceedings only if (1) it is substantive or (2) a watershed ruling bearing on "the fundamental fairness and accuracy of the criminal proceeding," like the Sixth Amendment right to counsel decision in *Gideon v. Wainwright*, 372 U.S. 335 (1963) (excerpted in Ch. 9). In *Whorton v. Bockting* (2007) (excerpted below), the Roberts Court adhered to *Teague* in holding that the decision in *Crawford v. Washington*, 541 U.S. 36 (2004) (discussed in Ch. 9), did not apply retroactively on collateral review. *Crawford* announced a new rule in ruling that "testimonial statements of witnesses absent from [a] trial" are admissible "only where the declarant is unavailable, and where the defendant has had a prior opportunity to cross-examine [the witness]," and overruled *Ohio v. Roberts*, 448 U.S. 56 (1980), as inconsistent with the Sixth Amendment's Confrontation Clause. In *Whorton*, writing for a unanimous Court Justice Alito held that although *Crawford* announced a new rule it was neither substantive nor a watershed ruling, like *Gideon*, and thus did not apply retroactively. See also *Davis v. United States*, 564 U.S. 229 (2011), (on the application of the exclusionary rule) and the ruling in *Linkletter v. Walker* (1965) (excerpted below). Likewise, writing for the majority in *Montgomery v. Louisiana*, 136 S.Ct. 718 (2016), Justice Kennedy held that the Court's ruling in *Miller v. Alabama*, 567 U.S. 460 (2012), that sentencing a juvenile to life without the possibility of parole without considering mitigating factors violates the Eighth Amendment, applies retroactively because it was a substantive ruling. This decision reversed a state supreme court's decision that *Miller* was merely a procedural ruling. However, in *Montgomery*, unlike *Whorton*, Justices Scalia, Thomas, and Alito disagreed and dissented.

The Court directly and indirectly encourages interest groups and the government to litigate issues of public policy. The Court selects and decides "only those cases which present questions whose resolution will have immediate importance far beyond the particular facts and parties

Members of the Burger Court shaking hands prior to going on the bench to hear oral arguments, in the tradition begun by Chief Justice Melville Fuller. (*Yoichi Okamoto/Science Source.*)

involved." Attorneys whose cases are accepted by the Court, Chief Justice Fred Vinson emphasized, "are, in a sense, prosecuting or defending class actions; that you represent your clients, but [more crucially] tremendously important principles, upon which are based the plans, hopes and aspirations of a great many people throughout the country."[5]

Interest groups from the entire political spectrum look to the Court to decide issues of public policy: from business organizations and corporations in the late nineteenth century to the Jehovah's Witnesses in the 1930s, to the ACLU and NAACP in the 1950s and 1960s, and to "liberal" women's rights groups and consumer and environmental protection groups—like the National Organization for Women (NOW), Common Cause, "Nader's Raiders," the Sierra Club, the Environmental Defense Fund, and the Natural Resources Defense Council—as well as to a growing number of conservative "public interest" law firms like the Pacific Legal Foundation, the Mountain States Legal Foundation, and the Washington Legal Foundation. "This is government by lawsuit," Justice Robert Jackson declared; "these constitutional lawsuits are the stuff of power politics in America."[6]

Interest group activities and public interest law firms offer a number of advantages for litigating policy disputes. They command greater financial resources than the average individual. A single suit may settle a large number of claims, and the issues are not as likely to be compromised or settled out of court. Interest group law firms typically specialize in particular kinds of lawsuits. They are, therefore, able to litigate more skillfully and over a longer period of time. There are also tactical opportunities. Litigants may be chosen to bring test cases, and those cases may be coordinated with other litigation and the activities of other organizations.

The Court is an instrument of political power, but the justices remain dependent on the attitudes and actions of their immediate constituents, elected officials, and the dynamics of pressure-group politics and public opinion. Implementation and compliance largely depend on lower courts, Congress, and the president. Compliance with the Court's decisions by lower courts is invariably uneven. They may extend or limit decisions in anticipation of later rulings by the high Court. Following the watershed ruling on privacy in *Griswold v. Connecticut*, 381 U.S. 479 (1965) (see Ch. 4), lower courts interpreted the newfound constitutional right of privacy to strike down a wide range of laws, from those limiting the length of male employees' and students' hair to ones forbidding certain sexual acts between consenting adults and the use of marijuana, to laws requiring psychological tests of applicants for government jobs, and to laws governing access to financial and medical records. The Court reversed or would not approve the extension of the right of privacy in many of these areas.

A simple model of compliance is not very useful: Decisions handed down by the Court are not necessarily or readily applied by lower courts. Ambiguity and plurality or 5–4 decisions invite lower courts to pursue their own policy goals. Crucial language in an opinion may be treated as *dicta*. Differences between the facts on which the Court ruled and the circumstances of a case at hand may be emphasized so as to distinguish or reach the opposite result of the Court's decision.

Lower federal courts may thus effectively delay implementation and compliance. Open defiance is infrequent but not unprecedented. *Jaffree v. Board of School Commissioners of Mobile County* (1983) (see excerpt below) is extreme but illustrative of lower court defiance. There, a federal district court judge in Alabama directly challenged the legitimacy of the Court in its public school prayer rulings. A majority of the Court rebuffed the lower court when it decided an appeal of the ruling and struck down the "moment of silence" law in *Wallace v. Jaffree*, 472 U.S. 38 (1985) (see Ch. 6).

On the other hand, lower federal courts may anticipate the Court's future rulings, based on recent changes in its direction, in what has been termed *"anticipatory compliance." Brzonkala v. Virginia Polytechnic Institute and State University,* 169 F.3d 820 (1999), for example, is based on the Court's rulings on federalism (see Vol. 1, Chs. 6 and 7), handed down after the passage of the Violence Against Women Act of 1994. The Court of Appeals for the Fourth Circuit struck down provisions of that law; subsequently, a bare majority of the Court affirmed that decision and extended its previous rulings in *United States v. Morrison* (2000) (excerpted in Vol. 1, Ch. 6).

In addition, as the Burger, Rehnquist, and Roberts Courts moved in more conservative directions in areas of civil rights and liberties, state supreme courts increasingly refused to follow the Court's construction of federal law and recognized new rights or extended protection on the basis of state constitutions to claims that the Supreme Court has declined to embrace (see Vol. 1, Ch. 7). State courts may do so if they base their decisions on their state constitutions and make a *"plain statement"* of *"adequate and independent state grounds"*; see *Michigan v. Long,* 463 U.S. 1032 (1983) (excerpted in Ch. 7). In *Bowers v. Hardwick,* 478 U.S. 186 (1986), for instance, a bare majority of the Court refused to extend the constitutional right of privacy in a challenge to Georgia's law punishing sodomy. But in *Commonwealth of Kentucky v. Jeffrey Wasson,* 842 S.W.2d 487 (1992) (see excerpt below), Kentucky's supreme court, as did other state courts, expressly declined to follow *Bowers* when striking down its state law against homosexual sodomy. Moreover, the trend in the last forty years of state supreme courts not following the Court's rulings but instead basing their decisions solely on the state's constitution, as in *Wasson,* has been called "the new judicial federalism."

Major confrontations between Congress and the Court have occurred a number of times. With the election of Thomas Jefferson in 1800, Republicans gained control of Congress. Defeated President John Adams and the outgoing Federalists in Congress passed the Judiciary Act of 1801, creating new circuit court judgeships and stipulating that when the next vacancy on the Court occurred it should go unfilled. That attempt to maintain influence in the judiciary was quickly countered. In 1802, the Republican Congress repealed the Act of 1801, abolishing the judgeships and returning the number of justices to six. Congress also postponed the Court's next term to preclude it from immediately hearing a challenge, in *Stuart v. Laird,* 5 U.S. 299 (1803), to its repealing legislation. When the Court decided *Stuart,* it upheld Congress's power to repeal the Judiciary Act of 1801. The Jeffersonian-Republicans then impeached Justice Samuel Chase for expounding federalist doctrine.

Although the Senate acquitted him, it would not confirm nominees for federal judgeships unless they were Republicans.

The Marshall Court approved the expansion of national governmental power, but in response Congress in the 1820s and 1830s threatened to remove the Court's jurisdiction over disputes involving states' rights. After the Civil War, Congress succeeded in repealing the Court's jurisdiction over certain denials of writs of *habeas corpus*—orders commanding that a prisoner be brought before a judge and cause shown for his imprisonment. In *Ex parte McCardle*, 74 U.S. 506 (1869), the Court upheld the repeal of its jurisdiction and thus avoided deciding a controversial case attacking the constitutionality of Reconstruction legislation. But most Court watchers and recent rulings indicate that the Court would likely strike down legislation stripping jurisdiction over areas involving fundamental rights; see, for example, *Boumediene v. Bush*, 553 U.S. 723 (2008) (excerpted in Vol. 1, Ch. 3).

At the turn of the century, Progressives in Congress unsuccessfully sought to pressure the Court—dominated at the time by advocates of laissez-faire social and economic policy. They proposed requiring a two-thirds vote by the justices when striking down federal statutes and permitting Congress to overrule the Court's decisions by a two-thirds majority. The confrontation escalated with the Court's invalidation of President Franklin D. Roosevelt's early New Deal program passed by Congress in the 1930s. FDR retaliated by attempting to pack the Court by increasing the number of justices. Even though it was upset by the Court's invalidation of the New Deal, Congress would not accept FDR's Court-packing plan. It did, though, pass legislation allowing justices to retire, after ten years of service at age seventy, with full rather than half salary. Congress thus made retirement more financially attractive and gave FDR opportunities to appoint justices who shared his political philosophy.

Congress may pressure the Court in a number of ways. The Senate may try to influence judicial appointments, and justices may be impeached. More often, institutional and jurisdictional changes are used as weapons against the Court. Congress has tried to pressure the Court when setting its terms and size and when authorizing appropriations for salaries, law clerks, secretaries, and office technology. Only once, in 1802 when repealing the Judiciary Act of 1801 and abolishing a session for a year, did Congress actually set the Court's term to delay and influence a particular decision.

The size of the Court is not preordained, and changes generally reflect attempts to control the Court. The Jeffersonian-Republicans' quick repeal of the act passed by the Federalists in 1801 reducing the number of justices was the first of several attempts to influence the

Court. Presidents James Madison, James Monroe, and John Adams all claimed that the country's geographical expansion warranted enlarging the size of the Court. But Congress refused to do so until the last day of Andrew Jackson's term in 1837. During the Civil War, the number of justices increased to ten ostensibly due to the creation of a tenth circuit in the West. This gave Abraham Lincoln his fourth appointment and a chance to secure a pro-Union majority on the bench. Antagonism toward President Andrew Johnson's Reconstruction policies following the Civil War led to a reduction from ten justices to seven. After General Ulysses S. Grant was elected president, Congress again authorized nine justices—the number that has prevailed. In the nineteenth century at least, Congress rather successfully denied presidents additional appointments to preserve the Court's policies and increased the number of justices as a way to change the ideological composition of the Court.

Although Article III of the Constitution forbids reducing justices' salaries, Congress may withhold salary increases as punishment, especially in times of high inflation. More direct attacks are possible. Under Article III, Congress is authorized "to make exceptions" to the appellate jurisdiction of the Court. That authorization has been viewed as a way of denying the Court review of certain kinds of cases. Congress succeeded with the 1868 repeal of jurisdiction over writs of *habeas corpus*, which the Court upheld in *Ex parte McCardle*, 7 Wall. (74 U.S.) 506 (1869). More recently, in response to the rulings that "enemy combatants" held in Guantánamo Bay, Cuba, had a right to file a writ of *habeas corpus* and to trials by independent tribunals, in *Rasul v. Bush*, 542 U.S. 466 (2004) (excerpted in Vol. 1, Ch. 3) and *Hamdi v. Rumsfeld*, 542 U.S. 507 (2004), Congress enacted the Detainee Treatment Act (DTA) of 2005, which, among other things, withdrew jurisdiction over *habeas* writs filed by aliens detained outside the United States. However, in *Hamdan v. Rumsfeld*, 548 U.S. 557 (2006), without ruling on the constitutionality of that law, the Court held that enemy detainees whose *habeas* applications were pending at the time of the enactment of the DTA could invoke the judiciary's jurisdiction and ruled that they must be tried by civilian courts, courts martial, or military commissions as authorized by Congress. Subsequently, Congress passed and President George W. Bush signed into law the Military Commissions Act of 2006, which denies federal courts jurisdiction over *habeas* applications filed by "unlawful enemy combatants." Democrats opposed that court-stripping jurisdiction and Senator Arlen Specter (R–PA), chair of the judiciary committee, also deemed it unconstitutional but nonetheless voted for the bill. The Court struck down that jurisdiction-stripping legislation in *Boumediene v. Bush*, 553 U.S. 723 (2008) (excerpted in Vol. 1, Ch. 3).

Court-curbing legislation is not a very viable weapon. Rather than limiting judicial review, Congress has given the Court the power to set its own agenda and decide major issues of public law and policy—precisely the kinds of issues that Congress then seeks to deny the Court review. The Court has also suggested that it would not approve repeals of its jurisdiction that are merely attempts to dictate how particular kinds of cases should be decided.[7] Most proposals to curb the Court, of course, are simply that. During the McCarthy era, for instance, Republican Senator William Jenner spearheaded a drive to forbid review of cases challenging legislative committees investigating un-American activities. Another unsuccessful attempt was made in 1968 to amend the Omnibus Crime Control and Safe Streets Act so as to prevent the Court from reviewing state criminal cases raising *Miranda* issues.

Congress has had somewhat greater success in reversing the Court by constitutional amendment. Congress must pass a constitutional amendment that three-fourths of the states must then ratify. The process is cumbersome, and thousands of amendments to overrule the Court have failed. But four decisions have been overturned by constitutional amendment. *Chisholm v. Georgia*, 2 U.S. 419 (1793), holding that citizens of one state could sue another state in federal courts, was reversed by the Eleventh Amendment, guaranteeing sovereign immunity for states from suits by citizens of another state. The Thirteenth and Fourteenth Amendments, abolishing slavery and making blacks citizens of the United States, technically overturned the ruling in *Dred Scott v. Sandford* (1857) that blacks were not persons under the Constitution. With the ratification in 1913 of the Sixteenth Amendment, Congress reversed *Pollock v. Farmers' Loan and Trust Company*, 157 U.S. 429 (1895), which had invalidated a federal income tax. In 1970 an amendment to the Voting Rights Act of 1965 lowered the voting age to eighteen years for all elections. Though he signed the act into law, President Richard Nixon had his attorney general challenge the validity of lowering the voting age by simple legislation, rather than by constitutional amendment. Within six months, in *Oregon v. Mitchell*, 400 U.S. 112 (1970), a bare majority of the Court held that Congress exceeded its power by lowering the voting age for state and local elections. Less than a year later the Twenty-sixth Amendment was ratified extending the franchise to eighteen-year-olds in all elections.

More successful than Court curbing and amending the Constitution are congressional enactments and rewriting of legislation in response to the Court's rulings. Congressional reversals usually relate to both statutory and nonstatutory matters involving administrative policies.

Congress cannot overturn the Court's interpretations of the Constitution by mere legislation, as the Court underscored in *City of Boerne v.*

Flores, 521 U.S. 507 (1997) (excerpted in Ch. 6). But Congress can enhance or thwart compliance with the Court's rulings. After the Warren Court's landmark decision in *Gideon v. Wainwright*, 372 U.S. 335 (1963) (see Ch. 9), that indigents have a right to counsel, Congress provided attorneys for indigents charged with federal offenses. By contrast, in the Crime Control and Safe Streets Act of 1968, Congress permitted federal courts to use evidence obtained from suspects who had not been read their *Miranda* rights, if their testimony appeared voluntary based on the "totality of the circumstances" surrounding their interrogation. Congress thus attempted to return to a pre-*Miranda* standard for federal agents' questioning of criminal suspects. Democratic and Republican administrations, however, declined to enforce that provision and instead complied with *Miranda* in federal prosecutions. Finally, in *Dickerson v. United States*, 530 U.S. 428 (2000) (excerpted in Ch. 8), the Court rebuffed Congress's attempt to make an end run around *Miranda* and ruled that that decision applies to both federal and state police questioning of suspects.

Congress indubitably has the power to delay and undercut implementation of the Court's rulings. On major issues of public policy Congress is likely to prevail or, at least, temper the impact of the Court's rulings. But the Court forges public policy not only when invalidating federal legislation. No less importantly, the Court makes policy by overturning state and local laws and practices. The continuing controversies over decisions striking down state laws on school desegregation, school prayer, and abortion are a measure of the Court's influence on American life.

Charged with the responsibility of taking "care that the laws be faithfully executed," the president is the chief executive officer under the Constitution. As the only nationally elected public official, the president represents the views of the dominant national political coalition. A president's obligation to faithfully execute the laws, including decisions of the Court, thus may collide with his or her own perceived electoral mandate.

The Court has often been the focus of presidential campaigns and power struggles. But presidents rarely openly defy particular decisions by the Court. Presidential defiance is, perhaps, symbolized by the famous remark attributed to Andrew Jackson: "John Marshall has made his decision, now let him enforce it." Jackson's refusal to enforce the decision in *Worcester v. Georgia*, 31 U.S. 515 (1832), which denied state courts jurisdiction over crimes committed on Indian lands, in fact simply left enforcement problems up to the courts and legislatures. During the Civil War, however, Lincoln ordered his military commanders to refuse to obey writs of *habeas corpus* issued by Chief Justice Taney.

In major confrontations, presidents generally yield to the Court. Richard Nixon complied with the ruling in *New York Times Co. v. United States*, 403 U.S. 713 (1971) (see Vol. 1, Ch. 4), which struck down, as a prior restraint on freedom of the press, an injunction against the publication of the Pentagon Papers—a top secret report detailing the history of America's involvement in Vietnam. Then, during the Watergate scandal in 1974, Nixon submitted to the Court's decision in *United States v. Nixon*, 418 U.S. 683 (1974) (see Vol. 1, Ch. 4) ordering the release of White House tape recordings pertinent to the trial of his former attorney general John Mitchell and other presidential aides for conspiracy and obstruction of justice.

Although seldom directly defying the Court, in the short and long run presidents may undercut Supreme Court policy making. By giving contradictory directives to federal agencies and assigning low priority for enforcement by the Department of Justice, presidents may limit the Court's decisions. Presidents may also make broad moral appeals in response to the Court's rulings, and those appeals may transcend their limited time in office. The Court put school desegregation and abortion on the national agenda. But President John F. Kennedy's appeal for civil rights captivated a generation and encouraged public acceptance of the Court's rulings. Similarly, President Ronald Reagan's opposition to abortion focused attention on "traditional family values" and served to legitimize resistance to the Court's decisions.

Presidential influence over the Court in the long run remains contingent on appointments to the Court. Vacancies occur on the average of one every twenty-two months. Four presidents—including Jimmy Carter—had no opportunity to appoint members of the Court. There is no guarantee how a justice will vote or whether that vote will prove sufficient in limiting or reversing past rulings with which a president disagrees. But through their appointments presidents may leave their mark on Supreme Court policy-making and possibly align the Court and the country or precipitate later confrontations.

For much of the Court's history, the work of the justices has not involved major issues of public policy. In most areas of public law and policy, the fact that the Court decides an issue is more important than what it decides. Relatively few of the major issues of public policy that arise in government reach the Court. When the Court does decide major questions of public policy, its rulings decide only the instant case and not the larger surrounding political controversies. Major confrontations in constitutional politics, like those over school desegregation and abortion, are determined as much by what is possible in a system of free government and pluralistic society as by what the Court says about the meaning of the Constitution. And on those controversial issues of public policy, constitutional law frames the political debate in the ongoing dialogue between the Court and the country. The Court's rulings and interpretation of the Constitution rest, in Chief Justice Edward White's words, "solely upon the approval of a free people."[8]

NOTES

1. Robert Dahl, "Decision-Making in a Democracy: The Supreme Court as a National Policy-Maker," 6 *Journal of Public Law* 293 (1957).

2. See Richard Funston, "The Supreme Court and Critical Elections," 69 *American Political Science Review* 795 (1975); Jonathan Casper, "The Supreme Court and National Policymaking," 70 *American Political Science Review* 5066 (1976); William Mishler and Reginald Sheehan, "The Supreme Court as a Countermajoritarian Institution?" 87 *American Political Science Review* 87 (1993); and Thomas Marshall, *Public Opinion and the Supreme Court* (New York: Longman, 1989).

3. See, for example, Walter Murphy, J. Tananhaus, and D. Kastner, *Public Evaluations of Constitutional Courts* (Beverly Hills, CA: Sage, 1973).

4. *Williams v. United States*, 401 U.S. 646 (1971).

5. Fred Vinson, speech given before the American Bar Association, September 7, 1949, reprinted in 69 S.Ct. vi (1949).

6. Robert Jackson, *The Struggle for Judicial Supremacy* (New York: Knopf, 1951), 287.

7. *United States v. Klein*, 80 U.S. 128 (1872).

8. Edward White, "The Supreme Court of the United States," 7 *American Bar Association Journal* 341 (1921).

SELECTED BIBLIOGRAPHY

Banks, Christopher, and David M O'Brien. *The Judicial Process: Law, Courts, and Judicial Politics*. 2nd ed. St. Paul, MN: West Academic, 2020.

Barnes, Jeb. *Overruled? Legislative Overrides, Pluralism, and Contemporary Court-Congress Relations*. Palo Alto, CA: Stanford University Press, 2004.

Canon, Bradley, and Charles Johnson. *Judicial Policies: Implementation and Impact*. 2nd ed. Washington, DC: C.Q. Press, 1999.

Cooper, Phillip. *Hard Judicial Choices*. New York: Oxford University Press, 1988.

Dinan, John. *The American State Constitutional Tradition*. Lawrence: University Press of Kansas, 2006.

Epstein, Lee, and Joseph Kobylka. *The Supreme Court & Legal Change*. Chapel Hill: University of North Carolina Press, 1992.

Gates, John. *The Supreme Court and Partisan Realignment*. Boulder, CO: Westview, 1992.

Hall, Kermit, ed. *The Oxford Companion to the Supreme Court*. 2nd ed. New York: Oxford University Press, 2005.

McGuire, Kevin. *The Supreme Court Bar*. Charlottesville: University Press of Virginia, 1993.

Murphy, Walter. *Elements of Judicial Strategy*. Chicago: University of Chicago Press, 1964.

O'Brien, David M. *Storm Center: The Supreme Court in American Politics.* 12th ed. New York: W. W. Norton & Company, 2020.

Pacelle, Richard. *The Transformation of the Supreme Court's Agenda.* Boulder, CO: Westview, 1991.

Pickerill, J. Mitchell. *Constitutional Deliberations in Congress.* Durham, NC: Duke University Press, 2004.

Rosen, Jeffrey. *The Most Democratic Branch: How the Courts Serve America.* New York: Oxford University Press, 2006.

Rosenberg, Gerald. *The Hollow Hope.* 2nd ed. Chicago: University of Chicago Press, 2008.

Shaman, Jeffrey. *Equity and Liberty in the Golden Age of State Constitutional Law.* New York: Oxford University Press, 2008.

Segal, Jeffrey, and Harold Spaeth. *The Supreme Court and the Attitudinal Model.* 2nd ed. Cambridge, MA: Cambridge University Press, 2002.

Supreme Court Historical Society. *Journal of Supreme Court History.* Washington, DC: SCHS, 1976–present.

Urofsky, Melvin, ed. *The Public Debate Over Controversial Supreme Court Decisions.* Washington, DC: C.Q. Press, 2006.

Linkletter v. Walker

381 U.S. 618, 85 S.Ct. 1731 (1965)

Victor Linkletter was tried and convicted in state court on evidence illegally obtained by police prior to *Mapp v. Ohio*, 367 U.S. 643 (1961) (see Ch. 7), which barred states from using illegally obtained evidence at trial under the Fourth Amendment's exclusionary rule. Linkletter contended that *Mapp* should apply retroactively and he should be retried with the illegally obtained evidence excluded. A federal district court disagreed, and after a court of appeals affirmed that ruling, Linkletter appealed to the Supreme Court.

The Court's decision was 7–2; with the majority's opinion announced by Justice Clark. The dissent was by Justice Black, who was joined by Justice Douglas.

■ ■ ■

☐ *Justice CLARK delivers the opinion of the Court.*

In *Mapp v. Ohio*, 367 U.S. 643 (1961), we held that the exclusion of evidence seized in violation of the search and seizure provisions of the Fourth Amendment was required of the States by the Due Process Clause of the Fourteenth Amendment. In so doing we overruled *Wolf v. People of*

State of Colorado, 338 U.S. 25 (1949), to the extent that it failed to apply the exclusionary rule to the States. This case presents the question of whether this requirement operates retrospectively upon cases finally decided in the period prior to *Mapp*. The Court of Appeals for the Fifth Circuit held that it did not, and we granted *certiorari* in order to settle what has become a most troublesome question in the administration of justice. We agree with the Court of Appeals. . . .

At common law there was no authority for the proposition that judicial decisions made law only for the future. Blackstone stated the rule that the duty of the court was not to "pronounce a new law, but to maintain and expound the old one." 1 Blackstone, *Commentaries* 69 (15th ed. 1809). . . .

In the case of the overruled decision, *Wolf v. People of State of Colorado, supra*, here, it was thought to be only a failure at true discovery and was consequently never the law; while the overruling one, *Mapp*, was not "new law but an application of what is, and theretofore had been, the true law." . . .

On the other hand, [the late-nineteenth century legal philosopher John] Austin maintained that judges do in fact do something more than discover law; they make it interstitially by filling in with judicial interpretation the vague, indefinite, or generic statutory or common-law terms that alone are but the empty crevices of the law. Implicit in such an approach is the admission when a case is overruled that the earlier decision was wrongly decided. However, rather than being erased by the later overruling decision it is considered as an existing juridical fact until overruled, and intermediate cases finally decided under it are not to be disturbed.

The Blackstonian view ruled English jurisprudence and cast its shadow over our own. . . . However, some legal philosophers continued to insist that such a rule was out of tune with actuality largely because judicial repeal ofttime did "work hardship to those who [had] trusted to its existence." CARDOZO, Address to the N.Y. Bar Assn. (1932). . . .

It is true that heretofore, without discussion, we have applied new constitutional rules to cases finalized before the promulgation of the rule. Petitioner contends that our method of resolving those prior cases demonstrates that an absolute rule of retroaction prevails in the area of constitutional adjudication. However, we believe that the Constitution neither prohibits nor requires retrospective effect. As Justice CARDOZO said, "We think the Federal Constitution has no voice upon the subject." . . .

Since *Weeks v. United States*, 232 U.S. 383 (1914) this Court has adhered to the rule that evidence seized by federal officers in violation of the Fourth Amendment is not admissible at trial in a federal court. In 1949 in *Wolf v. People of State of Colorado, supra*, the Court decided that while the right to privacy—"the core of the Fourth Amendment"—was such a basic right as to be implicit in "the concept of ordered liberty" and thus enforceable against the States through the Fourteenth Amendment, "the ways of enforcing such a basic right raise questions of a different order. How such arbitrary conduct should be checked, what remedies against it should be afforded, the means by which the right should be made effective, are all questions that are not to be so dogmatically answered as to preclude the varying solutions which spring from an allowable range of judgment on issues not susceptible of quantitative solution."

Mapp was announced in 1961. The Court in considering "the current validity of the factual grounds upon which *Wolf* was based" pointed out that prior to *Wolf* "almost two-thirds of the States were opposed to the use of the exclusionary rule, now, despite the *Wolf* case, more than half of those since passing upon it . . . have wholly or partly adopted or adhered to the *Weeks* rule." . . .

We believe that the existence of the *Wolf* doctrine prior to *Mapp* is "an operative fact and may have consequences which cannot justly be ignored. The past cannot always be erased by a new judicial declaration." The thousands of cases that were finally decided on *Wolf* cannot be obliterated. The "particular conduct, private and official," must be considered. Here "prior determinations deemed to have finality and acted upon accordingly" have "become vested." And finally, "public policy in the light of the nature both of the [*Wolf* doctrine] and of its previous application" must be given its proper weight. In short, we must look to the purpose of the *Mapp* rule; the reliance placed upon the *Wolf* doctrine; and the effect on the administration of justice of a retrospective application of *Mapp*.

It is clear that the *Wolf* Court, once it had found the Fourth Amendment's unreasonable Search and Seizure Clause applicable to the States through the Due Process Clause of the Fourteenth Amendment, turned its attention to whether the exclusionary rule was included within the command of the Fourth Amendment. This was decided in the negative. It is clear that based upon the factual considerations heretofore discussed the *Wolf* Court then concluded that it was not necessary to the enforcement of the Fourth Amendment for the exclusionary rule to be extended to the States as a requirement of due process. *Mapp* had as its prime purpose the enforcement of the Fourth Amendment through the inclusion of the exclusionary rule within its rights. This, it was found, was the only effective deterrent to lawless police action. Indeed, all of the cases since *Wolf* requiring the exclusion of illegal evidence have been based on the necessity for an effective deterrent to illegal police action. We cannot say that this purpose would be advanced by making the rule retrospective. The misconduct of the police prior to *Mapp* has already occurred and will not be corrected by releasing the prisoners involved. Nor would it add harmony to the delicate state-federal relationship of which we have spoken as part and parcel of the purpose of *Mapp*. Finally, the ruptured privacy of the victims' homes and effects cannot be restored. Reparation comes too late. . . .

Finally, there are interests in the administration of justice and the integrity of the judicial process to consider. To make the rule of *Mapp* retrospective would tax the administration of justice to the utmost. Hearings would have to be held on the excludability of evidence long since destroyed, misplaced or deteriorated. If it is excluded, the witnesses available at the time of the original trial will not be available or if located their memory will be dimmed. To thus legitimate such an extraordinary procedural weapon that has no bearing on guilt would seriously disrupt the administration of justice. . . .

All that we decide today is that though the error complained of might be fundamental it is not of the nature requiring us to overturn all final convictions based upon it. After full consideration of all the factors we are not able to say that the *Mapp* rule requires retrospective application.

Affirmed.

☐ *Justice BLACK, with whom Justice DOUGLAS joins, dissenting.*

The Court offers no defense based on any known principle of justice for discriminating among defendants who were similarly convicted by use of evidence unconstitutionally seized. It certainly cannot do so as between Linkletter and Miss Mapp. The crime with which she was charged took place more than a year before his, yet the decision today seems to rest on the fanciful concept that the Fourth Amendment protected her 1957 offense against conviction by use of unconstitutional evidence but denied its protection to Linkletter for his 1958 offense. In making this ruling the Court assumes for itself the virtue of acting in harmony with a comment of Justice HOLMES that "[t]he life of the law has not been logic: it has been experience." Justice HOLMES was not there talking about the Constitution; he was talking about the evolving judge-made law of England and of some of our States whose judges are allowed to follow in the common law tradition. It should be remembered in this connection that no member of this Court has ever more seriously criticized it than did Justice HOLMES for reading its own predilections into the "vague contours" of the Due Process Clause. But quite apart from that, there is no experience of the past that justifies a new Court-made rule to perpetrate a grossly invidious and unfair discrimination against Linkletter simply because he happened to be prosecuted in a State that was evidently well up with its criminal court docket. If this discrimination can be excused at all it is not because of experience but because of logic—sterile and formal at that—not, according to Justice HOLMES, the most dependable guide in law-making. . . .

As the Court concedes, this is the first instance on record where this Court, having jurisdiction, has ever refused to give a previously convicted defendant the benefit of a new and more expansive Bill of Rights interpretation. I am at a loss to understand why those who suffer from the use of evidence secured by a search and seizure in violation of the Fourth Amendment should be treated differently from those who have been denied other guarantees of the Bill of Rights. . . .

Whorton v. Bockting

549 U.S. 406, 127 S.CT. 1173 (2007)

The facts and the issue of application of the retroactivity doctrine are discussed in Justice Alito's unanimous opinion for the Court, reversing the judgment of the Court of Appeals for the Ninth Circuit.

■ ■ ■

☐ *Justice ALITO delivered the opinion of the Court.*

This case presents the question whether, under the rules set out in *Teague v. Lane,* 489 U.S. 288 (1989), our decision in *Crawford v. Washington,* 541 U.S. 36 (2004), is retroactive to cases already final on direct review. We hold that it is not.

Respondent Marvin Bockting lived in Las Vegas, Nevada, with his wife, Laura Bockting, their 3-year-old daughter Honesty, and Laura's 6-year-old daughter from a previous relationship, Autumn. One night, while respondent was at work, Autumn awoke from a dream crying, but she refused to tell her mother what was wrong, explaining: "[D]addy said you would make him leave and that he would beat my butt if I told you." After her mother reassured her, Autumn said that respondent had frequently forced her to engage in numerous and varied sexual acts with him. . . .

[Subsequently, Bockting was charged and tried for sexual assault, but his step-daughter did not testify, rather her mother and a police detective recounted her out-of-court statements.] The jury found respondent guilty of three counts of sexual assault on a minor under the age of 14, and the trial court imposed two consecutive life sentences and another concurrent life sentence.

Respondent took an appeal to the Nevada Supreme Court, which handed down its final decision in 1993, more than a decade before *Crawford*. In analyzing respondent's contention that the admission of Autumn's out-of-court statements had violated his Confrontation Clause rights, the Nevada Supreme Court looked to *Ohio v. Roberts*, 448 U.S. 56 (1980), which was then the governing precedent of this Court. *Roberts* had held that the Confrontation Clause permitted the admission of a hearsay statement made by a declarant who was unavailable to testify if the statement bore sufficient indicia of reliability, either because the statement fell within a firmly rooted hearsay exception or because there were "particularized guarantees of trustworthiness" relating to the statement in question. . . .

Respondent then filed a petition for a writ of *habeas corpus* with the United States District Court for the District of Nevada, arguing that the Nevada Supreme Court's decision violated his Confrontation Clause rights. The District Court denied the petition [and Bockting] appealed to the United States Court of Appeals for the Ninth Circuit.

While this appeal was pending, we issued our opinion in *Crawford*, in which we overruled *Roberts* and held that "[t]estimonial statements of witnesses absent from trial" are admissible "only where the declarant is unavailable, and only where the defendant has had a prior opportunity to cross-examine [the witness]." We noted that the outcome in *Roberts*—as well as the outcome in all similar cases decided by this Court—was consistent with the rule announced in *Crawford*, but we concluded that the interpretation of the Confrontation Clause set out in *Roberts* was unsound in several respects. First, we observed that *Roberts* potentially excluded too much testimony because it imposed Confrontation Clause restrictions on nontestimonial hearsay not governed by that Clause. At the same time, we noted, the *Roberts* test was too "malleable" in permitting the admission of *ex parte* testimonial statements. . . .

In *Teague* and subsequent cases, we have laid out the framework to be used in determining whether a rule announced in one of our opinions should be applied retroactively to judgments in criminal cases that are already final on direct review. Under the *Teague* framework, an old rule applies both on direct and collateral review, but a new rule is generally applicable only to cases that are still on direct review. See *Griffith v. Kentucky*, 479 U.S. 314 (1987). A new rule applies retroactively in a collateral proceeding only if (1) the rule is substantive or (2) the rule is a "'watershed rul[e] of criminal procedure' implicating the fundamental fairness and accuracy of the criminal proceeding."

In this case, it is undisputed that respondent's conviction became final on direct appeal well before *Crawford* was decided. We therefore turn to the question whether *Crawford* applied an old rule or announced a new one. A new rule is defined as "a rule that . . . was not 'dictated by precedent existing at the time the defendant's conviction became final.' "

Applying this definition, it is clear that *Crawford* announced a new rule. The *Crawford* rule was not "dictated" by prior precedent. Quite the opposite is true: The *Crawford* rule is flatly inconsistent with the prior governing precedent, *Roberts*, which *Crawford* overruled. . . .

Because *Crawford* announced a "new rule" and because it is clear and undisputed that the rule is procedural and not substantive, that rule cannot be applied in this collateral attack on respondent's conviction unless it is a " 'watershed rul[e] of criminal procedure' implicating the fundamental fairness and accuracy of the criminal proceeding." This exception is "extremely narrow," *Schriro v. Summerlin*, 542 U.S. 348 (2004). . . .

In order to qualify as watershed, a new rule must meet two requirements. First, the rule must be necessary to prevent "an 'impermissibly large risk' " of an inaccurate conviction. Second, the rule must "alter our understanding of the bedrock procedural elements essential to the fairness of a proceeding."

The *Crawford* rule does not satisfy the first requirement relating to an impermissibly large risk of an inaccurate conviction. To be sure, the *Crawford* rule reflects the Framers' preferred mechanism (cross-examination) for ensuring that inaccurate out-of-court testimonial statements are not used to convict an accused. But in order for a new rule to meet the accuracy requirement at issue here, "[i]t is . . . not enough . . . to say that [the] rule is aimed at improving the accuracy of trial," or that the rule "is directed toward the enhancement of reliability and accuracy in some sense." Instead, the question is whether the new rule remedied "an 'impermissibly large risk' " of an inaccurate conviction.

Guidance in answering this question is provided by *Gideon v. Wainwright*, 372 U.S. 335 (1963), to which we have repeatedly referred in discussing the meaning of the *Teague* exception at issue here. In *Gideon*, the only case that we have identified as qualifying under this exception, the Court held that counsel must be appointed for any indigent defendant charged with a felony. When a defendant who wishes to be represented by counsel is denied representation, *Gideon* held, the risk of an unreliable verdict is intolerably high. The new rule announced in *Gideon* eliminated this risk.

The *Crawford* rule is in no way comparable to the *Gideon* rule. The *Crawford* rule is much more limited in scope, and the relationship of that rule to the accuracy of the fact finding process is far less direct and profound. *Crawford* overruled *Roberts* because *Roberts* was inconsistent with the original understanding of the meaning of the Confrontation Clause, not because the Court reached the conclusion that the overall effect of the *Crawford* rule would be to improve the accuracy of fact finding in criminal trials. . . .

The *Crawford* rule also did not "alter our understanding of the bedrock procedural elements essential to the fairness of a proceeding." . . . We have frequently held that the *Teague* bar to retroactivity applies to new rules that are based on "bedrock" constitutional rights. Similarly, "[t]hat a new procedural rule is 'fundamental' in some abstract sense is not enough."

Instead, in order to meet this requirement, a new rule must itself constitute a previously unrecognized bedrock procedural element that is essential to the fairness of a proceeding. In applying this requirement, we again have looked to the example of *Gideon*, and "we have not hesitated to hold that less sweeping and fundamental rules" do not qualify.

In this case, it is apparent that the rule announced in *Crawford*, while certainly important, is not in the same category with *Gideon*. *Gideon* effected a profound and "sweeping" change. The *Crawford* rule simply lacks the "primacy" and "centrality" of the *Gideon* rule, and does not qualify as a rule that "alter[ed] our understanding of the bedrock procedural elements essential to the fairness of a proceeding."

In sum, we hold that *Crawford* announced a "new rule" of criminal procedure and that this rule does not fall within the *Teague* exception for watershed rules. We therefore reverse the judgment of the Court of Appeals and remand the case for further proceedings consistent with this opinion.

Jaffree v. Board of School Commissioners of Mobile County

554 F.Supp. 1104 (1983)

Ishmael Jaffree challenged the constitutionality of Alabama's law authorizing teachers to lead students in a moment of "silent meditation or voluntary prayer" as a violation of the First Amendment guarantees for religious freedom. Federal District Court Judge Brevard Hand rejected Jaffree's complaint in an opinion sharply critical of the Supreme Court's rulings on the First Amendment establishment clause. His ruling was subsequently appealed by Jaffree and overturned by a court of appeals. Governor George Wallace then appealed that ruling to the Supreme Court in *Wallace v. Jaffree*, 472 U.S. 38 (1985) (see Ch. 6), which affirmed the appellant court's decision overturning Judge Hand's decision.

■ ■ ■

MEMORANDUM OPINION

☐ *Chief Judge BREVARD HAND.*

The United States Supreme Court has previously addressed itself in many cases to the practice of prayer and religious services in the public schools. As courts are wont to say, this court does not write upon a clean slate when it addresses the issue of school prayer.

Viewed historically, three decisions have lately provided general rules for school prayer. In *Engel v. Vitale*, 370 U.S. 421 [(1962)], *Abington v. Schempp*, 374 U.S. 203 (1963), and *Murray v. Curlett*, 374 U.S. 203 (1963) the Supreme Court established the basic considerations. As stated, the rule is that "[t]he First Amendment has erected a wall between church and state. That wall must be kept high and impregnable. We could not approve the slightest breach." *Everson v. Board of Education*, 330 U.S. 1 (1947).

The principles enunciated in *Engel v. Vitale, Abington v. Schempp,* and *Murray v. Curlett* have been distilled to this: "To pass muster under the Establishment Clause, the governmental activity must, first, reflect a clearly secular governmental purpose; second, have a primary effect that neither advances nor inhibits religion; and third, avoid excessive government entanglement with religion. *Committee for Public Education & Religious Liberty v. Nyquist,* 413 U.S. 756 (1973)." . . .

In sum, under present rulings the use of officially-authorized prayers or Bible readings for motivational purposes constitutes a direct violation of the establishment clause. Through a series of decisions, the courts have held that the establishment clause was designed to avoid any official sponsorship or approval of religious beliefs. Even though a practice may not be coercive, active support of a particular belief raises the danger, under the rationale of the Court, that state-approved religious views may be eventually established. . . .

In the face of this precedent the defendants argue that school prayers as they are employed are constitutional. The historical argument which they advance takes two tacks. First, the defendants urge that the first amendment to the U.S. Constitution was intended only to prohibit the *federal government* from establishing a *national* religion. Read in its proper historical context, the defendants contend that the first amendment has no application to the states. The intent of the drafters and adoptors of the first amendment was to prevent the establishment of a national church or religion, and to prevent any single religious sect or denomination from obtaining a preferred position under the auspices of the federal government. . . .

Second, the defendants argue that whatever prohibitions were initially placed upon the federal government by the first amendment that those prohibitions were not incorporated against the states when the fourteenth amendment became law on July 19, 1868. The defendants have introduced the Court to a mass of historical documentation which all point to the intent of the Thirty-ninth Congress to narrowly restrict the scope of the fourteenth amendment. In particular, these historical documents, according to the defendants, clearly demonstrate that the first amendment was never intended to be incorporated through the fourteenth amendment to apply against the states. The Court [subsequently] examine[d] each historical argument in turn. . . .

[The Court concluded that] the establishment clause, as ratified in 1791, was intended only to prohibit the federal government from establishing a national religion. The function of the establishment clause was two-fold. First, it guaranteed to each individual that Congress would not impose a national religion. Second, the establishment clause guaranteed to each state that the states were free to define the meaning of religious establishment under their own constitutions and laws.

The historical record clearly establishes that when the fourteenth amendment was ratified in 1868 that its ratification did not incorporate the first amendment against the states. . . .

What is a court to do when faced with a direct challenge to settled precedent? In most types of cases "it is more important that the applicable rule of law be settled than that it be settled right." *Burnet v. Coronado Oil & Gas Co.,* 285 U.S. 393 (1932) (BRANDEIS, J., dissenting). This general rule holds even where the court is persuaded that it has made a serious error of interpretation in cases involving a statute. However, in cases involving the federal constitution, where correction through legislative action is practically impossible, a court should be willing to examine earlier precedent and to overrule it if the court is persuaded that the earlier precedent was wrongly decided. . . .

This Court's review of the relevant legislative history surrounding the adoption of both the first amendment and of the fourteenth amendment, together with the plain language of those amendments, leaves no doubt that those amendments were not intended to forbid religious prayers in the schools which the states and their political subdivisions mandate. . . .

If the appellate courts disagree with this Court in its examination of history and conclusion of constitutional interpretation thereof, then this Court will look again at the record in this case and reach conclusions which it is not now forced to reach.

Commonwealth of Kentucky v. Jeffrey Wasson

SUPREME COURT OF KENTUCKY, 842 S.W. 2D 487 (1992)

Jeffrey Wasson was arrested in a public parking lot and charged with soliciting an undercover police officer to engage in "deviate sexual intercourse." Under a Kentucky statute (KRS 510.100), "deviate sexual intercourse with another person of the same sex" is a criminal offense; the statute also provides that "consent of the other person shall not be a defense." At Wasson's trial, however, a district judge dismissed the charge and held that the statute violated provisions in the Kentucky Constitution that guarantee a "right of privacy" and the equal protection of the laws. A state appellate court affirmed and the Commonwealth of Kentucky appealed that ruling to its supreme court.

■ ■ ■

☐ Opinion of the Court by Justice LEIBSON

The Commonwealth maintains that the United States Supreme Court's decision in *Bowers v. Hardwick*, [478 U.S. 186 (1986)], is dispositive of the right to privacy issue; that the "Kentucky Constitution did not intend to confer any greater right to privacy than was afforded by the U.S. Constitution." Turning to the equal protection argument raised by a statute which criminalizes oral or anal intercourse between persons of the same sex, but not between persons of different sexes, which was not addressed in the *Bowers* case, the Commonwealth argues there is "a rational basis for making such a distinction." . . . The thrust of the argument advanced by the Commonwealth as a rational basis for criminalizing consensual intercourse between persons of the same sex, when the same acts between persons of the opposite sex are not punished, is that the level of moral indignation felt by the majority of society against the sexual preference of homosexuals justifies having their legislative representative criminalize these sexual activities. The Commonwealth believes that homosexual intercourse is immoral, and that what is beyond the pale of majoritarian morality is beyond the limits of constitutional protection.

The grounds stated by the District Court for striking down the statute as unconstitutional are: "KRS 510.100 clearly seeks to regulate the profoundly private conduct and in so doing impermissibly invades the privacy of the citizens of this state." . . . The Fayette Circuit Court "agreed with that conclusion," and further held the statute "unjustifiably discriminates, and thus is unconstitutional under Sections 2 and 3 of our Kentucky Constitution." These Sections are:

> Section 2. Absolute and arbitrary power over the lives, liberty and property of freemen exists nowhere in a republic, not even in the largest majority.

> Section 3. All men, when they form a social compact, are equal. . . .

These Sections [together with other provisions of the Kentucky constitution] express the guarantee of equal treatment provided by the law in our Kentucky Constitution. The lower courts' judgments limit their finding of unconstitutionality to state constitutional grounds. *Bowers v. Hardwick* speaks neither to rights of privacy under the state constitution nor to equal protection rights under either federal or state constitutions. *Bowers* addressed the constitutionality of a Georgia statute prohibiting acts of consensual sodomy between persons of the same sex or the opposite sex. Because the Georgia statute embraced both heterosexual and homosexual conduct, the *Bowers* opinion did not involve the Equal Protection Clause of the Fourteenth Amendment.

For reasons that follow, we hold the guarantees of individual liberty provided in our 1891 Kentucky Constitution offer greater protection of the right of privacy than provided by the Federal constitution as interpreted by the United States Supreme Court, and that the statute in question is a violation of such rights; and, further, we hold that the statute in question violates rights of equal protection as guaranteed by our Kentucky Constitution.

■ I. Rights of Privacy

No language specifying "rights of privacy," as such, appears in either the federal or State Constitution. The Commonwealth recognizes such rights exist, but takes the position that, since they are implicit rather than explicit, our Court should march in lock step with the United States Supreme Court in declaring when such rights exist. Such is not the formulation of federalism. On the contrary, under our system of dual sovereignty, it is our responsibility to interpret and apply our state constitution independently. We are not bound by decisions of the United States Supreme Court when deciding whether a state statute impermissibly infringes upon individual rights guaranteed in the State Constitution so long as state constitutional protection does not fall below the federal floor, meaning the minimum guarantee of individual rights under the United States Constitution as interpreted by the United States Supreme Court. . . .

Kentucky cases recognized a legally protected right of privacy based on our own constitution and common law tradition long before the United States Supreme Court first took notice of whether there were any rights of privacy inherent in the Federal Bill of Rights. . . .

[Moreover,] the United States Supreme Court is extremely reticent in extending the reach of the Due Process Clauses in substantive matters [pertaining to privacy]. . . . *Bowers v. Hardwick* decides that rights protected by the Due Process Clauses in the Fifth and Fourteenth Amendments to the United States Constitution do not "extend a fundamental right to homosexuals to engage in acts of consensual sodomy."

Bowers decides nothing beyond this. But state constitutional jurisprudence in this area is not limited by the constraints inherent in federal due process analysis. Deviate sexual intercourse conducted in private by consenting adults is not beyond the protections of the guarantees of individual liberty in our Kentucky Constitution simply because "proscriptions against that conduct have ancient roots." Kentucky constitutional guarantees against government intrusion address substantive rights. . . . [T]he Kentucky Constitution of 1891 . . . amplifies [its guarantee of individual liberty] with a Bill of Rights in 26 sections, the first of which states:

> Section 1. All men are, by nature, free and equal, and have certain inherent and inalienable rights, among which may be reckoned:
>
> First: The right of enjoying and defending their lives and liberties. . . .
>
> Third: The right of seeking and pursuing their safety and happiness. . . .
>
> Section 2. Absolute and arbitrary power over the lives, liberty and property of freemen exists nowhere in a republic, not even in the largest majority. . . .

The leading case on this subject is *Commonwealth v. Campbell*, [133 Ky. 50 (1909)]. At issue was an ordinance that criminalized possession of intoxicating liquor, even for "private use." Our Court held that the Bill of Rights in the 1891 Constitution prohibited state action thus intruding upon the "inalienable rights possessed by the citizens" of Kentucky. Our Court interpreted the Kentucky Bill of Rights as defining a right of privacy, even though the constitution did not say so in that terminology. . . .

In the *Campbell* case our Court quoted at length from the "great work" *On Liberty* of the nineteenth-century English philosopher and economist, John Stuart Mill. . . . Mill's premise is that "physical force in the form of legal penalties," i.e., criminal sanctions, should not be used as a means to improve the citizen. The majority has no moral right to dictate how everyone else should live. Public indignation, while given due weight, should be subject to the overriding test of rational and critical analysis, drawing the line at harmful consequences to others. Modern legal philosophers who follow Mill temper this test with an enlightened paternalism, permitting the law to intervene to stop self-inflicted harm such as the result of drug taking, or failure to use seat belts or crash helmets, not to enforce majoritarian or conventional morality, but because the victim of such self-inflicted harm becomes a burden on society.

Based on the *Campbell* opinion, and on the Comments of the 1891 Convention Delegates, there is little doubt but that the views of John Stuart Mill, which were then held in high esteem, provided the philosophical underpinnings for the reworking and broadening of protection of individual rights that occurs throughout the 1891 constitution.

We have recognized protection of individual rights greater than the federal floor in a number of cases, most recently: *Ingram v. Commonwealth, Ky.*, 801

S.W.2d 321 (1900), involving protection against double jeopardy and *Dean v. Commonwealth, Ky.*, 777 S.W.2d 900 (1989), involving the right of confrontation. Perhaps the most dramatic recent example of protection of individual rights under the state constitution where the United States Supreme Court had refused to afford protection under the Federal Constitution is *Rose v. Council for Better Educ., Inc., Ky.*, 790 S.W.2d 186 (1989). In *Rose*, our Court recognized our Kentucky Constitution afforded individual school children from property poor districts a fundamental right to an adequate education such as provided in wealthier school districts, even though sixteen years earlier the United States Supreme Court held the Federal Constitution provided no such protection in *San Antonio Independent School District v. Rodriguez*, 411 U.S. 1 (1973). . . .

We view the United States Supreme Court decision in *Bowers v. Hardwick* as a misdirected application of the theory of original intent. To illustrate: as a theory of majoritarian morality, miscegenation was an offense with ancient roots. It is highly unlikely that protecting the rights of persons of different races to copulate was one of the considerations behind the Fourteenth Amendment. Nevertheless, in *Loving v. Virginia*, 388 U.S. 1 (1967), the United States Supreme Court recognized that a contemporary, enlightened interpretation of the liberty interest involved in the sexual act made its punishment constitutionally impermissible.

According to *Bowers v. Hardwick*, "until 1961, all fifty States outlawed sodomy, and today, twenty-five States and District of Columbia continue to provide criminal penalties for sodomy performed in private and between consenting adults." In the space of three decades half the states decriminalized this conduct. . . . Two states [New York and Pennsylvania] by court decisions hold homosexual sodomy statutes of this nature unconstitutional for reasons similar to those stated here. . . . Thus our decision, rather than being the leading edge of change, is but a part of the moving stream. . . .

■ II. EQUAL PROTECTION

As stated earlier, in *Bowers v. Hardwick*, the Equal Protection Clause was not implicated because the Georgia statute criminalized both heterosexual and homosexual sodomy. Unlike the due Process Clause analysis provided in *Bowers v. Hardwick*, equal protection analysis does not turn on whether the law (KRS 510.100) transgresses "liberties that are 'deeply rooted in this Nation's history and tradition.'" *Bowers v. Hardwick*. . . .

Certainly, the practice of deviate sexual intercourse violates traditional morality. But so does the same act between heterosexuals, which activity is decriminalized. Going one step further, all sexual activity between consenting adults outside of marriage violates our traditional morality. The issue here is not whether sexual activity traditionally viewed as immoral can be punished by society, but whether it can be punished solely on the basis of sexual preference. . . .

We need not speculate as to whether male and/or female homosexuals will be allowed status as a protected class if and when the United States Supreme Court confronts this issue. They are a separate and identifiable class for Kentucky constitutional law analysis because no class of persons can be discriminated against under the Kentucky Constitution. All are entitled to equal treatment, unless there is a substantial governmental interest, a rational basis, for different treatment.

In the final analysis we can attribute no legislative purpose to this statute except to single out homosexuals for different treatment for indulging their sexual preference by engaging in the same activity heterosexuals are now at liberty to perform. By 1974 there had already been a sea change in societal values insofar as attaching criminal penalties to extramarital sex. The question is whether a society that no longer criminalizes adultery, fornication, or deviate sexual intercourse between heterosexuals has a rational basis to single out homosexual acts for different treatment. Is there a rational basis for declaring this one type of sexual immorality so destructive of family values as to merit criminal punishment whereas other acts of sexual immorality which were likewise forbidden by the same religious and traditional heritage of Western civilization are now decriminalized? If there is a rational basis for different treatment it has yet to be demonstrated in this case.

The purpose of the present statute is not to protect the marital relationship against sexual activity outside of marriage, but only to punish one aspect of it while other activities similarly destructive of the marital relationship, if not more so, go unpunished. Sexual preference, and not the act committed, determines criminality, and is being punished. Simply because the majority, speaking through the General Assembly, finds one type of extramarital intercourse more offensive than another, does not provide a rational basis for criminalizing the sexual preference of homosexuals.

For the reasons stated, we affirm the decision of the Fayette Circuit Court, and the judgment on appeal from the Fayette District Court.

☐ *Justices LAMBERT, WINTERSHEIMBER, and REYNOLDS dissented.*

■ THE DEVELOPMENT OF LAW

Oklahoma Supreme Court Rules Ten Commandments Monument on State Capitol Grounds Unconstitutional

---

In 2009 the Oklahoma legislature passed the Ten Commandments Monument Display Act, authorizing the State Capitol Preservation Commission to place on the state capitol grounds "a suitable monument displaying the Ten Commandments." A member of the state house of representatives donated such a monument, which was erected on capitol grounds in 2012. Shortly thereafter a group of citizens sought the removal of the monument on the ground that Article II, Section 5 of the state constitution forbids any use of public property for the benefit of religion. A district court rejected that claim and the plaintiffs appealed that decision to the state supreme court.

In June 2015, the Oklahoma Supreme Court, in *Prescott v. Oklahoma Capitol Preservation Commission,* 2015 WL 3982750 (Okla., 2015), reversed upon concluding that the "plain intent of Article 2, Section 5 is to ban State Government, its officials, and its subdivisions from using public money or property for the benefit of any religious purpose." That provision states:

> No public money or property shall ever be appropriated, applied, donated, or used, directly or indirectly, for the use, benefit, or support of any sect, church, denomination, or system of religion, or for the use, benefit, or support of any priest, preacher, minister, or other religious teacher or dignitary, or sectarian institution as such.

Besides emphasizing the plain language of that "broad and expansive" prohibition on governmental support of religion, the court rejected the claim that the placement of the monument had "a non-religious historic purpose," observing that "the Ten Commandments are obviously religious in nature and are an integral part of the Jewish and Christian faiths." Moreover, the court's *per curiam* opinion acknowledged that the U.S. Supreme Court, in *Van Orden v. Perry,* 545 U.S. 677 (2005) (excerpted in Vol. 2, Ch. 6), ruled that a similar Ten Commandments monument on Texas's state capitol grounds did not violate the First Amendment's (dis)establishment clause. However, it underscored that "the issue in the case at hand is whether the Oklahoma Ten Commandments monument violates the Oklahoma Constitution, *not whether it violates the Establishment Clause.* Our opinion rests solely on the Oklahoma Constitution with no regard for federal jurisprudence. See *Michigan v. Long,* 463 U.S. 1032 (1983)" (which is excerpted in Ch. 7, and ruled that state courts must make a "plain statement" that their decisions rest on "adequate and independent state grounds," when declining to follow the U.S. Supreme Court rulings).

In a concurring opinion, Chief Justice Reif emphasized the plain meaning of Article II, Section 5's text in discerning its intent, but also noted and compared the applicability of the court's ruling *Meyer v. Oklahoma City,* 496 P.2d 789 (Okla., 1972), holding that a fifty-foot Latin Cross on municipal fairgrounds did not violate the state constitution. In his view, *Meyer* differed because the fairgrounds, unlike that of the state capitol, were a "commercial setting" with a "distinctly secular environment." Furthermore, the Latin Cross merely conveyed a "symbolic message," whereas the Ten Commandments monument "explicitly 'display[ed]' and 'articulate[d]' ideas that directly pertain to the Judeo-Christian system of religion."

3

ECONOMIC RIGHTS AND AMERICAN CAPITALISM

Private property is not mentioned in the Constitution even though its protection was one of the central purposes of the Constitution. Sections 8 and 10 of Article I and Section 1 of Article IV govern various matters related to private property—taxes, duties, imposts, excises, commerce, bankruptcies, bills of credit, debts, the impairment of contracts, and the rights of authors and inventors. Yet private property did not receive specific protection until the ratification in 1791 of the Fifth Amendment. The due process and takings clauses of that amendment provide that "No person shall . . . be deprived of life, liberty, or property without due process of law; nor shall private property be taken for public use without just compensation."

Liberty and property were, nevertheless, closely tied together in the minds of the Framers of the Constitution. Property conditioned suffrage and was closely linked with representation (see Vol. 1, Chs. 5 and 8). When defending the Constitution in the *Federalist Papers*, Alexander Hamilton sought to show that it would provide security "to liberty and to property." Noah Webster, a prominent New York publisher, even more bluntly claimed "that *property* is the basis of *power*" when differentiating America from England and Europe, where property was concentrated in the hands of a few:

> [I]n America, and here alone, we have gone at once to the *founda-tion of liberty*, and raised the people to their true dignity. Let the lands be possessed by the people in fee-simple, let the fountain be kept pure, and the streams will be pure of course. Our jealousy of *trial by jury, the liberty of the press, &c.*, is totally groundless. Such rights are inseparably connected with the *power* and *dignity* of the

people, which rest on their *property*. They cannot be abridged. All *other* [free] nations have wrested *property* and *freedom* from *barons* and *tyrants; we* begin our empire with full possession of property and all its attending rights.[1]

The Framers took to heart the teaching of the English philosopher John Locke, in his *Second Treatise of Government*, that property is a natural right—a right preceding the establishment of government—and its preservation one of the chief ends of government. On Locke's labor theory of value, property was but an extension of liberty. "The *labour* that was mine, removing [objects] out of that common state [of nature] they were in, hath *fixed* my *Property* in them," argued Locke. "Thus the Grass my Horse has bit; the Turfs my Servant has cut; and the Ore I have digg'd in any place where I have a right to them in common with others, become my *Property*."[2] No less influential than Locke on the Framers was Sir William Blackstone, who also maintained in his *Commentaries on the Laws of England* that property was an "absolute right, inherent in every Englishman."[3]

Given this background and understanding of the fundamental nature of property, it is perhaps not surprising that the Supreme Court emerged within a generation of the ratification of the Constitution as a defender of property rights and economic liberty. Through an expansive interpretation of the contract clause in the early nineteenth century, and the creation of a "liberty of contract" in the latter part of that century, the Court laid the basis in constitutional law for the growth of American capitalism, and a source of limits and constraints on the exercise of national, state, and local government.

NOTES

1. Noah Webster, "An Examination into the Leading Principles of the Federal Constitution" (October 10, 1787), in *The Founders' Constitution*, Vol. 1, eds. Philip Kurland and Ralph Lerner (Chicago: University of Chicago Press, 1987), 596–597.

2. John Locke, "Second Treatise of Government" (1689), in *Two Treatises of Government*, ed. Peter Laslett (New York: Mentor Books, 1960), 330.

3. Sir William Blackstone, *Commentaries on the Laws of England* (1765–1769) (Chicago: University of Chicago Press, 1979).

SELECTED BIBLIOGRAPHY

Ely, James W. *The Guardian of Every Other Right: A Constitutional History of Property Rights.* New York: Oxford University Press, 1992.

Paul, Ellen F., and Dickman, Howard. *Liberty, Property, and the Future of Constitutional Development.* Albany: State University of New York Press, 1990.

A | *The Contract Clause and Vested Interests in Property*

Article I, Section 10, forbids the states from "impairing the Obligation of Contracts." That provision was ostensibly aimed at preventing the states from reneging on private contracts (such as loans made by banks) and passing laws favoring debtors, as was done in the 1780s in the aftermath of the Revolutionary War. As such, the guarantee presumably covered only private contracts. But in a series of rulings, the Marshall Court (1801–1836) broadly interpreted the contract clause to apply to public contracts (that is, contracts between a governmental agency and private individuals) and to safeguard vested interests in private property.

The famous "*Yazoo* case," *Fletcher v. Peck* (1810) (excerpted below), was the first important ruling of the Marshall Court in which the contract clause was turned into a guarantee for public contracts, in addition to a limitation on states' powers over private contracts. Notice that besides broadly construing the contract clause, Chief Justice Marshall notes that Georgia's law revoking its earlier land grants contravened "general principles, which are common to our free institutions, or by the particular provisions of the constitution of the United States." Chief Justice Marshall pushed his theory further two years later in *New Jersey v. Wilson*, 7 Cr. 164 (11 U.S.) (1812). New Jersey had made Indian lands tax-exempt, but when the land was sold to a non–Indian the state sought to tax the new owner. However, the Marshall Court ruled that the original contract with the Indians was still valid and the state could not tax the land. In one of the few cases involving private contracts, *Sturges v. Crowninshield*, 4 Wheat. (17 U.S.) 122 (1819), Chief Justice Marshall struck down a New York bankruptcy law as applied to a contract made before the law was passed. However, he found himself in the minority in *Ogden v. Sanders*, 12 Wheat. (25 U.S.) 213 (1827), when the Court upheld another bankruptcy law that had been enacted before a contested contract was made.

Next to *Fletcher v. Peck*, the second most important Marshall Court ruling on the contract clause is *Trustees of Dartmouth College v. Woodward* (1819) (see excerpt below). Again, the clause was expansively read to protect the vested interests in a corporate charter granted by the English Crown in 1769, prior to the Revolutionary War.

The Marshall Court's interpretation of the contract clause was controversial and was viewed as a severe limitation on states' regulatory powers. Yet it remained the dominant feature in the early development of constitutional law and the vehicle by which the power of judicial review was asserted and established. Indeed, the contract clause was used in almost 40 percent of the cases challenging state legislation before 1889, and the Court and lower federal courts used it to strike down some seventy-five state laws.[1]

The Court under Chief Justice Roger Taney (1836–1864) maintained respect for proprietary interests but was more deferential to the powers of states. In its leading ruling on the contract clause, *Charles River Bridge Co. v. Warren Bridge Co.* (1837) (see excerpt below), notice that Chief Justice Taney emphasizes that "[w]hile the rights of private property are sacredly guarded, we must not forget that the community also have rights, and that the happiness and well-being of every citizen depends on their faithful preservation." Taney thus established the principle that public contracts were to be strictly construed on the recognition that states have an important role in promoting the general welfare and technological advances in the public interest.

Despite the expansive interpretation given the contract clause in the early and mid-nineteenth century, its protection for proprietary interests did not override state police powers or the power of eminent domain (the government's taking of private property for public use without just compensation) (see Section C, in this chapter). Nor did it foreclose the possibility of state regulations aimed at promoting public morals, health, safety, and welfare. In *Stone v. Mississippi*, 101 U.S. 814 (1880), for instance, the Court unanimously upheld state police power over John Stone's claim of vested property rights. Stone had been granted by the Mississippi legislature a twenty-five-year franchise to sell lottery tickets, but two years later the state adopted a new constitution prohibiting the sale of lottery tickets. When Stone sought to evade prosecution for selling lottery tickets, the Court rejected his invocation of the contract clause, just as it did when state prohibition laws were attacked for infringing on contracts for the sale of beer,[2] and when employment contracts were superseded by workmen's compensation laws.[3] As Justice Mahlon Pitney, in *Atlantic Coastline Railroad Co. v. City of Goldsboro*, 232 U.S. 548 (1914), explained for a unanimous Court, when affirming that states may delegate to cities the power to regulate health, safety, and welfare:

> [I]t is settled that neither the "contract" clause nor the "due process" clause has the effect of overriding the power of the state to establish all regulations that are reasonably necessary to secure the health, safety, good order, comfort, or general welfare of the community; that this power can neither be abdicated nor bargained away, and is inalienable even by express grant; and that all contract and property rights are held subject to its fair exercise.

Justice Pitney expressed the modern view of the contract clause. *Home Building & Loan Association v. Blaisdell* (1934) (see excerpt below) illustrates how far the Court in the twentieth century moved away from its earlier application of the contract clause. There a bare majority of the Hughes Court upheld Minnesota's law, passed during the Great Depression, preventing the repossession of mortgaged property. The principle of judicial deference to legislative regulation of private contracts asserted in *Blaisdell* was reaffirmed in *City of El Paso v. Simmons* (1965) (see excerpt below). However, *United States Trust Co. of New York v. State of New Jersey*, 379 U.S. 479 (1977) indicates that the Court gives heightened scrutiny and greater weight to claims under the contract clause in controversies involving a state's impairment of its own contracts, in contrast with private contracts. More recently, in one of the rare contract clause cases granted review, the Roberts Court confronted the retroactive application of a change in state estate law. Minnesota enacted a statute that provides when a marriage is dissolved or annulled the designated beneficiary of an insurance policy made to a former spouse is revoked, and the proceeds go to a contingent beneficiary or to the policyholder's estate. A federal court found that the retroactive application of the law violated the contract clause but was reversed in *Sveen v. Melin,* 138 S.Ct. 1815 (2018), holding that not all retroactive applications of changes in state laws run afoul of the contract clause. Writing for the Court, Justice Kagan reaffirmed that there are two conditions for finding a violation: (1) does a law substantially impair an existing contractual relationship; and, if so, (2) whether it appropriately and reasonably advances a significant and legitimate governmental interest. Justice Gorsuch dissented.

Why did the Court's reliance on and enforcement of the contract clause decline in the late nineteenth and twentieth centuries? In historical perspective, a number of reasons. For one thing, the Industrial Revolution brought a growth in the number of corporations and economic problems that could not be accommodated even with a broad reading of the contract clause. Second, the Court developed its contract clause jurisprudence in the absence of congressional legislation. But in the late nineteenth century Congress responded to the social and economic pressures that accompanied industrialization and urbanization. Finally, as discussed below, the Court invented and enforced a "liberty of contract" under the Fourteenth Amendment's due process clause in defense of vested property rights against progressive economic legislation.

NOTES

1. Benjamin Wright, *The Contract Clause of the Constitution* (Cambridge, MA: Harvard University Press, 1938), 95.
2. See *Boston Beer Co. v. Massachusetts*, 97 U.S. 25 (1878).
3. *New York Central Railroad Co. v. White*, 243 U.S. 188 (1917).

SELECTED BIBLIOGRAPHY

Hobson, Charles. *The Great Yazoo Lands Sale*. Lawrence: University of Kansas, 2016.

Kutler, Stanley I. *Privilege and Creative Destruction: The Charles River Bridge Case*. 2nd ed. Baltimore, MD: Johns Hopkins University Press, 1990.

Magrath, C. Peter. *Yazoo: The Case of Fletcher v. Peck*. New York: W. W. Norton & Company, 1967.

Stites, Francis. *Private Interest and Public Gain: The Dartmouth College Case*. Amherst: University of Massachusetts, 1972.

Fletcher v. Peck

6 CR. (10 U.S.) 87 (1810)

Robert Fletcher sued John Peck for the breach of a covenant on land that Peck had sold him. The land was part of a larger land grant in 1795 of the Georgia legislature to four land-holding companies, which had bribed several members of the legislature to win passage of the land grant. The next year, however, the state enacted legislation declaring the 1795 law and all rights and claims to it null and void. Peck had acquired the land in 1800 and sold it three years later to Fletcher, at which time he claimed that all past sales of the land had been lawful. Fletcher, though, contended that because the original sale of the land had been declared invalid by the Georgia legislature, Peck could not legally sell the land and was guilty of breach of contract. A federal circuit court found in favor of Peck, and Fletcher appealed directly to the Supreme Court.

The Court's decision was 6–1, and the opinion was announced by Chief Justice Marshall. A separate opinion was delivered by Justice Johnson.

■ ■ ■

☐ *Chief Justice MARSHALL delivered the opinion of the Court.*

The suit was instituted on several covenants contained in a deed made by John Peck, the defendant in error, conveying to Robert Fletcher, the plaintiff in error, certain lands which were part of a large purchase made by

James Gunn and others, in the year 1795, from the state of Georgia, the contract for which was made in the form of a bill passed by the legislature of that state. . . .

Titles which, according to every legal test, are perfect, are acquired with that confidence which is inspired by the opinion that the purchaser is safe. If there be any concealed defect, arising from the conduct of those who had held the property long before he acquired it, of which he had no notice, that concealed defect cannot be set up against him. He has paid his money for a title good at law, he is innocent, whatever may be the guilt of others, and equity will not subject him to the penalties attached to that guilt. All titles would be insecure, and the intercourse between man and man would be very seriously obstructed, if this principle be overturned. . . .

If the legislature felt itself absolved from those rules of property which are common to all the citizens of the United States, and from those principles of equity which are acknowledged in all our courts, its act is to be supported by its power alone, and the same power may devest any other individual of his lands, if it shall be the will of the legislature so to exert it.

It is not intended to speak with disrespect of the legislature of Georgia, or of its acts. Far from it. The question is a general question and is treated as one. For although such powerful objections to a legislative grant, as are alleged against this, may not again exist, yet the principle, on which alone this rescinding act is to be supported, may be applied to every case to which it shall be the will of any legislature to apply it. The principle is this: that a legislature may, by its own act, devest the vested estate of any man whatever, for reasons which shall, by itself, be deemed sufficient. . . .

Is the power of the legislature competent to the annihilation of such title, and to a resumption of the property thus held?

The principle asserted is, that one legislature is competent to repeal any act which a former legislature was competent to pass; and that one legislature cannot abridge the powers of a succeeding legislature.

The correctness of this principle, so far as respects general legislation, can never be controverted. But, if an act be done under a law, a succeeding legislature cannot undo it. The past cannot be recalled by the most absolute power. Conveyances have been made; those conveyances have vested legal estates, and, if those estates may be seized by the sovereign authority, still, that they originally vested is a fact, and cannot cease to be a fact.

When, then, a law is in its nature a contract, when absolute rights have vested under that contract; a repeal of the law cannot devest those rights; and the act of annulling them, if legitimate, is rendered so by a power applicable to the case of every individual in the community. . . .

It is the peculiar province of the legislature to prescribe general rules for the government of society; the application of those rules to individuals in society would seem to be the duty of other departments. How far the power of giving the law may involve every other power, in cases where the constitution is silent, never has been, and perhaps never can be, definitely stated.

The validity of this rescinding act, then, might well be doubted, were Georgia a single sovereign power. But Georgia cannot be viewed as a single, unconnected, sovereign power, on whose legislature no other restrictions are imposed than may be found in its own constitution. She is a part of a large empire; she is a member of the American Union; and that Union has a constitution the supremacy of which all acknowledge, and which imposes limits to the legislatures of the several states, which none claim a right to pass. The constitution of the United States declares that no state shall pass any bill of attainder, ex post facto law or law impairing the obligation of contracts.

Does the case now under consideration come within this prohibitory section of the constitution?

In considering this very interesting question, we immediately ask ourselves what is a contract? Is a grant a contract?

A contract is a compact between two or more parties, and is either executory or executed. An executory contract is one in which a party binds himself to do, or not to do, a particular thing; such was the law under which the conveyance was made by the governor. A contract executed is one in which the object of contract is performed; and this, says Blackstone, differs in nothing from a grant. The contract between Georgia and the purchasers was executed by the grant. A contract executed, as well as one which is executory, contains obligations binding on the parties. A grant, in its own nature, amounts to an extinguishment of the right of the grantor, and implies a contract not to reassert that right. A party is, therefore, always estopped by his own grant.

Since, then, in fact, a grant is a contract executed, the obligation of which still continues, and since the constitution uses the general term contract, without distinguishing between those which are executory and those which are executed, it must be construed to comprehend the latter as well as the former. A law annulling conveyances between individuals, and declaring that the grantors should stand seized of their former estates, notwithstanding those grants, would be as repugnant to the constitution as a law discharging the vendors of property from the obligation of executing their contracts by conveyances. It would be strange if a contract to convey was secured by the constitution, while an absolute conveyance remained unprotected.

If, under a fair construction of the constitution, grants are comprehended under the term contracts, is a grant from the state excluded from the operation of the provision? Is the clause to be considered as inhibiting the state from impairing the obligation of contracts between two individuals, but as excluding from that inhibition contracts made with itself?

The words themselves contain no such distinction. They are general, and are applicable to contracts of every description. . . .

It is, then, the unanimous opinion of the court, that, in this case, the estate having passed into the hands of a purchaser for a valuable consideration, without notice, the state of Georgia was restrained, either by general principles, which are common to our free institutions, or by the particular provisions of the constitution of the United States, from passing a law whereby the estate of the plaintiff in the premises so purchased could be constitutionally and legally impaired and rendered null and void. . . .

Trustees of Dartmouth College v. Woodward
4 WHEAT. (17 U.S.) 518 (1819)

Dartmouth College was incorporated in 1769 under a charter granted by the English Crown, which authorized a twelve-member board of trustees to govern the college and to appoint their successors. The New Hampshire legislature, however, amended the charter in 1816 with legislation increasing the size of the board of trustees to twenty-one, establishing a board of overseers, and authorizing the governor to appoint new trustees and members of the board of overseers. The incumbent trustees refused to recognize the legislation as binding and sued William Woodward, the college's treasurer, to recover corporate property that was temporarily entrusted to him under the legislation. A trial court failed to resolve the question of the constitutionality of the legislation, but it was upheld by a state superior court. The trustees of Dartmouth College then appealed to the Supreme Court. As was the practice through most of the nineteenth century, they hired a member of the Supreme Court's bar, Daniel Webster, to argue their case. As was also the practice, attorneys for both sides were given unlimited time to present their arguments. Webster was one of the greatest orators and rather dramatically concluded his argument before the bench, observing,

> Sir, you may destroy this little institution. It is weak. It is in your hands! I know it is one of the lesser lights in the literary horizon of the country. You may put it out. But if you do so, you must carry through your work. You must extinguish, one after another, all those great lights of science which, for more than a century, have thrown their radiance over our land.

> It is, Sir, as I have said, a small college and yet, there are those who love it. . . .

> Sir, I care not how others may feel, but, for myself, when I see my Alma Mater surrounded, like Caesar in the senate-house, by those who are reiterating stab on stab, I would not, for this right hand, have her turn to me, and say *et tu quoque, mi fili!*

The Court's decision was 6–1; the opinion was announced by Chief Justice Marshall. Justices Washington and Story concurred, and Justice Duvall dissented.

■ ■ ■

☐ *Chief Justice MARSHALL delivered the opinion of the Court.*

It can require no argument to prove that the circumstances of this case constitute a contract. An application is made to the crown for a charter to incorporate a religious and literary institution. In the application, it is stated that large contributions have been made for the object, which will be conferred on the corporation as soon as it shall be created. The charter is granted, and on its faith the property is conveyed. Surely in this transaction every ingredient of a complete and legitimate contract is to be found.

The points for consideration are:

1. Is this contract protected by the constitution of the United States?

2. Is it impaired by the acts under which the defendant holds?

1. On the first point it . . . becomes, then, the duty of the court most seriously to examine this charter, and to ascertain its true character. . . .

From [a] review of the charter, it appears that Dartmouth College is an eleemosynary institution, incorporated for the purpose of perpetuating the application of the bounty of the donors, to the specified objects of that bounty; that its trustees or governors were originally named by the founder, and invested with the power of perpetuating themselves; that they are not public officers, nor is it a civil institution, participating in the administration of government; but a charity school, or a seminary of education, incorporated for the preservation of its property, and the perpetual application of that property to the objects of its creation.

Yet a question remains to be considered, of more real difficulty, on which more doubt has been entertained than on all that have been discussed. The founders of the college, at least those whose contributions were in money, have parted with the property bestowed upon it, and their representatives have no interest in that property. The donors of land are equally without interest, so long as the corporation shall exist. Could they be found, they are unaffected by any alteration in its constitution, and probably regardless of its form, or even of its existence. The students are fluctuating, and no individual among our youth has a vested interest in the institution, which can be asserted in a court of justice. Neither the founders of the college nor the youth for whose benefit it was founded, complain of the alteration made in its charter, or think themselves injured by it. The trustees alone complain, and the trustees have no beneficial interest to be protected. Can this be such a contract as the constitution intended to withdraw from the power of state legislation? Contracts, the parties to which have a vested beneficial interest, and those only, it has been said, are the objects about which the constitution is solicitous, and to which its protection is extended.

The court has bestowed on this argument the most deliberate consideration, and the result will be stated. Dr. Wheelock, acting for himself, and for those who, at his solicitation, had made contributions to his school, applied for this charter, as the instrument which should enable him, and them, to perpetuate their beneficent intention. It was granted. An artificial, immortal being, was created by the crown, capable of receiving and distributing forever, according to the will of the donors, the donations which should be made to it. On this being, the contributions which had been collected were immediately bestowed. These gifts were made, not, indeed, to make a profit

for the donors, or their posterity, but for something in their opinion of inestimable value; for something which they deemed a full equivalent for the
money with which it was purchased. The consideration for which they
stipulated, is the perpetual application of the fund to its object, in the mode
prescribed by themselves. Their descendants may take no interest in the
preservation of this consideration. But in this respect their descendants are
not their representatives. They are represented by the corporation. The corporation is the assignee of their rights, stands in their place, and distributes
their bounty, as they would themselves have distributed it, had they been
immortal. So with respect to the students who are to derive learning from
this source. The corporation is a trustee for them also. Their potential rights,
which, taken distributively, are imperceptible, amount collectively to a most
important interest. These are, in the aggregate, to be exercised, asserted and
protected, by the corporation. They were as completely out of the donors, at
the instant of their being vested in the corporation, and as incapable of being
asserted by the students, as at present. . . .

   This is plainly a contract to which the donors, the trustees, and the
crown (to whose rights and obligations New Hampshire succeeds), were the
original parties. It is a contract made on a valuable consideration. It is a
contract for the security and disposition of property. It is a contract, on the
faith of which real and personal estate has been conveyed to the corporation. It is then a contract within the letter of the constitution, and within
its spirit also, unless the fact that the property is invested by the donors in
trustees for the promotion of religion and education, for the benefit of
persons who are perpetually changing, though the objects remain the
same, shall create a particular exception, taking this case out of the prohibition contained in the constitution.

   It is more than possible that the preservation of rights of this description
was not particularly in the view of the framers of the constitution when the
clause under consideration was introduced into that instrument. It is probable that interferences of more frequent recurrence, to which the temptation
was stronger, and of which the mischief was more extensive, constituted the
great motive for imposing this restriction on the state legislatures. But
although a particular and a rare case may not, in itself, be of sufficient magnitude to induce a rule, yet it must be governed by the rule, when established unless some plain and strong reason for excluding it can be given. It is
not enough to say that this particular case was not in the mind of the convention when the article was framed, nor of the American people when it
was adopted. It is necessary to go farther, and to say that, had this particular
case been suggested, the language would have been so varied, as to exclude
it, or it would have been made a special exception. The case being within
the words of the rule, must be within its operation likewise, unless there be
something in the literal construction so obviously absurd, or mischievous,
or repugnant to the general spirit of the instrument, as to justify those who
expound the constitution in making it an exception.

   On what safe and intelligible ground can this exception stand? There is
no exception in the constitution, no sentiment delivered by its contemporaneous expounders, which would justify us in making it. In the absence of all
authority of this kind, is there, in the nature and reason of the case itself, that
which would sustain a construction of the constitution, not warranted by its

words? Are contracts of this description of a character to excite so little interest that we must exclude them from the provisions of the constitution, as being unworthy of the attention of those who framed the instrument? Or does public policy so imperiously demand their remaining exposed to legislative alteration, as to compel us, or rather permit us to say that these words, which were introduced to give stability to contracts, and which in their plain import comprehend this contract, must yet be so construed as to exclude it?

Almost all eleemosynary corporations, those which are created for the promotion of religion, of charity, or of education, are of the same character. The law of this case is the law of all. . . .

The opinion of the court, after mature deliberation, is, that this is a contract, the obligation of which cannot be impaired without violating the constitution of the United States. This opinion appears to us to be equally supported by reason, and by the former decisions of this court.

2. We next proceed to the inquiry whether its obligation has been impaired by those acts of the legislature of New Hampshire to which the special verdict refers.

From the review of this charter, which has been taken, it appears that the whole power of governing the college, of appointing and removing tutors, of fixing their salaries, of directing the course of study to be pursued by the students, and of filling up vacancies created in their own body, was vested in the trustees. On the part of the crown it was expressly stipulated that this corporation, thus constituted, should continue forever; and that the number of trustees should forever consist of twelve, and no more. By this contract the crown was bound, and could have made no violent alteration in its essential terms, without impairing its obligation. . . .

It has been already stated that the act "to amend the charter, and enlarge and improve the corporation of Dartmouth College," increases the number of trustees to twenty-one, gives the appointment of the additional members to the executive of the state, and creates a board of overseers, to consist of twenty-five persons, of whom twenty-one are also appointed by the executive of New Hampshire, who have power to inspect and control the most important acts of the trustees. . . .

The whole power of governing the college is transferred from trustees appointed according to the will of the founder, expressed in the charter, to the executive of New Hampshire. The management and application of the funds of this eleemosynary institution, which are placed by the donors in the hands of trustees named in the charter, and empowered to perpetuate themselves, are placed by this act under the control of the government of the state. The will of the state is substituted for the will of the donors in every essential operation of the college. This is not an immaterial change. The founders of the college contracted, not merely for the perpetual application of the funds which they gave, to the objects for which those funds were given; they contracted also to secure that application by the constitution of the corporation. They contracted for a system which should, as far as human foresight can provide, retain forever the government of the literary institution they had formed, in the hands of persons approved by themselves. This system is totally changed. The charter of 1769 exists no longer. It is reorganized; and reorganized in such a manner as to convert a literary institution, moulded according to the will of its founders, and placed under the control of private literary men, into a machine entirely subservient to the will of government. This may be for the advantage of this college in particular, and may be for the advantage of literature in general, but it is not according to the will of the donors, and is subversive of that contract, on the faith of which their property was given. . . .

It results from this opinion, that the acts of the legislature of New Hampshire, which are stated in the special verdict found in this cause, are repugnant to the constitution of the United States; and that the judgment on this special verdict ought to have been for the plaintiffs. The judgment of the State Court must therefore be reversed.

Charles River Bridge Co. v. Warren Bridge Co.

11 PET. (36 U.S.) 420 (1837)

In 1785, the Massachusetts legislature incorporated the Charles River Bridge Company and authorized it to build a toll bridge over the Charles River. The company was obligated to pay Harvard College £200 annually as compensation in lieu of its right to operate a ferry that had been granted the college in 1650. In 1792, the charter was extended for another seventy years. But in 1832 the legislature incorporated the Warren Bridge Company and authorized it to build a bridge for free public use just 275 yards away from the Charles River Bridge. That prompted the owners of the Charles River Bridge Company to seek an injunction against the construction of the Warren Bridge. The Massachusetts Supreme Judicial Court dismissed the complaint and Charles River Bridge Company appealed to the Supreme Court.

The Court's decision was 5–2, and the majority's opinion was announced by Chief Justice Taney. Justice McLean concurred. Dissent was by Justice Story, who was joined by Justice Thompson.

■ ■ ■

☐ *Chief Justice TANEY delivered the opinion of the Court.*

[On] what ground can the plaintiffs in error contend that the ferry rights of the college have been transferred to the proprietors of the bridge? If they have been thus transferred, it must be by some mode of transfer known to the law, and the evidence relied on to prove it can be pointed out in the record. How was it transferred? It is not suggested that there ever was in point of fact, a deed of conveyance executed by the college to the bridge company. Is there any evidence in the record from which such a conveyance may, upon legal principle, be presumed? The testimony before the court, so far from laying the foundation for such a presumption, repels it in the most positive terms. The petition to the Legislature in 1785, on which the charter was granted, does not suggest an assignment, nor any agreement or consent on the part of the college; and the petitioners do not appear to have regarded the wishes of that institution, as by any means necessary to insure their success. They place their application entirely on considerations of public interest and public convenience, and the superior advantages of a communication across Charles River by a bridge instead of a ferry. The Legislature, in granting the charter, show, by the language of the law, that they acted on the principles assumed by the petitioners. The preamble recites that the bridge "will be of great public utility"; and that is the only reason they assign for passing the law which incorporates this company. The validity of the charter is not made to depend on the consent of the college, nor of any assignment or surrender on their part; and the Legislature deal with the subject, as if it were one exclusively within their own power, and as if the ferry right were not to be transferred to the bridge company, but to be extinguished; and they appear to have acted on the principle that the State, by virtue of its sovereign powers and eminent domain, had a right to take away the franchise of the ferry; because in their judgment, the public interest and convenience would be better promoted by a bridge in the same place; and upon that principle they proceed to make a pecuniary compensation to the college for the franchise thus taken away. . . .

It does not, by any means, follow that because the legislative power in Massachusetts, in 1650, may have granted to a justly favored seminary of learning, the exclusive right of ferry between Boston and Charlestown, they would, in 1785, give the same extensive privilege to another corporation, who were about to erect a bridge in the same place. The fact that such a right was granted to the college cannot, by any sound rule of construction, be used to extend the privileges of the bridge company beyond what the words of the charter naturally and legally import. Increased population longer experienced in legislation, the different character of the corporations which owned the ferry from that which owned the bridge, might well have induced a change in the policy of the State in this respect; and as the franchise of the ferry and that of the bridge are different in their nature. . . .

[T]here is no rule of legal interpretation which would authorize the court to associate these grants together, and to infer that any privilege was intended to be given to the bridge company, merely because it had been conferred on the ferry. The charter to the bridge is a written instrument which must speak for itself, and be interpreted by its own terms.

This brings us to the Act of the Legislature of Massachusetts of 1785, by which the plaintiffs were incorporated by the name of "The Proprietors of the Charles River Bridge"; and it is here, and in the law of 1792, prolonging their charter, that we must look for the extent and nature of the franchise conferred upon the plaintiffs. . . .

"This, like many other cases, is a bargain between a company of adventurers and the public, the terms of which are expressed in the statute; and the rule of construction in all such cases, is now fully established to be this— that any ambiguity in the terms of the contract, must operate against the adventurers, and in favor of the public, and the plaintiffs can claim nothing that is not clearly given them by the act." And the doctrine thus laid down is abundantly sustained by the authorities referred to, in this decision. . . .

[T]he object and end of all government is to promote the happiness and prosperity of the community by which it is established, and it can never be assumed that the government intended to diminish its power of accomplishing the end for which it was created. And in a country like ours, free, active and enterprising, continually advancing in numbers and wealth; new channels of communication are daily found necessary, both for travel and trade, and are essential to the comfort, convenience, and prosperity of the people. A State ought never to be presumed to surrender this power, because, like the taxing power, the whole community have an interest in preserving it undiminished. And when a corporation alleges that a State has surrendered for seventy years its power of improvement and public accommodation, in a great and important line of travel, along which a vast number of its citizens must daily pass; the community have a right to insist, in the language of this court above quoted, "that its abandonment ought not to be presumed, in a case in which the deliberate purpose of the State to abandon it does not appear." The continued existence of a government would be of no great value, if by implications and presumptions, it was disarmed of the powers necessary to accomplish the ends of its creation, and the functions it was designed to perform, transferred to the hands of privileged corporations. The rule of construction announced by the court was not confined to the taxing power, nor is it so limited in the opinion delivered. On the contrary, it was distinctly placed on the ground that the interests of the community were concerned in preserving, undiminished, the power then in question; and whenever any power of the State is said to be surrendered or diminished, whether it be the taxing power or any other affecting the public interest, the same principle applies, and the rule of construction must be the same. No one will question that the interests of the great body of the people of the State, would, in this instance, be affected by the surrender of this great line of travel to a single corporation, with the right to exact toll, and exclude competition for seventy years. While the rights of private property are sacredly guarded, we must not forget that the community also have rights, and that the happiness and well being of every citizen depends on their faithful preservation.

Adopting the rule of construction above stated as the settled one, we proceed to apply it to the charter of 1785, to the proprietors of the Charles River Bridge. This act of incorporation is in the usual form, and the privileges such as are commonly given to corporations of that kind. It confers on them the ordinary faculties of a corporation, for the purpose of building the bridge; and establishes certain rates of toll, which the company are authorized to take. This is the whole grant. There is no exclusive privilege given to them over the waters of Charles River, above or below their bridge. No right to erect another bridge themselves, nor to prevent other persons from erecting one. No engagement from the State that another shall not be erected, and no undertaking not to sanction competition, nor to make improvements that may diminish the amount of its income. Upon all these subjects the charter is silent, and nothing is said in it about a line of travel, so much insisted on in the argument, in which they are to have exclusive privileges. No words are used from which an intention to grant any of these rights can be inferred. If the plaintiff is entitled to them, it must be implied simply from the nature of the grant, and cannot be inferred from the words by which the grant is made.

The relative position of the Warren Bridge has already been described. It does not interrupt the passage over the Charles River Bridge, nor make the way to it or from it less convenient. None of the faculties or franchises granted to that corporation have been revoked by the Legislature; and its right to take the tolls granted by the charter remains unaltered. In short, all the franchises and rights of property enumerated in the charter, and there mentioned to have been granted to it, remain unimpaired. But its income is destroyed by the Warren Bridge; which, being free, draws off the passengers and property which would have gone over it, and renders their franchise of no value. This is the gist of the complaint. For it is not pretended that the erection of the Warren Bridge would have done them any injury, or in any degree affected their right of property, if it had not diminished the amount of their tolls. In order, then, to entitle themselves to relief, it is necessary to show that the Legislature contracted not to do the act of which they complain; and that they impaired, or in other words violated, that contract, by the erection of the Warren Bridge.

The inquiry then is, does the charter contain such a contract on the part of the State? Is there any such stipulation to be found in that instrument? It must be admitted on all hands, that there is none—no words that even relate to another bridge, or to the diminution of their tolls, or to the line of travel. If a contract on that subject can be gathered from the charter, it must be by implication, and cannot be found in the words used. Can such an agreement be implied? The rule of construction before stated is an answer to the question. In charters of this description, no rights are taken from the public or given to the corporation, beyond those which the words of the charter, by their natural and proper construction, purport to convey. There are no words which import such a contract as the plaintiffs in error contend for, and none can be implied. . . .

Indeed, the practice and usage of almost every State in the Union, old enough to have commenced the work of internal improvement, is opposed to the doctrine contended for on the part of the plaintiffs in error. Turnpike roads have been made in succession, on the same line of travel; the latter ones interfering materially with the profits of the first. These corporations have, in some instances, been utterly ruined by the introduction of newer and better modes of transportation and traveling. In some cases railroads have rendered the turnpike roads on the same line of travel so entirely useless, that the franchise of the turnpike corporation is not worth preserving. Yet in none of these cases have the corporations supposed that their privileges were invaded, or any contract violated on the part of the State. . . .

If this court should establish the principles now contended for, what is to become of the numerous railroads established on the same line of travel with turnpike companies; and which have rendered the franchises of the turnpike corporations of no value? Let it once be understood that such charters carry with them these implied contracts, and give this unknown and undefined property in a line of traveling, and you will soon find the old turnpike corporations awakening from their sleep, and calling upon this court to put down the improvements which have taken their place. The millions of property which have been invested in railroads and canals, upon lines of travel which had been before occupied by turnpike corporations, will be put in jeopardy. We shall be thrown back to the improvements of the last century, and obliged to stand still until the claims of the old turnpike corporations shall be satisfied, and they shall consent to permit these States to avail themselves of the lights of modern science, and to partake of the benefit of those improvements which are now adding to the wealth and prosperity, and the convenience and comfort, of every other part of the civilized world. . . .

The judgment of the Supreme Judicial Court of the Commonwealth of Massachusetts, dismissing the plaintiffs' bill, must, therefore, be affirmed with costs.

☐ *Justice McLEAN concurred in a separate opinion, expressing his view that the case should be dismissed for lack of jurisdiction.*

☐ *Justice STORY, dissenting.*

I admit that where the terms of a grant are to impose burdens upon the public, or to create a restraint injurious to the public interest, there is sound reason for interpreting the terms, if ambiguous, in favor of the public. But at the same time, I insist that there is not the slightest reason for saying, even in such a case, that the grant is not to be construed favorably to the grantee, so as to secure him in the enjoyment of what is actually granted. . . .

This charter is not . . . any restriction upon the legislative power, unless it be true that because the Legislature cannot grant again what it has already granted, the legislative power is restricted. If so, then every grant of the public land is a restriction upon that power; a doctrine that has never yet been established, nor (as far as I know) ever contended for. Every grant of a franchise is, so far as that grant extends, necessarily exclusive; and cannot be resumed, or interfered with. All the learned judges in the State court admitted that the franchise of Charles River Bridge, whatever it be, could not be resumed or interfered with. The Legislature could not recall its grant or destroy it. It is a contract, whose obligation cannot be constitutionally impaired. In this respect, it does not differ from a grant of lands. In each case, the particular land, or the particular franchise, is withdrawn from the legislative operation. . . .

Then, again, how is it established that this is a grant in derogation of the rights and interests of the people? No individual citizen has any right to build a bridge over navigable waters; and consequently he is deprived of no right, when a grant is made to any other persons for that purpose. Whether it promotes or injures the particular interest of an individual citizen, constitutes no ground for judicial or legislative interference, beyond what his own rights justify. When, then, it is said that such a grant is in derogation of the rights and interests of the people, we must understand that reference is had to the rights and interests common to the whole people, as such (such as the right of navigation), or belonging to them as a political body; or, in other words, the rights and interests of the State. Now, I cannot understand how any grant of a franchise is a derogation from the rights of the people of the State, any more than a grant of public land. The right, in each case, is gone to the extent of the thing granted, and so far may be said to derogate from, that is to say, to lessen the rights of the people, or of the State. But that is not the sense in which the argument is pressed; for, by derogation, is here meant an injurious or mischievous detraction from the sovereign rights of the State. On the other hand, there can be no derogation from the rights of the people, as such, except it applies to rights common there before; which the building of a bridge over navigable waters certainly is not. If it had been said that the grant of this bridge was in derogation of the common right of navigating the Charles River, by reason of its obstructing, pro tanto, a free and open passage, the ground would have been intelligible. So, if it had been an exclusive grant of the navigation of that stream. But, if at the same time, equivalent public rights of a different nature, but of greater public accommodation and use, had been obtained; it could hardly have been said, in a correct sense, that there was any derogation from the rights of the people, or the rights of the State. It would be a mere exchange of one public right for another. . . .

No sound lawyer will, I presume, assert that the grant of a right to erect a bridge over a navigable stream, is a grant of a common right. Before such grant, had all the citizens of the State a right to erect bridges over navigable streams? Certainly they had not; and, therefore, the grant was no restriction of any common right. It was neither a monopoly, nor, in a legal sense, had it any tendency to a monopoly. It took from no citizen what he possessed before, and had no tendency to take it from him. It took, indeed, from the Legislature the power of granting the same identical privilege or franchise to any other persons. But this made it no more a monopoly than the grant of the public stock or funds of a State for a valuable consideration. Even in cases of monopolies, strictly so called, if the nature of the grant be such that it is for the public good, as in cases of patents for inventions, the rule has always been to give them a favorable construction in support of the patent. . . .

I have thus endeavored to answer, and I think I have successfully answered all the arguments (which indeed run into each other) adduced to justify a strict construction of the present charter. I go further, and maintain not only that it is not a case for strict construction, but that the charter upon its very face, by its terms, and for its professed objects, demands from the court, upon undeniable principles of law, a favorable construction for the grantees. In the first place, the Legislature has declared that the erecting of the bridge will be of great public utility; and this exposition of its own motives for the grant requires the court to give a liberal interpretation, in order to promote, and not to destroy an enterprise of great public utility. In the next place, the grant is a contract for a valuable consideration, and a full and adequate consideration. The proprietors are to lay out a large sum of money (and in those times it was a very large outlay of capital) in erecting a bridge; they are to keep it in repair during the whole period of forty years; they are to surrender it in good repair at the end of that period to the State, as its own property; they are to pay, during the whole period, an annuity of two hundred pounds to Harvard College; and they are to incur other heavy expenses and burdens, for the public accommodation. In return for all these charges, they are entitled to no more than the receipt of the tolls during the forty years, for their reimbursement of capital, interest and expenses. With all this they are to take upon themselves the chances of success; and if the enterprise fails, the loss is exclusively their own. Nor let any man imagine that there was not, at the time when this charter was granted, much solid ground for doubting success. In order to entertain a just view of this subject, we must go back to that period of general bankruptcy, and distress and difficulty. The Constitution of the United States was not only not then in existence, but it was not then even dreamed of. The union of the States was crumbling into ruins, under the old confederation. Agriculture, manufactures and commerce were at their lowest ebb. There was infinite danger to all the States from local interests and jealousies, and from the apparent impossibility of a much longer adherence to that shadow of a government the Continental Congress. And even four years afterwards, when every evil had been greatly aggravated, and civil war was added to other calamities, the Constitution of the United States was all but shipwrecked in passing through the State conventions. It was adopted by very slender majorities. These are historical facts which required no coloring to give them effect, and admitted of no concealment to seduce men into schemes of future aggrandizement. I would even now put it to the common sense of every man, whether, if the Constitution of the United States had not been adopted, the charter would have been worth a forty years' purchase of the tolls. . . .

Now, I put it to the common sense of every man, whether if at the moment of granting the charter the Legislature had said to the proprietors—you shall build the bridge; you shall bear the burdens; you shall be bound by the charges; and your sole reimbursement shall be from the tolls of forty years: and yet we will not even guaranty you any certainty of receiving any tolls. On the contrary, we reserve to ourselves the full power and authority to erect other bridges, toll or free bridges, according to our own free will and pleasure, contiguous to yours, and having the same termini with yours; and if you are successful we may thus supplant you, divide, destroy your profits, and annihilate your tolls, without annihilating your burdens: if, I say, such had been the language of the Legislature, is there a man living of ordinary discretion or prudence, who would have accepted such a charter upon such terms? I fearlessly answer no. . . .

Yet, this is the very form and pressure of the present case. It is not an imaginary and extravagant case. Warren Bridge has been erected, under such a supposed reserved authority, in the immediate neighborhood of Charles River Bridge; and with the same termini, to accommodate the same line of travel. For a half dozen years it was to be a toll bridge for the benefit of the proprietors, to reimburse them for their expenditures. At the end of that period, the bridge is to become the property of the State, and free of toll, unless the Legislature should hereafter impose one. In point of fact, it has since become, and now is, under the sanction of the act of incorporation, and other subsequent acts, a free bridge without the payment of any tolls for all persons. So that, in truth, here now is a free bridge, owned by and erected under the authority of the Commonwealth, which necessarily takes away all the tolls from Charles River Bridge, while its prolonged charter has twenty years to run. And yet the act of the Legislature establishing Warren Bridge is said to be no violation of the franchise granted to the Charles River Bridge. . . .

To sum up, then, the whole argument on this head, I maintain that, upon the principles of common reason and legal interpretation, the present grant carries with it a necessary implication that the Legislature shall do no act to destroy or essentially to impair the franchise: that (as one of the learned judges of the State court expressed it) there is an implied agreement that the State will not grant another bridge between Boston and Charlestown, so near as to draw away the custom from the old one: and (as another learned judge expressed it) that there is an implied agreement of the State to grant the undisturbed use of the bridge and its tolls, so far as respects any acts of its own, or of any persons acting under its authority. In other words, the State, impliedly, contracts not to resume its grant, or to do any act to the prejudice or destruction of its grant.

Home Building & Loan Association v. Blaisdell

290 U.S. 398, 54 S.Ct. 231 (1934)

In response to the social pressures arising from the economic depression in the early 1930s, Minnesota's legislature passed the Minnesota Moratorium Act of 1934. The law authorized state courts to postpone the payments of homeowners and farmers on mortgages to prevent their foreclosures. Under the act, John Blaisdell sought an extension of time on the payment of his mortgage to Home Building & Loan Association. But a trial court granted a motion to dismiss Blaisdell's petition. The Minnesota Supreme Court reversed and the trial court subsequently granted Blaisdell an extension of time on his mortgage payments. Home Building & Loan Association appealed, contending that Minnesota's moratorium law violated state and federal protections for private contracts and the taking of property without the due process of law.

The Court's decision was 5–4; the majority's opinion was announced by Chief Justice Hughes. Justice Sutherland dissented and was joined by Justices Van Devanter, McReynolds, and Butler.

■ ■ ■

☐ *Chief Justice HUGHES delivered the opinion of the Court.*

In determining whether the provision for this temporary and conditional relief exceeds the power of the state by reason of the clause in the Federal Constitution prohibiting impairment of the obligations of contracts, we must consider the relation of emergency to constitutional power, the historical setting of the contract clause, the development of the jurisprudence of this Court in the construction of that clause, and the principles of construction which we may consider to be established.

Emergency does not create power. Emergency does not increase granted power or remove or diminish the restrictions imposed upon power granted or reserved. The Constitution was adopted in a period of grave emergency. Its grants of power to the federal government and its limitations of the power of the States were determined in the light of emergency, and they are not altered by emergency. What power was thus granted and what limitations were thus imposed are questions which have always been, and always will be, the subject of close examination under our constitutional system.

While emergency does not create power, emergency may furnish the occasion for the exercise of power. . . . The constitutional question presented in the light of an emergency is whether the power possessed embraces the particular exercise of it in response to particular conditions. . . .

In the construction of the contract clause, the debates in the Constitutional Convention are of little aid. But the reasons which led to the adoption of that clause, and of the other prohibitions of section 10 of article 1, are not left in doubt, and have frequently been described with eloquent emphasis. The widespread distress following the revolutionary period and the plight of debtors had called forth in the States an ignoble array of legislative schemes for the defeat of creditors and the invasion of contractual obligations. Legislative interferences had been so numerous and extreme that the confidence essential to prosperous trade had been undermined and the utter destruction of credit was threatened. "The sober people of America" were convinced that some "thorough reform" was needed which would "inspire a general prudence and industry, and give a regular course to the business of society." *The Federalist*, No. 44. It was necessary to interpose the restraining power of a central authority in order to secure the foundations even of "private faith." The occasion and general purpose of the contract clause are summed up in the terse statement of Chief Justice MARSHALL in *Ogden v. Saunders*, 12 Wheat. 213 [1827]. "The power of changing the relative situation of debtor and creditor, of interfering with contracts, a power which comes home to every man, touches the interest of all, and controls the conduct of every individual in those things which he supposes to be proper for his own exclusive management, had been used to such an excess by the state legislatures, as to break in upon the ordinary intercourse of society, and destroy all confidence between man and man. This mischief had become so great, so alarming, as not only to impair commercial intercourse, and threaten the existence of credit, but to sap the morals of the people, and destroy the sanctity of private faith. To guard against the continuance of the evil, was an object of deep interest with all the truly wise, as well as the virtuous, of this great community, and was one of the important benefits expected from a reform of the government." . . .

The obligation of a contract is the law which binds the parties to perform their agreement. This Court has said that "the laws which subsist at the time and place of the making of a contract, and where it is to be performed, enter into and form a part of it, as if they were expressly referred to or incorporated in its terms." This principle embraces alike those which affect its validity, construction, discharge, and enforcement. . . .

Not only is the constitutional provision qualified by the measure of control which the state retains over remedial processes, but the state also continues to possess authority to safeguard the vital interests of its people. It does not matter that legislation appropriate to that end "has the result of modifying or abrogating contracts already in effect." Not only are existing laws read into contracts in order to fix obligations as between the parties, but the reservation of essential attributes of sovereign power is also read into contracts as a postulate of the legal order. The policy of protecting contracts against impairment presupposes the maintenance of a government by virtue of which contractual relations are worthwhile—a government which retains adequate authority to secure the peace and good order of society. This principle of harmonizing the constitutional prohibition with the necessary residuum of state power has had progressive recognition in the decisions of this Court. . . .

The question is not whether the legislative action affects contracts incidentally, or directly or indirectly, but whether the legislation is addressed to a legitimate end and the measures taken are reasonable and appropriate to that end. . . .

Undoubtedly, whatever is reserved of state power must be consistent with the fair intent of the constitutional limitation of that power. The

A "Hooverville," named after President Herbert Hoover, in New York City during the Great Depression. Hoover was president from 1928 to 1932, when he lost the presidential election to Democrat Franklin D. Roosevelt. The economic collapse that began in Hoover's first year as president led to the Great Depression. (*Bettmann/Corbis via Getty Images.*)

reserved power cannot be construed so as to destroy the limitation, nor is the limitation to be construed to destroy the reserved power in its essential aspects. They must be construed in harmony with each other. This principle precludes a construction which would permit the state to adopt as its policy the repudiation of debts or the destruction of contracts or the denial of means to enforce them. But it does not follow that conditions may not arise in which a temporary restraint of enforcement may be consistent with the spirit and purpose of the constitutional provision and thus be found to be within the range of the reserved power of the state to protect the vital interests of the community. It cannot be maintained that the constitutional prohibition should be so construed as to prevent limited and temporary interpositions with respect to the enforcement of contracts if made necessary by a great public calamity such as fire, flood, or earthquake. . . .

Where, in earlier days, it was thought that only the concerns of individuals or of classes were involved, and that those of the state itself were touched only remotely, it has later been found that the fundamental interests of the state are directly affected; and that the question is no longer merely that of one party to a contract as against another, but of the use of reasonable means to safeguard the economic structure upon which the good of all depends.

It is no answer to say that this public need was not apprehended a century ago, or to insist that what the provision of the Constitution meant to the vision of that day it must mean to the vision of our time. If by the statement that what the Constitution meant at the time of its adoption it means today, it is intended to say that the great clauses of the Constitution must be confined to the interpretation which the framers, with the conditions and outlook of their time, would have placed upon them, the statement carries its own refutation. It was to guard against such a narrow conception that Chief Justice MARSHALL uttered the memorable warning: "We must never forget, that it is *a constitution* we are expounding . . . a constitution intended to endure for ages to come, and, consequently, to be adapted to the various *crises* of human affairs." . . . (*McCulloch v. Maryland*, 4 Wheat. 316 [1819]) When we are dealing with the words of the Constitution, said this Court in *Missouri v. Holland*, 252 U.S. 416 [1920], "we must realize that they have called into life a being the development of which could not have been foreseen completely by the most gifted of its begetters. . . . The case before us must be considered in the light of our whole experience and not merely in that of what was said a hundred years ago."

Nor is it helpful to attempt to draw a fine distinction between the intended meaning of the words of the Constitution and their intended application. When we consider the contract clause and the decisions which have expounded it in harmony with the essential reserved power of the states to protect the security of their peoples, we find no warrant for the conclusion that the clause has been warped by these decisions from its proper significance or that the founders of our government would have interpreted the clause differently had they had occasion to assume that responsibility in the conditions of the later day. The vast body of law which has been developed was unknown to the fathers, but it is believed to have preserved the essential content and the spirit of the Constitution. With a growing recognition of public needs and the relation of individual right to public security, the court has sought to prevent the perversion of the clause through its use as an instrument to throttle the capacity of the states to protect their fundamental interests. This development is a growth from the seeds which the fathers planted. It is a development forecast by the prophetic words of Justice JOHNSON in *Ogden v. Saunders*, already quoted. And the germs of the later decisions are found in the early cases of the *Charles River Bridge* [11 Pet. 420 (1837)] and the *West River Bridge* [*Co. v. Dix*, 6 How. (47 U.S.) 506 (1848)], which upheld the public right against strong insistence upon the contract clause. The principle of this development is, as we have seen, that the reservation of the reasonable exercise of the protective power of the state is read into all contracts, and there is no greater reason for refusing to apply this principle to Minnesota mortgages. . . .

Applying the criteria established by our decisions, we conclude:

1. An emergency existed in Minnesota which furnished a proper occasion for the exercise of the reserved power of the state to protect the vital interests of the community. The declarations of the existence of this emergency by the Legislature and by the Supreme Court of Minnesota cannot be regarded as a subterfuge or as lacking in adequate basis. . . .

2. The legislation was addressed to a legitimate end; that is, the legislation was not for the mere advantage of particular individuals but for the protection of a basic interest of society.

3. In view of the nature of the contracts in question—mortgages of unquestionable validity—the relief afforded and justified by the emergency, in order not to contravene the constitutional provision, could only be of a character appropriate to that emergency, and could be granted only upon reasonable conditions.

4. The conditions upon which the period of redemption is extended do not appear to be unreasonable. . . .

5. The legislation is temporary in operation. It is limited to the exigency which called it forth. While the postponement of the period of redemption from the foreclosure sale is to May 1, 1935, that period may be reduced by the order of the court under the statute, in case of a change in circumstances, and the operation of the statute itself could not validly outlast the emergency or be so extended as virtually to destroy the contracts.

We are of the opinion that the Minnesota statute as here applied does not violate the contract clause of the Federal Constitution. Whether the legislation is wise or unwise as a matter of policy is a question with which we are not concerned.

☐ *Justice SUTHERLAND dissenting, joined by Justices VAN DEVANTER, McREYNOLDS, and BUTLER.*

Few questions of greater moment than that just decided have been submitted for judicial inquiry during this generation. He simply closes his eyes to the necessary implications of the decision who fails to see in it the potentiality of future gradual but ever-advancing encroachments upon the sanctity of private and public contracts. . . .

A provision of the Constitution, it is hardly necessary to say, does not admit of two distinctly opposite interpretations. It does not mean one thing at one time and an entirely different thing at another time. If the contract impairment clause, when framed and adopted, meant that the terms of a contract for the payment of money could not be altered *in invitum* by a state statute enacted for the relief of hardly pressed debtors to the end and with the effect of postponing payment or enforcement during and because of an economic or financial emergency, it is but to state the obvious to say that it means the same now. . . .

[W]e are here dealing, not with a power granted by the Federal Constitution, but with the state police power, which exists in its own right. Hence the question is, not whether an emergency furnishes the occasion for the exercise of that state power, but whether an emergency furnishes an occasion for the relaxation of the restrictions upon the power imposed by the contract impairment clause; and the difficulty is that the contract impairment clause forbids state action under any circumstances, if it have the effect of impairing the obligation of contracts. That clause restricts every state power in the particular specified, no matter what may be the occasion. It does not contemplate that an emergency shall furnish an occasion for softening the restriction or making it any the less a restriction upon state action in that contingency than it is under strictly normal conditions.

The Minnesota statute either impairs the obligation of contracts or it does not. If it does not, the occasion to which it relates becomes immaterial, since then the passage of the statute is the exercise of a normal, unrestricted, state power and requires no special occasion to render it effective. If it does, the emergency no more furnishes a proper occasion for its exercise than if the emergency were nonexistent. And so, while, in form, the suggested distinction seems to put us forward in a straight line, in reality it simply carries us back in a circle, like bewildered travelers lost in a wood, to the point where we parted company with the view of the state court.

If what has now been said is sound, as I think it is, we come to what really is the vital question in the case: Does the Minnesota statute constitute an impairment of the obligation of the contract now under review? . . .

It is quite true . . . that "the reservation of essential attributes of sovereign power is also read into contracts"; and that the Legislature cannot "bargain away the public health or the public morals." General statutes to put an end to lotteries, the sale or manufacture of intoxicating liquors, the maintenance of nuisances, to protect the public safety, etc., although they have the indirect effect of absolutely destroying private contracts previously made in contemplation of a continuance of the state of affairs then in existence but subsequently prohibited, have been uniformly upheld as not violating the contract impairment clause. The distinction between legislation of that character and the Minnesota statute, however, is readily observable. . . .

[T]he statute denies appellant for a period of two years the ownership and possession of the property—an asset which, in any event, is of substantial character, and which possibly may turn out to be of great value. The statute, therefore, is not merely a modification of the remedy; it effects a material and injurious change in the obligation.

B | *The Development and Demise of a "Liberty of Contract"*

Ratification of the Fourteenth Amendment in 1868 provided the Supreme Court with a new basis for protecting economic rights. The amendment overturned the Taney Court's ruling in *Dred Scott v. Sandford*, 60 U.S. 393 (1857) (see Ch. 12), that blacks were not citizens of the United States. Section 1 of the amendment aimed at ensuring that states would not deny blacks their citizenship by providing that "[n]o State shall make or enforce any law which shall abridge the privileges or immunities of citizens of the United States; nor shall any State deprive any person of life, liberty, or property, without due process of law; nor deny to any person within its jurisdiction the equal protection of the laws." The drafters of the amendment in the Thirty-ninth Congress thought that the privileges or immunities clause was the most important guarantee, because it expressly prohibited states from denying the privileges and immunities of being a citizen of the United States. Its importance is underscored by its almost literal repetition of the privileges and immunities clause of Article IV, Section 2, which provides that "[t]he Citizens of each State shall be entitled to all Privileges and Immunities of Citizens in the several States."

What counted among the privileges and immunities, however, was far from certain. In *Dred Scott*, Chief Justice Taney construed Article IV to protect only the privileges and immunities of citizens of states who were also citizens of the United States and who were temporarily in a state other than their own. The Fourteenth Amendment overturned this interpretation by extending citizenship to blacks, but offered no further clarification.

An obvious, although narrow, view is that the privileges or immunities clause simply forbids states from discriminating against citizens of other states.[1] Yet during the House and Senate debates on the amendment's adoption a frequently cited opinion was that of Justice Bushrod Washington. While sitting on a circuit court, he had interpreted the privileges and immunities clause in *Corfield v. Coryell*, 6 Fed. Cases 3230 (1825), upholding a New Jersey statute prohibiting nonresidents from gathering oysters in the state. Gathering oysters was not among the privileges and immunities of citizenship, but Washington added that citizens were guaranteed those rights "which are, in their nature, fundamental; which belong of right, to the citizens of all free governments." He listed (notably without mentioning the Bill of Rights) a rather wide-ranging set of fundamental rights; among others, he included the right to possess property, to travel from one state to another, to be protected by the government, to be exempt from higher taxes than paid by other citizens, and the right to bring suits in courts of law.

Whatever potential the Fourteenth Amendment's privileges or immunities clause had was soon dashed in *Butchers' Benevolent Association v. Crescent City Livestock Landing & Slaughterhouse Co.* (1873) (*The Slaughterhouse Cases*) (see excerpt below). When upholding a Louisiana law that created a monopoly on the operation of slaughterhouses, Justice Samuel Miller construed citizenship in the states and the United States to be distinct and separate and the Fourteenth Amendment to apply only to national citizenship. The independent butchers who opposed the legislative creation of a monopoly thus could not claim protection under the Fourteenth Amendment.

Four dissenters in *The Slaughterhouse Cases* disagreed. Justice Stephen Field rejected the majority's notion of dual citizenship, while Justice Joseph Bradley contended that the butchers had a right to practice their profession under the due process clauses of the Fifth and

Fourteenth Amendments. Bradley was the only one to accept the interpretation of the amendment advanced by the butchers' attorney, John Campbell, a former member of the Court who resigned when his state seceded from the Union.

Campbell had argued that the Fourteenth Amendment had a grander purpose than just guaranteeing the rights of former slaves. Its due process clause guaranteed individual freedom, free enterprise, and laissez-faire individualism. His argument was an invitation for the Court to interpret the due process clause as something more than a mere procedural guarantee. Although Campbell failed to carry the day, his argument proved prophetic of what would come.

Due process was generally understood to mean "the law of the land," but the law of the land and due process were on the brink of transformation. The due process clauses of the Fifth and Fourteenth Amendments were rooted in the English common law, running back to the Magna Carta of 1215. The Magna Carta granted that "[n]o free-man shall be arrested, or imprisoned, or disseized, or outlawed, or exiled, or in any way molested; nor will [the Crown] proceed against him, unless by lawful judgment of his peers or by the law of the land." That guarantee was reaffirmed and reformed in the Petition of Right in 1628, which specified that freemen could "be imprisoned or detained only by the law of the land, or by due process of law, and not by the King's special command without any charge." Later, colonial charters and state constitutions incorporated this provision as well.

The Court's first opportunity to interpret the Fifth Amendment's due process clause had come in 1856. *Murray's Lessee v. Hoboken Land & Improvement Company*, 18 How. (59 U.S.) 272 (1856), upheld a congressional statute authorizing the Treasury Department to issue administrative warrants (without prior judicial approval) for the property of revenue collectors found to be indebted to the United States. The Taney Court rejected the claim that this amounted to the taking of property without due process because it found no conflict between this procedure and any guarantee of the Bill of Rights or settled common-law practices.

The following year in *Dred Scott*, Chief Justice Taney relied in part on the Fifth Amendment's due process clause when upholding slave owners' proprietary interests in slaves. Taney thereby suggested that the due process of law included substantive rights as well as procedural guarantees. Moreover, state courts were beginning to acknowledge protection for property rights and economic liberties as a matter of due process of law. In *Wynehamer v. New York*, 13 N.Y. 378 (1856), New York's highest court struck down a law prohibiting the possession of liquor as a denial of due process of law.[2]

Campbell's due process argument and Justice Bradley's dissent in *The Slaughterhouse Cases* were thus early manifestations of the legal movement toward extending greater protection to economic liberties under constitutional guarantees other than that of the contract clause. In 1870, the Legal Tender Act of 1862 was invalidated, partially on the grounds that it deprived creditors of property without the due process of law, in *Hepburn v. Griswold*, 8 Wall. 603 (1870). Five years later, in *Loan Association v. Topeka*, 20 Wall. (87 U.S.) 655 (1875), a Kansas tax designed to help local industries was overturned, in Justice Miller's words, as an "unauthorized invasion of [the] private right [of property which grows] . . . out of the essential nature of free government."

By 1877, the Court under Chief Justice Morrison Waite (1874–1888) was prepared to acknowledge the due process clause's *substantive* protection for economic liberty. Although upholding Illinois's law regulating grain elevators as "clothed with the public interest" in *Munn v. Illinois* (1877) (see excerpt below), Waite conceded that economic legislation might constitute the taking of property without due process of law. And while he cautioned that "[f]or protection against abuses by legislatures, the people must resort to the polls, not to the courts," *Munn* signaled that the Court might be persuaded to supervise legislation regulating economic activities. In any event, the Court faced a growing stream of litigation attacking legislation on due process grounds. In *Davidson v. New Orleans*, 96 U.S. 97 (1878), Justice Miller was thus moved to complain that

> the docket of this court is crowded with cases in which we are asked to hold that State courts and State legislatures have deprived their own citizens of life, liberty, or property without due process of law. There is here abundant evidence that there exists some strange misconception of the scope of this provision as found in the Fourteenth Amendment. In fact, it would seem, from the character of many of the cases before us, and the arguments made in them, that the clause under consideration is looked upon as means of bringing to the test of the decision of this court the abstract opinions of every unsuccessful litigant in a State court of justice of the decision against him, and of the merits of the legislation on which such a decision may be founded.

"The great tides and currents which engulf the rest of men," as Justice Benjamin Cardozo observed, "do not turn aside in their course, and pass the judges by."[3] The country's economic expansion in the late nineteenth century was reinforced by the intellectual currents of Conservative Social Darwinism—the philosophy of the survival of the fittest as applied to social and economic relations and perpetuating the myth of rugged individualism and laissez-faire capitalism.

Cartoon depicting the Supreme Court's backlog of cases in 1883 due to the growing amount of litigation challenging government regulations. (*Puck Magazine*/*Library of Congress.*)

The Court was gradually infused with this philosophy of laissez-faire capitalism, as its composition changed between 1877 and 1890 with the elevation of corporate lawyers to the ranks of justices.[4] And its assumption of the guardianship of economic liberty manifested itself in various ways. Notably, in an otherwise uninteresting tax case, *Santa Clara County v. Southern Pacific Railroad Company*, 118 U.S. 394 (1886), corporations were proclaimed to be "legal persons" entitled to full protection of the Fourteenth Amendment. Chief Justice Waite evidently thought this was so self-evident that he did not bother to emphasize it in his opinion, and the reporter of the Court's decisions decided on his own initiative that it merited special note in the headnotes accompanying the Court's opinion. The significance of that ruling, of course, was not lost on lawyers for railroads, corporations, and other businesses attacking government regulations.

Ten years after *Santa Clara County*, the Court explicitly held that the Fourteenth Amendment's due process clause protects a substantive, but unenumerated, "liberty of contract." *Allgeyer v. Louisiana*, 165 U.S. 578 (1897), invalidated a Louisiana law restricting the issuance of insurance policies and imposing a $1,000 fine on anyone having an illegal policy. Allgeyer & Company had a maritime insurance policy with a New York insurance firm in violation of Louisiana's law and appealed a ruling of that state's supreme court upholding the law and a fine on Allgeyer. When striking down the law, Justice Rufus Peckham boldly announced the doctrine of a liberty of contract:

> The "liberty" mentioned in [the Fourteenth] Amendment means not only the right of the citizen to be free from the mere physical restraint of his person, as by incarceration, but the term is deemed to embrace the right of the citizen to be free in the enjoyment of all his faculties; to be free to use them in all lawful ways; to live and work where he will; to earn his livelihood by any lawful calling; to pursue any livelihood or avocation, and for that purpose to enter into all contracts which may be proper, necessary and essential to his carrying out to a successful conclusion the purposes above mentioned.

Allgeyer ushered in what became known as the *Lochner* era of substantive due process economic protectionism, after one of the most notorious rulings on the liberty of contract, *Lochner v. New York* (1905) (see excerpt below). There, speaking for a bare majority, Justice Peckham struck down New York's labor law limiting the number of hours bakers could work as an interference with their liberty of contract. And in one of his most famous dissenting opinions, Justice Oliver Wendell Holmes sharply criticized his brethren for reading their own conservative economic philosophy into the Constitution. Under the guise of a liberty of contract and its substantive due process analysis, Holmes charged, the Court had become a superlegislature in overseeing economic regulations.

Justice Holmes's dissent brought the insights of "American legal realism" to bear on the majority's ruling in *Lochner* and embodies the principal liberal and progressive criticism of the *Lochner* era: the majority in *Lochner* was making rather than interpreting the law, and through its creation and enforcement of an unenumerated "liberty of contract" imposed its own conservative economic philosophy on the country. But note that the other dissenting opinion filed in *Lochner* by Justice Harlan, and joined by Justices White and Day, represents a rival interpretation of the ruling in and the era associated with *Lochner*. Justice Harlan considered the liberty of contract a vital constitutional guarantee, rooted in the Reconstruction Amendments and the antislavery movement's emphasis on self-ownership. That liberty, though, as Harlan reminded his colleagues, remained subject to legislation aimed at promoting public health, safety, and general welfare. The majority in *Lochner*, on Harlan's view, mistakenly construed New York's law as a protectionist measure for bakery workers, rather than as a legitimate piece of health and safety legislation promoting the general welfare. That is why Justice Harlan marshaled empirical studies showing that working long hours in bakeries may indeed be injurious to workers' health. In other words, the majority in *Lochner* failed to see how New York's law promoted the general welfare and got carried away with its stand against protectionist legislation favoring one occupation or group over another.[5]

Lochner and the era that it represents, in sum, invites two rival interpretations. On the Holmesian view, *Lochner* represents the Court's purblind imposition of a laissez-faire economic philosophy against the growing forces of economic progressives. Alternatively, the *Lochner* era was a time of great class conflict and political struggles during which the Court tried to draw (not always successfully) a principled distinction between, on the one hand, legitimate economic legislation promoting health, safety, and the general welfare; and, on the other hand, economic legislation that was invalid because it was deemed to advance the special interests of particular groups or classes.

For four decades (from 1897 to 1937) the philosophy of laissez-faire capitalism and defensive stand against special interests' protective economic legislation held sway with a majority of the Court under Chief Justices Waite, Melville Fuller (1888–1910), Edward White (1910–1921), William Howard Taft (1921–1930), and Charles Evans Hughes (1930–1941). Never before or since were economic regulations more severely scrutinized. Close to 200 state and federal laws were overturned during the *Lochner* era.

The Court did not strike down all legislation, however, as Justice Harlan's dissent in *Lochner* emphasized. Where legislation sought to enforce health, safety, or moral standards with little or no impact on economic liberty, the Court deferred to the states and Congress. In *Mugler v. Kansas*, 123 U.S. 623 (1887), for instance, when sustaining a state prohibition law, Justice John Harlan explained that

> [t]here is no justification for holding that the State, under the guise merely of police regulation, is here aiming to deprive the citizen of his constitutional rights; for we cannot shut out of view the fact, within the knowledge of all, that the public health, the public morals, and the public safety, may be endangered by the general use of intoxicating drinks; nor the fact, established by statistics accessible to everyone, that the idleness, disorder, pauperism, and crime existing in the country are, in some degree at least, traceable to this evil.

But Harlan also cautioned that not every law enacted for the promotion of public welfare would survive or

> be accepted as a legitimate exertion of the police powers of the State. There are, of necessity, limits beyond which legislation cannot rightfully go. . . . The courts are not bound by mere forms,

nor are they to be misled by mere pretenses. They are at liberty—indeed, are under a solemn duty—to look at the substance of things, whenever they enter upon the inquiry whether the legislature has transcended the limits of its authority. If, therefore, a statute purporting to have been enacted to protect the public health, the public morals, or the public safety, has no real or substantial relation to those objects, or is a palpable invasion of rights secured by the fundamental law, it is the duty of the courts to so adjudge, and thereby give effect to the Constitution.

On this reasoning, the Court also upheld federal laws prohibiting the sale of liquor[6] and state laws banning sales and advertisements for cigarettes,[7] as well as zoning and land-use laws.[8]

The extent to which the Court was predisposed to defer to states when regulations had no direct economic impact is underscored in two further rulings during the *Lochner* era. In *Jacobson v. Massachusetts*, 197 U.S. 11 (1905), the Court refused to question the basis for a state law requiring smallpox vaccinations. In Justice Harlan's words:

> We must assume that when the statute in question was passed, the legislature of Massachusetts was not unaware of . . . opposing theories [of the effectiveness of vaccinations], and was compelled, of necessity, to choose between them. It was not compelled to commit a matter involving the public health and safety to the final decision of a court or jury. It is no part of the function of a court or a jury to determine which one of two modes was likely to be the most effective for the protection of the public against disease. That was for the legislative department to determine in the light of all the information it had or could obtain.

Nor was the Court inclined to scrutinize the basis for Virginia's law, passed in response to the eugenics movement, requiring the sterilization of those who were mentally defective or afflicted with epilepsy. It affirmed the compulsory sterilization of Carrie Buck, a seventeen-year-old, "feebleminded" female in a state mental institution, whose mother had also been an inmate and who had already given birth to a mentally defective child. Justice Holmes's opinion for the Court revealed not only his deference to legislatures but his acceptance of the tooth and claw of Social Darwinism. In *Buck v. Bell*, 274 U.S. 200 (1927) (excerpted in Ch. 11), he observed that

> [w]e have seen more than once that the public welfare may call upon the best citizens for their lives. It would be strange if it could not call upon those who already sap the strength of the State for these lesser sacrifices, often not felt to be such by those concerned, in order to prevent our being swamped with incompetence. It is better for all the world, if instead of waiting to execute degenerate

offspring for crime, or to let them starve for the imbecility, society can prevent those who are manifestly unfit from continuing their kind. The principle that sustains compulsory vaccination is broad enough to cover cutting the Fallopian tubes. . . . Three generations of imbeciles are enough.

When legislation aimed at promoting health, safety, or welfare *and* directly affected economic activities, the Court did not automatically strike it down. But the Court had to be convinced of the reasonableness of the regulations. In *Holden v. Hardy*, 169 U.S. 366 (1898), with only Justices Peckham and David Brewer dissenting, the Court upheld Utah's law limiting the number of hours in a day miners could work in mines and smelters to eight.

In *Muller v. Oregon* (1908) (excerpted below), the Court unanimously approved a state law limiting the workday for women in industries to ten hours per day. There the Court was persuaded by what became known as "the Brandeis brief." When defending Oregon's law, the progressive and highly regarded labor lawyer, Louis Brandeis, filed an extraordinary brief, containing only two pages of legal argument and more than a hundred pages of statistics and social science studies showing how long hours of labor endangered the health of women and thus the reasonableness of the state's law.[9] (Notably, after Brandeis was named to the Court in 1916, he never cited social science materials when writing an opinion for the Court upholding state legislation. Instead, he only cited these materials when writing dissenting opinions, criticizing the majority for overturning state laws and showing the reasonableness of the legislation.)

Although upholding state regulations in cases like *Muller* and *Bunting v. Oregon*, 243 U.S. 426 (1917), sustaining a labor law limiting workdays to ten hours a day for men and women, the Court's prevailing practice was nevertheless to strike down economic regulations. The problem for the Court and the country was that while the development of the doctrine of a liberty of contract may have been in response, in Holmes's classic phrase, "to the felt necessities of the time," it ran against the political currents of the early twentieth century. Reform Social Darwinism had replaced Conservative Social Darwinism in teaching that humans not only adapt to the environment but may change it as well.[10] Under pressure from reformers, labor unions, and the progressive movement, legislatures were passing new laws in response to the plight of workers in sweatshops, child labor, and generally dismal working conditions as depicted in novels by Upton Sinclair. The justices were no longer in tune with the times. The Court and the country were on a collision course in constitutional politics.

In *Adair v. United States*, 208 U.S. 161 (1908), for example, the Court, with only Justices Holmes and McKenna dissenting, struck down a section of a congressional labor-relations law banning yellow-dog contracts—contracts signed by workers promising they would not join labor unions—and forbidding the firing of employees who belonged to unions. When approving of Adair's firing of O. B. Coppage from the Louisville & Nashville Railroad Company because he was a union member, Justice Harlan disabused any thought of abandoning the liberty of contract:

> While . . . the right of liberty and property guaranteed by the Constitution against deprivation without due process of law is subject to such reasonable restraints as the common good or the general welfare may require, it is not within the functions of government—at least, in the absence of contract between the parties—to compel any person, in the course of his business and against his will, to accept or retain the personal services of another, or to compel any person, against his will, to perform personal services for another. The right of a person to sell his labor upon such terms as he deems proper is, in its essence, the same as the right of the purchaser of labor to prescribe the conditions upon which he will accept such labor from the person offering to sell it. So the right of the employee to quit the service of the employer, for whatever reason, is the same as the right of the employer, for whatever reason, to dispense with the services of such employee. It was the legal right of the defendant Adair—however unwise such a course might have been—to discharge Coppage because of his being a member of a labor organization, as it was the legal right of Coppage, if he saw fit to do so—however unwise such a course on his part might have been—to quit the service in which he was engaged, because the defendant employed some persons who were not members of a labor organization. In all such particulars the employer and the employee have equality of right, and any legislation that disturbs that equality is an arbitrary interference with the liberty of contract which no government can legally justify in a free land.

In *Coppage v. Kansas*, 236 U.S. 1 (1915), with Justices Holmes, Rufus Day, and Charles Evans Hughes dissenting, the Court struck down a state law outlawing yellow-dog contracts. The Kansas state supreme court had upheld the law and the conviction of T. B. Coppage for firing a switchman for the St. Louis & San Francisco Railway Company because the employee refused to give up his union membership. In another vintage expression of the doctrine of a liberty of contract, Justice Mahlon Pitney explained that

> it is said by the Kansas supreme court to be a matter of common knowledge that "employees, as a rule, are not financially able to be

as independent in making contracts for the sale of their labor as are employers in making a contract of purchase thereof." No doubt; wherever the right of private property exists, there must and will be inequalities of fortune; and thus it naturally happens that parties negotiating about a contract are not equally unhampered by circumstances. This applies to all contracts, and not merely to that between employer and employee. Indeed, a little reflection will show that wherever the right of private property and the right of a free contract coexist, each party when contracting is inevitably more or less influenced by the question whether he has much property, or little, or none; for the contract is made to the very end that each may gain something that he needs or desires more urgently than that which he proposes to give in exchange. And, since it is self-evident that, unless all things are held in common, some persons must have more property than others, it is from the nature of things impossible to uphold freedom of contract and the right of private property without at the same time recognizing as legitimate those inequalities of fortune that are the necessary result of the exercise of those rights. But the 14th Amendment, in declaring that a state shall not "deprive any person of life, liberty, or property without due process of law," gives to each of these an equal sanction; it recognizes "liberty" and "property" as coexistent human rights, and debars the states from any unwarranted interference with either.

And since a state may not strike them down directly, it is clear that it may not do so indirectly, as by declaring in effect that the public good requires the removal of those inequalities that are but the normal and inevitable result of their exercise. . . . The police power is broad, and not easily defined, but it cannot be given the wide scope that is here asserted for it, without in effect nullifying the constitutional guaranty.

In the 1920s the Court's defense of the liberty of contract reached the high-water mark and the controversy was exacerbated by the Great Depression. In *Adkins v. Children's Hospital*, 261 U.S. 525 (1923), a bare majority struck down the District of Columbia's minimum wage law for women and again made clear that *Lochner* was still alive. The minimum wage law, according to Justice George Sutherland, was "simply and exclusively a price-fixing law." "Women," he added, "are legally as capable of contracting for themselves as men." In dissent, Chief Justice Taft maintained that *Muller*, not *Lochner*, should control the decision and questioned whether *Lochner* had not been "overruled *sub silentio*," that is, overruled without expressly saying so. But *Wolff Packing Co. v. Court of Industrial Relations*, 262 U.S. 522 (1923), with none other than Taft delivering the Court's opinion, underscored that economic liberty was a "preferred freedom," when striking down Kansas's law creating an industrial-relations court to handle labor-management disputes. And there remained a die-hard majority on the Court into the 1930s for defending the vestiges of laissez-faire capitalism. In *Morehead v. Tipaldo*, 298 U.S. 587 (1936), the four remaining justices from *Adkins*'s majority—Sutherland, Pierce Butler, Willis Van Devanter, and James McReynolds—were thus joined by Owen Roberts in overturning New York's minimum wage law.

The controversy over the Court finally erupted into the most serious crisis in constitutional politics since *Dred Scott.* During President Franklin Delano Roosevelt's first term, the Court invalidated most of his early New Deal programs thereby thwarting his plans for the country's recovery from the Great Depression. After FDR's landslide reelection in 1936, he boldly proposed judicial reforms that would allow him to expand the size of the Court to fifteen by appointing a new member for every justice over seventy years of age. Then in the spring of 1937 when the Senate Judiciary Committee was debating his Court-packing plan, the Court abruptly upheld major pieces of the New Deal legislation. The Court had become badly split 5–4 in striking down progressive New Deal legislation. Sutherland, McReynolds, Butler, and Van Devanter—the "Four Horsemen"—voted as a bloc against economic legislation for violating economic liberty, while Stone and Cardozo followed Brandeis in supporting progressive legislation. Hughes and Roberts were the swing votes, although the latter, more conservative justice, had cast the crucial fifth vote to strike down FDR's programs. Roberts, however, was persuaded by Hughes to change his mind. In March he abandoned the Four Horsemen in *West Coast Hotel Co. v. Parrish* (1937) (see excerpt below) to uphold Washington State's minimum wage law. Two weeks later, in *National Labor Relations Board v. Jones & Laughlin Steel Corporation*, 301 U.S. 1 (1937) (see Vol. 1, Ch. 6), Roberts again switched sides to affirm a major piece of New Deal legislation, the National Labor Relations Act.

The Court's "switch in time that saved nine" was widely speculated to have been due to FDR's Court-packing plan. But even though the rulings did not come down until the spring, Roberts had switched his vote at conference in December 1936, two months before FDR announced his plan. The reversal of the Court's position nonetheless contributed to the Senate Judiciary Committee's rejection of FDR's proposal in May. Then Van Devanter—one of the president's staunchest opponents—told the president that he would resign at the end of the next term. FDR had the first of eight appointments in the next six years to infuse his own political philosophy into the Court.

The Court's about-face in 1937 ended a constitutional crisis and an era. With the Court's abandonment of the liberty of contract and turning its back on substantive due process came a virtual abdication of judicial supervision of economic regulations. *Lincoln Federal Labor Union v. Northwestern Iron & Metal Co.*, 335 U.S. 525 (1949), which expressly repudiated *Adair* and *Coppage*, is illustrative. As FDR's first appointee to the Court, Justice Hugo Black, in *Ferguson v. Skrupa*, 372 U.S. 726 (1963), exclaimed, "[I]t is up to legislatures, not courts, to decide on the wisdom and utility of legislation."[11] The Burger Court, when upholding a state law requiring employees to be compensated when on jury duty by their employers, in *Dean v. Gadsden Times Publishing Corporation*, 412 U.S. 543 (1973), underscored that "[i]f our recent cases mean anything, they leave debatable issues as respects business, economic, and social affairs to legislative decision. We could strike down this law only if we returned to the philosophy of *Lochner, Coppage*, and *Adkins* cases."

Since the 1937 revolution in constitutional politics, the Court has evolved a proverbial double standard: it gives economic regulation only minimal scrutiny, requiring only that it have some rational basis, while giving that affecting civil liberties heightened scrutiny, often upholding legislation only if the government's interest in regulation is compelling. And since 1937 the Court has assumed a special role in overseeing voting rights and access to the political process (see Vol. 1, Ch. 8); the freedom of speech, press, and association (see Ch. 5); and invidious forms of racial and nonracial discrimination (see Ch. 12).

It appears highly unlikely that the Court will once again heighten its scrutiny of economic legislation under the due process clause, let alone return to the days of the liberty of contract. Justice William Rehnquist, for example, in *United States Railroad Retirement Board v. Fritz*, 449 U.S. 166 (1980), rebuffed a due process attack on legislation eliminating railroad retirees' social security and retirement benefits with the observation that "[t]he plain language [of the statute] marks the beginning and end of our inquiry."

Finally, it bears noting that although the Court turned its back on the doctrine of a liberty of contract in 1937, it did not abandon reading substantive guarantees into the due process clause of the Fourteenth Amendment, as further discussed in Chapters 4 and 12.

Notes

1. For further discussion, see Charles Fairman, "Does the Fourteenth Amendment Incorporate the Bill of Rights?" 2 *Stanford Law Review* 5 (1949); and William Crosskey, "Charles Fairman, 'Legislative History,' and the Constitutional Limitations on State Authority," 22 *University of Chicago Law Review* 1 (1954).

2. See Edward Corwin, *Liberty against Government: The Rise, Flowering and Decline of a Famous Judicial Concept* (Baton Rouge: Louisiana State University Press, 1948).

3. Benjamin Cardozo, *The Nature of the Judicial Process* (New Haven, CT: Yale University Press, 1921), 168.

4. For further discussion, see Benjamin Twiss, *Lawyers and the Constitution: How Laissez Faire Came to the Supreme Court* (Princeton, NJ: Princeton University Press, 1942); Robert McCloskey, *American Conservatism in the Age of Enterprise* (Cambridge, MA: Harvard University Press, 1951); and James Willard Hurst, *Law and the Conditions of Freedom in the Nineteenth-Century United States* (Madison: University of Wisconsin Press, 1956).

5. For further discussion, see Howard Gillman, *The Constitution Besieged: The Rise and Demise of Lochner Era Police Powers Jurisprudence* (Durham, NC: Duke University Press, 1993).

6. *Hamilton v. Kentucky Distilleries and Warehouse Co.*, 251 U.S. 146 (1919).

7. See *Austin v. Tennessee*, 179 U.S. 343 (1900); and *Packer Corporation v. Utah*, 285 U.S. 105 (1932).

8. A leading case is *Euclid v. Ambler Realty Co.*, 272 U.S. 365 (1926). See also *Welch v. Swasey*, 214 U.S. 91 (1909); *Cusack v. Chicago*, 242 U.S. 526 (1917); and *Berman v. Parker*, 348 U.S. 26 (1954).

9. Other rulings upholding labor laws for women include *Cotting v. Godard*, 183 U.S. 79 (1901); *German Alliance Insurance Co. v. Lewis*, 233 U.S. 389 (1914); and *Townsend v. Yeomans*, 301 U.S. 441 (1937).

10. For further discussion, see Morton White, *Social Thought in America: The Revolt against Formalism* (New York: Viking Press, 1949).

11. See also *Williamson v. Lee Optical of Oklahoma*, 348 U.S. 483 (1955); and *Olsen v. Nebraska*, 313 U.S. 236 (1941).

SELECTED BIBLIOGRAPHY

Bernstein, David. *Rehabilitating Lochner: Defending Individual Rights against Progressive Reform.* Chicago: University of Chicago Press, 2011.

Gillman, Howard. *The Constitution Besieged: The Rise and Demise of Lochner Era Police Powers Jurisprudence.* Durham, NC: Duke University Press, 1993.

Kens, Paul. *Judicial Power and Reform Politics: The Anatomy of Lochner v. New York.* Lawrence: University Press of Kansas, 1990.

Labbé, Ronald, and Jonathan Lurie. *The Slaughterhouse Cases.* Lawrence: University Press of Kansas, 2003.

Paul, Arnold. *Conservative Crisis and the Rule of Law: Attitudes of Bench and Bar, 1887–1895.* Ithaca, NY: Cornell University Press, 1960.

Twiss, Benjamin. *Lawyers and the Constitution: How Laissez Faire Came to the Supreme Court.* Princeton, NJ: Princeton University Press, 1942.

Butchers' Benevolent Association v. Crescent City Livestock Landing & Slaughterhouse Co. (The Slaughterhouse Cases)

16 WALL. (83 U.S.) 36 (1873)

In 1869 due to the pollution and the spread of cholera, the Louisiana legislature passed a law aimed at cleaning up the Mississippi River by prohibiting all slaughtering of livestock in the City of New Orleans and surrounding parishes except at one slaughterhouse, which was given an exclusive franchise for twenty-five years. The Butchers' Benevolent Association, a group of independent slaughterers, challenged the constitutionality of the legislation on the grounds that it violated the Thirteenth and Fourteenth Amendments by depriving them of their livelihood. A state court and the Louisiana State Supreme Court upheld the law, and the Butchers' Benevolent Association appealed to the Supreme Court.

The Court's decision was 5–4, with the majority's opinion announced by Justice Miller. Justices Field, Bradley, and Swayne dissented, joined by Chief Justice Chase.

■ ■ ■

□ *Justice MILLER delivered the opinion of the Court.*

The plaintiffs . . . allege that the statute is a violation of the Constitution of the United States in these several particulars:

That it creates an involuntary servitude forbidden by the 13th article of amendment;

That it abridges the privileges and immunities of citizens of the United States;

That it denies to the plaintiffs the equal protection of the laws; and,

That it deprives them of their property without due process of law; contrary to the provisions of the 1st section of the 14th article of amendment.

This court is thus called upon for the first time to give construction to these articles. . . .

The most cursory glance at these articles discloses a unity of purpose, when taken in connection with the history of the times, which cannot fail to have an important bearing on any question of doubt concerning their true meaning. . . .

[N]o one can fail to be impressed with the one pervading purpose found in [the 13th, 14th and 15th Amendments], lying at the foundation of each, and without which none of them would have been even suggested; we mean the freedom of the slave race, the security and firm establishment of that freedom, and the protection of the newly made freemen and citizens from the oppressions of those who had formerly exercised unlimited dominion over him. It is true that only the 15th Amendment, in terms, mentions the negro by speaking of his color and his slavery. But it is just as true that each of the other articles was addressed to the grievances of that race, and designed to remedy them as the fifteenth.

We do not say that no one else but the negro can share in this protection. Both the language and spirit of these articles are to have their fair and just weight in any question of construction. Undoubtedly, while negro slavery alone was in the mind of the Congress which proposed the 13th article, it forbids any other kind of slavery, now or hereafter. . . .

The next observation is more important in view of the arguments of counsel in the present case. It is that the distinction between citizenship of the United States and citizenship of a state is clearly recognized and established. Not only may a man be a citizen of the United States without being a citizen of a state, but an important element is necessary to convert the former into the latter. He must reside within the state to make him a citizen of it, but it is only necessary that he should be born or naturalized in the United States to be a citizen of the Union.

It is quite clear, then, that there is a citizenship of the United States and a citizenship of a state, which are distinct from each other and which depend upon different characteristics or circumstances in the individual.

We think this distinction and its explicit recognition in this Amendment of great weight in this argument, because the next paragraph of this same section, which is the one mainly relied on by the plaintiffs in error, speaks only of privileges and immunities of citizens of the United States, and does not speak of those of citizens of the several states. The argument, however, in favor of the plaintiffs, rests wholly on the assumption that the citizenship is the same and the privileges and immunities guaranteed by the clause are the same.

The language is: "No state shall make or enforce any law which shall abridge the privileges or immunities of citizens of the United States." It is a little remarkable, if this clause was intended as a protection to the citizen of a state against the legislative power of his own state, that the words "citizen of the state" should be left out when it is so carefully used, and used in contradistinction to "citizens of the United States" in the very sentence which precedes it. It is too clear for argument that the change in phraseology was adopted understandingly and with a purpose.

Of the privileges and immunities of the citizens of the United States, and of the privileges and immunities of the citizen of the state, and what they respectively are, we will presently consider; but we wish to state here that it is only the former which are placed by this clause under the protection of the Federal Constitution, and that the latter, whatever they may be, are not intended to have any additional protection by this paragraph of the Amendment.

If, then, there is a difference between the privileges and immunities belonging to a citizen of the United States as such, and those belonging to the citizen of the state as such, the latter must rest for their security and protection where they have heretofore rested; for they are not embraced by this paragraph of the Amendment. . . .

In the Constitution of the United States, which superseded the Articles of Confederation, the corresponding provision is found in section two of the 4th article, in the following words: The citizens of each state shall be entitled to all the privileges and immunities of citizens of the several states.

There can be but little question that the purpose of both these provisions is the same, and that the privileges and immunities intended are the same in each. In the Articles of the Confederation we have some of these specifically mentioned, and enough perhaps to give some general idea of the class of civil rights meant by the phrase. . . .

The constitutional provision there alluded to did not create those rights, which it called privileges and immunities of citizens of the states. It threw around them in that clause no security for the citizen of the state in which they were claimed or exercised. Nor did it profess to control the power of the state governments over the rights of its own citizens.

Its sole purpose was to declare to the several states, that whatever those rights, as you grant or establish them to your own citizens, or as you limit or qualify, or impose restrictions on their exercise, the same, neither more nor less, shall be the measure of the rights of citizens of other states within your jurisdiction. . . .

The argument has not been much pressed in these cases that the defendant's charter deprives the plaintiffs of their property without due process of law, or that it denies to them the equal protection of the law. The first of these paragraphs has been in the Constitution since the adoption of the 5th Amendment, as a restraint upon the Federal power. It is also to be found in some form of expression in the constitutions of nearly all the states, as a restraint upon the power of the states. This law, then, has practically been the same as it now is during the existence of the government, except so far as the present Amendment may place the restraining power over the states in this matter in the hands of the Federal government.

We are not without judicial interpretation, therefore, both state and national, of the meaning of this clause. And it is sufficient to say that under no construction of that provision that we have ever seen, or any that we deem admissible, can the restraint imposed by the state of Louisiana upon the exercise of their trade by the butchers of New Orleans be held to be a deprivation of property within the meaning of that provision.

"Nor shall any state deny to any person within its jurisdiction the equal protection of the laws."

In the light of the history of these amendments, and the pervading purpose of them, which we have already discussed, it is not difficult to give a meaning to this clause. The existence of laws in the states where the newly emancipated negroes resided, which discriminated with gross injustice and hardship against them as a class, was the evil to be remedied by this clause, and by it such laws are forbidden.

☐ *Justice FIELD, dissenting.*

The question presented is . . . nothing less than the question whether the recent Amendments to the Federal Constitution protect the citizens of the United States against the deprivation of their common rights by state legislation. In my judgment the 14th Amendment does afford such protection, and was so intended by the Congress which framed and the states which adopted it.

The counsel for the plaintiffs in error have contended, with great force, that the act in question is also inhibited by the 13th Amendment.

That Amendment prohibits slavery and involuntary servitude, except as a punishment for crime, but I have not supposed it was susceptible of a construction which would cover the enactment in question. I have been so accustomed to regard it as intended to meet that form of slavery which had previously prevailed in this country, and to which the recent Civil War owed its existence, that I was not prepared, nor am I yet, to give to it the extent and force ascribed by counsel. Still it is evident that the language of the Amendment is not used in a restrictive sense. It is not confined to African slavery alone. It is general and universal in its application. Slavery of white men as well as of black men is prohibited, and not merely slavery in the strict sense of the term, but involuntary servitude in every form. . . .

The first clause of the fourteenth amendment . . . recognizes in express terms, if it does not create, citizens of the United States, and it makes the citizenship dependent upon the place of the birth, or the fact of their adoption, and not upon the Constitution or laws of any state or the condition of their ancestry. A citizen of a state is now only a citizen of the United States residing in that state. The fundamental rights, privileges, and immunities which belong to him as a free man and a free citizen, now belong to him as a citizen of the United States, and are not dependent upon his citizenship of any state. . . .

The Amendment does not attempt to confer any new privileges or immunities upon citizens or to enumerate or define those already existing. It assumes that there are such privileges and immunities which belong of right to citizens as such, and ordains that they shall not be abridged by state legislation. If this inhibition has no reference to privileges and immunities of this character, but only refers, as held by the majority of the court in their opinion, to such privileges and immunities as were before its adoption specially designated in the Constitution or necessarily implied as belonging to citizens of the United States, it was a vain and idle enactment, which accomplished nothing, and most unnecessarily excited Congress and the people on its passage. With privileges and immunities thus designated no state could ever have interfered by its laws, and no new constitutional provision was required to inhibit such interference. The supremacy of the Constitution and the laws of the United States always controlled any state legislation of that character. But if the Amendment refers to the natural and inalienable rights which belong to all citizens, the inhibition has a profound significance and consequence.

What, then, are the privileges and immunities which are secured against abridgement by state legislation? . . .

The privileges and immunities designated are those which of right belong to the citizens of all free governments. Clearly among these must be placed the right to pursue a lawful employment in a lawful manner, without other restraint than such as equally affects all persons. . . .

This equality of right, with exemption from all disparaging and partial enactments, in the lawful pursuits of life, throughout the whole country, is the distinguishing privilege of citizens of the United States. To them, everywhere, all pursuits, all professions, all avocations are open without other restrictions than such as are imposed equally upon all others of the same age, sex and condition. The state may prescribe such regulations for every pursuit and calling of life as will promote the public health, secure the good order and advance the general prosperity of society, but when once prescribed, the pursuit or calling must be free to be followed by every citizen who is within the conditions designated, and will conform to the regulations. This is the fundamental idea upon which our institutions rest, and unless adhered to in the legislation of the country our government will be a Republic only in name. The 14th Amendment, in my judgment, makes it essential to the validity of the legislation of every state that this equality of right should be respected. . . .

I am authorized by Chief Justice CHASE, Justice SWAYNE and Justice BRADLEY, to state that they concur with me in this dissenting opinion.

□ *Justice BRADLEY, dissenting.*

In my view, a law which prohibits a large class of citizens from adopting a lawful employment, or from following a lawful employment previously adopted, does deprive them of liberty as well as property, without due process of law. Their right of choice is a portion of their liberty; their occupation is their property. Such a law also deprives those citizens of the equal protection of the laws, contrary to the last clause of the section. . . .

It is futile to argue that none but persons of the African race are intended to be benefited by this Amendment. They may have been the primary cause of the Amendment, but its language is general, embracing all citizens, and I think it was purposely so expressed.

Munn v. Illinois
4 Otto (94 U.S.) 113, 24 L.Ed. 77 (1877)

In 1871 in response to the Granger movement—a movement to promote the interests of independent farmers in Midwest states—and pressures to stop the exploitation of farmers by grain-elevator operators, Illinois's legislature enacted a law requiring operating licenses and setting the maximum rates that grain warehouses and elevators could charge for the storage of grain. Ira Munn was found in violation of the law and attacked its constitutionality as a violation of the commerce clause and the due process clause of the Fourteenth Amendment. The Illinois State Supreme Court, however, upheld Munn's conviction and Munn appealed to the Supreme Court.

The Court's decision was 7–2, with the majority's opinion announced by Chief Justice Waite. Justices Field and Strong dissented.

■ ■ ■

□ *Chief Justice WAITE delivered the opinion of the Court.*

Every statute is presumed to be constitutional. The courts ought not to declare one to be unconstitutional, unless it is clearly so. If there is doubt, the expressed will of the Legislature should be sustained.

The Constitution contains no definition of the word "deprive," as used in the Fourteenth Amendment. To determine its signification, therefore, it is necessary to ascertain the effect which usage has given it, when employed in the same or a like connection.

While this provision of the amendment is new in the Constitution of the United States as a limitation upon the powers of the States, it is old as a principle of civilized government. It is found in Magna Charta, and, in substance if not in form, in nearly or quite all the constitutions that have been from time to time adopted by the several States of the Union. By the Fifth Amendment, it was introduced into the Constitution of the United States as a limitation upon the powers of the National Government, and by the Fourteenth, as a guaranty against any encroachment upon an acknowledged right of citizenship by the Legislatures of the States. . . .

This Act was passed at a time when Magna Charta had been recognized as the fundamental law of England for hundreds of years.

This great charter embodied the principle that no person shall be deprived of life, liberty or property, but by the judgment of his peers or the law of the land, which is an equivalent for the modern phrase, "due process of law." . . .

[I]t is apparent that, down to the time of the adoption of the Fourteenth Amendment, it was not supposed that statutes regulating the use, or even the price of the use, of private property necessarily deprived an owner of his property without due process of law. Under some circumstances they may, but not under all. The Amendment does not change the law in this particular; it simply prevents the States from doing that which will operate as such a deprivation.

This brings us to inquire as to the principles upon which this power of regulation rests, in order that we may determine what is within and what without its operative effect. Looking, then, to the common law, from whence came the right which the Constitution protects, we find that when private property is "affected with a public interest, it ceases to be *juris privati* only." This was said by Lord Chief Justice Hale more than two hundred years ago, in his treatise *De Portibus Maris*, and has been accepted without objection as an essential element in the law of property ever since. Property does become clothed with a public interest when used in a manner to make it of public consequence, and affect the community at large. When, therefore, one devotes his property to a use in which the public has an interest, he, in effect, grants to the public an interest in that use, and must submit to be controlled by the public for the common good, to the extent of the interest he has thus created. He may withdraw his grant by discontinuing the use; but, so long as he maintains the use, he must submit to the control. . . .

It remains only to ascertain whether the warehouses of these plaintiffs in error, and the business which is carried on there, come within the operation of this principle. . . .

[I]t is difficult to see why, if the common carrier, or the miller, or the ferryman, or the innkeeper, or the wharfinger, or the baker, or the cartman, or the hackney-coachman, pursues a public employment and exercises "a sort of public office," these plaintiffs in error do not. They stand, to use again the language of their counsel, in the very "gateway of commerce," and take toll from all who pass. Their business most certainly "tends to a common charge, and is become a thing of public interest and use." Every bushel of grain for its passage "pays a toll, which is a common charge," and, therefore, according to Lord Hale, every such warehouseman "ought to be under public regulation, viz.: that he . . . take but reasonable toll." Certainly, if any business can be clothed "with a public interest, and cease to be *juris privati* only," this has been. It may not be made so by the operation of the Constitution of Illinois or this statute, but it is by the facts. . . .

We know that this is a power which may be abused; but that is no argument against its existence. For protection against abuses by Legislatures the people must resort to the polls; not to the courts. . . .

We come now to consider the effect upon this statute of the power of Congress to regulate commerce. . . . The warehouses of these plaintiffs in error are situated and their business carried on exclusively within the limits of the State of Illinois. They are used as instruments by those engaged in State as well as those engaged in interstate commerce, but they are no more necessarily a part of commerce itself than the dray or the cart by which, but for them, grain would be transferred from one railroad station to another. Incidentally they may become connected with interstate commerce, but not necessarily so. Their regulation is a thing of domestic concern and, certainly, until Congress acts in reference to their interstate relations, the State may exercise all the powers of government over them, even though in so doing it may indirectly operate upon commerce outside its immediate jurisdiction. We do not say that a case may not arise in which it will be found that a State, under the form of regulating its own affairs, has encroached upon the exclusive domain of Congress in respect to interstate commerce, but we do say that, upon the facts as they are represented to us in this record, that has not been done. . . .

The judgment is affirmed.

☐ *Justice FIELD, dissenting.*

There is nothing in the character of the business of the defendants as warehousemen which called for the interference complained of in this case. Their buildings are not nuisances; their occupation of receiving and storing grain infringes upon no rights of others, disturbs no neighborhood, infects not the air, and in no respect prevents others from using and enjoying their property as to them may seem best. The legislation in question is nothing less than a bold assertion of absolute power by the State to control, at its discretion, the property and business of the citizen, and fix the compensation he shall receive. . . .

The business of a warehouseman was, at common law, a private business, and is so in its nature. It has no special privileges connected with it, nor did the law ever extend to it any greater protection than it extended to all other private business. No reason can be assigned to justify legislation interfering with the legitimate profits of that business, that would not equally justify an intermeddling with the business of every man in the community, so soon, at least, as his business became generally useful.

I am of opinion that the judgment of the Supreme Court of Illinois should be reversed.

Lochner v. New York

198 U.S. 45, 25 S.CT. 539 (1905)

Joseph Lochner was found guilty and fined $50 for violating an 1897 New York law prohibiting employers from having their employees work more than sixty hours a week in a bakery. Lochner's conviction was affirmed by two state courts and he applied for a writ of error from the Supreme Court.

The Court's decision was 5–4; the majority's opinion was announced by Justice Peckham. Dissents were by Justices Holmes and Harlan, who were joined by Justices White and Day.

■ ■ ■

☐ *Justice PECKHAM delivered the opinion of the Court.*

The mandate of the statute, that "no employee shall be required or permitted to work," is the substantial equivalent of an enactment that "no employee shall contract or agree to work," more than ten hours per day; and, as there is no provision for special emergencies, the statute is mandatory in all cases. It is not an act merely fixing the number of hours which shall constitute a legal day's work, but an absolute prohibition upon the employer permitting, under any circumstances, more than ten hours' work to be done in his establishment. The employee may desire to earn the extra money which would arise from his working more than the prescribed time, but this statute forbids the employer from permitting the employee to earn it.

The statute necessarily interferes with the right of contract between the employer and employees, concerning the number of hours in which the latter may labor in the bakery of the employer. The general right to make a contract in relation to his business is part of the liberty of the individual protected by the 14th Amendment of the Federal Constitution. *Allgeyer v. Louisiana*, 165 U.S. 578 [1897]. Under that provision no state can deprive any person of life, liberty, or property without due process of law. The right to purchase or to sell labor is part of the liberty protected by this amendment, unless there are circumstances which exclude the right. There are, however, certain powers, existing in the sovereignty of each state in the Union, somewhat vaguely termed police powers, the exact description and limitation of which have not been attempted by the courts. Those powers, broadly stated, and without, at present, any attempt at a more specific limitation, relate to the safety, health, morals, and general welfare of the public. Both property and liberty are held on such reasonable conditions as may be imposed by the governing power of the state in the exercise of those powers, and with such conditions the 14th Amendment was not designed to interfere. . . .

The state, therefore, has power to prevent the individual from making certain kinds of contracts, and in regard to them the Federal Constitution offers no protection. If the contract be one which the state, in the legitimate exercise of its police power, has the right to prohibit, it is not prevented from prohibiting it by the 14th Amendment. Contracts in violation of a statute, either of the Federal or state government, or a contract to let one's property for immoral purposes, or to do any other unlawful act, could obtain no protection from the Federal Constitution, as coming under the liberty of person or of free contract. Therefore, when the state, by its legislature, in the assumed exercise of its police powers, has passed an act which seriously limits the right to labor or the right of contract in regard to their means of livelihood between persons who are *sui juris* (both employer and employee), it becomes of great importance to determine which shall prevail,—the right of the individual to labor for such time as he may choose, or the right of the state to prevent the individual from laboring, or from entering into any contract to labor, beyond a certain time prescribed by the state.

This court has recognized the existence and upheld the exercise of the police powers of the states in many cases which might fairly be considered as border ones, and it has, in the course of its determination of questions regarding the asserted invalidity of such statutes, on the ground of their violation of the rights secured by the Federal Constitution, been guided by rules of a very liberal nature, the application of which has resulted, in numerous instances, in upholding the validity of state statutes thus assailed. . . .

It must, of course, be conceded that there is a limit to the valid exercise of the police power by the state. . . . Otherwise the 14th Amendment would have no efficacy and the legislatures of the states would have unbounded power, and it would be enough to say that any piece of legislation was

Joseph Lochner in his bakery. (*Collection of the Supreme Court of the United States.*)

enacted to conserve the morals, the health, or the safety of the people; such legislation would be valid, no matter how absolutely without foundation the claim might be. The claim of the police power would be a mere pretext,— become another and delusive name for the supreme sovereignty of the state to be exercised free from constitutional restraint. . . . In every case that comes before this court, therefore, where legislation of this character is concerned, and where the protection of the Federal Constitution is sought, the question necessarily arises: Is this a fair, reasonable, and appropriate exercise of the police power of the state, or is it an unreasonable, unnecessary, and arbitrary interference with the right of the individual to his personal liberty, or to enter into those contracts in relation to labor which may seem to him appropriate or necessary for the support of himself and his family? Of course the liberty of contract relating to labor includes both parties to it. The one has as much right to purchase as the other to sell labor.

This is not a question of substituting the judgment of the court for that of the legislature. If the act be within the power of the state it is valid, although the judgment of the court might be totally opposed to the enactment of such a law. . . .

The question whether this act is valid as a labor law, pure and simple, may be dismissed in a few words. There is no reasonable ground for interfering with the liberty of person or the right of free contract, by determining the hours of labor, in the occupation of a baker. There is no contention that bakers as a class are not equal in intelligence and capacity to men in other trades or manual occupations, or that they are not able to assert their rights and care for themselves without the protecting arm of the state, interfering with their independence of judgment and of action. They are in no sense wards of the state. Viewed in the light of a purely labor law, with no reference whatever to the question of health, we think that a law like the one before us involves neither the safety, the morals, nor the welfare, of the public, and that the interest of the public is not in the slightest degree affected by such an act. The law must be upheld, if at all, as a law pertaining to the health of the individual engaged in the occupation of a baker. It does not affect any other portion of the public than those who are engaged in that occupation. Clean and wholesome bread does not depend upon whether the baker works but ten hours per day or only sixty hours a week. The limitation of the hours of labor does not come within the police power on that ground.

It is a question of which of two powers or rights shall prevail,—the power of the state to legislate or the right of the individual to liberty of person and freedom of contract. The mere assertion that the subject relates, though but in a remote degree, to the public health, does not necessarily render the enactment valid. The act must have a more direct relation, as a means to an end, and the end itself must be appropriate and legitimate, before an act can be held to be valid which interferes with the general right of an individual to be free in his person and in his power to contract in relation to his own labor. . . .

We think that there can be no fair doubt that the trade of a baker, in and of itself, is not an unhealthy one to that degree which would authorize the legislature to interfere with the right to labor, and with the right of free contract on the part of the individual, either as employer or employee. In looking through statistics regarding all trades and occupations, it may be true that the trade of a baker does not appear to be as healthy as some other trades, and is also vastly more healthy than still others. To the common understanding the trade of a baker has never been regarded as an unhealthy one. . . .

It seems to us that the real object and purpose were simply to regulate the hours of labor between the master and his employees (all being men, *sui juris*), in a private business, not dangerous in any degree to morals, or in any real and substantial degree to the health of the employees. Under such circumstances the freedom of master and employee to contract with each other in relation to their employment, and in defining the same, cannot be prohibited or interfered with, without violating the Federal Constitution.

☐ *Justice HOLMES, dissenting.*

This case is decided upon an economic theory which a large part of the country does not entertain. If it were a question whether I agreed with that theory, I should desire to study it further and long before making up my mind. But I do not conceive that to be my duty, because I strongly believe that my agreement or disagreement has nothing to do with the right of a majority to embody their opinions in law. It is settled by various decisions of this court that state constitutions and state laws may regulate life in many ways which we as legislators might think as injudicious, or if you like as tyrannical, as this, and which equally with this, interfere with the liberty to contract. Sunday laws and usury laws are ancient examples. A more modern one is the prohibition of lotteries. The liberty of the citizen to do as he likes so long as he does not interfere with the liberty of others to do the same, which has been a shibboleth for some well-known writers, is interfered with by school laws, by the Post Office, by every state or municipal institution which takes his money for purposes thought desirable, whether he likes it or not. The 14th Amendment does not enact Mr. Herbert Spencer's *Social Statics*. The other day we sustained the Massachusetts vaccination law. *Jacobson v. Massachusetts*, 197 U.S. 11 [1905]. United States and state statutes and decisions cutting down the liberty to contract by way of combination are familiar to this court. *Northern Securities Co. v. United States*, 193 U.S. 197 [1904]. Two years ago we upheld the prohibition of sales of stock on margins, or for future delivery, in the Constitution of California. *Otis v. Parker*, 187 U.S. 606 [1903]. The decision sustaining an eight-hour law for miners is still recent. *Holden v. Hardy* [169 U.S. 366 (1898)]. Some of these laws embody convictions or prejudices which judges are likely to share. Some may not. But a Constitution is not intended to embody a particular economic theory, whether of paternalism and the organic relation of the citizen to the state or of *laissez faire*. It is made for people of fundamentally differing views, and the accident of our finding certain opinions natural and familiar, or novel, and even shocking, ought not to conclude our judgment upon the question whether statutes embodying them conflict with the Constitution of the United States.

General propositions do not decide concrete cases. The decision will depend on a judgment or intuition more subtle than any articulate major premise. But I think that the proposition just stated, if it is accepted, will carry us far toward the end. Every opinion tends to become a law. I think that the word "liberty," in the 14th Amendment, is perverted when it is held to prevent the natural outcome of a dominant opinion, unless it can be said that a rational and fair man necessarily would admit that the statute proposed would infringe fundamental principles as they have been understood by the traditions of our people and our law. It does not need research to show that no such sweeping condemnation can be passed upon the statute before us. A reasonable man might think it a proper measure on the score of health. Men whom I certainly could not pronounce unreasonable would uphold it as a first installment of a general regulation of the hours of work. Whether in the latter aspect it would be open to the charge of inequality I think it unnecessary to discuss.

☐ *Justice HARLAN, with whom Justices WHITE and DAY join, dissenting.*

[Granting] that there is a liberty of contract which cannot be violated even under the sanction of direct legislative enactment, but assuming, as according to settled law we may assume, that such liberty of contract is subject to such regulations as the State may reasonably prescribe for the common good and the well-being of society, what are the conditions under which the judiciary may declare such regulations to be in excess of legislative authority and void? Upon this point there is no room for dispute; for, the rule is universal that a legislative enactment, Federal or state, is never to be disregarded or held invalid unless it be, beyond question, plainly and palpably in excess of legislative power. . . .

Let these principles be applied to the present case. By the statute in question it is provided that, "No employee shall be required or permitted to work in a biscuit, bread or cake bakery or confectionery establishment more than sixty hours in any one week, or more than ten hours in any one day, unless for the purpose of making a shorter work day on the last day of the week; nor more hours in any one week than will make an average of ten hours per day for the number of days during such week in which such employee shall work."

It is plain that this statute was enacted in order to protect the physical well-being of those who work in bakery and confectionery establishments. It may be that the statute had its origin, in part, in the belief that employers and employees in such establishments were not upon an equal footing, and that the necessities of the latter often compelled them to submit to such exactions as unduly taxed their strength. Be this as it may, the statute must be taken as expressing the belief of the people of New York that, as a general rule, and in the case of the average man, labor in excess of sixty hours during a week in such establishments may endanger the health of those who thus labor. Whether or not this be wise legislation it is not the province of the court to inquire. Under our systems of government the courts are not concerned with the wisdom or policy of legislation. So that in determining the question of power to interfere with liberty of contract, the court may inquire whether the means devised by the State are germane to an end which may be lawfully accomplished and have a real or substantial relation to the protection of health, as involved in the daily work of the persons, male and female, engaged in bakery and confectionery establishments.

But when this inquiry is entered upon I find it impossible, in view of common experience, to say that there is here no real or substantial relation between the means employed by the State and the end sought to be accomplished by its legislation. Nor can I say that the statute has no appropriate or direct connection with that protection to health which each State owes to her citizens, or that it is not promotive of the health of the employees in question, or that the regulation prescribed by the State is utterly unreasonable and extravagant or wholly arbitrary. Still less can I say that the statute is, beyond question, a plain, palpable invasion of rights secured by the fundamental law. Therefore I submit that this court will transcend its functions if it assumes to annul the statute of New York. It must be remembered that this statute does not apply to all kinds of business. It applies only to work in bakery and confectionery establishments, in which, as all know, the air constantly breathed by workmen is not as pure and healthful as that to be found in some other establishments or out of doors.

Professor Hirt in his treatise on the *Diseases of the Workers* has said: "The labor of the bakers is among the hardest and most laborious imaginable, because it has to be performed under conditions injurious to the health of those engaged in it. . . ." Another writer says: "The constant inhaling of flour dust causes inflammation of the lungs and of the bronchial tubes. The eyes also suffer through this dust, which is responsible for the many cases of running eyes among the bakers. The long hours of toil to which all bakers are subjected produce rheumatism, cramps and swollen legs. The intense heat in the workshops induces the workers to resort to cooling drinks, which together with their habit of exposing the greater part of their bodies to the change in the atmosphere, is another source of a number of diseases of various organs. Nearly all bakers are pale-faced and of more delicate health than the workers of other crafts, which is chiefly due to their hard work and their irregular and unnatural mode of living whereby the power of resistance against disease is greatly diminished. The average age of a baker is below that of other workmen; they seldom live over their fiftieth year, most of them dying between the ages of forty and fifty. During periods of epidemic diseases the bakers are generally the first to succumb to the disease, and the number swept away during such periods far exceeds the number of other crafts in comparison to the men employed in the respective industries. . . ."

We judicially know that the question of the number of hours during which a workman should continuously labor has been, for a long period, and is yet, a subject of serious consideration among civilized peoples, and by those having special knowledge of the laws of health. Suppose the statute prohibited labor in bakery and confectionery establishments in excess of eighteen hours each day. No one, I take it, could dispute the power of the State to enact such a statute. But the statute before us does not embrace extreme or exceptional cases. It may be said to occupy a middle ground in respect of the hours of labor. What is the true ground for the State to take between legitimate protection, by legislation, of the public health and liberty of contract is not a question easily solved, nor one in respect of which there is or can be absolute certainty. There are very few, if any, questions in political economy about which entire certainty may be predicated. . . .

We also judicially know that the number of hours that should constitute a day's labor in particular occupations involving the physical strength and safety of workmen has been the subject of enactments by Congress and by nearly all of the States. Many, if not most, of those enactments fix eight hours as the proper basis of a day's labor. . . .

If such reasons exist that ought to be the end of this case, for the State is not amenable to the judiciary, in respect of its legislative enactments, unless such enactments are plainly, palpably, beyond all question, inconsistent with the Constitution of the United States. We are not to presume that the State of New York has acted in bad faith. Nor can we assume that its legislature acted without due deliberation, or that it did not determine this question upon the fullest attainable information, and for the common good. We cannot say that the State has acted without reason nor ought we to proceed upon the theory that its action is a mere sham. Our duty, I submit, is to sustain the statute as not being in conflict with the Federal Constitution, for the reason—and such is an all-sufficient reason—it is not shown to be plainly and palpably inconsistent with that instrument. . . .

The judgment in my opinion should be affirmed.

Muller v. Oregon
208 U.S. 412, 28 S.CT. 324 (1908)

At the dawn of the twentieth century, the Progressive Movement, led by organizations such as the National Consumers' League (NCL), promoted legislation setting maximum working hours and minimum wages. After *Lochner v. New York* (1905), however, many such state laws appeared in jeopardy. When the owner of a laundry, Curt Muller, challenged the constitutionality of his conviction for violating Oregon's law limiting the number of hours women could work to ten hours per day, the NCL decided to make a "test case" out of the suit and recruited the well-known Progressive reformer and advocate Louis D. Brandeis to argue the case on appeal. In light of *Lochner*, his strategy was to try to persuade the Court of the reasonableness of, and factual basis for, Oregon's law. Accordingly, he had the NCL gather extensive social, economic, and public health information on the effect of women working long hours. Nearly thirty reports from other countries and states were compiled and quoted in the 113-page brief submitted to the Court. It later became known as the "Brandeis brief" because it contained only two pages of legal arguments, the rest being data and expert opinion supporting the position that "Long hours of labor are dangerous for women primarily because of their special physical organization."

The Court's decision was unanimous in affirming the state supreme court's ruling upholding Oregon's law. Justice Brewer delivered the opinion of the Court.

■ ■ ■

☐ *Justice BREWER delivered the opinion of the court.*

It is the law of Oregon that women, whether married or single, have equal contractual and personal rights with men. [P]utting to one side the elective franchise, in the matter of personal and contractual rights they stand on the same plane as the other sex. Their rights in these respects can no more be infringed than the equal rights of their brothers. We held in *Lochner v. New York*, 198 U.S. 45 [(1905)], that a law providing that no laborer shall be required or permitted to work in a bakery more than sixty hours in a week or ten hours in a day was not as to men a legitimate exercise of the police power of the State, but an unreasonable, unnecessary and arbitrary interference with the right and liberty of the individual to contract in relation to his labor, and as such was in conflict with, and void under, the Federal Constitution. That decision is invoked by plaintiff in error as decisive of the question before us. But this assumes that the difference between the sexes does not justify a different rule respecting a restriction of the hours of labor.

It may not be amiss, in the present case, before examining the constitutional question, to notice the course of legislation as well as expressions of opinion from other than judicial sources. In the brief filed by Mr. Louis D. Brandeis, for the defendant in error, is a very copious collection of all these matters, an epitome of which is found in the margin.

In foreign legislation Mr. Brandeis calls attention to these statutes: Great Britain: Factories Act of 1844; Factory and Workshop Act of 1901. France, 1848; Act Nov. 2, 1892, and March 30, 1900. Switzerland, Canton of Glarus, 1848; Federal Law 1877. Austria, 1855; Acts 1897. Holland, 1889; art. 5, Sec. 1. Italy, June 19, 1902, art. 7. Germany, Laws 1891.

Then follow extracts from over ninety reports of committees, bureaus of statistics, commissioners of hygiene, inspectors of factories, both in this country and in Europe, to the effect that long hours of labor are dangerous for women, primarily because of their special physical organization. The matter is discussed in these reports in different aspects, but all agree as to the danger. It would of course take too much space to give these reports in detail. Following them are extracts from similar reports discussing the general benefits of short hours from an economic aspect of the question. In many of these reports individual instances are given tending to support the general conclusion. Perhaps the general scope and character of all these reports may be summed up in what an inspector for Hanover says: "The reasons for the reduction of the working day to ten hours—(a) the physical organization of women, (b) her maternal functions, (c) the rearing and education of the children, (d) the maintenance of the home—are all so important and so far reaching that the need for such reduction need hardly be discussed." . . .

The legislation and opinions referred to in the margin may not be, technically speaking, authorities, and in them is little or no discussion of the constitutional question presented to us for determination, yet they are significant of a widespread belief that woman's physical structure, and the functions she performs in consequence thereof, justify special legislation restricting or qualifying the conditions under which she should be permitted to toil. Constitutional questions, it is true, are not settled by even a consensus of present public opinion, for it is the peculiar value of a written constitution that it places in unchanging form limitations upon legislative action, and thus gives a permanence and stability to popular government which otherwise would be lacking. At the same time, when a question of fact is debated and debatable, and the extent to which a special constitutional limitation goes is affected by the truth in respect to that fact, a widespread and long continued belief concerning it is worthy of consideration. We take judicial cognizance of all matters of general knowledge.

It is undoubtedly true, as more than once declared by this court, that the general right to contract in relation to one's business is part of the liberty of the individual, protected by the Fourteenth Amendment to the Federal Constitution; yet it is equally well settled that this liberty is not absolute and extending to all contracts, and that a State may, without conflicting with the provisions of the Fourteenth Amendment, restrict in many respects the individual's power of contract. Without stopping to discuss at length the extent to which a State may act in this respect, we refer to the following cases in which the question has been considered: *Allgeyer v. Louisiana*, 165 U.S. 578 [1897]; *Lochner v. New York*.

That woman's physical structure and the performance of maternal functions place her at a disadvantage in the struggle for subsistence is obvious. This is especially true when the burdens of motherhood are upon her. Even when they are not, by abundant testimony of the medical fraternity continuance for a long time on her feet at work, repeating this from day to day, tends to injurious effects upon the body, and as healthy mothers are essential to vigorous offspring, the physical well-being of woman becomes an object of public interest and care in order to preserve the strength and vigor of the race.

Still again, history discloses the fact that woman has always been dependent upon man. . . . As minors, though not to the same extent, she has been looked upon in the courts as needing especial care that her rights may be preserved. Education was long denied her, and while now the doors of the school room are opened and her opportunities for acquiring knowledge are great, yet even with that and the consequent increase of capacity for business affairs it is still true that in the struggle for subsistence she is not an equal competitor with her brother. Though limitations upon personal and contractual rights may be removed by legislation, there is that in her disposition and habits of life which will operate against a full assertion of those rights. She will still be where some legislation to protect her seems necessary to secure a real equality of right. Doubtless there are individual exceptions, and there are many respects in which she has an advantage over him; but looking at it from the viewpoint of the effort to maintain an independent position in life, she is not upon an equality. Differentiated by these matters from the other sex, she is properly placed in a class by herself, and legislation designed for her protection may be sustained, even when like legislation is not necessary for men and could not be sustained. It is impossible to close one's eyes to the fact that she still looks to her brother and depends upon him. . . . Many words cannot make this plainer. The two sexes differ in structure of body, in the functions to be performed by each, in the amount of physical strength, in the capacity for long-continued labor, particularly when done standing, the influence of vigorous health upon the future well-being of the race, the self-reliance which enables one to assert full rights, and in the capacity to maintain the struggle for subsistence. This difference justifies a difference in legislation and upholds that which is designed to compensate for some of the burdens which rest upon her. . . .

For these reasons, and without questioning in any respect the decision in *Lochner v. New York*, we are of the opinion that it cannot be adjudged that the act in question is in conflict with the Federal Constitution, so far as it respects the work of a female in a laundry, and the judgment of the Supreme Court of Oregon is

Affirmed.

West Coast Hotel Co. v. Parrish

300 U.S. 379, 57 S.Ct. 578 (1937)

An employee of the West Coast Hotel Company, Elsie Parrish, sued to recover the difference between her wage and the minimum wage of $14.50 per forty-eight-hour week as set by the Industrial Welfare Committee of Washington State. In 1913, Washington's legislature passed legislation to protect the health and welfare of women and minors by setting a minimum wage. But the trial court denied Parrish's claim. When the Washington Supreme Court reversed, attorneys for West Coast Hotel Company appealed to the Supreme Court, arguing that the law ran afoul of the Fourteenth Amendment's due process clause.

The Court's decision was 5–4, with the majority's opinion announced by Chief Justice Hughes. Justice Sutherland dissented and was joined by Justices Van Devanter, McReynolds, and Butler.

■ ■ ■

☐ *Chief Justice HUGHES delivered the opinion of the Court.*

This case presents the question of the constitutional validity of the minimum wage law of the state of Washington. . . .

The appellant conducts a hotel. The appellee Elsie Parrish was employed as a chambermaid and (with her husband) brought this suit to recover the difference between the wages paid her and the minimum wage fixed pursuant to the state law. The minimum wage was $14.50 per week of 48 hours. The appellant challenged the act as repugnant to the due process clause of the Fourteenth Amendment of the Constitution of the United States. The Supreme Court of the state, reversing the trial court, sustained the statute and directed judgment for the plaintiffs. *Parrish v. West Coast Hotel Co.*, 185 Wash. 581, 55 P.(2d) 1083 [1936]. The case is here on appeal.

The appellant relies upon the decision of this Court in *Adkins v. Children's Hospital*, 261 U.S. 525 [1923], which held invalid the District of Columbia Minimum Wage Act (40 Stat. 960) which was attacked under the due process clause of the Fifth Amendment. . . .

The recent case of *Morehead v. New York ex rel. Tipaldo*, 298 U.S. 587 [1936], came here on *certiorari* to the New York court which had held the New York minimum wage act for women to be invalid. A minority of this

Court thought that the New York statute was distinguishable in a material feature from that involved in the *Adkins* Case and that for that and other reasons the New York statute should be sustained. But the Court of Appeals of New York had said that it found no material difference between the two statutes and this Court held that the "meaning of the statute" as fixed by the decision of the state court "must be accepted here as if the meaning had been specifically expressed in the enactment." That view led to the affirmance by this Court of the judgment in the *Morehead* Case, as the Court considered that the only question before it was whether the *Adkins* Case was distinguishable and that reconsideration of that decision had not been sought. . . .

We think that the question which was not deemed to be open in the *Morehead* Case is open and is necessarily presented here. . . .

The principle which must control our decision is not in doubt. The constitutional provision invoked is the due process clause of the Fourteenth Amendment governing the states, as the due process clause invoked in the *Adkins* Case governed Congress. In each case the violation alleged by those attacking minimum wage regulation for women is deprivation of freedom of contract. What is this freedom? The Constitution does not speak of freedom of contract. It speaks of liberty and prohibits the deprivation of liberty without due process of law. In prohibiting that deprivation, the Constitution does not recognize an absolute and uncontrollable liberty. Liberty in each of its phases has its history and connotation. But the liberty safe-guarded is liberty in a social organization which requires the protection of law against the evils which menace the health, safety, morals, and welfare of the people. Liberty under the Constitution is thus necessarily subject to the restraints of due process, and regulation which is reasonable in relation to its subject and is adopted in the interests of the community is due process.

This essential limitation of liberty in general governs freedom of contract in particular. More than twenty-five years ago we set forth the applicable principle in these words, after referring to the cases where the liberty guaranteed by the Fourteenth Amendment had been broadly described. . . .

This power under the Constitution to restrict freedom of contract has had many illustrations. That it may be exercised in the public interest with respect to contracts between employer and employee is undeniable. Thus statutes have been sustained limiting employment in underground mines and smelters to eight hours a day; in requiring redemption in cash of store orders or other evidences of indebtedness issued in the payment of wages; in forbidding the payment of seamen's wages in advance; in making it unlawful to contract to pay miners employed at quantity rates upon the basis of screened coal instead of the weight of the coal as originally produced in the mine; in prohibiting contracts limiting liability for injuries to employees; in limiting hours of work of employees in manufacturing establishments; and in maintaining workmen's compensation laws. In dealing with the relation of employer and employed, the Legislature has necessarily a wide field of discretion in order that there may be suitable protection of health and safety, and that peace and good order may be promoted through regulations designed to insure wholesome conditions of work and freedom from oppression. . . .

This array of precedents and the principles they applied were thought by the dissenting Justices in the *Adkins* Case to demand that the minimum wage statute be sustained. The validity of the distinction made by the

Court between a minimum wage and a maximum of hours in limiting liberty of contract was especially challenged. That challenge persists and is without any satisfactory answer. . . .

We think that the views thus expressed are sound and that the decision in the *Adkins* Case was a departure from the true application of the principles governing the regulation by the state of the relation of employer and employed. . . .

There is an additional and compelling consideration which recent economic experience has brought into a strong light. The exploitation of a class of workers who are in an unequal position with respect to bargaining power and are thus relatively defenseless against the denial of a living wage is not only detrimental to their health and well being, but casts a direct burden for their support upon the community. What these workers lose in wages the taxpayers are called upon to pay. The bare cost of living must be met. We may take judicial notice of the unparalleled demands for relief which arose during the recent period of depression and still continue to an alarming extent despite the degree of economic recovery which has been achieved. It is unnecessary to cite official statistics to establish what is of common knowledge through the length and breadth of the land. While in the instant case no factual brief has been presented, there is no reason to doubt that the state of Washington has encountered the same social problem that is present elsewhere. The community is not bound to provide what is in effect a subsidy for unconscionable employers. The community may direct its law-making power to correct the abuse which springs from their selfish disregard of the public interest. . . .

Our conclusion is that the case of *Adkins v. Children's Hospital* should be, and it is, overruled. The judgment of the Supreme Court of the state of Washington is

Affirmed.

☐ *Justice SUTHERLAND, dissenting.*

Justice VAN DEVANTER, Justice McREYNOLDS, Justice BUTLER, and I think the judgment of the court below should be reversed.

It is urged that the question involved should now receive fresh consideration, among other reasons, because of "the economic conditions which have supervened"; but the meaning of the Constitution does not change with the ebb and flow of economic events. We frequently are told in more general words that the Constitution must be construed in the light of the present. If by that it is meant that the Constitution is made up of living words that apply to every new condition which they include, the statement is quite true. But to say, if that be intended, that the words of the Constitution mean today what they did not mean when written—that is, that they do not apply to a situation now to which they would have applied then—is to rob that instrument of the essential element which continues it in force as the people have made it until they, and not their official agents, have made it otherwise. . . .

The judicial function is that of interpretation; it does not include the power of amendment under the guise of interpretation. To miss the point of difference between the two is to miss all that the phrase "supreme law of the land" stands for and to convert what was intended as inescapable and enduring mandates into mere moral reflections.

If the Constitution, intelligently and reasonably construed in the light of these principles, stands in the way of desirable legislation, the blame must rest upon that instrument, and not upon the court for enforcing it according to its terms. The remedy in that situation—and the only true remedy— is to amend the Constitution. . . .

In the *Adkins* Case we . . . said that while there was no such thing as absolute freedom of contract, but that it was subject to a great variety of restraints, nevertheless, freedom of contract was the general rule and restraint the exception; and that the power to abridge that freedom could only be justified by the existence of exceptional circumstances. This statement of the rule has been many times affirmed; and we do not understand that it is questioned by the present decision.

C | *The "Takings Clause" and Just Compensation*

A final source for the Court's protection of proprietary interests is the Fifth Amendment's provision that "private property [shall not] be taken for public use, without just compensation." The takings clause broadly guarantees government the power of eminent domain—the power to take private property for public purposes—subject to the just compensation of the owners. But what is a "public purpose"? What constitutes the "taking" of property? And what amounts to "just" compensation?

The requirement that government put private property to public use has been rather loosely interpreted. The only limitations appear to be that government may not take property for the sole purpose of making money for itself or for a private enterprise. However, governments may take property and then resell it to private companies for such purposes as urban renewal, the development of industrial parks, or shopping centers, and for use by (even privately owned) public utilities. In *Hawaii Housing Authority v. Midkiff*, 467 U.S. 229 (1984) (excerpted below), for example, the Burger Court approved a state land reform act. As a vestige of Hawaiian feudalism, 96 percent of the state was owned by seventy-two landowners or state and federal governments. In 1967, Hawaii's legislature authorized the use of the power of eminent domain to condemn residential lots and to sell and transfer ownership to existing tenants on the land. The Court unanimously rejected the contention that this program constituted a taking of private property for private, not public, purposes.

General benefit to the public, not public ownership, is what matters, and the Court tends to be highly deferential to legislatures as to what benefits the public. "Subject to specific constitutional limitations," as the Court observed in *Berman v. Parker*, 348 U.S. 26 (1954), "when the legislature has spoken, the public interest has been declared in terms well-nigh conclusive."

Private property does not have to be physically taken by the government for an individual to win compensation. However, *Loretto v. Teleprompter Manhattan CATV*, 458 U.S. 419 (1982), held that permanent physical occupation of property by the government is per se taking and *First English Evangelical Lutheran Church v. County of Los Angeles*, 482 U.S. 304 (1987), ruled that temporary land-use laws may constitute a taking of private property, so-called *regulatory takings*. In the classic case of *United States v. Causby*, 328 U.S. 256 (1946), the Court upheld a demand for compensation by a farmer whose land was adjacent to a military airport. The noise of airplane flights over the farm rendered it virtually worthless and the Court upheld the farmer's claim that the government was using his farmland as an extension of its runway and had to pay for it.

Not everyone next to an airport or highway, however, may demand compensation because of the accompanying noise or, for that matter, inconvenience of government regulations. Instead, for property to be "taken" in a constitutional sense, an owner must show a nearly total loss of the use of the property. In *Pennsylvania Coal Co. v. Mahon*, 260 U.S. 393 (1922), Justice Holmes formulated a practical rule, when holding that "property may be regulated to a certain extent, [but] if regulation goes too far it will be recognized as a taking." There is no "brightline rule," but rather, the burden is placed on the property owner of showing a virtually complete loss of the use of his or her property to win compensation.

In another important ruling in *Penn Central Transportation Co. v. New York*, 438 U.S. 104 (1978), the Burger Court affirmed a historic preservation law prohibiting the owners of Grand Central Station in New York City from building a high-rise office tower above the station.

Finally, the Court largely avoided controversies over whether a property owner has received just compensation. In general, just compensation means what, in the absence of the government's acquisition of the property, a willing buyer would pay, or the fair market value. As the Court observed in *Backus v. Fort Street Union Depot Co.*, 169 U.S. 557 (1898): "All that is essential is that in some appropriate way, before some properly constituted tribunal, inquiry shall be made as to the amount of compensation, and when this has been provided there is that due process of law which is required by the Federal Constitution."

The Rehnquist Court signaled renewed interest in, and invited litigation over, regulatory takings–clause jurisprudence in its 1987 rulings in *Nollan v. California Coastal Commission*, 483 U.S. 825 (1987), and *First*

English Evangelical Lutheran Church v. County of Los Angeles, as well as revisited challenges to land-use regulations in several other cases. In *Nollan*, Justice Scalia commanded a bare majority for holding that the just compensation clause was violated by California's regulation requiring homeowners of beachfront property to agree to a public easement across their property as a condition of receiving a building permit. However, a majority of the Court appears unwilling to further extend *Nollan's* analysis. In the leading regulatory "takings clause" case after *Nollan, Lucas v. South Carolina Coastal Council* (1992) (excerpted below), the owner of beachfront property appealed a decision of the South Carolina Supreme Court that upheld a regulation barring the rebuilding of houses on the shoreline. Writing for the majority in *Lucas*, Justice Scalia held, on the one hand, that property owners who suffer total economic loss of the value of their land may have a takings-clause claim. Historically, the Court recognized takings claims only when the government actually took physical possession of a property, as in an eminent domain proceeding. But, in *Nollan* and *Lucas*, the Court recognized regulatory takings requiring the government to pay compensation when its regulations diminish the value of private property. In *Lucas*, Scalia held that it is not enough for the government to defend its environmental, land-use, and zoning regulations as in the "public interest." Governments must also defend their regulations as necessary to avoid a public harm or the "harmful or noxious use" of private property; thus a property owner might be denied a permit to run a landfill operation because it would result in flooding of nearby land. Because the state courts failed to identify the public nuisances that would justify the building restrictions in this case, the court remanded *Lucas* for further consideration.

Justice Scalia's opinion, on the other hand, limited its takings-clause analysis to apply only when property owners are totally deprived of the economic value of their land. As he put it, "When the owner of real property has been called upon to sacrifice *all* economically beneficial uses in the name of the common good, that is, to leave his property economically idle, he has suffered a taking." That, however, significantly limited the Court's holding because, as dissenting Justice Stevens observed, "A land-owner whose property is diminished in value 95 percent recovers nothing, while an owner whose property is diminished 100 percent recovers the land's full value." Since most environmental and land-use regulations do not deprive property owners of all economic use or value of their property, Justice Scalia's analysis in *Lucas* is severely limited. The Roberts Court revisited a regulatory-takings question left open after *Lucas,* namely, the so-called denominator problem of who and what defines the boundaries of property alleged taken by government and entitling compensation, in *Murr v. Wisconsin*, 137 S. Ct. 1933

(2017). The Murrs were given two adjacent riverfront lots—lots E and F—by their parents, who bought them separately, but when the titles were transferred, under state and local law, they were considered "merged." They later wanted to sell Lot E and make improvements on the other. But they were denied doing so because the lots were deemed merged, and hence could only be sold or built on as a combined parcel. Writing for the Court, Justice Kennedy affirmed *Lucas*'s holding that "with certain qualifications . . . a regulation which 'denies all economically beneficial or productive use of land' will require" compensation; and, second, whether a regulatory takings occurs depends on "a complex of factors," including the economic impact, the extent to which there is interference with the property owners' investment expectations, and the character of the governmental action. While emphasizing "flexibility" in applying those considerations, Kenney concluded that courts should (1) objectively consider the owner's expectations about dividing a property, (2) consider the property's physical nature, and (3) assess the property's value in relation to that of other holdings. Here, Kennedy concluded that the Murrs' property should be considered a single parcel because the two lots had been merged, they were contiguous, and Lot E added to the value of Lot F; thus, the Murrs were not entitled to compensation. Chief Justice Roberts, joined by Justices Thomas and Alito, dissented, criticizing the majority for its elaborate test and maintained, "State law defines the boundaries of distinct parcels of law, and those boundaries should determine the 'private property' at issue in regulatory takings cases."

In a major ruling with wide-ranging ramifications for urban planners and homeowners, by a 5–4 vote the Court upheld the use of the government's power of eminent domain and to condemn and take, with just compensation, private property for the purpose of advancing the economic development of the community. Writing for the Court in *Kelo v. City of New London* (excerpted below), Justice Stevens held that "public use" was not limited to the use of public domain to build a road or a bridge; or to redistribute land ownership, as in *Hawaii Housing Authority v. Midkiff*; but includes "promoting economic development," even if the property was taken and sold for development by private developers. Justice Stevens emphasized that courts should be deferential to the decisions of state and local authorities. Justice Kennedy cast the pivotal fifth vote and filed a concurring opinion, underscoring that courts should still exercise review in such cases in order to ensure that governments do not use their power of eminent domain to simply reward or advance the interests of businesses and powerful private interests. Justice O'Connor filed a dissenting opinion which was joined by Chief Justice Rehnquist, and Justices Scalia and Thomas dissented.

Finally, the Roberts Court ruled that the government may not force farmers to give up part of their annual crop for less than it is worth in *Horne v. Department of Agriculture*, 135 S.Ct. 2419 (2015). By an 8–1 vote, a 1940s-era program enacted initially during the Great Depression was invalidated because it allowed federal officials to seize personal property from farmers without fully compensating them, even though the goal of the program was to benefit farmers by stabilizing market prices. The Agricultural Marketing Agreement Act of 1937 authorized issuing "marketing orders" in order to stabilize markets for particular crops. A market order for raisins established a Raisins Administrative Committee, which imposed a requirement that growers set aside a certain percentage of their crop for the government. The government then sold the raisins in noncompetitive markets, donated them, or otherwise disposed of them. If there were any profits left over, the net proceeds were paid to the farmers. In 2002–2003, for example, raisin growers were required to set aside 47 percent of their crop. Marvin Horne refused to set aside any raisins on the ground that this would constitute a taking of private property without just compensation as guaranteed by the Fifth Amendment. Horne was later fined the fair market value of the raisins and given a civil penalty. On appeal, the Court of Appeals for the Ninth Circuit held that the requirement was not a taking because personal property is afforded less protection than *real* property.

Writing for the Court in *Horne*, Chief Justice Roberts reversed the appellate court in holding that the government must pay just compensation as a condition for not selling the raisins in interstate commerce. Notably, *Wickard v. Filburn*, 317 U.S. 111 (1942) (excerpted in Vol. 1, Ch. 6), upheld the act under Congress's power to regulate interstate commerce, even though Wickard grew 239 bushels of wheat more than his allocated 222 bushels in order to feed his livestock, because of the aggregative effect on the market. That ruling was limited by Chief Justice Roberts in *National Federation of Independent Business v. Sebelius*, 567 U.S. 519 (2012) (excerpted in Vol. 1, Ch. 6), which upheld the "individual mandate" for health insurance in the Affordable Care Act based on Congress's spending and tax power but not its power under the interstate commerce clause. In *Horne*, Chief Justice Roberts reasoned that the just compensation clause applies to personal property no less than to real property; and the government has a duty to pay just compensation for taking personal property just like taking your car or home. The Chief Justice traced this principle back to the Magna Carta, and it was incorporated in the Fifth Amendment, due to the taking of property by both sides in the Revolutionary War. Here, he concluded that the government could simply limit the production of raisins—as with wheat in *Wickard v. Filburn*—but the Raisin Committee took personal and physical property by transferring the raisins from the grower to the government. Only Justice Sotomayor dissented on the merits. *Horne* was a significant victory for property owners in limiting the powers of the federal government, but it may have little immediate impact since only a few other crops—such as California dried prunes, dates, almonds, and walnuts—are regulated in the same way.

SELECTED BIBLIOGRAPHY

Adler, Jonathan, ed. *Business and the Roberts Court*. New York: Oxford University Press, 2016.

Bernstein, Jeff. *Little Pink House: A True Story of Defiance and Courage (Kelo v. City of New London)*. New York: Grand Central Publishing, 2009.

Fischel, William. *Regulatory Takings: Law, Economics, and Politics*. Cambridge, MA: Harvard University Press, 1995.

Levy, Leonard. *A License to Steal: Forfeiture of Property*. Chapel Hill: University of North Carolina Press, 1996.

Somin, Ilya. *The Grasping Hand: Kelo v. City of New London and the Limits of Eminent Domain*. Chicago: University of Chicago Press, 2015.

Wolf, Michael Allan. *The Zoning of America: Euclid v. Ambler*. Lawrence: University Press of Kansas, 2008.

■ INSIDE THE COURT

Hawaii Housing Authority v. Midkiff (1984) and Kelo v. City of New London, Connecticut (2005)

A major controversy erupted over the Court's ruling in *Kelo v. City of New London, Connecticut* (2005) (excerpted in this chapter), holding that private property may be taken by the government, with just compensation, in order to promote economic development, even if the property is then turned over for development by private businesses. Some states and local governments responded with constitutional amendments and ordinances prohibiting such takings whereas other cities moved to condemn property in order to promote economic revitalization. Yet, *Hawaii Housing Authority v. Midkiff* (1984) (excerpted in this chapter) upheld a state land reform that transferred ownership of law from feudal owners to tenants. While *Kelo* was widely criticized, *Midkiff* was praised for promoting equality and the redistribution of the wealth, even though both upheld the government's taking of private property for "public use" and selling it to private developers and owners.

Ironically, Justice O'Connor delivered the opinion for the Court in *Midkiff* but issued a stinging dissent in *Kelo*. Moreover, Justice O'Connor circulated a draft opinion in *Midkiff* that swept very broadly in justifying the government's taking of property for public use for virtually any social purpose. In response, Justice Lewis F. Powell suggested some modifying language to narrow the opinion. On May 18, 1984, Justice Powell sent the following memo to Justice O'Connor:[1]

Dear Sandra:

This refers to our brief conversation yesterday. I should have been in touch with you sooner. My suggested changes, set forth below, do not affect your basic analysis. I have been concerned by the sweep of language that can be read as saying that any "social" purpose may justify the taking of private property. The language to this effect is primarily on page 14.

I suggest the following as a substitute for the next to the last sentence in the paragraph on p. 14 that carries over from p. 13:

As the unique way titles were held in Hawaii skewed the land market, exercise of the power of eminent domain was justified. The Act advances its purposes without the state taking actual possession of the land. In such cases,

The paragraph that begins on p. 14 also can be read broadly to the effect that "social problems" may be addressed by taking private property pursuant to "social legislation". I suggest revisions of some of the language of this paragraph, beginning with the second sentence, along the following lines:

Judicial deference is required here because, in our system of government, legislatures are better able to assess what public purposes should be advanced by an exercise of the taking power. State legislatures are as capable as Congress of making such determinations within their respective spheres of authority. See *Berman v. Parker*, 348 U.S. [26 (1954)], at 32. Thus, if there are substantial reasons for an exercise of the taking power, courts must . . .

(continues)

■ INSIDE THE COURT
Hawaii Housing Authority v. Midkiff (1984) and
Kelo v. City of New London, Connecticut (2005) *(continued)*

The first full sentence on page 13 states that "redistribution offered simply to reduce the economic and social evils . . . is a rational exercise of the power of eminent domain." Again, I am troubled by the emphasis without limits on "economic and social evils". In this case we are concerned only with a very specific and unique evil. I would suggest omission of the phrase "reduce the economic evils", replacing it with "correct deficiencies in the market".

This *is* a unique case, and I think we may regret language that could encourage Congress and state legislatures to justify taking private property for any perceived social evil.

I am not sending this letter to the Conference, in the hope that changes along these lines will be acceptable to you. If not, I probably will write briefly.

I do appreciate your willingness to consider these.

Sincerely,
[LFP]

Justice Powell's suggested changes were incorporated by Justice O'Connor, though her opinion still swept broadly on the government's power of eminent domain. See and compare her opinion (for a unanimous Court, with Justice Marshall not participating) in *Midkiff*, along with her dissenting opinion (joined by Chief Justice Rehnquist and Justices Scalia and Thomas) in *Kelo*, and consider how to define "public use," for what purposes, and whether courts or state and local governments should determine the justification for the government's taking of private property.

1. Justice Lewis F. Powell Jr., Papers, Washington & Lee University School of Law, Lexington, Virginia.

Hawaii Housing Authority v. Midkiff

467 U.S. 229, 104 S.CT. 2321 (1984)

The Hawaiian islands were originally settled by Polynesian immigrants from the western Pacific. These settlers developed an economy around a feudal land-tenure system in which one island high chief controlled the land and assigned it for development to subchiefs. Beginning in the early 1800s, Hawaiian leaders and American settlers attempted to divide the lands of the kingdom among the crown, the chiefs, and the common people. These efforts proved largely unsuccessful, however. Finally, in the mid-1960s the Hawaii legislature held hearings and discovered that while the state and federal governments owned almost 49 percent of the state's land, another 47 percent was owned by seventy-two landholders. The legislature concluded that such concentrated land ownership was responsible for skewing the state's land prices and injuring the public tranquillity and welfare. Accordingly, the legislature enacted legislation in order to compel the large landowners to break up their estates. The Land Reform Act of 1967 created a mechanism for condemning residential tracts and for transferring ownership of condemned land to lessees. Under the act's condemnation scheme, tenants living on single-family lots within development tracts at least five acres in size were entitled to ask the Hawaii Housing Authority (HHA) to condemn the property on which they lived. When twenty-five eligible tenants, or tenants on half of the lots in the tract, whichever was less, filed appropriate applications, the act authorized the HHA to hold a public hearing to determine whether the acquisition of the land would "effectuate the public purposes" of the law. If the HHA found that these purposes would be served, it was authorized to acquire the land, at prices set either by a condemnation trial or by negotiations with the landowners.

After HHA held a public hearing on the proposed acquisition of appellees' lands and found that such acquisition would effectuate the act's public purposes, it directed appellees to negotiate with certain lessees concerning the sale of the designated properties. When these negotiations failed, HHA ordered appellees to submit to compulsory arbitration as provided by the act. Rather than comply with this order, appellees filed suit in federal district court, asking that the act be declared unconstitutional. That court held that act to be constitutional under the public use clause of the Fifth Amendment. But the Court of Appeals for the Ninth Circuit reversed, holding that the law violated the Fifth Amendment. The HHA appealed and the Supreme Court granted review and reversed the appellate court.

The Court's decision, with Justice Marshall not participating, was unanimous and delivered by Justice O'Connor.

■ ■ ■

☐ *Justice O'CONNOR delivered the opinion of the Court.*

The Fifth Amendment of the United States Constitution provides, in pertinent part, that "private property [shall not] be taken for public use, without just compensation." These cases present the question whether the Public Use Clause of that Amendment, made applicable to the States through the Fourteenth Amendment, prohibits the State of Hawaii from taking, with just compensation, title in real property from lessors and transferring it to lessees in order to reduce the concentration of ownership of fees simple in the State. We conclude that it does not. . . .

The starting point for our analysis of the Act's constitutionality is the Court's decision in *Berman v. Parker*, 348 U.S. 26 (1954). In *Berman*, the Court held constitutional the District of Columbia Redevelopment Act of 1945. That Act provided both for the comprehensive use of the eminent domain power to redevelop slum areas and for the possible sale or lease of the condemned lands to private interests. In discussing whether the takings authorized by that Act were for a "public use," the Court stated:

> We deal, in other words, with what traditionally has been known as the police power. An attempt to define its reach or trace its outer limits is fruitless, for each case must turn on its own facts. The definition is essentially the product of legislative determinations addressed to the purposes of government, purposes neither abstractly nor historically capable of complete definition. Subject to specific constitutional limitations, when the legislature has spoken, the public interest has been declared in terms well-nigh conclusive. In such cases the legislature, not the judiciary, is the main guardian of the public needs to be served by social legislation, whether it be Congress legislating concerning the District of Columbia . . . or the States legislating concerning local affairs. . . . This principle admits of no exception merely because the power of eminent domain is involved. . . .

The Court explicitly recognized the breadth of the principle it was announcing, noting:

> Once the object is within the authority of Congress, the right to realize it through the exercise of eminent domain is clear. For the power of eminent domain is merely the means to the end. . . . Once the object is within the authority of Congress, the means by which it will be attained is also for Congress to determine. Here one of the means chosen is the use of private enterprise for redevelopment of the area. Appellants argue that this makes the project a taking from one businessman for the benefit of another businessman. But the means of executing the project are for Congress and Congress alone to determine, once the public purpose has been established.

The "public use" requirement is thus coterminous with the scope of a sovereign's police powers. There is, of course, a role for courts to play in reviewing a legislature's judgment of what constitutes a public use, even when the eminent domain power is equated with the police power. But the Court in *Berman* made clear that it is "an extremely narrow" one. The Court in *Berman* cited with approval the Court's decision in *Old Dominion Co. v. United States*, 269 U.S. 55 (1925), which held that deference to the legislature's "public use" determination is required "until it is shown to involve an impossibility." . . . To be sure, the Court's cases have repeatedly stated that "one person's property may not be taken for the benefit of another private person without a justifying public purpose, even though compensation be paid." *Thompson v. Consolidated Gas Corp.*, 300 U.S. 55 (1937). Thus, in *Missouri Pacific R. Co. v. Nebraska*, 164 U.S. 403 (1896), where the "order in question was not, and was not claimed to be, . . . a taking of private property for a public use under the right of eminent domain," the Court invalidated a compensated taking of property for lack of a justifying public purpose. But where the exercise of the eminent domain power is rationally related to a conceivable public purpose, the Court has never held a compensated taking to be proscribed by the Public Use Clause. On this basis, we have no trouble concluding that the Hawaii Act is constitutional. The people of Hawaii have attempted, much as the settlers of the original 13 Colonies did, to reduce the perceived social and economic evils of a land oligopoly traceable to their monarchs. The land oligopoly has, according to the Hawaii Legislature, created artificial deterrents to the normal functioning of the State's residential land market and forced thousands of individual homeowners to lease, rather than buy, the land underneath their homes. Regulating oligopoly and the evils associated with it is a classic exercise of a State's police powers. We cannot disapprove of Hawaii's exercise of this power. . . .

The State of Hawaii has never denied that the Constitution forbids even a compensated taking of property when executed for no reason other than to confer a private benefit on a particular private party. A purely private taking could not withstand the scrutiny of the public use requirement; it would serve no legitimate purpose of government and would thus be void. But no purely private taking is involved in these cases. The Hawaii Legislature enacted its Land Reform Act not to benefit a particular class of identifiable individuals but to attack certain perceived evils of concentrated property ownership in Hawaii—a legitimate public purpose. Use of the condemnation power to achieve this purpose is not irrational. Since we assume for purposes of these appeals that the weighty demand of just compensation has been met, the requirements of the Fifth and Fourteenth Amendments have been satisfied. Accordingly, we reverse the judgment of the Court of Appeals, and remand these cases for further proceedings in conformity with this opinion.

Lucas v. South Carolina Coastal Council
505 U.S. 1003, 112 S.CT. 2886 (1992)

In 1986, petitioner David H. Lucas paid $975,000 for two residential lots on the Isle of Palms in Charleston County, South Carolina, on which he intended to build single-family homes. In 1988, however, the South Carolina Legislature enacted the Beachfront Management Act, which had the effect of barring Lucas from building on the land. A state trial court found that this prohibition rendered Lucas's parcels "valueless," for which he was entitled to just compensation. On appeal, the state supreme court reversed and Lucas appealed to the U.S. Supreme Court.

The state supreme court's decision was reversed by a vote of 6–3. Justice Scalia delivered the opinion for the Court. Justice Kennedy filed a concurring opinion. Justices Blackmun and Stevens filed separate dissenting opinions, and Justice Souter filed a statement indicating that case should have been dismissed as improvidently granted.

■ ■ ■

☐ *Justice SCALIA delivered the opinion of the Court.*

Prior to Justice HOLMES's exposition in *Pennsylvania Coal Co. v. Mahon*, 260 U.S. 393 (1922), it was generally thought that the Takings Clause reached only a "direct appropriation" of property, *Legal Tender Cases*, 79 U.S. (12 Wall.) 457 (1871), or the functional equivalent of a "practical ouster of [the owner's] possession," *Transportation Co. v. Chicago*, 99 U.S. 635 (1879). Justice HOLMES recognized in *Mahon*, however, that if the protection against physical appropriations of private property was to be meaningfully enforced, the government's power to redefine the range of interests included in the ownership of property was necessarily constrained by constitutional limits. If, instead, the uses of private property were subject to unbridled, uncompensated qualification under the police power, "the natural tendency of human nature [would be] to extend the qualification more and more until at last private property disappeared." These considerations gave birth in that case to the oft-cited maxim that, "while property may be regulated to a certain extent, if regulation goes too far it will be recognized as a taking."

Nevertheless, our decision in *Mahon* offered little insight into when, and under what circumstances, a given regulation would be seen as going "too far" for purposes of the Fifth Amendment. In 70-odd years of succeeding "regulatory takings" jurisprudence, we have generally eschewed any "set formula" for determining how far is too far, preferring to "engage in . . . essentially ad hoc, factual inquiries." *Penn Central Transportation Co. v. New York City*, 438 U.S. 104 (1978). We have, however, described at least two discrete categories of regulatory action as compensable without case-specific inquiry into the public interest advanced in support of the restraint. The first encompasses regulations that compel the property owner to suffer a physical "invasion" of his property. In general (at least with regard to permanent invasions), no matter how minute the intrusion, and no matter how weighty the public purpose behind it, we have required compensation. For example, in *Loretto v. Teleprompter Manhattan CATV Corp.*, 458 U.S. 419 (1982), we determined that New York's law requiring landlords to allow television cable companies to emplace cable facilities in their apartment buildings constituted a taking, even though the facilities occupied at most only 1½ cubic feet of the landlords' property.

The second situation in which we have found categorical treatment appropriate is where regulation denies all economically beneficial or productive use of land. As we have said on numerous occasions, the Fifth Amendment is violated when land-use regulation "does not substantially advance legitimate state interests or denies an owner economically viable use of his land."

We have never set forth the justification for this rule. Perhaps it is simply, as Justice BRENNAN suggested, that total deprivation of beneficial use is, from the landowner's point of view, the equivalent of a physical appropriation. See *San Diego Gas & Electric Co. v. San Diego*, 450 U.S. [627] (1981). . . . We think . . . that there are good reasons for our frequently expressed belief that when the owner of real property has been called upon to sacrifice all economically beneficial uses in the name of the common good, that is, to leave his property economically idle, he has suffered a taking.

The trial court found Lucas's two beachfront lots to have been rendered valueless by respondent's enforcement of the coastal-zone construction ban. Under Lucas's theory of the case, which rested upon our "no economically viable use" statements, that finding entitled him to compensation. . . . The South Carolina Supreme Court, however, thought otherwise. In its view, the Beachfront Management Act was no ordinary enactment, but involved an exercise of South Carolina's "police powers" to mitigate the harm to the public interest that petitioner's use of his land might occasion. . . . In the court's view, these concessions brought petitioner's challenge within a long line of this Court's cases sustaining against Due Process and Takings Clause challenges the State's use of its "police powers" to enjoin a property owner from activities akin to public nuisances. See *Mugler v. Kansas*, 123 U.S. 623 (1887) (law prohibiting manufacture of alcoholic beverages).

For a number of reasons, however, we think the South Carolina Supreme Court was too quick to conclude that that principle decides the present case. The "harmful or noxious uses" principle was the Court's early attempt to describe in theoretical terms why government may, consistent with the Takings Clause, affect property values by regulation without incurring an obligation to compensate—a reality we nowadays acknowledge explicitly with respect to the full scope of the State's police power. . . . "Harmful or noxious use" analysis was, in other words, simply the progenitor of our more contemporary statements that "land-use regulation does not effect a taking if it 'substantially advances legitimate state interests' . . ."

The transition from our early focus on control of "noxious" uses to our contemporary understanding of the broad realm within which government may regulate without compensation was an easy one, since the distinction between "harm-preventing" and "benefit-conferring" regulation is often in the eye of the beholder. It is quite possible, for example, to describe in either fashion the ecological, economic, and esthetic concerns that inspired the South Carolina Legislature in the present case. One could say that imposing a servitude on Lucas's land is necessary in order to prevent his use of it from "harming" South Carolina's ecological resources; or, instead, in order to achieve the "benefits" of an ecological preserve. Whether one or the other of the competing characterizations will come to one's lips in a particular case depends primarily upon one's evaluation of the worth of competing uses of real estate. A given restraint will be seen as mitigating "harm" to the adjacent parcels or securing a "benefit" for them, depending upon the observer's evaluation of the relative importance of the use that the restraint favors. Whether Lucas's construction of single-family residences on his parcels should be described as bringing "harm" to South Carolina's adjacent ecological resources thus depends principally upon whether the describer believes that the State's use interest in nurturing those resources is so important that any competing adjacent use must yield.

When it is understood that "prevention of harmful use" was merely our early formulation of the police power justification necessary to sustain (without compensation) any regulatory diminution in value; and that the distinction between regulation that "prevents harmful use" and that which "confers benefits" is difficult, if not impossible, to discern on an objective, value-free basis; it becomes self-evident that noxious-use logic cannot serve as a touchstone to distinguish regulatory "takings"—which require compensation—from regulatory deprivations that do not require compensation. . . .

Where the State seeks to sustain regulation that deprives land of all economically beneficial use, we think it may resist compensation only if the logically antecedent inquiry into the nature of the owner's estate shows that the proscribed use interests were not part of his title to begin with. This accords, we think, with our "takings" jurisprudence, which has traditionally been guided by the understandings of our citizens regarding the content of, and the State's power over, the "bundle of rights" that they acquire when they obtain title to property. It seems to us that the property owner necessarily expects the uses of his property to be restricted, from time to time, by various measures newly enacted by the State in legitimate exercise of its police powers; "as long recognized, some values are enjoyed under an implied limitation and must yield to the police power." *Pennsylvania Coal Co. v. Mahon.* And in the case of personal property, by reason of the State's traditionally high degree of control over commercial dealings, he ought to be aware of the possibility that new regulation might even render his property economically worthless (at least if the property's only economically productive use is sale or manufacture for sale). In the case of land, however, we think the notion pressed by the Council that title is somehow held subject to the "implied limitation" that the State may subsequently eliminate all economically valuable use is inconsistent with the historical compact recorded in the Takings Clause that has become part of our constitutional culture.

Where "permanent physical occupation" of land is concerned, we have refused to allow the government to decree it anew (without compensation), no matter how weighty the asserted "public interests" involved, *Loretto v.*

Teleprompter Manhattan CATV Corp.—though we assuredly would permit the government to assert a permanent easement that was a pre-existing limitation upon the landowner's title. We believe similar treatment must be accorded confiscatory regulations, i.e., regulations that prohibit all economically beneficial use of land: Any limitation so severe cannot be newly legislated or decreed (without compensation), but must inhere in the title itself, in the restrictions that background principles of the State's law of property and nuisance already place upon land ownership. A law or decree with such an effect must, in other words, do no more than duplicate the result that could have been achieved in the courts—by adjacent landowners (or other uniquely affected persons) under the State's law of private nuisance, or by the State under its complementary power to abate nuisances that affect the public generally, or otherwise.

On this analysis, the owner of a lakebed, for example, would not be entitled to compensation when he is denied the requisite permit to engage in a landfilling operation that would have the effect of flooding others' land. . . . Such regulatory action may well have the effect of eliminating the land's only economically productive use, but it does not proscribe a productive use that was previously permissible under relevant property and nuisance principles. The use of these properties for what are now expressly prohibited purposes was always unlawful, and (subject to other constitutional limitations) it was open to the State at any point to make the implication of those background principles of nuisance and property law explicit. In light of our traditional resort to "existing rules or understandings that stem from an independent source such as state law" to define the range of interests that qualify for protection as "property" under the Fifth and Fourteenth Amendments, this recognition that the Takings Clause does not require compensation when an owner is barred from putting land to a use that is proscribed by those "existing rules or understandings" is surely unexceptional. When, however, a regulation that declares "off-limits" all economically productive or beneficial uses of land goes beyond what the relevant background principles would dictate, compensation must be paid to sustain it.

The "total taking" inquiry we require today will ordinarily entail (as the application of state nuisance law ordinarily entails) analysis of, among other things, the degree of harm to public lands and resources, or adjacent private property, posed by the claimant's proposed activities, the social value of the claimant's activities and their suitability to the locality in question, and the relative ease with which the alleged harm can be avoided through measures taken by the claimant and the government (or adjacent private landowners) alike. The fact that a particular use has long been engaged in by similarly situated owners ordinarily imports a lack of any common-law prohibition (though changed circumstances or new knowledge may make what was previously permissible no longer so. So also does the fact that other landowners, similarly situated, are permitted to continue the use denied to the claimant.

It seems unlikely that common-law principles would have prevented the erection of any habitable or productive improvements on petitioner's land; they rarely support prohibition of the "essential use" of land. The question, however, is one of state law to be dealt with on remand. We emphasize that to win its case South Carolina must do more than proffer the legislature's declaration that the uses Lucas desires are inconsistent with the public interest, or the conclusory assertion that they violate a common-law maxim. . . . As we have said, a "State, by *ipse dixit*, may not transform private property into public property without compensation. . . ." *Webb's Fabulous Pharmacies, Inc. v. Beckwith*, 449 U.S. 155 (1980). Instead, as it would be required to do if it sought to restrain Lucas in a common-law action for public nuisance, South Carolina must identify background principles of nuisance and property law that prohibit the uses he now intends in the circumstances in which the property is presently found. Only on this showing can the State fairly claim that, in proscribing all such beneficial uses, the Beachfront Management Act is taking nothing.

The judgment is reversed, and the case is remanded for proceedings not inconsistent with this opinion.

☐ *Justice BLACKMUN, dissenting.*

Today the Court launches a missile to kill a mouse.

The State of South Carolina prohibited petitioner Lucas from building a permanent structure on his property from 1988 to 1990. Relying on an unreviewed (and implausible) state trial court finding that this restriction left Lucas' property valueless, this Court granted review to determine whether compensation must be paid in cases where the State prohibits all economic use of real estate. According to the Court, such an occasion never has arisen in any of our prior cases, and the Court imagines that it will arise "relatively rarely" or only in "extraordinary circumstances." Almost certainly it did not happen in this case.

Nonetheless, the Court presses on to decide the issue, and as it does, it ignores its jurisdictional limits, remakes its traditional rules of review, and creates simultaneously a new categorical rule and an exception (neither of which is rooted in our prior case law, common law, or common sense). I protest not only the Court's decision, but each step taken to reach it. More fundamentally, I question the Court's wisdom in issuing sweeping new rules to decide such a narrow case. [T]he Court could have reached the result it wanted without inflicting this damage upon our Takings Clause jurisprudence. . . .

☐ *Justice STEVENS, dissenting.*

In addition to lacking support in past decisions, the Court's new rule is wholly arbitrary. A landowner whose property is diminished in value 95% recovers nothing, while an owner whose property is diminished 100% recovers the land's full value. The case at hand illustrates this arbitrariness well. The Beachfront Management Act not only prohibited the building of new dwellings in certain areas, it also prohibited the rebuilding of houses that were "destroyed beyond repair by natural causes or by fire." Thus, if the homes adjacent to Lucas' lot were destroyed by a hurricane one day after the Act took effect, the owners would not be able to rebuild, nor would they be assured recovery. Under the Court's categorical approach, Lucas (who has lost the opportunity to build) recovers, while his neighbors (who have lost both the opportunity to build and their homes) do not recover. The arbitrariness of such a rule is palpable.

Moreover, because of the elastic nature of property rights, the Court's new rule will also prove unsound in practice. In response to the rule, courts may define "property" broadly and only rarely find regulations to effect total takings. This is the approach the Court itself adopts in its revisionist reading of venerable precedents. We are told that—notwithstanding the Court's findings to the contrary in each case—the brewery in *Mugler*—could be put to "other uses" and that, therefore, those cases did not involve total regulatory takings. . . .

Finally, the Court's justification for its new categorical rule is remarkably thin. The Court mentions in passing three arguments in support of its rule; none is convincing. First, the Court suggests that "total deprivation of feasible use is, from the landowner's point of view, the equivalent of a physical appropriation." This argument proves too much. From the "landowner's point of view," a regulation that diminishes a lot's value by 50% is as well "the equivalent" of the condemnation of half of the lot. Yet, it is well established that a 50% diminution in value does not by itself constitute a taking. Thus, the landowner's perception of the regulation cannot justify the Court's new rule.

Second, the Court emphasizes that because total takings are "relatively rare" its new rule will not adversely affect the government's ability to "go on." This argument proves too little. Certainly it is true that defining a small class of regulations that are per se takings will not greatly hinder important governmental functions—but this is true of any small class of regulations. The Court's suggestion only begs the question of why regulations of this particular class should always be found to effect takings. . . .

In short, the Court's new rule is unsupported by prior decisions, arbitrary and unsound in practice, and theoretically unjustified. In my opinion, a categorical rule as important as the one established by the Court today should be supported by more history or more reason than has yet been provided. . . .

Kelo v. City of New London, Connecticut
545 U.S. 469, 125 S.Ct. 2655 (2005)

The city of New London is at the junction of the Thames River and the Long Island Sound in southeastern Connecticut. Decades of economic decline led the state in 1990 to designate the city a "distressed municipality." In 1996, the federal government closed the Naval Undersea Warfare Center, which had been located in the Fort Trumbull area of the city and had employed over 1,500 people. In 1998, the city's unemployment rate was nearly double that of the state, and its population of just under 24,000 residents was at its lowest since 1920. These conditions prompted state and local officials to target New London, and particularly its Fort Trumbull area, for economic revitalization. The New London Development Corporation (NLDC), a private nonprofit entity, was authorized to assist the city in planning economic development. In January 1998, Connecticut approved a $5.35 million bond issue to support the NLDC's planning activities and a $10 million bond issue for the creation of a Fort Trumbull State Park. In February, the pharmaceutical company Pfizer announced that it would build a $300 million research facility in the Fort Trumbull area, and the NLDC hoped that that would draw new business to the area. The Fort Trumbull area is on a peninsula that juts into the Thames River and includes approximately 115 privately owned properties, as well as the thirty-two acres of land formerly occupied by the naval facility. The NLDC's development plan called for the creation of a waterfront conference hotel at the center of a "small urban village," including restaurants and stores, as well as a pedestrian "riverwalk" that would continue down the coast, along with a new U.S. Coast Guard Museum, a renovated marina, and research and development office space. The NLDC's development plan aimed to capitalize on the arrival of the Pfizer facility and the new commerce it would attract. In addition to creating jobs and generating tax revenue, the plan sought to create recreational opportunities on the waterfront and in the park. The city council approved the plan in January 2000, and designated the NLDC its development agent. The city council also authorized the NLDC to purchase property or to acquire property by exercising eminent domain in the city's name. The NLDC successfully negotiated the purchase of most of the real estate in the ninety-acre area, but its negotiations with some homeowners failed and the NLDC initiated the condemnation proceedings against them.

Susette Kelo lived in the Fort Trumbull area and had made extensive improvements to her well-maintained house, which overlooks the Thames River. In December 2000, Kelo and a few other homeowners of condemned property sued New London, claiming that the taking of their properties, even with just compensation, violated the "public use" restriction in the Fifth Amendment, because their properties would not be used for a public purpose, like building a road, but instead sold to private parties for development—development that the city claimed would economically benefit the community. A trial court granted a restraining order prohibiting New London's taking of some of the properties, but on appeal the state supreme court ruled that the city could take all of the properties. Kelo appealed that decision and the Supreme Court granted review.

The state supreme court's decision was affirmed by a 5–4 vote. Justice Stevens delivered the opinion of the Court. Justice Kennedy filed a concurring opinion. Justice O'Connor, joined by Chief Justice Rehnquist and Justices Scalia and Thomas, dissented. Justice Thomas also filed a dissenting opinion.

■ ■ ■

☐ *Justice STEVENS delivered the opinion of the Court.*

We granted *certiorari* to determine whether a city's decision to take property for the purpose of economic development satisfies the "public use" requirement of the Fifth Amendment. Two polar propositions are perfectly clear. On the one hand, it has long been accepted that the sovereign may not take the property of A for the sole purpose of transferring it to another private party B, even though A is paid just compensation. On the other hand, it is equally clear that a State may transfer property from one private party to another if future "use by the public" is the purpose of the taking; the condemnation of land for a railroad with common-carrier duties is a familiar example. Neither of these propositions, however, determines the disposition of this case.

As for the first proposition, the City would no doubt be forbidden from taking petitioners' land for the purpose of conferring a private benefit on a particular private party. See [*Hawaii Housing Authority v.*] *Midkiff,* 467 U.S. [229 (1984)] ("A purely private taking could not withstand the scrutiny of the public use requirement; it would serve no legitimate purpose of government and would thus be void"). Nor would the City be allowed to take property under the mere pretext of a public purpose, when its actual purpose was to bestow a private benefit. The takings before us, however, would be executed pursuant to a "carefully considered" development plan. The trial judge and all the members of the Supreme Court of Connecticut agreed that there was no evidence of an illegitimate purpose in this case. Therefore, as was true of the statute challenged in *Midkiff,* the City's development plan was not adopted "to benefit a particular class of identifiable individuals."

On the other hand, this is not a case in which the City is planning to open the condemned land—at least not in its entirety—to use by the general public. Nor will the private lessees of the land in any sense be required to operate like common carriers, making their services available to all corners. But although such a projected use would be sufficient to satisfy the public use requirement, this "Court long ago rejected any literal requirement that condemned property be put into use for the general public." Indeed, while many state courts in the mid-nineteenth century endorsed "use by the public" as the proper definition of public use, that narrow view steadily eroded over time. Not only was the "use by the public" test difficult to administer (e.g., what proportion of the public need have access to the property? at what price?), but it proved to be impractical given the diverse and always evolving needs of society. Accordingly, when this Court began applying the Fifth Amendment to the States at the close of the nineteenth century, it embraced the broader and more natural interpretation of public use as "public purpose." Thus, in a case upholding a mining company's use of an aerial bucket line to transport ore over property it did not own, Justice HOLMES' opinion for the Court stressed "the inadequacy of use by the general public as a universal test." *Strickley v. Highland Boy Gold Mining Co.,* 200 U.S. 527 (1906). We have repeatedly and consistently rejected that narrow test ever since.

The disposition of this case therefore turns on the question whether the City's development plan serves a "public purpose." Without exception, our cases have defined that concept broadly, reflecting our longstanding policy of deference to legislative judgments in this field.

In *Berman v. Parker*, 348 U.S. 26 (1954), this Court upheld a redevelopment plan targeting a blighted area of Washington, DC, in which most of the housing for the area's 5,000 inhabitants was beyond repair. Under the plan, the area would be condemned and part of it utilized for the construction of streets, schools, and other public facilities. The remainder of the land would be leased or sold to private parties for the purpose of redevelopment, including the construction of low-cost housing.

The owner of a department store located in the area challenged the condemnation, pointing out that his store was not itself blighted and arguing that the creation of a "better balanced, more attractive community" was not a valid public use. Writing for a unanimous Court, Justice DOUGLAS refused to evaluate this claim in isolation, deferring instead to the legislative and agency judgment that the area "must be planned as a whole" for the plan to be successful. The Court explained that "community redevelopment programs need not, by force of the Constitution, be on a piecemeal basis—lot by lot, building by building." The public use underlying the taking was unequivocally affirmed: "We do not sit to determine whether a particular housing project is or is not desirable. The concept of the public welfare is broad and inclusive. . . . The values it represents are spiritual as well as physical, aesthetic as well as monetary. It is within the power of the legislature to determine that the community should be beautiful as well as healthy, spacious as well as clean, well-balanced as well as carefully patrolled. In the present case, the Congress and its authorized agencies have made determinations that take into account a wide variety of values. It is not for us to reappraise them. If those who govern the District of Columbia decide that the Nation's Capital should be beautiful as well as sanitary, there is nothing in the Fifth Amendment that stands in the way."

In *Hawaii Housing Authority v. Midkiff*, the Court considered a Hawaii statute whereby fee title was taken from lessors and transferred to lessees (for just compensation) in order to reduce the concentration of land ownership. We unanimously upheld the statute and rejected the Ninth Circuit's view that it was "a naked attempt on the part of the state of Hawaii to take the property of A and transfer it to B solely for B's private use and benefit." Reaffirming *Berman*'s deferential approach to legislative judgments in this field, we concluded that the State's purpose of eliminating the "social and economic evils of a land oligopoly" qualified as a valid public use. Our opinion also rejected the contention that the mere fact that the State immediately transferred the properties to private individuals upon condemnation somehow diminished the public character of the taking. . . .

Those who govern the City were not confronted with the need to remove blight in the Fort Trumbull area, but their determination that the area was sufficiently distressed to justify a program of economic rejuvenation is entitled to our deference. The City has carefully formulated an economic development plan that it believes will provide appreciable benefits to the community, including—but by no means limited to—new jobs and increased tax revenue. As with other exercises in urban planning and development, the City is endeavoring to coordinate a variety of commercial, residential, and recreational uses of land, with the hope that they will form a whole greater than the sum of its parts. To effectuate this plan, the City has invoked a state statute that specifically authorizes the use of eminent domain to promote economic development. . . . Because that plan unquestionably serves a public purpose, the takings challenged here satisfy the public use requirement of the Fifth Amendment.

To avoid this result, petitioners urge us to adopt a new bright-line rule that economic development does not qualify as a public use. Putting aside the unpersuasive suggestion that the City's plan will provide only purely economic benefits, neither precedent nor logic supports petitioners' proposal. Promoting economic development is a traditional and long accepted function of government. There is, moreover, no principled way of distinguishing economic development from the other public purposes that we have recognized. . . .

Petitioners contend that using eminent domain for economic development impermissibly blurs the boundary between public and private takings. Again, our cases foreclose this objection. Quite simply, the government's pursuit of a public purpose will often benefit individual private parties. For example, in *Midkiff*, the forced transfer of property conferred a direct and significant benefit on those lessees who were previously unable to purchase their homes. . . .

It is further argued that without a bright-line rule nothing would stop a city from transferring citizen A's property to citizen B for the sole reason that citizen B will put the property to a more productive use and thus pay more taxes. Such a one-to-one transfer of property, executed outside the confines of an integrated development plan, is not presented in this case. While such an unusual exercise of government power would certainly raise a suspicion that a private purpose was afoot, the hypothetical cases posited by petitioners can be confronted if and when they arise. They do not warrant the crafting of an artificial restriction on the concept of public use.

Alternatively, petitioners maintain that for takings of this kind we should require a "reasonable certainty" that the expected public benefits will actually accrue. Such a rule, however, would represent an even greater departure from our precedent. "When the legislature's purpose is legitimate and its means are not irrational, our cases make clear that empirical debates over the wisdom of takings—no less than debates over the wisdom of other kinds of socioeconomic legislation—are not to be carried out in the federal courts." *Midkiff*. . . .

Just as we decline to second-guess the City's considered judgments about the efficacy of its development plan, we also decline to second-guess the City's determinations as to what lands it needs to acquire in order to effectuate the project. "It is not for the courts to oversee the choice of the boundary line nor to sit in review on the size of a particular project area. Once the question of the public purpose has been decided, the amount and character of land to be taken for the project and the need for a particular tract to complete the integrated plan rests in the discretion of the legislative branch."

In affirming the City's authority to take petitioners' properties, we do not minimize the hardship that condemnations may entail, notwithstanding the payment of just compensation. We emphasize that nothing in our opinion precludes any State from placing further restrictions on its exercise of the takings power. Indeed, many States already impose "public use" requirements that are stricter than the federal baseline. Some of these requirements have been established as a matter of state constitutional law, while others are expressed in state eminent domain statutes that carefully limit the grounds upon which takings may be exercised. . . .

The judgment of the Supreme Court of Connecticut is affirmed.

☐ *Justice O'CONNOR, with whom THE CHIEF JUSTICE, Justice SCALIA, and Justice THOMAS join, dissenting.*

Over two centuries ago, just after the Bill of Rights was ratified, Justice CHASE wrote: "An act of the Legislature (for I cannot call it a law) contrary to the great first principles of the social compact, cannot be considered a rightful exercise of legislative authority. . . . A few instances will suffice to explain what I mean. . . . [A] law that takes property from A, and gives it to B: It is against all reason and justice, for a people to entrust a Legislature with such powers; and, therefore, it cannot be presumed that they have done it." *Calder v. Bull*, 3 Dall. 386 (1798). Today the Court abandons this long-held, basic limitation on government power. Under the banner of economic development, all private property is now vulnerable to being taken and transferred to another private owner, so long as it might be upgraded—i.e., given to an owner who will use it in a way that the legislature deems more beneficial to the public—in the process. To reason, as the Court does, that the incidental public benefits resulting from the subsequent ordinary use of private property render economic development takings "for public use" is to wash out any distinction between private and public use of property—and thereby effectively to delete the words "for public use" from the Takings Clause of the Fifth Amendment. Accordingly I respectfully dissent. . . .

[W]e have read the Fifth Amendment's language to impose two distinct conditions on the exercise of eminent domain: "the taking must be for a 'public use' and 'just compensation' must be paid to the owner." *Brown v. Legal Foundation of Wash.*, 538 U.S. 216 (2003). These two limitations serve to protect "the security of Property," which Alexander Hamilton described to the Philadelphia Convention as one of the "great obj[ects] of Gov[ernment]." Together they ensure stable property ownership by providing safeguards against excessive, unpredictable, or unfair use of the government's eminent domain power—particularly against those owners who, for whatever reasons, may be unable to protect themselves in the political process against the majority's will.

While the Takings Clause presupposes that government can take private property without the owner's consent, the just compensation requirement spreads the cost of condemnations and thus "prevents the public from loading upon one individual more than his just share of the burdens of government." *Monongahela Nav. Co. v. United States*, 148 U.S. 312 (1893). The public use requirement, in turn, imposes a more basic limitation, circumscribing the very scope of the eminent domain power: Government may compel an individual to forfeit her property for the public's use, but not for the benefit of another private person. This requirement promotes fairness as well as security.

Where is the line between "public" and "private" property use? We give considerable deference to legislatures' determinations about what governmental activities will advantage the public. But were the political branches the sole arbiters of the public-private distinction, the Public Use Clause would amount to little more than hortatory fluff. An external, judicial check on how the public use requirement is interpreted, however limited, is necessary if this constraint on government power is to retain any meaning.

Our cases have generally identified three categories of takings that comply with the public use requirement, though it is in the nature of things that the boundaries between these categories are not always firm. Two are relatively straightforward and uncontroversial. First, the sovereign may transfer private property to public ownership—such as for a road, a hospital, or a military base. Second, the sovereign may transfer private property to private parties, often common carriers, who make the property available for the public's use—such as with a railroad, a public utility, or a stadium. But "public ownership" and "use-by-the-public" are sometimes too constricting and impractical ways to define the scope of the Public Use Clause. Thus we have allowed that, in certain circumstances and to meet certain exigencies, takings that serve a public purpose also satisfy the Constitution even if the property is destined for subsequent private use.

This case returns us for the first time in over 20 years to the hard question of when a purportedly "public purpose" taking meets the public use requirement. It presents an issue of first impression: Are economic development takings constitutional? I would hold that they are not. We are guided by two precedents about the taking of real property by eminent domain. In *Berman*, we upheld takings within a blighted neighborhood of Washington, DC. The neighborhood had so deteriorated that, for example, 64.3% of its dwellings were beyond repair. . . .

In *Midkiff*, we upheld a land condemnation scheme in Hawaii whereby title in real property was taken from lessors and transferred to lessees. At that time, the State and Federal Governments owned nearly 49% of the State's land, and another 47% was in the hands of only 72 private landowners. Concentration of land ownership was so dramatic that on the State's most urbanized island, Oahu, 22 landowners owned 72.5% of the fee simple titles. The Hawaii Legislature had concluded that the oligopoly in land ownership was "skewing the State's residential fee simple market, inflating land prices, and injuring the public tranquility and welfare," and therefore enacted a condemnation scheme for redistributing title.

In those decisions, we emphasized the importance of deferring to legislative judgments about public purpose. Because courts are ill-equipped to evaluate the efficacy of proposed legislative initiatives, we rejected as unworkable the idea of courts' "deciding on what is and is not a governmental function and . . . invalidating legislation on the basis of their view on that question at the moment of decision, a practice which has proved impracticable in other fields." Likewise, we recognized our inability to evaluate whether, in a given case, eminent domain is a necessary means by which to pursue the legislature's ends.

Yet for all the emphasis on deference, *Berman* and *Midkiff* hewed to a bedrock principle without which our public use jurisprudence would collapse: "A purely private taking could not withstand the scrutiny of the public use requirement; it would serve no legitimate purpose of government and would thus be void." *Midkiff.* To protect that principle, those decisions reserved "a role for courts to play in reviewing a legislature's judgment of what constitutes a public use . . . [though] the Court in *Berman* made clear that it is 'an extremely narrow' one."

The Court's holdings in *Berman* and *Midkiff* were true to the principle underlying the Public Use Clause. In both those cases, the extraordinary, precondemnation use of the targeted property inflicted affirmative harm on society—in *Berman* through blight resulting from extreme poverty and in *Midkiff* through oligopoly resulting from extreme wealth. And in both cases, the relevant legislative body had found that eliminating the existing property use was necessary to remedy the harm. Thus a public purpose was realized when the harmful use was eliminated. Because each taking directly achieved a public benefit, it did not matter that the property was turned over to private use. Here, in contrast, New London does not claim that Susette Kelo's . . . well-maintained [home is] the source of any social harm. Indeed, it could not so claim without adopting the absurd argument that any single-family home that might be razed to make way for an apartment building, or any church that might be replaced with a retail store, or any small business that might be more lucrative if it were instead part of a national franchise, is inherently harmful to society and thus within the government's power to condemn.

In moving away from our decisions sanctioning the condemnation of harmful property use, the Court today significantly expands the meaning of public use. It holds that the sovereign may take private property currently put to ordinary private use, and give it over for new, ordinary private use, so long as the new use is predicted to generate some secondary benefit for the public—such as increased tax revenue, more jobs, maybe even aesthetic pleasure. But nearly any lawful use of real private property can be said to generate some incidental benefit to the public. Thus, if predicted (or even guaranteed) positive side-effects are enough to render transfer from one private party to another constitutional, then the words "for public use" do not realistically exclude any takings, and thus do not exert any constraint on the eminent domain power. . . .

It was possible after *Berman* and *Midkiff* to imagine unconstitutional transfers from A to B. Those decisions endorsed government intervention when private property use had veered to such an extreme that the public was suffering as a consequence. Today nearly all real property is susceptible to condemnation on the Court's theory. Any property may now be taken for the benefit of another private party, but the fallout from this decision will not be random. The beneficiaries are likely to be those citizens with disproportionate influence and power in the political process, including large corporations and development firms. As for the victims, the government now has license to transfer property from those with fewer resources to those with more. . . .

☐ *Justice THOMAS, dissenting.*

Long ago, William Blackstone wrote that "the law of the land . . . postpone[s] even public necessity to the sacred and inviolable rights of private property." *Commentaries on the Laws of England* (1765). The Framers embodied that principle in the Constitution, allowing the government to take property not for "public necessity," but instead for "public use." Amdt. 5. Defying this understanding, the Court replaces the Public Use Clause with a "[P]ublic [P]urpose" Clause, a restriction that is satisfied, the Court instructs, so long as the purpose is "legitimate" and the means "not irrational." This deferential shift in phraseology enables the Court to hold, against all common sense, that a costly urban-renewal project whose stated purpose is a vague promise of new jobs and increased tax revenue, but which is also suspiciously agreeable to the Pfizer Corporation, is for a "public use."

I cannot agree. If such "economic development" takings are for a "public use," any taking is, and the Court has erased the Public Use Clause from our Constitution, as Justice O'CONNOR powerfully argues in dissent. I do not believe that this Court can eliminate liberties expressly enumerated in the Constitution and therefore join her dissenting opinion. Regrettably, however, the Court's error runs deeper than this. Today's decision is simply the latest in a string of our cases construing the Public Use Clause to be a virtual nullity, without the slightest nod to its original meaning. In my view, the Public Use Clause, originally understood, is a meaningful limit on the government's eminent domain power. Our cases have strayed from the Clause's original meaning, and I would reconsider them. . . .

The consequences of today's decision are not difficult to predict, and promise to be harmful. So-called "urban renewal" programs provide some compensation for the properties they take, but no compensation is possible for the subjective value of these lands to the individuals displaced and the indignity inflicted by uprooting them from their homes. Allowing the government to take property solely for public purposes is bad enough, but extending the concept of public purpose to encompass any economically beneficial goal guarantees that these losses will fall disproportionately on poor communities. Those communities are not only systematically less likely to put their lands to the highest and best social use, but are also the least politically powerful. If ever there were justification for intrusive judicial review of constitutional provisions that protect "discrete and insular minorities," *United States v. Carolene Products Co.*, 304 U.S. 144 (1938), surely that principle would apply with great force to the powerless groups and individuals the Public Use Clause protects. The deferential standard this Court has adopted for the Public Use Clause is therefore deeply perverse. It encourages "those citizens with disproportionate influence and power in the political process, including large corporations and development firms" to victimize the weak.

Those incentives have made the legacy of this Court's "public purpose" test an unhappy one. In the 1950's, no doubt emboldened in part by the expansive understanding of "public use" this Court adopted in *Berman*, cities "rushed to draw plans" for downtown development. "Of all the families displaced by urban renewal from 1949 through 1963, 63 percent of those whose race was known were nonwhite, and of these families, 56 percent of nonwhites and 38 percent of whites had incomes low enough to qualify for public housing, which, however, was seldom available to them." Public works projects in the 1950's and 1960's destroyed predominantly minority communities in St. Paul, Minnesota, and Baltimore, Maryland. In 1981, urban planners in Detroit, Michigan, uprooted the largely "lower-income and elderly" Poletown neighborhood for the benefit of the General Motors Corporation. Urban renewal projects have long been associated with the displacement of blacks; "[i]n cities across the country, urban renewal came to be known as 'Negro removal.'" Over 97 percent of the individuals forcibly removed from their homes by the "slum-clearance" project upheld by this Court in *Berman* were black. Regrettably, the predictable consequence of the Court's decision will be to exacerbate these effects. . . .

4

THE NATIONALIZATION OF THE BILL OF RIGHTS

This chapter examines the constitutional basis for civil liberties and civil rights and the controversy over the nationalization of the Bill of Rights—that is, the Supreme Court's extension of those guarantees as limitations on the states. The original Constitution contained few explicit guarantees for civil liberties and civil rights. But with the adoption of the Bill of Rights, the first ten amendments to the Constitution, the basis for civil liberties and civil rights was laid. The Bill of Rights, however, limited the powers of only the national government, not the states. With the ratification of the Fourteenth Amendment in 1868, though, there was a new basis for applying the Bill of Rights to the states. Its due process clause provides that "No state shall . . . deprive any person of life, liberty, or property without due process of law." This chapter examines the controversy over the Supreme Court's reading into the Fourteenth Amendment's due process clause guarantees of the Bill of Rights to make them applicable to the states. Subsequent chapters examine how the Supreme Court has interpreted and applied specific provisions of the Bill of Rights. Chapter 5 considers the First Amendment's guarantees for free speech, press, and association and Chapter 6, its provisions for religious freedom. Chapters 7 through 10 then examine guarantees for the rights of the accused in the criminal justice system. Chapter 11 takes up the right of privacy and Chapter 12, the Fourteenth Amendment's guarantee for the equal protection of the laws.

Unamended, the Constitution contains only five provisions for civil liberties. Article 1 forbids Congress and the states from passing *ex post facto* laws (laws making some activity retroactively a crime) and bills of attainder (legislation punishing specific individuals or members of a group without a trial). It also provides that Congress may not, except in times of rebellion or invasion, suspend writs of *habeas corpus*. A writ of *habeas corpus* is an ancient order (which is Latin for "you should have the body") aimed at safeguarding against unlawful arrests and imprisonment of individuals. (A prisoner in jail may petition a court for a writ of *habeas corpus* that then requires the government to explain to a judge why the prisoner is being held, of what crimes he or she is accused, and the basis for continuing imprisonment.) In addition (as dealt with in Ch. 3), states are also forbidden in Article I from "impairing the Obligation of Contract," and in Article IV from denying the privileges and immunities of citizenship.

The Constitution was itself deemed to be a bill of rights, at least by the Federalists. James Wilson and Alexander Hamilton, among others, argued that civil rights and civil liberties would remain secure because the powers of the national government are limited to those expressly granted, and the states would continue to safeguard individuals' civil rights and liberties.

Those opposing the Constitution, the Anti-Federalists, were not persuaded. They feared that the national government's power was too great and would further expand at the expense of the powers of (and the protections for individual liberty afforded by) the states. A leading New York Anti-Federalist, Brutus, for example, warned that the federal judiciary would "extend the limits of the general government gradually, and by insensible degrees . . . facilitate the abolition of the state governments."[1] Nor did the Anti-Federalists trust Congress, let alone the executive branch, to respect civil rights and liberties. As Richard Henry Lee wrote to Samuel Adams in 1787:

> The corrupting nature of power, and its insatiable appetite for increase, hath proved the necessity, and procured the adoption of the strongest and most express declarations of that *Residuum* of natural rights, which is not intended to be given up to Society; and which indeed is not necessary to be given for any good social purpose. In a government therefore, when the power of judging what shall be for the *general welfare*, which goes to every object of human legislation; and where the laws of such Judges shall be the *supreme Law of the Land*: it seems to be of the last consequence to declare in most explicit terms the reservations above alluded to.[2]

Although the Anti-Federalists unsuccessfully fought against the Constitution's ratification, they succeeded in insisting on the addition of the Bill of Rights. Delaware unanimously ratified the document on December 7, 1787. Within weeks Pennsylvania, New Jersey, Georgia, and

Connecticut gave their approval. Massachusetts followed in February 1788, but with a closely divided vote of 187 to 168. In the spring, Maryland and South Carolina gave their overwhelming endorsements. Then in June, close votes in New Hampshire and Virginia secured the requisite nine states for ratification. But the battle in the New York convention was fierce and crucial, for this large commercial state separated New England from the Southern states. Largely due to the leadership of Hamilton, a Federalist, New York finally voted in favor. The price of winning ratification there and in Massachusetts and Virginia, however, was agreement that the First Congress would adopt a declaration of rights and promptly send it to the states for ratification. North Carolina did not ratify until November 1789 and Rhode Island held out until May 1790.

During the debate over New York's ratification, Hamilton tried to popularize the counterarguments to those made by the Anti-Federalists. "[T]he Constitution itself, in every rational sense, and to every useful purpose, is a bill of rights," he insisted in *Federalist*, No. 84, when contending that the addition of a declaration of rights was "not only unnecessary . . . but would even be dangerous." In arguing that a bill of rights was unnecessary, Hamilton pointed to the Preamble of the Constitution:

> We the people of the United States, to secure the blessings of liberty to ourselves and our posterity, do *ordain* and *establish* this constitution for the United States of America." Here is a better recognition of popular rights than volumes of those aphorisms which make the principal figure in several of our state bills of rights, and which would sound much better in a treatise of ethics than in a constitution of government.

A bill of rights might also prove dangerous, Hamilton contended, because it

> would contain various exceptions to powers which are not granted; and on this very account, would afford a colourable pretext to claim more than were granted. For why declare that things shall not be done which there is no power to do? Why for instance, should it be said, that the liberty of the press shall not be restrained, when no power is given by which restrictions may be imposed? I will not contend that such a provision would confer a regulating power; but it is evident that it would furnish, to men disposed to usurp, a plausible pretence for claiming that power. They might urge with a semblance of reason, that the constitution ought not to be charged with the absurdity of providing against the abuse of an authority, which was not given, and that provision against restraining the liberty of press afforded a clear implication, that a

power to prescribe proper regulations concerning it, was intended to be vested in the national government.

Furthermore, Hamilton suggested the problems of which rights to include and exclude and how to define those rights specified in a declaration of rights:

> On the subject of the liberty of the press, as much has been said, I cannot forbear adding a remark or two: In the first place, I observe that there is not a syllable concerning it in the constitution of this state [New York], and in the next I contend that whatever has been said about it in that of any other state, amounts to nothing. What signifies a declaration that "the liberty of the press shall be inviolably preserved?" What is the liberty of the press? Who can give it any definition which would not leave the utmost latitude for evasion? I hold it to be impracticable; and from this, I infer, that its security, whatever fine declarations may be inserted in any constitution respecting it, must altogether depend on public opinion, and on the general spirit of the people and of the government.

Despite their success in securing the ratification of the Constitution, the Federalists failed to turn the tide of public opinion running in favor of a bill of rights. As Thomas Jefferson noted in a letter to James Madison on December 20, 1787, "a bill of rights is what the people are entitled to against every government on earth, general or particular, and what no just government should refuse, or rest on inference."[3] Madison was not initially inclined toward the addition of a declaration of rights.

In a letter to Jefferson, Madison gave four reasons for his ambivalence. First, he accepted the Federalists' argument that "the rights in question are reserved by the manner in which the federal powers are granted." Second, he feared "that a positive declaration of some of the most essential rights could not be obtained in the requisite latitude." In particular, "the rights of Conscience" might be narrowed by any formal-legal definition. Third, republican liberty was guarded against Congress by its constitutionally "limited powers" and "the jealousy" of the states. Finally, he maintained that "experience proves the inefficacy of a bill of rights on those occasions when its controul is most needed."[4]

However, Madison came to side with Jefferson and the Anti-Federalists and provided some of the strongest arguments for a bill of rights. They, too, worried about what to include and exclude in a bill of rights. In 1788, Madison explained that he had not viewed a bill of rights "in an important light . . . [b]ecause there is great reason to fear that a positive declaration of some of the most essential rights could not be obtained in the requisite latitude."[5] But Jefferson responded that "Half a loaf is better than no bread. If we cannot secure all our rights, let's secure what we can."[6] He and Madison, furthermore, came to view a bill of rights as putting into "the hands of the judiciary" an additional check on the coercive powers of government. "This is a body," observed Jefferson, "which if rendered independent, and kept strictly to their own department merits great confidence for their learning and integrity."[7]

In the First Congress in 1789, as a member of the House of Representatives Madison championed the cause of adding a declaration of rights to the Constitution. His aim was "to satisfy the public mind that their liberties will be perpetual, and this without endangering any part of the constitution."[8] With parliamentary skill, Madison steered the amendments through Congress and the Bill of Rights was ratified by the states in 1791. Madison, however, was forced to compromise and failed to achieve two goals. He had proposed that the amendments be incorporated into the body of the original Constitution, because he did not want them to be perceived as inferior or less important than the document itself. But he was defeated on that as well as on proposing that the amendments bind the states along with the national government.

NOTES

1. Brutus, in *New York Journal*, in *The Complete Anti-Federalist*, Vol. 2, ed. Herbert Storing (Chicago: University of Chicago Press, 1981), 441.

2. Richard Henry Lee to Samuel Adams (October 5, 1787), in *The Founders' Constitution*, Vol. 1, eds. Philip Kurland and Ralph Lerner (Chicago: University of Chicago Press, 1987), 448.

3. Thomas Jefferson, *The Papers of Thomas Jefferson*, Vol. 12, ed. Julian Boyd (Princeton, NJ: Princeton University Press, 1950–), 440.

4. James Madison, *The Papers of James Madison*, Vol. 11, ed. R. Rutland (Charlottesville: University Press of Virginia, 1977), 295–298.

5. Madison, *The Papers of James Madison*, Vol. 11, 295–298.

6. Jefferson, *The Papers of Thomas Jefferson*, Vol. 14, 659.

7. Jefferson, *The Papers of Thomas Jefferson*, Vol. 14, 659.

8. Madison, *The Papers of James Madison*, Vol. 12, 196–209.

SELECTED BIBLIOGRAPHY

Cogan, Neil H. *The Complete Bill of Rights: The Drafts, Debates, Sources, & Origins.* New York: Oxford University Press, 1997.

Lash, Kurt. *The Lost History of the Ninth Amendment.* New York: Oxford University Press, 2009.

Levy, Leonard W. *Original Intent and the Framers' Constitution.* New York: Macmillan, 1988.

———. *Origins of the Bill of Rights.* New Haven, CT: Yale University Press, 1999.

A | *The Selective Nationalization of Guarantees of the Bill of Rights Plus Other Fundamental Rights*

The Bill of Rights did not limit the powers of the states until the twentieth century. The Supreme Court's nationalization—or application to the states—of the Bill of Rights and its interpretative basis for doing so remain controversial. The prevailing view of the Bill of Rights in the nineteenth century was well stated in 1833 by Chief Justice John Marshall. In *Barron v. The Mayor and City Council of Baltimore* (1833) (see excerpt below), after reviewing the history of the Bill of Rights, Marshall concluded there was "no expression indicating an intention to apply [guarantees of the Bill of the Rights] to the State governments. This court cannot so apply them."

Barron was reaffirmed in *Permoli v. New Orleans*, 3 How. (44 U.S.) 589 (1845), and in *Mattox v. United States*, 156 U.S. 237 (1895). As late as 1922 the Court maintained that "the Constitution of the United States imposes upon the states no obligation to confer upon those within its jurisdiction . . . the right to free speech" in *Prudential Insurance Company v. Cheek*, 259 U.S. 530 (1922). Indeed, despite the Court's eventual nationalization of most of the guarantees of the Bill of Rights, *Barron* has never been expressly overturned.

Ratification of the Fourteenth Amendment in 1868, however, changed the constitutional landscape and laid a new basis for applying the Bill of Rights to the states. It specifically denied the states the power to "make or enforce any law which shall abridge the privileges or immunities of citizens of the United States . . . [or] deprive any person of life, liberty, or property, without due process of law . . . [or] deny to any person within its jurisdiction the equal protection of the laws." Two of the principal leaders in the Thirty-ninth Congress proposing the amendment, Ohio Representative John A. Bingham and Michigan Senator Jacob M. Howard, suggested during floor debates that an objective was the extension of the Bill of Rights to the states (thereby overturning *Barron*). The Fourteenth Amendment, Senator Howard claimed, would bar the states from denying citizens their privileges and immunities guaranteed by the Constitution, including "the personal rights guaranteed and secured by the first eight amendments of the Constitution."[1]

Whether Congress intended the Fourteenth Amendment to incorporate and apply guarantees of the Bill of Rights to the states, however, is a long-running controversy. The record of the Thirty-ninth

Congress and of the states' ratification of the Fourteenth Amendment is far from complete and unambiguous.[2] Justices, historians, and legal scholars are unlikely to agree on the historical basis for the Court's reading provisions of the Bill of Rights into the Fourteenth Amendment. Justices Felix Frankfurter and (the second) John Harlan, as well as some law professors, maintain that the amendment was not intended to apply the Bill of Rights to the states.[3] By contrast, Justices Hugo Black and William Douglas, along with other leading historians and legal scholars, championed an interpretation of the legislative record pointing in the opposite direction.[4] And it seems fair to conclude that "the legislative argument is one neither side can win."[5]

History, though, is not the only thing that divided the Court when interpreting the Fourteenth Amendment. No less important are the politics of interpretation and rival judicial and political philosophies. And those differences, as much as different readings of history, account for the continuing controversy over turning the Fourteenth Amendment into a vehicle for nationalizing the Bill of Rights.

When initially confronted with the question of extending the Bill of Rights to the states in *The Slaughterhouse Cases* (1873) (see Ch. 3), the justices split 5–4. The majority rejected the view that the Fourteenth Amendment's privileges or immunities clause incorporated the Bill of Rights. Yet the four dissenters (Chief Justice Chase and Justices Bradley, Field, and Swayne) took the opposite view. The Court's narrow reading of the amendment, in Swayne's words, turned "what was meant for bread into stone."

The Slaughterhouse Cases, as dissenting Justice Field remarked, rendered the Fourteenth Amendment "a vain and idle enactment, which accomplished nothing, and most unnecessarily excited Congress and the people on its passage." The majority's opinion, however, dealt primarily with the privileges or immunities clause. And that left open the possibility that the Court might eventually be persuaded to incorporate or absorb the Bill of Rights into the amendment's due process clause.

With two exceptions in the late nineteenth century, the Court remained unmoved from its interpretation in *The Slaughterhouse Cases*. Both rulings involved the Fifth Amendment's prohibition against the taking of private property for public use without just compensation, and registered the Court's embrace of laissez-faire capitalism and the priority given to economic liberties (see THE DEVELOPMENT OF LAW box in this section and, there, *Missouri Pacific Railway Co. v. Nebraska* and *Chicago, Burlington & Quincy Railway Co. v. Chicago*).

Despite refusing to nationalize the Bill of Rights, the Court could not escape responsibility for giving meaning to the Fourteenth Amendment's due process clause. That meant coming up with standards or tests for determining what state practices and procedures denied individuals their rights under the Fourteenth Amendment due process clause. So long as the Court held that the due process clause did not include the guarantees afforded by the Bill of Rights, the justices had to create their own standards and rationalizations for what process is due under the Fourteenth Amendment.

The Court faced the question of what process is due in *Hurtado v. California* (1884) (see excerpt below). In holding that states need not honor the Fifth Amendment's requirement that individuals be indicted by a grand jury before being tried for a crime, Justice Matthews proclaimed the states free to experiment with their own criminal justice procedures. They, he said, were free "to draw on the wells of justice, so long as they don't go too far." On this standard, each case would have to be considered on its own merits. But as dissenting Justice John Marshall Harlan suggested, whether states ran afoul of the due process clause also turned on each justice's conception of what process is due, rather than on enumerated guarantees. In Harlan's opinion the Bill of Rights were incorporated lock, stock, and barrel into the due process clause. His position of *total incorporation*, nevertheless, failed to command a majority. Accordingly, state practices and procedures falling short of the requirements of the Bill of Rights were upheld. In *Maxwell v. Dow*, 176 U.S. 581 (1900), for example, the Court ruled that states were free to convict individuals before juries composed of fewer than twelve members and on less than a unanimous verdict. And *Twining v. New Jersey*, 211 U.S. 78 (1908), held that states need not honor an accused's Fifth Amendment's privilege against self-incrimination.

Forty years passed before the Court was prepared to extend guarantees of the Bill of Rights to the states. Then when confronted with a spate of litigation challenging state laws punishing subversive speech, the Court merely assumed (in spite of its previous denials) that the First Amendment freedoms of speech and press limited the states, no less than the national government. In *Gilbert v. Minnesota*, 254 U.S. 325 (1920), the Court granted that individuals might challenge the constitutionality of state laws making it a crime falsely or maliciously to criticize the government. In *Gitlow v. New York*, 268 U.S. 652 (1925) (see Ch. 5), Justice Edward Sanford noted in *dictum* that "[w]e may and do assume that freedom of speech and of the press . . . are among the fundamental rights and liberties protected . . . from impairment by the states." By the 1940s, the other First Amendment freedoms were construed to be so fundamental as to constrain the states as well.

Still, in the area of criminal procedure, the Court remained reluctant to impose the guarantees of the Fourth through the Eighth Amendments on the states. Indicative of the Court's deference to the states is the infamous Scottsboro Case, *Powell v. Alabama*, 287 U.S. 45 (1932) (see

In 1909, the National Association for the Advancement of Colored People (NAACP) was founded to protest various forms of racial discrimination—discrimination in the criminal justice system, in voting rights, and in education and employment. In the 1920s and 1930s, one of the NAACP's major initiatives was to lobby Congress to enact a federal law against lynching, as well as to participate in bringing "test cases" like the famous Scottsboro Boys Case, *Powell v. Alabama* (1932) (excerpted in Ch. 9). But, because the NAACP was involved in lobbying, it was denied tax-exempt status by the Internal Revenue Service. As a result, in 1938 under the direction of Thurgood Marshall, the NAACP's litigation activities were separated and carried forth with the formation of the NAACP Legal Defense and Educational Fund, Inc., known later as the LDF. Here, in 1934 NAACP members picket a crime conference in Washington, D.C., in protest of lynching. (*Bettman/Corbis via Getty Images.*)

Ch. 9). There nine black teenagers were tried and convicted for raping a white woman (a capital offense), without the representation of counsel, before an all-white jury in Scottsboro, Alabama. In ordering that they be retried and appointed an attorney, the Court ruled that they had been denied due process and subjected to a fundamentally unfair trial. But it declined to make the Fifth and Sixth Amendments applicable to the states. Instead, the Court relied on general principles of "natural justice" and "ordered liberty," as it also did in *Norris v. Alabama*, 294 U.S. 587 (1935), holding jury trials are required in criminal cases, and *Brown v. Mississippi*, 297 U.S. 278 (1936), holding that confessions coerced by third-degree police tactics violate due process.

In *Palko v. Connecticut* (1937) (excerpted below), Justice Benjamin Cardozo rationalized the selective application of some but not all guaran-

■ THE DEVELOPMENT OF LAW

The Selective Nationalization of the Bill of Rights plus Other Fundamental Rights

GUARANTEE/RIGHT	AMENDMENT	YEAR	CASE
Public use and just compensation provisions condition the taking of private property by the government	5	1896	*Missouri Pacific Railway Co. v. Nebraska*, 164 U.S. 403
		1897	*Chicago, Burlington & Quincy Railway Co. v. Chicago*, 166 U.S. 226
Freedom of speech	1	1927	*Fiske v. Kansas*, 274 U.S. 380 (also earlier in *dictum: Gitlow v. New York*, 268 U.S. 652 (1925); and *Gilbert v. Minnesota*, 254 U.S. 325 (1920)
Freedom of the press	1	1931	*Near v. Minnesota*, 283 U.S. 697
Fair trial and right to counsel in capital cases	6	1932	*Powell v. Alabama*, 287 U.S. 45
Freedom of religion	1	1934	*Hamilton v. Regents of the University of California*, 293 U.S. 245 (in *dictum*)
Freedom of assembly (and implicitly freedom to petition for redress of grievances)	1	1937	*De Jonge v. Oregon*, 299 U.S. 353
Free exercise of religion	1	1940	*Cantwell v. Connecticut*, 310 U.S. 296
Separation of church and state	1	1947	*Everson v. Board of Education*, 330 U.S. 1

GUARANTEE/RIGHT	AMENDMENT	YEAR	CASE
Right to a public trial	6	1948	*In re Oliver*, 333 U.S. 257
Right against unreasonable searches and seizures	4	1949	*Wolf v. Colorado*, 338 U.S. 25
Freedom of association	1	1958	*NAACP v. Alabama*, 357 U.S. 449
Exclusionary rule	4	1961	*Mapp v. Ohio*, 367 U.S. 643
Ban against cruel and unusual punishments	8	1962	*Robinson v. California*, 370 U.S. 660
Right to counsel in all felony cases	6	1963	*Gideon v. Wainwright*, 372 U.S. 335
Right against self-incrimination	5	1964	*Malloy v. Hogan*, 378 U.S. 1
Right to confront witness (and by implication the right to be informed of the nature and cause of the accusation)	6	1965	*Pointer v. Texas*, 380 U.S. 400
Right to privacy	penumbra of 1, 3, 4, 5, and 14	1965	*Griswold v. Connecticut*, 381 U.S. 479
Right to impartial jury	6	1966	*Parker v. Gladden*, 385 U.S. 363
Right to speedy trial	6	1967	*Klopfer v. North Carolina*, 386 U.S. 213
Right to compulsory process for obtaining witnesses	6	1967	*Washington v. Texas*, 388 U.S. 14
Right to jury trial in nonpetty cases	6	1968	*Duncan v. Louisiana*, 391 U.S. 145

(continues)

■ The Development of Law

*The Selective Nationalization of the Bill of Rights plus
Other Fundamental Rights (continued)*

GUARANTEE/RIGHT	AMENDMENT	YEAR	CASE
Right against double jeopardy	5	1969	*Benton v. Maryland*, 395 U.S. 784
Right to counsel in all criminal cases involving a jail term	6	1972	*Argersinger v. Hamlin*, 407 U.S. 25
Right to keep and bear arms	2	2010	*McDonald v. City of Chicago*, 561 U.S. 742

tees of the Bill of Rights. According to his theory of *selective incorporation*, some rights are "so rooted in the traditions and conscience of our people as to be ranked as fundamental" and "implicit in the concept of ordered liberty." Among those he deemed applicable to the states were the First Amendment freedoms, the Fifth Amendment's eminent domain provision, and the Sixth Amendment right to counsel in capital cases. Other guarantees of the Bill of Rights were simply formal rights not binding on the states. Cardozo's honor roll of preferred freedoms thus created a constitutional double standard for enforcing the Bill of Rights.

Cardozo's theory of selective incorporation stood for almost twenty-five years, until the 1960s when the Warren Court forged a constitutional revolution in criminal procedure by extending virtually all the guarantees of the Fourth through the Eighth Amendments to the states. In the 1940s and 1950s, the Court remained sharply divided over whether and how to nationalize the Bill of Rights.

The divisiveness within the Court arising from the debate over the nationalization of the Bill of Rights and the politics of interpretation is exemplified by *Adamson v. California* (1947) (see excerpt below). There Justice Reed, writing for the majority, adhered to the theory of selective incorporation. But concurring Justice Frankfurter maintained that the requirements of the due process clause in the Fifth Amendment and those of the due process clause in the Fourteenth Amendment were completely independent and that when enforcing the latter the justices should balance the rights of the accused against the interests of the states in prosecuting crime. Frankfurter urged the Court to look at what *fundamental fairness* requires in each case when balancing these competing interests. Dissenting Justices Black and Douglas, however, countered that that standard was no improvement over the theory of selective incorporation; it was as ambiguous as other natural law formulations in giving the Court unbridled power. For that reason, along with his own reading of the history of the Fourteenth Amendment, Black continued to press for total incorporation, based on the privileges or immunities clause. The two other dissenters in *Adamson*, Justices Frank Murphy and Wiley Rutledge, went further in advancing an even broader libertarian position, that of *total incorporation plus* any other fundamental rights not enumerated in the Bill of Rights.

In response to Justice Black's criticisms, Justice Frankfurter in *Rochin v. California* (1952) (excerpted below) relied on a "shocks-the-conscience" test for determining when police practices violate the due process clause. In other words, the guarantees of the Bill of Rights for the rights of the accused did not apply (even) on the basis of selective incorporation, but rather only in particular cases on a case-by-case basis. Frankfurter's test was actually a slight refinement from that of Justice Holmes. Frankfurter once asked Holmes about how he decided when due process was violated. Holmes response was when it "made him puke."[6] Yet, as Black pointed out, that was subjective and problematic in application. Two years after *Rochin*, in Chief Justice Earl Warren's first term, the Court again relied on the test. But in *Irvine v. California*, 347 U.S. 128 (1954), the majority failed to find police bugging of an entire house for over a month, without obtaining a search warrant, to either violate the Fourth Amendment or shock their consciences.

The Warren Court remained until the 1960s split between Frankfurter's approach and Black's insistence on total incorporation. That intellectual struggle would not be decisively settled until the Court's composition changed. In *Mapp v. Ohio*, 367 U.S. 643 (1961) (see Ch. 7), the Court finally agreed to extend to the states the Fourth Amendment's

■ CONSTITUTIONAL HISTORY

Guarantees of the Bill of Rights That Have Not Been Applied to the States

Third Amendment limitation on the quartering of soldiers in a person's house.
Fifth Amendment right to indictment by a grand jury.
Seventh Amendment right to a jury trial in civil cases.

exclusionary rule, requiring that illegally obtained evidence be excluded from use at trial. Then the following year Justices Frankfurter and Whittaker retired. With their replacements, Justices Byron White and Arthur Goldberg, there was finally a solid majority supporting the nationalization of the major guarantees of the Bill of Rights.

By the end of Chief Justice Warren's tenure in 1969, nearly all the guarantees of the Bill of Rights were applied to the states. In addition, in *Griswold v. Connecticut* (1965) (see excerpt below), the Court created out of whole constitutional cloth a right of privacy, which Justice Douglas found in the penumbras, or shadows, of the First, Third, Fourth, Fifth, and Ninth Amendments, and made applicable to the states by the Fourteenth Amendment. While joining the decision announced in Douglas's opinion, concurring Justice Goldberg, joined by Chief Justice Warren and Justice Brennan, staked out yet another theory of incorporation—that of *selective incorporation plus* other fundamental yet unenumerated rights. The Court in *Griswold* went too far for Justices Black and Stewart. In dissent, Black again warned that whenever the justices substitute their own interpretative language for that of the Constitution, they threaten to become "a day-to-day constitutional convention."

■ THE DEVELOPMENT OF LAW

Approaches to Nationalization of the Bill of Rights under the Fourteenth Amendment

---

Total incorporation of all guarantees—Justice Harlan's opinion, dissenting in *Hurtado v. California* (1884).

Selective incorporation of "preferred freedoms" and those rights "implicit in the concept of ordered liberty"—Justice Benjamin Cardozo's opinion in *Palko v. Connecticut* (1937).

Fundamental fairness application of guarantees on a case-by-case basis—Justice Felix Frankfurter, concurring in *Adamson v. California* (1947); and majority opinion in *Rochin v. California* (1952).

Total incorporation plus other fundamental rights not expressly granted in the Bill of Rights—Justices Frank Murphy and Wiley Rutledge, dissenting in *Adamson v. California* (1947).

Selective incorporation plus other fundamental rights not expressly granted in the Bill of Rights—Justices Arthur Goldberg, Chief Justice Earl Warren, and Justice William J. Brennan, concurring in *Griswold v. Connecticut* (1965).

The Court's rulings extending to the states the rights of the accused afforded in the Bill of Rights made for a larger struggle in constitutional politics. They effectively raised the issue of "law and order" and "crime control" to the national political agenda as well. During their presidential campaigns, Richard Nixon, Ronald Reagan, George H. W. Bush, and George W. Bush effectively criticized the Court for "liberal judicial activism." Subsequently, they appointed more conservative justices, which in turn changed the internal dynamics of the Court. The Court, though, did not turn back the constitutional clock on the incorporation of the Bill of Rights. Rather than disincorporate those guarantees, the Court (as further discussed in later chapters) in some cases limited their reach and carved out exceptions for state compliance with the commands of the Bill of Rights.[7] Moreover, the Roberts Court incorporated into the due process clause of the Fourteenth Amendment the "right to keep and bear arms" of the Second Amendment and extended it to state and local governments in *McDonald v. City of Chicago* (2010) (excerpted below), though it left open the kinds of gun regulations that are permissible and invited further litigation.

In *Timbs v. Indiana* (2019), the Court unanimously found that the Eighth Amendment's ban on excessive fines applies to the states through the due process clause of Fourteenth Amendment, removing an important source of revenue for many states and local governments.

NOTES

1. *Congressional Globe*, 39th Cong., 1st sess., 1865–1866, 2765.

2. For further discussion see Howard J. Graham, "The 'Conspiracy Theory' of the Fourteenth Amendment," 47 *Yale Law Journal* 371 (1938); and Walter F. Murphy, "Constitutional Interpretation: The Art of the Historian, Magician, or Statesman?" 87 *Yale Law Journal* 1752 (1978).

3. Besides the cases discussed and reprinted here see Felix Frankfurter, "Memorandum on 'Incorporation' of the Bill of Rights into the Due Process Clause of the Fourteenth Amendment," 78 *Harvard Law Review* 746 (1965); Charles Fairman, "Does the Fourteenth Amendment Incorporate the Bill of Rights?" 2 *Stanford Law Review* 1 (1949); Charles Fairman, "A Reply to Professor Crosskey," 22 *University of Chicago Law Review* 145 (1954); Raoul Berger, *Government by Judiciary: The Transformation of the Fourteenth Amendment* (Cambridge, MA: Harvard University Press, 1977).

4. See Hugo Black, "The Bill of Rights," 35 *New York University Law Review* 865 (1960); Alfred Avins, "Incorporation of the Bill of Rights: The Crosskey-Fairman Debates Revisited," 6 *Harvard Journal on Legislation* 1 (1968); William Crosskey, "Charles Fairman, 'Legislative History,' and the Constitutional Limitations on State Authority," 22 *University of Chicago Law Review* 1 (1954); Horace Flack, *The Adoption of the Fourteenth Amendment* (Baltimore, MD: Johns Hopkins University Press, 1908); and Jacobus tenBroek, *Equal under Law* (London: Collier Books, 1965).

5. John Hart Ely, *Democracy and Distrust: A Theory of Judicial Review* (Cambridge, MA: Harvard University Press, 1981), 27.

6. Quoted, for example, in Memorandum to Justice Burton with respect to *Louisiana v. Resweber* (December 13, 1946), in Justice Robert H. Jackson Papers, Box 138, Manuscripts Room, Library of Congress.

7. However, see Rehnquist's dissenting opinion in *Wallace v. Jaffree*, 472 U.S. 38 (1985) (see Ch. 6), raising questions about the Court's extension of the First Amendment establishment clause to the states. Justice Thomas has also taken that position in a number of opinions.

Selected Bibliography

Amar, Akhil Reed. *The Bill of Rights: Creation and Reconstruction*. New Haven, CT: Yale University Press, 1998.

Cortner, Richard C. *The Supreme Court and the Second Bill of Rights: The Fourteenth Amendment and the Nationalization of Civil Liberties*. Madison: University of Wisconsin Press, 1981.

Farber, Daniel. *Retained by the People: The 'Silent' Ninth Amendment and the Constitutional Rights Americans Don't Know They Have*. New York: Perseus Books, 2007.

Flack, Horace. *The Adoption of the Fourteenth Amendment*. Baltimore, MD: Johns Hopkins University Press, 1908.

Graham, Howard. *Everyman's Constitution: Historical Essays on the Fourteenth Amendment, the "Conspiracy Theory," and American Constitutionalism*. Madison, WI: State Historical Society of Madison, 1968.

Labbè, Ronald, and Jonathan Lurie. *The Slaughterhouse Cases: Regulation, Reconstruction, and the Fourteenth Amendment*. Lawrence: University Press of Kansas, 2005.

Lash, Kurt. *The Fourteenth Amendment and the Privileges and Immunities of American Citizenship*. New York: Cambridge University Press, 2014.

Magliocca, Gerald. *The Heart of The Constitution: How the Bill of Rights Became the Bill of Rights*. New York: Oxford University Press, 2017.

Orth, John V. *Due Process of Law: A Brief History*. Lawrence: University Press of Kansas, 2005.

tenBroek, Jacobus. *The Antislavery Origins of the Fourteenth Amendment*. Berkeley: University of California Press, 1951.

Barron v. The Mayor and City of Baltimore

7 Pet. (32 U.S.) 243, 8 L.Ed. 672 (1833)

John Barron inherited and was co-owner of a wharf in the eastern harbor of Baltimore. The wharf had been highly profitable because it was surrounded by some of the deepest water in the harbor. But city improvements (the diversion of certain streams and the paving of streets) resulted in large deposits of sand accumulating around the wharf. The waters became too shallow for ships to gain access to the wharf and Barron faced a major financial loss.

Barron sued the mayor and city council of Baltimore for damages in county court. He did so on the grounds that the Fifth Amendment forbids the states as well as the national government from taking private property for public use without just compensation. The trial court agreed and awarded Barron $4,500 in damages. That decision was reversed by an appellate court, and Barron appealed to the Supreme Court. When Barron's attorney appeared before the high bench, Chief Justice Marshall asked him to confine his argument to whether the Fifth Amendment was applicable to the states and thus gave the Court jurisdiction over the case. After hearing his arguments, the chief justice announced that the Court need not bother hearing the attorneys representing the city of Baltimore.

The Court's decision and opinion were unanimous.

■ ■ ■

☐ *Chief Justice MARSHALL delivered the opinion of the Court.*

The question thus presented is, we think, of great importance, but not of much difficulty.

The Constitution was ordained and established by the people of the United States for themselves, for their own government, and not for the government of the individual States. Each State established a constitution for itself, and in that constitution provided such limitations and restrictions on the powers of its particular government as its judgment dictated. The people of the United States framed such a government for the United States as they supposed best adapted to their situation, and best calculated to promote their interests. The powers they conferred on this government were to be exercised by itself; and the limitations on power, if expressed in general terms, are naturally, and, we think, necessarily applicable to the government created by the instrument. They are limitations of power granted in the instrument itself; not of distinct governments, framed by different persons and for different purposes.

If these propositions be correct, the fifth amendment must be understood as restraining the power of the general government, not as applicable to the States. In their several constitutions they have imposed such restrictions on their respective governments as their own wisdom suggested; such as they deemed most proper for themselves. It is a subject on which they judge exclusively, and with which others interfere no further than they are supposed to have a common interest.

The counsel for the plaintiff in error insists that the Constitution was intended to secure the people of the several States against the undue exercise of power by their respective State governments; as well as against that which might be attempted by their general government. In support of this argument he relies on the inhibitions contained in the tenth section of the first article.

We think that section affords a strong if not a conclusive argument in support of the opinion already indicated by the court.

The preceding section contains restrictions which are obviously intended for the exclusive purpose of restraining the exercise of power by the departments of the general government. Some of them use language applicable only to Congress, others are expressed in general terms. The third clause, for example, declares that "no bill of attainder or ex post facto law shall be passed." No language can be more general; yet the demonstration is complete that it applies solely to the government of the United States. . . .

If the original Constitution, in the ninth and tenth sections of the first article, draws this plain and marked line of discrimination between the limitations it imposes on the powers of the general government and on those of the States; if in every inhibition intended to act on State power, words are employed which directly express that intent, some strong reason must be assigned for departing from this safe and judicious course in framing the amendments, before that departure can be assumed.

We search in vain for that reason. . . .

Had the framers of these amendments intended them to be limitations on the powers of the State governments they would have imitated the framers of the original Constitution, and have expressed that intention. Had Congress engaged in the extraordinary occupation of improving the constitutions of the several States by affording the people additional protection from the exercise of power by their own governments in matters which concerned themselves alone, they would have declared this purpose in plain and intelligible language.

But it is universally understood, it is a part of the history of the day, that the great revolution which established the Constitution of the United States was not effected without immense opposition. Serious fears were extensively entertained that those powers which the patriot statesmen who then watched over the interests of our country, deemed essential to union, and to the attainment of those invaluable objects for which union was sought, might be exercised in a manner dangerous to liberty. In almost every convention by which the Constitution was adopted, amendments to guard against the abuse of power were recommended. These amendments demanded security against the apprehended encroachments of the general government—not against those of the local governments.

In compliance with a sentiment thus generally expressed, to quiet fears thus extensively entertained, amendments were proposed by the required majority in Congress, and adopted by the States. These amendments contain no expression indicating an intention to apply them to the State governments. This court cannot so apply them.

We are of opinion that the provision in the fifth amendment to the Constitution, declaring that private property shall not be taken for public use without just compensation, is intended solely as a limitation on the exercise of power by the government of the United States, and is not applicable to the legislation of the States. . . .

This court, therefore, has no jurisdiction of the case, and is dismissed.

The Slaughterhouse Cases (reprise)

16 WALL. (83 U.S.) 36, 21 L.ED. 394 (1873)

See Chapter 3, where this decision is discussed and reprinted in part.

■ ■ ■

Hurtado v. California

110 U.S. 516, 4 S.Ct. 111 (1884)

On Saturday, February 4, 1882, Joseph Hurtado assaulted Jose Estuardo in a saloon brawl in Sacramento, California. He was arrested and scheduled for trial the following Monday. But the city attorney was unable to appear, the trial was postponed, and Hurtado released. He headed for a nearby bar. Later, Hurtado saw Estuardo approaching the bar and walked out and shot him in the chest. As Estuardo tried to flee, Hurtado shot him again in the back, and a third time as Estuardo lay on the ground. Hurtado was arrested and subsequently tried and convicted of murder, and sentenced to death.

If Hurtado had been tried in federal court, he would have been indicted by a grand jury before being tried for his crime. The Fifth Amendment requires indictment by a grand jury before a person accused of a capital offense may be tried. By contrast, the California Constitution of 1879 provided that prosecutions of criminal defendants could proceed on a prosecutor's filing a statement of information (a formal statement of accusation of the crimes committed, but not submitted to a grand jury). On appeal, Hurtado's attorney challenged the constitutionality of this procedure as a violation of the Fifth Amendment and the due process clause of the Fourteenth Amendment. After two state courts upheld his conviction, Hurtado petitioned the Supreme Court for a writ of error, claiming that the state had denied him his rights under the Bill of Rights. But the justices rejected that plea.

The Court's decision was 7–1, with Justice Field not participating; the majority's opinion was announced by Justice Matthews. Justice Harlan dissented.

■ ■ ■

☐ *Justice MATTHEWS delivered the opinion of the Court.*

It is claimed on behalf of the prisoner that the conviction and sentence are void, on the ground that they are repugnant to that clause of the fourteenth article of amendment to the constitution of the United States, which is in these words: "Nor shall any state deprive any person of life, liberty, or property without due process of law." The proposition of law we are asked to affirm is that an indictment or presentment by a grand jury, as known to the common law of England, is essential to that "due process of law," when applied to prosecutions for felonies, which is secured and guaranteed by this provision of the constitution of the United States, and which accordingly it is forbidden to the states, respectively, to dispense with in the administration of criminal law. . . .

[I]t is maintained that the phrase "due process of law" is equivalent to "law of the land," as found in the twenty-ninth chapter of *Magna Charta*; that by immemorial usage it has acquired a fixed, definite, and technical meaning; that it refers to and includes, not only the general principles of public liberty and private right, which lie at the foundation of all free government, but the very institutions which, venerable by time and custom, have been tried by experience and found fit and necessary for the preservation of those principles, and which, having been the birthright and inheritance of every English subject, crossed the Atlantic with the colonists and were transplanted and established in the fundamental laws of the state; that, having been originally introduced into the constitution of the United States as a limitation upon the powers of the government, brought into being by that instrument, it has now been added as an additional security to the individual against oppression by the states themselves; that one of these institutions is that of the grand jury, an indictment or presentment by which against the accused in cases of alleged felonies is an essential part of due process of law, in order that he may not be harassed and destroyed by prosecutions founded only upon private malice or popular fury.

It is urged upon us, however, in argument, that the claim made in behalf of the plaintiff in error is supported by the decision of this court in *Murray's Lessee v. Hoboken Land & Imp. Co.* [18 How. (59 U.S.) 272 (1856)]. There, Justice CURTIS, delivering the opinion of the court, after showing that due process of law must mean something more than the actual existing law of the land, for otherwise it would be no restraint upon legislative power, proceeds as follows: "To what principle, then, are we to resort to ascertain whether this process, enacted by congress, is due process? To this the answer must be twofold. We must examine the constitution itself to see whether this process be in conflict with any of its provisions. If not found to be so, we must look to those settled usages and modes of proceeding existing in the common and statute law of England before the emigration of our ancestors, and which are shown not to have been unsuited to their civil and political condition by having been acted on by them after the settlement of this country." . . .

We are to construe this phrase in the fourteenth amendment by the *usus loquendi* of the constitution itself. The same words are contained in the fifth amendment. That article makes specific and express provision for perpetuating the institution of the grand jury, so far as relates to prosecutions for the more aggravated crimes under the laws of the United States. It declares that "no person shall be held to answer for a capital or otherwise infamous crime, unless on a presentment or indictment of a grand jury, except in cases arising in the land or naval forces, or in the militia when in actual service in time of war or public danger; nor shall any person be subject for the same offense to be twice put in jeopardy of life or limb; nor shall he be compelled in any criminal case to be a witness against himself." It then immediately adds: "nor be deprived of life, liberty, or property without due process of law." According to a recognized canon of interpretation, especially applicable to formal and solemn instruments of constitutional law, we are forbidden to assume, without clear reason to the contrary, that any part of this most important amendment is superfluous. The natural and obvious inference is that, in the sense of the constitution, "due process of law" was not meant or intended to include, *ex vi termini*, the institution and procedure of a grand jury in any case. The conclusion is equally irresistible, that when the same phrase was employed in the fourteenth amendment to restrain the action of the states, it was used in the same sense and with no greater extent; and that if in the adoption of that amendment it had been part of its purpose to perpetuate the institution of the grand jury in all the states, it would have embodied, as did the fifth amendment, express declarations to that effect. Due process of law in the latter refers to that law of the land which derives its authority from the legislative powers conferred upon congress by the constitution of the United States, exercised within the limits therein prescribed, and interpreted according to the principles of the common law. In the fourteenth amendment, by parity of reason, it refers to that law of the land in each state which derives its authority from the inherent and reserved powers of the state, exerted within the limits of those fundamental principles of liberty and justice which lie at the base of all our civil and political institutions.

But it is not to be supposed that these legislative powers are absolute and despotic, and that the amendment prescribing due process of law is too vague and indefinite to operate as a practical restraint. It is not every act, legislative in form, that is law. Law is something more than mere will exerted as an act of power. It must be not a special rule for a particular person or a particular case, but, in the language of Mr. Webster, in his familiar definition, "the general law, a law which hears before it condemns, which proceeds upon inquiry, and renders judgment only after trial," so "that every citizen shall hold his life, liberty, property, and immunities under the protection of the general rules which govern society," and thus excluding, as not due process of law, acts of attainder, bills of pains and penalties, acts of confiscation, acts reversing judgments, and acts directly transferring one man's estate to another, legislative judgments and decrees, and other similar special, partial, and arbitrary exertions of power under the forms of legislation. Arbitrary power, enforcing its edicts to the injury of the persons and property of its subjects, is not law, whether manifested as the decree of a personal monarch or of an impersonal multitude. And the limitations imposed by our constitutional law upon the action of the governments, both state and national, are essential to the preservation of public and private rights, notwithstanding the representative character of our political institutions. The enforcement of these limitations by judicial process is the device of self-governing communities to protect the rights of individuals and minorities, as well against the power of numbers, as against the violence of public agents transcending the limits of lawful authority, even when acting in the name and wielding the force of the government. . . .

Tried by these principles, we are unable to say that the substitution for a presentment or indictment by a grand jury of the proceeding by information after examination and commitment by a magistrate, certifying to the probable guilt of the defendant, with the right on his part to the aid of counsel, and to the cross-examination of the witnesses produced for the prosecution, is not due process of law. It is, as we have seen, an ancient proceeding at common law, which might include every case of an offense of less grade than a felony, except misprision of treason; and in every circumstance of its administration, as authorized by the statute of California, it carefully considers and guards the substantial interest of the prisoner. It is merely a preliminary proceeding, and can result in no final judgment, except as the consequence of a regular judicial trial, conducted precisely as in cases of indictments. . . .

For these reasons, finding no error therein, the judgment of the supreme court of California is affirmed.

☐ *Justice HARLAN, dissenting.*

"Due process of law," within the meaning of the national Constitution, does not import one thing with reference to the powers of the states and another with reference to the powers of the general government. If particular proceedings, conducted under the authority of the general government, and involving life, are prohibited because not constituting that due process of law required by the Fifth Amendment of the Constitution of the United States, similar proceedings, conducted under the authority of a state, must be deemed illegal, as not being due process of law within the meaning of the Fourteenth Amendment. The words "due process of law," in the latter amendment, must receive the same interpretation they had at common law from which they were derived, and which was given to them at the formation of the general government. What was that interpretation? . . .

"The words 'due process of law' were undoubtedly intended," said this Court, in *Murray's Lessee v. Hoboken, etc. Co.* [18 How (59 U.S.) 272 (1856)], "to convey the same meaning as the words 'by the law of the land' in Magna Charta." Whether the phrase in our American constitutions, national or state, be "law of the land" or "due process of law," it means in every case the same thing. . . .

It seems to me that too much stress is put upon the fact that the framers of the Constitution made express provision for the security of those rights which at common law were protected by the requirement of due process of law, and, in addition, declared, generally, that no person shall "be deprived of life, liberty or property without due process of law." The rights, for the security of which these express provisions were made, were of a character so essential to the safety of the people that it was deemed wise to avoid the possibility that Congress, in regulating the processes of law, would impair or destroy them. Hence, their specific enumeration in the earlier amendments of the Constitution, in connection with the general requirement of due process of law, the latter itself being broad enough to cover every right of life, liberty or property secured by the settled usages and modes of proceeding existing under the common and statute law of England at the time our government was founded. . . .

[I]t is a fact of momentous interest in this discussion, that, when the Fourteenth Amendment was submitted and adopted, the Bill of Rights and the constitutions of twenty-seven States expressly forbade criminal prosecutions, by information, for capital cases [including the California Constitution of 1849]; while, in the remaining ten States, they were impliedly forbidden by a general clause declaring that no person should be deprived of life otherwise than by "the judgment of his peers or the law of the land," or "without due process of law." It may be safely affirmed that, when that Amendment was adopted, a criminal prosecution, by information, for a crime involving life, was not permitted in any one of the States composing the Union. So that the court, in this case, while conceding that the requirement of due process of law protects the fundamental principles of liberty and justice, adjudges, in effect, that an immunity or right, recognized at the common law to be essential to personal security, jealously guarded by our

Justice Benjamin Cardozo and Chief Justice Charles Evans Hughes in 1937. Justice Cardozo's opinion in *Palko v. Connecticut* (1937) set the stage for the Court's selective nationalization of the Bill of Rights. (*Bettmann/Corbis via Getty Images*)

national Constitution against violation by any tribunal or body exercising authority under the general government, and expressly or impliedly recognized, *when the Fourteenth Amendment was adopted*, in the Bill of Rights or Constitution of every State in the Union, is, yet, not a fundamental principle in governments established, as those of the States of the Union are, to secure to the citizen liberty and justice, and, therefore, is not involved in that due process of law required in proceedings conducted under the sanction of a State. My sense of duty constrains me to dissent from this interpretation of the supreme law of the land.

Palko v. Connecticut

302 U.S. 319, 58 S.Ct. 149 (1937)

Frank Jacob Palko was a man wanted for killing two police officers in Bridgeport, Connecticut, in September 1935. He had been stopped by them for questioning about the burglary of a music store and when confronted shot them both and then escaped. A month later, he was arrested in New York and confessed to the Bridgeport murders. Palko was subsequently indicted by a grand jury on the charge of first-degree premeditated murder; tried before a jury, which found him guilty of second-degree murder; and sentenced to life imprisonment.

After his trial, the prosecution persisted in seeking the death penalty and appealed Palko's trial and sentence. Under Connecticut law, a criminal sentence could be appealed by the state if the trial judge made errors prejudicial to the prosecution and the judge granted his permission for an appeal. The prosecution objected to the judge's orders forbidding the use of Palko's confession as evidence and of certain questioning during the trial, as well as the judge's characterization of what constitutes premeditated murder in his instructions to the jury on the difference between first- and second-degree murder. The state supreme court of appeals agreed the trial judge had erred, reversed Palko's conviction, and ordered a retrial.

At Palko's second trial, his attorney objected that retrial violated the Fifth Amendment guarantee against holding a person in double jeopardy for the same offense. The trial judge overruled that objection. Palko was convicted for first-degree murder and sentenced to be electrocuted. After unsuccessfully appealing to the state supreme court, Palko's attorney petitioned the Supreme Court. In claiming that Palko's retrial violated the double jeopardy clause of the Fifth Amendment, he argued that historical evidence showed that the Bill of Rights was applicable to the states under the Fourteenth Amendment.

The Court's decision was 8–1; the majority's opinion was delivered by Justice Cardozo. Justice Butler dissented without opinion.

■ ■ ■

☐ *Justice CARDOZO delivered the opinion of the Court.*

The . . . appellant [contends] that whatever is forbidden by the Fifth Amendment is forbidden by the Fourteenth also. The Fifth Amendment, which is not directed to the States, but solely to the federal government, creates immunity from double jeopardy. No person shall be "subject for the same offense to be twice put in jeopardy of life or limb." The Fourteenth Amendment ordains, "nor shall any State deprive any person of life, liberty, or property, without due process of law." To retry a defendant, though under one indictment and only one, subjects him, it is said, to double jeopardy in violation of the Fifth Amendment, if the prosecution is one on behalf of the United States. From this the consequence is said to follow that there is a denial of life or liberty without due process of law, if the prosecution is one on behalf of the people of a state. . . .

We have said that in appellant's view the Fourteenth Amendment is to be taken as embodying the prohibitions of the Fifth. His thesis is even broader. Whatever would be a violation of the original bill of rights (Amendments 1 to 8) if done by the federal government is now equally unlawful by force of the Fourteenth Amendment if done by a state. There is no such general rule.

The Fifth Amendment provides, among other things, that no person shall be held to answer for a capital or otherwise infamous crime unless on presentment or indictment of a grand jury. This court has held that, in prosecutions by a state, presentment or indictment by a grand jury may give way to informations at the instance of a public officer. *Hurtado v. California*, 110 U.S. 516 [1884]. The Fifth Amendment provides also that no person shall be compelled in any criminal case to be a witness against himself. This court has said that, in prosecutions by a state, the exemption will fail if the state elects to end it. The Sixth Amendment calls for a jury trial in criminal cases and the Seventh for a jury trial in civil cases at common law where the value in controversy shall exceed $20. This court has ruled that consistently with those amendments trial by jury may be modified by a state or abolished altogether. . . .

On the other hand, the due process clause of the Fourteenth Amendment may make it unlawful for a state to abridge by its statutes the freedom of speech which the First Amendment safeguards against encroachment by the Congress (*De Jonge v. Oregon*, 299 U.S. 353 [1937] or the like freedom of the press (*Grosjean v. American Press Co.*, 297 U.S. 233 [1936]; *Near v. Minnesota*, 283 U.S. 697 [1931], or the free exercise of religion (*Hamilton v. Regents of University*, 293 U.S. 245 [1934], or the right of peaceable assembly, without which speech would be unduly trammeled . . . or the right of one accused of crime to the benefit of counsel (*Powell v. Alabama*, 287 U.S. 45 [1932]. In these and other situations immunities that are valid as against the federal government by force of the specific pledges of particular amendments have been found to be implicit in the concept of ordered liberty, and thus, through the Fourteenth Amendment, become valid as against the states.

The line of division may seem to be wavering and broken if there is a hasty catalogue of the cases on the one side and the other. Reflection and analysis will induce a different view. There emerges the perception of a rationalizing principle which gives to discrete instances a proper order and coherence. The right to trial by jury and the immunity from prosecution except as the result of an indictment may have value and importance. Even so, they are not of the very essence of a scheme of ordered liberty. To abolish them is not to violate a "principle of justice so rooted in the traditions and conscience of our people as to be ranked as fundamental." What is true of jury trials and indictments is true also, as the cases show, of the immunity from compulsory self-incrimination. *Twining v. New Jersey* [211 U.S. 78 (1908)]. This too might be lost, and justice still be done. . . .

We reach a different plane of social and moral values when we pass to the privileges and immunities that have been taken over from the earlier articles of the Federal Bill of Rights and brought within the Fourteenth Amendment by a process of absorption. These in their origin were effective against the federal government alone. If the Fourteenth Amendment has absorbed them, the process of absorption has had its source in the belief that neither liberty nor justice would exist if they were sacrificed. This is true, for illustration, of freedom of thought and speech. Of that freedom one may say that it is the matrix, the indispensable condition, of nearly every other form of freedom. With rare aberrations a pervasive recognition of that truth can be traced in our history, political and legal. So it has come about that the domain of liberty, withdrawn by the Fourteenth Amendment from encroachment by the states, has been enlarged by latter-day judgments to include liberty of the mind as well as liberty of action. The extension became, indeed, a logical imperative when once it was recognized, as long ago it was, that liberty is something more than exemption from physical restraint, and that even in the field of substantive rights and duties the legislative judgment, if oppressive and arbitrary, may be overridden by the courts. Fundamental too in the concept of due process, and so in that of liberty, is the thought that condemnation shall be rendered only after trial. The hearing, moreover, must be a real one, not a sham or a pretense. For that reason, ignorant defendants in a capital case were held to have been condemned unlawfully when in truth, though not in form, they were refused the aid of counsel. *Powell v. Alabama*. The decision did not turn upon the fact that the benefit of counsel would have been guaranteed to the defendants by the provisions of the Sixth Amendment if they had been prosecuted in a federal court. The decision turned upon the fact that in the particular situation laid before us in the evidence the benefit of counsel was essential to the substance of a hearing.

Our survey of the cases serves, we think, to justify the statement that the dividing line between them, if not unfaltering throughout its course, has been true for the most part to a unifying principle. On which side of the line the case made out by the appellant has appropriate location must be the next inquiry and the final one. Is that kind of double jeopardy to which the statute has subjected him a hardship so acute and shocking that our polity will not endure it? Does it violate those "fundamental principles of liberty and justice which lie at the base of all our civil and political institutions"? The answer surely must be "no." What the answer would have to be if the state were permitted after a trial free from error to try the accused over again or to bring another case against him, we have no occasion to consider. We deal with the statute before us and no other. The state is not attempting to wear the accused out by a multitude of cases with accumulated trials. It asks no more than this, that the case against him shall go on until there shall be a trial free from the corrosion of substantial legal error. This is not cruelty at all, nor even vexation in any immoderate degree. . . . The judgment is affirmed.

Adamson v. California
332 U.S. 46, 67 S.Ct. 1672 (1947)

Admiral Dewey Adamson, a forty-three-year-old black man with a prior criminal record, was arrested and tried for breaking into the Los Angeles apartment of a sixty-four-year-old widow and then murdering her. At his trial, Adamson refused to testify in his own defense because of his prior criminal record. If he had, the prosecution could impeach his credibility as a witness based on his previous convictions for robbery and burglary. The Fifth Amendment guarantees the accused a right against self-incrimination and being "compelled in any criminal case to be a witness against himself." But California's state constitution permitted prosecutors to comment on a defendant's failure to testify. At Adamson's trial, the district attorney told the jury that Adamson's refusal to testify stripped him of a presumption of innocence. He told the jury in summation, "Counsel asked you to find this defendant not guilty. But does the defendant get on the stand and say, under oath, 'I am not guilty'? Not one word from him, and not one word from a single witness. I leave the case in your hands." The jury convicted Adamson on both counts. He was sentenced, as a habitual criminal, to life imprisonment on the burglary count and to death in the gas chamber on the murder count. Adamson's attorney appealed unsuccessfully to the state supreme court and then to the Supreme Court.

Adamson's attorney asked the Supreme Court to strike down California's law permitting prosecutorial comment. It penalized the defendant for exercising his Fifth Amendment rights which, he also argued, were applicable to the states under the Fourteenth Amendment's privileges or immunities clause and due process clause. That meant overturning *Twining v. New Jersey*, 211 U.S. 78 (1908), which upheld New Jersey's practice of allowing juries to draw unfavorable inferences from a defendant's failure to testify. But Adamson's attorney urged the Court to reconsider and adopt dissenting Justice Harlan's opinion there and in *Hurtado*. At conference, the justices voted five to three to affirm Adamson's conviction, with Justice Black initially passing because he was unsure prosecutorial comments violated the Fifth Amendment, although he was certain that the amendment and others of the Bill of Rights should apply to the states. In the end, Black joined the dissenters writing one of his major opinions disputing the majority's reading of the history and purposes of the Bill of Rights and the Fourteenth Amendment. Justice Reed's opinion for the majority paid little attention to the privileges or immunities claim and concentrated instead on the due process claim.

The Court's decision was 5–4, and the majority's opinion was announced by Justice Reed. Justice Frankfurter concurred. Dissents were delivered by Justices Murphy and Black, joined by Justices Rutledge and Douglas.

■ ■ ■

☐ *Justice REED delivered the opinion of the Court.*

[The appellant contends that] the due process clause of the Fourteenth Amendment protects his privilege against self-incrimination. The due process clause of the Fourteenth Amendment, however, does not draw all the rights of the federal Bill of Rights under its protection. That contention was made and rejected in *Palko v. Connecticut* [302 U.S. 319 (1937)]. *Palko* held that such provisions of the Bill of Rights as were "implicit in the concept of ordered liberty" became secure from state interference by the clause. But it held nothing more. . . .

For a state to require testimony from an accused is not necessarily a breach of a state's obligation to give a fair trial. Therefore, we must examine the effect of the California law applied in this trial to see whether the comment on failure to testify violates the protection against state action that the due process clause does grant to an accused. The due process clause forbids compulsion to testify by fear of hurt, torture or exhaustion. It forbids any other type of coercion that falls within the scope of due process. California follows Anglo-American legal tradition in excusing defendants in criminal prosecutions from compulsory testimony. That is a matter of legal policy and not because of the requirements of due process under the Fourteenth Amendment. So our inquiry is directed, not at the broad question of the constitutionality of compulsory testimony from the accused under the due process clause, but to the constitutionality of the provision of the California law that permits comment upon his failure to testify. . . .

Generally, comment on the failure of an accused to testify is forbidden in American jurisdictions. . . . California, however, is one of a few states that permit limited comment upon a defendant's failure to testify. That permission is narrow. . . . This does not involve any presumption, rebuttable or irrebuttable, either of guilt or of the truth of any fact, that is offered in evidence.

It allows inferences to be drawn from proven facts. Because of this clause, the court can direct the jury's attention to whatever evidence there may be that a defendant could deny and the prosecution can argue as to inferences that may be drawn from the accused's failure to testify. . . . California has prescribed a method for advising the jury in the search for truth. However sound may be the legislative conclusion that an accused should not be compelled in any criminal case to be a witness against himself, we see no reason why comment should not be made upon his silence. It seems quite natural that when a defendant has opportunity to deny or explain facts and determines not to do so, the prosecution should bring out the strength of the evidence by commenting upon defendant's failure to explain or deny it. The prosecution evidence may be of facts that may be beyond the knowledge of the accused. If so, his failure to testify would have little if any weight. But the facts may be such as are necessarily in the knowledge of the accused. In that case a failure to explain would point to an inability to explain.

☐ *Justice FRANKFURTER, concurring.*

For historical reasons a limited immunity from the common duty to testify was written into the Federal Bill of Rights, and I am prepared to agree that, as part of that immunity, comment on the failure of an accused to take the witness stand as forbidden in federal prosecutions. . . .

But to suggest that such a limitation can be drawn out of "due process" in its protection of ultimate decency in a civilized society is to suggest that the Due Process Clause fastened fetters of unreason upon the States. . . .

Between the incorporation of the Fourteenth Amendment into the Constitution and the beginning of the present membership of the Court—a period of 70 years—the scope of that Amendment was passed upon by 43 judges. Of all these judges, only one, who may respectfully be called an eccentric exception, ever indicated the belief that the Fourteenth Amendment was a shorthand summary of the first eight Amendments theretofore limiting only the Federal Government, and that due process incorporated those eight Amendments as restrictions upon the powers of the States. . . .

The notion that the Fourteenth Amendment was a covert way of imposing upon the States all the rules which it seemed important to Eighteenth Century statesmen to write into the Federal Amendments, was rejected by judges who were themselves witnesses of the process by which the Fourteenth Amendment became part of the Constitution. Arguments that may now be adduced to prove that the first eight Amendments were concealed within the historic phrasing of the Fourteenth Amendment were not unknown at the time of its adoption. A surer estimate of their bearing was possible for judges at the time than distorting distance is likely to vouchsafe. Any evidence of design or purpose not contemporaneously known could hardly have influenced those who ratified the Amendment. Remarks of a particular proponent of the Amendment, no matter how influential, are not to be deemed part of the Amendment. What was submitted for ratification was his proposal, not his speech. Thus, at the time of the ratification of the Fourteenth Amendment the constitutions of nearly half of the ratifying States did not have the rigorous requirements of the Fifth Amendment for instituting criminal proceedings through a grand jury. It could hardly have occurred to these States that by ratifying the Amendment they uprooted their established methods for prosecuting crime and fastened upon themselves a new prosecutorial system. . . .

It may not be amiss to restate the pervasive function of the Fourteenth Amendment in exacting from the States observance of basic liberties. The Amendment neither comprehends the specific provisions by which the founders deemed it appropriate to restrict the federal government nor is it confined to them. The Due Process Clause of the Fourteenth Amendment has an independent potency, precisely as does the Due Process Clause of the Fifth Amendment in relation to the Federal Government. It ought not to require argument to reject the notion that due process of law meant one thing in the Fifth Amendment and another in the Fourteenth. The Fifth Amendment specifically prohibits prosecution of an "infamous crime" except upon indictment; it forbids double jeopardy; it bars compelling a person to be a witness against himself in any criminal case; it precludes deprivation of "life, liberty, or property, without due process of law." Are Madison and his contemporaries in the framing of the Bill of Rights to be charged with writing into it a meaningless clause? To consider "due process of law" as merely a shorthand statement of other specific clauses in the same amendment is to attribute to the authors and proponents of this Amendment ignorance of, or indifference to, a historic conception which was one of the great instruments in the arsenal of constitutional freedom which the Bill of Rights was to protect and strengthen. . . .

And so, when, as in a case like the present, a conviction in a State court is here for review under a claim that a right protected by the Due Process Clause of the Fourteenth Amendment has been denied, the issue is not whether an infraction of one of the specific provisions of the first eight Amendments is disclosed by the record. The relevant question is whether the criminal proceedings which resulted in conviction deprived the accused of the due process of law to which the United States Constitution entitled him. Judicial review of that guaranty of the Fourteenth Amendment inescapably imposes upon this Court an exercise of judgment upon the whole course of the proceedings in order to ascertain whether they offend those canons of decency and fairness which express the notions of justice of English-speaking peoples even toward those charged with the most heinous offenses. These standards of justice are not authoritatively formulated anywhere as though they were prescriptions in a pharmacopoeia. But neither does the application of the Due Process Clause imply that judges are wholly at large. The judicial judgment in applying the Due Process Clause must move within the limits of accepted notions of justice and is not to be based upon the idiosyncrasies of a merely personal judgment.

☐ *Justice MURPHY, with whom Justice RUTLEDGE joins, dissenting.*

While in substantial agreement with the views of Justice BLACK, I have one reservation and one addition to make.

I agree that the specific guarantees of the Bill of Rights should be carried over intact into the first section of the Fourteenth Amendment. But I am not prepared to say that the latter is entirely and necessarily limited by the Bill of Rights. Occasions may arise where a proceeding falls so far short of conforming to fundamental standards of procedure as to warrant constitutional condemnation in terms of a lack of due process despite the absence of a specific provision in the Bill of Rights.

☐ *Justice BLACK, dissenting.*

My study of the historical events that culminated in the Fourteenth Amendment, and the expressions of those who sponsored and favored, as well as those who opposed its submission and passage, persuades me that one of the chief objects that the provisions of the Amendment's first section, separately, and as a whole, were intended to accomplish was to make the Bill of Rights, applicable to the states. With full knowledge of the import of the *Barron* [*v. Baltimore* (1833)] decision, the framers and backers of the Fourteenth Amendment proclaimed its purpose to be to overturn the constitutional rule that case had announced. This historical purpose has never received full consideration or exposition in any opinion of this Court interpreting the Amendment. . . .

For this reason, I am attaching to this dissent, an appendix which contains a resumé, by no means complete, of the Amendment's history. In my judgment that history conclusively demonstrates that the language of the first section of the Fourteenth Amendment, taken as a whole, was thought by those responsible for its submission to the people, and by those who opposed its submission, sufficiently explicit to guarantee that thereafter no state could deprive its citizens of the privileges and protections of the Bill of Rights. Whether this Court ever will, or whether it now should, in the light of past decisions, give full effect to what the Amendment was intended to accomplish is not necessarily essential to a decision here. However that may be, our prior decisions, including *Twining* [*v. New Jersey*, 211 U.S. 78 (1908)], do not prevent our carrying out that purpose, at least to the extent of making applicable to the states, not a mere part, as the Court has, but the full protection of the Fifth Amendment's provision against compelling evidence from an accused to convict him of crime. And I further contend that the "natural law" formula which the Court uses to reach its conclusion in this case should be abandoned as an incongruous excrescence on our Constitution. I believe that formula to be itself a violation of our Constitution, in that it subtly conveys to courts, at the expense of legislatures, ultimate power over public policies in fields where no specific provision of the Constitution limits legislative power. . . .

I cannot consider the Bill of Rights to be an outworn 18th Century "strait jacket" as the *Twining* opinion did. Its provisions may be thought outdated abstractions by some. And it is true that they were designed to meet ancient evils. But they are the same kind of human evils that have emerged from century to century wherever excessive power is sought by the few at the expense of the many. In my judgment the people of no nation can lose their liberty so long as a Bill of Rights like ours survives and its basic purposes are conscientiously interpreted, enforced and respected so as to afford continuous protection against old, as well as new, devices and practices which might thwart those purposes. I fear to see the consequences of the Court's practice of substituting its own concepts of decency and fundamental justice for the language of the Bill of Rights as its point of departure in interpreting and enforcing that Bill of Rights. If the choice must be between the selective process of the *Palko* decision applying some of the Bill of Rights to the States, or the *Twining* rule applying none of them, I would choose the *Palko* selective process. But rather than accept either of these choices. I would follow what I believe was the original purpose of the Fourteenth Amendment—to extend to all the people of the nation the complete protection of the Bill of Rights.

Justice DOUGLAS joined in this opinion.

346 | THE NATIONALIZATION OF THE BILL OF RIGHTS

Rochin v. California

342 U.S. 165, 72 S.CT. 205 (1952)

Antonio Richard Rochin was sitting in his bedroom when three Los Angeles county deputy sheriffs crashed through the door, armed, without a search or arrest warrant. He quickly grabbed and swallowed two morphine capsules lying on a nightstand. The deputies immediately tried to force him to vomit the pills by choking and sticking their fingers down his throat. When that failed, they rushed Rochin to a hospital, where a doctor inserted a tube and an emetic solution down his throat. At that, he finally vomited the pills into a pail. Rochin was later charged, tried, and convicted for violating a state narcotics law. His conviction was upheld on appeal by a state appellate court, and the California State Supreme Court denied a further appeal. Rochin's attorney petitioned the Supreme Court on the ground that the police denied Rochin's rights under the Fourth and Fifth Amendments and the due process clause of the Fourteenth Amendment. The petition was granted, and the Court reversed the two California State court rulings.

The Court's decision was unanimous; the opinion was announced by Justice Frankfurter, with Justice Minton not participating. Concurrences were by Justices Black and Douglas.

■ ■ ■

☐ *Justice FRANKFURTER delivered the opinion of the Court.*

In our federal system the administration of criminal justice is predominantly committed to the care of the States. The power to define crimes belongs to Congress only as an appropriate means of carrying into execution its limited grant of legislative powers. U.S. Const. Art. I, Sec. 8, cl. 18. Broadly speaking, crimes in the United States are what the laws of the individual States make them, subject to the limitations of Art. I, Sec. 10, cl. 1, in the original Constitution, prohibiting bills of attainder and *ex post facto* laws, and of the Thirteenth and Fourteenth Amendments.

These limitations, in the main, concern not restrictions upon the powers of the States to define crime, except in the restricted area where federal authority has pre-empted the field, but restrictions upon the manner in which the States may enforce their penal codes. Accordingly, in reviewing a State criminal conviction under a claim of right guaranteed by the Due Process Clause of the Fourteenth Amendment, from which is derived the most far-reaching and most frequent federal basis of challenging State criminal justice, "we must be deeply mindful of the responsibilities of the States for the enforcement of criminal laws, and exercise with due humility our merely negative function in subjecting convictions from state courts to the very narrow scrutiny which the Due Process Clause of the Fourteenth Amendment authorizes." . . .

However, this Court too has its responsibility. Regard for the requirements of the Due Process Clause "inescapably imposes upon this Court an exercise of judgment upon the whole course of the proceedings [resulting in a conviction] in order to ascertain whether they offend those canons of decency and fairness which express the notions of justice of English-speaking peoples even toward those charged with the most heinous offenses." These standards of justice are not authoritatively formulated anywhere as though they were specifics. Due process of law is a summarized constitutional guarantee of respect for those personal immunities which, as Justice CARDOZO twice wrote for the Court, are "so rooted in the tradition and conscience of our people as to be ranked as fundamental," or are "implicit in the concept of ordered liberty." *Palko v. State of Connecticut* [302 U.S. 319 (1937)].

The Due Process Clause places upon this Court the duty of exercising a judgment, within the narrow confines of judicial power in reviewing State convictions, upon interests of society pushing in opposite directions.

Due process of law thus conceived is not to be derided as resort to a revival of "natural law." To believe that this judicial exercise of judgment could be avoided by freezing "due process of law" at some fixed stage of time or thought is to suggest that the most important aspect of constitutional adjudication is a function for inanimate machines and not for judges, for whom the independence safeguarded by Article III of the Constitution was designed and who are presumably guided by established standards of judicial behavior. Even cybernetics has not yet made that haughty claim. To practice the requisite detachment and to achieve sufficient objectivity no doubt demands of judges the habit of self-discipline and self-criticism, incertitude that one's own views are incontestable and alert tolerance toward views not shared. But these are precisely the presuppositions of our judicial process. They are precisely the qualities society has a right to expect from those entrusted with ultimate judicial power.

Restraints on our jurisdiction are self-imposed only in the sense that there is from our decisions no immediate appeal short of impeachment or constitutional amendment. But that does not make due process of law a matter of judicial caprice. The faculties of the Due Process Clause may be indefinite and vague, but the mode of their ascertainment is not self-willed. In each case "due process of law" requires an evaluation based on a disinterested inquiry pursued in the spirit of science, on a balanced order of facts exactly and fairly stated, on the detached consideration of conflicting claims, on a judgment not *ad hoc* and episodic but duly mindful of reconciling the needs both of continuity and of change in a progressive society.

Applying these general considerations to the circumstances of the present case, we are compelled to conclude that the proceedings by which this conviction was obtained do more than offend some fastidious squeamishness or private sentimentalism about combatting crime too energetically. This is conduct that shocks the conscience. Illegally breaking into the privacy of the petitioner, the struggle to open his mouth and remove what was there, the forcible extraction of his stomach's contents—this course of proceeding by agents of government to obtain evidence is bound to offend even hardened sensibilities. They are methods too close to the rack and the screw to permit of constitutional differentiation. . . .

On the facts of this case the conviction of the petitioner has been obtained by methods that offend the Due Process Clause. The judgment below must be reversed.

Reversed.

☐ *Justice BLACK, concurring.*

Adamson v. People of State of California, 332 U.S. 46 [1947], sets out reasons for my belief that state as well as federal courts and law enforcement officers must obey the Fifth Amendment's command that "No person . . . shall be compelled in any criminal case to be a witness against himself." I think a person is compelled to be a witness against himself not only when he is compelled to testify, but also when as here, incriminating evidence is forcibly taken from him by a contrivance of modern science. . . .

In the view of a majority of the Court, however, the Fifth Amendment imposes no restraint of any kind on the states. They nevertheless hold that California's use of this evidence violated the Due Process Clause of the Fourteenth Amendment. Since they hold as I do in this case, I regret my inability to accept their interpretation without protest. But I believe that faithful adherence to the specific guarantees in the Bill of Rights insures a more permanent protection of individual liberty than that which can be afforded by the nebulous standards stated by the majority.

What the majority hold is that the Due Process Clause empowers this Court to nullify any state law if its application "shocks the conscience," offends "a sense of justice" or runs counter to the "decencies of civilized conduct." . . . We are further admonished to measure the validity of state practices, not by our reason, or by the traditions of the legal profession, but by "the community's sense of fair play and decency"; by the "traditions and conscience of our people"; or by "those canons of decency and fairness which express the notions of justice of English-speaking peoples." These canons are made necessary, it is said, because of "interests of society pushing in opposite directions." . . .

[O]ne may well ask what avenues of investigation are open to discover "canons" of conduct so universally favored that this Court should write them into the Constitution? All we are told is that the discovery must be made by an evaluation based on a disinterested inquiry pursued in the spirit of science, on a balanced order of facts." . . .

I long ago concluded that the accordion-like qualities of this philosophy must inevitably imperil all the individual liberty safeguards specifically enumerated in the Bill of Rights.

☐ *Justice DOUGLAS, concurring.*

I think that words taken from [Rochin's] lips, capsules taken from his stomach, blood taken from his veins are all inadmissible provided they are taken from him without his consent. They are inadmissible because of the command of the Fifth Amendment.

That is an unequivocal, definite and workable rule of evidence for state and federal courts. But we cannot in fairness free the state courts from that command and yet excoriate them for flouting the "decencies of civilized conduct" when they admit the evidence. That is to make the rule turn not on the Constitution but on the idiosyncrasies of the judges who sit here.

■ INSIDE THE COURT

The Theory and Drafting of Justice Douglas's Opinion in Griswold v. Connecticut

After the justices' conference, Chief Justice Earl Warren assigned Justice Douglas the task of drafting an opinion to announce the Court's decision in *Griswold v. Connecticut*. His initial draft, however, did not develop the theory that a constitutional right of privacy was based on penumbrae of various guarantees of the Bill of Rights, as eventually announced in *Griswold*. Rather, Douglas sought to justify the decision based on earlier cases recognizing a First Amendment right of associational privacy. The analogy and precedents, he admitted, "do not decide this case. . . . Marriage does not fit precisely any of the categories of First Amendment rights. But it is a form of association as vital in the life of a man or a woman as any other, and perhaps more so."

Both Black and Brennan strongly objected to Douglas's extravagant reliance on First Amendment precedents. In a three-page letter, Brennan detailed an alternative approach, as the following excerpt indicates:

> I have read your draft opinion in *Griswold v. Connecticut*, and, while I agree with a great deal of it, I should like to suggest a substantial change in emphasis for your consideration. It goes without saying, of course, that your rejection of any approach based on *Lochner v. New York* is absolutely right. [In *Lochner*, a majority read into the Fourteenth Amendment a "liberty of contract" to strike down economic legislation. Although the Court later abandoned the doctrine of a liberty of contract, *Lochner* continues to symbolize the original sin of constitutional interpretation—that is, the Court's creation and enforcement of unenumerated rights.] And I agree that the association of husband and wife is not mentioned in the Bill of Rights, and that that is the obstacle we must hurdle to effect a reversal in this case.

> But I hesitate to bring the husband–wife relationship within the right to association we have constructed in the First Amendment context. . . . In the First Amendment context, in situations like *NAACP v. Alabama*, privacy is necessary to protect the capacity of an association for fruitful advocacy. In the present context, it seems to me that we are really interested in the privacy of married couples quite apart from any interest in advocacy. . . . Instead of expanding the First

(continues)

■ Inside the Court
The Theory and Drafting of Justice Douglas's Opinion in Griswold v. Connecticut *(continued)*

> Amendment right of association to include marriage, why not say that what has been done for the First Amendment can also be done for some of the other fundamental guarantees of the Bill of Rights? In other words, where fundamentals are concerned, the Bill of Rights guarantees are but expressions or examples of those rights, and do not preclude applications or extensions of those rights to situations unanticipated by the Framers.

The restriction on the dissemination and use of contraceptives, Brennan explained, "would, on this reasoning, run afoul of a right to privacy created out of the Fourth Amendment and the self-incrimination clause of the Fifth, together with the Third, in much the same way as the right of association has been created out of the First. Taken together, those amendments indicate a fundamental concern with the sanctity of the home and the right of the individual to be alone." "With this change of emphasis," Brennan concluded, the opinion "would be most attractive to me because it would require less departure from the specific guarantes and because I think there is a better chance it will command a Court."

Douglas subsequently revised his opinion and based the right of privacy on the penumbrae of the First, Third, Fourth, Fifth, Ninth, and Fourteenth Amendments. In the end, his opinion was joined by only a plurality of the Court. Justice Goldberg, joined by Chief Justice Warren and Justice Brennan, wrote a separate concurring opinion, as did Justices Harlan and White. Justices Black and Stewart each wrote separate dissenting opinions.

Source: Library of Congress, William J. Brennan Jr., Letter of April 24, 1965, in Justice William J. Brennan Jr., Papers.

Griswold v. Connecticut

381 U.S. 479, 85 S.Ct. 1678 (1965)

Estelle Griswold, executive director of the Planned Parenthood League of Connecticut, and Dr. C. Lee Buxton were part of a movement to repeal Connecticut's 1879 law prohibiting the dissemination of information about and the use of contraceptives. In the 1940s, after unsuccessfully seeking a repeal of the law by the state legislature, the league turned to the courts for a declaratory judgment finding the law unconstitutional. When the state supreme court upheld the law, a doctor appealed its ruling to the Supreme Court. In *Tileston v. Ullman*, 318 U.S. 44 (1943) (discussed in Ch. 2), however, the Court ruled that the doctor had no standing alone, without his patients, to challenge the constitutionality of the law under the Fourteenth Amendment. Almost twenty years later, Dr. Buxton and two of his female patients, both of whom had previously experienced difficult pregnancies, decided again to ask the Court for a declaratory judgment striking down the law. Once again, in *Poe v. Ullman*, 367 U.S. 497 (1961) (discussed in Ch. 2), a majority of the Court denied standing, largely because the law (with one exception) had gone unenforced for more than three-quarters of a century. But four justices dissented and the next year two of the justices in the majority, Justices Frankfurter and Whittaker, retired. Because Justice Frankfurter's opinion in *Poe* had stressed the unenforceability of the law, Griswold and Buxton decided that they would have to get arrested to gain standing to challenge Connecticut's law. They opened a birth control clinic, ten days later were arrested, and subsequently convicted in state courts. They thereupon made another appeal to the Supreme Court, which granted review.

The Court's decision was 7–2, and the majority's opinion was announced by Justice Douglas. Concurrences were by Justice Goldberg, joined by Chief Justice Warren and Justice Brennan, and by Justices Harlan and White. Justices Black and Stewart dissented.

■ ■ ■

☐ *Justice DOUGLAS delivered the opinion of the Court.*

[W]e are met with a wide range of questions that implicate the Due Process Clause of the Fourteenth Amendment. Overtones of some arguments suggest that *Lochner v. State of New York*, 198 U.S. 45 [(1905)], should be our guide. But we decline that invitation as we did in *West Coast Hotel Co. v. Parrish*, 300 U.S. 379 [(1937)]; *Olsen v. State of Nebraska*, 313 U.S. 236 [(1941)]; *Lincoln Federal Labor Union v. Northwestern Co.*, 335 U.S. 525 [(1949)]; *Williamson v. Lee Optical Co.*, 348 U.S. 483 [(1955)]; [and] *Giboney v. Empire Storage Co.*, 336 U.S. 490 [(1949)]. We do not sit as a super-legislature to determine the wisdom, need, and propriety of laws that touch economic problems, business affairs, or social conditions. This law, however, operates directly on an intimate relation of husband and wife and their physician's role in one aspect of that relation.

The association of people is not mentioned in the Constitution nor in the Bill of Rights. The right to educate a child in a school of the parents' choice—whether public or private or parochial—is also not mentioned. Nor is the right to study any particular subject or any foreign language. Yet the First Amendment has been construed to include certain of those rights.

By *Pierce v. Society of Sisters*, [268 U.S. 510 (1925)], the right to educate one's children as one chooses is made applicable to the States by the force of

Estelle Griswold (left), whose case led to the landmark ruling on the right of privacy, and Cornelia Jahncke, president of the Planned Parenthood League of Connecticut, celebrating news of the Court's ruling. (*The Granger Collection, New York.*)

the First and Fourteenth Amendments. By *Meyer v. State of Nebraska*, [262 U.S. 390 (1923)], the same dignity is given the right to study the German language in a private school. In other words, the State may not, consistently with the spirit of the First Amendment, contract the spectrum of available knowledge. The right of freedom of speech and press includes not only the right to utter or to print, but the right to distribute, the right to receive, the right to read; and freedom of inquiry, freedom of thought, and freedom to teach—indeed the freedom of the entire university community. *Sweezy v. State of New Hampshire*, 354 U.S. 234 [(1958)]. Without those peripheral rights the specific rights would be less secure. And so we reaffirm the principle of the *Pierce* and the *Meyer* cases.

In *NAACP v. State of Alabama* [357 U.S. 44 (1958)], we protected the "freedom to associate and privacy in one's associations," noting that freedom of association was a peripheral First Amendment right. Disclosure of membership lists of a constitutionally valid association, we held, was invalid "as entailing the likelihood of a substantial restraint upon the exercise by petitioner's members of their right to freedom of association." In other words, the First Amendment has a penumbra where privacy is protected from governmental intrusion. In like context, we have protected forms of "association" that are not political in the customary sense but pertain to the social, legal, and economic benefit of the members. . . .

Those cases involved more than the "right of assembly"—a right that extends to all irrespective of their race or idealogy. . . . The right of "association" like the right of belief (*West Virginia State Board of Education v. Barnette*, 319 U.S. 624 [(1943)], is more than the right to attend a meeting; it includes the right to express one's attitudes or philosophies by membership in a group or by affiliation with it or by other lawful means. Association in that context is a form of expression of opinion; and while it is not expressly included in the First Amendment its existence is necessary in making the express guarantees fully meaningful.

The foregoing cases suggest that specific guarantees in the Bill of Rights have penumbras, formed by emanations from those guarantees that help give them life and substance. See *Poe v. Ullman*, 367 U.S. 497 [(1961)] (dissenting opinion). Various guarantees create zones of privacy. The right of association contained in the penumbra of the First Amendment is one, as we have seen. The Third Amendment in its prohibition against the quartering of soldiers "in any house" in time of peace without the consent of the owner is another facet of that privacy. The Fourth Amendment explicitly affirms the "right of the people to be secure in their persons, houses, papers, and effects, against unreasonable searches and seizures." The Fifth Amendment in its Self-Incrimination Clause enables the citizen to create a zone of privacy which government may not force him to surrender to his detriment. The Ninth Amendment provides: "The enumeration in the Constitution, of certain rights, shall not be construed to deny or disparage others retained by the people."

The Fourth and Fifth Amendments were described in *Boyd v. United States*, 116 U.S. 616 [(1886)], as protection against all governmental invasions "of the sanctity of a man's home and the privacies of life."

We recently referred in *Mapp v. Ohio*, 367 U.S. 643 [(1961)], to the Fourth Amendment as creating a "right to privacy, no less important than any other right carefully and particularly reserved to the people." . . .

We have had many controversies over these penumbral rights of "privacy and repose." These cases bear witness that the right of privacy which presses for recognition here is a legitimate one.

The present case, then, concerns a relationship lying within the zone of privacy created by several fundamental constitutional guarantees. And it concerns a law which, in forbidding the *use* of contraceptives rather than regulating their manufacture or sale, seeks to achieve its goals by means having a maximum destructive impact upon that relationship. Such a law cannot stand in light of the familiar principle, so often applied by this Court, that a "governmental purpose to control or prevent activities constitutionally subject to state regulation may not be achieved by means which sweep unnecessarily broadly and thereby invade the area of protected freedoms." *NAACP v. Alabama*. . . . Would we allow the police to search the sacred precincts of marital bedrooms for telltale signs of the use of contraceptives? The very idea is repulsive to the notions of privacy surrounding the marriage relationship.

We deal with a right of privacy older than the Bill of Rights—older than our political parties, older than our school system. Marriage is a coming together for better or for worse, hopefully enduring, and intimate to the degree of being sacred. It is an association that promotes a way of life, not causes; a harmony in living, not political faiths; a bilateral loyalty, not commercial or social projects. Yet it is an association for as noble a purpose as any involved in our prior decisions.

Reversed.

☐ *Justice GOLDBERG, with whom THE CHIEF JUSTICE and Justice BRENNAN join, concurring.*

I agree with the Court that Connecticut's birth-control law unconstitutionally intrudes upon the right of marital privacy, and I join in its opinion and judgment. Although I have not accepted the view that "due process" as used in the Fourteenth Amendment includes all of the first eight Amendments (see my concurring opinion in *Pointer v. Texas*, 380 U.S. 400 [(1965)], and the dissenting opinion of Justice BRENNAN in *Cohen v. Hurley*, 366 U.S. 117 [(1961)]. I do agree that the concept of liberty protects those personal rights that are fundamental, and is not confined to the specific terms of the Bill of Rights. My conclusion that the concept of liberty is not so restricted and that it embraces the right of marital privacy though that right is not mentioned explicitly in the Constitution is supported both by numerous decisions of this Court, referred to in the Court's opinion, and by the language and history of the Ninth Amendment. In reaching the conclusion that the right of marital privacy is protected, as being within the protected penumbra of specific guarantees of the Bill of Rights, the Court refers to the Ninth Amendment. I add these words to emphasize the relevance of that Amendment to the Court's holding. . . .

The language and history of the Ninth Amendment reveal that the Framers of the Constitution believed that there are additional fundamental rights, protected from governmental infringement, which exist alongside those fundamental rights specifically mentioned in the first eight constitutional amendments.

The Ninth Amendment reads, "The enumeration in the Constitution, of certain rights, shall not be construed to deny or disparage others retained by the people." The Amendment is almost entirely the work of James Madison. It was introduced in Congress by him and passed the House and Senate with little or no debate and virtually no change in language. It was proffered to quiet expressed fears that a bill of specifically enumerated rights could not be sufficiently broad to cover all essential rights and that the specific mention of certain rights would be interpreted as a denial that others were protected.

In presenting the proposed Amendment, Madison said:

> It has been objected also against a bill of rights, that, by enumerating particular exceptions to the grant of power, it would disparage those rights which were not placed in that enumeration; and it might follow by implication, that those rights which were not singled out, were intended to be assigned into the hands of the General Government, and were consequently insecure. This is one of the most plausible arguments I have ever heard urged against the admission of a bill of rights into this system; but, I conceive, that it may be guarded against. I have attempted it, as gentlemen

may see by turning to the last clause of the fourth resolution [the Ninth Amendment]. I *Annals of Congress* 439 (Gales and Seaton ed. 1834). . . .

While this Court has had little occasion to interpret the Ninth Amendment, "[i]t cannot be presumed that any clause in the constitution is intended to be without effect." *Marbury v. Madison*, 1 Cranch 137 [(1803)]. To hold that a right so basic and fundamental and so deep-rooted in our society as the right of privacy in marriage may be infringed because that right is not guaranteed in so many words by the first eight amendments to the Constitution is to ignore the Ninth Amendment and to give it no effect whatsoever. . . .

I do not mean to imply that the Ninth Amendment is applied against the States by the Fourteenth. Nor do I mean to state that the Ninth Amendment constitutes an independent source of rights protected from infringement by either the States or the Federal Government. Rather, the Ninth Amendment shows a belief of the Constitution's authors that fundamental rights exist that are not expressly enumerated in the first eight amendments and an intent that the list of rights included there not be deemed exhaustive. . . . The Ninth Amendment simply shows the intent of the Constitution's authors that other fundamental personal rights should not be denied such protection or disparaged in any other way simply because they are not specifically listed in the first eight constitutional amendments. . . .

In determining which rights are fundamental, judges are not left at large to decide cases in light of their personal and private notions. Rather, they must look to the "traditions and [collective] conscience of our people" to determine whether a principle is "so rooted [there] . . . as to be ranked as fundamental." *Snyder v. Com. of Massachusetts*, 291 U.S. 97 [(1934)]. The inquiry is whether a right involved "is of such a character that it cannot be denied without violating those 'fundamental principles of liberty and justice which lie at the base of all our civil and political institutions' . . ." *Powell v. State of Alabama*, 287 U.S. 45 [(1932)]. . . .

The entire fabric of the Constitution and the purposes that clearly underlie its specific guarantees demonstrate that the rights to marital privacy and to marry and raise a family are of similar order and magnitude as the fundamental rights specifically protected.

Although the Constitution does not speak in so many words of the right of privacy in marriage, I cannot believe that it offers these fundamental rights no protection. The fact that no particular provision of the Constitution explicitly forbids the State from disrupting the traditional relation of the family—a relation as old and as fundamental as our entire civilization— surely does not show that the Government was meant to have the power to do so. Rather, as the Ninth Amendment expressly recognizes, there are fundamental personal rights such as this one, which are protected from abridgment by the Government though not specifically mentioned in the Constitution. . . .

The logic of the dissents would sanction federal or state legislation that seems to me even more plainly unconstitutional than the statute before us. Surely the Government, absent a showing of a compelling subordinating state interest, could not decree that all husbands and wives must be sterilized after two children have been born to them. Yet by their reasoning such an invasion of marital privacy would not be subject to constitutional challenge because, while it might be "silly," no provision of the Constitution specifically prevents the Government from curtailing the marital right to bear children and raise a family. While it may shock some of my Brethren that the Court today holds that the Constitution protects the right of marital privacy, in my view it is far more shocking to believe that the personal liberty guaranteed by the Constitution does not include protection against such totalitarian limitation of family size, which is at complete variance with our constitutional concepts. . . .

In a long series of cases this Court has held that where fundamental personal liberties are involved, they may not be abridged by the States simply on a showing that a regulatory statute has some rational relationship to the effectuation of a proper state purpose. "Where there is a significant encroachment upon personal liberty, the State may prevail only upon showing a subordinating interest which is compelling," *Bates v. City of Little Rock*, 361 U.S. 516 [(1960)]. . . .

Although the Connecticut birth-control law obviously encroaches upon a fundamental personal liberty, the State does not show that the law serves any "subordinating [state] interest which is compelling" or that it is "necessary . . . to the accomplishment of a permissible state policy." The State, at most, argues that there is some rational relation between this statute and what is admittedly a legitimate subject of state concern—the discouraging of extramarital relations. It says that preventing the use of birth-control devices by married persons helps prevent the indulgence by some in such extramarital relations. The rationality of this justification is dubious, particularly in light of the admitted widespread availability to all persons in the State of Connecticut, unmarried as well as married, of birth-control devices for the prevention of disease, as distinguished from the prevention of conception. . . . But, in any event, it is clear that the state interest in safeguarding marital fidelity can be served by a more discriminately tailored statute, which does not, like the present one, sweep unnecessarily broadly, reaching far beyond the evil sought to be dealt with and intruding upon the privacy of all married couples. . . . The law must be shown "necessary, and not merely rationally related to, the accomplishment of a permissible state policy." . . .

In sum, I believe that the right of privacy in the marital relation is fundamental and basic—a personal right "retained by the people" within the meaning of the Ninth Amendment. Connecticut cannot constitutionally abridge this fundamental right, which is protected by the Fourteenth Amendment from infringement by the States. I agree with the Court that petitioners' convictions must therefore be reversed.

☐ *Justice HARLAN, concurring.*

I fully agree with the judgment of reversal, but find myself unable to join the Court's opinion. The reason is that it seems to me to evince an approach to this case very much like that taken by my Brothers BLACK and STEWART in dissent, namely: the Due Process Clause of the Fourteenth Amendment does not touch this Connecticut statute unless the enactment is found to violate some right assured by the letter or penumbra of the Bill of Rights.

In other words, what I find implicit in the Court's opinion is that the "incorporation" doctrine may be used to *restrict* the reach of Fourteenth Amendment Due Process. For me this is just as unacceptable constitutional doctrine as is the use of the "incorporation" approach to *impose* upon the States all the requirements of the Bill of Rights as found in the provisions of the first eight amendments and in the decisions of this Court interpreting them.

In my view, the proper constitutional inquiry in this case is whether this Connecticut statute infringes the Due Process Clause of the Fourteenth Amendment because the enactment violates basic values "implicit in the concept of ordered liberty," *Palko v. State of Connecticut*, 302 U.S. 319 [(1937)]. For reasons stated at length in my dissenting opinion in *Poe v. Ullman*, [367 U.S. 497 (1961)], I believe that it does. While the relevant inquiry may be aided by resort to one or more of the provisions of the Bill of Rights, it is not dependent on them or any of their radiations. The Due Process Clause of the Fourteenth Amendment stands, in my opinion, on its own bottom. . . .

While I could not more heartily agree that judicial "self restraint" is an indispensable ingredient of sound constitutional adjudication, I do submit that the formula suggested for achieving it is more hollow than real. "Specific" provisions of the Constitution, no less than "due process," lend themselves as readily to "personal" interpretations by judges whose constitutional outlook is simply to keep the Constitution in supposed "tune with the times." . . .

Judicial self–restraint will not, I suggest, be brought about in the "due process" area by the historically unfounded incorporation formula long advanced by my Brother BLACK, and now in part espoused by my Brother STEWART. It will be achieved in this area, as in other constitutional areas, only by continual insistence upon respect for the teachings of history, solid recognition of the basic values that underlie our society, and wise appreciation of the great roles that the doctrines of federalism and separation of powers have played in establishing and preserving American freedoms. . . . Adherence to these principles will not, of course, obviate all constitutional differences of opinion among judges, nor should it. Their continued recognition will, however, go farther toward keeping most judges from roaming at large in the constitutional field than will the interpolation into the Constitution of an artificial and largely illusory restriction on the content of the Due Process Clause.

☐ *Justice WHITE, concurring.*

In my view this Connecticut law as applied to married couples deprives them of "liberty" without due process of law as that concept is used in the Fourteenth Amendment. I therefore concur in the judgment of the Court reversing these convictions under Connecticut's aiding and abetting statute.

☐ *Justice BLACK, with whom Justice STEWART joins, dissenting.*

The Court talks about a constitutional "right of privacy" as though there is some constitutional provision or provisions forbidding any law ever to be passed which might abridge the "privacy" of individuals. But there is not. There are, of course, guarantees in certain specific constitutional provisions which are designed in part to protect privacy at certain times and places with respect to certain activities. Such, for example, is the Fourth Amendment's guarantee against "unreasonable searches and seizures." But I think it belittles that Amendment to talk about it as though it protects nothing but "privacy." . . .

One of the most effective ways of diluting or expanding a constitutionally guaranteed right is to substitute for the crucial word or words of a constitutional guarantee another word or words, more or less flexible and more or less restricted in meaning. This fact is well illustrated by the use of the term "right of privacy" as a comprehensive substitute for the Fourth Amendment's guarantee against "unreasonable searches and seizures." "Privacy" is a broad, abstract and ambiguous concept which can easily be shrunken in meaning but which can also, on the other hand, easily be interpreted as a constitutional ban against many things other than searches and seizures. I have expressed the view many times that First Amendment freedoms, for example, have suffered from a failure of the courts to stick to the simple language of the First Amendment in construing it, instead of invoking multitudes of words substituted for those the Framers used. For these reasons I get nowhere in this case by talk about a constitutional "right of privacy" as an emanation from one or more constitutional provisions. I like my privacy as well as the next one, but I am nevertheless compelled to admit that government has a right to invade it unless prohibited by some specific constitutional provision. For these reasons I cannot agree with the Court's judgment and the reasons it gives for holding this Connecticut law unconstitutional. . . .

I think that if properly construed neither the Due Process Clause nor the Ninth Amendment, nor both together, could under any circumstances be a proper basis for invalidating the Connecticut law. I discuss the due process and Ninth Amendment arguments together because on analysis they turn out to be the same thing—merely using different words to claim for this Court and the federal judiciary power to invalidate any legislative act which the judges find irrational, unreasonable or offensive.

The due process argument which my Brothers HARLAN and WHITE adopt here is based, as their opinions indicate, on the premise that this Court is vested with power to invalidate all state laws that it considers to be arbitrary, capricious, unreasonable, or oppressive, or this Court's belief that a particular state law under scrutiny has no "rational or justifying" purpose, or is offensive to a "sense of fairness and justice." If these formulas based on "natural justice," or others which mean the same thing, are to prevail, they require judges to determine what is or is not constitutional on the basis of their own appraisal of what laws are unwise or unnecessary. The power to make such decisions is of course that of a legislative body. . . . I do not believe that we are granted power by the Due Process Clause or any other constitutional provision or provisions to measure constitutionality by our belief that legislation is arbitrary, capricious or unreasonable, or accomplishes no justifiable purpose, or is offensive to our own notions of "civilized standards of conduct." Such an appraisal of the wisdom of legislation is an attribute of the power to make laws, not of the power to interpret them. . . .

My Brother GOLDBERG has adopted the recent discovery that the Ninth Amendment as well as the Due Process Clause can be used by this

Court as authority to strike down all state legislation which this Court thinks violates "fundamental principles of liberty and justice," or is contrary to the "traditions and [collective] conscience of our people." He also states, without proof satisfactory to me, that in making decisions on this basis judges will not consider "their personal and private notions." One may ask how they can avoid considering them. Our Court certainly has no machinery with which to take a Gallup Poll. . . .

I realize that many good and able men have eloquently spoken and written, sometimes in rhapsodical strains, about the duty of this Court to keep the Constitution in tune with the times. The idea is that the Constitution must be changed from time to time and that this Court is charged with a duty to make those changes. For myself, I must with all deference reject that philosophy. The Constitution makers knew the need for change and provided for it. Amendments suggested by the people's elected representatives can be submitted to the people or their selected agents for ratification. That method of change was good for our Fathers, and being somewhat old-fashioned I must add it is good enough for me. And so, I cannot rely on the Due Process Clause or the Ninth Amendment or any mysterious and uncertain natural law concept as a reason for striking down this state law. The Due Process Clause with an "arbitrary and capricious" or "shocking to the conscience" formula was liberally used by this Court to strike down economic legislation in the early decades of this century, threatening, many people thought, the tranquility and stability of the Nation. See, e. g., *Lochner v. State of New York*, 198 U.S. 45 [(1905)]. That formula, based on subjective considerations of "natural justice," is no less dangerous when used to enforce this Court's views about personal rights than those about economic rights. I had thought that we had laid that formula, as a means for striking down state legislation, to rest once and for all in cases like *West Coast Hotel Co. v. Parrish*, [300 U.S. 379 (1937)], and many other opinions.

☐ *Justice STEWART, whom Justice BLACK joins, dissenting.*

Since 1879 Connecticut has had on its books a law which forbids the use of contraceptives by anyone. I think this is an uncommonly silly law. . . . But we are not asked in this case to say whether we think this law is unwise, or even asinine. We are asked to hold that it violates the United States Constitution. And that I cannot do.

In the course of its opinion the Court refers to no less than six Amendments to the Constitution: the First, the Third, the Fourth, the Fifth, the Ninth, and the Fourteenth. But the Court does not say which of these Amendments, if any, it thinks is infringed by this Connecticut law.

We *are* told that the Due Process Clause of the Fourteenth Amendment is not, as such, the "guide" in this case. With that much I agree. . . .

As to the First, Third, Fourth, and Fifth Amendments, I can find nothing in any of them to invalidate this Connecticut law, even assuming that all those Amendments are fully applicable against the States. . . .

[And] to say that the Ninth Amendment has anything to do with this case is to turn somersaults with history. The Ninth Amendment, like its companion the Tenth, which this Court held "states but a truism that all is retained which has not been surrendered," *United States v. Darby*, 312 U.S. 100 [(1941)], was framed by James Madison and adopted by the States simply to make clear that the adoption of the Bill of Rights did not alter the plan that the *Federal* Government was to be a government of express and limited powers, and that all rights and powers not delegated to it were retained. . . .

What provision of the Constitution, then, does make this state law invalid? The Court says it is the right of privacy "created by several fundamental constitutional guarantees." With all deference, I can find no such general right of privacy in the Bill of Rights, in any other part of the Constitution, or in any case ever before decided by this Court.

Duncan v. Louisiana

391 U.S. 145, 88 S.Ct. 1444 (1968)

Gary Duncan, a nineteen-year-old black man, was driving in Plaquemines Parish, Louisiana, a community in which racial tensions ran high and opposition to school desegregation remained heated in 1966. He saw four white boys confronting two of his younger cousins and stopped to pick his cousins up. At that point, there apparently was some sort of exchange in which Duncan "touched" or "slapped" the arm of one of the white boys, Herman Landry, and then drove away. The head of a private school, established in opposition to the desegregation of the local public schools, saw the incident and called the sheriff. Duncan was intercepted and questioned by a deputy sheriff, but allowed to leave. Three days later, he was arrested on a charge of cruelty to minors. Believing that the arrest was racial harassment, Duncan's parents sought help from the Lawyers' Constitutional Defense Committee (LCDC), an organization providing attorneys for civil rights litigation. While the LCDC was initially reluctant to take what appeared to be a minor case, further developments led to an important ruling by the Supreme Court.

At Duncan's preliminary hearing, his attorney Richard Sobol moved to quash the charge since Louisiana's law governing cruelty to minors applied only to those with parental control or responsibility over an abused minor (which clearly did not apply to Duncan). Before the judge ruled on that motion, however, Landry's parents signed an affidavit charging Duncan with assault and battery. Duncan was rearrested and scheduled for another trial on the battery charge, which carried a maximum sentence of two years in prison. This time, Sobol asked the judge for a jury trial on the grounds that the Sixth Amendment provision for jury trials applied to the states and that jury trials were required whenever an accused faces a serious charge and the possibility of being sentenced to six months or more in jail. That request was denied by the trial judge. The basis was thus laid for a test case for determining whether the Sixth Amendment applied to the states. Duncan was convicted for battery, fined $150, and sentenced to sixty days in prison. Sobol appealed Duncan's conviction to the supreme court of Louisiana, which upheld the lower court, and then to the Supreme Court. The fundamental issue in this case, as Duncan's attorney told the Court, is "whether the Due Process Clause of the Fourteenth Amendment secures the right to trial by jury in state criminal cases."

The Court's decision was 7–2, with the majority's opinion announced by Justice White. Justice Black, joined by Justice Douglas and Justice Fortas, concurred. Justice Harlan dissented and was joined by Justice Stewart.

■ ■ ■

☐ *Justice WHITE delivered the opinion of the Court.*

The Fourteenth Amendment denies the States the power to "deprive any person of life, liberty, or property, without due process of law." In resolving conflicting claims concerning the meaning of this spacious language, the Court has looked increasingly to the Bill of Rights for guidance; many of the rights guaranteed by the first eight Amendments to the Constitution have been held to be protected against state action by the Due Process Clause of the Fourteenth Amendment. That clause now protects the right to compensation for property taken by the State; the rights of speech, press, and religion covered by the First Amendment; the Fourth Amendment rights to be free from unreasonable searches and seizures and to have excluded from criminal trials any evidence illegally seized; the right guaranteed by the Fifth Amendment to be free of compelled self-incrimination; and the Sixth Amendment rights to counsel, to a speedy and public trial, to confrontation of opposing witnesses, and to compulsory process for obtaining witnesses.

The test for determining whether a right extended by the Fifth and Sixth Amendments with respect to federal criminal proceedings is also protected against state action by the Fourteenth Amendment has been phrased in a variety of ways in the opinions of this Court. The question has been asked whether a right is among those "fundamental principles of liberty and justice which lie at the base of all our civil and political institutions"; whether it is "basic in our system of jurisprudence"; and whether it is "a fundamental right, essential to a fair trial." . . . Because we believe that trial by jury in criminal cases is fundamental to the American scheme of justice, we hold that the Fourteenth Amendment guarantees a right of jury trial in all criminal cases which—were they to be tried in a federal court—would come within the Sixth Amendment's guarantee. . . .

We are aware of prior cases in this Court in which the prevailing opinion contains statements contrary to our holding today that the right to jury trial in serious criminal cases is a fundamental right and hence must be recognized by the States as part of their obligation to extend due process of law to all persons within their jurisdiction. . . . Respectfully, we reject the prior *dicta* regarding jury trial in criminal cases.

The guarantees of jury trial in the Federal and State Constitutions reflect a profound judgment about the way in which law should be enforced and justice administered. A right to jury trial is granted to criminal defendants in order to prevent oppression by the Government. Those who wrote our constitutions knew from history and experience that it was necessary to protect against unfounded criminal charges brought to eliminate enemies and against judges too responsive to the voice of higher authority. The framers of the constitutions strove to create an independent judiciary but insisted upon further protection against arbitrary action. Providing an accused with the right to be tried by a jury of his peers gave him an inestimable safeguard against the corrupt or overzealous prosecutor and against the compliant, biased, or eccentric judge. If the defendant preferred the common-sense judgment of a jury to the more tutored but perhaps less sympathetic reaction of the single judge, he was to have it. Beyond this, the jury trial provisions in the Federal and State Constitutions reflect a fundamental decision about the exercise of official power—a reluctance to entrust plenary powers over the life and liberty of the citizen to one judge or to a group of judges. Fear of unchecked power, so typical of our State and Federal Governments in other respects, found expression in the criminal law in this insistence upon community participation in the determination of guilt or innocence. The deep commitment of the Nation to the right of jury trial in serious criminal cases as a defense against arbitrary law enforcement qualifies for protection under the Due Process Clause of the Fourteenth Amendment, and must therefore be respected by the States. . . .

Louisiana's final contention is that even if it must grant jury trials in serious criminal cases, the conviction before us is valid and constitutional because here the petitioner was tried for simple battery and was sentenced to only 60 days in the parish prison. We are not persuaded. It is doubtless true that there is a category of petty crimes or offenses which is not subject to the Sixth Amendment jury trial provision and should not be subject to the Fourteenth Amendment jury trial requirement here applied to the States. Crimes carrying possible penalties up to six months do not require a jury trial if they otherwise qualify as petty offenses. But the penalty authorized for a particular crime is of major relevance in determining whether it is serious or not and may in itself, if severe enough, subject the trial to the mandates of the Sixth Amendment. . . .

We need not, however, settle in this case the exact location of the line between petty offenses and serious crimes. It is sufficient for our purposes to hold that a crime punishable by two years in prison is, based on past and contemporary standards in this country, a serious crime and not a petty offense.

☐ *Justice BLACK, with whom Justice DOUGLAS joins, concurring.*

I want to emphasize that I believe as strongly as ever that the Fourteenth Amendment was intended to make the Bill of Rights applicable to the States. I have been willing to support the selective incorporation doctrine, however, as an alternative, although perhaps less historically supportable than complete incorporation. The selective incorporation process, if used properly, does limit the Supreme Court in the Fourteenth Amendment field to specific Bill of Rights' protections only and keeps judges from roaming at will in their own notions of what policies outside the Bill of Rights are desirable and what are not. And, most importantly for me, the selective incorporation process has the virtue of having already worked to make most of the Bill of Rights' protections applicable to the States. . . .

□ *Justice HARLAN whom Justice STEWART joins, dissenting.*

The Civil War Amendments dramatically altered the relation of the Federal Government to the States. The first section of the Fourteenth Amendment imposes highly significant restrictions on state action. But the restrictions are couched in very broad and general terms: citizenship; privileges and immunities; due process of law; equal protection of the laws. . . . The question has been, Where does the Court properly look to find the specific rules that define and give content to such terms as "life, liberty, or property" and "due process of law"?

A few members of the Court have taken the position that the intention of those who drafted the first section of the Fourteenth Amendment was simply, and exclusively, to make the provisions of the first eight Amendments applicable to state action. This view has never been accepted by this Court. In my view, often expressed elsewhere, the first section of the Fourteenth Amendment was meant neither to incorporate nor to be limited to, the specific guarantees of the first eight Amendments. The overwhelming historical evidence demonstrates, to me conclusively, that the Congressmen and state legislators who wrote, debated, and ratified the Fourteenth Amendment did not think they were "incorporating" the Bill of Rights.

Although I therefore fundamentally disagree with the total incorporation view of the Fourteenth Amendment, it seems to me that such a position does at least have the virtue, lacking in the Court's selective incorporation approach of internal consistency: we look to the Bill of Rights, word for word, clause for clause, precedent for precedent because it is said, the men who wrote the Amendment wanted it that way. . . .

Apart from the approach taken by the absolute incorporationists, I can see only one method of analysis that has an internal logic. That is to start with the words "liberty" and "due process of law" and attempt to define them in a way that accords with American traditions and our system of government. This approach, involving a much more discriminating process of adjudication than does "incorporation," is, albeit difficult, the one that was followed throughout the 19th and most of the present century. It entails a "gradual progress of judicial inclusion and exclusion," seeking, with due recognition of constitutional tolerance for state experimentation and disparity, to ascertain those "immutable principles . . . of justice which inhere in the very idea of free government which no member of the Union may disregard." . . .

The relationship of the Bill of Rights to this "gradual process" seems to me to be twofold. In the first place it has long been clear that the Due Process Clause imposes some restrictions on state action that parallel Bill of Rights restrictions on federal action. Second, and more important than this accidental overlap, is the fact that the Bill of Rights is evidence, at various points, of the content Americans find in the term "liberty" and of American standards of fundamental fairness. . . .

Today's Court still remains unwilling to accept the total incorporationists' view of the history of the Fourteenth Amendment. This, if accepted, would afford a cogent reason for applying the Sixth Amendment to the States. The Court is also, apparently, unwilling to face the task of determining whether denial of trial by jury in the situation before us, or in other situations, is fundamentally unfair. Consequently, the Court has compromised on the ease of the incorporationist position, without its internal logic. It has simply assumed that the question before us is whether the Jury Trial Clause of the Sixth Amendment should be incorporated into the Fourteenth, jot-for-jot and case-for-case, or ignored. Then the Court merely declares that the clause in question is "in" rather than "out."

The Court has justified neither its starting place nor its conclusion. If the problem is to discover and articulate the rules of fundamental fairness in criminal proceedings, there is no reason to assume that the whole body of rules developed in this Court constituting Sixth Amendment jury trial must be regarded as a unit. The requirement of trial by jury in federal criminal cases has given rise to numerous subsidiary questions respecting the exact scope and content of the right. It surely cannot be that every answer the Court has given, or will give, to such a question is attributable to the Founders; or even that every rule announced carries equal conviction of this Court; still less can it be that every such subprinciple is equally fundamental to ordered liberty.

Examples abound. I should suppose it obviously fundamental to fairness that a "jury" means an "impartial jury." I should think it equally obvious that the rule, imposed long ago in the federal courts, that "jury" means "jury of exactly twelve," is not fundamental to anything: there is no significance except to mystics in the number 12. Again, trial by jury has been held to require a unanimous verdict of jurors in the federal courts, although unanimity has not been found essential to liberty in Britain, where the requirement has been abandoned. . . .

The argument that jury trial is not a requisite of due process is quite simple. The central proposition of *Palko* [*v. Connecticut*, 302 U.S. 319 (1937)], . . . is that "due process of law" requires only that criminal trials be fundamentally fair. As stated above, apart from the theory that it was historically intended as a mere shorthand for the Bill of Rights, I do not see what else "due process of law" can intelligibly be thought to mean. If due process of law requires only fundamental fairness, then the inquiry in each case must be whether a state trial process was a fair one. The Court has held, properly I think, that in an adversary process it is a requisite of fairness, for which there is no adequate substitute, that a criminal defendant be afforded a right to counsel and to cross-examine opposing witnesses. But it simply has not been demonstrated, nor, I think, can it be demonstrated, that trial by jury is the only fair means of resolving issues of fact. . . .

In sum, there is a wide range of views on the desirability of trial by jury, and on the ways to make it most effective when it is used; there is also considerable variation from State to State in local conditions such as the size of the criminal caseload, the ease or difficulty of summoning jurors, and other trial conditions bearing on fairness. We have before us, therefore, an almost perfect example of a situation in which the celebrated *dictum* of Justice BRANDEIS should be invoked. It is, he said, "one of the happy incidents of the federal system that a single courageous state may, if its citizens choose, serve as a laboratory. . . ." *New State Ice Co. v. Liebmann*, 285 U.S. 262 [(1932)]. This Court, other courts, and the political process are available to correct any experiments in criminal procedure that prove fundamentally unfair to defendants. That is not what is being done today: instead, and quite without reason, the Court has chosen to impose upon every State one means of trying criminal cases; it is a good means, but it is not the only fair means, and it is not demonstrably better than the alternatives States might devise.

I would affirm the judgment of the Supreme Court of Louisiana.

McDonald v. City of Chicago
561 U.S. 742 (2010)

In 1983, the city of Chicago enacted, in response to a number of killings, an ordinance banning the possession of unregistered firearms. Under the ordinance, gun owners had to register with police their possession of firearms, and annually reregister their ownership and/or sale of the arms. A first violation of the regulation is punishable by a fine of $300 to $500, incarceration for ten to ninety days, or both. In light of the Supreme Court's ruling in *District of Columbia v. Heller*, 554 U.S. 570 (2008), striking down the District of Columbia's firearm regulations, four residents challenged Chicago's regulation. A three-judge panel of the Court of Appeals for the Seventh Circuit upheld Chicago's ordinances.

The appellate court's decision was reversed by a 5–4 vote. Justice Alito delivered the opinion of the Court for a plurality. Justices Scalia and Thomas each filed concurring opinions. Justices Stevens and Breyer each filed dissenting opinions. Justices Ginsburg and Sotomayor joined the latter's dissent.

■ ■ ■

□ *Justice ALITO announced the judgment of the Court and delivered the opinion of the Court with respect to Parts I, II-A, II-B, II-D, III-A, and III-B, in which THE CHIEF JUSTICE, Justice SCALIA, Justice KENNEDY, and Justice THOMAS join, and an opinion with respect to Parts II-C, IV, and V, in which THE CHIEF JUSTICE, Justice SCALIA, and Justice KENNEDY join.*

Two years ago, in *District of Columbia v. Heller* (2008), we held that the Second Amendment protects the right to keep and bear arms for the purpose of self-defense, and we struck down a District of Columbia law that banned the possession of handguns in the home. The city of Chicago (City) and the village of Oak Park, a Chicago suburb, have laws that are similar to the District of Columbia's, but Chicago and Oak Park argue that their laws are constitutional because the Second Amendment has no application to the States. We have previously held that most of the provisions of the Bill of Rights apply with full force to both the Federal Government and the States. Applying the standard that is well established in our case law, we hold that the Second Amendment right is fully applicable to the States. . . .

- II

- A

Petitioners argue that the Chicago and Oak Park laws violate the right to keep and bear arms for two reasons. Petitioners' primary submission is that this right is among the "privileges or immunities of citizens of the United States" and that the narrow interpretation of the Privileges or Immunities Clause adopted in the *Slaughter-House Cases*, 6 Wall. 86 (1873), should now be rejected. As a secondary argument, petitioners contend that the Fourteenth Amendment's Due Process Clause "incorporates" the Second Amendment right. . . .

- B

The Bill of Rights, including the Second Amendment, originally applied only to the Federal Government.

The constitutional Amendments adopted in the aftermath of the Civil War fundamentally altered our country's federal system. The provision at issue in this case, Section 1 of the Fourteenth Amendment, provides, among other things, that a State may not abridge "the privileges or immunities of citizens of the United States" or deprive "any person of life, liberty, or property, without due process of law."

Four years after the adoption of the Fourteenth Amendment, this Court was asked to interpret the Amendment's reference to "the privileges or immunities of citizens of the United States." *The Slaughter-House Cases* involved challenges to a Louisiana law permitting the creation of a state-sanctioned monopoly on the butchering of animals within the city of New Orleans. Justice SAMUEL MILLER's opinion for the Court concluded that the Privileges or Immunities Clause protects only those rights "which owe their existence to the Federal government, its National character, its Constitution, or its laws." The Court held that other fundamental rights—rights that predated the creation of the Federal Government and that "the State governments were created to establish and secure"—were not protected by the Clause.

In drawing a sharp distinction between the rights of federal and state citizenship, the Court relied on two principal arguments. First, the Court emphasized that the Fourteenth Amendment's Privileges or Immunities Clause spoke of "the privileges or immunities of citizens of the United States," and the Court contrasted this phrasing with the wording in the first sentence of the Fourteenth Amendment and in the Privileges and Immunities Clause of Article IV, both of which refer to state citizenship. Second, the Court stated that a contrary reading would "radically chang[e] the whole theory of the relations of the State and Federal governments to each other and of both these governments to the people," and the Court refused to conclude that such a change had been made "in the absence of language which expresses such a purpose too clearly to admit of doubt." Finding the phrase "privileges or immunities of citizens of the United States" lacking by this high standard, the Court reasoned that the phrase must mean something more limited.

Under the Court's narrow reading, the Privileges or Immunities Clause protects such things as the right "to come to the seat of government to assert any claim [a citizen] may have upon that government, to transact any business he may have with it, to seek its protection, to share its offices, to engage in administering its functions . . . [and to] become a citizen of any State of the Union by a bonafide residence therein, with the same rights as other citizens of that State." . . .

Today, many legal scholars dispute the correctness of the narrow *Slaughter-House* interpretation.

Three years after the decision in the *Slaughter-House Cases*, the Court decided *Cruikshank* [92 U.S. 542 (1876)], the first of the three 19th-century cases on which the Seventh Circuit relied. In that case, the Court reviewed convictions stemming from the infamous Colfax Massacre in Louisiana on Easter Sunday 1873. Dozens of blacks, many unarmed, were slaughtered by a rival band of armed white men. Cruikshank himself allegedly marched unarmed African-American prisoners through the streets and then had them summarily executed. Ninety-seven men were indicted for participating in the massacre, but only nine went to trial. Six of the nine were acquitted of all charges; the remaining three were acquitted of murder but convicted under the Enforcement Act of 1870, for banding and conspiring together to deprive their victims of various constitutional rights, including the right to bear arms.

The Court reversed all of the convictions, including those relating to the deprivation of the victims' right to bear arms. The Court wrote that the right of bearing arms for a lawful purpose "is not a right granted by the Constitution" and is not "in any manner dependent upon that instrument for its existence." "The second amendment," the Court continued, "declares that it shall not be infringed; but this . . . means no more than that it shall not be infringed by Congress." "Our later decisions in *Presser v. Illinois*, 116 U.S. 252 (1886), and *Miller v. Texas*, 153 U.S. 535 (1894), reaffirmed that the Second Amendment applies only to the Federal Government."

- C

As previously noted, the Seventh Circuit concluded that *Cruikshank*, *Presser*, and *Miller* doomed petitioners' claims at the Court of Appeals level. Petitioners argue, however, that we should overrule those decisions and hold that the right to keep and bear arms is one of the "privileges or immunities of citizens of the United States." In petitioners' view, the Privileges or Immunities Clause protects all of the rights set out in the Bill of Rights, as well as some others, but petitioners are unable to identify the Clause's full scope. Nor is there any consensus on that question among the scholars who agree that the *Slaughter-House Cases'* interpretation is flawed.

We see no need to reconsider that interpretation here. For many decades, the question of the rights protected by the Fourteenth Amendment against state infringement has been analyzed under the Due Process Clause of that Amendment and not under the Privileges or Immunities Clause. We therefore decline to disturb the *Slaughter-House* holding.

At the same time, however, this Court's decisions in *Cruikshank*, *Presser*, and *Miller* do not preclude us from considering whether the Due Process

Clause of the Fourteenth Amendment makes the Second Amendment right binding on the States. . . .

■ D

In the late 19th century, the Court began to consider whether the Due Process Clause prohibits the States from infringing rights set out in the Bill of Rights. See *Hurtado v. California*, 110 U.S. 516 (1884) (due process does not require grand jury indictment); *Chicago, B. & Q. R. Co. v. Chicago*, 166 U.S. 226 (1897) (due process prohibits States from taking of private property for public use without just compensation). Five features of the approach taken during the ensuing era should be noted.

First, the Court viewed the due process question as entirely separate from the question of whether a right was a privilege or immunity of national citizenship.

Second, the Court explained that the only rights protected against state infringement by the Due Process Clause were those rights "of such a nature that they are included in the conception of due process of law."

Third, in some cases decided during this era the Court "can be seen as having asked, when inquiring into whether some particular procedural safeguard was required of a State, if a civilized system could be imagined that would not accord the particular protection." *Duncan v. Louisiana*, 391 U.S. 145 (1968). Thus, in holding that due process prohibits a State from taking private property without just compensation, the Court described the right as "a principle of natural equity, recognized by all temperate and civilized governments, from a deep and universal sense of its justice." Similarly, the Court found that due process did not provide a right against compelled incrimination in part because this right "has no place in the jurisprudence of civilized and free countries outside the domain of the common law."

Fourth, the Court during this era was not hesitant to hold that a right set out in the Bill of Rights failed to meet the test for inclusion within the protection of the Due Process Clause. The Court found that some such rights qualified. See, e.g., *Gitlow v. New York*, 268 U.S. 652 (1925) (freedom of speech and press); *Near v. Minnesota ex rel. Olson*, 283 U.S. 697 (1931) (same); *Powell* (assistance of counsel in capital cases); *De Jonge* (freedom of assembly); *Cantwell v. Connecticut*, 310 U.S. 296 (1940) (free exercise of religion). But others did not. See, e.g., *Hurtado* (grand jury indictment requirement); *Twining* (privilege against self-incrimination).

Finally, even when a right set out in the Bill of Rights was held to fall within the conception of due process, the protection or remedies afforded against state infringement sometimes differed from the protection or remedies provided against abridgment by the Federal Government. To give one example, in *Betts* the Court held that, although the Sixth Amendment required the appointment of counsel in all federal criminal cases in which the defendant was unable to retain an attorney, the Due Process Clause required appointment of counsel in state criminal proceedings only where "want of counsel in [the] particular case . . . result[ed] in a conviction lacking in . . . fundamental fairness."

An alternative theory regarding the relationship between the Bill of Rights and Section 1 of the Fourteenth Amendment was championed by Justice BLACK. This theory held that Section 1 of the Fourteenth Amendment totally incorporated all of the provisions of the Bill of Rights. As Justice BLACK noted, the chief congressional proponents of the Fourteenth Amendment espoused the view that the Amendment made the Bill of Rights applicable to the States and, in so doing, overruled this Court's decision in *Barron*. Nonetheless, the Court never has embraced Justice BLACK's "total incorporation" theory.

While Justice BLACK's theory was never adopted, the Court eventually moved in that direction by initiating what has been called a process of "selective incorporation," i.e., the Court began to hold that the Due Process Clause fully incorporates particular rights contained in the first eight Amendments.

The decisions during this time abandoned three of the previously noted characteristics of the earlier period. The Court made it clear that the governing standard is not whether any "civilized system [can] be imagined that would not accord the particular protection." Instead, the Court inquired whether a particular Bill of Rights guarantee is fundamental to our scheme of ordered liberty and system of justice.

The Court also shed any reluctance to hold that rights guaranteed by the Bill of Rights met the requirements for protection under the Due Process Clause. The Court eventually incorporated almost all of the provisions of the Bill of Rights. Only a handful of the Bill of Rights protections remain unincorporated.

Finally, the Court abandoned "the notion that the Fourteenth Amendment applies to the States only a watered-down, subjective version of the individual guarantees of the Bill of Rights," stating that it would be "incongruous" to apply different standards "depending on whether the claim was asserted in a state or federal court." Instead, the Court decisively held that incorporated Bill of Rights protections "are all to be enforced against the States under the Fourteenth Amendment according to the same standards that protect those personal rights against federal encroachment."

Employing this approach, the Court overruled earlier decisions in which it had held that particular Bill of Rights guarantees or remedies did not apply to the States.

■ III

With this framework in mind, we now turn directly to the question whether the Second Amendment right to keep and bear arms is incorporated in the concept of due process. In answering that question, as just explained, we must decide whether the right to keep and bear arms is fundamental to our scheme of ordered liberty, or as we have said in a related context, whether this right is "deeply rooted in this Nation's history and tradition."

■ A

Our decision in *Heller* points unmistakably to the answer. Self-defense is a basic right, recognized by many legal systems from ancient times to the present day, and in *Heller*, we held that individual self-defense is "the central component" of the Second Amendment right. Explaining that "the need for defense of self, family, and property is most acute" in the home, we found that this right applies to handguns because they are "the most preferred firearm in the nation to 'keep' and use for protection of one's home and family."

Heller makes it clear that this right is "deeply rooted in this Nation's history and tradition." *Heller* explored the right's origins, noting that the 1689 English Bill of Rights explicitly protected a right to keep arms for self-defense, and that by 1765, Blackstone was able to assert that the right to keep and bear arms was "one of the fundamental rights of Englishmen."

Blackstone's assessment was shared by the American colonists. As we noted in *Heller*, King George III's attempt to disarm the colonists in the 1760's and 1770's "provoked polemical reactions by Americans invoking their rights as Englishmen to keep arms."

The right to keep and bear arms was considered no less fundamental by those who drafted and ratified the Bill of Rights. "During the 1788 ratification debates, the fear that the federal government would disarm the people in order to impose rule through a standing army or select militia was pervasive in Antifederalist rhetoric." *Heller*.

This understanding persisted in the years immediately following the ratification of the Bill of Rights. In addition to the four States that had adopted Second Amendment analogues before ratification, nine more States adopted state constitutional provisions protecting an individual right to keep and bear arms between 1789 and 1820. Founding-era legal commentators confirmed the importance of the right to early Americans. St. George Tucker, for example, described the right to keep and bear arms as "the true palladium of liberty" and explained that prohibitions on the right would place liberty "on the brink of destruction."

▪ B

By the 1850's, the perceived threat that had prompted the inclusion of the Second Amendment in the Bill of Rights—the fear that the National Government would disarm the universal militia—had largely faded as a popular concern, but the right to keep and bear arms was highly valued for purposes of self-defense. And when attempts were made to disarm "Free-Soilers" in "Bloody Kansas," Senator Charles Sumner, who later played a leading role in the adoption of the Fourteenth Amendment, proclaimed that "[n]ever was [the rifle] more needed in just self-defense than now in Kansas." Indeed, the 1856 Republican Party Platform protested that in Kansas the constitutional rights of the people had been "fraudulently and violently taken from them" and the "right of the people to keep and bear arms" had been "infringed."

After the Civil War, many of the over 180,000 African Americans who served in the Union Army returned to the States of the old Confederacy, where systematic efforts were made to disarm them and other blacks. The laws of some States formally prohibited African Americans from possessing firearms. For example, a Mississippi law provided that "no freedman, free negro or mulatto, not in the military service of the United States government, and not licensed so to do by the board of police of his or her county, shall keep or carry fire-arms of any kind, or any ammunition, dirk or bowie knife." . . .

Union Army commanders took steps to secure the right of all citizens to keep and bear arms, but the 39th Congress concluded that legislative action was necessary. Its efforts to safeguard the right to keep and bear arms demonstrate that the right was still recognized to be fundamental.

The most explicit evidence of Congress' aim appears in Section 14 of the Freedmen's Bureau Act of 1866, which provided that "the right . . . to have full and equal benefit of all laws and proceedings concerning personal liberty, personal security, and the acquisition, enjoyment, and disposition of estate, real and personal, including the constitutional right to bear arms, shall be secured to and enjoyed by all the citizens . . . without respect to race or color, or previous condition of slavery." Section 14 thus explicitly guaranteed that "all the citizens," black and white, would have "the constitutional right to bear arms."

The Civil Rights Act of 1866, which was considered at the same time as the Freedmen's Bureau Act, similarly sought to protect the right of all citizens to keep and bear arms. Section 1 of the Civil Rights Act guaranteed the "full and equal benefit of all laws and proceedings for the security of person and property, as is enjoyed by white citizens."

Congress, however, ultimately deemed these legislative remedies insufficient. Southern resistance, Presidential vetoes, and this Court's pre-Civil-War precedent persuaded Congress that a constitutional amendment was necessary to provide full protection for the rights of blacks. Today, it is generally accepted that the Fourteenth Amendment was understood to provide a constitutional basis for protecting the rights set out in the Civil Rights Act of 1866.

In debating the Fourteenth Amendment, the 39th Congress referred to the right to keep and bear arms as a fundamental right deserving of protection. Senator Samuel Pomeroy described three "indispensable" "safeguards of liberty under our form of Government." One of these, he said, was the right to keep and bear arms: "Every man . . . should have the right to bear arms for the defense of himself and family and his homestead. And if the cabin door of the freedman is broken open and the intruder enters for purposes as vile as were known to slavery, then should a well-loaded musket be in the hand of the occupant to send the polluted wretch to another world, where his wretchedness will forever remain complete."

Evidence from the period immediately following the ratification of the Fourteenth Amendment only confirms that the right to keep and bear arms was considered fundamental. In an 1868 speech addressing the disarmament of freedmen, Representative Stevens emphasized the necessity of the right: "Disarm a community and you rob them of the means of defending life. Take away their weapons of defense and you take away the inalienable right of defending liberty." . . .

The right to keep and bear arms was also widely protected by state constitutions at the time when the Fourteenth Amendment was ratified. . . .

In sum, it is clear that the Framers and ratifiers of the Fourteenth Amendment counted the right to keep and bear arms among those fundamental rights necessary to our system of ordered liberty. . . .

■ IV

Municipal respondents' remaining arguments are at war with our central holding in *Heller*: that the Second Amendment protects a personal right to keep and bear arms for lawful purposes, most notably for self-defense within the home. Municipal respondents, in effect, ask us to treat the right recognized in *Heller* as a second-class right, subject to an entirely different body of rules than the other Bill of Rights guarantees that we have held to be incorporated into the Due Process Clause.

Municipal respondents' main argument is nothing less than a plea to disregard 50 years of incorporation precedent and return (presumably for this case only) to a bygone era. Municipal respondents submit that the Due Process Clause protects only those rights "recognized by all temperate and civilized governments, from a deep and universal sense of [their] justice." According to municipal respondents, if it is possible to imagine any civilized legal system that does not recognize a particular right, then the Due Process Clause does not make that right binding on the States. Therefore, the municipal respondents continue, because such countries as England, Canada, Australia, Japan, Denmark, Finland, Luxembourg, and New Zealand either ban or severely limit handgun ownership, it must follow that no right to possess such weapons is protected by the Fourteenth Amendment.

This line of argument is, of course, inconsistent with the long-established standard we apply in incorporation cases. And the present-day implications of municipal respondents' argument are stunning. For example, many of the rights that our Bill of Rights provides for persons accused of criminal offenses are virtually unique to this country. If our understanding of the right to a jury trial, the right against self-incrimination, and the right to counsel were necessary attributes of any civilized country, it would follow that the United States is the only civilized Nation in the world.

Municipal respondents attempt to salvage their position by suggesting that their argument applies only to substantive as opposed to procedural rights. But even in this trimmed form, municipal respondents' argument flies in the face of more than a half-century of precedent. For example, in *Everson v. Board of Ed. of Ewing*, 330 U.S. 1 (1947), the Court held that the Fourteenth Amendment incorporates the Establishment Clause of the First Amendment. Yet several of the countries that municipal respondents recognize as civilized have established state churches. If we were to adopt municipal respondents' theory, all of this Court's Establishment Clause precedents involving actions taken by state and local governments would go by the boards.

Municipal respondents maintain that the Second Amendment differs from all of the other provisions of the Bill of Rights because it concerns the right to possess a deadly implement and thus has implications for public safety. And they note that there is intense disagreement on the question whether the private possession of guns in the home increases or decreases gun deaths and injuries.

The right to keep and bear arms, however, is not the only constitutional right that has controversial public safety implications. . . . Municipal respondents cite no case in which we have refrained from holding that a provision of the Bill of Rights is binding on the States on the ground that the right at issue has disputed public safety implications.

We likewise reject municipal respondents' argument that we should depart from our established incorporation methodology on the ground that making the Second Amendment binding on the States and their subdivisions is inconsistent with principles of federalism and will stifle experimentation. Municipal respondents point out—quite correctly—that conditions and problems differ from locality to locality and that citizens in different jurisdictions have divergent views on the issue of gun control. Municipal respondents therefore urge us to allow state and local governments to enact any gun control law that they deem to be reasonable, including a complete ban on the possession of handguns in the home for self-defense.

There is nothing new in the argument that, in order to respect federalism and allow useful state experimentation, a federal constitutional right should not be fully binding on the States. This argument was made repeatedly and eloquently by Members of this Court who rejected the concept of incorporation and urged retention of the two-track approach to incorporation. Throughout the era of "selective incorporation," Justice HARLAN in particular, invoking the values of federalism and state experimentation, fought a determined rearguard action to preserve the two-track approach.

Time and again, however, those pleas failed. Unless we turn back the clock or adopt a special incorporation test applicable only to the Second Amendment, municipal respondents' argument must be rejected. Under our precedents, if a Bill of Rights guarantee is fundamental from an American perspective, then, unless *stare decisis* counsels otherwise, that guarantee is fully binding on the States and thus limits (but by no means eliminates) their ability to devise solutions to social problems that suit local needs and values. As noted by the 38 States that have appeared in this case as *amici* supporting petitioners, "[s]tate and local experimentation with reasonable firearms regulations will continue under the Second Amendment."

Municipal respondents and their *amici* complain that incorporation of the Second Amendment right will lead to extensive and costly litigation, but this argument applies with even greater force to constitutional rights and remedies that have already been held to be binding on the States. . . .

Municipal respondents argue, finally, that the right to keep and bear arms is unique among the rights set out in the first eight Amendments "because the reason for codifying the Second Amendment (to protect the militia) differs from the purpose (primarily, to use firearms to engage in self-defense) that is claimed to make the right implicit in the concept of ordered liberty." Municipal respondents suggest that the Second Amendment right differs from the rights heretofore incorporated because the latter were "valued for [their] own sake." But we have never previously suggested that incorporation of a right turns on whether it has intrinsic as opposed to instrumental value, and quite a few of the rights previously held to be incorporated—for example the right to counsel and the right to confront and subpoena witnesses—are clearly instrumental by any measure. Moreover, this contention repackages one of the chief arguments that we rejected in *Heller*, i.e., that the scope of the Second Amendment right is defined by the immediate threat that led to the inclusion of that right in the Bill of Rights. In *Heller*, we recognized that the codification of this right was prompted by fear that the Federal Government would disarm and thus disable the militias, but we rejected the suggestion that the right was valued only as a means of preserving the militias. On the contrary, we stressed that the right was also valued because the possession of firearms was thought to be essential for self-defense. As we put it, self-defense was "the central component of the right itself."

■ V

■ A

We turn, finally, to the two dissenting opinions. Justice STEVENS' eloquent opinion covers ground already addressed, and therefore little need be added in response. Justice STEVENS would "ground the prohibitions against state action squarely on due process, without intermediate reliance on any of the first eight Amendments." The question presented in this case, in his view, "is whether the particular right asserted by petitioners applies to the States because of the Fourteenth Amendment itself, standing on its own bottom." He would hold that "[t]he rights protected against state infringement by the Fourteenth Amendment's Due Process Clause need not be identical in shape or scope to the rights protected against Federal Government infringement by the various provisions of the Bill of Rights."

As we have explained, the Court, for the past half-century, has moved away from the two-track approach. If we were now to accept Justice STEVENS' theory across the board, decades of decisions would be undermined. We assume that this is not what is proposed. What is urged instead, it appears, is that this theory be revived solely for the individual right that *Heller* recognized, over vigorous dissents. . . .

■ B

Justice BREYER's dissent makes several points to which we briefly respond. To begin, while there is certainly room for disagreement about *Heller*'s analysis of the history of the right to keep and bear arms, nothing written since *Heller* persuades us to reopen the question there decided. Few other questions of original meaning have been as thoroughly explored.

Justice BREYER's conclusion that the Fourteenth Amendment does not incorporate the right to keep and bear arms appears to rest primarily on four factors: First, "there is no popular consensus" that the right is fundamental; second, the right does not protect minorities or persons neglected by those holding political power; third, incorporation of the Second Amendment right would "amount to a significant incursion on a traditional and important area of state concern, altering the constitutional relationship between the States and the Federal Government" and preventing local variations; and fourth, determining the scope of the Second Amendment right in cases involving state and local laws will force judges to answer difficult empirical questions regarding matters that are outside their area of expertise. Even if we believed that these factors were relevant to the incorporation inquiry, none of these factors undermines the case for incorporation of the right to keep and bear arms for self-defense. . . .

In *Heller*, we held that the Second Amendment protects the right to possess a handgun in the home for the purpose of self-defense. Unless considerations of *stare decisis* counsel otherwise, a provision of the Bill of Rights that protects a right that is fundamental from an American perspective applies equally to the Federal Government and the States. We therefore hold that the Due Process Clause of the Fourteenth Amendment incorporates the Second Amendment right recognized in *Heller*. The judgment of the Court of Appeals is reversed, and the case is remanded for further proceedings.

☐ *Justice SCALIA, concurring.*

I join the Court's opinion. Despite my misgivings about Substantive Due Process as an original matter, I have acquiesced in the Court's incorporation of certain guarantees in the Bill of Rights "because it is both long established and narrowly limited." This case does not require me to reconsider that view, since straightforward application of settled doctrine suffices to decide it. . . .

☐ *Justice THOMAS, concurring in part and concurring in the judgment.*

I agree with the Court that the Fourteenth Amendment makes the right to keep and bear arms set forth in the Second Amendment "fully applicable to the States." I write separately because I believe there is a more straightforward path to this conclusion, one that is more faithful to the Fourteenth Amendment's text and history.

Applying what is now a well-settled test, the plurality opinion concludes that the right to keep and bear arms applies to the States through the Fourteenth Amendment's Due Process Clause because it is "fundamental" to the American "scheme of ordered liberty," and "deeply rooted in this Nation's history and Tradition." I agree with that description of the right. But I cannot agree that it is enforceable against the States through a clause that speaks only to "process." Instead, the right to keep and bear arms is a privilege of American citizenship that applies to the States through the Fourteenth Amendment's Privileges or Immunities Clause. . . .

[E]vidence plainly shows that the ratifying public understood the Privileges or Immunities Clause to protect constitutionally enumerated rights, including the right to keep and bear arms. As the Court demonstrates, there can be no doubt that Section 1 was understood to enforce the Second Amendment against the States. In my view, this is because the right to keep and bear arms was understood to be a privilege of American citizenship guaranteed by the Privileges or Immunities Clause. . . .

I agree with the Court that the Second Amendment is fully applicable to the States. I do so because the right to keep and bear arms is guaranteed by the Fourteenth Amendment as a privilege of American citizenship.

☐ *Justice STEVENS, dissenting.*

In *District of Columbia v. Heller* (2008) the Court answered the question whether a federal enclave's "prohibition on the possession of usable handguns in the home violates the Second Amendment to the Constitution." The question we should be answering in this case is whether the Constitution "guarantees individuals a fundamental right," enforceable against the States, "to possess a functional, personal firearm, including a handgun, within the home." That is a different—and more difficult—inquiry than asking if the Fourteenth Amendment "incorporates" the Second Amendment. The so-called incorporation question was squarely and, in my view, correctly resolved in the late 19th century. . . .

This is a substantive due process case. . . .

If text and history are inconclusive on this point, our precedent leaves no doubt: It has been "settled" for well over a century that the Due Process Clause "applies to matters of substantive law as well as to matters of procedure." Time and again, we have recognized that in the Fourteenth Amendment as well as the Fifth, the "Due Process Clause guarantees more than fair process, and the 'liberty' it protects includes more than the absence of physical restraint." "The Clause also includes a substantive component that 'provides heightened protection against government interference with certain fundamental rights and liberty interests.'" Some of our most enduring precedents, accepted today by virtually everyone, were substantive due process decisions. See, e.g., *Loving v. Virginia*, 388 U.S. 1 (1967) (recognizing a due-process as well as equal-protection-based right to marry person of another race); *Bolling v. Sharpe*, 347 U.S. 497 (1954) (outlawing racial segregation in District of Columbia public schools); *Pierce v. Society of Sisters*, 268 U.S. 510 (1925) (vindicating right of parents to direct upbringing and education of their children); *Meyer v. Nebraska*, 62 U.S. 390 (1923) (striking down prohibition on teaching of foreign languages).

The second principle woven through our cases is that substantive due process is fundamentally a matter of personal liberty. For it is the liberty clause of the Fourteenth Amendment that grounds our most important holdings in this field. It is the liberty clause that enacts the Constitution's "promise" that a measure of dignity and self-rule will be afforded to all persons. . . .

[I]t is . . . an overstatement to say that the Court has "abandoned" a "two-track approach to incorporation." The Court moved away from that approach in the area of criminal procedure. But the Second Amendment differs in fundamental respects from its neighboring provisions in the Bill of Rights; and if some 1960's opinions purported to establish a general method of incorporation, that hardly binds us in this case. The Court has not hesitated to cut back on perceived WARREN Court excesses in more areas than I can count. . . .

Furthermore, there is a real risk that, by demanding the provisions of the Bill of Rights apply identically to the States, federal courts will cause those provisions to "be watered down in the needless pursuit of uniformity." *Duncan v. Louisiana*, 391 U.S. 145 (1968) (HARLAN, J., dissenting). When one legal standard must prevail across dozens of jurisdictions with disparate needs and customs, courts will often settle on a relaxed standard. This watering-down risk is particularly acute when we move beyond the narrow realm of criminal procedure and into the relatively vast domain of substantive rights. So long as the requirements of fundamental fairness are always and everywhere respected, it is not clear that greater liberty results from the jot-for-jot application of a provision of the Bill of Rights to the States. Indeed, it is far from clear that proponents of an individual right to keep and bear arms ought to celebrate today's decision.

Our precedents have established, not an exact methodology, but rather a framework for decisionmaking. In this respect, too, the Court's narrative fails to capture the continuity and flexibility in our doctrine.

The basic inquiry was described by Justice CARDOZO more than 70 years ago. When confronted with a substantive due process claim, we must ask whether the allegedly unlawful practice violates values "implicit in the concept of ordered liberty." *Palko v. Connecticut*, 302 U.S. 319 (1937). If the practice in question lacks any "oppressive and arbitrary" character, if judicial enforcement of the asserted right would not materially contribute to "a fair and enlightened system of justice," then the claim is unsuitable for substantive due process protection. Implicit in Justice CARDOZO's test is a recognition that the postulates of liberty have a universal character. Liberty claims that are inseparable from the customs that prevail in a certain region, the idiosyncratic expectations of a certain group, or the personal preferences of their champions, may be valid claims in some sense; but they are not of constitutional stature. Whether conceptualized as a "rational continuum" of legal precepts, or a seamless web of moral commitments, the rights embraced by the liberty clause transcend the local and the particular.

Justice CARDOZO's test undeniably requires judges to apply their own reasoned judgment, but that does not mean it involves an exercise in abstract philosophy. In addition to other constraints . . . historical and empirical data of various kinds ground the analysis. Textual commitments laid down elsewhere in the Constitution, judicial precedents, English common law, legislative and social facts, scientific and professional developments, practices of other civilized societies, and, above all else, the "traditions and conscience of our people," are critical variables. They can provide evidence about which rights really are vital to ordered liberty, as well as a spur to judicial action.

The Court errs both in its interpretation of *Palko* and in its suggestion that later cases rendered *Palko's* methodology defunct. . . .

A rigid historical test is inappropriate in this case, most basically, because our substantive due process doctrine has never evaluated substantive rights in purely, or even predominantly, historical terms. When the Court applied many of the procedural guarantees in the Bill of Rights to the States in the 1960's, it often asked whether the guarantee in question was "fundamental in the context of the criminal processes maintained by the American States." That inquiry could extend back through time, but it was focused not so much on historical conceptions of the guarantee as on its functional significance within the States' regimes. This contextualized approach made sense, as the choice to employ any given trial-type procedure means little in the abstract. It is only by inquiring into how that procedure intermeshes with other procedures and practices in a criminal justice system that its relationship to "liberty" and "due process" can be determined.

Yet when the Court has used the Due Process Clause to recognize rights distinct from the trial context—rights relating to the primary conduct of free individuals—Justice CARDOZO's test has been our guide. The right to free speech, for instance, has been safeguarded from state infringement not because the States have always honored it, but because it is "essential to free government" and "to the maintenance of democratic institutions"— that is, because the right to free speech is implicit in the concept of ordered liberty. While the verbal formula has varied, the Court has largely been consistent in its liberty-based approach to substantive interests outside of the adjudicatory system. As the question before us indisputably concerns such an interest, the answer cannot be found in a granular inspection of state constitutions or congressional debates. . . .

[T]he liberty safeguarded by the Fourteenth Amendment is not merely preservative in nature but rather is a "dynamic concept." Its dynamism provides a central means through which the Framers enabled the Constitution to "endure for ages to come," a central example of how they "wisely spoke in general language and left to succeeding generations the task of applying that language to the unceasingly changing environment in which they would live." "The task of giving concrete meaning to the term 'liberty,'" I have elsewhere explained at some length, "was a part of the work assigned to future generations." The judge who would outsource the interpretation of "liberty" to historical sentiment has turned his back on a task the Constitution assigned to him and drained the document of its intended vitality.

At this point a difficult question arises. In considering such a majestic term as "liberty" and applying it to present circumstances, how are we to do justice to its urgent call and its open texture—and to the grant of interpretive discretion the latter embodies—without injecting excessive subjectivity or unduly restricting the States' "broad latitude in experimenting with possible solutions to problems of vital local concern"? One part of the answer, already discussed, is that we must ground the analysis in historical experience and reasoned judgment, and never on "merely personal and private notions." Our precedents place a number of additional constraints on the decisional process. Although "guideposts for responsible decisionmaking in this unchartered area are scarce and open-ended."

The most basic is that we have eschewed attempts to provide any all-purpose, top-down, totalizing theory of "liberty." . . .

Yet while "the 'liberty' specially protected by the Fourteenth Amendment" is "perhaps not capable of being fully clarified," it is capable of being refined and delimited. . . .

Rather than seek a categorical understanding of the liberty clause, our precedents have thus elucidated a conceptual core. The clause safeguards, most basically, "the ability independently to define one's identity," "the individual's right to make certain unusually important decisions that will affect his own, or his family's, destiny," and the right to be respected as a human being. Self-determination, bodily integrity, freedom of conscience, intimate relationships, political equality, dignity and respect—these are the central values we have found implicit in the concept of ordered liberty.

Another key constraint on substantive due process analysis is respect for the democratic process. . . .

This sensitivity is an aspect of a deeper principle: the need to approach our work with humility and caution. Because the relevant constitutional language is so "spacious," I have emphasized that "[t]he doctrine of judicial self-restraint requires us to exercise the utmost care whenever we are asked to break new ground in this field." . . .

Several rules of the judicial process help enforce such restraint. In the substantive due process field as in others, the Court has applied both the doctrine of *stare decisis*—adhering to precedents, respecting reliance interests, prizing stability and order in the law—and the common-law method-taking cases and controversies as they present themselves, proceeding slowly and incrementally, building on what came before. This restrained methodology was evident even in the heyday of "incorporation" during the 1960's. Although it would have been much easier for the Court simply to declare certain Amendments in the Bill of Rights applicable to the States in toto, the Court took care to parse each Amendment into its component guarantees, evaluating them one by one. This piecemeal approach allowed the Court to scrutinize more closely the right at issue in any given dispute, reducing both the risk and the cost of error. . . .

The question in this case, then, is not whether the Second Amendment right to keep and bear arms (whatever that right's precise contours) applies to the States because the Amendment has been incorporated into the Fourteenth Amendment. It has not been. The question, rather, is whether the particular right asserted by petitioners applies to the States because of the Fourteenth Amendment itself, standing on its own bottom. And to answer that question, we need to determine, first, the nature of the right that has been asserted and, second, whether that right is an aspect of Fourteenth Amendment "liberty." Even accepting the Court's holding in *Heller*, it remains entirely possible that the right to keep and bear arms identified in that opinion is not judicially enforceable against the States, or that only part of the right is so enforceable. It is likewise possible for the Court to find in this case that some part of the *Heller* right applies to the States, and then to find in later cases that other parts of the right also apply, or apply on different terms. . . .

[W]hile the utility of firearms, and handguns in particular, to the defense of hearth and home is certainly relevant to an assessment of petitioners' asserted right, there is no freestanding self-defense claim in this case. The question we must decide is whether the interest in keeping in the home a firearm of one's choosing—a handgun, for petitioners—is one that is "comprised within the term liberty" in the Fourteenth Amendment.

While I agree with the Court that our substantive due process cases offer a principled basis for holding that petitioners have a constitutional right to possess a usable firearm in the home, I am ultimately persuaded that a better reading of our case law supports the city of Chicago. I would not foreclose the possibility that a particular plaintiff—say, an elderly widow who lives in a dangerous neighborhood and does not have the strength to operate a long gun—may have a cognizable liberty interest in possessing a handgun. But I cannot accept petitioners' broader submission. A number of factors, taken together, lead me to this conclusion.

First, firearms have a fundamentally ambivalent relationship to liberty. Just as they can help homeowners defend their families and property from intruders, they can help thugs and insurrectionists murder innocent victims. The threat that firearms will be misused is far from hypothetical, for gun crime has devastated many of our communities. . . .

Hence, in evaluating an asserted right to be free from particular gun-control regulations, liberty is on both sides of the equation. Guns may be useful for self-defense, as well as for hunting and sport, but they also have a unique potential to facilitate death and destruction and thereby to destabilize ordered liberty. Your interest in keeping and bearing a certain firearm may diminish my interest in being and feeling safe from armed violence. And while granting you the right to own a handgun might make you safer on any given day— assuming the handgun's marginal contribution to self-defense outweighs its marginal contribution to the risk of accident, suicide, and criminal mischief— it may make you and the community you live in less safe overall, owing to the increased number of handguns in circulation. It is at least reasonable for a democratically elected legislature to take such concerns into account in considering what sorts of regulations would best serve the public welfare. . . .

Second, the right to possess a firearm of one's choosing is different in kind from the liberty interests we have recognized under the Due Process Clause. Despite the plethora of substantive due process cases that have been decided in the post-*Lochner* century, I have found none that holds, states, or even suggests that the term "liberty" encompasses either the common-law right of self-defense or a right to keep and bear arms. I do not doubt for a moment that many Americans feel deeply passionate about firearms, and see them as critical to their way of life as well as to their security. Nevertheless, it does not appear to be the case that the ability to own a handgun, or any particular type of firearm, is critical to leading a life of autonomy, dignity, or political equality: The marketplace offers many tools for self-defense, even if they are imperfect substitutes, and neither petitioners nor their *amici* make such a contention. Petitioners' claim is not the kind of substantive interest, accordingly, on which a uniform, judicially enforced national standard is presumptively appropriate. . . .

Third, the experience of other advanced democracies, including those that share our British heritage, undercuts the notion that an expansive right to keep and bear arms is intrinsic to ordered liberty. Many of these countries place restrictions on the possession, use, and carriage of firearms far more onerous than the restrictions found in this Nation (England, Canada, Australia, Japan, Denmark, Finland, Luxembourg, and New Zealand). That the United States is an international outlier in the permissiveness of its approach to guns does not suggest that our laws are bad laws. It does suggest that this Court may not need to assume responsibility for making our laws still more permissive. . . .

Fourth, the Second Amendment differs in kind from the Amendments that surround it, with the consequence that its inclusion in the Bill of Rights is not merely unhelpful but positively harmful to petitioners' claim. Generally, the inclusion of a liberty interest in the Bill of Rights points toward the conclusion that it is of fundamental significance and ought to be enforceable against the States. But the Second Amendment plays a peculiar role within the Bill, as announced by its peculiar opening clause. Even accepting the *Heller* Court's view that the Amendment protects an individual right to keep and bear arms disconnected from militia service, it remains undeniable that "the purpose for which the right was codified" was "to prevent elimination of the militia." It was the States, not private persons, on whose immediate behalf the Second Amendment was adopted. Notwithstanding the *Heller* Court's efforts to write the Second Amendment's preamble out of the Constitution, the Amendment still serves the structural function of protecting the States from encroachment by an overreaching Federal Government.

The Second Amendment, in other words, "is a federalism provision." It is directed at preserving the autonomy of the sovereign States, and its logic therefore "resists" incorporation by a federal court against the States. No one suggests that the Tenth Amendment, which provides that powers not given to the Federal Government remain with "the States," applies to the States; such a reading would border on incoherent, given that the Tenth Amendment exists (in significant part) to safeguard the vitality of state governance. The Second Amendment is no different. . . .

Fifth, although it may be true that Americans' interest in firearm possession and state-law recognition of that interest are "deeply rooted" in some important senses, it is equally true that the States have a long and unbroken history of regulating firearms. The idea that States may place substantial restrictions on the right to keep and bear arms short of complete disarmament is, in fact, far more entrenched than the notion that the Federal Constitution protects any such right. Federalism is a far "older and more deeply rooted tradition than is a right to carry," or to own, "any particular kind of weapon." . . .

Finally, even apart from the States' long history of firearms regulation and its location at the core of their police powers, this is a quintessential area in which federalism ought to be allowed to flourish without this Court's meddling. Whether or not we can assert a plausible constitutional basis for intervening, there are powerful reasons why we should not do so.

Across the Nation, States and localities vary significantly in the patterns and problems of gun violence they face, as well as in the traditions and cultures of lawful gun use they claim. The city of Chicago, for example, faces a pressing challenge in combating criminal street gangs. Most rural areas do not. The city of Chicago has a high population density, which increases the potential for a gunman to inflict mass terror and casualties. Most rural areas do not. The city of Chicago offers little in the way of hunting opportunities. Residents of rural communities are, one presumes, much more likely to stock the dinner table with game they have personally felled.

Given that relevant background conditions diverge so much across jurisdictions, the Court ought to pay particular heed to state and local legislatures' "right to experiment." . . .

The fact that the right to keep and bear arms appears in the Constitution should not obscure the novelty of the Court's decision to enforce that right against the States. By its terms, the Second Amendment does not apply to the States; read properly, it does not even apply to individuals outside of the militia context. The Second Amendment was adopted to protect the States from federal encroachment. And the Fourteenth Amendment has never been understood by the Court to have "incorporated" the entire Bill of Rights. There was nothing foreordained about today's outcome.

Although the Court's decision in this case might be seen as a mere junct to its decision in *Heller*, the consequences could prove far more destructive— quite literally—to our Nation's communities and to our constitutional structure. Thankfully, the Second Amendment right identified in *Heller* and its newly minted Fourteenth Amendment analogue are limited, at least for now, to the home. But neither the "assurances" provided by the plurality, nor the many historical sources cited in its opinion should obscure the reality that today's ruling marks a dramatic change in our law—or that the Justices who have joined it have brought to bear an awesome amount of discretion in resolving the legal question presented by this case. . . .

Accordingly, I respectfully dissent.

☐ *Justice BREYER, with whom Justice GINSBURG and Justice SOTOMAYOR join, dissenting.*

In my view, Justice STEVENS has demonstrated that the Fourteenth Amendment's guarantee of "substantive due process" does not include a general right to keep and bear firearms for purposes of private self-defense. As he argues, the Framers did not write the Second Amendment with this objective in view. Unlike other forms of substantive liberty, the carrying of arms for that purpose often puts others' lives at risk. And the use of arms for private self-defense does not warrant federal constitutional protection from state regulation.

382 | THE NATIONALIZATION OF THE BILL OF RIGHTS

The Court, however, does not expressly rest its opinion upon "substantive due process" concerns. Rather, it directs its attention to this Court's "incorporation" precedents and asks whether the Second Amendment right to private self-defense is "fundamental" so that it applies to the States through the Fourteenth Amendment. . . .

[H]istorians now tell us . . . that the right to which Blackstone referred had, not nothing, but everything, to do with the militia. As properly understood at the time of the English Civil Wars, the historians claim, the right to bear arms "ensured that Parliament had the power" to arm the citizenry: "to defend the realm" in the case of a foreign enemy, and to "secure the right of 'self-preservation,'" or "self-defense," should "the sovereign usurp the English Constitution." *English Historians' Brief.* Thus, the Declaration of Right says that private persons can possess guns only "as allowed by law." Moreover, when Blackstone referred to "the right of having and using arms for self-preservation and defence," he was referring to the right of the people "to take part in the militia to defend their political liberties," and to the right of Parliament (which represented the people) to raise a militia even when the King sought to deny it that power. Nor can the historians find any convincing reason to believe that the Framers had something different in mind than what Blackstone himself meant. The historians concede that at least one historian takes a different position, but the Court, they imply, would lose a poll taken among professional historians of this period, say, by a vote of 8 to 1.

If history, and history alone, is what matters, why would the Court not now reconsider *Heller* in light of these more recently published historical views?

My aim in referring to this history is to illustrate the reefs and shoals that lie in wait for those nonexpert judges who place virtually determinative weight upon historical considerations. In my own view, the Court should not look to history alone but to other factors as well—above all, in cases where the history is so unclear that the experts themselves strongly disagree. It should, for example, consider the basic values that underlie a constitutional provision and their contemporary significance. And it should examine as well the relevant consequences and practical justifications that might, or might not, warrant removing an important question from the democratic decisionmaking process.

In my view, taking *Heller* as a given, the Fourteenth Amendment does not incorporate the Second Amendment right to keep and bear arms for purposes of private self-defense. Under this Court's precedents, to incorporate the private self-defense right the majority must show that the right is, e.g., "fundamental to the American scheme of justice," *Duncan v. Louisiana*, 391 U.S. 145 (1968).

The majority here, like that in *Heller*, relies almost exclusively upon history to make the necessary showing. But to do so for incorporation purposes is both wrong and dangerous. As Justice STEVENS points out, our society has historically made mistakes—for example, when considering certain 18th- and 19th-century property rights to be fundamental. And in the incorporation context, as elsewhere, history often is unclear about the answers.

Accordingly, this Court, in considering an incorporation question, has never stated that the historical status of a right is the only relevant consideration. Rather, the Court has either explicitly or implicitly made clear in its opinions that the right in question has remained fundamental over time.

I thus think it proper, above all where history provides no clear answer, to look to other factors in considering whether a right is sufficiently "fundamental" to remove it from the political process in every State. I would include among those factors the nature of the right; any contemporary disagreement about whether the right is fundamental; the extent to which incorporation will further other, perhaps more basic, constitutional aims; and the extent to which incorporation will advance or hinder the Constitution's structural aims, including its division of powers among different governmental institutions (and the people as well). Is incorporation needed, for example, to further the Constitution's effort to ensure that the government treats each individual with equal respect? Will it help maintain the democratic form of government that the Constitution foresees? In a word, will incorporation prove consistent, or inconsistent, with the Constitution's efforts to create governmental institutions well suited to the carrying out of its constitutional promises?

Finally, I would take account of the Framers' basic reason for believing the Court ought to have the power of judicial review. Alexander Hamilton feared granting that power to Congress alone, for he feared that Congress, acting as judges, would not overturn as unconstitutional a popular statute that it had recently enacted, as legislators. *The Federalist* No. 78 ("This independence of the judges is equally requisite to guard the constitution and the rights of individuals from the effects of those ill humours, which" can, at times, lead to "serious oppressions of the minor part in the community"). Judges, he thought, may find it easier to resist popular pressure to suppress the basic rights of an unpopular minority. That being so, it makes sense to ask whether that particular comparative judicial advantage is relevant to the case at hand.

How do these considerations apply here? For one thing, I would apply them only to the private self-defense right directly at issue. After all, the Amendment's militia-related purpose is primarily to protect States from federal regulation, not to protect individuals from militia-related regulation. Moreover, the Civil War Amendments, the electoral process, the courts, and numerous other institutions today help to safeguard the States and the people from any serious threat of federal tyranny. How are state militias additionally necessary? It is difficult to see how a right that, as the majority concedes, has "largely faded as a popular concern" could possibly be so fundamental that it would warrant incorporation through the Fourteenth Amendment. Hence, the incorporation of the Second Amendment cannot be based on the militia-related aspect of what *Heller* found to be more extensive Second Amendment rights.

For another thing, as *Heller* concedes, the private self-defense right that the Court would incorporate has nothing to do with "the reason" the Framers "codified" the right to keep and bear arms "in a written Constitution." *Heller* immediately adds that the self-defense right was nonetheless "the central component of the right." In my view, this is the historical equivalent of a claim that water runs uphill. . . .

Further, there is no popular consensus that the private self-defense right described in *Heller* is fundamental. . . .

Moreover, there is no reason here to believe that incorporation of the private self-defense right will further any other or broader constitutional objective. . . .

Finally, incorporation of the right will work a significant disruption in the constitutional allocation of decisionmaking authority, thereby interfering with the Constitution's ability to further its objectives.

First, on any reasonable accounting, the incorporation of the right recognized in *Heller* would amount to a significant incursion on a traditional and important area of state concern, altering the constitutional relationship between the States and the Federal Government. Private gun regulation is the quintessential exercise of a State's "police power"—i.e., the power to "protec[t] . . . the lives, limbs, health, comfort, and quiet of all persons, and the protection of all property within the State," by enacting "all kinds of restraints and burdens" on both "persons and property." . . .

Second, determining the constitutionality of a particular state gun law requires finding answers to complex empirically based questions of a kind that legislatures are better able than courts to make. . . .

Third, the ability of States to reflect local preferences and conditions—both key virtues of federalism—here has particular importance. The incidence of gun ownership varies substantially as between crowded cities and uncongested rural communities, as well as among the different geographic regions of the country. Thus, approximately 60 percent of adults who live in the relatively sparsely populated Western States of Alaska, Montana, and Wyoming report that their household keeps a gun, while fewer than 15 percent of adults in the densely populated Eastern States of Rhode Island, New Jersey, and Massachusetts say the same. . . .

Fourth, although incorporation of any right removes decisions from the democratic process, the incorporation of this particular right does so without strong offsetting justification—as the example of Oak Park's handgun ban helps to show. Oak Park decided to ban handguns in 1983, after a local attorney was shot to death with a handgun that his assailant had smuggled into a courtroom in a blanket. A citizens committee spent months gathering information about handguns. It secured 6,000 signatures from community residents in support of a ban. And the village board enacted a ban into law. . . .

Given the empirical and local value-laden nature of the questions that lie at the heart of the issue, why, in a Nation whose Constitution foresees democratic decisionmaking, is it so fundamental a matter as to require taking that power from the people? What is it here that the people did not know? What is it that a judge knows better?

In sum, the police power, the superiority of legislative decisionmaking, the need for local decisionmaking, the comparative desirability of democratic decisionmaking, the lack of a manageable judicial standard, and the life-threatening harm that may flow from striking down regulations all argue against incorporation. Where the incorporation of other rights has been at issue, some of these problems have arisen. But in this instance all these problems are present, all at the same time, and all are likely to be present in most, perhaps nearly all, of the cases in which the constitutionality of a gun regulation is at issue. At the same time, the important factors that favor incorporation in other instances—e.g., the protection of broader constitutional objectives—are not present here. The upshot is that all factors militate against incorporation—with the possible exception of historical factors. . . .

With respect, I dissent.

■ CONSTITUTIONAL HISTORY

The Second and Third Amendments

The Second and Third Amendments register the concerns of the revolutionary period during which state militias defeated the British and there was vehement opposition to the British practice of quartering troops in private homes. The Second Amendment states, "A well regulated Militia being necessary to the security of a free State, the right of the people to keep and bear Arms shall not be infringed." The Third Amendment provides that "No Soldier shall, in time of peace be quartered in any house, without the consent of the Owner, nor in time of war, but in a manner to be prescribed by law."

The guarantees of both amendments were part of some state constitutions and bills of rights, prior to the ratification of the Bill of Rights. Pennsylvania's Constitution of 1776, for example, provided in Article 13 of its Declaration of Rights "[t]hat the people have a right to bear arms for the defense of themselves and the state; and as standing armies in the time of peace are dangerous to liberty, they ought not to be kept up; And that the military should be kept under strict subordination to, and governed by, the civil power." Delaware's Declaration of Rights and Fundamental Rules of 1776 provided "[t]hat no Soldier ought to be quartered in any House in Time of Peace without the Consent of the Owner; and in Time of War in such Manner only as the Legislature shall direct."

The controversy over the right to bear arms has intensified in recent decades, and neither amendment was interpreted by the Supreme Court to limit state regulations; see *Presser v. Illinois*, 116 U.S. 252 (1886). The principal decision, *United States v. Miller*, 307 U.S. 174 (1939), construing the Second Amendment upheld a congressional statute, the National Firearms Act of 1934, requiring the registration of sawed-off shotguns. There, the Court reviewed the constitutional provisions pertaining to militias and observed, "With the obvious purpose to assure the continuation and render possible the effectiveness of such forces the declaration and guarantee of the Second Amendment were made. It must be interpreted and applied with that end in view." On that basis the Court concluded, "In the absence of any evidence tending to show that possession or use of a 'shotgun having a barrel of less than 18 inches in length' at this time has some reasonable relationship to the preservation or efficiency of a

(continues)

■ CONSTITUTIONAL HISTORY
The Second and Third Amendments (continued)

well regulated militia, we cannot say that the Second Amendment guarantees the right to keep and bear such an instrument. Certainly it is not within judicial notice that this weapon is any part of the ordinary military equipment or that its use could contribute to the common defense."

However, in a historic ruling in *District of Columbia v. Heller*, 554 U.S. 570 (2008), the Court struck down two key provisions of the District of Columbia's 1976 ban on handguns, the strictest in the nation: (1) a flat ban on possessing a handgun in one's home; and (2) a requirement that any gun, except one kept at a business, must be unloaded and disassembled or have a trigger lock in place. The Court left intact other provisions, such as the requirement that guns must be registered and licensed.

Writing for a bare majority, Justice Scalia advanced several arguments—textualist, intratextualist, and based on the original understanding of the amendment—for invalidating the ban on handguns. First, he separated the prefatory and operative clauses of the amendment, observing that "The Second Amendment is naturally divided into two parts: its prefatory clause [a well regulated Militia] and its operative clause [the right of the people to keep and bear Arms]. . . . [A] prefatory clause does not limit or expand the scope of the operative clause. . . . The prefatory clause does not suggest that preserving the militia was the only reason Americans valued the ancient right; most undoubtedly thought it even more important for self-defense and hunting." Turning to the operative clause—"to keep and bear Arms"—he added: "Although the phrase implies that the carrying of the weapon is for the purpose of 'offensive or defensive action,' it in no way connotes participation in a structured military organization. . . . [T]he most natural reading of 'keep Arms' in the Second Amendment is to have weapons." After separating those clauses, he focused on "the right of the people" and offered an intratextualist analysis, emphasizing that "in all six other provisions of the Constitution that mention 'the people,' the term unambiguously refers to all members of the political community, not an unspecified subset. . . . Putting all of these textual elements together, we find that they guarantee the individual right to possess and carry weapons in case of confrontation." Finally, Justice Scalia drew on the "original understanding" of the amendment, which he asserted applied "to weapons that were not specifically designed for military use and were not employed in a military capacity." "In sum," he concluded, "the District's ban on handgun possession in the home violates the Second Amendment, as does its prohibition against rendering any lawful firearm in the home operable for the purpose of immediate self-defense. Assuming that Heller is not disqualified from the exercise of Second Amendment rights, the District must permit him to register his handgun and must issue him a license to carry it in the home."

Justice Scalia's opinion for the Court, however, emphasized that "the right secured by the Second Amendment is not unlimited." More specifically, Justice Scalia expressly emphasized that the amendment only applies to federal regulations and does not apply to the states under the Fourteenth Amendment. In underscoring that the decision applied only to the possession of handguns in one's home for purposes of self defense, he noted that "we do not read the Second Amendment to protect the right of citizens to carry arms for any sort of confrontation, just as we do not read the First Amendment to protect the right of citizens to speak for any purpose." Justice Scalia also noted that the decision did not apply to other long-standing restrictions, such as prohibitions on the possession of firearms by felons and the mentally ill and the carrying of concealed weapons, as well as to bans on the carrying of firearms into schools and government buildings, and to conditions imposed on the commercial sale of firearms. In addition, he emphasized the narrowness of the ruling as applying only to "the sorts of weapons protected . . . 'in common use at the time'" of the ratification of the amendment, thus, leaving open the regulation of semiautomatic, assault, and other weapons.

Subsequently, after *Heller* the Roberts Court inexorably confronted the issue of whether the Second Amendment applies to the states and limits their powers over gun control. The Court took up that issue in *McDonald v. Chicago* (2010) (excerpted in this chapter), and held that the Second Amendment applies to the state and local governments and is incorporated in the Fourteenth Amendment due process clause. In a *per curiam* opinion, *Caetano v. Massachusetts*, 136 S.Ct. 1027 (2016), the Court also overturned a state supreme court holding that the Second Amendment does not protect possession of stun guns. In reversing the Massachusetts supreme court, it rejected its reasons for ruling that the amendment does not protect possession of stun guns: (1) stun guns were not available when the amendment was adopted, (2) they are dangerous and unusual, and (3) stun guns are not readily adaptable for military use. In addition, the Court reiterated that the amendment "extends, prima facie, to all Instruments that constitute bearable arms, even those that were not in existence at the time of the founding." Justices Alito and Thomas concurred but also have struck down the state's law barring possession of electronic weapons.

For further reading see Saul Cornell, *A Well-Regulated Militia: The Founding Fathers and the Origins of Gun Control in America*, New York: Oxford University Press, 2008; Mark Tushnet, *Out of Range: Why the Constitution Can't End the Battle Over Guns*, New York: Oxford University Press, 2007; Saul Cornell and Nathan Kozuskanich, eds., *Up in Arms: The Second Amendment in the Modern Republic*, Amherst: University of Massachusetts Press, 2013; and Michael Waldman, *The Second Amendment: A Biography*, New York: Simon & Schuster, 2014.

B | *The Rise and (Partial) Retreat of the "Due Process Revolution"*

The due process revolution forged during the latter Warren Court years (1962–1969) by extending the major guarantees of the Bill of Rights to the states took on a life of its own. In the early 1970s, the Burger Court continued to expand the protection of the due process clause to require trial-type hearings prior to the infringement of individuals' rights and entitlements. Notably, in *Goldberg v. Kelly*, 397 U.S. 254 (1970), the Court held that the due process clause of the Fourteenth Amendment requires a trial-type hearing for recipients of Aid to Families with Dependent Children (AFDC) prior to the termination of their benefits under the AFDC program.

The Court, for example, extended due process-based require-ments in *Wisconsin v. Constantineau*, 400 U.S. 433 (1971), for the public posting of the names of people deemed unfit to consume alcoholic beverages; *Richardson v. Wright*, 405 U.S. 208 (1972), requiring the opportunity to offer oral evidence and to cross-examine witnesses in a hearing before the termination of disability benefits; *Morrissey v. Brewer*, 408 U.S. 471 (1972), requiring a hearing before the revoca-tion of parole; *Gibson v. Berryhill*, 411 U.S. 564 (1973), requiring an impartial hearing by officers on a state optometry board; *Weinberger v. Hynson, Westcott & Dunning, Inc.*, 412 U.S. 609 (1973), requiring a hearing prior to the Food and Drug Administration's withdrawal of new drug applications; and *Arnett v. Kennedy*, 416 U.S. 134 (1974), holding that federal employees must be accorded minimal procedural guarantees as afforded by federal law before having their employment terminated.

In Justice William O. Douglas's last term after more than thirty-six years on the bench, a bare majority of the Court signaled that the due process revolution was coming to an end in *Goss v. Lopez*, 419 U.S. 565 (1975). There President Nixon's four appointees—Chief Jus-tice Burger and Justices Blackmun, Powell, and Rehnquist—dissented from the majority's view that due process requires a conversation, and not a hearing, prior to the temporary suspension of students from school, and that they must receive at least notice of the charges against them, an explanation of the evidence authorities have, and an opportu-nity to tell their side of the story. In Justice Byron White's words for the majority:

Even truncated trial-type procedures might well overwhelm administrative facilities in many places and, in diverting resources, cost more than it would save in educational effectiveness. Moreover, further formalizing the suspension process and escalating its formality and adversary nature may not only make it too costly as a regular disciplinary tool but also destroy its effectiveness as part of the teaching process. On the other hand, requiring effective notice and informal hearing permitting the student to give his version of the events will provide a meaningful hedge against erroneous action.

The Burger Court's rulings on the substantive and procedural rights of individuals committed to mental institutions further illustrate its movement away from an expansive reading of the constitutional protection afforded by the due process clause. Along with *Goss v. Lopez* in 1975, the Burger Court held, in *O'Connor v. Donaldson*, 422 U.S. 563 (1975), that individuals who are not dangerous to others may not be confined in institutions against their will, if they can survive outside with the aid of relatives or friends and are not receiving special therapy. At the same time, the Court refused to embrace a constitutional "right to treatment." Kenneth Donaldson was confined to the Florida State Hospital, following commitment proceedings initiated by his father who said that he suffered from delusions. For almost fifteen years, Donaldson repeatedly requested to be released, claiming that he was not receiving any special treatment justifying his confinement and that he could survive outside the institution with the help of friends and relatives. But, the hospital superintendent, Dr. J. B. O'Connor, denied his release. Finally, Donaldson filed a lawsuit charging that O'Connor was depriving him of his constitutional right to liberty under the Fourteenth Amendment.

Although declining to read a substantive "right to treatment" into the Fourteenth Amendment due process clause in *O'Connor v. Donaldson*, Justice Potter Stewart ruled that "a State cannot constitutionally confine without more a nondangerous individual who is capable of surviving safely in freedom by himself or with the help of willing and responsible family members or friends."

Subsequently, the Court held that due process requires a standard of proof in civil commitment proceedings greater than the "preponderance of the evidence" standard used in other civil proceedings, but less rigorous than the "beyond a reasonable doubt" standard used in criminal cases. *Addington v. Texas*, 441 U.S. 418 (1979), created a new (middle level) standard requiring clear and convincing evidence to justify an individual's involuntary hospitalization. In cases involving the commitment of children to mental health institutions, the Court also held that a commitment hearing before a "neutral fact finder" (who, however, need not be legally trained) is required under the due process clause.[1] Notice, a hearing, and the opportunity to call and cross-examine witnesses before a neutral fact finder are also required before inmates in a state prison may be transferred to a mental institution.[2] Moreover, *Youngberg v. Romeo*, 457 U.S. 307 (1982), held that developmentally disabled individuals still enjoy certain constitutionally protected liberty interests. In *Youngberg*, the Court unanimously ruled that individuals confined to state mental institutions may assert under the Fourteenth Amendment due process clause "constitutionally protected interests in the conditions of reasonable care and safety, reasonably nonrestrictive confinement conditions, and such training as may be required by these interests." Thus while *O'Connor v. Donaldson* declined to embrace a broad right to treatment under the due process clause, the Court nevertheless held that individuals have some constitutionally protected procedural and substantive liberty interests in commitment proceedings and in the conditions of their hospitalization.

With the Senate's confirmation of Justice Douglas's successor, Justice John Paul Stevens, the Court took a more restrictive, less expansive view of what process is due under the due process clause. In *Mathews v. Eldridge*, 424 U.S. 319 (1976), the Court held that an evidentiary hearing is not required prior to the termination of disability benefits. In a number of other cases, the Court denied claims to procedural guarantees under the due process clause: *Meachum v. Fano*, 427 U.S. 215 (1976), rejected a due process argument for a hearing prior to the transfer of a prisoner from one prison to another. *Bishop v. Wood*, 426 U.S. 341 (1976), approved the dismissal of a city police officer without a pretermination hearing. *Codd v. Velger*, 429 U.S. 624 (1977), held that a hearing need not be held for the dismissal of policemen who challenged materials placed in their files as damaging. *Dixon v. Love*, 431 U.S. 105 (1977), upheld Illinois's summary revocation of drivers' licenses for repeated traffic violations, holding that *Eldridge* does not require a pretermination hearing. And in *Ingraham v. Wright*, 430 U.S. 651 (1977), the justices split 5–4 when holding that no hearing is necessary prior to the "paddling" of students in public schools. In *Board of Curators of University of Missouri v. Horowitz*, 435 U.S. 78 (1978), a bare majority of the Court affirmed that the dismissal of a medical student did not require an elaborate procedural hearing before the school's decision-making body. *Greenholtz v. Inmates*, 442 U.S. 1 (1979), ruled that an oral hearing for parole decisions was not needed and that a parole board could rely simply on the files on an inmate.

Barry v. Barchi, 443 U.S. 55 (1979), upheld the summary dismissal of harness racing trainers.

The Burger Court, however, upheld claims for procedural due process in a few cases. In *Memphis Light, Gas & Water Division v. Craft*, 436 U.S. 1 (1978), for example, the Court held that the due process clause requires public utilities to establish an administrative procedure for hearing complaints before disconnecting gas, water, and electric services. And *Vitek v. Jones*, 445 U.S. 480 (1980), ruled that a hearing was required before the transfer of prisoners to state mental health institutions for involuntary commitment. *Cleveland Board of Education v. Loudermill*, 470 U.S. 532 (1985), also held that in the dismissal of an employee for cause the state must afford a hearing on the charges during the pretermination process.

The Court, nevertheless, has tended to cut back on further readings of substantive rights into the due process clause. The due process clause has been interpreted only to prevent government "from abusing [its] power, or employing it as an instrument of oppression."[3]

As Chief Justice Rehnquist explained, in *DeShaney v. Winnebago County Department of Social Services*, 489 U.S. 189 (1989), "the Due Process Clauses generally confer no affirmative right to governmental aid, even where such aid may be necessary to secure life, liberty, or property interests of which the government itself may not deprive the individual." In *DeShaney* (with Justices Brennan, Blackmun, and Marshall dissenting) the Court held that

> [i]n the substantive due process analysis, it is the State's affirmative act of restraining the individual's freedom to act on his own behalf—through incarceration, institutionalization, or other similar restraint of personal liberty—which is the "deprivation of liberty" triggering the protections of the Due Process Clause, not its failure to act to protect his liberty interests against harms inflicted by other means.

In that case, Chief Justice Rehnquist rejected the claim of Melody DeShaney that welfare workers were liable for the repeated beatings by the natural father of her son, Joshua, which left the four-year-old boy brain damaged. As Chief Justice Rehnquist observed,

> [T]he harms Joshua suffered did not occur while he was in the State's custody, but while he was in the custody of his natural father, who was in no sense a state actor. While the State may have been aware of the dangers that Joshua faced in the free world, it played no part in their creation, nor did it do anything to render him any more vulnerable to them. That the State once took

temporary custody of Joshua does not alter the analysis, for when it returned him to his father's custody, it placed him in no worse position than that in which he would have been had it not acted at all; the State does not become the permanent guarantor of an individual's safety by having once offered him shelter. Under these circumstances, the State had no constitutional duty to protect Joshua. . . .

The people of Wisconsin may well prefer a system of liability which would place upon the State and its officials the responsibility for failure to act in situations such as the present one. They may create such a system, if they do not have it already, by changing the tort law of the State in accordance with the regular law-making process. But they should not have it thrust upon them by this Court's expansion of the Due Process Clause of the Fourteenth Amendment.

In another decision, *Michael H. v. Gerald D.*, 491 U.S. 110 (1989), the Rehnquist Court split 5–4 in rejecting the substantive due process argument that the natural (unwed) father of the child of a married woman had a right to file to establish paternity and for visitation rights. Under California law, which the majority upheld, the legal husband of a married woman who bears a child is presumptively the legal father. Writing for a bare majority, Justice Scalia explained that

the legal issue in the present case reduces to whether the relationship between persons in the situation of Michael and Victoria has been treated as a protected family unit under the historic practices of our society, or whether on any other basis it has been accorded special protection. We think it impossible to find that it has. In fact, quite to the contrary, our traditions have protected the marital family. . . .

The presumption of legitimacy was a fundamental principle of the common law. . . . [W]hat is at issue here is not entitlement to a state pronouncement that Victoria was begotten by Michael. It is no conceivable denial of constitutional right for a State to decline to declare facts unless some legal consequence hinges upon the requested declaration. What Michael asserts here is a right to have himself declared the natural father *and thereby to obtain parental prerogatives*. What he must establish, therefore, is not that our society has traditionally allowed a natural father in his circumstances to establish paternity, but that it has traditionally accorded such a father parental rights, or at least has not traditionally denied them. Even if the law in all States had always been that the entire world could challenge the marital presumption and obtain a declaration as to who was the natural father, that would not advance Michael's claim. Thus, it is ultimately irrelevant, even for purposes of determining *current* social attitudes towards the alleged substantive right Michael asserts, that the present law in a number of States appears to allow the natural father—including the natural father who has not established a relationship with the child—the theoretical power to rebut the marital presumption.

By contrast, dissenting Justice Brennan argued that

it would be comforting to believe that a search for "tradition" involves nothing more idiosyncratic or complicated than poring through dusty volumes on American history. . . . "What the deeply rooted traditions of the country are is arguable." Indeed, wherever I would begin to look for an interest "deeply rooted in the country's traditions," one thing is certain: I would not stop (as does the plurality) at Bracton, or Blackstone, or Kent, or even the American Law Reports in conducting my search. Because reasonable people can disagree about the content of particular traditions, and because they can disagree even about which traditions are relevant to the definition of "liberty," the plurality has not found the objective boundary that it seeks.

Even if we could agree, moreover, on the content and significance of particular traditions, we still would be forced to identify the point at which a tradition becomes firm enough to be relevant to our definition of liberty and the moment at which it becomes too obsolete to be relevant any longer. The plurality supplies no objective means by which we might make these determinations. Indeed, as soon as the plurality sees signs that the tradition upon which it bases its decision (the laws denying putative fathers like Michael standing to assert paternity) is crumbling, it shifts ground and says that the case has nothing to do with that tradition, after all. "What is at issue here," the plurality asserts after canvassing the law on paternity suits, "is not entitlement to a state pronouncement that Victoria was begotten by Michael." But that is precisely what is at issue here, and the plurality's last-minute denial of this fact dramatically illustrates the subjectivity of its own analysis.

It is ironic that an approach so utterly dependent on tradition is so indifferent to our precedents. Citing barely a handful of this Court's numerous decisions defining the scope of the liberty protected by the Due Process Clause to support its reliance on tradition, the plurality acts as though English legal treatises and the American Law Reports always have provided the sole source for our constitutional principles. They have not. Just as common-law notions no longer define the "property" that the Constitution protects, see *Goldberg v. Kelly*, 397 U.S. 254 [(1970)], neither do they circumscribe the "liberty" that it guarantees. On the contrary, " '[l]iberty' and 'property' are broad and majestic terms. . . ."

The plurality's interpretive method is more than novel; it is misguided. It ignores the good reasons for limiting the role of "tradition" in interpreting the Constitution's deliberately capacious language. In the plurality's constitutional universe, we may not take notice of the fact that the original reasons for the conclusive presumption of paternity are out of place in a world in which blood tests can prove virtually beyond a shadow of a doubt who sired a particular child and in which the fact of illegitimacy no longer plays the burdensome and stigmatizing role it once did. Nor, in the plurality's world, may we deny "tradition" its full scope by pointing out that the rationale for the conventional rule has changed over the years; instead, our task is simply to identify a rule denying the asserted interest and not to ask whether the basis for that rule—which is the true reflection of the values undergirding it—has changed too often or too recently to call the rule embodying that rationale a "tradition." Moreover, by describing the decisive question as whether Michael and Victoria's interest is one that has been "traditionally *protected by* our society" (emphasis added) rather than one that society traditionally has thought important (with or without protecting it), and by suggesting that our sole function is to "*discern* the society's views" (emphasis added), the plurality acts as if the only purpose of the Due Process Clause is to confirm the importance of interests already protected by a majority of the States. Transforming the protection afforded by the Due Process Clause into a redundancy mocks those who, with care and purpose, wrote the Fourteenth Amendment.

In construing the Fourteenth Amendment to offer shelter only to those interests specifically protected by historical practice, moreover, the plurality ignores the kind of society in which our Constitution exists. We are not an assimilative, homogeneous society, but a facilitative, pluralistic one, in which we must be willing to abide someone else's unfamiliar or even repellant practice because the same tolerant impulse protects our own idiosyncracies. Even if we can agree, therefore, that "family" and "parenthood" are part of the good life, it is absurd to assume that we can agree on the content of those terms and destructive to pretend that we do. In a community such as ours, "liberty" must include the freedom not to conform. The plurality today squashes this freedom by requiring specific approval from history before protecting anything in the name of liberty.

The document that the plurality construes today is unfamiliar to me. It is not the living charter that I have taken to be our Constitution; it is instead a stagnant, archaic, hidebound document steeped in the prejudices and superstitions of a time long past. *This* Constitution does not recognize that times change, does not see that sometimes a practice or rule outlives its foundations. I cannot accept an interpretive method that does such violence to the charter that I am bound by oath to uphold.

The question before us . . . is whether California has an interest so powerful that it justifies granting Michael *no* hearing before terminating his parental rights. . . .

Make no mistake: to say that the State must provide Michael with a hearing to prove his paternity is not to express any opinion of the ultimate state of affairs between Michael and Victoria and Carole and Gerald. In order to change the current situation among these people, Michael first must convince a court that he is Victoria's father, and even if he is able to do this, he will be denied visitation rights if that would be in Victoria's best interests. It is elementary that a determination that a State must afford procedures before it terminates a given right is not a prediction about the end result of those procedures.

In addition, in *Washington v. Harper*, 494 U.S. 210 (1990), the Rehnquist Court held that mentally ill prison inmates may be treated with antipsychotic drugs against their will and without a prior judicial proceeding. In his opinion for the Court, Justice Kennedy held that such treatment does not violate substantive due process where the prisoner is deemed to be dangerous to himself or others and the treatment is in the prisoner's medical interest. Justice Kennedy also held that the due process clause does not require a judicial hearing prior to such treatment of prisoners. The requirements of "procedural due process," according to Justice Kennedy, are satisfied by prison policies requiring administrative panels, composed of corrections officials and medical professionals, to review decisions to treat prisoners with antipsychotic drugs.

However, in *Foucha v. Louisiana*, 504 U.S. 71 (1992) Justice White sharply divided the Court when commanding a bare majority for asserting substantive and procedural due process protection under the Fourteenth Amendment. There, he struck down Louisiana's law permitting the continued institutionalization of an individual who was criminally acquitted by reason of insanity and who subsequently regained his sanity but was still deemed to pose a threat to society. Chief Justice Rehnquist and Justice Scalia joined a bitter dissent written by Justice Thomas denouncing the majority's due process analysis, while Justice Kennedy dissented separately. However, in *Kansas v. Hendricks*, 521 U.S. 346 (1997) (see THE DEVELOPMENT OF LAW box in this section), writing for a bare majority, Justice Thomas rejected a substantive due process challenge to Kansas's 1994 law for institutionalizing sexual predators after they have served their prison time.

Notably, a bare majority of the Court revived economic substantive due process in holding that large punitive damage awards that are "grossly excessive" violate the Fourteenth Amendment in *BMW of North America v. Gore* (1996) (excerpted below). Subsequent rulings have reaffirmed the decision of *BMW v. Gore*, but without providing any clearer standard. In *State Farm Mutual Automobile Insurance v. Campbell*, 538 U.S. 408 (2003), for instance, by a 6–3 vote the Court overturned a $145 million jury award that was 145 times the amount of injury as "an irrational and arbitrary deprivation of the property of the defendant." Writing for the majority Justice Kennedy emphasized that damage awards greater than a nine-to-one ratio were constitutionally suspect. And a bare majority of the Roberts Court, in *Philip Morris USA v. Williams*, 549 U.S. 346 (2007), held that a jury award of $79.5 million to a smoker, a roughly 100-to-one ratio to actual damages, was "grossly excessive" for the injuries shared by people who were not parties to the litigation. See also the other cases summarized in THE DEVELOPMENT OF LAW box in this section.

Finally, the Court underscored the continuing viability of and controversy over substantive due process in *County of Sacramento v. Lewis* (1998) (excerpted below). Although rejecting the specific claim presented, the Court did not entirely rule out substantive due process protection for innocent people injured by police action. Writing for the Court and drawing on the test first put forth in *Rochin v. California* (1952) (excerpted in Section A of this chapter), Justice Souter held that police who cause accidents that kill innocent bystanders during high-speed pursuit of criminal suspects are not liable unless their actions "shock the conscience." In his words, "Only a purpose to cause harm unrelated to the legitimate object of arrest will satisfy the element of arbitrary conduct shocking to the conscience, necessary for a due process violation." (Subsequently, the Roberts Court, with Justice Stevens dissenting, in *Scott v. Harris*, 550 U.S. 372 (2007), ruled that under the Fourth Amendment it was reasonable for police to ram a speeding motorist off the road, leaving him permanently paralyzed, in light of the need to protect pedestrians and other drivers from a high-speed car chase.)

NOTES

1. See *Parham v. J. R.*, 442 U.S. 584 (1979).

2. See *Vitek v. Jones*, 445 U.S. 480 (1980).

3. *Davidson v. Cannon*, 474 U.S. 344 (1986). See also *Parratt v. Taylor*, 451 U.S. 527 (1981).

SELECTED BIBLIOGRAPHY

Curry, Lynne. *The DeShaney Case: Child Abuse, Family Rights, and the Dilemma of State Intervention*. Lawrence: University Press of Kansas, 2007.

Keynes, Edward. *Liberty, Property, and Privacy: Toward a Jurisprudence of Substantive Due Process*. University Park: Pennsylvania State University Press, 1996.

Orth, John, V. *Due Process of Law: A Brief History*. Lawrence: University Press of Kansas, 2003.

■ THE DEVELOPMENT OF LAW
Other Recent Rulings on Substantive and Procedural Due Process

CASE	VOTE	RULING
Sigert v. Gilley, 500 U.S. 226 (1991)	6–3	Reaffirmed the holding in *Paul v. Davis*, 424 U.S. 693 (1976), that injury to a person's reputation is neither a liberty interest protected by the due process clauses nor the constitutional right of privacy. Justices Blackmun, Marshall, and Stevens dissented.
Pacific Mutual Life Insurance Company v. Haslip, 499 U.S. 1 (1991)	8–1	Rejected a Fourteenth Amendment substantive due process challenge to the common law method for assessing punitive damages against corporations for the fraudulent activities of their employees. Justice O'Connor dissented.
Foucha v. Louisiana, 504 U.S. 71 (1992)	5–4	Writing for the Court, Justice White struck down Louisiana's law permitting the continued institutionalization of an individual who was criminally acquitted by reason of insanity and who subsequently regained his sanity, but was still deemed to pose a threat to society. Chief Justice Rehnquist and Justices Kennedy, Scalia, and Thomas dissented.
Collins v. Harker Heights, 503 U.S. 115 (1992)	9–0	Unanimously rejected the claims of a city sanitation worker's survivors that the Fourteenth Amendment embraces the right of workers to be free from "unreasonable risk of harm."
Reno v. Flores, 507 U.S. 292 (1993)	7–2	Rejected a substantive due process challenge to the Immigration and Naturalization Service's policy of placing children entering the country illegally in detention centers, and releasing them only to parents or close relatives, pending their deportation hearings.

(continues)

■ THE DEVELOPMENT OF LAW
*Other Recent Rulings on Substantive and Procedural
Due Process (continued)*

CASE	VOTE	RULING
TXO Production Corporation v. Alliance Resources Corporation, 509 U.S. 443 (1993)	6–3	For the third time in five years, the Court revisited the issue of whether large punitive damage awards violate due process. At issue was a jury's

punitive damage award, along with $19,000 in actual damages, to Alliance Resources, after the company countersued TXO Production Corporation for filing suit against it in order to force Alliance Resources to sell mineral rights to TXO. A jury found that TXO's initial suit was frivolous and awarded $10 million in punitive damages—approximately 526 times the amount of actual damages. Although upholding the award and rejecting a substantive due process challenge, the Court was badly splintered. Justice Stevens's opinion for the Court commanded only a plurality, with only Chief Justice Rehnquist and Justice Blackmun joining in its entirety. He reaffirmed the position, in *Pacific Mutual Life Insurance v. Haslip*, 498 U.S. 1306 (1991), that the Court could not "draw a mathematical bright line" between constitutionally acceptable and unacceptable jury awards. Instead of focusing on the disparity between punitive and compensatory awards, Justice Stevens maintained that the Court should focus on the general "reasonableness" of an award. Here, TXO's "bad faith" and "larger pattern of fraud, trickery, and deceit" justified the jury's award.

United States v. James Daniel Good Real Property, 510 U.S. 43 (1993)	5–4	Writing for the Court, Justice Kennedy ruled that convicted drug dealers must be given a hearing before the

government seizes their property under forfeiture laws. Separate opinions, concurring and dissenting, were filed by Chief Justice Rehnquist and Justices O'Connor and Thomas.

Honda Motor Co. v. Oberg, 512 U.S. 415 (1994)	7–2	Writing for the Court, Justice Stevens struck down Oregon's limitation on judicial review

of jury awards of punitive damages as a violation of due process. Justice Ginsburg, joined by Chief Justice Rehnquist, dissented.

CASE	VOTE	RULING

Sandin v. Conner, 515 U.S. 472 (1995) — 5–4 — Writing for the majority, Chief Justice Rehnquist rejected a prison inmate's claim that officials deprived him of procedural due process when they refused to allow him to present witnesses during a disciplinary hearing that resulted in his isolated confinement for alleged misconduct. Justices Breyer, Ginsburg, Souter, and Stevens dissented.

Bennis v. Michigan, 516 U.S. 442 (1996) — 5–4 — Writing for the majority, Chief Justice Rehnquist rejected the claim that the government violates due process and the Fifth Amendment's taking clause when it undertakes the forfeiture of an innocent person's property, which was used in an illegal activity. Justices Breyer, Kennedy, Souter, and Stevens dissented.

Cooper v. Oklahoma, 517 U.S. 348 (1996) — 9–0 — Justice Stevens struck down Oklahoma's law presuming that a defendant is competent to stand trial unless proven incompetent by "clear and convincing evidence." Finding that the state's presumption and procedures violated "fundamental fairness" and due process, Justice Stevens reaffirmed that states may presume a defendant's competence and require proof of incompetence based on the lower standard of "the preponderance of the evidence."

United States v. Armstrong, 517 U.S. 456 (1996) — 8–1 — Writing for the Court, Chief Justice Rehnquist reversed a lower federal court's holding that several black defendants, charged with drug trafficking, had met the threshold requirement for arguing that federal prosecutors engaged in the selective prosecution of blacks and for requiring the government to turn over records on its prosecutorial policies and practices. Their attorneys presented evidence that all the defendants in twenty-four crack cocaine cases resolved in 1991 were black. However, the chief justice held that lower courts should defer to the government's interests in prosecutorial discretion and that under the federal rules of evidence and the equal protection component of the Fifth Amendment's due process clause, claimants must demonstrate that federal prosecution policy "had a discriminatory effect and that it was motivated by a discriminatory purpose."

(continues)

■ The Development of Law
*Other Recent Rulings on Substantive and Procedural
Due Process (continued)*

CASE	VOTE	RULING
BMW of North America v. Gore, 517 U.S. 559 (1996)	5–4	Writing for the Court, Justice Stevens held that a punitive damages award of 500 times the amount of the actual damages was "grossly excessive" and violated the Fourteenth Amendment's due process clause. Chief Justice Rehnquist and Justices Scalia, Ginsburg, and Thomas dissented.
Montana v. Egelhoff, 518 U.S. 37 (1996)	5–4	Writing for a plurality, Justice Scalia held that due process was not violated by a Montana law instructing juries that an intoxicated condition should not be considered in determining the mental state of a person accused of deliberate homicide.
Young v. Harper, 520 U.S. 143 (1997)	9–0	Writing for the Court, Justice Thomas held that the summary reinstitutionalization of a state prisoner who had been released under a preparole program aimed at reducing prison overcrowding, deprived him of liberty without the due process of law under the Fourteenth Amendment and that the prisoner was entitled to the procedural protections for parole hearings set forth in *Morrissey v. Brewer*, 408 U.S. 471 (1972).
Kansas v. Hendricks, 521 U.S. 346 (1997)	5–4	Upheld Kansas's law providing for the involuntary civil commitment of sexual predators, even after they have served their prison sentences, over due process objections. Agreeing with that part of the Court's analysis, Justices Breyer, Ginsburg, Souter, and Stevens dissented on other grounds.
Sacramento County v. Lewis, 523 U.S. 833 (1998)	9–0	Held that police who cause accidents that kill even innocent bystanders during high-speed pursuit of criminal suspects are not liable unless their actions "shock the conscience." As Justice Souter explained, "Only a purpose to cause harm unrelated to the legitimate object of arrest will satisfy the element of arbitrary conduct shocking to the conscience, necessary for a due process violation."

CASE	VOTE	RULING
Chicago v. Morales, 527 U.S. 41 (1999)	6–3	In an opinion for the Court joined only by a plurality, Justice Stevens held that an

ordinance prohibiting "criminal street gang members" from loitering in public places was impermissibly vague in defining "loitering" and, therefore, failed to give citizens adequate notice of what was forbidden. Justices Scalia and Thomas filed dissenting opinions; Chief Justice Rehnquist joined the latter's dissent.

| *Troxel v. Granville,* 530 U.S. 57 (2000) | 6–3 | Reaffirming that the Fourteenth Amendment has a substantive component pro- |

viding "heightened protection against governmental interference with certain fundamental rights and liberty interests," including those of parents to make decisions concerning the care of their children, the Court held that Washington's statute allowing "any person" "at any time" to petition for visitation rights infringed on parents' "fundamental right to rear children."

| *Cooper Industries, Inc. v. Leatherman Tool Group, Inc.* 532 U.S. 424 (2001) | 8–1 | Held that due process requires federal appellate courts to use a de novo, rather than an abuse of discretion, standard |

when reviewing for "grossly excessive" damage awards. A jury awarded Leatherman Tool Group $50,000 in compensatory damages and $4.5 million dollars in punitive damages for Cooper Industries' unfair competition and false advertising. Writing for the Court, Justice Stevens reasoned that de novo review was appropriate because determining whether damages awards are excessive requires courts to determine the reasonableness of the award based on the facts in each case. Justice Ginsburg dissented.

| *Dusenbery v. United States,* 534 U.S. 161 (2002) | 5–4 | Writing for the Court, Chief Justice Rehnquist upheld the forfeiture of private property |

of a prison inmate, who was served notice by certified mail and in the absence of a response to the notice of forfeiture, and held that due process does not require "actual notice," only "an attempt to provide actual notice" of forfeiture. Justices Ginsburg, Stevens, Souter, and Breyer dissented.

(continues)

■ The Development of Law
*Other Recent Rulings on Substantive and Procedural
Due Process (continued)*

CASE	VOTE	RULING
Kansas v. Crane, 534 U.S. 407 (2002)	7–2	In *Kansas v. Hendricks,* 521 U.S. 346 (1997) (excerpted in this chapter) the Court

upheld the state's Sexually Violent Predator Act, authorizing the continued civil commitment of convicted sexual offenders who have a "mental abnormality or personality disorder" that renders them dangerous to themselves or others. Subsequently, Kansas sought the continued commitment of Michael Crane, but the state supreme court ruled that due process requires a finding that the defendant "cannot control his dangerous behavior." Justice Breyer held that there must be a hearing and finding that a dangerous sexual offender lacks self-control, but also emphasized that under Hendricks there is no narrow or technical meaning of "lack of control" and that that depends on the circumstances and individual psychiatric evaluations. Justices Scalia and Thomas dissented.

CASE	VOTE	RULING
Connecticut Department of Public Safety v. Doe, 538 U.S. 1 (2003)	9–0	Writing for a unanimous Court, Chief Justice Rehnquist held that due process is not violated by states' requiring

convicted sex offenders to register personal information, including addresses and photographs, which are then posted on a website, because the registry requirement is based on a prior conviction, not the sex offender's current dangerousness.

CASE	VOTE	RULING
State Farm Mutual Automobile Insurance v. Campbell, 538 U.S. 408 (2003)	6–3	Writing for the Court, Justice Kennedy held that punitive damage awards must be proportionate to the wrong

committed and that "the wealth of a defendant cannot justify an otherwise unconstitutional punitive damages award." Here, the majority overturned a $145 million jury award against State Farm that was 145 times the amount of the injury as "an irrational and arbitrary deprivation of the property of the defendant." Justice Kennedy emphasized that damage awards greater than a nine-to-one ratio were constitutionally suspect. Justices Scalia, Thomas, and Ginsburg dissented.

CASE	VOTE	RULING
Demore v. Kim, 538 U.S. 510 (2003)	5–4	Writing for the Court, Chief Justice Rehnquist upheld a 1996 federal law authorizing

the detention of immigrants, including permanent residents or "green card holders," who have committed certain crimes and served their sentences while the government decides whether to deport them. The majority rejected the due process claim that they are entitled to a hearing on whether they would jump bail or posed a danger to society. In the chief justice's words, "Congress may make rules as to aliens that would be unacceptable if applied to citizens." Justice Souter, joined by Justices Stevens and Ginsburg, filed an opinion in part concurring and dissenting that endorsed the substantive and procedural due process claim. In a separate opinion, Justice Breyer concurred and dissented in part.

Overton v. Bazetta, 539 U.S. 126 (2003)	9–0	Held that prison regulations limiting inmate visitations do not violate freedom of association or substantive due process, and are rationally related to penal interests.

Sell v. United States, 539 U.S. 166 (2003)	6–3	Writing for the Court, Justice Breyer held that antipsychotic drugs may be administered to

a mentally ill defendant without his or her consent if the forced medication (1) is necessary to an "important governmental interest," (2) significantly furthers that interest, (3) is medically necessary without a less intrusive alternative, and (4) is medically appropriate.

Lawrence v. Texas, 539 U.S. 558 (2003)	6–3	Writing for the Court, Justice Kennedy invalidated Texas's law criminalizing homosexual sodomy; the case is excerpted in Chapter 11.

Deck v. Mississippi, 544 U.S. 622 (2005)	7–2	Writing for the Court, Justice Breyer held that the shackling of a defendant during the

sentencing phase of a capital trial is inherently prejudicial and runs afoul of due process, unless the use of visible shackles is justified by an "essential state interest." Justices Scalia and Thomas dissented.

(continues)

■ The Development of Law
Other Recent Rulings on Substantive and Procedural
Due Process (continued)

CASE	VOTE	RULING
Town of Castle Rock v. Gonzales, 545 U.S. 748 (2005)	7–2	Writing for the Court, Justice Scalia ruled that due process does not protect everything deemed to be a governmental

"benefit." Jessica Gonzales filed for damages because the town's police failed to enforce restraining orders and argued that that was an entitlement and governmental benefit. Justices Stevens and Ginsburg dissented.

Jones v. Flowers, 547 U.S. 220 (2006)	5–3	Writing for the Court, Chief Justice Roberts held that Arkansas violated due process in

selling private property after a notice to the property owner was returned unclaimed and then took no further steps to notify the owner of the forfeiture. Justice Thomas dissented and was joined by Justices Scalia and Kennedy.

Philip Morris USA v. Williams, 549 U.S. 346 (2007)	5–4	Writing for the Court, Justice Breyer reaffirmed *BMW v. Gore and State Farm,* holding that "grossly excessive" puni-

tive damages run afoul of the due process clause. Here, the majority held that the roughly 100-to-1 ratio of the $79.5 million award to a smoker was a "grossly excessive" punitive award for injuries inflicted on strangers to the litigation. Justices Stevens, Thomas, and Ginsburg each filed dissenting opinions, which Justice Scalia joined.

Caperton v. A.T. Massey Coal Co., Inc., 556 U.S. 868 (2009)	5–4	By a five-to-four vote, the Court held that it is unconstitutional for a state supreme court justice to sit on a

case involving the financial interests of a major donor to the justice's election campaign. Justice Kennedy held that West Virginia Supreme Court Chief Justice Brent Benjamin should have recused himself from a case that overturned a $50 million verdict against a company headed by a man who contributed $3 million to the justice's election. The failure to do so ran afoul of the due process clause which incorporates the common-law

CASE	VOTE	RULING

rule requiring recusal when a judge has "a direct, personal, substantial, pecuniary interest" in a case and, according to the Court's precedents, recusal is required where "the probability of actual bias on the part of the judge or decision-maker is too high to be constitutionally tolerable."

District Attorney's Office for Third District v. Osborne, 557 U.S. 52 (2009)	5–4	Alaska is one of three states that does not allow postconviction access to DNA and other biological evidence in

order to challenge a defendant's conviction. Chief Justice Roberts rejected a due process challenge and held that it was up to the states and Congress to decide who has a right to testing that might prove innocence. Justices Stevens, Souter, Ginsburg, and Breyer dissented.

Skinner v. Switzer, 562 U.S. 521 (2011)	6–3	Distinguishing the ruling in *District Attorney's Office v. Osborne,* 557 U.S. 52 (2009), the

Court held that Texas's denial of all DNA evidence, specifically unused evidence at trial, to a death row inmate violated procedural due process and thus permits Section 1983 civil rights suits. The dissenters—Justices Kennedy, Thomas, and Alito—protested that the ruling provided a "road map" for state inmates to reopen DNA-access claims after having lost in habeas corpus appeals, and therefore opened the "floodgate" for such lawsuits.

Turner v. Rogers, 564 U.S. 431 (2011)	5–4	Writing for the Court, Justice Breyer held that due process does not require

states to provide attorneys for indigents in civil proceedings, even if they may result in incarceration for willful contempt in repeatedly failing to make child-support payments. However, the majority ruled that in such proceedings states should provide "substitute procedural safeguards," such as (1) notice to the defendant that his ability to pay is a critical issue in contempt proceedings; (2) the use of a form to elicit relevant financial information; (3) an opportunity at the hearing to respond to statements and questions about financial status; and (4) an express finding by the court that the defendant has the ability to pay. Chief Justice Roberts and Justices Scalia, Thomas, and Alito dissented.

(continues)

■ The Development of Law
Other Recent Rulings on Substantive and Procedural
Due Process (continued)

CASE	VOTE	RULING
FCC v. Fox Television Stations, Inc., 567 U.S. 239 (2012)	8–0	Writing for the Court, Justice Kennedy held that the FCC violated the Due Process Clause

when it sanctioned broadcasters for "fleeting indecent" broadcasts without providing them with fair notice of the Commission's change in policy regarding "fleeting expletives" on the airways. Justice Sotomayor did not participate in the decision. It thus avoided the constitutional challenge.

| *Kerry v. Din,* 135 S.Ct. 2128 (2015) | 5–4 | Fauzia Din, a naturalized U.S. citizen, sued the government for violating her |

constitutional rights after her husband was denied a visa. Din claimed that her due process rights were violated because the government interfered with her "liberty interest in her marriage." Din's husband had been found ineligible for a visa because he was once a member of the Taliban and those involved in "terrorist activities" are barred from entry. Justice Scalia, writing for a plurality, with only Chief Justice Roberts and Justice Thomas joining, held that Din was deprived of "life, liberty or property" when her husband was denied a visa. Concurring, Justice Kennedy, joined by Justice Alito, concluded that there was no need to decide whether Din had a protected liberty interest because, even assuming she did, the notice she received satisfied due process. Justices Ginsburg, Breyer, Sotomayor, and Kagan dissented.

| *Johnson v. United States,* 135 S.Ct. 2551 (2015) | 8–1 | Writing for the Court, Justice Scalia held that a provision of the Armed |

Career Criminal Act was too vague to survive due process analysis and, hence, rejected the government's attempt to obtain an enhanced sentence for Samuel Johnson, who had pled guilty to being a felon in possession of a firearm. Justice Alito dissented.

CASE	VOTE	RULING
Nelson v. Colorado, 137 S.Ct. 1249 (2017)	7–1	Writing for the Court, Justice Ginsburg held that Colorado's Exoneration

Act, governing refunds of the costs, fees, and restitution of defendants who were tried and convicted but later acquitted or not retried after the reversal of their convictions, violated procedural due process. Justices Thomas dissented, and Judge Gorsuch did not participate.

BMW of North America v. Gore
517 U.S. 559, 116 S.Ct. 1589 (1996)

Dr. Ira Gore Jr., purchased a BMW sedan for $40,750.88. After driving the car for about nine months, he took it to "Slick Finish" to make it look "snazzier than it normally would appear." Mr. Slick detected evidence that the car had been repainted. Convinced that he had been cheated, Gore sued BMW of North America (BMW), alleging that the failure to disclose that the car had been repainted constituted suppression of a material fact. He asked for $500,000 in compensatory and punitive damages. During the trial, BMW acknowledged that it had a policy of selling damaged new cars as "new" if the cost of repairing them was less than 3 percent of their retail price. Because the $601.37 cost of repainting Gore's car was only about 1.5 percent of its suggested retail price, BMW did not disclose the damage or repair. Gore countered that his repainted car was worth less than a car that had not been refinished. To prove his actual damages of $4,000, he relied on the testimony of a former BMW dealer who estimated that the value of a repainted BMW was approximately 10 percent less than the value of a new car that had not been damaged and repaired. To support his claim for punitive damages, Dr. Gore introduced evidence that since 1983 BMW had sold 983 refinished cars as new, including fourteen in Alabama, without disclosing that the cars had been repainted at a cost of more than $300 per vehicle. Using the actual damage estimate of $4,000 per vehicle, Gore argued that a punitive award of $4 million would provide an appropriate penalty for selling approximately 1,000 cars for more than they were worth. The jury returned a verdict finding BMW liable for compensatory damages of $4,000. In addition, the jury assessed $4 million in punitive damages, based on a determination that the nondisclosure policy constituted "gross, oppressive or malicious" fraud. On appeal, the Alabama Supreme Court rejected BMW's claim that the award exceeded the constitutionally permissible amount, but ruled that the jury improperly computed the amount of punitive damages by multiplying Gore's compensatory damages by the number of similar sales in other jurisdictions. The court held that "a constitutionally reasonable punitive damages award in this case is $2,000,000." BMW appealed that decision to the Supreme Court.

The state supreme court's decision was reversed by a 5–4 vote. Justice Stevens delivered the opinion for the Court. Justice Breyer filed a concurring opinion. Justice Scalia filed a dissenting opinion, which Justice Thomas joined. Justice Ginsburg filed a dissenting opinion, which Chief Justice Rehnquist joined. On remand, the state supreme court reduced the punitive award to $50,000.

■ ■ ■

☐ *Justice STEVENS delivered the opinion of the Court.*

The Due Process Clause of the Fourteenth Amendment prohibits a State from imposing a "grossly excessive" punishment on a tortfeasor. *TXO Production Corp. v. Alliance Resources Corp.*, 509 U.S. 443 (1993). The wrongdoing involved in this case was the decision by a national distributor of automobiles not to advise its dealers, and hence their customers, of predelivery damage to new cars when the cost of repair amounted to less than 3 percent of the car's suggested retail price. The question presented is whether a $2 million punitive damages award exceeds the constitutional limit. . . .

Punitive damages may properly be imposed to further a State's legitimate interests in punishing unlawful conduct and deterring its repetition. *Gertz v. Robert Welch, Inc.*, 418 U.S. 323 (1974). In our federal system, States necessarily have considerable flexibility in determining the level of punitive damages that they will allow in different classes of cases and in any particular case. Most States that authorize exemplary damages afford the jury similar latitude, requiring only that the damages awarded be reasonably necessary to vindicate the State's legitimate interests in punishment and deterrence. Only when an award can fairly be categorized as "grossly excessive" in relation to these interests does it enter the zone of arbitrariness that violates the Due Process Clause of the Fourteenth Amendment. For that reason, the federal excessiveness inquiry appropriately begins with an identification of the state interests that a punitive award is designed to serve. We therefore focus our attention first on the scope of Alabama's legitimate interests in punishing BMW and deterring it from future misconduct.

No one doubts that a State may protect its citizens by prohibiting deceptive trade practices and by requiring automobile distributors to disclose presale repairs that affect the value of a new car. But the States need not, and in fact do not, provide such protection in a uniform manner. Some States rely on the judicial process to formulate and enforce an appropriate disclosure requirement by applying principles of contract and tort law. Other States have enacted various forms of legislation that define the disclosure obligations of automobile manufacturers, distributors, and dealers. The result is a patchwork of rules representing the diverse policy judgments of lawmakers in 50 States. . . .

We think it follows from these principles of state sovereignty and comity that a State may not impose economic sanctions on violators of its laws with the intent of changing the tortfeasors' lawful conduct in other States. Before this Court Dr. Gore argued that the large punitive damages award was necessary to induce BMW to change the nationwide policy that it adopted in 1983. But by attempting to alter BMW's nationwide policy, Alabama would be infringing on the policy choices of other States. To avoid such encroachment, the economic penalties that a State such as Alabama inflicts on those who transgress its laws, whether the penalties take the form of legislatively authorized fines or judicially imposed punitive damages, must be supported by the State's interest in protecting its own consumers and its own economy. Alabama may insist that BMW adhere to a particular disclosure policy in that State. Alabama does not have the power, however, to punish BMW for conduct that was lawful where it occurred and that had no impact on Alabama or its residents. Nor may Alabama impose sanctions on BMW in order to deter conduct that is lawful in other jurisdictions. . . .

When the scope of the interest in punishment and deterrence that an Alabama court may appropriately consider is properly limited, it is apparent—for reasons that we shall now address—that this award is grossly excessive.

Elementary notions of fairness enshrined in our constitutional juris-prudence dictate that a person receive fair notice not only of the conduct that will subject him to punishment, but also of the severity of the penalty that a State may impose. Three guideposts, each of which indicates that BMW did not receive adequate notice of the magnitude of the sanction that Alabama might impose for adhering to the nondisclosure policy adopted in 1983, lead us to the conclusion that the $2 million award against BMW is grossly excessive: the degree of reprehensibility of the nondisclo-sure; the disparity between the harm or potential harm suffered by Dr. Gore and his punitive damages award; and the difference between this remedy and the civil penalties authorized or imposed in comparable cases. We discuss these considerations in turn.

Perhaps the most important indicium of the reasonableness of a punitive damages award is the degree of reprehensibility of the defendant's conduct. This principle reflects the accepted view that some wrongs are more blame-worthy than others. In *TXO*, both the West Virginia Supreme Court and the Justices of this Court placed special emphasis on the principle that punitive damages may not be "grossly out of proportion to the severity of the offense."

In this case, none of the aggravating factors associated with particularly reprehensible conduct is present. The harm BMW inflicted on Dr. Gore was purely economic in nature. The presale refinishing of the car had no effect on its performance or safety features, or even its appearance for at least nine months after his purchase. BMW's conduct evinced no indiffer-ence to or reckless disregard for the health and safety of others. . . .

Finally, the record in this case discloses no deliberate false statements, acts of affirmative misconduct, or concealment of evidence of improper motive. . . .

That conduct is sufficiently reprehensible to give rise to tort liability, and even a modest award of exemplary damages does not establish the high degree of culpability that warrants a substantial punitive damages award. Because this case exhibits none of the circumstances ordinarily associated with egregiously improper conduct, we are persuaded that BMW's conduct was not sufficiently reprehensible to warrant imposition of a $2 million exemplary damages award.

The second and perhaps most commonly cited indicium of an unreasonable or excessive punitive damages award is its ratio to the actual harm inflicted on the plaintiff. The principle that exemplary damages must bear a reasonable relationship to compensatory damages has a long pedigree. . . .

The $2 million in punitive damages awarded to Dr. Gore by the Alabama Supreme Court is 500 times the amount of his actual harm as determined by the jury. Moreover, there is no suggestion that Dr. Gore or any other BMW purchaser was threatened with any additional potential harm by BMW's nondisclosure policy. . . .

Comparing the punitive damages award and the civil or criminal penalties that could be imposed for comparable misconduct provides a third indicium of excessiveness. . . . In this case the $2 million economic sanction imposed on BMW is substantially greater than the statutory fines available in Alabama and elsewhere for similar malfeasance.

The maximum civil penalty authorized by the Alabama Legislature for a violation of its Deceptive Trade Practices Act is $2,000; other States authorize more severe sanctions, with the maxima ranging from $5,000 to $10,000. . . . Moreover, at the time BMW's policy was first challenged, there does not appear to have been any judicial decision in Alabama or elsewhere indicating that application of that policy might give rise to such severe punishment.

The sanction imposed in this case cannot be justified on the ground that it was necessary to deter future misconduct without considering whether less drastic remedies could be expected to achieve that goal. The fact that a multimillion dollar penalty prompted a change in policy sheds no light on the question whether a lesser deterrent would have adequately protected the interests of Alabama consumers. In the absence of a history of noncompliance with known statutory requirements, there is no basis for assuming that a more modest sanction would not have been sufficient to motivate full compliance with the disclosure requirement imposed by the Alabama Supreme Court in this case.

[W]e of course accept the Alabama courts' view that the state interest in protecting its citizens from deceptive trade practices justifies a sanction in addition to the recovery of compensatory damages. We cannot, however, accept the conclusion of the Alabama Supreme Court that BMW's conduct was sufficiently egregious to justify a punitive sanction that is tantamount to a severe criminal penalty.

The fact that BMW is a large corporation rather than an impecunious individual does not diminish its entitlement to fair notice of the demands that the several States impose on the conduct of its business. Indeed, its status as an active participant in the national economy implicates the federal interest in preventing individual States from imposing undue burdens on interstate commerce. While each State has ample power to protect its own consumers, none may use the punitive damages deterrent as a means of imposing its regulatory policies on the entire Nation.

[W]e are not prepared to draw a bright line marking the limits of a constitutionally acceptable punitive damages award. [H]owever, we are fully convinced that the grossly excessive award imposed in this case transcends the constitutional limit. . . .

☐ *Justice SCALIA, with whom Justice THOMAS joins, dissenting.*

Today we see the latest manifestation of this Court's recent and increasingly insistent "concern about punitive damages that 'run wild.'" *Pacific Mut. Life Ins. Co. v. Haslip*, 499 U.S. 1 (1991). Since the Constitution does not make that concern any of our business, the Court's activities in this area are an unjustified incursion into the province of state governments. . . .

I do not regard the Fourteenth Amendment's Due Process Clause as a secret repository of substantive guarantees against "unfairness"—neither the unfairness of an excessive civil compensatory award, nor the unfairness of an "unreasonable" punitive award. What the Fourteenth Amendment's procedural guarantee assures is an opportunity to contest the reasonableness of a damages judgment in state court; but there is no federal guarantee a damages award actually be reasonable. . . .

The most significant aspects of today's decision—the identification of a "substantive due process" right against a "grossly excessive" award, and the concomitant assumption of ultimate authority to decide anew a matter of "reasonableness" resolved in lower court proceedings—are of course not new. *Haslip* and *TXO* revived the notion . . . that the measure of civil punishment poses a question of constitutional dimension to be answered by this Court. Neither of those cases, however, nor any of the precedents upon which they relied, actually took the step of declaring a punitive award unconstitutional simply because it was "too big."

At the time of adoption of the Fourteenth Amendment, it was well understood that punitive damages represent the assessment by the jury, as the voice of the community, of the measure of punishment the defendant deserved. Today's decision, though dressed up as a legal opinion, is really no more than a disagreement with the community's sense of indignation or outrage expressed in the punitive award of the Alabama jury, as reduced by the State Supreme Court. . . .

One might understand the Court's eagerness to enter this field, rather than leave it with the state legislatures, if it had something useful to say. In fact, however, its opinion provides virtually no guidance to legislatures, and to state and federal courts, as to what a "constitutionally proper" level of punitive damages might be. . . .

[T]he Court identifies "three guideposts" that lead it to the conclusion that the award in this case is excessive: degree of reprehensibility, ratio between punitive award and plaintiff's actual harm, and legislative sanctions provided for comparable misconduct. The legal significance of these "guideposts" is nowhere explored, but their necessary effect is to establish federal standards governing the hitherto exclusively state law of damages. Apparently (though it is by no means clear) all three federal "guideposts" can be overridden if "necessary to deter future misconduct"—a loophole that will encourage state reviewing courts to uphold awards as necessary for the adequat[e] protect[ion]" of state consumers. By effectively requiring state reviewing courts to concoct rationalizations—whether within the "guideposts" or through the loophole—to justify the intuitive punitive reactions of state juries, the Court accords neither category of institution the respect it deserves.

Of course it will not be easy for the States to comply with this new federal law of damages, no matter how willing they are to do so. In truth, the "guideposts" mark a road to nowhere; they provide no real guidance at all. . . . For the foregoing reasons, I respectfully dissent.

☐ *Justice GINSBURG, with whom THE CHIEF JUSTICE joins, dissenting.*

The Court, I am convinced, unnecessarily and unwisely ventures into territory traditionally within the States' domain, and does so in the face of reform measures recently adopted or currently under consideration in legislative arenas. The Alabama Supreme Court, in this case, endeavored to follow this Court's prior instructions; and, more recently, Alabama's highest court has installed further controls on awards of punitive damages. I would therefore leave the state court's judgment undisturbed, and resist unnecessary intrusion into an area dominantly of state concern. . . .

County of Sacramento v. Lewis
523 U.S. 833, 118 S.Ct. 1708 (1998)

On May 22, 1990, James Smith, a Sacramento County sheriff's deputy, along with another officer, Murray Stapp, responded to a call to break up a fight. Upon returning to his patrol car, Stapp saw a motorcycle approaching at high speed. It was operated by Brian Willard and carried Philip Lewis as a passenger. Neither had anything to do with the fight that prompted the call to the police. Stapp turned on his rotating lights, yelled to the boys to stop, and pulled his patrol car closer to Smith's, attempting to pen the motorcycle in. Instead, Willard slowly maneuvered the cycle between the two police cars and sped off. Smith immediately began pursuit at high speed. They wove in and out of oncoming traffic, reaching speeds up to 100 miles an hour. The chase ended after the motorcycle tipped. By the time Smith slammed on his brakes, Willard was out of the way, but Lewis was not. The patrol car skidded into him at 40 miles an hour, propelling him some 70 feet down the road. Lewis was pronounced dead at the scene.

Lewis's parents sued the Sacramento County Sheriff's Department and Deputy Smith, alleging a deprivation of Philip Lewis's Fourteenth Amendment substantive due process right to life. The district court granted summary judgment for Smith, reasoning that even if he violated the Constitution, he was entitled to qualified immunity. The Court of Appeals for the Ninth Circuit reversed and the city appealed to the Supreme Court which granted review and reversed the appellate court.

The Court's decision was unanimous and opinion delivered by Justice Souter. Concurring opinions were filed by Chief Justice Rehnquist and Justices Breyer, Kennedy, Scalia, and Stevens.

■ ■ ■

☐ *Justice SOUTER delivered the opinion of the Court.*

The issue in this case is whether a police officer violates the Fourteenth Amendment's guarantee of substantive due process by causing death through deliberate or reckless indifference to life in a high-speed automobile chase aimed at apprehending a suspected offender. We answer no, and hold that in such circumstances only a purpose to cause harm unrelated to the legitimate object of arrest will satisfy the element of arbitrary conduct shocking to the conscience, necessary for a due process violation. . . .

Our prior cases have held the provision that "no State shall . . . deprive any person of life, liberty, or property, without due process of law," U.S. Const., Amdt. 14, Sec. 1, to "guarantee more than fair process," *Washington v. Glucksberg*, [521 U.S. 702] (1997), and to cover a substantive sphere as well, "barring certain government actions regardless of the fairness of the procedures used to implement them," *Daniels v. Williams*, 474 U.S. 327 (1986). . . .

Since the time of our early explanations of due process, we have understood the core of the concept to be protection against arbitrary action . . . *Hurtado v. California*, 110 U.S. 516 (1884).

We have emphasized time and again that "the touchstone of due process is protection of the individual against arbitrary action of government," *Wolff v. McDonnell*, 418 U.S. 539 (1974), whether the fault lies in a denial of fundamental procedural fairness, or in the exercise of power without any reasonable justification in the service of a legitimate governmental objective. While due process protection in the substantive sense limits what the government may do in both its legislative, see, e.g., *Griswold v. Connecticut*, 381 U.S. 479 (1965), and its executive capacities, see, e.g., *Rochin v. California*, 342 U.S. 165 (1952), criteria to identify what is fatally arbitrary differ depending on whether it is legislation or a specific act of a governmental officer that is at issue.

Our cases dealing with abusive executive action have repeatedly emphasized that only the most egregious official conduct can be said to be "arbitrary in the constitutional sense," *Collins v. Harker Heights*, 503 U.S. [112 (1992)], thereby recognizing the point made in different circumstances by Chief Justice MARSHALL, "that it is a constitution we are expounding," *McCulloch v. Maryland*, 4 Wheat. 316 (1819). . . .

To this end, for half a century now we have spoken of the cognizable level of executive abuse of power as that which shocks the conscience. We first put the test this way in *Rochin v. California*, where we found the forced pumping of a suspect's stomach enough to offend due process as conduct "that shocks the conscience" and violates the "decencies of civilized conduct." In the intervening years we have repeatedly adhered to *Rochin*'s benchmark. . . .

It should not be surprising that the constitutional concept of conscience-shocking duplicates no traditional category of common-law fault, but rather points clearly away from liability, or clearly toward it, only at the ends of the tort law's spectrum of culpability. Thus, we have made it clear that the due process guarantee does not entail a body of constitutional law imposing liability whenever someone cloaked with state authority causes harm. . . .

Whether the point of the conscience-shocking is reached when injuries are produced with culpability falling within the middle range, following from something more than negligence but "less than intentional conduct, such as recklessness or 'gross negligence'" is a matter for closer calls. . . .

Rules of due process are not, however, subject to mechanical application in unfamiliar territory. Deliberate indifference that shocks in one environment may not be so patently egregious in another, and our concern with preserving the constitutional proportions of substantive due process demands an exact analysis of circumstances before any abuse of power is condemned as conscience-shocking. What we have said of due process in the procedural sense is just as true here:

> The phrase [due process of law] formulates a concept less rigid and more fluid than those envisaged in other specific and particular provisions of the Bill of Rights. Its application is less a matter of rule. Asserted denial is to be tested by an appraisal of the totality of facts in a given case. That which may, in one setting, constitute a denial of fundamental fairness, shocking to the universal sense of justice, may, in other circumstances, and in the light of other considerations, fall short of such denial. *Betts v. Brady*, 316 U.S. 455 (1942).

Thus, attention to the markedly different circumstances of normal pretrial custody and high-speed law enforcement chases shows why the deliberate indifference that shocks in the one case is less egregious in the other (even assuming that it makes sense to speak of indifference as deliberate in the case of sudden pursuit). As the very term "deliberate indifference" implies, the standard is sensibly employed only when actual deliberation is practical, and in the custodial situation of a prison, forethought about an inmate's welfare is not only feasible but obligatory under a regime that incapacitates a prisoner to exercise ordinary responsibility for his own welfare. . . .

But just as the description of the custodial prison situation shows how deliberate indifference can rise to a constitutionally shocking level, so too does it suggest why indifference may well not be enough for liability in the different circumstances of a case like this one. We have, indeed, found that deliberate indifference does not suffice for constitutional liability (albeit under the Eighth Amendment) even in prison circumstances when a prisoner's claim arises not from normal custody but from response to a violent disturbance. . . .

Like prison officials facing a riot, the police on an occasion calling for fast action have obligations that tend to tug against each other. Their duty is to restore and maintain lawful order, while not exacerbating disorder more than necessary to do their jobs. They are supposed to act decisively and to show restraint at the same moment, and their decisions have to be made "in haste, under pressure, and frequently without the luxury of a second chance." A police officer deciding whether to give chase must balance on one hand the need to stop a suspect and show that flight from the law is no way to freedom, and, on the other, the high-speed threat to everyone within stopping range, be they suspects, their passengers, other drivers, or bystanders.

To recognize a substantive due process violation in these circumstances when only mid-level fault has been shown would be to forget that liability for deliberate indifference to inmate welfare rests upon the luxury enjoyed by prison officials of having time to make unhurried judgments, upon the chance for repeated reflection, largely uncomplicated by the pulls of competing obligations. . . . Just as a purpose to cause harm is needed for Eighth Amendment liability in a riot case, so it ought to be needed for Due Process liability in a pursuit case. Accordingly, we hold that high-speed chases with no intent to harm suspects physically or to worsen their legal plight do not give rise to liability under the Fourteenth Amendment, redressible by an action under Section 1983. . . .

The judgment below is accordingly reversed.

☐ *Justice SCALIA, with whom Justice THOMAS joins, concurring in the judgment.*

Today's opinion gives the lie to those cynics who claim that changes in this Court's jurisprudence are attributable to changes in the Court's membership. It proves that the changes are attributable to nothing but the passage of time (not much time, at that), plus application of the ancient maxim, "That was then, this is now."

Just last Term, in *Washington v. Glucksberg*, the Court specifically rejected the method of substantive-due-process analysis employed by Justice SOUTER in his concurrence in that case, which is the very same method employed by Justice SOUTER in his opinion for the Court today. . . .

Today, so to speak, the stone that the builders had rejected has become the foundation-stone of our substantive-due-process jurisprudence. The atavistic methodology that Justice SOUTER announces for the Court is the very same methodology that the Court called atavistic when it was proffered by Justice SOUTER in *Glucksberg*. In fact, if anything, today's opinion is even more of a throw-back to highly subjective substantive-due-process methodologies than the concurrence in *Glucksberg* was. Whereas the latter said merely that substantive due process prevents "arbitrary impositions" and "purposeless restraints" (without any objective criterion as to what is arbitrary or purposeless), today's opinion resuscitates the *ne plus ultra*, the Napoleon Brandy, the Mahatma Ghandi, the Celophane of subjectivity, th' ol' "shocks-the-conscience" test. According to today's opinion, this is the measure of arbitrariness when what is at issue is executive rather than legislative action. *Glucksberg*, of course, rejected "shocks-the-conscience," just as it rejected the less subjective "arbitrary action" test. A 1992 executive-action case, *Collins v. Harker Heights*, which had paid lip-service to "shocks-the-conscience," was cited in *Glucksberg* for the proposition that "our Nation's history, legal traditions, and practices . . . provide the crucial 'guideposts for responsible decisionmaking.'" In fact, even before *Glucksberg* we had characterized the last "shocks-the-conscience" claim to come before us as "nothing more than [a] bald assertion," and had rejected it on the objective ground that the petitioner "failed to proffer any historical, textual, or controlling precedential support for [his alleged due process right], and we decline to fashion a new due process right out of thin air." *Carlisle v. United States*, 517 U.S. 416 (1996).

Respondents provide no textual or historical support for this alleged due process right, and, as in *Carlisle*, I would "decline to fashion a new due process right out of thin air." Nor have respondents identified any precedential support. . . .

I would reverse the judgment of the Ninth Circuit, not on the ground that petitioners have failed to shock my still, soft voice within, but on the ground that respondents offer no textual or historical support for their alleged due process right. Accordingly, I concur in the judgment of the Court.

5

FREEDOM OF EXPRESSION AND ASSOCIATION

A connection between freedom of speech, press, and association and the exigencies of a self-governing society was acknowledged by the colonists and the Framers of the Constitution and Bill of Rights. Yet in the seventeenth and eighteenth centuries those freedoms were more circumscribed than today and were still emerging from a protracted struggle that began in England in the Middle Ages.

Government censorship stems from the 1275 enactment of *De Scandalis Magnatum*, imposing penalties for any false talk about the king.[1] The law punished what a later amendment in 1559 termed "seditious words" (criticism of the government subject to criminal penalties) for contributing to public disorder and lawlessness. In the sixteenth and seventeenth centuries, censorship expanded with the enforcement of *Scandalum Magnatum* by the King's Council, which sat in the "starred chambre" at Westminster and became infamously known as the Star Chamber. The Star Chamber was especially merciless in cases such as that of the *Trial of William Prynn*.[2] Prynn had published a book expressing disdain for actors and acting, which was viewed as an attack on the queen, who had recently appeared in a play, and, therefore, as seditious libel against the government. Prynn was fined £10,000, sentenced to life imprisonment, branded on the forehead, and had his nose slit and his ears cut off!

The Star Chamber left a legacy of human tragedy and an imprint on the English heritage from which the drafters of the Bill of Rights drew their principles of free government. The Star Chamber was abolished in 1641, but its precedents continued to be applied by common-reasons, Madison not only rejected the application of Blackstonian common-law principles to freedom of speech and press but proposed as another constitutional amendment that "no State shall violate the equal rights of conscience, or the freedom of the press."

Madison advanced perhaps the broadest possible view of free speech and press. Considering a vigorous press essential to free government, he rejected the imposition of any sanctions for the licentiousness accompanying the exercise of free speech and press. In Madison's words:

> Among those principles deemed sacred in America, among those sacred rights considered as forming the bulwark of liberty, which the Government contemplates with awful reverence and would approach only with the most cautious circumspection, there is no one of which the importance is more deeply impressed on the public mind than the liberty of the press. That this *liberty* is often carried to excess; that it has sometimes degenerated into *licentiousness*, is seen and lamented, *but the remedy has not yet been discovered. Perhaps it is an evil inseparable from the good with which it is allied; perhaps it is a shoot which cannot be stripped from the stalk without wounding vitally the plant from which it is torn. However desirable those measures might be which might correct without enslaving the press, they have never yet been devised in America.*[8]

Still, as Madison acknowledged, his understanding of freedom of speech and press was not representative of that in the founding period.[9] Colonial experiences with censorship by the Crown had fostered agreement that free speech and press should be protected. Also, there was little debate in the First Congress on adopting a provision guaranteeing the freedom of speech and press. But those, including Thomas Jefferson, who feared the abuse of these freedoms also expected the states to continue common-law restrictions on libel and other licentious publications.

Madison's proposal for expressly prohibiting the states from limiting the freedom of speech and press did not survive. Ratified on December 15, 1791, the First Amendment provides, "Congress shall make no law respecting an establishment of religion, or prohibiting the free exercise thereof; or abridging the freedom of speech, or of the press; or the right of the people peaceably to assemble." The amendment was thought to protect only against prior restraint by the national government; it did not provide absolute immunity for what speakers or publishers might utter or print. Thus the First Amendment was in Hamiltonian terms superfluous (because the Constitution did not give Congress the power to regulate speech and press in the first place), whereas from Madison's vantage point it did not sufficiently safeguard individuals' freedom (particularly from state regulation) and from Jefferson's perspective the amendment simply reaffirmed both the limits of the national government's power and the reserved powers of the states.

Less than a decade later, a constitutional crisis over the First Amendment arose when Congress passed the Alien and Sedition Acts of 1798. The Sedition Act imposed criminal sanctions for "any false, scandalous writing against the government of the United States." It was passed by the Federalist Congress to censure political criticism and turn public opinion against the Jeffersonian-Republicans. The ensuing controversy revealed, once again, that the predominant view of freedom of speech and press was that the First Amendment incorporated traditional Blackstonian common-law principles, rather than broader libertarian principles.

The congressional reports on the repeal of the Sedition Act on February 25, 1799, amply illustrate the acceptance of Blackstonian principles. The constitutionality of the act was defended in the majority's report to Congress on four grounds. First, punishment of seditious libel did not constitute an abridgement of freedom of speech and press, because those freedoms never included "a license for every man to publish what he pleases without being liable to punishment." Second, although little more than a restatement of the first point, the laws of the states and national government never extended "to the publication of false, scandalous, and malicious writings against the Government." Third, the Sedition Act was "merely declaratory of the common law, and useful for rendering that law more generally known, and more easily understood." Fourth, the committee drew a distinction between the religious and the speech and press freedoms protected by the First Amendment. The amendment provides that "*Congress shall make no law respecting* an establishment of religion, *or prohibiting* the free exercise thereof," implying that the national government is absolutely barred from legislating on religious matters. By comparison, the amendment forbids Congress only from passing laws "*abridging* the freedom of speech, or of the press." From that language, the committee surmised that Congress was not precluded from passing legislation *respecting* speech and press.[10]

In the House of Representatives, Albert Gallatin and others had argued against the constitutionality of the Sedition Act on the grounds that "the States have complete power on the subject." Likewise, Thomas Jefferson, in the Kentucky Resolutions of 1798 and 1799 (see Ch. 1), insisted that the states alone possessed the power to initiate libel actions. But the minority report filed in Congress on the repeal of the Sedition Act drew on Madison's understanding of the importance of political speech and guaranteeing the freedom of political debate and criticism:

The most important and necessary information for the people to receive is, of the misconduct of the Government; because their good deeds, although they will produce affection and gratitude to public officers, will only confirm the existing confidence, and will, therefore, make no change in the conduct of the people. The question, whether the Government ought to have control over the persons who alone can give information throughout the country, is nothing more than this, whether men interested in suppressing information necessary for the people to have, ought to be entrusted with the power, or whether they ought to have a power which their personal interest leads to the abuse of?[11]

On this basis, Jeffersonian-Republicans and libertarians, who were a minority in Congress, rejected the majority's report on the constitutionality of the Sedition Act. But their arguments proved unpersuasive, in part because they were neither in complete agreement nor consistent in their views of the scope of freedom of speech and press. The Jeffersonian-Republicans waxed and waned in maintaining that the only permissible restrictions on speech and press could come from the states. And the continued prosecutions for seditious libel after the Sedition Act expired underscores how deeply rooted was the common-law understanding of the freedom of speech and press.

There were no prosecutions under the Sedition Act after 1801, when the act expired and Thomas Jefferson became president. But seditious libel remained a crime in common law. In 1804, President Jefferson wrote to Mrs. John Adams and explained his pardoning of those convicted under the Sedition Act, insisting that the "law [was] a nullity as absolute and as palpable as if Congress had ordered us to fall down and worship a golden image." Eloquent in describing his rage against the Federalists' prosecutions under the act, Jefferson was no less vengeful in recommending prosecutions by the states of Federalist editors![12] In New York courts, in *People v. Croswell*, 3 Johnson's (N.Y.) Cases 336 (1804), Republicans prosecuted a Federalist editor for seditious libel against President Jefferson. Three years later, they were still relying on state and federal courts to try individuals for seditious libel against the president. Not until 1812, in another action for libel against the president, did the Supreme Court finally rule that there was no federal common law of crimes, including the crime of seditious libel. *United States v. Hudson and Goodwin*, 1 Cr. 21 (1812).

In 1833, the most widely read commentator on the Constitution within a generation of the founding period and a Supreme Court justice, Joseph Story, observed that "there is a good deal of loose reasoning on the subject of the liberty of the press, as if its inviolability were constitutionally such." Story endorsed Blackstone's view of free speech and press, remained uncertain whether the First Amendment prohibited Congress from "punishing the licentiousness of the press," and had no doubt that the states could punish individuals for libelous and "other mischievous publications."[13]

By the late nineteenth century, another influential authority on the Constitution, Thomas Cooley, acknowledged that the press had assumed an increasingly important role in society as a result of technological innovations and urbanization. Cooley agreed with Madison that "repression of full and free discussion is dangerous in any government resting upon the will of the people." However, like Story, Cooley continued to view the First Amendment in terms of common-law principles and practices. The amendment, as he put it, guaranteed "a right to freely utter and publish whatever the citizen may please, and to be protected against any responsibility for so doing, except so far as such publications, from their blasphemy, obscenity, or scandalous character, may be a public offense, or as by their falsehood and malice they may injuriously affect the standing, reputation, or pecuniary interests of individuals."[14]

From the founding period and throughout the nineteenth century, the First Amendment was thus comprehended in terms of developing common-law principles and practices. That meant that Blackstone's definition of free speech and press served as the touchstone for understanding those freedoms. Blackstone's view was that liberty of speech and press meant the absence of prior restraints but also the permissibility of subsequent punishment for speech or print that was deemed "improper, mischievous or illegal." While Blackstone distinguished between liberty and licentiousness—or protected and unprotected communications—he failed to articulate the criteria for determining what and when speech and print constituted an abuse of liberty, assuming that common-law judges would defer to legislatures when defining the nature of licentiousness.

In the absence of constitutional restraints imposed by the Supreme Court under the First Amendment, the struggle for free speech and press became a legacy of suppression. In the nineteenth century, lower courts, legislatures, government officials, and ultimately the shifting tides of public opinion enjoyed broad power to punish speech and press and thereby the power to deprive the rights of minorities to express unpopular views.

After the public outcry against the Sedition Act, the national government in the first half of the nineteenth century largely left the suppression of licentious publications to the states. Beginning in the 1830s, the dissemination of information about slavery was punished in the North and the South by enthusiasts both of abolition and of the institution of slavery. In the North, crusading vigilantes fomented mob action, leading to the tarring and feathering, clubbing, whipping, and shooting of abolitionists. William Lloyd Garrison, for one, was stripped half naked and paraded through the streets of Boston. In Illinois, Elijah Lovejoy died at the hands of a mob, while resisting the destruction of his printing press. In the South, legislation punished abolitionist sentiments as "incendiary," "inflammatory," and "provoking servile insurrection." That legislation was reinforced by censorship of the mails. Censorship of the mails began in 1835 with the refusal of a Charleston, South Carolina, postmaster to deliver abolitionist mail in the South. The postmaster general, along with President Andrew Jackson and John C. Calhoun, endeavored to get Congress to pass a law authorizing such actions. Congress refused and passed a law to the contrary, at the urging of Daniel Webster and Henry Clay, that such legislation would abridge free speech and press. But states effectively nullified federal law. During the Civil War, major newspapers in the North and the South criticized President Abraham Lincoln's conduct of the war, and Lincoln reluctantly ordered the New York *World* and the New York *Journal of Commerce* closed and their editors arrested.

While abolitionist sentiments sparked government censorship in the early nineteenth century, allegedly lewd and obscene materials were the object of censorship in the latter part of the century. In 1865, Congress authorized punishment for purveyors of obscenity and further expanded the law with the Comstock Act of 1873, named after Anthony Comstock, a tireless crusader against impure and lustful publications. Into this century, federal courts upheld congressional power to suppress obscene materials. Likewise, state courts affirmed bans against publishing, importing, mailing, and purchasing of pornographic materials, as well as supposedly objectionable books by noted authors such as Honoré de Balzac, Gustav Flaubert, James Joyce, and D. H. Lawrence, as well as Theodore Dreiser's *An American Tragedy!*

Along with a growing number of obscenity prosecutions, actions for criminal libel increased in the last quarter of the nineteenth century, with more than 100 prosecutions between 1890 and 1900. By the turn of the century, public opinion was aroused by the doctrines of socialism, anarchism, syndicalism, and the specter of violent revolution raised by radical political groups, especially Communists. The assassination of President William McKinley by a reputed anarchist dramatized for the public the dangers of such doctrines. Consequently, there was resumption of legislation punishing seditious libel. By the end of World War I, no less than thirty-two states had laws against criminal syndicalism or sedition; more than 1,900 individuals were prosecuted for seditious libel; and more than 100 newspapers, pamphlets, and other periodicals were censored.[15]

The Espionage Act of 1917 was the primary source of federal restrictions on speech and press in the early twentieth century. That act rested on the traditional dichotomy of liberty versus licentiousness in imposing criminal liability on any individual who, when the country was at war, would "make or convey false reports or false statements with the intent to interfere with the operations or success of the military or naval forces of the United States or to promote the success of its enemies," or to "willfully cause or attempt to cause insubordination, disloyalty, mutiny, or refusal of duty, in the military or naval forces of the United States," or to "willfully obstruct the recruiting or enlistment service of the United States, to the injury of the service of the United States."[16]

When challenges to the Espionage Act and other state laws punishing dissident and subversive individuals and groups finally reached the Supreme Court, the justices faced the vexing responsibility of giving meaning to the First Amendment by developing standards and tests for determining the scope of constitutionally protected free speech and press. As discussed in the next section and as the cases excerpted there illustrate, in the first half of the twentieth century the Court employed "the clear and present danger" test and other techniques of ad hoc balancing of free speech claims against competing governmental interests. In the second half of the twentieth century, however, the Court evolved a "two-level theory" or definitional balancing approach to the First Amendment: political and other kinds of speech receive full protection unless they fall into one of *four categories of unprotected speech* ("obscenity," "libel," "fighting words," and "commercial speech"). But as discussed and as the cases excerpted show in other sections of this chapter, more recently some of these categories ("fighting words" and "commercial speech," for instance) have been given expanded First Amendment protection, and depending on the *context*—public schools, airwaves and broadcasts versus the print media and the Internet—the Court has denied protection for indecent and offensive speech in balancing free speech claims against competing governmental interests.

In sum, the justices and the country remain locked in a dialogue over how free "free speech" should be and how it should be balanced with such competing governmental interests as promoting moral decency, national security, equality, and the social order. In other words, the Court and the country continue to debate why we value and should value free speech over other competing values. Is free speech valuable because it is *instrumental* to self-governance and the democratic process? Does free speech have *intrinsic value* because individual expression is related to self-determination and human dignity? Should speech be protected because we are agnostic and, as Justice Holmes in *Abrams v. United States*, 250 U.S. 616 (1919), observed, "the best test of truth is the power of the thought to get itself accepted in the competition of the market"? Or should we value free speech over governmental restrictions due to the "slippery slope" of governmental censorship?

NOTES

1. See Fredrick Siebert, *Freedom of the Press in England, 1476–1776* (Urbana: University of Illinois, 1965).

2. *Trial of William Prynn*, 3 Howell's State Trials 561 (1632).

3. Sir William Blackstone, *Commentaries on the Laws of England*, Vol. 4 (Oxford, UK: Clarendon Press, 1766), 151–152.

4. John P. Roche, *Shadow and Substance* (New York: Macmillan, 1964), 11.

5. John Milton, *Areopagitica*, in *The Works of John Milton*, Vol. 4, ed. William Haller (New York: Columbia University Press, 1931); and see William Clyde, *The Struggle for the Freedom of the Press from Caxton to Cromwell* (London: Oxford University Press, 1934).

6. John Locke, "A Letter Concerning Toleration," in *The Works of John Locke*, Vol. 4, 11th ed. (London: W. Otridge, 1905–1907), 45–46.

7. Cato, "Reflections on Libelling," in *Freedom of the Press from Zenger to Jefferson*, ed. Leonard Levy (New York: Bobbs-Merrill, 1966), 12.

8. *Annals of Congress: First Congress, 1789–1791*, Vol. 1 (Washington, DC: Gales and Seaton, 1834), 453; and James Madison, *The Writings of James Madison*, Vol. 6, ed. Haillard Hunt (New York: Putnam's Sons, 1906–1910), 336.

9. See James Madison to Edward Everett (August 28, 1830), in Madison, *The Writings of James Madison*, Vol. 9, 383.

10. "Majority Report on Repeal of the Sedition Act," *Annals of Congress*, 5th Cong., 3rd Sess., February 25, 1799, 2987–2990.

11. "Majority Report," *Annals of Congress*, 3003–3014.

12. Letters from Thomas Jefferson to Abigail Adams (September 11, 1804), and to Thomas McKean (February 19, 1803) in *The Writings of Thomas Jefferson*, Vol. 8, ed. Paul Ford (New York: Putnam's Sons, 1892–1899), 310 and 218–219.

13. Joseph Story, *Commentaries on the Constitution of the United States* (Boston: Little, Brown, 1833), 735.

14. Thomas Cooley, *A Treatise on the Constitutional Limitations*, Vol. 2 (Boston: Little, Brown, 1868), 886 and 931–940.

15. See Fredrick Siebert, *The Rights and Privileges of the Press* (New York: D. Appleton-Century, 1934), 271; and James Paul and Murray Schwartz, *Federal Censorship: Obscenity in the Mail* (New York: Free Press, 1961), 17–24.

16. The Espionage Act of June 15, 1917, 40 Stat. 217. See also Act of May 16, 1918, 40 Stat. 553.

SELECTED BIBLIOGRAPHY

Abrams, Floyd. *Speaking Freely: Trials of the First Amendment*. New York: Viking, 2005.

Bird, Wendell. *Press and Speech Under Attack: The Early Supreme Court Justices, the Sedition Act of 1798, and the Campaign against Dissent*. New York: Oxford University Press, 2016.

Cronin, Mary M. *An Indispensible Liberty: The Fight for Free Speech in Nineteenth Century America.* Carbondale: Southern Illinois University Press, 2016.

Delgado, Richard, and Jean Stefancic. *Must We Defend Nazis? Why the First Amendment Should Not Protect Hate Speech and White Supremacy.* New York: New York University Press, 2018.

Kluger, Richard. *Indelible Ink: The Trials of John Peter Zenger and the Birth of America's Free Press.* New York: W. W. Norton, 2016.

Knowles, Helen, and Steven Lichtman. *Judging Free Speech: First Amendment Jurisprudence and the U.S. Supreme Court.* New York: Palgrave/Macmillan, 2015.

Lendier, Marc. *Gitlow v. New York: Every Idea an Incitement.* Lawrence: University of Kansas Press, 2014.

Levy, Leonard. *Emergence of a Free Press.* New York: Oxford University Press, 1985.

Levy, Leonard, ed. *Freedom of Press from Zenger to Jefferson.* New York: Bobbs-Merrill, 1966.

Lewis, Anthony. *Freedom for the Thought That We Hate: A Biography of the First Amendment.* New York: Basic Books, 2010.

Magarian, Gregory. *Managed Speech: The Roberts Court's First Amendment.* New York: Oxford University Press, 2017.

Meiklejohn, Alexander. *Political Freedom: The Constitutional Powers of the People.* New York: Harper & Row, 1948.

Stone, Goffrey, and Lee Bollinger, eds. *The Free Speech Century.* New York: Oxford University Press, 2018.

Strossen, Nadine. *Hate: Why We Should Resist It with Free Speech, Not Censorship.* New York: Oxford University Press, 2017.

A | *Judicial Approaches to the First Amendment*

When First Amendment challenges to state and federal sedition laws reached the Supreme Court in the aftermath of World War I, the convictions were upheld. This litigation, however, forced the Court to confront two long-avoided tasks: first, deciding whether the First Amendment applied equally against the states and the national government and, second, articulating standards for defining the scope of constitutionally protected free speech and press. Once the Court held the First Amendment applied to the states (see Ch. 3), it could no longer avoid the even more difficult task of giving constitutional meaning to the amendment. Initially, the Court took for granted that Blackstone's common-law principles governed the First Amendment's guarantees of free speech and press. But gradually members of the Court pressed for the development of constitutional principles that would define the scope of protected speech and press. By 1936, in *Grosjean v. American Press Co.,* 297 U.S. 233 (1936), Justice George Sutherland finally noted, as Madison more than a century before had urged, that constitutional principles (not the English common law) governed the scope of protected speech and press. In Sutherland's words,

> It is impossible to concede that by the words "freedom of the press" the framers of the amendment intended to adopt merely the narrow view then reflected by the law of England that such freedom consisted only in immunity from previous censorship. . . . Undoubtedly, the range of a constitutional provision phrased in terms of the common law sometimes may be fixed by recourse to the applicable rules of law. But the doctrine which justifies such recourse, like other canons of construction, must yield to more compelling reasons whenever they exist.

Still, it took decades for the Court to respond to those "more compelling reasons" for breaking away from common-law principles and articulating the constitutional principles that now govern the application of

Justices Oliver Wendell Holmes (left) and Louis D. Brandeis. In the 1920s, Justices Brandeis and Holmes dissented from the Court's upholding the convictions of individuals for expressing unpopular, and what was considered subversive, political ideas. In an effort to extend First Amendment protection for free speech, Justice Holmes invented the clear and present danger test. (*Bettmann/Corbis via Getty Images.*)

the First Amendment. For the justices that meant reconciling rival interpretative approaches to the First Amendment and a political struggle within the Court, as well as between the Court and the country over the freedoms of speech and press.

■ (1) FIFTY YEARS OF "CLEAR AND PRESENT DANGER"

The surge of litigation challenging convictions under the Espionage Act and state sedition laws necessitated that the Court develop its own interpretative standards for protecting the freedom of speech and press. In *Schenck v. United States* (1919) (see excerpt below), Justice Oliver Wendell Holmes initially intimated what would become one of the best-known tests for defining the scope of constitutionally protected free speech and press: *"the clear and present danger"* test—"whether the words used are used in such circumstances and are of such a nature as to create a clear and present danger that they will bring about the substantive evils that Congress has a right to prevent." However, Holmes retreated and based his opinion on the old common-law presumption of the "reasonableness of legislation" and whether the proscribed speech had a *"bad tendency"*—"whether the statements contained in the [communication] had a natural tendency to produce the forbidden consequences."[1] Within a week, in two more unanimous rulings, Holmes again upheld convictions under the Espionage Act on the bad tendency standard.[2]

But in a fourth case in 1919, *Abrams v. United States*, 250 U.S. 616 (1919), Holmes broke with the majority over using the clear and present danger test as an alternative to the bad tendency test. *Abrams* involved the conviction of five individuals under the Espionage Act for distributing leaflets condemning the government's war effort and intervention in Russia and calling for a general strike of workers in protest. When rejecting the majority's reliance on the bad tendency test, in dissent with Justice Louis Brandeis, Holmes proclaimed that "only the emergency that makes it immediately dangerous to leave the correction of evil counsels to time warrants making any exception to the sweeping command, 'Congress shall make no law . . . abridging the freedom of speech.'" His dissent in *Abrams* was followed by four other biting dissents and one concurring opinion, establishing the foundations for the evolution of this most famous of judicial approaches to the First Amendment.[3]

In the 1920s, the Court continued to hold that the First Amendment did not protect speech and press that might have pernicious effects on society. *Gitlow v. People of the State of New York* (1925) (excerpted below) is illustrative. There Justice Edward Sanford reaffirmed the traditional common-law principles governing the punishment of subversive speech:

Such utterances, by their very nature, involve danger to the public peace and to the security of the State. They threaten breaches of the peace and ultimate revolution. And the immediate danger is none the less real and substantial, because the effect of a given utterance cannot be accurately foreseen. The State cannot reasonably be required to measure the danger from every such utterance in the nice balance of a jeweler's scale. A single revolutionary spark may kindle a fire that, smoldering for a time, may burst into a sweeping and destructive conflagration.

In another illustrious dissent in *Gitlow*, Holmes reiterated his clear and present danger test. Two years later, in *Whitney v. California*, 274 U.S. 357 (1927), involving the conviction of a Communist under a state syndicalism act, Brandeis endeavored to further sharpen the clear and present danger test. Even in the face of legislation, the First Amendment forbids restrictions short of demonstrating an *imminent* clear and present danger; in Brandeis's words, "Only an emergency can justify repression."

In the two decades following *Abrams*, the clear and present danger test was virtually abandoned. Under the leadership of Chief Justice Charles Evans Hughes in the 1930s, however, the Court also substantially undermined reliance on the reasonableness of legislation and bad tendency approach. A series of rulings extended First Amendment protection to pamphlets and leaflets,[4] and peaceful picketing,[5] because its guarantees were construed to safeguard "the liberty to discuss publicly and truthfully all matters of public concern without previous restraint or fear of subsequent punishment."[6]

In the 1940s, the clear and present danger test enjoyed a kind of renaissance, buttressed by the Hughes Court's precedents expanding the scope of the First Amendment. The test, though, was fundamentally transformed during the tenures of Chief Justices Harlan Stone and Fred Vinson (respectively, 1941–1946 and 1946–1953).

Holmes and Brandeis formulated the clear and present danger test as an evidentiary rule for determining the permissibility of applying statutory prohibitions in particular circumstances; it did not purport to establish a standard for reviewing the constitutionality of legislation per se. Moreover, they invoked the test only in cases involving alleged threats to national security.

By contrast, in the 1940s the Court turned the clear and present danger test into a standard for judging both the application and constitutionality per se of statutes. It also became a basis for reviewing a wide range of restrictions on speech and the press, including state laws restricting or prohibiting handbill distributions and solicitations,[7] and requiring compulsory saluting of the American flag,[8] as well as contempt-of-court convictions and individuals' speeches before public assemblies.[9]

As the scope of the First Amendment expanded in the 1940s, some justices pushed for an even more libertarian approach. Chief Justice Stone and Justices Black, Douglas, Murphy, and Rutledge claimed the amendment enjoyed a "preferred position," virtually foreclosing the possibility of upholding any restrictions on free speech and press. As Stone observed, "The First Amendment is not confined to safeguarding freedom of speech and freedom of religion against discriminatory attempts to wipe them out. On the contrary, the Constitution, by virtue of the First and Fourteenth Amendments, has put those freedoms in a *preferred position.*"[10]

The reformulation of the clear and present danger test and articulation of the preferred position approach toward the First Amendment were not without opposition from within the Court. Throughout his twenty-three years on the bench (1939–1962), Justice Frankfurter criticized his colleagues for their "idle play on words" and "perversion" of the Holmesian-Brandeis formulation and ridiculed those embracing a "preferred position" for devising a "deceptive formula . . . [that] makes for mechanical jurisprudence."[11]

Divisions within the Court were further exacerbated by the political currents in the 1940s and 1950s. Beginning in the early 1940s, political passions again swept the country with dire warnings about fascism and communism. In 1940, Congress enacted the Alien Registration Act, or Smith Act, the first federal peacetime sedition act since the Alien and Sedition Acts of 1798. Less restrictive than the Sedition Act, the Smith Act made it a crime to advocate or to belong to any organization that advocated the forceful overthrow of the government. Subsequently, Congress required loyalty oaths and statements of non-Communist affiliation from public- and private-sector employees, with the Labor-Management Relations Act of 1947. The paranoia over Communists continued through the 1950s. Over President Harry Truman's veto, Congress passed the Internal Security Act of 1950, also known as the McCarran Act, which required members of the Communist Party to register with the U.S. attorney general. Senator Joseph McCarthy's subcommittee and the Special House Committee on Un-American Activities as well as numerous legislative committees held hearings and investigations of individuals' loyalty.

Bitterly divided, the Court affirmed the constitutionality of both the Smith Act and the McCarran Act in, respectively, *Dennis v. United States* (1951) (see excerpt below) and *Communist Party v. Subversive Activities Control Board*, 367 U.S. 203 (1961). *Dennis* remains the watershed case in which the Vinson Court's reformulation of the clear and present danger test rendered futile further reliance on the test.

Dennis was presaged by Chief Justice Vinson's opinion in *American Communications Association v. Douds*, 339 U.S. 382 (1950), upholding a requirement for the filing of non-Communist affidavits in the Labor-Management Relations Act. In their briefs before the Court, the unions argued that it was difficult "to conceive how the expression of belief, or the joining of a political party, without more, could ever constitute [a clear and present] danger." Chief Justice Vinson thought otherwise: the threat of communism was substantial, considerably greater than when Holmes proposed his clear and present danger test and, therefore, justified congressional action. No less important, Vinson indicated that the clear and present danger test was not a mechanical rule, but rather a balancing technique:

> [E]ven harmful conduct cannot justify restrictions upon speech unless substantial interests of society are at stake. But in suggesting that the substantive evil must be serious and substantial, it was never the intention of this Court to lay down an absolutist test measured in terms of danger to the Nation. When the effect of a statute or ordinance upon the exercise of First Amendment freedoms is relatively small and the public interest to be protected is substantial, it is obvious that a rigid test requiring a showing of imminent danger to the security of the Nation is an absurdity.

In Vinson's hands, the clear and present danger test became a balancing technique for rationalizing restrictions on speech and the press.[12]

The opinions in *Dennis* reveal the internal politics of the Vinson Court and the competing interpretive approaches toward the First Amendment. When a second opportunity to interpret the Smith Act arose with *Yates v. United States*, 354 U.S. 178 (1957), it was anticipated that the result would be different from that in *Dennis*. Oleta Yates and thirteen other second-string functionaries of the Communist Party were prosecuted shortly after *Dennis* was announced; each was found guilty, fined $10,000, and sentenced to five years in prison. By the time their appeal was granted in 1955, Vinson and his three supporters in *Dennis* were gone. President Dwight Eisenhower in 1953 had appointed Earl Warren as chief justice, and Justices Reed, Jackson, and Minton had been replaced by Whittaker, Harlan, and Brennan. Still, the Warren Court (with newly appointed Justices Whittaker and Brennan not participating) declined to strike down the Smith Act in *Yates*. However, it reversed five of the convictions and ordered retrials for the others, setting forth certain conditions for applying the Smith Act that made future convictions exceedingly difficult.

Justice Harlan's opinion for the Court in *Yates* abandoned the clear and present danger test and substituted instead a *balancing approach* according to which First Amendment freedoms were weighed against society's right of self-preservation. He claimed that was the essence of *Dennis* in distinguishing between advocacy of abstract doctrines (which receives First Amendment protection) and the advocacy of violence and unlawful action. Two years later, he again provided the voice for a bare majority and reasserted his balancing approach to the First Amendment in *Barenblatt v. United States*, 360 U.S. 109 (1959).

By the 1960s, the clear and present danger test had evolved into a rhetorical technique and then gave way to Harlan's explicit balancing of First Amendment freedoms against legislative restrictions. Harlan's balancing approach, however, enjoyed the support only of a bare majority of the Court. In the early 1960s, the Warren Court was split 5–4 over balancing First Amendment freedoms, with Justice Potter Stewart as the swing vote. A bare majority, in *Scales v. United States*, 367 U.S. 203 (1961), upheld the Smith Act's prohibition on membership in subversive organizations, and in *Communist Party of the United States v. Subversives Activities Control Board (SACB)*, 367 U.S. 1 (1961), the registration requirements for all members of subversive organizations, as established by the Internal Security Act of 1950. In *Scales*, Harlan upheld the membership clause by distinguishing between mere, passive members (the "foolish, deluded, or perhaps merely optimistic") and those knowing, active members whose intent was "to bring about the overthrow of the government as speedily as circumstances would permit." Over the four dissenters' objections that the Court had legitimated "guilt by association," Harlan's opinion for the majority concluded that there was enough evidence that Scales was an "active" member engaged in illegal advocacy. In the second case upholding the SACB, Frankfurter performed the delicate task of writing an opinion for another bare majority. In both cases, Chief Justice Warren and Justices Black, Douglas, and Brennan dissented. One week later, though, Justice Stewart swung over to the dissenters' side to form a majority for reversing the conviction of an individual found in contempt for refusing to answer questions before a subcommittee of the House Committee on Un-American Activities, *Deutch v. United States*, 367 U.S. 456 (1961).

Following *Scales*, prosecutions for subversive activities under the Smith Act sharply declined, and by the mid-1960s (with the appointments of Abe Fortas and Thurgood Marshall as associate justices) there was a solid majority on the Warren Court for striking down portions of the McCarran Act. Because Congress refused to appropriate funds, the SACB was finally shut down in 1973, over the objections of President Richard Nixon, who as a congressman in 1950 had been one of its sponsors. A year later, the Special House Committee on Un-American Activities was abolished and its duties transferred to the House Judicial Committee.

In Chief Justice Earl Warren's last term, the Court handed down a *per curiam* opinion in *Brandenburg v. Ohio* (1969) (see excerpt below), finally laying to rest the long line of cases upholding convictions for so-called subversive speech and activities advocating unpopular political doctrines. Justices Black and Douglas gave their final requiem for the clear and present danger test in brief concurring opinions. But see and compare the Court's ruling on the constitutionality of criminalizing cross-burning in *Virginia v. Black* (2003) (in Section B of this chapter).

NOTES

1. *Pierce v. United States*, 252 U.S. 239 (1920).

2. *Debs v. United States*, 249 U.S. 211 (1919); and *Frowerk v. United States*, 249 U.S. 204 (1919).

3. See *Schaefer v. United States*, 251 U.S. 466 (1920); *Pierce v. United States*, 252 U.S. 239 (1920); *Gilbert v. Minnesota*, 254 U.S. 325 (1920); *Gitlow v. New York*, 268 U.S. 652 (1925); and *Whitney v. California*, 274 U.S. 357 (1927).

4. See *Lovell v. City of Griffin*, 303 U.S. 444 (1938); *Schneider v. New Jersey*, 308 U.S. 147 (1939); *Marsh v. Alabama*, 326 U.S. 501 (1946); *Cantwell v. Connecticut*, 310 U.S. 296 (1940); and *Cox v. New Hampshire*, 312 U.S. 569 (1941).

5. *Cantwell v. Connecticut*, 310 U.S. 296 (1940).

6. *Thornhill v. Alabama*, 310 U.S. 88 (1940).

7. See *Cantwell v. Connecticut*, 310 U.S. 296 (1940); *Douglas v. City of Jeanette*, 319 U.S. 157 (1943); *Jones v. Opelika*, 319 U.S. 103 (1943); *Murdock v. Pennsylvania*, 319 U.S. 105 (1943); and *Follet v. Town of McCormick*, 321 U.S. 573 (1944).

8. See and compare *Minersville School District v. Gobitis*, 310 U.S. 586 (1940), with *West Virginia Board of Education v. Barnette*, 319 U.S. 624 (1943).

9. *Bridges v. California*, 314 U.S. 252 (1941); *Pennekamp v. Florida*, 328 U.S. 331 (1946); *Craig v. Harney*, 331 U.S. 367 (1947) (contempt-of-court citations for publications concerning pending trials); and *Terminello v. Chicago*, 337 U.S. 1 (1949) (conviction for public speech).

10. *Jones v. Opelika*, 316 U.S. 584, 608 (1942) (Stone, J., dissenting opinion), adopted on rehearing, *Jones v. Opelika*, 319 U.S. 103 (1943).

11. See *Bridges v. California*, 314 U.S. 252, 295 (1941); *Craig v. Harney*, 331 U.S. 367, 391 (1947); and *Kovacs v. Cooper*, 336 U.S. 77, 96 (1949).

12. See *Niemotko v. Maryland*, 340 U.S. 268 (1951); and *Feiner v. New York*, 340 U.S. 315 (1951).

Selected Bibliography

Black, Hugo. *A Constitutional Faith*. New York: Knopf, 1968.

Blumberg, Phillip. *Repressive Jurisprudence in the Early American Republic: The First Amendment and the Legacy of English Law*. New York: Cambridge University Press, 2010.

Collins, Ronald, and Sam Chaltain. *We Must Not Be Afraid to Be Free*. New York: Oxford University Press, 2011.

Emerson, Thomas. *The System of Freedom of Expression*. New York: Random House, 1970.

Finan, Christopher. *From the Palmer Raids to the Patriot Act: A History of the Fight for Free Speech in America*. Boston: Beacon Press, 2007.

Haynes, Charles, Sam Chaltain, and Susan Glisson, eds. *First Freedoms: A Documentary History of First Amendment Rights in America*. New York: Oxford University Press, 2006.

Healy, Thomas. *The Great Dissent: How Oliver Wendell Holmes Changed His Mind—and Changed the History of Free Speech in America*. New York: Metropolitan Books, 2013.

Polenberg, Richard. *Fighting Faiths: The Abrams Case, the Supreme Court, and Free Speech*. New York: Viking, 1987.

Stone, Geoffrey. *Perilous Times: Free Speech in Wartime from the Sedition Act of 1798 to the War on Terrorism*. New York: W. W. Norton & Company, 2004.

Strum, Phillippa. *Speaking Freely: Whitney v. California and American Speech*. Lawrence: University of Kansas Press, 2016.

Tushnet, Marc, Alan Chen, Joseph Blocher. *Free Speech Beyond Words: The Surprising Reach of the First Amendment*. New York: New York University Press, 2017.

Schenck v. United States
249 U.S. 47, 39 S.Ct. 247 (1919)

As secretary of the Socialist Party, Charles Schenck was responsible for the printing, distributing, and mailing to men eligible for the draft leaflets that advocated opposition to the government's involvement in World War I and urged them to resist conscription. He was arrested, tried, and convicted in federal courts for violating the Espionage Act of 1917. That act was passed amid the so-called Red (communist) scare, prompted by economic dislocations due to the war and growing distrust of aliens and foreign-born radicals because of the Bolshevik revolution in Russia. Schenck's appeal was the first of several cases challenging the Espionage Act to reach the Supreme Court.

The Court's decision was unanimous, and the opinion was announced by Justice Holmes.

■ ■ ■

☐ *Justice HOLMES delivered the opinion of the Court.*

The document in question upon its first printed side recited the first section of the Thirteenth Amendment, said that the idea embodied in it was violated by the conscription act and that a conscript is little better than a convict. In impassioned language it intimated that conscription was despotism in its worst form and a monstrous wrong against humanity in the interest of Wall Street's chosen few. It said, "Do not submit to intimidation," but in form at least confined itself to peaceful measures such as a petition for the repeal of the act. The other and later printed side of the sheet was headed "Assert Your Rights." It stated reasons for alleging that anyone violated the Constitution when he refused to recognize "your right to assert your opposition to the draft," and went on, "If you do not assert and support your rights, you are helping to deny or disparage rights which it is the solemn duty of all citizens and residents of the United States to retain." It described the arguments on the other side as coming from cunning politicians and a mercenary capitalist press, and even silent consent to the conscription law as helping to support an infamous conspiracy. It denied the power to send our citizens away to foreign shores to shoot up the people of other lands, and added that words could not express the condemnation such cold-blooded ruthlessness deserves, &c., &c., winding up, "You must do your share to maintain, support and uphold the rights of the people of this country." Of course the document would not have been sent unless it had been intended to have some effect, and we do not see what effect it could be expected to have upon persons subject to the draft except to influence them to obstruct the carrying of it out. The defendants do not deny that the jury might find against them on this point.

But it is said, suppose that that was the tendency of this circular, it is protected by the First Amendment to the Constitution. Two of the strongest expressions are said to be quoted respectively from well-known public men. It well may be that the prohibition of laws abridging the freedom of speech is not confined to previous restraints, although to prevent them may have been the main purpose, as intimated in *Patterson v. Colorado*, 205 U.S. 454 [1907]. We admit that in many places and in ordinary times the defendants in saying all that was said in the circular would have been within their constitutional rights. But the character of every act depends upon the circumstances in which it is done. *Aikens v. Wisconsin*, 195 U.S. 194 [1904]. The most stringent protection of free speech would not protect a man in falsely shouting fire in a theatre and causing a panic. It does not even protect a man from an injunction against uttering words that may have all the effect of force. The question in every case is whether the words used are used in such circumstances and are of such a nature as to create a clear and present danger that they will bring about the substantive evils that Congress has a right to prevent. It is a question of proximity and degree. When a nation is at war many things that might be said in time of peace are such a hindrance to its effort that their utterance will not be endured so long as men fight and that no Court could regard them as protected by any constitutional right. It seems to be admitted that if an actual obstruction of the recruiting service were proved, liability for words that produced that effect might be enforced. The statute of 1917 in section 4 punishes conspiracies to obstruct as well as actual obstruction. If the act, (speaking, or circulating a paper,) its tendency and the intent with which it is done are the same, we perceive no ground for saying that success alone warrants making the act a crime. . . .

Judgments affirmed.

Gitlow v. People of the State of New York
268 U.S. 652, 45 S.Ct. 625 (1925)

On November 8, 1919, police arrested Benjamin Gitlow, a twenty-eight-year-old son of Russian-Jewish immigrants, who a year before was elected to the New York legislature as a Socialist and who was well known as a leader of the left-wing faction of the Socialist Party—which would later form the American Communist Party. Gitlow was arrested and tried under the New York Criminal Anarchy Act of 1902, prohibiting the advocacy of criminal anarchy—"the doctrine that organized governments should be overthrown by force or violence, or by the assassination of the executive head or of any of the executive officials of government, or by any unlawful means." Gitlow's crime was publishing a pamphlet, *Left Wing Manifesto*, proclaiming the inevitability of a proletarian revolution. Although no evidence was introduced at trial that his publication had led to any unlawful action, Gitlow was convicted by a jury and given the maximum sentence of five to ten years in prison. Gitlow unsuccessfully appealed his conviction in state courts on the grounds that the New York law was unconstitutional under the First and Fourteenth Amendments. The recently formed American Civil Liberties Union (ACLU) then came to Gitlow's defense and appealed his case to the Supreme Court.

The Court's decision was 7–2, with the majority's opinion announced by Justice Sanford. Justice Holmes dissented and was joined by Justice Brandeis.

■ ■ ■

☐ *Justice SANFORD delivered the opinion of the Court.*

Benjamin Gitlow was indicted in the Supreme Court of New York, with three others, for the statutory crime of criminal anarchy. He was separately tried, convicted, and sentenced to imprisonment. . . .

The contention here is that the statute, by its terms and as applied in this case, is repugnant to the due process clause of the Fourteenth Amendment. Its material provisions are: . . .

"Sec. 161. *Advocacy of Criminal Anarchy.* Any person who:

Benjamin Gitlow and William Z. Foster, the Communist Workers' Party 1928 candidates for president and vice president, three years after the Supreme Court upheld Gitlow's conviction for publishing an article calling for workers to overthrow capitalism. (*Bettmann/Corbis via Getty Images.*)

"1. By word of mouth or writing advocates, advises or teaches the duty, necessity or propriety of overthrowing or overturning organized government by force or violence, or by assassination of the executive head or of any of the executive officials of government, or by any unlawful means; or,

"2. Prints, publishes, edits, issues or knowingly circulates, sells, distributes or publicly displays any book, paper, document, or written or printed matter in any form, containing or advocating, advising or teaching the doctrine that organized government should be overthrown by force, violence or any unlawful means, . . .

"Is guilty of a felony and punishable" by imprisonment or fine, or both. . . .

The defendant is a member of the Left Wing Section of the Socialist Party, a dissenting branch or faction of that party formed in opposition to its dominant policy of "moderate Socialism." Membership in both is open to aliens as well as citizens. The Left Wing Section was organized nationally at a conference in New York City in June, 1919, attended by ninety delegates from twenty different States. The conference elected a National Council, of which the defendant was a member, and left to it the adoption of a "Manifesto." This was published in *The Revolutionary Age*, the official organ of the Left Wing. The defendant was on the board of managers of the paper and was its business manager. He arranged for the printing of the paper and took to the printer the manuscript of the first issue which contained the Left Wing Manifesto, and also a Communist Program and a Program of the Left Wing that had been adopted by the conference. Sixteen thousand copies were printed, which were delivered at the premises in New York City used as the office of the Revolutionary Age and the headquarters of the Left Wing, and occupied by the defendant and other officials. . . .

There was no evidence of any effect resulting from the publication and circulation of the Manifesto.

No witnesses were offered in behalf of the defendant. . . .

The sole contention here is, essentially, that as there was no evidence of any concrete result flowing from the publication of the Manifesto or of circumstances showing the likelihood of such result, the statute as construed and applied by the trial court penalizes the mere utterance, as such, of "doctrine" having no quality of incitement, without regard either to the circumstances of its utterance or to the likelihood of unlawful consequences. . . .

The statute does not penalize the utterance or publication of abstract "doctrine" or academic discussion having no quality of incitement to any concrete action. It is not aimed against mere historical or philosophical essays. It does not restrain the advocacy of changes in the form of government by constitutional and lawful means. What it prohibits is language advocating, advising or teaching the overthrow of organized government by unlawful means. These words imply urging to action. . . .

The Manifesto, plainly, is neither the statement of abstract doctrine nor, as suggested by counsel, mere prediction that industrial disturbances and revolutionary mass strikes will result spontaneously in an inevitable process of evolution in the economic system. It advocates and urges in fervent language mass action which shall progressively foment industrial disturbances and through political mass strikes and revolutionary mass action overthrow and destroy organized parliamentary government. It concludes with a call to action in these words:

> The proletariat revolution and the Communist reconstruction of society—*the struggle for these*—is now indispensable. . . . The Communist International calls the proletariat of the world to the final struggle!

This is not the expression of philosophical abstraction, the mere prediction of future events; it is the language of direct incitement. . . .

For present purposes we may and do assume that freedom of speech and of the press—which are protected by the First Amendment from abridgment by Congress—are among the fundamental personal rights and "liberties" protected by the due process clause of the Fourteenth Amendment from impairment by the States. . . .

It is a fundamental principle, long established, that the freedom of speech and of the press which is secured by the Constitution, does not confer an absolute right to speak or publish, without responsibility, whatever one may choose, or an unrestricted and unbridled license that gives immunity for every possible use of language and prevents the punishment of those who abuse this freedom. . . .

That a State in the exercise of its police power may punish those who abuse this freedom by utterances inimical to the public welfare, tending to corrupt public morals, incite to crime, or disturb the public peace, is not open to question. . . .

By enacting the present statute the State has determined, through its legislative body, that utterances advocating the overthrow of organized government by force, violence and unlawful means, are so inimical to the general welfare and involve such danger of substantive evil that they may be penalized in the exercise of its police power. That determination must be given great weight. Every presumption is to be indulged in favor of the validity of the statute. *Mugler v. Kansas*. . . . And the case is to be considered "in the light of the principle that the State is primarily the judge of regulations required in the interest of public safety and welfare"; and that its police "statutes may only be declared unconstitutional where they are arbitrary or unreasonable attempts to exercise authority vested in the State in the public interest." *Great Northern Ry. v. Clara City* [246 U.S. 434 (1918)]. That utterances inciting to the overthrow of organized government by unlawful means, present a sufficient danger of substantive evil to bring their punishment within the range of legislative discretion, is clear. Such utterances, by their very nature, involve danger to the public peace and to the security of the State. They threaten breaches of the peace and ultimate revolution. And the immediate danger is none the less real and substantial, because the effect of a given utterance cannot be accurately foreseen. The State cannot reasonably be required to measure the danger from every such utterance in the nice balance of a jeweler's scale. A single revolutionary spark may kindle a fire that, smouldering for a time, may burst into a sweeping and destructive conflagration. It cannot be said that the State is acting arbitrarily or unreasonably when in the exercise of its judgment as to the measures necessary to protect the public peace and safety, it seeks to extinguish the spark without waiting until it has enkindled the flame or blazed into the conflagration. It cannot reasonably be required to defer the adoption of measures for its own peace and safety until the revolutionary utterances lead to actual disturbances of the public peace or imminent and immediate danger of its own destruction; but it may, in the exercise of its judgment, suppress the threatened danger in its incipiency. . . .

We cannot hold that the present statute is an arbitrary or unreasonable exercise of the police power of the State unwarrantably infringing the freedom of speech or press; and we must and do sustain its constitutionality.

This being so it may be applied to every utterance—not too trivial to be beneath the notice of the law—which is of such a character and used with such intent and purpose as to bring it within the prohibition of the statute. . . .

In other words, when the legislative body has determined generally, in the constitutional exercise of its discretion, that utterances of a certain kind involve such danger of substantive evil that they may be punished, the question whether any specific utterance coming within the prohibited class is likely, in and of itself, to bring about the substantive evil, is not open to consideration. It is sufficient that the statute itself be constitutional and that the use of the language comes within its prohibition.

It is clear that the question in such cases is entirely different from that involved in those cases where the statute merely prohibits certain acts involving the danger of substantive evil, without any reference to language itself, and it is sought to apply its provisions to language used by the defendant for the purpose of bringing about the prohibited results. There, if it be contended that the statute cannot be applied to the language used by the defendant because of its protection by the freedom of speech or press, it must necessarily be found, as an original question, without any previous determination by the legislative body, whether the specific language used involved such likelihood of bringing about the substantive evil as to deprive it of the constitutional protection. In such case it has been held that the general provisions of the statute may be constitutionally applied to the specific utterance of the defendant if its natural tendency and probable effect was to bring about the substantive evil which the legislative body might prevent. *Schenck v. United States*, [249 U.S. 47 (1919)]; *Debs v. United States*, [249 U.S. 211 (1919)]. And the general statement in the *Schenck* Case that the "question in every case is whether the words used are used in such circumstances and are of such a nature as to create a clear and present danger that they will bring about the substantive evils,"—upon which great reliance is placed in the defendant's argument—was manifestly intended, as shown by the context, to apply only in cases of this class, and has no application to those like the present, where the legislative body itself has previously determined the danger of substantive evil arising from utterances of a specified character. . . .

Affirmed.

☐ *Justice HOLMES, dissenting.*

Justice BRANDEIS and I are of the opinion that this judgment should be reversed. The general principle of free speech, it seems to me, must be taken to be included in the Fourteenth Amendment, in view of the scope that has been given to the word "liberty" as there used, although perhaps it may be accepted with a somewhat larger latitude of interpretation than is allowed to Congress by the sweeping language that governs or ought to govern the laws of the United States. If I am right then I think that the criterion sanctioned by the full Court in *Schenck v. United States*, applies:

> The question in every case is whether the words used are used in such circumstances and are of such a nature as to create a clear and present danger that they will bring about the substantive evils that [the State] has a right to prevent. . . .

If what I think the correct test is applied it is manifest that there was no present danger of an attempt to overthrow the government by force on the part of the admittedly small minority who shared the defendant's views. It is said that this manifesto was more than a theory, that it was an incitement. Every idea is an incitement. It offers itself for belief and if believed it is acted on unless some other belief outweighs it or some failure of energy stifles the movement at its birth. The only difference between the expression of an opinion and an incitement in the narrower sense is the speaker's enthusiasm for the result. Eloquence may set fire to reason. But whatever may be thought of the redundant discourse before us it had no chance of starting a present conflagration. If in the long run the beliefs expressed in proletarian dictatorship are destined to be accepted by the dominant forces of the community, the only meaning of free speech is that they should be given their chance and have their way.

If the publication of this document had been laid as an attempt to induce an uprising against government at once and not at some indefinite time in the future it would have presented a different question. The object would have been one with which the law might deal, subject to the doubt whether there was any danger that the publication could produce any result, or in other words, whether it was not futile and too remote from possible consequences. But the indictment alleges the publication and nothing more.

Dennis v. United States
341 U.S. 494, 71 S.Ct. 857 (1951)

Eugene Dennis and ten other leaders of the American Communist Party were indicted under the Smith Act of 1940 for willfully and knowingly conspiring to teach and advocate the forceful and violent overthrow and destruction of the government. After a nine-month trial, Dennis and the others were found guilty and, thereafter, appealed their convictions in a federal appeals court. That court upheld their convictions with a scholarly opinion written by prominent Judge Learned Hand. Reviewing the evolution of the clear and present danger test since *Schenck*, Hand concluded that it was no more than a balancing technique. But he also ventured to give the test greater precision by adding that courts must consider "whether the gravity of the 'evil,' discounted by its improbability, justifies such invasion of free speech as is necessary to avoid the danger." According to Hand, restrictions on speech and press were permissible only if they posed a clear and, not merely present but, imminent and probable danger. As refashioned, the clear and present danger test was sharper than Justice Holmes's initial formulation, yet it permitted changing political circumstances to determine the scope of the First Amendment. Turning to international events and the threat of communism, Judge Hand could not imagine "a more probable danger, unless one must wait till the actual eve of hostilities." Dennis's attorneys promptly appealed Judge Hand's ruling to the Supreme Court. The Court granted review (with newly appointed Justice Tom Clark recusing himself, because he had been attorney general when the government began prosecuting Dennis).

The Court's decision was 6–2, with Justice Clark not participating, and the plurality's opinion announced by Chief Justice Vinson. Concurrences were by Justices Frankfurter and Jackson, dissents by Justices Black and Douglas.

■ ■ ■

☐ *Chief Justice VINSON, with whom Justice REED, Justice BURTON, and Justice MINTON join, delivered the opinion of the Court.*

Petitioners were indicted in July, 1948, for violation of the conspiracy provisions of the Smith Act, during the period of April, 1945 to July, 1948. . . . A verdict of guilty as to all the petitioners was returned by the jury on October 14, 1949. The Court of Appeals affirmed the convictions. We granted *certiorari* [to decide] . . . the following two questions: (1) Whether either Sec. 2 or Sec. 3 of the Smith Act, inherently or as construed and applied in the instant case, violates the First Amendment and other provisions of the Bill of Rights; (2) whether either Sec. 2 or Sec. 3 of the Act, inherently or as construed and applied in the instant case, violates the First and Fifth Amendments because of indefiniteness.

Sections 2 and 3 of the Smith Act provide as follows:

Sec. 2.

(a) It shall be unlawful for any person—
(1) to knowingly or willfully advocate, abet, advise, or teach the duty, necessity, desirability, or propriety of overthrowing or destroying any government in the United States by force or violence, or by the assassination of any officer of any such government. . . .

Sec. 3. It shall be unlawful for any person to attempt to commit, or to conspire to commit, any of the acts prohibited by the provisions of . . . this title.

The indictment charged the petitioners with wilfully and knowingly conspiring (1) to organize as the Communist Party of the United States of America a society, group and assembly of persons who teach and advocate the overthrow and destruction of the Government of the United States by force and violence, and (2) knowingly and wilfully to advocate and teach the duty and necessity of overthrowing and destroying the Government of the United States by force and violence. . . .

The trial of the case extended over nine months, six of which were devoted to the taking of evidence, resulting in a record of 16,000 pages. Our limited grant of the writ of *certiorari* has removed from our consideration any question as to the sufficiency of the evidence to support the jury's determination that petitioners are guilty of the offense charged. Whether on this record petitioners did in fact advocate the overthrow of the Government by force and violence is not before us, and we must base any discussion of this point upon the conclusions stated in the opinion of the Court of Appeals, which treated the issue in great detail. That court held that the record in this case amply supports the necessary finding of the jury that petitioners, the leaders of the Communist Party in this country, were unwilling to work within our framework of democracy, but intended to initiate a violent revolution whenever the propitious occasion appeared. . . .

The obvious purpose of the statute is to protect existing Government, not from change by peaceable, lawful and constitutional means, but from change by violence, revolution and terrorism. That it is within the *power* of the Congress to protect the Government of the United States from armed rebellion is a proposition which requires little discussion. Whatever theoretical merit there may be to the argument that there is a "right" to rebellion against dictatorial governments is without force where the existing structure of the government provides for peaceful and orderly change. We reject any principle of governmental helplessness in the face of preparation for revolution, which principle, carried to its logical conclusion, must lead to anarchy. No one could conceive that it is not within the power of Congress to prohibit acts intended to overthrow the Government by force and violence. The question with which we are concerned here is not whether Congress has such *power*, but whether the *means* which it has employed conflict with the First and Fifth Amendments to the Constitution. . . .

[The petitioners attack] the statute on the grounds that by its terms it prohibits academic discussion of the merits of Marxism-Leninism, that it stifles ideas and is contrary to all concepts of a free speech and a free press. . . .

The very language of the Smith Act negates the interpretation which petitioners would have us impose on that Act. It is directed at advocacy, not discussion. Thus, the trial judge properly charged the jury that they could not convict if they found that petitioners did "no more than pursue peaceful studies and discussions or teaching and advocacy in the realm of ideas." . . . Congress did not intend to eradicate the free discussion of political theories, to destroy the traditional rights of Americans to discuss and evaluate ideas without fear of governmental sanction. Rather Congress was concerned with the very kind of activity in which the evidence showed these petitioners engaged.

But although the statute is not directed at the hypothetical cases which petitioners have conjured, its application in this case has resulted in convictions for the teaching and advocacy of the overthrow of the Government by force and violence, which, even though coupled with the intent to accomplish that overthrow, contains an element of speech. For this reason, we must pay special heed to the demands of the First Amendment marking out the boundaries of speech. . . .

The rule we deduce from [*Schenck v. United States* and the other Espionage Act] cases is that where an offense is specified by a statute in nonspeech or nonpress terms, a conviction relying upon speech or press as evidence of violation may be sustained only when the speech or publication created a "clear and present danger" of attempting or accomplishing the prohibited crime, e.g., interference with enlistment. The dissents, in emphasizing the value of speech, were addressed to the argument of the sufficiency of the evidence. . . .

Although no case subsequent to *Whitney* [*v. California*, 274 U.S. 421 (1927)] and *Gitlow* [*v. New York* (1925)] has expressly overruled the majority opinions in those cases, there is little doubt that subsequent opinions have inclined toward the HOLMES-BRANDEIS rationale. . . . But . . . neither Justice HOLMES nor Justice BRANDEIS ever envisioned that a shorthand phrase should be crystallized into a rigid rule to be applied inflexibly without regard to the circumstances of each case. Speech is not an absolute, above and beyond control by the legislature when its judgment, subject to review here, is that certain kinds of speech are so undesirable as to warrant criminal sanction. . . .

In this case we are squarely presented with the application of the "clear and present danger" test, and must decide what that phrase imports. We first note that many of the cases in which this Court has reversed convictions by use of this or similar tests have been based on the fact that the interest which the State was attempting to protect was itself too insubstantial to warrant restriction of speech. . . . Overthrow of the Government by force and violence is certainly a substantial enough interest for the Government to limit speech. . . . If, then, this interest may be protected, the literal problem which is presented is what has been meant by the use of the phrase "clear and present danger" of the utterances bringing about the evil within the power of Congress to punish.

Obviously, the words cannot mean that before the Government may act, it must wait until the *putsch* is about to be executed, the plans have been laid and the signal is awaited. If Government is aware that a group aiming at its overthrow is attempting to indoctrinate its members and to commit them to a course whereby they will strike when the leaders feel the circumstances permit, action by the Government is required. The argument that there is no need for Government to concern itself, for Government is strong, it possesses ample powers to put down a rebellion, it may defeat the revolution with ease needs no answer. For that is not the question. Certainly an attempt to overthrow the Government by force, even though doomed from the outset because of inadequate numbers or power of the revolutionists, is a sufficient evil for Congress to prevent. The damage which such attempts create both physically and politically to a nation makes it impossible to measure the validity in terms of the probability of success, or the immediacy of a successful attempt. In the instant case the trial judge charged the jury that they could not convict unless they found that petitioners intended to overthrow the Government "as speedily as circumstances would permit." This does not mean, and could not properly mean, that they would not strike until there was certainty of success. What was meant was that the revolutionists would strike when they thought the time was ripe. We must therefore reject the contention that success or probability of success is the criterion.

The situation with which Justices HOLMES and BRANDEIS were concerned in *Gitlow* was a comparatively isolated event, bearing little relation in their minds to any substantial threat to the safety of the community. . . . They were not confronted with any situation comparable to the instant one—the development of an apparatus designed and dedicated to the overthrow of the Government, in the context of world crisis after crisis.

Chief Judge Learned Hand, writing for the majority below, interpreted the phrase as follows: "In each case [courts] must ask whether the gravity of the 'evil,' discounted by its improbability, justifies such invasion of free speech as is necessary to avoid the danger." We adopt this statement of the rule. As articulated by Chief Judge Hand, it is as succinct and inclusive as any other we might devise at this time. It takes into consideration those factors which we deem relevant, and relates their significances. More we cannot expect from words.

Likewise, we are in accord with the court below, which affirmed the trial court's finding that the requisite danger existed. The mere fact that from the period 1945 to 1948 petitioners' activities did not result in an attempt to overthrow the Government by force and violence is of course no answer to the fact that there was a group that was ready to make the attempt. The formation by petitioners of such a highly organized conspiracy, with rigidly disciplined members subject to call when the leaders, these petitioners, felt that the time had come for action, coupled with the inflammable nature of world conditions, similar uprisings in other countries, and the touch-and-go nature of our relations with countries with whom petitioners were in the very least ideo-logically attuned, convince us that their convictions were justified on this score. And this analysis disposes of the contention that a conspiracy to advo-cate, as distinguished from the advocacy itself, cannot be constitutionally restrained, because it comprises only the preparation. It is the existence of the conspiracy which creates the danger. . . . If the ingredients of the reaction are present, we cannot bind the Government to wait until the catalyst is added. . . .

When facts are found that establish the violation of a statute, the protec-tion against conviction afforded by the First Amendment is a matter of law. The doctrine that there must be a clear and present danger of a substantive evil that Congress has a right to prevent is a judicial rule to be applied as a matter of law by the courts. The guilt is established by proof of facts. Whether the First Amendment protects the activity which constitutes the violation of the statute must depend upon a judicial determination of the scope of the First Amendment applied to the circumstances of the case. . . .

[I]n the very case in which the phrase was born, *Schenck*, this Court itself examined the record to find whether the requisite danger appeared, and the issue was not submitted to a jury. And in every later case in which the Court has measured the validity of a statute by the "clear and present danger" test, that determination has been by the court, the question of the danger not being submitted to the jury.

The question in this case is whether the statute which the legislature has enacted may be constitutionally applied. In other words, the Court must examine judicially the application of the statute to the particular situ-ation, to ascertain if the Constitution prohibits the conviction. We hold that the statute may be applied where there is a "clear and present danger" of the substantive evil which the legislature had the right to prevent.

☐ Justice *FRANKFURTER, concurring.*

Primary responsibility for adjusting the interests which compete in the situation before us of necessity belongs to the Congress. . . . We are to set aside the judgment of those whose duty it is to legislate only if there is no reasonable basis for it. . . .

"Great cases," it is appropriate to remember, "like hard cases make bad law. For great cases are called great, not by reason of their real importance in shaping the law of the future, but because of some accident of immediate overwhelming interest which appeals to the feelings and distorts the judg-ment. These immediate interests exercise a kind of hydraulic pressure which makes what previously was clear seem doubtful, and before which even well settled principles of law will bend." Justice HOLMES, dissenting in *Northern Securities Co. v. United States*, 193 U.S. 197 [1904].

This is such a case. Unless we are to compromise judicial impartiality and subject these defendants to the risk of an *ad hoc* judgment influenced by the impregnating atmosphere of the times, the constitutionality of their conviction must be determined by principles established in cases decided in more tranquil periods. . . .

First. Free-speech cases are not an exception to the principle that we are not legislators, that direct policy-making is not our province. How best to reconcile competing interests is the business of legislatures, and the balance they strike is a judgment not to be displaced by ours, but to be respected unless outside the pale of fair judgment. . . .

Second. A survey of the relevant decisions indicates that the results which we have reached are on the whole those that would ensue from careful weighing of conflicting interests. . . .

Third. Not every type of speech occupies the same position on the scale of values. There is no substantial public interest in permitting certain kinds of utterances: "the lewd and obscene, the profane, the libelous, and the insulting or 'fighting' words—those which by their very utterance inflict injury or tend to incite an immediate breach of the peace." *Chaplinsky v. State of New Hampshire,* 315 U.S. 568 [1942]. It is pertinent to the decision before us to consider where on the scale of values we have in the past placed the type of speech now claiming constitutional immunity.

The defendants have been convicted of conspiring to organize a party of persons who advocate the overthrow of the Government by force and violence. The jury has found that the object of the conspiracy is advocacy as "a rule or principle of action," "by language reasonably and ordinarily calculated to incite persons to such action," and with the intent to cause the overthrow "as speedily as circumstances would permit."

On any scale of values which we have hitherto recognized, speech of this sort ranks low. . . .

But there is underlying validity in the distinction between advocacy and the interchange of ideas, and we do not discard a useful tool because it may be misused. That such a distinction could be used unreasonably by those in power against hostile or unorthodox views does not negate the fact that it may be used reasonably against an organization wielding the power of the centrally controlled international Communist movement. The object of the conspiracy before us is so clear that the chance of error in saying that the defendants conspired to advocate rather than to express ideas is slight. Justice DOUGLAS quite properly points out that the conspiracy before us is not a conspiracy to overthrow the Government. But it would be equally wrong to treat it as a seminar in political theory.

These general considerations underlie decision of the case before us.

On the one hand is the interest in security. The Communist Party was not designed by these defendants as an ordinary political party. For the circumstances of its organization, its aims and methods, and the relation of the defendants to its organization and aims we are concluded by the jury's verdict. The jury found that the Party rejects the basic premise of our political system—that change is to be brought about by nonviolent constitutional process. The jury found that the Party advocates the theory that there is a duty and necessity to overthrow the Government by force and violence. It found that the Party entertains and promotes this view, not as a prophetic insight or as a bit of unworldly speculation, but as a program for winning adherents and as a policy to be translated into action. . . .

On the other hand is the interest in free speech. The right to exert all governmental powers in aid of maintaining our institutions and resisting their physical overthrow does not include intolerance of opinions and speech that cannot do harm although opposed and perhaps alien to dominant, traditional opinion. . . .

A public interest is not wanting in granting freedom to speak their minds even to those who advocate the overthrow of the Government by force. For, as the evidence in this case abundantly illustrates, coupled with such advocacy is criticism of defects in our society. . . . Suppressing advocates of overthrow inevitably will also silence critics who do not advocate overthrow but fear that their criticism may be so construed. No matter how clear we may be that the defendants now before us are preparing to overthrow our Government at the propitious moment, it is self-delusion to think that we can punish them for their advocacy without adding to the risks run by loyal citizens who honestly believe in some of the reforms these defendants advance. It is a sobering fact that in sustaining the convictions before us we can hardly escape restriction on the interchange of ideas. . . .

It is not for us to decide how we would adjust the clash of interests which this case presents were the primary responsibility for reconciling it ours. Congress has determined that the danger created by advocacy of overthrow justifies the ensuing restriction on freedom of speech. . . .

To make validity of legislation depend on judicial reading of events still in the womb of time—a forecast, that is, of the outcome of forces at best appreciated only with knowledge of the topmost secrets of nations—is to charge the judiciary with duties beyond its equipment.

☐ *Justice JACKSON, concurring.*

The Communist Party . . . does not seek its strength primarily in numbers. Its aim is a relatively small party whose strength is in selected, dedicated, indoctrinated, and rigidly disciplined members. From established policy it tolerates no deviation and no debate. It seeks members that are, or may be, secreted in strategic posts in transportation, communications, industry, government, and especially in labor unions where it can compel employers to accept and retain its members. It also seeks to infiltrate and control organizations of professional and other groups. Through these placements in positions of power it seeks a leverage over society that will make up in power of coercion what it lacks in power of persuasion.

The Communists have no scruples against sabotage, terrorism, assassination, or mob disorder; but violence is not with them, as with the anarchists, an end in itself. The Communist Party advocates force only when prudent and profitable. Their strategy of stealth precludes premature or uncoordinated outbursts of violence, except, of course, when the blame will be placed on shoulders other than their own. They resort to violence as to truth, not as a principle but as an expedient. Force or violence, as they would resort to it, may never be necessary, because infiltration and deception may be enough. . . .

The foregoing is enough to indicate that, either by accident or design, the Communist strategem outwits the anti-anarchist pattern of statute aimed against "overthrow by force and violence" if qualified by the doctrine that only "clear and present danger" of accomplishing that result will sustain the prosecution.

The "clear and present danger" test was an innovation by Justice HOLMES in the *Schenck* case, reiterated and refined by him and Justice BRANDEIS in later cases, all arising before the era of World War II revealed the subtlety and efficacy of modernized revolutionary techniques used by totalitarian parties. In those cases, they were faced with convictions under so-called criminal syndicalism statutes aimed at anarchists but which, loosely construed, had been applied to punish socialism, pacifism, and left-wing ideologies, the charges often resting on far-fetched inferences which, if true, would establish only technical or trivial violations. They proposed "clear and present danger" as a test for the sufficiency of evidence in particular cases.

I would save it, unmodified, for application as a "rule of reason" in the kind of case for which it was devised. When the issue is criminality of a hot-headed speech on a street corner, or circulation of a few incendiary pamphlets, or parading by some zealots behind a red flag, or refusal of a handful of school children to salute our flag, it is not beyond the capacity of the judicial process to gather, comprehend, and weigh the necessary materials for decision whether it is a clear and present danger of substantive evil or a harmless letting off of steam. It is not a prophecy, for the danger in such cases has matured by the time of trial or it was never present. The test applies and has meaning where a conviction is sought to be based on a speech or writing which does not directly or explicitly advocate a crime but to which such tendency is sought to be attributed by construction or by implication from external circumstances. The formula in such cases favors freedoms that are vital to our society, and, even if sometimes applied too generously, the consequences cannot be grave. But its recent expansion has extended, in particular to Communists, unprecedented immunities. Unless we are to hold our Government captive in a judge-made verbal trap, we must approach the problem of a well-organized, nation-wide conspiracy, such as I have described, as realistically as our predecessors faced the trivialities that were being prosecuted until they were checked with a rule of reason.

I think reason is lacking for applying that test to this case.

If we must decide that this Act and its application are constitutional only if we are convinced that petitioner's conduct creates a "clear and present danger" of violent overthrow, we must appraise imponderables, including international and national phenomena which baffle the best informed foreign offices and our most experienced politicians. We would have to foresee and predict the effectiveness of Communist propaganda, opportunities for infiltration, whether, and when, a time will come that they consider propitious for action, and whether and how fast our existing government will deteriorate. And we would have to speculate as to whether an approaching Communist *coup* would not be anticipated by a nationalistic fascist movement. No doctrine can be sound whose application requires us to make a prophecy of that sort in the guise of a legal decision. The judicial process simply is not adequate to a trial of such far-flung issues. The answers given would reflect our own political predilections and nothing more.

The authors of the clear and present danger test never applied it to a case like this, nor would I. If applied as it is proposed here, it means that the Communist plotting is protected during its period of incubation; its preliminary stages of organization and preparation are immune from the law; the Government can move only after imminent action is manifest, when it would, of course, be too late.

The highest degree of constitutional protection is due to the individual acting without conspiracy. But even an individual cannot claim that the Constitution protects him in advocating or teaching overthrow of government by force or violence. I should suppose no one would doubt that Congress has power to make such attempted overthrow a crime. But the contention is that one has the constitutional right to work up a public desire and will to do what it is a crime to attempt. I think direct incitement by speech or writing can be made a crime, and I think there can be a conviction without also proving that the odds favored its success by 99 to 1, or some other extremely high ratio. . . .

Of course, it is not always easy to distinguish teaching or advocacy in the sense of incitement from teaching or advocacy in the sense of exposition or explanation. It is a question of fact in each case.

What really is under review here is a conviction of conspiracy, after a trial for conspiracy, on an indictment charging conspiracy, brought under a statute outlawing conspiracy. With due respect to my colleagues, they seem to me to discuss anything under the sun except the law of conspiracy. . . .

The Constitution does not make conspiracy a civil right. The Court has never before done so and I think it should not do so now. . . .

The reasons underlying the doctrine that conspiracy may be a substantive evil in itself, apart from any evil it may threaten, attempt or accomplish, are peculiarly appropriate to conspiratorial Communism. . . .

I do not suggest that Congress could punish conspiracy to advocate something, the doing of which it may not punish. Advocacy or exposition of the doctrine of communal property ownership, or any political philosophy unassociated with advocacy of its imposition by force or seizure of government by unlawful means could not be reached through conspiracy prosecution. But it is not forbidden to put down force or violence, it is not forbidden to punish its teaching or advocacy, and the end being punishable, there is no doubt of the power to punish conspiracy for the purpose.

☐ *Justice BLACK, dissenting.*

At the outset I want to emphasize what the crime involved in this case is, and what it is not. These petitioners were not charged with an attempt to overthrow the Government. They were not charged with overt acts of any kind designed to overthrow the Government. They were not even charged with saying anything or writing anything designed to overthrow the Government. The charge was that they agreed to assemble and to talk and publish certain ideas at a later date: The indictment is that they conspired to organize the Communist Party and to use speech or newspapers and other publications in the future to teach and advocate the forcible overthrow of the Government. No matter how it is worded, this is a virulent form of prior censorship of speech and press, which I believe the First Amendment forbids. I would hold Section 3 of the Smith Act authorizing this prior restraint unconstitutional on its face and as applied. . . .

So long as this Court exercises the power of judicial review of legislation, I cannot agree that the First Amendment permits us to sustain laws suppressing freedom of speech and press on the basis of Congress' or our own notions of mere "reasonableness." Such a doctrine waters down the First Amendment so that it amounts to little more than an admonition to Congress. . . .

Public opinion being what it now is, few will protest the conviction of these Communist petitioners. There is hope, however, that in calmer times, when present pressures, passions and fears subside, this or some later Court will restore the First Amendment liberties to the high preferred place where they belong in a free society.

☐ *Justice DOUGLAS, dissenting.*

If this were a case where those who claimed protection under the First Amendment were teaching the techniques of sabotage, the assassination of the President, the filching of documents from public files, the planting of bombs, the art of street warfare, and the like, I would have no doubts. The freedom to speak is not absolute; the teaching of methods of terror and other seditious conduct should be beyond the pale along with obscenity and immorality. This case was argued as if those were the facts. . . . But the fact is that no such evidence was introduced at the trial. There is a statute which makes a seditious conspiracy unlawful. Petitioners, however, were not charged with a "conspiracy to overthrow" the Government. They were charged with a conspiracy to form a party and groups and assemblies of people who teach and advocate the overthrow of our Government by force or violence and with a conspiracy to advocate and teach its overthrow by force and violence. It may well be that indoctrination in the techniques of terror to destroy the Government would be indictable under either statute. But the teaching which is condemned here is of a different character.

So far as the present record is concerned, what petitioners did was to organize people to teach and themselves teach the Marxist-Leninist doctrine contained chiefly in four books: *Foundations of Leninism* by Stalin (1924); *The Communist Manifesto* by Marx and Engels (1848); *State and Revolution* by Lenin (1917); *History of the Communist Party of the Soviet Union* (1939).

Those books are to Soviet Communism what *Mein Kampf* was to Nazism. If they are understood, the ugliness of Communism is revealed, its deceit and cunning are exposed, the nature of its activities becomes apparent, and the chances of its success less likely. That is not, of course, the reason why petitioners chose these books for their classrooms. They are fervent Communists to whom these volumes are gospel. They preached the creed with the hope that some day it would be acted upon.

The opinion of the Court does not outlaw these texts nor condemn them to the fire, as the Communists do literature offensive to their creed. But if the books themselves are not outlawed, if they can lawfully remain on library shelves, by what reasoning does their use in a classroom become a crime? It would not be a crime under the Act to introduce these books to a class, though that would be teaching what the creed of violent overthrow of the Government is. The Act, as construed, requires the element of intent— that those who teach the creed believe in it. The crime then depends not on what is taught but on who the teacher is. That is to make freedom of speech turn not on *what is said*, but on the *intent* with which it is said. Once we start down that road we enter territory dangerous to the liberties of every citizen. . . .

Intent, of course, often makes the difference in the law. An act otherwise excusable or carrying minor penalties may grow to an abhorrent thing if the evil intent is present. We deal here, however, not with ordinary acts but with speech, to which the Constitution has given a special sanction. . . .

There comes a time when even speech loses its constitutional immunity. Speech innocuous one year may at another time fan such destructive flames that it must be halted in the interests of the safety of the Republic. That is the meaning of the clear and present danger test. When conditions are so critical that there will be no time to avoid the evil that the speech threatens, it is time to call a halt. Otherwise, free speech which is the strength of the Nation will be the cause of its destruction.

Yet free speech is the rule, not the exception. The restraint to be constitutional must be based on more than fear, on more than passionate opposition against the speech, on more than a revolted dislike for its contents. There must be some immediate injury to society that is likely if speech is allowed. The classic statement of these conditions was made by Justice BRANDEIS in his concurring opinion in *Whitney v. People of State of California*, 274 U.S. 357 [1927].

> Fear of serious injury cannot alone justify suppression of free speech and assembly. Men feared witches and burnt women. It is the function of speech to free men from the bondage of irrational fears. To justify suppression of free speech there must be reasonable ground to fear that serious evil will result if free speech is practiced. There must be reasonable ground to believe that the danger apprehended is imminent. There must be reasonable ground to believe that the evil to be prevented is a serious one. Every denunciation of existing law tends in some measure to increase the probability that there will be violation of it. Condonation of a breach enhances the probability. Expressions of approval add to the probability. Propagation of the criminal state of mind by teaching syndicalism increases it. Advocacy of law-breaking heightens it still further. But even advocacy of violation, however, reprehensible morally, is not a justification for denying free speech where the advocacy falls short of incitement and there is nothing to indicate that the advocacy would be immediately acted on. The wide difference between advocacy and incitement, between preparation and attempt, between assembling and conspiracy, must be borne in mind. In order to support a finding of clear and present danger it must be shown either that immediate serious violence was to be expected or was advocated, or that the past conduct furnished reason to believe that such advocacy was then contemplated.

Brandenburg v. Ohio
395 U.S. 444, 89 S.Ct. 1827 (1969)

Clarence Brandenburg, the leader of a Ku Klux Klan group, was arrested, tried, and convicted under the Ohio Criminal Syndicalism statute for "advocat[ing] . . . the duty, necessity, or propriety of crime, sabotage, violence, or unlawful methods of terrorism as a means of accomplishing industrial or political reform" and for "voluntarily assembl[ing] with any society, group, or assemblage or persons formed to teach or advocate the doctrines of criminal syndicalism." He had addressed a small rally of hooded men, some of whom carried firearms, standing before a burning cross and declared, among other things, that if the president, Congress, and the Court continued "to suppress the white, Caucasian race, it's possible that there might have to be revengenance [*sic*] taken." The major evidence introduced against Brandenburg at trial were two films of his speeches at rallies. Brandenburg unsuccessfully appealed his conviction in a state appellate court and then to the state supreme court, which denied review. On further appeal to the Supreme Court, Brandenburg's case was granted review. At conference, the justices unanimously voted to overturn his conviction. Subsequently, Chief Justice Warren assigned Justice Abe Fortas to draft an opinion for the Court. But Justice Fortas was pressed into resigning in May, and hence the Court's opinion came on June 9 as an unsigned (*per curiam*) opinion.

The Court's decision was unanimous, and the opinion was announced *per curiam*, with Justice Fortas not participating. Concurrences were by Justices Black and Douglas.

■ ■ ■

PER CURIAM.

The appellant, a leader of a Ku Klux Klan group, was convicted under the Ohio Criminal Syndicalism statute for "advocat[ing] . . . the duty, necessity, or propriety of crime, sabotage, violence, or unlawful methods of terrorism as a means of accomplishing industrial or political reform" and for "voluntarily assembl[ing] with any society, group, or assemblage of persons formed to teach or advocate the doctrines of criminal syndicalism." He was fined $1,000 and sentenced to one to 10 years' imprisonment. The appellant challenged the constitutionality of the criminal syndicalism statute under the First and Fourteenth Amendments to the United States Constitution, but the intermediate appellate court of Ohio affirmed his conviction without opinion. . . . We reverse.

The record shows that a man, identified at trial as the appellant, telephoned an announcer-reporter on the staff of a Cincinnati television station and invited him to come to a Ku Klux Klan "rally" to be held at a farm in Hamilton County. With the cooperation of the organizers, the reporter and a cameraman attended the meeting and filmed the events. Portions of the films were later broadcast on the local station and on a national network. . . .

One film showed 12 hooded figures, some of whom carried firearms. They were gathered around a large wooden cross, which they burned. No one was present other than the participants and the newsmen who made the film. Most of the words uttered during the scene were incomprehensible when the film was projected, but scattered phrases could be understood that were derogatory of Negroes and, in one instance, of Jews. . . .

The second film showed six hooded figures one of whom, later identified as the appellant, repeated a speech very similar to that recorded on the first film. The reference to the possibility of "revengeance" was omitted, and one sentence was added: "Personally, I believe the nigger should be returned to Africa, the Jew returned to Israel." Though some of the figures in the films carried weapons, the speaker did not. . . .

[The Court's] decisions have fashioned the principle that the constitutional guarantees of free speech and free press do not permit a State to forbid or proscribe advocacy of the use of force or of law violation except where such advocacy is directed to inciting or producing imminent lawless action and is likely to incite or produce such action. As we said in *Noto v. United States*, 367 U.S. 290 (1961), "the mere abstract teaching . . . of the moral propriety or even moral necessity for a resort to force and violence, is not the same as preparing a group for violent action and steeling it to such action." A statute which fails to draw this distinction impermissibly intrudes upon the freedoms guaranteed by the First and Fourteenth Amendments. It sweeps within its condemnation speech which our Constitution has immunized from governmental control.

Measured by this test, Ohio's Criminal Syndicalism Act cannot be sustained. The Act punishes persons who "advocate or teach the duty, necessity, or propriety" of violence "as a means of accomplishing industrial or political reform"; or who publish or circulate or display any book or paper containing such advocacy; or who "justify" the commission of violent acts "with intent to exemplify, spread or advocate the propriety of the doctrines of criminal syndicalism"; or who "voluntarily assemble" with a group formed "to teach or advocate the doctrines of criminal syndicalism." Neither the indictment nor the trial judge's instructions to the jury in any way refined the statute's bald definition of the crime in terms of mere advocacy not distinguished from incitement to imminent lawless action.

Accordingly, we are here confronted with a statute which, by its own words and as applied, purports to punish mere advocacy and to forbid, on pain of criminal punishment, assembly with others merely to advocate the described type of action. Such a statute falls within the condemnation of the First and Fourteenth Amendments. The contrary teaching of *Whitney v. California*, [274 U.S. 357 (1927)], cannot be supported, and that decision is therefore overruled.

Reversed.

□ *Justice BLACK, concurring.*

I agree with the views expressed by Justice DOUGLAS in his concurring opinion in this case that the "clear and present danger" doctrine should have no place in the interpretation of the First Amendment.

□ *Justice DOUGLAS, concurring.*

While I join the opinion of the Court, I desire to enter a *caveat.* . . .

I see no place in the regime of the First Amendment for any "clear and present danger" test, whether strict and tight as some would make it, or free-wheeling as the Court in *Dennis* [*v. United States* (1951)] rephrased it.

When one reads the opinions closely and sees when and how the "clear and present danger" test has been applied, great misgivings are aroused. First, the threats were often loud but always puny and made serious only by judges

Brandenburg v. Ohio was perhaps the climax of the many Court decisions in the 1960s that significantly expanded First Amendment freedoms. Clarence Branden-burg was a member of the Ku Klux Klan who violated an Ohio syndicalism statute by advocating racial strife during a televised rally. (*AP Photo*)

so wedded to the *status quo* that critical analysis made them nervous. Second, the test was so twisted and perverted in *Dennis* as to make the trial of those teachers of Marxism an all-out political trial which was part and parcel of the cold war that has eroded substantial parts of the First Amendment. . . .

The line between what is permissible and not subject to control and what may be made impermissible and subject to regulation is the line between ideas and overt acts.

The example usually given by those who would punish speech is the case of one who falsely shouts fire in a crowded theatre.

This is, however, a classic case where speech is brigaded with action. They are indeed inseparable and a prosecution can be launched for the overt acts actually caused. Apart from rare instances of that kind, speech is, I think, immune from prosecution.

■ (2) JUDICIAL LINE DRAWING: *AD HOC* AND DEFINITIONAL BALANCING

The internal struggle within the Court over rival interpretive approaches to the First Amendment registered not merely differences over the history and principles of free speech and press. There were profound differences as well in judicial self-perception and philosophy over the role of the Court in a constitutional democracy and why free speech is important to defend. How deferential should the Court be to legislative majorities in defining the line between constitutionally protected and unprotected speech and press? What standards and principles should guide the Court's line drawing? What kinds of speech should, and should not, receive First Amendment protection? Why does free speech matter?—(1) because free speech has an *instrumental* value in promoting and maintaining democracy; (2) because free speech has *intrinsic value* and is essential to individual self-expression and self-determination; (3) because the best test of truth is determined by "the marketplace of ideas"; and/or (4) because once speech is regulated, censored, and punished we invite the proverbial "slippery slope" of governmental censorship.

The clear and present danger test was initially formulated as an alternative to the traditional presumption of the reasonableness of legislation and the bad tendency test, which was used by the Court to rationalize legislative restrictions on speech and press. Although potentially a basis for protecting free speech and press, the clear and present danger test gradually evolved into a balancing technique for upholding restrictions on speech and press. After fifty years, the clear and present danger test was laid to rest in *Brandenburg v. Ohio* (1969) (excerpted above), and since then survives primarily in *dicta.*[1] A majority of the Warren Court also eventually repudiated the *ad hoc* or case-by-case balancing approach advanced by Justice Harlan. Two years before *Brandenburg,* in a 6–2 decision (with Harlan and White in dissent and newly appointed Justice Thurgood Marshall not participating), Chief Justice Warren struck down as unconstitutional a provision of the McCarran Act forbidding any member of the Communist party to be employed in a defense facility. Joined by Black, Douglas, Stewart, Fortas, and Brennan in *United States v. Robel,* 389 U.S. 258 (1967), Warren used the occasion expressly to reject *ad hoc* balancing of First Amendment freedoms:

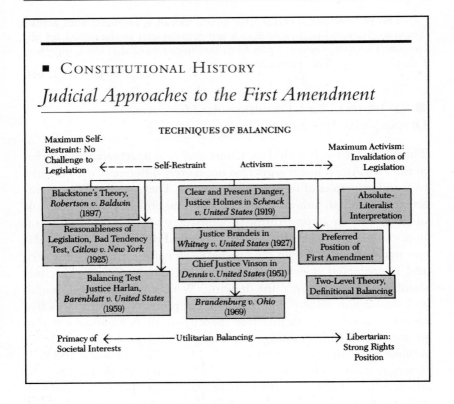

■ CONSTITUTIONAL HISTORY

Judicial Approaches to the First Amendment

TECHNIQUES OF BALANCING

Maximum Self-Restraint: No Challenge to Legislation ←------ Self-Restraint   Activism ------→ Maximum Activism: Invalidation of Legislation

Blackstone's Theory, *Robertson v. Baldwin* (1897)

Clear and Present Danger, Justice Holmes in *Schenck v. United States* (1919)

Absolute-Literalist Interpretation

Reasonableness of Legislation, Bad Tendency Test, *Gitlow v. New York* (1925)

Justice Brandeis in *Whitney v. United States* (1927)

Preferred Position of First Amendment

Balancing Test Justice Harlan, *Barenblatt v. United States* (1959)

Chief Justice Vinson in *Dennis v. United States* (1951)

Two-Level Theory, Definitional Balancing

Brandenburg v. Ohio (1969)

Primacy of ← ------- Utilitarian Balancing -------→ Libertarian: Societal Interests   Strong Rights Position

Faced with a clear conflict between a federal statute enacted in the interests of national security and an individual's exercise of his First Amendment rights, we have confined our analysis to whether Congress has adopted a constitutional means in achieving its concededly legitimate legislative goal. In making this determination we have found it necessary to measure the validity of the means adopted by Congress against both the goal it has sought to achieve and the specific prohibitions of the First Amendment. But we have in no way "balanced" those respective interests. We have ruled only that the Constitution requires that the conflict between congressional power and individual rights be accommodated by legislation drawn more narrowly to avoid the conflict.

Ad hoc balancing, whether under the clear and present danger test or as advocated by Harlan, was widely criticized within and without the Court for three principal reasons: (1) it was ambiguous and unpredictable in application, (2) it failed to establish a constitutional standard for adjudicating claims in a principled fashion, and (3) it tended to legitimate restrictions on speech and press because First Amendment claims were construed as simply private interests to be juxtaposed with public interests in self-preservation and punishing licentiousness.[2]

During his more than thirty years on the high bench, Justice Black remained one of the sharpest critics of balancing First Amendment freedoms and championed an "absolutist-literalist" interpretation. As he summarized his approach in 1968, when giving the James Carpenter Lectures at Columbia University School of Law,

> My view is, without deviation, without exception, without any ifs, buts, or whereas, that freedom of speech means that government shall not do anything to people, or, in the words of the Magna Carta, move against people, either for the views they have or the views they express or the words they speak or write. Some people would have you believe that this is a very radical position, and maybe it is. But all I am doing is following what to me is the clear wording of the First Amendment that "Congress shall make no law . . . abridging the freedom of speech[,] or of the press."[3]

The Court's abandonment of *ad hoc* balancing is a measure of Black's contribution to the constitutional politics of the First Amendment. Still, a majority of the Court has never been persuaded to embrace his absolutist-literalist position.

Instead of *ad hoc* balancing and Black's absolutism, the Court gradually developed a "principled, or definitional, balancing" approach to the First Amendment—that is, the Court has defined certain categories of speech as protected or unprotected per se. The Court's definitional-balancing approach to, or two-level theory of, the First Amendment was initially intimated by Justice Murphy, when writing for a unanimous Court in *Chaplinsky v. New Hampshire*, 315 U.S. 568 (1942). There the Court upheld the conviction under a statute forbidding the use of offensive or derisive language in public. Chaplinsky, at the time of his arrest for creating a public disturbance, called the arresting officer "a Goddamned racketeer" and "a damned Fascist." In contemplating these "fighting words," Murphy held that the First Amendment provides no protection for such words because they "are no essential part of any exposition of ideas." Certain categories of speech—the insulting or fighting words, the obscene, and libelous—have minimal, if any, social value and, therefore, are not worthy of constitutional protection. In Justice Murphy's words:

> There are certain well-defined and narrowly limited classes of speech, the prevention and punishment of which has never been thought to raise any constitutional problem. These include the lewd and the obscene, the profane, the libelous, and the insulting or "fighting words"—those which by their very utterance inflict injury or tend to incite an immediate breach of the peace. It has been observed that such utterances are no essential part of any exposition of ideas, and are of such slight social value as a step to

Justice Hugo Black in his chambers. Black was President Roosevelt's first appointee to the Court and a leader of the liberals on the Court. Justice Black is also known for his view that the First Amendment is absolute, that "Congress shall make no law . . . abridging the freedom of speech, or of the press" means what it says. (*Collection of the Supreme Court of the United States.*)

truth that any benefit that may be derived from them is clearly outweighed by the social interest in law and order.

Justice Murphy thus implied a two-level theory of the First Amendment: the amendment safeguards communications that have social value, but not those categories of (unprotected) speech that are "clearly outweighed by the social interest in order and morality."

Definitional balancing remains no less problematic than *ad hoc* balancing, because the Court must with some precision define the categories of and the standards for determining unprotected speech (fighting words, obscenity, libel, and commercial speech). Because of the Court's preoccupation with subversive political speech in the early part of the twentieth century and due to its deference to legislative and common-law proscriptions on speech and press, the task of further defining these categories of unprotected speech was largely avoided until the era of the

Warren Court. Since then the Court has faced the problems of refining and defining the tests for those narrow categories of speech that fall outside the scope of First Amendment protection: the four unprotected categories of speech are (1) the obscene or pornographic, (2) "fighting words" and other offensive expression, (3) libel, and (4) commercial speech. It is those and other problems of how the Court has drawn and redrawn those categories that the following sections of this chapter address.

But note that the Court is not of one mind on the application of categories of unprotected speech. Indeed, in the "hate-speech" case, *R.A.V. v. City of St. Paul, Minnesota,* 505 U.S. 377 (1992) (excerpted in Section B), concurring Justice Stevens draws into question the Court's definitional balancing or categorical approach to the First Amendment. See also *Virginia v. Black* (2003) (excerpted below) on the constitutionality of criminalizing cross-burning.

In addition, there are other areas of expression that do not receive First Amendment protection. But they are not categorically constitutionally unprotected. There is no protection, for example, for perjury, plagiarism, contempt of court, fraud and false advertising, insider trading and price fixing, trademark infringements, antitrust, copyright, or harassment in the workplace. Until the Roberts Court's decision in *Matal v. Tam,* 137 S. Ct. 1744 (2017) (discussed further in Section B of this chapter), trademarks were also deemed unprotected freedom of expression. There, the Court struck down the disparagement clause of the federal trademark law, prohibiting trademarks insulting to any individual or group. An Asian-American rock band known as the Slants was turned down by the U.S. Patent and Trademark Office for a trademark on its name because it was deemed offensive and to disparage people or groups. Writing for a unanimous Court (with Gorsuch not participating), Justice Alito held that ran afoul of the First Amendment because "[it]t offends a bedrock First Amendment principle: Speech may not be banned on the ground that it expresses ideas that offend."

The Court has also recognized restrictions on prisoners' communications, government employees' speech—particularly pertaining to military secrets—and *government-funded expression* (see, e.g., *Rust v. Sullivan,* 500 U.S. 173 (1991); *Rosenberger v. Rector and Visitors of the University of Virginia,* 515 U.S. 819 (1995); and *Pleasant Grove City v. Summum,* 555 U.S. 460 (2009) [holding that a small religious group could not compel a city to erect a monument in a public park]), along with students' rights, as well as upheld limitations to protect captive audiences. In addition, the Court has upheld "reasonable *time, place, and manner*" and noise regulations on expression.

A majority of the Roberts Court has continued in a series of decisions to defend the First Amendment guarantee for freedom of expression and to refuse to carve out exceptions or create more categories of unprotected speech. In *United States v. Alvarez*, 567 U.S. 709 (2012), for example, a plurality declared unconstitutional the Stolen Valor Act, which made it a crime to lie about receiving a military decoration or medal, punishable by up to a year in prison. Writing for the Court, Justice Kennedy held that the government had "not demonstrated that false statements generally should constitute a new category of unprotected speech." Underscoring its defense of the First Amendment, Justice Kennedy continued: "The remedy for speech that is false is speech that is true. This is the ordinary course in a free society. The response to the unreasoned is the rational; to the uninformed, the enlightened; to the straight-out lie, the simple truth. . . . The First Amendment itself ensures the right to respond to speech we do not like, and for good reason. Freedom of speech and thought flows not from the beneficence of the state but from the inalienable rights of the person."

By a 7–2 vote in *Brown v. Entertainment Merchants Association* (2011) (excerpted below in Section B(2)), the Court also struck down California's law punishing the sale of violent video games to minors. Justice Scalia's opinion for the Court swept broadly in reaffirming the broad protection of the First Amendment and refusing to carve out another category of unprotected speech. Justice Alito, joined by Chief Justice Roberts, concurred but left open the possibility of upholding such a law if properly framed. Justices Thomas and Breyer dissented. Notably, Justice Thomas would have upheld the law based on the "original understanding" of freedom of speech, while Justice Breyer would have done so based on social science data and the projected consequences of violent video games.

In sum, a categorical or definitional balancing approach defines the contemporary Court's basic framework for First Amendment protected and unprotected expression. But other areas of expression exist, and within each category of unprotected expression the Court has balanced freedom of expression and perceived harms—harms both public and private—based on the *context* and medium of expression, as further discussed in this chapter.

Notes

1. See, for example, *Detroit Edison Company v. National Labor Relations Board*, 440 U.S. 301 (1979); *Federal Communications Commission v. Pacifica Foundation*, 438 U.S. 726 (1978); *Landmark Communications, Inc. v. Virginia*, 435 U.S. 829 (1978); *Nebraska Press Association v. Stuart*, 427 U.S. 539 (1976); *Greer v. Spock*, 424 U.S. 828 (1976); *Pell v. Procunier*, 417 U.S. 817 (1974); *Cohen v. California*, 403 U.S. 15 (1971); and *Younger v. Harris*, 401 U.S. 37 (1971).

■ INSIDE THE COURT

"Absolutists" v. "Balancers": A Dialogue

A DIALOGUE
(With Apologies to Gertrude Stein)

L(ibertarian) L(ads):
  Speech is speech is speech.
F(rivolous) F(rankfurter):
  Crying-fire-in-theatre is speech is speech is not "speech."
  Libel is speech is speech is not "speech."
  Picketing is speech is speech is not "speech."
  Pornographic film is speech is speech is not "speech."

–Anonymous

Source: Undated memo from Justice Frankfurter to Justice Douglas, in Justice William O. Douglas Papers, Box 330, Manuscripts Room, Library of Congress.

2. For criticism of the *ad hoc* balancing approach, see Thomas I. Emerson, "Toward a General Theory of the First Amendment," 72 *Yale Law Journal* 854 (1963); Laurent Frantz, "The First Amendment in the Balance," 71 *Yale Law Journal* 1424 (1962); Robert McKay, "The Preference for Freedom," 34 *New York University Law Review* 1182 (1959); Samuel Krislov, "From *Ginzburg* to *Ginsberg*: The Unhurried Children's Hour in Obscenity Litigation," in *Supreme Court Review*, ed. Philip Kurland (Chicago: University of Chicago Press, 1968); and Harry Kalven, "Uninhibited, Robust, and Wide-Open—A Note on Free Speech and the Warren Court," 67 *Minnesota Law Review* 289 (1968). For defenses of balancing, see Wallace Mendelson, "On the Meaning of the First Amendment: Absolutes in the Balance," 50 *California Law Review* 821 (1962); and Dean Alfange Jr., "The Balancing of Interests in Free Speech Cases: In Defense of an Abused Doctrine," 2 *Law in Transition Quarterly* 35 (1965).

3. Hugo L. Black, *A Constitutional Faith* (New York: Alfred Knopf, 1968), 45.

SELECTED BIBLIOGRAPHY

Berns, Walter. *Freedom, Virtue and the First Amendment.* Baton Rouge: Louisiana State University Press, 1957.

————. *The First Amendment and the Future of American Democracy.* New York: Basic Books, 1976.

Black, Hugo. *A Constitutional Faith.* New York: Alfred Knopf, 1968.

Bollinger Lee C. *Uninhibited, Robust, and Wide-Open: A Free Press for a New Century.* New York: Oxford University Press, 2010.

Bollinger, Lee C., and Geoffrey R. Stone, eds. *Eternally Vigilant: Free Speech in the Modern Era*. Chicago: University of Chicago Press, 2002.

Brettschneider, Corey. *When the State Speaks, What Should It Say? How Democracies Can Protect Expression and Promote Equality*. Princeton: Princeton University Press, 2016.

Emerson, Thomas. *The System of Freedom of Expression*. New York: Random House, 1970.

Gelber, Katharine. *Free Speech After 9/11*. New York: Oxford University Press, 2016.

Lewis, Anthony. *Freedom for the Thought We Hate: A Biography of the First Amendment*. New York: Basic Books, 2008.

Meiklejohn, Alexander. *Political Freedom: The Constitutional Powers of the People*. New York: Harper & Row, 1965.

Redish, Martin. *The Logic of Persecution: Free Speech and the McCarthy Era*. Palo Alto: Stanford University Press, 2004.

Strassel, Kimberley. *The Intimidation Game: How the Left Is Silencing Free Speech*. New York: Twelve, 2016.

B | *Obscenity, Pornography, and Offensive Speech*

The problem of defining and dealing with obscenity, pornography, and other offensive speech is a continuing controversy in the constitutional politics of interpreting the First Amendment. Perhaps, as political scientist Harry Clor proposed:

> In the ideal system of legal control . . . wise men would solemnly weigh three considerations: the moral evils of obscenity, the virtues of art, and the requirements of public consensus in a regime of rational liberty. Each consideration would be given its full weight in the light of the common good. No work which is grossly obscene would ever be publicly circulated in society. No work which is not obscene would ever be censored.[1]

But such an "ideal system," as Clor concedes, "cannot be achieved among us." In a pluralistic society, people disagree over what is obscene, pornographic, and offensive; no consensus is likely. "One man's vulgarity is another man's lyric," as Justice Harlan put it in *Cohen v. California*, (1971) (see excerpt below). Or as Justice Stewart quipped in *Jacobellis v. Ohio*, 378 U.S. 184 (1964), "I know it [pornography] when I see it." Yet, for that very reason, Justice Black and Harvard Law School professor Alan Dershowitz, among others, argued, "To deny constitutional protection to a genre of speech that is incapable of precise definition is to endanger all freedom of expression. . . . Pornography should be included within the protection of the First Amendment, if for no other reason than by excluding it we give too much definitional power to the voracious censor."[2]

The Supreme Court in maintaining that obscenity, pornography, and fighting words fall outside the scope of First Amendment protection continues to confront the vexing definitional problems presented by its own line drawing. So too, as the Court's composition has changed, the tests and boundaries drawn defining *obscenity* and other forms of constitutionally unprotected offensive speech have evolved.

■ (1) Obscenity and Pornography

From the late nineteenth to the twentieth century, federal courts upheld congressional and state power to suppress allegedly obscene materials by applying the extremely restrictive English common-law test set forth in *Regina v. Hicklin*, L.R. 2 Q.B. 360 (1868). The so-called *Hicklin* test was "whether the tendency of the matter charged as obscenity is to deprive and corrupt those whose minds are open to such immoral influences and into whose hands a publication of this sort might fall." Under this test, books by Honoré de Balzac, Gustave Flaubert, James Joyce, D. H. Lawrence, and Arthur Miller were banned based on isolated passages and the influence they might have on the weakest members of society (children and the mentally impaired). As Justice Frankfurter was moved to observe, "the incidence of this standard is to reduce the adult population of [the country] to reading only what is fit for children."[3]

Not until *Roth v. United States* and its companion case, *Alberts v. California* (1957) (excerpted below) was the *Hicklin* test finally repudiated. There with Justices Black, Douglas, and Harlan in dissent over the holding that obscenity is "utterly without redeeming social value" and without First Amendment protection, Justice Brennan proposed a constitutional test for obscenity—"whether to the average person, applying contemporary community standards, the dominant theme of the material taken as a whole appeals to the prurient interests." As the opinions of the dissenters point out, though, the *Roth* test was problematic. Who is an "average person," what are "contemporary community standards," how and where are those standards to be determined, and, finally, what is "prurient interest"?

The Warren Court subsequently expanded the *Roth* test in three other important rulings. In *Kingsley International Corporation v. Regents of University of New York*, 360 U.S. 684 (1959), overturning the denial of a license to exhibit the movie *Lady Chatterley's Lover*, Justice Stewart held that books and films could not be banned for "thematic obscenity"—their dealing primarily with sexual themes. In *Manual Enterprises, Inc. v. Day*, 370 U.S. 478 (1962), Justice Harlan interpreted the prurient interest element of *Roth* to require that materials appeal to prurient interests in a "patently offensive way." Again writing for the Court in *Jacobellis v. State of Ohio*, 378 U.S. 184 (1964), Justice Brennan reversed the convictions of the makers and distributors of a film *The Lovers* and added to the *Roth* test the requirement that a book or film must be shown to lack "redeeming social importance" according to "national contemporary standards." Finally, in *A Book Named "John Cleland's Memoirs of a Woman of Pleasure" v. Massachusetts*, 383 U.S. 413 (1966), Justice Brennan combined all three of the above requirements in holding that obscene materials are excluded from First Amendment protection only if they fail all three requirements—that is, they (1) have a prurient interest that (2) appeal in a patently offensive way and (3) lack a redeeming social value.

As a result of the Warren Court's rulings only hard-core pornography fell outside of the scope of protected speech. This encouraged the proliferation of sexually oriented publications during the 1960s, the decade of the sexual revolution, and, in turn, elevated pornography to an issue in national politics. In 1968, for example, one of the charges made against Justice Fortas during his ill-fated nomination to be chief justice was that he had sided with the majority on the Warren Court in expansively reading the protection afforded by the First Amendment. Richard Nixon then made an issue of pornography in his 1968 presidential election campaign, pledging to return law and order to the country and appoint only "strict constructionists" to the Court.[4]

The Warren Court responded to the increased legislation and law enforcement efforts to control the "explosion" in the dissemination of sexually oriented and pornographic materials. The Court, for instance, upheld the conviction of Ralph Ginzburg for pandering by advertising the sale and mailing of his magazine *Eros* from such places as Middlesex, New Jersey; Blue Balls, Montana; and Intercourse, Pennsylvania, in *Ginzburg v. United States*, 383 U.S. 463 (1966). Selective prosecutions and bans on the sales of sexually oriented magazines to minors were also upheld in *Ginsberg v. New York*, 390 U.S. 629 (1968), sustaining the conviction of Sam Ginsberg for selling two "girlie" magazines to a sixteen-year-old boy. See also *United States v. Williams*, 553 U.S. 285 (2008) (excerpted in Section F), upholding a congressional act making it a federal crime to pander child pornography. In addition, permit systems and local censorship boards for screening sexually oriented films were approved so long as they afforded the film's distributors due process and abided by the Court's standards for determining what is obscene.[5]

However, even in Chief Justice Earl Warren's last term, the Court stood by its expansive reading of the First Amendment. *Stanley v.*

Georgia (1969) (see excerpt below) struck down a statute prohibiting the possession of obscene materials even in an individual's own house; as Justice Marshall put it, "Whatever may be the justifications for other statutes regulating obscenity, we do not think they reach into the privacy of one's home."

The year after *Stanley*, however, President Nixon's first appointee, Chief Justice Warren Burger, came to the Court. Already critical of the Warren Court's rulings on obscenity, he quickly tried to persuade his colleagues that the *Roth* line of rulings should be reconsidered. Initially unsuccessful, Burger was forced to voice his disagreement in dissenting opinions, questioning the propriety of "the national community standard" for obscenity in *Hoyt v. Minnesota*, 399 U.S. 524 (1970), and criticizing the Court for becoming a "super-censorship board" in *Cain v. Kentucky*, 387 U.S. 319 (1970), and *Walker v. Ohio*, 398 U.S. 434 (1970).

By 1973, Nixon's last two appointees, Justices Lewis Powell and William Rehnquist, were on the Court. And Burger finally got a bare majority to agree on a new test for obscenity, giving states and localities greater flexibility and control over sexually oriented materials. In *Miller v. California* (1973) (excerpted below), Burger set out more concrete rules for obscenity prosecutions. While maintaining the prurient interest test, he redefined it as "whether the work depicts or describes, in a patently offensive way sexual conduct specifically defined by state law," thus inviting states precisely to define obscenity in legislation. He also rejected as too broad the utterly without redeeming social value test and devised his own more precise test—"whether the work, taken as a whole, lacks serious literary, artistic, political or scientific value." Finally, the contemporary community standards test was reinterpreted to mean local, not national standards.

Ten companion cases coming down on a 5–4 vote with *Miller* buttressed the Burger Court's renewed deference to states and localities in controlling sexually oriented materials. *Paris Adult Theatre I v. Slaton* 413 U.S. 49 (1973), for example, limited the ruling in *Stanley v. Georgia*, by upholding state regulation of adult movie houses. Prior to *Paris Adult Theatre I*, the Court had held that the First Amendment and the right of privacy did not preclude searches of luggage for obscene materials by U.S. customs officials at airports in *United States v. 37 Photographs*, 402 U.S. 363 (1971). Subsequently, in *United States v. 12-1200 Foot Reels of Super 8mm Film*, 413 U.S. 123 (1973), the Court held that an individual does not have a First Amendment or privacy right to purchase obscene materials.

The test for obscenity announced in *Miller* was problematic, and the four dissenters remained adamant in their opposition. But the politics of the Court had changed. As Justice Stevens, in an unusual concurring opinion to the denial of review of an appeal of one of the hundreds of obscenity convictions following *Miller*, explained, "[T]here is no reason to believe that the majority of the Court which decided *Miller v. California* . . . is any less adamant than the minority. Accordingly, regardless of how I might vote on the merits after full argument, it would be pointless to grant *certiorari* in case after case of this character only to have *Miller* reaffirmed time after time."[6]

The most troubling problems with *Miller* arose because obscenity prosecutions under the ruling turned on varying local community standards. At the federal level this allowed prosecutors to "forum shop"—that is, they could initiate prosecutions in a district court in a geographical area with the most restrictive community standards. The Court declined to review this practice. At the state level, materials deemed obscene in one state might not be obscene in another. Consequently, the Court frequently cannot avoid rendering a final decision on the matter, notwithstanding that obscenity under *Miller* is determined according to local community standards. The Court thus held, in *Jenkins v. Georgia*, 418 U.S. 153 (1973), that the movie *Carnal Knowledge* was not obscene, despite lower court rulings to the contrary.

The Court tried to clarify some of the ambiguous aspects of *Miller*. *Pinkus v. United States*, 436 U.S. 293 (1978), held that children are not part of the "community," but "sensitive persons" and deviant groups are and should be considered in determining whether sexually oriented materials run afoul of local community standards. In *Pope v. Illinois*, 481 U.S. 497 (1987), the Court ruled that *Miller*'s third prong—requiring the showing that a work lacks serious literary, artistic, political, or scientific value—be applied based on standards set by a "reasonable" person, not an "ordinary" person. In addition, in *New York v. Ferber* (1982) (see excerpt below) the Court unanimously, although with four separate concurring opinions, upheld New York's ban on child pornography. Subsequently, in *Osborne v. Ohio*, 495 U.S. 103 (1990), the Rehnquist Court upheld Ohio's statute banning the possession and viewing of child pornography. However, in *Ashcroft v. Free Speech Coalition* (2002) (excerpted below) the Court held that Congress may not make it a crime to create, distribute, or possess "virtual child pornography" generated by computer images of young adults or simulated images, rather than of actual children.

Besides trying to clarify the application of *Miller*'s tests for obscenity, the Burger and Rehnquist Courts were more receptive to restrictions on the availability of sexually oriented materials. Over First Amendment objections, for example, restrictions on the mailing of obscene materials have been upheld. *Rowan v. U.S. Post Office Department*, 397 U.S. 728 (1970), sustained a federal obscenity statute allowing individuals to request that the post office not deliver unsolicited mailings to their homes of materials they find offensive. *United States v. Reidel*, 402 U.S. 351 (1971) upheld a federal obscenity statute prohibiting the mailing of certain pornographic materials, but *Bolger v. Youngs Drug Product Corp.*, 463 U.S. 60 (1983), struck down another statute as applied to the unsolicited mailing of advertisements for contraceptives.

Restrictions on adult bookstores, nude dancing, and other forms of live sexually oriented entertainment have also been approved. *California v. LaRue*, 409 U.S. 109 (1972), sustained California's law prohibiting sexually explicit live entertainment and films in bars. Although striking down a law prohibiting nude dancers in places of adult-only entertainment in *Schad v. Borough of Mount Ephraim*, 452 U.S. 61 (1981), the Court upheld New York's prohibition on nude dancing on the basis of the state's power to regulate liquor under the Twenty-first Amendment.[7] *Arcara v. Cloud Books, Inc.*, 478 U.S. 697 (1986), also allowed the closing of an adult bookstore whose premises were used for the purpose of soliciting for prostitution.

One of the principal ways that cities and localities control and regulate adult theaters and nightclubs is through exclusionary zoning, that is, restricting the operation of such businesses to certain areas of a community. In *Young v. American Mini Theatres*, 327 U.S. 50 (1976), the justices (5–4) upheld the barring of adult theaters from within 1,000 feet of each other or 500 feet from a residential area. *Larkin v. Grendel's Den, Inc.*, 459 U.S. 116 (1982), however, struck down a Massachusetts statute giving the power to churches to veto applications for liquor licenses for running afoul of the First Amendment establishment clause. In *City of Renton v. Playtime Theatres, Inc.*, 475 U.S. 41 (1986), the Court approved the use of exclusionary zoning in regulating adult entertainment establishments. Subsequently, in *Barnes v. Glen Theatre, Inc.*, 501 U.S. 560 (1991), a bare majority of the Rehnquist Court upheld Indiana's ban on "totally nude dancing." But the Court was badly fragmented and almost a decade later it revisited the issue of First Amendment protection for nude dancing in *City of Erie v. Pap's A.M.* (2000) (excepted below), again upholding bans on totally nude dancing. There Justice O'Connor held that a ban on totally nude dancing was not aimed at regulating expression per se but instead at curbing the "secondary effects," such as prostitution, associated with adult entertainment establishments. On that basis, Justice O'Connor also upheld an ordinance barring more than one adult establishment from operating at the same location, but only a plurality joined her opinion in *City of Los Angeles v. Alameda Books, Inc.*, 535 U.S. 425 (2002).

By contrast, in *Reno v. American Civil Liberties Union*, 521 U.S. 844 (1997) (excerpted below), the Court struck down the Communications

Decency Act of 1996, in which Congress had sought to protect minors from "obscene or indecent" material on the Internet. The following term, though, in *National Endowment for the Arts v. Finley*, 524 U.S. 569 (1998), the Court upheld a 1990 "public decency" amendment to the National Foundation for the Arts and Humanities Act, requiring the NEA to take "general standards of decency" into account when awarding grants to artists. Writing for Court, Justice O'Connor relied on and extended the ruling in *Rust v. Sullivan*, 500 U.S. 173 (1991). Both decisions involved *government-funded speech* (discussed further in the second half of this section).

However, in *Ashcroft v. Free Speech Coalition* (2002) (excerpted below) the Court struck down provisions of the Child Pornography Prevention Act of 1996 that criminalized the creation, possession, and distribution of "virtual child pornography." But see also the discussion in Section F of this chapter of *Ashcroft v. American Civil Liberties Union*, 535 U.S. 564 (2002), upholding the use of "community standards" to define what material on the Internet is "harmful to minors" in the Child Online Protection Act of 1998, but also allowing the law to be enjoined from going into effect until other questions about its impact on free speech are resolved; the Third Circuit subsequently struck down the law and the Court denied review of that decision. *United States v. American Library Association*, 539 U.S. 194 (2003), upheld the Children's Internet Protection Act of 2001, authorizing public libraries that receive federal funding to install pornography filters on computers that provide public access to the Internet. In addition, in *United States v. Williams*, 553 U.S. 285 (2008) (excerpted in Section F of this chapter), the Roberts Court upheld the so-called PROTECT Act of 2003 (Prosecutorial Remedies and Other Tools to end the Exploitation of Children Today Act), which Congress enacted in response to the ruling in *Ashcroft v. Free Speech Coalition* (2002), and made it a crime to pander child pornography.

Notes

1. Harry Clor, *Obscenity and Public Morality* (Chicago: University of Chicago Press, 1969), 272.

2. Alan Dershowitz, "What Is Porn?" *ABA Journal* 36 (November 1, 1986).

3. *Butler v. Michigan*, 352 U.S. 380 (1957).

4. See David M. O'Brien, *Storm Center: The Supreme Court in American Politics*, 11th ed. (New York: W. W. Norton & Company, 2017), chap. 2.

5. See, for example, *Kingsley Books v. Brown*, 354 U.S. 436 (1957) (city may get injunction against sale of indecent books with appeal and trial within two days); *Times Film Corporation v. City of Chicago*, 365 U.S. 43 (1961) (no absolute right to exhibit, even

once, any and every kind of film; no prior censorship of permit system); *Bantam Books, Inc. v. Sullivan*, 372 U.S. 58 (1963) (held Rhode Island Committee on Morality constituted prior restraint in providing no hearing on books banned for youths); *A Quantity of Copies of Books v. Kansas*, 378 U.S. 205 (1964) (procedure for impoundment of books was unconstitutional); *Freedman v. Maryland*, 380 U.S. 51 (1965) (held state motion picture censorship statute failed to provide adequate safeguards against undue repression of speech); *Teitel Film Corporation v. Cusack*, 390 U.S. 139 (1968) (held censorship board for review of films was unconstitutional, where fifty days passed before completion of administrative process and no provision was made for prompt judicial decision); *Rabe v. Washington*, 405 U.S. 313 (1972) (held state's obscenity statute, proscribing showing of pictures at drive-ins, which could be shown in adult theaters, was unconstitutional and vague); *Heller v. New York*, 413 U.S. 483 (1973) (held because judge saw entire film before issuing warrant for seizure for obscene film, no adversary hearing prior to seizure was required); *Roaden v. Kentucky*, 413 U.S. 496 (1973) (holding seizure of film in public distribution without warrant was prior restraint and violated Fourth Amendment); *Southeastern Promotions, Ltd. v. Conrad*, 420 U.S. 546 (1975) (held denial of city-leased theater for production of *Hair* was prior restraint because it was imposed without procedural safeguards); *Vance v. Universal Amusement Co.*, 445 U.S. 308 (1980) (struck down as prior restraint restriction on an exhibition of obscene motion pictures). Most recently, in *City of Littleton v. Z. J. Gifts D-4, LLC*, 541 U.S. 774 (2004), the Court reaffirmed that ordinances requiring the licensing of adult businesses must provide access to judicial review and a prompt judicial decision.

6. *Liles v. Oregon*, 425 U.S. 963 (1976).

7. *New York State Liquor Authority v. Bellanca*, 452 U.S. 714 (1981); reaffirmed in *City of Newport, Kentucky v. Iacobucci*, 479 U.S. 92 (1986).

SELECTED BIBLIOGRAPHY

de Grazia, Edward. *Girls Lean Back Everywhere: The Law of Obscenity and the Assault on Genius.* New York: Random House, 1992.

Geltzer, Jeremy. *Dirty Words and Filthy Pictures: Film and the First Amendment.* Austin: University of Texas Press, 2015.

Hunt, Lynn, ed. *The Invention of Pornography.* New York: Zone Books, 1993.

Kendrick, Walter. *The Secret Museum: Pornography in Modern Culture.* New York: Viking, 1987.

MacKinnon, Catharine. *Only Words.* Cambridge, MA: Harvard University Press, 1993.

MacKinnon, Catharine, and Dworkin, Andrea. *In Harm's Way: The Pornography Civil Rights Hearings.* Cambridge, MA: Harvard University Press, 1997.

Stone, Geoffrey. *Sexing the Constitution.* New York: W.W. Norton, 2017.

Strossen, Nadine. *Defending Pornography.* New York: Scribner, 1995.

Strub, Whitney. *Obscenity Rules: Roth v. United States and the Long Struggle over Sexual Expression.* Lawrence: University of Kansas Press, 2015.

Williams, Susan H. *Truth, Autonomy, and Speech: Feminist Theory and the First Amendment.* New York: New York University Press, 2004.

Roth v. United States and *Alberts v. California*

354 U.S. 476, 77 S.Ct. 1304 (1957)

Samuel Roth was charged with violating a federal statute making it a crime to send "obscene, lewd, lascivious, or filthy" materials or advertisements through the mail. He was convicted for advertising and selling a quarterly publication, *American Aphrodite*, dealing with literary erotica and containing nude photographs, but acquitted on the charge that the photographs were obscene. David Alberts was indicted and convicted under California's obscenity law for publishing pictures of "nude and scantily-clad women"; his works made no claim to literary aspirations. On their appeal of their convictions to the Supreme Court, their cases were consolidated in the Warren Court's landmark ruling and opinion by Justice Brennan, who was still in his freshman year, having arrived at the Court only nine months before.

The Court's decision was 6–3 in *Roth* and 7–2 in *Alberts*, with the majority's opinion announced by Justice Brennan. Chief Justice Warren concurred. A separate opinion, concurring in *Alberts* and dissenting in *Roth*, was delivered by Justice Harlan. Justice Douglas dissented and was joined by Justice Black.

■ ■ ■

☐ *Justice BRENNAN delivered the opinion of the Court.*

Roth conducted a business in New York in the publication and sale of books, photographs and magazines. He used circulars and advertising matter to solicit sales. He was convicted by a jury in the District Court for the Southern District of New York upon 4 counts of a 26-count indictment charging him with mailing obscene circulars and advertising, and an obscene book, in violation of the federal obscenity statute. His conviction was affirmed by the Court of Appeals for the Second Circuit. . . .

Alberts conducted a mail-order business from Los Angeles. He was convicted . . . under a misdemeanor complaint which charged him with lewdly keeping for sale obscene and indecent books, and with writing, composing and publishing an obscene advertisement of them, in violation of the California Penal Code. The conviction was affirmed by the Appellate Department of the Superior Court of the State of California in and for the County of Los Angeles. . . .

The dispositive question is whether obscenity is utterance within the area of protected speech and press. . . .

All ideas having even the slightest redeeming social importance—unorthodox ideas, controversial ideas, even ideas hateful to the prevailing climate of opinion—have the full protection of the guaranties, unless excludable because they encroach upon the limited area of more important interests. But implicit in the history of the First Amendment is the rejection of obscenity as utterly without redeeming social importance. This rejection for that reason is mirrored in the universal judgment that obscenity should be restrained, reflected in the international agreement of over 50 nations, in the obscenity laws of all of the 48 States, and in the 20 obscenity laws enacted by the Congress from 1842 to 1956. This is the same judgment expressed by this Court in *Chaplinsky v. New Hampshire* [315 U.S. 568 (1942)]. We hold that obscenity is not within the area of constitutionally protected speech or press. . . .

[S]ex and obscenity are not synonymous. Obscene material is material which deals with sex in a manner appealing to prurient interest. The portrayal of sex, e.g., in art, literature and scientific works, is not itself sufficient reason to deny material the constitutional protection of freedom of speech and press. Sex, a great and mysterious motive force in human life, has indisputably been a subject of absorbing interest to mankind through the ages; it is one of the vital problems of human interest and public concern. . . .

It is therefore vital that the standards for judging obscenity safeguard the protection of freedom of speech and press for material which does not treat sex in a manner appealing to prurient interest.

The early leading standard of obscenity allowed material to be judged merely by the effect of an isolated excerpt upon particularly susceptible persons. *Regina v. Hicklin*, [1868] L.R. 3 Q.B. 360. Some American courts adopted this standard but later decisions have rejected it and substituted this test: whether to the average person, applying contemporary community standards, the dominant theme of the material taken as a whole appeals to prurient interest. The *Hicklin* test, judging obscenity by the effect of isolated passages upon the most susceptible persons, might well encompass material legitimately treating with sex, and so it must be rejected as unconstitutionally restrictive of the freedoms of speech and press. On the other hand, the substituted standard provides safeguards adequate to withstand the charge of constitutional infirmity.

Both trial courts below sufficiently followed the proper standard. Both courts used the proper definition of obscenity. . . .

In summary, then, we hold that these statutes, applied according to the proper standard for judging obscenity, do not offend constitutional safeguards against convictions based upon protected material, or fail to give men in acting adequate notice of what is prohibited.

☐ *Justice HARLAN, concurring in part and dissenting in part.*

In the final analysis, the problem presented by these cases is how far, and on what terms, the state and federal government have power to punish individuals for disseminating books considered to be undesirable because of their nature of supposed deleterious effect upon human conduct. Proceeding from the premise that "no issue is presented in either case concerning the obscenity of the material involved," the Court finds the "dispositive question" to be "whether obscenity is utterance within the area of protected speech and press," and then holds that "obscenity" is not so protected because it is "utterly without redeeming social importance." This sweeping formula appears to me to beg the very question before us. The Court seems to assume that "obscenity" is a peculiar *genus* of "speech and press," which is as distinctly recognizable, and classifiable as poison ivy is among other plants. On this basis the *constitutional* question before us simply becomes, as the Court says, whether "obscenity," as an abstraction is protected by the First and Fourteenth Amendments, and the question whether a *particular* book may be suppressed becomes a mere matter of classification, of "fact," to be entrusted to a fact-finder and insulated from independent constitutional judgment. But surely the problem cannot be solved in such a generalized fashion. Every communication has an individuality and "value" of its own. The suppression of a particular writing or other tangible form of expression is, therefore, an *individual* matter, and in the nature of things every such suppression raises an individual constitutional problem, in which a reviewing court must determine for *itself* whether the attacked expression is suppressable within constitutional standards. Since those standards do not readily lend themselves to generalized definitions, the constitutional problem in the last analysis becomes one of particularized judgments which appellate courts must make for themselves. . . .

I concur in the judgment of the Court in No. 61, *Alberts v. People of State of California*.

The question in this case is whether the defendant was deprived of liberty without due process of law when he was convicted for selling certain materials found by the judge to be obscene because they would have a "tendency to deprave or corrupt its readers by exciting lascivious thoughts or arousing lustful desire." . . .

Since the domain of sexual morality is pre-eminently a matter of state concern, this Court should be slow to interfere with state legislation calculated to protect that morality. It seems to me that nothing in the broad and flexible command of the Due Process Clause forbids California to prosecute one who sells books whose dominant tendency might be to "deprave or corrupt" a reader. I agree with the Court, of course, that the books must be judged as a whole and in relation to the normal adult reader.

What has been said, however, does not dispose of the case. It still remains for us to decide whether the state court's determination that this material should be suppressed is consistent with the Fourteenth Amendment; and that, of course, presents a federal question as to which we, and not the state court, have the ultimate responsibility. And so, in the final analysis, I concur in the judgment because, upon an independent perusal of the material involved, and in light of the considerations discussed above, I cannot say that its suppression would so interfere with the communication of "ideas" in any proper sense of that term that it would offend the Due Process Clause. I therefore agree with the Court that appellant's conviction must be affirmed.

I dissent in No. 582, *Roth v. United States*.

We are faced here with the question whether the federal obscenity statute, as construed and applied in this case, violates the First Amendment to the Constitution. To me, this question is of quite a different order than one where we are dealing with state legislation under the Fourteenth Amendment. I do not think it follows that state and federal powers in this area are the same, and that just because the State may suppress a particular utterance, it is automatically permissible for the Federal Government to do the same. . . .

The Federal Government has, for example, power to restrict seditious speech directed against it, because that Government certainly has the substantive authority to protect itself against revolution. But in dealing with obscenity we are faced with the converse situation, for the interests which obscenity statutes purportedly protect are primarily entrusted to the care, not of the Federal Government, but of the States. Congress has no substantive power over sexual morality. Such powers as the Federal Government has in this field are but incidental to its other powers, here the postal power, and are not of the same nature as those possessed by the States, which bear direct responsibility for the protection of the local moral fabric. . . .

Not only is the federal interest in protecting the Nation against pornography attenuated, but the dangers of federal censorship in this field are far greater than anything the States may do. It has often been said that one of the great strengths of our federal system is that we have, in the forty-eight States, forty-eight experimental social laboratories. Different States will have different attitudes toward the same work of literature. The same book which is freely read in one State might be classed as obscene in another. And it seems to me that no overwhelming danger to our freedom to experiment and to gratify our tastes in literature is likely to result from the suppression of a borderline book in one of the States, so long as there is no uniform nationwide suppression of the book, and so long as other States are free to experiment with the same or bolder books.

Quite a different situation is presented, however, where the Federal Government imposes the ban. The danger is perhaps not great if the people of one State, through their legislature, decide that "Lady Chatterley's Lover" goes so far beyond the acceptable standards of candor that it will be deemed offensive and non-sellable, for the State next door is still free to make its own choice. At least we do not have one uniform standard. But the dangers to free thought and expression are truly great if the Federal Government imposes a blanket ban over the Nation on such a book. The prerogative of the States to differ on their ideas of morality will be destroyed, the ability of States to experiment will be stunted. The fact that the people of one State cannot read some of the works of D. H. Lawrence seems to me, if not wise or desirable, at least acceptable. But that no person in the United States should be allowed to do so seems to me to be intolerable, and violative of both the letter and spirit of the First Amendment.

I judge this case, then, in view of what I think is the attenuated federal interest in this field, in view of the very real danger of a deadening uniformity which can result from nation-wide federal censorship, and in view of the fact that the constitutionality of this conviction must be weighed against the First and not the Fourteenth Amendment. So viewed, I do not think that this conviction can be upheld.

☐ *Justice DOUGLAS, with whom Justice BLACK joins, dissenting.*

I do not think that the problem can be resolved by the Court's statement that "obscenity is not expression protected by the First Amendment." . . . I reject too the implication that problems of freedom of speech and of the press are to be resolved by weighing against the values of free expression, the judgment of the Court that a particular form of that expression has "no redeeming social importance." The First Amendment, its prohibition in terms absolute, was designed to preclude courts as well as legislatures from weighing the values of speech against silence. The First Amendment puts free speech in the preferred position.

Stanley v. Georgia
394 U.S. 557, 89 S.Ct. 1243 (1969)

Robert Eli Stanley was charged in Fulton County, Georgia, for violating the state's law making it a crime to possess obscene materials. His arrest arose from a search of his home by police who had a warrant to seize evidence of bookmaking activities, but discovered in a desk drawer in Stanley's bedroom three reels of 8-millimeter film. After viewing the films in his living room, the police arrested Stanley, and he was later convicted for the possession of allegedly obscene materials in a state superior court. Stanley appealed a decision by the state supreme court upholding his conviction to the Supreme Court, which granted *certiorari*.

The Court's decision was unanimous, and the opinion was announced by Justice Marshall. Concurrences were by Justices Black and Stewart, who were joined by Justices Brennan and White.

■ ■ ■

☐ *Justice MARSHALL delivered the opinion of the Court.*

[The] appellant is asserting . . . the right to read or observe what he pleases—the right to satisfy his intellectual and emotional needs in the privacy of his own home. He is asserting the right to be free from state inquiry into the contents of his library. Georgia contends that appellant does not have these rights, that there are certain types of materials that the individual may not read or even possess. Georgia justifies this assertion by arguing that the films in the present case are obscene. But we think that mere categorization of these films as "obscene" is insufficient justification for such a drastic invasion of personal liberties guaranteed by the First and Fourteenth Amendments. Whatever may be the justifications for other statutes regulating obscenity, we do not think they reach into the privacy of one's own home. If the First Amendment means anything, it means that a State has no business telling a man, sitting alone in his own house, what books he may read or what films he may watch. Our whole constitutional heritage rebels at the thought of giving government the power to control men's minds. . . .

We hold that the First and Fourteenth Amendments prohibit making mere private possession of obscene material a crime. *Roth [v. United States* (1957)] and the cases following that decision are not impaired by today's holding. As we have said, the States retain broad power to regulate obscenity; that power simply does not extend to mere possession by the individual in the privacy of his own home. Accordingly, the judgment of the court below is reversed and the case is remanded for proceedings not inconsistent with this opinion.

■ INSIDE THE COURT

Letter from Justice Black to Justice Harlan, December 10, 1969

Because the Supreme Court held that obscene materials fall outside of the protection of the First Amendment, when hearing appeals of convictions under state and federal obscenity laws, the justices had to examine the evidence in each case, including screening sexually explicit films in a room in the basement of the Court. Because of Justice Hugo Black's absolutist interpretation of the First Amendment, he declined to join the other justices in screening allegedly obscene films, as the following letter indicates.

Supreme Court of the United States
Washington, D. C. 20543

CHAMBERS OF
JUSTICE HUGO L. BLACK

December 10, 1969

Dear John,

I have your note advising that arrangements have been made for the Court to see "I, a Woman" and "I Am Curious (Yellow)" at 11 A.M. next Monday morning. I cannot see that looking at the pictures would change my view that the First Amendment would be violated by barring the showing of these pictures. Consequently I shall not be present.

Sincerely,

Hugo J.

Mr. Justice Harlan

cc: Members of the Conference

Source: Library of Congress, Justice William J. Brennan Jr., Papers.

Miller v. California

413 U.S. 15, 93 S.CT. 2607 (1973)

By the 1970s, as a result of the *Roth* line of cases, there was a proliferation of sexually oriented materials and there were renewed attempts
by states and localities to regulate and ban obscene and pornographic
materials. That in turn meant a large number of appeals of obscenity
convictions coming to the Supreme Court. In 1971–1972, there were
more than sixty such cases on the Court's docket, and the justices heard
oral arguments in eight cases in the 1972 term. One of these cases
involved the conviction of Marvin Miller for violating California's
obscenity law. He was found guilty of mailing unsolicited materials
advertising adult books and films, which included pictures of men
and women engaged in sexual acts and displaying their genitals.

When the justices discussed *Miller* and other obscenity cases in
May and June 1972, they were dissatisfied with *Roth* yet pulled in
opposite directions. In particular, Chief Justice Burger and Justice
Brennan each wanted to take the Court in a different direction on
the obscenity problem.

Chief Justice Burger had come to the Court in 1969 believing
that the *Roth* line of cases was mistaken; it was too permissive and
failed to give states and localities enough power over sexually explicit
materials. He urged a reconsideration of *Roth* and tougher standards.
"In short," as he put in a June 14, 1972, memorandum, "a little
'chill' will do some of the 'pornos' no great harm and it might be
good for the country."

Justice Brennan, who authored *Roth* and other opinions in this
area for the Warren Court, was no less concerned and had come to
reevaluate his earlier position in *Roth*. In his view, however, *Roth* was
mistaken in not going far enough; it allowed too much censorship. As
he explained in a memorandum for the justices on May 22, 1972:

> With all respect, the Chief Justice's proposed solution to the
> obscenity quagmire will, in my view, worsen an already intoler-
> able mess. I've been thinking for some time that only a drastic
> change in applicable constitutional principles promises a way
> out. I've decided that I shall use this case as a vehicle for saying
> that I'm prepared to make that change. I'll write in effect that
> it has proved impossible to separate expression concerning sex,
> called obscenity, from other expression concerning sex, whether
> the material takes the form of words, photographs or film; . . .
> that we should treat obscenity not as expression concerning sex
> except from First Amendment speech but as expression, although
> constituting First Amendment speech, that is regulable to the
> extent of legislating against its offensive exposure to unwilling
> adults and dissemination to juveniles.

Both Burger and Brennan began working on draft opinions in the hope of winning a majority over to their side. That proved impossible so late in the term, so *Miller* was carried over for reargument in the October 1972 term. Both continued to compete for votes, but in the end, on June 21, 1973, a bare majority accepted Burger's analysis and more restrictive tests for obscenity based on local community standards. Brennan's draft became a dissenting opinion.

The Court's decision was 5–4, with the majority's opinion announced by Chief Justice Burger. Dissents were by Justices Douglas and Brennan, who were joined by Justices Stewart and Marshall.

■ ■ ■

☐ *Chief Justice BURGER delivered the opinion of the Court.*

This is one of a group of "obscenity-pornography" cases being reviewed by the Court in a re-examination of standards enunciated in earlier cases involving what Justice HARLAN called "the intractable obscenity problem." . . .

Appellant conducted a mass mailing campaign to advertise the sale of illustrated books, euphemistically called "adult" material. After a jury trial, he was convicted of violating California Penal Code Sec. 311.2(a), a misdemeanor, by knowingly distributing obscene matter, and the Appellate Department, Superior Court of California, County of Orange, summarily affirmed the judgment without opinion. Appellant's conviction was specifically based on his conduct in causing five unsolicited advertising brochures . . . [containing] pictures and drawings very explicitly depicting men and women in groups of two or more engaging in a variety of sexual activities, with genitals often prominently displayed.

This case involves the application of a State's criminal obscenity statute to a situation in which sexually explicit materials have been thrust by aggressive sales action upon unwilling recipients who had in no way indicated any desire to receive such materials. . . .

[O]bscene material is unprotected by the First Amendment. . . . We acknowledge, however, the inherent dangers of undertaking to regulate any form of expression. State statutes designed to regulate obscene materials must be carefully limited. As a result, we now confine the permissible scope of such regulation to works which depict or describe sexual conduct. That conduct must be specifically defined by the applicable state law, as written or authoritatively construed. A state offense must also be limited to works which, taken as a whole, appeal to the prurient interest in sex, which portray sexual conduct in a patently offensive way, and which, taken as a whole, do not have serious literary, artistic, political, or scientific value.

The basic guidelines for the trier of fact must be: (a) whether "the average person, applying contemporary community standards" would find that the work, taken as a whole, appeals to the prurient interest; (b) whether the work depicts or describes, in a patently offensive way, sexual conduct specifically defined by the applicable state law; and (c) whether the work, taken as a whole, lacks serious literary, artistic, political, or scientific value. We do not adopt as a constitutional standard the "*utterly* without redeeming social value" test of *Memoirs v. Massachusetts* [383 U.S. 413 (1966)].

We emphasize that it is not our function to propose regulatory schemes for the States. That must await their concrete legislative efforts. It is possible, however, to give a few plain examples of what a state statute could define for regulation under part (b) of the standard announced in this opinion, *supra*:

(a) Patently offensive representations or descriptions of ultimate sexual acts, normal or perverted, actual or simulated.

(b) Patently offensive representation or descriptions of masturbation, excretory functions, and lewd exhibition of the genitals.

Sex and nudity may not be exploited without limit by films or pictures exhibited or sold in places of public accommodation any more than live sex and nudity can be exhibited or sold without limit in such public places. At a minimum, prurient, patently offensive depiction or description of sexual conduct must have serious literary, artistic, political, or scientific value to merit First Amendment protection. . . . For example, medical books for the education of physicians and related personnel necessarily use graphic illustrations and descriptions of human anatomy. In resolving the inevitably sensitive questions of fact and law, we must continue to rely on the jury system, accompanied by the safeguards that judges, rules of evidence, presumption of innocence, and other protective features provide, as we do with rape, murder, and a host of other offenses against society and its individual members.

Justice BRENNAN has abandoned his former position and now maintains that no formulation of this Court, the Congress, or the States can adequately distinguish obscene material unprotected by the First Amendment from protected expression. . . .

[But under] the holdings announced today, no one will be subject to prosecution for the sale or exposure of obscene materials unless these materials depict or describe patently offensive "hard core" sexual conduct specifically defined by the regulating state law, as written or construed. We are satisfied that these specific prerequisites will provide fair notice to a dealer in such materials that his public and commercial activities may bring prosecution.

Justice BRENNAN also emphasizes "institutional stress" in justification of his change of view. Noting that "[t]he number of obscenity cases on our docket gives ample testimony to the burden that has been placed upon this Court," he quite rightly remarks that the examination of contested materials "is hardly a source of edification to the members of this Court." He also notes, and we agree, that "uncertainty of the standards creates a continuing source of tension between state and federal courts. . . ."

But today, for the first time since *Roth* was decided in 1957, a majority of this Court has agreed on concrete guidelines to isolate "hard core" pornography from expression protected by the First Amendment. Now we may abandon the casual practice of *Redrup v. New York*, 386 U.S. 767 (1967), and attempt to provide positive guidance to federal and state courts alike.

This may not be an easy road, free from difficulty. But no amount of "fatigue" should lead us to adopt a convenient "institutional" rationale—an absolutist, "anything goes" view of the First Amendment—because it will lighten our burdens. . . .

Under a National Constitution, fundamental First Amendment limitations on the powers of the States do not vary from community to community, but this does not mean that there are, or should or can be, fixed, uniform national standards of precisely what appeals to the "prurient interest" or is "patently offensive." These are essentially questions of fact, and our Nation is simply too big and too diverse for this Court to reasonably expect that such standards could be articulated for all 50 States in a single formulation, even assuming the prerequisite consensus exists. When triers of fact are asked to decide whether "the average person, applying contemporary community standards" would consider certain materials "prurient," it would be unrealistic to require that the answer be based on some abstract formulation. The adversary system, with lay jurors as the usual ultimate fact-finders in criminal prosecutions, has historically permitted triers of fact to draw on the standards of their community, guided always by limiting instructions on the law. To require a State to structure obscenity proceedings around evidence of a *national* "community standard" would be an exercise in futility. . . .

We conclude that neither the state's alleged failure to offer evidence of "national standards," nor the trial court's charge that the jury consider state community standards, were constitutional errors. Nothing in the First Amendment requires that a jury must consider hypothetical and unascertainable "national standards" when attempting to determine whether certain materials are obscene as a matter of fact. . . . It is neither realistic nor constitutionally sound to read the First Amendment as requiring that the people of Maine or Mississippi accept public depiction of conduct found tolerable in Las Vegas, or New York City. . . . People in different States vary in their tastes and attitudes, and this diversity is not to be strangled by the absolutism of imposed uniformity. . . . We hold that the requirement that the jury evaluate the materials with reference to "contemporary standards of the State of California" serves this protection purpose and is constitutionally adequate. . . .

In sum, we (a) reaffirm the *Roth* holding that obscene material is not protected by the First Amendment; (b) hold that such material can be regulated by the States, subject to the specific safeguards enunciated above, without a showing that the material is *"utterly* without redeeming social value"; and (c) hold that obscenity is to be determined by applying "contemporary community standards," . . . not "national standards." . . .

Vacated and remanded.

☐ *Justice DOUGLAS, dissenting.*

Today the Court retreats from the earlier formulations of the constitutional test and undertakes to make new definitions. This effort, like the earlier ones, is earnest and well intentioned. The difficulty is that we do not deal with constitutional terms, since "obscenity" is not mentioned in the Constitution or Bill of Rights. And the First Amendment makes no such exception from "the press" which it undertakes to protect nor, as I have said on other occasions, is an exception necessarily implied, for there was no recognized exception to the free press at the time the Bill of Rights was adopted which treated "obscene" publications differently from other types of papers, magazines, and books. So there are no constitutional guidelines for deciding what is and what is not "obscene." The Court is at large because we deal with tastes and standards of literature. What shocks me may be sustenance for my neighbor. What causes one person to boil up in rage over one pamphlet or movie may reflect only his neurosis, not shared by others. We deal here with a regime of censorship which, if adopted, should be done by constitutional amendment after full debate by the people. . . .

The idea that the First Amendment permits government to ban publications that are "offensive" to some people puts an ominous gloss on freedom of the press. That test would make it possible to ban any paper or any journal or magazine in some benighted place. . . . The idea that the First Amendment permits punishment for ideas that are "offensive" to the particular judge or jury sitting in judgment is astounding. No greater leveler of speech or literature has ever been designed. . . .

I do not think we, the judges, were ever given the constitutional power to make definitions of obscenity. If it is to be defined, let the people debate and decide by a constitutional amendment what they want to ban as obscene and what standards they want the legislatures and the courts to apply. Perhaps the people will decide that the path towards a mature, integrated society requires that all ideas competing for acceptance must have no censor. Perhaps they will decide otherwise. Whatever the choice, the courts will have some guidelines. Now we have none except our own predilections.

□ *Justice BRENNAN, with whom Justice STEWART and Justice MARSHALL join, dissenting.*

In my dissent in *Paris Adult Theatre I v. Slaton*, 413 U.S. 49 [1973], I noted that I had no occasion to consider the extent of state power to regulate the distribution of sexually oriented material to juveniles or the offensive exposure of such material to unconsenting adults. . . . I need not now decide whether a statute might be drawn to impose, within the requirements of the First Amendment, criminal penalties for the precise conduct at issue here. For it is clear that under my dissent in *Paris Adult Theatre I*, the statute under which the prosecution was brought is unconstitutionally overbroad, and therefore invalid on its face.

New York v. Ferber

458 U.S. 747, 102 S.Ct. 3348 (1982)

Paul Ferber, the proprietor of a Manhattan adult bookstore, sold to an undercover police officer two films almost exclusively showing young boys masturbating. He was arrested, tried, and convicted under New York's law prohibiting anyone from knowingly promoting a sexual performance by a child under the age of sixteen by distributing materials depicting such activities. The New York Court of Appeals, however, overturned the conviction and found the statute overly broad and that it ran afoul of the First Amendment. The state, thereupon, appealed to the Supreme Court.

The Court's decision was unanimous, with the opinion announced by Justice White. Concurrences were by Justices Blackmun, O'Connor, Brennan, and Stevens.

■ ■ ■

☐ *Justice WHITE delivered the opinion of the Court.*

At issue in this case is the constitutionality of a New York criminal statute which prohibits persons from knowingly promoting sexual performances by children under the age of 16 by distributing material which depicts such performances. . . .

In *Miller v. California* [1973], a majority of the Court agreed that "a state offense must also be limited to works which, taken as a whole, appeal to the prurient interest in sex, which portray sexual conduct in a patently offensive way, and which, taken as a whole, do not have serious literary, artistic, political, or scientific value." Over the past decade, we have adhered to the guidelines expressed in *Miller,* which subsequently has been followed in the regulatory schemes of most states.

The *Miller* standard, like its predecessors, was an accommodation between the state's interests in protecting the "sensibilities of unwilling recipients" from exposure to pornographic material and the dangers of censorship inherent in unabashedly content-based laws. Like obscenity statutes, laws directed at the dissemination of child pornography run the risk of suppressing protected expression by allowing the hand of the censor to become unduly heavy. For the following reasons, however, we are persuaded that the States are entitled to greater leeway in the regulation of pornographic depictions of children.

First. It is evident beyond the need for elaboration that a state's interest in "safeguarding the physical and psychological well being of a minor" is "compelling." . . .

The legislative judgment, as well as the judgment found in the relevant literature, is that the use of children as subjects of pornographic materials is harmful to the physiological, emotional, and mental health of the child. That judgment, we think, easily passes muster under the First Amendment.

Second. The distribution of photographs and films depicting sexual activity by juveniles is intrinsically related to the sexual abuse of children in at least two ways. First, the materials produced are a permanent record of the children's participation and the harm to the child is exacerbated by their circulation. Second, the distribution network for child pornography must be closed if the production of material which requires the sexual exploitation of children is to be effectively controlled. . . .

Third. The advertising and selling of child pornography provides an economic motive for and is thus an integral part of the production of such materials, an activity illegal throughout the nation. . . . We note that were the statutes outlawing the employment of children in these films and photographs fully effective, and the constitutionality of these laws have not been questioned, the First Amendment implications would be no greater than that presented by laws against distribution: enforceable production laws would leave no child pornography to be marketed.

Fourth. The value of permitting live performances and photographic reproductions of children engaged in lewd sexual conduct is exceedingly modest, if not *de minimis.* We consider it unlikely that visual depictions of children performing sexual acts or lewdly exhibiting their genitals would often constitute an important and necessary part of a literary performance or scientific or educational work. As the trial court in this case observed, if it were necessary for literary or artistic value, a person over the statutory age who perhaps looked younger could be utilized. Simulation outside of the prohibition of the statute could provide another alternative. Nor is there any question here of censoring a particular literary theme or portrayal of sexual activity. The First Amendment interest is limited to that of rendering the portrayal somewhat more "realistic" by utilizing or photographing children.

Fifth. Recognizing and classifying child pornography as a category of material outside the protection of the First Amendment is not incompatible with our earlier decisions. . . .

[I]t is not rare that a content-based classification of speech has been accepted because it may be appropriately generalized that within the confines of the given classification, the evil to be restricted so overwhelmingly outweighs the expressive interests, if any, at stake, that no process of case-by-case adjudication is required. When a definable class of material, such as that covered by Sec. 263.15, bears so heavily and pervasively on the welfare of children engaged in its production, we think the balance of competing interests is clearly struck and that it is permissible to consider these materials as without the protection of the First Amendment.

There are, of course, limits on the category of child pornography which, like obscenity, is unprotected by the First Amendment. As with all legislation in this sensitive area, the conduct to be prohibited must be adequately defined by the applicable state law, as written or authoritatively construed. Here the nature of the harm to be combatted requires that the state offense be limited to works that *visually* depict sexual conduct by children below a specified age. The category of "sexual conduct" proscribed must also be suitably limited and described.

The test for child pornography is separate from the obscenity standard enunciated in *Miller*, but may be compared to it for purpose of clarity. The *Miller* formulation is adjusted in the following respects: A trier of fact need not find that the material appeals to the prurient interest of the average person; it is not required that sexual conduct portrayed be done so in a patently offensive manner; and the material at issue need not be considered as a whole. We note that the distribution of descriptions of other depictions of sexual conduct, not otherwise obscene, which do not involve live performance or photographic or other visual reproduction of live performances, retain First Amendment protection. . . .

It is therefore clear that there is nothing unconstitutionally "under-inclusive" about a statute that singles out this category of material for proscription. It also follows that the State is not barred by the First Amendment from prohibiting the distribution of unprotected materials produced outside the State.

It remains to address the claim that the New York statute is unconstitutionally overbroad because it would forbid the distribution of material with serious literary, scientific or educational value or material which does not threaten the harms sought to be combatted by the State. . . .

The scope of the First Amendment overbreadth doctrine, like most exceptions to established principles, must be carefully tied to the circumstances in which facial invalidation of a statute is truly warranted. Because of the wide-reaching effects of striking a statute down on its face at the request of one whose own conduct may be punished despite the First Amendment, we have recognized that the overbreadth doctrine is "strong medicine" and have employed it with hesitation, and then "only as a last resort." We have, in consequence, insisted that the overbreadth involved be "substantial" before the statute involved will be invalidated on its face. . . .

The requirement of substantial overbreadth is directly derived from the purpose and nature of the doctrine. While a sweeping statute, or one incapable of limitation, has the potential to repeatedly chill the exercise of expressive activity by many individuals, the extent of deterrence of protected speech can be expected to decrease with the declining reach of the regulation. This observation appears equally applicable to the publication of books and films as it is to activities, such as picketing or participation in election campaigns, which have previously been categorized as involving conduct plus speech. . . .

Applying these principles, Sec. 263.15 is not substantially overbroad. We consider this the paradigmatic case of a state statute whose legitimate reach dwarfs its arguably impermissible applications. . . . While the reach of the statute is directed at the hard core of child pornography, the Court of Appeals was understandably concerned that some protected expression, ranging from medical textbooks to pictorials in National Geographic would fall prey to the statute. How often, if ever, it may be necessary to employ children to engage in conduct clearly within the reach of the Sec. 263.15 in order to produce educational, medical or artistic works cannot be known with certainty. Yet we seriously doubt, and it has not been suggested, that these arguably impermissible applications of the statute amount to more than a tiny fraction of the materials within the statute's reach. . . .

As applied to Paul Ferber and to others who distribute similar material, the statute does not violate the First Amendment as applied to the States through the Fourteenth. The decision of the New York Court of Appeals is reversed and the case is remanded to that Court for further proceedings not inconsistent with this opinion.

☐ *Justice BRENNAN, with whom Justice MARSHALL joins, concurring.*

I agree with much of what is said in the Court's opinion. . . .

But in my view application of Sec. 263.15 or any similar statute to depictions of children that in themselves do have serious literary, artistic, scientific or medical value, would violate the First Amendment. As the Court recognizes, the limited classes of speech, the suppression of which does not raise serious First Amendment concerns, have two attributes. They are of exceedingly "slight social value," and the State has a compelling interest in their regulation. See *Chaplinsky v. New Hampshire* [315 U.S. 568] (1942). The First Amendment value of depictions of children that are in themselves serious contributions to art, literature or science, is, by definition, simply not "*de minimis*." At the same time, the State's interest in suppression of such materials is likely to be far less compelling. For the Court's assumption of harm to the child resulting from the "permanent record" and "circulation" of the child's "participation," lacks much of its force where the depiction is a serious contribution to art or science.

City of Erie v. Pap's A.M.

529 U.S. 277, 120 S.Ct. 1382 (2000)

Following the Supreme Court's ruling in *Barnes v. Glen Theatre, Inc.*, 501 U.S. 560 (1991), that Indiana's law against public nudity could apply to nude dancing in adult clubs and require dancers to wear G-strings and pasties instead of dancing totally nude, the city of Erie, Pennsylvania, enacted an ordinance making it an offense to appear in public in a "state of nudity." Two days after the law went into effect, Pap's A.M., the owner of Kandyland, a club that featured totally nude dancing, sought an injunction against the enforcement of the law. The trial court granted an injunction upon finding the ordinance unconstitutional, but an appellate court reversed. Subsequently, the Pennsylvania Supreme Court overruled that decision, holding that nude dancing was expressive conduct protected by the First Amendment. The state supreme court noted that that was the view of eight members of the Supreme Court in *Barnes*, counting four members in the majority and the four dissenters. But it also concluded that *Barnes* provided no clear precedent because the Court's decision was 5–4 and its plurality opinion fragmented the justices with four separate and conflicting opinions. Erie appealed and the Supreme Court granted review.

The Court reversed, and its decision was seven-and-a-half to two-and-a-half. Justice O'Connor delivered the opinion for the Court. Justice Scalia, joined by Justice Thomas, filed a concurring opinion. Justice Souter filed a separate opinion, concurring and dissenting in part. Justice Stevens filed a dissent, which Justice Ginsburg joined.

■ ■ ■

☐ *Justice O'CONNOR announced the judgment of the Court, delivered the opinion of the Court with respect to Parts I and II, and delivered an opinion with respect to Parts III and IV, in which Chief Justice REHNQUIST, Justice KENNEDY, and Justice BREYER joined.*

■ III

Being "in a state of nudity" is not an inherently expressive condition. As we explained in *Barnes* [*v. Glen Theatre, Inc.*, 501 U.S. 560 (1991)], however, nude dancing of the type at issue here is expressive conduct, although we think that it falls only within the outer ambit of the First Amendment's protection.

To determine what level of scrutiny applies to the ordinance at issue here, we must decide "whether the State's regulation is related to the suppression of expression." *Texas v. Johnson*, 491 U.S. 397 (1989). If the governmental purpose in enacting the regulation is unrelated to the suppression of expression, then the regulation need only satisfy the "less stringent" standard from [*United States v.*] *O'Brien* [391 U.S. 367 (1968)] for evaluating restrictions on symbolic speech. If the government interest is related to the content of the expression, however, then the regulation falls outside the scope of the *O'Brien* test and must be justified under a more demanding standard.

In *Barnes*, we analyzed an almost identical statute, holding that Indiana's public nudity ban did not violate the First Amendment, although no five Members of the Court agreed on a single rationale for that conclusion. We now clarify that government restrictions on public nudity such as the ordinance at issue here should be evaluated under the framework set forth in *O'Brien* for content-neutral restrictions on symbolic speech.

The ordinance here, like the statute in *Barnes*, is on its face a general prohibition on public nudity. By its terms, the ordinance regulates conduct alone. It does not target nudity that contains an erotic message; rather, it bans all public nudity, regardless of whether that nudity is accompanied by expressive activity. . . . As Justice SOUTER noted in *Barnes*, "on its face, the governmental interest in combating prostitution and other criminal activity is not at all inherently related to expression." In that sense, this case is similar to *O'Brien*. O'Brien burned his draft registration card as a public statement of his antiwar views, and he was convicted under a statute making it a crime to knowingly mutilate or destroy such a card. This Court rejected his claim that the statute violated his First Amendment rights, reasoning that the law punished him for the "noncommunicative impact of his conduct, and for nothing else." . . . So too here, the ordinance prohibiting public nudity is aimed at combating crime and other negative secondary effects caused by the presence of adult entertainment establishments like Kandyland and not at suppressing the erotic message conveyed by this type of nude dancing. Put another way, the ordinance does not attempt to regulate the primary effects of the expression, i.e., the effect on the audience of watching nude erotic dancing, but rather the secondary effects, such as the impacts on public health, safety, and welfare, which we have previously recognized are "caused by the presence of even one such" establishment. *Renton v. Playtime Theatres, Inc.*, 475 U.S. 41 (1986). . . .

[E]ven if Erie's public nudity ban has some minimal effect on the erotic message by muting that portion of the expression that occurs when the last stitch is dropped, the dancers at Kandyland and other such establishments are free to perform wearing pasties and G-strings. Any effect on the overall expression is *de minimis*. . . .

We conclude that Erie's asserted interest in combating the negative secondary effects associated with adult entertainment establishments like Kandyland is unrelated to the suppression of the erotic message conveyed by nude dancing. The ordinance prohibiting public nudity is therefore valid if it satisfies the four-factor test from *O'Brien* for evaluating restrictions on symbolic speech.

■ IV

Applying that standard here, we conclude that Erie's ordinance is justified under *O'Brien*. The first factor of the *O'Brien* test is whether the government regulation is within the constitutional power of the government to enact. Here, Erie's efforts to protect public health and safety are clearly within the city's police powers. The second factor is whether the regulation furthers an important or substantial government interest. The asserted interests of regulating conduct through a public nudity ban and of combating the harmful secondary effects associated with nude dancing are undeniably important. And in terms of demonstrating that such secondary effects pose a threat, the city need not "conduct new studies or produce evidence independent of that already generated by other cities" to demonstrate the problem of secondary effects, "so long as whatever evidence the city relies upon is reasonably believed to be relevant to the problem that the city addresses." *Renton v. Playtime Theatres, Inc.* Because the nude dancing at Kandyland is of the same character as the adult entertainment at issue in *Renton, Young v. American Mini Theatres, Inc.*, 427 U.S. 50 (1976), and *California v. LaRue*, 409 U.S. 109 (1972), it was reasonable for Erie to conclude that such nude dancing was likely to produce the same secondary effects. . . .

In any event, Erie also relied on its own findings. The preamble to the ordinance states that "the Council of the City of Erie has, at various times over more than a century, expressed its findings that certain lewd, immoral activities carried on in public places for profit are highly detrimental to the public health, safety and welfare, and lead to the debasement of both women and men, promote violence, public intoxication, prostitution and other serious criminal activity." The city council members, familiar with commercial downtown Erie, are the individuals who would likely have had first-hand knowledge of what took place at and around nude dancing establishments in Erie, and can make particularized, expert judgments about the resulting harmful secondary effects. Here, Kandyland has had ample opportunity to contest the council's findings about secondary effects—before the council itself, throughout the state proceedings, and before this Court. Yet to this day, Kandyland has never challenged the city council's findings or cast any specific doubt on the validity of those findings. . . .

The ordinance also satisfies *O'Brien*'s third factor, that the government interest is unrelated to the suppression of free expression. The fourth and final *O'Brien* factor—that the restriction is no greater than is essential to the furtherance of the government interest—is satisfied as well. The ordinance regulates conduct, and any incidental impact on the expressive element of nude dancing is *de minimis*. The requirement that dancers wear pasties and G-strings is a minimal restriction in furtherance of the asserted government interests, and the restriction leaves ample capacity to convey the dancer's erotic message. Justice SOUTER points out that zoning is an alternative means of addressing this problem. It is far from clear, however, that zoning imposes less of a burden on expression than the minimal requirement implemented here. In any event, since this is a content-neutral restriction, least restrictive means analysis is not required.

We hold, therefore, that Erie's ordinance is a content-neutral regulation that is valid under *O'Brien*. Accordingly, the judgment of the Pennsylvania Supreme Court is reversed, and the case is remanded for further proceedings not inconsistent with this opinion.

☐ *Justice SCALIA, with whom Justice THOMAS joins, concurring in the judgment.*

I agree that the decision of the Pennsylvania Supreme Court must be reversed, but disagree with the mode of analysis the Court has applied.

The city of Erie self-consciously modeled its ordinance on the public nudity statute we upheld against constitutional challenge in *Barnes v. Glen Theatre, Inc.*, calculating (one would have supposed reasonably) that the courts of Pennsylvania would consider themselves bound by our judgment on a question of federal constitutional law. In *Barnes*, I voted to uphold the challenged Indiana statute "not because it survives some lower level of First Amendment scrutiny, but because, as a general law regulating conduct and not specifically directed at expression, it is not subject to First Amendment scrutiny at all." Erie's ordinance, too, by its terms prohibits not merely nude dancing, but the act—irrespective of whether it is engaged in for expressive purposes—of going nude in public. The facts that a preamble to the ordinance explains that its purpose, in part, is to "limi[t] a recent increase in nude live entertainment," that city councilmembers in supporting the ordinance commented to that effect, and that the ordinance includes in the definition of nudity the exposure of devices simulating that condition, neither make the law any less general in its reach nor demonstrate that what the municipal authorities really find objectionable is expression rather than public nakedness. As far as appears (and as seems overwhelmingly likely), the preamble, the council members' comments, and the chosen definition of the prohibited conduct simply reflect the fact that Erie had recently been having a public nudity problem not with streakers, sunbathers or hot-dog vendors, but with lap dancers. . . .

Moreover, even were I to conclude that the city of Erie had specifically singled out the activity of nude dancing, I still would not find that this regulation violated the First Amendment unless I could be persuaded (as on this record I cannot) that it was the communicative character of nude dancing that prompted the ban. When conduct other than speech itself is regulated, it is my view that the First Amendment is violated only "[w]here the government prohibits conduct precisely because of its communicative attributes." Here, even if one hypothesizes that the city's object was to suppress only nude dancing, that would not establish an intent to suppress what (if anything) nude dancing communicates. I do not feel the need, as the Court does, to identify some "secondary effects" associated with nude dancing that the city could properly seek to eliminate. (I am highly skeptical, to tell the truth, that the addition of pasties and G-strings will at all reduce the tendency of establishments such as Kandyland to attract crime and prostitution, and hence to foster sexually transmitted disease.) The traditional power of government to foster good morals (*bonos mores*), and the acceptability of the traditional judgment (if Erie wishes to endorse it) that nude public dancing itself is immoral, have not been repealed by the First Amendment.

☐ *Justice SOUTER, concurring in part and dissenting in part.*

Erie's stated interest in combating the secondary effects associated with nude dancing establishments is an interest unrelated to the suppression of expression under *United States v. O'Brien*, and the city's regulation is thus properly considered under the *O'Brien* standards. I do not believe, however, that the current record allows us to say that the city has made a sufficient evidentiary showing to sustain its regulation, and I would therefore vacate the decision of the Pennsylvania Supreme Court and remand the case for further proceedings. . . .

[T]he record before us today is deficient in its failure to reveal any evidence on which Erie may have relied, either for the seriousness of the threatened harm or for the efficacy of its chosen remedy. The plurality does the best it can with the materials to hand, but the pickings are slim. . . .

There is one point, however, on which an evidentiary record is not quite so hard to find, but it hurts, not helps, the city. The final *O'Brien* requirement is that the incidental speech restriction be shown to be no greater than essential to achieve the government's legitimate purpose. To deal with this issue, we have to ask what basis there is to think that the city would be unsuccessful in countering any secondary effects by the significantly lesser restriction of zoning to control the location of nude dancing, thus allowing for efficient law enforcement, restricting effects on property values, and limiting exposure of the public. The record shows that for 23 years there has been a zoning ordinance on the books to regulate the location of establishments like Kandyland, but the city has not enforced it. One councilor remarked that "I think there's one of the problems. The ordinances are on the books and not enforced. Now this takes place. You really didn't need any other ordinances." Another commented, "I felt very, very strongly, and I feel just as strongly right now, that this is a zoning matter." Even on the plurality's view of the evidentiary burden, this hurdle to the application of *O'Brien* requires an evidentiary response.

The record suggests that Erie simply did not try to create a record of the sort we have held necessary in other cases, and the suggestion is confirmed by the course of this litigation. The evidentiary question was never decided (or, apparently, argued) below, nor was the issue fairly joined before this Court. . . . Accordingly, although I join with the plurality in adopting the *O'Brien* test, I respectfully dissent from the Court's disposition of the case.

☐ *Justice STEVENS, with whom Justice GINSBURG joins, dissenting.*

Far more important than the question whether nude dancing is entitled to the protection of the First Amendment are the dramatic changes in legal doctrine that the Court endorses today. Until now, the "secondary effects" of commercial enterprises featuring indecent entertainment have justified only the regulation of their location. For the first time, the Court has now held that such effects may justify the total suppression of protected speech. Indeed, the plurality opinion concludes that admittedly trivial advancements of a State's interests may provide the basis for censorship. The Court's commendable attempt to replace the fractured decision in *Barnes v. Glen Theatre, Inc.*, with a single coherent rationale is strikingly unsuccessful; it is supported neither by precedent nor by persuasive reasoning.

The Court relies on the so-called "secondary effects" test to defend the ordinance. The present use of that rationale, however, finds no support whatsoever in our precedents. Never before have we approved the use of that doctrine to justify a total ban on protected First Amendment expression. On the contrary, we have been quite clear that the doctrine would not support that end.

In *Young v. American Mini Theatres, Inc.*, 427 U.S. 50 (1976), we upheld a Detroit zoning ordinance that placed special restrictions on the location of motion picture theaters that exhibited "adult" movies. The "secondary effects" of the adult theaters on the neighborhoods where they were located—

lower property values and increases in crime (especially prostitution) to name a few—justified the burden imposed by the ordinance. Essential to our holding, however, was the fact that the ordinance was "nothing more than a limitation on the place where adult films may be exhibited" and did not limit the size of the market in such speech.

In *Renton v. Playtime Theatres, Inc.*, 475 U.S. 41 (1986), we upheld a similar ordinance, again finding that the "secondary effects of such theaters on the surrounding community" justified a restrictive zoning law. We noted, however, that "[t]he Renton ordinance, like the one in *American Mini Theatres*, does not ban adult theaters altogether," but merely "circumscribe[s] their choice as to location." Indeed, in both *Renton* and *American Mini Theatres*, the zoning ordinances were analyzed as mere "time, place, and manner" regulations. Because time, place, and manner regulations must "leave open ample alternative channels for communication of information," *Ward v. Rock Against Racism*, 491 U.S. 781 (1989), a total ban would necessarily fail that test. . . .

The reason we have limited our secondary effects cases to zoning and declined to extend their reasoning to total bans is clear and straightforward: A dispersal that simply limits the places where speech may occur is a minimal imposition whereas a total ban is the most exacting of restrictions. The State's interest in fighting presumed secondary effects is sufficiently strong to justify the former, but far too weak to support the latter, more severe burden. . . . The fact that this censorship may have a laudable ulterior purpose cannot mean that censorship is not censorship. For these reasons, the Court's holding rejects the explicit reasoning in *American Mini Theatres* and *Renton*. . . .

The Court's mishandling of our secondary effects cases is not limited to its approval of a total ban. It compounds that error by dramatically reducing the degree to which the State's interest must be furthered by the restriction imposed on speech, and by ignoring the critical difference between secondary effects caused by speech and the incidental effects on speech that may be caused by a regulation of conduct.

In what can most delicately be characterized as an enormous understatement, the plurality concedes that "requiring dancers to wear pasties and G-strings may not greatly reduce these secondary effects." To believe that the mandatory addition of pasties and a G-string will have any kind of noticeable impact on secondary effects requires nothing short of a titanic surrender to the implausible. . . .

Of course, the line between governmental interests aimed at conduct and unrelated to speech, on the one hand, and interests arising out of the effects of the speech, on the other, may be somewhat imprecise in some cases. In this case, however, we need not wrestle with any such difficulty because Erie has expressly justified its ordinance with reference to secondary effects. Indeed, if Erie's concern with the effects of the message were unrelated to the message itself, it is strange that the only means used to combat those effects is the suppression of the message. For these reasons, the Court's argument that "this case is similar to *O'Brien*" is quite wrong. . . . The Court cannot have its cake and eat it too—either Erie's ordinance was not aimed at speech and the Court may attempt to justify the regulation under the incidental burdens test, or Erie has aimed its law at the secondary effects of speech, and the Court can try to justify the law under that doctrine. But it cannot conflate the two with the expectation that Erie's interests aimed at secondary effects will be rendered unrelated to speech by virtue of this doctrinal polyglot. . . .

The censorial purpose of Erie's ordinance precludes reliance on the judgment in *Barnes* as sufficient support for the Court's holding today. Several differences between the Erie ordinance and the statute at issue in *Barnes* belie the Court's assertion that the two laws are "almost identical." . . . To begin with, the preamble to Erie's ordinance candidly articulates its agenda, declaring: "Council specifically wishes to adopt the concept of Public Indecency prohibited by the laws of the State of Indiana, which was approved by the U.S. Supreme Court in *Barnes v. Glen Theatre Inc.*, for the purpose of limiting a recent increase in nude live entertainment within the City." . . .

It is clear beyond a shadow of a doubt that the Erie ordinance was a response to a more specific concern than nudity in general, namely, nude dancing of the sort found in Kandyland. Given that the Court has not even tried to defend the ordinance's total ban on the ground that its censorship of protected speech might be justified by an overriding state interest, it should conclude that the ordinance is patently invalid. For these reasons, as well as the reasons set forth in Justice WHITE's dissent in *Barnes*, I respectfully dissent.

Reno v. American Civil Liberties Union
521 U.S. 844, 117 S.Ct. 2329 (1997)

When enacting the Communications Decency Act of 1996 (CDA), Congress sought to protect minors from harmful material on the Internet. The law, among other things, in Section 223(a) criminalized the "knowing" transmission of "obscene or indecent" messages to any recipient under eighteen years of age. Section 223(d) prohibited the "knowing" sending or displaying to a person under eighteen of any message "that, in context, depicts or describes, in terms patently offensive as measured by contemporary community standards, sexual or excretory activities or organs." Affirmative defenses were provided for those who take "good faith, . . . effective . . . actions" to restrict access by minors to the prohibited communications (Section 223(e)(5)(A)), and those who restrict such access by requiring certain designated forms of proof of age, such as a verified credit card or an adult identification number (Section 223(e)(5)(B)).

Following the law's enactment, the American Civil Liberties Union and a number of businesses and interest groups filed suit challenging the constitutionality of Sections 223(a)(1) and 223(d). Subsequently, a federal district court entered a preliminary injunction against enforcement of both challenged provisions and the government appealed to the Supreme Court.

The Court's decision was 7–2 and its opinion delivered by Justice Stevens. Justice O'Connor filed an opinion concurring in the judgment in part and dissenting in part, which Chief Justice Rehnquist joined.

Roger Baldwin on the campus of Washington University, St. Louis, Missouri, in 1906. A Boston aristocrat and a Progressive Era social reformer, Baldwin founded the Civil Liberties Bureau of the American Union against Militarism in 1917 to defend draft resisters during World War I. In 1920, that organization was reorganized as the American Civil Liberties Union (ACLU), based on nationwide local chapters. The ACLU is credited with spearheading the drive to defend and expand the scope of First Amendment freedoms in the twentieth century. (*Roger Nash Baldwin Papers; Public Policy Papers, Department of Special Collections, Princeton University Library.*)

■ ■ ■

☐ *Justice STEVENS delivered the opinion of the Court.*

At issue is the constitutionality of two statutory provisions enacted to protect minors from "indecent" and "patently offensive" communications on the Internet. Notwithstanding the legitimacy and importance of the congressional goal of protecting children from harmful materials, we agree with the three-judge District Court that the statute abridges "the freedom of speech" protected by the First Amendment.

The Internet is an international network of interconnected computers. It is the outgrowth of what began in 1969 as a military program called "ARPA-NET," which was designed to enable computers operated by the military, defense contractors, and universities conducting defense-related research to communicate with one another by redundant channels even if some portions of the network were damaged in a war. While the ARPANET no longer exists, it provided an example for the development of a number of civilian networks that, eventually linking with each other, now enable tens of millions of people to communicate with one another and to access vast amounts of information from around the world. The Internet is "a unique and wholly new medium of worldwide human communication." . . .

Sexually explicit material on the Internet includes text, pictures, and chat and "extends from the modestly titillating to the hardest-core." These files are created, named, and posted in the same manner as material that is not sexually explicit, and may be accessed either deliberately or unintentionally during the course of an imprecise search. "Once a provider posts its content on the Internet, it cannot prevent that content from entering any community." . . . Some of the communications over the Internet that originate in foreign countries are also sexually explicit.

Though such material is widely available, users seldom encounter such content accidentally. . . . For that reason, the "odds are slim" that a user would enter a sexually explicit site by accident. Unlike communications received by radio or television, "the receipt of information on the Internet requires a series of affirmative steps more deliberate and directed than merely turning a dial. A child requires some sophistication and some ability to read to retrieve material and thereby to use the Internet unattended."

Systems have been developed to help parents control the material that may be available on a home computer with Internet access. A system may either limit a computer's access to an approved list of sources that have been identified as containing no adult material, it may block designated inappropriate sites, or it may attempt to block messages containing identifiable objectionable features. "Although parental control software currently can screen for certain suggestive words or for known sexually explicit sites, it cannot now screen for sexually explicit images." Nevertheless, the evidence indicates that "a reasonably effective method by which parents can prevent their children from accessing sexually explicit and other material which parents may believe is inappropriate for their children will soon be available."

The problem of age verification differs for different uses of the Internet. The District Court categorically determined that there "is no effective way to determine the identity or the age of a user who is accessing material through e-mail, mail explorers, newsgroups or chat rooms." The Government offered no evidence that there was a reliable way to screen recipients and participants in such forums for age. Moreover, even if it were technologically feasible to block minors' access to newsgroups and chat rooms containing discussions of art, politics, or other subjects that potentially elicit "indecent" or "patently offensive" contributions, it would not be possible to block their access to that material and "still allow them access to the remaining content, even if the overwhelming majority of that content was not indecent."

Technology exists by which an operator of a Web site may condition access on the verification of requested information such as a credit card number or an adult password. Credit card verification is only feasible, however, either in connection with a commercial transaction in which the card is used, or by payment to a verification agency. Using credit card possession as a surrogate for proof of age would impose costs on non-commercial Web sites that would require many of them to shut down. For that reason, at the time of the trial, credit card verification was "effectively unavailable to a substantial number of Internet content providers." Moreover, the imposition of such a requirement "would completely bar adults who do not have a credit card and lack the resources to obtain one from accessing any blocked material." . . .

In arguing for reversal, the Government contends that the CDA is plainly constitutional under three of our prior decisions: (1) *Ginsberg v. New York*, 390 U.S. 629 (1968); (2) *FCC v. Pacifica Foundation*, 438 U.S. 726 (1978); and (3) *Renton v. Playtime Theatres, Inc.*, 475 U.S. 41 (1986). A close look at these cases, however, raises—rather than relieves—doubts concerning the constitutionality of the CDA.

In *Ginsberg*, we upheld the constitutionality of a New York statute that prohibited selling to minors under 17 years of age material that was considered obscene as to them even if not obscene as to adults. We rejected the defendant's broad submission that "the scope of the constitutional freedom of expression secured to a citizen to read or see material concerned with sex cannot be made to depend on whether the citizen is an adult or a minor." In four important respects, the statute upheld in *Ginsberg* was narrower than the CDA. First, we noted in *Ginsberg* that "the prohibition against sales to minors does not bar parents who so desire from purchasing the magazines for their children." Under the CDA, by contrast, neither the parents' consent—nor even their participation—in the communication would avoid the application of the statute. Second, the New York statute applied only to commercial transactions, whereas the CDA contains no such limitation. Third, the New York statute combined its definition of material that is harmful to minors with the requirement that it be "utterly without redeeming social importance for minors." The CDA fails to provide us with any definition of the term "indecent" as used in Section 223(a)(1) and, importantly, omits any requirement that the "patently offensive" material covered by Section 223(d) lack serious literary, artistic, political, or scientific value. Fourth, the New York statute defined a minor as a person under the age of 17, whereas the CDA, in applying to all those under 18 years, includes an additional year of those nearest majority.

In *Pacifica*, we upheld a declaratory order of the Federal Communications Commission, holding that the broadcast of a recording of a 12-minute monologue entitled "Filthy Words" that had previously been delivered to a live audience "could have been the subject of administrative sanctions." The Commission had found that the repetitive use of certain words referring to excretory or sexual activities or organs "in an afternoon broadcast when children are in the audience was patently offensive" and concluded that the monologue was indecent "as broadcast." The respondent did not quarrel with the finding that the afternoon broadcast was patently offensive, but contended that it was not "indecent" within the meaning of the relevant statutes because it contained no prurient appeal. After rejecting respondent's statutory arguments, we confronted its two constitutional arguments: (1) that the Commission's construction of its authority to ban indecent speech was so broad that its order had to be set aside even if the broadcast at issue was unprotected; and (2) that since the recording was not obscene, the First Amendment forbade any abridgment of the right to broadcast it on the radio.

In the portion of the lead opinion not joined by Justices POWELL and BLACKMUN, the plurality stated that the First Amendment does not prohibit all governmental regulation that depends on the content of speech. Accordingly, the availability of constitutional protection for a vulgar and offensive monologue that was not obscene depended on the context of the broadcast. Relying on the premise that "of all forms of communication" broadcasting had received the most limited First Amendment protection, the Court concluded that the ease with which children may obtain access to broadcasts, "coupled with the concerns recognized in *Ginsberg*," justified special treatment of indecent broadcasting.

As with the New York statute at issue in *Ginsberg*, there are significant differences between the order upheld in *Pacifica* and the CDA. First, the order in *Pacifica*, issued by an agency that had been regulating radio stations for decades, targeted a specific broadcast that represented a rather dramatic departure from traditional program content in order to designate when—rather than whether—it would be permissible to air such a program in that particular medium. The CDA's broad categorical prohibitions are not limited to particular times and are not dependent on any evaluation by an agency familiar with the unique characteristics of the Internet. Second, unlike the CDA, the Commission's declaratory order was not punitive; we expressly refused to decide whether the indecent broadcast "would justify a criminal prosecution." Finally, the Commission's order applied to a medium which as a matter of history had "received the most limited First Amendment protection" in large part because warnings could not adequately protect the listener from unexpected program content. The Internet, however, has no comparable history.

In *Renton*, we upheld a zoning ordinance that kept adult movie theaters out of residential neighborhoods. The ordinance was aimed, not at the content of the films shown in the theaters, but rather at the "secondary effects"— such as crime and deteriorating property values—that these theaters fostered: "It is the secondary effect which these zoning ordinances attempt to avoid, not the dissemination of 'offensive' speech." According to the Government, the CDA is constitutional because it constitutes a sort of "cyberzoning" on the Internet. But the CDA applies broadly to the entire universe of cyberspace. And the purpose of the CDA is to protect children from the primary effects of "indecent" and "patently offensive" speech, rather than any "secondary" effect of such speech. Thus, the CDA is a content-based blanket restriction on speech, and, as such, cannot be "properly analyzed as a form of time, place, and manner regulation."

These precedents, then, surely do not require us to uphold the CDA and are fully consistent with the application of the most stringent review of its provisions. . . .

Neither before nor after the enactment of the CDA have the vast democratic forums of the Internet been subject to the type of government supervision and regulation that has attended the broadcast industry. Moreover, the Internet is not as "invasive" as radio or television. The District Court specifically found that "communications over the Internet do not 'invade' an individual's home or appear on one's computer screen unbidden. Users seldom encounter content 'by accident.'" It also found that "almost all sexually explicit images are preceded by warnings as to the content," and cited testimony that "'odds are slim' that a user would come across a sexually explicit sight by accident." . . .

Regardless of whether the CDA is so vague that it violates the Fifth Amendment, the many ambiguities concerning the scope of its coverage render it problematic for purposes of the First Amendment. For instance, each of the two parts of the CDA uses a different linguistic form. The first uses the word "indecent," while the second speaks of material that "in context, depicts or describes, in terms patently offensive as measured by contemporary community standards, sexual or excretory activities or organs." Given the absence of a definition of either term, this difference in language will provoke uncertainty among speakers about how the two standards relate to each other and just what they mean. Could a speaker confidently assume that a serious discussion about birth control practices, homosexuality, the First Amendment issues raised by the Appendix to our *Pacifica* opinion, or the consequences of prison rape would not violate the CDA? This uncertainty undermines the likelihood that the CDA has been carefully tailored to the congressional goal of protecting minors from potentially harmful materials.

The vagueness of the CDA is a matter of special concern for two reasons. First, the CDA is a content-based regulation of speech. The vagueness of such a regulation raises special First Amendment concerns because of its obvious chilling effect on free speech. Second, the CDA is a criminal statute. In addition to the opprobrium and stigma of a criminal conviction, the CDA threatens violators with penalties including up to two years in prison for each act of violation. The severity of criminal sanctions may well cause speakers to remain silent rather than communicate even arguably unlawful words, ideas, and images. . . .

We are persuaded that the CDA lacks the precision that the First Amendment requires when a statute regulates the content of speech. In order to deny minors access to potentially harmful speech, the CDA effectively suppresses a large amount of speech that adults have a constitutional right to receive and to address to one another. That burden on adult speech is unacceptable if less restrictive alternatives would be at least as effective in achieving the legitimate purpose that the statute was enacted to serve.

In evaluating the free speech rights of adults, we have made it perfectly clear that "sexual expression which is indecent but not obscene is protected by the First Amendment." *Sable* [*Communications v. Federal Communications Commission*, 492 U.S. 115 (1989)]. Indeed, *Pacifica* itself admonished that "the fact that society may find speech offensive is not a sufficient reason for suppressing it."

It is true that we have repeatedly recognized the governmental interest in protecting children from harmful materials. But that interest does not justify an unnecessarily broad suppression of speech addressed to adults. As we have explained, the Government may not "reduce the adult population . . . to . . . only what is fit for children." "Regardless of the strength of the government's interest" in protecting children, "the level of discourse reaching a mailbox simply cannot be limited to that which would be suitable for a sandbox." *Bolger v. Youngs Drug Products Corp.*, 463 U.S. 60 (1983).

In arguing that the CDA does not so diminish adult communication, the Government relies on the incorrect factual premise that prohibiting a transmission whenever it is known that one of its recipients is a minor would not interfere with adult-to-adult communication. The findings of the District Court make clear that this premise is untenable. Given the size of the potential audience for most messages, in the absence of a viable age-verification process, the sender must be charged with knowing that one or more minors will likely view it. Knowledge that, for instance, one or more members of a 100-person chat group will be minor—and therefore that it would be a crime to send the group an indecent message—would surely burden communication among adults. . . .

For the purposes of our decision, we need neither accept nor reject the Government's submission that the First Amendment does not forbid a blanket prohibition on all "indecent" and "patently offensive" messages communicated to a 17-year-old—no matter how much value the message may contain and regardless of parental approval. It is at least clear that the strength of the Government's interest in protecting minors is not equally strong throughout the coverage of this broad statute. Under the CDA, a parent allowing her 17-year-old to use the family computer to obtain information on the Internet that she, in her parental judgment, deems appropriate could face a lengthy prison term. Similarly, a parent who sent his 17-year-old college freshman [child] information on birth control via e-mail could be incarcerated even though neither he, his child, nor anyone in their home community, found the material "indecent" or "patently offensive," if the college town's community thought otherwise.

The breadth of this content-based restriction of speech imposes an especially heavy burden on the Government to explain why a less restrictive provision would not be as effective as the CDA. It has not done so. The arguments in this Court have referred to possible alternatives such as requiring that indecent material be "tagged" in a way that facilitates parental control of material coming into their homes, making exceptions for messages with artistic or educational value, providing some tolerance for parental choice, and regulating some portions of the Internet—such as commercial Web sites—differently than others, such as chat rooms. Particularly in the light of the absence of any detailed findings by the Congress, or even hearings addressing the special problems of the CDA, we are persuaded that the CDA is not narrowly tailored if that requirement has any meaning at all. . . .

For the foregoing reasons, the judgment of the district court is affirmed.

☐ *Justice O'CONNOR, with whom THE CHIEF JUSTICE joins, concurring in the judgment in part and dissenting in part.*

I write separately to explain why I view the Communications Decency Act of 1996 (CDA) as little more than an attempt by Congress to create "adult zones" on the Internet. Our precedent indicates that the creation of such zones can be constitutionally sound. Despite the soundness of its purpose, however, portions of the CDA are unconstitutional because they stray from the blueprint our prior cases have developed for constructing a "zoning law" that passes constitutional muster. . . .

The Court in *Ginsberg* concluded that the New York law created a constitutionally adequate adult zone simply because, on its face, it denied access only to minors. The Court did not question—and therefore necessarily assumed—that an adult zone, once created, would succeed in preserving adults' access while denying minors' access to the regulated speech. Before today, there was no reason to question this assumption, for the Court has previously only considered laws that operated in the physical world, a world with two characteristics that make it possible to create "adult zones": geography and identity. . . .

The electronic world is fundamentally different. Because it is no more than the interconnection of electronic pathways, cyberspace allows speakers and listeners to mask their identities. Cyberspace undeniably reflects some form of geography; chat rooms and Web sites, for example, exist at fixed "locations" on the Internet. Since users can transmit and receive messages on the Internet without revealing anything about their identities or ages, however, it is not currently possible to exclude persons from accessing certain messages on the basis of their identity.

Cyberspace differs from the physical world in another basic way: Cyberspace is malleable. Thus, it is possible to construct barriers in cyberspace and use them to screen for identity, making cyberspace more like the physical world and, consequently, more amenable to zoning laws. This transformation of cyberspace is already underway. Internet speakers (users who post material on the Internet) have begun to zone cyberspace itself through the use of "gateway" technology. Such technology requires Internet users to enter information about themselves—perhaps an adult identification number or a credit card number—before they can access certain areas of cyberspace, much like a bouncer checks a person's driver's license before admitting him to a nightclub. Internet users who access information have not attempted to zone cyberspace itself, but have tried to limit their own power to access information in cyberspace, much as a parent controls what her children watch on television by installing a lock box. This user-based zoning is accomplished through the use of screening software (such as Cyber Patrol or SurfWatch) or browsers with screening capabilities, both of which search addresses and text for keywords that are associated with "adult" sites and, if the user wishes, blocks access to such sites. The Platform for Internet Content Selection (PICS) project is designed to facilitate user-based zoning by encouraging Internet speakers to rate the content of their speech using codes recognized by all screening programs. . . .

Although the prospects for the eventual zoning of the Internet appear promising, I agree with the Court that we must evaluate the constitutionality of the CDA as it applies to the Internet as it exists today. Given the present state of cyberspace, I agree with the Court that the "display" provision cannot pass muster. . . .

The "indecency transmission" and "specific person" provisions present a closer issue, for they are not unconstitutional in all of their applications. As discussed above, the "indecency transmission" provision makes it a crime to transmit knowingly an indecent message to a person the sender knows is under 18 years of age. The "specific person" provision proscribes the same conduct, although it does not as explicitly require the sender to know that the intended recipient of his indecent message is a minor. Appellant urges the Court to construe the provision to impose such a knowledge requirement and I would do so.

So construed, both provisions are constitutional as applied to a conversation involving only an adult and one or more minors—e.g., when an adult speaker sends an e-mail knowing the addressee is a minor, or when an adult and minor converse by themselves or with other minors in a chat room. In this context, these provisions are no different from the law we sustained in *Ginsberg*. Restricting what the adult may say to the minors in no way restricts the adult's ability to communicate with other adults. He is not prevented from speaking indecently to other adults in a chat room (because there are no other adults participating in the conversation) and he remains free to send indecent e-mails to other adults. The relevant universe contains only one adult, and the adult in that universe has the power to refrain from using indecent speech and consequently to keep all such speech within the room in an "adult" zone.

The analogy to *Ginsberg* breaks down, however, when more than one adult is a party to the conversation. If a minor enters a chat room otherwise occupied by adults, the CDA effectively requires the adults in the room to asstop using indecent speech. If they did not, they could be prosecuted under the "indecency transmission" and "specific person" provisions for any indecent statements they make to the group, since they would be transmitting an indecent message to specific persons, one of whom is a minor. The CDA is therefore akin to a law that makes it a crime for a bookstore owner to sell pornographic magazines to anyone once a minor enters his store. Even assuming such a law might be constitutional in the physical world as a reasonable alternative to excluding minors completely from the store, the absence of any means of excluding minors from chat rooms in cyberspace restricts the rights of adults to engage in indecent speech in those rooms. The "indecency transmission" and "specific person" provisions share this defect.

But these two provisions do not infringe on adults' speech in all situations. I do not find that the provisions are overbroad in the sense that they restrict minors' access to a substantial amount of speech that minors have the right to read and view. Accordingly, the CDA can be applied constitutionally in some situations. . . .

[T]he constitutionality of the CDA as a zoning law hinges on the extent to which it substantially interferes with the First Amendment rights of adults. Because the rights of adults are infringed only by the "display" provision and by the "indecency transmission" and "specific person" provisions as applied to communications involving more than one adult, I would invalidate the CDA only to that extent. Insofar as the "indecency transmission" and "specific person" provisions prohibit the use of indecent speech in communications between an adult and one or more minors, however, they can and should be sustained. The Court reaches a contrary conclusion, and from that holding that I respectfully dissent.

Ashcroft v. Free Speech Coalition
535 U.S. 234, 122 S.Ct. 1389 (2002)

In 1996 Congress enacted the Child Pornography Prevention Act (CPPA), making it a crime to create, distribute, or possess "virtual child pornography" generated by computer images of young adults rather than actual children. The constitutionality of the law was challenged by the Free Speech Coalition—a coalition of artists, photographers, and adult entertainment businesses. A federal district court upheld its provisions but the Court of Appeals for the Ninth Circuit reversed and found that the CPPA violated the First Amendment. Attorney General John D. Ashcroft appealed that decision and the Supreme Court granted review.

The decision of the appellate court was affirmed in a six-and-a-half to two-and-a-half vote. Justice Kennedy delivered the opinion for the Court. Justice Thomas filed a concurring opinion, indicating that a more narrowly drawn statute might pass constitutional muster. Chief Justice Rehnquist filed a dissenting opinion, which Justice Scalia joined. Justice O'Connor filed a separate opinion in part concurring and dissenting.

■ ■ ■

☐ *Justice KENNEDY delivered the opinion of the Court.*

We consider in this case whether the Child Pornography Prevention Act of 1996 (CPPA) abridges the freedom of speech. . . . By prohibiting child pornography that does not depict an actual child, the statute goes beyond *New York v. Ferber*, 458 U.S. 747 (1982), which distinguished child pornography from other sexually explicit speech because of the State's interest in protecting the children exploited by the production process. As a general rule, pornography can be banned only if obscene, but under *Ferber*, pornography showing minors can be proscribed whether or not the images are obscene under the definition set forth in *Miller v. California*, 413 U.S. 15 (1973). . . .

The CPPA, however, is not directed at speech that is obscene; Congress has proscribed those materials through a separate statute. Like the law in *Ferber*, the CPPA seeks to reach beyond obscenity, and it makes no attempt to conform to the *Miller* standard. For instance, the statute would reach visual depictions, such as movies, even if they have redeeming social value.

The principal question to be resolved, then, is whether the CPPA is constitutional where it proscribes a significant universe of speech that is neither obscene under *Miller* nor child pornography under *Ferber*.

Before 1996, Congress defined child pornography as the type of depictions at issue in *Ferber*, images made using actual minors. The CPPA retains that prohibition at 18 U.S.C. Sec. 2256(8)(A) and adds three other prohibited categories of speech, of which the first, Sec. 2256(8)(B), and the third, Sec. 2256(8)(D), are at issue in this case. Section 2256(8)(B) prohibits "any visual depiction, including any photograph, film, video, picture, or computer or computer-generated image or picture" that "is, or appears to be, of a minor engaging in sexually explicit conduct." The prohibition on "any visual depiction" does not depend at all on how the image is produced. The section captures a range of depictions, sometimes called "virtual child pornography," which include computer-generated images, as well as images produced by more traditional means. For instance, the literal terms of the statute embrace a Renaissance painting depicting a scene from classical mythology, a "picture" that "appears to be, of a minor engaging in sexually explicit conduct." The statute also prohibits Hollywood movies, filmed without any child actors, if a jury believes an actor "appears to be" a minor engaging in "actual or simulated . . . sexual intercourse."

These images do not involve, let alone harm, any children in the production process; but Congress decided the materials threaten children in other, less direct, ways. Pedophiles might use the materials to encourage children to participate in sexual activity. Furthermore, pedophiles might "whet their own sexual appetites" with the pornographic images, "thereby increasing the creation and distribution of child pornography and the sexual abuse and exploitation of actual children." Under these rationales, harm flows from the content of the images, not from the means of their production. In addition, Congress identified another problem created by computer-generated images: their existence can make it harder to prosecute pornographers who do use real minors. As imaging technology improves, Congress found, it becomes more difficult to prove that a particular picture was produced using actual children.

Section 2256(8)(C) prohibits a more common and lower tech means of creating virtual images, known as computer morphing. Rather than creating original images, pornographers can alter innocent pictures of real children so that the children appear to be engaged in sexual activity. Although morphed images may fall within the definition of virtual child pornography, they implicate the interests of real children and are in that sense closer to the images in *Ferber*. Respondents do not challenge this provision, and we do not consider it.

Respondents do challenge Sec. 2256(8)(D). Like the text of the "appears to be" provision, the sweep of this provision is quite broad. Section 2256(8) (D) defines child pornography to include any sexually explicit image that was "advertised, promoted, presented, described, or distributed in such a manner that conveys the impression" it depicts "a minor engaging in sexually explicit conduct." The statute is not so limited in its reach, however, as it punishes even those possessors who took no part in pandering. . . .

The CPPA's penalties are indeed severe. A first offender may be imprisoned for 15 years. A repeat offender faces a prison sentence of not less than 5 years and not more than 30 years in prison. While even minor punishments can chill protected speech, this case provides a textbook example of why we permit facial challenges to statutes that burden expression. With these severe penalties in force, few legitimate movie producers or book publishers, or few other speakers in any capacity, would risk distributing images in or near the uncertain reach of this law. . . .

Under *Miller v. California*, 413 U.S. 15(1973), the Government must prove that the work, taken as a whole, appeals to the prurient interest, is patently offensive in light of community standards, and lacks serious literary, artistic, political, or scientific value. The CPPA, however, extends to images that appear to depict a minor engaging in sexually explicit activity without regard to the *Miller* requirements. The materials need not appeal to the prurient interest. Any depiction of sexually explicit activity, no matter how it is presented, is proscribed. The CPPA applies to a picture in a psychology manual, as well as a movie depicting the horrors of sexual abuse. It is not necessary, moreover, that the image be patently offensive. Pictures of what appear to be 17-year-olds engaging in sexually explicit activity do not in every case contravene community standards.

The CPPA prohibits speech despite its serious literary, artistic, political, or scientific value. The statute proscribes the visual depiction of an idea—that of teenagers engaging in sexual activity—that is a fact of modern society and has been a theme in art and literature throughout the ages. Under the CPPA, images are prohibited so long as the persons appear to be under 18 years of age. This is higher than the legal age for marriage in many States, as well as the age at which persons may consent to sexual relations.

Both themes—teenage sexual activity and the sexual abuse of children—have inspired countless literary works. William Shakespeare created the most famous pair of teenage lovers, one of whom is just 13 years of age. See *Romeo and Juliet*, act I, sc. 2, l. 9 ("She hath not seen the change of fourteen years"). In the drama, Shakespeare portrays the relationship as something splendid and innocent, but not juvenile. The work has inspired no less than 40 motion pictures, some of which suggest that the teenagers consummated their relationship. Shakespeare may not have written sexually explicit scenes for the Elizabethan audience, but were modern directors to adopt a less conventional approach, that fact alone would not compel the conclusion that the work was obscene. . . .

In contrast to the speech in *Ferber*, speech that itself is the record of sexual abuse, the CPPA prohibits speech that records no crime and creates no victims by its production. Virtual child pornography is not "intrinsically related" to the sexual abuse of children, as were the materials in *Ferber*. While the Government asserts that the images can lead to actual instances of child abuse, the causal link is contingent and indirect. The harm does not necessarily follow from the speech, but depends upon some unquantified potential for subsequent criminal acts.

The Government says these indirect harms are sufficient because, as *Ferber* acknowledged, child pornography rarely can be valuable speech. This argument, however, suffers from two flaws. First, *Ferber's* judgment about child pornography was based upon how it was made, not on what it communicated. The case reaffirmed that where the speech is neither obscene nor the product of sexual abuse, it does not fall outside the protection of the First Amendment.

The second flaw in the Government's position is that *Ferber* did not hold that child pornography is by definition without value. On the contrary, the Court recognized some works in this category might have significant value, but relied on virtual images—the very images prohibited by the CPPA—as an alternative and permissible means of expression: "[I]f it were necessary for literary or artistic value, a person over the statutory age who perhaps looked younger could be utilized. Simulation outside of the prohibition of the statute could provide another alternative." *Ferber*, then, not only referred to the distinction between actual and virtual child pornography, it relied on it as a reason supporting its holding. *Ferber* provides no support for a statute that eliminates the distinction and makes the alternative mode criminal as well.

The CPPA, for reasons we have explored, is inconsistent with *Miller* and finds no support in *Ferber*. The Government seeks to justify its prohibitions in other ways. It argues that the CPPA is necessary because pedophiles may use virtual child pornography to seduce children. There are many things innocent in themselves, however, such as cartoons, video games, and candy, that might be used for immoral purposes, yet we would not expect those to be prohibited because they can be misused. The Government, of course, may punish adults who provide unsuitable materials to children, see *Ginsberg v. New York*, 390 U.S. 629 (1968), and it may enforce criminal penalties for unlawful solicitation. The precedents establish, however, that speech within the rights of adults to hear may not be silenced completely in an attempt to shield children from it. *Butler v. Michigan*, 352 U.S. 380 (1957). . . .

In sum, Sec. 2256(8)(B) covers materials beyond the categories recognized in *Ferber* and *Miller*, and the reasons the Government offers in support of limiting the freedom of speech have no justification in our precedents or in the law of the First Amendment. The provision abridges the freedom to engage in a substantial amount of lawful speech. For this reason, it is overbroad and unconstitutional.

Respondents challenge Sec. 2256(8)(D) as well. This provision bans depictions of sexually explicit conduct that are "advertised, promoted, presented, described, or distributed in such a manner that conveys the impression that the material is or contains a visual depiction of a minor engaging in sexually explicit conduct." The parties treat the section as nearly identical to the provision prohibiting materials that appear to be child pornography.

In the Government's view, the difference between the two is that "the 'conveys the impression' provision requires the jury to assess the material at issue in light of the manner in which it is promoted."

We disagree with this view. The CPPA prohibits sexually explicit materials that "conve[y] the impression" they depict minors. While that phrase may sound like the "appears to be" prohibition in Sec. 2256(8)(B), it requires little judgment about the content of the image. Under Sec. 2256(8)(D), the work must be sexually explicit, but otherwise the content is irrelevant. Even if a film contains no sexually explicit scenes involving minors, it could be treated as child pornography if the title and trailers convey the impression that the scenes would be found in the movie. The determination turns on how the speech is presented, not on what is depicted. While the legislative findings address at length the problems posed by materials that look like child pornography, they are silent on the evils posed by images simply pandered that way. . . .

[T]he CPPA does more than prohibit pandering. It prohibits possession of material described, or pandered, as child pornography by someone earlier in the distribution chain. The provision prohibits a sexually explicit film containing no youthful actors, just because it is placed in a box suggesting a prohibited movie. Possession is a crime even when the possessor knows the movie was mislabeled. The First Amendment requires a more precise restriction. For this reason, Sec. 2256(8)(D) is substantially overbroad and in violation of the First Amendment.

For the reasons we have set forth, the prohibitions of Sections 2256(8) (B) and 2256(8)(D) are overbroad and unconstitutional. . . .

☐ *Chief Justice REHNQUIST, with whom Justice SCALIA joins in part, dissenting.*

Congress has a compelling interest in ensuring the ability to enforce prohibitions of actual child pornography, and we should defer to its findings that rapidly advancing technology soon will make it all but impossible to do so.

I also agree with Justice O'CONNOR that serious First Amendment concerns would arise were the Government ever to prosecute someone for simple distribution or possession of a film with literary or artistic value, such as "Traffic" or "American Beauty." I write separately, however, because the Child Pornography Prevention Act of 1996 (CPPA) need not be construed to reach such materials. . . .

Other than computer generated images that are virtually indistinguishable from real children engaged in sexually explicit conduct, the CPPA can be limited so as not to reach any material that was not already unprotected before the CPPA. The CPPA's definition of "sexually explicit conduct" is quite explicit in this regard. It makes clear that the statute only reaches "visual depictions." . . . [I] think the definition reaches only the sort of "hard core of child pornography" that we found without protection in *Ferber*. So construed, the CPPA bans visual depictions of youthful looking adult actors engaged in actual sexual activity; mere suggestions of sexual activity, such as youthful looking adult actors squirming under a blanket, are more akin to written descriptions than visual depictions, and thus fall outside the purview of the statute. . . .

To the extent the CPPA prohibits possession or distribution of materials that "convey the impression" of a child engaged in sexually explicit conduct, that prohibition can and should be limited to reach "the sordid business of pandering" which lies outside the bounds of First Amendment protection. *Ginzburg v. United States,* 383 U.S. 463 (1966). . . .

For these reasons, I would construe the CPPA in a manner consistent with the First Amendment, reverse the Court of Appeals' judgment, and uphold the statute in its entirety.

☐ *Justice O'CONNOR, with whom THE CHIEF JUSTICE and Justice SCALIA join, concurring in the judgment and dissenting in part.*

Because the Government may already prohibit obscenity without violating the First Amendment, see *Miller v. California* (1973), what the Government asks this Court to rule is that it may also prohibit youthful-adult and virtual-adult pornography that is merely indecent without violating that Amendment. Although such pornography looks like the material at issue in *New York v. Ferber,* no children are harmed in the process of creating such pornography. Therefore, *Ferber* does not support the Government's ban on youthful-adult and virtual-child pornography. . . .

I also agree with the Court's decision to strike down the CPPA's ban on material presented in a manner that "conveys the impression" that it contains pornographic depictions of actual children ("actual-child pornography"). The Government fails to explain how this ban serves any compelling state interest. . . .

Finally, I agree with the Court that the CPPA's ban on youthful-adult pornography is overbroad. . . .

I disagree with the Court, however, that the CPPA's prohibition of virtual-child pornography is overbroad. . . . Although Section 2256(8)(B) does not distinguish between youthful-adult and virtual-child pornography, the CPPA elsewhere draws a line between these two classes of speech. The statute provides an affirmative defense for those who produce, distribute, or receive pornographic images of individuals who are actually adults, Sec. 2252A(c), but not for those with pornographic images that are wholly computer generated. This is not surprising given that the legislative findings enacted by Congress contain no mention of youthful-adult pornography. Those findings focus explicitly only on actual-child pornography and virtual-child pornography. Drawing a line around, and striking just, the CPPA's ban on youthful-child pornography not only is consistent with Congress' understanding of the categories of speech encompassed by Section 2256(8)(B), but also preserves the CPPA's prohibition of the material that Congress found most dangerous to children.

In sum, I would strike down the CPPA's ban on material that "conveys the impression" that it contains actual-child pornography, but uphold the ban on pornographic depictions that "appea[r] to be" of minors so long as it is not applied to youthful-adult pornography.

■ (2) FIGHTING WORDS AND OFFENSIVE SPEECH

Although fighting words is a category of unprotected First Amendment speech, the Court so narrowly applies the category as virtually to eliminate it. Even an invitation to a brawl no longer appears excluded from First Amendment protection. The Court, for example, reversed the conviction of a man who, while being arrested, rather unambiguously invited a fight by calling a police officer a son of a bitch and threatening to kill him.[1] *Lewis v. New Orleans*, 415 U.S. 130 (1974), struck down an ordinance prohibiting the cursing of policemen, and *City of Houston, Texas v. Hill*, 482 U.S. 451 (1987), invalidated a law that made it unlawful to interfere with a police officer while performing his duties.

Offensive speech may convey a political statement and hence be entitled to protection. In *Watts v. United States*, 395 U.S. 705 (1969), for instance, the Court overturned the conviction of an individual who, at a protest rally against the Vietnam War, shouted, "If they ever make me carry a rifle, the first man I want to get is LBJ [President Lyndon Johnson]." The justices agreed (6–3) that the federal statute criminalizing threats against the life of the president must be strictly construed and the statement here was an expression of political views, rather than an actual threat. The Rehnquist Court, however, was more sharply split in *Rankin v. McPherson*, 483 U.S. 378 (1987), holding that a public employee could not be fired for remarking during a private conversation, after hearing of the 1981 assassination attempt on President Reagan, "If they go for him again, I hope they get him." Dissenting Justice Scalia, joined by Chief Justice Rehnquist and Justices O'Connor and White, contended that such speech conveys no "public concerns" entitled to First Amendment protection.

The landmark ruling in *Cohen v. California* (1969) (see excerpt below) held that four-letter words, however offensive, are not per se excluded from First Amendment protection. Over the objections of three dissenters, Justice Harlan rejected arguments that privacy interests justified the conviction, under California's penal code punishing disturbances of the peace and offensive conduct, of an individual who wore a jacket emblazoned with the words *Fuck the Draft* in the corridor of a Los Angeles County courthouse. Notice that Harlan weighed the competing claims of privacy and free speech not on the basis of the content of the speech (whether some individuals regard certain speech as obscene or offensive), but in terms of the manner of the intrusion and the context in which individuals claim that they have reasonable expectations of privacy against being made a "captive audience" for offensive speech.

When weighing free speech claims against interests in privacy and safeguards against offensive intrusions, the Court considers the context and relative intrusiveness of different modes of communication. Justice Brandeis in *Packer Corporation v. Utah*, 285 U.S. 105 (1932) suggested this approach when upholding a statute forbidding all advertising of cigarettes on billboards and streetcar signs but permitting such ads in newspapers, magazines, and storefront windows:

Billboards, street car signs, and placards and such are in a class by themselves. . . . [They] are constantly before the eyes of observers on the streets and in street cars to be seen without the exercise of choice or violation on their part. Other forms of advertising are ordinarily seen as a matter of choice on the part of the observer. The young people as well as the adults have the message of the billboard thrust upon them by all the arts and devices that skill can produce. In the case of newspapers and magazines, there must be some seeking by the one who is to see and read the advertisement. The radio can be turned off, but not so the billboard or street car placard.

In the *Handbills Cases* of 1939, however, the Court ruled that Jehovah's Witnesses and others seeking to engage in religious or political canvassing could not be barred from ringing doorbells and knocking on the doors of private residencies.[2] As the Court, in *Martin v. City of Struthers*, 319 U.S. 141 (1943), observed, "[T]he ordinance was designed to protect a legitimate interest, that of privacy in the home, but in balancing the interests, the considerations of free speech and the free exercise of religion out-weighed this interest." Subsequently, the owners of a company town were forbidden from prohibiting the door-to-door circulation of religious and political literature.[3] Those rulings were reaffirmed in *Watchtower Bible & Tract Society of New York, Inc. v. Village of Stratton*, 536 U.S. 150 (2002).

By contrast, *Kovacs v. Cooper*, 336 U.S. 77 (1949), upheld an ordinance outlawing sound trucks emitting "loud and raucous noises" because their intrusiveness was such that an individual "is practically helpless to escape this interference with his privacy by loudspeakers." Two years later, *Breard v. Alexandria*, 341 U.S. 622 (1951), sustained a prohibition on solicitors, peddlers, and transient vendors of merchandise from going onto private property without the owner's permission. There the Court distinguished the solicitations for religious purposes from that of the door-to-door salesmen in finding that the latter did not outweigh the intrusion on individuals' privacy in their homes.

As in *Cohen*, the Court in *Public Utilities Commission v. Pollak*, 343 U.S. 451 (1952), ruled that individuals have greater privacy interests against offensive intrusions in their homes than in public places. There the Court sustained a privately owned transit company's use of radio loudspeakers in its streetcars and buses for the purpose of providing "music as you ride." In rejecting the arguments of patrons who found the music offensive and intrusive on their privacy, Justice Burton observed,

> The Court below has emphasized the claim that the radio programs are an invasion of the constitutional rights of privacy of the passengers. . . . This position wrongly assumes that . . . each passenger on a public vehicle regulated by the Federal Government

[has] a right of privacy substantially equal to the privacy to which he is entitled in his own home. However complete his right of privacy may be at home, it is substantially limited by the rights of others when its possessor travels on a public thoroughfare or rides in a public conveyance.

Still, balancing free speech claims against interests in privacy and freedom from offensive speech is often difficult for the Court. Over the dissent of Chief Justice Burger and Justices White and Rehnquist, *Erzoznik v. City of Jacksonville*, 422 U.S. 205 (1975), struck down an ordinance making it a public nuisance to show any motion picture containing nudity in a drive-in theater where the screen was visible from a public street. In rejecting the privacy claims of homeowners who could see the movie screen from their backyards and of drivers of cars passing by on a highway, Justice Powell reasoned that

[t]his discrimination cannot be justified as a means of preventing significant intrusions on privacy. The ordinance seeks to keep these films from being seen from public streets and places where the offended viewer can avert his eyes. In short, the screen of a drive-in theater is not "so unobtrusive as to make it impossible for an unwilling individual to avoid exposure to it." . . . Thus, we conclude that the limited privacy interest of persons on the public streets cannot justify this censorship of otherwise protected speech on the basis of its content.

Compare the reasoning in cases such as *Cohen* and *Erzoznik* with that in Justice Stevens's plurality opinion and the dissenters' opinions in *Federal Communications Commission v. Pacifica Foundation* (1976) (see excerpt below). There a bare majority upheld the Federal Communication Commission's regulations banning indecent, but not obscene, speech on the radio, in a case arising from a twelve-minute monologue by satiric humorist George Carlin on seven dirty words that cannot be said on the radio or television. In *Sable Communications v. Federal Communications Commission*, 492 U.S. 115 (1989), though, the Court unanimously struck down a 1988 congressional statute banning indecent telephone "dial-a-porn" services when holding that only hard-core obscene messages may be outlawed. A fragmented Court also struck down a similar requirement, under the Cable Television Consumer Protection and Competition Act of 1992, that cable companies block access to sexually explicit material unless viewers request access in advance and in writing. See *Denver Area Education Telecommunications Consortium, Inc. v. Federal Communications Commission*, 518 U.S. 727 (1996).

Controversy over indecent and offensive speech has also led to some important rulings on the rights of students in primary and secondary schools.[4] In *Board of Education, Island Trees Union Free School District v.*

Pico, 457 U.S. 853 (1985), the Court ruled that local school boards could not remove books from school libraries because they were deemed offensive. Although not addressing the power of school boards to select books for its libraries, Justice Brennan emphasized that "[o]ur Constitution does not permit the official suppression of *ideas*. . . . [L]ocal school boards may not remove books from school library shelves simply because they dislike the ideas contained in those books and seek by their removal to prescribe what shall be orthodox in politics, nationalism, religion, or other matters of opinion."

In *Bethel School District No. 403 v. Fraser* (1986) (see excerpt below), however, the Court (voting 7–2) upheld the authority of a principal to discipline a student for using suggestive (possibly indecent, but not obscene) language in a speech at a student rally. Consider the opinions in this case with those in *Tinker v. Des Moines Independent Community School District*, 393 U.S. 503 (1969) (see Section H, in this chapter). Following *Bethel*, the Court upheld over First Amendment objections a high school principal's censorship of articles on teenage pregnancy scheduled to appear in a student newspaper.[5] See also the Roberts Court's upholding of sanctions for a student who held a banner "Bong Hits 4 Jesus" at a school event held off school grounds in *Morse v. Frederick* (2007) (excerpted in Section H). By a 5–4 vote the Court again rejected a claim to a student's First Amendment protection.

The Court also could not escape reviewing challenges to so-called hate-speech codes and laws enacted by more than thirty states and numerous localities and colleges in the late 1980s and 1990s. The laws basically took two forms: (1) some made it a crime to arouse "anger, alarm, or resentment in others on the basis of race, color, creed, religion, or gender"; while (2) others provided enhanced sentences for individuals found guilty of criminal assault or vandalism, mandating longer prison sentences for those convicted of such crimes when the victim was selected out of racial, religious, gender, or ethnic bias.

When confronted with an attack on the first kind of hate-speech law in *R.A.V. v. City of St. Paul, Minnesota*, 505 U.S. 377 (1992) (see excerpt below), the Court unanimously invalidated St. Paul's hate-speech ordinance. In announcing the decision Justice Scalia held that even within the category of fighting words—a category of unprotected speech—governments may not bar or penalize the expression of some but not other words based on their content. Yet, only Chief Justice Rehnquist and Justices Kennedy, Souter, and Thomas agreed with Scalia's analysis and joined his opinion. In concurring opinions that read like dissents, Justices Blackmun, Stevens, and White, whom O'Connor joined, accused the majority of rewriting First Amendment doctrine. They would have overturned the ordinance as "fatally overbroad because it criminalizes not only unprotected expression but expression protected by the First Amendment."

Despite unanimity on the result in *R.A.V.*, the fragmentation of the justices contributed, perhaps, to the Court's willingness to revisit the controversy over hate-speech laws the following term in *Wisconsin v. Mitchell*, 508 U.S. 476 (1993) (see excerpt below). Here, unlike *R.A.V.*, the justices unanimously joined Chief Justice Rehnquist's opinion upholding the second sort of hate-speech law, which mandates longer sentences for individuals convicted of assault or vandalism when the crime was committed and the victim was selected because of racial, religious, gender, or ethnic bias. Subsequently, in *Virginia v. Black* (2003) (excerpted below), a majority of the Court indicated that a properly drawn statute criminalizing cross-burning, if clearly aimed at punishing intimidation rather than political expression, would survive constitutional muster.

Notably, the Supreme Court's defense of broad First Amendment protection for hate speech and other offensive speech contrasts with that in other countries. See, for example, the IN COMPARATIVE PERSPECTIVE box in this section on the Canadian Supreme Court's rulings on hate speech and pornography. In Germany, France, Romania, Poland, Israel, and Hungary, it is against the law to deny the Holocaust. In 2006 a Council of Europe resolution took effect that requires member states to make it a criminal offense to distribute racist and other biased materials over the Internet. In 2009 President Barack Obama signed a new federal law that expanded the definition of a hate crime to include violence committed not only on the basis of race, color, ethnicity, and religion but also gender identity and sexual orientation. All but five states have some form of hate-crime laws that were revised after the Court's rulings.

Finally, in recent years another major source of controversy has been governmental financing and grants for speech deemed offensive or politically objectionable. In *Rust v. Sullivan*, 500 U.S. 173 (1991), a bare majority of the Court upheld the Reagan administration's regulation prohibiting family-planning clinics that receive federal funding from also providing medical counseling on abortion. Writing for the majority, Chief Justice Rehnquist contended that probation was simply a choice of government-funded speech, while for the dissenters, Justice Blackmun countered that the regulation impinged on freedom of speech and limited women's freedom of choice over abortion. In *National Endowment for the Arts v. Finley*, 524 U.S. 569 (1998), the Court upheld a "public decency" amendment to the National Foundation for the Arts and Humanities Act, requiring the NEA to take "general standards of decency" into account when awarding grants to artists. See also *United States v. American Library Association*, 539 U.S. 194 (2003), upholding a federal statute requiring public libraries that receive federal funding for

providing Internet access to install software to block obscene and pornographic images and to prevent minors from accessing such materials.

Rust, however, was subsequently limited and distinguished in *Legal
Services Corporation v. Velazquez*, 351 U.S. 533 (2001), striking down a
restriction on the kinds of lawsuits that the federally funded Legal Services Corporation (LSC), which represent poor people, may engage in.
Justice Kennedy distinguished *Rust* while reaffirming that the *Rust* ban
on abortion counseling amounted to *governmental speech*, even though it
was using private speakers to communicate its message. By contrast, the
LSC program, like that challenged in *Rosenberger v. Rector and Visitors of
the University of Virginia*, 515 U.S. 819 (1995), was deemed to facilitate
private speech, not to promote a governmental message. In addition, the
Court upheld the constitutionality of the so-called Solomon Amendment, a federal law requiring the cutoff of federal funding to colleges
and universities that refuse to permit the military to recruit their students, because of the American Law School's policy of nondiscrimination against sexual orientation and opposition to the military's "don't
ask, don't tell" policy. Writing for the Court, in *Rumsfeld v. Forum for
Academic and Institutional Rights*, 547 U.S. 47 (2006), Chief Justice
Roberts rejected the First Amendment challenge on the grounds that
law schools had other ways to communicate their position. In *Pleasant
Grove City v. Summum*, 555 U.S. 460 (2009), the Roberts Court further
extended the doctrine that the First Amendment does not apply to
government-sponsored speech. Justice Alito held that under the First
Amendment free speech clause a small religious sect, the Summum,
could not compel a city to erect a statue, which contained a monument
inscribed with the Ten Commandments, and several other public displays in a public park.

Subsequently, *Walker v. Texas Division, Sons of Confederate Veterans,
Inc.*, 135 S.Ct. 2239 (2015), reaffirmed that the First Amendment does
not apply to government speech and that the government may "select
the views it wants to express." At issue was Texas's refusal to allow the
Confederate Flag on specialty ("vanity") automobile license plates,
which is permitted in nine other states, because of the flag's offensive
symbolism. Writing for a bare majority, which included the three other
most liberal justices and Justice Thomas, Justice Breyer held: "As a
general matter when the government speaks it is entitled to promote a
program, to espouse a policy or to take a position." Otherwise, he reasoned, the government could not encourage vaccinations or recycling,
and people may still "display [their] message in question in larger letters
on a bumper sticker right next to the plate." In so holding, Justice
Breyer relied on the decision in *Pleasant Grove City v. Summum*, that a city
could exclude a particular sect's monument from a public land and

distinguished the ruling in *Wooley v. Maynard*, 430 U.S. 705 (1977), holding that New Hampshire could not compel people (with religious objections) to display license plates with the state's motto, "Live Free or Die." Writing for the dissenters, Justice Alito, who wrote the opinion in *Summum*, accused the majority of distorting that precedent and of failing to recognize that monuments are different in terms of their history and "spatial limitations." In the dissenters' view, the majority "establishes a precedent that threatens private speech that the government finds displeasing."

By contrast, on the same day, the Court struck down an ordinance limiting the kinds of messages that may be displayed on billboards and other outdoor signs in *Reed v. Town of Gilbert, Arizona*, 135 S.Ct. 2218 (2015). Writing for the unanimous Court, Justice Thomas reasoned that laws that address different forms of public expression and that treat them differently amount to discrimination and cannot survive "strict scrutiny"—the Court's most demanding test. At issue was a dispute between the small Good News Community Church, which had no permanent location and held services in different places, and the town of Gilbert over the posting of signs directing congregants to where church meetings were to be held each week. Attorneys for the church argued that the town's barring of these signs was discriminatory because the town allowed signs for political candidates, homeowners associations, and builders. The Court agreed that the ordinance was not content neutral, though concurring Justices Kennedy, Alito, and Sotomayor contended that the majority's opinion swept too broadly and that very few bans on public signs were likely to survive scrutiny.

The Roberts Court underscored its defense of freedom of expression when striking down regulations of potentially offensive trademarks in *Matal v. Tam*, 137 S. Ct. 1744 (2017). There, the Court struck down the disparagement clause of the federal trademark law, the Lanham Act of 1947, prohibiting trademarks insulting to any individual or group. An Asian-American rock band known as the Slants was turned down by the U.S. Patent and Trademark Office for a trademark on its name because it was deemed offensive and insulting to people or groups. Writing for a unanimous Court (with Gorsuch not participating), Justice Alito held that ran afoul of the First Amendment because "[i]t offends a bedrock First Amendment principle: Speech may not be banned on the ground that it expresses ideas that offend." In ruling that "immoral," "scandalous," or "disparaging" trademarks are private, not government, speech, Alito added:

> There is also a deeper problem with the argument that commercial speech may be cleaned of any expression likely to cause offense. The commercial market is well stocked with merchandise

that disparages prominent figures and groups, and the line between commercial and non-commercial speech is not always clear, as this case illustrates. If affixing the commercial label permits the suppression of any speech that may lead to political or social "volatility," free speech would be endangered.

In 2019, the Court continued to fortify its resistance to viewpoint discrimination, striking down another part of the Lanham Act in *Iancu v. Brunetti*, 139 S.Ct. 2294 (2019), holding that the government could not refuse to register immoral or "scandalous" trademarks. At issue in *Iancu* was a clothing brand named F-U-C-T, meant to stand for "Friends U Can't Trust," which was deemed vulgar. Ruling that the Constitution forbids the government to take sides or engage in viewpoint discrimination, the Court overturned regulations that blocked the issuance of trademarks that might be deeply offensive. The problem for the Court was that the trademark office registered marks for brands with distinctly pro-religious messages but rejected those that disparaged religion. Here the Court developed its resistance to viewpoint discrimination, addressed in *R.A.V. v. City of St. Paul, Minnesota* (excerpted in this chapter). In dissent, Chief Justice Roberts argued that the First Amendment protects free speech but it "does not require the government to give aid and comfort to those using obscene, vulgar and profane modes of expression."

The Court, however, also continues to grapple with the problem of defining the scope of freedom of expression with respect to *government-funded speech* in *Agency for International Development v. Alliance for Open Society International, Inc.*, 570 U.S. 205 (2013). Writing for the majority, Chief Justice Roberts ruled that government runs afoul of the First Amendment when it requires that recipients publicly endorse its policies as a condition of receiving federal funds. In 2003 Congress enacted the United States Leadership Against HIV/AIDS, Tuberculosis, and Malaria Act, establishing a broad range of programs and appropriating billions of dollars for nongovernmental organizations to combat HIV/AIDS worldwide. The law also imposed two conditions: (1) no funds could be used to advocate the legalization of prostitution, (2) nor awarded unless an organization had "a policy explicitly opposing prostitution." A number of organizations challenged the constitutionality of the latter requirement. They did not advocate prostitution but wanted to remain neutral, because otherwise their efforts to educate prostitutes about the spread of HIV/AIDS might be hindered, and hence they claimed that this requirement violated their freedom of speech. A majority of the Court agreed and distinguished *Rust v. Sullivan*'s upholding Congress's denial of federal funds for the purpose of advocating abortion. That was acceptable, Chief Justice Roberts reasoned, because Congress may impose limitations on how its appropriations are spent. In *Rust*, organizations receiving funding could still use private funds (just not federal funds) for their advocacy, whereas here, Congress compelled the advocacy of a particular message as a condition of receiving funding. And the First Amendment forbids government from dictating what people may say. As the chief justice put it, "By requiring recipients to profess a specific belief, the [command of what people say] goes beyond defining the limits of the federally funded program to defining the recipient." Justice Scalia, joined by Justice Thomas, dissented. (See also Chapter 6, dealing with the (dis)establishment clause and governmental support for religion.)

More recently, the Roberts Court split 5–4 when striking down a state law requiring "crisis pregnancy centers," operated by religious groups opposed to abortion, to post notices about the availability of contraception and low-cost abortion services as government-compelled speech in violation of the First Amendment, in *National Institute of Family and Life Advocates v. Becerra,* 138 S. Ct. 2361 (2018). The California Reproductive Freedom, Accountability, Comprehensive Care, and Transparency Act (FACT Act) of 2015 required some 200 "crisis pregnancy centers," pro-life centers offering prenatal-related services, to post notices notifying women that the state provides free or low-cost services, including abortions, and provide phone numbers for those services; unlicensed clinics also were required to give notice that they did not provide medical services, such as abortions. Both regulations were invalidated because they targeted the content of speech and failed to survive the strict scrutiny test since they compelled speech about abortion services that the clinics opposed on religious grounds. Writing for the majority, Justice Thomas observed: "Licensed clinics must provide a government-drafted script about the availability of state-sponsored services, as well as contact information for how to obtain them. One of those services is abortion—the very practice that petitioners are devoted to opposing." California had other means of informing women about the availability of abortion and could not "co-opt the licensed facilities to deliver its message." In a concurring opinion, Justice Kennedy added that the First Amendment bars compelling people to betray their beliefs: "Governments must not be allowed to force persons to express a message contrary to their deepest convictions. Freedom of speech secures freedom of thought and belief. This law imperils those liberties." Writing for the dissenters—Justices Ginsburg, Sotomayor, and Kagan—Justice Breyer criticized the majority for inconsistency, since a bare majority upheld provisions of a Pennsylvania law requiring doctors who perform abortions to inform patients about abortion and alternatives, in *Planned Parenthood of Southeastern Pennsylvania v. Casey,* 505 U.S. 833 (1992) (excerpted in Ch. 11); and upheld federal regulations banning abortion counseling by organizations receiving federal funding, in *Rust v. Sullivan,* 500 U.S. 173 (1991). In Justice Breyer's words: "If a state can lawfully require a doctor to tell a woman seeking an abortion about adoption services, why should it not be able, as here, to require a medical counselor to tell a woman seeking prenatal care or other reproductive health care about childbirth and abortion services? As the question suggests, there is no convincing reason to distinguish between information about adoption and information about abortion in this context. After all, the rule of law embodies evenhandedness, and 'what is sauce for the goose is normally sauce for the gander.'" Justice Thomas, in the opinion for the Court, responded that *Casey* was different because it dealt with a medical procedure, and prompted Breyer to counter: "Really? No one doubts that choosing an abortion is a medical procedure that involves certain health risks. But the same is true of carrying a child to term and giving birth." Moreover, Breyer challenged Thomas's use of the strict scrutiny test to invalidate California's regulation, pointing out: "Using the First Amendment to strike down economic and social laws that legislatures long would have thought themselves free to enact will, for the American public, obscure, not clarify, the true value of protecting freedom of speech."

NOTES

1. *Gooding v. Wilson,* 405 U.S. 518 (1972).
2. *Schneider v. New Jersey,* 308 U.S. 147 (1939).
3. *Marsh v. Alabama,* 326 U.S. 501 (1946).
4. In *Papish v. Board of Curators,* 410 U.S. 667 (1973), the Court held that a graduate student could not be expelled from a university for distributing a publication that included a cartoon of the Statue of Liberty with the word "motherfucker."
5. *Hazelwood School District v. Kuhlmeirer,* 484 U.S. 260 (1988).

SELECTED BIBLIOGRAPHY

Cleary, Edward J. *Beyond the Burning Cross: The First Amendment and the Landmark R.A.V. Case.* New York: Random House, 1994.

Downs, Donald A. *Restoring Free Speech and Liberty on Campus.* New York: Cambridge University Press, 2004.

Gould, Jon. *Speak No Evil: The Triumph of Hate Speech Regulation.* Chicago: University of Chicago Press, 2006.

Jacobs, James, and Kimberly Potter. *Hate Crimes: Criminal Law and Identity Politics.* New York: Oxford University Press, 1998.

Lewis, Anthony. *Freedom for the Thought We Hate: A Biography of the First Amendment.* New York: Basic Books, 2010.

Matsuda, Mari, Charles Lawrence, Richard Delgado, and Kimberle Crenshaw. *Words That Wound: Critical Race Theory, Assaultive Speech, and the First Amendment.* Boulder, CO: Westview Press, 1993.

Slater, Adam, ed. *Unsafe Space: The Crisis of Free Speech on Campus.* New York: Palgrave, 2016.

Waldron, Jeremy. *The Harm in Hate Speech.* Cambridge, MA: Harvard University Press, 2012.

Cohen v. California

403 U.S. 15, 91 S.Ct. 1780 (1971)

Justice Harlan's opinion for the Court recounts the facts that led to this important ruling announcing the First Amendment principle that four-letter words are not obscene per se and may express political ideas as well. His position was controversial within the Court, however. In a circulated but unpublished dissenting opinion, Chief Justice Burger protested "that this Court's limited resources of time should be devoted to such a case as this. It is a measure of a lack of a sense of priorities. . . . It is nothing short of absurd nonsense that juvenile delinquents and their emotionally unstable outbursts should command the attention of this Court. The appeal should be dismissed for failure to present a substantial federal question." By the time the decision came down, Burger decided to withhold his draft and to join with Justice Black in a dissenting opinion filed by Justice Blackmun.

The Court's decision was 6–3, with the majority's opinion announced by Justice Harlan. Justice Blackmun dissented and was joined by Chief Justice Burger and Justice Black.

■ ■ ■

☐ *Justice HARLAN delivered the opinion of the Court.*

This case may seem at first blush too inconsequential to find its way into our books, but the issue it presents is of no small constitutional significance.

Appellant Paul Robert Cohen was convicted in the Los Angeles Municipal Court of violating that part of California Penal Code Section 415 which prohibits "maliciously and willfully disturb[ing] the peace or quiet of any neighborhood or person . . . by . . . offensive conduct. . . ." He was given 30 days' imprisonment. The facts upon which his conviction rests are detailed in the opinion of the Court of Appeal of California, Second Appellate District, as follows:

> On April 26, 1968, the defendant was observed in the Los Angeles County Courthouse in the corridor outside of division 20 of the municipal court wearing a jacket bearing the words 'Fuck the Draft' which were plainly visible. There were women and children present in the corridor. The defendant was arrested. The defendant testified that he wore the jacket knowing that the words were

on the jacket as a means of informing the public of the depth of his feelings against the Vietnam War and the draft.

The defendant did not engage in, nor threaten to engage in, nor did anyone as the result of his conduct in fact commit or threaten to commit any act of violence. The defendant did not make any loud or unusual noise, nor was there any evidence that he uttered any sound prior to his arrest. . . .

In order to lay hands on the precise issue which this case involves, it is useful first to canvass various matters which this record does *not* present.

The conviction quite clearly rests upon the asserted offensiveness of the *words* Cohen used to convey his message to the public. The only "conduct" which the State sought to punish is the fact of communication. Thus, we deal here with a conviction resting solely upon "speech." . . . [T]he state certainly lacks power to punish Cohen for the underlying content of the message the inscription conveyed. At least so long as there is no showing of an intent to incite disobedience to or disruption of the draft, Cohen could not, consistently with the First and Fourteenth Amendments, be punished for asserting the evident position on the inutility or immorality of the draft his jacket reflected. . . .

In the second place, as it comes to us, this case cannot be said to fall within those relatively few categories of instances where prior decisions have established the power of government to deal more comprehensively with certain forms of individual expression simply upon a showing that such a form was employed. This is not, for example, an obscenity case. Whatever else may be necessary to give rise to the States' broader power to prohibit obscene expression, such expression must be, in some significant way, erotic. *Roth v. United States*, 354 U.S. 476 (1957). It cannot plausibly be maintained that this vulgar allusion to the Selective Service System would conjure up such psychic stimulation in anyone likely to be confronted with Cohen's crudely defaced jacket.

This Court has also held that the States are free to ban the simple use, without a demonstration of additional justifying circumstances, of so-called "fighting words," those personally abusive epithets which, when addressed to the ordinary citizen, are, as a matter of common knowledge, inherently likely to provoke violent reaction. *Chaplinsky v. New Hampshire*, 315 U.S. 568 (1942). While the four-letter word displayed by Cohen in relation to the draft is not uncommonly employed in a personally provocative fashion, in this instance it was clearly not "directed to the person of the hearer." No individual actually or likely to be present could reasonably have regarded the words on appellant's jacket as a direct personal insult. Nor do we have here an instance of the exercise of the State's police power to prevent a speaker from intentionally provoking a given group to hostile reaction.

There is, as noted above, no showing that anyone who saw Cohen was in fact violently aroused or that appellant intended such a result.

Finally, in arguments before this Court much has been made of the claim that Cohen's distasteful mode of expression was thrust upon unwilling or unsuspecting viewers, and that the State might therefore legitimately act as it did in order to protect the sensitive from otherwise unavoidable exposure to appellant's crude form of protest. Of course, the mere presumed presence of unwitting listeners or viewers does not serve automatically to justify curtailing all speech capable of giving offense. While this Court has recognized that government may properly act in many situations to prohibit

516 | FREEDOM OF EXPRESSION AND ASSOCIATION

intrusion into the privacy of the home of unwelcome views and ideas which cannot be totally banned from the public dialogue, e.g., *Rowan v. United States Post Office Dept.*, 397 U.S. 728 (1970), we have at the same time consistently stressed that "we are often 'captives' outside the sanctuary of the home and subject to objectionable speech." The ability of government, consonant with the Constitution, to shut off discourse solely to protect others from hearing it is, in other words, dependent upon a showing that substantial privacy interests are being invaded in an essentially intolerable manner. Any broader view of this authority would effectively empower a majority to silence dissidents simply as a matter of personal predilections.

In this regard, persons confronted with Cohen's jacket were in a quite different posture than, say, those subjected to the raucous emissions of sound trucks blaring outside their residences. Those in the Los Angeles courthouse could effectively avoid further bombardment of their sensibilities simply by averting their eyes. And, while it may be that one has a more substantial claim to a recognizable privacy interest when walking through a courthouse corridor than, for example, strolling through Central Park, surely it is nothing like the interest in being free from unwanted expression in the confines of one's own home. Given the subtlety and complexity of the factors involved, if Cohen's "speech" was otherwise entitled to constitutional protection, we do not think the fact that some unwilling "listeners" in a public building may have been briefly exposed to it can serve to justify this breach of the peace conviction where, as here, there was no evidence that persons powerless to avoid appellant's conduct did in fact object to it, and where that portion of the statute upon which Cohen's conviction rests evinces no concern, either on its face or as construed by the California courts with the special plight of the captive auditor, but, instead, indiscriminately sweeps within its prohibitions all "offensive conduct" that disturbs "any neighborhood or person." . . .

Against this background, the issue flushed by this case stands out in bold relief. It is whether California can excise, as "offensive conduct," one particular scurrilous epithet from the public discourse, either upon the theory of the court below that its use is inherently likely to cause violent reaction or upon a more general assertion that the States, acting as guardians of public morality, may properly remove this offensive word from the public vocabulary.

The rationale of the California Court is plainly untenable. At most it reflects an "undifferentiated fear or apprehension of disturbance [which] is not enough to overcome the right to freedom of expression." *Tinker v. Des Moines Indep. Community School Dist.*, 393 U.S. 503 (1969). We have been shown no evidence that substantial numbers of citizens are standing ready to strike out physically at whoever may assault their sensibilities with execrations like that uttered by Cohen. There may be some persons about with such lawless and violent proclivities, but that is an insufficient base upon which to erect, consistently with constitutional values, a governmental power to force persons who wish to ventilate their dissident views into avoiding particular forms of expression. . . .

At the outset, we cannot overemphasize that, in our judgment, most situations where the State has a justifiable interest in regulating speech will fall within one or more of the various established exceptions, discussed above but not applicable here, to the usual rule that governmental bodies may not prescribe the form or content of individual expression. Equally important to our conclusion is the constitutional backdrop against which our decision must be made. The constitutional right of free expression is powerful medicine in a society as diverse and populous as ours. It is designed and intended to remove governmental restraints from the arena of public discussion, putting the decision as to what views shall be voiced largely into the hands of each of us, in the hope that use of such freedom will ultimately produce a more capable citizenry and more perfect polity and in the belief that no other approach would comport with the premise of individual dignity and choice upon which our political system rests. . . .

To many, the immediate consequence of this freedom may often appear to be only verbal tumult, discord, and even offensive utterance. These are, however, within established limits, in truth necessary side effects of the broader enduring values which the process of open debate permits us to achieve. That the air may at times seem filled with verbal cacophony is, in this sense not a sign of weakness but of strength. . . .

Against this perception of the constitutional policies involved, we discern certain more particularized considerations that peculiarly call for reversal of this conviction. First, the principle contended for by the State seems inherently boundless. How is one to distinguish this from any other offensive word? Surely the State has no right to cleanse public debate to the point where it is grammatically palatable to the most squeamish among us. Yet no readily ascertainable general principle exists for stopping short of that result were we to affirm the judgment below. For, while the particular four-letter word being litigated here is perhaps more distasteful than most others of its genre, it is nevertheless often true that one man's vulgarity is another's lyric. Indeed, we think it is largely because governmental officials cannot make principled distinctions in this area that the Constitution leaves matters of taste and style so largely to the individual.

Additionally, we cannot overlook the fact, because it is well illustrated by the episode involved here, that much linguistic expression serves a dual communicative function: it conveys not only ideas capable of relatively precise, detached explication, but otherwise inexpressible emotions as well. In fact, words are often chosen as much for their emotive as their cognitive force. We cannot sanction the view that the Constitution, while solicitous of the cognitive content of individual speech has little or no regard for that emotive function which practically speaking, may often be the more important element of the overall message sought to be communicated. . . .

Finally, and in the same vein, we cannot indulge the facile assumption that one can forbid particular words without also running a substantial risk of suppressing ideas in the process. Indeed, governments might soon seize upon the censorship of particular words as a convenient guise for banning the expression of unpopular views. We have been able, as noted above, to discern little social benefit that might result from running the risk of opening the door to such grave results.

It is, in sum, our judgment that absent a more particularized and compelling reason for its actions, the State may not, consistently with the First and Fourteenth Amendments, make the simple public display here involved of this single four-letter expletive a criminal offense. Because that is the only arguably sustainable rationale for the conviction here at issue, the judgment below must be
   Reversed.

☐ *Justice BLACKMUN, with whom THE CHIEF JUSTICE and Justice BLACK join, dissenting.*

I dissent [because] . . . Cohen's absurd and immature antics, in my view, was mainly conduct and little speech. . . . Further, the case appears to me to be well within the sphere of *Chaplinsky v. New Hampshire*, where Justice MURPHY, a known champion of First Amendment freedoms, wrote for a unanimous bench. As a consequence, this Court's agonizing over First Amendment values seems misplaced and unnecessary.

Federal Communications Commission v. Pacifica Foundation
438 U.S. 726, 98 S.CT. 3026 (1978)

Justice Stevens explains the facts in this case, involving satiric humorist George Carlin and the FCC's regulation of indecent language on radio and television, at the outset of his plurality opinion announcing the decision of the Court.

The Court's decision was 5–4, with the plurality's opinion announced by Justice Stevens. Justice Powell concurred and was joined by Justice Blackmun. Dissents were by Justices Brennan and Stewart, who were joined by Justices Marshall and White.

■ ■ ■

☐ *Justice STEVENS delivered the opinion of the Court, with whom THE CHIEF JUSTICE and Justice REHNQUIST joined.*

This case requires that we decide whether the Federal Communications Commission has any power to regulate a radio broadcast that is indecent but not obscene.

A satiric humorist named George Carlin recorded a 12-minute monologue entitled "Filthy Words" before a live audience in a California theater. He began by referring to his thoughts about "the words you couldn't say on the public, ah, airwaves, um, the ones you definitely wouldn't say, ever." He proceeded to list those words and repeat them over and over again in a variety of colloquialisms. The transcript of the recording, which is appended to this opinion, indicates frequent laughter from the audience. [The words that Carlin said could not be said on television or the radio, were "shit, piss, fuck, cunt, cocksucker, motherfucker, and tits."]

At about 2 o'clock in the afternoon on Tuesday, October 30, 1973, a New York radio station, owned by respondent Pacifica Foundation, broadcast the "Filthy Words" monologue. A few weeks later a man, who stated that he had heard the broadcast while driving with his young son, wrote a letter complaining to the Commission. . . .

The complaint was forwarded to the station for comment. In its response, Pacifica explained that the monologue had been played during a program about contemporary society's attitude toward language and that, immediately before its broadcast, listeners had been advised that it included "sensitive language which might be regarded as offensive to some." Pacifica characterized George Carlin as "a significant social satirist" who "like Twain and Sahl before him, examines the language of ordinary people. . . . Carlin is not mouthing obscenities, he is merely using words to satirize as harmless and essentially silly our attitudes towards those words."

Pacifica stated that it was not aware of any other complaints about the broadcast.

On February 21, 1975, the Commission issued a declaratory order granting the complaint and holding that Pacifica "could have been the subject of administrative sanctions." The Commission did not impose formal sanctions, but it did state that the order would be "associated with the station's license file, and in the event that subsequent complaints are received, the Commission will then decide whether it should utilize any of the available sanctions it has been granted by Congress." . . .

The Commission characterized the language used in the Carlin monologue as "patently offensive," though not necessarily obscene, and expressed the opinion that it should be regulated by principles analogous to those found in the law of nuisance where the "law generally speaks to *channeling* behavior more than actually prohibiting it. . . . [T]he concept of 'indecent' is intimately connected with the exposure of children to language that describes, in terms patently offensive as measured by contemporary community standards for the broadcast medium, sexual or excretory activities and organs at times of the day when there is a reasonable risk that children may be in the audience." . . .

The United States Court of Appeals for the District of Columbia reversed. . . . [We now reverse that ruling and uphold the F.C.C.'s action.]

The question in this case is whether a broadcast of patently offensive words dealing with sex and excretion may be regulated because of its content. Obscene materials have been denied the protection of the First Amendment because their content is so offensive to contemporary moral standards. *Roth v. United States*, 354 U.S. 476 [(1957)]. But the fact that society may find speech offensive is not a sufficient reason for suppressing it. Indeed, if it is the speaker's opinion that gives offense, that consequence is a reason for according it constitutional protection. For it is a central tenet of the First Amendment that the government must remain neutral in the marketplace of ideas. If there were any reason to believe that the Commission's characterization of the Carlin monologue as offensive could be traced to its political content—or even to the fact that it satirized contemporary attitudes about four-letter words—First Amendment protection might be required. But that is simply not this case. These words offend for the same reasons that obscenity offends. Their place in the hierarchy of First Amendment values was aptly sketched by Justice MURPHY when he said: "[S]uch utterances are no essential part of any exposition of ideas, and are of such slight social value as a step to truth that any benefit that may be derived from them is clearly outweighed by the social interest in order and morality." *Chaplinsky v. New Hampshire* [315 U.S. 568 (1942)]. . . .

Although these words ordinarily lack literary, political, or scientific value, they are not entirely outside the protection of the First Amendment. Some uses of even the most offensive words are unquestionably protected. See, e.g., *Hess v. Indiana*, 414 U.S. 105 [(1973)]. Indeed, we may assume, *arguendo*, that this monologue would be protected in other contexts. Nonetheless, the constitutional protection accorded to a communication containing such patently offensive sexual and excretory language need not be the same in every context. It is a characteristic of speech such as this that both its capacity to offend and its "social value," to use Justice MURPHY's term, vary with the circumstances. Words that are commonplace in one setting are shocking in another. To paraphrase Justice HARLAN, one occasion's lyric is another's vulgarity. Cf. *Cohen v. California*, 403 U.S. 15 [(1971)].

In this case it is undisputed that the content of Pacifica's broadcast was "vulgar," "offensive," and "shocking." Because content of that character is not entitled to absolute constitutional protection under all circumstances, we must consider its context in order to determine whether the Commission's action was constitutionally permissible.

We have long recognized that each medium of expression presents special First Amendment problems. And of all forms of communication, it is broadcasting that has received the most limited First Amendment protection. Thus, although other speakers cannot be licensed except under laws that carefully define and narrow official discretion, a broadcaster may be deprived of his license and his forum if the Commission decides that such an action would serve "the public interest, convenience, and necessity." Similarly, although the First Amendment protects newspaper publishers from being required to print the replies of those whom they criticize, *Miami Herald Publishing Co. v. Tornillo*, 418 U.S. 241 [(1974)], it affords no such protection to broadcasters; on the contrary, they must give free time to the victims of their criticism. *Red Lion Broadcasting Co. v. FCC*, 395 U.S. 367 [(1969)].

The reasons for these distinctions are complex, but two have relevance to the present case. First, the broadcast media have established a uniquely pervasive presence in the lives of all Americans. Patently offensive, indecent material presented over the airwaves confronts the citizen, not only in public, but also in the privacy of the home, where the individual's right to be left alone plainly outweighs the First Amendment rights of an intruder. *Rowan v. Post Office Dept.*, 397 U.S. 728. [(1970)]. Because the broadcast audience is constantly tuning in and out, prior warnings cannot completely protect the listener or viewer from unexpected program content. To say that one may avoid further offense by turning off the radio when he hears indecent language is like saying that the remedy for an assault is to run away after the first blow. One may hang up on an indecent phone call, but that option does not give the caller a constitutional immunity or avoid a harm that has already taken place.

Second, broadcasting is uniquely accessible to children, even those too young to read. Although Cohen's written message might have been incomprehensible to a first grader, Pacifica's broadcast could have enlarged a child's vocabulary in an instant. Other forms of offensive expression may be withheld from the young without restricting the expression at its source. Bookstores and motion picture theaters, for example, may be prohibited from making indecent material available to children. We held in *Ginsberg v. New York*, 390 U.S. 629 [(1968)], that the government's interest in the "well-being of its youth" and in supporting "parents' claim to authority in their own household" justified the regulation of otherwise protected expression. The ease with which children may obtain access to broadcast material, coupled with the concerns recognized in *Ginsberg*, amply justify special treatment of indecent broadcasting.

It is appropriate, in conclusion, to emphasize the narrowness of our holding. This case does not involve a two-way radio conversation between a cab driver and a dispatcher, or a telecast of an Elizabethan comedy. We have not decided that an occasional expletive in either setting would justify any sanction or, indeed, that this broadcast would justify a criminal prosecution. The Commission's decision rested entirely on a nuisance rationale under which context is all-important. The concept requires consideration of a host of variables. The time of day was emphasized by the Commission. The content of the program in which the language is used will also affect the composition of the audience, and differences between radio, television, and perhaps closed-circuit transmissions, may also be relevant. As Justice SUTHERLAND wrote, a "nuisance may be merely a right thing in the wrong place,—like a pig in the parlor instead of the barnyard." *Euclid v. Ambler Realty Co.*, 272 U.S. 365 [(1926)]. We simply hold that when the Commission finds that a pig has entered the parlor, the exercise of its regulatory power does not depend on proof that the pig is obscene.

The judgment of the Court of Appeals is reversed.

It is so ordered.

☐ *Justice BRENNAN, with whom Justice MARSHALL joins, dissenting.*

Without question, the privacy interests of an individual in his home are substantial and deserving of significant protection. In finding these interests sufficient to justify the content regulation of protected speech, however, the Court commits two errors. First, it misconceives the nature of the privacy interests involved where an individual voluntarily chooses to admit radio communications into his home. Second, it ignores the constitutionally protected interests of both those who wish to transmit and those who desire to receive broadcasts that many—including the FCC and this Court—might find offensive. . . .

Even if an individual who voluntarily opens his home to radio communications retains privacy interests of sufficient moment to justify a ban on protected speech if those interests are "invaded in an essentially intolerable manner," *Cohen v. California*, [403 U.S. 15 (1971)], the very fact that those interests are threatened only by a radio broadcast precludes any intolerable invasion of privacy; for unlike other intrusive modes of communication, such as sound trucks, "[t]he radio can be turned off," *Lehman v. Shaker Heights*, 418 U.S. 298 (1974)—and with a minimum of effort. . . .

The Court's balance, of necessity, fails to accord proper weight to the interests of listeners who wish to hear broadcasts the FCC deems offensive. It permits majoritarian tastes completely to preclude a protected message from entering the homes of a receptive, unoffended minority. No decision of this Court supports such a result. Where the individuals constituting the offended majority may freely choose to reject the material being offered, we have never found their privacy interests of such moment to warrant the suppression of speech on privacy grounds. . . .

Most parents will undoubtedly find understandable as well as commendable the Court's sympathy with the FCC's desire to prevent offensive broadcasts from reaching the ears of unsupervised children. Unfortunately, the facial appeal of this justification for radio censorship masks its constitutional insufficiency. . . .

Because the Carlin monologue is obviously not an erotic appeal to the prurient interests of children, the Court, for the first time, allows the government to prevent minors from gaining access to materials that are not obscene, and are therefore protected, as to them. It thus ignores our recent admonition that "[s]peech that is neither obscene as to youths nor subject to some other legitimate proscription cannot be suppressed solely to protect the young from ideas or images that a legislative body thinks unsuitable for them." The Court's refusal to follow its own pronouncements is especially lamentable since it has the anomalous subsidiary effect, at least in the radio context at issue here, of making completely unavailable to adults material which may not constitutionally be kept even from children. This result violates in spades the principle of *Butler v. Michigan*, [352 U.S. 380 (1957)]. *Butler* involved a challenge to a Michigan statute that forbade the publication, sale, or distribution of printed material "tending to incite minors to violent or depraved or immoral acts, manifestly tending to the corruption of the morals of youth." Although *Roth v. United States* [357 U.S. 476

Cartoon depicting the right to free speech. *Washington Post*, January 15, 2012, A18. (TOLES © 2012, The Washington Post. *Used by permission of Universal Uclick. All rights reserved.*)

(1957)], had not yet been decided, it is at least arguable that the material the statute in *Butler* was designed to suppress could have been constitutionally denied to children. Nevertheless, this Court found the statute unconstitutional. Speaking for the Court, Justice FRANKFURTER reasoned:

> The incidence of this enactment is to reduce the adult population of Michigan to reading only what is fit for children. It thereby arbitrarily curtails one of those liberties of the individual, now enshrined in the Due Process Clause of the Fourteenth Amendment, that history has attested as the indispensable conditions for the maintenance and progress of a free society. . . .

Where, as here, the government may not prevent the exposure of minors to the suppressed material, the principle of *Butler* applies *a fortiori*. . . .

☐ *Justice STEWART, with whom Justice BRENNAN, Justice WHITE, and Justice MARSHALL join, dissenting.*

I think that "indecent" should properly be read as meaning no more than "obscene." Since the Carlin monologue concededly was not "obscene," I believe that the Commission lacked statutory authority to ban it. Under this construction of the statute, it is unnecessary to address the difficult and important issue of the Commission's constitutional power to prohibit speech that would be constitutionally protected outside the context of electronic broadcasting.

Bethel School District No. 403 v. Fraser
478 U.S. 675, 106 S.Ct. 3159 (1986)

The facts in this case involving lewd speech at a school assembly are given in Chief Justice Burger's opinion for the Court, Justice Brennan's concurring opinion, and Justice Stevens's dissenting opinion. Notice how each emphasizes particular facts and views differently the context and circumstances that gave rise to this case.

The Court's decision was 7–2, with the majority's opinion announced by Chief Justice Burger. Concurrences were by Justices Blackmun and Brennan, dissents by Justices Marshall and Stevens.

■ ■ ■

☐ *Chief Justice BURGER delivered the opinion of the Court.*

On April 26, 1983, respondent Matthew N. Fraser, a student at Bethel High School in Bethel, Washington, delivered a speech nominating a fellow student for student elective office. Approximately 600 high school students, many of whom were 14-year-olds, attended the assembly. Students were required to attend the assembly or to report to the study hall. The assembly was part of a school-sponsored educational program in self-government. Students who elected not to attend the assembly were required to report to study hall. During the entire speech, Fraser referred to his candidate in terms of an elaborate, graphic, and explicit sexual metaphor.

Two of Fraser's teachers, with whom he discussed the contents of his speech in advance, informed him that the speech was "inappropriate and that he probably should not deliver it," and that his delivery of the speech might have "severe consequences." . . .

A Bethel High School disciplinary rule prohibiting the use of obscene language in the school provides:

> Conduct which materially and substantially interferes with the educational process is prohibited, including the use of obscene, profane language or gestures.

The morning after the assembly, the Assistant Principal called Fraser into her office and notified him that the school considered his speech to have been a violation of this rule. . . . Fraser served two days of his suspension, and was allowed to return to school on the third day. . . .

This Court acknowledged in *Tinker v. Des Moines Independent Community School Dist.*, [393 U.S. 503 (1969)], that students do not "shed their constitutional rights to freedom of speech or expression at the schoolhouse gate." The Court of Appeals read that case as precluding any discipline of Fraser for indecent speech and lewd conduct in the school assembly. That court appears to have proceeded on the theory that the use of lewd and obscene speech in order to make what the speaker considered to be a point in a nominating speech for a fellow student was essentially the same as the wearing of an armband in *Tinker* as a form of protest or the expression of a political position.

The marked distinction between the political "message" of the armbands in *Tinker* and the sexual content of respondent's speech in this case seems to have been given little weight by the Court of Appeals. In upholding the students' right to engage in a nondisruptive, passive expression of a political viewpoint in *Tinker*, this Court was careful to note that the case did "not concern speech or action that intrudes upon the work of the schools or the rights of other students." . . .

It is against this background that we turn to consider the level of First Amendment protection accorded to Fraser's utterances and actions before an official high school assembly attended by 600 students.

The role and purpose of the American public school system was well described by two historians, saying "public education must prepare pupils for citizenship in the Republic. . . . It must inculcate the habits and manners of civility as values in themselves conducive to happiness and as indispensable to the practice of self-government in the community and the nation." . . .

These fundamental values of "habits and manners of civility" essential to a democratic society must, of course, include tolerance of divergent political and religious views, even when the views expressed may be unpopular. But these "fundamental values" must also take into account consideration of the sensibilities of others, and, in the case of a school, the sensibilities of fellow students. The undoubted freedom to advocate unpopular and controversial views in schools and classrooms must be balanced against the society's countervailing interest in teaching students the boundaries of socially appropriate behaviour. Even the most heated political discourse in a democratic society requires consideration for the personal sensibilities of the other participants and audiences. . . .

Surely it is a highly appropriate function of public school education to prohibit the use of vulgar and offensive terms in public discourse. Indeed, the "fundamental values necessary to the maintenance of a democratic political system" disfavor the use of terms of debate highly offensive or highly threatening to others. Nothing in the Constitution prohibits the states from insisting that certain modes of expression are inappropriate and subject to sanctions. The inculcation of these values is truly the "work of the schools." The determination of what manner of speech in the classroom or in school assembly is inappropriate properly rests with the school board. . . .

This Court's First Amendment jurisprudence has acknowledged limitations on the otherwise absolute interest of the speaker in reaching an unlimited audience where the speech is sexually explicit and the audience may include children. . . .

We hold that petitioner School District acted entirely within its permissible authority in imposing sanctions upon Fraser in response to his offensively lewd and indecent speech. Unlike the sanctions imposed on the students wearing armbands in *Tinker*, the penalties imposed in this case were unrelated to any political viewpoint. The First Amendment does not prevent the school officials from determining that to permit a vulgar and lewd speech such as respondent's would undermine the school's basic educational mission. A high school assembly or classroom is no place for a sexually explicit monologue directed towards an unsuspecting audience of teenage students. Accordingly, it was perfectly appropriate for the school to disassociate itself to make the point to the pupils that vulgar speech and lewd conduct is wholly inconsistent with the "fundamental values" of public school education.

☐ *Justice BRENNAN, concurring.*

Respondent gave the following speech at a high school assembly in support of a candidate for student government office:

> I know a man who is firm—he's firm in his pants, he's firm in his shirt, his character is firm—but most . . . of all, his belief in you, the students of Bethel, is firm.
>
> Jeff Kuhlman is a man who takes his point and pounds it in. If necessary, he'll take an issue and nail it to the wall. He doesn't attack things in spurts—he drives hard, pushing and pushing until finally—he succeeds.
>
> Jeff is a man who will go to the very end—even the climax, for each and every one of you.
>
> So vote for Jeff for A.S.B. vice-president—he'll never come between you and the best our high school can be.

The Court, referring to these remarks as "obscene," "vulgar," "lewd," and "offensively lewd," concludes that school officials properly punished respondent for uttering the speech. Having read the full text of respondent's remarks, I find it difficult to believe that it is the same speech the Court describes. To my mind, the most that can be said about respondent's speech—and all that need be said—is that in light of the discretion school officials have to teach high school students how to conduct civil and effective public discourse, and to prevent disruption of school educational activities, it was not unconstitutional for school officials to conclude, under the circumstances of this case, that respondent's remarks exceeded permissible limits. Thus, while I concur in the Court's judgment, I write separately to express my understanding of the breadth of the Court's holding. . . .

In the present case, school officials sought only to ensure that a high school assembly proceed in an orderly manner. There is no suggestion that school officials attempted to regulate respondent's speech because they disagreed with the views he sought to express. Nor does this case involve an attempt by school officials to ban written materials they consider "inappropriate" for high school students, or to limit what students should hear, read, or learn about. Thus, the Court's holding concerns only the authority that school officials have to restrict a high school student's use of disruptive language in a speech given to a high school assembly.

☐ *Justice MARSHALL, dissenting.*

I agree with the principles that Justice BRENNAN sets out in his opinion concurring in the judgment. I dissent from the Court's decision, however, because in my view the school district failed to demonstrate that respondent's remarks were indeed disruptive.

☐ *Justice STEVENS, dissenting.*

"Frankly, my dear, I don't give a damn."

When I was a high school student, the use of those words in a public forum shocked the Nation. Today Clark Gable's four-letter expletive is less offensive than it was then. Nevertheless, I assume that high school administrators may prohibit the use of that word in classroom discussion and even in extracurricular activities that are sponsored by the school and held on school premises. For I believe a school faculty must regulate the content as well as the style of student speech in carrying out its educational mission. It does seem to me, however, that if a student is to be punished for using offensive speech, he is entitled to fair notice of the scope of the prohibition and the consequences of its violation. The interest in free speech protected by the First Amendment and the interest in fair procedure protected by the Due Process Clause of the Fourteenth Amendment combine to require this conclusion.

This respondent was an outstanding young man with a fine academic record. The fact that he was chosen by the student body to speak at the school's commencement exercises demonstrates that he was respected by his peers. This fact is relevant for two reasons. It confirms the conclusion that the discipline imposed on him—a three-day suspension and ineligibility to speak at the school's graduation exercises—was sufficiently serious to justify invocation of the School District's grievance procedures. More importantly, it indicates that he was probably in a better position to determine whether an audience composed of 600 of his contemporaries would be offended by the use of a four-letter word—or a sexual metaphor—than is a group of judges who are at least two generations and 3,000 miles away from the scene of the crime.

The fact that the speech may not have been offensive to his audience—or that he honestly believed that it would be inoffensive—does not mean that he had a constitutional right to deliver it. For the school—not the student—must prescribe the rules of conduct in an educational institution. But it does mean that he should not be disciplined for speaking frankly in a school assembly if he had no reason to anticipate punitive consequences.

One might conclude that respondent should have known that he would be punished for giving this speech on three quite different theories: (1) It violated the "Disruptive Conduct" rule published in the student handbook; (2) he was specifically warned by his teachers; or (3) the impropriety is so obvious that no specific notice was required. . . .

The fact that respondent reviewed the text of his speech with three different teachers before he gave it does indicate that he must have been aware of the possibility that it would provoke an adverse reaction, but the teachers' responses certainly did not give him any better notice of the likelihood of discipline than did the student handbook itself. In my opinion, therefore, the most difficult question is whether the speech was so obviously offensive that an intelligent high school student must be presumed to have realized that he would be punished for giving it. . . .

It seems fairly obvious that respondent's speech would be inappropriate in certain classroom and formal social settings. On the other hand, in a locker room or perhaps in a school corridor the metaphor in the speech might be regarded as rather routine comment. If this be true, and if respondent's audience consisted almost entirely of young people with whom he conversed on a daily basis, can we—at this distance—confidently assert that he must have known that the school administration would punish him for delivering it?

For three reasons, I think not. First, it seems highly unlikely that he would have decided to deliver the speech if he had known that it would result in his suspension and disqualification from delivering the school commencement address. Second, I believe a strong presumption in favor of free expression should apply whenever an issue of this kind is arguable. Third, because the Court has adopted the policy of applying contemporary community standards in evaluating expression with sexual connotations, this Court should defer to the views of the district and circuit judges who are in a much better position to evaluate this speech than we are.

R.A.V. v. City of St. Paul, Minnesota

505 U.S. 377, 112 S.Ct. 2538 (1992)

Robert A. Viktora, a white teenager, and several other white youths burned a cross after midnight on the lawn of the only black family in a St. Paul, Minnesota, neighborhood. He was subsequently arrested and charged with violating a 1989 city ordinance making it a crime to place on public or private property a burning cross, swastika, or other symbol likely to arouse "anger, alarm, or resentment in others on the basis of race, color, creed, religion or gender." A state juvenile court, however, dismissed the complaint on the grounds that the ordinance was overly broad and unconstitutional. But the Minnesota State Supreme Court reversed upon concluding that the ordinance applied only to conduct "outside First Amendment protection." In determining that the ordinance only prohibited "fighting words," or speech that threatens "imminent lawless action"—categories of speech that have historically fallen outside the scope of the First Amendment—the state court observed that "[t]he burning of a cross is itself an unmistakable symbol of violence and hatred based on virulent notions of racial supremacy. It is the responsibility, even the obligation, of diverse communities to confront such notions in whatever form they appear." The state high court also distinguished St. Paul's ordinance from Texas's flag-burning law, which was struck down by a bare majority in *Texas v. Johnson*, 491 U.S. 397 (1989) (see Ch. 5). St. Paul did not ban cross-burning per se, the Minnesota court reasoned, "but only those displays that one knows or should know will create anger, alarm or resentment based on racial, ethnic, gender or religious bias." Robert A. Viktora appealed that ruling to the Supreme Court.

The state court's decision was reversed and the Court's decision was unanimous; Justice Scalia announced the opinion. Justice O'Connor joined Justice White's concurrence, as did Justices Blackmun and Stevens, who also delivered concurring opinions.

■ ■ ■

☐ *Justice SCALIA delivered the opinion of the Court.*

The First Amendment generally prevents government from proscribing speech, see, e.g., *Cantwell v. Connecticut*, 310 U.S. 296 (1940), or even expressive conduct, see, e.g., *Texas v. Johnson*, 491 U.S. 397 (1989), because of disapproval of the ideas expressed. Content-based regulations are presumptively invalid. From 1791 to the present, however, our society, like other free but civilized societies, has permitted restrictions upon the content of speech in a few limited areas, which are "of such slight social value as a step to truth that any benefit that may be derived from them is clearly outweighed by the social interest in order and morality." *Chaplinsky* [*v. New Hampshire*, 315 U.S. 568 (1942)]. We have recognized that "the freedom of speech" referred to by the First Amendment does not include a freedom to disregard these traditional limitations. Our decisions since the 1960's have narrowed the scope of the traditional categorical exceptions for defamation, and for obscenity, but a limited categorical approach has remained an important part of our First Amendment jurisprudence.

We have sometimes said that these categories of expression are "not within the area of constitutionally protected speech," or that the "protection of the First Amendment does not extend" to them. Such statements must be taken in context, however, and are no more literally true than is the occasionally repeated shorthand characterizing obscenity "as not being speech at all." What they mean is that these areas of speech can, consistently with the First Amendment, be regulated because of their constitutionally proscribable content (obscenity, defamation, etc.)—not that they are categories of speech entirely invisible to the Constitution, so that they may be made the vehicles for content discrimination unrelated to their distinctively proscribable content. Thus, the government may proscribe libel; but it may not make the further content discrimination of proscribing only libel critical of the government. . . .

The proposition that a particular instance of speech can be proscribable on the basis of one feature (e.g., obscenity) but not on the basis of another (e.g., opposition to the city government) is commonplace, and has found application in many contexts. We have long held, for example, that nonverbal expressive activity can be banned because of the action it entails, but not because of the ideas it expresses—so that burning a flag in violation of an ordinance against outdoor fires could be punishable, whereas burning a flag in violation of an ordinance against dishonoring the flag is not. Similarly, we have upheld reasonable "time, place, or manner" restrictions, but only if they are "justified without reference to the content of the regulated speech." *Ward v. Rock Against Racism*, 491 U.S. 781 (1989). And just as the power to proscribe particular speech on the basis of a noncontent element (e.g., noise) does not entail the power to proscribe the same speech on the basis of a content element; so also, the power to proscribe it on the basis of one content element (e.g., obscenity) does not entail the power to proscribe it on the basis of other content elements.

In other words, the exclusion of "fighting words" from the scope of the First Amendment simply means that, for purposes of that Amendment, the unprotected features of the words are, despite their verbal character, essentially a "nonspeech" element of communication. Fighting words are thus analogous to a noisy sound truck: Each is, as Justice FRANKFURTER recognized, a "mode of speech," *Niemotko v. Maryland*, 340 U.S. 268 (1951); both can be used to convey an idea; but neither has, in and of itself, a claim upon the First Amendment. As with the sound truck, however, so also with fighting words: The government may not regulate use based on hostility— or favoritism—towards the underlying message expressed. . . .

Even the prohibition against content discrimination that we assert the First Amendment requires is not absolute. It applies differently in the context of proscribable speech than in the area of fully protected speech. The rationale of the general prohibition, after all, is that content discrimination "raises the specter that the Government may effectively drive certain ideas or viewpoints from the marketplace," *Simon & Schuster* [*Inc. v. Members of the New York State Crime Victims Board*, 502 U.S. 105] (1991). But content discrimination among various instances of a class of proscribable speech often does not pose this threat.

When the basis for the content discrimination consists entirely of the very reason the entire class of speech at issue is proscribable, no significant danger of idea or viewpoint discrimination exists. Such a reason, having been adjudged neutral enough to support exclusion of the entire class of speech from First Amendment protection, is also neutral enough to form the basis of distinction within the class. To illustrate: A State might choose to prohibit only that obscenity which is the most patently offensive in its prurience—i.e., that which involves the most lascivious displays of sexual activity. But it may not prohibit, for example, only that obscenity which includes offensive political messages. And the Federal Government can criminalize only those threats of violence that are directed against the President—since the reasons why threats of violence are outside the First Amendment (protecting individuals from the fear of violence, from the disruption that fear engenders, and from the possibility that the threatened violence will occur) have special force when applied to the person of the President. . . . But the Federal Government may not criminalize only those threats against the President that mention his policy on aid to inner cities. And to take a final example, a State may choose to regulate price advertising in one industry but not in others, because the risk of fraud (one of the characteristics of commercial speech that justifies depriving it of full First Amendment protection, see *Virginia State Board of Pharmacy v. Virginia Citizens Consumer Council, Inc.*, 425 U.S. 748 (1976)) is in its view greater there.

Another valid basis for according differential treatment to even a content-defined subclass of proscribable speech is that the subclass happens to be associated with particular "secondary effects" of the speech, so that the regulation is "justified without reference to the content of the . . . speech," *Renton v. Playtime Theatres, Inc.*, 475 U.S. 41 (1986). A State could, for example, permit all obscene live performances except those involving minors. Moreover, since words can in some circumstances violate laws directed not against speech but against conduct (a law against treason, for example, is violated by telling the enemy the nation's defense secrets), a particular content-based subcategory of a proscribable class of speech can be swept up incidentally within the reach of a statute directed at conduct rather than speech. Where the government does not target conduct on the basis of its expressive content, acts are not shielded from regulation merely because they express a discriminatory idea or philosophy. . . .

Applying these principles to the St. Paul ordinance, we conclude that, even as narrowly construed by the Minnesota Supreme Court, the ordinance is facially unconstitutional. Although the phrase in the ordinance, "arouses anger, alarm or resentment in others," has been limited by the Minnesota Supreme Court's construction to reach only those symbols or displays that amount to "fighting words," the remaining, unmodified terms make clear that the ordinance applies only to "fighting words" that insult, or provoke violence, "on the basis of race, color, creed, religion or gender." Displays containing abusive invective, no matter how vicious or severe, are permissible unless they are addressed to one of the specified disfavored topics. Those who wish to use "fighting words" in connection with other ideas—to express hostility, for example, on the basis of political affiliation, union membership, or homosexuality—are not covered. The First Amendment does not permit St. Paul to impose special prohibitions on those speakers who express views on disfavored subjects. In its practical operation, moreover, the ordinance goes even beyond mere content discrimination, to actual viewpoint discrimination. Displays containing some words—odious racial epithets, for example—would be prohibited to proponents of all views. But "fighting words" that do not themselves invoke race, color, creed, religion, or gender—aspersions upon a person's mother, for example—would seemingly be usable ad libitum in the placards of those arguing in favor of race, color, etc., tolerance and equality, but could not be used by that speaker's opponents. One could hold up a sign saying, for example, that all "anti-Catholic bigots" are misbegotten; but not that all "papists" are, for that would insult and provoke violence "on the basis of religion." St. Paul has no such authority to license one side of a debate to fight freestyle, while requiring the other to follow Marquis of Queensbury Rules.

What we have here, it must be emphasized, is not a prohibition of fighting words that are directed at certain persons or groups (which would be facially valid if it met the requirements of the Equal Protection Clause); but rather, a prohibition of fighting words that contain (as the Minnesota Supreme Court repeatedly emphasized) messages of "bias-motivated" hatred and in particular, as applied to this case, messages "based on virulent notions of racial supremacy." . . .

The content-based discrimination reflected in the St. Paul ordinance comes within neither any of the specific exceptions to the First Amendment prohibition we discussed earlier, nor within a more general exception for content discrimination that does not threaten censorship of ideas. It assuredly does not fall within the exception for content discrimination based on the very reasons why the particular class of speech at issue (here, fighting words) is proscribable. As explained earlier, the reason why fighting words are categorically excluded from the protection of the First Amendment is not that their content communicates any particular idea, but that their content embodies a particularly intolerable (and socially unnecessary) mode of expressing whatever idea the speaker wishes to convey. St. Paul has not singled out an especially offensive mode of expression—it has not, for example, selected for prohibition only those fighting words that communicate ideas in a threatening (as opposed to a merely obnoxious) manner. Rather, it has proscribed fighting words of whatever manner that communicate messages of racial, gender, or religious intolerance. Selectivity of this sort creates the possibility that the city is seeking to handicap the expression of particular ideas. That possibility would alone be enough to render the ordinance presumptively invalid, but St. Paul's comments and concessions in this case elevate the possibility to a certainty. . . .

Let there be no mistake about our belief that burning a cross in someone's front yard is reprehensible. But St. Paul has sufficient means at its disposal to prevent such behavior without adding the First Amendment to the fire.

The judgment of the Minnesota Supreme Court is reversed, and the case is remanded for proceedings not inconsistent with this opinion.

☐ *Justice WHITE, with whom Justice BLACKMUN and
Justice O'CONNOR join, and with whom Justice STEVENS
joins except as to Part I(A), concurring in the judgment.*

I agree with the majority that the judgment of the Minnesota Supreme
Court should be reversed. However, our agreement ends there.

[T]he majority casts aside long-established First Amendment doctrine
without the benefit of briefing and adopts an untried theory. This is hardly
a judicious way of proceeding, and the Court's reasoning in reaching its
result is transparently wrong.

Today, . . . the Court announces that earlier Courts did not mean their
repeated statements that certain categories of expression are "not within the
area of constitutionally protected speech." The present Court submits that
such clear statements "must be taken in context" and are not "literally true."

To the contrary, those statements meant precisely what they said: The
categorical approach is a firmly entrenched part of our First Amendment
jurisprudence. Indeed, the Court in *Roth* [*v. United States*, 354 U.S. 476
(1952)], reviewed the guarantees of freedom of expression in effect at the
time of the ratification of the Constitution and concluded, "in light of this
history, it is apparent that the unconditional phrasing of the First Amendment was not intended to protect every utterance."

In its decision today, the Court points to "[n]othing . . . in this Court's
precedents warranting disregard of this longstanding tradition." Nevertheless, the majority holds that the First Amendment protects those narrow
categories of expression long held to be undeserving of First Amendment
protection—at least to the extent that lawmakers may not regulate some
fighting words more strictly than others because of their content. The
Court announces that such content-based distinctions violate the First
Amendment because "the government may not regulate use based on hostility—or favoritism—towards the underlying message expressed." Should
the government want to criminalize certain fighting words, the Court now
requires it to criminalize all fighting words.

To borrow a phrase, "Such a simplistic, all-or-nothing-at-all approach
to First Amendment protection is at odds with common sense and with our
jurisprudence as well." It is inconsistent to hold that the government may
proscribe an entire category of speech because the content of that speech is
evil, . . . but that the government may not treat a subset of that category
differently without violating the First Amendment; the content of the subset is by definition worthless and undeserving of constitutional protection.

The majority's observation that "fighting words are quite expressive
indeed" is no answer. Fighting words are not a means of exchanging views,
rallying supporters, or registering a protest; they are directed against individuals to provoke violence or to inflict injury. Therefore, a ban on all
fighting words or on a subset of the fighting words category would restrict
only the social evil of hate speech, without creating the danger of driving
viewpoints from the marketplace.

Therefore, the Court's insistence on inventing its brand of First Amendment underinclusiveness puzzles me. The overbreadth doctrine has the
redeeming virtue of attempting to avoid the chilling of protected expression,
but the Court's new "underbreadth" creation serves no desirable function.

Instead, it permits, indeed invites, the continuation of expressive conduct that in this case is evil and worthless in First Amendment terms, until the city of St. Paul cures the underbreadth by adding to its ordinance a catch-all phrase such as "and all other fighting words that may constitutionally be subject to this ordinance."

Any contribution of this holding to First Amendment jurisprudence is surely a negative one, since it necessarily signals that expressions of violence, such as the message of intimidation and racial hatred conveyed by burning a cross on someone's lawn, are of sufficient value to outweigh the social interest in order and morality that has traditionally placed such fighting words outside the First Amendment. Indeed, by characterizing "fighting words as a form of debate," the majority legitimates hate speech as a form of public discussion.

Furthermore, the Court obscures the line between speech that could be regulated freely on the basis of content (i.e., the narrow categories of expression falling outside the First Amendment) and that which could be regulated on the basis of content only upon a showing of a compelling state interest (i.e., all remaining expression). By placing fighting words, which the Court has long held to be valueless, on at least equal constitutional footing with political discourse and other forms of speech that we have deemed to have the greatest social value, the majority devalues the latter category.

- I

- B

In a second break with precedent, the Court refuses to sustain the ordinance even though it would survive under the strict scrutiny applicable to other protected expression. Assuming, *arguendo*, that the St. Paul ordinance is a content-based regulation of protected expression, it nevertheless would pass First Amendment review under settled law upon a showing that the regulation "is necessary to serve a compelling state interest and is narrowly drawn to achieve that end." *Simon & Schuster*. St. Paul has urged that its ordinance, in the words of the majority, "helps to ensure the basic human rights of members of groups that have historically been subjected to discrimination. . . ." The Court expressly concedes that this interest is compelling and is promoted by the ordinance. Nevertheless, the Court treats strict scrutiny analysis as irrelevant to the constitutionality of the legislation. . . .

Although the First Amendment does not apply to categories of unprotected speech, such as fighting words, the Equal Protection Clause requires that the regulation of unprotected speech be rationally related to a legitimate government interest. A defamation statute that drew distinctions on the basis of political affiliation or "an ordinance prohibiting only those legally obscene works that contain criticism of the city government," would unquestionably fail rational basis review.

Turning to the St. Paul ordinance and assuming *arguendo*, as the majority does, that the ordinance is not constitutionally overbroad, there is no question that it would pass equal protection review. The ordinance proscribes a subset of "fighting words," those that injure "on the basis of race, color, creed, religion or gender." This selective regulation reflects the City's judgment that harms based on race, color, creed, religion, or gender are more pressing public concerns than the harms caused by other fighting words. In light of our Nation's long and painful experience with discrimination, this determination is plainly reasonable. Indeed, as the majority concedes, the interest is compelling. . . .

Although I disagree with the Court's analysis, I do agree with its conclusion: The St. Paul ordinance is unconstitutional. However, I would decide the case on overbreadth grounds. . . .

☐ *Justice STEVENS, with whom Justice WHITE and Justice BLACKMUN join as to Part I, concurring in the judgment.*

[M]y colleagues today wrestle with two broad principles: first, that certain "categories of expression [including 'fighting words'] are not within the area of constitutionally protected speech"; and second, that "content-based regulations [of expression] are presumptively invalid." Although in past opinions the Court has repeated both of these maxims, it has—quite rightly—adhered to neither with the absolutism suggested by my colleagues. Thus, while I agree that the St. Paul ordinance is unconstitutionally overbroad for the reasons stated in Part II of Justice WHITE's opinion, I write separately to suggest how the allure of absolute principles has skewed the analysis of both the majority and concurring opinions.

■ I

The Court today revises this categorical approach. It is not, the Court rules, that certain "categories" of expression are "unprotected," but rather that certain "elements" of expression are wholly "proscribable." To the Court, an expressive act, like a chemical compound, consists of more than one element. Although the act may be regulated because it contains a proscribable element, it may not be regulated on the basis of another (nonproscribable) element it also contains. Thus, obscene antigovernment speech may be regulated because it is obscene, but not because it is antigovernment. It is this revision of the categorical approach that allows the Court to assume that the St. Paul ordinance proscribes only fighting words, while at the same time concluding that the ordinance is invalid because it imposes a content-based regulation on expressive activity.

As an initial matter, the Court's revision of the categorical approach seems to me something of an adventure in a doctrinal wonderland, for the concept of "obscene antigovernment" speech is fantastical. The category of the obscene is very narrow; to be obscene, expression must be found by the trier of fact to "appeal to the prurient interest, . . . depict or describe, in a patently offensive way, sexual conduct, [and] taken as a whole, lack serious literary, artistic, political or scientific value." *Miller v. California*, 413 U.S. 15 (1973). "Obscene antigovernment" speech, then, is a contradiction in terms: If expression is antigovernment, it does not "lac[k] serious . . . political . . . value" and cannot be obscene. . . .

I am, however, even more troubled by the second step of the Court's analysis—namely, its conclusion that the St. Paul ordinance is an unconstitutional content-based regulation of speech. Drawing on broadly worded *dicta*, the Court establishes a near-absolute ban on content-based regulations of expression and holds that the First Amendment prohibits the regulation of fighting words by subject matter. Thus, while the Court rejects the "all-or-nothing-at-all" nature of the categorical approach, it promptly embraces an absolutism of its own: within a particular "proscribable" category of expression, the Court holds, a government must either proscribe all speech or no speech at all. This aspect of the Court's ruling fundamentally misunderstands the role and constitutional status of content-based regulations on speech, conflicts with the very nature of First Amendment jurisprudence, and disrupts well-settled principles of First Amendment law. . . .

Our First Amendment decisions have created a rough hierarchy in the constitutional protection of speech. Core political speech occupies the highest, most protected position; commercial speech and nonobscene, sexually explicit speech are regarded as a sort of second-class expression; obscenity and fighting words receive the least protection of all. Assuming that the Court is correct that this last class of speech is not wholly "unprotected," it certainly does not follow that fighting words and obscenity receive the same sort of protection afforded core political speech. Yet in ruling that proscribable speech cannot be regulated based on subject matter, the Court does just that. Perversely, this gives fighting words greater protection than is afforded commercial speech. . . .

In sum, the central premise of the Court's ruling—that "[c]ontent-based regulations are presumptively invalid"—has simplistic appeal, but lacks support in our First Amendment jurisprudence. To make matters worse, the Court today extends this overstated claim to reach categories of hitherto unprotected speech and, in doing so, wreaks havoc in an area of settled law. Finally, although the Court recognizes exceptions to its new principle, those exceptions undermine its very conclusion that the St. Paul ordinance is unconstitutional. Stated directly, the majority's position cannot withstand scrutiny.

▪ II

Although I agree with much of Justice WHITE's analysis, I do not join Part I-A of his opinion because I have reservations about the "categorical approach" to the First Amendment. . . .

[T]his approach sacrifices subtlety for clarity and is, I am convinced, ultimately unsound. As an initial matter, the concept of "categories" fits poorly with the complex reality of expression. Few dividing lines in First Amendment law are straight and unwavering, and efforts at categorization inevitably give rise only to fuzzy boundaries. Our definitions of "obscenity" illustrate this all too well. The quest for doctrinal certainty through the definition of categories and subcategories is, in my opinion, destined to fail.

Moreover, the categorical approach does not take seriously the importance of context. The meaning of any expression and the legitimacy of its regulation can only be determined in context. Whether, for example, a picture or a sentence is obscene cannot be judged in the abstract, but rather only in the context of its setting, its use, and its audience. . . .

Perhaps sensing the limits of such an all-or-nothing approach, the Court has applied its analysis less categorically than its doctrinal statements suggest. The Court has recognized intermediate categories of speech (for example, for indecent nonobscene speech and commercial speech) and geographic categories of speech (public fora, limited public fora, nonpublic fora) entitled to varying levels of protection. The Court has also stringently delimited the categories of unprotected speech. While we once declared that "libelous utterances [are] not . . . within the area of constitutionally protected speech," *Beauharnais v. Illinois*, 343 U.S. 250 (1952), our rulings in *New York Times Co. v. Sullivan*, 376 U.S. 254 (1964); *Gertz v. Robert Welch, Inc.*, 418 U.S. 323 (1974), and *Dun & Bradstreet, Inc. v. Greenmoss Builders, Inc.*, 472 U.S. 749 (1985), have substantially qualified this broad claim. Similarly, we have consistently construed the "fighting words" exception set forth in *Chaplinsky* narrowly. . . . In short, the history of the categorical approach is largely the history of narrowing the categories of unprotected speech.

This evolution, I believe, indicates that the categorical approach is unworkable and the quest for absolute categories of "protected" and "unprotected" speech ultimately futile. . . .

■ III

Unlike the Court, I do not believe that all content-based regulations are equally infirm and presumptively invalid; unlike Justice WHITE, I do not believe that fighting words are wholly unprotected by the First Amendment. To the contrary, I believe our decisions establish a more complex and subtle analysis, one that considers the content and context of the regulated speech, and the nature and scope of the restriction on speech. Applying this analysis and assuming *arguendo* (as the Court does) that the St. Paul ordinance is not overbroad, I conclude that such a selective, subject-matter regulation on proscribable speech is constitutional. . . .

In sum, the St. Paul ordinance (as construed by the Court) regulates expressive activity that is wholly proscribable and does so not on the basis of viewpoint, but rather in recognition of the different harms caused by such activity. Taken together, these several considerations persuade me that the St. Paul ordinance is not an unconstitutional content-based regulation of speech. Thus, were the ordinance not overbroad, I would vote to uphold it.

Wisconsin v. Mitchell
508 U.S. 476, 113 S.CT. 2194 (1993)

One evening in 1989 Todd Mitchell and several other black men and youths were talking about a scene in the movie *Mississippi Burning* in which a white man beats a young black man. Later, as the group moved outside to the street, Mitchell asked them, "Do you all feel hyped up to move on some white people?" Shortly thereafter a young white boy appeared on the other side of the street. And as he walked by, Mitchell counted "one, two, three" and said, "There goes a white boy; go get him!" After rushing the boy, Mitchell and the others beat him unconscious and stole his tennis shoes.

Subsequently, Mitchell was convicted of battery, which carries a maximum sentence of two years imprisonment. But under

Wisconsin's "hate-speech" law an enhanced sentence may be given whenever the defendant "intentionally selects the person against whom the crime . . . is committed . . . because of the race, religion, color, disability, sexual orientation, national origin or ancestry of that person." Accordingly, Mitchell was sentenced to four years imprisonment. His challenge to the state's "hate-speech" law was initially unsuccessful, but on appeal the state supreme court agreed that the law violated "the First Amendment directly by punishing what the legislature has deemed to be offensive thought." But that ruling was appealed by the state, and the Supreme Court granted review.

The Court's decision was unanimous. Chief Justice Rehnquist announced the opinion.

■ ■ ■

☐ *Chief Justice REHNQUIST delivered the opinion of the Court.*

The State argues that the statute does not punish bigoted thought, as the Supreme Court of Wisconsin said, but instead punishes only conduct. While this argument is literally correct, it does not dispose of Mitchell's First Amendment challenge. To be sure, our cases reject the "view that an apparently limitless variety of conduct can be labeled 'speech' whenever the person engaging in the conduct intends thereby to express an idea." *United States v. O'Brien*, 391 U.S. 367 (1968); accord, *R.A.V. [v. City of St. Paul, Minnesota*, 505 U.S. 377 (1992)]. Thus, a physical assault is not by any stretch of the imagination expressive conduct protected by the First Amendment. See *Roberts v. United States Jaycees*, 468 U.S. 609 (1984) ("Violence or other types of potentially expressive activities that produce special harms distinct from their communicative impact . . . are entitled to no constitutional protection").

But the fact remains that under the Wisconsin statute the same criminal conduct may be more heavily punished if the victim is selected because of his race or other protected status than if no such motive obtained. Thus, although the statute punishes criminal conduct, it enhances the maximum penalty for conduct motivated by a discriminatory point of view more severely than the same conduct engaged in for some other reason or for no reason at all. Because the only reason for the enhancement is the defendant's discriminatory motive for selecting his victim, Mitchell argues (and the Wisconsin Supreme Court held) that the statute violates the First Amendment by punishing offenders' bigoted beliefs.

Traditionally, sentencing judges have considered a wide variety of factors in addition to evidence bearing on guilt in determining what sentence to impose on a convicted defendant. Thus, in many States the commission of a murder, or other capital offense, for pecuniary gain is a separate aggravating circumstance under the capital-sentencing statute. . . .

[But] Mitchell argues that the Wisconsin penalty-enhancement statute is invalid because it punishes the defendant's discriminatory motive, or reason, for acting. But motive plays the same role under the Wisconsin statute as it does under federal and state antidiscrimination laws, which we have previously upheld against constitutional challenge.

Nothing in our decision last Term in *R.A.V.* compels a different result here. That case involved a First Amendment challenge to a municipal ordinance prohibiting the use of " 'fighting words' that insult, or provoke violence, 'on the basis of race, color, creed, religion or gender.' " Because the ordinance only proscribed a class of "fighting words" deemed particularly offensive by the city—i.e., those "that contain . . . messages of 'bias-motivated' hatred"—we held that it violated the rule against content-based discrimination. But whereas the ordinance struck down in *R.A.V.* was explicitly directed at expression (i.e., "speech" or "messages") the statute in this case is aimed at conduct unprotected by the First Amendment. . . .

Finally, there remains to be considered Mitchell's argument that the Wisconsin statute is unconstitutionally overbroad because of its "chilling effect" on free speech. Mitchell argues (and the Wisconsin Supreme Court agreed) that the statute is "overbroad" because evidence of the defendant's prior speech or associations may be used to prove that the defendant intentionally selected his victim on account of the victim's protected status. Consequently, the argument goes, the statute impermissibly chills free expression with respect to such matters by those concerned about the possibility of enhanced sentences if they should in the future commit a criminal offense covered by the statute. We find no merit in this contention.

The sort of chill envisioned here is far more attenuated and unlikely than that contemplated in traditional "overbreadth" cases. We must conjure up a vision of a Wisconsin citizen suppressing his unpopular bigoted opinions for fear that if he later commits an offense covered by the statute, these opinions will be offered at trial to establish that he selected his victim on account of the victim's protected status, thus qualifying him for penalty-enhancement. To stay within the realm of rationality, we must surely put to one side minor misdemeanor offenses covered by the statute, such as negligent operation of a motor vehicle, for it is difficult, if not impossible, to conceive of a situation where such offenses would be racially motivated. We are left, then, with the prospect of a citizen suppressing his bigoted beliefs for fear that evidence of such beliefs will be introduced against him at trial if he commits a more serious offense against person or property. This is simply too speculative a hypothesis to support Mitchell's overbreadth claim. . . .

For the foregoing reasons, we hold that Mitchell's First Amendment rights were not violated by the application of the Wisconsin penalty-enhancement provision in sentencing him. The judgment of the Supreme Court of Wisconsin is therefore reversed, and the case is remanded for further proceedings not inconsistent with this opinion.

Virginia v. Black

538 U.S. 343, 123 S.CT. 1536 (2003)

In 1998, Barry Elton Black led a Ku Klux Klan rally at which a twenty-five-foot cross was burned on private property with the owner's permission, but which was clearly visible to nearby home-owners and motorists on a state road. He was convicted under

Virginia's fifty-year-old law making cross-burning a crime and fined $2,500. Also in 1998, Richard J. Elliott and Jonathan O'Mara burned a cross in the yard of James Jubilee, an African American, because they were angry with him. Both were convicted and sentenced to ninety days in jail and fined $2,500. On appeal in 2001, the Virginia Supreme Court overturned their convictions and struck down the state's law in holding that it ran afoul of the First Amendment's guarantee for freedom of expression. The state appealed and the Supreme Court granted *certiorari*.

Justice O'Connor's opinion for the Court commanded only a plurality, but by a vote of 6–3 the Court held that a properly drafted law punishing cross-burning would survive a First Amendment challenge. Justice O'Connor's opinion, joined by Chief Justice Rehnquist and Justices Stevens and Breyer, held that the state may make it a crime to burn a cross because it is "a particularly virulent form of intimidation." Justice Scalia, in a separate opinion in part concurring and dissenting, and Justice Thomas, in a dissenting opinion, agreed. However, Justice O'Connor also ruled that Virginia's law was unconstitutional because a section of the law dealing with jury instructions permitting an inference of intent to intimidate invited juries to ignore "all of the contextual factors that are necessary to decide whether a particular cross burning [was] intended to intimidate" instead of to express a political message. Justice Scalia disagreed with that part of her analysis and holding, in contending that under the statute a jury could be properly instructed and the inference of intimidation rebutted. In his dissent, Justice Thomas contended that the plurality went too far and that cross-burning could never receive First Amendment protection because its sole message was one of terror and lawlessness. Justice Souter, joined by Justices Kennedy and Ginsburg, filed another separate opinion in part concurring and dissenting. These three justices agreed that Virginia's law was unconstitutional but maintained that the First Amendment forbids all content-based regulations of speech. Cross-burning, in their view, was inherently symbolic and might convey not only a message of terror but also of political ideology. Accordingly, they would have held that any law punishing cross-burning could not survive First Amendment scrutiny.

■ ■ ■

☐ *Justice O'CONNOR announced the judgment of the Court and delivered the opinion of the Court with respect to Parts I, II, and III, and an opinion with respect to Parts IV and V, in which THE CHIEF JUSTICE, Justice STEVENS, and Justice BREYER join.*

In this case we consider whether the Commonwealth of Virginia's statute banning cross burning with "an intent to intimidate a person or group of persons" violates the First Amendment. We conclude that while a State, consistent with the First Amendment, may ban cross burning carried out with the intent to intimidate, the provision in the Virginia statute treating any cross burning as prima facie evidence of intent to intimidate renders the statute unconstitutional in its current form. . . .

■ II

Cross burning originated in the 14th century as a means for Scottish tribes to signal each other. . . . Cross burning in this country, however, long ago became unmoored from its Scottish ancestry. Burning a cross in the United States is inextricably intertwined with the history of the Ku Klux Klan.

The first Ku Klux Klan began in Pulaski, Tennessee, in the spring of 1866. Although the Ku Klux Klan started as a social club, it soon changed into something far different. The Klan fought Reconstruction and the corresponding drive to allow freed blacks to participate in the political process. Soon the Klan imposed "a veritable reign of terror" throughout the South. The Klan employed tactics such as whipping, threatening to burn people at the stake, and murder. The Klan's victims included blacks, southern whites who disagreed with the Klan and "carpetbagger" northern whites.

The activities of the Ku Klux Klan prompted legislative action at the national level. . . . Congress passed what is now known as the Ku Klux Klan Act. President Grant used these new powers to suppress the Klan in South Carolina, the effect of which severely curtailed the Klan in other States as well. By the end of Reconstruction in 1877, the first Klan no longer existed.

The genesis of the second Klan began in 1905, with the publication of Thomas Dixon's *The Clansmen: An Historical Romance of the Ku Klux Klan.* Dixon's book was a sympathetic portrait of the first Klan, depicting the Klan as a group of heroes "saving" the South from blacks and the "horrors" of Reconstruction. Although the first Klan never actually practiced cross burning, Dixon's book depicted the Klan burning crosses to celebrate the execution of former slaves. Cross burning thereby became associated with the first Ku Klux Klan. When D. W. Griffith turned Dixon's book into the movie *The Birth of a Nation* in 1915, the association between cross burning and the Klan became indelible. . . .

From the inception of the second Klan, cross burnings have been used to communicate both threats of violence and messages of shared ideology. The first initiation ceremony occurred on Stone Mountain near Atlanta, Georgia. While a 40-foot cross burned on the mountain, the Klan members took their oaths of loyalty. This cross burning was the second recorded instance in the United States. The first known cross burning in the country had occurred a little over one month before the Klan initiation, when a Georgia mob celebrated the lynching of Leo Frank by burning a "gigantic cross" on Stone Mountain that was "visible throughout" Atlanta. . . .

The Klan continued to use cross burnings to intimidate after World War II. . . . The decision of this Court in *Brown v. Board of Education,* 347 U.S. 483 (1954), along with the civil rights movement of the 1950's and 1960's, sparked another outbreak of Klan violence. These acts of violence included bombings, beatings, shootings, stabbings, and mutilations. . . .

To this day, regardless of whether the message is a political one or whether the message is also meant to intimidate, the burning of a cross is a "symbol of hate." And while cross burning sometimes carries no intimidating message, at other times the intimidating message is the only message conveyed. . . .

In sum, while a burning cross does not inevitably convey a message of intimidation, often the cross burner intends that the recipients of the message fear for their lives. And when a cross burning is used to intimidate, few if any messages are more powerful.

■ III

The First Amendment affords protection to symbolic or expressive conduct as well as to actual speech. See, e.g., *R.A.V. v. City of St. Paul*, 505 U.S. [377 (1992)]; *Texas v. Johnson*, [491 U.S. 397 (1989)]; *United States v. O'Brien*, 391 U.S. 367 (1968); *Tinker v. Des Moines Independent Community School Dist.*, 393 U.S. 503 (1969).

The protections afforded by the First Amendment, however, are not absolute, and we have long recognized that the government may regulate certain categories of expression consistent with the Constitution. See, e.g., *Chaplinsky v. New Hampshire*, 315 U.S. 568 (1942).

We have consequently held that fighting words—"those personally abusive epithets which, when addressed to the ordinary citizen, are, as a matter of common knowledge, inherently likely to provoke violent reaction"—are generally proscribable under the First Amendment. *Cohen v. California*, 403 U.S. 15 (1971). Furthermore, "the constitutional guarantees of free speech and free press do not permit a State to forbid or proscribe advocacy of the use of force or of law violation except where such advocacy is directed to inciting or producing imminent lawless action and is likely to incite or produce such action." *Brandenburg v. Ohio*, 395 U.S. 444 (1969). And the First Amendment also permits a State to ban a "true threat." *Watts v. United States*, 394 U.S. 705 (1969); accord, *R.A.V.* ("[T]hreats of violence are outside the First Amendment").

"True threats" encompass those statements where the speaker means to communicate a serious expression of an intent to commit an act of unlawful violence to a particular individual or group of individuals. The speaker need not actually intend to carry out the threat. Rather, a prohibition on true threats "protect[s] individuals from the fear of violence" and "from the disruption that fear engenders," in addition to protecting people "from the possibility that the threatened violence will occur." Intimidation in the constitutionally proscribable sense of the word is a type of true threat, where a speaker directs a threat to a person or group of persons with the intent of placing the victim in fear of bodily harm or death. . . .

The fact that cross burning is symbolic expression, however, does not resolve the constitutional question. The Supreme Court of Virginia relied upon *R.A.V.* to conclude that once a statute discriminates on the basis of this type of content, the law is unconstitutional. We disagree.

In *R.A.V.*, we held that a local ordinance that banned certain symbolic conduct, including cross burning, when done with the knowledge that such conduct would "arouse anger, alarm or resentment in others on the basis of race, color, creed, religion or gender" was unconstitutional. We held that the ordinance did not pass constitutional muster because it discriminated on the basis of content by targeting only those individuals who "provoke violence" on a basis specified in the law.

We did not hold in *R.A.V.* that the First Amendment prohibits *all* forms of content-based discrimination within a proscribable area of speech. Rather, we specifically stated that some types of content discrimination did not violate the First Amendment. Indeed, we noted that it would be constitutional to ban only a particular type of threat: "[T]he Federal Government can criminalize only those threats of violence that are directed against the President . . . since the reasons why threats of violence are outside the First Amendment . . . have special force when applied to the person of the President." And a State may "choose to prohibit only that obscenity which is the most patently offensive in its prurience—i.e., that which involves the most lascivious displays of sexual activity." Consequently, while the holding of *R.A.V.* does not permit a State to ban only obscenity based on "offensive political messages," or "only those threats against the President that mention his policy on aid to inner cities," the First Amendment permits content discrimination "based on the very reasons why the particular class of speech at issue . . . is proscribable."

Similarly, Virginia's statute does not run afoul of the First Amendment insofar as it bans cross burning with intent to intimidate. Unlike the statute at issue in *R.A.V.*, the Virginia statute does not single out for opprobrium only that speech directed toward "one of the specified disfavored topics." . . .

The First Amendment permits Virginia to outlaw cross burnings done with the intent to intimidate because burning a cross is a particularly virulent form of intimidation. Instead of prohibiting all intimidating messages, Virginia may choose to regulate this subset of intimidating messages in light of cross burning's long and pernicious history as a signal of impending violence. Thus, just as a State may regulate only that obscenity which is the most obscene due to its prurient content, so too may a State choose to prohibit only those forms of intimidation that are most likely to inspire fear of bodily harm. A ban on cross burning carried out with the intent to intimidate is fully consistent with our holding in *R.A.V.* and is proscribable under the First Amendment.

■ IV

The Supreme Court of Virginia ruled in the alternative that Virginia's cross-burning statute was unconstitutionally overbroad due to its provision stating that "[a]ny such burning of a cross shall be prima facie evidence of an intent to intimidate a person or group of persons." . . . In this Court, as in the Supreme Court of Virginia, respondents do not argue that the prima facie evidence provision is unconstitutional as applied to any one of them. Rather, they contend that the provision is unconstitutional on its face. . . .

As construed by the jury instruction, the prima facie provision strips away the very reason why a State may ban cross burning with the intent to intimidate. The prima facie evidence provision permits a jury to convict in every cross-burning case in which defendants exercise their constitutional right not to put on a defense. And even where a defendant like Black presents a defense, the prima facie evidence provision makes it more likely that the jury will find an intent to intimidate regardless of the particular facts of the case. The provision permits the Commonwealth to arrest, prosecute, and convict a person based solely on the fact of cross burning itself. . . .

As the history of cross burning indicates, a burning cross is not always intended to intimidate. Rather, sometimes the cross burning is a statement of ideology, a symbol of group solidarity. . . . Thus, "[b]urning a cross at a political rally would almost certainly be protected expression." *R.A.V.* . . .

The prima facie provision makes no effort to distinguish among these different types of cross burnings. . . . For these reasons, the prima facie evidence provision, as interpreted through the jury instruction and as applied in Barry Black's case, is unconstitutional on its face. . . .

■ V

With respect to Barry Black, we agree with the Supreme Court of Virginia that his conviction cannot stand, and we affirm the judgment of the Supreme Court of Virginia. With respect to Elliott and O'Mara, we vacate the judgment of the Supreme Court of Virginia, and remand the case for further proceedings. It is so ordered.

☐ *Justice STEVENS, concurring.*

Cross burning with "an intent to intimidate" unquestionably qualifies as the kind of threat that is unprotected by the First Amendment. For the reasons stated in the separate opinions that Justice WHITE and I wrote in *R.A.V.*, that simple proposition provides a sufficient basis for upholding the basic prohibition in the Virginia statute even though it does not cover other types of threatening expressive conduct. With this observation, I join Justice O'CONNOR's opinion.

☐ *Justice THOMAS, dissenting.*

Although I agree with the majority's conclusion that it is constitutionally permissible to "ban . . . cross burning carried out with intent to intimidate," I believe that the majority errs in imputing an expressive component to the activity in question. In my view, whatever expressive value cross burning has, the legislature simply wrote it out by banning only intimidating conduct undertaken by a particular means. A conclusion that the statute prohibiting cross burning with intent to intimidate sweeps beyond a prohibition on certain conduct into the zone of expression overlooks not only the words of the statute but also reality. . . .

[T]his statute prohibits only conduct, not expression. And, just as one cannot burn down someone's house to make a political point and then seek refuge in the First Amendment, those who hate cannot terrorize and intimidate to make their point. In light of my conclusion that the statute here addresses only conduct, there is no need to analyze it under any of our First Amendment tests.

Even assuming that the statute implicates the First Amendment, in my view, the fact that the statute permits a jury to draw an inference of intent to intimidate from the cross burning itself presents no constitutional problems. Therein lies my primary disagreement with the plurality. . . .

Because I would uphold the validity of this statute, I respectfully dissent.

☐ *Justice SCALIA, with whom Justice THOMAS joins, concurring in part, concurring in the judgment in part, and dissenting in part.*

I agree with the Court that, under our decision in *R.A.V.*, a State may, without infringing the First Amendment, prohibit cross burning carried out with the intent to intimidate. Accordingly, I join Parts I–III of the Court's opinion. I also agree that we should vacate and remand the judgment of the Virginia Supreme Court so that that Court can have an opportunity authoritatively to construe the prima-facie-evidence provision of Section 18.2-423. I write separately, however, to describe what I believe to be the correct interpretation of Sec. 18.2-423, and to explain why I believe there is no justification for the plurality's apparent decision to invalidate that provision on its face.

In order to determine whether this component of the statute violates the Constitution, it is necessary, first, to establish precisely what the presentation of prima facie evidence accomplishes. . . . [P]resentation of evidence that a defendant burned a cross in public view is automatically sufficient, on its own, to support an inference that the defendant intended to intimidate only until the defendant comes forward with some evidence in rebuttal.

The question presented, then, is whether, given this understanding of the term "prima facie evidence," the cross-burning statute is constitutional. The Virginia Supreme Court answered that question in the negative. It stated that "[Sec.] 18.2-423 sweeps within its ambit for arrest and prosecution, both protected and unprotected speech." "The enhanced probability of prosecution under the statute chills the expression of protected speech sufficiently to render the statute overbroad."

This approach toward overbreadth analysis is unprecedented. We have never held that the mere threat that individuals who engage in protected conduct will be subject to arrest and prosecution suffices to render a statute overbroad. Rather, our overbreadth jurisprudence has consistently focused on whether the prohibitory terms of a particular statute extend to protected conduct; that is, we have inquired whether individuals who engage in protected conduct can be convicted under a statue, not whether they might be subject to arrest and prosecution. . . .

In deeming Sec. 18.2-423 facially invalid, the plurality presumably means to rely on some species of overbreadth doctrine. But it must be a rare species indeed. . . . The class of persons that the plurality contemplates could impermissibly be convicted under Sec. 18.2-423 includes only those individuals who (1) burn a cross in public view, (2) do not intend to intimidate, (3) are nonetheless charged and prosecuted, and (4) refuse to present a defense.

Conceding (quite generously, in my view) that this class of persons exists, it cannot possibly give rise to a viable facial challenge, not even with the aid of our First Amendment overbreadth doctrine.

I believe the prima-facie-evidence provision in Virginia's cross-burning statute is constitutionally unproblematic. . . .

☐ *Justice SOUTER, with whom Justice KENNEDY and Justice GINSBURG join, concurring in the judgment in part and dissenting in part.*

I agree with the majority that the Virginia statute makes a content-based distinction within the category of punishable intimidating or threatening expression, the very type of distinction we considered in *R.A.V.* I disagree that any exception should save Virginia's law from unconstitutionality under the holding in *R.A.V.* or any acceptable variation of it.

As the majority points out, the burning cross can broadcast threat and ideology together, ideology alone, or threat alone, as was apparently the choice of respondents Elliott and O'Mara.

The issue is whether the statutory prohibition restricted to this symbol falls within one of the exceptions to R.A.V.'s general condemnation of limited content-based proscription within a broader category of expression proscribable generally. Because of the burning cross's extraordinary force as a method of intimidation, the *R.A.V.* exception most likely to cover the statute is the first of the three mentioned there, which the *R.A.V.* opinion called an exception for content discrimination on a basis that "consists entirely of the very reason the entire class of speech at issue is proscribable." *R.A.V.* This is the exception the majority speaks of here as covering statutes prohibiting "particularly virulent" proscribable expression.

I do not think that the Virginia statute qualifies for this virulence exception as *R.A.V.* explained it. The statute fits poorly with the illustrative examples given in *R.A.V.*, none of which involves communication generally associated with a particular message, and in fact, the majority's discussion of a special virulence exception here moves that exception toward a more flexible conception than the version in *R.A.V.* I will reserve judgment on that doctrinal development, for even on a pragmatic conception of *R.A.V.* and its exceptions the Virginia statute could not pass muster, the most obvious hurdle being the statute's prima facie evidence provision. That provision is essential to understanding why the statute's tendency to suppress a message disqualifies it from any rescue by exception from R.A.V.'s general rule. . . .

[N]o content-based statute should survive even under a pragmatic recasting of *R.A.V.* without a high probability that no "official suppression of ideas is afoot," *R.A.V.* I believe the prima facie evidence provision stands in the way of any finding of such a high probability here. . . .

To the extent the prima facie evidence provision skews prosecutions, then, it skews the statute toward suppressing ideas. Thus, the appropriate way to consider the statute's prima facie evidence term, in my view, is not as if it were an overbroad statutory definition amenable to severance or a narrowing construction. The question here is not the permissible scope of an arguably overbroad statute, but the claim of a clearly content-based statute to an exception from the general prohibition of content-based proscriptions, an exception that is not warranted if the statute's terms show that suppression of ideas may be afoot. Accordingly, the way to look at the prima facie evidence provision is to consider it for any indication of what is afoot. And if we look at the provision for this purpose, it has a very obvious significance as a mechanism for bringing within the statute's prohibition some expression that is doubtfully threatening though certainly distasteful. . . .

I conclude that the statute under which all three of the respondents were prosecuted violates the First Amendment, since the statute's content-based distinction was invalid at the time of the charged activities, regardless of whether the prima facie evidence provision was given any effect in any respondent's individual case. In my view, severance of the prima facie evidence provision now could not eliminate the unconstitutionality of the whole statute at the time of the respondents' conduct. I would therefore affirm the judgment of the Supreme Court of Virginia vacating the respondents' convictions and dismissing the indictments. Accordingly, I concur in the Court's judgment as to respondent Black and dissent as to respondents Elliott and O'Mara.

Brown v. Entertainment Merchants Association
564 U.S. 786, 131 S.CT. 2729 (2011)

In 2005 California enacted a law requiring the labeling of video games containing violence and restricting the sales of such videos to minors, with fines up to $1,000 for violations. When the constitutionality of the law was challenged, the state argued for the extension of a constitutional standard, created for cases involving the protection of minors from obscene materials, to violent materials, rather than obscenity. That standard derives from *Ginsberg v. New York*, 390 U.S. 629 (1968), which defines a violent video game as one depicting the "killing, maiming, dismembering, or sexually assaulting the image of a human being" in a manner that a reasonable person would find appeals to "a deviant or morbid interest" of minors, and is "patently offensive" to prevailing standards of what is suitable for minors and causes the game—as a whole—to lack "serious, artistic, political or scientific value" for minors. The Court of Appeals for the Ninth Circuit found the statute to run afoul of the First Amendment, rejecting the proposed extension of the *Ginsberg* standard and using instead the strict scrutiny test. In that there was no proof that playing such games harms minors, physically or psychologically. The state appealed and the Court granted review.

The appellate court's ruling was affirmed by a 7–2 vote. Justice Scalia delivered the opinion for the Court. Justice Alito filed a concurrence, joined by Chief Justice Roberts. Justices Thomas and Breyer each issued dissenting opinions.

■ ■ ■

☐ *Justice SCALIA delivered the opinion of the Court.*

Like the protected books, plays, and movies that preceded them, video games communicate ideas—and even social messages—through many familiar literary devices (such as characters, dialogue, plot, and music) and through features distinctive to the medium (such as the player's interaction with the virtual world). That suffices to confer First Amendment protection. . . . And whatever the challenges of applying the Constitution to ever-advancing technology, "the basic principles of freedom of speech and the press, like the First Amendment's command, do not vary" when a new and different medium for communication appears. *Joseph Burstyn, Inc. v. Wilson*, 343 U.S. 495 (1952).

The most basic of those principles is this: "[A]s a general matter, . . . government has no power to restrict expression because of its message, its ideas, its subject matter, or its content." *Ashcroft v. American Civil Liberties Union*, 535 U.S. 564 (2002). There are of course exceptions. " 'From 1791 to the present,' . . . the First Amendment has 'permitted restrictions upon the content of speech in a few limited areas,' and has never 'include[d] a freedom to disregard these traditional limitations.' " *United States v. Stevens*, [130 S.Ct. 1577] (2010). These limited areas—such as obscenity, *Roth v. United States*, 354 U.S. 476, 483 (1957); incitement, *Brandenburg v. Ohio*, 395 U.S. 444 (1969); and fighting words, *Chaplinsky v. New Hampshire*, 315 U.S. 568 (1942)—represent "well-defined and narrowly limited classes of speech, the prevention and punishment of which have never been thought to raise any Constitutional problem."

Last Term, in *Stevens*, we held that new categories of unprotected speech may not be added to the list by a legislature that concludes certain speech is too harmful to be tolerated. *Stevens* concerned a federal statute purporting to criminalize the creation, sale, or possession of certain depictions of animal cruelty. . . .

That holding controls this case. As in *Stevens*, California has tried to make violent-speech regulation look like obscenity regulation by appending a saving clause required for the latter. That does not suffice. Our cases have been clear that the obscenity exception to the First Amendment does not cover whatever a legislature finds shocking, but only depictions of "sexual conduct," *Miller* [*v. California*, 413 U.S. 15 (1973)]. . . .

Because speech about violence is not obscene, it is of no consequence that California's statute mimics the New York statute regulating obscenity for minors that we upheld in *Ginsberg v. New York*, 390 U.S. 629 (1968). That case approved a prohibition on the sale to minors of sexual material that would be obscene from the perspective of a child. . . .

The California Act is something else entirely. It does not adjust the boundaries of an existing category of unprotected speech to ensure that a definition designed for adults is not uncritically applied to children. . . . Instead, it wishes to create a wholly new category of content-based regulation that is permissible only for speech directed at children. . . .

California's argument would fare better if there were a longstanding tradition in this country of specially restricting children's access to depictions of violence, but there is none. Certainly the books we give children to read—or read to them when they are younger—contain no shortage of gore. *Grimm's Fairy Tales*, for example, are grim indeed. As her just deserts for trying to poison Snow White, the wicked queen is made to dance in red hot slippers "till she fell dead on the floor, a sad example of envy and jealousy." Cinderella's evil stepsisters have their eyes pecked out by doves. And Hansel and Gretel (children!) kill their captor by baking her in an oven.

High school reading lists are full of similar fare. Homer's Odysseus blinds Polyphemus the Cyclops by grinding out his eye with a heated stake. . . . And Golding's *Lord of the Flies* recounts how a schoolboy called Piggy is savagely murdered by *other children* while marooned on an island.

This is not to say that minors' consumption of violent entertainment has never encountered resistance. In the 1800s, dime novels depicting crime and "penny dreadfuls" (named for their price and content) were blamed in some quarters for juvenile delinquency. . . . When motion pictures came along, they became the villains instead. . . For a time, our Court did permit broad censorship of movies because of their capacity to be "used for evil," . . . but we eventually reversed course. *Joseph Burstyn, Inc.* Radio dramas were next, and then came comic books. . . Many in the late 1940's and early 1950's blamed comic books for fostering a "preoccupation with violence and horror" among the young, leading to a rising juvenile crime rate.

California claims that video games present special problems because they are "interactive," in that the player participates in the violent action on screen and determines its outcome. The latter feature is nothing new: Since at least the publication of *The Adventures of You: Sugarcane Island* in 1969, young readers of choose-your-own-adventure stories have been able to make decisions that determine the plot by following instructions about which page to turn to. . . .

Because the Act imposes a restriction on the content of protected speech, it is invalid unless California can demonstrate that it passes strict scrutiny—that is, unless it is justified by a compelling government interest and is narrowly drawn to serve that interest. . . .

California cannot meet that standard. . . .

The State's evidence is not compelling. California relies primarily on the research of Dr. Craig Anderson and a few other research psychologists whose studies purport to show a connection between exposure to violent video games and harmful effects on children. These studies have been rejected by every court to consider them, and with good reason: They do not prove that violent video games cause minors to act aggressively (which would at least be a beginning). Instead, "[n]early all of the research is based on correlation, not evidence of causation, and most of the studies suffer from significant, admitted flaws in methodology." . . . They show at best some correlation between exposure to violent entertainment and minuscule real-world effects, such as children's feeling more aggressive or making louder noises in the few minutes after playing a violent game than after playing a nonviolent game. . . .

The Act is also seriously underinclusive in another respect—and a respect that renders irrelevant the contentions of the concurrence and the dissents that video games are qualitatively different from other portrayals of violence. The California Legislature is perfectly willing to leave this dangerous, mind-altering material in the hands of children so long as one parent (or even an aunt or uncle) says it's OK. And there are not even any requirements as to how this parental or avuncular relationship is to be verified; apparently the child's or putative parent's, aunt's, or uncle's say-so suffices. That is not how one addresses a serious social problem. . . .

California's legislation straddles the fence between (1) addressing a serious social problem and (2) helping concerned parents control their children. Both ends are legitimate, but when they affect First Amendment rights they must be pursued by means that are neither seriously underinclusive nor seriously overinclusive. See *Church of Lukumi Babalu Aye, Inc. v. Hialeah*, 508 U.S. 520 (1993). As a means of protecting children from portrayals of violence, the legislation is seriously underinclusive, not only because it excludes portrayals other than video games, but also because it permits a parental or avuncular veto. And as a means of assisting concerned parents it is seriously overinclusive because it abridges the First Amendment rights of young people whose parents (and aunts and uncles) think violent video games are a harmless pastime. . . .

☐ *Justice ALITO, with whom THE CHIEF JUSTICE joins, concurring in the judgment.*

I disagree, however, with the approach taken in the Court's opinion. In considering the application of unchanging constitutional principles to new and rapidly evolving technology, this Court should proceed with caution. We should make every effort to understand the new technology. We should take into account the possibility that developing technology may have important societal implications that will become apparent only with time. We should not jump to the conclusion that new technology is fundamentally the same as some older thing with which we are familiar. And we should not hastily dismiss the judgment of legislators, who may be in a better position than we are to assess the implications of new technology. The opinion of the Court exhibits none of this caution. . . .

There are reasons to suspect that the experience of playing violent video games just might be very different from reading a book, listening to the radio, or watching a movie or a television show. . . .

Here, the California law does not define "violent video games" with the "narrow specificity" that the Constitution demands. . . .

Although our society does not generally regard all depictions of violence as suitable for children or adolescents, the prevalence of violent depictions in children's literature and entertainment creates numerous opportunities for reasonable people to disagree about which depictions may excite "deviant" or "morbid" impulses. . . .

For these reasons, I conclude that the California violent video game law fails to provide the fair notice that the Constitution requires. And I would go no further. I would not express any view on whether a properly drawn statute would or would not survive First Amendment scrutiny. We should address that question only if and when it is necessary to do so. . . .

Today's most advanced video games create realistic alternative worlds in which millions of players immerse themselves for hours on end. These games feature visual imagery and sounds that are strikingly realistic, and in the near future video-game graphics may be virtually indistinguishable from actual video footage. Many of the games already on the market can produce high definition images, and it is predicted that it will not be long before video-game images will be seen in three dimensions. It is also forecast that video games will soon provide sensory feedback. By wearing a special vest or other device, a player will be able to experience physical sensations supposedly felt by a character on the screen. Some *amici* who support respondents foresee the day when "virtual-reality shoot-'em-ups" will allow children to "actually feel the splatting blood from the blown-off head" of a victim. . . .

If the technological characteristics of the sophisticated games that are likely to be available in the near future are combined with the characteristics of the most violent games already marketed, the result will be games that allow troubled teens to experience in an extraordinarily personal and vivid way what it would be like to carry out unspeakable acts of violence. . . .

For all these reasons, I would hold only that the particular law at issue here fails to provide the clear notice that the Constitution requires. . . . If differently framed statutes are enacted by the States or by the Federal Government, we can consider the constitutionality of those laws when cases challenging them are presented to us.

☐ *Justice THOMAS, dissenting.*

The Court's decision today does not comport with the original public understanding of the First Amendment. The majority strikes down, as facially unconstitutional, a state law that prohibits the direct sale or rental of certain video games to minors because the law "abridg[es] the freedom of speech." But I do not think the First Amendment stretches that far. The practices and beliefs of the founding generation establish that "the freedom of speech," as originally understood, does not include a right to speak to minors (or a right of minors to access speech) without going through the minors' parents or guardians. I would hold that the law at issue is not facially unconstitutional under the First Amendment, and reverse and remand for further proceedings. . . .

As originally understood, the First Amendment's protection against laws "abridging the freedom of speech" did not extend to *all* speech. "There are certain well-defined and narrowly limited classes of speech, the prevention and punishment of which have never been thought to raise any Constitutional problem." *Chaplinsky v. New Hampshire*, 315 U.S. 568 (1942). Laws regulating such speech do not "abridg[e] the freedom of speech" because such speech is understood to fall outside "the freedom of speech."

In my view, the "practices and beliefs held by the Founders" reveal another category of excluded speech: speech to minor children bypassing their parents. The historical evidence shows that the founding generation believed parents had absolute authority over their minor children and expected parents to use that authority to direct the proper development of their children. It would be absurd to suggest that such a society understood "the freedom of speech" to include a right to speak to minors (or a corresponding right of minors to access speech) without going through the minors' parents. . . The founding generation would not have considered it an abridgment of "the freedom of speech" to support parental authority by restricting speech that bypasses minors' parents. . . .

In the Puritan tradition common in the New England colonies, fathers ruled families with absolute authority. . . The Puritans rejected many customs, such as godparenthood, that they considered inconsistent with the patriarchal structure. . .

Part of the father's absolute power was the right and duty "to fill his children's minds with knowledge and . . . make them apply their knowledge in right action." . . .

The Revolution only amplified these concerns. The Republic would require virtuous citizens, which necessitated proper training from childhood. . .

Based on these views of childhood, the founding generation understood parents to have a right and duty to govern their children's growth. Parents were expected to direct the development and education of their children and ensure that bad habits did not take root. . . .

The law at the time reflected the founding generation's understanding of parent-child relations. According to Sir William Blackstone, parents were responsible for maintaining, protecting, and educat[ing] their children, and therefore had "power" over their children. *Commentaries on the Laws of England* (1765). . . .

"The freedom of speech," as originally understood, does not include a right to speak to minors without going through the minors' parents or guardians. Therefore, I cannot agree that the statute at issue is facially unconstitutional under the First Amendment.

I respectfully dissent.

☐ *Justice BREYER, dissenting.*

The majority's claim that the California statute, if upheld, would create a "new categor[y] of unprotected speech is overstated. No one here argues that depictions of violence, even extreme violence, *automatically* fall outside the First Amendment's protective scope as, for example, do obscenity and depictions of child pornography. We properly speak of *categories* of expression that lack protection when, like "child pornography," the category is broad, when it applies automatically, and when the State can prohibit everyone, including adults, from obtaining access to the material within it. But where, as here, careful analysis must precede a narrower judicial conclusion (say, denying protection to a shout of "fire" in a crowded theater, or to an effort to teach a terrorist group how to peacefully petition the United Nations), we do not normally describe the result as creating a "new category of unprotected speech." . . .

The interest that California advances in support of the statute is compelling. . . . As to the need to help parents guide their children, the Court noted in 1968 that "parental control or guidance cannot always be provided." Today, 5.3 million grade-school-age children of working parents are routinely home alone. Thus, it has, if anything, become more important to supplement parents' authority to guide their children's development.

As to the State's independent interest, we have pointed out that juveniles are more likely to show a "lack of maturity" and are "more vulnerable or susceptible to negative influences and outside pressures," and that their "character . . . is not as well formed as that of an adult." *Roper v. Simmons*, 543 U.S. 551 (2005). And we have therefore recognized "a compelling interest in protecting the physical and psychological well-being of minors."

At the same time, there is considerable evidence that California's statute significantly furthers this compelling interest. . . . There are many scientific studies that support California's views. Social scientists, for example, have found *causal* evidence that playing these games results in harm. Longitudinal studies, which measure changes over time, have found that increased exposure to violent video games causes an increase in aggression over the same period.

Experimental studies in laboratories have found that subjects randomly assigned to play a violent video game subsequently displayed more characteristics of aggression than those who played nonviolent games. . . .

Surveys of 8th and 9th grade students have found a correlation between playing violent video games and aggression. . . .

And "meta-analysis," *i.e.*, studies of all the studies, have concluded that exposure to violent video games "was positively associated with aggressive

■ IN COMPARATIVE PERSPECTIVE

Communitarianism, Feminism, and the Canadian Supreme Court's Rulings on Hate Speech and Pornography

Since the enactment of the Canadian Charter of Rights and Freedoms in 1982, the Canadian Supreme Court has actively interpreted its provisions, frequently citing rulings of the U.S. Supreme Court in support of its decisions. Indeed, on the Charter's tenth anniversary, in an interview with the *Toronto Globe and Mail* (April 17, 1992), Chief Justice Antonio Lamer observed that the Charter had "Americanized" the Canadian Supreme Court.

When dealing with challenges to laws punishing hate speech and pornographic materials, however, the Canadian Supreme Court charted a different course, expressly rejecting the principal tenets of the U.S. Supreme Court's doctrine of free speech in favor of the more communitarian approach grounded in a theory of equality. In doing so, the Canadian Supreme Court embraced the controversial position advanced unsuccessfully in the United States by some American feminists, such as Catharine MacKinnon and Andrea Dworkin. MacKinnon also participated in filing "friend of the court" briefs for the Women's Legal Education and Action Fund in both of the major cases decided by the Canadian Supreme Court.

Notably, the Canadian Charter combines a commitment to social equality and multiculturalism with a guarantee for freedom of expression. Section 1 specifies that the Charter "guarantees the rights and freedoms set out in it subject only to such reasonable limits prescribed by law as can be demonstratively justified in a free and democratic society." Freedom of expression is guaranteed in Section 2(b)'s provision that "Everyone has the following fundamental freedoms: . . . freedom of thought, belief, opinion and expression, including freedom of the press and other media of communication." That guarantee, though, appears qualified by not only the first section but also a detailed provision for equality in Section 15, which reads:

> (1) Every individual is equal before and under the law and has the right to the equal protection and equal benefit of the law without discrimination and, in particular, without discrimination based on race, national or ethnic origin, colour, religion, sex, age or physical or mental disability.
>
> (2) Subsection (1) does not preclude any law, program or activity that has as its object the amelioration of conditions of

disadvantaged individuals or groups including those that are disadvantaged because of race, national or ethnic origin, colour, religion, sex, age or mental or physical disability.

In addition, two other sections underscore the commitment to multiculturalism and gender equality. Section 27 provides that the Charter "shall be interpreted in a manner consistent with the preservation and enhancement of the multicultural heritage of Canadians." And Section 28 stipulates that, "Notwithstanding anything in this Charter, the rights and freedoms referred to in it are guaranteed equally to male and female persons."

In *Regina v. Keegstra*, 3 SCR 697 (1990), the Canadian Supreme Court confronted the application of those guarantees in a challenge to the constitutionality of a provision in the criminal code prohibiting the communication, other than in private conversation, of "hatred against any identifiable group . . . distinguished by colour, race, religion or ethnic origin." James Keegstra, a high school teacher, was tried and convicted for communicating anti-Semitic teachings to his students. His conviction, however, was overturned by the Alberta Court of Appeals on the grounds that the provision punishing hate speech violated the Charter's guarantee for freedom of expression. That decision was in turn reversed by the Canadian Supreme Court, which upheld Canada's hate-speech law. Writing for the majority, Chief Justice Dickson explained,

> Where [Section] 1 operates to accentuate a uniquely Canadian vision of a free and democratic society, however, we must not hesitate to part from the path taken in the United States. Far from requiring a less solicitous protection of Charter rights and freedoms, such independence of vision protects these rights and freedoms in a different way. As will be seen below, in my view the international commitment to eradicate hate propaganda and, most importantly, the special role given equality and multiculturalism in the Canadian Constitution necessitate a departure from the view, reasonably prevalent in America at present, that the suppression of hate propaganda is incompatible with the guarantee of free expression. . . .
>
> In my opinion, a response of humiliation and degradation from an individual targeted by hate propaganda is to be expected. A person's sense of human dignity and belonging to the community at large is closely linked to the concern and respect accorded the groups to which he or she belongs. The derision, hostility and abuse encouraged by hate propaganda therefore have a severely negative impact on the individual's sense of self-worth and acceptance. This impact may cause target group members to take drastic measures in reaction, perhaps avoiding activities which bring them into contact with non-group members or adopting attitudes and postures directed

(continues)

■ In Comparative Perspective
Communitarianism, Feminism, and the Canadian Supreme Court's Rulings on Hate Speech and Pornography (continued)

towards blending in with the majority. Such consequences bear heavily in a nation that prides itself on tolerance and the fostering of human dignity. . . .

At the core of freedom of expression lies the need to ensure that truth and the common good are attained, whether in scientific and artistic endeavors or in the process of determining the best course to take in our political affairs. Since truth and the ideal form of political and social organization can rarely, if at all, be identified with absolute certainty, it is difficult to prohibit expression without impeding the free exchange of potentially valuable information. Nevertheless, the argument from truth does not provide convincing support for the protection of hate propaganda. Taken to its extreme, this argument would require us to permit the communication of all expression, it being impossible to know with *absolute* certainty which factual statements are true, or which ideas obtain the greatest good. The problem with this extreme position, however, is that the greater the degree of certainty that a statement is erroneous or mendacious, the less the value in the quest for truth. Indeed, expression can be used to the detriment of our search for truth; the state should not be the sole arbiter of truth, but neither should we overplay the view that rationality will overcome all falsehoods in the unregulated marketplace of ideas. There is very little chance that statements intended to promote hatred against an identifiable group are true, or that their vision of society will lead to a better world. To portray such statements as crucial to truth and the betterment of the political and social milieu is therefore misguided. . . .

The connection between freedom of expression and the political process is perhaps the linchpin of the s. 2(b) guarantee, and the nature of this connection is largely derived from the Canadian commitment to democracy. Nonetheless, expression can work to undermine our commitment to democracy where employed to propagate ideas anathemic to democratic values. Hate propaganda works in just such a way, arguing as it does for a society in which the democratic process is subverted and individuals are denied respect and dignity simply because of racial or religious characteristics. This brand of expressive activity is thus wholly inimical to the democratic aspirations of the free expression guarantee. . . .

Two years after handing down the ruling in *Keegstra*, the Canadian Supreme Court then faced, in *Regina v. Butler*, 1 SCR 452 (1992), a constitutional challenge to the criminal code's provision penalizing the possession and distribution of obscenity. The code defines obscenity as "any publication a dominant characteristic of which is the undue exploitation of sex, or of sex and any one or more of . . . crime, horror, cruelty, and violence, shall be deemed to be obscene." Donald Victor Butler challenged the constitutionality of that provision after he was tried for and convicted of selling "hard core" videotapes and magazines at his "adult video" store in Winnipeg, Manitoba. In rejecting his claim that the law ran afoul of the Charter's guarantee of freedom of expression, Justice Sopinka explained:

> In determining when the exploitation of sex will be considered "undue," the courts have attempted to formulate workable tests. The most important of these is the "community standard of tolerance" test. . . . The community standards test has been the subject of extensive judicial analysis. It is the standards of the community as a whole which must be considered and not the standards of a small segment of that community such as a university community where a film was shown. . . .
>
> [T]he community standards test is concerned not with what Canadians would not tolerate being exposed to themselves, but what they would not tolerate *other* Canadians being exposed to. . . . There has been a growing recognition in recent cases that material which may be said to exploit sex in a "degrading or dehumanizing" manner will necessarily fail the community standards test. . . .
>
> Among other things, degrading or dehumanizing materials place women (and sometimes men) in positions of subordination, servile submission or humiliation. They run against the principles of equality and dignity of all human beings. In the appreciation of whether material is degrading or dehumanizing, the appearance of consent is not necessarily determinative. Consent cannot save materials that otherwise contain degrading or dehumanizing scenes. Sometimes the very appearance of consent makes the depicted acts even more degrading or dehumanizing.
>
> This type of material would, apparently, fail the community standards test not because it offends against morals but because it is perceived by public opinion to be harmful to society, particularly to women. While the accuracy of this perception is not susceptible of exact proof, there is a substantial body of opinion that holds that the portrayal of persons being subjected to degrading or dehumanizing sexual treatment results in harm, particularly to women and therefore to society as a whole. . . .
>
> The courts must determine as best they can what the community would tolerate others being exposed to on the basis of the degree of harm that may flow from such exposure. Harm in this

(continues)

■ IN COMPARATIVE PERSPECTIVE

Communitarianism, Feminism, and the Canadian Supreme Court's Rulings on Hate Speech and Pornography (continued)

context means that it predisposes persons to act in an anti-social manner as, for example, the physical or mental mistreatment of women by men, or what is perhaps debatable, the reverse. Anti-social conduct for this purpose is conduct which society formally recognizes as incompatible with its proper functioning. The stronger the inference of a risk of harm the lesser the likelihood of tolerance. The inference may be drawn from the material itself or from the material and other evidence. Similarly evidence as to the community standards is desirable but not essential.

In making this determination with respect to the three categories of pornography referred to above, the portrayal of sex coupled with violence will almost always constitute the undue exploitation of sex. Explicit sex which is degrading or dehumanizing may be undue if the risk of harm is substantial. Finally, explicit sex that is not violent and neither degrading nor dehumanizing is generally tolerated in our society and will not qualify as the undue exploitation of sex unless it employs children in its production. . . .

For further reading on Canadian constitutional politics, see Stephen Newman, ed., *Constitutional Politics in Canada and the United States* (Ithaca: State University of New York, 2004). On the debate over the censorship of pornography, see Catharine MacKinnon, *Only Words* (Cambridge, MA: Harvard University Press, 1993); Andrea Dworkin, *Intercourse* (New York: Free Press, 1987); and compare Nadine Strossen, *Defending Pornography: Free Speech, Sex, and the Fight for Women's Rights* (New York: Scribner, 1995).

behavior, aggressive cognition, and aggressive affect," and that "playing violent video games is a *causal* risk factor for long-term harmful outcomes.". . .

The upshot is that California's statute, as applied to its heartland of applications (*i.e.*, buyers under 17; extremely violent, realistic video games), imposes a restriction on speech that is modest at most. That restriction is justified by a compelling interest (supplementing parents' efforts to prevent their children from purchasing potentially harmful violent, interactive material). And there is no equally effective, less restrictive alternative. California's statute is consequently constitutional on its face—though litigants remain free to challenge the statute as applied in particular instances, including any effort by the State to apply it to minors aged 17. . . . For these reasons, I respectfully dissent.

C | *Libel*

Libel is defamation of character by print or visual presentation; slander is defamation by oral presentation. Libel prosecutions may be either criminal or civil. Criminal prosecutions for libel against the government and groups repair and maintain the peace and order of a community, whereas civil suits brought by victims of libel are for monetary damages.

English common law permitted prosecutions for seditious libel (libel of the government and government officials), as did the Alien and Sedition Acts in 1798. But in the landmark libel ruling *New York Times v. Sullivan* (1964) (excerpted below), the Court had occasion to declare the Sedition Act and seditious libel unconstitutional and inconsistent with the First Amendment.

Some states also provided criminal penalties for group libel, attacks on groups. In *Beauharnais v. Illinois*, 343 U.S. 250 (1952), the Court upheld an Illinois law making it unlawful to publish or exhibit any writing or picture portraying the "depravity, criminality, unchastity, or lack of virtue of a class of citizens, of any race, color, creed or religion."

Beauharnais, head of the White Circle League, had circulated on the streets of Chicago a leaflet containing derogatory statements about blacks and urging the police to protect whites from their "rapes, knives, guns, and marijuana." But dissenting Justice Douglas warned: "Today a white man stands convicted for protesting in unseemly language against our decisions invalidating restrictive covenants. Tomorrow a Negro will be hauled before a court for denouncing lynch law in heated terms." Indeed, *Beauharnais* was widely criticized for failing to consider the close relationship between group libel and seditious libel, and allowing an important area of public discussion—the role of interest groups in American politics—to fall outside of First Amendment protection. Still, although in *Ashton v. Kentucky*, 384 U.S. 195 (1966), Justice Douglas struck down a criminal libel law as unconstitutionally vague, the Court has never expressly repudiated *Beauharnais* or the concept of group libel. Indeed, the Court often cites *Beauharnais* in support of maintaining that libel or defamation receives no First Amendment protection; thus, *Beauharnais* was cited approvingly in *R.A.V. v. City of St. Paul*, 505 U.S. 377 (1992) (see excerpt above), even though the Court struck down St. Paul's "hate-speech" law. Moreover, dissenting in *Smith v. Collin*, 436 U.S. 916 (1978), Justices Blackmun and Rehnquist underscored that "*Beauharnais* has never been overruled or formally limited in any way."

Civil libel suits may seek two kinds of damages: (1) compensatory damages as reimbursement for an individual's actual financial loss resulting from, for example, loss of employment or reputation as a result of being libeled; and (2) punitive damages, awarded as compensation for mental suffering due to a libelous attack, that aim to punish the publisher.

Awards for libel by public officials are virtually impossible to win. Members of Congress enjoy absolute immunity under the speech and debate clause, subject to the ruling in *Hutchinson v. Proxmire*, 443 U.S. 111 (1979) (see Vol. 1, Ch. 5). In *Barr v. Matteo*, 360 U.S. 564 (1959), the Court extended immunity to all federal administrative officials for statements made within the "outer perimeter" of their official duties.

Not until *New York Times v. Sullivan* (1964) (excerpted below) did the Court set down a constitutional standard for determining libel of public officials and "public figures." There Justice Brennan declared that public officials may win libel suits only on showing "actual malice," that is, "with knowledge that it was false or with reckless disregard of whether it was false or not."

The *New York Times* ruling proved controversial and makes it exceedingly difficult for public officials and public figures to win libel suits. Some critics, following Justices Black and Douglas in their concurring opinion in *New York Times*, argue that the Court did not go far enough toward safeguarding First Amendment freedoms and predict problems in applying the test. Other critics counter that the *New York Times* rule renders public officials defenseless against all but the most vicious attacks. As Justice Fortas observed in *St. Amant v. Thompson*, 390 U.S. 727 (1968), "The First Amendment does not require that we license shotgun attacks on public officials in virtually unlimited open-season. The occupation of public officeholder does not forfeit one's membership in the human race."

Following *New York Times*, the Court confronted the problems in defining "public officials" and "public figures" and over whether the actual malice test should apply to both. In *Rosenblatt v. Baer*, 383 U.S. 75 (1966), the Court held that a former ski instructor and county commissioner was a public figure, who had to prove actual malice in a libel suit over reports alleging his involvement in city corruption. A year later in two cases, *Associated Press v. Walker*, 388 U.S. 130 (1967), and *Curtis Publishing Company v. Butts*, 388 U.S. 130 (1967), both involving public figures, the Warren Court split 5–4, with the chief justice as the swing vote.

In the *Associated Press* case, Edwin A. Walker, a well-known, retired, right-wing general, sought libel damages for a news report that he personally "took command" of a violent crowd protesting the enrollment of James Meredith, a black man, at the University of Mississippi. Walker claimed to have been libeled as a private individual and won a jury award of $500,000 in compensatory damages and $300,000 in punitive damages. However, the trial judge found no malice in the publication and struck down the latter award, which an appellate court affirmed. The Supreme Court unanimously reversed, but disagreed on the standard to be applied. Justices Brennan, Douglas, Black, and White, along with Chief Justice Warren, thought that the actual malice test should apply. But Justices Clark, Stewart, and Fortas joined an opinion by Justice Harlan allowing public figures (unlike public officials) to recover damages on showing only a "highly unreasonable conduct constituting an extreme departure from the standards of investigation and reporting ordinarily adhered to by responsible publishers." However, in *Curtis Publishing Company*, Harlan and three supporters in *Walker* were joined by Chief Justice Warren in upholding Wally Butts's libel award of $460,000 for an article in *The Saturday Evening Post*, alleging that Butts, a coach at the University of Georgia, conspired to rig a football game between his team and the University of Alabama. Although Butts, like Walker, was found to be a public figure, Harlan reasoned that here the publication was not "hot news" and, therefore, his standard of highly unreasonable conduct in the investigation and reporting of the story should apply. Although Chief Justice Warren concurred, he nevertheless agreed with the four dissenters that the actual malice test should apply to both public officials and public figures.

The Warren Court failed to reach complete agreement on the application of the actual malice test and, moreover, it never found a private individual who was not a public figure.[1] Finally, in *Gertz v. Robert Welch, Inc.* (1974) (excerpted below), the Burger Court found a "private individual" and announced a new libel standard for that category of persons—private individuals must prove only that a publisher was negligent in failing to exercise normal care in reporting. Two years later in *Time Inc. v. Firestone*, 424 U.S. 448 (1976), Justice Rehnquist reaffirmed that ruling in holding that a divorcée of the heir to the fortune of the Firestone Corporation was not a public figure, even though she had held news conferences about her divorce. *Time* magazine mistakenly referred to her as an "adulteress," when the divorce decree had not specifically found that she had committed adultery.[2]

In *Gertz*, Justice Powell emphasized that "under the First Amendment there is no such thing as a false idea. However pernicious an opinion may seem, we depend for its correction not on the conscience of judges and juries but on the competition of other ideas. But there is no constitutional value in false statements of fact." He thereby suggested that statements of "opinion" might be exempt from state libel laws. But in *Milkovich v. Lorain Journal Co.*, 497 U.S. 1 (1990), the Rehnquist Court rejected that implication. Michael Milkovich Sr., a high school wrestling coach, sued a small daily newspaper, owned by the Lorain Journal Company, for an article that asserted that he had lied under oath during an investigation of a melee in the school's gymnasium. The newspaper contended that its sportswriter was merely stating an "opinion" for which under *Gertz* he could not be held libel. Writing for the Court, however, Chief Justice Rehnquist rejected that interpretation of *Gertz*:

> [W]e do not think this passage from *Gertz* was intended to create a wholesale defamation exemption for anything that might be labeled "opinion." . . . Not only would such an interpretation be contrary to the tenor and context of the passage, but it would also ignore the fact that expressions of "opinion" may often imply an assertion of objective fact.
>
> If a speaker says, "In my opinion John Jones is a liar," he implies a knowledge of facts which lead to the conclusion that Jones told an untruth. Even if the speaker states the facts upon which he bases his opinion, if those facts are either incorrect or incomplete, or if his assessment of them is erroneous, the statement may still imply a false assertion of fact. Simply couching such statements in terms of opinion does not dispel these implications; and the statement, "In my opinion Jones is a liar," can cause as much damage to reputation as the statement, "Jones is a liar." . . .
>
> Apart from their reliance on the *Gertz dictum*, respondents do not really contend that a statement such as, "In my opinion John Jones is a liar," should be protected by a separate privilege for "opinion" under the First Amendment. But they do contend that in every defamation case the First Amendment mandates an inquiry into whether a statement is "opinion" or "fact," and that only the latter statements may be actionable.
>
> They propose that a number of factors developed by the lower courts (in what we hold was a mistaken reliance on the *Gertz dictum*) be considered in deciding which is which. But we think the "breathing space" which "freedoms of expression require in order to survive," [*Philadelphia Newspapers, Inc. v.*] *Hepps*, [475 U.S. 767 (1986)] (quoting *New York Times*), is adequately secured by existing constitutional doctrine without the creation of an artificial dichotomy between "opinion" and "fact."
>
> Foremost, we think *Hepps* stands for the proposition that a statement on matters of public concern must be provable as false before there can be liability under state defamation law, at least in situations, like the present, where a media defendant is involved.
>
> Thus, unlike the statement, "In my opinion Mayor Jones is a liar," the statement, "In my opinion Mayor Jones shows abysmal ignorance by accepting the teachings of Marx and Lenin," would not be actionable.

In other rulings the Court has made it somewhat easier for public officials and public figures, while somewhat more difficult for private individuals, to win libel awards. *Herbert v. Lando*, 441 U.S. 153 (1979), for example, held that at trial attorneys could probe the editorial process, questioning editors and reporters, to prove actual malice; members of the press have no privilege from testifying in libel cases and answering questions about editorial prepublication decisions. In *Philadelphia Newspapers, Inc. v. Hepps*, 475 U.S. 767 (1986), a bare majority agreed that private individuals bringing libel actions have the burden of showing the falsity in reports or stories that touch on matters of public concern. Subsequently, in *Masson v. The New Yorker Magazine*, 501 U.S. 496 (1991), the Court dealt with the complicated question of whether actual malice may be inferred in a libel suit based on evidence of fabricated quotations. Writing for the Court, Justice Kennedy held that the First Amendment does not provide a shield for writers who fabricate quotations and that the "actual malice" test applies.

The Court, however, continues to refuse to recognize in its First Amendment jurisprudence the difference between libel actions and suits over invasion of privacy. In tort law and common law, individuals may sue for basically four kinds of privacy interests: (1) intrusions into their private affairs, causing mental distress; (2) public disclosure of embarrassing facts damaging to their reputation; (3) publicity placing them in a false light; and (4) appropriation of their name or likeness without their permission.[3] In suits for invasion of privacy, unlike those for libel, truth is no defense; indeed, that is the basic difference between the two—truth is always a defense against libel, whereas in privacy suits it is the actual intrusion on, and truthful disclosure of, private affairs per se that causes mental suffering and injury to reputation.

In giving priority to First Amendment freedoms, the Court applies its tests for libel in cases involving invasion of privacy as well. As the Court explained, in *Time, Inc. v. Hill*, 385 U.S. 374 (1967), "We create a risk of serious impairment of the indispensable service of a free press in a free society if we saddle the press with the impossible burden of verifying to a certainty the facts associated with news articles with a person's name, picture, or portrait, particularly as related to nondefamatory matter." In this case, the Hill family sued *Life* magazine for a pictorial essay on the opening of a play, *The Desperate Hours*, which was based on the Hill family's experiences as hostages of three escaped convicts. The *Life* account, though, failed to differentiate between the truth and fiction in the play, and the Hills sued for invasion of privacy and portrayal of them in false light. The Court (with only Justice Fortas dissenting) reversed a lower court's award to the Hills on the grounds that the opening of the play was a matter of public interest.

Seven years later, in *Cantrell v. Forest City Publishing Company*, 419 U.S. 245 (1974), Margaret Cantrell and her children brought an invasion of privacy suit against the Forest City Publishing Company for a follow-up story on a bridge disaster that a year before had claimed the life of her husband. The story inaccurately portrayed the Cantrells as destitute after the bridge collapsed, and Mrs. Cantrell sued for invasion of privacy and misrepresentation. At trial, the judge instructed the jury to find the publisher liable on the *New York Times* actual malice test. On appeal, the Court refused to consider whether states may constitutionally apply more relaxed standards of liability for invasion of privacy than for libel.

In *Cox Broadcasting Corporation v. Cohn* (1975) (excerpted below), however, the Court struck down a privacy statute making it a misdemeanor to name or identify a rape victim, in a case brought by the father of a deceased rape victim against Cox Broadcasting Corporation for identifying his daughter as a rape victim in a television broadcast.[4] On a vote of 6–3 in *The Florida Star v. B.J.F.*, 491 U.S. 524 (1989), the justices also overturned a civil award against a newspaper for truthfully reporting, in violation of a state statute, the name of a rape victim. But there the Court suggested that *Cohn* was limited to actual public records.

Notes

1. See *Greenbelt Co-op. v. Bresler*, 398 U.S. 6 (1970) (use of term *blackmail* when characterizing the conduct of a real estate developer, who was deemed to be a public figure, seeking zoning variances was not libel); *Monitor Patriot Co. v. Roy*, 401 U.S. 265, (1971) (held candidates for elective office were public officials or public figures subject to actual malice test); *Rosenbloom v. Metromedia*, 403 U.S. 29 (1971) (held that a distributor of nudist magazines, who was called a "smut peddler," but was later acquitted of obscenity charges, had to prove actual malice).

2. See also *Wolston v. Reader's Digest*, 443 US 157 (1979) (holding alleged KGB spy not a public figure).

3. See William Prosser, "Privacy," 48 *California Law Review* 383 (1960).

4. See, however, *Zacchini v. Scripps-Howard Broadcasting Corporation*, 433 U.S. 562 (1977) (holding 5–4 that the First Amendment does not immunize news media from a suit brought by a "human cannonball" for appropriation of names and likeness in media coverage of the stunt that arguably diminished its value).

Selected Bibliography

Gertz, Elmer. *Gertz v. Robert Welch, Inc.: The Story of a Landmark Libel Case*. Carbondale: Southern Illinois University Press, 1992.

Hall, Kermit, and Urofsky, Melvin. *New York Times v. Sullivan: Civil Rights, Libel Law, and the Free Press*. Lawrence: University of Kansas Press, 2014.

Levine, Lee, and Wermiel, Stephen. *The Progeny: Justice William J. Brennan's Fight to Save New York Times v. Sullivan.* Chicago: ABN Press, 2014.

Lewis, Anthony. *Make No Law: The Sullivan Case and the First Amendment.* New York: Random House, 1991.

Milo, Dario. *Defamation and Freedom of Speech.* New York: Oxford University Press, 2008.

Robinson, Eric. *Reckless Disregard: St. Amant v. Thompson and the Transformation of Libel Law.* Baton Rouge: Louisiana State University Press, 2018.

Smolla, Rodney. *Jerry Falwell v. Larry Flynt: The First Amendment on Trial.* New York: St. Martin's, 1988.

Solove, Daniel. *The Future of Reputation: Gossip, Rumor, and Privacy on the Internet.* New Haven, CT: Yale University Press, 2007.

Spicer, Robert. *Free Speech and False Speech: Political Deception and Its Legal Limits.* New York: Macmillan, 2018.

■ THE DEVELOPMENT OF LAW
Other Important Rulings on Libel

CASE	VOTE	RULING
Herbert v. Lando, 441 U.S. 153 (1979)	5–4	Trial attorneys may probe the editorial process, questioning editors and reporters, to prove "actual malice." In the preparation of news stories, reporters have no privilege from testifying in libel cases and answering questions about prepublication decisions.
Keeton v. Hustler Magazine, Inc., 465 U.S. 770 (1984)	6–3	Libel suits may be brought in any jurisdiction in which a magazine is sold, allowing forum shopping.
Anderson v. Liberty Lobby 477 U.S. 242 (1986)	6–3	Libel actions should go to trial only if there is clear and convincing evidence of actual malice.

(continues)

■ THE DEVELOPMENT OF LAW
Other Important Rulings on Libel (continued)

CASE	VOTE	RULING
Philadelphia Newspapers, Inc. v. Hepps, 475 U.S. 767 (1986)	5–4	Held that private individuals bringing libel actions have the burden of showing the falsity in reports

or stories that touch on matters of public concern. The majority thus shifted the burden of showing falsity in stories of public concern to the plaintiff. Chief Justice Burger and Justices Stevens, White, and Rehnquist dissented.

CASE	VOTE	RULING
Masson v. The New Yorker, 501 U.S. 496 (1991)	8–1	The First Amendment does not provide a shield for writers who fabricate quotes and the "actual

malice" test of "knowing or reckless disregard" of the truth or falsity of a quotation applies.

CASE	VOTE	RULING
Hustler Magazine v. Falwell, 485 U.S. 46 (1988)	9–0	Public figure forbidden from recovering damages for emotional distress due to advertisement parody.

CASE	VOTE	RULING
Milkovich v. Lorain Journal Co., 497 U.S. 1 (1990)	7–2	Held that there is no exception in the application of libel laws for statements

of opinion, although defendants may not be held liable for statements that cannot be proved true or false. The First Amendment, in Chief Justice Rehnquist's words, does not create "a wholesale defamation exemption for anything that might be labeled opinion."

New York Times Company v. Sullivan

376 U.S. 254, 84 S.CT. 710 (1964)

Justice Brennan sets forth the pertinent facts at the outset of his opinion for the Court. The advertisement that gave rise to the litigation leading to this landmark ruling is reprinted here.

The Court's decision was unanimous, and the opinion was announced by Justice Brennan. Justices Black and Goldberg concurred and were joined by Justice Douglas.

■ ■ ■

☐ *Justice BRENNAN delivered the opinion of the Court.*

We are required in this case to determine for the first time the extent to which the constitutional protections for speech and press limit a State's power to award damages in a libel action brought by a public official against critics of his official conduct.

Respondent L. B. Sullivan is one of the three elected Commissioners of the City of Montgomery, Alabama. . . . He brought this civil libel action against the four individual petitioners, who are Negroes and Alabama clergymen, and against petitioner the New York Times Company, a New York corporation which publishes the *New York Times*, a daily newspaper. . . .

Respondent's complaint alleged that he had been libeled by statements in a full-page advertisement that was carried in the *New York Times* on March 29, 1960. Entitled "Heed Their Rising Voices," the advertisement began by stating that "As the whole world knows by now, thousands of Southern Negro students are engaged in widespread non-violent demonstrations in positive affirmation of the right to live in human dignity as guaranteed by the U.S. Constitution and the Bill of Rights." . . . The text concluded with an appeal for funds for three purposes: support of the student movement, "the struggle for the right-to-vote," and the legal defense of Dr. Martin Luther King Jr., leader of the movement, against a perjury indictment then pending in Montgomery. . . .

Of the 10 paragraphs of text in the advertisement, the third and a portion of the sixth were the basis of respondent's claim of libel. They read as follows:

Third paragraph:

> In Montgomery, Alabama, after students sang "My Country, 'Tis of Thee" on the State Capitol steps, their leaders were expelled from school, and truckloads of police armed with shotguns and tear-gas ringed the Alabama State College Campus. When the entire student body protested to state authorities by refusing to re-register, their dining hall was padlocked in an attempt to starve them into submission.

Sixth paragraph:

> Again and again the Southern violators have answered Dr. King's peaceful protests with intimidation and violence. They

have bombed his home almost killing his wife and child. They have assaulted his person. They have arrested him seven times—for "speeding," "loitering" and similar "offenses." And now they have charged him with "perjury"—a *felony* under which they could imprison him for *ten years.* . . .

Although neither of these statements mentions respondent by name, he contended that the word "police" in the third paragraph referred to him as the Montgomery Commissioner who supervised the Police Department, so that he was being accused of "ringing" the campus with police. He further claimed that the paragraph would be read as imputing to the police, and hence to him, the padlocking of the dining hall in order to starve the students into submission. As to the sixth paragraph, he contended that since arrests are ordinarily made by the police, the statement "They have arrested [Dr. King] seven times" would be read as referring to him. . . .

It is uncontroverted that some of the statements contained in the two paragraphs were not accurate descriptions of events which occurred in Montgomery. Although Negro students staged a demonstration on the State Capital steps, they sang the National Anthem and not "My Country, 'Tis of Thee." Although nine students were expelled by the State Board of Education, this was not for leading the demonstration at the Capitol, but for demanding service at a lunch counter in the Montgomery County Courthouse on another day. Not the entire student body, but most of it, had protested the expulsion, not by refusing to register, but by boycotting classes on a single day; virtually all the students did register for the ensuing semester. . . . Although the police were deployed near the campus in large numbers on three occasions, they did not at any time "ring" the campus, and they were not called to the campus in connection with the demonstration on the State Capitol steps, as the third paragraph implied. Dr. King had not been arrested seven times, but only four. . . .

Respondent made no effort to prove that he suffered actual pecuniary loss as a result of the alleged libel.★ . . .

The trial judge submitted the case to the jury under instructions that the statements in the advertisement were "libelous per se" and were not privileged, so that petitioners might be held liable if the jury found that they had published the advertisement and that the statements were made "of and concerning" respondent. The jury was instructed that, because the statements were libelous *per se,* "the law . . . implies legal injury from the bare fact of publication itself," "falsity and malice are presumed," "general damages need not be alleged or proved but are presumed," and "punitive damages may be awarded by the jury even though the amount of actual damages is neither found nor shown." [The jury found for the respondent and awarded $500,000 in damages.] . . .

We reverse the judgment. We hold that the rule of law applied by the Alabama courts is constitutionally deficient for failure to provide the safeguards for freedom of speech and of the press that are required by the First and Fourteenth Amendments in a libel action brought by a public official

---

★Approximately 394 copies of the edition of the *Times* containing the advertisement were circulated in Alabama. Of these, about 35 copies were distributed in Montgomery County. The total circulation of the *Times* for that day was approximately 650,000 copies.

against critics of his official conduct. We further hold that under the proper safeguards the evidence presented in this case is constitutionally insufficient to support the judgment for respondent.

■ I

We may dispose at the outset of two grounds asserted to insulate the judgment of the Alabama courts from constitutional scrutiny. The first is the proposition relied on by the State Supreme Court—that "The Fourteenth Amendment is directed against State action and not private action." That proposition has no application to this case. Although this is a civil lawsuit between private parties, the Alabama courts have applied a state rule of law which petitioners claim to impose invalid restrictions on their constitutional freedoms of speech and press. . . .

The second contention is that the constitutional guarantees of freedom of speech and of the press are inapplicable here, at least so far as the *Times* is concerned, because the allegedly libelous statements were published as part of a paid, "commercial" advertisement. The argument relies on *Valentine v. Chrestensen*, 316 U.S. 52 [(1942)], where the Court held that a city ordinance forbidding street distribution of commercial and business advertising matter did not abridge the First Amendment freedoms, even as applied to a handbill having a commercial message on one side but a protest against certain official action on the other. The reliance is wholly misplaced. . . .

The publication here was not a "commercial" advertisement in the sense in which the word was used in *Chrestensen*. It communicated information, expressed opinion, recited grievances, protested claimed abuses, and sought financial support on behalf of a movement whose existence and objectives are matters of the highest public interest and concern. . . . That the *Times* was paid for publishing the advertisement is as immaterial in this connection as is the fact that newspapers and books are sold. Any other conclusion would discourage newspapers from carrying "editorial advertisements" of this type, and so might shut off an important outlet for the promulgation of information and ideas by persons who do not themselves have access to publishing facilities—who wish to exercise their freedom of speech even though they are not members of the press. . . .

■ II

[W]e consider this case against the background of a profound national commitment to the principle that debate on public issues should be uninhibited, robust, and wide-open, and that it may well include vehement, caustic, and sometimes unpleasantly sharp attacks on government and public officials. The present advertisement, as an expression of grievance and protest on one of the major public issues of our time, would seem clearly to qualify for the constitutional protection. The question is whether it forfeits that protection by the falsity of some of its factual statements and by its alleged defamation of respondent.

Authoritative interpretations of the First Amendment guarantees have consistently refused to recognize an exception for any test of truth—whether administered by judges, juries, or administrative officials—and especially one that puts the burden of proving truth on the speaker. The constitutional protection does not turn upon "the truth, popularity, or social utility of the ideas and beliefs which are offered." . . .

Injury to official reputation error affords no more warrant for repressing speech that would otherwise be free than does factual error. Where judicial officers are involved, this Court has held that concern for the dignity and reputation of the courts does not justify the punishment as criminal contempt of criticism of the judge or his decision. This is true even though the utterance contains "half-truths" and "misinformation." Such repression can be justified, if at all, only by a clear and present danger of the obstruction of justice. . . .

If neither factual error nor defamatory content suffices to remove the constitutional shield from criticism of official conduct, the combination of the two elements is no less inadequate. This is the lesson to be drawn from the great controversy over the Sedition Act of 1798, which first crystallized a national awareness of the central meaning of the First Amendment. . . .

Although the Sedition Act was never tested in this Court, the attack upon its validity has carried the day in the court of history. Fines levied in its prosecution were repaid by Act of Congress on the ground that it was unconstitutional. . . . Jefferson, as President, pardoned those who had been convicted and sentenced under the Act and remitted their fines. . . .

There is no force in respondent's argument that the constitutional limitations implicit in the history of the Sedition Act apply only to Congress and not to the States. It is true that the First Amendment was originally addressed only to action by the Federal Government. . . . But this distinction was eliminated with the adoption of the Fourteenth Amendment and the application to the States of the First Amendment's restrictions.

What a State may not constitutionally bring about by means of a criminal statute is likewise beyond the reach of its civil law of libel. The fear of damage awards under a rule such as that invoked by the Alabama courts here may be markedly more inhibiting than the fear of prosecution under a criminal statute. Alabama, for example, has a criminal libel law which subjects to prosecution "any person who speaks, writes, or prints of and concerning another any accusation falsely and maliciously importing the commission by such person of a felony, or any other indictable offense involving moral turpitude," and which allows as punishment upon conviction a fine not exceeding $500 and a prison sentence of six months. Presumably a person charged with violation of this statute enjoys ordinary criminal-law safeguards such as the requirements of an indictment and of proof beyond a reasonable doubt. These safeguards are not available to the defendant in a civil action. The judgment awarded in this case—without the need for any proof of actual pecuniary loss—was one thousand times greater than the maximum fine provided by the Alabama criminal statute, and one hundred times greater than that provided by the Sedition Act. . . . Whether or not a newspaper can survive a succession of such judgments, the pall of fear and timidity imposed upon those who would give voice to public criticism is an atmosphere in which the First Amendment freedoms cannot survive. . . .

The state rule of law is not saved by its allowance of the defense of truth. . . . A rule compelling the critic of official conduct to guarantee the truth of all his factual assertions—and to do so on pain of libel judgments virtually unlimited in amount—leads to a comparable "self-censorship." Allowance of the defense of truth, with the burden of proving it on the defendant, does not mean that only false speech will be deterred. . . . Under such a rule, would-be critics of official conduct may be deterred from voicing their criticism, even though it is believed to be true and even though it is in fact true, because of doubt whether it can be proved in court or fear of the expense of having to do so. They tend to make only statements which "steer far wider of the unlawful zone." The rule thus dampens the vigor and limits the variety of public debate. It is inconsistent with the First and Fourteenth Amendments.

The constitutional guarantees require, we think, a federal rule that prohibits a public official from recovering damages for a defamatory falsehood relating to his official conduct unless he proves that the statement was made with "actual malice"—that is, with knowledge that it was false or with reckless disregard of whether it was false or not. . . .

Such a privilege for criticism of official conduct is appropriately analogous to the protection accorded a public official when *he* is sued for libel by a private citizen. In *Barr v. Matteo*, 360 U.S. 564 [(1959)], this Court held the utterance of a federal official to be absolutely privileged if made "within the outer perimeter" of his duties. The States accord the same immunity to statements of their highest officers, although some differentiate their lesser officials and qualify the privilege they enjoy. But all hold that all officials are protected unless actual malice can be proved. The reason for the official privilege is said to be that the threat of damage suits would otherwise "inhibit the fearless, vigorous, and effective administration of policies of government" and "dampen the ardor of all but the most resolute, or the most irresponsible, in the unflinching discharge of their duties." Analogous considerations support the privilege for the citizen-critic of government. It is as much his duty to criticize as it is the official's duty to administer. As Madison said, "the censorial power is in the people over the Government, and not in the Government over the people." It would give public servants an unjustified preference over the public they serve, if critics of official conduct did not have a fair equivalent of the immunity granted to the officials themselves.

We conclude that such a privilege is required by the First and Fourteenth Amendments.

■ III

We hold today that the Constitution delimits a State's power to award damages for libel in actions brought by public officials against critics of their official conduct. Since this is such an action, the rule requiring proof of actual malice is applicable. . . .

[T]he proof presented to show actual malice lacks the convincing clarity which the constitutional standard demands, and hence that it would not constitutionally sustain the judgment for respondent under the proper rule of law. . . .

We also think the evidence was constitutionally defective in another respect: it was incapable of supporting the jury's finding that the allegedly libelous statements were made "of and concerning" respondent. . . . There was no reference to respondent in the advertisement, either by name or official position. A number of the allegedly libelous statements—the charges that the dining hall was padlocked and that Dr. King's home was bombed, his person assaulted, and a perjury prosecution instituted against him—did not even concern the police; despite the ingenuity of the arguments which would attach this significance to the word "They," it is plain that these statements could not reasonably be read as accusing respondent of personal involvement in the acts in question. . . .

The judgment of the Supreme Court of Alabama is reversed and the case is remanded to that court for further proceedings not inconsistent with this opinion.

Reversed and remanded.

☐ *Justice BLACK, with whom Justice DOUGLAS joins, concurring.*

I base my vote to reverse on the belief that the First and Fourteenth Amendments not merely "delimit" a State's power to award damages to "public officials against critics of their official conduct" but completely prohibit a State from exercising such a power. The Court goes on to hold that a State can subject such critics to damages if "actual malice" can be proved against them. "Malice," even as defined by the Court, is an elusive, abstract concept, hard to prove and hard to disprove. The requirement that malice be proved provides at best an evanescent protection for the right critically to discuss public affairs and certainly does not measure up to the sturdy safeguard embodied in the First Amendment. Unlike the Court, therefore, I vote to reverse exclusively on the ground that the *Times* and the individual defendants had an absolute, unconditional constitutional right to publish in the *Times* advertisement their criticisms of the Montgomery agencies and officials.

Gertz v. Robert Welch, Inc.

418 U.S. 323, 94 S.CT. 2997 (1974)

Elmer Gertz was a Chicago lawyer hired to sue a policeman by a family whose son had been killed by the officer. The John Birch Society in its magazine *American Opinion* charged that Gertz was a "Leninist" and "Communist-fronter" and that the lawsuit against the policeman was part of a nationwide communist conspiracy to discredit law enforcement. Gertz sued Robert Welch, publisher of the magazine, for libel in federal district court. That court held for the publisher on applying the *New York Times v. Sullivan* actual malice rule. Gertz appealed to the United States Court of Appeals for the Seventh Circuit, which affirmed the lower court's ruling, and finally to the Supreme Court.

The Court's decision was 5–4, and the majority's opinion was announced by Justice Powell. Justice Blackmun concurred. Dissents were by Chief Justice Burger and Justices Douglas, Brennan, and White.

■ ■ ■

☐ *Justice POWELL delivered the opinion of the Court.*

We begin with the common ground. Under the First Amendment there is no such thing as a false idea. However pernicious an opinion may seem, we depend for its correction not on the conscience of judges and juries but on the competition of other ideas. But there is no constitutional value in false statements of fact. Neither the intentional lie nor the careless error materially advances society's interest in "uninhibited, robust, and wide-open" debate on public issues. *New York Times Co. v. Sullivan*, [376 U.S. 254 (1964)]. They belong to that category of utterances which "are no essential part of any exposition of ideas, and are of such slight social value as a step to truth that any benefit that may be derived from them is clearly outweighed by the social interest in order and morality." *Chaplinsky v. New Hampshire* [315 U.S. 568] (1942).

Although the erroneous statement of fact is not worthy of constitutional protection, it is nevertheless inevitable in free debate. . . . And punishment of error runs the risk of inducing a cautious and restrictive exercise of the constitutionally guaranteed freedoms of speech and press. Our decisions recognize that a rule of strict liability that compels a publisher or broadcaster to guarantee the accuracy of his factual assertions may lead to intolerable self-censorship. . . . The First Amendment requires that we protect some falsehood in order to protect speech that matters.

The need to avoid self-censorship by the news media is, however, not the only societal value at issue. If it were, this Court would have embraced long ago the view that publishers and broadcasters enjoy an unconditional and indefeasible immunity from liability for defamation.

The legitimate state interest underlying the law of libel is the compensation of individuals for the harm inflicted on them by defamatory falsehood. We would not lightly require the State to abandon this purpose, for, as Justice STEWART has reminded us, the individual's right to the protection of his own good name

> reflects no more than our basic concept of the essential dignity and worth of every human being—a concept at the root of any decent system of ordered liberty. The protection of private personality, like the protection of life itself, is left primarily to the individual States under the Ninth and Tenth Amendments. But this does not mean that the right is entitled to any less recognition by this Court as a basic of our constitutional system. *Rosenblatt v. Baer*, 383 U.S. 75 (1966) (concurring opinion). . . .

The *New York Times* standard defines the level of constitutional protection appropriate to the context of defamation of a public person. . . . For the reasons stated below, we conclude that the state interest in compensating-injury to the reputation of private individuals requires that a different rule should obtain with respect to them. . . .

[W]e have no difficulty in distinguishing among defamation plaintiffs. The first remedy of any victim of defamation is self-help—using available opportunities to contradict the lie or correct the error and thereby to minimize its adverse impact on reputation. Public officials and public figures usually enjoy significantly greater access to the channels of effective communication and hence have a more realistic opportunity to counteract false statements then private individuals normally enjoy. Private individuals are therefore more vulnerable to injury, and the state interest in protecting them is correspondingly greater.

More important than the likelihood that private individuals will lack effective opportunities for rebuttal, there is a compelling normative consideration underlying the distinction between public and private defamation plaintiffs. An individual who decides to seek governmental office must accept certain necessary consequences of that involvement in public affairs. He runs the risk of closer public scrutiny than might otherwise be the case. . . .

Those classed as public figures stand in a similar position. Hypothetically, it may be possible for someone to become a public figure through no purposeful action of his own, but the instances of truly involuntary public figures must be exceedingly rare. For the most part those who attain this status have assumed roles of especial prominence in the affairs of society. Some occupy positions of such persuasive power and influence that they are deemed public figures for all purposes. More commonly, those classed as public figures have thrust themselves to the forefront of particular public controversies in order to influence the resolution of the issues involved. In either event, they invite attention and comment.

Even if the foregoing generalities do not obtain in every instance, the communications media are entitled to act on the assumption that public officials and public figures have voluntarily exposed themselves to increased risk of injury from defamatory falsehood concerning them. No such assumption is justified with respect to a private individual. He has not accepted public office or assumed an "influential role in ordering society." He has relinquished no part of his interest in the protection of his own good name, and consequently he has a more compelling call on the courts for redress of injury inflicted by defamatory falsehood. Thus, private individuals are not only more vulnerable to injury than public officials and public figures: they are also more deserving of recovery.

For these reasons we conclude that the States should retain substantial latitude in their efforts to enforce a legal remedy for defamatory falsehood injurious to the reputation of a private individual. The extension of the *New York Times* test . . . would abridge this legitimate state interest to a degree that we find unacceptable. And it would occasion the additional difficulty of forcing state and federal judges to decide on an *ad hoc* basis which publications address issues of "general or public interest" and which do not—to determine, in the words of Justice MARSHALL, "what information is relevant to self-government," *Rosenbloom v. Metromedia, Inc.*, [403 U.S. 29 (1971)]. We doubt the wisdom of committing this task to the conscience of judges. . . .

We hold that, so long as they do not impose liability without fault, the States may define for themselves the appropriate standard of liability for a publisher or broadcaster of defamatory falsehood injurious to a private individual. This approach provides a more equitable boundary between the competing concerns involved here. It recognizes the strength of the legitimate state interest in compensating private individuals for wrongful injury to reputation, yet shields the press and broadcast media from the rigors of strict liability for defamation. At least this conclusion obtains where, as here, the substance of the defamatory statement "makes substantial danger to reputation apparent." This phrase places in perspective the conclusion we announce today. . . .

Our accommodation of the competing values at stake in defamation suits by private individuals allows the States to impose liability on the publisher or broadcaster of defamatory falsehood on a less demanding showing than that required by *New York Times*. This conclusion is not based on a belief that the considerations which prompted the adoption of the *New York Times* privilege for defamation of public officials and its extension to public figures are wholly inapplicable to the context of private individuals. Rather, we endorse this approach in recognition of the strong and legitimate state interest in compensating private individuals for injury to reputation. But this counter-vailing state interest extends no further than compensation for actual injury. For the reasons stated below, we hold that the States may not permit recovery of presumed or punitive damages, at least when liability is not based on a showing of knowledge of falsity or reckless disregard for the truth.

The common law of defamation is an oddity of tort law, for it allows recovery of purportedly compensatory damages without evidence of actual loss. Under the traditional rules pertaining to actions for libel, the existence of injury is presumed from the fact of publication. Juries may award substan-tial sums as compensation for supposed damage to reputation without any proof that such harm actually occurred. The largely uncontrolled discretion of juries to award damages where there is no loss unnecessarily compounds the potential of any system of liability for defamatory falsehood to inhibit the vigorous exercise of First Amendment freedoms. Additionally, the doctrine of presumed damages invites juries to punish unpopular opinion rather than to compensate individuals for injury sustained by the publication of a false fact. More to the point, the States have no substantial interest in securing for plaintiffs such as this petitioner gratuitous awards of money damages far in excess of any actual injury.

We would not, of course, invalidate state law simply because we doubt its wisdom, but here we are attempting to reconcile state law with a compet-ing interest grounded in the constitutional command of the First Amend-ment. It is therefore appropriate to require that state remedies for defamatory falsehood reach no farther than is necessary to protect the legitimate interest involved. It is necessary to restrict defamation plaintiffs who do not prove knowledge of falsity or reckless disregard for the truth to compensation for actual injury. We need not define "actual injury," as trial courts have wide experience in framing appropriate jury instructions in tort actions. Suffice it to say that actual injury is not limited to out-of-pocket loss. Indeed, the more customary types of actual harm inflicted by defamatory falsehood include impairment of reputation and standing in the community, personal humilia-tion, and mental anguish and suffering. Of course, juries must be limited by appropriate instructions, and all awards must be supported by competent evi-dence concerning the injury, although there need be no evidence which assigns an actual dollar value to the injury.

We also find no justification for allowing awards of punitive damages against publishers and broadcasters held liable under state-defined standards of liability for defamation. In most jurisdictions jury discretion over the amounts awarded is limited only by the gentle rule that they not be excessive. Conse-quently, juries assess punitive damages in wholly unpredictable amounts bear-ing no necessary relation to the actual harm caused. And they remain free to use their discretion selectively to punish expressions of unpopular views. Like the doctrine of presumed damages, jury discretion to award punitive damages unnecessarily exacerbates the danger of media self-censorship, but, unlike the former rule, punitive damages are wholly irrelevant to the state interest that justifies a negligence standard for private defamation actions. They are not compensation for injury. Instead, they are private fines levied by civil juries to punish reprehensible conduct and to deter its future occurrence. In short, the private defamation plaintiff who establishes liability under a less demanding standard than that stated by *New York Times* may recover only such damages as are sufficient to compensate him for actual injury.

Notwithstanding our refusal to extend the *New York Times* privilege to defamation of private individuals, respondent contends that we should affirm the judgment below on the ground that petitioner is either a public official or a public figure. There is little basis for the former assertion. Several years prior to the present incident, petitioner had served briefly on housing committees appointed by the mayor of Chicago, but at the time of publication he had never held any remunerative governmental position. Respondent admits this but argues that petitioner's appearance at the coroner's inquest rendered him a "de facto public official." Our cases recognized no such concept. Respondent's suggestion would sweep all lawyers under the *New York Times* rule as officers of the court and distort the plain meaning of the "public official" category beyond all recognition. We decline to follow it. . . .

Petitioner has long been active in community and professional affairs. He has served as an officer of local civic groups and of various professional organizations, and he has published several books and articles on legal subjects. Although petitioner was consequently well known in some circles, he had achieved no general fame or notoriety in the community. None of the prospective jurors called at the trial had ever heard of petitioner prior to this litigation, and respondent offered no proof that this response was atypical of the local population. We would not lightly assume that a citizen's participation in community and professional affairs rendered him a public figure for all purposes. Absent clear evidence of general fame or notoriety in the community and pervasive involvement in the affairs of society, an individual should not be deemed a public personality for all aspects of his life. It is preferable to reduce the public-figure question to a more meaningful context by looking to the nature and extent of an individual's participation in the particular controversy giving rise to the defamation.

In this context it is plain that petitioner was not a public figure. He played a minimal role at the coroner's inquest, and his participation related solely to his representation of a private client. He took no part in the criminal prosecution of Officer Nuccio. Moreover, he never discussed either the criminal or civil litigation with the press and was never quoted as having done so. He plainly did not thrust himself into the vortex of this public issue, nor did he engage the public's attention in an attempt to influence its outcome. We are persuaded that the trial court did not err in refusing to characterize petitioner as a public figure for the purpose of this litigation.

We therefore conclude that the *New York Times* standard is inapplicable to this case and that the trial court erred in entering judgment for respondent. Because the jury was allowed to impose liability without fault and was permitted to presume damages without proof of injury, a new trial is necessary. We reverse and remand for further proceedings in accord with this opinion.

It is so ordered.

☐ *Justice BLACKMUN, concurring.*

The Court today refuses to apply *New York Times* to the private individual, as contrasted with the public official and the public figure. . . . I sense some illogic in this. . . . [Still] I am willing to join, and do join, the Court's opinion and its judgment for two reasons:

1. By removing the specters of presumed and punitive damages in the absence of *New York Times* malice, the Court eliminates significant and powerful motives for self-censorship that otherwise are present in the traditional libel action. By so doing, the Court leaves what should prove to be sufficient and adequate breathing space for a vigorous press. What the Court has done, I believe, will have little, if any, practical effect on the functioning of responsible journalism.

2. The Court was sadly fractionated in *Rosenbloom* [*v. Metromedia, Inc.,* 403 U.S. 29 (1971)]. A result of that kind inevitably leads to uncertainty. I feel that it is of profound importance for the Court to come to rest in the defamation area and to have a clearly defined majority position that eliminates the unsureness engendered by *Rosenbloom's* diversity. If my vote were not needed to create a majority, I would adhere to my prior view. A definitive ruling, however, is paramount.

☐ *Chief Justice BURGER, dissenting.*

I am frank to say I do not know the parameters of a "negligence" doctrine as applied to the news media. Conceivably this new doctrine could inhibit some editors, as the dissents of Justice DOUGLAS and Justice BRENNAN suggest. But I would prefer to allow this area of law to continue to evolve as it has up to now with respect to private citizens rather than embark on a new doctrinal theory which has no jurisprudential ancestry.

☐ *Justice DOUGLAS, dissenting.*

The Court describes this case as a return to the struggle of "defin[ing] the proper accommodation between the law of defamation and the freedoms of speech and press protected by the First Amendment." It is indeed a struggle, once described by Justice BLACK as "the same quagmire" in which the Court "is now helplessly struggling in the field of obscenity." I would suggest that the struggle is a quite hopeless one, for, in light of the command of the First Amendment, no "accommodation" of its freedoms can be "proper" except those made by the Framers themselves.

☐ *Justice BRENNAN, dissenting.*

I cannot agree . . . that free and robust debate—so essential to the proper functioning of our system of government—is permitted adequate "breathing space," when, as the Court holds, the States may impose all but strict liability for defamation if the defamed party is a private person and "the substance of the defamatory statement 'makes substantial danger to reputation apparent.'" I adhere to my view expressed in *Rosenbloom v. Metromedia, Inc., supra,* that we strike the proper accommodation between avoidance of media self-censorship and protection of individual reputations only when we require States to apply the *New York Times Co. v. Sullivan* "knowing or reckless falsity" standard in civil libel actions concerning media reports of the involvement of private individuals in events of public or general interest. . . .

☐ *Justice WHITE, dissenting.*

For some 200 years—from the very founding of the Nation—the law of defamation and right of the ordinary citizen to recover for false publication injurious to his reputation have been almost exclusively the business of state courts and legislatures. Under typical state defamation law, the defamed private citizen had to prove only a false publication that would subject him to hatred, contempt, or ridicule. Given such publication, general damage to reputation was presumed, while punitive damages required proof of additional facts. The law governing the defamation of private citizens remained untouched by the First Amendment because until relatively recently, the consistent view of the Court was that libelous words constitute a class of speech wholly unprotected by the First Amendment, subject only to limited exceptions carved out since 1964.

But now, using that Amendment as the chosen instrument, the Court, in a few printed pages, has federalized major aspects of libel law by declaring unconstitutional in important respects the prevailing defamation law in all or most of the 50 States. . . .

These are radical changes in the law and severe invasions of the prerogatives of the States. They should at least be shown to be required by the First Amendment or necessitated by our present circumstances. Neither has been demonstrated. . . .

Scant, if any, evidence exists that the First Amendment was intended to abolish the common law of libel, at least to the extent of depriving ordinary citizens of meaningful redress against their defamers. . . .

[T]he law has heretofore put the risk of falsehood on the publisher where the victim is a private citizen and no grounds of special privilege are invoked. The Court would now shift this risk to the victim, even though he has done nothing to invite the calumny, is wholly innocent of fault, and is helpless to avoid his injury. I doubt that jurisprudential resistance to liability without fault is sufficient ground for employing the First Amendment to revolutionize the law of libel, and in my view, that body of legal rules poses no realistic threat to the press and its service to the public. The press today is vigorous and robust. To me, it is quite incredible to suggest that threats of libel suits from private citizens are causing the press to refrain from publishing the truth. I know of no hard facts to support that proposition, and the Court furnishes none.

Cox Broadcasting Corporation v. Cohn

420 U.S. 469, 95 S.CT. 1029 (1975)

In August 1971, Martin Cohn's seventeen-year-old daughter was raped; she died as result of the incident. Subsequently, a television report on the incident and the arrest of six youths charged with her rape and murder identified Cohn's daughter as the victim, on the basis of police reports and other public records. Cohn thereupon sued the owner of the television station, Cox Broadcasting Corporation, under a Georgia privacy statute making it a misdemeanor to broadcast the name or identity of a rape victim. The trial judge rejected arguments of Cox Broadcasting Corporation that its broadcast was protected under the First and Fourteenth Amendments. On appeal, the state supreme court upheld Georgia's statute as a legitimate limitation on the First Amendment. Cox Broadcasting Corporation subsequently appealed that ruling to the Supreme Court.

The state court's decision was reversed; the Court's decision was 8–1, and the majority's opinion was announced by Justice White. Concurrence was by Chief Justice Burger and Justices Powell and Douglas. Justice Rehnquist dissented.

■ ■ ■

☐ *Justice WHITE delivered the opinion of the Court.*

The issue before us in this case is whether, consistently with the First and Fourteenth Amendments, a State may extend a cause of action for damages for invasion of privacy caused by the publication of the name of a deceased rape victim which was publicly revealed in connection with the prosecution of the crime. . . .

Georgia stoutly defends both [Section] 26-9901 and the State's common-law privacy action challenged here. Its claims are not without force, for powerful arguments can be made, and have been made, that however it may be ultimately defined, there *is* a zone of privacy surrounding every individual, a zone within which the State may protect him from intrusion by the press, with all its attendant publicity. Indeed, the central thesis of the root article by Warren and Brandeis, The Right to Privacy, 4 *Harv.L.Rev.* 193, 196 (1890), was that the press was overstepping its prerogatives by publishing essentially private information and that there should be a remedy for the alleged abuses.

More compellingly, the century has experienced a strong tide running in favor of the so-called right of privacy. In 1967, we noted that "[i]t has been said that a 'right of privacy' has been recognized at common law in 30 States plus the District of Columbia and by statute in four States." *Time, Inc. v. Hill*, 385 U.S. 374 [(1967)]. . . .

In this sphere of collision between claims of privacy and those of the free press, the interests on both sides are plainly rooted in the traditions and significant concerns of our society. Rather than address the broader question whether truthful publications may ever be subjected to civil or criminal liability consistently with the First and Fourteenth Amendments, or to put it another way, whether the State may ever define and protect an area of privacy free from unwanted publicity in the press, it is appropriate to focus on the narrower interface between press and privacy that this case presents, namely, whether the State may impose sanctions on the accurate publication of the name of a rape victim obtained from public records—more specifically, from judicial records which are maintained in connection with a public prosecution and which themselves are open to public inspection. We are convinced that the State may not do so.

In the first place, in a society in which each individual has but limited time and resources with which to observe at first hand the operations of his government, he relies necessarily upon the press to bring to him in convenient form the facts of those operations. Great responsibility is accordingly placed upon the news media to report fully and accurately the proceedings of government, and official records and documents open to the public are the basic data of governmental operations. Without the information provided by the press most of us and many of our representatives would be unable to vote intelligently or to register opinions on the administration of government generally. With respect to judicial proceedings in particular, the function of the press serves to guarantee the fairness of trials and to bring to bear the beneficial effects of public scrutiny upon the administration of justice. . . .

[E]ven the prevailing law of invasion of privacy generally recognizes that the interests in privacy fade when the information involved already appears on the public record. The conclusion is compelling when viewed in terms of the First and Fourteenth Amendments and in light of the public interest in a vigorous press. The Georgia cause of action for invasion of privacy through public disclosure of the name of a rape victim imposes sanctions on pure expression—the content of a publication—and not conduct or a combination of speech and nonspeech elements that might otherwise be open to regulation or prohibition. The publication of truthful information available on the public record contains none of the indicia of those limited categories of expression, such as "fighting" words, which "are no essential part of any exposition of ideas, and are of such slight social value as a step to truth that any benefit that may be derived from them is clearly outweighed by the social interest in order and morality." *Chaplinsky v. New Hampshire,* 315 U.S. 568 (1942).

By placing the information in the public domain on official court records, the State must be presumed to have concluded that the public interest was thereby being served. Public records by their very nature are of interest to those concerned with the administration of government, and a public benefit is performed by the reporting of the true contents of the records by the media. The freedom of the press to publish that information appears to us to be of critical importance to our type of government in which the citizenry is the final judge of the proper conduct of public business. In preserving that form of government the First and Fourteenth Amendments command nothing less than that the States may not impose sanctions on the publication of truthful information contained in official court records open to public inspection.

We are reluctant to embark on a course that would make public records generally available to the media but forbid their publication if offensive to the sensibilities of the supposed reasonable man. Such a rule would make it very difficult for the media to inform citizens about the public business and yet stay within the law. The rule would invite timidity and self-censorship and very likely lead to the suppression of many items that would otherwise be published and that should be made available to the public. At the very least, the First and Fourteenth Amendments will not allow exposing the press to liability for truthfully publishing information released to the public in official court records. If there are privacy interests to be protected in judicial proceedings, the States must respond by means which avoid public documentation or other exposure of private information. Their political institutions must weigh the interests in privacy with the interests of the public to know and of the press to publish. Once true information is disclosed in public court documents open to public inspection, the press cannot be sanctioned for publishing it. In this instance as in others reliance must rest upon the judgment of those who decide what to publish or broadcast. . . .

Reversed.

■ IN COMPARATIVE PERSPECTIVE

Blasphemy and Other Hate Speech

A major controversy erupted in 2005–2006 when the Danish newspaper *Jyllands-Posten* published twelve cartoons depicting the Islamic Prophet Muhammad, including one with a bomb under his turban. As other European newspapers reprinted the cartoons and the cartoons circulated on the Internet, the controversy grew, particularly in Muslim countries. Riots broke out in Pakistan; the Danish and Norwegian embassies in Syria as well as the Danish General Consulate in Beirut, Lebanon, were burned. The same kind of controversy reemerged in 2015 when *Charlie Hebdo*, a French satirical magazine, published similar cartoons; in response, Islamic extremists targeted and murdered its editors.

In Denmark, blasphemy—the defamation of the name of God— remains a crime, but the law has been unenforced since 1938. France abolished its blasphemy laws in 1881 during its struggle with the Catholic Church, but speech that incites racial or religious hatred remains a crime. Holocaust denial and, as of 2014, "apology for terrorism" are also outlawed. By contrast, Pakistan has one of the harshest blasphemy laws, punishing "defiling the Holy Qu'ran" with life imprisonment. Other countries with blasphemy laws include Austria, Australia, Canada, Finland, Germany, India, Ireland, Israel, Italy, the Netherlands, South Africa, Spain, Switzerland, and the United Kingdom. In 2006, for instance, a German court convicted Manfred von H. (whose full name was not released) for sending to mosques and the media rolls of toilet paper on which he had stamped "Qu'ran, the Holy Qu'ran." He was sentenced to one year in prison but placed on probation.

In some countries, blasphemy has been expanded to include non-religious hate speech. A number of European and other countries, for example, criminalize the denial of the Holocaust. Austria, Australia, Belgium, Canada, the Czech Republic, France, Germany, Israel,

(continues)

■ IN COMPARATIVE PERSPECTIVE
Blasphemy and Other Hate Speech (continued)

Lithuania, New Zealand, Poland, Romania, Slovakia, and Switzerland have such laws. In 2006, English historian and author of *Hitler's War*, David Irving, was sentenced to three years imprisonment by an Austrian court for speeches he had previously made in the country asserting that only 74,000 Jews died of natural causes and millions were sent to Palestine during World War II.

In the United States, the Supreme Court struck down New York's blasphemy law as an unconstitutional prior restraint in *Joseph Burstyn v. Wilson*, 343 U.S. 495 (1952). New York had banned Roberto Rossellini's film *The Miracle*, about a peasant woman who believed she was the Virgin Mary. The Catholic Church denounced the film as sacrilegious, but the Supreme Court struck down the state's law, observing, "It is not the business of government in our nation to suppress real or imagined attacks upon a particular religious doctrine." Still, a number of states—Oklahoma, Massachusetts, Michigan, and North Carolina, for example—retain laws against blasphemy, but they are rarely enforced.

For further reading see Ronald Krotosynski, *The First Amendment in Cross-Cultural Perspective: A Comparative Legal Analysis of the Freedom of Speech*, New York: New York University Press, 2006; Georg Nolte, ed., *European and US Constitutionalism*, New York: Cambridge University Press, 2005; Michael Ignatieff, ed., *American Exceptionalism and Human Rights*, Princeton, NJ: Princeton University Press, 2005; and the Annual State Department Report on International Religious Freedom at www.state.gov/reports/2018-report-on-international-religious-freedom. See also Laura Witten-Keller and Raymond Haberski, *The Miracle Case: Film Censorship and the Supreme Court*, Lawrence: University Press of Kansas, 2008; Alan Dershowitz, *Blasphemy: How the Religious Right Is Hijacking the Declaration of Independence*, New York: Wiley, 2008; and Leonard Levy, *Blasphemy*, Chapel Hill: University of North Carolina Press, 1995.

D | *Commercial Speech*

In contrast with the toughening of obscenity standards, the Court has moved in the direction of extending greater protection to commercial speech, although not without sharp criticism. Commercial speech involves the advertising of goods and services, such as the costs of toothpaste or attorney's fees, as well as that of corporations and businesses that aim at influencing public policy.

That commercial speech should be "less protected" than other kinds of speech was first suggested in *Valentine v. Chrestensen*, 316 U.S. 52 (1942). There the Court upheld a New York ordinance prohibiting the distribution of "commercial and business advertising matter." Lewis Chrestensen was convicted under the ordinance for distributing handbills that on one side advertised his submarine and, on the other, printed the First Amendment as a protest against the ordinance. The justices unanimously held there was no "restraint on the government as respects purely commercial advertising." It remained unclear, though, whether commercial speech was unprotected per se (like obscenity) or simply less protected, and why it fell outside of First Amendment protection—was it the commercial motive, the content, or the method of distribution?

The problems with *Valentine* became more apparent in later cases. When confronted with the issue of whether the ad, "Heed Their Rising Voices," in *New York Times v. Sullivan* (1964) (see Section C in this chapter) fell under the commercial speech doctrine, Justice Brennan ducked the issue, observing that (unlike Chrestensen's handbill) the *New York Times* ad "communicated information, expressed opinion, recited grievances, protested claimed abuses, and sought financial support on behalf of a movement whose existence and objectives are matters of the highest public interest and concern. . . . That the *Times* was paid for publishing the advertisement is as immaterial in this connection as is the fact that newspapers and books are sold." In *New York Times v. Sullivan*, Brennan thus implied that the motive of a publisher might be used to define the scope of the First Amendment. But in *Pittsburgh Press v. Pittsburgh Commission on Human Rights*, 413 U.S. 376 (1973), the Court went the opposite way, suggesting that editorial motives may diminish a publication's status and First Amendment protection as well. There the *Pittsburgh Press* was found in violation of an ordinance against discriminatory hiring on the basis of gender, due to its carrying help-wanted advertisements in gender-designated columns. The publishers contended the First Amendment protected their editorial judgments; they had a right to decide whether to accept an ad in the first place and, once accepted, where to place it in the newspaper. A majority of the Court (with Chief Justice Burger and Justice Douglas dissenting) rejected that argument. Justice Powell, writing for the majority, found no impairment of editorial freedom and emphasized that "[t]he advertisements, as embroidered by their placement, signaled that the advertisers were likely to show an illegal sex preference in their hiring decisions."

In *Bigelow v. Virginia* (1975) (excerpted below) the Court finally limited *Valentine*, in holding that the "commercial aspects" and "publisher's motives of financial gain" in advertisements do not "negate all

First Amendment guarantees." Compare the rationale for extending First Amendment protection to commercial speech given in Justice Blackmun's opinion with the competing arguments of Justice Rehnquist in his dissenting opinion.

Two years after *Bigelow*, a ban on lawyer advertising of routine legal services was struck down in *Bates v. State Bar of Arizona*, 433 U.S. 350 (1977). But the Court did not end the controversy over lawyer advertising in *Bates*. *In re Primus*, 436 U.S. 412 (1978), held that the First Amendment protects lawyers who solicit clients for a nonprofit organization (there, the American Civil Liberties Union), but in *Ohralik v. Ohio State Bar Association*, 436 U.S. 447 (1978), the Court upheld disciplining an attorney for ambulance chasing and soliciting clients on a contingency basis (that is, if a lawyer wins the case for his client, he gets a percentage of the award). In *Zauderer v. Office of Disciplinary Counsel of Supreme Court of Ohio*, 471 U.S. 626 (1985), when holding that lawyers may not be disciplined for advertising in newspapers, the Court ruled that advertisements for contingency-fee services must disclose the difference between legal fees and costs (the latter are paid by the client regardless of the outcome of a case). *Shapero v. Kentucky Bar Association*, 486 U.S. 466 (1988), held that direct-mail solicitation by an attorney was protected First Amendment–commercial speech, and that a state bar association could not prevent the lawyer from soliciting clients in this way.

The Court's expansion of First Amendment protection for commercial speech based on a public interest rationale came with strong opposition from Chief Justice Rehnquist. As Justice Blackmun explained in *Virginia State Board of Pharmacy v. Virginia Citizen Consumer Council*, 425 U.S. 748 (1976), "So long as we preserve a predominantly free enterprise economy, the allocation of our resources in large measure will be made through numerous private economic decisions. It is a matter of public interest that those decisions in the aggregate, be intelligent and well informed. To this end, the free flow of commercial information is indispensable." The Court thereby ostensibly overturned *Valentine v. Chrestensen*. But, dissenting from that ruling, Rehnquist retorted, "I cannot distinguish between the public's right to know the price of drugs and its right to know the price of title searches or physical examinations or other professional services for which standardized fees are charged."

Again, with only Rehnquist dissenting in *Central Hudson Gas & Electric Corp. v. Public Service Commission of New York*, 447 U.S. 557 (1980), the Burger Court upheld First Amendment protection for a public utility's promotional ads and set forth a four-factor test for protecting commercial speech: (1) whether the speech concerns lawful activity and is lawful; (2) whether the asserted governmental interest in banning the speech is substantial; and, if so, (3) whether the regulation directly advances the government's interests; and (4) whether the regulation is no more extensive than necessary to serve the government's interests.

Although Rehnquist failed to carry the Court in *Central Hudson*, he massed a bare majority in *Posadas de Puerto Rico v. Tourism Company of Puerto Rico*, 478 U.S. 328 (1986), for upholding Puerto Rico's ban on advertising casino gambling to local residents. He did so largely on the ground that Puerto Rico could ban gambling altogether and that this power included the lesser power of regulating advertising for gambling.

However, subsequent rulings failed to follow *Posadas* and even the *Central Hudson* test. (For further discussion and a summary of other recent rulings, see THE DEVELOPMENT OF LAW box below.) Finally, a decade after handing down *Posadas*, the Court reconsidered that ruling in *44 Liquormart v. Rhode Island* (excerpted below). In that case, Justice Stevens struck down a state's ban on advertising the price of liquor and threw into question other governmental attempts to regulate advertising for alcohol, tobacco, and other "vices." While Justice Stevens cast further doubt on the ruling and reasoning in *Posadas*, concurring Justices Scalia and Thomas also questioned the Court's continued use of *Central Hudson*. The First Amendment's protection for commercial speech was, again, reaffirmed in *Lorillard Tobacco Co. v. Reilly*, 533 U.S. 525 (2001), striking down state restrictions on advertising for tobacco products, as well as other recent rulings. Notably in *Lorillard*, concurring Justice Thomas reiterated his opposition to the *Central Hudson* test and accorded commercial speech "lesser" First Amendment protection.

In 2017, The Roberts Court underscored the expanded protection for commercial speech when striking down a section of the 1947 Lanham Act, prohibiting trademarks disparaging individuals or groups. Writing for the Court in *Matal v. Tam,* 137 S. Ct. 1744 (2017) discussed in Section B of this chapter, Justice Alito emphasized that trademarks are private, commercial speech—not government speech that receives First Amendment protection. Finally, in *Iancu v. Brunetti*, 588 U.S. ___ (2019), the Court struck down the Lanham Act's provision permitting the denial of trademark if the subject covers "immoral, deceptive, or scandalous matter," arguing that this provision otherwise would permit the trademark office to exercise viewpoint discrimination, which is prohibited by the First Amendment.

■ THE DEVELOPMENT OF LAW

Other Important Rulings on Commercial Speech and the First Amendment

CASE	VOTE	RULING
Virginia State Board of Pharmacy v. Virginia Citizen Consumer Council, 425 U.S. 748 (1976)	7–1	Upheld advertising of prescription drug prices, ostensibly overturning *Valentine v. Chrestensen* (1942).
Bates v. State Bar of Arizona, 433 U.S. 350 (1977)	5–4	Struck down Arizona's disciplinary rule that restricted advertising by lawyers of their

services. Chief Justice Burger and Justices Powell and Stewart in part concurred and dissented. Justice Rehnquist dissented.

CASE	VOTE	RULING
First National Bank of Boston v. Bellotti, 435 U.S. 765 (1978)	5–4	Held corporations enjoy First Amendment protection in publicizing their views on an income tax referendum.
Friedman v. Rogers, 440 U.S. 1 (1979)	7–2	Upheld ban on advertising of optometrists under trade names.
Consolidated Edison Company v. Public Service Commission, 447 U.S. 530 (1980)	7–2	Upheld insertion of handbills on nuclear energy with billing statements.
Central Hudson Gas & Electric Corp. v. Public Service Commission of New York, 447 U.S. 557 (1980)	8–1	Upheld promotional ads of a public utility and electrical monopoly.
Bolger v. Youngs Drug Products Corporation, 463 U.S. 60 (1983)	9–0	Held unconstitutional a statute barring unsolicited mailings of ads for contraceptives.

CASE	VOTE	RULING
Pacific Gas & Electric v. Public Utilities Commission of California, 475 U.S. 1 (1986)	5–4	A state may not force a public utility company to include in its newsletter the material of a third party.
Posadas de Puerto Rico Associates v. Tourism Company of Puerto Rico, 479 U.S. 328 (1986)	5–4	Over First Amendment objections, Justice Rehnquist upheld Puerto Rico's ban on advertising for gambling casinos to residents, while per-

mitting such advertising to residents of the fifty states. Writing for a bare majority, Justice Rehnquist reasoned that, because Puerto Rico could completely ban gambling, it could regulate and restrict advertising for gambling operations.

Board of Trustees of the State University of New York v. Fox, 492 U.S. 469 (1989)	6–3	Held that officials of a university did not violate students' First Amendment free speech rights by banning

Tupperware parties in dormitories; commercial speech need not meet the least drastic means test that applies when reviewing regulations of noncommercial speech.

Peel v. Attorney Registration and Disciplinary Commission of Illinois, 496 U.S. 91 (1990)	5–4	In a plurality opinion, Justice Stevens held that Illinois had improperly censured an attorney for printing on his letter-

head that he was a certified civil trial specialist, because the letterhead was nondeceptive and protected commercial speech. Justices White, O'Connor, and Scalia, along with Chief Justice Rehnquist, dissented.

Edenfield v. Fane, 507 U.S. 761 (1993)	8–1	Struck down a ban on soliciting by certified public accountants (CPAs) on the

ground that "[s]olicitation by a CPA does not entail the coercive force of the personal presence of a trained advocate." Writing for the majority, Justice Kennedy distinguished prior rulings that limited protection for attorneys' solicitations on the ground that "a CPA is not a professional trained in the art of persuasion" and CPAs solicit business in ways conducive to long-term relationships with their clients, rather than engaging in "high pressure sales tactics." Only Justice O'Connor dissented.

(continues)

■ THE DEVELOPMENT OF LAW
*Other Important Rulings on Commercial Speech and the
First Amendment (continued)*

CASE	VOTE	HOLDING
United States v. Edge Broadcasting Company, 509 U.S. 418 (1993)	7–2	Under federal law, lottery advertisements are generally prohibited, but broadcasters may advertise state-run lotteries on stations licensed in a state that conducts lotteries.

A North Carolina company, Edge Broadcasting Company, challenged the application of those restrictions because it wanted to broadcast advertisements for Virginia's lottery. As the company broadcasts close to the Virginia and North Carolina border, approximately 90 percent of Edge's listeners reside in the former state, though it is licensed in the latter. Writing for the majority Justice White applied the four-factor test for commercial speech set forth in *Central Hudson Gas & Electric Corp. v. Public Service Commission of New York*, 447 U.S. 557 (1980), and upheld the federal restrictions as applied to Edge Broadcasting Company, since they advanced the federal government's interest in supporting nonlottery states' antigambling policies and did so in an effective and nonexcessive way. Justices Stevens and Blackmun dissented.

Ibanez v. Florida Department of Professional Regulation, 512 U.S. 136 (1994)	7–2	Struck down Florida's ban on the use of the appellations CPA (certified public accountant) and CFP (certified financial planner) on lawyers' business cards and letterheads, as well as

telephone listings. Writing for the majority, Justice Ginsburg reaffirmed that states may "ban such speech only if it is false, deceptive, or misleading," and rejected Florida's claim that the use of "CPA" in advertisements was "inherently misleading." By contrast, dissenting Justice O'Connor, along with Chief Justice Rehnquist, contended that "States may prohibit inherently misleading speech entirely."

City of Ladue v. Gilleo, 512 U.S. 43 (1994)	9–0	Struck down an ordinance that banned homeowners from posting any signs, except

for real estate sale signs, on their property. In 1990, during the United States' clash with Iraq, Margaret Gilleo ran afoul of the law by placing an 8½-by-11-inch sign, "For Peace in Gulf," in a second-floor window of her home. Writing for the Court, Justice Stevens held that the ordinance was overinclusive and too restrictive of the freedoms guaranteed by the First Amendment.

CASE	VOTE	HOLDING
Rubin v. Coors Brewing Co., 514 U.S. 476 (1995)	9–0	Writing for the Court, Justice Thomas affirmed a lower court's striking down the pro-

visions of a 1935 federal statute imposing labeling restrictions on the alcohol content of malt beverages. Under federal law, the disclosure of alcohol is required on distilled spirits and wines, while the alcohol content of beer could be shown on billboards but not on bottle labels. The government had defended its labeling restrictions on the ground that they prevented "strength wars" in advertising the sale of beer. The Court, however, held that the government's interest failed the test set forth in *Central Hudson Gas & Electric Corp. v. Public Service Commission of New York*, 447 U.S. 557 (1980), requiring the government's interest in regulating commercial speech to be "substantial" and "not more extensive than is necessary to serve that interest."

Florida Bar v. Went For It, 515 U.S. 618 (1995)	5–4	Writing for the majority, Justice O'Connor upheld Florida's prohibition on personal

lawyers making written solicitations to victims or victims' relatives within thirty days of an accident or natural disaster, upon concluding that the government's interests in the restriction met the test set forth in *Central Hudson*. By contrast, dissenting Justices Ginsburg, Kennedy, Souter, and Stevens strongly disagreed with the majority's analysis and failure to recognize the First Amendment's protection for attorney advertising.

Glickman v. Wileman Brothers & Elliott, Inc., 521 U.S. 457 (1997)	5–4	Upheld regulations pursuant to the Agricultural Marketing Agreement Act of 1937 re- quiring fruit producers to

contribute financially toward generic advertising for fruit in certain markets. Wileman Brothers & Elliott, Inc., challenged the constitutionality of that regulation as compelled speech in violation of the First Amendment's protection for commercial speech. In rejecting that claim, Justice Stevens observed that "requiring respondents to pay the assessments can not be said to engender any crisis of conscience. None of the advertising in this record promotes any particular message other than encouraging consumers to buy California tree fruit."

(continues)

■ THE DEVELOPMENT OF LAW
*Other Important Rulings on Commercial Speech and the
First Amendment (continued)*

CASE	VOTE	HOLDING
Greater New Orleans Broadcasting Association v. United States, 527 U.S. 173 (1999)	9–0	In *United States v. Edge Broadcasting Co.*, 509 U.S. 418 (1993), the Court upheld the application of a section of the Communications Act of 1934,

forbidding the broadcasting of advertisements for gambling, to bar a radio station in North Carolina, where lotteries are illegal, from broadcasting ads for Virginia's lotteries. Here, however, the Court held that the prohibition infringed on First Amendment interests as applied to radio and television broadcasts for private casino gambling in Louisiana, where gambling is legal. Writing for the Court, Justice Stevens emphasized that federal law regulating gambling advertisements is inconsistent and crosscutting. Among the numerous exceptions to the Communications Act's ban on advertisements of gambling, for instance, were Congress's 1975 exemption of the broadcasting of ads for state-run lotteries and its 1988 exemption of those for gambling operations run by Native American tribes. Because of these exemptions to, and the incoherence of, federal law, Justice Stevens ruled that the government failed to satisfy the four-factor test for regulating commercial speech laid down in *Central Hudson Gas & Electric Corp. v. Public Service Commission of New York*, 447 U.S. 557 (1980). Chief Justice Rehnquist and Justice Thomas filed concurring opinions.

Los Angeles Police Department v. United Reporting Publishing Corporation, 528 U.S. 32 (1999)	7–2	Writing for the Court, Chief Justice Rehnquist upheld a California law that permits police departments to give journalists, scholars, and

others access to arrest records, but forbids their release to companies that would use the information for commercial purposes; the law was enacted to safeguard privacy interests and to protect arrestees and victims from solicitations, lawyers, and other businesses.

United States v. United Foods, 533 U.S. 405 (2001)	6–3	Writing for the Court, Justice Kennedy struck down a 1990 federal statute mandating that mushroom handlers pay an

assessment that was used to fund advertisements promoting the sale of mushrooms. In holding that the law violates the First Amendment, the Court distinguished *Glickman v. Wileman Brothers & Elliott, Inc.*, 521 U.S. 457 (1997), upholding the constitutionality of a series of agricultural marketing orders that required producers of certain California fruits to pay a fee used for product advertising. In Glickman, according to Justice Kennedy, the mandated fee was part of a larger regulatory marketing scheme, whereas here the forced subsidy for generic advertising was not part of a larger economic regulatory scheme and, thus, ran afoul of the First Amendment protection for commercial speech, relying on *Abood v. Detroit Board of Education*, 431 U.S. 209 (1977).

CASE	VOTE	HOLDING
Lorillard Tobacco Co. v. Reilly, 533 U.S. 525 (2001)	5–4	Writing for the Court, Justice O'Connor held that federal regulations of cigarette

advertising preempted Massachusetts's regulations, and that the state's regulation of advertisements for smokeless tobacco products, which are not covered by federal law, violated the First Amendment.

Thompson v. Western States Medical Center, 535 U.S. 357 (2002)	5–4	Writing for the Court, Justice O'Connor struck down a federal restriction on the advertising of "compound drugs."

Chief Justice Rehnquist and Justices Stevens, Ginsburg, and Breyer dissented.

Johanns v. Livestock Marketing Association, 544 U.S. 550 (2005)	6–3	Writing for the Court, Justice Scalia upheld the Beef Promotion and Research Act of 1985, which requires cattle

producers to pay $1 for each head of cattle in order to finance a marketing campaign, "Beef: It's What's for Dinner." Although the Court invalidated a similar program for the marketing of mushrooms, in *United States v. United Foods*, 533 U.S. 405 (2001), it did not address the question of whether such programs are "government speech." Some independent cattle producers objected to the program, contending that it constituted unconstitutionally "compelled speech." Justice Scalia, however, ruled that "government speech" is not subject to ordinary First Amendment analysis. In his words, "Compelled funding of government speech does not alone raise First Amendment concerns. . . . Citizens may challenge compelled support of private speech, but have no First Amendment right not

(continues)

■ The Development of Law
*Other Important Rulings on Commercial Speech and the
First Amendment (continued)*

---

to fund government speech." Justices Stevens, Kennedy, and Souter
dissented.

CASE	VOTE	HOLDING
Sorrell v. IMS Health Inc., 564 U.S. 552 (2011)	6–3	Writing for the Court, Justice Kennedy invalidated Vermont's Prescription Confidentiality Law of 2007, restricting the disclosure and sale of

pharmacy records that reveal the prescribing practices of individual
doctors. The law was challenged by some pharmaceutical manufacturers
and "data mining" firms that collect such data and analyze it to
produce reports on prescribers' behavior. Data miners lease these reports
to pharmaceutical manufacturers, whose sales representatives use
the reports to refine their marketing tactics and increase sales. The
majority held that, "Speech in aid of pharmaceutical marketing . . . is
a form of expression protected by the Free Speech Clause of the First
Amendment," because it is a content-based restriction aimed at particular
speakers and therefore cannot satisfy "heightened judicial scrutiny."
In Justice Kennedy's words, "The Constitution 'does not enact
Mr. Herbert Spencer's Social Statics.' *Lochner v. New York* (1905)
(Holmes, J., dissenting). It does enact the First Amendment." Justices
Breyer, Ginsburg, and Kagan dissented.

Selected Bibliography

Collins, Ronald, and Skover, David. *The Death of Discourse.* 2nd ed. Boulder, CO:
Westview, 2004.

Lessig, Lawrence. *Free Culture: How Big Media Uses Technology and the Law to Lock
Down Culture and Control Creativity.* New York: Penguin Press, 2004.

Postman, Neil. *Amusing Ourselves to Death: Public Discourse in the Age of Show Business.*
New York: Viking, 1985.

Shiner, Roger A. *Freedom of Commercial Expression.* New York: Oxford University
Press, 2004.

Twitchell, James. *Carnival Culture: The Trashing of Taste in America.* New York:
Columbia University Press, 1992.

———. *Adcult USA: The Triumph of Advertising in American Culture.* New York:
Columbia University Press, 1995.

Bigelow v. Virginia

421 U.S. 809, 95 S.CT. 2222 (1975)

Justice Blackmun in his opinion for the Court sets forth the facts in this case involving a Virginia State prohibition against advertising the availability of abortion services and clinics, even those in other states.

The Court's decision was 7–2, and the majority's opinion was announced by Justice Blackmun. Dissent was by Justice Rehnquist, who was joined by Justice White.

■ ■ ■

☐ *Justice BLACKMUN delivered the opinion of the Court.*

An advertisement carried in appellant's newspaper led to his conviction for a violation of a Virginia statute that made it a misdemeanor, by the sale or circulation of any publication, to encourage or prompt the procuring of an abortion. The issue here is whether the editor-appellant's First Amendment rights were unconstitutionally abridged by the statute. . . .

The *Virginia Weekly* was a newspaper published by the Virginia Weekly Associates of Charlottesville. . . . Jeffrey C. Bigelow, was a director and the managing editor and responsible officer of the newspaper.

On February 8, 1971, the *Weekly*'s Vol. V, No. 6, was published and circulated under the direct responsibility of the appellant. On page 2 of that issue was the following advertisement:

> UNWANTED PREGNANCY
> LET US HELP YOU
> Abortions are now legal in New York
> There are no residency requirements.
> FOR IMMEDIATE PLACEMENT IN
> ACCREDITED HOSPITALS AND
> CLINICS AT LOW COST
> Contact
> WOMEN'S PAVILION
> 515 Madison Avenue
> New York, N.Y. 10022
> or call any time
> (212) 371-6670 or (212) 371-6650
> AVAILABLE 7 DAYS A WEEK
> STRICTLY CONFIDENTIAL. We
> will make all arrangements for you
> and help you with information and
> counseling.

It is to be observed that the advertisement announced that the Women's Pavilion of New York City would help women with unwanted pregnancies to obtain "immediate placement in accredited hospitals and clinics at low cost" and would "make all arrangements" on a "strictly confidential" basis; that it offered "information and counseling"; that it gave the organization's address and telephone numbers; and that it stated that abortions "are now legal in New York" and there "are no residency requirements." Although the advertisement did not contain the name of any licensed physician, the "placement" to which it referred was to "accredited hospitals and clinics."

Bigelow was charged with [and convicted for] violating . . . [a statute that provided]:

"If any person, by publication, lecture, advertisement, or by the sale or circulation of any publication, or in any other manner, encourage or prompt the procuring of abortion or miscarriage, he shall be guilty of a misdemeanor." [The Supreme Court of Virginia upheld Bigelow's conviction.] . . .

The central assumption made by the Supreme Court of Virginia was that the First Amendment guarantees of speech and press are inapplicable to paid commercial advertisements. Our cases, however, clearly establish that speech is not stripped of First Amendment protection merely because it appears in that form. . . .

The appellee, as did the Supreme Court of Virginia, relies on *Valentine v. Chrestensen*, 316 U.S. 52 (1942), where a unanimous Court, in a brief opinion, sustained an ordinance which had been interpreted to ban the distribution of a handbill advertising the exhibition of a submarine. The handbill solicited customers to tour the ship for a fee. The promoter-advertiser had first attempted to distribute a single-faced handbill consisting only of the advertisement, and was denied permission to do so. He then had printed, on the reverse side of the handbill, a protest against official conduct refusing him the use of wharfage facilities. The Court found that the message of asserted "public interest" was appended solely for the purpose of evading the ordinance and therefore did not constitute an "exercise of the freedom of communicating information and disseminating opinion." . . .

But the holding is distinctly a limited one: the ordinance was upheld as a reasonable regulation of the manner in which commercial advertising could be distributed. The fact that it had the effect of banning a particular handbill does not mean that *Chrestensen* is authority for the proposition that all statutes regulating commercial advertising are immune from constitutional challenge. The case obviously does not support any sweeping proposition that advertising is unprotected *per se*.

This Court's cases decided since *Chrestensen* clearly demonstrate as untenable any reading of that case that would give it so broad an effect. In *New York Times Co. v. Sullivan*, [376 U.S. 254 (1964)], a city official instituted a civil libel action against four clergymen and the *New York Times*. The suit was based on an advertisement carried in the newspaper criticizing police action against members of the civil rights movement and soliciting contributions for the movement. The Court held that this advertisement, although containing factually erroneous defamatory content, was entitled to the same degree of constitutional protection as ordinary speech. . . .

The principle that commercial advertising enjoys a degree of First Amendment protection was reaffirmed in *Pittsburgh Press Co. v. Human Rel. Comm'n*, 413 U.S. 376 (1973). There, the Court, although divided, sustained an ordinance that had been construed to forbid newspapers to carry help-wanted advertisements in sex-designated columns except where based upon a bona fide occupational exemption. The Court did describe the advertisements at issue as "classic examples of commercial speech," for each was "no more than a proposal of possible employment." But the Court indicated that the advertisements would have received some degree of First Amendment protection if the commercial proposal had been legal. . . .

The legitimacy of appellant's First Amendment claim in the present case is demonstrated by the important differences between the advertisement presently at issue and those involved in *Chrestensen* and in *Pittsburgh Press*. The advertisement published in appellant's newspaper did more than simply propose a commercial transaction. It contained factual material of clear "public interest." Portions of its message, most prominently the lines, "Abortions are now legal in New York. There are no residency requirements," involve the exercise of the freedom of communicating information and disseminating opinion.

Viewed in its entirety, the advertisement conveyed information of potential interest and value to a diverse audience—not only to readers possibly in need of the services offered, but also to those with a general curiosity about, or genuine interest in, the subject matter or the law of another State and its development, and to readers seeking reform in Virginia. . . .

Advertising, like all public expression, may be subject to reasonable regulation that serves a legitimate public interest. To the extent that commercial activity is subject to regulation, the relationship of speech to that activity may be one factor, among others, to be considered in weighing the First Amendment interest against the governmental interest alleged. Advertising is not thereby stripped of all First Amendment protection. The relationship of speech to the marketplace of products or of services does not make it valueless in the marketplace of ideas. . . .

If . . . this statute were upheld . . . Virginia might exert the power sought here over a wide variety of national publications or interstate newspapers carrying advertisements similar to the one that appeared in Bigelow's newspaper or containing articles on the general subject matter to which the advertisement referred. Other States might do the same. The burdens thereby imposed on publications would impair, perhaps severely, their proper functioning. We know from experience that "liberty of the press is in peril as soon as the government tries to compel what is to go into a newspaper." The policy of the First Amendment favors dissemination of information and opinion, and "[t]he guarantees of freedom of speech and press were not designed to prevent 'the censorship of the press merely, but any action of the government by means of which it might prevent such free and general discussion of public matters as seems absolutely essential.' . . ."

We conclude that Virginia could not apply Va.Code Ann. Sec. 18.1-63 (1960), as it read in 1971, to appellant's publication of the advertisement in question without unconstitutionally infringing upon his First Amendment rights. The judgment of the Supreme Court of Virginia is therefore reversed.

☐ *Justice REHNQUIST, with whom Justice WHITE joins, dissenting.*

Since the Court concludes, apparently from two lines of the advertisement, that it conveyed information of value to those interested in the "subject matter or the law of another State and its development" and to those "seeking reform in Virginia," and since the ad relates to abortion, elevated to constitutional stature by the Court, it concludes that this advertisement is entitled to something more than the limited constitutional protection traditionally accorded commercial advertising. Although recognizing that "[a]dvertising, like all public expression, may be subject to reasonable regulation that serves a legitimate public interest," the Court for reasons not entirely clear to me concludes that Virginia's interest is of "little, if any, weight." . . .

If the Court's decision does, indeed, turn upon its conclusion that the advertisement here in question was protected by the First and Fourteenth Amendments, the subject of the advertisement ought to make no difference. It will not do to say, as the Court does, that this advertisement conveyed information about the "subject matter or the law of another State and its development" to those "seeking reform in Virginia," and that it related to abortion, as if these factors somehow put it on a different footing from other commercial advertising. This was a proposal to furnish services on a commercial basis, and since we have always refused to distinguish for First Amendment purposes on the basis of content, it is no different from an advertisement for a bucket shop operation or a Ponzi scheme which has its headquarters in New York. If Virginia may not regulate advertising of commercial abortion agencies because of the interest of those seeking to reform Virginia's abortion laws, it is difficult to see why it is not likewise precluded from regulating advertising for an out-of-state bucket shop on the ground that such information might be of interest to those interested in repealing Virginia's "blue sky" laws. . . .

[T]he advertisement appears to me, as it did to the courts below, to be a classic commercial proposition directed toward the exchange of services rather than the exchange of ideas. . . . Whatever slight factual content the advertisement may contain and whatever expression of opinion may be laboriously drawn from it does not alter its predominantly commercial content. . . . I am unable to perceive any relationship between the instant advertisement and that for example in issue in *New York Times Co. v. Sullivan.* . . .

Assuming *arguendo* that this advertisement is something more than a normal commercial proposal, I am unable to see why Virginia does not have a legitimate public interest in its regulation. The Court apparently concedes . . . that the States have a strong interest in the prevention of commercial advertising in the health field—both in order to maintain high ethical standards in the medical profession and to protect the public from unscrupulous practices.

Without denying the power of either New York or Virginia to prohibit advertising such as that in issue where both publication of the advertised activity and the activity itself occur in the same State, the Court instead focuses on the multistate nature of this transaction. . . .

The source of this rigid territorial limitation on the power of the States in our federal system to safeguard the health and welfare of their citizens is not revealed. . . . [W]e have consistently recognized that irrespective of a State's power to regulate extraterritorial commercial transactions in which its citizens participate it retains an independent power to regulate the business of commercial solicitation and advertising within its borders. . . .

Were the Court's statements taken literally, they would presage a standard of the lowest common denominator for commercial ethics and business conduct. . . . Loan sharks might well choose States with unregulated small loan industries, luring the unwary with immune commercial advertisements. And imagination would place the only limit on the use of such a "no-man's land" together with artificially created territorial contacts to bilk the public and circumvent long-established state schemes of regulation.

44 Liquormart, Inc. v. Rhode Island

517 U.S. 484, 116 S.CT. 1495 (1996)

In 1956, Rhode Island enacted two prohibitions against advertising the retail price of alcoholic drinks. The first prohibits "advertising in any manner whatsoever" of the price of alcoholic drinks, with the exception of price tags, and the second categorically forbids any ads making "reference to the price of any alcoholic beverages." In 1991, complaints from competitors about an ad placed by 44 Liquormart in a newspaper generated enforcement proceedings under the statute. Notably, the ad did not state the price of any alcoholic beverages and, indeed, noted that "State law prohibits advertising liquor prices." Rather, the ad listed 44 Liquormart's low prices for peanuts, potato chips, and Schweppes mixers and identified various brands of packaged liquor as well as including the word "WOW" in large letters next to pictures of vodka and rum bottles. Subsequently, after being fined $400, 44 Liquormart filed a suit seeking a declaratory judgment that the state's restrictions violated the First Amendment. A federal district court agreed that the advertising ban was unconstitutional because it did not "directly advance" the government's interest in reducing alcohol consumption and was "more extensive than necessary to serve that interest." But a federal appellate court reversed this decision and 44 Liquormart appealed to the Supreme Court.

The appellate court's decision was reversed by a unanimous Court and its opinion was delivered by Justice Stevens. Justices Scalia, Thomas, and O'Connor filed concurring opinions.

■ ■ ■

> ☐ *Justice STEVENS delivered the opinion of the Court with respect to Parts I, II, and VII, in which Justices SCALIA, KENNEDY, SOUTER, THOMAS, and GINSBURG joined; the opinion of the Court with respect to Part VIII, in which Justices SCALIA, KENNEDY, SOUTER, and GINSBURG joined; an opinion with respect to Parts III and V, in which Justices KENNEDY, SOUTER, and GINSBURG joined; an opinion with respect to Part VI, in which Justices KENNEDY, THOMAS, and GINSBURG joined; and an opinion with respect to Part IV, in which Justices KENNEDY and GINSBURG joined.*

■ III

Advertising has been a part of our culture throughout our history. Even in colonial days, the public relied on "commercial speech" for vital information about the market. Early newspapers displayed advertisements for goods and services on their front pages, and town criers called out prices in public squares. Indeed, commercial messages played such a central role in public life prior to the Founding that Benjamin Franklin authored his early defense of a free press in support of his decision to print, of all things, an advertisement for voyages to Barbados. . . .

It was not until the 1970's, however, that this Court held that the First Amendment protected the dissemination of truthful and nonmisleading commercial messages about lawful products and services. In *Bigelow v. Virginia*, 421 U.S. 809 (1975), we held that it was error to assume that commercial speech was entitled to no First Amendment protection or that it was without value in the marketplace of ideas. The following Term in *Virginia Bd. of Pharmacy v. Virginia Citizens Consumer Council, Inc.*, 425 U.S. 748 (1976), we expanded on our holding in *Bigelow* and held that the State's blanket ban on advertising the price of prescription drugs violated the First Amendment. *Virginia Pharmacy Bd.* reflected the conclusion that the same interest that supports regulation of potentially misleading advertising, namely the public's interest in receiving accurate commercial information, also supports an interpretation of the First Amendment that provides constitutional protection for the dissemination of accurate and nonmisleading commercial messages. . . . The opinion further explained that a State's paternalistic assumption that the public will use truthful, nonmisleading commercial information unwisely cannot justify a decision to suppress it. . . .

At the same time, our early cases recognized that the State may regulate some types of commercial advertising more freely than other forms of protected speech. Specifically, we explained that the State may require commercial messages to "appear in such a form, or include such additional information, warnings, and disclaimers, as are necessary to prevent its being deceptive," *Virginia Pharmacy Bd.*, and that it may restrict some forms of aggressive sales practices that have the potential to exert "undue influence" over consumers. See *Bates v. State Bar of Ariz.*, 433 U.S. 350 (1977). . . .

In *Central Hudson Gas & Electric Corp. v. Public Service Commission of New York*, 447 U.S. 557 (1980), we took stock of our developing commercial speech jurisprudence. In that case, we considered a regulation "completely" banning all promotional advertising by electric utilities. Our decision acknowledged the special features of commercial speech but identified the serious First Amendment concerns that attend blanket advertising prohibitions that do not protect consumers from commercial harms. . . . In reaching its conclusion, the majority explained that although the special nature of commercial speech may require less than strict review of its regulation, special concerns arise from "regulations that entirely suppress commercial speech in order to pursue a nonspeech-related policy." In those circumstances, "a ban on speech could screen from public view the underlying governmental policy." As a result, the Court concluded that "special care" should attend the review of such blanket bans, and it pointedly remarked that "in recent years this Court has not approved a blanket ban on commercial speech unless the speech itself was flawed in some way, either because it was deceptive or related to unlawful activity."

■ IV

When a State regulates commercial messages to protect consumers from misleading, deceptive, or aggressive sales practices, or requires the disclosure of beneficial consumer information, the purpose of its regulation is consistent with the reasons for according constitutional protection to commercial speech and therefore justifies less than strict review. However, when a State entirely prohibits the dissemination of truthful, nonmisleading commercial messages for reasons unrelated to the preservation of a fair bargaining process, there is far less reason to depart from the rigorous review that the First Amendment generally demands.

Sound reasons justify reviewing the latter type of commercial speech regulation more carefully. Most obviously, complete speech bans, unlike content-neutral restrictions on the time, place, or manner of expression . . . are particularly dangerous because they all but foreclose alternative means of disseminating certain information. . . .

It is the State's interest in protecting consumers from "commercial harms" that provides "the typical reason why commercial speech can be subject to greater governmental regulation than noncommercial speech." *Cincinnati v. Discovery Network, Inc.*, 507 U.S. 410 (1993). Yet bans that target truthful, nonmisleading commercial messages rarely protect consumers from such harms. Instead, such bans often serve only to obscure an "underlying governmental policy" that could be implemented without regulating speech. *Central Hudson*. In this way, these commercial speech bans not only hinder consumer choice, but also impede debate over central issues of public policy.

Precisely because bans against truthful, nonmisleading commercial speech rarely seek to protect consumers from either deception or overreaching, they usually rest solely on the offensive assumption that the public will respond "irrationally" to the truth. The First Amendment directs us to be especially skeptical of regulations that seek to keep people in the dark for what the government perceives to be their own good. That teaching applies equally to state attempts to deprive consumers of accurate information about their chosen products: "The commercial market-place, like other spheres of our social and cultural life, provides a forum where ideas and information flourish. Some of the ideas and information are vital, some of slight worth. But the general rule is that the speaker and the audience, not the government, assess the value of the information presented." . . .

■ V

The State argues that the price advertising prohibition should nevertheless be upheld because it directly advances the State's substantial interest in promoting temperance, and because it is no more extensive than necessary. Although there is some confusion as to what Rhode Island means by temperance, we assume that the State asserts an interest in reducing alcohol consumption. . . .

Although the record suggests that the price advertising ban may have some impact on the purchasing patterns of temperate drinkers of modest means, the State has presented no evidence to suggest that its speech prohibition will significantly reduce market-wide consumption. . . . In addition, as the District Court noted, the State has not identified what price level would lead to a significant reduction in alcohol consumption, nor has it identified the amount that it believes prices would decrease without the ban. Thus, the State's own showing reveals that any connection between the ban and a significant change in alcohol consumption would be purely fortuitous. . . .

The State also cannot satisfy the requirement that its restriction on speech be no more extensive than necessary. It is perfectly obvious that alternative forms of regulation that would not involve any restriction on speech would be more likely to achieve the State's goal of promoting temperance. As the State's

own expert conceded, higher prices can be maintained either by direct regulation or by increased taxation. Per capita purchases could be limited as is the case
with prescription drugs. Even educational campaigns focused on the problems
of excessive, or even moderate, drinking might prove to be more effective.

As a result, even under the less than strict standard that generally applies
in commercial speech cases, the State has failed to establish a "reasonable fit"
between its abridgment of speech and its temperance goal. . . . It necessarily
follows that the price advertising ban cannot survive the more stringent
constitutional review that *Central Hudson* itself concluded was appropriate
for the complete suppression of truthful, nonmisleading commercial speech.

■ VI

The State responds by arguing that it merely exercised appropriate "legislative
judgment" in determining that a price advertising ban would best promote
temperance. Relying on the *Central Hudson* analysis set forth in *Posadas de Puerto
Rico Associates v. Tourism Co. of P.R.*, 478 U.S. 328 (1986), and *United States v.
Edge Broadcasting Co.*, 509 U.S. 418 (1993), Rhode Island first argues that,
because expert opinions as to the effectiveness of the price advertising ban "go
both ways," the Court of Appeals correctly concluded that the ban constituted
a "reasonable choice" by the legislature. The State next contends that precedent requires us to give particular deference to that legislative choice because
the State could, if it chose, ban the sale of alcoholic beverages outright. Finally,
the State argues that deference is appropriate because alcoholic beverages are
so-called "vice" products. We consider each of these contentions in turn.

The State's first argument fails to justify the speech prohibition at issue.
Our commercial speech cases recognize some room for the exercise of legislative judgment. However, Rhode Island errs in concluding that *Edge* and
Posadas establish the degree of deference that its decision to impose a price
advertising ban warrants. . . . [In] *Posadas*, . . . a five-Member majority held
that, under the *Central Hudson* test, it was "up to the legislature" to choose
to reduce gambling by suppressing in-state casino advertising rather than
engaging in educational speech. Rhode Island argues that this logic demonstrates the constitutionality of its own decision to ban price advertising
in lieu of raising taxes or employing some other less speech-restrictive
means of promoting temperance.

The reasoning in *Posadas* does support the State's argument, but, on
reflection, we are now persuaded that *Posadas* erroneously performed the
First Amendment analysis. The casino advertising ban was designed to
keep truthful, nonmisleading speech from members of the public for fear
that they would be more likely to gamble if they received it. As a result, the
advertising ban served to shield the State's antigambling policy from the
public scrutiny that more direct, nonspeech regulation would draw.

Given our longstanding hostility to commercial speech regulation of this
type, *Posadas* clearly erred in concluding that it was "up to the legislature" to
choose suppression over a less speech-restrictive policy. The *Posadas* majority's
conclusion on that point cannot be reconciled with the unbroken line of prior
cases striking down similarly broad regulations on truthful, nonmisleading
advertising when non-speech-related alternatives were available.

Because the 5-to-4 decision in *Posadas* marked such a sharp break from
our prior precedent, and because it concerned a constitutional question

about which this Court is the final arbiter, we decline to give force to its highly deferential approach. Instead, in keeping with our prior holdings, we conclude that a state legislature does not have the broad discretion to suppress truthful, nonmisleading information for paternalistic purposes that the *Posadas* majority was willing to tolerate. . . . We also cannot accept the State's second contention, which is premised entirely on the "greater-includes-the-lesser" reasoning endorsed toward the end of the majority's opinion in *Posadas*. There, the majority stated that "the greater power to completely ban casino gambling necessarily includes the lesser power to ban advertising of casino gambling." . . .

In *Rubin v. Coors Brewing Co.*, [514 U.S. 476] (1995), the United States advanced a similar argument as a basis for supporting a statutory prohibition against revealing the alcoholic content of malt beverages on product labels. We rejected the argument, noting that the statement in the *Posadas* opinion was made only after the majority had concluded that the Puerto Rican regulation "survived the *Central Hudson* test." Further consideration persuades us that the "greater-includes-the-lesser" argument should be rejected for the additional and more important reason that it is inconsistent with both logic and well-settled doctrine.

Although we do not dispute the proposition that greater powers include lesser ones, we fail to see how that syllogism requires the conclusion that the State's power to regulate commercial activity is "greater" than its power to ban truthful, nonmisleading commercial speech. Contrary to the assumption made in *Posadas*, we think it quite clear that banning speech may sometimes prove far more intrusive than banning conduct. As a venerable proverb teaches, it may prove more injurious to prevent people from teaching others how to fish than to prevent fish from being sold. Similarly, a local ordinance banning bicycle lessons may curtail freedom far more than one that prohibits bicycle riding within city limits. In short, we reject the assumption that words are necessarily less vital to freedom than actions, or that logic somehow proves that the power to prohibit an activity is necessarily "greater" than the power to suppress speech about it. . . .

Finally, we find unpersuasive the State's contention that, under *Posadas* and *Edge*, the price advertising ban should be upheld because it targets commercial speech that pertains to a "vice" activity. The appellees premise their request for a so-called "vice" exception to our commercial speech doctrine on language in *Edge* which characterized gambling as a "vice." Respondents misread our precedent. Our decision last Term striking down an alcohol-related advertising restriction effectively rejected the very contention respondents now make. See *Rubin v. Coors Brewing Co.*

Moreover, the scope of any "vice" exception to the protection afforded by the First Amendment would be difficult, if not impossible, to define. Almost any product that poses some threat to public health or public morals might reasonably be characterized by a state legislature as relating to "vice activity." Such characterization, however, is anomalous when applied to products such as alcoholic beverages, lottery tickets, or playing cards, that may be lawfully purchased on the open market. . . . For these reasons, a "vice" label that is unaccompanied by a corresponding prohibition against the commercial behavior at issue fails to provide a principled justification for the regulation of commercial speech about that activity.

■ VII

As is clear, the text of the Twenty-first Amendment supports the view that, while it grants the States authority over commerce that might otherwise be reserved to the Federal Government, it places no limit whatsoever on other constitutional provisions. Nevertheless, Rhode Island argues, and the Court of Appeals agreed, that in this case the Twenty-first Amendment tilts the First Amendment analysis in the State's favor.

In reaching its conclusion, the Court of Appeals relied on our decision in *California v. LaRue*, 409 U.S. 109 (1972). In *LaRue*, five Members of the Court relied on the Twenty-first Amendment to buttress the conclusion that the First Amendment did not invalidate California's prohibition of certain grossly sexual exhibitions in premises licensed to serve alcoholic beverages. Specifically, the opinion stated that the Twenty-first Amendment required that the prohibition be given an added presumption in favor of its validity. We are now persuaded that the Court's analysis in *LaRue* would have led to precisely the same result if it had placed no reliance on the Twenty-first Amendment. . . .

Without questioning the holding in *LaRue*, we now disavow its reasoning insofar as it relied on the Twenty-first Amendment. As we explained in a case decided more than a decade after *LaRue*, although the Twenty-first Amendment limits the effect of the dormant Commerce Clause on a State's regulatory power over the delivery or use of intoxicating beverages within its borders, "the Amendment does not license the States to ignore their obligations under other provisions of the Constitution." *Capital Cities Cable, Inc. v. Crisp*, 467 U.S. 691 (1984). That general conclusion reflects our specific holdings that the Twenty-first Amendment does not in any way diminish the force of the Supremacy Clause. . . . We see no reason why the First Amendment should not also be included in that list. Accordingly, we now hold that the Twenty-first Amendment does not qualify the constitutional prohibition against laws abridging the freedom of speech embodied in the First Amendment. The Twenty-first Amendment, therefore, cannot save Rhode Island's ban on liquor price advertising.

■ VIII

Because Rhode Island has failed to carry its heavy burden of justifying its complete ban on price advertising, we conclude that [the state's restrictions on liquor advertising] abridge speech in violation of the First Amendment as made applicable to the States by the Due Process Clause of the Fourteenth Amendment. The judgment of the Court of Appeals is therefore reversed.

☐ *Justice SCALIA, concurring in part and concurring in the judgment.*

Since I do not believe we have before us the wherewithal to declare *Central Hudson* wrong—or at least the wherewithal to say what ought to replace it—I must resolve this case in accord with our existing jurisprudence, which all except Justice THOMAS agree would prohibit the challenged regulation. I am not disposed to develop new law, or reinforce old, on this issue, and accordingly I merely concur in the judgment of the Court. I believe, however, that Justice STEVENS' treatment of the application of the Twenty-First Amendment to this case is correct, and accordingly join Parts I, II, VII, and VIII of Justice STEVENS' opinion.

☐ *Justice THOMAS, concurring in Parts I, II, VI, and VII, and concurring in the judgment.*

In cases such as this, in which the government's asserted interest is to keep legal users of a product or service ignorant in order to manipulate their choices in the marketplace, the balancing test adopted in *Central Hudson* should not be applied, in my view. Rather, such an "interest" is *per se* illegitimate and can no more justify regulation of "commercial" speech than it can justify regulation of "noncommercial" speech. . . .

I do not see a philosophical or historical basis for asserting that "commercial" speech is of "lower value" than "noncommercial" speech. . . . Nor do I believe that the only explanations that the Court has ever advanced for treating "commercial" speech differently from other speech can justify restricting "commercial" speech in order to keep information from legal purchasers so as to thwart what would otherwise be their choices in the marketplace.

I do not join the principal opinion's application of the *Central Hudson* balancing test because I do not believe that such a test should be applied to a restriction of "commercial" speech, at least when, as here, the asserted interest is one that is to be achieved through keeping would-be recipients of the speech in the dark. Application of the advancement-of-state-interest prong of *Central Hudson* makes little sense to me in such circumstances. Faulting the State for failing to show that its price advertising ban decreases alcohol consumption "significantly," seems to imply that if the State had been more successful at keeping consumers ignorant and thereby decreasing their consumption, then the restriction might have been upheld. This contradicts *Virginia Pharmacy Bd.*'s rationale for protecting "commercial" speech in the first instance. . . .

☐ *Justice O'CONNOR, with whom THE CHIEF JUSTICE, Justice SOUTER, and Justice BREYER join, concurring in the judgment.*

I agree with the Court that Rhode Island's price-advertising ban is invalid. I would resolve this case more narrowly, however, by applying our established *Central Hudson* test to determine whether this commercial-speech regulation survives First Amendment scrutiny.

Under that test, we first determine whether the speech at issue concerns lawful activity and is not misleading, and whether the asserted governmental interest is substantial. If both these conditions are met, we must decide whether the regulation "directly advances the governmental interest asserted, and whether it is not more extensive than is necessary to serve that interest." *Central Hudson*. . . . Rhode Island's regulation fails the final prong; that is, its ban is more extensive than necessary to serve the State's interest. . . .

Rhode Island offers one, and only one, justification for its ban on price advertising. Rhode Island says that the ban is intended to keep alcohol prices high as a way to keep consumption low. . . .

The fit between Rhode Island's method and this particular goal is not reasonable. If the target is simply higher prices generally to discourage consumption, the regulation imposes too great, and unnecessary, a prohibition on speech in order to achieve it. The State has other methods at its disposal— methods that would more directly accomplish this stated goal without intruding on sellers' ability to provide truthful, nonmisleading information to customers. . . .

E | *Freedom of the Press*

The Supreme Court articulated constitutional principles for freedom of the press based on the recognition that "speech concerning public affairs . . . is the essence of self-government."[1] Consistent with "the assumption that the widest possible dissemination of information from diverse and antagonistic sources is essential to the welfare of the public," in *Associated Press v. United States*, 326 U.S. 1 (1945), the Court reaffirmed that "Any system of prior restraint of expression . . . [bears] a heavy presumption against its constitutional validity" in *New York Times v. United States*, 403 U.S. 713 (1971) (excerpted below).

At the same time, First Amendment protection for the press also extends to various modes of disseminating information—pamphlets, leaflets, signs, magazines, advertisements, books, motion pictures, and radio and television broadcasts.[2] Accordingly, the "lonely pamphleteer" and the "citizen-critic" are protected along with the "institutional press." This is because the speech and press clauses have traditionally been viewed as inseparable, coterminous, and thus a constitutional redundancy. As the Court in *Thornhill v. Alabama*, 310 U.S. 88 (1940), observed,

> The freedom of speech and of the press guaranteed by the Constitution embraces at least the liberty to discuss publicly and truthfully all matters of public concern without previous restraint or fear of subsequent punishment. The exigencies of the colonial period and the efforts to secure freedom from oppressive administration developed a broadened conception of these liberties as adequate to supply the public need for information and education with respect to the significant issues of the times. . . . Freedom of discussion, if it would fulfill its historical function in this nation, must embrace all issues about which information is needed or appropriate to enable the members of society to cope with the exigencies of their period.

In the last five decades, though, there has been a movement to further enlarge the scope of the First Amendment by recognizing the "institutional status" of the press, such recognition to include affirmative rights to acquire information and special press privileges shielding reporters from indirect restraints on their freedom. Justice Stewart, among others, argued that the First Amendment "is, in essence, a *structural* provision of the Constitution" that confers preferred constitutional status on "the organized press" and "the daily newspapers and other established news media." The "primary purpose" of the amendment, in his words, "was to create a fourth institution outside the

Government as an additional check on the three official branches. . . .
The publishing business is, in short, the only organized private business that is given explicit constitutional protection."[3]

A dilemma posed by such a structuralist interpretation of the First
Amendment and special privileges for the institutional press lies in how
to define *the press*. As Justice White notes in *Branzburg v. Hayes* (1972)
(discussed below), press privileges "present practical and conceptual difficulties of a high order." The Court could fashion constitutional press
privileges by following the lines drawn by some legislatures in drafting
press shield laws (which, in some instances, protect reporters from having
to reveal their sources), defining members of the institutional press
according to either their employer, work schedule, or publication record. Alternatively, immunity could be given for all who write profes-
sionally. But both approaches threaten to deny constitutional protection
for the citizen-critic, and broader definitions of "the press" might prove
so overinclusive as to render meaningless special privileges carved out
for the press in the first place.

Is the First Amendment guarantee against "abridging the freedom
of speech, or of the press" redundant? Should the press be accorded
special constitutional status? And who, in the age of the Internet and
i-reporters, constitutes "the press"? These are some of the underlying
issues confronting the Court in cases arising from direct and indirect
restraints on press freedom.

NOTES

1. *Garrison v. Louisiana*, 379 U.S. 64 (1964).

2. See *Lovell v. City of Griffin*, 303 U.S. 444 (1938) (pamphlets); *Schneider v. New
Jersey*, 308 U.S. 147 (1939) (leaflets); *Thornhill v. Alabama*, 310 U.S. 88 (1940) (signs);
Roth v. United States, 354 U.S. 376 (1957) (*dicta*, books); *Joseph Burstyn, Inc. v. Wilson*,
343 U.S. 495 (1952) (motion pictures); *New York Times Co. v. Sullivan*, 376 U.S. 254
(1964) (noncommercial advertisements); *Virginia State Board of Pharmacy v. Virginia
Citizens Consumer Council*, 425 U.S. 748 (1976) (commercial advertisements); *Green-
belt Cooperative Publishing Association v. Bresler*, 398 U.S. 6 (1970) (newspapers); *Time,
Inc. v. Hill*, 385 U.S. 374 (1967) (magazines); *Red Lion Broadcasting Co. v. Federal
Communications Commission*, 395 U.S. 367 (1969) (radio); and *Estes v. Texas*, 381 U.S.
532 (1965) (*dicta*, television).

3. Potter Stewart, "Or of the Press," 26 *Hastings Law Journal* 631 (1975). See also
Floyd Abrams, "The Press *Is* Different: Reflections on Justice Stewart and the
Autonomous Press," 7 *Hofstra Law Review* 559 (1979). But see also Anthony Lewis, "A
Public Right to Know about Public Institutions: The First Amendment as Sword," in
The Supreme Court Review, eds. Philip Kurland and Gerhard Casper (Chicago: Uni-
versity of Chicago Press, 1981).

■ (1) THE DOCTRINE OF NO PRIOR RESTRAINT

The doctrine of no prior restraint was the touchstone for freedom of the press in English common law and generally assumed to be incorporated into the First Amendment. As Justice Holmes, *Patterson v. Colorado*, 205 U.S. 454 (1907), observed, "[T]he main purpose of [the Free Speech and Press] provisions is to 'prevent all such *previous restraints* upon publications as had been practiced by other governments,' and they do not prevent the subsequent punishment of such as may be deemed contrary to the public welfare."

In *Near v. State of Minnesota ex rel. Olson* (1931) (excerpted below), Chief Justice Hughes wrote the doctrine into the developing law of the First Amendment. Subsequently, *Grosjean v. American Press Company*, 297 U.S. 233 (1936), held that taxes may not impose a discriminatory burden on newspapers. There, Governor Huey Long and his political machine in the Louisiana legislature passed a license tax of 2 percent of the gross income of newspapers selling more than 2,000 copies a week, to stifle their opponents. The principle that taxes may not operate as a prior restraint was reaffirmed in *Minneapolis Star and Tribune v. Minneapolis Commissioner of Revenue*, 460 U.S. 575 (1983), and again, in the Court's striking down a law imposing a sales tax on magazines, but not newspapers, in *Arkansas Writers' Project v. Ragland*, 481 U.S. 221 (1987).

Notably, in *Simon & Schuster, Inc. v. Members of the New York State Crime Victims Board*, 502 U.S. 105 (1991), the Rehnquist Court struck down New York's "Son-of-Sam" law. The law was adopted in order to prevent criminals from profiting from their notoriety and the sale of stories of their criminal activities. In 1977, David Berkowitz, a serial killer popularly known as the "Son of Sam," murdered five women and later agreed to have his story of terror published for a substantial advance on royalties. New York's legislature immediately responded by passing its "Son-of-Sam" law, requiring publishers to deposit with the Victims Control Board all royalties and earnings from its contracts with accused or convicted criminals. The board in turn was authorized to hold the money for five years, during which time victims could bring civil actions against a convicted defendant, and to make payments to victims of a crime. The act also covered individuals who were not criminally charged, tried, and convicted but who admitted committing crimes in a book or other commercial communications. In 1987, the Victims Control Board notified Simon & Schuster that it had violated the law by not turning over its contract with and the royalties owed Henry Hill, who retold his life in organized crime in *Wiseguy*. Attorneys for Simon & Schuster and Hill countered that New York's law violated the First Amendment's guarantee of freedom of speech and press.

Writing for the Court in *Simon & Schuster*, Justice O'Connor struck down New York's law as "presumptively inconsistent with the First Amendment" for imposing "a financial burden on speakers because of the content of their speech." "In the context of financial regulation," O'Connor underscored, "the Government's ability to impose content-based burdens on speech raises the specter that the Government may effectively drive certain ideas or viewpoints from the marketplace. The First Amendment presumptively places this sort of discrimination beyond the power of the Government." Nor did the Court find New York's statute either to serve a "compelling state interest" or to have been "narrowly drawn to achieve that end."

Under the doctrine of no prior restraint, *Mills v. Alabama*, 384 U.S. 214 (1966), invalidated a law barring editorial comments on election days. In *Landmark Communications, Inc. v. Virginia*, 435 U.S. 829 (1978), the Court struck down a Virginia law forbidding the disclosure of confidential information about the proceedings of the state's Judicial Inquiry and Review Commission. So too in *Smith v. Daily Mail Publishing Company*, 443 U.S. 97 (1979), a statute barring the disclosure of the names of juveniles arrested by police was struck down as a prior restraint. And *Butterworth v. Smith*, 494 U.S. 624 (1990), overturned a Florida statute barring witnesses before grand juries from later disclosing their testimony.

Further underscoring the First Amendment's outweighing of interests in personal privacy and law enforcement, *Bartnicki v. Vopper*, 532 U.S. 514 (2001), held that the amendment protects lawfully obtained information even when the original source acquired the information through unlawful means. At issue was the reach of federal and state wiretapping laws aimed at preventing people from intercepting private communications versus the First Amendment's protection for the dissemination of information. The case stemmed from heated contract negotiations between a teachers' union and a school board, when the union's president on her cell phone angrily told the union's chief negotiator that if the school board members did not accept its offer, the teachers were going to "blow off the front porches" of their homes. An opponent of the union said that he found a recording of that conversation in his mailbox and turned it over to a local radio station, which broadcast it. Yet, in balancing the government's interests, in deterring unlawful wiretapping and protecting the privacy of personal communications, against the communication of matters of public importance and criticisms of public officials, Justice Stevens concluded that the government's interests were not so great as to override the First Amendment's protection for the dissemination of information lawfully obtained, even though the original acquisition of the information was unlawful.

Notice that Chief Justice Hughes in *Near v. Minnesota* does not deny that "a government might prevent actual obstruction of the sailing dates of transports or the number or location of troops," implying that there might be a "national security" exception to the First Amendment doctrine of no prior restraint. "On similar grounds," he also notes that "the primary requirements of decency may be enforced against obscene publications" and "[t]he security of the community life may be protected against incitements to acts of violence." In these areas there remains controversy over the application of the doctrine of no prior restraint. In *New York Times Co. v. United States*, 403 U.S. 713 (1971) (see excerpt below) the Court denied as a prior restraint the government's attempt to enjoin the publication of the "Pentagon Papers." In *Southeastern Promotions v. Conrad*, 420 U.S. 546 (1975), the Court required the municipal board of Chattanooga, Tennessee, to make its city Memorial Auditorium available for the stage production of *Hair*, a theatrical performance that included nudity, simulated sex, and vulgar language. A majority of the Court concluded that denying the use of the facility constituted a prior restraint and reaffirmed that "a system of prior restraint 'avoids constitutional infirmity only if it takes place under procedural safeguards designed to obviate the dangers of a censorship system.'"

SELECTED BIBLIOGRAPHY

Committee to Protect Journalists. *Attacks on the Press: The New Face of Censorhip.* New York: Bloomberg Press, 2017.

Ellsberg, Daniel. *Secrets: A Memoir of Vietnam and the Pentagon Papers.* New York: Viking, 2003.

Friendly, Fred. *Minnesota Rag: The Dramatic Story of the Landmark Supreme Court That Gave New Meaning to Freedom of the Press.* New York: Random House, 1981.

Levy, Leonard. *Emergence of a Free Press.* New York: Oxford University Press, 1985.

Millar, Gavin, and Andrew Scott. *Newsgathering: Law, Regulation and the Public Interest.* New York: Oxford University Press, 2015.

O'Brien, David. *The Public's Right to Know: The Supreme Court and the First Amendment.* New York: Praeger, 1981.

Prados, John, and Margaret P. Porter, eds. *Inside the Pentagon Papers.* Lawrence: University Press of Kansas, 2004.

Rudenstine, David. *The Day the Presses Stopped: A History of the Pentagon Papers Case.* Berkeley: University of California Press, 1996.

Schudson, Michael. *The Rise of the Right to Know: Politics and the Culture of Transparency, 1945–1975.* Cambridge: Harvard University Press, 2015.

Snepp, Frank. *Irreparable Harm: A First Hand Account of How One Agent Took on the CIA in an Epic Battle over Secrecy and Free Speech.* New York: Random House, 1999.

Near v. State of Minnesota ex rel. Olson

283 U.S. 697, 51 S.Ct. 625 (1931)

Jay Near was the editor of a muckraking newspaper, the *Saturday Press*, that gave vent to his anti-Semitic, antiblack, anti-Catholic, and antilabor views. In 1927, his newspaper was closed under a 1925 Minnesota abatement statute for any newspaper, magazine, or periodical creating a public nuisance by "malicious, scandalous and defamatory" publication. Under the law, Near could be permanently enjoined from publishing, with a penalty of $1,000 as a fine or a year in jail for violating the injunction against publishing. Near contended the law was unconstitutional, but the state supreme court disagreed, and subsequently a district court and the state supreme court upheld the closing of Near's newspaper. But Near's case came to be championed by Colonel Robert McCormick, the publisher of the Chicago *Tribune*, who paid for an appeal to the Supreme Court.

The Court's decision was 5–4, and the majority's opinion was announced by Chief Justice Hughes. Dissent was by Justice Butler, who was joined by Justices Van Devanter, McReynolds, and Sutherland.

■ ■ ■

☐ *Chief Justice HUGHES delivered the opinion of the Court.*

Chapter 285 of the Session Laws of Minnesota for the year 1925 provides for the abatement, as a public nuisance, of a "malicious, scandalous and defamatory newspaper, magazine or other periodical." Section 1 of the act is as follows:

> Section 1. Any person who, as an individual, or as a member or employee of a firm, or association or organization, or as an officer, director, member or employee of a corporation, shall be engaged in the business of regularly or customarily producing, publishing or circulating, having in possession, selling or giving away
>
> (a) an obscene, lewd and lascivious newspaper, magazine, or other periodical, or
>
> (b) a malicious, scandalous and defamatory newspaper, magazine or other periodical,
>
> —is guilty of a nuisance, and all persons guilty of such nuisance may be enjoined, as hereinafter provided. . . .

Under this statute (clause b), the county attorney of Hennepin County brought this action to enjoin the publication of what was described as a "malicious, scandalous and defamatory newspaper, magazine or other periodical," known as the *Saturday Press*, published by the defendants in the city of Minneapolis. . . .

Without attempting to summarize the contents of the voluminous exhibits attached to the complaint, we deem it sufficient to say that the articles charged, in substance, that a Jewish gangster was in control of gambling, bootlegging, and racketeering in Minneapolis, and that law enforcing officers and agencies were not energetically performing their duties. . . .

If we cut through mere details of procedure, the operation and effect of the statute in substance is that public authorities may bring the owner or publisher of a newspaper or periodical before a judge upon a charge of conducting a business of publishing scandalous and defamatory matter—in particular that the matter consists of charges against public officers of official dereliction—and, unless the owner or publisher is able and disposed to bring competent evidence to satisfy the judge that the charges are true and are published with good motives and for justifiable ends, his newspaper or periodical is suppressed and further publication is made punishable as a contempt. This is of the essence of censorship.

The question is whether a statute authorizing such proceedings in restraint of publication is consistent with the conception of the liberty of the press as historically conceived and guaranteed. In determining the extent of the constitutional protection, it has been generally, if not universally, considered that it is the chief purpose of the guaranty to prevent previous restraints upon publication. The struggle in England, directed against the legislative power of the licenser, resulted in renunciation of the censorship of the press. The liberty deemed to be established was thus described by Blackstone: "The liberty of the press is indeed essential to the nature of a free state; but this consists in laying no *previous* restraints upon publications, and not in freedom from censure for criminal matter when published. Every freeman has an undoubted right to lay what sentiments he pleases before the public; to forbid this, is to destroy the freedom of the press; but if he publishes what is improper, mischievous or illegal, he must take the consequence of his own temerity." The distinction was early pointed out between the extent of the freedom with respect to censorship under our constitutional system and that enjoyed in England. Here, as Madison said, "the great and essential rights of the people are secured against legislative as well as against executive ambition. They are secured, not by laws paramount to prerogative, but by constitutions paramount to laws. This security of the freedom of the press requires that it should be exempt not only from previous restraint by the Executive, as in Great Britain, but from legislative restraint also." Report on the Virginia Resolutions, *Madison's Works*, vol. IV, p. 543. . . .

The criticism upon Blackstone's statement has not been because immunity from previous restraint upon publication has not been regarded as deserving of special emphasis, but chiefly because that immunity cannot be deemed to exhaust the conception of the liberty guaranteed by State and Federal Constitutions. . . . [I]t is recognized that punishment for the abuse of the liberty accorded to the press is essential to the protection of the public, and that the common-law rules that subject the libeler to responsibility for the public offense, as well as for the private injury, are not abolished by the protection extended in our constitutions. The law of criminal libel rests upon that secure foundation. There is also the conceded authority of courts to punish for contempt when publications directly tend to prevent the proper discharge of judicial functions. In the present case, we have no occasion to inquire as to the permissible scope of subsequent punishment.

For whatever wrong the appellant has committed or may commit, by his publications, the state appropriately affords both public and private redress by its libel laws. As has been noted, the statute in question does not deal with punishments; it provides for no punishment, except in case of contempt for violation of the court's order, but for suppression and injunction— that is, for restraint upon publication.

The objection has also been made that the principle as to immunity from previous restraint is stated too broadly, if every such restraint is deemed to be prohibited. That is undoubtedly true; the protection even as to previous restraint is not absolutely unlimited. But the limitation has been recognized only in exceptional cases. "When a nation is at war many things that might be said in time of peace are such a hindrance to its effort that their utterance will not be endured so long as men fight and that no Court could regard them as protected by any constitutional right." *Schenck v. United States.* [249 U.S. 47 (1919)]. No one would question but that a government might prevent actual obstruction to its recruiting service or the publication of the sailing dates of transports or the number and location of troops. On similar grounds, the primary requirements of decency may be enforced against obscene publications. The security of the community life may be protected against incitements to acts of violence and the overthrow by force of orderly government. The constitutional guaranty of free speech does not "protect a man from an injunction against uttering words that may have all the effect of force. *Gompers v. Buck's Stove & Range Co.*, 221 U.S. 418 [(1911)]. . . ." *Schenck v. United States, supra.* These limitations are not applicable here. . . .

The fact that, for approximately one hundred and fifty years, there has been almost an entire absence of attempts to impose previous restraints upon publications relating to the malfeasance of public officers is significant of the deep-seated conviction that such restraints would violate constitutional right. Public officers, whose character and conduct remain open to debate and free discussion in the press, find their remedies for false accusations in actions under libel laws providing for redress and punishment, and not in proceedings to restrain the publication of newspapers and periodicals. The general principle that the constitutional guaranty of the liberty of the press gives immunity from previous restraints has been approved in many decisions under the provisions of state constitutions. . . .

For these reasons we hold the statute, so far as it authorized the proceedings in this action under clause (b) of section 1, to be an infringement of the liberty of the press guaranteed by the Fourteenth Amendment.

☐ *Justice BUTLER, with whom Justices VAN DEVANTER, McREYNOLDS, and SUTHERLAND join, dissenting.*

The decision of the Court in this case . . . gives to freedom of the press a meaning and a scope not heretofore recognized, and construes "liberty" in the due process clause of the Fourteenth Amendment to put upon the states a federal restriction that is without precedent. . . .

The Minnesota statute does not operate as a *previous* restraint on publication within the proper meaning of that phrase. It does not authorize administrative control in advance such as was formerly exercised by the licensers and censors, but prescribes a remedy to be enforced by a suit in equity. In this case there was previous publication made in the course of the business of regularly producing malicious, scandalous, and defamatory periodicals. The business and publications unquestionably constitute an abuse of the right of free press. The statute denounces the things done as a nuisance on the ground, as stated by the state Supreme Court, that they threaten morals, peace, and good order. There is no question of the power of the state to denounce such transgressions. The restraint authorized is only in respect of continuing to do what has been duly adjudged to constitute a nuisance.

New York Times Company v. United States

403 U.S. 713, 91 S.CT. 2140 (1971)

In 1971, amid growing opposition to the undeclared Vietnam War, the Nixon administration sought to enjoin the *New York Times* and the *Washington Post* from publishing a series of articles based on a forty-seven-volume study, *History of U.S. Decision-Making Process on Vietnam Policy.* The study was prepared in 1968 and classified as "Top Secret—Sensitive." The *New York Times* received copies of the study—known as the Pentagon Papers—from Daniel Ellsberg, who had secretly copied them while working for a think tank after his unsuccessful efforts to persuade leading politicians to publicize the study.

After several months of reviewing the documents, the *New York Times* commenced publication of selected items on June 13, 1971. Following the third installment the Department of Justice sought an injunction against publication of the balance of the series and obtained a temporary restraining order prohibiting further publication until June 19. On June 18 the *Washington Post* also printed two articles based on the study and by five o'clock that day the government had filed a similar suit against its further publication of the material.

The next morning a district court denied the government's request for a preliminary injunction, but later in the day a circuit court judge extended the temporary restraining order until noon, June 21, to give a panel of the circuit court the opportunity to consider the government's application. On June 22, the circuit court remanded the case to the district court to determine whether any of the other materials posed such grave and immediate danger to the security of the country as to warrant prior restraint and a continued stay on publication until June 25. The *New York Times* promptly appealed to the Supreme Court to vacate the stay on publication and to expedite consideration of the case. On June 25 the Court granted *certiorari* and heard arguments the next day.

Notably, during the oral arguments, Solicitor General Erwin Griswold, who had not been told by the Nixon administration exactly what in the volumes was potentially injurious to national security, argued, "You [Justice Black, known for his absolutism or strict constructionism] say that no law means no law, and that should be obvious. I can only say, Mr. Justice, that to me it is equally obvious that 'no law' does not mean 'no law,' and I would seek to persuade the Court that that is true." (Years later he would reflect that he should have said, "Yes, Mr. Justice, and the Constitution says 'Congress shall make no law . . . .' And *Congress* has made no law in this case.") Remarkably, four days later the Court issued no fewer than ten opinions. Although a majority of the Burger Court held that the injunction against publication constituted a prior restraint, and thus permitted publication of the excerpts of the Pentagon Papers, it was not until June 13, 2011, that the full set of the forty-seven volumes was released, because the government refused to reveal eleven words it deemed would compromise national security.

The Court's decision was 6–3, and the opinion was announced *per curiam*. There were concurrences by Justices Black, Douglas, Brennan, Stewart, White, and Marshall and dissents by Chief Justice Burger and Justices Harlan and Blackmun.

■ ■ ■

PER CURIAM.

We granted *certiorari* in these cases in which the United States seeks to enjoin the *New York Times* and the *Washington Post* from publishing the contents of a classified study entitled "*History of U.S. Decision-Making Process on Vietnam Policy.*"

"Any system of prior restraints of expression comes to this Court bearing a heavy presumption against its constitutional validity." *Bantam Books, Inc. v. Sullivan*, 372 U.S. 58 (1963); see also *Near v. Minnesota ex rel. Olson*, 283 U.S. 697 (1931). The Government "thus carries a heavy burden of showing justification for the imposition of such a restraint." *Organization for a Better Austin v. Keefe*, 402 U.S. 415 (1971). The District Court for the Southern District of New York in the *New York Times* case, 328 F.Supp. 324, and the District Court for the District of Columbia and the Court of Appeals for the District of Columbia Circuit, 446 F.2d 1327, in the *Washington Post* case held that the Government had not met that burden. We agree.

The judgment of the Court of Appeals for the District of Columbia Circuit is therefore affirmed. The order of the Court of Appeals for the Second Circuit is reversed and the case is remanded with directions to enter a judgment affirming the judgment of the District Court for the Southern District of New York. The stays entered June 25, 1971, by the Court are vacated.

☐ *Justice BLACK, with whom Justice DOUGLAS joins, concurring.*

I believe that every moment's continuance of the injunctions against these newspapers amounts to a flagrant, indefensible, and continuing violation of the First Amendment. . . . In my view it is unfortunate that some of my Brethren are apparently willing to hold that the publication of news may sometimes be enjoined. Such a holding would make a shambles of the First Amendment. . . .

In seeking injunctions against these newspapers and in its presentation to the Court, the Executive Branch seems to have forgotten the essential purpose and history of the First Amendment. When the Constitution was adopted, many people strongly opposed it because the document contained no Bill of Rights to safeguard certain basic freedoms. They especially feared that the new powers granted to a central government might be interpreted to permit the government to curtail freedom of religion, press, assembly, and speech. . . . Madison and the other Framers of the First Amendment, able men that they were, wrote in language they earnestly believed could never be misunderstood: "Congress shall make no law . . . abridging the freedom . . . of the press. . . ." Both the history and language of the First Amendment support the view that the press must be left free to publish news, whatever the source, without censorship, injunctions, or prior restraints. . . .

In other words, we are asked to hold that despite the First Amendment's emphatic command, the Executive Branch, the Congress, and the Judiciary can make laws enjoining publication of current news and abridging freedom of the press in the name of "national security." The Government does not even attempt to rely on any act of Congress. Instead it makes the bold and dangerously far-reaching contention that the courts should take it upon themselves to "make" a law abridging freedom of the press in the name of equity, presidential power and national security. . . . To find that the President has "inherent power" to halt the publication of news by resort to the courts would wipe out the First Amendment and destroy the fundamental liberty and security of the very people the Government hopes to make "secure." No one can read the history of the adoption of the First Amendment without being convinced beyond any doubt that it was injunctions like those sought here that Madison and his collaborators intended to outlaw in this Nation for all time.

The word "security" is a broad, vague generality whose contours should not be invoked to abrogate the fundamental law embodied in the First Amendment. The guarding of military and diplomatic secrets at the expense of informed representative government provides no real security for our Republic. The Framers of the First Amendment, fully aware of both the need to defend a new nation and the abuses of the English and Colonial Governments, sought to give this new society strength and security by providing that freedom of speech, press, religion, and assembly should not be abridged.

□ *Justice DOUGLAS, with whom Justice BLACK joins, concurring.*

The Government says that it has inherent powers to go into court and obtain an injunction to protect the national interest, which in this case is alleged to be national security.

Near v. Minnesota ex rel. Olson, 283 U.S. 697 [(1931)], repudiated that expansive doctrine in no uncertain terms. . . .

Secrecy in government is fundamentally anti-democratic, perpetuating bureaucratic errors. Open debate and discussion of public issues are vital to our national health. On public questions there should be "uninhibited, robust, and wide-open" debate.

□ *Justice BRENNAN, concurring.*

I write separately in these cases only to emphasize what should be apparent that our judgments in the present cases may not be taken to indicate the propriety, in the future, of issuing temporary stays and restraining orders to block the publication of material sought to be suppressed by the Government. So far as I can determine, never before has the United States sought to enjoin a newspaper from publishing information in its possession. The relative novelty of the questions presented, the necessary haste with which decisions were reached, the magnitude of the interests asserted, and the fact that all the parties have concentrated their arguments upon the question whether permanent restraints were proper may have justified at least some of the restraints heretofore imposed in these cases. . . . But even if it be assumed that some of the interim restraints were proper in the two cases before us, that assumption has no bearing upon the propriety of similar judicial action in the future. . . . More important, the First Amendment stands as an absolute bar to the imposition of judicial restraints in circumstances of the kind presented by these cases.

☐ *Justice STEWART, with whom Justice WHITE joins, concurring.*

In the governmental structure created by our Constitution, the Executive is endowed with enormous power in the two related areas of national defense and international relations. This power, largely unchecked by the Legislative and Judicial branches, has been pressed to the very hilt since the advent of the nuclear missile age. For better or for worse, the simple fact is that a President of the United States possesses vastly greater constitutional independence in these two vital areas of power than does, say, a prime minister of a country with a parliamentary form of government.

In the absence of the governmental checks and balances present in other areas of our national life, the only effective restraint upon executive policy and power in the areas of national defense and international affairs may lie in an enlightened citizenry—in an informed and critical public opinion which alone can here protect the values of democratic government. For this reason, it is perhaps here that a press that is alert, aware, and free most vitally serves the basic purpose of the First Amendment. For without an informed and free press there cannot be an enlightened people.

Yet it is elementary that the successful conduct of international diplomacy and the maintenance of an effective national defense require both confidentiality and secrecy. Other nations can hardly deal with this Nation in an atmosphere of mutual trust unless they can be assured that their confidences will be kept. And within our own executive departments, the development of considered and intelligent international policies would be impossible if those charged with their formulation could not communicate with each other freely, frankly, and in confidence. In the area of basic national defense the frequent need for absolute secrecy is, of course, self-evident.

I think there can be but one answer to this dilemma, if dilemma it be. The responsibility must be where the power is. If the Constitution gives the Executive a large degree of unshared power in the conduct of foreign affairs and the maintenance of our national defense, then under the Constitution the Executive must have the largely unshared duty to determine and preserve the degree of internal security necessary to exercise that power successfully. It is an awesome responsibility, requiring judgment and wisdom of a high order. I should suppose that moral, political, and practical considerations would dictate that a very first principle of that wisdom would be an insistence upon avoiding secrecy for its own sake. For when everything is classified, then nothing is classified, and the system becomes one to be disregarded by the cynical or the careless, and to be manipulated by those intent on self-protection or self-promotion. I should suppose, in short, that the hallmark of a truly effective internal security system would be the maximum possible disclosure, recognizing that secrecy can best be preserved only when credibility is truly maintained. But be that as it may, it is clear to me that it is the constitutional duty of the Executive—as a matter of sovereign prerogative and not as a matter of law as the courts know law—through the promulgation and enforcement of executive regulations, to protect the confidentiality necessary to carry out its responsibilities in the fields of international relations and national defense.

This is not to say that Congress and the courts have no role to play. Undoubtedly Congress has the power to enact specific and appropriate criminal laws to protect government property and preserve government secrets. . . . Moreover, if Congress should pass a specific law authorizing civil proceedings in this field, the courts would likewise have the duty to decide the constitutionality of such a law as well as its applicability to the facts proved.

But in the cases before us we are asked neither to construe specific regulations nor to apply specific laws. We are asked, instead, to perform a function that the Constitution gave to the Executive, not the Judiciary. We are asked, quite simply, to prevent the publication by two newspapers of material that the Executive Branch insists should not, in the national interest, be published. I am convinced that the Executive is correct with respect to some of the documents involved. But I cannot say that disclosure of any of them will surely result in direct, immediate, and irreparable damage to our Nation or its people. That being so, there can under the First Amendment be but one judicial resolution of the issues before us. I join the judgments of the Court.

☐ *Justice WHITE, with whom Justice STEWART joins, concurring.*

I concur in today's judgments, but only because of the concededly extraordinary protection against prior restraints enjoyed by the press under our constitutional system. I do not say that in no circumstances would the First Amendment permit an injunction against publishing information about government plans or operations. Nor, after examining the materials the Government characterizes as the most sensitive and destructive, can I deny that revelation of these documents will do substantial damage to public interests. Indeed, I am confident that their disclosure will have that result. But I nevertheless agree that the United States has not satisfied the very heavy burden that it must meet to warrant an injunction against publication in these cases, at least in the absence of express and appropriately limited congressional authorization for prior restraints in circumstances such as these.

The Government's position is simply stated: The responsibility of the Executive for the conduct of the foreign affairs and for the security of the Nation is so basic that the President is entitled to an injunction against publication of a newspaper story whenever he can convince a court that the information to be revealed threatens "grave and irreparable" injury to the public interest; and the injunction should issue whether or not the material to be published is classified, whether or not publication would be lawful under relevant criminal statutes enacted by Congress, and regardless of the circumstances by which the newspaper came into possession of the information.

At least in the absence of legislation by Congress, based on its own investigations and findings, I am quite unable to agree that the inherent powers of the Executive and the courts reach so far as to authorize remedies having such sweeping potential for inhibiting publications by the press. Much of the difficulty inheres in the "grave and irreparable danger" standard suggested by the United States. If the United States were to have judgment under such a standard in these cases, our decision would be of little guidance to other courts in other cases, for the material at issue here would not be available from the Court's opinion or from public records, nor would it be published by the press. Indeed, even today where we hold that the United States has not met its burden, the material remains sealed in court records and it is properly not discussed in today's opinions. Moreover, because the material poses substantial dangers to national interests and because of the hazards of criminal sanctions, a responsible press may choose never to publish the more sensitive materials. To sustain the Government in these cases would start the courts down a long and hazardous road that I am not willing to travel, at least without congressional guidance and direction.

☐ *Justice MARSHALL, concurring.*

The problem here is whether in these particular cases the Executive Branch has authority to invoke the equity jurisdiction of the courts to protect what it believes to be the national interest. See *In re Debs*, 158 U.S. 564 (1895). The Government argues that in addition to the inherent power of any government to protect itself, the President's power to conduct foreign affairs and his position as Commander in Chief give him authority to impose censorship on the press to protect his ability to deal effectively with foreign nations and to conduct the military affairs of the country. Of course, it is beyond cavil that the President has broad powers by virtue of his primary responsibility for the conduct of our foreign affairs and his position as Commander in Chief. . . .

It would, however, be utterly inconsistent with the concept of separation of powers for this Court to use its power of contempt to prevent behavior that Congress has specifically declined to prohibit. There would be a similar damage to the basic concept of these co-equal branches of Government if when the Executive Branch has adequate authority granted by Congress to protect "national security" it can choose instead to invoke the contempt power of a court to enjoin the threatened conduct. The Constitution provides that Congress shall make laws, the President execute laws, and courts interpret laws. It did not provide for government by injunction in which the courts and the Executive Branch can "make law" without regard to the action of Congress. It may be more convenient for the Executive Branch if it need only convince a judge to prohibit conduct rather than ask the Congress to pass a law, and it may be more convenient to enforce a contempt order than to seek a criminal conviction in a jury trial. Moreover, it may be considered politically wise to get a court to share the responsibility for arresting those who the Executive Branch has probable cause to believe are violating the law. But convenience and political considerations of the moment do not justify a basic departure from the principles of our system of government.

☐ *Chief Justice BURGER, dissenting.*

I suggest . . . these cases have been conducted in unseemly haste. . . .

Here, moreover, the frenetic haste is due in large part to the manner in which the Times proceeded from the date it obtained the purloined documents. It seems reasonably clear now that the haste precluded reasonable and deliberate judicial treatment of these cases and was not warranted. . . .

☐ *Justice HARLAN, with whom THE CHIEF JUSTICE and Justice BLACKMUN join, dissenting.*

With all respect, I consider that the Court has been almost irresponsibly feverish in dealing with these cases.

Both the Court of Appeals for the Second Circuit and the Court of Appeals for the District of Columbia Circuit rendered judgment on June 23. The *New York Times*' petition for *certiorari*, its motion for accelerated consideration thereof, and its application for interim relief were filed in this Court on June 24 at about 11 A.M. The application of the United States for interim relief in the *Post* case was also filed here on June 24 at about 7:15 P.M. This Court's order setting a hearing before us on June 26 at 11 A.M., a course which I joined only to avoid the possibility of even more peremptory action by the Court, was issued less than 24 hours before. The record in the *Post* case was filed with the Clerk shortly before 1 P.M. on June 25; the record in the *Times* case did not arrive until 7 or 8 o'clock that same night. The briefs of the parties were received less than two hours before argument on June 26.

This frenzied train of events took place in the name of the presumption against prior restraints created by the First Amendment. Due regard for the extraordinarily important and difficult questions involved in these litigations should have led the Court to shun such a precipitate timetable. In order to decide the merits of these cases properly, some or all of the following questions should have been faced:

1. Whether the Attorney General is authorized to bring these suits in the name of the United States. . . .

2. Whether the First Amendment permits the federal courts to enjoin publication of stories which would present a serious threat to national security. . . .

3. Whether the threat to publish highly secret documents is of itself a sufficient implication of national security to justify an injunction on the theory that regardless of the contents of the documents, harm enough results simply from the demonstration of such a breach of secrecy.

4. Whether the unauthorized disclosure of any of these particular documents would seriously impair the national security.

5. What weight should be given to the opinion of high officers in the Executive Branch of the Government with respect to questions 3 and 4.

6. Whether the newspapers are entitled to retain and use the documents notwithstanding the seemingly uncontested facts that the documents, or the originals of which they are duplicates, were purloined from the Government's possession and that the newspapers received them with knowledge that they had been feloniously acquired. . . .

7. Whether the threatened harm to the national security or the Government's possessory interest in the documents justifies the issuance of an injunction against publication in light of—

a. The strong First Amendment policy against prior restraints on publication;

b. The doctrine against enjoining conduct in violation of criminal statutes; and

c. The extent to which the materials at issue have apparently already been otherwise disseminated.

These are difficult questions of fact, of law, and of judgment: the potential consequences of erroneous decision are enormous. The time which has been available to us, to the lower courts, and to the parties has been wholly inadequate for giving these cases the kind of consideration they deserve. It is a reflection on the stability of the judicial process that these great issues—as important as any that have arisen during my time on the Court—should have been decided under the pressures engendered by the torrent of publicity that has attended these litigations from their inception.

Forced as I am to reach the merits of these cases, I dissent from the opinion and judgments of the Court. . . .

It is plain to me that the scope of the judicial function in passing upon the activities of the Executive Branch of the Government in the field of foreign affairs is very narrowly restricted. This view is, I think, dictated by the concept of separation of powers upon which our constitutional system rests.

In a speech on the floor of the House of Representatives, Chief Justice John MARSHALL, then a member of that body, stated:

> The President is the sole organ of the nation in its external relations, and its sole representative with foreign nations. 10 *Annals of Cong.* 613.

From that time, shortly after the founding of the Nation, to this, there has been no substantial challenge to this description of the scope of executive power. . . . I agree that, in performance of its duty to protect the values of the First Amendment against political pressures, the judiciary must review the initial Executive determination to the point of satisfying itself that the subject matter of the dispute does lie within the proper compass of the President's foreign relations power. Constitutional considerations forbid "a complete abandonment of judicial control." Moreover the judiciary may properly insist that the determination that disclosure of the subject matter would irreparably impair the national security be made by the head of the Executive Department concerned—here the Secretary of State or the Secretary of Defense—after actual personal consideration by that officer. This safeguard is required in the analogous area of executive claims of privilege for secrets of state. . . .

But in my judgment the judiciary may not properly go beyond these two inquiries and redetermine for itself the probable impact of disclosure on the national security.

☐ *Justice BLACKMUN, dissenting.*

The country would be none the worse off were the cases tried quickly, to be sure, but in the customary and properly deliberative manner. The most recent of the material, it is said, dates no later than 1968, already about three years ago, and the Times itself took three months to formulate its plan of procedure and, thus, deprived its public for that period.

The First Amendment, after all, is only one part of an entire Constitution. Article II of the great document vests in the Executive Branch primary power over the conduct of foreign affairs and places in that branch the responsibility for the Nation's safety. Each provision of the Constitution is important, and I cannot subscribe to a doctrine of unlimited absolutism for the First Amendment at the cost of downgrading other provisions. First Amendment absolutism has never commanded a majority of this Court. . . .

What is needed here is a weighing, upon properly developed standards, of the broad right of the press to print and of the very narrow right of the Government to prevent.

■ (2) Indirect Prior Restraints

Besides direct prior restraints, the press may be subject to indirect restraints and requirements that arguably have a chilling effect on the exercise of free speech and press. In *Snepp v. United States*, 444 U.S. 507 (1980), for example, the Court summarily dismissed a First Amendment challenge to the Central Intelligence Agency requiring employees and former employees to submit any (fiction or nonfiction) writings for prepublication review. In *Meese v. Keene*, 481 U.S. 465 (1987), over the objections of three dissenters (Justices Blackmun, Brennan, and Marshall), the Rehnquist Court upheld the labeling as "political propaganda" of three documentary films (dealing with acid rain and the environment) under the Foreign Agents Registration Act.

In three companion cases in 1972, *Branzburg v. Hayes, In re Pappas*, and *United States v. Caldwell*, 408 U.S. 665 (1972), Justice White, writing for a bare majority of the Court, rejected reporters' claims that the First Amendment guarantees them a testimonial privilege against discussing their sources before grand juries and at trials. After this ruling, many states subsequently adopted "press shield" laws, protecting reporters from revealing their sources. Justice White, again, wrote for the Court in *Zurcher v. The Stanford Daily*, 436 U.S. 547 (1978), holding that newspaper offices are not exempt from searches by police for photographs and other mere evidence of crime. The ruling in *Zurcher*, however, was undercut by Congress's passing the Privacy Protection Act of 1980, which prohibits the unannounced searches of newsrooms by federal, state, and local law enforcement officers, except in certain narrowly defined circumstances. As discussed in Section H of this chapter, the Court has also substantially cut back on the First Amendment freedoms of students and student newspapers in cases such as *Hazelwood School District v. Kuhlmeier*, 484 U.S. 260 (1988).

Members of the press also unsuccessfully sought to have the Court vindicate a First Amendment right of access to acquire information. In *dicta* in a number of rulings the Court had suggested that the amendment conveys a "right to receive" as a corollary of the freedom to disseminate information.[1] But a bare majority of the Court rebuffed a further expansion of the First Amendment when members of the press pushed for an "affirmative right of access" in challenging prohibitions of personal interviews between reporters and inmates in state and federal prisons, in *Pell v. Procunier*, 417 U.S. 817 (1974), and *Saxbe v. Washington Post*, 417 U.S. 843 (1974). There Justice Stewart reaffirmed that "the First Amendment does not guarantee the press a constitutional right of special access to information not available to the public generally." In dissent with Justices Brennan and Marshall, Justice Douglas argued that the First Amendment confers special privileges on the press so it may vindicate the public's interests in information about the operation of government. Justice Powell also dissented, finding that the prohibition "significantly impairs the right of the people to a free flow of information and ideas on the conduct of Government." He explained, "The underlying right is the right of the public generally. The press is the necessary representative of the public's interests in this context and the instrumentality which effects the public's rights." When the issue again arose in *Houchins v. KQED, Inc.*, 438 U.S. 1 (1978), the Court remained sharply divided, but it still rejected the claim to a First Amendment right of access. However, see *Globe Newspaper Co. v. Superior Court for the County of Norfolk* (1982) (excerpted in Section G of this chapter).

Cohen v. Cowles Media Co., 501 U.S. 663 (1991), raised an issue bearing on indirect prior restraints on the press. *Cohen* posed the question of whether newspapers may be sued for disclosing the names of their confidential sources. Dan Cohen, a political consultant, was fired from his job after two newspapers identified him as the confidential source of damaging information about the criminal record of another candidate. He had been promised anonymity by reporters, but their editors overrode their objections to naming him and revised their stories to point to the fact that Cohen was the source of the damaging information. Cohen sued for breach of contract, and a jury awarded him $700,000. The Minnesota Supreme Court, however, overturned that award when holding that the First Amendment's guarantee for freedom of the press outweighed "the common law interest in protecting a promise of anonymity."

By a 5–4 vote, the Court held that the First Amendment does not provide a shield against suits for damages, under state promissory estoppel law, for a newspaper's breach of a promise of confidentiality. Writing for the bare majority, Justice White observed that generally applicable laws do not offend the First Amendment simply because their enforcement against the press has incidental effect on its ability to gather and report the news. . . . [T]ruthful information sought to be published must have been lawfully acquired. The press may not with impunity break and enter an office or dwelling to gather news. Neither does the First Amendment relieve a newspaper reporter of the obligation shared by all citizens to respond to a grand jury subpoena and answer questions relevant to a criminal investigation, even though the reporter might be required to reveal a confidential source. . . . It is therefore beyond dispute that "[t]he publisher of a newspaper has no special immunity from the application of general laws. He has no special privilege to invade the rights and liberties of others." Accordingly, enforcement of such general laws against the press is not subject to stricter scrutiny than would be applied to enforcement against other persons or organizations.

In *United States v. National Treasury Employees Union*, 513 U.S. 454 (1995), the Court struck down provisions of the Ethics Reform Act of 1989 that banned federal employees from receiving honoraria for giving speeches and publishing articles and books. Writing for the Court, Justice Stevens explained,

> Federal employees who write for publication in their spare time have made significant contributions to the marketplace of ideas. They include literary giants like Nathaniel Hawthorne and Herman Melville, who were employed by the Customs Service; Walt Whitman, who worked for the Departments of Justice and Interior; and Bret Harte, an employee of the mint. . . .
> The large-scale disincentive to Government employees' expression also imposes a significant burden on the public's right to read and hear what the employees would otherwise have written and said. We have no way to measure the true cost of that burden, but we cannot ignore the risk that it might deprive us of the work of a future Melville or Hawthorne. The honoraria ban imposes the kind of burden that abridges speech under the First Amendment.

Finally, extending prior rulings that the First Amendment does not convey a right to receive information, in *Beard v. Banks*, 548 U.S. 521 (2006), the Court upheld a prison policy of conditioning access to nonreligious periodicals upon inmates' good behavior. Writing for the Court, Justice Breyer held that prisons may impose reasonable restrictions on the constitutional rights of inmates. Justices Stevens and Ginsburg dissented.

NOTE

1. See *Martin v. City of Struthers*, 319 U.S. 141, 143 (1943); *Thomas v. Collins*, 323 U.S. 516 (1945); *Procunier v. Martinez*, 416 U.S. 396 (1974); and *Kleindienst v. Mandel*, 408 U.S. 753 (1972).

F | *Regulating the Broadcast, Cable Media, and the Internet*

Radio, television, cable, and other electronic media have posed special First Amendment problems. This is because they were considered a scarce public resource that should be licensed and regulated in "the public interest." In 1934, the Federal Communications Commission (FCC) was created to regulate broadcast and telecommunications systems based on considerations of "public interest, convenience and necessity." While the FCC is forbidden from exercising censorship per se, it has the authority to license every radio and television station, subject to renewal every three years, and to revoke or suspend those licenses for violations of its rules or other statutory requirements, including antitrust laws. Among the regulations imposed are those requiring "equal time" for opponents of political candidates who are given air time and a "family hour" on television (during which programs are shown that have little or no violence or suggestive sexual material), bans against broadcasting obscene and indecent language, and limitations on the co-ownership of newspapers and broadcasting systems.

In the past several decades, however, regulations were gradually cut back. This was partially in response to technological developments, such as cable television and satellite transmissions. These advances increased the multiplicity of channels and held the potential for greater public access. This, in turn, undermined the traditional rationale for regulating radio and television as a scarce public resource, and exempted from First Amendment protection. In addition, in the last several decades, there was a movement toward deregulation to promote economic competition and efficiency. Because the radio market, for example, had grown and competition increased since the 1930s, the FCC relaxed some of its regulations and did away with others—such as requiring maximum time limits for commercials and minimum requirements for news and public affairs programming.

One of the most controversial requirements imposed on the broadcast media in 1949, and finally eliminated in 1987, was the "fairness doctrine" requiring stations to notify and provide air time for individuals personally attacked or made the subject of political editorials. *Red Lion Broadcasting Co., Inc. v. Federal Communications Commission*, 395 U.S. 367 (1969), upheld the fairness doctrine based on a crucial distinction between the broadcast media (governed as a public utility) and print media (a private business) in terms of the First Amendment. *Red*

622 | Freedom of Expression and Association

Lion's distinctions were underscored by the Court's striking down Florida's "right to reply" law, requiring newspapers to print the reply of any political candidate who was subject to a personal attack by a newspaper. In *Miami Herald Publishing Company v. Tornillo*, 418 U.S. 241 (1974), Justice White explained that "this [right to reply] law runs afoul of the elementary First Amendment proposition that government may not force a newspaper to print copy which, in its journalistic discretion, it chooses to leave on the newspaper floor."

In *Columbia Broadcasting System v. Democratic National Committee*, 412 U.S. 94 (1973), the Court also ruled that the FCC was not required to ensure a "private right of access to the broadcast media," when sustaining CBS's policy of refusing paid editorial advertisements. In *CBS, Inc. v. FCC*, 453 U.S. 367 (1981), however, the Court affirmed a "right of access" for legally qualified candidates for federal office when ruling that CBS should not have refused to sell air time in 1979 to the Democratic National Committee for President Carter's reelection bid because it deemed it too early for the presidential campaign of 1980 to begin.

While the FCC abandoned the fairness doctrine, in 1987 it also moved to enforce more strictly its regulations against "indecent" broadcasts. This followed the ruling in *Federal Communications Commission v. Pacifica Foundation* (1978) (see excerpt in Section B) and from a change in the views of a majority of the commissioners, who were appointed by President Reagan. As a result, some new First Amendment controversies have arisen over the reading on the radio of literary works, such as Allen Ginsberg's poem "Howl," and fleeting "indecent" images and language on broadcast television.

The Court upheld as well the FCC's rules banning the acquisition of radio and television stations by newspapers in *FCC v. National Citizens Committee*, 436 U.S. 775 (1978), and the FCC's decision not to consider changes in the entertainment format of radio stations when reviewing applications for renewal or transfer of broadcasting licenses in *FCC v. WNCN Listeners Guild*, 450 U.S. 582 (1981).

The Court accords greater First Amendment protection to cable and electronic media because of the multiplicity of channels and greater access brought about by the development of cable television and more satellite and telecommunications systems. In *United States v. Midwest Video Corporation*, 406 U.S. 649 (1972), the justices (5–4) upheld the FCC's regulation of television antennae and cable systems. But in *FCC v. Midwest Video Corporation*, 440 U.S. 689 (1979), the Court (6–3) struck down the FCC's regulations requiring major cable systems (with twenty or more channel capacities) to provide up to four channels for free public expression and public affairs programming. "Under the [FCC's] rules," Justice White observed, "cable operators [were] deprived of all discretion regarding who may exploit their access channels and what may be transmitted over such channels."

Due to the Court's ruling in *Midwest Video Corporation* (II), the FCC has less jurisdiction over cable television systems than over radio and broadcast television. The Court, though, held the FCC's technical standards governing the quality of cable television signals to preempt those of states and localities. *City of New York v. FCC*, 486 U.S. 57 (1988). The powers of states and localities over cable television were also sharply limited in *Capital Cities Cable, Inc. v. Crisp*, 467 U.S. 691 (1984), overturning an Oklahoma law barring the broadcasting of advertisements for alcoholic beverages as applied to cable television operators. Without hearing oral arguments or issuing a written opinion, the Court also affirmed a lower federal court ruling striking down Utah's law restricting cable telecasts of nudity, sex acts, and other "indecent" images in *Wilkinson v. Jones*, 480 U.S. 926 (1987). But in *Leathers v. Medlock*, 499 U.S. 439 (1991), the Court upheld a state's 4 percent tax on cable television, though not on similar communications services. In her opinion for the Court, Justice O'Connor reaffirmed that states may neither single out the press as a whole for special taxes nor discriminate among different kinds of media on the basis of content or for the purpose of censorship. Nonetheless, O'Connor held that states may apply general taxes to some kinds of media, and not others, so long as the taxes do not discriminate "on the basis of ideas."

In *Turner Broadcasting System, Inc. v. Federal Communications Commission*, 512 U.S. 622 (1994) (*Turner Broadcasting I*), the Court held for the first time that the First Amendment extends some protection to the cable industry and requires heightened judicial scrutiny of any regulation or restriction, in light of the differences between broadcast and cable technologies. In 1992, Congress overrode a presidential veto to enact the Cable Television Consumer Protection and Competition Act. That legislation subjects the cable industry to rate regulation by the FCC and by municipal franchising authorities; prohibits municipalities from awarding exclusive franchises to cable operators; imposes various restrictions on cable programmers; and directs the FCC to develop and promulgate regulations imposing minimum technical standards for cable operators. Turner Broadcasting System challenged two "must-carry provisions" of the law as a violation of the First Amendment. Section 4 of the act requires cable companies to carry "local commercial television stations," other than those qualifying as "noncommercial educational" stations under Section 5, that operate within the same television market as the cable system. Cable systems with more than twelve active channels, and more than three hundred subscribers, are required to set aside up to one-third of their channels for commercial broadcast stations that request carriage. Cable systems with more than three hundred subscribers, but only twelve or fewer active channels, must carry the signals of three commercial broadcast stations. Section 5 of the act imposes similar requirements regarding the carriage of local public broadcasting television stations.

Writing for the Court in *Turner Broadcasting I,* Justice Kennedy held that the First Amendment extends protection to the cable industry. On that issue, the justices were unanimous. However, Justice Kennedy commanded only four other votes—those of Chief Justice Rehnquist and Justices Blackmun, Souter, and Stevens—on the central issue of the constitutionality of the "must-carry provisions." On that issue a bare majority declined to strike down the regulations and remanded the case back to the lower court for reconsideration.

But, subsequently in *Turner Broadcasting System, Inc. v. Federal Communications Commissions,* 520 U.S. 180 (1997) (*Turner Broadcasting II*), Justice Kennedy commanded a bare majority for upholding the must-carry provisions. The provisions, according to Justice Kennedy, were "content neutral" and therefore had to pass only an intermediate level of scrutiny; namely, whether the regulations advance an "important government interest" without unnecessarily burdening speech. Turning to the economic theory advanced in *Turner Broadcasting I* as a justification for the provisions, Justice Kennedy ruled that it was reasonable for Congress to conclude that local broadcast stations needed special protection. In his words, "Congress has an independent interest in preserving a multiplicity of broadcasters to ensure that all households have access to information and entertainment on an equal footing with those who subscribe to cable."

The Court, then, further extended First Amendment protection for cable television when striking down two restrictions on the programming of "indecent material" that Congress had imposed in the Cable Television Consumer Protection and Competition Act of 1992. Although upholding the act's authorization for cable operators to forbid the programmers of privately "leased cable channels" from programming "patently offensive" material, the Court invalidated the act's similar authorization for cable operators with respect to "public, educational, and governmental channels." The Court also invalidated another provision that required cable operators to isolate "patently offensive" programming on a single channel and require viewers to request access in advance and in writing in *Denver Area Telecommunications Consortium v. Federal Communications Commissions,* 518 U.S. 727 (1996).

In a related controversy over Congress's regulation of indecent and obscene material on cable, the Court struck down a provision of the Telecommunications Act of 1966, in *United States v. Playboy Entertainment Group, Inc.,* 529 U.S. 803 (2000). That act required, in part, cable television operators providing channels "primarily dedicated to sexually-oriented programming" to either fully scramble those channels or limit their transmission to hours between 10 P.M. and 6 A.M., when young viewers were unlikely. Scrambling proved inexact, however, and audio or visual portions could often be heard or viewed in what is known as "signal bleed." As a result, most cable operators adopted the "time channeling" approach, which in turn meant that for two-thirds of the day no viewers in their service could watch sexually oriented programming. Writing for the Court, Justice Kennedy ruled that that section of the act could not survive strict scrutiny because it was content based and therefore had to advance a compelling governmental interest in the least restrictive way. Here, Justice Kennedy emphasized the key difference between broadcast and cable television: cable television may block unwanted channels on a household–by–household basis and, thus, time-channeling on cable television sweeps too broadly.

Finally, in its first major ruling on free speech and the Internet, in *Reno v. American Civil Liberties Union* (1997) (excerpted in Section B of this chapter), the Court unanimously struck down provisions of the Communications Decency Act of 1996, which had made a federal crime the transmission of "obscene or indecent" messages to anyone under the age of eighteen. In doing so, the Court also held that the Internet is a unique medium unlike broadcast and cable communications. Subsequently, the Court, in *Ashcroft v. Free Speech Coalition*, 534 U.S. 234 (2002) (excerpted in Section B of this chapter), struck down provisions of the Child Pornography Prevention Act of 1996, which made it a crime to distribute "virtual child pornography." And in *Ashcroft v. American Civil Liberties Union*, 542 U.S. 656 (2004), it affirmed lower court orders enjoining the enforcement of the Child Online Protection Act of 1998, which Congress enacted in response to the ruling in *Reno v. ACLU*. However, in *United States v. American Library Association*, 539 U.S. 194 (2003), it upheld the Children's Internet Protection Act of 2001, authorizing public libraries to install pornography filters on computers that provide public access to the Internet. In addition, in *United States v. Williams*, 553 U.S. 285 (2008) (excerpted below), the Roberts Court upheld the so-called PROTECT Act of 2003 (Prosecutorial Remedies and Other Tools to end the Exploitation of Children Today Act), which Congress enacted in response to the ruling in *Ashcroft v. Free Speech Coalition* (2002) that made it a crime to pander child pornography. The Roberts Court, however, struck down North Carolina's law making it a felony for registered sex offenders to access social media on the Internet that "permits minor children to become members or create or maintain Web pages." Writing for the Court in *Packingham v. North Carolina*, 137 S.Ct. 1730 (2017), Justice Kennedy held that the law impermissibly restricted freedom of speech because of its overreach and application to sites such as Facebook, LinkedIn, and Twitter; as well, it was not narrowly tailored to prohibiting sexual offenders from engaging in conduct that may lead to sexual abuse of children.

Selected Bibliography

Bernal, Paul. *The Internet Warts and All: Free Speech, Privacy, and Truth.* New York: Cambridge University Press, 2018.

Chris, Cynthia. *The Indecent Screen: Regulating Television in the Twenty-First Century.* Newark, NJ: Rutgers University Press, 2019.

Biegel, Stuart. *Beyond Our Control? Confronting the Limits of Our Legal System in the Age of Cyberspace.* Cambridge, MA: MIT Press, 2001.

Friendly, Fred W. *The Good Guys, the Bad Guys and the First Amendment.* New York: Random House, 1976.

Gant, Scott. *We're All Journalists Now: The Transformation of the Press and the Reshaping of Law in the Internet Age.* New York: Simon & Schuster, 2007.

Goodale, James C., and Frieden, Rob. *All About Cable and Broadband.* New York: Law Journal Press, 2015.

Lessig, Lawrence. *Code and Other Laws of Cyberspace.* New York: Basic Books, 2000.

Levmore, Saul, and Nussbaum, Martha, eds. *The Offensive Internet: Speech, Privacy, and Reputation.* Cambridge, MA: Harvard University Press, 2011.

Powe, Lucas. *Media Law: A Very Short Introduction.* New York: Oxford University Press, 2017.

Shariff, Shaheen. *Sexting and Cyberbullying: Defining the Line for Digitally Empowered Kids.* New York: Cambridge University Press, 2015.

Solove, Daniel. *The Future of Reputation: Gossip, Rumor, and Privacy on the Internet.* New Haven, CT: Yale University Press, 2007.

Federal Communications Commission v. Pacifica Foundation (reprise)

438 U.S. 726, 98 S.Ct. 3026 (1978)

In this case, the Court upheld the FCC's power to ban indecent language on the radio. The case is reprinted in part in Section B of this chapter.

■ ■ ■

Reno v. American Civil Liberties Union (reprise)
521 U.S. 844, 117 S.CT. 2329 (1997)

This case is excerpted in Section B of this chapter.

■ ■ ■

United States v. Williams
553 U.S. 285, 128 S.CT. 1830 (2008)

In response to the Court's ruling in *Ashcroft v. Free Speech Coalition*, 534 U.S. 234 (2002), which struck down provisions of the Child Pornography Prevention Act of 1996 that made it a crime to distribute or possess "virtual child pornography," Congress enacted the Prosecutorial Remedies and Other Tools to end the Exploitation of Children Today Act of 2003 (the PROTECT Act). Part of that law, Section 2252(a)(3)(B), makes it a federal crime for any person who "knowingly . . . advertises, promotes, or solicits . . . any material or purported material in a manner that reflects the belief, or that is intended to cause another to believe, that the material or purported material is, or contains—(i) an obscene visual depiction of a minor engaging in sexually explicit conduct; or (ii) a visual depiction of an actual minor engaging in sexually explicit conduct." Subsequently, in 2004, Michael Williams, using a sexually explicit screen name, signed in to an Internet chat room. A Secret Service agent had also signed in to the chat room under the moniker "Lisa n Miami." The agent noticed that Williams had posted a message that read: "Dad of toddler has 'good' pics of her an [sic] me for swap of your toddler pics, or live cam." The agent struck up a conversation with Williams, leading to an electronic exchange of nonpornographic pictures of children. Later, Williams messaged that he had photographs of men molesting his four-year-old daughter. Suspicious that "Lisa n Miami" was a law-enforcement agent, before proceeding further Williams demanded that the agent produce additional pictures. When he did not, Williams posted the following public message in the chat room: "HERE ROOM; I CAN PUT UPLINK CUZ IM FOR REAL—SHE CANT." Appended to this declaration was a hyperlink that led to seven pictures of actual children, aged approximately five to fifteen, engaging in sexually explicit conduct and displaying their genitals. The Secret Service then obtained a search warrant for Williams's home, where agents seized two hard drives containing twenty-two images of real children engaged in sexually explicit conduct. Williams was charged with one count of pandering child pornography under Section 2252A(a)(3)(B) and one count of possessing child pornography under Section 2252A(a)(5)(B). He pleaded guilty to both counts but reserved the right to challenge the constitutionality of the pandering conviction. The district court rejected his challenge and sentenced him to concurrent sixty-month sentences. The Court of Appeals for the Eleventh Circuit reversed the pandering conviction, holding that the statute was both overbroad and impermissibly vague. In its view, the statute was broad enough to include any "braggart, exaggerator, or outright liar" who claimed to have child pornography. The government appealed and the Supreme Court granted *certiorari*.

The appellate court's decision was reversed by a 7–2 vote. Justice Scalia delivered the opinion of the Court. Justice Stevens filed a concurring opinion, while Justice Souter, joined by Justice Ginsburg, issued a dissenting opinion.

■ ■ ■

☐ *Justice SCALIA delivered the opinion of the Court.*

Section 2252A(a)(3)(B) of Title 18, United States Code, criminalizes, in certain specified circumstances, the pandering or solicitation of child pornography. This case presents the question whether that statute is overbroad under the First Amendment or impermissibly vague under the Due Process Clause of the Fifth Amendment.

We have long held that obscene speech—sexually explicit material that violates fundamental notions of decency—is not protected by the First Amendment. See *Roth v. United States*, 354 U.S. 476 (1957). But to protect explicit material that has social value, we have limited the scope of the obscenity exception, and have overturned convictions for the distribution of sexually graphic but nonobscene material. See *Miller v. California*, 413 U.S. 15 (1973); see also, e.g., *Jenkins v. Georgia*, 418 U.S. 153 (1974).

Over the last 25 years, we have confronted a related and overlapping category of proscribable speech: child pornography. See *Ashcroft v. Free Speech Coalition*, 535 U.S. 234 (2002); *New York v. Ferber*, 458 U.S. 747 (1982). This consists of sexually explicit visual portrayals that feature children. We have held that a statute which proscribes the distribution of all child pornography, even material that does not qualify as obscenity, does not on its face violate the First Amendment. Moreover, we have held that the government may criminalize the possession of child pornography, even though it may not criminalize the mere possession of obscene material involving adults.

The broad authority to proscribe child pornography is not, however, unlimited. Four Terms ago, we held facially overbroad two provisions of the federal Child Pornography Prevention Act of 1996 (CPPA). *Free Speech Coalition*. The first of these banned the possession and distribution of "any visual depiction" that "is, or appears to be, of a minor engaging in sexually explicit conduct," even if it contained only youthful-looking adult actors or virtual images of children generated by a computer. This was invalid, we explained, because the child-protection rationale for speech restriction does not apply to materials produced without children. The second provision at issue in *Free Speech Coalition* criminalized the possession and distribution of material that had been pandered as child pornography, regardless of whether it actually was that. A person could thus face prosecution for possessing unobjectionable material that someone else had pandered. We held that this prohibition, which did "more than prohibit pandering," was also facially overbroad.

After our decision in *Free Speech Coalition*, Congress went back to the drawing board and produced legislation with the unlikely title of the Prosecutorial Remedies and Other Tools to end the Exploitation of Children Today Act of 2003. We shall refer to it as the Act. Section 503 of the Act amended 18 U.S.C. Section 2252A to add a new pandering and solicitation provision, relevant portions of which now read as follows:

(a) Any person who—
(3)knowingly—
(B)advertises, promotes, presents, distributes, or solicits through the mails, or in interstate or foreign commerce by any means, including by computer, any material or purported material in a manner that reflects the belief, or that is intended to cause another to believe, that the material or purported material is, or contains—
(i)an obscene visual depiction of a minor engaging in sexually explicit conduct; or
(ii) a visual depiction of an actual minor engaging in sexually explicit conduct, shall be punished as provided in subsection (b).

Section 2256(2)(A) defines "sexually explicit conduct" as "actual or simulated—

(i)sexual intercourse, including genital-genital, oral-genital, anal-genital, or oral-anal, whether between persons of the same or opposite sex;
(ii)bestiality;
(iii)masturbation;
(iv)sadistic or masochistic abuse; or
(v)lascivious exhibition of the genitals or pubic area of any person.

Violation of Section 2252A(a)(3)(B) incurs a minimum sentence of 5 years imprisonment and a maximum of 20 years.

The Act's express findings indicate that Congress was concerned that limiting the child-pornography prohibition to material that could be proved to feature actual children, as our decision in *Free Speech Coalition* required, would enable many child pornographers to evade conviction. The emergence of new technology and the repeated retransmission of picture files over the Internet could make it nearly impossible to prove that a particular image was produced using real children—even though "[t]here is no substantial evidence that any of the child pornography images being trafficked today were made other than by the abuse of real children," virtual imaging being prohibitively expensive. . . .

According to our First Amendment overbreadth doctrine, a statute is facially invalid if it prohibits a substantial amount of protected speech. The doctrine seeks to strike a balance between competing social costs. *Virginia v.*

Hicks, 539 U.S. 113 (2003). On the one hand, the threat of enforcement of an overbroad law deters people from engaging in constitutionally protected speech, inhibiting the free exchange of ideas. On the other hand, invalidating a law that in some of its applications is perfectly constitutional—particularly a law directed at conduct so antisocial that it has been made criminal—has obvious harmful effects. In order to maintain an appropriate balance, we have vigorously enforced the requirement that a statute's overbreadth be substantial, not only in an absolute sense, but also relative to the statute's plainly legitimate sweep.

The first step in overbreadth analysis is to construe the challenged statute; it is impossible to determine whether a statute reaches too far without first knowing what the statute covers. Generally speaking, Section 2252A(a)(3)(B) prohibits offers to provide and requests to obtain child pornography. The statute does not require the actual existence of child pornography. In this respect, it differs from the statutes in *Ferber*, and *Free Speech Coalition*, which prohibited the possession or distribution of child pornography. Rather than targeting the underlying material, this statute bans the collateral speech that introduces such material into the child-pornography distribution network. Thus, an Internet user who solicits child pornography from an undercover agent violates the statute, even if the officer possesses no child pornography. Likewise, a person who advertises virtual child pornography as depicting actual children also falls within the reach of the statute.

The statute's definition of the material or purported material that may not be pandered or solicited precisely tracks the material held constitutionally proscribable in *Ferber* and *Miller*: obscene material depicting (actual or virtual) children engaged in sexually explicit conduct, and any other material depicting actual children engaged in sexually explicit conduct. . . .

We now turn to whether the statute, as we have construed it, criminalizes a substantial amount of protected expressive activity.

Offers to engage in illegal transactions are categorically excluded from First Amendment protection. *Pittsburgh Press Co. v. Pittsburgh Comm'n on Human Relations*, 413 U.S. 376 (1973). One would think that this principle resolves the present case, since the statute criminalizes only offers to provide or requests to obtain contraband—child obscenity and child pornography involving actual children, both of which are proscribed, and the proscription of which is constitutional. The Eleventh Circuit, however, believed that the exclusion of First Amendment protection extended only to commercial offers to provide or receive contraband.

This mistakes the rationale for the categorical exclusion. It is based not on the less privileged First Amendment status of commercial speech, see *Central Hudson Gas & Elec. Corp. v. Public Serv. Comm'n of N. Y.*, 447 U.S. 557 (1980), but on the principle that offers to give or receive what it is unlawful to possess have no social value and thus, like obscenity, enjoy no First Amendment protection. Many long established criminal proscriptions—such as laws against conspiracy, incitement, and solicitation—criminalize speech (commercial or not) that is intended to induce or commence illegal activities. Offers to provide or requests to obtain unlawful material, whether as part of a commercial exchange or not, are similarly undeserving of First Amendment protection. It would be an odd constitutional principle that permitted the government to prohibit offers to sell illegal drugs, but not offers to give them away for free. . . .

In sum, we hold that offers to provide or requests to obtain child pornography are categorically excluded from the First Amendment. . . .

Child pornography harms and debases the most defenseless of our citizens. Both the State and Federal Governments have sought to suppress it for many years, only to find it proliferating through the new medium of the Internet. This Court held unconstitutional Congress's previous attempt to meet this new threat, and Congress responded with a carefully crafted attempt to eliminate the First Amendment problems we identified. As far as the provision at issue in this case is concerned, that effort was successful.

☐ *Justice SOUTER, with whom Justice GINSBURG joins, dissenting.*

Dealing in obscenity is penalized without violating the First Amendment, but as a general matter pornography lacks the harm to justify prohibiting it. If, however, a photograph (to take the kind of image in this case) shows an actual minor child as a pornographic subject, its transfer and even its possession may be made criminal. *New York v. Ferber*, 458 U.S. 747 (1982). The exception to the general rule rests not on the content of the picture but on the need to foil the exploitation of child subjects, and the justification limits the exception: only pornographic photographs of actual children may be prohibited, see *Ashcroft v. Free Speech Coalition*, 535 U.S. 234 (2002). Thus, just six years ago the Court struck down a statute outlawing particular material merely represented to be child pornography, but not necessarily depicting actual children. . . .

I accept the Court's explanation that Congress may criminalize proposals unrelated to any extant image. I part ways from the Court, however, on the regulation of proposals made with regard to specific, existing representations. Under the new law, the elements of the pandering offense are the same, whether or not the images are of real children. As to those that do not show real children, of course, a transaction in the material could not be prosecuted consistently with the First Amendment, and I believe that

---

■ IN COMPARATIVE PERSPECTIVE

Death Threats and Other Offensive Speech on the Internet: India's Supreme Court Ruling

In a widely watched First Amendment challenge to the conviction of Anthony Elonis, who was sentenced to forty-four months in prison under a 1939 federal communications statute for posting death threats to his estranged wife on Facebook, there was speculation that the Court would clarify what exactly constitutes a "true threat," a category

(continues)

■ IN COMPARATIVE PERSPECTIVE
*Death Threats and Other Offensive Speech on the Internet:
India's Supreme Court Ruling (continued)*

of speech not protected by the First Amendment, on the Internet. Among other posts, Elonis wrote: "There's one way to love ya, but a thousand ways to kill ya,/ And I'am not going to rest until your body is a mess,/ Soaked in blood and dying from all the little cuts./ Hurry up and die bitch." But the Roberts Court evaded the First Amendment question and instead decided *Elonis v. United States*, 135 S.Ct. 2001 (2015), on statutory grounds; the Court ruled that the appellate court's holding, which would require only a display of negligence with respect to a threat posted on the Internet, was not sufficient to support a criminal conviction. In other words, a showing of negligence or recklessness—that is, the failure of the accused to refrain even with awareness of the legal risk—was not enough. Rather, Chief Justice Roberts held that a higher standard must be met. Prosecutors must prove that the threat was consciously made, based on the "mental state" of the accused, for the expression to be criminal. He left the constitutional question of what constitutes a "true threat" on the Internet unanswered.

By contrast, in *Shreya Singhal v. Union of India*, No. 167 of 2012 (2015), India's Supreme Court struck down a section of its Information Technology Act, as amended in 2009, as unconstitutional on the grounds that it was too vague and had a "chilling effect" on free speech. The offending section provided the government with broad authority to prosecute those who posted content deemed false or "grossly offensive" on the Internet, a crime punishable with a fine and three years imprisonment. The law, Judge Rohinton Fali Nariman ruled, was "cast so widely that virtually any opinion on any subject would be covered by it," adding, "If it is to withstand the test of constitutionality, the chilling effect on free speech must be total."

However, while freedom of speech is enshrined in India's post-World War constitution, India's free speech rights remain less extensive overall than those in the United States. Books and movies are often banned or censored in India out of consideration for religious and minority groups; whereas blasphemy in the United States is protected by the First Amendment (see the IN COMPARATIVE PERSPECTIVE box on blasphemy earlier in Section C of this chapter).

maintaining the First Amendment protection of expression we have previously held to cover fake child pornography requires a limit to the law's criminalization of pandering proposals. In failing to confront the tension between ostensibly protecting the material pandered while approving prosecution of the pandering of that same material, and in allowing the new pandering prohibition to suppress otherwise protected speech, the Court undermines *Ferber* and *Free Speech Coalition* in both reasoning and result. This is the significant element of today's holding, and I respectfully dissent from it. . . .

G | *Fair Trial/Free Press Controversies*

Television, along with newspapers, and their coverage of sensational trials, led to a series of "fair trial/free press" controversies. Adverse, prejudicial pretrial and trial publicity ostensibly creates a conflict between the defendant's Sixth Amendment right to a fair trial and the First Amendment freedoms of speech and press, as well as the public's interest in information about the operation of the criminal justice system. But because constitutional rights are assertable only against the government, not other individuals, fair trial/free press controversies actually involve determining what process is due and how to reconcile governmental attempts to limit publicity or access to judicial proceedings with First Amendment principles.

The Sixth Amendment specifically provides that "in all criminal prosecutions the accused shall enjoy the right to a speedy and *public trial*" (emphasis added). A presumption of openness is rooted in common-law practice, stemming from earlier Anglo-Saxon customs. Open, public trials have traditionally been viewed as an essential safeguard against judicial abuse of power and miscarriages of justice. Also, publicity may both educate people about the operation of the judiciary and provide an opportunity for members of the public to scrutinize the administration of justice.

Despite the language of the Sixth Amendment and generally accepted practice of having open trials, neither the press nor the public could compel openness. While acknowledging the public's interests in open trials, the Court maintained that the Sixth Amendment guarantees only the rights of the accused, not the public. However, the Court also noted that "although a defendant can, under some circumstances, waive his constitutional right to a public trial, he has no absolute right to compel a private trial" in *Singer v. United States*, 380 U.S. 24 (1965). In short, under the Sixth Amendment, members of the public have no constitutional claim to compel open trials, but neither do defendants have a right to a closed trial.

Because the Sixth Amendment guarantees an accused person's rights, and only secondarily the public's interests, judges may restrict public access and publicity to ensure due process and procedural fairness.[1] But as judges began increasingly to restrict media coverage of judicial proceedings, lawyers turned to the First Amendment claiming, as Justice Douglas once put it, "The trial is a public event. What transpires in the courtroom is public property."[2] Because the First Amendment, unlike the Sixth Amendment, comprehends the public's broad interests in freedom of information, it provides a basis for challenging restraints on publicity and access to trials.

Prior to the 1960s, the Court tended to overturn contempt charges of the press for editorials and news stories concerning pretrial and trial proceedings.[3] But extensive publicity and, in one case, the videotaping and playing of a confession on television prior to the accused's trial, led to the Court's reconsideration and insistence that judges exercise their powers to ensure fair trials.[4] Then in *Estes v. Texas*, 381 U.S. 532 (1965), when the Court first tackled the controversy over televising of criminal trials, the justices were deeply split. Justice Stewart's initial draft failed to command a majority. He was relegated to writing a dissenting opinion, joined by three others. Justice Tom Clark wrote the majority's opinion holding that cameras in the courtroom were too disruptive and denied the defendant's right to a fair trial.

The year after *Estes*, with an even more controversial ruling, in *Sheppard v. Maxwell*, 384 U.S. 333 (1966), the Warren Court overturned the conviction of Dr. Sam Sheppard for murdering his wife because the trial judge failed to ensure the decorum essential to a fair trial. There the press had what Justice Clark characterized as "a Roman holiday," with live broadcasting of the coroner's inquest from a high school gymnasium. During the trial, the judge reserved three of the four rows of benches in the courtroom for news reporters and permitted the erection of a press table inside the bar of the courtroom, which allowed journalists to overhear all of Sheppard's conversations with his attorneys.

In *Sheppard*, Justice Clark's opinion for the Court suggested that in sensational trials judges should adopt rules governing reporters' access to the courtroom and insulating witnesses from journalists, as well as issue gag orders barring police, witnesses, and counsel from talking with reporters about trial proceedings. But this ruling only intensified the fair trial/free press controversy. Immediately, the American Bar Association adopted as part of its Canons of Professional Ethics rules limiting attorneys' permissible statements about pending trials and recommendations that judges use their contempt power to inhibit prejudicial publicity. The American Newspaper Publishers Association countered that such interference with news reporting constituted a prior restraint.

Following *Sheppard*, trial courts' increasing reliance on gag orders was vigorously contested by the press as a prior restraint in violation of the First Amendment. The Court finally addressed the constitutionality of gag orders in *Nebraska Press Association v. Stuart*, 427 U.S. 539 (1976). In striking down the gag order there, Chief Justice Burger's opinion did not hold gag orders unconstitutional per se, which prompted Justice Brennan's concurring opinion expressing the view that all gag orders run afoul of the First Amendment. Chief Justice Burger indicated alternatives to issuing gag orders, including changes of venue (that is, moving a trial to another locality where there is less public interest in or publicity about the trial), postponing trials to permit adverse publicity to die down, permitting rigorous examination of potential jurors to check against prejudice, instructing juries emphatically of their responsibility to consider admitted evidence only, and even sequestering juries. In addition, mistrials for adverse publicity may be granted and convictions overturned on appeal.

Although the Court in *Nebraska Press Association* did not rule out gag orders in all circumstances, it made them extremely difficult to defend against First Amendment challenges.[5] As a result, when confronted with the difficulties of controlling for prejudicial publicity, trial judges simply closed pretrial hearings and trials. That generated a new controversy over the right of the press and the public to attend judicial proceedings under the First and Sixth Amendments.

When the Court initially confronted the issue of closed judicial proceedings in *Gannett Co. v. DePasquale*, 443 U.S. 368 (1979), involving the closure of a pretrial hearing, the justices split 5–4, and even those in the majority were not in agreement on interpreting the First and Sixth Amendments. Justice Stewart's opinion announcing the decision upholding the closure there, moreover, further fueled the controversy, prompting five justices later publicly to try to explain the ruling.[6] Stewart expressly rejected the view that the Sixth Amendment embodies a right of the public to attend criminal trials and declined to decide "in the abstract . . . whether there is any such constitutional right" under the First Amendment. But because he also stated twelve times in his opinion that the public and press have no constitutional right of access to *either pretrial hearings or trials*, there was confusion over the scope of the Court's ruling.

Gannett's ambiguity and confusion had considerable impact on public and press access to judicial proceedings. One year after *Gannett*, the Court tried to clear up some of the confusion, but a majority of the justices still could not agree on the rationale for and scope of the Court's ruling in *Richmond Newspapers, Inc. v. Virginia*, 488 U.S. 555 (1980). Only Justices Stevens and White joined Chief Justice Burger's opinion announcing the Court's overturning the closure of a criminal trial. Both the First and Sixth Amendments, according to Burger, run together to make trials analogous to other "public forums" in which members of the press and public have historically enjoyed access, and distinguishable from places not generally recognized as open to the public (such as prisons, jails, and military bases). For this reason, Burger held that the press and public enjoy a "right of visitation" that precludes, except in extraordinary circumstances, the closing of criminal trials in contrast with pretrial hearings. But Burger did not go far enough for concurring Justices Brennan, Marshall, and Stevens, who contended that the First Amendment has an "affirmative side" requiring public access to pretrial hearings and trials in every circumstance.

Three years after *Gannett*, Justice Brennan was able to mass a solid majority behind his opinion in *Globe Newspaper Company v. Superior Court for the County of Norfolk* (1982) (see excerpt below), holding that the First Amendment guarantees the press and the public access to pretrial hearings and trials. Subsequently, the Court reaffirmed the principle of openness when overturning the closure of *voir dire* examinations, in *Press-Enterprise Co. v. Superior Court of California*, 464 U.S. 501 (1984). In *Waller v. Georgia*, 467 U.S. 39 (1984), Justice Powell held, for a unanimous Court, that the entire closure of pretrial hearings on the suppression of evidence violated the Sixth Amendment. *Press-Enterprise Co. v. Superior Court of California*, 477 U.S. 648 (1986), reaffirmed the First Amendment right of the press and the public to attend pretrial hearings in virtually all cases. The Roberts Court in *per curiam* opinion, in *Presley v. Georgia*, 130 S.Ct. 721 (2010), with Justices Thomas and Scalia dissenting, reaffirmed the holding in *Press-Enterprise Co.* that the public has a right to attend *voir dire* examinations of potential juries, but did so on the basis of the Sixth Amendment guarantee of a public trial, rather than on the First Amendment.

Controversies over ensuring both fair trials and freedom of the press evolved with the struggles within the Court over reaching agreement on the scope of the First Amendment. At the same time, though, television coverage of trials became more responsible, and television technology became more sophisticated and less intrusive. In the 1970s, a number of states began once again allowing television coverage of state criminal trials. The Court reconsidered *Estes* and *Sheppard* in *Chandler v. Florida*, 449 U.S. 560 (1981), and upheld television coverage of criminal trials over the objections of the defendants.

The most recent rulings bearing on the "fair trial/free press" controversy came in *Mu'Min v. Virginia*, 500 U.S. 415 (1991) (further discussed in Ch. 9). Writing for a bare majority, Chief Justice Rehnquist held that in a murder case that had received substantial pretrial publicity the Sixth

Amendment does not require judges to question potential jurors about what information each has seen or read about the crime. In addition, in *Skilling v. United States*, 130 S.Ct. 2896 (2010), the Court reaffirmed that the media prominence of the defendant does not necessarily produce prejudice, that juror impartiality does not require ignorance of the case, and that a presumption of prejudice arises only in an extreme case. The case grew out of the collapse of the Enron Corporation in 2001 and the indictment of Jeffrey Skilling, Enron's chief executive officer, for manipulating publicly reported financial records and making false and misleading statements. In response to the publicity over Enron's collapse, Skilling had moved for a change of venue because of the hostility toward him in Houston and because the extensive pretrial publicity poisoned potential jurors. Writing for the Court, Justice Ginsburg rejected that argument.

NOTES

1. *Illinois v. Allen*, 397 U.S. 337 (1970).

2. *Craig v. Harney*, 331 U.S. 367 (1947).

3. See *Pennekamp v. Florida*, 328 U.S. 331 (1946); and *Craig v. Harney*, 331 U.S. 367 (1947).

4. See *Irvin v. Dowd*, 366 U.S. 717 (1961); and *Rideau v. Louisiana*, 373 U.S. 723 (1963) (videotaping and televising of confessions denied due process).

5. See *Oklahoma Press Publishing Company v. District Court*, 430 U.S. 308 (1977) (striking down gag orders); and *Seattle Times Co. v. Rhinehart*, 467 U.S. 20 (1984) (upholding a protective order on pretrial discovery proceedings so long as it did not preclude dissemination of the same information gathered from other sources).

6. See David M. O'Brien, "The Trials and Tribulations of Courtroom Secrecy and Judicial Craftsmanship: Reflections on *Gannett* and *Richmond Newspapers*," 3 *Communications and the Law* 3–33 (1981).

Globe Newspaper Company v. Superior Court for the County of Norfolk

457 U.S. 596, 102 S.CT. 2613 (1982)

Under a Massachusetts statute, trial courts were required to exclude members of the press and public from the courtroom in cases involving certain sexual offenses and during the testimony of victims under the age of eighteen. Citing the statute, a trial judge excluded reporters from Globe Newspapers at a preliminary hearing for a person charged with raping three minor girls and ordered the trial closed. The newspaper moved to have the court revoke its order. When that failed, the newspaper immediately sought injunctive relief from the Supreme Judicial Court of Massachusetts, which was denied. Attorneys for Globe Newspapers, then, filed an appeal to the full court, but before its decision came down, the rape trial proceeded and the defendant was acquitted. Nine months later, the Supreme Judicial Court found the case moot but nevertheless proceeded to rule that the statute did not require the closure of entire trials, only the exclusion of the press and public during the testimony of a minor rape victim. Globe Newspapers Company appealed that ruling to the Supreme Court.

The Court's decision was 6–3, and the majority's opinion was announced by Justice Brennan. Justice O'Connor concurred. Dissents were by Justice Stevens and Chief Justice Burger, who was joined by Justice Rehnquist.

■ ■ ■

☐ *Justice BRENNAN delivered the opinion of the Court.*

Section 16A of Chapter 278 of the Massachusetts General Laws, as construed by the Massachusetts Supreme Judicial Court, requires trial judges, at trials for specified sexual offenses involving a victim under the age of 18, to exclude the press and general public from the courtroom during the testimony of that victim. The question presented is whether the statute thus construed violates the First Amendment as applied to the States through the Fourteenth Amendment. . . .

The Court's recent decision in *Richmond Newspapers* [*Inc. v. Virginia*, 448 U.S. 555 (1980)], firmly established for the first time that the press and general public have a constitutional right of access to criminal trials. Although there was no opinion of the Court in that case, seven Justices recognized that this right of access is embodied in the First Amendment, and applied to the States through the Fourteenth Amendment. . . .

Two features of the criminal justice system, emphasized in the various opinions in *Richmond Newspapers*, together serve to explain why a right of access to *criminal trials* in particular is properly afforded protection by the First Amendment. First, the criminal trial historically has been open to the press and general public. "[A]t the time when our organic laws were adopted, criminal trials both here and in England had long been presumptively open." *Richmond Newspapers, Inc. v. Virginia, supra.* . . .

Second, the right of access to criminal trials plays a particularly significant role in the functioning of the judicial process and the government as a whole. Public scrutiny of a criminal trial enhances the quality and safeguards the integrity of the factfinding process, with benefits to both the defendant and to society as a whole. Moreover, public access to the criminal trial fosters an appearance of fairness, thereby heightening public respect for the judicial process. And in the broadest terms, public access to criminal trials permits the public to participate in and serve as a check upon the judicial process—an essential component in our structure of self-government. In sum, the institutional value of the open criminal trial is recognized in both logic and experience.

Although the right of access to criminal trials is of constitutional stature, it is not absolute. See *Richmond Newspapers, Inc. v. Virginia* (plurality opinion); *Nebraska Press Assn. v. Stuart*, 427 U.S. [539 (1976)]. But the circumstances under which the press and public can be barred from a criminal trial are limited; the State's justification in denying access must be a weighty one. Where, as in the present case, the State attempts to deny the right of access in order to inhibit the disclosure of sensitive information, it must be shown that the denial is necessitated by a compelling governmental interest, and is narrowly tailored to serve that interest. . . .

The state interests asserted to support Section 16A, though articulated in various ways, are reducible to two: the protection of minor victims of sex crimes from further trauma and embarrassment; and the encouragement of such victims to come forward and testify in a truthful and credible manner. We consider these interests in turn.

We agree with appellee that the first interest—safeguarding the physical and psychological well-being of a minor—is a compelling one. But as compelling as that interest is, it does not justify a *mandatory* closure rule, for it is clear that the circumstances of the particular case may affect the significance of the interest. . . .

Nor can Section 16A be justified on the basis of the Commonwealth's second asserted interest—the encouragement of minor victims of sex crimes to come forward and provide accurate testimony. The Commonwealth has offered no empirical support for the claim that the rule of automatic closure contained in Section 16A will lead to an increase in the number of minor sex victims coming forward and cooperating with state authorities. Not only is the claim speculative in empirical terms, but it is also open to serious question as a matter of logic and common sense. Although Section 16A bars the press and general public from the courtroom during the testimony of minor sex victims, the press is not denied access to the transcript, court personnel, or any other possible source that could provide an account of the minor victim's testimony. Thus Section 16A cannot prevent the press from publicizing the substance of a minor victim's testimony, as well as his or her identity. . . .

For the foregoing reasons, we hold that Section 16A, as construed by the Massachusetts Supreme Judicial Court, violates the First Amendment to the Constitution. Accordingly, the judgment of the Massachusetts Supreme Judicial Court is Reversed.

☐ *Chief Justice BURGER, with whom Justice REHNQUIST joins, dissenting.*

Historically our society has gone to great lengths to protect minors *charged* with crime, particularly by prohibiting the release of the names of offenders, barring the press and public from juvenile proceedings, and sealing the records of those proceedings. Yet today the Court holds unconstitutional a state statute designed to protect not the *accused*, but the minor *victims* of sex crimes. In doing so, it advances a disturbing paradox. Although states are permitted, for example, to mandate the closure of all proceedings in order to protect a 17-year-old charged with rape, they are not permitted to require the closing of part of criminal proceedings in order to protect an innocent child who has been raped or otherwise sexually abused. . . .

I cannot agree with the Court's expansive interpretation of our decision in *Richmond Newspapers, Inc. v. Virginia* (1980), or its cavalier rejection of the serious interests supporting Massachusetts' mandatory closure rule. Accordingly, I dissent. . . .

H | *Symbolic Speech and Speech-Plus-Conduct*

Besides the First Amendment protection accorded pure speech (except, as discussed above, for those categories and contexts of unprotected speech), the Supreme Court has extended protection to "symbolic speech"—symbols, signs, and other means of expression— and to "speech-plus-conduct"—activities such as sit-ins, picketing, and demonstrating. The Court has done so because symbolic speech and speech-plus-conduct are, in Justice Harlan's words, in *Garner v. Louisiana*, 368 U.S. 157 (1961),

> as much a part of the "free trade in ideas" . . . as in verbal expres-
> sion, more commonly thought of as "speech." It, like speech,
> appeals to good sense and to "the power of reason as applied
> through public discussion" . . . just as much as, if not more than, a
> public oration delivered from a soapbox at a street corner. This
> Court has never limited the right to speak, a protected "liberty"
> under the Fourteenth Amendment . . . to mere verbal expression.

Justice Harlan, however, also pointed out that it is often necessary to weigh these First Amendment claims against the competing interests and rights of property owners, for example, and the government's interests in preserving the public safety and order in public streets, parks, and buildings. In these cases, the Court must determine whether symbols or conduct in fact serve to express or communicate ideas; whether the government's interests in regulating or prohibiting expression is content neutral, rather than an effort to suppress particular ideas; and how great an inhibition particular ordinances and statutes impose on the exercise of First Amendment freedoms. By extending First Amendment protection in these and other areas, the Court has created a complex "system of freedom of expression."

SELECTED BIBLIOGRAPHY

Bishop, Ronald. *Taking the Pledge of Allegiance: The Media and Michael Newdow's Constitutional Challenge.* Albany: SUNY Press, 2007.

Cleary, Edward. *Beyond the Burning Cross: The First Amendment and the Landmark R.A.V. Case.* New York: Random House, 1994.

Driver, Justin. *The Schoolhouse Gate: Public Education, the Supreme Court, and the Battle for the American Mind.* New York: Pantheon, 2018.

Ellis, Richard J. *To the Flag: The Unlikely History of the Pledge of Allegiance.* Lawrence: University Press of Kansas, 2007.

Foster, James. *Bong Hits 4 Jesus.* Fairbanks: University of Alaska Press, 2010.

Goldstein, Justin. *Burning the Flag: The Great 1989–1990 American Flag Desecration Controversy.* Kent, OH: Kent State University Press, 1996.

Shiell, Timothy. *Campus Hate Speech on Trial,* 2d ed. Lawrence: University of Kansas Press, 2009.

Strum, Philippa. *When the Nazis Came to Skokie.* Lawrence: University Press of Kansas, 1999.

Zick, Timothy. *Speech Out of Doors: Preserving First Amendment Liberties in Public Places.* New York: Cambridge University Press, 2008.

■ (1) SYMBOLIC SPEECH

The Court initially acknowledged that symbols and symbolic speech may receive First Amendment protection in *Stromberg v. California*, 283 U.S. 359 (1931). There Chief Justice Hughes struck down a state law prohibiting the display of a red flag as a symbol of opposition to the government and overturned the conviction of a director of a Communist youth camp who raised a red flag every morning as part of the camp's daily activities.

In *West Virginia State Board of Education v. Barnette* (1943) (excerpted below), striking down a state law compelling schoolchildren to salute the American flag, the Court reaffirmed that nonverbal expressions receive First Amendment protection and that an individual may not be forced to participate in symbolic activities. In this case, compare Justice Jackson's interpretation of the First Amendment with Justice Frankfurter's impassioned dissenting opinion.

The Court underscored the principles announced in *Barnette* in *Wooley v. Maynard*, 430 U.S. 705 (1977), when striking down New Hampshire's statute requiring passenger cars to carry license plates inscribed with the state's motto, Live Free or Die. The Court found the state's justifications not sufficiently compelling to override First Amendment interests. Specifically, Chief Justice Burger rejected the state's arguments that requiring the motto on the license plates of passengers cars, but not commercial vehicles, was an aid to police; and that the state had an interest in inculcating respect for history and authority. But dissenting Justice Rehnquist countered that the state had not compelled Maynard to do anything and that there were other ways for him to express his views. Moreover, he questioned how far protection for free speech principles should extend: should the First Amendment protect an atheist's objections to the motto "In God We Trust" on coins and currency?

First Amendment protection for other symbols and nonverbal expression has been extended as well. *Tinker v. Des Moines Independent*

642 | FREEDOM OF EXPRESSION AND ASSOCIATION

Community School District (1969) (see excerpt below) upheld the right of children to wear black armbands to school when protesting America's involvement in the Vietnam War. But compare the Court's opinion there with the ruling and opinions in *Bethel School District No. 403 v. Fraser* (1986) (in Section B), as well as in *Morse v. Frederick* (2007) (excerpted below); see also the CONSTITUTIONAL HISTORY box on students' First Amendment rights in this section.

The Court also found, in *Brown v. Louisiana*, 383 U.S. 131 (1966), that the protest of a group of black students standing silently in a "whites-only" library to be constitutionally protected symbolic speech. But in *Clark v. Community for Creative Non-Violence*, 468 U.S. 288 (1984), over the objections of Justices Brennan and Marshall, the Court held that the National Park Service's regulations against camping in national parks not designated as campsites do not violate the First Amendment as applied to demonstrators who erected and slept in a tent city in Lafayette Park, Washington, D.C., as a way of dramatizing the plight of the needy and homeless. In reaffirming that not all forms of symbolic speech and nonverbal expression are protected, the Court applied a test created in *United States v. O'Brien*, 391 U.S. 367 (1968).

In *United States v. O'Brien*, the Court held that burning draft cards at protest rallies against the Vietnam War was not protected symbolic speech. There Chief Justice Earl Warren set out certain guidelines for differentiating between protected and unprotected symbolic speech. Those guidelines are often referred to as the *O'Brien* four-prong test: (1) Is the regulation within Congress's authority to enact? (2) Does the regulation further a legitimate governmental interest? (3) Is the regulation unrelated to the suppression of speech? (4) Is the regulation only an incidental restriction on speech? Chief Justice Warren concluded that the ban on draft card burning survived all of those concerns. Congress had the authority because it has the power to raise an army, and the ban promoted the efficiency of the system. He also deemed the regulation to be unrelated to the suppression of speech per se, and to be only a minor incidental restriction, since antiwar protests could be expressed in other ways. He further explained:

> We cannot accept the view that an apparently limitless variety of conduct can be labelled "speech" whenever the person engaging in the conduct intends thereby to express an idea. . . . This Court has held that when "speech" and "nonspeech" elements are combined in the same course of conduct, a sufficiently important governmental interest in regulating the nonspeech element can justify incidental limitations on First Amendment freedoms. To characterize the quality of the governmental interest which must appear, the Court has employed a variety of descriptive terms: compelling; substantial; subordinating; paramount; cogent; strong. Whatever imprecision

inheres in these terms, we think it clear that a government regulation is sufficiently justified if it is within the constitutional power of the Government; if it furthers an important or substantial governmental interest; if the governmental interest is unrelated to the suppression of free expression; and if the incidental restriction on alleged First Amendment freedoms is no greater than is essential to the furtherance of that interest.

One of the most potent national political symbols is the American flag, and the Court has often faced controversies over not just the government's forcing individuals to participate in symbolic acts honoring the flag, as in *Barnette*, but also over punishing individuals who use and abuse the flag as a way of expressing their political views. In *Street v. New York*, 394 U.S. 576 (1969), the justices split 5–4 when overturning the conviction of a protestor who burned the flag, in violation of a law making it a misdemeanor to publicly mutilate, deface, or cast contempt on the flag "by words or act." There Chief Justice Warren and Justices Black, Fortas, and White dissented. Over the dissent of Chief Justice Burger and Justices Blackmun and Rehnquist, the Court, in *Smith v. Goguen*, 415 U.S. 566 (1974), overturned the conviction of an individual wearing a small United States flag on the seat of his pants. With those three justices in dissent again, *Spence v. Washington*, 418 U.S. 405 (1974), held that the First Amendment protected a student who hung the American flag upside down with a peace symbol attached on the window of his dormitory room.

In another surprising and controversial 5–4 decision, the Court once again upheld the First Amendment protection for symbolic speech in *Texas v. Johnson* (1989) (see excerpt below), prompting President George H. W. Bush and numerous congressmen to call for a constitutional amendment overturning that decision. Congress, however, passed instead the Federal Flag Protection Act of 1989, authorizing the prosecution of those who desecrate the American flag. That law was immediately challenged and was overturned by the Court in *United States v. Eichman*, 496 U.S. 310 (1990). As in *Johnson*, the justices split 5–4 in holding that the federal statute "suffer[ed] from the same fundamental flaw" as the earlier state laws in aiming at "suppressing expression." Following that ruling, a further attempt to overturn *Texas v. Johnson* by passing a constitutional amendment failed. The Senate in 2006 rejected, again, a proposed constitutional amendment giving Congress the power to ban flag desecration by a vote of 66-to-34, one vote short of the two-thirds majority required.

However, in *Virginia v. Black* (2003) (excerpted in Section B) the Court held that states may criminalize cross-burning, unlike burning the American flag. Although striking down Virginia's law making it a crime to burn a cross, a majority of the Court indicated that a properly drawn statute criminalizing cross-burning might survive First Amendment scrutiny because of the unique history and intimidation associated with cross-burning.

West Virginia State Board of Education v. Barnette
319 U.S. 624, 63 S.CT. 1178 (1943)

During World War I and throughout World War II, patriotism and fear of communism, socialism, and fascism led states and localities to enact statutes requiring, among other things, students to salute the flag and recite the pledge of allegiance. When Jehovah's Witnesses challenged the constitutionality of a small Pennsylvania town's 1914 ordinance compelling students to salute the American flag (in a manner similar to that in Nazi Germany, with right arm extended and the palm of the hand pointing upward), the Court upheld the flag-salute statute in *Minersville School District v. Gobitis*, 310 U.S. 586 (1940), with an opinion by Justice Frankfurter and only Justice Stone dissenting.

Following *Gobitis*, the West Virginia state legislature enacted a law requiring all schools to offer history and civics courses, and pursuant to that legislation the State Board of Education directed all teachers and students to salute the flag as part of the daily activities of the school. Failure to comply with this requirement could lead to students being expelled, and parents were liable for prosecution with a penalty of thirty days in jail and a $50 fine.

Walter Barnette, a Jehovah's Witness, sought in federal district court an injunction against the enforcement of compulsory flag salutes in school on the grounds that it violated his and his children's religious belief that they should not worship any graven image and the First Amendment free exercise clause. The State Board of Education moved to dismiss the complaint, but a federal district judge granted the injunction. The State Board of Education appealed that decision to the Supreme Court.

By the time the justices heard *Barnette*, the Court's composition had changed from that when *Gobitis* was decided three years earlier. Chief Justice Hughes and Justice McReynolds retired in 1941, and President Franklin Roosevelt elevated Justice Stone to chief justice, appointed his attorney general, Robert Jackson, to fill Stone's seat as associate justice, and named James Byrnes to replace McReynolds. Justice Byrnes served only one year and was succeeded by FDR's last appointee, Wiley Rutledge. Moreover, FDR's three earlier appointees, Justices Black, Douglas, and Murphy, who had voted with the majority in *Gobitis*, switched their positions and voted with FDR's last three appointees in *Barnette*. Chief Justice Stone assigned Jackson to write the opinion for the Court striking down compulsory flag salutes as a violation of the First Amendment guarantee for free speech, instead of on the free exercise clause. Justices Black, Douglas, and Murphy wrote separate concurring opinions explaining their reversing of positions. Justice Frankfurter wrote an impassioned dissenting opinion and, along with Justices Reed and Roberts, maintained the views expressed in *Gobitis.*

The Court's decision was 6–3, and the majority's opinion was announced by Justice Jackson. Concurrences were by Justices Murphy and Black, who were joined by Justice Douglas. Justices Reed and Roberts dissented without opinion. There was also a dissent by Justice Frankfurter.

■ ■ ■

☐ *Justice JACKSON delivered the opinion of the Court.*

The freedom asserted by these appellees does not bring them into collision with rights asserted by any other individual. It is such conflicts which most frequently require intervention of the State to determine where the rights of one end and those of another begin. But the refusal of these persons to participate in the ceremony does not interfere with or deny rights of others to do so. Nor is there any question in this case that their behavior is peaceable and orderly. The sole conflict is between authority and rights of the individual. The State asserts power to condition access to public education on making a prescribed sign and profession and at the same time to coerce attendance by punishing both parent and child. The latter stand on a right of self-determination in matters that touch individual opinion and personal attitude.

As the present CHIEF JUSTICE said in dissent in the *Gobitis* case, the State may "require teaching by instruction and study of all in our history and in the structure and organization of our government, including the guaranties of civil liberty which tend to inspire patriotism and love of country." Here, however, we are dealing with a compulsion of students to declare a belief. They are not merely made acquainted with the flag salute so that they may be informed as to what it is or even what it means. The issue here is whether this slow and easily neglected route to aroused loyalties constitutionally may be short-cut by substituting a compulsory salute and slogan. . . .

There is no doubt that, in connection with the pledges, the flag salute is a form of utterance. Symbolism is a primitive but effective way of communicating ideas. The use of an emblem or flag to symbolize some system, idea, institution, or personality is a short cut from mind to mind. Causes and nations, political parties, lodges and ecclesiastical groups seek to knit the loyalty of their followings to a flag or banner, a color or design. The State announces rank, function, and authority through crowns and maces, uniforms and black robes; the church speaks through the Cross, the Crucifix, the altar and shrine, and clerical raiment. Symbols of State often convey political ideas just as religious symbols come to convey theological ones. Associated with many of these symbols are appropriate gestures of acceptance or respect: a salute, a bowed or bared head, a bended knee. A person gets from a symbol the meaning he puts into it, and what is one man's comfort and inspiration is another's jest and scorn.

Over a decade ago Chief Justice HUGHES led this Court in holding that the display of a red flag as a symbol of opposition by peaceful and legal means to organized government was protected by the free speech guaranties of the Constitution. *Stromberg v. California*, 283 U.S. 359 [(1931)]. Here it is the State that employs a flag as a symbol of adherence to government as presently organized. It requires the individual to communicate by word and sign his acceptance of the political ideas it thus bespeaks. Objection to this form of communication when coerced is an old one, well known to the framers of the Bill of Rights. . . .

[H]ere, the power of compulsion is invoked without any allegation that remaining passive during a flag salute ritual creates a clear and present danger that would justify an effort even to muffle expression. To sustain the compulsory flag salute we are required to say that a Bill of Rights which guards the individual's right to speak his own mind left it open to public authorities to compel him to utter what is not in his mind.

Whether the First Amendment to the Constitution will permit officials to order observance of ritual of this nature does not depend upon whether as a voluntary exercise we would think it to be good, bad or merely innocuous. . . .

Nor does the issue, as we see it, turn on one's possession of particular religious views or the sincerity with which they are held. While religion supplies appellees' motive for enduring the discomforts of making the issue in this case, many citizens who do not share these religious views hold such a compulsory rite to infringe constitutional liberty of the individual. It is not necessary to inquire whether non-conformist beliefs will exempt from the duty to salute unless we first find power to make the salute a legal duty.

The *Gobitis* decision, however, *assumed*, as did the argument in that case and in this, that power exists in the State to impose the flag salute discipline upon school children in general. The Court only examined and rejected a claim based on religious beliefs of immunity from an unquestioned general rule. The question which underlies the flag salute controversy is whether such a ceremony so touching matters of opinion and political attitude may be imposed upon the individual by official authority under powers committed to any political organization under our Constitution. We examine rather than assume existence of this power and, against this broader definition of issues in this case, reexamine specific grounds assigned for the *Gobitis* decision.

1. It was said that the flag-salute controversy confronted the Court with "the problem which Lincoln cast in memorable dilemma: 'Must a government of necessity be too *strong* for the liberties of its people, or too *weak* to maintain its own existence?'" and that the answer must be in favor of strength. . . .

We think these issues may be examined free of pressure or restraint growing out of such considerations.

It may be doubted whether Mr. Lincoln would have thought that the strength of government to maintain itself would be impressively vindicated by our confirming power of the state to expel a handful of children from school. Such oversimplification, so handy in political debate, often lacks the precision necessary to postulates of judicial reasoning. If validly applied to this problem, the utterance cited would resolve every issue of power in favor of those in authority and would require us to override every liberty thought to weaken or delay execution of their policies. . . .

2. It was also considered in the *Gobitis* case that functions of educational officers in states, counties and school districts were such that to interfere with their authority "would in effect make us the school board for the country." . . .

The Fourteenth Amendment, as now applied to the States, protects the citizen against the State itself and all of its creatures—Boards of Education not excepted. These have, of course, important, delicate, and highly discretionary functions, but none that they may not perform within the limits of the Bill of Rights. That they are educating the young for citizenship is reason for scrupulous protection of constitutional freedoms of the individual, if we are not to strangle the free mind at its source and teach youth to discount important principles of our government as mere platitudes. . . .

3. The *Gobitis* opinion reasoned that this is a field "where courts possess no marked and certainly no controlling competence," that it is committed to the legislatures as well as the courts to guard cherished liberties and that it is constitutionally appropriate to "fight out the wise use of legislative authority in the forum of public opinion and before legislative assemblies rather than to transfer such a contest to the judicial arena," since all the "effective means of inducing political changes are left free." . . .

The very purpose of a Bill of Rights was to withdraw certain subjects from the vicissitudes of political controversy, to place them beyond the reach of majorities and officials and to establish them as legal principles to be applied by the courts. One's right to life, liberty, and property, to free speech, a free press, freedom of worship and assembly, and other fundamental rights may not be submitted.

4. Lastly, and this is the very heart of the *Gobitis* opinion, it reasons that "National unity is the basis of national security," that the authorities have "the right to select appropriate means for its attainment," and hence reaches the conclusion that such compulsory measures toward "national unity" are constitutional. Upon the verity of this assumption depends our answer in this case.

Struggles to coerce uniformity of sentiment in support of some end thought essential to their time and country have been waged by many good as well as by evil men. Nationalism is a relatively recent phenomenon but at other times and places the ends have been racial or territorial security, support of a dynasty or regime, and particular plans for saving souls. As first and moderate methods to attain unity have failed, those bent on its accomplishment must resort to an ever-increasing severity. As governmental pressure toward unity becomes greater, so strife becomes more bitter as to whose unity it shall be. Probably no deeper division of our people could proceed from any provocation than from finding it necessary to choose what doctrine and whose program public educational officials shall compel youth to unite in embracing. Ultimate futility of such attempts to compel coherence is the lesson of every such effort from the Roman drive to stamp out Christianity as a disturber of its pagan unity, the Inquisition, as a means to religious and dynastic unity, the Siberian exiles as a means to Russian unity, down to the fast failing efforts of our present totalitarian enemies. Those who begin coercive elimination of dissent soon find themselves exterminating dissenters. Compulsory unification of opinion achieves only the unanimity of the graveyard.

It seems trite but necessary to say that the First Amendment to our Constitution was designed to avoid these ends by avoiding these beginnings. There is no mysticism in the American concept of the State or of the nature or origin of its authority. We set up government by consent of the governed, and the Bill of Rights denies those in power any legal opportunity to coerce that consent. Authority here is to be controlled by public opinion, not public opinion by authority. . . .

If there is any fixed star in our constitutional constellation, it is that no official, high or petty, can prescribe what shall be orthodox in politics, nationalism, religion, or other matters of opinion or force citizens to confess by word or act their faith therein. If there are any circumstances which permit an exception, they do not now occur to us.

We think the action of the local authorities in compelling the flag salute and pledge transcends constitutional limitations on their power and invades the sphere of intellect and spirit which it is the purpose of the First Amendment to our Constitution to reserve from all official control.

☐ *Justice ROBERTS and Justice REED adhere to the views expressed by the Court in* Minersville School District v. Gobitis, *and are of the opinion that the judgment below should be reversed.*

☐ *Justice FRANKFURTER, dissenting.*

One who belongs to the most vilified and persecuted minority in history is not likely to be insensible to the freedoms guaranteed by our Constitution. Were my purely personal attitude relevant I should wholeheartedly associate myself with the general libertarian views in the Court's opinion, representing as they do the thought and action of a lifetime. But as judges we are neither Jew nor Gentile, neither Catholic nor agnostic. We owe equal attachment to the Constitution and are equally bound by our judicial obligations whether we derive our citizenship from the earliest or the latest immigrants to these shores. As a member of this Court I am not justified in writing my private notions of policy into the Constitution, no matter how deeply I may cherish them or how mischievous I may deem their disregard. The duty of a judge who must decide which of two claims before the Court shall prevail, that of a State to enact and enforce laws within its general competence or that of an individual to refuse obedience because of the demands of his conscience, is not that of the ordinary person. It can never be emphasized too much that one's own opinion about the wisdom or evil of a law should be excluded altogether when one is doing one's duty on the bench. The only opinion of our own even looking in that direction that is material is our opinion whether legislators could in reason have enacted such a law. In the light of all the circumstances, including the history of this question in this Court, it would require more daring than I possess to deny that reasonable legislators could have taken the action which is before us for review. Most unwillingly, therefore, I must differ from my brethren with regard to legislation like this. I cannot bring my mind to believe that the "liberty" secured by the Due Process Clause gives this Court authority to deny to the State of West Virginia the attainment of that which we all recognize as a legitimate legislative end, namely, the promotion of good citizenship, by employment of the means here chosen.

Not so long ago we were admonished that "the only check upon our own exercise of power is our own sense of self-restraint. For the removal of unwise laws from the statute books appeal lies, not to the courts, but to the ballot and to the processes of democratic government." We have been told that generalities do not decide concrete cases. But the intensity with which a general principle is held may determine a particular issue, and whether we put first things first may decide a specific controversy.

The admonition that judicial self-restraint alone limits arbitrary exercise of our authority is relevant every time we are asked to nullify legislation. The Constitution does not give us greater veto power when dealing with one phase of "liberty" than with another, or when dealing with grade school regulations than with college regulations that offend conscience, as was the case in *Hamilton v. Regents*, 293 U.S. 245 [(1934)]. In neither situation is our function comparable to that of a legislature or are we free to act as though we were a super-legislature. Judicial self-restraint is equally necessary whenever an exercise of political or legislative power is challenged. There is no warrant in the constitutional basis of this Court's authority for attributing different roles to it depending upon the nature of the challenge to the legislation. Our power does not vary according to the particular provision of the Bill of Rights which is invoked. The right not to have property taken without just compensation has, so far as the scope of judicial power is concerned, the same constitutional dignity as the right to be protected against unreasonable searches and seizures, and the latter has no less claim than freedom of the press or freedom of speech or religious freedom. In no instance is this Court the primary protector of the particular liberty that is invoked. . . .

When Justice HOLMES, speaking for this Court, wrote that "it must be remembered that legislatures are ultimate guardians of the liberties and welfare of the people in quite as great a degree as the courts," he went to the very essence of our constitutional system and the democratic conception of our society. He did not mean that for only some phases of civil government this Court was not to supplant legislatures and sit in judgment upon the right or wrong of a challenged measure. He was stating the comprehensive judicial duty and role of this Court in our constitutional scheme whenever legislation is sought to be nullified on any ground, namely, that responsibility for legislation lies with legislatures, answerable as they are directly to the people, and this Court's only and very narrow function is to determine whether within the broad grant of authority vested in legislatures they have exercised a judgment for which reasonable justification can be offered.

The framers of the federal Constitution might have chosen to assign an active share in the process of legislation to this Court. . . . But the framers of the Constitution denied such legislative powers to the federal judiciary. They chose instead to insulate the judiciary from the legislative function. They did not grant to this Court supervision over legislation.

The reason why from the beginning even the narrow judicial authority to nullify legislation has been viewed with a jealous eye is that it serves to prevent the full play of the democratic process. The fact that it may be an undemocratic aspect of our scheme of government does not call for its rejection or its disuse. But it is the best of reasons, as this Court has frequently recognized, for the greatest caution in its use.

The precise scope of the question before us defines the limits of the constitutional power that is in issue. The State of West Virginia requires all pupils to share in the salute to the flag as part of school training in citizenship. The present action is one to enjoin the enforcement of this requirement by those in school attendance. We have not before us any attempt by the State to punish disobedient children or visit penal consequences on their parents. All that is in question is the right of the state to compel participation in this exercise by those who choose to attend the public schools.

We are not reviewing merely the action of a local school board. The flag salute requirement in this case comes before us with the full authority of the State of West Virginia. We are in fact passing judgment on "the power of the State as a whole." Practically we are passing upon the political power of each of the forty-eight states. Moreover, since the First Amendment has been read into the Fourteenth, our problem is precisely the same as it would be if we had before us an Act of Congress for the District of Columbia. To suggest that we are here concerned with the heedless action of some village tyrants is to distort the augustness of the constitutional issue and the reach of the consequences of our decision. . . .

We are told that symbolism is a dramatic but primitive way of communicating ideas. Symbolism is inescapable. Even the most sophisticated live by symbols. But it is not for this Court to make psychological judgments as to the effectiveness of a particular symbol in inculcating concededly indispensable feelings, particularly if the state happens to see fit to utilize the symbol that represents our heritage and our hopes. And surely only flippancy could be responsible for the suggestion that constitutional validity of a requirement to salute our flag implies equal validity of a requirement to salute a dictator. The significance of a symbol lies in what it represents. To reject the swastika does not imply rejection of the Cross. And so it bears repetition to say that it mocks reason and denies our whole history to find in the allowance of a requirement to salute our flag on fitting occasions the seeds of sanction for obeisance to a leader. To deny the power to employ educational symbols is to say that the state's educational system may not stimulate the imagination because this may lead to unwise stimulation. . . .

Of course patriotism cannot be enforced by the flag salute. But neither can the liberal spirit be enforced by judicial invalidation of illiberal legislation. Our constant preoccupation with the constitutionality of legislation rather than with its wisdom tends to preoccupation of the American mind with a false value. The tendency of focusing attention on constitutionality is to make constitutionality synonymous with wisdom, to regard a law as all right if it is constitutional. Such an attitude is a great enemy of liberalism. Particularly in legislation affecting freedom of thought and freedom of speech much which should offend a free-spirited society is constitutional. Reliance for the most precious interests of civilization, therefore, must be found outside of their vindication in courts of law. Only a persistent positive translation of the faith of a free society into the convictions and habits and actions of a community is the ultimate reliance against unabated temptations to fetter the human spirit.

Tinker v. Des Moines Independent Community School District
393 U.S. 503, 89 S.CT. 733 (1969)

In December 1965, a group of adults and students in Des Moines, Iowa, held a meeting and decided to publicize their objections to the war in Vietnam by wearing black armbands during the Christmas holiday season. The principals of the Des Moines schools became aware of the plan and promptly adopted a policy forbidding the wearing of armbands in school and suspending any student who refused to comply.

John Tinker, a fifteen-year-old high-school student, and his sister, Mary Beth, a thirteen-year-old junior-high-school student, along with three other students in the 15,000 district student body, wore black armbands to school and were sent home and suspended until they agreed no longer to wear the armbands. They and their parents asked a federal district court for an injunction restraining school officials from enforcing the policy against wearing black armbands. The court, however, upheld the school's authority. On appeal to the Court of Appeals for the Eighth Circuit, the judges were evenly divided and accordingly upheld the lower court's ruling without issuing an opinion. The Tinkers, thereupon, appealed to the Supreme Court, which granted *certiorari*.

The Court's decision was 7–2, and the majority's opinion was announced by Justice Fortas. Justices Stewart and White concurred; Justices Black and Harlan dissented.

■ ■ ■

☐ *Justice FORTAS delivered the opinion of the Court.*

[T]he wearing of an armband for the purpose of expressing certain views is the type of symbolic act that is within the Free Speech Clause of the First Amendment. . . . It [is] closely akin to "pure speech" which, we have repeatedly held, is entitled to comprehensive protection under the First Amendment.

First Amendment rights, applied in light of the special characteristics of the school environment, are available to teachers and students. It can hardly be argued that either students or teachers shed their constitutional rights to freedom of speech or expression at the schoolhouse gate. This has been the unmistakable holding of this Court for almost 50 years. In *Meyer v. Nebraska*, 262 U.S. 390 (1923), and *Bartels v. Iowa*, 262 U.S. 404 (1923), this Court, in opinions by Justice McREYNOLDS, held that the Due Process Clause of the Fourteenth Amendment prevents States from forbidding the teaching of a foreign language to young students. Statutes to this effect,

In 1965, in support of Senator Robert Kennedy's call for an extension of a Christmas truce in Vietnam, several public schoolchildren in Des Moines, Iowa, decided to wear black armbands with peace symbols to school in order to mourn the war casualties and to protest the war. The students were suspended and allowed to return to school without the armbands. John and Mary Beth Tinker, shown here, became the name parties in the case testing the constitutional rights of children in school. (*Bettman/ Corbis via Getty Images.*)

the Court held, unconstitutionally interfere with the liberty of teacher, student, and parent. . . .

The problem posed by the present case does not relate to regulation of the length of skirts or the type of clothing, to hair style, or deportment. It does not concern aggressive, disruptive action or even group demonstrations. Our problem involves direct, primary First Amendment rights akin to "pure speech."

The school officials banned and sought to punish petitioners for a silent, passive expression of opinion, unaccompanied by any disorder or disturbance on the part of petitioners. There is here no evidence whatever of petitioners' interference, actual or nascent, with the schools' work or of collision with the rights of other students to be secure and to be let alone. Accordingly, this case does not concern speech or action that intrudes upon the work of the schools or the rights of other students. . . .

[T]he school authorities did not purport to prohibit the wearing of all symbols of political or controversial significance. The record shows that students in some of the schools wore buttons relating to national political campaigns, and some even wore the Iron Cross, traditionally a symbol of Nazism. The order prohibiting the wearing of armbands did not extend to these. Instead, a particular symbol—black armbands worn to exhibit opposition to this Nation's involvement in Vietnam—was singled out for prohibition. Clearly, the prohibition of expression of one particular opinion, at least without evidence that it is necessary to avoid material and substantial interference with schoolwork or discipline, is not constitutionally permissible. . . .

We reverse and remand for further proceedings consistent with this opinion.

☐ *Justice BLACK, dissenting.*

Even a casual reading of the record shows that this armband did divert students' minds from the regular lessons, and that talk, comments, etc., made John Tinker "self-conscious" in attending school with his armband. While the absence of obscene remarks or boisterous and loud disorder perhaps justifies the Court's statement that the few armband students did not actually "disrupt" the classwork, I think the record overwhelmingly shows that the armbands did exactly what the elected school officials and principals foresaw they would, that is, took the students' minds off their classwork and diverted them to thoughts about the highly emotional subject of the Vietnam war. And I repeat that if the time has come when pupils of state-supported schools, kindergartens, grammar schools, or high schools, can defy and flout orders of school officials to keep their minds on their own schoolwork, it is the beginning of a new revolutionary era of permissiveness in this country fostered by the judiciary.

■ CONSTITUTIONAL HISTORY

Major Rulings on Students' First Amendment Rights

CASE	RULING
West Virginia State Board of Education v. Barnette, 319 U.S. 624 (1943) (excerpted in this chapter)	Held that students could not be compelled, over free speech and free religious exercise claims, to salute the American flag, and overruled *Minersville School District v. Gobitis,* 310 U.S. 586 (1940).
Keyishian v. Board of Regents, 385 U.S. 589 (1967)	Noted the importance of the free flow of ideas in schools: "The Classroom is peculiarly the 'marketplace of ideas.' The Nation's future depends upon leaders trained through wide exposure to that robust exchange of ideas."

(continues)

■ CONSTITUTIONAL HISTORY
Major Rulings on Students' First Amendment Rights (continued)

Tinker v. Des Moines Independent School District, 393 U.S. 503 (1969) (excerpted in this chapter)	Held that the First Amendment protects school children, protesting the Vietnam War, wearing black armbands with a peace symbol.
Board of Education, Island Trees Union Free School District v. Pico, 457 U.S. 853 (1985)	Held that schools may not remove books from school libraries because they are deemed offensive.
Bethel School District No. 403 v. Fraser, 478 U.S. 675 (1986) (excerpted in this chapter)	Held that school officials did not violate a student's rights when they suspended him for using crude (but not obscene) language in a speech to a school assembly.
Hazelwood School District v. Kuhlmeier, 484 U.S. 260 (1988)	Held that high schools may censor articles in student newspapers because, unlike

the protected speech in *Tinker*, schools are sponsors of student newspapers and thus not passive observers in the speech.

Board of Education of the Westside Community Schools v. Mergens, 496 U.S. 226 (1990)	Upheld the Equal Access Act of 1984, which forbids public schools from discriminating against student meetings on

school grounds on the basis of "religious, political, philosophical or other content of the speech at such meetings."

Lee v. Weisman, 505 U.S. 577 (1992) (excerpted in Ch. 6)	Held that the First Amendment forbids school-sponsored invocations and benedictions at graduation ceremonies.
Lamb's Chapel v. Center Moriches Union Free School District, 508 U.S. 384 (1993)	Held that a school district's denial of a religious group's use of school facilities for meetings after school hours violated the First Amendment.

CASE	RULING
Santa Fe Independent School District v. Doe, 530 U.S. 290 (2000)	Held that schools may not sponsor prayers at the start of football games.
Good News Club v. Milford Central School, 533 U.S. 98 (2001)	Held that when public schools establish a limited public forum they may not deny access

to religious groups seeking to use facilities for after-school meetings.

Morse v. Frederick, 551 U.S. 393 (2007) (excerpted in this chapter)	Held that the First Amendment does not protect a student who held a banner, "Bong Hits 4 Jesus," off school grounds but

during a school event, and the student was subsequently suspended.

For further reading, see Catherine Ross, *Lessons in Censorship: How Schools and Courts Subvert Students' First Amendment Rights* (Cambridge, MA: Harvard University Press, 2015); and Jamin H. Raskin, *We the Students: Supreme Court Decisions For and About Students*, 2d ed. (Washington, DC: C.Q. Press, 2003). See also John Johnson, *The Struggle for Student Rights: Tinker v. Des Moines and the 1960s* (Lawrence: University Press of Kansas, 1997); and Anne P. Dupre, *Speaking Up: The Unintended Costs of Free Speech in Public Schools* (Cambridge, MA: Harvard University Press, 2008).

Students rallying on the steps of the Supreme Court in support of free speech. (*Mark Wilson, Getty Images.*)

Morse v. Frederick

551 U.S. 393, 127 S.Ct. 2618 (2007)

Juneau-Douglas High School, in Juneau, Alaska, released its students to observe the "Winter Olympics Torch Relay," sponsored by Coca-Cola and other private sponsors. Joseph Frederick, and some other students, stood on the sidewalk across from the school to observe the event. When television cameras could view it, they unfurled a banner that read "Bong Hits 4 Jesus." Deborah Morse, the school principal, promptly crossed over the street, grabbed, and crumpled up the banner. Subsequently, she suspended Frederick for ten days for violating the school's policy against displaying offensive material and promoting the use of illegal drugs. Frederick countered that the display was humorous and meaningless. After appealing to the local school board, he filed a lawsuit in federal district court, contending that his First Amendment rights had been violated and asking that the suspension be removed from his high school records. A federal district court rejected Frederick's claims, reasoning that *Bethel School District No. 403 v. Fraser*, 478 U.S. 675 (1986) (excerpted in Chapter 5) (holding that schools may sanction students for offensive speech at a school assembly), and not *Tinker v. Des Moines Independent Community School District*, 393 U.S. 503 (1969) (excerpted in this chapter) (holding that students retain First Amendment rights of freedom of expression that may be suppressed only if officials reasonably "forecast substantial disruptions of or material interference with school activities"). On appeal, a panel of the Court of Appeals for the Ninth Circuit reversed, reasoning that the precedent in *Fraser* embraced only offensive speech that was "sexual in nature" and that the circumstances here were different from those in *Hazelwood School District v. Kuhlmeier*, 484 U.S. 260 (1988), which upheld school authorities' censorship of a student newspaper. As a result, the precedent in *Tinker* was controlling, and Frederick could not be punished for speech that did not disrupt the school's functioning. Morse appealed that decision and the Supreme Court granted review.

The appellate court's decision was reversed. Chief Justice Roberts issued the opinion for the Court. Justices Thomas and Alito filed concurring opinions. Justice Stevens filed a dissenting opinion, which Justices Souter and Ginsburg joined. Justice Breyer filed a separate opinion, concurring and dissenting in part.

■ ■ ■

☐ *Chief Justice ROBERTS delivered the opinion of the Court.*

Our cases make clear that students do not "shed their constitutional rights to freedom of speech or expression at the schoolhouse gate." *Tinker v.*

Des Moines Independent Community School Dist., 393 U.S. 503 (1969). At the same time, we have held that "the constitutional rights of students in public school are not automatically coextensive with the rights of adults in other settings," *Bethel School Dist. No. 403 v. Fraser*, 478 U.S. 675 (1986), and that the rights of students "must be 'applied in light of the special characteristics of the school environment.'" *Hazelwood School Dist. v. Kuhlmeier*, 484 U.S. 260 (1988). Consistent with these principles, we hold that schools may take steps to safeguard those entrusted to their care from speech that can reasonably be regarded as encouraging illegal drug use. We conclude that the school officials in this case did not violate the First Amendment by confiscating the pro-drug banner and suspending the student responsible for it . . . .

The message on Frederick's banner is cryptic. It is no doubt offensive to some, perhaps amusing to others. To still others, it probably means nothing at all. Frederick himself claimed "that the words were just nonsense meant to attract television cameras." But Principal Morse thought the banner would be interpreted by those viewing it as promoting illegal drug use, and that interpretation is plainly a reasonable one. . . .

The question thus becomes whether a principal may, consistent with the First Amendment, restrict student speech at a school event, when that speech is reasonably viewed as promoting illegal drug use. We hold that she may.

In *Tinker*, this Court made clear that "First Amendment rights, applied in light of the special characteristics of the school environment, are available to teachers and students." *Tinker* involved a group of high school students who decided to wear black armbands to protest the Vietnam War. School officials learned of the plan and then adopted a policy prohibiting students from wearing armbands. When several students nonetheless wore armbands to school, they were suspended. The students sued, claiming that their First Amendment rights had been violated, and this Court agreed.

Tinker held that student expression may not be suppressed unless school officials reasonably conclude that it will "materially and substantially disrupt the work and discipline of the school." . . .

This Court's next student speech case was *Fraser*. . . . The mode of analysis employed in *Fraser* is not entirely clear. The Court was plainly attuned to the content of Fraser's speech, citing the "marked distinction between the political 'message' of the armbands in Tinker and the sexual content of [Fraser's] speech." But the Court also reasoned that school boards have the authority to determine "what manner of speech in the classroom or in school assembly is inappropriate."

We need not resolve this debate to decide this case. For present purposes, it is enough to distill from *Fraser* two basic principles. First, *Fraser's* holding demonstrates that "the constitutional rights of students in public school are not automatically coextensive with the rights of adults in other settings." Had Fraser delivered the same speech in a public forum outside the school context, it would have been protected. See *Cohen v. California*, 403 U.S. 15 (1971). In school, however, Fraser's First Amendment rights were circumscribed "in light of the special characteristics of the school environment." Second, *Fraser* established that the mode of analysis set forth in *Tinker* is not absolute. Whatever approach *Fraser* employed, it certainly did not conduct the "substantial disruption" analysis prescribed by *Tinker*.

Our most recent student speech case, *Kuhlmeier*, concerned "expressive activities that students, parents, and members of the public might reasonably perceive to bear the imprimatur of the school." Staff members of a high school newspaper sued their school when it chose not to publish two of their articles. The Court of Appeals analyzed the case under *Tinker,* ruling in favor of the students because it found no evidence of material disruption to class-work or school discipline. This Court reversed, holding that "educators do not offend the First Amendment by exercising editorial control over the style and content of student speech in school-sponsored expressive activities so long as their actions are reasonably related to legitimate pedagogical concerns." *Kuhlmeier* does not control this case because no one would reasonably believe that Frederick's banner bore the school's imprimatur. The case is nevertheless instructive because it confirms both principles cited above. *Kuhlmeier* acknowledged that schools may regulate some speech "even though the government could not censor similar speech outside the school." And, like *Fraser,* it confirms that the rule of *Tinker* is not the only basis for restricting student speech. . . .

☐ *Justice STEVENS, with whom Justice SOUTER and Justice GINSBURG join, dissenting.*

A significant fact barely mentioned by the Court sheds a revelatory light on the motives of both the students and the principal of Juneau-Douglas High School (JDHS). On January 24, 2002, the Olympic Torch Relay gave those Alaska residents a rare chance to appear on national television. As Joseph Frederick repeatedly explained, he did not address the curious message—"BONG HiTS 4 JESUS"—to his fellow students. He just wanted to get the camera crews' attention. Moreover, concern about a nationwide evaluation of the conduct of the JDHS student body would have justified the principal's decision to remove an attention-grabbing 14-foot banner, even if it had merely proclaimed "Glaciers Melt!"

I agree with the Court that the principal should not be held liable for pulling down Frederick's banner. I would hold, however, that the school's interest in protecting its students from exposure to speech "reasonably regarded as promoting illegal drug use" cannot justify disciplining Frederick for his attempt to make an ambiguous statement to a television audience simply because it contained an oblique reference to drugs. The First Amendment demands more, indeed, much more. . . .

In my judgment, the First Amendment protects student speech if the message itself neither violates a permissible rule nor expressly advocates conduct that is illegal and harmful to students. This nonsense banner does neither, and the Court does serious violence to the First Amendment in upholding—indeed, lauding—a school's decision to punish Frederick for expressing a view with which it disagreed. . . .

☐ *Justice BREYER, concurring in the judgment in part and dissenting in part.*

This holding, based as it is on viewpoint restrictions, raises a host of serious concerns. One concern is that, while the holding is theoretically limited to speech promoting the use of illegal drugs, it could in fact authorize further viewpoint-based restrictions. . . .

Legal principles must treat like instances alike. Those principles do not permit treating "drug use" separately without a satisfying explanation of why drug use is *sui generis*. To say that illegal drug use is harmful to students, while surely true, does not itself constitute a satisfying explanation because there are many such harms. During a real war, one less metaphorical than the war on drugs, the Court declined an opportunity to draw narrow subject-matter-based lines. *West Virginia Bd. of Ed. v. Barnette*, 319 U.S. 624 (1943) (holding students cannot be compelled to recite the Pledge of Allegiance during World War II). We should decline this opportunity today. . . .

In some instances, it is appropriate to decide a constitutional issue in order to provide "guidance" for the future. But I cannot find much guidance in today's decision. The Court makes clear that school officials may "restrict" student speech that promotes "illegal drug use" and that they may "take steps" to "safeguard" students from speech that encourages "illegal drug use." Beyond "steps" that prohibit the unfurling of banners at school outings, the Court does not explain just what those "restrict[ions]" or those "steps" might be.

Nor, if we are to avoid the risk of interpretations that are too broad or too narrow, is it easy to offer practically valuable guidance. Students will test the limits of acceptable behavior in myriad ways better known to school teachers than to judges; school officials need a degree of flexible authority to respond to disciplinary challenges; and the law has always considered the relationship between teachers and students special. Under these circumstances, the more detailed the Court's supervision becomes, the more likely its law will engender further disputes among teachers and students. Consequently, larger numbers of those disputes will likely make their way from the schoolhouse to the courthouse. Yet no one wishes to substitute courts for school boards, or to turn the judge's chambers into the principal's office. . . .

Texas v. Johnson

491 U.S. 397, 109 S.Ct. 2533 (1989)

During the 1984 Republican National Convention, Gregory Johnson participated in a political demonstration in Dallas, Texas, to protest the policies of the Reagan administration. After a march through the streets, Johnson burned the American flag while protesters chanted. No one was physically injured or threatened with injury. Johnson was arrested, tried, and convicted of flag desecration in violation of a Texas statute, and a state appeals court affirmed. However, the Texas Court of Criminal Appeals reversed, holding that Johnson's flag burning was expressive conduct protected by the First Amendment. The state appealed that decision to the Supreme Court.

The state court's decision was affirmed; the Court's decision was 5–4, and the majority's opinion was announced by Justice Brennan. Justice Kennedy concurred; dissents were by Justice Stevens and Chief Justice Rehnquist, who were joined by Justices White and O'Connor.

■ ■ ■

Justice BRENNAN delivered the opinion of the Court.

Johnson was convicted of flag desecration for burning the flag rather than for uttering insulting words. This fact somewhat complicates our consideration of his conviction under the First Amendment. We must first determine whether Johnson's burning of the flag constituted expressive conduct, permitting him to invoke the First Amendment in challenging his conviction. If his conduct was expressive, we next decide whether the State's regulation is related to the suppression of free expression. See, e.g., *United States v. O'Brien*, 391 U.S. 367 (1968). If the State's regulation is not related to expression, then the less stringent standard we announced in *United States v. O'Brien* for regulations of noncommunicative conduct controls. If it is, then we are outside of *O'Brien's* test, and we must ask whether this interest justifies Johnson's conviction under a more demanding standard. A third possibility is that the State's asserted interest is simply not implicated on these facts, and in that event the interest drops out of the picture. . . .

The First Amendment literally forbids the abridgement only of "speech," but we have long recognized that its protection does not end at the spoken or written word. While we have rejected "the view that an apparently limitless variety of conduct can be labeled 'speech' whenever the person engaging in the conduct intends thereby to express an idea," *United States v. O'Brien*, we have acknowledged that conduct may be "sufficiently imbued with elements

Gregory Johnson being arrested after setting fire to the American flag during a protest at the Republican party's 1984 national convention. His arrest and conviction were appealed and overturned in *Texas v. Johnson* (1989). (*David Leeson/Images Works/The LIFE Images Collection/Getty Images.*)

of communication to fall within the scope of the First and Fourteenth Amendments." . . .

Especially pertinent to this case are our decisions recognizing the communicative nature of conduct relating to flags. Attaching a peace sign to the flag, *Spence* [*v. Washington*, 418 U.S. 405 (1974)], saluting the flag, [*West Virginia State Board of Education v. Barnette*, 319 U.S. 624 (1943)], and displaying a red flag, *Stromberg v. California*, 283 U.S. 359 (1931), we have held, all may find shelter under the First Amendment. See also *Smith v. Goguen*, 415 U.S. 566 (1974) (WHITE, J., concurring in judgment) (treating flag "contemptuously" by wearing pants with small flag sewn into their seat is expressive conduct). That we have had little difficulty identifying an expressive element in conduct relating to flags should not be surprising. The very purpose of a national flag is to serve as a symbol of our country; it is, one might say, "the one visible manifestation of two hundred years of nationhood." Thus, we have observed:

> [T]he flag salute is a form of utterance. Symbolism is a primitive but effective way of communicating ideas. The use of an emblem or flag to symbolize some system, idea, institution, or personality, is a short cut from mind to mind. Causes and nations, political parties, lodges and ecclesiastical groups seek to knit the loyalty of their followings to a flag or banner, a color or design. *Barnette*. . . .

We have not automatically concluded, however, that any action taken with respect to our flag is expressive. Instead, in characterizing such action for First Amendment purposes, we have considered the context in which it occurred. . . .

The State of Texas conceded for purposes of its oral argument in this case that Johnson's conduct was expressive conduct. . . . Johnson burned an American flag as part—indeed, as the culmination—of a political demonstration that coincided with the convening of the Republican Party and its renomination of Ronald Reagan for President. The expressive, overtly political nature of this conduct was both intentional and overwhelmingly apparent. At his trial, Johnson explained his reasons for burning the flag as follows: "The American Flag was burned as Ronald Reagan was being renominated as President. And a more powerful statement of symbolic speech, whether you agree with it or not, couldn't have been made at that time. It's quite a just position [juxtaposition]. We had new patriotism and no patriotism." In these circumstances, Johnson's burning of the flag was conduct "sufficiently imbued with elements of communication," to implicate the First Amendment.

The Government generally has a freer hand in restricting expressive conduct than it has in restricting the written or spoken word. . . . It may not, however, proscribe particular conduct *because* it has expressive elements. . . . It is, in short, not simply the verbal or nonverbal nature of the expression, but the governmental interest at stake, that helps to determine whether a restriction on that expression is valid.

Thus, although we have recognized that where " 'speech' and 'nonspeech' elements are combined in the same course of conduct, a sufficiently important governmental interest in regulating the nonspeech element can justify incidental limitations on First Amendment freedoms," *O'Brien*, we have limited the applicability of *O'Brien*'s relatively lenient standard to those cases in which "the governmental interest is unrelated to the suppression of free expression." . . .

In order to decide whether *O'Brien*'s test applies here, therefore, we must decide whether Texas has asserted an interest in support of Johnson's conviction that is unrelated to the suppression of expression. If we find that an interest asserted by the State is simply not implicated on the facts before us, we need not ask whether *O'Brien*'s test applies. The State offers two separate interests to justify this conviction: preventing breaches of the peace, and preserving the flag as a symbol of nationhood and national unity. We hold that the first interest is not implicated on this record and that the second is related to the suppression of expression.

Texas claims that its interest in preventing breaches of the peace justifies Johnson's conviction for flag desecration. However, no disturbance of the peace actually occurred or threatened to occur because of Johnson's burning of the flag. Although the State stresses the disruptive behavior of the protestors during their march toward City Hall, it admits that "no actual breach of the peace occurred at the time of the flagburning or in response to the flagburning." . . .

The State also asserts an interest in preserving the flag as a symbol of nationhood and national unity. In *Spence*, we acknowledged that the Government's interest in preserving the flag's special symbolic value "is directly related to expression in the context of activity" such as affixing a peace symbol to a flag. We are equally persuaded that this interest is related to expression in the case of Johnson's burning of the flag. The State, apparently, is concerned that such conduct will lead people to believe either that the flag does not stand for nationhood and national unity, but instead reflects other, less positive concepts, or that the concepts reflected in the flag do not in fact exist, that is, we do not enjoy unity as a Nation. These concerns blossom only when a person's treatment of the flag communicates some message, and thus are related "to the suppression of free expression" within the meaning of *O'Brien*. We are thus outside of *O'Brien*'s test altogether.

It remains to consider whether the State's interest in preserving the flag as a symbol of nationhood and national unity justifies Johnson's conviction. . . .

Whether Johnson's treatment of the flag violated Texas law thus depended on the likely communicative impact of his expressive conduct. Our decision in *Boos v. Barry*, [485 U.S. 312 (1988)], tells us that this restriction on Johnson's expression is content-based. In *Boos*, we considered the constitutionality of a law prohibiting "the display of any sign within 500 feet of a foreign embassy if that sign tends to bring that foreign government into 'public odium' or 'public disrepute.'" Rejecting the argument that the law was content-neutral because it was justified by "our international law obligation to shield diplomats from speech that offends their dignity," we held that "[t]he emotive impact of speech on its audience is not a 'secondary effect'" unrelated to the content of the expression itself.

According to the principles announced in *Boos*, Johnson's political expression was restricted because of the content of the message he conveyed. We must therefore subject the State's asserted interest in preserving the special symbolic character of the flag to "the most exacting scrutiny." *Boos v. Barry*. . . .

The State's argument is not that it has an interest simply in maintaining the flag as a symbol of *something*, no matter what it symbolizes; indeed, if that were the State's position, it would be difficult to see how that interest is endangered by highly symbolic conduct such as Johnson's. Rather, the State's claim is that it has an interest in preserving the flag as a symbol of *nationhood* and *national unity*, a symbol with a determinate range of meanings. According to Texas, if one physically treats the flag in a way that would tend to cast doubt on either the idea that nationhood and national unity are the flag's referents or that national unity actually exists, the message conveyed thereby is a harmful one and therefore may be prohibited.

If there is a bedrock principle underlying the First Amendment, it is that the Government may not prohibit the expression of an idea simply because society finds the idea itself offensive or disagreeable. . . .

We have not recognized an exception to this principle even where our flag has been involved. In *Street v. New York*, 394 U.S. 576 (1969), we held that a State may not criminally punish a person for uttering words critical of the flag. Rejecting the argument that the conviction could be sustained on the ground that Street had "failed to show the respect for our national symbol which may properly be demanded of every citizen," we concluded that "the constitutionally guaranteed 'freedom to be intellectually . . . diverse or even contrary,' and the 'right to differ as to things that touch the heart of the existing order,' encompass the freedom to express publicly one's opinions about our flag, including those opinions which are defiant or contemptuous." Nor may the Government, we have held, compel conduct that would evince respect for the flag. "To sustain the compulsory flag salute we are required to say that a Bill of Rights which guards the individual's right to speak his own mind, left it open to public authorities to compel him to utter what is not in his mind." . . .

In short, nothing in our precedents suggests that a State may foster its own view of the flag by prohibiting expressive conduct relating to it. To bring its argument outside our precedents, Texas attempts to convince us that even if its interest in preserving the flag's symbolic role does not allow it to prohibit words or some expressive conduct critical of the flag, it does permit it to forbid the outright destruction of the flag. The State's argument cannot depend here on the distinction between written or spoken words and nonverbal conduct. That distinction, we have shown, is of no moment where the nonverbal conduct is expressive, as it is here, and where the regulation of that conduct is related to expression, as it is here. . . .

There is, moreover, no indication—either in the text of the Constitution or in our cases interpreting it—that a separate juridical category exists for the American flag alone. Indeed, we would not be surprised to learn that the persons who framed our Constitution and wrote the Amendment that we now construe were not known for their reverence for the Union Jack. The First Amendment does not guarantee that other concepts virtually sacred to our Nation as a whole—such as the principle that discrimination on the basis of race is odious and destructive—will go unquestioned in the marketplace of ideas. See *Brandenburg v. Ohio*, 395 U.S. 444 (1969). We decline, therefore, to create for the flag an exception to the joust of principles protected by the First Amendment. . . .

The way to preserve the flag's special role is not to punish those who feel differently about these matters. It is to persuade them that they are wrong. . . .

Johnson was convicted for engaging in expressive conduct. The State's interest in preventing breaches of the peace does not support his conviction because Johnson's conduct did not threaten to disturb the peace. Nor does the State's interest in preserving the flag as a symbol of nationhood and national unity justify his criminal conviction for engaging in political expression. The judgment of the Texas Court of Criminal Appeals is therefore Affirmed.

☐ *Justice KENNEDY, concurring.*

I write not to qualify the words Justice BRENNAN chooses so well, for he says with power all that is necessary to explain our ruling. I join his opinion without reservation, but with a keen sense that this case, like others before us from time to time, exacts its personal toll. This prompts me to add to our pages these few remarks. . . .

The hard fact is that sometimes we must make decisions we do not like. We make them because they are right, right in the sense that the law and the Constitution, as we see them, compel the result. And so great is our commitment to the process that, except in the rare case, we do not pause to express distaste for the result, perhaps for fear of undermining a valued principle that dictates the decision. This is one of those rare cases. . . .

With all respect to those views, I do not believe the Constitution gives us the right to rule as the dissenting members of the Court urge, however painful this judgment is to announce. Though symbols often are what we ourselves make of them, the flag is constant in expressing beliefs Americans share, beliefs in law and peace and that freedom which sustains the human spirit. The case here today forces recognition of the costs to which those beliefs commit us. It is poignant but fundamental that the flag protects those who hold it in contempt. . . .

☐ *Chief Justice REHNQUIST, with whom Justice WHITE and Justice O'CONNOR join, dissenting.*

For more than 200 years, the American flag has occupied a unique position as the symbol of our Nation, a uniqueness that justifies a governmental prohibition against flag burning in the way respondent Johnson did here. . . .

No other American symbol has been as universally honored as the flag. In 1931, Congress declared "The Star Spangled Banner" to be our national anthem. In 1949, Congress declared June 14th to be Flag Day. In 1987, John Philip Sousa's "The Stars and Stripes Forever" was designated as the national march. Congress has also established "The Pledge of Allegiance to the Flag" and the manner of its deliverance. The flag has appeared as the principal symbol on approximately 33 United States postal stamps and in the design of at least 43 more, more times than any other symbol.

Both Congress and the States have enacted numerous laws regulating misuse of the American flag. Until 1967, Congress left the regulation of misuse of the flag up to the States. Now, however, Title 18 U.S.C. Sec. 700(a), provides that:

> Whoever knowingly casts contempt upon any flag of the United States by publicly mutilating, defacing, defiling, burning, or trampling upon it shall be fined not more than $1,000 or imprisoned for not more than one year, or both.

Congress has also prescribed detailed rules for the design of the flag, the time and occasion of flag's display, the position and manner of its display, respect for the flag, and conduct during hoisting, lowering and passing of the flag. With the exception of Alaska and Wyoming, all of the States now have statutes prohibiting the burning of the flag. . . .

The American flag, then, throughout more than 200 years of our history, has come to be the visible symbol embodying our Nation. It does not represent the views of any particular political party, and it does not represent any particular political philosophy. The flag is not simply another "idea" or "point of view" competing for recognition in the marketplace of ideas. Millions and millions of Americans regard it with an almost mystical reverence regardless of what sort of social, political, or philosophical beliefs they may have. I cannot agree that the First Amendment invalidates the Act of Congress, and the laws of 48 of the 50 States, which make criminal the public burning of the flag. . . .

Here it may equally well be said that the public burning of the American flag by Johnson was no essential part of any exposition of ideas, and at the same time it had a tendency to incite a breach of the peace. Johnson was free to make any verbal denunciation of the flag that he wished; indeed, he was free to burn the flag in private. He could publicly burn other symbols of the Government or effigies of political leaders. He did lead a march through the streets of Dallas, and conducted a rally in front of the Dallas City Hall. He engaged in a "die-in" to protest nuclear weapons. He shouted out various slogans during the march, including: "Reagan, Mondale which will it be? Either one means World War III"; "Ronald Reagan, killer of the hour, Perfect example of U.S. power"; and "red, white and blue, we spit on you, you stand for plunder, you will go under." For none of these acts was he arrested or prosecuted; it was only when he proceeded to burn publicly an American flag stolen from its rightful owner that he violated the Texas statute. . . .

The result of the Texas statute is obviously to deny one in Johnson's frame of mind one of many means of "symbolic speech." Far from being a case of "one picture being worth a thousand words," flag burning is the equivalent of an inarticulate grunt or roar that, it seems fair to say, is most likely to be indulged in not to express any particular idea, but to antagonize others. . . .

☐ *Justice STEVENS, dissenting.*

The Court is . . . quite wrong in blandly asserting that respondent "was prosecuted for his expression of dissatisfaction with the policies of this country, expression situated at the core of our First Amendment values." Respondent was prosecuted because of the method he chose to express his dissatisfaction with those policies. Had he chosen to spray paint—or perhaps convey with a motion picture projector—his message of dissatisfaction on the facade of the Lincoln Memorial, there would be no question about the power of the Government to prohibit his means of expression. The prohibition would be supported by the legitimate interest in preserving the quality of an important national asset. Though the asset at stake in this case is intangible, given its unique value, the same interest supports a prohibition on the desecration of the American flag.

Virginia v. Black (reprise)

538 U.S. 343, 123 S.CT. 1536 (2006)

This case is excerpted in Section B of this chapter.

■ ■ ■

■ (2) SPEECH-PLUS-CONDUCT

Speech-plus-conduct includes activities such as peaceful picketing, boycotts, and demonstrations. Individuals engaged in these activities may receive some First Amendment protection, but it depends on the circumstances, and they do not enjoy the same freedom as those "who communicate ideas by pure speech."[1] Moreover, individuals remain subject to laws making it illegal to trespass on private property without the owner's permission, for example, and laws forbidding the "breach of the peace," disorderly conduct, blocking traffic, resisting arrest, and inciting to riot.

The Court extended First Amendment protection to speech-plus-conduct initially by developing the "public forum" doctrine in recognition of the importance of discussion of public affairs in public streets, parks, and facilities. The concept of a public forum was introduced into constitutional law by Justice Roberts in *Hague v. Committee for Industrial Organization (CIO)*, 307 U.S. 496 (1939). There the CIO was denied permission to use public halls for a rally in Jersey City, New Jersey, and its members were arrested and removed from the city for publicly discussing and distributing leaflets on the labor movement. When striking down the city's ordinance prohibiting assemblies "in or upon the public streets, highways, public parks or public buildings" without a permit from the director of public safety, Justice Roberts observed,

> Wherever the title of streets and parks may rest, they have immemorially been held in trust for the use of the public and, time out of mind, have been used for purposes of assembly, communicating thoughts between citizens, and discussing public questions. Such use of the streets and public places has, from ancient times, been a part of the privileges, immunities, rights and liberties of citizens. The privilege of a citizen of the United States to use the streets and parks for communication of views on national questions may be regulated in the interest of all; it is not absolute, but relative, and must be exercised in consonance with peace and good order; but it must not, in the guise of regulation, be abridged or denied.

Subsequently, the concept of a public forum was expanded to include municipal auditoriums, sidewalks, shopping centers, criminal trials, and the public areas surrounding schools, courthouses, embassies, and state capitol buildings. *The Development Law* box in this section. In *Forsyth County v. The Nationalist Movement*, 505 U.S. 123 (1992), a bare majority struck down an ordinance imposing a fee of up to $1,000 per day for parades, which was adopted after a clash between civil rights demonstrators and Ku Klux Klan members. Writing for the majority, Justice Blackmun found the ordinance to (1) give "unbridled discretion" to city administrators; (2) discriminate against groups on the basis of the content of their speech, since unpopular groups had to pay higher fees; and (3) impose a $1,000 ceiling on fees that was irrelevant in light of the competing First Amendment values.

Access to a public forum, however, is conditional. States and localities may impose reasonable "time, place, and manner" restrictions governing the use of public streets, parks, and other public facilities. They may also require permits for parades, marches, and demonstrations, so long as those restrictions are evenly applied and not overly broad so as to allow local officials to censor particular groups. In *Cox v. New Hampshire*, 312 U.S. 569 (1941), for example, the Court unanimously upheld the convictions of a group of Jehovah's Witnesses who marched single file along a downtown street, carrying placards, without first obtaining a special permit for "parades or processions."[2] Moreover, in *Ward v. Rock Against Racism*, 491 U.S. 781 (1989), the Court indicated that it was prepared to give states and localities greater leeway in imposing time, place, and manner restrictions. By a vote of 6–3, New York's ordinance requiring concerts in Central Park to use a city-owned sound system and engineer to operate the system was upheld. And the majority ruled that time, place, and manner restrictions do not have to meet the least restrictive alternative test that the Court applies in other areas of regulation imposing on First Amendment freedoms. Subsequently, *United States v. Kokinda*, 497 U.S. 720 (1990), held that post offices may ban all solicitations on their property. Four members of the Court—Chief Justice Rehnquist and Justices O'Connor, White, and Scalia—also held that a sidewalk on postal property was not a public forum, and thus solicitations could be banned there as well. Justice Kennedy, casting the crucial fifth vote, however, concluded that the Court need not address the public forum issue, because the post office's ban on solicitations was a reasonable time, place, and manner restriction. By contrast, dissenting Justices Brennan, Marshall, Blackmun, and Stevens contended that the public sidewalks outside of post offices constituted public forums entitled to First Amendment protection. The Court also held that certain public places are non-public forums (see THE DEVELOPMENT OF LAW box in this section). Most recently, the Roberts Court held that polling places on election days may be regulated over

■ THE DEVELOPMENT OF LAW

Rulings Extending the Concept of a Public Forum

CASE	RULING
Hague v. CIO, 307 U.S. 496 (1939)	Public streets and meeting halls.
Edwards v. South Carolina, 372 U.S. 229 (1963)	Steps of state capitol building.
Cox v. Louisiana, 379 U.S. 536 (1965)	Streets surrounding state capitol.
Cox v. Louisiana, 379 U.S. 559 (1965)	Streets and sidewalk near courthouse.
Police Department of City of Chicago v. Mosley, 408 U.S. 92 (1972)	Sidewalks and streets in front of school.
Chief of the Capitol Police v. Jeanette Rankin Brigade, 409 U.S. 972 (1972)	Peaceful protests in Lafayette Park.
Southeastern Promotions v. Conrad, 420 U.S. 546 (1975)	Municipal auditorium.
Richmond Newspapers, Inc. v. Virginia, 448 U.S. 555 (1980)	Criminal trials.
Widmar v. Vincent, 454 U.S. 263 (1981)	State university facilities that have been established as an open forum cannot be denied to religious groups.
United States v. Grace, 461 U.S. 171 (1982)	Steps of the Supreme Court of the United States.
Board of Airport Commissioners of Los Angeles v. Jews for Jesus, Inc., 482 U.S. 569 (1987)	Struck down a "First Amendment free zone," which banned all First Amendment expression, solicitations, and canvassing in a central airport terminal.
Boos v. Barry, 485 U.S. 312 (1988)	Struck down statute prohibiting protests within 500 feet of an embassy.
Lehman v. City of Shaker Heights, 418 U.S. 298 (1974)	Bus placards.

■ THE DEVELOPMENT OF LAW

Places That Have Been Held Not to Be Public Forums

CASE	RULING
Adderly v. Florida, 385 U.S. 39 (1966)	Area surrounding jails.
Flower v. United States, 407 U.S. 197 (1972)	Army bases.
Greer v. Spock, 424 U.S. 828 (1976)	Military bases.
United States v. Kokinda, 497 U.S. 720 (1990)	Sidewalks on property of U.S. post offices (plurality holding).
International Society for Krishna Consciousness v. Lee, 505 U.S. 830 (1992)	Airports (bare majority holding).
Arkansas Educational Television Commission v. Forbes, 523 U.S. 666 (1998)	Public televisions may exclude "marginal" candidates from televised debates of major candidates for political office. In

refusing to extend the concept of a "public forum" to such debates, Justice Kennedy ruled that the televised debate was a "nonpublic forum" and that the decision to exclude Steve Forbes, an independent candidate, was under the circumstances a reasonable, viewpoint-neutral exercise of journalistic discretion consistent with the First Amendment. Justices Stevens, Ginsburg, and Souter dissented.

United States v. American Library Association, 539 U.S. 126 (2003)	In upholding the Children's Internet Protection Act of 2001, which authorizes public

libraries that receive federal funding to install pornography filters on computers providing Internet access, Chief Justice Rehnquist held that providing Internet access does not turn a library into a public forum.

Pleasant Grove City v. Summum, 555 U.S. 460 (2009)	Unlike speech in a public park or other public forum, the Court held that a city's decision

about what kinds of permanent monuments to permit constituted government speech, and thus, the public forum doctrine does not apply.

Minnesota Voters Alliance v. Mansky, 138 S. Ct. 1876_(2018)	Polling places are non-public forums, and restrictions on "political apparel" are permissible if they are not vague

or overly broad for reasonable application.

First Amendment objections because they are non-public forums, in *Minnesota Voters Alliance v. Mansky,* 138 S. Ct. 1876 (2018). A Minnesota law prohibited individuals from wearing a "political badge, political button, or other political insignia" inside a polling place on election days. Writing for the Court, Chief Justice Roberts ruled that polling places are subject to such regulations but struck down Minnesota's law as too vague and overly broad for reasonable application.

It bears emphasizing that the concept of public forum and time, place, and manner restrictions apply only to public streets and other public places not otherwise restricted to the public. Generally, individuals have no First Amendment rights to intrude on private property and may be prosecuted for trespass or nuisance.[3] However, in *Amalgamated Food Employees Union v. Logan Valley Plaza,* 391 U.S. 308 (1968), the Court (6–3) upheld the right of a labor union to picket outside a store in a privately owned shopping center on the grounds that the Logan Valley Plaza was the only shopping center in the community and, hence, was functionally equivalent for First Amendment purposes to a downtown business district and the only forum available for the union to publicize its labor dispute. But after Nixon's four appointees joined the Court, the justices 5–4 (with Justices Brennan, Douglas, Marshall, and Stewart dissenting) held that a privately owned shopping center could prohibit the distribution of handbills protesting the draft and the Vietnam War. In *Lloyd Corporation v. Tanner,* 407 U.S. 551 (1972), Justice Powell, writing for the majority, thought that there were "adequate alternative avenues of communication" available. Then in *Hudgens v. National Labor Relations Board,* 424 U.S. 507 (1976), involving another labor picketing dispute, the justices (voting 6-to-2) rejected the *Logan Valley* ruling, and Justice Stewart's opinion for the Court contended that the First Amendment guarantee for freedom of expression was inapplicable to shopping centers. But, finally, in *PruneYard Shopping Center v. Robins,* 447 U.S. 74 (1980), the Court unanimously held that California could under its own state constitution permit the distribution of pamphlets and petitions in shopping malls and confer greater freedom of expression than the Court does when interpreting and applying the First Amendment.

In addition to time, place, and manner restrictions, as well as required parade permits, the courts may issue injunctions against or limiting demonstrations, marches, and parades. The Court in *Walker v. City of Birmingham,* 388 U.S. 307 (1967), arising from Martin Luther King's defiance of a court order against a march in Birmingham, Alabama, upheld the power of courts to enjoin particular marches and to find those who fail to comply with their orders in contempt of court.

In an important ruling on freedom of speech and speech-plus-conduct, growing out of the continuing controversy over abortion, the Rehnquist Court confronted the issue of antiabortion protesters' First Amendment rights in *Madsen v. Women's Health Center*, 512 U.S. 753 (1994). *Madsen* presented the issue of whether a Florida trial judge's injunction against antiabortion protesters constituted a suppression of their message or, as the Florida state supreme court held, aimed at protecting constitutionally guaranteed interests in medical care and patients' privacy.

Splitting 6–3 and 5–4 on different parts of the ruling in *Madsen*, the Court held that injunctions restraining antiabortion protesters must be evaluated for "content neutrality" and must not burden protesters' speech more than necessary to achieve the government's legitimate interests, as well as be framed in the narrowest possible terms to achieve its pinpoint objective. Writing for the majority, Chief Justice Rehnquist upheld the thirty-six-foot buffer zone around the clinic's entrances and driveway, along with the limitations on noise around the clinic during surgery and recovery periods. However, he rejected as too broad and as an infringement on First Amendment freedoms the injunction's (1) thirty-six-foot buffer zone as applied to private property, (2) blanket ban on "observable images" on pickets, and (3) three-hundred-foot-no-approach zone around the clinic.

Subsequently, in *Schenck v. Pro-Choice Network of Western New York*, 519 U.S. 357 (1997), the Court upheld a lower court's creation of a "fifteen-foot fixed buffer zone" around doorways and parking lot entrances to an abortion clinic, but also permitted two antiabortion counselors to enter the zone at any one time. The problem of antiabortion protests and clinic blockades diminished following the enactment of the Freedom of Access to Clinic Entrances Act (FACE) in 1994, which makes it a federal crime to obstruct access to clinics and imposes stiff prison sentences for doing so. Nonetheless, returning to the issue of restrictions on antiabortion protesters, the Court upheld Colorado's law making it unlawful for a person within 100 feet of a health care facility's entrance to "knowingly approach" within eight feet another person, without permission, in order to pass out leaflets or engage in oral protest. Writing for the Court in *Hill v. Colorado*, 530 U.S. 703 (2000), Justice Stevens found the statute to be a "narrowly tailored" time, place, and manner regulation, under *Ward v. Rock Against Racism*, 491 U.S. 781 (1989).

Most recently, the Roberts Court unanimously struck down Massachusetts's 2007 law establishing thirty-five-foot buffer zones, including public sidewalks, around any abortion clinic. Massachusetts's was the only such statewide law; most buffer zones are enacted as local ordinances in response to antiabortion protesters. In *McCullen v. Coakley*, 573 U.S. 464 (2014), the Court split 5–4 in their reasoning. Chief

Justice Roberts wrote for the majority, holding that while the law did not target the content or viewpoint of expression, it was not "narrowly tailored" enough to survive First Amendment scrutiny. The chief justice reasoned that protesters could be arrested, without saying anything, simply because they were within a buffer zone, and precisely for that reason the law swept too broadly. By contrast, in a concurring opinion that reads like a sharp dissent, Justice Scalia, joined by Justices Kennedy and Thomas, countered that the law did indeed target specific speech—antiabortion advocacy—and therefore was content-based discrimination that could not survive strict scrutiny under the First Amendment.

In *Hurley v. Irish-American Gay, Lesbian, and Bisexual Group of Boston*, 515 U.S. 557 (1995), the justices unanimously reversed a Massachusetts state court decision holding that the veteran groups organizing Boston's St. Patrick Day parade could not exclude gay, lesbian, and bisexual marchers. The state court had ruled that the parade's organizers could not discriminate on the basis of sexual orientation and that the parade, although privately organized, was nonetheless subject to the state's public accommodations law. Writing for the Court, Justice Souter explained,

> [T]he Massachusetts law has been applied in a peculiar way. Its enforcement does not address any dispute about the participation of openly gay, lesbian, or bisexual individuals in various units admitted to the parade. The petitioners disclaim any intent to exclude homosexuals as such, and no individual member of GLIB claims to have been excluded from parading as a member of any group that the Council has approved to march. Instead, the disagreement goes to the admission of GLIB as its own parade unit carrying its own banner. Since every participating unit affects the message conveyed by the private organizers, the state court's application of the statute produced an order essentially requiring petitioners to alter the expressive content of their parade. . . . Under this approach any contingent of protected individuals with a message would have the right to participate in petitioners' speech, so that the communication produced by the private organizers would be shaped by all those protected by the law who wished to join in with some expressive demonstration of their own. But this use of the State's power violates the fundamental rule of protection under the First Amendment, that a speaker has the autonomy to choose the content of his own message. . . .
>
> Rather like a composition, the Council selects the expressive units of the parade from potential participants, and though the score may not produce a particularized message, each contingent's expression in the Council's eyes comports with what merits celebration on that day. Even if this view gives the Council credit for a more con-

sidered judgment than it actively made, the Council clearly decided to exclude a message it did not like from the communication it chose to make, and that is enough to invoke its right as a private speaker to shape its expression by speaking on one subject while remaining silent on another. The message it disfavored is not difficult to identify. . . . But whatever the reason, it boils down to the choice of a speaker not to propound a particular point of view, and that choice is presumed to lie beyond the government's power to control.

Finally, in a widely watched and emotional case, *Snyder v. Phelps*, 562 U.S. 443 (2011), the Court upheld First Amendment protection for picketers at military funerals in protest of tolerance for homosexuals, particularly in the military. Although reaffirming broad First Amendment protection for freedom of expression, the Court's opinion was narrowly tailored to the facts in the case. In 1955 Fred Phelps founded the Westboro Baptist Church, a small family-run church in Topeka, Kansas. The church preaches that God hates and punishes the United States for its tolerance of homosexuality, particularly in the military. During the last twenty-five years the church has publicized its message by picketing nearly 600 military funerals. One of those was for Marine Lance Corporal Matthew Snyder, who was killed in Iraq. Phelps read about Snyder's funeral and decided to travel to Maryland with six other Westboro Baptist parishioners to picket. The church notified authorities in advance of its intent and complied with police instructions in picketing, which took place within a ten- by twenty-five-foot plot of public land adjacent to a public street, behind a temporary fence, approximately 1,000 feet from where the funeral was held. Several buildings also separated the picket site from the funeral and none of the picketers went into the cemetery. Chief Justice Roberts delivered the opinion of the Court, with only Justice Alito dissenting.

NOTES

1. *Cox v. Louisiana*, 379 U.S. 536 (1965).

2. See also *Niemotko v. Maryland*, 340 U.S. 268 (1951); *Poulos v. New Hampshire*, 345 U.S. 395 (1951); *Kunz v. New York*, 340 U.S. 290 (1951); and *Cameron v. Johnson*, 381 U.S. 741 (1965).

3. But see *Gregory v. Chicago*, 394 U.S. 111 (1969) (upholding the picketing by black activists on the sidewalk outside of the home of Chicago's Mayor Richard Daley).

I | *Freedom of Association*

The First Amendment's provision for "the right of the people to peaceably assemble, and to petition the Government for a redress of grievances" provides the textual basis for the Court's recognition of a right of association and associational privacy. But the Court also recognized that the freedom of association is implicit in the very structure of the First Amendment's guarantees for a "system of freedom of expression" and the Constitution's framework for the operation of free government. In *Sweezy v. New Hampshire*, 354 U.S. 234 (1957), the Court thus observed that "[o]ur form of government is built on the premise that every citizen shall have the right to engage in political expression and association. This right was enshrined in the First Amendment of the Bill of Rights." More than a century before, Alexis de Tocqueville found that in "no country in the world has the principle of association been more successfully used or more unsparingly applied to a multitude of different objects, than in America," when proclaiming, "The most natural privilege of a man next to the right of acting for himself, is that of combining his exertions with those of his fellow creatures and of acting in common with them. The right of association therefore appears to be as almost inalienable in its nature as the right of personal liberty. No legislator can attack it without impairing the foundations of society."[1]

The Court formally proclaimed a First Amendment right of association and associational privacy in *National Association for the Advancement of Colored People v. Alabama* (1958) (see excerpt below), when unanimously reversing a contempt citation for the NAACP's refusal to turn over lists of members to Alabama's state attorney general. The Court in the 1950s and 1960s, however, remained divided over the scope of freedom of association, especially when confronted with First Amendment challenges to congressional investigations (see Vol. 1, Ch. 5) and state and federal prosecutions of members of the Communist Party and other "subversive" organizations (see Section A, in this chapter). The year after *NAACP v. Alabama*, for example, the justices split 5–4 in *Uphaus v. Wyman*, 360 U.S. 72 (1959), holding that New Hampshire could compel the production of membership lists of "Communist front" organizations. But the next year in *Bates v. City of Little Rock*, 361 U.S. 516 (1960), and *Shelton v. Tucker*, 364 U.S. 479 (1960), the Court reaffirmed that compelled disclosure of membership lists denies individuals' freedom of association and associational privacy. *Shelton* struck down as overly broad an Arkansas statute requiring teachers to file affidavits listing all organizations to which they had belonged in the preceding five years. Still, the justices, divided 5–4 as in *Uphaus*, upheld the provisions of the Internal Security Act of 1950, making it unlawful to be a member of the Communist Party and requiring members of subversive organizations to register with the Subversive Activities Control Board, in *Communist Party v. Subversive Activities Control Board (SACB)*, 367 U.S. 1 (1961), and *Scales v. United States*, 367 U.S. 203 (1961).[2]

The Warren Court's rulings in the 1950s and early 1960s extended First Amendment protection to groups and organizations formed or associated for lawful purposes, but not to those, such as the Communist Party, which were deemed to have subversive purposes. In *NAACP v. Alabama*, the Court thus distinguished an earlier ruling, *Bryant v. Zimmerman*, 278 U.S. 63 (1928), upholding a New York anti–Ku Klux Klan statute requiring oath-bound organizations to submit membership lists on the basis of the Klan's illegal activities. This was the basis for the Court's denial of First Amendment claims whenever associations were found or deemed to have unlawful purposes. As the Court explained, in *DeJonge v. Oregon*, 299 U.S. 353 (1937), "The right of peaceable assembly is a right cognate to those of free speech and free press and is equally fundamental," but it did not extend to associations that "incite[d] violence and crime," which could also be prosecuted under laws punishing criminal conspiracies, among other illegal activities.

The Court's dichotomy between nonsubversive and subversive organizations was problematic because organizations may have both legal and illegal goals, and thus individual members might be punished for knowing but guiltless behavior; their only crime being guilt by association. In addition, states could thwart the activities of organizations, such as the NAACP, by claiming they were subversive or infiltrated by other subversive organizations.

The balance on the Warren Court, though, shifted in 1962 when Justice Goldberg, a prominent union lawyer and a successful labor negotiator, was named to the bench. He sided with Chief Justice Warren and Justices Black, Brennan, and Douglas in forming a solid majority for extending greater First Amendment protection, which held even after Goldberg's resignation in 1965 with President Johnson's appointments of Justices Fortas (in 1965) and Marshall (in 1967). *Gibson v. Florida Legislative Investigation Committee*, 372 U.S. 539 (1963) (see Vol. 1, Ch. 5), signaled that the Court would no longer presume the validity of governmental inquiries but require that the government establish an "immediate, substantial, and subordinating state interest necessary to sustain its right of inquiry into the membership lists of a nonsubversive organization." Along with that ruling, in *NAACP v. Button*, 371 U.S. 415 (1963), the Court held that the NAACP's litigation activities aimed

676 | Freedom of Expression and Association

at forcing desegregation were protected under the First Amendment. In Justice Brennan's words, litigation is a "form of political expression" and "for such a group, association for litigation may be the most effective form of political association." Subsequently, the Court held that the Subversive Activities Control Board (SACB) could not revoke the passports of individuals who registered, as required under the Internal Security Act of 1950, as members of the Communist Party.[3] And the SACB's ordering all Communists to register with the federal government was overturned in *American Committee for Protection of Foreign Born v. SACB*, 380 U.S. 503 (1965). Finally, in *United States v. Robel*, 389 U.S. 258 (1967), a section of the Internal Security Act making it unlawful for a member of a Communist-action organization to work in a defense facility was held to violate the First Amendment. The statute, in the Court's view, swept too broadly and "indiscriminately across all types of associations with Communist-action groups, without regard to the quality or degree of membership. . . . The statute quite literally establishes guilt by association alone, without any need to establish that an individual's association poses the threat feared by the Government in proscribing it."

The scope of First Amendment protection for freedom of association and expression was also expanded in cases challenging the constitutionality of loyalty oaths and the firing of public employees for their political beliefs, associations, and activities. However, over First Amendment objections the Court approved restrictions on political activities imposed on federal career civil servants under the Hatch Act or Federal Lobbying Act, forbidding active participation in political campaigns. The law was upheld in *United States v. Harriss*, 347 U.S. 612 (1954), and again in *United States Civil Service Commission v. National Association of Letter Carriers*, 413 U.S. 548 (1973). In the words of Justice White, who authored the majority's opinion in the latter 6–3 ruling, "It is in the best interest of the country, indeed essential, that federal service should depend upon meritorious performance rather than political service, and that the political influence of federal employees on others and on the electoral process should be limited." In *Lyng v. International Union, United Automobile, Aerospace and Agricultural Workers of America*, 485 U.S. 360 (1988), the Court upheld over the First Amendment objections of the union a 1981 amendment to the Food Stamp Act, which makes households ineligible for food stamps if a member of the household is on a strike.

In another highly controversial ruling in *Elrod v. Burns*, 427 U.S. 347 (1976), the justices (voting 5-to-3 and with Stevens not participating) struck down the practice of patronage dismissals as an unconstitutional restriction on city employees' First Amendment freedoms. The controversy and struggle within the Court over systems of political patronage and dismissal of public employees continued in *Branti v. Finkel*, 445 U.S. 507 (1980). In that case, the justices, 6–3 (with Justices Stewart, Powell, and Rehnquist in dissent), held that the First Amendment protects district attorneys from being discharged for expressing their political views. After Stewart retired and was replaced by O'Connor, however, the Court held (5–4, with Justices Brennan, Blackmun, Marshall, and Stevens now in dissent) that the firing of state attorneys general for political reasons does not violate the First Amendment.[4] But then Justice Brennan marshaled a bare majority, in *Rutan v. Republican Party of Illinois*, 497 U.S. 62 (1990), for eliminating political patronage in the hiring and firing of most public employees (see Vol. 1, Ch. 8).

The protection accorded freedom of association extends to a broad range of groups, associations, and organizations, including public interest groups,[5] unions,[6] political parties,[7] and married couples.[8] But the right of association and associational privacy does not extend to individuals' claims to anonymity. In *Laird v. Tatum*, 408 U.S. 1 (1972), the Burger Court, over the sharp dissents of Justices Douglas, Brennan, Marshall, and Stewart, upheld the army's surveillance of political protesters at rallies, demonstrations, and marches against America's involvement in the Vietnam War.

Nor does the First Amendment right of association present a barrier to state and federal laws prohibiting invidious discrimination in privately owned businesses serving the public or private associations and clubs. The freedom of association is basically the freedom to discriminate—the freedom to choose with whom one associates and in what context and for what purpose. But the Court has held that not all private associations and discriminations receive First Amendment protection; those associations discriminating against racial minorities and women may not find a haven in the First Amendment right of association.

While the Court broadened the First Amendment to include a right of association and associational privacy in cases such as *NAACP v. Alabama*, it was reluctant to tackle the competing First Amendment claims of those who protested segregation with sit-ins, and those who discriminated against blacks in their private businesses and associations. Over the objections of dissenting Justices Black and Douglas, the Court upheld a lower court's ordering the integration of the Wisconsin state bar association in *Lathrop v. Donahue*, 367 U.S. 820 (1961). But when it came to cases challenging the convictions for trespass of blacks who demonstrated with sit-ins at racially segregated lunch counters, and raising the claim of owners of segregated restaurants that they had a right to decide whom to serve, the Court split three ways. In *Bell v. Maryland*, 378 U.S. 226 (1964), Justice Brennan's opinion for the Court simply declined to confront the issue when it remanded the case back to the Maryland Supreme Court. Justices Douglas and Goldberg, along with Chief Justice Warren, however, were prepared to hold that individuals have no First Amendment right to discriminate racially in their accommodations open to the public. They were unable to forge a majority, though, because Justices Clark and Stewart were unwilling to go that far and joined Brennan instead. Dissenting Justices Black, Harlan, and White agreed that individuals could associate and racially discriminate in their private affairs, but they did not think that either the Fourteenth Amendment's equal protection clause forbade private discrimination in public accommodations or that the First Amendment protected the protesters of segregated lunch counters. In Black's words:

> The right to freedom of expression is a right to express views— not a right to force other people to supply a platform or a pulpit. It is argued that this supposed constitutional right to invade other people's property would not mean that a man's home, his private club, or his church could be forcibly entered or used against his will—only his store or place of business which he has himself "opened to the public" by selling goods or services for money. . . . But the whole quarrel . . . [here is] that instead of being open to all, the restaurant refused service to Negroes.

Times change, and the Warren Court was at a great turning point in the history of constitutional politics. In 1964, Congress passed the Civil Rights Act, or Public Accommodations Act, banning racial discrimination or segregation in public accommodations. The Court upheld that legislation in *Heart of Atlanta Motel v. United States*, 379 U.S. 241 (1964) (see Vol. 1, Ch. 6) and avoided becoming further entangled with the remaining issues of discrimination in private clubs and associations. Exempted from the Civil Rights Act are boardinghouses renting fewer than five rooms, and private clubs and other enterprises not open to the general public.

With states and localities pushing to eliminate discrimination based on race and gender, the Court finally confronted the issue of whether freedom of association extended to private clubs discriminating racially or against women. In *Roberts v. United States Jaycees* 468 U.S. 609 (1984), the First Amendment freedom of association argument of the Jaycees was rejected by the Court in upholding a Minnesota human rights law, compelling the Jaycees to accept women as regular members. On the basis of *United States Jaycees*, the Court subsequently upheld state laws barring all-male clubs from discriminating against women, in *Board of Directors of Rotary International v. Rotary Club of Duarte*, 481 U.S. 537 (1987), and *New York State Club Association, Inc. v. City of New York*,

487 U.S. 1 (1988). *City of Dallas v. Stanglin,* 490 U.S. 19 (1989), held that an ordinance limiting certain dance halls to only fourteen-through-eighteen-year-olds did not deny adults' freedom of association under the First Amendment.

The Court further held in *Boy Scouts of America v. Dale* (2000) (excerpted below) that homosexuals may be excluded from the Boy Scouts; otherwise, the latter's First Amendment right to *expressive association* would be violated. A long-running controversy over public-employee unions and freedom of association was finally revisited by the Roberts Court in *Janus v. American Federation of State, County, and Municipal Employees (AFSCME),* 138 S. Ct. 2448 (2018). In *Abood v. Detroit Board of Education,* 431 U.S. 209 (1977), the Burger Court held that public-employee unions—firefighters and teachers, for instance—may collect fees from nonmembers to cover the cost of workplace negotiations over salaries and benefits, but not a union's political activities, such as lobbying or campaign contributions. Critics, however, argued that it violated nonmembers' freedom of association and was coercive and unworkable, since unions often advocate raising taxes to achieve public employees' salary increases; almost half of the states allow public-employee unions to charge nonmember employees such "fair share" fees to prevent them being free riders. A long-time critic of public-employee unions, writing for the Court's majority in *Janis,* Justice Alito overturned *Abood,* observing: "States and public-sector unions may no longer extract agency fees from nonconsenting employees. . . . This procedure violates the First Amendment and cannot continue." Alito also dismissed the argument that nonmembers were getting a free ride from union activities, asserting it overlooked they were rendered "captive riders" who "don't want to make the trip at all." Dissenting Justice Kagan, joined by Ginsburg, Breyer, and Sotomayor, countered that the ruling "prevents the American people, acting through their state and local officials, from making important choices about workplace governance."

NOTES

1. Alexis de Tocqueville, *Democracy in America,* Vol. 2, ed. Phillips Bradley (New York: Vintage Books, 1954), 196.

2. In *Cramp v. Board of Public Instruction,* 368 U.S. 278 (1961), the Court also upheld a state regulation requiring an affidavit for public employees that they are not members of a subversive organization.

3. *Aptheker v. United States,* 378 U.S. 500 (1964).

4. *Connick v. Myers,* 461 U.S. 138 (1983).

5. See *NAACP v. Button,* 371 U.S. 415 (1963).

6. In *International Association of Machinists v. Street*, 367 U.S. 740 (1961), the Court upheld closed union shops. See also *Brotherhood of Railway Trainmen v. Virginia State Bar*, 377 U.S. 1 (1964). In *Jones v. North Carolina Prisoners' Labor Union, Inc.*, 433 U.S. 119 (1977), however, the Court upheld restrictions on a prison inmate's "labor union" mailings for membership and solicitations. In *Minnesota State Board for Community Colleges v. Knight*, 465 U.S. 271 (1984), the Court held that a state's requiring public employees to engage in official exchanges of views only through their professional representatives did not violate the First Amendment. In *Knox v. Service Employees International*, 132 S.Ct. 2277 (2012), the Court held that unions in making mid-year assessments must give nonmember employees notice of the opportunity to opt out of paying the special fee.

7. In *Cousins v. Wigoda*, 419 U.S. 477 (1975), the Court upheld the national political party's power to specify how delegates from a state political party will be selected. In *Democratic Party of the United States v. Wisconsin*, 450 U.S. 107 (1981), Wisconsin's rule on binding primaries was found to violate the First Amendment. In *Brown v. Socialist Workers 74 Campaign Committee*, 459 U.S. 87 (1982), the Court held that disclosure of membership lists of the Socialist Workers party violated the First Amendment. However, the Court upheld the disclosure provisions of the Federal Election Campaign Act in *Buckley v. Valeo*, 424 U.S. 1 (1976), which is reprinted in part in Vol. 1, Ch. 8.

8. See *Griswold v. Connecticut*, 381 U.S. 479 (1965) (see Chs. 2 and 11).

Selected Bibliography

Ellis, Richard. *Judging the Boy Scouts of America: Gay Rights, Freedom of Association, and the Dale Case*. Lawrence: University of Kansas Press, 2014.

Kalven, Harry, Jr. *The Negro and The First Amendment*. Chicago: University of Chicago Press, 1965.

Koppelman, Andrew, and Tobias Wolff. *A Right to Discriminate? How the Case of Boy Scouts of America v. James Dale Warped the Law of Free Association*. New Haven: Yale University Press, 2009.

Schmidt, Christopher. *The Sit-Ins: Protest and Legal Change in the Civil Rights Era*. Chicago: University of Chicago Press, 2018.

National Association for the Advancement of Colored People v. Alabama
357 U.S. 449, 78 S.Ct. 1163 (1958)

The National Association for the Advancement of Colored People (NAACP) encountered bitter opposition in the South for bringing litigation challenging racial discrimination. Hostility mounted following its victory in the landmark school desegregation ruling in *Brown v. Board of Education*, 347 U.S. 483 (1954) (see Ch. 12). As the NAACP sought to force compliance with *Brown*, southern hostility led to efforts by the states to prevent the NAACP from bringing

In *NAACP v. Alabama* (1958), a unanimous Court held unconstitutional Alabama's demand that the NAACP reveal the names and addresses of all its members and agents in the state. The decision markedly broadened the horizons of the First Amendment. (*Everett Collection/Newscom.*)

more litigation. In 1956, Alabama's state attorney general sought to enjoin the NAACP from conducting business in the state under a law requiring out-of-state corporations to register and satisfy certain reporting requirements before doing business in the state. The NAACP was incorporated in New York and considered itself exempt from Alabama's law requiring, among other things, filing with the state certain records and membership lists, including the names and addresses of all members residing in the state. While filing the registration forms, the NAACP refused to give up its membership lists. For that it was found in contempt and fined $100,000. The state supreme court declined to review an appeal, and the NAACP appealed to the Supreme Court.

The court's decision was unanimous, and the opinion was announced by Justice Harlan.

■ ■ ■

☐ *Justice HARLAN delivers the opinion of the Court.*

We review from the standpoint of its validity under the Federal Constitution a judgment of civil contempt entered against petitioner, the National

Association for the Advancement of Colored People, in the courts of Alabama. The question presented is whether Alabama, consistently with the Due Process Clause of the Fourteenth Amendment, can compel petitioner to reveal to the State's Attorney General the names and addresses of all its Alabama members and agents, without regard to their positions or functions in the Association. The judgment of contempt was based upon petitioner's refusal to comply fully with a court order requiring in part the production of membership lists. . . .

Alabama has a statute similar to those of many other States which requires a foreign corporation, except as exempted, to qualify before doing business by filing its corporate charter with the Secretary of State and designating a place of business and an agent to receive service of process. . . . [The NAACP] has never complied with the qualification statute, from which it considered itself exempt.

In 1956 the Attorney General of Alabama brought an equity suit in the State Circuit Court, Montgomery County, to enjoin the Association from conducting further activities within, and to oust it from, the State. . . .

[T]he State moved for the production of a large number of the Association's records and papers, including bank statements, leases, deeds, and records containing the names and addresses of all Alabama "members" and "agents" of the Association. It alleged that all such documents were necessary for adequate preparation for the hearing, in view of petitioner's denial of the conduct of intrastate business within the meaning of the qualification statute. Over petitioner's objections, the court ordered the production of a substantial part of the requested records, including the membership lists. . . .

Thereafter petitioner . . . produced substantially all the data called for by the production order except its membership lists, as to which it contended that Alabama could not constitutionally compel disclosure, and moved to modify or vacate the contempt judgment, or stay its execution pending appellate review. This motion was denied. While a similar stay application, which was later denied, was pending before the Supreme Court of Alabama, the Circuit Court made a further order adjudging petitioner in continuing contempt and increasing the fine already imposed to $100,000. . . .

It is beyond debate that freedom to engage in association for the advancement of beliefs and ideas is an inseparable aspect of the "liberty" assured by the Due Process Clause of the Fourteenth Amendment, which embraces freedom of speech. . . .

The fact that Alabama, so far as is relevant to the validity of the contempt judgment presently under review, has taken no direct action, to restrict the right of petitioner's members to associate freely, does not end inquiry into the effect of the production order. In the domain of these indispensable liberties; whether of speech, press, or association, the decisions of this Court recognize that abridgement of such rights, even though unintended, may inevitably follow from varied forms of governmental action. . . .

It is hardly a novel perception that compelled disclosure of affiliation with groups engaged in advocacy may constitute as effective a restraint on freedom of association as the forms of governmental action in the cases above were thought likely to produce upon the particular constitutional rights there involved. This Court has recognized the vital relationship between freedom to associate and privacy in one's associations. . . . Inviolability of privacy in group association may in many circumstances be indispensable to preservation of freedom of association, particularly where a group espouses dissident beliefs.

We think that the production order, in the respects here drawn in question, must be regarded as entailing the likelihood of a substantial restraint upon the exercise by petitioner's members of their right to freedom of association. Petitioner has made an uncontroverted showing that on past occasions revelation of the identity of its rank-and-file members has exposed these members to economic reprisal, loss of employment, threat of physical coercion, and other manifestations of public hostility. Under these circumstances, we think it apparent that compelled disclosure of petitioner's Alabama membership is likely to affect adversely the ability of petitioner and its members to pursue their collective effort to foster beliefs which they admittedly have the right to advocate, in that it may induce members to withdraw from the Association and dissuade others from joining it because of fear of exposure of their beliefs shown through their associations and of the consequences of this exposure. . . .

We turn to the final question whether Alabama has demonstrated an interest in obtaining the disclosures it seeks from petitioner which is sufficient to justify the deterrent effect which we have concluded these disclosures may well have on the free exercise by petitioner's members of their constitutionally protected right of association. Such a ". . . subordinating interest of the State must be compelling," *Sweezy v. New Hampshire*, 354 U.S. 234 [(1957)] (concurring opinion). . . .

Whether there was "justification" in this instance turns solely on the substantiality of Alabama's interest in obtaining the membership lists. . . . The exclusive purpose was to determine whether petitioner was conducting intrastate business in violation of the Alabama foreign corporation registration statute, and the membership lists were expected to help resolve this question. . . . Without intimating the slightest view upon the merits of these issues, we are unable to perceive that the disclosure of the names of petitioner's rank-and-file members has a substantial bearing. As matters stand in the state court, petitioner (1) has admitted its presence and conduct of activities in Alabama since 1918; (2) has offered to comply in all respects with the state qualification statute, although preserving its contention that the statute does not apply to it; and (3) has apparently complied satisfactorily with the production order, except for the membership lists, by furnishing the Attorney General with varied business records, its charter and statement of purposes, the names of all of its directors and officers, and with the total number of its Alabama members and the amount of their dues. . . .

We hold that the immunity from state scrutiny of membership lists which the Association claims on behalf of its members is here so related to the right of the members to pursue their lawful private interests privately and to associate freely with others in so doing as to come within the protection of the Fourteenth Amendment. And we conclude that Alabama has fallen short of showing a controlling justification for the deterrent effect on the free enjoyment of the right to associate which disclosure of membership lists is likely to have. Accordingly, the judgment of civil contempt and the $100,000 fine which resulted from petitioner's refusal to comply with the production order in this respect must fall.

Boy Scouts of America v. Dale
530 U.S. 640, 120 S.Ct. 2446 (2000)

Founded in 1910, the Boy Scouts of America is a federally chartered corporation that, as of 1992, included more than 4 million youths and 1 million adults as active members in more than 44,000 Boy Scout troops throughout the country. In 1991 the New Jersey legislature amended its Law Against Discrimination (LAD) to include protection from discrimination based on "affectional or sexual orientation." Subsequently, the Boy Scouts revoked James Dale's Boy Scout Adult membership, upon learning that he was a homosexual, and he sued the Boy Scouts for violating the provisions of LAD.

In 1978, at the age of eight, James Dale joined a Cub Scout Pack and remained a member until 1981, when he became a member of a Boy Scout Troop. He remained a youth member until he reached age eighteen in 1988. During that time he earned more than twenty-five merit badges. In 1989 he sought and received adult membership and became an Assistant Scoutmaster, a position that he held for about a year and a half. About that time, he left home to attend Rutgers University and, while at college, acknowledged for the first time that he was gay. Shortly thereafter Dale became copresident of the Rutgers University Lesbian/Gay Alliance. Then, in July 1990, while attending a seminar on the health needs of lesbian and gay teenagers, Dale was interviewed by the *Star-Ledger*, which subsequently published an article that included Dale's photograph and identified him as the "copresident of the Rutgers University Lesbian/Gay Alliance." Later that month, Dale received from the Boy Scouts a letter revoking his membership and asking him to "sever any relations [he] may have with the Boy Scouts of America." Dale appealed unsuccessfully, and finally, in 1992, he filed a lawsuit in state court against the Boy Scouts of America for discriminating against him in violation of LAD.

The trial court concluded that Dale was "a sexually active homosexual" and the Boy Scouts had always excluded "active homosexual[s]." The court also ruled that the provisions of LAD did not apply to the Boy Scouts because it was not a "public accommodation." A state appellate court reversed and remanded upon concluding that the Boy Scouts were a "public accommodation." The state supreme court affirmed that decision, and the Boy Scouts appealed to the Supreme Court, which granted review.

The decision of the state supreme court was reversed in a 5–4 decision, and the opinion for the Court was delivered by Chief Justice Rehnquist. Justices Stevens and Souter each filed dissenting opinions, and were joined by Justices Ginsburg and Breyer.

■ ■ ■

☐ *Chief Justice REHNQUIST delivered the opinion of the Court.*

In *Roberts v. United States Jaycees,* 468 U.S. 609 (1984), we observed that "implicit in the right to engage in activities protected by the First Amendment" is "a corresponding right to associate with others in pursuit of a wide variety of political, social, economic, educational, religious, and cultural ends." This right is crucial in preventing the majority from imposing its views on groups that would rather express other, perhaps unpopular, ideas. Government actions that may unconstitutionally burden this freedom may take many forms, one of which is "intrusion into the internal structure or affairs of an association" like a "regulation that forces the group to accept members it does not desire." Forcing a group to accept certain members may impair the ability of the group to express those views, and only those views, that it intends to express. Thus, "[f]reedom of association plainly presupposes a freedom not to associate."

The forced inclusion of an unwanted person in a group infringes the group's freedom of expressive association if the presence of that person affects in a significant way the group's ability to advocate public or private viewpoints. *New York State Club Assn., Inc. v. City of New York,* 487 U.S. 1 (1988). But the freedom of expressive association, like many freedoms, is not absolute. We have held that the freedom could be overridden "by regulations adopted to serve compelling state interests, unrelated to the suppression of ideas, that cannot be achieved through means significantly less restrictive of associational freedoms." *Roberts.*

To determine whether a group is protected by the First Amendment's expressive associational right, we must determine whether the group engages in "expressive association." The First Amendment's protection of expressive association is not reserved for advocacy groups. But to come within its ambit, a group must engage in some form of expression, whether it be public or private.

Because this is a First Amendment case where the ultimate conclusions of law are virtually inseparable from findings of fact, we are obligated to independently review the factual record to ensure that the state court's judgment does not unlawfully intrude on free expression. The record reveals the following. The Boy Scouts is a private, nonprofit organization. According to its mission statement: "It is the mission of the Boy Scouts of America to serve others by helping to instill values in young people and, in other ways, to prepare them to make ethical choices over their lifetime in achieving their full potential." "The values we strive to instill are based on those found in the Scout Oath and Law." . . .

Thus, the general mission of the Boy Scouts is clear: "[T]o instill values in young people." The Boy Scouts seeks to instill these values by having its adult leaders spend time with the youth members, instructing and engaging them in activities like camping, archery, and fishing. During the time spent with the youth members, the scoutmasters and assistant scoutmasters inculcate them with the Boy Scouts' values—both expressly and by example. It seems indisputable that an association that seeks to transmit such a system of values engages in expressive activity.

Given that the Boy Scouts engages in expressive activity, we must determine whether the forced inclusion of Dale as an assistant scoutmaster would significantly affect the Boy Scouts' ability to advocate public or private viewpoints. This inquiry necessarily requires us first to explore, to a limited extent, the nature of the Boy Scouts' view of homosexuality.

The values the Boy Scouts seeks to instill are "based on" those listed in the Scout Oath and Law. The Boy Scouts explains that the Scout Oath and Law provide "a positive moral code for living; they are a list of do's rather than don'ts." The Boy Scouts asserts that homosexual conduct is inconsistent with the values embodied in the Scout Oath and Law, particularly with the values represented by the terms "morally straight" and "clean."

Obviously, the Scout Oath and Law do not expressly mention sexuality or sexual orientation. And the terms "morally straight" and "clean" are by no means self-defining. Different people would attribute to those terms very different meanings. For example, some people may believe that engaging in homosexual conduct is not at odds with being "morally straight" and "clean." And others may believe that engaging in homosexual conduct is contrary to being "morally straight" and "clean." The Boy Scouts says it falls within the latter category. . . .

The Boy Scouts asserts that it "teach[es] that homosexual conduct is not morally straight," *Brief for Petitioners*, and that it does "not want to promote homosexual conduct as a legitimate form of behavior." We accept the Boy Scouts' assertion. We need not inquire further to determine the nature of the Boy Scouts' expression with respect to homosexuality. . . .

The Boy Scouts publicly expressed its views with respect to homosexual conduct by its assertions in prior litigation. For example, throughout a California case with similar facts filed in the early 1980's, the Boy Scouts consistently asserted the same position with respect to homosexuality that it asserts today. We cannot doubt that the Boy Scouts sincerely holds this view.

We must then determine whether Dale's presence as an assistant scoutmaster would significantly burden the Boy Scouts' desire to not "promote homosexual conduct as a legitimate form of behavior." As we give deference to an association's assertions regarding the nature of its expression, we must also give deference to an association's view of what would impair its expression. That is not to say that an expressive association can erect a shield against antidiscrimination laws simply by asserting that mere acceptance of a member from a particular group would impair its message. But here Dale, by his own admission, is one of a group of gay Scouts who have "become leaders in their community and are open and honest about their sexual orientation." Dale was the copresident of a gay and lesbian organization at college and remains a gay rights activist. Dale's presence in the Boy Scouts would, at the very least, force the organization to send a message, both to the youth members and the world, that the Boy Scouts accepts homosexual conduct as a legitimate form of behavior.

Hurley [v. Irish-American Gay, Lesbian, and Bisexual Group of Boston, 515 U.S. 557 (1995)], is illustrative on this point. There we considered whether the application of Massachusetts' public accommodations law to require the organizers of a private St. Patrick's Day parade to include among the marchers an Irish-American gay, lesbian, and bisexual group, GLIB, violated the parade organizers' First Amendment rights. We noted that the parade organizers did not wish to exclude the GLIB members because of their sexual orientations, but because they wanted to march behind a GLIB banner. We observed: "[A] contingent marching behind the organization's banner would at least bear witness to the fact that some Irish are gay, lesbian, or bisexual, and the presence of the organized marchers would suggest their view that people of their sexual orientations have as much claim to unqualified social acceptance as heterosexuals. The parade's organizers may not believe these facts about Irish sexuality to be so, or they may object to unqualified social acceptance of gays and lesbians or have some other reason for wishing to keep GLIB's message out of the parade. But whatever the reason, it boils down to the choice of a speaker not to propound a particular point of view, and that choice is presumed to lie beyond the government's power to control." Here, we have found that the Boy Scouts believes that homosexual conduct is inconsistent with the values it seeks to instill in its youth members; it will not "promote homosexual conduct as a legitimate form of behavior." As the presence of GLIB in Boston's St. Patrick's Day parade would have interfered with the parade organizers' choice not to propound a particular point of view, the presence of Dale as an assistant scoutmaster would just as surely interfere with the Boy Scouts' choice not to propound a point of view contrary to its beliefs. . . .

Having determined that the Boy Scouts is an expressive association and that the forced inclusion of Dale would significantly affect its expression, we inquire whether the application of New Jersey's public accommodations law to require that the Boy Scouts accept Dale as an assistant scoutmaster runs afoul of the Scouts' freedom of expressive association. We conclude that it does.

State public accommodations laws were originally enacted to prevent discrimination in traditional places of public accommodation—like inns and trains. Many on the list are what one would expect to be places where the public is invited. For example, the statute includes as places of public accommodation taverns, restaurants, retail shops, and public libraries. But the statute also includes places that often may not carry with them open invitations to the public, like summer camps and roof gardens. In this case, the New Jersey Supreme Court went a step further and applied its public accommodations law to a private entity without even attempting to tie the term "place" to a physical location. As the definition of "public accommodation" has expanded from clearly commercial entities, such as restaurants, bars, and hotels, to membership organizations such as the Boy Scouts, the potential for conflict between state public accommodations laws and the First Amendment rights of organizations has increased.

We recognized in cases such as *Roberts* and *Duarte* that States have a compelling interest in eliminating discrimination against women in public accommodations. But in each of these cases we went on to conclude that the enforcement of these statutes would not materially interfere with the ideas that the organization sought to express. In *Roberts*, we said "[i]ndeed, the Jaycees has failed to demonstrate any serious burden on the male members' freedom of expressive association." We thereupon concluded in each of these cases that the organizations' First Amendment rights were not violated by the application of the States' public accommodations laws.

In *Hurley*, we said that public accommodations laws "are well within the State's usual power to enact when a legislature has reason to believe that a given group is the target of discrimination, and they do not, as a general matter, violate the First or Fourteenth Amendments." But we went on to note that in that case "the Massachusetts [public accommodations] law has been applied in a peculiar way" because "any contingent of protected individuals with a message would have the right to participate in petitioners' speech, so that the communication produced by the private organizers would be shaped by all those protected by the law who wish to join in with some expressive demonstration of their own." And in the associational freedom cases such as *Roberts, Duarte,* and *New York State Club Assn.,* after finding a compelling state interest, the Court went on to examine whether or not the application of the state law would impose any "serious burden" on the organization's rights of expressive association. So in these cases, the associational interest in freedom of expression has been set on one side of the scale, and the State's interest on the other. . . .

The judgment of the New Jersey Supreme Court is reversed, and the cause remanded for further proceedings not inconsistent with this opinion.

☐ *Justice STEVENS, with whom Justice SOUTER, Justice GINSBURG, and Justice BREYER join, dissenting.*

The majority holds that New Jersey's law violates BSA's right to associate and its right to free speech. But that law does not "impos[e] any serious burdens" on BSA's "collective effort on behalf of [its] shared goals," *Roberts v. United States Jaycees,* 468 U.S. 609 (1984), nor does it force BSA to communicate any message that it does not wish to endorse. New Jersey's law, therefore, abridges no constitutional right of the Boy Scouts. . . .

In light of BSA's self-proclaimed ecumenism, furthermore, it is even more difficult to discern any shared goals or common moral stance on homosexuality. Insofar as religious matters are concerned, BSA's bylaws state that it is "absolutely nonsectarian in its attitude toward religious training." "The BSA does not define what constitutes duty to God or the practice of religion. This is the responsibility of parents and religious leaders." In fact, many diverse religious organizations sponsor local Boy Scout troops. Because a number of religious groups do not view homosexuality as immoral or wrong and reject discrimination against homosexuals, it is exceedingly difficult to believe that BSA nonetheless adopts a single particular religious or moral philosophy when it comes to sexual orientation. This is especially so in light of the fact that Scouts are advised to seek guidance on sexual matters from their religious leaders (and Scoutmasters are told to refer Scouts to them); BSA surely is aware that some religions do not teach that homosexuality is wrong.

The Court seeks to fill the void by pointing to a statement of "policies and procedures relating to homosexuality and Scouting" signed by BSA's President and Chief Scout Executive in 1978 and addressed to the members of the Executive Committee of the national organization. [However, four] aspects of the 1978 policy statement are relevant to the proper disposition of this case. First, at most this letter simply adopts an exclusionary membership policy. But simply adopting such a policy has never been considered sufficient, by itself, to prevail on a right to associate claim.

Second, the 1978 policy was never publicly expressed—unlike, for example, the Scout's duty to be "obedient." It was an internal memorandum, never circulated beyond the few members of BSA's Executive Committee. It remained, in effect, a secret Boy Scouts policy.

Third, it is apparent that the draftsmen of the policy statement foresaw the possibility that laws against discrimination might one day be amended to protect homosexuals from employment discrimination. Their statement clearly provided that, in the event such a law conflicted with their policy, a Scout's duty to be "obedient" and "obe[y] the laws," even if "he thinks [the laws] are unfair" would prevail in such a contingency. In 1978, however, BSA apparently did not consider it to be a serious possibility that a State might one day characterize the Scouts as a "place of public accommodation" with a duty to open its membership to all qualified individuals. The portions of the statement dealing with membership simply assume that membership in the Scouts is a "privilege" that BSA is free to grant or to withhold. The statement does not address the question whether the publicly proclaimed duty to obey the law should prevail over the private discriminatory policy if, and when, a conflict between the two should arise—as it now has in New Jersey. At the very least, then, the statement reflects no unequivocal view on homosexuality. . . .

Fourth, the 1978 statement simply says that homosexuality is not "appropriate." It makes no effort to connect that statement to a shared goal or expressive activity of the Boy Scouts. Whatever values BSA seeks to instill in Scouts, the idea that homosexuality is not "appropriate" appears entirely unconnected to, and is mentioned nowhere in, the myriad of publicly declared values and creeds of the BSA. That idea does not appear to be among any of the principles actually taught to Scouts. Rather, the 1978 policy appears to be no more than a private statement of a few BSA executives that the organization wishes to exclude gays—and that wish has nothing to do with any expression BSA actually engages in. . . .

It is clear, then, that nothing in these policy statements supports BSA's claim. The only policy written before the revocation of Dale's membership was an equivocal, undisclosed statement that evidences no connection between the group's discriminatory intentions and its expressive interests. The later policies demonstrate a brief—though ultimately abandoned—attempt to tie BSA's exclusion to its expression, but other than a single sentence, BSA fails to show that it ever taught Scouts that homosexuality is not "morally straight" or "clean," or that such a view was part of the group's collective efforts to foster a belief. Furthermore, BSA's policy statements fail to establish any clear, consistent, and unequivocal position on homosexuality. . . .

BSA's claim finds no support in our cases. We have recognized "a right to associate for the purpose of engaging in those activities protected by the First Amendment—speech, assembly, petition for the redress of grievances, and the exercise of religion." *Roberts.* And we have acknowledged that "when the State interferes with individuals' selection of those with whom they wish to join in a common endeavor, freedom of association may be implicated." But "[t]he right to associate for expressive purposes is not absolute"; rather, "the nature and degree of constitutional protection afforded freedom of association may vary depending on the extent to which the constitutionally protected liberty is at stake in a given case." Indeed, the right to associate does not mean "that in every setting in which individuals exercise some discrimination in choosing associates, their selective process of inclusion and exclusion is protected by the Constitution." *New York State Club Assn., Inc. v. City of New York,* 487 U.S. 1 (1988). . . .

Several principles are made perfectly clear by *Jaycees* and [*Board of Directors of Rotary Int'l v.*] *Rotary Club*. First, to prevail on a claim of expressive association in the face of a State's antidiscrimination law, it is not enough simply to engage in some kind of expressive activity. Both the Jaycees and the Rotary Club engaged in expressive activity protected by the First Amendment, yet that fact was not dispositive. Second, it is not enough to adopt an openly avowed exclusionary membership policy. Both the Jaycees and the Rotary Club did that as well. Third, it is not sufficient merely to articulate some connection between the group's expressive activities and its exclusionary policy. The Rotary Club, for example, justified its male-only membership policy by pointing to the "aspect of fellowship that is enjoyed by the [exclusively] male membership" and by claiming that only with an exclusively male membership could it "operate effectively" in foreign countries.

Rather, in *Jaycees*, we asked whether Minnesota's Human Rights Law requiring the admission of women "impose[d] any serious burdens" on the group's "collective effort on behalf of [its] shared goals." Notwithstanding the group's obvious publicly stated exclusionary policy, we did not view the inclusion of women as a "serious burden" on the Jaycees' ability to engage in the protected speech of its choice. . . . The relevant question is whether the mere inclusion of the person at issue would "impose any serious burden," "affect in any significant way," or be "a substantial restraint upon" the organization's "shared goals," "basic goals," or "collective effort to foster beliefs." Accordingly, it is necessary to examine what, exactly, are BSA's shared goals and the degree to which its expressive activities would be burdened, affected, or restrained by including homosexuals.

The evidence before this Court makes it exceptionally clear that BSA has, at most, simply adopted an exclusionary membership policy and has no shared goal of disapproving of homosexuality. BSA's mission statement and federal charter say nothing on the matter; its official membership policy is silent; its Scout Oath and Law—and accompanying definitions—are devoid of any view on the topic; its guidance for Scouts and Scoutmasters on sexuality declare that such matters are "not construed to be Scouting's proper area," but are the province of a Scout's parents and pastor; and BSA's posture respecting religion tolerates a wide variety of views on the issue of homosexuality. Moreover, there is simply no evidence that BSA otherwise teaches anything in this area, or that it instructs Scouts on matters involving homosexuality in ways not conveyed in the Boy Scout or Scoutmaster Handbooks. In short, Boy Scouts of America is simply silent on homosexuality. There is no shared goal or collective effort to foster a belief about homosexuality at all—let alone one that is significantly burdened by admitting homosexuals. . . .

Equally important is BSA's failure to adopt any clear position on homosexuality. BSA's temporary, though ultimately abandoned, view that homosexuality is incompatible with being "morally straight" and "clean" is a far cry from the clear, unequivocal statement necessary to prevail on its claim. Despite the solitary sentences in the 1991 and 1992 policies, the group continued to disclaim any single religious or moral position as a general matter and actively eschewed teaching any lesson on sexuality. It also continued to define "morally straight" and "clean" in the Boy Scout and Scoutmaster Handbooks without any reference to homosexuality. As noted earlier, nothing in our cases suggests that a group can prevail on a right to expressive association if it, effectively, speaks out of both sides of its mouth. A State's antidiscrimination law does not impose a "serious burden" or a "substantial restraint" upon the group's "shared goals" if the group itself is unable to identify its own stance with any clarity. . . .

The majority's argument relies exclusively on *Hurley v. Irish-American Gay, Lesbian and Bisexual Group of Boston, Inc.*, 515 U.S. 557 (1995). In that case, petitioners John Hurley and the South Boston Allied War Veterans Council ran a privately operated St. Patrick's Day parade. Respondent, an organization known as "GLIB," represented a contingent of gays, lesbians, and bisexuals who sought to march in the petitioners' parade "as a way to express pride in their Irish heritage as openly gay, lesbian, and bisexual individuals." When the parade organizers refused GLIB's admission, GLIB brought suit under Massachusetts' antidiscrimination law. That statute, like New Jersey's law, prohibited discrimination on account of sexual orientation in any place of public accommodation, which the state courts interpreted to include the parade. Petitioners argued that forcing them to include GLIB in their parade would violate their free speech rights. . . .

Furthermore, it is not likely that BSA would be understood to send any message, either to Scouts or to the world, simply by admitting someone as a member. Over the years, BSA has generously welcomed over 87 million young Americans into its ranks. In 1992 over one million adults were active BSA members. The notion that an organization of that size and enormous prestige implicitly endorses the views that each of those adults may express in a non-Scouting context is simply mind-boggling. . . .

Unfavorable opinions about homosexuals "have ancient roots." *Bowers v. Hardwick*, 478 U.S. 186 (1986). Like equally atavistic opinions about certain racial groups, those roots have been nourished by sectarian doctrine. Over the years, however, interaction with real people, rather than mere adherence to traditional ways of thinking about members of unfamiliar classes, have modified those opinions. A few examples: The American Psychiatric Association's and the American Psychological Association's removal of "homosexuality" from their lists of mental disorders; a move toward greater understanding within some religious communities; Justice BLACKMUN's classic opinion in *Bowers*; Georgia's invalidation of the statute upheld in *Bowers*; and New Jersey's enactment of the provision at issue in this case.

That such prejudices are still prevalent and that they have caused serious and tangible harm to countless members of the class New Jersey seeks to protect are established matters of fact that neither the Boy Scouts nor the Court disputes. That harm can only be aggravated by the creation of a constitutional shield for a policy that is itself the product of a habitual way of thinking about strangers. As Justice BRANDEIS so wisely advised, "we must be ever on our guard, lest we erect our prejudices into legal principles."

If we would guide by the light of reason, we must let our minds be bold. I respectfully dissent.

6

FREEDOM FROM AND
OF RELIGION

Religious freedom is guaranteed in the two opening clauses of the
First Amendment: "Congress shall make no law respecting an
establishment of religion, or prohibiting the free exercise thereof."
Together, the clauses guarantee freedom from and of religion by pointing in opposite directions. The establishment clause points toward a
principle of the separation of government from religion; neither should
involve itself with the other. The free exercise clause suggests a principle of voluntarism—freedom from coercion in choosing a religion or no
religion.

Religious freedom has never been absolute, however. The First
Amendment, as the Court observed in *Cantwell v. Connecticut*, 310 U.S.
296 (1940), "embraces two concepts—freedom to believe and freedom
to act. The first is absolute but, in the nature of things, the second cannot be. Conduct remains subject to regulation of society." Drawing on
the distinction between belief and action, the Court thus wrote into
constitutional law a third principle of religious freedom that runs back
to Thomas Jefferson, who, in his *Bill for Establishing Religious Freedom* for
the state of Virginia in 1779, observed that "the acts of the body," unlike
"the operations of the mind, are subject to the coercion of the laws."[1]

Nor does the text and historical record of the First Amendment
provide simple interpretative solutions for the continuing controversies
in constitutional politics over religious freedom. What is "an establishment of religion," for example, and what is a "law respecting" the establishment of religion? What is and who defines *religion*? Many of the
contemporary disputes over the separation of government and religion,
moreover, could not have been foreseen during the founding period;

there was no controversy over school prayer, for example, because there was no system of public education.

The traditions and aspirations of religious freedom from the colonial through the revolutionary period and to the time the First Amendment was adopted and ratified in 1791 were complex and occasionally conflicting. Although populated by many escaping religious persecution in England or on the European continent, colonial settlements remained religious enclaves, discriminating against those of other faiths. In Massachusetts, the established Congregational Church taxed and harassed Quakers, Baptists, and others. In Virginia and four other southern colonies, the (Anglican) Church of England was established.

As the colonies developed and their leaders moved toward the Declaration of Independence, religious freedom grew and began to take on new meaning. With that conceptual change came a rejection of the European understanding of established church-states. England, Scotland, and Germany had established churches, while the Roman Catholic Church was established in Italy, Spain, and elsewhere. But in 1774 when the British Parliament passed a statute establishing both Anglicanism and Catholicism in Canada, the Continental Congress protested with "astonishment, that a British Parliament should ever consent to establish in that country a religion that has deluged [England] in blood, and dispersed bigotry, persecution, murder and rebellion through every part of the world."[2]

By the 1770s, the original thirteen colonies, always predominantly Protestant, were on their way to a new form of establishmentism, unlike the European single state-church denomination. Christianity or Protestantism, in contrast with Judaism, Islam, and Hinduism (as well as, for some colonists, Catholicism), was established in the northern colonies but allowed for multiple churches and denominations. Maryland's "declaration of rights" in 1776, hence, recognized the religious freedom of "persons professing the Christian religion." In 1778, South Carolina's constitution proclaimed that "the Christian Protestant religion shall be deemed . . . the established religion of this state." Notably, four colonies (Rhode Island, Pennsylvania, Delaware, and New Jersey) never established a state religion.[3] The established churches—Congregationalists in New England and Episcopalians in the South—bitterly confronted dissenting churches—Baptists in the North and Evangelicals in the South. The principal conflict between these denominations revolved around governmental financial support for churches, which Evangelicals fought to end. In the 1770s, Patrick Henry championed *nonpreferentialism*, that is, no governmental aid for particular religions but aid for all religions equally. Nonpreferentialism, however, was rejected in the South due to opposition from Evangelicals and fell out of favor in the 1790s and early nineteenth century as states abandoned established churches and religions as well as religious qualifications for holding state office. The controversy over governmental support for religion, nonetheless, again intensified with the great Catholic immigration in the nineteenth century. Widespread anti-Catholicism at this time (indeed, Catholic children were beaten and churches burned) reinforced opposition to government funding for religious schools.

Religious freedom found expression in Article VI of the Constitution, providing that "no religious Test shall ever be required as a Qualification to any Office or public Trust under the United States." But that was not enough to silence critics pressing for the addition of a bill of rights. When defending the Constitution during Virginia's ratifying convention on June 12, 1788, Madison sought to reassure those fearing government would deny religious freedom:

> If there were a majority of one sect, a bill of rights would be a poor protection for liberty. Happily for the states, they enjoy the utmost freedom of religion. This freedom arises from that multiplicity of sects, which pervades America, and which is the best and only security for religious liberty in any society. For where there is such a variety of sects, there cannot be a majority of any one sect to oppress and persecute the rest. . . . A particular state might concur in one religious project. But the United States abound in such a variety of sects, that it is a strong security against religious persecution, and it is sufficient to authorize a conclusion, that no one sect will ever be able to outnumber or depress the rest.[4]

Madison failed to dissuade those seeking further protection for religious freedom. While ratifying the Constitution, the Virginia convention proposed the addition of a bill of rights, including the following:

> That religion or the duty which we owe to our Creator, and the manner of discharging it can be directed only by reason and conviction, not by force or violence, and therefore all men have an equal, natural and unalienable right to the free exercise of religion according to the dictates of conscience, and that no particular religious sect or society ought to be favored or established by Law in preference to others.[5]

Defenders of religious freedom, however, were never of one mind. Some maintained that disestablishment of church and state was necessary to safeguard religion from the corrosive influence of politics. When celebrating the purity of evangelical faith in 1644, Roger Williams proclaimed that God commanded that "the most Paganish, Jewish, Turkish, or Antichristian consciences and worships, be granted to all men in all Nations and Countries." And he invoked the metaphor of a "wall of separation" in defense of the integrity of religion.

First, the faithful labors of many witnesses of Jesus Christ, extant to the world, abundantly proving that the church of the Jews under the Old Testament in the antitype were both separate from the world; and that when they have opened a gap in the hedge or *wall of separation* between the garden of the church and the wilderness of the world, God hath ever broke down the wall itself, removed the candlestick, and made His garden a wilderness, as at this day. And that therefore if He will ever please to restore His garden and paradise again, it must of necessity be walled in peculiarly unto Himself from the world; and that all that shall be saved out of the world are to be transplanted out of the wilderness of the world, and added unto His church or garden.[6]

More than 150 years later, President Jefferson again relied on the metaphor of a wall of separation in his famous letter to the Danbury Baptist Association in 1802:

Believing with you that religion is a matter which lies solely between man and his God, that he owes account to none other for his faith or his worship, that the legislative powers of government reach actions only, and not opinions, I contemplate with sovereign reverence that act of the whole American people which declared that their legislature should "make no law respecting an establishment of religion, or prohibiting the free exercise thereof," thus building a wall of separation between Church and State.[7]

Unlike those who shared Roger Williams's view that the entanglement of religion and the state would compromise the former, Jefferson was more concerned about insulating government from the influences of religion and religious fervor. In his home state of Virginia, Jefferson had fought for religious freedom—freedom not just for Protestants or Christians. As he reflected about the opposition in 1779 to his "Bill for Establishing Religious Freedom":

Where the preamble declares, that coercion is a departure from the plan of the holy author of our religion, an amendment was proposed, by inserting the word "Jesus Christ," that it should read, "a departure from the plan of Jesus Christ, the holy author of our religion"; the insertion was rejected by a great majority, in proof that they meant to comprehend, within the mantle of its protection, the Jew and the Gentile, the Christian and Mohometan, the Hindoo, and Infidel of every denomination.[8]

James Madison agreed that a wall of separation would help preserve the integrity of government, but he also thought that it might benefit religion as well. Madison, along with Jefferson, opposed proposals to establish religious taxes in Virginia. In his famous "Memorial and Remonstrance against Religious Assessments" in 1785, he persuasively argued against government support of religion. Governmental assistance to religious establishments, Madison maintained, tended to divide society into factions and produce "pride and indolence in the clergy; ignorance and servility in the laity; in both, superstition, bigotry and persecution." Nor did Madison think government depended on the support of religion. "That is not a just government," he wrote in 1792, in which "a man's religious rights are violated by penalties, or fettered by tests, or taxes by a hierarchy."[9]

But Madison proved unsuccessful in persuading the First Congress that the states as well as the federal government should be barred from passing laws respecting the establishment of religion and religious freedom. On June 8, 1789, in the House of Representatives, Madison introduced a series of proposed amendments to the Constitution, among them: "The civil rights of none shall be abridged on account of religious belief or worship, nor shall any national religion be established, nor shall the full and equal rights of conscience be in any manner, or on any pretext, infringed." And another: "No State shall violate the equal rights of conscience, or the freedom of the press, or the trial by jury in criminal cases."[10]

Without debate, Madison's proposals were referred to a special committee, of which he was a member. Within a week, the committee reported back to the full House. Madison's proposals remained intact, except for some editing: the words "civil rights" and "national" were deleted. The House devoted a single day to considering the amendment. As a result of a motion by Fisher Ames, and further stylistic changes, the revised amendment read: "Congress shall make no law establishing religion, or prohibiting the free exercise thereof, nor shall the rights of conscience be infringed."

The House's proposed amendments were debated in secret by the Senate in September. The *Senate Journal*, however, records three unsuccessful motions to change the amendment on September 3. All would have narrowed the amendment to ban establishments preferring "one religious sect or society," or "any particular denomination of religion in preference to another." But six weeks later, the Senate voted to amend the House's version to read, "Congress shall make no law establishing articles of faith or a mode of worship, or prohibiting the free exercise of religion." This change narrowed the religion clauses to barring Congress only from endorsing a single denomination or national religion. Under it, Congress could provide nondiscriminatory government aid to all religions (something Baptists bitterly opposed).

The Senate's changes provoked opposition in the House. A joint conference committee, chaired by Madison, was created to resolve the differences between the House and Senate versions of the proposed amendments. Finally, on September 24, the House agreed to accept the Senate's version of other amendments on the condition that the amendment on religion be changed to its present form: "Congress shall make no laws respecting an establishment of religion, or prohibiting the free exercise thereof." The Senate agreed; Congress adopted the religion clauses.

Madison's efforts to guarantee "the full and equal rights of conscience" and to forbid the states from violating "the equal rights of conscience" nevertheless failed. States continued vestiges of establishment and restrictions on religious freedom. Massachusetts, for one, denied Jews the right to hold public office until 1828 and did not remove its final vestiges of the establishment of Congregationalism until 1833.

Not until *Cantwell v. Connecticut*, 310 U.S. 296 (1940), did the Hughes Court hold the free exercise clause applicable to the states. In Justice Roberts's words, "The Fourteenth Amendment has rendered the legislatures of the states as incompetent as Congress to enact" laws denying the free exercise of religion. Seven years later, the Vinson Court made the establishment clause applicable to the states in *Everson v. Board of Education of Ewing Township* (1947) (excerpted below), in which Justice Black, for a bare majority, wrote the high-wall theory of the separation of government from religion into constitutional law but upheld the reimbursement of the costs of transporting children to private religious schools.

Since *Cantwell* and *Everson*, controversy has infused and surrounded the Court's interpretation of the religion clauses. But before turning to the Court's rulings and rival interpretations of the religion clauses, it may be helpful to consider two different theoretical approaches to religious freedom that have animated constitutional politics: nonpreferentialism and the high-wall theory of the separation of government and religion.

President Ronald Reagan's attorney general, Edwin Meese III, championed a revival of the *nonpreferentialism position*, advocated over 200 years ago by Patrick Henry, among others, when he wrote,

> the First Amendment forbade the establishment of a particular religion or a particular church. It also precluded the federal government from favoring one church, or one church group over another. That's what the First Amendment did, but it did not go further. It did not, for example, preclude federal aid to religious groups so long as that assistance furthered a public purpose and so long as it did not discriminate in favor of one religious group against another.[11]

Chief Justices Burger and Rehnquist, along with other justices, shared this view, as well as political scientist Walter Berns. "There was no dispute with respect to the principles on which the Constitution was built," Berns claims, when observing that "stated in its most radical form, [the Framers] all agreed that our institutions do *not* presuppose a providential Supreme Being." But, he adds, "whereas our institutions do not presuppose a Supreme Being, their preservation does." And on that basis Berns reasoned that "[l]iberal democracy must preserve what it cannot itself generate, and it must do this without jeopardizing the private character of religion." In short, nonpreferentialism holds that government may aid religion, but not support or endorse any particular religion.

Everson, from the perspective of Berns and others, wrongly launched "an interpretation under which the First Amendment forbids precisely what many a man in the First Congress went to such pains to protect— namely, public support of religion, albeit on a nondiscriminatory basis."[12] However, Justice Black's opinion, although writing the high-wall theory into constitutional law, allowed reimbursement for the cost of busing children to private religious schools on a *child benefit* or *benevolent neutrality*. In other words, the Court should enforce a *strict separation* between government and religion, striking down direct aid for religion but permitting indirect aid, as in *Everson*.

By contrast, the four dissenters in *Everson* argued for a *"strict neutrality"* interpretation of Jefferson's high-wall theory of separation of government and religion. Historian Leonard Levy supports this interpretation when attacking the nonpreferentialist's approach to the religion clauses:

> The fundamental defect of the nonpreferential interpretation is that it results in the unhistorical contention that the First Amendment augmented a nonexistent congressional power to legislate in the field of religion [since Article I does not give Congress any legislative powers over religion]. . . . Preferring 'religion over irreligion' is a red herring; the question of such a preference was not an issue. The government possessed no power to aid irreligion or religion. . . .
>
> Nonpreferentialism, unfortunately, is but a pose for those who think that religion needs to be patronized and promoted by government. When they speak of nonpreferential aid, they speak euphemistically as if they are not partisan. In fact they really are preferentialists. . . . Nonpreferentialists prefer government sponsorship and subsidy of religion rather than allow it to compete on its merits against irreligion and indifference. They prefer government nurture of religion because they mistakenly dread government neutrality as too risky, and so they condemn it as hostility. They prefer what they call, again euphemistically, accommodation.[13]

Conflicts in constitutional politics over religious freedom involve not only deciding between and applying the nonpreferentialist or accommodationist approach versus a high-wall theory of separation of government and religion. In the contemporary administrative state, laws and exemptions from laws may be challenged for violating either the establishment clause or the free exercise clause. There is an essential tension between these two guarantees. Scholarships, grants, tax credits, or reimbursements have been viewed as infringing on, alternatively, one or the other religion clauses. In *Witters v. Washington Department of Services for the Blind*, 474 U.S. 481 (1986), for example, the Court confronted a controversy over the denial of aid for vocational rehabilitation, available under state law, to Larry Witters by the Washington State Commission for the Blind. Witters's application for financial aid was denied because he wanted to pursue a Bible studies degree at a private Christian college. The commission's denial of financial aid might have been viewed as infringing on Witters's free exercise of religion, but the Washington State Supreme Court ruled that giving assistance to Witters would have the primary effect of advancing religion and so violated the establishment clause. On appeal, the Supreme Court reversed that decision and held that such assistance does not violate the establishment clause. On remand, however, the Washington supreme court held that Witters could still not use the scholarship to attend a Bible college under a vocational scholarship for the blind because that would violate the state constitution's provision for the separation of church and state, which erected a higher wall of separation than the Supreme Court's interpretation of the First Amendment.

Subsequently, a bare majority of the Rehnquist Court extended that ruling in *Zobrest v. Catalina Foothills School District*, 509 U.S. 1 (1993) (excerpted in Section A), when upholding public funding for a sign-language interpreter for a deaf high school student who attended a religious school. The Court, then, extended *Witters* and *Zobrest* to uphold the loan of computer software and hardware to private religious schools, in *Mitchell v. Helms*, 530 U.S. 793 (2000); and in *Zelman v. Simmons-Harris* 536 U.S. 639 (2003) upheld vouchers for public school students in failing inner-city schools in Cleveland, Ohio, to attend schools outside of the city, even though 96 percent of the funding went to religious schools.

The Court drew a line, however, and addressed the tensions between the (dis)establishment and free exercise clauses in *Locke v. Davey* (2004) (excerpted below in Section B). There, the Court held that a student awarded a state scholarship who wanted to earn degrees in theology and business administration could be barred from using it for that purpose, under Washington state's constitutional bar against public expenditures for religion, over his objections that that violated the First Amendment guarantee for the free exercise of religion. Writing for the Court, Chief Justice Rehnquist distinguished *Zelman* and other (dis)establishment clause rulings permitting indirect aid for religious schools, whether through vouchers, computer software, or scholarships, on the ground that those programs directly benefit students and turned on individual student choices. Thus, although in *Witters*, the Court held that the (dis)establishment clause was not violated by permitting Witters to use a Washington state scholarship to pursue biblical studies, Witters never received the scholarship because on remand, state courts held that the state constitution imposed a more strict separation of government from religion than the federal constitution. When Joshua Davey subsequently argued that Washington's constitutional provision barring his use of a scholarship to pursue a pastoral degree violated the First Amendment free exercise clause in *Locke v. Davey*, the Court ruled that the free exercise clause does not compel what the (dis)establishment clause would permit. In *Locke* Justices Scalia and Thomas dissented and objected to the majority's permitting states to discriminate against religion.

    Locke v. Davey, however, was distinguished and qualified by the Roberts Court in *Trinity Lutheran Church of Columbia, Inc. v. Comer*, 137 S.Ct. 2012 (2017) (excerpted in Section B of this chapter). There, Chief Justice Roberts held that the denial of a grant to a religious organization for playground resurfacing violated the free exercise clause and was permissible under recent rulings on the (dis)establishment clause. Chief Justice Roberts distinguished *Locke* on the ground that the issue was Washington State's denial of a scholarship based on the *status* of Joshua Davey's pursuing a degree in pastoral ministries (a religious activity), for which the free exercise clause did not compel public funding for, and Davey could still pursue the degree without the scholarship; whereas, in *Trinity Lutheran* Missouri discriminated against a religious organization's *use* of a grant—available to all but religious organizations—for resurfacing a playground (a nonreligious activity), in violation of the free exercise clause. In other words, in *Locke* the denial of the scholarship was permissible because public funding would go for a theological activity, which the free exercise clause does not compel, while in *Trinity Lutheran* the denial of the grant to a religious organization for a non-theological purpose—resurfacing a playground— did violate the free exercise clause.

Notes

1. Thomas Jefferson, in *The Writings of Thomas Jefferson*, Vol. 2, ed. Paul Ford (New York: Putnam's Sons, 1892–1899), 237–239.

2. "Continental Congress to the People of Great Britain, October 21, 1774," in *The Founders' Constitution*, Vol. 5, ed. Philip Kurland and Ralph Lerner (Chicago: University of Chicago Press, 1987), 61.

3. See Leonard Levy, *The Establishment Clause: Religion and the First Amendment* (New York: Macmillan, 1986), 61.

4. James Madison, in *The Founders' Constitution*, Vol. 5, ed. Kurland and Lerner, 88.

5. "Virginia Ratifying Convention," in *The Founders' Constitution*, Vol. 5, ed. Kurland and Lerner, 89.

6. Quoted in Levy, *The Establishment Clause*, 184.

7. Thomas Jefferson, "Letter to Danbury Baptist Association, January 1, 1802," in *The Founders' Constitution*, Vol. 5, ed. Kurland and Lerner, 96.

8. Thomas Jefferson, in *The Founders' Constitution*, Vol. 5, ed. Kurland and Lerner, 85.

9. James Madison, *The Papers of James Madison*, Vol. 14, ed. Robert Rutland (Chicago: University of Chicago Press, 1983), 266–267.

10. Joseph Gales and W. W. Seaton, *The Debates and Proceedings in the Congress of the United States*, Vol. 1 (Washington, DC: Gales and Seaton, 1834–1856), 451–452.

11. Edwin Meese III, "Address before the Christian Legal Society," given in San Diego, CA, September 29, 1985.

12. Walter Berns, *The First Amendment and the Future of American Democracy* (New York: Basic Books, 1976), 10, 12, 34, and 60.

13. Levy, *The Establishment Clause*, 93–94 and 118.

SELECTED BIBLIOGRAPHY

Barry, John M. *Roger Williams and the Creation of the American Soul.* New York: Viking, 2012.

Brown, Steven P. *Trumping Religion: The New Christian Right, The Free Speech Clause, and the Courts.* Tuscaloosa: University of Alabama Press, 2002.

Curry, Thomas. *The First Freedoms: Church and State in America to the Passage of the First Amendment.* New York: Oxford University Press, 1986.

Hamilton, Marci. *God vs. the Gavel: Religion and the Rule of Law.* New York: Cambridge University Press, 2005.

Holmes, David. *The Faiths of the Founding Fathers.* New York: Oxford University Press, 2006.

Howe, Mark DeWolfe. *The Garden and the Wilderness: Religion and Government in American Constitutional History.* Chicago: University of Chicago Press, 1965.

Kramnick, Isaac, and Moore, Laurence. *The Godless Constitution: The Case against Religious Correctness.* New York: W. W. Norton & Company, 2005.

Levy, Leonard. *The Establishment Clause: Religion and the First Amendment.* New York: Macmillan, 1986.

Meacham, Jon. *American Gospel: God, the Founding Fathers, and the Making of a Nation.* New York: Random House, 2006.

Rogosta, John. *Religious Freedom: Jefferson's Legacy, America's Creed.* Charlottesville: University of Virginia Press, 2013.

Waldman, Steven. *Founding Faith: Providence, Politics, and the Birth of Religious Freedom in America.* New York: Random House, 2008.

A | *The (Dis)Establishment of Religion*

In the constitutional politics of interpreting and applying the establishment clause, the Court has been divided over four rival interpretative principles and tests for the separation of government from religion: (1) *strict separation* requires state neutrality with respect to particular religions and a secular purpose for legislation but may permit some benefits or indirect support for religion; (2) *strict neutrality* requires not merely a secular purpose for legislation but bars all laws that either aid or hinder religion (directly or indirectly); (3) a *nonpreferentialist approach* allows that government may (indirectly or directly) aid religion but not any particular religion; and closely related to the latter, (4) an *accommodationist* approach, while maintaining that laws must have a secular purpose, allows for governmental accommodation of religion without endorsing a particular religion. Both *nonpreferentialism* and *accommodationism* of religion advance the view that government should not be hostile toward religion. However, *nonpreferentialism* maintains that government may support religion, just not any particular religion, under the First Amendment's (dis)establishment clause; whereas, *accommodationists* contend that the government should make exceptions for religious minorities from generally applicable laws because of the First Amendment's free exercise clause (as in *Sherbert v. Verner*, 374 U.S. 398 (1963), and *Wisconsin v. Yoder*, 406 U.S. 205 (1972); both excerpted in Section B of this chapter).

Strict separation of government and religion holds "that government can do nothing which involves governmental support of religion or which is favorable to the cultivation of religious interests."[1] In *Everson v. Board of Education of Ewing Township* (1947) (see excerpt below), the Vinson Court embraced this theory and wrote Jefferson's metaphor of a wall of separation into constitutional law. However, the justices split 5–4 because the majority decided to construe New Jersey's program of reimbursing parents for the cost of busing children to private schools, including parochial schools, as a "subsidy to parents not churches." Justice Black's opinion for the majority suggested that strict separation need not preclude "child benefits" or a state's "benevolent neutrality" toward religion. So too, in *Corporation of Presiding Bishops v. Amos*, 483 U.S. 327 (1987), the Rehnquist Court ruled that the establishment clause was not violated by allowing nonprofit (Mormon) industries to hire only religiously faithful employees.

The four dissenters in *Everson* agreed that the establishment clause embodies a high-wall principle of separation, but viewed the majority's holding as a breach of the wall. In their view, strict neutrality was required; that is, religion "may not be used as a basis for classification for

purposes of governmental action, whether that action t~~~~
of rights or privileges or the imposition of duties or obl~~~~
A year after *Everson*, the Court struck down a "rel~~~~
gram," allowing public school children to attend religiou~~~~
campus grounds, in *McCollum v. Board of Education*, 333 U~~~~
The religious instructors were not paid by the city, but the ~~~~
rooms in public schools was held to violate the establishm~~~~
second case, involving students going off campus for religio~~~~
however, the Court upheld a released-time program becaus~~~~
instruction did not occur on school property and did no~~~~
expenditure of public funds, and there was no evidence that the ~~~~
were being compelled to attend the off-campus classes on religion.
Zorach v. Clauson, 343 U.S. 306 (1952), dissenting Justices Black, Jackson,
and Frankfurter contended that even this released-time program breached
the high wall of separation between government and religion.

The Vinson Court thus agreed that the establishment clause requires
state neutrality and that governmental programs must have a secular purpose, but disagreed over whether religion might indirectly benefit or
receive assistance from government. As the Court's composition changed,
the Warren Court moved constitutional law in the direction of a "strict
neutrality" version of the high wall of separation, and then the Burger and
Rehnquist Courts swung back toward a nonpreferentialist position,
allowing governmental accommodation of and support for religion. Since
Everson, though, the justices have remained split on the tests for determining whether public school facilities may be used for religious purposes and
in what other ways government may accommodate religion.

The Warren Court generated a continuing storm of controversy
when holding that public school systems may not require children to
recite either nondenominational prayers or the Lord's Prayer, in *Engel v.
Vitale* (1962) (excerpted below) and *Abington School District v. Schempp*
(1963) (excerpted below). In *Schempp*, the Court drew on its earlier rationale, in *McGowan v. State of Maryland*, 366 U.S. 420 (1961), for upholding
blue laws, or Sunday closing laws, and formulated a two-part test for laws
under the establishment clause: whether laws have "a secular legislative
purpose and a primary effect that neither advances nor inhibits religion."

By the end of the Warren Court era, the wall of separation appeared
firmly entrenched in constitutional law. In charting the boundaries
between religion and government, the Warren Court had pushed constitutional law in the direction of strict neutrality when applying *Schempp*'s
secular purpose–secular effect test, much as the dissenters in *Everson* had
urged. In Chief Justice Warren's last term, the Court unanimously
struck down Arkansas's law forbidding the teaching of evolution in
public schools in *Epperson v. Arkansas*, 393 U.S. 97 (1968).

ction of constitutional law, however, began to shift when
e Burger came to the Court in 1969. As the composition of the
rther changed with the appointees of Republican Presidents
Reagan, and George H. W. Bush, the balance on the Court
toward greater accommodation of government support of religion.
f Justice Burger took an activist role in redirecting the interpretation
application of the establishment clause. He signaled his disagreement
th the Warren Court's strict interpretation in *Walz v. Tax Commission of
City of New York*, 397 U.S. 664 (1971). There the Court rejected a challenge to New York's tax exemption for "real or personal property used
exclusively for religious, educational or charitable purposes." And Burger
found occasion to stress that *Everson*'s majority upheld governmental
benevolent neutrality, as well as to advance his accommodationist interpretation of the religion clauses. "[T]here is room for play in the joints
productive of a benevolent neutrality which will permit religious exercise to exist without sponsorship and without interference." Chief Justice
Burger, however, went a step further by suggesting that government support of religion was permissible so long as there was "no excessive governmental entanglement with religion"—hence, the accommodation of
religion without preference for any particular religion.

When introducing the idea of "excessive governmental entanglement with religion" in *Walz*, Burger failed to mention the Warren
Court's *Schempp* test. But the following year in *Lemon v. Kurtzman* (1971)
(excerpted below), which involved reimbursement of the cost of teachers' salaries and instructional materials in secular subjects for private
religious schools, he turned *Schempp's* two-prong test (whether a statute
has a secular purpose and its primary effect neither advances nor inhibits religion) into a three-prong test by adding that a "statute must not
foster 'an excessive government entanglement with religion.' "

The *Lemon* test allowed the Burger Court to move in the direction of
permitting governmental accommodation of religion. But the *Lemon* test
requires the Court to distinguish sharply between the level of educational
institutions (primary and secondary schools versus institutions of higher
education) and the particular kinds of assistance, services, and benefits
extended by the government. At the same time, the line of separation
between government and religion became less clear, turning on the
degree of entanglement, and thus the particular facts of any kind of entanglement presented in each case. Reliance on *Lemon* also meant that
whether governmental support of religion survives establishment clause
objections depends on the policy goals of the majority on the Court. In a
companion ruling handed down with *Lemon*, for example, the justices
voted 5–4 in upholding a federal program providing construction grants
to colleges and universities. The majority in *Tilton v. Richardson*, 403 U.S.

672 (1971), had no problem with these grants going to religiously affiliated schools and, in contrast to *Lemon*, held that the program survived *Lemon's* three-prong test as follows: (1) The buildings to be constructed had a secular purpose and were to be used only for nonreligious purposes. (2) Unlike the primary and secondary schools in *Lemon*, in the view of the majority, church-related colleges are not "permeated" with religion and students are "less impressionable and less susceptible to church indoctrination." Finally, (3) the grants were on a one-time basis and, hence, did not give rise to excessive government entanglement with religion.

The difficulties in and disagreements about applying *Lemon* further divided the Court over whether *Lemon* should be abandoned in favor of another accommodationist approach or in favor of returning to a strict interpretation of the wall of separation between government and religion. In *Wolman v. Walter*, 433 U.S. 229 (1977), for example, when upholding certain diagnostic and therapeutic testing services to be provided to primary and secondary schools affiliated with particular religions in Ohio, the justices could not agree on the application of the *Lemon* test, and Blackmun's opinion for the Court simply failed to mention it. Only Burger, Powell, and Stewart continued to support *Lemon*. Rehnquist, O'Connor, White, and Scalia, although inclined toward an accommodationist approach to the establishment clause, criticized the *Lemon* tests. Brennan, Marshall, and Stevens, while relying on *Lemon* in some of their opinions for the Court, also suggested abandoning *Lemon*. Dissenting in *Committee for Public Education and Religious Liberty v. Regan*, 444 U.S. 646 (1980), Justice Stevens observed that

> the entire enterprise of trying to justify various types of subsidies to nonpublic schools should be abandoned. Rather than continuing with the Sisyphean task of trying to patch together the "blurred, indistinct, and variable barrier" described in *Lemon v. Kurtzman*, . . . I would resurrect the "high and impregnable" wall between church and state constructed by the Framers of the First Amendment. See *Everson v. Board of Education*.

In *Widmar v. Vincent*, 454 U.S. 263 (1981), the Burger Court struck down a Missouri statute prohibiting the use of university buildings and grounds "for purposes of religious worship," which had been used to deny a student religious group access to the facilities of a state university. There, the Court observed that "[u]niversity students are . . . less impressionable than younger students and should be able to appreciate that the university's policy is one of neutrality towards religion." The Court's holding in *Widmar* that an equal access policy at the level of universities did not violate the establishment clause encouraged Congress to extend that principle to primary and secondary schools. Congress did so with the passage of the Equal Access Act of 1984, which bars public schools from discriminating against meetings of student activity groups on school grounds on the basis of "religious, political, philosophical or other content of the speech at such meetings."

When the constitutionality of the Equal Access Act was challenged in *Board of Education of the Westside Community Schools v. Mergens*, 496 U.S. 226 (1990), the Court upheld the law, with only Justice Stevens dissenting. In that case, the school board had prohibited a Christian Bible club from meeting on school grounds. The board contended that if the religious club was allowed to meet it would have to have a faculty sponsor, which in turn would violate the establishment clause. But, writing for the Court, Justice O'Connor held that the school board had violated the provisions of the Equal Access Act and that those provisions did not violate the establishment clause. In her view, the act neither had a primary effect of advancing religion nor excessively entangled government and religion, even though the student religious meetings would be held on school grounds and under the school's aegis.

Subsequently, in *Lamb's Chapel v. Center Moriches Union Free School District*, 508 U.S. 384 (1993), the Court unanimously held that a school district's denial of a religious group's use of school facilities for meetings after school hours violated the First Amendment's guarantee of free speech. Although resting the decision on free speech grounds, Justice White's opinion for the Court also held that permitting religious groups access to school grounds did not run afoul of the First Amendment's (dis)establishment clause. *Lamb's Chapel*, then, was reaffirmed and extended in *Good News Club v. Milford Central School*, 533 U.S. 98 (2001).

As a result of the Court's failure to agree on an interpretative approach and test for applying the establishment clause, the justices sometimes invoke *Lemon's* three-prong test[3] and at other times pay little or no attention to it.[4] *Stone v. Graham*, 449 U.S. 39 (1980), is illustrative. There in a *per curiam* opinion for a bare majority, the *Lemon* tests were recited verbatim, but the Court struck down Kentucky's law requiring the posting of the Ten Commandments in school classrooms simply because it lacked a secular purpose. *Stone v. Graham* also underscored the importance of whether the justices construe the legislative purpose of a law to be secular or religious. In *Stone*, the majority held that posting the Ten Commandments "serves no . . . educational function."

The continuing struggle within the Court is registered in several important rulings. Splitting 5–4 in *Lynch v. Donnelly*, 465 U.S. 668 (1984), the Burger Court upheld the Pawtucket, Rhode Island, display of the crèche during the Christmas holiday season. Notably, the majority interpreted the crèche to be a secular, not a religious, symbol and found no excessive government entanglement with religion. The following year, then, the justices divided 6–3 in *Wallace v. Jaffree* (1985) (see excerpt below) in striking down Alabama's law requiring a moment of silence in public schools for meditation or voluntary prayer. Along with Stevens's opinion for the Court, relying on *Lemon*, compare O'Connor's concurring opinion and Burger's dissenting opinion, both criticizing reliance on and application of *Lemon*. The dissenting opinion of Rehnquist is also notable in attacking not only *Lemon* but the Court's understanding of the establishment clause since *Everson*.

Edwards v. Aguillard, 482 U.S. 578 (1987), overturned Louisiana's law requiring the teaching of creationism, and *County of Allegheny v. American Civil Liberties Union Greater Pittsburgh Chapter*, 492 U.S. 573 (1989), held that the display of a crèche inside a city building violated the establishment clause and limited *Lynch v. Donnelly*, as well as rejected Chief Justice Burger's analysis there. At the same time, the Court upheld the display of the menorah next to a Christmas tree outside a city/county office building. In both *Lynch* and *County of Allegheny*, Justice O'Connor cast the crucial vote in determining the outcome and drawing the Court's line between religion and government.

In *Lee v. Weisman*, 505 U.S. 577 (1992) (excerpted below), a bare majority of the Court held that the First Amendment forbids school-sponsored invocations and benedictions at graduation ceremonies. Justice Kennedy announced the decision because he cast the deciding vote in a ruling that otherwise split the justices four to four. The school district's supervision of graduation ceremonies, according to Kennedy, "places public pressure, as well as peer pressure, on attending students to stand as a group or, at least, maintain respectful silence during the Invocation and Benediction." Yet, in suggesting a "governmental coercion" test, his opinion held out the possibility that government may endorse religion in other ways. In that regard, Justice Kennedy conceded too much for the four other justices—Justices Souter, O'Connor, Blackmun, and Stevens—in the majority. In separate concurrences, those four justices emphasized that in their view government may no more endorse religion than, as in *Lee*, coerce participation in a religious practice. By contrast, the four dissenters—Chief Justice Rehnquist and Justices Scalia, Thomas, and White—derided Justice Kennedy's analysis of the psychological coercion of students forced to attend benedictions as "psychology practiced by amateurs."

The ruling in *Lee v. Weisman* provoked considerable protest, including school-sponsored prayers at the outset of high school football games. When that practice was challenged in *Santa Fe Independent School District v. Doe*, 530 U.S. 290 (2000), the Court reaffirmed *Weisman* by a 6–3 vote in holding that schools may not sponsor prayers at football games. Chief Justice Rehnquist and Justices Scalia and Thomas dissented from Justice Stevens's opinion for the Court.

In sum, despite bitter disagreements, the Court continues to occasionally rely on the *Lemon* test and expressly declined to overrule it in

Lee v. Weisman. Moreover, in *Board of Education of Kiryas Joel v. Grumet,* 512 U.S. 687 (1994), the Court's majority again declined to jettison *Lemon.* Dividing 6–3 when striking down New York's law creating a special school district for Kiryas Joel, a community inhabited solely by Hasidic Jews, Justice Souter's opinion for the Court approvingly cited *Lemon* twice. Justice Blackmun's concurrence strongly supported the *Lemon* test, while Justice O'Connor's concurrence called for abandoning *Lemon,* as did dissenting Justice Scalia, whose dissent was joined by that of Chief Justice Rehnquist and Justice Thomas.

In addition, the Court has grappled with the issue of the interrelationship among First Amendment doctrines for free speech, the (dis)establishment of religion, and the free exercise of religion. During the last couple of decades, a number of Christian groups have challenged a variety of public schools' policies based on the (dis)establishment clause and the Court's interpretations of that clause. They have argued that those policies restrict their freedom of religious expression and violate their First Amendment right of free speech; in other words, in order to achieve their free exercise goals, they have sued on the basis of the First Amendment's guarantee for free speech and press. In the so-called *Wide Awake* case, *Rosenberger v. The Rector and Visitors of the University of Virginia,* 515 U.S. 819 (1995), the editor of a university Christian student group's magazine sued the university, based on the (dis)establishment clause's prohibition of governmental sponsorship of religion, over its policy of denying student-activity funds for the magazine. Rosenberger contended that the policy was discriminatory and a violation of the First Amendment guarantee for free speech. Writing for the Court, Justice Kennedy agreed, holding that discrimination against the expression of religious viewpoints violates the First Amendment's guarantee for free speech and that the amendment's (dis)establishment clause did not compel or justify the university's policy. By contrast, Justice Souter, joined by Justices Breyer, Ginsburg, and Stevens, countered that for the first time the Court had approved direct government expenditures for religious activities, which ran afoul of the First Amendment's (dis)establishment clause and "strict neutrality."

Following *Rosenberger,* some New Christian Right students objected to the use of their student fees to support gay and lesbian organizations at the University of Wisconsin. Writing for the Court in *Board of Regents of the University of Wisconsin System v. Southworth,* 529 U.S. 217 (2000), Justice Kennedy upheld the requiring of mandatory student activity fees, but ruled that here the allocation of those funds for extracurricular activities based on a student referendum mechanism was not viewpoint neutral and thus ran afoul of the First Amendment. Subsequently, a bare majority of the Roberts Court held that public universities may require officially recognized student groups to accept all students who want to join, and such a requirement does not violate the constitutional rights of religious groups that want to exclude homosexuals. Writing the majority in *Christian Legal Society v. Martinez*, 561 U.S. 661 (2010), Justice Ginsburg ruled that the University of California's Hastings College of Law's non-discrimination policy did not unfairly target faith-based groups. In her words, "CLS, it bears emphasis, seeks not parity with other organizations, but a preferential exemption from Hastings' policy" in being officially recognized but with an exemption from the university's nondiscrimination policy with regard to homosexuals. Justice Ginsburg distinguished prior rulings on discrimination against a group's viewpoints and emphasized that Hastings solved that problem by its protecting "all comers" policy: "It is, after all, hard to imagine a more view-point-neutral policy than one requiring *all* student groups to accept *all* comers."

The Court's continuing reassessment of its (dis)establishment clause jurisprudence is underscored by the bare majority's ruling in *Agostini v. Felton*, 521 U.S. 203 (1997), overruling two twelve-year-old precedents set in *Aguilar v. Felton*, 473 U.S. 402 (1985) and *School District of Grand Rapids v. Ball*, 473 U.S. 373 (1985); both of those decisions were also decided by bare majorities. In *Aguilar v. Felton*, the Court held impermissible New York's providing teachers for handicapped students in parochial schools. As a result, New York instituted a program whereby the students walked from their classrooms to state vans parked on the street, outside of the parochial school grounds, and were given remedial education by public school teachers. In light of the Rehnquist Court's rulings and evolving jurisprudence, however, a district court held that those two 1985 rulings had been effectively overruled. An appellate court reversed that decision but in turn was reversed by a bare majority of the Court in *Agostini v. Felton*. The bare majority in *Agostini* held that, contrary to *Aguilar*, the (dis)establishment clause does not bar state-funded teachers for handicapped students who attend parochial schools.

Further underscoring the Court's reassessment of prior decisions in the area, by a 6–3 vote the justices overruled two other rulings, *Meek v. Pittenger*, 421 U.S. 349 (1975), and *Wolman v. Walter*, 433 U.S. 229 (1977), in *Mitchell v. Helms* 530 U.S. 793 (2000). Relying on *Agostini v. Felton* and extending *Witters v. Washington Department of Services for the Blind*, 474 U.S. 481 (1986), and *Zobrest v. Catalina Foothills School District*, 509 U.S. 1 (1993), Justice Thomas held that public school districts may lend computer software, as well as other forms of aid, to private religious schools. Notably, Justice Thomas also wrote for the Court in the 6–3 three decision in *Good News Club v. Milford Central School* 533 U.S. 98 (2001), holding that when public schools establish limited public forums they may not deny access to religious groups seeking to use their facilities for after-school meetings, thereby reaffirming and extending the prior rulings in *Lamb's Chapel v. Center Moriches Union Free School District* and *Rosenberger v. The Rector and Visitors of the University of Virginia*. Moreover, in *Zelman v. Simmons-Harris* 536 U.S. 639 (2003) a bare majority of the Court extended *Witters, Agostini,* and *Zobrest* in upholding public-funded vouchers for students to attend private religious schools because the voucher system had a secular purpose by providing funding for students in failing inner-city schools to attend better schools outside of the city, even though 96 percent of the funding went to religious schools. Although in those cases the Court held that governmental aid to religious schools in the form of student scholarships, remedial teachers, sign interpreters, and vouchers does not violate the (dis)establishment clause, in *Locke v. Davey* (2004) (excerpted in Section B of this chapter) the Court held that the free exercise clause does not provide a basis for compelling a state to allow a student to use a scholarship to pursue a pastoral degree when the state's constitution forbids such aid and imposes a more rigorous separation of government from religion than the Court's interpretation of the First Amendment. In sum, such aid to religion is permitted under the (dis)establishment clause but not required and cannot be compelled under the free exercise clause.

Notably, the Court avoided the heated controversy over whether requiring school children to recite the Pledge of Allegiance violates the First Amendment by denying standing to raise the issue in *Elk Grove Unified School District v. Newdow* (2004) (excerpted in Chapter 2). Writing for the Court, Justice Stevens held that Michael A. Newdow, who challenged the policy on behalf of his daughter, though he was not her legal custodian, lacked "prudential standing" to bring the suit. In other words, when legal claims are made on behalf of another person based on domestic relations law, a field largely left to states, "the prudent course is for the federal court to stay its hand rather than reach out to resolve a weighty question of federal constitutional law." But in separate concurring opinions Chief Justice Rehnquist and Justices O'Connor and Thomas would have granted standing and rejected Newdow's claims, though for different reasons. Chief Justice Rehnquist contended that *Lee v. Weisman,* invalidating school-sponsored prayer at graduation ceremonies, could be distinguished and that the words "under God" are "not endorsement of any religion." Justice O'Connor agreed; however, she deemed teacher-led recitations of "under God" as simply "ceremonial deism."

The Roberts Court revisited the controversy over prayers before governmental meetings in *Town of Greece, New York v. Galloway* (2014) (excerpted below), in holding that prayers—predominately Christian prayers—before town council meetings do not violate the First Amendment. Writing for the Court, though only Chief Justice Roberts and Justice Alito joined the opinion, Justice Kennedy shifted the test for "the separation of church and state" from the "endorsement test" for a particular religion to the "coercion test"—whether "dissidents" who do not share the prayer's belief are "coerced" by the opening of public meetings with a prayer. In doing so Justice Kennedy reinterpreted and extended the ruling in *Marsh v. Chambers*, 463 U.S. 783 (1983), that prayers were permissible before legislative sessions of Congress and state legislatures to local government meetings. Justice Kennedy's opinion was actually a kind of middle ground between that of Justices Thomas and Scalia, on the one hand, and the four dissenters, on the other. Justice Kennedy made clear that the ruling was narrow: (1) prayers may be given not only at opening sessions of Congress but also at all state and local governmental meetings; but (2) only in the ceremonial part of the governing body's session; (3) prayer practices must allow anyone in the community to deliver a prayer; (4) while also not dictating what is in the prayers, though they need not embrace the beliefs of any or multiple faiths. Yet (5) such prayers may not "proselytize"—promote one faith as the true path—or criticize those of other faiths; and (6) the prayers are permissible if most of the audience is made up of adults. Finally, (7) in reviewing challenges to governmental prayer practices, courts should examine "the pattern of prayer" and not second-guess the content of the individual prayers given. Justice Thomas, joined by Justice Scalia, maintained that the First Amendment (dis)establishment clause did not apply to the states in the first place, and states and localities are free to include or exclude prayers from their meetings. In the major dissenting opinion, Justice Kagan, joined by Justices Ginsburg, Breyer, and Sotomayor, disputed Justice Kennedy's reinterpretation of *Marsh* and view of the underlying factual circumstances and application of the First Amendment.

The Roberts Court also reconsidered the controversy over the public display of the Ten Commandments and other religious symbols, addressed in *Stone v. Graham*, 449 U.S. 39 (1980), which held unconstitutional a Kentucky statute requiring the posting of the Ten Commandments in every public schoolroom; and in *County of Allegheny v. American Civil Liberties Union, Greater Pittsburgh Chapter*, 492 U.S. 573 (1989). In both cases, the Court split 5–4. In *Van Orden v. Perry* (excerpted below), writing for a plurality Chief Justice Rehnquist held that the erection of a six-foot granite monument on which the Ten Commandments were chiseled did not violate the First Amendment (dis)establishment clause. However, in *McCreary v. American Civil Liberties Union of Kentucky* (excerpted below), Justice Souter ruled that two Kentucky counties violated the First Amendment by prominently displaying the Ten Commandments in their courthouses. In both cases, Justice Breyer cast the pivotal vote and formed bare majorities. He did so on pragmatic grounds, reasoning that the Texas monument had stood unchallenged for over forty years, whereas the Kentucky displays immediately sparked controversy and appeared to clearly aim at endorsing religion. See also and compare THE DEVELOPMENT OF LAW: Oklahoma Supreme Court Rules Ten Commandments Monument on State Capitol Grounds Unconstitutional (in Ch. 2).

Subsequently, the Roberts Court again revisited the controversy over the public display of religious displays in *Salazar v. Buono*, 559 U.S. 700 (2010), involving whether an eight-foot cross in the Mojave National Preserve was an unconstitutional governmental endorsement of religion. Erected in 1934 by the Veterans of Foreign Wars, the cross had been maintained as a war memorial by the National Park Service. The American Civil Liberties Union filed a suit in 2001 on behalf of a former park service officer, Frank Buono, a Catholic, who alleged that the cross violated the establishment clause of the First Amendment. The suit also noted that the park service had denied a request to have a Buddhist shrine erected near the cross. A federal district court agreed with Buono, ruling in 2002 that the "primary effect of the presence of the cross" was to "advance religion." Congress responded in 2004 by enacting legislation directing the Department of the Interior to transfer about an acre of land to the Veterans of Foreign Wars in exchange for a privately owned plot nearby. A three-judge panel of the U.S. Court of Appeals for the Ninth Circuit upheld the lower court's decision and invalidated the land transfer, observing that "carving out a tiny parcel of property in the midst of this vast preserve—like a donut hole with the cross atop it—will do nothing to minimize the impermissible government endorsement" of a religious symbol. That ruling was appealed to the Supreme Court, contending that it would require the government to "tear down a cross that has stood without incident for 70 years as a memorial to fallen service members." In a fragmented, 5–4 decision the Court reversed the appellate court and reopened the possibility of maintaining the cross as a war memorial. Writing for a plurality, Justice Kennedy, joined only by Chief Justice Roberts and Justice Alito, overturned the district court's order rejecting Congress's solution to the earlier ruling that the cross conveyed a constitutionally impermissible endorsement of religion and remanded the case for further consideration. Justice Stevens dissented, joined by Justices Ginsburg and Sotomayor, emphasizing that a "solitary cross . . . conveys an inescapably sectarian message" in violation of the First Amendment. In a separate dissent, Justice Breyer contended that the district court should have been allowed to decide whether the land-transfer law violated its earlier injunctions and would have not reached the First Amendment claim.

The Court returned to the question of a publicly maintained Christian cross in *American Legion v. American Humanist Association*, 239 S.Ct. 2067 (2019), where the Court voted 7–2 in favor of allowing the state of Maryland to continue to maintain a World War I memorial carved into a forty-foot-tall stone-and-brick cross perched above a busy highway in Maryland. But the 7–2 decision was far less clear than the numbers suggest, since the seven justices in the majority were split on the rationale for their decision. Underlying these divisions was the continuing struggle over *Lemon v. Kurtzman*. Some, including Justice Alito who wrote the opinion of the Court, have signaled they are ready to overturn *Lemon*. Others would tweak and adjust *Lemon* by weighing cases individually, while Justice Thomas, writing separately, said the establishment clause was never meant to apply to the states but only to the federal government. In dissent were Justices Ginsburg and Sotomayor, who took a more traditional separation of church and state view that would have disentangled the state and the cross. In short, the Court continues to be deeply divided over the limits on state involvement with religious symbols.

Notes

1. Paul Kauper, *Religion and the Constitution* (Baton Rouge: Louisiana State University Press, 1964), 59.

2. Philip Kurland, "Of Church and State and the Supreme Court," 29 *University of Chicago Law Review* 5 (1961).

3. See, for example, *Stone v. Graham*, 449 U.S. 39 (1980); *Committee for Public Education and Religious Liberty v. Regan*, 444 U.S. 646 (1980); *Larkin v. Grendel's Den, Inc.*, 459 U.S. 116 (1982); *Aguilar v. Felton*, 473 U.S. 402 (1985); and *Texas Monthly, Inc. v. Bullock*, 489 U.S. 1 (1989).

4. See, for example, *Larson v. Valente*, 456 U.S. 228 (1982); and *Marsh v. Chambers*, 463 U.S. 783 (1983).

Selected Bibliography

Dierenfield, Bruce. *The Battle Over School Prayer: How Engel v. Vitale Changed America*. Lawrence: University Press of Kansas, 2007.

Dreisbach, Daniel. *Thomas Jefferson and the Wall of Separation between Church and State*. New York: New York University Press, 2002.

Feldman, Stephen, ed. *Law and Religion: A Critical Anthology*. New York: New York University Press, 2000.

Grumet, Louis. *The Curious Case of Kiryas Joel: The Rise of a Village Theocracy and the Battle to Defend the Separation of Church and State*. Chicago: Chicago Review Press, 2016.

Hamburger, Philip. *Separation of Church and State*. Cambridge, MA: Harvard University Press, 2002.

Howe, Mark De Wolfe. *The Garden and the Wilderness: Religion and Government in American Constitutional History*. Chicago: University of Chicago Press, 1965.

Kramnick, Isaac, and Moore, R. Lawrence. *The Godless Constitution: A Moral Defense of the Secular State*. New York: W. W. Norton & Company, 2005.

Larson, Edward. *Summer for the Gods: The Scopes Trial and America's Continuing Debate over Science and Religion*. New York: Basic Books, 1997.

Levy, Leonard. *The Establishment Clause: Religion and the First Amendment*. New York: Macmillan, 1986.

■ THE DEVELOPMENT OF LAW

Major Rulings Upholding Governmental Aid or Support of Religion over Establishment Clause Objections

CASE	VOTE	KIND OF AID/SUPPORT FOR RELIGION UPHELD
Everson v. Board of Education of Ewing Township, New Jersey, 330 U.S. 1 (1947)	5–4	Bus fare reimbursement for parents of children attending private religious schools.
Zorach v. Clauson, 343 U.S. 306 (1952)	6–3	Released-time program for religious instruction in class held off campus.
Walz v. Tax Commission of the City of New York, 397 U.S. 664 (1970)	7–1	Tax exemption for property used solely for religious purposes as permissible benevolent neutrality.
Tilton v. Richardson, 403 U.S. 672 (1971)	5–4	Most of a $240 million federal funding program for the construction of academic buildings on private sectarian and secular colleges; not enough entanglement of church and state to violate establishment clause.
Hunt v. McNair, 413 U.S. 734 (1973)	6–3	South Carolina's state issue bond for construction of academic buildings for nonreligious purposes by private religious schools.
Meek v. Pittenger, 421 U.S. 349 (1975)	6–3	Loan of secular textbooks from public schools to private and parochial schools.
Roemer v. Maryland Public Works Board, 426 U.S. 736 (1976)	5–4	General-purpose funds for nonsectarian purposes to colleges and universities with religious affiliations.

CASE	VOTE	KIND OF AID/SUPPORT FOR RELIGION UPHELD
Wolman v. Walter, 433 U.S. 229 (1977)	8–1	Diagnostic and therapeutic testing services provided to private religiously affiliated primary and secondary schools.
Committee for Public Education and Religious Liberty v. Regan, 444 U.S. 646 (1980)	5–4	Reimbursement for certain expenses for record-keeping and testing incurred by private schools due to state regulations.
Mueller v. Allen, 463 U.S. 388 (1983)	5–4	Annual tax deduction of $700 for parents of children in elementary and secondary schools run by religious organizations: a neutral accommodation.
Marsh v. Chambers, 463 U.S. 783 (1983)	5–4	State practice of a chaplain opening sessions of legislature.
Lynch v. Donnelly, 465 U.S. 688 (1984)	5–4	Crèche as part of city-sponsored Christmas display in park; accommodation and crèche viewed as a secular symbol.
Bowen v. Kendrick, 487 U.S. 589 (1988)	5–4	Authorization of federal funds for public and private organizations under Adolescent Family

Life Act for premarital counseling services by organizations affiliated with established churches.

County of Allegheny v. American Civil Liberties Union Greater Pittsburgh Chapter, 492 U.S. 573 (1989)	5–4	Writing for the majority, Justice Blackmun held that the display of a crèche inside a city building violated the (dis)establishment clause and limited

the earlier ruling in *Lynch v. Donnelly*, 465 U.S. 688 (1984), which had upheld a city-sponsored display of a crèche as part of a Christmas exhibit

(continues)

■ THE DEVELOPMENT OF LAW
Major Rulings Upholding Governmental Aid or Support of Religion over Establishment Clause Objections (continued)

in a park. At the same time, Justice Blackmun upheld the display of the menorah next to a Christmas tree outside of a city-county office building. Justice O'Connor cast the deciding vote and issued a concurring opinion.

CASE	VOTE	KIND OF AID/SUPPORT FOR RELIGION UPHELD
Zobrest v. Catalina Foothills School District, 509 U.S. 1 (1993)	5–4	Upheld public funding for a sign-language interpreter for a deaf student attending a private religious high school.
Lamb's Chapel v. Center Moriches Union Free School District, 508 U.S. 384 (1993)	9–0	Held that public schools that provide after-hours access to other groups may not deny access to facilities to religious groups.
Rosenberger v. The Rector and Visitors of the University of Virginia, 515 U.S. 819 (1995)	5–4	Writing for the majority, Justice Kennedy held that the University of Virginia's policy, denying student-activities

funds to groups that advocate particular religions, discriminated against the expression of religious viewpoints in violation of the First Amendment's guarantee for free speech, and that the amendment's (dis)establishment clause did not compel or justify the university's policy. The four dissenters— Justices Breyer, Ginsburg, Souter, and Stevens—thought otherwise.

CASE	VOTE	KIND OF AID/SUPPORT FOR RELIGION UPHELD
Agostini v. Felton, 521 U.S. 203 (1997)	5–4	Overruling two precedents, *Aguilar v. Felton*, 473 U.S. 402 (1985), and *School District of*

Grand Rapids v. Ball, 473 U.S. 373 (1985), in an opinion delivered by Justice O'Connor, the Court held that public school teachers could be sent into parochial schools to provide remedial education. Justices Souter and Ginsburg filed dissenting opinions, which were joined by Justices Stevens and Breyer.

Mitchell v. Helms, 530 U.S. 793 (2000)	6–3	Overturning *Meek v. Pittenger*, 421 U.S. 349 (1975), and *Wolman v. Walter*, 433 U.S. 229

(1977), Justice Thomas held that the First Amendment does not bar public schools from lending computer software and hardware to private religious schools. Justices Souter, Stevens, and Ginsburg dissented.

Good News Club v. Milford Central School, 533 U.S. 98 (2001)	6–3	Writing for the Court, Justice Thomas held that when public schools established limited public forums they may not

deny access to religious groups seeking to use their facilities for after-school meetings.

Zelman v. Simmons-Harris, 536 U.S. 639 (2002)	5–4	Writing for the Court, Chief Justice Rehnquist upheld Ohio's voucher program per-

mitting students of Cleveland's inner-city schools to attend private religious schools over First Amendment objections, despite that 96 percent of the vouchers went to parochial schools. Justices Stevens, Souter, Ginsburg, and Breyer dissented.

■ THE DEVELOPMENT OF LAW

Major Rulings Striking Down Laws and Policies for Violating the Establishment Clause

CASE	VOTE	ACTIVITY/ASSISTANCE HELD UNCONSTITUTIONAL
McCollum v. Board of Education, 333 U.S. 203 (1948)	8–1	Released-time program for religious instruction held on school grounds.
Engel v. Vitale, 370 U.S. 421 (1962)	6–1	A twenty-two-word nondenominational prayer written for students in public school.
Abington School District v. Schempp and *Murray v. Curlett,* 374 U.S. 203 (1963)	8–1	Reading of the Lord's Prayer and Bible verses in public schools.
Epperson v. Arkansas, 393 U.S. 97 (1968)	9–0	Arkansas's "monkey law," forbidding the teaching of evolutionary theory.
Lemon v. Kurtzman, 403 U.S. 602 (1971)	8–0	Direct aid to parochial schools, including use of public funds to pay salaries of parochial teachers.
Levitt v. Committee for Public Education and Religious Liberty, 413 U.S. 472 (1973); *Committee for Public Education and Religious Liberty v. Nyquist,* 413 U.S. 756 (1973); *Sloan v. Lemon,* 413 U.S. 825 (1973)	6–3	Financial aid for parochial schools, including tuition reimbursement, tax exemptions, and special counseling services and loan of educational equipment.
Meek v. Pittenger, 421 U.S. 349 (1975)	6–3	Counseling, testing, remedial classes, equipment, and other auxiliary services given to

schools affiliated with religious organizations. Overruled by *Mitchell v. Helms*, 530 U.S. 793 (2000).

CASE	VOTE	ACTIVITY/ASSISTANCE HELD UNCONSTITUTIONAL
Wolman v. Walter, 433 U.S. 229 (1977)	5–4	Financial aid for field trips and class paraphernalia provided to private schools affili-

ated with religious organizations. Overruled by *Mitchell v. Helms*, 530 U.S. 793 (2000).

New York v. Cathedral Academy, 434 U.S. 125 (1977)	6-3	Direct reimbursement to parochial schools for record-keeping and testing services.
Stone v. Graham, 449 U.S. 39 (1980)	5–4	Kentucky law requiring the posting of the Ten Commandments in classrooms.
Widmar v. Vincent, 454 U.S. 263 (1981)	8–1	Missouri's prohibition of the use of state university buildings for "religious worship."
Larkin v. Grendel's Den, 459 U.S. 116 (1982)	5–4	Law giving churches veto over issuance of liquor licenses.
Wallace v. Jaffree, 472 U.S. 38 (1985)	6–3	Alabama law authorizing one minute of silence in public schools for meditation or voluntary prayer.
Aguilar v. Felton, 473 U.S. 402 (1985)	5–4	Instructional services provided on grounds of parochial schools. Overruled by *Agostini v. Felton*, 521 U.S. 203 (1997).
School District of Grand Rapids v. Ball, 473 U.S. 373 (1985)	5–4	Invalidated a "shared time" program that provided remedial classes, at public expense,

to students attending religious schools. This ruling, along with *Aguilar v. Felton* (above), was overruled in *Agostini v. Felton*, 521 U.S. 203 (1997).

(continues)

■ THE DEVELOPMENT OF LAW
Major Rulings Striking Down Laws and Policies for
Violating the Establishment Clause (continued)

CASE	VOTE	ACTIVITY/ASSISTANCE HELD UNCONSTITUTIONAL
Edwards v. Aguillard, 482 U.S. 578 (1987)	7–2	Louisiana law requiring teaching of creationism to balance teaching of evolution.
Texas Monthly, Inc. v. Bullock, 489 U.S. 1 (1989)	6–3	Texas law giving tax exemption to religious periodicals.
County of Allegheny v. American Civil Liberties Union Greater Pittsburgh Chapter, 492 U.S. 573 (1989)	5–4	Writing for the majority, Justice Blackmun held that the display of a crèche inside a city building violated the (dis)establishment

clause and limited the earlier ruling in *Lynch v. Donnelly*, 465 U.S. 688 (1984), which had upheld a city-sponsored display of a crèche as part of a Christmas exhibit in a park. At the same time, Justice Blackmun upheld the display of the menorah next to a Christmas tree outside of a city-county office building. Justice O'Connor cast the deciding vote and issued a concurring opinion. Separate opinions, in part concurring and dissenting, were filed by Justices Brennan and Stevens, and joined by Justice Marshall. Justice Kennedy also issued a separate opinion, concurring and dissenting in part, and was joined by Chief Justice Rehnquist and Justices Scalia and White.

Lee v. Weisman, 505 U.S. 577 (1992)	5–4	Invocations and benedictions at public school graduation ceremonies supervised by school authorities.
Board of Education of Kiryas Joel v. Grumet, 512 U.S. 687 (1994)	6–3	Writing for the Court, Justice Souter struck down New York's law creating a

special school district in Kiryas Joel, a community inhabited solely by Hasidic Jews of the Satmar sect, one of the most orthodox and conservative Jewish sects. That law was passed after the Court, in *Aguilar v.*

CASE	VOTE	ACTIVITY/ASSISTANCE HELD UNCONSTITUTIONAL

Felton, 473 U.S. 402 (1985), prohibited New York from paying for remedial classes for handicapped children attending private religious schools. Notably, Justice Souter's opinion declined to jettison the three-prong test set forth in *Lemon v. Kurtzman*, 403 U.S. 602 (1971), and commanded only a plurality in parts. Justice Blackmun concurred, in an opinion strongly supporting *Lemon*, while Justice O'Connor's concurrence suggested that *Lemon* should be abandoned. Joined by Chief Justice Rehnquist and Justice Thomas, Justice Scalia rejected the majority's analysis and decision, as well as renewed his call for discarding *Lemon*.

Santa Fe Independent School District v. Doe, 530 U.S. 290 (2000)	6:3	Writing for the Court and reaffirming *Lee v. Weisman*, 505 U.S. 577 (1992), Justice Stevens held that having

school-sponsored prayers prior to high school football games violates the First Amendment. Chief Justice Rehnquist and Justices Scalia and Thomas dissented.

Peters, Shawn F. *Judging Jehovah's Witnesses.* Lawrence: University Press of Kansas, 2000.

Pfeffer, Leo. *God, Caesar and the Constitution.* Boston: Beacon Press, 1975.

———. *Church, State, and Freedom.* Boston: Beacon Press, 1953.

Stokes, Anson, and Pfeffer, Leo. *Church and State in the United States.* New York: Harper and Row, 1965.

Sullivan, Winnifred Fallers. *Paying the Words Extra: Religious Discourse in the Supreme Court of the United States.* Cambridge, MA: Harvard University Press, 1995.

Wenger, Tisa. *Religious Freedom: The Contested History of an American Ideal.* Chapel Hill: University of North Carolina Press, 2017.

Everson v. Board of Education of Ewing Township

330 U.S. 1, 67 S.Ct. 504 (1947)

Arch Everson filed a suit challenging the constitutionality of an authorization for reimbursement to parents with children in private schools for the cost of busing their children. The Board of Education of Ewing Township had adopted the plan under a New Jersey statute permitting local school districts to make their own rules for the transportation of children to and from schools. Most of the private schools in the area were Catholic parochial schools. A state court struck down the program. The New Jersey Court of Errors and Appeals reversed, holding that neither the state law nor the school board's resolution violated the state or federal Constitution. Everson then turned to the Supreme Court, which granted review.

The Court's decision was 5–4, and the majority's opinion was announced by Justice Black. A dissent by Justice Rutledge was joined by Justices Jackson, Frankfurter, and Burton.

■ ■ ■

☐ *Justice BLACK delivered the opinion of the Court.*

The New Jersey statute is challenged as a "law respecting an establishment of religion." . . . These words of the First Amendment reflected in the minds of early Americans a vivid mental picture of conditions and practices which they fervently wished to stamp out in order to preserve liberty for themselves and for their posterity. Doubtless their goal has not been entirely reached; but so far has the Nation moved toward it that the expression "law respecting an establishment of religion," probably does not so vividly remind present-day Americans of the evils, fears, and political problems that caused that expression to be written into our Bill of Rights. Whether this New Jersey law is one respecting the "establishment of religion" requires an understanding of the meaning of that language, particularly with respect to the imposition of taxes. Once again, therefore, it is not inappropriate briefly to review the background and environment of the period in which that constitutional language was fashioned and adopted.

A large proportion of the early settlers of this country came here from Europe to escape the bondage of laws which compelled them to support and attend government favored churches. The centuries immediately before and contemporaneous with the colonization of America had been filled with turmoil, civil strife, and persecutions, generated in large part by established sects determined to maintain their absolute political and religious supremacy. With the power of government supporting them, at various times and places, Catholics had persecuted Protestants, Protestants had persecuted Catholics, Protestant sects had persecuted other Protestant sects, Catholics of one shade of belief had persecuted Catholics of another shade of belief, and all of these had from time to time persecuted Jews. In efforts to force loyalty to whatever religious group happened to be on top and in league with the government of a particular time and place, men and women had been fined, cast in jail, cruelly tortured, and killed. . . .

These practices of the old world were transplanted to and began to thrive in the soil of the new America. The very characters granted by the English Crown to the individuals and companies designated to make the laws which would control the destinies of the colonials authorized these individuals and companies to erect religious establishments which all, whether believers or non-believers, would be required to support and attend. An exercise of this authority was accompanied by a repetition of many of the old world practices and persecutions. Catholics found themselves hounded and proscribed because of their faith; Quakers who followed their conscience went to jail; Baptists were peculiarly obnoxious to certain dominant Protestant sects; men and women of varied faiths who happened to be in a minority in a particular locality were persecuted because they steadfastly persisted in worshipping God only as their own consciences dictated. And all of these dissenters were compelled to pay tithes and taxes to support government-sponsored churches whose ministers preached inflammatory sermons designed to strengthen and consolidate the established faith by generating a burning hatred against dissenters.

These practices became so commonplace as to shock the freedom-loving colonials into a feeling of abhorrence. The imposition of taxes to pay ministers' salaries and to build and maintain churches and church property aroused their indignation. It was these feelings which found expression in the First Amendment. No one locality and no one group throughout the Colonies can rightly be given entire credit for having aroused the sentiment that culminated in adoption of the Bill of Rights' provisions embracing religious liberty. But Virginia, where the established church had achieved a dominant influence in political affairs and where many excesses attracted wide public attention, provided a great stimulus and able leadership for the movement. The people there, as elsewhere, reached the conviction that individual religious liberty could be achieved best under a government which was stripped of all power to tax, to support, or otherwise to assist any or all religions, or to interfere with the beliefs of any religious individual or group.

The movement toward this end reached its dramatic climax in Virginia in 1785–86 when the Virginia legislative body was about to renew Virginia's tax levy for the support of the established church. Thomas Jefferson and James Madison led the fight against this tax. Madison wrote his great Memorial and Remonstrance against the law. In it, he eloquently argued that a true religion did not need the support of law; that no person, either believer or non-believer, should be taxed to support a religious institution of any kind; that the best interest of a society required that the minds of men always be wholly free; and that cruel persecutions were the inevitable result of government-established religions. Madison's Remonstrance received strong support throughout Virginia, and the Assembly postponed consideration of the proposed tax measure until its next session. When the proposal came up for consideration at that session, it not only died in committee, but the Assembly enacted the famous "Virginia Bill for Religious Liberty" originally written by Thomas Jefferson. The preamble to that Bill stated among other things that

> Almighty God hath created the mind free; that all attempts to influence it by temporal punishments, or burthens, or by civil incapacitations, tend only to beget habits of hypocrisy and meanness, and are a departure from the plan of the Holy author of our religion who being Lord both of body and mind, yet chose not to propagate it by coercions on either; . . . that to compel a man to furnish contributions of money for the propagation of opinions which he disbelieves, is sinful and tyrannical; that even the forcing him to support this or that teacher of his own religious persuasion, is depriving him of the comfortable liberty of giving his contributions to the particular pastor, whose morals he would make his pattern. . . .

And the statute itself enacted

> [t]hat no man shall be compelled to frequent or support any religious worship, place, or ministry whatsoever, nor shall be enforced, restrained, molested, or burthened, in his body or goods, nor shall otherwise suffer on account of his religious opinions or belief. . . .

This Court has previously recognized that the provisions of the First Amendment, in the drafting and adoption of which Madison and Jefferson played such leading roles, had the same objective and were intended to provide the same protection against governmental intrusion on religious liberty as the Virginia statute.

Prior to the adoption of the Fourteenth Amendment, the First Amendment did not apply as a restraint against the states. Most of them did soon provide similar constitutional protections for religious liberty. But some states persisted for about half a century in imposing restraints upon the free exercise of religion and in discriminating against particular religious groups. In recent years, so far as the provision against the establishment of a religion is concerned, the question has most frequently arisen in connection with proposed state aid to church schools and efforts to carry on religious teachings in the public schools in accordance with the tenets of a particular sect. Some churches have either sought or accepted state financial support for their schools. Here again the efforts to obtain state aid or acceptance of it have not been limited to any one particular faith. The state courts, in the main, have remained faithful to the language of their own constitutional provisions designed to protect religious freedom and to separate religious and governments. Their decisions, however, show the difficulty in drawing the line between tax legislation which provides funds for the welfare of the general public and that which is designed to support institutions which teach religion.

The meaning and scope of the First Amendment, preventing establishment of religion or prohibiting the free exercise thereof, in the light of its history and the evils it was designed forever to suppress, have been several times elaborated by the decisions of this Court prior to the application of the First Amendment to the states by the Fourteenth. The broad meaning given the Amendment by these earlier cases has been accepted by this Court in its decisions concerning an individual's religious freedom rendered since the Fourteenth Amendment was interpreted to make the prohibitions of the First applicable to state action abridging religious freedom. There is every reason to give the same application and broad interpretation to the "establishment of religion" clause. . . .

The "establishment of religion" clause of the First Amendment means at least this: Neither a state nor the Federal Government can set up a church. Neither can pass laws which aid one religion, aid all religions, or prefer one religion over another. Neither can force nor influence a person to go to or to remain away from church against his will or force him to profess a belief or disbelief in any religion. No person can be punished for entertaining or professing religious beliefs or disbeliefs, for church attendance or non-attendance. No tax in any amount, large or small, can be levied to support any religious activities or institutions, whatever they may be called, or whatever form they may adopt to teach or practice religion. Neither a state nor the Federal Government can, openly or secretly, participate in the affairs of any religious organizations or groups and vice versa. In the words of Jefferson, the clause against establishment of religion by law was intended to erect "a wall of separation between Church and State."

We must consider the New Jersey statute in accordance with the foregoing limitations imposed by the First Amendment. But we must not strike that state statute down if it is within the state's constitutional power even though it approaches the verge of that power. New Jersey cannot consistently with the "establishment of religion" clause of the First Amendment contribute tax-raised funds to the support of an institution which teaches the tenets and faith of any church. On the other hand, other language of the amendment commands that New Jersey cannot hamper its citizens in the free exercise of their own religion. Consequently, it cannot exclude individual Catholics, Lutherans, Mohammedans, Baptists, Jews, Methodists, Nonbelievers, Presbyterians, or the members of any other faith, *because of their faith, or lack of it,* from receiving the benefits of public welfare legislation. While we do not mean to intimate that a state could not provide transportation only to children attending public schools, we must be careful, in protecting the citizens of New Jersey against state-established churches, to be sure that we do not inadvertently prohibit New Jersey from extending its general State law benefits to all its citizens without regard to their religious belief.

Measured by these standards, we cannot say that the First Amendment prohibits New Jersey from spending tax-raised funds to pay the bus fares of parochial school pupils as a part of a general program under which it pays the fares of pupils attending public and other schools. It is undoubtedly true that children are helped to get to church schools. There is even a possibility that some of the children might not be sent to the church schools if the parents were compelled to pay their children's bus fares out of their own pockets when transportation to a public school would have been paid for by the State. The same possibility exists where the state requires a local transit company to provide reduced fares to school children including those attending parochial schools, or where a municipally owned transportation system undertakes to carry all school children free of charge. Moreover, state-paid policemen, detailed to protect children going to and from church schools from the very real hazards of traffic, would serve much the same purpose and accomplish much the same result as state provisions intended to guarantee free transportation of a kind which the state deems to be best for the school children's welfare. And parents might refuse to risk their children to the serious danger of traffic accidents going to and from parochial schools, the approaches to which were not protected by policemen. Similarly, parents might be reluctant to permit their children to attend schools which the state had cut off from such general government services as ordinary police and fire protection, connections for sewage disposal, public highways and sidewalks. Of course, cutting off church schools from these services, so separate and so indisputably marked off from the religious function, would make it far more difficult for the schools to operate. But such is obviously not the purpose of the First Amendment. That Amendment requires the state to be a neutral in its relations with groups of religious believers and non-believers; it does not require the state to be their adversary. State power is no more to be used so as to handicap religions, than it is to favor them. . . .

The First Amendment has erected a wall between church and state. That wall must be kept high and impregnable. We could not approve the slightest breach. New Jersey has not breached it here.

Affirmed.

☐ *Justice RUTLEDGE, with whom Justice FRANKFURTER,*
Justice JACKSON, and Justice BURTON join, dissenting.

The Amendment's purpose was not to strike merely at the official establishment of a single sect, creed or religion, outlawing only a formal relation such as had prevailed in England and some of the colonies. Necessarily it was to uproot all such relationships. But the object was broader than separating church and state in this narrow sense. It was to create a complete and permanent separation of the spheres of religious activity and civil authority by comprehensively forbidding every form of public aid or support for religion. In proof the Amendment's wording and history unite with this Court's consistent utterances whenever attention has been fixed directly upon the question.

"Religion" appears only once in the Amendment. But the word governs two prohibitions and governs them alike. It does not have two meanings, one narrow to forbid "an establishment" and another, much broader, for securing "the free exercise thereof." "Thereof" brings down "religion" with its entire and exact content, no more and no less, from the first into the second guaranty, so that Congress and now the states are as broadly restricted concerning the one as they are regarding the other. . . .

Compulsory attendance upon religious exercises went out early in the process of separating church and state, together with forced observance of religious forms and ceremonies. Test oaths and religious qualification for office followed later. These things none devoted to our great tradition of religious liberty would think of bringing back. Hence today, apart from efforts to inject religious training or exercises and sectarian issues into the public schools, the only serious surviving threat to maintaining that complete and permanent separation of religion and civil power which the First Amendment commands is through use of the taxing power to support religion, religious establishments, or establishments having a religious foundation whatever their form or special religious function.

Does New Jersey's action furnish support for religion by use of the taxing power? Certainly it does, if the test remains undiluted as Jefferson and Madison made it, that money taken by taxation from one is not to be used or given to support another's religious training or belief, or indeed one's own. Today as then the furnishing of "contributions of money for the propagation of opinions which he disbelieves" is the forbidden exaction; and the prohibition is absolute for whatever measure brings that consequence and whatever mount may be sought or given to that end.

The funds used here were raised by taxation. The Court does not dispute nor could it that their use does in fact give aid and encouragement to religious instruction. It only concludes that this aid is not "support" in law. But Madison and Jefferson were concerned with aid and support in fact not as a legal conclusion "entangled in precedents." Remonstrance. Here parents pay money to send their children to parochial schools and funds raised by taxation are used to reimburse them. This not only helps the children to get to school and the parents to send them. It aids them in a substantial way to get the very thing which they are sent to the particular school to secure, namely, religious training and teaching. . . .

To say that New Jersey's appropriation and her use of the power of taxation for raising the funds appropriated are not for public purposes but are for private ends, is to say that they are for the support of religion and religious teaching. Conversely, to say that they are for public purposes is to say that they are not for religious ones.

This is precisely for the reason that education which includes religious training and teaching, and its support, have been made matters of private right and function not public, by the very terms of the First Amendment. That is the effect not only in its guaranty of religion's free exercise, but also in the prohibition of establishments. . . .

The reasons underlying the Amendment's policy have not vanished with time or diminished in force. Now as when it was adopted the price of religious freedom is double. It is that the church and religion shall live both within and upon that freedom. There cannot be freedom of religion, safeguarded by the state, and intervention by the church or its agencies in the state's domain or dependency on its largesse. Madison's Remonstrance. The great condition of religious liberty is that it be maintained free from sustenance, as also from other interferences, by the state. For when it comes to rest upon that secular foundation it vanishes with the resting. Public money devoted to payment of religious costs, educational or other, brings the quest for more. It brings too the struggle of sect against sect for the larger share or for any. Here one by numbers alone will benefit most, there another. That is precisely the history of societies which have had an established religion and dissident groups. It is the very thing Jefferson and Madison experienced and sought to guard against, whether in its blunt or in its more screened forms. . . .

No one conscious of religious values can be unsympathetic toward the burden which our constitutional separation puts on parents who desire religious instruction mixed with secular for their children. They pay taxes for others' children's education, at the same time the added cost of instruction for their own. Nor can one happily see benefits denied to children which others receive, because in conscience they or their parents for them desire a different kind of training others do not demand.

But if those feelings should prevail, there would be an end to our historic constitutional policy and command. No more unjust or discriminatory in fact is it to deny attendants at religious schools the cost of their transportation than it is to deny them tuitions, sustenance for their teachers, or any other educational expense which others receive at public cost. Hardship in fact there is which none can blink. But, for assuring to those who undergo it the greater, the most comprehensive freedom, it is one written by design and firm intent into our basic law. . . .

That policy necessarily entails hardship upon persons who forego the right to educational advantages the state can supply in order to secure others it is precluded from giving. Indeed this may hamper the parent and the child forced by conscience to that choice. But it does not make the state unneutral to withhold what the Constitution forbids it to give. On the contrary it is only by observing the prohibition rigidly that the state can maintain its neutrality and avoid partisanship in the dissensions inevitable when sect opposes sect over demands for public moneys to further religious education, teaching or training in any form or degree, directly or indirectly. . . .

The judgment should be reversed.

Engel v. Vitale

370 U.S. 421, 82 S.Ct. 1261 (1962)

Steven Engel and several other parents of school-age children sued the principal and the Board of Education of Union Free School District No. 9, in New Hyde Park, New York, for requiring students to recite at the beginning of each school day a nondenominational prayer. The prayer, written by the State Board of Regents, was as follows: "Almighty God, we acknowledge our dependence upon Thee, and we beg Thy blessings upon us, our parents, our teachers and our country." An order upholding the power of New York to adopt and require children to recite this prayer was issued by a state court and affirmed by the New York Court of Appeals. Engel made a final appeal to the Supreme Court.

The Court's decision was 6–1, and the majority's opinion was announced by Justice Black, with Justices Frankfurter and White not participating. Concurrence was by Justice Douglas and dissent by Justice Stewart.

■ ■ ■

☐ *Justice BLACK delivered the opinion of the Court.*

We think that by using its public school system to encourage recitation of the Regents' prayer, the State of New York has adopted a practice wholly inconsistent with the Establishment Clause. There can, of course, be no doubt that New York's program of daily classroom invocation of God's blessings as prescribed in the Regents' prayer is a religious activity. . . .

It is a matter of history that this very practice of establishing governmentally composed prayers for religious services was one of the reasons which caused many of our early colonists to leave England and seek religious freedom in America. *The Book of Common Prayer*, which was created under governmental direction and which was approved by Acts of Parliament in 1548 and 1549, set out in minute detail the accepted form and content of prayer and other religious ceremonies to be used in the established, tax-supported Church of England. . . .

[G]roups, lacking the necessary political power to influence the Government on the matter, decided to leave England and its established church and seek freedom in America from England's governmentally ordained and supported religion.

It is an unfortunate fact of history that when some of the very groups which had most strenuously opposed the established Church of England found themselves sufficiently in control of colonial governments in this country to write their own prayers into law, they passed laws making their own religion the official religion of their respective colonies. Indeed, as late as the time of the Revolutionary War, there were established churches in at least eight of the thirteen former colonies and established religions in at least four of the other five. But the successful Revolution against English political domination was shortly followed by intense opposition to the practice of establishing religion by law. This opposition crystallized rapidly into an effective political force in Virginia where the minority religious groups such as Presbyterians, Lutherans, Quakers and Baptists had gained such strength that the adherents to the established Episcopal Church were actually a minority themselves. In 1785–1786, those opposed to the established Church, led by James Madison and Thomas Jefferson, who, though themselves not members of any of these dissenting religious groups, opposed all religious establishments by law on grounds of principle, obtained the enactment of the famous "Virginia Bill for Religious Liberty" by which all religious groups were placed on an equal footing so far as the State was concerned. Similar though less far-reaching legislation was being considered and passed in other States.

By the time of the adoption of the Constitution, our history shows that there was a widespread awareness among many Americans of the dangers of a union of Church and State. These people knew, some of them from bitter personal experience, that one of the greatest dangers to the freedom of the individual to worship in his own way lay in the Government's placing its official stamp of approval upon one particular kind of prayer or one particular form of religious services. They knew the anguish, hardship and bitter strife that could come when zealous religious groups struggled with one another to obtain the Government's stamp of approval from each King, Queen, or Protector that came to temporary power. The Constitution was intended to avert a part of this danger by leaving the government of this country in the hands of the people rather than in the hands of any monarch. But this safeguard was not enough. Our Founders were no more willing to let the content of their prayers and their privilege of praying whenever they pleased be influenced by the ballot box than they were to let these vital matters of personal conscience depend upon the succession of monarchs. The First Amendment was added to the Constitution to stand as a guarantee that neither the power nor the prestige of the Federal Government would be used to control, support or influence the kinds of prayer the American people can say—that the people's religions must not be subjected to the pressures of government for change each time a new political administration is elected to office. Under that Amendment's prohibition against governmental establishment of religion, as reinforced by the provisions of the Fourteenth Amendment, government in this country, be it state or federal, is without power to prescribe by law any particular form of prayer which is to be used as an official prayer in carrying on any program of governmentally sponsored religious activity.

There can be no doubt that New York's state prayer program officially establishes the religious beliefs embodied in the Regents' prayer. The respondents' argument to the contrary, which is largely based upon the contention that the Regents' prayer is "nondenominational" and the fact that the program, as modified and approved by state courts, does not require all pupils to recite the prayer but permits those who wish to do so to remain silent or be excused from the room, ignores the essential nature of the program's constitutional defects. Neither the fact that the prayer may be denominationally neutral nor the fact that its observance on the part of the students is voluntary can serve to free it from the limitations of the Establishment Clause, as it might from the Free Exercise Clause, of the First Amendment, both of which are operative against the States by virtue of the Fourteenth Amendment. Although these two clauses may in certain instances overlap, they forbid two quite different kinds of governmental encroachment upon religious freedom. The Establishment Clause, unlike the Free Exercise Clause, does not depend upon any showing of direct governmental compulsion and is violated by the enactment of laws which establish an official religion whether those laws operate directly to coerce nonobserving individuals or not. This is not to say, of course, that laws officially prescribing a particular form of religious worship do not involve coercion of such individuals. When the power, prestige and financial support of government is placed behind a particular religious belief, the indirect coercive pressure upon religious minorities to conform to the prevailing officially approved religion is plain. But the purposes underlying the Establishment Clause go much further than that. Its first and most immediate purpose rested on the belief that a union of government and religion tends to destroy government and to degrade religion. The history of governmentally established religion, both in England and in this country, showed that whenever government had allied itself with one particular form of religion, the inevitable result had been that it had incurred the hatred, disrespect and even contempt of those who held contrary beliefs. That same history showed that many people had lost their respect for any religion that had relied upon the support of government to spread its faith. The Establishment Clause thus stands as an expression of principle on the part of the Founders of our Constitution that religion is too personal, too sacred, too holy, to permit its "unhallowed perversion" by a civil magistrate. Another purpose of the Establishment Clause rested upon an awareness of the historical fact that governmentally established religions and religious persecutions go hand in hand. . . . The New York laws officially prescribing the Regents' prayer are inconsistent both with the purposes of the Establishment Clause and with the Establishment Clause itself.

It has been argued that to apply the Constitution in such a way as to prohibit state laws respecting an establishment of religious services in public schools is to indicate a hostility toward religion or toward prayer. Nothing, of course, could be more wrong. . . . It is neither sacrilegious nor antireligious to say that each separate government in this country should stay out of the business of writing or sanctioning official prayers and leave that purely religious function to the people themselves and to those the people choose to look to for religious guidance. . . .

To those who may subscribe to the view that because the Regents' official prayer is so brief and general there can be no danger to religious freedom in its governmental establishment, however, it may be appropriate to say in the words of James Madison, the author of the First Amendment:

> [I]t is proper to take alarm at the first experiment on our liberties. . . . Who does not see that the same authority which can establish Christianity, in exclusion of all other Religions, may establish with the same ease any particular sect of Christians, in exclusion of all other Sects? That the same authority which can force a citizen to contribute three pence only of his property for the support of any one establishment, may force him to conform to any other establishment in all cases whatsoever?

The judgment of the Court of Appeals of New York is reversed and the cause remanded for further proceedings not inconsistent with this opinion. Reversed and remanded.

☐ *Justice DOUGLAS, concurring.*

In New York the teacher who leads in prayer is on the public payroll; and the time she takes seems minuscule as compared with the salaries appropriated by state legislatures and Congress for chaplains to conduct prayers in the legislative halls. Only a bare fraction of the teacher's time is given to reciting this short 22-word prayer, about the same amount of time that our Crier spends announcing the opening of our sessions and offering a prayer for this Court. Yet for me the principle is the same, no matter how briefly the prayer is said, for in each of the instances given the person praying is a public official on the public payroll, performing a religious exercise in a governmental institution. It is said that the element of coercion is inherent in the giving of this prayer. If that is true here, it is also true of the prayer with which this Court is convened, and of those that open the Congress. Few adults, let alone children, would leave our courtroom or the Senate or the House while those prayers are being given. Every such audience is in a sense a "captive" audience.

At the same time I cannot say that to authorize this prayer is to establish a religion in the strictly historic meaning of those words. A religion is not established in the usual sense merely by letting those who choose to do so say the prayer that the public school teacher leads. Yet once government finances a religious exercise it inserts a divisive influence into our communities. . . .

By reason of the First Amendment government is commanded "to have no interest in theology or ritual" for on those matters "government must be neutral." The First Amendment leaves the Government in a position not of hostility to religion but of neutrality. The philosophy is that the atheist or agnostic—the non-believer—is entitled to go his own way. The philosophy is that if government interferes in matters spiritual, it will be a divisive force. The First Amendment teaches that a government neutral in the field of religion better serves all religious interests. . . .

I therefore join the Court in reversing the judgment below.

☐ *Justice STEWART, dissenting.*

With all respect, I think the Court has misapplied a great constitutional principle. I cannot see how an "official religion" is established by letting those who want to say a prayer say it. On the contrary, I think that to deny the wish of these school children to join in reciting this prayer is to deny them the opportunity of sharing in the spiritual heritage of our nation. . . .

At the opening of each day's Session of this Court we stand, while one of our officials invokes the protection of God. Since the days of JOHN MARSHALL our Crier has said, "God save the United States and this Honorable Court." Both the Senate and the House of Representatives open their daily Sessions with prayer. . . .

I do not believe that this Court, or the Congress, or the President has by the actions and practices I have mentioned established an "official religion" in violation of the Constitution. And I do not believe the State of New York has done so in this case.

Abington School District v. Schempp and Murray v. Curlett

374 U.S. 203, 83 S.CT. 1560 (1963)

The Supreme Court granted and consolidated these two cases. Each involved disputes arising from state laws requiring schools to begin each day with readings from the Bible. Edward Schempp challenged Pennsylvania's law, which declared that "at least ten verses from the Holy Bible shall be read, without comment, at the opening of each public school day. Any child shall be excused from such Bible reading, or attending such Bible reading, upon written request of his parent or guardian." A three-judge federal district court struck down the state's law as a violation of the First Amendment, and the school board appealed directly to the Supreme Court. The companion case was brought by Madalyn Murray and her son, both professed atheists. They challenged the constitutionality of a rule of the school board of Baltimore, Maryland, requiring students to recite the Lord's Prayer at the opening of each school day. A state court and the Maryland Court of Appeals had upheld the school board.

The Court's decision was 8–1, and the majority's opinion was announced by Justice Clark. Concurrences were by Justices Douglas, Brennan, and Goldberg, who were joined by Justice Harlan. Justice Stewart dissented.

■ ■ ■

☐ *Justice CLARK delivered the opinion of the Court.*

The wholesome "neutrality" of which this Court's cases speak . . . stems from a recognition of the teachings of history that powerful sects or groups might bring about a fusion of governmental and religious functions or a concert or dependency of one upon the other to the end that official support of the State or Federal Government would be placed behind the tenets of one or of all orthodoxies. This the Establishment Clause prohibits. And a further reason for neutrality is found in the Free Exercise Clause, which recognizes the value of religious training, teaching and observance and, more particularly, the right of every person to freely choose his own course with reference thereto, free of any compulsion from the state. This the Free Exercise Clause guarantees. Thus . . . the two clauses may overlap. . . . [T]he Establishment Clause has been directly considered by this Court eight times in the past score of years and, with only one Justice dissenting on the point, it has consistently held that the clause withdrew all legislative power respecting religious belief or the expression thereof. The test may be stated as follows: what are the purpose and the primary effect of the enactment? If either is the advancement or inhibition of religion then the enactment exceeds the scope of legislative power as circumscribed by the Constitution. That is to say that to withstand the strictures of the Establishment Clause there must be a secular legislative purpose and a primary effect that neither advances nor inhibits religion. The Free Exercise Clause, likewise considered many times here, withdraws from legislative power, state and federal, the exertion of any restraint on the free exercise of religion. Its purpose is to secure religious liberty in the individual by prohibiting any invasions thereof by civil authority. Hence it is necessary in a free exercise case for one to show the coercive effect of the enactment as it operates against him in the practice of his religion. The distinction between the two clauses is apparent—a violation of the Free Exercise Clause is predicated on coercion while the Establishment Clause violation need not be so attended.

Applying the Establishment Clause principles to the cases at bar we find that the States are requiring the selection and reading at the opening of the school day of verses from the *Holy Bible* and the recitation of the Lord's Prayer by the students in unison. These exercises are prescribed as part of the curricular activities of students who are required by law to attend school. They are held in the school buildings under the supervision and with the participation of teachers employed in those schools. . . . The trial court in [*Schempp*] has found that such an opening exercise is a religious ceremony and was intended by the State to be so. We agree with the trial court's finding as to the religious character of the exercises. Given that finding, the exercises and the law requiring them are in violation of the Establishment Clause.

There is no such specific finding as to the religious character of the exercises in [*Murray*] and the State contends (as does the State in [*Schempp*]) that the program is an effort to extend its benefits to all public school children without regard to their religious belief. Included within its secular purposes, it says, are the promotion of moral values, the contradiction to the materialistic trends of our times, the perpetuation of our institutions and the teaching of literature. The case came up on demurrer, of course, to a petition which alleged that the uniform practice under the rule had been to read from the King James version of the *Bible* and that the exercise was sectarian. The short answer, therefore, is that the religious character of the exercise was admitted by the State. But even if its purpose is not strictly religious, it is sought to be accomplished through readings, without comment, from the *Bible*. Surely the place of the *Bible* as an instrument of religion cannot be gainsaid, and the State's recognition of the pervading religious character of the ceremony is evident from the rule's specific permission of the alternative use of the Catholic Douay version as well as the recent amendment permitting nonattendance at the exercises. None of these factors is consistent with the contention that the *Bible* is here used either as an instrument for non-religious moral inspiration or as a reference for the teaching of secular subjects.

The conclusion follows that in both cases the laws require religious exercises and such exercises are being conducted in direct violation of the rights of the appellees and petitioners. Nor are these required exercises mitigated by the fact that individual students may absent themselves upon parental request, for that fact furnishes no defense to a claim of unconstitutionality under the Establishment Clause. . . . Further, it is no defense to urge that the religious practices here may be relatively minor encroachments on the First Amendment. The breach of neutrality that is today a trickling stream may all too soon become a raging torrent and, in the words of Madison, "it is proper to take alarm at the first experiment on our liberties." . . .

It is insisted that unless these religious exercises are permitted a "religion of secularism" is established in the schools. We agree of course that the State may not establish a "religion of secularism" in the sense of affirmatively opposing or showing hostility to religion, thus "preferring those who believe in no religion over those who do believe." We do not agree, however, that this decision in any sense has that effect. In addition, it might well be said that one's education is not complete without a study of comparative religion or the history of religion and its relationship to the advancement of civilization. It certainly may be said that the *Bible* is worthy of study for its literary and historic qualities. Nothing we have said here indicates that such study of the *Bible* or of religion, when presented objectively as part of a secular program of education, may not be effected consistently with the First Amendment. But the exercises here do not fall into those categories. They are religious exercises, required by the States in violation of the command of the First Amendment that the Government maintain strict neutrality, neither aiding nor opposing religion.

Finally, we cannot accept that the concept of neutrality, which does not permit a State to require a religious exercise even with the consent of the majority of those affected, collides with the majority's right to free exercise of religion. While the Free Exercise Clause clearly prohibits the use of state action to deny the rights of free exercise to *anyone*, it has never meant that a majority could use the machinery of the State to practice its beliefs. Such a contention was effectively answered by Justice JACKSON for the Court in *West Virginia Board of Education v. Barnette*, 319 U.S. 624 (1943). . . .

The place of religion in our society is an exalted one, achieved through a long tradition of reliance on the home, the church and the inviolable citadel of the individual heart and mind. We have come to recognize through bitter experience that it is not within the power of government to invade that citadel, whether its purpose or effect be to aid or oppose, to advance or retard. In the relationship between man and religion, the State is firmly committed to a position of neutrality. Though the application of that rule requires interpretation of a delicate sort, the rule itself is clearly and concisely stated in the words of the First Amendment.

Lemon v. Kurtzman, Earley v. DiCenso, and *Robinson v. DiCenso*
403 U.S. 602, 91 S.CT. 2105 (1971)

These three cases brought controversies over laws in Pennsylvania and Rhode Island that provided for direct and indirect financial support of private primary and secondary schools, some of which were run by religious organizations. The cases were consolidated for oral argument and decision. Chief Justice Burger discusses the programs of each state at the outset of his opinion for the Court.

The Court's decision was unanimous, and the opinion was announced by Chief Justice Burger, with Justice Marshall not participating in *Lemon*. Justice Douglas concurred and was joined by Justice Black.

■ ■ ■

☐ *Chief Justice BURGER delivered the opinion of the Court.*

Pennsylvania has adopted a statutory program that provides financial support to nonpublic elementary and secondary schools by way of reimbursement for the cost of teachers' salaries, textbooks, and instructional materials in specified secular subjects. Rhode Island has adopted a statute under which the State pays directly to teachers in nonpublic elementary schools a supplement of 15% of their annual salary. Under each statute state aid has been given to church-related educational institutions. We hold that both statutes are unconstitutional.

The Rhode Island Statute The Rhode Island Salary Supplement Act was enacted in 1969. It rests on the legislative finding that the quality of education available in nonpublic elementary schools has been jeopardized by the rapidly rising salaries needed to attract competent and dedicated teachers. The Act authorizes state officials to supplement the salaries of teachers of secular subjects in nonpublic elementary schools by paying directly to a teacher an amount not in excess of 15% of his current annual salary. As supplemented, however, a nonpublic school teacher's salary cannot exceed the maximum paid to teachers in the State's public schools, and the recipient must be certified by the state board of education in substantially the same manner as public school teachers.

In order to be eligible for the Rhode Island salary supplement, the recipient must teach in a nonpublic school at which the average per-pupil expenditure on secular education is less than the average in the State's public schools during a specified period. Appellant State Commissioner of Education also requires eligible schools to submit financial data. If this information indicates a per-pupil expenditure in excess of the statutory limitation, the records of the school in question must be examined in order to assess how much of the expenditure is attributable to secular education and how much to religious activity.

The Act also requires that teachers eligible for salary supplements must teach only those subjects that are offered in the State's public schools. They must use "only teaching materials which are used in the public schools." Finally, any teacher applying for a salary supplement must first agree in writing "not to teach a course in religion for so long as or during such time as he or she receives any salary supplements" under the Act. . . .

A three-judge federal court found that Rhode Island's nonpublic elementary schools accommodated approximately 25% of the State's pupils. About 95% of these pupils attended schools affiliated with the Roman Catholic church. To date some 250 teachers have applied for benefits under the Act. All of them are employed by Roman Catholic schools. . . .

The District Court concluded that the Act violated the Establishment Clause, holding that it fostered "excessive entanglement" between government and religion. In addition two judges thought that the Act had the impermissible effect of giving "significant aid to a religious enterprise." We affirm.

The Pennsylvania Statute Pennsylvania has adopted a program that has some but not all of the features of the Rhode Island program. The Pennsylvania Nonpublic Elementary and Secondary Education Act was passed in 1968 in response to a crisis that the Pennsylvania Legislature found existed in the State's nonpublic schools due to rapidly rising costs. . . .

The statute authorizes appellee state Superintendent of Public Instruction to "purchase" specified "secular educational services" from nonpublic schools. Under the "contracts" authorized by the statute, the State directly reimburses nonpublic schools solely for their actual expenditures for teachers' salaries, textbooks, and instructional materials. A school seeking reimbursement must maintain prescribed accounting procedures that identify the "separate" cost of the "secular educational service." These accounts are subject to state audit. . . .

There are several significant statutory restrictions on state aid. Reimbursement is limited to courses "presented in the curricula of the public schools." It is further limited "solely" to courses in the following "secular" subjects: mathematics, modern foreign languages, physical science, and physical education. Textbooks and instructional materials included in the program must be approved by the state Superintendent of Public Instruction. Finally, the statute prohibits reimbursement for any course that contains "any subject matter expressing religious teaching, or the morals or forms of worship of any sect." . . .

It appears that some $5 million has been expended annually under the Act. The State has now entered into contracts with some 1,181 nonpublic elementary and secondary schools with a student population of some 535,215 pupils—more than 20% of the total number of students in the State. More than 96% of these pupils attend church-related schools, and most of these schools are affiliated with the Roman Catholic church. . . .

A three-judge federal court . . . held that the Act violated neither the Establishment nor the Free Exercise Clause. . . . We reverse. . . .

The language of the Religion Clauses of the First Amendment is at best opaque, particularly when compared with other portions of the Amendment. Its authors did not simply prohibit the establishment of a state church or a state religion, an area history shows they regarded as very important and fraught with great dangers. Instead they commanded that there should be "no law *respecting* an establishment of religion." A law may be one "respecting" the forbidden objective while falling short of its total realization. A law "respecting" the proscribed result, that is, the establishment of religion, is not always easily identifiable as one violative of the Clause. A given law might not *establish* a state religion but nevertheless be one "respecting" that end in the sense of being a step that could lead to such establishment and hence offend the First Amendment. . . .

Every analysis in this area must begin with consideration of the cumulative criteria developed by the Court over many years. Three such tests may be learned from our cases. First, the statute must have a secular legislative purpose; second, its principal or primary effect must be one that neither advances or inhibits religion; finally, the statute must not foster "an excessive government Entanglement with religion." . . .

Inquiry into the legislative purposes of the Pennsylvania and Rhode Island statutes affords no basis for a conclusion that the legislative intent was to advance religion. On the contrary, the statutes themselves clearly state that they are intended to enhance the quality of the secular education in all schools covered by the compulsory attendance laws. There is no reason to believe the legislatures meant anything else. . . .

The legislatures of Rhode Island and Pennsylvania have concluded that secular and religious education are identifiable and separable. In the abstract we have no quarrel with this conclusion.

The two legislatures, however, have also recognized that church-related elementary and secondary schools have a significant religious mission and that a substantial portion of their activities is religiously oriented. They have therefore sought to create statutory restrictions designed to guarantee the separation between secular and religious educational functions and to ensure that State financial aid supports only the former. All these provisions are precautions taken in candid recognition that these programs approached, even if they did not intrude upon, the forbidden areas under the Religion Clauses. We need not decide whether these legislative precautions restrict the principal or primary effect of the programs to the point where they do not offend the Religion Clauses, for we conclude that the cumulative impact of the entire relationship arising under the statutes in each State involves excessive entanglement between government and religion.

In *Walz v. Tax Commission*, [397 U.S. 664 (1970)], the Court upheld state tax exemptions for real property owned by religious organizations and used for religious worship. That holding, however, tended to confine rather than enlarge the area of permissible state involvement with religious institutions by calling for close scrutiny of the degree of entanglement involved in the relationship. The objective is to prevent, as far as possible, the intrusion of either into the precincts of the other.

Our prior holdings do not call for total separation between church and state; total separation is not possible in an absolute sense. Some relationship between government and religious organizations is inevitable. . . . Fire inspections, building and zoning regulations, and state requirements under compulsory school-attendance laws are examples of necessary and permissible contacts. . . . Judicial caveats against entanglement must recognize that the line of separation, far from being a "wall," is a blurred, indistinct, and variable barrier depending on all the circumstances of a particular relationship. . . .

In order to determine whether the government entanglement with religion is excessive, we must examine the character and purposes of the institutions that are benefited, the nature of the aid that the State provides, and the resulting relationship between the government and the religious authority. . . . Here we find that both statutes foster an impermissible degree of entanglement.

(a) *Rhode Island program* The church schools involved in the program are located close to parish churches. . . . The school buildings contain identifying religious symbols such as crosses on the exterior and crucifixes, and religious paintings and statutes either in the classrooms or hallways. Although only approximately 30 minutes a day are devoted to direct religious instruction, there are religiously oriented extracurricular activities. Approximately two-thirds of the teachers in these schools are nuns of various religious orders. Their dedicated efforts provide an atmosphere in which religious instruction and religious vocations are natural and proper parts of life in such schools. . . .

This process of inculcating religious doctrine is, of course, enhanced by the impressionable age of the pupils, in primary schools particularly. In short, parochial schools involve substantial religious activity and purpose.

The substantial religious character of these church-related schools gives rise to entangling church-state relationships of the kind the Religion Clauses sought to avoid. . . .

The dangers and corresponding entanglements are enhanced by the particular form of aid that the Rhode Island Act provides. Our decisions from *Everson* to *Allen* have permitted the States to provide church-related schools with secular, neutral, or nonideological services, facilities, or materials. Bus transportation, school lunches, public health services, and secular textbooks supplied in common to all students were not thought to offend the Establishment Clause. . . .

In [*Board of Education v. Allen*, 392 U.S. 236 (1968)] the Court refused to make assumptions, on a meager record, about the religious content of the textbooks that the State would be asked to provide. We cannot, however, refuse here to recognize that teachers have a substantially different ideological character from books. In terms of potential for involving some aspect of faith or morals in secular subjects, a textbook's content is ascertainable, but a teacher's handling of a subject is not. We cannot ignore the danger that a teacher under religious control and discipline poses to the separation of the religious from the purely secular aspects of precollege education. The conflict of functions inheres in the situation.

In our view the record shows these dangers are present to a substantial degree. . . .

The schools are governed by the standards set forth in a "Handbook of School Regulations," which has the force of synodal law in the diocese. It emphasizes the role and importance of the teacher in parochial schools: "The prime factor for the success or the failure of the school is the spirit and personality, as well as the professional competency, of the teacher. . . ." The Handbook also states that: "Religious formation is not confined to formal courses; nor is it restricted to a single subject area." . . .

Several teachers testified, however, that they did not inject religion into their secular classes. . . . But what has been recounted suggests the potential if not actual hazards of this form of state aid. The teacher is employed by a religious organization, subject to the direction and discipline of religious authorities, and works in a system dedicated to rearing children in a particular faith. These controls are not lessened by the fact that most of the lay teachers are of the Catholic faith. Inevitably some of a teacher's responsibilities hover on the border between secular and religious orientation. . . .

The Rhode Island Legislature has not, and could not, provide state aid on the basis of a mere assumption that secular teachers under religious discipline can avoid conflicts. The State must be certain, given the Religion Clauses, that subsidized teachers do not inculcate religion—indeed the State here has undertaken to do so. To ensure that no trespass occurs, the State has therefore carefully conditioned its aid with pervasive restrictions. . . .

A comprehensive, discriminating, and continuing state surveillance will inevitably be required to ensure that these restrictions are obeyed and the First Amendment otherwise respected. Unlike a book, a teacher cannot be inspected once so as to determine the extent and intent of his or her personal beliefs and subjective acceptance of the limitations imposed by the First Amendment. These prophylactic contacts will involve excessive and enduring entanglement between state and church.

There is another area of entanglement in the Rhode Island program that gives concern. The statute excludes teachers employed by nonpublic schools whose average per-pupil expenditures on secular education equal or exceed the comparable figures for public schools. In the event that the total expenditures of an otherwise eligible school exceed this norm, the program requires the government to examine the school's records in order to determine how much of the total expenditures is attributable to secular education and how much to religious activity. This kind of state inspection and evaluation of the religious content of a religious organization is fraught with the sort of entanglement that the Constitution forbids. It is a relationship pregnant with dangers of excessive government direction of church schools and hence of churches. . . .

(b) *Pennsylvania program* As we noted earlier, the very restrictions and surveillance necessary to ensure that teachers play a strictly nonideological role give rise to entanglements between church and state. The Pennsylvania statute, like that of Rhode Island, fosters this kind of relationship. . . .

The Pennsylvania statute, moreover, has the further defect of providing state financial aid directly to the church-related schools. This factor distinguishes both *Everson* and *Allen*, for in both those cases the Court was careful to point out that state aid was provided to the student and his parents—not to the church-related school. . . . The history of government grants of a continuing cash subsidy indicates that such programs have almost always been accompanied by varying measures of control and surveillance. The government cash grants before us now provide no basis for predicting that comprehensive measures of surveillance and controls will not follow. . . .

A broader base of entanglement of yet a different character is presented by the devisive political potential of these state programs. In a community where such a large number of pupils are served by church-related schools, it can be assumed that state assistance will entail considerable political activity. Partisans of parochial schools, understandably concerned with rising costs and sincerely dedicated to both the religious and secular educational missions of their schools, will inevitably champion this cause and promote political action to achieve their goals. Those who oppose state aid, whether for constitutional, religious, or fiscal reasons, will inevitably respond and employ all of the usual political campaign techniques to prevail. Candidates will be forced to declare and voters to choose. . . .

Ordinarily political debate and division, however vigorous or even partisan, are normal and healthy manifestations of our democratic system of government, but political division along religious lines was one of the principal evils against which the First Amendment was intended to protect. The potential divisiveness of such conflict is a threat to the normal political process. It conflicts with our whole history and tradition to permit questions of the Religion Clauses to assume such importance in our legislatures and in our elections that they could divert attention from the myriad issues and problems that confront every level of government. . . .

The merit and benefits of these schools . . . are not the issue before us in these cases. The sole question is whether state aid to these schools can be squared with the dictates of the Religion Clauses. Under our system the choice has been made that government is to be entirely excluded from the area of religious instruction and churches excluded from the affairs of government. The Constitution decrees that religion must be a private matter for the individual, the family, and the institutions of private choice, and that while some involvement and entanglement are inevitable, lines must be drawn.

Wallace v. Jaffree

472 U.S. 38, 105 S.CT. 2479 (1985)

The pertinent facts in this controversy, involving a challenge to Alabama's law requiring that each school day begin with a moment of silent prayer or meditation, are stated by Justice Stevens in his opinion for the Court. (Excerpts from the lower court's opinion are reprinted in Ch. 2.)

The Court's decision was 6–3, and the majority's opinion was announced by Justice Stevens. Concurrences were by Justices Powell and O'Connor, dissents by Chief Justice Burger and Justices White and Rehnquist.

■ ■ ■

☐ Justice STEVENS delivered the opinion of the Court.

Appellee Ishmael Jaffree is a resident of Mobile County, Alabama. On May 28, 1982, he filed a complaint on behalf of three of his minor children; two of them were second-grade students and the third was then in kindergarten. The complaint named members of the Mobile County School Board, various school officials, and the minor plaintiffs' three teachers as defendants. The complaint alleged that the appellees brought the action "seeking principally a declaratory judgment and an injunction restraining the Defendants and each of them from maintaining or allowing the maintenance of regular religious prayer services or other forms of religious observances in the Mobile County Public Schools in violation of the First Amendment as made applicable to states by the Fourteenth Amendment to the United States Constitution." The complaint further alleged that two of the children had been subjected to various acts of religious indoctrination "from the beginning of the school year in September, 1981"; that the defendant teachers had "on a daily basis" led their classes in saying certain prayers in unison; that the minor children were exposed to ostracism from their peer group class members if they did not participate; and that Ishmael Jaffree had repeatedly but unsuccessfully requested that the devotional services be stopped. . . .

In its lengthy conclusions of law, the District Court reviewed a number of opinions of this Court interpreting the Establishment Clause of the First Amendment, and then embarked on a fresh examination of the question whether the First Amendment imposes any barrier to the establishment of an official religion by the State of Alabama. After reviewing at length what it perceived to be newly discovered historical evidence, the District Court concluded that "the establishment clause of the first amendment to the United States Constitution does not prohibit the state from establishing a religion." In a separate opinion, the District Court dismissed appellees' challenge to the three Alabama statutes because of a failure to state any claim for which relief could be granted. The court's dismissal of this challenge was also based on its conclusion that the Establishment Clause did not bar the States from establishing a religion.

The Court of Appeals . . . , not surprisingly, reversed. . . .

Our unanimous affirmance of the Court of Appeals' judgment . . . makes it unnecessary to comment at length on the District Court's remarkable conclusion that the Federal Constitution imposes no obstacle to Alabama's establishment of a state religion. Before analyzing the precise issue that is presented to us, it is nevertheless appropriate to recall how firmly embedded in our constitutional jurisprudence is the proposition that the several States have no greater power to restrain the individual freedoms protected by the First Amendment than does the Congress of the United States. . . .

When the Court has been called upon to construe the breadth of the Establishment Clause, it has examined the criteria developed over a period of years. Thus, in *Lemon v. Kurtzman*, 403 U.S. 602 (1972), we wrote:

> Every analysis in this area must begin with consideration of the cumulative criteria developed by the Court over many years. Three such tests may be gleaned from our cases. First, the statute must have a secular legislative purpose; second, its principal or primary effect must be one that neither advances nor inhibits religion . . . finally, the statute must not foster "an excessive government entanglement with religion." . . . It is the first of these three criteria that is most plainly implicated by this case. As the District Court correctly recognized, no consideration of the second or third criteria is necessary if a statute does not have a clearly secular purpose. For even though a statute that is motivated in part by a religious purpose may satisfy the first criterion, see, e.g., *Abington School Dist. v. Schempp*, . . . the First Amendment requires that a statute must be invalidated if it is entirely motivated by a purpose to advance religion.

In applying the purpose test, it is appropriate to ask "whether government's actual purpose is to endorse or disapprove of religion." In this case, the answer to that question is dispositive. For the record not only provides us with an unambiguous affirmative answer, but it also reveals that the enactment of [the Alabama law] was not motivated by any clearly secular purpose—indeed, the statute had *no* secular purpose.

The sponsor of the bill that became [law], Senator Donald Holmes, inserted into the legislative record—apparently without dissent—a statement indicating that the legislation was an "effort to return voluntary prayer" to the public schools. Later Senator Holmes confirmed this purpose before the District Court. In response to the question whether he had any purpose for the legislation other than returning voluntary prayer to public schools, he stated, "No, I did not have no other purpose in mind." The State did not present evidence of *any* secular purpose. . . .

We must, therefore, conclude that the Alabama Legislature intended to change existing law and that it was motivated by the same purpose that the Governor's Answer to the Second Amended Complaint expressly admitted; that the statement inserted in the legislative history revealed; and that Senator Holmes' testimony frankly described. The Legislature enacted [the statute authorizing teachers to lead students in a moment of "silent meditation or voluntary prayer"] despite the existence of [an earlier law permitting teachers to begin each school day with a period of silence "for meditation"] for the sole purpose of expressing the State's endorsement of prayer activities for one minute at the beginning of each school day. The addition of "or voluntary prayer" indicates that the State intended to characterize prayer as a favored practice. Such an endorsement is not consistent with the established principle that the Government must pursue a course of complete neutrality toward religion. . . .

Keeping in mind, as we must, "both the fundamental place held by the Establishment Clause in our constitutional scheme and the myriad, subtle ways in which Establishment Clause values can be eroded," we conclude that [the statute] violates the First Amendment.

The judgment of the Court of Appeals is affirmed. . . .

☐ *Justice O'CONNOR, concurring.*

I write separately to identify the peculiar features of the Alabama law that render it invalid, and to explain why moment of silence laws in other States do not necessarily manifest the same infirmity. . . .

[R]eligious liberty protected by the Establishment Clause is infringed when the government makes adherence to religion relevant to a person's standing in the political community. Direct government action endorsing religion or a particular religious practice is invalid under this approach because it "sends a message to nonadherents that they are outsiders, not full members of the political community, and an accompanying message to adherents that they are insiders, favored members of the political community." Under this view, *Lemon's* inquiry as to the purpose and effect of a statute requires courts to examine whether government's purpose is to endorse religion and whether the statute actually conveys a message of endorsement.

The endorsement test is useful because of the analytic content it gives to the *Lemon*-mandated inquiry into legislative purpose and effect. In this country, church and state must necessarily operate within the same community. Because of this co-existence, it is inevitable that the secular interests of Government and the religious interests of various sects and their adherents will frequently intersect, conflict, and combine. A statute that ostensibly promotes a secular interest often has an incidental or even a primary effect of helping or hindering a sectarian belief. Chaos would ensue if every such statute were invalid under the Establishment Clause. For example, the State could not criminalize murder for fear that it would thereby promote the Biblical command against killing. The task for the Court is to sort out those statutes and government practices whose purpose and effect go against the grain of religious liberty protected by the First Amendment. . . .

☐ *Justice REHNQUIST, dissenting.*

Thirty-eight years ago this Court, in *Everson v. Board of Education* [330 U.S. 1] (1947) summarized its exegesis of Establishment Clause doctrine thus:

> In the words of Jefferson, the clause against establishment of religion by law was intended to erect 'a wall of separation between church and State.' *Reynolds v. United States*, [98 U.S. 145 (1879)].

This language from *Reynolds*, a case involving the Free Exercise Clause of the First Amendment rather than the Establishment Clause, quoted from Thomas Jefferson's letter to the Danbury Baptist Association the phrase "I contemplate with sovereign reverence that act of the whole American people which declared that their legislature should 'make no law respecting an establishment of religion, or prohibiting the free exercise thereof,' thus building a wall of separation between church and State."

It is impossible to build sound constitutional doctrine upon a mistaken understanding of constitutional history, but unfortunately the Establishment Clause has been expressly freighted with Jefferson's misleading metaphor for nearly forty years. Thomas Jefferson was of course in France at the time the constitutional amendments known as the Bill of Rights were passed by Congress and ratified by the states. His letter to the Danbury Baptist Association was a short note of courtesy, written fourteen years after the amendments were passed by Congress. He would seem to any detached observer as a less than ideal source of contemporary history as to the meaning of the Religion Clauses of the First Amendment.

Jefferson's fellow Virginian James Madison, with whom he was joined in the battle for the enactment of the Virginia Statute of Religious Liberty of 1786, did play as large a part as anyone in the drafting of the Bill of Rights. He had two advantages over Jefferson in this regard: he was present in the United States, and he was a leading member of the First Congress. But when we turn to the record of the proceedings in the First Congress leading up to the adoption of the Establishment Clause of the Constitution, including Madison's significant contributions thereto, we see a far different picture of its purpose than the highly simplified "wall of separation between church and State." . . .

On the basis of the record of these proceedings in the House of Representatives, James Madison was undoubtedly the most important architect among the members of the House of the amendments which became the Bill of Rights, but it was James Madison speaking as an advocate of sensible legislative compromise, not as an advocate of incorporating the Virginia Statute of Religious Liberty into the United States Constitution. During the ratification debate in the Virginia Convention, Madison had actually opposed the idea of any Bill of Rights. His sponsorship of the amendments in the House was obviously not that of a zealous believer in the necessity of the Religion Clauses, but of one who felt it might do some good, could do no harm, and would satisfy those who had ratified the Constitution on the condition that Congress propose a Bill of Rights. His original language "nor shall any national religion be established" obviously does not conform to the "wall of separation" between church and State idea which latter day commentators have ascribed to him. His explanation on the floor of the meaning of his language—"that Congress should not establish a religion, and enforce the legal observation of it by law" is of the same ilk. When he replied to Huntington in the debate over the proposal which came from the Select Committee of the House, he urged that the language "no religion shall be established by law" should be amended by inserting the word "national" in front of the word "religion."

It seems indisputable from these glimpses of Madison's thinking, as reflected by actions on the floor of the House in 1789, that he saw the amendment as designed to prohibit the establishment of a national religion, and perhaps to prevent discrimination among sects. He did not see it as requiring neutrality on the part of government between religion and irreligion. Thus the Court's opinion in *Everson*—while correct in bracketing Madison and Jefferson together in their exertions in their home state leading to the enactment of the Virginia Statute of Religious Liberty—is totally incorrect in suggesting that Madison carried these views onto the floor of the United States House of Representatives when he proposed the language which would ultimately become the Bill of Rights.

The repetition of this error in the Court's opinion in [*McCollum v. Board of Education* (1948) and *Engel v. Vitale* (1962)] does not make it any sounder historically. Finally, in *Abington School Board District v. Schempp* [(1963)], the Court made the truly remarkable statement that "the views of Madison and Jefferson, preceded by Roger Williams came to be incorporated not only in the Federal Constitution but likewise in those of most of our States" (footnote omitted). On the basis of what evidence we have, this statement is demonstrably incorrect as a matter of history. And its repetition in varying forms in succeeding opinions of the Court can give it no more authority than it possesses as a matter of fact; *stare decisis* may bind courts as to matters of law, but it cannot bind them as to matters of history. . . .

The actions of the First Congress, which reenacted the Northwest Ordinance for the governance of the Northwest Territory in 1789, confirm the view that Congress did not mean that the Government should be neutral between religion and irreligion. The House of Representatives took up the Northwest Ordinance on the same day as Madison introduced his proposed amendments which became the Bill of Rights; while at that time the Federal Government was of course not bound by draft amendments to the Constitution which had not yet been proposed by Congress, say nothing of ratified by the States, it seems highly unlikely that the House of Representatives would simultaneously consider proposed amendments to the Constitution and enact an important piece of territorial legislation which conflicted with the intent of those proposals. The Northwest Ordinance, 1 Stat. 50, reenacted the Northwest Ordinance of 1787 and provided that "[r]eligion, morality, and knowledge, being necessary to good government and the happiness of mankind, schools and the means of education shall forever be encouraged." . . .

As the United States moved from the 18th into the 19th century, Congress appropriated time and again public moneys in support of sectarian Indian education carried on by religious organizations. Typical of these was Jefferson's treaty with the Kaskaskia Indians, which provided annual cash support for the Tribe's Roman Catholic priest and church. It was not until 1897, when aid to sectarian education for Indians had reached $500,000 annually, that Congress decided thereafter to cease appropriating money for education in sectarian schools. . . . This history shows the fallacy of the notion found in *Everson* that "no tax in any amount" may be levied for religious activities in any form. . . .

Notwithstanding the absence of an historical basis for this theory of rigid separation, the wall idea might well have served as a useful albeit misguided analytical concept, had it led this Court to unified and principled results in Establishment Clause cases. The opposite, unfortunately, has been true; in the 38 years since *Everson* our Establishment Clause cases have been neither principaled nor unified. Our recent opinions, many of them hopelessly divided pluralities, have with embarrassing candor conceded that the "wall of separation" is merely a "blurred, indistinct, and variable barrier," which "is not wholly accurate" and can only be "dimly perceived." . . .

Whether due to its lack of historical support or its practical workability, the *Everson* "wall" has proven all but useless as a guide to sound constitutional adjudication. . . .

But the greatest injury of the "wall" notion is its mischievous diversion of judges from the actual intentions of the drafters of the Bill of Rights. The "crucible of litigation," is well adapted to adjudicating factual disputes on the basis of testimony presented in court, but no amount of repetition of historical errors in judicial opinions can make the errors true. The "wall of separation between church and State" is a metaphor based on bad history, a metaphor which has proved useless as a guide to judging. It should be frankly and explicitly abandoned.

The Court has more recently attempted to add some mortar to *Everson's* wall through the three-part test of *Lemon*, which served at first to offer a more useful test for purposes of the Establishment Clause than did the "wall" metaphor. Generally stated, the *Lemon* test proscribes state action that has a sectarian purpose or effect, or causes an impermissible governmental entanglement with religion. . . .

Lemon cited *Board of Education v. Allen*, [392 U.S. 236] (1968), as the source of the "purpose" and "effect" prongs of the three-part test. The *Allen* opinion explains, however, how it inherited the purpose and effect elements from *Schempp* and *Everson*, both of which contain the historical errors described above. Thus the purpose and effect prongs have the same historical deficiencies as the wall concept itself: they are in no way based on either the language or intent of the drafters.

The secular purpose prong has proven mercurial in application because it has never been fully defined, and we have never fully stated how the test is to operate. If the purpose prong is intended to void those aids to sectarian institutions accompanied by a stated legislative purpose to aid religion, the prong will condemn nothing so long as the legislature utters a secular purpose and says nothing about aiding religion. Thus the constitutionality of a statute may depend upon what the legislators put into the legislative history and, more importantly, what they leave out. The purpose prong means little if it only requires the legislature to express any secular purpose and omit all sectarian references, because legislators might do just that. Faced with a valid legislative secular purpose, we could not properly ignore that purpose without a factual basis for doing so.

However, if the purpose prong is aimed to void all statutes enacted with the intent to aid sectarian institutions, whether stated or not, then most statutes providing any aid, such as textbooks or bus rides for sectarian school children, will fail because one of the purposes behind every statute, whether stated or not, is to aid the target of its largesse. In other words, if the purpose prong requires an absence of *any* intent to aid sectarian institutions, whether or not expressed, few state laws in this area could pass the test, and we would be required to void some state aids to religion which we have already upheld.

The entanglement prong of the *Lemon* test came from *Walz v. Tax Commission*. . . . We have not always followed *Walz's* reflective inquiry into entanglement, however. One of the difficulties with the entanglement prong is that, when divorced from the logic of *Walz*, it creates an "insoluable paradox" in school aid cases: we have required aid to parochial schools to be closely watched lest it be put to sectarian use, yet this close supervision itself will create an entanglement. . . .

The entanglement test ... also ignores the myriad state administrative regulations properly placed upon sectarian institutions such as curriculum, attendance, and certification requirements for sectarian schools, or fire and safety regulations for churches. Avoiding entanglement between church and State may be an important consideration in a case like *Walz*, but if the entanglement prong were applied to all state and church relations in the automatic manner in which it has been applied to school aid cases, the State could hardly require anything of church-related institutions as a condition for receipt of financial assistance.

These difficulties arise because the *Lemon* test has no more grounding in the history of the First Amendment than does the wall theory upon which it rests. The three-part test represents a determined effort to craft a workable rule from an historically faulty doctrine; but the rule can only be as sound as the doctrine it attempts to service. The three-part test has simply not provided adequate standards for deciding. Establishment Clause cases, as this Court has slowly come to realize. Even worse, the *Lemon* test has caused this Court to fracture into unworkable plurality opinions, depending upon how each of the three factors applies to a certain state action. The results from our school services cases show the difficulty we have encountered in making the *Lemon* test yield principled results. . . .

These results violate the historically sound principle "that the Establishment Clause does not forbid governments . . . to [provide] general welfare under which benefits are distributed to private individuals, even though many of those individuals may elect to use those benefits in ways that 'aid' religious instruction or worship." . . .

The Framers intended the Establishment Clause to prohibit the designation of any church as a "national" one. The Clause was also designed to

---

■ INSIDE THE COURT

Justice Kennedy Switches Positions and the Outcome in Lee v. Weisman

On Wednesday, November 6, 1991, oral arguments were heard in *Lee v. Weisman*, challenging the constitutionality of school-sponsored prayers at graduation ceremonies. Two days later at their Friday conference, the justices split five to four to reverse the lower court decision holding that the First Amendment (dis)establishment clause bars state-sponsored prayers in schools.

Chief Justice Rehnquist led the discussion, observing that there was "no harm here" and that the case was simply "an extension of *Marsh*" v. *Chambers*, 463 U.S. 783 (1983), which by a 5-to-4 vote upheld the practice of chaplains opening sessions of state legislatures

with a prayer. He voted to reverse, as did Justice White, who emphasized that the practice survived the three-prong test set down in
Lemon v. Kurtzman (1971) (excerpted in this chapter). Justices Marshall and Blackmun disagreed and voted to affirm the lower court.
Justice Stevens then emphasized that when interpreting the First
Amendment, to rely on history "is a dangerous policy" because of
the problem of "holy wars" in Ireland and the Near East. He stressed
the need for religious tolerance and for him the close connection
between the case and prior rulings forbidding state-sponsored prayers
in public schools; see *Engel v. Vitale* (1962) (excerpted in this chapter).
Justice O'Connor spoke next and shared the concerns about "encouraging a practice of tolerance," as expressed by Blackmun and Stevens.
She also thought that the appellate court had "applied *Lemon* faithfully," even though she disagreed with the test set forth there. In short,
O'Connor was inclined to reverse. Justice Scalia came down firmly
on the chief's side. He said he respected "evolving traditions," but
insisted that the issue here was not remotely establishing religion. He
also reminded the others that "the country went bananas when [the
Court] took prayer out of the schools." And he rejected the suggestion that psychological coercion has "anything to do with the Establishment Clause" and would leave that as consideration solely for
free exercise claims. Justice Kennedy followed by emphasizing his
coercion test but indicating that he did not find benedictions at graduation ceremonies coercive. In his view, the lower court could be
reversed on the basis of either *Marsh* or *Lemon*. Finally, the most recent
appointee, Justice Souter, spoke. In his view, the practice failed the
Lemon test and, in any event, the case should be resolved in a way
that did not "undermine *Engel*." He voted to affirm.

With the justices so closely divided, Chief Justice Rehnquist
subsequently assigned the opinion for the Court to Justice Kennedy,
who appeared inclined to his view and was pivotal to holding on to
a bare majority. Almost immediate thereafter Souter wrote Blackmun, telling him that he would write a dissent and, as the newest
justice on the bench, "stake out my ground" on the First Amendment. Blackmun, however, urged him to wait until he circulated his
own dissenting opinion and Souter agreed to let that opinion serve as
"the flagship on our side."

Over the next three months Justice Kennedy and his law clerks
worked on drafting an opinion for the Court. In the process, though, he
changed his mind and produced a draft affirming, rather than reversing,
the lower court, based on the psychological coercion of students forced

(continues)

■ Inside the Court
Justice Kennedy Switches Positions and the Outcome in
Lee v. Weisman *(continued)*

---

to observe school-sponsored prayers. On Friday, March 27, 1992, he met with the chief justice and told him his draft reached a result contrary to the opinion assignment. Rehnquist nonetheless agreed to his circulating it to the other justices. The following Monday, March 30, Kennedy sent Blackmun a note giving him advance notice and explaining his change in course:

> Dear Harry:
>   After writing to reverse in the high school graduation prayer case, my draft looked quite wrong. So I have written it to rule in favor of the objecting student, both at middle school and high school exercises. The Chief said to go ahead and circulate, and I thought as the senior member of those who voted for this result you should have brief advance notice. I will accompany the draft with a memo confirming that I circulate with the Chief's consent, though he had desired a different result. . . . I thought it most important to write something that you and I and the others who voted this way can join. That is why this took me a longer [sic] than it should have and, of course, I will be most attentive to your criticisms. . . .
>
>   Sincerely,
>   Tony

The next day Chief Justice Rehnquist gave the opinion assignment to Blackmun, the senior associate now in the new majority, and he reassigned the opinion to Kennedy. During the next two months, Kennedy circulated six drafts and accommodated changes suggested by Blackmun, Stevens, and O'Connor. The latter, in particular, urged him to tone down his reliance on *Lemon.* Justice Scalia in turn drafted a scathing dissent, which Chief Justice Rehnquist and Justices White and Thomas joined. The decision announced from the bench on June 24, 1992, thus, reached a result contrary to the vote originally cast at conference.

Source: Docket book pages and memos in Box 586, Justice Harry A. Blackmun Papers, Library of Congress.

stop the Federal Government from asserting a preference for one religious denomination or sect over others. Given the "incorporation" of the Establishment Clause as against the States via the Fourteenth Amendment in *Everson*, States are prohibited as well from establishing a religion or discriminating between sects. As its history abundantly shows, however, nothing in the Establishment Clause requires government to be strictly neutral between religion and irreligion, nor does that Clause prohibit Congress or the States from pursuing legitimate secular ends through nondiscriminatory sectarian means. . . .

Lee v. Weisman

505 U.S. 577, 112 S.CT. 2649 (1992)

Daniel Weisman, who is Jewish and the father of two school students in Providence, Rhode Island, initially objected to the middle and high schools allowing prayers during their commencement ceremonies when his first daughter graduated. He renewed his complaints when his second daughter graduated. At that graduation ceremony, Rabbi Leslie Gutterman offered an invocation thanking God "for the legacy of America where diversity is celebrated" and a benediction in which he observed, "O God, we are grateful for the learning which we have celebrated on this joyous commencement. . . . We give thanks to you, Lord, for keeping us alive, sustaining us and allowing us to reach this special, happy occasion." Subsequently, Weisman sued school officials, and federal district and appellate courts ruled that mentioning God during public school graduation ceremonies violates the First Amendment establishment clause. In appealing that decision, attorneys for the school board countered that such prayers do not constitute governmental endorsement or promotion of religion. Moreover, in a brief supporting the school board, the Bush administration asked the justices to abandon the three-prong test established in *Lemon v. Kurtzman*. Under that test, laws and government practices run afoul of the establishment clause if they (1) fail to have a secular purpose, (2) have the primary effect of advancing religion, or (3) promote "an excessive government entanglement with religion." The district and appellate courts concluded that the graduation prayers constituted an "advancement of religion." And the George H. W. Bush administration urged the Court to "jettison the framework erected by *Lemon* in circumstances where, as here, the practice under assault is a non-coercive, ceremonial acknowledgement of the heritage of a deeply religious people."

The Court's decision was 5–4. The majority's opinion was announced by Justice Kennedy. Justices Blackmun and Souter's concurrences were joined by Justices Stevens and O'Connor. Justice

Scalia's dissent was joined by Chief Justice Rehnquist and Justices White and Thomas.

■ ■ ■

☐ *Justice KENNEDY delivered the opinion of the court.*

This case does not require us to revisit the difficult questions dividing us in recent cases, questions of the definition and full scope of the principles governing the extent of permitted accommodation by the State for the religious beliefs and practices of many of its citizens. See *Allegheny County v. Greater Pittsburgh ACLU*, 492 U.S. 573 (1989); *Wallace v. Jaffree*, 472 U.S. 38 (1985); *Lynch v. Donnelly*, 465 U.S. 668 (1984). For without reference to those principles in other contexts, the controlling precedents as they relate to prayer and religious exercise in primary and secondary public schools compel the holding here that the policy of the city of Providence is an unconstitutional one. We can decide the case without reconsidering the general constitutional framework by which public schools' efforts to accommodate religion are measured. Thus we do not accept the invitation of petitioners and *amicus* of the United States to reconsider our decision in *Lemon v. Kurtzman*, [403 U.S. 602 (1971)]. The government involvement with religious activity in this case is pervasive, to the point of creating a state-sponsored and state-directed religious exercise in a public school. Conducting this formal religious observance conflicts with settled rules pertaining to prayer exercises for students, and that suffices to determine the question before us.

The principle that government may accommodate the free exercise of religion does not supersede the fundamental limitations imposed by the establishment Clause. It is beyond dispute that, at a minimum, the Constitution guarantees that "government may not coerce anyone to support or participate in religion or its exercise, or otherwise act in a way which establishes a [state] religion or religious faith, or tends to do so." *Lynch*. The State's involvement in the school prayers challenged today violates these central principles. . . .

We need not look beyond the circumstances of this case to see the phenomenon at work. The undeniable fact is that the school district's supervision and control of a high school graduation ceremony places public pressure, as well as peer pressure, on attending students to stand as a group or, at least, maintain respectful silence during the Invocation and Benediction. This pressure, though subtle and indirect, can be as real as any overt compulsion. Of course, in our culture standing or remaining silent can signify adherence to a view or simple respect for the views of others. And no doubt some persons who have no desire to join a prayer have little objection to standing as a sign of respect for those who do. But for the dissenter of high school age, who has a reasonable perception that she is being forced by the State to pray in a manner her conscience will not allow, the injury is no less real. There can be no doubt that for many, if not most, of the students at the graduation, the act of standing or remaining silent was an expression of participation in the Rabbi's prayer. That was the very point of the religious exercise. It is of little comfort to a dissenter, then, to be told that for her the act of standing or remaining in silence signifies mere respect, rather than participation. What matters is that, given our social conventions, a reasonable dissenter in this milieu could believe that the group exercise signified her own participation or approval of it. . . .

The injury caused by the government's action, and the reason why Daniel and Deborah Weisman object to it, is that the State, in a school setting, in effect required participation in a religious exercise. It is, we concede, a brief exercise during which the individual can concentrate on joining its message, meditate on her own religion, or let her mind wander. But the embarrassment and the intrusion of the religious exercise cannot be refuted by arguing that these prayers, and similar ones to be said in the future, are of a de minimis character. To do so would be an affront to the Rabbi who offered them and to all those for whom the prayers were an essential and profound recognition of divine authority. And for the same reason, we think that the intrusion is greater than the two minutes or so of time consumed for prayers like these. . . .

Inherent differences between the public school system and a session of a State Legislature distinguish this case from *Marsh v. Chambers*, 463 U.S. 783 (1983). The considerations we have raised in objection to the invocation and benediction are in many respects similar to the arguments we considered in *Marsh*. But there are also obvious differences. The atmosphere at the opening of a session of a state legislature where adults are free to enter and leave with little comment and for any number of reasons cannot compare with the constraining potential of the one school event most important for the student to attend. The influence and force of a formal exercise in a school graduation are far greater than the prayer exercise we condoned in *Marsh*. The *Marsh* majority in fact gave specific recognition to this distinction and placed particular reliance on it in upholding the prayers at issue there. Today's case is different. At a high school graduation, teachers and principals must and do retain a high degree of control over the precise contents of the program, the speeches, the timing, the movements, the dress, and the decorum of the students. In this atmosphere the state-imposed character of an invocation and benediction by clergy selected by the school combine to make the prayer a state-sanctioned religious exercise in which the student was left with no alternative but to submit. . . .

For the reasons we have stated, the judgment of the Court of Appeals is Affirmed.

☐ *Justice SCALIA, with whom THE CHIEF JUSTICE,*
Justice WHITE, and Justice THOMAS join, dissenting.

From our Nation's origin, prayer has been a prominent part of governmental ceremonies and proclamations. The Declaration of Independence, the document marking our birth as a separate people, "appealed to the Supreme Judge of the world for the rectitude of our intentions" and avowed "a firm reliance on the protection of divine Providence." In his first inaugural address, after swearing his oath of office on a *Bible*, George Washington deliberately made a prayer a part of his first official act as President. . . . Such supplications have been a characteristic feature of inaugural addresses ever since. . . .

[A] tradition of Thanksgiving Proclamations—with their religious theme of prayerful gratitude to God—has been adhered to by almost every President. . . .

The Court presumably would separate graduation invocations and benedictions from other instances of public "preservation and transmission of religious beliefs" on the ground that they involve "psychological coercion." I find it a sufficient embarrassment that our Establishment Clause jurisprudence regarding holiday displays, has come to "require scrutiny more commonly associated with interior decorators than with the judiciary." *American Jewish Congress v. Chicago*, 827 F. 2d 120 (Easterbrook, J., dissenting). But interior decorating is a rock-hard science compared to psychology practiced by amateurs. A few citations of "research in psychology" that have no particular bearing upon the precise issue here, cannot disguise the fact that the Court has gone beyond the realm where judges know what they are doing. The Court's argument that state officials have "coerced" students to take part in the invocation and benediction at graduation ceremonies is, not to put too fine a point on it, incoherent.

The Court identifies two "dominant facts" that it says dictate its ruling that invocations and benedictions at public-school graduation ceremonies violate the Establishment Clause. Neither of them is in any relevant sense true.

The Court declares that students' "attendance and participation in the [invocation and benediction] are in a fair and real sense obligatory." But what exactly is this "fair and real sense"? According to the Court, students at graduation who want "to avoid the fact or appearance of participation," in the invocation and benediction are psychologically obligated by "public pressure, as well as peer pressure, . . . to stand as a group or, at least, maintain respectful silence" during those prayers. This assertion—the very linchpin of the Court's opinion—is almost as intriguing for what it does not say as for what it says. It does not say, for example, that students are psychologically coerced to bow their heads, place their hands in a Dürer-like prayer position, pay attention to the prayers, utter "Amen," or in fact pray. (Perhaps further intensive psychological research remains to be done on these matters.) It claims only that students are psychologically coerced "to stand . . . or, at least, maintain respectful silence." Both halves of this disjunctive (both of which must amount to the fact or appearance of participation in prayer if the Court's analysis is to survive on its own terms) merit particular attention.

To begin with the latter: The Court's notion that a student who simply sits in "respectful silence" during the invocation and benediction (when all others are standing) has somehow joined—or would somehow be perceived as having joined—in the prayers is nothing short of ludicrous. We indeed live in a vulgar age. But surely "our social conventions," have not coarsened to the point that anyone who does not stand on his chair and shout obscenities can reasonably be deemed to have assented to everything said in his presence. Since the Court does not dispute that students exposed to prayer at graduation ceremonies retain (despite "subtle coercive pressures") the free will to sit, there is absolutely no basis for the Court's decision. It is fanciful enough to say that "a reasonable dissenter," standing head erect in a class of bowed heads, "could believe that the group exercise signified her own participation or approval of it." It is beyond the absurd to say that she could entertain such a belief while pointedly declining to rise.

But let us assume the very worst, that the nonparticipating graduate is "subtly coerced" . . . to stand! Even that half of the disjunctive does not remotely establish a "participation" (or an "appearance of participation") in a religious exercise. The Court acknowledges that "in our culture standing . . . can signify adherence to a view or simple respect for the views of others." (Much more often the latter than the former, I think, except perhaps in the proverbial town meeting, where one votes by standing.) But if it is a permissible inference that one who is standing is doing so simply out of respect for the prayers of others that are in progress, then how can it possibly be said that a "reasonable dissenter . . . could believe that the group exercise signified her own participation or approval"? Quite obviously, it cannot. I may add, moreover, that maintaining respect for the religious observances of others is a fundamental civic virtue that government (including the public schools) can and should cultivate—so that even if it were the case that the displaying of such respect might be mistaken for taking part in the prayer, I would deny that the dissenter's interest in avoiding even the false appearance of participation constitutionally trumps the government's interest in fostering respect for religion generally.

The opinion manifests that the Court itself has not given careful consideration to its test of psychological coercion. For if it had, how could it observe, with no hint of concern or disapproval, that students stood for the Pledge of Allegiance, which immediately preceded Rabbi Gutterman's invocation? The government can, of course, no more coerce political orthodoxy than religious orthodoxy. *West Virginia Board of Education v. Barnette*, 319 U.S. 624 (1943). Moreover, since the Pledge of Allegiance has been revised since *Barnette* to include the phrase "under God," recital of the Pledge would appear to raise the same Establishment Clause issue as the invocation and benediction. If students were psychologically coerced to remain standing during the invocation, they must also have been psychologically coerced, moments before, to stand for (and thereby, in the Court's view, take part in or appear to take part in) the Pledge. Must the Pledge therefore be barred from the public schools (both from graduation ceremonies and from the classroom)? In *Barnette* we held that a public-school student could not be compelled to recite the Pledge; we did not even hint that she could not be compelled to observe respectful silence—indeed, even to stand in respectful silence—when those who wished to recite it did so. Logically, that ought to be the next project for the Court's bulldozer. . . .

The deeper flaw in the Court's opinion does not lie in its wrong answer to the question whether there was state-induced "peer-pressure" coercion; it lies, rather, in the Court's making violation of the Establishment Clause hinge on such a precious question. The coercion that was a hallmark of historical establishments of religion was coercion of religious orthodoxy and of financial support by force of law and threat of penalty. Typically, attendance at the state church was required; only clergy of the official church could lawfully perform sacraments; and dissenters, if tolerated, faced an array of civil disabilities. . . .

Our religion-clause jurisprudence has become bedeviled (so to speak) by reliance on formulaic abstractions that are not derived from, but positively conflict with, our long-accepted constitutional traditions. Foremost among these has been the so-called *Lemon* test, see *Lemon v. Kurtzman*, 403 U.S. 602 (1971), which has received well-earned criticism from many members of this Court. The Court today demonstrates the irrelevance of *Lemon* by essentially ignoring it, and the interment of that case may be the one happy byproduct of the Court's otherwise lamentable decision. Unfortunately, however, the Court has replaced *Lemon* with its psychological coercion test, which suffers the double disability of having no roots whatever in our people's historic practice, and being as infinitely expandable as the reasons for psychotherapy itself. . . . For the foregoing reasons, I dissent.

Zobrest v. Catalina Foothills School District

509 U.S. 1, 113 S.CT. 2462 (1993)

The parents of James Zobrest, a deaf child, sued the Catalina Foothills School District after it refused to provide a sign-language interpreter to accompany James Zobrest to classes at a Roman Catholic high school. They alleged that the Individuals with Disabilities Education Act (IDEA) and the First Amendment's free exercise clause required the school district to provide the interpreter and that the amendment's (dis)establishment clause did not present an insurmountable barrier. After a federal district and appellate court disagreed, the Zobrests appealed to the Supreme Court, which granted *certiorari*.

The Court's decision was 5–4; the majority's opinion was announced by Chief Justice Rehnquist. Justice Blackmun's dissent was joined by Justice Souter and in part by Justices Stevens and O'Connor. Justice O'Connor, joined by Justice Stevens, also delivered a dissenting opinion.

■ ■ ■

☐ *Chief Justice REHNQUIST delivered the opinion of the Court.*

We have never said that "religious institutions are disabled by the First Amendment from participating in publicly sponsored social welfare programs." *Bowen v. Kendrick*, 487 U.S. 589 (1988). For if the Establishment Clause did bar religious groups from receiving general government benefits, then "a church could not be protected by the police and fire departments, or have its public sidewalk kept in repair." *Widmar v. Vincent*, 454 U.S. 263 (1981). Given that a contrary rule would lead to such absurd results, we have consistently held that government programs that neutrally provide benefits to a broad class of citizens defined without reference to religion are not readily subject to an Establishment Clause challenge just because sectarian institutions may also receive an attenuated financial benefit. Nowhere have we stated this principle more clearly than in *Mueller v. Allen*, 463 U.S. 388 (1983), and *Witters v. Washington Dept. of Services for Blind*, 474 U.S. 481 (1986), two cases dealing specifically with government programs offering general educational assistance.

In *Mueller*, we rejected an Establishment Clause challenge to a Minnesota law allowing taxpayers to deduct certain educational expenses in computing their state income tax, even though the vast majority of those deductions (perhaps over 90%) went to parents whose children attended sectarian schools. Two factors, aside from States' traditionally broad taxing authority, informed our decision. We noted that the law "permits all parents—whether their children attend public school or private—to deduct their children's educational expenses." We also pointed out that under Minnesota's scheme, public funds become available to sectarian schools "only as a result of numerous private choices of individual parents of school-age children," thus distinguishing *Mueller* from our other cases involving "the direct transmission of assistance from the State to the schools themselves."

Witters was premised on virtually identical reasoning. In that case, we upheld against an Establishment Clause challenge the State of Washington's extension of vocational assistance, as part of a general state program, to a blind person studying at a private Christian college to become a pastor, missionary, or youth director. Looking at the statute as a whole, we observed that "any aid provided under Washington's program that ultimately flows to religious institutions does so only as a result of the genuinely independent and private choices of aid recipients." The program, we said, "creates no financial incentive for students to undertake sectarian education." We also remarked that, much like the law in *Mueller*, "Washington's program is 'made available generally without regard to the sectarian-nonsectarian, or public-nonpublic nature of the institution benefited.'" In light of these factors, we held that Washington's program—even as applied to a student who sought state assistance so that he could become a pastor—would not advance religion in a manner inconsistent with the Establishment Clause.

That same reasoning applies with equal force here. . . . Respondent contends, however, that this case differs from *Mueller* and *Witters*, in that petitioners seek to have a public employee physically present in a sectarian school to assist in James' religious education. In light of this distinction, respondent argues that this case more closely resembles *Meek v. Pittenger*, 421 U.S. 349 (1975), and *School Dist. of Grand Rapids v. Ball*, 473 U.S. 373 (1985). In *Meek*, we struck down a statute that provided "massive aid" to private schools—more than 75% of which were church related—through a direct loan of teaching material and equipment. The material and equipment covered by the statute included maps, charts, and tape recorders. . . . *Ball* similarly involved two public programs that provided services on private school premises; there, public employees taught classes to students in private school classrooms. We found that those programs likewise violated the Constitution, relying largely on *Meek*. According to respondent, if the government could not provide educational services on the premises of sectarian schools in *Meek* and *Ball*, then it surely cannot provide James with an interpreter on the premises of Salpointe.

Respondent's reliance on *Meek* and *Ball* is misplaced for two reasons. First, the programs in *Meek* and *Ball*—through direct grants of government aid—relieved sectarian schools of costs they otherwise would have borne in educating their students. For example, the religious schools in *Meek* received teaching material and equipment from the State, relieving them of an otherwise necessary cost of performing their educational function. "This kind of direct aid," we determined, "is indistinguishable from the provision of a direct cash subsidy to the religious school." The extension of aid to petitioners, however, does not amount to "an impermissible 'direct subsidy'" of Salpointe. For Salpointe is not relieved of an expense that it otherwise would have assumed in educating its students. . . .

Second, the task of a sign-language interpreter seems to us quite different from that of a teacher or guidance counselor. . . . Nothing in this record suggests that a sign-language interpreter would do more than accurately interpret whatever material is presented to the class as a whole. . . . James' parents have chosen of their own free will to place him in a pervasively sectarian environment. The sign-language interpreter they have requested will neither add to nor subtract from that environment, and hence the provision of such assistance is not barred by the Establishment Clause. . . .

☐ *Justice BLACKMUN, with whom Justice SOUTER joins, and with whom Justice STEVENS and Justice O'CONNOR join as to Part I, dissenting.*

I disagree both with the Court's decision to reach this question and with its disposition on the merits. I therefore dissent. . . .

At Salpointe [High School, a private Roman Catholic school], where the secular and the sectarian are "inextricably intertwined," governmental assistance to the educational function of the school necessarily entails governmental participation in the school's inculcation of religion. A state-employed sign-language interpreter would be required to communicate the material covered in religion class, the nominally secular subjects that are taught from a religious perspective, and the daily Masses at which Salpointe encourages attendance for Catholic students. In an environment so pervaded by discussions of the divine, the interpreter's every gesture would be infused with religious significance. Indeed, petitioners willingly concede this point: "That the interpreter conveys religious messages is a given in the case." Brief for Petitioners. By this concession, petitioners would seem to surrender their constitutional claim.

The majority attempts to elude the impact of the record by offering three reasons why this sort of aid to petitioners survives Establishment Clause scrutiny. First, the majority observes that provision of a sign-language interpreter occurs as "part of a general government program that distributes benefits neutrally to any child qualifying as 'handicapped' under the IDEA, without regard to the 'sectarian-nonsectarian, or public-nonpublic' nature of the school the child attends." Second, the majority finds significant the fact that aid is provided to pupils and their parents, rather than directly to sectarian schools. And, finally, the majority opines that "the task of a sign-language interpreter seems to us quite different from that of a teacher or guidance counselor."

But the majority's arguments are unavailing. As to the first two, even a general welfare program may have specific applications that are constitutionally forbidden under the Establishment Clause. For example, a general program granting remedial assistance to disadvantaged school-children attending public and private, secular and sectarian schools alike would clearly offend the Establishment Clause insofar as it authorized the provision of teachers. See *Aguilar v. Felton*, 473 U.S. 402 (1985); *Grand Rapids School District v. Ball*, 473 U.S. 373 (1985); *Meek v. Pittenger*, 421 U.S. 349 (1975). Such a program would not be saved simply because it supplied teachers to secular as well as sectarian schools. Nor would the fact that teachers were furnished to pupils and their parents, rather than directly to sectarian schools, immunize such a program from Establishment Clause scrutiny. The majority's decision must turn, then, upon the distinction between a teacher and a sign-language interpreter. . . .

[O]ur cases make clear that government crosses the boundary when it furnishes the medium for communication of a religious message. If petitioners receive the relief they seek, it is beyond question that a state-employed sign-language interpreter would serve as the conduit for petitioner's religious education, thereby assisting Salpointe in its mission of religious indoctrination. But the Establishment Clause is violated when a sectarian school enlists "the machinery of the State to enforce a religious orthodoxy." *Lee v. Weisman*, [505 U.S. 577] (1992). . . .

[The majority's] distinction between the provision of funds and the provision of a human being is not merely one of form. It goes to the heart of the principles animating the Establishment Clause. As *amicus* Council on Reli-

gious Freedom points out, the provision of a state-paid sign-language interpreter may pose serious problems for the church as well as for the state. Many
sectarian schools impose religiously based rules of conduct, as Salpointe has
in this case. A traditional Hindu school would be likely to instruct its students and staff to dress modestly, avoiding any display of their bodies. And an
orthodox Jewish yeshiva might well forbid all but kosher food upon its premises. To require public employees to obey such rules would impermissibly
threaten individual liberty, but to fail to do so might endanger religious
autonomy. For such reasons, it long has been feared that "a union of government and religion tends to destroy government and to degrade religion." *Engel
v. Vitale*, 370 U.S. 421 (1962). The Establishment Clause was designed to avert
exactly this sort of conflict.

Van Orden v. Perry

545 U.S. 677, 125 S.CT. 2854 (2005)

In the 1950s and 1960s, the Fraternal Order of Eagles, a national
civic organization, erected hundreds of granite Ten Commandments
monuments around the country. One of these was among twenty-
one historical markers and seventeen monuments in a twenty-two-
acre public park surrounding the Texas State Capitol in Austin. On
a six-foot high monolith is inscribed the Ten Commandments, which
the Eagles erected and donated to the city in an effort to combat
juvenile delinquency. Thomas Van Orden, a lawyer who was homeless and who frequently visited the Capitol, where he spent his days
in the law library of the state supreme court building, filed a lawsuit
in 2001, contending that the monument violated the First Amendment (dis)establishment clause. A federal district court held that, amid
the other monuments, the display of the Ten Commandments had a
secular purpose. That decision was affirmed by the Court of Appeals
for the Fifth Circuit, and Van Orden appealed.

The appellate court's decision was affirmed by a 5–4 vote. Chief
Justice Rehnquist delivered a plurality opinion for the Court, which
Justices Scalia, Kennedy, and Thomas joined. Justices Scalia, Thomas,
and Breyer each filed concurring opinions. Justices Stevens, O'Connor,
Souter, and Ginsburg dissented.

■ ■ ■

☐ *Chief Justice REHNQUIST announced the judgment of the Court and
delivered an opinion, in which Justice SCALIA, Justice KENNEDY,
and Justice THOMAS join.*

Our cases, Januslike, point in two directions in applying the Establishment Clause. One face looks toward the strong role played by religion and

religious traditions throughout our Nation's history. . . . The other face looks toward the principle that governmental intervention in religious matters can itself endanger religious freedom.

This case, like all Establishment Clause challenges, presents us with the difficulty of respecting both faces. Our institutions presuppose a Supreme Being, yet these institutions must not press religious observances upon their citizens. One face looks to the past in acknowledgment of our Nation's heritage, while the other looks to the present in demanding a separation between church and state. Reconciling these two faces requires that we neither abdicate our responsibility to maintain a division between church and state nor evince a hostility to religion by disabling the government from in some ways recognizing our religious heritage. . . .

These two faces are evident in representative cases both upholding and invalidating laws under the Establishment Clause. Over the last 25 years, we have sometimes pointed to *Lemon v. Kurtzman*, 403 U.S. 602 (1971), as providing the governing test in Establishment Clause challenges. Compare *Wallace v. Jaffree*, 472 U.S. 38 (1985) (applying *Lemon*), with *Marsh v. Chambers*, 463 U.S. 783 (1983) (not applying *Lemon*). Yet, just two years after *Lemon* was decided, we noted that the factors identified in *Lemon* serve as "no more than helpful signposts." *Hunt v. McNair*, 413 U.S. 734 (1973). Many of our recent cases simply have not applied the *Lemon* test. See, e.g., *Zelman v. Simmons-Harris*, 536 U.S. 639 (2002); *Good News Club v. Milford Central School*, 533 U.S. 98 (2001). Others have applied it only after concluding that the challenged practice was invalid under a different Establishment Clause test.

Whatever may be the fate of the *Lemon* test in the larger scheme of Establishment Clause jurisprudence, we think it not useful in dealing with the sort of passive monument that Texas has erected on its Capitol grounds. Instead, our analysis is driven both by the nature of the monument and by our Nation's history. As we explained in *Lynch v. Donnelly*, 465 U.S. 668 (1984): "There is an unbroken history of official acknowledgment by all three branches of government of the role of religion in American life from at least 1789." For example, both Houses passed resolutions in 1789 asking President George Washington to issue a Thanksgiving Day Proclamation to "recommend to the people of the United States a day of public thanksgiving and prayer, to be observed by acknowledging, with grateful hearts, the many and signal favors of Almighty God." President Washington's proclamation directly attributed to the Supreme Being the foundations and successes of our young Nation. . . .

In this case we are faced with a display of the Ten Commandments on government property outside the Texas State Capitol. Such acknowledgments of the role played by the Ten Commandments in our Nation's heritage are common throughout America. We need only look within our own Courtroom. Since 1935, Moses has stood, holding two tablets that reveal portions of the Ten Commandments written in Hebrew, among other lawgivers in the south frieze. Representations of the Ten Commandments adorn the metal gates lining the north and south sides of the Courtroom as well as the doors leading into the Courtroom. Moses also sits on the exterior east facade of the building holding the Ten Commandments tablets. . . .

Our opinions, like our building, have recognized the role the Decalogue plays in America's heritage. The Executive and Legislative Branches have also acknowledged the historical role of the Ten Commandments.

These displays and recognitions of the Ten Commandments bespeak the rich American tradition of religious acknowledgments.

Of course, the Ten Commandments are religious—they were so viewed at their inception and so remain. The monument, therefore, has religious significance. According to Judeo-Christian belief, the Ten Commandments were given to Moses by God on Mt. Sinai. But Moses was a lawgiver as well as a religious leader. And the Ten Commandments have an undeniable historical meaning, as the foregoing examples demonstrate. Simply having religious content or promoting a message consistent with a religious doctrine does not run afoul of the Establishment Clause.

There are, of course, limits to the display of religious messages or symbols. For example, we held unconstitutional a Kentucky statute requiring the posting of the Ten Commandments in every public schoolroom. *Stone v. Graham*, 449 U.S. 39 (1980). In the classroom context, we found that the Kentucky statute had an improper and plainly religious purpose. As evidenced by *Stone*'s almost exclusive reliance upon two of our school prayer cases (citing *School Dist. of Abington Township v. Schempp*, 374 U.S. 203 (1963), and *Engel v. Vitale*, 370 U.S. 421 (1962)), it stands as an example of the fact that we have "been particularly vigilant in monitoring compliance with the Establishment Clause in elementary and secondary schools," *Edwards v. Aguillard*, 482 U.S. 578 (1987). Indeed, *Edwards v. Aguillard* recognized that *Stone*—along with *Schempp* and *Engel*—was a consequence of the "particular concerns that arise in the context of public elementary and secondary schools." Neither *Stone* itself nor subsequent opinions have indicated that *Stone*'s holding would extend to a legislative chamber or to capitol grounds.

The placement of the Ten Commandments monument on the Texas State Capitol grounds is a far more passive use of those texts than was the case in *Stone*, where the text confronted elementary school students every day. Indeed, Van Orden, the petitioner here, apparently walked by the monument for a number of years before bringing this lawsuit. The monument is therefore also quite different from the prayers involved in *Schempp* and *Lee v. Weisman* [505 U.S. 577 (1992)]. Texas has treated her Capitol grounds monuments as representing the several strands in the State's political and legal history. The inclusion of the Ten Commandments monument in this group has a dual significance, partaking of both religion and government. We cannot say that Texas' display of this monument violates the Establishment Clause of the First Amendment.

☐ *Justice BREYER, concurring in the judgment.*

In *School Dist. of Abington Township v. Schempp*, 374 U.S. 203 (1963), Justice GOLDBERG, joined by Justice HARLAN, wrote, in respect to the First Amendment's Religion Clauses, that there is "no simple and clear measure which by precise application can readily and invariably demark the permissible from the impermissible." One must refer instead to the basic purposes of those Clauses. They seek to "assure the fullest possible scope of religious liberty and tolerance for all." They seek to avoid that divisiveness based upon religion that promotes social conflict, sapping the strength of government and religion alike. They seek to maintain that "separation of church and state" that has long been critical to the "peaceful dominion that religion exercises in [this] country," where the "spirit of religion" and the "spirit of freedom" are productively "united," "reign[ing] together" but in separate spheres "on the same soil." A. de Tocqueville, *Democracy in America* (1835).

The Court has made clear, as Justices GOLDBERG and HARLAN noted, that the realization of these goals means that government must "neither engage in nor compel religious practices," that it must "effect no favoritism among sects or between religion and nonreligion," and that it must "work deterrence of no religious belief." The government must avoid excessive interference with, or promotion of, religion. But the Establishment Clause does not compel the government to purge from the public sphere all that in any way partakes of the religious. Such absolutism is not only inconsistent with our national traditions, but would also tend to promote the kind of social conflict the Establishment Clause seeks to avoid.

Thus, as Justice GOLDBERG and HARLAN pointed out, the Court has found no single mechanical formula that can accurately draw the constitutional line in every case. Where the Establishment Clause is at issue, tests designed to measure "neutrality" alone are insufficient, both because it is sometimes difficult to determine when a legal rule is "neutral," and because "untutored devotion to the concept of neutrality can lead to invocation or approval of results which partake not simply of that noninterference and noninvolvement with the religious which the Constitution commands, but of a brooding and pervasive devotion to the secular and a passive, or even active, hostility to the religious."

Neither can this Court's other tests readily explain the Establishment Clause's tolerance, for example, of the prayers that open legislative meetings; certain references to, and invocations of, the Deity in the public words of public officials; the public references to God on coins, decrees, and buildings; or the attention paid to the religious objectives of certain holidays, including Thanksgiving. If the relation between government and religion is one of separation, but not of mutual hostility and suspicion, one will inevitably find difficult borderline cases. And in such cases, I see no test-related substitute for the exercise of legal judgment. That judgment is not a personal judgment. Rather, as in all constitutional cases, it must reflect and remain faithful to the underlying purposes of the Clauses, and it must take account of context and consequences measured in light of those purposes. While the Court's prior tests provide useful guideposts—and might well lead to the same result the Court reaches today—no exact formula can dictate a resolution to such fact-intensive cases.

The case before us is a borderline case. It concerns a large granite monument bearing the text of the Ten Commandments located on the grounds of the Texas State Capitol. On the one hand, the Commandments' text undeniably has a religious message, invoking, indeed emphasizing, the Deity. On the other hand, focusing on the text of the Commandments alone cannot conclusively resolve this case. Rather, to determine the message that the text here conveys, we must examine how the text is used. And that inquiry requires us to consider the context of the display.

In certain contexts, a display of the tablets of the Ten Commandments can convey not simply a religious message but also a secular moral message (about proper standards of social conduct). And in certain contexts, a display of the tablets can also convey a historical message (about a historic relation between those standards and the law)—a fact that helps to explain the display of those tablets in dozens of courthouses throughout the Nation, including the Supreme Court of the United States.

Here the tablets have been used as part of a display that communicates not simply a religious message, but a secular message as well. The circumstances surrounding the display's placement on the capitol grounds and its physical setting suggest that the State itself intended the latter, nonreligious aspects of the tablets' message to predominate. And the monument's 40-year history on the Texas state grounds indicates that that has been its effect.

The group that donated the monument, the Fraternal Order of Eagles, a private civic (and primarily secular) organization, while interested in the religious aspect of the Ten Commandments, sought to highlight the Commandments' role in shaping civic morality as part of that organization's efforts to combat juvenile delinquency. The Eagles' consultation with a committee composed of members of several faiths in order to find a nonsectarian text underscores the group's ethics-based motives. The tablets, as displayed on the monument, prominently acknowledge that the Eagles donated the display, a factor which, though not sufficient, thereby further distances the State itself from the religious aspect of the Commandments' message.

The physical setting of the monument, moreover, suggests little or nothing of the sacred. The monument sits in a large park containing 17 monuments and 21 historical markers, all designed to illustrate the "ideals" of those who settled in Texas and of those who have lived there since that time. . . .

If these factors provide a strong, but not conclusive, indication that the Commandments' text on this monument conveys a predominantly secular message, a further factor is determinative here. As far as I can tell, 40 years passed in which the presence of this monument, legally speaking, went unchallenged (until the single legal objection raised by petitioner). And I am not aware of any evidence suggesting that this was due to a climate of intimidation. Hence, those 40 years suggest more strongly than can any set of formulaic tests that few individuals, whatever their system of beliefs, are likely to have understood the monument as amounting, in any significantly detrimental way, to a government effort to favor a particular religious sect, primarily to promote religion over nonreligion, to "engage in" any "religious practic[e]," to "compel" any "religious practic[e]," or to "work deterrence" of any "religious belief." *Schempp* (GOLDBERG, J., concurring). Those 40 years suggest that the public visiting the capitol grounds has considered the religious aspect of the tablets' message as part of what is a broader moral and historical message reflective of a cultural heritage.

This case, moreover, is distinguishable from instances where the Court has found Ten Commandments displays impermissible. The display is not on the grounds of a public school, where, given the impressionability of the young, government must exercise particular care in separating church and state. This case also differs from *McCreary County*, where the short (and stormy) history of the courthouse Commandments' displays demonstrates the substantially religious objectives of those who mounted them, and the effect of this readily apparent objective upon those who view them. . . .

For these reasons, I believe that the Texas display—serving a mixed but primarily nonreligious purpose, not primarily "advanc[ing]" or "inhibit[ing] religion," and not creating an "excessive government entanglement with religion,"—might satisfy this Court's more formal Establishment Clause tests. *Lemon.* But, as I have said, in reaching the conclusion that the Texas display falls on the permissible side of the constitutional line, I rely less upon a literal application of any particular test than upon consideration of the basic purposes of the First Amendment's Religion Clauses themselves. This display has stood apparently uncontested for nearly two generations. That experience helps us understand that as a practical matter of degree this display is unlikely to prove divisive. And this matter of degree is, I believe, critical in a borderline case such as this one.

At the same time, to reach a contrary conclusion here, based primarily upon the religious nature of the tablets' text would, I fear, lead the law to exhibit a hostility toward religion that has no place in our Establishment Clause traditions. Such a holding might well encourage disputes concerning the removal of longstanding depictions of the Ten Commandments from public buildings across the Nation. And it could thereby create the very kind of religiously based divisiveness that the Establishment Clause seeks to avoid. . . .

In light of these considerations, I cannot agree with today's plurality's analysis. Nor can I agree with Justice SCALIA's dissent in *McCreary County*. I do agree with Justice O'CONNOR's statement of principles in *McCreary County*, though I disagree with her evaluation of the evidence as it bears on the application of those principles to this case.

☐ *Justice STEVENS, with whom Justice GINSBURG joins, dissenting.*

The sole function of the monument on the grounds of Texas' State Capitol is to display the full text of one version of the Ten Commandments. The monument is not a work of art and does not refer to any event in the history of the State. It is significant because, and only because, it communicates the following message:

I AM the Lord thy God.
Thou shalt have no other gods before me.
Thou shalt not make to thyself any graven images.
Thou shalt not take the Name of the Lord thy God in vain.
Remember the Sabbath day, to keep it holy.
Honor thy father and thy mother, that thy days may be long upon the land which the Lord thy God giveth thee.
Thou shalt not kill.
Thou shalt not commit adultery.
Thou shalt not steal.
Thou shalt not bear false witness against thy neighbor.
Thou shalt not covet thy neighbor's house.
Thou shalt not covet thy neighbor's wife, nor his manservant, nor his maidservant, nor his cattle, nor anything that is thy neighbor's.

Viewed on its face, Texas' display has no purported connection to God's role in the formation of Texas or the founding of our Nation; nor does it provide the reasonable observer with any basis to guess that it was erected to honor any individual or organization. The message transmitted by Texas' chosen display is quite plain: This State endorses the divine code of the "Judeo-Christian" God.

For those of us who learned to recite the King James version of the text long before we understood the meaning of some of its words, God's Commandments may seem like wise counsel. The question before this Court, however, is whether it is counsel that the State of Texas may proclaim without violating the Establishment Clause of the Constitution. If any fragment of Jefferson's metaphorical "wall of separation between church and State" is to be preserved—if there remains any meaning to the "wholesome 'neutrality' of which this Court's [Establishment Clause] cases speak," *School Dist. of Abington Township v. Schempp*, 374 U.S. 203 (1963)—a negative answer to that question is mandatory.

In my judgment, at the very least, the Establishment Clause has created a strong presumption against the display of religious symbols on public property. The adornment of our public spaces with displays of religious symbols and messages undoubtedly provides comfort, even inspiration, to many individuals who subscribe to particular faiths. Unfortunately, the practice also runs the risk of "offend[ing] nonmembers of the faith being advertised as well as adherents who consider the particular advertisement disrespectful."

Government's obligation to avoid divisiveness and exclusion in the religious sphere is compelled by the Establishment and Free Exercise Clauses, which together erect a wall of separation between church and state. This metaphorical wall protects principles long recognized and often recited in this Court's cases. The first and most fundamental of these principles, one that a majority of this Court today affirms, is that the Establishment Clause demands religious neutrality—government may not exercise a preference for one religious faith over another. This essential command, however, is not merely a prohibition against the government's differentiation among religious sects. We have repeatedly reaffirmed that neither a State nor the Federal Government "can constitutionally pass laws or impose requirements which aid all religions as against non-believers, and neither can aid those religions based on a belief in the existence of God as against those religions founded on different beliefs." *Torcaso v. Watkins*, 367 U.S. 488 (1961). This principle is based on the straightforward notion that governmental promotion of orthodoxy is not saved by the aggregation of several orthodoxies under the State's banner. . . .

The judgment of the Court in this case stands for the proposition that the Constitution permits governmental displays of sacred religious texts. This makes a mockery of the constitutional ideal that government must remain neutral between religion and irreligion. If a State may endorse a particular deity's command to "have no other gods before me," it is difficult to conceive of any textual display that would run afoul of the Establishment Clause. . . . I respectfully dissent.

McCreary v. American Civil Liberties Union of Kentucky

545 U.S. 844, 125 S.Ct. 2722 (2005)

Two Kentucky counties, McCreary and Pulaski, in 1999 installed in their courthouses large copies of the King James version of the Ten Commandments. The constitutionality of those public displays was immediately challenged by the American Civil Liberties Union

(ACLU) chapter in the state. Subsequently, the counties passed resolutions declaring the Ten Commandments a "precedent legal code" for Kentucky's laws, and directing the addition of other historical documents, such as President Abraham Lincoln's declaration of a national prayer in 1863. After a federal district court found that display to run afoul of the First Amendment in 2000, the counties added several other secular documents, including the Magna Carta and the lyrics of "The Star Spangled Banner." That third display of the Ten Commandments, surrounded by other historical documents, was again challenged by the ACLU. In 2000, a district court ordered the removal of the displays. The counties appealed, arguing that the displays had a secular and educational purpose, but the Court of Appeals for the Sixth Circuit disagreed and affirmed the trial court. Whereupon, McCreary county appealed and the Supreme Court granted review.

The appellate court's decision was affirmed on a 5–4 vote. Justice Souter delivered the opinion for the Court. Justice O'Connor filed a concurring opinion. Justice Scalia filed a dissenting opinion, which Chief Justice Rehnquist and Justices Kennedy and Thomas joined.

■ ■ ■

☐ *Justice SOUTER delivered the opinion of the Court.*

Twenty-five years ago in a case prompted by posting the Ten Commandments in Kentucky's public schools, this Court recognized that the Commandments "are undeniably, a sacred text in the Jewish and Christian faiths" and held that their display in public classrooms violated the First Amendment's bar against establishment of religion. *Stone* [*v. Graham*] 449 U.S. [39 (1980)]. *Stone* found a predominantly religious purpose in the government's posting of the Commandments, given their prominence as "an instrument of religion" (quoting *School Dist. of Abington Township v. Schempp,* 374 U.S. 203 (1963)). The Counties ask for a different approach here by arguing that official purpose is unknowable and the search for it inherently vain. In the alternative, the Counties would avoid the District Court's conclusion by having us limit the scope of the purpose enquiry so severely that any trivial rationalization would suffice, under a standard oblivious to the history of religious government action like the progression of exhibits in this case. . . .

The touchstone for our analysis is the principle that the "First Amendment mandates governmental neutrality between religion and religion, and between religion and nonreligion." *Epperson v. Arkansas,* 393 U.S. 97 (1968); *Everson v. Board of Ed. of Ewing,* 330 U.S. 1 (1947); *Wallace v. Jaffree.* When the government acts with the ostensible and predominant purpose of advancing religion, it violates that central Establishment Clause value of official religious neutrality, there being no neutrality when the government's ostensible object is to take sides. . . .

Indeed, the purpose apparent from government action can have an impact more significant than the result expressly decreed: when the government maintains Sunday closing laws, it advances religion only minimally because many working people would take the day as one of rest regardless, but if the government justified its decision with a stated desire for all Americans to honor Christ, the divisive thrust of the official action would be inescapable. This is the teaching of *McGowan v. Maryland*, 366 U.S. 420 (1961), which upheld Sunday closing statutes on practical, secular grounds after finding that the government had forsaken the religious purposes behind centuries-old predecessor laws.

Despite the intuitive importance of official purpose to the realization of Establishment Clause values, the Counties ask us to abandon *Lemon*'s purpose test, or at least to truncate any enquiry into purpose here. Their first argument is that the very consideration of purpose is deceptive: according to them, true "purpose" is unknowable, and its search merely an excuse for courts to act selectively and unpredictably in picking out evidence of subjective intent. The assertions are as seismic as they are unconvincing.

Examination of purpose is a staple of statutory interpretation that makes up the daily fare of every appellate court in the country, and governmental purpose is a key element of a good deal of constitutional doctrine. *Church of Lukumi Babalu Aye, Inc. v. Hialeah*, 508 U.S. 520 (1993) (discriminatory purpose raises level of scrutiny required by free exercise claim). With enquiries into purpose this common, if they were nothing but hunts for mares' nests deflecting attention from bare judicial will, the whole notion of purpose in law would have dropped into disrepute long ago.

But scrutinizing purpose does make practical sense, as in Establishment Clause analysis, where an understanding of official objective emerges from readily discoverable fact, without any judicial psychoanalysis of a drafter's heart of hearts. The eyes that look to purpose belong to an "objective observer," one who takes account of the traditional external signs that show up in the "text, legislative history, and implementation of the statute," or comparable official act. There is, then, nothing hinting at an unpredictable or disingenuous exercise when a court enquires into purpose after a claim is raised under the Establishment Clause.

The cases with findings of a predominantly religious purpose point to the straightforward nature of the test. In *Wallace*, for example, we inferred purpose from a change of wording from an earlier statute to a later one, each dealing with prayer in schools. . . .

After declining the invitation to abandon concern with purpose wholesale, we also have to avoid the Counties' alternative tack of trivializing the enquiry into it. The Counties would read the cases as if the purpose enquiry were so naive that any transparent claim to secularity would satisfy it, and they would cut context out of the enquiry, to the point of ignoring history, no matter what bearing it actually had on the significance of current circumstances. There is no precedent for the Counties' arguments, or reason supporting them. . . .

Lemon said that government action must have "a secular . . . purpose," and after a host of cases it is fair to add that although a legislature's stated reasons will generally get deference, the secular purpose required has to be genuine, not a sham, and not merely secondary to a religious objective. . . .

We take *Stone* as the initial legal benchmark, our only case dealing with the constitutionality of displaying the Commandments. *Stone* recognized that the Commandments are an "instrument of religion" and that, at least on the facts before it, the display of their text could presumptively be understood as meant to advance religion: although state law specifically required their posting in public school classrooms, their isolated exhibition did not leave room even for an argument that secular education explained their being there. But *Stone* did not purport to decide the constitutionality of every possible way the Commandments might be set out by the government, and under the Establishment Clause detail is key. *County of Allegheny v. American Civil Liberties Union, Greater Pittsburgh Chapter*, 492 U.S. 573 (1989) (opinion of BLACKMUN, J.) ("[T]he question is what viewers may fairly understand to be the purpose of the display. That inquiry, of necessity, turns upon the context in which the contested object appears"). Hence, we look to the record of evidence showing the progression leading up to the third display of the Commandments.

The display rejected in *Stone* had two obvious similarities to the first one in the sequence here: both set out a text of the Commandments as distinct from any traditionally symbolic representation, and each stood alone, not part of an arguably secular display. *Stone* stressed the significance of integrating the Commandments into a secular scheme to forestall the broadcast of an otherwise clearly religious message, and for good reason, the Commandments being a central point of reference in the religious and moral history of Jews and Christians. They proclaim the existence of a monotheistic god (no other gods). . . . The reasonable observer could only think that the Counties meant to emphasize and celebrate the Commandments' religious message.

This is not to deny that the Commandments have had influence on civil or secular law; a major text of a majority religion is bound to be felt. The point is simply that the original text viewed in its entirety is an unmistakably religious statement dealing with religious obligations and with morality subject to religious sanction. When the government initiates an effort to place this statement alone in public view, a religious object is unmistakable.

Once the Counties were sued, they modified the exhibits and invited additional insight into their purpose in a display that hung for about six months. This new one was the product of forthright and nearly identical Pulaski and McCreary County resolutions listing a series of American historical documents with theistic and Christian references, which were to be posted in order to furnish a setting for displaying the Ten Commandments and any "other Kentucky and American historical document[t]" without raising concern about "any Christian or religious references" in them. As mentioned, the resolutions expressed support for an Alabama judge who posted the Commandments in his courtroom, and cited the fact the Kentucky Legislature once adjourned a session in honor of "Jesus Christ, Prince of Ethics."

In this second display, unlike the first, the Commandments were not hung in isolation, merely leaving the Counties' purpose to emerge from the pervasively religious text of the Commandments themselves. Instead, the second version was required to include the statement of the government's purpose expressly set out in the county resolutions, and underscored it by juxtaposing the Commandments to other documents with highlighted references to God as their sole common element. The display's unstinting focus was on religious passages, showing that the Counties were posting the Commandments precisely because of their secretarian content. That demonstration of the government's objective was enhanced by serial religious references and the accompanying resolution's claim about the embodiment of ethics in Christ. Together, the display and resolution presented an indisputable, and undisputed, showing of an impermissible purpose.

Today, the Counties make no attempt to defend their undeniable objective, but instead hopefully describe version two as "dead and buried." Their refusal to defend the second display is understandable, but the reasonable observer could not forget it. After the Counties changed lawyers, they mounted a third display, without a new resolution or repeal of the old one. The result was the "Foundations of American Law and Government" exhibit, which placed the Commandments in the company of other documents the Counties thought especially significant in the historical foundation of American government. In trying to persuade the District Court to lift the preliminary injunction, the Counties cited several new purposes for the third version, including a desire "to educate the citizens of the county regarding some of the documents that played a significant role in the foundation of our system of law and government." The Counties' claims did not, however, persuade the court, intimately familiar with the details of this litigation, or the Court of Appeals, neither of which found a legitimizing secular purpose in this third version of the display. The conclusions of the two courts preceding us in this case are well warranted. . . .

In holding the preliminary injunction adequately supported by evidence that the Counties' purpose had not changed at the third stage, we do not decide that the Counties' past actions forever taint any effort on their part to deal with the subject matter. We hold only that purpose needs to be taken seriously under the Establishment Clause and needs to be understood in light of context; an implausible claim that governmental purpose has changed should not carry the day in a court of law any more than in a head with common sense. . . .

Nor do we have occasion here to hold that a sacred text can never be integrated constitutionally into a governmental display on the subject of law, or American history. We do not forget, and in this litigation have frequently been reminded, that our own courtroom frieze was deliberately designed in the exercise of governmental authority so as to include the figure of Moses holding tablets exhibiting a portion of the Hebrew text of the later, secularly phrased Commandments; in the company of 17 other lawgivers, most of them secular figures, there is no risk that Moses would strike an observer as evidence that the National Government was violating neutrality in religion.

The importance of neutrality as an interpretive guide is no less true now than it was when the Court broached the principle in *Everson v. Board of Ed. of Ewing*, 330 U.S. 1 (1947), and a word needs to be said about the different view taken in today's dissent. We all agree, of course, on the need for some interpretative help. The First Amendment contains no textual definition of "establishment," and the term is certainly not self-defining. No one contends that the prohibition of establishment stops at a designation of a national (or with Fourteenth Amendment incorporation, *Cantwell v. Connecticut*, 310 U.S. 296 (1940), a state) church, but nothing in the text says just how much more it covers. There is no simple answer, for more than one reason.

The prohibition on establishment covers a variety of issues from prayer in widely varying government settings, to financial aid for religious individuals and institutions, to comment on religious questions. In these varied settings, issues of interpreting inexact Establishment Clause language, like difficult interpretative issues generally, arise from the tension of competing values, each constitutionally respectable, but none open to realization to the logical limit. . . .

Given the variety of interpretative problems, the principle of neutrality has provided a good sense of direction: the government may not favor one religion over another, or religion over irreligion, religious choice being the prerogative of individuals under the Free Exercise Clause. The principle has been helpful simply because it responds to one of the major concerns that prompted adoption of the Religion Clauses. The Framers and the citizens of their time intended not only to protect the integrity of individual conscience in religious matters, *Wallace v. Jaffree*, but to guard against the civic divisiveness that follows when the Government weighs in on one side of religious debate; nothing does a better job of roiling society, a point that needed no explanation to the descendants of English Puritans and Cavaliers (or Massachusetts Puritans and Baptists). A sense of the past thus points to governmental neutrality as an objective of the Establishment Clause, and a sensible standard for applying it. To be sure, given its generality as a principle, an appeal to neutrality alone cannot possibly lay every issue to rest, or tell us what issues on the margins are substantial enough for constitutional significance, a point that has been clear from the Founding era to modern times. But invoking neutrality is a prudent way of keeping sight of something the Framers of the First Amendment thought important. . . .

[W]e affirm the Sixth Circuit in upholding the preliminary injunction.

☐ *Justice SCALIA, with whom THE CHIEF JUSTICE and Justice THOMAS join, and with whom Justice KENNEDY joins [in part], dissenting.*

[O]ne model of the relationship between church and state [is] a model spread across Europe by the armies of Napoleon, and reflected in the Constitution of France, which begins "France is [a] . . . secular . . . Republic." Religion is to be strictly excluded from the public forum. This is not, and never was, the model adopted by America. George Washington added to the form of Presidential oath prescribed by Art. II, Sec. 1, cl. 8, of the Constitution, the concluding words "so help me God." The Supreme Court under John MARSHALL opened its sessions with the prayer, "God save the United States and this Honorable Court." The First Congress instituted the practice of beginning its legislative sessions with a prayer. *Marsh v. Chambers*, 463 U.S. 783 (1983). The same week that Congress submitted the Establishment Clause as part of the Bill of Rights for ratification by the States, it enacted legislation providing for paid chaplains in the House and Senate. The day after the First Amendment was proposed, the same Congress that had proposed it requested the President to proclaim "a day of public thanksgiving and prayer, to be observed, by acknowledging, with grateful hearts, the many and signal favours of Almighty God." President Washington offered the first Thanksgiving Proclamation shortly thereafter, devoting November 26, 1789 on behalf of the American people "to the service of that great and glorious Being who is the beneficent author of all the good that is, that was, or that will be," thus beginning a tradition of offering gratitude to God that continues today. The same Congress also reenacted the Northwest Territory Ordinance of 1787, 1 Stat. 50, Article III of which provided: "Religion, morality, and knowledge, being necessary to good government and the happiness of mankind, schools and the means of education shall forever be encouraged." And of course the First Amendment itself accords religion (and no other manner of belief) special constitutional protection.

These actions of our First President and Congress and the MAR-SHALL Court were not idiosyncratic; they reflected the beliefs of the period. Those who wrote the Constitution believed that morality was essential to the well-being of society and that encouragement of religion was the best way to foster morality. . . .

Nor have the views of our people on this matter significantly changed. Presidents continue to conclude the Presidential oath with the words "so help me God." Our legislatures, state and national, continue to open their sessions with prayer led by official chaplains. The sessions of this Court continue to open with the prayer "God save the United States and this Honorable Court." Invocation of the Almighty by our public figures, at all levels of government, remains commonplace. Our coinage bears the motto "IN GOD WE TRUST." And our Pledge of Allegiance contains the acknowledgment that we are a Nation "under God." As one of our Supreme Court opinions rightly observed, "We are a religious people whose institutions presuppose a Supreme Being." *Zorach v. Clauson*, 343 U.S. 306 (1952), repeated with approval in *Lynch v. Donnelly*, 465 U.S. 668 (1984).

With all of this reality (and much more) staring it in the face, how can the Court possibly assert that "the First Amendment mandates governmental neutrality between . . . religion and nonreligion," and that "[m]anifesting a purpose to favor . . . adherence to religion generally," is unconstitutional? Who says so? Surely not the words of the Constitution. Surely not the history and traditions that reflect our society's constant understanding of those words. Surely not even the current sense of our society. . . . Nothing stands behind the Court's assertion that governmental affirmation of the society's belief in God is unconstitutional except the Court's own say-so, citing as support only the unsubstantiated say-so of earlier Courts going back no farther than the mid-20th century. . . .

What distinguishes the rule of law from the dictatorship of a shifting Supreme Court majority is the absolutely indispensable requirement that judicial opinions be grounded in consistently applied principle. That is what prevents judges from ruling now this way, now that—thumbs up or thumbs down—as their personal preferences dictate. Today's opinion forthrightly (or actually, somewhat less than forthrightly) admits that it does not rest upon consistently applied principle. In a revealing footnote, the Court acknowledges that the "Establishment Clause doctrine" it purports to be applying "lacks the comfort of categorical absolutes." What the Court means by this lovely euphemism is that sometimes the Court chooses to decide cases on the principle that government cannot favor religion, and sometimes it does not. The footnote goes on to say that "[i]n special instances we have found good reason" to dispense with the principle, but "[n]o such reasons present themselves here." It does not identify all of those "special instances," much less identify the "good reason" for their existence. . . .

Besides appealing to the demonstrably false principle that the government cannot favor religion over irreligion, today's opinion suggests that the posting of the Ten Commandments violates the principle that the government cannot favor one religion over another. That is indeed a valid principle where public aid or assistance to religion is concerned, see *Zelman v. Simmons-Harris*, 536 U.S. 639 (2002), or where the free exercise of religion is at issue, *Church of Lukumi Babalu Aye, Inc. v. Hialeah*, 508 U.S. 520 (1993), but it necessarily applies in a more limited sense to public acknowledgment of the Creator. If religion in the public forum had to be entirely nondenominational, there could be no religion in the public forum at all. One cannot say the word "God," or "the Almighty," one cannot offer public supplication or thanksgiving, without contradicting the beliefs of some people that there are many gods, or that God or the gods pay no attention to human affairs. With respect to public acknowledgment of religious belief, it is entirely clear from our Nation's historical practices that the Establishment Clause permits this disregard of polytheists and believers in unconcerned deities, just as it permits the disregard of devout atheists. The Thanksgiving Proclamation issued by George Washington at the instance of the First Congress was scrupulously nondenominational—but it was monotheistic. In *Marsh v. Chambers*, we said that the fact the particular prayers offered in the Nebraska Legislature were "in the Judeo-Christian tradition," posed no additional problem, because "there is no indication that the prayer opportunity has been exploited to proselytize or advance any one, or to disparage any other, faith or belief."

Historical practices thus demonstrate that there is a distance between the acknowledgment of a single Creator and the establishment of a religion. The former is, as *Marsh v. Chambers* put it, "a tolerable acknowledgment of beliefs widely held among the people of this country." The three most popular religions in the United States, Christianity, Judaism, and Islam—which combined account for 97.7% of all believers—are monotheistic. All of them, moreover (Islam included), believe that the Ten Commandments were given by God to Moses, and are divine prescriptions for a virtuous life. Publicly honoring the Ten Commandments is thus indistinguishable, insofar as discriminating against other religions is concerned, from publicly honoring God. . . .

To any person who happened to walk down the hallway of the McCreary or Pulaski County Courthouse during the roughly nine months when the Foundations Displays were exhibited, the displays must have seemed unremarkable—if indeed they were noticed at all. The walls of both courthouses were already lined with historical documents and other assorted portraits; each Foundations Display was exhibited in the same format as these other displays and nothing in the record suggests that either County took steps to give it greater prominence.

Entitled "The Foundations of American Law and Government Display," each display consisted of nine equally sized documents: the original version of the Magna Carta, the Declaration of Independence, the Bill of Rights, the Star Spangled Banner, the Mayflower Compact of 1620, a picture of Lady Justice, the National Motto of the United States ("In God We Trust"), the Preamble to the Kentucky Constitution, and the Ten Commandments. The displays did not emphasize any of the nine documents in any way: The frame holding the Ten Commandments was of the same size and had the same appearance as that which held each of the other documents.

Posted with the documents was a plaque, identifying the display, and explaining that it "contains documents that played a significant role in the foundation of our system of law and government." [T]he Foundations Displays manifested the purely secular purpose. . . .

In sum: The first displays did not necessarily evidence an intent to further religious practice; nor did the second displays, or the resolutions authorizing them; and there is in any event no basis for attributing whatever intent motivated the first and second displays to the third. Given the presumption of regularity that always accompanies our review of official action, the Court has identified no evidence of a purpose to advance religion in a way that is inconsistent with our cases. The Court may well be correct in identifying the third displays as the fruit of a desire to display the Ten Commandments, but neither our cases nor our history support its assertion that such a desire renders the fruit poisonous.

■ THE DEVELOPMENT OF LAW

Oklahoma Supreme Court Rules Ten Commandments Monument on State Capitol Grounds Unconstitutional

Reprise and excerpted in Ch. 2

Town of Greece, New York v. Galloway
572 U.S. 565, 134 S.CT. 1811 (2014)

Since 1999, the monthly town board meetings in Greece, New York, opened with a roll call, a recitation of the Pledge of Allegiance, and a prayer given by clergy selected from the congregations listed in a local directory. While the prayer program is open to all creeds, nearly all the local congregations were Christian. Susan Galloway and Linda Stephens, among others, attended meetings to speak on local issues and filed a lawsuit, alleging that the town violated the First Amendment's establishment clause by preferring Christians over other prayer givers and by sponsoring sectarian prayers. The plaintiffs sought to limit the town to "inclusive and ecumenical" prayers that referred only to a "generic God." A federal district court upheld the prayer practice, but the U.S. Court of Appeals for the Second Circuit reversed the decision, holding that some aspects of the prayer program, viewed in their totality by a reasonable observer, conveyed the message that the Town of Greece was endorsing Christianity. Attorneys for the town appealed that decision and the Supreme Court granted review.

The appellate court's decision was reversed by a 5–4 vote. Justice Kennedy delivered the opinion for the Court, which only Chief Justice Roberts and Justice Alito joined. Justice Alito filed a concurring opinion, as did Justice Thomas, whose concurrence was joined by Justice Scalia. Justices Breyer and Kagan filed dissenting opinions— Kagan's opinion was joined by Justices Ginsburg, Breyer, and Sotomayor.

■ ■ ■

☐ *Justice KENNEDY delivered the opinion of the Court.*

In *Marsh v. Chambers*, 463 U.S. 783 (1983), the Court found no First Amendment violation in the Nebraska Legislature's practice of opening its sessions with a prayer delivered by a chaplain paid from state funds. The decision concluded that legislative prayer, while religious in nature, has long been understood as compatible with the Establishment Clause. As practiced by Congress since the framing of the Constitution, legislative prayer lends gravity to public business, reminds lawmakers to transcend petty differences in pursuit of a higher purpose, and expresses a common aspiration to a just and peaceful society. The Court has considered this symbolic expression to be a "tolerable acknowledgement of beliefs widely held," rather than a first, treacherous step towards establishment of a state church.

Marsh is sometimes described as "carving out an exception" to the Court's Establishment Clause jurisprudence, because it sustained legislative prayer without subjecting the practice to "any of the formal 'tests' that have traditionally structured" this inquiry. The Court in *Marsh* found those tests unnecessary because history supported the conclusion that legislative invocations are compatible with the Establishment Clause. The First Congress made it an early item of business to appoint and pay official chaplains, and both the House and Senate have maintained the office virtually uninterrupted since that time. . . .

Marsh stands for the proposition that it is not necessary to define the precise boundary of the Establishment Clause where history shows that the specific practice is permitted. Any test the Court adopts must acknowledge a practice that was accepted by the Framers and has withstood the critical scrutiny of time and political change. A test that would sweep away what has so long been settled would create new controversy and begin anew the very divisions along religious lines that the Establishment Clause seeks to prevent.

The Court's inquiry, then, must be to determine whether the prayer practice in the town of Greece fits within the tradition long followed in Congress and the state legislatures. Respondents assert that the town's prayer exercise falls outside that tradition and transgresses the Establishment Clause for two independent but mutually reinforcing reasons. First, they argue that *Marsh* did not approve prayers containing sectarian language or themes, such as the prayers offered in Greece that referred to the "death, resurrection, and ascension of the Savior Jesus Christ," and the "saving sacrifice of Jesus Christ on the cross." Second, they argue that the setting and conduct of the town board meetings create social pressures that force nonadherents to remain in the room or even feign participation in order to avoid offending the representatives who sponsor the prayer and will vote on matters citizens bring before the board. The sectarian content of the prayers compounds the subtle coercive pressures, they argue, because the nonbeliever who might tolerate ecumenical prayer is forced to do the same for prayer that might be inimical to his or her beliefs.

Respondents maintain that prayer must be nonsectarian, or not identifiable with any one religion; and they fault the town for permitting guest chaplains to deliver prayers that "use overtly Christian terms" or "invoke specifics of Christian theology." A prayer is fitting for the public sphere, in their view, only if it contains the "'most general, nonsectarian reference to God,'" and eschews mention of doctrines associated with any one faith. They argue that prayer which contemplates "the workings of the Holy Spirit, the events of Pentecost, and the belief that God 'has raised up the Lord Jesus' and 'will raise us, in our turn, and put us by His side'" would be impermissible, as would any prayer that reflects dogma particular to a single faith tradition.

An insistence on nonsectarian or ecumenical prayer as a single, fixed standard is not consistent with the tradition of legislative prayer outlined in the Court's cases. The Court found the prayers in *Marsh* consistent with the First Amendment not because they espoused only a generic theism but because our history and tradition have shown that prayer in this limited context could "coexis[t] with the principles of disestablishment and religious freedom." The Congress that drafted the First Amendment would have been accustomed to invocations containing explicitly religious themes of the sort respondents find objectionable. . . .

The contention that legislative prayer must be generic or nonsectarian derives from *dictum* in *County of Allegheny* as disputed when written and has been repudiated by later cases. There the Court held that a crèche placed on the steps of a county courthouse to celebrate the Christmas season violated the Establishment Clause because it had "the effect of endorsing a patently Christian message." Four dissenting Justices disputed that endorsement could be the proper test, as it likely would condemn a host of traditional practices that recognize the role religion plays in our society, among them legislative prayer and the "forthrightly religious" Thanksgiving proclamations issued by nearly every President since Washington. The Court sought to counter this criticism by recasting *Marsh* to permit only prayer that contained no overtly Christian references . . . .

Marsh nowhere suggested that the constitutionality of legislative prayer turns on the neutrality of its content. *Marsh* did not suggest that Nebraska's prayer practice would have failed had the chaplain not acceded to the legislator's request. Nor did the Court imply the rule that prayer violates the Establishment Clause any time it is given in the name of a figure deified by only one faith or creed. To the contrary, the Court instructed that the "content of the prayer is not of concern to judges," provided "there is no indication that the prayer opportunity has been exploited to proselytize or advance any one, or to disparage any other, faith or belief."

To hold that invocations must be nonsectarian would force the legislatures that sponsor prayers and the courts that are asked to decide these cases to act as supervisors and censors of religious speech, a rule that would involve government in religious matters to a far greater degree than is the case under the town's current practice of neither editing or approving prayers in advance nor criticizing their content after the fact. Our Government is prohibited from prescribing prayers to be recited in our public institutions in order to promote a preferred system of belief or code of moral behavior. *Engel v. Vitale*, 370 U.S. 421 (1962). . . .

In rejecting the suggestion that legislative prayer must be nonsectarian, the Court does not imply that no constraints remain on its content. The relevant constraint derives from its place at the opening of legislative sessions, where it is meant to lend gravity to the occasion and reflect values long part of the Nation's heritage. Prayer that is solemn and respectful in tone, that invites lawmakers to reflect upon shared ideals and common ends before they embark on the fractious business of governing, serves that legitimate function. If the course and practice over time shows that the invocations denigrate nonbelievers or religious minorities, threaten damnation, or preach conversion, many present may consider the prayer to fall short of the desire to elevate the purpose of the occasion and to unite lawmakers in their common effort. That circumstance would present a different case than the one presently before the Court.

The tradition reflected in *Marsh* permits chaplains to ask their own God for blessings of peace, justice, and freedom that find appreciation among people of all faiths. That a prayer is given in the name of Jesus, Allah, or Jehovah, or that it makes passing reference to religious doctrines, does not remove it from that tradition. These religious themes provide particular means to universal ends. . . .

Respondents point to other invocations that disparaged those who did not accept the town's prayer practice. One guest minister characterized objectors as a "minority" who are "ignorant of the history of our country," while another lamented that other towns did not have "God-fearing" leaders. Although these two remarks strayed from the rationale set out in *Marsh*, they do not despoil a practice that on the whole reflects and embraces our tradition. Absent a pattern of prayers that over time denigrate, proselytize, or betray an impermissible government purpose, a challenge based solely on the content of a prayer will not likely establish a constitutional violation. *Marsh*, indeed, requires an inquiry into the prayer opportunity as a whole, rather than into the contents of a single prayer.

Finally, the Court disagrees with the view taken by the Court of Appeals that the town of Greece contravened the Establishment Clause by inviting a predominantly Christian set of ministers to lead the prayer. The town made reasonable efforts to identify all of the congregations located within its borders and represented that it would welcome a prayer by any minister or layman who wished to give one. That nearly all of the congregations in town turned out to be Christian does not reflect an aversion or bias on the part of town leaders against minority faiths. . . .

Respondents further seek to distinguish the town's prayer practice from the tradition upheld in *Marsh* on the ground that it coerces participation by nonadherents. They and some *amici* contend that prayer conducted in the intimate setting of a town board meeting differs in fundamental ways from the invocations delivered in Congress and state legislatures, where the public remains segregated from legislative activity and may not address the body except by occasional invitation. Citizens attend town meetings, on the other hand, to accept awards; speak on matters of local importance; and petition the board for action that may affect their economic interests, such as the granting of permits, business licenses, and zoning variances. Respondents argue that the public may feel subtle pressure to participate in prayers that violate their beliefs in order to please the board members from whom they are about to seek a favorable ruling. In their view the fact that board members in small towns know many of their constituents by name only increases the pressure to conform.

It is an elemental First Amendment principle that government may not coerce its citizens "to support or participate in any religion or its exercise." On the record in this case the Court is not persuaded that the town of Greece, through the act of offering a brief, solemn, and respectful prayer to open its monthly meetings, compelled its citizens to engage in a religious observance. The inquiry remains a fact-sensitive one that considers both the setting in which the prayer arises and the audience to whom it is directed.

The prayer opportunity in this case must be evaluated against the backdrop of historical practice. As a practice that has long endured, legislative prayer has become part of our heritage and tradition, part of our expressive idiom, similar to the Pledge of Allegiance, inaugural prayer, or the recitation of "God save the United States and this honorable Court" at the opening of this Court's sessions. It is presumed that the reasonable observer is acquainted with this tradition and understands that its purposes are to lend gravity to public proceedings and to acknowledge the place religion holds in the lives of many private citizens, not to afford government an opportunity to proselytize or force truant constituents into the pews.

The principal audience for these invocations is not, indeed, the public but lawmakers themselves, who may find that a moment of prayer or quiet reflection sets the mind to a higher purpose and thereby eases the task of governing. . . .

The analysis would be different if town board members directed the public to participate in the prayers, singled out dissidents for opprobrium, or indicated that their decisions might be influenced by a person's acquiescence in the prayer opportunity. No such thing occurred in the town of Greece. Although board members themselves stood, bowed their heads, or made the sign of the cross during the prayer, they at no point solicited similar gestures by the public. . . .

In their declarations in the trial court, respondents stated that the prayers gave them offense and made them feel excluded and disrespected. Offense, however, does not equate to coercion. Adults often encounter speech they find disagreeable; and an Establishment Clause violation is not made out any time a person experiences a sense of affront from the expression of contrary religious views in a legislative forum, especially where, as here, any member of the public is welcome in turn to offer an invocation reflecting his or her own convictions. If circumstances arise in which the pattern and practice of ceremonial, legislative prayer is alleged to be a means to coerce or intimidate others, the objection can be addressed in the regular course. But the showing has not been made here, where the prayers neither chastised dissenters nor attempted lengthy disquisition on religious dogma. Courts remain free to review the pattern of prayers over time to determine whether they comport with the tradition of solemn, respectful prayer approved in *Marsh*, or whether coercion is a real and substantial likelihood. . . .

This case can be distinguished from the conclusions and holding of *Lee v. Weisman*. There the Court found that, in the context of a graduation where school authorities maintained close supervision over the conduct of the students and the substance of the ceremony, a religious invocation was coercive as to an objecting student. Four Justices dissented in *Lee*, but the circumstances the Court confronted there are not present in this case and do not control its outcome. Nothing in the record suggests that members of the public are dissuaded from leaving the meeting room during the prayer, arriving late, or even, as happened here, making a later protest. In this case, as in *Marsh*, board members and constituents are "free to enter and leave with little comment and for any number of reasons." . . .

In the town of Greece, the prayer is delivered during the ceremonial portion of the town's meeting. Board members are not engaged in policy-making at this time, but in more general functions, such as swearing in new police officers, inducting high school athletes into the town hall of fame, and presenting proclamations to volunteers, civic groups, and senior citizens. . . .

Ceremonial prayer is but a recognition that, since this Nation was founded and until the present day, many Americans deem that their own existence must be understood by precepts far beyond the authority of government to alter or define and that willing participation in civic affairs can be consistent with a brief acknowledgment of their belief in a higher power, always with due respect for those who adhere to other beliefs. The prayer in this case has a permissible ceremonial purpose. It is not an unconstitutional establishment of religion. . . .

☐ *Justice ALITO, with whom Justice SCALIA joins, concurring.*

I write separately to respond to the principal dissent, which really consists of two very different but intertwined opinions. One is quite narrow; the other is sweeping. I will address both. . . .

I turn now to the narrow aspect of the principal dissent, and what we find here is that the principal dissent's objection, in the end, is really quite niggling. According to the principal dissent, the town could have avoided any constitutional problem in either of two ways.

First, the principal dissent writes, "[i]f the Town Board had let its chaplains know that they should speak in nonsectarian terms, common to diverse religious groups, then no one would have valid grounds for complaint." "Priests and ministers, rabbis and imams," the principal dissent continues, "give such invocations all the time" without any great difficulty.

Both Houses of Congress now advise guest chaplains that they should keep in mind that they are addressing members from a variety of faith traditions, and as a matter of policy, this advice has much to recommend it. But any argument that nonsectarian prayer is constitutionally required runs headlong into a long history of contrary congressional practice. From the beginning, as the Court notes, many Christian prayers were offered in the House and Senate, and when rabbis and other non-Christian clergy have served as guest chaplains, their prayers have often been couched in terms particular to their faith traditions.

Not only is there no historical support for the proposition that only generic prayer is allowed, but as our country has become more diverse, composing a prayer that is acceptable to all members of the community who hold religious beliefs has become harder and harder. It was one thing to compose a prayer that is acceptable to both Christians and Jews; it is much harder to compose a prayer that is also acceptable to followers of Eastern religions that are now well represented in this country. . . .

If a town wants to avoid the problems associated with this first option, the principal dissent argues, it has another choice: It may "invit[e] clergy of many faiths." "When one month a clergy member refers to Jesus, and the next to Allah or Jehovah," the principal dissent explains, "the government does not identify itself with one religion or align itself with that faith's citizens, and the effect of even sectarian prayer is transformed."

If, as the principal dissent appears to concede, such a rotating system would obviate any constitutional problems, then despite all its high rhetoric, the principal dissent's quarrel with the town of Greece really boils down to this: The town's clerical employees did a bad job in compiling the list of potential guest chaplains. For that is really the only difference between what the town did and what the principal dissent is willing to accept. . . .

The informal, imprecise way in which the town lined up guest chaplains is typical of the way in which many things are done in small and medium-sized units of local government. In such places, the members of the governing body almost always have day jobs that occupy much of their time. The town almost never has a legal office and instead relies for legal advice on a local attorney whose practice is likely to center on such things as land-use regulation, contracts, and torts. When a municipality like the town of Greece seeks in good faith to emulate the congressional practice on which our holding in *Marsh v. Chambers* was largely based, that municipality should not be held to have violated the Constitution simply because its method of recruiting guest chaplains lacks the demographic exactitude that might be regarded as optimal. . . .

While the principal dissent, in the end, would demand no more than a small modification in the procedure that the town of Greece initially followed, much of the rhetoric in that opinion sweeps more broadly. Indeed, the logical thrust of many of its arguments is that prayer is never permissible prior to meetings of local government legislative bodies. At Greece Town Board meetings, the principal dissent pointedly notes, ordinary citizens (and even children!) are often present. The guest chaplains stand in front of the room facing the public. "[T]he setting is intimate," and ordinary citizens are permitted to speak and to ask the board to address problems that have a direct effect on their lives. The meetings are "occasions for ordinary citizens to engage with and petition their government, often on highly individualized matters." Before a session of this sort, the principal dissent argues, any prayer that is not acceptable to all in attendance is out of bounds.

The features of Greece meetings that the principal dissent highlights are by no means unusual. It is common for residents to attend such meetings, either to speak on matters on the agenda or to request that the town address other issues that are important to them. Nor is there anything unusual about the occasional attendance of students, and when a prayer is given at the beginning of such a meeting, I expect that the chaplain generally stands at the front of the room and faces the public. To do otherwise would probably be seen by many as rude. Finally, although the principal dissent attaches importance to the fact that guest chaplains in the town of Greece often began with the words "Let us pray," that is also commonplace and for many clergy, I suspect, almost reflexive. In short, I see nothing out of the ordinary about any of the features that the principal dissent notes. . . .

There can be little doubt that the decision in *Marsh* reflected the original understanding of the First Amendment. It is virtually inconceivable that the

First Congress, having appointed chaplains whose responsibilities prominently included the delivery of prayers at the beginning of each daily session, thought that this practice was inconsistent with the Establishment Clause. And since this practice was well established and undoubtedly well known, it seems equally clear that the state legislatures that ratified the First Amendment had the same understanding. In the case before us, the Court of Appeals appeared to base its decision on one of the Establishment Clause "tests" set out in the opinions of this Court, but if there is any inconsistency between any of those tests and the historic practice of legislative prayer, the inconsistency calls into question the validity of the test, not the historic practice. . . .

☐ *Justice THOMAS, with whom Justice SCALIA joins, concurring.*

The Establishment Clause provides that "Congress shall make no law respecting an establishment of religion." As I have explained before, the text and history of the Clause "resis[t] incorporation" against the States. [*Elk Grove Unified School District v. Newdow*, 542 U.S. 1 (2004) (THOMAS, con. op.). If the Establishment Clause is not incorporated, then it has no application here, where only municipal action is at issue.

As an initial matter, the Clause probably prohibits Congress from establishing a national religion. . . . That choice of language—"Congress shall make no law"—effectively denied Congress any power to regulate state establishments.

Construing the Establishment Clause as a federalism provision accords with the variety of church-state arrangements that existed at the Founding. At least six States had established churches in 1789. New England States like Massachusetts, Connecticut, and New Hampshire maintained local-rule establishments whereby the majority in each town could select the minister and religious denomination (usually Congregationalism, or "Puritanism"). In the South, Maryland, South Carolina, and Georgia eliminated their exclusive Anglican establishments following the American Revolution and adopted general establishments, which permitted taxation in support of all Christian churches (or, as in South Carolina, all Protestant churches). Virginia, by contrast, had recently abolished its official state establishment and ended direct government funding of clergy after a legislative battle led by James Madison. Other States—principally Rhode Island, Pennsylvania, and Delaware, which were founded by religious dissenters—had no history of formal establishments at all, although they still maintained religious tests for office.

The import of this history is that the relationship between church and state in the fledgling Republic was far from settled at the time of ratification. Although the remaining state establishments were ultimately dismantled—Massachusetts, the last State to disestablish, would do so in 1833—that outcome was far from assured when the Bill of Rights was ratified in 1791. That lack of consensus suggests that the First Amendment was simply agnostic on the subject of state establishments; the decision to establish or disestablish religion was reserved to the States.

The Federalist logic of the original Establishment Clause poses a special barrier to its mechanical incorporation against the States through the Fourteenth Amendment. Unlike the Free Exercise Clause, which "plainly protects individuals against congressional interference with the right to exercise their religion," the Establishment Clause "does not purport to protect individual rights." Instead, the States are the particular beneficiaries of the

Clause. Incorporation therefore gives rise to a paradoxical result: Applying the Clause against the States eliminates their right to establish a religion free from federal interference, thereby "prohibit[ing] exactly what the Establishment Clause protected."

Put differently, the structural reasons that counsel against incorporating the Tenth Amendment also apply to the Establishment Clause. To my knowledge, no court has ever suggested that the Tenth Amendment, which "reserve[s] to the States" powers not delegated to the Federal Government, could or should be applied against the States. To incorporate that limitation would be to divest the States of all powers not specifically delegated to them, thereby inverting the original import of the Amendment. Incorporating the Establishment Clause has precisely the same effect. . . .

Even if the Establishment Clause were properly incorporated against the States, the municipal prayers at issue in this case bear no resemblance to the coercive state establishments that existed at the founding. "The coercion that was a hallmark of historical establishments of religion was coercion of religious orthodoxy and of financial support by force of law and threat of penalty." *Lee v. Weisman*, 505 U.S. 577(1992) (SCALIA, J., dissenting). In a typical case, attendance at the established church was mandatory, and taxes were levied to generate church revenue. Dissenting ministers were barred from preaching, and political participation was limited to members of the established church. . . .

Thus, to the extent coercion is relevant to the Establishment Clause analysis, it is actual legal coercion that counts—not the "subtle coercive pressures" allegedly felt by respondents in this case. The majority properly concludes that "[o]ffense . . . does not equate to coercion," since "[a]dults often encounter speech they find disagreeable[,] and an Establishment Clause violation is not made out any time a person experiences a sense of affront from the expression of contrary religious views in a legislative forum." I would simply add, in light of the foregoing history of the Establishment Clause, that "[p]eer pressure, unpleasant as it may be, is not coercion" either.

☐ *Justice BREYER, dissenting.*

As we all recognize, this is a "fact-sensitive" case. The Court of Appeals did not believe that the Constitution forbids legislative prayers that incorporate content associated with a particular denomination. Rather, the court's holding took that content into account simply because it indicated that the town had not followed a sufficiently inclusive "prayer-giver selection process." It also took into account related "actions (and inactions) of prayer-givers and town officials." Those actions and inactions included (1) a selection process that led to the selection of "clergy almost exclusively from places of worship located within the town's borders," despite the likelihood that significant numbers of town residents were members of congregations that gather just outside those borders; (2) a failure to "infor[m] members of the general public that volunteers" would be acceptable prayer givers; and (3) a failure to "infor[m] prayer-givers that invocations were not to be exploited as an effort to convert others to the particular faith of the invocational speaker, nor to disparage any faith or belief different than that of the invocational speaker."

The Court of Appeals further emphasized what it was not holding. It did not hold that "the town may not open its public meetings with a prayer," or that "any prayers offered in this context must be blandly 'nonsectarian.'" In essence, the Court of Appeals merely held that the town must do more than it had previously done to try to make its prayer practices inclusive of other faiths. And it did not prescribe a single constitutionally required method for doing so.

In my view, the Court of Appeals' conclusion and its reasoning are convincing. Justice KAGAN's dissent is consistent with that view, and I join it. . . .

☐ *Justice KAGAN, with whom Justice GINSBURG, Justice BREYER, and Justice SOTOMAYOR join, dissenting.*

For centuries now, people have come to this country from every corner of the world to share in the blessing of religious freedom. Our Constitution promises that they may worship in their own way, without fear of penalty or danger, and that in itself is a momentous offering. Yet our Constitution makes a commitment still more remarkable—that however those individuals worship, they will count as full and equal American citizens. A Christian, a Jew, a Muslim (and so forth)—each stands in the same relationship with her country, with her state and local communities, and with every level and body of government. So that when each person performs the duties or seeks the benefits of citizenship, she does so not as an adherent to one or another religion, but simply as an American.

I respectfully dissent from the Court's opinion because I think the Town of Greece's prayer practices violate that norm of religious equality—the breathtakingly generous constitutional idea that our public institutions belong no less to the Buddhist or Hindu than to the Methodist or Episcopalian. I do not contend that principle translates here into a bright separationist line. To the contrary, I agree with the Court's decision in *Marsh v. Chambers* upholding the Nebraska Legislature's tradition of beginning each session with a chaplain's prayer. And I believe that pluralism and inclusion in a town hall can satisfy the constitutional requirement of neutrality; such a forum need not become a religion-free zone. But still, the Town of Greece should lose this case. The practice at issue here differs from the one sustained in *Marsh* because Greece's town meetings involve participation by ordinary citizens, and the invocations given—directly to those citizens—were predominantly sectarian in content. Still more, Greece's Board did nothing to recognize religious diversity: In arranging for clergy members to open each meeting, the Town never sought (except briefly when this suit was filed) to involve, accommodate, or in any way reach out to adherents of non-Christian religions. So month in and month out for over a decade, prayers steeped in only one faith, addressed toward members of the public, commenced meetings to discuss local affairs and distribute government benefits. In my view, that practice does not square with the First Amendment's promise that every citizen, irrespective of her religion, owns an equal share in her government.

To begin to see what has gone wrong in the Town of Greece, consider several hypothetical scenarios in which sectarian prayer—taken straight from this case's record—infuses governmental activities. None involves, as this case does, a proceeding that could be characterized as a legislative session, but they are useful to elaborate some general principles. In each instance, assume (as was true in Greece) that the invocation is given pursuant to government policy and is representative of the prayers generally offered in the designated setting:

- You are a party in a case going to trial; let's say you have filed suit against the government for violating one of your legal rights. The judge bangs his gavel to call the court to order, asks a minister to come to the front of the room, and instructs the 10 or so individuals present to rise for an opening prayer. The clergyman faces those in attendance and says: "Lord, God of all creation, ... We acknowledge the saving sacrifice of Jesus Christ on the cross. We draw strength . . . from his resurrection at Easter. Jesus Christ, who took away the sins of the world, destroyed our death, through his dying and in his rising, he has restored our life. Blessed are you, who has raised up the Lord Jesus, you who will raise us, in our turn, and put us by His side. . . . Amen." The judge then asks your lawyer to begin the trial.

- It's election day, and you head over to your local polling place to vote. As you and others wait to give your names and receive your ballots, an election official asks everyone there to join him in prayer. He says: "We pray this [day] for the guidance of the Holy Spirit as [we vote] . . . . Let's just say the Our Father together. 'Our Father, who art in Heaven, hallowed be thy name; thy Kingdom come, thy will be done, on earth as it is in Heaven. . . .'" And after he concludes, he makes the sign of the cross, and appears to wait expectantly for you and the other prospective voters to do so too.

- You are an immigrant attending a naturalization ceremony to finally become a citizen. The presiding official tells you and your fellow applicants that before administering the oath of allegiance, he would like a minister to pray for you and with you. The pastor steps to the front of the room, asks everyone to bow their heads, and recites: "[F]ather, son, and Holy Spirit—it is with a due sense of reverence and awe that we come before you [today] seeking your blessing . . . . You are . . . a wise God, oh Lord, . . . as evidenced even in the plan of redemption that is fulfilled in Jesus Christ. We ask that you would give freely and abundantly wisdom to one and to all . . . in the name of the Lord and Savior Jesus Christ, who lives with you and the Holy Spirit, one God for ever and ever. Amen."

I would hold that the government officials responsible for the above practices—that is, for prayer repeatedly invoking a single religion's beliefs in these settings—crossed a constitutional line. I have every confidence the Court would agree. Why?

The reason, of course, has nothing to do with Christianity as such. This opinion is full of Christian prayers, because those were the only invocations offered in the Town of Greece. But if my hypotheticals involved the prayer of some other religion, the outcome would be exactly the same. . . .

And making matters still worse: They have done so in a place where individuals come to interact with, and participate in, the institutions and processes of their government. A person goes to court, to the polls, to a naturalization ceremony—and a government official or his hand-picked minister asks her, as the first order of official business, to stand and pray with others in a way conflicting with her own religious beliefs. Perhaps she feels sufficient pressure to go along—to rise, bow her head, and join in whatever others are saying: After all, she wants, very badly, what the judge or poll worker or immigration official has to offer. Or perhaps she is made of stronger mettle, and she opts not to participate in what she does not believe—indeed, what would, for her, be something like blasphemy. She then must make known her dissent from the common religious view, and place herself apart from other citizens, as well as from the officials responsible for the invocations. And so a civic function of some kind brings religious differences to the fore: That public proceeding becomes (whether intentionally or not) an instrument for dividing her from adherents to the community's majority religion, and for altering the very nature of her relationship with her government.

That is not the country we are, because that is not what our Constitution permits. Here, when a citizen stands before her government, whether to perform a service or request a benefit, her religious beliefs do not enter into the picture. . . .

[N]o one can fairly read the prayers from Greece's Town meetings as anything other than explicitly Christian—constantly and exclusively so. From the time Greece established its prayer practice in 1999 until litigation loomed nine years later, all of its monthly chaplains were Christian clergy. And after a brief spell surrounding the filing of this suit (when a Jewish layman, a Wiccan priestess, and a Baha'i minister appeared at meetings), the Town resumed its practice of inviting only clergy from neighboring Protestant and Catholic churches. About two-thirds of the prayers given over this decade or so invoked "Jesus," "Christ," "Your Son," or "the Holy Spirit"; in the 18 months before the record closed, 85% included those references. And the prayers usually close with phrases like "in the name of Jesus Christ" or "in the name of Your son."

Still more, the prayers betray no understanding that the American community is today, as it long has been, a rich mosaic of religious faiths. The monthly chaplains appear almost always to assume that everyone in the room is Christian (and of a kind who has no objection to government-sponsored worship). . . .

To recap: *Marsh* upheld prayer addressed to legislators alone, in a proceeding in which citizens had no role—and even then, only when it did not "proselytize or advance" any single religion. It was that legislative prayer practice (not every prayer in a body exercising any legislative function) that the Court found constitutional given its "unambiguous and unbroken history." But that approved practice, as I have shown, is not Greece's. None of the history *Marsh* cited—and none the majority details today—supports calling on citizens to pray, in a manner consonant with only a single religion's beliefs, at a participatory public proceeding, having both legislative and adjudicative components. Or to use the majority's phrase, no "history shows that th[is] specific practice is permitted." And so, contra the majority, Greece's prayers cannot simply ride on the constitutional coattails of the legislative tradition *Marsh* described. . . .

None of this means that Greece's town hall must be religion- or prayer-free. "[W]e are a religious people," *Marsh* observed, and prayer draws some warrant from tradition in a town hall, as well as in Congress or a state legislature. What the circumstances here demand is the recognition that we are a pluralistic people too. When citizens of all faiths come to speak to each other and their elected representatives in a legislative session, the government must take especial care to ensure that the prayers they hear will seek to include, rather than serve to divide. No more is required—but that much is crucial—to treat every citizen, of whatever religion, as an equal participant in her government.

And contrary to the majority's (and Justice ALITO's) view, that is not difficult to do. If the Town Board had let its chaplains know that they should speak in nonsectarian terms, common to diverse religious groups, then no one would have valid grounds for complaint. Priests and ministers, rabbis and imams give such invocations all the time; there is no great mystery to the project. Or if the Board preferred, it might have invited clergy of many faiths to serve as chaplains, as the majority notes that Congress does. When one month a clergy member refers to Jesus, and the next to Allah or Jehovah—as the majority hopefully though counterfactually suggests happened here—the government does not identify itself with one religion or align itself with that faith's citizens, and the effect of even sectarian prayer is transformed. So Greece had multiple ways of incorporating prayer into its town meetings—reflecting all the ways that prayer (as most of us know from daily life) can forge common bonds, rather than divide.

But Greece could not do what it did: infuse a participatory government body with one (and only one) faith, so that month in and month out, the citizens appearing before it become partly defined by their creed—as those who share, and those who do not, the community's majority religious belief. In this country, when citizens go before the government, they go not as Christians or Muslims or Jews (or what have you), but just as Americans (or here, as Grecians). That is what it means to be an equal citizen, irrespective of religion. And that is what the Town of Greece precluded by so identifying itself with a single faith.

How, then, does the majority go so far astray, allowing the Town of Greece to turn its assemblies for citizens into a forum for Christian prayer? The answer does not lie in first principles: I have no doubt that every member of this Court believes as firmly as I that our institutions of government belong equally to all, regardless of faith. Rather, the error reflects two kinds of blindness. First, the majority misapprehends the facts of this case, as distinct from those characterizing traditional legislative prayer. And second, the majority misjudges the essential meaning of the religious worship in Greece's town hall, along with its capacity to exclude and divide.

The facts here matter to the constitutional issue; indeed, the majority itself acknowledges that the requisite inquiry—a "fact-sensitive" one— turns on "the setting in which the prayer arises and the audience to whom it is directed." But then the majority glides right over those considerations—at least as they relate to the Town of Greece. When the majority analyzes the "setting" and "audience" for prayer, it focuses almost exclusively on Congress and the Nebraska Legislature, it does not stop to analyze how far those factors differ in Greece's meetings. The majority thus gives short shrift to the gap—more like, the chasm—between a legislative floor session involving only elected officials and a town hall revolving around ordinary citizens. And similarly the majority neglects to consider how the prayers in Greece are mostly addressed to members of the public, rather than (as in the forums it discusses) to the lawmakers. "The District Court in *Marsh*," the majority expounds, "described the prayer exercise as 'an internal act' directed at the Nebraska Legislature's 'own members.'" Well, yes, so it is in Lincoln, and on Capitol Hill. But not in Greece, where as I have described, the chaplain faces the Town's residents—with the Board watching from on high—and calls on them to pray together.

And of course—as the majority sidesteps as well—to pray in the name of Jesus Christ. In addressing the sectarian content of these prayers, the majority again changes the subject, preferring to explain what happens in other government bodies. The majority notes, for example, that Congress "welcom[es] ministers of many creeds," who commonly speak of "values that count as universal," and in that context, the majority opines, the fact "[t]hat a prayer is given in the name of Jesus, Allah, or Jehovah . . . does not remove it from" *Marsh's* protection. But that case is not this one, as I have shown, because in Greece only Christian clergy members speak, and then mostly in the voice of their own religion; no Allah or Jehovah ever is mentioned. So all the majority can point to in the Town's practice is that the Board "maintains a policy of nondiscrimination," and "represent[s] that it would welcome a prayer by any minister or layman who wishe[s] to give one." But that representation has never been publicized; nor has the Board (except for a few months surrounding this suit's filing) offered the chaplain's role to any non-Christian clergy or layman, in either Greece or its environs; nor has the Board ever provided its chaplains with guidance about reaching out to members of other faiths, as most state legislatures and Congress do. The majority thus errs in assimilating the Board's prayer practice to that of Congress or the Nebraska Legislature. Unlike those models, the Board is determinedly—and relentlessly—noninclusive.

And the month in, month out sectarianism the Board chose for its meetings belies the majority's refrain that the prayers in Greece were "ceremonial" in nature. Ceremonial references to the divine surely abound: The majority is right that "the Pledge of Allegiance, inaugural prayer, or the recitation of 'God save the United States and this honorable Court'" each fits the bill. But prayers evoking "the saving sacrifice of Jesus Christ on the cross," "the plan of redemption that is fulfilled in Jesus Christ," "the life and death, resurrection and ascension of the Savior Jesus Christ," the workings of the Holy Spirit, the events of Pentecost, and the belief that God "has raised up the Lord Jesus" and "will raise us, in our turn, and put us by His side"? No. These are statements of profound belief and deep meaning, subscribed to by many, denied by some. . . .

The content of Greece's prayers *is* a big deal, to Christians and non-Christians alike. A person's response to the doctrine, language, and imagery contained in those invocations reveals a core aspect of identity—who that person is and how she faces the world. And the responses of different individuals, in Greece and across this country, of course vary. Contrary to the majority's apparent view, such sectarian prayers are not "part of our expressive idiom" or "part of our heritage and tradition," assuming the word "our" refers to all Americans. They express beliefs that are fundamental to some, foreign to others—and because that is so they carry the ever-present potential to both exclude and divide. The majority, I think, assesses too lightly the significance of these religious differences, and so fears too little the "religiously based divisiveness that the Establishment Clause seeks to avoid." I would treat more seriously the multiplicity of Americans' religious commitments, along with the challenge they can pose to the project—the distinctively American project—of creating one from the many, and governing all as united. . . .

When the citizens of this country approach their government, they do so only as Americans, not as members of one faith or another. And that means that even in a partly legislative body, they should not confront government-sponsored worship that divides them along religious lines. I believe, for all the reasons I have given, that the Town of Greece betrayed that promise. . . .

B | *Free Exercise of Religion*

The free exercise clause embodies the principle of freedom from governmental coercion in choosing a religion or no religion. That guarantee is not absolute, however. Individuals may be prosecuted for certain religious practices (handling poisonous snakes or taking illegal drugs) and compelled to comply with regulations and laws (such as Sunday closing laws) that contravene their religious beliefs. Still, the Court has interpreted the free exercise clause to require state neutrality with regard to religion. A law may not discriminate on the basis of religion or have a religious purpose. On this basis, in *Torcaso v. Watkins*, 367 U.S. 488 (1961), the Court struck down Maryland's law requiring that individuals take an oath declaring their "belief in the existence of God" as a condition of holding public office. In *McDaniel v. Paty*, 435 U.S. 618 (1978), a Tennessee statute forbidding ministers and priests from serving as delegates to state constitutional conventions was overturned. Over free exercise objections, the Court has also upheld laws that have a secular purpose but which forbid Mormons from practicing polygamy, *Reynolds v. United States*, 98 U.S. 145 (1890); required smallpox vaccinations, *Jacobson v. Massachusetts*, 197 U.S. 11 (1905); required the closing of businesses on Sundays, *Braunfeld v. Brown*, 366 U.S. 599 (1961); and prohibited the distribution of handbills and solicitations on fairgrounds, *Heffron v. International Society for Krishna Consciousness*, 452 U.S. 640 (1981).

State neutrality and rigid enforcement of the secular regulation principle, however, has been criticized for being too harsh, taking little or no account of the impact of coercive laws on individuals' religious lives. As an alternative, or exception to strict state neutrality, the Court invented the "least drastic means test," when striking down a South Carolina law denying unemployment compensation to a Seventh Day Adventist who refused to work on the Sabbath, in *Sherbert v. Verner* (1963) (see excerpt below). On this test, the Court considers whether states might achieve their objectives through other, less drastic means.

In *Wisconsin v. Yoder* (1972) (see excerpt below), Chief Justice Burger advanced his *accommodationist* approach in carving out an exception for the Amish from compulsory school attendance beyond the eighth grade. When accommodating free exercise claims the Court basically balances those claims against competing governmental interests, taking into consideration the nature of the regulation, the centrality of a religious belief, and the equality in treatment of religion. In *Cruz v. Beto*, 405 U.S. 319 (1972), for instance, the Court ruled that where Catholic, Protestant, and Jewish prison inmates were allowed to hold religious services, the state could not deny the same right of free exercise to Buddhists. By contrast, in *O'Lone v. Shabazz*, 482 U.S. 342 (1987), a bare majority of the Rehnquist Court held that Islamic prisoners could be denied the right to attend services in jail for security reasons.

The Court, however, has also held that governmental interests may simply outweigh free exercise claims, despite their coercive effect on religious beliefs and practices. In *Goldman v. Weinberger*, 475 U.S. 503 (1986), the justices (6–3) upheld the air force's prohibition of wearing yarmulkes by Orthodox Jewish officers. The following year, Congress passed a law permitting members of the military to wear religious apparel indoors, while on duty, so long as it does not interfere with their military duties and is "neat and conservative." In *Lyng v. Northwest Indian Cemetery Protective Association*, 485 U.S. 439 (1988), the Court upheld the forest service's permitting road constructions and timber harvests in areas of the national forest that were traditionally used for religious purposes by Indian tribes.

When confronted with free exercise claims, the Court may not be able to avoid the issue of what is religion. And who should define *religious beliefs*—the government, the Court, or the individual? When upholding a congressional statute banning and punishing polygamy, which Mormons practiced as a religious belief, in *Reynolds v. United States*, 98 U.S. 145 (1879), Chief Justice Waite observed, "The word 'religion' is not defined in the Constitution. We must go elsewhere, therefore, to ascertain its meaning, and nowhere more appropriately, we think, than to the history of the times in the midst of which the provision was adopted." After surveying the founding period, Waite found no religious support for the practice of polygamy (the Church of Jesus Christ of Latter-day Saints—the Mormon Church—was not established until the late nineteenth century) and found support for the statute, which had the secular purpose of enforcing the standards of "civilized society," in Jefferson's "Bill for Establishing Religious Freedom," allowing government to "interfere when [religious] principles break out into overt acts against peace and good order." But dissenting in *Everson*, Justice Rutledge cautioned against the Court's trying to define religion for free exercise purposes, while refusing to do so under the establishment clause:

> "Religion" appears only once in the [First] Amendment. But the word governs two prohibitions and governs them alike. It does not have two meanings, one narrow to forbid "an establishment" and another, much broader, for securing "the free exercise thereof." "Thereof" brings down "religion" with its entire and exact con-

tent, no more and no less, from the first into the second guaranty, so that Congress and now the states are broadly restricted concerning the one as they are regarding the other.

The Court, again, confronted the problem in *United States v. Ballard*, 322 U.S. 78 (1944), involving the prosecution of the leaders of the "I Am" religion for mail fraud. Guy Ballard, the founder of the religion, claimed to be the messenger of a Master Saint Germain and to have powers to cure diseases. Ballard's widow and son were charged with making claims about curing diseases, which they knew were false. But the Court held that at their trial the jury could not be allowed to determine the truth or falsity of the Ballards' claims; it could determine only whether the Ballards sincerely believed their claims, or instead were deceitful and guilty of misrepresentations. "Men may believe what they cannot prove," Justice Douglas wrote, adding, "They may not be put to the proof of their religious doctrines or beliefs. . . . The First Amendment does not select any one group or any one type of religion for preferred treatment." The majority did not go far enough for dissenting Justice Jackson, who argued:

> In the first place, as a matter of either practice or philosophy I do not see how we can separate an issue as to what is believed from considerations as to what is believable. . . . In the second place, any inquiry into intellectual honesty in religion raises profound psychological problems. . . . And then I do not know what degree of skepticism or disbelief in a religious representation amounts to actionable fraud.

In a dissenting opinion, Chief Justice Stone found it hard "to say that freedom of thought and worship includes freedom to procure money by making knowingly false statements about one's religious experiences" and explained that

> if it were shown that a defendant in this case had asserted as a part of the alleged fraudulent scheme, that he had physically shaken hands with St. Germain in San Francisco on a day named, or that, as the indictment here alleges, by the exertion of his spiritual power he "had in fact cured . . . hundreds of persons afflicted with diseases and ailments," I should not doubt that it would be open to the Government to submit to the jury proof that he had never been in San Francisco and that no such cures had ever been effected.

Stone and Jackson agreed that the Ballards could have been prosecuted for misrepresenting "that funds are being used to build a church when in fact they are being used for personal purposes."

While the government may prosecute religious leaders and their followers for crimes such as tax evasion, fraud, misrepresentations, and child abuse, the Court has suggested that it may be futile for the government to try to define religion for free exercise purposes. At least the Court gave an expansive reading to religion in the conscientious objector cases arising from a federal statute allowing exemptions from military service for an individual "who, by reason of religious training or belief, is conscientiously opposed to participation in war in any form." *Religious training and belief* was defined by Congress as "an individual's belief in relation to a Supreme Being involving duties superior to those arising from any human relation, but . . . not any essentially political, sociological, or philosophical views or a merely personal moral code." When hearing an appeal of three men who did not subscribe to a traditional religion but claimed not to be "irreligious or aetheists," in *United States v. Seeger*, 380 U.S. 163 (1965), the Court unanimously held that they were entitled to conscientious exemption because the test of one's religious belief "in relation to a Supreme Being" is "whether a given belief that is sincere and meaningful occupies a place in the life of its possessor parallel to that filled by the orthodox belief in God of one who clearly qualifies for the exemption. Where such beliefs have parallel positions in the lives of their respective holders we cannot say that one is 'in relation to a Supreme Being' and the other is not." Congress responded to *Seeger* by deleting the language "in relation to a Supreme Being." But the Court went even further in *Welsh v. United States*, 398 U.S. 333 (1970), holding that an individual who denied that his beliefs opposing war were religious, nonetheless, was entitled to conscientious objector status because his ethical and moral beliefs were parallel to and just as strong as religious convictions.

Finally, the Court applied *Sherbert*'s balancing test in several cases to prohibit the denial of unemployment compensation to individuals who lost their jobs because of their religious beliefs. See THE DEVELOPMENT OF LAW box in this section. However, in *Employment Division, Department of Human Resources of Oregon v. Smith* (1990) (see excerpt below), Justice Scalia rejected further application of *Sherbert*'s balancing test and its requirement that states show a compelling interest in regulations to justify overriding free exercise claims.

The ruling in *Oregon v. Smith* was sharply criticized from within and without the Court. Moreover, compare *Smith* with the so-called animal sacrifice case, *Church of the Lukumi Babalu Aye v. City of Hialeah*, 508 U.S. 520 (1993) (excerpted below), in which the Court unanimously rejected the City of Hialeah's arguments that its ban on ritual animal sacrifices was a "generally applicable law" that satisfied the analysis and test set forth in *Smith*; instead the Court held that the ordinances targeted a specific religion and violated the principle of religious nondiscrimination. Subsequently, Congress sought to override *Smith* and to reestablish the *Sherbert v. Verner* test with the enactment of the Religious Freedom Restoration Act of 1993. But, when that act was challenged in *City of Boerne v. Flores*, 521 U.S. 507 (1997) (excerpted below), the Court ruled that Congress did not have the power, under the Fourteenth Amendment's enforcement power in Section 5, to enforce constitutional rights broader than previously interpreted by the Court.

In response to the invalidation of the Religious Freedom Restoration Act (RFRA) of 1993 in *City of Boerne v. Flores*, Congress enacted the Religious Land Use and Institutionalized Persons Act (RLUIPA) of 2000. Congress passed the narrower RLUIPA based on its powers under the spending and commerce clauses. The RLUIPA specifies that state and local governments that receive federal funding for services may not "impose a substantial burden on the religious exercise of a person residing in or confined to an institution," unless the burden is necessary to achieving a "compelling" governmental purpose. When inmates in Ohio prisons were denied special services for their observance of rituals associated with Wicca, Satanism, Asatru, and the Church of Jesus Christ Christian, a clinical legal program at the Ohio State University Moritz College of Law took up their representation and sued the state for violating the RLUIPA. The state countered that the RLUIPA violated the (dis)establishment clause, would compromise prison security, and would prove costly. In *Cutter v. Wilkinson*, 544 U.S. 709 (2005), the Court unanimously upheld the act and Congress's power to enact the law under its spending and commerce clauses.

In addition, although in *City of Boerne v. Flores* the Court ruled that the RFRA's application to state laws exceeded Congress's power, in *Gonzales v. O Centro Espirita Beneficente Uniao do Vegetal*, 546 U.S. 418 (2006), the Roberts Court unanimously held that the RFRA permitted federal courts to make exceptions for religious minorities on a case-by-case basis from generally applicable federal laws on the use of drugs, if used in a "sincere exercise of religion." Writing for the Court, Chief Justice Roberts noted that peyote, a hallucinogen, had been made an exception to the Controlled Substances Act (CSA) for use by Native Americans for thirty-five years. And in permitting the importation of *hoasca* (pronounced "wass-ca") for use by a small sect originating in the Amazon Rainforest, observed, "If such use is permitted . . . for hundreds of thousands of Native Americans practicing their faith, it is difficult to see how those same findings alone can preclude any consideration of a similar exception for the 130 or so American members of the [O Centro Espirita Beneficente Uniao do Vegetal] who want to practice theirs." In so holding, Chief Justice Roberts rejected the Bush administration's arguments that it had compelling governmental interests in forbidding the importation of *hoasca* based on (1) protecting the health of users, (2) preventing the diversion of the drug to recreational users, and (3) complying with the 1971 U.N. Convention on Psychotropic Substances.

In sum, in several recent rulings the Court has attempted to clarify the contours of the free exercise clause and to address the tensions between it and the (dis)establishment clause; the Court has also moved toward a more *nonpreferentialist* interpretation of the (dis)establishment clause and *accommodation* of religion with respect to religious minorities and generally applicable laws. On the one hand, under *Oregon v. Smith*, religious minorities are not protected under the free exercise clause from otherwise neutral and generally applicable laws that indirectly burden their religious faith and practices. Yet, on the other hand, under *Church of the Lukumi Babalu Aye v. City Hialeah*, the free exercise clause protects religious minorities from overt discrimination and bars legislation that specifically targets them with penalties for their religious practices. *Locke v. Davey* (2004) (excerpted below) illustrated the dilemma in holding that the free exercise clause does not override state constitutional provisions barring governmental aid to religion and compel such support for religion, even though such aid would be permissible under the Court's interpretation of the (dis)establishment clause. In other words, the free exercise clause does not exempt religious minorities from neutral and generally applicable laws that impose indirect burdens, but only forbids direct religious discrimination, while providing no basis for compelling governmental support for religion even when such support has been allowed over (dis)establishment clause objections in cases like *Witters v. Washington Department of Services for the Blind*, 474 U.S. 481 (1986); and *Zobrest v. Catalina Foothills School District* (1993) and (excerpted in Section A of this chapter), *Zelman v. Simmons-Harris* (2002).

A majority of the Roberts Court underscored their more expansive reading of the protection for freedom of religion under both the (dis)establishment and free exercise clauses in *Trinity Lutheran Church of Columbia, Inc. v. Comer* (2017) (excerpted below). Writing for the Court, Chief Justice Roberts distinguished *Locke v. Davey* in ruling that the denial of a grant to a religious organization for playground resurfacing violated the free exercise clause. *Locke* was distinguished on the ground that the state of Washington offered a scholarship to students in religious and non-religious schools alike—but recipients could not use the funds to pursue a degree in devotional theology. The Court argued that in the *Trinity* case, the student would have to choose between their religious beliefs and receiving a government benefit. But in *Locke,* the student was denied support because of what he proposed to do, rather than because of who he was. The chief justice, however, emphasized the narrowness of the ruling in footnote 3, stating: "This case involves express discrimination based on religious identity . . . . We do not address religious uses of funding or other forms of discrimination." Concurring Justices Thomas and Gorsuch would have more broadly construed the free exercise clause and refused to join footnote 3. In particular, Justice Gorsuch deemed the distinction between *status* (religious activity) and *use* (nonreligious activity) in determining permissible public expenditures to be a distinction without a difference. Justices Ginsburg and Sotomayor dissented.

Notably, after a bare majority of the Roberts Court upheld, in *National Federation of Independent Business v. Sebelius*, 567 U.S. 519 (2012) (excerpted in Vol. 1, Ch. 6), the main provisions of President Obama's signature piece of legislation—the Patient Protection and Affordable Care Act (ACA) of 2010 (otherwise known as "Obamacare")—conservatives, Catholics, and Evangelical Christians maintained their opposition, specifically to its requirement that heath care programs include coverage for contraception and abortion. As a result, when implementing the law the Obama administration exempted religious groups and businesses from the contraceptive coverage provisions. Still, conservatives and some Evangelical Christians continued to oppose the law's requirement that employers provide health-insurance coverage for contraception—such as IUDs and morning-after pills—because they contend that there is no difference between certain kinds of contraception and abortion. In particular, the Becket Fund for Religious Liberty spearheaded a challenge to the law based on the RFRA. The Evangelical owners of Hobby Lobby Stores, a multimillion dollar for-profit corporation with over 17,000 employees in some 600 arts and crafts stores, joined forces with the Becket Fund in challenging the law because of their religious objections. At issue was whether a for-profit corporation may be exempted from the ACA's requirements for contraceptive coverage because of the guarantees for religious freedom under the RFRA.

In a bitter 5–4 decision in *Burwell v. Hobby Lobby Stores, Inc.*, 134 U.S. 2751 (2014), Justice Alito held that the RFRA's religious freedom exemptions apply to "closely held for-profit corporations," like Hobby Lobby Stores, and they are exempt from providing employees with contraceptive coverage under the ACA. Justice Alito underscored in a 49-page opinion that the ruling did not apply to large corporations not controlled by a family or small group with religious objections to contraceptives and abortion. Nor did the ruling, Justice Alito emphasized, apply to health care coverage for blood transfusions, vaccinations, or other medical procedures objected to on religious grounds. But Justice Ginsburg's 35-page dissent—joined by Justices Breyer, Sotomayor, and

Kagan—countered that the Roberts Court's bare majority had indeed rendered a "decision of startling breadth" in (1) acknowledging that corporations, like individuals, may claim religious exemption from regulations and (2) permitting employers to deny women certain health care benefits because of a "closely held corporation's" religious objections. Although the ruling in *Hobby Lobby Stores* was only a statutory (not a constitutional) decision, it is certain to invite further litigation.

The Roberts Court also considered the application of another statute bearing on religious freedom in *Holt v. Hobbs*, 574 U.S. 352 (2015). After the Court struck down portions of the RFRA in *City of Bourne v. Flores* (1997) (excerpted below), Congress enacted the Religious Land Use and Institutional Persons Act of 2000 (RLUIPA), which provides that "No government shall impose a substantial burden on the religious exercise" of an institutionalized person without demonstrating that its restriction "is the least restrictive means of furthering [a] compelling governmental interest." Aka Muhammad Holt, a devout Muslim serving a sentence in an Arkansas prison, claimed that this provision along with the First Amendment free exercise clause was violated when correction officials refused to let him grow a half-inch beard in accord with his religious beliefs. Avoiding the constitutional claim and reaching only the RLUIPA claim, Justice Alito wrote for a unanimous court to uphold Holt's claim and reject the government's asserted interests—in maintaining security and preventing contraband in the prison—as "underinclusive" and "not the least restrictive means" of achieving its goals. Justice Alito noted, for example, that the prison's policy permitted inmates with skin conditions to grow four-inch beards, and there was no limitation on the length of hair on the head. In short, the prison could advance its interests simply by checking a half-inch beard for weapons and contraband, instead of altogether prohibiting such beards.

Finally, a majority of the Roberts Court failed to come together to address the First Amendment free speech and religious exercise claims of a baker who refused to make a wedding cake for a same-sex couple because of religious convictions, and who was found to run afoul of a state antidiscrimination law, in *Masterpiece Cakeshop v. Colorado Civil Rights Commission* (2018) (excerpted in Ch. 12). Writing for the majority, Justice Kennedy reversed the state court's decision and remanded the case for reconsideration because the Colorado Civil Rights Commission had not considered Masterpiece Cakeshop's claims with religious neutrality. Justices Kagan, Gorsuch, and Thomas issued concurring opinions; Justice Ginsburg, joined by Justice Sotomayor, dissented.

■ THE DEVELOPMENT OF LAW

Major Rulings Denying Free Exercise Claims

CASE	VOTE	RULING
Reynolds v. United States, 98 U.S. 145 (1878)	9–0	Upheld a congressional statute banning polygamy over the religious objections of Mormons.
Hamilton v. Regents of the University of California, 293 U.S. 245 (1934)	9–0	Upheld compulsory courses in military science over the religious objections of religious students.
Minersville v. Gobitis, 310 U.S. 586 (1940)	8–1	Upheld compulsory flag salute over the objections of Jehovah's Witnesses.
Prince v. Massachusetts, 321 U.S. 158 (1944)	8–1	Upheld statute forbidding minors from selling newspapers on streets over the objections of Jehovah's Witnesses.
McGowan v. Maryland, 366 U.S. 420 (1961); *Braunfeld v. Brown,* 366 U.S. 599 (1961)	6–3 7–2	Upheld Sunday closing laws over the objections of Orthodox Jews who recognize Saturday as the Sabbath.
Garber v. Kansas, 389 U.S. 51 (1967)	6–3	Rejected Amish claim of a right to refuse to send children to public schools.
Gillette v. United States and *Negre v. Larsen,* 401 U.S. 437 (1971)	8–1	Denied conscientious objection status to those opposing certain wars and "unjust" wars.
Heffron v. International Society for Krishna Consciousness, 452 U.S. 640 (1981)	5–4	Upheld law banning sales and solicitations at fairgrounds by a religious group.

(continues)

■ THE DEVELOPMENT OF LAW
Major Rulings Denying Free Exercise Claims (continued)

CASE	VOTE	RULING
United States v. Lee, 455 U.S. 252 (1982)	8–0	Amish employers must pay social security taxes, even though Congress exempted self-employed Amish.
Bob Jones University and Goldsboro Christian School v. United States, 461 U.S. 574 (1983)	8–1	Upheld IRS's withdrawing of tax-exempt status for educational institutions that discriminate racially.
Tony and Susan Alamo Foundation v. Secretary of Labor, 471 U.S. 290 (1985)	9–0	Religious organizations must comply with federal minimum wage laws.
Goldman v. Weinberger, 475 U.S. 503 (1986)	5–4	Orthodox Jewish rabbi and air force captain may not wear yarmulke contrary to military dress code.
Bowen v. Roy, 476 U.S. 693 (1986)	8–1	Government may use social security numbers despite religious objections.
O'Lone v. Shabazz, 482 U.S. 342 (1987)	5–4	For security reasons, Islamic prisoners may be denied the right to attend religious services.
Lyng v. Northwest Indian Cemetery Protective Association, 485 U.S. 439 (1988)	5–3	With Scalia not participating, Court held that the forest service may permit road construction and timber har-

vesting in areas of national parks traditionally used for religious purposes by Indian tribes.

Hernandez v. Commissioner of Internal Revenue, 490 U.S. 680 (1989)	5–2	Upheld IRS decision that fixed donations to Church of Scientology by members are not tax-deductible contributions.
Jimmy Swaggart Ministries v. Board of Equalization of California, 493 U.S. 378 (1990)	9–0	Upheld California's 6 percent sales tax as applied to sales of religious materials sold by Jimmy Swaggart Ministries

at "evangelistic crusades" in the state and through mail-order sales to state residents.

CASE	VOTE	RULING
Employment Division, Department of Human Resources of Oregon v. Smith, 494 U.S. 872 (1990)	6–3	Held that the free exercise clause does not prohibit the application of Oregon's drug laws to the ceremonial use of peyote by members of the

Native American Church and that members of the church could be denied unemployment compensation after they were fired from their jobs as drug-rehabilitation counselors because of their ceremonial use of peyote.

Minnesota v. Hershberger, 495 U.S. 901 (1990)	7–2	Vacated a decision of the Minnesota Supreme Court that exempted the Amish from highway safety laws.
City of Boerne v. Flores, 521 U.S. 507 (1997)	6–3	Writing for the Court, Justice Kennedy invalidated the Religious Freedom Restoration Act of 1993,

which sought to reestablish the test, set forth in *Sherbert v. Verner*, 374 U.S. 398 (1963), for balancing claims to religious freedom against governmental interests in generally applicable laws, which the Court discarded in *Employment Division, Dept. of Human Resources of Oregon v. Smith*, 494 U.S. 872 (1990). Justices O'Connor, Souter, and Breyer dissented.

SELECTED BIBLIOGRAPHY

Brown, Steven P. *Trumping Religion: The New Christian Right, the Free Speech Clause, and the Courts.* Tuscaloosa: University of Alabama Press, 2002.

Epps, Garrett. *To an Unknown God: Religious Freedom on Trial.* New York: St. Martin's, 2001.

Long, Carolyn. *Religious Freedom and Indian Rights: The Case of Oregon v. Smith.* Lawrence: University of Kansas Press, 2000.

Manwaring, David. *Render unto Caesar: The Flag Salute Controversy.* Chicago: University of Chicago Press, 1962.

O'Brien, David M. *Animal Sacrifice and Religious Freedom: Church of Lukumi Babalu Aye, Inc. v. City of Hialeah.* Lawrence: University Press of Kansas, 2004.

Peters, Shawn Francis. *Judging Jehovah's Witnesses: Religious Persecution and the Dawn of the Rights Revolution.* Lawrence: University of Kansas Press, 2000.

————. *The Yoder Case.* Lawrence: University Press of Kansas, 2003.

Smith, Steven. *Foreordained Failure: The Quest for a Constitutional Principle of Religious Freedom.* New York: Oxford University Press, 1995.

Sherbert v. Verner

374 U.S. 398, 83 S.Ct. 1790 (1963)

In his opinion announcing the decision of the Court, Justice Brennan discusses the facts in this case, involving a claim that the denial of unemployment benefits to an individual who refused to work on her Sabbath violated the free exercise clause.

The Court's decision was 7–2, and the majority's opinion was announced by Justice Brennan. Concurrences were by Justices Douglas and Stewart and dissent was by Justice Harlan, who was joined by Justice White.

■ ■ ■

☐ *Justice BRENNAN delivered the opinion of the Court.*

Appellant, a member of the Seventh-day Adventist Church was discharged by her South Carolina employer because she would not work on Saturday, the Sabbath Day of her faith. When she was unable to obtain other employment because from conscientious scruples she would not take Saturday work, she filed a claim for unemployment compensation benefits under the South Carolina Unemployment Compensation Act. . . .

The appellee Employment Security Commission, in administrative proceedings under the statute, found that appellant's restriction upon her availability for Saturday work brought her within the provision disqualifying for benefits insured workers who fail, without good cause, to accept "suitable work when offered . . . by the employment office or the employer. . . ." The Commission's finding was sustained by the Court of Common Pleas for Spartanburg County. That court's judgment was in turn affirmed by the South Carolina Supreme Court, which rejected appellant's contention that, as applied to her, the disqualifying provisions of the South Carolina statute abridged her right to the free exercise of her religion secured under the Free Exercise Clause of the First Amendment through the Fourteenth Amendment. . . . We reverse the judgment of the South Carolina Supreme Court and remand for further proceedings not inconsistent with this opinion. . . .

We turn first to the question whether the disqualification for benefits imposes any burden on the free exercise of appellant's religion. We think it is clear that it does. In a sense the consequences of such a disqualification to religious principles and practices may be only an indirect result of welfare legislation within the State's general competence to enact; it is true that no criminal sanctions directly compel appellant to work a six-day week. But this is only the beginning, not the end, of our inquiry. For "[i]f the purpose or effect of a law is to impede the observance of one or all religions or is to discriminate invidiously between religions, that law is constitutionally invalid even though the burden may be characterized as being only indirect." *Braunfeld v. Brown.* Here not only is it apparent that appellant's declared in eligibility for benefits derives solely from the practice of her religion, but the pressure upon her to forego that practice is unmistakable. The ruling forces her to choose between following the precepts of her religion and forfeiting benefits, on the one hand, and abandoning one of the precepts of her religion in order to accept work, on the other hand. Governmental imposition of such a choice puts the same kind of burden upon the free exercise of religion as would a fine imposed against appellant for her Saturday worship.

Nor may the South Carolina court's construction of the statute be saved from constitutional infirmity on the ground that unemployment compensation benefits are not appellant's "right" but merely a "privilege." It is too late in the day to doubt that the liberties of religion and expression may be infringed by the denial of or placing of conditions upon a benefit or privilege. . . .

- III

We must next consider whether some compelling state interest enforced in the eligibility provisions of the South Carolina statute justifies the substantial infringement of appellant's First Amendment right. It is basic that no showing merely of a rational relationship to some colorable state interest would suffice; in this highly sensitive constitutional area, "[o]nly the gravest abuses, endangering paramount interests, give occasion for permissible limitation," *Thomas v. Collins,* 323 U.S. 516 [1945]. No such abuse or danger has been advanced in the present case. The appellees suggest no more than a possibility that the filing of fraudulent claims by unscrupulous claimants feigning religious objections to Saturday work might not only dilute the unemployment compensation fund but also hinder the scheduling by employers of necessary Saturday work. But that possibility is not apposite here because no such objection appears to have been made before the South Carolina Supreme Court, and we are unwilling to assess the importance of an asserted state interest without the views of the state court. Nor, if the contention had been made below, would the record appear to sustain it. . . . For even if the possibility of spurious claims did threaten to dilute the fund and disrupt the scheduling of work, it would plainly be incumbent upon the appellees to demonstrate that no alternative forms of regulation would combat such abuses without infringing First Amendment rights.

In these respects, then, the state interest asserted in the present case is wholly dissimilar to the interests which were found to justify the less direct burden upon religious practices in *Braunfeld v. Brown,* [366 U.S. 599 (1961)]. The Court recognized that the Sunday closing law which that decision sustained undoubtedly served "to make the practice of [the Orthodox Jewish merchants'] religious beliefs more expensive." But the statute was nevertheless saved by a countervailing factor which finds no equivalent in the instant case—a strong state interest in providing one uniform day of rest for all workers. That secular objective could be achieved, the Court found, only by declaring Sunday to be that day of rest. Requiring exemptions for Sabbatarians, while theoretically possible, appeared to present an administrative problem of such magnitude, or to afford the exempted class so great a competitive advantage, that such a requirement would have rendered the entire statutory scheme unworkable. In the present case no such justifications underlie the determination of the state court that appellant's religion makes her ineligible to receive benefits.

■ IV

In holding as we do, plainly we are not fostering the "establishment" of the Seventh-day Adventist religion in South Carolina, for the extension of unemployment benefits to Sabbatarians in common with Sunday worshippers reflects nothing more than the governmental obligation of neutrality in the face of religious differences, and does not represent that involvement of religious with secular institutions which it is the object of the Establishment Clause to forestall. See School District of *Abington Township v. Schempp*, 374 U.S. 203 [(1963)]. Nor does the recognition of the appellant's right to unemployment benefits under the state statute serve to abridge any other person's religious liberties. Nor do we, by our decision today, declare the existence of a constitutional right to unemployment benefits on the part of all persons whose religious convictions are the cause of their unemployment. This is not a case in which an employee's religious convictions serve to make him a nonproductive member of society. Finally, nothing we say today constrains the States to adopt any particular form or scheme of unemployment compensation. Our holding today is only that South Carolina may not constitutionally apply the eligibility provisions so as to constrain a worker to abandon his religious convictions respecting the day of rest.

☐ *Justice HARLAN with whom Justice WHITE joins, dissenting.*

In the present case all that the state court has done is to apply . . . accepted principles. Since virtually all of the mills in the Spartanburg area were operating on a six-day week, the appellant was "unavailable for work," and thus ineligible for benefits, when personal considerations prevented her from accepting employment on a full-time basis in the industry and locality in which she had worked. The fact that these personal considerations sprang from her religious convictions was wholly without relevance to the state court's application of the law. Thus in no proper sense can it be said that the State discriminated against the appellant on the basis of her religious beliefs or that she was denied benefits *because* she was a Seventh-day Adventist. She was denied benefits just as any other claimant would be denied benefits who was not "available for work" for personal reasons.

With this background, this Court's decision comes into clearer focus. What the Court is holding is that if the State chooses to condition unemployment compensation on the applicant's availability for work, it is constitutionally compelled to *carve out an exception*—and to provide benefits—for those whose unavailability is due to their religious convictions. Such a holding has particular significance in two respects.

First. Despite the Court's protestations to the contrary, the decision necessarily overrules *Braunfeld v. Brown*, which held that it did not offend the "Free Exercise" Clause of the Constitution for a State to forbid a Sabbatarian to do business on Sunday. The secular purpose of the statute before us today is even clearer than that involved in *Braunfeld*. And just as in *Braunfeld*—where exceptions to the Sunday closing laws for Sabbatarians would have been inconsistent with the purpose to achieve a uniform day of rest and would have required case-by-case inquiry into religious beliefs—so here, an exception to the rules of eligibility based on religious convictions would necessitate judicial examination of those convictions and would be at odds with the limited purpose of the statute to smooth out the economy during periods of industrial instability. Finally, the indirect financial burden of the present law is far less than that involved in *Braunfeld*. . . .

Second. The implications of the present decision are far more troublesome than its apparently narrow dimensions would indicate at first glance. The meaning of today's holding, as already noted, is that the State must furnish unemployment benefits to one who is unavailable for work if the unavailability stems from the exercise of religious convictions. The State, in other words, must *single out* for financial assistance those whose behavior is religiously motivated, even though it denies such assistance to others whose identical behavior (in this case, inability to work no Saturdays) is not religiously motivated.

It has been suggested that such singling out of religious conduct for special treatment may violate the constitutional limitations on state action. My

---

■ THE DEVELOPMENT OF LAW

Major Rulings Upholding Free Exercise Claims

CASE	VOTE	RULING
Cantwell v. Connecticut, 310 U.S. 296 (1940)	9–0	Struck down permit requirement for soliciting funds on public streets challenged by Jehovah's Witnesses.
Murdock v. Commonwealth of Pennsylvania, 319 U.S. 105 (1943)	5–4	Struck down license tax on canvassing and soliciting as applied to Jehovah's Witnesses.
Martin v. Struthers, 319 U.S. 141 (1943)	5–4	Overturned ordinance forbidding door-to-door solicitations as applied to Jehovah's Witnesses.

(continues)

■ THE DEVELOPMENT OF LAW
Major Rulings Upholding Free Exercise Claims (continued)

CASE	VOTE	RULING
Douglas v. City of Jeanette, 319 U.S. 157 (1943)	9–0	After citizens' complaints, police may not stop Jehovah's Witnesses from proselytizing on Sundays.
West Virginia State Board of Education v. Barnette, 319 U.S. 624 (1943)	6–3	Overturned compulsory flag salute statute.
Jamison v. Texas, 318 U.S. 413 (1943)	8–0	Overturned statute barring handbill distributions as related to religious activities.
United States v. Ballard, 322 U.S. 78 (1944)	5–4	The truth of religious beliefs may not be judged by jury at trials.
Girouard v. United States, 328 U.S. 61 (1946)	5–3	Naturalization may not be denied to conscientious objectors.
Marsh v. Alabama, 326 U.S. 501 (1946)	5–3	Distribution of religious literature cannot be banned in private company town.
Niemotko v. Maryland, 340 U.S. 268 (1951)	9–0	Use of public parks may not be denied to Jehovah's Witnesses.
Torcaso v. Watkins, 367 U.S. 488 (1961)	9–0	Struck down required oath declaring belief in God for public office.
Sherbert v. Verner, 374 U.S. 398 (1963)	7–2	Overturned the denial of unemployment compensation to a Seventh Day

Adventist who was fired for refusing to work on the Sabbath.

■ THE DEVELOPMENT OF LAW
Major Rulings Upholding Free Exercise Claims (continued)

CASE	VOTE	RULING
United States v. Seeger, 380 U.S. 163 (1965)	9–0	Broadly interpreted religious training and belief in according conscientious objector status.
Wisconsin v. Yoder, 406 U.S. 205 (1972)	6–1	Amish are exempt from sending children to school beyond the eighth grade.

Wooley v. Maynard, 430 U.S. 705 (1977)   7–2 | Upheld claim of Jehovah's Witnesses that they could not be compelled to bare license plates reading Live Free or Die.

McDaniel v. Paty, 435 U.S. 618 (1978)   8–0 | Religious leaders may not be disqualified from serving as delegates to state constitutional conventions.

Thomas v. Review Board of Indiana Employment Security Division, 450 U.S. 707 (1981)   8–1 | State may not deny unemployment compensation to individual who terminated employment because of religious objection to working in the production of armaments.

Hobbie v. Unemployment Appeals Commission of Florida, 480 U.S. 136 (1987)   8–1 | Applied *Sherbert* in holding that denial of unemployment compensation benefits must withstand strict scrutiny and that it is immaterial that claimant had a religious conversion during course of employment. Chief Justice Rehnquist dissented.

Frazee v. Illinois Department of Employment Security, 489 U.S. 829 (1989)   9–0 | Held that denial of unemployment compensation to worker who refused to work on Sabbath violated the free exercise clause, even though refusal was not based on a religious sect's doctrines.

(continues)

■ THE DEVELOPMENT OF LAW
Major Rulings Upholding Free Exercise Claims (continued)

CASE	VOTE	RULING
Church of the Lukumi Babalu Aye v. City of Hialeah, 508 U.S. 520 (1993)	9–0	Struck down a ban on animal sacrifice as impermissibly religiously motivated and infringing on the free exercise of religion.
Watchtower Bible & Tract Society of New York, Inc. v. Village of Stratton, 536 U.S. 150 (2002)	8–1	Reaffirming a line of rulings, from *Murdock v. Commonwealth of Pennsylvania,* 319 U.S. 105 (1943),

extending First Amendment to the door-to-door canvassing of Jehovah's Witnesses, the Court struck down an ordinance requiring a permit for solicitations on private property. Chief Justice Rehnquist dissented.

---

own view, however, is that at least under the circumstances of this case it would be a permissible accommodation of religion for the State, if it *chose* to do so, to create an exception to its eligibility requirements for persons like the appellant. The constitutional obligation of "neutrality," see *School District of Abington Township v. Schempp,* is not so narrow a channel that the slightest deviation from an absolutely straight course leads to condemnation. . . .

The State violates its obligation of neutrality when, for example, it mandates a daily religious exercise in its public schools, with all the attendant pressures on the school children that such an exercise entails. See *Engel v. Vitale,* 370 U.S. 421 [(1962)]. *School District of Abington Township v. Schempp, supra.* But there is, I believe, enough flexibility in the Constitution to permit a legislative judgment accommodating an unemployment compensation law to the exercise of religious beliefs such as appellant's.

For very much the same reasons, however, I cannot subscribe to the conclusion that the State is constitutionally *compelled* to carve out an exception to its general rule of eligibility in the present case. Those situations in which the Constitution may require special treatment on account of religion are, in my view, few and far between, and this view is amply supported by the course of constitutional litigation in this area.

Wisconsin v. Yoder

406 U.S. 205, 92 S.Ct. 1527 (1972)

Jonas Yoder and Wallace Miller, members of the Old Order Amish religion, and Adin Yutzy, a member of the Conservative Amish Mennonite Church, were charged, tried, and convicted of violating the compulsory school-attendance law in Green County Court, Wisconsin, and fined $5 each. Under Wisconsin's compulsory school-attendance law, children were required to attend public or private school until reaching the age of sixteen. Yoder, Miller, and Yutzy, however, refused to send their children, ages fourteen and fifteen, to public school after they completed the eighth grade. And when defending their actions, they claimed the compulsory-attendance law violated their free exercise of religion under the First and Fourteenth Amendments. A state appeals court affirmed their convictions, but the Wisconsin Supreme Court reversed and found that the application of the law denied the Amish's First Amendment rights. The state of Wisconsin appealed to the Supreme Court.

The Court's decision was six and one-half to one-half, and the majority's opinion was announced by Chief Justice Burger, with Justices Powell and Rehnquist not participating. The concurrence by Justice Stewart was joined by Justice Brennan. There was a separate opinion, in part dissenting, by Justice Douglas.

■ ■ ■

☐ *Chief Justice BURGER delivered the opinion of the Court.*

Formal high school education beyond the eighth grade is contrary to Amish beliefs, not only because it places Amish children in an environment hostile to Amish beliefs with increasing emphasis on competition in class work and sports and with pressure to conform to the styles, manners, and ways of the peer group, but also because it takes them away from their community, physically and emotionally, during the crucial and formative adolescent period of life. During this period, the children must acquire Amish attitudes favoring manual work and self-reliance and the specific skills needed to perform the adult role of an Amish farmer or housewife. They must learn to enjoy physical labor. Once a child has learned basic reading, writing, and elementary mathematics, these traits, skills, and attitudes admittedly fall within the category of those best learned through example and "doing" rather than in a classroom. And, at this time in life, the Amish child must also grow in his faith and his relationship to the Amish community if he is to be prepared to accept the heavy obligations imposed by adult baptism. . . .

The Amish do not object to elementary education through the first eight grades as a general proposition because they agree that their children must have basic skills in the "three R's" in order to read the Bible, to be good farmers and citizens, and to be able to deal with non-Amish people when necessary in the course of daily affairs. They view such a basic education as acceptable because it does not significantly expose their children to worldly values or interfere with their development in the Amish community during the crucial adolescent period. While Amish accept compulsory elementary education generally, wherever possible they have established their own elementary schools in many respects like the small local schools of the past. In the Amish belief higher learning tends to develop values they reject as influences that alienate man from God. . . .

There is no doubt as to the power of a State, having a high responsibility for education of its citizens, to impose reasonable regulations for the control and duration of basic education. . . .

[A] State's interest in universal education, however highly we rank it, is not totally free from a balancing process when it impinges on fundamental rights and interests, such as those specifically protected by the Free Exercise Clause of the First Amendment, and the traditional interest of parents with respect to the religious upbringing of their children. . . .

It follows that in order for Wisconsin to compel school attendance beyond the eighth grade against a claim that such attendance interferes with the practice of a legitimate religious belief, it must appear either that the State does not deny the free exercise of religious belief by its requirement, or that there is a state interest of sufficient magnitude to override the interest claiming protection under the Free Exercise Clause. . . .

We come then to the quality of the claims of the respondents concerning the alleged encroachment of Wisconsin's compulsory school-attendance statute on their rights and the rights of their children to the free exercise of the religious beliefs they and their forbears have adhered to for almost three centuries. In evaluating those claims we must be careful to determine whether the Amish religious faith and their mode of life are, as they claim, inseparable and interdependent. A way of life, however virtuous and admirable, may not be interposed as a barrier to reasonable state regulation of education if it is based on purely secular considerations; to have the protection of the Religion Clauses, the claims must be rooted in religious belief. Although a determination of what is a "religious" belief or practice entitled to constitutional protection may present a most delicate question, the very concept of ordered liberty precludes allowing every person to make his own standards on matters of conduct in which society as a whole has important interests. Thus, if the Amish asserted their claims because of their subjective evaluation and rejection of the contemporary secular values accepted by the majority, much as Thoreau rejected the social values of his time and isolated himself at Walden Pond, their claims would not rest on a religious basis. Thoreau's choice was philosophical and personal rather than religious, and such belief does not rise to the demands of the Religion Clauses.

Giving no weight to such secular considerations, however, we see that the record in this case abundantly supports the claim that the traditional way of life of the Amish is not merely a matter of personal preference, but one of deep religious conviction, shared by an organized group, and intimately related to daily living. . . .

We turn, then, to the State's broader contention that its interest in its system of compulsory education is so compelling that even the established religious practices of the Amish must give way. Where fundamental claims of religious freedom are at stake, however, we cannot accept such a sweeping claim; despite its admitted validity in the generality of cases, we must search-ingly examine the interests that the State seeks to promote by its requirement for compulsory education to age 16, and the impediment to those objectives that would flow from recognizing the claimed Amish exemption. . . .

The State advances two primary arguments in support of its system of compulsory education. It notes, as Thomas Jefferson pointed out early in our history, that some degree of education is necessary to prepare citizens to participate effectively and intelligently in our open political system if we are to preserve freedom and independence. Further, education prepares indi-viduals to be self-reliant and self-sufficient participants in society. We accept these propositions.

However, the evidence adduced by the Amish in this case is persua-sively to the effect that an additional one or two years of formal high school for Amish children in place of their long-established program of informal vocational education would do little to serve those interests. Respondents' experts testified at trial, without challenge, that the value of all education must be assessed in terms of its capacity to prepare the child for life. It is one thing to say that compulsory education for a year or two beyond the eighth grade may be necessary when its goal is the preparation of the child for life in modern society as the majority live, but it is quite another if the goal of education be viewed as the preparation of the child for life in the separated agrarian community that is the keystone of the Amish faith. . . .

Our holding in no way determines the proper resolution of possible competing interests of parents, children, and the State in an appropriate state court proceeding in which the power of the State is asserted on the theory that Amish parents are preventing their minor children from attending high school despite their expressed desires to the contrary. Recognition of the claim of the State in such a proceeding would, of course, call into question traditional concepts of parental control over the religious upbringing and education of their minor children recognized in this Court's past decisions. It is clear that such an intrusion by a State into family decisions in the area of religious training would give rise to grave questions of religious freedom. . . . On this record we neither reach nor decide those issues. . . .

For the reasons stated we hold, with the Supreme Court of Wisconsin, that the First and Fourteenth Amendments prevent the State from compelling respondents to cause their children to attend formal high school to age 16. . . .

☐ *Justice DOUGLAS, dissenting in part.*

Religion is an individual experience. It is not necessary, nor even appro-priate, for every Amish child to express his views on the subject in a prosecu-tion of a single adult. Crucial, however, are the views of the child whose parent is the subject of the suit. Frieda Yoder has in fact testified that her own religious views are opposed to high-school education. I therefore join the judgment of the Court as to respondent Jonas Yoder. But Frieda Yoder's views may not be those of Vernon Yutzy or Barbara Miller. I must dissent, therefore, as to respondents Adin Yutzy and Wallace Miller as their motion to dismiss also raised the question of their children's religious liberty. . . .

On this important and vital matter of education, I think the children should be entitled to be heard. While the parents, absent dissent, normally speak for the entire family, the education of the child is a matter on which the child will often have decided views. He may want to be a pianist or an astronaut or an ocean geographer. To do so he will have to break from the Amish tradition.

It is the future of the student, not the future of the parents, that is imperiled in today's decision. If a parent keeps his child out of school beyond the grade school, then the child will be forever barred from entry into the new and amazing world of diversity that we have today. The child may decide that that is the preferred course, or he may rebel. It is the student's judgment, not his parent's, that is essential if we are to give full meaning to what we have said about the Bill of Rights and of the right of students to be masters of their own destiny. If he is harnessed to the Amish way of life by those in authority over him and if his education is truncated, his entire life may be stunted and deformed. The child, therefore, should be given an opportunity to be heard before the State gives the exemption which we honor today.

Employment Division, Department of Human Resources of Oregon v. Smith
494 U.S. 872, 110 S.Ct. 1595 (1990)

Two Native Americans, Alfred Smith and Galen Black, were fired from their jobs with a private drug rehabilitation organization because they took peyote (an intoxicating drug produced from mescal cacti). Both were members of the Native American Church and ingested peyote for sacramental purposes in religious ceremonies. When they later applied for unemployment compensation, Oregon's Employment Division denied them benefits on the grounds that their discharge was for work-related "misconduct." A state appellate court reversed that decision, holding that the denial of benefits violated Smith's and Black's rights under the First Amendment free exercise clause. The state then appealed to the Oregon Supreme Court, which affirmed the lower court. It did so, however, on construing the purpose of the misconduct provision, under which Smith was denied benefits, to be one of preserving the financial integrity of the state's compensation fund and not that of enforcing the state's criminal laws against drug usage. Citing *Sherbert v. Verner* (1963) (see excerpt above), the Oregon Supreme Court concluded that Smith was entitled to unemployment benefits because the state's interest in the compensation fund did not outweigh the burden imposed on Smith's religious beliefs and practices.

In 1987, Oregon appealed the ruling of its state's supreme court to the U.S. Supreme Court, contending that its criminal laws against peyote consumption were relevant to balancing the state's interests in denying benefits and Smith's First Amendment claims. In *Employment Division, Department of Human Resources of Oregon v. Smith*, 485 U.S. 660 (1988) (*Smith I*), a majority of the Court agreed, when vacating the decision and remanding the case back to the Oregon Supreme Court. But when doing so, the Court noted that the state supreme court had not decided whether the sacramental use of peyote was in fact proscribed under state law. Until the state court ruled on that issue, the Supreme Court declined to address the question of "whether the practice is protected by the Federal Constitution." On remand, the Oregon Supreme Court held that its state laws made no exception for the sacramental use of peyote but interpreted the First Amendment to protect such usage and reaffirmed its previous ruling that Smith was entitled to unemployment benefits. The state, again, appealed to the U.S. Supreme Court, which granted *certiorari.*

The Court's decision was 6–3, and the majority's opinion was announced by Justice Scalia. Justice O'Connor concurred, agreeing with the majority's result but rejecting its reasoning and abandonment of *Sherbert*'s analysis. Justices Brennan and Marshall concurred in her reasoning but disagreed with her conclusion that Smith was not entitled to benefits. Justice Blackmun dissented and was joined by Justices Brennan and Marshall.

■ ■ ■

☐ *Justice SCALIA delivered the opinion of the Court.*

This case requires us to decide whether the Free Exercise Clause of the First Amendment permits the State of Oregon to include religiously inspired peyote use within the reach of its general criminal prohibition on use of that drug, and thus permits the State to deny unemployment benefits to persons dismissed from their jobs because of such religiously inspired use. . . .

Respondents' claim for relief rests on our decisions in *Sherbert v. Verner,* [374 U.S. 398 (1963)]; *Thomas v. Review Board, Indiana Employment Security Div.,* [450 U.S. 707 (1981)]; and *Hobbie v. Unemployment Appeals Comm'n of Florida,* 480 U.S. 136 (1987), in which we held that a State could not condition the availability of unemployment insurance on an individual's willingness to forgo conduct required by his religion. As we observed in *Smith I,* however, the conduct at issue in those cases was not prohibited by law. We held that distinction to be critical, for "if Oregon does prohibit the religious use of peyote, and if that prohibition is consistent with the Federal Constitution, there is no federal right to engage in that conduct in Oregon," and "the State is free to withhold unemployment compensation from respondents for engaging in work-related misconduct, despite its religious motivation." Now that the Oregon Supreme Court has confirmed that Oregon does prohibit the religious use of peyote, we proceed to consider whether that prohibition is permissible under the Free Exercise Clause. . . .

The free exercise of religion means, first and foremost, the right to believe and profess whatever religious doctrine one desires. Thus, the First Amendment obviously excludes all "governmental regulation of religious *beliefs* as such." *Sherbert v. Verner, supra.* . . .

But the "exercise of religion" often involves not only belief and profession but the performance of (or abstention from) physical acts: assembling with others for a worship service, participating in sacramental use of bread and wine, proselytizing, abstaining from certain foods or certain modes of transportation. It would be true, we think (though no case of ours has involved the point), that a state would be "prohibiting the free exercise [of religion]" if it sought to ban such acts or abstentions only when they are engaged in for religious reasons, or only because of the religious belief that they display. It would doubtless be unconstitutional, for example, to ban the casting of "statues that are to be used for worship purposes," or to prohibit bowing down before a golden calf.

Respondents in the present case, however, seek to carry the meaning of "prohibiting the free exercise [of religion]" one large step further. They contend that their religious motivation for using peyote places them beyond the reach of a criminal law that is not specifically directed at their religious practice, and that is concededly constitutional as applied to those who use the drug for other reasons. They assert, in other words, that "prohibiting the free exercise [of religion]" includes requiring any individual to observe a generally applicable law that requires (or forbids) the performance of an act that his religious belief forbids (or requires). As a textual matter, we do not think the words must be given that meaning. It is no more necessary to regard the collection of a general tax, for example, as "prohibiting the free exercise [of religion]" by those citizens who believe support of organized government to be sinful, than it is to regard the same tax as "abridging the freedom . . . of the press" of those publishing companies that must pay the tax as a condition of staying in business. It is a permissible reading of the text, in the one case as in the other, to say that if prohibiting the exercise of religion (or burdening the activity of printing) is not the object of the tax but merely the incidental effect of a generally applicable and otherwise valid provision, the First Amendment has not been offended. . . .

Our decisions reveal that the latter reading is the correct one. We have never held that an individual's religious beliefs excuse him from compliance with an otherwise valid law prohibiting conduct that the State is free to regulate. [Citing *Minersville School District Bd. of Ed. v. Gobitis*, 310 U.S. 586 (1940), *Reynolds v. United States*, 98 U.S. 145 (1879), *Prince v. Massachusetts*, 321 U.S. 158 (1944), *Braunfeld v. Brown*, 366 U.S. 599 (1961), and *Gillette v. United States*, 410 U.S. 437 (1971).] . . .

The only decisions in which we have held that the First Amendment bars application of a neutral, generally applicable law to religiously motivated action have involved not the Free Exercise Clause alone, but the Free Exercise Clause in conjunction with other constitutional protections, such as freedom of speech and of the press, see *Cantwell v. Connecticut*, [310 U.S. 296 (1940)], (invalidating a licensing system for religious and charitable solicitations under which the administrator had discretion to deny a license to any cause he deemed nonreligious); *Murdock v. Pennsylvania*, 319 U.S. 105 (1943) (invalidating a flat tax on solicitation as applied to the dissemination of religious ideas); *Follett v. McCormick*, 321 U.S. 573 (1944) (same), or the right of parents, acknowledged in *Pierce v. Society of Sisters*, 268 U.S. 510 (1925), to direct the education of their children, see *Wisconsin v. Yoder*, 406 U.S. 208 (1972) (invalidating compulsory school-attendance laws as applied to Amish parents who refused on religious grounds to send their children to school). Some of our cases prohibiting compelled expression, decided exclusively upon free speech grounds, have also involved freedom of religion, cf. *Wooley v. Maynard*, 430 U.S. 705 (1977) (invalidating compelled display of a license plate slogan that offended individual religious beliefs); *West Virginia Board of Educa-*

tion v. Barnette, 319 U.S. 624 (1943) (invalidating compulsory flag salute statute challenged by religious objectors). . . .

The present case does not present such a hybrid situation, but a free exercise claim unconnected with any communicative activity or parental right. Respondents urge us to hold, quite simply, that when otherwise prohibitable conduct is accompanied by religious convictions, not only the convictions but the conduct itself must be free from governmental regulation. . . .

Respondents argue that even though exemption from generally applicable criminal laws need not automatically be extended to religiously motivated actors, at least the claim for a religious exemption must be evaluated under the balancing test set forth in *Sherbert v. Verner* (1963). Under the *Sherbert* test, governmental actions that substantially burden a religious practice must be justified by a compelling governmental interest. . . . Applying that test we have, on three occasions, invalidated state unemployment compensation rules that conditioned the availability of benefits upon an applicant's willingness to work under conditions forbidden by his religion. See *Sherbert v. Verner, supra; Thomas v. Review Board, Indiana Employment Div.* (1981); *Hobbie v. Unemployment Appeals Comm'n of Florida* (1987). We have never invalidated any governmental action on the basis of the *Sherbert* test except the denial of unemployment compensation. . . .

Even if we were inclined to breathe into *Sherbert* some life beyond the unemployment compensation field, we would not apply it to require exemptions from a generally applicable criminal law. . . .

We conclude today that the sounder approach, and the approach in accord with the vast majority of our precedents, is to hold the test inapplicable to such challenges. The government's ability to enforce generally applicable prohibitions of socially harmful conduct, like its ability to carry out other aspects of public policy, "cannot depend on measuring the effects of a governmental action on a religious objector's spiritual development." *Lyng* [*v. Northwest Indian Cemetery Association*, 485 U.S. 439 (1988)]. To make an individual's obligation to obey such a law contingent upon the law's coincidence with his religious beliefs, except where the State's interest is "compelling"—permitting him, by virtue of his beliefs, "to become a law unto himself,"*Reynolds v. United States*—contradicts both constitutional tradition and common sense.

The "compelling government interest" requirement seems benign, because it is familiar from other fields. But using it as the standard that must be met before the government may accord different treatment on the basis of race, see, e.g., *Palmore v. Sidoti*, 466 U.S. 429 (1984), or before the government may regulate the content of speech, see, e.g., *Sable Communications of California v. FCC*, 492 U.S. 115 (1989), is not remotely comparable to using it for the purpose asserted here. What it produces in those other fields—equality of treatment, and an unrestricted flow of contending speech—are constitutional norms; what it would produce here—a private right to ignore generally applicable laws—is a constitutional anomaly.

Nor is it possible to limit the impact of respondents' proposal by requiring a "compelling state interest" only when the conduct prohibited is "central" to the individual's religion. It is no more appropriate for judges to determine the "centrality" of religious beliefs before applying a "compelling interest" test in the free exercise field, than it would be for them to determine the "importance" of ideas before applying the "compelling interest" test in the free speech field. What principle of law or logic can be brought to bear to contradict a believer's assertion that a particular act is "central" to his personal faith? . . .

If the "compelling interest" test is to be applied at all, then, it must be applied across the board, to all actions thought to be religiously commanded. Moreover, if "compelling interest" really means what it says (and watering it down here would subvert its rigor in the other fields where it is applied), many laws will not meet the test. Any society adopting such a system would be courting anarchy, but that danger increases in direct proportion to the society's diversity of religious beliefs, and its determination to coerce or suppress none of them. . . .

Values that are protected against government interference through enshrinement in the Bill of Rights are not thereby banished from the political process. Just as a society that believes in the negative protection accorded to the press by the First Amendment is likely to enact laws that affirmatively foster the dissemination of the printed word, so also a society that believes in the negative protection accorded to religious belief can be expected to be solicitous of that value in its legislation as well. It is therefore not surprising that a number of States have made an exception to their drug laws for sacramental peyote use. But to say that a nondiscriminatory religious-practice exemption is permitted, or even that it is desirable, is not to say that it is constitutionally required, and that the appropriate occasions for its creation can be discerned by the courts. It may fairly be said that leaving accommodation to the political process will place at a relative disadvantage those religious practices that are not widely engaged in; but that unavoidable consequence of democratic government must be preferred to a system in which each conscience is a law unto itself or in which judges weigh the social importance of all laws against the centrality of all religious beliefs. . . .

Because respondents' ingestion of peyote was prohibited under Oregon law, and because that prohibition is constitutional, Oregon may, consistent with the Free Exercise Clause, deny respondents unemployment compensation when their dismissal results from use of the drug. The decision of the Oregon Supreme Court is accordingly reversed.

It is so ordered.

☐ *Justice O'CONNOR, with whom Justice BRENNAN, Justice MARSHALL, and Justice BLACKMUN join in parts I and II, concurring.*

Although I agree with the result the Court reaches in this case, I cannot join its opinion. In my view, today's holding dramatically departs from well-settled First Amendment jurisprudence, appears unnecessary to resolve the question presented, and is incompatible with our Nation's fundamental commitment to individual religious liberty. . . .

■ II

The Court today extracts from our long history of free exercise precedents the single categorical rule that "if prohibiting the exercise of religion . . . is . . . merely the incidental effect of a generally applicable and otherwise valid provision, the First Amendment has not been offended."

Indeed, the Court holds that where the law is a generally applicable criminal prohibition, our usual free exercise jurisprudence does not even apply. To reach this sweeping result, however, the Court must not only give a strained reading of the First Amendment but must also disregard our consistent application of free exercise doctrine to cases involving generally applicable regulations that burden religious conduct. . . .

The Court today . . . interprets the Clause to permit the government to prohibit, without justification, conduct mandated by an individual's religious beliefs, so long as that prohibition is generally applicable. But a law that prohibits certain conduct—conduct that happens to be an act of worship for someone—manifestly does prohibit that person's free exercise of his religion. A person who is barred from engaging in religiously motivated conduct is barred from freely exercising his religion. Moreover, that person is barred from freely exercising his religion regardless of whether the law prohibits the conduct only when engaged in for religious reasons, only by members of that religion, or by all persons. It is difficult to deny that a law that prohibits religiously motivated conduct, even if the law is generally applicable, does not at least implicate First Amendment concerns.

The Court responds that generally applicable laws are "one large step" removed from laws aimed at specific religious practices. The First Amendment, however, does not distinguish between laws that are generally applicable and laws that target particular religious practices. Indeed, few States would be so naive as to enact a law directly prohibiting or burdening a religious practice as such. Our free exercise cases have all concerned generally applicable laws that had the effect of significantly burdening a religious practice. If the First Amendment is to have any vitality, it ought not be construed to cover only the extreme and hypothetical situation in which a State directly targets a religious practice. . . .

To say that a person's right to free exercise has been burdened, of course, does not mean that he has an absolute right to engage in the conduct. Under our established First Amendment jurisprudence, we have recognized that the freedom to act, unlike the freedom to believe, cannot be absolute. Instead, we have respected both the First Amendment's express textual mandate and the governmental interest in regulation of conduct by requiring the Government to justify any substantial burden on religiously motivated conduct by a compelling state interest and by means narrowly tailored to achieve that interest. . . .

The compelling interest test effectuates the First Amendment's command that religious liberty is an independent liberty, that it occupies a preferred position, and that the Court will not permit encroachments upon this liberty, whether direct or indirect, unless required by clear and compelling governmental interests "of the highest order," [*Wisconsin v.*] *Yoder* [406 U.S. 208 (1972)]. . . .

In my view, however, the essence of a free exercise claim is relief from a burden imposed by government on religious practices or beliefs, whether the burden is imposed directly through laws that prohibit or compel specific religious practices, or indirectly through laws that, in effect, make abandonment of one's own religion or conformity to the religious beliefs of others the price of an equal place in the civil community. . . .

Indeed, we have never distinguished between cases in which a State conditions receipt of a benefit on conduct prohibited by religious beliefs and cases in which a State affirmatively prohibits such conduct. The *Sherbert* compelling interest test applies in both kinds of cases. . . .

Finally, the Court today suggests that the disfavoring of minority religions is an "unavoidable consequence" under our system of government and that accommodation of such religions must be left to the political process. In my view, however, the First Amendment was enacted precisely to protect the rights of those whose religious practices are not shared by the majority and may be viewed with hostility. The history of our free exercise doctrine amply demonstrates the harsh impact majoritarian rule has had on unpopular or emerging religious groups such as the Jehovah's Witnesses and the Amish. . . .

■ III

The Court's holding today not only misreads settled First Amendment precedent; it appears to be unnecessary to this case. I would reach the same result applying our established free exercise jurisprudence. . . .

[T]he critical question in this case is whether exempting respondents from the State's general criminal prohibition "will unduly interfere with fulfillment of the governmental interest." Although the question is close, I would conclude that uniform application of Oregon's criminal prohibition is "essential to accomplish," its overriding interest in preventing the physical harm caused by the use of a Schedule I controlled substance. Oregon's criminal prohibition represents that State's judgment that the possession and use of controlled substances, even by only one person, is inherently harmful and dangerous. Because the health effects caused by the use of controlled substances exist regardless of the motivation of the user, the use of such substances, even for religious purposes, violates the very purpose of the laws that prohibit them. . . .

For these reasons, I believe that granting a selective exemption in this case would seriously impair Oregon's compelling interest in prohibiting possession of peyote by its citizens. Under such circumstances, the Free Exercise Clause does not require the State to accommodate respondents' religiously motivated conduct. . . .

☐ *Justice BLACKMUN, with whom Justice BRENNAN and Justice MARSHALL join, dissenting.*

This Court over the years painstakingly has developed a consistent and exacting standard to test the constitutionality of a state statute that burdens the free exercise of religion. Such a statute may stand only if the law in general, and the State's refusal to allow a religious exemption in particular, are justified by a compelling interest that cannot be served by less restrictive means.

Until today, I thought this was a settled and inviolate principle of this Court's First Amendment jurisprudence. The majority, however, perfunctorily dismisses it as a "constitutional anomaly." As carefully detailed in Justice O'CONNOR's concurring opinion . . . the majority is able to arrive at this view only by mischaracterizing this Court's precedents. The Court discards leading free exercise cases such as *Cantwell v. Connecticut* (1940), and *Wisconsin v. Yoder* (1972), as "hybrid." . . . The Court views traditional free exercise analysis as somehow inapplicable to criminal prohibitions (as opposed to conditions on the receipt of benefits), and to state laws of general applicability (as opposed, presumably, to laws that expressly single out religious practices). The Court cites cases in which, due to various exceptional circumstances, we found strict scrutiny inapposite, to hint that the Court has repudiated that standard altogether. In short, it effectuates a wholesale overturning of settled law concerning the Religion Clauses of our Constitution. One hopes that the Court is aware of the consequences, and that its result is not a product of overreaction to the serious problems the country's drug crisis has generated.

This distorted view of our precedents leads the majority to conclude that strict scrutiny of a state law burdening the free exercise of religion is a "luxury" that a well-ordered society cannot afford, and that the repression of minority religions is an "unavoidable consequence of democratic government." I do not believe the Founders thought their dearly bought freedom from religious persecution a "luxury," but an essential element of liberty—and they could not have thought religious intolerance "unavoidable," for they drafted the Religion Clauses precisely in order to avoid that intolerance.

For these reasons, I agree with Justice O'CONNOR's analysis of the applicable free exercise doctrine, and I join parts I and II of her opinion. As she points out, "the critical question in this case is whether exempting respondents from the State's general criminal prohibition: 'will unduly interfere with fulfillment of the governmental interest.'" I do disagree, however, with her specific answer to that question. . . .

The State's interest in enforcing its prohibition, in order to be sufficiently compelling to outweigh a free exercise claim, cannot be merely abstract or symbolic. The State cannot plausibly assert that unbending application of a criminal prohibition is essential to fulfill any compelling interest, if it does not, in fact, attempt to enforce that prohibition. In this case, the State actually has not evinced any concrete interest in enforcing its drug laws against religious users of peyote. Oregon has never sought to prosecute respondents, and does not claim that it has made significant enforcement efforts against other religious users of peyote. The State's asserted interest thus amounts only to the symbolic preservation of an unenforced prohibition. . . .

I dissent.

Church of the Lukumi Babalu Aye v. City of Hialeah

508 U.S. 520, 113 S.Ct. 2217 (1993)

In 1987, the Church of the Lukumi Babalu Aye leased land in Hialeah, Florida, and announced plans to establish a church, school, and cultural center there, which would bring its practice of Santeria, including the ritual sacrifice of animals, into the open. Santeria originated with the Yoruba people of western Africa who were brought as slaves to Cuba and other parts of the Caribbean. Santeria teaches that individuals have a destiny from God, but a destiny only fulfilled with the aid of spirits, or *orishas*, symbolized through the iconography of Catholic saints and who depend for survival on animal sacrifice. The practice of animal sacrifice is part of rituals performed at birth, marriage, and death rites; for the cure of the sick; at initiation ceremonies, and at an annual celebration. Chickens, pigeons, doves, ducks, guinea pigs, goats, sheep, and turtles are sacrificed by the cutting of the carotid arteries in the neck. The animals are then cooked and eaten, except after healing and death rituals.

The church's announcement sparked immediate controversy and public outcry over the sacrifice of animals. As a result, Hialeah's city council passed several ordinances prohibiting animal sacrifice, including:

> Resolution 87-66, expressing "concern" over religious practices inconsistent with public morals, peace, or safety, and declaring the city's "commitment" to prohibiting such practices;
>
> Ordinance 87-40, punishing "whoever . . . unnecessarily or cruelly . . . kills any animal";
>
> Ordinance 87-52, which defines "sacrifice" as "to unnecessarily kill . . . an animal in a . . . ritual . . . not for the primary purpose of food consumption," and prohibits the "possession, sacrifice, or slaughter" of an animal if it is killed in "any type of ritual" and there is an intent to use it for food, but exempts "any licensed [food] establishment" if the killing is otherwise permitted by law;
>
> Ordinance 87-71, prohibiting the sacrifice of animals; and
>
> Ordinance 87-72, which defines "slaughter" as "the killing of animals for food," and prohibits slaughter outside of areas zoned for slaughterhouses, but includes an exemption for "small numbers of hogs and/or cattle" when exempted by state law.
>
> Church attorneys immediately attacked the constitutionality of the ordinances for abrogating the First Amendment's guarantee of free exercise of religion. After a federal district and appellate court upheld the ordinances, the church appealed to the Supreme Court.
>
> The Court's decision was unanimous, with Justice Kennedy announcing the opinion. Concurring opinions were delivered by Justice Scalia, who was joined by Chief Justice Rehnquist; by Justice Souter; and by Justice Blackmun, who was joined by Justice O'Connor.

■ ■ ■

☐ *Justice KENNEDY delivered the opinion for the Court with respect to Parts I, III, and IV, which Chief Justice REHNQUIST and Justices WHITE, STEVENS, SCALIA, SOUTER, and THOMAS join; Part II-B, which Chief Justice REHNQUIST and Justices WHITE, STEVENS, SCALIA, and THOMAS join; Parts II-A-1 and II-A-3, which Chief Justice REHNQUIST and Justices STEVENS, SCALIA, and THOMAS join; and Part II-A-2, which Justice STEVENS joins.*

We invalidate the challenged enactments and reverse the judgment of the Court of Appeals. . . .

■ II

In addressing the constitutional protection for free exercise of religion, our cases establish the general proposition that a law that is neutral and of general applicability need not be justified by a compelling governmental interest even if the law has the incidental effect of burdening a particular religious practice. *Employment Div., Dept. of Human Resources of Oregon v. Smith*, [492 U.S. 872 (1992)]. Neutrality and general applicability are interrelated, and, as becomes apparent in this case, failure to satisfy one requirement is a likely indication that the other has not been satisfied. A law failing to satisfy these requirements must be justified by a compelling governmental interest and must be narrowly tailored to advance that interest. These ordinances fail to satisfy the *Smith* requirements. We begin by discussing neutrality. . . .

■ A

At a minimum, the protections of the Free Exercise Clause pertain if the law at issue discriminates against some or all religious beliefs or regulates or prohibits conduct because it is undertaken for religious reasons. See, e.g., *Braunfeld v. Brown*, 366 U.S. 599 (1961). . . .

■ 1

Although a law targeting religious beliefs as such is never permissible, if the object of a law is to infringe upon or restrict practices because of their religious motivation, the law is not neutral, *Smith*; and it is invalid unless it is justified by a compelling interest and is narrowly tailored to advance that interest. There are, of course, many ways of demonstrating that the object or purpose of a law is the suppression of religion or religious conduct. To determine the object of a law, we must begin with its text, for the minimum requirement of neutrality is that a law not discriminate on its face. A law lacks facial neutrality if it refers to a religious practice without a secular meaning discernable from the language or context. Petitioners contend that three of the ordinances fail this test of facial neutrality because they use the words "sacrifice" and "ritual," words with strong religious connotations. We agree that these words are consistent with the claim of facial discrimination, but the argument is not conclusive. The words "sacrifice" and "ritual" have a religious origin, but current use admits also of secular meanings. The ordinances, furthermore, define "sacrifice" in secular terms, without referring to religious practices.

We reject the contention advanced by the city that our inquiry must end with the text of the laws at issue. Facial neutrality is not determinative. The Free Exercise Clause, like the Establishment Clause, extends beyond facial discrimination. The Clause "forbids subtle departures from neutrality," *Gillette v. United States*, 401 U.S. 437 (1971), and "covert suppression of particular religious beliefs." Official action that targets religious conduct for distinctive treatment cannot be shielded by mere compliance with the requirement of facial neutrality. . . .

The record in this case compels the conclusion that suppression of the central element of the Santeria worship service was the object of the ordinances. First, though use of the words "sacrifice" and "ritual" does not compel a finding of improper targeting of the Santeria religion, the choice of these words is support for our conclusion. There are further respects in which the text of the city council's enactments discloses the improper attempt to target Santeria. Resolution 87-66, adopted June 9, 1987, recited that "residents and citizens of the City of Hialeah have expressed their concern that certain religions may propose to engage in practices which are inconsistent with public morals, peace of safety," and "reiterated" the city's commitment to prohibit "any and all [such] acts of any and all religious groups." No one suggests, and on this record it cannot be maintained, that city officials had in mind a religion other than Santeria.

It becomes evident that these ordinances target Santeria sacrifice when the ordinances' operation is considered. . . . It is a necessary conclusion that almost the only conduct subject to [Hialeah's] Ordinances is the religious exercise of Santeria church members. The texts show that they were drafted in tandem to achieve this result. . . .

The legitimate governmental interests in protecting the public health and preventing cruelty to animals could be addressed by restrictions stopping far short of a flat prohibition of all Santeria sacrificial practice. If improper disposal, not the sacrifice itself, is the harm to be prevented, the city could have imposed a general regulation on the disposal of organic garbage. It did not do so. . . .

Under similar analysis, narrower regulation would achieve the city's interest in preventing cruelty to animals. With regard to the city's interest in ensuring the adequate care of animals, regulation of conditions and treatment, regardless of why an animal is kept, is the logical response to the city's concern, not a prohibition on possession for the purpose of sacrifice. The same is true for the city's interest in prohibiting cruel methods of killing. . . . If the city has a real concern that other methods are less humane, however, the subject of the regulation should be the method of slaughter itself, not a religious classification that is said to be some general relation to it. . . .

■ B

We turn next to a second requirement of the Free Exercise Clause, the rule that laws burdening religious practice must be of general applicability. *Smith*. . . .

The principle that government, in pursuit of legitimate interests, cannot in a selective manner impose burdens only on conduct motivated by religious belief is essential to the protection of the rights guaranteed by the Free Exercise Clause. The principle underlying the general applicability requirement has parallels in our First Amendment jurisprudence. In this case we need not define with precision the standard used to evaluate whether a prohibition is of general application, for these ordinances fall well below the minimum standard necessary to protect First Amendment rights.

Respondent claims that Ordinances 87-40, 87-52, and 87-71 advance two interests: protecting the public health and preventing cruelty to animals. The ordinances are underinclusive for those ends. They fail to prohibit non-religious conduct that endangers these interests in a similar or greater degree than Santeria sacrifice does. The underinclusion is substantial, not inconsequential. Despite the city's proffered interest in preventing cruelty to animals, the ordinances are drafted with care to forbid few killings but those occasioned by religious sacrifice. Many types of animal deaths or kills for nonreligious reasons are either not prohibited or approved by express provision. For example, fishing—which occurs in Hialeah—is legal. Extermination of mice and rats within a home is also permitted. . . .

The ordinances are also underinclusive with regard to the city's interest in public health, which is threatened by the disposal of animal carcasses in open public places and the consumption of uninspected meat. Neither interest is pursued by respondent with regard to conduct that is not motivated by religious conviction. The health risks posed by the improper disposal of animal carcasses are the same whether Santeria sacrifice or some nonreligious killing preceded it. The city does not, however, prohibit hunters from bringing their kill to their houses, nor does it regulate disposal after their activity. Despite substantial testimony at trial that the same public health hazards result from improper disposal of garbage by restaurants, restaurants are outside the scope of the ordinances. Improper disposal is a general problem that causes substantial health risks, but which respondent addresses only when it results from religious exercise.

The ordinances are underinclusive as well with regard to the health risk posed by consumption of uninspected meat. Under the city's ordinances, hunters may eat their kill and fishermen may eat their catch without undergoing governmental inspection. Likewise, state law requires inspection of meat that is sold but exempts meat from animals raised for the use of the owner and "members of his household and nonpaying guests and employees." The asserted interest in inspected meat is not pursued in contexts similar to that of religious animal sacrifice. . . .

We conclude, in sum, that each of Hialeah's ordinances pursues the city's governmental interests only against conduct motivated by religious belief. The ordinances "have every appearance of a prohibition that society is prepared to impose upon [Santeria worshippers] but not upon itself." *The Florida Star v. B.J.F.*, 491 U.S. 524 (1989) (SCALIA, J., concurring in part and concurring in judgment). This precise evil is what the requirement of general applicability is designed to prevent.

■ III

A law burdening religious practice that is not neutral or not of general application must undergo the most rigorous of scrutiny. To satisfy the commands of the First Amendment, a law restrictive of religious practice must advance "interests of the highest order" and must be narrowly tailored in pursuit of those interests. The compelling interest standard that we apply once a law

818 | F<small>REEDOM</small> F<small>ROM AND</small> O<small>F</small> R<small>ELIGION</small>

fails to meet the *Smith* requirements is not "watered . . . down" but "really means what it says." *Smith.* A law that targets religious conduct for distinctive treatment or advances legitimate governmental interests only against conduct with a religious motivation will survive strict scrutiny only in rare cases. It follows from what we have already said that these ordinances cannot withstand this scrutiny.

First, even were the governmental interests compelling, the ordinances are not drawn in narrow terms to accomplish those interests. . . . Respondent has not demonstrated, moreover, that, in the context of these ordinances, its governmental interests are compelling. . . . The laws here in question were enacted contrary to these constitutional principles, and they are void.

☐ *Justice SCALIA, with whom Chief Justice REHNQUIST joins, concurring in part and concurring in the judgment.*

The Court analyzes the "neutrality" and the "general applicability" of the Hialeah ordinances in separate sections (Parts II–A and II–B, respectively), and allocates various invalidating factors to one or the other of those sections. If it were necessary to make a clear distinction between the two terms, I would draw a line somewhat different from the Court's. But I think it is not necessary, and would frankly acknowledge that the terms are not only "interrelated," but substantially overlap. . . .

In my view, the defect of lack of neutrality applies primarily to those laws that by their terms impose disabilities on the basis of religion (e.g., a law excluding members of a certain sect from public benefits); whereas the defect of lack of general applicability applies primarily to those laws which, though neutral in their terms, through their design, construction, or enforcement target the practices of a particular religion for discriminatory treatment. But certainly a law that is not of general applicability (in the sense I have described) can be considered "nonneutral"; and certainly no law that is nonneutral (in the relevant sense) can be thought to be of general applicability. Because I agree with most of the invalidating factors set forth in Part II of the Court's opinion, and because it seems to me a matter of no consequence under which rubric ("neutrality," Part II–A, or "general applicability," Part II–B) each invalidating factor is discussed, I join the judgment of the Court and all of its opinion except section 2 of Part II–A.

I do not join that section because it departs from the opinion's general focus on the object of the laws at issue to consider the subjective motivation of the lawmakers, i.e., whether the Hialeah City Council actually intended to disfavor the religion of Santeria. As I have noted elsewhere, it is virtually impossible to determine the singular "motive" of a collective legislative body, and this Court has a long tradition of refraining from such inquiries. . . .

☐ *Justice SOUTER, concurring in part and concurring in the judgment.*

This case turns on a principle about which there is no disagreement, that the Free Exercise Clause bars government action aimed at suppressing religious belief or practice. The Court holds that Hialeah's animal-sacrifice laws violate that principle, and I concur in that holding without reservation.

Because prohibiting religious exercise is the object of the laws at hand, this case does not present the more difficult issue addressed in our last free-exercise case, *Smith*, which announced the rule that a "neutral, generally applicable" law does not run afoul of the Free Exercise Clause even when it prohibits religious exercise in effect. The Court today refers to that rule in *dicta*, and despite my general agreement with the Court's opinion I do not join Part II, where the *dicta* appear, for I have doubts about whether the *Smith* rule merits adherence. I write separately to explain why the *Smith* rule is not germane to this case and to express my view that, in a case presenting the issue, the Court should reexamine the rule *Smith* declared. . . .

The *Smith* rule, in my view, may be reexamined consistently with principles of *stare decisis*. To begin with, the *Smith* rule was not subject to "full-dress argument" prior to its announcement. . . . The *Smith* rule's vitality as precedent is limited further by the seeming want of any need of it in resolving the question presented in that case. . . .

Nor did *Smith* consider the original meaning of the Free Exercise Clause, though overlooking the opportunity was no unique transgression. Save in a handful of passing remarks, the Court has not explored the history of the Clause since its early attempts in 1879 and 1890, see *Reynolds v. United States*, 98 U.S. [245 (1879)], attempts that recent scholarship makes clear were incomplete. The curious absence of history from our free-exercise decisions creates a stark contrast with our cases under the Establishment Clause, where historical analysis has been so prominent. . . .

Our cases now present competing answers to the question when government, while pursuing secular ends, may compel disobedience to what one believes religion commands. The case before us is rightly decided without resolving the existing tension, which remains for another day when it may be squarely faced.

City of Boerne v. Flores
521 U.S. 507, 117 S.CT. 2157 (1997)

Situated on a hill in the city of Boerne, Texas, is St. Peter Catholic Church, built in 1923 and replicating the mission style of the region's earlier history. The church seats about 230 worshippers, but in the 1990s became too small to accommodate the growing number of parishioners. Accordingly, the Archbishop of San Antonio gave permission to the parish to enlarge the building. Shortly afterward, however, the Boerne City Council passed an ordinance authorizing the city's Historic Landmark Commission to prepare a preservation plan with proposed historic landmarks and districts. Under the ordinance, the Commission must preapprove construction affecting historic landmarks or buildings in a historic district. When the Archbishop applied for a building permit so construction could proceed, city authorities, relying on the ordinance and the designation of the church as a historic landmark, denied the application. The Archbishop in turn challenged that decision in federal district court, claiming that the city violated the church's religious freedom as guaranteed by the Religious Freedom Restoration Act of 1993 (RFRA). Congress enacted that law following the Supreme Court's ruling in *Employment Division, Department of Human Resources of Oregon v. Smith*, 494 U.S. 872 (1990), and established as a matter of federal statutory law the pre-*Smith* test for balancing claims to religious freedom against governmental interests in otherwise generally applicable laws, like Boerne's zoning ordinance. And in defending the decision to deny the church a building permit, attorneys for the city countered that Congress had exceeded its enforcement powers under Section 5 of the Fourteenth Amendment in enacting the RFRA. The district court held the RFRA unconstitutional as a violation of the separation of powers. When the Court of Appeals for the Fifth Circuit reversed, the city of Boerne appealed to the Supreme Court, which granted *certiorari*.

The Court's decision was 6–3 and its opinion delivered by Justice Kennedy. Justices Stevens and Scalia filed concurring opinions. Justice O'Connor filed a dissenting opinion, which Justices Souter and Breyer joined in part. In a brief dissent omitted here, Justice Souter reiterated his doubts, expressed in *Church of Lukumi Babalu Aye, Inc. v. Hialeah*, 508 U.S. 520 (1990), about the precedential value of *Smith*, and indicated that the Court here should have either reconsidered the soundness of the *Smith* rule or dismissed this case as improvidently granted. In another brief dissent, Justice Breyer expressed agreement with Justice O'Connor's dissent except for her views of Congress's enforcement power under Section 5 of the Fourteenth Amendment, an issue which he would not have reached in this case.

■ ■ ■

☐ *Justice KENNEDY delivered the opinion of the Court, in which Chief Justice REHNQUIST and Justices STEVENS, THOMAS, and GINSBURG joined, and in all but Part III-A-1 of which Justice SCALIA joined.*

A decision by local zoning authorities to deny a church a building permit was challenged under the Religious Freedom Restoration Act of 1993 (RFRA). The case calls into question the authority of Congress to enact RFRA. We conclude the statute exceeds Congress' power. . . .

■ II

Congress enacted RFRA in direct response to the Court's decision in *Employment Div., Dept. of Human Resources of Ore. v. Smith*, 494 U.S. 872 (1990). There we considered a Free Exercise Clause claim brought by members of the Native American Church who were denied unemployment benefits when they lost their jobs because they had used peyote. In evaluating the claim, we declined to apply the balancing test set forth in *Sherbert v.*

Verner, 374 U.S. 398 (1963), under which we would have asked whether Oregon's prohibition substantially burdened a religious practice and, if it did, whether the burden was justified by a compelling government interest. . . . The application of the *Sherbert* test, the *Smith* decision explained, would have produced an anomaly in the law, a constitutional right to ignore neutral laws of general applicability. The anomaly would have been accentuated, the Court reasoned, by the difficulty of determining whether a particular practice was central to an individual's religion. . . .

Many criticized the Court's reasoning, and this disagreement resulted in the passage of RFRA. Congress announced:

> (1) [T]he framers of the Constitution, recognizing free exercise of religion as an unalienable right, secured its protection in the First Amendment to the Constitution;
> (2) laws "neutral" toward religion may burden religious exercise as surely as laws intended to interfere with religious exercise;
> (3) governments should not substantially burden religious exercise without compelling justification;
> (4) in *Employment Division v. Smith*, 494 U.S. 872 (1990), the Supreme Court virtually eliminated the requirement that the government justify burdens on religious exercise imposed by laws neutral toward religion; and
> (5) the compelling interest test as set forth in prior Federal court rulings is a workable test for striking sensible balances between religious liberty and competing prior governmental interests.

The Act's stated purposes are:

> (1) to restore the compelling interest test as set forth in *Sherbert v. Verner*, 374 U.S. 398 (1963) and *Wisconsin v. Yoder*, 406 U.S. 205 (1972) and to guarantee its application in all cases where free exercise of religion is substantially burdened; and
> (2) to provide a claim or defense to persons whose religious exercise is substantially burdened by government.

RFRA prohibits "[g]overnment" from "substantially burden[ing]" a person's exercise of religion even if the burden results from a rule of general applicability unless the government can demonstrate the burden "(1) is in furtherance of a compelling governmental interest; and (2) is the least restrictive means of furthering that compelling governmental interest." The Act's mandate applies to any "branch, department, agency, instrumentality, and official (or other person acting under color of law) of the United States," as well as to any "State, or . . . subdivision of a State." . . .

- III

- A

The parties disagree over whether RFRA is a proper exercise of Congress' Section 5 power "to enforce" by "appropriate legislation" the constitutional guarantee that no State shall deprive any person of "life, liberty, or property, without due process of law" nor deny any person "equal protection of the laws." . . .

All must acknowledge that Section 5 is "a positive grant of legislative power" to Congress, *Katzenbach v. Morgan*, 384 U.S. 641 (1966). In *Ex parte Virginia*, 100 U.S. 339 (1880), we explained the scope of Congress' Section 5 power in the following broad terms: "Whatever legislation is appropriate, that is, adapted to carry out the objects the amendments have in view, whatever tends to enforce submission to the prohibitions they contain, and to secure to all persons the enjoyment of perfect equality of civil rights and the equal protection of the laws against State denial or invasion, if not prohibited, is brought within the domain of congressional power." Legislation which deters or remedies constitutional violations can fall within the sweep of Congress' enforcement power even if in the process it prohibits conduct which is not itself unconstitutional and intrudes into "legislative spheres of autonomy previously reserved to the States." *Fitzpatrick v. Bitzer*, 427 U.S. 445 (1976). For example, the Court upheld a suspension of literacy tests and similar voting requirements under Congress' parallel power to enforce the provisions of the Fifteenth Amendment, see U.S. Const., Amdt. 15, Sec. 2, as a measure to combat racial discrimination in voting, *South Carolina v. Katzenbach*, 383 U.S. 301 (1966), despite the facial constitutionality of the tests under *Lassiter v. Northampton County Bd. of Elections*, 360 U.S. 45 (1959). We have also concluded that other measures protecting voting rights are within Congress' power to enforce the Fourteenth and Fifteenth Amendments, despite the burdens those measures placed on the States. . . .

Congress' power under Section 5, however, extends only to "enforcing" the provisions of the Fourteenth Amendment. The Court has described this power as "remedial," *South Carolina v. Katzenbach*. The design of the Amendment and the text of Section 5 are inconsistent with the suggestion that Congress has the power to decree the substance of the Fourteenth Amendment's restrictions on the States. Legislation which alters the meaning of the Free Exercise Clause cannot be said to be enforcing the Clause. Congress does not enforce a constitutional right by changing what the right is. It has been given the power "to enforce," not the power to determine what constitutes a constitutional violation. Were it not so, what Congress would be enforcing would no longer be, in any meaningful sense, the "provisions of [the Fourteenth Amendment]." . . .

■ 1

The Fourteenth Amendment's history confirms the remedial, rather than substantive, nature of the Enforcement Clause. The Joint Committee on Reconstruction of the 39th Congress began drafting what would become the Fourteenth Amendment in January 1866. The objections to the Committee's first draft of the Amendment, and the rejection of the draft, have a direct bearing on the central issue of defining Congress' enforcement power. In February, Republican Representative John Bingham of Ohio reported the following draft amendment to the House of Representatives on behalf of the Joint Committee: "The Congress shall have power to make all laws which shall be necessary and proper to secure to the citizens of each State all privileges and immunities of citizens in the several States, and to all persons in the several States equal protection in the rights of life, liberty, and property."

The proposal encountered immediate opposition, which continued through three days of debate. Members of Congress from across the political spectrum criticized the Amendment, and the criticisms had a common theme: The proposed Amendment gave Congress too much legislative power at the expense of the existing constitutional structure. Democrats and conservative Republicans argued that the proposed Amendment would give Congress a power to intrude into traditional areas of state responsibility, a power inconsistent with the federal design central to the Constitution. . . .

As a result of these objections having been expressed from so many different quarters, the House voted to table the proposal until April. The Amendment in its early form was not again considered. Instead, the Joint Committee began drafting a new article of Amendment, which it reported to Congress on April 30, 1866.

Section 1 of the new draft Amendment imposed self-executing limits on the States. Section 5 prescribed that "the Congress shall have power to enforce, by appropriate legislation, the provisions of this article." The revised Amendment proposal did not raise the concerns expressed earlier regarding broad congressional power to prescribe uniform national laws with respect to life, liberty, and property. After revisions not relevant here, the new measure passed both Houses and was ratified in July 1868 as the Fourteenth Amendment. . . .

■ 2

The remedial and preventive nature of Congress' enforcement power, and the limitation inherent in the power, were confirmed in our earliest cases on the Fourteenth Amendment. In the *Civil Rights Cases*, 109 U.S. 3 (1883), the Court invalidated sections of the Civil Rights Act of 1875 which prescribed criminal penalties for denying to any person "the full enjoyment of" public accommodations and conveyances, on the grounds that it exceeded Congress' power by seeking to regulate private conduct. The Enforcement Clause, the Court said, did not authorize Congress to pass "general legislation upon the rights of the citizen, but corrective legislation; that is, such as may be necessary and proper for counteracting such laws as the States may adopt or enforce, and which, by the amendment, they are prohibited from making or enforcing. . . ." Although the specific holdings of these early cases might have been superseded or modified, see, e.g., *Heart of Atlanta Motel, Inc. v. United States*, 379 U.S. 241 (1964), their treatment of Congress' Section 5 power as corrective or preventive, not definitional, has not been questioned. . . .

■ 3

Any suggestion that Congress has a substantive, non-remedial power under the Fourteenth Amendment is not supported by our case law. In *Oregon v. Mitchell*, a majority of the Court concluded Congress had exceeded its enforcement powers by enacting legislation lowering the minimum age of voters from 21 to 18 in state and local elections. The five Members of the Court who reached this conclusion explained that the legislation intruded into an area reserved by the Constitution to the States. . . .

If Congress could define its own powers by altering the Fourteenth Amendment's meaning, no longer would the Constitution be "superior paramount law, unchangeable by ordinary means." It would be "on a level with ordinary legislative acts, and, like other acts, . . . alterable when the legislature shall please to alter it." *Marbury v. Madison.* Under this approach, it is difficult to conceive of a principle that would limit congressional power. Shifting legislative majorities could change the Constitution and effectively circumvent the difficult and detailed amendment process contained in Article V.

We now turn to consider whether RFRA can be considered enforcement legislation under Section 5 of the Fourteenth Amendment.

- III

- B

Regardless of the state of the legislative record, RFRA cannot be considered remedial, preventive legislation, if those terms are to have any meaning. RFRA is so out of proportion to a supposed remedial or preventive object that it cannot be understood as responsive to, or designed to prevent, unconstitutional behavior. It appears, instead, to attempt a substantive change in constitutional protections. Preventive measures prohibiting certain types of laws may be appropriate when there is reason to believe that many of the laws affected by the congressional enactment have a significant likelihood of being unconstitutional. Remedial legislation under Section 5 "should be adapted to the mischief and wrong which the [Fourteenth] Amendment was intended to provide against." *Civil Rights Cases.*

RFRA is not so confined. Sweeping coverage ensures its intrusion at every level of government, displacing laws and prohibiting official actions of almost every description and regardless of subject matter. RFRA's restrictions apply to every agency and official of the Federal, State, and local Governments. RFRA has no termination date or termination mechanism. Any law is subject to challenge at any time by any individual who alleges a substantial burden on his or her free exercise of religion.

The reach and scope of RFRA distinguish it from other measures passed under Congress' enforcement power, even in the area of voting rights. In *South Carolina v. Katzenbach*, the challenged provisions were confined to those regions of the country where voting discrimination had been most flagrant and affected a discrete class of state laws, i.e., state voting laws. Furthermore, to ensure that the reach of the Voting Rights Act was limited to those cases in which constitutional violations were most likely (in order to reduce the possibility of overbreadth), the coverage under the Act would terminate "at the behest of States and political subdivisions in which the danger of substantial voting discrimination has not materialized during the preceding five years." . . .

The stringent test RFRA demands of state laws reflects a lack of proportionality or congruence between the means adopted and the legitimate end to be achieved. If an objector can show a substantial burden on his free exercise, the State must demonstrate a compelling governmental interest and show that the law is the least restrictive means of furthering its interest. Claims that a law substantially burdens someone's exercise of religion will often be difficult to contest. Laws valid under *Smith* would fall under RFRA without regard to whether they had the object of stifling or punishing free exercise. . . .

The substantial costs RFRA exacts, both in practical terms of imposing a heavy litigation burden on the States and in terms of curtailing their traditional general regulatory power, far exceed any pattern or practice of unconstitutional conduct under the Free Exercise Clause as interpreted in *Smith*. Simply put, RFRA is not designed to identify and counteract state laws likely to be unconstitutional because of their treatment of religion. In most cases, the state laws to which RFRA applies are not ones which will have been motivated by religious bigotry. If a state law disproportionately burdened a particular class of religious observers, this circumstance might be evidence of an impermissible legislative motive. RFRA's substantial burden test, however, is not even a discriminatory effects or disparate impact test. It is a reality of the modern regulatory state that numerous state laws, such as the zoning regulations at issue here, impose a substantial burden on a large class of individuals. When the exercise of religion has been burdened in an incidental way by a law of general application, it does not follow that the persons affected have been burdened any more than other citizens, let alone burdened because of their religious beliefs. In addition, the Act imposes in every case a least restrictive means requirement—a requirement that was not used in the pre-*Smith* jurisprudence RFRA purported to codify—which also indicates that the legislation is broader than is appropriate if the goal is to prevent and remedy constitutional violations. . . .

Broad as the power of Congress is under the Enforcement Clause of the Fourteenth Amendment, RFRA contradicts vital principles necessary to maintain separation of powers and the federal balance. The judgment of the Court of Appeals sustaining the Act's constitutionality is reversed.

☐ *Justice STEVENS, concurring.*

In my opinion, the Religious Freedom Restoration Act of 1993 (RFRA) is a "law respecting an establishment of religion" that violates the First Amendment to the Constitution. . . .

☐ *Justice O'CONNOR, with whom Justice BREYER joins except as to a portion of Part I, dissenting.*

I dissent from the Court's disposition of this case. I agree with the Court that the issue before us is whether the Religious Freedom Restoration Act (RFRA) is a proper exercise of Congress' power to enforce Section 5 of the Fourteenth Amendment. But as a yardstick for measuring the constitutionality of RFRA, the Court uses its holding in *Employment Div., Dept. of Human Resources of Ore. v. Smith*, 494 U.S. 872 (1990), the decision that prompted Congress to enact RFRA as a means of more rigorously enforcing the Free Exercise Clause. I remain of the view that *Smith* was wrongly decided, and I would use this case to reexamine the Court's holding there. . . . If the Court were to correct the misinterpretation of the Free Exercise Clause set forth in *Smith*, it would simultaneously put our First Amendment jurisprudence back on course and allay the legitimate concerns of a majority in Congress who believed that *Smith* improperly restricted religious liberty. We would then be in a position to review RFRA in light of a proper interpretation of the Free Exercise Clause. . . .

Locke v. Davey

540 U.S. 712, 124 S.CT. 1307 (2004)

Washington created a Promise Scholarship Program to assist academically gifted students, from low-income families, with postsecondary education expenses of up to $1,125 per year. In accord with the state constitution, students could not use such a scholarship to pursue a degree in theology. Article I, Section 11 of the state constitution goes beyond the First Amendment in providing that "No public money or property shall be appropriated for or applied to any religious worship, exercise or instruction, or the support of any religious establishment."

Joshua Davey was awarded a Promise Scholarship and chose to attend Northwest College, a church-affiliated institution, in order to pursue a double major in pastoral ministries and business administration. But he was told that he could not use his scholarship to pursue a pastoral degree, and he sued Governor Gary Locke and other state officials. Davey argued that the denial of the scholarship violated the First Amendment's free exercise clause. A federal district court rejected Davey's claims, but the Court of Appeals for the Ninth Circuit reversed, concluding that the state had singled out religion for unfavorable treatment and its exclusion of theology majors ran afoul of the ruling in *Church of Lukumi Babalu Aye, Inc. v. Hialeah*, 508 U.S. 520 (1993) (excerpted in this chapter), as well as declared the program unconstitutional. Locke appealed that decision to the Supreme Court.

The appellate court's decision was reversed by a 7–2 vote. Chief Justice Rehnquist delivered the opinion for the Court. Justices Scalia and Thomas each delivered dissenting opinions.

■ ■ ■

☐ *Chief Justice REHNQUIST delivered the opinion of the Court.*

The Religion Clauses of the First Amendment . . . are frequently in tension. Yet we have long said that "there is room for play in the joints" between them. *Walz v. Tax Comm'n of City of New York*, 397 U.S. 664 (1970). In other words, there are some state actions permitted by the Establishment Clause but not required by the Free Exercise Clause.

This case involves that "play in the joints" described above. Under our Establishment Clause precedent, the link between government funds and religious training is broken by the independent and private choice of recipients. See *Zelman v. Simmons-Harris*, 536 U.S. 639 (2002); *Zobrest v. Catalina Foothills School Dist.*, 509 U.S. 1 (1993); *Witters v. Washington Dept. of Servs. for Blind*, 474 U.S. 481 (1986); *Mueller v. Allen*, 463 U.S. 388 (1983). As such, there is no doubt that the State could, consistent with the Federal Constitution, permit Promise Scholars to pursue a degree in devotional theology, *Witters*, and the State does not contend otherwise. The question before us,

dom of conscience" has no logical limit and can justify the singling out of religion for exclusion from public programs in virtually any context. . . .

The Court has not approached other forms of discrimination this way. When we declared racial segregation unconstitutional, we did not ask whether the State had originally adopted the regime, not out of "animus" against blacks, but because of a well-meaning but misguided belief that the races would be better off apart. It was sufficient to note the current effect of segregation on racial minorities. Similarly, the Court does not excuse statutes that facially discriminate against women just because they are the vestigial product of a well-intentioned view of women's appropriate social role. . . .

It may be that Washington's original purpose in excluding the clergy from public benefits was benign, [b]ut those singled out for disfavor can be forgiven for suspecting more invidious forces at work. Let there be no doubt: This case is about discrimination against a religious minority. Most citizens of this country identify themselves as professing some religious belief, but the State's policy poses no obstacle to practitioners of only a tepid, civic version of faith. Those the statutory exclusion actually affects—those whose belief in their religion is so strong that they dedicate their study and their lives to its ministry—are a far narrower set. One need not delve too far into modern popular culture to perceive a trendy disdain for deep religious conviction. In an era when the Court is so quick to come to the aid of other disfavored groups, see, *Romer v. Evans*, 517 U.S. 620 (1996), its indifference in this case, which involves a form of discrimination to which the Constitution actually speaks, is exceptional. . . . I respectfully dissent.

Trinity Lutheran Church of Columbia, Inc. v. Comer
137 S.Ct. 2012 (2017)

The Trinity Lutheran Church Child Learning Center is a Missouri preschool and daycare center. Its playground had a coarse, pea-gravel surface, and the Center sought to replace the gravel with a rubber surface by participating in Missouri's Scrap Tire Program. Missouri's Department of Natural Resources offered grants to qualifying nonprofit organizations to install playground surfaces made from recycled tires. The department had a policy of denying grants to any applicant owned or controlled by a church or other religious entity and hence denied the Center's application. In a letter rejecting the application, the department explained that Article I, Section 7 of the Missouri Constitution prohibited financial assistance to a church.

Trinity Lutheran sued, alleging the denial of its application violated the free exercise clause of the First Amendment. A federal district court dismissed the suit, based on interpreting the free exercise clause to prohibit the government from outlawing or restricting a religious practice but not to prohibit withholding a benefit on account of religion. The district court relied on *Locke v. Davey*, 540 U.S. 712 (2004), upholding a state's decision not to fund scholarly degrees in devotional theology as part of a scholarship program. An appellate court affirmed, reasoning that although the state could award a grant to the Center without running afoul of the establishment clause of the Constitution, it did not follow that the free exercise clause compelled the state to disregard the antiestablishment principle in Missouri's Constitution.

The appellate court's decision was reversed by a 7–2 vote. Chief Justice Roberts delivered the opinion for the Court. Justices Thomas, Gorsuch, and Breyer issued concurring opinions. Justice Sotomayor issued a dissenting opinion, which Justice Ginsburg joined.

☐ *Chief Justice ROBERTS delivered the opinion of the Court, except as to footnote 3. Justices KENNEDY, ALITO, and KAGAN, joined that opinion in full, and Justices THOMAS and GORSUCH joined except as to footnote 3.*

Due to limited resources, the Department cannot offer grants to all applicants and so awards them on a competitive basis to those scoring highest based on several criteria, such as the poverty level of the population in the surrounding area and the applicant's plan to promote recycling. When the Center applied, the Department had a strict and express policy of denying grants to any applicant owned or controlled by a church or other religious entity. That policy, in the Department's view, was compelled by Article I, Section 7 of the Missouri Constitution, which provides:

> That no money shall ever be taken from the public treasury, directly or indirectly, in aid of any church, sect or denomination of religion, or in aid of any priest, preacher, minister or teacher thereof, as such; and that no preference shall be given to nor any discrimination made against any church, sect or creed of religion, or any form of religious faith or worship.

In its application, the Center disclosed its status as a ministry of Trinity Lutheran Church and specified that the Center's mission was "to provide a safe, clean, and attractive school facility in conjunction with an educational program structured to allow a child to grow spiritually, physically, socially, and cognitively." . . .

The parties agree that the Establishment Clause of that Amendment does not prevent Missouri from including Trinity Lutheran in the Scrap Tire Program. That does not, however, answer the question under the Free Exercise Clause, because we have recognized that there is "play in the joints" between what the Establishment Clause permits and the Free Exercise Clause compels. *Locke [v. Davey]*.

The Free Exercise Clause "protect[s] religious observers against unequal treatment" and subjects to the strictest scrutiny laws that target the religious for "special disabilities" based on their "religious status." *Church of Lukumi*

Babalu Aye, Inc. v. Hialeah, 508 U.S. 520 (1993). Applying that basic principle, this Court has repeatedly confirmed that denying a generally available benefit solely on account of religious identity imposes a penalty on the free exercise of religion that can be justified only by a state interest "of the highest order."

In *Everson v. Board of Education of Ewing*, 330 U. S. 1 (1947), for example, we upheld against an Establishment Clause challenge a New Jersey law enabling a local school district to reimburse parents for the public transportation costs of sending their children to public and private schools, including parochial schools. In the course of ruling that the Establishment Clause allowed New Jersey to extend that public benefit to all its citizens regardless of their religious belief, we explained that a State "cannot hamper its citizens in the free exercise of their own religion. Consequently, it cannot exclude individual Catholics, Lutherans, Mohammedans, Baptists, Jews, Methodists, Non-believers, Presbyterians, or the members of any other faith, *because of their faith, or lack of it*, from receiving the benefits of public welfare legislation."

Three decades later, in *McDaniel* [*v. Paty* 435 U.S. 618 (1978)], the Court struck down under the Free Exercise Clause a Tennessee statute disqualifying ministers from serving as delegates to the State's constitutional convention. . . .

In recent years, when this Court has rejected free exercise challenges, the laws in question have been neutral and generally applicable without regard to religion. We have been careful to distinguish such laws from those that single out the religious for disfavored treatment. . . .

In *Employment Division, Department of Human Resources of Oregon v. Smith*, 494 U. S. 872 (1990), we rejected a free exercise claim brought by two members of a Native American church denied unemployment benefits because they had violated Oregon's drug laws by ingesting peyote for sacramental purposes. . . .

Finally, in *Church of Lukumi Babalu Aye, Inc. v. Hialeah*, we struck down three facially neutral city ordinances that outlawed certain forms of animal slaughter. Members of the Santeria religion challenged the ordinances under the Free Exercise Clause, alleging that despite their facial neutrality, the ordinances had a discriminatory purpose easy to ferret out: prohibiting sacrificial rituals integral to Santeria but distasteful to local residents. We agreed. A law, we said, may not discriminate against "some or all religious beliefs." Nor may a law regulate or outlaw conduct because it is religiously motivated. And, citing *McDaniel* and *Smith*, we restated the now-familiar refrain: The Free Exercise Clause protects against laws that "'impose[] special disabilities on the basis of . . . religious status.'"

Like the disqualification statute in *McDaniel*, the Department's policy puts Trinity Lutheran to a choice: It may participate in an otherwise available benefit program or remain a religious institution. Of course, Trinity Lutheran is free to continue operating as a church, just as McDaniel was free to continue being a minister. But that freedom comes at the cost of automatic and absolute exclusion from the benefits of a public program for which the Center is otherwise fully qualified. And when the State conditions a benefit in this way, *McDaniel* says plainly that the State has punished the free exercise of religion: "To condition the availability of benefits . . . upon [a recipient's] willingness to . . . surrender[] his religiously impelled [status] effectively penalizes the free exercise of his constitutional liberties."

The Department contends that merely declining to extend funds to Trinity Lutheran does not prohibit the Church from engaging in any religious conduct or otherwise exercising its religious rights. In this sense, says the Department, its policy is unlike the ordinances struck down in *Lukumi*, which outlawed rituals central to Santeria. Here the Department has simply declined to allocate to Trinity Lutheran a subsidy the State had no obligation to provide in the first place. That decision does not meaningfully burden the Church's free exercise rights. . . .

It is true the Department has not criminalized the way Trinity Lutheran worships or told the Church that it cannot subscribe to a certain view of the Gospel. But, as the Department itself acknowledges, the Free Exercise Clause protects against "indirect coercion or penalties on the free exercise of religion, not just outright prohibitions." *Lyng* [*v. Northwest Indian Cemetery Protective Association*, 485 U.S. 439 (1988)]. As the Court put it more than 50 years ago, "[i]t is too late in the day to doubt that the liberties of religion and expression may be infringed by the denial of or placing of conditions upon a benefit or privilege." *Sherbert* [*v. Verner*, 374 U.S. 398 (1963)]. . . .

[W]ithout having to disavow its religious character. . . .

The Department attempts to get out from under the weight of our precedents by arguing that the free exercise question in this case is instead controlled by our decision in *Locke v. Davey*. It is not. In *Locke*, the State of Washington created a scholarship program to assist high-achieving students with the costs of postsecondary education. The scholarships were paid out of the State's general fund, and eligibility was based on criteria such as an applicant's score on college admission tests and family income. While scholarship recipients were free to use the money at accredited religious and non-religious schools alike, they were not permitted to use the funds to pursue a devotional theology degree—one "devotional in nature or designed to induce religious faith." Davey was selected for a scholarship but was denied the funds when he refused to certify that he would not use them toward a devotional degree. He sued, arguing that the State's refusal to allow its scholarship money to go toward such degrees violated his free exercise rights.

This Court disagreed. It began by explaining what was not at issue. Washington's selective funding program was not comparable to the free exercise violations found in the "*Lukumi* line of cases," including those striking down laws requiring individuals to "choose between their religious beliefs and receiving a government benefit." At the outset, then, the Court made clear that *Locke* was not like the case now before us.

Washington's restriction on the use of its scholarship funds was different. According to the Court, the State had "merely chosen not to fund a distinct category of instruction." Davey was not denied a scholarship because of who he was; he was denied a scholarship because of what he proposed to do—use the funds to prepare for the ministry. Here there is no question that Trinity Lutheran was denied a grant simply because of what it is—a church. . . .

The Court in *Locke* also stated that Washington's choice was in keeping with the State's antiestablishment interest in not using taxpayer funds to pay for the training of clergy; in fact, the Court could "think of few areas in which a State's antiestablishment interests come more into play." The claimant in *Locke* sought funding for an "essentially religious endeavor . . . akin to a religious calling as well as an academic pursuit," and opposition to such funding "to support church leaders" lay at the historic core of the Religion Clauses. Here nothing of the sort can be said about a program to use recycled tires to resurface playgrounds. . . .

The judgment of the United States Court of Appeals for the Eighth Circuit is reversed, and the case is remanded for further proceedings consistent with this opinion.

☐ *Justice GORSUCH, with whom Justice THOMAS joins, concurring in part.*

I agree this violates the First Amendment and I am pleased to join nearly all of the Court's opinion. I offer only two modest qualifications.

First, the Court leaves open the possibility a useful distinction might be drawn between laws that discriminate on the basis of religious status and religious use. Respectfully, I harbor doubts about the stability of such a line. Does a religious man say grace before dinner? Or does a man begin his meal in a religious manner? Is it a religious group that built the playground? Or did a group build the playground so it might be used to advance a religious mission? The distinction blurs in much the same way the line between acts and omissions can blur when stared at too long, leaving us to ask (for example) whether the man who drowns by awaiting the incoming tide does so by act (coming upon the sea) or omission (allowing the sea to come upon him). Often enough the same facts can be described both ways.

Neither do I see why the First Amendment's Free Exercise Clause should care. After all, that Clause guarantees the free exercise of religion, not just the right to inward belief (or status). And this Court has long explained that government may not "devise mechanisms, overt or disguised, designed to persecute or oppress a religion or its practices." *Church of Lukumi Babalu Aye, Inc. v. Hialeah* (1993). Generally the government may not force people to choose between participation in a public program and their right to free exercise of religion. I don't see why it should matter whether we describe that benefit, say, as closed to Lutherans (status) or closed to people who do Lutheran things (use). It is free exercise either way.

For these reasons, reliance on the status-use distinction does not suffice for me to distinguish *Locke v. Davey*. In that case, this Court upheld a funding restriction barring a student from using a scholarship to pursue a degree in devotional theology. But can it really matter whether the restriction in *Locke* was phrased in terms of use instead of status (for was it a student who wanted a vocational degree in religion? or was it a religious student who wanted the necessary education for his chosen vocation?). If that case can be correct and distinguished, it seems it might be only because of the opinion's claim of a long tradition against the use of public funds for training of the clergy, a tradition the Court correctly explains has no analogue here.

Second and for similar reasons, I am unable to join the footnoted observation, n. 3, that "[t]his case involves express discrimination based on religious identity with respect to playground resurfacing." Of course the footnote is entirely correct, but I worry that some might mistakenly read it to suggest that only "playground resurfacing" cases, or only those with some association with children's safety or health, or perhaps some other social good we find sufficiently worthy, are governed by the legal rules recounted in and faithfully applied by the Court's opinion. Such a reading would be unreasonable for our cases are "governed by general principles, rather than ad hoc improvisations." *Elk Grove Unified School Dist. v. Newdow*, 542 U. S. 1, (2004) (REHNQUIST, C. J., concurring in judgment). And the general principles here do not permit discrimination against religious exercise—whether on the playground or anywhere else.

☐ *Justice SOTOMAYOR, with whom Justice GINSBURG joins, dissenting.*

To hear the Court tell it, this is a simple case about recycling tires to resurface a playground. The stakes are higher. This case is about nothing less than the relationship between religious institutions and the civil government—that is, between church and state. The Court today profoundly changes that relationship by holding, for the first time, that the Constitution requires the government to provide public funds directly to a church. Its decision slights both our precedents and our history, and its reasoning weakens this country's longstanding commitment to a separation of church and state beneficial to both. . . .

Properly understood . . . this is a case about whether Missouri can decline to fund improvements to the facilities the Church uses to practice and spread its religious views. This Court has repeatedly warned that funding of exactly this kind—payments from the government to a house of worship—would cross the line drawn by the Establishment Clause. . . .

The government may not directly fund religious exercise. See *Everson v. Board of Ed. of Ewing*, 330 U. S. 1 (1947). Put in doctrinal terms, such funding violates the Establishment Clause because it impermissibly "advanc[es] . . . religion."

Nowhere is this rule more clearly implicated than when funds flow directly from the public treasury to a house of worship. A house of worship exists to foster and further religious exercise. Within its walls, worshippers gather to practice and reaffirm their faith. And from its base, the faithful reach out to those not yet convinced of the group's beliefs. When a government funds a house of worship, it underwrites this religious exercise. . . .

The Church seeks state funds to improve the Learning Center's facilities, which, by the Church's own avowed description, are used to assist the spiritual growth of the children of its members and to spread the Church's faith to the children of nonmembers. The Church's playground surface—like a Sunday School room's walls or the sanctuary's pews—are integrated with and integral to its religious mission. The conclusion that the funding the Church seeks would impermissibly advance religion is inescapable. . . .

When the Court last addressed direct funding of religious institutions, in *Mitchell* [*v. Helms*, 530 U.S. 793 (2000)], it adhered to the rule that the Establishment Clause prohibits the direct funding of religious activities. At issue was a federal program that helped state and local agencies lend educational materials to public and private schools, including religious schools. The controlling concurrence assured itself that the program would not lead to the public funding of religious activity. It pointed out that the program allocated secular aid, that it did so "on the basis of neutral, secular criteria," that the aid would not "supplant non-[program] funds," that "no . . . funds ever reach the coffers of religious schools," that "evidence of actual diversion is *de minimis*," and that the program had "adequate safeguards" to police violations. (O'CONNOR, J., concurring in judgment). Those factors, it concluded, were "sufficient to find that the program . . . [did] not have the impermissible effect of advancing religion." . . .

Today's opinion suggests the Court has made the leap the *Mitchell* plurality could not. For if it agrees that the funding here will finance religious activities, then only a rule that considers that fact irrelevant could support a conclusion of constitutionality. . . . It permits direct subsidies for religious indoctrination, with all the attendant concerns that led to the Establishment Clause. And it favors certain religious groups, those with a belief system that allows them to compete for public dollars and those well-organized and well-funded enough to do so successfully. . . .

Even assuming the absence of an Establishment Clause violation and proceeding on the Court's preferred front—the Free Exercise Clause—the Court errs. It claims that the government may not draw lines based on an entity's religious "status." But we have repeatedly said that it can. When confronted with government action that draws such a line, we have carefully considered whether the interests embodied in the Religion Clauses justify that line. The question here is thus whether those interests support the line drawn in Missouri's Article I, Sec. 7, separating the State's treasury from those of houses of worship. They unquestionably do. . . .

The Establishment Clause prohibits laws "respecting an establishment of religion" and the Free Exercise Clause prohibits laws "prohibiting the free exercise thereof." Even in the absence of a violation of one of the Religion Clauses, the interaction of government and religion can raise concerns that sound in both Clauses. For that reason, the government may sometimes act to accommodate those concerns, even when not required to do so by the Free Exercise Clause, without violating the Establishment Clause. And the government may sometimes act to accommodate those concerns, even when not required to do so by the Establishment Clause, without violating the Free Exercise Clause. "[T]here is room for play in the joints productive of a benevolent neutrality which will permit religious exercise to exist without sponsorship and without interference." [*Waltz v. Tax Comm'n of City of New York,* 397 U.S. 664 (1970).] This space between the two Clauses gives government some room to recognize the unique status of religious entities and to single them out on that basis for exclusion from otherwise generally applicable laws.

Invoking this principle, this Court has held that the government may sometimes relieve religious entities from the requirements of government programs. A State need not, for example, require nonprofit houses of worship to pay property taxes. . . . Invoking this same principle, this Court has held that the government may sometimes close off certain government aid programs to religious entities. The State need not, for example, fund the training of a religious group's leaders, those "who will preach their beliefs, teach their faith, and carry out their mission." It may instead avoid the historic "antiestablishment interests" raised by the use of "taxpayer funds to support church leaders." *Locke v. Davey* (2004).

When reviewing a law that, like this one, singles out religious entities for exclusion from its reach, we thus have not myopically focused on the fact that a law singles out religious entities, but on the reasons that it does so.

Missouri has decided that the unique status of houses of worship requires a special rule when it comes to public funds. Its Constitution reflects that choice . . . . Missouri's decision, which has deep roots in our Nation's history, reflects a reasonable and constitutional judgment. . . .

Those who fought to end the public funding of religion based their opposition on a powerful set of arguments, all stemming from the basic premise that the practice harmed both civil government and religion. . . . After the Revolution, Virginia debated and rejected a general religious assessment. The proposed bill would have allowed taxpayers to direct payments to a Christian church of their choice to support a minister, exempted "Quakers and Menonists," and sent undirected assessments to the public treasury for "seminaries of learning." A Bill Establishing a Provision for Teachers of the Christian Religion, reprinted in *Everson* (supplemental appendix to dissent of RUTLEDGE, J.).

In opposing this proposal, James Madison authored his famous *Memorial and Remonstrance Against Religious Assessments* (1785), in which he condemned the bill as hostile to religious freedom. Believing it "proper to take alarm," despite the bill's limits, he protested "that the same authority which can force a citizen to contribute three pence only of his property for the support of any one establishment, may force him to conform to any other establishment." Religion had "flourished, not only without the support of human laws, but in spite of every opposition from them." Compelled support for religion, he argued, would only weaken believers' "confidence in its innate excellence," strengthen others' "suspicion that its friends are too conscious of its fallacies to trust in its own merits," and harm the "purity and efficacy" of the supported religion. He ended by deeming the bill incompatible with Virginia's guarantee of "'free exercise of . . . Religion according to the dictates of conscience.'" . . .

In *Locke*, this Court expressed an understanding of, and respect for, this history. *Locke* involved a provision of the State of Washington's Constitution that, like Missouri's nearly identical Article I, Sec. 7, barred the use of public funds for houses of worship or ministers. Consistent with this denial of funds to ministers, the State's college scholarship program did not allow funds to be used for devotional theology degrees. When asked whether this violated the would-be minister's free exercise rights, the Court invoked the play in the joints principle and answered no. The Establishment Clause did not require the prohibition because "the link between government funds and religious training [was] broken by the independent and private choice of [scholarship] recipients." Nonetheless, the denial did not violate the Free Exercise Clause because a "historic and substantial state interest" supported the constitutional provision. The Court could "think of few areas in which a State's antiestablishment interests come more into play" than the "procuring [of] taxpayer funds to support church leaders."

The same is true of this case, about directing taxpayer funds to houses of worship. Like the use of public dollars for ministers at issue in *Locke*, turning over public funds to houses of worship implicates serious antiestablishment and free exercise interests. . . .

At bottom, the Court creates the following rule today: The government may draw lines on the basis of religious status to grant a benefit to

A | *Requirements for a Warrant and Reasonable Searches and Seizures*

As a general rule (subject to the exceptions discussed in Section B, in this chapter), police must obtain search and arrest warrants from a "neutral and detached magistrate." The Court made this requirement applicable to the states in *Wolf v. Colorado*, 338 U.S. 25 (1949). In *Coolidge v. New Hampshire*, 403 U.S. 443 (1971), the Court underscored the importance of judicial approval of warrants when holding invalid a warrant issued by an attorney general[1]; and in *Connally v. Georgia*, 429 U.S. 245 (1977), declined to permit a justice of the peace to issue warrants when his salary was paid in part by warrant fees.

When obtaining warrants, police must demonstrate *probable cause* that a person has committed a crime if they are to obtain an arrest warrant, and show probable cause to believe that contraband or the instrumentalities of crime will be found in a particular place when they are seeking a search warrant. Although the Fourth Amendment does not specify the basis for warrantless searches and seizures by police, they too must generally be based on probable cause,[2] or a "reasonable suspicion" of criminal activities (as further discussed in Section B). Regardless of whether police seek an arrest or a search warrant, they must supply the same quantum of evidence when establishing probable cause.[3] Probable cause for making an arrest turns on "whether at that moment [of arrest] the facts and circumstances within [the officers'] knowledge and of which they [have] reasonably trustworthy information [are] sufficient to warrant a prudent man in believing that the [suspect] had committed or was committing an offense."[4] And the test is objective in the sense that a judge (or "reasonable" person) would agree that enough evidence exists to support a police officer's determination; in other words, the subjective judgment of an officer alone does not support a finding of probable cause.

In determining whether probable cause has been reasonably established, judges consider the *specificity* of what is to be searched and the *particularity* of what is to be seized. The Court reaffirmed that core principle in *Groh v. Ramirez*, 540 U.S. 551 (2004), in holding that a search warrant that failed to identify the items to be seized, and described only the defendant's house as the place to be searched, violated the Fourth Amendment. Because police often rely on informants, the Court also demands that police show that their information is *reliable*, not vague, and sufficient for judges to draw their own conclusions.[5] Hearsay evidence may be used,[6] yet police must attest to the reliability of informants, although they need not demonstrate their credibility.[7]

The Warren Court established a two-prong test for determining probable cause when holding that police failed to establish this in an affidavit for a warrant that simply claimed "reliable information from a credible person" indicated "narcotics and narcotics paraphernalia" were kept at a certain location. In that case, *Aguilar v. Texas*, 378 U.S. 108 (1964), the Court held that police must explain (1) how it is that an informant knows what he claims to know and (2) why they believe the information to be accurate and reliable. The more conservative Burger and Rehnquist Courts, however, abandoned that test. *Illinois v. Gates*, 462 U.S. 213 (1983), held that the *Aguilar* factors—showing the basis and veracity of informers' tips—were "relevant considerations" but no longer independent requirements. "[A] deficiency in one may be compensated for . . . by a strong showing as to the other." In *Gates* and *Massachusetts v. Upton*, 466 U.S. 727 (1984), the Court ruled that judges may determine whether "*the totality of the circumstances*" presented by police justifies a finding of probable cause.[8]

Although search warrants authorize police to search only particular locations and to seize specific items, police had long been allowed to conduct searches when making arrests, with or without arrest warrants. Until the Warren Court era, moreover, police were permitted to undertake rather sweeping searches when armed with only an arrest warrant. *Harris v. United States*, 331 U.S. 145 (1947), for instance, allowed the search of a four-room apartment based only on an arrest warrant for the occupant. The Warren Court, however, signaled a change in *Chapman v. United States*, 365 U.S. 610 (1961), when disapproving of a warrantless search of a rented house, which police entered through an unlocked window with the owner's (but not the renter's) consent. There, Justice Charles Whittaker observed that

> [n]o reason is offered for not obtaining a search warrant except the inconvenience of the officers and some slight delay necessary to prepare papers and present the evidence to a magistrate. These are never very convincing reasons and, in these circumstances, certainly are not enough to by-pass the constitutional requirement. No suspect was fleeing or likely to take flight. The search was of a permanent premises, not of a movable vehicle. No evidence or contraband was threatened with removal or destruction.

Harris was finally expressly overruled in *Chimel v. California* (1969) (see excerpt below). More recently, *Muehler v. Mena*, 544 U.S. 93 (2005), held that when executing a search warrant police may handcuff and detain occupants in order to minimize the risk of harm to police.

Chimel's ruling that police, armed with only an arrest warrant or when they have probable cause to make an arrest, are constrained in searching only what is in "plain view" and in "the immediate area" surrounding an arrestee has been repeatedly reaffirmed. But the Court's rulings usually turn on the particular circumstances of each case.[9]

As *Arizona v. Hicks* (1987) (excerpted below), indicates, the Court, although occasionally sharply split, continues to draw a line limiting the scope of warrantless searches made in connection with arrests. In *Yabarra v. Illinois*, 444 U.S. 85 (1979), the Court also held that a warrant authorizing police to search a small tavern and the bartender for narcotics did not justify a pat-down search of patrons of the bar. In *Payton v. New York*, 445 U.S. 573 (1980), the justices struck down a state statute authorizing police to enter private residences without a warrant to make routine felony arrests. In *Steagald v. United States*, 451 U.S. 204 (1981), the Court held that police needed a search warrant to enter the home of a third party when attempting to arrest a person for whom they had a valid arrest warrant. And in *Welsh v. Wisconsin*, 466 U.S. 470 (1984), the Court rejected a warrantless nighttime entry into a house by police to arrest an individual for driving under the influence of alcohol. But in *Horton v. California*, 496 U.S. 128 (1990), the Court ruled that a warrantless search and seizure was permissible under the *plain view doctrine*, because the defendant's criminal conduct was observable and immediately apparent to police officers.

Moreover, fingerprints, mug shots, and DNA swabs may be taken from suspects arrested (but not yet tried and convicted) for "serious" violent crimes. Writing for the Court in *Maryland v. King*, 569 U.S. 435 (2013), Justice Kennedy likened DNA sampling to fingerprinting during a suspect's booking, calling it "a safe and secure way to process and identify the persons and possessions they must take into custody." Justice Kennedy rejected privacy claims, observing that "once an individual has been arrested on probable cause for a dangerous offense that may require detention before trial, his or her expectations of privacy and freedom from police scrutiny are reduced." By contrast, dissenting Justice Scalia, joined by Justices Ginsburg, Sotomayor, and Kagan, countered that the DNA swabs amounted to a general search warrant meant to possibly solve "cold cases," and thus lacked reasonable individualized suspicion. Alonzo Jay King Jr. was arrested for assault when police took a DNA sample that ultimately linked him to a six-year-old unresolved rape case, for which he was subsequently tried, convicted, and sentenced to life imprisonment.

In *Maryland v. Buie*, 494 U.S. 325 (1990), the Court gave police authority to make "protective sweeps" of the premises when arresting a person in his home if they reasonably believe (although do not have probable cause to believe) that the area may harbor another individual who poses a danger to them. Police had arrest warrants for Jerome Buie and a suspected accomplice in the robbery of a Godfather's Pizza restaurant by two men, one of whom wore a red running suit. They had a secretary call his home to see if he was there before they arrived. When the police arrived at Buie's house, they quickly entered and fanned out through the first and second floors. Failing to find Buie, the police shouted down to the basement and ordered anyone there to come out. Buie soon appeared. And an officer then went down into the basement to see if "there was someone else" there, whereupon he discovered a red running suit. At his trial, Buie's attorney argued that the running suit had been seized pursuant to an illegal search and should be excluded as evidence. On appeal to the Supreme Court, Justice White upheld such protective searches, observing,

> To reach our conclusion today, . . . we need not disagree with the Court's statement in *Chimel* that "the invasion of privacy that results from a top-to-bottom search of a man's house [cannot be characterized] as 'minor,'" . . . The type of search we authorize today is far removed from the "top-to-bottom" search involved in *Chimel*; moreover, it is decidedly not "automati[c]" but may be conducted only when justified by a reasonable, articulable suspicion that the house is harboring a person posing a danger to those on the arrest scene.

But dissenting Justice Brennan, joined by Justice Marshall, countered that the Court had extended the holding in *Terry v. Ohio* (1968) (excerpted below) "into the home, dispensing with the Fourth Amendment's general requirements of a warrant and probable cause and carving a 'reasonable suspicion' exception for protective sweeps in private dwellings."

In *United States v. Grubbs*, 547 U.S. 90 (2006), the Court held that judges may issue "anticipatory" search warrants based on probable cause that a crime is about to be committed. The case involved a warrant for a parcel containing a videotape of child pornography that would not be executed until the parcel arrived and was taken into possession. An undercover postal agent alerted police that Grubbs had ordered the videotape. Justice Scalia upheld such "anticipatory" search warrants based on the traditional standard of probable cause when "there is a fair probability that contraband or evidence of crime" will be found, even though the warrant is issued in advance of the particular item deemed evidence of a crime. In short, the triggering event is not necessary for a warrant because the Fourth Amendment requires only that a warrant specifies the "place to be searched" and "the persons or things to be seized."

In addition, the Roberts Court rejected a claim that the Fourth Amendment was violated by police who were executing a valid warrant but mistakenly searched an innocent couple's home. With only Justice Souter dissenting in *Los Angeles County v. Rettele*, 550 U.S. 609 (2007), the Court held that "[i]n executing a search warrant, officers may take reasonable action to secure the premises and to ensure their own safety and the efficacy of the search." Police had search warrants for two houses in an attempt to locate four known African Americans suspected of engaging in identity theft. When they arrived at 7 A.M. at the first residence, the police were let in by a white couple's seventeen-year-old son, who was immediately ordered to lie face down. The officers proceeded into a bedroom, where Max Rettele and Judy Sadler were naked in bed. At gunpoint, they were ordered to stand up and show their hands, over their protests. The police, then, apologized for their mistake and for not knowing that Rettele and Sadler had moved into the house three months earlier. Rettele subsequently sued the police, but the Court ruled that the Fourth Amendment's guarantee against unreasonable searches and seizures was not violated, observing, "Valid warrants will issue to search the innocent, and people like Rettele and Sadler unfortunately bear the cost."

However, when executing an arrest warrant on private property, police may not invite members of the media to come along and film or photograph the arrest. The Court drew the line on that practice in recognition of homeowners' Fourth Amendment protection for privacy interests in *Wilson v. Layne*, 526 U.S. 603 (1999).

The obligation of police to obtain a search warrant (if circumstances permit and when a search is not incident to an arrest) holds. But the more conservative Burger and Rehnquist Courts tended to be more receptive to law enforcement interests (as further discussed in the next section). The Warren Court held in *Jones v. United States*, 382 U.S. 257 (1960), for instance, that to search the house of a man arrested two blocks away was not permissible as a search incident to arrest. In *Hill v. California*, 401 U.S. 797 (1974), the Burger Court held that the arrest of the wrong man permitted a search of the immediate area surrounding him as a search incident to his arrest. In *Mincey v. Arizona*, 437 U.S. 385 (1978), the Court disallowed a warrantless search of the murder scene in an accused's apartment four days after his arrest. That decision was unanimously reaffirmed in *Flippo v. West Virginia*, 528 U.S. 11 (1999), again rejecting a "murder crime scene" exception for warrantless searches. But in *United States v. Edwards*, 415 U.S. 800 (1974), a bare majority of the Court allowed the warrantless search of an accused's bodily clothing ten hours after his arrest and after substitute clothing had been given to him. The Court also permits warrantless searches of individuals arrested and taken into custody,[10] as well as delayed searches of automobiles that are impounded after the drivers' arrest.[11] In *Soldal v. Cook County*, 506 U.S. 56 (1992), however, the Court upheld the application of the Fourth Amendment to the seizure and removal of a mobile home from a trailer park by the landowner, who removed the mobile home without an eviction order, while police prevented the homeowner from interfering with the eviction. Writing for the Court, Justice White observed that

> [a] "seizure" of property . . . occurs when "there is some meaningful interference with an individual's possessory interests in that property." *United States v. Jacobsen.* 466 U.S. 109 (1984). In addition, we have emphasized that "at the very core" of the Fourth Amendment "stands the right of a man to retreat into his own home." *Silverman v. United States,* 365 U.S. 505 (1961). As a result of the state action in this case, the Soldals' domicile was not only seized, it literally was carried away, giving a new meaning to the term "mobile home." We fail to see how being unceremoniously dispossessed of one's home in the manner alleged to have occurred here can be viewed as anything but a seizure invoking the protection of the Fourth Amendment.

In *Florence v. Board of Chosen Freeholders*, 566 U.S. 318 (2012), the Roberts Court held that the Fourth Amendment was not violated by the strip search of an individual, who was arrested for a minor offense, when jailed, even though there was no reasonable suspicion that he possessed contraband or was dangerous. A New Jersey state trooper had stopped a car in which Albert Florence was a passenger and arrested him on the basis of an outstanding warrant. Florence contested the validity of the warrant but was taken to the Burlington county jail, where he was subjected to the jail's routine strip and body cavity search. He was held for six days, transferred to another correctional facility, and underwent another strip search. The following day, the charges against him were dismissed. Subsequently, Florence sued, contending that his Fourth Amendment rights had been violated. Writing for the majority Justice Kennedy deemed the jail's search procedures for all inmates was reasonable in balancing the needs of correctional facilities and inmates' privacy, and that the creation of an exception for nonviolent offenders would be unworkable. Correction officials have significant interests in conducting thorough searches of new inmates in order to minimize risks to staff and to guard against the introduction of drugs and weapons, as well as to prevent gang violence. Justice Breyer, joined by Justices Ginsburg, Sotomayor, and Kagan, dissented. The Court had previously upheld the strip search of pretrial detainees in federal correctional facilities in order to discover and deter the smuggling of drugs and weapons in *Bell v. Wolfish*, 441 U.S. 520 (1979).

A bare majority of the Roberts Court, however, underscored the Fourth Amendment's protection for homes in a ruling on the use of drug-sniffing dogs in *Florida v. Jardines* (2013) (excerpted below), in contrast to automobiles (see the discussion of *Illinois v. Caballes*, 543 U.S. 405 (2005), and *Florida v. Harris*, 568 U.S. 237 (2013), in Section C of this chapter). Note that Justice Scalia's opinion for the Court relies on the traditional trespass theory of a "constitutionally protected area," whereas Justice Kagan's concurrence would reach the same result based on an analysis of "reasonable expectations of privacy"; the dissenters rejected both approaches and the application of the Fourth Amendment's guarantees.

Moreover, in a major ruling on the application of the Fourth Amendment in the twenty-first century digital age, the Roberts Court unanimously held that police must generally obtain a search warrant for searching cell phones even after arresting a person and taking them into custody in *Riley v. California* (2014) (excerpted below).

Notes

1. However, *Shadwick v. City of Tampa*, 407 U.S. 345 (1972), permitted the delegation of responsibility for issuing warrants to municipal county clerks.

2. See *Wong Sun v. United States*, 371 U.S. 471 (1963).

3. See *Spinelli v. United States*, 393 U.S. 410 (1969), and *Draper v. United States*, 358 U.S. 307 (1959).

4. *Beck v. Ohio*, 379 U.S. 89 (1964).

5. *Jones v. United States*, 362 U.S. 257 (1960).

6. See *McCray v. Illinois*, 386 U.S. 300 (1967).

7. See *United States v. Harris*, 403 U.S. 573 (1971), and *Adams v. Williams*, 407 U.S. 143 (1972).

8. At the same time, the Court holds that, notwithstanding its totality of circumstances approach to determining probable cause, the balance between individual rights and law enforcement interests that is struck in determining probable cause is not drawn on a case-by-case basis. See *Dunaway v. New York*, 442 U.S. 200 (1979).

9. See *Ker v. California*, 374 U.S. 23 (1963) (upholding an arrest for possession of marijuana based on police seeing the plants in a kitchen window); *Vale v. Louisiana*, 399 U.S. 30 (1970) (overturning a warrantless search of a house of a man arrested on its entry steps); and *Lo-Ji Sales v. New York*, 442 U.S. 319 (1979) (reaffirming that the Fourth Amendment forbids open-ended searches of a retail store).

10. *Gustafson v. Florida*, 414 U.S. 260 (1973) (allowing full-body search of a man arrested for a traffic violation and taken into custody).

11. See *Chambers v. Maroney*, 399 U.S. 42 (1970) (upholding search of a car taken to the police station by police who had probable cause to stop the car and believed it contained stolen guns and money); and *South Dakota v. Opperman*, 428 U.S. 364 (1976) (upheld a routine inventory search of a locked car that was impounded).

Chimel v. California

395 U.S. 752, 89 S.CT. 2034 (1969)

Late one afternoon in September 1965, three police officers arrived at Ted Chimel's home in Santa Ana, California. They had a warrant to arrest him for burglary of a coin shop. Chimel was not at home, but his wife allowed the police to wait in the house until he returned from work. When he arrived, police handed him the arrest warrant and asked whether they could look around his house. Chimel objected but was told that "on the basis of a lawful arrest" the police could conduct a search. The police searched the entire three-bedroom house, including the attic, the garage, and a small work-shop. They seized numerous coins, medals, and tokens, which were later used as evidence against Chimel at trial. Following his con-viction, Chimel unsuccessfully appealed to a state appellate court and the California Supreme Court, contending that the police had unlawfully searched his house. Failing in those efforts, Chimel appealed to the Supreme Court, which granted review.

The Court's decision was 7–2, and the majority's opinion was announced by Justice Stewart. Justice Harlan concurred, and Jus-tice White, joined by Justice Black, dissented.

■ ■ ■

☐ *Justice STEWART delivered the opinion of the Court.*

This case raises basic questions concerning the permissible scope under the Fourth Amendment of a search incident to a lawful arrest. . . .

In 1950, [the Court handed down] *United States v. Rabinowitz*, 339 U.S. 56 [(1950)], the decision upon which California primarily relies in the case now before us. In *Rabinowitz*, federal authorities had been informed that the defendant was dealing in stamps bearing forged overprints. On the basis of that information they secured a warrant for his arrest, which they executed at his one-room business office. At the time of the arrest, the officers "searched the desk, safe, and file cabinets in the office for about an hour and a half," and seized 573 stamps with forged overprints. The stamps were admitted into evi-dence at the defendant's trial, and this Court affirmed his conviction, rejecting the contention that the warrantless search had been unlawful. The Court held that the search in its entirety fell within the principle giving law enforcement authorities "[t]he right 'to search the place where the arrest is made in order to find and seize things connected with the crime. . . .'" The test, said the Court, "is not whether it is reasonable to procure a search warrant, but whether the search was reasonable." . . .

Rabinowitz has come to stand for the proposition, *inter alia*, that a warrant-less search "incident to a lawful arrest" may generally extend to the area that is considered to be in the "possession" or under the "control" of the person arrested. And it was on the basis of that proposition that the California courts upheld the search of the petitioner's entire house in this case. That doctrine, however, at least in the broad sense in which it was applied by the California courts in this case, can withstand neither historical nor rational analysis.

Even limited to its own facts, the *Rabinowitz* decision was, as we have seen, hardly founded on an unimpeachable line of authority. [Justice STEWART, after reviewing cases following *Rabinowitz*, concluded that the Fourth] Amendment was in large part a reaction to the general warrants and warrantless searches that had so alienated the colonists and had helped speed the movement for independence. In the scheme of the Amendment, therefore, the requirement that "no Warrants shall issue, but upon probable cause," plays a crucial part. . . .

A similar analysis underlies the "search incident to arrest" principle, and marks its proper extent. When an arrest is made, it is reasonable for the arresting officer to search the person arrested in order to remove any weapons that the latter might seek to use in order to resist arrest or effect his escape. Otherwise, the officer's safety might well be endangered, and the arrest itself frustrated. In addition, it is entirely reasonable for the arresting officer to search for and seize any evidence on the arrestee's person in order to prevent its concealment or destruction. And the area into which an arrestee might reach in order to grab a weapon or evidentiary items must, of course, be governed by a like rule. A gun on a table or in a drawer in front of one who is arrested can be as dangerous to the arresting officer as one concealed in the clothing of the person arrested. There is ample justification, therefore, for a search of the arrestee's person and the area "within his immediate control"—construing that phrase to mean the area from within which he might gain possession of a weapon or destructible evidence.

There is no comparable justification, however, for routinely searching any room other than that in which an arrest occurs—or, for that matter, for searching through all the desk drawers or other closed or concealed areas in that room itself. Such searches, in the absence of well-recognized exceptions, may be made only under the authority of a search warrant. The "adherence to judicial processes" mandated by the Fourth Amendment requires no less. . . .

It is argued in the present case that it is "reasonable" to search a man's house when he is arrested in it. But that argument is founded on little more than a subjective view regarding the acceptability of certain sorts of police conduct, and not on considerations relevant to Fourth Amendment interests. Under such an unconfined analysis, Fourth Amendment protection in this area would approach the evaporation point. It is not easy to explain why, for instance, it is less subjectively "reasonable" to search a man's house when he is arrested on his front lawn—or just down the street—than it is when he happens to be in the house at the time of arrest. . . .

The petitioner correctly points out that one result of decisions such as *Rabinowitz* and *Harris* [v. *United States*, 331 U.S. 14 (1947)], is to give law enforcement officials the opportunity to engage in searches not justified by probable cause, by the simple expedient of arranging to arrest suspects at home rather than elsewhere. We do not suggest that the petitioner is necessarily correct in his assertion that such a strategy was utilized here, but the fact remains that had he been arrested earlier in the day, at his place of employment rather than at home, no search of his house could have been made without a search warrant. . . .

Application of sound Fourth Amendment principles to the facts of this case produces a clear result. The search here went far beyond the petitioner's person and the area from within which he might have obtained either a weapon or something that could have been used as evidence against him. There was no constitutional justification, in the absence of a search warrant, for extending the search beyond that area. The scope of the search was, therefore, "unreasonable" under the Fourth and Fourteenth Amendments and the petitioner's conviction cannot stand.

Reversed.

Arizona v. Hicks

480 U.S. 321, 107 S.Ct. 1149 (1987)

Justice Antonin Scalia presented the pertinent facts in his opinion for the Court in this case, involving a police search and the application of the plain view doctrine.

The Court's decision was 6–3, and the majority's opinion was announced by Justice Scalia. Justice White concurred, and Justice O'Connor, joined by Chief Justice Rehnquist and Justice Powell, dissented.

■ ■ ■

☐ *Justice SCALIA delivered the opinion of the Court.*

In *Coolidge v. New Hampshire*, 403 U.S. 43 (1971), we said that in certain circumstances a warrantless seizure by police of an item that comes within plain view during their lawful search of a private area may be reasonable under the Fourth Amendment. . . . We granted *certiorari* . . . in the present case to decide whether this "plain view" doctrine may be invoked when the police have less than probable cause to believe that the item in question is evidence of a crime or is contraband.

On April 18, 1984, a bullet was fired through the floor of respondent's apartment, striking and injuring a man in the apartment below. Police officers arrived and entered respondent's apartment to search for the shooter, for other victims, and for weapons. They found and seized three weapons, including a sawed-off rifle, and in the course of their search also discovered a stocking-cap mask.

One of the policemen, Officer Nelson, noticed two sets of expensive stereo components, which seemed out of place in the squalid and otherwise ill-appointed four-room apartment. Suspecting that they were stolen, he read and recorded their serial numbers—moving some of the components, including a Bang and Olufsen turntable, in order to do so—which he then reported by phone to his headquarters. On being advised that the turntable had been taken in an armed robbery, he seized it immediately. It was later determined that some of the other serial numbers matched those on other stereo equipment taken in the same armed robbery, and a warrant was obtained and executed to seize that equipment as well. Respondent was subsequently indicted for the robbery. . . .

Officer Nelson's moving of the equipment . . . constitute[d] a "search" separate and apart from the search for the shooter, victims, and weapons that was the lawful objective of his entry into the apartment. Merely inspecting those parts of the turntable that came into view during the latter search would not have constituted an independent search, because it would have produced no additional invasion of respondent's privacy interest. But taking action, unrelated to the objectives of the authorized intrusion, which exposed to view concealed portions of the apartment or its contents, did produce a new invasion of respondent's privacy unjustified by the exigent circumstance that validated the entry. . . . It matters not that the search uncovered nothing of any great personal value to the respondent—serial numbers rather than (what might conceivably have been hidden behind or under the equipment) letters or photographs. A search is a search, even if it happens to disclose nothing but the bottom of a turntable.

The remaining question is whether the search was "reasonable" under the Fourth Amendment.

On this aspect of the case we reject, at the outset, the apparent position of the Arizona Court of Appeals that because the officers' action directed to the stereo equipment was unrelated to the justification for their entry into respondent's apartment, it was *ipso facto* unreasonable. That lack of relationship *always* exists with regard to action validated under the "plain view" doctrine; where action is taken for the purpose of justifying the entry, invocation of the doctrine is superfluous. . . .

We turn, then, to application of the doctrine to the facts of this case. "It is well established that under certain circumstances the police may *seize* evidence in plain view without a warrant," *Coolidge*. Those circumstances include situations "[w]here the initial intrusion that brings the police within plain view of such [evidence] is supported . . . by one of the recognized exceptions to the warrant requirement," such as the exigent-circumstances intrusion here. It would be absurd to say that an object could lawfully be seized and taken from the premises, but could not be moved for closer examination. It is clear, therefore, that the search here was valid if the "plain view" doctrine would have sustained a seizure of the equipment.

There is no doubt it would have done so if Officer Nelson had probable cause to believe that the equipment was stolen. The State has conceded, however, that he had only a "reasonable suspicion," by which it means something less than probable cause. . . .

We now hold that probable cause is required. To say otherwise would be to cut the "plain view" doctrine loose from its theoretical and practical moorings. The theory of that doctrine consists of extending to nonpublic places such as the home, where searches and seizures without a warrant are presumptively unreasonable, the police's longstanding authority to make warrantless seizures in public places of such objects as weapons and contraband. And the practical justification for that extension is the desirability of sparing police, whose viewing of the object in the course of a lawful search is as legitimate as it would have been in a public place, the inconvenience and the risk—to themselves or to preservation of the evidence—of going to obtain a warrant. . . . Dispensing with the need for a warrant is worlds apart from permitting a lesser standard of *cause* for the seizure than a warrant would require, *i.e.*, the standard of probable cause. No reason is apparent why an object should routinely be seizable on lesser grounds, during an unrelated search and seizure, than would have been needed to obtain a warrant for that same object if it had been known to be on the premises.

We do not say, of course, that a seizure can never be justified on less than probable cause. We have held that it can—where, for example, the seizure is minimally intrusive and operational necessities render it the only practicable means of detecting certain types of crime. See, e.g., *United States v. Cortez*, 449 U.S. 411 (1981) (investigative detention of vehicle suspected to be transporting illegal aliens); *United States v. Place*, 462 U.S. 696 [1983] (seizure of suspected drug dealer's luggage at airport to permit exposure to specially trained dog). No special operational necessities are relied on here, however—but rather the mere fact that the items in question came lawfully within the officer's plain view. That alone cannot supplant the requirement of probable cause. . . .

For the reasons stated, the judgment of the Court of Appeals of Arizona is affirmed.

Florida v. Jardines
569 U.S. 1, 133 S.CT. 1409 (2013)

In 2006, William Pedraja of the Miami-Dade Police Department received an unverified tip that marijuana was being grown in the home of Joelis Jardines. One month later, the Department and the Drug Enforcement Administration sent a team to Jardines's home. Detective Pedraja watched the home for fifteen minutes and saw no vehicles in the driveway or activity around the home, and could not see inside because the blinds were drawn. He then approached Jardines's home accompanied by detective Douglas Bartelt, a trained canine handler who had arrived with his drug-sniffing dog. Detective Bartelt had the dog on a six-foot leash, owing in part to the dog's "wild" nature and tendency to dart around erratically. As the dog approached Jardines's front porch, he apparently sensed one of the odors he had been trained to detect and began energetically exploring the area for the strongest point source of that odor. After sniffing the base of the front door, the dog sat—the trained behavior upon discovering the odor's strongest point—and Bartelt pulled the dog away from the door and returned to his vehicle. He then left after informing Pedraja that there had been a positive alert for narcotics. On the basis of what he had learned, Pedraja got a warrant to search the residence. When the warrant was executed later that day, Jardines was arrested and a search revealed marijuana plants. Subsequently, he was charged with trafficking in cannabis. At trial, Jardines moved to suppress the marijuana plants on the ground that the canine investigation was an unreasonable search. The trial court granted the motion, but a state appellate court reversed. On appeal the Florida

Supreme Court held that the use of the trained narcotics dog was a Fourth Amendment search unsupported by probable cause, rendering invalid the warrant based upon information gathered in that search.

The Supreme Court granted review and affirmed the state supreme court's decision by a 5–4 vote. Justice Scalia delivered the opinion of the Court. Justice Kagan filed a concurring opinion, joined by Justices Ginsburg and Sotomayor. Justice Alito filed a dissenting opinion, which Chief Justice Roberts and Justices Kennedy and Breyer joined.

■ ■ ■

☐ *Justice SCALIA delivered the opinion of the Court.*

The Fourth Amendment provides in relevant part that the "right of the people to be secure in their persons, houses, papers, and effects, against unreasonable searches and seizures, shall not be violated." The Amendment establishes a simple baseline, one that for much of our history formed the exclusive basis for its protections: When "the Government obtains information by physically intruding" on persons, houses, papers, or effects, "a 'search' within the original meaning of the Fourth Amendment" has "undoubtedly occurred." *United States v. Jones* (2012). By reason of our decision in *Katz v. United States*, 389 U.S. 276 (1967), property rights "are not the sole measure of Fourth Amendment"—but—though *Katz* may add to the baseline, it does not subtract anything from the Amendment's protections "when the Government does engage in [a] physical intrusion of a constitutionally protected area," *United States v. Knotts*, 460 U.S. 276 (1983).

That principle renders this case a straightforward one. The officers were gathering information in an area belonging to Jardines and immediately surrounding his house—in the curtilage of the house, which we have held enjoys protection as part of the home itself. And they gathered that information by physically entering and occupying the area to engage in conduct not explicitly or implicitly permitted by the homeowner.

The Fourth Amendment "indicates with some precision the places and things encompassed by its protections": persons, houses, papers, and effects. *Oliver v. United States*, 466 U.S. 170 (1984). The Fourth Amendment does not, therefore, prevent all investigations conducted on private property; for example, an officer may (subject to *Katz*) gather information in what we have called "open fields"—even if those fields are privately owned—because such fields are not enumerated in the Amendment's text. *Hester v. United States*, 265 U.S. 57 (1924).

But when it comes to the Fourth Amendment, the home is first among equals. At the Amendment's "very core" stands "the right of a man to retreat into his own home and there be free from unreasonable governmental intrusion." *Silverman v. United States*, 365 U.S. 505 (1961). This right would be of little practical value if the State's agents could stand in a home's porch or side garden and trawl for evidence with impunity; the right to retreat would be significantly diminished if the police could enter a man's property to observe his repose from just outside the front window.

We therefore regard the area "immediately surrounding and associated with the home"—what our cases call the curtilage—as "part of the home itself for Fourth Amendment purposes." That principle has ancient and durable roots. Just as the distinction between the home and the open fields is "as old as the common law," *Hester*, so too is the identity of home and what Blackstone called the "curtilage or homestall," for the "house protects and privileges all its branches and appurtenants." This area around the home is "intimately linked to the home, both physically and psychologically," and is where "privacy expectations are most heightened." *California v. Ciraolo*, 476 U.S. 207 (1986).

While the boundaries of the curtilage are generally "clearly marked," the "conception defining the curtilage" is at any rate familiar enough that it is "easily understood from our daily experience." Here there is no doubt that the officers entered it: The front porch is the classic exemplar of an area adjacent to the home and "to which the activity of home life extends."

Since the officers' investigation took place in a constitutionally protected area, we turn to the question of whether it was accomplished through an unlicensed physical intrusion. While law enforcement officers need not "shield their eyes" when passing by the home "on public thoroughfares," an officer's leave to gather information is sharply circumscribed when he steps off those thoroughfares and enters the Fourth Amendment's protected areas. In permitting, for example, visual observation of the home from "public navigable airspace," we were careful to note that it was done "in a physically nonintrusive manner." *Entick v. Carrington*, 95 Eng. Rep. 807 (K.B. 1765), a case "undoubtedly familiar" to "every American statesman" at the time of the Founding. *Boyd v. United States*, 116 U.S. 616 (1886), states the general rule clearly: "[O]ur law holds the property of every man so sacred, that no man can set his foot upon his neighbour's close without his leave." As it is undisputed that the detectives had all four of their feet and all four of their companion's firmly planted on the constitutionally protected extension of Jardines' home, the only question is whether he had given his leave (even implicitly) for them to do so. He had not. . . .

[And] introducing a trained police dog to explore the area around the home in hopes of discovering incriminating evidence is something else. There is no customary invitation to do that. An invitation to engage in canine forensic investigation assuredly does not inhere in the very act of hanging a knocker. To find a visitor knocking on the door is routine (even if sometimes unwelcome); to spot that same visitor exploring the front path with a metal detector, or marching his bloodhound into the garden before saying hello and asking permission, would inspire most of us to—well, call the police. The scope of a license—express or implied—is limited not only to a particular area but also to a specific purpose. Consent at a traffic stop to an officer's checking out an anonymous tip that there is a body in the trunk does not permit the officer to rummage through the trunk for narcotics. Here, the background social norms that invite a visitor to the front door do not invite him there to conduct a search. . . .

The State argues that investigation by a forensic narcotics dog by definition cannot implicate any legitimate privacy interest. The State cites for authority our decisions in *United States v. Place*, 462 U.S. 696 (1983), *United States v. Jacobsen*, 466 U.S. 109 (1984), and *Illinois v. Caballes*, 543 U.S. 405 (2005), which held, respectively, that canine inspection of luggage in an airport, chemical testing of a substance that had fallen from a parcel in transit, and canine inspection of an automobile during a lawful traffic stop, do not violate the "reasonable expectation of privacy" described in *Katz*.

Just last Term, we considered an argument much like this. [*United States v.*] *Jones* [131 S.Ct. 945 (2012)] held that tracking an automobile's whereabouts using a physically-mounted GPS receiver is a Fourth Amendment search. The Government argued that the *Katz* standard "show[ed] that no search occurred," as the defendant had "no 'reasonable expectation of privacy'"—a proposition with at least as much support in our case law as the one the State marshals here. But because the GPS receiver had been physically mounted on the defendant's automobile (thus intruding on his "effects"), we held that tracking the vehicle's movements was a search: a person's "rights do not rise or fall with the *Katz* formulation." The *Katz* reasonable-expectations test "has been added to, not substituted for," the traditional property-based understanding of the Fourth Amendment, and so is unnecessary to consider when the government gains evidence by physically intruding on constitutionally protected areas.

Thus, we need not decide whether the officers' investigation of Jardines' home violated his expectation of privacy under *Katz*. One virtue of the Fourth Amendment's property-rights baseline is that it keeps easy cases easy. That the officers learned what they learned only by physically intruding on Jardines' property to gather evidence is enough to establish that a search occurred.

For a related reason we find irrelevant the State's argument (echoed by the dissent) that forensic dogs have been commonly used by police for centuries. This argument is apparently directed to our holding in *Kyllo v. United States*, 533 U.S. 27 (2001), that surveillance of the home is a search where "the Government uses a device that is not in general public use" to "explore details of the home that would previously have been unknowable without physical intrusion." But the implication of that statement is that when the government uses a physical intrusion to explore details of the home (including its curtilage), the antiquity of the tools that they bring along is irrelevant.

The government's use of trained police dogs to investigate the home and its immediate surroundings is a "search" within the meaning of the Fourth Amendment. The judgment of the Supreme Court of Florida is therefore affirmed.

□ *Justice KAGAN, with whom Justice GINSBURG and Justice SOTOMAYOR join, concurring.*

For me, a simple analogy clinches this case—and does so on privacy as well as property grounds. A stranger comes to the front door of your home carrying super-high-powered binoculars. He doesn't knock or say hello. Instead, he stands on the porch and uses the binoculars to peer through your windows, into your home's furthest corners. It doesn't take long (the binoculars are really very fine): In just a couple of minutes, his uncommon behavior allows him to learn details of your life you disclose to no one. Has your "visitor" trespassed on your property, exceeding the license you have granted to members of the public to, say, drop off the mail or distribute campaign flyers? Yes, he has. And has he also invaded your "reasonable expectation of privacy," by nosing into intimacies you sensibly thought protected from disclosure? *Katz v. United States* (1967) (HARLAN, J., concurring). Yes, of course, he has done that too.

That case is this case in every way that matters. Here, police officers came to Joelis Jardines' door with a super-sensitive instrument, which they deployed to detect things inside that they could not perceive unassisted. The equipment they used was animal, not mineral. But contra the dissent (noting the ubiquity of dogs in American households), that is of no significance in determining whether a search occurred. Detective Bartelt's dog was not your neighbor's pet, come to your porch on a leisurely stroll. As this Court discussed earlier this Term, drug-detection dogs are highly trained tools of law enforcement, geared to respond in distinctive ways to specific scents so as to convey clear and reliable information to their human partners. See *Florida v. Harris* (2013). They are to the poodle down the street as high-powered binoculars are to a piece of plain glass. Like the binoculars, a drug-detection dog is a specialized device for discovering objects not in plain view (or plain smell). And as in the hypothetical above, that device was aimed here at a home—the most private and inviolate (or so we expect) of all the places and things the Fourth Amendment protects. Was this activity a trespass? Yes, as the Court holds today. Was it also an invasion of privacy? Yes, that as well.

The Court today treats this case under a property rubric; I write separately to note that I could just as happily have decided it by looking to Jardines' privacy interests. A decision along those lines would have looked . . . well, much like this one. It would have talked about "the right of a man to retreat into his own home and there be free from unreasonable governmental intrusion." It would have insisted on maintaining the "practical value" of that right by preventing police officers from standing in an adjacent space and "trawl[ing] for evidence with impunity." It would have explained that "privacy expectations are most heightened" in the home and the surrounding area. And it would have determined that police officers invade those shared expectations when they use trained canine assistants to reveal within the confines of a home what they could not otherwise have found there.

It is not surprising that in a case involving a search of a home, property concepts and privacy concepts should so align. The law of property "naturally enough influence[s]" our "shared social expectations" of what places should be free from governmental incursions. And so the sentiment "my home is my own," while originating in property law, now also denotes a common understanding—extending even beyond that law's formal protections—about an especially private sphere. Jardines' home was his property; it was also his most intimate and familiar space. The analysis proceeding from each of those facts, as today's decision reveals, runs mostly along the same path.

I can think of only one divergence: If we had decided this case on privacy grounds, we would have realized that *Kyllo v. United States*, 533 U.S. 27 (2001), already resolved it. The *Kyllo* Court held that police officers conducted a search when they used a thermal-imaging device to detect heat emanating from a private home, even though they committed no trespass. Highlighting our intention to draw both a "firm" and a "bright" line at "the entrance to the house," we announced the following rule: "Where, as here, the Government uses a device that is not in general public use, to explore details of the home that would previously have been unknowable without physical intrusion, the surveillance is a 'search' and is presumptively unreasonable without a warrant."

That "firm" and "bright" rule governs this case: The police officers here conducted a search because they used a "device . . . not in general public use" (a trained drug-detection dog) to "explore details of the home" (the presence of certain substances) that they would not otherwise have discovered without entering the premises. . . .

☐ *Justice ALITO, with whom THE CHIEF JUSTICE,*
Justice KENNEDY, and Justice BREYER join, dissenting.

The Court's decision in this important Fourth Amendment case is based on a putative rule of trespass law that is nowhere to be found in the annals of Anglo-American jurisprudence.

The law of trespass generally gives members of the public a license to use a walkway to approach the front door of a house and to remain there for a brief time. This license is not limited to persons who intend to speak to an occupant or who actually do so. (Mail carriers and persons delivering packages and flyers are examples of individuals who may lawfully approach a front door without intending to converse.) Nor is the license restricted to categories of visitors whom an occupant of the dwelling is likely to welcome; as the Court acknowledges, this license applies even to "solicitors, hawkers and peddlers of all kinds." And the license even extends to police officers who wish to gather evidence against an occupant (by asking potentially incriminating questions).

According to the Court, however, the police officer in this case, Detective Bartelt, committed a trespass because he was accompanied during his otherwise lawful visit to the front door of respondent's house by his dog, Franky. Where is the authority evidencing such a rule? Dogs have been domesticated for about 12,000 years; they were ubiquitous in both this country and Britain at the time of the adoption of the Fourth Amendment; and their acute sense of smell has been used in law enforcement for centuries. Yet the Court has been unable to find a single case—from the United States or any other common-law nation—that supports the rule on which its decision is based. Thus, trespass law provides no support for the Court's holding today.

The Court's decision is also inconsistent with the reasonable-expectations-of-privacy test that the Court adopted in *Katz v. United States.* A reasonable person understands that odors emanating from a house may be detected from locations that are open to the public, and a reasonable person will not count on the strength of those odors remaining within the range that, while detectible by a dog, cannot be smelled by a human.

For these reasons, I would hold that no search within the meaning of the Fourth Amendment took place in this case, and I would reverse the decision below. . . .

The concurring opinion attempts to provide an alternative ground for today's decision, namely, that Detective Bartelt's conduct violated respondent's reasonable expectations of privacy. But we have already rejected a very similar, if not identical argument, see *Illinois v. Caballes,* 543 U.S. 405 (2005), and in any event I see no basis for concluding that the occupants of a dwelling have a reasonable expectation of privacy in odors that emanate from the dwelling and reach spots where members of the public may lawfully stand. . . .

The concurrence suggests that a *Kyllo*-based decision would be "much like" the actual decision of the Court, but that is simply not so. The holding of the Court is based on what the Court sees as a "physical intrusion of a constitutionally protected area." As a result, it does not apply when a dog alerts while on a public sidewalk or street or in the corridor of a building to which the dog and handler have been lawfully admitted.

The concurrence's *Kyllo*-based approach would have a much wider reach. When the police used the thermal imaging device in *Kyllo*, they were on a public street and "committed no trespass." Therefore, if a dog's nose is just like a thermal imaging device for Fourth Amendment purposes, a search would occur if a dog alerted while on a public sidewalk or in the corridor of an apartment building. And the same would be true if the dog was trained to sniff, not for marijuana, but for more dangerous quarry, such as explosives or for a violent fugitive or kidnapped child. I see no ground for hampering legitimate law enforcement in this way.

The conduct of the police officer in this case did not constitute a trespass and did not violate respondent's reasonable expectations of privacy. I would hold that this conduct was not a search, and I therefore respectfully dissent.

Riley v. California
573 U.S. 373, 134 S.CT. 2473 (2014)

David Riley was stopped for a traffic violation and arrested on weapons charges. An officer searching Riley incident to the arrest seized a cell phone from Riley's pants pocket. The officer accessed information on the phone and noticed the repeated use of a term associated with a street gang. At the police station two hours later, a detective specializing in gangs further examined the phone's digital contents. Based in part on photographs and videos that the detective found, Riley was charged with a gang-related shooting. Riley's attorney moved to suppress all evidence that the police had obtained from his cell phone. The trial court denied the motion, Riley was convicted, and that decision was affirmed by a California state appellate court.

Brima Wurie was arrested after police observed him making a drug sale. At the police station, the officers seized a cell phone from Wurie's person and noticed that the phone was receiving multiple calls from a source identified as "my house." The officers opened the phone, accessed its call log, determined the number associated with the "my house" label, and traced that number to what they suspected was Wurie's apartment. They secured a search warrant and found drugs, a firearm and ammunition, and cash. Wurie was then charged with drug and firearm offenses. He moved to suppress the evidence obtained from the search of the apartment. A federal district court denied the motion, Wurie was convicted, and a federal appellate court reversed the denial of the motion to suppress and vacated Wurie's convictions.

On appeal, the Supreme Court reversed the state court's decision in Riley's case and affirmed the federal appellate court's decision in Wurie's case. Chief Justice Roberts delivered the opinion of a unanimous Court. Justice Alito filed a concurring opinion.

■ ■ ■

☐ *Chief Justice ROBERTS delivered the opinion of the Court.*

The Fourth Amendment provides: "The right of the people to be secure in their persons, houses, papers, and effects, against unreasonable searches and seizures, shall not be violated, and no Warrants shall issue, but upon probable cause, supported by Oath or affirmation, and particularly describing the place to be searched, and the persons or things to be seized."

As the text makes clear, "the ultimate touchstone of the Fourth Amendment is 'reasonableness.'" Our cases have determined that "[w]here a search is undertaken by law enforcement officials to discover evidence of criminal wrongdoing . . . reasonableness generally requires the obtaining of a judicial warrant." *Vernonia School Dist. 47J v. Acton*, 515 U.S. 646 (1995). Such a warrant ensures that the inferences to support a search are "drawn by a neutral and detached magistrate instead of being judged by the officer engaged in the often competitive enterprise of ferreting out crime." *Johnson v. United States*, 333 U.S. 10 (1948). In the absence of a warrant, a search is reasonable only if it falls within a specific exception to the warrant requirement.

The two cases before us concern the reasonableness of a warrantless search incident to a lawful arrest. In 1914, this Court first acknowledged in dictum "the right on the part of the Government, always recognized under English and American law, to search the person of the accused when legally arrested to discover and seize the fruits or evidences of crime." *Weeks v. United States*, 232 U.S. 383. Since that time, it has been well accepted that such a search constitutes an exception to the warrant requirement. Indeed, the label "exception" is something of a misnomer in this context, as warrantless searches incident to arrest occur with far greater frequency than searches conducted pursuant to a warrant.

Although the existence of the exception for such searches has been recognized for a century, its scope has been debated for nearly as long. See *Arizona v. Gant*, 556 U.S. 332 (2009). That debate has focused on the extent to which officers may search property found on or near the arrestee. Three related precedents set forth the rules governing such searches:

The first, *Chimel v. California*, 395 U.S. 752 (1969), laid the groundwork for most of the existing search incident to arrest doctrine. Police officers in that case arrested Chimel inside his home and proceeded to search his entire three-bedroom house, including the attic and garage. In particular rooms, they also looked through the contents of drawers.

The Court crafted the following rule for assessing the reasonableness of a search incident to arrest: "When an arrest is made, it is reasonable for the arresting officer to search the person arrested in order to remove any weapons that the latter might seek to use in order to resist arrest or effect his escape. Otherwise, the officer's safety might well be endangered, and the arrest itself frustrated. In addition, it is entirely reasonable for the arresting officer to search for and seize any evidence on the arrestee's person in order to prevent its concealment or destruction. . . . There is ample justification, therefore, for a search of the arrestee's person and the area 'within his immediate control'—construing that phrase to mean the area from within which he might gain possession of a weapon or destructible evidence."

The extensive warrantless search of Chimel's home did not fit within this exception, because it was not needed to protect officer safety or to preserve evidence. Four years later, in *United States* v. *Robinson*, 414 U.S. 218 (1973), the Court applied the *Chimel* analysis in the context of a search of the arrestee's person. A police officer had arrested Robinson for driving with a revoked license. The officer conducted a patdown search and felt an object that he could not identify in Robinson's coat pocket. He removed the object, which turned out to be a crumpled cigarette package, and opened it. Inside were 14 capsules of heroin. . . .

[T]he search of Robinson was reasonable even though there was no concern about the loss of evidence, and the arresting officer had no specific concern that Robinson might be armed. In doing so, the Court did not draw a line between a search of Robinson's person and a further examination of the cigarette pack found during that search. It merely noted that, "[h]aving in the course of a lawful search come upon the crumpled package of cigarettes, [the officer] was entitled to inspect it." A few years later, the Court clarified that this exception was limited to "personal property . . . immediately associated with the person of the arrestee." *United States* v. *Chadwick*, 433 U.S. 1(1977) (200-pound, locked footlocker could not be searched incident to arrest), abrogated on other grounds by *California* v. *Acevedo*, 500 U.S. 565 (1991).

The search incident to arrest trilogy concludes with *Gant*, which analyzed searches of an arrestee's vehicle. *Gant*, like *Robinson*, recognized that the *Chimel* concerns for officer safety and evidence preservation underlie the search incident to arrest exception. As a result, the Court concluded that *Chimel* could authorize police to search a vehicle "only when the arrestee is unsecured and within reaching distance of the passenger compartment at the time of the search." *Gant* added, however, an independent exception for a warrantless search of a vehicle's passenger compartment "when it is 'reasonable to believe evidence relevant to the crime of arrest might be found in the vehicle.'" That exception stems not from *Chimel*, the Court explained, but from "circumstances unique to the vehicle context."

These cases require us to decide how the search incident to arrest doctrine applies to modern cell phones, which are now such a pervasive and insistent part of daily life that the proverbial visitor from Mars might conclude they were an important feature of human anatomy. A smart phone of the sort taken from Riley was unheard of ten years ago; a significant majority of American adults now own such phones. Even less sophisticated phones like Wurie's, which have already faded in popularity since Wurie was arrested in 2007, have been around for less than 15 years. Both phones are based on technology nearly inconceivable just a few decades ago, when *Chimel* and *Robinson* were decided.

Absent more precise guidance from the founding era, we generally determine whether to exempt a given type of search from the warrant requirement "by assessing, on the one hand, the degree to which it intrudes upon an individual's privacy and, on the other, the degree to which it is needed for the promotion of legitimate governmental interests." Such a balancing of interests supported the search incident to arrest exception in *Robinson*, and a mechanical application of *Robinson* might well support the warrantless searches at issue here.

But while *Robinson*'s categorical rule strikes the appropriate balance in the context of physical objects, neither of its rationales has much force with respect to digital content on cell phones. On the government interest side, *Robinson* concluded that the two risks identified in *Chimel*—harm to officers and destruction of evidence—are present in all custodial arrests. There are no comparable risks when the search is of digital data. In addition, *Robinson* regarded any privacy interests retained by an individual after arrest as significantly diminished by the fact of the arrest itself. Cell phones, however, place vast quantities of personal information literally in the hands of individuals. A search of the information on a cell phone bears little resemblance to the type of brief physical search considered in *Robinson*.

We therefore decline to extend *Robinson* to searches of data on cell phones, and hold instead that officers must generally secure a warrant before conducting such a search. . . .

Digital data stored on a cell phone cannot itself be used as a weapon to harm an arresting officer or to effectuate the arrestee's escape. Law enforcement officers remain free to examine the physical aspects of a phone to ensure that it will not be used as a weapon—say, to determine whether there is a razor blade hidden between the phone and its case. Once an officer has secured a phone and eliminated any potential physical threats, however, data on the phone can endanger no one.

Perhaps the same might have been said of the cigarette pack seized from Robinson's pocket. Once an officer gained control of the pack, it was unlikely that Robinson could have accessed the pack's contents. But unknown physical objects may always pose risks, no matter how slight, during the tense atmosphere of a custodial arrest. The officer in *Robinson* testified that he could not identify the objects in the cigarette pack but knew they were not cigarettes. Given that, a further search was a reasonable protective measure. No such unknowns exist with respect to digital data. . . .

The United States and California focus primarily on the second *Chimel* rationale: preventing the destruction of evidence.

Both Riley and Wurie concede that officers could have seized and secured their cell phones to prevent destruction of evidence while seeking a warrant. That is a sensible concession. And once law enforcement officers have secured a cell phone, there is no longer any risk that the arrestee himself will be able to delete incriminating data from the phone.

The United States and California argue that information on a cell phone may nevertheless be vulnerable to two types of evidence destruction unique to digital data—remote wiping and data encryption. . . . As an initial matter, these broader concerns about the loss of evidence are distinct from *Chimel*'s focus on a defendant who responds to arrest by trying to conceal or destroy evidence within his reach. With respect to remote wiping, the Government's primary concern turns on the actions of third parties who are not present at the scene of arrest. And data encryption is even further afield. There, the Government focuses on the ordinary operation of a phone's security features, apart from *any* active attempt by a defendant or his associates to conceal or destroy evidence upon arrest. . . .

In any event, as to remote wiping, law enforcement is not without specific means to address the threat. Remote wiping can be fully prevented by disconnecting a phone from the network. There are at least two simple ways to do this: First, law enforcement officers can turn the phone off or remove its battery. Second, if they are concerned about encryption or other potential problems, they can leave a phone powered on and place it in an enclosure that isolates the phone from radio waves. Such devices are commonly called "Faraday bags," after the English scientist Michael Faraday. They are essentially sandwich bags made of aluminum foil: cheap, lightweight, and easy to use. They may not be a complete answer to the problem, but at least for now they provide a reasonable response. In fact, a number of law enforcement agencies around the country already encourage the use of Faraday bags.

To the extent that law enforcement still has specific concerns about the potential loss of evidence in a particular case, there remain more targeted ways to address those concerns. If "the police are truly confronted with a 'now or never' situation,"—for example, circumstances suggesting that a defendant's phone will be the target of an imminent remote-wipe attempt—they may be able to rely on exigent circumstances to search the phone immediately.

The search incident to arrest exception rests not only on the heightened government interests at stake in a volatile arrest situation, but also on an arrestee's reduced privacy interests upon being taken into police custody. *Robinson* focused primarily on the first of those rationales. The fact that an arrestee has diminished privacy interests does not mean that the Fourth Amendment falls out of the picture entirely. Not every search "is acceptable solely because a person is in custody." To the contrary, when "privacy-related concerns are weighty enough" a "search may require a warrant, notwithstanding the diminished expectations of privacy of the arrestee." *Ibid.* One such example, of course, is *Chimel*. *Chimel* refused to "characteriz[e] the invasion of privacy that results from a top-to-bottom search of a man's house as 'minor.' " Because a search of the arrestee's entire house was a substantial invasion beyond the arrest itself, the Court concluded that a warrant was required.

Robinson is the only decision from this Court applying *Chimel* to a search of the contents of an item found on an arrestee's person. . . .

The United States asserts that a search of all data stored on a cell phone is "materially indistinguishable" from searches of these sorts of physical items. That is like saying a ride on horseback is materially indistinguishable from a flight to the moon. . . .

Cell phones differ in both a quantitative and a qualitative sense from other objects that might be kept on an arrestee's person. The term "cell phone" is itself misleading shorthand; many of these devices are in fact minicomputers that also happen to have the capacity to be used as a telephone. They could just as easily be called cameras, video players, rolodexes, calendars, tape recorders, libraries, diaries, albums, televisions, maps, or newspapers.

One of the most notable distinguishing features of modern cell phones is their immense storage capacity. Before cell phones, a search of a person was limited by physical realities and tended as a general matter to constitute only a narrow intrusion on privacy. Most people cannot lug around every piece of mail they have received for the past several months, every picture they have taken, or every book or article they have read—nor would they have any reason to attempt to do so. And if they did, they would have to drag behind them a trunk of the sort held to require a search warrant in *Chadwick*, rather than a container the size of the cigarette package in *Robinson*.

But the possible intrusion on privacy is not physically limited in the same way when it comes to cell phones. The current top-selling smart phone has a standard capacity of 16 gigabytes (and is available with up to 64 gigabytes). Sixteen gigabytes translates to millions of pages of text, thousands of pictures, or hundreds of videos. Cell phones couple that capacity with the ability to store many different types of information: Even the most basic phones that sell for less than $20 might hold photographs, picture messages, text messages, Internet browsing history, a calendar, a thousand-entry phone book, and so on. We expect that the gulf between physical practicability and digital capacity will only continue to widen in the future.

The storage capacity of cell phones has several interrelated consequences for privacy. First, a cell phone collects in one place many distinct types of information—an address, a note, a prescription, a bank statement, a video—that reveal much more in combination than any isolated record. Second, a cell phone's capacity allows even just one type of information to convey far more than previously possible. The sum of an individual's private life can be reconstructed through a thousand photographs labeled with dates, locations, and descriptions; the same cannot be said of a photograph or two of loved ones tucked into a wallet. Third, the data on a phone can date back to the purchase of the phone, or even earlier. A person might carry in his pocket a slip of paper reminding him to call Mr. Jones; he would not carry a record of all his communications with Mr. Jones for the past several months, as would routinely be kept on a phone.

Finally, there is an element of pervasiveness that characterizes cell phones but not physical records. Prior to the digital age, people did not typically carry a cache of sensitive personal information with them as they went about their day. Now it is the person who is not carrying a cell phone, with all that it contains, who is the exception. According to one poll, nearly three-quarters of smart phone users report being within five feet of their phones most of the time, with 12% admitting that they even use their phones in the shower. A decade ago police officers searching an arrestee might have occasionally stumbled across a highly personal item such as a diary. But those discoveries were likely to be few and far between. Today, by contrast, it is no exaggeration to say that many of the more than 90% of American adults who own a cell phone keep on their person a digital record of nearly every aspect of their lives—from the mundane to the intimate. Allowing the police to scrutinize such records on a routine basis is quite different from allowing them to search a personal item or two in the occasional case.

Although the data stored on a cell phone is distinguished from physical records by quantity alone, certain types of data are also qualitatively different. An Internet search and browsing history, for example, can be found on an Internet-enabled phone and could reveal an individual's private interests or concerns—perhaps a search for certain symptoms of disease, coupled with frequent visits to WebMD. Data on a cell phone can also reveal where a person has been. Historic location information is a standard feature on many smart phones and can reconstruct someone's specific movements down to the minute, not only around town but also within a particular building . . .

We cannot deny that our decision today will have an impact on the ability of law enforcement to combat crime. Cell phones have become important tools in facilitating coordination and communication among members of criminal enterprises, and can provide valuable incriminating information about dangerous criminals. Privacy comes at a cost.

Our holding, of course, is not that the information on a cell phone is immune from search; it is instead that a warrant is generally required before such a search, even when a cell phone is seized incident to arrest. Our cases have historically recognized that the warrant requirement is "an important working part of our machinery of government," not merely "an inconvenience to be somehow 'weighed' against the claims of police efficiency." *Coolidge* v. *New Hampshire*, 493 U.S. 443 (1971). Recent technological advances similar to those discussed here have, in addition, made the process of obtaining a warrant itself more efficient.

Moreover, even though the search incident to arrest exception does not apply to cell phones, other case-specific exceptions may still justify a warrantless search of a particular phone. "One well-recognized exception applies when 'the exigencies of the situation' make the needs of law enforcement so compelling that [a] warrantless search is objectively reasonable under the Fourth Amendment." . . . In light of the availability of the exigent circumstances exception, there is no reason to believe that law enforcement officers will not be able to address some of the more extreme hypotheticals that have been suggested: a suspect texting an accomplice who, it is feared, is preparing to detonate a bomb, or a child abductor who may have information about the child's location on his cell phone. The defendants here recognize—indeed, they stress—that such fact-specific threats may justify a warrantless search of cell phone data. The critical point is that, unlike the search incident to arrest exception, the exigent circumstances exception requires a court to examine whether an emergency justified a warrantless search in each particular case. . . .

B | *Exceptions to the Warrant Requirement*

There are a number of exceptions to the Fourth Amendment's command that police obtain a warrant prior to conducting a search. Besides conducting *searches incident to an arrest* after taking a person into custody (as discussed in Section A of this chapter), police may undertake *consent searches*—searches of persons and their property after being given their consent. While it seems obvious that individuals may waive their rights, whose and what kind of consent is necessary for a police search has proven problematic.

The Court maintains that police may not conduct a warrantless search of an apartment or hotel room without the occupant's consent, despite having the owner's permission.[1] However, in *Michigan v. Summers*, 452 U.S. 692 (1981), the Court held that police when executing a search warrant may "detain the occupants of the premises while a proper search is conducted." That ruling was further qualified and clarified in *Bailey v. United States*, 568 U.S. 186 (2013), in holding that the *Summers* rule was limited to the immediate vicinity of the premises. In *Bailey*, police followed and detained Chunon Bailey about one mile from an apartment where narcotics were found in plain view and then arrested him. Justices

Breyer, Thomas, and Alito dissented. In *Illinois v. Rodriguez*, 497 U.S. 177 (1990), the Court also held that incriminating evidence may be used at trial even though it was seized during a warrantless entry into a home by police officers who were let in by a person they mistakenly thought was authorized to consent to a search. "What we hold today does not suggest that law enforcement officers may always accept a person's invitation to enter," wrote Justice Scalia, when holding that "consent to enter must be judged against an objective standard: would the facts available to the officer . . . warrant a man of reasonable caution in the belief that the consenting party had authority over the premises?" In addition, in *Minnesota v. Carter* (1998) (excerpted in Section E of this chapter), the Court held that temporary visitors in homes (unlike homeowners, apartment renters, and even overnight guests) have no "reasonable expectations of privacy" and Fourth Amendment protection.

Traditionally, consent searches were justified on the theory that individuals could waive their Fourth Amendment rights. But in *Schneckloth v. Bustamonte*, 412 U.S. 218 (1973), the Burger Court appeared to dismiss that theory in holding that the underlying issue is whether consent may be reasonably deemed to be "voluntary" based on the circumstances surrounding a particular search. There the Court ruled that, when a suspect is not in custody but police make a consent search, the state must show only that the consent was voluntarily given, even though the suspect had no knowledge that he could refuse to agree to the search. The next year, *United States v. Matlock*, 415 U.S. 164 (1974), held that police could search a bedroom inhabited by two persons so long as they obtained the consent of one of the two. When distinguishing earlier rulings denying consent searches based on a landlord's consent, Justice White explained that "it is reasonable to recognize that any of the co-inhabitants has the right to permit the inspection in his own common area to be searched." However, *Georgia v. Randolph*, 547 U.S. 103 (2006), held that police may not search a home without a warrant based on the consent of one spouse over the objections of another. Writing for the Court, Justice Souter distinguished *Matlock*'s holding that the consent of one cotenant was sufficient when the other was not present to object, because of the burden on police of obtaining the latter's consent, in ruling that the consent of both cotenants present must be obtained before conducting a warrantless search. Chief Justice Roberts and Justices Scalia and Thomas dissented.

In *Illinois v. Batchelder*, 463 U.S. 1112 (1983), the Court also upheld *implied consent* laws requiring drivers to submit to breathalyzer tests or else have their licenses automatically revoked. In *Birchfield v. North Dakota*, 136 S.Ct. 614 (2015), however, the Roberts Court held that the Fourth Amendment, while permitting warrantless breath tests as a *search-incident-to-an-arrest,* does not permit warrantless blood tests and drivers may not be held criminally liable for refusing to submit to blood tests. Writing for the Court, Justice Alito reasoned that breath tests do not implicate significant privacy interests, whereas blood tests do since they involve piercing and extracting part of a person's body. Moreover, motorists may not be criminally punished for refusing to submit to a blood (unlike a breath) test and a warrant must be obtained for such searches. Dissenting in part, Justices Ginsburg and Sotomayor would have barred both warrantless breath and blood tests without a driver's explicit consent. Notably, when police make a warrantless arrest, *Gerstein v. Pugh*, 420 U.S. 103 (1975), held that authorities must provide their arrestees "promptly" with a fair and reliable determination of the probable cause for their arrest. However, in *County of Riverside v. McLaughlin*, 500 U.S. 44 (1991), a bare majority of the Rehnquist Court reinterpreted *Gerstein* and held that states may hold individuals who have been arrested without a warrant for up to forty-eight hours without a hearing to determine whether police had probable cause to make an arrest and incarcerate an individual. Notably, in dissent Justice Scalia sharply criticized the majority for its reinterpretation of *Gerstein* and departure from the common law and constitutional jurisprudence underlying the adoption of the Fourth Amendment in 1791.

Another exception is the so-called *open fields doctrine*—allowing police to search and seize illegal items that are in open public view—announced in *Hester v. United States*, 265 U.S. 57 (1924). On this doctrine, the Court upheld a warrantless search of land on which marijuana was growing in *Oliver v. United States*, 466 U.S. 170 (1984) and two years later, in *California v. Ciraolo* (1986) (see excerpt in Section E). The justices also rejected the Fourth Amendment arguments of Dow Chemical Company, which objected to the Environmental Protection Agency's aerial photography of its site when inspecting for pollution violations in *Dow Chemical Company v. United States*, 476 U.S. 227 (1986). *United States v. Dunn*, 480 U.S. 294 (1987), further extended the open fields doctrine when permitting a search of a barn in an open field at night by police armed with a flashlight but no warrant. And in *Florida v. Riley*, 488 U.S. 445 (1988), the Court again rejected Fourth Amendment privacy claims when holding that police do not need a search warrant for searches of private property by helicopters flying 400 feet above ground.

More controversial is the exception the Warren Court carved out in *Terry v. Ohio* (1968) (excerpted below), allowing police without either a warrant or probable cause to *stop and frisk* individuals who look suspicious. There the Court explicitly balanced Fourth Amendment interests against those of law enforcement. Notice, though, Chief Justice Warren approved of such searches only to the extent that they were "limited to outer clothing . . . in an attempt to discover weapons which might be used to assault [a police officer]." A companion ruling, *Sibron v. New York*, 392 U.S. 40 (1968), underscored *Terry*'s limited holding in refusing to permit the search of a drug suspect who police had no reason to believe was armed or dangerous; as Chief Justice Warren emphasized, "the police officer is not entitled to seize and search every person whom he sees on the street."

The *Terry* exception has been enlarged by the Burger, Rehnquist, and Roberts Courts to allow greater leeway for police to stop and search suspicious individuals. In *Adams v. Williams*, 407 U.S. 143 (1972), the Court permitted the stopping and frisking of an individual by an officer, who had no personal knowledge of him and merely relied on a tip from a known informant that he was carrying narcotics and had a gun. The officer went to a vehicle in which the man was sitting and, as the man rolled down the door window, the officer reached in and grabbed the man's loaded gun. However, in *Florida v. J.L.*, 529 U.S. 266 (2000), the Court held unconstitutional the stopping and frisking of an individual for a gun based on a police officer's receiving an anonymous tip that a young black male wearing a plaid shirt at a bus stop was carrying a gun. Justice Ginsburg ruled that anonymous tips, unless accompanied by other specific indicators of reliability, fall short of providing a basis for reasonable suspicion to justify the stopping and frisking of individuals. As with other recent decisions, however, that exception has been expanded with respect to traffic stops. In *Arizona v. Johnson*, 555 U.S. 323 (2009), the Roberts Court further extended the "stop and frisk" exception to the Fourth Amendment laid down in *Terry v. Ohio*. Justice Ginsburg held for a unanimous Court that police may order a passenger out of a stopped vehicle and conduct a pat-down search if they have reason to believe that the rider is armed and dangerous, and therefore poses a threat to police and the public. In *Brendlin v. California*, 551 U.S. 249 (2007), the Roberts Court held that during a traffic stop police may seize "everyone in the vehicle"—the driver and all passengers.

United States v. Sokolow (1989) (excerpted below) underscores that the police no longer need to have probable cause to stop and frisk suspicious individuals. When upholding law enforcement officers' investigative stop of a suspected drug courier at an airport, Chief Justice Rehnquist ruled that there need be only a "reasonable suspicion" for stopping a suspect—something more than a "hunch" and considerably less than probable cause.[2] The ruling in *Sokolow* permitting "drug courier profiles" has not been followed by some state supreme courts when construing their state constitutions (see THE DEVELOPMENT OF LAW box, "Other Recent State Supreme Court Decisions Declining to Follow the U.S. Supreme Court's Rulings" in Ch. 2), and civil rights groups complained that it encourages racial profiling. In response, in

2003 President George W. Bush issued guidelines governing seventy federal law enforcement agencies that bar the use of race and ethnicity in routine investigations. Under the policy federal agents may not focus, for example, on specific neighborhoods because of their racial composition; however, the policy does not cover state police and permits the use of race and ethnicity to "identify terrorist threats and stop potential catastrophic attacks."

In a series of rulings, the Rehnquist Court pushed even further a narrow reading of the Fourth Amendment's proscription against "unreasonable searches and seizures." *California v. Hodari D.*, 499 U.S. 621 (1991), for example, posed an inexorable question given prior rulings on the permissibility of police officers stopping and frisking individuals whom they have probable cause to believe are engaged or a reasonable suspicion that they are engaged in criminal activities. Specifically, the question presented was whether police made an unlawful "seizure" when they chased a man who ran away at the sight of them, and then recovered abandoned evidence (drugs) which was used at trial. By a 7–1 vote, however, the Rehnquist Court held that even though police did not have a "reasonable suspicion" for them to question or detain Hodari D. that did not matter.

Writing for the Court in *Hodari D.*, Justice Scalia held that Hodari D. had not been "seized" within the meaning of the Fourth Amendment. In his view, criminal suspects are "seized" for Fourth Amendment purposes only at the point at which officers either use physical force or the suspect complies with their "show of authority." "We do not think it desirable," as he put it, "to stretch the Fourth Amendment beyond its words. . . . Street pursuits always place the public at some risk, and compliance with police orders to stop should therefore be encouraged. . . . Since policemen do not command 'Stop!' expecting to be ignored, or give chase hoping to be outrun, it fully suffices to apply deterrent to their genuine, successful seizures."

In a footnote, Scalia further added that states need not bother to show that police even had a "reasonable suspicion" to justify their pursuit of an individual fleeing from them, since they need not meet that standard within the context of an individual fleeing their presence. "That it would be unreasonable to stop, for brief inquiry, young men who scatter in panic upon the mere sighting of the police is not self-evident, and arguably contradicts proverbial common sense," he noted, quoting the biblical saying, "The wicked flee when no man pursueth."

The facts in *Hodari D.* are important because they are replayed virtually every day in urban areas of the country. Hodari D., a teenager, was standing with several other youths around a car in a high-crime area of Oakland, California. At some point, they spotted an unmarked police car approaching, and they started running away. With the police in chase, Hodari D. tossed away a small rock of crack cocaine, which the police subsequently recovered. Seconds later Hodari D. was tackled to the ground by a police officer; he was found to be also carrying a pager and $130 in cash. At a preliminary hearing, Hodari D.'s attorney argued that the cocaine had to be excluded at his trial because it was obtained in violation of the Fourth Amendment. The trial judge disagreed but was overturned by a state appellate court, which relied on the Court's previous rulings that police must have "reasonable suspicion" to stop and question people.

The ruling in *Hodari D.* was subsequently underscored by a bare majority in upholding the search and seizure of an individual who held an opaque bag and fled upon seeing a police caravan in *Illinois v. Wardlow* (2000) (excerpted below). Subsequently, the Roberts Court, with Justice Stevens dissenting, in *Scott v. Harris*, 550 U.S. 372 (2007), ruled that under the Fourth Amendment it was reasonable for police to ram a speeding motorist off the road, leaving him permanently paralyzed, in light of the need to protect pedestrians and other drivers from a high-speed car chase.

The Court has also confronted the issue of how far police may go when conducting suspicionless searches of passengers' belongings on public buses and trains. In *Florida v. Bostick*, 501 U.S. 429 (1991), by a 6–3 vote the justices upheld random police questioning of bus and train passengers. *Bostick* originated with the "war on drugs" as waged in Broward County, Florida. There, sheriff's department officers routinely board buses at scheduled stops and ask passengers for permission to search their luggage. As it happened, two officers boarded a bus on which Terrance Bostick was traveling and, without reasonable suspicion or probable cause, questioned him and other passengers at a scheduled bus stop. They asked for his consent to search two of his bags and advised him of his right to deny consent, but he contested both that he was in a position to deny their request and that he in fact consented to their search. In any event, police searched his bags, and upon finding some cocaine, they arrested him. At a pretrial hearing he unsuccessfully moved to suppress the introduction of the cocaine as evidence on the grounds that it had been seized in violation of his Fourth Amendment rights. And Bostick later pleaded guilty but reserved the right to appeal the trial court's denial of his motion to suppress the contraband.

Writing for the Court in *Bostick*, Justice O'Connor reaffirmed that "the Fourth Amendment permits police officers to approach individuals at random in airport lobbies and other public places to ask them questions and to request consent to search their luggage, so long as a reasonable person would understand that he or she could refuse to cooperate." And O'Connor found no basis for distinguishing random searches and seizures in airport terminals from those in buses and trains. In her words:

Since *Terry*, we have held repeatedly that mere police questioning does not constitute a seizure. . . . There is no doubt that if this same encounter had taken place before Bostick boarded the bus or in the lobby of the bus terminal, it would not rise to the level of a seizure. . . .

[T]he mere fact that Bostick did not feel free to leave the bus does not mean that the police seized him. Bostick was a passenger on a bus that was scheduled to depart. He would not have felt free to leave the bus even if the police had not been present. Bostick's movements were "confined" in a sense, but this was the natural result of his decision to take the bus; it says nothing about whether or not the police conduct at issue was coercive. . . .

Concluding, Justice O'Connor also rejected Bostick's claim that he was "seized" because no reasonable person would freely consent to a search of luggage that he or she knows contains drugs. That argument, observed O'Connor, could not prevail because the "reasonable person" test presupposes "an innocent person." But dissenting in *Bostick*, Justices Marshall, Blackmun, and Stevens countered that "the Fourth Amendment clearly condemns the suspicionless, dragnet-style sweep of intrastate or interstate buses."

The Court, finally, drew a line on searches of passengers' luggage on public transport in *Bond v. United States* (2000) (excerpted below), with only Justice Breyer and Scalia dissenting from Chief Justice Rehnquist's opinion for the Court, drawing a line at suspicionless physical inspection of luggage on public buses. Moreover, in *United States v. Drayton*, 536 U.S. 194 (2002), the Court reaffirmed three earlier interrelated rulings bearing on searches of people in public places: (1) that the "consent" of a passenger on a bus to a request by an officer to a patdown search for contraband (*Minnesota v. Dickerson*, 508 U.S. 366 [1993] [excerpted below]) (2) "presupposes an innocent person" would consent (*Florida v. Bostick*, 501 U.S. 429 [1991]), and (3) that the officers are not required to inform citizens of their right to refuse to consent (*Ohio v. Robinette*, 519 U.S. 33 [(1996)]). In *Drayton*, three law enforcement officers boarded a bus in Tallahassee, Florida, which was bound for Detroit, Michigan. One sat in the driver's seat, another in the back of the bus, and the third questioned passengers. Two young men wearing jackets and baggy pants, in the summer, were questioned and consented to pat downs, which revealed plastic bags of cocaine under their clothing. Writing for the Court in *Drayton*, Justice Kennedy observed:

Law enforcement officers do not violate the Fourth Amendment's prohibition of unreasonable seizures merely by approaching individuals on the street or in other public places and putting questions to them if they are willing to listen. Even when law enforcement officers have no basis for suspecting a particular individual, they may pose questions, ask for identification, and request consent to search luggage—provided they do not induce cooperation by coercive means. See *Florida v. Bostick*, 501 U.S. [429 (1991)]. If a reasonable person would feel free to terminate the encounter, then he or she has not been seized. . . .

The Court also broadened *Terry*'s stop-and-frisk exception in *Minnesota v. Dickerson*, 508 U.S. 366 (1993) (excerpted below). In this case the Court was invited to approve yet another exception—a "plain feel" exception—to the Fourth Amendment's warrant requirement. In appealing a ruling of its state supreme court that rejected that exception, Minnesota argued that a "plain feel" exception was analogous to the "plain view" exception and a logical extension of *Terry v. Ohio*. Although partially rejecting the state's arguments and finding that here police went too far in squeezing a small object in the suspect's jacket pocket, the Court nevertheless expanded *Terry*'s stop-and-frisk exception to include searches and seizures of "nonthreatening contraband," as well as weapons (which was the basis for *Terry*'s exception) that are identifiable by touch during a police patdown.

A bare majority also ruled, in *Hiibel v. Sixth Judicial District of Nevada*, 542 U.S. 177 (2004), that neither the Fourth nor Fifth Amendment is violated by the arrest of a person who refuses to identify himself or herself during a *Terry*-stop by police.

Still another exception pertains to when police conduct a search within the context of *hot pursuit* and other *exigent circumstances* to prevent the destruction of evidence. *United States v. Santana*, 427 U.S. 38 (1976), indicates how fine a line the Court sometimes draws in permitting the warrantless entry into private homes and in distinguishing prior rulings allowing for warrantless arrests in exigent situations[3] and where police are in hot pursuit chasing an automobile.[4] Along with *Santana* the Court held, in *United States v. Watson*, 423 U.S. 411 (1976), that an arrest may be made in a public place without a warrant, even if police have time to obtain one. But subsequently the Court limited *Santana* and *Watson* in ruling that except where there are truly exigent circumstances, police must obtain a warrant before entering private premises to make an arrest.[5] Still, in *Illinois v. McArthur*, 531 U.S. 326 (2001), the Court ruled that police, while waiting for a search warrant, may secure a dwelling and not allow the resident to enter unaccompanied, without violating the Fourth Amendment, if they have probable cause to believe that there is contraband on the premises and the resident would destroy it if allowed unrestricted entry. Moreover, in a unanimous opinion in *Brigham City, Utah v. Stuart*, 547 U.S. 398 (2006), the Court held that police may enter a homeowner's dwelling without a warrant or probable cause when there is a "need to assist persons who are seriously injured or threatened with such an injury." In Chief Justice Roberts's words: "Law enforcement officers may enter a home without a warrant to render emergency assistance to an injured occupant or to protect an occupant from imminent injury."

By an 8–1 vote the Roberts Court tried to clarify the *exigencies of the circumstances* exception to the requirement for a warrant for a search and seizure of property. Following *United States v. Santana,* lower courts were conflicted over the standards for judging police searches pursuant to the exigencies of the circumstances and whether police created the exigencies as a pretext for a warrantless search. In *Kentucky v. King,* 563 U.S. 452 (2011), the Court approved a warrantless search and seizure based on "a police-created exigency" because evidence might be destroyed, so long as police do not "engag[e] or threaten to engage in conduct that violates the Fourth Amendment." In adopting that rule the Court rejected alternative tests, such as whether police acted in "bad faith" because that test turns on subjective motives. A test of "reasonable foreseeability" of the destruction of evidence was dismissed as too unpredictable, while drawing a line at whether police had time to obtain a warrant and didn't was deemed too restrictive. Under the new test, police could knock on a door and if they hear or see evidence being destroyed inside, their entry would be permissible. By contrast, police may not break down a door if the person inside won't open the door, since that violates the Fourth Amendment. Justice Alito delivered the opinion of the Court in *Kentucky v. King,* and Justice Ginsburg dissented arguing that the test should be whether the urgency arose prior to police arriving on the scene, rather than afterward as a pretext for a warrantless search. See also *Collins v. Virginia,* 138 S. Ct. 1663 (2018) (excerpted in the next section).

In addition, in *Wilson v. Arkansas,* 514 U.S. 927 (1995), the Court reaffirmed that when police enter a home armed with search and arrest warrants, they must generally announce their presence and entry. Writing for the Court, however, Justice Thomas declined to set forth a rigid bright-line rule and instead left it for the lower courts to determine under what circumstances police may reasonably enter a house without first knocking and announcing their entry. Subsequently, *Richards v. Wisconsin,* 520 U.S. 385 (1997), held that exceptions for drug-related cases may be made to the knock-and-announce requirement, if police have a "reasonable suspicion" that announcing their entry would result in the destruction of drugs or otherwise inhibit their investigation. In *United States v. Ramirez,* 523 U.S. 65 (1998), then, the Court unanimously ruled that police armed with a search warrant do not need extra justification to enter a home without knocking first, even if the entry results in property damage. The Court reaffirmed its view that police have flexibility, because of potential physical harm and the risk that suspects may destroy evidence, when announcing their presence and entry into the home of suspected drug dealers, in *United States v. Banks,*

540 U.S. 31 (2003). Writing for a unanimous Court, Justice Souter held that the reasonableness of a forced entry under the "knock and announce" rule depends on the "totality of the circumstances," not how long police wait; here, police entered a house fifteen to twenty seconds after announcing. The Court reaffirmed its view that police have flexibility because of the circumstances of their presence. In addition, *United States v. Verdugo-Urquidez*, 494 U.S. 259 (1990), held that the Fourth Amendment does not forbid warrantless searches and seizures by government agents of the property in foreign countries of aliens who have been arrested and are jailed in the United States. Chief Justice Rehnquist reasoned that, unlike the Fifth Amendment, which applies to criminal trials, the Fourth Amendment does not apply to aliens or their property outside the United States. He did so by construing the Fourth Amendment right "of the people to be secure in their persons, houses, papers, and effects" to carve out for constitutional protection only those persons who are part of the national community and to exclude those who are aliens outside U.S. territory.

The Court once maintained, but no longer does, that police could not seize, with or without a warrant, mere evidence—clothing, private papers, and the like—but only illegal items, such as weapons, contraband, and such. In *Gouled v. United States*, 255 U.S. 298 (1921), the Court ruled that unlawfully seized papers could be suppressed at trial on the grounds that the Fourth Amendment permitted the government to seize only that property over which it could also assert a property interest at common law, as with the seizure of stolen goods. Applications of the rule, however, led to inconsistent, sometimes illogical, results,[6] and eventually to the Court's reconsideration of the rule.[7] The mere evidence rule was finally abandoned in *Warden v. Hayden*, 387 U.S. 294 (1967), in which the Court explained that

> [t]he premise that property interests control the right of the Government to search and seize has been discredited. Searches and seizures may be "unreasonable" within the Fourth Amendment even though the Government asserts a superior property interest at common law. We have recognized that the principal object of the Fourth Amendment is the protection of privacy rather than property, and have increasingly discarded fictional and procedural barriers rested on property concepts.

Ironically, the Court's abandonment of the mere evidence rule resulted in less Fourth Amendment protection for individuals' privacy interests in their private papers. The Court subsequently held that the Fourth Amendment does not bar the government from obtaining through a subpoena *duces tecum* (an order requiring the production of papers and documents) individuals' private papers held by their accountants, attorneys, and banks.[8]

The Court also recognizes exceptions for *automobile searches* (examined in Section C) and *administrative searches* (examined in Section D). Finally, though even more contentious, was the George W. Bush and Barack Obama administrations' warrantless electronic surveillance of foreign communications with alleged terrorists based on a *special needs exception* (discussed in Section D of this chapter).

NOTES

1. *Chapman v. United States*, 365 U.S. 610 (1961) (landlord's consent for search of tenant's room was not enough); *Stoner v. California*, 376 U.S. 483 (1964) (striking down a search of a hotel room without the consent of the occupant, although the hotel clerk gave permission for the search).

2. In *United States v. Mendenhall*, 446 U.S. 544 (1980), the Court also upheld the stopping and search of a woman at an airport based on her fitting a "drug courier profile." A bare majority found that her agreeing to accompany agents to their office was voluntary, and thus she had not been "seized" for the purposes of the Fourth Amendment. However, in *Florida v. Royer*, 460 U.S. 491 (1983), the Court rejected the arrest of a person based on a drug courier profile as unreasonable, observing "that a person has been 'seized' within the meaning of the Fourth Amendment only if, in view of all the circumstances surrounding the incident, a reasonable person would have believed that he was not free to leave."

3. See *Warden v. Hayden*, 387 U.S. 294 (1967).

4. See *Johnson v. United States*, 333 U.S. 10 (1948).

5. *Payton v. New York*, 445 U.S. 573 (1980).

■ INSIDE THE COURT

Memorandum from Justice William J. Brennan to Chief Justice Earl Warren on Terry v. Ohio

March 14, 1968

RE: *The "Stop and Frisk" Cases*

Dear Chief:

I have heard from Bill [Douglas] and Abe [Fortas] something of their comments upon your opinions, and other suggestions for changes. I've read also, of course, the views stated by Hugo [Black], John [Harlan] and Byron [White] in their circulations. All of this has prompted me to do some extended and hard thinking which I hope I may share with you.

I'm attaching a rather extensive suggested revision of your *Terry* opinion with explanatory notes outlining my reasons, and also a rather extensively foot-noted memorandum stating my reasons for the conviction I've reached (contrary to my previous view) that we should not handle this question as a matter of "probable cause" and the Warrant Clause, but as a matter of the Reasonableness Clause. I hope you won't think me presumptuous to submit my thoughts in this form. I do it only because I think it's the best way for me to state them. . . .

I've become acutely concerned that the mere fact of our affirmance in *Terry* will be taken by police all over the country as our license to them to carry on, indeed widely expand, present "aggressive surveillance" techniques which the press tells us are being deliberately employed in Miami, Chicago, Detroit and other ghetto cities. This is happening, of course, in response to the "crime in the streets" alarums [*sic*] being sounded in this election year in the Congress, the White House and every Governor's office. Much of what I suggest be omitted from your opinion strikes me as susceptible to being read as sounding the same note. This seems to me to be particularly unfortunate since our affirmance surely does this: from here on out, it becomes entirely unnecessary for the police to establish "probable cause to *arrest*" to support weapons charges; an officer can move against anyone he *suspects* has a weapon and get a conviction if he "frisks" him and finds one. In this lies the terrible risk that police will conjure up "suspicious circumstances," and courts will credit their versions. It will not take much of this to aggravate the already white heat resentment of ghetto Negroes against the police—and the Court will become the scapegoat.

The alternative would of course mean a reversal of this conviction—a holding that there is no constitutional authority to frisk for weapons unless the officer has probable cause to *arrest* for the crime of carrying a weapon. I recognize that police will frisk anyway and try to make a case that the frisk was incident to an arrest for public drunkenness, vagrancy, loitering, breach of the peace, etc.—but at times I think these abuses would be more tolerable than those I apprehend may follow our legitimating of frisks on the basis of suspicious circumstances.

This states frankly my worries. But if we are to affirm *Terry*, I think the tone of our opinion may be even more important than what we say. If I have exceeded the proprieties, I hope you will forgive me—I am truly worried.

Sincerely,
Bill [Brennan]

Source: Library of Congress, Papers of Chief Justice Earl Warren, Manuscripts Room.

6. Compare *Marron v. United States*, 275 U.S. 192 (1927), with *United States v. Lefkowitz*, 285 U.S. 452 (1932).

7. See *Jones v. United States*, 362 U.S. 257 (1960).

8. See *Couch v. United States*, 409 U.S. 322 (1973); *United States v. Miller*, 425 U.S. 435 (1976); *California Bankers Association v. Shultz*, 416 U.S. 21 (1974).

Terry v. Ohio
392 U.S. 1, 88 S.CT. 1868 (1968)

Chief Justice Earl Warren discusses the facts in this case, upholding a police officer's stopping and frisking individuals whom he had a reasonable suspicion might be contemplating a robbery, at the outset of his opinion for the Court.

The Court's decision was 8–1, and the majority's opinion was announced by Chief Justice Warren. Concurrences were by Justices Black, Harlan, and White. Justice Douglas dissented.

■ ■ ■

☐ *Chief Justice WARREN delivered the opinion of the Court.*

This case presents serious questions concerning the role of the Fourth Amendment in the confrontation on the street between the citizen and the policeman investigating suspicious circumstances.

Petitioner Terry was convicted of carrying a concealed weapon and sentenced to the statutorily prescribed term of one to three years in the penitentiary. Following the denial of a pretrial motion to suppress, the prosecution introduced in evidence two revolvers and a number of bullets seized from Terry and a codefendant, Richard Chilton, by Cleveland Police Detective Martin McFadden. At the hearing on the motion to suppress this evidence, Officer McFadden testified that while he was patrolling in plain clothes in downtown Cleveland at approximately 2:30 in the afternoon of October 31, 1963, his attention was attracted by two men, Chilton and Terry, standing on the corner of Huron Road and Euclid Avenue. He had never seen the two men before, and he was unable to say precisely what first drew his eye to them. However, he testified that he had been a policeman for 39 years and a detective for 35 and that he had been assigned to patrol this vicinity of downtown Cleveland for shoplifters and pickpockets for 30 years. He explained that he had developed routine habits of observation over the years and that he would "stand and watch people or walk and watch people at many intervals of the day." He added: "Now, in this case when I looked over they didn't look right to me at the time."

His interest aroused, Officer McFadden took up a post of observation in the entrance to a store 300 to 400 feet away from two men. . . . He saw one of the men leave the other one and walk southwest on Huron Road, past some stores. The man paused for a moment and looked in a store window, then walked on a short distance, turned around and walked back toward the corner, pausing once again to look in the same store window. He rejoined his companion at the corner, and the two conferred briefly. Then the second man went through the same series of motions, strolling down Huron Road, looking in the same window, walking on a short distance, turning back, peering in the store window again, and returning to confer with the first man at the corner. The two men repeated this ritual alternately between five and six times apiece—in all, roughly a dozen trips. At one point, while the two were standing together on the corner, a third man approached them and engaged them briefly in conversation. This man then left the two others and walked west on Euclid Avenue. Chilton and Terry resumed their measured pacing, peering and conferring. After this had gone on for 10 to 12 minutes, the two men walked off together, heading west on Euclid Avenue, following the path taken earlier by the third man.

By this time Officer McFadden had become thoroughly suspicious. He . . . suspected the two men of "casing a job, a stick-up," and . . . he considered it his duty as a police officer to investigate further. . . . Thus, Officer McFadden followed Chilton and Terry and saw them stop in front of Zucker's store to talk to the same man who had conferred with them earlier on the street corner. Deciding that the situation was ripe for direct action, Officer McFadden approached the three men, identified himself as a police officer and asked for their names. At this point his knowledge was confined to what he had observed. . . . When the men "mumbled something" in response to his inquiries, Officer McFadden grabbed petitioner Terry, spun him around so that they were facing the other two, with Terry between McFadden and the others, and patted down the outside of his clothing. In the left breast pocket of Terry's overcoat Officer McFadden felt a pistol. He reached inside the overcoat pocket, but was unable to remove the gun. At this point, keeping Terry between himself and the others, the officer ordered all three men to enter Zucker's store. As they went in, he removed Terry's overcoat completely, removed a .38-caliber revolver from the pocket and ordered all three men to face the wall with their hands raised. Officer McFadden proceeded to pat down the outer clothing of Chilton and the third man, Katz. He discovered another revolver in the outer pocket of Chilton's overcoat, but no weapons were found on Katz. The officer testified that he only patted the men down to see whether they had weapons, and that he did not put his hands beneath the outer garments of either Terry or Chilton until he felt their guns. . . .

On the motion to suppress the guns the prosecution took the position that they had been seized following a search incident to a lawful arrest. The trial court rejected this theory, stating that it "would be stretching the facts beyond reasonable comprehension" to find that Officer McFadden had had probable cause to arrest the men before he patted them down for weapons. However, the court denied the defendants' motion on the ground that Officer McFadden, on the basis of his experience, "had reasonable cause to believe . . . that the defendants were conducting themselves suspiciously, and some interrogation should be made of their action." Purely for his own protection, the court held, the officer had the right to pat down the outer clothing of these men, who he had reasonable cause to believe might be armed. . . . We granted *certiorari* to determine whether the admission of the revolvers in evidence violated petitioner's rights under the Fourth Amendment, made applicable to the States by the Fourteenth. We affirm the conviction. . . .

[Here,] the question is whether in all the circumstances of this on-the-street encounter, [the individual's] right to personal security was violated by an unreasonable search and seizure. . . .

Our first task is to establish at what point in this encounter the Fourth Amendment becomes relevant. That is, we must decide whether and when Officer McFadden "seized" Terry and whether and when he conducted a "search." . . . It is quite plain that the Fourth Amendment governs "seizures" of the person which do not eventuate in a trip to the station house and prosecution for crime—"arrests" in traditional terminology. It must be recognized that whenever a police officer accosts an individual and restrains his freedom to walk away, he has "seized" that person. And it is nothing less than sheer torture of the English language to suggest that a careful exploration of the outer surfaces of a person's clothing all over his or her body in an attempt to find weapons is not a "search." Moreover, it is simply fantastic to urge that such a procedure performed in public by a policeman while the citizen stands helpless, perhaps facing a wall with his hands raised, is a "petty indignity." It is a serious intrusion upon the sanctity of the person, which may inflict great indignity and arouse strong resentment, and it is not to be undertaken lightly.

The danger in the logic which proceeds upon distinctions between a "stop" and an "arrest," or "seizure" of the person, and between a "frisk" and a "search" is twofold. It seeks to isolate from constitutional scrutiny the initial stages of the contact between the policeman and the citizen. And by suggesting a rigid all-or-nothing model of justification and regulation under the Amendment, it obscures the utility of limitations upon the scope, as well as the initiation, of police action as a means of constitutional regulation. . . .

The distinctions of classical "stop-and-frisk" theory thus serve to divert attention from the central inquiry under the Fourth Amendment—the reasonableness in all the circumstances of the particular governmental invasion of a citizen's personal security. "Search" and "seizure" are not talismans. We therefore reject the notions that the Fourth Amendment does not come into play at all as a limitation upon police conduct if the officers stop short of something called a "technical arrest" or a "full-blown search." . . .

The crux of this case . . . is not the propriety of Officer McFadden's taking steps to investigate petitioner's suspicious behavior, but rather, whether there was justification for McFadden's invasion of Terry's personal security by searching him for weapons in the course of that investigation. We are now concerned with more than the governmental interest in investigating crime; in addition, there is the more immediate interest of the police officer in taking steps to assure himself that the person with whom he is dealing is not armed with a weapon that could unexpectedly and fatally be used against him. Certainly it would be unreasonable to require that police officers take unnecessary risks in the performance of their duties. American criminals have a long tradition of armed violence, and every year in this country many law enforcement officers are killed in the line of duty, and thousands more are wounded. Virtually all of these deaths and a substantial portion of the injuries are inflicted with guns and knives.

In view of these facts, we cannot blind ourselves to the need for law enforcement officers to protect themselves and other prospective victims of violence in situations where they may lack probable cause for an arrest. When an officer is justified in believing that the individual whose suspicious behavior he is investigating at close range is armed and presently dangerous to the officer or to others, it would appear to be clearly unreasonable to deny the officer the power to take necessary measures to determine whether the person is in fact carrying a weapon and to neutralize the threat of physical harm. . . .

We conclude that the revolver seized from Terry was properly admitted in evidence against him. At the time he seized petitioner and searched him for weapons, Officer McFadden had reasonable grounds to believe that petitioner was armed and dangerous, and it was necessary for the protection of himself and others to take swift measures to discover the true facts and neutralize the threat of harm if it materialized. The policeman carefully restricted his search to what was appropriate to the discovery of the particular items which he sought. Each case of this sort will, of course, have to be decided on its own facts. We merely hold today that where a police officer observes unusual conduct which leads him reasonably to conclude in light of his experience that criminal activity may be afoot and that the persons with whom he is dealing may be armed and presently dangerous, where in the course of investigating this behavior he identifies himself as a policeman and makes reasonable inquiries, and where nothing in the initial stages of the encounter serves to dispel his reasonable fear for his own or others' safety, he is entitled for the protection of himself and others in the area to conduct a carefully limited search of the outer clothing of such persons in an attempt to discover weapons which might be used to assault him.

Such a search is a reasonable search under the Fourth Amendment, and any weapons seized may properly be introduced in evidence against the person from whom they were taken.

Affirmed.

☐ *Justice DOUGLAS, dissenting.*

I agree that petitioner was "seized" within the meaning of the Fourth Amendment. I also agree that frisking petitioner and his companions for guns was a "search." But it is a mystery how that "search" and that "seizure" can be constitutional by Fourth Amendment standards, unless there was "probable cause" to believe that (1) a crime had been committed or (2) a crime was in the process of being committed or (3) a crime was about to be committed.

The opinion of the Court disclaims the existence of "probable cause." If loitering were in issue and that was the offense charged, there would be "probable cause" shown. But the crime here is carrying concealed weapons; and there is no basis for concluding that the officer had "probable cause" for believing that that crime was being committed. Had a warrant been sought, a magistrate would, therefore, have been unauthorized to issue one, for he can act only if there is a showing of "probable cause." We hold today that the police have greater authority to make a "seizure" and conduct a "search" than a judge has to authorize such action. We have said precisely the opposite over and over again. . . .

The infringement on personal liberty of any "seizure" of a person can only be "reasonable" under the Fourth Amendment if we require the police to possess "probable cause" before they seize him. Only that line draws a meaningful distinction between an officer's mere inkling and the presence of facts within the officer's personal knowledge which would convince a reasonable man that the person seized has committed, is committing, or is about to commit a particular crime. . . .

United States v. Sokolow

490 U.S. 1, 109 S.Ct. 1581 (1989)

Chief Justice William H. Rehnquist reviews the circumstances giving rise to this case, involving a warrantless search and seizure of Andrew Sokolow at the Honolulu, Hawaii, airport by drug enforcement agents, in his opinion for the Court.

The Court's decision was 7–2, and the majority's opinion was announced by Chief Justice Rehnquist. The dissent by Justice Marshall was joined by Justice Brennan.

■ ■ ■

☐ *Chief Justice REHNQUIST delivered the opinion of the Court.*

Respondent Andrew Sokolow was stopped by Drug Enforcement Administration (DEA) agents upon his arrival at Honolulu International Airport. The agents found 1,063 grams of cocaine in his carry-on luggage. When respondent was stopped, the agents knew, *inter alia*, that (1) he paid $2,100 for two airplane tickets from a roll of $20 bills; (2) he traveled under a name that did not match the name under which his telephone number was listed; (3) his original destination was Miami, a source city for illicit drugs; (4) he stayed in Miami for only 48 hours, even though a round-trip flight from Honolulu to Miami takes 20 hours; (5) he appeared nervous during his trip; and (6) he checked none of his luggage. A divided panel of the United States Court of Appeals for the Ninth Circuit held that the DEA agents did not have a reasonable suspicion to stop respondent, as required by the Fourth Amendment. We take the contrary view.

This case involves a typical attempt to smuggle drugs through one of the Nation's airports. On a Sunday in July 1984, respondent went to the United Airlines ticket counter at Honolulu Airport, where he purchased two round-trip tickets for a flight to Miami leaving later that day. The tickets were purchased in the names of "Andrew Kray" and "Janet Norian," and had open return dates. Respondent paid $2,100 for the tickets from a large roll of $20 bills, which appeared to contain a total of $4,000. He also gave the ticket agent his home telephone number. The ticket agent noticed that respondent seemed nervous; he was about 25 years old; he was dressed in a black jumpsuit and wore gold jewelry; and he was accompanied by a woman, who turned out to be Janet Norian. Neither respondent nor his companion checked any of their four pieces of luggage.

After the couple left for their flight, the ticket agent informed Officer John McCarthy of the Honolulu Police Department of respondent's cash purchase of tickets to Miami. Officer McCarthy determined that the telephone number respondent gave to the ticket agent was subscribed to a "Karl Herman," who resided at 348-A Royal Hawaiian Avenue in Honolulu. Unbeknownst to McCarthy (and later to the DEA agents), respondent was Herman's roommate. The ticket agent identified respondent's voice on the answering machine at Herman's number. Officer McCarthy was unable to find any listing under the name "Andrew Kray" in Hawaii. McCarthy subsequently learned that return reservations from Miami to Honolulu had been made in the names of Kray and Norian, with their arrival scheduled for July 25, three days after respondent and his companion had left. He also learned that Kray and Norian were scheduled to make stopovers in Denver and Los Angeles.

On July 25, during the stopover in Los Angeles, DEA agents identified respondent. He "appeared to be very nervous and was looking all around the waiting area." . . . Later that day, at 6:30 P.M., respondent and Norian arrived in Honolulu. As before, they had not checked their luggage. Respondent was still wearing a black jumpsuit and gold jewelry. The couple proceeded directly to the street and tried to hail a cab, where Agent Richard Kempshall and three other DEA agents approached them. Kempshall displayed his credentials, grabbed respondent by the arm and moved him back onto the sidewalk. Kempshall asked respondent for his airline ticket and identification; respondent said that he had neither. He told the agents that his name was "Sokolow," but that he was traveling under his mother's maiden name, "Kray."

Respondent and Norian were escorted to the DEA office at the airport. There, the couple's luggage was examined by "Donker," a narcotics detector dog, which alerted to respondent's brown shoulder bag. The agents arrested respondent. He was advised of his constitutional rights and declined to make any statements. The agents obtained a warrant to search the shoulder bag. They found no illicit drugs, but the bag did contain several suspicious documents indicating respondent's involvement in drug trafficking. The agents had Donker reexamine the remaining luggage, and this time the dog alerted to a medium sized Louis Vuitton bag. By now, it was 9:30 P.M., too late for the agents to obtain a second warrant. They allowed respondent to leave for the night, but kept his luggage. The next morning, after a second dog confirmed Donker's alert, the agents obtained a warrant and found 1,063 grams of cocaine inside the bag.

Respondent was indicted for possession with the intent to distribute cocaine in violation of 21 U.S.C. Sec. 841(a)(1). The United States District Court for Hawaii denied his motion to suppress the cocaine and other evidence seized from his luggage, finding that the DEA agents had a reasonable suspicion that he was involved in drug trafficking when they stopped him at the airport. Respondent then entered a conditional plea of guilty to the offense charged.

The United States Court of Appeals for the Ninth Circuit reversed respondent's conviction by a divided vote, holding that the DEA agents did not have a reasonable suspicion to justify the stop. . . .

The Court of Appeals held that the DEA agents seized respondent when they grabbed him by the arm and moved him back onto the sidewalk. The Government does not challenge that conclusion, and we assume—without deciding—that a stop occurred here. Our decision, then, turns on whether the agents had a reasonable suspicion that respondent was engaged in wrong-doing when they encountered him on the sidewalk. In *Terry v. Ohio*, [392 U.S. 1] (1968), we held that the police can stop and briefly detain a person for investigative purposes if the officer has a reasonable suspicion supported by articulable facts that criminal activity "may be afoot," even if the officer lacks probable cause.

The officer, of course, must be able to articulate something more than an "inchoate and unparticularized suspicion or 'hunch'." The Fourth

Amendment requires "some minimal level of objective justification" for making the stop. *INS v. Delgado*, 466 U.S. 210 (1984). That level of suspicion is considerably less than proof of wrongdoing by a preponderance of the evidence. We have held that probable cause means "a fair probability that contraband or evidence of a crime will be found," *Illinois v. Gates*, 462 U.S. 213 (1983), and the level of suspicion required for a *Terry* stop is obviously less demanding than that for probable cause. See *United States v. Montoya de Hernandez*, 473 U.S. 531 (1985).

The concept of reasonable suspicion like probable cause is not readily or even usefully, reduced to a neat set of legal rules." *Gates, supra.* We think the Court of Appeals' effort to refine and elaborate the requirements of "reasonable suspicion" in this case create unnecessary difficulty in dealing with one of the relatively simple concepts embodied in the Fourth Amendment. In evaluating the validity of a stop such as this, we must consider "the totality of the circumstances—the whole picture." . . .

We hold that the agents had a reasonable basis to suspect that respondent was transporting illegal drugs on these facts. The judgment of the Court of Appeals is therefore reversed and the case remanded for further proceedings consistent with our decision.

☐ *Justice MARSHALL, with whom Justice BRENNAN joins, dissenting.*

The Fourth Amendment cabins government's authority to intrude on personal privacy and security by requiring that searches and seizures usually be supported by a showing of probable cause. The reasonable-suspicion standard is a derivation of the probable cause command, applicable only to those brief detentions which fall short of being full-scale searches and seizures and which are necessitated by law-enforcement exigencies such as the need to stop ongoing crimes, to prevent imminent crimes, and to protect law-enforcement officers in highly charged situations. *Terry v. Ohio* (1968). By requiring reasonable suspicion as a prerequisite to such seizures, the Fourth Amendment protects innocent persons from being subjected to "overbearing or harassing" police conduct carried out solely on the basis of imprecise stereotypes of what criminals look like, or on the basis of irrelevant personal characteristics such as race. . . .

To deter such egregious police behavior, we have held that a suspicion is not reasonable unless officers have based it on "specific and articulable facts." [See *Terry* and] also *United States v. Brignoni-Ponce*, 422 U.S. 873 (1975). It is not enough to suspect that an individual has committed crimes in the past, harbors unconsummated criminal designs, or has the propensity to commit crimes. On the contrary, before detaining an individual, law enforcement officers must reasonably suspect that he is engaged in, or poised to commit, a criminal act *at that moment.*

The rationale for permitting brief, warrantless seizures is, after all, that it is impractical to demand strict compliance with the Fourth Amendment's ordinary probable-cause requirement in the face of ongoing or imminent criminal activity demanding "swift action predicated upon the on-the-spot observations of the officer on the beat." *Terry, supra.* Observations raising suspicions of past criminality demand no such immediate action, but instead should appropriately trigger routine police investigation, which may ultimately generate sufficient information to blossom into probable cause.

Evaluated against this standard, the facts about Andrew Sokolow known to the DEA agents at the time they stopped him fall short of reasonably indicating that he was engaged at the time in criminal activity. It is highly significant that the DEA agents stopped Sokolow because he matched one of the DEA's "profiles" of a paradigmatic drug courier. In my view, a law enforcement officer's mechanistic application of a formula of personal and behavioral traits in deciding whom to detain can only dull the officer's ability and determination to make sensitive and fact-specific inferences "in light of his experience," *Terry*, particularly in ambiguous or borderline cases. Reflexive reliance on a profile of drug courier characteristics runs a far greater risk than does ordinary, case-by-case police work, of subjecting innocent individuals to unwarranted police harassment and detention. . . .

Illinois v. Wardlow

528 U.S. 119, 120 S.Ct. 673 (2000)

Around noon in an area of Chicago known for drug trafficking, two uniformed police officers were riding in the last of a four-car police caravan when they noticed William Wardlow holding an opaque bag. After looking in their direction, Wardlow fled down an alley and the officers followed, eventually cornering him. During a pat-down search for weapons, one of the officers squeezed the bag and felt a heavy object, which turned out to be a .38-caliber handgun. At his trial, Wardlow's attorney moved to suppress the use of the gun as evidence on the ground that the officer did not have a "reasonable suspicion" to justify the search and seizure under *Terry v. Ohio*, 392 U.S. 1 (1968). The trial court disagreed, but a state appellate court reversed Wardlow's conviction and the Illinois Supreme Court affirmed, concluding that a sudden flight from police, even in a high crime area, does not create a "reasonable suspicion" to justify a *Terry* stop. The state appealed and the Supreme Court granted review.

The state supreme court's decision was reversed in a 5–4 decision, with the opinion delivered by Chief Justice Rehnquist. Justice Stevens filed an opinion in part concurring and dissenting, which Justices Breyer, Ginsburg, and Souter joined.

■ ■ ■

☐ *Chief Justice REHNQUIST delivered the opinion of the Court.*

This case, involving a brief encounter between a citizen and a police officer on a public street, is governed by the analysis we first applied in *Terry* [*v. Ohio*]. In *Terry*, we held that an officer may, consistent with the Fourth Amendment, conduct a brief, investigatory stop when the officer has a reasonable, articulable suspicion that criminal activity is afoot. While "reasonable suspicion" is a less demanding standard than probable cause and requires a showing considerably less than preponderance of the evidence, the Fourth Amendment requires at least a minimal level of objective justification for making the stop. . . .

An individual's presence in an area of expected criminal activity, standing alone, is not enough to support a reasonable, particularized suspicion that the person is committing a crime. But officers are not required to ignore the relevant characteristics of a location in determining whether the circumstances are sufficiently suspicious to warrant further investigation. . . .

In this case, moreover, it was not merely respondent's presence in an area of heavy narcotics trafficking that aroused the officers' suspicion but his unprovoked flight upon noticing the police. Our cases have also recognized that nervous, evasive behavior is a pertinent factor in determining reasonable suspicion. Headlong flight—wherever it occurs—is the consummate act of evasion: it is not necessarily indicative of wrongdoing, but it is certainly suggestive of such. In reviewing the propriety of an officer's conduct, courts do not have available empirical studies dealing with inferences drawn from suspicious behavior, and we cannot reasonably demand scientific certainty from judges or law enforcement officers where none exists. Thus, the determination of reasonable suspicion must be based on commonsense judgments and inferences about human behavior. We conclude Officer Nolan was justified in suspecting that Wardlow was involved in criminal activity, and, therefore, in investigating further. . . .

☐ *Justice STEVENS, with whom Justice SOUTER, Justice GINSBURG, and Justice BREYER join, concurring in part and dissenting in part.*

Guided by that totality-of-the-circumstances test, the Court concludes that Officer Nolan had reasonable suspicion to stop respondent. In this respect, my view differs from the Court's. The entire justification for the stop is articulated in the brief testimony of Officer Nolan. Some facts are perfectly clear; others are not. This factual insufficiency leads me to conclude that the Court's judgment is mistaken. . . .

Nolan was part of an eight-officer, four-car caravan patrol team. The officers were headed for "one of the areas in the 11th District [of Chicago] that's high [in] narcotics traffic." The reason why four cars were in the caravan was that "[n]ormally in these different areas there's an enormous amount of people, sometimes lookouts, customers." Officer Nolan testified that he was in uniform on that day, but he did not recall whether he was driving a marked or an unmarked car.

Officer Nolan and his partner were in the last of the four patrol cars that "were all caravaning eastbound down Van Buren." Nolan first observed respondent "in front of 4035 West Van Buren." Wardlow "looked in our direction and began fleeing." Nolan then "began driving southbound down the street observing [respondent] running through the gangway and the alley southbound," and observed that Wardlow was carrying a white, opaque bag under his arm. After the car turned south and intercepted respondent as he "ran right towards us," Officer Nolan stopped him and conducted a "protective search," which revealed that the bag under respondent's arm contained a loaded handgun.

This terse testimony is most noticeable for what it fails to reveal. Though asked whether he was in a marked or unmarked car, Officer Nolan could not recall the answer. He was not asked whether any of the other three cars in the caravan were marked, or whether any of the other seven officers were in uniform. Though he explained that the size of the caravan was because "[n]ormally in these different areas there's an enormous amount of people, sometimes lookouts, customers," Officer Nolan did not testify as to whether anyone besides Wardlow was nearby 4035 West Van Buren. Nor is it clear that that address was the intended destination of the caravan. As the Appellate Court of Illinois interpreted the record, "it appears that the officers were simply driving by, on their way to some unidentified location, when they noticed defendant standing at 4035 West Van Buren." Officer Nolan's testimony also does not reveal how fast the officers were driving. It does not indicate whether he saw respondent notice the other patrol cars. And it does not say whether the caravan, or any part of it, had already passed Wardlow by before he began to run. . . .

No other factors sufficiently support a finding of reasonable suspicion. . . . Officer Nolan did testify that he expected to find "an enormous amount of people," including drug customers or lookouts, and the Court points out that "[i]t was in this context that Officer Nolan decided to investigate Wardlow after observing him flee." This observation, in my view, lends insufficient weight to the reasonable suspicion analysis; indeed, in light of the absence of testimony that anyone else was nearby when respondent began to run, this observation points in the opposite direction. . . .

It is the State's burden to articulate facts sufficient to support reasonable suspicion. In my judgment, Illinois has failed to discharge that burden. I am not persuaded that the mere fact that someone standing on a sidewalk looked in the direction of a passing car before starting to run is sufficient to justify a forcible stop and frisk.

Bond v. United States

529 U.S. 334, 120 S.Ct. 1462 (2000)

The facts are stated by Chief Justice Rehnquist in the opinion of the Court, reversing the appellate court's decision. Justice Breyer filed a dissenting opinion, which Justice Scalia joined.

■ ■ ■

☐ *Chief Justice REHNQUIST delivered the opinion of the Court.*

Petitioner Steven Dewayne Bond was a passenger on a Greyhound bus that left California bound for Little Rock, Arkansas. The bus stopped, as it was required to do, at the permanent Border Patrol checkpoint in Sierra Blanca, Texas. Border Patrol Agent Cesar Cantu boarded the bus to check the immigration status of its passengers. After reaching the back of the bus, having satisfied himself that the passengers were lawfully in the United States, Agent Cantu began walking toward the front. Along the way, he squeezed the soft luggage which passengers had placed in the overhead storage space above the seats. . . .

As Agent Cantu inspected the luggage in the compartment above petitioner's seat, he squeezed a green canvas bag and noticed that it contained a "brick-like" object. Petitioner admitted that the bag was his and agreed to allow Agent Cantu to open it. Upon opening the bag, Agent Cantu discovered a "brick" of methamphetamine. The brick had been wrapped in duct tape until it was oval-shaped and then rolled in a pair of pants.

Petitioner was indicted for conspiracy to possess, and possession with intent to distribute, methamphetamine. He moved to suppress the drugs, arguing that Agent Cantu conducted an illegal search of his bag. Petitioner's motion was denied, and the District Court found him guilty on both counts and sentenced him to 57 months in prison. On appeal, he conceded that other passengers had access to his bag, but contended that Agent Cantu manipulated the bag in a way that other passengers would not. The Court of Appeals rejected this argument. . . . We granted *certiorari*, and now reverse.

[T]he Government asserts that by exposing his bag to the public, petitioner lost a reasonable expectation that his bag would not be physically manipulated. The Government relies on our decisions in *California v. Ciraolo*, [476 U.S. 207 (1986)], and *Florida v. Riley*, 488 U.S. 445 (1989), for the proposition that matters open to public observation are not protected by the Fourth Amendment. In *Ciraolo*, we held that police observation of a backyard from a plane flying at an altitude of 1,000 feet did not violate a reasonable expectation of privacy. Similarly, in *Riley*, we relied on *Ciraolo* to hold that police observation of a greenhouse in a home's curtilage from a helicopter passing at an altitude of 400 feet did not violate the Fourth Amendment. We reasoned that the property was "not necessarily protected from inspection that involves no physical invasion," and determined that because any member of the public could have lawfully observed the defendants' property by flying overhead, the defendants' expectation of privacy was "not reasonable and not one 'that society is prepared to honor.'"

But *Ciraolo* and *Riley* are different from this case because they involved only visual, as opposed to tactile, observation. Physically invasive inspection is simply more intrusive than purely visual inspection. For example, in *Terry v. Ohio*, 392 U.S. 1 (1968), we stated that a "careful [tactile] exploration of the outer surfaces of a person's clothing all over his or her body" is a "serious intrusion upon the sanctity of the person, which may inflict great indignity and arouse strong resentment, and is not to be undertaken lightly." Although Agent Cantu did not "frisk" petitioner's person, he did conduct a probing tactile examination of petitioner's carry-on luggage. Obviously, petitioner's bag was not part of his person. But travelers are particularly concerned about their carry-on luggage; they generally use it to transport personal items that, for whatever reason, they prefer to keep close at hand. . . .

Our Fourth Amendment analysis embraces two questions. First, we ask whether the individual, by his conduct, has exhibited an actual expectation of privacy; that is, whether he has shown that "he [sought] to preserve [something] as private." Here, petitioner sought to preserve privacy by using an opaque bag and placing that bag directly above his seat. Second, we inquire whether the individual's expectation of privacy is "one that society is prepared to recognize as reasonable." When a bus passenger places a bag in an overhead bin, he expects that other passengers or bus employees may move it for one reason or another. Thus, a bus passenger clearly expects that his bag may be handled. He does not expect that other passengers or bus employees will, as a matter of course, feel the bag in an exploratory manner. But this is exactly what the agent did here. We therefore hold that the agent's physical manipulation of petitioner's bag violated the Fourth Amendment.

☐ *Justice BREYER, with whom Justice SCALIA joins, dissenting.*

Does a traveler who places a soft-sided bag in the shared overhead storage compartment of a bus have a "reasonable expectation" that strangers will not push, pull, prod, squeeze, or otherwise manipulate his luggage? Unlike the majority, I believe that he does not. . . .

[A]n individual cannot reasonably expect privacy in respect to objects or activities that he "knowingly exposes to the public." Indeed, the Court has said that it is not objectively reasonable to expect privacy if "[a]ny member of the public could have" used his senses to detect "everything that th[e] officers observed." *California v. Ciraolo.* Thus, it has held that the fact that strangers may look down at fenced-in property from an aircraft or sift through garbage bags on a public street can justify a similar police intrusion. Consider, too, the accepted police practice of using dogs to sniff for drugs hidden inside luggage. . . .

Of course, the agent's purpose here—searching for drugs—differs dramatically from the intention of a driver or fellow passenger who squeezes a bag in the process of making more room for another parcel. But in determining whether an expectation of privacy is reasonable, it is the effect, not the purpose, that matters. . . .

If we are to depart from established legal principles, we should not begin here. At best, this decision will lead to a constitutional jurisprudence of "squeezes," thereby complicating further already complex Fourth Amendment law, increasing the difficulty of deciding ordinary criminal matters, and hindering the administrative guidance (with its potential for control of unreasonable police practices) that a less complicated jurisprudence might provide. . . .

Minnesota v. Dickerson

508 U.S. 366, 113 S.CT. 2130 (1993)

One evening in 1989 two Minneapolis police officers patrolling the city in an unmarked squad car noticed Timothy Dickerson leaving an apartment building. They had previously responded to complaints of drug sales in the building and considered it a "crack house." Dickerson was walking toward the police but upon spotting the squad car abruptly turned in the opposite direction. One of the police officers watched as Dickerson entered an alley and, based upon his seemingly evasive actions and the fact that he had just left a building known for cocaine traffic, the officers decided to stop him. Pulling their squad car into the alley, they ordered Dickerson to stop and submit to a patdown search. That search revealed no weapons, but the officer conducting the search felt a small lump in Dickerson's nylon jacket, reached into a pocket, and retrieved a small plastic bag containing one-fifth of one gram of crack cocaine. Dickerson was immediately arrested and charged with the possession of a controlled substance.

Before trial Dickerson's attorney moved to suppress the cocaine, but the trial judge, after concluding that the officers were justified under *Terry v. Ohio*, 392 U.S. 1 (1968), in stopping and frisking Dickerson, rejected the motion on the grounds that the officers' search of Dickerson's pocket was analogous to the "plain-view" exception. The trial court's decision, however, was reversed by an appellate court, and that decision was affirmed by the state supreme court, which agreed that the police overstepped *Terry* in seizing the cocaine and "declined to adopt the plain feel exception" to the Fourth Amendment's warrant requirement. Minnesota appealed to the Supreme Court, which granted review and affirmed the state supreme court's ruling, but also recognized a "plain feel" exception to Fourth Amendment searches.

The Court's decision was 6–3, with Justice White announcing the majority's opinion. Justice Scalia concurred. In a separate opinion Chief Justice Rehnquist, joined by Justices Blackmun and Thomas, in part concurred and in part dissented.

■ ■ ■

☐ *Justice WHITE delivered the opinion of the Court.*

Terry [*v. Ohio*, 392 U.S. 1 (1968)] held that "when an officer is justified in believing that the individual whose suspicious behavior he is investigating at close range is armed and presently dangerous to the officer or to others," the officer may conduct a patdown search "to determine whether the person is in fact carrying a weapon." Rather, a protective search—permitted without a warrant and on the basis of reasonable suspicion less than probable cause—must be strictly "limited to that which is necessary for the discovery of weapons which might be used to harm the officer or others nearby." If the protective search goes beyond what is necessary to determine if the suspect is armed, it is no longer valid under *Terry* and its fruits will be suppressed. *Sibron v. New York*, 392 U.S. 40 (1968).

These principles were settled 25 years ago when, on the same day, the Court announced its decisions in *Terry* and *Sibron*. The question presented today is whether police officers may seize nonthreatening contraband detected during a protective patdown search of the sort permitted by *Terry*. We think the answer is clearly that they may, so long as the officers' search stays within the bounds marked by *Terry*.

We have already held that police officers, at least under certain circumstances, may seize contraband detected during the lawful execution of a *Terry* search. In *Michigan v. Long* [463 U.S. 1032 (1983)], for example, police approached a man who had driven his car into a ditch and who appeared to be under the influence of some intoxicant. As the man moved to reenter the car from the roadside, police spotted a knife on the floorboard. The officers stopped the man, subjected him to a patdown search, and then inspected the interior of the vehicle for other weapons. During the search of the passenger compartment, the police discovered an open pouch containing marijuana and seized it. This Court upheld the validity of the search and seizure under *Terry*. The Court held first that, in the context of a roadside encounter, where police have reasonable suspicion based on specific and articulate facts to believe that a driver may be armed and dangerous, they may conduct a protective search for weapons not only of the driver's person but also of the passenger compartment of the automobile. Of course, the protective search of the vehicle, being justified solely by the danger that weapons stored there could be used against the officers or bystanders, must be "limited to those areas in which a weapon may be placed or hidden." The Court then held: "If, while conducting a legitimate *Terry* search of the interior of the automobile, the officer should, as here, discover contraband other than weapons, he clearly cannot be required to ignore the contraband, and the Fourth Amendment does not require its suppression in such circumstances."

The Court in *Long* justified this latter holding by reference to our cases under the "plain-view" doctrine. If, however, the police lack probable cause to believe that an object in plain view is contraband without conducting some further search of the object—i.e., if "its incriminating character [is not] 'immediately apparent'"—the plain-view doctrine cannot justify its seizure. *Arizona v. Hicks*, 480 U.S. 321 (1987).

We think that this doctrine has an obvious application by analogy to cases in which an officer discovers contraband through the sense of touch during an otherwise lawful search. The rationale of the plain-view doctrine is that if contraband is left in open view and is observed by a police officer from a lawful vantage point, there has been no invasion of a legitimate expectation of privacy and thus no "search" within the meaning of the Fourth Amendment—or at least no search independent of the initial intrusion that gave the officers their vantage point. The warrantless seizure of contraband that presents itself in this manner is deemed justified by the realization that resort to a neutral magistrate under such circumstances would often be impracticable and would do little to promote the objectives of the Fourth Amendment. The same can be said of tactile discoveries of contraband. If a police officer lawfully pats down a suspect's outer clothing and feels an object whose contour or mass makes its identity immediately apparent, there has been no invasion of the suspect's privacy beyond that already authorized by the officer's search for weapons; if the object is contraband, its warrantless seizure would be justified by the same practical considerations that inhere in the plain view context. . . .

It remains to apply these principles to the facts of this case. Respondent has not challenged the finding made by the trial court and affirmed by both the Court of Appeals and the State Supreme Court that the police were justified under *Terry* in stopping him and frisking him for weapons. Thus, the dispositive question before this Court is whether the officer who conducted the search was acting within the lawful bounds marked by *Terry* at the time he gained probable cause to believe that the lump in respondent's jacket was contraband. . . . The Minnesota Supreme Court, after "a close examination of the record," held that the officer's own testimony "belies any notion that he 'immediately'" recognized the lump as crack cocaine. Rather, the court concluded, the officer determined that the lump was contraband only after "squeezing, sliding and otherwise manipulating the contents of the defendant's pocket"—a pocket which the officer already knew contained no weapon.

Under the State Supreme Court's interpretation of the record before it, it is clear that the court was correct in holding that the police officer in this case overstepped the bounds of the "strictly circumscribed" search for weapons allowed under *Terry*. Where, as here, "an officer who is executing a valid search for one item seizes a different item," this Court rightly "has been sensitive to the danger . . . that officers will enlarge a specific authorization, furnished by a warrant or an exigency, into the equivalent of a general warrant to rummage and seize at will." *Texas v. Brown*, 460 U.S. [730 (1983)] (STEVENS, J., concurring in judgment). Here, the officer's continued exploration of respondent's pocket after having concluded that it contained no weapon was unrelated to "the sole justification of the search [under *Terry*:] . . . the protection of the police officer and others nearby." It therefore amounted to the sort of evidentiary search that *Terry* expressly refused to authorize, and that we have condemned in subsequent cases. . . .

☐ *Justice SCALIA, concurring.*

My problem with the present case is that I am not entirely sure that the physical search—the "frisk"—that produced the evidence at issue here complied with [the Fourth Amendment's] constitutional standard. The decision of ours that gave approval to such searches, *Terry v. Ohio*, 392 U.S. 1 (1968), made no serious attempt to determine compliance with traditional standards, but rather, according to the style of this Court at the time, simply adjudged that such a search was "reasonable" by current estimations.

There is good evidence, I think, that the "stop" portion of the *Terry* "stop-and-frisk" holding accords with the common law—that it had long been considered reasonable to detain suspicious persons for the purpose of demanding that they give an account of themselves. . . .

I am unaware, however, of any precedent for a physical search of a person thus temporarily detained for questioning. Sometimes, of course, the temporary detention of a suspicious character would be elevated to a full custodial arrest on probable cause—as, for instance, when a suspect was unable to provide a sufficient accounting of himself. At that point, it is clear that the common law would permit not just a protective "frisk," but a full physical search incident to the arrest. When, however, the detention did not rise to the level of a full-blown arrest (and was not supported by the degree of cause needful for that purpose), there appears to be no clear support at common law for physically searching the suspect. I frankly doubt, moreover, whether the fiercely proud men who adopted our Fourth Amendment would have allowed themselves to be subjected, on mere suspicion of being armed and dangerous, to such indignity. . . .

On the other hand, even if a "frisk" prior to arrest would have been considered impermissible in 1791, perhaps it was considered permissible by 1868, when the Fourteenth Amendment (the basis for applying the Fourth Amendment to the States) was adopted. Or perhaps it is only since that time that concealed weapons capable of harming the interrogator quickly and from beyond arm's reach have become common—which might alter the judgment of what is "reasonable" under the original standard. But technological changes were no more discussed in *Terry* than was the original state of the law.

If I were of the view that *Terry* was (insofar as the power to "frisk" is concerned) incorrectly decided, I might—even if I felt bound to adhere to that case—vote to exclude the evidence incidentally discovered, on the theory that half a constitutional guarantee is better than none. I might also vote to exclude it if I agreed with the original-meaning-is-irrelevant, good-policy-is-constitutional-law school of jurisprudence that the *Terry* opinion represents. As a policy matter, it may be desirable to permit "frisks" for weapons, but not to encourage "frisks" for drugs by admitting evidence other than weapons.

I adhere to original meaning, however. And though I do not favor the mode of analysis in *Terry*, I cannot say that its result was wrong. Constitutionality of the "frisk" in the present case was neither challenged nor argued. Assuming, therefore, that the search was lawful, I agree with the Court's premise that any evidence incidentally discovered in the course of it would be admissible, and join the Court's opinion in its entirety.

United States v. Santana

427 U.S. 38, 96 S. CT. 2406 (1976)

The facts are discussed by Justice Rehnquist in the opinion announcing the Court's decision, upholding the warrantless search and seizure of Ms. Santana inside her home based on the "exigent circumstances" and the fact that police were in "hot pursuit" of her and had probable cause to suspect her of drug dealing.

The appellate court's decision was reversed by a 7–2 vote. Chief Justice Rehnquist delivered the opinion of the Court. Justices White and Stevens filed concurring opinions, and Justice Marshall, joined by Justice Brennan, issued a dissenting opinion.

■ ■ ■

☐ *Justice REHNQUIST delivered the opinion of the Court.*

Michael Gilletti, an undercover officer with the Philadelphia Narcotics Squad arranged a heroin "buy" with one Patricia McCafferty (from whom he had purchased narcotics before). McCafferty told him it would cost $115 "and we will go down to Mom Santana's for the dope."

Gilletti notified his superiors of the impending transaction, recorded the serial numbers of $110 (*sic*) in marked bills, and went to meet McCafferty at a prearranged location. She got in his car and directed him to drive to 2311 North Fifth Street, which, as she had previously informed him, was respondent Santana's residence.

McCafferty took the money and went inside the house, stopping briefly to speak to respondent Alejandro who was sitting on the front steps. She came out shortly afterwards and got into the car. Gilletti asked for the heroin; she thereupon extracted from her bra several glassine envelopes containing a brownish-white powder and gave them to him.

Gilletti then stopped the car, displayed his badge, and placed McCafferty under arrest. He told her that the police were going back to 2311 North Fifth Street and that he wanted to know where the money was. She said, "Mom has the money." At this point Sergeant Pruitt and other officers came up to the car. Gilletti showed them the envelope and said, "Mom Santana has the money." Gilletti then took McCafferty to the police station.

[Gilletti and several other police] then drove approximately two blocks back to 2311 North Fifth Street. They saw Santana standing in the doorway of the house with a brown paper bag in her hand. They pulled up to within 15 feet of Santana and got out of their van, shouting "police," and displaying their identification. As the officers approached, Santana retreated into the vestibule of her house.

The officers followed through the open door, catching her in the vestibule. As she tried to pull away, the bag tilted and "two bundles of glazed paper packets with a white powder" fell to the floor. Respondent Alejandro tried to make off with the dropped envelopes but was forcibly restrained. When Santana was told to empty her pockets, she produced $135, $70 of which could be identified as Gilletti's marked money. The white powder in the bag was later determined to be heroin. . . .

In *United States v. Watson*, 423 U.S. 411 (1976), we held that the warrantless arrest of an individual in a public place upon probable cause did not violate the Fourth Amendment. Thus the first question we must decide is whether, when the police first sought to arrest Santana, she was in a public place.

While it may be true that under the common law of property the threshold of one's dwelling is "private," as is the yard surrounding the house, it is nonetheless clear that under the cases interpreting the Fourth Amendment Santana was in a "public" place. She was not in an area where she had any expectation of privacy. "What a person knowingly exposes to the public, even in his own house or office, is not a subject of Fourth Amendment protection." *Katz v. United States*, 389 U.S. 347 (1967). She was not merely visible to the public but was as exposed to public view, speech, hearing, and touch as if she had been standing completely outside her house. *Hester v. United States*, 265 U.S. 57 (1924). Thus, when the police, who concededly had probable cause to do so, sought to arrest her, they merely intended to perform a function which we have approved in *Watson*.

The only remaining question is whether her act of retreating into her house could thwart an otherwise proper arrest. We hold that it could not. In *Warden v. Hayden*, 387 U.S. 294 (1967), we recognized the right of police, who had probable cause to believe that an armed robber had entered a house a few minutes before, to make a warrantless entry to arrest the robber and to search for weapons. This case, involving a true "hot pursuit," is clearly governed by *Warden*; the need to act quickly here is even greater than in that case while the intrusion is much less. The District Court was correct in concluding that "hot pursuit" means some sort of a chase, but it need not be an extended hue and cry "in and about (the) public streets." The fact that the pursuit here ended almost as soon as it began did not render it any the less a "hot pursuit" sufficient to justify the warrantless entry into Santana's house. Once Santana saw the police, there was likewise a realistic expectation that any delay would result in destruction of evidence.

We thus conclude that a suspect may not defeat an arrest which has been set in motion in a public place, and is therefore proper under *Watson*, by the expedient of escaping to a private place.

☐ *Justice MARSHALL, with whom Mr. Justice BRENNAN joins, dissenting.*

[I]f I correctly read the Court's citation to the "open fields" doctrine of *Hester v. United States* (1924), the Court holds that the police may enter upon private property to make warrantless arrests of persons who are in plain view and outdoors; and the Court applies that doctrine today to persons who are arguably within their homes but who are "as exposed" to the public as if they were outside. But the Court's encroachment upon the reserved question is limited. Thus, the Court's citation of *Katz v. United States* (1967) does not suggest that a plain view of a suspect is alone sufficient to justify warrantless entry and seizure in the home. Indeed, the Court's rejection of sight alone as a basis for warrantless entry and arrest is made patent by negative implication from the Court's need to elaborate a hot pursuit justification for the police following Santana into her home. Presumably, if plain view were the touchstone, Santana would have been just as liable to warrantless arrest as she retreated several feet inside her open door as she was when standing in the doorway. . . .

The Court's doctrine, then, appears *sui generis*, useful only in arresting persons who are "as exposed to public view, speech, hearing, and touch," as though in the unprotected outdoors. Narrow though it may be, however, the Court's approach does not depend on whether exigency justifies an arrest on private property, and thus I cannot join it. . . .

I do not believe that these exigent circumstances automatically validate Santana's arrest. The *exigency* that justified the entry and arrest *was solely a product of police conduct*. Had Officer Gilletti driven McCafferty to a more remote location before arresting her, it appears that no exigency would have been created by the arrest; in such an event a warrant would have been necessary, in my view, before Santana could have been arrested. It is not apparent on this record why Officer Gilletti arrested McCafferty so close to Santana's home when the arresting officers were clearly aware that such a nearby arrest would necessitate the prompt arrest of Santana. While a police decision that the time is right to arrest a suspect should properly be given great deference, the power to arrest is an awesome one and is subject to abuse. An arrest may permit a search of premises incident to the arrest, a search that otherwise could be carried out only upon probable cause and pursuant to a search warrant. Likewise, an arrest in circumstances such as those presented here may create exigency that may justify a search or another arrest. When an arrest is so timed that it is no more than an attempt to circumvent the warrant requirement, I would hold the subsequent arrest or search unlawful. . . .

C | The Special Problems of Automobiles in a Mobile Society

Automobiles pose special Fourth Amendment problems. This is because of their mobility and the possibility of criminal suspects escaping and destroying evidence. The Court's rulings have made automobile searches and seizures not just another exception to the warrant requirement, but virtually a "whole new ball game" as to what is an unreasonable search and seizure.

The leading case distinguishing automobiles from "houses, papers, and effects" for Fourth Amendment purposes is *Carroll v. United States*, 267 U.S. 132 (1925). There Chief Justice William Howard Taft observed that

> [t]he guaranty of freedom from unreasonable searches and seizures by the Fourth Amendment has been construed, practically since the beginning of government, as recognizing a necessary difference between a search of a store, dwelling house, or other structure in respect of which a proper official warrant readily may be obtained and a search of a ship, motor boat, wagon, or automobile for contraband goods, where it is not practicable to secure a warrant, because the vehicle can be quickly moved out of the locality or jurisdiction in which the warrant must be sought.

But in finding warrantless searches and seizures of automobiles permissible, Taft added,

> It would be intolerable and unreasonable if [police] were authorized to stop every automobile on the chance of finding [illegal goods], and thus subject all persons lawfully using the highways to the inconvenience and indignity of such a search. Travelers may be so stopped in crossing an international boundary because of national self-protection reasonably requiring one entering the country to identify himself as entitled to come in, and his belongings as effects which may be lawfully brought in. But those lawfully within the country, entitled to use the public highways, have a right to free passage without interruption or search unless there is known to a competent official, authorized to search, probable cause for believing that their vehicles are carrying contraband or illegal merchandise.

Subsequently, in *Chambers v. Maroney*, 399 U.S. 42 (1970), the Court reaffirmed that warrantless searches of automobiles and their contents are permissible under the Fourth Amendment on the rationale given in *Carroll*.

Following the *Carroll-Chambers* doctrine, controversy revolved around how far police could go in stopping and searching vehicles and their occupants. In *United States v. Robinson*, 414 U.S. 218 (1973), the Court held that police, without a warrant but based on probable cause, could conduct a rather extensive search of a driver arrested for a traffic offense. There, the majority extended *Terry v. Ohio* (1968) (excerpted above) to permit a patdown and search of a driver's coat pocket and a crumpled cigarette pack that contained heroin.

A companion case, *Gustafson v. Florida*, 414 U.S. 260 (1973), upheld the full-body search of a driver who was arrested and taken into custody. In *Pennsylvania v. Mimms*, 434 U.S. 106 (1977), the justices (6–3) also upheld an officer's frisking a driver who, after stopping a car with an expired license plate, asked the driver to step out of his car and produce his driver's license. At that point, the officer noticed that the driver had a large "bulge" in his sports jacket and patted him down. In two other rulings on drivers and passengers, the Court held, first, that police, after making a routine traffic stop and ticketing the driver, do not have to inform the driver that he or she is "legally free to go," before engaging in further questioning. The Ohio Supreme Court had held contrariwise but the Court reversed in *Ohio v. Robinette*, 519 U.S. 33 (1996). Second, *Maryland v. Wilson*, 519 U.S. 408 (1997), extended the ruling in *Pennsylvania v. Mimms* to permit police to order both drivers and passengers out of a car stopped for routine traffic violations.

However, in *Missouri v. McNeely*, 569 U.S. 141 (2013), the Court limited the *exigencies of circumstances* exception to the warrant requirement (discussed in Section B of this chapter), and rejected a per se rule that police have drivers suspected of driving while intoxicated (DWI) of alcohol submit to a blood test without their consent or a warrant; about half of the states require a warrant for DWI suspects. Tyler McNeely was stopped by a police officer for speeding and crossing the centerline. After declining to take a breath test to measure his blood alcohol concentration, he was arrested and taken to a nearby hospital for blood testing. The officer never attempted to secure a search warrant. McNeely refused to consent to the blood test, but the officer directed a lab technician to take a sample. McNeely tested well above the legal limit, and he was charged with driving while intoxicated. He moved to suppress the blood test result, arguing that taking his blood without a warrant violated his Fourth Amendment rights. The trial court agreed, concluding that the exigency exception to the warrant requirement did not apply because, apart from the fact that McNeely's blood alcohol was dissipating, no circumstances suggested that the officer faced an emergency. The Missouri Supreme Court affirmed, relying on *Schmerber v. California*, 384 U.S. 757 (1966), in which the Court upheld a DWI suspect's warrantless blood test where

■ THE DEVELOPMENT OF LAW
Automobiles and Border Patrol Searches

CASE	VOTE	RULING
Almeida-Sanchez v. United States, 413 U.S. 266 (1973)	5–4	Warrantless search of cars without probable cause by border patrol agents twenty miles north of the border violated the Fourth Amendment.
United States v. Brignoni Ponce, 422 U.S. 873 (1975)	9–0	Except at the border, roving border patrol agents may stop cars only if they

have reasonable suspicion and specific and articulable facts indicating that a vehicle contains illegal aliens; Mexican ancestry of occupants alone is not grounds for reasonable suspicion.

United States v. Ortiz, 422 U.S. 891 (1975)	9–0	Fourth Amendment forbids border patrol searches at fixed checkpoints distantly removed from the border and requires probable cause for searches.
United States v. Martinez-Fuerte, 428 U.S. 543 (1976)	7–2	Vehicles may be stopped at a fixed checkpoint for brief questioning of occu-

pants, and vehicles may be directed selectively to a secondary inspection point, even when the basis for doing so is the "apparent Mexican ancestry" of occupants of the vehicle.

United States v. Arvizu, 534 U.S. 266 (2002)	9–0	Writing for the Court, Chief Justice Rehnquist held that under *Terry v.*

Ohio, 392 U.S. 1 (1968), based on "the totality of the circumstances" an experienced border patrol officer had "reasonable suspicion" to stop on an unpaved road in a remote area of Arizona an otherwise innocuous automobile, which in turn led to a search that uncovered over 100 pounds of marijuana.

CASE	VOTE	RULING
United States v. Flores-Montano, 541 U.S. 149 (2004)	9–0	International border customs officers may, without reasonable suspicion,

search, remove, disassemble, and reassemble a vehicle's gas tank in order to search for drugs or other contraband. Writing for the Court, Chief Justice Rehnquist held that the government's interests in protecting the border is at its "zenith" at international borders and paramount to any privacy interests in an automobile.

the officer "might reasonably have believed that he was confronted with an emergency, in which the delay necessary to obtain a warrant, under the circumstances, threatened 'the destruction of evidence.'" This case, the state court found, involved a routine DWI investigation where no factors other than the natural dissipation of blood alcohol suggested that there was an emergency, and, thus, the nonconsensual warrantless test violated McNeely's right to be free from unreasonable searches of his person. Writing for the Court in *McNeely*, Justice Sotomayor affirmed and concluded that in drunk-driving investigations, the natural dissipation of alcohol in the bloodstream does not constitute an exigency in every case to justify a warrantless blood test. Justice Sotomayor held that only in exceptional circumstances may a warrantless blood test be conducted and that should be determined on a case-by-case basis based on "the totality of circumstances." In her words: "cases will arise when anticipated delays in obtaining a warrant will justify a blood test without judicial authorization. . . . [But our decision that consent or warrants must generally be obtained underscores] our recognition that any compelled intrusion into the human body implicates significant, constitutionally protected privacy interests." Only dissenting Justice Thomas would permit warrantless blood tests of drivers suspected of DWI.

In *Delaware v. Prouse*, 440 U.S. 648 (1978), the Court drew a line at police making routine stops of vehicles for the purpose of checking drivers' licenses and car registrations, holding that police must have probable cause or a reasonable suspicion to believe that a vehicle or its occupants have violated some law. However, in *Alabama v. White*, 496 U.S. 325 (1990), the Rehnquist Court held that police may stop and question individuals traveling in their automobiles based on anonymous tips and if they obtain some corroboration that establishes a reasonable suspicion of the occupants' criminal activity. Justices Stevens, Marshall, and Brennan dissented from that ruling, as they also did in *Michigan State Police v. Sitz*, 496 U.S. 444 (1990). In *Sitz*, the Court ruled that highway sobriety checkpoints were permissible, even though police had no reasonable suspicion to believe that drivers were intoxicated. Unlike *Prouse*, Chief Justice Rehnquist emphasized that this case did not involve random highway stops, and statistical evidence showed that about 1.5 percent of the drivers stopped were arrested for alcohol impairment. "The balance of the state's interest in preventing drunken driving," he concluded, "and the degree of intrusion upon individual motorists who are briefly stopped weighs in favor of the state program."

The Court, nonetheless, refused to extend *Sitz* in *Indianapolis v. Edmond*, 531 U.S. 32 (2000). Writing for the Court, Justice O'Connor struck down the use of fixed checkpoints to interdict unlawful drugs on the ground that they lacked individualized suspicion of the drivers' criminal activity and aimed only to advance states' "general interest in crime control," in contrast with sobriety checkpoints. However, *Edmond* was subsequently distinguished and limited in *Illinois v. Lidster* (2004) (excerpted below), in which the Court upheld "informational checkpoints"—checkpoints at which all cars are stopped in order to inquire whether drivers have information pertaining to a recent crime, such as the location of a missing person or the identity of the perpetrator of a crime.

Moreover, a bare majority of the Roberts Court broadened police powers to stop drivers of cars based on anonymous tips from otherwise uncorroborated 911 phone calls in holding that a 911 phone call is enough to establish a "reasonable suspicion" for police to make an investigatory stop. The ruling in *Navarette v. California*, 572 U.S. 393 (2014), not only continued the trend in recent decades of decoupling the Fourth Amendment's "reasonableness clause" from the "warrants clause" requirements of a search and seizure, but also broadened the automobile exception. The decision expanded police discretion to make warrantless stops and searches based on "the totality of circumstances" standard for whether they have a "reasonable suspicion" of criminal activities. Writing for the Court, Justice Thomas held that police may make such stops based on the following reasoning and construction of the facts in this case: First, the tipster made a 911 call about the careless and erratic driving of a truck and reported its license number. Second, the fact that the tip came from a 911 call added to its reliability, because new technology allows police to identify 911 callers and go after them, if necessary, for making false reports. Third, the fact that a tipster described a near accident was enough for police to conclude that the driver might be drunk. Fourth, the suspicion of drunken driving, along with its hazards to the public, justified the stop; even though police did not witness any erratic driving while following the vehicle, this did not prove that the driver was not drunk. Fifth, the suspicion of drunk driving was enough, under the Fourth Amendment, for police to stop the vehicle. The police officers smelled marijuana during the traffic stop, which justified a search of the truck. The officers found bags of marijuana, for which the driver and passengers were arrested and prosecuted. Chief Justice Roberts and Justices Kennedy, Breyer, and Alito joined Justice Thomas's opinion.

In a sharp dissent in *Navarette* Justice Scalia, joined by Justices Ginsburg, Sotomayor, and Kagan, took strong exception to Justice Thomas's construction of the facts and sequence of events, as well as the ultimate conclusion. In Justice Scalia's words:

> The Court's opinion serves up a freedom-destroying cocktail consisting of two parts patent falsity: (1) that anonymous 911 reports of traffic violations are reliable so long as they correctly identify a car and its location, and (2) that a single instance of careless or reckless driving necessarily supports a reasonable suspicion of drunkenness. All the malevolent 911 caller need do is assert a traffic violation, and the targeted car will be stopped, forcibly if necessary, by the police. If the driver turns out not to be drunk (which will almost always be the case), the caller need fear no consequences, even if 911 knows his identity. After all, he never alleged drunkenness, but merely called in a traffic violation—and on that point his word is as good as his victim's.
>
> Drunken driving is a serious matter, but so is the loss of our freedom to come and go as we please without police interference. To prevent and detect murder we do not allow searches without probable cause or targeted Terry stops without reasonable suspicion. We should not do so for drunken driving either. After today's opinion all of us on the road, and not just drug dealers, are at risk of having our freedom of movement curtailed on suspicion of drunkenness, based upon a phone tip, true or false, of a single instance of careless driving.

The Roberts Court considered another case involving the basis for automobile traffic stops with *Heien v. North Carolina*, 135 S.Ct. 530 (2014), in which the issue of concern was whether an officer's mistaken understanding of a statute may nonetheless create a "reasonable suspicion" justifying a traffic stop. In this case, a police officer had pulled over Nicholas Brady Heien after noticing that only one of his car's brake lights was working. While issuing a warning ticket for the broken brake light, the officer became suspicious of the occupants and asked the driver, Heien, for permission to search the vehicle. Heien gave permission and the officer discovered cocaine. Heien was then arrested for drug trafficking. Subsequently, a trial court denied Heien's motion to suppress the seized evidence on Fourth Amendment grounds, concluding that the car's faulty brake light gave the officer reasonable suspicion to stop the car. A state appellate court reversed in holding that the state's code requiring cars to be "equipped with a stop lamp" required only a single light (which Heien's vehicle had), and therefore the stop was unreasonable. However, that decision was reversed by the state's supreme court on the basis that the officer's mistaken understanding of the law was reasonable, and thus the stop was valid. On appeal that ruling was affirmed by a vote of 8-to-1, with only Justice Sotomayor dissenting.

Writing for the Court in *Heien* Chief Justice Roberts held that the Fourth Amendment only requires officials to act reasonably, not perfectly, and gives them "fair leeway for enforcing the law." Searches and seizures based on mistakes of fact may be reasonable, subject to the limitation that "the mistakes [are] those of reasonable men." Likewise, mistakes about the law are no less compatible with the concept of reasonable suspicion. Whether an officer is reasonably mistaken about the facts or the law, the result is the same. In the chief justice's view, there was little difficulty in concluding that the officer's mistaken view of the law was reasonable, because the state's vehicle code requires "a stop lamp" but also provides that the lamp "may be incorporated into a unit with one or more rear lamps." Although the state appellate court held that "rear lamps" do not include brake lights, the word "other" in the code made it objectively reasonable to think that a faulty brake light constituted a violation, and thus basis for stopping the car. Chief Justice Roberts, though, also emphasized that an exception to the Fourth Amendment for reasonable mistakes about the law does not give police a "Fourth Amendment advantage through a sloppy study of the laws he is duty-bound to enforce." Furthermore, in *Illinois v. Caballes*, 543 U.S. 405 (2005), the Court held that after police stop a car they may use drug-sniffing dogs around a car stopped for a routine traffic violation and prosecutors may introduce evidence of contraband that was found as a result.

That decision was reaffirmed in *Florida v. Harris*, 568 U.S. 237 (2013). After stopping Harris for driving with expired tags, a police officer asked him for permission to search the vehicle. When Harris refused, the officer retrieved Aldo, a highly trained and certified narcotics detection dog. The dog sniffed the driver's door handle and indicated the presence of narcotics. And a search revealed all of the materials necessary to make methamphetamine but no actual narcotics. In an opinion for the Court, Justice Kagan held: "The question—similar to every inquiry into probable cause—is whether all the facts surrounding a dog's alert, viewed through the lens of common sense, would make a reasonably prudent person think that a search would reveal contraband or evidence of a crime. . . . A sniff is up to snuff when it meets that test. . . . Aldo's did."

Subsequently, though, the Roberts Court sought to limit its ruling in *Illinois v. Caballes* (2005). In *Rodriguez v. United States*, 135 S.Ct. 1609 (2015), the Court held that police may not drag out a routine traffic stop in order to buy time for a dog to search a vehicle for drugs. Writing for the Court, Justice Ginsburg, who had dissented in *Caballes*, held, "A police stop exceeding the time needed to handle the matter for which the stop was made violates the Constitution's shield against unreasonable seizures," and emphasized that an officer's authority for stopping a car "ends when tasks tied to the traffic infraction are—or reasonably should have been—completed." In this case, a police officer had seen a car veer onto the shoulder of the highway and then jerk back onto the road. The officer, accompanied by his dog, stopped the car and asked the driver, Denny Rodriguez, for his license, registration, and proof of insurance. The officer ran a records check and then wrote Rodriguez a warning ticket. But the officer was also suspicious of Rodriguez and a passenger, and asked for consent to search the car. When Rodriguez refused, the officer told him to get out of the car. After a second officer arrived, he then circled his drug-sniffing dog twice around the car, and the dog alerted to the presence of drugs. A search uncovered a "large bag of methamphetamine" and Rodriguez was arrested. "All told, seven or eight minutes had elapsed from the time [the officer] issued the written warning until the dog indicated the presence of drugs," Justice Ginsburg underscored in holding that the "line drawn" in *Caballes* was that a dog sniff may not prolong a routine traffic stop. Justices Kennedy, Thomas, and Alito dissented. Justice Thomas argued that the majority's ruling would lead to arbitrary results: "Under its reasoning, a traffic stop made by a rookie could be executed in a reasonable manner, whereas the same traffic stop made by a knowledgeable veteran officer in *precisely the same circumstances* might not, if in fact his knowledge and experience made him capable of completing the stop faster." And Justice Alito charged that the ruling would lead to police workarounds, such as conducting the dog sniff while running a records check and before issuing a ticket or warning for the original infraction. In his words, "Most officers will learn the prescribed sequence of events even if they cannot fathom the reason for the requirement. (I would love to be the proverbial fly on the wall when police instructors teach this rule to officers who make traffic stops.)" However, by a unanimous vote the Roberts Court held that passengers, no less the driver, may challenge the constitutionality of police officers' stopping a vehicle, in *Brendlin v. California*, 551 U.S. 249 (2007). Writing for the Court, Justice Souter observed:

A person is seized by the police and thus entitled to challenge the government's action under the Fourth Amendment when the officer "by means of physical force or show of authority," terminates or restrains his freedom of movement, *Florida v. Bostick*, 501 U.S. 429 (1991) (quoting *Terry v. Ohio*, 392 U.S. 1 (1968)), "through means intentionally applied." Thus, an "unintended person . . . [may be] the object of the detention," so long as the detention is "willful" and not merely the consequence of "an unknowing act." *County of Sacramento v. Lewis*, 523 U.S. 833 (1998). A police officer may make a seizure by show of authority and without the use of physical force, but there is no seizure without actual submission; otherwise, there is at most an attempted seizure, so far as the Fourth Amendment is concerned. *California v. Hodari D.*, 499 U.S. 621 (1991).

When the actions of the police do not show an unambiguous intent to restrain or when an individual's submission to a show of governmental authority takes the form of passive acquiescence, there needs to be some test for telling when a seizure occurs in response to authority, and when it does not. The test was devised by Justice STEWART in *United States v. Mendenhall*, 446 U.S. 544 (1980), who wrote that a seizure occurs if "in view of all of the circumstances surrounding the incident, a reasonable person would have believed that he was not free to leave."

The law is settled that in Fourth Amendment terms a traffic stop entails a seizure of the driver "even though the purpose of the stop is limited and the resulting detention quite brief." *Delaware v. Prouse*, 440 U.S. 648 (1979). And although we have not, until today, squarely answered the question whether a passenger is also seized, we have said over and over in *dicta* that during a traffic stop an officer seizes everyone in the vehicle, not just the driver . . . .

Once police stop a vehicle, they may search the area in plain view around the driver, and if they have a reasonable suspicion of finding illegal items or make a protective search to discover weapons, they may search the entire interior of the vehicle.[1] In *New York v. Class*, 475 U.S. 106 (1986), for example, the justices upheld a search of a car based on an officer's spotting a gun under the front seat, when looking through the front window to see the vehicle identification number on the dashboard. The Court underscored how far police may go in *California v. Carney*, 471 U.S. 386 (1985), upholding a warrantless search of the entire interior of a mobile home that was parked in a public parking lot, where police had probable cause to believe that the occupant was selling marijuana. Warrantless searches of the exterior of vehicles[2] and inventory searches of impounded automobiles are also permissible.[3]

A series of cases presented the Court with another line-drawing problem, namely, how far police may go in searching containers found in a vehicle. Initially, in *United States v. Chadwick*, 433 U.S. 1 (1977), the Court held that a locked footlocker that had been loaded into the trunk of an automobile could not be searched without a warrant. On Joseph Chadwick's arrival by train in Boston from San Diego, he was arrested at a waiting vehicle by federal agents, who had been alerted that he was a possible drug trafficker. They arrested Chadwick and seized the automobile and the footlocker, which they had probable cause to believe contained narcotics. At a federal building an hour and half after the arrest, the agents opened the footlocker without Chadwick's consent or a search warrant. The Court disallowed that search, observing that "[b]y placing personal effects inside a double-locked footlocker, [Chadwick] manifested an expectation that the contents would remain free from public examination. No less than one who locks the doors of his home against intruders, one who safeguards his personal possessions in this manner is due the protection of the Fourth Amendment Warrant Clause."

Two years later, *Arkansas v. Sanders*, 442 U.S. 753 (1979), again addressed the issue of whether luggage could be searched without a warrant along with the rest of a vehicle. There, Little Rock, Arkansas, police had a tip that Lonnie Sanders would arrive at the airport carrying a green suitcase, holding marijuana. After he arrived, police watched him retrieve the suitcase from the baggage claim area and place it in the trunk of a taxi. The officers followed the taxi a short distance and then stopped it. Without Sanders's permission, they opened the suitcase containing marijuana. The issue in *Sanders* was "whether the warrantless search of [Sanders's] suitcase falls on the *Chadwick* or the *Chambers-Carroll* side of the Fourth Amendment line."

Writing for the Court, Justice Powell held that *Chadwick* was controlling. In *Robbins v. California*, 453 U.S. 420 (1981), the Court then held that an opaque container in the trunk of a car could not be searched without a warrant, even though police had probable cause to search the vehicle and the container. In this case, police had stopped a station wagon that was being driven erratically, and when the driver opened the door of the vehicle they smelled marijuana. A search of the passenger compartment yielded some marijuana. After arresting Jeffrey Robbins, the police then opened the tailgate of the station wagon and searched a recessed luggage compartment, where they found two green garbage bags containing marijuana.

But in *United States v. Ross*, 456 U.S. 798 (1982), following Justice O'Connor's appointment, the Burger Court overturned *Robbins*. Subsequently, as the composition of the bench changed further in the late 1980s and 1990s, the Rehnquist Court incrementally broadened the scope of police searches of automobile occupants and their belongings.[4] Finally, *California v. Acevedo* (excerpted below), expressly overruled *Chadwick* and *Arkansas v. Sanders*.

After over a decade of rulings cutting back on the scope of the Fourth Amendment's application to automobile searches, however, the Court held that police may not conduct full searches of cars stopped for minor traffic violations and whose drivers are issued citations, rather than arrested. The ruling in *Knowles v. Iowa*, 525 U.S. 113 (1998), was unanimous and handed down by Chief Justice Rehnquist, who drew a "bright line" limiting automobile searches in a short opinion for the Court.

Nonetheless, the Court underscored in a brief *per curiam* opinion, in *Maryland v. Dyson*, 527 U.S. 465 (1999), that the automobile exception to the Fourth Amendment's warrant requirement does not require police to obtain a warrant to search a car when they have probable cause to believe that it contains contraband. By a 6–3 vote in *Wyoming v. Houghton*, 526 U.S. 295 (1999), the Court also reaffirmed that police may search the belongings of passengers in cars if they have probable cause for doing so. In *Florida v. White*, 526 U.S. 559 (1999), the Court held that the Fourth Amendment does not require police to obtain a warrant before seizing an automobile from a public place when they have probable cause to believe that it is forfeitable contraband. Moreover, in *Atwater v. Lago Vista*, 532 U.S. 318 (2001) a bare majority held that police may arrest and hold drivers stopped for routine misdemeanor traffic violations, such as driving without a buckled seatbelt, which are punishable only by fines. The Court also reaffirmed and extended its ruling in *New York v. Belton*, 453 U.S. 454 (1981), holding that after police make a custodial arrest of a driver, they may search the car as a contemporaneous incident of the arrest. In *Thornton v. United States*, 541 U.S. 615 (2004), Chief Justice Rehnquist held that under *Belton* police could permissibly search the passenger compartment of a car—even after the driver got out and a patdown revealed drugs in his pocket, for which he was arrested. A subsequent search of the car revealed a handgun under the driver's seat, for which Thorton was also prosecuted. Justices Stevens and Souter dissented.

The Roberts Court limited warrantless car searches and reaffirmed the holding in *Chimel v. California* (1969) (excerpted in Section A), as extended to cars in *New York v. Belton*, and, in *Arizona v. Gant*, 556 U.S. 332 (2009), holding that police may search only the immediate area in order to protect the safety of officers in a search-incident-to-arrest situation; however the police must have a warrant to search a car after the driver or passenger is taken into custody and may conduct a warrantless search only for evidence related to the arrest. On the other hand, the Roberts Court ruled unanimously that police do not act unconstitutionally in conducting a search of a driver following an arrest based on probable cause, even if the arrest violates a state law. Delivering the opinion for the Court in *Virginia v. Moore*, 553 U.S. 164 (2008), Justice

Scalia upheld the conviction of David Moore for possession of cocaine after he was stopped for driving on a suspended license, which under state law authorized a traffic citation, not an arrest. As long as police have probable cause to make an arrest, Justice Scalia held, it makes no difference that a state law bars police from making an arrest when the crime involved is only a misdemeanor traffic offense.

More recently, in *Byrd v. United States,* 138 S. Ct. 1518 (2018), the Roberts Court unanimously held that the driver of a rental car, who was not listed on the rental agreement but had lawful possession of the car, had "a reasonable expectation of privacy" in the car and invalidated a warrantless search of the car by police without probable cause. Writing for the Court, Justice Kennedy distinguished *Rakas v. Illinois,* 439 U.S. 128 (1978), which held that passengers in an automobile, in which the driver was permissibly stopped, searched, and found in possession of drugs, had a far more limited expectation of privacy since they had no property interest in the vehicle. In *Byrd*, Kennedy found the lawful driver of the rental car shared a proprietary interest in the car and, hence, had a reasonable expectation of privacy.

Moreover, the Roberts Court rejected the view that the *automobile exception* is a categorical exception justifying warrantless searches on the curtilage of one's home. Writing for the Court in *Collins v. Virginia* (2018) (excerpted below), Justice Sotomayor underscored that the automobile exception is not absolute, holding unconstitutional a warrantless search, based on a posting on Facebook, for a stolen motorbike parked in the driveway of a home, and sharply distinguished the exigencies of circumstances exception to the Fourth Amendment (discussed in the preceding section).

Notes

1. *New York v. Belton*, 453 U.S. 454 (1981); *Michigan v. Long*, 463 U.S. 1032 (1983); and *Whren v. United States*, 517 U.S. 806 (1996).

2. *Cardwell v. Lewis*, 417 U.S. 583 (1974) (with probable cause, warrantless inspection of exterior of car is permissible). *Harris v. United States*, 390 U.S. 234 (1968) upheld the use of an automobile registration card found in plain view in an impounded car. See *Texas v. Brown*, 460 U.S. 730 (1983).

3. In *Preston v. United States*, 376 U.S. 364 (1964), however, the Warren Court held that a search of a car, after the driver's arrest and the car was taken to a garage, was too remote to be a search incident to an arrest. But *Chambers v. Maroney*, 399 U.S. 42 (1970), upheld the search of a car in a police station, and *South Dakota v. Opperman*, 428 U.S. 364 (1976), upheld routine inventory searches of locked cars impounded by police.

4. See *United States v. Johns*, 469 U.S. 478 (1985); and *Colorado v. Bertine*, 479 U.S. 367 (1987); but see *Florida v. Wells*, 495 U.S. 1 (1990).

Illinois v. Lidster

540 U.S. 419, 124 S.CT. 885 (2004)

Shortly after midnight in Lombard, Illinois, a seventy-year-old bicyclist was killed in a hit-and-run accident. A week later, at about the same time and same place, police set up a highway checkpoint. Drivers were stopped, asked whether they had witnessed the incident, and given a flyer requesting assistance in identifying the vehicle and driver. As Robert Lidster approached the checkpoint, his van swerved, nearly hitting an officer, and subsequently he failed a sobriety test. Following his arrest and conviction for driving under the influence of alcohol, his attorney challenged the lawfulness of the arrest and conviction on the ground that the informational checkpoint stop violated the Fourth Amendment. The trial court dismissed the challenge, but the Illinois state supreme court disagreed and held that, under *Indianapolis v. Edmond*, 531 U.S. 32 (2000), such informational checkpoint stops lack individual suspicion and, hence, run afoul of the Fourth Amendment.

The state supreme court's decision was reversed by a vote of 6–3. Justice Breyer delivered the opinion for the Court. Justice Stevens, joined by Justices Souter and Ginsburg, filed an opinion in part concurring and dissenting.

■ ■ ■

☐ *Justice BREYER delivered the opinion of the Court.*

This Fourth Amendment case focuses upon a highway checkpoint where police stopped motorists to ask them for information about a recent hit-and-run accident. We hold that the police stops were reasonable, hence, constitutional. . . .

The Illinois Supreme Court basically held that our decision in [*Indianapolis v.*] *Edmond*, [531 U.S. 32 (2000)] governs the outcome of this case. We do not agree. *Edmond* involved a checkpoint at which police stopped vehicles to look for evidence of drug crimes committed by occupants of those vehicles. After stopping a vehicle at the checkpoint, police would examine (from outside the vehicle) the vehicle's interior; they would walk a drug-sniffing dog around the exterior; and, if they found sufficient evidence of drug (or other) crimes, they would arrest the vehicle's occupants. We found that police had set up this checkpoint primarily for general "crime control" purposes, i.e., "to detect evidence of ordinary criminal wrongdoing." We noted that the stop was made without individualized suspicion. And we held that the Fourth Amendment forbids such a stop, in the absence of special circumstances.

The checkpoint stop here differs significantly from that in *Edmond*. The stop's primary law enforcement purpose was not to determine whether a vehicle's occupants were committing a crime, but to ask vehicle occupants, as members of the public, for their help in providing information about a crime in all likelihood committed by others. The police expected the information elicited to help them apprehend, not the vehicle's occupants, but other individuals.

Edmond's language, as well as its context, makes clear that the constitutionality of this latter, information-seeking kind of stop was not then before the Court. . . . We concede that *Edmond* describes the law enforcement objective there in question as a "general interest in crime control," but it specifies that the phrase "general interest in crime control" does not refer to every "law enforcement" objective. We must read this and related general language in *Edmond* as we often read general language in judicial opinions—as referring in context to circumstances similar to the circumstances then before the Court and not referring to quite different circumstances that the Court was not then considering.

Neither do we believe, *Edmond* aside, that the Fourth Amendment would have us apply an *Edmond*-type rule of automatic unconstitutionality to brief, information-seeking highway stops of the kind now before us. For one thing, the fact that such stops normally lack individualized suspicion cannot by itself determine the constitutional outcome. The Fourth Amendment does not treat a motorist's car as his castle. And special law enforcement concerns will sometimes justify highway stops without individualized suspicion. See *Michigan Dept. of State Police v. Sitz*, 496 U.S. 444 (1990) (sobriety checkpoint); [*United States v.*] *Martinez-Fuerte*, [428 U.S. 543 (1976)] (Border Patrol checkpoint). Moreover, unlike *Edmond*, the context here (seeking information from the public) is one in which, by definition, the concept of individualized suspicion has little role to play. Like certain other forms of police activity, say, crowd control or public safety, an information-seeking stop is not the kind of event that involves suspicion, or lack of suspicion, of the relevant individual.

For another thing, information-seeking highway stops are less likely to provoke anxiety or to prove intrusive. The stops are likely brief. The police are not likely to ask questions designed to elicit self-incriminating information. . . .

Finally, we do not believe that an *Edmond*-type rule is needed to prevent an unreasonable proliferation of police checkpoints. Practical considerations—namely, limited police resources and community hostility to related traffic tie-ups—seem likely to inhibit any such proliferation. And, of course, the Fourth Amendment's normal insistence that the stop be reasonable in context will still provide an important legal limitation on police use of this kind of information-seeking checkpoint. . . .

We now consider the reasonableness of the checkpoint stop before us in light of the factors just mentioned. . . . We hold that the stop was constitutional.

The relevant public concern was grave. Police were investigating a crime that had resulted in a human death. . . . The stop advanced this grave public concern to a significant degree. Most importantly, the stops interfered only minimally with liberty of the sort the Fourth Amendment seeks to protect. Viewed objectively, each stop required only a brief wait in line—a very few minutes at most. . . . Viewed subjectively, the contact provided little reason for anxiety or alarm. The police stopped all vehicles systematically. And there is no allegation here that the police acted in a discriminatory or otherwise unlawful manner while questioning motorists during stops.

For these reasons we conclude that the checkpoint stop was constitutional.

California v. Acevedo

500 U.S. 565, 111 S.CT. 1982 (1991)

In October 1987, police in Santa Ana, California, received a telephone call from a federal drug-enforcement agent in Hawaii, informing them that he had seized a package of marijuana that was to have been delivered by Federal Express to a house in Santa Ana. It was decided that the agent would send the package to the police instead and they would take it to the local Federal Express office and arrest the person who claimed it. A few days later, Jamie Daza claimed the package and then drove to his apartment, taking the package in with him. While still staked out at his apartment an hour later, police observed Daza leave to throw away the box and paper that had contained the marijuana into a trash bin. At that point, one of the officers left the scene to get a search warrant, but before the officer returned, police saw Richard St. George leave the apartment carrying a blue knapsack that appeared to be half full. The officers stopped him as he was driving off, searched the knapsack, and found twelve pounds of marijuana. A little later, Charles Acevedo arrived at the apartment and, after about ten minutes, reappeared carrying a brown paper bag that looked full. Acevedo walked to a silver Honda in the parking lot and placed the bag in the trunk of the car and started the car's engine. Fearing the loss of evidence, officers in a marked police car stopped him and subsequently, without a warrant, opened the trunk and the bag and found marijuana.

Acevedo was charged with possession of marijuana. At his trial he moved to suppress the introduction of the marijuana as evidence against him on the grounds that it was obtained in violation of his Fourth Amendment rights. After his motion was denied, he pleaded guilty and, after his conviction and sentence, appealed the court's denial of his motion to suppress the marijuana as evidence. A state appellate court concluded that the marijuana should have been suppressed on the grounds that the officers had probable cause to believe that the paper bag contained drugs but lacked probable cause to suspect that Acevedo's car, itself, otherwise contained contraband. Because the officers' probable cause was directed specifically at the bag, the court held that the case was controlled by *United States v.*

Chadwick, 433 U.S. 1 (1977), which held that under similar circumstances police needed a warrant to search a large piece of luggage placed in the back of a car, rather than by *United States v. Ross*, 456 U.S. 798 (1982), which upheld a warrantless search of containers in the trunk of a car that police had probable cause to believe was being used by a drug dealer. Although the court agreed that the officers could seize the paper bag, it held that, under *Chadwick*, they could not open the bag without first obtaining a warrant for that purpose. Subsequently, the state of California appealed that ruling to the state supreme court, which denied review, and to the Supreme Court, which granted review.

The Court's decision was 6–3. Justice Blackmun announced the majority opinion, with which Justice Scalia concurred. Justice White delivered a dissenting opinion, as did Justice Stevens, who was joined by Justice Marshall.

■ ■ ■

☐ *Justice BLACKMUN delivered the opinion of the Court.*

In *Carroll v. United States*, 267 U.S. 132 (1925) this Court . . . held that a warrantless search of an automobile based upon probable cause to believe that the vehicle contained evidence of crime in the light of an exigency arising out of the likely disappearance of the vehicle did not contravene the Warrant Clause of the Fourth Amendment.

The Court refined the exigency requirement in *Chambers v. Maroney*, 399 U.S. 42 (1970), when it held that the existence of exigent circumstances was to be determined at the time the automobile is seized. . . . Following *Chambers*, if the police have probable cause to justify a warrantless seizure of an automobile on a public roadway, they may conduct either an immediate or a delayed search of the vehicle.

In *United States v. Ross*, 456 U.S. 798, decided in 1982, we held that a warrantless search of an automobile under the *Carroll* doctrine could include a search of a container or package found inside the car when such a search was supported by probable cause. . . . In *Ross*, therefore, we clarified the scope of the *Carroll* doctrine as properly including a "probing search" of compartments and containers within the automobile so long as the search is supported by probable cause.

In addition to this clarification, *Ross* distinguished the *Carroll* doctrine from the separate rule that governed the search of closed containers. The Court had announced this separate rule, unique to luggage and other closed packages, bags, and containers, in *United States v. Chadwick*, 433 U.S. 1 (1977). In *Chadwick*, federal narcotics agents had probable cause to believe that a 200-pound double-locked footlocker contained marijuana. The agents tracked the locker as the defendants removed it from a train and carried it through the station to a waiting car. As soon as the defendants lifted the locker into the trunk of the car, the agents arrested them, seized the locker, and searched it. In this Court . . . the United States urged that the search of movable luggage could be considered analogous to the search of an automobile. The Court rejected this argument because, it reasoned, a person expects more privacy in his luggage and personal effects than he does in his automobile. . . .

In *Arkansas v. Sanders*, 442 U.S. 753 (1979), the Court extended *Chadwick*'s rule to apply to a suitcase actually being transported in the trunk of a car. In *Sanders*, the police had probable cause to believe a suitcase contained marijuana. They watched as the defendant placed the suitcase in the trunk of a taxi and was driven away. The police pursued the taxi for several blocks, stopped it, found the suitcase in the trunk, and searched it. Although the Court had applied the *Carroll* doctrine to searches of integral parts of the automobile itself, indeed, in *Carroll*, contraband whiskey was in the upholstery of the seats, it did not extend the doctrine to the warrantless search of personal luggage "merely because it was located in an automobile lawfully stopped by the police." Again, the *Sanders* majority stressed the heightened privacy expectation in personal luggage and concluded that the presence of luggage in an automobile did not diminish the owner's expectation of privacy in his personal items.

In *Ross*, the Court endeavored to distinguish between *Carroll*, which governed the *Ross* automobile search, and *Chadwick*, which governed the *Sanders* automobile search. It held that the *Carroll* doctrine covered searches of automobiles when the police had probable cause to search an entire vehicle but that the *Chadwick* doctrine governed searches of luggage when the officers had probable cause to search only a container within the vehicle. Thus, in a *Ross* situation, the police could conduct a reasonable search under the Fourth Amendment without obtaining a warrant, whereas in a *Sanders* situation, the police had to obtain a warrant before they searched. . . .

The facts in this case closely resemble the facts in *Ross*. . . . This Court in *Ross* rejected *Chadwick*'s distinction between containers and cars. . . . [But w]e now must decide the question deferred in *Ross*: whether the Fourth Amendment requires the police to obtain a warrant to open the sack in a movable vehicle simply because they lack probable cause to search the entire car. We conclude that it does not. . . .

We now agree that a container found after a general search of the automobile and a container found in a car after a limited search for the container are equally easy for the police to store and for the suspect to hide or destroy. In fact, we see no principled distinction in terms of either the privacy expectation or the exigent circumstances between the paper bag found by the police in *Ross* and the paper bag found by the police here. Furthermore, by attempting to distinguish between a container for which the police are specifically searching and a container which they come across in a car, we have provided only minimal protection for privacy and have impeded effective law enforcement. . . .

We conclude that it is better to adopt one clear-cut rule to govern automobile searches and eliminate the warrant requirement for closed containers set forth in *Sanders*. The interpretation of the *Carroll* doctrine set forth in *Ross* now applies to all searches of containers found in an automobile. In other words, the police may search without a warrant if their search is supported by probable cause.

☐ *Justice STEVENS, with whom Justice MARSHALL* dissenting.

In its opinion today, the Court recognizes that the pol̶ probable cause to search respondent's vehicle and that a seal̶ not have but the paper bag that respondent had carried from Daza's ̶nything placed in the trunk of his car would have been unconstitution̶t and as I read the opinion, the Court assumes that the police could n̶ over, a warrantless inspection of the bag before it was placed in the car.̶de Court also does not question the fact that, under our prior case̶ have been lawful for the police to seize the container and deta̶ respondent) until they obtained a search warrant. Thus, all of the̶ facts that governed our decisions in *Chadwick* and *Sanders* are pres̶ whereas the relevant fact that justified the vehicle search in *Ross* is n̶ ent. The Court does not attempt to identify any exigent circumstanc̶ would justify its refusal to apply the general rule against warrantless sea̶ Instead, it advances these three arguments: First, the rules identified ir̶ foregoing cases are confusing and anomalous. Second, the rules do not pro̶ tect any significant interest in privacy. And, third, the rules impede effective law enforcement. None of these arguments withstands scrutiny.

■ THE "CONFUSION"

In the nine years since *Ross* was decided, the Court has considered three cases in which the police had probable cause to search a particular container and one in which they had probable cause to search two vehicles. The decisions in all four of those cases were perfectly straightforward and provide no evidence of confusion in the state or lower federal courts.

In *United States v. Place*, 462 U.S. 696 (1983), we held that, although reasonable suspicion justifies the temporary detention of an airline passenger's luggage, the seizure in that particular case was unreasonable because of the prolonged delay in ascertaining the existence of probable cause. . . . In *Oklahoma v. Castleberry*, 471 U.S. 146 (1985), police officers had probable cause to believe the defendant carried narcotics in blue suitcases in the trunk of his car. After arresting him, they opened the trunk, seized the suitcases, and searched them without a warrant. The state court held that the search was invalid. . . . This Court affirmed by an equally divided court. In the case the Court decides today, the California Court of Appeal also had no difficulty applying the critical distinction. . . .

In the case in which the police had probable cause to search two vehicles, *United States v. Johns*, 469 U.S. 478 (1985), we rejected the respondent's reliance on *Chadwick* with a straightforward explanation of why that case, unlike *Ross*, did not involve an exception to the warrant requirement. We first expressed our agreement with the Court of Appeals that the Customs officers who had conducted the search had probable cause to search the vehicles. We then explained:

> Under the circumstances of this case, respondents' reliance
> on *Chadwick* is misplaced. . . . *Chadwick*. . . . did not involve the
> exception to the warrant requirement recognized in *Carroll v.*
> *United States*, because the police had no probable cause to believe

...tomobile, as contrasted to the footlocker, contained that d'd. This point is underscored by our decision in *Ross*, con eld that notwithstanding *Chadwick* police officers may ... t a warrantless search of containers discovered in the course wful vehicle search. Given our conclusion that the Customs ers had probable cause to believe that the pickup trucks con- ed contraband, *Chadwick* is simply inapposite.

The decided cases thus provide no support for the Court's concern about fusion." The Court instead relies primarily on predictions that were de by Justice BLACKMUN in his dissenting opinions in *Chadwick* and *Sanders*. The Court, however, cites no evidence that these predictions have in act materialized or that anyone else has been unable to understand the "inherent opaqueness," of this uncomplicated issue. . . .

To the extent there was any "anomaly" in our prior jurisprudence, the Court has "cured" it at the expense of creating a more serious paradox. For, surely it is anomalous to prohibit a search of a briefcase while the owner is carrying it exposed on a public street yet to permit a search once the owner has placed the briefcase in the locked trunk of his car. . . .

- ## THE PRIVACY ARGUMENT

The Court's statement that *Chadwick* and *Sanders* provide only "minimal protection to privacy," is also unpersuasive. Every citizen clearly has an interest in the privacy of the contents of his or her luggage, briefcase, hand-bag or any other container that conceals private papers and effects from public scrutiny. That privacy interest has been recognized repeatedly in cases spanning more than a century. Under the Court's holding today, the privacy interest that protects the contents of a suitcase or a briefcase from a warrantless search when it is in public view simply vanishes when its owner climbs into a taxicab. . . .

- ## THE BURDEN ON LAW ENFORCEMENT

In the years since *Ross* was decided, the Court has heard argument in 30 Fourth Amendment cases involving narcotics. In all but one, the govern-ment was the petitioner. All save two involved a search or seizure without a warrant or with a defective warrant. And, in all except three, the Court upheld the constitutionality of the search or seizure. In the meantime, the flow of narcotics cases through the courts has steadily and dramatically increased. . . . No impartial observer could criticize this Court for hinder-ing the progress of the war on drugs. On the contrary, decisions like the one the Court makes today will support the conclusion that this Court has become a loyal foot soldier in the Executive's fight against crime. Even if the warrant requirement does inconvenience the police to some extent, that fact does not distinguish this constitutional requirement from any other procedural protection secured by the Bill of Rights. It is merely a part of the price that our society must pay in order to preserve its freedom. . . .

I respectfully dissent.

Collins v. Virginia

138 S. Ct. 1663 (2018)

Officer Matthew McCall of the Albemarle County Police Department in Virginia saw a driver of an orange and black motorcycle with an extended frame, which is a traffic infraction. The driver eluded his attempt to stop the motorcycle. A few weeks later, another police officer, David Rhodes, saw an orange and black motorcycle traveling well over the speed limit, but the driver again got away. The officers compared notes and concluded that the two incidents involved the same motorcyclist. Upon further investigation, the officers learned that the motorcycle likely was stolen and in the possession of Ryan Collins. After discovering photographs on Collins's Facebook profile that featured an orange and black motorcycle parked at the top of the driveway of a house, Rhodes tracked down the address of the house, drove there, and parked on the street.

From the street, Rhodes saw what appeared to be a motorcycle with an extended frame covered with a white tarp, parked in the same location on the driveway as in the Facebook photograph. Without a warrant, Rhodes walked toward the house, stopping to take a photograph of the covered motorcycle from the sidewalk. He then walked onto the residential property of Collins's girlfriend to where the motorcycle was parked, where he pulled off the tarp, revealing a motorcycle. He then ran a search of the license plate and vehicle identification numbers, which confirmed that the motorcycle was stolen. After gathering this information, Rhodes took photographs of the uncovered motorcycle, put the tarp back on, and returned to his car to wait for Collins. Shortly thereafter, Collins returned to the house, and Rhodes walked to the front door and knocked. Collins answered and admitted that the motorcycle was his and he had bought it without a title. Whereupon, Rhodes arrested Collins.

Collins was indicted by a grand jury for receiving stolen property. At a pretrial hearing, Collins's lawyer moved to suppress the evidence on the ground that Rhodes had made a warrantless search and had trespassed on the curtilage of the house in violation of the Fourth Amendment. The trial court denied the motion, and Collins was convicted. An appellate court and the state supreme court affirmed on the basis of its interpretation of a categorical *automobile exception* to the Fourth Amendment.

The state supreme court was reversed by a vote of 8–1. Justice Sotomayor delivered the opinion of the Court. Justice Thomas filed a concurring opinion, and Justice Alito filed a dissenting opinion.

■ ■ ■

☐ *Justice SOTOMAYOR delivered the opinion of the Court.*

This case arises at the intersection of two components of the Court's Fourth Amendment jurisprudence: the automobile exception to the warrant requirement and the protection extended to the curtilage of a home.

The Court has held that the search of an automobile can be reasonable without a warrant. The Court first articulated the so-called automobile exception in *Carroll* v. *United States*, 267 U. S. 132 (1925). In that case, law enforcement officers had probable cause to believe that a car they observed traveling on the road contained illegal liquor. The Court upheld the warrantless search and seizure, explaining that a "necessary difference" exists between searching "a store, dwelling house or other structure" and searching "a ship, motor boat, wagon or automobile" because a "vehicle can be quickly moved out of the locality or jurisdiction in which the warrant must be sought."

The "ready mobility" of vehicles served as the core justification for the automobile exception for many years. As the Court explained in *South Dakota* v. *Opperman*, 428 U. S. 364 (1976):

> Automobiles, unlike homes, are subjected to pervasive and continuing governmental regulation and controls, including periodic inspection and licensing requirements. As an everyday occurrence, police stop and examine vehicles when license plates or inspection stickers have expired, or if other violations, such as exhaust fumes or excessive noise, are noted, or if headlights or other safety equipment are not in proper working order.

In announcing each of these two justifications, the Court took care to emphasize that the rationales applied only to automobiles and not to houses, and therefore supported "treating automobiles differently from houses" as a constitutional matter.

When these justifications for the automobile exception "come into play," officers may search an automobile without having obtained a warrant so long as they have probable cause to do so.

Like the automobile exception, the Fourth Amendment's protection of curtilage has long been black letter law. "[W]hen it comes to the Fourth Amendment, the home is first among equals." *Florida* v. *Jardines*, 569 U. S. 1 (2013). To give full practical effect to that right, the Court considers curtilage—"the area 'immediately surrounding and associated with the home'"—to be "'part of the home itself for Fourth Amendment purposes.'" *Jardines*. "The protection afforded the curtilage is essentially a protection of families and personal privacy in an area intimately linked to the home, both physically and psychologically, where privacy expectations are most heightened." *California* v. *Ciraolo*, 476 U. S. 207 (1986).

When a law enforcement officer physically intrudes on the curtilage to gather evidence, a search within the meaning of the Fourth Amendment has occurred. Such conduct thus is presumptively unreasonable absent a warrant.

With this background in mind, we turn to the application of these doctrines in the instant case. As an initial matter, we decide whether the part of the driveway where Collins' motorcycle was parked and subsequently searched is curtilage.

According to photographs in the record, the driveway runs alongside the front lawn and up a few yards past the front perimeter of the house. The top portion of the driveway that sits behind the front perimeter of the house is enclosed on two sides by a brick wall about the height of a car and on a third side by the house. A side door provides direct access between this partially enclosed section of the driveway and the house. A visitor endeavoring to reach the front door of the house would have to walk partway up the driveway, but would turn off before entering the enclosure and instead proceed up a set of steps leading to the front porch. When Officer Rhodes searched the motorcycle, it was parked inside this partially enclosed top portion of the driveway that abuts the house. . . .

In physically intruding on the curtilage of Collins' home to search the motorcycle, Officer Rhodes not only invaded Collins' Fourth Amendment interest in the item searched, *i.e.,* the motorcycle, but also invaded Collins' Fourth Amendment interest in the curtilage of his home. The question before the Court is whether the automobile exception justifies the invasion of the curtilage. The answer is no.

Applying the relevant legal principles to a slightly different factual scenario confirms that this is an easy case. Imagine a motorcycle parked inside the living room of a house, visible through a window to a passerby on the street. Imagine further that an officer has probable cause to believe that the motorcycle was involved in a traffic infraction. Can the officer, acting without a warrant, enter the house to search the motorcycle and confirm whether it is the right one? Surely not.

The reason is that the scope of the automobile exception extends no further than the automobile itself. . . . Similarly, it is a "settled rule that warrantless arrests in public places are valid," but, absent another exception such as exigent circumstances, officers may not enter a home to make an arrest without a warrant, even when they have probable cause. *Payton* v. *New York*, 445 U. S. 573 (1980). That is because being "'arrested in the home involves not only the invasion attendant to all arrests but also an invasion of the sanctity of the home.'" Likewise, searching a vehicle parked in the curtilage involves not only the invasion of the Fourth Amendment interest in the vehicle but also an invasion of the sanctity of the curtilage. . . .

For the foregoing reasons, we conclude that the automobile exception does not permit an officer without a warrant to enter a home or its curtilage in order to search a vehicle therein.

☐ *Justice ALITO, dissenting.*

The Fourth Amendment prohibits "unreasonable" searches. What the police did in this case was entirely reasonable. The Court's decision is not. . . .

An ordinary person of common sense would react to the Court's decision the way Mr. Bumble famously responded when told about a legal rule that did not comport with the reality of everyday life. If that is the law, he exclaimed, "the law is a ass—a idiot." C. Dickens, *Oliver Twist* 277 (1867).

The Fourth Amendment is neither an "ass" nor an "idiot." Its hallmark is reasonableness, and the Court's strikingly unreasonable decision is based on a misunderstanding of Fourth Amendment basics.

The Fourth Amendment protects "[t]he right of the people to be secure in their persons, houses, papers, and effects." A "house," for Fourth Amendment purposes, is not limited to the structure in which a person lives, but by the same token, it also does not include all the real property surrounding a dwelling. Instead, a person's "house" encompasses the dwelling and a circumscribed area of surrounding land that is given the name "curtilage." Land outside the curtilage is called an "open field," and a search conducted in that area is not considered a search of a "house" and is therefore not governed by the Fourth Amendment. Ascertaining the boundaries of the curtilage thus determines only whether a search is governed by the Fourth Amendment. The concept plays no other role in Fourth Amendment analysis.

In this case, there is no dispute that the search of the motorcycle was governed by the Fourth Amendment, and therefore whether or not it occurred within the curtilage is not of any direct importance. The question before us is not whether there was a Fourth Amendment search but whether the search was reasonable. And the only possible argument as to why it might not be reasonable concerns the need for a warrant. For nearly a century, however, it has been well established that officers do not need a warrant to search a motor vehicle on public streets so long as they have probable cause. *Carroll.* Thus, the issue here is whether there is any good reason why this same rule should not apply when the vehicle is parked in plain view in a driveway just a few feet from the street.

In considering that question, we should ask whether the reasons for the "automobile exception" are any less valid in this new situation. Is the vehicle parked in the driveway any less mobile? Are any greater privacy interests at stake? If the answer to those questions is "no," then the automobile exception should apply. And here, the answer to each question is emphatically "no." The tarp-covered motorcycle parked in the driveway could have been uncovered and ridden away in a matter of seconds. And Officer Rhodes's brief walk up the driveway impaired no real privacy interests. . . .

I would affirm the decision below and therefore respectfully dissent.

D | *Other Governmental Searches in the Administrative State*

The Supreme Court permits a lower standard than probable cause for the issuance of warrants for *administrative searches*—searches by public officials other than police, such as housing, health, safety, and welfare inspectors.

The Court also allows for some types of warrantless administrative searches, depending on the kind of search and the manner in which it is conducted. Whether an administrative warrant is required turns on the Court's balancing of individuals' privacy interests against competing governmental interests in conducting various types of searches—housing inspections, for example, welfare visitations, or inspections for violation of health, safety, and environmental regulations.

Initially, in *Frank v. Maryland*, 359 U.S. 360 (1959), the Court held that administrative searches were outside the purview of the Fourth Amendment, when permitting warrantless housing inspections conducted at reasonable times and aimed at enforcing health regulations. Justice Felix Frankfurter held that only searches aimed at obtaining evidence of criminal activity required prior judicial approval. But dissenting Chief Justice Warren and Justices Black, Douglas, and Brennan complained that the majority's distinction between criminal and civil searches diluted Fourth Amendment-protected privacy interests. The amendment, in Justice Douglas's words,

> was designed to protect the citizen against uncontrolled invasion of his privacy. It does not make the home a place of refuge from the law. It only requires the sanction of the judiciary rather than the executive before that privacy may be invaded. History shows that all officers tend to be officious; and health inspectors, making out a case for criminal prosecution of the citizen are no exception. . . . One invasion of privacy by an official of the government can be as oppressive as another. . . . It would seem that the public interest in protecting privacy is equally as great in one case as another.

Frank's dissenters continued objecting to the formalistic dichotomy between criminal and civil searches, but they could not win a majority over to their side until the Court's composition changed. Finally, they were joined by Justices Byron White and Abe Fortas, who had replaced on the bench two members of the *Frank* majority. In two companion 1967 cases—*Camara v. Municipal Court*, 387 U.S. 523 (1967), and *See v. City of Seattle*, 387 U.S. 541 (1967)—the Court held that a search warrant was required when an owner denies permission for entry and search of his premises by housing and safety inspectors.

Writing for the Court in *Camera*, Justice White ruled, on the one hand, that the Fourth Amendment bars prosecution of a person for refusing to permit administrative officials to conduct warrantless inspections and, on the other hand, that administrative warrants may be issued on showing less than probable cause, as required in criminal cases. The standard for issuing administrative warrants, he explained,

> will vary with the municipal program being enforced, may be based upon the passage of time, the nature of the building (e.g., a multifamily apartment house), or the condition of the entire area, but they will not necessarily depend upon specific knowledge of the conditions of the particular dwelling. It has been suggested that to so vary the probable cause test from the standard applied in criminal cases would be to authorize a "synthetic search warrant" and thereby to lessen the overall protections of the Fourth Amendment. . . . But we do not agree. The warrant procedure is designed to guarantee that a decision to search private property is justified by a reasonable governmental interest. But reasonableness is still the ultimate standard. If a valid public interest justifies the intrusion contemplated, there is probable cause to issue a suitably restricted search warrant.

Probable cause remains required for search warrants aimed at uncovering evidence of criminal activity, but administrative searches may be based "balancing the need to search against the invasions which the search entails."

Whether an administrative warrant is required depends on the government's interests and the type and manner of the search, as well as the competing interests in personal privacy. In *Marshall v. Barlow's Inc.*, 436 U.S. 307 (1978), for example, the Court struck down a provision in the Occupational Safety and Health Act authorizing warrantless inspections of workplaces for safety violations. When holding that the businessman's right of privacy included the right to have a magistrate determine the reasonableness of a search according to an "administrative plan containing neutral criteria," Justice White emphasized that "[i]f the government intrudes on a person's property, the privacy interest suffers whether the government's motivation is to investigate violations of criminal laws or breaches of other statutory or regulatory standards."

Warrantless searches of mines and heavily regulated commercial business are permissible, however. In *New York v. Burger*, 482 U.S. 691 (1987), the Court upheld the warrantless search of an automobile junkyard. There Justice Blackmun explained:

> An owner or operator of a business thus has an expectation of privacy in commercial property, which society is prepared to consider to be reasonable, see *Katz v. United States*, 389 U.S. 347 (1967) (HARLAN, J., concurring). . . . An expectation of privacy in commercial premises, however, is different from, and indeed less

than, a similar expectation in an individual's home. . . . Because the owner or operator of commercial premises in a "closely regulated" industry has a reduced expectation of privacy, the warrant and probable-cause requirements, which fulfill the traditional Fourth Amendment standard of reasonableness for a government search . . . have lessened application in this context. Rather, we conclude that, as in other situations of "special need," see *New Jersey v. T.L.O.*, 469 U.S. 325 (1985) [holding that a high school principal may search the belongings of students], where the privacy interests of the owner are weakened and the government interests in regulating particular businesses are concomitantly heightened, a warrantless inspection of commercial premises may well be reasonable within the meaning of the Fourth Amendment.

Blackmun proceeded to hold that warrantless administrative searches would "be deemed to be reasonable only so long as three criteria are met":

> First, there must be a "substantial" government interest that informs the regulatory scheme pursuant to which the inspection is made. . . . Second, the warrantless inspections must be "necessary to further [the] regulatory scheme." . . . Finally, "the statute's inspection program, in terms of the certainty and regularity of its application, [must] provid[e] a constitutionally adequate substitute for a warrant." . . . In other words, the regulatory scheme must perform the two basic functions of a warrant: it must advise the owner of the commercial premises that the search is being made pursuant to the law and has a properly limited scope, and it must limit the discretion of the inspecting officers.

The Court has been sharply split on according Fourth Amendment privacy protection to students and public employees, having held that, in certain contexts, there are *special needs* that justify warrantless searches. In *New Jersey v. T.L.O.*, 469 U.S. 325 (1985), by a 6–3 vote the Court upheld the warrantless search of a student's backpack on the grounds that (1) it was "reasonable at its inception" and (2) permissible in scope. The Court continues to rely on *T.L.O.*'s two-prong test in other cases dealing with not only students' rights but also drug testing, in spite of the controversy over the test and its application.

T.L.O.'s special needs exception was subsequently applied to random drug testing of high school student athletes in *Vernonia School District No. 47J v. Acton*, 515 U.S. 646 (1995) (excerpted below), as well as to all students involved in extracurricular activities in *Board of Education of Independent School District No. 92 of Pottawatomie City v. Earls*, 536 U.S. 822 (2002) (excerpted below). But the Court drew the line on applying the "special needs" rationale in *Ferguson v. Charleston*, 532 U.S. 67 (2001), in ruling that the results of nonconsensual hospital drug testing of pregnant women was impermissibly turned over to police for possible arrest and prosecution for child abuse. Writing for the majority, Justice Stevens emphasized that all prior cases involved the element of consent and unlike prior cases there was the possibility of criminal prosecution. In addition, the special needs situations involved in prior cases were unrelated to the government's interests in law enforcement, whereas here they were directly related to criminal conduct. Also, *Ferguson v. Charlestown*, 532 U.S. 67 (2011), struck down a state policy of testing pregnant women for cocaine use, without their consent, and informing police of those who tested positive. In *Safford Unified School District No. 1 v. Redding*, 129 S.Ct. 2633 (2009) (excerpted below), the Court also found the strip search of a thirteen-year-old student for possession of prescription drugs unreasonable.

In the context of employment, a bare majority upheld a state hospital supervisor's warrantless search of an employee's office for work-related items in *O'Connor v. Ortega*, 480 U.S. 709 (1987), and subsequently extended that rationale to employees' text messaging, for example; see THE DEVELOPMENT OF LAW box in this section.

Even more controversial for the Court and the country is the issue of drug and alcohol testing of public employees. In *National Treasury Employees Union v. Von Raab* (1989) (see excerpt below), the Rehnquist Court split 5–4 when upholding the U.S. Customs Service's drug-testing program for employees. In another ruling, in *Skinner v. Railway Labor Executives' Association*, 489 U.S. 602 (1989), the justices divided 6–3 over allowing mandatory drug and alcohol tests for railroad workers involved in serious accidents. Following those rulings, more than forty federal agencies began conducting drug tests under an executive order for a drug-free federal workplace. Carl Willner, an attorney in the antitrust division of the Department of Justice (DoJ), challenged the DoJ's drug-testing requirement as a violation of his Fourth Amendment guarantee against unreasonable searches and seizures. In 1990, a federal district court ruled that "suspicionless testing" of employees was unconstitutional and should be limited to only public employees in jobs "affecting public safety, and those working directly with aspects of drug enforcement." But a three-judge panel of the Court of Appeals for the District of Columbia Circuit reversed, and the Rehnquist Court denied review to an appeal of that ruling in *Willner v. Barr*, 502 U.S. 1020 (1992).

■ THE DEVELOPMENT OF LAW

Searches by Government Officials in the Administrative State

CASE	VOTE	RULING
Frank v. Maryland, 359 U.S. 360 (1959)	5–4	Warrant requirement does not apply to housing and health inspections, if conducted at reasonable times.
Abel v. United States, 362 U.S. 217 (1960)	5–4	Immigration officers may seize allegedly forged birth certificates without warrant.
Ohio ex rel. Eaton v. Price, 364 U.S. 263 (1960)	4–4	Affirmed by an equally divided Court a lower court ruling upholding ordinance authorizing housing inspectors to enter homes without warrants.
Camara v. Municipal Court, 387 U.S. 523 (1967); **and** *See v. City of Seattle,* 387 U.S. 541 (1967)	6–3	Search warrant required for housing and safety inspections.
Colonnade Catering Corporation v. United States, 397 U.S. 72 (1970)	6–3	Inspection for liquor license by IRS agents did not justify breaking and entering locked storeroom.
Wyman v. James, 400 U.S. 309 (1971)	6–3	Social workers may make warrantless searches of welfare recipients' homes.
United States v. Biswell, 406 U.S. 311 (1972)	8–1	Upheld warrantless search of a gun dealer's locked storeroom during business hours under the Gun Control Act of 1968.

(continues)

■ THE DEVELOPMENT OF LAW
Searches by Government Officials in the
Administrative State (continued)

CASE	VOTE	RULING
Air Pollution Variance Board of State of Colorado v. Western Alfalfa Corporation, 416 U.S. 861 (1974)	9–0	Upheld health inspector's entry of outdoor premises without consent of owner to observe smoke plumes.
California Bankers Association v. Shultz, 416 U.S. 21 (1974)	6–3	Upheld record keeping and mandatory reporting of depositors' financial transactions under the Bank Secrecy Act.
United States v. Bisceglia, 420 U.S. 141 (1975)	7–2	The IRS may issue "John Doe" summons to banks to identify depositors who filed fraudulent tax returns.
United States v. Miller, 425 U.S. 435 (1976)	7–2	Held depositors have no Fourth Amendment–protected interests in bank deposits.
United States v. Ramsey, 431 U.S. 606 (1977)	6–3	Customs officials may open mail without a warrant in search for narcotics.
Marshall v. Barlow's, Inc., 436 U.S. 307 (1978)	5–3	Struck down section of the Occupational Safety and Health Act authorizing agents to make warrantless inspections for safety violations.
Michigan v. Tyler, 436 U.S. 499 (1978)	6–3	Firefighters need no warrant to enter premises to fight a fire, but thereafter must obtain a warrant when investigating the cause of a fire.
Donovan v. Dewey, 452 U.S. 594 (1981)	8–1	Upheld warrantless inspection of mines.

CASE	VOTE	RULING
Michigan v. Clifford, 464 U.S. 287 (1984)	5–4	Administrative warrant required for a postfire search; criminal warrant necessary if the object of search is evidence of criminal activity.
Hudson v. Palmer, 468 U.S. 517 (1984)	6–3	Prison inmates have no reasonable expectation of privacy in prison cells from searches by guards.
New Jersey v. T.L.O., 469 U.S. 325 (1985)	6–3	Upheld principal's search of student's purse.
United States v. Jones, 469 U.S. 478 (1985); and *United States v. Sharpe,* 470 U.S. 675 (1985)	7–2	U.S. Customs officials may search a trunk with probable cause but no warrant; and a drug enforcement agent may delay a passenger at the airport without a warrant.
O'Connor v. Ortega, 480 U.S. 709 (1987)	5–4	State hospital supervisor's warrantless search of employee's office for work-related items upheld.
New York v. Burger, 482 U.S. 691 (1987)	6–3	Warrantless administrative search of "heavily regulated" commercial premises—here, a junkyard—permissible.
Griffin v. Wisconsin, 483 U.S. 868 (1987)	5–4	Upheld warrantless search of probationer's home on "reasonable grounds," rather than probable cause, for search.
National Treasury Employees Union v. Von Raab, 489 U.S. 656 (1989)	5–4	Upheld U.S. Customs Service's drug-testing program for employees.
Skinner v. Railway Labor Executives' Association, 489 U.S. 602 (1989)	6–3	Mandatory drug and alcohol testing for employees involved in accidents upheld.

(continues)

■ The Development of Law
Searches by Government Officials in the
Administrative State (continued)

CASE	VOTE	RULING
Vernonia School District 47J v. Acton, 515 U.S. 646 (1995)	6–3	Upheld a public school district's policy requiring all students signing up for

interscholastic sports to submit to a drug test and to remain subject to random tests throughout the year.

Chandler v. Miller, 520 U.S. 305 (1997)	8–1	Writing for the Court, Justice Ginsburg struck down Georgia's 1990 law

requiring candidates for public office to submit to drug testing or to certify that they are drug free. Chief Justice Rehnquist dissented.

Ferguson v. Charleston, 532 U.S. 67 (2001)	6–3	Held that a hospital's drug testing of pregnant women without their consent for

law enforcement purposes was an unreasonable search and seizure. Chief Justice Rehnquist and Justices Scalia and Thomas dissented.

Board of Education of Independent School District No. 92 of Pottawatomie City v. Earls, 536 U.S. 822 (2002)	6–3	Upheld school district's requirement that students who participate in any extracurricular program submit to random drug tests. Justices O'Connor, Stevens, and Souter dissented.

City of Ontario v. Quon, 500 U.S. 746 (2010)	9–0	The Court held that a police department's review of text messages sent and

received by Sergeant Jeff Quon, under departmental general policy about computer and Internet use indicating it reserved the right to monitor e-mail messages and Internet usage, was permissible because the government was reasonably investigating violations of workplace rules. The Court did not decide whether Quon had a reasonable expectation of privacy in his text messages because the search had a legitimate work-related purpose and was not excessive.

CASE	VOTE	RULING
City of Los Angeles, California v. Patel, 135 S.Ct. 2443 (2015)	5–4	The majority struck down an ordinance requiring hotel managers to record and keep specific informa-

tion about their guests for ninety days; the records were also to be available to police, and the failure or refusal to do so was made a criminal misdemeanor. Writing for the Court, Justice Sotomayor held that the ordinance was unconstitutional because it failed to provide hotel operators with the opportunity for precompliance review. Quoting *Arizona v. Gant*, 556 U.S. 332 (2009), she reaffirmed that "searches conducted outside of the judicial process . . . are per se unreasonable . . . subject only to a few . . . exceptions." While one exception is administrative searches to the Fourth Amendment, an administrative search must nevertheless afford an opportunity for precompliance review before a neutral decision making. But, she also emphasized the narrowness of the ruling in that police may obtain administrative subpoenas without probable cause that a regulation has been violated. Chief Justice Roberts and Justices Scalia, Thomas, and Alito dissented.

National Treasury Employees Union v. Von Raab
489 U.S. 656, 109 S.Ct. 1384 (1989)

Justice Anthony Kennedy discusses the facts in this case, arising from a challenge to the U.S. Customs Service's mandatory drug-testing program, at the outset of his opinion for the Court.

The Court's decision was 5–4, and the majority's opinion was announced by Justice Kennedy. Justices Marshall and Scalia dissented and were joined by Justices Brennan and Stevens.

■ ■ ■

☐ *Justice KENNEDY delivered the opinion of the Court.*

We granted *certiorari* to decide whether it violates the Fourth Amendment for the United States Customs Service to require a urinalysis test from employees who seek transfer or promotion to certain positions. The United States Customs Service, a bureau of the Department of the Treasury, is the federal agency responsible for processing persons, carriers, cargo, and mail into the United States, collecting revenue from imports, and enforcing customs and related laws. An important responsibility of the Service is the interdiction and seizure of contraband, including illegal drugs. . . . In the routine discharge of their duties, many Customs employees have direct contact with those who traffic in drugs for profit. Drug import operations, often directed by sophisticated criminal syndicates, *United States v. Mendenhall*, 446 U.S. 544 (1980) (POWELL, J., concurring), may be effected by violence or its threat. As a necessary response, many Customs operatives carry and use firearms in connection with their official duties. . . .

In December 1985, respondent, the Commissioner of Customs, established a Drug Screening Task Force to explore the possibility of implementing a drug screening program within the Service. After extensive research and consultation with experts in the field, the Task Force concluded "that drug screening through urinalysis is technologically reliable, valid and accurate." Citing this conclusion, the Commissioner announced his intention to require drug tests of employees who applied for, or occupied, certain positions within the Service. . . .

In May 1986, the Commissioner announced implementation of the drug-testing program. Drug tests were made a condition of placement or employment for positions that meet one or more of three criteria. The first is direct involvement in drug interdiction or enforcement of related laws, an activity the Commissioner deemed fraught with obvious dangers to the mission of the agency and the lives of Customs agents. The second criterion is a requirement that the incumbent carry firearms, as the Commissioner concluded that "[p]ublic safety demands that employees who carry deadly arms and are prepared to make instant life or death decisions be drug free." The third criterion is a requirement for the incumbent to handle "classified" material, which the Commissioner determined might fall into the hands of smugglers if accessible to employees who, by reason of their own illegal drug use, are susceptible to bribery or blackmail. . . .

After an employee qualifies for a position covered by the Customs testing program, the Service advises him by letter that his final selection is contingent upon successful completion of drug screening. An independent contractor contacts the employee to fix the time and place for collecting the sample. On reporting for the test, the employee must produce photographic identification and remove any outer garments, such as a coat or a jacket, and personal belongings. The employee may produce the sample behind a partition, or in the privacy of a bathroom stall if he so chooses. To ensure against adulteration of the specimen, or substitution of a sample from another person, a monitor of the same sex as the employee remains close at hand to listen for the normal sounds of urination. Dye is added to the toilet water to prevent the employee from using the water to adulterate the sample. . . .

Customs employees who test positive for drugs and who can offer no satisfactory explanation are subject to dismissal from the Service. Test results may not, however, be turned over to any other agency, including criminal prosecutors, without the employee's written consent. . . .

We have recognized before that requiring the Government to procure a warrant for every work-related intrusion "would conflict with 'the common-sense realization that government offices could not function if every employment decision became a constitutional matter.'" *O'Connor v. Ortega*, [480 U.S. 709 (1987)]; *New Jersey v. T.L.O.*, [469 U.S. 325 (1985)] (noting that "[t]he warrant requirement . . . is unsuited to the school environment: requiring a teacher to obtain a warrant before searching a child suspected of an infraction of school rules (or of the criminal law) would unduly interfere with the maintenance of the swift and informal disciplinary procedures needed in the schools"). Even if Customs Service employees are more likely to be familiar with the procedures required to obtain a warrant than most other Government workers, requiring a warrant in this context would serve only to divert valuable agency resources from the Service's primary mission. The Customs Service has been entrusted with pressing responsibilities, and its mission would be compromised if it were required to seek search warrants in connection with routine, yet sensitive, employment decisions.

Furthermore, a warrant would provide little or nothing in the way of additional protection of personal privacy. A warrant serves primarily to advise the citizen that an intrusion is authorized by law and limited in its permissible scope and to interpose a neutral magistrate between the citizen and the law enforcement officer "engaged in the often competitive enterprise of ferreting out crime." *Johnson v. United States*, 333 U.S. 10 (1948). But in the present context, "the circumstances justifying toxicological testing and the permissible limits of such intrusions are defined narrowly and specifically . . . and doubtless are well known to covered employees." . . .

Even where it is reasonable to dispense with the warrant requirement in the particular circumstances, a search ordinarily must be based on probable cause. Our cases teach, however, that the probable-cause standard "is peculiarly related to criminal investigations." In particular, the traditional probable-cause standard may be unhelpful in analyzing the reasonableness of routine administrative functions especially where the Government seeks to *prevent* the development of hazardous conditions or to detect violations that rarely generate articulable grounds for searching any particular place or person. . . . Our precedents have settled that, in certain limited circumstances, the Government's need to discover such latent or hidden conditions, or to prevent their development, is sufficiently compelling to justify the intrusion on privacy entailed by conducting such searches without any measure of individualized suspicion. We think the Government's need to conduct the suspicionless searches required by the Customs program outweighs the privacy interests of employees engaged directly in drug interdiction, and of those who otherwise are required to carry firearms.

The Customs Service is our Nation's first line of defense against one of the greatest problems affecting the health and welfare of our population. . . .

It is readily apparent that the Government has a compelling interest in ensuring that front-line interdiction personnel are physically fit, and have unimpeachable integrity and judgment. Indeed, the Government's interest here is at least as important as its interest in searching travelers entering the country. We have long held that travelers seeking to enter the country may be stopped and required to submit to a routine search without probable cause, or even founded suspicion, "because of national self protection reasonably requiring one entering the country to identify himself as entitled to come in, and his belongings as effects which may be lawfully brought in." *Carroll v. United States*, 267 U.S. 132 (1925). This national interest in self protection could be irreparably damaged if those charged with safeguarding it were, because of their own drug use, unsympathetic to their mission of interdicting narcotics. A drug user's indifference to the Service's basic mission or, even worse, his active complicity with the malefactors, can facilitate importation of sizable drug shipments or block apprehension of dangerous criminals. The public interest demands effective measures to bar drug users from positions directly involving the interdiction of illegal drugs. . . .

Against these valid public interests we must weigh the interference with individual liberty that results from requiring these classes of employees to undergo a urine test. The interference with individual privacy that results from the collection of a urine sample for subsequent chemical analysis could be substantial in some circumstances. We have recognized, however, that the "operational realities of the workplace" may render entirely reasonable certain work-related intrusions by supervisors and co-workers that might be viewed as unreasonable in other contexts. See *O'Connor v. Ortega.* . . . [Indeed] employment may diminish privacy expectations even with respect to such personal searches. . . .

We think Customs employees who are directly involved in the interdiction of illegal drugs or who are required to carry firearms in the line of duty likewise have a diminished expectation of privacy in respect to the intrusions occasioned by a urine test. Unlike most private citizens or government employees in general, employees involved in drug interdiction reasonably should expect effective inquiry into their fitness and probity. Much the same is true of employees who are required to carry firearms. Because successful performance of their duties depends uniquely on their judgment and dexterity, these employees cannot reasonably expect to keep from the Service personal information that bears directly on their fitness. . . .

We hold that the suspicionless testing of employees who apply for promotion to positions directly involving the interdiction of illegal drugs, or to positions which require the incumbent to carry a firearm, is reasonable. The Government's compelling interests in preventing the promotion of drug users to positions where they might endanger the integrity of our Nation's borders or the life of the citizenry outweigh the privacy interests of those who seek promotion to these positions, who enjoy a diminished expectation of privacy by virtue of the special, and obvious, physical and ethical demands of those positions. We do not decide whether testing those who apply for promotion to positions where they would handle "classified" information is reasonable because we find the record inadequate for this purpose.

The judgment of the Court of Appeals for the Fifth Circuit is affirmed in part and vacated in part, and the case is remanded for further proceedings consistent with this opinion.

It is so ordered.

□ *Justice MARSHALL, with whom Justice BRENNAN joins, dissenting.*

For the reasons stated in my dissenting opinion in *Skinner v. Railway Labor Executives Association,* [489 U.S. 602 (1989)], I also dissent from the Court's decision in this case. Here, as in *Skinner,* the Court's abandonment of the Fourth Amendment's express requirement that searches of the person rest on probable cause is unprincipled and unjustifiable. But even if I believed that balancing analysis was appropriate under the Fourth Amendment, I would still dissent from today's judgment, for the reasons stated by Justice SCALIA in his dissenting opinion.

☐ *Justice SCALIA, with whom Justice STEVENS joins, dissenting.*

The issue in this case is not whether Customs Service employees can constitutionally be denied promotion, or even dismissed, for a single instance of unlawful drug use, at home or at work. They assuredly can. The issue here is what steps can constitutionally be taken to *detect* such drug use. . . .

Until today this Court had upheld a bodily search separate from arrest and without individualized suspicion of wrongdoing only with respect to prison inmates, relying upon the uniquely dangerous nature of that environment. See *Bell v. Wolfish*, 441 U.S. 520 (1979). Today, in *Skinner [v. Railway Labor Executives' Association*, 489 U.S. 602 (1989)], we allow a less intrusive bodily search of railroad employees involved in train accidents. I joined the Court's opinion there because the demonstrated frequency of drug and alcohol use by the targeted class of employees, and the demonstrated connection between such use and grave harm, rendered the search a reasonable means of protecting society. I decline to join the Court's opinion in the present case because neither frequency of use nor connection to harm is demonstrated or even likely. In my view the Customs Service rules are a kind of immolation of privacy and human dignity in symbolic opposition to drug use.

The Fourth Amendment protects the "right of the people to be secure in their persons, houses, papers, and effects, against unreasonable searches and seizures." While there are some absolutes in Fourth Amendment law, as soon as those have been left behind and the question comes down to whether a particular search has been "reasonable," the answer depends largely upon the social necessity that prompts the search. . . .

The Court's opinion in the present case, however, will be searched in vain for real evidence of a real problem that will be solved by urine testing of Customs Service employees. Instead, there are assurances that "[t]he Customs Service is our Nation's first line of defense against one of the greatest problems affecting the health and welfare of our population," that "[m]any of the Service's employees are often exposed to [drug smugglers] and to the controlled substances they seek to smuggle into the country," that "Customs officers have been the targets of bribery by drug smugglers on numerous occasions, and several have been removed from the Service for accepting bribes and other integrity violations." . . .

What is absent in the Government's justifications—notably absent, revealingly absent, and as far as I am concerned dispositively absent—is the recitation of *even a single instance* in which any of the speculated horribles actually occurred: an instance, that is, in which the cause of bribe-taking, or of poor aim, or of unsympathetic law enforcement, or of compromise of classified information, was drug use. . . .

The Court's response to this lack of evidence is that "[t]here is little reason to believe that American workplaces are immune from [the] pervasive social problem" of drug abuse. Perhaps such a generalization would suffice if the workplace at issue could produce such catastrophic social harm that no risk whatever is tolerable—the secured areas of a nuclear power plant, for example. But if such a generalization suffices to justify demeaning bodily searches, without particularized suspicion, to guard against the bribing or blackmailing of a law enforcement agent, or the careless use of a firearm, then the Fourth Amendment has become frail protection indeed. . . .

Today's decision would be wrong, but at least of more limited effect, if its approval of drug testing were confined to that category of employees assigned specifically to drug interdiction duties. Relatively few public employees fit that description. But in extending approval of drug testing to that category consisting of employees who carry firearms, the Court exposes vast numbers of public employees to this needless indignity. . . .

There is only one apparent basis that sets the testing at issue here apart from all these other situations—but it is not a basis upon which the Court is willing to rely. I do not believe for a minute that the driving force behind these drug-testing rules was any of the feeble justifications put forward by counsel here and accepted by the Court. The only plausible explanation, in my view, is what the Commissioner himself offered in the concluding sentence of his memorandum to Customs Service employees announcing the program: "Implementation of the drug screening program would set an important example in our country's struggle with this most serious threat to our national health and security." Or as respondent's brief to this Court asserted: "if a law enforcement agency and its employees do not take the law seriously, neither will the public on which the agency's effectiveness depends." What better way to show that the Government is serious about its "war on drugs" than to subject its employees on the front line of that war to this invasion of their privacy and affront to their dignity? To be sure, there is only a slight chance that it will prevent some serious public harm resulting from Service employee drug use, but it will show to the world that the Service is "clean," and—most important of all—will demonstrate the determination of the Government to eliminate this scourge of our society! I think it obvious that this justification is unacceptable; that the impairment of individual liberties cannot be the means of making a point; that symbolism, even symbolism for so worthy a cause as the abolition of unlawful drugs, cannot validate an otherwise unreasonable search.

Vernonia School District 47J v. Acton
515 U.S. 646, 115 S.CT. 2386 (1995)

The parents of James Acton, a twelve-year-old seventh-grader with no indication of drug use, challenged the constitutionality of the Vernonia School District's drug-testing policy for students participating in school athletic programs. Teachers and school officials in Vernonia, a small logging community in Oregon, noticed a sharp increase in drug use and disciplinary problems in the late 1980s. Between 1988 and 1989, for instance, the number of disciplinary referrals doubled that reported in the early 1980s. In addition, school officials later testified during the trial that student athletes were not only among the drug users but were leaders of the drug culture. As a result, in the fall of 1989, the school board approved a drug-testing policy under which athletes had to sign a form consenting to drug testing and obtain the written consent of their parents. At the beginning of each season, every student athlete was tested for drugs. Throughout the season, then, 10 percent of the student athletes were randomly tested each week.

A federal district court rejected the Actons' claim that the school district's policy of random drug testing violated the Fourth Amendment's guarantee against "unreasonable searches and seizures." But the Court of Appeals for the Ninth Circuit reversed and school officials appealed to the Supreme Court.

The Court's decision was 6–3 and the opinion was delivered by Justice Scalia. Justice O'Connor filed a dissenting opinion, which was joined by Justices Stevens and Souter.

■ ■ ■

☐ *Justice SCALIA delivered the opinion of the Court.*

We have held that the Fourteenth Amendment extends this constitutional guarantee to searches and seizures by state officers, including public school officials, *New Jersey v. T. L. O.*, 469 U.S. 325 (1985). In *Skinner v. Railway Labor Executives' Assn.*, 489 U.S. 602 (1989), we held that state-compelled collection and testing of urine, such as that required by the Student Athlete Drug Policy, constitutes a "search" subject to the demands of the Fourth Amendment. See also [*National Treasury Employees Union*] *v. Von Raab*, 489 U.S. 656 (1989).

As the text of the Fourth Amendment indicates, the ultimate measure of the constitutionality of a governmental search is "reasonableness." At least in a case such as this, where there was no clear practice, either approving or disapproving the type of search at issue, at the time the constitutional provision was enacted, whether a particular search meets the reasonableness standard "is judged by balancing its intrusion on the individual's Fourth Amendment interests against its promotion of legitimate governmental interests." *Skinner*. . . . A search unsupported by probable cause can be constitutional, we have said, "when special needs, beyond the normal need for law enforcement, make the warrant and probable-cause requirement impracticable." *Griffin v. Wisconsin*, 483 U.S. 868 (1987).

We have found such "special needs" to exist in the public-school context. There, the warrant requirement "would unduly interfere with the maintenance of the swift and informal disciplinary procedures [that are] needed," and "strict adherence to the requirement that searches be based upon probable cause" would undercut "the substantial need of teachers and administrators for freedom to maintain order in the schools." *T. L. O.* The school search we approved in *T. L. O.*, while not based on probable cause, was based on individualized suspicion of wrongdoing. As we explicitly acknowledged, however, "the Fourth Amendment imposes no irreducible requirement of such suspicion." We have upheld suspicionless searches and seizures to conduct drug testing of railroad personnel involved in train accidents, *Skinner*; to conduct random drug testing of federal customs officers who carry arms or are involved in drug interdiction, *Von Raab*; and to maintain automobile checkpoints looking for illegal immigrants and contraband, and drunk drivers, *Michigan Dept. of State Police v. Sitz*, 496 U.S. 444 (1990).

The first factor to be considered is the nature of the privacy interest upon which the search here at issue intrudes. The Fourth Amendment does not protect all subjective expectations of privacy, but only those that society recognizes as "legitimate." What expectations are legitimate varies, of course, with context, depending, for example, upon whether the individual asserting the privacy interest is at home, at work, in a car, or in a public park. In addition, the legitimacy of certain privacy expectations vis-a-vis the State may depend upon the individual's legal relationship with the State. . . . Central, in our view, to the present case is the fact that the subjects of the policy are (1) children, who (2) have been committed to the temporary custody of the State as schoolmaster. . . .

Fourth Amendment rights, no less than First and Fourteenth Amendment rights, are different in public schools than elsewhere; the "reasonableness" inquiry cannot disregard the schools' custodial and tutelary responsibility for children. For their own good and that of their classmates, public school children are routinely required to submit to various physical examinations, and to be vaccinated against various diseases. . . .

Legitimate privacy expectations are even less with regard to student athletes. School sports are not for the bashful. They require "suiting up" before each practice or event, and showering and changing afterwards. Public school locker rooms, the usual sites for these activities, are not notable for the privacy they afford. The locker rooms in Vernonia are typical: no individual dressing rooms are provided; shower heads are lined up along a wall, un-separated by any sort of partition or curtain; not even all the toilet stalls have doors. . . .

There is an additional respect in which school athletes have a reduced expectation of privacy. By choosing to "go out for the team," they voluntarily subject themselves to a degree of regulation even higher than that imposed on students generally. In Vernonia's public schools, they must submit to a preseason physical exam (James testified that his included the giving of a urine sample), they must acquire adequate insurance coverage or sign an insurance waiver, maintain a minimum grade point average, and comply with any "rules of conduct, dress, training hours and related matters as may be established for each sport by the head coach and athletic director with the principal's approval." . . .

Finally, we turn to consider the nature and immediacy of the governmental concern at issue here, and the efficacy of this means for meeting it. In both *Skinner* and *Von Raab*, we characterized the government interest motivating the search as "compelling." . . . It is a mistake, however, to think that the phrase "compelling state interest," in the Fourth Amendment context, describes a fixed, minimum quantum of governmental concern, so that one can dispose of a case by answering in isolation the question: Is there a compelling state interest here? Rather, the phrase describes an interest which appears important enough to justify the particular search at hand, in light of other factors which show the search to be relatively intrusive upon a genuine expectation of privacy. Whether that relatively high degree of government concern is necessary in this case or not, we think it is met.

That the nature of the concern is important—indeed, perhaps compelling—can hardly be doubted. Deterring drug use by our Nation's schoolchildren is at least as important as enhancing efficient enforcement of the Nation's laws against the importation of drugs, which was the governmental concern in *Von Raab*, or deterring drug use by engineers and trainmen, which was the governmental concern in *Skinner*. . . .

Taking into account all the factors we have considered above—the decreased expectation of privacy, the relative unobtrusiveness of the search, and the severity of the need met by the search—we conclude Vernonia's Policy is reasonable and hence constitutional. . . .

☐ *Justice O'CONNOR, with whom Justice STEVENS and Justice SOUTER join, dissenting.*

The population of our Nation's public schools, grades 7 through 12, numbers around 18 million. By the reasoning of today's decision, the millions of these students who participate in interscholastic sports, an overwhelming majority of whom have given school officials no reason whatsoever to suspect they use drugs at school, are open to an intrusive bodily search.

In justifying this result, the Court dispenses with a requirement of individualized suspicion on considered policy grounds. First, it explains that precisely because every student athlete is being tested, there is no concern that school officials might act arbitrarily in choosing who to test. Second, a broad-based search regime, the Court reasons, dilutes the accusatory nature of the search. In making these policy arguments, of course, the Court sidesteps powerful, countervailing privacy concerns. Blanket searches, because they can involve "thousands or millions" of searches, "pose a greater threat to liberty" than do suspicion-based ones, which "affect one person at a time," *Illinois v. Krull*, 480 U.S. 340 (1987) (O'CONNOR, J., dissenting). Searches based on individualized suspicion also afford potential targets considerable control over whether they will, in fact, be searched because a person can avoid such a search by not acting in an objectively suspicious way. And given that the surest way to avoid acting suspiciously is to avoid the underlying wrongdoing, the costs of such a regime, one would think, are minimal.

But whether a blanket search is "better" than a regime based on individualized suspicion is not a debate in which we should engage. In my view, it is not open to judges or government officials to decide on policy grounds which is better and which is worse. For most of our constitutional history, mass, suspicionless searches have been generally considered per se unreasonable within the meaning of the Fourth Amendment. And we have allowed exceptions in recent years only where it has been clear that a suspicion-based regime would be ineffectual. Because that is not the case here, I dissent. . . .

The view that mass, suspicionless searches, however evenhanded, are generally unreasonable remains inviolate in the criminal law enforcement context, see *Ybarra v. Illinois*, 444 U.S. 85 (1979) (invalidating evenhanded, nonaccusatory patdown for weapons of all patrons in a tavern in which there was probable cause to think drug dealing was going on), at least where the search is more than minimally intrusive, see *Michigan Dept. of State Police v. Sitz*, 496 U.S. 444 (1990) (upholding the brief and easily avoidable detention, for purposes of observing signs of intoxication, of all motorists approaching a roadblock). . . .

Thus, it remains the law that the police cannot, say, subject to drug testing every person entering or leaving a certain drug-ridden neighborhood in order to find evidence of crime. And this is true even though it is hard to think of a more compelling government interest than the need to fight the scourge of drugs on our streets and in our neighborhoods. Nor could it be otherwise, for if being evenhanded were enough to justify evaluating a search regime under an open-ended balancing test, the Warrant Clause, which presupposes that there is some category of searches for which individualized suspicion is non-negotiable would be a dead letter. . . .

One searches today's majority opinion in vain for recognition that history and precedent establish that individualized suspicion is "usually required" under the Fourth Amendment (regardless of whether a warrant and probable cause are also required) and that, in the area of intrusive personal searches, the only recognized exception is for situations in which a suspicion-based scheme would be likely ineffectual. Far from acknowledging anything special about individualized suspicion, the Court treats a suspicion-based regime as if it were just any run-of-the-mill, less intrusive alternative—that is, an alternative that officials may bypass if the lesser intrusion, in their reasonable estimation, is outweighed by policy concerns unrelated to practicability. . . .

The great irony of this case is that most (though not all) of the evidence the District introduced to justify its suspicionless drug-testing program consisted of first- or secondhand stories of particular, identifiable students acting in ways that plainly gave rise to reasonable suspicion of in-school drug use—and thus that would have justified a drug-related search under our *T. L. O.* decision. Small groups of students, for example, were observed by a teacher "passing joints back and forth" across the street at a restaurant before school and during school hours. Another group was caught skipping school and using drugs at one of the student's houses. Several students actually admitted their drug use to school officials (some of them being caught with marijuana pipes). . . .

In light of all this evidence of drug use by particular students, there is a substantial basis for concluding that a vigorous regime of suspicion-based testing would have gone a long way toward solving Vernonia's school drug problem while preserving the Fourth Amendment rights of James Acton and others like him. . . .

Board of Education of Independent School District No. 92 of Pottawatomie City v. Earls

536 U.S. 822, 122 S.Ct. 2559 (2002)

Following the Court's upholding of random drug testing of high school athletes, in *Vernonia School District No. 47J v. Acton*, 515 U.S. 646 (1995), in 1998 the school district of Tecumseh, Oklahoma, a rural community about forty miles from Oklahoma City, adopted a policy of requiring all middle and high school students who participate in any extracurricular activities to consent to random drug testing. Lindsay Earls, a member of the choir and the marching band, challenged the constitutionality of the policy for violating the Fourth

Amendment guarantee against unreasonable searches and seizures. A federal district court rejected her claim, but the Court of Appeals for the Tenth Circuit reversed and the school board appealed.

The appellate court's decision was reversed by a 5–4 vote. Justice Thomas delivered the opinion of the Court. Justice Breyer filed a concurring opinion. Justices O'Connor and Ginsburg filed dissenting opinions, which Justices Stevens and Souter joined.

■ ■ ■

☐ *Justice THOMAS delivered the opinion of the Court.*

The Fourth Amendment to the United States Constitution protects "[t]he right of the people to be secure in their persons, houses, papers, and effects, against unreasonable searches and seizures." Searches by public school officials, such as the collection of urine samples, implicate Fourth Amendment interests. See *Vernonia; New Jersey v. T. L. O.*, 469 U.S. 325 (1985). We must therefore review the School District's Policy for "reasonableness," which is the touchstone of the constitutionality of a governmental search.

In the criminal context, reasonableness usually requires a showing of probable cause. See, e.g., *Skinner v. Railway Labor Executives' Assn.*, 489 U.S. 602 (1989). The probable-cause standard, however, "is peculiarly related to criminal investigations" and may be unsuited to determining the reasonableness of administrative searches where the "Government seeks to prevent the development of hazardous conditions." *Treasury Employees v. Von Raab*, 489 U.S. 656 (1989).

Given that the School District's Policy is not in any way related to the conduct of criminal investigations, respondents do not contend that the School District requires probable cause before testing students for drug use. Respondents instead argue that drug testing must be based at least on some level of individualized suspicion. It is true that we generally determine the reasonableness of a search by balancing the nature of the intrusion on the individual's privacy against the promotion of legitimate governmental interests. But we have long held that "the Fourth Amendment imposes no irreducible requirement of [individualized] suspicion." *United States v. Martinez-Fuerte*, 428 U.S. 543 (1976).

Significantly, this Court has previously held that "special needs" inhere in the public school context. While schoolchildren do not shed their constitutional rights when they enter the schoolhouse, see *Tinker v. Des Moines Independent Community School Dist.*, 393 U.S. 503 (1969), "Fourth Amendment rights . . . are different in public schools than elsewhere; the 'reasonableness' inquiry cannot disregard the schools' custodial and tutelary responsibility for children." *Vernonia*. In particular, a finding of individualized suspicion may not be necessary when a school conducts drug testing.

In *Vernonia*, this Court held that the suspicionless drug testing of athletes was constitutional. Applying the principles of *Vernonia* to the somewhat different facts of this case, we conclude that Tecumseh's Policy is also constitutional.

We first consider the nature of the privacy interest allegedly compromised by the drug testing. . . . A student's privacy interest is limited in a public school environment where the State is responsible for maintaining discipline, health, and safety. Schoolchildren are routinely required to submit to physical examinations and vaccinations against disease. Securing order in the school environment sometimes requires that students be subjected to greater controls than those appropriate for adults.

Respondents argue that because children participating in nonathletic extracurricular activities are not subject to regular physicals and communal undress, they have a stronger expectation of privacy than the athletes tested in *Vernonia*. This distinction, however, was not essential to our decision in *Vernonia*, which depended primarily upon the school's custodial responsibility and authority.

In any event, students who participate in competitive extracurricular activities voluntarily subject themselves to many of the same intrusions on their privacy as do athletes. Some of these clubs and activities require occasional off-campus travel and communal undress. All of them have their own rules and requirements for participating students that do not apply to the student body as a whole. . . .

Next, we consider the character of the intrusion imposed by the Policy. Urination is "an excretory function traditionally shielded by great privacy." *Skinner*. But the "degree of intrusion" on one's privacy caused by collecting a urine sample "depends upon the manner in which production of the urine sample is monitored." *Vernonia*.

Under the Policy, a faculty monitor waits outside the closed restroom stall for the student to produce a sample and must "listen for the normal sounds of urination in order to guard against tampered specimens and to insure an accurate chain of custody." The monitor then pours the sample into two bottles that are sealed and placed into a mailing pouch along with a consent form signed by the student. This procedure is virtually identical to that reviewed in *Vernonia*, except that it additionally protects privacy by allowing male students to produce their samples behind a closed stall. Given that we considered the method of collection in *Vernonia* a "negligible" intrusion, the method here is even less problematic. . . .

Finally, this Court must consider the nature and immediacy of the government's concerns and the efficacy of the Policy in meeting them. This Court has already articulated in detail the importance of the governmental concern in preventing drug use by schoolchildren. The drug abuse problem among our Nation's youth has hardly abated since *Vernonia* was decided in 1995. In fact, evidence suggests that it has only grown worse. As in *Vernonia*, "the necessity for the State to act is magnified by the fact that this evil is being visited not just upon individuals at large, but upon children for whom it has undertaken a special responsibility of care and direction." The health and safety risks identified in *Vernonia* apply with equal force to Tecumseh's children. Indeed, the nationwide drug epidemic makes the war against drugs a pressing concern in every school. . . .

Finally, we find that testing students who participate in extracurricular activities is a reasonably effective means of addressing the School District's legitimate concerns in preventing, deterring, and detecting drug use. . . . Accordingly, we reverse the judgment of the Court of Appeals. It is so ordered.

☐ *Justice GINSBURG, with whom Justice STEVENS,*
Justice O'CONNOR, and Justice SOUTER join, dissenting.

This case presents circumstances dispositively different from those of *Vernonia*. True, as the Court stresses, Tecumseh students participating in competitive extracurricular activities other than athletics share two relevant characteristics with the athletes of *Vernonia*. First, both groups attend public schools. "[O]ur decision in *Vernonia*," the Court states, "depended primarily upon the school's custodial responsibility and authority." Concern for student health and safety is basic to the school's caretaking, and it is undeniable that "drug use carries a variety of health risks for children, including death from overdose."

Those risks, however, are present for *all* schoolchildren. *Vernonia* cannot be read to endorse invasive and suspicionless drug testing of all students upon any evidence of drug use, solely because drugs jeopardize the life and health of those who use them. Many children, like many adults, engage in dangerous activities on their own time; that the children are enrolled in school scarcely allows government to monitor all such activities. If a student has a reasonable subjective expectation of privacy in the personal items she brings to school, surely she has a similar expectation regarding the chemical composition of her urine. Had the *Vernonia* Court agreed that public school attendance, in and of itself, permitted the State to test each student's blood or urine for drugs, the opinion in *Vernonia* could have saved many words.

The second commonality to which the Court points is the voluntary character of both interscholastic athletics and other competitive extracurricular activities. "By choosing to 'go out for the team,' [school athletes] voluntarily subject themselves to a degree of regulation even higher than that imposed on students generally." Comparably, the Court today observes, "students who participate in competitive extracurricular activities voluntarily subject themselves to" additional rules not applicable to other students. . . .

Voluntary participation in athletics has a distinctly different dimension: Schools regulate student athletes discretely because competitive school sports by their nature require communal undress and, more important, expose students to physical risks that schools have a duty to mitigate. For the very reason that schools cannot offer a program of competitive athletics without intimately affecting the privacy of students, *Vernonia* reasonably analogized school athletes to "adults who choose to participate in a closely regulated industry." Industries fall within the closely regulated category when the nature of their activities requires substantial government oversight. Interscholastic athletics similarly require close safety and health regulation; a school's choir, band, and academic team do not.

In short, *Vernonia* applied, it did not repudiate, the principle that "the legality of a search of a student should depend simply on the reasonableness, under all the circumstances, of the search." *T. L. O.* Enrollment in a public school, and election to participate in school activities beyond the bare minimum that the curriculum requires, are indeed factors relevant to reasonableness, but they do not on their own justify intrusive, suspicionless searches. *Vernonia*, accordingly, did not rest upon these factors; instead, the Court performed what today's majority aptly describes as a "fact-specific balancing." Balancing of that order, applied to the facts now before the Court, should yield a result other than the one the Court announces today. . . .

Nationwide, students who participate in extracurricular activities are significantly less likely to develop substance abuse problems than are their less-involved peers. Even if students might be deterred from drug use in order to preserve their extracurricular eligibility, it is at least as likely that other students might forgo their extracurricular involvement in order to avoid detection of their drug use. Tecumseh's policy thus falls short doubly if deterrence is its aim: It invades the privacy of students who need deterrence least, and risks steering students at greatest risk for substance abuse away from extracurricular involvement that potentially may palliate drug problems.

To summarize, this case resembles *Vernonia* only in that the School Districts in both cases conditioned engagement in activities outside the obligatory curriculum on random subjection to urinalysis. The defining characteristics of the two programs, however, are entirely dissimilar. The *Vernonia* district sought to test a subpopulation of students distinguished by their reduced expectation of privacy, their special susceptibility to drug-related injury, and their heavy involvement with drug use. The Tecumseh district seeks to test a much larger population associated with none of these factors. It does so, moreover, without carefully safeguarding student confidentiality and without regard to the program's untoward effects. A program so sweeping is not sheltered by *Vernonia*; its unreasonable reach renders it impermissible under the Fourth Amendment. . . . For the reasons stated, I would affirm the judgment of the Tenth Circuit declaring the testing policy at issue unconstitutional.

Safford Unified School District No. 1 v. Redding

557 U.S. 364, 129 S.CT. 2633 (2009)

The facts are discussed in the excerpt below. The Court affirmed the Court of Appeals for the Ninth Circuit's holding that a strip search of a middle school student for ibuprofen pills violated the Fourth Amendment, but reversed the appellate court's holding that school officials did not enjoy qualified immunity from a suit for damages.

Justice Souter delivered the opinion for the Court. Justices Stevens, Ginsburg, and Thomas each issued separate opinions, in part concurring and dissenting.

■ ■ ■

☐ *Justice SOUTER delivered the opinion of the Court.*

The issue here is whether a 13-year-old student's Fourth Amendment right was violated when she was subjected to a search of her bra and underpants by school officials acting on reasonable suspicion that she had brought forbidden prescription and over-the-counter drugs to school. Because there were no reasons to suspect the drugs presented a danger or were concealed in her underwear, we hold that the search did violate the Constitution, but because there is reason to question the clarity with which the right was established, the official who ordered the unconstitutional search is entitled to qualified immunity from liability.

The events immediately prior to the search in question began in 13-year-old Savana Redding's math class at Safford Middle School one October day in 2003. The assistant principal of the school, Kerry Wilson, came into the room and asked Savana to go to his office. There, he showed her a day planner, unzipped and open flat on his desk, in which there were several knives, lighters, a permanent marker, and a cigarette. Wilson asked Savana whether the planner was hers; she said it was, but that a few days before she had lent it to her friend, Marissa Glines. Savana stated that none of the items in the planner belonged to her.

Wilson then showed Savana four white prescription-strength ibuprofen 400-mg pills, and one over-the-counter blue naproxen 200-mg pill, all used for pain and inflammation but banned under school rules without advance permission. He asked Savana if she knew anything about the pills. Savana answered that she did not. Wilson then told Savana that he had received a report that she was giving these pills to fellow students; Savana denied it and agreed to let Wilson search her belongings. Helen Romero, an administrative assistant, came into the office, and together with Wilson they searched Savana's backpack, finding nothing.

At that point, Wilson instructed Romero to take Savana to the school nurse's office to search her clothes for pills. Romero and the nurse, Peggy Schwallier, asked Savana to remove her jacket, socks, and shoes, leaving her in stretch pants and a T-shirt (both without pockets), which she was then asked to remove. Finally, Savana was told to pull her bra out and to the side and shake it, and to pull out the elastic on her underpants, thus exposing her breasts and pelvic area to some degree. No pills were found.

Savana's mother filed suit against Safford Unified School District No. 1, Wilson, Romero, and Schwallier for conducting a strip search in violation of Savana's Fourth Amendment rights. The individuals (hereinafter petitioners) moved for summary judgment, raising a defense of qualified immunity. The District Court for the District of Arizona granted the motion on the ground that there was no Fourth Amendment violation, and a panel of the Ninth Circuit affirmed.

A closely divided Circuit sitting *en banc*, however, reversed. Following the two-step protocol for evaluating claims of qualified immunity, the Ninth Circuit held that the strip search was unjustified under the Fourth Amendment test for searches of children by school officials set out in *New Jersey v. T.L.O.*, 469 U.S. 325 (1985). . . . In *T.L.O.*, we recognized that the school setting "requires some modification of the level of suspicion of illicit activity needed to justify a search," and held that for searches by school officials "a careful balancing of governmental and private interests suggests that the public interest is best served by a Fourth Amendment standard of reasonableness that stops short of probable cause." We have thus applied a standard of reasonable suspicion to determine the legality of a school administrator's search of a student, and have held that a school search "will be permissible in its scope when the measures adopted are reasonably related to the objectives of the search and not excessively intrusive in light of the age and sex of the student and the nature of the infraction." . . .

In this case, the school's policies strictly prohibit the nonmedical use, possession, or sale of any drug on school grounds, including "[a]ny prescription or over-the-counter drug, except those for which permission to use in school has been granted pursuant to Board policy." A week before Savana was searched, another student, Jordan Romero (no relation of the school's administrative assistant), told the principal and Assistant Principal Wilson that "certain students were bringing drugs and weapons on campus," and that he had been sick after taking some pills that "he got from a classmate." On the morning of October 8, the same boy handed Wilson a white pill that he said Marissa Glines had given him. He told Wilson that students were planning to take the pills at lunch.

Wilson learned from Peggy Schwallier, the school nurse, that the pill was ibuprofen 400 mg, available only by prescription. Wilson then called Marissa out of class. Outside the classroom, Marissa's teacher handed Wilson the day planner, found within Marissa's reach, containing various contraband items. Wilson escorted Marissa back to his office.

In the presence of Helen Romero, Wilson requested Marissa to turn out her pockets and open her wallet. Marissa produced a blue pill, several white ones, and a razor blade. Wilson asked where the blue pill came from, and Marissa answered, "I guess it slipped in when she gave me the IBU 400s." When Wilson asked whom she meant, Marissa replied, "Savana Redding." Wilson then enquired about the day planner and its contents; Marissa denied knowing anything about them. Wilson did not ask Marissa any followup questions to determine whether there was any likelihood that Savana presently had pills: neither asking when Marissa received the pills from Savana nor where Savana might be hiding them.

Schwallier did not immediately recognize the blue pill, but information provided through a poison control hotline indicated that the pill was a 200-mg dose of an antiinflammatory drug, generically called naproxen, available over the counter. At Wilson's direction, Marissa was then subjected to a search of her bra and underpants by Romero and Schwallier, as Savana was later on. The search revealed no additional pills.

It was at this juncture that Wilson called Savana into his office and showed her the day planner. Their conversation established that Savana and Marissa were on friendly terms: while she denied knowledge of the contraband, Savana admitted that the day planner was hers and that she had lent it to Marissa. Wilson had other reports of their friendship from staff members, who had identified Savana and Marissa as part of an unusually rowdy group at the school's opening dance in August, during which alcohol and cigarettes were found in the girls' bathroom. Wilson had reason to connect the girls with this contraband, for Wilson knew that Jordan Romero had told the principal that before the dance, he had been at a party at Savana's house where alcohol was served. Marissa's statement that the pills came from Savana was thus sufficiently plausible to warrant suspicion that Savana was involved in pill distribution.

This suspicion of Wilson's was enough to justify a search of Savana's backpack and outer clothing. If a student is reasonably suspected of giving out contraband pills, she is reasonably suspected of carrying them on her person and in the carryall that has become an item of student uniform in most places today. If Wilson's reasonable suspicion of pill distribution were not understood to support searches of outer clothes and backpack, it would not justify any search worth making. And the look into Savana's bag, in her presence and in the relative privacy of Wilson's office, was not excessively intrusive, any more than Romero's subsequent search of her outer clothing.

Here it is that the parties part company, with Savana's claim that extending the search at Wilson's behest to the point of making her pull out her underwear was constitutionally unreasonable. The exact label for this final step in the intrusion is not important, though strip search is a fair way to speak of it. Romero and Schwallier directed Savana to remove her clothes down to her underwear, and then "pull out" her bra and the elastic band on her underpants. Although Romero and Schwallier stated that they did not see anything when Savana followed their instructions, we would not define strip search and its Fourth Amendment consequences in a way that would guarantee litigation about who was looking and how much was seen. The very fact of Savana's pulling her underwear away from her body in the presence of the two officials who were able to see her necessarily exposed her breasts and pelvic area to some degree, and both subjective and reasonable societal expectations of personal privacy support the treatment of such a search as categorically distinct, requiring distinct elements of justification on the part of school authorities for going beyond a search of outer clothing and belongings.

Savana's subjective expectation of privacy against such a search is inherent in her account of it as embarrassing, frightening, and humiliating. The reasonableness of her expectation (required by the Fourth Amendment standard) is indicated by the consistent experiences of other young people similarly searched, whose adolescent vulnerability intensifies the patent intrusiveness of the exposure.

The indignity of the search does not, of course, outlaw it, but it does implicate the rule of reasonableness as stated in *T.L.O.,* that "the search as actually conducted [be] reasonably related in scope to the circumstances which justified the interference in the first place." The scope will be permissible, that is, when it is "not excessively intrusive in light of the age and sex of the student and the nature of the infraction."

Here, the content of the suspicion failed to match the degree of intrusion. Wilson knew beforehand that the pills were prescription-strength ibuprofen and over-the-counter naproxen, common pain relievers equivalent to two Advil, or one Aleve. He must have been aware of the nature and limited threat of the specific drugs he was searching for, and while just about anything can be taken in quantities that will do real harm, Wilson had no reason to suspect that large amounts of the drugs were being passed around, or that individual students were receiving great numbers of pills.

Nor could Wilson have suspected that Savana was hiding common painkillers in her underwear. . . .

In sum, what was missing from the suspected facts that pointed to Savana was any indication of danger to the students from the power of the drugs or their quantity, and any reason to suppose that Savana was carrying pills in her underwear. We think that the combination of these deficiencies was fatal to finding the search reasonable. . . .

We do mean . . . to make it clear that the concern to limit a school search to reasonable scope requires the support of reasonable suspicion of danger or of resort to underwear for hiding evidence of wrongdoing before a search can reasonably make the quantum leap from outer clothes and backpacks to exposure of intimate parts. The meaning of such a search, and the degradation its subject may reasonably feel, place a search that intrusive in a category of its own demanding its own specific suspicions. . . .

☐ *Justice STEVENS, with whom Justice GINSBURG joins, concurring in part and dissenting in part.*

In *New Jersey v. T.L.O.*, 469 U.S. 325 (1985), the Court established a two-step inquiry for determining the reasonableness of a school official's decision to search a student. First, the Court explained, the search must be "justified at its inception" by the presence of "reasonable grounds for suspecting that the search will turn up evidence that the student has violated or is violating either the law or the rules of the school." Second, the search must be "permissible in its scope," which is achieved "when the measures adopted are reasonably related to the objectives of the search and not excessively intrusive in light of the age and sex of the student and the nature of the infraction."

Nothing the Court decides today alters this basic framework. It simply applies *T.L.O.* to declare unconstitutional a strip search of a 13-year-old honors student that was based on a groundless suspicion that she might be hiding medicine in her underwear. This is, in essence, a case in which clearly established law meets clearly outrageous conduct. I have long believed that "[i]t does not require a constitutional scholar to conclude that a nude search of a 13-year-old child is an invasion of constitutional rights of some magnitude." The strip search of Savana Redding in this case was both more intrusive and less justified than the search of the student's purse in *T. L.O.* . . .

☐ *Justice THOMAS, concurring in the judgment in part and dissenting in part.*

I agree with the Court that the judgment against the school officials with respect to qualified immunity should be reversed. Unlike the majority, however, I would hold that the search of Savana Redding did not violate the Fourth Amendment. The majority imposes a vague and amorphous standard on school administrators. It also grants judges sweeping authority to second-guess the measures that these officials take to maintain discipline in their schools and ensure the health and safety of the students in their charge. This deep intrusion into the administration of public schools exemplifies why the Court should return to the common-law doctrine of *in loco parentis* under which "the judiciary was reluctant to interfere in the routine business of school administration, allowing schools and teachers to set and enforce rules and to maintain order." *Morse v. Frederick*, 551 U.S. 393 (2007) (THOMAS, J., concurring). But even under the prevailing Fourth Amendment test established by *New Jersey v. T.L.O.*(1985), all petitioners, including the school district, are entitled to judgment as a matter of law in their favor. . . .

E | *Wiretapping, Bugging, and Police Surveillance*

Advances in science and technology often generate controversies that the Framers never envisioned and that challenge established constitutional doctrine. The telephone and radio, for example, were such a technological change in the early twentieth century, for with them came the possibility of eavesdropping on private conversations at great distances. Governmental intrusions by means of wiretapping and other electronic monitoring devices eventually led to a new interpretative approach to the Fourth Amendment.

Fourth Amendment protection for personal privacy was initially discussed in *Boyd v. United States*, 116 U.S. 616 (1886). When declaring unconstitutional a statute allowing the government to order individuals to produce private papers and invoices as mere evidence of illegally imported goods, the Court laid the basis for a liberal construction of the Fourth Amendment. In *Boyd*, the Court observed that "constitutional provisions for the security of person and property should be liberally construed. A close and literal construction deprives them of half their efficacy, and leads to gradual depreciation of the right." In his opinion for the Court, Justice Joseph Bradley reasoned that individuals have an "indefeasible" right of private property in the common law and under the Fourth Amendment, which renders "unreasonable" any governmental search or seizure of private papers and other property as mere evidence of criminal activities. In an often-quoted passage, he explained that

> [t]he principles laid down in *Entick v. Carrington* [19 Howard State Records 1029 (K.B. 1765), holding general warrants to be illegal] affect the very essence of constitutional liberty and security. They reach farther than the concrete form of the case then before the court, with its adventitious circumstances; they apply to all invasions on the part of the government and its employees of the sanctity of a man's home and the privacies of life. It is not the breaking of his doors, and the rummaging of his drawers, that constitutes the essence of the offence; but it is the invasion of his indefeasible right of personal security, personal liberty and private property, where that right has never been forfeited by his conviction of some public offense,—it is the invasion of this sacred right which underlies and constitutes the essence of Lord Camden's judgment. Breaking into a house and opening boxes and drawers are circumstances of aggravation; but any forcible and compulsory extortion of a man's own testimony or of his private papers to be used as evidence to convict him of crime or to forfeit his goods, is within the

condemnation of that judgment. In this regard, the Fourth and Fifth Amendments run almost into each other.

   Boyd stood as a watershed ruling for not only laying the basis for a liberal construction of Fourth Amendment-protected privacy but also in defining constitutionally protected privacy interests in terms of common-law property rights. As a result, the scope of Fourth Amendment protection extended beyond "persons, houses, papers, and effects" to include other "constitutionally protected areas"—business offices,[1] stores,[2] hotel rooms,[3] apartments,[4] automobiles,[5] and taxicabs.[6]

   The Court's analysis in *Boyd* and other cases of constitutionally protected areas greatly expanded protection for privacy interests and did so on an objective standard: Individuals' privacy interests were protected against unreasonable searches and seizures in those areas where they had proprietary interests as well. But by linking privacy interests to common-law property rights, the Court created an obstacle for dealing with Fourth Amendment challenges to governmental intrusions by means of wiretaps and electronic surveillance. Traditionally, common law recognized no "search" unless there was an actual physical trespass on private property and no "seizure" unless tangible items were taken. Wiretapping, of course, involves neither a physical trespass nor the taking of tangible property.

   When first confronted with the issue of wiretapping in *Olmstead v. United States* (1928) (excerpted below), the justices split 5–4 on holding that because the interception of telephone conversations occurs without entry into private premises there is no "search" of a constitutionally protected area, and further that conversations are not things that can be "seized" under the Fourth Amendment. But compare Chief Justice Taft's strict construction and application of the underlying property principles of the Fourth Amendment with the interpretations offered in the dissenting opinions of Justices Pierce Butler and Louis Brandeis. Attempting to combine a strict construction with a liberal application of common-law principles, Butler finds proprietary interests in the wire violated by the tap. By contrast, Brandeis advances both a liberal construction and application of the Fourth Amendment in contending that constitutionally protected privacy interests should not be confined to traditional categories of searches involving physical trespass and seizures of tangible materials.

   Olmstead stood for almost forty years. For a time, the Court evaded ruling again on the constitutionality of wiretaps by treating the issue as a matter of interpreting the Federal Communications Act of 1934, which prohibited the interception and divulgence of telephone and telegraph communications.[7] In *Nardone v. United States*, 308 U.S. 338 (1939), the Court ruled that that law made wiretapped communications inadmissible in federal courts. However, the government took the position that wiretaps remained permissible if the communications were not introduced at trial. As a result, federal and state wiretapping continued, especially in cases involving national security. Subsequently, the Court extended *Olmstead*'s trespass theory to the use of detectaphones—devices placed against a wall that detect sounds on the other side. In *Goldman v. United States*, 316 U.S. 129 (1942), federal agents without a warrant entered a suspect's office and planted a dictaphone with wires leading to an office next door, but the next day the dictaphone broke and the agents used a detectaphone instead, which was placed on the outside wall of the room and did not involve police entering the office. The Court held that evidence obtained by the use of detectaphone was admissible because no physical trespass was involved; whereas, evidence gathered from the dictaphone would have been inadmissible.

Although still relying on *Olmstead-Goldman*'s trespass theory in 1961, the Court rejected *Olmstead*'s holding that conversations per se have no Fourth Amendment protection because they are not tangible objects that may be seized. In *Silverman v. United States*, 365 U.S. 505 (1961), federal agents without a warrant drove a "spike mike" into a wall to overhear conversations. They made contact with a heating duct serving the house and, thereby, were able to monitor conversations throughout the house. The mike's penetration of the duct, the Court held, constituted "an actual intrusion of a constitutionally protected area." The Court remained unwilling, though, to overturn *Olmstead*. Writing for the majority, Justice Potter Stewart claimed to "find no occasion to re-examine *Goldman* here, but we decline to go beyond it, by even a fraction of an inch." Concurring Justice Douglas urged abandonment of *Olmstead*'s trespass theory of Fourth Amendment protection:

> The depth of the penetration of the electronic device—even the degree of its remoteness from the inside of the house—is not the measure of the injury. . . . Our concern should not be with the trivialities of the local law of trespass, as the opinion of the Court indicates. But neither should the command of the Fourth Amendment be limited by nice distinctions turning on the kind of electronic equipment employed. Rather the sole concern should be with whether the privacy of the home is invaded.

Finally, in the landmark ruling *Katz v. United States* (1967) (excerpted below), *Olmstead*'s trespass theory was overturned. In holding that police must first obtain a warrant before undertaking a wiretap, even of a public telephone, Justice Stewart advanced a new standard for triggering the guarantees of the Fourth Amendment in declaring that the Fourth

Amendment "protects people, not places," requiring probable cause and judicial approval of wiretaps. Notice that this standard is more subjective than that in *Boyd* and *Olmstead*, which made proprietary rights the basis for defining "constitutionally protected areas" under the Fourth Amendment. For that reason, concurring Justice John Harlan endeavored to clarify and qualify the majority's holding by proposing a two-prong test—"first that a person have exhibited an actual (subjective) expectation of privacy and, second, that the expectation be one that society is prepared to recognize as 'reasonable.'"

Katz's theory of "reasonable expectations of privacy" and Harlan's two-prong test for applying that standard made the reasonableness of searches context dependent. As the Court in *Terry v. Ohio* (1968) (excerpted in Section B of this chapter) observed, "wherever an individual may harbor a reasonable 'expectation of privacy,' . . . he is entitled to be free from unreasonable governmental intrusion" but "the specific content and incidents of this right [of privacy] must be shaped by the context in which it is asserted." As a result, the Court faces the task of deciding whether an expectation of privacy is "reasonable" and one "society is prepared to recognize as 'reasonable.'" While the Warren Court tended to expand Fourth Amendment protection along these lines, the more conservative Burger and Rehnquist Courts cut back by narrowly construing "reasonable expectations of privacy" under the Fourth Amendment. In cases like *United States v. Santana*, 427 U.S. 38 (1976) (excerpted in Section B) warrantless arrests and searches were upheld, despite individuals being in areas in which they have proprietary interests, because of the "exigencies of the circumstances" and the Court found no "reasonable expectation of privacy."[8]

So too, the Court contracted the scope of Fourth Amendment protection by denying that individuals have reasonable expectations of privacy against warrantless searches of private papers held by their attorneys[9] and bank records.[10] "*Katz* has not eliminated property considerations—ownership, possession, occupancy—but has changed their role from legal touchstones for the Fourth Amendment to standards by which expectations of privacy are evaluated."[11]

California v. Ciraolo (1986) (excerpted below) illustrates the Court's analysis in holding that people have no reasonable expectation of privacy against warrantless police surveillance by helicopters. In other rulings, the Court has denied that individuals have Fourth Amendment–protected expectations of privacy against police placing beepers on packages being transported[12] and against warrantless searches of their garbage left in containers for collection.[13] Underscoring the Rehnquist Court's use of the Warren Court's liberal standard of "reasonable expectations of privacy" for determining the scope of the Fourth Amendment is *Minnesota v.*

Carter, 525 U.S. 83 (1998). There, the Court held that temporary visitors in a home, unlike the homeowner, do not have "reasonable expectations of privacy" or Fourth Amendment protection, when they sought to exclude incriminating evidence that was discovered as a result of a police officer's observing them, from a sidewalk, through gaps in an apartment's closed window blind.

However, in an unusual lineup in a 5–4 decision in *Kyllo v. United States* (2001) (excerpted below), the Court held that the use by federal agents of thermal imagers, in order to detect heat radiations from a house that was suspected of being used to grow marijuana, without a warrant violated the Fourth Amendment.

Along with *Katz,* in *Berger v. State of New York,* 388 U.S. 41 (1967), the Court decided the question left unanswered by *Silverman*'s holding that conversations receive Fourth Amendment protection: namely, what constitutes a reasonable search and seizure by electronic eavesdropping. When striking down New York's eavesdropping statute and acknowledging that "eavesdropping involves an intrusion on privacy that is broad in scope," the Court established specific constitutional requirements: Police may be authorized by a judge to eavesdrop only on (1) showing probable cause, (2) describing with specificity the object to be seized, and (3) giving notice to the subject of the search; (4) authorization must be for a limited time only; and (5) police are required to return to the magistrate the specific items seized.

As for government informants and secret agents, the Court maintains that individuals simply assume the risk that they are dealing with undercover police and that their conversations are being recorded.[14] In *United States v. White,* 401 U.S. 745 (1971), for example, the Court adhered to its *assumption of risk rule* when upholding a conviction based on evidence obtained by an informer who carried an electronic transmitter. Justice White, for the majority, found no constitutionally significant difference between electronically equipped and nonequipped informers, explaining that

> [o]ur problem is not what the privacy expectations of particular defendants in particular situations may be or the extent to which they may in fact have relied on the discretion of their companions. Very probably, individual defendants neither know nor suspect that their colleagues have gone or will go to the police or are carrying recorders or transmitters. Otherwise, conversation would cease and our problem with these encounters would be nonexistent or far different from those now before us. Our problem, in terms of the principles announced in *Katz,* is what expectations of privacy are constitutionally "justifiable"—what expectations the Fourth Amendment will protect in the absence of a warrant. So far, the law permits the frustration of actual expectations of privacy

by permitting authorities to use the testimony of those associates who for one reason or another have determined to turn to the police, as well as by authorizing the use of informants. . . . If the law gives no protection to the wrongdoer whose trusted accomplice is or becomes a police agent, neither should it protect him when that same agent has recorded or transmitted the conversations which are later offered in evidence to prove the State's case.

But dissenting Justices Harlan, Douglas, and Marshall countered that the majority "ignored the differences occasioned by third-party monitoring and recording which insures full and accurate disclosure of all that is said," and warned that

[i]t is too easy to forget—and, hence, too often forgotten—that the issue here is whether to interpose a search warrant procedure between law enforcement agencies engaging in electronic eavesdropping and the public generally. By casting its "risk analysis" solely in terms of the expectations and risks that "wrongdoers" or "one contemplating illegal activities" ought to bear, the plurality opinion, I think, misses the mark entirely. . . . Interposition of a warrant requirement is designed not to shield "wrongdoers," but to secure a measure of privacy and a sense of personal security throughout our society.

Finally, the Roberts Court's first encounter with the Fourth Amendment's application in the digital age of the twenty-first century left more questions unanswered than addressed and, thus, invited decades of litigation. Moreover, although unanimous in the ruling, the Court actually split four to four to one and decided the narrowest-minimalist question. Justice Scalia's opinion for the Court commanded only the support of a plurality—Chief Justice Roberts and Justices Kennedy and Thomas—in holding that the planting of a global positioning system (GPS) tracking device on a car for almost a month constituted a "search" for Fourth Amendment purposes. The opinion turned on the fact that a trespass on private property was involved and only secondarily did "reasonable expectations of privacy" come into consideration. By contrast, Justice Alito's concurrence, joined by Justices Ginsburg, Breyer, and Kagan, did not concede that a "search" had occurred and quarreled with that focus of analysis, emphasizing instead that the issue should be analyzed in terms of "reasonable expectations of privacy" under the amendment. Neither Justice Scalia's opinion for the Court nor Justice Alito's concurrence, however, reached the issue of whether a warrant, probable cause, or a "reasonable suspicion" of criminality was required. Both also held out the possibility that the warrantless installation of GPS devices might be permissible depending on the length of the period of tracking and/or the investigatory purpose (e.g., monitoring drug trafficking versus combating potential terrorist attacks). In a separate concurring opinion, Justice Sotomayor indicated the need to reassess privacy in light of twenty-first century developments, but joined in the ruling because it was all that was needed to dispose of the case, *United States v. Jones* (2012) (excerpted below).

The Roberts Court, however, was sharply split in *Carpenter v. United States* (2019) (excerpted below), ruling that law enforcement requires a warrant to acquire the records of individuals' cellphone usage and locations, or cell-site locations information (CSLI), from wireless carriers, like Sprint. Chief Justice Roberts delivered the opinion of the Court, while Justices Kennedy, Thomas, Alito, and Gorsuch each issued dissenting opinions.

Notes

1. *Silverthorne Lumber Co. v. United States*, 251 U.S. 385 (1920).

2. *Amos v. United States*, 255 U.S. 313 (1921).

3. *Stoner v. California*, 376 U.S. 483 (1964); *United States v. Jeffers*, 342 U.S. 48 (1951); and *Lustig v. United States*, 338 U.S. 74 (1949).

4. *Jones v. United States*, 362 U.S. 257 (1960).

5. *Henry v. United States*, 361 U.S. 98 (1959).

6. *Rios v. United States*, 364 U.S. 253 (1960).

7. *Nardone v. United States*, 302 U.S. 379 (1937). However, in *Schwartz v. Texas*, 344 U.S. 199 (1952), the Court held, assuming that Congress had not preempted the area of wiretap legislation, that wiretapped evidence could be "divulged" in state courts if obtained by state agents. Five years later the Court nevertheless extended the act to exclude illegally state-gathered wiretap evidence in federal courts. *Benanti v. United States*, 355 U.S. 96 (1957). Finally, in *Lee v. Florida*, 392 U.S. 378 (1968), the Court overturned *Schwartz* when holding that the Act prohibited the admission of state-gathered evidence even in state courts.

8. See *Rakas v. Illinois*, 439 U.S. 128 (1978), holding that passengers in an automobile have no valid Fourth Amendment claims or legitimate expectations of privacy against searches of automobiles or seizures of evidence therein. See also *Brown v. United States*, 411 U.S. 223 (1973). But see *Byrd v. United States*, 138 S.Ct. 1518 (2018), holding that driver of a rental car, who is not listed on the rental agreement but has lawful possession, has a "reasonable expectation of privacy."

9. See *United States v. Miller*, 425 U.S. 435 (1976).

10. *California Bankers Association v. Shultz*, 416 U.S. 21 (1974).

11. Comment, "Government Access to Bank Records," 83 *Yale Law Journal* 1461 (1974).

12. *United States v. Knotts*, 460 U.S. 276 (1983).

13. *California v. Greenwood*, 486 U.S. 35 (1988).

14. See *Lee v. United States*, 343 U.S. 747 (1952); *Hoffa v. United States*, 385 U.S. 293 (1966); *Lewis v. United States*, 385 U.S. 206 (1966); and *Osborn v. United States*, 385 U.S. 323 (1966).

■ INSIDE THE COURT

Letter from Chief Justice Taft on Olmstead v. United States, *Holmes, Prohibition, and the Supreme Court*

On June 12, 1928, Chief Justice William Howard Taft sent his brother, Horace Taft, the following letter:

> I am interested in what you say as to the comment on our decision and opinion in the wiretapping case. Holmes has written the nastiest opinion in dissent and Brandeis is fuller of eloquence and idealism. Someone sent me an editorial from *The World* [a newspaper], I think it is. The truth is that Holmes wrote it the other way till Brandeis got after him and induced him to change on the ground that a state law in Washington forbids wiretapping. Holmes in his opinion really admits that the Fourth Amendment does not cover wiretapping. If it does not, then the law is all against his conclusion on which he rests his case, but he is a law unto himself if Brandeis says yes. It has an element of humor for me that the public seemed to be affected by the fact that it is against the bootleggers and assumes that it was that which carried the day. Of course that had nothing to do with the conclusion. The telephone might just as well have been used to carry on a conspiracy to rob, to murder, to commit treason. The truth is we have to face the problems presented by new inventions. Many of them are most useful to the criminals in their war against society and are at once availed of, and these idealist gentlemen urge a conclusion which facilitates the crime by their use and furnishes immunity from conviction by seeking to bring its use by government officers within the obstruction of the Bill of Rights and the Fourth Amendment. I have a very violent attack on me this morning from Mississippi by someone who only signs Alexander Hamilton and Patrick Henry. I fear he is a bootlegger. I have some supporting letters, but on the whole I look most for condemnation. Holmes says the misdemeanor of the State of Washington is a crime but he does not realise or consider that the admissibility of evidence in the federal courts is determined not by a statute but by the common law. More than this, a large majority of the state supreme courts refuse to follow the *Weeks* case [proclaiming the exclusionary rule, prohibiting the use of illegally obtained evidence in federal courts] decided by our Court as to the inadmissibility of evidence secured in violation of the Fourth Amendment. Chief Judge Cardozo speak-

---

■ INSIDE THE COURT
Letter from Chief Justice Taft on Olmstead v. United States,
Holmes, Prohibition, and the Supreme Court (continued)

---

ing for the Court of Appeals of New York writes an opinion
showing that 31 state supreme courts are against it and only 14
for it. They have had in New York a case decided by their
Appellate Division following the same principle in which the
evidence of the policemen who listened in by wiretapping
was held to be admissible although the law of New York forbids wiretapping as a misdemeanor. Of course one does not
like to be held up as one who favors the worst morals, but we
have to put up with such attacks in our efforts to follow the
old time common law recognized by all authorities, English
and American, that if evidence is pertinent it is admissible
however obtained. Cardozo argues that this view is the proper
one in defense of society. We have hard enough time to convict without presenting immunity to worst advanced and
progressive criminals. I shall continue to be worried by
attacks from all the academic lawyers who write college law
journals, but I suppose it is not a basis for impeachment. We
pointed out that Congress can change the rule if it sees fit. It
will be of interest to see whether Congress will do it. Here
it may be that the Prohibitionists in Congress will oppose
such legislation not because of their sensitiveness to the
scope of the Fourth Amendment but just because they are in
favor of convicting bootleggers. Indeed most of the opposing views are due and will be due to that issue solely.

In 1934, Congress passed the Federal Communications Act,
prohibiting the interception and divulgence of telephone and telegraph communications.

Source: Justice Oliver Wendell Holmes Papers, Manuscripts Room, Harvard
Law School.

Olmstead v. United States

277 U.S. 438, 48 S.CT. 564 (1928)

Roy Olmstead was indicted and convicted in federal district court of
illegally importing and selling liquor in violation of the National
Prohibition Act. At his trial, prosecutors introduced incriminating

evidence obtained by wiretaps on telephone lines between his home and office. Olmstead challenged the constitutionality of using this evidence on the grounds that it was obtained in violation of the Fourth Amendment guarantee against unreasonable searches and seizures and the Fifth Amendment guarantee against being compelled to testify against oneself. But an appellate court affirmed his conviction, and Olmstead appealed to the Supreme Court.

The Court's decision was 5–4, and the majority's opinion was announced by Chief Justice Taft. Justices Brandeis, Holmes, Stone, and Butler dissented.

■ ■ ■

☐ *Chief Justice TAFT delivered the opinion of the Court.*

There is no room in the present case for applying the Fifth Amendment, unless the Fourth Amendment was first violated. There was no evidence of compulsion to induce the defendants to talk over their many telephones. They were continually and voluntarily transacting business without knowledge of the interception. Our consideration must be confined to the Fourth Amendment. . . .

The well-known historical purpose of the Fourth Amendment, directed against general warrants and writs of assistance, was to prevent the use of governmental force to search a man's house, his person, his papers, and his effects, and to prevent their seizure against his will. . . .

The amendment itself shows that the search is to be of material things—the person, the house, his papers, or his effects. The description of the warrant necessary to make the proceeding lawful is that it must specify the place to be searched and the person or *things* to be seized. . . .

The amendment does not forbid what was done here. There was no searching. There was no seizure. The evidence was secured by the use of the sense of hearing and that only. There was no entry of the houses or offices of the defendants. . . .

The language of the amendment cannot be extended and expanded to include telephone wires, reaching to the whole world from the defendant's house or office. The intervening wires are not part of his house or office, any more than are the highways along which they are stretched. . . .

Congress may, of course, protect the secrecy of telephone messages by making them, when intercepted, inadmissible in evidence in federal criminal trials, by direct legislation, and thus depart from the common law of evidence. But the courts may not adopt such a policy by attributing an enlarged and unusual meaning to the Fourth Amendment. The reasonable view is that one who installs in his house a telephone instrument with connecting wires intends to project his voice to those quite outside, and that the wires beyond his house, and messages while passing over them, are not within the protection of the Fourth Amendment. Here those who intercepted the projected voices were not in the house of either party to the conversation. . . .

We think, therefore, that the wire tapping here disclosed did not amount to a search or seizure within the meaning of the Fourth Amendment.

☐ *Justice BRANDEIS, dissenting.*

The government makes no attempt to defend the methods employed by its officers. Indeed, it concedes that, if wire tapping can be deemed a search and seizure within the Fourth Amendment, such wire tapping as was practiced in the case at bar was an unreasonable search and seizure, and that the evidence thus obtained was inadmissible. But it relies on the language of the amendment, and it claims that the protection given thereby cannot properly be held to include a telephone conversation. . . .

When the Fourth and Fifth Amendments were adopted, "the form that evil had theretofore taken" had been necessarily simple. Force and violence were then the only means known to man by which a government could directly effect self-incrimination. It could compel the individual to testify—a compulsion effected, if need be, by torture. It could secure possession of his papers and other articles incident to his private life—a seizure effected, if need be, by breaking and entry. Protection against such invasion of "the sanctities of a man's home and the privacies of life" was provided in the Fourth and Fifth Amendments by specific language. *Boyd v. United States*, 116 U.S. 616 [(1886)]. But "time works changes, brings into existence new conditions and purposes." Subtler and more far-reaching means of invading privacy have become available to the government. Discovery and invention have made it possible for the government, by means far more effective than stretching upon the rack, to obtain disclosure in court of what is whispered in the closet.

Moreover, "in the application of a Constitution, our contemplation cannot be only of what has been, but of what may be." The progress of science in furnishing the government with means of espionage is not likely to stop with wire tapping. Ways may some day be developed by which the government, without removing papers from secret drawers, can reproduce them in court, and by which it will be enabled to expose to a jury the most intimate occurrences of the home. Advances in the psychic and related sciences may bring means of exploring unexpressed beliefs, thoughts and emotions. . . . Can it be that the Constitution affords no protection against such invasions of individual security? . . .

Time and again this Court, in giving effect to the principle underlying the Fourth Amendment, has refused to place an unduly literal construction upon it. . . .

The protection guaranteed by the amendments is much broader in scope. The makers of our Constitution undertook to secure conditions favorable to the pursuit of happiness. They recognized the significance of man's spiritual nature, of his feelings and of his intellect. They knew that only a part of the pain, pleasure and satisfactions of life are to be found in material things. They sought to protect Americans in their beliefs, their thoughts, their emotions and their sensations. They conferred, as against the government, the right to be let alone—the most comprehensive of rights and the right most valued by civilized men. To protect that right, every unjustifiable intrusion by the government upon the privacy of the individual, whatever the means employed, must be deemed a violation of the Fourth Amendment. And the use, as evidence in a criminal proceeding, of facts ascertained by such intrusion must be deemed a violation of the Fifth.

Applying to the Fourth and Fifth Amendments the established rule of construction, the defendants' objections to the evidence obtained by wire tapping must, in my opinion, be sustained. It is, of course, immaterial where the physical connection with the telephone wires leading into the defendants' premises was made. And it is also immaterial that the intrusion was in aid of law enforcement. Experience should teach us to be most on our guard to protect liberty when the government's purposes are beneficent. Men born to freedom are naturally alert to repel invasion of their liberty by evil-minded rulers. The greatest dangers to liberty lurk in insidious encroachment by men of zeal, well-meaning but without understanding. . . .

Decency, security, and liberty alike demand that government officials shall be subjected to the same rules of conduct that are commands to the citizen. In a government of laws, existence of the government will be imperiled if it fails to observe the law scrupulously. Our government is the potent, the omnipresent teacher. For good or for ill, it teaches the whole people by its example. Crime is contagious. If the government becomes a lawbreaker, it breeds contempt for law; it invites every man to become a law unto himself; it invites anarchy. To declare that in the administration of the criminal law the end justifies the means—to declare that the government may commit crimes in order to secure the conviction of a private criminal—would bring terrible retribution. Against that pernicious doctrine this court should resolutely set its face.

☐ *Justice BUTLER, dissenting.*

The single question for consideration is this: May the government, consistently with that clause, have its officers whenever they see fit, tap wires, listen to, take down, and report the private messages and conversations transmitted by telephones? . . .

Telephones are used generally for transmission of messages concerning official, social, business and personal affairs including communications that are private and privileged—those between physician and patient, lawyer and client, parent and child, husband and wife. The contracts between telephone companies and users contemplate the private use of the facilities employed in the service. The communications belong to the parties between whom they pass. During their transmission the exclusive use of the wire belongs to the persons served by it. Wire tapping involves interference with the wire while being used. Tapping the wires and listening in by the officers literally constituted a search for evidence. As the communications passed, they were heard and taken down. . . .

This Court has always construed the Constitution in the light of the principles upon which it was founded. The direct operation or literal meaning of the words used do not measure the purpose or scope of its provisions. Under the principles established and applied by this court, the Fourth Amendment safeguards against all evils that are like and equivalent to those embraced within the ordinary meaning of its words. . . .

When the facts in these cases are truly estimated, a fair application of that principle decides the constitutional question in favor of the petitioners. With great deference, I think they should be given a new trial.

■ INSIDE THE COURT

Justice Potter Stewart, Katz v. United States, *and the Right of Privacy*

The justices initially split four to four at conference when considering the appeal of the U.S. Court of Appeals for the Ninth Circuit in *Katz v. United States.* The appellate court had upheld the warrantless wiretapping of a public telephone booth that Charles Katz used to make gambling bets, because there was no actual trespass and the booth was public. Justice Stewart voted to affirm, while Justice Thurgood Marshall recused himself because he had participated in the case when serving as solicitor general.

Justice Stewart, however, had a memo on the case prepared by one his law clerks, Laurence Tribe, who later became a leading constitutional scholar at Harvard Law School. Tribe's memo swept broadly in embracing a right to privacy and recommended reversing the Ninth Circuit. In response, Justice Stewart penciled in language rejecting the idea that the Constitution recognized a general right of privacy. In his words:

> I do not believe there is any such thing as a general *Constitutional* "right to privacy." The Fourth Amendment protects against certain specific governmental intrusions upon a person's privacy. But its protections go further, and often have nothing to do with privacy at all. . . . And the protection of a person's *general* right to privacy is, like the protection of the right to his property, and his very life, left to the law of the individual states.

In addition, elsewhere, Tribe wrote that "the Fourth Amendment secures personal privacy—and not simply 'protected areas,'" but Justice Stewart changed that line to "the Fourth Amendment protects people—and not simply 'areas.'"

Justice Stewart, then, had the memorandum circulated to other chambers and, after further revisions, it commanded a majority, with only Justice Black dissenting from the reversal of the Ninth Circuit's decision. Still, Justice Stewart retained his reluctance to recognize a general constitutional right of privacy and, with slight modification, his original qualifications appear in the final published opinion for the Court:

(continues)

■ INSIDE THE COURT
Justice Potter Stewart, Katz v. United States,
and the Right of Privacy (continued)

[T]he Fourth Amendment cannot be translated into a general constitutional "right of privacy." That Amendment protects individual privacy against certain kinds of governmental intrusions, but its protections go further, and often have nothing to do with privacy at all. Other provisions of the Constitution protect personal privacy from other forms of governmental invasion. But the protection of a person's *general* right of privacy—his right to be left alone by other people—is, like the protection of his property and of his very life, left largely to the law of the individual states.

Source: Justice Potter Stewart Papers (MS 1367), Box 48, Folder 423, Manuscripts and Archives, Yale University Library.

Katz v. United States

389 U.S. 347, 88 S.Ct. 507 (1967)

Charles Katz was convicted in federal district court of violating federal law for placing bets and wagers from a public telephone booth in Los Angeles to bookies in Boston and Miami. Federal Bureau of Investigation agents had recorded his conversations with an electronic listening device placed outside the booth, and those recorded conversations were used against him at trial. After a federal appellate court rejected an appeal of his conviction, Katz appealed to the Supreme Court.

The Court's decision was 7–1, and the majority's opinion was announced by Justice Stewart. There were concurrences by Justices White, Harlan, and Douglas, who were joined by Justice Brennan. Justice Black dissented.

■ ■ ■

☐ *Justice STEWART delivered the opinion of the Court.*

The petitioner was convicted in the District Court for the Southern District of California under an eight-count indictment charging him with transmitting wagering information by telephone from Los Angeles to Miami and Boston in violation of a federal statute. At trial the Government was permitted, over the petitioner's objection, to introduce evidence of the petitioner's end of telephone conversations, overheard by FBI agents who had attached an electronic listening and recording device to the outside of the public telephone booth from which he had placed his calls. In affirming his conviction, the Court of Appeals rejected the contention that the recordings had been obtained in violation of the Fourth Amendment. . . .

We granted *certiorari* in order to consider the constitutional questions thus presented.

The petitioner has phrased those questions as follows:

A. Whether a public telephone booth is a constitutionally protected area so that evidence obtained by attaching an electronic listening recording device to the top of such a booth is obtained in violation of the right to privacy of the user of the booth.

B. Whether physical penetration of a constitutionally protected area is necessary before a search and seizure can be said to be violative of the Fourth Amendment to the United States Constitution.

We decline to adopt this formulation of the issues. In the first place the correct solution of Fourth Amendment problems is not necessarily promoted by incantation of the phrase "constitutionally protected area." Secondly, the Fourth Amendment cannot be translated into a general constitutional "right to privacy." That Amendment protects individual privacy against certain kinds of governmental intrusion, but its protections go further, and often have nothing to do with privacy at all. Other provisions of the Constitution protect personal privacy from other forms of governmental invasion. But the protection of a person's *general* right to privacy—his right to be let alone by other people—is, like the protection of his property and of his very life, left largely to the law of the individual States.

Because of the misleading way the issues have been formulated, the parties have attached great significance to the characterization of the telephone booth from which the petitioner placed his calls. The petitioner has strenuously argued that the booth was a "constitutionally protected area." The Government has maintained with equal vigor that it was not. But this effort to decide whether or not a given "area," viewed in the abstract, is "constitutionally protected" deflects attention from the problem presented by this case. For the Fourth Amendment protects people, not places. What a person knowingly exposes to the public, even in his own home or office, is not a subject of Fourth Amendment protection. But what he seeks to preserve as private, even in an area accessible to the public, may be constitutionally protected. . . .

The Government stresses the fact that the telephone booth from which the petitioner made his calls was constructed partly of glass, so that he was as visible after he entered it as he would have been if he had remained outside. But what he sought to exclude when he entered the booth was not the intruding eye—it was the uninvited ear. He did not shed his right to do so simply because he made his calls from a place where he might be seen. . . . One who occupies it, shuts the door behind him, and pays the toll that permits him to place a call is surely entitled to assume that the words he utters into the mouthpiece will not be broadcast to the world. To read the Constitution more narrowly is to ignore the vital role that the public telephone has come to play in private communication. . . .

We conclude that the underpinnings of *Olmstead* and *Goldman* have been so eroded by our subsequent decisions that the "trespass" doctrine there enunciated can no longer be regarded as controlling. The Government's activities in electronically listening to and recording the petitioner's words violated the privacy upon which he justifiably relied while using the telephone booth and thus constituted a "search and seizure" within the meaning of the Fourth Amendment. The fact that the electronic device employed to achieve that end did not happen to penetrate the wall of the booth can have no constitutional significance.

The question remaining for decision, then, is whether the search and seizure conducted in this case complied with constitutional standards. In that regard, the Government's position is that its agents acted in an entirely defensible manner: They did not begin their electronic surveillance until investigation of the petitioner's activities had established a strong probability that he was using the telephone in question to transmit gambling information to persons in other States, in violation of federal law. Moreover, the surveillance was limited, both in scope and in duration, to the specific purpose of establishing the contents of the petitioner's unlawful telephonic communications. The agents confined their surveillance to the brief periods during which he used the telephone booth, and they took great care to overhear only the conversations of the petitioner himself. . . .

It is apparent that the agents in this case acted with restraint. Yet the inescapable fact is that this restraint was imposed by the agents themselves, not by a judicial officer. They were not required, before commencing the search to present their estimate of probable cause for detached scrutiny by a neutral magistrate. They were not compelled during the conduct of the search itself, to observe precise limits established in advance by a specific court order. Nor were they directed, after the search had been completed, to notify the authorizing magistrate in detail of all that had been seized. In the absence of such safeguards, this Court has never sustained a search upon the sole ground that officers reasonably expected to find evidence of a particular crime and voluntarily confined their activities to the least intrusive means consistent with that end. . . .

Wherever a man may be, he is entitled to know that he will remain free from unreasonable searches and seizures. The government agents here ignored "the procedure of antecedent justification . . . that is central to the Fourth Amendment," a procedure that we hold to be a constitutional precondition of the kind of electronic surveillance involved in this case. Because the surveillance here failed to meet that condition, and because it led to the petitioner's conviction, the judgment must be reversed.

☐ *Justice HARLAN, concurring.*

I join the opinion of the Court, which I read to hold only (a) that an enclosed telephone booth is an area where, like a home, *Weeks v. United States*, 232 U.S. 383 (1914), and unlike a field, *Hester v. United States*, 265 U.S. 57 (1924), a person has a constitutionally protected reasonable expectation of privacy; (b) that electronic as well as physical intrusion into a place that is in this sense private may constitute a violation of the Fourth Amendment; and (c) that the invasion of a constitutionally protected area by federal authorities is, as the Court has long held, presumptively unreasonable in the absence of a search warrant.

As the Court's opinion states, "the Fourth Amendment protects people, not places." The question, however, is what protection it affords to those people. Generally, as here, the answer to that question requires reference to a "place." My understanding of the rule that has emerged from prior decisions is that there is a twofold requirement, first that a person have exhibited an actual (subjective) expectation of privacy and, second, that the expectation be one that society is prepared to recognize as "reasonable." Thus a man's home is, for most purposes, a place where he expects privacy, but objects, activities, or statements that he exposes to the "plain view" of outsiders are not "protected" because no intention to keep them to himself has been exhibited. On the other hand, conversations in the open would not be protected against being overheard, for the expectation of privacy under the circumstances would be unreasonable.

☐ *Justice BLACK, dissenting.*

My basic objection is twofold: (1) I do not believe that the words of the Amendment will bear the meaning given them by today's decision, and (2) I do not believe that it is the proper role of this Court to rewrite the Amendment in order "to bring it into harmony with the times" and thus reach a result that many people believe to be desirable. . . .

The Fourth Amendment says that

> The right of the people to be secure in their persons, houses, papers, and effects, against unreasonable searches and seizures, shall not be violated, and no Warrants shall issue, but upon probable cause, supported by Oath or affirmation, and particularly describing the place to be searched, and the persons or things to be seized.

The first clause protects "persons, houses, papers, and effects, against unreasonable searches and seizures. . . ." These words connote the idea of tangible things with size, form, and weight, things capable of being searched, seized, or both. The second clause of the Amendment still further establishes its Framers' purpose to limit its protection to tangible things by providing that no warrants shall issue but those "particularly describing the place to be searched, and the persons or things to be seized." A conversation overheard by eavesdropping, whether by plain snooping or wiretapping, is not tangible and, under the normally accepted meanings of the words, can neither be searched nor seized. . . .

Tapping telephone wires, of course, was an unknown possibility at the time the Fourth Amendment was adopted. But eavesdropping (and wiretapping is nothing more than eavesdropping by telephone) was. . . . There can be no doubt that the Framers were aware of this practice, and if they had desired to outlaw or restrict the use of evidence obtained by eavesdropping, I believe that they would have used the appropriate language to do so in the Fourth Amendment. They certainly would not have left such a task to the ingenuity of language-stretching judges. . . .

Since I see no way in which the word of the Fourth Amendment can be construed to apply to eavesdropping, that closes the matter for me. In interpreting the Bill of Rights, I willingly go as far as a liberal construction of the language takes me, but I simply cannot in good conscience give a meaning to words which they have never before been thought to have and which they certainly do not have in common ordinary usage. I will not distort the words of the Amendment in order to "keep the Constitution up to date" or "to bring it into harmony with the times." It was never meant that this Court have such power, which in affect would make us a continuously functioning constitutional convention.

California v. Ciraolo

476 U.S. 207, 106 S.CT. 1809 (1986)

Chief Justice Warren Burger discusses the facts of this case, involving a warrantless search for marijuana plants by police helicopter, at the outset of his opinion for the Court.

The Court's decision was 5–4, and the majority's opinion was announced by Chief Justice Burger. Justice Powell's dissent was joined by Justices Brennan, Marshall, and Blackmun.

■ ■ ■

☐ *Chief Justice BURGER delivered the opinion of the Court.*

We granted *certiorari* to determine whether the Fourth Amendment is violated by aerial observation without a warrant from an altitude of 1,000 feet of a fenced-in backyard within the curtilage of a home.

On September 2, 1982, Santa Clara Police received an anonymous telephone tip that marijuana was growing in respondent's backyard. Police were unable to observe the contents of respondent's yard from ground level because of a 6-foot outer fence and a 10-foot inner fence completely enclosing the yard. Later that day, Officer Shutz, who was assigned to investigate, secured a private plane and flew over respondent's house at an altitude of 1,000 feet, within navigable airspace; he was accompanied by Officer Rodriguez. Both officers were trained in marijuana identification. From the overflight, the officers readily identified marijuana plants 8 feet to 10 feet in height growing in a 15-by-25 foot plot in respondent's yard; they photographed the area with a standard 35mm camera.

On September 8, 1982, Officer Shutz obtained a search warrant on the basis of an affidavit describing the anonymous tip and their observations; a photograph depicting respondent's house, the backyard, and neighboring homes was attached to the affidavit as an exhibit. The warrant was executed the next day and 73 plants were seized; it is not disputed that these were marijuana.

After the trial court denied respondent's motion to suppress the evidence of the search, respondent pleaded guilty to a charge of cultivation of marijuana. The California Court of Appeals reversed, however, on the ground that the warrantless aerial *observation* of respondent's yard which led to the issuance of the warrant violated the Fourth Amendment. That court held first that respondent's backyard marijuana garden was within the "curtilage" of his home, under *Oliver v. United States*, 466 U.S. 170 (1984). The court emphasized that the height and existence of the two fences constituted "objective criteria from which we may conclude he manifested a reasonable expectation of privacy by any standard." . . .

The touchstone of Fourth Amendment analysis is whether a person has a "constitutionally protected reasonable expectation of privacy." *Katz v. United States*, 389 U.S. 347 (1967) (HARLAN, J., concurring). *Katz* posits a two-part inquiry: first, has the individual manifested a subjective expectation of privacy in the object of the challenged search? Second, is society willing to recognize that expectation as reasonable?

Clearly—and understandably—respondent has met the test of manifesting his own subjective intent and desire to maintain privacy as to his unlawful agricultural pursuits. . . . It can reasonably be assumed that the 10-foot fence was placed to conceal the marijuana crop from at least street level views. . . .

Yet a 10-foot fence might not shield these plants from the eyes of a citizen or a policeman perched on the top of a truck or a 2-level bus. Whether respondent therefore manifested a subjective expectation of privacy from *all* observations of his backyard, or whether instead he manifested merely a hope that no one would observe his unlawful gardening pursuits, is not entirely clear in these circumstances. . . .

We turn, therefore, to the second inquiry under *Katz*, i.e., whether that expectation is reasonable. In pursuing this inquiry, we must keep in mind that "[t]he test of legitimacy is not whether the individual chooses to conceal assertedly 'private' activity," but instead "whether the government's intrusion infringes upon the personal and societal values protected by the Fourth Amendment." . . .

Respondent argues that because his yard was in the curtilage of his home, no governmental aerial observation is permissible under the Fourth Amendment without a warrant. . . . The protection afforded the curtilage is essentially a protection of families and personal privacy in an area intimately linked to the home, both physically and psychologically, where privacy expectations are most heightened. The claimed area here was immediately adjacent to a suburban home, surrounded by high double fences. This close nexus to the home would appear to encompass this small area within the curtilage. . . .

That the area is within the curtilage does not itself bar all police observation. The Fourth Amendment protection of the home has never been extended to require law enforcement officers to shield their eyes when passing by a home on public thoroughfares. Nor does the mere fact that an individual has taken measures to restrict some views of his activities preclude an officer's observations from a public vantage point where he has a right to be and which renders the activities clearly visible. . . .

The observations by Officers Shutz and Rodriquez in this case took place within public navigable airspace in a physically nonintrusive manner; from this point they were able to observe plants readily discernable to the naked eye as marijuana. That the observation from aircraft was directed at identifying the plants and the officers were trained to recognize marijuana is irrelevant. Such observation is precisely what a judicial officer needs to provide a basis for a warrant. Any member of the public flying in this airspace who glanced down could have seen everything that these officers observed. On this record, we readily conclude that respondent's expectation that his garden was protected from such observation is unreasonable and is not an expectation that society is prepared to honor.

Justice POWELL, with whom Justice BRENNAN, Justice MARSHALL, and Justice BLACKMUN join, dissenting.

Concurring in *Katz v. United States*, 389 U.S. 347 (1967), Justice HARLAN warned that any decision to construe the Fourth Amendment as proscribing only physical intrusions by police onto private property "is, in the present day, bad physics as well as bad law, for reasonable expectations of privacy may be defeated by electronic as well as physical invasion." Because the Court today ignores that warning in an opinion that departs significantly from the standard developed in *Katz* for deciding when a Fourth Amendment violation has occurred, I dissent. . . .

Our decisions following the teaching of *Katz* illustrate that this inquiry "normally embraces two discrete questions." "The first is whether the individual, by his conduct, has 'exhibited an actual (subjective) expectation of privacy.'" The second is whether that subjective expectation "is 'one that society is prepared to recognize as "reasonable."'" . . .

While the Court today purports to reaffirm this analytical framework, its conclusory rejection of respondent's expectation of privacy in the yard of his residence as one that "is unreasonable," represents a turning away from the principles that have guided our Fourth Amendment inquiry. . . .

■ THE DEVELOPMENT OF LAW

Other Important Rulings on Governmental Wiretapping and Electronic Surveillance

CASE	VOTE	RULING
United States v. United States District Court, 407 U.S. 297 (1972)	8–0	Rejects claim of the Nixon administration that there was a national security exception to the requirement that judges approve warrants for wiretaps upon the request of the attorney general, as required by the Omnibus Crime Control and Safe Streets Act (OCCSS Act) of 1968.
United States v. Kahn, 415 U.S. 143 (1974)	6–3	Upheld use of wiretapped evidence, obtained pursuant to a wiretap as authorized by the OCCSS Act, against the wife of a man who was the subject of a warrant for wiretapping.
United States v. Giordano, 416 U.S. 505 (1974)	5–4	Authority for issuing wiretaps under the OCCSS Act cannot be delegated from the attorney general to the assistant attorney general.

CASE	VOTE	RULING
United States v. Donovan, 429 U.S. 413 (1977)	6–3	Under the OCCSS Act, police must identify all persons for whom they

have probable cause to obtain a wiretap warrant, but failure to do so did not trigger suppression of evidence under the statute.

United States v. New York Telephone Company, 434 U.S. 159 (1977)	5–4	OCCSS Act does not cover "pen registers"—devices that record the numbers dialed from a phone.
Scott v. United States, 436 U.S. 128 (1978)	7–2	Upheld wiretapping of all phone calls under a warrant issued pursuant to OCCSS Act.
Dalia v. United States, 441 U.S. 238 (1979)	6–3	No need to obtain separate warrant to make a covert entry to plant an authorized wiretap.
Smith v. Maryland, 442 U.S. 735 (1979)	6–3	Upheld use of pen registers.
United States v. Karo, 468 U.S. 705 (1984)	6–3	Planting of beepers does not require authorization of search warrant.

Kyllo v. United States

533 U.S. 27, 121 S.Ct. 2038 (2001)

In 1992, federal agents suspected Danny Kyllo of growing marijuana in his home and decided to use an Agema Thermovision 210 thermal imager to scan his house. The imagers detect infrared radiation, which virtually all objects emit, and converts the radiation into images based on their relative warmth. From the passenger's seat of their car across the street from the house, the agents scanned the house and found that the roof over the garage and a side wall of the house were relatively hot. The agents concluded that Kyllo was using halide, high-intensity lights to grow marijuana and, on that basis, along with an informant's tip and utility bills, obtained a warrant to search the house, where they found more than 100 marijuana plants. Kyllo sought to suppress that evidence on the ground that the use of the thermal imager constituted a warrantless search in violation of the Fourth Amendment. A federal district court rejected that motion and its decision was affirmed by an appellate court.

The appellate court's decision was reversed by a 5–4 vote and the opinion for the Court was delivered by Justice Scalia. Justice Stevens filed a dissenting opinion, which Chief Justice Rehnquist and Justice O'Connor and Kennedy joined.

■ ■ ■

☐ *Justice SCALIA delivered the opinion of the Court.*

This case presents the question whether the use of a thermal-imaging device aimed at a private home from a public street to detect relative amounts of heat within the home constitutes a "search" within the meaning of the Fourth Amendment. . . .

"At the very core" of the Fourth Amendment "stands the right of a man to retreat into his own home and there be free from unreasonable governmental intrusion." *Silverman v. United States,* 365 U.S. 505 (1961). . . . On the other hand, the antecedent question of whether or not a Fourth Amendment "search" has occurred is not so simple under our precedent. The permissibility of ordinary visual surveillance of a home used to be clear because, well into the 20th century, our Fourth Amendment jurisprudence was tied to common-law trespass. See, e.g., *Goldman v. United States,* 316 U.S. 129 (1942); *Olmstead v. United States,* 277 U.S. 438 (1928). Visual surveillance was unquestionably lawful because "the eye cannot by the laws of England be guilty of a trespass." *Boyd v. United States,* 116 U.S. 616 (1886). We have since decoupled violation of a person's Fourth Amendment rights from trespassory violation of his property, see *Rakas v. Illinois,* 439 U.S. 128 (1978), but the lawfulness of warrantless visual surveillance of a home has still been preserved. As we observed in *California v. Ciraolo,* 476 U.S. 207 (1986), "[t]he Fourth Amendment protection of the home has never been extended to require law enforcement officers to shield their eyes when passing by a home on public thoroughfares."

One might think that the new validating rationale would be that examining the portion of a house that is in plain public view, while it is a "search" despite the absence of trespass, is not an "unreasonable" one under the Fourth Amendment. But in fact we have held that visual observation is no "search" at all—perhaps in order to preserve somewhat more intact our doctrine that warrantless searches are presumptively unconstitutional. See *Dow Chemical Co. v. United States,* 476 U.S. 227 (1986). In assessing when a search is not a search, we have applied somewhat in reverse the principle first enunciated in *Katz v. United States,* 389 U.S. 347 (1967) . . . that a Fourth Amendment search does not occur—even when the explicitly protected location of a house is concerned—unless "the individual manifested a subjective expectation of privacy in the object of the challenged search," and "society [is] willing to recognize that expectation as reasonable." *Ciraolo.* . . .

The present case involves officers on a public street engaged in more than naked-eye surveillance of a home. We have previously reserved judgment as to how much technological enhancement of ordinary perception from such a vantage point, if any, is too much. While we upheld enhanced aerial photography of an industrial complex in *Dow Chemical,* we noted that we found "it important that this is not an area immediately adjacent to a private home, where privacy expectations are most heightened."

It would be foolish to contend that the degree of privacy secured to citizens by the Fourth Amendment has been entirely unaffected by the advance of technology. For example, as the cases discussed above make clear, the technology enabling human flight has exposed to public view (and hence, we have said, to official observation) uncovered portions of the house and its curtilage that once were private. The question we confront today is what limits there are upon this power of technology to shrink the realm of guaranteed privacy.

The *Katz* test—whether the individual has an expectation of privacy that society is prepared to recognize as reasonable—has often been criticized as circular, and hence subjective and unpredictable. While it may be difficult to refine *Katz* when the search of areas such as telephone booths, automobiles, or even the curtilage and uncovered portions of residences are at issue, in the case of the search of the interior of homes—the prototypical and hence most commonly litigated area of protected privacy—there is a ready criterion, with roots deep in the common law, of the minimal expectation of privacy that exists, and that is acknowledged to be reasonable. To withdraw protection of this minimum expectation would be to permit police technology to erode the privacy guaranteed by the Fourth Amendment. We think that obtaining by sense-enhancing technology any information regarding the interior of the home that could not otherwise have been obtained without physical "intrusion into a constitutionally protected area," *Silverman,* constitutes a search—at least where (as here) the technology in question is not in general public use. This assures preservation of that degree of privacy against government that existed when the Fourth Amendment was adopted. On the basis of this criterion, the information obtained by the thermal imager in this case was the product of a search.

The Government maintains, however, that the thermal imaging must be upheld because it detected "only heat radiating from the external surface of the house." The dissent makes this its leading point, contending that there is a fundamental difference between what it calls "off-the-wall" observations and "through-the-wall surveillance." But just as a thermal imager captures only heat emanating from a house, so also a powerful directional microphone picks up only sound emanating from a house—and a satellite capable of scanning from many miles away would pick up only visible light emanating from a house. We rejected such a mechanical interpretation of the Fourth Amendment in *Katz,* where the eavesdropping device picked up only sound waves that reached the exterior of the phone booth. Reversing that approach would leave the homeowner at the mercy of advancing technology—including imaging technology that could discern all human activity in the home. While the technology used in the present case was relatively crude, the rule we adopt must take account of more sophisticated systems that are already in use or in development. . . .

We have said that the Fourth Amendment draws "a firm line at the entrance to the house," *Payton*. That line, we think, must be not only firm but also bright—which requires clear specification of those methods of surveillance that require a warrant. While it is certainly possible to conclude from the videotape of the thermal imaging that occurred in this case that no "significant" compromise of the homeowner's privacy has occurred, we must take the long view, from the original meaning of the Fourth Amendment forward. Where, as here, the Government uses a device that is not in general public use, to explore details of the home that would previously have been unknowable without physical intrusion, the surveillance is a "search" and is presumptively unreasonable without a warrant.

Since we hold the Thermovision imaging to have been an unlawful search, it will remain for the District Court to determine whether, without the evidence it provided, the search warrant issued in this case was supported by probable cause—and if not, whether there is any other basis for supporting admission of the evidence that the search pursuant to the warrant produced.

☐ *Justice STEVENS, with whom THE CHIEF JUSTICE,*
Justice O'CONNOR, and Justice KENNEDY join, dissenting.

There is, in my judgment, a distinction of constitutional magnitude between "through-the-wall surveillance" that gives the observer or listener direct access to information in a private area, on the one hand, and the thought processes used to draw inferences from information in the public domain, on the other hand. The Court has crafted a rule that purports to deal with direct observations of the inside of the home, but the case before us merely involves indirect deductions from "off-the-wall" surveillance, that is, observations of the exterior of the home. Those observations were made with a fairly primitive thermal imager that gathered data exposed on the outside of petitioner's home but did not invade any constitutionally protected interest in privacy. Moreover, I believe that the supposedly "bright-line" rule the Court has created in response to its concerns about future technological developments is unnecessary, unwise, and inconsistent with the Fourth Amendment.

There is no need for the Court to craft a new rule to decide this case, as it is controlled by established principles from our Fourth Amendment jurisprudence. One of those core principles, of course, is that "searches and seizures inside a home without a warrant are presumptively unreasonable." *Payton v. New York,* 445 U.S. 573 (1980). But it is equally well settled that searches and seizures of property in plain view are presumptively reasonable. Whether that property is residential or commercial, the basic principle is the same: "What a person knowingly exposes to the public, even in his own home or office, is not a subject of Fourth Amendment protection." *California v. Ciraolo,* 476 U.S. 207 (1986). . . .

[T]he notion that heat emissions from the outside of a dwelling is a private matter implicating the protections of the Fourth Amendment is not only unprecedented but also quite difficult to take seriously. Heat waves, like aromas that are generated in a kitchen, or in a laboratory or opium den, enter the public domain if and when they leave a building. A subjective expectation that they would remain private is not only implausible but also surely not "one that society is prepared to recognize as 'reasonable.'" *Katz* (HARLAN, J., concurring).

To be sure, the homeowner has a reasonable expectation of privacy concerning what takes place within the home, and the Fourth Amendment's protection against physical invasions of the home should apply to their functional equivalent. But the equipment in this case did not penetrate the walls of petitioner's home, and while it did pick up "details of the home" that were exposed to the public, it did not obtain "any information regarding the interior of the home." In the Court's own words, based on what the thermal imager "showed" regarding the outside of petitioner's home, the officers "concluded" that petitioner was engaging in illegal activity inside the home. It would be quite absurd to characterize their thought processes as "searches," regardless of whether they inferred (rightly) that petitioner was growing marijuana in his house, or (wrongly) that "the lady of the house [was taking] her daily sauna and bath." In either case, the only conclusions the officers reached concerning the interior of the home were at least as indirect as those that might have been inferred from the contents of discarded garbage, see *California v. Greenwood,* 486 U.S. 35 (1988), or pen register data, see *Smith v. Maryland,* 442 U.S. 735 (1979). . . .

Since what was involved in this case was nothing more than drawing inferences from off-the-wall surveillance, rather than any "through-the-wall" surveillance, the officers' conduct did not amount to a search and was perfectly reasonable. . . .

Despite the Court's attempt to draw a line that is "not only firm but also bright," the contours of its new rule are uncertain because its protection apparently dissipates as soon as the relevant technology is "in general public use." Yet how much use is general public use is not even hinted at by the Court's opinion, which makes the somewhat doubtful assumption that the thermal imager used in this case does not satisfy that criterion. In any event, putting aside its lack of clarity, this criterion is somewhat perverse because it seems likely that the threat to privacy will grow, rather than recede, as the use of intrusive equipment becomes more readily available. . . .

The two reasons advanced by the Court as justifications for the adoption of its new rule are both unpersuasive. First, the Court suggests that its rule is compelled by our holding in *Katz,* because in that case, as in this, the surveillance consisted of nothing more than the monitoring of waves emanating from a private area into the public domain. Yet there are critical differences between the cases. In *Katz,* the electronic listening device attached to the outside of the phone booth allowed the officers to pick up the content of the conversation inside the booth, making them the functional equivalent of intruders because they gathered information that was otherwise available only to someone inside the private area; it would be as if, in this case, the thermal imager presented a view of the heat-generating activity inside petitioner's home. By contrast, the thermal imager here disclosed only the relative amounts of heat radiating from the house; it would be as if, in *Katz,* the listening device disclosed only the relative volume of sound leaving the booth, which presumably was discernible in the public domain. Surely, there is a significant difference between the general and well-settled expectation that strangers will not have direct access to the contents of private communications, on the one hand, and the rather theoretical expectation that an occasional homeowner would even care if anybody noticed the relative amounts of heat emanating from the walls of his house, on the other. It is pure hyperbole for the Court to suggest that refusing to extend the holding of *Katz* to this case would leave the homeowner at the mercy of "technology that could discern all human activity in the home."

Second, the Court argues that the permissibility of "through-the-wall surveillance" cannot depend on a distinction between observing "intimate details" such as "the lady of the house [taking] her daily sauna and bath," and noticing only "the nonintimate rug on the vestibule floor" or "objects no smaller than 36 by 36 inches." This entire argument assumes, of course, that the thermal imager in this case could or did perform "through-the-wall surveillance" that could identify any detail "that would previously have been unknowable without physical intrusion." In fact, the device could not and did not enable its user to identify either the lady of the house, the rug on the vestibule floor, or anything else inside the house. . . .

Although the Court is properly and commendably concerned about the threats to privacy that may flow from advances in the technology available to the law enforcement profession, it has unfortunately failed to heed the tried and true counsel of judicial restraint. Instead of concentrating on the rather mundane issue that is actually presented by the case before it, the Court has endeavored to craft an all-encompassing rule for the future. It would be far wiser to give legislators an unimpeded opportunity to grapple with these emerging issues rather than to shackle them with prematurely devised constitutional constraints.

I respectfully dissent.

United States v. Jones

565 U.S. 400, 132 S.Ct. 945 (2012)

Antoine Jones, the owner of a nightclub in the District of Columbia, was the target of a law enforcement investigation of drug trafficking. Officers used various investigative techniques, including visual surveillance and the installation of a camera focused on the front door of the nightclub, a pen register (to record the numbers of telephone calls), and a wiretap covering Jones's cellular phone. Based on those sources, the government sought a warrant authorizing the use of a global positioning system (GPS) tracking device for the Jeep Grand Cherokee registered to Jones's wife. A warrant was issued for the installation of the GPS device in the District of Columbia within ten days. However, not until the eleventh day, and not in the District of Columbia but in Maryland, did agents install the device on the undercarriage of the Jeep while parked in a public parking lot. Over the next twenty-eight days, agents tracked the Jeep's movements and once replaced the device's battery when the vehicle was in a public lot in Maryland. The device tracked the Jeep's location within fifty to one hundred feet and transmitted that location by cellular phone to a government computer. The government ultimately obtained a multiple-count indictment charging Jones with conspiracy to distribute cocaine. Before trial, Jones filed a motion to suppress evidence obtained through the GPS device. The district court granted the motion in part, suppressing the data obtained while the vehicle was parked in the garage adjoining Jones's residence but holding the remaining data admissible, because "[a] person traveling in an automobile on public thoroughfares has no reasonable expectation of privacy in his movements from one place to another." Jones's trial ended with a hung jury but a second trial found him guilty and he was sentenced to life imprisonment. On appeal, however, the United States Court of Appeals for the District of Columbia Circuit reversed on the ground that the conviction was based on the warrantless use of the GPS device, which violated the Fourth Amendment. The government appealed and the Supreme Court granted *certiorari*.

The appellate court's decision was affirmed. Justice Scalia delivered the opinion for the Court. Justices Alito and Sotomayor each filed concurring opinions; Justices Ginsburg, Breyer, and Kagan joined Justice Alito's concurrence.

■ ■ ■

☐ *Justice SCALIA delivered the opinion of the Court.*

The Fourth Amendment provides in relevant part that "[t]he right of the people to be secure in their persons, houses, papers, and effects, against unreasonable searches and seizures, shall not be violated." It is beyond dispute that a vehicle is an "effect" as that term is used in the Amendment. We hold that the Government's installation of a GPS device on a target's vehicle, and its use of that device to monitor the vehicle's movements, constitutes a "search."

It is important to be clear about what occurred in this case: The Government physically occupied private property for the purpose of obtaining information. We have no doubt that such a physical intrusion would have been considered a "search" within the meaning of the Fourth Amendment when it was adopted. *Entick v. Carrington*, 95 Eng. Rep. 807 (C.P. 1765), is a "case we have described as a 'monument of English freedom' 'undoubtedly familiar' to 'every American statesman' at the time the Constitution was adopted, and considered to be 'the true and ultimate expression of constitutional law'" with regard to search and seizure. In that case, Lord Camden expressed in plain terms the significance of property rights in search-and-seizure analysis: "[O]ur law holds the property of every man so sacred, that no man can set his foot upon his neighbour's close without his leave; if he does he is a trespasser, though he does no damage at all; if he will tread upon his neighbour's ground, he must justify it by law."

The text of the Fourth Amendment reflects its close connection to property, since otherwise it would have referred simply to "the right of the people to be secure against unreasonable searches and seizures"; the phrase "in their persons, houses, papers, and effects" would have been superfluous.

Consistent with this understanding, our Fourth Amendment jurisprudence was tied to common-law trespass, at least until the latter half of the 20th century. Thus, in *Olmstead v. United States*, 277 U.S. 438 (1928), we held that wiretaps attached to telephone wires on the public streets did not constitute a Fourth Amendment search because "[t]here was no entry of the houses or offices of the defendants."

Our later cases, of course, have deviated from that exclusively property-based approach. In *Katz v. United States*, 389 U.S. 347 (1967), we said that "the Fourth Amendment protects people, not places," and found a violation in attachment of an eavesdropping device to a public telephone booth. Our later cases have applied the analysis of Justice HARLAN's concurrence in that case, which said that a violation occurs when government officers violate a person's "reasonable expectation of privacy." The Government contends that the HARLAN standard shows that no search occurred here, since Jones had no "reasonable expectation of privacy" in the area of the Jeep accessed by Government agents (its underbody) and in the locations of the Jeep on the public roads, which were visible to all. But we need not address the Government's contentions, because Jones's Fourth Amendment rights do not rise or fall with the *Katz* formulation. At bottom, we must "assur[e] preservation of that degree of privacy against government that existed when the Fourth Amendment was adopted." *Kyllo* [*v. United States*, 533 U.S. 27 (2001)]. As explained, for most of our history the Fourth Amendment was understood to embody a particular concern for government trespass upon the areas ("persons, houses, papers, and effects") it enumerates.

Katz did not repudiate that understanding. . . . *Katz* did not narrow the Fourth Amendment's scope. The Government contends that several of our post-*Katz* cases foreclose the conclusion that what occurred here constituted a search. It relies principally on two cases in which we rejected Fourth Amendment challenges to "beepers," electronic tracking devices that represent another form of electronic monitoring. The first case, [*United States v.*] *Knotts*, [460 U.S. 276 (1983)], upheld against Fourth Amendment challenge the use of a "beeper" that had been placed in a container of chloroform, allowing law enforcement to monitor the location of the container. We said that there had been no infringement of Knotts' reasonable expectation of privacy since the information obtained—the location of the automobile carrying the container on public roads, and the location of the off-loaded container in open fields near Knotts' cabin—had been voluntarily conveyed to the public. But as we have discussed, the *Katz* reasonable-expectation-of-privacy test has been added to, not substituted for, the common-law trespassory test. . . . The second "beeper" case, *United States v. Karo*, 468 U.S. 705 (1984), does not suggest a different conclusion. . . .

Finally, the Government's position gains little support from our conclusion in *Oliver v. United States*, 466 U.S. 170 (1984), that officers' information-gathering intrusion on an "open field" did not constitute a Fourth Amendment search even though it was a trespass at common law. Quite simply, an open field, unlike the curtilage of a home, is not one of those protected areas enumerated in the Fourth Amendment. The Government's physical intrusion on such an area—unlike its intrusion on the "effect" at issue here—is of no Fourth Amendment significance.

The concurrence begins by accusing us of applying "18th century tort law." That is a distortion. What we apply is an 18th century guarantee against unreasonable searches, which we believe must provide at a minimum the degree of protection it afforded when it was adopted. The concurrence does not share that belief. It would apply exclusively *Katz*'s reasonable-expectation-of-privacy test, even when that eliminates rights that previously existed.

The concurrence faults our approach for "present[ing] particularly vexing problems" in cases that do not involve physical contact, such as those that involve the transmission of electronic signals. We entirely fail to understand that point. For unlike the concurrence, which would make *Katz* the exclusive test, we do not make trespass the exclusive test. Situations involving merely the transmission of electronic signals without trespass would remain subject to *Katz* analysis.

In fact, it is the concurrence's insistence on the exclusivity of the *Katz* test that needlessly leads us into "particularly vexing problems" in the present case. This Court has to date not deviated from the understanding that mere visual observation does not constitute a search. . . . Thus, even assuming that the concurrence is correct to say that "[t]raditional surveillance" of Jones for a 4-week period "would have required a large team of agents, multiple vehicles, and perhaps aerial assistance," our cases suggest that such visual observation is constitutionally permissible. It may be that achieving the same result through electronic means, without an accompanying trespass, is an unconstitutional invasion of privacy, but the present case does not require us to answer that question. And answering it affirmatively leads us needlessly into additional thorny problems. The concurrence posits that "relatively short-term monitoring of a person's movements on public streets" is okay, but that "the use of longer term GPS monitoring in investigations of most offenses" is no good. That introduces yet another novelty into our jurisprudence.

There is no precedent for the proposition that whether a search has occurred depends on the nature of the crime being investigated. And even accepting that novelty, it remains unexplained why a 4-week investigation is "surely" too long and why a drug-trafficking conspiracy involving substantial amounts of cash and narcotics is not an "extraordinary offens[e]," which may permit longer observation. What of a 2-day monitoring of a suspected purveyor of stolen electronics? Or of a 6-month monitoring of a suspected terrorist? We may have to grapple with these "vexing problems" in some future case where a classic trespassory search is not involved and resort must be had to *Katz* analysis; but there is no reason for rushing forward to resolve them here. . . .

☐ *Justice ALITO, with whom Justice GINSBURG, Justice BREYER, and Justice KAGAN join, concurring in the judgment.*

This case requires us to apply the Fourth Amendment's prohibition of unreasonable searches and seizures to a 21st-century surveillance technique, the use of a Global Positioning System (GPS) device to monitor a vehicle's movements for an extended period of time. Ironically, the Court has chosen to decide this case based on 18th-century tort law. By attaching a small GPS device to the underside of the vehicle that respondent drove, the law enforcement officers in this case engaged in conduct that might have provided grounds in 1791 for a suit for trespass to chattels. And for this reason, the Court concludes, the installation and use of the GPS device constituted a search.

This holding, in my judgment, is unwise. It strains the language of the Fourth Amendment; it has little if any support in current Fourth Amendment case law; and it is highly artificial. I would analyze the question presented in this case by asking whether respondent's reasonable expectations of privacy were violated by the long-term monitoring of the movements of the vehicle he drove.

The Fourth Amendment prohibits "unreasonable searches and seizures," and the Court makes very little effort to explain how the attachment or use of the GPS device fits within these terms. The Court does not contend that there was a seizure. . . .

The Court does claim that the installation and use of the GPS constituted a search, but this conclusion is dependent on the questionable proposition that these two procedures cannot be separated for purposes of Fourth Amendment analysis. If these two procedures are analyzed separately, it is not at all clear from the Court's opinion why either should be regarded as a search. It is clear that the attachment of the GPS device was not itself a search; if the device had not functioned or if the officers had not used it, no information would have been obtained. And the Court does not contend that the use of the device constituted a search either. On the contrary, the Court accepts the holding in *United States v. Knotts*, 460 U.S. 276 (1983), that the use of a surreptitiously planted electronic device to monitor a vehicle's movements on public roads did not amount to a search.

The Court argues—and I agree—that "we must 'assur[e] preservation of that degree of privacy against government that existed when the Fourth Amendment was adopted.'" But it is almost impossible to think of late 18th-century situations that are analogous to what took place in this case. (Is it possible to imagine a case in which a constable secreted himself somewhere in a coach and remained there for a period of time in order to monitor the movements of the coach's owner?) The Court's theory seems to be that the concept of a search, as originally understood, comprehended any technical trespass that led to the gathering of evidence, but we know that this is incorrect. At common law, any unauthorized intrusion on private property was actionable, but a trespass on open fields, as opposed to the "curtilage" of a home, does not fall within the scope of the Fourth Amendment because private property outside the curtilage is not part of a "hous[e]" within the meaning of the Fourth Amendment.

The Court's reasoning in this case is very similar to that in the Court's early decisions involving wiretapping and electronic eavesdropping, namely, that a technical trespass followed by the gathering of evidence constitutes a search. In the early electronic surveillance cases, the Court concluded that a Fourth Amendment search occurred when private conversations were monitored as a result of an "unauthorized physical penetration into the premises occupied" by the defendant. *Silverman v. United States*, 365 U.S. 505 (1961). In *Silverman*, police officers listened to conversations in an attached home by inserting a "spike mike" through the wall that this house shared with the vacant house next door. This procedure was held to be a search because the mike made contact with a heating duct on the other side of the wall and thus "usurp[ed] . . . an integral part of the premises."

By contrast, in cases in which there was no trespass, it was held that there was no search. Thus, in *Olmstead v. United States* (1928), the Court found that the Fourth Amendment did not apply because "[t]he taps from house lines were made in the streets near the houses." Similarly, the Court concluded that no search occurred in *Goldman v. United States*, 316 U.S. 129 (1942), where a "detectaphone" was placed on the outer wall of defendant's office for the purpose of overhearing conversations held within the room.

This trespass-based rule was repeatedly criticized. In *Olmstead*, Justice BRANDEIS wrote that it was "immaterial where the physical connection with the telephone wires was made." Although a private conversation transmitted by wire did not fall within the literal words of the Fourth Amendment, he argued, the Amendment should be understood as prohibiting "every unjustifiable intrusion by the government upon the privacy of the individual."

Katz v. United States finally did away with the old approach, holding that a trespass was not required for a Fourth Amendment violation. *Katz* involved the use of a listening device that was attached to the outside of a public telephone booth and that allowed police officers to eavesdrop on one end of the target's phone conversation. This procedure did not physically intrude on the area occupied by the target, but the *Katz* Court "repudiate[ed]" the old doctrine and held that "[t]he fact that the electronic device employed . . . did not happen to penetrate the wall of the booth can have no constitutional significance." What mattered, the Court now held, was whether the conduct at issue "violated the privacy upon which [the defendant] justifiably relied while using the telephone booth." Under this approach, as the Court later put it when addressing the relevance of a technical trespass, "an actual trespass is neither necessary nor sufficient to establish a constitutional violation." *United States v. Karo*, 468 U.S. 705 (1984). . . .

In sum, the majority is hard pressed to find support in post-*Katz* cases for its trespass-based theory.

Disharmony with a substantial body of existing case law is only one of the problems with the Court's approach in this case.

I will briefly note four others. First, the Court's reasoning largely disregards what is really important (the use of a GPS for the purpose of long-term tracking) and instead attaches great significance to something that most would view as relatively minor (attaching to the bottom of a car a small, light object that does not interfere in any way with the car's operation). Attaching such an object is generally regarded as so trivial that it does not provide a basis for recovery under modern tort law. But under the Court's reasoning, this conduct may violate the Fourth Amendment. By contrast, if long-term monitoring can be accomplished without committing a technical trespass—suppose, for example, that the Federal Government required or persuaded auto manufacturers to include a GPS tracking device in every car—the Court's theory would provide no protection.

Second, the Court's approach leads to incongruous results. If the police attach a GPS device to a car and use the device to follow the car for even a brief time, under the Court's theory, the Fourth Amendment applies. But if the police follow the same car for a much longer period using unmarked cars and aerial assistance, this tracking is not subject to any Fourth Amendment constraints.

In the present case, the Fourth Amendment applies, the Court concludes, because the officers installed the GPS device after respondent's wife, to whom the car was registered, turned it over to respondent for his exclusive use. But if the GPS had been attached prior to that time, the Court's theory would lead to a different result. The Court proceeds on the assumption that respondent "had at least the property rights of a bailee," but a bailee may sue for a trespass to chattel only if the injury occurs during the term of the bailment. So if the GPS device had been installed before respondent's wife gave him the keys, respondent would have no claim for trespass—and, presumably, no Fourth Amendment claim either.

Third, under the Court's theory, the coverage of the Fourth Amendment may vary from State to State. If the events at issue here had occurred in a community property State or a State that has adopted the Uniform Marital Property Act, respondent would likely be an owner of the vehicle, and it would not matter whether the GPS was installed before or after his wife turned over the keys. In non-community-property States, on the other hand, the registration of the vehicle in the name of respondent's wife would generally be regarded as presumptive evidence that she was the sole owner.

Fourth, the Court's reliance on the law of trespass will present particularly vexing problems in cases involving surveillance that is carried out by making electronic, as opposed to physical, contact with the item to be tracked. For example, suppose that the officers in the present case had followed respondent by surreptitiously activating a stolen vehicle detection system that came with the car when it was purchased. Would the sending of a radio signal to activate this system constitute a trespass to chattels? Trespass to chattels has traditionally required a physical touching of the property. In recent years, courts have wrestled with the application of this old tort in cases involving unwanted electronic contact with computer systems, and some have held that even the transmission of electrons that occurs when a communication is sent from one computer to another is enough. But may such decisions be followed in applying the Court's trespass theory? Assuming that what matters under the Court's theory is the law of trespass as it existed at the time of the adoption of the Fourth Amendment, do these recent decisions represent a change in the law or simply the application of the old tort to new situations?

The *Katz* expectation-of-privacy test avoids the problems and complications noted above, but it is not without its own difficulties. It involves a degree of circularity, and judges are apt to confuse their own expectations of privacy with those of the hypothetical reasonable person to which the *Katz* test looks. In addition, the *Katz* test rests on the assumption that this hypothetical reasonable person has a well-developed and stable set of privacy expectations. But technology can change those expectations. Dramatic technological change may lead to periods in which popular expectations are in flux and may ultimately produce significant changes in popular attitudes. New technology may provide increased convenience or security at the expense of privacy, and many people may find the trade-off worthwhile. And even if the public does not welcome the diminution of privacy that new technology entails, they may eventually reconcile themselves to this development as inevitable. . . .

Recent years have seen the emergence of many new devices that permit the monitoring of a person's movements. In some locales, closed-circuit television video monitoring is becoming ubiquitous. On toll roads, automatic toll collection systems create a precise record of the movements of motorists who choose to make use of that convenience. Many motorists purchase cars that are equipped with devices that permit a central station to ascertain the car's location at any time so that roadside assistance may be provided if needed and the car may be found if it is stolen.

Perhaps most significant, cell phones and other wireless devices now permit wireless carriers to track and record the location of users—and as of June 2011, it has been reported, there were more than 322 million wireless devices in use in the United States. For older phones, the accuracy of the location information depends on the density of the tower network, but new "smart phones," which are equipped with a GPS device, permit more precise tracking. . . .

In the pre-computer age, the greatest protections of privacy were neither constitutional nor statutory, but practical. Traditional surveillance for any extended period of time was difficult and costly and therefore rarely undertaken. The surveillance at issue in this case—constant monitoring of the location of a vehicle for four weeks—would have required a large team of agents, multiple vehicles, and perhaps aerial assistance. Only an investigation of unusual importance could have justified such an expenditure of law enforcement resources. Devices like the one used in the present case, however, make long-term monitoring relatively easy and cheap. In circumstances involving dramatic technological change, the best solution to privacy concerns may be legislative. A legislative body is well situated to gauge changing public attitudes, to draw detailed lines, and to balance privacy and public safety in a comprehensive way.

To date, however, Congress and most States have not enacted statutes regulating the use of GPS tracking technology for law enforcement purposes. The best that we can do in this case is to apply existing Fourth Amendment doctrine and to ask whether the use of GPS tracking in a particular case involved a degree of intrusion that a reasonable person would not have anticipated.

Under this approach, relatively short-term monitoring of a person's movements on public streets accords with expectations of privacy that our society has recognized as reasonable. But the use of longer term GPS monitoring in investigations of most offenses impinges on expectations of privacy. For such offenses, society's expectation has been that law enforcement agents and others would not—and indeed, in the main, simply could not—secretly monitor and catalogue every single movement of an individual's car for a very long period. In this case, for four weeks, law enforcement agents tracked every movement that respondent made in the vehicle he was driving. We need not identify with precision the point at which the tracking of this vehicle became a search, for the line was surely crossed before the 4-week mark. Other cases may present more difficult questions. But where uncertainty exists with respect to whether a certain period of GPS surveillance is long enough to constitute a Fourth Amendment search, the police may always seek a warrant. We also need not consider whether prolonged GPS monitoring in the context of investigations involving extraordinary offenses would similarly intrude on a constitutionally protected sphere of privacy. In such cases, long-term tracking might have been mounted using previously available techniques.

For these reasons, I conclude that the lengthy monitoring that occurred in this case constituted a search under the Fourth Amendment. I therefore agree with the majority that the decision of the Court of Appeals must be affirmed.

☐ *Justice SOTOMAYOR, concurring.*

I join the Court's opinion because I agree that a search within the meaning of the Fourth Amendment occurs, at a minimum, "[w]here, as here, the Government obtains information by physically intruding on a constitutionally protected area." . . .

Of course, the Fourth Amendment is not concerned only with trespassory intrusions on property. Rather, even in the absence of a trespass, "a Fourth Amendment search occurs when the government violates a subjective expectation of privacy that society recognizes as reasonable." In *Katz*, this Court enlarged its then prevailing focus on property rights by announcing that the reach of the Fourth Amendment does not "turn upon the presence or absence of a physical intrusion." As the majority's opinion makes clear, however, *Katz*'s reasonable-expectation-of-privacy test augmented, but did not displace or diminish, the common-law trespassory test that preceded it. Thus, "when the Government *does* engage in physical intrusion of a constitutionally protected area in order to obtain information, that intrusion may constitute a violation of the Fourth Amendment." *United States v. Knotts*, 460 U.S. 276 (1983) (BRENNAN, J., concurring in judgment). Justice ALITO's approach, which discounts altogether the constitutional relevance of the Government's physical intrusion on Jones' Jeep, erodes that longstanding protection for privacy expectations inherent in items of property that people possess or control. By contrast, the trespassory test applied in the majority's opinion reflects an irreducible constitutional minimum: When the Government physically invades personal property to gather information, a search occurs. The reaffirmation of that principle suffices to decide this case.

Nonetheless, as Justice ALITO notes, physical intrusion is now unnecessary to many forms of surveillance. With increasing regularity, the Government will be capable of duplicating the monitoring undertaken in this case by enlisting factory- or owner-installed vehicle tracking devices or GPS-enabled smartphones. In cases of electronic or other novel modes of surveillance that do not depend upon a physical invasion on property, the majority opinion's trespassory test may provide little guidance. But "[s]ituations involving merely the transmission of electronic signals without trespass would *remain* subject to *Katz* analysis." As Justice ALITO incisively observes, the same technological advances that have made possible nontrespassory surveillance techniques will also affect the *Katz* test by shaping the evolution of societal privacy expectations. Under that rubric, I agree with Justice ALITO that, at the very least, "longer term GPS monitoring in investigations of most offenses impinges on expectations of privacy."

In cases involving even short-term monitoring, some unique attributes of GPS surveillance relevant to the *Katz* analysis will require particular attention. GPS monitoring generates a precise, comprehensive record of a person's public movements that reflects a wealth of detail about her familial, political, professional, religious, and sexual associations. The Government can store such records and efficiently mine them for information years into the future. And because GPS monitoring is cheap in comparison to conventional surveillance techniques and, by design, proceeds surreptitiously, it evades the ordinary checks that constrain abusive law enforcement practices: "limited police resources and community hostility." *Illinois v. Lidster,* 540 U.S. 419 (2004).

Awareness that the Government may be watching chills associational and expressive freedoms. And the Government's unrestrained power to assemble data that reveal private aspects of identity is susceptible to abuse. The net result is that GPS monitoring—by making available at a relatively low cost such a substantial quantum of intimate information about any person whom the Government, in its unfettered discretion, chooses to track— may "alter the relationship between citizen and government in a way that is inimical to democratic society."

I would take these attributes of GPS monitoring into account when considering the existence of a reasonable societal expectation of privacy in the sum of one's public movements. I would ask whether people reasonably expect that their movements will be recorded and aggregated in a manner that enables the Government to ascertain, more or less at will, their political and religious beliefs, sexual habits, and so on. I do not regard as dispositive the fact that the Government might obtain the fruits of GPS monitoring through lawful conventional surveillance techniques. I would also consider the appropriateness of entrusting to the Executive, in the absence of any oversight from a coordinate branch, a tool so amenable to misuse, especially in light of the Fourth Amendment's goal to curb arbitrary exercises of police power to and prevent "a too permeating police surveillance."

More fundamentally, it may be necessary to reconsider the premise that an individual has no reasonable expectation of privacy in information voluntarily disclosed to third parties. This approach is ill suited to the digital age, in which people reveal a great deal of information about themselves to third parties in the course of carrying out mundane tasks. People disclose the phone numbers that they dial or text to their cellular providers; the URLs that they visit and the e-mail addresses with which they correspond to their Internet service providers; and the books, groceries, and medications they purchase to online retailers. Perhaps, as Justice ALITO notes, some people may find the "trade-off" of privacy for convenience "worthwhile," or come to accept this "diminution of privacy" as "inevitable," and perhaps not. I for one doubt that people would accept without complaint the warrantless disclosure to the Government of a list of every Web site they had visited in the last week, or month, or year. But whatever the societal expectations, they can attain constitutionally protected status only if our Fourth Amendment jurisprudence ceases to treat secrecy as a prerequisite for privacy. I would not assume that all information voluntarily disclosed to some member of the public for a limited purpose is, for that reason alone, disentitled to Fourth Amendment protection.

Resolution of these difficult questions in this case is unnecessary, however, because the Government's physical intrusion on Jones' Jeep supplies a narrower basis for decision. I therefore join the majority's opinion.

Carpenter v. United States

138 S. CT. 2206 (2018)

Police arrested four men suspected of robbing a series of Radio Shack and T-Mobile stores in Detroit. One of the men confessed that during the past four months they had robbed nine different stores in Michigan and Ohio. He identified accomplices and gave the FBI some of their cell phone numbers. The FBI then reviewed his call records to identify additional numbers that he had called around the time of the robberies. Based on that information, the prosecutors applied for court orders under the Stored Communications Act to obtain cell phone records for Timothy Carpenter. That statute, as amended in 1994, permits the government to compel the disclosure of certain telecommunications records when it "offers specific and articulable facts showing that there are reasonable grounds to believe" that the records sought "are relevant and material to an ongoing criminal investigation." Federal judges issued two orders directing Carpenter's wireless carriers—MetroPCS and Sprint—to disclose cell-site location information (CSLI) for his phone's incoming and outgoing calls during the four-month period when the robberies occurred. The first order sought 152 days of cell-site records from MetroPCS, which produced records spanning 127 days. The second order for CSLI from Sprint produced two days of records covering the period when Carpenter's phone was "roaming" in northeastern Ohio. Altogether the government obtained 12,898 location points cataloging Carpenter's movements—an average of 101 data points per day.

Carpenter was charged with robbery and an additional six counts of carrying a firearm during a federal crime. At a pretrial hearing, Carpenter's attorney moved to suppress the cell-site data, arguing that the seizure of the records violated the Fourth Amendment because they were obtained without a warrant supported by probable cause. A district court denied the motion. At trial, an FBI agent testified about the cell-site data, explaining that each time a cell phone taps into the wireless network, the carrier logs a time-stamped record of the cell site. Based on that information, the agent produced maps placing Carpenter's phone near four of the robberies. The prosecutors argued the location records demonstrated that Carpenter was "right where the . . . robbery was at the exact time of the robbery." Carpenter was convicted and sentenced to more than 100 years in prison. The Court of Appeals for the Sixth Circuit affirmed, holding that Carpenter lacked a reasonable expectation of privacy in the CSLI collected by the FBI because he had shared that information with his (third-party) wireless carriers.

Since cell phone users voluntarily convey cell-site data to their carriers as "a means of establishing communication," the court concluded that the resulting business records are not entitled to Fourth Amendment protection. Carpenter appealed to the Supreme Court, which granted *certiorari*.

The appellate court's decision was reversed by a 5–4 vote. Chief Justice Roberts delivered the opinion for the Court. Justices Kennedy, Thomas, Alito, and Gorsuch each filed dissenting opinions.

■ ■ ■

☐ *Chief Justice ROBERTS delivered the opinion of the Court.*

This case presents the question whether the Government conducts a search under the Fourth Amendment when it accesses historical cell phone records that provide a comprehensive chronicle of the user's past movements.

There are 396 million cell phone service accounts in the United States—for a Nation of 326 million people. Cell phones perform their wide and growing variety of functions by connecting to a set of radio antennas called "cell sites." . . . Cell phones continuously scan their environment looking for the best signal, which generally comes from the closest cell site. Most modern devices, such as smartphones, tap into the wireless network several times a minute whenever their signal is on, even if the owner is not using one of the phone's features. Each time the phone connects to a cell site, it generates a time-stamped record known as cell-site location information (CSLI).

Wireless carriers collect and store CSLI for their own business purposes, including finding weak spots in their network and applying "roaming" charges when another carrier routes data through their cell sites. In addition, wireless carriers often sell aggregated location records to data brokers, without individual identifying information of the sort at issue here. While carriers have long retained CSLI for the start and end of incoming calls, in recent years phone companies have also collected location information from the transmission of text messages and routine data connections. Accordingly, modern cell phones generate increasingly vast amounts of increasingly precise CSLI. . . .

The Founding generation crafted the Fourth Amendment as a "response to the reviled 'general warrants' and 'writs of assistance' of the colonial era, which allowed British officers to rummage through homes in an unrestrained search for evidence of criminal activity."

For much of our history, Fourth Amendment search doctrine was "tied to common-law trespass" and focused on whether the Government "obtains information by physically intruding on a constitutionally protected area." *United States* v. *Jones*, 565 U. S. 400 (2012). More recently, the Court has recognized that "property rights are not the sole measure of Fourth Amendment violations." In *Katz* v. *United States*, 389 U. S. 347 (1967), we established that "the Fourth Amendment protects people, not places," and expanded our conception of the Amendment to protect certain expectations of privacy as well. When an individual "seeks to preserve something as private," and his expectation of privacy is "one that society is prepared to recognize as reasonable," we have held that official intrusion into that private sphere generally qualifies as a search and requires a warrant supported by probable cause. *Smith* [*v. Maryland,* 442 U.S. 735 (1979)].

Although no single rubric definitively resolves which expectations of privacy are entitled to protection, the analysis is informed by historical understandings "of what was deemed an unreasonable search and seizure when [the Fourth Amendment] was adopted." *Carroll* v. *United States,* 267 U. S. 132 (1925). On this score, our cases have recognized some basic guideposts. First, that the Amendment seeks to secure "the privacies of life" against "arbitrary power." *Boyd* v. *United States,* 116 U. S. 616 (1886). Second, and relatedly, that a central aim of the Framers was "to place obstacles in the way of a too permeating police surveillance."

We have kept this attention to Founding-era understandings in mind when applying the Fourth Amendment to innovations in surveillance tools. As technology has enhanced the Government's capacity to encroach upon areas normally guarded from inquisitive eyes, this Court has sought to "assure[ ] preservation of that degree of privacy against government that existed when the Fourth Amendment was adopted." *Kyllo* v. *United States,* 533 U. S. 27 (2001). For that reason, we rejected in *Kyllo* a "mechanical interpretation" of the Fourth Amendment and held that use of a thermal imager to detect heat radiating from the side of the defendant's home was a search. Because any other conclusion would leave homeowners "at the mercy of advancing technology," we determined that the Government—absent a warrant—could not capitalize on such new sense-enhancing technology to explore what was happening within the home. . . .

The case before us involves the Government's acquisition of wireless carrier cell-site records revealing the location of Carpenter's cell phone whenever it made or received calls. This sort of digital data—personal location information maintained by a third party—does not fit neatly under existing precedents. Instead, requests for cell-site records lie at the intersection of two lines of cases, both of which inform our understanding of the privacy interests at stake.

The first set of cases addresses a person's expectation of privacy in his physical location and movements. In *United States* v. *Knotts,* 460 U. S. 276 (1983), we considered the Government's use of a "beeper" to aid in tracking a vehicle through traffic. Police officers in that case planted a beeper in a container of chloroform before it was purchased by one of Knotts's co-conspirators. The officers (with intermittent aerial assistance) then followed the automobile carrying the container from Minneapolis to Knotts's cabin in Wisconsin, relying on the beeper's signal to help keep the vehicle in view. The Court concluded that the "augment[ed]" visual surveillance did not constitute a search because "[a] person traveling in an automobile on public thoroughfares has no reasonable expectation of privacy in his movements from one place to another." Since the movements of the vehicle and its final destination had been "voluntarily conveyed to anyone who wanted to look," Knotts could not assert a privacy interest in the information obtained.

This Court in *Knotts,* however, was careful to distinguish between the rudimentary tracking facilitated by the beeper and more sweeping modes of surveillance. The Court emphasized the "limited use which the government made of the signals from this particular beeper" during a discrete "automotive journey." Significantly, the Court reserved the question whether "different constitutional principles may be applicable" if "twenty-four hour surveillance of any citizen of this country [were] possible."

Three decades later, the Court considered more sophisticated surveillance of the sort envisioned in *Knotts* and found that different principles did indeed apply. In *United States* v. *Jones*, FBI agents installed a GPS tracking device on Jones's vehicle and remotely monitored the vehicle's movements for 28 days. The Court decided the case based on the Government's physical trespass of the vehicle. At the same time, five Justices [with Justices ALITO and SOTOMAYOR concurring] agreed that related privacy concerns would be raised by, for example, "surreptitiously activating a stolen vehicle detection system" in Jones's car to track Jones himself, or conducting GPS tracking of his cell phone. Since GPS monitoring of a vehicle tracks "every movement" a person makes in that vehicle, the concurring Justices concluded that "longer term GPS monitoring in investigations of most offenses impinges on expectations of privacy"—regardless whether those movements were disclosed to the public at large.

In a second set of decisions, the Court has drawn a line between what a person keeps to himself and what he shares with others. We have previously held that "a person has no legitimate expectation of privacy in information he voluntarily turns over to third parties." *Smith*. That remains true "even if the information is revealed on the assumption that it will be used only for a limited purpose." *United States* v. *Miller*, 425 U. S. 435 (1976). As a result, the Government is typically free to obtain such information from the recipient without triggering Fourth Amendment protections.

This third-party doctrine largely traces its roots to *Miller*. While investigating Miller for tax evasion, the Government subpoenaed his banks, seeking several months of canceled checks, deposit slips, and monthly statements. The Court rejected a Fourth Amendment challenge to the records collection. For one, Miller could "assert neither ownership nor possession" of the documents; they were "business records of the banks." For another, the nature of those records confirmed Miller's limited expectation of privacy, because the checks were "not confidential communications but negotiable instruments to be used in commercial transactions," and the bank statements contained information "exposed to [bank] employees in the ordinary course of business." The Court thus concluded that *Miller* had "take[n] the risk, in revealing his affairs to another, that the information [would] be conveyed by that person to the Government."

Three years later, *Smith* applied the same principles in the context of information conveyed to a telephone company. The Court ruled that the Government's use of a pen register—a device that recorded the outgoing phone numbers dialed on a landline telephone—was not a search. . . .

The question we confront today is how to apply the Fourth Amendment to a new phenomenon: the ability to chronicle a person's past movements through the record of his cell phone signals. Such tracking partakes of many of the qualities of the GPS monitoring we considered in *Jones*. Much like GPS tracking of a vehicle, cell phone location information is detailed, encyclopedic, and effortlessly compiled.

At the same time, the fact that the individual continuously reveals his location to his wireless carrier implicates the third-party principle of *Smith* and *Miller.* But while the third-party doctrine applies to telephone numbers and bank records, it is not clear whether its logic extends to the qualitatively different category of cell-site records. After all, when *Smith* was decided in 1979, few could have imagined a society in which a phone goes wherever its owner goes, conveying to the wireless carrier not just dialed digits, but a detailed and comprehensive record of the person's movements.

We decline to extend *Smith* and *Miller* to cover these novel circumstances. Given the unique nature of cell phone location records, the fact that the information is held by a third party does not by itself overcome the user's claim to Fourth Amendment protection. Whether the Government employs its own surveillance technology as in *Jones* or leverages the technology of a wireless carrier, we hold that an individual maintains a legitimate expectation of privacy in the record of his physical movements as captured through CSLI. The location information obtained from Carpenter's wireless carriers was the product of a search.

A person does not surrender all Fourth Amendment protection by venturing into the public sphere. To the contrary, "what [one] seeks to preserve as private, even in an area accessible to the public, may be constitutionally protected." *Katz.* A majority of this Court has already recognized that individuals have a reasonable expectation of privacy in the whole of their physical movements. *Jones.* Prior to the digital age, law enforcement might have pursued a suspect for a brief stretch, but doing so "for any extended period of time was difficult and costly and therefore rarely undertaken." For that reason, "society's expectation has been that law enforcement agents and others would not—and indeed, in the main, simply could not—secretly monitor and catalogue every single movement of an individual's car for a very long period."

Allowing government access to cell-site records contravenes that expectation. Although such records are generated for commercial purposes, that distinction does not negate Carpenter's anticipation of privacy in his physical location. Mapping a cell phone's location over the course of 127 days provides an all-encompassing record of the holder's whereabouts. As with GPS information, the time-stamped data provides an intimate window into a person's life, revealing not only his particular movements, but through them his "familial, political, professional, religious, and sexual associations." These location records "hold for many Americans the 'privacies of life.'" . . .

In fact, historical cell-site records present even greater privacy concerns than the GPS monitoring of a vehicle we considered in *Jones.* Unlike the bugged container in *Knotts* or the car in *Jones,* a cell phone—almost a "feature of human anatomy"—tracks nearly exactly the movements of its owner. While individuals regularly leave their vehicles, they compulsively carry cell phones with them all the time. A cell phone faithfully follows its owner beyond public thoroughfares and into private residences, doctor's offices, political headquarters, and other potentially revealing locales.

Moreover, the retrospective quality of the data here gives police access to a category of information otherwise unknowable. In the past, attempts to reconstruct a person's movements were limited by a dearth of records and the frailties of recollection. With access to CSLI, the Government can now travel back in time to retrace a person's whereabouts, subject only to the retention polices of the wireless carriers, which currently maintain records for up to five years. . . .

Accordingly, when the Government accessed CSLI from the wireless carriers, it invaded Carpenter's reasonable expectation of privacy in the whole of his physical movements.

The Government's primary contention to the contrary is that the third-party doctrine governs this case. In its view, cell-site records are fair game because they are "business records" created and maintained by the wireless carriers. The Government (along with Justice KENNEDY) recognizes that this case features new technology, but asserts that the legal question nonetheless turns on a garden-variety request for information from a third-party witness.

The Government's position fails to contend with the seismic shifts in digital technology that made possible the tracking of not only Carpenter's location but also everyone else's, not for a short period but for years and years. Sprint Corporation and its competitors are not your typical witnesses. Unlike the nosy neighbor who keeps an eye on comings and goings, they are ever alert, and their memory is nearly infallible. There is a world of difference between the limited types of personal information addressed in *Smith* and *Miller* and the exhaustive chronicle of location information casually collected by wireless carriers today. The Government thus is not asking for a straightforward application of the third-party doctrine, but instead a significant extension of it to a distinct category of information. . . .

We therefore decline to extend *Smith* and *Miller* to the collection of CSLI. Given the unique nature of cell phone location information, the fact that the Government obtained the information from a third party does not overcome Carpenter's claim to Fourth Amendment protection. The Government's acquisition of the cell-site records was a search within the meaning of the Fourth Amendment.

Our decision today is a narrow one. We do not express a view on matters not before us: real-time CSLI or "tower dumps" (a download of information on all the devices that connected to a particular cell site during a particular interval). We do not disturb the application of *Smith* and *Miller* or call into question conventional surveillance techniques and tools, such as security cameras. Nor do we address other business records that might incidentally reveal location information. Further, our opinion does not consider other collection techniques involving foreign affairs or national security.

Having found that the acquisition of Carpenter's CSLI was a search, we also conclude that the Government must generally obtain a warrant supported by probable cause before acquiring such records. Although the "ultimate measure of the constitutionality of a governmental search is 'reasonableness,'" our cases establish that warrantless searches are typically unreasonable where "a search is undertaken by law enforcement officials to discover evidence of criminal wrongdoing." *Vernonia School Dist. 47J v. Acton*, 515 U. S. 646 (1995). Thus, "[i]n the absence of a warrant, a search is reasonable only if it falls within a specific exception to the warrant requirement."

The Government acquired the cell-site records pursuant to a court order issued under the Stored Communications Act, which required the Government to show "reasonable grounds" for believing that the records were "relevant and material to an ongoing investigation." That showing falls well short of the probable cause required for a warrant. The Court usually requires "some quantum of individualized suspicion" before a search or seizure may take place. Under the standard in the Stored Communications Act, however, law enforcement need only show that the cell-site evidence might be pertinent to an ongoing investigation—a "gigantic" departure from the probable cause rule, as the Government explained below. Consequently, an order issued under Section 2703(d) of the Act is not a permissible mechanism for accessing historical cell-site records. Before compelling a wireless carrier to turn over a subscriber's CSLI, the Government's obligation is a familiar one—get a warrant. . . .

This is certainly not to say that all orders compelling the production of documents will require a showing of probable cause. The Government will be able to use subpoenas to acquire records in the overwhelming majority of investigations. We hold only that a warrant is required in the rare case where the suspect has a legitimate privacy interest in records held by a third party. . . .

☐ *Justice KENNEDY, with whom Justice THOMAS and Justice ALITO join, dissenting.*

The new rule the Court seems to formulate puts needed, reasonable, accepted, lawful, and congressionally authorized criminal investigations at serious risk in serious cases, often when law enforcement seeks to prevent the threat of violent crimes. And it places undue restrictions on the lawful and necessary enforcement powers exercised not only by the Federal Government, but also by law enforcement in every State and locality throughout the Nation. . . .

Here the only question necessary to decide is whether the Government searched anything of Carpenter's when it used compulsory process to obtain cell-site records from Carpenter's cell phone service providers. This Court's decisions in *Miller* and *Smith* dictate that the answer is no, as every Court of Appeals to have considered the question has recognized.

Miller and *Smith* hold that individuals lack any protected Fourth Amendment interests in records that are possessed, owned, and controlled only by a third party. . . . The principle established in *Miller* and *Smith* is correct for two reasons, the first relating to a defendant's attenuated interest in property owned by another, and the second relating to the safeguards inherent in the use of compulsory process.

First, *Miller* and *Smith* placed necessary limits on the ability of individuals to assert Fourth Amendment interests in property to which they lack a "requisite connection." *Minnesota v. Carter*, 525 U. S. 83 (1998) (KENNEDY, J., concurring). Fourth Amendment rights, after all, are personal. The Amendment protects "[t]he right of the people to be secure in *their* . . . persons, houses, papers, and effects"—not the persons, houses, papers, and effects of others.

The concept of reasonable expectations of privacy, first announced in *Katz v. United States*, 389 U. S. 347 (1967), sought to look beyond the "arcane distinctions developed in property and tort law" in evaluating whether a person has a sufficient connection to the thing or place searched to assert Fourth Amendment interests in it. Yet "property concepts" are, nonetheless, fundamental "in determining the presence or absence of the privacy interests protected by that Amendment." This is so for at least two reasons. First, as a matter of settled expectations from the law of property, individuals often have greater expectations of privacy in things and places that belong to them, not to others. And second, the Fourth Amendment's protections must remain tethered to the text of that Amendment, which, again, protects only a person's own "persons, houses, papers, and effects." . . .

Miller and *Smith* set forth an important and necessary limitation on the *Katz* framework. They rest upon the commonsense principle that the absence of property law analogues can be dispositive of privacy expectations. The defendants in those cases could expect that the third-party businesses could use the records the companies collected, stored, and classified as their own for any number of business and commercial purposes. The businesses were not bailees or custodians of the records, with a duty to hold the records for the defendants' use. The defendants could make no argument that the records were their own papers or effects. The records were the business entities' records, plain and simple. The defendants had no reason to believe the records were owned or controlled by them and so could not assert a reasonable expectation of privacy in the records.

The second principle supporting *Miller* and *Smith* is the longstanding rule that the Government may use compulsory process to compel persons to disclose documents and other evidence within their possession and control. A subpoena is different from a warrant in its force and intrusive power. While a warrant allows the Government to enter and seize and make the examination itself, a subpoena simply requires the person to whom it is directed to make the disclosure. A subpoena, moreover, provides the recipient the "opportunity to present objections" before complying, which further mitigates the intrusion.

For those reasons this Court has held that a subpoena for records, although a "constructive" search subject to Fourth Amendment constraints, need not comply with the procedures applicable to warrants—even when challenged by the person to whom the records belong. . . . Persons with no meaningful interests in the records sought by a subpoena, like the defendants in *Miller* and *Smith*, have no rights to object to the records' disclosure—much less to assert that the Government must obtain a warrant to compel disclosure of the records.

Based on *Miller* and *Smith* and the principles underlying those cases, it is well established that subpoenas may be used to obtain a wide variety of records held by businesses, even when the records contain private information. Credit cards are a prime example. . . .

In my respectful view the majority opinion misreads this Court's precedents, old and recent, and transforms *Miller* and *Smith* into an unprincipled and unworkable doctrine. The Court's newly conceived constitutional standard will cause confusion; will undermine traditional and important law enforcement practices; and will allow the cell phone to become a protected medium that dangerous persons will use to commit serious crimes. . . .

☐ *Justice THOMAS, dissenting.*

This case should not turn on "whether" a search occurred. It should turn, instead, on *whose* property was searched. The Fourth Amendment guarantees individuals the right to be secure from unreasonable searches of "*their* persons, houses, papers, and effects." In other words, "*each* person has the right to be secure against unreasonable searches . . . in *his own* person, house, papers, and effects." *Minnesota* v. *Carter*, 525 U. S. 83 (1998) (SCALIA, J., concurring). By obtaining the cell-site records of MetroPCS and Sprint, the Government did not search Carpenter's property. He did not create the records, he does not maintain them, he cannot control them, and he cannot destroy them. Neither the terms of his contracts nor any provision of law makes the records his. The records belong to MetroPCS and Sprint. . . .

The more fundamental problem with the Court's opinion, however, is its use of the "reasonable expectation of privacy" test, which was first articulated by Justice Harlan in *Katz* v. *United States*. The *Katz* test has no basis in the text or history of the Fourth Amendment. And, it invites courts to make judgments about policy, not law. Until we confront the problems with this test, *Katz* will continue to distort Fourth Amendment jurisprudence. I respectfully dissent. . . .

☐ *Justice ALITO, with whom Justice THOMAS joins, dissenting.*

The Court's reasoning fractures two fundamental pillars of Fourth Amendment law, and in doing so, it guarantees a blizzard of litigation while threatening many legitimate and valuable investigative practices upon which law enforcement has rightfully come to rely.

First, the Court ignores the basic distinction between an actual search (dispatching law enforcement officers to enter private premises and root through private papers and effects) and an order merely requiring a party to look through its own records and produce specified documents. The former, which intrudes on personal privacy far more deeply, requires probable cause; the latter does not. Treating an order to produce like an actual search, as today's decision does, is revolutionary. It violates both the original understanding of the Fourth Amendment and more than a century of Supreme Court precedent. . . .

Second, the Court allows a defendant to object to the search of a third party's property. This also is revolutionary. The Fourth Amendment protects "[t]he right of the people to be secure in *their* persons, houses, papers, and effects," not the persons, houses, papers, and effects of others.

By departing dramatically from these fundamental principles, the Court destabilizes long-established Fourth Amendment doctrine. We will be making repairs—or picking up the pieces—for a long time to come.

Today the majority holds that a court order requiring the production of cell-site records may be issued only after the Government demonstrates probable cause. That is a serious and consequential mistake. The Court's holding is based on the premise that the order issued in this case was an actual "search" within the meaning of the Fourth Amendment, but that premise is inconsistent with the original meaning of the Fourth Amendment and with more than a century of precedent.

The order in this case was the functional equivalent of a subpoena for documents, and there is no evidence that these writs were regarded as "searches" at the time of the founding. Subpoenas *duces tecum* and other forms of compulsory document production were well known to the founding generation. . . .

The Fourth Amendment does not regulate all methods by which the Government obtains documents. Rather, it prohibits only those "searches and seizures" of "persons, houses, papers, and effects" that are "unreasonable." Consistent with that language, "at least until the latter half of the 20th century" "our Fourth Amendment jurisprudence was tied to common-law trespass." *United States* v. *Jones* (2012). So by its terms, the Fourth Amendment does not apply to the compulsory production of documents, a practice that involves neither any physical intrusion into private space nor any taking of property by agents of the state.

Compliance with a subpoena *duces tecum* requires none of that. A subpoena *duces tecum* permits a subpoenaed individual to conduct the search for the relevant documents himself, without law enforcement officers entering his home or rooting through his papers and effects. As a result, subpoenas avoid the many incidental invasions of privacy that necessarily accompany any actual search. And it was *those* invasions of privacy—which, although incidental, could often be extremely intrusive and damaging—that led to the adoption of the Fourth Amendment. . . .

As a matter of original understanding, the Fourth Amendment does not regulate the compelled production of documents at all. Here the Government received the relevant cell-site records pursuant to a court order compelling Carpenter's cell service provider to turn them over. That process is thus immune from challenge under the original understanding of the Fourth Amendment. . . .

Compounding its initial error, the Court also holds that a defendant has the right under the Fourth Amendment to object to the search of a third party's property. This holding flouts the clear text of the Fourth Amendment, and it cannot be defended under either a property-based interpretation of that Amendment or our decisions applying the reasonable-expectations-of-privacy test adopted in *Katz*. By allowing Carpenter to object to the search of a third party's property, the Court threatens to revolutionize a second and independent line of Fourth Amendment doctrine. . . .

The desire to make a statement about privacy in the digital age does not justify the consequences that today's decision is likely to produce.

☐ *Justice GORSUCH, dissenting.*

In the late 1960s this Court suggested for the first time that a search triggering the Fourth Amendment occurs when the government violates an "expectation of privacy" that "society is prepared to recognize as 'reasonable.'" *Katz* v. *United States.* Then, in a pair of decisions in the 1970s applying the *Katz* test, the Court held that a "reasonable expectation of privacy" *doesn't* attach to information shared with "third parties." See *Smith* v. *Maryland (1979); United States* v. *Miller* (1976). By these steps, the Court came to conclude, the Constitution does nothing to limit investigators from searching records you've entrusted to your bank, accountant, and maybe even your doctor.

What's left of the Fourth Amendment? Today we use the Internet to do most everything. Smartphones make it easy to keep a calendar, correspond with friends, make calls, conduct banking, and even watch the game.

Countless Internet companies maintain records about us and, increasingly, *for* us. Even our most private documents—those that, in other eras, we would have locked safely in a desk drawer or destroyed—now reside on third party servers. *Smith* and *Miller* teach that the police can review all of this material, on the theory that no one reasonably expects any of it will be kept private. But no one believes that, if they ever did.

What to do? It seems to me we could respond in at least three ways. The first is to ignore the problem, maintain *Smith* and *Miller,* and live with the consequences. If the confluence of these decisions and modern technology means our Fourth Amendment rights are reduced to nearly nothing, so be it. The second choice is to set *Smith* and *Miller* aside and try again using the *Katz* "reasonable expectation of privacy" jurisprudence that produced them. The third is to look for answers elsewhere. . . .

What if we dropped *Smith* and *Miller's* third party doctrine and retreated to the root *Katz* question whether there is a "reasonable expectation of privacy" in data held by third parties? Rather than solve the problem with the third party doctrine, I worry this option only risks returning us to its source: After all, it was *Katz* that produced *Smith* and *Miller* in the first place.

Katz's problems start with the text and original understanding of the Fourth Amendment, as Justice THOMAS thoughtfully explains today. (dissenting opinion). The Amendment's protections do not depend on the breach of some abstract "expectation of privacy" whose contours are left to the judicial imagination. Much more concretely, it protects your "person," and your "houses, papers, and effects." Nor does your right to bring a Fourth Amendment claim depend on whether a judge happens to agree that your subjective expectation to privacy is a "reasonable" one. Under its plain terms, the Amendment grants you the right to invoke its guarantees whenever one of your protected things (your person, your house, your papers, or your effects) is unreasonably searched or seized. Period. . . .

Even taken on its own terms, *Katz* has never been sufficiently justified. In fact, we still don't even know what its "reasonable expectation of privacy" test *is.* Is it supposed to pose an empirical question (what privacy expectations do people *actually* have) or a normative one (what expectations *should* they have)? Either way brings problems. If the test is supposed to be an empirical one, it's unclear why judges rather than legislators should conduct it. Legislators are responsive to their constituents and have institutional resources designed to help them discern and enact majoritarian preferences. Politically insulated judges come armed with only the attorneys' briefs, a few law clerks, and their own idiosyncratic experiences. They are hardly the representative group you'd expect (or want) to be making empirical judgments for hundreds of millions of people. Unsurprisingly, too, judicial judgments often fail to reflect public views.

Maybe, then, the *Katz* test should be conceived as a normative question. But if that's the case, why (again) do judges, rather than legislators, get to determine whether society *should be* prepared to recognize an expectation of privacy as legitimate? . . . Answering questions like that calls for the exercise of raw political will belonging to legislatures, not the legal judgment proper to courts. When judges abandon legal judgment for political will we not only risk decisions where "reasonable expectations of privacy" come to bear "an uncanny resemblance to those expectations of privacy" shared by Members of this Court. . . .

Katz has yielded an often unpredictable—and sometimes unbelievable—jurisprudence. *Smith* and *Miller* are only two examples; there are many others. Take *Florida* v. *Riley*, 488 U. S. 445 (1989), which says that a police helicopter hovering 400 feet above a person's property invades no reasonable expectation of privacy. Try that one out on your neighbors. Or *California* v. *Greenwood*, 486 U. S. 35 (1988), which holds that a person has no reasonable expectation of privacy in the garbage he puts out for collection. In that case, the Court said that the homeowners forfeited their privacy interests because "[i]t is common knowledge that plastic garbage bags left on or at the side of a public street are readily accessible to animals, children, scavengers, snoops, and other members of the public." But the habits of raccoons don't prove much about the habits of the country. . . .

Resorting to *Katz* in data privacy cases threatens more of the same. . . . Nor is this the end of it. After finding a reasonable expectation of privacy, the Court says there's still more work to do. Courts must determine whether to "extend" *Smith* and *Miller* to the circumstances before them. So apparently *Smith* and *Miller* aren't quite left for dead; they just no longer have the clear reach they once did. How do we measure their new reach? The Court says courts now must conduct a *second Katz*-like balancing inquiry, asking whether the fact of disclosure to a third party outweighs privacy interests in the "category of information" so disclosed. But how are lower courts supposed to weigh these radically different interests? Or assign values to different categories of information? All we know is that historical cell-site location information (for seven days, anyway) escapes *Smith* and *Miller*'s shorn grasp, while a lifetime of bank or phone records does not. As to any other kind of information, lower courts will have to stay tuned. . . .

There is another way. . . . It was tied to the law. The Fourth Amendment protects "the right of the people to be secure in their persons, houses, papers and effects, against unreasonable searches and seizures." True to those words and their original understanding, the traditional approach asked if a house, paper or effect was *yours* under law. No more was needed to trigger the Fourth Amendment. Though now often lost in *Katz*'s shadow, this traditional understanding persists. *Katz* only "supplements, rather than displaces the traditional property-based understanding of the Fourth Amendment."

What does all this mean for the case before us? . . . I do not agree with the Court's decision today to keep *Smith* and *Miller* on life support and supplement them with a new and multilayered inquiry that seems to be only *Katz*-squared. Returning there, I worry, promises more trouble than help. Instead, I would look to a more traditional Fourth Amendment approach. Even if *Katz* may still supply one way to prove a Fourth Amendment interest, it has never been the only way. Neglecting more traditional approaches may mean failing to vindicate the full protections of the Fourth Amendment. . . .

■ THE DEVELOPMENT OF LAW

The USA PATRIOT Act, Wiretaps, and the Foreign Intelligence Surveillance Court

Enacted in response to the terrorist attacks of September 11, 2001, the USA PATRIOT Act authorized sweeping changes in law enforcement, notably lowering the standards for searching and seizing individuals suspected of terrorism, for example, as well as expanding investigatory powers. Among the changes, the law authorized:

- Roving wiretaps—wiretaps on any telephone used by a person suspected of terrorism—and the use of key-logger devices, which register every stroke made on a computer, and Internet wiretaps.
- Police searches of private property without prior notification of the owners and without a search warrant.
- A lower standard for judicial approval of wiretaps for individuals suspected of terrorist activities.
- The attorney general to designate domestic groups as terrorist organizations and to block the entry into the country of foreigners aligned with them.
- The Central Intelligence Agency to investigate Americans suspected of having connections to terrorism.
- The Department of Treasury to monitor financial transactions— bank accounts, mutual funds, and brokerage deals—and to obtain medical and other electronic records on individuals.
- The detention and deportation of foreigners suspected of having connections to terrorist organizations.

At the time one of the most controversial provisions of the USA PATRIOT Act removed restrictions on information sharing and foreign intelligence gathering. Section 203 requires the attorney general to disclose to the director of the Central Intelligence Agency (CIA) "foreign intelligence" obtained from a federal criminal investigation, including wiretaps and grand jury hearings. The CIA may also share information with domestic law enforcement agencies.

Critics charged that the broad language of the act's disclosure requirements permits the Department of Justice (DoJ) to give the CIA all information related to a foreigner or to a citizen's contacts with a foreign government or organization, not merely pertaining to international terrorism. Moreover, the act did not establish any standards or safeguards for restricting the disclosure of "foreign intelligence information." Critics therefore contended that the intelligence community may collect information about individuals who have committed no crimes but who are involved in lawful protests of American foreign policies.

Furthermore, the USA PATRIOT Act changed the Foreign Intelligence Surveillance Act (FISA) of 1978, which created a special FISA court, staffed by sitting federal judges on special assignments, to approve wiretaps and to ensure that "the sole purpose" of domestic intelligence gathering was to obtain foreign intelligence information. That law was enacted because of abuses in domestic surveillance of anti-Vietnam War protesters and leaders of the civil rights movement in the 1960s and 1970s. Section 218 of the USA PATRIOT Act, however, changed the law so the DoJ need only show that the collection of foreign intelligence information has "a significant purpose," instead of being "the sole purpose" of an investigation.

Based on those provisions in 2002, Attorney General John Ashcroft issued new guidelines allowing federal prosecutors to consult with law enforcement agents conducting foreign intelligence surveillance. Those guidelines were in turn challenged as a violation of the Fourth Amendment and for permitting the use of special FISA wiretaps for investigating and prosecuting ordinary criminals, and not just spies and terrorists. In May 2002, the FISA Court unanimously rejected the new guidelines and for the first time in the history of the court released a published opinion, *In re All Matters Submitted to the Foreign Intelligence Surveillance Court*, No. Multiple 02-429 F.Supp. 2d C (U.S. Foreign Intel. Surv. Ct., 17 May 2002). Emphasizing the special and intrusive nature of FISA surveillance, the seven judges on the court maintained that the "walls" prohibiting criminal prosecutors from conducting investigations of suspected foreign spies and terrorists should not be torn down and that the DoJ's new guidelines were not "reasonably designed."

However, the DoJ successfully appealed that decision to a special three-judge court of appeals, as authorized by the FISA and whose judges are assigned from other federal appellate courts by the chief justice of the Supreme Court. Subsequently, the FISA Appellate Court upheld the DoJ's new guidelines, in *In re: Sealed Case* (U.S. Foreign Intelligence Surveillance Court of Review No. 02-001 and 02-002). In doing so, the appellate court stressed that the USA PATRIOT Act aimed to eliminate "walls" between foreign intelligence and domestic law enforcement agencies. As a result, federal criminal prosecutors may use information against citizens obtained from wiretaps authorized by the FISA Court, based on less than probable cause and on more searching surveillance than permitted under traditional wiretaps.

The principal provisions of the USA PATRIOT Act were renewed in 2006, and again in 2010 and 2011. Yet another controversy erupted over the revelation that President George W. Bush issued a secret executive

(continues)

■ THE DEVELOPMENT OF LAW
The USA PATRIOT Act, Wiretaps, and the
Foreign Intelligence Surveillance Court (continued)

order authorizing the National Security Agency (NSA) to conduct war-rantless electronic surveillance of "communications where one . . . party to the communication is outside of the United States" and there is "a reasonable basis to conclude that one party" is a member of or supporting Al Qaeda or other terrorists. The surveillance involves monitoring e-mails, through Google-like searches, and tracking cell phone calls and other Internet and satellite communications. Foreign intelligence surveillance was supposed to be governed by the FISA, but the Bush administration defended the NSA's warrantless surveillance on three grounds. First, the president has the inherent power and power as commander in chief to do so during times of war. Prior presidents made similar claims. President Abraham Lincoln ordered the warrantless wiretapping of telegraph wires during the Civil War. Likewise, during World Wars I and II Presidents Woodrow Wilson and Franklin D. Roosevelt ordered the interception of international communications. Similar claims to presidential power were made by subsequent administrations, including those of Presidents Jimmy Carter and Bill Clinton.

Second, the joint resolution for the Authorization for the Use of Military Force (AUMF) of 2001 provided for the use of "all necessary and appropriate" force to combat terrorists, and thus justifies the president's action. Third, the AUMF justifies not complying with the provisions of the FISA, since it superseded FISA. In addition, *Smith v. Maryland*, 442 U.S. 735 (1979), upheld the use of pen registers, which record the telephone numbers called from phones but not the conversations. Accordingly, by extension the NSA's collection of "metadata"—the phone numbers and e-mail addresses, the time and duration of the contacts, but not their content—was permissible.

By contrast, some members of Congress and civil liberties groups countered that the president has no inherent power to authorize warrant-less domestic security surveillance; that neither the AUMF nor the FISA permit such a program; and that *United States v. United States District Court*, 407 U.S. 297 (1972), the so-called *Keith* case, held that domestic intelligence surveillance requires prior judicial approval of a warrant in order to satisfy the Fourth Amendment's guarantee against unreasonable searches and seizures, though the decision left open the matter of warrantless foreign surveillance. After months of negotiations in 2006 Congress enacted legislation reasserting the authority of the FISA Court, while permitting wiretapping without a warrant for up to forty-five days but requiring the attorney general to certify and explain why such warrantless surveillance is necessary to a subcommittee of the Senate Intelligence Committee.

Subsequently, in 2006 it was also revealed that the NSA had been monitoring the phone numbers dialed by millions of U.S. citizens in order to search for telephone calling patterns and possible links to terrorists, as well as that the CIA and the Department of Treasury had been mining the transactions of 7,800 financial institutions worldwide. In 2006, a federal district court declared the NSA program unconstitutional. Then, in 2007 a FISA Court judge held that the Bush administration overstepped its authority in monitoring telephone calls and e-mails that pass through U.S. networks between foreign nationals. In response, however, Congress enacted and President Bush signed into law the Protect America Act of 2007, which expanded the administration's authority to conduct warrantless wiretaps without FISA approval, including telephone calls and e-mails of U.S. citizens, so long as officials indicate that they are targeting someone overseas suspected of terrorism. The constitutionality of that law was immediately challenged by the Center for Constitutional Rights as a violation of the First and Fourth Amendments.

In 2008, Congress revised the FISA, which was created to issue warrants for domestic spying cases related to espionage and terrorism. It did so because of controversies over the Bush administration's bypassing the court and conducting warrantless searches of electronic communications. The major provisions of the law provide:

(1) Telecommunication companies that assisted the government in warrantless surveillance on the Internet after the September 11, 2001 (9/11), terrorist attacks are shielded from lawsuits for invasion of privacy.

(2) Procedures for monitoring telephone calls and e-mails of foreigners must be approved by the Foreign Intelligence Surveillance Court, and the government's surveillance of U.S. citizens, including those abroad, require that court's approval of individual warrants.

(3) The government is prohibited from targeting a foreigner in order to secretly eavesdrop on a U.S. citizen's telephone calls and e-mails without court approval.

(4) The government may conduct emergency eavesdropping without a court-approved warrant but must seek approval within one week.

President Obama subsequently signed a renewal of the USA PATRIOT Act, which expanded the use of warrantless electronic surveillance. The administration also increased the number of applications to the FISA Court for secret warrants for the surveillance of individuals and organizations suspected of aiding potential terrorists and hostile organizations.

In 2013, however, a former NSA contractor, Edward J. Snowden, revealed that the NSA was collecting metadata on all U.S. citizens'

(continues)

■ THE DEVELOPMENT OF LAW
The USA PATRIOT Act, Wiretaps, and the
Foreign Intelligence Surveillance Court (continued)

phone calls and e-mails—tracking their contacts, the duration of calls, and patterns of correspondence—without obtaining a warrant (the content of communications were not recorded). This renewed a major controversy and debate over how to balance liberty and security. That debate disclosed that since its inception in 1979, the FISA Court had received almost 34,000 warrant applications and denied only 11 requests. In addition, it was revealed that the FISA Court broadly interpreted the "special needs" exception to the Fourth Amendment warrant requirement (further discussed in Ch. 7, Section D) to permit the NSA to conduct warrantless surveillance of all communications and e-mails.

The mood in Congress and the country was quite different from the mood immediately after 9/11 when, in 2015, major provisions of the USA PATRIOT Act were due to expire or be renewed. Both Democrats and Republicans called for more restrictions on governmental surveillance, and a kind of national debate over governmental surveillance and liberty versus national security ensued.

Finally, in June 2015 Congress enacted and President Obama signed into law the USA Freedom Act. While the law permits continued governmental surveillance, there are new restrictions—called a "milestone" and "landmark" in the post-9/11 world. Among the major restrictions are (1) the storage of metadata would be kept by phone companies and service providers, not the NSA; (2) the government now must go to the FISA Court for an order to search those companies' databases; and (3) the FISA Court is now, for the first time, required to declassify its most significant decisions and in certain cases permit third parties to argue for the protection of privacy rights. The NSA, however, may obtain two "hops" with one court order—that is, the first "hop" grants access to the phone numbers directly linked to the target's number, and then those numbers may be sent to phone companies for a second "hop" to expand further the numbers obtained. Still, there remain other limits to the usefulness of the data gathered because of the growing use of apps on smartphones that make calls over the Internet—via Skype, Whatsapp, or Google—since phone companies do not have data on those calls. In addition, wireless companies are increasingly adopting flat-rate plans that do not bill each call, and hence do not maintain records on the numbers dialed or their call durations.

*The full title of the law is Uniting and Strengthening America by Providing Appropriate Tools Required to Intercept and Obstruct Terrorism (USA PATRIOT) Act of 2001.

F | *The Exclusionary Rule*

If police do not honor the commands of the Fourth Amendment and make an unreasonable search and seizure, what is to be done? In England and some other countries, illegally obtained evidence may be used against a defendant and is not grounds for appealing a conviction. But he or she has the right to sue for civil damages or call for criminal proceedings against the officers who violated the law.[1] In *Weeks v. United States*, 232 U.S. 383 (1914), however, the Court adopted the exclusionary rule—prohibiting the admission of illegally seized evidence at the trial.

The basis for and application of the exclusionary rule has been a source of continuing controversy. Some justices and scholars defend the rule as a *constitutional principle* essential to the rights guaranteed by the Fourth Amendment. But this rationale has been criticized for "making the tail of the exclusionary rule wag the dog of the Fourth Amendment."[2] Others claim that the rule is simply an *evidentiary rule* that should be limited or eliminated based on considerations of public policy. One policy argument for the exclusionary rule is that it preserves *judicial integrity*; the judiciary's prestige would be damaged if judges were complacent about allowing the use of illegally obtained evidence by prosecutors in convicting defendants for breaking the law. Critics of the constitutional status of the exclusionary rule more often argue that the rule is defensible only if it succeeds in promoting a policy of deterring police from illegal searches and seizures.[3] The *deterrence rationale*, in turn, has generated debate over whether the exclusionary rule indeed deters police, whether it has a direct or indirect effect on police misconduct, and how significant empirical studies are and should be for determining the fate of the exclusionary rule.[4]

Writing for the majority in *Weeks v. United States*, Justice William Day refused to distinguish between the seizure and introduction at trial of illegally obtained evidence, but he was ambiguous about whether the exclusionary rule was a constitutional requirement or simply an evidentiary rule that could be expanded or contracted depending on public policy considerations. To allow the use of illegally seized evidence, Day observed, "would be to affirm by judicial decision a manifest neglect if not an open defiance of the prohibitions . . . of the Constitution." And he suggested that the exclusionary rule was essential to the personal rights secured by the Fourth Amendment, observing that without it claims against unreasonable "invasions of the home and privacy of the citizens" would have little practical feasibility; "[i]f letters and private documents can thus be seized and held and used in evidence against a citizen accused of an offense, the protection of the Fourth Amendment declaring his right to be secure against such searches and seizures is of no value, and, so far as those thus placed are concerned, might as well be stricken from the Constitution." Yet Day also noted that the exclusionary rule expressed the Court's disapproval of illegal police conduct and recognition of the need to preserve the integrity of the judicial system. In his words, "The tendency of those who execute the criminal laws of the country to obtain conviction by means of unlawful seizures and enforced confessions . . . should find no sanction in the judgments of the courts . . . charged at all times with the support of the Constitution." As a result of Day's ambiguous opinion, it was debatable whether the exclusionary rule expressed a constitutional principle or simply registered a policy aimed at enhancing judicial integrity and deterring police misconduct.

The status of the exclusionary rule remained problematic thirty-five years later when the Court made the Fourth Amendment but not the exclusionary rule applicable to the states under the Fourteenth Amendment. (For further discussion of federal-state relations and the Court's nationalization of the Bill of Rights, see Ch. 4, in this volume, and Vol. 1, Ch. 7.) In *Wolf v. Colorado*, 338 U.S. 25 (1949), Justice Frankfurter observed that "[t]he security of one's privacy against arbitrary intrusion by the police—which is at the core the Fourth Amendment—is basic to a free society. It is therefore implicit in 'the concept of ordered liberty' and as such enforceable against the states through the Due Process Clause." But he held the exclusionary rule to be a nonconstitutional remedy and took a dim view of Justice Day's rationale for the rule, terming it a mere "judicial implication" without foundation in the Fourth Amendment. Likewise, Justice Hugo Black reiterated that the "federal exclusionary rule is not a command of the Fourth Amendment but is a judicially created rule of evidence which Congress might negate."

Wolf's dissenters (Justices Douglas, Murphy, and Rutledge) had quite a different interpretation. They contended that the Fourth Amendment's guarantee of a right of privacy required the exclusion of illegally obtained evidence and that the exclusionary rule was the only means of giving "content to the commands of the Fourth Amendment."

As a consequence of *Wolf*'s holding that the Fourth Amendment but not the exclusionary rule applied to the states, the Court had to decide on a case-by-case basis whether illegal searches and seizures by state police violated the due process clause of the Fourteenth Amendment.[5] In addition, because the exclusionary rule applied only if federal agents were guilty of unlawful searches and seizures, state police who illegally obtained evidence could turn it over on a "silver platter" to federal prosecutors for use in federal courts. The Warren Court finally abandoned what became known as the silver platter doctrine in *Elkins v. United States*, 364 U.S. 206 (1960).

In *Elkins*, a bare majority agreed with *Wolf*'s dissenters on the application of the exclusionary rule, but not its underlying rationale. The distinction drawn in *Wolf* between the Fourth Amendment's requirements imposed on the federal government and those of the due process clause of the Fourteenth Amendment imposed on the states was finally eliminated. And the Court held that evidence illegally seized by state police could no longer be turned over to federal agents and used in federal courts. But the majority declined to make the exclusionary rule fully applicable to the states and accepted *Wolf*'s reasoning that "[t]he rule is calculated to prevent, not repair. Its purpose is to deter—to compel respect for the constitutional guaranty in the only effectively available way—by removing the incentive to disregard it."

Two years after *Elkins*, the Warren Court nevertheless held in a landmark ruling in *Mapp v. Ohio* (1961) (excerpted below) that the exclusionary rule limits the states as well as the federal government. Notice that Justice Tom Clark's opinion for the majority rationalized the exclusionary rule in terms of constitutional principles, including the right of privacy, as well as the policies of preserving judicial integrity and deterring police misconduct. However, in *Linkletter v. Walker* (see Ch. 2), the Court identified deterrence as the principal rationale for the exclusionary rule, when denying retroactivity to its holding in *Mapp*. There, Justice Clark observed that "[w]e cannot say that this purpose [deterrence] would be advanced by making the rule retrospective. . . . Nor would it add harmony to the delicate state-federal relationship of which we have spoken as part and parcel of the purpose of *Mapp*. Finally, the ruptured privacy of the victims' homes and effects cannot be restored. Reparation comes too late."

Subsequent rulings have not only focused on deterrence as the rationale for the rule but also on that basis criticized the rule and limited its scope. In *United States v. Calandra*, 414 U.S. 338 (1974), for example, the Court held that the exclusionary rule did not apply to questions asked of a grand jury witness that were based on evidence obtained by an illegal search and seizure of his papers. By divorcing the exclusionary rule from its rationale as a safeguard for Fourth Amendment rights, the rule's role in safeguarding privacy interests diminished. As Justice Powell viewed it in his opinion for the Court: "[T]he rule is a judicially created remedy designed to safeguard Fourth Amendment rights generally through its deterrent effect, rather than a personal constitutional right of the party aggrieved."

The Burger and Rehnquist Courts cut back on the application of the exclusionary rule in a number of other ways as well. In *United States v. Janis*, 428 U.S. 433 (1976), a suit to recover unpaid federal income taxes, the Court held that illegally obtained evidence may be used in civil trials. And in a sweeping ruling in *Stone v. Powell*, 428 U.S. 465 (1976), the Court ruled that state prisoners may no longer petition for a writ of *habeas corpus* in federal district courts to review their convictions, when they already have had the opportunity on direct appeal to argue that their Fourth Amendment rights were violated. Writing for the majority, Justice Powell held that the costs of overturning convictions in cases where illegally obtained evidence was used at trial simply outweighed whatever benefits the exclusionary rule has in deterring police misconduct.

Although the Court has not expressly overturned *Mapp* or abandoned the exclusionary rule, it has carved out exceptions to the application of the rule. One long-standing exception to the exclusionary rule, however, permits prosecutors to introduce at trial illegally obtained evidence for the purpose of discrediting the defendant's *own* testimony.[6] In *United States v. Havens*, 446 U.S. 620 (1980), the Burger Court expanded this exception to allow prosecutors to use illegally obtained evidence to impeach the testimony during cross–examination of an accomplice called to testify for the defendant. But a bare majority in *James v. Illinois*, 493 U.S. 307 (1990), barred further expansion of this exception to the exclusionary rule. In this case, Justice Brennan held that the prosecution may not introduce illegally obtained evidence to impeach the testimony of *any* witness called by a defendant.

In *Nix v. Williams* (1984) (excerpted below), the Court upheld an *inevitable discovery* exception to the exclusionary rule. In a companion ruling, *Segura v. United States*, 468 U.S. 796 (1984), the justices split 5–4 on holding that the exclusionary rule does not prohibit the use of illegally obtained evidence that police would have later found as a result of other independent sources. A bare majority of the Roberts Court also held in *Hudson v. Michigan,* 547 U.S. 586 (2006), that a violation of the amendment's "knock and announce" rule does not trigger the exclusionary rule.

In still two more rulings, *United States v. Leon* and *Massachusetts v. Sheppard* (excerpted below), the Court legitimized a *good faith* exception to the exclusionary rule. Subsequently, in *Arizona v. Evans*, 514 U.S. 1 (1995), the Rehnquist Court expanded the "good faith" exception to the exclusionary rule to include police reliance on mistaken computer records of outstanding arrest warrants. And a bare majority of the Roberts Court in *Herring v. United States* (2009) (excerpted below) held that negligent errors and illegal seizures do not automatically trigger the exclusionary rule. Writing for the Court, Chief Justice Roberts emphasized, "Our cases establish that suppression [of illegally obtained evidence] is not an automatic consequence of a Fourth Amendment violation. Instead, the question turns on the culpability of the police and the potential of exclusion to deter wrongful police conduct." In other words, if police make an objectively reasonable mistake (i.e., are merely negligent), the exclusionary rule does not apply to whatever evidence is found. In so holding, the majority extended the "good faith" exception to ordinary police conduct; see *United States v. Leon* and *Massachusetts v. Sheppard* (1984) (excerpted below), *Arizona v. Evans*, 514 U.S. 1 (1995), and *Herring v. United States* (2009) (excerpted below). In addition, in *Pearson v. Callahan*, 555 U.S. 223 (2009), the Roberts Court unanimously held that police may not be sued for entering a house without a warrant after receiving a signal from an informant on the inside that a drug transaction was taking place. Writing for the Court, Justice Alito observed that the law in this area was not "clearly established" and therefore police are immune from liability for entering the house without a warrant. Together, *Herring* and *Pearson* further cut back on the scope and application of the exclusionary rule.

Subsequently, a solid majority of the Roberts Court held that warrantless searches of cars incident to an arrest of occupants made with reasonable reliance on binding precedents do not trigger the exclusionary rule, even if the kind of search conducted is later found to violate the Fourth Amendment. Writing for the Court in *Davis v. United States*, 564 U.S. 229 (2011), Justice Alito's opinion swept broadly with regard to "good faith" exceptions to the exclusionary rule and to the retroactivity to pending cases of new rulings on impermissible searches and seizures. Notably, the majority expressly reaffirmed that the exclusionary rule is merely a judicially created remedy and not a principle commanded by the Fourth Amendment. Justices Ginsburg and Breyer dissented.

Finally, in an important ruling in *Utah v. Strieff* (2016) (excerpted below) with wide-ranging implications for law enforcement and society, as emphasized by dissenting Justice Sotomayor, the Roberts Court held that if officers make a suspicionless or random stop of an individual and discover there is an outstanding arrest warrant (even for a minor traffic ticket) for that person, they may make a search incident to arrest. If illegal substances are discovered during the search, that evidence may be used at trial (and not excluded even though the search was illegal).

NOTES

1. In his dissenting opinion in *Bivens v. Six-Unknown Named Agents*, 403 U.S. 388 (1971), Chief Justice Burger urged that the exclusionary rule be abandoned and that in its place a system of tort remedies be established, permitting defendants to sue police for unlawful searches and seizures while allowing illegally obtained evidence to be used.

2. Anthony Amsterdam, "Perspectives on the Fourth Amendment," 58 *Minnesota Law Review* 369 (1974).

3. See Dallin Oaks, "Studying the Exclusionary Rule in Search and Seizure," 37 *University of Chicago Law Review* 665 (1970); and Stephen Schlesinger, *Exclusionary Injustice: The Problem of Illegally Obtained Evidence* (New York: Dekker, 1977).

4. See Stephen Schlesinger, "The Exclusionary Rule: Have Proponents Proven That It Is a Deterrent to Police?" 62 *Judicature* 404 (1979); and Bradley Canon, "The Exclusionary Rule: Have Critics Proven That It Doesn't Deter Police?" 62 *Judicature* 398 (1979).

5. See *Rochin v. California* (1952), in Vol. 2, Ch. 4.

6. See *Walder v. United States*, 347 U.S. 62 (1954).

SELECTED BIBLIOGRAPHY

Amsterdam, Anthony. *Perspectives on the Fourth Amendment.* St. Paul: Minnesota Law Review Foundation, 1974.

Long, Carolyn. *Mapp v. Ohio: Guarding against Unreasonable Searches and Seizures.* Lawrence: University Press of Kansas, 2005.

Maclin, Tracey. *The Supreme Court and the Fourth Amendment's Exclusionary Rule.* New York: Oxford University Press, 2012.

Zotti, Priscilla H. Machado. *Injustice for All: Mapp v. Ohio and the Fourth Amendment.* New York: Peter Lang, 2005.

Mapp v. Ohio
367 U.S. 643, 81 S.CT. 1684 (1961)

Justice Tom Clark discusses the facts in his opinion for the Court, which made the Fourth Amendment exclusionary rule applicable in state as well as federal courts.

The Court's decision was 6–3, and the majority's opinion was announced by Justice Clark. Concurrences were by Justices Black and Douglas. Justice Stewart issued a memorandum. Justice Harlan dissented and was joined by Justices Frankfurter and Whittaker.

■ ■ ■

□ *Justice CLARK delivered the opinion of the Court.*

Appellant stands convicted of knowingly having had in her possession and under her control certain lewd and lascivious books, pictures, and photographs in violation of Sec. 2905.34 of Ohio's Revised Code. . . .

On May 23, 1957, three Cleveland police officers arrived at appellant's residence in that city pursuant to information that "a person [was] hiding out in the home, who was wanted for questioning in connection with a recent bombing, and that there was a large amount of policy paraphernalia being hidden in the home." Miss Mapp and her daughter by a former marriage lived on the top floor of the two-family dwelling. Upon their arrival at that house, the officers knocked on the door and demanded entrance but appellant, after telephoning her attorney, refused to admit them without a search warrant. They advised their headquarters of the situation and undertook a surveillance of the house.

The officers again sought entrance some three hours later when four or more additional officers arrived on the scene. When Miss Mapp did not come to the door immediately, at least one of the several doors to the house was forcibly opened and the policemen gained admittance. Meanwhile Miss Mapp's attorney arrived, but the officers, having secured their own entry, and continuing in their defiance of the law, would permit him neither to see Miss Mapp nor to enter the house. It appears that Miss Mapp was halfway down the stairs from the upper floor to the front door when the officers, in this high-handed manner, broke into the hall. She demanded to see the search warrant. A paper, claimed to be a warrant, was held up by one of the officers. She grabbed the "warrant" and placed it in her bosom. A struggle ensued in which the officers recovered the piece of paper and as a result of which they handcuffed appellant because she had been "belligerent" in resisting their official rescue of the "warrant" from her person. Running roughshod over appellant, a policeman "grabbed" her, "twisted [her] hand," and she "yelled [and] pleaded with him" because "it was hurting." Appellant, in handcuffs, was then forcibly taken upstairs to her bedroom where the officers searched a dresser, a chest of drawers, a closet and some suitcases. They also looked into a photo album and through personal papers belonging to the appellant. The search spread to the rest of the second floor including the child's bedroom, the living room, the kitchen and a dinette. The basement of the building and a trunk found therein were also searched. The obscene materials for possession of which she was ultimately convicted were discovered in the course of that widespread search. . . .

The State says that even if the search were made without authority, or otherwise unreasonably, it is not prevented from using the unconstitutionally seized evidence at trial, citing *Wolf v. People of State of Colorado*, [338 U.S. 25] 1949, in which this Court did indeed hold "that in a prosecution in a State court for a State crime the Fourteenth Amendment does not forbid the admission of evidence obtained by an unreasonable search and seizure." . . .

[I]t is urged once again that we review that holding.

Seventy-five years ago, in *Boyd v. United States*, [116 U.S. 616] 1886, considering the Fourth and Fifth Amendments as running "almost into each other" on the facts before it, this Court held that the doctrines of those Amendments

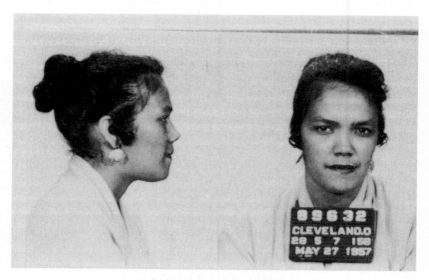

Dollree Mapp. (*AP Photo*)

apply to all invasions on the part of the government and its employ-ees of the sanctity of a man's home and the privacies of life. It is not the breaking of his doors, and the rummaging of his drawers, that constitutes the essence of the offence; but it is the invasion of his indefeasible right of personal security, personal liberty and private property. . . . Breaking into a house and opening boxes and drawers are circumstances of aggravation; but any forcible and compulsory extortion of a man's own testimony or of his private papers to be used as evidence to convict him of crime or to forfeit his goods, is within the condemnation . . . [of those Amendments].

The Court noted that

constitutional provisions for the security of person and property should be liberally construed. . . . It is the duty of courts to be watchful for the constitutional rights of the citizen, and against any stealthy encroachments thereon. . . .

In this jealous regard for maintaining the integrity of individual rights, the Court gave life to Madison's prediction that "independent tribunals of justice . . . will be naturally led to resist every encroachment upon rights expressly stipulated for in the Constitution by the declaration of rights." I *Annals of Cong.* 439 (1789). . . .

Less than 30 years after *Boyd*, this Court, in *Weeks v. United States*, [232 U.S. 383] 1914, stated that

the 4th Amendment, . . . put the courts of the United States and Federal officials, in the exercise of their power and authority, under limitations and restraints [and] . . . forever secure[d] the people, their persons, houses, papers, and effects, against all unreasonable searches and seizures under the guise of law . . . and the duty of giving to it force and effect is obligatory upon all entrusted under our Federal system with the enforcement of the laws. . . .

[T]he Court in that case clearly stated that use of the seized evidence involved "a denial of the constitutional rights of the accused." Thus, in the year 1914, in the *Weeks* case, this Court "for the first time" held that "in a federal prosecution the Fourth Amendment barred the use of evidence secured through an illegal search and seizure." This Court has ever since required of federal law officers a strict adherence to that command which this Court has held to be a clear, specific, and constitutionally required— even if judicially implied—deterrent safeguard without insistence upon which the Fourth Amendment would have been reduced to "a form of words." . . .

In 1949, 35 years after *Weeks* was announced, this Court, in *Wolf v. People of State of Colorado*, again for the first time, discussed the effect of the Fourth Amendment upon the States through the operation of the Due Process Clause of the Fourteenth Amendment. It said:

[W]e have no hesitation in saying that were a State affirmatively to sanction such police incursion into privacy it would run counter to the guaranty of the Fourteenth Amendment.

Nevertheless, after declaring that the "security of one's privacy against arbitrary intrusion by the police" is "implicit in 'the concept of ordered liberty' and as such enforceable against the States through the Due Process Clause," cf. *Palko v. State of Connecticut*, [302 U.S. 319] 1937, and announcing that it "stoutly adhere[d]" to the *Weeks* decision, the Court decided that the *Weeks* exclusionary rule would not then be imposed upon the States as "an essential ingredient of the right." The Court's reasons for not considering essential to the right to privacy, as a curb imposed upon the States by the Due Process Clause, that which decades before had been posited as part and parcel of the Fourth Amendment's limitation upon federal encroachment of individual privacy, were bottomed on factual considerations.

While they are not basically relevant to a decision that the exclusionary rule is an essential ingredient of the Fourth Amendment as the right it embodies is vouchsafed against the States by the Due Process Clause, we will consider the current validity of the factual grounds upon which *Wolf* was based.

The Court in *Wolf* first stated that "[t]he contrariety of views of the States" on the adoption of the exclusionary rule of *Weeks* was "particularly impressive," and, in this connection, that it could not "brush aside the experience of States which deem the incidence of such conduct by the police too slight to call for a deterrent remedy . . . by overriding the [States'] relevant rules of evidence." While in 1949, prior to the *Wolf* case, almost two-thirds of the States were opposed to the use of the exclusionary rule, now, despite the *Wolf* case, more than half of those since passing upon it, by their own legislative or judicial decision, have wholly or partly adopted or adhered to the *Weeks* rule. . . . Significantly, among those now following the rule is California, which, according to its highest court, was "compelled to reach that conclusion because other remedies have completely failed to secure compliance with the constitutional provisions. . . ." In connection with this California case, we note that the second basis elaborated in *Wolf* in support of its failure to enforce the exclusionary doctrine against the States was that "other means of protection" have been afforded "the right to privacy." The experience of California that such other remedies have been worthless and futile is buttressed by the experience of other States. . . .

[Notably,] the force of [the] reasoning [in *Wolf*] has been largely vitiated by later decisions of this Court. These include the recent discarding of the "silver platter" doctrine which allowed federal judicial use of evidence seized in violation of the Constitution by state agents, *Elkins v. United States*, [364 U.S. 206 (1960)], the relaxation of the formerly strict requirements as to standing to challenge the use of evidence thus seized, so that now the procedure of exclusion, "ultimately referable to constitutional safeguards," is available to anyone even "legitimately on [the] premises" unlawfully searched, *Jones v. United States*, [362 U.S. 257] 1960; and finally, the formulation of a method to prevent state use of evidence unconstitutionally seized by federal agents, *Rea v. United States*, [350 U.S. 214] 1956. . . .

It, therefore, plainly appears that the factual considerations supporting the failure of the *Wolf* Court to include the *Weeks* exclusionary rule when it recognized the enforceability of the right to privacy against the States in 1949, while not basically relevant to the constitutional consideration, could not, in any analysis, now be deemed controlling. . . .

Today we once again examine *Wolf*'s constitutional documentation of the right to privacy free from unreasonable state intrusion, and, after its dozen years on our books, are led by it to close the only courtroom door remaining open to evidence secured by official lawlessness in flagrant abuse of that basic right, reserved to all persons as a specific guarantee against that very same unlawful conduct. We hold that all evidence obtained by searches and seizures in violation of the Constitution is, by that same authority, inadmissible in a state court.

Since the Fourth Amendment's right of privacy has been declared enforceable against the States through the Due Process Clause of the Fourteenth, it is enforceable against them by the same sanction of exclusion as is used against the Federal Government. Were it otherwise, then just as without the *Weeks* rule the assurance against unreasonable federal searches and seizures would be "a form of words," valueless and undeserving of mention in a perpetual charter of inestimable human liberties, so too, without that rule the freedom from state invasions of privacy would be so ephemeral and so neatly severed from its conceptual nexus with the freedom from all brutish means of coercing evidence as not to merit this Court's high regard as a freedom "implicit in 'the concept of ordered liberty.'" At the time that the Court held in *Wolf* that the Amendment was applicable to the States through the Due Process Clause, the cases of this Court, as we have seen, have steadfastly held that as to federal officers the Fourth Amendment included the exclusion of the evidence seized in violation of its provisions. Even *Wolf* "stoutly adhered" to that proposition. The right to privacy, when conceded operatively enforceable against the States, was not susceptible of destruction by avulsion of the sanction upon which its protection and enjoyment had always been deemed dependent under the *Boyd, Weeks* and *Silverthorne* [*Lumber Co. v. United States*, 251 U.S. 385 (1920)], cases. Therefore, in extending the substantive protections of due process to all constitutionally unreasonable searches—state or federal—it was logically and constitutionally necessary that the exclusion doctrine—an essential ingredient of the right newly recognized by the *Wolf* case. In short, the admission of the new constitutional right by *Wolf* could not consistently tolerate denial of its most important constitutional privilege, namely, the exclusion of the evidence which an accused had been forced to give by reason of the unlawful seizure. To hold otherwise is to grant the right but in reality to withhold its privilege and enjoyment. Only last year the Court itself recognized that the purpose of the exclusionary rule "is to deter—to compel respect for the constitutional guarantee in the only effectively available way—by removing the incentive to disregard it." *Elkins v. United States. . . ."*

Indeed, we are aware of no restraint, similar to that rejected today conditioning the enforcement of any other basic constitutional right. The right to privacy, no less important than any other right carefully and particularly reserved to the people, would stand in marked contrast to all other rights declared as "basic to a free society." *Wolf v. People of State of Colorado.* This Court has not hesitated to enforce as strictly against the States as it does against the Federal Government the rights of free speech and of a free press, the rights to notice and to a fair, public trial, including, as it does, the right not to be convicted by use of a coerced confession, however logically relevant it be, and without regard to its reliability. And nothing could be more certain than that when a coerced confession is involved, "the relevant rules of evidence" are overridden without regard to "the incidence of such conduct by the police," slight or frequent. Why should not the same rule apply to what is tantamount to coerced testimony by way of unconstitutional seizure of goods, papers, effects, documents, etc.? . . .

Moreover, our holding that the exclusionary rule is an essential part of both the Fourth and Fourteenth Amendments is not only the logical dictate of prior cases, but it also makes very good sense. There is no war between the Constitution and common sense. Presently, a federal prosecutor may make no use of evidence illegally seized, but a State's attorney across the street may, although he supposedly is operating under the enforceable prohibitions of the same Amendment. Thus the State, by admitting evidence unlawfully seized, serves to encourage disobedience to the Federal Constitution which it is bound to uphold. . . .

In non-exclusionary States, federal officers, being human, were by it invited to and did, as our cases indicate, step across the street to the State's attorney with their unconstitutionally seized evidence. Prosecution on the basis of that evidence was then had in a state court in utter disregard of the enforceable Fourth Amendment. If the fruits of an unconstitutional search had been inadmissible in both state and federal courts, this inducement to evasion would have been sooner eliminated. . . .

There are those who say, as did Justice (then Judge) CARDOZO, that under our constitutional exclusionary doctrine "[t]he criminal is to go free because the constable has blundered." *People v. Defore*, [242 N.Y. 13 (1926)]. In some cases this will undoubtedly be the result. But, as was said in *Elkins*, "there is another consideration—the imperative of judicial integrity." The criminal goes free, if he must, but it is the law that sets him free. Nothing can destroy a government more quickly than its failure to observe its own laws, or worse, its disregard of the character of its own existence. . . .

The ignoble shortcut to conviction left open to the State tends to destroy the entire system of constitutional restraints on which the liberties of the people rest. Having once recognized that the right to privacy embodied in the Fourth Amendment is enforceable against the States, and that the right to be secure against rude invasions of privacy by state officers is, therefore, constitutional in origin, we can no longer permit that right to remain an empty promise. Because it is enforceable in the same manner and to like effect as other basic rights secured by the Due Process Clause, we can no longer permit it to be revocable at the whim of any police officer who, in the name of law enforcement itself, chooses to suspend its enjoyment. Our decision, founded on reason and truth, gives to the individual no more than that which the Constitution guarantees him, to the police officer no less than that to which honest law enforcement is entitled, and, to the courts, that judicial integrity so necessary in the true administration of justice.

The judgment of the Supreme Court of Ohio is reversed and the cause remanded for further proceedings not inconsistent with this opinion.

Reversed and remanded.

☐ *Justice BLACK, concurring.*

I am still not persuaded that the Fourth Amendment, standing alone, would be enough to bar the introduction into evidence against an accused of papers and effects seized from him in violation of its commands. For the Fourth Amendment does not itself contain any provision expressly precluding the use of such evidence, and I am extremely doubtful that such a provision could properly be inferred from nothing more than the basic command against unreasonable searches and seizures. Reflection on the problem, however, in the light of cases coming before the Court since *Wolf*, has led me to conclude that when the Fourth Amendment's ban against unreasonable searches and seizures is considered together with the Fifth Amendment's ban against compelled self-incrimination, a constitutional basis emerges which not only justifies but actually requires the exclusionary rule.

☐ *Justice HARLAN, with whom Justice FRANKFURTER and Justice WHITTAKER join, dissenting.*

I would not impose upon the States this federal exclusionary remedy. The reasons given by the majority for now suddenly turning its back on *Wolf* seem to me notably unconvincing.

First, it is said that "the factual grounds upon which *Wolf* was based" have since changed, in that more States now follow the *Weeks* exclusionary rule than was so at the time *Wolf* was decided. While that is true, a recent survey indicates that at present one-half of the States still adhere to the common-law non-exclusionary rule, and one, Maryland, retains the rule as to felonies. But in any case surely all this is beside the point, as the majority itself indeed seems to recognize. Our concern here, as it was in *Wolf*, is not with the desirability of that rule but only with the question whether the States are Constitutionally free to follow it or not as they may themselves determine, and the relevance of the disparity of views among the States on

■ INSIDE THE COURT

Letter from Justice Stewart to Justice Clark on Mapp v. Ohio

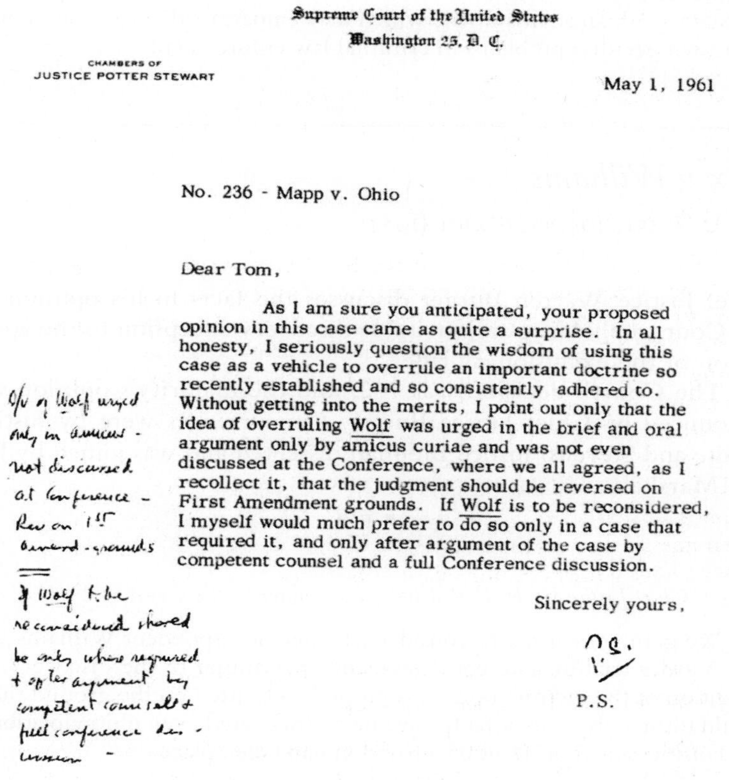

Supreme Court of the United States
Washington 25, D. C.

CHAMBERS OF
JUSTICE POTTER STEWART

May 1, 1961

No. 236 - Mapp v. Ohio

Dear Tom,

      As I am sure you anticipated, your proposed opinion in this case came as quite a surprise. In all honesty, I seriously question the wisdom of using this case as a vehicle to overrule an important doctrine so recently established and so consistently adhered to. Without getting into the merits, I point out only that the idea of overruling <u>Wolf</u> was urged in the brief and oral argument only by amicus curiae and was not even discussed at the Conference, where we all agreed, as I recollect it, that the judgment should be reversed on First Amendment grounds. If <u>Wolf</u> is to be reconsidered, I myself would much prefer to do so only in a case that required it, and only after argument of the case by competent counsel and a full Conference discussion.

                            Sincerely yours,

                            P.S.

[handwritten margin notes:] O/r of Wolf urged only in amicus - not discussed at Conference - Rev on 1st onward - grounds — If Wolf to be reconsidered should be only where required + after argument by competent counsel + full conference discussion -

Mr. Justice Clark

Source: Justice Tom C. Clark Papers, Rare Books and Special Collections, Tarlton Law Library, University of Texas at Austin. See also Justice Potter Stewart Papers (MS 1376), Box 11, Folders 99–100, Manuscripts and Archives, Yale University Library.

this point lies simply in the fact that the judgment involved is a debatable one. Moreover, the very fact on which the majority relies, instead of lending support to what is now being done, points away from the need of replacing voluntary state action with federal compulsion.

The preservation of a proper balance between state and federal responsibility in the administration of criminal justice demands patience on the part of those who might like to see things move faster among the States in this respect. Problems of criminal law enforcement vary widely from State to State. . . . For us the question remains, as it has always been, one of state power, not one of passing judgment on the wisdom of one state course or another. In my view this Court should continue to forbear from fettering the States with an adamant rule which may embarrass them in coping with their own peculiar problems in criminal law enforcement. . . .

Nix v. Williams

467 U.S. 431, 104 S.Ct. 2501 (1984)

Chief Justice Warren Burger discusses the facts in his opinion for the Court, upholding an inevitable discovery exception to the application of the exclusionary rule.

The Court's decision was 7–2, and the majority's opinion was announced by Chief Justice Burger. Concurrences were by Justices White and Stevens. Justice Brennan dissented and was joined by Justice Marshall.

■ ■ ■

☐ *Chief Justice BURGER delivers the opinion of the Court.*

We granted *certiorari* to consider whether, at respondent Williams' second murder trial in state court, evidence pertaining to the discovery and condition of the victim's body was properly admitted on the ground that it would ultimately or inevitably have been discovered even if no violation of any constitutional or statutory provision had taken place.

■ I

■ A

On December 24, 1968, 10-year-old Pamela Powers disappeared from a YMCA building in Des Moines, Iowa, where she had accompanied her parents to watch an athletic contest. Shortly after she disappeared, Williams was seen leaving the YMCA carrying a large bundle wrapped in a blanket; a 14-year-old boy who had helped Williams open his car door reported that he had seen "two legs in it and they were skinny and white."

Williams' car was found the next day 160 miles east of Des Moines in Davenport, Iowa. Later several items of clothing belonging to the child, some of Williams' clothing, and an army blanket like the one used to wrap the bundle that Williams carried out of the YMCA were found at a rest stop on Interstate 80 near Grinnell, between Des Moines and Davenport. A warrant was issued for Williams' arrest.

Police surmised that Williams had left Pamela Powers or her body somewhere between Des Moines and the Grinnell rest stop where some of the young girl's clothing had been found. On December 26, the Iowa Bureau of Criminal Investigation initiated a large-scale search. . . . Meanwhile, Williams surrendered to local police in Davenport, where he was promptly arraigned. Williams contacted a Des Moines attorney who arranged for an attorney in Davenport to meet Williams at the Davenport police station. Des Moines police informed counsel they would pick Williams up in Davenport and return him to Des Moines without questioning him. Two Des Moines detectives then drove to Davenport, took Williams into custody, and proceeded to drive him back to Des Moines.

During the return trip, one of the policemen, Detective Leaming, began a conversation with Williams, saying:

> I want to give you something to think about while we're traveling down the road. . . . They are predicting several inches of snow for tonight, and I feel that you yourself are the only person that knows where this little girl's body is . . . and if you get a snow on top of it you yourself may be unable to find it. And since we will be going right past the area [where the body is] on the way into Des Moines, I feel that we could stop and locate the body, that the parents of this little girl should be entitled to a Christian burial for the little girl who was snatched away from them on Christmas [E]ve and murdered. . . . [A]fter a snow storm [we may not be] able to find it at all.

Leaming told Williams he knew the body was in the area of Mitchellville—a town they would be passing on the way to Des Moines. He concluded the conversation by saying "I do not want you to answer me. . . . Just think about it. . . ."

Later, as the police car approached Grinnell, Williams asked Leaming whether the police had found the young girl's shoes. After Leaming replied that he was unsure, Williams directed the police to a point near a service station where he said he had left the shoes; they were not found. As they continued to drive to Des Moines, Williams asked whether the blanket had been found and then directed the officers to a rest area in Grinnell where he said he had disposed of the blanket; they did not find the blanket. At this point Leaming and his party were joined by the officers in charge of the search. As they approached Mitchellville, Williams, without any further conversation, agreed to direct the officers to the child's body.

The officers directing the search had called off the search at 3 P.M., when they left the Grinnell Police Department to join Leaming at the rest area. At that time, one search team near the Jasper County-Polk County line was only two and one-half miles from where Williams soon guided Leaming and his party to the body. The child's body was found next to a culvert in a ditch beside a gravel road in Polk County, about two miles south of Interstate 80, and essentially within the area to be searched.

■ B

First Trial: In February 1969 Williams was indicted for first-degree murder. Before trial in the Iowa court, his counsel moved to suppress evidence of the body and all related evidence including the condition of the body as shown by the autopsy. The ground for the motion was that such evidence was the "fruit" or product of Williams' statements made during the automobile ride from Davenport to Des Moines and prompted by Leaming's statements. The motion to suppress was denied.

The jury found Williams guilty of first-degree murder; the judgment of conviction was affirmed by the Iowa Supreme Court. Williams then sought release on *habeas corpus* in the United States District Court for the Southern District of Iowa. That court concluded that the evidence in question had been wrongly admitted at Williams' trial, a divided panel of the Court of Appeals for the Eighth Circuit agreed. . . .

We granted *certiorari*, and a divided Court affirmed, holding that Detective Leaming had obtained incriminating statements from Williams by what was viewed as interrogation in violation of his right to counsel. *Brewer v. Williams,* 430 U.S. 387 (1977). This Court's opinion noted, however, that although Williams' incriminating statements could not be introduced into evidence at a second trial, evidence of the body's location and condition "might well be admissible on the theory that the body would have been discovered in any event, even had incriminating statements not been elicited from Williams."

■ C

Second Trial: At Williams' second trial in 1977 in the Iowa court, the prosecution did not offer Williams' statements into evidence, nor did it seek to show that Williams had directed the police to the child's body. However, evidence of the condition of her body as it was found, articles and photographs of her clothing, and the results of post mortem medical and chemical tests on the body were admitted. The trial court concluded that the State had proved by a preponderance of the evidence that, if the search had not been suspended and Williams had not led the police to the victim, her body would have been discovered *"within a short time"* in essentially the same condition as it was actually found. . . .

On appeal, the Supreme Court of Iowa again affirmed. That court held that there was in fact a "hypothetical independent source" exception to the exclusionary rule:

> After the defendant has shown unlawful conduct on the part of the police, the State has the burden to show by a preponderance of the evidence that (1) the police did not act in bad faith for the purpose of hastening discovery of the evidence in question, and (2) that the evidence in question would have been discovered by lawful means. . . .

In 1980 Williams renewed his attack on the state-court conviction by seeking a writ of *habeas corpus* in the United States District Court for the Southern District of Iowa. The District Court conducted its own independent review of the evidence and concluded, as had the state courts, that the body would inevitably have been found by the searchers in essentially the same condition it was in when Williams led police to its discovery. The District Court denied Williams' petition. . . .

The Court of Appeals for the Eighth Circuit reversed. . . .

We granted the State's petition for *certiorari*, and we reverse.

■ II

■ A

The Iowa Supreme Court correctly stated that the "vast majority" of all courts, both state and federal, recognize an inevitable discovery exception to the exclusionary rule. We are now urged to adopt and apply the so-called ultimate or inevitable discovery exception to the exclusionary rule. . . .

Williams contends that evidence of the body's location and condition is "fruit of the poisonous tree," *i.e.*, the "fruit" or product of Detective Leaming's plea to help the child's parents give her "a Christian burial," which this Court had already held equated to interrogation. He contends that admitting the challenged evidence violated the Sixth Amendment whether it would have been inevitably discovered or not. Williams also contends that, if the inevitable discovery doctrine is constitutionally permissible, it must include a threshold showing of police good faith.

■ B

The doctrine requiring courts to suppress evidence as the tainted "fruit" of unlawful governmental conduct had its genesis in *Silverthorne Lumber Co. v. United States*, 251 U.S. 385 (1920); there, the Court held that the exclusionary rule applies not only to the illegally obtained evidence itself, but also to other incriminating evidence derived from the primary evidence. . . .

The core rationale consistently advanced by this Court for extending the exclusionary rule to evidence that is the fruit of unlawful police conduct has been that this admittedly drastic and socially costly course is needed to deter police from violations of constitutional and statutory protections. This Court has accepted the argument that the way to ensure such protections is to exclude evidence seized as a result of such violations notwithstanding the high social cost of letting persons obviously guilty go unpunished for their crimes. On this rationale, the prosecution is not to be put in a better position than it would have been in if no illegality had transpired.

By contrast, the derivative evidence analysis ensures that the prosecution is not put in a *worse* position simply because of some earlier police error or misconduct. The independent source doctrine allows admission of evidence that has been discovered by means wholly independent of any constitutional violation. That doctrine, although closely related to the inevitable discovery doctrine, does not apply here; Williams' statements to Leaming indeed led police to the child's body, but that is not the whole story. The independent source doctrine teaches us that the interest of society in deterring unlawful police conduct and the public interest in having juries receive all probative evidence of a crime are properly balanced by putting the police in the same, not a *worse*, position than they would have been in if no police error or misconduct had occurred. When the challenged evidence has an independent source, exclusion of such evidence would put the police in a worse position than they would have been in absent any error or violation. There is a functional similarity between these two doctrines in that exclusion of evidence that would inevitably have been discovered would also put the government in a worse position, because the police would have obtained that evidence if no misconduct had taken place. Thus, while the independent source exception would not justify admission of evidence in this case, its rationale is wholly consistent with and justifies our adoption of the ultimate or inevitable discovery exception to the exclusionary rule. . . .

The requirement that the prosecution must prove the absence of bad faith, imposed here by the Court of Appeals, would place courts in the position of withholding from juries relevant and undoubted truth that would have been available to police absent any unlawful police activity. Of course, that view would put the police in a *worse* position than they would have been in if no unlawful conduct had transpired. And, of equal importance, it wholly fails to take into account the enormous societal cost of excluding truth in the search for truth in the administration of justice. Nothing in this court's prior holdings supports any such formalistic, pointless, and punitive approach. . . .

Exclusion of physical evidence that would inevitably have been discovered adds nothing to either the integrity or fairness of a criminal trial. The Sixth Amendment right to counsel protects against unfairness by preserving the adversary process in which the reliability of proffered evidence may be tested in cross-examination. Here, however, Detective Leaming's conduct did nothing to impugn the reliability of the evidence in question—the body of the child and its condition as it was found, articles of clothing found on the body, and the autopsy. No one would seriously contend that the presence of counsel in the police car when Leaming appealed to Williams' decent human instincts would have had any bearing on the reliability of the body as evidence. Suppression, in these circumstances, would do nothing whatever to promote the integrity of the trial process, but would inflict a wholly unacceptable burden on the administration of criminal justice. . . .

■ C

On this record it is clear that the search parties were approaching the actual location of the body, and we are satisfied, along with three courts earlier, that the volunteer search teams would have resumed the search had Williams not earlier led the police to the body and the body inevitably would have been found. The evidence asserted by Williams as newly discovered, *i.e.*, certain photographs of the body and deposition testimony of Agent Ruxlow made in connection with the federal *habeas* proceeding, does not demonstrate that the material facts were inadequately developed in the suppression hearing in state court or that Williams was denied a full, fair, and adequate opportunity to present all relevant facts at the suppression hearing.

The judgment of the Court of Appeals is reversed, and the case is remanded for further proceedings consistent with this opinion.

It is so ordered.

☐ *Justice BRENNAN, with whom Justice MARSHALL joins, dissenting.*

I agree that in these circumstances the "inevitable discovery" exception to the exclusionary rule is consistent with the requirements of the Constitution.

In its zealous efforts to emasculate the exclusionary rule, however, the Court loses sight of the crucial difference between the "inevitable discovery" doctrine and the "independent source" exception from which it is derived. When properly applied, the "independent source" exception allows the prosecution to use evidence only if it was, in fact, obtained by fully lawful means. It therefore does no violence to the constitutional protections that the exclusionary rule is meant to enforce. The "inevitable discovery" exception is likewise compatible with the Constitution, though it differs in one key respect from its next of kin: specifically, the evidence sought to be introduced at trial has not actually been obtained from an independent source, but rather would have been discovered as a matter of course if independent investigations were allowed to proceed.

In my view, this distinction should require that the government satisfy a heightened burden of proof before it is allowed to use such evidence. The inevitable discovery exception necessarily implicates a hypothetical finding that differs in kind from the factual finding that precedes application of the independent source rule. To ensure that this hypothetical finding is narrowly confined to circumstances that are functionally equivalent to an independent source, and to protect fully the fundamental rights served by the exclusionary rule, I would require clear and convincing evidence before concluding that the government had met its burden of proof on this issue.

United States v. Leon
468 U.S. 897, 104 S.Ct. 3405 (1984)

and

Massachusetts v. Sheppard
468 U.S. 981, 104 S.Ct. 3424 (1984)

In August 1981, a confidential informant told a police officer in Burbank, California, that two persons he knew as "Armando" and "Patsy" were selling cocaine and methaqualone at their home. The informant gave the police their address but also claimed that they generally kept only small quantities of drugs there and stored the rest at another location. On the basis of this information, police initiated an extensive investigation focusing on the residence of Armando Sanchez, who had previously been arrested for possessing marijuana, and Patsy Stewart, who had no prior criminal record. Later, two other residences were also staked out.

In the course of the investigation, officers observed a car belonging to Richardo Del Castillo, who had previously been arrested for possessing fifty pounds of marijuana, arriving at Sanchez's house. The driver entered the house, leaving shortly thereafter carrying a small paper bag. A check of Del Castillo's probation records led police to Alberto Leon. Leon had been arrested in 1980 on drug charges, and one of his companions informed police that Leon was heavily involved with importing drugs into the country. Police in Burbank also learned from police in Glendale, California, that Leon was living in a house on South Sunset Canyon in Burbank.

One day during their surveillance of Sanchez and Stewart, police observed them board separate flights for Miami, Florida, and later return to Los Angeles together. At the airport, Sanchez and Stewart were stopped and agreed to a search of their luggage. A small amount of marijuana was discovered, but they were allowed to leave the airport.

Based on these and other observations, officer Cyril Rombach applied for a warrant to search the residences of Sanchez, Stewart, and Leon for a long list of items related to drug trafficking. A warrant was issued in September 1981 by a judge, and the ensuing search produced a large quantity of drugs. All three were indicted by a grand jury and charged with conspiracy to possess and distribute cocaine and other drugs.

Leon and the others filed motions to suppress the evidence seized pursuant to the warrant. A district court judge granted part of their motions to suppress on concluding that the police had failed to establish probable cause in their application for a warrant. In response to a request from the government, the court made clear that Officer Rombach had acted in good faith, but rejected the government's argument that the Fourth Amendment exclusionary rule should not apply where evidence is seized by police who reasonably and in good faith rely on a search warrant.

Subsequently, a divided panel of the Court of Appeals for the Ninth Circuit affirmed, finding that Officer Rombach's affidavit failed to meet the two-prong test for establishing probable cause as required in *Aguilar v. Texas*, 378 U.S. 108 (1964), and *Spinelli v. United States*, 393 U.S. 410 (1969), but that test and those rulings were overturned in *Illinois v. Gates*, 462 U.S. 213 (1983) (as discussed in Section A of this chapter).

The Reagan administration appealed the appellate court's decision and asked the Supreme Court to decide "[w]hether the Fourth Amendment exclusionary rule should be modified so as not to bar the admission of evidence seized in reasonable, good-faith reliance on a search warrant that is subsequently held to be defective."

The Court granted *certiorari* in this case, along with another, *Massachusetts v. Sheppard*, and upheld the good-faith exception to the exclusionary rule. In the *Massachusetts* case, police relied on good faith on a warrant usually issued for searches for controlled substances, instead of an arrest warrant, when making an arrest. A judge signed the wrong warrant after finding that police had established probable cause in their application, even though they used the wrong application form because their office had run out of (and on Sunday they could not obtain) the proper warrant forms.

The Court's decision was 6–3 in *Leon* and 7–2 in *Sheppard*, and the majority's opinion was announced by Justice White. Justice Blackmun concurred, and Justice Brennan, joined by Justice Marshall, dissented. In a separate opinion, Justice Stevens dissented in *Leon* and concurred in *Sheppard*.

■ ■ ■

Justice WHITE delivered the opinion of the Court.

This case presents the question whether the Fourth Amendment exclusionary rule should be modified so as not to bar the use in the prosecution's case in chief of evidence obtained by officers acting in reasonable reliance on a search warrant issued by a detached and neutral magistrate but ultimately found to be unsupported by probable cause. To resolve this question, we must consider once again the tension between the sometimes competing goals of, on the one hand, deterring official misconduct and removing inducements to unreasonable invasions of privacy and, on the other, establishing procedures under which criminal defendants are "acquitted or convicted on the basis of all the evidence which exposes the truth." . . .

The Fourth Amendment contains no provision expressly precluding the use of evidence obtained in violation of its commands, and an examination of its origin and purposes makes clear that the use of fruits of a past unlawful search or seizure "work[s] no new Fourth Amendment wrong." *United States v. Calandra*, 414 U.S. 338 (1974). The wrong condemned by the Amendment is "fully accomplished" by the unlawful search or seizure itself, and the exclusionary rule is neither intended nor able to "cure the invasion of the defendant's rights which he has already suffered." *Stone v. Powell*, [428 U.S. 465 (1976)] (WHITE, J., dissenting). The rule thus operates as "a judicially created remedy designed to safeguard Fourth Amendment rights generally through its deterrent effect, rather than a personal constitutional right of the party aggrieved." *United States v. Calandra*. . . .

The substantial social costs exacted by the exclusionary rule for the vindication of Fourth Amendment rights have long been a source of concern. "Our cases have consistently recognized that unbending application of the exclusionary sanction to enforce ideals of governmental rectitude would impede unacceptably the truth-finding functions of judge and jury." *United States v. Payne*, 447 U.S. 727 (1980). An objectionable collateral consequence of this interference with the criminal justice system's truth-finding function is that some guilty defendants may go free or receive reduced sentences as a result of favorable plea bargains. Particularly when law enforcement officers have acted in objective good faith or their transgressions have been minor, the magnitude of the benefit conferred on such guilty defendants offends basic concepts of the criminal justice system. Indiscriminate application of the exclusionary rule, therefore, may well "generat[e] disrespect for the law and administration of justice." Accordingly, "[a]s with any remedial device, the application of the rule has been restricted to those areas where its remedial objectives are thought most efficaciously served."

Close attention to those remedial objectives has characterized our recent decisions concerning the scope of the Fourth Amendment exclusionary rule. The Court has, to be sure, not seriously questioned, "in the absence of a more efficacious sanction, the continued application of the rule to suppress evidence from the [prosecution's] case where a Fourth Amendment violation has been substantial and deliberate. . . ." *Franks v. Delaware*, 438 U.S. 154 (1978); *Stone v. Powell, supra.* Nevertheless, the balancing approach that has evolved in various contexts—including criminal trials—"forcefully suggest[s] that the exclusionary rule be more generally modified to permit the introduction of evidence obtained in the reasonable good-faith belief that a search or seizure was in accord with the Fourth Amendment." *Illinois v. Gates . . .* (WHITE, J., concurring in judgment). . . .

As yet, we have not recognized any form of good-faith exception to the Fourth Amendment exclusionary rule. But the balancing approach that has evolved during the years of experience with the rule provides strong support for the modification currently urged upon us. As we discuss below, our evaluation of the costs and benefits of suppressing reliable physical evidence seized by officers reasonably relying on a warrant issued by a detached and neutral magistrate leads to the conclusion that such evidence should be admissible in the prosecution's case in chief.

Because a search warrant "provides the detached scrutiny of a neutral magistrate, which is a more reliable safeguard against improper searches than the hurried judgment of a law enforcement officer 'engaged in the often competitive enterprise of ferreting out crime,'" *United States v. Chadwick*, 433 U.S. 1 (1977) (quoting *Johnson v. United States*, 333 U.S. 10 (1948)), we have expressed a strong preference for warrants and declared that "in a doubtful or marginal case a search under a warrant may be sustainable where without one it would fall." *United States v. Ventresca*, 380 U.S. 102 (1965). Reasonable minds frequently may differ on the question whether a particular affidavit establishes probable cause, and we have thus concluded that the preference for warrants is most appropriately effectuated by according "great deference" to a magistrate's determination.

Deference to the magistrate, however, is not boundless. It is clear, first, that the deference accorded to a magistrate's finding of probable cause does not preclude inquiry into the knowing or reckless falsity of the affidavit on which that determination was based. Second, the courts must also insist that the magistrate purport to "perform his 'neutral and detached' function and not serve merely as a rubber stamp for the police." A magistrate failing to "manifest that neutrality and detachment demanded of a judicial officer when presented with a warrant application" and who acts instead as "an adjunct law enforcement officer" cannot provide valid authorization for an otherwise unconstitutional search.

Third, reviewing courts will not defer to a warrant based on an affidavit that does not "provide the magistrate with a substantial basis for determining the existence of probable cause." *Illinois v. Gates.* "Sufficient information must be presented to the magistrate to allow that official to determine probable cause; his action cannot be a mere ratification of the bare conclusions of others." Even if the warrant application was supported by more than a "bare bones" affidavit, a reviewing court may properly conclude that, notwithstanding the deference that magistrates deserve, the warrant was invalid because the magistrate's probable-cause determination reflected an improper analysis of the totality of the circumstances, or because the form of the warrant was improper in some respect.

Only in the first of these three situations, however, has the Court set forth a rationale for suppressing evidence obtained pursuant to a search warrant; in the other areas, it has simply excluded such evidence without considering whether Fourth Amendment interests will be advanced. To the extent that proponents of exclusion rely on its behavioral effects on judges and magistrates in these areas, their reliance is misplaced. First, the exclusionary rule is designed to deter police misconduct rather than to punish the errors of judges and magistrates. Second, there exists no evidence suggesting that judges and magistrates are inclined to ignore or subvert the Fourth Amendment or that lawlessness among these actors requires application of the extreme sanction of exclusion.

Third, and most important, we discern no basis, and are offered none, for believing that exclusion of evidence seized pursuant to a warrant will have a significant deterrent effect on the issuing judge or magistrate. Many of the factors that indicate that the exclusionary rule cannot provide an effective "special" or "general" deterrent for individual offending law enforcement officers apply as well to judges or magistrates. And, to the extent that the rule is thought to operate as a "systemic" deterrent on a wider audience, it clearly can have no such effect on individuals empowered to issue search warrants. Judges and magistrates are not adjuncts to the law enforcement team; as neutral judicial officers, they have no stake in the outcome of particular criminal prosecutions. The threat of exclusion thus cannot be expected significantly to deter them. Imposition of the exclusionary sanction is not necessary meaningfully to inform judicial officers of their errors, and we cannot conclude that admitting evidence obtained pursuant to a warrant while at the same time declaring that the warrant was somehow defective will in any way reduce judicial officers' professional incentives to comply with the Fourth Amendment, encourage them to repeat their mistakes, or lead to the granting of all colorable warrant requests.

If exclusion of evidence obtained pursuant to a subsequently invalidated warrant is to have any deterrent effect, therefore, it must alter the behavior of individual law enforcement officers or the policies of their departments. One could argue that applying the exclusionary rule in cases where the police failed to demonstrate probable cause in the warrant application deters future inadequate presentations or "magistrate shopping" and thus promotes the ends of the Fourth Amendment. Suppressing evidence obtained pursuant to a technically defective warrant supported by probable cause also might encourage officers to scrutinize more closely the form of the warrant and to point out suspected judicial errors. We find such arguments speculative and conclude that suppression of evidence obtained pursuant to a warrant should be ordered only on a case-by-case basis and only in those unusual cases in which exclusion will further the purposes of the exclusionary rule.

We have frequently questioned whether the exclusionary rule can have any deterrent effect when the offending officers acted in the objectively reasonable belief that their conduct did not violate the Fourth Amendment. "No empirical researcher, proponent or opponent of the rule, has yet been able to establish with any assurance whether the rule has a deterrent effect. . . ." *United States v. Janis* [428 U.S. 433 (1976)]. But even assuming that the rule effectively deters some police misconduct and provides incentives for the law enforcement profession as a whole to conduct itself in accord with the Fourth Amendment, it cannot be expected, and should not be applied, to deter objectively reasonable law enforcement activity. . . .

In short, where the officer's conduct is objectively reasonable, "excluding the evidence will not further the ends of the exclusionary rule in any appreciable way; for it is painfully apparent that . . . the officer is acting as a reasonable officer would and should act in similar circumstances. Excluding the evidence can in no way affect his future conduct unless it is to make him less willing to do his duty." *Stone v. Powell* (WHITE, J., dissenting).

This is particularly true, we believe, when an officer acting with objective good faith has obtained a search warrant from a judge or magistrate and acted within its scope. In most such cases, there is no police illegality and thus nothing to deter. It is the magistrate's responsibility to determine whether the officer's allegations establish probable cause and, if so, to issue a warrant comporting in form with the requirements of the Fourth Amendment. In the ordinary case, an officer cannot be expected to question the magistrate's probable-cause determination or his judgment that the form of the warrant is technically sufficient. Penalizing the officer for the magistrate's error, rather than his own, cannot logically contribute to the deterrence of Fourth Amendment violations.

We conclude that the marginal or nonexistent benefits produced by suppressing evidence obtained in objectively reasonable reliance on a subsequently invalidated search warrant cannot justify the substantial costs of exclusion. We do not suggest, however, that exclusion is always inappropriate in cases where an officer has obtained a warrant and abided by its terms. . . . [T]he officer's reliance on the magistrate's probable-cause determination and on the technical sufficiency of the warrant he issues must be objectively reasonable, and it is clear that in some circumstances the officer will have no reasonable grounds for believing that the warrant was properly issued.

Suppression therefore remains an appropriate remedy if the magistrate or judge in issuing a warrant was misled by information in an affidavit that the affiant knew was false or would have known was false except for his reckless disregard of the truth. . . . The exception we recognize today will also not apply in cases where the issuing magistrate wholly abandoned his judicial role in the manner condemned in *Lo-Ji Sales, Inc. v. New York*, 442 U.S. 319 (1979); in such circumstances, no reasonably well trained officer should rely on the warrant. Nor would an officer manifest objective good faith in relying on a warrant based on an affidavit "so lacking in indicia of probable cause as to render official belief in its existence entirely unreasonable." Finally, depending on the circumstances of the particular case, a warrant may be so facially deficient—*i.e.*, in failing to particularize the place to be searched or the things to be seized—that the executing officers cannot reasonably presume it to be valid. . . .

In so limiting the suppression remedy, we leave untouched the probable-cause standard and the various requirements for a valid warrant. Other objections to the modification of the Fourth Amendment exclusionary rule

judge *can* do is wring his hands and hope that perhaps by excluding such evidence he can deter future transgressions by the police.

Such a reading appears plausible, because, as critics of the exclusionary rule never tire of repeating, the Fourth Amendment makes no express provision for the exclusion of evidence secured in violation of its commands. A short answer to this claim, of course, is that many of the Constitution's most vital imperatives are stated in general terms and the task of giving meaning to these precepts is therefore left to subsequent judicial decision-making in the context of concrete cases. . . .

A more direct answer may be supplied by recognizing that the Amendment, like other provisions of the Bill of Rights, restrains the power of the government as a whole; it does not specify only a particular agency and exempt all others. The judiciary is responsible, no less than the executive, for ensuring that constitutional rights are respected. . . .

According to the Court, the substantive protections of the Fourth Amendment are wholly exhausted at the moment when police unlawfully invade an individual's privacy and thus no substantive force remains to those protections at the time of trial when the government seeks to use evidence obtained by the police.

I submit that such a crabbed reading of the Fourth Amendment casts aside the teaching of those Justices who first formulated the exclusionary rule, and rests ultimately on an impoverished understanding of judicial responsibility in our constitutional scheme. For my part, "[t]he right of the people to be secure in their persons, houses, papers, and effects, against unreasonable searches and seizures" comprises a personal right to exclude all evidence secured by means of unreasonable searches and seizures. The right to be free from the initial invasion of privacy and the right of exclusion are coordinate components of the central embracing right to be free from unreasonable searches and seizures.

Such a conception of the rights secured by the Fourth Amendment was unquestionably the original basis of what has come to be called the exclusionary rule when it was first formulated in *Weeks v. United States*, 232 U.S. 383 (1914). . . . As the Court in *Weeks* clearly recognized, the obligations cast upon government by the Fourth Amendment are not confined merely to the police. In the words of Justice HOLMES: "If the search and seizure are unlawful as invading personal rights secured by the Constitution those rights would be infringed yet further if the evidence were allowed to be used." *Dodge v. United States*, 272 U.S. 530 (1926). . . .

That conception of the rule, in my view, is more faithful to the meaning and purpose of the Fourth Amendment and to the judiciary's role as the guardian of the people's constitutional liberties. In contrast to the present Court's restrictive reading, the Court in *Weeks* recognized that, if the Amendment is to have any meaning, police and the courts cannot be regarded as constitutional strangers to each other; because the evidence-gathering role of the police is directly linked to the evidence-admitting function of the courts, an individual's Fourth Amendment rights may be undermined as completely by one as by the other. . . .

After today's decisions, however, that institutional incentive will be lost. Indeed, the Court's "reasonable mistake" exception to the exclusionary rule will tend to put a premium on police ignorance of the law. Armed with the assurance provided by today's decisions that evidence will always be admissible whenever an officer has "reasonably" relied upon a warrant, police departments will be encouraged to train officers that if a warrant has simply been signed, it is reasonable, without more, to rely on it. Since in close cases there will no longer be any incentive to err on the side of constitutional behavior, police would have every reason to adopt a "let's-wait-until-it's-decided" approach in situations in which there is a question about a warrant's validity or the basis for its issuance.

Although the Court brushes these concerns aside, a host of grave consequences can be expected to result from its decision to carve this new exception out of the exclusionary rule. A chief consequence of today's decisions will be to convey a clear and unambiguous message to magistrates that their decisions to issue warrants are now insulated from subsequent judicial review. Creation of this new exception for good-faith reliance upon a warrant implicitly tells magistrates that they need not take much care in reviewing warrant applications, since their mistakes will from now on have virtually no consequence: If their decision to issue a warrant was correct, the evidence will be admitted; if their decision was incorrect but the police relied in good faith on the warrant, the evidence will also be admitted. Inevitably, the care and attention devoted to such an inconsequential chore will dwindle. Although the Court is correct to note that magistrates do not share the same stake in the outcome of a criminal case as the police, they nevertheless need to appreciate that their role is of some moment in order to continue performing the important task of carefully reviewing warrant applications. Today's decisions effectively remove that incentive.

Herring v. United States

555 U.S. 135, 129 S.Ct. 695 (2009)

In July 2004, police investigator Mark Anderson learned that Bennie Dean Herring had gone to the Coffee County Sheriff's Department to retrieve something from his impounded truck. Herring was no stranger to law enforcement, and Anderson asked the county's warrant clerk to check for any outstanding warrants for Herring's arrest. When she found none, Anderson asked the clerk to check with her counterpart in neighboring Dale County. After checking Dale County's computer database, the clerk replied that there was an active arrest warrant for Herring's failure to appear on a felony charge, and information was relayed to Anderson, while a request was made for a fax copy of the warrant as confirmation. Subsequently, Anderson and a deputy followed Herring as he left the impound lot, pulled him over, and arrested him. A search incident to the arrest revealed methamphetamine in his pocket and a pistol (which as a felon he could not possess) in his vehicle. There was, however, a mistake about the warrant. The Dale County sheriff's computer records were supposed to correspond to actual arrest warrants, which the office also maintains. But the clerk discovered that the warrant had been recalled five months earlier. Normally when a warrant is recalled, the court clerk's office or a judge's chambers calls the clerk, who enters the information in the sheriff's computer database and disposes of the physical copy. For whatever reason, the information about the recall of the warrant for Herring did not appear in the database.

After Herring was indicted in federal district court for illegally possessing the gun and drugs, he moved to suppress the evidence on the ground that his initial arrest had been illegal because the warrant had been rescinded. A magistrate judge recommended denying the motion because the arresting officers had acted in a good-faith belief that the warrant was still outstanding. Thus, even if a Fourth Amendment violation existed, there was "no reason to believe that application of the exclusionary rule here would deter the occurrence of any future mistakes." The district court adopted that recommendation and the Court of Appeals for the Eleventh Circuit affirmed. Herring appealed that decision and the Supreme Court granted review.

The appellate court's decision was affirmed by a 5–4 vote. Chief Justice Roberts delivered the opinion for the Court. Justices Ginsburg and Breyer issued dissenting opinions, which Justices Stevens and Souter joined.

■ ■ ■

☐ *Chief Justice ROBERTS delivered the opinion of the Court.*

The Fourth Amendment forbids "unreasonable searches and seizures," and this usually requires the police to have probable cause or a warrant before making an arrest. What if an officer reasonably believes there is an outstanding arrest warrant, but that belief turns out to be wrong because of a negligent bookkeeping error by another police employee? The parties here agree that the ensuing arrest is still a violation of the Fourth Amendment, but dispute whether contraband found during a search incident to that arrest must be excluded in a later prosecution.

Our cases establish that such suppression is not an automatic consequence of a Fourth Amendment violation. Instead, the question turns on the culpability of the police and the potential of exclusion to deter wrongful police conduct. Here the error was the result of isolated negligence attenuated from the arrest. We hold that in these circumstances the jury should not be barred from considering all the evidence. . . .

When a probable-cause determination was based on reasonable but mistaken assumptions, the person subjected to a search or seizure has not necessarily been the victim of a constitutional violation. The very phrase "probable cause" confirms that the Fourth Amendment does not demand all possible precision. And whether the error can be traced to a mistake by a state actor or some other source may bear on the analysis. For purposes of deciding this case, however, we accept the parties' assumption that there was a Fourth

Amendment violation. The issue is whether the exclusionary rule should be applied. . . .

The fact that a Fourth Amendment violation occurred—i.e., that a search or arrest was unreasonable—does not necessarily mean that the exclusionary rule applies. *Illinois v. Gates*, 462 U.S. 213 (1983). Indeed, exclusion "has always been our last resort, not our first impulse," *Hudson v. Michigan*, 547 U.S. 586 (2006), and our precedents establish important principles that constrain application of the exclusionary rule.

First, the exclusionary rule is not an individual right and applies only where it "result[s] in appreciable deterrence." *Leon*. We have repeatedly rejected the argument that exclusion is a necessary consequence of a Fourth Amendment violation. *Leon*, [*Arizona v.*] *Evans*, [514 U.S. 1 (1995)]. Instead we have focused on the efficacy of the rule in deterring Fourth Amendment violations in the future. See *Stone v. Powell*, 428 U.S. 465 (1976).

In addition, the benefits of deterrence must outweigh the costs. "[T]o the extent that application of the exclusionary rule could provide some incremental deterrent, that possible benefit must be weighed against [its] substantial social costs." *Illinois v. Krull*, 480 U.S. 340 (1987). The principal cost of applying the rule is, of course, letting guilty and possibly dangerous defendants go free—something that "offends basic concepts of the criminal justice system." *Leon*.

These principles are reflected in the holding of *Leon*: When police act under a warrant that is invalid for lack of probable cause, the exclusionary rule does not apply if the police acted "in objectively reasonable reliance" on the subsequently invalidated search warrant. We (perhaps confusingly) called this objectively reasonable reliance "good faith." In a companion case, *Massachusetts v. Sheppard*, 468 U.S. 981 (1984), we held that the exclusionary rule did not apply when a warrant was invalid because a judge forgot to make "clerical corrections" to it.

Shortly thereafter we extended these holdings to warrantless administrative searches performed in good-faith reliance on a statute later declared unconstitutional. Finally, in *Evans*, we applied this good-faith rule to police who reasonably relied on mistaken information in a court's database that an arrest warrant was outstanding. We held that a mistake made by a judicial employee could not give rise to exclusion for three reasons: The exclusionary rule was crafted to curb police rather than judicial misconduct; court employees were unlikely to try to subvert the Fourth Amendment; and "most important, there [was] no basis for believing that application of the exclusionary rule in [those] circumstances" would have any significant effect in deterring the errors. *Evans* left unresolved "whether the evidence should be suppressed if police personnel were responsible for the error," an issue not argued by the State in that case, but one that we now confront.

The extent to which the exclusionary rule is justified by these deterrence principles varies with the culpability of the law enforcement conduct. As we said in *Leon*, "an assessment of the flagrancy of the police misconduct constitutes an important step in the calculus" of applying the exclusionary rule. . . .

Indeed, the abuses that gave rise to the exclusionary rule featured intentional conduct that was patently unconstitutional. In *Weeks*, a foundational exclusionary rule case, the officers had broken into the defendant's home (using a key shown to them by a neighbor), confiscated incriminating papers, then returned again with a U.S. Marshal to confiscate even more.

Not only did they have no search warrant, which the Court held was required, but they could not have gotten one had they tried. They were so lacking in sworn and particularized information that "not even an order of court would have justified such procedure."

Equally flagrant conduct was at issue in *Mapp v. Ohio*, 367 U.S. 643 (1961), which overruled *Wolf v. Colorado*, 338 U.S. 25 (1949), and extended the exclusionary rule to the States. Officers forced open a door to Ms. Mapp's house, kept her lawyer from entering, brandished what the court concluded was a false warrant, then forced her into handcuffs and canvassed the house for obscenity. An error that arises from nonrecurring and attenuated negligence is thus far removed from the core concerns that led us to adopt the rule in the first place. And in fact since *Leon*, we have never applied the rule to exclude evidence obtained in violation of the Fourth Amendment, where the police conduct was no more intentional or culpable than this.

To trigger the exclusionary rule, police conduct must be sufficiently deliberate that exclusion can meaningfully deter it, and sufficiently culpable that such deterrence is worth the price paid by the justice system. As laid out in our cases, the exclusionary rule serves to deter deliberate, reckless, or grossly negligent conduct, or in some circumstances recurring or systemic negligence. The error in this case does not rise to that level. . . .

The pertinent analysis of deterrence and culpability is objective, not an "inquiry into the subjective awareness of arresting officers." We have already held that "our good-faith inquiry is confined to the objectively ascertainable question whether a reasonably well trained officer would have known that the search was illegal" in light of "all of the circumstances." *Leon*. These circumstances frequently include a particular officer's knowledge and experience, but that does not make the test any more subjective than the one for probable cause, which looks to an officer's knowledge and experience, but not his subjective intent.

We do not suggest that all recordkeeping errors by the police are immune from the exclusionary rule. In this case, however, the conduct at issue was not so objectively culpable as to require exclusion. In *Leon* we held that "the marginal or nonexistent benefits produced by suppressing evidence obtained in objectively reasonable reliance on a subsequently invalidated search warrant cannot justify the substantial costs of exclusion." The same is true when evidence is obtained in objectively reasonable reliance on a subsequently recalled warrant.

If the police have been shown to be reckless in maintaining a warrant system, or to have knowingly made false entries to lay the groundwork for future false arrests, exclusion would certainly be justified under our cases should such misconduct cause a Fourth Amendment violation. We said as much in *Leon*, explaining that an officer could not "obtain a warrant on the basis of a 'bare bones' affidavit and then rely on colleagues who are ignorant of the circumstances under which the warrant was obtained to conduct the search." . . .

Petitioner's claim that police negligence automatically triggers suppression cannot be squared with the principles underlying the exclusionary rule, as they have been explained in our cases. In light of our repeated holdings that the deterrent effect of suppression must be substantial and outweigh any harm to the justice system, we conclude that when police mistakes are the result of negligence such as that described here, rather than systemic error or reckless disregard of constitutional requirements, any marginal deterrence does not "pay its way." In such a case, the criminal should not "go free because the constable has blundered." *People v. Defore,* 242 N.Y. 13 (1926) (opinion of the Court by CARDOZO, J.).

☐ *Justice GINSBURG, with whom Justice STEVENS, Justice SOUTER, and Justice BREYER join, dissenting.*

The exclusionary rule provides redress for Fourth Amendment violations by placing the government in the position it would have been in had there been no unconstitutional arrest and search. The rule thus strongly encourages police compliance with the Fourth Amendment in the future. The Court, however, holds the rule inapplicable because careless record-keeping by the police—not flagrant or deliberate misconduct—accounts for Herring's arrest.

I would not so constrict the domain of the exclusionary rule and would hold the rule dispositive of this case: "[I]f courts are to have any power to discourage [police] error of [the kind here at issue], it must be through the application of the exclusionary rule." *Arizona v. Evans,* 514 U.S. 1 (1995) (STEVENS, J., dissenting). The unlawful search in this case was contested in court because the police found methamphetamine in Herring's pocket and a pistol in his truck. But the "most serious impact" of the Court's holding will be on innocent persons "wrongfully arrested based on erroneous information [carelessly maintained] in a computer data base." . . .

Beyond doubt, a main objective of the rule "is to deter—to compel respect for the constitutional guaranty in the only effectively available way—by removing the incentive to disregard it." *Elkins v. United States,* 364 U.S. 206 (1960). But the rule also serves other important purposes: It "enabl[es] the judiciary to avoid the taint of partnership in official lawlessness," and it "assur[es] the people—all potential victims of unlawful government conduct—that the government would not profit from its lawless behavior, thus minimizing the risk of seriously undermining popular trust in government." *United States v. Calandra,* 414 U.S. 338 (1974) (BRENNAN, J., dissenting). . . .

The Court maintains that Herring's case is one in which the exclusionary rule could have scant deterrent effect and therefore would not "pay its way." I disagree.

The exclusionary rule, the Court suggests, is capable of only marginal deterrence when the misconduct at issue is merely careless, not intentional or reckless. The suggestion runs counter to a foundational premise of tort law—that liability for negligence, i.e., lack of due care, creates an incentive to act with greater care. The Government so acknowledges.

That the mistake here involved the failure to make a computer entry hardly means that application of the exclusionary rule would have minimal value. . . .

Is the potential deterrence here worth the costs it imposes? In light of the paramount importance of accurate recordkeeping in law enforcement, I would answer yes, and next explain why, as I see it, Herring's motion presents a particularly strong case for suppression.

Electronic databases form the nervous system of contemporary criminal justice operations. In recent years, their breadth and influence have dramatically expanded. Police today can access databases that include not only the updated National Crime Information Center (NCIC), but also terrorist watchlists, the Federal Government's employee eligibility system, and various commercial databases. . . . As a result, law enforcement has an increasing supply of information within its easy electronic reach.

The risk of error stemming from these databases is not slim. Herring's *amici* warn that law enforcement databases are insufficiently monitored and often out of date. Government reports describe, for example, flaws in NCIC databases, terrorist watchlist databases, and databases associated with the Federal Government's employment eligibility verification system.

Inaccuracies in expansive, interconnected collections of electronic information raise grave concerns for individual liberty. . . .

First, by restricting suppression to bookkeeping errors that are deliberate or reckless, the majority leaves Herring, and others like him, with no remedy for violations of their constitutional rights. There can be no serious assertion that relief is available under 42 U.S.C. Section 1983. The arresting officer would be sheltered by qualified immunity, and the police department itself is not liable for the negligent acts of its employees. Moreover, identifying the department employee who committed the error may be impossible.

Second, I doubt that police forces already possess sufficient incentives to maintain up-to-date records. The Government argues that police have no desire to send officers out on arrests unnecessarily, because arrests consume resources and place officers in danger. The facts of this case do not fit that description of police motivation. Here the officer wanted to arrest Herring and consulted the Department's records to legitimate his predisposition.

Third, even when deliberate or reckless conduct is afoot, the Court's assurance will often be an empty promise: How is an impecunious defendant to make the required showing? If the answer is that a defendant is entitled to discovery (and if necessary, an audit of police databases), then the Court has imposed a considerable administrative burden on courts and law enforcement.

Negligent recordkeeping errors by law enforcement threaten individual liberty, are susceptible to deterrence by the exclusionary rule, and cannot be remedied effectively through other means. Such errors present no occasion to further erode the exclusionary rule. The rule "is needed to make the Fourth Amendment something real; a guarantee that does not carry with it the exclusion of evidence obtained by its violation is a chimera." *Calandra*. (BRENNAN, J., dissenting). In keeping with the rule's "core concerns" suppression should have attended the unconstitutional search in this case.

For the reasons stated, I would reverse the judgment of the Eleventh Circuit.

Utah v. Strieff

136 S.Ct. 2056 (2016)

A narcotics detective surveilling a house based on an anonymous tip about drug activity became suspicious that the occupants were dealing drugs because of the number of people entering and leaving the house. When Edward Strieff left the house, the officer detained him in a nearby parking lot and asked him what he was doing at the house. He then requested Strieff's identification and relayed the information to a police dispatcher, who told him that Strieff had an outstanding arrest warrant for a traffic violation. Whereupon the officer arrested him, searched him, and found drugs. Strieff's attorney moved to suppress the evidence, arguing that it was obtained from an illegal investigatory stop. A trial court denied the motion and an appellate court affirmed, the Utah Supreme Court reversed and ordered the evidence suppressed.

On appeal, the state supreme court's decision was reversed by a vote of 6–2. Justice Thomas delivered the Court's opinion and Justice Sotomayor issued a dissent, joined in part by Justice Ginsburg.

■ ■ ■

☐ *Justice THOMAS delivered the opinion of the Court.*

To enforce the Fourth Amendment's prohibition against "unreasonable searches and seizures," this Court has at times required courts to exclude evidence obtained by unconstitutional police conduct. But the Court has also held that, even when there is a Fourth Amendment violation, this exclusionary rule does not apply when the costs of exclusion outweigh its deterrent benefits. In some cases, for example, the link between the unconstitutional conduct and the discovery of the evidence is too attenuated to justify suppression. The question in this case is whether this attenuation doctrine applies when an officer makes an unconstitutional investigatory stop; learns during that stop that the suspect is subject to a valid arrest warrant; and proceeds to arrest the suspect and seize incriminating evidence during a search incident to that arrest. We hold that the evidence the officer seized as part of the search incident to arrest is admissible because the officer's discovery of the arrest warrant attenuated the connection between the unlawful stop and the evidence seized incident to arrest. . . .

Under the Court's precedents, the exclusionary rule encompasses both the "primary evidence obtained as a direct result of an illegal search or seizure" and, relevant here, "evidence later discovered and found to be derivative of an illegality," the so-called "'fruit of the poisonous tree.'" *Segura* v. *United States*, 468 U.S. 796 (1984). But the significant costs of this rule have led us to deem it "applicable only . . . where its deterrence benefits outweigh its substantial social costs." *Hudson* v. *Michigan*, 547 U.S. 586 (2006).

We have accordingly recognized several exceptions to the rule. Three of these exceptions involve the causal relationship between the unconstitutional act and the discovery of evidence. First, the independent source doctrine allows trial courts to admit evidence obtained in an unlawful search if officers independently acquired it from a separate, independent source. See *Murray* v. *United States*, 487 U.S. 533 (1988). Second, the inevitable discovery doctrine allows for the admission of evidence that would have been discovered even without the unconstitutional source. See *Nix* v. *Williams*, 467 U.S. 431 (1984). Third, and at issue here, is the attenuation doctrine: Evidence is admissible when the connection between unconstitutional police conduct and the evidence is remote or has been interrupted by some intervening circumstance, so that "the interest protected by the constitutional guarantee that has been violated would not be served by suppression of the evidence obtained." *Hudson.*

Turning to the application of the attenuation doctrine to this case, we first address a threshold question: whether this doctrine applies at all to a case like this, where the intervening circumstance that the State relies on is the discovery of a valid, pre-existing, and untainted arrest warrant. The Utah Supreme Court declined to apply the attenuation doctrine because it read our precedents as applying the doctrine only "to circumstances involving an independent act of a defendant's 'free will' in confessing to a crime or consenting to a search." In this Court, Strieff has not defended this argument, and we disagree with it, as well. The attenuation doctrine evaluates the causal link between the government's unlawful act and the discovery of evidence, which often has nothing to do with a defendant's actions. And the logic of our prior attenuation cases is not limited to independent acts by the defendant.

It remains for us to address whether the discovery of a valid arrest warrant was a sufficient intervening event to break the causal chain between the unlawful stop and the discovery of drug-related evidence on Strieff's person. The three factors articulated in *Brown* v. *Illinois*, 422 U.S. 590 (1975), guide our analysis. First, we look to the "temporal proximity" between the unconstitutional conduct and the discovery of evidence to determine how closely the discovery of evidence followed the unconstitutional search. Second, we consider "the presence of intervening circumstances." Third, and "particularly" significant, we examine "the purpose and flagrancy of the official misconduct." In evaluating these factors, we assume without deciding (because the State conceded the point) that Officer Fackrell lacked reasonable suspicion to initially stop Strieff. And, because we ultimately conclude that the warrant breaks the causal chain, we also have no need to decide whether the warrant's existence alone would make the initial stop constitutional even if Officer Fackrell was unaware of its existence.

The first factor, temporal proximity between the initially unlawful stop and the search, favors suppressing the evidence. Our precedents have declined to find that this factor favors attenuation unless "substantial time" elapses between an unlawful act and when the evidence is obtained. *Kaupp* v. *Texas*, 538 U.S. 626 (2003). Here, however, Officer Fackrell discovered drug contraband on Strieff's person only minutes after the illegal stop. As the Court explained in *Brown*, such a short time interval counsels in favor of suppression; there, we found that the confession should be suppressed, relying in part on the "less than two hours" that separated the unconstitutional arrest and the confession.

In contrast, the second factor, the presence of intervening circumstances, strongly favors the State. In *Segura*, the Court addressed similar facts to those here and found sufficient intervening circumstances to allow the admission of evidence. There, agents had probable cause to believe that apartment occupants were dealing cocaine. They sought a warrant. In the meantime, they entered the apartment, arrested an occupant, and discovered evidence of drug activity during a limited search for security reasons. The next evening, the Magistrate Judge issued the search warrant. This Court deemed the evidence admissible notwithstanding the illegal search because the information supporting the warrant was "wholly unconnected with the [arguably illegal] entry and was known to the agents well before the initial entry."

Segura, of course, applied the independent source doctrine because the unlawful entry "did not contribute in any way to discovery of the evidence seized under the warrant." But the *Segura* Court suggested that the existence of a valid warrant favors finding that the connection between unlawful conduct and the discovery of evidence is "sufficiently attenuated to dissipate the taint." That principle applies here.

In this case, the warrant was valid, it predated Officer Fackrell's investigation, and it was entirely unconnected with the stop. And once Officer Fackrell discovered the warrant, he had an obligation to arrest Strieff. "A warrant is a judicial mandate to an officer to conduct a search or make an arrest, and the officer has a sworn duty to carry out its provisions." *United States* v. *Leon,* 468 U.S. 897 (1984). Officer Fackrell's arrest of Strieff thus was a ministerial act that was independently compelled by the pre-existing warrant. And once Officer Fackrell was authorized to arrest Strieff, it was undisputedly lawful to search Strieff as an incident of his arrest to protect Officer Fackrell's safety.

Finally, the third factor, "the purpose and flagrancy of the official misconduct," also strongly favors the State. The exclusionary rule exists to deter police misconduct. *Davis* v. *United States,* 564 U.S. 229 (2011). The third factor of the attenuation doctrine reflects that rationale by favoring exclusion only when the police misconduct is most in need of deterrence—that is, when it is purposeful or flagrant.

Officer Fackrell was at most negligent. In stopping Strieff, Officer Fackrell made two good-faith mistakes. First, he had not observed what time Strieff entered the suspected drug house, so he did not know how long Strieff had been there. Officer Fackrell thus lacked a sufficient basis to conclude that Strieff was a short-term visitor who may have been consummating a drug transaction. Second, because he lacked confirmation that Strieff was a short-term visitor, Officer Fackrell should have asked Strieff whether he would speak with him, instead of demanding that Strieff do so. Officer Fackrell's stated purpose was to "find out what was going on [in] the house." Nothing prevented him from approaching Strieff simply to ask. See *Florida* v. *Bostick,* 501 U.S. 429 (1991) ("[A] seizure does not occur simply because a police officer approaches an individual and asks a few questions"). But these errors in judgment hardly rise to a purposeful or flagrant violation of Strieff's Fourth Amendment rights.

While Officer Fackrell's decision to initiate the stop was mistaken, his conduct thereafter was lawful. The officer's decision to run the warrant check was a "negligibly burdensome precautio[n]" for officer safety. And Officer Fackrell's actual search of Strieff was a lawful search incident to arrest.

Moreover, there is no indication that this unlawful stop was part of any systemic or recurrent police misconduct. To the contrary, all the evidence suggests that the stop was an isolated instance of negligence that occurred in connection with a bona fide investigation of a suspected drug house. Officer Fackrell saw Strieff leave a suspected drug house. And his suspicion about the house was based on an anonymous tip and his personal observations.

Applying these factors, we hold that the evidence discovered on Strieff's person was admissible because the unlawful stop was sufficiently attenuated by the pre-existing arrest warrant. Although the illegal stop was close in time to Strieff's arrest, that consideration is outweighed by two factors supporting the State. The outstanding arrest warrant for Strieff's arrest is a critical intervening circumstance that is wholly independent of the illegal stop. The discovery of that warrant broke the causal chain between the unconstitutional stop and the discovery of evidence by compelling Officer Fackrell to arrest Strieff. And, it is especially significant that there is no evidence that Officer Fackrell's illegal stop reflected flagrantly unlawful police misconduct. . . .

☐ *Justice SOTOMAYOR, with whom Justice GINSBURG joins in part, dissenting.*

The Court today holds that the discovery of a warrant for an unpaid parking ticket will forgive a police officer's violation of your Fourth Amendment rights. Do not be soothed by the opinion's technical language: This case allows the police to stop you on the street, demand your identification, and check it for outstanding traffic warrants—even if you are doing nothing wrong. If the officer discovers a warrant for a fine you forgot to pay, courts will now excuse his illegal stop and will admit into evidence anything he happens to find by searching you after arresting you on the warrant. Because the Fourth Amendment should prohibit, not permit, such misconduct, I dissent.

Minutes after Edward Strieff walked out of a South Salt Lake City home, an officer stopped him, questioned him, and took his identification to run it through a police database. The officer did not suspect that Strieff had done anything wrong. Strieff just happened to be the first person to leave a house that the officer thought might contain "drug activity."

As the State of Utah concedes, this stop was illegal. App. 24. The Fourth Amendment protects people from "unreasonable searches and seizures." An officer breaches that protection when he detains a pedestrian to check his license without any evidence that the person is engaged in a crime. *Delaware* v. *Prouse*, 440 U.S. 648 (1979); *Terry* v. *Ohio*, 392 U.S. 1 (1968). The officer deepens the breach when he prolongs the detention just to fish further for evidence of wrongdoing. . . .

It is tempting in a case like this, where illegal conduct by an officer uncovers illegal conduct by a civilian, to forgive the officer. After all, his instincts, although unconstitutional, were correct. But a basic principle lies at the heart of the Fourth Amendment: Two wrongs don't make a right. See *Weeks* v. *United States*, 232 U.S. 383 (1914). When "lawless police conduct" uncovers evidence of lawless civilian conduct, this Court has long required later criminal trials to exclude the illegally obtained evidence. *Terry; Mapp* v. *Ohio* (1961). For example, if an officer breaks into a home and finds a forged check lying around, that check may not be used to prosecute the homeowner for bank fraud. We would describe the check as "'fruit of the poisonous tree.'" *Wong Sun* v. *United States,* 371 U.S. 471 (1963). Fruit that must be cast aside includes not only evidence directly found by an illegal search but also evidence "come at by exploitation of that illegality."

This "exclusionary rule" removes an incentive for officers to search us without proper justification. *Terry.* It also keeps courts from being "made party to lawless invasions of the constitutional rights of citizens by permitting unhindered governmental use of the fruits of such invasions." When courts admit only lawfully obtained evidence, they encourage "those who formulate law enforcement polices, and the officers who implement them, to incorporate Fourth Amendment ideals into their value system." *Stone* v. *Powell,* 428 U.S. 465 (1976). But when courts admit illegally obtained evidence as well, they reward "manifest neglect if not an open defiance of the prohibitions of the Constitution." *Weeks.* . . .

The officer did not ask Strieff to volunteer his name only to find out, days later, that Strieff had a warrant against him. The officer illegally stopped Strieff and immediately ran a warrant check. The officer's discovery of a warrant was not some intervening surprise that he could not have anticipated. Utah lists over 180,000 misdemeanor warrants in its database, and at the time of the arrest, Salt Lake County had a "backlog of outstanding warrants" so large that it faced the "potential for civil liability." The officer's violation was also calculated to procure evidence. His sole reason for stopping Strieff, he acknowledged, was investigative—he wanted to discover whether drug activity was going on in the house Strieff had just exited.

The warrant check, in other words, was not an "intervening circumstance" separating the stop from the search for drugs. It was part and parcel of the officer's illegal "expedition for evidence in the hope that something might turn up." *Brown.* Under our precedents, because the officer found Strieff's drugs by exploiting his own constitutional violation, the drugs should be excluded.

The Court sees things differently. To the Court, the fact that a warrant gives an officer cause to arrest a person severs the connection between illegal policing and the resulting discovery of evidence. This is a remarkable proposition: The mere existence of a warrant not only gives an officer legal cause to arrest and search a person, it also forgives an officer who, with no knowledge of the warrant at all, unlawfully stops that person on a whim or hunch. . . .

The majority likewise misses the point when it calls the warrant check here a "'negligibly burdensome precautio[n]'" taken for the officer's "safety." . . . We allow such checks during legal traffic stops because the legitimacy of a person's driver's license has a "close connection to roadway safety." A warrant check of a pedestrian on a sidewalk, "by contrast, is a measure aimed at 'detect[ing] evidence of ordinary criminal wrongdoing.'" Surely we would not allow officers to warrant-check random joggers, dog walkers, and lemonade vendors just to ensure they pose no threat to anyone else.

The majority also posits that the officer could not have exploited his illegal conduct because he did not violate the Fourth Amendment on purpose. Rather, he made "good-faith mistakes." Never mind that the officer's sole purpose was to fish for evidence. The majority casts his unconstitutional actions as "negligent" and therefore incapable of being deterred by the exclusionary rule.

But the Fourth Amendment does not tolerate an officer's unreasonable searches and seizures just because he did not know any better. Even officers prone to negligence can learn from courts that exclude illegally obtained evidence. Indeed, they are perhaps the most in need of the education, whether by the judge's opinion, the prosecutor's future guidance, or an updated manual on criminal procedure. If the officers are in doubt about what the law requires, exclusion gives them an "incentive to err on the side of constitutional behavior." *United States* v. *Johnson*, 457 U.S. 537 (1982).

Most striking about the Court's opinion is its insistence that the event here was "isolated," with "no indication that this unlawful stop was part of any systemic or recurrent police misconduct." Respectfully, nothing about this case is isolated.

Outstanding warrants are surprisingly common. When a person with a traffic ticket misses a fine payment or court appearance, a court will issue a warrant. The States and Federal Government maintain databases with over 7.8 million outstanding warrants, the vast majority of which appear to be for minor offenses.

Justice Department investigations across the country have illustrated how these astounding numbers of warrants can be used by police to stop people without cause. In a single year in New Orleans, officers "made nearly 60,000 arrests, of which about 20,000 were of people with outstanding traffic or misdemeanor warrants from neighboring parishes for such infractions as unpaid tickets." . . .

I do not doubt that most officers act in "good faith" and do not set out to break the law. That does not mean these stops are "isolated instance[s] of negligence," however. Many are the product of institutionalized training procedures. . . .

Writing only for myself, and drawing on my professional experiences, I would add that unlawful "stops" have severe consequences much greater than the inconvenience suggested by the name. This Court has given officers an array of instruments to probe and examine you. When we condone officers' use of these devices without adequate cause, we give them reason to target pedestrians in an arbitrary manner. We also risk treating members of our communities as second-class citizens.

Although many Americans have been stopped for speeding or jaywalking, few may realize how degrading a stop can be when the officer is looking for more. This Court has allowed an officer to stop you for whatever reason he wants—so long as he can point to a pretextual justification after the fact. That justification must provide specific reasons why the officer suspected you were breaking the law, *Terry*, but it may factor in your ethnicity, *United States* v. *Brignoni-Ponce*, 422 U.S. 873 (1975), where you live, *Adams* v. *Williams*, 407 U.S. 143 (1972), what you were wearing, *United States* v. *Sokolow*, 490 U.S. 1 (1989), and how you behaved, *Illinois* v. *Wardlow*, 528 U.S. 119 (2000). The officer does not even need to know which law you might have broken so long as he can later point to any possible infraction—even one that is minor, unrelated, or ambiguous.

The indignity of the stop is not limited to an officer telling you that you look like a criminal. The officer may next ask for your "consent" to inspect your bag or purse without telling you that you can decline. Regardless of your answer, he may order you to stand "helpless, perhaps facing a wall with [your] hands raised." *Terry.* If the officer thinks you might be dangerous, he may then "frisk" you for weapons. This involves more than just a pat down. As onlookers pass by, the officer may "'feel with sensitive fingers every portion of [your] body. A thorough search [may] be made of [your] arms and armpits, waistline and back, the groin and area about the testicles, and entire surface of the legs down to the feet.'"

The officer's control over you does not end with the stop. If the officer chooses, he may handcuff you and take you to jail for doing nothing more than speeding, jaywalking, or "driving [your] pickup truck . . . with [your] 3-year-old son and 5-year-old daughter . . . without [your] seatbelt fastened." *Atwater* v. *Lago Vista*, 532 U.S. 318 (2001). At the jail, he can fingerprint you, swab DNA from the inside of your mouth, and force you to "shower with a delousing agent" while you "lift [your] tongue, hold out [your] arms, turn around, and lift [your] genitals." *Florence* v. *Board of Chosen Freeholders of County of Burlington,* [132 S.Ct. 1510] (2012); *Maryland* v. *King,* [133 S.Ct. 1958] (2013). Even if you are innocent, you will now join the 65 million Americans with an arrest record and experience the "civil death" of discrimination by employers, landlords, and whoever else conducts a background check. And, of course, if you fail to pay bail or appear for court, a judge will issue a warrant to render you "arrestable on sight" in the future.

This case involves a *suspicionless* stop, one in which the officer initiated this chain of events without justification. . . . . We must not pretend that the countless people who are routinely targeted by police are "isolated." They are the canaries in the coal mine whose deaths, civil and literal, warn us that no one can breathe in this atmosphere. They are the ones who recognize that unlawful police stops corrode all our civil liberties and threaten all our lives. Until their voices matter too, our justice system will continue to be anything but.

I dissent.

8

THE FIFTH AMENDMENT
GUARANTEE AGAINST
SELF-ACCUSATION

The Fifth Amendment's provision that "[n]o person . . . shall be compelled in any criminal case to be a witness against himself" gave constitutional effect to an old common-law maxim: "No man is bound to betray [accuse] himself."[1] That maxim can be traced to Englishman John Lambert, an obdurate heretic, who in 1537, while chained to a stake, protested the inquisitorial practices of ecclesiastical courts. Not until the middle of the seventeenth century, however, did the principle that no man is bound to accuse himself become firmly embedded in English common law. Yet by the close of that century, the principle had become part of the legal systems in the colonies. Six of the original thirteen states included the guarantee in their state constitutions or bills of rights, and in the remaining it was recognized by their courts.

Although the common-law maxim provided the historical basis for the Fifth Amendment, the drafters of the Bill of Rights were apparently unsure of its precise scope. Initially, George Mason, as author of the Virginia Declaration of Rights, urged the constitutionality of this rule of evidence as part of accepted accusatorial criminal procedure:

> That in all capital or criminal prosecutions a man hath a right to demand the cause and nature of his accusation, to be confronted with the accusers and witnesses, to call for evidence in favor, and to a speedy trial by an impartial jury of twelve men of his vicinage, without whose unanimous consent he cannot be found guilty; *nor can he be compelled to give evidence against himself*; that no man be deprived of his liberty, except by the law of the land or the judgment of his peers.[2]

Mason's formulation, however, fell short of the common-law protection for witnesses as well as for the accused.

By comparison, James Madison's draft of the proposed amendment embraced the broad scope of the traditional common-law maxim: "No person shall be subject, except in cases of impeachment, to more than one punishment or trial for the same offense; *nor shall be compelled to be a witness against himself*; nor be deprived of life, liberty, or property, without due process of law; nor be obliged to relinquish his property, where it may be necessary for public use, without just compensation."

Madison's proposal broadly applied to civil and criminal proceedings as well as to all stages of the legal process, including both legislative and judicial inquiries. Indeed, because Madison collapsed the maxim "No man is bound to accuse himself" with another—"No man should be a witness in his own case"—his formulation would have applied "to any testimony that fell short of making one vulnerable, but that nevertheless exposed him to public disgrace or obloquy, or other injury to name of reputation," and would have extended protection to third-party witnesses in civil and criminal proceedings.[3]

In the House committee assigned to finalize the Bill of Rights, John Lawrence suggested that the clause constituted "a general declaration in some degree contrary to laws passed" and should be "confined to criminal cases." The clause was amended without discussion and adopted unanimously.[4] Inclusion of the phrase "in any criminal case" limited the scope of the guarantee, ostensibly precluding invocation of the right during police interrogations and by parties and witnesses in civil and equity suits as well as in nonjudicial proceedings, such as grand jury and legislative investigations.

But the Supreme Court has interpreted the guarantee to be "as broad as the mischief against which it seeks to guard."[5] The scope of the amendment extends beyond criminal trials to grand jury proceedings;[6] to legislative investigations;[7] and, in some circumstances, to witnesses in civil and criminal cases where truthful assertions might result in forfeiture, penalty, or criminal prosecution.[8] The Warren Court's landmark ruling in *Miranda v. Arizona* (1966) (excerpted in Section A) "expanded the right beyond all precedent, yet not beyond its historical spirit and purpose"[9] in extending the guarantee to police interrogations. As a consequence, the Fifth Amendment's guarantee applies from the time police begin "to focus on a particular suspect" through "custodial interrogation"[10] to the trial itself as well as to other quasi-judicial and nonjudicial proceedings.[11] In addition, individuals may not be disbarred or lose their jobs simply because they plead their Fifth Amendment right to remain silent.[12] In *United States v. Aloyzas Balsys*, 524 U.S. 666 (1998), however, the Court held that individuals may not claim the privilege simply because of a fear that incriminating statements may result in deportation and prosecution by a foreign nation.

Although, historically, rejecting a strict construction of the amendment, the Court has imposed two crucial restrictions by loosely construing the guarantee to confer "a privilege against self-incrimination." First, the inference that the amendment grants only a *privilege* rather than a *right* has great jurisprudential significance. Privileges differ from rights: whereas privileges are granted (and revocable) by the government, rights do not derive from the government and limit the exercise of governmental power. As historian Leonard W. Levy observes, "to speak of the 'privilege' against self-incrimination, degrades it, inadvertently, in comparison to other constitutional rights."[13] Second, the amendment literally does not protect merely self-incrimination. As Levy points out:

> [T]o speak of a right against self-incrimination stunts the wide right not to give evidence against oneself. . . . The "right against self-incrimination" is a shorthand gloss of modern origin that implies a restriction not in the constitutional clause. The right not to be witness against oneself imports a principle of wider reach, applicable at least in criminal cases, to the self-production of any adverse evidence, including evidence that made one the herald of his own infamy, thereby publicly disgracing him. The clause extended, in other words, to all the injurious as well as incriminating consequences of disclosures.[14]

In sum, the shorthand version of the guarantee as a privilege against self-incrimination unnecessarily limits the scope of the Fifth Amendment.

The primary effect of the Fifth Amendment remains that in criminal trials the accused cannot be compelled to take the witness stand. It is also improper for judges to comment on a defendant's refusal to testify.[15] Witnesses must explicitly claim the right to remain silent; otherwise, they are considered to have tacitly waived it.[16] Judges ultimately decide whether a claim to exercise the right is valid.[17] Even in criminal cases, the accused may refuse to answer only questions tantamount to admissions of guilt but not when self-incrimination is "of an imaginary and unsubstantial character, having reference to some extraordinary and barely possible contingency, so improbable that no reasonable man would suffer it to influence his conduct."[18]

The scope of the Fifth Amendment, however, depends on the Supreme Court's construction of the purposes and policies behind the amendment, which in turn depends on the politics of the Court and its composition. *Murphy v. Waterfront Commission*, 387 U.S. 52 (1964), concisely elucidated the "complex of values" underlying the right against self-accusation:

> It reflects many of our fundamental values and most noble aspirations: our unwillingness to subject those suspected of crime to the cruel trilemma of self-accusation, perjury, or contempt; our preference for an accusatorial rather than an inquisitorial system of criminal justice; our fear that self-incrimination will be elicited by inhumane treatment and abuses; our sense of fair play which dictates a "fair state-individual balance by requiring the government . . . in its contest with the individual to shoulder the entire load," . . . our respect for the inviolability of the human personality and of the right of each individual "to a private enclave where he may lead a private life," . . . our distrust of self-deprecatory statements; and our realization that the privilege while "a shelter to the guilty," has often [been] "a protection to the innocent."

From this complex of values, three basic rationales stand out: the guarantee's role in (1) maintaining a responsible accusatorial system, (2) preventing cruel and inhumane treatment of suspects, and (3) offering protection for personal privacy. Each implies a different interpretative approach toward the amendment. Together, they define the jurisprudential basis for the struggle within the Court over defining the scope of the Fifth Amendment.

The "fox hunter's reason" was how Jeremy Bentham, an eighteenth-century English legal reformer, characterized the first rationale for the privilege against self-incrimination. Just as in a fox hunt certain rules governed the ways by which fox hunters may capture the fox, so too evidentiary rules define an acceptable process for prosecuting suspects of criminal activity in an accusatorial system. Both the rules of fox hunting and of the criminal justice system are predicated on the notion of fairness—fair treatment of the fox and the criminal suspect. In Bentham's words, "[I]t consists in introducing upon the carpet of legal procedure the ideal of *fairness*, in the sense in which the word is used by sportsmen. The fox is to have a fair chance for his life: he must have (so close is the analogy) what is called *law*: leave to run a certain length of way, for the express purpose of giving him a chance for escape."[19]

How does the Fifth Amendment's guarantee serve the ideal of justice as fair treatment in accusatory systems? Justice Abe Fortas explained that

> [t]o maintain a "fair state-individual balance," to require the government "to shoulder the entire load," . . . to respect the inviolability of the human personality, our accusatory system of criminal justice demands that the government seeking to punish an individual produce the evidence by its own independent labors, rather than by the cruel, simple expedient of compelling it from his own mouth. . . . The principle that a man is not obliged to furnish the state with ammunition to use against him is basic to this concep-

tion. Equals, meeting in battle, owe no such duty to one another, regardless of the obligations that they may be under prior to battle. A sovereign state has the right to defend itself, and within the limits of accepted procedure, to punish infractions of the rules that govern its relationships with its sovereign individual to surrender or impair his right of self-defense.[20]

On this interpretation, the Fifth Amendment has instrumental value in securing a "fair fight" and a "fair state-individual balance"; the right against compelled self-incrimination is not an end in itself. But if the amendment has only instrumental value, then its scope is limited to those contexts in which individuals face the threat of prosecution. And the government is forbidden from only exerting "genuine compulsion" in securing a suspect's self-incriminating statements. Where disclosures are not incriminating (merely embarrassing) or when incriminating testimony is given in exchange for a grant of immunity, the amendment offers no protection. This was the view taken in *United States v. Washington*, 431 U.S. 181 (1977): "Absent some officially coerced self-accusation the Fifth Amendment privilege is not violated by even the most damning admissions. . . . The constitutional guarantee is only that the witness be not *compelled* to give self-incriminating testimony. The test is whether, considering the totality of the circumstances, the free will of the witness was overborne."

A rival interpretation is grounded in what Bentham termed "an old woman's reason"; namely, the belief that it is cruel and inhumane to force a person to partake in his own undoing. From this perspective, the Fifth Amendment embodies an end in itself—respect for the moral dignity of the individual—and confers a right to remain silent. "The essence of [the old woman's] reason," as Bentham put it, "is contained in the word *hard*: 'tis hard upon a man to be obliged to criminate himself.'" And Bentham viewed dimly "this plea of tenderness, this double-distilled and treble-refined sentimentality," claiming that it served only the guilty: "Hard it is upon a man, it must be confessed, to be obliged to do anything that he does not like. That he should not much like to do what is meant by his [in]criminating himself, is natural enough; for what it leads to, is, his being punished. What is not less hard is in a man's being punished, that, and no more, is there in his thus being made to incriminate himself."

History, however, shows that respect for human dignity played an important role in the development of a right against self-accusation. In the late sixteenth century, Puritan leaders attacked the *ex officio* oath on the grounds that "[m]uch more is it equall that a mans owne private faults should remayne private to God and himselfe till the Lord discover them. And in regard of this righte consider howe the Lord ordained wittnesses where by the magistrate should seeke into the offences of his subjects and not by oathe rifle the secrets of theare hearts."[21] Colonial common law also offered protection "against physical compulsion and against the moral compulsion that an oath to a revengeful God commands of a pious soul."[22] It is to this history and interpretation that Justice Douglas appealed when dissenting, in *Ullmann v. United States*, 350 U.S. 422 (1956), from the Court's upholding the constitutionality of grants of immunity:

> The guarantee against self-incrimination contained in the Fifth Amendment is not only a protection against conviction and prosecution but a safeguard of conscience and human dignity and freedom of expression as well. . . . [T]he Framers put it well beyond the power of Congress to *compel* anyone to confess his crimes. The evil to be guarded against was partly self-accusation under legal compulsion. But that was only a part of the evil. The conscience and dignity of man were also involved.

Notwithstanding the moral appeal of the old woman's rationale, critics charge that it "confronts the clear fact that the rule against self-incrimination is psychologically and morally unacceptable as a general governing principle in human relations."[23] Court of Appeals Judge Henry J. Friendly, for one, argued that "[n]o parent would teach such a doctrine to his children; the lesson parents preach is that a misdeed, even a serious one, will generally be forgiven; a failure to make a clean breast of it will not be. Every day people are being asked to explain their conduct to parents, employers, and teachers."[24] However, there is a vast difference between the state's compelling a person to incriminate himself and a person's revelations to his or her lover, parents, friends, or employer, as well as between the kinds of sanctions that may result from those self-revelations.

Finally, "the hermit's rationale" draws attention to the amendment's protection for personal privacy. This view of the amendment was often advanced during the Warren Court era. In particular, in *Warden v. Hayden*, 387 U.S. 294 (1967), Justice Douglas observed that "[p]rivacy involves the choice of the individual to disclose or to reveal what he believes, what he thinks, what he possesses. . . . That dual aspect of privacy means that the individual should have the freedom to select for himself the time and circumstances when he will share his secrets with others and decide the extent of that sharing. This is his prerogative, not the State's."

The importance of these competing rationales is underscored by Justice Harlan's observation, dissenting in *Garrity v. New Jersey*, 385 U.S. 493 (1967): "The Constitution contains no formulae within which we can calculate the areas . . . to which the privilege should extend, and the Court has therefore been obliged to fashion for itself standards for the application of the privilege." Consider how these competing rationales enter into the Court's rulings on coerced confessions and police inter-rogations, grants of immunity, and its distinction between "real" and "testimonial" evidence, as well as on claims to Fifth Amendment pro-tection for required records and private papers, in the following sections of this chapter.

NOTES

1. See Leonard Levy, *The Origins of the Fifth Amendment* (New York: Oxford University Press, 1968).

2. "Virginia Declaration of Rights," in *The Federal and State Constitutions, Colonial Charters, and Other Organic Laws*, ed. F. Thorpe (New York: Harper & Brothers, 1898). Emphasis added.

3. Levy, *The Origins of the Fifth Amendment*, 243–244.

4. "Amendments Reported by the House Select Committee, July 28, 1789," in *Documentary History of the Constitution of the United States*, Vol. 5, 186.

5. *Counselman v. Hitchcock*, 142 U.S. 547 (1892).

6. See *Lefkowitz v. Cunningham*, 431 U.S. 801 (1977); *California v. Byers*, 402 U.S. 424 (1971); *United States v. Kordel*, 397 U.S. 1 (1970); and *Marbury v. Madison*, 5 U.S. 137 (1803).

7. See *Watkins v. United States*, 354 U.S. 178 (1957); and *Bart v. United States*, 349 U.S. 219 (1955).

8. *McCarthy v. Arndstein*, 266 U.S. 34 (1924). But see *Chavez v. Martinez*, 538 U.S. 760 (2003), holding that violations of *Miranda* do not apply to civil suits for damages.

9. Levy, *The Origins of the Fifth Amendment*, 38.

10. *Escobedo v. Illinois*, 378 U.S. 478 (1964).

11. See *Miranda v. Arizona*, 384 U.S. 436 (police interrogations); *Emspack v. United States*, 349 U.S. 190 (1955), and *Quinn v. United States*, 349 U.S. 155 (1955) (legislative investigations); *McCarthy v. Arndstein*, 266 U.S. 34 (1924) (civil proceedings); *ICC v. Brimson*, 154 U.S. 447 (1894) (administrative investigations); *Counselman v. Hitchcock*, 142 U.S. 547 (1892) (grand jury proceedings).

12. See *Regan v. New York*, 349 U.S. 58 (1954); *Slochower v. Board of Education*, 350 U.S. 551 (1956); *Spavack v. Klein*, 385 U.S. 511 (1967); *Gardner v. Broderick*, 392 U.S. 273 (1968); *Uniformed Sanitation Men's Association v. Commissioner of Sanitation of the City of New York*, 392 U.S. 280 (1968); *Lefkowitz v. Turley*, 414 U.S. 70 (1973); and *Lefkowitz v. Cunningham*, 431 U.S. 801 (1977).

13. Leonard W. Levy, "The Right against Self-Incrimination," 29 *Journal of Politics* 3 (1969).

14. Levy, *The Origins of the Fifth Amendment*, 425–427.

15. See *Griffin v. California*, 380 U.S. 609 (1965). But also see *United States v. Young*, 470 U.S. 1 (1985) (a 5–4 ruling upholding a prosecutor's statements that the defendant was guilty and urging the jury to do its job).

16. *California v. Byers*, 402 U.S. 424 (1971); *Rogers v. United States*, 340 U.S. 367 (1951); and *United States v. Monia*, 317 U.S. 424 (1943).

17. *Mackey v. United States*, 401 U.S. 667 (1971); *Hoffman v. United States*, 341 U.S. 479 (1955); and *Mason v. United States*, 244 U.S. 362 (1917).

18. *Emspack v. United States*, 349 U.S. 190 (1955).

19. Jeremy Bentham, *A Rationale of Judicial Evidence* (1827), 238–239. The discussion in this section draws on David M. O'Brien, "The Fifth Amendment: Fox Hunters, Old Women, Hermits, and the Burger Court," 54 *Notre Dame Lawyer* 26 (1978).

20. Abe Fortas, "The Fifth Amendment: *Nemo Tenetur Prodere Seipsum*," 25 *Cleveland Bar Association Journal* 95 (1954).

21. Quoted in Levy, *The Origins of the Fifth Amendment*, 177.

22. R. Carter Pittman, "The Colonial and Constitutional History of the Privilege against Self-Incrimination," 21 *Virginia Law Review* 783 (1935).

23. David Louisell, "Criminal Discovery and Self-Incrimination," 53 *California Law Review* 95 (1965).

24. Henry J. Friendly, "The Fifth Amendment Tomorrow: The Case for Constitutional Change," 37 *Cincinnati Law Review* 673 (1968).

Selected Bibliography

Baker, Liva. *Miranda: Crime, Law and Politics*. New York: Atheneum, 1983.

Levy, Leonard W. *Origins of the Fifth Amendment*. New York: Oxford University Press, 1968.

Simon, David. *Homicide: A Year on the Killing Streets*. Boston: Houghton Mifflin, 1991.

Stuart, Gary. *Miranda: The Story of America's Right to Remain Silent*. Tucson: University of Arizona Press, 2004.

Tanenhaus, David. *The Constitutional Rights of Children: In re Gault and Juvenile Justice*. Lawrence: University of Kansas Press, 2011.

Thomas, George, III. *Confessions of Guilt: From Torture to Miranda and Beyond*. New York: Oxford University Press, 2012.

White, Welsh S. *Miranda's Waning Protections*. Ann Arbor: University of Michigan Press, 2003.

A | *Coerced Confessions and Police Interrogations*

The issues that arise with police interrogations and coerced confessions were long avoided by the Court until the Fifth Amendment was applied to the states in *Malloy v. Hogan*, 378 U.S. 1 (1964). However, in the 1930s and 1940s the Court confronted police practices and the rights of the accused under the due process clause of the Fourteenth Amendment. In *Brown v. Mississippi*, 297 U.S. 278 (1936), for example, police physically tortured a suspect, and Chief Justice Charles Evans Hughes responded with a unanimous opinion warning that "the freedom of constitutional government . . . is limited by the requirement of due process of law. Because a State may dispense with a jury trial, it does not follow that it may substitute trial by ordeal. The rack and torture chamber may not be substituted for the witness stand." Subsequently, *Ashcraft v. Tennessee*, 322 U.S. 143 (1944), held that the use of some confessions violates the due process clause because they are the result of "inherently coercive" police interrogations; here, Ashcraft's confession came after thirty-six hours of continuous police questioning under electric lights. On a case-by-case basis in the 1950s, the Court found a number of police interrogations so psychologically coercive as to run afoul of the due process clause.[1] And in *Mallory v. United States*, 354 U.S. 449 (1957), the Court held that a confession was improper when the defendant had not been properly arraigned first.

The problem with the Court's looking at the *totality of the circumstances* in each case to determine whether a confession was coerced and for a violation of a suspect's Fifth Amendment rights (and the Sixth Amendment right to counsel) was that it provided little guidance for police and lower courts. In the 1940s and 1950s police in many areas of the country were still not required to be high school graduates and the quality of state court judges was much lower than today. Still, the Court remained reluctant to establish a "bright line" ruling on how far police could go when interrogating suspects. In *Crooker v. California*, 357 U.S. 433 (1958), for instance, the justices split 5–4 in holding that the denial of the presence of an attorney during police questioning did not violate the rights of an accused man who had a college degree and some law school training. Yet in the following year the Court unanimously held that the presence of counsel was required when the defendant confessed during a three-o'clock-in-the-morning interrogation by police in *Spano v. New York*, 360 U.S. 315 (1959).

A solid majority on the Warren Court (after the appointment of Justice Arthur Goldberg in 1962) finally came together in establishing a bright line rule for police interrogations.[2] In *Massiah v. United States*, 377 U.S. 201 (1964), the Court held that a defendant's Fifth and Sixth Amendment rights were violated by a prosecutor's use as evidence of his incriminating statements made to a codefendant after being indicted and which were overheard by police on a radio with the codefendant's permission. Splitting 5–4 in *Escobedo v. Illinois*, 378 U.S. 478 (1964), the Court went even further. For a bare majority, Justice Goldberg held that no "meaningful distinction" could be drawn between police interrogations before and after a suspect's formal indictment. Individuals have the right to the presence of an attorney at the time they become suspects and the focus of police investigations.

Escobedo laid the basis for the 5–4 ruling in *Miranda v. Arizona* (1966) (excerpted below) in which Chief Justice Earl Warren set down a code of conduct for police interrogations, requiring police to inform suspects of their rights to remain silent and to have an attorney present during police questioning. As a result, the totality of circumstances standard was replaced by *Miranda*'s bright line rule.

The year after *Miranda*, the Court carried its protection for the rights of the accused even further when holding that the requirements of the due process clause apply to juvenile courts.[3] Historically, juveniles were treated differently from adults on the theory that the state is not an adversary but rather represents parental authority (*parens patriae*) in bringing civil (not criminal) proceedings against them.[4] *In re Gault*, 387 U.S. 1 (1967), extended to juvenile courts the rights of notification of charges, timely hearings, representation by counsel, and the right to confront accusers, as well as the Fifth Amendment's right to remain silent. Subsequently, the Court ruled that the same standard of proof for guilt must apply in juvenile courts as in other criminal proceedings[5] and that the prohibition against double jeopardy also applies.[6] But *Fare v. Michael C.*, 442 U.S. 707 (1979), held that whether a juvenile's confession may be used as evidence in court, when he asked to see his probation officer rather than an attorney, depends on the totality of circumstances. *Schall v. Martin*, 467 U.S. 253 (1984), upheld the pretrial detention of juveniles deemed by a judge to be a "serious risk."

Miranda ignited a long-running political controversy. Congress responded in the Crime Control and Safe Streets Act of 1968 by providing that in federal courts confessions are admissible based on the totality of circumstances rule (not *Miranda*, which still applies in state courts). The Department of Justice in both Democratic and Republican administrations, however, disregarded that provision and complied with *Miranda*'s guidelines. But as the Court became more conservative (with the addition of appointees of presidents Richard Nixon, Ronald Reagan, and George H. W. Bush, as well as George W. Bush's two appointees), the justices reevaluated the necessity of full *Miranda* warnings in every circumstance and distinguished *Miranda* requirements as mere "prophylactic rules" from the Fifth Amendment's guarantee, thereby limiting the contexts and circumstances in which police must honor *Miranda*. Finally, the constitutionality of *Miranda* was directly challenged in *Dickerson v. United States* (2000) (excerpted below), which held that Congress could not override the ruling and that *Miranda* applies in both federal and state interrogations.

Because the Court construes *Miranda* to be basically a procedural ruling, it allows prosecutorial use of incriminating statements made without the benefit of full *Miranda* warnings and without a "knowing and intelligent" waiver of a defendant's Fifth Amendment rights.[7] *Harris v. New York*, 401 U.S. 222 (1971), for example, held that statements, otherwise inadmissible against the defendant because of the failure to satisfy *Miranda*, may be used to impeach the defendant's testimony at trial. In *Oregon v. Hass*, 420 U.S. 714 (1975), *Harris* was extended to permit the defendant's impeachment by use of statements obtained while he was in police custody and after he requested an attorney but before the lawyer arrived. And *Michigan v. Tucker*, 417 U.S. 433 (1975), held that the Fifth Amendment was not violated by the prosecution's use of testimony of a witness discovered as the result of the defendant's statements to police given in the absence of *Miranda* warnings. Again, in *Michigan v. Mosley*, 423 U.S. 96 (1975), the Court sustained a police interrogation, after a two-hour interval, of a suspect who had earlier claimed his right to remain silent.

Although reaffirming *Miranda*, the Court significantly limited its application by distinguishing the circumstances in which it applies on a case-by-case basis. In doing so, the Court redefined the nature of *personal compulsion* that triggers the Fifth Amendment's protection and returned to the pre-*Miranda* standard of "considering the totality of circumstances, [whether] the free will of the witness is overborne."[8] Three cases—*Rhode Island v. Innis* (1980), *Duckworth v. Eagan* (1989), and *McNeil v. Wisconsin* (1991) (all excerpted below)—illustrate the Court's recent analysis. In addition, *Florida v. Powell,* 130 S.Ct. 1195 (2010), held that police need not give the precise language of informing a suspect of the right to counsel during an interrogation as laid down in *Miranda*, as interpreted in *Duckworth v. Egan*. Writing for the Court in *Florida v. Powell*, Justice Ginsburg reaffirmed *Duckworth's* holding that the precise language of *Miranda* need not be followed. In this case police officers informed a suspect of "the right to talk to a lawyer before answering any of [the law enforcement officers'] questions," and that he could invoke that right "at anytime . . . during th[e] interview." That was held to satisfy *Miranda*. By contrast, dissenting Justices Stevens and Breyer countered that *Miranda* mandated that suspects be informed of "the right to consult with a lawyer *and to have the lawyer with him during interrogation*" (emphasis added). In addition, *Berghuis v. Thompkins*, 130 U.S. 2250 (2010), held that a suspect must unambiguously and unequivocally invoke the right to remain silent, and if incriminating statements are made, they may be considered a waiver of the right to remain silent.

Still, in *Minnick v. Mississippi*, 498 U.S. 146 (1990), the Court reinforced *Miranda*'s protections by reaffirming that once an accused person in police custody requests an attorney, police may not initiate further questioning until an attorney is available and present during the questioning. An earlier decision, *Edwards v. Arizona*, 451 U.S. 477 (1981), held that under *Miranda*, once an accused asks for an attorney, he may not be subjected to another round of questioning "until counsel has been made available to him." That ruling was reaffirmed in *Minnick v. Mississippi*. Writing for the majority, Justice Anthony Kennedy explained that

> [t]o protect the privilege against self-incrimination guaranteed by the Fifth Amendment, we have held that police must terminate interrogation of an accused in custody if the accused requests the assistance of counsel. *Miranda v. Arizona*, 384 U.S. 436 (1966). We reinforced the protections of *Miranda* in *Edwards v. Arizona*, 451 U.S. 477 (1981), which held that once the accused requests counsel, officials may not reinitiate questioning "until counsel has been made available" to him. The issue in the case before us is whether *Edwards*'s protection ceases once the suspect has consulted with an attorney. . . .
>
> *Edwards* is "designed to prevent police from badgering a defendant into waiving his previously asserted *Miranda* rights." *Michigan v. Harvey*, [494 U.S. 344] (1990). The rule ensures that any statement made in subsequent interrogation is not the result of coercive pressures. *Edwards* conserves judicial resources which would otherwise be expended in making difficult determinations of voluntariness, and implements the protections of *Miranda* in practical and straightforward terms.
>
> The merit of the *Edwards* decision lies in the clarity of its command and the certainty of its application. . . .
>
> We consider our ruling to be an appropriate and necessary application of the *Edwards* rule. A single consultation with an attorney does not remove the suspect from persistent attempts by officials to persuade him to waive his rights, or from the coercive pressures that accompany custody and that may increase as custody is prolonged. . . . We decline to remove protection from police-initiated questioning based on isolated consultations with counsel who is absent when the interrogation resumes.

However, in *Maryland v. Shatzer,* 559 U.S. 98 (2010), the Roberts Court ruled that a suspect's incriminating statements could be used at trial, even though they were made in a second interrogation in which he waived his right to counsel and which took place more than two weeks after he was first interrogated and informed of his right to counsel. Writing for the Court, Justice Scalia held that the break in his custody, even though he was in jail, satisfied the rulings in *Edwards v. Arizona,* 451 U.S. 477 (1981), and *Minnick v. Mississippi,* 498 U.S. 146 (1990).

Still, *McNeil v. Wisconsin,* 501 U.S. 171 (1991), held that police do not violate a suspect's Fifth Amendment *Miranda* right if they question him about a crime when his Sixth Amendment court-appointed lawyer in another criminal case is not present. Here, Paul McNeil was in police custody and had previously appeared in court with his attorney on another charge when he was subsequently questioned about a different crime without the presence of his attorney. The narrow question posed, thus, was whether a suspect's Sixth Amendment right to counsel implicitly carries with it the Fifth Amendment right, as construed in *Miranda,* not to be questioned about any other crime in the absence of a suspect's attorney. By a 6–3 vote the Court held that the Sixth Amendment does not convey *Miranda*'s guarantee against being questioned by police about another crime while in police custody and in the absence of a suspect's attorney. A decade later, a bare majority extended *McNeil v. Wisconsin* in *Texas v. Cobb,* 532 U.S. 162 (2001). Cobb was arrested on burglary charges and confessed to that crime in 1994 but denied any knowledge of the disappearance of the mother and child at the residence. Counsel was appointed to represent him on that charge. But subsequently in 1995 while in custody in response to police questioning, Cobb waived his *Miranda* rights and confessed to the murders. He was later convicted and sentenced to death. Chief Justice Rehnquist held that, pursuant to *McNeil,* the Sixth Amendment right to counsel is offense-specific and cannot be invoked for all future prosecutions. In addition, Chief Justice Rehnquist reasoned that because burglary and murder are separate offenses, the Sixth Amendment did not prohibit the police from interrogating Cobb about the murders and, therefore, his confession was admissible. However, in *Fellers v. United States,* 540 U.S. 519 (2004), a unanimous Court reaffirmed that the Sixth Amendment bars the use of incriminating statements elicited by police from an accused after he has waived his *Miranda* rights and after he has been indicted for an offense. Writing for the Court, Justice O'Connor reaffirmed that the Sixth Amendment right to counsel bars interrogations or the deliberate elicitation of information, out of the presence of counsel, once judicial proceedings have begun, whether by a formal charge, preliminary hearing, indictment, or arraignment.

The Court has also cut back on the basis for federal appellate courts to review alleged *Miranda* violations. In *Arizona v. Fulminante* (excerpted below), the Rehnquist Court significantly undercut a 1967 Warren Court ruling in *Chapman v. California*, 386 U.S. 18 (1967). *Chapman* drew a line on the extension of the so-called *harmless error doctrine*—under which appellate courts will not reverse the judgments of trial courts on the ground that minor procedural errors were made during a trial. In *Chapman*, adverse comments by the prosecutor and trial judge about a defendant's refusal to testify in his own defense at trial were held not to be constitutionally "harmless errors." Writing for the Court, Justice Black also ruled that "before a federal constitutional error can be held harmless, [an appellate court] must be able to declare a belief that it was harmless beyond a reasonable doubt." Moreover, Justice Black noted that three kinds of constitutional errors were not subject to the "harmless error" doctrine; namely, when a defendant submits to a coerced confession, faces a criminal trial without the assistance of counsel, and is tried before a biased judge. As a result of *Chapman*, prosecutorial use of coerced confessions was not considered a "harmless error" and invariably resulted in reversals of defendants' convictions. But, five members of the Rehnquist Court held otherwise in *Fulminante*.

In *Withrow v. Williams*, 507 U.S. 680 (1993), however, a bare majority declined to extend the ruling in *Stone v. Powell*, 428 U.S. 465 (1976) (see Ch. 7) so as to withdraw federal *habeas corpus* jurisdiction from cases involving state prisoners' claims of *Miranda* violations. In *Stone v. Powell*, the Court held that the landmark ruling on the Fourth Amendment's exclusionary rule, in *Mapp v. Ohio*, 367 U.S. 643 (1961) (see Ch. 7), did not recognize "a personal constitutional right," rather merely a prudential rule geared toward deterring illegal searches and seizures. On that basis, *Stone* held that prisoners could no longer file for a writ of *habeas corpus* in federal courts for review of convictions in state courts that they claimed were based on illegally obtained evidence. Notably, writing for the majority in *Withrow*, Justice Souter refused to extend *Stone*'s reasoning and ruled that *Miranda* guarantees "a fundamental trial right" justifying federal *habeas* review. *Withrow* thus underscores the Court's differing evaluation of *Mapp*'s exclusionary rule and *Miranda*'s safeguards, as well as the continuing division within the Court over *Miranda*; in *Withrow*, Chief Justice Rehnquist and Justices O'Connor, Scalia, and Thomas dissented.

Dickerson v. United States (2000) (excerpted below), as noted earlier, reaffirmed the constitutionality of *Miranda*. Nonetheless the Court continued to limit the scope of *Miranda*. In *Chavez v. Martinez*, 538 U.S. 760 (2003), for example, the Court held that violations of *Miranda* do not run afoul of the Fifth Amendment in civil cases seeking an award for damages as a result of persistent police questioning. *United States v. Patane*, 542 U.S. 630 (2004), held that, notwithstanding the ruling in *Dickerson* that *Miranda* was constitutionally based, the *Miranda* warnings are merely prophylactic rules, and if a suspect during police questioning without being given the *Miranda* warnings makes statements that lead police to incriminating evidence, that evidence may be used at trial and its introduction does not violate the Fifth Amendment. Samuel Patane violated a restraining order for harassing his ex-girlfriend and was questioned by police about his illegal possession of a pistol. The officer attempted to advise him of his *Miranda* rights, but Patane interrupted and said he knew his rights. Patane was then questioned about the pistol and said, "I am not sure I should tell you anything about the [pistol] because I don't want you to take it away from me." But on further questioning Patane told the officer where the pistol was and gave his permission to get it. Writing for a bare majority, Justice Thomas observed that "the *Miranda* rule is a prophylactic employed to protect against violations of the Self-Incrimination Clause. The Self-Incrimination Clause, however, is not implicated by the admission into evidence of the physical fruit of a voluntary statement." In short, the failure to provide full *Miranda* warnings is not itself a constitutional violation and there was no reason to fashion a "fruit of the poisonous tree" rule in order to deter un-*Miranda* police questioning. Justice Kennedy cast the pivotal vote. Justices Stevens, Souter, Ginsburg, and Breyer dissented and would have applied the "fruit of the poisonous tree" doctrine in order to provide an "incentive" for police to provide full *Miranda* warnings before custodial interrogations.

However, the Court held in *Missouri v. Seibert*, 542 U.S. 600 (2004) that the practice of police first questioning suspects without reading them their *Miranda* rights and obtaining confessions, then giving them the *Miranda* warnings and again obtaining incriminating statements, is unconstitutional. Such mid-interrogation warnings are invalid under *Miranda*; the first confession must be excluded because the suspect was not read the *Miranda* rights, and the second must be excluded because it was obtained by police using the first confession. Yet, in *Berghuis v. Thompkins,* 130 U.S. 2250 (2010), a bare majority held that a suspect must unambiguously and unequivocally invoke the right to remain silent, and if the suspect answers any questions that amount to a confession, it may be considered a waiver of the right to remain silent.

In two rulings different majorities of the Roberts Court reconsidered what constitutes being in "police custody" for the purpose of triggering the requirement of giving *Miranda* warnings of the right to remain silent. In *J.D.B. v. North Carolina*, 564 U.S. 261 (2011), a bare majority held that in determining whether minors are in "policy custody" for the purpose of determining whether they should be read their *Miranda* rights, their age may be taken into consideration. At issue was the police questioning and the confession of a thirteen-year old at school, who was not informed of the right to remain silent. Justice Alito, joined by Chief Justice Roberts and Justices Scalia and Thomas, dissented, contending that the majority was departing from *Miranda*'s "bright-line rule" on when an individual becomes a "suspect" and reverting to the older "totality of circumstances" rule for determining coerced confessions. Notably, neither Justice Sotomayor's opinion for the Court nor Justice Alito's dissent mentioned *In re Gault*, 387 U.S. 1 (1967), the landmark ruling on minors' rights to remain silent and have the assistance of counsel.

In *Howes v. Fields*, 565 U.S. 499 (2012), however, a majority of the Roberts Court went toward further weakening *Miranda*. There, the majority now joined Justice Alito in holding that courts in determining whether a person is in "custody," and thus entitled to *Miranda* warnings, should consider "all of the circumstances surrounding the interrogation" when determining whether a prisoner is in "custody" for *Miranda* purposes. In *Miranda* the Court observed that "the very fact of custodial interrogation exacts a heavy toll on individual liberty, and trades on the weaknesses of individuals." But *Howes v. Fields* held that courts should consider how an interrogated prisoner would have gauged his freedom of movement and that not all restraints on freedom of movement amount to *Miranda* custody. Randall Fields, a prisoner, was taken from his prison cell and questioned by two sheriffs about criminal activities prior to going to prison. At no time was he given *Miranda* warnings or advised that he had a right to remain silent. During more than five hours of questioning he was told that he could return to his cell, and although several times he told the deputies he did not want to speak to them, he never asked to return to his cell. Fields eventually confessed and that confession was used against him at trial.

In addition, in light of the decision in *Missouri v. Seibert* and other rulings, the Obama administration advocated a *public safety* exception from *Miranda* with respect to the interrogation of suspected terrorists. Under such an exception, terrorist suspects may be questioned about co-conspirators and connections with international terrorist organizations prior to being given *Miranda* warnings, and their confessions may be used for further investigations but not introduced at trial.

Also writing for the Court in *Salinas v. Texas*, 570 U.S. 178 (2013), Justice Alito held that prosecutors may comment at trial on a defendant's unwillingness to respond to an officer's questions about a murder, even though as a suspect he had not yet been arrested, taken into custody, or received *Miranda* warnings. In doing so, Justice Alito distinguished *Griffin v. California*, 380 U.S. 609 (1965), from other precedents supporting the right to remain silent, because here the individual had not invoked the Fifth Amendment privilege against self-incrimination. Concurring justices would have overturned *Griffin* as inconsistent with "the Constitution's text, history, or logic." By contrast, dissenting Justice Breyer, joined by Justices Ginsburg, Sotomayor, and Kagan, countered that the ruling was inconsistent with a range of precedents, as well as *Miranda* and the Fifth Amendment guarantee. In Justice Breyer's words: "The Fifth Amendment prohibits prosecutors from commenting on an individual's silence where that silence amounts to an effort to avoid becoming 'a witness against himself.' This Court has specified that 'a rule of evidence' permitting 'commen[t] . . . by counsel' in a criminal case upon a defendant's failure to testify 'violates the Fifth Amendment.'"

NOTES

1. See *Leyra v. Denno*, 347 U.S. 556 (1954); *Fikes v. Alabama*, 352 U.S. 191 (1957); and *Payne v. Arkansas*, 356 U.S. 560 (1958).

2. See *Haynes v. Washington*, 373 U.S. 503 (1963) (holding that a written confession was involuntary because the accused had been held incommunicado); and *Jackson v. Denno*, 378 U.S. 368 (1964).

3. In *Gallegos v. Colorado*, 370 U.S. 49 (1962), the Court held that the due process clause was violated by a confession of a fourteen-year-old boy held by police for five days before sending for his parents.

4. Relying on the theory of *parens patriae* in according juveniles less protection under the Bill of Rights than adults, the Court in *Ingraham v. Wright*, 430 U.S. 651 (1977), upheld corporal punishment in public schools. The Court also upheld laws permitting parents to admit their minor children to mental hospitals without a hearing. *O'Connor v. Donaldson*, 422 U.S. 563 (1975), held that adults may not be committed to a mental institution under the due process clause without a hearing on their commitment, at which time they may contest their institutionalization. But see *Secretary of Public Welfare v. Institutionalized Juveniles*, 422 U.S. 640 (1979); and *Parham v. J.R.*, 422 U.S. 584 (1979).

5. *In re Winship*, 397 U.S. 358 (1970).

6. *Breed v. Jones*, 421 U.S. 519 (1975).

7. See *Harris v. New York*, 401 U.S. 222 (1971); *Michigan v. Tucker*, 417 U.S. 433 (1974); *Michigan v. Mosley*, 423 U.S. 96 (1975); *Oregon v. Hass*, 420 U.S. 714 (1975); *Doyle v. New York*, 426 U.S. 610 (1976); *Oregon v. Mathiason*, 429 U.S. 492 (1977); and *United States v. Wong*, 431 U.S. 174 (1977).

8. *United States v. Wong*, 431 U.S. 174 (1977).

■ INSIDE THE COURT

Chief Justice Earl Warren, Miranda v. Arizona, *and the Attack on the Court*

The Warren Court was sharply criticized for "being soft on criminals" because of its rulings on the rights of the accused. During the 1968 presidential election, Richard Nixon made law and order a campaign issue, promising if elected to appoint strict constructionists to the Court who would overturn the controversial rulings of the Warren Court. Warren and Nixon knew each other from the 1950s, when Warren was the popular governor of California and Nixon was a young Republican congressman from that state. Fearing that Nixon would win the election, Warren offered to retire in 1968 so Democratic President Lyndon Johnson could appoint his successor. But LBJ's nomination of Justice Abe Fortas for chief justice met opposition in the Senate, and Fortas was forced to withdraw from consideration. Warren stayed on the Court until after the election, and then President Nixon nominated Warren E. Burger to become chief justice in 1969.

Years later in his memoirs, Chief Justice Warren reflected on the campaign against the Court and *Miranda,* observing that the

> attack centered on the case of *Miranda v. Arizona.* . . . [But there] was really nothing new in this except to require police and prosecutors to advise the poor, the ignorant, and the unwary of a basic constitutional right in a manner which had been followed by the Federal Bureau of Investigation procedures for many years. It was of no assistance to hardened underworld types because they already know what their rights are and demand them. And so it is with all sophisticated criminals and affluent prisoners who had ready access to their lawyers. However, because so many people who are arrested are poor and illiterate, short-cut methods and often cruelties are perpetrated to obtain convictions.[1]

1. Earl Warren, *The Memoirs of Earl Warren* (Garden City, NY: Doubleday, 1977), 316–317.

Before going to the Court in 1953, Warren had worked his way up in politics by serving as California's attorney general. And he had a keen understanding of law enforcement practices that influenced the drafting of his opinion in *Miranda*. When working on *Miranda*, Warren specifically recalled a controversy involving a law professor's seminar for Minneapolis-area police and Minnesota's state attorney general (and later senator and vice president) Walter Mondale. At the seminar, police were told how to adhere to the Court's decisions and still maintain past interrogation practices. "For instance, you're supposed to arraign a prisoner before a magistrate without unreasonable delay," the law professor advised. "But if the magistrate goes hunting for the weekend on a Friday afternoon at 3:00 P.M., you can arrange to arrest your suspect at 3:30. That way you've got the whole weekend." Mondale took the law professor to task at a news conference, responding, "Some persons claim the Supreme Court has gone too far. Others claim to know how constitutional protections may be avoided by tricky indirection. Both viewpoints are wrong—this [seminar] was called to assist us in better fulfilling our sworn duty to uphold the Constitution. It was not called to second guess the Supreme Court." Warren, though, knew full well that not all state attorneys general and police would support the Court's rulings. He, therefore, strove to outline in *Miranda* a code for police procedures governing the interrogation of criminal suspects that police could not easily evade.

After Warren circulated his draft of *Miranda* to the other justices, his trusted ally on the Court, William Brennan, responded with a twenty-one-page list of suggested revisions. At the outset, Brennan emphasized the importance of careful drafting in *Miranda*. "[T]his will be one of the most important opinions of our time," Brennan explained when making "one major suggestion": "It goes to the basic trust of the approach to be taken. In your very first sentence you state that the root problem is 'the *role* society must *assume*, consistent with the federal Constitution, in prosecuting individuals for crime.' I would suggest that the root issue is 'the *restraints* society must *observe*, consistent with the federal Constitution, in prosecuting individuals for crime.'" Warren made that and numerous other changes before handing down the opinion for the Court in *Miranda v. Arizona*.

Sources: Library of Congress, Materials in the Earl Warren Papers and William J. Brennan Jr., Papers, Manuscripts Room.

Miranda v. Arizona

384 U.S. 436, 86 S.CT. 1602 (1966)

On March 3, 1963, an eighteen-year-old girl was kidnapped and raped on the outskirts of Phoenix, Arizona. Ten days later, police arrested Ernesto A. Miranda, a twenty-three-year-old indigent with a ninth-grade education. (A doctor who later examined Miranda diagnosed him as schizophrenic, although "alert and oriented as to time, place, and person" and competent to stand trial.) At the police station, the rape victim identified Miranda standing in a police lineup as her attacker. Two officers subsequently took Miranda to a separate room and interrogated him. At first denying his guilt, Miranda eventually confessed and wrote out and signed a brief statement admitting and describing the crime. Following Miranda's trial and conviction, his attorneys appealed on the grounds that Miranda's confession had been coerced and that police had violated his Fifth Amendment rights. The Supreme Court granted review, along with three other cases raising the issue of the admissibility into evidence of confessions obtained during police interrogations.

The Court's decision was five and one-half to three and one-half, and the majority's opinion was announced by Chief Justice Warren. There was a separate opinion, in part concurring and dissenting, by Justice Clark. Justices Harlan and White, joined by Justice Stewart, dissented.

■ ■ ■

☐ *Chief Justice WARREN delivered the opinion of the Court.*

The cases before us raise questions which go to the roots of our concepts of American criminal jurisprudence: the restraints society must observe consistent with the Federal Constitution in prosecuting individuals for crime. More specifically, we deal with the admissibility of statements obtained from an individual who is subjected to custodial police interrogation and the necessity for procedures which assure that the individual is accorded his privilege under the Fifth Amendment to the Constitution not to be compelled to incriminate himself.

We dealt with certain phases of this problem recently in *Escobedo v. State of Illinois,* 378 U.S. 478 (1964). There, as in the four cases before us, law enforcement officials took the defendant into custody and interrogated him in a police station for the purpose of obtaining a confession. The police did not effectively advise him of his right to remain silent or of his right to consult with his attorney. Rather, they confronted him with an alleged accomplice who accused him of having perpetrated a murder. When the defendant denied the accusation and said "I didn't shoot Manuel, you did it," they handcuffed him and took him to an interrogation room. There, while handcuffed and standing, he was questioned for four hours until he confessed. During this interrogation, the police denied his request to speak to his attorney, and they prevented his retained attorney, who had come to the police station, from consulting with him. At his trial, the State, over his objection, introduced the confession against him. We held that the statements thus made were constitutionally inadmissible. . . .

We granted *certiorari* in these cases in order further to explore some facets of the problems, thus exposed, of applying the privilege against self-incrimination to in-custody interrogation, and to give concrete constitutional guidelines for law enforcement agencies and courts to follow.

We start here, as we did in *Escobedo*, with the premise that our holding is not an innovation in our jurisprudence, but is an application of principles long recognized and applied in other settings. We have undertaken a thorough re-examination of the *Escobedo* decision and the principles it announced, and we reaffirm it. That case was but an explication of basic rights that are enshrined in our Constitution—that "No person . . . shall be compelled in any criminal case to be a witness against himself," and that "the accused shall . . . have the Assistance of Counsel"—rights which were put in jeopardy in that case through official overbearing. . . .

Our holding will be spelled out with some specificity in the pages which follow but briefly stated it is this: the prosecution may not use statements, whether exculpatory or inculpatory, stemming from custodial interrogation of the defendant unless it demonstrates the use of procedural safeguards effective to secure the privilege against self-incrimination. By custodial interrogation, we mean questioning initiated by law enforcement officers after a person has been taken into custody or otherwise deprived of his freedom of action in any significant way. As for the procedural safeguards to be employed, unless other fully effective means are devised to inform accused persons of their right of silence and to assure a continuous opportunity to exercise it, the following measures are required. Prior to any questioning, the person must be warned that he has a right to remain silent, that any statement he does make may be used as evidence against him, and that he has a right to the presence of an attorney, either retained or appointed. The defendant may waive effectuation of these rights, provided the waiver is made voluntarily, knowingly and intelligently. If, however, he indicates in any manner and at any stage of the process that he wishes to consult with an attorney before speaking there can be no questioning. Likewise, if the individual is alone and indicates in any manner that he does not wish to be interrogated, the police may not question him. The mere fact that he may have answered some questions or volunteered some statements on his own does not deprive him of the right to refrain from answering any further inquiries until he has consulted with an attorney and thereafter consents to be questioned.

The constitutional issue we decide in each of these cases is the admissibility of statements obtained from a defendant questioned while in custody or otherwise deprived of his freedom of action in any significant way. In each, the defendant was questioned by police officers, detectives, or a prosecuting attorney in a room in which he was cut off from the outside world. In none of these cases was the defendant given a full and effective warning of his rights at the outset of the interrogation process. In all the cases, the questioning elicited oral admissions, and in three of them, signed

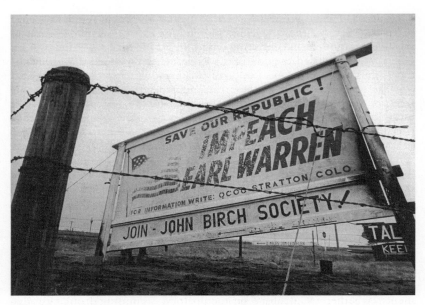

An early "Impeach Earl Warren" sign in 1962. The sign was constructed by those who thought the Warren Court had gone too far in defending civil rights and liberties. (*Duane Howell/The Denver Post via Getty Images*)

statements as well which were admitted at their trials. They all thus share salient features—incommunicado interrogation of individuals in a police-dominated atmosphere, resulting in self-incriminating statements without full warnings of constitutional rights.

An understanding of the nature and setting of this in-custody interrogation is essential to our decisions today. The difficulty in depicting what transpires at such interrogations stems from the fact that in this country they have largely taken place incommunicado. From extensive factual studies undertaken in the early 1930's, including the famous Wickersham Report to Congress by a Presidential Commission, it is clear that police violence and the "third degree" flourished at that time. In a series of cases decided by this Court long after these studies, the police resorted to physical brutality—beatings, hanging, whipping—and to sustained and protracted questioning incommunicado in order to extort confessions. The Commission on Civil Rights in 1961 found much evidence to indicate that "some policemen still resort to physical force to obtain confessions." . . .

Unless a proper limitation upon custodial interrogation is achieved—such as these decisions will advance—there can be no assurance that practices of this nature will be eradicated in the foreseeable future. . . .

[W]e stress that the modern practice of in-custody interrogation is psychologically rather than physically oriented. As we have stated before, "Since *Chambers v. State of Florida*, 309 U.S. 227, [(1940)], this Court has recognized that coercion can be mental, as well as physical, and that the blood of the accused is not the only hallmark of an unconstitutional inquisition." *Blackburn v. State of Alabama*, 361 U.S. 199 (1960). Interrogation still takes place in privacy. Privacy results in secrecy and this in turn results in a gap in our knowledge as to what in fact goes on in the interrogation rooms. A valuable source of information about present police practices, however, may be found in various police manuals and texts which document procedures employed with success in the past, and which recommend various other effective tactics. These texts are used by law enforcement agencies themselves as guides. . . .

[T]he setting prescribed by the manuals and observed in practice [is] clear. In essence, it is this: To be alone with the subject is essential to prevent distraction and to deprive him of any outside support. The aura of confidence in his guilt undermines his will to resist. He merely confirms the preconceived story the police seek to have him describe. Patience and persistence, at times relentless questioning, are employed. To obtain a confession, the interrogator must "patiently maneuver himself or his quarry into a position from which the desired objective may be attained." When normal procedures fail to produce the needed result, the police may resort to deceptive stratagems such as giving false legal advice. It is important to keep the subject off balance, for example, by trading on his insecurity about himself or his surroundings. The police then persuade, trick, or cajole him out of exercising his constitutional rights.

Even without employing brutality, the "third degree" or the specific stratagems described above, the very fact of custodial interrogation exacts a heavy toll on individual liberty and trades on the weakness of individuals. . . .

The potentiality for compulsion is forcefully apparent, for example, in *Miranda*, where the indigent Mexican defendant was a seriously disturbed individual with pronounced sexual fantasies. . . . To be sure, the records do not evince overt physical coercion or patent psychological ploys. The fact remains that in none of these cases did the officers undertake to afford appropriate safeguards at the outset of the interrogation to insure that the statements were truly the product of free choice.

It is obvious that such an interrogation environment is created for no purpose other than to subjugate the individual to the will of his examiner. This atmosphere carries its own badge of intimidation. To be sure, this is not physical intimidation, but it is equally destructive of human dignity. The current practice of incommunicado interrogation is at odds with one of our Nation's most cherished principles—that the individual may not be compelled to incriminate himself. Unless adequate protective devices are employed to dispel the compulsion inherent in custodial surroundings, no statement obtained from the defendant can truly be the product of his free choice. . . .

[T]he constitutional foundation underlying the privilege is the respect a government—state or federal—must accord to the dignity and integrity of its citizens. To maintain a "fair state-individual balance," to require the government "to shoulder the entire load," to respect the inviolability of the human personality, our accusatory system of criminal justice demands that the government seeking to punish an individual produce the evidence against him by its own independent labors, rather than by the cruel, simple expedient of compelling it from his own mouth. In sum, the privilege is fulfilled only when the person is guaranteed the right "to remain silent unless he chooses to speak in the unfettered exercise of his own will." . . .

The question in these cases is whether the privilege is fully applicable during a period of custodial interrogation. . . . We are satisfied that all the principles embodied in the privilege apply to informal compulsion exerted by law-enforcement officers during in-custody questioning. An individual swept from familiar surroundings into police custody, surrounded by antagonistic forces, and subjected to the techniques of persuasion described above cannot be otherwise than under compulsion to speak. As a practical matter, the compulsion to speak in the isolated setting of the police station may well be greater than in courts or other official investigations, where there are often impartial observers to guard against intimidation or trickery. . . .

Today, then, there can be no doubt that the Fifth Amendment privilege is available outside of criminal court proceedings and serves to protect persons in all settings in which their freedom of action is curtailed in any significant way from being compelled to incriminate themselves. We have concluded that without proper safeguards the process of in-custody interrogation of persons suspected or accused of crime contains inherently compelling pressures which work to undermine the individual's will to resist and to compel him to speak where he would not otherwise do so freely. In order to combat these pressures and to permit a full opportunity to exercise the privilege against self-incrimination, the accused must be adequately and effectively apprised of his rights and the exercise of those rights must be fully honored.

It is impossible for us to foresee the potential alternatives for protecting the privilege which might be devised by Congress or the States in the exercise of their creative rule-making capacities. Therefore we cannot say that the Constitution necessarily requires adherence to any particular solution for the inherent compulsions of the interrogation process as it is presently conducted. Our decision in no way creates a constitutional straitjacket which will handicap sound efforts at reform, nor is it intended to have this effect. We encourage Congress and the States to continue their laudable search for increasingly effective ways of protecting the rights of the individual while promoting efficient enforcement of our criminal laws. However, unless we are shown other procedures which are at least as effective in apprising accused persons of their right of silence and in assuring a continuous opportunity to exercise it, the following safeguards must be observed.

At the outset, if a person in custody is to be subjected to interrogation, he must first be informed in clear and unequivocal terms that he has the right to remain silent. For those unaware of the privilege, the warning is needed simply to make them aware of it—the threshold requirement for an intelligent decision as to its exercise. More important, such a warning is an absolute prerequisite in overcoming the inherent pressures of the interrogation atmosphere. It is not just the subnormal or woefully ignorant who succumb to an interrogator's imprecations, whether implied or expressly stated, that the interrogation will continue until a confession is obtained or that silence in the face of accusation is itself damning and will bode ill when presented to a jury. Further, the warning will show the individual that his interrogators are prepared to recognize his privilege should he choose to exercise it. . . .

The warning of the right to remain silent must be accompanied by the explanation that anything said can and will be used against the individual in court. This warning is needed in order to make him aware not only of the privilege, but also of the consequences of forgoing it. It is only through an awareness of these consequences that there can be any assurance of real understanding and intelligent exercise of the privilege. . . .

[T]he right to have counsel present at the interrogation is indispensable to the protection of the Fifth Amendment privilege under the system we delineate today. Our aim is to assure that the individual's right to choose between silence and speech remains unfettered throughout the interrogation process. . . . Thus, the need for counsel to protect the Fifth Amendment privilege comprehends not merely a right to consult with counsel prior to questioning, but also to have counsel present during any questioning if the defendant so desires. . . .

If an individual indicates that he wishes the assistance of counsel before any interrogation occurs, the authorities cannot rationally ignore or deny his request on the basis that the individual does not have or cannot afford a retained attorney. The financial ability of the individual has no relationship to the scope of the rights involved here. The privilege against self-incrimination secured by the Constitution applies to all individuals. . . . The cases before us as well as the vast majority of confession cases with which we have dealt in the past involve those unable to retain counsel. While authorities are not required to relieve the accused of his poverty, they have the obligation not to take advantage of indigence in the administration of justice. . . .

In order fully to apprise a person interrogated of the extent of his rights under this system then, it is necessary to warn him not only that he has the right to consult with an attorney, but also that if he is indigent a lawyer will be appointed to represent him. Without this additional warning, the admonition of the right to consult with counsel would often be understood as meaning only that he can consult with a lawyer if he has one or has the funds to obtain one. The warning of a right to counsel would be hollow if not couched in terms that would convey to the indigent—the person most often subjected to interrogation—the knowledge that he too has a right to have counsel present. . . .

Once warnings have been given, the subsequent procedure is clear. If the individual indicates in any manner, at any time prior to or during questioning, that he wishes to remain silent, the interrogation must cease. At this point he has shown that he intends to exercise his Fifth Amendment privilege; any statement taken after the person invokes his privilege cannot be other than the product of compulsion, subtle or otherwise. Without the right to cut off questioning, the setting of in-custody interrogation operates on the individual to overcome free choice in producing a statement after the privilege has been once invoked. If the individual states that he wants an attorney, the interrogation must cease until an attorney is present. At that time, the individual must have an opportunity to confer with the attorney and to have him present during any subsequent questioning. If the individual cannot obtain an attorney and he indicates that he wants one before speaking to police, they must respect his decision to remain silent. . . .

The principles announced today deal with the protection which must be given to the privilege against self-incrimination when the individual is first subjected to police interrogation while in custody at the station or otherwise deprived of his freedom of action in any significant way. It is at this point that our adversary system of criminal proceedings commences, distinguishing itself at the outset from the inquisitorial system recognized in some countries. Under the system of warnings we delineate today or under any other system which may be devised and found effective, the safeguards to be erected about the privilege must come into play at this point.

Our decision is not intended to hamper the traditional function of police officers in investigating crime. When an individual is in custody on probable cause, the police may, of course, seek out evidence in the field to be used at trial against him. Such investigation may include inquiry of persons not under restraint. General on-the-scene questioning as to facts surrounding a crime or other general questioning of citizens in the fact-finding process is not affected by our holding. It is an act of responsible citizenship for individuals to give whatever information they may have to aid in law enforcement. In such situations the compelling atmosphere inherent in the process of in-custody interrogation is not necessarily present.

In dealing with statements obtained through interrogation, we do not purport to find all confessions inadmissible. Confessions remain a proper element in law enforcement. Any statement given freely and voluntarily without any compelling influences is, of course, admissible in evidence. The fundamental import of the privilege while an individual is in custody is not whether he is allowed to talk to the police without the benefit of warnings and counsel, but whether he can be interrogated. There is no requirement that police stop a person who enters a police station and states that he wishes to confess to a crime, or a person who calls the police to offer a confession or any other statement he desires to make. Volunteered statements of any kind are not barred by the Fifth Amendment and their admissibility is not affected by our holding today.

To summarize, we hold that when an individual is taken into custody or otherwise deprived of his freedom by the authorities in any significant way and is subjected to questioning, the privilege against self-incrimination is jeopardized. Procedural safeguards must be employed to protect the privilege and unless other fully effective means are adopted to notify the person of his right of silence and to assure that the exercise of the right will be scrupulously honored, the following measures are required. He must be warned prior to any questioning that he has the right to remain silent, that anything he says can be used against him in a court of law, that he has the right to the presence of an attorney, and that if he cannot afford an attorney one will be appointed for him prior to any questioning if he so desires. Opportunity to exercise these rights must be afforded to him throughout the interrogation. After such warnings have been given, and such opportunity afforded him, the individual may knowingly and intelligently waive these rights and agree to answer questions or make a statement. But unless and until such warnings and waiver are demonstrated by the prosecution at trial, no evidence obtained as a result of interrogation can be used against him. . . .

In announcing these principles, we are not unmindful of the burdens which law enforcement officials must bear, often under trying circumstances. We also fully recognize the obligation of all citizens to aid in enforcing the criminal laws. This Court, while protecting individual rights, has always given ample latitude to law enforcement agencies in the legitimate exercise of their duties. The limits we have placed on the interrogation process should not constitute an undue interference with a proper system of law enforcement. . . .

Over the years the Federal Bureau of Investigation has compiled an exemplary record of effective law enforcement while advising any suspect or arrested person, at the outset of an interview, that he is not required to make a statement, that any statement may be used against him in court, that the individual may obtain the services of an attorney of his own choice and, more recently, that he has a right to free counsel if he is unable to pay. A letter received from the Solicitor General in response to a question from the Bench makes it clear that the present pattern of warnings and respect for the rights of the individual followed as a practice by the FBI is consistent with the procedure which we delineate today. . . .

Because of the nature of the problem and because of its recurrent significance in numerous cases, we have to this point discussed the relationship of the Fifth Amendment privilege to police interrogation without specific concentration on the facts of the cases before us. We turn now to these facts to consider the application to these cases of the constitutional principles discussed above. In each instance, we have concluded that statements were obtained from the defendant under circumstances that did not meet constitutional standards for protection of the privilege.

☐ *Justice CLARK, concurring and dissenting in part.*

I am unable to join the majority because its opinion goes too far on too little, while my dissenting brethren do not go quite far enough. Nor can I join in the Court's criticism of the present practices of police and investigatory agencies as to custodial interrogation. The materials it refers to as "police manuals" are, as I read them, merely writings in this field by professors and some police officers. . . .

The rule prior to today—as Justice GOLDBERG, the author of the Court's opinion in *Escobedo*, stated it in *Haynes v. Washington*, [373 U.S. 503 (1963)]—depended upon "a totality of circumstances evidencing an involuntary . . . admission of guilt." . . .

I would continue to follow that rule. Under the "totality of circumstances" rule of which my Brother GOLDBERG spoke in *Haynes*, I would consider in each case whether the police officer prior to custodial interrogation added the warning that the suspect might have counsel present at the interrogation and, further, that a court would appoint one at his request if he was too poor to employ counsel. In the absence of warnings, the burden would be on the State to prove that counsel was knowingly and intelligently waived or that in the totality of the circumstances, including the failure to give the necessary warnings, the confession was clearly voluntary. . . .

☐ *Justice HARLAN, with whom Justice STEWART and Justice WHITE join, dissenting.*

Without at all subscribing to the generally black picture of police conduct painted by the Court, I think it must be frankly recognized at the outset that police questioning allowable under due process precedents may inherently entail some pressure on the suspect and may seek advantage in his ignorance or weaknesses. The atmosphere and questioning techniques, proper and fair though they be, can in themselves exert a tug on the suspect to confess, and in this light "[t]o speak of any confessions of crime made after arrest as being 'voluntary' or 'uncoerced' is somewhat inaccurate, although traditional. A confession is wholly and incontestably voluntary only if a guilty person gives himself up to the law and becomes his own accuser." *Ashcraft v.*

State of Tennessee, 322 U.S. 143 [(1944)] (JACKSON, J., dissenting). Until today, the role of the Constitution has been only to sift out *undue* pressure, not to assure spontaneous confessions. . . .

What the Court largely ignores is that its rules impair, if they will not eventually serve wholly to frustrate, an instrument of law enforcement that has long and quite reasonably been thought worth the price paid for it. There can be little doubt that the Court's new code would markedly decrease the number of confessions. To warn the suspect that he may remain silent and remind him that his confession may be used in court are minor obstructions. To require also an express waiver by the suspect and an end to questioning whenever he demurs must heavily handicap questioning. And to suggest or provide counsel for the suspect simply invites the end of the interrogation. . . .

In conclusion: Nothing in the letter or the spirit of the Constitution or in the precedents squares with the heavy-handed and one-sided action that is so precipitously taken by the Court in the name of fulfilling its constitutional responsibilities.

☐ *Justice WHITE, with whom Justice HARLAN and Justice STEWART join, dissenting.*

That the Court's holding today is neither compelled nor even strongly suggested by the language of the Fifth Amendment, is at odds with American and English legal history, and involves a departure from a long line of precedent does not prove either that the Court has exceeded its powers or that the Court is wrong or unwise in its present reinterpretation of the Fifth Amendment. It does, however, underscore the obvious—that the Court has not discovered or found the law in making today's decision, nor has it derived it from some irrefutable sources; what it has done is to make new law and new public policy in much the same way that it has in the course of interpreting other great clauses of the Constitution. This is what the Court historically has done. Indeed, it is what it must do and will continue to do until and unless there is some fundamental change in the constitutional distribution of governmental powers.

But if the Court is here and now to announce new and fundamental policy to govern certain aspects of our affairs, it is wholly legitimate to examine the mode of this or any other constitutional decision in this Court and to inquire into the advisability of its end product in terms of the long-range interest of the country. At the very least, the Court's text and reasoning should withstand analysis and be a fair exposition of the constitutional provision which its opinion interprets. Decisions like these cannot rest alone on syllogism, metaphysics or some ill-defined notions of natural justice, although each will perhaps play its part. In proceeding to such constructions as it now announces, the Court should also duly consider all the factors and interests bearing upon the cases, at least insofar as the relevant materials are available; and if the necessary considerations are not treated in the record or obtainable from some other reliable source, the Court should not proceed to formulate fundamental policies based on speculation alone.

First, we may inquire what are the textual and factual bases of this new fundamental rule. To reach the result announced on the grounds it does, the Court must stay within the confines of the Fifth Amendment, which forbids self-incrimination only if *compelled*. Hence the core of the Court's opinion is that because of the "compulsion inherent in custodial surroundings, no statement obtained from [a] defendant [in custody] can truly be the product of his free choice," absent the use of adequate protective devices as described by the Court. However, the Court does not point to any sudden inrush of new knowledge requiring the rejection of 70 years' experience. . . . Rather than asserting new knowledge, the Court concedes that it cannot truly know what occurs during custodial questioning, because of the innate secrecy of such proceedings. It extrapolates a picture of what it conceives to be the norm from police investigatorial manuals, published in 1959 and 1962 or earlier, without any attempt to allow for adjustments in police practices that may have occurred in the wake of more recent decisions of state appellate tribunals or this Court. . . . Insofar as appears from the Court's opinion, it has not examined a single transcript of any police interrogation, let alone the interrogation that took place in any one of these cases which it decides today. Judged by any of the standards for empirical investigation utilized in the social sciences the factual basis for the Court's premise is patently inadequate. . . .

[E]ven if one assumed that there was an adequate factual basis for the conclusion that all confessions obtained during in-custody interrogation are the product of compulsion, the rule propounded by the Court will still be irrational, for, apparently, it is only if the accused is also warned of his right to counsel and waives both that right and the right against self-incrimination that the inherent compulsiveness of interrogation disappears. But if the defendant may not answer without a warning a question such as "Where were you last night?" without having his answer be a compelled one, how can the Court ever accept his negative answer to the question of whether he wants to consult his retained counsel or counsel whom the court will appoint? And why if counsel is present and the accused nevertheless confesses, or counsel tells the accused to tell the truth, and that is what the accused does, is the situation any less coercive insofar as the accused is concerned? The Court apparently realizes its dilemma of foreclosing questioning without the necessary warnings but at the same time permitting the accused, sitting in the same chair in front of the same policemen, to waive his right to consult an attorney. It expects, however, that the accused will not often waive the right; and if it is claimed that he has, the State faces a severe, if not impossible burden of proof.

All of this makes very little sense in terms of the compulsion which the Fifth Amendment proscribes. That amendment deals with compelling the accused himself. It is his free will that is involved. Confessions and incriminating admissions, as such, are not forbidden evidence; only those which are compelled are banned. I doubt that the Court observes these distinctions today. By considering any answers to any interrogation to be compelled regardless of the content and course of examination and by escalating the requirements to prove waiver, the Court not only prevents the use of compelled confessions but for all practical purposes forbids interrogation except in the presence of counsel. . . .

Criticism of the Court's opinion, however, cannot stop with a demonstration that the factual and textual bases for the rule it propounds are, at best, less than compelling. Equally relevant is an assessment of the rule's consequences measured against community values. . . .

In some unknown number of cases the Court's rule will return a killer, a rapist or other criminal to the streets and to the environment which produced him, to repeat his crime whenever it pleases him. As a consequence, there will not be a gain, but a loss, in human dignity. The real concern is not the unfortunate consequences of this new decision on the criminal law as an abstract, disembodied series of authoritative proscriptions, but the impact on those who rely on the public authority for protection and who without it can only engage in violent self-help with guns, knives and the help of their neighbors similarly inclined. . . .

Much of the trouble with the Court's new rule is that it will operate indiscriminately in all criminal cases, regardless of the severity of the crime or the circumstances involved. It applies to every defendant, whether the professional criminal or one committing a crime of momentary passion who is not part and parcel of organized crime. It will slow down the investigation and the apprehension of confederates in those cases where time is of the essence, such as kidnapping; those involving national security; and some of those involving organized crime. . . .

Rhode Island v. Innis

446 U.S. 291, 100 S.Ct. 1682 (1980)

In his opinion for the Court, Justice Potter Stewart discusses the facts, involving the issue of what a police interrogation is, and when a confession compelled by police is in violation of *Miranda*.

The Court's decision was 6–3, and the majority's opinion was announced by Justice Stewart. Concurrences were by Chief Justice Burger and Justice White. Dissents were by Justices Stevens and Marshall; Justice Brennan joined Justice Marshall's dissent.

■ ■ ■

☐ *Justice STEWART delivered the opinion of the Court.*

On the night of January 12, 1975, John Mulvaney, a Providence, R.I., taxicab driver, disappeared after being dispatched to pick up a customer. His body was discovered four days later buried in a shallow grave in Coventry, R.I. He had died from a shotgun blast aimed at the back of his head.

On January 17, 1975, shortly after midnight, the Providence police received a telephone call from Gerald Aubin, also a taxicab driver, who reported that he had just been robbed by a man wielding a sawed-off shotgun. Aubin further reported that he had dropped off his assailant near Rhode Island College in a section of Providence known as Mount Pleasant. While at the Providence police station waiting to give a statement, Aubin noticed a picture of his assailant on a bulletin board. Aubin so informed one of the police officers present. The officer prepared a photo array, and again Aubin identified a picture of the same person. That person was the respondent. Shortly thereafter, the Providence police began a search of the Mount Pleasant area.

At approximately 4:30 A.M. on the same date, Patrolman Lovell, while cruising the streets of Mount Pleasant in a patrol car, spotted the respondent standing in the street facing him. When Patrolman Lovell stopped his car, the respondent walked towards it. Patrolman Lovell then arrested the respondent, who was unarmed, and advised him of his so-called *Miranda* rights. While the two men waited in the patrol car for other police officers to arrive, Patrolman Lovell did not converse with the respondent other than to respond to the latter's request for a cigarette.

Within minutes, Sergeant Sears arrived at the scene of the arrest, and he also gave the respondent the *Miranda* warnings. Immediately thereafter, Captain Leyden and other police officers arrived. Captain Leyden advised the respondent of his *Miranda* rights. The respondent stated that he understood those rights and wanted to speak with a lawyer. Captain Leyden then directed that the respondent be placed in a "caged wagon," a four-door police car with a wire screen mesh between the front and rear seats, and be driven to the central police station. . . .

While en route to the central station, Patrolman Gleckman initiated a conversation with Patrolman McKenna concerning the missing shotgun. . . . Patrolman McKenna apparently shared his fellow officer's concern. . . . While Patrolman Williams said nothing, he overheard the conversation between the two officers:

> A. He [Gleckman] said it would be too bad if the little—I believe he said a girl—would pick up the gun, maybe kill herself.

The respondent then interrupted the conversation, stating that the officers should turn the car around so he could show them where the gun was located. At this point, Patrolman McKenna radioed back to Captain Leyden that they were returning to the scene of the arrest and that the respondent would inform them of the location of the gun. At the time the respondent indicated that the officers should turn back, they had traveled no more than a mile, a trip encompassing only a few minutes.

The police vehicle then returned to the scene of the arrest where a search for the shotgun was in progress. There, Captain Leyden again advised the respondent of his *Miranda* rights. The respondent replied that he understood those rights but that he "wanted to get the gun out of the way because of the kids in the area in the school." The respondent then led the police to a nearby field, where he pointed out the shotgun under some rocks by the side of the road. . . .

It was the view of the state appellate court that, even though the police officers may have been genuinely concerned about the public safety and even though the respondent had not been addressed personally by the police officers, the respondent nonetheless had been subjected to "subtle coercion" that was the equivalent of "interrogation" within the meaning of the *Miranda* opinion. . . .

We granted *certiorari* to address for the first time the meaning of "interrogation" under *Miranda v. Arizona.* . . .

In the present case, the parties are in agreement that the respondent was fully informed of his *Miranda* rights and that he invoked his *Miranda* right to counsel when he told Captain Leyden that he wished to consult with a lawyer. It is also uncontested that the respondent was "in custody" while being transported to the police station.

The issue, therefore, is whether the respondent was "interrogated" by the police officers in violation of the respondent's undisputed right under *Miranda* to remain silent until he had consulted with a lawyer. In resolving this issue, we first define the term "interrogation" under *Miranda* before turning to a consideration of the facts of this case.

The starting point for defining "interrogation" in this context is, of course, the Court's *Miranda* opinion. There the Court observed that "[b]y custodial interrogation, we mean *questioning* initiated by law enforcement officers after a person has been taken into custody or otherwise deprived of his freedom of action in any significant way." (emphasis added). This passage and other references throughout the opinion to "questioning" might suggest that the *Miranda* rules were to apply only to those police interrogation practices that involve express questioning of a defendant while in custody.

We do not, however, construe the *Miranda* opinion so narrowly. The concern of the Court in *Miranda* was that the "interrogation environment" created by the interplay of interrogation and custody would "subjugate the individual to the will of his examiner" and thereby undermine the privilege against compulsory self-incrimination. The police practices that evoked this concern included several that did not involve express questioning. For example, one of the practices discussed in *Miranda* was the use of line-ups in which a coached witness would pick the defendant as the perpetrator. . . .

This is not to say, however, that all statements obtained by the police after a person has been taken into custody are to be considered the product of interrogation. As the Court in *Miranda* noted:

> Confessions remain a proper element in law enforcement. Any statement given freely and voluntarily without any compelling influences is, of course, admissible in evidence. *The fundamental import of the privilege while an individual is in custody is not whether he is allowed to talk to the police without the benefit of warnings and counsel, but whether he can be interrogated.* . . . Volunteered statements of any kind are not barred by the Fifth Amendment and their admissibility is not affected by our holding today. (emphasis added).

It is clear, therefore, that the special procedural safeguards outlined in *Miranda* are required not where a suspect is simply taken into custody, but rather where a suspect in custody is subjected to interrogation. "Interrogation," as conceptualized in the *Miranda* opinion, must reflect a measure of compulsion above and beyond that inherent in custody itself.

We conclude that the *Miranda* safeguards come into play whenever a person in custody is subjected to either express questioning or its functional equivalent. That is to say, the term "interrogation" under *Miranda* refers not only to express questioning, but also to any words or actions on the part of the police (other than those normally attendant to arrest and custody) that the police should know are reasonably likely to elicit an incriminating response from the suspect. . . .

Turning to the facts of the present case, we conclude that the respondent was not "interrogated" within the meaning of *Miranda*. It is undisputed that the first prong of the definition of "interrogation" was not satisfied, for the conversation between Patrolmen Gleckman and McKenna included no express questioning of the respondent. Rather, that conversation was, at least in form, nothing more than a dialogue between the two officers to which no response from the respondent was invited.

Moreover, it cannot be fairly concluded that the respondent was subjected to the "functional equivalent" of questioning. It cannot be said, in short, that Patrolmen Gleckman and McKenna should have known that their conversation was reasonably likely to elicit an incriminating response from the respondent. There is nothing in the record to suggest that the officers were aware that the respondent was peculiarly susceptible to an appeal to his conscience concerning the safety of handicapped children. Nor is there anything in the record to suggest that the police knew that the respondent was unusually disoriented or upset at the time of his arrest.

The case thus boils down to whether, in the context of a brief conversation, the officers should have known that the respondent would suddenly be moved to make a self-incriminating response. Given the fact that the entire conversation appears to have consisted of no more than a few off-hand remarks, we cannot say that the officers should have known that it was reasonably likely that Innis would so respond. . . .

For the reasons stated, the judgment of the Supreme Court of Rhode Island is vacated, and the case is remanded to that court for further proceedings not inconsistent with this opinion.

It is so ordered.

☐ *Justice MARSHALL, with whom Justice BRENNAN joins, dissenting.*

I am substantially in agreement with the Court's definition of "interrogation" within the meaning of *Miranda v. Arizona*. . . . In my view, the *Miranda* safeguards apply whenever police conduct is intended or likely to produce a response from a suspect in custody. As I read the Court's opinion, its definition of "interrogation" for *Miranda* purposes is equivalent, for practical purposes, to my formulation, since it contemplates that "where a police practice is designed to elicit an incriminating response from the accused, it is unlikely that the practice will not also be one which the police should have known was reasonably likely to have that effect." Thus, the Court requires an objective inquiry into the likely effect of police conduct on a typical individual, taking into account any special susceptibility of the suspect to certain kinds of pressure of which the police know or have reason to know.

I am utterly at a loss, however, to understand how this objective standard as applied to the facts before us can rationally lead to the conclusion that there was no interrogation. . . .

The Court attempts to characterize Gleckman's statements as "no more than a few off hand remarks" which could not reasonably have been expected to elicit a response. If the statements had been addressed to respondent, it would be impossible to draw such a conclusion. The simple message of the "talking back and forth" between Gleckman and McKenna was that they had to find the shotgun to avert a child's death.

One can scarcely imagine a stronger appeal to the conscience of a suspect—*any* suspect—than the assertion that if the weapon is not found an innocent person will be hurt or killed. And not just any innocent person, but an innocent child—a little girl—a helpless, handicapped little girl on her way to school. The notion that such an appeal could not be expected to have any effect unless the suspect were known to have some special interest in handicapped children verges on the ludicrous. As a matter of fact, the appeal to a suspect to confess for the sake of others, to "display some evidence of decency and honor," is a classic interrogation technique. . . . This is not a case where police officers speaking among themselves are accidentally overheard by a suspect. These officers were "talking back and forth" in close quarters with the handcuffed suspect, traveling past the very place where they believed the weapon was located. They knew petitioner would hear and attend to their conversation, and they are chargeable with knowledge of and responsibility for the pressures to speak which they created.

I firmly believe that this case is simply an aberration, and that in future cases the Court will apply the standard adopted today in accordance with its plain meaning.

Duckworth v. Eagan

492 U.S. 195, 109 S.CT. 2875 (1989)

When first questioned by police about the stabbing of a woman, Gary Eagan made an exculpatory statement after being read, and then signing, a waiver form that provided that if he could not afford a lawyer, one would be appointed for him "if and when you go to court." But a day later when being questioned again and after signing a different waiver form, Eagan confessed to the stabbing and led officers to a site where they recovered pertinent physical evidence. Over Eagan's attorney's objections, his two statements were admitted into evidence during trial. Following his conviction, Eagan unsuccessfully appealed to the Indiana Supreme Court and then applied for a writ of *habeas corpus* in federal district court. Eagan claimed, among other things, that his confession was inadmissible because the first waiver form did not comply with the requirements of *Miranda v. Arizona* (see excerpt above). The court denied his petition, holding that the record showed adherence to *Miranda*. But the Court of Appeals for the Seventh Circuit reversed on the grounds that the police informing Eagan that counsel would be appointed "if and when you go to court" was constitutionally defective, since it failed to make a clear and unequivocal warning that Eagan had a right to an appointed attorney before interrogation and because the police warning linked the right to counsel to a future event. The state appealed that ruling to the Supreme Court, which granted review.

The Court's decision was 5–4, and the majority's opinion was announced by Chief Justice Rehnquist. Justice O'Connor's concurrence was joined by Justice Scalia. Justice Marshall dissented and was joined by Justices Brennan, Blackmun, and Stevens.

■ ■ ■

☐ *Chief Justice REHNQUIST delivered the opinion of the Court.*

[*C*]*ertiorari* . . . [was granted] to resolve a conflict among the lower courts as to whether informing a suspect that an attorney would be appointed for him "if and when you go to court" renders *Miranda* warnings inadequate. We agree with the majority of the lower courts that it does not.

In *Miranda v. Arizona*, 384 U.S. 436 (1966), the Court established certain procedural safeguards that require police to advise criminal suspects of their rights under the Fifth and Fourteenth Amendments before commencing custodial interrogation. In now-familiar words, the Court said that the suspect must be told that "he has the right to remain silent, that anything he says can be used against him in a court of law, that he has the right to the presence of an attorney, and that if he cannot afford an attorney one will be appointed for him prior to any questioning if he so desires." The Court in *Miranda* "presumed that interrogation in certain custodial circumstances is inherently coercive and . . . that statements made under those circumstances are inadmissible unless the suspect is specifically warned of his *Miranda* rights and freely decides to forgo those rights." *New York v. Quarles*, 467 U.S. 649 (1984). . . .

We have never insisted that *Miranda* warnings be given in the exact form described in that decision. In *Miranda* itself, the Court said that "[t]he warnings required and the waiver necessary in accordance with our opinion today are, *in the absence of a fully effective equivalent*, prerequisites to the admissibility of any statement made by a defendant." . . .

Miranda has not been limited to stationhouse questioning, see *Rhode Island v. Innis*, [446 U.S. 291 (1980)] (police car), and the officer in the field may not always have access to printed *Miranda* warnings, or he may inadvertently depart from routine practice, particularly if a suspect requests an elaboration of the warnings. The prophylactic *Miranda* warnings are "not themselves rights protected by the Constitution but [are] instead measures to insure that the right against compulsory self-incrimination [is] protected." *Michigan v. Tucker*, 417 U.S. 433 (1974). Reviewing courts therefore need not examine *Miranda* warnings as if construing a will or defining the terms of an easement. The inquiry is simply whether the warnings reasonably "conve[y] to [a suspect] his rights as required by *Miranda*." [*California v.*] *Prysock*, [453 U.S. 355 (1981)] . . .

We think the initial warnings given to respondent touched all of the bases required by *Miranda*. The police told respondent that he had the right to remain silent, that anything he said could be used against him in court, that he had the right to speak to an attorney before and during questioning, that he had "this right to the advice and presence of a lawyer even if [he could] not afford to hire one," and that he had the "right to stop answering at any time until [he] talked to a lawyer." . . . [T]he police also added that they could not provide respondent with a lawyer, but that one would be appointed "if and when you go to court." The Court of Appeals thought this "if and when you go to court" language suggested that "only those accused who can afford an attorney have the right to have one present before answering any questions," and "implie[d] that if the accused does not 'go to court,' *i.e.*[,] the government does not file charges, the accused is not entitled to [counsel] at all." . . .

In our view, the Court of Appeals misapprehended the effect of the inclusion of "if and when you go to court" language in *Miranda* warnings.

First, this instruction accurately described the procedure for the appointment of counsel in Indiana. . . . We think it must be relatively commonplace for a suspect, after receiving *Miranda* warnings, to ask *when* he will obtain counsel. The "if and when you go to court" advice simply anticipates that question. Second, *Miranda* does not require that attorneys be producible on call, but only that the suspect be informed, as here, that he has the right to an attorney before and during questioning, and that an attorney would be appointed for him if he could not afford one. The Court in *Miranda* emphasized that it was not suggesting that "each police station must have a 'station house lawyer' present at all times to advise prisoners." If the police cannot provide appointed counsel, *Miranda* requires only that the police not question a suspect unless he waives his right to counsel. Here, respondent did just that. . . .

The judgment of the Court of Appeals is accordingly reversed, and the case is remanded for further proceedings not inconsistent with our decision. It is so ordered.

☐ *Justice MARSHALL, with whom Justice BRENNAN joins, and with whom Justice BLACKMUN and Justice STEVENS join as to Part I, dissenting.*

The majority holds today that a police warning advising a suspect that he is entitled to an appointed lawyer only "if and when he goes to court" satisfies the requirements of *Miranda v. Arizona*, 384 U.S. 436 (1966). The majority reaches this result by seriously mischaracterizing that decision. Under *Miranda*, a police warning must "clearly infor[m]" a suspect taken into custody "that if he cannot afford an attorney one will be appointed for him *prior to any questioning* if he so desires." A warning qualified by an "if and when you go to court" caveat does nothing of the kind; instead, it leads the suspect to believe that a lawyer will not be provided until some indeterminate time in the future *after questioning*. I refuse to acquiesce in the continuing debasement of this historic precedent, and therefore dissent. I also write to express my disagreement with Justice O'CONNOR's uninvited suggestion that the rationale of *Stone v. Powell*, 428 U.S. 465 (1976), should be extended to bar federal *habeas* review of *Miranda* claims. . . .

■ I

In concluding that the first warning given to respondent Eagan satisfies the dictates of *Miranda*, the majority makes a mockery of that decision. Eagan was initially advised that he had the right to the presence of counsel before and during questioning. But in the very next breath, the police informed Eagan that, if he could not afford a lawyer, one would be appointed to represent him only "if and when" he went to court. As the Court of Appeals found, Eagan could easily have concluded from the "if and when" caveat that only "those accused who can afford an attorney have the right to have one present before answering any questions; those who are not so fortunate must wait." Eagan was, after all, never told that questioning would be *delayed* until a lawyer was appointed "if and when" Eagan did, in fact, go to court. Thus, the "if and when" caveat may well have had the effect of negating the initial promise that counsel could be present. At best, a suspect like Eagan "would not know . . . whether or not he had a right to the services of a lawyer."

In lawyer-like fashion, THE CHIEF JUSTICE parses the initial warnings given Eagan and finds that the most plausible interpretation is that Eagan would not be questioned until a lawyer was appointed when he later appeared in court. What goes wholly overlooked in THE CHIEF JUSTICE's analysis is that the recipients of police warnings are often frightened suspects unlettered in the law, not lawyers or judges or others schooled in interpreting legal or semantic nuance. Such suspects can hardly be expected to interpret, in as facile a manner as THE CHIEF JUSTICE, "the pretzellike warnings here—intertwining, contradictory, and ambiguous as they are." The majority thus refuses to recognize that "[t]he warning of a right to counsel would be hollow if not couched in terms that would convey to the indigent—the person most often subjected to interrogation—the knowledge that he too has the right to have counsel present." *Miranda.* . . .

Even if the typical suspect could draw the inference the majority does—that questioning will not commence until a lawyer is provided at a later court appearance—a warning qualified by an "if and when" caveat still fails to give a suspect any indication of *when* he will be taken to court. Upon hearing the warnings given in this case, a suspect would likely conclude that no lawyer would be provided until trial. In common parlance, "going to court" is synonymous with "going to trial." Furthermore, the negative implication of the caveat is that, if the suspect is never taken to court, he "is not entitled to an attorney at all." An unwitting suspect harboring uncertainty on this score is precisely the sort of person who may feel compelled to talk "voluntarily" to the police, without the presence of counsel, in an effort to extricate himself from his predicament. . . .

Miranda, it is true, does not require the police to have a "station house lawyer" ready at all times to counsel suspects taken into custody. But if a suspect does not understand that a lawyer will be made available within a reasonable period of time after he has been taken into custody and advised of his rights, the suspect may decide to talk to the police *for that reason alone*. The threat of an indefinite deferral of interrogation, in a system like Indiana's, thus constitutes an effective means by which the police can pressure a suspect to speak without the presence of counsel. . . .

The majority's misreading of *Miranda*—stating that police warnings need only "touc[h] all of the bases required by *Miranda*," that *Miranda* warnings need only be "reasonably conve[yed]" to a suspect, and that *Miranda* warnings are to be measured not point by point but "in their totality"—is exacerbated by its interpretation of *California v. Prysock*, 453 U.S. 355 (1981) (*per curiam*), a decision that squarely supports Eagan's claim in this case. The juvenile suspect in *Prysock* was initially told that he had the right to have a lawyer present before and during questioning. He then was told that he had the right to have his parents present as well. At this point the suspect was informed that a lawyer would be appointed to represent him at no cost if he could not afford one. The California Court of Appeal ruled these warnings insufficient because the suspect was not expressly told of his right to an appointed attorney before and during questioning. This Court reversed, finding that "nothing in the warnings given respondent suggested any limitation on the right to the presence of appointed counsel." . . .

It poses no great burden on law enforcement officers to eradicate the confusion stemming from the "if and when" caveat. Deleting the sentence containing the offending language is all that needs to be done. Purged of this language, the warning tells the suspect in a straightforward fashion that he has the right to the presence of a lawyer before and during questioning, and that a lawyer will be appointed if he cannot afford one. The suspect is given no reason to believe that the appointment of an attorney may come after interrogation. . . .

Arizona v. Fulminante

499 U.S. 279, 111 S.CT. 1246 (1991)

While serving time in a federal prison for another crime, Oreste C. Fulminante made an incriminating confession to a fellow inmate, Anthony Sarivola, who was actually an informer for the Federal Bureau of Investigation (FBI). He did so because the informer offered to protect him from violence in the prison, but only on the condition that he give him a full account of the murder of Fulminante's eleven-year-old stepdaughter. Fulminante agreed and told Sarivola how he had murdered his stepdaughter. His confession to Sarivola, along with another, less detailed confession made to Sarivola's wife after his release from prison, was later introduced as evidence against him in a trial for murdering his stepdaughter. Following his conviction, Fulminante's attorney appealed to the Arizona Supreme Court, which overturned the conviction. Based on rulings of the Supreme Court of the United States, the state supreme court found that Fulminante's confession was involuntary and coerced, that the use of the confession at his trial was not a harmless error, and thus Fulminante was entitled to a retrial. The state then appealed that decision to the Supreme Court, which granted review.

The Court's decision was 5–4 and 5–3. The justices were extraordinarily divided on the opinion announced by Justice White, who commanded only a bare majority on just two of the three issues presented. A separate opinion by Chief Justice Rehnquist, in part dissenting and commanding another majority on the central issue, was joined by Justice O'Connor and in parts by Justices Kennedy, Souter, and Scalia. Justice White's opinion held (1) that Fulminante's confession was coerced and (2) that its use as evidence against him at trial was not harmless beyond a reasonable doubt. His opinion on both of those issues was joined by Justices Blackmun, Marshall, and Stevens. And White commanded a bare majority by picking up the vote of Justice Scalia on (1) and the vote of Justice Kennedy on (2).

On the latter issue, Chief Justice Rehnquist and Justices O'Connor and Scalia dissented, and Justice Souter failed to indicate how or even whether he voted on that issue. The separate opinion by Chief Justice Rehnquist in turn commanded four votes (O'Connor, Kennedy, Souter, and Scalia) for another bare majority holding that (3) the admission at trial of coerced confessions may be excused as a harmless error if there is other evidence that adequately supports a guilty verdict.

■ ■ ■

☐ *Justice WHITE delivered the opinion of the Court.*

Although the question is a close one, we agree with the Arizona Supreme Court's conclusion that Fulminante's confession was coerced. . . . Accepting the Arizona court's finding, permissible on this record, that there was a credible threat of physical violence, we agree with its conclusion that Fulminante's will was overborne in such a way as to render his confession the product of coercion.

Four of us, Justices MARSHALL, BLACKMUN, STEVENS, and myself, would affirm the judgment of the Arizona Supreme Court on the ground that the harmless-error rule is inapplicable to erroneously admitted coerced confessions. We thus disagree with the Justices who have a contrary view.

The majority today abandons what until now the Court has regarded as the "axiomatic [proposition] that a defendant in a criminal case is deprived of due process of law if his conviction is founded, in whole or in part, upon an involuntary confession, without regard for the truth or falsity of the confession, and even though there is ample evidence aside from the confession to support the conviction." *Jackson v. Denno*, 378 U.S. 368 (1964). . . .

In extending to coerced confessions the harmless-error rule of *Chapman v. United States*, 386 U.S. 18 (1967), the majority declares that because the Court has applied that analysis to numerous other "trial errors," there is no reason that it should not apply to an error of this nature as well. The four of us remain convinced, however, that we should abide by our cases that have refused to apply the harmless-error rule to coerced confessions, for a coerced confession is fundamentally different from other types of erroneously admitted evidence to which the rule has been applied. . . .

Chapman specifically noted three constitutional errors that could not be categorized as harmless error: using a coerced confession against a defendant in a criminal trial, depriving a defendant of counsel, or trying a defendant before a biased judge. The majority attempts to distinguish the use of a coerced confession from the other two errors listed in *Chapman* first by distorting the decision in *Payne v. Arkansas* [356 U.S. 560 (1958)] and then by drawing a meaningless dichotomy between "trial errors" and "structural defects" in the trial process. . . .

The search for truth is indeed central to our system of justice, but "certain constitutional rights are not, and should not be, subject to harmless-error analysis because those rights protect important values that are unrelated to the truth-seeking function of the trial." *Rose v. Clark*, 478 U.S. 570 (1986). The right of a defendant not to have his coerced confession used against him is among those rights, for using a coerced confession "abort[s] the fair trial process" and "render[s] a trial fundamentally unfair." *Id.*

For the foregoing reasons the four of us would adhere to the consistent line of authority that has recognized as a basic tenet of our criminal justice system, before and after both *Miranda* and *Chapman*, the prohibition against using a defendant's coerced confession against him at his criminal trial. *Stare decisis* is "of fundamental importance to the rule of law." *Welch v. Texas Highways and Public Transp.*, 483 U.S. 468 (1987); the majority offers no convincing reason for overturning our long line of decisions requiring the exclusion of coerced confessions.

Since five Justices have determined that harmless-error analysis applies to coerced confessions, it becomes necessary to evaluate under that ruling the admissibility of Fulminante's confession to Sarivola. . . . Five of us are of the view that the State has not carried its burden and accordingly affirm the judgment of the court below reversing petitioner's conviction. . . .

Our review of the record leads us to conclude that the State has failed to meet its burden of establishing, beyond a reasonable doubt, that the admission of Fulminante's confession to Anthony Sarivola was harmless error. Three considerations compel this result.

First, the transcript discloses that both the trial court and the State recognized that a successful prosecution depended on the jury believing the two confessions. Absent the confessions, it is unlikely that Fulminante would have been prosecuted at all. . . .

Second, the jury's assessment of the confession to Donna Sarivola could easily have depended in large part on the presence of the confession to Anthony Sarivola. Absent the admission at trial of the first confession, the jurors might have found Donna Sarivola's story unbelievable. . . .

Third, the admission of the first confession led to the admission of other evidence prejudicial to Fulminante. For example, the State introduced evidence that Fulminante knew of Sarivola's connections with organized crime in an attempt to explain why Fulminante would have been motivated to confess to Sarivola in seeking protection. Absent the confession, this evidence would have no relevance and would have been inadmissible at trial. . . .

In declaring that Fulminante "acted with an especially heinous and depraved state of mind," the sentencing judge relied solely on the two confessions. Although the sentencing judge might have reached the same conclusions even without the confession to Anthony Sarivola, it is impossible to say so beyond a reasonable doubt. . . . Because a majority of the Court has determined that Fulminante's confession to Anthony Sarivola was coerced and because a majority has determined that admitting this confession was not harmless beyond a reasonable doubt, we agree with the Arizona Supreme Court's conclusion that Fulminante is entitled to a new trial at which the confession is not admitted. Accordingly the judgment of the Arizona Supreme Court is

Affirmed.

☐ *Chief Justice REHNQUIST, with whom Justice O'CONNOR joins, Justice KENNEDY and Justice SOUTER join as to parts I and II, and Justice SCALIA joins as to parts II and III, concurring as to part II, and dissenting as to parts I and III.*

■ II

Since this Court's landmark decision in *Chapman v. California*, 386 U.S. 18 (1967), in which we adopted the general rule that a constitutional error does not automatically require reversal of a conviction, the Court has applied harmless-error analysis to a wide range of errors and has recognized that most constitutional errors can be harmless. . . .

The admission of an involuntary confession—a classic "trial error"—is markedly different from the other two constitutional violations referred to in the *Chapman* footnote as not being subject to harmless-error analysis. One of those cases, *Gideon v. Wainwright*, 372 U.S. 335 (1963), involved the total deprivation of the right to counsel at trial. The other, *Turney v. Ohio*, 273 U.S. 510 (1927), involved a judge who was not impartial. These are structural defects in the constitution of the trial mechanism, which defy analysis by "harmless-error" standards. The entire conduct of the trial from beginning to end is obviously affected by the absence of counsel for a criminal defendant, just as it is by the presence on the bench of a judge who is not impartial. Since our decision in *Chapman*, other cases have added to the category of constitutional errors which are not subject to harmless error the following: unlawful exclusion of members of the defendant's race from a grand jury, *Vasquez v. Hillery*, 474 U.S. 254 (1986); the right to self-representation at trial, *McKaskle v. Wiggins*, 465 U.S. 168 (1984); and the right to public trial, *Waller v. Georgia*, 467 U.S. 39 (1984). Each of these constitutional deprivations is a similar structural defect affecting the framework within which the trial proceeds, rather than simply an error in the trial process itself. . . .

It is evident from a comparison of the constitutional violations which we have held subject to harmless error, and those which we have held not, that involuntary statements or confessions belong in the former category. The admission is a "trial error," similar in both degree and kind to the erroneous admission of other types of evidence. The evidentiary impact of an involuntary confession, and its effect upon the composition of the record, is indistinguishable from that of a confession obtained in violation of the Sixth Amendment—of evidence seized in violation of the Fourth Amendment—or [as in *Chapman*] of a prosecutor's improper comment on a defendant's silence at trial in violation of the Fifth Amendment.

■ III

I would agree with the finding of the Supreme Court of Arizona in its initial opinion—in which it believed harmless-error analysis was applicable to the admission of involuntary confessions—that the admission of Fulminante's confession was harmless. Indeed, this seems to me to be a classic case of harmless error; a second confession giving more details of the crime than the first was admitted in evidence and found to be free of any constitutional objection.

Dickerson v. United States

530 U.S. 428, 120 S.Ct. 2326 (2000)

In *Miranda v. Arizona*, 384 U.S. 436 (1966), the Supreme Court held that before police question criminal suspects, they must warn them of their Fifth and Sixth Amendment rights to remain silent and to have an attorney present; otherwise, any incriminating statements are considered involuntary and excluded at trial. That decision applied to all state courts and remains controversial. Two years later, Congress enacted the Crime Control and Safe Streets Act of 1968, in which Section 3501 specified that the pre-*Miranda* standard of "the totality of circumstances" for determining the voluntariness of a confession would apply in federal courts, not whether a defendant had been given the *Miranda* warnings. Subsequently, the Department of Justice, in both Republican and Democratic administrations, except in a couple of cases during the administration of Republican President Ronald Reagan, maintained the position that *Miranda* governed in both state and federal criminal prosecutions.

In 1997 Thomas Dickerson was arrested and indicted for bank robbery. At a pretrial hearing, his attorney moved to suppress an incriminating statement made at a Federal Bureau of Investigation office on the ground that the agents failed to read Dickerson his *Miranda* rights. A federal district court agreed that *Miranda* applied, but the Court of Appeals for the Fourth Circuit reversed, holding that *Miranda* was not a constitutional ruling and therefore Congress could determine the standard for voluntary confessions admitted into evidence in federal courts. That decision was appealed, and the Supreme Court granted review.

The appellate court's decision was reversed in a 7–2 decision, and opinion for the Court was delivered by Chief Justice Rehnquist. Justice Scalia filed a dissenting opinion, which Justice Thomas joined.

■ ■ ■

☐ *Chief Justice REHNQUIST delivered the opinion of the Court.*

We hold that *Miranda*, being a constitutional decision of this Court, may not be in effect overruled by an Act of Congress, and we decline to overrule *Miranda* ourselves. We therefore hold that *Miranda* and its progeny in this Court govern the admissibility of statements made during custodial interrogation in both state and federal courts. . . .

In *Miranda*, we noted that the advent of modern custodial police interrogation brought with it an increased concern about confessions obtained by coercion. Because custodial police interrogation, by its very nature, isolates and pressures the individual, we stated that "[e]ven without employing brutality, the 'third degree' or [other] specific stratagems, custodial interrogation exacts a heavy toll on individual liberty and trades on the weakness of individuals." We concluded that the coercion inherent in custodial interrogation blurs the line between voluntary and involuntary statements, and thus heightens the risk that an individual will not be "accorded his privilege under the Fifth Amendment not to be compelled to incriminate himself." Accordingly, we laid down "concrete constitutional guidelines for law enforcement agencies and courts to follow." Those guidelines established that the admissibility in evidence of any statement given during custodial interrogation of a suspect would depend on whether the police provided the suspect with four warnings. These warnings (which have come to be known colloquially as "*Miranda* rights") are: a suspect "has the right to remain silent, that anything he says can be used against him in a court of law, that he has the right to the presence of an attorney, and that if he cannot afford an attorney one will be appointed for him prior to any questioning if he so desires."

Two years after *Miranda* was decided, Congress enacted Section 3501. Given Section 3501's express designation of voluntariness as the touchstone of admissibility, its omission of any warning requirement, and the instruction for trial courts to consider a nonexclusive list of factors relevant to the circumstances of a confession, we agree with the Court of Appeals that Congress intended by its enactment to overrule *Miranda*. Because of the obvious conflict between our decision in *Miranda* and Section 3501, we must address whether Congress has constitutional authority to thus supersede *Miranda*. If Congress has such authority, Section 3501's totality-of-the-circumstances approach must prevail over *Miranda*'s requirement of warnings; if not, that section must yield to *Miranda*'s more specific requirements.

The law in this area is clear. This Court has supervisory authority over the federal courts, and we may use that authority to prescribe rules of evidence and procedure that are binding in those tribunals. However, the power to judicially create and enforce nonconstitutional "rules of procedure and evidence for the federal courts exists only in the absence of a relevant Act of Congress." Congress retains the ultimate authority to modify or set aside any judicially created rules of evidence and procedure that are not required by the Constitution.

But Congress may not legislatively supersede our decisions interpreting and applying the Constitution. See, e.g., *City of Boerne v. Flores*, 521 U.S. 507 (1997). This case therefore turns on whether the *Miranda* Court announced a constitutional rule or merely exercised its supervisory authority to regulate evidence in the absence of congressional direction. Recognizing this point, the Court of Appeals surveyed *Miranda* and its progeny to determine the constitutional status of the *Miranda* decision. Relying on the fact that we have created several exceptions to *Miranda*'s warnings requirement and that we have repeatedly referred to the *Miranda* warnings as "prophylactic," *New York v. Quarles*, 467 U.S. 649 (1984), and "not themselves rights protected by the Constitution," *Michigan v. Tucker*, 417 U.S. 433 (1974), the Court of Appeals concluded that the protections announced in *Miranda* are not constitutionally required.

We disagree with the Court of Appeals' conclusion, although we concede that there is language in some of our opinions that supports the view taken by that court. But first and foremost of the factors on the other side—that *Miranda* is a constitutional decision—is that both *Miranda* and two of its companion cases applied the rule to proceedings in state courts—to wit, Arizona, California, and New York. Since that time, we have consistently applied *Miranda*'s rule to prosecutions arising in state courts. It is beyond dispute that we do not hold a supervisory power over the courts of the several States. . . .

The *Miranda* opinion itself begins by stating that the Court granted *certiorari* "to explore some facets of the problems of applying the privilege against self-incrimination to in-custody interrogation, and to give concrete constitutional guidelines for law enforcement agencies and courts to follow." In fact, the majority opinion is replete with statements indicating that the majority thought it was announcing a constitutional rule. Indeed, the Court's ultimate conclusion was that the unwarned confessions obtained in the four cases before the Court in *Miranda* "were obtained from the defendant under circumstances that did not meet constitutional standards for protection of the privilege." . . .

Whether or not we would agree with *Miranda*'s reasoning and its resulting rule, were we addressing the issue in the first instance, the principles of *stare decisis* weigh heavily against overruling it now.

We do not think there is such justification for overruling *Miranda*. *Miranda* has become embedded in routine police practice to the point where the warnings have become part of our national culture. See *Mitchell v. United States*, 526 U.S. 314 (1999) (SCALIA, J., dissenting) (stating that the fact that a rule has found "wide acceptance in the legal culture" is "adequate reason not to overrule" it). While we have overruled our precedents when subsequent cases have undermined their doctrinal underpinnings, we do not believe that this has happened to the *Miranda* decision. If anything, our subsequent cases have reduced the impact of the *Miranda* rule on legitimate law enforcement while reaffirming the decision's core ruling that unwarned statements may not be used as evidence in the prosecution's case in chief. . . .

In sum, we conclude that *Miranda* announced a constitutional rule that Congress may not supersede legislatively. Following the rule of *stare decisis*, we decline to overrule *Miranda* ourselves. The judgment of the Court of Appeals is therefore Reversed.

☐ *Justice SCALIA, with whom Justice THOMAS joins, dissenting.*

Those to whom judicial decisions are an unconnected series of judgments that produce either favored or disfavored results will doubtless greet today's decision as a paragon of moderation, since it declines to overrule *Miranda v. Arizona*. Those who understand the judicial process will appreciate that today's decision is not a reaffirmation of *Miranda*, but a radical revision of the most significant element of *Miranda* (as of all cases): the rationale that gives it a permanent place in our jurisprudence. . . .

It takes only a small step to bring today's opinion out of the realm of power-judging and into the mainstream of legal reasoning: The Court need only go beyond its carefully couched iterations that "*Miranda* is a constitutional decision," that "*Miranda* is constitutionally based," that *Miranda* has "constitutional underpinnings," and come out and say quite clearly: "We reaffirm today that custodial interrogation that is not preceded by *Miranda* warnings or their equivalent violates the Constitution of the United States." It cannot say that, because a majority of the Court does not believe it. The Court therefore acts in plain violation of the Constitution when it denies effect to this Act of Congress. . . .

It was once possible to characterize the so-called *Miranda* rule as resting (however implausibly) upon the proposition that what the statute here before us permits—the admission at trial of un-Mirandized confessions—violates the Constitution. That is the fairest reading of the *Miranda* case itself. The Court began by announcing that the Fifth Amendment privilege against self-incrimination applied in the context of extrajudicial custodial interrogation—itself a doubtful proposition as a matter both of history and precedent. Having extended the privilege into the confines of the station house, the Court liberally sprinkled throughout its sprawling 60-page opinion suggestions that, because of the compulsion inherent in custodial interrogation, the privilege was violated by any statement thus obtained that did not conform to the rules set forth in *Miranda*, or some functional equivalent. . . .

[*Miranda*] was objectionable for innumerable reasons, not least the fact that cases spanning more than 70 years had rejected its core premise that, absent the warnings and an effective waiver of the right to remain silent and of the (thitherto unknown) right to have an attorney present, a statement obtained pursuant to custodial interrogation was necessarily the product of compulsion. Moreover, history and precedent aside, the decision in *Miranda*, if read as an explication of what the Constitution requires, is preposterous. There is, for example, simply no basis in reason for concluding that a response to the very first question asked, by a suspect who already knows all of the rights described in the *Miranda* warning, is anything other than a volitional act. And even if one assumes that the elimination of compulsion absolutely requires informing even the most knowledgeable suspect of his right to remain silent, it cannot conceivably require the right to have counsel present. There is a world of difference, which the Court recognized under the traditional voluntariness test but ignored in *Miranda*, between compelling a suspect to incriminate himself and preventing him from foolishly doing so of his own accord. Only the latter (which is *not* required by the Constitution) could explain the Court's inclusion of a right to counsel and the requirement that it, too, be knowingly and intelligently waived. Counsel's presence is not required to tell the suspect that he *need* not speak; the interrogators can do that. The only good reason for having counsel there is that he can be counted on to advise the suspect that he *should* not speak.

Preventing foolish (rather than compelled) confessions is likewise the only conceivable basis for the rules that courts must exclude any confession elicited by questioning conducted, without interruption, after the suspect has indicated a desire to stand on his right to remain silent, see *Michigan v. Mosley*, 423 U.S. 96 (1975), or initiated by police after the suspect has expressed a desire to have counsel present, see *Edwards v. Arizona*, 451 U.S. 477 (1981). Nonthreatening attempts to persuade the suspect to reconsider that initial decision are not, without more, enough to render a change of heart the product of anything other than the suspect's free will. Thus, what is most remarkable about the *Miranda* decision—and what made it unacceptable as a matter of straightforward constitutional interpretation in the *Marbury* tradition—is its palpable hostility toward the act of confession per se, rather than toward what the Constitution abhors, compelled confession.

For these reasons, and others more than adequately developed in the *Miranda* dissents and in the subsequent works of the decision's many critics, any conclusion that a violation of the *Miranda* rules necessarily amounts to a violation of the privilege against compelled self-incrimination can claim no support in history, precedent, or common sense, and as a result would at least presumptively be worth reconsidering even at this late date. But that is unnecessary, since the Court has (thankfully) long since abandoned the notion that failure to comply with *Miranda*'s rules is itself a violation of the Constitution. . . .

I dissent from today's decision, and, until Section 3501 is repealed, will continue to apply it in all cases where there has been a sustainable finding that the defendant's confession was voluntary.

B | *Grants of Immunity*

Grants of immunity—immunizing a person from prosecution in exchange for incriminating testimony—have been upheld since *Brown v. United States*, 161 U.S. 221 (1896). There the Court ruled that the primary function of the Fifth Amendment is "to secure the witness against prosecution which might be aided directly or indirectly by his disclosure." Consequently, individuals may be forced to forgo their Fifth Amendment rights when offered immunity, even though their testimony opens them to infamy and disgrace; see *Ullmann v. United States*, 350 U.S. 422 (1956). Refusing to testify after being granted immunity constitutes contempt of court, for which a person may be punished.

Traditionally, individuals received complete immunity, or "transactional immunity," barring prosecution for crimes related to their testimony. In *Ullmann v. United States*, the Court upheld the Federal Immunity Act of 1954 and subsequently held that grants of immunity are as broad as the privilege against self-incrimination that individuals forfeit. The Court also held, in *Murphy v. Waterfront Commission*, 378 U.S. 52 (1964), that defendants granted immunity by states may not later be prosecuted under federal law on the basis of their incriminating testimony.

Congress, however, cut back on the scope of immunity grants in the Omnibus Crime Control and Safe Streets Act of 1968 by providing for only "use" or "testimonial" immunity. Transactional immunity accords full immunity from prosecution for an offense about which an individual testifies. By contrast, use immunity does not foreclose the possibility of prosecution based on other independently obtained evidence. Use or testimonial immunity was upheld in *Kastigar v. United States*, 406 U.S. 441 (1972). Most recently, the Court split 5–4 in *McKune v. Lile*, 536 U.S. 24 (2002), in upholding Kansas's Sexual Abuse Treatment Program, which requires sexual offenders to sign a form taking responsibility for their sexual offenses as part of their treatment, without also granting them immunity from further prosecution.

C | *Real versus Testimonial Evidence*

The Supreme Court has limited the scope of the Fifth Amendment by drawing a distinction between "real" and "testimonial" evidence. No protection is afforded real or physical evidence, such as blood, handwriting, or voice samples. Only testimonial evidence (oral testimony) receives protection. As the Court observed in *Fisher v. United States*, 425 U.S. 391 (1976), the amendment "prohibits compelling a person to *speak* and incriminate himself but it does not prohibit compelled revelation of *written* thoughts."

The distinction between real and testimonial evidence derives from a 1910 ruling that a suspect may be compelled to cooperate with police by putting on a blouse to determine whether it fits. In *Holt v. United States*, 218 U.S. 245 (1910), the Court explained that "the prohibition of compelling a man to be a witness against himself is a prohibition of physical or moral compulsion to *extort communications* from him, not an exclusion of his body as evidence when it may be material." The distinction was not further elaborated until *Schmerber v. California*, 384 U.S. 757 (1966), upholding the taking of blood samples from a driver at the time of his arrest following an automobile accident.

Since *Schmerber*, handwriting samples, voice samples, and scrapings from under a suspect's fingernails, among other physical evidence, have been held not to violate the Fifth Amendment. (See the box, THE DEVELOPMENT OF LAW: Rulings on Real versus Testimonial Evidence, in this section.)

The Roberts Court, however, clarified and qualified *Schmerber* in *Missouri v. McNeely*, 569 U.S. 141 (2013), in rejecting a *per se* rule that police have drivers suspected of driving while intoxicated (DWI) from alcohol submit to a blood test without their consent or a warrant; about half of the states require a warrant for DWI suspects. Tyler McNeely was stopped by a police officer for speeding and crossing the centerline. After declining to take a breath test to measure his blood alcohol concentration, he was arrested and taken to a nearby hospital for blood testing. The officer never attempted to secure a search warrant. McNeely refused to consent to the blood test, but the officer directed a lab technician to take a sample. McNeely tested well above the legal limit, and he was charged with driving while intoxicated. He moved to suppress the blood test result, arguing that taking his blood without a warrant violated his Fourth Amendment rights. The trial court agreed, concluding that the exigency exception to the warrant requirement did not apply because, apart from the fact that McNeely's blood alcohol was dissipating, no circumstances suggested that the officer faced an emergency. The Missouri Supreme Court affirmed, relying on *Schmerber,* in which the Court upheld a DWI suspect's warrantless blood test where the officer "might reasonably have believed that he was confronted with an emergency, in which the delay necessary to obtain a warrant, under the circumstances, threatened 'the destruction of evidence.'" The state court found, however, that this case involved a routine DWI investigation where no factors other than

---

■ The Development of Law

Rulings on Real versus Testimonial Evidence[1]

CASE	VOTE	RULING
Breithaupt v. Abram, 352 U.S. 432 (1957)	6–3	Upheld police taking blood sample from a driver involved in an automobile accident.
Schmerber v. California, 384 U.S. 757 (1966)	5–4	Upheld taking blood sample in a hospital from a driver who appeared intoxicated.
United States v. Wade, 388 U.S. 218 (1967)	5–4	Held that compelling a suspect to voice the words of a bank robber in a postindictment lineup was permissible.
Gilbert v. California, 388 U.S. 263 (1967)	5–4	Upheld taking of handwriting sample from suspect in absence of counsel.
United States v. Dionisio, 410 U.S. 1 (1973)	6–3	Upheld use of voice samples presented to grand jury.
Cupp v. Murphy, 412 U.S. 291 (1973)	9–0	Upheld police taking a sample of fingernails scraping from an individual who was not under arrest and who had voluntarily gone to police station.

1. See also the drug testing cases in Chapter 7.

CASE	VOTE	RULING
Estelle v. Williams, 425 U.S. 501 (1976)	7–2	Accused cannot be compelled to stand trial dressed in prison clothes; but here,

the failure to raise an objection negated any compulsion that would have violated the Fifth Amendment.

Wyrick v. Fields, 459 U.S. 42 (1982)	8–1	A defendant who agrees, on the advice of counsel, to submit to a polygraph test may be subsequently questioned about the test's results.

Pennsylvania v. Muniz, 496 U.S. 582 (1990)	8–1	Upheld the admissibility at trial of videotapes of suspects answering questions of police

at the time of their booking. Writing for the majority, Justice Brennan said that the videotapes, showing slurred speech and other signs of intoxication, were physical—not testimonial—evidence and, therefore, not covered by the Fifth Amendment's privilege against self-incrimination; Justice Marshall dissented.

Maryland v. King, 569 U.S. 435 (2013)	5–4	The majority held that police may take DNA swabs from suspects arrested, but not yet

tried and convicted, for "serious" violent crimes. Writing for the Court, Justice Kennedy likened DNA sampling to fingerprinting during a suspect's booking, calling it "a safe and secure way to process and identify the persons and possessions they must take into custody." By contrast, dissenting Justice Scalia, joined by Justices Ginsburg, Sotomayor, and Kagan, countered that the DNA swabs amounted to a general search warrant meant to possibly solve "cold cases" and thus lacked reasonable individualized suspicion in violation of the Fourth Amendment. Alonzo Jay King Jr. was under arrest for assault when police took a DNA sample that ultimately linked him to a six-year-old unresolved rape case, for which he was subsequently tried, convicted, and sentenced to life imprisonment.

■ THE DEVELOPMENT OF LAW

Other Court Rulings on Coerced Confessions and Limiting Miranda

CASE	VOTE	RULING
Parker v. North Carolina, 397 U.S. 790 (1970)	6–3	Defendant's guilty plea was voluntary where, after an allegedly coercive interrogation, it was given one month later and he testified at trial that it was voluntary.
Harris v. New York, 401 U.S. 222 (1971)	5–4	Incriminating statements without being given *Miranda* warnings may be used to impeach accused's testimony at trial.
Lego v. Twomey, 404 U.S. 477 (1972)	4–3	Preponderance of evidence is the standard for proving that a confession is voluntary.
Michigan v. Tucker, 417 U.S. 433 (1974)	8–1	Upheld the use of a witness at trial who was discovered as a result of questioning a defendant who had not received *Miranda* warnings.
Oregon v. Hass, 420 U.S. 714 (1975)	6–2	Upheld use of incriminating statements made by defendant in police car after being given *Miranda*

warnings and requesting the presence of counsel, but where defendant was told that counsel could not be telephoned until they reached police station.

| *Michigan v. Mosley,* 423 U.S. 96 (1975) | 7–2 | Once *Miranda* warnings are given and accused indicates desire to remain silent, any police |

questioning must be in presence of an attorney. But here, questioning stopped and was resumed two hours later, and the incriminating statements that were thereby elicited could be used at trial.

CASE	VOTE	RULING

Oregon v. Mathiason,   6–3   *Miranda* is not violated where a
429 U.S. 492 (1977)   person on parole voluntarily
goes to police station at officer's
request, agrees to a thirty-minute interview, and is allowed to leave but is
later arrested based on incriminating statements made in the interview.

Brewer v. Williams,   5–4   Writing for a bare majority, Jus-
430 U.S. 387 (1977)   tice Stewart held that a police
officer's "Christmas burial
speech" about finding the body of a murdered girl amounted to indirect
interrogation of the suspect and ran afoul of *Miranda.* In a dissent, Chief
Justice Burger contended that the body could still be introduced as evidence in spite of the majority's holding, based on an "inevitable discovery" exception to the exclusionary rule, which the Court subsequently
recognized in *Nix v. Williams,* 467 U.S. 431 (1984) (excerpted in Ch. 8,
and further discussed in *Brewer v. Williams;* see also *Rhode Island v. Innis,*
446 U.S. 291 (1980), excerpted in this chapter).

United States v. Washington,   7–2   Held that prosecutors may use at
431 U.S. 181 (1977); and   trial incriminating statements
United States v. Wong,   made by a witness before a
431 U.S. 174 (1977)   grand jury even though the
witness was not told that he was
in danger of being indicted; as a result, perjured testimony before grand
jury may be used at trial even though defendant had not received an effective warning of his rights.

North Carolina v. Butler,   6–3   Held that it is not necessary for a
441 U.S. 369 (1979)   suspect to expressly waive rights
during a custodial interrogation.

Rhode Island v. Innis,   6–3   *Miranda* comes into operation at
446 U.S. 291 (1980)   time of actual police
"interrogation."

California v. Prysock,   6–3   Precise language of *Miranda*
453 U.S. 355 (1981)   warning is not necessary when
informing suspects of their
rights.

(continues)

■ THE DEVELOPMENT OF LAW
*Other Court Rulings on Coerced Confessions and
Limiting* Miranda *(continued)*

CASE	VOTE	RULING
Oregon v. Bradshaw, 462 U.S. 1039 (1983)	5–4	Held that the initiation of a conversation with the police by a defendant amounts to a waiver of *Miranda* rights.
California v. Beheler, 463 U.S. 1121 (1983)	6–3	*Miranda* is not required when a suspect voluntarily goes to a police station for questioning, is allowed to leave, and later is arrested.
Minnesota v. Murphy, 465 U.S. 420 (1984)	6–3	Probation officer who obtained incriminating information from parolee was not obliged to give *Miranda* warnings.
Oregon v. Elstad, 470 U.S. 298 (1985)	6–3	Upheld the use of an initial culpatory statement, made in violation of *Miranda*, because it was voluntarily given by the defendant in his home.
Allen v. Illinois, 478 U.S. 364 (1986)	5–4	Fifth Amendment does not apply to incriminating statements made in proceedings to commit to a psychiatric prison a person said to be sexually dangerous.
Colorado v. Connelly, 479 U.S. 157 (1986)	7–2	Fifth Amendment not violated by the confession of a mentally ill man who told police that the "voice of God" told him to confess to a murder.
Arizona v. Mauro, 481 U.S. 520 (1987)	5–4	*Miranda* not violated when defendant was informed of rights,

requested an attorney, and was allowed to have a telephone conversation with his wife, which the police recorded and later introduced as evidence against the defendant.

CASE	VOTE	RULING
Pennsylvania v. Burder, 488 U.S. 9 (1988)	7–2	Held that ordinary traffic stops are not custodial stops for the purposes of *Miranda*, and police do not have to read drivers their *Miranda* rights.
Duckworth v. Eagan, 492 U.S. 195 (1989)	5–4	When advising suspects of their rights, the police may depart from the actual wording of the rights set down in *Miranda*.
Illinois v. Perkins, 496 U.S. 292 (1990)	8–1	The Court held that a defendant, who was jailed but not yet arraigned, had no right to be

informed of his *Miranda* rights by an undercover police agent seeking to elicit his incriminating statements by posing as a fellow inmate; Justice Marshall dissented.

McNeil v. Wisconsin, 501 U.S. 171 (1991)	6–3	Held that the Sixth Amendment right to counsel does not convey *Miranda*'s guarantees nor bar

police from questioning a defendant about a separate crime in the absence of his attorney.

Arizona v. Fulminante, 499 U.S. 279 (1991)	5–4	Although Justice White delivered an opinion for the Court, Chief Justice Rehnquist com-

manded four other votes for holding that the admission at trial of coerced confessions may be excused as a harmless error if it can be shown that other evidence, obtained independently of the confession, was also used at trial and was adequate to support a guilty verdict. Justice Souter provided the key vote to form a majority on that issue. But the lineup of the justices changed and was complicated by their stands on the other questions presented in the case as well. Notably, Justice White's opinion commanded a majority on the two other issues in the case. White deemed the circumstances of Fulminante's confession to constitute a coerced confession,

(continues)

■ The Development of Law
Other Court Rulings on Coerced Confessions and
Limiting Miranda *(continued)*

whereas Rehnquist, O'Connor, Kennedy, and Souter disagreed. On that issue, Scalia joined White's opinion, along with Blackmun, Marshall, and Stevens. On the third issue of whether the use of Fulminante's confession was harmless beyond a reasonable doubt, White commanded a majority for affirming the state supreme court's judgment that Fulminante's confession may not be used against him. On that issue, White was joined by Blackmun, Marshall, Stevens, and Kennedy; Rehnquist, O'Connor, and Scalia dissented; and Souter gave no indication of whether or how he voted.

CASE	VOTE	RULING
Brecht v. Abrahamson, 507 U.S. 619 (1993)	5–4	Held that on *habeas corpus* review federal courts may set aside convictions that are challenged

for alleged trial errors in violation of *Miranda* only when the errors have a "substantial and injurious effect or influence" that results in "actual prejudice" against the defendant.

| *Stansbury v. California,* 511 U.S. 318 (1994) | 9–0 | Held that when trial courts determine whether a person was "in custody" for *Miranda* pur- |

poses, the objective circumstances of the police interrogation should be controlling, not the officers' subjective views as to whether the suspect should be given *Miranda* warnings.

| *Davis v. United States,* 512 U.S. 452 (1994) | 9–0 | Upheld the use of incriminating statements made by a suspect who said, "Maybe I should talk |

to a lawyer," during a police interrogation that then continued. Writing for the Court, Justice O'Connor observed, "If the suspect effectively waives his right to counsel after receiving Miranda warnings, law enforcement officers are free to question him. . . . We decline the petitioner's invitation to extend *Edwards* [*v. Arizona,* 451 U.S. 477 (1981)] and require law enforcement officers to cease questioning immediately upon the making of an ambiguous or equivocal reference to an attorney."

| *Yarborough v. Alvarado,* 541 U.S. 652 (2004) | 5–4 | Writing for the Court, Justice Kennedy held that a juvenile, who was brought by his parents |

to the police station and in a two-hour-long interview made incriminating statements about a robbery and murder, then allowed to leave, but a month later was arrested and charged, was not in police custody for the purposes of *Miranda*, and his incriminating statements could be used against him even though he had not been given the *Miranda* warning about his rights. According to Justice Kennedy, the fact that he was a juvenile and other psychological considerations was deemed not relevant to whether he was in police custody. Justices Stevens, Souter, Ginsburg, and Breyer dissented.

CASE	VOTE	RULING

United States v. Patane,
542 U.S. 630 (2004)

5–4

Writing for the Court, Justice Thomas held that a gun discovered as a result of the suspect's incriminating statements could be used as evidence, even though he had not been given *Miranda* warnings, and characterized the warning as "prophylactic rules." The dissenters would have applied "the fruit of the poisonous tree" doctrine and excluded the use of the evidence.

Florida v. Powell,
559 U.S. 50 (2010)

7–2

The Roberts Court held that police need not give the precise language of informing a suspect of the right to counsel during an interrogation as laid down in *Miranda*, as interpreted in *Duckworth v. Egan*, 492 U.S. 195 (1989). Writing for the Court, Justice Ginsburg reaffirmed *Duckworth*'s holding that the precise language of Miranda need not be followed. In this case police officers informed a suspect of "the right to talk to a lawyer before answering any of [the law enforcement officers'] questions," and that he could invoke that right "at anytime . . . during th[e] interview." That was held to satisfy *Miranda*. By contrast, dissenting Justices Stevens and Breyer countered that *Miranda* mandated that suspects be informed of "the right to consult with a *lawyer and to have the lawyer with him during interrogation*" (emphasis added).

Maryland v. Shatzer,
559 U.S. 98 (2010)

9–0

Justice Scalia ruled that a suspect's incriminating statements could be used at trial, even though they were made in a second interrogation in which he waived his right to counsel and which took place more than two weeks after he was first interrogated and informed of his right to counsel. Justice Scalia held that the break in his custody, even though he was in jail, satisfied the rulings in *Edwards v. Arizona*, 451 U.S. 477 (1981), and *Minnick v. Mississippi*, 498 U.S. 146 (1990).

(continues)

■ THE DEVELOPMENT OF LAW
*Other Court Rulings on Coerced Confessions and
Limiting* Miranda *(continued)*

CASE	VOTE	RULING
Berghuis v. Thompkins, 560 U.S. 370 (2010)	5–4	Writing for a bare Majority, Justice Kennedy ruled that (1) a suspect must say un-

equivocally and unambiguously that he or she is invoking the right to remain silent; and (2) if the suspect answers any questions—even with a one-word response—that amount to a confession, it may be considered a waiver of the right to remain silent and may be used as evidence at trial. In short, police need not obtain an explicit waiver of a suspect's *Miranda* rights. Justices Stevens, Ginsburg, Breyer, and Sotomayor dissented.

CASE	VOTE	RULING
Howes v. Fields, 565 U.S. 499 (2012)	6–3	Writing for the Court, Justice Alito held that in determining when a prisoner is in

custody for *Miranda* purposes, courts should consider "all of the circumstances surrounding the interrogation," specifically how a suspect would have gauged his freedom of movement, and that not all restraints on freedom of movement amount to custody. Fields, a prisoner, was taken from his prison cell and questioned by two sheriffs about his criminal activities prior to going to prison. At no time was he given *Miranda* warnings. Although during more than five hours of questioning he was told that he could return to his cell, and several times he told the sheriffs he no longer wanted to talk, he never asked to return to his cell. Fields eventually confessed and that confession was used against him at trial. Justices Ginsburg, Breyer, and Sotomayor concurred and dissented in part.

CASE	VOTE	RULING
Salinas v. Texas, 570 U.S. 178 (2013)	5–4	Justice Alito held that prosecutors may comment at trial on a defendant's unwilling-

ness to respond to an officer's questions about a murder, even though as a suspect he had not yet been arrested, taken into custody, or received *Miranda* warnings. In doing so, Justice Alito distinguished *Griffin v. California*, 380 U.S. 609 (1965), from other precedents supporting the right to remain silent, because here the individual had not invoked the Fifth Amendment privilege against self-incrimination.

> Concurring justices would have overturned Griffin as inconsistent
> with "the Constitution's text, history, or logic." By contrast, dissent-
> ing Justice Breyer, joined by Justices Ginsburg, Sotomayor, and Ka-
> gan, countered that the ruling was inconsistent with a range of
> precedents, as well as *Miranda* and the Fifth Amendment guarantee.

the natural dissipation of blood alcohol suggested that there was an
emergency, and, thus, the nonconsensual warrantless test violated
McNeely's right to be free from unreasonable searches of his person.
Writing for the Court in *Missouri v. McNeely,* Justice Sotomayor affirmed
and concluded that in drunk-driving investigations, the natural dissipation of alcohol in the bloodstream does not constitute an exigency in
every case to justify a warrantless blood test. Justice Sotomayor held that
only in exceptional circumstances may a warrantless blood test be conducted, and that should be determined on a case-by-case basis based on
"the totality of circumstances." In her words, "cases will arise when
anticipated delays in obtaining a warrant will justify a blood test without
judicial authorization. . . . [But our decision that consent or warrants
must generally be obtained underscores] our recognition that any compelled intrusion into the human body implicates significant, constitutionally protected privacy interests." Only dissenting Justice Thomas
would permit warrantless blood tests of drivers suspected of DWI.

D | *Required Records, Private Papers, and Custodial Possession*

Another limitation on the Fifth Amendment is the *required records*
doctrine—that is, records required to be kept to provide information
for regulatory agencies receive no Fifth Amendment protection. *Shapiro v. United States,* 335 U.S. 1 (1948), held that required records have
"public aspects" that foreclose protection for personal information also
contained therein. Twenty years later, in *Grosso v. United States,* 390
U.S. 62 (1968), the Court clarified the doctrine:

> The premises of the doctrine, as it is described in *Shapiro,* are evidently
> these: first, the purpose of the United States's inquiry must be essen-
> tially regulatory; second, information is to be obtained by requiring
> the preservation of records of a kind which the regulated party has
> customarily kept; and third, the records themselves must have issued
> "public aspects" which render them analogous to public documents.

Income tax returns are required records, according to *United States v. Sullivan*, 274 U.S. 259 (1927), and the Fifth Amendment is no defense against prosecution for failing to file tax returns. The problem posed by illegal-income earners and the reporting requirements in filing tax returns, however, continued to be presented to the Court. In *United States v. Murdock*, 284 U.S. 141 (1931), a taxpayer filed a return claiming certain deductions but refused on Fifth Amendment grounds to answer questions concerning them, for which he was prosecuted for willful failure to supply necessary information. Although the taxpayer's Fifth Amendment claim was invalid, the Court held that a good faith claim of the amendment bars conviction for willfully failing to answer the IRS's questions. But in *Marchetti v. United States*, 390 U.S. 39 (1968), the Court struck down an IRS regulation requiring gamblers to register and to submit monthly information concerning their wagering activities. It did so on the grounds that the information was not customarily kept, the reports had no public records aspects, and the requirements were directed at a "select group inherently suspect of criminal activities."

A series of rulings on claims to Fifth Amendment protection for private papers firmly established that "a party is privileged from producing . . . evidence, but not from its production," *Johnson v. United States*, 228 U.S. 457 (1913). Individuals may claim Fifth Amendment privacy interests and, for example, quash an administrative subpoena directing them to produce papers or documents in which they have privacy interests. But they have no Fifth Amendment protection against the government subpoenaing their papers held by a bank, accountant, or attorney.

In *Couch v. United States*, 409 U.S. 322 (1973), for instance, Mrs. Couch was denied any reasonable expectation of privacy under the Fifth Amendment to intervene with an IRS summons of her accountant to turn over her business records. There the Court stressed that "no Fourth or Fifth Amendment claim can prevail where . . . there exists no legitimate expectation of privacy and no semblance of governmental compulsion against the person of the accused. . . . The criterion for Fifth Amendment immunity remains not the ownership of property, but the 'physical or moral compulsion exerted.'"

Two dissenters in *Couch* took quite a different view of the Fifth Amendment's protection for privacy. Justice Douglas urged that a "Fifth Amendment claim [is] valid *even in the absence of personal compulsion* so long as [the] accused has a reasonable expectation of privacy in [the] articles subpoenaed."

A majority of the Court, however, rejected such a broad interpretation of the Fifth Amendment. Three years after *Couch, Fisher v. United States*, 425 U.S. 391 (1976), held that individuals have no valid Fifth Amendment claims against their attorneys turning over documents related to their tax returns to the IRS, because that does "not 'compel' the taxpayer to do anything—and certainly [does] not compel him to be a 'witness against himself.'"

Following *Couch* and *Fisher*, in *United States v. Doe*, 465 U.S. 605 (1984), the Court reached the same conclusion with respect to an individual's own papers. In short, the amendment protects only testimonial components of an individual's actual production of personal materials.

In *Baltimore City Department of Social Services v. Bouknight*, 493 U.S. 549 (1990), the Court further extended the *Schmerber* line of cases on real (physical) versus testimonial evidence (as discussed in Section C) and those dealing with the production of required records and private papers. There, the Court held that a mother could not invoke the Fifth Amendment when resisting a juvenile court order to produce a child who was in her custody. Maurice Bouknight was an abused child who was taken for a time by social workers from his mother, Jacqueline Bouknight. After a subsequent hearing in juvenile court, the child was returned to her custody on certain conditions, including that she attend a parental training program, and under a protective supervision order. Eight months later, after determining that Mrs. Bouknight was violating the conditions for custody of her child and that the child might be dead, social workers filed petitions to remove the child and to force Mrs. Bouknight to produce her child in court. Mrs. Bouknight in turn claimed that her Fifth Amendment guarantee against self-incrimination barred the juvenile court from compelling her to produce her child in court.

Writing for the majority in *Bouknight*, Chief Justice Rehnquist conceded that the order to produce the child compelled Mrs. Bouknight to make testimonial assertions, but that here, in a civil proceeding, she could not rely on the Fifth Amendment. The guarantee against self-incrimination was inapplicable because (1) Mrs. Bouknight had assumed custodial duties related to the child's production analogous to those assumed with the production of required records; and (2) the production was part of a noncriminal proceeding.

In dissent, Justice Marshall, joined by Justice Brennan, rejected the majority's reasoning and reliance on earlier cases. On the one hand, Bouknight was "not acting as a custodian in the traditional sense of that word because she is not acting *on behalf of the State*." On the other hand, prior cases upholding diminished Fifth Amendment protection for the production of required records and private papers dealt with purely civil regulatory systems and regulations aimed at the general public. But here, Marshall contended that the civil proceeding against Mrs. Bouknight "*inevitably* intersects with criminal sanctions" for child abuse.

■ The Development of Law

Rulings on Required Records and Private Papers

CASE	VOTE	RULING
United States v. Sullivan, 274 U.S. 259 (1927)	9–0	Rejected Fifth Amendment objection to filing federal income tax return.
Shapiro v. United States, 335 U.S. 1 (1948)	5–4	Records required to be kept under the regulatory powers of Congress acquire a "public aspect" and have no Fifth Amendment protection.
Marchetti v. United States, 390 U.S. 39 (1968), and *Grosso v. United States,* 390 U.S. 62 (1968)	8–1	Internal Revenue Service requirement that individuals register as gamblers violates Fifth Amendment since gambling is illegal.
Haynes v. United States, 390 U.S. 85 (1968)	8–1	Fifth Amendment not violated by requirement that gun owners register their guns.
Leary v. United States, 395 U.S. 6 (1969)	9–0	No Fifth Amendment protection against registering and tax on importation of marijuana.
Minor v. United States, 396 U.S. 87 (1969)	7–2	Narcotic seller's rights were not violated by requirement to register and pay sales tax.
United States v. U.S. Coin and Currency, 401 U.S. 715 (1971)	5–4	Upheld Marchetti; Fifth Amendment bars IRS from requiring gamblers to register with federal government.

CASE	VOTE	RULING
California v. Byers, 402 U.S. 424 (1971)	5–4	Upheld a "hit–and–run" statute that required drivers who hit a parked car to stop and leave their name and driver's license number.
Bellis v. United States, 417 U.S. 85 (1974)	8–1	Fifth Amendment applies to only personal production of private papers—papers held by third

parties (accountants, lawyers, etc.) are not protected, even if they incriminate the custodian of the papers.

California Bankers Association v. Shultz, 416 U.S. 21 (1974)	6–3	Upheld the Bank Secrecy Act giving the IRS access to individuals' bank records.
Garner v. United States, 424 U.S. 648 (1976)	9–0	Held that an individual who could have but failed to raise a Fifth Amendment objection on

a tax return was foreclosed from subsequently invoking the Fifth Amendment.

Braswell v. United States, 487 U.S. 99 (1988)	5–4	The president (and sole shareholder) of a corporation cannot claim the Fifth Amendment in refusing to turn over corporate documents.
Doe v. United States, 487 U.S. 201 (1988)	8–1	Contents of foreign bank accounts are not protected by the Fifth Amendment.

9

THE RIGHT TO COUNSEL AND OTHER PROCEDURAL GUARANTEES

A long with the Fourth Amendment and the Fifth Amendment's right against self-accusation and the due process clause, a number of other guarantees of the Fifth, Sixth, Seventh, and Eighth Amendments protect the rights of the accused. The Fifth Amendment provides for indictment by a grand jury and forbids holding defendants in double jeopardy. The Sixth Amendment guarantees an accused the assistance of counsel, the rights to be informed of charges and to confront accusers, as well as a right to a speedy and public trial by an impartial jury in all criminal cases. The Seventh Amendment guarantees a jury trial in civil cases where the controversy exceeds twenty dollars. The Eighth Amendment prohibits the imposition of excessive bail and fines, besides banning cruel and unusual punishments (see Ch. 10).

A | *The Right to Counsel*

The Sixth Amendment guarantees the accused "the assistance of counsel for his defense." Literally, the guarantee confers a right of which one may avail him- or herself but which the government is not obliged to ensure in all criminal cases. The year after the adoption and before the ratification of the Bill of Rights, Congress further indicated that the assistance of counsel was not mandatory in all criminal cases. The Federal Crimes Act of 1790 imposed a statutory duty on courts to assign counsel to represent defendants only in capital cases. In noncapital cases, the accused had a right to hire counsel but, if too poor to afford one, the government was not obligated to appoint one for his defense.

In *Johnson v. Zerbst*, 304 U.S. 458 (1938), the Hughes Court fundamentally changed the right to counsel in federal courts. There, in an appeal from a conviction for counterfeiting, the Court noted that the "right to be heard would be, in many cases, of little avail if it did not comprehend the right to be heard by counsel" and ruled that "the Sixth Amendment withholds from federal courts, in all criminal proceedings, the power and authority to deprive an accused of his life or liberty unless he has or waives the assistance of counsel."

The Court remained reluctant to impose the right to counsel on state courts, however. In its first confrontation with that issue in the famous *Scottsboro* case—*Powell v. Alabama* (1932) (see excerpt below)—the Hughes Court declined to apply the Sixth Amendment to state criminal courts. The Court did hold that under the circumstances of the case the due process clause of the Fifth Amendment required the trial court "to make an effective appointment of counsel." In this case, the "Scottsboro boys," as the several young black defendants were known, were accused of the capital offense of raping two white women. They were tried before an all-white jury, without the assistance of counsel, in a small southern town, Scottsboro, Alabama.

In the 1940s and 1950s, the Stone and Vinson Courts continued to defer to the states but ruled on a case-by-case basis that some defendants had to be retried and given the assistance of counsel. In *Betts v. Brady*, 316 U.S. 455 (1942), the Stone Court interpreted *Powell* to require the appointment of counsel only in "special circumstances" and in capital cases. There, Betts, an indigent white man indicted for robbery, requested but was denied counsel. Conceding that a layman might encounter difficulties with courtroom procedures when defending himself, Justice Owen Roberts nonetheless held that Betts was "of ordinary intelligence and ability to take care of his own interests on the trial of [a] narrow issue." Three dissenters, Justices Black, Douglas, and Murphy, protested the refusal to extend the right to counsel to all indigents. "[A]ny other practice seems to me to defeat the promise of our democratic society to provide equal justice under the law," charged Justice Black. "A practice cannot be reconciled with 'common and fundamental ideas of fairness and right,' which subjects innocent men to increased dangers of conviction merely because of their poverty."

Although adhering to the *special circumstances rule* and upholding several convictions obtained without the defendant's assistance of counsel,[1] the Vinson Court held that counsel was required in capital cases;[2] when the conduct of a trial judge was questionable;[3] where defendants were young, ignorant, or otherwise handicapped;[4] and in legally complex cases.[5]

Finally, in *Gideon v. Wainwright* (1963) (excerpted below), the Warren Court overturned *Betts* and extended the right to counsel to the accused in all states in all criminal cases. *Argersinger v. Hamlin* (1972) (excerpted below) then applied the right to counsel to all offenses involving the possibility of imprisonment, regardless of whether they were petty, misdemeanor, or felony offenses. As a result of a series of rulings, the right to counsel now extends to virtually every stage of the criminal justice system: from when police make a quasi-arrest or arrest, to preindictment preliminary hearings and confessions before and after indictment, as well as to preliminary hearings, arraignment proceedings, police lineups, the trial, and subsequent proceedings on sentencing, appeals, and probation hearings. In addition, *Faretta v. California*, 422 U.S. 806 (1975), held that defendants may waive the right to counsel and represent themselves, if a trial judge finds them competent to do so.[6]

The Scottsboro boys with their attorney, Samuel S. Leibowitz. The Scottsboro boys were initially tried before an all-white jury, without the assistance of counsel in a small town in Scottsboro, Alabama, for allegedly raping two white women. They were sentenced to death, but their convictions were appealed and led to the Supreme Court's important ruling in *Powell v. Alabama* (1932). (*Brown Brothers.*)

■ THE DEVELOPMENT OF LAW

Rulings Extending the Right to Counsel throughout the Criminal Justice System

STAGE OF CRIMINAL JUSTICE SYSTEM	CASE
Quasi-arrest	*Orozco v. Texas*, 394 U.S. 324 (1969)
Arrest	*Miranda v. Arizona*, 384 U.S. 436 (1966)
Preindictment preliminary hearing	*Coleman v. Alabama*, 399 U.S. 1 (1970)
Preindictment confession	*Escobedo v. Illinois*, 378 U.S. 478 (1964)
Postindictment	*Massiah v. United States*, 377 U.S. 201 (1964)
Preliminary hearings	*White v. Maryland*, 373 U.S. 59 (1963)
Arraignment	*Hamilton v. Alabama*, 368 U.S. 52 (1961)
Lineups	*United States v. Wade*, 388 U.S. 218 (1967), and *Gilbert v. California*, 388 U.S. 263 (1967)
Plea bargaining	*Missouri v. Frye*, 132 S.Ct. 1399 (2012), and *Lafler v. Cooper*, 132 S.Ct. 1376 (2012)
Trials	*Gideon v. Wainwright*, 372 U.S. 335 (1963), as modified by *Argersinger v. Hamlin*, 407 U.S. 25 (1972), and *Scott v. Illinois*, 440 U.S. 367 (1979)
Appeals	*Douglas v. California*, 372 U.S. 353 (1963)
Probation hearings	*Mempa v. Rhay*, 389 U.S. 128 (1967)
Revocation of probation or parole	*Gagnon v. Scarpelli*, 411 U.S. 778 (1973)

The Burger and Rehnquist Courts qualified the application of the right to counsel in a number of areas. Besides the exceptions for the presence of counsel during police questioning and interrogation (see Ch. 8), counsel is not required during hearings on the competency of witnesses testifying against the defendant,[7] nor need counsel be present at preindictment lineups[8] or at photo-identification hearings.[9] *Scott v. Illinois*, 440 U.S. 367 (1979), limited *Argersinger* to require court-appointed attorneys only in cases where defendants are in fact sentenced to jail terms.[10] The right to counsel on appeal was limited in *Ross v. Moffitt*, 417 U.S. 600 (1974), holding that the assistance of counsel applies only to the first appeal and not to further discretionary appeals. *Pennsylvania v. Finley*, 481 U.S. 551 (1987), further ruled that defendants have no right to court-appointed attorneys in postconviction proceedings or to insist that a court-appointed lawyer follow certain procedures when withdrawing from their appeals because the lawyer deems further appeals "frivolous."[11] And there is no right to counsel at disciplinary hearings in prison[12] and proceedings on revoking parole.[13] Finally, in *McNeil v. Wisconsin*, 501 U.S. 171 (1991), the Court held that the Sixth Amendment right to counsel does not convey the same protection as *Miranda*'s guarantee of counsel and that an accused who is in police custody may be questioned about another crime in the absence of his attorney without violating the Sixth Amendment, even though such questioning would be in violation of *Miranda*. However, in *Fellers v. United States*, 540 U.S. 519 (2004), a unanimous Court reaffirmed that the Sixth Amendment bars the use of incriminating statements elicited by police from an accused, after waiving his *Miranda* rights, and after he has been indicted for an offense. Writing for the Court, Justice O'Connor reaffirmed that the Sixth Amendment right to counsel bars interrogations or the deliberate elicitation of information, out of the presence of counsel, once judicial proceedings have begun, whether by a formal charge, preliminary hearing, indictment, or arraignment. A bare majority in *United States v. Gonzalez-Lopez*, 548 U.S. 140 (2006), also reaffirmed that the Sixth Amendment guarantees the right to have a paid counsel of the defendant's choosing and that the violation of that right entails a reversal of the defendant's conviction. Justice Scalia delivered the opinion of the Court. Justice Alito filed a dissent, which Chief Justice Roberts and Justices Kennedy and Thomas joined.

The Roberts Court held in *Indiana v. Edwards*, 554 U.S. 164 (2008), that states may require a criminal defendant who suffers from mental illness to have a court-appointed lawyer at trial, rather than acting in his own defense, even when the defendant is deemed competent to stand trial. Edwards, who suffered from schizophrenia, was deemed by the trial court competent to stand trial but not competent to defend himself. He appealed that ruling, arguing that it violated his Sixth Amendment right to counsel and the Court's holding in *Faretta v. California*, 422 U.S. 806 (1975), that a defendant deemed competent to stand trial has a right to self-representation. Justice Breyer delivered the opinion of the Court, which declined to overrule *Faretta* on the ground that states have some flexibility and that there was "no empirical research" showing "that *Faretta's* holding has proven counterproductive in practice" or that the right of representing oneself "furthers or inhibits" the fairness of a trial.

In another 7–2 decision, the Roberts Court held that a defendant's incriminating statements, made in violation of the Sixth Amendment right to counsel, to a governmental informant in a prison cell may be used to impeach the defendant's trial testimony. Writing for the Court in *Kansas v. Ventris*, 556 U.S. 586 (2009), Justice Scalia held that the core of the Sixth Amendment right to counsel is a trial right and covers pretrial interrogations only to ensure that the defendant has "effective representation by counsel at the only stage when legal aid and advice would help him" (quoting *Massiah v. United States*, 377 U.S. 201 [1964]). But, the right to be free of uncounseled interrogation applies only at the time of police interrogation, and not when a confession is admitted as evidence against the defendant. Justices Stevens and Ginsburg dissented.

Writing for a bare majority in *Montejo v. Louisiana*, 556 U.S. 778 (2009), Justice Scalia also overturned a long-standing decision in *Michigan v. Jackson*, 475 U.S. 625 (1986), that barred police from initiating questions unless a suspect's lawyer is present. *Michigan v. Jackson* had held that police may not question a suspect who has a lawyer or who has asked for one unless an attorney is present, even if a suspect agreed to talk with officers in the absence of an attorney. Writing for the Court in *Montejo*, Justice Scalia dismissed the prior ruling as "poorly reasoned" because police could not even ask a suspect who had been appointed an attorney if he wanted to talk. In his words, "It would be completely unjustified to presume that a defendant's consent to police-initiated interrogation was involuntary or coerced simply because he had previously been appointed a lawyer." Dissenting Justice Stevens, who had delivered the decision in *Michigan v. Jackson*, joined by Justices Souter, Ginsburg, and Breyer, countered, "The police interrogation in this case clearly violated petitioner's Sixth Amendment right to counsel," and would "only diminish the public's confidence in the reliability and fairness of our system of justice."

Notes

1. See *Canizio v. New York*, 327 U.S. 82 (1946); and *Bute v. Illinois*, 333 U.S. 640 (1948).

2. *Tomkins v. Missouri*, 323 U.S. 485 (1945).

3. *Townsend v. Burke*, 334 U.S. 736 (1948); and *White v. Ragen*, 324 U.S. 760 (1945).

4. *De Meerleer v. Michigan*, 329 U.S. 663 (1947); *Marino v. Ragen*, 332 U.S. 561 (1947); *Moore v. Michigan*, 355 U.S. 155 (1957); *Massey v. Moore*, 348 U.S. 105 (1954); *Hudson v. North Carolina*, 363 U.S. 697 (1960); and *Culombe v. Connecticut*, 367 U.S. 568 (1961).

5. *Cash v. Culver*, 358 U.S. 633 (1959).

6. *McKaskle v. Wiggins*, 465 U.S. 168 (1984); however, held that the defendant's right to counsel in his own defense was not violated by the unsolicited participation of a standby counsel.

7. *Kentucky v. Stincer*, 482 U.S. 730 (1987), holding that the Sixth Amendment was not violated by denial of attendance of counsel during competency hearings for two minor victims whom the defendant was accused of sodomizing.

8. *Kirby v. Illinois*, 405 U.S. 682 (1972).

9. *United States v. Ash*, 413 U.S. 300 (1973). *Moore v. Illinois*, 434 U.S. 220 (1977); however, held that counsel must be present during a one-on-one corporeal identification of the defendant.

10. Notably, in *Herring v. New York*, 422 U.S. 853 (1975), the Court held that judges may not deny the right to counsel in nonjury trials.

11. In *Anders v. California*, 386 U.S. 738 (1967), the Court held that a court-appointed attorney who seeks to withdraw from a case because he deems further appeals frivolous must file a brief explaining the meritlessness of an appeal as well as anything that might be arguable on appeal, and a court must then determine that there are no nonfrivolous issues. *Penson v. Ohio*, 488 U.S. 75 (1988), reaffirmed that a defendant's attorney after making a first appeal must file an *Anders* brief showing that further appeals are frivolous and justifying the attorney's request to withdraw.

12. *Baxter v. Palmigiano*, 425 U.S. 308 (1976).

13. *Gagnon v. Scarpelli*, 411 U.S. 778 (1973).

Selected Bibliography

Chemerinsky, Erwin. *Closing the Court House Door: How Your Constitutional Rights Became Unenforceable.* New Haven: Yale University Press, 2017.

Cole, David. *No Equal Justice.* New York: New Press, 1999.

Goodman, James. *Stories of Scottsboro.* New York: Pantheon, 1994.

Lewis, Anthony. *Gideon's Trumpet.* New York: Random House, 1964.

Norris, C., and Washington, S. *The Last of the Scottsboro Boys.* New York: Putnam, 1979.

Powell v. Alabama

287 U.S. 45, 53 S.Ct. 55 (1932)

In Scottsboro, Alabama, Ozie Powell and eight other black youths were arrested, charged, and tried before an all-white jury for raping two white women traveling on a train. Each was tried separately without the assistance of counsel, and on conviction they were sentenced to death. Their trials and convictions received wide publicity, and lawyers affiliated with the International Labor Defense, a Communist-front organization in New York, volunteered to represent them on appeal. After the Alabama Supreme Court affirmed their convictions, an appeal was made to the Supreme Court, which granted review. Justice George Sutherland's opinion for the majority discusses some additional facts in the case.

The Court's decision was 7–2, with Justices Butler and McReynolds dissenting.

■ ■ ■

☐ *Justice SUTHERLAND delivered the opinion of the Court.*

Before the train reached Scottsboro, Ala., a sheriff's posse seized the defendants and two other negroes. Both girls and the negroes then were taken to Scottsboro, the county seat. Word of their coming and of the alleged assault had preceded them, and they were met at Scottsboro by a large crowd. It does not sufficiently appear that the defendants were seriously threatened with, or that they were actually in danger of, mob violence; but it does appear that the attitude of the community was one of great hostility. The sheriff thought it necessary to call for the militia to assist in safeguarding the prisoners. Chief Justice Anderson pointed out in his opinion that every step taken from the arrest and arraignment to the sentence was accompanied by the military. Soldiers took the defendants to Gadsden for safe-keeping, brought them back to Scottsboro for arraignment, returned them to Gadsden for safe-keeping while awaiting trial, escorted them to Scottsboro for trial a few days later, and guarded the courthouse and grounds at every stage of the proceedings. It is perfectly apparent that the proceedings, from beginning to end, took place in an atmosphere of tense, hostile, and excited public sentiment. During the entire time, the defendants were closely confined or were under military guard. The record does not disclose their ages, except that one of them was nineteen; but the record clearly indicates that most, if not all, of them were truthful, and they are constantly referred to as "the boys." They were ignorant and illiterate. All of them were residents of other states, where alone members of their families or friends resided. . . .

[W]e confine ourselves . . . to the inquiry whether the defendants were in substance denied the right of counsel, and if so, whether such denial infringes the due process clause of the Fourteenth Amendment.

First. The record shows that immediately upon the return of the indictment defendants were arraigned and pleaded not guilty. Apparently they were not asked whether they had, or were able to employ, counsel, or wished to have counsel appointed; or whether they had friends or relatives who might assist in that regard if communicated with. That it would not have been an idle ceremony to have given the defendants reasonable opportunity to communicate with their families and endeavor to obtain counsel is demonstrated by the fact that very soon after conviction, able counsel appeared in their behalf. . . .

It is hardly necessary to say that the right to counsel being conceded, a defendant should be afforded a fair opportunity to secure counsel of his own choice. Not only was that not done here, but such designation of counsel as was attempted was either so definite or so close upon the trial as to amount to a denial of effective and substantial aid in that regard. . . .

[U]ntil the very morning of the trial no lawyer had been named or definitely designated to represent the defendants. Prior to that time, the trial judge had "appointed all the members of the bar" for the limited "purpose of arraigning the defendants." Whether they would represent the defendants thereafter, if no counsel appeared in their behalf, was a matter of speculation only, or, as the judge indicated, of mere anticipation on the part of the court. Such a designation, even if made for all purposes, would, in our opinion, have fallen far short of meeting, in any proper sense, a requirement for the appointment of counsel. How many lawyers were members of the bar does not appear; but, in the very nature of things, whether many or few, they would not, thus collectively named, have been given that clear appreciation of responsibility or impressed with that individual sense of duty which should and naturally would accompany the appointment of a selected member of the bar, specifically named and assigned.

That this action of the trial judge in respect of appointment of counsel was little more than an expansive gesture, imposing no substantial or definite obligation upon any one. . . . [D]uring perhaps the most critical period of the proceedings against these defendants, that is to say, from the time of their arraignment until the beginning of their trial, when consultation, thorough-going investigation and preparation were vitally important, the defendants did not have the aid of counsel in any real sense, although they were as much entitled to such aid during that period as at the trial itself. . . .

The defendants, young, ignorant, illiterate, surrounded by hostile sentiment, haled back and forth under guard of soldiers, charged with an atrocious crime regarded with especial horror in the community where they were to be tried, were thus put in peril of their lives within a few moments after counsel for the first time charged with any degree of responsibility began to represent them. . . .

Under the circumstances disclosed, we hold that defendants were not accorded the right of counsel in any substantial sense. To decide otherwise, would simply be to ignore actualities. . . .

Second. The Constitution of Alabama provides that in all criminal prosecutions the accused shall enjoy the right to have the assistance of counsel; and a state statute requires the court in a capital case, where the defendant is

DIVISION OF CORRECTIONS
CORRESPONDENCE REGULATIONS

MAIL WILL NOT BE DELIVERED WHICH DOES NOT CONFORM WITH THESE RULES

No. 1 -- Only 2 letters each week, not to exceed 2 sheets letter-size 8 1/2 x 11" and written *on one side only,* and if ruled paper, do not write between lines. *Your complete name* must be signed at the close of your letter. *Clippings, stamps, letters* from other people, *stationery or cash must not be enclosed* in your letters.

No. 2 -- All *letters* must be addressed in the *complete prison name* of the inmate. *Cell number,* where applicable, and *prison number* must be placed in lower left corner of envelope, with your complete name and address in the upper left corner.

No. 3 -- *Do not send any packages without a Package Permit.* Unauthorized *packages* will be destroyed.

No. 4 -- *Letters* must be written in English only.

No. 5 -- *Books, magazines, pamphlets,* and *newspapers* of reputable character will be delivered *only if* mailed direct from the publisher.

No. 6 -- *Money* must be sent in the form of *Postal Money Orders* only, in the inmate's complete prison name and prison number.

INSTITUTION _____ CELL NUMBER _____

NAME _____ NUMBER _____

In The Supreme Court of The United States
Washington D.C.

Clarence Earl Gideon
    Petitioner | Petition for a writ
    vs. | of Certiorari Directed
H.G. Cochran, Jr, as | to The Supreme Court
Director, Divisions | State of Florida.
of corrections state
of Florida   No. - **890** Misc.

OCT. TERM 1961
U.S. Supreme Court

To. The Honorable Earl Warren, Chief
Justice of the United States
    Comes now The petitioner, Clarence
Earl Gideon, a citizen of The United states
of America, in proper person, and appearing
as his own counsel. Who petitions this
Honorable Court for a Writ of Certiorari
directed to The Supreme Court of The state
of Florida. To review the order and Judge-
ment of the court below denying The
petitioner a writ of Habeus Corpus.
    Petitioner submits That The Supreme
Court of The United States has The authority
and jurisdiction to review The final Judge-
ment of The Supreme Court of The State
of Florida The highest court of The State
Under sec. 344 (B) Title 28 U.S.C.A. and
Because The "Due process clause" of the

Clarence Gideon's petition to the Supreme Court, which led to the Warren Court's landmark ruling on the right to counsel. (*Collection of the Supreme Court of the United States.*)

unable to employ counsel, to appoint counsel for him. The state Supreme Court held that these provisions had not been infringed, and with that holding we are powerless to interfere. The question, however, which it is our duty, and within our power, to decide, is whether the denial of the assistance of counsel contravenes the due process clause of the Fourteenth Amendment to the Federal Constitution. . . .

In the light of the facts outlined in the forepart of this opinion—the ignorance and illiteracy of the defendants, their youth, the circumstances of public hostility, the imprisonment and the close surveillance of the defendants by the military forces, the fact that their friends and families were all in other states and communication with them necessarily difficult, and above all that they stood in deadly peril of their lives—we think the failure of the trial court to give them reasonable time and opportunity to secure counsel was a clear denial of due process.

But passing that, and assuming their inability, even if opportunity had been given, to employ counsel, as the trial court evidently did assume, we are of the opinion that, under the circumstances just stated, the necessity of counsel was so vital and imperative that the failure of the trial court to make an effective appointment of counsel was likewise a denial of due process within the meaning of the Fourteenth Amendment. Whether this would be so in other criminal prosecutions, or under other circumstances, we need not determine. All that it is necessary now to decide, as we do decide, is that in a capital case, where the defendant is unable to employ counsel, and is incapable adequately of making his own defense because of ignorance, feeblemindedness, illiteracy, or the like, it is the duty of the court, whether requested or not, to assign counsel for him as a necessary requisite of due process of law; and that duty is not discharged by an assignment at such a time or under such circumstances as to preclude the giving of effective aid in the preparation and trial of the case. To hold otherwise would be to ignore the fundamental postulate, already adverted to, "that there are certain immutable principles of justice which inhere in the very idea of free government which no member of the Union may disregard."

Gideon v. Wainwright

372 U.S. 335, 83 S.CT. 792 (1963)

Clarence Earl Gideon, a fifty-one-year-old rambler who was in and out of jails for most of his life, was convicted of breaking and entering into the Bay Harbor Poolroom in Panama City, Florida. At his trial, he claimed he was too poor to afford an attorney and requested that one be provided. The judge refused, and Gideon was convicted and sentenced. But Gideon persisted. While serving a five-year sentence for petty larceny in the Florida State Prison, he mailed a petition,

Clarence Gideon after his release from a Panama City, Florida, jail. Gideon's petition sparked the landmark ruling by the Supreme Court holding that all defendants accused of serious crimes have a right to representation by counsel. (*AP Photo*)

printed on lined paper obtained from a prison guard, to the Supreme Court.

Gideon did not know that he was asking the Court to reverse itself. In *Betts v. Brady* (1942), the Court had held that only in special circumstances, like those in the *Scottsboro* case, was counsel required. Justice Hugo Black, along with Justices Douglas and Murphy, had dissented in *Betts.* Only three members of the Court that decided *Betts*, however, remained when Gideon's petition was granted: two of the dissenters—Black and Douglas—and Felix Frankfurter, who was eighty years old, ill, and in his last year on the bench. They had been joined by Tom Clark and President Eisenhower's appointees— Warren, Harlan, Brennan, Whittaker, and Stewart. By the time *Gideon* was handed down, Frankfurter and Whittaker had retired.

They had been replaced by President Kennedy's appointees—Arthur Goldberg and Byron White.

Gideon fit the agenda of the Warren Court. In fact, Chief Justice Warren had told his law clerks to look for a case that would enable the Court to overrule *Betts*'s special circumstance rule for when the assistance of counsel was required for defendants in criminal cases. After granting Gideon's case, Warren asked prominent Washington, D.C., lawyer (and later Supreme Court justice) Abe Fortas to act as counsel for Gideon on his appeal. Because of Justice Black's long-standing interest in overturning *Betts*, Warren assigned him to write the opinion announcing the Court's decision.

The Court's decision was unanimous; the opinion was announced by Justice Black. Concurrences were by Justices Douglas, Clark, and Harlan.

■ ■ ■

☐ *Justice BLACK delivered the opinion of the Court.*

Since 1942, when *Betts v. Brady*, 316 U.S. 455, was decided by a divided Court, the problem of a defendant's federal constitutional right to counsel in a state court has been a continuing source of controversy and litigation in both state and federal courts. To give this problem another review here, we granted *certiorari*. Since Gideon was proceeding *in forma pauperis*, we appointed counsel to represent him and requested both sides to discuss in their briefs and oral arguments the following: "Should this Court's holding in *Betts v. Brady*, be reconsidered?"

The facts upon which Betts claimed that he had been unconstitutionally denied the right to have counsel appointed to assist him are strikingly like the facts upon which Gideon here bases his federal constitutional claim. . . . Treating due process as "a concept less rigid and more fluid than those envisaged in other specific and particular provisions of the Bill of Rights," the Court held that refusal to appoint counsel under the particular facts and circumstances in the *Betts* case was not so "offensive to the common and fundamental ideas of fairness" as to amount to a denial of due process. Since the facts and circumstances of the two cases are so nearly indistinguishable, we think the *Betts v. Brady* holding if left standing would require us to reject Gideon's claim that the Constitution guarantees him the assistance of counsel. Upon full reconsideration we conclude that *Betts v. Brady* should be overruled. . . .

We accept *Betts v. Brady*'s assumption, based as it was on our prior cases, that a provision of the Bill of Rights which is "fundamental and essential to a fair trial" is made obligatory upon the States by the Fourteenth Amendment. We think the Court in *Betts* was wrong, however, in concluding that the Sixth Amendment's guarantee of counsel is not one of these fundamental rights. Ten years before *Betts v. Brady*, this Court, after full consideration of all the historical data examined in *Betts*, had unequivocally declared that "the right to the aid of counsel is of this fundamental character." *Powell v. Alabama*. . . . While the Court at the close of its *Powell* opinion did by its language, as this Court frequently does, limit its holding to the particular facts and circumstances of that case, its conclusions about the fundamental nature of the right to counsel are unmistakable. . . .

In light of these and many other prior decisions of this Court, it is not surprising that the *Betts* Court, when faced with the contention that "one charged with crime, who is unable to obtain counsel, must be furnished counsel by the state," conceded that "[e]xpressions in the opinions of this court lend color to the argument. . . ." The fact is that in deciding as it did—that "appointment of counsel is not a fundamental right, essential to a fair trial"—the Court in *Betts v. Brady* made an abrupt break with its own well-considered precedents. In returning to these old precedents, sounder we believe than the new, we but restore constitutional principles established to achieve a fair system of justice. Not only these precedents but also reason and reflection require us to recognize that in our adversary system of criminal justice, any person haled into court, who is too poor to hire a lawyer, cannot be assured a fair trial unless counsel is provided for him. This seems to us to be an obvious truth. Governments, both state and federal, quite properly spend vast sums of money to establish machinery to try defendants accused of crime. Lawyers to prosecute are everywhere deemed essential to protect the public's interest in an orderly society. Similarly, there are few defendants charged with crime, few indeed, who fail to hire the best lawyers they can get to prepare and present their defenses. That government hires lawyers to prosecute and defendants who have the money hire lawyers to defend are the strongest indications of the widespread belief that lawyers in criminal courts are necessities, not luxuries. The right of one charged with crime to counsel may not be deemed fundamental and essential to fair trials in some countries, but it is in ours. From the very beginning, our state and national constitutions and laws have laid great emphasis on procedural and substantive safeguards designed to assure fair trials before impartial tribunals in which every defendant stands equal before the law. This noble ideal cannot be realized if the poor man charged with crime has to face his accusers without a lawyer to assist him. . . . The Court in *Betts v. Brady* departed from the sound wisdom upon which the Court's holding in *Powell v. Alabama* rested. Florida, supported by two other States, has asked that *Betts v. Brady* be left intact. Twenty-two States, as friends of the Court, argue that *Betts* was "an anachronism when handed down" and that it should now be overruled. We agree.

Argersinger v. Hamlin

407 U.S. 25, 92 S.CT. 2006 (1972)

In his opinion for the Court, Justice William O. Douglas discusses the pertinent facts involving the appeal of an individual's conviction for carrying a concealed weapon, a crime that was punishable by imprisonment for up to six months, in holding that defendants accused of petty offenses that carry punishments of six months or more of imprisonment are entitled to representation by counsel.

The Court's decision was unanimous; the opinion was announced by Justice Douglas. Chief Justice Burger and Justices Brennan and Powell concurred, with whom Justice Rehnquist joined.

■ ■ ■

☐ *Justice DOUGLAS delivered the opinion of the Court.*

Petitioner, an indigent, was charged in Florida with carrying a concealed weapon, an offense punishable by imprisonment up to six months, a $1,000 fine, or both. The trial was to a judge, and petitioner was unrepresented by counsel. He was sentenced to serve 90 days in jail, and brought this *habeas corpus* action in the Florida Supreme Court, alleging that, being deprived of his right to counsel, he was unable as an indigent layman properly to raise and present to the trial court good and sufficient defenses to the charge for which he stands convicted. The Florida Supreme Court by a four-to-three decision, in ruling on the right to counsel, followed the line we marked out in *Duncan v. Louisiana*, 391 U.S. 145 [(1968)], as respects the right to trial by jury and held that the right to court-appointed counsel extends only to trials "for non-petty offenses punishable by more than six months imprisonment." . . .

We reverse. . . .

Both *Powell* [*v. Alabama*, 287 U.S. 45 (1932)] and *Gideon* [*v. Wainwright*, 372 U.S. 335 (1963)] involved felonies. But their rationale has relevance to any criminal trial, where an accused is deprived of his liberty. *Powell* and *Gideon* suggest that there are certain fundamental rights applicable to all such criminal prosecutions. . . .

The requirement of counsel may well be necessary for a fair trial even in a petty-offense prosecution. We are by no means convinced that legal and constitutional questions involved in a case that actually leads to imprisonment even for a brief period are any less complex than when a person can be sent off for six months or more. . . .

The trial of vagrancy cases is illustrative. While only brief sentences of imprisonment may be imposed, the cases often bristle with thorny constitutional questions. . . .

In addition, the volume of misdemeanor cases, far greater in number than felony prosecutions, may create an obsession for speedy dispositions, regardless of the fairness of the result. . . .

That picture is seen in almost every report. "The misdemeanor trial is characterized by insufficient and frequently irresponsible preparation on the part of the defense, the prosecution, and the court. Everything is rush, rush." . . .

There is evidence of the prejudice which results to misdemeanor defendants from this "assembly-line justice." One study concluded that "[m]isdemeanants represented by attorneys are five times as likely to emerge from police court with all charges dismissed as are defendants who face similar charges without counsel." American Civil Liberties Union, *Legal Counsel for Misdemeanants, Preliminary Report* 1 (1970). . . .

We hold, therefore, that absent a knowing and intelligent waiver, no person may be imprisoned for any offense, whether classified as petty, misdemeanor, or felony, unless he was represented by counsel at his trial.

☐ *Justice POWELL, with whom Justice REHNQUIST joins, concurring.*

There is a middle course, between the extremes of Florida's six-month rule and the Court's rule, which comports with the requirements of the Fourteenth Amendment. I would adhere to the principle of due process that requires fundamental fairness in criminal trials, a principle which I believe encompasses the right to counsel in petty cases whenever the assistance of counsel is necessary to assure a fair trial. . . .

I would hold that the right to counsel in petty-offense cases is not absolute but is one to be determined by the trial courts exercising a judicial discretion on a case-by-case basis. The determination should be made before the accused formally pleads; many petty cases are resolved by guilty pleas in which the assistance of counsel may be required. If the trial court should conclude that the assistance of counsel is not required in any case, it should state its reasons so that the issue could be preserved for review. The trial court would then become obligated to scrutinize carefully the subsequent proceedings for the protection of the defendant. If an unrepresented defendant sought to enter a plea of guilty, the Court should examine the case against him to insure that there is admissible evidence tending to support the elements of the offense. If a case went to trial without defense counsel, the court should intervene, when necessary, to insure that the defendant adequately brings out the facts in his favor and to prevent legal issues from being overlooked. Formal trial rules should not be applied strictly against unrepresented defendants. Finally, appellate courts should carefully scrutinize all decisions not to appoint counsel and the proceedings which follow.

It is impossible, as well as unwise, to create a precise and detailed set of guidelines for judges to follow in determining whether the appointment of counsel is necessary to assure a fair trial. Certainly three general factors should be weighed. First, the court should consider the complexity of the offense charged. . . .

Second, the court should consider the probable sentence that will follow if a conviction is obtained. The more serious the likely consequences, the greater is the probability that a lawyer should be appointed. . . .

Third, the court should consider the individual factors peculiar to each case. These, of course, would be the most difficult to anticipate. One relevant factor would be the competency of the individual defendant to present his own case. The attitude of the community toward a particular defendant or particular incident would be another consideration. But there might be other reasons why a defendant would have a peculiar need for a lawyer which would compel the appointment of counsel in a case where the court would normally think this unnecessary. Obviously, the sensitivity and diligence of individual judges would be crucial to the operation of a rule of fundamental fairness requiring the consideration of the varying factors in each case.

B | *Plea Bargaining and the Right to Effective Counsel*

Plea bargaining is the practice of prosecutors and defense attorneys agreeing to terms on which the defendant agrees to plead guilty to a lesser charge than the one originally charged in exchange for a reduced sentence. Over 90 percent of all guilty pleas are the result of this practice. The advantage for the government is that it cuts the time and costs of attorneys, trials, and other resources of the criminal justice system. While the defendant receives a reduced sentence, he forgoes several constitutional rights, including, among others, the Fifth Amendment right against self-accusation and the Sixth Amendment rights to a public trial and to confront one's accusers as well as the presumption of innocence.

Brady v. United States, 397 U.S. 742 (1970), upheld the constitutionality of plea bargaining as having a "mutuality of advantage." The state, observed Justice White in his opinion for the Court, conserves "scarce judicial and prosecutorial resources" and achieves "more promptly imposed punishment"; while for the defendant, "his exposure is reduced, the correctional process can begin immediately, and the practical burdens of a trial are eliminated."

Critics of plea bargaining, though, question the constitutionality of defendants forgoing their constitutional rights and whether they are compelled to do so. The 5–4 ruling in *Bordenkircher v. Hayes* (1978) (excerpted below) illustrates the issue and how it has divided the Court.

Another issue arising with plea bargaining (and more generally with court-appointed attorneys) is whether defendants have a right to *effective* counsel. In *McMann v. Richardson*, 397 U.S. 759 (1970), three defendants claimed that their confessions were coerced and their court-appointed attorney had incompetently represented them. But the Court held that their attorney was "reasonably competent" and they must assume the risk of "ordinary error" by their attorneys. *Henderson v. Morgan*, 426 U.S. 637 (1976), however, set aside a conviction because the defendant pled guilty to second-degree murder without being informed of the consequences. The Court, nonetheless, remains reluctant to find attorneys incompetent, even when they have little or no time to confer with their clients[1] and when they misinform their clients on plea bargaining.[2]

The right to counsel includes a right to effective counsel, as Justice Stevens explained in *United States v. Cronic*, 466 U.S. 648 (1984), because competent counsel is essential to the accusatory system and "the reliability of the trial process."[3] Accordingly, public defenders do not enjoy absolute immunity from being sued for incompetent representation.[4] The test for determining when the right to effective counsel has been denied was set forth by Justice O'Connor in *Strickland v. Washington,* 466 U.S. 668 (1984):

> A convicted defendant's claim that counsel's assistance was so defective as to require reversal of a conviction or death sentence has two components. First, the defendant must show that counsel's performance was deficient. This requires showing that counsel made errors so serious that counsel was not functioning as the "counsel" guaranteed the defendant by the Sixth Amendment. Second, the defendant must show that the deficient performance prejudiced the defense. This requires showing that counsel's errors were so serious as to deprive the defendant of a fair trial, a trial whose result is reliable. Unless a defendant makes both showings, it cannot be said that the conviction or death sentence resulted from a breakdown in the adversary process that renders the result unreliable. . . .

Subsequently, the Court held that defendants have a right to effective counsel on their first appeal, *Evitts v. Lucey,* 469 U.S. 387 (1985). But when defendants tell their attorneys that they are going to lie on the witness stand, attorneys may withdraw from their cases without denying the right to effective counsel.[5] In *Mallard v. U.S. District Court,* 490 U.S. 296 (1989), the Court also held that a judge may not compel a lawyer to serve as a defendant's court-appointed counsel. The Court ruled that if a defendant insists on maintaining his or her innocence, counsel may not tell a jury the contrary—in this case, that the defendant committed three murders. In *McCoy v. Louisiana,* 138 S. Ct. 1500 (2018), Justice Ginsburg held that the Sixth Amendment right to assistance of counsel is fulfilled when counsel provides advice to a client: to follow or not follow that advice is a choice for accused to make. This case was distinguished from an earlier ruling in *Florida v. Nelson,* 543 U.S. 175 (2004), which held that counsel could concede a client's guilt when that client had refused to either consent or object to counsel's recommended action. In *McCoy,* Justices Alito, Thomas and Gorsuch dissented.

However, a bare majority in *Davila v. Davis,* 137 S. Ct. 2058 (2018), ruled that when a prisoner fails to challenge the effectiveness of counsel in a state-court proceeding, he may not raise that claim in a federal *habeas* petition. Writing for the Court, Justice Thomas reaffirmed *Coleman v. Thompson,* 501 U.S. 722 (1991), that the right to counsel does not extend to state postconviction proceedings and emphasized that there are only "narrow" and "highly circumscribed equitable" exceptions, as recognized in *Martinez v. Ryan,* 566 U.S. 1 (2012), to *Coleman's* general rule.

In two landmark rulings on the Sixth Amendment right to effective counsel, a bare majority of the Roberts Court ruled that the accused has a right to effective counsel with respect to plea bargains. In both cases, Justice Kennedy wrote for the majority and Chief Justice Roberts and Justices Scalia, Thomas, and Alito dissented. In *Missouri v. Frye* (2012) (excerpted below), the Court held that "the constitutional right to counsel extends to the negotiation and consideration of plea offers that lapse or are rejected" and that defendants must show that prejudice due to ineffective counsel based on "a reasonable probability they would have accepted the earlier plea offer had they been afforded effective counsel" and "a reasonable probability the plea would have been entered without the prosecution canceling it or the trial court refusing to accept it." In doing so, Justice Kennedy emphasized that "[c]riminal justice today is for the most part a system of pleas, not a system of trials," in light of the fact that 97 percent of convictions in federal courts and 94 percent in state courts are the result of plea bargains. In a companion ruling, *Lafler v. Cooper,* 566 U.S. 156 (2012), involved a defendant's attorney reporting a favorable plea offer but recommending a rejection of the offer that resulted in a trial and a harsher sentence than would have been obtained by agreeing to a plea bargain. In such circumstances, Justice Kennedy held that "a defendant must show that but for the ineffective advice of counsel there is a reasonable probability that the plea offer would have been presented to the court, that the court would have accepted its terms, and that the conviction or sentence, or both, under the offer's terms would have been less severe than under the judgment and sentence that in fact were imposed." In addition, *Lafler* held that the appropriate remedy must "neutralize the taint" of the constitutional violation but not provide a "windfall" to the defendant. In some situations the trial court may conduct an evidentiary hearing and exercise its discretion in resentencing the defendant. In other situations, Justice Kennedy suggested, "the prosecution [might] reoffer the plea proposal. Once this has occurred, the judge can then exercise discretion in deciding whether to vacate the conviction from trial and accept the plea or leave the conviction undisturbed." For the dissenters, Justice Scalia complained that the majority's ruling was inconsistent with precedents and invited "a whole new field of constitutionalized criminal procedure: plea-bargaining law."

- IN COMPARATIVE PERSPECTIVE

Plea Bargaining in Western Europe

In the United States, less than 5 percent of all state and federal criminal cases go to trial; about 90 percent of all violent crimes in state courts end with plea bargains and 96 percent of property charges do. Plea bargaining practices in Western Europe and elsewhere differ from those in the United States. Germany, for example, did not permit plea bargains (*absprachen*) until the 1970s, when they were introduced in a response to rising caseloads and longer trials. Plea bargains are negotiated before or during trial; defendants confess to crimes, but unlike "guilty pleas" in the United States, these pleas only shorten the trial but do not determine guilt or innocence. In addition, unlike in the United States, defense counsel has access to the complete pretrial investigation. Hence, the prosecution and defense are on more equal terms during plea negotiations. Moreover, German judges are active participants in plea negotiations, whereas in the United States the prosecution and defense counsel negotiate pleas.

In Italy, plea bargaining (*patteggiamento*) is more similar to that in this country since its adoption in 1989. The prosecution and defense counsel conduct their own pretrial investigations, and may propose "sentence bargains," reducing a sentence by up to one-third in minor cases, if a crime does not entail five years' imprisonment. Unlike in the United States, however, the charges may not be dropped. A plea bargain is also not considered a guilty plea, and Italian judges retain the power to enforce a sentence if there are insufficient grounds for acquittal or if the sentence is not proportionate to the crime.

In France, plea bargaining (*composition*) was introduced in 1999. At the beginning of formal proceedings the prosecutor may move to divert the case from the standard criminal process in exchange for an admission of guilt and an agreement to perform certain conditions, such as paying a fine. Such plea bargains do not establish guilt and if the defendant fulfills the conditions, the case is dismissed. Defendants may only accept the prosecution's offer and such plea bargains are considered an act of case diversion by the prosecutor rather than a confession of guilt to a lesser offense.

For further readings, see Maximo Langer, "From Legal Transplants to Legal Translations: The Globalization of Plea Bargaining and the Americanization Thesis in Criminal Procedure," 45 *Harvard International Law Journal* 1 (2004); and George Fisher, *Plea Bargaining Triumph: A History of Plea Bargaining in America* (Palo Alto, CA: Stanford University Press, 2003).

■ The Development of Law

Rulings on Plea Bargaining and Effective Counsel

CASE	VOTE	RULING
McCarthy v. United States, 394 U.S. 459 (1969)	9–0	Held that guilty pleas must be personally presented to a judge and the latter must assess their voluntariness.
McMann v. Richardson, 397 U.S. 759 (1970)	6–3	A defendant who enters a guilty plea is not compelled to plead guilty under the Fifth Amendment merely because the plea was a way of avoiding the death penalty.
North Carolina v. Alford, 400 U.S. 25 (1970)	6–3	A guilty plea prevents a defendant from subsequently making a habeas corpus claim that his confession was coerced.
Santobello v. New York, 404 U.S. 257 (1971)	6–3	Once a state agrees to a plea bargain it must be honored; here, the state reneged on a bargain struck due to a change in prosecutors.
Rummel v. Estelle, 445 U.S. 263 (1980)	5–4	The Eighth Amendment ban on cruel and unusual punishment was not violated when a prosecutor threatened a defendant, who insisted on his right to a jury trial, that if he did not agree to a plea bargain he would be indicted and tried under the state's criminal recidivist statute for having committed three prior felonies, and the defendant was sentenced to lifetime imprisonment.
Alabama v. Smith, 490 U.S. 794 (1989)	8–1	Held there is no presumption of unfairness when a judge imposes a harsher sentence on a criminal defendant who is convicted after a trial, and after backing out of a plea-bargain agreement that had called for a lighter sentence.

CASE	VOTE	RULING
Williams v. Taylor, 529 U.S. 362 (2000)	6–3 & 5–4	Writing for the Court, Justice Stevens held that Terry Williams was denied his consti-

tutionally guaranteed right to effective counsel, as defined in *Strickland v. Washington,* 466 U.S. 668 (1984), because his attorney failed to investigate and to present substantial mitigating evidence to the jury. Justices O'Connor, Kennedy, Souter, Ginsburg, and Breyer joined portions of that opinion. Justice O'Connor delivered an opinion for the Court holding that the Anti-terrorism and Effective Death Penalty Act of 1996 places a new constraint on federal courts in granting writs of *habeas corpus* review; they may grant review only if the state court's adjudication was "contrary to" or "involved an unreasonable application of clearly established federal law." Chief Justice Rehnquist and Justices Kennedy, Scalia, and Thomas joined that opinion.

Mickens v. Taylor, 535 U.S. 162 (2002)	5–4	Rejected a death row inmate's claim that his Sixth Amendment right to effec-

tive counsel was violated because his court-appointed attorney had previously represented the murder victim.

Wiggins v. Smith, 539 U.S. 510 (2003)	7–2	Overturned a death sentence upon finding that the defendant's attorney failed to in-

vestigate and to introduce mitigating factors related to sexual abuse and that the failure to do so violated the Sixth Amendment right to effective counsel under *Strickland v. Washington,* 466 U.S. 668 (1984).

Iowa v. Tovar, 541 U.S. 77 (2004)	9–0	Writing for the Court, Justice Ginsburg held that the Sixth Amendment right to

counsel is not violated by an accused pleading guilty in a plea bargain without the assistance of an attorney, because he waived the right, was informed of the consequences of pleading guilty, and made a knowing and intelligent act.

United States v. Dominguez *Benitez,* 542 U.S. 74 (2004)	9–0	Justice Souter rejected a claim that a sentence should be overturned because a federal dis-

trict court judge failed to warn the defendant that if the court did not accept a plea bargain he could not withdraw his guilty plea, since it was stipulated in the signed agreement and made no difference in the outcome.

(continues)

■ The Development of Law
Rulings on Plea Bargaining and Effective Counsel (continued)

CASE	VOTE	RULING
Florida v. Nixon, 543 U.S. 175 (2004)	8–0	Writing for the Court, Justice Ginsburg held that the Sixth Amendment right to

effective counsel was not violated by an attorney's confessing his client's guilt in a gruesome murder case, without the client's consent, in order to maintain his credibility with the jury and to subsequently argue for a lifetime sentence rather than the imposition of the death penalty. Justice Ginsburg noted, "In a capital case, counsel must consider in conjunction both the guilt and penalty phases in determining how best to proceed."

| *Missouri v. Frye,* 566 U.S. 134 (2012) | 5–4 | Writing for the majority, Justice Kennedy held that "the constitutional right to |

counsel extends to the negotiation and consideration of plea offers that lapse or are rejected," and that defendants must show evidence of prejudice due to ineffective counsel based on "a reasonable probability they would have accepted the earlier plea offer had they been afforded effective counsel" and "a reasonable probability the plea would have been entered without the prosecution canceling it or the trial court refusing to accept it." In doing so, Justice Kennedy emphasized that "[c]riminal justice today is for the most part a system of pleas, not a system of trials," in light of the fact that 97 percent of convictions in federal courts and 94 percent in state courts are the result of plea bargains.

| *Lafler v. Cooper,* 566 U.S. 156 (2012) | 5–4 | Writing for the Court, Justice Kennedy held that the defendant's Sixth Amend- |

ment right was denied when the defendant's attorney reported a favorable plea offer but recommended a rejection of the offer that resulted in a trial and a harsher sentence than would have been obtained by agreeing to a plea bargain. In such circumstances, Justice Kennedy held that "a defendant must show that but for the ineffective advice of counsel there is a reasonable probability that the plea offer would have been presented to the court, that the court would have accepted its terms, and that the conviction or sentence, or both, under the offer's terms would have been less severe than under the judgment and sentence that in fact were imposed." For the dissenters, Justice Scalia complained that the majority's ruling invited "a whole new field of constitutionalized criminal procedure: plea-bargaining law."

NOTES

1. See *Morris v. Slappy*, 461 U.S. 1 (1983); and *Chambers v. Maroney*, 399 U.S. 42 (1970).

2. See *North Carolina v. Alford*, 400 U.S. 25 (1970); and *Tollett v. Henderson*, 411 U.S. 258 (1973).

3. See also *Entsminger v. Iowa*, 386 U.S. 748 (1967), holding that defendant was denied the right to effective counsel when the court-appointed attorney failed to file the entire record on appeal.

4. *Ferri v. Ackerman*, 444 U.S. 193 (1979).

5. *Nix v. Whiteside*, 475 U.S. 157 (1986).

SELECTED BIBLIOGRAPHY

Fisher, George. *Plea Bargaining's Triumph: A History of Plea Bargaining in America.* Palo Alto, CA: Stanford University Press, 2003.

Packer, Herbert. *The Limits of the Criminal Sanction.* Palo Alto, CA: Stanford University Press, 1968.

Vogel, Mary. *Coercion to Compromise: Social Conflict and the Emergence of Plea Bargaining.* New York: Oxford University Press, 2001.

Bordenkircher v. Hayes

434 U.S. 357, 98 S.CT. 663 (1978)

Justice Potter Stewart discusses the facts in his opinion for the Court, upholding a prosecutor's threat of indictment and conviction of Paul Hayes under Kentucky's Habitual Criminal Act because Mr. Hayes refused to agree to a plea bargain and insisted on a trial when he was charged with forging a check in the amount of $88.30.

The Court's decision was 5–4, and the majority's opinion was announced by Justice Stewart. Dissents were by Justices Powell and Blackmun, who were joined by Justices Brennan and Marshall.

■ ■ ■

☐ *Justice STEWART delivered the opinion of the Court.*

The question in this case is whether the Due Process Clause of the Fourteenth Amendment is violated when a state prosecutor carries out a threat made during plea negotiations to reindict the accused on more serious charges if he does not plead guilty to the offense with which he was originally charged.

The respondent, Paul Lewis Hayes, was indicted by a Fayette County, Ky., grand jury on a charge of uttering a forged instrument in the amount of $88.30, an offense then punishable by a term of two to ten years in prison. Ky.Rev.Stat. Sec. 434.130 (repealed 1974). After arraignment, Hayes, his retained counsel, and the Commonwealth's attorney met in the presence of the clerk of the court to discuss a possible plea agreement. During these conferences the prosecutor offered to recommend a sentence of five years in prison if Hayes would plead guilty to the indictment. He also said that if Hayes did not plead guilty and "save the court the inconvenience and necessity of a trial," he would return to the grand jury to seek an indictment under the Kentucky Habitual Criminal Act, then Ky.Rev.Stat. Sec. 431.190 (repealed 1975), which would subject Hayes to a mandatory sentence of life imprisonment by reason of his two prior felony convictions. Hayes chose not to plead guilty, and the prosecutor did obtain an indictment charging him under the Habitual Criminal Act. . . .

A jury found Hayes guilty on the principal charge of uttering a forged instrument and, in a separate proceeding, further found that he had twice before been convicted of felonies. As required by the habitual offender statute, he was sentenced to a life term in the penitentiary. . . .

It may be helpful to clarify at the outset the nature of the issue in this case. While the prosecutor did not actually obtain the recidivist indictment until after the plea conferences had ended, his intention to do so was clearly put forth at the outset of the plea negotiations. Hayes was thus fully informed of the true terms of the offer when he made his decision to plead not guilty. This is not a situation, therefore, where the prosecutor without notice brought an additional and more serious charge after plea negotiations relating only to the original indictment had ended with the defendant's insistence on pleading not guilty. As a practical matter, in short, this case would be no different if the grand jury had indicted Hayes as a recidivist from the outset, and the prosecutor had offered to drop that charge as part of the plea bargain.

The Court of Appeals nonetheless drew a distinction between "concessions relating to prosecution under an existing indictment," and threats to bring more severe charges not contained in the original indictment—a line it thought necessary in order to establish a prophylactic rule to guard against the evil of prosecutorial vindictiveness. . . .

We have recently had occasion to observe that "[w]hatever might be the situation in an ideal world, the fact is that the guilty plea and the often concomitant plea bargain are important components of this country's criminal justice system. Properly administered, they can benefit all concerned." *Blackledge v. Allison*, 431 U.S. 63 [1977]. The open acknowledgment of this previously clandestine practice has led this Court to recognize the importance of counsel during plea negotiations, *Brady v. United States*, 397 U.S. 742 [1970]. The need for a public record indicating that a plea was knowingly and voluntarily made, *Boykin v. Alabama*, 395 U.S. 238 [1969]. And the requirement that a prosecutor's plea bargaining promise must be kept, *Santobello v. New York*, 404 U.S. 257 [1971]. . . .

Plea bargaining flows from "the mutuality of advantage" to defendants and prosecutors, each with his own reasons for wanting to avoid trial. *Brady v. United States*. Defendants advised by competent counsel and protected by other procedural safeguards are presumptively capable of intelligent choice in response to prosecutorial persuasion, and unlikely to be driven to false self-condemnation. Indeed, acceptance of the basic legitimacy of plea bargaining necessarily implies rejection of any notion that a guilty plea is involuntary in a constitutional sense simply because it is the end result of the bargaining process. By hypothesis, the plea may have been induced by promises of a recommendation of a lenient sentence or a reduction of charges, and thus by fear of the possibility of a greater penalty upon conviction after a trial. . . .

While confronting a defendant with the risk of more severe punishment clearly may have a "discouraging effect on the defendant's assertion of his trial rights, the imposition of these difficult choices [is] an inevitable"—and permissible—"attribute of any legitimate system which tolerates and encourages the negotiation of pleas." It follows that, by tolerating and encouraging the negotiation of pleas, this Court has necessarily accepted as constitutionally legitimate the simple reality that the prosecutor's interest at the bargaining table is to persuade the defendant to forego his right to plead not guilty.

It is not disputed here that Hayes was properly chargeable under the recidivist statute, since he had in fact been convicted of two previous felonies. In our system, so long as the prosecutor has probable cause to believe that the accused committed an offense defined by statute, the decision whether or not to prosecute, and what charge to file or bring before a grand jury, generally rests entirely in his discretion. . . .

There is no doubt that the breadth of discretion that our country's legal system vests in prosecuting attorneys carries with it the potential for both individual and institutional abuse. And broad though that discretion may be, there are undoubtedly constitutional limits upon its exercise. We hold only that the course of conduct engaged in by the prosecutor in this case, which no more than openly presented the defendant with the unpleasant alternatives of foregoing trial or facing charges on which he was plainly subject to prosecution, did not violate the Due Process Clause of the Fourteenth Amendment.

Accordingly, the judgment of the Court of Appeals is Reversed.

☐ *Justice POWELL, dissenting.*

Although I agree with much of the Court's opinion, I am not satisfied that the result in this case is just or that the conduct of the plea bargaining met the requirements of due process.

Respondent was charged with the uttering of a single forged check in the amount of $88.30. Under Kentucky law, this offense was punishable by a prison term of from two to 10 years, apparently without regard to the amount of the forgery. During the course of plea bargaining, the prosecutor offered respondent a sentence of five years in consideration of a guilty plea. I observe, at this point, that five years in prison for the offense charged hardly could be characterized as a generous offer. Apparently respondent viewed the offer in this light and declined to accept it; he protested that he was innocent and insisted on going to trial. . . .

In most cases a court could not know why the harsher indictment was sought, and an inquiry into the prosecutor's motive would neither be indicated nor likely to be fruitful. In those cases, I would agree with the majority that the situation would not differ materially from one in which the higher charge was brought at the outset.

But this is not such a case. Here, any inquiry into the prosecutor's purpose is made unnecessary by his candid acknowledgement that he threatened to procure and in fact procured the habitual criminal indictment because of respondent's insistence on exercising his constitutional rights. . . .

The plea-bargaining process, as recognized by this Court, is essential to the functioning of the criminal-justice system. It normally affords genuine benefits to defendants as well as to society. And if the system is to work effectively, prosecutors must be accorded the widest discretion, within constitutional limits, in conducting bargaining. This is especially true when a defendant is represented by counsel and presumably is fully advised of his rights. Only in the most exceptional case should a court conclude that the scales of the bargaining are so unevenly balanced as to arouse suspicion. In this case, the prosecutor's actions denied respondent due process because their admitted purpose was to discourage and then to penalize with unique severity his exercise of constitutional rights. Implementation of a strategy calculated solely to deter the exercise of constitutional rights is not a constitutionally permissible exercise of discretion. I would affirm the opinion of the Court of Appeals on the facts of this case.

Missouri v. Frye
566 U.S. 134, 132 S.Ct. 1399 (2012)

Galin Frye was charged with driving with a revoked license and, because he had three other convictions for the same offense, was charged with a felony, carrying a maximum four-year prison sentence. The prosecutor offered Frye's counsel two possible plea bargains, including one to reduce the charge to a misdemeanor and recommending a ninety-day sentence. The attorney, however, failed to tell Frye about the offers and they expired. Less than a week before his preliminary hearing, Frye was again arrested for driving with a revoked license. He subsequently pleaded guilty without a plea agreement and was sentenced to three years in prison. But on appeal, Frye alleged that his attorney's failure to inform him of the plea offers deprived him of his Sixth Amendment right to an effective assistance of counsel, and testified that he would have pleaded guilty to the misdemeanor had he known of the offer. The trial court denied his motion but the Missouri appellate court reversed, holding that Frye met both requirements for showing a Sixth Amendment violation under *Strickland v. Washington*, 466 U.S. 668 (1984). That court found that Frye's counsel was ineffective in not communicating the plea offers to him and concluded that he had shown that counsel's deficient performance caused prejudice because he pleaded guilty to a felony instead of a misdemeanor. The state appealed that decision.

Justice Kennedy delivered the opinion of the Court. Justice Scalia filed a dissenting opinion, joined by Chief Justice Roberts and Justices Thomas and Alito.

■ ■ ■

☐ *Justice KENNEDY delivered the opinion of the Court.*

The right to counsel is the right to effective assistance of counsel. See *Strickland v. Washington*, 466 U.S. 668 (1984). This case arises in the context of claimed ineffective assistance that led to the lapse of a prosecution offer of a plea bargain, a proposal that offered terms more lenient than the terms of the guilty plea entered later. The initial question is whether the constitutional right to counsel extends to the negotiation and consideration of plea offers that lapse or are rejected. If there is a right to effective assistance with respect to those offers, a further question is what a defendant must demonstrate in order to show that prejudice resulted from counsel's deficient performance. Other questions relating to ineffective assistance with respect to plea offers, including the question of proper remedies, are considered in a second case decided today. See *Lafler v. Cooper*, [132 S.Ct. 1376 (2012)]. . . .

It is well settled that the right to the effective assistance of counsel applies to certain steps before trial. Critical stages include arraignments, postindictment interrogations, postindictment lineups, and the entry of a guilty plea.

With respect to the right to effective counsel in plea negotiations, a proper beginning point is to discuss two cases from this Court considering the role of counsel in advising a client about a plea offer and an ensuing guilty plea: *Hill v. Lockhart*, 474 U.S. 52 (1985); and *Padilla v. Kentucky*, [130 S.Ct. 1473] (2010).

Hill established that claims of ineffective assistance of counsel in the plea bargain context are governed by the two-part test set forth in *Strickland*. [T]he Missouri Court of Appeals, applying the two part test of *Strickland*, determined first that defense counsel had been ineffective and second that there was resulting prejudice.

In *Hill*, the decision turned on the second part of the *Strickland* test. There, a defendant who had entered a guilty plea claimed his counsel had misinformed him of the amount of time he would have to serve before he became eligible for parole. But the defendant had not alleged that, even if adequate advice and assistance had been given, he would have elected to plead not guilty and proceed to trial. Thus, the Court found that no prejudice from the inadequate advice had been shown or alleged.

In *Padilla*, the Court again discussed the duties of counsel in advising a client with respect to a plea offer that leads to a guilty plea. Padilla held that a guilty plea, based on a plea offer, should be set aside because counsel misinformed the defendant of the immigration consequences of the conviction. The Court made clear that "the negotiation of a plea bargain is a critical phase of litigation for purposes of the Sixth Amendment right to effective assistance of counsel." It also rejected the argument made by petitioner in this case that a knowing and voluntary plea supersedes errors by defense counsel.

In the case now before the Court, the State, as petitioner, points out that the legal question presented is different from that in *Hill* and *Padilla*. In those cases the claim was that the prisoner's plea of guilty was invalid because counsel had provided incorrect advice pertinent to the plea. In the instant case, by contrast, the guilty plea that was accepted, and the plea proceedings concerning it in court, were all based on accurate advice and information from counsel. The challenge is not to the advice pertaining to the plea that was accepted but rather to the course of legal representation that preceded it with respect to other potential pleas and plea offers. . . .

The State is correct to point out that *Hill* and *Padilla* concerned whether there was ineffective assistance leading to acceptance of a plea offer, a process involving a formal court appearance with the defendant and all counsel present. Before a guilty plea is entered, the defendant's understanding of the plea and its consequences can be established on the record. This affords the State substantial protection against later claims that the plea was the result of inadequate advice. . . .

When a plea offer has lapsed or been rejected, however, no formal court proceedings are involved. This underscores that the plea-bargaining process is often in flux, with no clear standards or timelines and with no judicial supervision of the discussions between prosecution and defense. Indeed, discussions between client and defense counsel are privileged. . . .

Ninety-seven percent of federal convictions and ninety-four percent of state convictions are the result of guilty pleas. The reality is that plea bargains have become so central to the administration of the criminal justice system that defense counsel have responsibilities in the plea bargain process, responsibilities that must be met to render the adequate assistance of counsel that the Sixth Amendment requires in the criminal process at critical stages. Because ours "is for the most part a system of pleas, not a system of trials," *Lafler*, it is insufficient simply to point to the guarantee of a fair trial as a backstop that inoculates any errors in the pretrial process. In today's criminal justice system, therefore, the negotiation of a plea bargain, rather than the unfolding of a trial, is almost always the critical point for a defendant. . . .

The inquiry then becomes how to define the duty and responsibilities of defense counsel in the plea bargain process. This is a difficult question. Bargaining is, by its nature, defined to a substantial degree by personal style. The alternative courses and tactics in negotiation are so individual that it may be neither prudent nor practicable to try to elaborate or define detailed standards for the proper discharge of defense counsel's participation in the process. . . .

Here the question is whether defense counsel has the duty to communicate the terms of a formal offer to accept a plea on terms and conditions that may result in a lesser sentence, a conviction on lesser charges, or both.

This Court now holds that, as a general rule, defense counsel has the duty to communicate formal offers from the prosecution to accept a plea on terms and conditions that may be favorable to the accused. Any exceptions to that rule need not be explored here, for the offer was a formal one with a fixed expiration date. When defense counsel allowed the offer to expire without advising the defendant or allowing him to consider it, defense counsel did not render the effective assistance the Constitution requires.

Though the standard for counsel's performance is not determined solely by reference to codified standards of professional practice, these standards can be important guides. The American Bar Association recommends defense counsel "promptly communicate and explain to the defendant all plea offers made by the prosecuting attorney," and this standard has been adopted by numerous state and federal courts over the last 30 years. . . .

Here defense counsel did not communicate the formal offers to the defendant. As a result of that deficient performance, the offers lapsed. Under *Strickland*, the question then becomes what, if any, prejudice resulted from the breach of duty.

To show prejudice from ineffective assistance of counsel where a plea offer has lapsed or been rejected because of counsel's deficient performance, defendants must demonstrate a reasonable probability they would have accepted the earlier plea offer had they been afforded effective assistance of counsel. Defendants must also demonstrate a reasonable probability the plea would have been entered without the prosecution canceling it or the trial court refusing to accept it, if they had the authority to exercise that discretion under state law. To establish prejudice in this instance, it is necessary to show a reasonable probability that the end result of the criminal process would have been more favorable by reason of a plea to a lesser charge or a sentence of less prison time.

This application of *Strickland* to the instances of an uncommunicated, lapsed plea does nothing to alter the standard laid out in *Hill*. In cases where a defendant complains that ineffective assistance led him to accept a plea offer as opposed to proceeding to trial, the defendant will have to show "a reasonable probability that, but for counsel's errors, he would not have pleaded guilty and would have insisted on going to trial." . . . *Strickland*'s inquiry into whether "the result of the proceeding would have been different," requires looking not at whether the defendant would have proceeded to trial absent ineffective assistance but whether he would have accepted the offer to plead pursuant to the terms earlier proposed.

In order to complete a showing of *Strickland* prejudice, defendants who have shown a reasonable probability they would have accepted the earlier plea offer must also show that, if the prosecution had the discretion to cancel it or if the trial court had the discretion to refuse to accept it, there is a reasonable probability neither the prosecution nor the trial court would have prevented the offer from being accepted or implemented. This further showing is of particular importance because a defendant has no right to be offered a plea, nor a federal right that the judge accept it. . . .

These standards must be applied to the instant case. As regards the deficient performance prong of *Strickland*, the Court of Appeals found the "record is void of any evidence of any effort by trial counsel to communicate the [formal] offer to Frye during the offer window, let alone any evidence that Frye's conduct interfered with trial counsel's ability to do so." On this record, it is evident that Frye's attorney did not make a meaningful attempt to inform the defendant of a written plea offer before the offer expired. The Missouri Court of Appeals was correct that "counsel's representation fell below an objective standard of reasonableness."

The Court of Appeals erred, however, in articulating the precise standard for prejudice in this context. As noted, a defendant in Frye's position must show not only a reasonable probability that he would have accepted the lapsed plea but also a reasonable probability that the prosecution would have adhered to the agreement and that it would have been accepted by the trial court. Frye can show he would have accepted the offer, but there is strong reason to doubt the prosecution and the trial court would have permitted the plea bargain to become final.

There appears to be a reasonable probability Frye would have accepted the prosecutor's original offer of a plea bargain if the offer had been communicated to him, because he pleaded guilty to a more serious charge, with no promise of a sentencing recommendation from the prosecutor. . . .

The Court of Appeals failed, however, to require Frye to show that the first plea offer, if accepted by Frye, would have been adhered to by the prosecution and accepted by the trial court. Whether the prosecution and trial court are required to do so is a matter of state law, and it is not the place of this Court to settle those matters. The Court has established the minimum requirements of the Sixth Amendment as interpreted in *Strickland*, and states have the discretion to add procedural protections under state law if they choose. A state may choose to preclude the prosecution from withdrawing a plea offer once it has been accepted or perhaps to preclude a trial court from rejecting a plea bargain. . . .

 ☐ *Justice SCALIA, with whom THE CHIEF JUSTICE,
Justice THOMAS, and Justice ALITO join, dissenting.*

This is a companion case to *Lafler v. Cooper*. The principal difference between the cases is that the fairness of the defendant's conviction in *Lafler* was established by a full trial and jury verdict, whereas Frye's conviction here was established by his own admission of guilt, received by the court after the usual colloquy that assured it was voluntary and truthful. In *Lafler* all that could be said (and as I discuss there it was quite enough) is that the fairness of the conviction was clear, though a unanimous jury finding beyond a reasonable doubt can sometimes be wrong. Here it can be said not only that the process was fair, but that the defendant acknowledged the correctness of his conviction. . . .

Counsel's mistake did not deprive Frye of any substantive or procedural right; only of the opportunity to accept a plea bargain to which he had no entitlement in the first place. So little entitlement that, had he known of and accepted the bargain, the prosecution would have been able to withdraw it right up to the point that his guilty plea pursuant to the bargain was accepted. . . .

While the inadequacy of counsel's performance in this case is clear enough, whether it was prejudicial (in the sense that the Court's new version of *Strickland* requires) is not. The Court's description of how that question is to be answered on remand is alone enough to show how unwise it is to constitutionalize the plea-bargaining process. Prejudice is to be determined, the Court tells us, by a process of retrospective crystal-ball gazing posing as legal analysis. First of all, of course, we must estimate whether the defendant would have accepted the earlier plea bargain. Here that seems an easy question, but as the Court acknowledges, it will not always be. Next, since Missouri, like other states, permits accepted plea offers to be withdrawn by the prosecution (a reality which alone should suffice, one would think, to demonstrate that Frye had no entitlement to the plea bargain), we must estimate whether the prosecution would have withdrawn the plea offer. And finally, we must estimate whether the trial court would have approved the plea agreement. These last two estimations may seem easy in the present case, since Frye committed a new infraction before the hearing at which the agreement would have been presented; but they assuredly will not be easy in the mine run of cases. . . .

The plea-bargaining process is a subject worthy of regulation, since it is the means by which most criminal convictions are obtained. It happens not to be, however, a subject covered by the Sixth Amendment, which is concerned not with the fairness of bargaining but with the fairness of conviction. "The Constitution . . . is not an all-purpose tool for judicial construction of a perfect world; and when we ignore its text in order to make it that, we often find ourselves swinging a sledge where a tack hammer is needed." *Padilla v. Kentucky* (2010) (SCALIA, J., dissenting). In this case and its companion, the Court's sledge may require the reversal of perfectly valid, eminently just, convictions. A legislature could solve the problems presented by these cases in a much more precise and efficient manner. It might begin, for example, by penalizing the attorneys who made such grievous errors. That type of sub-constitutional remedy is not available to the Court, which is limited to penalizing (almost) everyone else by reversing valid convictions or sentences. Because that result is inconsistent with the Sixth Amendment and decades of our precedent, I respectfully dissent.

C | *Indictment by a Grand Jury*

Embedded in the colonies as part of the English common law was the right to a jury trial. But in the 1760s and 1770s, colonists deeply resented royalist judges and were hostile to the legal profession that defended the system. The institution of indictment by a grand jury grew out of colonial hostility toward royalist courts. Prosecuting officers had to make a prima facie case to a body of laymen that an individual violated criminal law, and if the grand jury was persuaded it would vote for an indictment on the charges presented. The original thirteen states, however, varied in the power given to juries. As Alexander Hamilton noted in *The Federalist*, No. 83, "no general rule could have been fixed by the Convention which would have corresponded with the circumstances of all the States."

The Fifth Amendment provides that "no person shall be held to answer for a capital [crime, which carries the death penalty] or otherwise infamous crime, unless on a presentment or indictment of a Grand Jury." This guarantee applies to only the national government because the Court has never reversed *Hurtado v. California*, 110 U.S. 516 (1884) (see Ch. 4), which ruled that the guarantee for an indictment by a grand jury does not apply to the states under the Fourteenth Amendment's due process clause. A grand jury consists of twelve to twenty-three laymen— typically selected by lot from voting rolls or chosen by local officials. The district attorney meets with the grand jury in secret sessions and has the power to inquire into any alleged offense as directed by the district attorney or as charged by a judge.

Writing for a bare majority in *United States v. Williams*, 504 U.S. 6 (1992), Justice Scalia held that when seeking a grand jury's indictment charging an accused with a criminal offense, federal prosecutors need not present exculpatory evidence—facts favorable to the accused and which might result in the grand jury's refusal to hand down an indictment.

In holding that federal courts have no power to dismiss an indictment because prosecutors withheld "substantially exculpatory evidence" from a grand jury, Scalia emphasized that the role of a grand
jury—unlike a trial jury—is to "assess whether there is adequate basis
for bringing a criminal charge," not to determine an accused's ultimate guilt or innocence. "Imposing on the prosecutor a legal obligation to present exculpatory evidence in his possession would be
incompatible with this system," claimed Scalia, even though prosecutors must turn over such exculpatory evidence to a defendant's attorney before going to trial.

Hurtado v. California (reprise)
110 U.S. 516, 4 S.Ct. 111 (1884)

The pertinent sections of this case are reprinted in Chapter 4.

■ ■ ■

D | The Right to an Impartial Jury Trial

The jury is a fact-finding institution that determines the guilt or innocence of defendants. Because juries are composed of laypeople or "peers"
drawn from the community of the accused, juries also represent the
democratic subculture within the judicial system. Juries, as Justice
White observed in *Duncan v. Louisiana*, 391 U.S. 145 (1968), "prevent
oppression by the Government . . . [and] safeguard against the corrupt
or overzealous prosecutor and against the compliant, biased, or eccentric
judge."

The Sixth Amendment (and Article III, Section 2 of the Constitution) provides that the accused "shall enjoy the right" to a jury trial in
criminal cases. The Seventh Amendment guarantees a jury trial in civil
cases "where the value in controversy shall exceed twenty dollars." *Granfi-
anciera v. Nordberg*, 492 U.S. 33 (1989), extended the Seventh Amendment
right to a jury trial to defendants charged with bankruptcy fraud. The right
to jury trials may be waived but "the consent of the government counsel
and the sanction of the court must be had, in addition to the express and
intelligent consent of the defendant."[1]

In federal courts, the right to a jury trial is limited to those cases subject to the Fifth Amendment's provision for a grand jury indictment. Consequently, jury trials are not required for some petty crimes.[2] Nor may jury trials be required on charges of being in contempt of court,[3] on petitions for the writ of *habeas corpus*, and in certain other civil and administrative proceedings, such as those for disbarment and deportation. Neither does the Sixth Amendment's guarantee apply to courts–martial.[4]

Duncan v. Louisiana made the right to a jury trial in all nonpetty cases applicable to the states. Nonpetty cases were defined in *Baldwin v. New York*, 399 U.S. 66 (1970), as those carrying a potential sentence of six months or more imprisonment. However, in *Lewis v. United States*, 518 U.S. 322 (1996), the Court held that a defendant has no Sixth Amendment right to a jury trial when prosecuted in a single proceeding for multiple petty offenses—offenses that each carry a maximum of six or fewer months—even though the aggregate prison term exceeds six months. Writing for the Court, Justice O'Connor held that "[t]he Sixth Amendment's guarantee of the right to a jury trial does not extend to petty offenses, and its scope does not change where a defendant faces a potential aggregate prison term in excess of six months for petty offenses charged."

The requirement that a jury be "impartial" has given rise to numerous questions. In addition to the fair trial/free press controversy (discussed in Ch. 5), the composition and method of selecting of juries has often been contested. In the "second *Scottsboro* case," *Norris v. Alabama*, 294 U.S. 587 (1935), the Hughes Court held that the due process and equal protection clauses of the Fourteenth Amendment do not permit the exclusion of blacks from juries.[5] But in *Fay v. New York*, 322 U.S. 261 (1947), the Vinson Court ruled that the Sixth Amendment does not require proportional representation of a community when upholding "blue ribbon" juries selected from "the upper economic and social stratum" and excluding manual workers.

The basic protection against racial, economic, and gender bias is the principle that juries must reflect a "cross-section of the community." In *Smith v. Texas*, 311 U.S. 128 (1940), the Court observed that "it is part of the established tradition in the use of juries as instruments of public justice that the jury be a body truly representative of the community." When holding that women could not be excluded as potential jurors in *Taylor v. Louisiana*, 419 U.S. 522 (1975), the fair cross–section requirement was reaffirmed "as fundamental to the jury trial guaranteed by the Sixth Amendment." Accordingly, the Court has struck down various methods for selecting jurors because they worked toward "the total exclusion" of blacks and women,[6] but also maintained that there is no right to include the presence of blacks or women on juries.[7] The principle of a fair cross-section of the community in jury selection is also included in the Federal Jury Selection and Service Act of 1974, barring the exclusion of potential jurors on account of race, color, religion, gender, national origin, and economic status.[8]

Defense attorneys may use their peremptory challenges to exclude potential jurors who they believe might harbor racial prejudice. During *voir dire* examination of potential jurors, when the victim and the defendant are members of different racial groups, defense attorneys may also ask potential jurors questions about whether they have any racial bias.[9] Specifically, *Turner v. Murray*, 476 U.S. 28 (1986), held that where a black man was sentenced to death for murdering a white jeweler, the defendant had a right to have prospective jurors informed of the victim's race and questioned about racial bias. *Batson v. Kentucky* (1986) (excerpted below) held that the Fourteenth Amendment forbids prosecutors from challenging potential jurors solely on the basis of race to secure an all-white jury. However, in *Holland v. Illinois*, 493 U.S. 474 (1990), writing for a bare majority, Justice Scalia held that a prosecutor's use of peremptory challenges so as to exclude all potential black jurors from a jury did not deny a white defendant's right to an impartial jury trial under the Sixth Amendment. But then in *Powers v. Ohio*, 499 U.S. 400 (1991), Justice Kennedy held that prosecutors' use of peremptory challenges to exclude blacks from juries trying white defendants violates the equal protection clause. In so doing, he distinguished *Holland* on the basis that the Fourteenth Amendment "prohibits a prosecutor from using the State's peremptory challenges to exclude otherwise qualified and unbiased persons from the . . . jury solely by reason of their race, a practice that forecloses a significant opportunity to participate in civil life." "The suggestion," added Kennedy, "that racial classifications may survive when visited upon all persons is no more authoritative today than the case which advanced the theorem, *Plessy v. Ferguson*, 163 U.S. 537 (1896). The idea has no place in our modern equal protection jurisprudence." Still, Justice Scalia, dissenting along with Chief Justice Rehnquist, claimed that he was "unmoved" by white defendants' claims that their rights are violated when they are tried by all-white juries.

In his first major decision after a contentious nomination hearing, Justice Kavanaugh, writing for a 7–2 majority in *Flowers v. Mississippi*, reasserted the Court's decision in *Batson*, that race is one criterion that is not acceptable as grounds for a peremptory challenge. Across six trials of Curtis Flowers in a quadruple murder case, the same white prosecutor used peremptory challenges to exclude forty-one of the forty-two black prospective jurors. The Court identified "critical facts" that required reversal of the lower court's decision, including the sheer number of blacks excluded across six trials, the use of disparate questioning of black and white potential jurors, and striking at least one black potential juror who was similarly situated to white prospective jurors who were not struck by the state. "We need not and do not decide that any one of these . . . facts alone would require reversal," Kavanaugh wrote. In reaching this conclusion, he added, "we break no new legal ground. We simply enforce and reinforce *Batson* by applying it to the extraordinary facts of this case."

By a 6–3 vote in *Edmonson v. Leesville Concrete Co.*, 500 U.S. 614 (1991) (further discussed in Ch. 12), the Court also extended *Batson* to the use of peremptory challenges to exclude blacks from juries in civil trials. And the Court again revisited in *Georgia v. McCollum*, 505 U.S. 42 (1992), the issue of using race as a basis for excluding potential jurors from criminal trials and further extended the *Batson*, *Powers*, and *Edmunson* line of rulings. *Batson* barred prosecutors from disqualifying jurors on the basis of race and, as noted above, *Powers* held that criminal defendants of any race may challenge prosecutors' racially based peremptory challenges, while *Edmonson* held that lawyers in civil trials may not exclude potential jurors on the basis of race either. *Georgia v. McCollum*, thus, raised the issue of whether two white defendants charged with criminally assaulting two blacks could exclude blacks from serving on the jury.

Writing for the majority in *McCollum*, Justice Blackmun concluded that it was unconstitutional in criminal trials for defendants' attorneys, no less than for prosecutors, to exclude jurors solely on the basis of their race. In his words, it is "an affront to justice to argue that a fair trial includes the right to discriminate against a group of citizens on the basis of their race." As a result, all-white juries in racially charged cases, such as that of the white police officers tried for beating motorist Rodney King in Los Angeles, will be much more difficult to obtain. At the same time, *McCollum* also makes it more difficult for minority defendants to exclude white jurors in order to secure some minorities on their juries. Only Justices O'Connor and Scalia dissented. Subsequently, with Justices Scalia and Thomas dissenting, the Court further extended the *Batson* line of cases in *Campbell v. Louisiana*, 523 U.S. 392 (1998), holding that the selection process for grand jury forepersons could be challenged for racial bias.

The issue of juror bias has posed special problems in jury selection for capital cases. Historically, potential jurors having constitutional objections to the death penalty were excluded from capital cases. But *Witherspoon v. Illinois*, 391 U.S. 510 (1968), held that jurors opposed to the death penalty were impermissibly excluded; otherwise, in Justice Potter Stewart's words, every jury would be a "hanging jury." *Maxwell v. Bishop*, 398 U.S. 262 (1970), ruled that the death penalty may not be imposed when prospective jurors are removed due to their opposition to capital punishment. But the Burger and Rehnquist Courts reconsidered the issue. In *Darden v. Wainwright*, 477 U.S. 168 (1986), the justices held 5–4 that potential jurors who have religious objections to the death penalty may be excluded, and *A. L. Lockhart v. McCree* (1986) (excerpted below) held that "death qualified" juries are permissible.[10] Indeed, in *Morgan v. Illinois*, 504 U.S. 719 (1992) (see Ch. 10), the Court held that defendants' attorneys in capital cases during *voir dire* examinations must be allowed to ask whether a potential juror would automatically vote to impose a death sentence upon the defendant's conviction. Denial of such questioning during jury selection, the Court ruled, violates the Fourteenth Amendment's due process clause.

Traditionally, a common-law jury was composed of twelve persons, and *Thompson v. Utah*, 170 U.S. 343 (1898), held that the Sixth Amendment jury was "constituted, as it was in common law, of twelve persons, neither more nor less." *Duncan v. Louisiana* implicitly posed the issue of whether states had to adhere to twelve-member juries as well, or whether they were still free to experiment with jury size. In 1967, Florida enacted a law providing for six-member juries in all criminal cases, except for capital crimes. That law was immediately challenged and upheld in *Williams v. Florida* (1970) (excerpted below). In federal district courts, six-member juries had been used in *civil* cases, even before *Williams*. This was so despite the fact that the Seventh Amendment specifically refers to the common-law jury in providing for jury trials in civil cases. A bare majority of the Court in *Colegrove v. Battin*, 413 U.S. 149 (1973), nevertheless, upheld six-member juries in civil cases. Writing for the majority, Justice Brennan deemed the common-law jury not to be frozen into the Constitution. Justices Douglas, Marshall, Stewart, and Powell dissented from what Marshall termed the majority's upholding of a "six-man mutation . . . a different institution which functions differently, produces different results, and was wholly unknown to the Framers of the Seventh Amendment."

Once the Court abandoned the history and principle of twelve-member juries, it faced the question of where to draw a line on jury size. *Ballew v. Georgia*, 435 U.S. 223 (1978), finally drew the line at six when rejecting Georgia's use of five-member juries in criminal cases.

A related controversy arose with *Johnson v. Louisiana*, 406 U.S. 356 (1972), and *Apodaca v. Oregon*, 406 U.S. 404 (1972), holding that nonunanimous jury verdicts in criminal cases did not violate the Fourteenth Amendment's due process and equal protection clauses. In *Johnson*, a bare majority approved Louisiana's law permitting convictions based on a vote of nine out of twelve jurors. *Apodaca* upheld an Oregon statute under which two defendants were found guilty by jury votes of eleven to one and ten to two. In both, Justice White dismissed the history of unanimous verdicts and applied his *Williams* analysis of the function of juries in concluding that nonunanimous and unanimous juries were "functionally equivalent." His opinion was so sweeping in rejecting the history of unanimity, dating back to 1367 and an accepted part of federal jury trials, that Justice Powell, although joining the majority, was moved to point out in a concurring opinion that unanimity in federal courts was "mandated by history."

Together, *Williams v. Florida, Johnson,* and *Apodaca* presented the issue of where the Court would draw the line on the permissibility of nonunanimous verdicts rendered by juries composed of less than twelve members. That issue was met in *Burch v. Louisiana* (1979) (see excerpt below), holding that unanimous verdicts are required in six-member juries.

In *Sullivan v. Louisiana,* 508 U.S. 275 (1993), the Court unanimously reaffirmed that in criminal cases juries must find the accused guilty beyond a reasonable doubt. Although the Rehnquist Court has expanded the "harmless error doctrine" in other areas—for example, *Arizona v. Fulminante* (1991) (in Ch. 8)—here it declined to hold that a judge's instructions to a jury that it must find the defendant "probably guilty" constituted merely a harmless error. Writing for the Court, Justice Scalia observed, "the Fifth Amendment requirement of proof beyond a reasonable doubt and the Sixth Amendment requirement of a jury verdict are interrelated. It would not satisfy the Sixth Amendment to have a jury determine that the defendant is probably guilty. . . . In other words, the jury verdict required by the Sixth Amendment is a jury verdict of guilty beyond a reasonable doubt."

Finally, the Court has cast increasing doubt about the constitutional permissibility of federal and state mandatory sentencing guidelines. In *Apprendi v. New Jersey,* 530 U.S. 466 (2000), the Court struck down New Jersey's law permitting judges to hand down longer sentences for "hate crimes" based on the "preponderance of evidence" standard. A bare majority ruled that enhanced sentences may be imposed only by a jury and on the basis of the stricter "beyond a reasonable doubt" standard. In *Ring v. Arizona,* 536 U.S. 584 (2002), the Court applied the *Apprendi* principle to require juries, not judges, to determine the aggravating circumstances for imposing death sentences. Then, in *Blakely v. Washington,* 542 U.S. 296 (2004), a bare majority struck down Washington's sentencing system for permitting judges to make findings that increase a convicted defendant's sentence beyond the ordinary range for violating the right to trial by a jury. Writing for the Court, Justice Scalia reaffirmed that "any fact that increases the penalty for a crime beyond the prescribed statutory maximum must be submitted to a jury and proved beyond a reasonable doubt." Although Scalia added that "the federal guidelines are not before us, and we express no opinion on them," dissenting Justice O'Connor warned, "Over 20 years of sentencing reform are all but lost, and tens of thousands of criminal judgments are in jeopardy." Justice O'Connor proved prophetic because in *United States v. Booker*, 543 U.S. 220 (2005), a bare majority ruled that the federal guidelines violate the Sixth Amendment because federal judges may impose enhanced sentences based on facts that a jury did not consider.

The Court was badly fragmented in *Booker*, however, and two opinions for the Court were delivered for different bare majorities. On the one hand, Justice Stevens, joined by Justices Scalia, Souter, Thomas, and Ginsburg, ruled that federal judges are no longer bound by the guidelines. On the other hand, Justice Breyer, joined by Chief Justice Rehnquist and Justices O'Connor, Kennedy, and Ginsburg, held that the guidelines should still be consulted and that judges' sentences are subject to reversal if appellate courts find them unreasonable and defendants deserve longer or shorter sentences. The federal guidelines, in the words of Justice Breyer, who helped write them, serve to "avoid excessive sentencing disparities while maintaining flexibility sufficient to individualize sentences where necessary." Justice Ginsburg cast the crucial fifth vote for both opinions but issued no separate opinion. But by a 6–3 vote the Roberts Court, in *Cunningham v. California*, 549 U.S. 270 (2007), struck down California's determinate sentencing law that permitted sentencing judges to impose enhanced sentences based on aggravating factors that had not been submitted to a jury. Based on the reasoning in *Apprendi, Blakely*, and *Booker*, Justice Ginsburg held that the statute ran afoul of the Sixth Amendment. Justices Kennedy, Breyer, and Alito dissented.

In *Kimbrough v. United States*, 552 U.S. 85 (2007), the Roberts Court reaffirmed the earlier ruling in *Booker* 220 (2005) that the federal mandatory sentencing guidelines were only advisory for federal judges in sentencing. The federal guidelines, in the words of Justice Breyer, who helped write them, serve to "avoid excessive sentencing disparities while maintaining flexibility sufficient to individualize sentences where necessary." In a related case the Roberts Court reinforced that ruling. In *Gall v. United States*, 552 U.S. 38 (2007), Justice Stevens writing for the Court, with Justices Thomas and Alito dissenting, held that appellate courts must review all sentences under the "deferential abuse of discretion standard" regardless of the range of variance between the sentence imposed and the guideline's recommendations. The Roberts Court also limited the line of cases following *Apprendi v. New Jersey*, 536 U.S. 466 (2000), limiting federal judges' discretion in sentencing, in holding that enhanced sentences may not be imposed unless based on facts found by a jury. In *Oregon v. Ice*, 555

U.S. 160 (2009), a bare majority held that the Sixth Amendment jury trial right limits judges' discretion to decide to require that sentences be served separately rather than simultaneously. However, in *Southern Union Company v. United States*, 567 U.S. 343 (2012), the Court further extended its ruling in *Apprendi v. New Jersey*, that enhanced sentences, which go beyond mandatory sentencing guidelines, may be imposed only by juries (and not judges) to criminal fines as a penalty. A bare majority also overturned its decision in *Harris v. United States*, 536 U.S. 545 (2002), in which the Court had upheld judicial fact-finding that increases a mandatory minimum sentence for a crime under the Sixth Amendment. Writing for the Court in *Alleyne v. United States*, 570 U.S. 99 (2013), Justice Thomas held that *Harris* was inconsistent with *Apprendi* and the original meaning of the Sixth Amendment because here the jury had not decided the actual sentence, but rather the sentencing judge increased the sentence from five to seven years based on mandatory guidelines.

Justice Thomas reaffirmed the Sixth Amendment and *Apprendi* to require juries to determine the facts beyond a reasonable doubt that justify a sentence.

Chief Justice Roberts dissented and was joined by Justices Scalia and Kennedy; Justice Alito dissented in a separate opinion.

NOTES

1. *Patton v. United States*, 281 U.S. 276 (1930). See also *Singer v. United States*, 380 U.S. 24 (1965).

2. See *Cheff v. Schnackenberg*, 384 U.S. 373 (1966).

3. But see also *United States v. Barnett*, 376 U.S. 681 (1964); and *Cheff v. Schnackenberg*, 384 U.S. 373 (1966).

4. See *Ex parte Milligan*, 4 Wall. 2 (1866) (see Vol. 1, Ch. 3).

5. *Hernandez v. Texas*, 347 U.S. 475 (1954), extended the ruling in *Norris* to prohibit states from excluding Hispanics from juries. *Eubanks v. Louisiana*, 356 U.S. 584 (1958) overturned the conviction of a black man by an all-white jury.

6. See *Turner v. Fouche*, 396 U.S. 346 (1970); *Avery v. Georgia*, 345 U.S. 559 (1952); and *Whitus v. Georgia*, 385 U.S. 545 (1967).

7. See *Swain v. Alabama*, 380 U.S. 202 (1965); *Carter v. Jury Commission of Greene County*, 396 U.S. 320 (1970).

8. See *Test v. United States*, 420 U.S. 28 (1975), allowing a defendant to inspect jury lists to determine whether a disproportionate number of people with Hispanic surnames have been excluded.

9. See *Ham v. South Carolina*, 409 U.S. 524 (1973); *Ristanino v. Ross*, 424 U.S. 589 (1976); and *Rosales-Lopez v. United States*, 451 U.S. 182 (1981).

10. See also *Wainwright v. Witt*, 469 U.S. 412 (1985). *Buchanan v. Kentucky*, 483 U.S. 402 (1987), further upheld the use of death-qualified juries in a joint trial where a death sentence was sought for only one of the codefendants.

Selected Bibliography

Abramson, Jeffrey. *We, The Jury: The Jury System and the Ideal of Democracy: With a New Preface.* Cambridge, MA: Harvard University Press, 2000.

Bodenhamer, David. *Fair Trial: Rights of the Accused in American History.* New York: Oxford University Press, 1992.

Burns, Robert P. *A Theory of the Trial.* Princeton, NJ: Princeton University Press, 1999.

Hale, Dennis. *The Jury in America: Triumph and Decline.* Lawrence: University of Kansas Press, 2016.

Jonakait, Randolph. *The American Jury System.* New Haven, CT: Yale University Press, 2003.

Kadri, Sadakat. *The Trial: A History, from Socrates to O.J. Simpson.* New York: Random House, 2005.

Levy, Leonard W. *The Palladium of Justice: Origins of Trial by Jury.* Chicago: Ivan R. Dee, 1999.

Vidmar, Neil, ed., *World Jury Systems.* New York: Oxford University Press, 2000.

Vidmar, Neil, and Hans, Valerie. *American Juries: The Verdict.* New York: Prometheus Books, 2007.

Batson v. Kentucky

476 U.S. 79, 106 S.Ct. 1712 (1986)

James Kirkland Batson, a black man, was tried for second-degree burglary and receiving stolen goods. Before his trial, the judge conducted a *voir dire* examination of the jury venire and excused certain potential jurors. The prosecutor then used his peremptory challenges to strike all four black persons in the venire to secure an all-white jury. Batson's attorney moved to dismiss the jury for violating his client's Sixth and Fourteenth Amendments guarantees of a jury drawn from a cross-section of the community. The trial judge denied the motion and Batson was tried and convicted. The Kentucky Supreme Court affirmed and Batson's attorney made a further appeal to the Supreme Court of the United States.

The Court's decision was 7–2, and the majority's opinion was announced by Justice Powell. Justices White, Stevens, and O'Connor concurred; Chief Justice Burger and Justice Rehnquist dissented.

■ ■ ■

☐ *Justice POWELL delivered the opinion of the Court.*

In *Swain v. Alabama,* [380 U.S. 202 (1965)], this Court recognized that a "State's purposeful or deliberate denial to Negroes on account of race of participation as jurors in the administration of justice violates the Equal Protection Clause." This principle has been "consistently and repeatedly" reaffirmed in numerous decisions of this Court both preceding and following *Swain.* We reaffirm the principle today.

More than a century ago, the Court decided that the State denies a black defendant equal protection of the laws when it puts him on trial before a jury from which members of his race have been purposefully excluded. *Strauder v. West Virginia,* 100 U.S. 303 (1880). . . .

In holding that racial discrimination in jury selection offends the Equal Protection Clause, the Court in *Strauder* recognized, however, that a defendant has no right to a "petit jury composed in whole or in part of persons of his own race." "The number of our races and nationalities stands in the way of evolution of such a conception" of the demand of equal protection. *Akins v. Texas,* 325 U.S. 398 (1945). But the defendant does have the right to be tried by a jury whose members are selected pursuant to nondiscriminatory criteria. The Equal Protection Clause guarantees the defendant that the State will not exclude members of his race from the jury venire on account of race, *Strauder,* or on the false assumption that members of his race as a group are not qualified to serve as jurors. . . .

The harm from discriminatory jury selection extends beyond that inflicted on the defendant and the excluded juror to touch the entire community. Selection procedures that purposefully exclude black persons from juries undermine public confidence in the fairness of our system of justice. . . .

In *Strauder,* the Court invalidated a state statute that provided that only white men could serve as jurors. We can be confident that no state now has such a law. The Constitution requires, however, that we look beyond the face of the statute defining juror qualifications and also consider challenged selection practices to afford "protection against action of the State through its administrative officers in effecting the prohibited discrimination." . . .

Accordingly, the component of the jury selection process at issue here, the State's privilege to strike individual jurors through peremptory challenges, is subject to the commands of the Equal Protection Clause. Although a prosecutor ordinarily is entitled to exercise permitted peremptory challenges "for any reason at all, as long as that reason is related to his view concerning the outcome" of the case to be tried, the Equal Protection Clause forbids the prosecutor to challenge potential jurors solely on account of their race or on the assumption that black jurors as a group will be unable impartially to consider the State's case against a black defendant.

The principles announced in *Strauder* never have been questioned in any subsequent decision of this Court. Rather, the Court has been called upon repeatedly to review the application of those principles to particular facts. A recurring question in these cases, as in any case alleging a violation of the Equal Protection Clause, was whether the defendant had met his burden of proving purposeful discrimination on the part of the State. . . .

The showing necessary to establish a prima facie case of purposeful discrimination in selection of the venire may be discerned in this Court's decisions. The defendant initially must show that he is a member of a racial group capable of being singled out for differential treatment. In combination with that evidence, a defendant may then make a prima facie case by proving that in the particular jurisdiction members of his race have not been summoned for jury service over an extended period of time. Proof of systematic exclusion from the venire raises an inference of purposeful discrimination because the "result bespeaks discrimination."

Since the ultimate issue is whether the State has discriminated in selecting the defendant's venire, however, the defendant may establish a prima facie case "in other ways than by evidence of long-continued unexplained absence" of members of his race "from many panels." In cases involving the venire, this Court has found a prima facie case on proof that members of the defendant's race were substantially underrepresented on the venire from which his jury was drawn and that the venire was selected under a practice providing "the opportunity for discrimination." This combination of factors raises the necessary inference of purposeful discrimination because the Court has declined to attribute to chance the absence of black citizens on a particular jury array where the selection mechanism is subject to abuse. When circumstances suggest the need, the trial court must undertake a "factual inquiry" that "takes into account all possible explanatory factors" in the particular case. . . .

While we recognize, of course, that the peremptory challenge occupies an important position in our trial procedures, we do not agree that our decision today will undermine the contribution the challenge generally makes to the administration of justice. The reality of practice, amply reflected in many state and federal court opinions, shows that the challenge may be, and unfortunately at times has been, used to discriminate against black jurors. By requiring trial courts to be sensitive to the racially discriminatory use of peremptory challenges, our decision enforces the mandate of equal protection and furthers the ends of justice. In view of the heterogeneous population of our nation, public respect for our criminal justice system and the rule of law will be strengthened if we ensure that no citizen is disqualified from jury service because of his race.

A. L. Lockhart v. McCree

476 U.S. 162, 106 S.Ct. 1758 (1986)

A. L. Lockhart, the director of the Arkansas Department of Correction, appealed the Court of Appeals for the Eighth Circuit's affirmance of a federal district court's ruling. The district court had held that Ardia McCree's Sixth and Fourteenth Amendment rights were violated in a capital case by a state trial judge's removal, over McCree's objections, of prospective jurors who stated that they would not under any circumstance vote to impose the death penalty. The Supreme Court granted review.

The Court's decision was 6–3, and the majority's opinion was announced by Justice Rehnquist. Justice Blackmun delivered a concurring opinion. Justice Marshall dissented and was joined by Justices Brennan and Stevens.

■ ■ ■

☐ *Justice REHNQUIST delivered the opinion of the Court.*

In this case we address the question left open by our decision nearly 18 years ago in *Witherspoon v. Illinois*, 391 U.S. 510 (1968): Does the Constitution prohibit the removal for cause, prior to the guilt phase of a bifurcated capital trial, of prospective jurors whose opposition to the death penalty is so strong that it would prevent or substantially impair the performance of their duties as jurors at the sentencing phase of the trial? We hold that it does not. . . .

Before turning to the legal issues in the case, we are constrained to point out what we believe to be several serious flaws in the evidence upon which the courts below reached the conclusion that "death qualification" produces "conviction-prone" juries. McCree introduced into evidence some fifteen social science studies in support of his constitutional claims, but only six of the studies even purported to measure the potential effects on the guilt-innocence determination of the removal from the jury of "*Witherspoon* excludables." . . .

Of the six studies introduced by McCree that at least purported to deal with the central issue in this case, namely, the potential effects on the determination of guilt or innocence of excluding "*Witherspoon* excludables" from the jury, three were also before this Court when it decided *Witherspoon, supra.* There, this Court reviewed the studies and concluded:

> The data adduced by the petitioner . . . are too tentative and fragmentary to establish that jurors not opposed to the death penalty tend to favor the prosecution in the determination of guilt. We simply cannot conclude, either on the basis of the record now before us or as a matter of judicial notice, that the exclusion of jurors opposed to capital punishment results in an unrepresentative jury on the issue of guilt or substantially increases the risk of conviction. In light of the presently available information, we are not prepared to announce a *per se* constitutional rule requiring the reversal of every conviction returned by a jury selected as this one was. . . .

It goes almost without saying that, if these studies were "too tentative and fragmentary" to make out a claim of constitutional error in 1968, the same studies, unchanged but for having aged some eighteen years, are still insufficient to make out such a claim in this case.

Nor do the three post-*Witherspoon* studies introduced by McCree on the "death qualification" issue provide substantial support for the "*per se* constitutional rule" McCree asks this Court to adopt. All three of the "new" studies were based on the responses of individuals randomly selected from some segment of the population, but who were not actual jurors sworn under oath to apply the law to the facts of an actual case involving the fate of an actual capital defendant. We have serious doubts about the value of these studies in predicting the behavior of actual jurors.

Finally, and most importantly, only one of the six "death qualification" studies introduced by McCree even attempted to identify and account for the presence of so-called "nullifiers," or individuals who, because of their deep-seated opposition to the death penalty, would be unable to decide a capital defendant's guilt or innocence fairly and impartially. McCree concedes, as he must, that "nullifiers" may properly be excluded from the guilt-phase jury, and studies that fail to take into account the presence of such "nullifiers" thus are fatally flawed. Surely a "*per se* constitutional rule" as far-reaching as the one McCree proposes should not be based on the results of the lone study that avoids this fundamental flaw.

Having identified some of the more serious problems with McCree's studies, however, we will assume for purposes of this opinion that the studies are both methodologically valid and adequate to establish that "death qualification" in fact produces juries somewhat more "conviction-prone" than "non-death-qualified" juries. We hold, nonetheless, that the Constitution does not prohibit the States from "death qualifying" juries in capital cases. . . .

Even if we were willing to extend the fair cross-section requirement to petit juries, we would still reject the Eighth Circuit's conclusion that "death qualification" violates that requirement. The essence of a "fair cross-section" claim is the systematic exclusion of "a 'distinctive' group in the community." . . .

We have never attempted to precisely define the term "distinctive group," and we do not undertake to do so today. But we think it obvious that the concept of "distinctiveness" must be linked to the purposes of the fair cross-section requirement. In *Taylor* [*v. Louisiana*, 419 U.S. 522 (1975)] we identified those purposes as (1) "guard[ing] against the exercise of arbitrary power" and ensuring that the "commonsense judgment of the community" will act as "a hedge against the overzealous or mistaken prosecutor," (2) preserving "public confidence in the fairness of the criminal justice system," and (3) implementing our belief that "sharing in the administration of justice is a phase of civic responsibility." . . .

Our prior jury-representativeness cases, whether based on the fair cross-section component of the Sixth Amendment or the Equal Protection Clause of the Fourteenth Amendment, have involved such groups as blacks, see *Peters v. Kiff*, 407 U.S. 493 (1972) (plurality opinion) (equal protection), women, see *Taylor, supra* (same), and Mexican-Americans, see *Castaneda v. Partida*, 430 U.S. 482 (1977) (equal protection). The wholesale exclusion of these large groups from jury service clearly contravened all three of the aforementioned purposes of the fair cross-section requirement. Because these groups were excluded for reasons completely unrelated to the ability of members of the group to serve as jurors in a particular case, the exclusion raised at least the possibility that the composition of juries would be arbitrarily skewed in such a way as to deny criminal defendants the benefit of the common-sense judgment of the community. In addition, the exclusion from jury service of large groups of individuals not on the basis of their inability to serve as jurors, but on the basis of some immutable characteristic such as race, gender, or ethnic background, undeniably gave rise to an "appearance of unfairness." Finally, such exclusion improperly deprived members of these often historically disadvantaged groups of their right as citizens to serve on juries in criminal cases.

The group of *"Witherspoon* excludables" involved in the case at bar differs significantly from the groups we have previously recognized as "distinctive." "Death qualification," unlike the wholesale exclusion of blacks, women, or Mexican-Americans from jury service, is carefully designed to serve the State's concededly legitimate interest in obtaining a single jury that can properly and impartially apply the law to the facts of the case at both the guilt and sentencing phases of a capital trial. There is very little danger, therefore, and McCree does not even argue, that "death qualification" was instituted as a means for the State to arbitrarily skew the composition of capital-case juries.

Furthermore, unlike blacks, women, and Mexican-Americans, *"Witherspoon* excludables" are singled out for exclusion in capital cases on the basis of an attribute that is within the individual's control. It is important to remember that not all who oppose the death penalty are subject to removal for cause in capital cases; those who firmly believe that the death penalty is unjust may nevertheless serve as jurors in capital cases so long as they state clearly that they are willing to temporarily set aside their own beliefs in deference to the rule of law. Because the group of *"Witherspoon* excludables" includes only those who cannot and will not conscientiously obey the law with respect to one of the issues in a capital case, "death qualification" hardly can be said to create an "appearance of unfairness."

Finally, the removal for cause of *"Witherspoon* excludables" in capital cases does not prevent them from serving as jurors in other criminal cases, and thus leads to no substantial deprivation of their basic rights of citizenship. They are treated no differently than any juror who expresses the view that he would be unable to follow the law in a particular case. . . .

In our view, it is simply not possible to define jury impartiality, for constitutional purposes, by reference to some hypothetical mix of individual viewpoints. Prospective jurors come from many different backgrounds, and have many different attitudes and predispositions. But the Constitution presupposes that a jury selected from a fair cross-section of the community is impartial, regardless of the mix of individual viewpoints actually represented on the jury, so long as the jurors can conscientiously and properly carry out their sworn duty to apply the law to the facts of the particular case. We hold that McCree's jury satisfied both aspects of this constitutional standard.

☐ *Justice MARSHALL, with whom Justice BRENNAN and Justice STEVENS join, dissenting.*

Respondent contends here that the "death-qualified" jury that convicted him, from which the State, as authorized by *Witherspoon*, had excluded all venire persons unwilling to consider imposing the death penalty, was in effect "organized to return a verdict" of guilty. In support of this claim; he has presented overwhelming evidence that death-qualified juries are substantially more likely to convict or to convict on more serious charges than juries on which unalterable opponents of capital punishment are permitted to serve. Respondent does not challenge the application of *Witherspoon* to the jury in the sentencing stage of bifurcated capital cases. Neither does he demand that individuals unable to assess culpability impartially ("nullifiers") be permitted to sit on capital juries. All he asks is the chance to have his guilt or innocence determined by a jury like those that sit in non-capital cases—one whose composition has not been tilted in favor of the prosecution by the exclusion of a group of prospective jurors uncommonly aware of an accused's constitutional rights but quite capable of determining his culpability without favor or bias. . . .

In the wake of *Witherspoon*, a number of researchers set out to supplement the data that the Court had found inadequate in that case. The results of these studies were exhaustively analyzed by the District Court in this case, and can be only briefly summarized here. The data strongly suggest that death qualification excludes a significantly large subset—at least 11% to 17%—of potential jurors who could be impartial during the guilt phase of trial. Among the members of this excludable class are a disproportionate number of blacks and women.

The perspectives on the criminal justice system of jurors who survive death qualification are systematically different from those of the excluded jurors. Death-qualified jurors are, for example, more likely to believe that a defendant's failure to testify is indicative of his guilt, more hostile to the insanity defense, more mistrustful of defense attorneys, and less concerned about the danger of erroneous convictions. This pro-prosecution bias is reflected in the greater readiness of death-qualified jurors to convict or to convict on more serious charges. And, finally, the very process of death qualification—which focuses attention on the death penalty before the trial has even begun—has been found to predispose the jurors that survive it to believe that the defendant is guilty. . . .

Faced with the near unanimity of authority supporting respondent's claim that death qualification gives the prosecution a particular advantage in the guilt phase of capital trials, the majority here makes but a weak effort to contest that proposition. Instead, it merely assumes for the purposes of this opinion "that 'death-qualification' in fact produces juries somewhat more 'conviction-prone' than 'non-death-qualified' juries," and then holds that this result does not offend the Constitution. This disregard for the clear import of the evidence tragically misconstrues the settled constitutional principles that guarantee a defendant the right to a fair trial and an impartial jury whose composition is not biased toward the prosecution. . . .

One need not rely on the analysis and assumptions of . . . *Witherspoon* to demonstrate that the exclusion of opponents of capital punishment capable of impartially determining culpability infringes a capital defendant's constitutional right to a fair and impartial jury. For the same conclusion is compelled by the analysis that in *Ballew v. Georgia*, 435 U.S. 223 (1978) led a majority of this Court to hold that a criminal conviction rendered by a five-person jury violates the Sixth and Fourteenth Amendments. . . .

The principle of "impartiality" invoked in *Witherspoon* is thus not the only basis for assessing whether the exclusion of jurors unwilling to consider the death penalty but able impartially to determine guilt infringes a capital defendant's constitutional interest in a fair trial. By identifying the critical concerns that are subsumed in that interest, the *Ballew* Court pointed to an alternative approach to the issue, drawing on the very sort of empirical data that respondent has presented here. And viewed in light of the concerns articulated in *Ballew*, the evidence is sufficient to establish that death qualification constitutes a substantial threat to a defendant's Sixth and Fourteenth Amendment right to a fair jury trial—a threat constitutionally acceptable only if justified by a sufficient state interest. . . .

Williams v. Florida
399 U.S. 78, 90 S.Ct. 1893 (1970)

Johnny Williams was tried by a six-member jury and convicted of robbery in Dade County, Florida. His attorneys appealed the conviction, but a state appellate court affirmed. They made an appeal to the Supreme Court, which granted *certiorari*.

The Court's decision was 5–3, and the majority's opinion was announced by Justice White, with Justice Blackmun not participating. Chief Justice Burger concurred. A separate opinion, in part dissenting and concurring, was delivered by Justice Black and joined by Justice Douglas. Justice Marshall dissented, in part.

■ ■ ■

☐ *Justice WHITE delivered the opinion of the Court.*

In *Duncan v. Louisiana*, 391 U.S. 79 (1968), we held that the Fourteenth Amendment guarantees a right to trial by jury in all criminal cases that— were they to be tried in a federal court—would come within the Sixth Amendment's guarantee. Petitioner's trial for robbery . . . clearly falls within the scope of that holding. The question in this case then is whether the constitutional guarantee of a trial by "jury" necessarily requires trial by exactly 12 persons, rather than some lesser number—in this case six. We hold that the 12-man panel is not a necessary ingredient of "trial by jury," and that respondent's refusal to impanel more than the six members provided for by Florida law did not violate petitioner's Sixth Amendment rights as applied to the States through the Fourteenth.

We had occasion in *Duncan v. Louisiana*, to review briefly the oft-told history of the development of trial by jury in criminal cases. That history revealed a long tradition attaching great importance to the concept of relying on a body of one's peers to determine guilt or innocence as a safeguard against arbitrary law enforcement. That same history, however, affords little insight into the considerations that gradually led the size of that body to be generally fixed at 12. . . . [W]hile sometime in the 14th century the size of the jury at common law came to be fixed generally at 12, that particular feature of the jury system appears to have been a historical accident, unrelated to the great purposes which gave rise to the jury in the first place. The question before us is whether this accidental feature of the jury has been immutably codified into our Constitution. . . .

While "the intent of the Framers" is often an elusive quarry, the relevant constitutional history casts considerable doubt on the easy assumption in our past decisions that if a given feature existed in a jury at common law in 1789, then it was necessarily preserved in the Constitution. Provisions for jury trial were first placed in the Constitution in Article III's provision that "[t]he Trial of all Crimes . . . shall be by Jury; and such Trial shall be held in the State where the said Crimes shall have been committed." The "very scanty history [of this provision] in the records of the Constitutional Convention" sheds little light either way on the intended correlation between Article III's "jury" and the features of the jury at common law. . . .

We do not pretend to be able to divine precisely what the word "jury" imported to the Framers, the First Congress, or the States in 1789. It may well be that the usual expectation was that the jury would consist of 12, and that hence, the most likely conclusion to be drawn is simply that little thought was actually given to the specific question we face today. But there is absolutely no indication in "the intent of the Framers" of an explicit decision to equate the constitutional and common-law characteristics of the jury. Nothing in this history suggests, then, that we do violence to the letter of the Constitution by turning to other than purely historical considerations to determine which features of the jury system, as it existed at common law, were preserved in the Constitution. The relevant inquiry, as we see it, must be the function that the particular feature performs and its relation to the purposes of the jury trial. Measured by this standard, the 12-man requirement cannot be regarded as an indispensable component of the Sixth Amendment.

The purpose of the jury trial, as we noted in *Duncan*, is to prevent oppression by the Government. . . . Given this purpose, the essential feature of a jury obviously lies in the interposition between the accused and his accuser of the commonsense judgment of a group of laymen, and in the community participation and shared responsibility that results from that group's determination of guilt or innocence. The performance of this role is not a function of the particular number of the body that makes up the jury. To be sure, the number should probably be large enough to promote group deliberation, free from outside attempts at intimidation, and to provide a fair possibility for obtaining a representative cross-section of the community. But we find little reason to think that these goals are in any meaningful sense less likely to be achieved when the jury numbers six, than when it numbers 12—particularly if the requirement of unanimity is retained. And, certainly the reliability of the jury as a factfinder hardly seems likely to be a function of its size. . . .

We conclude, in short, as we began: the fact that the jury at common law was composed of precisely 12 is a historical accident, unnecessary to effect the purposes of the jury system and wholly without significance "except to mystics." *Duncan v. Louisiana* (HARLAN, J., dissenting). To read the Sixth Amendment as forever codifying a feature so incidental to the real purpose of the Amendment is to ascribe a blind formalism to the Framers which would require considerably more evidence than we have been able to discover in the history and language of the Constitution or in the reasoning of our past decisions. . . . Legislatures may well have their own views about the relative value of the larger and smaller juries, and may conclude that, wholly apart from the jury's primary function, it is desirable to spread the collective responsibility for the determination of guilt among the larger group. In capital cases, for example, it appears that no State provides for less than 12 jurors—a fact that suggests implicit recognition of the value of the larger body as a means of legitimating society's decision to impose the death penalty. Our holding does no more than leave these considerations to Congress and the States, unrestrained by an interpretation of the Sixth Amendment that would forever dictate the precise number that can constitute a jury. Consistent with this holding, we conclude that petitioner's Sixth Amendment rights, as applied to the States through the Fourteenth Amendment, were not violated by Florida's decision to provide a six-man rather than a 12-man jury. . . .

Burch v. Louisiana

441 U.S. 130, 99 S.Ct. 1623 (1979)

Daniel Burch was tried for exhibiting two obscene motion pictures. The six-member jury found him guilty by a 5–1 vote. He was sentenced to two consecutive seven-month prison terms, which were suspended, and fined $1,000. Burch's attorney appealed the constitutionality of nonunanimous six-member jury verdicts. The Louisiana Supreme Court affirmed and Burch's attorney appealed to the Supreme Court.

The Court's decision was 6–3, and the majority's opinion was announced by Justice Rehnquist. Justice Stevens concurred. A separate opinion, in part dissenting and concurring, was delivered by Justice Brennan and joined by Justices Stewart and Marshall.

■ ■ ■

☐ *Justice REHNQUIST delivered the opinion of the Court.*

[W]e believe that conviction by a nonunanimous six-member jury in a state criminal trial for a nonpetty offense deprives an accused of his constitutional right to trial by jury.

Only in relatively recent years has this Court had to consider the practices of the several States relating to jury size and unanimity. . . .

The Court in *Duncan* [*v. Louisiana*, 391 U.S. 145 (1968)], held that because trial by jury in "serious" criminal cases is "fundamental to the American scheme of justice" and essential to due process of law, the Fourteenth Amendment guarantees a state criminal defendant the right to a jury trial in any case, which, if tried in a federal court, would require a jury under the Sixth Amendment. . . .

Two terms later in *Williams v. Florida*, 399 U.S. 78 (1970), the Court held that this constitutional guarantee of trial by jury did not require a State to provide an accused with a jury of 12 members and that Florida did not violate the jury trial rights of criminal defendants charged with nonpetty offenses by affording them jury panels comprised of only six persons. . . .

[I]n *Apodaca v. Oregon* 106 U.S. 404 (1972), we upheld a state statute providing that only 10 members of a 12-person jury need concur to render a verdict in certain noncapital cases. In terms of the role of the jury as a safeguard against oppression, the plurality opinion perceived no difference between those juries required to act unanimously and those permitted to act by votes of 10 to two. . . . Nor was unanimity viewed by the plurality as contributing materially to the exercise of the jury's commonsense judgment or as a necessary precondition to effective application of the requirement that jury panels represent a fair cross-section of the community. . . .

[I]n *Ballew v. Georgia*, 135 U.S. 223 (1978), we held that conviction by a unanimous five-person jury in a trial for a nonpetty offense deprives an accused of his right to trial by jury. While readily admitting that the line between six members and five was not altogether easy to justify, at least five Members of the Court believed that reducing a jury to five persons in non-petty cases raised sufficiently substantial doubts as to the fairness of the proceeding and proper functioning of the jury to warrant drawing the line at six. . . .

[T]his case lies at the intersection of our decisions concerning jury size and unanimity. As in *Ballew*, we do not pretend the ability to discern *a priori* a bright line below which the number of jurors participating in the trial or in the verdict would not permit the jury to function in the manner required by our prior cases. But having already departed from the strictly historical requirements of jury trial, it is inevitable that lines must be drawn some-where if the substance of the jury trial right is to be preserved. . . . [M]uch the same reasons that led us in *Ballew* to decide that use of a five-member jury threatened the fairness of the proceeding and the proper role of the jury, lead us to conclude now that conviction for a nonpetty offense by only five members of a six-person jury presents a similar threat to preservation of the substance of the jury trial guarantee and justifies our requiring verdicts rendered by six-person juries to be unanimous. We are buttressed in this view by the current jury practices of the several States. It appears that of those States that utilize six-member juries in trials of nonpetty offenses, only two, including Louisiana, also allow nonunanimous verdicts. We think that this near uniform judgment of the Nation provides a useful guide in delimiting the line between those jury practices that are constitu-tionally permissible and those that are not. . . .

[O]n this record, any benefits that might accrue by allowing five mem-bers of a six-person jury to render a verdict, as compared with requiring unanimity of a six-member jury, are speculative, at best. More importantly, we think that when a State has reduced the size of its juries to the minimum number of jurors permitted by the Constitution, the additional authorization of nonunanimous verdicts by such juries sufficiently threatens the constitu-tional principles that led to the establishment of the size threshold that any countervailing interest of the State should yield.

■ IN COMPARATIVE PERSPECTIVE

Juries around the World

Juries trace their roots to the common law jury system that evolved in England over 900 years ago, after the Norman Conquest in 1066. The Normans had a practice of putting a group of individuals under oath (and thus the term "juror") to tell the truth. Contrary to modern practice, jurors were chosen because of their knowledge of the case. They were eventually allowed to question witnesses, in contrast to the passivity of most contemporary juries. Later, the principle of impartiality emerged and by 1367 unanimous verdicts were required. Subsequently, jury trials became the only form of trials used by English courts. That lasted until the mid-nineteenth century when they were reserved for only the most serious crimes, but they continued to predominate in civil cases until the early twentieth century.

With British colonization, the jury system was introduced elsewhere—in colonies in North America, the Caribbean, and parts of Africa and Asia—though taking different forms. Nowhere did the jury system become as entrenched as in the United States. The right to a jury trial was enshrined in the constitutions of the original thirteen states and in the Sixth and Seventh Amendments of the Bill of Rights. Juries were deemed an important political institution and a check on governmental power. Although until the twentieth century juries generally excluded women and minorities, they were far more representative than in England.

In England and Wales, juries became more representative in the twentieth century. The Juries Act of 1974 required jurors to be selected randomly from all registered voters. Ironically, though, the English jury was transformed in other ways that rendered it a less important institution. The Criminal Justice Act of 1967 did away with unanimous verdicts and authorized convictions based on a majority vote of ten of the twelve jurors. The incremental reclassification of crimes also resulted in having jury trials in less than 2 percent of all criminal cases. The vast majority of criminal cases are now tried by magistrates' courts, composed of three lay magistrates. Because of the cost of jury trials, legislation gave judges the power to refuse jury trials in civil cases and less than 1 percent of all civil cases are now tried before juries. The Supreme Court Act of 1981 preserves a qualified right to a jury trial in only four kinds of civil cases: libel and slander, fraud, malicious prosecution, and false imprisonment.

(continues)

Whereas in England the use of juries declined, in Canada juries in serious criminal cases remain generally used. A jury trial is constitutionally guaranteed in the 1982 Charter of Rights and Freedoms. That constitutional guarantee, though, is qualified by the criminal code, based on the Criminal Code of 1892. Basically, in Canada criminal offenses are defined as three types: (1) *indictable* offenses are the most serious crimes, like murder and treason, and tried before a judge and jury; (2) *summary conviction* offenses are less serious, carrying a maximum sentence of two years in jail or a fine of less than $5,000, and tried before a judge alone; and (3) *hybrid* offenses may be treated either as an indictable or a summary conviction offense, and hence may or may not entail a jury trial. In the latter instance, the public prosecutor decides how to charge hybrid offenses and therefore effectively decides whether the accused is accorded a jury trial.

Like the traditional common law jury, Canadian juries are composed of twelve members and render unanimous verdicts; sentencing, however, is the responsibility of judges. Since Canada has two official languages, English and French, the accused has the right to be tried by a judge and jury who speak his or her language. Juries were once composed almost exclusively of white males but are now selected randomly from the electoral rolls. As in England, however, juries in civil cases have virtually disappeared.

Juries took a different twist in Australia because four of its six states originated as penal colonies. Initially, juries were composed of six military officers and later free settlers who had migrated from Britain; convicts and former convicts were excluded. But because former convicts stayed they eventually outnumbered the free settlers, and a controversy arose over the rights of citizenship focusing on who could serve on juries. By the 1830s, it became settled in a few (and by the end of the nineteenth century in all) colonies for former convicts to serve on juries. When the six federated states became the Commonwealth of Australia in 1901, the new states retained their powers over criminal law, including the jury trial process. Notably, the Australian Constitution, which contains no bill of rights, does provide for a jury trial for any crimes against the Commonwealth.

The introduction of juries varied considerably elsewhere, depending on the indigenous culture. In Sierra Leone, England's oldest African colony, juries were used in both civil and criminal cases. But they were deemed not to guarantee fair trials because jurors confronted tribal rivalries. Within a couple of generations, juries in civil cases were abandoned and a two-thirds majority for conviction was required in criminal trials. A modified jury trial was implemented in Gambia in 1845, while the Gold Coast (Ghana) authorized the attorney general to order a jury trial if eligible English-speaking jurors could be found and to permit nonunanimous verdicts. Juries, typically composed of nine white males, were introduced into South Africa in 1828, but this usage gradually declined and was abolished in 1969. In other African countries, jury systems were not established until the twentieth century.

In nineteenth-century Western Europe, the Napoleonic Criminal Code of 1808 first introduced elements of the jury system into the French inquisitorial system with trials combining judges and lay jurors. Subsequently, Austria, parts of Germany, Belgium, Greece, Hungary, Portugal, and Spain adopted various elements of the jury system.

As a result of Portuguese and Spanish colonialization, the jury system was also introduced in the nineteenth century in South American countries, including Brazil (1822), Uruguay (1830), Argentina (1853), Chile (1872), Ecuador (1890), and Venezuela (1898).

In sum, the "traditional common law jury," composed of twelve members who render unanimous verdicts, was neither uniform nor standard. Juries varied and continue to vary in terms of their size, permissible verdicts, and representation. By the twenty-first century, the use of juries, particularly in civil cases, had declined or been abandoned in many parts of the world because juries were criticized as too costly, incompetent in dealing with complex litigation, and subject to bias due to preemptory challenges and to the influence of media coverage of trials. Nevertheless, although diminished in their usage, they survive in Australia, Canada, England and Wales, Ireland, New Zealand, the United States, and some forty-six other countries, including parts of the Mediterranean (Gibraltar and Malta), Africa (Ghana and Malawi), Asia (Hong Kong and Sri Lanka), the South Pacific (Tonga and the Marshall Islands), South America (Brazil and Guyana), and the Caribbean (Barbados, Jamaica, and Montserrat). Variations of the jury system also remain in use in Austria, Belgium, Denmark, and Norway; and in the 1990s Russia and Spain reintroduced juries in criminal cases.

For further reading, see Neal Vidmar, ed., *World Jury Systems* (New York: Oxford University Press, 2000).

E | *A Speedy and Public Trial*

A "speedy and public trial" is also a guarantee of the Sixth Amendment, which was made applicable to the states in *Klopfer v. North Carolina*, 386 U.S. 213 (1967). But what is a *speedy* trial? In *Dickey v. Florida*, 398 U.S. 30 (1970), the Court found that a defendant was denied the right to a speedy trial when his trial took place eight years after an alleged offense, and he was available in the state for prosecution during that time. *Barker v. Wingo*, 407 U.S. 514 (1972), however, held that a five-year delay between arrest and trial did not violate the Sixth Amendment. Congress responded with the federal Speedy Trial Act of 1974, requiring persons arrested to be charged within thirty days, arraigned ten days later, and tried within two months of arraignment. Charges may be dismissed if a defendant moves for dismissal after the speedy trial period has elapsed and no trial has commenced. *Doggett v. United States*, 505 U.S. 647 (1992), held that the Sixth Amendment right to a speedy trial was violated by the prosecution of an individual who had been indicted eight and one-half years earlier for importing cocaine, but who had left the country before he could be arrested. Based on the facts in the case, the Court chided the federal government for failing to pursue the accused vigorously and accord him a speedy trial.

In *Vermont v. Brillon*, 556 U.S. 81 (2009) the Roberts Court held that trial delays caused by defense counsel, whether privately retained or appointed by a court, are attributable to the defendant unless the delays are the result of a "systematic breakdown in the public defenders system." At issue was whether a three-year delay in bringing a defendant to trial violated the Sixth Amendment right to a speedy trial. Brillon was arrested and charged with felony domestic violence and as a habitual offender. During the three years prior to his trial, he was assigned six different public defenders. He was eventually found guilty and sentenced to twelve to twenty years in prison, and he appealed. Writing for the Court, Justice Ginsburg ruled that assigned counsel "act on behalf of their clients, and delays sought by counsel are ordinarily attributable to the defendants they represent." Finally, the Roberts Court in *per curiam* opinion, in *Presley v. Georgia*, 558 U.S. 209 (2010), with Justices Thomas and Scalia dissenting, reaffirmed that the public has a right to attend *voir dire* examinations of potential juries, but did so on the basis of the Sixth Amendment guarantee of a public trial rather than on the First Amendment.

The Sixth Amendment also embodies a presumption against trials *in absentia* of the defendant, although the Federal Rules of Criminal Procedure permit a waiver of the accused's right to be present at the trial "whenever a defendant initially present is voluntarily absent after the trial has commenced." And in *Crosby v. United States*, 506 U.S. 255 (1993), involving an appeal of the government's trial of a defendant *in absentia*, the Court unanimously ruled that Rule 43 of the Federal Rules of Criminal Procedure forbids the federal government's trying a defendant who is absent at the trial's beginning.

Notably, the Roberts Court unanimously held that the Sixth Amendment speedy trial clause does not apply to the sentencing phase, regardless of how long time passes between the trial and conviction and a judge's handing down a sentence, in *Betterman v. Montana*, 136 S.Ct. 1609 (2016).

F | *The Rights to Be Informed of Charges and to Confront Accusers*

The accused has a right "to be informed of the nature and cause of the accusation against" him under the Sixth Amendment. This provision aims at ensuring defendants the opportunity to prepare adequate defenses. More often, though, defense attorneys challenge the constitutionality of criminal statutes for being "void for vagueness" under the due process clause. This principle—that a statute must specifically define and give notice of the kind of activity proscribed—was well-stated in *Connally v. General Construction Co.*, 269 U.S. 385 (1926):

> That the terms of a penal statute . . . must be sufficiently explicit to inform those who are subject to it what conduct on their part will render them liable to its penalties, is a well-recognized requirement, consonant alike with ordinary notions of fair play and the settled rules of law. And a statute which either forbids or requires the doing of an act in terms so vague that men of common intelligence must necessarily guess at its meaning and differ as to its application, violates the first essential of due process of law.

The accused also has, under the Sixth Amendment, the right "to be confronted with the witnesses against him." This provision was made applicable to the states in *Pointer v. Texas*, 380 U.S. 400 (1965), where a transcript of a witness's testimony made at a preliminary hearing was introduced at trial because the witness had left the state. The accused also has the right to compel witnesses to appear in his favor in federal and state courts. *Lee v. Illinois*, 476 U.S. 530 (1986), held 5–4 that the use of a codefendant's confession as evidence of a defendant's guilt violated the confrontation clause and was presumptively unreliable because the confession was given after the codefendant was told that the defendant had implicated her in criminal activity. In *Olden v. Kentucky*, 488 U.S. 227 (1988), the Court held that a trial judge's refusal to permit a black defendant in a kidnapping, rape, and sodomy trial to cross-examine the white victim regarding her cohabitation with a black boyfriend violated the defendant's Sixth Amendment right to a confrontation of witnesses. So, too, in *Gray v. Maryland*, 521 U.S. 185 (1998), the Court ruled that the Sixth Amendment right to confront witnesses was violated by the introduction of an edited confession of a codefendant as evidence without giving the defendant an opportunity to cross-examine. The Court in *Crawford v. Washington*, 541 U.S. 36 (2004), also overturned the ruling in *Ohio v. Roberts*, 448 U.S. 56 (1980), that statements from a witness who was not available for cross-examination could nevertheless be admitted at trial if the judge deemed them reliable. Writing for a unanimous Court, Justice Scalia held that the standard of "reliability" was too subjective and amorphous. In his words, "Dispensing with confrontation because testimony is obviously reliable is akin to dispensing with jury trial because a defendant is obviously guilty. This is not what the Sixth Amendment prescribes." Under the Court's new rule, the prosecution may use statements of absent witnesses only if they were previously cross-examined by the defense at a deposition or in a prior trial.

In two bitterly divided 5–4 decisions involving the right of defendants to confront accusers in cases involving alleged child abuse, Justice O'Connor held the balance. Writing for a bare majority in *Maryland v. Craig*, 497 U.S. 836 (1990), Justice O'Connor held that individuals charged with child abuse have no constitutional right to confront, at least once, their young accusers. In that case, O'Connor upheld the state's allowing four children to testify out of the presence of the defendant over a one-way, closed-circuit television. In her words, "A state's interest in the physical and psychological well-being of child-abuse victims may be sufficiently important to outweigh, at least in some cases, a defendant's right to face his or her accusers in court." But Justice Scalia countered in a dissenting opinion, joined by Justices Brennan, Marshall, and Stevens, that "[t]o say that a defendant loses his right to confront a witness when that would cause the witness not to testify is rather like saying that the defendant loses his right to counsel when counsel would save him."

In the second case, the four dissenters from *Craig* joined Justice O'Connor for another bare majority ruling in *Idaho v. Wright*, 497

U.S. 805 (1990). In that case, Justice O'Connor rejected as hearsay evidence the testimony of a doctor who had interviewed a two-and-a-half-year-old child about alleged sexual abuse. Although O'Connor refused to establish a bright-line rule for when such testimony, in the absence of the victim's own testimony, could be introduced, she emphasized that such hearsay evidence must be so trustworthy as to render a cross-examination of the victim of marginal utility.

Left unanswered by *Craig* and *Wright*, however, was whether judges may exclude all testimony by alleged victims who are capable of testifying, thereby allowing juries to determine a defendant's guilt entirely on the basis of hearsay testimony of those who questioned the children out of court. The following term, *White v. Illinois*, 502 U.S. 346 (1992), unanimously held that the Sixth Amendment's confrontation clause permits, in a trial of a defendant accused of sexually abusing a four-year-old child, the introduction as testimony of the victim's "spontaneous declaration" made to police and doctors, along with the results of a medical examination. The Court also rejected the claim that an accused's right to confront witnesses against him requires the prosecution either to produce the victim at trial or establish the victim's unavailability. Writing for the Court, Chief Justice Rehnquist explained that

> [g]iven the evidentiary value of such statements, their reliability, and that establishing a generally applicable unavailability rule would have few practical benefits while imposing pointless litigation costs, we see no reason to treat the out-of-court statements in this case differently from those we found admissible in [cases not involving child abuse]. . . . We therefore see no basis . . . for excluding from trial, under the aegis of the Confrontation Clause, evidence embraced within such exceptions to the hearsay rule as those for spontaneous declarations and statements made for medical treatment.

In addition, in *Michigan v. Lucas*, 500 U.S. 145 (1991), the Court upheld Michigan's rape-shield law, which mandates that evidence of past sexual conduct be barred at trial if a defendant fails to give notice of its introduction at least ten days prior to the trial. Writing for the Court in *Lucas*, Justice O'Connor held that a defendant's right to confront accusers does not permit courts to adopt per se rules barring trial courts from allowing the introduction at trial of evidence of rape victims' prior sexual relationship with criminal defendants. Nor are states precluded from requiring defendants to give notification, within ten days of their arraignment, of their plans to present evidence about the alleged victim's past sexual conduct and on that basis ban in some cases the introduction of such evidence at trial. Michigan's ten-day deadline for such notification is the shortest in the country; the federal rape-shield law requires such notice 15 days before a trial commences.

In *Davis v. Washington*, 547 U.S. 813 (2006), the Roberts Court held that statements made during a 911 call may be introduced at trial without affording the defendant the opportunity to confront the accuser because such statements are not "testimonial" and thus not subject to the Sixth Amendment's confrontation clause. Writing for the Court, Justice Scalia ruled that statements made in a 911 call were not "testimonial" because they were made in reporting an immediate emergency and demanding police assistance, whereas statements made by a victim to police at the crime scene are "testimonial" and may not be introduced at a trial unless the defendant has the opportunity to confront the witness.

In a 5–4 ruling in *Melendez-Diaz v. Massachusetts*, 557 U.S. 305 (2009), the majority held that chemists and other scientists who prepare crime lab reports may be summoned as witnesses in criminal trials to defend their analyses in order not to violate defendants' Sixth Amendment right to confront witnesses against them. Writing for the Court, Justice Scalia observed that "There is little reason to believe that confrontation will be useless in testing analysts' honesty, proficiency, and methodology—the features that are commonly the focus in the cross-examination of experts." In doing so, he recited reports about the defectiveness of crime labs and their results, and dismissed claims that crime lab reports are a product of "neutral scientific testing." "Forensic evidence," Justice Scalia wrote, "is not uniquely immune from the risk of manipulation." Chief Justice Roberts and Justices Kennedy, Breyer, and Alito dissented.

The Roberts Court continued to confront litigation over the ruling in *Crawford v. Washington*, 541 U.S. 36 (2004). There, writing for a unanimous Court, Justice Scalia ostensibly laid down a bright-line rule that the prosecution may use statements of an absent witness against the accused at trial only if they were previously cross-examined by the defense counsel at a deposition or in a prior trial. But since *Crawford*, the Court has carved out some exceptions, dealing, for example, with the use of child abuse victims' statements against defendants, in balancing the Sixth Amendment's guarantee of defendants' right to confront witnesses and the introduction of hearsay evidence at trial. In *Michigan v. Bryant*, 562 U.S. 344 (2011), a majority of the Court held that a dying victim's statements identifying the assailant could be introduced at trial against the defendant. Richard Bryant, who had been shot in a parking lot, identified his assailant to police investigating the crime scene and died shortly afterward. His statements were introduced at trial but were held by the state supreme court to violate the Sixth Amendment and run afoul of the ruling in

Crawford. But writing for a majority, Justice Sotomayor distinguished the application of *Crawford*'s ruling and the statements here as "nontestimonial" because they were made to police at the time they were responding to "an ongoing emergency" and there was a "potential threat to the responding police and the public at large." By contrast, statements to police that amount to "testimony" about the accused are not allowed to be used at trial. Dissenting Justice Scalia, the author of the decision in *Crawford*, sharply rejected the majority's distinction between nontestimonial and testimonial in limiting the holding in *Crawford*.

In *Bullcoming v. New Mexico*, 564 U.S. 647 (2011), the Court confronted the issue of whether crime lab reports may be introduced as evidence against the defendant even though the author of the report is unavailable to testify against the defendant. Donald Bullcoming struck a car at a stop sign and was later alleged to have been driving under the influence of alcohol. After leaving the crime scene, he allegedly went for drinks with friends and failed a gas chromatograph test for blood alcohol content after he was subsequently located again by police. The analyst who signed the forensic report was unavailable to testify at trial, and prosecutors called another analyst from the lab to testify. At issue, thus, was if a lab machine provides the incriminating evidence against the accused, does it matter which lab analyst testifies about the lab results and confronts the accused? Writing for a bare majority, Justice Ginsburg held that the confrontation clause does not permit the prosecution to introduce a forensic report, containing a testimonial certification, and call an analyst who did not conduct, observe, or certify the test reported. The accused has the right to confront the analyst who made the certification and, if unavailable at trial, the accused must have an opportunity during a pretrial hearing to cross-examine that particular scientist.

A bare majority in *Williams v. Illinois*, 567 U.S. 50 (2012), ruled that it was constitutionally permissible for an expert witness to discuss others' testimonial statements if they were not themselves admitted as evidence. Sandra Lambatos, a forensic specialist in the state police lab, testified that she matched a DNA profile produced by an outside laboratory, Cellmark, to a profile the state lab produced using a sample of the petitioner's blood. She offered no other statement for the purpose of identifying the sample used for Cellmark's profile or establishing how it tested the sample. The defense moved to exclude Lambatos's testimony but the prosecution countered that the defendant's confrontation rights were satisfied because he had the opportunity to cross-examine the expert who had testified as to the match. The trial judge admitted the evidence and found the defendant guilty, which on appeal was affirmed by a state appellate and supreme court. The Supreme Gourt affirmed that decision. Justice Kagan dissented and was joined by Justices Scalia, Ginsburg, and Sotomayor. Justice Kagan contended that the majority was trying to apply an eighteenth-century conception of the right to confront one's accusers to twenty-first century evidence, such as DNA testing. Writing for a plurality, Justice Alito maintained that Lambatos's testimony about the lab report was not offered to prove that it was true, and that Cellmark's report was not the sort of evidence to which the confrontation clause applies because it was made "for the purpose of finding a rapist who was on the loose." Justice Thomas cast the deciding vote and, disagreeing with Justice Alito's opinion for the Court, contended that "the confrontation clause . . . [applies] to a narrow class of statements bearing indicia of solemnity." But, Justice Kagan countered that "would turn the confrontation clause into a constitutional geegaw—nice for show, but of little value."

The Roberts Court narrowed the holding a decade earlier in *Crawford v. Washington*, 541 U.S. 36 (2004), with its holding in *Ohio v. Clark*, 135 S.Ct. 2173 (2015). The Court addressed a question left unanswered after *Crawford*, namely, whether the ban on out-of-court statements introduced as evidence when the person who made the accusations does not confront the accused at trial may still be applied when those statements were made to someone other than a police officer. The case involved a three-year-old boy who told his preschool teacher that he had been sexually abused by his mother's boyfriend. Writing for the Court, Justice Alito held that such statements may be introduced without violating the Sixth Amendment Confrontation Clause.

G | *The Guarantee against Double Jeopardy*

The Fifth Amendment provides that defendants may not be twice held "in jeopardy of life or limb" for the same offense. The purpose of this guarantee, Justice Hugo Black explained in *Green v. United States*, 355 U.S. 184 (1957), is that "the State with all its resources and power should not be allowed to make repeated attempts to convict an individual for an alleged offense, thereby subjecting him to embarrassment, expense and ordeal and compelling him to live in a continuing state of anxiety and insecurity, as well as enhancing the possibility that even though innocent he may be found guilty."

The double jeopardy clause, however, was not deemed to be "fundamental" to the "concept of ordered liberty" so as to apply to the states in *Palko v. Connecticut* (1937) (see Ch. 4). But a solid majority of the Warren Court made the states bound by the double jeopardy clause in *Benton v. Maryland*, 395 U.S. 784 (1969). *Crist v. Bretz*, 437 U.S. 28 (1978), further held that states must observe the federal rule that the jeopardy clause is triggered once a jury is empanelled, and thus the defendant may not be retried for the same offense.

Like some other guarantees, the double jeopardy clause is not self-explanatory; much depends on how *jeopardy* is interpreted in the context of a legal proceeding and how the *same offense* is viewed. Defendants who have been acquitted or convicted and then retried by the same court, of course, have been placed in double jeopardy. *Waller v. Florida*, 397 U.S. 387 (1970), also held that defendants may not be retried for a different crime based on the same evidence. If a jury fails to reach a verdict and is dismissed, a second trial is permissible as a continuation of the first trial.[1] But the government may not appeal an acquittal, even if egregious errors led to the acquittal.[2] The government may, though, retry a defendant who wins a motion for mistrial,[3] except when a mistrial is declared by a judge on his own, due to improper procedures.[4] An accused may waive the right against being held in double jeopardy when requesting a new trial or appealing a guilty verdict, but if the conviction is set aside on appeal, a retrial for the same offense is permissible.[5]

Whether defendants are tried for the same offense depends on whether the trial takes place in the same jurisdiction and based on the same evidence. In *United States v. Lara*, 541 U.S. 193 (2004), for instance, the Court held that the federal government may prosecute a Native-American Indian in federal court, even after a conviction in a tribal court for virtually the same offense, assaulting a federal officer. Writing for the Court, Justice Breyer held that the double jeopardy clause does not bar prosecutions by two sovereign governments, and reaffirmed "the inherent power of Indian tribes . . . to exercise criminal jurisdiction over all Indians." Justices Scalia and Souter dissented. In 2019, the Court affirmed a long-standing practice of allowing separate prosecutions in state and federal court for the same crime. In a 7–2 decision in *Gamble v. United States*, Justice Alito said the Court had no reason "to break a chain of precedent linking dozens of cases over 170 years." Alito explained this practice was not an exception to the double jeopardy rule, but rather it follows from the text of the Fifth Amendment. "Where there are two sovereigns, there are two laws and two 'offenses,'" Alito wrote. Thus, to be tried by two sovereigns for violations against each is not to be tried twice for the same crime. This case had particular resonance when handed down in June 2019 since it would make possible state prosecutions even if the accused had been issued an executive pardon by the president. Such a pardon would apply only to a federal conviction and would not preclude a state prosecution.

If two charges grow out of the same evidence, retrial on separate charges other than that litigated at the first trial is permissible.[6] *United States v. Halper*, 490 U.S. 435 (1989), unanimously held that civil fines may not be placed on top of criminal penalties for the same offense. However, almost a decade later in *Hudson v. United States*, 522 U.S. 93 (1997), a bare majority overturned *Halper* and held that individuals may face criminal prosecution for banking violations for which they have already been fined. In holding that fines are civil, not criminal, and therefore do not trigger the double jeopardy clause, Chief Justice Rehnquist reaffirmed an earlier rule, set forth in *United States v. Ward*, 448 U.S. 242 (1980), that the threshold question in such cases is whether the legislature intended a successive punishment to be "civil" or "criminal."

The test for whether the double jeopardy clause is violated remains whether the same evidence is introduced in both trials.[7] Under *Blockburger v. United States*, 284 U.S. 299 (1932), successive prosecutions of criminal conduct under different statutes is forbidden, if they include identical statutory elements or lesser included offenses. In *Grady v. Corbin*, 495 U.S. 508 (1990), a bare majority of the Court expanded the scope of the double jeopardy clause to bar a subsequent prosecution under a different statute when the government must show that the defendant's conduct constituted an offense for which the defendant had already been prosecuted under another statute.

In *United States v. Felix*, 503 U.S. 378 (1992), the Court then held that the Fifth Amendment's double jeopardy clause is not violated by two separate federal prosecutions of a defendant for the crime of manufacturing illegal drugs and then for conspiracy to manufacture and distribute the same illegal drugs in a different jurisdiction. The Rehnquist Court unanimously agreed that the two prosecutions were not for "the same offense," despite the use of some of the same evidence against the defendant in both trials.

Following the retirements of Justices Brennan and Marshall, a bare majority was finally mustered to overturn the Court's 1990 ruling in *Grady v. Corbin*. In *United States v. Dixon*, 509 U.S. 688 (1993), another bare majority held that the double jeopardy clause does not bar the prosecution of an individual who has already been subject to prosecution for contempt for defying a judge's order for conduct that led to conviction for contempt of court in the first place. Writing for the Court, Justice Scalia, who had dissented in *Grady*, reaffirmed the test set forth in *Blockburger*, which inquires whether each offense contains an element not contained in the other; and, if not, whether they are the "same offense" for the purposes of the double jeopardy clause. However, he also overruled *Grady's* "same conduct" test as inconsistent with earlier precedents and the history of the double jeopardy clause. *Dixon* thus reestablished the traditional view that under the double jeopardy clause the question is not whether two prosecutions require proof of the same conduct but, instead, whether the two offenses have the same "elements."

Moreover, *Dowling v. United States*, 493 U.S. 342 (1990), held that prosecutors may introduce at trial evidence relating to crimes for which the defendant in a prior trial had been acquitted. Notably, the double jeopardy clause does not bar defendants from receiving a more severe sentence on retrial.[8] Nor does it forbid both federal and state governments to prosecute the same offense.[9] *Poland v. Arizona*, 476 U.S. 147 (1986), construed the double jeopardy clause not to bar defendants from being retried and given capital punishment after they appealed their first conviction for first-degree murder and where an appellate court had reversed and ordered their retrial because of evidentiary problems even though it found that sufficient evidence had been presented for imposing a death sentence. But the Rehnquist Court split 5–4 in *Quinn v. Millsap*, 491 U.S. 95 (1989). There, a defendant was sentenced to prison for two crimes—fifteen years for attempted robbery and life imprisonment for felony murder—stemming from the same offense. By the time a state court held invalid the multiple sentences for the same offense, the robbery sentence had been commuted and the time served credited to the life sentence. But a federal court of appeals threw out the life sentence on appeal. Writing for a bare majority, Justice Kennedy reversed, observing that "[n]either the Double Jeopardy Clause nor any other constitutional provision exists to provide unjustified windfalls." Siding with Justices Brennan, Marshall, and Stevens in dissent, Justice Scalia countered that "[a] technical rule with equitable exceptions is no rule at all. Three strikes is out. The state broke the rules here, and must abide by the result."

In *Department of Revenue of Montana v. Kurth Ranch*, 511 U.S. 747 (1994), however, a bare majority of the Rehnquist Court struck down Montana's tax on illegal drugs as a violation of the double jeopardy clause, because it imposed an additional penalty inflicted on those convicted of possessing illegal drugs and thus unconstitutionally punished people twice for the same offense. Along with more than twenty other states, Montana imposed a tax on illegal drugs confiscated in drug raids. But, writing for the majority, Justice Stevens rejected the state's claim that the tax was simply a revenue-raising measure, and observed, "This tax, imposed on criminals and no others, departs so far from normal revenue laws as to become a form of punishment." In *United States v. Ursery*, 518 U.S. 267 (1996), the Court nevertheless held that civil forfeiture proceedings, which since the 1980s have become common for defendants who have been criminally convicted for drug trafficking, do not violate the Double Jeopardy Clause when the defendant has also been tried for the same offense on criminal charges. Writing for the Court, Chief Justice Rehnquist held simply that civil forfeitures "do not constitute 'punishment' for purposes of the Double Jeopardy Clause."

Finally, in *Evans v. Michigan*, 568 U.S. 313 (2013), the Court held that the double-jeopardy clause bars a retrial after an acquittal, even if the acquittal was erroneous. However, in *Currier v. Virginia,* 138 S. Ct. 2144 (2018), by a 5-to-4 vote the Roberts Court held that the double jeopardy clause is not violated when a defendant and the prosecutor agree to separate trials for two separate charges related to the same crime. In this instance, the result was an acquittal in the first trial on a burglary charge but a conviction in the second on felon in possession of a gun during a burglary.

NOTES

1. *United States v. Perez*, 9 Wheat. 579 (1824).

2. *Sanabria v. United States*, 437 U.S. 54 (1978); and *Oregon v. Washington*, 434 U.S. 497 (1978).

3. See *United States v. Dinitz*, 424 U.S. 600 (1976); and *Oregon v. Kennedy*, 456 U.S. 667 (1987). See also *Blueford v. Arkansas*, 132 S.Ct. 2044 (2012).

4. Compare *United States v. Jorn*, 400 U.S. 470 (1971) with *Illinois v. Somerville*, 410 U.S. 458 (1973).

5. See *United States v. Ball*, 163 U.S. 662 (1896) and compare *Burks v. United States*, 437 U.S. 1 (1978); *Hudson v. Louisiana*, 450 U.S. 40 (1981); and *Tibbs v. Florida*, 457 U.S. 31 (1982).

6. See *Morgan v. Devine*, 237 U.S. 632 (1915); and *United States v. Ewell*, 383 U.S. 116 (1966).

7. See *Hoag v. New York*, 356 U.S. 464 (1958); *Ashe v. Swenson*, 397 U.S. 436 (1970); and *United States v. Halper*, 490 U.S. 435 (1989). *Lockhart v. Nelson*, 488 U.S. 33 (1988) held that the double jeopardy clause does not bar retrial after an appellate court has determined that evidence at the first trial was erroneously admitted.

8. See *United States v. DiFrancesco*, 449 U.S. 117 (1980); and *Chaffin v. Stynchcombem*, 412 U.S. 17 (1973). But compare *North Carolina v. Pierce*, 395 U.S. 711 (1969); and *Bullington v. Missouri*, 451 U.S. 430 (1981). See also *Witte v. United States*, 515 U.S. 389 (1995) (holding that the double jeopardy clause does not bar prosecution for a crime even though the same criminal conduct was previously used to raise the defendant's prison sentence for a different offense).

9. See *United States v. Lanza*, 260 U.S. 377 (1922); *Abbate v. United States*, 359 U.S. 187 (1959); *Bartkus v. Illinois*, 359 U.S. 121 (1959). The Court, however, has overturned the prosecution by local and state governments in the same jurisdiction of a defendant based on the same evidence. See *Waller v. Florida*, 397 U.S. 387 (1970); and *Missouri v. Hunter*, 459 U.S. 359 (1983).

H | *The Guarantee against Excessive Bail and Fines*

The Eighth Amendment's provisions that "excessive bail shall not be required, nor excessive fines imposed" gave constitutional effect to rights dating back to the English Bill of Rights in 1689. Bail is a pledge of money or property by an accused that ostensibly guarantees his appearance at trial; it enables the accused to remain free while awaiting trial. The provision limits both Congress and federal courts in setting bail. Under the Bail Reform Act of 1966, those accused of noncapital federal offenses may be released on their own recognizance or on an unsecured bond, unless a judge deems that release would "not reasonably assure" their appearance in court.

Because of the concern over the number of crimes committed by repeat offenders while on bail and the battle against importers of drugs and narcotics, Congress passed the Bail Reform Act of 1984. It authorizes the pretrial detention of defendants who are deemed to pose a threat to the community. By a vote of 6–3 in *United States v. Salerno*, 481 U.S. 739 (1987), the Court upheld pretrial detention as "regulatory, not penal." Chief Justice Rehnquist's opinion for the Court explained,

> The Bail Reform Act . . . operates only on individuals who have been arrested for a specific category of extremely serious offenses. Congress specifically found that these individuals are far more likely to be responsible for dangerous acts in the community after arrest. . . . While the government's general interest in preventing is compelling, even this interest is heightened when the government musters convincing proof that the arrestee, already indicted or held to answer for a serious crime, presents a demonstrable danger to the community. Under these narrow circumstances, society's interest in crime prevention is at its greatest.

> On the other side of the scale, of course, is the individual's strong interest in liberty. We do not minimize the importance and fundamental nature of this right. But, as our cases hold, this right

may, in circumstances where the government's interest is sufficiently weighty, be subordinated to the greater needs of society.

Two years later, in *Caplin & Drysdale v. United States* and *United States v. Monsanto*, 491 U.S. 600 (1989), the Rehnquist Court held 5–4 that the Department of Justice may seize the money and property illegally acquired by criminal defendants who are facing trial even if they claim that those assets would be used to pay the costs of their defense at trial. In Justice White's words for the majority, "A defendant has no Sixth Amendment right to spend another person's money for services rendered by an attorney, even if those funds are the only way that the defendant will be able to retain the attorney of his choice."

In recent years, the Court has faced a series of challenges to state and federal laws authorizing the seizure and forfeiture of property of individuals who have been convicted of criminal activities. Forfeiture has become a major weapon in the federal government's so-called drug war. But in two Eighth Amendment challenges to forfeitures as constituting "excessive fines," in *Alexander v. United States*, 509 U.S. 544 (1993), and *Austin v. United States*, 509 U.S. 602 (1993), the Court rebuffed the federal government's argument that forfeiture is not punitive but "remedial" and that the guilt or innocence of the property owner is "constitutionally irrelevant."

Notably, in *Austin v. United States*, the Court unanimously held that the guarantee against excessive fines requires the government to show a relationship between the seriousness of the offense and the forfeiture of property. Richard Austin, after having been convicted of selling cocaine, argued that the government's filing of a civil forfeiture complaint against his mobile home and auto-body shop abridged the Eighth Amendment. The government, however, countered that the amendment applies only to criminal proceedings and not civil actions, like forfeiture, even though related to a criminal conviction. In rejecting the government's arguments for the Court, Justice Blackmun observed,

> Fundamentally, even assuming that [the forfeiture provisions here] serve some remedial purpose, the Government's argument fails. . . . In light of the historical understanding of forfeiture as punishment, the clear focus of [the forfeiture provisions] on the culpability of the owner, and the evidence that Congress understood those provisions as serving to deter and to punish, we cannot conclude that forfeiture under Sections 881(a)(4) and (a)(7) [of the U.S. Code] serves solely a remedial purpose. We therefore conclude that forfeiture under these provisions constitutes "payment to a sovereign as punishment for some offense," and, as such, is subject to the limitations of the Eighth Amendment's Excessive Fines Clause.

In *Austin*, Justice Blackmun nevertheless declined to lay down guidelines for when the government's seizure of property is unconstitutionally excessive. Instead, the Court remanded *Austin* back to the lower courts for reconsideration. Consequently, that issue will percolate in the lower federal courts, allowing them to develop their own rules, and allow the Court eventually to revisit the issue of when forfeitures constitute "excessive fines" under the Eighth Amendment.

I | *Indigents and the Criminal Justice System*

Beginning in the 1950s, the Warren Court held in a number of cases that the Fourteenth Amendment due process and equal protection clauses require states to provide indigents with certain resources for their defense at trial and on appeal. *Griffin v. Illinois*, 351 U.S. 12 (1956), is the leading case in which the Court struck down a statute granting free trial transcripts to indigents only for review of constitutional questions and where the defendant was given a death sentence. There, the Court held that the right of indigents to meaningful appellate review was denied unless they were furnished trial transcripts in any appeals. *Gideon v. Wainwright* (1963) (excerpted in Section A), of course, extended the right to counsel to indigents at trial. However, the Burger and Rehnquist Courts have upheld constraints on indigents' access to the judicial system in several, although not all, rulings. Some of the major rulings on the rights of indigents are summarized in the following THE DEVELOPMENT OF LAW box.

■ The Development of Law

Rulings on Indigents and the Judicial System

CASE	VOTE	RULING
Burns v. Ohio, 360 U.S. 252 (1959)	7–2	Indigents have the right to file an appeal.
Lane v. Brown, 372 U.S. 477 (1963)	9–0	Right to have trial transcript on appeal.
Hardy v. United States, 375 U.S. 277 (1964)	8–1	Court-appointed attorney is entitled to trial transcript.
Long v. District Court of Iowa, 385 U.S. 192 (1966)	9–0	Transcripts must be provided for *habeas corpus* proceedings on appeal.
Roberts v. LaVallee, 389 U.S. 40 (1967)	8–1	Indigents have a right to transcripts even after exhaustion of state appeals.
Gardner v. California, 393 U.S. 367 (1969)	6–3	Right to free trial transcript for preparation of *habeas corpus* petition.
Williams v. Oklahoma City, 395 U.S. 458 (1969)	9–0	States that permit appeals for any conviction may not deny right of appeal to indigents.
Williams v. Illinois, 399 U.S. 235 (1970)	9–0	Fourteenth Amendment forbids states from converting fines into prison sentences.
Mayer v. City of Chicago, 404 U.S. 189 (1971)	9–0	Struck down Illinois's law providing trial transcripts only in felony cases as constituting an "unreasonable distinction"; required transcripts in felony and nonfelony cases.

Tate v. Short, 401 U.S. 395 (1971)	9–0	An indigent convicted of traffic offenses may not be committed to a municipal prison farm because of the inability to pay a fine.
Boddie v. Connecticut, 401 U.S. 371 (1971)	8–1	Struck down filing fee required to have access to divorce court.
Schilb v. Kuebel, 404 U.S. 357 (1971)	6–3	States may require accused to pay 10 percent of bail bond or $25, whichever is greater, to secure pretrial release from jail.
United States v. Kras, 409 U.S. 434 (1973)	5–4	Upheld a $50 filing fee for access to bankruptcy court.
Ortwein v. Schwab, 410 U.S. 656 (1973)	5–4	Upheld Oregon's $25 filing fee for those seeking an appeal of an adverse welfare benefits decision.
Fuller v. Oregon, 417 U.S. 40 (1974)	7–2	Upheld a probationary system requiring reimbursement of the state for fees and the expenses of attorneys.
Ross v. Moffitt, 417 U.S. 600 (1974)	6–3	Held that after the first appeal as of right, indigents have no right to a court-appointed at-

torney on further appeals to a state's highest court or to the United States Supreme Court.

Bounds v. Smith, 430 U.S. 817 (1977)	6–3	Prisons must provide adequate law libraries for prisoners who want to make a "meaningful appeal."
Ake v. Oklahoma, 470 U.S. 68 (1986)	8–1	If sanity is an issue at a defendant's trial, the state must provide a psychiatrist.

(continues)

■ The Development of Law
Rulings on Indigents and the Judicial System (continued)

CASE	VOTE	RULING
Pennsylvania v. Finley, 481 U.S. 551 (1987)	5–4	There is no constitutional right to a court-appointed attorney in postconviction proceedings.
Murray v. Giarratano, 492 U.S. 1 (1989)	5–4	States are not required to furnish lawyers for indigents on death row who lost initial rounds of appeals.
In re Amendment to Rule 34, 500 U.S. 13 (1991)	6–3	Amended the Supreme Court's rules to authorize the denial of *in forma pau-*

peris petitions if a majority deems them "frivolous or malicious." Justices Blackmun, Marshall, and Stevens dissented.

Lewis v. Casey, 518 U.S. 343 (1996)	8–1	Writing for the Court, Justice Scalia reinterpreted the ruling in *Bounds v. Smith,*

430 U.S. 817 (1977) to limit the standing of prison inmates to sue, and the remedial powers of federal courts in ordering changes in prison law libraries and legal assistance programs so as to facilitate inmates' "right of access to the courts."

10

CRUEL AND UNUSUAL
PUNISHMENT

The ban on "cruel and unusual punishments" is another guarantee of the Bill of Rights rooted in the history of English common law. In 1583, the Archbishop of Canterbury turned the High Commission into an Ecclesiastical Court for punishing heretics and critics of the Crown. Torture was used to extract confessions, and death was imposed for a large number of crimes. Opposition gradually mounted and led to the English Bill of Rights of 1689. Among those rights, the ban on "cruel and unusual punishments" registered not only opposition to the practices of the High Commission but also the imposition of punishments unauthorized by statute and disproportionate to the offense. The phrasing of the English guarantee against "cruel and unusual punishments" reappeared in Virginia's Declaration of Rights in 1776. It was later incorporated verbatim in the Eighth Amendment.

Prior to the 1960s, the Supreme Court had little occasion to interpret the guarantee against "cruel and unusual punishments." But in the 1960s there was an organized legal attack orchestrated by the American Civil Liberties Union and the National Association for the Advancement of Colored People (NAACP) Legal Defense Fund, among other organizations, on the constitutionality of capital punishment. In response to these pressures and litigation in the 1970s the Court began erecting barriers to the imposition of the death sentence. But that in turn made capital punishment a major political issue and invited the mobilization of forces pushing for a renewal of executions. With changes in the composition of the high bench, the Court again responded and shifted direction.

The nation's last public hanging in 1936. Rainey Bethea was executed in Owensboro, Kentucky, before a crowd of about 20,000 people. (*Keystone-France/Gamma-Keystone via Getty Images*)

Certain themes in the Court's initial interpretation of the guarantee against cruel and unusual punishments, however, laid the basis for its eventual application of the amendment in the area of capital punishment. First, the Court indicated that the amendment does not ban unusual punishments but rather those that are barbaric in their cruelty. The Court's initial encounters with Eighth Amendment claims involved whether novel methods of execution ran afoul of the amendment. *Wilkerson v. Utah*, 99 U.S. 130 (1878), unanimously upheld public execution by musketry, and *In re Kemmler*, 136 U.S. 436 (1890), upheld electrocution, which though unusual at the time was more "humane" than hanging and other forms of execution. As Justice Stephen Field, in *O'Neil v. Vermont*, 144 U.S. 323 (1892), summarized:

> That designation [cruel and unusual punishments], it is true, is usually applied to punishments which inflict torture, such as the rack, the thumbscrew, the iron boot, the stretching of limbs and the like, which are attended with acute pain and suffering. . . . The inhibition is directed, not only against punishments of the character mentioned, but against all punishments which by their excessive length or severity are greatly disproportionate to the offenses charged. The whole inhibition is against that which is excessive.

Second, the Court indicated that the intentions of those who carry out executions may not be controlling in applying the amendment. In the case of Willy Francis, a mechanical failure of the electric chair frustrated the state's first attempt to put him to death. And Francis appealed to the Court, contending that a second trip to the electric chair constituted cruel and unusual punishment. The justices by a vote of 5–4 rejected his claim, finding the unsuccessful execution an "unforeseeable accident" but not intentional cruelty. *Louisiana ex rel. Francis v. Resweber*, 329 U.S. 459 (1947).

Finally, the Court indicated that punishments that are grossly disproportionate to the offense might violate the Eighth Amendment. The first ruling overturning a punishment under the amendment, in *Weems v. United States*, 217 U.S. 349 (1910), involved a Coast Guard officer, stationed in the Philippines, who was convicted of falsifying public documents and sentenced to twelve years of incarceration, chained, and put under perpetual surveillance, as well as stripped of all civil liberties. *Trop v. Dulles*, 356 U.S. 86 (1958), held that the loss of citizenship as a result of a court-martial for wartime desertion constituted cruel and unusual punishment. In controversial although often-cited *dicta*, Chief Justice Warren added that "[t]he amendment must draw its meaning from evolving standards of decency that mark the progress of a maturing society."

SELECTED BIBLIOGRAPHY

Abu-Jamal, Mumia. *Live from Death Row.* Reading, MA: Addison-Wesley, 1995.

Banner, Stuart. *The Death Penalty: An American History.* Cambridge, MA; Harvard University Press, 2002.

Bedau, Hugo, and Paul Cassell, eds. *Debating the Death Penalty.* New York: Oxford University Press, 2004.

Berns, Walter. *For Capital Punishment.* New York: Basic Books, 1979.

Black, Charles, Jr. *Capital Punishment: The Inevitability of Caprice and Mistake.* New York: W. W. Norton & Company, 1974.

Bowers, William J. et al. *Legal Homicide: Death as Punishment in America, 1864–1982.* Boston: Northeastern University Press, 1984.

Hirsch, James. *Hurricane: The Miraculous Journey of Rubin Carter.* Boston: Houghton Mifflin, 2000.

Hood, Roger. *The Death Penalty: A World Wide Perspective.* 3rd ed. New York: Oxford University Press, 2002.

Kirchmeier, Jeffrey. *Imprisoned by the Past: Warren McCleskey and the American Death Penalty.* New York: Oxford University Press, 2015.

Mandery, Evan. *A Wild Justice: The Death and Resurrection of Capital Punishment.* New York: W. W. Norton, 2013.

Mello, Michael. *Dead Wrong: A Death Row Lawyer Speaks Out against Capital Punishment.* Madison: University of Wisconsin Press, 1997.

Moran, Richard. *Executioner's Current: Thomas Edison, George Westinghouse, and Invention of the Electric Chair.* New York: Knopf, 2002.

Ogletree, Charles, and Austin Sarat, eds. *From Lynch Mobs to the Killing State: Race and the Death Penalty in America.* New York: New York University Press, 2006.

Oshinsky, David. *Capital Punishment on Trial: Furman v. Georgia and the Death Penalty in Modern America.* Lawrence: University Press of Kansas, 2010.

Prettyman, Barrett, Jr. *Death and the Supreme Court.* New York: Harcourt, Brace & World, 1961.

Sarat, Austin. *Gruesome Spectacles: Botched Executions and America's Death Penalty.* Stanford: Stanford University Press, 2014.

Scheck, Barry, Peter Neufeld, and Jim Dwyer. *Actual Innocence: Five Days to Execution, and Other Dispatches from the Wrongly Convicted.* New York: Doubleday, 2000.

Zimring, Franklin. *The Contradictions of American Capital Punishment.* New York: Oxford University Press, 2003.

A | *Noncapital Punishment*

In *Robinson v. California*, 370 U.S. 660 (1962), the Warren Court struck down a statute making narcotics addiction per se a criminal offense, with at least a mandatory ninety-day jail sentence. Besides finding the punishment disproportionate, the Warren Court indicated that the amendment might have broader application outside of the area of capital punishment. However, a bare majority of the Court refused to extend *Robinson* when upholding a conviction for public drunkenness of an ex-alcoholic, and finding alcoholism not to be a "disease," in *Powell v. Texas*, 392 U.S. 514 (1968). The Court subsequently held that the conditions of prison isolation cells and prison officials' indifference to the illness of inmates may violate the Eighth Amendment,[1] but also refused to apply the amendment to corporal punishment in public schools,[2] and to the shooting without warning of a prisoner during the quelling of a prison riot.[3] In addition, the Court was reluctant to strike down noncapital punishments as disproportionate to the crime. By a vote of 5–4 in *Rummel v. Estelle*, 445 U.S. 263, (1980), for example, Texas's habitual criminal offenders act was upheld as applied to a man convicted of three thefts totaling $289. Three years later, however, Justice Blackmun, who cast the crucial fifth vote in *Rummel*, joined *Rummel*'s four dissenters in *Solem v. Helm*, 463 U.S. 277 (1983), striking down as cruel and unusual punishment a life sentence imposed on a defendant convicted for writing a $100 bad check and who had six prior nonviolent offenses. However, a bare majority in *Harmelin v. Michigan*, 501 U.S. 957 (1991), rejected the claim that a lifetime sentence, without the possibility of parole, for possessing 650 grams of cocaine violated the Eighth Amendment. And in *Ewing v. California* (2003) (excerpted below), a bare majority upheld California's "three-strikes-and-you're-out" law, imposing sentences of twenty-five years to life for those convicted of three felonies and, unlike such laws in other states, permits counting certain misdemeanors as felonies. Gary Ewing, who had previous convictions for burglary and robbery, received a twenty-five-year-to-life sentence for stealing three golf clubs, each valued at $399. Writing for the Court, Justice O'Connor held that Ewing's sentence was not grossly disproportionate and therefore did not violate the Eighth Amendment. Justices Scalia and Thomas, concurring, disagreed that disproportionate analysis has any place in Eighth Amendment jurisprudence. Justices Stevens, Souter, Ginsburg, and Breyer dissented.

More recently, the Roberts Court, in *Graham v. Florida*, 560 U.S. 48 (2010), held that the Eighth Amendment bars juvenile offenders from receiving life sentences without parole for nonhomicide crimes. Writing for the Court, Justice Kennedy ruled that societal views did not support lifetime sentences for juveniles and that juvenile nonhomicide offenders must be given the opportunity to reform. In his words: "By denying the defendant the right to reenter the community, the state makes an irrevocable judgment about that person's value and place in society. . . . This judgment is not appropriate in light of a juvenile nonhomicide offender's capacity for change and limited moral culpability." Chief Justice Roberts concurred but would have decided such cases on a case-by-case basis and emphasized, "Some crimes are so heinous, and some juvenile offenders so highly culpable, that a sentence of life without parole may be entirely justified under the Constitution." Justice Thomas dissented, joined by Justices Scalia and Alito. However, the Court upheld the constitutionality of the Adam Walsh Child Protection and Safety Act of 2006, which authorizes the indefinite civil commitment of mentally ill, sexual federal offenders, even if they have served their sentences, in *United States v. Comstock*, 560 U.S. 126 (2010). Similar state laws were upheld in *Kansas v. Hendricks*, 521 U.S. 346 (1997), which rejected a due process challenge. Writing for the Court, Justice Breyer held that Congress had the authority under Article I's necessary and proper clause, reasoning, "As a federal custodian, it has the constitutional power to act in order to protect nearby (and other) communities from the danger federal prisoners may pose." In addition, the majority rejected a Tenth Amendment challenge to the law for infringing on states' rights in holding that the statute did not invade states' interests.

The issue of the Eighth Amendment's applicability to the confinement and treatment of prison inmates is one area that has continued to haunt the Court. In *Hudson v. McMillian*, 503 U.S. 1 (1992), the Court split 7–2 in holding that a prison inmate's Eighth Amendment rights were violated by prison guards' use of excessive force. Keith Hudson was punched and kicked by two guards while he remained handcuffed and a supervisor instructed the guards not to "have too much fun." He sustained loosened teeth and a split lip but no "significant injury." After initially winning $800 in damages, Hudson's claims were dismissed by an appellate court on the grounds that he failed to show a "significant injury" from "objectively and clearly unnecessary" use of excessive force aimed at "an unnecessary and wanton infliction of pain."

When reversing the lower court's ruling in *Hudson*, Justice O'Connor ruled that the touchstone for the Court's analysis in such cases was "whether force was applied in a good-faith effort to maintain or restore discipline, or maliciously and sadistically to cause harm." O'Connor thereupon distinguished *Whitley v. Albers*, 475 U.S. 312 (1986), which held that an inmate's Eighth Amendment rights were not violated by a prison guard's shooting him during a prison riot. The settled rule, in O'Connor's view, was whether guards "unnecessarily and wanton[ly]" inflict pain. O'Connor, though, rejected the argument that inmates must also show a "significant injury."

The "objective component" of the Eighth Amendment's guarantee against "cruel and unusual punishment," Justice O'Connor observed in *Hudson*, was (1) contextually dependent on the kind of claim raised and (2) draws "its meaning from evolving standards of decency that mark the progress of a maturing society," citing *Trop v. Dulles*, 356 U.S. 86 (1958). On that basis, O'Connor distinguished other cases involving conditions-of-confinement claims and whether the denial of inmates' medical needs constituted "cruel and unusual punishment." In such cases, inmates must show "deliberate indifference" of prison authorities and that the inmates' deprivations or injuries are "serious." By contrast, inmates claiming constitutional deprivations due to excessive force must show that "prison officials maliciously and sadistically use[d] force to cause harm."

A majority of the Court, nonetheless, buttressed the ruling in *Hudson v. McMillian*, with Justices Thomas and Scalia dissenting, in *Helling v. McKinney*, 509 U.S. 25 (1993). There, Justice White held that a prison inmate could raise an Eighth Amendment claim against prison authorities who Donald Helling said showed "deliberate indifference" to his objections to being housed with another cellmate who smoked five packs of cigarettes a day and, thus, involuntarily exposed Helling to health risks. As to the amendment's applicability to such conditions of imprisonment, Justice White observed:

> Contemporary standards of decency require no less. In *Estelle* [*v. Gamble*, 429 U.S. 97 (1976)], we concluded that although accidental or inadvertent failure to provide adequate medical care to a prisoner would not violate the Eighth Amendment, "deliberate indifference to serious medical needs of prisoners" violates the Amendment because it constitutes the unnecessary and wanton infliction of pain contrary to contemporary standards of decency. . . .

For the same reasons expressed in their dissenting opinion in *Hudson*— namely, that the Eighth Amendment only applies to sentencing and not to the conditions of imprisonment and rejecting the "evolving standard of decency"—Justices Thomas and Scalia dissented in *Helling*. However, the justices unanimously reinstated a suit for damages brought by a transsexual prison inmate in *Farmer v. Brennan*, 511 U.S. 825 (1994). Dee Farmer, who is serving a twenty-year sentence for credit card fraud, was born male but underwent estrogen therapy, had breast implants, and had unsuccessful surgery to remove his testicles. In prison, Farmer was raped and subsequently claimed that prison officials should not have put him with the general prison population because they should have known that a transgender woman "who projects feminine characteristics" would be vulnerable to sexual assaults. In holding for the Court that Farmer could sue for damages based on showing that prison officials exhibited "deliberate indifference" to his safety, Justice Souter observed, "Being violently assaulted in prison is simply not part of the penalty that criminal offenders pay for their offenses against society." Although concurring in the judgment in a separate opinion, Justice Thomas maintained his position that the Eighth Amendment does not extend to brutality among prisoners or inflicted by guards. As Justice Thomas put it, "Punishment, from the time of the founding through the present day, has always meant a fine, penalty or confinement inflicted upon a person by the authority of the law and the judgment and sentence of a court, for some crime or offense committed by him. . . . Because the unfortunate attack that befell the petitioner was not part of his sentence, it did not constitute 'punishment' under the Eighth Amendment."

Finally, in *Brown v. Plata*, 563 U.S. 493 (2011), a bare majority of the Roberts Court affirmed a court order for the release of approximately 40,000 inmates in California's prison system due to overcrowding that created conditions of cruel and unusual punishment. The system was designed to house about 80,000, but at various times held up to 160,000 prisoners; and the lower court ordered a reduction of the prison population to 100,000. In affirming the lower court, the majority emphasized, "As many as 200 prisoners may live in a gymnasium, monitored by as few as two or three correctional officers . . . [and that as] many as 54 prisoners may share a single toilet," as well as that about one prisoner per week commits suicide. Writing for the Court, Justice Kennedy acknowledged, "The release of prisoners in large numbers—assuming the state finds no other way to comply with the order—is a matter of undoubted, grave concern." "Yet," he stressed, "so too is the continuing injury and harm resulting from these serious constitutional violations. . . . A prison that deprives prisoners of basic sustenance, including adequate medical care, is incompatible with the concept of human dignity and has no place in civilized society." Justice Kennedy underscored that the state could achieve the reduction by a variety of means, including releasing the least dangerous convicts, transferring inmates to other prisons, and building more prisons. Justices Ginsburg, Breyer, Sotomayor, and Kagan joined his opinion. By contrast, dissenting Justice Scalia blasted the majority for affirming "perhaps the most radical injunction issued by a court in our nation's history." They emphasized that courts exceed their authority and are ill-equipped to bring about such major changes through "structural injunctions" and "institutional-reform litigation." In a separate dissent, Justice Alito, joined by Chief Justice Roberts, lamented the impact on public safety: "I fear that today's decision, like prior prisoner-release orders, will lead to a grim roster of victims. I hope that I am wrong. In a few years, we will see."

In sum, the Eighth Amendment applies to the conditions and treatment of prison inmates. But the standard varies depending on the nature of the case. In conditions of imprisonment cases, like *Farmer v. Brennan*, the standard is whether prison officials showed a "deliberate indifference" to the conditions and safety of inmates. In cases involving prison officials' use of excessive force, as in *Hudson v. McMillian*, the standard is whether "prison officials maliciously and sadistically use[d] force to cause harm." The Roberts Court reaffirmed that decision in *Wilkins v. Gaddy*, 559 U.S. 34 (2010).

NOTES

1. *Hutto v. Finney*, 437 U.S. 678 (1978); and *Estelle v. Gamble*, 429 U.S. 97 (1976).
2. *Ingraham v. Wright*, 430 U.S. 651 (1977).
3. *Whitley v. Albers*, 475 U.S. 312 (1986).

Ewing v. California
538 U.S. 11, 123 S.CT. 1179 (2003)

In the 1990s, about half the states enacted "three-strikes-and-you're-out" laws, requiring mandatory sentences, including life imprisonment, for individuals convicted of three felonies. California's 1994 law provides that a defendant who has two or more prior felony convictions must receive "an indeterminate term of life imprisonment," with the possibility of parole after twenty-five years of imprisonment. In addition, the law gives prosecutors and judges the discretion to treat certain offenses—known as "wobblers"—as either felonies or misdemeanors, and some crimes that would otherwise be misdemeanors may become wobblers and counted as felonies under the law. For example, a petty theft, a misdemeanor, may become a wobbler and treated as a felony when the defendant previously served prison time for committing a theft-related crime.

In 2000, when on parole from serving a nine-year prison term for committing three burglaries and a robbery, Gary Ewing walked into a pro golf shop and walked out with three golf clubs, priced at $399 each, concealed in his pants leg. An employee observed him limp out of the shop and called the police. The police apprehended him in the parking lot and arrested him. Ewing was charged with and convicted of one count of a felony grand theft of personal property in excess of $400. As required under California's three-strikes law, the prosecutor sought a lifetime prison sentence. At sentencing, Ewing asked the court to reduce the conviction for grand theft, a "wobbler," to a misdemeanor so as to avoid a three-strikes sentence. The trial judge, however, determined that the theft of the golf clubs should remain a felony and that the four prior strikes for burglary and robbery should stand. Ewing was sentenced to twenty-five years to life in prison. A state appellate court affirmed and the Supreme Court of California denied review, whereupon Ewing appealed to the Supreme Court.

The judgment was affirmed by a 5–4 vote. Justice O'Connor delivered the opinion for the Court, which Chief Justice Rehnquist and Justice Kennedy joined. Justices Scalia and Thomas filed concurring opinions. Justices Stevens and Breyer filed dissenting opinions, which Justices Souter and Ginsburg joined.

■ ■ ■

☐ *Justice O'CONNOR announced the judgment of the Court and delivered an opinion in which THE CHIEF JUSTICE and Justice KENNEDY join.*

The Eighth Amendment, which forbids cruel and unusual punishments, contains a "narrow proportionality principle" that "applies to noncapital sentences." *Harmelin v. Michigan*, 501 U.S. 957 (1991). We have most recently addressed the proportionality principle as applied to terms of years in a series of cases beginning with *Rummel v. Estelle*, [445 U.S. 263 (1980)].

In *Rummel*, we held that it did not violate the Eighth Amendment for a State to sentence a three-time offender to life in prison with the possibility of parole. Like Ewing, Rummel was sentenced to a lengthy prison term under a recidivism statute. Rummel's two prior offenses were a 1964 felony for "fraudulent use of a credit card to obtain $80 worth of goods or services," and a 1969 felony conviction for "passing a forged check in the amount of $28.36." His triggering offense was a conviction for felony theft—"obtaining $120.75 by false pretenses."

This Court ruled that "[h]aving twice imprisoned him for felonies, Texas was entitled to place upon Rummel the onus of one who is simply unable to bring his conduct within the social norms prescribed by the criminal law of the State." The recidivism statute "is nothing more than a societal decision that when such a person commits yet another felony, he should be subjected to the admittedly serious penalty of incarceration for life, subject only to the State's judgment as to whether to grant him parole." . . .

In *Hutto v. Davis*, 454 U.S. 370 (1982), the defendant was sentenced to two consecutive terms of 20 years in prison for possession with intent to distribute nine ounces of marijuana and distribution of marijuana. We held that such a sentence was constitutional: "In short, *Rummel* stands for the proposition that federal courts should be reluctant to review legislatively mandated terms of imprisonment, and that successful challenges to the proportionality of particular sentences should be exceedingly rare."

Three years after *Rummel*, in *Solem v. Helm*, 463 U.S. 277 (1983), we held that the Eighth Amendment prohibited "a life sentence without possibility of parole for a seventh nonviolent felony." The triggering offense in *Solem* was "uttering a 'no account' check for $100." We specifically stated that the Eighth Amendment's ban on cruel and unusual punishments "prohibits . . . sentences that are disproportionate to the crime committed," and that the "constitutional principle of proportionality has been recognized explicitly in this Court for almost a century." The *Solem* Court then explained that three factors may be relevant to a determination of whether a sentence is so disproportionate that it violates the Eighth Amendment: "(i) The gravity of the offense and the harshness of the penalty; (ii) the sentences imposed on other criminals in the same jurisdiction; and (iii) the sentences imposed for commission of the same crime in other jurisdictions."

Applying these factors in *Solem*, we struck down the defendant's sentence of life without parole. We specifically noted the contrast between that sentence and the sentence in *Rummel*, pursuant to which the defendant was eligible for parole. . . .

The proportionality principles in our cases . . . guide our application of the Eighth Amendment in the new context that we are called upon to consider.

For many years, most States have had laws providing for enhanced sentencing of repeat offenders. Yet between 1993 and 1995, three strikes laws effected a sea change in criminal sentencing throughout the Nation. These laws responded to widespread public concerns about crime by targeting the class of offenders who pose the greatest threat to public safety: career criminals. . . .

Throughout the States, legislatures enacting three strikes laws made a deliberate policy choice that individuals who have repeatedly engaged in serious or violent criminal behavior, and whose conduct has not been deterred by more conventional approaches to punishment, must be isolated from society in order to protect the public safety. Though three strikes laws may be relatively new, our tradition of deferring to state legislatures in making and implementing such important policy decisions is longstanding.

Our traditional deference to legislative policy choices finds a corollary in the principle that the Constitution "does not mandate adoption of any one penological theory." A sentence can have a variety of justifications, such as incapacitation, deterrence, retribution, or rehabilitation. Some or all of these justifications may play a role in a State's sentencing scheme. Selecting the sentencing rationales is generally a policy choice to be made by state legislatures, not federal courts.

When the California Legislature enacted the three strikes law, it made a judgment that protecting the public safety requires incapacitating criminals who have already been convicted of at least one serious or violent crime. Nothing in the Eighth Amendment prohibits California from making that choice. . . .

Against this backdrop, we consider Ewing's claim that his three strikes sentence of 25 years to life is unconstitutionally disproportionate to his offense of "shoplifting three golf clubs." We first address the gravity of the offense compared to the harshness of the penalty. At the threshold, we note that Ewing incorrectly frames the issue. The gravity of his offense was not merely "shoplifting three golf clubs." Rather, Ewing was convicted of felony grand theft for stealing nearly $1,200 worth of merchandise after previously having been convicted of at least two "violent" or "serious" felonies. Even standing alone, Ewing's theft should not be taken lightly. His crime was certainly not "one of the most passive felonies a person could commit." To the contrary, the Supreme Court of California has noted the "seriousness" of grand theft in the context of proportionality review. That grand theft is a "wobbler" under California law is of no moment. Though California courts have discretion to reduce a felony grand theft charge to a misdemeanor, it remains a felony for all purposes "unless and until the trial court imposes a misdemeanor sentence." . . .

Ewing's sentence is justified by the State's public-safety interest in incapacitating and deterring recidivist felons, and amply supported by his own long, serious criminal record. Ewing has been convicted of numerous misdemeanor and felony offenses, served nine separate terms of incarceration, and committed most of his crimes while on probation or parole. His prior "strikes" were serious felonies including robbery and three residential burglaries. To be sure, Ewing's sentence is a long one. But it reflects a rational legislative judgment, entitled to deference, that offenders who have committed serious or violent felonies and who continue to commit felonies must be incapacitated. . . .

We hold that Ewing's sentence of 25 years to life in prison, imposed for the offense of felony grand theft under the three strikes law, is not grossly disproportionate and therefore does not violate the Eighth Amendment's prohibition on cruel and unusual punishments. The judgment of the California Court of Appeal is affirmed.

☐ *Justice SCALIA, concurring in the judgment.*

In my concurring opinion in *Harmelin v. Michigan*, I concluded that the Eighth Amendment's prohibition of "cruel and unusual punishments" was aimed at excluding only certain modes of punishment, and was not a "guarantee against disproportionate sentences." Out of respect for the principle of *stare decisis*, I might nonetheless accept the contrary holding of *Solem v. Helm*—that the Eighth Amendment contains a narrow proportionality principle—if I felt I could intelligently apply it. This case demonstrates why I cannot. . . .

☐ *Justice STEVENS, with whom Justice SOUTER, Justice GINSBURG and Justice BREYER join, dissenting.*

The concurrences prompt this separate writing to emphasize that proportionality review is not only capable of judicial application but also required by the Eighth Amendment.

"The Eighth Amendment succinctly prohibits 'excessive' sanctions." *Atkins v. Virginia*, 536 U.S. 304 (2002). It "would be anomalous indeed" to suggest that the Eighth Amendment makes proportionality review applicable in the context of bail and fines but not in the context of other forms of punishment, such as imprisonment. *Solem v. Helm.* Rather, by broadly prohibiting excessive sanctions, the Eighth Amendment directs judges to exercise their wise judgment in assessing the proportionality of all forms of punishment.

The absence of a black-letter rule does not disable judges from exercising their discretion in construing the outer limits on sentencing authority that the Eighth Amendment imposes. After all, judges are "constantly called upon to draw . . . lines in a variety of contexts," and to exercise their judgment to give meaning to the Constitution's broadly phrased protections. For example, the Due Process Clause directs judges to employ proportionality review in assessing the constitutionality of punitive damages awards on a case-by-case basis. See, e.g., *BMW of North America, Inc. v. Gore*, 517 U.S. 559 (1996). . . . Throughout most of the Nation's history—before guideline sentencing became so prevalent—federal and state trial judges imposed specific sentences pursuant to grants of authority that gave them uncabined discretion within broad ranges. Likewise, I think it clear that the Eighth Amendment's prohibition of "cruel and unusual punishments" expresses a broad and basic proportionality principle that takes into account all of the justifications for penal sanctions. It is this broad proportionality principle that would preclude reliance on any of the justifications for punishment to support, for example, a life sentence for overtime parking. Accordingly, I respectfully dissent.

B | *Capital Punishment*

Social forces and litigation aimed at persuading the Court to declare capital punishment unconstitutional under the Eighth Amendment and the Fourteenth Amendment's equal protection clause finally reached the justices in the early 1970s. There had been a steady decline in the number of executions since the 1930s, when more than 165 convicts were annually put to death. Between 1960 and 1967, there were fewer than fifty-two executions per year, and after 1967, when most states adopted a moratorium on carrying out death sentences, there were no executions until 1977, when Gary Gilmore was executed by shooting. The moratorium and growing controversy over capital punishment were largely due to the pressures of the NAACP Legal Defense Fund, the American Civil Liberties Union (ACLU), and the American Bar Association (ABA). These groups pointed out the fact that black convicts disproportionately received death sentences, especially when convicted for rape. Variations among state laws and the absence of standards for imposing capital punishment raised the issue of whether executions violated the Fourteenth Amendment equal protection clause as well as whether they constituted cruel and unusual punishment under the Eighth Amendment. These concerns have been underscored with a number of states instituting moratoriums on executions because in recent years more death row inmates were released from prison (often because new DNA evidence proved their innocence) than were executed. Opposition to the death penalty is also growing among a wide range of organizations, including the American Bar Association, the Conference of Catholic Bishops, and the Christian Coalition.

The controversy over capital punishment proved divisive for the Court. Initially, in *McGautha v. California* and *Crampton v. Ohio*, 402 U.S. 183 (1971), the justices split 6–3 when holding that states need not specify in their statutes the factors that juries must consider when imposing death sentences. The Court also indicated that bifurcated trials—that is, a two-stage trial in which juries first determine a defendant's guilt and second decide on a sentence—are preferable to single trials in which juries simultaneously convict and sentence, but held that bifurcated trials are not constitutionally required.

Despite the rulings in *McGautha* and *Crampton* just the year before, the imposition of capital punishment in one murder and two rape cases was held to violate the Eighth and Fourteenth Amendments in *Furman v. Georgia* (1972) (excerpted below) and two companion cases.

The justices were sharply divided, however. The opinion announcing the Court's decision was a brief *per curiam* opinion followed by 231 pages of separate opinions filed by all nine justices, five concurring and four dissenting. Notice in the excerpts reprinted here that even those justices in the majority could not agree on the basis for the Court's ruling. Justices Douglas, Stewart, and White take an analytical approach, interpreting the Eighth Amendment in light of the commands of the Fourteenth Amendment's due process and equal protection clauses. Only Justices Brennan and Marshall address the normative question in maintaining that capital punishment is unconstitutional due to its severity, finality, excessiveness, and denial of human dignity. By contrast, the four dissenters question the role of the Court in overturning capital punishment laws and contend that it should defer to the states on the matter. Rehnquist's dissenting opinion, though, also takes up the normative question and justifies capital punishment on a theory of society's retribution.

Furman immediately escalated the controversy over capital punishment. Thirty-five states enacted new legislation specifying the factors that juries must consider when issuing death sentences. Georgia, Florida, Texas, and twenty-two other states adopted laws requiring juries to consider specific *aggravating factors* (justifying the imposition of capital punishment) and *mitigating factors* (justifying the imposition of an alternative sentence to the death penalty). Louisiana, North Carolina, Oklahoma, and seven other states mandated capital punishment for particular crimes.

By 1976 there were over 600 people on death row under the post-*Furman* laws, and the Court faced numerous challenges to their constitutionality. In a batch of rulings handed down in 1976, the Court squarely ruled that capital punishment is not unconstitutional. In the leading case, *Gregg v. Georgia*, 428 U.S. 153 (1976), with only Brennan and Marshall dissenting, the Court upheld Georgia's statute specifying the aggravating and mitigating circumstances for imposing the death penalty and providing for bifurcated trials.

Woodson v. North Carolina, 428 U.S. 280 (1976), and *Roberts v. Louisiana*, 428 U.S. 325 (1976), however, on a 5–4 vote struck down laws requiring mandatory death sentences for certain crimes. There, a plurality of justices (Stewart, Powell, and Stevens) were joined by Brennan and Marshall (who continued to maintain their position that capital punishment is unconstitutional per se). Stewart's plurality opinion struck down mandatory death sentences for four reasons: (1) there was evidence that juries often fail to convict under mandatory death sentence statutes; (2) these laws provide no standards for guiding juries in their sentencing and fail to allow them to show mercy; (3) the laws also fail to provide for the "particularized consideration" of the accused and the circumstances of the crime, and, (4) because capital punishment is different from every other form of punishment (in its finality), its imposition requires individualized sentencing.

The Court's insistence on individualized sentencing was further underscored in *Lockett v. Ohio* (1978) (see excerpt below), holding that states may not limit the kinds of mitigating factors that juries may consider when deciding whether to impose the death penalty.

While the Court continued to confront numerous procedural challenges to the execution of death sentences, the 1976 rulings made clear that there was not a majority on the Court for striking down capital punishment per se. In what was widely regarded as the last major broadside attack on the wholesale imposition of the death penalty in *McCleskey v. Kemp* (1987) (excerpted below), the justices split 5–4 in holding that statistics, showing that blacks who murder whites receive the death penalty more often than whites who kill blacks, did not prove racial bias in the imposition of capital punishment.

One particularly controversial practice in the imposition of capital punishment was prosecutorial use during sentencing of so-called victim-impact statements (describing the victim and the impact of his or her murder on relatives). By a 5–4 vote, *Booth v. Maryland*, 482 U.S. 496 (1987), disapproved of the use of victim-impact statements. Justice Powell, the author of the Court's opinion, cast the deciding vote. When he retired at the end of the 1986 term, there was speculation that his replacement, Justice Anthony Kennedy, would tip the balance on the Court toward reconsidering and upholding victim-impact statements. Yet, Justice White, who dissented in *Booth*, switched sides in *South Carolina v. Gathers*, 490 U.S. 805 (1989), joining a bare majority for again disallowing the use of victim-impact statements. But, following Justice Brennan's retirement in 1990, the balance on the high bench shifted further. And in *Payne v. Tennessee*, 501 U.S. 808 (1991) (excerpted below), the Rehnquist Court overturned both *Booth* and *Gathers*, deciding to permit the use of victim-impact statements at the sentencing stage of capital trials.

Two other recurrent controversies involved the execution of mentally disabled persons and minors. The execution of mentally impaired convicts was first confronted in *Ford v. Wainwright*, 477 U.S. 399. There, the Eighth Amendment was held to bar the execution of convicts who were (or had gone while on death row) insane. However, a 5–4 ruling in *Penry v. Lynaugh*, 492 U.S. 302 (1989), the Court the execution of convicted murderers who are mildly or moderately mentally disabled. But the Court reversed that decision in Virginia (2002) (excerpted below).

- CONSTITUTIONAL HISTORY

The Imposition and Execution of Capital Punishment

After a ten-year moratorium on executions in the late 1960s and early 1970s, the Supreme Court ruled that the death penalty is not cruel and unusual punishment. More states added the death penalty, and the federal government increased the number of crimes for which the death penalty may be imposed. As a result, the number of persons on death row increased dramatically. But more recently the number of people on death row and annually executed has declined due to a number of factors. DNA tests established the innocence of a sizable number of those convicted of murder, and a number of Republican and Democratic governors declared moratoriums on executions. Groups like the U.S. Conference of Catholic Bishops, who oppose the death penalty on moral grounds, renewed the debate. The American Bar Association (ABA) also called for a halt to executions because capital punishment carried out in arbitrary and capricious ways, in violation of due process and the equal protection of the law. In addition, there has a rise in the number of life-without-parole sentences instead of

Number of Death Row Inmates, 1953–2018

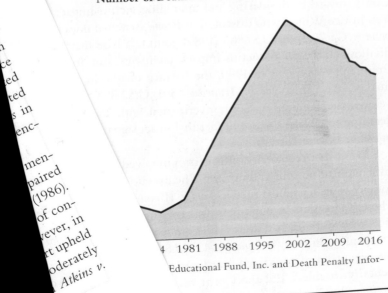

1981   1988   1995   2002   2009   2016

Educational Fund, Inc. and Death Penalty Infor-

capital punishment. Prosecutors seek the death penalty in less than 5 percent of all murder cases. Currently, twenty-one states and the District of Columbia ban capital punishment. In four states (California, Colorado, Pennsylvania, and Oregon) the governor has imposed a moratorium on the death penalty. In the twenty-nine states maintaining capital punishment, all permit execution by lethal injection, and nine of those allow execution by the electric chair and by gas chamber, and three by firing squad (Utah, Oklahoma, and Mississippi).

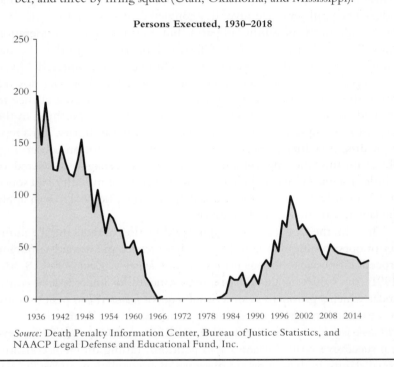

Persons Executed, 1930–2018

Source: Death Penalty Information Center, Bureau of Justice Statistics, and NAACP Legal Defense and Educational Fund, Inc.

As for the execution of minors, initially, a bare majority vacated the death sentence of a sixteen-year-old in *Eddings v. Oklahoma*, 455 U.S. 104 (1982), and then ruled in *Thompson v. Oklahoma*, 487 U.S. 815 (1988), that the Eighth Amendment forbids the execution of those fifteen years old or younger at the time of their crimes. But with Justice O'Connor casting the deciding vote in *Stanford v. Kentucky*, 492 U.S. 361 (1989), the Court held that the death penalty may be imposed on convicts who are sixteen years old and older. However, that decision was subsequently overturned in *Roper v. Simmons*, 543 U.S. 551 (2005) based essentially on the same reasoning as in *Atkins v. Virginia* (2002).

Continuing a trend in the last couple of decades, a bare majority of the Court struck down mandatory life sentences without the possibility of parole for juvenile murderers in *Miller v. Alabama*, 567 U.S. 460 (2012), invalidating a federal statute and mandatory-sentencing laws in twenty-eight states. Writing for the Court, Justice Kagan held, "Mandatory life without parole for a juvenile precludes consideration of his chronological age and its hallmark features—among them, immaturity, impetuosity, and failure to appreciate risks and consequences. . . . It prevents taking into account the family and home environment that surrounds him—and from which he cannot usually extricate himself—no matter how brutal or dysfunctional." In doing so, the Court ruled that judges may still sentence juveniles convicted of murder to a life sentence without the possibility of parole but must take into consideration mitigating circumstances. Chief Justice Roberts and Justices Scalia, Thomas, and Alito dissented. Dissenting Justice Alito countered, "Even a 17½-year-old who sets off a bomb in a crowded mall or guns down a dozen students and teachers is a 'child' and must be given a chance to persuade a judge to permit his release into society. . . . Nothing in the Constitution supports this arrogation of legislative authority." In a separate dissent, Chief Justice Roberts echoed that position, observing: "Determining the appropriate sentence for a teenager convicted of murder presents grave and challenging questions of morality and social policy [that legislatures should decide]. Our role, however, is to apply the law, not to answer such questions."

In sum, the Court has pressed in the direction of reducing the number of opportunities for appealing death sentences and toward removing procedural obstacles to executions. In *McCleskey v. Zant*, 499 U.S. 467 (1991), the Court handed down a new standard for lower federal courts under which a prisoner's second or subsequent *habeas corpus* petition must be dismissed except in exceptional circumstances. The importance of *McCleskey v. Zant* lies in the fact that death row inmates typically file several successive writ of *habeas corpus* petitions, raising different constitutional claims, in their efforts to overturn their convictions and sentences. Approximately 40 percent of all death sentences have been overturned by lower courts upon finding constitutional errors in the conviction and sentencing of death-row inmates. By limiting lower courts' consideration of successive petitions in *McCleskey v. Zant*, the Rehnquist Court thus enabled states to carry out death sentences more quickly; under federal law, though, there is no limit on the number of *habeas corpus* petitions that may be filed by inmates in federal prisons. Moreover, the Antiterrorism and Effective Death Penalty Act of 1996, which basically limits state death row inmates to one *habeas corpus* review in federal courts unless new claims are presented, was upheld in *Felker v. Turpin*, 518 U.S. 651 (1996).

Finally, in a sharply fragmented ruling, in *Baze v. Rees*, 553 U.S. 35 (2008), the Roberts Court concluded that the most common method of execution by lethal injection does not violate the Eighth Amendment. Writing for a plurality, joined by only Justices Kennedy and Alito, Chief Justice Roberts adopted as a standard for assessing the validity of an execution method whether it poses a "substantial risk of serious harm," and rejected the death row inmate's claim that the standard should be "unnecessary risk." Chief Justice Roberts's opinion left open the possibility of further challenges to the use of lethal drugs under a specific procedure of other states; lethal injection is used in twenty-nine other states and the federal government. Especially, he noted that states are free to choose a procedure for carrying out executions so long as they are shown to be "feasible, readily implemented, and in fact significantly reduce a substantial risk of severe pain." But Chief Justice Roberts also added that "[i]f a state refuses to adopt such an alternative in the face of these documented advantages, without a legitimate penological justification for adhering to its current method of execution, then a state's refusal to change its method can be viewed as 'cruel and unusual punishment' under the Eighth Amendment." In a concurring opinion, Justice Stevens contended that the ruling, instead of ending the controversy over the use of a three-drug protocol injection, would only invite more litigation. He also noted that based on his experience, the imposition of capital punishment constituted a pointless and needless extinction of life with only negligible social benefits.

In a no less sharply divided ruling, a bare majority struck down death penalty laws in Louisiana and five other states that imposed capital punishment for crimes like child rape. Writing for the majority in *Kennedy v. Louisiana*, 554 U.S. 407 (2008), Justice Kennedy categorically ruled out the death penalty for individual crimes "where the victim's life was not taken," but did not rule out capital punishment for "offenses against the state" such as treason, terrorism, or espionage. The Court had previously overruled laws imposing the death penalty for the crime of rape of an adult woman as disproportionate to the offense in *Coker v. Georgia*, 433 U.S. 584 (1977). Justice Kennedy based the decision on "evolving standards of decency" and the Court's "own independent judgment." Writing for the dissenters, Justice Alito, joined by Chief Justice Roberts and Justices Scalia and Thomas, sharply criticized the majority's reasoning and maintained that the issue should be left to the states.

In a narrow yet very divisive ruling in *Glossip v. Gross*, 135 S.Ct. 2726 (2015), a bare majority of the Court rejected a challenge to the use of midazolam in executions. After *Baze v. Rees,* most states started using three-drug "cocktails." However, some of these drugs became unavailable due to European companies' refusal to sell them for executions, and

■ IN COMPARATIVE PERSPECTIVE

Capital Punishment around the World

Countries and Territories That Have Abolished the Death Penalty for All Crimes (N = 105)

Albania	Dominican Republic	Malta	São Tomé and Príncipe
Andorra	Ecuador	Marshall Islands	Senegal
Angola	Estonia	Mauritius	Serbia
Argentina	Finland	Mexico	Seychelles
Armenia	Fiji	Micronesia	Slovak Republic
Australia	France	Moldova	Slovenia
Austria	Gabon	Monaco	Solomon Islands
Azerbaijan	Georgia	Montenegro	South Africa
Belgium	Germany	Mozambique	Spain
Benin	Greece	Namibia	Suriname
Bhutan	Guinea	Nauru	Sweden
Bolivia	Guinea-Bissau	Nepal	Switzerland
Bosnia-Herzegovina	Haiti	Netherlands	Timor-Leste
	Holy See	New Zealand	Togo
Bulgaria	Honduras	Nicaragua	Turkey
Burundi	Hungary	Niue	Turkmenistan
Cambodia	Iceland	Norway	Tuvalu
Canada	Ireland	Palau	Ukraine
Cape Verde	Italy	Panama	United Kingdom
Colombia	Kiribati	Paraguay	Uruguay
Cook Islands	Kyrgyzstan	Philippines	Uzbekistan
Congo	Latvia	Poland	Vanuatu
Costa Rica	Liberia	Portugal	Vatican City State
Côte d'Ivoire	Lichtenstein	Romania	Venezuela
Croatia	Lithuania	Rwanda	
Cyprus	Luxembourg	Samoa	
Czech Republic	Macedonia	San Marino	
Denmark	Madagascar		
Djibouti			

Countries and Territories That Have Abolished the Death Penalty for Ordinary Crimes (N = 5)

Chile	Kazakhstan	Peru
El Salvador	Israel	

Countries and Territories That Have De Facto Abolished the Death Penalty (N = 30)

Algeria	Ghana	Mongolia	Sierra Leone
Brunei	Grenada	Morocco	South Korea
Burkina Faso	Kenya	Myanmar (Burma)	Sri Lanka
Cameroon	Laos	Niger	Swaziland
Central African	Liberia	Papua New	Tajikistan
Republic	Malawi	Guinea	Tanzania
Eritrea	Maldives	Russian Federation	Tonga
	Mali		Tunisia
	Mauritania		Zambia

Countries and Territories That Retain the Death Penalty (N = 57)

Afghanistan	Egypt	Lebanon	Singapore
Antigua and	Equatorial	Lesotho	Somalia
Barbuda	Guinea	Libya	South Sudan
Bahamas	Ethiopia	Malaysia	Sudan
Bahrain	Gambia	Nigeria	Syria
Bangladesh	Guatemala	North Korea	Taiwan
Barbados	Guyana	Oman	Thailand
Belarus	India	Pakistan	Trinidad and
Belize	Indonesia	Palestinian	Tobago
Botswana	Iran	Authority	Uganda
Chad	Iraq	Qatar	United Arab
China	Jamaica	Saint Kitts and	Emirates
Comoros	Japan	Nevis	United States
Cuba	Jordan	Saint Lucia	Vietnam
Dominica	Kuwait	Saint Vincent	Yemen
		Saudi Arabia	Zimbabwe

Source: Amnesty International, "The Death Penalty: List of Abolitionist and Retentionist Countries," as of July, 2018. See also Andrew Novak, *The Global Decline of the Mandatory Death Penalty* (Burlington, VT: Ashgate, 2014).

■ INSIDE THE COURT

Justice Arthur Goldberg's Role in the Controversy over Capital Punishment and Opinion in Rudolph v. Alabama

At the end of his first term on the Court (1962–1963), Justice Arthur Goldberg circulated to the other members of the Warren Court an unpublished twenty-page "Memorandum to the Conference from Mr. Justice Goldberg." In it he pointed out that a number of cases on the Court's docket involved capital punishment, but not one challenged its constitutionality per se. The "petitioners' failure to urge [the unconstitutionality of the death penalty] should not preclude this Court from considering this matter," observed Goldberg at the outset, pointing out that

> [t]his Court has never explicitly considered whether, and under what circumstances, the Eighth and Fourteenth Amendments to the United States Constitution proscribe the imposition of the death penalty. The Court has, of course, implicitly decided (in every case affirming a capital conviction) that the death penalty is constitutional. But in light of the worldwide trend toward abolition, I think this Court should now request argument and explicitly consider this constantly recurring issue.

Citing various studies on the imposition of capital punishment in the states and in other countries, Goldberg tried to persuade his brethren to adopt his position on capital punishment: "I am convinced that whatever may be said of times past, 'the evolving standards of decency that mark the progress of [our] maturing society' now condemn as barbaric and inhuman the deliberate institutionalized taking of human life by the state." But, except for Justice Brennan, no other member of the Warren Court yet wanted to confront the issue of capital punishment, nor strike it down as unconstitutional.

Failing to persuade other justices to reach out and tackle the constitutionality of capital punishment, Goldberg filed the following dissent from the denial of *certiorari* in *Rudolph v. Alabama*, 375 U.S. 917 (1963), a case appealing a death sentence imposed on a convicted rapist. This opinion is generally credited with sending a signal to lawyers around the country to challenge the constitutionality of capital punishment in their appeals and thereby force the Court's hand. Goldberg left the Court in 1965, but his position became championed by Justice Brennan in *Furman v. Georgia* (1972) (excerpted below) and in his subsequent opinions on capital punishment.

SUPREME COURT OF THE UNITED STATES

No. 308, Misc.—October Term, 1963.

| Frank Lee Rudolph, Petitioner. v. State of Alabama. | On Petition for Writ of Certiorari and Affidavit In Forma Pauperis to the Supreme Court of Alabama. |

[October 21, 1963.]

Mr. Justice Goldberg, with whom Mr. Justice Douglas and Mr. Justice Brennan join, dissenting.

I would grant certiorari in this case and in *Snider* v. *Cunningham*, 169, Misc., to consider whether the Eighth and Fourteenth Amendments to the United States Constitution permit the imposition of the death penalty on a convicted rapist who has neither taken nor endangered human life.

The following questions, *inter alia*, seem relevant and worthy of argument and consideration:

(1) In light of the trend both in this country and throughout the world against punishing rape by death,[1]

---

[1] The United Nations recently conducted a survey on the laws, regulations and practices relating to capital punishment throughout the world. In addition to the United States, 65 countries and territories responded. All but five—Nationalist China, Northern Rhodesia, Nyasaland, Republic of South Africa, and the United States— reported that their laws no longer permit the imposition of the death penalty for rape.

The following of the United States reported that their laws no longer permit the imposition of the death penalty for rape: Alaska, Arizona, California, Colorado, Connecticut, Delaware, Hawaii, Idaho, Illinois, Indiana, Iowa, Kansas, Maine, Massachusetts, Michigan, Minnesota, Montana, Nebraska, New Hampshire, New Jersey, New Mexico, New York, North Dakota, Ohio, Oregon, Pennsylvania,

(continues)

■ INSIDE THE COURT
*Justice Arthur Goldberg's Role in the Controversy over Capital
Punishment and Opinion in* Rudolph v. Alabama *(continued)*

RUDOLPH *v.* ALABAMA.

does the imposition of the death penalty by those States
which retain it for rape violate "evolving standards of
decency that mark the progress of [our] maturing society," [2] or "standards of decency more or less universally
accepted?" [3]

(2) Is the taking of human life to protect a value other
than human life consistent with the constitutional proscription against "punishments which by their exces-

---

South Dakota, Tennessee, Utah, Vermont, Washington, Wisconsin
and Wyoming. The laws of the remaining States permit the imposition of the death penalty for rape, but some States do not, in fact,
impose it. United Nations, Capital Punishment (prepared by Mr.
Marc Ancel, Justice of the French Supreme Court) (N. Y. 1962)
38, 71–75.

[2] *Trop* v. *Dulles,* 356 U. S. 86, 101 (opinion of WARREN, C. J., joined
by Justices BLACK, DOUGLAS, and Whittaker).

[3] *Francis* v. *Resweber,* 329 U. S. 495, 469 (Frankfurter, J., concurring). See *Weems* v. *United States,* 217 U. S. 349, 373:

"Legislation, both statutory and constitutional, is enacted, it is true,
from an experience of evils, but its general language should not, therefore, be necessarily confined to the form that evil had theretofore
taken. Time works changes, brings into existence new conditions
and purpose. Therefore, a principle to be vital must be capable of
wider application than the mischief which gave it birth. This is
peculiarly true of constitutions. They are not ephemeral enactments,
designed to meeting passing occasions. They are, to use the words
of Chief Justice Marshall, 'designed to approach immortality as
nearly as human institutions can approach it.' The future is their
care and provision for events of good and bad tendencies of which no
prophecy can be made. In the application of a constitution, therefore, our contemplation cannot be only of what has been but of what
may be. Under any other rule a constitution would indeed be as
easy of application as it would be deficient in efficacy and power. Its
general principles would have little value and be converted by prece-

RUDOLPH v. ALABAMA.

sive . . . severity are greatly disproportioned to the offenses charged?"[4]

(3) Can the permissible aims of punishment (e. g., deterrence, isolation, rehabilitation)[5] be achieved as effectively by punishing rape less severely than by death (e. g., by life imprisonment);[6] if so, does the imposition of the death penalty for rape constitute "unnecessary cruelty?"[7]

---

dent into impotent and lifeless formulas. Rights declared in words might be lost in reality."

Also see *Ex parte Wilson*, 114 U. S. 417, 427–428:

"What punishments may be considered as infamous may be affected by the changes of opinions from one age to another. In former times, being put in the stocks was not considered as necessarily infamous . . . . But at the present day [it] might be thought an infamous punishment."

[4] *Weems* v. *United States*, 217 U. S. 349, 371. Cf. *Lambert* v. *California*, 355 U. S. 225, 231 (dissenting opinion of Frankfurter, J.).

[5] See, e. g., *Williams* v. *New York*, 337 U. S. 241; *Trop* v. *Dulles*, 356 U. S. 86, 111 (concurring opinion of BRENNAN, J.); *Blyew* v. *United States*, 13 Wall. 581, 600.

[6] The United Nations Report on Capital Punishment noted: "In Canada, rape ceased to be punishable with death in 1954: it is reported that there were 37 convictions for rape in 1950, 44 in 1953 and only 27 in 1954, the year of abolition; from 1957 to 1959 a steady decrease in convictions was noted (from 56 to 44), while in the same period the population of Canada increased by 27 per cent." United Nations, Capital Punishment, *supra*, note 1, at 54–55.

Such statistics must of course be regarded with caution. See, e. g., Royall Commission Report on Capital Punishment (1953) 24; Hart, Murder and Its Punishment, 12 N. W. L. Rev. 433, 457 (1957); Allen, Review, 10 Stan. L. Rev. 595, 600 (1958). In Canada, for example, the death sentence was rarely imposed for rape even prior to its formal abolition in 1954. In 1961 there was a slight increase in the number of convictions for rape. See United Nations, Capital Punishment, *supra*, note 1, at 55.

[7] *Weems* v. *United States*, 217 U. S. 349, 370. See *Robinson* v. *California*, 370 U. S. 660, 677 (concurring opinion of DOUGLAS, J.).

Oklahoma, among a few other states, switched to using midazolam as a replacement. Thereafter followed several well-publicized botched executions. One condemned man kicked and grimaced for forty-three minutes, only to die after the injection had been halted. Oklahoma death row inmates sued, claiming that the drug was not reliable, and hence cruel and unusual punishment. Writing for the majority, Justice Alito rejected their claims for (1) failing to show that states had better options than using midazolam, and (2) failing to prove that its use "is sure or likely to result in needless suffering." Of the four dissenters, Justice Breyer provocatively suggested reopening the old debate over the constitutionality of the death penalty, observing that "it is highly likely that the death penalty violates the Eighth Amendment," and adding, "At the very least, the Court should call for full briefing on the basic question." To which Justice Scalia shot back, calling his arguments "gobbleddy-gook," and charging, "Justice Breyer does not just reject the death penalty, he rejects the Enlightenment." No less scathing, though, Justice Sotomayor's dissent accused the majority of being "factually wrong" in determining that midazolam does not cause an intolerable risk of severe pain. And requiring inmates to identify, in her words, an "available alternative means by which the state may kill them is legally indefensible." Justice Alito countered that her "resort to this outlandish rhetoric reveals the weakness of its legal arguments."

Furman v. Georgia, Jackson v. Georgia, and *Branch v. Texas*
408 U.S. 238, 92 S.CT. 2726 (1972)

William Furman was convicted and sentenced to death for murder. Lucious Jackson was sentenced to death after being convicted for rape. And Elmer Branch was sentenced to death on his conviction for rape. After unsuccessful appeals in the Georgia and Texas supreme courts, their attorneys appealed to the Supreme Court, which granted review and consolidated the cases for decision. The Court struck down Georgia's and Texas's laws for imposing capital punishment. Excerpts from the concurring and dissenting opinions are reprinted here.

The Court's decision was 5–4, and the majority's opinion *per curiam.* Justices Douglas, Brennan, Stewart, White, and Marshall concurred; Chief Justice Burger and Justices Blackmun, Powell, and Rehnquist dissented.

■ ■ ■

☐ *Justice DOUGLAS, concurring.*

That the requirements of due process ban cruel and unusual punishment is now settled. *Louisiana ex rel. Francis v. Resweber*, 329 U.S. 459 [1947] (BURTON, J., dissenting): *Robinson v. California*, 370 U.S. 660 [1962]. It is also settled that the proscription of cruel and unusual punishments forbids the judicial imposition of them as well as their imposition by the legislature. *Weems v. United States*, 217 U.S. 349 [1910]. . . .

It has been assumed in our decisions that punishment by death is not cruel, unless the manner of execution can be said to be inhuman and barbarous. *In re Kemmler*, 136 U.S. 436 [1890]. It is also said in our opinions that the proscription of cruel and unusual punishments "is not fastened to the obsolete, but may acquire meaning as public opinion becomes enlightened by a humane justice." *Weems v. United States, supra.* A like statement was made in *Trop v. Dulles*, 356 U.S. 86 [1958], that the Eighth Amendment "must draw its meaning from the evolving standards of decency that mark the progress of a maturing society." . . .

It would seem to be incontestable that the death penalty inflicted on one defendant is "unusual" if it discriminates against him by reason of his race, religion, wealth, social position, or class, or if it is imposed under a procedure that gives room for the play of such prejudices. . . .

The words "cruel and unusual" certainly include penalties that are barbaric. But the words, at least when read in light of the English proscription against selective and irregular use of penalties, suggest that it is "cruel and unusual" to apply the death penalty—or any other penalty—selectively to minorities whose numbers are few, who are outcasts of society, and who are unpopular, but whom society is willing to see suffer though it would not countenance general application of the same penalty across the board. . . .

In a Nation committed to equal protection of the laws there is no permissible "caste" aspect of law enforcement. Yet we know that the discretion of judges and juries in imposing the death penalty enables the penalty to be selectively applied, feeding prejudices against the accused if he is poor and despised, and lacking political clout, or if he is a member of a suspect or unpopular minority, and saving those who by social position may be in a more protected position. In ancient Hindu law a Brahman was exempt from capital punishment, and under that law, "[g]enerally, in the law books, punishment increased in severity as social status diminished." We have, I fear, taken in practice the same position, partially as a result of making the death penalty discretionary and partially as a result of the ability of the rich to purchase the services of the most respected and most resourceful legal talent in the Nation.

The high service rendered by the "cruel and unusual" punishment clause of the Eighth Amendment is to require legislatures to write penal laws that are evenhanded, nonselective, and nonarbitrary, and to require judges to see to it that general laws are not applied sparsely, selectively, and spottily to unpopular groups. . . .

Any law which is nondiscriminatory on its face may be applied in such a way as to violate the Equal Protection Clause of the Fourteenth Amendment. *Yick Wo v. Hopkins*, 118 U.S. 356 [1886]. Such conceivably might be the fate of a mandatory death penalty, where equal or lesser sentences were imposed on the elite, a harsher one on the minorities or members of the lower castes. Whether a mandatory death penalty would otherwise be constitutional is a question I do not reach.

I concur in the judgments of the Court.

☐ *Justice BRENNAN, concurring.*

Ours would indeed be a simple task were we required merely to measure a challenged punishment against those that history has long condemned. That narrow and unwarranted view of the Clause, however, was left behind with the 19th century. Our task today is more complex. We know "that the words of the [Clause] are not precise, and that their scope is not static." We know, therefore, that the Clause "must draw its meaning from the evolving standards of decency that mark the progress of a maturing society." That knowledge, of course, is but the beginning of the inquiry.

In *Trop v. Dulles*, it was said that "[t]he question is whether [a] penalty subjects the individual to a fate forbidden by the principle of civilized treatment guaranteed by the [Clause]." It was also said that a challenged punishment must be examined "in light of the basic prohibition against inhuman treatment" embodied in the Clause. It was said, finally, that:

> The basic concept underlying the [Clause] is nothing less than the dignity of man. While the State has the power to punish, the [Clause] stands to assure that this power be exercised within the limits of civilized standards.

At bottom, then, the Cruel and Unusual Punishments Clause prohibits the infliction of uncivilized and inhuman punishments. The State, even as it punishes, must treat its members with respect for their intrinsic worth as human beings. A punishment is "cruel and unusual," therefore, if it does not comport with human dignity.

This formulation, of course, does not of itself yield principles for assessing the constitutional validity of particular punishments. Nevertheless, even though "[t]his Court has had little occasion to give precise content to the [Clause]," there are principles recognized in our cases and inherent in the Clause sufficient to permit a judicial determination whether a challenged punishment comports with human dignity.

The primary principle is that a punishment must not be so severe as to be degrading to the dignity of human beings. Pain, certainly, may be a factor in the judgment. The infliction of an extremely severe punishment will often entail physical suffering. See *Weems v. United States*. Yet the Framers also knew "that there could be exercises of cruelty by laws other than those which inflicted bodily pain or mutilation." Even though "[t]here may be involved no physical mistreatment, no primitive torture," *Trop v. Dulles, supra*, severe mental pain may be inherent in the infliction of a particular punishment. See *Weems v. United States, supra*, . . . That, indeed, was one of the conclusions underlying the holding of the plurality in *Trop v. Dulles* that the punishment of expatriation violates the Clause. And the physical and mental suffering inherent in the punishment of *cadena temporal*, was an obvious basis for the Court's decision in *Weems v. United States* that the punishment was "cruel and unusual."

More than the presence of pain, however, is comprehended in the judgment that the extreme severity of a punishment makes it degrading to the dignity of human beings. The barbaric punishments condemned by history, "punishments which inflict torture, such as the rack, the thumb-screw, the iron boot, the stretching of limbs, and the like," are, of course, "attended with acute pain and suffering." *O'Neil v. Vermont*, 144 U.S. 323 (1892) (FIELD, J., dissenting). When we consider why they have been condemned, however, we realize that the pain involved is not the only reason. The true significance of these punishments is that they treat members of the human race as nonhumans, as objects to be toyed with and discarded. They are thus inconsistent with the fundamental premise of the Clause that even the vilest criminal remains a human being possessed of common human dignity. . . .

In determining whether a punishment comports with human dignity, we are aided also by a second principle inherent in the Clause—that the State must not arbitrarily inflict a severe punishment. This principle derives from the notion that the State does not respect human dignity when, without reason, it inflicts upon some people a severe punishment that it does not inflict upon others. Indeed, the very words "cruel and unusual punishments" imply condemnation of the arbitrary infliction of severe punishments. And, as we now know, the English history of the Clause reveals a particular concern with the establishment of a safeguard against arbitrary punishments. . . .

A third principle inherent in the Clause is that a severe punishment must not be unacceptable to contemporary society. Rejection by society, of course, is a strong indication that a severe punishment does not comport with human dignity. In applying this principle, however, we must make certain that the judicial determination is as objective as possible. Thus, for example, *Weems v. United States*, and *Trop v. Dulles*, suggest that one factor that may be considered is the existence of the punishment in jurisdictions other than those before the Court. *Wilkerson v. Utah* suggests that another factor to be considered is the historic usage of the punishment. *Trop v. Dulles, supra*, combined present acceptance with past usage by observing that "the death penalty has been employed throughout our history, and, in a day when it is still widely accepted, it cannot be said to violate the constitutional concept of cruelty." In *Robinson v. California*, [370 U.S. 660 (1962)], which involved the infliction of punishment for narcotics addiction, the Court went a step further, concluding simply that "in the light of contemporary human knowledge, a law which made a criminal offense of such a disease would doubtless be universally thought to be an infliction of cruel and unusual punishment." . . .

The final principle inherent in the Clause is that a severe punishment must not be excessive. A punishment is excessive under this principle if it is unnecessary: The infliction of a severe punishment by the State cannot comport with human dignity when it is nothing more than the pointless infliction of suffering. If there is a significantly less severe punishment adequate to achieve the purposes for which the punishment is inflicted, cf. *Robinson v. California, supra*, (DOUGLAS, J., concurring); *Trop v. Dulles, supra*, (BRENNAN, J., concurring), the punishment inflicted is unnecessary and therefore excessive. . . .

Thus, although "the death penalty has been employed throughout our history," *Trop v. Dulles* . . . in fact the history of this punishment is one of successive restriction. What was once a common punishment has become, in the context of a continuing moral debate, increasingly rare. The evolution of this punishment evidences, not that it is an inevitable part of the American scene, but that it has proved progressively more troublesome to the national conscience. The result of this movement is our current system of administering the punishment, under which death sentences are rarely imposed and death is even more rarely inflicted. It is, of course, "We, the People" who are responsible for the rarity both of the imposition and the carrying out of this punishment. Juries, "express[ing] the conscience of the community on the ultimate question of life or death," *Witherspoon v. Illinois,* [391 U.S. 510 (1968)], have been able to bring themselves to vote for death in a mere 100 or so cases among the thousands tried each year where the punishment is available. Governors, elected by and acting for us, have regularly commuted a substantial number of those sentences. And it is our society that insists upon due process of law to the end that no person will be unjustly put to death, thus ensuring that many more of those sentences will not be carried out. In sum, we have made death a rare punishment today.

The progressive decline in, and the current rarity of, the infliction of death demonstrate that our society seriously questions the appropriateness of this punishment today. The States point out that many legislatures authorize death as the punishment for certain crimes and that substantial segments of the public, as reflected in opinion polls and referendum votes, continue to support it. Yet the availability of this punishment through statutory authorization, as well as the polls and referenda, which amount simply to approval of that authorization, simply underscores the extent to which our society has in fact rejected this punishment. When an unusually severe punishment is authorized for wide-scale application but not, because of society's refusal, inflicted save in a few instances, the inference is compelling that there is a deep-seated reluctance to inflict it. Indeed, the likelihood is great that the punishment is tolerated only because of its disuse. The objective indicator of society's view of an unusually severe punishment is what society does with it, and today society will inflict death upon only a small sample of the eligible criminals. Rejection could hardly be more complete without becoming absolute. At the very least, I must conclude that contemporary society views this punishment with substantial doubt. . . .

In sum, the punishment of death is inconsistent with all four principles: Death is an unusually severe and degrading punishment; there is a strong probability that it is inflicted arbitrarily; its rejection by contemporary society is virtually total; and there is no reason to believe that it serves any penal purpose more effectively than the less severe punishment of imprisonment. The function of these principles is to enable a court to determine whether a punishment comports with human dignity. Death, quite simply, does not.

☐ *Justice STEWART, concurring.*

The penalty of death differs from all other forms of criminal punishment, not in degree but in kind. It is unique in its total irrevocability. It is unique in its rejection of rehabilitation of the convict as a basic purpose of criminal justice. And it is unique, finally, in its absolute renunciation of all that is embodied in our concept of humanity.

For these and other reasons, at least two of my Brothers have concluded that the infliction of the death penalty is constitutionally impermissible in all circumstances under the Eighth and Fourteenth Amendments.

Their case is a strong one. But I find it unnecessary to reach the ultimate question they would decide. See *Ashwander v. Tennessee Valley Authority*, 297 U.S. 288 [1936] (BRANDEIS, J., concurring). . . .

These death sentences are cruel and unusual in the same way that being struck by lightning is cruel and unusual. For, of all the people convicted of rapes and murders in 1967 and 1968, many just as reprehensible as these, the petitioners are among a capriciously selected random handful upon whom the sentence of death has in fact been imposed. My concurring Brothers have demonstrated that, if any basis can be discerned for the selection of these few to be sentenced to die, it is the constitutionally impermissible basis of race. See *McLaughlin v. Florida*, 379 U.S. 184 [1964]. But racial discrimination has not been proved, and I put it to one side. I simply conclude that the Eighth and Fourteenth Amendments cannot tolerate the infliction of a sentence of death under legal systems that permit this unique penalty to be so wantonly and so freakishly imposed.

☐ *Justice WHITE, concurring.*

In joining the Court's judgments . . . I do not at all intimate that the death penalty is unconstitutional *per se* or that there is no system of capital punishment that would comport with the Eighth Amendment. That question, ably argued by several of my Brethren, is not presented by these cases and need not be decided. . . .

I add only that past and present legislative judgment with respect to the death penalty loses much of its force when viewed in light of the recurring practice of delegating sentencing authority to the jury and the fact that a jury, in its own discretion and without violating its trust or any statutory policy, may refuse to impose the death penalty no matter what the circumstances of the crime. Legislative "policy" is thus necessarily defined not by what is legislatively authorized but by what juries and judges do in exercising the discretion so regularly conferred upon them. In my judgment what was done in these cases violated the Eighth Amendment.

☐ *Justice MARSHALL, concurring.*

In order to assess whether or not death is an excessive or unnecessary penalty, it is necessary to consider the reasons why a legislature might select it as punishment for one or more offenses, and examine whether less severe penalties would satisfy the legitimate legislative wants as well as capital punishment. If they would, then the death penalty is unnecessary cruelty, and, therefore, unconstitutional.

There are six purposes conceivably served by capital punishment: retribution, deterrence, prevention of repetitive criminal acts, encouragement of guilty pleas and confessions, eugenics, and economy. . . .

[After examining and rejecting each rationale for capital punishment, Justice MARSHALL concluded:] [E]ven if capital punishment is not excessive, it nonetheless violates the Eighth Amendment because it is morally unacceptable to the people of the United States at this time in their history.

In judging whether or not a given penalty is morally acceptable, most courts have said that the punishment is valid unless "it shocks the conscience and sense of justice of the people."

Judge Frank once noted the problems inherent in the use of such a measuring stick:

> [The court,] before it reduces a sentence as "cruel and unusual," must have reasonably good assurances that the sentence offends the "common conscience." And, in any context, such a standard—the community's attitude—is usually an unknowable. It resembles a slithery shadow, since one can seldom learn, at all accurately, what the community, or a majority, actually feels. Even a carefully-taken "public opinion poll" would be inconclusive in a case like this.

While a public opinion poll obviously is of some assistance in indicating public acceptance or rejection of a specific penalty, its utility cannot be very great. This is because whether or not a punishment is cruel and unusual depends, not on whether its mere mention "shocks the conscience and sense of justice of the people," but on whether people who were fully informed as to the purposes of the penalty and its liabilities would find the penalty shocking, unjust, and unacceptable.

In other words, the question with which we must deal is not whether a substantial proportion of American citizens would today, if polled, opine that capital punishment is barbarously cruel, but whether they would find it to be so in the light of all information presently available.

This is not to suggest that with respect to this test of unconstitutionality people are required to act rationally; they are not. With respect to this judgment, a violation of the Eighth Amendment is totally dependent on the predictable subjective, emotional reactions of informed citizens.

It has often been noted that American citizens know almost nothing about capital punishment. Some of the conclusions arrived at in the preceding section and the supporting evidence would be critical to an informed judgment on the morality of the death penalty: e.g., that the death penalty is no more effective a deterrent than life imprisonment, that convicted murderers are rarely executed, but are usually sentenced to a term in prison; that convicted murderers usually are model prisoners, and that they almost always become law-abiding citizens upon their release from prison; that the costs of executing a capital offender exceed the costs of imprisoning him for life; that while in prison, a convict under sentence of death performs none of the useful functions that life prisoners perform; that no attempt is made in the sentencing process to ferret out likely recidivists for execution; and that the death penalty may actually stimulate criminal activity.

This information would almost surely convince the average citizen that the death penalty was unwise, but a problem arises as to whether it would convince him that the penalty was morally reprehensible. This problem arises from the fact that the public's desire for retribution, even though this is a goal that the legislature cannot constitutionally pursue as its sole justification for capital punishment, might influence the citizenry's view of the morality of capital punishment. The solution to the problem lies in the fact that no one has ever seriously advanced retribution as a legitimate goal of our society. Defenses of capital punishment are always mounted on deterrent or other similar theories. This should not be surprising. It is the people of this country who have urged in the past that prison rehabilitate as well as isolate offenders, and it is the people who have injected a sense of purpose into our penology. I cannot believe that at this stage in our history, the American people would ever knowingly support purposeless vengeance. Thus, I believe that the great mass of citizens would conclude on the basis of the material already considered that the death penalty is immoral and therefore unconstitutional.

But, if this information needs supplementing, I believe that the following facts would serve to convince even the most hesitant of citizens to condemn death as a sanction: capital punishment is imposed discriminatorily against certain identifiable classes of people; there is evidence that innocent people have been executed before their innocence can be proved; and the death penalty wreaks havoc with our entire criminal justice system. . . .

Assuming knowledge of all the facts presently available regarding capital punishment, the average citizen would, in my opinion, find it shocking to his conscience and sense of justice. For this reason alone capital punishment cannot stand.

☐ *Chief Justice BURGER, with whom Justice BLACKMUN, Justice POWELL, and Justice REHNQUIST join, dissenting.*

Today the Court has not ruled that capital punishment is *per se* violative of the Eighth Amendment: nor has it ruled that the punishment is barred for any particular class or classes of crimes. The substantially similar concurring opinions of Justice STEWART and Justice WHITE, which are necessary to support the judgment setting aside petitioners' sentences, stop short of reaching the ultimate question. . . .

The critical factor in the concurring opinions of both Justice STEWART and Justice WHITE is the infrequency with which the penalty is imposed. This factor is taken not as evidence of society's abhorrence of capital punishment—the inference that petitioners would have the Court draw—but as the earmark of a deteriorated system of sentencing. It is concluded that petitioners' sentences must be set aside, not because the punishment is impermissibly cruel, but because juries and judges have failed to exercise their sentencing discretion in acceptable fashion. . . .

While I would not undertake to make a definitive statement as to the parameters of the Court's ruling, it is clear that if state legislatures and the Congress wish to maintain the availability of capital punishment, significant statutory changes will have to be made. Since the two pivotal concurring opinions turn on the assumption that the punishment of death is now meted out in a random and unpredictable manner, legislative bodies may seek to bring their laws into compliance with the Court's ruling by providing standards for juries and judges to follow in determining the sentence in capital cases or by more narrowly defining the crimes for which the penalty is to be imposed. If such standards can be devised or the crimes more meticulously defined, the result cannot be detrimental. . . .

Since there is no majority of the Court on the ultimate issue presented in these cases, the future of capital punishment in this country has been left in an uncertain limbo. Rather than providing a final and unambiguous answer on the basic constitutional question, the collective impact of the majority's ruling is to demand an undetermined measure of change from the various state legislatures and the Congress. While I cannot endorse the process of decision making that has yielded today's result and the restraints that that result imposes on legislative action, I am not altogether displeased that legislative bodies have been given the opportunity, and indeed unavoidable responsibility, to make a thorough reevaluation of the entire subject of capital punishment. If today's opinions demonstrate nothing else, they starkly show that this is an area where legislatures can act far more effectively than courts.

The legislatures are free to eliminate capital punishment for specific crimes or to carve out limited exceptions to a general abolition of the penalty, without adherence to the conceptual strictures of the Eighth Amendment. The legislatures can and should make an assessment of the deterrent influence of capital punishment, both generally and as affecting the commission of specific types of crimes. If legislatures come to doubt the efficacy of capital punishment, they can abolish it, either completely or on a selective basis. If new evidence persuades them that they have acted unwisely, they can reverse their field and reinstate the penalty to the extent it is thought warranted. An Eighth Amendment ruling by judges cannot be made with such flexibility or discriminating precision.

☐ *Justice POWELL, with whom THE CHIEF JUSTICE,*
Justice BLACKMUN, and Justice REHNQUIST join,
dissenting.

With deference and respect for the views of the Justices who differ, it seems to me that all these studies—both in this country and elsewhere—suggest that, as a matter of policy and precedent, this is a classic case for the exercise of our oft-announced allegiance to judicial restraint. I know of no case in which greater gravity and delicacy have attached to the duty that this Court is called on to perform whenever legislation—state or federal—is challenged on constitutional grounds. It seems to me that the sweeping judicial action undertaken today reflects a basic lack of faith and confidence in the democratic process. Many may regret, as I do, the failure of some legislative bodies to address the capital punishment issue with greater frankness or effectiveness. Many might decry their failure either to abolish the penalty entirely or selectively, or to establish standards for its enforcement. But impatience with the slowness, and even the unresponsiveness, of legislatures is no justification for judicial intrusion upon their historic powers. . . .

☐ *Justice REHNQUIST, with whom THE CHIEF JUSTICE,*
Justice BLACKMUN, and Justice POWELL join, dissenting.

Whatever its precise rationale, today's holding necessarily brings into sharp relief the fundamental question of the role of judicial review in a democratic society. How can government by the elected representatives of the people coexist with the power of the federal judiciary, whose members are constitutionally insulated from responsiveness to the popular will, to declare invalid laws duly enacted by the popular branches of government?

The answer, of course, is found in Hamilton's *Federalist* Paper No. 78 and in Chief Justice MARSHALL's classic opinion in *Marbury v. Madison*, 1 Cranch 137, (1803). An oft-told story since then, it bears summarization once more. Sovereignty resides ultimately in the people as a whole and, by adopting through their States a written Constitution for the Nation and subsequently adding amendments to that instrument, they have both granted certain powers to the National Government, and denied other powers to the National and the State Governments. Courts are exercising no more than the judicial function conferred upon them by Art. III of the Constitution when they assess, in a case before them, whether or not a particular legislative enactment is within the authority granted by the Constitution to the enacting body, and whether it runs afoul of some limitation placed by the Constitution on the authority of that body. For the theory is that the people themselves have spoken in the Constitution, and therefore its commands are superior to the commands of the legislature, which is merely an agent of the people.

The Founding Fathers thus wisely sought to have the best of both worlds, the undeniable benefits of both democratic self-government and individual rights protected against possible excesses of that form of government.

The courts in cases properly before them have been entrusted under the Constitution with the last word, short of constitutional amendment, as to whether a law passed by the legislature conforms to the Constitution. But just because courts in general, and this Court in particular, do have the last word, the admonition of Justice STONE dissenting in *United States v. Butler*, [297 U.S. 1 (1936)], must be constantly borne in mind:

> [W]hile unconstitutional exercise of power by the executive and legislative branches of the government is subject to judicial restraint, the only check upon our own exercise of power is our own sense of self-restraint. . . .

The very nature of judicial review, as pointed out by Justice STONE in his dissent in the *Butler* case, makes the courts the least subject to Madisonian check in the event that they shall, for the best of motives, expand judicial authority beyond the limits contemplated by the Framers. It is for this reason that judicial self-restraint is surely an implied, if not an expressed, condition of the grant of authority of judicial review. The Court's holding in these cases has been reached, I believe, in complete disregard of that implied condition.

Lockett v. Ohio

438 U.S. 586, 98 S.Ct. 2954 (1978)

Chief Justice Warren Burger discusses the facts in his opinion for the Court, striking down that portion of Ohio's capital punishment law that restricted the mitigating factors to be considered when imposing the death penalty.

The Court's decision was seven and one-half to one-half, and the majority's opinion was announced by Chief Justice Burger, with Justice Brennan not participating. Concurrences were by Justices

Blackmun and Marshall. A separate opinion, in part concurring and in part dissenting, was delivered by Justice Rehnquist.

■ ■ ■

☐ *Chief Justice BURGER delivered the opinion of the Court.*

Lockett was charged with aggravated murder with the aggravating specifications (1) that the murder was "committed for the purpose of escaping detection, apprehension, trial, or punishment" for aggravated robbery, and (2) that the murder was "committed . . . while committing, attempting to commit, or fleeing immediately after committing or attempting to commit aggravated robbery." That offense was punishable by death in Ohio. . . .

Lockett became acquainted with Parker and Nathan Earl Dew while she and a friend, Joanne Baxter, were in New Jersey. Parker and Dew then accompanied Lockett, Baxter, and Lockett's brother back to Akron, Ohio, Lockett's home town. After they arrived in Akron, Parker and Dew needed money for the trip back to New Jersey. Dew suggested that he pawn his ring. Lockett overheard his suggestion, but felt that the ring was too beautiful to pawn, and suggested instead that they could get some money by robbing a grocery store and a furniture store in the area. . . .

The next day Parker, Dew, Lockett, and her brother gathered at Baxter's apartment. Lockett's brother asked if they were "still going to do it," and everyone, including Lockett, agreed to proceed. The four then drove by the pawnshop several times and parked the car. Lockett's brother and Dew entered the shop. Parker then left the car and told Lockett to start it again in two minutes. The robbery proceeded according to plan until the pawnbroker grabbed the gun when Parker announced the "stickup." The gun went off with Parker's finger on the trigger firing a fatal shot into the pawnbroker.

Parker went back to the car where Lockett waited with the engine running. While driving away from the pawnshop, Parker told Lockett what had happened. She took the gun from the pawnshop and put it into her purse. Lockett and Parker drove to Lockett's aunt's house and called a taxicab. Shortly thereafter, while riding away in a taxicab, they were stopped by the police. . . .

[At the conclusion of her trial, the judge] instructed the jury that, before it could find Lockett guilty, it had to find that she purposely had killed the pawnbroker while committing or attempting to commit aggravated robbery. The jury was further charged that one who

purposely aids, helps, associates himself or herself with another for the purpose of committing a crime is regarded as if he or she were the principal offender and is just as guilty as if the person performed every act constituting the offense. . . .

The jury found Lockett guilty as charged.

Once a verdict of aggravated murder with specifications had been returned, the Ohio death penalty statute required the trial judge to impose a death sentence unless, after "considering the nature and circumstances of the offense" and Lockett's "history, character, and condition," he found by a preponderance of the evidence that (1) the victim had induced or facilitated the offense, (2) it was unlikely that Lockett would have committed the offense but for the fact that she "was under duress, coercion, or strong provocation," or (3) the offense was "primarily the product of [Lockett's] psychosis or mental deficiency." . . .

In accord with the Ohio statute, the trial judge requested a presentence report as well as psychiatric and psychological reports. The reports contained detailed information about Lockett's intelligence, character, and background. The psychiatric and psychological reports described her as a 21-year-old with low average or average intelligence, and not suffering from a mental deficiency. . . .

After considering the reports and hearing argument on the penalty issue, the trial judge concluded that the offense had not been primarily the product of psychosis or mental deficiency. Without specifically addressing the other two statutory mitigating factors, the judge said that he had "no alternative, whether [he] like[d] the law or not" but to impose the death penalty. He then sentenced Lockett to death. . . .

Prior to *Furman v. Georgia*, 408 U.S. 238 (1972), every State that authorized capital punishment had abandoned mandatory death penalties, and instead permitted the jury unguided and unrestrained discretion regarding the imposition of the death penalty in a particular capital case. Mandatory death penalties had proved unsatisfactory, as the plurality noted in *Woodson v. North Carolina*, 428 U.S. 280 (1976), in part because juries, "with some regularity, disregarded their oaths and refused to convict defendants where a death sentence was the automatic consequence of a guilty verdict."

This Court had never intimated prior to *Furman* that discretion in sentencing offended the Constitution. See *Pennsylvania ex rel. Sullivan v. Ashe*, 302 U.S. 51 (1937); *Williams v. New York*, 337 U.S. 241 (1949); *Williams v. Oklahoma*, 358 U.S. 576 (1959). As recently as *McGautha v. California*, 402 U.S. 183 (1971), the Court had specifically rejected the contention that discretion in imposing the death penalty violated the fundamental standards of fairness embodied in Fourteenth Amendment due process . . . and had asserted that States were entitled to assume that "jurors confronted with the truly awesome responsibility of decreeing death for a fellow human [would] act with due regard for the consequences of their decision." . . .

The constitutional status of discretionary sentencing in capital cases changed abruptly, however, as a result of the separate opinions supporting the judgment in *Furman*. The question in *Furman* was whether "the imposition and carrying out of the death penalty [in the cases before the Court] constitute[d] cruel and unusual punishment in violation of the Eighth and Fourteenth Amendments." Two Justices concluded that the Eighth Amendment prohibited the death penalty altogether and on that ground voted to reverse the judgments sustaining the death penalties. (BRENNAN, J., concurring); (MARSHALL, J., concurring). Three Justices were unwilling to hold the death penalty *per se* unconstitutional under the Eighth and Fourteenth Amendments, but voted to reverse the judgments on other grounds. In separate opinions, the three concluded that discretionary sentencing, unguided by legislatively defined standards, violated the Eighth Amendment because it was "pregnant with discrimination," (DOUGLAS, J., concurring), because it permitted the death penalty to be "wantonly" and "freakishly" imposed, (STEWART, J., concurring), and because it imposed the death penalty with "great infrequency" and afforded "no meaningful basis for distinguishing the few cases in which it [was] imposed from the many cases in which it [was] not," (WHITE, J., concurring). Thus, what had been approved under the Due Process Clause of the Fourteenth Amendment in *McGautha* became impermissible under the Eighth and Fourteenth Amendments by virtue of the judgment in *Furman*. See, *Gregg v. Georgia*, 428 U.S. 153 (1976) (opinion of STEWART, POWELL, and STEVENS, JJ.).

Predictably, the variety of opinions supporting the judgment in *Furman* engendered confusion as to what was required in order to impose the death penalty in accord with the Eighth Amendment. Some States responded to what was thought to be the command of *Furman* by adopting mandatory death penalties for a limited category of specific crimes thus eliminating all discretion from the sentencing process in capital cases. Other States attempted to continue the practice of individually assessing the culpability of each individual defendant convicted of a capital offense and, at the same time, to comply with *Furman*, by providing standards to guide the sentencing decision.

Four years after *Furman*, we considered Eighth Amendment issues posed by five of the post-*Furman* death penalty statutes. Four Justices took the position that all five statutes complied with the Constitution; two Justices took the position that none of them complied. Hence, the disposition of each case varied according to the votes of three Justices who delivered a joint opinion in each of the five cases upholding the constitutionality of the statutes of Georgia, Florida, and Texas, and holding those of North Carolina and Louisiana unconstitutional.

The joint opinion reasoned that, to comply with *Furman*, sentencing procedures should not create "a substantial risk that the [death penalty will] be inflicted in an arbitrary and capricious manner." *Gregg v. Georgia, supra.* In the view of the three Justices, however, *Furman* did not require that all sentencing discretion be eliminated, but only that it be "directed and limited," so that the death penalty would be imposed in a more consistent and rational manner and so that there would be a "meaningful basis for distinguishing the . . . cases in which it is imposed from . . . the many cases in which it is not." The plurality concluded, in the course of invalidating North Carolina's mandatory death penalty statute, that the sentencing process must permit consideration of the "character and record of the individual offender and the circumstances of the particular offense as a constitutionally indispensable part of the process of inflicting the penalty of death." *Woodson v. North Carolina.* In order to ensure the reliability, under Eighth Amendment standards, of the determination that "death is the appropriate punishment in a specific case." . . .

We are now faced with those questions and we conclude that the Eighth and Fourteenth Amendments require that the sentencer, in all but the rarest kind of capital case, not be precluded from considering, *as a mitigating factor*, any aspect of a defendant's character or record and any of the circumstances of the offense that the defendant proffers as a basis for a sentence less than death. We recognize that, in noncapital cases, the established practice of individualized sentences rests not on constitutional commands, but on public policy enacted into statutes. The considerations that account for the wide acceptance of individualization of sentences in noncapital cases surely cannot be thought less important in capital cases. Given that the imposition of death by public authority is so profoundly different from all other penalties, we cannot avoid the conclusion that an individualized decision is essential in capital cases. The need for treating each defendant in a capital case with that degree of respect due the uniqueness of the individual is far more important than in noncapital cases. A variety of flexible techniques—probation, parole, work furloughs, to name a few—and various postconviction remedies may be available to modify an initial sentence of confinement in noncapital cases. The nonavailability of corrective or modifying mechanisms with respect to an executed capital sentence underscores the need for individualized consideration as a constitutional requirement in imposing the death sentence.

There is no perfect procedure for deciding in which cases governmental authority should be used to impose death. But a statute that prevents the sentencer in all capital cases from giving independent mitigating weight to aspects of the defendant's character and record and to circumstances of the offense proffered in mitigation creates the risk that the death penalty will be imposed in spite of factors which may call for a less severe penalty. When the choice is between life and death, that risk is unacceptable and incompatible with the commands of the Eighth and Fourteenth Amendments.

The Ohio death penalty statute does not permit the type of individualized consideration of mitigating factors we now hold to be required by the Eighth and Fourteenth Amendments in capital cases. . . .

We see, therefore, that once it is determined that the victim did not induce or facilitate the offense, that the defendant did not act under duress or coercion, and that the offense was not primarily the product of the defendant's mental deficiency, the Ohio statute mandates the sentence of death. The absence of direct proof that the defendant intended to cause the death of the victim is relevant for mitigating purposes only if it is determined that it sheds some light on one of the three statutory mitigating factors. Similarly, consideration of a defendant's comparatively minor role in the offense, or age, would generally not be permitted, as such, to affect the sentencing decision.

The limited range of mitigating circumstances which may be considered by the sentencer under the Ohio statute is incompatible with the Eighth and Fourteenth Amendments. To meet constitutional requirements, a death penalty statute must not preclude consideration of relevant mitigating factors.

Accordingly, the judgment under review is reversed to the extent that it sustains the imposition of the death penalty; the case is remanded for further proceedings.

☐ *Justice REHNQUIST, concurring in part and dissenting in part.*

THE CHIEF JUSTICE states: "We do not write on a 'clean slate.' " But it can scarcely be maintained that today's decision is the logical application of a coherent doctrine first espoused by the opinions leading to the Court's judgment in *Furman*, and later elaborated in the *Woodson* series of cases. . . .

If a defendant as a matter of constitutional law is to be permitted to offer as evidence in the sentencing hearing any fact, however bizarre, which he wishes, even though the most sympathetically disposed trial judge could conceive of no basis upon which the jury might take it into account in imposing a sentence, the new constitutional doctrine will not eliminate arbitrariness or freakishness in the imposition of sentences, but will codify and institutionalize it. By encouraging defendants in capital cases, and presumably sentencing judges and juries, to take into consideration any-thing under the sun as a "mitigating circumstance," it will not guide sen-tencing discretion but will totally unleash it. . . .

I continue to view *McGautha* as a correct exposition of the limits of our authority to revise state criminal procedures in capital cases under the Eighth and Fourteenth Amendments. Sandra Lockett was fairly tried, and was found guilty of aggravated murder. I do not think Ohio was required to receive any sort of mitigating evidence which an accused or his lawyer wishes to offer, and therefore I disagree with [that part] of the plurality's opinion [which holds contrariwise].

McCleskey v. Kemp

481 U.S. 279, 107 S.CT. 1756 (1987)

Justice Lewis F. Powell discusses the facts in his opinion announc-ing the decision of a majority of the Court. The Court rejected the argument that statistical studies—showing that black defendants who murder white victims are more likely to receive the death penalty than white defendants charged with murdering white or black victims—establish the basis for declaring the death sentence imposed on Warren McCleskey, a black man, unconstitutional under the Eighth and Fourteenth Amendments.

The Court's decision was 5–4, and the majority's opinion was announced by Justice Powell. Dissents were by Justices Brennan, Blackmun, and Stevens and joined by Justice Marshall.

■ ■ ■

☐ *Justice POWELL delivered the opinion of the Court.*

This case presents the question whether a complex statistical study that indicates a risk that racial considerations enter into capital sentencing determinations proves that petitioner McCleskey's capital sentence is unconstitutional under the Eighth or Fourteenth Amendment.

McCleskey, a black man, was convicted of two counts of armed rob-bery and one count of murder. . . .

On appeal, the Supreme Court of Georgia affirmed the convictions and sentences. . . .

McCleskey next filed a petition for a writ of *habeas corpus* in the federal District Court for the Northern District of Georgia. His petition raised 18 claims, one of which was that the Georgia capital sentencing process is administered in a racially discriminatory manner in violation of the Eighth and Fourteenth Amendments to the United States Constitution. In support of his claim, McCleskey proffered a statistical study performed by Profes-sors David C. Baldus, George Woodworth, and Charles Pulaski (the Baldus study) that purports to show a disparity in the imposition of the death sen-tence in Georgia based on the race of the murder victim and, to a lesser extent, the race of the defendant. The Baldus study is actually two sophisticated statistical studies that examine over 2,000 murder cases that occurred in Georgia during the 1970s. The raw numbers collected by Professor Baldus indicate that defendants charged with killing white persons received the death penalty in 11% of the cases, but defendants charged with killing blacks received the death penalty in only 1% of the cases. The raw numbers also indicate a reverse racial disparity according to the race of the defendant: 4% of the black defendants received the death penalty, as opposed to 7% of the white defendants.

Baldus also divided the cases according to the combination of the race of the defendant and the race of the victim. He found that the death penalty was assessed in 22% of the cases involving black defendants and white victims; 8% of the cases involving white defendants and white victims; 1% of the cases involving black defendants and black victims; and 3% of the cases involving white defendants and black victims. Similarly, Baldus found that prosecutors sought the death penalty in 70% of the cases involving black defendants and white victims; 32% of the cases involving white defendants and white victims; 15% of the cases involving black defendants and black victims; and 19% of the cases involving white defendants and black victims.

Baldus subjected his data to an extensive analysis, taking account of 230 variables that could have explained the disparities on nonracial grounds. One of his models concludes that, even after taking account of 39 nonracial variables, defendants charged with killing white victims were 4.3 times as likely to receive a death sentence as defendants charged with killing blacks. According to this model, black defendants were 1.1 times as likely to receive a death sentence as other defendants. Thus, the Baldus study indicates that black defendants, such as McCleskey, who kill white victims have the greatest likelihood of receiving the death penalty. . . .

McCleskey's first claim is that the Georgia capital punishment statute violates the Equal Protection Clause of the Fourteenth Amendment. He argues that race has infected the administration of Georgia's statute in two ways: persons who murder whites are more likely to be sentenced to death than persons who murder blacks, and black murderers are more likely to be sentenced to death than white murderers. As a black defendant who killed a white victim, McCleskey claims that the Baldus study demonstrates that he was discriminated against because of his race and because of the race of his victim. . . .

We agree with the Court of Appeals, and every other court that has considered such a challenge, that this claim must fail.

Our analysis begins with the basic principle that a defendant who alleges an equal protection violation has the burden of proving "the existence of purposeful discrimination." A corollary to this principle is that a criminal defendant must prove that the purposeful discrimination "had a discriminatory effect" on him. Thus, to prevail under the Equal Protection Clause, McCleskey must prove that the decisionmakers in *his* case acted with discriminatory purpose. He offers no evidence specific to his own case that would support an inference that racial considerations played a part in his sentence. Instead, he relies solely on the Baldus study. . . .

The Court has accepted statistics as proof of intent to discriminate in certain limited contexts. First, this Court has accepted statistical disparities as proof of an equal protection violation in the selection of the jury venire in a particular district. Although statistical proof normally must present a "stark" pattern to be accepted as the sole proof of discriminatory intent under the Constitution, *Arlington Heights v. Metropolitan Housing Dev. Corp.*, 429 U.S. 252 (1977), "[b]ecause of the nature of the jury-selection task, we have permitted a finding of constitutional violation even when the statistical pattern does not approach [such] extremes." . . . Second, this Court has accepted statistics in the form of multiple regression analysis to prove statutory violations under Title VII. *Bazemore v. Friday*, [478 U.S. 385 (1986)] (opinion of BRENNAN. J., concurring in part).

But the nature of the capital sentencing decision, and the relationship of the statistics to that decision, are fundamentally different from the corresponding elements in the venire-selection or Title VII cases. Most importantly, each particular decision to impose the death penalty is made by a petit jury selected from a properly constituted venire. Each jury is unique in its composition, and the Constitution requires that its decision rest on consideration of innumerable factors that vary according to the characteristics of the individual defendant and the facts of the particular capital offense. Thus, the application of an inference drawn from the general statistics to a specific decision in a trial and sentencing simply is not comparable to the application of an inference drawn from general statistics to a specific venire-selection or Title VII case. In those cases, the statistics relate to fewer entities, and fewer variables are relevant to the challenged decisions. . . .

Finally, McCleskey's statistical proffer must be viewed in the context of his challenge. McCleskey challenges decisions at the heart of the State's criminal justice system. . . .

Implementation of these laws necessarily requires discretionary judgments. Because discretion is essential to the criminal justice process, we would demand exceptionally clear proof before we would infer that the discretion has been abused. The unique nature of the decisions at issue in this case also counsel against adopting such an inference from the disparities indicated by the Baldus study. Accordingly, we hold that the Baldus study is clearly insufficient to support an inference that any of the decisionmakers in McCleskey's case acted with discriminatory purpose.

McCleskey also suggests that the Baldus study proves that the State as a whole has acted with a discriminatory purpose. He appears to argue that the State has violated the Equal Protection Clause by adopting the capital punishment statute and allowing it to remain in force despite its allegedly discriminatory application. But "'[d]iscriminatory purpose' . . . implies more than intent as volition or intent as awareness of consequences. It implies that the decisionmaker, in this case a state legislature, selected or reaffirmed a particular course of action at least in part 'because of,' not merely 'in spite of,' its adverse effects upon an identifiable group." . . .

For this claim to prevail, McCleskey would have to prove that the Georgia Legislature enacted or maintained the death penalty statute *because of* an anticipated racially discriminatory effect. In *Gregg v. Georgia*, 428 U.S. 153 (1976), this Court found that the Georgia capital sentencing system could operate in a fair and neutral manner. There was no evidence then, and there is none now, that the Georgia Legislature enacted the capital punishment statute to further a racially discriminatory purpose. . . .

McCleskey also argues that the Baldus study demonstrates that the Georgia capital sentencing system violates the Eighth Amendment. . . .

Two principal decisions guide our resolution of McCleskey's Eighth Amendment claim. In *Furman v. Georgia*, 408 U.S. 238 (1972), the Court concluded that the death penalty was so irrationally imposed that any particular death sentence could be presumed excessive. Under the statutes at issue in *Furman*, there was no basis for determining in any particular case whether the penalty was proportionate to the crime: "the death penalty [was] exacted with great infrequency even for the most atrocious crimes and . . . there [was] no meaningful basis for distinguishing the few cases in which it [was] imposed from the many cases in which it [was] not." . . .

In *Gregg*, the Court specifically addressed the question left open in *Furman*—whether the punishment of death for murder is "under all circumstances, 'cruel and unusual' in violation of the Eighth and Fourteenth Amendments of the Constitution." We noted that the imposition of the death penalty for the crime of murder "has a long history of acceptance both in the United States and in England." During the 4-year period between *Furman* and *Gregg*, at least 35 states had reenacted the death penalty, and Congress had authorized the penalty for aircraft piracy. . . .

The second question before the Court in *Gregg* was the constitutionality of the particular procedures embodied in the Georgia capital punishment statute. We explained the fundamental principle of *Furman*, that "where discretion is afforded a sentencing body on a matter so grave as the determination of whether a human life should be taken or spared, that discretion must be suitably directed and limited so as to minimize the risk of wholly arbitrary and capricious action." Numerous features of the then new Georgia statute met the concerns articulated in *Furman*. The Georgia system bifurcates guilt and sentencing proceedings so that the jury can receive all relevant information for sentencing without the risk that evidence irrelevant to the defendant's guilt will influence the jury's consideration of that issue. The statute narrows the class of murders subject to the death penalty to cases in which the jury finds at least one statutory aggravating circumstance beyond a reasonable doubt. Conversely, it allows the defendant to introduce any relevant mitigating evidence that might influence the jury not to impose a death sentence. The procedures also require a particularized inquiry into "the circumstances of the offense together with the character and propensities of the offender." Thus, "while some jury discretion still exists, 'the discretion to be exercised is controlled by clear and objective standards so as to produce nondiscriminatory application.'" Moreover, the Georgia system adds "an important additional safeguard against arbitrariness and caprice" in a provision for automatic appeal of a death sentence to the State Supreme Court. The statute requires that court to review each sentence to determine whether it was imposed under the influence of passion or prejudice, whether the evidence supports the jury's finding of a statutory aggravating circumstance, and whether the sentence is disproportionate to sentences imposed in generally similar murder cases. To aid the court's review, the trial judge answers a questionnaire about the trial, including detailed questions as to "the quality of the defendant's representation [and] whether race played a role in the trial." . . .

In the cases decided after *Gregg*, the Court has imposed a number of requirements on the capital sentencing process to ensure that capital sentencing decisions rest on the individualized inquiry contemplated in *Gregg*. . . .

In contrast to the carefully defined standards that must narrow a sentencer's discretion to *impose* the death sentence, the Constitution limits a

State's ability to narrow a sentencer's discretion to consider relevant evidence that might cause it to *decline to impose* the death sentence. . . .

Although our constitutional inquiry has centered on the procedures by which a death sentence is imposed, we have not stopped at the face of a statute, but have probed the application of statutes to particular cases. For example, in *Godfrey v. Georgia*, 446 U.S. 420 (1980), the Court invalidated a Georgia Supreme Court interpretation of the statutory aggravating circumstance that the murder be "outrageously or wantonly vile, horrible or inhuman in that it involved torture, depravity of mind, or an aggravated battery to the victim." . . . Although that court had articulated an adequate limiting definition of this phrase, we concluded that its interpretation in *Godfrey* was so broad that it may have vitiated the role of the aggravating circumstance in guiding the sentencing jury's discretion.

Finally, where the objective indicia of community values have demonstrated a consensus that the death penalty is disproportionate as applied to a certain class of cases, we have established substantive limitations on its application. In *Coker v. Georgia*, 433 U.S. 584 (1977), the Court held that a State may not constitutionally sentence an individual to death for the rape of an adult woman. . . .

In sum, our decisions since *Furman* have identified a constitutionally permissible range of discretion in imposing the death penalty. First, there is a required threshold below which the death penalty cannot be imposed. In this context, the State must establish rational criteria that narrow the decisionmaker's judgment as to whether the circumstances of a particular defendant's case meet the threshold. Moreover, a societal consensus that the death penalty is disproportionate to a particular offense prevents a State from imposing the death penalty for that offense. Second, States cannot limit the sentencer's consideration of any relevant circumstance that could cause it to decline to impose the penalty. In this respect, the State cannot channel the sentencer's discretion, but must allow it to consider any relevant information offered by the defendant.

In light of our precedents under the Eighth Amendment, McCleskey cannot argue successfully that his sentence is "disproportionate to the crime in the traditional sense." See *Pulley v. Harris*, 465 U.S. 37 (1984). He does not deny that he committed a murder in the course of a planned robbery, a crime for which this Court has determined that the death penalty constitutionally may be imposed. *Gregg v. Georgia*. . . . His disproportionality claim "is of a different sort." *Pulley v. Harris*. McCleskey argues that the sentence in his case is disproportionate to the sentences in other murder cases.

On the one hand, he cannot base a constitutional claim on an argument that his case differs from other cases in which defendants *did* receive the death penalty. On automatic appeal, the Georgia Supreme Court found that McCleskey's death sentence was not disproportionate to other death sentences imposed in the State. . . .

On the other hand, absent a showing that the Georgia capital punishment system operates in an arbitrary and capricious manner, McCleskey cannot prove a constitutional violation by demonstrating that other defendants who may be similarly situated did *not* receive the death penalty. In *Gregg*, the Court confronted the argument that "the opportunities for discretionary action that are inherent in the processing of any murder case under Georgia law," specifically the opportunities for discretionary leniency, rendered the capital sentences imposed arbitrary and capricious. We rejected this contention. . . .

Because McCleskey's sentence was imposed under Georgia sentencing procedures that focus discretion "on the particularized nature of the crime and the particularized characteristics of the individual defendant," we lawfully may presume that McCleskey's death sentence was not "wantonly and freakishly" imposed and thus that the sentence is not disproportionate within any recognized meaning under the Eighth Amendment. . . .

☐ *Justice BRENNAN, with whom Justice MARSHALL joins, and with whom Justice BLACKMUN and Justice STEVENS join in part, dissenting.*

Adhering to my view that the death penalty is in all circumstances cruel and unusual punishment forbidden by the Eighth and Fourteenth Amendments, I would vacate the decision below insofar as it left undisturbed the death sentence imposed in this case. . . .

The Court today holds that Warren McCleskey's sentence was constitutionally imposed. It finds no fault in a system in which lawyers must tell their clients that race casts a large shadow on the capital sentencing process. The Court arrives at this conclusion by stating that the Baldus Study cannot "*prove* that race enters into any capital sentencing decisions or that race was a factor in McCleskey's particular case." Since, according to Professor Baldus, we cannot say "to a moral certainty" that race influenced a decision, we can identify only "a likelihood that a particular factor entered into some decisions," and "a discrepancy that appears to correlate with race." This "likelihood" and "discrepancy," holds the Court, is insufficient to establish a constitutional violation. The Court reaches this conclusion by placing four factors on the scales opposite McCleskey's evidence: the desire to encourage sentencing discretion, the existence of "statutory safeguards" in the Georgia scheme, the fear of encouraging widespread challenges to other sentencing decisions, and the limits of the judicial role. The Court's evaluation of the significance of petitioner's evidence is fundamentally at odds with our consistent concern for rationality in capital sentencing, and the considerations that the majority invokes to discount that evidence cannot justify ignoring its force. . . .

[O]ur inquiry under the Eighth Amendment has not been directed to the validity of the individual sentences before us. In *Godfrey*, for instance, the Court struck down the petitioner's sentence because the vagueness of the statutory definition of heinous crimes created a *risk* that prejudice or other impermissible influences *might have infected* the sentencing decision. In vacating the sentence, we did not ask whether it was likely that Godfrey's own sentence reflected the operation of irrational considerations. Nor did we demand a demonstration that such considerations had actually entered into other sentencing decisions involving heinous crimes. . . .

Defendants challenging their death sentences thus never have had to prove that impermissible considerations have actually infected sentencing decisions. We have required instead that they establish that the system under which they were sentenced posed a significant risk of such an occurrence. McCleskey's claim does differ, however, in one respect from these earlier cases: it is the first to base a challenge not on speculation about how a system *might* operate, but on empirical documentation of how it *does* operate.

The Court assumes the statistical validity of the Baldus study and acknowledges that McCleskey has demonstrated a risk that racial prejudice plays a role in capital sentencing in Georgia. Nonetheless, it finds the probability of prejudice insufficient to create constitutional concern. Close analysis of the Baldus study, however, in light of both statistical principles and human experience, reveals that the risk that race influenced McCleskey's sentence is intolerable by any imaginable standard.

The Baldus study indicates that, after taking into account some 230 nonracial factors that might legitimately influence a sentencer, the jury *more likely than not* would have spared McCleskey's life had his victim been black. The study distinguishes between those cases in which (1) the jury exercises virtually no discretion because the strength or weakness of aggravating factors usually suggests that only one outcome is appropriate; and (2) cases reflecting an "intermediate" level of aggravation, in which the jury has considerable discretion in choosing a sentence. McCleskey's case falls into the intermediate range. In such cases, death is imposed in 34% of white-victim crimes and 14% of black-victim crimes, a difference of 139% in the rate of imposition of the death penalty. In other words, just under 59%—almost 6 in 10—defendants comparable to McCleskey would not have received the death penalty if their victims had been black.

Furthermore, even examination of the sentencing system as a whole, factoring in those cases in which the jury exercises little discretion, indicates the influence of race on capital sentencing. For the Georgia system as a whole, race accounts for a six percentage point difference in the rate at which capital punishment is imposed. Since death is imposed in 11% of all white-victim cases, the rate in comparably aggravated black-victim cases is 5%. The rate of capital sentencing in a white-victim case is thus 120% greater than the rate in a black-victim case. Put another way, over half— 55%—of defendants in white-victim crimes in Georgia would not have been sentenced to die if their victims had been black. Of the more than 200 variables potentially relevant to a sentencing decision, race of the victim is a powerful explanation for variation in death sentence rates—as powerful as nonracial aggravating factors such as a prior murder conviction or acting as the principal planner of the homicide.

These adjusted figures are only the most conservative indication of the risk that race will influence the death sentences of defendants in Georgia. Data unadjusted for the mitigating or aggravating effect of other factors show an even more pronounced disparity by race. The capital sentencing rate for all white-victim cases was almost *11 times* greater than the rate for black-victim cases. Furthermore, blacks who kill whites are sentenced to death at nearly *22 times* the rate of blacks who kill blacks, and more than 7 *times* the rate of whites who kill blacks. *Ibid.* In addition, prosecutors seek the death penalty for 70% of black defendants with white victims, but for only 15% of black defendants with black victims, and only 19% of white defendants with black victims. Since our decision upholding the Georgia capital-sentencing system in *Gregg*, the State has executed 7 persons. All of the 7 were convicted of killing whites, and 6 of the 7 executed were black. Such execution figures are especially striking in light of the fact that, during the period encompassed by the Baldus study, only 9.2% of Georgia homicides involved black defendants and white victims, while 60.7% involved black victims.

McCleskey's statistics have particular force because most of them are the product of sophisticated multiple-regression analysis. Such analysis is designed precisely to identify patterns in the aggregate, even though we may not be able to reconstitute with certainty any individual decision that goes to make up that pattern. Multiple-regression analysis is particularly well-suited to identify the influence of impermissible considerations in sentencing, since it is able to control for permissible factors that may explain an apparent arbitrary pattern. While the decision-making process of a body such as a jury may be complex, the Baldus study provides a massive compilation of the details that are most relevant to that decision. . . .

The statistical evidence in this case thus relentlessly documents the risk that McCleskey's sentence was influenced by racial considerations. This evidence shows that there is a better than even chance in Georgia that race will influence the decision to impose the death penalty: a majority of defendants in white-victim crimes would not have been sentenced to die if their victims had been black. In determining whether this risk is acceptable, our judgment must be shaped by the awareness that "[t]he risk of racial prejudice infecting a capital sentencing proceeding is especially serious in light of the complete finality of the death sentence." . . .

Evaluation of McCleskey's evidence cannot rest solely on the numbers themselves. We must also ask whether the conclusion suggested by those numbers is consonant with our understanding of history and human experience. Georgia's legacy of a race-conscious criminal justice system, as well as this Court's own recognition of the persistent danger that racial attitudes may affect criminal proceedings, indicate that McCleskey's claim is not a fanciful product of mere statistical artifice.

For many years, Georgia operated openly and formally precisely the type of dual system the evidence shows is still effectively in place. The criminal law expressly differentiated between crimes committed by and against blacks and whites, distinctions whose lineage traced back to the time of slavery. During the colonial period, black slaves who killed whites in Georgia, regardless of whether in self-defense or in defense of another, were automatically executed. . . .

By the time of the Civil War, a dual system of crime and punishment was well established in Georgia. The state criminal code contained separate sections for "Slaves and Free Persons of Color," and for all other persons. . . .

Formal dual criminal laws may no longer be in effect, and intentional discrimination may no longer be prominent. Nonetheless, "subtle, less consciously held racial attitudes" continue to be of concern, and the Georgia system gives such attitudes considerable room to operate. The conclusions drawn from McCleskey's statistical evidence are therefore consistent with the lessons of social experience.

The majority thus misreads our Eighth Amendment jurisprudence in concluding that McCleskey has not demonstrated a degree of risk sufficient to raise constitutional concern. The determination of the significance of his evidence is at its core an exercise in human moral judgment, not a mechanical statistical analysis. It must first and foremost be informed by awareness of the fact that death is irrevocable, and that as a result "the qualitative difference of death from all other punishments requires a greater degree of scrutiny of the capital sentencing determination." For this reason, we have demanded a uniquely high degree of rationality in imposing the death

■ INSIDE THE COURT:

Justice Scalia's Unpublished Memorandum on McCleskey v. Kemp, *Indicating that Statistics Show Racial Prejudice in Death Penalty Sentencing*

Supreme Court of the United States
Washington, D. C. 20543

CHAMBERS OF
JUSTICE ANTONIN SCALIA

January 6, 1987

Re: No. 84-6811 - McCleskey v. Kemp

MEMORANDUM TO THE CONFERENCE:

I plan to join Lewis's opinion in this case, with two reservations. I disagree with the argument that the inferences that can be drawn from the Baldus study are weakened by the fact that each jury and each trial is unique, or by the large number of variables at issue. And I do not share the view, implicit in the opinion, that an effect of racial factors upon sentencing, if it could only be shown by sufficiently strong statistical evidence, would require reversal. Since it is my view that the unconscious operation of irrational sympathies and antipathies, including racial, upon jury decisions and (hence) prosecutorial decisions is real, acknowledged in the decisions of this court, and ineradicable, I cannot honestly say that all I need is more proof. I expect to write separately to make these points, but not until I see the dissent.

Sincerely,

[signature]

For a further discussion, see Denis D. Dorin, "Far Right of the Mainstream: Racism, Right, and Remedies from the Perspective of Justice Antonin Scalia's *McCleskey Memorandum,*" 45 Mercer Law Review 1035 (1994). (*Library of Congress, Justice Thurgood Marshall Papers.*)

penalty. A capital-sentencing system in which race more likely than not plays a role does not meet this standard. It is true that every nuance of decision cannot be statistically captured, nor can any individual judgment be plumbed with absolute certainty. Yet the fact that we must always act without the illumination of complete knowledge cannot induce paralysis when we confront what is literally an issue of life and death. Sentencing data, history, and experience all counsel that Georgia has provided insufficient assurance of the heightened rationality we have required in order to take a human life. . . .

Payne v. Tennessee

501 U.S. 808, 111 S.Ct. 2597 (1991)

Pervis Payne, a developmentally disabled man with no previous criminal record, was tried and convicted of stabbing to death a twenty-eight-year-old woman and her two-year-old daughter, as well as attempting to murder her three-year-old son. During closing arguments at his trial, the prosecutor asked the jury to impose the death sentence and told them, "There obviously is nothing you can do for Charisse or Lacie. But there is something you can do for Nicholas. . . . He is going to want to know what type of justice was done." Payne was sentenced to death and his attorney immediately appealed the sentence on the grounds that the trial judge impermissibly allowed the prosecution's use of victim-impact statements and failed to comply with the Court's rulings in *Booth v. Maryland*, 482 U.S. 496 (1987), and *South Carolina v. Gathers*, 490 U.S. 805 (1989). But when the Court granted review, it directed the attorneys specifically to address the question of whether *Booth* and *Gathers* should be overturned, even though neither party had raised that question in the original petitions and briefs.

The Court's decision was 6–3. Chief Justice Rehnquist announced the majority's opinion, with which Justices O'Connor, Scalia, and Souter each concurred. Justice Blackmun joined dissents by Justices Marshall and Stevens.

■ ■ ■

☐ *Chief Justice REHNQUIST delivered the opinion of the Court.*

In this case we reconsider our holdings in *Booth v. Maryland*, 482 U.S. 496 (1987), and *South Carolina v. Gathers*, 490 U.S. 805 (1989), that the Eighth Amendment bars the admission of victim impact evidence during the penalty phase of a capital trial. . . .

Booth and *Gathers* were based on two premises: that evidence relating to a particular victim or to the harm that a capital defendant causes a victim's family do not in general reflect on the defendant's "blameworthiness," and that only evidence relating to "blameworthiness" is relevant to the capital sentencing decision. However, the assessment of harm caused by the defendant as a result of the crime charged has understandably been an important concern of the criminal law, both in determining the elements of the offense and in determining the appropriate punishment. Thus, two equally blameworthy criminal defendants may be guilty of different offenses solely because their acts cause differing amounts of harm. . . .

Payne echoes the concern voiced in Booth's case that the admission of victim impact evidence permits a jury to find that defendants whose victims were assets to their community are more deserving of punishment than those whose victims are perceived to be less worthy. As a general matter, however, victim impact evidence is not offered to encourage comparative judgments of this kind—for instance, that the killer of a hardworking, devoted parent deserves the death penalty, but that the murderer of a reprobate does not. It is designed to show instead each victim's "uniqueness as an individual human being," whatever the jury might think the loss to the community resulting from his death might be. . . .

Under our constitutional system, the primary responsibility for defining crimes against state law, fixing punishments for the commission of these crimes, and establishing procedures for criminal trials rests with the States. The state laws respecting crimes, punishments, and criminal procedure are of course subject to the overriding provisions of the United States Constitution. Where the State imposes the death penalty for a particular crime, we have held that the Eighth Amendment imposes special limitations upon that process.

"First, there is a required threshold below which the death penalty cannot be imposed. In this context, the State must establish rational criteria that narrow the decisionmaker's judgment as to whether the circumstances of a particular defendant's case meet the threshold. Moreover, a societal consensus that the death penalty is disproportionate to a particular offense prevents a State from imposing the death penalty for that offense. Second, States cannot limit the sentencer's consideration of any relevant circumstance that could cause it to decline to impose the penalty. In this respect, the State cannot challenge the sentencer's discretion, but must allow it to consider any relevant information offered by the defendant." *McCleskey v. Kemp*, 481 U.S. 279 (1987).

But, as we noted in *California v. Ramos*, 463 U.S. 992 (1983), "[b]eyond these limitations . . . the Court has deferred to the State's choice of substantive factors relevant to the penalty determination." . . .

The States remain free, in capital cases, as well as others, to devise new procedures and new remedies to meet felt needs. Victim impact evidence is simply another form or method of informing the sentencing authority about the specific harm caused by the crime in question, evidence of a general type long considered by sentencing authorities. We think the *Booth* Court was wrong in stating that this kind of evidence leads to the arbitrary imposition of the death penalty. In the majority of cases, and in this case, victim impact evidence serves entirely legitimate purposes. In the event that evidence is introduced that is so unduly prejudicial that it renders the trial fundamentally unfair, the Due Process Clause of the Fourteenth Amendment provides a mechanism for relief. . . .

We thus hold that if the State chooses to permit the admission of victim impact evidence and prosecutional argument on that subject, the Eighth Amendment erects no per se bar. . . .

Stare decisis is not an inexorable command; rather, it "is a principle of policy and not a mechanical formula of adherence to the latest decision." *Helvering v. Hallock*, 309 U.S. 106 (1940). This is particularly true in constitutional cases, because in such cases "correction through legislative action is practically impossible." *Burnet v. Coronado Oil & Gas Co.*, [285 U.S. 393 (1932)] (BRANDEIS, J., dissenting). Considerations in favor of *stare decisis* are at their acme in cases involving property and contract rights, where reliance interests are involved, see *Swift & Co. v. Wickham*, 382 U.S. 111 (1965); *Burnet v. Coronado Oil & Gas Co.*, *supra*; the opposite is true in cases such as the present one involving procedural and evidentiary rules. . . .

Booth and *Gathers* were decided by the narrowest of margins, over spirited dissents challenging the basic underpinnings of those decisions. . . . Reconsidering these decisions now, we conclude for the reasons heretofore stated, that they were wrongly decided and should be, and now are, overruled. We accordingly affirm the judgment of the Supreme Court of Tennessee.

Affirmed.

☐ *Justice MARSHALL, with whom Justice BLACKMUN joins, dissenting.*

Power, not reason, is the new currency of this Court's decisionmaking. . . . Neither the law nor the facts supporting *Booth* and *Gathers* underwent any change in the last four years. Only the personnel of this Court did.

In dispatching *Booth* and *Gathers* to their graves, today's majority ominously suggests that an even more extensive upheaval of this Court's precedents may be in store. Renouncing this Court's historical commitment to a conception of "the judiciary as a source of impersonal and reasoned judgments," *Moragne v. States Marine Lines*, 398 U.S. 375 (1970), the majority declares itself free to discard any principle of constitutional liberty which was recognized or reaffirmed over the dissenting votes of four Justices and with which five or more Justices now disagree. The implications of this radical new exception to the doctrine of *stare decisis* are staggering. The majority today sends a clear signal that scores of established constitutional liberties are now ripe for reconsideration, thereby inviting the very type of open defiance of our precedents that the majority rewards in this case. Because I believe that this Court owes more to its constitutional precedents in general and to *Booth* and *Gathers* in particular, I dissent. . . .

[T]his Court has never departed from precedent without "special justification." *Arizona v. Rumsey*, 467 U.S. 203 (1984). Such justifications include the advent of "subsequent changes or development in the law" that undermine a decision's rationale, *Patterson v. McLean Credit Union*, [491 U.S. 164 (1989)]; the need "to bring [a decision] into agreement with experience and with facts newly ascertained," *Burnet*, *supra*; and a showing that a particular precedent has become a "detriment to coherence and consistency in the law," *Patterson*.

The majority cannot seriously claim that any of these traditional bases for overruling a precedent applies to *Booth* or *Gathers*. The majority does not suggest that the legal rationale of these decisions has been undercut by changes or developments in doctrine during the last two years. Nor does the majority claim that experience over that period of time has discredited the principle that "any decision to impose the death sentence be, and appear to be, based on reason rather than caprice or emotion," *Gardner v. Florida*,

430 U.S. 349 (1977) (plurality opinion), the larger postulate of political morality on which *Booth* and *Gathers* rest. . . .

It takes little real detective work to discern just what has changed since this Court decided *Booth* and *Gathers*: this Court's own personnel. . . .

In addition, the majority points out, "*Booth* and *Gathers* were decided by the narrowest of margins, over spirited dissents" and thereafter were "questioned by members of the Court." Taken together, these considerations make it legitimate, in the majority's view, to elevate the position of the *Booth* and *Gathers* dissenters into the law of the land.

This truncation of the Court's duty to stand by its own precedents is astonishing. By limiting full protection of the doctrine of *stare decisis* to "cases involving property and contract rights," the majority sends a clear signal that essentially all decisions implementing the personal liberties protected by the Bill of Rights and the Fourteenth Amendment are open to reexamination. Taking into account the majority's additional criterion for overruling—that a case either was decided or reaffirmed by a 5–4 margin "over spirited dissen[t],"—the continued vitality of literally scores of decisions must be understood to depend on nothing more than the proclivities of the individuals who now comprise a majority of this Court.★ See, e.g., *Metro Broadcasting v. FCC*, [497 U.S. 547] (1990) (authority of Federal government to set aside broadcast licenses for minority applicants); *Grady v. Corbin*, [495 U.S. 508] (1990) (right under Double Jeopardy Clause not to be subjected twice to prosecution for same criminal conduct); *Mills v. Maryland*, *supra* (Eighth Amendment right to jury instructions that do not preclude consideration of nonunanimous mitigating factors in capital sentencing); *United States v. Paradise*, 480 U.S. 149 (1987) (right to promotions as remedy for racial discrimination in government hiring); *Ford v. Wainwright*, 477 U.S. 399 (1986) (Eighth Amendment right not to be executed if insane); *Thornburgh v. American College of Obstetricians and Gynecologists*, 476 U.S. 747 (1986) (reaffirming right to abortion recognized in *Roe v. Wade*, 410 U.S. 113 (1973)); *Aguilar v. Felton*, 473 U.S. 402 (1985) (Establishment Clause bar on governmental financial assistance to parochial schools).

In my view, this impoverished conception of *stare decisis* cannot possibly be reconciled with the values that inform the proper judicial function.

★Based on the majority's new criteria for overruling, these decisions, too, must be included on the "endangered precedents" list: *Rutan v. Republican Party of Illinois*, [497 U.S. 62] (1990) (First Amendment right not to be denied public employment on the basis of party affiliation); *Peel v. Attorney Registration and Disciplinary Comm'n*, [496 U.S. 91] (1990) (First Amendment right to advertise legal specialization); *Zinermon v. Burch*, 494 U.S. 113 (1990) (due process right to procedural safeguards aimed at assuring voluntariness of decision to commit oneself to mental hospital); *James v. Illinois*, 493 U.S. 307 (1990) (Fourth Amendment right to exclusion of illegally obtained evidence introduced for impeachment of defense witness); *Rankin v. McPherson*, 483 U.S. 378 (1987) (First Amendment right of public employee to express views on matter of public importance); *Rock v. Arkansas*, 483 U.S. 44 (1987) (Fifth Amendment and Sixth Amendment right of criminal defendant to provide hypnotically refreshed testimony on his own behalf); *Gray v. Mississippi*, 481 U.S. 648 (1987) (rejecting applicability of harmless error analysis to Eighth Amendment right not to be sentenced to death by "death qualified" jury); *Maine v. Moulton*, 474 U.S. 159 (1985) (Sixth Amendment right to counsel violated by introduction of statements made to government informant-codefendant in course of preparing defense strategy); *Garcia v. San Antonio Metropolitan Transit Auth.*, 469 U.S. 528 (1985) (rejecting theory that Tenth Amendment provides immunity to states from federal regulation); *Pulliam v. Allen*, 466 U.S. 522 (1984) (right to obtain injunctive relief from constitutional violations committed by judicial officials).

Contrary to what the majority suggests, *stare decisis* is important not merely because individuals rely on precedent to structure their commercial activity but because fidelity to precedent is part and parcel of a conception of "the judiciary as a source of impersonal and reasoned judgments."

Atkins v. Virginia

536 U.S. 304, 122 S.CT. 2242 (2002)

In *Ford v. Wainwright*, 477 U.S. 399 (1986), the Court held that the Eighth Amendment bars the execution of death row inmates who are (or who have gone while on death row) insane. However, in *Penry v. Lynaugh*, 492 U.S. 302 (1989), a bare majority upheld the execution of an individual who was mentally disabled. In her opinion for the Court, Justice O'Connor emphasized that at the time, only one state banned the execution of the mentally disabled and that even when added to the fourteen states that had rejected capital punishment that did "not provide sufficient evidence at present of a national consensus" against executing mentally disabled convicts. Subsequently, seventeen other states of the thirty-eight states that imposed the death penalty at the time enacted laws barring executions of the mentally disabled. And opponents of the death penalty continued to raise the issue in an effort to persuade the Court to reconsider the matter.

In 1998, Daryl Renard Atkins, who has an IQ of 59—that of a nine- to twelve-year-old—was convicted and sentenced to death for participating in the robbery and murder of a U.S. airman in Virginia. The Virginia Supreme Court affirmed his sentence and an appeal was made to the Supreme Court. Notably, a number of friend of court briefs highlighted the controversy and urged the Court to abandon its earlier ruling; among those filing *amicus* briefs were the European Union, the U.S. Catholic Conference, and the American Psychological Association.

The state supreme court's decision was reversed on a 6–3 vote and Justice Stevens delivered the opinion of the Court. Chief Justice Rehnquist and Justice Scalia filed dissenting opinions, which Justice Thomas joined.

■ ■ ■

☐ *Justice STEVENS delivers the opinion of the Court.*

Those mentally retarded persons who meet the law's requirements for criminal responsibility should be tried and punished when they commit crimes. Because of their disabilities in areas of reasoning, judgment, and control of their impulses, however, they do not act with the level of moral culpability that characterizes the most serious adult criminal conduct.

Moreover, their impairments can jeopardize the reliability and fairness of capital proceedings against mentally retarded defendants. Presumably for these reasons, in the 13 years since we decided *Penry v. Lynaugh*, 492 U.S. 302 (1989), the American public, legislators, scholars, and judges have deliberated over the question whether the death penalty should ever be imposed on a mentally retarded criminal. The consensus reflected in those deliberations informs our answer to the question presented by this case: whether such executions are "cruel and unusual punishments" prohibited by the Eighth Amendment to the Federal Constitution. . . .

The Eighth Amendment succinctly prohibits "excessive" sanctions. . . . A claim that punishment is excessive is judged not by the standards that prevailed in 1685 when Lord Jeffreys presided over the "Bloody Assizes" or when the Bill of Rights was adopted, but rather by those that currently prevail. As Chief Justice WARREN explained in his opinion in *Trop v. Dulles*, 356 U.S. 86 (1958): "The basic concept underlying the Eighth Amendment is nothing less than the dignity of man. . . . The Amendment must draw its meaning from the evolving standards of decency that mark the progress of a maturing society."

Proportionality review under those evolving standards should be informed by "objective factors to the maximum possible extent." We have pinpointed that the "clearest and most reliable objective evidence of contemporary values is the legislation enacted by the country's legislatures." *Penry*. Relying in part on such legislative evidence, we have held that death is an impermissibly excessive punishment for the rape of an adult woman, *Coker v. Georgia*, 433 U.S. 584 (1977), or for a defendant who neither took life, attempted to take life, nor intended to take life, *Enmund v. Florida*, 458 U.S. 782 (1982). In *Coker*, we focused primarily on the then-recent legislation that had been enacted in response to our decision 10 years earlier in *Furman v. Georgia*, 408 U.S. 238 (1972) (*per curiam*), to support the conclusion that the "current judgment," though "not wholly unanimous," weighed very heavily on the side of rejecting capital punishment as a "suitable penalty for raping an adult woman." The "current legislative judgment" relevant to our decision in *Enmund* was less clear than in *Coker* but "nevertheless weigh[ed] on the side of rejecting capital punishment for the crime at issue." . . .

Guided by our approach in these cases, we shall first review the judgment of legislatures that have addressed the suitability of imposing the death penalty on the mentally retarded and then consider reasons for agreeing or disagreeing with their judgment.

The parties have not called our attention to any state legislative consideration of the suitability of imposing the death penalty on mentally retarded offenders prior to 1986. In that year, the public reaction to the execution of a mentally retarded murderer in Georgia apparently led to the enactment of the first state statute prohibiting such executions. In 1988, when Congress enacted legislation reinstating the federal death penalty, it expressly provided that a "sentence of death shall not be carried out upon a person who is mentally retarded." In 1989, Maryland enacted a similar prohibition. It was in that year that we decided *Penry*, and concluded that those two state enactments, "even when added to the 14 States that have rejected capital punishment completely, do not provide sufficient evidence at present of a national consensus."

Much has changed since then. [S]tate legislatures across the country began to address the issue. In 1990 Kentucky and Tennessee enacted statutes similar to those in Georgia and Maryland, as did New Mexico in 1991, and Arkansas, Colorado, Washington, Indiana, and Kansas in 1993 and 1994. In 1995, when New York reinstated its death penalty, it emulated the Federal Government by expressly exempting the mentally retarded. Nebraska followed suit in 1998. There appear to have been no similar enactments during the next two years, but in 2000 and 2001 six more States—South Dakota, Arizona, Connecticut, Florida, Missouri, and North Carolina—joined the procession. The Texas Legislature unanimously adopted a similar bill, and bills have passed at least one house in other States, including Virginia and Nevada.

It is not so much the number of these States that is significant, but the consistency of the direction of change. Given the well-known fact that anti-crime legislation is far more popular than legislation providing protections for persons guilty of violent crime, the large number of States prohibiting the execution of mentally retarded persons (and the complete absence of States passing legislation reinstating the power to conduct such executions) provides powerful evidence that today our society views mentally retarded offenders as categorically less culpable than the average criminal. . . .

To the extent there is serious disagreement about the execution of mentally retarded offenders, it is in determining which offenders are in fact retarded. In this case, for instance, the Commonwealth of Virginia disputes that Atkins suffers from mental retardation. Not all people who claim to be mentally retarded will be so impaired as to fall within the range of mentally retarded offenders about whom there is a national consensus. As was our approach in *Ford v. Wainwright*, with regard to insanity, "we leave to the State[s] the task of developing appropriate ways to enforce the constitutional restriction upon its execution of sentences." . . .

[O]ur death penalty jurisprudence provides two reasons consistent with the legislative consensus that the mentally retarded should be categorically excluded from execution. First, there is a serious question as to whether either justification that we have recognized as a basis for the death penalty applies to mentally retarded offenders. *Gregg v. Georgia*, 428 U.S. 153 (1976), identified "retribution and deterrence of capital crimes by prospective offenders" as the social purposes served by the death penalty. Unless the imposition of the death penalty on a mentally retarded person "measurably contributes to one or both of these goals, it 'is nothing more than the purposeless and needless imposition of pain and suffering,' and hence an unconstitutional punishment." *Enmund*.

With respect to retribution—the interest in seeing that the offender gets his "just deserts"—the severity of the appropriate punishment necessarily depends on the culpability of the offender. Since *Gregg*, our jurisprudence has consistently confined the imposition of the death penalty to a narrow category of the most serious crimes. For example, in *Godfrey v. Georgia*, 446 U.S. 420 (1980), we set aside a death sentence because the petitioner's crimes did not reflect "a consciousness materially more 'depraved' than that of any person guilty of murder." If the culpability of the average murderer is insufficient to justify the most extreme sanction available to the State, the lesser culpability of the mentally retarded offender surely does not merit that form of retribution. Thus, pursuant to our narrowing jurisprudence, which seeks to ensure that only the most deserving of execution are put to death, an exclusion for the mentally retarded is appropriate.

With respect to deterrence—the interest in preventing capital crimes by prospective offenders—"it seems likely that 'capital punishment can serve as a deterrent only when murder is the result of premeditation and deliberation,'" *Enmund*. Exempting the mentally retarded from that punishment will not affect the "cold calculus that precedes the decision" of other potential murderers. Indeed, that sort of calculus is at the opposite end of the spectrum from behavior of mentally retarded offenders. . . . Nor will exempting the mentally retarded from execution lessen the deterrent effect of the death penalty with respect to offenders who are not mentally retarded. Such individuals are unprotected by the exemption and will continue to face the threat of execution. Thus, executing the mentally retarded will not measurably further the goal of deterrence. . . .

The judgment of the Virginia Supreme Court is reversed and the case is remanded for further proceedings not inconsistent with this opinion. It is so ordered.

☐ *Justice SCALIA, with whom THE CHIEF JUSTICE and Justice THOMAS join, dissenting.*

Today's decision is the pinnacle of our Eighth Amendment death-is-different jurisprudence. Not only does it, like all of that jurisprudence, find no support in the text or history of the Eighth Amendment; it does not even have support in current social attitudes regarding the conditions that render an otherwise just death penalty inappropriate. Seldom has an opinion of this Court rested so obviously upon nothing but the personal views of its members. . . .

The Court makes no pretense that execution of the mildly mentally retarded would have been considered "cruel and unusual" in 1791. Only the severely or profoundly mentally retarded, commonly known as "idiots," enjoyed any special status under the law at that time. They, like lunatics, suffered a "deficiency in will" rendering them unable to tell right from wrong. W. Blackstone, *Commentaries on the Laws of England* (1769). Due to their incompetence, idiots were "excuse[d] from the guilt, and of course from the punishment, of any criminal action committed under such deprivation of the senses." Instead, they were often committed to civil confinement or made wards of the State, thereby preventing them from "go[ing] loose, to the terror of the king's subjects." Mentally retarded offenders with less severe impairments—those who were not "idiots"—suffered criminal prosecution and punishment, including capital punishment.

The Court is left to argue, therefore, that execution of the mildly retarded is inconsistent with the "evolving standards of decency that mark the progress of a maturing society." *Trop v. Dulles*. Before today, our opinions consistently emphasized that Eighth Amendment judgments regarding the existence of social "standards" "should be informed by objective factors to the maximum possible extent" and "should not be, or appear to be, merely the subjective views of individual Justices." *Coker v. Georgia*.

The Court pays lipservice to these precedents as it miraculously extracts a "national consensus" forbidding execution of the mentally retarded from the fact that 18 States—less than half (47%) of the 38 States that permit capital punishment (for whom the issue exists)—have very recently enacted legislation barring execution of the mentally retarded. Even that 47% figure is a distorted one. If one is to say, as the Court does today, that all executions of the mentally retarded are so morally repugnant as to violate our national "standards of decency," surely the "consensus" it points to must be one that has set its righteous face against all such executions. Not 18 States, but only seven—18% of death penalty jurisdictions—have legislation of that scope. Eleven of those that the Court counts enacted statutes prohibiting execution of mentally retarded defendants convicted after, or convicted of crimes committed after, the effective date of the legislation; those already on death row, or consigned there before the statute's effective date, or even (in those States using the date of the crime as the criterion of retroactivity) tried in the future for murders committed many years ago, could be put to death. That is not a statement of absolute moral repugnance, but one of current preference between two tolerable approaches. . . .

But let us accept, for the sake of argument, the Court's faulty count. That bare number of States alone—18—should be enough to convince any reasonable person that no "national consensus" exists. How is it possible that agreement among 47% of the death penalty jurisdictions amounts to "consensus"? Our prior cases have generally required a much higher degree of agreement before finding a punishment cruel and unusual on "evolving standards" grounds. . . .

Moreover, a major factor that the Court entirely disregards is that the legislation of all 18 States it relies on is still in its infancy. The oldest of the statutes is only 14 years old; five were enacted last year; over half were enacted within the past eight years. Few, if any, of the States have had sufficient experience with these laws to know whether they are sensible in the long term. . . .

The Court's thrashing about for evidence of "consensus" includes reliance upon the margins by which state legislatures have enacted bans on execution of the retarded. Presumably, in applying our Eighth Amendment "evolving-standards-of-decency" jurisprudence, we will henceforth weight not only how many States have agreed, but how many States have agreed by how much. Of course if the percentage of legislators voting for the bill is significant, surely the number of people represented by the legislators voting for the bill is also significant: the fact that 49% of the legislators in a State with a population of 60 million voted against the bill should be more impressive than the fact that 90% of the legislators in a state with a population of 2 million voted for it. (By the way, the population of the death penalty States that exclude the mentally retarded is only 44% of the population of all death penalty States.) This is quite absurd. . . .

But the Prize for the Court's Most Feeble Effort to fabricate "national consensus" must go to its appeal (deservedly relegated to a footnote) to the views of assorted professional and religious organizations, members of the so-called "world community," and respondents to opinion polls. I agree with THE CHIEF JUSTICE that the views of professional and religious organizations and the results of opinion polls are irrelevant. Equally irrelevant are the practices of the "world community," whose notions of justice are (thankfully) not always those of our people. . . .

Today's opinion adds one more to the long list of substantive and procedural requirements impeding imposition of the death penalty imposed under this Court's assumed power to invent a death-is-different jurisprudence. None of those requirements existed when the Eighth Amendment was adopted, and some of them were not even supported by current moral consensus. . . .

This newest invention promises to be more effective than any of the others in turning the process of capital trial into a game. One need only read the definitions of mental retardation adopted by the American Association of Mental Retardation and the American Psychiatric Association to realize that the symptoms of this condition can readily be feigned. And whereas the capital defendant who feigns insanity risks commitment to a mental institution until he can be cured (and then tried and executed), *Jones v. United States*, 463 U.S. 354 (1983), the capital defendant who feigns mental retardation risks nothing at all. The mere pendency of the present case has brought us petitions by death row inmates claiming for the first time, after multiple *habeas* petitions, that they are retarded. . . .

■ IN COMPARATIVE PERSPECTIVE

The South African Constitutional Court Declares Capital Punishment Unconstitutional

On June 17, 1995, the Constitutional Court of the Republic of South Africa declared capital punishment to violate the provisional 1993 Constitution, which was subsequently superceded by the Constitution of 1996. The decision in *The State v. T Makwanyane and M Mchunu*, 1995 (3)SA 391 (Const. Ct.), was unanimous, though there were ten concurring opinions filed along with President Chaskalson's opinion for the Court, for a total of 130 pages. In the excerpt below, note President Chaskalson's approach to constitutional interpretation and reliance on comparative constitutional law.

President CHASKALSON:

[2] Section 277(1)(a) of the Criminal Procedure Act No. 51 of 1977 prescribes that the death penalty is a competent sentence for murder. Counsel for the accused was invited by the Appellate Division to consider whether this provision was consistent with the Republic of South Africa Constitution, 1993, which had come into force subsequent to the conviction and sentence by the trial court. He argued that it was not, contending that it was in conflict with the provisions of sections 9 and 11(2) of the Constitution. . . .

[8] Chapter Three of the Constitution sets out the fundamental rights to which every person is entitled under the Constitution and also contains provisions dealing with the

way in which the Chapter is to be interpreted by the Courts. It does not deal specifically with the death penalty, but in section 11(2), it prohibits "cruel, inhuman or degrading treatment or punishment." There is no definition of what is to be regarded as "cruel, inhuman or degrading" and we therefore have to give meaning to these words ourselves. . . .

[27] The principal arguments advanced by counsel for the accused in support of their contention that the imposition of the death penalty for murder is a "cruel, inhuman or degrading punishment," were that the death sentence is an affront to human dignity, is inconsistent with the unqualified right to life entrenched in the Constitution, cannot be corrected in case of error or enforced in a manner that is not arbitrary, and that it negates the essential content of the right to life and the other rights that flow from it. The Attorney General argued that the death penalty is recognised as a legitimate form of punishment in many parts of the world, it is a deterrent to violent crime, it meets society's need for adequate retribution for heinous offences, and it is regarded by South African society as an acceptable form of punishment. He asserted that it is, therefore, not cruel, inhuman or degrading within the meaning of section 11(2) of the Constitution. These arguments for and against the death sentence are well known and have been considered in many of the foreign authorities and cases to which we were referred. We must deal with them now in the light of the provisions of our own Constitution. . . .

[33] The death sentence is a form of punishment which has been used throughout history by different societies. It has long been the subject of controversy. As societies became more enlightened, they restricted the offences for which this penalty could be imposed. The movement away from the death penalty gained momentum during the second half of the present century with the growth of the abolitionist movement. . . . According to Amnesty International, 1,831 executions were carried out throughout the world in 1993 as a result of sentences of death, of which 1,419 were in China, which means that only 412 executions were carried out in the rest of the world in that year. Today, capital punishment has been abolished as a penalty for murder either specifically or in practice by almost half the countries of the world including the democracies of Europe and our neighbouring countries, Namibia, Mozambique and Angola. In most of those countries where it is retained, as the Amnesty International statistics show, it is seldom used. . . .

[40] The earliest litigation on the validity of the death sentence seems to have been pursued in the courts of the

(continues)

■ IN COMPARATIVE PERSPECTIVE
The South African Constitutional Court Declares
Capital Punishment Unconstitutional (continued)

United States of America. . . . Statutes providing for mandatory death sentences, or too little discretion in sentencing, have been rejected by the Supreme Court because they do not allow for consideration of factors peculiar to the convicted person facing sentence, which may distinguish his or her case from other cases. For the same reason, statutes which allow too wide a discretion to judges or juries have also been struck down on the grounds that the exercise of such discretion leads to arbitrary results. In sum, therefore, if there is no discretion, too little discretion, or an unbounded discretion, the provision authorising the death sentence has been struck down as being contrary to the Eighth Amendment; where the discretion has been "suitably directed and limited so as to minimise the risk of wholly arbitrary and capricious action," the challenge to the statute has failed. . . .

[47] There seems to me to be little difference between the guided discretion required for the death sentence in the United States, and the criteria laid down by the Appellate Division for the imposition of the death sentence. The fact that the Appellate Division, a court of experienced judges, takes the final decision in all cases is, in my view, more likely to result in consistency of sentencing, than will be the case where sentencing is in the hands of jurors who are offered statutory guidance as to how that discretion should be exercised.

[48] The argument that the imposition of the death sentence under section 277 is arbitrary and capricious does not, however, end there. It also focuses on what is alleged to be the arbitrariness inherent in the application of section 277 in practice. Of the thousands of persons put on trial for murder, only a very small percentage are sentenced to death by a trial court, and of those, a large number escape the ultimate penalty on appeal. At every stage of the process there is an element of chance. The outcome may be dependent upon factors such as the way the case is investigated by the police, the way the case is presented by the prosecutor, how effectively the accused is defended, the personality and particular attitude to capital punishment of the trial judge and, if the matter

goes on appeal, the particular judges who are selected to hear the case. Race and poverty are also alleged to be factors. . . .

[58] Under our constitutional order the right to human dignity is specifically guaranteed. It can only be limited by legislation which passes the stringent test of being 'necessary.' The weight given to human dignity by Justice BRENNAN is wholly consistent with the values of our Constitution and the new order established by it. It is also consistent with the approach to extreme punishments followed by courts in other countries.

[59] In Germany, the Federal Constitutional Court has stressed this aspect of punishment. "Respect for human dignity especially requires the prohibition of cruel, inhuman, and degrading punishments. [The state] cannot turn the offender into an object of crime prevention to the detriment of his constitutionally protected right to social worth and respect." [*Life Imprisonment Case [1977] 45 BVerfGE 187*]. . . .

[80] The unqualified right to life vested in every person by section 9 of our Constitution is another factor crucially relevant to the question whether the death sentence is cruel, inhuman or degrading punishment within the meaning of section 11(2) of our Constitution. In this respect our Constitution differs materially from the Constitutions of the United States and India. . . .

[95] The carrying out of the death sentence destroys life, which is protected without reservation under section 9 of our Constitution, it annihilates human dignity which is protected under section 10, elements of arbitrariness are present in its enforcement and it is irremediable. Taking these factors into account . . . and giving the words of section 11(2) the broader meaning to which they are entitled at this stage of the enquiry, rather than a narrow meaning, I am satisfied that in the context of our Constitution the death penalty is indeed a cruel, inhuman and degrading punishment. . . .

[144] The rights to life and dignity are the most important of all human rights, and the source of all other personal rights in Chapter Three. By committing ourselves to a society founded on the recognition of human rights we are required to value these two rights above all others. And this must be demonstrated by the State in everything that it does, including the way it punishes criminals. This is not achieved by objectifying murderers and putting them to death to serve as an example to others in the expectation that they might possibly be deterred thereby. . . .

11

THE RIGHT OF PRIVACY

A right of privacy is not specifically provided for in the Constitution or the Bill of Rights. Yet both embody the principle of limited government and hence the idea that individuals in some degree enjoy a "right to be let alone." As Justice Louis Brandeis, dissenting from the Court's initial denial of Fourth Amendment protection against wiretaps in *Olmstead v. United States* (1928) (see Ch. 7), observed:

> The makers of our Constitution undertook to secure conditions favorable to the pursuit of happiness. They recognized the significance of man's spiritual nature, of his feelings and of his intellect. They knew that only part of the pain, pleasure, and satisfactions of life are to be found in material things. They sought to protect Americans in their beliefs, their thoughts, their emotions and their sensations. They conferred as against the Government, the right to be let alone—the most comprehensive of rights and the right most valued by civilized man.

Neither common law nor constitutional law, however, recognized a right of privacy until the late nineteenth century. In his treatise, *The Law of Torts* (1888), Judge Thomas Cooley planted the seed for the development of a right of privacy by noting for the first time a right to be let alone. Two years later, writing in the *Harvard Law Review*, Samuel Warren and Louis Brandeis cultivated the idea by arguing that common-law protection for property rights was evolving toward a "recognition of man's spiritual nature."[1] Their analysis of privacy as the right to be let alone sparked the development of a right of privacy in tort law (law dealing with private injuries, such as the public revelations of embarrassing personal facts and the appropriation for commercial purposes of an individual's name or likeness). Between 1890 and 1941, state courts in twelve states recognized a right of privacy;

the number increased to eighteen by 1956 and then to more than thirty-one states by 1960.[2]

The Supreme Court initially acknowledged protection for privacy interests under the Fourth and Fifth Amendments in *Boyd v. United States*, 116 U.S. 616 (1886) (see Ch. 7), when holding that those amendments apply "to all invasions on the part of the government and its employees of the sanctity of a man's home and the privacies of life. It is not the breaking of his doors, and the rummaging of his drawers, that constitutes the essence of the offense, but it is the invasion of his indefeasible right of personal security, personal liberty and private property." Subsequently, the Court incorporated an analysis of individuals' "reasonable expectations of privacy" into Fourth Amendment jurisprudence. *Katz v. United States*, 389 U.S. 347 (1967) (see Ch. 7), and *Terry v. Ohio*, 392 U.S. 1 (1968) (see Ch. 7), for example, reaffirmed that "wherever an individual may harbor a reasonable 'expectation of privacy,' . . . he is entitled to be free from unreasonable governmental intrusion," when explaining that "the specific content and incidents of this right [of privacy] must be shaped by the context in which it is asserted."

In a series of other rulings, the Court also acknowledged protection for privacy interests under the Fifth Amendment (see Ch. 8). In addition, by the 1960s the Court had also affirmed First Amendment protection for privacy interests. As early as 1920, Justice Brandeis, dissenting from the Court's upholding of a law forbidding the teaching and advocacy of pacifism in *Gilbert v. Minnesota*, 254 U.S. 325 (1920), contended that the amendment protects "the privacy and freedom of the home. Father and mother may follow the promptings of religious belief, of conscience or of conviction, and teach son or daughter the doctrine of pacifism." When holding that individuals may possess obscenity in their homes in *Stanley v. Georgia* (1969) (see Ch. 5), the Court reaffirmed that individuals have First Amendment–protected privacy interests in their homes.[3] The Court as well formally acknowledged a First Amendment right of associational privacy in *National Association for the Advancement of Colored People v. Alabama* (1958) (see Ch. 5) and extended its protection to a broad range of religious, economic, political, and social activities and associations.

Still, the Warren Court's declaration of a constitutional right of privacy in *Griswold v. Connecticut* (1965) (in Ch. 4) provoked a continuing controversy in constitutional politics. The right of privacy, according to Justice William Douglas, may be found in the penumbras, or shadows, of the First, Third, Fourth, Fifth, and Ninth Amendments and applied to the states under the Fourteenth Amendment due process clause. Dissenting Justices Hugo Black and Potter Stewart countered that *Griswold*'s majority was turning "somersaults with history" and becoming a "super-legislature" by creating a right of privacy out of whole-constitutional cloth. Notice, however, that at the outset of his opinion in *Griswold*, Justice Douglas disclaims undertaking the kind of substantive due process analysis associated with the discredited *Lochner* era. During that era the Court created and enforced a "liberty of contract" and ultimately precipitated the 1937 constitutional crisis over its invalidation of New Deal and progressive economic legislation (see Ch. 3). Still, Black and Stewart, and a good number of Court watchers, remained unpersuaded.

No less controversial, as Justices Black and Stewart suggest, is the reliance of Justice Douglas and concurring Justice Arthur Goldberg on the Ninth Amendment. That amendment provides that "[t]he enumeration in the Constitution of certain rights shall not be construed to deny or disparage others retained by the people." Despite the criticism of Justices Black and Stewart, though, neither Douglas nor Goldberg contends that the Ninth Amendment provides an independent basis for the Court's articulation of unenumerated rights. Instead, they maintain that the amendment only provides a *rule of construction* for ensuring the "requisite latitude" of guarantees of the Bill of Rights. As Justice Douglas later explained, "The Ninth Amendment obviously does not create federally enforceable rights. . . . [b]ut a catalogue of these customary, traditional, and time-honored rights, amenities, privileges and immunities. . . . Many of them in my view come within the meaning of the term 'liberty' as used in the Fourteenth Amendment."[4] When defending this interpretation of the Ninth Amendment, justices and commentators frequently turn to the correspondence between James Madison and Thomas Jefferson over the adoption of the Bill of Rights. Both initially feared "that a positive declaration of some of the most essential rights could not be obtained in the requisite latitude" but eventually agreed that a bill of rights would put "into the hands of the judiciary" a "legal check" on the exercise of governmental power (see Ch. 4). When proposing amendments to the Constitution in the first Congress, Madison thus argued:

> It has been objected also against a bill of rights, that, by enumerating particular exceptions to the grant of power, it would disparage those rights which were not placed in that enumeration; and it might follow by implication, that those rights which were not singled out, were intended to be assigned into the hands of the General Government, and were consequently insecure. This is one of the most plausible arguments I have ever heard urged against the admission of a bill of rights into this system; but, I conceive, that it may be guarded against. I have attempted it, as gentlemen may see by turning to the [proposed amendment that eventually became the Ninth Amendment].[5]

Still, critics counter that there is a difference in kind, rather than simply degree, between the Court's recognition of protection for personal privacy as part of the "requisite latitude," for example, of the Fourth Amendment and the creation of a broad constitutional right of privacy.

The debate sparked by the Warren Court's ruling on the right of privacy in *Griswold* erupted into a major political controversy with the Burger Court's 1973 ruling in *Roe v. Wade* (1973) (excerpted in Section A of this chapter), striking down a Texas law that sharply limited the availability of abortions. The Burger and Rehnquist Courts limited the application of the right of privacy to areas primarily involving reproductive freedom. While the Rehnquist Court (as indicated in the next section) was more willing to uphold state laws restricting access to abortions, the Court did not consider overturning *Griswold*. Moreover, while the Court has generally refused to extend the right of privacy, in *Lawrence v. Texas* (2003) (excerpted in Section B) a majority finally acknowledged that the right of privacy extends to personal autonomy and intimate consensual sexual relations, when striking down Texas's law criminalizing homosexual sodomy.

Notes

1. S. Warren and L. Brandeis, "The Right of Privacy," 4 *Harvard Law Review* 193 (1890).

2. See William Prosser, "Privacy," 48 *California Law Review* 383 (1960).

3. See also *Cohen v. California* (1971) and *Federal Communications v. Pacific Foundation* (1978), both in Ch. 5.

4. *Doe v. Bolton*, 410 U.S. 179 (1973).

5. James Madison, House of Representatives, in *The Debates and Proceedings in the Congress of the United States*, Vol. 1 (Washington, DC: Gales and Seaton, 1834), 455.

Selected Bibliography

Farber, Daniel. *Retained by the People: The 'Silent' Ninth Amendment and the Constitutional Rights Americans Don't Know They Have.* New York: Perseus Books, 2007.

Lash, Kurt. *The Lost History of the Ninth Amendment.* New York: Oxford University Press, 2009.

O'Brien, David M. *Privacy, Law, and Public Policy.* New York: Praeger, 1979.

Richards, Neil. *Intellectual Privacy: Rethinking Civil Liberties in the Digital Age.* New York: Oxford University Press, 2015.

Westin, Alan F. *Privacy and Freedom.* New York: Atheneum, 1970.

A | *Privacy and Reproductive Freedom*

The Supreme Court initially acknowledged protection under the Fourteenth Amendment due process clause for personal privacy and freedom from governmental intrusions into the areas of marriage, reproduction, and child-rearing in the 1920s, during the height of the *Lochner* era (see Ch. 3). In *Meyer v. Nebraska*, 262 U.S. 390 (1923), the Court struck down a state law, passed shortly after World War I and amid opposition to peace negotiations with Germany, forbidding the teaching of German and modern languages other than English in private and public schools. There, Justice James McReynolds observed,

> Without a doubt, [the Fourteenth Amendment guarantee that "No state . . . shall deprive any person of life, liberty or property without due process of law"] denotes not merely freedom from bodily restraint but also the right of the individual to contract, to engage in any of the common occupations of life, to acquire useful knowledge, to marry, establish a home and bring up children, to worship God according to the dictates of his own conscience, and generally to enjoy these privileges long recognized at common law as essential to the orderly pursuit of happiness by free men.

Two years later, *Pierce v. Society of Sisters*, 268 U.S. 510 (1925), overturned an Oregon law requiring primary and secondary school children to attend public rather than private schools on the grounds that it interfered "with the liberty of parents and guardians to direct the upbringing and education of children under their control." However, in *Buck v. Bell* (1927) (excerpted below) the Court rejected a substantive due process challenge to Virginia's law on the compulsory sterilization of those deemed mentally defective.

The first major ruling extending protection to reproductive freedom, however, came in *Skinner v. Oklahoma*, 316 U.S. 535 (1942). *Buck v. Bell*, 274 U.S. 200 (1927) (excerpted below) had upheld a Virginia law, passed in response to the eugenics movement, requiring the sterilization of persons confined to state mental health institutions. But in *Skinner* the Court unanimously overturned a state law providing for the sterilization of "habitual criminals." Jack Skinner had been convicted of stealing chickens in 1926, of robbery in 1929, and again in 1934. In 1936, the state attorney general instituted proceedings against Skinner under Oklahoma's 1935 Habitual Criminal Sterilization Act, which authorized the sterilization of individuals who had been convicted two or more times of certain "felonies involving moral turpitude." Skinner challenged the constitutionality of Oklahoma's law as a violation of the Fourteenth Amendment due process and equal protection clauses. When striking down the law for running afoul of the equal protection clause because it permitted the sterilization of those convicted of crimes such as embezzlement but not those convicted of larceny, Justice Douglas explained,

> We are dealing here with legislation which involves one of the basic civil rights of man. Marriage and procreation are fundamental to the very existence and survival of the race. The power to sterilize, if exercised, may have subtle, far-reaching and devastating effects. In evil or reckless hands it can cause races or types which are inimical to the dominant group to wither and disappear. There is no redemption for the individual whom the law touches. Any experiment which the State conducts is to his irreparable injury. He is forever deprived of a basic liberty.

Later, *Loving v. Virginia*, 388 U.S. 1 (1967) (see the box, CONSTITU-TIONAL HISTORY: *Loving v. Virginia* and Bans on Interracial Marriage, in Ch. 12), struck down a state miscegenation law that criminalized interracial marriages. And when holding that states may not deny parents, who failed to meet child-support obligations, the right to remarry without a court's permission, the Court "reaffirm[ed] the fundamental character of the right to marry" in *Zablocki v. Redhail*, 434 U.S. 374 (1978).

Beginning in the 1940s, individuals began attacking the constitutionality of laws prohibiting the use of contraceptives, but the Court refused to hear their appeals. (See INSIDE THE COURT: Standing and the Connecticut Birth Control Cases, in Ch. 2.) Finally, in *Griswold v. Connecticut* (1965) (see Ch. 4) the Court struck down Connecticut's statute as a denial of the right of privacy of married couples. Seven years later, over the dissent of Chief Justice Burger, *Eisenstadt v. Baird*, 405 U.S. 438 (1972), overturned a Massachusetts law forbidding the use of contraceptives by unmarried individuals. In his opinion for the Court, Justice Brennan observed that

> [w]hatever the rights of the individual to access to contraceptives may be, the rights must be the same for the unmarried and the married alike. If under *Griswold* the distribution of contraceptives to married persons cannot be prohibited, a ban on distribution to unmarried persons would be equally impermissible. It is true that in *Griswold* the right of privacy in question inhered in the marital relationship. Yet the marital couple is not an independent entity

with a mind and heart of its own, but an association of two individuals each with a separate intellectual and emotional makeup. If the right of privacy means anything, it is the right of the *individual*, married or single, to be free from unwarranted governmental intrusion into matters so fundamentally affecting a person as the decision whether to bear or beget a child.

A year before *Eisenstadt*, a bare majority of the Burger Court upheld the District of Columbia's law allowing abortions not only to save a woman's life but also to maintain her physical and psychological well-being. But in *United States v. Vuitch*, 402 U.S. 62 (1971), the Court declined to rule on whether a woman's right of privacy included her decision to terminate or carry an unwanted pregnancy to term. Yet the Court could not escape deciding that question. Just one month after deciding *Vuitch*, the Court granted review to abortion cases, *Roe v. Wade* (1973) (see excerpt below) and *Doe v. Bolton*, 410 U.S. 179 (1973). A movement to liberalize abortion laws had grown throughout the turbulent 1960s with demands for women's rights. The legal reforms pushed by women's pro-choice advocates were in some respects little more than a return to the legal status of abortions a century earlier. Until the mid-nineteenth century, most states permitted abortions, except after quickening—the first movement of the fetus—and then an abortion was usually considered only a minor offense. After the Civil War, the American Medical Association, in opposition to the use of midwives, and other antiabortionists persuaded states to toughen their laws. By 1910 every state, except Kentucky, had made abortion a felony. But by the late 1960s, fourteen states had liberalized laws to permit abortions when the woman's health was in danger, when there was a likelihood of fetal abnormality, and when the woman was a victim of rape or incest. Four states—Alaska, Hawaii, New York, and Washington—had gone so far as to repeal all criminal penalties for abortions performed in early pregnancy.

When handing down *Roe v. Wade* the Court elevated the issue of abortion to the national political agenda and sparked a larger political struggle in the country. States could no longer categorically proscribe abortions or make them unnecessarily difficult to obtain. The promotion of maternal care and the preservation of the life of a fetus were not sufficiently "compelling state interests" to justify restrictive abortion laws. During roughly the first trimester (three months) of a pregnancy, the decision on abortion is that of a woman and her doctor. During the second, the Court ruled, states may regulate abortions, but only in ways reasonably related to its interest in safeguarding the health of women. In the third trimester, states' interests in preserving the life of the unborn become compelling, and they may limit, even ban, abortions, except when necessary to save a woman's life. *Roe* was thus controversial in not only extending the right of privacy in this area, but in Justice Blackmun's trimester approach to balancing the interests of women seeking abortions and those of the states.

In the years immediately after *Roe*, thirty-four states passed new abortion laws. Some were in conformity with the Court's ruling—requiring, for example, that abortions be performed by licensed physicians—but others sought to limit the impact of *Roe*. States tried to restrict the availability of abortions in several ways: by requiring the informed consent of a husband or that of parents for a minor's abortion, by forbidding the advertising of abortion clinics, and by withholding state funds for abortions not medically necessary. In addition, ten states passed laws or resolutions pledging to ban or severely restrict abortions, and fifteen others left their pre-*Roe* laws on the books, in anticipation of *Roe*'s being eventually overturned.

Initially, the Burger Court basically stood its ground, striking down most state and local attempts to limit *Roe*. However, in three 1977 decisions the Court (dividing 6–3) upheld some state restrictions on the availability of abortions. In *Beal v. Doe*, 432 U.S. 438 (1977), and *Maher v. Roe* (1977) (see excerpt below), a majority of the Court approved restrictions on the public funding of nontherapeutic abortions. In *Poelker v. Doe*, 432 U.S. 519 (1977), the Court upheld a city's policy of refusing nontherapeutic abortions in public hospitals. As the Court's composition changed in the 1980s, pressure mounted with speculation that *Roe* might be further restricted, if not reversed.

Opposition came not only from the states, but also from Congress and the president. Congress failed to pass a constitutional amendment overturning *Roe* but succeeded in limiting the reach of the Court's ruling in a number of ways. In the decade and a half following *Roe*, Congress enacted over thirty laws restricting the availability of abortions. Among these statutes, Congress barred the use of funds for programs in which abortion is included as a method of family planning; barred government officials from ordering recipients of federal funds to perform abortions; barred lawyers working in federally funded legal aid programs from giving assistance to those seeking "nontherapeutic" abortions; provided that employees are not required to pay health insurance benefits for abortions, except to save a woman's life; prohibited the use of federal employee health benefits to pay for abortions, except when a woman's life is imperiled; prohibited the use of foreign aid funds for abortions; and prohibited federal prisons from paying for pregnant inmates' abortions. In *Harris v. McRae*, 448 U.S. 297 (1980), the Court split 5–4 when upholding the so-called Hyde Amendment (named after its sponsor, Republican Representative Henry Hyde of Illinois), forbidding federal funding of nontherapeutic abortions under the Medicaid program. Again, voting 5–4 in *Bowen v. Kendrick*, 487 U.S. 589 (1988), the Court upheld the Adolescent Family Life Act, which prohibits federal funding of organizations involved with abortions, while allowing the funding of religious groups advocating self-discipline as a form of birth control.

By the 1980s, abortion was an issue in presidential politics as well. The 1980, 1984, and 1988 Republican platforms supported a constitutional amendment "to restore protection of the right to life for unborn children." The strategy of Ronald Reagan's administration was twofold: appoint to the federal bench only those opposed to abortion, and initiate litigation that might ultimately lead to overturning *Roe*. But even after the retirements of Justices Douglas and Stewart—and the appointments of Stevens in 1975 and O'Connor in 1981—the Court continued to reaffirm its basic ruling in *Roe*. In *City of Akron v. Akron Center for Reproductive Health*, 462 U.S. 416 (1983), for example, the Court struck down several restrictions imposed on women seeking abortions, including requirements that they sign informed consent forms and wait at least twenty-four hours afterward before having an abortion, along with requiring doctors to perform abortions after the first trimester in a hospital and dispose of fetal remains "in a humane and sanitary way."

In *City of Akron*, Reagan's solicitor general asked the justices to reconsider *Roe* but stopped short of urging its reversal. Still, only Justice O'Connor, joined by Justices Rehnquist and White, was willing to reconsider, if not overturn, *Roe*. In her dissenting opinion in *City of Akron*, Justice O'Connor strongly attacked the constitutional theory and trimester approach of *Roe*, explaining that

> [t]he trimester or "three-stage" approach adopted by the Court in *Roe*, and, in a modified form, employed by the Court to analyze the state regulations in these cases, cannot be supported as a legitimate or useful framework for accommodating the woman's right and the State's interests. The decision of the Court today graphically illustrates why the trimester approach is a completely unworkable method of accommodating the conflicting personal rights and compelling state interests that are involved in the abortion context.
>
> As the Court indicates today, the State's compelling interest in maternal health changes as medical technology changes, and any health regulation must not "depart from accepted medical practice." . . . In applying this standard, the Court holds that "the safety of second-trimester abortions has increased dramatically" since 1973, when *Roe* was decided. . . . Although a regulation such as one requiring that all second-trimester abortions be performed

in hospitals "had strong support" in 1973 "as a reasonable health regulation," . . . this regulation can no longer stand because, according to the Court's diligent research into medical and scientific literature, the dilation and evacuation procedure (D & E), used in 1973 only for first-trimester abortions, "is now widely and successfully used for second trimester abortions." Further, the medical literature relied on by the Court indicates that the D & E procedure may be performed in an appropriate non-hospital setting for "at least . . . the early weeks of the second trimester. . . ." The Court then chooses the period of 16 weeks of gestation as that point at which D & E procedures may be performed safely in a non-hospital setting, and thereby invalidates the Akron hospitalization regulation. . . .

Just as improvement in medical technology inevitably will move *forward* the point at which the State may regulate for reasons of maternal health, different technological improvements will move *backwards* the point of viability at which the State may proscribe abortions except when necessary to preserve the life and health of the mother. . . .

The *Roe* framework, then, is clearly on a collision course with itself. As the medical risks of various abortion procedures decrease, the point at which the State may regulate for reasons of maternal health is moved further forward to actual childbirth. As medical science becomes better able to provide for the separate existence of the fetus, the point of viability is moved further back toward conception. . . . The *Roe* framework is inherently tied to the state of medical technology that exists whenever particular litigation ensues. Although legislatures are better suited to make necessary factual judgments in this area, the Court's framework forces legislatures, as a matter of constitutional law, to speculate about what constitutes "accepted medical practice" at any given time. Without the necessary expertise or ability, courts must then pretend to act as science review boards and examine those legislative judgments. . . .

Justice O'Connor also proposed that the Court abandon *Roe*'s trimester approach and adopt the test of whether state regulations place an "undue burden" on women seeking abortions:

The "undue burden" required in the abortion cases represents the required threshold inquiry that must be conducted before this Court can require a State to justify its legislative actions under the exacting "compelling state interest" standard. . . .

The "unduly burdensome" standard is particularly appropriate in the abortion context because of the *nature* and *scope* of the right that is involved. The privacy right involved in the abortion context "cannot be said to be absolute." *Roe* . . . Rather, the *Roe* right is intended to protect against state action "drastically limiting the availability and safety of the desired service," . . . or against "official interference" and "coercive restraint" imposed on the abortion decision. . . . That a state regulation may "inhibit" abortions to some degree does not require that we find that the regulation is invalid. . . .

In two companion cases handed down along with *City of Akron*, the justices split 5–4 (with Justice Powell casting the crucial fifth vote) in upholding a Missouri law requiring pathology reports for all abortions, the presence of a second physician during abortions performed after viability, and parental consent for minors seeking abortions. They also sustained the constitutionality of a Virginia statute mandating that second-trimester abortions be performed in licensed outpatient clinics in *Planned Parenthood Association of Kansas City, Missouri v. Ashcroft*, 462 U.S. 476 (1983), and *Simopoulos v. Virginia*, 462 U.S. 506 (1983).

Three years after *City of Akron*, the Reagan administration renewed its attack on *Roe*. This time, Reagan's second solicitor general, Harvard Law School professor Charles Fried, dared to do what his predecessor refused: he questioned the Court's wisdom and argued that *Roe* be overturned. But a majority of the Court again rebuffed the Reagan administration when handing down *Thornburgh v. American College of Obstetricians*, 476 U.S. 747 (1986). A majority of the Court, moreover, appeared impatient with the administration's persistence in trying to undo *Roe*. When announcing the decision from the bench, Blackmun exclaimed, "We reaffirm *once again* the general principles of *Roe*." However, Chief Justice Burger broke with *Roe*'s supporters in *Thornburgh*, joining Justices O'Connor, Rehnquist, and White in dissent and indicated that *Roe* should be "reexamined."

The 5–4 split in *Thornburgh* further escalated speculation about how another Reagan appointee might affect the Court and *Roe*. As the Court's composition changed in the late 1980s, support for *Roe* among the justices appeared to decline from 7–2, to 6–3, and to 5–4. Then within a week of the ruling on *Thornburgh*, Chief Justice Burger announced that he would step down from the Court. Reagan immediately responded by shrewdly elevating Justice Rehnquist, one of *Roe*'s sharpest critics, to the chief justiceship and naming Antonin Scalia to his seat on the bench.

As long as Justice Powell remained on the Court, he held the pivotal vote for upholding *Roe*. When he announced his retirement in June 1987, Reagan's nomination of Judge Robert H. Bork—one of *Roe*'s harshest critics—set off a political firestorm. After a bitter Senate battle, Judge Bork's nomination was rejected by the widest margin (58-to-42) of any Supreme Court nominee. Reagan's second nominee, Judge Douglas Ginsburg, was forced to withdraw, but his third nominee, Judge Anthony Kennedy, won easy Senate confirmation.

In the final days of the Reagan administration, the Court thus seemed poised to reconsider, and possibly overturn, *Roe.* Indeed, a few weeks before the Senate confirmed Justice Kennedy, the justices split 4-to-4, thereby affirming by an equally divided Court a lower court's ruling striking down a law requiring parental notification for teenagers seeking abortions. *Hartigan v. Zbaraz*, 484 U.S. 171 (1987). Subsequently, during the summer of 1988, Reagan's Department of Justice talked Missouri's attorney general William Webster into seizing an opportunity afforded by appealing another appellate court's invalidation of that state's restrictions on abortions. Webster's legal strategy was to defend Missouri's law as "nothing more than regulat[ing] abortions within the parameters allowed by *Roe v. Wade.*" But he was persuaded to repeat word for word in his brief filed before the Court the language Fried used in his *Thornburgh* brief demanding *Roe*'s reversal, in *Webster v. Reproductive Health Services*, 492 U.S. 490 (1989).

Webster badly fragmented the Rehnquist Court. Although a bare majority supported the result, Chief Justice Rehnquist's opinion was joined only by Justices Kennedy and White. Notwithstanding its ruling in *Thornburgh*, just three years earlier, a bare majority of the Court upheld the principal provisions of Missouri's 1986 abortion law (1) decreeing that life begins at conception and that "unborn children have protectable interests in life, health, and well-being," (2) requiring doctors, prior to performing an abortion on a woman believed to be twenty or more weeks pregnant, to test the fetus's "gestational age, weight, and lung maturity," (3) prohibiting public employees and facilities from being used to perform abortions not necessary to save a woman's life, and (4) making it unlawful to use public funds, employees, and facilities for the purpose of "encouraging or counseling" a woman to have an abortion except when her life is in danger. In separate concurring opinions, Justice Scalia decried Justice O'Connor's refusal to vote to overturn *Roe*, while for her part, O'Connor claimed that there would be other occasions to reconsider that ruling.

Following another 5–4 split in *Rust v. Sullivan*, 500 U.S. 173 (1991), which upheld the Reagan administration's restrictions on organizations that receive federal funding from providing counseling on abortion, and the retirements of two of *Roe*'s staunchest supporters—Justices Brennan and Marshall—speculation again mounted that the Rehnquist Court would overrule *Roe* in *Planned Parenthood of Southeastern Pennsylvania v. Casey*, 505 U.S. 833 (1992) (see excerpt below). Yet, in an extraordinary joint opinion signed by Justices O'Connor, Kennedy, and Souter (and joined in part by Justices Blackmun and Stevens), a controlling majority emerged that claimed to uphold "the essence of *Roe*," while also redefining the standards for reviewing restrictive abortion laws. In caustic dissenting opinions, joined by Justices Thomas and White, Chief Justice Rehnquist and Justice Scalia criticized the plurality's analysis, particularly its refashioning of the doctrine of *stare decisis* in order to justify its refusal to completely jettison *Roe*.

After *Casey*, Nebraska and several other states enacted so-called late-term or partial-birth abortion laws (political, not medical, terms), forbidding a rare procedure known as "dilation and extraction" (D&X) or "intact dilation and evacuation" (D&E). Writing for a bare majority in *Stenberg v. Carhart*, 530 U.S. 914 (2000) (*Carhart I*), Justice Breyer held that the law placed an "undue burden" on women and provided no exception for instances when the procedure was necessary to preserve a woman's health. In his words:

> Three established principles determine the issue before us. We shall set them forth in the language of the joint opinion in *Casey*. First, before "viability . . . the woman has a right to choose to terminate her pregnancy."
>
> Second, "a law designed to further the State's interest in fetal life which imposes an undue burden on the woman's decision before fetal viability" is unconstitutional. An "undue burden is . . . shorthand for the conclusion that a state regulation has the purpose or effect of placing a substantial obstacle in the path of a woman seeking an abortion of a nonviable fetus."
>
> Third, "'subsequent to viability, the State in promoting its interest in the potentiality of human life may, if it chooses, regulate, and even proscribe, abortion except where it is necessary, in appropriate medical judgment, for the preservation of the life or health of the mother.'"
>
> We apply these principles to a Nebraska law banning "partial birth abortion." . . . The law classifies violation of the statute as a "Class III felony" carrying a prison term of up to 20 years, and a fine of up to $25,000.
>
> We hold that this statute violates the Constitution. . . .
>
> 1. About 90% of all abortions performed in the United States take place during the first trimester of pregnancy, before 12 weeks of gestational age. During the first trimester, the predominant abortion method is "vacuum aspiration," which involves insertion of a vacuum tube (cannula) into the uterus to evacuate the contents. . . .
>
> 2. Approximately 10% of all abortions are performed during the second trimester of pregnancy (12 to 24 weeks). . . . The most commonly used procedure is called "dilation and evacuation" (D&E). That procedure (together with a modified form of vacuum aspiration used in the early second trimester) accounts for about 95% of all abortions performed from 12 to 20 weeks of gestational age.
>
> 3. D&E "refers generically to transcervical procedures performed at 13 weeks gestation or later." . . . There are variations in

D&E operative strategy. However, the common points are that D&E involves (1) dilation of the cervix; (2) removal of at least some fetal tissue using nonvacuum instruments; and (3) (after the 15th week) the potential need for instrumental disarticulation or dismemberment of the fetus or the collapse of fetal parts to facilitate evacuation from the uterus. . . .

6. At trial, Dr. Carhart and Dr. Stubblefield described a variation of the D&E procedure, which they referred to as an "intact D&E." Like other versions of the D&E technique, it begins with induced dilation of the cervix. The procedure then involves removing the fetus from the uterus through the cervix "intact," i.e., in one pass, rather than in several passes. It is used after 16 weeks at the earliest, as vacuum aspiration becomes ineffective and the fetal skull becomes too large to pass through the cervix. . . .

8. The American College of Obstetricians and Gynecologists describes the D&X procedure in a manner corresponding to a breech-conversion intact D&E, including the following steps: "1. deliberate dilatation of the cervix, usually over a sequence of days; 2. instrumental conversion of the fetus to a footling breech; 3. breech extraction of the body excepting the head; and 4. partial evacuation of the intracranial contents of a living fetus to effect vaginal delivery of a dead but otherwise intact fetus." Despite the technical differences we have just described, intact D&E and D&X are sufficiently similar for us to use the terms interchangeably. . . .

The question before us is whether Nebraska's statute, making criminal the performance of a "partial birth abortion," violates the Federal Constitution, as interpreted in *Planned Parenthood of Southeastern Pa. v. Casey*, and *Roe v. Wade*. We conclude that it does for at least two independent reasons. First, the law lacks any exception "for the preservation of the health of the mother." Second, it "imposes an undue burden on a woman's ability" to choose a D&E abortion, thereby unduly burdening the right to choose abortion itself. . . .

Justice O'Connor, concurring, emphasized: "First, the Nebraska statute is inconsistent with *Casey* because it lacks an exception for those instances when the banned procedure is necessary to preserve the health of the mother. . . . Second, Nebraska's statute is unconstitutional on the alternative and independent ground that it imposes an undue burden on a woman's right to choose to terminate her pregnancy before viability. Nebraska's ban covers not just the dilation and extraction (D&X) procedure, but also the dilation and evacuation (D&E) procedure, 'the most commonly used method for performing previability second trimester abortions.' " Chief Justice Rehnquist and Justices Scalia, Kennedy, and Thomas dissented.

Stenberg v. Carhart (Carhart I) did not lay the controversy to rest, however. Proponents of banning the procedure kept pressure on

Justice William O. Douglas. Justice Douglas was the author of the Court's controversial ruling in *Griswold v. Connecticut* (1965) proclaiming a constitutional right of privacy. (*Bettmann/Corbis via Getty Images*)

Congress to enact a federal law, the Partial-Birth Abortion Ban Act, which in spite of *Carhart I* did not provide an exception for when a woman's health is endangered. In 2003, the Republican-controlled Congress passed and President George W. Bush signed into law the first federal restriction on an abortion procedure since *Roe v. Wade*; Congress had twice before passed similar laws, but President Clinton vetoed them. The statute was immediately challenged in federal courts. In *Gonzales v. Carhart (Carhart II)* 550 U.S. 124 (2007), a bare majority of the Roberts Court upheld the federal law, though did not overturn *Carhart I*. Justices Stevens, Souter, Ginsburg, and Breyer dissented.

Over forty years after *Roe v. Wade*, the struggles continue at the national level and across the country. The 2016 Republican Party platform continued three-decades-old opposition, though notably, now even in cases of rape and incest. In spite of *Carhart I* striking down Nebraska's law, the Roberts Court's subsequent upholding in *Carhart II* of the federal law banning so-called late-term abortions has led numerous states to reenact new restrictions. Because Planned Parenthood operates clinics that perform abortions—and most abortions now are in clinics rather than hospitals—it remains a focus of opposition: it was denied a license to operate a clinic in Kansas, defunded in Texas, and some states now require doctors who perform abortions to have an affiliation with a local hospital. In recent years, over half of the states enacted legislation extending waiting periods, requiring ultrasound tests, and imposing zoning requirements on the operation of clinics in order to force their closure, and nine states banned abortions twenty weeks after pregnancy. In 2013, North Dakota enacted the most restrictive law, banning abortions if a fetal heartbeat can be detected, which may occur as early as six weeks into pregnancy, and abortions based on genetic defects such as Down syndrome. Such state and local legislation aim not only to restrict access to abortion but also create the basis for the next test case that would invite the Court to overrule *Roe* and *Casey*.

In the first major ruling on new restrictions on abortion in twenty-five years, in *Whole Woman's Health v. Hellerstedt* (2016) (excerpted below), a majority of the Court (dividing 5–3) struck down Texas's restrictions requiring abortion clinics to (1) have their doctors have admitting privileges at a hospital within thirty miles of the clinic's location, and (2) to meet the facility standards of surgical centers and hospitals. Proponents maintained that the regulations were in the interests of the health and safety of women; whereas, opponents countered that they were medically unnecessary, burdensome, costly, and simply aimed at limiting the availability of abortions. Almost half of the state's clinics were forced to close due to these regulations. Writing for the majority, Justice Breyer held that the restrictions imposed an "undue burden" on women seeking an abortion and that standard, established in *Casey*, "requires that courts consider the burdens a law imposes on abortion access together with the benefits those laws confer." Chief Justice Roberts and Justices Thomas and Alito dissented. The Roberts Court also split 5–4 when striking down a state law requiring "crisis pregnancy centers," operated by religious groups opposed to abortion, to post notices about the availability of contraception and low-cost abortion services, in *National Institute of Family and Life Advocates v. Becerra,* 138 S. Ct. 2361 (2018). The California Reproductive Freedom, Accountability, Comprehensive Care, and Transparency Act (FACT Act) of 2015 required some 200 crisis pregnancy centers, pro-life centers offering prenatal-related services, to notify women that the state provides free or low-cost services, including abortions, and to provide phone numbers for those services; unlicensed clinics also were required to give notice that they did not provide medical services, such as abortions. Both regulations were invalidated because they targeted the content of speech and failed to survive the strict scrutiny test since they compelled speech about abortion services that the clinics opposed on religious grounds. Writing for the majority, Justice Thomas observed: "Licensed clinics must provide a government-drafted script about the availability of state-sponsored services, as well as contact information for how to obtain them. One of those services is abortion—the very practice that petitioners are devoted to opposing." California had other means of informing women about the availability of abortions and could not "co-opt the licensed facilities to deliver its message." In a concurring opinion, Justice Kennedy added that the First Amendment bars compelling people to betray their religious beliefs: "Governments must not be allowed to force persons to express a message contrary to their deepest convictions. Freedom of speech secures freedom of thought and belief. This law imperils those liberties." Writing for the dissenters—Justices Ginsburg, Sotomayor, and Kagan—Justice Breyer criticized the majority for inconsistency, since a bare majority upheld provisions of a Pennsylvania law requiring doctors who perform abortions to inform patients about abortion and alternatives, in *Planned Parenthood of Southeastern Pennsylvania v. Casey,* 505 U.S. 833 (1992) (excerpted below); and upheld federal regulations banning counseling on abortion by organizations receiving federal funding, in *Rust v. Sullivan,* 500 U.S. 173 (1991). In Justice Breyer's words: "If a state can lawfully require a doctor to tell a woman seeking an abortion about adoption services, why should it not be able, as here, to require a medical counselor to tell a woman seeking prenatal care or other reproductive health care about childbirth and abortion services? As the question suggests, there is no convincing reason to distinguish between information about adoption and information about abortion in this context. After all, the rule of law embodies evenhandedness, and 'what is sauce for the goose is normally sauce for the gander.'" Justice Thomas responded that *Casey* was different because it dealt with a medical procedure, and prompted Breyer to counter: "Really? No one doubts that choosing an abortion is a medical procedure that involves certain health risks. But the same is true of carrying a child to term and giving birth." Moreover, Breyer challenged Thomas's use of the strict scrutiny test in invalidating California's regulation, pointing out: "Using the First Amendment to strike down economic and social laws that legislatures long would have thought themselves free to enact will, for the American public, obscure, not clarify, the true value of protecting freedom of speech."

Selected Bibliography

Cohen, Adam. *Im★be★ciles: The Supreme Court, American Eugenics, and the Sterilization of Carrie Buck.* New York: Penguin Press, 2016.

Craig, Barbara, and O'Brien, David. *Abortion and American Politics.* Chatham, NJ: Chatham House, 1993.

Garrow, David. *Liberty & Sexuality: The Right to Privacy and the Making of Roe v. Wade.* New York: Macmillan, 1994.

Haugeberg, Karissa. *Women against Abortion: Inside the Longest Moral Reform Movement of the 20th Century.* Carbondale: University of Illinois Press, 2017.

Hull, N. E. H., and Hoffer, Charles. *Roe v. Wade: The Abortion Rights Controversy in American History.* Lawrence: University Press of Kansas, 2001.

Johnson, John. *Griswold v. Connecticut: Birth Control and the Right of Privacy.* Lawrence: University Press of Kansas, 2005.

Kaplin, Laura. *The Story of Jane: The Legendary Underground Feminist Abortion Service.* New York: Pantheon, 1996.

Lombardo, Paul. *Three Generations, No Imbeciles: Eugenics, the Supreme Court, and Buck v. Bell.* Baltimore: Johns Hopkins University Press, 2010.

Mohr, James. *Abortion in America.* New York: Oxford University Press, 1978.

Reagan, Leslie. *When Abortion Was a Crime: Women, Medicine, and Law in the United States, 1867–1973.* Berkeley: University of California Press, 1997.

Sanger, Carol. *About Abortion: Terminating Pregnancy in the 21st Century.* Cambridge, MA: Harvard University Press, 2017.

Weddington, Sarah. *A Question of Choice.* New York: Grosset/Putnam, 1992.

Williams, Daniel K. *Defenders of the Unborn: The Pro-Life Movement Before* Roe v. Wade. New York: Oxford University Press, 2016.

Ziegler, Mary. *Beyond Abortion: Roe v. Wade and the Battle for Privacy.* Cambridge, MA: Harvard University Press, 2018.

Buck v. Bell

274 U.S. 200, 47 S.Ct. 584 (1927)

In 1924, Virginia enacted a law permitting the sterilization of individuals, male and female, who were deemed "mentally defective" and committed to a State Colony for Epileptics and Feeble Minded. The law, like those in other states, was part of the eugenics movement and a reflection of the late-nineteenth-century philosophy of Social Darwinism. Compulsory sterilization was justified as being in the interests of both the individual and society. Subsequently, attorneys challenged the constitutionality of the law as a violation of the Fourteenth Amendment's guarantees for due process and the equal protection of the law. Carrie Buck, an eighteen-year-old "feeble-minded" woman was the daughter of a woman in the same institution. A state court rejected the challenge and Virginia's highest court affirmed, whereupon Buck's attorneys appealed to the Supreme Court.

The Court affirmed the decision below by a vote of eight to one. Justice Holmes delivered the opinion of the Court. Justice Butler dissented without an opinion.

■ ■ ■

☐ *Justice HOLMES delivered the opinion of the Court.*

An Act of Virginia approved March 20, 1924, recites that the health of the patient and the welfare of society may be promoted in certain cases by the sterilization of mental defectives, under careful safeguard, etc. . . . ; that the Commonwealth is supporting in various institutions many defective persons who if now discharged would become a menace but if incapable of procreating might be discharged with safety and become self-supporting with benefit to themselves and to society; and that experience has shown that heredity plays an important part in the transmission of insanity, imbecility, etc. The statute then enacts that whenever the superintendent of certain institutions including the above named State Colony shall be of the opinion that it is for the best interest of the patients and of society that an inmate under his care should be sexually sterilized, he may have the operation performed upon any patient afflicted with hereditary forms of insanity, imbecility, etc. . . . The superintendent first presents a petition to the special board of directors of his hospital or colony, stating the facts and the grounds for his opinion, verified by affidavit. Notice of the petition and of the time and place of the hearing in the institution is to be served upon the inmate, and also upon his guardian, and if there is no guardian the superintendent is to apply to the Circuit Court of the County to appoint one. . . . The evidence is all to be reduced to writing, and after the board has made its order for or against the operation, the superintendent, or the inmate, or his guardian, may appeal to the Circuit Court of the County. . . . Finally any party may apply to the Supreme Court of Appeals, which, if it grants the appeal, is to hear the case upon the record of the trial in the Circuit Court and may enter such order as it thinks the Circuit Court should have entered. There can be no doubt that so far as procedure is concerned the rights of the patient are most carefully considered. . . .

The attack is not upon the procedure but upon the substantive law. It seems to be contended that in no circumstances could such an order be justified. It certainly is contended that the order cannot be justified upon the existing grounds. The judgment finds the facts that have been recited and that Carrie Buck "is the probable potential parent of socially inadequate offspring, likewise afflicted, that she may be sexually sterilized without detriment to her general health and that her welfare and that of society will be promoted by her sterilization," and thereupon makes the order. In view of the general declarations of the Legislature and the specific findings of the Court obviously we cannot say as a matter of law that the grounds do not exist, and if they exist they justify the result. We have seen more than once that the public welfare may call upon the best citizens for their lives. It would be strange if it could not call upon those who already sap the strength of the State for these lesser sacrifices, often not felt to be such by those concerned, in order to prevent our being swamped with incompetence. It is better for all the world, if instead of waiting to execute degenerate offspring for crime, or to let them starve for their imbecility, society can prevent those who are manifestly unfit from continuing their kind. The principle that sustains compulsory vaccination is broad enough to cover cutting the Fallopian tubes. *Jacobson v. Massachusetts*, 197 U.S. 11 (1905). Three generations of imbeciles are enough. . . .

Griswold v. Connecticut (reprise)
381 U.S. 479 (1965)

See Chapter 4, where *Griswold v. Connecticut* is reprinted in part. See also INSIDE THE COURT: Standing and the Connecticut Birth Control Cases (in Ch. 2) and INSIDE THE COURT: The Theory and Drafting of Justice Douglas's Opinion in *Griswold v. Connecticut* (in Ch. 4).

■ ■ ■

Roe v. Wade
410 U.S. 113, 93 S.Ct. 705 (1973)

In 1969, a high-school dropout, Norma McCorvey, who was divorced and had a five-year-old daughter and little money, unsuccessfully sought an abortion in Texas. Texas, like most other states at the time, prohibited abortions unless necessary to save a woman's life. McCorvey carried her pregnancy and gave up the child she bore for adoption. The lawyer who arranged for the adoption also introduced McCorvey to two recent graduates of the University of Texas Law School, Sarah Weddington and Linda Coffee. The three women decided to challenge the constitutionality of Texas's law and McCorvey became "Jane Roe" in a test case against Henry Wade, the criminal district attorney for Dallas County, Texas. Wade appealed to the Supreme Court the decision of a three-judge federal district court striking down Texas's law. The Court granted review and heard oral arguments in 1971 and then carried the case over for rearguments in 1972. Justice Blackmun finally handed down the Court's opinion on January 23, 1973.

The Court's decision was 7–2, and the majority's opinion was announced by Justice Blackmun. Chief Justice Burger and Justices Douglas and Stewart concurred; Justices Rehnquist and White dissented.

■ ■ ■

☐ *Justice BLACKMUN delivers the opinion of the Court.*

This Texas federal appeal . . . present[s] constitutional challenges to state criminal abortion legislation. The Texas statutes under attack here are typical of those that have been in effect in many States for approximately a century. . . .

The Texas statutes that concern us here make it a crime to "procure an abortion," as therein defined, or to attempt one, except with respect to "an abortion procured or attempted by medical advice for the purpose of saving the life of the mother." Similar statutes are in existence in a majority of the States. . . .

The principal thrust of appellant's attack on the Texas statutes is that they improperly invade a right, said to be possessed by the pregnant woman, to choose to terminate her pregnancy. Appellant would discover this right in the concept of personal "liberty" embodied in the Fourteenth Amendment's Due Process Clause; or in personal, marital, familial, and sexual privacy said to be protected by the Bill of Rights or its penumbras, see *Griswold v. Connecticut*; or among those rights reserved to the people by the Ninth Amendment, *Griswold v. Connecticut*, [381 U.S. 479 (1965)] (GOLDBERG, J., concurring). Before addressing this claim, we feel it desirable briefly to survey, in several aspects, the history of abortion, for such insight as that history may afford us, and then to examine the state purposes and interests behind the criminal abortion laws.

It perhaps is not generally appreciated that the restrictive criminal abortion laws in effect in a majority of States today are of relatively recent vintage. Those laws, generally proscribing abortion or its attempt at any time during pregnancy except when necessary to preserve the pregnant woman's life, are not of ancient or even of common-law origin. Instead, they derive from statutory changes effected, for the most part, in the latter half of the 19th century. . . .

[A]bortion was practiced in Greek times as well as in the Roman Era. . . . Greek and Roman Law afforded little protection to the unborn. . . .

It is undisputed that at common law, abortion performed *before* "quickening"—the first recognizable movement of the fetus *in utero*, appearing usually from the 16th to the 18th week of pregnancy—was not an indictable offense. . . . In this country, the law in effect in all but a few States until mid-19th century was the pre-existing English common law. Connecticut, the first State to enact abortion legislation, adopted in 1821 that part of Lord Ellenborough's Act that related to a woman "quick with child." The death penalty was not imposed. Abortion before quickening was made a crime in that State only in 1860. In 1828, New York enacted legislation that, in two respects, was to serve as a model for early anti-abortion statutes. First, while barring destruction of an unquickened fetus as well as a quick fetus, it made the former only a misdemeanor, but the latter second-degree manslaughter. Second, it incorporated a concept of therapeutic abortion by providing that an abortion was excused if it "shall have been necessary to preserve the life of such mother, or shall have been advised by two physicians to be necessary for such purpose." By 1840, when Texas had received the common law, only eight American States had statutes dealing with abortion. It was not until after the War Between the States that legislation began generally to replace the common law. Most of these initial statutes dealt severely with abortion after quickening but were lenient with it before quickening. . . .

Gradually, in the middle and late 19th century the quickening distinction disappeared from the statutory law of most States and the degree of the offense and the penalties were increased. By the end of the 1950's a large majority of the jurisdictions banned abortion, however and whenever performed, unless done to save or preserve the life of the mother. . . .

It is thus apparent that at common law, at the time of the adoption of our Constitution, and throughout the major portion of the 19th century, abortion was viewed with less disfavor than under most American statutes currently in effect. Phrasing it another way, a woman enjoyed a substantially broader right to terminate a pregnancy than she does in most States today. . . .

Three reasons have been advanced to explain historically the enactment of criminal abortion laws in the 19th century and to justify their continued existence.

It has been argued occasionally that these laws were the product of a Victorian social concern to discourage illicit sexual conduct. Texas, however, does not advance this justification in the present case. . . .

A second reason is concerned with abortion as a medical procedure. When most criminal abortion laws were first enacted, the procedure was a hazardous one for the woman. . . . Thus, it has been argued that a State's real concern in enacting a criminal abortion law was to protect the pregnant woman, that is, to restrain her from submitting to a procedure that placed her life in serious jeopardy.

Modern medical techniques have altered this situation. Appellants and various *amici* refer to medical data indicating that abortion in early pregnancy, that is, prior to the end of the first trimester, although not without its risk, is now relatively safe. Mortality rates for women undergoing early abortions, where the procedure is legal, appear to be as low as or lower than the rates for normal childbirth. Consequently, any interest of the State in protecting the woman from an inherently hazardous procedure, except when it would be equally dangerous for her to forgo it, has largely disappeared. Of course, important state interests in the areas of health and medical standards do remain. The State has a legitimate interest in seeing to it that abortion, like any other medical procedure, is performed under circumstances that insure maximum safety for the patient. This interest obviously extends at least to the performing physician and his staff, to the facilities involved, to the availability of aftercare, and to adequate provision for any complication or emergency that might arise. The prevalence of high mortality rates at illegal "abortion mills" strengthens, rather than weakens, the State's interest in regulating the conditions under which abortions are performed. Moreover, the risk to the

Norma McCorvey, who became well known as "Jane Roe," the appellant in *Roe v. Wade*. (*Bettmann/Corbis via Getty Images.*)

woman increases as her pregnancy continues. Thus, the State retains a definite interest in protecting the woman's own health and safety when an abortion is proposed at a late stage of pregnancy.

The third reason is the State's interest—some phrase it in terms of duty—in protecting prenatal life. Some of the argument for this justification rests on the theory that a new human life is present from the moment of conception. The State's interest and general obligation to protect life then extends, it is argued, to prenatal life. Only when the life of the pregnant mother herself is at stake, balanced against the life she carries within her, should the interest of the embryo or fetus not prevail. Logically, of course, a legitimate state interest in this area need not stand or fall on acceptance of the belief that life begins at conception or at some other point prior to live birth. In assessing the State's interest, recognition may be given to the less rigid claim that as long as at least *potential* life is involved, the State may assert interests beyond the protection of the pregnant woman alone. . . .

The Constitution does not explicitly mention any right of privacy. In a line of decisions, however, going back perhaps as far as *Union Pacific R. Co. v. Botsford*, 141 U.S. 250 (1891), the Court has recognized that a right of personal privacy, or a guarantee of certain areas or zones of privacy, does exist under the Constitution. In varying contexts, the Court or individual Justices have, indeed, found at least the roots of that right in the First Amendment, *Stanley v. Georgia*, 394 U.S. 557 (1969); in the Fourth and Fifth Amendments, *Terry v. Ohio*, 392 U.S. 1 (1968), *Katz v. United States*, 389 U.S. 347 (1967); *Boyd v. United States*, 116 U.S. 616 (1886), see *Olmstead v. United States*, 277 U.S. 438 (1928) (BRANDEIS, J., dissenting); in the penumbras of the Bill of Rights, *Griswold v. Con-*

necticut; in the Ninth Amendment, *id.* (GOLDBERG, J., concurring); or in the concept of liberty guaranteed by the first section of the Fourteenth Amendment, see *Meyer v. Nebraska*, 262 U.S. 390 (1923). These decisions make it clear that only personal rights that can be deemed "fundamental" or "implicit in the concept of ordered liberty," *Palko v. Connecticut*, [302 U.S. 319] (1937), are included in this guarantee of personal privacy. They also make it clear that the right has some extension to activities relating to marriage, *Loving v. Virginia*, 388 U.S. 1 (1967); procreation, *Skinner v. Oklahoma*, 316 U.S. 535 (1942); contraception, *Eisenstadt v. Baird*, [405 U.S. 438 (1972)]; family relationships, *Prince v. Massachusetts*, 321 U.S. 158 (1944); and child rearing and education, *Pierce v. Society of Sisters*, 268 U.S. 510 (1925). . . .

This right of privacy, whether it be founded in the Fourteenth Amendment's concept of personal liberty and restrictions upon state action, as we feel it is, or, as the District Court determined, in the Ninth Amendment's reservation of rights to the people, is broad enough to encompass a woman's decision whether or not to terminate her pregnancy. The detriment that the State would impose upon the pregnant woman by denying this choice altogether is apparent. Specific and direct harm medically diagnosable even in early pregnancy may be involved. Maternity, or additional offspring, may force upon the woman a distressful life and future. Psychological harm may be imminent. Mental and physical health may be taxed by child care. There is also the distress, for all concerned, associated with the unwanted child, and there is the problem of bringing a child into a family already unable, psychologically and otherwise, to care for it. In other cases, as in this one, the additional difficulties and continuing stigma of unwed motherhood may be involved. All these are factors the woman and her responsible physician necessarily will consider in consultation.

On the basis of elements such as these, appellant and some *amici* argue that the woman's right is absolute and that she is entitled to terminate her pregnancy at whatever time, in whatever way, and for whatever reason she alone chooses. With this we do not agree. . . . The Court's decisions recognizing a right of privacy also acknowledge that some state regulation in areas protected by that right is appropriate. As noted above, a State may properly assert important interests in safeguarding health, in maintaining medical standards, and in protecting potential life. . . .

We, therefore, conclude that the right of personal privacy includes the abortion decision, but that this right is not unqualified and must be considered against important state interests in regulation. . . .

Where certain "fundamental rights" are involved, the Court has held that regulation limiting these rights may be justified only by a "compelling state interest," and that legislative enactments must be narrowly drawn to express only the legitimate state interests at stake. . . .

The appellee and certain *amici* argue that the fetus is a "person" within the language and meaning of the Fourteenth Amendment. In support of this, they outline at length and in detail the well-known facts of fetal development. If this suggestion of personhood is established, the appellant's case, of course, collapses, for the fetus' right to life would then be guaranteed specifically by the Amendment. The appellant conceded as much on reargument. On the other hand, the appellee conceded on reargument that no case could be cited that holds that a fetus is a person within the meaning of the Fourteenth Amendment.

The Constitution does not define "person" in so many words. Section 1 of the Fourteenth Amendment contains three references to "person." The first, in defining "citizens," speaks of "persons born or naturalized in the United States." The word also appears both in the Due Process Clause and in the Equal Protection Clause. "Person" is used in other places in the Constitution: in the listing of qualifications for Representatives and Senators, Art. I, Sec. 2, cl. 2, and Sec. 3, cl. 3; in the Apportionment Clause, Art. I, Sec. 2, cl. 3; in the Migration and Importation provision, Art. I, Sec. 9, cl. 1; in the Emolument Clause, Art. I, Sec. 9, cl. 8; in the Electors provisions, Art. II, Sec. 1, cl. 2, and the superseded cl. 3; in the provision outlining qualifications for the office of President, Art. II, Sec. 9, cl. 5; in the Extradition provisions, Art. IV, Sec. 2, cl. 2, and the superseded Fugitive Slave Clause 3; and in the Fifth, Twelfth, and Twenty-second Amendments, as well as in Sections 2 and 3 of the Fourteenth Amendment. But in nearly all these instances, the use of the word is such that it has application only postnatally. None indicates, with any assurance, that it has any possible prenatal application.

All this, together with our observation, *supra*, that throughout the major portion of the 19th century prevailing legal abortion practices were far freer than they are today, persuades us that the word "person," as used in the Fourteenth Amendment, does not include the unborn. . . .

This conclusion, however, does not of itself fully answer the contentions raised by Texas, and we pass on to other considerations.

The pregnant woman cannot be isolated in her privacy. She carries an embryo and, later, a fetus, if one accepts the medical definitions of the developing young in the human uterus. The situation therefore is inherently different from marital intimacy, or bedroom possession of obscene material, or marriage, or procreation, or education, with which *Eisenstadt* and *Griswold*, *Stanley*, *Loving*, *Skinner* and *Pierce* and *Meyer* were respectively concerned. As we have intimated above, it is reasonable and appropriate for a State to decide that at some point in time another interest, that of health of the mother or that of potential human life, becomes significantly involved. The woman's privacy is no longer sole and any right of privacy she possesses must be measured accordingly.

Texas urges that, apart from the Fourteenth Amendment, life begins at conception and is present throughout pregnancy, and that, therefore, the State has a compelling interest in protecting that life from and after conception. We need not resolve the difficult question of when life begins. When those trained in the respective disciplines of medicine, philosophy, and theology are unable to arrive at any consensus, the judiciary, at this point in the development of man's knowledge, is not in a position to speculate as to the answer.

It should be sufficient to note briefly the wide divergence of thinking on this most sensitive and difficult question. There has always been strong support for the view that life does not begin until live birth. This was the belief of the Stoics. It appears to be the predominant, though not the unanimous, attitude of the Jewish faith. It may be taken to represent also the position of a large segment of the Protestant community, insofar as that can be ascertained; organized groups that have taken a formal position on the abortion issue have generally regarded abortion as a matter for the conscience of the individual and her family. As we have noted, the common law found greater significance in quickening. Physicians and their scientific colleagues have regarded that event with less interest and have tended to focus either upon conception, upon live birth, or upon the interim point at which the fetus becomes "viable," that is, potentially able to live outside the mother's womb, albeit with artificial aid. Viability is usually placed at about seven months (28 weeks) but may occur earlier, even at 24 weeks. The Aristotelian theory of "mediate animation," that held sway throughout the Middle Ages and the Renaissance in Europe, continued to be official Roman Catholic dogma until the 19th century, despite opposition to this "ensoulment" theory from those in the Church who would recognize the existence of life from the moment of conception. . . .

In areas other than criminal abortion, the law has been reluctant to endorse any theory that life, as we recognize it, begins before live birth or to accord legal rights to the unborn except in narrowly defined situations and except when the rights are contingent upon live birth. . . .

In view of all this, we do not agree that, by adopting one theory of life, Texas may override the rights of the pregnant woman that are at stake. We repeat, however, that the State does have an important and legitimate interest in preserving and protecting the health of the pregnant woman, whether she be a resident of the State or a nonresident who seeks medical consultation and treatment there, and that it has still *another* important and legitimate interest in protecting the potentiality of human life. These interests are separate and distinct. Each grows in substantiality as the woman approaches term and, at a point during pregnancy, each becomes "compelling."

With respect to the State's important and legitimate interest in the health of the mother, the "compelling" point, in the light of present medical knowledge, is at approximately the end of the first trimester. This is so because of the now-established medical fact that until the end of the first trimester mortality in abortion may be less than mortality in normal childbirth. It follows that, from and after this point, a State may regulate the abortion procedure to the extent that the regulation reasonably relates to the preservation and protection of maternal health. Examples of permissible state regulation in this area are requirements as to the qualifications of the person who is to perform the abortion; as to the licensure of that person; as to the facility in which the procedure is to be performed, that is, whether it must be a hospital or may be a clinic or some other place of less-than-hospital status; as to the licensing of the facility; and the like.

This means, on the other hand, that, for the period of pregnancy prior to this "compelling" point, the attending physician, in consultation with his patient, is free to determine, without regulation by the State, that, in his medical judgment, the patient's pregnancy should be terminated. If that decision is reached, the judgment may be effectuated by an abortion free of interference by the State.

With respect to the State's important and legitimate interest in potential life, the "compelling" point is at viability. This is so because the fetus then presumably has the capability of meaningful life outside the mother's womb. State regulation protective of fetal life after viability thus has both logical and biological justifications. If the State is interested in protecting fetal life after viability, it may go so far as to proscribe abortion during that period, except when it is necessary to preserve the life or health of the mother.

Measured against these standards, Art. 1196 of the Texas Penal Code . . . sweeps too broadly. The statute makes no distinction between abortions performed early in pregnancy and those performed later, and it limits to a single reason, "saving" the mother's life, the legal justification for the procedure. The statute, therefore, cannot survive the constitutional attack made upon it here. . . .

To summarize and to repeat:

> 1. A state criminal abortion statute of the current Texas type, that excepts from criminality only a life saving procedure on behalf of the mother, without regard to pregnancy stage and without recognition of the other interests involved, is violative of the Due Process Clause of the Fourteenth Amendment.
>
> (a) For the stage prior to approximately the end of the first trimester, the abortion decision and its effectuation must be left to the medical judgment of the pregnant woman's attending physician.
>
> (b) For the stage subsequent to approximately the end of the first trimester, the State, in promoting its interest in the health of the mother, may, if it chooses, regulate the abortion procedure in ways that are reasonably related to maternal health.
>
> (c) For the stage subsequent to viability, the State in promoting its interest in the potentiality of human life may, if it chooses, regulate, and even proscribe, abortion except where it is necessary, in appropriate medical judgment, for the preservation of the life or health of the mother. . . .

This holding, we feel, is consistent with the relative weights of the respective interests involved, with the lessons and examples of medical and legal history, with the lenity of the common law, and with the demands of the profound problems of the present day.

☐ *Justice STEWART, concurring.*

[I]t was clear to me then, and it is equally clear to me now, that the *Griswold* decision can be rationally understood only as a holding that the Connecticut statute substantively invaded the "liberty" that is protected by the Due Process Clause of the Fourteenth Amendment. As so understood, *Griswold* stands as one in a long line of . . . cases decided under the doctrine of substantive due process, and I now accept it as such. . . .

[T]he Court today is correct in holding that the right asserted by Jane Roe is embraced within the personal liberty protected by the Due Process Clause of the Fourteenth Amendment. . . .

☐ *Justice REHNQUIST, dissenting.*

I have difficulty in concluding, as the Court does, that the right of "privacy" is involved in this case. Texas, by the statute here challenged, bars the performance of a medical abortion by a licensed physician on a plaintiff such as Roe. A transaction resulting in an operation such as this is not "private" in the ordinary usage of that word. Nor is the "privacy" that the Court finds here even a distant relative of the freedom from searches and seizures protected by the Fourth Amendment to the Constitution, which the Court has referred to as embodying a right to privacy. . . .

If the Court means by the term "privacy" no more than that the claim of a person to be free from unwanted state regulation of consensual transactions may be a form of "liberty" protected by the Fourteenth Amendment, there is no doubt that similar claims have been upheld in our earlier decisions on the basis of that liberty. I agree with the statement of Justice STEWART in his concurring opinion that the "liberty," against deprivation of which without due process the Fourteenth Amendment protects, embraces more than the rights found in the Bill of Rights. But that liberty is not guaranteed absolutely against deprivation, only against deprivation without due process of law. The test traditionally applied in the area of social and economic legislation is whether or not a law such as that challenged has a rational relation to a valid state objective. *Williamson v. Lee Optical Co.*, 348 U.S. 483 (1955).

The Due Process Clause of the Fourteenth Amendment undoubtedly does place a limit, albeit a broad one, on legislative power to enact laws such as this. If the Texas statute were to prohibit an abortion even where the mother's life is in jeopardy, I have little doubt that such a statute would lack a rational relation to a valid state objective under the test stated in *Williamson, supra*. But the Court's sweeping invalidation of any restrictions on abortion during the first trimester is impossible to justify under that standard, and the conscious weighing of competing factors that the Court's opinion apparently substitutes for the established test is far more appropriate to a legislative judgment than to a judicial one. . . .

While the Court's opinion quotes from the dissent of Justice HOLMES in *Lochner v. New York*, 198 U.S. 45 (1905), the result it reaches is more closely attuned to the majority opinion of Justice PECKHAM in that case. As in *Lochner* and similar cases applying substantive due process standards to economic and social welfare legislation, the adoption of the compelling state interest standard will inevitably require this Court to examine the legislative policies and pass on the wisdom of these policies in the very process of deciding whether a particular state interest put forward may or may not be "compelling." The decision here to break pregnancy into three distinct terms and to outline the permissible restrictions the State may impose in each one, for example, partakes more of judicial legislation than it does of a determination of the intent of the drafters of the Fourteenth Amendment.

The fact that a majority of the States reflecting, after all the majority sentiment in those States, have had restrictions on abortions for at least a century is a strong indication, it seems to me, that the asserted right to an abortion is not "so rooted in the traditions and conscience of our people as to be ranked as fundamental." . . .

To reach its result, the Court necessarily has had to find within the scope of the Fourteenth Amendment a right that was apparently completely unknown to the drafters of the Amendment. As early as 1821, the first state law dealing directly with abortion was enacted by the Connecticut Legislature. By the time of the adoption of the Fourteenth Amendment in 1868, there were at least 36 laws enacted by state or territorial legislatures limiting abortion. . . .

The only conclusion possible from this history is that the drafters did not intend to have the Fourteenth Amendment withdraw from the States the power to legislate with respect to this matter.

☐ *Justice WHITE, with whom Justice REHNQUIST joins, dissenting.*

With all due respect, I dissent. I find nothing in the language or history of the Constitution to support the Court's judgment. The Court simply fashions and announces a new constitutional right for pregnant mothers and, with scarcely any reason or authority for its action, invests that right with sufficient substance to override most existing state abortion statutes. The upshot is that the people and the legislatures of the 50 States are constitutionally disentitled to weigh the relative importance of the continued existence and development of the fetus, on the one hand, against a spectrum of possible impacts on the mother, on the other hand. As an exercise of raw judicial power, the Court perhaps has authority to do what it does today; but in my view its judgment is an improvident and extravagant exercise of the power of judicial review that the Constitution extends to this Court. . . .

Maher v. Roe

432 U.S. 464, 97 S.Ct. 2376 (1977)

Two indigent women, known as Susan Roe and Mary Poe, sued Edward Maher, the commissioner of Connecticut's Department of Social Services, and challenged the constitutionality of a state regulation prohibiting the funding of abortions that are not medically necessary. The state interpreted Title XIX of the Social Security Act, which establishes the Medicaid program under which participating states may provide federally funded medical assistance to needy persons, to forbid the funding of nontherapeutic abortions. Roe, an unmarried mother of three children, was unable to obtain an abortion because her doctor refused to certify that an abortion was medically necessary. Poe, a sixteen-year-old high school junior, had an abortion but, because she failed to obtain a certificate of medical necessity, the Department of Social Services refused to reimburse the hospital for Poe's $244 hospital bill.

A federal district court rejected Connecticut's interpretation of Title XIX when holding that the Social Security Act not only allowed funding of nontherapeutic abortions, but required it. On appeal, the Court of Appeals for the Second Circuit ruled that the Social Security Act permitted (but did not require) state funding of abortions and remanded the case back to the district court, which then overturned Connecticut's regulation forbidding the funding of nontherapeutic abortions.

Maher appealed that ruling to the Supreme Court, which granted review. The Court handed down its decision along with *Beal v. Doe*, 432 U.S. 438 (1977), which held that the Social Security Act does not require states to pay for nontherapeutic abortions as a condition of their participating in the Medicaid program.

The Court's decision was 6–3, and the majority's opinion was announced by Justice Powell. Chief Justice Burger filed a concurring opinion. Separate dissenting opinions were filed by Justices Brennan, Blackmun, and Marshall.

■ ■ ■

☐ *Justice POWELL delivers the opinion of the Court.*

[W]e hold today that Title XIX of the Social Security Act does not require the funding of nontherapeutic abortions as a condition of participation in the joint federal–state medicaid program established by that statute. . . .

The Constitution imposes no obligation on the States to pay the pregnancy-related medical expenses of indigent women, or indeed to pay any of the medical expenses of indigents. But when a State decides to alleviate some of the hardships of poverty by providing medical care, the manner in which it dispenses benefits is subject to constitutional limitations. Appellees' claim is that Connecticut must accord equal treatment to both abortion and childbirth, and may not evidence a policy preference by funding only the medical expenses incident to childbirth. This challenge to the classifications established by the Connecticut regulation presents a question arising under the Equal Protection Clause of the Fourteenth Amendment. . . .

This case involves no discrimination against a suspect class. An indigent woman desiring an abortion does not come within the limited category of disadvantaged classes so recognized by our cases. Nor does the fact that the impact of the regulation falls upon those who cannot pay lead to a different conclusion. In a sense, every denial of welfare to an indigent creates a wealth classification as compared to nonindigents who are able to pay for the desired goods or services. But this Court has never held that financial need alone identifies a suspect class for purposes of equal protection analysis. . . . Accordingly, the central question in this case is whether the regulation "impinges upon a fundamental right explicitly or implicitly protected by the Constitution." . . .

At issue in *Roe* [*v. Wade*, 410 U.S. 113 (1973)], was the constitutionality of a Texas law making it a crime to procure or attempt to procure an abortion, except on medical advice for the purpose of saving the life of the mother. . . . [W]e concluded that the Fourteenth Amendment's concept of personal liberty affords constitutional protection against state interference with certain aspects of an individual's personal "privacy," including a woman's decision to terminate her pregnancy. . . .

The Texas law in *Roe* was a stark example of impermissible interference with the pregnant woman's decision to terminate her pregnancy. In subsequent cases, we have invalidated other types of restrictions, different in form but similar in effect, on the woman's freedom of choice. . . .

The Connecticut regulation before us is different in kind from the laws invalidated in our previous abortion decisions. The Connecticut regulation places no obstacles—absolute or otherwise—in the pregnant woman's path to an abortion. An indigent woman who desires an abortion suffers no disadvantage as a consequence of Connecticut's decision to fund childbirth; she continues as before to be dependent on private sources for the service she desires. The State may have made childbirth a more attractive alternative, thereby influencing the woman's decision, but it has imposed no restriction on access to abortions that was not already there. The indigency that may make it difficult—and in some cases, perhaps, impossible—for some women to have abortions is neither created nor in any way affected by the Connecticut regulation. We conclude that the Connecticut regulation does not impinge upon the fundamental right recognized in *Roe*.

Our conclusion signals no retreat from *Roe* or the cases applying it. There is a basic difference between direct state interference with a protected activity and state encouragement of an alternative activity consonant with legislative policy. Constitutional concerns are greatest when the State attempts to impose its will by force of law; the State's power to encourage actions deemed to be in the public interest is necessarily far broader. . . .

The question remains whether Connecticut's regulation can be sustained under the less demanding test of rationality that applies in the absence of a suspect classification or the impingement of a fundamental right. This test requires that the distinction drawn between childbirth and nontherapeutic abortion by the regulation be "rationally related" to a "constitutionally permissible" purpose. We hold that the Connecticut funding scheme satisfies this standard.

Roe itself explicitly acknowledged the State's strong interest in protecting the potential life of the fetus. That interest exists throughout the pregnancy, "grow[ing] in substantiality as the woman approaches term." Because the pregnant woman carries a potential human being she "cannot be isolated in her privacy. . . . [Her] privacy is no longer sole and any right of privacy she possesses must be measured accordingly." . . . The State unquestionably has a "strong and legitimate interest in encouraging normal childbirth," . . . an interest honored over the centuries. Nor can there be any question that the Connecticut regulation rationally furthers that interest. The medical costs associated with childbirth are substantial, and have increased significantly in recent years. As recognized by the District Court in this case, such costs are significantly greater than those normally associated with elective abortions during the first trimester. The subsidizing of costs incident to childbirth is a rational means of encouraging childbirth.

Pro-life demonstrators marching near the Supreme Court. (*AP Photo/Haraz N. Ghanbari*)

We certainly are not unsympathetic to the plight of an indigent woman who desires an abortion, but "the Constitution does not provide judicial remedies for every social and economic ill."

Justice BRENNAN, with whom Justice MARSHALL and Justice BLACKMUN join, dissenting.

[A] distressing insensitivity to the plight of impoverished pregnant women is inherent in the Court's analysis. The stark reality for too many, not just "some," indigent pregnant women is that indigency makes access to competent licensed physicians not merely "difficult" but "impossible." As a practical matter, many indigent women will feel they have no choice but to carry their pregnancies to term because the State will pay for the associated medical services, even though they would have chosen to have abortions if the State had also provided funds for that procedure, or indeed if the State had provided funds for neither procedure. This disparity in funding by the State clearly operates to coerce indigent pregnant women to bear children they would not otherwise choose to have, and just as clearly, this coercion can only operate upon the poor, who are uniquely the victims of this form of financial pressure. . . .

The Court's premise is that only an equal protection claim is presented here. Claims of interference with enjoyment of fundamental rights have, however, occupied a rather protean position in our constitutional jurisprudence. Whether or not the Court's analysis may reasonably proceed under the Equal Protection Clause, the Court plainly errs in ignoring, as it does, the unanswerable argument of appellee, and holding of the District Court, that the regulation unconstitutionally impinges upon her claim of privacy derived from the Due Process Clause.

    Roe v. Wade and cases following it hold that an area of privacy invulnerable to the State's intrusion surrounds the decision of a pregnant woman whether or not to carry her pregnancy to term. The Connecticut scheme clearly infringes upon that area of privacy by bringing financial pressures on indigent women that force them to bear children they would not otherwise have. That is an obvious impairment of the fundamental right established by *Roe.* . . .

■ THE DEVELOPMENT OF LAW

*Other Post-*Roe *Rulings on Abortion*

CASE	VOTE	RULING
Doe v. Bolton, 410 U.S. 179 (1973)	7–2	A companion case decided along with *Roe v. Wade*, which extended *Roe*, in

holding that states may not criminalize abortions, or make abortions unreasonably difficult to obtain. *Doe* struck down state requirements that abortions be performed in licensed hospitals; that abortions be approved beforehand by a hospital committee; and that two physicians concur in the abortion decision.

CASE	VOTE	RULING
Planned Parenthood of Central Missouri v. Danforth, 428 U.S. 52 (1976)	5–4	Ruled that informed consent statutes, requiring doctors to obtain the written consent of a woman

after informing her of the dangers of abortion and possible alternatives, were permissible if the requirements were related to maternal health and not overbearing; the requirements must also be narrowly drawn so as not to unduly interfere with the physician–patient relationship; and in addition, the Court upheld requiring doctors to provide information to states on each abortion performed, so long as the reporting requirements related to maternal health remain confidential and are not overbearing. The Court, however, struck down fetal-protection statutes that pertain only to previable fetuses and require doctors to use available means to save the lives of fetuses; finally, the Court held that "it is not the proper function of the legislature or the courts to place viability, which is essentially a medical concept, at a specific point in the gestation period. The time when viability is achieved may vary with each pregnancy, and the determination of whether a particular fetus is viable is, and must be, a matter for the judgment of the attending physician."

CASE	VOTE	RULING
Bellotti v. Baird, 428 U.S. 132 (1976)	9–0	Overturned a law requiring parental consent for minors seeking abortions.
Beal v. Doe, 432 U.S. 438 (1977)	6–3	Held that nothing in the language or history of Title XIX of the Social Security Act required the funding of nontherapeutic abortions as a condition of a state's participating in the Medicaid program established under the act; the Court indicated that Title XIX left states free to include coverage for nontherapeutic abortions if they choose to do so, but also that they could refuse to fund unnecessary medical services.
Maher v. Roe, 432 U.S. 464 (1977)	6–3	Upheld Connecticut's refusal to reimburse Medicaid recipients for abortion expenses except where the attending physician certifies that an abortion is medically or psychiatrically necessary.
Poelker v. Doe, 432 U.S. 519 (1977)	6–3	Upheld the policy of the city of St. Louis, Missouri, to deny indigent pregnant women access to nontherapeutic abortions in public hospitals.
Bellotti v. Baird, 443 U.S. 622 (1979)	9–0	Ruled that while states may require minors to obtain parental consent, they must provide an alternative judicial procedure for procuring authorization of a minor's abortion, if parental consent is denied or the minor does not want to seek it.
Harris v. McRae, 448 U.S. 297 (1980)	5–4	Upheld the Hyde Amendment to the Medicaid program that limited federal

(continues)

■ THE DEVELOPMENT OF LAW
*Other Post-*Roe *Rulings on Abortion (continued)*

funding for nontherapeutic abortions; the Court also upheld the right of a state to fund only those medically necessary abortions for which it received federal reimbursement.

CASE	VOTE	RULING

H. L. v. Matheson, 450 U.S. 398 (1981) — 6–3 — Upheld a Utah statute requiring physicians to notify parents, "if possible," prior to performing an abortion on their minor daughter (1) when the girl is living with and dependent on her parents, (2) when she is not emancipated by marriage or otherwise, and (3) when she has made no claim or showing as to her maturity or as to her relationship with her parents.

Akron v. Akron Center for Reproductive Health, 462 U.S. 416 (1983) — 6–3 — Struck down five sections of a city ordinance for unduly restricting a woman's right to obtain an abortion; the sections provided that (1) after the first trimester of a pregnancy, all abortions be performed in a hospital; (2) there be notification of consent by parents before abortions are performed on unmarried minors; (3) the attending physician make certain specified statements to a patient so that the patient's consent for an abortion would amount to "informed consent"; (4) there be a twenty-four-hour waiting period between the time a patient signs the consent form and when an abortion is performed; and (5) fetal remains be disposed of in a "humane and sanitary manner."

Planned Parenthood Association of Kansas City v. Ashcroft, 462 U.S. 476 (1983) — 6–3 & 5–4 — Invalidated Missouri's second-trimester hospitalization requirement, but a bare majority struck down the state's requirement that after twelve weeks of pregnancy, all abortions be performed in a hospital and (voting 5–4) upheld three other sections of Missouri's law—they required (1) pathological reports for each abortion performed, (2) the presence of a second doctor during abortions performed after viability, and (3) parental consent or consent from a juvenile court for minors before obtaining an abortion.

Simopoulos v. Virginia, 462 U.S. 506 (1983) — 8–1 — Upheld Virginia's mandatory hospitalization requirement for abortions performed in the second trimester.

CASE	VOTE	RULING

Thornburgh v. American College of Obstetricians & Gynecologists, 476 U.S. 747 (1986) — 5–4 — Struck down a Pennsylvania law requiring (1) women to be advised of medical assistance and that the natural father is responsible for child support, (2) physicians to inform women of the detrimental effects and risks of abortion, (3) doctors to report all abortions to the state, (4) a higher degree of care in postviability abortions in an attempt to save the life of the fetus, and (5) the presence of a second physician during the performance of all abortions.

Bowen v. Kendrick, 487 U.S. 589 (1988) — 5–4 — Upheld the Adolescent Family Life Act, which prohibits federal funding of organizations involved with abortions, while permitting funding of religious groups advocating self-discipline as a form of birth control.

Webster v. Reproductive Health Services, 492 U.S. 490 (1989) — 5–4 — Upheld the constitutionality of Missouri's 1986 restrictive abortion law, which (1) decreed that life begins at conception; (2) requires a doctor, before performing an abortion on a woman believed to be twenty or more weeks pregnant, to test the fetus's "gestational age, weight, and lung maturity"; (3) prohibits public employees or facilities from being used to perform abortions not necessary to save a woman's life; and (4) made it unlawful to use public funds, employees, or facilities for the purpose of "encouraging or counseling" a woman to have an abortion, except when her life is endangered. Justices Brennan, Stevens, Marshall, and Blackmun dissented.

Hodgson v. Minnesota, 497 U.S. 417 (1990) — 5–4 — With Justice O'Connor casting the crucial vote, a bare majority agreed that, without a judicial bypass option, the state's requirement that minors notify both parents before obtaining an abortion was unconstitutional—on that issue, Justice O'Connor joined Justices Brennan, Blackmun, Marshall, and Stevens. But O'Connor also joined Chief Justice Rehnquist and Justices Scalia, Kennedy, and White in upholding the constitutionality of the parental consent law.

(continues)

■ THE DEVELOPMENT OF LAW
*Other Post-*Roe *Rulings on Abortion (continued)*

CASE	VOTE	RULING
Planned Parenthood of Southeastern Pennsylvania v. Casey, 500 U.S. 833 (1992)	5–4	In an unusual opinion for the Court issued by Justices O'Connor, Kennedy, and Souter, and joined in part

by Justices Blackmun and Stevens, the Court upheld most of the provisions of Pennsylvania's 1988 abortion law, requiring (1) doctors to discuss the risks and consequences of abortion and to obtain a woman's written consent for an abortion; (2) women to wait, after giving their informed consent, twenty-four hours before having an abortion; (3) unmarried women under the age of eighteen to obtain the written consent of at least one parent or a judge before having an abortion; and (4) doctors to report to public health authorities on each abortion performed. A bare majority struck down the additional requirement that women, under most circumstances, certify that they have notified their spouses of their intent to have an abortion. That requirement was deemed to constitute an "undue burden" on women, and on that score and the majority's refusal to discard *Roe*, Chief Justice Rehnquist and Justices Scalia, Thomas, and White dissented.

| *Stenberg v. Carhart I*, 530 U.S. 914 (2000) | 5–4 | Writing for the Court, Justice Breyer held that a Nebraska statute banning |

certain late-term or "partial birth" abortions was vague and failed to provide an exception for when a woman's health is endangered. Justice O'Connor cast the deciding vote. Chief Justice Rehnquist and Justices Scalia, Kennedy, and Thomas dissented.

| *Gonzales v. Carhart II*, 550 U.S. 124 (2007) | 5–4 | Writing for the Court, Justice Kennedy upheld the federal law, the Partial- |

Birth Abortion Ban Act of 2003, banning so-called late-term abortions. Justices Stevens, Souter, Ginsburg, and Breyer dissented.

■ INSIDE THE COURT

Drafting the Opinion for the Court in Planned Parenthood of Southeastern Pennsylvania v. Casey

Planned Parenthood's petition for review asked the Court to rule on whether *Roe*'s "holding that a woman's right to choose abortion is a fundamental right" had been overruled by subsequent decisions. But when voting to grant review at conference on January 12, 1992, Justice O'Connor remained in no mood to do so and Souter pushed for a reformulation of the question presented. He followed up by proposing that attorneys brief and direct arguments to whether "the 'undue burden' standard of review [is] the appropriate standard of review" and whether the appellate court correctly applied it. Although agreeing on a rephrasing of the questions, Stevens suggested instead that counsel be asked simply whether the lower court erred in upholding certain provisions and "what weight is due to *stare decisis* in evaluating the constitutional right to abortion." Justice Souter agreed but others disagreed with the latter question, even though it was central to the continuing controversy. As a result, when granting review the Court limited the issues to whether the appellate court erred in upholding provisions of the law and in striking down its requirement for spousal consent.

At the Wednesday conference two days after hearing oral arguments in *Casey* on April 4, Chief Justice Rehnquist led the discussion and voted to uphold all the state's requirements. Justice White agreed, while Stevens thought the requirement for a twenty-four-hour waiting period was "an insult" and the spousal consent requirement was "outrageous." Blackmun would have struck down all the provisions but "passed." O'Connor remained in no mood to overrule *Roe* but said that the appellate court had "got most [of it] right." Kennedy agreed, while Scalia and Thomas were firmly with the chief justice and would have gone further to overrule *Roe*. Rehnquist thus had a majority and a few days later assigned himself the job of writing the opinion for the Court, as he had done in *Webster v. Reproductive Health Services*, 492 U.S. 490 (1989), and other major cases.

Not quite a month later, on May 27, Chief Justice Rehnquist circulated his draft, upholding all of Pennsylvania's restrictions as having a rational basis. The only concession he made was in noting that women were exempt from the notice and consent requirements when

(continues)

■ INSIDE THE COURT
Drafting the Opinion for the Court in Planned Parenthood
of Southeastern Pennsylvania v. Casey *(continued)*

confronted with a "significant threat to [their] life or health," though
he also concluded that due process did not require states to include in
such a "medical emergency" exception "all insignificant and negligible threats to a woman's health." That outcome, as in *Webster*, had
been anticipated and Souter and O'Connor had been privately talking
with Kennedy about not following the chief in *Casey* as he had done
in *Webster*. They urged him to reaffirm *Roe*'s central holding on a
woman's right to choose, while upholding most of Pennsylvania's
restrictions based on O'Connor's "undue burden" test. Souter had
already been working on a draft dealing with *stare decisis* and why *Roe*
should be upheld, based on societal expectations and the damage that
would be done to the Court's institutional prestige if it were overturned. Kennedy agreed and two days after the chief justice circulated
his first draft he sent Blackmun a note telling him that he wanted to
talk about some "welcome news."

On June 3, Justices O'Connor, Kennedy, and Souter circulated
their draft opinion, concurring and dissenting in part from the chief's
draft opinion for the Court. Justice Stevens followed up by joining
certain sections of their opinion and urging Blackmun to do the same.
Rehnquist circulated a second draft of his opinion for the Court on
June 17, which now included a new section taking issue with the analysis of *stare decisis* in the opinion circulated by the "troika," as law clerks
referred to O'Connor, Kennedy, and Souter. He dismissed their analysis as "*dicta*" and reaffirmed *Webster*'s rejection of a woman's "fundamental right" to abortion and heightened scrutiny analysis. But it
proved too late. Stevens and Blackmun agreed to join portions of the
O'Connor-Kennedy-Souter draft and thereby formed a new bare
majority. Five days later, on June 22, the second draft opinion by
O'Connor-Kennedy-Souter circulated but now as the opinion for the
Court. Subsequently, on June 26, Rehnquist circulated his third and
revised draft, but one that now concurred and dissented in part, rather
than spoke for the Court. The next day, the final draft of the opinion
for the Court that would come down on June 29 circulated, reaffirming *Roe*'s "central holding" while upholding all of Pennsylvania's
restrictions except for that requiring spousal consent.

Source: Justice Harry A. Blackmun Papers, Box 151, Manuscripts Room,
Library of Congress, Washington, DC.

Planned Parenthood of Southeastern Pennsylvania v. Casey

505 U.S. 833, 112 S.Ct. 2791 (1992)

In 1988 and 1989, following the Supreme Court's ruling in *Webster v. Reproductive Health Services*, 492 U.S. 490 (1989), Pennsylvania amended its state abortion law by enacting more restrictive provisions conditioning access to abortions. Planned Parenthood of Southeastern Pennsylvania immediately challenged the constitutionality of those provisions. Subsequently, the Court of Appeals for the Third Circuit upheld most of those restrictions, except for a spousal notification provision. In doing so, the Third Circuit adopted Justice O'Connor's undue burden analysis, in her dissenting opinion in *Akron v. Akron Center for Reproductive Health, Inc.*, 462 U.S. 416 (1983). Accordingly, the appellate court gave strict scrutiny to any restriction that unduly burdened women and held that abortion restrictions that do not pose an undue burden are permissible so long as they have a rational basis. And on that basis, the Third Circuit upheld Pennsylvania's restrictions requiring women to (1) be informed by doctors about fetal development; (2) give their consent or, if they were minors, obtain parental consent; and (3) wait at least twenty-four hours after giving their informed consent before obtaining an abortion as well as (4) imposing certain reporting and public disclosure requirements on doctors who perform abortions. Despite the fact that virtually identical requirements were struck down by a bare majority of the Burger Court in *Thornburgh v. American College of Obstetricians and Gynecologists*, 476 U.S. 747 (1986), the Third Circuit noted that the Rehnquist Court had substantially altered its analysis and undercut support for a woman's fundamental right to obtain an abortion in *Webster v. Reproductive Health Services*, 492 U.S. 490 (1989). The appellate court, moreover, did not deem any of the above restrictions to constitute an undue burden and, therefore, applied the rational basis test when upholding these requirements. Pennsylvania, however, also required married women to notify their spouses of their desire to obtain an abortion, and the appellate court overturned that requirement as an undue burden on women. When strictly scrutinizing that provision, the Third Circuit concluded that it unduly burdened women by potentially exposing them to spousal abuse, violence, and economic duress at the hands of their husbands. Both sides of the abortion controversy appealed the appellate court's decision.

The Court's decision was 5–4, but the justices split 3–2–4. The opinion was announced by Justices O'Connor, Kennedy, and Souter.

Justices Blackmun and Stevens delivered separate opinions in part concurring and in part dissenting. Chief Justice Rehnquist and Justice Scalia joined each other and were joined by Justices Thomas and White.

■ ■ ■

☐ *Justice O'CONNOR, Justice KENNEDY, and Justice SOUTER announced the judgment of the Court and delivered the opinion of the Court with respect to Parts I, II, III, V-A, V-C, and VI, an opinion with respect to Part V-E, in which Justice STEVENS joins, and an opinion with respect to Parts IV, V-B, and V-D.*

■ I

After considering the fundamental constitutional questions resolved by *Roe* [*v. Wade*, 410 U.S. 113 (1973)], principles of institutional integrity, and the rule of *stare decisis*, we are led to conclude this: the essential holding of *Roe v. Wade* should be retained and once again reaffirmed.

It must be stated at the outset and with clarity that *Roe*'s essential holding, the holding we reaffirm, has three parts. First is a recognition of the right of the woman to choose to have an abortion before viability and to obtain it without undue interference from the State. Before viability, the State's interests are not strong enough to support a prohibition of abortion or the imposition of a substantial obstacle to the woman's effective right to elect the procedure. Second is a confirmation of the State's power to restrict abortions after fetal viability, if the law contains exceptions for pregnancies which endanger a woman's life or health. And third is the principle that the State has legitimate interests from the outset of the pregnancy in protecting the health of the woman and the life of the fetus that may become a child. These principles do not contradict one another; and we adhere to each. . . .

■ III

■ A

[W]hen this Court reexamines a prior holding, its judgment is customarily informed by a series of prudential and pragmatic considerations designed to test the consistency of overruling a prior decision with the ideal of the rule of law, and to gauge the respective costs of reaffirming and overruling a prior case. Thus, for example, we may ask whether the rule has proved to be intolerable simply in defying practical workability; whether the rule is subject to a kind of reliance that would lend a special hardship to the consequences of overruling and add inequity to the cost of repudiation; whether related principles of law have so far developed as to have left the old rule no more than a remnant of abandoned doctrine; or whether facts have so changed, or come to be seen so differently, as to have robbed the old rule of significant application or justification, e.g., *Burnet v. Coronado Oil Gas Co.*, 285 U.S. 393 (1932) (BRANDEIS, J., dissenting). . . .

Although *Roe* has engendered opposition, it has in no sense proven "unworkable," representing as it does a simple limitation beyond which a state law is unenforceable. . . .

We have seen how time has overtaken some of *Roe*'s factual assumptions: advances in maternal health care allow for abortions safe to the mother later in pregnancy than was true in 1973, and advances in neonatal care have advanced viability to a point somewhat earlier. But these facts go only to the scheme of time limits on the realization of competing interests, and the divergences from the factual premises of 1973 have no bearing on the validity of *Roe*'s central holding, that viability marks the earliest point at which the State's interest in fetal life is constitutionally adequate to justify a legislative ban on nontherapeutic abortions. The soundness or unsoundness of that constitutional judgment in no sense turns on whether viability occurs at approximately 28 weeks, as was usual at the time of *Roe*, at 23 to 24 weeks, as it sometimes does today, or at some moment even slightly earlier in pregnancy, as it may if fetal respiratory capacity can somehow be enhanced in the future. Whenever it may occur, the attainment of viability may continue to serve as the critical fact, just as it has done since *Roe* was decided; which is to say that no change in *Roe*'s factual underpinning has left its central holding obsolete, and none supports an argument for overruling it.

▪ B

In a less significant case, *stare decisis* analysis could, and would, stop at the point we have reached. But the sustained and widespread debate *Roe* has provoked calls for some comparison between that case and others of comparable dimension that have responded to national controversies and taken on the impress of the controversies addressed. Only two such decisional lines from the past century present themselves for examination, and in each instance the result reached by the Court accorded with the principles we apply today.

The first example is that line of cases identified with *Lochner v. New York*, 198 U.S. 45 (1905), which imposed substantive limitations on legislation limiting economic autonomy in favor of health and welfare regulation, adopting, in Justice HOLMES' view, the theory of laissez-faire. The *Lochner* decisions were exemplified by *Adkins v. Children's Hospital of D.C.*, 261 U.S. 525 (1923), in which this Court held it to be an infringement of constitutionally protected liberty of contract to require the employers of adult women to satisfy minimum wage standards. Fourteen years later, *West Coast Hotel Co. v. Parrish*, 300 U.S. 379 (1937), signaled the demise of *Lochner* by overruling *Adkins*. In the meantime, the Depression had come and, with it, the lesson that seemed unmistakable to most people by 1937, that the interpretation of contractual freedom protected in *Adkins* rested on fundamentally false factual assumptions about the capacity of a relatively unregulated market to satisfy minimal levels of human welfare. . . .

The second comparison that 20th century history invites is with the cases employing the separate-but-equal rule for applying the Fourteenth Amendment's equal protection guarantee. They began with *Plessy v. Ferguson*,

163 U.S. 537 (1896), holding that legislatively mandated racial segregation in public transportation works no denial of equal protection. . . . The *Plessy* Court considered "the underlying fallacy of the plaintiff's argument to consist in the assumption that the enforced separation of the two races stamps the colored race with a badge of inferiority. If this be so, it is not by reason of anything found in the act, but solely because the colored race chooses to put that construction upon it." Whether, as a matter of historical fact, the Justices in the *Plessy* majority believed this or not, this understanding of the implication of segregation was the stated justification for the Court's opinion. But this understanding of the facts and the rule it was stated to justify were repudiated in *Brown v. Board of Education*, 347 U.S. 483 (1954). . . .

The Court in *Brown* addressed these facts of life by observing that whatever may have been the understanding in *Plessy*'s time of the power of segregation to stigmatize those who were segregated with a "badge of inferiority," it was clear by 1954 that legally sanctioned segregation had just such an effect, to the point that racially separate public educational facilities were deemed inherently unequal. Society's understanding of the facts upon which a constitutional ruling was sought in 1954 was thus fundamentally different from the basis claimed for the decision in 1896. While we think *Plessy* was wrong the day it was decided, we must also recognize that the *Plessy* Court's explanation for its decision was so clearly at odds with the facts apparent to the Court in 1954 that the decision to reexamine *Plessy* was on this ground alone not only justified but required.

West Coast Hotel and *Brown* each rested on facts, or an understanding of facts, changed from those which furnished the claimed justifications for the earlier constitutional resolutions. . . . In constitutional adjudication as elsewhere in life, changed circumstances may impose new obligations, and the thoughtful part of the Nation could accept each decision to overrule a prior case as a response to the Court's constitutional duty.

Because the case before us presents no such occasion it could be seen as no such response. Because neither the factual underpinnings of *Roe*'s central holding nor our understanding of it has changed (and because no other indication of weakened precedent has been shown) the Court could not pretend to be reexamining the prior law with any justification beyond a present doctrinal disposition to come out differently from the Court of 1973. . . .

■ C

The examination of the conditions justifying the repudiation of *Adkins* by *West Coast Hotel* and *Plessy* by *Brown* is enough to suggest the terrible price that would have been paid if the Court had not overruled as it did. In the present case, however, as our analysis to this point makes clear, the terrible price would be paid for overruling. Our analysis would not be complete, however, without explaining why overruling *Roe*'s central holding would not only reach an unjustifiable result under principles of *stare decisis*, but would seriously weaken the Court's capacity to exercise the judicial power and to function as the Supreme Court of a Nation dedicated to the rule of law. . . .

The underlying substance of [the Court's] legitimacy is . . . expressed in the Court's opinions, and our contemporary understanding is such that a decision without principled justification would be no judicial act at all. . . . The Court must take care to speak and act in ways that allow people to accept its decisions on the terms the Court claims for them, as grounded truly in principle, not as compromises with social and political pressures having, as such, no bearing on the principled choices that the Court is obliged to make. Thus, the Court's legitimacy depends on making legally principled decisions under circumstances in which their principled character is sufficiently plausible to be accepted by the Nation. . . .

The Court's duty in the present case is clear. In 1973, it confronted the already-divisive issue of governmental power to limit personal choice to undergo abortion, for which it provided a new resolution based on the due process guaranteed by the Fourteenth Amendment. Whether or not a new social consensus is developing on that issue, its divisiveness is no less today than in 1973, and pressure to overrule the decision, like pressure to retain it, has grown only more intense. A decision to overrule *Roe*'s essential holding under the existing circumstances would address error, if error there was, at the cost of both profound and unnecessary damage to the Court's legitimacy, and to the Nation's commitment to the rule of law. It is therefore imperative to adhere to the essence of *Roe*'s original decision, and we do so today.

■ IV

We conclude that the basic decision in *Roe* was based on a constitutional analysis which we cannot now repudiate. The woman's liberty is not so unlimited, however, that from the outset the State cannot show its concern for the life of the unborn, and at a later point in fetal development the State's interest in life has sufficient force so that the right of the woman to terminate the pregnancy can be restricted.

That brings us, of course, to the point where much criticism has been directed at *Roe*, a criticism that always inheres when the Court draws a specific rule from what in the Constitution is but a general standard. . . . And it falls to us to give some real substance to the woman's liberty to determine whether to carry her pregnancy to full term.

We conclude the line should be drawn at viability, so that before that time the woman has a right to choose to terminate her pregnancy. We adhere to this principle for two reasons. First, as we have said, is the doctrine of *stare decisis*. Any judicial act of line-drawing may seem somewhat arbitrary, but *Roe* was a reasoned statement, elaborated with great care. We have twice reaffirmed it in the face of great opposition. Although we must overrule those parts of *Thornburgh* and *Akron I* which, in our view, are inconsistent with *Roe*'s statement that the State has a legitimate interest in promoting the life or potential life of the unborn, the central premise of those cases represents an unbroken commitment by this Court to the essential holding of *Roe*. It is that premise which we reaffirm today.

The second reason is that the concept of viability, as we noted in *Roe*, is the time at which there is a realistic possibility of maintaining and nourishing a life outside the womb, so that the independent existence of the second life can in reason and all fairness be the object of state protection that now overrides the rights of the woman. Consistent with other constitutional norms, legislatures may draw lines which appear arbitrary without the necessity of offering a justification. But courts may not. We must justify the lines we draw. And there is no line other than viability which is more workable. . . .

The woman's right to terminate her pregnancy before viability is the most central principle of *Roe v. Wade.* It is a rule of law and a component of liberty we cannot renounce. . . .

Though the woman has a right to choose to terminate or continue her pregnancy before viability, it does not at all follow that the State is prohibited from taking steps to ensure that this choice is thoughtful and informed. Even in the earliest stages of pregnancy, the State may enact rules and regulations designed to encourage her to know that there are philosophic and social arguments of great weight that can be brought to bear in favor of continuing the pregnancy to full term and that there are procedures and institutions to allow adoption of unwanted children as well as a certain degree of state assistance if the mother chooses to raise the child herself. "The Constitution does not forbid a State or city, pursuant to democratic processes, from expressing a preference for normal childbirth." *Webster v. Reproductive Health Services* [1989]. It follows that States are free to enact laws to provide a reasonable framework for a woman to make a decision that has such profound and lasting meaning. This, too, we find consistent with *Roe*'s central premises, and indeed the inevitable consequence of our holding that the State has an interest in protecting the life of the unborn.

We reject the trimester framework, which we do not consider to be part of the essential holding of *Roe.* . . . The trimester framework suffers from these basic flaws: in its formulation it misconceives the nature of the pregnant woman's interest; and in practice it undervalues the State's interest in potential life, as recognized in *Roe.* . . .

Because we set forth a standard of general application to which we intend to adhere, it is important to clarify what is meant by an undue burden. . . . We give this summary:

> (a) To protect the central right recognized by *Roe v. Wade* while at the same time accommodating the State's profound interest in potential life, we will employ the undue burden analysis as explained in this opinion. An undue burden exists, and therefore a provision of law is invalid, if its purpose or effect is to place a substantial obstacle in the path of a woman seeking an abortion before the fetus attains viability.
>
> (b) We reject the rigid trimester framework of *Roe v. Wade.* To promote the State's profound interest in potential life, throughout pregnancy the State may take measures to ensure that the woman's choice is informed, and measures designed to advance this interest will not be invalidated as long as their purpose is to persuade the woman to choose childbirth over abortion. These measures must not be an undue burden on the right.

(c) As with any medical procedure, the State may enact regulations to further the health or safety of a woman seeking an abortion. Unnecessary health regulations that have the purpose or effect of presenting a substantial obstacle to a woman seeking an abortion impose an undue burden on the right.

(d) Our adoption of the undue burden analysis does not disturb the central holding of *Roe v. Wade*, and we reaffirm that holding. Regardless of whether exceptions are made for particular circumstances, a State may not prohibit any woman from making the ultimate decision to terminate her pregnancy before viability.

(e) We also reaffirm *Roe*'s holding that "subsequent to viability, the State in promoting its interest in the potentiality of human life may, if it chooses, regulate, and even proscribe, abortion except where it is necessary, in appropriate medical judgment, for the preservation of the life or health of the mother."

These principles control our assessment of the Pennsylvania statute, and we now turn to the issue of the validity of its challenged provisions.

- **V**

- **A**

Because it is central to the operation of various other requirements, we begin with the statute's definition of medical emergency. Under the statute, a medical emergency is "that condition which, on the basis of the physician's good faith clinical judgment, so complicates the medical condition of a pregnant woman as to necessitate the immediate abortion of her pregnancy to avert her death or for which a delay will create serious risk of substantial and irreversible impairment of a major bodily function." . . .

We conclude that, as construed by the Court of Appeals, the medical emergency definition imposes no undue burden on a woman's abortion right. . . .

- **B**

Our prior decisions establish that as with any medical procedure, the State may require a woman to give her written informed consent to an abortion. In this respect, the statute is unexceptional. Petitioners challenge the statute's definition of informed consent because it includes the provision of specific information by the doctor and the mandatory 24-hour waiting period. The conclusions reached by a majority of the Justices in the separate opinions filed today and the undue burden standard adopted in this opinion require us to overrule in part some of the Court's past decisions, decisions driven by the trimester framework's prohibition of all previability regulations designed to further the State's interest in fetal life. . . .

To the extent *Akron I* and *Thornburgh* find a constitutional violation when the government requires, as it does here, the giving of truthful, nonmisleading information about the nature of the procedure, the attendant health risks and those of childbirth, and the "probable gestational age" of the fetus, those cases go too far, are inconsistent with *Roe*'s acknowledgment of an important interest in potential life, and are overruled. . . .

■ C

Section 3209 of Pennsylvania's abortion law provides, except in cases of medical emergency, that no physician shall perform an abortion on a married woman without receiving a signed statement from the woman that she has notified her spouse that she is about to undergo an abortion. The woman has the option of providing an alternative signed statement certifying that her husband is not the man who impregnated her; that her husband could not be located; that the pregnancy is the result of spousal sexual assault which she has reported; or that the woman believes that notifying her husband will cause him or someone else to inflict bodily injury upon her. A physician who performs an abortion on a married woman without receiving the appropriate signed statement will have his or her license revoked, and is liable to the husband for damages. . . .

[T]here are millions of women in this country who are the victims of regular physical and psychological abuse at the hands of their husbands. Should these women become pregnant, they may have very good reasons for not wishing to inform their husbands of their decision to obtain an abortion. Many may have justifiable fears of physical abuse, but may be no less fearful of the consequences of reporting prior abuse to the Commonwealth of Pennsylvania. Many may have a reasonable fear that notifying their husbands will provoke further instances of child abuse; these women are not exempt from Section 3209's notification requirement. Many may fear devastating forms of psychological abuse from their husbands, including verbal harassment, threats of future violence, the destruction of possessions, physical confinement to the home, the withdrawal of financial support, or the disclosure of the abortion to family and friends. These methods of psychological abuse may act as even more of a deterrent to notification than the possibility of physical violence, but women who are the victims of the abuse are not exempt from Section 3209's notification requirement. And many women who are pregnant as a result of sexual assaults by their husbands will be unable to avail themselves of the exception for spousal sexual assault, because the exception requires that the woman have notified law enforcement authorities within 90 days of the assault, and her husband will be notified of her report once an investigation begins. . . .

The unfortunate yet persisting conditions we document above will mean that in a large fraction of the cases in which Section 3209 is relevant, it will operate as a substantial obstacle to a woman's choice to undergo an abortion. It is an undue burden, and therefore invalid. . . .

■ D

We next consider the parental consent provision. . . .

We have been over most of this ground before. Our cases establish, and we reaffirm today, that a State may require a minor seeking an abortion to obtain the consent of a parent or guardian, provided that there is an adequate judicial bypass procedure. Under these precedents, in our view, the one-parent consent requirement and judicial bypass procedure are constitutional. . . .

■ E

In [*Planned Parenthood of Central Missouri v.*] *Danforth*, [428 U.S. 552 (1976)], we held that recordkeeping and reporting provisions "that are reasonably directed to the preservation of maternal health and that properly respect a patient's confidentiality and privacy are permissible." We think that under this standard, all the provisions at issue here except that relating to spousal notice are constitutional. . . .

Subsection (12) of the reporting provision requires the reporting of, among other things, a married woman's "reason for failure to provide notice" to her husband. This provision in effect requires women, as a condition of obtaining an abortion, to provide the Commonwealth with the precise information we have already recognized that many women have pressing reasons not to reveal. Like the spousal notice requirement itself, this provision places an undue burden on a woman's choice, and must be invalidated for that reason.

☐ *Justice BLACKMUN, concurring in part, concurring in the judgment in part, and dissenting in part.*

I join parts I, II, III, V-A, V-C, and VI of the joint opinion of Justice O'CONNOR, KENNEDY, and SOUTER. . . .

Make no mistake, the joint opinion of Justices O'CONNOR, KEN-NEDY, and SOUTER is an act of personal courage and constitutional principle. In contrast to previous decisions in which Justices O'CONNOR and KENNEDY postponed reconsideration of *Roe v. Wade*, the authors of the joint opinion today join Justice STEVENS and me in concluding that "the essential holding of *Roe* should be retained and once again reaffirmed." In brief, five Members of this Court today recognize that "the Constitution protects a woman's right to terminate her pregnancy in its early stages." . . .

Our precedents and the joint opinion's principles require us to subject all non-*de minimis* abortion regulations to strict scrutiny. Under this standard, the Pennsylvania statute's provisions requiring content-based counseling, a 24-hour delay, informed parental consent, and reporting of abortion-related information must be invalidated. . . .

If there is much reason to applaud the advances made by the joint opinion today, there is far more to fear from THE CHIEF JUSTICE's opinion.

THE CHIEF JUSTICE's criticism of *Roe* follows from his stunted conception of individual liberty. . . . He argues that the record in favor of a right to abortion is no stronger than the record in *Michael H. v. Gerald D.*, 491 U.S. 110 (1989), where the plurality found no fundamental right to visitation privileges by an adulterous father, or in *Bowers v. Hardwick*, 478 U.S. 186 (1986), where the Court found no fundamental right to engage in homosexual sodomy, or in a case involving the "firing of a gun . . . into another person's body." In THE CHIEF JUSTICE's world, a woman considering whether to terminate a pregnancy is entitled to no more protection than adulterers, murderers, and so-called "sexual deviates." Given THE CHIEF JUSTICE's exclusive reliance on tradition, people using contraceptives seem the next likely candidate for his list of outcasts. . . .

In one sense, the Court's approach is worlds apart from that of THE CHIEF JUSTICE and Justice SCALIA. And yet, in another sense, the distance between the two approaches is short—the distance is but a single vote.

I am 83 years old. I cannot remain on this Court forever, and when I do step down, the confirmation process for my successor well may focus on the issue before us today. That, I regret, may be exactly where the choice between the two worlds will be made.

□ *Justice STEVENS, in an opinion omitted here, concurred in part and dissented from Parts IV, V-B, and V-D of the joint opinion, voting to uphold the informed consent and reporting requirements, except for the provision for reporting on spousal notification, and voting to strike down as an undue burden the requirements for abortion counseling, a 24-hour waiting period, and spousal notification.*

□ *Chief Justice REHNQUIST, with whom Justice WHITE, Justice SCALIA, and Justice THOMAS joined, concurring in the judgment in part and dissenting in part.*

We think . . . that the Court was mistaken in *Roe* when it classified a woman's decision to terminate her pregnancy as a "fundamental right" that could be abridged only in a manner which withstood "strict scrutiny." . . .

The joint opinion of Justices O'CONNOR, KENNEDY, and SOUTER cannot bring itself to say that *Roe* was correct as an original matter, but the authors are of the view that "the immediate question is not the soundness of *Roe*'s resolution of the issue, but the precedential force that must be accorded to its holding." Instead of claiming that *Roe* was correct as a matter of original constitutional interpretation, the opinion therefore contains an elaborate discussion of *stare decisis*. This discussion of the principle of *stare decisis* appears to be almost entirely *dicta*, because the joint opinion does not apply that principle in dealing with *Roe*. *Roe* decided that a woman had a fundamental right to an abortion. The joint opinion rejects that view. *Roe* decided that abortion regulations were to be subjected to "strict scrutiny" and could be justified only in the light of "compelling state interests." The joint opinion rejects that view. *Roe* analyzed abortion regulation under a rigid trimester framework, a framework which has guided this Court's decisionmaking for 19 years. The joint opinion rejects that framework. . . .

In our view, authentic principles of *stare decisis* do not require that any portion of the reasoning in *Roe* be kept intact. . . .

The joint opinion discusses several *stare decisis* factors which, it asserts, point toward retaining a portion of *Roe.* Two of these factors are that the main "factual underpinning" of *Roe* has remained the same, and that its doctrinal foundation is no weaker now than it was in 1973. Of course, what might be called the basic facts which gave rise to *Roe* have remained the same—women become pregnant, there is a point somewhere, depending on medical technology, where a fetus becomes viable, and women give birth to children. But this is only to say that the same facts which gave rise to *Roe* will continue to give rise to similar cases. It is not a reason, in and of itself, why those cases must be decided in the same incorrect manner as was the first case to deal with the question. And surely there is no requirement, in considering whether to depart from *stare decisis* in a constitutional case, that a decision be more wrong now than it was at the time it was rendered. If that were true, the most outlandish constitutional decision could survive forever, based simply on the fact that it was no more outlandish later than it was when originally rendered. . . .

In the end, having failed to put forth any evidence to prove any true reliance, the joint opinion's argument is based solely on generalized assertions about the national psyche, on a belief that the people of this country have grown accustomed to the *Roe* decision over the last 19 years and have "ordered their thinking and living around" it. As an initial matter, one might inquire how the joint opinion can view the "central holding" of *Roe* as so deeply rooted in our constitutional culture, when it so casually uproots and disposes of that same decision's trimester framework. Furthermore, at various points in the past, the same could have been said about this Court's erroneous decisions that the Constitution allowed "separate but equal" treatment of minorities, or that "liberty" under the Due Process Clause protected "freedom of contract." The "separate but equal" doctrine lasted 58 years after *Plessy,* and *Lochner's* protection of contractual freedom lasted 32 years. However, the simple fact that a generation or more had grown used to these major decisions did not prevent the Court from correcting its errors in those cases, nor should it prevent us from correctly interpreting the Constitution here.

Apparently realizing that conventional *stare decisis* principles do not support its position, the joint opinion advances a belief that retaining a portion of *Roe* is necessary to protect the "legitimacy" of this Court. . . . [T]he joint opinion goes on to state that when the Court "resolves the sort of intensely divisive controversy reflected in *Roe* and those rare, comparable cases," its decision is exempt from reconsideration under established principles of *stare decisis* in constitutional cases. This is so, the joint opinion contends, because in those "intensely divisive" cases the Court has "called the contending sides of a national controversy to end their national division by accepting a common mandate rooted in the Constitution," and must therefore take special care not to be perceived as "surrendering to political pressure" and continued opposition. This is a truly novel principle. . . . Under this principle, when the Court has ruled on a divisive issue, it is apparently prevented from overruling that decision for the sole reason that it was incorrect, unless opposition to the original decision has died away. . . .

The joint opinion agrees that the Court's stature would have been seriously damaged if in *Brown* and *West Coast Hotel* it had dug in its heels and refused to apply normal principles of *stare decisis* to the earlier decisions. But the opinion contends that the Court was entitled to overrule *Plessy* and *Lochner* in those cases, despite the existence of opposition to the original decisions, only because both the Nation and the Court had learned new lessons in the interim. This is at best a feebly supported, post hoc rationalization for those decisions. . . .

The sum of the joint opinion's labors in the name of *stare decisis* and "legitimacy" is this: *Roe v. Wade* stands as a sort of judicial Potemkin Village, which may be pointed out to passersby as a monument to the importance of adhering to precedent. But behind the facade, an entirely new method of analysis, without any roots in constitutional law, is imported to decide the constitutionality of state laws regulating abortion. Neither *stare decisis* nor "legitimacy" are truly served by such an effort. . . .

For the reasons stated, we therefore would hold that each of the challenged provisions of the Pennsylvania statute is consistent with the Constitution.

☐ *Justice SCALIA, with whom THE CHIEF JUSTICE, Justice WHITE, and Justice THOMAS joined, concurring in the judgment in part and dissenting in part.*

My views on this matter are unchanged from those I set forth in my separate opinions in *Webster v. Reproductive Health Services*, 492 U.S. 490 (1989) (SCALIA, J., concurring in part and concurring in judgment), and *Ohio v. Akron Center for Reproductive Health*, 497 U.S. 502 (1990) (*Akron II*) (SCALIA, J., concurring). The States may, if they wish, permit abortion-on-demand, but the Constitution does not require them to do so. The permissibility of abortion, and the limitations upon it, are to be resolved like most important questions in our democracy: by citizens trying to persuade one another and then voting. . . . A State's choice between two positions on which reasonable people can disagree is constitutional even when (as is often the case) it intrudes upon a "liberty" in the absolute sense. Laws against bigamy, for example—which entire societies of reasonable people disagree with—intrude upon men and women's liberty to marry and live with one another. But bigamy happens not to be a liberty specially "protected" by the Constitution.

That is, quite simply, the issue in this case. . . . The issue is whether [a woman's claim to a constitutional right to have an abortion] is liberty protected by the Constitution of the United States. I am sure it is not. I reach that conclusion not because of anything so exalted as my views concerning the "concept of existence, of meaning, of the universe, and of the mystery of human life." Rather, I reach it for the same reason I reach the conclusion that bigamy is not constitutionally protected—because of two simple facts: (1) the Constitution says absolutely nothing about it, and (2) the longstanding traditions of American society have permitted it to be legally proscribed. . . .

The Court's reliance upon *stare decisis* can best be described as contrived. It insists upon the necessity of adhering not to all of *Roe*, but only to what it calls the "central holding." It seems to me that *stare decisis* ought to be applied even to the doctrine of *stare decisis*, and I confess never to have heard of this new, keep-what-you-want-and-throw-away-the-rest version. . . .

I am certainly not in a good position to dispute that the Court has saved the "central holding" of *Roe*, since to do that effectively I would have to know what the Court has saved, which in turn would require me to understand (as I do not) what the "undue burden" test means. I must confess, however, that I have always thought, and I think a lot of other people have always thought, that the arbitrary trimester framework, which the Court today discards, was quite as central to *Roe* as the arbitrary viability test, which the Court today retains. It seems particularly ungrateful to carve the trimester framework out of the core of *Roe*, since its very rigidity (in sharp contrast to the utter indeterminability of the "undue burden" test) is probably the only reason the Court is able to say, in urging *stare decisis*, that *Roe* "has in no sense proven 'unworkable.'" I suppose the Court is entitled to call a "central holding" whatever it wants to call a "central holding"—which is, come to think of it, perhaps one of the difficulties with this modified version of *stare decisis*. I thought I might note, however, that the following portions of *Roe* have not been saved:

- Under *Roe*, requiring that a woman seeking an abortion be provided truthful information about abortion before giving informed written consent is unconstitutional, if the information is designed to influence her choice, *Thornburgh, Akron I*. Under the joint opinion's "undue burden" regime (as applied today, at least) such a requirement is constitutional.
- Under *Roe*, requiring that information be provided by a doctor, rather than by nonphysician counselors, is unconstitutional, *Akron I*. Under the "undue burden" regime (as applied today, at least) it is not . . . Under *Roe*, requiring a 24-hour waiting period between the time the woman gives her informed consent and the time of the abortion is unconstitutional, *Akron I*. Under the "undue burden" regime (as applied today, at least) it is not. . . .
- Under *Roe*, requiring detailed reports that include demographic data about each woman who seeks an abortion and various information about each abortion is unconstitutional, *Thornburgh*. Under the "undue burden" regime (as applied today, at least) it generally is not. . . .

Roe fanned into life an issue that has inflamed our national politics in general, and has obscured with its smoke the selection of Justices to this Court in particular, ever since. And by keeping us in the abortion-umpiring business, it is the perpetuation of that disruption, rather than of any pax Roeana, that the Court's new majority decrees.

Whole Woman's Health v. Hellerstedt

136 S.CT. 2292 (2016)

In 2013, Texas enacted new regulations for abortion clinics, requiring (1) their doctors to have admitting privileges at a hospital within thirty miles of their location, and (2) that they meet the same facility standards as surgical centers and hospitals. Proponents argued that the regulations were in the interests of the health and safety of women; whereas, opponents countered that they were medically unnecessary, burdensome, costly, and simply aimed at limiting the availability of abortions. Almost half of the state's clinics were forced to close. A federal district court found the regulations to impose an "undue burden" on women, but the Court of Appeals for the Fifth Circuit reversed that decision and its decision was appealed.

The appellate court's decision was reversed by a 5–3 vote. Justice Breyer delivered the opinion for the Court, Justice Ginsburg filed a concurring opinion, and Justices Thomas and Alito each issued dissents, with Chief Justice Roberts joining the latter's dissenting opinion.

■ ■ ■

☐ *Justice BREYER delivered the opinion of the Court.*

In *Planned Parenthood of Southeastern Pa.* v. *Casey* (1992), a plurality of the Court concluded that there "exists" an "undue burden" on a woman's right to decide to have an abortion, and consequently a provision of law is constitutionally invalid, if the *"purpose or effect"* of the provision *"is to place a substantial obstacle* in the path of a woman seeking an abortion before the fetus attains viability." The plurality added that "[u]nnecessary health regulations that have the purpose or effect of presenting a substantial obstacle to a woman seeking an abortion impose an undue burden on the right."

We must here decide whether two provisions of Texas' House Bill 2 [H.R. 2] violate the Federal Constitution as interpreted in *Casey*. The first provision, which we shall call the*"admitting-privileges requirement,"* says that "[a] physician performing or inducing an abortion . . . must, on the date the abortion is performed or induced, have active admitting privileges at a hospital that . . . is located not further than 30 miles from the location at which the abortion is performed or induced."

The second provision, which we shall call the *"surgical-center requirement,"* says that "the minimum standards for an abortion facility must be equivalent to the minimum standards adopted under [the Texas Health and Safety Code section] for ambulatory surgical centers."

We conclude that neither of these provisions offers medical benefits sufficient to justify the burdens upon access that each imposes. Each places a substantial obstacle in the path of women seeking a previability abortion, each constitutes an undue burden on abortion access, *Casey*, and each violates the Federal Constitution. Amdt. 14, Sec. 1. . . .

■ *Undue Burden—Legal Standard*

We begin with the standard, as described in *Casey*. We recognize that the "State has a legitimate interest in seeing to it that abortion, like any other medical procedure, is performed under circumstances that insure maximum safety for the patient." *Roe* v. *Wade* (1973). But, we added, "a statute which, while furthering [a] valid state interest, has the effect of placing a substantial obstacle in the path of a woman's choice cannot be considered a permissible means of serving its legitimate ends." Moreover, "[u]necessary health regulations that have the purpose or effect of presenting a substantial obstacle to a woman seeking an abortion impose an undue burden on the right."

The Court of Appeals wrote that a state law is "constitutional if: (1) it does not have the purpose or effect of placing a substantial obstacle in the path of a woman seeking an abortion of a nonviable fetus; and (2) it is reasonably related to (or designed to further) a legitimate state interest." The Court of Appeals went on to hold that "the district court erred by substituting its own judgment for that of the legislature" when it conducted its "undue burden inquiry," in part because "medical uncertainty underlying a statute is for resolution by legislatures, not the courts."

The Court of Appeals' articulation of the relevant standard is incorrect. The first part of the Court of Appeals' test may be read to imply that a district court should not consider the existence or nonexistence of medical benefits when considering whether a regulation of abortion constitutes an undue burden. The rule announced in *Casey*, however, requires that courts consider the burdens a law imposes on abortion access together with the benefits those laws confer. And the second part of the test is wrong to equate the judicial review applicable to the regulation of a constitutionally protected personal liberty with the less strict review applicable where, for example, economic legislation is at issue. The Court of Appeals' approach simply does not match the standard that this Court laid out in *Casey*, which asks courts to consider whether any burden imposed on abortion access is "undue."

The statement that legislatures, and not courts, must resolve questions of medical uncertainty is also inconsistent with this Court's case law. Instead, the Court, when determining the constitutionality of laws regulating abortion procedures, has placed considerable weight upon evidence and argument presented in judicial proceedings. In *Casey,* for example, we relied heavily on the District Court's factual findings and the research-based submissions of *amici* in declaring a portion of the law at issue unconstitutional. . . .

■ *Undue Burden—Admitting-Privileges Requirement*

Turning to the lower courts' evaluation of the evidence, we first consider the admitting-privileges requirement. Before the enactment of H. B. 2, doctors who provided abortions were required to "have admitting privileges *or* have a working arrangement with a physician(s) who has admitting privileges at a local hospital in order to ensure the necessary back up for medical complications." The new law changed this requirement by requiring that a "physician performing or inducing an abortion . . . must, on the date the abortion is performed or induced, have active admitting privileges at a hospital that . . . is located not further than 30 miles from the location at which the abortion is performed or induced." The District Court held that the legislative change imposed an "undue burden" on a woman's right to have an abortion. We conclude that there is adequate legal and factual support for the District Court's conclusion.

The purpose of the admitting-privileges requirement is to help ensure that women have easy access to a hospital should complications arise during an abortion procedure. But the District Court found that it brought about no such health-related benefit. The court found that "[t]he great weight of evidence demonstrates that, before the act's passage, abortion in Texas was extremely safe with particularly low rates of serious complications and virtually no deaths occurring on account of the procedure." Thus, there was no significant health-related problem that the new law helped to cure. . . .

We add that, when directly asked at oral argument whether Texas knew of a single instance in which the new requirement would have helped even one woman obtain better treatment, Texas admitted that there was no evidence in the record of such a case. This answer is consistent with the findings of the other Federal District Courts that have considered the health benefits of other States' similar admitting-privileges laws.

At the same time, the record evidence indicates that the admitting-privileges requirement places a "substantial obstacle in the path of a woman's choice." The District Court found, as of the time the admitting-privileges requirement began to be enforced, the number of facilities providing abortions dropped in half, from about 40 to about 20. Eight abortion clinics closed in the months leading up to the requirement's effective date. Eleven more closed on the day the admitting-privileges requirement took effect.

Other evidence helps to explain why the new requirement led to the closure of clinics. We read that other evidence in light of a brief filed in this Court by the Society of Hospital Medicine. That brief describes the undisputed general fact that "hospitals often condition admitting privileges on reaching a certain number of admissions per year." Returning to the District Court record, we note that, in direct testimony, the president of Nova Health Systems, implicitly relying on this general fact, pointed out that it would be difficult for doctors regularly performing abortions at the El Paso clinic to obtain admitting privileges at nearby hospitals because "[d]uring the past 10 years, over 17,000 abortion procedures were performed at the El Paso clinic [and n]ot a single one of those patients had to be transferred to a hospital for emergency treatment, much less admitted to the hospital." In a word, doctors would be unable to maintain admitting privileges or obtain those privileges for the future, because the fact that abortions are so safe meant that providers were unlikely to have any patients to admit. . . .

In our view, the record contains sufficient evidence that the admitting-privileges requirement led to the closure of half of Texas' clinics, or thereabouts. Those closures meant fewer doctors, longer waiting times, and increased crowding. Record evidence also supports the finding that after the admitting-privileges provision went into effect, the "number of women of reproductive age living in a county . . . more than 150 miles from a provider increased from approximately 86,000 to 400,000 . . . and the number of women living in a county more than 200 miles from a provider from approximately 10,000 to 290,000." We recognize that increased driving distances do not always constitute an "undue burden." But here, those increases are but one additional burden, which, when taken together with others that the closings brought about, and when viewed in light of the virtual absence of any health benefit, lead us to conclude that the record adequately supports the District Court's "undue burden" conclusion. . . .

■ *Undue Burden—Surgical-Center Requirement*

The second challenged provision of Texas' new law sets forth the surgical-center requirement. Prior to enactment of the new requirement, Texas law required abortion facilities to meet a host of health and safety requirements. Under those pre-existing laws, facilities were subject to annual reporting and recordkeeping requirements; a quality assurance program; personnel policies and staffing requirements; physical and environmental requirements; infection control standards; disclosure requirements; patient-rights standards; and medical- and clinical-services standards; including anesthesia standards,. These requirements are policed by random and announced inspections, at least annually, as well as administrative penalties, injunctions, civil penalties, and criminal penalties for certain violations.

H. B. 2 added the requirement that an "abortion facility" meet the "minimum standards . . . for ambulatory surgical centers" under Texas law. The surgical-center regulations include, among other things, detailed specifications relating to the size of the nursing staff, building dimensions, and other building requirements. The nursing staff must comprise at least "an adequate number of [registered nurses] on duty to meet the following minimum staff requirements: director of the department (or designee), and supervisory and staff personnel for each service area to assure the immediate availability of [a registered nurse] for emergency care or for any patient when needed," as well as "a second individual on duty on the premises who is trained and currently certified in basic cardiac life support until all patients have been discharged from the facility" for facilities that provide moderate sedation, such as most abortion facilities. Facilities must include a full surgical suite with an operating room that has "a clear floor area of at least 240 square feet" in which "[t]he minimum clear dimension between built-in cabinets, counters, and shelves shall be 14 feet." There must be a preoperative patient holding room and a postoperative recovery suite. The former "shall be provided and arranged in a one-way traffic pattern so that patients entering from outside the surgical suite can change, gown, and move directly into the restricted corridor of the surgical suite," and the latter "shall be arranged to provide a one-way traffic pattern from the restricted surgical corridor to the postoperative recovery suite, and then to the extended observation rooms or discharge." Surgical centers must meet numerous other spatial requirements, including specific corridor widths. Surgical centers must also have an advanced heating, ventilation, and air conditioning system, and must satisfy particular piping system and plumbing requirements. Dozens of other sections list additional requirements that apply to surgical centers.

There is considerable evidence in the record supporting the District Court's findings indicating that the statutory provision requiring all abortion facilities to meet all surgical-center standards does not benefit patients and is not necessary. The District Court found that "risks are not appreciably lowered for patients who undergo abortions at ambulatory surgical centers as compared to nonsurgical-center facilities." The court added that women "will not obtain better care or experience more frequent positive outcomes at an ambulatory surgical center as compared to a previously licensed facility." And these findings are well supported.

The record makes clear that the surgical-center requirement provides no benefit when complications arise in the context of an abortion produced through medication. That is because, in such a case, complications would almost always arise only after the patient has left the facility. The record also contains evidence indicating that abortions taking place in an abortion facility are safe—indeed, safer than numerous procedures that take place outside hospitals and to which Texas does not apply its surgical-center requirements. The total number of deaths in Texas from abortions was five in the period from 2001 to 2012, or about one every two years (that is to say, one out of about 120,000 to 144,000 abortions). Nationwide, childbirth is 14 times more likely than abortion to result in death, but Texas law allows a midwife to oversee childbirth in the patient's own home. . . .

Moreover, many surgical-center requirements are inappropriate as applied to surgical abortions. Requiring scrub facilities; maintaining a one-way traffic pattern through the facility; having ceiling, wall, and floor finishes; separating soiled utility and sterilization rooms; and regulating air pressure, filtration, and humidity control can help reduce infection where doctors conduct procedures that penetrate the skin. But abortions typically involve either the administration of medicines or procedures performed through the natural opening of the birth canal, which is itself not sterile. . . .

The upshot is that this record evidence, along with the absence of any evidence to the contrary, provides ample support for the District Court's conclusion that "[m]any of the building standards mandated by the act and its implementing rules have such a tangential relationship to patient safety in the context of abortion as to be nearly arbitrary." That conclusion, along with the supporting evidence, provides sufficient support for the more general conclusion that the surgical-center requirement "will not [provide] better care or . . . more frequent positive outcomes." The record evidence thus supports the ultimate legal conclusion that the surgical-center requirement is not necessary. . . .

We agree with the District Court that the surgical-center requirement, like the admitting-privileges requirement, provides few, if any, health benefits for women, poses a substantial obstacle to women seeking abortions, and constitutes an "undue burden" on their constitutional right to do so. . . .

For these reasons the judgment of the Court of Appeals is reversed, and the case is remanded for further proceedings consistent with this opinion.

☐ *Justice GINSBURG, concurring.*

The Texas law called H. B. 2 inevitably will reduce the number of clinics and doctors allowed to provide abortion services. Texas argues that H. B. 2's restrictions are constitutional because they protect the health of women who experience complications from abortions. In truth, "complications from an abortion are both rare and rarely dangerous." *Planned Parenthood of Wis., Inc. v. Schimel,* 806 F. 3d 908, 912 (CA7 2015). Many medical procedures, including childbirth, are far more dangerous to patients, yet are not subject to ambulatory-surgical-center or hospital admitting-privileges requirements. Given those realities, it is beyond rational belief that H. B. 2 could genuinely protect the health of women, and certain that the law "would simply make it more difficult for them to obtain abortions." When a State severely limits access to safe and legal procedures, women in desperate circumstances may resort to unlicensed rogue practitioners, *faute de mieux*, at great risk to their health and safety. So long as this Court adheres to *Roe* v. *Wade* (1973), and *Planned Parenthood of Southeastern Pa.* v. *Casey* (1992), Targeted Regulation of Abortion Providers laws like H. B. 2 that "do little or nothing for health, but rather strew impediments to abortion," cannot survive judicial inspection.

☐ *Justice THOMAS, dissenting.*

Today the Court strikes down two state statutory provisions in all of their applications, at the behest of abortion clinics and doctors. That decision exemplifies the Court's troubling tendency "to bend the rules when any effort to limit abortion, or even to speak in opposition to abortion, is at issue." *Stenberg* v. *Carhart* (2000) (SCALIA, J., dissenting). . . . I write separately to emphasize how today's decision perpetuates the Court's habit of applying different rules to different constitutional rights—especially the putative right to abortion. . . .

Today's opinion also reimagines the undue-burden standard used to assess the constitutionality of abortion restrictions. Nearly 25 years ago, in *Planned Parenthood of Southeastern Pa.* v. *Casey*, a plurality of this Court invented the "undue burden" standard as a special test for gauging the permissibility of abortion restrictions. *Casey* held that a law is unconstitutional if it imposes an "undue burden" on a woman's ability to choose to have an abortion, meaning that it "has the purpose or effect of placing a substantial obstacle in the path of a woman seeking an abortion of a nonviable fetus." *Casey* thus instructed courts to look to whether a law substantially impedes women's access to abortion, and whether it is reasonably related to legitimate state interests. As the Court explained, "[w]here it has a rational basis to act, and it does not impose an undue burden, the State may use its regulatory power" to regulate aspects of abortion procedures, "all in furtherance of its legitimate interests in regulating the medical profession in order to promote respect for life, including life of the unborn."

I remain fundamentally opposed to the Court's abortion jurisprudence. Even taking *Casey* as the baseline, however, the majority radically rewrites the undue-burden test in three ways. First, today's decision requires courts to "consider the burdens a law imposes on abortion access together with the benefits those laws confer." Second, today's opinion tells the courts that, when the law's justifications are medically uncertain, they need not defer to the legislature, and must instead assess medical justifications for abortion restrictions by scrutinizing the record themselves. Finally, even if a law imposes no "substantial obstacle" to women's access to abortions, the law now must have more than a "reasonabl[e] relat[ion] to . . . a legitimate state interest." These precepts are nowhere to be found in *Casey* or its successors, and transform the undue-burden test to something much more akin to strict scrutiny. . . .

The majority's furtive reconfiguration of the standard of scrutiny applicable to abortion restrictions also points to a deeper problem. The undue-burden standard is just one variant of the Court's tiers-of-scrutiny approach to constitutional adjudication. And the label the Court affixes to its level of scrutiny in assessing whether the government can restrict a given right—be it "rational basis," intermediate, strict, or something else—is increasingly a meaningless formalism. As the Court applies whatever standard it likes to any given case, nothing but empty words separates our constitutional decisions from judicial fiat.

Though the tiers of scrutiny have become a ubiquitous feature of constitutional law, they are of recent vintage. Only in the 1960's did the Court begin in earnest to speak of "strict scrutiny" versus reviewing legislation for mere rationality, and to develop the contours of these tests. In short order, the Court adopted strict scrutiny as the standard for reviewing everything from race-based classifications under the Equal Protection Clause to restrictions on constitutionally protected speech. *Roe* v. *Wade* then applied strict scrutiny to a purportedly "fundamental" substantive due process right for the first time. *Casey*'s undue-burden test added yet another right-specific test on the spectrum between rational-basis and strict-scrutiny review.

The illegitimacy of using "made-up tests" to "displace longstanding national traditions as the primary determinant of what the Constitution means" has long been apparent. The Constitution does not prescribe tiers of scrutiny. The three basic tiers—"rational basis," intermediate, and strict scrutiny—"are no more scientific than their names suggest, and a further element of randomness is added by the fact that it is largely up to us which test will be applied in each case." . . .

Today's decision will prompt some to claim victory, just as it will stiffen opponents' will to object. But the entire Nation has lost something essential. The majority's embrace of a jurisprudence of rights-specific exceptions and balancing tests is "a regrettable concession of defeat—an acknowledgement that we have passed the point where 'law,' properly speaking, has any further application." SCALIA, The Rule of Law as a Law of Rules, 56 *U. Chi. L. Rev.* 1175 (1989). I respectfully dissent.

B | *Privacy and Personal Autonomy*

Griswold v. Connecticut invited further litigation aimed at expanding the right of privacy to include a broad and diverse range of interests in personal autonomy. State and lower federal courts broadly construed the right of privacy, for example, to allow cancer patients to use Laetrile, a drug that had not yet been approved by the Food and Drug Administration; and to outweigh state interests in requiring motorcyclists to wear helmets.

The Burger and Rehnquist Courts, however, largely declined to broaden the scope of the right of privacy. In *Kelly v. Johnson*, 425 U.S. 238 (1976), for instance, the Court upheld a regulation limiting the length of policemen's hair. In his opinion announcing the decision, Justice Rehnquist distinguished the " 'liberty' interest" claimed in *Kelly* from that in *Griswold* and *Roe* on the grounds that "those cases involved a substantial claim of infringement on the individual's freedom of choice with respect to certain basic matters of procreation, marriage, and family life."

In *Moore v. City of East Cleveland*, 431 U.S. 494 (1977), though, a bare majority overturned a city ordinance limiting the occupancy of any dwelling to members of the same "family" and narrowly defined "family" to include only a "few categories of related individuals." Inex Moore, a grandmother, was convicted of violating the ordinance and sentenced to five days in jail and fined $25 because she lived with her two grandsons, one of whom came to live with her after his mother's death. When striking down the ordinance, Justice Powell explained,

> When a city undertakes such intrusive regulation of the family . . . the usual judicial deference to the legislature is inappropriate. "This Court has long recognized that freedom of personal choice in matters of marriage and family life is one of the liberties protected by the Due Process Clause of the Fourteenth Amendment." [Citing *Meyer, Pierce, Skinner, Griswold,* and *Roe.*] . . . When government intrudes on choices concerning family living arrangements, this Court must examine carefully the importance of the governmental interests advanced and the extent to which they are served by the challenged regulation. When thus examined, this ordinance cannot survive. The city seeks to justify it as a means of preventing overcrowding, minimizing traffic and parking congestion, and avoiding an undue financial burden on the school system. Although these are legitimate goals, the ordinance serves them marginally, at best. . . .
>
> Substantive due process has at times been a treacherous field for this Court. There *are* risks when the judicial branch gives enhanced protection to certain substantive liberties without the guidance of the more specific provisions of the Bill of Rights. As the history of the *Lochner* era demonstrates, there is reason for concern lest the only limits to such judicial intervention become the predilections of those who happen at the time to be Members of this Court. That history counsels caution and restraint. But it does not counsel abandonment. . . .
>
> Our decisions establish that the Constitution protects the sanctity of the family precisely because the institution of the family is deeply rooted in this Nation's history and tradition. It is through the family that we inculcate and pass down many of our most cherished values, moral and cultural. . . . The tradition of uncles, aunts, cousins, and especially grandparents sharing a household along with parents has roots equally venerable and equally deserving of constitutional recognition. . . . The choice of relatives in this degree of kinship to live together may not lightly be denied by the State. . . . The Constitution prevents East Cleveland from

standardizing its children—and its adults—by forcing all to live in certain narrowly defined family patterns.

But dissenting Chief Justice Burger and Justices Rehnquist, Stewart, and White strongly objected to the majority's broad reading of the due process clause and exercise of judicial review, with Justice White observing:

> The ordinance . . . denies appellant the opportunity to live with all her grandchildren in this particular suburb; she is free to do so in other parts of the Cleveland metropolitan area. If there is power to maintain the character of a single-family neighborhood, as there surely is, some limit must be placed on the reach of the "family." Had it been our task to legislate, we might have approached the problem in a different manner than did the drafters of this ordinance; but I have no trouble in concluding that the normal goals of zoning regulation are present here and that the ordinance serves these goals by limiting, in identifiable circumstances, the number of people who can occupy a single household. The ordinance does not violate the Due Process Clause.

Moore v. City of East Cleveland underscores the struggles within the Court and the concern with limiting the application of the right of privacy to matters directly bearing on the "family—marriage; child-birth; the raising and education of children; and cohabitation with one's relatives." Accordingly, the Court has also rejected claims of "informational privacy"—that is, privacy interests in "avoiding disclosure of personal matters" in, for example, bank, tax, and medical records; and in "independence in making certain kinds of important decisions" that may be diminished due to developments in computer technology and telecommunications.

Whalen v. Roe, 429 U.S. 589 (1977), provided the Court's most comprehensive discussion of claims to informational privacy. There Justice Stevens upheld regulations requiring the reporting and maintaining of computerized records on individuals purchasing certain dangerous drugs. See also the treatment of privacy claims and the First Amendment in *Cox Broadcasting Co. v. Cohn* (1975) (in Ch. 5), *Federal Communications Commission v. Pacifica Foundation* (1978) (in Ch. 5), and Fourth Amendment–protected privacy interests (see Ch. 7), as well as Fifth Amendment–privacy claims with regard to private papers and required records (see Ch. 8). The problems of safeguarding interests in informational privacy remain largely matters for Congress and state legislatures. The Fair Credit Reporting Act of 1970 (regulating consumer reports), the Crime Control Act of 1973 (regulating access to individuals' criminal records), and the Family Educational Rights and

Privacy Act of 1974 (regulating access to student educational records), for instance, safeguard specific kinds of interests in informational privacy. The Privacy Act of 1974 embodies the most comprehensive statutory scheme for safeguarding privacy interests by regulating the collection and utilization of personal information by federal agencies.

Both *Moore* and *Whalen v. Roe* indicate the Court's reluctance to expand the right of privacy to provide broader protection for claims of sexual autonomy and personal lifestyle choices. In the 1980s, though, the movement to recognize homosexual rights prompted new legislation and litigation in the courts. Over twenty states repealed laws penalizing sexual activities between consenting adults, and several state supreme courts (in Georgia, Kentucky, Massachusetts, Montana, New York, Pennsylvania, and Tennessee) struck down laws punishing homosexual relations.

The Court avoided directly ruling on claims that the right of privacy includes sexual freedom between consenting adults in the privacy of their homes until *Bowers v. Hardwick*, 478 U.S. 186 (1986). Then the justices split 5–4, with Justice Powell casting the controlling vote, for upholding Georgia's law making heterosexual and homosexual sodomy a crime. (See the INSIDE THE COURT box below.) Notably, Justice Powell, after he retired, publicly regretted his vote in *Bowers*, and some state supreme courts rejected the Court's analysis as a matter of state constitutional law as well; see, for example, *Commonwealth of Kentucky v. Jeffrey Wasson*, 842 S.W.2d 487 (1992) (excerpted in Ch. 2). *Bowers* was finally reconsidered and overruled in *Lawrence v. Texas* (2003) (excerpted below). There, writing for the Court, Justice Kennedy struck down Texas's law, along with laws in twelve other states, that criminalized homosexual sodomy, holding that such laws violated the substantive privacy interests protected by the Fourteenth Amendment due process clause and implicated by the amendment's equal protection clause. By contrast, concurring Justice O'Connor would have struck down the law solely on equal protection grounds. Chief Justice Rehnquist and Justices Scalia and Thomas dissented.

The Court will certainly continue to confront claims of personal autonomy. For example, the Court faced for the first time the claim that the right of privacy includes a "right to die" in *Cruzan by Cruzan v. Director, Missouri Department of Health* (1990) (see excerpt below). There, the Court upheld the interests of the state of Missouri over the privacy claims of parents who sued to remove a feeding tube inserted in their daughter, Nancy Cruzan, who was brain dead and who doctors said would remain unconscious for the next thirty years unless the tube was removed and she was allowed to die. Writing for a bare majority, Chief Justice Rehnquist rejected further extension of the right of privacy into this vexing area of social policy. But he ruled that the Constitution permits, but does not require, states to demand "clear and convincing" evidence that an incompetent patient would have wanted to discontinue life-support equipment. Chief Justice Rehnquist also construed the Fourteenth Amendment's due process clause to guarantee a liberty interest that protects the right of individuals to terminate unwanted medical treatment, if they are able to express or have clearly expressed (in a living will, for example) their desire to have medical treatment terminated in the event that they become incompetent. With the exception of Justice Scalia, all the justices (including those in dissent) endorsed this interpretation of the Fourteenth Amendment's protection for individuals' liberty interests.

Subsequently, in *Washington v. Glucksberg* and *Vacco v. Quill* (1997) (excerpted below), the Court declined to extend the constitutional protection for the fundamental liberty interest recognized in *Cruzan* to terminally ill patients seeking "physician-assisted suicide"; that is, a right to have doctors prescribe lethal drugs. But note that Chief Justice Rehnquist's opinion for the Court and a number of the other justices' opinions did not completely rule out such a constitutional right, depending on the circumstances and future litigation.

SELECTED BIBLIOGRAPHY

Behuniak, Susan M., and Svenson, Arthur G. *Physician-Assisted Suicide: The Anatomy of a Constitutional Law Issue.* Lanham, MD: Rowman & Littlefield, 2003.

Dworkin, Ronald. *Life's Dominion: An Argument about Abortion, Euthanasia, and Individual Freedom.* New York: Knopf, 1993.

Gertsmann, Evan. *The Constitutional Underclass: Gays, Lesbians, and the Failure of Class-Based Equal Protection.* Chicago: University of Chicago Press, 1999.

Hendin, Herbert. *Seduced by Death.* New York: W. W. Norton & Company, 1997.

Humphrey, Derek, and Clement, Mary. *People, Politics and the Right-to-Die Movement.* New York: St. Martin's Press, 1998.

Koppleman, Andrew. *The Gay Rights Question in Contemporary American Law.* Chicago: University of Chicago Press, 2002.

Palmer, Larry. *Endings and Beginnings: Law, Medicine, and Society in Assisted Suicide.* Westport, CT: Praeger, 2000.

Quill, Timothy, and Battin, Margaret. *Physician-Assisted Dying: The Case for Palliative Care and Patient Choice.* Baltimore: Johns Hopkins University Press, 2004.

Richards, David A. J. *Identity and the Case for Gay Rights.* Chicago: University of Chicago Press, 1999.

———. *The Case for Gay Rights: From Bowers to Lawrence and Beyond.* Lawrence: University Press of Kansas, 2005.

———. *The Sodomy Cases: Bowers v. Hardwick and Lawrence v. Texas.* Lawrence: University Press of Kansas, 2009.

Robb, Graham. *Strangers: Homosexual Love in the Nineteenth Century*. New York: W. W. Norton & Company, 2004.

Schneider, Carl, ed. *Law at the End of Life: The Supreme Court and Assisted Suicide*. Ann Arbor: University Press of Michigan, 2000.

Urofsky, Melvin. *Lethal Judgments: Assisted Suicide and American Law*. Lawrence: University Press of Kansas, 1999.

■ INSIDE THE COURT

Vote Switching in Bowers v. Hardwick *and* Justice Powell's April 8, 1986 Memorandum

When the justices initially discussed *Bowers v. Hardwick* (1986) in con-ference, there were not four votes to grant review of the Court of Appeals for the Eleventh Circuit's ruling striking down Georgia's law proscribing heterosexual and homosexual sodomy. Almost a decade earlier, the Court had summarily affirmed a district court decision upholding Virginia's criminal sodomy law, in *Doe v. Commonwealth's Attorney for the City of Richmond*, 425 U.S. 901 (1976). Subsequently, in *Bowers* the appellate court held that because *Doe* was a summary affir-mance it was not controlling, and struck down Georgia's law. On appeal, when the Court considered that decision at conference, there were not four votes to grant review. But, on October 17, 1985, Justice White then circulated a proposed four-page dissent from the denial of *certiorari*, pointing out that the appellate court's decision conflicted with other circuits' rejection of claims that the right of privacy extends pro-tection to homosexual activities.

Justice White's proposed dissent drew quick responses from Justices Brennan and Rehnquist, who both joined his dissent. At conference the next day, October 18, Justice Marshall agreed and there thus emerged four votes to grant review. But Justices White and Rehnquist were steadfastly opposed to stretching the right of privacy to protect such activities, as were Chief Justice Burger and Justice O'Connor. And that left Justice Powell the pivotal vote. On the merits of the case, Justice Brennan worried, a majority might go the other way and reverse. After discussing the case with his law clerks, Justice Brennan circulated a memo explaining that he changed his vote to deny review. His strategy

(continues)

■ INSIDE THE COURT
Vote Switching in Bowers v. Hardwick *and Justice Powell's*
April 8, 1986 Memorandum (continued)

of vote switching, and thereby possibly minimizing the damage that a majority's rejection of Michael Hardwick's privacy claim might do to developing constitutional law, however, did not go unnoticed. The next day, Chief Justice Burger responded with a memo explaining that he now would vote to Join-3 in granting the case. At that week's Friday conference there thus remained four votes to grant: Chief Justice Burger and Justices Marshall, Rehnquist, and White, while the remaining five voted to deny review. On November 4, the Court announced it would hear oral arguments on March 31, 1986.

When the Court heard oral arguments, Hardwick was represented by Harvard Law School professor Laurence Tribe. Like Justice Brennan, Tribe knew that the Court would be sharply split when deciding the case and guessed that Justice Lewis Powell would likely cast the deciding vote. Just a year earlier, in Justice Powell's absence, the justices split 4-4 in *Board of Education of Oklahoma City v. National Gay Task Force*, 470 U.S. 903 (1985), leaving intact a lower-court ruling overturning an Oklahoma law providing for the dismissal of teachers who advocate homosexual relations. Tribe thus pitched his arguments for overturning Georgia's law at Justice Powell. "This case is about the limits of government power," he argued, reminding the justices they had held that individuals have constitutionally protected privacy interests in their homes. The question was whether states have a compelling interest in dictating "how every adult, married or unmarried, in every bedroom in Georgia will behave in the closest and most intimate personal association with another adult." But Powell interrupted from the bench to ask whether that meant that states could not proscribe consensual sodomy in "a motel room or the back of an automobile or [public] toilet or wherever." Knowing that a decade earlier the Court had summarily affirmed, in *Doe v. Commonwealth's Attorney for the City of Richmond* (1976), a man's conviction under Virginia's sodomy law for having homosexual relations in a public bathroom, Tribe was evasive. On Justice Powell's persistence and chiding him for avoiding his "public toilet" question, Tribe finally conceded that certain behavior in public places could be outlawed but underscored that "there is something special about a home."

Justice Powell was tentatively persuaded by Tribe's arguments. At the justices' private conference two days later, Chief Justice Burger began discussion of the case and voted to uphold Georgia's law. Justice Brennan countered that such laws violate individuals' privacy rights.

Justice White followed by siding with Burger, while Justices Marshall and Blackmun agreed with Brennan. Powell spoke next. He was troubled by the facts in this case. Powell agreed that individuals enjoy a right of privacy in their homes. But he was torn by two facts pointing in opposite directions. Punishment for sodomy in Georgia carried twenty years imprisonment, which seemed unfair. Still, Powell was concerned about overturning the law since Hardwick had not actually been tried and convicted. He would tentatively vote to strike the law down, but much turned on how the Court's opinion was written. Justice Rehnquist followed, voting to uphold Georgia's law, as did Justice O'Connor. Justice Stevens, then, voted to strike down the law. Since there appeared to be five votes to affirm the lower court's invalidation of Georgia's law, after conference Justice Brennan assigned Blackmun to write an opinion for the majority.

One week after the conference vote, though, Justice Powell circulated the memorandum reproduced here, in which he explains that he has reconsidered his position and would vote to reverse. As a result, the outcome in the case dramatically changed and there were five votes to reverse the lower court's decision. Powell's memo obviously troubled the four who had voted to affirm. And Justice Stevens tried to save that outcome by responding to Powell with a letter pointing out that, because Powell had expressed uncertainty about his vote, perhaps the Court ought to affirm with an order explaining that the Court was "equally divided," as the Court had done the year before in *Board of Education of Oklahoma City v. National Gay Task Force*. "Maybe we should follow a similar course in this case," wrote Stevens. But Powell was unmoved and could not in good conscience go along with that suggestion.

The day following Powell's circulation of his memorandum, on April 9, 1986, Chief Justice Burger assigned Justice White to write an opinion for the majority. In late April and May, he circulated three drafts of his proposed opinion. In June, Blackmun circulated his dissent, and Powell circulated his concurring opinion, explaining the importance for him of the fact that Hardwick had not been tried, convicted, and sentenced, as well as explaining his view that, if penalties for sodomy (such as the twenty-year sentence that Hardwick would have faced) were imposed, they might violate the Eighth Amendment's ban against "cruel and unusual punishment."

Supreme Court of the United States
Washington, D. C. 20543

CHAMBERS OF
JUSTICE LEWIS F. POWELL, JR.

April 8, 1986

85-140 Bowers v. Hardwick

MEMORANDUM TO THE CONFERENCE:

At Conference last week, I expressed the view that in some cases it would violate the Eighth Amendment to imprison a person for a private act of homosexual sodomy. I continue to think that in such cases imprisonment would constitute cruel and unusual punishment. I relied primarily on Robinson v. California.

At Conference, given my view as to the Eighth Amendment, my vote was to affirm but on this ground rather than the view of four other Justices that there was a violation of a fundamental substantive constitutional right - as CAll held. I did not agree that there is a substantive due process right to engage in conduct that for centuries has been recognized as deviant, and not in the best interest of preserving humanity. I may say generally, that I also hesitate to create another substantive due process right.

I write this memorandum today because upon further study as to exactly what is before us, I conclude that my "bottom line" should be to reverse rather than affirm. The only question presented by the parties is the substantive due process issue, and - as several of you noted at Conference - my Eighth Amendment view was not addressed by the court below or by the parties.

In sum, my more carefully considered view is that I will vote to reverse but will write separately to explain my view of this case generally. I will not know, until I see the writing, whether I can join an opinion finding no substantive due process right or simply join the judgment.

L.F.P., Jr.

ss

Source: Memos and correspondence in Justice Lewis F. Powell Jr. Papers, Washington and Lee Law School; Justice Thurgood Marshall Papers, Library of Congress; and Justice Byron White Papers, Box 50, Library of Congress.

Lawrence v. Texas

539 U.S. 558, 123 S.CT. 2472 (2003)

On the night of September 17, 1998, the Harris County Texas police department received a frantic call from someone who claimed that there was a man with a gun "going crazy" in the Houston apartment of John Geddes Lawrence. Officers responded and arrived and entered the apartment. They found no intruder, but instead found Lawrence and Tyron Garner engaged in sodomy. They arrested them for violating the state's "homosexual conduct" law, which made it a misdemeanor for any person to engage "in deviant sexual intercourse with another individual of the same sex." A few weeks later, Lawrence and Garner were tried and found guilty of "deviant homosexual conduct," and each was fined $200. They appealed and challenged the statute's constitutionality. A three-judge appeals panel ruled two to one that the convictions "impermissibly discriminate on the basis of sex," and violated the Equal Rights Amendment of the state constitution. But in March 2001, the full Texas Court of Appeals reversed and upheld the state's "homosexual conduct" law. Lawrence appealed that decision to the Texas Court of Criminal Appeals, which denied review, and subsequently filed an appeal to the U.S. Supreme Court, which granted review.

The state court's decision was reversed by a vote of 6–3. Justice Kennedy delivered the opinion of the Court. Justice O'Connor filed a concurring opinion. Justices Scalia and Thomas filed dissenting opinions, which Chief Justice Rehnquist joined.

■ ■ ■

☐ *Justice KENNEDY delivered the opinion of the Court.*

Liberty protects the person from unwarranted government intrusions into a dwelling or other private places. In our tradition the State is not omnipresent in the home. And there are other spheres of our lives and existence, outside the home, where the State should not be a dominant presence. Freedom extends beyond spatial bounds. Liberty presumes an autonomy of self that includes freedom of thought, belief, expression, and certain intimate conduct. The instant case involves liberty of the person both in its spatial and more transcendent dimensions.

The question before the Court is the validity of a Texas statute making it a crime for two persons of the same sex to engage in certain intimate sexual conduct. . . .

We conclude the case should be resolved by determining whether the petitioners were free as adults to engage in the private conduct in the exercise of their liberty under the Due Process Clause of the Fourteenth Amendment to the Constitution. For this inquiry we deem it necessary to reconsider the Court's holding in *Bowers* [*v. Hardwick*, 478 U.S. 186 (1986)].

There are broad statements of the substantive reach of liberty under the Due Process Clause in earlier cases, including *Pierce v. Society of Sisters*, 268 U.S. 510 (1925), and *Meyer v. Nebraska*, 262 U.S. 390 (1923); but the most pertinent beginning point is our decision in *Griswold v. Connecticut*, 381 U.S. 479 (1965).

In *Griswold* the Court invalidated a state law prohibiting the use of drugs or devices of contraception and counseling or aiding and abetting the use of

John Lawrence and Tyron Garner, right, were arrested under Texas's sodomy law. (*AP Photo/David J. Phillip.*)

contraceptives. The Court described the protected interest as a right to privacy and placed emphasis on the marriage relation and the protected space of the marital bedroom.

After *Griswold* it was established that the right to make certain decisions regarding sexual conduct extends beyond the marital relationship. In *Eisenstadt v. Baird*, 405 U.S. 438 (1972), the Court invalidated a law prohibiting the distribution of contraceptives to unmarried persons. The case was decided under the Equal Protection Clause, but with respect to unmarried persons, the Court went on to state the fundamental proposition that the law impaired the exercise of their personal rights. . . .

The opinions in *Griswold* and *Eisenstadt* were part of the background for the decision in *Roe v. Wade*, 410 U.S. 113 (1973). As is well known, the case involved a challenge to the Texas law prohibiting abortions, but the laws of other States were affected as well. Although the Court held the woman's rights were not absolute, her right to elect an abortion did have real and substantial protection as an exercise of her liberty under the Due Process Clause. The Court cited cases that protect spatial freedom and cases that go well beyond it. *Roe* recognized the right of a woman to make certain fundamental decisions affecting her destiny and confirmed once more that the protection of liberty under the Due Process Clause has a substantive dimension of fundamental significance in defining the rights of the person. . . .

This was the state of the law with respect to some of the most relevant cases when the Court considered *Bowers v. Hardwick*. The facts in *Bowers* had some similarities to the instant case. A police officer, whose right to enter seems not to have been in question, observed Hardwick, in his own bedroom, engaging in intimate sexual conduct with another adult male. The conduct was in violation of a Georgia statute making it a criminal offense to engage in sodomy. One difference between the two cases is that the Georgia statute prohibited the conduct whether or not the participants were of the same sex, while the Texas statute, as we have seen, applies only to participants of the same sex. Hardwick was not prosecuted, but he brought an action in federal court to declare the state statute invalid. He alleged he was a practicing homosexual and that the criminal prohibition violated rights guaranteed to him by the Constitution. The Court, in an opinion by Justice WHITE, sustained the Georgia law. Chief Justice BURGER and Justice POWELL joined the opinion of the Court and filed separate, concurring opinions. Four Justices dissented.

The Court began its substantive discussion in *Bowers* as follows: "The issue presented is whether the Federal Constitution confers a fundamental right upon homosexuals to engage in sodomy and hence invalidates the laws of the many States that still make such conduct illegal and have done so for a very long time." That statement, we now conclude, discloses the Court's own failure to appreciate the extent of the liberty at stake. To say that the issue in *Bowers* was simply the right to engage in certain sexual conduct demeans the claim the individual put forward, just as it would demean a married couple were it to be said marriage is simply about the right to have sexual intercourse. The laws involved in *Bowers* and here are, to be sure, statutes that purport to do no more than prohibit a particular sexual act. Their penalties and purposes, though, have more far-reaching consequences, touching upon the most private human conduct, sexual behavior, and in the most private of places, the home. The statutes do seek to control a personal relationship that, whether or not entitled to formal recognition in the law, is within the liberty of persons to choose without being punished as criminals.

This, as a general rule, should counsel against attempts by the State, or a court, to define the meaning of the relationship or to set its boundaries absent injury to a person or abuse of an institution the law protects. It suffices for us to acknowledge that adults may choose to enter upon this relationship in the confines of their homes and their own private lives and still retain their dignity as free persons. When sexuality finds overt expression in intimate conduct with another person, the conduct can be but one element in a personal bond that is more enduring. The liberty protected by the Constitution allows homosexual persons the right to make this choice. . . .

At the outset it should be noted that there is no longstanding history in this country of laws directed at homosexual conduct as a distinct matter. Beginning in colonial times there were prohibitions of sodomy derived from the English criminal laws passed in the first instance by the Reformation Parliament of 1533. The English prohibition was understood to include relations between men and women as well as relations between men and men. Thus early American sodomy laws were not directed at homosexuals as such but instead sought to prohibit nonprocreative sexual activity more generally. This does not suggest approval of homosexual conduct. It does tend to show that this particular form of conduct was not thought of as a separate category from like conduct between heterosexual persons.

Laws prohibiting sodomy do not seem to have been enforced against consenting adults acting in private. A substantial number of sodomy prosecutions and convictions for which there are surviving records were for predatory acts against those who could not or did not consent, as in the case of a minor or the victim of an assault. . . .

The policy of punishing consenting adults for private acts was not much discussed in the early legal literature. We can infer that one reason for this was the very private nature of the conduct. Despite the absence of prosecutions, there may have been periods in which there was public criticism of homosexuals as such and an insistence that the criminal laws be enforced to discourage their practices. But far from possessing "ancient roots," *Bowers*, American laws targeting same-sex couples did not develop until the last third of the 20th century. The reported decisions concerning the prosecution of consensual, homosexual sodomy between adults for the years 1880–1995 are not always clear in the details, but a significant number involved conduct in a public place.

It was not until the 1970's that any State singled out same-sex relations for criminal prosecution, and only nine States have done so. In summary, the historical grounds relied upon in *Bowers* are more complex than the majority opinion and the concurring opinion by Chief Justice BURGER indicate. Their historical premises are not without doubt and, at the very least, are overstated.

It must be acknowledged, of course, that the Court in *Bowers* was making the broader point that for centuries there have been powerful voices to condemn homosexual conduct as immoral. . . . The issue is whether the majority may use the power of the State to enforce these views on the whole society through operation of the criminal law. "Our obligation is to define the liberty of all, not to mandate our own moral code." *Planned Parenthood of Southeastern Pa. v. Casey*, 505 U.S. 833 (1992). . . .

In all events we think that our laws and traditions in the past half century are of most relevance here. These references show an emerging awareness that liberty gives substantial protection to adult persons in deciding how to conduct their private lives in matters pertaining to sex. . . .

In *Bowers* the Court referred to the fact that before 1961 all 50 States had outlawed sodomy, and that at the time of the Court's decision 24 States and the District of Columbia had sodomy laws. Justice POWELL pointed out that these prohibitions often were being ignored, however. Georgia, for instance, had not sought to enforce its law for decades.

The sweeping references by Chief Justice BURGER to the history of Western civilization and to Judeo-Christian moral and ethical standards did not take account of other authorities pointing in an opposite direction. A committee advising the British Parliament recommended in 1957 repeal of laws punishing homosexual conduct. *The Wolfenden Report* (1963). Parliament enacted the substance of those recommendations 10 years later.

Of even more importance, almost five years before *Bowers* was decided the European Court of Human Rights considered a case with parallels to *Bowers* and to today's case. An adult male resident in Northern Ireland alleged he was a practicing homosexual who desired to engage in consensual homosexual conduct. The laws of Northern Ireland forbade him that right. He alleged that he had been questioned, his home had been searched, and he feared criminal prosecution. The court held that the laws proscribing the conduct were invalid under the European Convention on Human

Rights. *Dudgeon v. United Kingdom*, 45 Eur. Ct. H. R. (1981). Authoritative in all countries that are members of the Council of Europe (21 nations then, 45 nations now), the decision is at odds with the premise in *Bowers* that the claim put forward was insubstantial in our Western civilization.

In our own constitutional system the deficiencies in *Bowers* became even more apparent in the years following its announcement. The 25 States with laws prohibiting the relevant conduct referenced in the *Bowers* decision are reduced now to 13, of which 4 enforce their laws only against homosexual conduct. In those States where sodomy is still proscribed, whether for same-sex or heterosexual conduct, there is a pattern of nonenforcement with respect to consenting adults acting in private. The State of Texas admitted in 1994 that as of that date it had not prosecuted anyone under those circumstances.

Two principal cases decided after *Bowers* cast its holding into even more doubt. In *Planned Parenthood of Southeastern Pa. v. Casey*, 505 U.S. 833 (1992), the Court reaffirmed the substantive force of the liberty protected by the Due Process Clause. The *Casey* decision again confirmed that our laws and tradition afford constitutional protection to personal decisions relating to marriage, procreation, contraception, family relationships, child rearing, and education. . . . Persons in a homosexual relationship may seek autonomy for these purposes, just as heterosexual persons do. The decision in *Bowers* would deny them this right.

The second post-*Bowers* case of principal relevance is *Romer v. Evans*, 517 U.S. 620 (1996). There the Court struck down class-based legislation directed at homosexuals as a violation of the Equal Protection Clause. *Romer* invalidated an amendment to Colorado's constitution which named as a solitary class persons who were homosexuals, lesbians, or bisexual either by "orientation, conduct, practices or relationships," and deprived them of protection under state antidiscrimination laws. We concluded that the provision was "born of animosity toward the class of persons affected" and further that it had no rational relation to a legitimate governmental purpose. . . .

Equality of treatment and the due process right to demand respect for conduct protected by the substantive guarantee of liberty are linked in important respects, and a decision on the latter point advances both interests. If protected conduct is made criminal and the law which does so remains unexamined for its substantive validity, its stigma might remain even if it were not enforceable as drawn for equal protection reasons. When homosexual conduct is made criminal by the law of the State, that declaration in and of itself is an invitation to subject homosexual persons to discrimination both in the public and in the private spheres. The central holding of *Bowers* has been brought in question by this case, and it should be addressed. Its continuance as precedent demeans the lives of homosexual persons. . . .

The foundations of *Bowers* have sustained serious erosion from our recent decisions in *Casey* and *Romer*. When our precedent has been thus weakened, criticism from other sources is of greater significance. In the United States criticism of *Bowers* has been substantial and continuing, disapproving of its reasoning in all respects, not just as to its historical assumptions. The courts of five different States have declined to follow it in interpreting provisions in their own state constitutions parallel to the Due Process Clause of the Fourteenth Amendment.

To the extent *Bowers* relied on values we share with a wider civilization, it should be noted that the reasoning and holding in *Bowers* have been rejected elsewhere. The European Court of Human Rights has followed not *Bowers* but its own decision in *Dudgeon v. United Kingdom*. Other nations, too, have taken action consistent with an affirmation of the protected right of homosexual adults to engage in intimate, consensual conduct. The right the petitioners seek in this case has been accepted as an integral part of human freedom in many other countries. There has been no showing that in this country the governmental interest in circumscribing personal choice is somehow more legitimate or urgent.

The doctrine of *stare decisis* is essential to the respect accorded to the judgments of the Court and to the stability of the law. It is not, however, an inexorable command. *Payne v. Tennessee*, 501 U.S. 808 (1991). In *Casey* we noted that when a Court is asked to overrule a precedent recognizing a constitutional liberty interest, individual or societal reliance on the existence of that liberty cautions with particular strength against reversing course. The holding in *Bowers*, however, has not induced detrimental reliance comparable to some instances where recognized individual rights are involved. Indeed, there has been no individual or societal reliance on *Bowers* of the sort that could counsel against overturning its holding once there are compelling reasons to do so. *Bowers* itself causes uncertainty, for the precedents before and after its issuance contradict its central holding.

The rationale of *Bowers* does not withstand careful analysis. . . . *Bowers* was not correct when it was decided, and it is not correct today. It ought not to remain binding precedent. *Bowers v. Hardwick* should be and now is overruled.

The present case does not involve minors. It does not involve persons who might be injured or coerced or who are situated in relationships where consent might not easily be refused. It does not involve public conduct or prostitution. It does not involve whether the government must give formal recognition to any relationship that homosexual persons seek to enter. The case does involve two adults who, with full and mutual consent from each other, engaged in sexual practices common to a homosexual lifestyle. The petitioners are entitled to respect for their private lives. The State cannot demean their existence or control their destiny by making their private sexual conduct a crime. Their right to liberty under the Due Process Clause gives them the full right to engage in their conduct without intervention of the government. The Texas statute furthers no legitimate state interest which can justify its intrusion into the personal and private life of the individual. . . .

The judgment of the Court of Appeals for the Texas Fourteenth District is reversed, and the case is remanded for further proceedings not inconsistent with this opinion.

It is so ordered.

☐ *Justice O'CONNOR, concurring in the judgment.*

The Court today overrules *Bowers v. Hardwick*. I joined *Bowers*, and do not join the Court in overruling it. Nevertheless, I agree with the Court that Texas' statute banning same-sex sodomy is unconstitutional. Rather than relying on the substantive component of the Fourteenth Amendment's Due Process Clause, as the Court does, I base my conclusion on the Fourteenth Amendment's Equal Protection Clause. . . .

A law branding one class of persons as criminal solely based on the State's moral disapproval of that class and the conduct associated with that class runs contrary to the values of the Constitution and the Equal Protection Clause, under any standard of review. I therefore concur in the Court's judgment that Texas' sodomy law banning "deviate sexual intercourse" between consenting adults of the same sex, but not between consenting adults of different sexes, is unconstitutional.

☐ *Justice SCALIA, with whom THE CHIEF JUSTICE and Justice THOMAS join, dissenting.*

"Liberty finds no refuge in a jurisprudence of doubt." *Planned Parenthood of Southeastern Pa. v. Casey,* 505 U.S. 833 (1992). That was the Court's sententious response, barely more than a decade ago, to those seeking to overrule *Roe v. Wade,* 410 U.S. 113 (1973). The Court's response today, to those who have engaged in a 17-year crusade to overrule *Bowers v. Hardwick,* 478 U.S. 186 (1986), is very different. The need for stability and certainty presents no barrier. . . .

I begin with the Court's surprising readiness to reconsider a decision rendered a mere 17 years ago in *Bowers v. Hardwick.* I do not myself believe in rigid adherence to *stare decisis* in constitutional cases; but I do believe that we should be consistent rather than manipulative in invoking the doctrine. Today's opinions in support of reversal do not bother to distinguish—or indeed, even bother to mention—the paean to *stare decisis* coauthored by three members of today's majority in *Planned Parenthood v. Casey.* There, when *stare decisis* meant preservation of judicially invented abortion rights, the widespread criticism of *Roe* was strong reason to reaffirm it. Today, however, the widespread opposition to *Bowers,* a decision resolving an issue as "intensely divisive" as the issue in *Roe,* is offered as a reason in favor of overruling it. Gone, too, is any "enquiry" (of the sort conducted in *Casey*) into whether the decision sought to be overruled has "proven 'unworkable.'" *Casey.*

Today's approach to *stare decisis* invites us to overrule an erroneously decided precedent (including an "intensely divisive" decision) if: (1) its foundations have been "eroded" by subsequent decisions; (2) it has been subject to "substantial and continuing" criticism; and (3) it has not induced "individual or societal reliance" that counsels against overturning. The problem is that *Roe* itself—which today's majority surely has no disposition to overrule—satisfies these conditions to at least the same degree as *Bowers.* . . .

What a massive disruption of the current social order, therefore, the overruling of *Bowers* entails. Not so the overruling of *Roe,* which would simply have restored the regime that existed for centuries before 1973, in which the permissibility of and restrictions upon abortion were determined legislatively State-by-State. *Casey,* however, chose to base its *stare decisis* determination on a different "sort" of reliance. "[P]eople," it said, "have organized intimate relationships and made choices that define their views of themselves and their places in society, in reliance on the availability of abortion in the event that contraception should fail." This falsely assumes that the consequence of overruling *Roe* would have been to make abortion unlawful. It would not; it would merely have permitted the States to do so. Many States would unquestionably have declined to prohibit abortion, and others would not have prohibited it within six months (after which the most significant reliance interests would have expired). Even for persons in States other than these, the choice would not have been between abortion and childbirth, but between abortion nearby and abortion in a neighboring State.

To tell the truth, it does not surprise me, and should surprise no one, that the Court has chosen today to revise the standards of *stare decisis* set forth in *Casey*. It has thereby exposed *Casey*'s extraordinary deference to precedent for the result-oriented expedient that it is.

Having decided that it need not adhere to *stare decisis*, the Court still must establish that *Bowers* was wrongly decided and that the Texas statute, as applied to petitioners, is unconstitutional. . . .

Our opinions applying the doctrine known as "substantive due process" hold that the Due Process Clause prohibits States from infringing fundamental liberty interests, unless the infringement is narrowly tailored to serve a compelling state interest. We have held repeatedly, in cases the Court today does not overrule, that only fundamental rights qualify for this so-called "heightened scrutiny" protection—that is, rights which are "deeply rooted in this Nation's history and tradition."

Bowers held, first, that criminal prohibitions of homosexual sodomy are not subject to heightened scrutiny because they do not implicate a "fundamental right" under the Due Process Clause. Noting that "[p]roscriptions against that conduct have ancient roots," that "[s]odomy was a criminal offense at common law and was forbidden by the laws of the original 13 States when they ratified the Bill of Rights," and that many States had retained their bans on sodomy, *Bowers* concluded that a right to engage in homosexual sodomy was not "deeply rooted in this Nation's history and tradition."

The Court today does not overrule this holding. Not once does it describe homosexual sodomy as a "fundamental right" or a "fundamental liberty interest," nor does it subject the Texas statute to strict scrutiny. Instead, having failed to establish that the right to homosexual sodomy is "deeply rooted in this Nation's history and tradition," the Court concludes that the application of Texas's statute to petitioners' conduct fails the rational-basis test, and overrules *Bowers'* holding to the contrary.

I shall address that rational-basis holding presently. First, however, I address some aspersions that the Court casts upon *Bowers'* conclusion that homosexual sodomy is not a "fundamental right"—even though, as I have said, the Court does not have the boldness to reverse that conclusion.

The Court's description of "the state of the law" at the time of *Bowers* only confirms that *Bowers* was right. The Court points to *Griswold v. Connecticut* (1965). But that case expressly disclaimed any reliance on the doctrine of "substantive due process," and grounded the so-called "right to privacy" in penumbras of constitutional provisions other than the Due Process Clause.

Roe v. Wade recognized that the right to abort an unborn child was a "fundamental right" protected by the Due Process Clause. The *Roe* Court, however, made no attempt to establish that this right was "deeply rooted in this Nation's history and tradition"; instead, it based its conclusion that "the Fourteenth Amendment's concept of personal liberty . . . is broad enough to encompass a woman's decision whether or not to terminate her pregnancy" on its own normative judgment that anti-abortion laws were undesirable. . . .

After discussing the history of antisodomy laws, the Court proclaims that, "it should be noted that there is no longstanding history in this country of laws directed at homosexual conduct as a distinct matter." This observation in no way casts into doubt the "definitive [historical] conclusion," on which *Bowers* relied: that our Nation has a longstanding history of laws prohibiting sodomy in general—regardless of whether it was performed by same-sex or opposite-sex couples. It is (as *Bowers* recognized) entirely irrelevant whether the laws in our long national tradition criminalizing homosexual sodomy were "directed at homosexual conduct as a distinct matter." Whether homosexual sodomy was prohibited by a law targeted at same-sex sexual relations or by a more general law prohibiting both homosexual and heterosexual sodomy, the only relevant point is that it was criminalized—which suffices to establish that homosexual sodomy is not a right "deeply rooted in our Nation's history and tradition." The Court today agrees that homosexual sodomy was criminalized and thus does not dispute the facts on which *Bowers* actually relied.

Next the Court makes the claim, again unsupported by any citations, that "[l]aws prohibiting sodomy do not seem to have been enforced against consenting adults acting in private." The key qualifier here is "acting in private"—since the Court admits that sodomy laws were enforced against consenting adults (although the Court contends that prosecutions were "infrequent.") I do not know what "acting in private" means; surely consensual sodomy, like heterosexual intercourse, is rarely performed on stage. . . . There are 203 prosecutions for consensual, adult homosexual sodomy reported in the West Reporting system and official state reporters from the years 1880–1995. There are also records of 20 sodomy prosecutions and 4 executions during the colonial period. *Bowers'* conclusion that homosexual sodomy is not a fundamental right "deeply rooted in this Nation's history and tradition" is utterly unassailable.

Realizing that fact, the Court instead says: "[W]e think that our laws and traditions in the past half century are of most relevance here. These references show an emerging awareness that liberty gives substantial protection to adult persons in deciding how to conduct their private lives in matters pertaining to sex." Apart from the fact that such an "emerging awareness" does not establish a "fundamental right," the statement is factually false. States continue to prosecute all sorts of crimes by adults "in matters pertaining to sex": prostitution, adult incest, adultery, obscenity, and child pornography. Sodomy laws, too, have been enforced "in the past half century," in which there have been 134 reported cases involving prosecutions for consensual, adult, homosexual sodomy. . . .

I turn now to the ground on which the Court squarely rests its holding: the contention that there is no rational basis for the law here under attack. This proposition is so out of accord with our jurisprudence—indeed, with the jurisprudence of any society we know—that it requires little discussion.

The Texas statute undeniably seeks to further the belief of its citizens that certain forms of sexual behavior are "immoral and unacceptable," *Bowers*—the same interest furthered by criminal laws against fornication, bigamy, adultery, adult incest, bestiality, and obscenity. *Bowers* held that this was a legitimate state interest. The Court today reaches the opposite conclusion. The Texas statute, it says, "furthers no legitimate state interest which can justify its intrusion into the personal and private life of the individual." The Court embraces instead Justice STEVENS' declaration in his *Bowers* dissent, that "the fact that the governing majority in a State has traditionally viewed a particular practice as immoral is not a sufficient reason for upholding a law prohibiting the practice." This effectively decrees the end of all morals legislation. If, as the Court asserts, the promotion of majoritarian sexual morality is not even a legitimate state interest, none of the above-mentioned laws can survive rational-basis review.

Finally, I turn to petitioners' equal-protection challenge, which no Member of the Court save Justice O'CONNOR embraces: On its face Section 21.06(a) applies equally to all persons. Men and women, heterosexuals and homosexuals, are all subject to its prohibition of deviate sexual intercourse with someone of the same sex. To be sure, Section 21.06 does distinguish between the sexes insofar as concerns the partner with whom the sexual acts are performed: men can violate the law only with other men, and women only with other women. But this cannot itself be a denial of equal protection, since it is precisely the same distinction regarding partners that is drawn in state laws prohibiting marriage with someone of the same sex while permitting marriage with someone of the opposite sex. . . .

Today's opinion is the product of a Court, which is the product of a law-profession culture, that has largely signed on to the so-called homosexual agenda, by which I mean the agenda promoted by some homosexual activists directed at eliminating the moral opprobrium that has traditionally attached to homosexual conduct. One of the most revealing statements in today's opinion is the Court's grim warning that the criminalization of homosexual conduct is "an invitation to subject homosexual persons to discrimination both in the public and in the private spheres." It is clear from this that the Court has taken sides in the culture war, departing from its role of assuring, as neutral observer, that the democratic rules of engagement are observed. Many Americans do not want persons who openly engage in homosexual conduct as partners in their business, as scoutmasters for their children, as teachers in their children's schools, or as boarders in their home. They view this as protecting themselves and their families from a lifestyle that they believe to be immoral and destructive. The Court views it as "discrimination" which it is the function of our judgments to deter. So imbued is the Court with the law profession's anti-anti-homosexual culture, that it is seemingly unaware that the attitudes of that culture are not obviously "mainstream"; that in most States what the Court calls "discrimination" against those who engage in homosexual acts is perfectly legal; that proposals to ban such "discrimination" under Title VII have repeatedly been rejected by Congress; that in some cases such "discrimination" is mandated by federal statute (mandating discharge from the armed forces of any service member who engages in or intends to engage in homosexual acts); and that in some cases such "discrimination" is a constitutional right, see *Boy Scouts of America v. Dale*, 530 U.S. 640 (2000).

Let me be clear that I have nothing against homosexuals, or any other group, promoting their agenda through normal democratic means. Social perceptions of sexual and other morality change over time, and every group has the right to persuade its fellow citizens that its view of such matters is the best. That homosexuals have achieved some success in that enterprise is attested to by the fact that Texas is one of the few remaining States that criminalize private, consensual homosexual acts. But persuading one's fellow citizens is one thing, and imposing one's views in absence of democratic majority will is something else. I would no more require a State to criminalize homosexual acts—or, for that matter, display any moral disapprobation of them—than I would forbid it to do so. What Texas has chosen to do is well within the range of traditional democratic action, and its hand should not be stayed through the invention of a brand-new "constitutional right" by a Court that is impatient of democratic change. It is indeed true that "later generations can see that laws once thought necessary and proper in fact serve only to oppress," and when that happens, later generations can repeal those laws. But it is the premise of our system that those judgments are to be made by the people, and not imposed by a governing caste that knows best.

☐ *Justice THOMAS, dissenting.*

I join Justice SCALIA's dissenting opinion. I write separately to note that the law before the Court today "is . . . uncommonly silly." *Griswold v. Connecticut* (1965) (STEWART, J., dissenting). If I were a member of the Texas Legislature, I would vote to repeal it. Punishing someone for expressing his sexual preference through noncommercial consensual conduct with another adult does not appear to be a worthy way to expend valuable law enforcement resources. . . .

Cruzan by Cruzan v. Director, Missouri Department of Health

497 U.S. 261, 110 S.CT. 2841 (1990)

Late in the night of January 11, 1983, Nancy Cruzan, at the age of twenty-five, was thrown from her car as it crashed off the road not far from her home in Carterville, Missouri. By the time police and paramedics arrived and restarted her heart and lungs, her brain had been deprived of oxygen for twelve to fourteen minutes. She never regained consciousness. In the hospital, Miss Cruzan's parents approved the surgical insertion of a feeding tube into her body to keep her alive. Her doctors agreed that she would never regain consciousness and that her cerebral cortex was atrophying. Without removing the feeding tube, they also agreed, Miss Cruzan could persist in a vegetative state for another thirty years.

In early 1987, Miss Cruzan's parents decided to seek permission to have the feeding tube removed. A year later, in 1988, a state trial judge granted the Cruzans permission, but the state appealed to the Missouri Supreme Court. By a vote of 4-3, the state supreme court reversed. The majority cited the preamble to the state's 1986 abortion law, which the U.S. Supreme Court upheld in *Webster v. Reproductive Health Services*, 492 U.S. 490 (1989) and which proclaims the state's "unqualified" interest in preserving the "sanctity of human life." The majority also held that the Cruzans could not assert a constitutional right of privacy to make a decision "for an incompetent in the absence of the formalities required under Missouri's Living Will statutes" or without establishing "clear and convincing evidence" that Miss Cruzan would have wanted the feeding tube removed.

The Cruzans appealed the Missouri Supreme Court's decision to the U.S. Supreme Court, which granted *certiorari*. The George H. W. Bush administration and various antiabortion rights groups filed briefs supporting the state, while the American Civil Liberties Union and other groups supported the Cruzans. In the meantime, while defending the state's decision, Missouri's attorney general, William Webster, endeavored to render the case moot. He drafted a bill, approved by Cruzan's attorneys, that would have allowed the Cruzans to remove the feeding tube from their daughter. The bill would have permitted the removal of life-support systems from patients (1) who were in a "persistent oblivious state" for at least thirty-six months, (2) whose family agreed to the removal of life-support systems, and (3) for which three physicians concurred that there was no likelihood of recovery. In addition, the bill would have provided that a patient's wishes to have such systems discontinued needed to be shown only on a "preponderance of the evidence," rather than the more rigorous standard of "clear and convincing" proof. But the Missouri state legislature refused to enact the bill into law. On June 25, 1990, the Supreme Court handed down its decision.

The Court's decision was 5–4, and the majority's opinion was announced by Chief Justice Rehnquist. Justices Scalia and O'Connor delivered concurring opinions. Dissents were by Justices Stevens and Brennan, who were joined by Justices Blackmun and Marshall.

■ ■ ■

☐ *Chief Justice REHNQUIST delivers the opinion of the Court.*

At common law, even the touching of one person by another without consent and without legal justification was a battery. Before the turn of the century, this Court observed that "[n]o right is held more sacred, or is more carefully guarded, by the common law, than the right of every individual to the possession and control of his own person, free from all restraint or interference of others, unless by clear and unquestionable authority of law." *Union Pacific R. Co. v. Botsford*, 141 U.S. 250, 251 (1891). . . .

The logical corollary of the doctrine of informed consent is that the patient generally possesses the right not to consent, that is, to refuse treatment. Until about 15 years ago and the seminal decision in *In re Quinlan*, 70 N. J. 10 [1976], *cert.* denied *sub nom., Garger v. New Jersey*, 429 U.S. 922 (1976), the number of right-to-refuse-treatment decisions were relatively few. Most of the earlier cases involved patients who refused medical treatment forbidden by their religious beliefs, thus implicating First Amendment rights as well as common law rights of self-determination. More recently, however, with the advance of medical technology capable of sustaining life well past the point where natural forces would have brought certain death in earlier times, cases involving the right to refuse life-sustaining treatment have burgeoned. . . .

[T]he common-law doctrine of informed consent is viewed as generally encompassing the right of a competent individual to refuse medical treatment. Beyond that, these decisions demonstrate both similarity and diversity in their approach to decision of what all agree is a perplexing question with unusually strong moral and ethical overtones. State courts have available to them for decision a number of sources—state constitutions, statutes, and common law—which are not available to us. In this Court, the question is simply and starkly whether the United States Constitution prohibits Missouri from choosing the rule of decision which it did. This is the first case in which we have been squarely presented with the issue of whether the United States Constitution grants what is in common parlance referred to as a "right to die." We follow the judicious counsel of our decision in *Twin City Bank v. Nebeker*, 167 U.S. 196 (1897), where we said that in deciding "a question of such magnitude and importance . . . it is the [better] part of wisdom not to attempt, by any general statement, to cover every possible phase of the subject."

The Fourteenth Amendment provides that no State shall "deprive any person of life, liberty, or property, without due process of law." The principle that a competent person has a constitutionally protected liberty interest in refusing unwanted medical treatment may be inferred from our prior decisions. In *Jacobson v. Massachusetts*, 197 U.S. 11 (1905), for instance, the Court balanced an individual's liberty interest in declining an unwanted smallpox vaccine against the State's interest in preventing disease. . . .

But determining that a person has a "liberty interest" under the Due Process Clause does not end the inquiry; "whether respondent's constitutional rights have been violated must be determined by balancing his liberty interests against the relevant state interests." *Youngberg v. Romeo*, 457 U.S. 307 (1982). . . .

[F]or purposes of this case, we assume that the United States Constitution would grant a competent person a constitutionally protected right to refuse lifesaving hydration and nutrition.

Petitioners go on to assert that an incompetent person should possess the same right in this respect as is possessed by a competent person. . . .

The difficulty with petitioners' claim is that in a sense it begs the question: an incompetent person is not able to make an informed and voluntary choice to exercise a hypothetical right to refuse treatment or any other right. Such a "right" must be exercised for her, if at all, by some sort of surrogate. Here, Missouri has in effect recognized that under certain circumstances a surrogate may act for the patient in electing to have hydration and nutrition withdrawn in such a way as to cause death, but it has established a procedural safeguard to assure that the action of the surrogate conforms as best it may to the wishes expressed by the patient while competent. Missouri requires that evidence of the incompetent's wishes as to the withdrawal of treatment be proved by clear and convincing evidence. The question, then, is whether the United States Constitution forbids the establishment of this procedural requirement by the State. We hold that it does not.

Whether or not Missouri's clear and convincing evidence requirement comports with the United States Constitution depends in part on what interests the State may properly seek to protect in this situation. Missouri relies on its interest in the protection and preservation of human life, and there can be no gainsaying this interest. As a general matter, the States—indeed, all civilized nations—demonstrate their commitment to life by treating homicide as serious crime. Moreover, the majority of States in this country have laws imposing criminal penalties on one who assists another to commit suicide. We do not think a State is required to remain neutral in the face of an informed and voluntary decision by a physically-able adult to starve to death.

But in the context presented here, a State has more particular interests at stake. The choice between life and death is a deeply personal decision of obvious and overwhelming finality. We believe Missouri may legitimately seek to safeguard the personal element of this choice through the imposition of heightened evidentiary requirements. It cannot be disputed that the Due Process Clause protects an interest in life as well as an interest in refusing life-sustaining medical treatment. Not all incompetent patients will have loved ones available to serve as surrogate decisionmakers. . . .

In our view, Missouri has permissibly sought to advance these interests through the adoption of a "clear and convincing" standard of proof to govern such proceedings. "The function of a standard of proof, as that concept is embodied in the Due Process Clause and in the realm of factfinding, is to 'instruct the factfinder concerning the degree of confidence our society thinks he should have in the correctness of factual conclusions for a particular type of adjudication.'" *Addington v. Texas*, 441 U.S. 418 (1979) (quoting *In re Winship*, 397 U.S. 358 (1970) (HARLAN, J., concurring)). . . .

We think it self-evident that the interests at stake in the instant proceedings are more substantial, both on an individual and societal level, than those involved in a run-of-the-mill civil dispute. But not only does the standard of proof reflect the importance of a particular adjudication, it also serves as "a societal judgment about how the risk of error should be distributed between the litigants." The more stringent the burden of proof a party must bear, the more that party bears the risk of an erroneous decision. We believe that Missouri may permissibly place an increased risk of an erroneous decision on those seeking to terminate an incompetent individual's life-sustaining treatment. An erroneous decision not to terminate results in a maintenance of the status quo; the possibility of subsequent developments such as advancements in medical science, the discovery of new evidence regarding the patient's intent, changes in the law, or simply the unexpected death of the patient despite the administration of life-sustaining treatment, at least create the potential that a wrong decision will eventually be corrected or its impact mitigated. An erroneous decision to withdraw life-sustaining treatment, however, is not susceptible of correction. . . .

In sum, we conclude that a State may apply a clear and convincing evidence standard in proceedings where a guardian seeks to discontinue nutrition and hydration of a person diagnosed to be in a persistent vegetative state. We note that many courts which have adopted some sort of substituted judgment procedure in situations like this, whether they limit consideration of evidence to the prior expressed wishes of the incompetent individual, or whether they allow more general proof of what the individual's decision would have been, require a clear and convincing standard of proof for such evidence. . . .

The judgment of the Supreme Court of Missouri is Affirmed.

☐ *Justice SCALIA, concurring.*

While I agree with the Court's analysis today, and therefore join in its opinion, I would have preferred that we announce, clearly and promptly, that the federal courts have no business in this field; that American law has always accorded the State the power to prevent, by force if necessary, suicide—including suicide by refusing to take appropriate measures necessary to preserve one's life; that the point at which life becomes "worthless," and the point at which the means necessary to preserve it become "extraordinary" or "inappropriate," are neither set forth in the Constitution nor known to the nine Justices of this Court any better than they are known to nine people picked at random from the Kansas City telephone directory; and hence, that even when it *is* demonstrated by clear and convincing evidence that a patient no longer wishes certain measures to be taken to preserve her life, it is up to the citizens of Missouri to decide, through their elected representatives, whether that wish will be honored. It is quite impossible (because the Constitution says nothing about the matter) that those citizens will decide upon a line less lawful than the one we would choose; and it is unlikely (because we know no more about "life-and-death" than they do) that they will decide upon a line less reasonable.

The text of the Due Process Clause does not protect individuals against deprivations of liberty *simpliciter*. It protects them against deprivations of liberty "without due process of law." To determine that such a deprivation would not occur if Nancy Cruzan were forced to take nourishment against her will, it is unnecessary to reopen the historically recurrent debate over whether "due process" includes substantive restrictions. . . . It is at least true that no "substantive due process" claim can be maintained unless the claimant demonstrates that the State has deprived him of a right historically and traditionally protected against State interference. . . .

I assert only that the Constitution has nothing to say about [a "right to die"]. To raise up a constitutional right here we would have to create out of nothing (for it exists neither in text nor tradition) some constitutional principle whereby, although the State may insist that an individual come in out of the cold and eat food, it may not insist that he take medicine; and although it may pump his stomach empty of poison he has ingested, it may not fill his stomach with food he has failed to ingest. Are there, then, no reasonable and humane limits that ought not to be exceeded in requiring an individual to preserve his own life? There obviously are, but they are not set forth in the Due Process Clause. What assures us that those limits will not be exceeded is the same constitutional guarantee that is the source of most of our protection—what protects us, for example, from being assessed a tax of 100% of our income above the subsistence level, from being forbidden to drive cars, or from being required to send our children to school for 10 hours a day, none of which horribles is categorically prohibited by the Constitution. Our salvation is the Equal Protection Clause, which requires the democratic majority to accept for themselves and their loved ones what they impose on you and me. This Court need not, and has no authority to, inject itself into every field of human activity where irrationality and oppression may theoretically occur, and if it tries to do so it will destroy itself.

☐ *Justice BRENNAN, with whom Justice MARSHALL and Justice BLACKMUN join, dissenting.*

Because I believe that Nancy Cruzan has a fundamental right to be free of unwanted artificial nutrition and hydration, which right is not outweighed by any interests of the State, and because I find that the improperly biased procedural obstacles imposed by the Missouri Supreme Court impermissibly burden that right, I respectfully dissent. Nancy Cruzan is entitled to choose to die with dignity. . . .

The question before this Court is a relatively narrow one: whether the Due Process Clause allows Missouri to require a now-incompetent patient in an irreversible persistent vegetative state to remain on life-support absent rigorously clear and convincing evidence that avoiding the treatment represents the patient's prior, express choice. . . .

The starting point for our legal analysis must be whether a competent person has a constitutional right to avoid unwanted medical care. Earlier this Term, this Court held that the Due Process Clause of the Fourteenth Amendment confers a significant liberty interest in avoiding unwanted medical treatment. *Washington v. Harper*, [494 U.S. 210] (1990). Today, the Court concedes that our prior decisions "support the recognition of a general liberty interest in refusing medical treatment." . . .

But if a competent person has a liberty interest to be free of unwanted medical treatment, as both the majority and Justice O'CONNOR concede, it must be fundamental. "We are dealing here with [a decision] which involves one of the basic civil rights of man." *Skinner v. Oklahoma ex rel. Williamson*, 316 U.S. 535 (1942) (invalidating a statute authorizing sterilization of certain felons).

The right to be free from medical attention without consent, to determine what shall be done with one's own body, *is* deeply rooted in this Nation's traditions, as the majority acknowledges. This right has long been "firmly entrenched in American tort law" and is securely grounded in the earliest common law. See also *Mills v. Rogers*, 457 U.S. 291 (1982) ("the right to refuse any medical treatment emerged from the doctrines of trespass and battery, which were applied to unauthorized touchings by a physician"). . . .

That there may be serious consequences involved in refusal of the medical treatment at issue here does not vitiate the right under our common law tradition of medical self-determination. . . .

There are also affirmative reasons why someone like Nancy might choose to forgo artificial nutrition and hydration under these circumstances. Dying is personal. And it is profound. For many, the thought of an ignoble end, steeped in decay, is abhorrent. A quiet, proud death, bodily integrity intact, is a matter of extreme consequence. . . .

I do not suggest that States must sit by helplessly if the choices of incompetent patients are in danger of being ignored. Even if the Court had ruled that Missouri's rule of decision is unconstitutional, as I believe it should have, States would nevertheless remain free to fashion procedural protections to safeguard the interests of incompetents under these circumstances. The Constitution provides merely a framework here: protections must be genuinely aimed at ensuring decisions commensurate with the will of the patient, and must be reliable as instruments to that end. Of the many States which have instituted such protections, Missouri is virtually the only one to have fashioned a rule that lessens the likelihood of accurate determinations. In contrast, nothing in the Constitution prevents States from reviewing the advisability of a family decision, by requiring a court proceeding or by appointing an impartial guardian *ad litem*. . . .

Finally, I cannot agree with the majority that where it is not possible to determine what choice an incompetent patient would make, a State's role as *parens patriae* permits the State automatically to make that choice itself. . . .

I respectfully dissent.

Washington v. Glucksberg
521 U.S. 702, 117 S.CT. 2258 (1997)

and

Vacco v. Quill
521 U.S. 793, 117 S.CT. 2293 (1997)

These cases arose from the growing controversy over the so-called right to die. In *Cruzan by Cruzan v. Director, Missouri Department of Health*, 497 U.S. 261 (1990), the Court held that individuals have a "fundamental liberty" interest under the Fourteenth Amendment in terminating life-support systems. In 1996, two federal appellate courts extended that ruling to forbid states from passing laws barring physicians from prescribing lethal dosages of drugs at the request of their terminally ill patients. At issue was not whether doctors like Jack Kevorkian may help the terminally ill end their lives, but rather whether they may prescribe lethal drugs to terminally ill patients. The Court of Appeals for the Ninth Circuit struck down Washington's law forbidding physician-assisted suicide on the ground that it violated individuals' "right of privacy" and substantive liberty protected by the due process clause of the Fourteenth Amendment. The Court of Appeals for the Second Circuit invalidated New York's law on the basis of the Fourteenth Amendment's equal protection clause upon rejecting the state's distinction between the terminally ill's right to terminate life-support systems and claim to a right to physician-assisted suicide.

Both appellate court decisions were unanimously reversed by the Supreme Court. Overturning the Second Circuit's decision in his opinion for the Court in *Vacco v. Quill*, Chief Justice Rehnquist rejected its equal protection analysis, observing that

> [t]he Equal Protection Clause commands that no State "deny to any person within its jurisdiction the equal protection of the laws." This provision creates no substantive rights. Instead, it

embodies a general rule that States must treat like cases alike but may treat unlike cases accordingly. If a legislative classification or distinction "neither burdens a fundamental right nor targets a suspect class, we will uphold [it] so long as it bears a rational relation to some legitimate end." *Romer v. Evans*, [517 U.S. 620] (1996). . . .

On their faces, neither New York's ban on assisting suicide nor its statutes permitting patients to refuse medical treatment treat anyone differently than anyone else or draw any distinctions between persons. Everyone, regardless of physical condition, is entitled, if competent, to refuse unwanted lifesaving medical treatment; no one is permitted to assist a suicide. Generally speaking, laws that apply evenhandedly to all "unquestionably comply" with the Equal Protection Clause.

Notably, though, in the penultimate paragraph of his opinion in *Vacco*, Chief Justice Rehnquist added a footnote leaving open the possible consideration of future due process claims to a right to physicians' assisted suicide:

> Justice STEVENS [in his opinions in *Vacco* and *Glucksberg*] . . . would not "foreclose the possibility that an individual plaintiff seeking to hasten her death, or a doctor whose assistance was sought, could prevail in a more particularized challenge." Our opinion does not absolutely foreclose such a claim. However, given our holding that the Due Process Clause of the Fourteenth Amendment does not provide heightened protection to the asserted liberty interest in ending one's life with a physician's assistance, such a claim would have been quite different from the ones advanced by respondents here.

The Court's unanimous decision in *Washington v. Glucksberg* was also delivered by Chief Justice Rehnquist but, as in *Vacco v. Quill*, only Justices O'Connor, Scalia, Kennedy, and Thomas joined his opinion for the Court. Moreover, in each case, four justices—Justices O'Connor, Stevens, Souter, and Breyer—issued concurring opinions rejecting some or all of Chief Justice Rehnquist's analysis and indicating that they might be prepared, depending on the particular circumstances of the case, to recognize a right to physician-assisted suicide, which the chief justice's opinion did not entirely rule out. For now, the justices agreed to let the controversy continue to play out in state legislatures and the lower courts.

■ ■ ■

☐ *Chief Justice REHNQUIST delivered the opinion of the Court.*

The question presented in this case is whether Washington's prohibition against "causing" or "aiding" a suicide offends the Fourteenth Amendment to the United States Constitution. We hold that it does not. . . .

We begin, as we do in all due-process cases, by examining our Nation's history, legal traditions, and practices. In almost every State—indeed, in almost every western democracy—it is a crime to assist a suicide. The States' assisted-suicide bans are not innovations. Rather, they are long-standing expressions of the States' commitment to the protection and preservation of all human life. . . .

Though deeply rooted, the States' assisted-suicide bans have in recent years been reexamined and, generally, reaffirmed. Because of advances in medicine and technology, Americans today are increasingly likely to die in institutions, from chronic illnesses. Public concern and democratic action are therefore sharply focused on how best to protect dignity and independence at the end of life, with the result that there have been many significant changes in state laws and in the attitudes these laws reflect. Many States, for example, now permit "living wills," surrogate health-care decision making, and the withdrawal or refusal of life-sustaining medical treatment. At the same time, however, voters and legislators continue for the most part to reaffirm their States' prohibitions on assisting suicide.

The Washington statute at issue in this case was enacted in 1975 as part of a revision of that State's criminal code. Four years later, Washington passed its Natural Death Act, which specifically stated that the "withholding or withdrawal of life-sustaining treatment . . . shall not, for any purpose, constitute a suicide" and that "nothing in this chapter shall be construed to condone, authorize, or approve mercy killing. . . ." In 1991, Washington voters rejected a ballot initiative which, had it passed, would have permitted a form of physician-assisted suicide. Washington then added a provision to the Natural Death Act expressly excluding physician-assisted suicide.

California voters rejected an assisted-suicide initiative similar to Washington's in 1993. On the other hand, in 1994, voters in Oregon enacted, also through ballot initiative, that State's "Death With Dignity Act," which legalized physician-assisted suicide for competent, terminally ill adults. Since the Oregon vote, many proposals to legalize assisted suicide have been and continue to be introduced in the States' legislatures, but none has been enacted. . . .

Thus, the States are currently engaged in serious, thoughtful examinations of physician-assisted suicide and other similar issues. . . .

The Due Process Clause guarantees more than fair process, and the "liberty" it protects includes more than the absence of physical restraint. The Clause also provides heightened protection against government interference with certain fundamental rights and liberty interests. In a long line of cases, we have held that, in addition to the specific freedoms protected by the Bill of Rights, the "liberty" specially protected by the Due Process Clause includes the rights to marry, *Loving v. Virginia*, 388 U.S. 1 (1967); to have children, *Skinner v. Oklahoma ex rel. Williamson*, 316 U.S. 535 (1942); to direct the education and upbringing of one's children, *Meyer v. Nebraska*, 262 U.S. 390 (1923); *Pierce v. Society of Sisters*, 268 U.S. 510 (1925); to marital privacy, *Griswold v. Connecticut*, 381 U.S. 479 (1965); to use contraception, *ibid; Eisenstadt v. Baird*, 405 U.S. 438 (1972); to bodily integrity, *Rochin v. California*, 342 U.S. 165 (1952), and to abortion, [*Planned Parenthood v.*] *Casey*, [505 U.S. 833 (1992)]. We have also assumed, and strongly suggested, that the Due Process Clause protects the traditional right to refuse unwanted lifesaving medical treatment. *Cruzan [by Cruzan v. Director, Missouri Dept. of Health*, 497 U.S. 261 (1990)].

But we "have always been reluctant to expand the concept of substantive due process because guideposts for responsible decision making in this uncharted area are scarce and open-ended." By extending constitutional protection to an asserted right or liberty interest, we, to a great extent, place the matter outside the arena of public debate and legislative action. We must therefore "exercise the utmost care whenever we are asked to break new ground in this field," lest the liberty protected by the Due Process Clause be subtly transformed into the policy preferences of the members of this Court.

Our established method of substantive-due-process analysis has two primary features: First, we have regularly observed that the Due Process Clause specially protects those fundamental rights and liberties which are, objectively, "deeply rooted in this Nation's history and tradition," *Snyder v. Massachusetts*, 291 U.S. 97 (1934) ("so rooted in the traditions and conscience of our people as to be ranked as fundamental"), and "implicit in the concept of ordered liberty," such that "neither liberty nor justice would exist if they were sacrificed," *Palko v. Connecticut*, 302 U.S. 319 (1937). Second, we have required in substantive-due-process cases a "careful description" of the asserted fundamental liberty interest. [*Reno v.*] *Flores* [507 U.S. 292 (1993)]; *Cruzan*. Our Nation's history, legal traditions, and practices thus provide the crucial "guideposts for responsible decision making" that direct and restrain our exposition of the Due Process Clause. As we stated recently in *Flores*, the Fourteenth Amendment "forbids the government to infringe . . . 'fundamental' liberty interests at all, no matter what process is provided, unless the infringement is narrowly tailored to serve a compelling state interest." . . .

We now inquire whether this asserted right has any place in our Nation's traditions. Here, as discussed above, we are confronted with a consistent and almost universal tradition that has long rejected the asserted right, and continues explicitly to reject it today, even for terminally ill, mentally competent adults. To hold for respondents, we would have to reverse centuries of legal doctrine and practice, and strike down the considered policy choice of almost every State. . . .

Respondents contend that in *Cruzan* we "acknowledged that competent, dying persons have the right to direct the removal of life-sustaining medical treatment and thus hasten death," and that "the constitutional principle behind recognizing the patient's liberty to direct the withdrawal of artificial life support applies at least as strongly to the choice to hasten impending death by consuming lethal medication."

The right assumed in *Cruzan*, however, was not simply deduced from abstract concepts of personal autonomy. Given the common-law rule that forced medication was a battery, and the long legal tradition protecting the decision to refuse unwanted medical treatment, our assumption was entirely consistent with this Nation's history and constitutional traditions. The decision to commit suicide with the assistance of another may be just as personal and profound as the decision to refuse unwanted medical treatment, but it has never enjoyed similar legal protection. Indeed, the two acts are widely and reasonably regarded as quite distinct. In *Cruzan* itself, we recognized that most States outlawed assisted suicide—and even more do today—and we certainly gave no intimation that the right to refuse unwanted medical treatment could be somehow transmuted into a right to assistance in committing suicide. . . .

The history of the law's treatment of assisted suicide in this country has been and continues to be one of the rejection of nearly all efforts to permit it. That being the case, our decisions lead us to conclude that the asserted "right" to assistance in committing suicide is not a fundamental liberty interest protected by the Due Process Clause. The Constitution also requires, however, that Washington's assisted-suicide ban be rationally related to legitimate government interests. See *Heller v. Doe*, 509 U.S. 312 (1993). This requirement is unquestionably met here. As the court below recognized, Washington's assisted-suicide ban implicates a number of state interests.

First, Washington has an "unqualified interest in the preservation of human life." *Cruzan.* The State's prohibition on assisted suicide, like all homicide laws, both reflects and advances its commitment to this interest. . . .

Relatedly, all admit that suicide is a serious public-health problem, especially among persons in otherwise vulnerable groups. Those who attempt suicide—terminally ill or not—often suffer from depression or other mental disorders. . . .

The State also has an interest in protecting the integrity and ethics of the medical profession. In contrast to the Court of Appeals' conclusion that "the integrity of the medical profession would [not] be threatened in any way by [physician-assisted suicide]," the American Medical Association, like many other medical and physicians' groups, has concluded that "physician-assisted suicide is fundamentally incompatible with the physician's role as healer."

Next, the State has an interest in protecting vulnerable groups—including the poor, the elderly, and disabled persons—from abuse, neglect, and mistakes. The Court of Appeals dismissed the State's concern that disadvantaged persons might be pressured into physician-assisted suicide as "ludicrous on its face." We have recognized, however, the real risk of subtle coercion and undue influence in end-of-life situations. *Cruzan.* . . . "The risk of harm is greatest for the many individuals in our society whose autonomy and well-being are already compromised by poverty, lack of access to good medical care, advanced age, or membership in a stigmatized social group" [New York Task Force on Life and the Law.] If physician-assisted suicide were permitted, many might resort to it to spare their families the substantial financial burden of end-of-life health-care costs.

The State's interest here goes beyond protecting the vulnerable from coercion; it extends to protecting disabled and terminally ill people from prejudice, negative and inaccurate stereotypes, and "societal indifference." The State's assisted-suicide ban reflects and reinforces its policy that the lives of terminally ill, disabled, and elderly people must be no less valued than the lives of the young and healthy, and that a seriously disabled person's suicidal impulses should be interpreted and treated the same way as anyone else's.

Finally, the State may fear that permitting assisted suicide will start it down the path to voluntary and perhaps even involuntary euthanasia. . . .

Throughout the Nation, Americans are engaged in an earnest and profound debate about the morality, legality, and practicality of physician-assisted suicide. Our holding permits this debate to continue, as it should in a democratic society. The decision of the *en banc* Court of Appeals is reversed, and the case is remanded for further proceedings consistent with this opinion.

☐ *Justice O'CONNOR, concurring.*

Death will be different for each of us. For many, the last days will be spent in physical pain and perhaps the despair that accompanies physical deterioration and a loss of control of basic bodily and mental functions. Some will seek medication to alleviate that pain and other symptoms.

The Court frames the issue in this case as whether the Due Process Clause of the Constitution protects a "right to commit suicide which itself includes a right to assistance in doing so," and concludes that our Nation's history, legal traditions, and practices do not support the existence of such a right. I join the Court's opinions because I agree that there is no generalized right to "commit suicide." . . .

Every one of us at some point may be affected by our own or a family member's terminal illness. There is no reason to think the democratic process will not strike the proper balance between the interests of terminally ill, mentally competent individuals who would seek to end their suffering and the State's interests in protecting those who might seek to end life mistakenly or under pressure. . . .

In sum, there is no need to address the question whether suffering patients have a constitutionally cognizable interest in obtaining relief from the suffering that they may experience in the last days of their lives. There is no dispute that dying patients in Washington and New York can obtain palliative care, even when doing so would hasten their deaths. The difficulty in defining terminal illness and the risk that a dying patient's request for assistance in ending his or her life might not be truly voluntary justifies the prohibitions on assisted suicide we uphold here.

☐ *Justice STEVENS, concurring in the judgments.*

The Court ends its opinion with the important observation that our holding today is fully consistent with a continuation of the vigorous debate about the "morality, legality, and practicality of physician-assisted suicide" in a democratic society. I write separately to make it clear that there is also room for further debate about the limits that the Constitution places on the power of the States to punish the practice.

History and tradition provide ample support for refusing to recognize an open-ended constitutional right to commit suicide. Much more than the State's paternalistic interest in protecting the individual from the irrevocable consequences of an ill-advised decision motivated by temporary concerns is at stake. There is truth in John Donne's observation that "No man is an island." The State has an interest in preserving and fostering the benefits that every human being may provide to the community—a community that thrives on the exchange of ideas, expressions of affection, shared memories and humorous incidents as well as on the material contributions that its members create and support. The value to others of a person's life is far too precious to allow the individual to claim a constitutional entitlement to complete autonomy in making a decision to end that life. Thus, I fully agree with the Court that the "liberty" protected by the Due Process Clause does not include a categorical "right to commit suicide which itself includes a right to assistance in doing so."

But just as our conclusion that capital punishment is not always unconstitutional did not preclude later decisions holding that it is sometimes impermissibly cruel, so is it equally clear that a decision upholding a general statutory prohibition of assisted suicide does not mean that every possible application of the statute would be valid. A State, like Washington, that has authorized the death penalty and thereby has concluded that the sanctity of human life does not require that it always be preserved, must acknowledge that there are situations in which an interest in hastening death is legitimate. Indeed, not only is that interest sometimes legitimate, I am also convinced that there are times when it is entitled to constitutional protection. . . .

While I agree with the Court that *Cruzan* does not decide the issue presented by these cases, *Cruzan* did give recognition, not just to vague, unbridled notions of autonomy, but to the more specific interest in making decisions about how to confront an imminent death. Although there is no absolute right to physician-assisted suicide, *Cruzan* makes it clear that some individuals who no longer have the option of deciding whether to live or to die because they are already on the threshold of death have a constitutionally protected interest that may outweigh the State's interest in preserving life at all costs. . . . There remains room for vigorous debate about the outcome of particular cases that are not necessarily resolved by the opinions announced today. How such cases may be decided will depend on their specific facts. In my judgment, however, it is clear that the so-called "unqualified interest in the preservation of human life," *Cruzan, Glucksberg*, is not itself sufficient to outweigh the interest in liberty that may justify the only possible means of preserving a dying patient's dignity and alleviating her intolerable suffering.

☐ *Justice SOUTER, concurring in the judgment.*

Three terminally ill individuals and four physicians who sometimes treat terminally ill patients brought this challenge to the Washington statute making it a crime "knowingly . . . [to] aid another person to attempt suicide," claiming on behalf of both patients and physicians that it would violate substantive due process to enforce the statute against a doctor who acceded to a dying patient's request for a drug to be taken by the patient to commit suicide. The question is whether the statute sets up one of those "arbitrary impositions" or "purposeless restraints" at odds with the Due Process Clause of the Fourteenth Amendment. *Poe v. Ullman*, 367 U.S. 497 (1961) (HARLAN, J., dissenting). I conclude that the statute's application to the doctors has not been shown to be unconstitutional, but I write separately to give my reasons for analyzing the substantive due process claims as I do, and for rejecting this one. . . .

Justice HARLAN's *Poe* dissent just cited, the conclusion of which was adopted in *Griswold v. Connecticut*, 381 U.S. 478 (1965), and the authority of which was acknowledged in *Planned Parenthood of Southeastern Pa. v. Casey*, 505 U.S. 833 (1992), . . . is important for three things that point to our responsibilities today. The first is Justice HARLAN's respect for the tradition of substantive due process review itself, and his acknowledgment of the Judiciary's obligation to carry it on. For two centuries American courts, and for much of that time this Court, have thought it necessary to provide some degree of review over the substantive content of legislation under constitutional standards of textual breadth. . . . This enduring tradition of American constitutional practice is, in Justice HARLAN's view, nothing more than what is required by the judicial authority and obligation to construe constitutional text and review legislation for conformity to that text. Like many judges who preceded him and many who followed, he found it impossible to construe the text of due process without recognizing substantive, and not merely procedural, limitations. "Were due process merely a procedural safeguard it would fail to reach those situations where the deprivation of life, liberty or property was accomplished by legislation which by operating in the future could, given even the fairest possible procedure in application to individuals, nevertheless destroy the enjoyment of all three." *Poe.* The text of the Due Process Clause thus imposes nothing less than an obligation to give substantive content to the words "liberty" and "due process of law."

The second of the dissent's lessons is a reminder that the business of such review is not the identification of extratextual absolutes but scrutiny of a legislative resolution (perhaps unconscious) of clashing principles, each quite possibly worthy in and of itself, but each to be weighed within the history of our values as a people. It is a comparison of the relative strengths of opposing claims that informs the judicial task, not a deduction from some first premise. Thus informed, judicial review still has no warrant to substitute one reasonable resolution of the contending positions for another, but authority to supplant the balance already struck between the contenders only when it falls outside the realm of the reasonable. [I deal below] with this second point, and also with the dissent's third, which takes the form of an object lesson in the explicit attention to detail that is no less essential to the intellectual discipline of substantive due process review than an understanding of the basic need to account for the two sides in the controversy and to respect legislation within the zone of reasonableness.

My understanding of unenumerated rights in the wake of the *Poe* dissent and subsequent cases avoids the absolutist failing of many older cases without embracing the opposite pole of equating reasonableness with past practice described at a very specific level. That understanding begins with a concept of "ordered liberty," comprising a continuum of rights to be free from "arbitrary impositions and purposeless restraints." . . . This approach calls for a court to assess the relative "weights" or dignities of the contending interests, and to this extent the judicial method is familiar to the common law. Common law method is subject, however, to two important constraints in the hands of a court engaged in substantive due process review. First, such a court is bound to confine the values that it recognizes to those truly deserving constitutional stature, either to those expressed in constitutional text, or those exemplified by "the traditions from which [the Nation] developed," or revealed by contrast with "the traditions from which it broke." *Poe* (HARLAN, J., dissenting). "We may not draw on our merely personal and private notions and disregard the limits . . . derived from considerations that are fused in the whole nature of our judicial process[,] . . . considerations deeply rooted in reason and in the compelling traditions of the legal profession." *Id.* (quoting *Rochin v. California*, 342 U.S. 165 (1952)); see also *Palko v. Connecticut* (looking to "principles of justice so rooted in the traditions and conscience of our people as to be ranked as fundamental") (quoting *Snyder v. Massachusetts*, 291 U.S. 97 (1934)).

The second constraint, again, simply reflects the fact that constitutional review, not judicial lawmaking, is a court's business here. The weighing or valuing of contending interests in this sphere is only the first step, forming the basis for determining whether the statute in question falls inside or outside the zone of what is reasonable in the way it resolves the conflict between the interests of state and individual. It is no justification for judicial intervention merely to identify a reasonable resolution of contending values that differs from the terms of the legislation under review. It is only when the legislation's justifying principle, critically valued, is so far from being commensurate with the individual interest as to be arbitrarily or pointlessly applied that the statute must give way. Only if this standard points against the statute can the individual claimant be said to have a constitutional right.

The *Poe* dissent thus reminds us of the nature of review for reasonableness or arbitrariness and the limitations entailed by it. But the opinion cautions against the repetition of past error in another way as well, more by its example than by any particular statement of constitutional method: it reminds us that the process of substantive review by reasoned judgment is one of close criticism going to the details of the opposing interests and to their relationships with the historically recognized principles that lend them weight or value. . . .

In my judgment, the importance of the individual interest here, as within that class of "certain interests" demanding careful scrutiny of the State's contrary claim cannot be gainsaid. Whether that interest might in some circumstances, or at some time, be seen as "fundamental" to the degree entitled to prevail is not, however, a conclusion that I need draw here, for I am satisfied that the State's interests . . . are sufficiently serious to defeat the present claim that its law is arbitrary or purposeless. . . .

12

THE EQUAL PROTECTION
OF THE LAWS

A guarantee for "the equal protection of the laws" did not find its
way into the Constitution until the ratification of the Fourteenth
Amendment in 1868. Then, over a half century lapsed before the
Supreme Court began enforcing it as a serious barrier to racial segregation and other kinds of nonracial discrimination as well. The Court,
though, never narrowly interpreted the Fourteenth Amendment simply
to require the evenhanded application of the laws. On such a view,
states could deny blond-haired individuals public employment or benefits so long as they rigorously denied all blond-haired applicants. But
such a narrow reading was rejected in *Yick Wo v. Hopkins*, 118 U.S. 356
(1886). When striking down San Francisco's "safety" ordinance, making it illegal to operate laundries in other than stone or brick buildings
(and which was used to put Chinese laundries out of business), the Court
observed that "[t]hough the law itself be fair on its face and impartial in
appearance, yet, if it is applied and administered by public authority
with an evil eye and an unjust hand, so as practically to make unjust
and illegal discrimination between persons in similar circumstances,
material to their rights, the denial of equal justice is . . . within the prohibition of the Constitution." At the same time, the equal protection
clause has never been broadly construed to forbid all discrimination or
inequities before the law. This is so because all laws—all legislative
classifications—discriminate and treat people differently.

The central problem for the Court lies in giving content and application to the principle of *legal equality*—equality before the law. Just as
controversial as whether the Fourteenth Amendment aimed to ensure

equal voting rights (see Vol. 1, Ch. 8), and whether it applied the guarantees of the Bill of Rights to the states (see Ch. 4), has been whether the amendment forbids racial segregation, as well as other kinds of nonracial discrimination. Justices, historians, and legal scholars have long debated the legislative history of the Fourteenth Amendment. Some contend that the Thirty-ninth Congress, which drafted and adopted the amendment, aimed to give the federal government broad powers to ensure the rights of blacks and to advance the political ideal of equality.[1] Others marshal evidence that the amendment was not designed to forbid racial segregation;[2] indeed, it neither granted voting rights to blacks nor prohibited racial segregation.[3] Still others conclude that the historical record "is not entirely consistent"[4] and that the amendment is "so broad and general that [it] could be used to support almost anything."[5]

As with other controversies in constitutional politics, the debate over the equal protection clause reflects rival interpretations of politics and the politics of interpretation.[6] Moreover, as historian and Harvard law school professor William Nelson points out, whether the equal protection clause applies to claims of nonracial discrimination that come before the Court in this century is "a question that never occurred to the Reconstruction generation and hence cannot be answered by examining the records of its actual thought." Even issues that Congress extensively debated, such as voting rights for blacks and segregation, went unresolved and inconsistencies remained. As Nelson underscores, "history can never tell us how the founding generation would have resolved inconsistencies that it did not, in fact, resolve."[7]

Once the Supreme Court turned to enforcing the equal protection clause in the twentieth century, it evolved standards for what legislative classifications are permissible and which discriminate in invidious, unconstitutional ways. Shortly after the Court's switch-in-time-that-saved-nine and abandonment of heightened review of economic legislation in 1937 (see Ch. 3), Justice Harlan F. Stone planted the seed for the modern Court's equal protection analysis. He did so in footnote four of *United States v. Carolene Products Co.*, 304 U.S. 144 (1938), which upheld Congress's power to ban the shipment in interstate commerce of skim milk compounded with fat or other nonmilk products. In his opinion, Justice Stone reaffirmed that no longer would heightened scrutiny be given to legislation regulating economic activities; instead the Court would presume "that it rests upon some rational basis." But at that point he added the following three-paragraph footnote, pointing out that heightened scrutiny might be given to legislation affecting fundamental rights or which singles out racial and other "discrete and insular minorities":

There may be narrower scope for operation of the presumption of constitutionality when legislation appears on its face to be within a specific prohibition of the Constitution, such as those of the first ten amendments, which are deemed equally specific when held to be embraced within the Fourteenth. See *Stromberg v. California*, 283 U.S. 359 [1931]; *Lovell v. Griffin*, 303 U.S. 444 [1938].

It is unnecessary to consider now whether legislation which restricts those political processes which can ordinarily be expected to bring about repeal of undesirable legislation is to be subjected to more exacting judicial scrutiny under the general prohibitions of the Fourteenth Amendment than are other types of legislation. On restrictions upon the right to vote, see *Nixon v. Herndon*, 273 U.S. 536 [1927]; *Nixon v. Condon*, 286 U.S. 73 [1932]; on restrictions upon the dissemination of information, see *Near v. Minnesota*, 283 U.S. 697 [1931]; *Grosjean v. American Press Co.*, 297 U.S. 233 [1936]; *Lovell v. Griffin* [1938]; on interferences with political organizations, see *Stromberg v. California* [1931]; *Fiske v. Kansas* [(1927)]; *Whitney v. California*, 274 U.S. 357 [1927]; *Herndon v. Lowry* [1937]; and see HOLMES, J., in *Gitlow v. New York*, 268 U.S. 652 [1925]; as to peaceable assembly, see *De Jonge v. Oregon*, 299 U.S. 353 [1937].

Nor need we inquire whether similar considerations enter into the review of statutes directed at particular religious, *Pierce v. Society of Sisters*, 268 U.S. 510 [1925], or national, *Meyer v. Nebraska*, 262 U.S. 390 [1923]; *Bartels v. Iowa*, 262 U.S. 404 [1923]; *Farrington v. Tokushige*, 273 U.S. 284 [1927], or racial minorities, *Nixon v. Herndon* [1927]; *Nixon v. Condon* [1932]; whether prejudices against discrete and insular minorities may be a special condition, which tends seriously to curtail the operation of those political processes ordinarily thought to be relied upon to protect minorities, and which may call for a correspondingly more searching judicial inquiry. . . .

The third paragraph of Justice Stone's footnote laid the basis for what evolved into a two- (and, later, a three-) tiered set of standards for judicial review under the equal protection clause.[8] By emphasizing the post–1937 Court's presumption of a rational basis for economic legislation, Justice Stone pointed the way toward heightened scrutiny (*strict scrutiny*) of legislation based on "suspect classifications," such as religion and race, or which impinged on "fundamental rights."

Justice Stone, though, used neither the phrase *fundamental rights* nor *strict scrutiny*. Four years later, in *Skinner v. Oklahoma*, 316 U.S. 535 (1942), Justice Douglas made the case for heightened judicial scrutiny of legislation affecting fundamental rights. Striking down a law requiring the forced sterilization of individuals convicted of two or more felonies involving moral turpitude, he observed that "[w]e are dealing here with legislation which involves one of the basic civil rights of man. Marriage and procreation are fundamental to the very existence and survival of the race." Ironically, the strict scrutiny test has its origins in an opinion by Justice Black, *upholding* the internment of Japanese-Americans during World War II. In *Korematsu v. United States*, 323 U.S. 214 (1944) (see Vol. 1, Ch. 3), Justice Black observed that "all legal restrictions which curtail the civil rights of a single racial group are immediately suspect. That is not to say that all such restrictions are unconstitutional. It is to say that courts must subject them to the most rigid scrutiny."

It remained for the Warren Court (1953–1969) to develop a two-tier approach to judicial review under the equal protection clause. When reviewing economic legislation, the Court gives *minimal scrutiny* and applies the *rational basis test*, asking simply whether legislation is reasonable and has a rational, conceivable basis. Under this test, legislation is invariably upheld. Indeed, only twice since 1937 have economic regulations been found irrational and unconstitutional under the Fourteenth Amendment. In *Morey v. Doud*, 354 U.S. 457 (1957), the Warren Court struck down Illinois's law exempting the American Express Company from licensing requirements for companies issuing money orders. In *Allegheny Pittsburgh Coal Co. v. County Commission*, 488 U.S. 336 (1989), the Rehnquist Court unanimously concluded that the equal protection clause was violated when a West Virginia county tax assessor valued real estate property "on the basis of its recent purchase price, but made only minor modifications in the assessments of land which had not been recently sold," resulting in the property of Allegheny Pittsburgh Coal Company to be "assessed at roughly 8 to 35 times more than comparable neighboring property." The county assessor's practice, in Chief Justice Rehnquist's words, was not "rationally related" to the state's law that property "be taxed at a rate uniform throughout the state according to its estimated market value."

Allegheny Pittsburgh Coal Co. appears to be the exception that proves the Court's predisposition to uphold economic legislation and to apply its minimal scrutiny test. The Rehnquist Court reviewed, in *Nordlinger v. Hahn*, 505 U.S. 1 (1992), an equal protection challenge to California's constitutional amendment—otherwise known as Proposition 13—that limits property-tax rates to 1 percent of assessed value. Under Proposition 13, properties bought before 1978 had their values rolled back to 1975 assessments, and properties purchased after the adoption of the amendment were assessed on the basis of their selling price. The immediate impact was a halt to rapidly rising tax increases, but the long-term consequence has been a growing disparity in the taxes paid by long-term owners and recent purchasers. As a result, some homeowners pay as much as 17 times more taxes than their neighbors who bought homes before 1978. The owner of a $3.8-million, 8,000-square-foot mansion in Beverly Hills who owned the property before 1978 paid about $3,200 in annual taxes, whereas a purchaser of that mansion would pay about

$38,000. At the same time, a recent buyer of a 1,000-square-foot bungalow that cost $370,000 pays $3,700 in taxes, or a little more than the owner of the mansion bought before 1978.

Writing for the Court in *Nordlinger*, Justice Blackmun upheld California's Proposition 13 and distinguished *Allegheny Pittsburgh*. In doing so, he underscored that

> [t]he appropriate standard of review is whether the difference in treatment between newer and older owners rationally furthers a legitimate state interest. In general, the Equal Protection Clause is satisfied so long as there is a plausible policy reason for the classification, the legislative facts on which the classification is apparently based rationally may have been considered to be true by the governmental decisionmaker, and the relationship of the classification to its goal is not so attenuated as to render the distinction arbitrary or irrational. This standard is especially deferential in the context of classifications made by complex tax laws. . . .

> We have no difficulty in ascertaining at least two rational or reasonable considerations of difference or policy that justify denying petitioner the benefits of her neighbors' lower assessments. First, the State has a legitimate interest in local neighborhood preservation, continuity, and stability. *Euclid v. Ambler Realty Co.*, 272 U.S. 265 (1926). The State therefore legitimately can decide to structure its tax system to discourage rapid turnover in ownership of homes and businesses, for example, in order to inhibit displacement of lower income families by the forces of gentrification or of established, "mom-and-pop" businesses by newer chain operations. . . .

> Second, the State legitimately can conclude that a new owner at the time of acquiring his property does not have the same reliance interest warranting protection against higher taxes as does an existing owner.

By a 6–3 vote in *Armour v. City of Indianapolis*, 566 U.S. 673 (2012), the Court reaffirmed that legislatures have broad authority to create classifications in tax systems. In 2005, Indianapolis abandoned apportioning the cost of sewer projects to the owners of improved property and switched to a bond system. Prior to the switch, landowners had the option of paying a lump sum or paying the assessment in installments. When the change was made, landowners paying in installments were forgiven their debt. Christine Armour had paid the lump sum and sought a partial refund. When denied, she sued, claiming a violation of the equal protection of the law. Writing for the Court, Justice Breyer held that the city had a rational basis for distinguishing between lot owners who had already paid their assessments and those who had not. And the line the city chose to draw, distinguishing past payments from future obligations, did not violate the Fourteenth Amendment, which requires a rational (not a perfect) line and, therefore, distinguishing between the two groups of taxpayers was not an equal protection violation. Chief Justice Roberts, joined by Justices Scalia and Alito, dissented.

By contrast, the strict scrutiny test applies to "suspect classifications," such as race, and legislation affecting fundamental rights. On this standard of review, legislation is sustained only if there is "a compelling state interest" in the legislative classification. *Korematsu* was the exception rather than the rule; when the Court applies this standard, legislation invariably falls.

The Warren Court's two-level analysis of equal protection claims proved as controversial as it was instrumental to forging an "egalitarian revolution" in constitutional law. Conservatives and strict constructionists criticized the Court for inventing new fundamental rights that they claimed lacked constitutional foundation.[9] Nor was the application of suspect classifications unproblematic. These classifications were "suspect" because they discriminated against individuals on the basis of immutable characteristics—characteristics such as race, gender, age, and illegitimacy—which people do not choose and cannot readily, if at all, change (although sex changes and notice of paternity are possible). By the end of the Warren Court era, the problem facing the justices was one of consistency in determining what classifications were suspect; notably, the Court was also split over whether gender, like race, was a suspect category. In addition, the Court was criticized for encouraging individuals to define their rights in terms of membership in groups and for inviting interest-group litigation. Finally, because legislation was invariably struck down under the strict scrutiny test and upheld under the rational basis test, the Warren Court's two-tier analysis was criticized for being too rigid, for being "strict in theory and fatal in fact."

By the 1970s and 1980s, the Court and the country were changing in response to the Warren Court's "egalitarian revolution." While litigation brought new claims of nonracial discrimination, the Court's composition also changed with the appointments of Republican Presidents Richard Nixon, Gerald Ford, and Ronald Reagan. As the high bench became more conservative, the Burger Court (1969–1986) and the Rehnquist Court (1986–2005) sought retrenchment, refusing to expand the list of fundamental rights, suspect classifications, and quasi-suspect categories like gender. Moreover, the Burger Court evolved a third, *intermediate* standard of judicial review: the "exacting scrutiny" or "strict rationality" test.[10] With this test, the Court looks for a "substantial relationship between the means and ends of legislation," and may or may not strike down legislation, for instance, discriminating on the basis of gender (see Section D, in this chapter). In addition, the

■ The Development of Law

The Supreme Court's Evolving Equal Protection Standards and Tests

TIERS OF ANALYSIS	STANDARD OF JUDICIAL REVIEW	LEGISLATIVE CLASSIFICATIONS	CLAIMS OF FUNDAMENTAL RIGHTS
Post-1937 Two-Tier Analysis			
Upper Tier Applies to suspect classifications and fundamental rights	Strict Scrutiny Test: Is there a compelling state interest in a legislative classification?	Race *See Brown v. Bd. of Education* (1954)	Right to Vote See Vol. 1, Ch. 8 Right to Travel *See Shapiro v. Thompson* (1969) Right to Marry *Obergefell v. Hodges* (2015)
Lower Tier Applies to economic regulation and nonsuspect classifications	Minimal Scrutiny/Rational Basis Test: Is there a rational basis for the legislation?	Economic Classifications	
The Burger Court's (1969–1986) Three-Tier Analysis			
Upper Tier	Strict Scrutiny Test	Racial classifications that impose burdens on minorities Alienage *See Plyler v. Doe* (1982)	
Intermediate Tier Applies to quasi-suspect categories	Exacting Scrutiny/Strict Rationality Test: Is there a substantial relationship in fact between the means and ends of legislation?	Gender *See Frontiero v. Richardson* (1973); *Craig v. Boren* (1976); *Michael M. v. Superior Court* (1981) (excerpted in this chapter)	

Lower Tier	Minimal Scrutiny Test/ Rational Basis Test	Affirmative Action See *Regents of the University of California v. Bakke* (1978) Illegitimacy See Section D(3) in this chapter Indigency, Education and Welfare See *San Antonio Independent School District v. Rodriguez* (excerpted below) Age and Alienage See the DEVELOPMENT OF LAW Box in Section D

THE REHNQUIST COURT'S (1986–2005) AND ROBERTS COURT'S (2005–) "NEW" TWO-TIER APPROACH[1]

Upper Tier	Strict Scrutiny Test	Right to Marry See *Obergefell v. Hodges* (2015) (excerpted in this chapter) Race and Affirmative Action See *City of Richmond v. J. A. Croson* (1989); *Gratz v. Bollinger* and *Grutter v. Bollinger* (2003); *Fisher v. University of Texas* (2016) (all excerpted in this chapter)
Lower Tier	Rational Basis Test	Economic Classifications Mental Retardation See *Heller v. Doe* (1993) Homosexuality and LGBTQ rights See *Romer v. Evans* (1996) (excerpted in this chapter); see also *Lawrence v. Texas* (2003) (excerpted in Chapter 11)

1. Note that the Court used an intermediate test—"exceedingly persuasive justification"—in striking down gender discrimination in *U.S. v. Virginia* (1996) (excerpted in this chapter), but there remained no majority for recognizing gender as a "suspect classification."

contemporary Court is resistant to attempts to heighten judicial review for new claims of quasi-suspect classifications. Indeed, the Rehnquist and Roberts Courts have been inclined to evaluate claims of racial discrimination under the strict scrutiny test and all other equal protection claims under the rational basis test.

Illustrative of the Court's equal protection analysis is *City of Cleburne, Texas v. Cleburne Living Center*, 473 U.S. 432 (1985), involving a challenge to a Texas zoning law. The law required a special city permit, renewable each year, for the construction of "hospitals for the insane or feeble-minded, or alcoholic or drug addicts, or penal or correctional institutions." The Cleburne Living Center wanted to operate a group home for thirteen mentally retarded men and women but was denied a permit because the city concluded that the home should be classified as a "hospital for the feeble-minded." A federal district court upheld the city's decision. But an appellate court reversed, holding "that mental retardation is a 'quasi-suspect' classification and that the ordinance violated the Equal Protection Clause because it did not substantially further an important governmental purpose." On appeal to the Supreme Court, Justice White held that the lower court erred in finding mental retardation to be a quasi-suspect classification justifying heightened judicial review. Although finding "a lesser standard of scrutiny [to be] appropriate," he nevertheless concluded "that under that standard the ordinance is invalid as applied in this case," explaining that

> where individuals in the group affected by a law have distinguishing characteristics relevant to interests the state has the authority to implement, the courts have been very reluctant, as they should be in our federal system, and with respect for our separation of powers, to closely scrutinize legislative choices as to whether, how and to what extent those interests should be pursued. In such cases, the Equal Protection Clause requires only a rational means to serve a legitimate end.

Heller v. Doe, 509 U.S. 312 (1993), further illustrates the Court's unwillingness to expand heightened scrutiny beyond the "rational basis" test. Writing for a bare majority, Justice Kennedy rejected an equal protection and due process challenge to Kentucky's law distinguishing between mentally retarded and mentally ill individuals and providing different procedures for their involuntary commitment.

Three years later, in *Romer v. Evans* (1996) (excerpted in Section D (2)), a majority of the Court affirmed a Colorado supreme court decision striking down a state constitutional amendment forbidding localities from enacting ordinances that outlaw discrimination against homosexuals. Notably, the state supreme court had applied the "strict scrutiny" test, whereas Justice Kennedy's opinion for the Court applies the "rational basis" test. As in *Cleburne Living Center* and *Heller v. Doe, Romer v. Evans* underscores the contemporary Court's reluctance, on the one hand, to expand heightened scrutiny under the Fourteenth Amendment and the Court's willingness, on the other hand, both to apply the "rational basis" test and to give that test more of a bite in dealing with challenges to nonracial discriminatory classifications.

The Court's analysis and evolving standards for judicial review under the equal protection clause are examined in this chapter in terms of the political struggles within the Court and the country over the historical quest for equality. The next section examines racial discrimination before and after the ratification of the Fourteenth Amendment and the role the Court played in the constitutional politics of racial segregation and desegregation. Section B turns to the Court's rulings on school desegregation. Section C takes up the controversy over affirmative action and reverse discrimination. Finally, Section D considers nonracial classifications and challenges to discrimination based on gender, homosexuality, indigency, illegitimacy, alienage, and age.

NOTES

1. See Horace Flack, *The Adoption of the Fourteenth Amendment* (Baltimore, MD: Johns Hopkins University Press, 1908); Jacobus tenBroek, *The Antislavery Origins of the Fourteenth Amendment* (Berkeley: University of California Press, 1951); William Wiecek, *The Sources of Antislavery Constitutionalism in America* (Ithaca, NY: Cornell University Press, 1977); and Howard Graham, *Everyman's Constitution: Historical Essays on the Fourteenth Amendment, the "Conspiracy Theory," and American Constitutionalism* (Madison: State Historical Society of Wisconsin, 1968).

2. See Alexander Bickel, "The Original Understanding and the Segregation Decision," 69 *Harvard Law Review* 1 (1955).

3. Raoul Berger, *Government by Judiciary: The Transformation of the Fourteenth Amendment* (Cambridge, MA: Harvard University Press, 1977).

4. See Earl Maltz, "The Fourteenth Amendment as Political Compromise— Section One in the Joint Committee on Reconstruction," 45 *Ohio State Law Journal* 933 (1984); and E. Maltz, "The Concept of Equal Protection of the Laws—A Historical Inquiry," 22 *San Diego Law Review* 499 (1985).

5. See Judith Baer, *Equality under the Constitution: Reclaiming the Fourteenth Amendment* (Ithaca, NY: Cornell University Press, 1983), 102–103.

6. See and compare William Brock, *An American Crisis: Congress and the Reconstruction* (New York: St. Martin's Press, 1963); Michael Les Benedict, *A Compromise of Principle: Congressional Republicans and Reconstruction* (New York: W. W. Norton & Company, 1974).

7. William Nelson, *The Fourteenth Amendment* (Cambridge, MA: Harvard University Press, 1988).

8. The footnote was actually initially drafted by Justice Stone's law clerk, Louis Lusky, and revised after Chief Justice Hughes made some suggestions. See Louis Lusky, *By What Right?* (Charlottesville, VA: Michie, 1975).

9. See, for example, the right to travel in *Shapiro v. Thompson* (excerpted in this chapter) and the right to privacy in *Griswold v. Connecticut* (in Ch. 4).

10. See Gerald Gunther, "In Search of Evolving Doctrine on a Changing Court: A Model for a New Equal Protection," 86 *Harvard Law Review* 1 (1972).

Selected Bibliography

Berger, Raoul. *Government by the Judiciary: The Transformation of the Fourteenth Amendment.* Cambridge, MA: Harvard University Press, 1977.

Brandon, Mark. *Free in the World: American Slavery and Constitutional Failure.* Princeton, NJ: Princeton University Press, 1998.

Graham, Hugh. *The Civil Rights Era.* New York: Oxford University Press, 1990.

West, Robin. *Progressive Constitutionalism: Reconstructing the Fourteenth Amendment.* Durham, NC: Duke University Press, 1994.

A | *Racial Discrimination and State Action*

"Our Constitution," in the words of Justice John Marshall Harlan dissenting alone in *Plessy v. Ferguson* (1896) (see excerpt below), "is color-blind, and neither knows nor tolerates classes among citizens." However, the history of constitutional politics, both before and after the ratification of the Fourteenth Amendment, belies that noble aspiration and appeal to future generations. While the Declaration of Independence proclaimed that "all men are created equal," the Constitution was far from color-blind.

Opposition to slavery emerged during the Revolutionary War, particularly after slaves served as soldiers in the colonial battle for freedom from the English Crown. After winning independence, several northern colonies passed laws abolishing slavery. Still Thomas Jefferson and others won approval of the Northwest Ordinance of 1787, forbidding slavery in western territories north of the Ohio River, only after agreeing that fugitive slaves "may be lawfully reclaimed." And even in New York, the state legislature did not order the mandatory emancipation of slaves until 1828.

The Constitutional Convention compromised on the question of slavery, even though the words *slavery* and *slaves* never appear in the document. Article I, Section 2 provides that, for the purposes of taxation and representation in the House of Representatives, "three fifths of all other [nonfree] Persons" were to be counted. This accommodated southern delegates' twin concerns that when levying taxes the federal government might discriminate against the South in the way it counted slaves and that the South would be underrepresented if slaves were not counted for the purposes of representation. The convention agreed as well to authorize Congress, in Article I, Section 9, to stop the "migration or importation" of slaves, although not before 1808. Finally, without much debate the convention endorsed (in Article IV, Section 2) the return of fugitive slaves to their owners.

Despite the efforts of some at the Constitutional Convention to limit the perpetuation of slavery, the Constitution registered the prejudices and white supremacy of the country.[1] Over a half century later, Chief Justice Roger Taney wrote those prejudices into constitutional law with his sweeping opinion in *Dred Scott v. Sandford* (1857) (see excerpt below), denying that blacks (not just slaves and temporarily freed slaves, but all blacks) could be citizens, and striking down the Missouri Compromise of 1820, in which Congress had sought to exclude slavery from federal territories north of the line 36°30'. When holding that blacks were excluded from "We the People of the United States," of which the preamble of the Constitution speaks, Chief Justice Taney laid bare the brute fact of white supremacy, explaining that blacks were "a subordinate and inferior class of beings, who had been subjugated by the dominant race, and, whether emancipated or not, yet remained subject to their authority."

Prior to the Civil War, the Court did little to undermine slavery. In *Prigg v. Pennsylvania*, 41 U.S. 539 (1842), though, the Court struck down a state law requiring masters to present to a magistrate proof of ownership of a runaway slave and upheld the federal Fugitive Slave Law of 1793, authorizing federal judges to certify a slaveholder's claim over a fugitive slave. In his opinion for the Court, Justice Joseph Story, however, also noted that states were not compelled by Congress to enforce the 1793 law. As a result, northern states were encouraged not to enforce fugitive slave laws, while southern states pushed for more stringent laws to protect their interests.

Although abolitionists attacked the constitutionality of fugitive slave laws, the Taney Court firmly defended the South's interests in slavery. In *Strader v. Graham*, 51 U.S. 82 (1851), for instance, the Taney Court unanimously upheld Kentucky's law making abettors of fugitive slaves liable for damages to slaveowners, even if slaves had been taken into free territory.[2]

With the outbreak of the Civil War in 1861, *Dred Scott*'s impact was limited. After the war, the ruling was technically overturned by the

Thirteenth Amendment (in 1865), which abolished slavery and "involuntary servitude," as well as gave Congress the "power to enforce this article by appropriate legislation." The Reconstruction Congress also considered how to ensure the voting rights and the civil rights of newly freed blacks. In 1862, Congress repealed the District of Columbia's "Black Codes," which limited the property rights of blacks and made certain offenses criminal for blacks only. But in 1865 President Andrew Johnson vetoed the passage of further civil rights legislation, contending that the protection of civil rights was a matter for the states, not the federal government. Congress, however, overrode the veto with a two-thirds vote and enacted the Civil Rights Act of 1866. Because controversy remained over the constitutionality of that legislation, one of the objectives of promoters of the Fourteenth Amendment in 1866 was to ensure the constitutional basis for the Civil Rights Act of 1866. The Fifteenth Amendment later specifically aimed at guaranteeing blacks equal voting rights (see Vol. 1, Ch. 8).

Both the Civil Rights Act of 1866 and the Fourteenth Amendment sought to ensure the citizenship of newly freed blacks and the equal protection of the laws. Congress was very explicit about the legal equality extended to blacks in the Civil Rights Act. It specifically guarantees

> citizens, of every race and color . . . the same right, in every State and Territory . . . to make and enforce contracts, to sue, be parties, and give evidence, to inherit, purchase, lease, sell, hold, and convey real and personal property, and to full and equal benefit of all laws and proceedings for the security of person and property, as is enjoyed by white citizens, and shall be subject to like punishments, pains, and penalties, and to no other.

Although the Fourteenth Amendment's equal protection clause is less detailed, Congress reaffirmed in Section 5 of that amendment its "power to enforce" the amendment with "appropriate legislation," such as the Civil Rights Act of 1866 and the Civil Rights Act of 1875, which barred racial discrimination in public accommodations.

In the face of congressional efforts to legislate away white prejudice, the Court defended and gave constitutional legitimacy to racial segregation. In *The Slaughterhouse Cases* (1873) (see Ch. 3), the Chase Court sharply limited the scope of the Fourteenth Amendment. There and in *Strauder v. West Virginia*, 100 U.S. 303 (1880), the Court gave the amendment narrow scope in eliminating racial discrimination. In *Strauder*, the Waite Court conceded the potential contributions of the Fourteenth Amendment. Strauder, a black man, sought to have his case moved from a state to a federal court because West Virginia barred blacks from serving on juries. When affirming his request, the Court observed that

> [t]he words of the amendment . . . contain a necessary implication of a positive immunity, or right, most valuable to the colored race—the right to exemption from unfriendly legislation against them distinctively as colored—exemption from legal distinctions, implying inferiority in civil society, lessening the security of their enjoyment of the rights which others enjoy, and discriminations which are steps towards reducing them to the condition of a subject race. . . . The very fact that colored people are singled out and expressly denied by statute all right to participate in the administration of the law, as jurors, because of their color, though they are citizens, and may be in other respects fully qualified, is practically a brand upon them, affixed by the law, an assertion of their inferiority, and a stimulant to that race prejudice which is an impediment to securing to individuals of that race that equal justice which the law aims to secure to all others.

That same year in *Ex Parte Virginia*, 100 U.S. 339 (1879), the Waite Court again indicated that practices might be made to conform to the promise "*No state* shall . . . deny to any person . . . the equal protection of the laws." This case involved a Virginia judge charged with violating federal law for excluding blacks from juries. He countered that, because the state had no law excluding blacks from juries, his actions though official did not constitute "state action" in violation of the amendment. Rejecting that argument, the Waite Court held that the amendment barred government "agencies" and "officials" from denying the equal protection of the laws.

Three years later, however, the Waite Court turned state action into a barrier for eliminating racial discrimination. In the *Civil Rights Cases* (1883) (see excerpt below), the Court held that Section 5 of the Fourteenth Amendment only authorized Congress to enact legislation barring racial discrimination that resulted from state action—state laws or actions done "under the color of state laws." Congress, in the Court's view, was not authorized to enact the Civil Rights Act of 1875 or to forbid racial discrimination by individuals and corporations in public accommodations.[3] The state action doctrine thus became a vehicle for perpetuating racial discrimination and segregation.

The *Civil Rights Cases* undercut congressional power and legitimated private racial discrimination. The Fuller Court, then, gave legitimacy to the doctrine of "separate but equal" facilities for blacks and whites in *Plessy v. Ferguson* (1896) (see excerpt below). Whereas forty years earlier in *Dred Scott* Chief Justice Taney had no doubts about the inferior status of blacks, in *Plessy* Justice Brown denied that the doctrine of separate but equal implied "the inferiority of either race."

The Court's rulings in the late nineteenth century returned control over race relations to the states. By the turn of the twentieth century, the states of the old Confederacy had largely disenfranchised blacks (see Vol. 1, Ch. 8) and erected a system of racial segregation. Blacks were separated from whites in public schools, government office buildings, public parks, and recreational areas, as well as hotels, restaurants, theaters, and other places of public accommodations.

The Court and the country did not begin to change until well into the twentieth century. In a few early cases, the Court led the way, striking down laws aimed at denying blacks' voting rights,[4] some racial zoning laws,[5] and recognizing the inequities of racially segregated educational facilities.[6] But only after the battle over the New Deal in 1937 and the period surrounding World War II did the federal government undertake the long process of dismantling the system of racial segregation. In 1939, Democratic president Franklin Roosevelt created a Civil Liberties Unit within the Department of Justice and later issued an executive order creating a Committee on Fair Employment Practices with authority over businesses working for the federal gov-

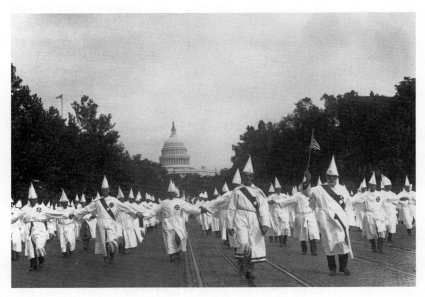

Founded in 1866 for the purpose of terrorizing black people, the Ku Klux Klan (KKK) experienced a rebirth in the early twentieth century. Here, in 1925 an estimated 40,000 KKK followers march in the nation's capital in celebration of white supremacy. (*Bettmann/Corbis via Getty Images.*)

ernment.[7] More significant were the executive orders issued by FDR's successor, President Harry Truman. In 1948, he boldly ordered an end to racial segregation in the military,[8] established the Fair Employment Board, and outlawed racial discrimination in the federal government.

Congress remained unwilling to act, and the actions of FDR and Truman provoked rebellion within the Democratic Party. In 1948 Alabama, Louisiana, Mississippi, and South Carolina left the Democratic Party to form the Dixiecrat Party. But Roosevelt's and Truman's appointments to the Court contributed to the shifting tide in constitutional politics after World War II. FDR elevated Justice Stone to the chief justiceship and named eight justices between 1937 and 1943: Hugo Black in 1937, Stanley Reed in 1938, Felix Frankfurter and William Douglas in 1939, Frank Murphy in 1940, James Byrnes and Robert Jackson in 1941, and Wiley Rutledge in 1943. Truman then appointed Chief Justice Fred Vinson in 1946 and Justices Harold Burton (in 1945) and Thomas Clark and Sherman Minton (in 1949).[9]

In the 1940s and 1950s, litigation brought by the National Association for the Advancement of Colored People (NAACP) pushed the Court into a leading role in the process of ending racial segregation. When striking down restrictive covenants in *Shelley v. Kraemer* (1948) (see excerpt below), the Court turned the state action doctrine into an instrument for prohibiting private racial discrimination.[10] The state action doctrine, which had supported systems of racial discrimination, became a tool for the Court to reach and ban private racial discrimination.

In the two decades following *Shelley*, the Court never denied relief on the grounds that no state action was present. In *Burton v. Wilmington Parking Authority*, 365 U.S. 715 (1961), for example, the Warren Court applied the state action doctrine to a restaurant denying service to blacks. It did so on the grounds that the restaurant, although privately owned, was located in a publicly owned parking garage and that public property could not be leased in a manner inconsistent with the Fourteenth Amendment. In *Evans v. Newton*, 382 U.S. 296 (1966), the Warren Court held that the equal protection clause was violated by Macon, Georgia's, "whites only" public park. The land for the park was deeded to the city in 1911 with the stipulation that it be used for a park "for whites only." Although the city resigned as the trustee for the park, and private trustees were appointed, the Court held that the Fourteenth Amendment applied under its new formulation of the state action doctrine. The Court then unanimously struck down Alabama's system of racially segregated prisons in *Lee v. Washington*, 390 U.S. 333 (1968), and in *Hunter v. Erickson*, 393 U.S. 385 (1969), overturned an ordinance barring fair housing practices.

The civil rights movement gathered momentum in the late 1950s and 1960s. Under the leadership of Dr. Martin Luther King Jr., thousands of protesting blacks defied segregation in restaurants and other public accommodations. When blacks started sit-ins at luncheon counters and restaurants, they were arrested for trespassing on private property or for breach of the peace. Media attention increasingly focused on the struggles of the civil rights movement following the arrest in Montgomery, Alabama, of Rosa Parks. Parks, a forty-two-year-old black woman, was arrested for taking a seat in the section reserved for whites on a public bus and became a symbol for generations. Yet, the Warren Court largely left it to the lower federal courts, the president, and Congress to deal with the controversy over segregated public accommodations. Even in its watershed ruling on school desegregation, in *Brown v. Board of Education of Topeka, Kansas,* 347 U.S. 483 (1954) (excerpted in Section B), the Court did not expressly overrule *Plessy v. Ferguson* (1896) (excerpted below). *Brown,* nonetheless, symbolically and effectively laid to rest *Plessy*'s doctrine of "separate but equal" facilities for blacks and whites. Two years after *Brown,* when Montgomery, Alabama's system of segregated seating on buses was challenged, in *Browder v. Gayle,* 142 F.Supp. 707 (M.D. Ala., 1956), a three-judge federal district court split 2-to-1 in holding that *Brown* had "impliedly, though not explicitly, overruled" *Plessy.* And when that ruling was appealed in *Gayle v. Browder,* 352 U.S. 903 (1956), the Warren Court simply affirmed the lower court in a one-line *per curiam* opinion, which notably cited *Brown.*

The Warren Court was reluctant to extend the state action doctrine to reach segregated lunch counters and restaurants. Although overturning convictions of civil rights "sitters-in," it did so without relying on the state action doctrine.[11] In *Bell v. Maryland,* 378 U.S. 226 (1964), for example, the convictions of twelve sit-in protesters were overturned on the grounds that Maryland's newly enacted antidiscrimination law might be applied by state courts to abate the prosecutions. Concurring Chief Justice Warren and Justices Douglas and Goldberg also argued that because the restaurant was "property that is serving the public" it could not discriminate against blacks. But dissenting Justice Black, joined by Justices Harlan and White, contended that Congress, not the Court, had the power under the Fourteenth Amendment to ban segregated public accommodations. Justice Black worried about the scope of the state action doctrine and remained unwilling to extend the equal protection clause to the practice of racial discrimination by owners of restaurants.

The controversy within the Warren Court over whether the state action doctrine applied to restaurants and other public accommodations was settled by the president and Congress. Almost a hundred years after the Civil Rights Act of 1875, Congress finally addressed the issue of segregated public accommodations. In response to the massive southern resistance to school desegregation and the violent reactions to the pressures for change brought by the civil rights movement, Democratic president John F. Kennedy proposed new aggressive civil rights legislation.[12] Following Kennedy's assassination, President Lyndon Johnson pushed the Civil Rights Act of 1964 and other legislation through Congress.[13] Besides limiting the use of literacy tests for voters (see Vol. 1, Ch. 8) and authorizing the Department of Justice to challenge segregated public facilities, the Civil Rights Act of 1964 in Title II forbade racial discrimination in public accommodations and in Title VII outlawed discrimination in employment.

Since the *Civil Rights Cases* had held that state action limited congressional power under the Fourteenth Amendment, Congress passed the Civil Rights Act of 1964 on its authority under the commerce clause (see Vol. 1, Ch. 6). When the constitutionality of the Civil Rights Act of 1964 was challenged, the Warren Court upheld it in *Heart of Atlanta Motel, Inc. v. United States* (1964) and *Katzenbach v. McClung* (1964) (both in Vol. 1, Ch. 6). The Court upheld as well the Voting Rights Act of 1965, banning racial discrimination in elections, in *South Carolina v. Katzenbach*, 383 U.S.301 (1966) (see Vol. 1, Ch. 8). Ironically, in the year that Congress passed the Civil Rights Act of 1968, forbidding discrimination in the sale, rental, financing, and advertising of housing, the Warren Court also construed the Civil Rights Act of 1866 to ban private racial discrimination in housing and affirmed Congress's authority to enact such legislation under the Thirteenth Amendment. In *Jones v. Alfred H. Mayer Co.*, 392 U.S. 409 (1968), the Court finally accepted the view of Justice Harlan dissenting in the *Civil Rights Cases*, that the Thirteenth Amendment proscribes all "badges and incidents" of slavery. In *McLaughlin v. Florida*, 379 U.S. 184 (1964), and *Loving v. Virginia*, 388 U.S. 1 (1967), the Court struck down state miscegenation laws, which barred interracial marriages.

The civil rights revolution embittered southern Democrats and some Republicans. In the 1968 presidential election, Republican candidate Richard Nixon campaigned against the "egalitarian jurisprudence" of the Warren Court, promising to appoint strict constructionists to the bench as part of his "southern strategy" to win the votes of southern white voters. With his election, a brief and dramatic period of social and legal change gradually came to an end. Nixon made his mark by appointing Chief Justice Warren Burger in 1969 and Justices Harry Blackmun in 1971 and Lewis F. Powell and William Rehnquist in 1972.

With the Burger Court (1969–1986) came changes. It drew the line on further extension of earlier rulings, but it also confronted new

■ CONSTITUTIONAL HISTORY

Loving v. Virginia *and Bans on Interracial Marriage*

In *Loving v. Virginia*, 388 U.S. 1 (1967), the Supreme Court struck down bans on interracial marriage; in many states it was a criminal offense. The Court held that states' refusal to recognize interracial marriages violated a fundamental right protected by the Fourteenth Amendment's due process and equal protection clauses.

Notably, in *Loving* the Court made no mention of the "full faith and credit" clause of Article IV of the Constitution, which requires states to honor court decisions of other states. Indeed, prior to the 1967 ruling there was a patchwork of laws on interracial marriages. In 1952, thirty states prohibited interracial marriages. But by the time *Loving* came down fourteen states had repealed their laws against interracial marriage. Moreover, states were not constitutionally compelled to recognize interracial marriages in other states. Some did and some did not, and it often depended on the circumstances and the issues at stake. State courts were almost evenly divided, for example, in recognizing legally married interracial couples in other states when the couple, after years of marriage, moved to a state barring interracial marriages. If a legally married interracial couple in one state, however, sought recognition in another state

controversies (involving, for example, affirmative action programs, as examined in Section C of this chapter) that would not have arisen were it not for the civil rights revolution of the 1960s. In *James v. Valtierra*, 402 U.S. 137 (1971), for instance, a bare majority upheld a law requiring qualified voters to approve low-cost housing projects, over the objection of the dissenters, that sanctioned racial segregation in housing. However, in *Hills v. Gautreaux*, 425 U.S. 284 (1976), the Court approved a lower court's order for the adoption of a comprehensive metropolitan plan for desegregating Chicago's public housing system.

The state action doctrine was given new twists and limited during the Burger Court years. The Court held that a restaurant's refusal to serve a white woman in the company of blacks was state action.[14] But *Evans v. Abney*, 396 U.S. 435 (1970), signaled that the Burger Court would limit the scope of the state action doctrine. There, once again

that barred interracial marriage for the purpose of suing for injuries, damage to property, or inheritance, state courts tended to recognize the interracial marriage, in spite of state laws against such marriages.

■ States with interracial marriage prohibition laws that were struck down in 1967.

■ States that had interracial marriage prohibitions in 1952 but repealed their laws before the 1967 decision.

□ States without interracial marriage prohibition laws.

the justices confronted the continuing controversy over Macon, Georgia's all-white park. After the Warren Court's ruling in *Evans v. Newton* (1966), the heirs of the donor of the park reclaimed the land on the grounds that the donor's will was not honored, because it expressly conditioned use of the land for whites only. The Burger Court upheld a state court's decision returning the land and found no state action to trigger the Fourteenth Amendment. In 1971, then, a bare majority of the Burger Court upheld the decision of Jackson, Mississippi, to close, rather than desegregate, the city's public swimming pools. Justices Douglas, Brennan, Marshall, and White dissented from that ruling in *Palmer v. Thompson*, 403 U.S. 217 (1971).

In *Moose Lodge No. 107 v. Irvis*, 407 U.S. 163 (1972), the Burger Court refused to apply the state action doctrine to a private club that refused to serve blacks, even though it had a state liquor license. Writing for the majority, Justice Rehnquist explained that

[t]he Court has never held, of course, that discrimination by an otherwise private entity would be violative of the equal protection clause if the private entity receives any sort of benefit or service at all from the State, or if it is subject to state regulation in any degree whatever. Since state-furnished services include such necessities of life as electricity, water, and police and fire protection, such a holding would utterly emasculate the distinction between private as distinguished from State conduct set forth in *The Civil Rights Cases* and adhered to in subsequent decisions. Our holdings indicate that where the impetus for the discrimination is private, the State must have "significantly involved itself with invidious discriminations," . . . in order for the discriminatory action to fall within the ambit of the constitutional prohibition.

By narrowing the scope of the state action doctrine, the Burger Court enlarged the range of private activities immune from suits under the Fourteenth Amendment. It did so by limiting the public function theory that underlies the doctrine of state action. Whereas the Warren Court looked at the totality of interrelationships between government and private activities, the Burger and Rehnquist Courts generally scrutinized and dismissed various arguments for extending the doctrine of state action. With those exceptions already noted, though, the Court has refused to extend the state action doctrine primarily in cases *not* involving claims of racial discrimination.

In one area—that of racially based peremptory challenges in jury selection—however, the Rehnquist Court vigorously enforced the Fourteenth Amendment and the state action doctrine. In *Batson v. Kentucky*, 476 U.S. 79 (1986) (excerpted in Ch. 9), dissenting Justice Rehnquist argued that "there is simply nothing 'unequal' about the State using its peremptory challenges to strike blacks from" juries trying black defendants. Yet, by a 7–2 vote (with Chief Justice Rehnquist and Justice Scalia dissenting) in *Powers v. Ohio*, 499 U.S. 400 (1991), the Court held that criminal defendants may claim a violation of the Fourteenth Amendment's equal protection when objecting to a prosecutor's race-based exclusion of jurors through the use of peremptory challenges during jury selection. A majority of the Court then went even further in *Edmonson v. Leesville Concrete Co.*, 500 U.S. 614 (1991), holding that parties in civil cases may not use peremptory challenges to exclude blacks from serving on juries. Writing for a six-member majority, Justice Kennedy found that the state action doctrine precludes such racial discrimination in civil cases and held that the Fifth Amendment's due process clause incorporated that holding and made it applicable to civil cases filed in federal courts as well.

Subsequently, in *Georgia v. McCollum*, 505 U.S. 42 (1992), the Court extended *Edmonson* to bar the use of peremptory challenges in criminal cases to exclude potential jurors on the basis of race. Once again, Justices O'Connor and Scalia dissented, while Chief Justice Rehnquist and Justice Thomas concurred even though they disagreed with the ruling there and in *Edmonson*. Yet only Justices Scalia and Thomas dissented from the further extension of the *Batson*-line of cases in *Campbell v. Louisiana*, 523 U.S. 392 (1998). There, Justice Kennedy held that a white defendant could challenge the selection process for grand jury forepersons for racial bias, because between 1976 and 1993 no black served as foreperson even though more than 20 percent of the voters in the Parish were black.

Another notable controversy arose in *Bob Jones University v. United States* and *Goldsboro Christian Schools, Inc. v. United States*, 461 U.S. 574 (1983). There the Court upheld the policy decision of the Internal Revenue Service denying tax-exempt status to private schools that racially discriminate. In his opinion for the Court, Chief Justice Burger conceded that the "[d]enial of tax benefits will inevitably have a substantial impact on the operation of private religious schools."

However, in *Bazemore v. Friday*, 478 U.S. 385 (1986), speaking for a bare majority Justice White held that the "affirmative duty to desegregate" had no application to 4-H and Homemaker Clubs, which were segregated until 1965 and run by the North Carolina Agricultural Extension Service. He observed that "[w]hile school children must go to school, there is no compulsion to join 4-H or Homemaker Clubs, and . . . there is no statutory or regulatory authority to deny a young person the right to join any Club he or she wishes to join."

The state action doctrine, nevertheless, became less important for striking down private racial discrimination after *Jones v. Alfred H. Mayer Co.*, 392 U.S. 409 (1968), held that Congress intended to forbid private racial discrimination in the Civil Rights Act of 1866 and that it had the authority to do so under the Thirteenth Amendment. The Court, furthermore, extended that ruling and reinforced the Civil Rights Act of 1866 as a barrier to private racial discrimination in housing, schools, and employment,[15] whenever there is proof of intentional discrimination.[16]

After *Alfred H. Mayer Co.*, the Court faced a number of important cases challenging the application of the Civil Rights Act of 1866. In *Runyon v. McCrary*, 427 U.S. 160 (1976), the Court held that the Civil Rights Act of 1866 extended to private schools that refuse to admit blacks. "It is now well established," Justice Stewart observed in his opinion for the Court, that the Civil Rights Act of 1866 "prohibits racial discrimination in the making and enforcement of private contracts."

Subsequently, the Court extended the protection of the Civil Rights Act of 1866 to Arabians and Jews upon concluding that "Jews and Arabs were among the people [in 1866] then considered to be distinct races and hence within the protection of the statute."[17] In 1987, however, the Rehnquist Court also indicated a move in more conservative directions by suggesting a willingness in *Patterson v. McLean Credit Union* to reconsider *Runyon v. McCrary.* But, ultimately, in *Patterson v. McLean Credit Union*, 491 U.S. 164 (1989), the Rehnquist Court decided that "no special justification has been shown for overruling *Runyon.*" In his opinion for the Court, Justice Kennedy explained that

> whether *Runyon*'s interpretation of [the Civil Rights Act of 1866] as prohibiting racial discrimination in the making and enforcement of private contracts is wrong or right as an original matter, it is certain that it is not inconsistent with the prevailing sense of justice in this country. To the contrary, *Runyon* is entirely consistent with our society's deep commitment to the eradication of discrimination based on a person's race or color of his or her skin.

Still, he refused to hold employers liable for racial harassment and discrimination as a condition of employment. The statute, in Justice Kennedy's words, covers "only conduct at the initial formation of the contract and conduct which impairs the right to enforce contract obligations through [the] legal process." Following *Patterson*, Congress expanded coverage of the Civil Rights Act of 1866 to forbid discrimination in all phases of employment and not merely in hiring practices.

■ The Development of Law

Other Rulings on State Action

CASE	VOTE	RULING
Jackson v. Metropolitan Edison Co., 419 U.S. 345 (1974)	6–3	Held that a privately owned electric company, operating under a state license, which terminated service to a customer, was not covered by the state action doctrine, in a suit brought by the customer, claiming a right to notice, a hearing, and the opportunity to pay past electric bills. Justices Douglas, Brennan, and Marshall dissented.

CASE	VOTE	RULING

Blum v. Yaretsky, 457 U.S. 991 (1982) — **7–2** — The Court rejected the argument that state subsidies to a private institution constituted state action and made the institution subject to the limitations of the Fourteenth Amendment; here, patients in a nursing home, who were transferred to another without notice or a hearing, claimed they were denied procedural due process; Justices Brennan and Marshall dissented.

San Francisco Arts & Athletics, Inc. v. United States Olympic Committee (USOC), 483 U.S. 522 (1987) — **5–4** — Held that the USOC was not a government actor, despite Congress's granting it the right to prohibit commercial and promotional uses of the word Olympic, and rejected the equal protection claims of the petitioner who was barred from calling its athletic competitions the "Gay Olympic Games"; Justices Brennan, Marshall, Blackmun, and O'Connor dissented.

National Collegiate Athletic Association (NCAA) v. Tarkanian, 488 U.S. 179 (1988) — **5–4** — Upheld the University of Nevada, Las Vegas's disciplinary actions against its head basketball coach in accordance with the NCAA's rules and ruled that the NCAA recommendations for disciplinary actions were not state action, and hence the NCAA was not liable for violating the coach's civil rights; Justice White, a former football player, was joined by Justices Brennan, Marshall, and O'Connor in dissent, finding the NCAA to be a state actor because it acted jointly with the University of Nevada.

Edmonson v. Leesville Concrete Co., 500 U.S. 614 (1991) — **6–3** — Held that the state action doctrine precludes the use of peremptory challenges to exclude blacks from serving on juries in civil cases. Justices O'Connor and Scalia, along with Chief Justice Rehnquist, dissented.

Brentwood Academy v. Tennessee Secondary School Athletic Association, 531 U.S. 288 (2001) — **5–4** — Held that the Tennessee Secondary Athletic Association is a "state actor" because of its pervasive en-

(continues)

■ The Development of Law
Other Rulings on State Action (continued)

---

twinement with state school officials. The association regulates interscholastic sports among Tennessee public and private high schools. Its
staff, although not state employees, may join the state retirement system, and the association sets membership standards and student eligibility rules, as well as has the power to penalize schools that violate its
rules. When the association penalized Brentwood Academy for violating its recruitment rules, Brentwood Academy sued, claiming that enforcement of the rule constituted state action that violated the First and
Fourteenth Amendments. Writing for the Court, Justice Souter reaffirmed that state action may be found when there exists a "close nexus
between the state and the challenged action" and when seemingly private behavior "may be fairly treated as that of the state itself," citing
Jackson v. Metropolitan Edison Co., 419 U.S. 345 (1974). Chief Justice
Rehnquist and Justices Kennedy, Scalia, and Thomas dissented.

Notes

1. See the excellent collection of writings of the Framers of the Constitution on
the matter of slavery in Philip Kurland and Ralph Lerner, eds., *The Founders' Constitution*, Vol. 1 (Chicago: University of Chicago Press, 1987), 495–576.

2. See also *Ableman v. Booth*, 62 U.S. 506 (1859).

3. See also *United States v. Cruikshank*, 92 U.S. 542 (1875).

4. See, for example, *Guinn v. United States*, 238 U.S. 347 (1915); and *Lane v. Wilson*,
307 U.S. 268 (1939) (striking down grandfather clauses denying voting rights to
most blacks). See also Vol. 1, Ch. 8.

5. See *Missouri ex. rel. Gaines v. Canada*, 305 U.S. 337 (1938).

6. See *Buchanan v. Warley*, 245 U.S. 60 (1917).

7. Exec. Order 8802, *Federal Register*, Vol. VI (1941), 3109.

8. Exec. Order 9981, *Federal Register*, Vol. XII (1948), 4313.

9. For a discussion of FDR's and Truman's appointments, see David M. O'Brien,
Storm Center: The Supreme Court in American Politics, 12th ed. (New York: W. W.
Norton & Company, 2020), chap. 2.

10. In *Reitman v. Mulkey*, 387 U.S. 369 (1967), a bare majority of the Warren Court
struck down California's restrictive covenant law.

11. See *Garner v. Louisiana*, 368 U.S. 157 (1961); *Bouie v. City of Columbia*, 378 U.S.
342 (1964); and *Barr v. City of Columbia*, 378 U.S. 146 (1964).

12. In 1957 and 1960, Congress enacted two other civil rights laws, but both
proved ineffective. See Carl Brauer, *John F. Kennedy and the Second Reconstruction*
(New York: Columbia University Press, 1977).

13. See James Harvey, *Black Civil Rights during the Johnson Administration* (Jackson: University and College Press of Mississippi, 1973).

14. *Adickes v. S. H. Kress & Co.*, 398 U.S. 144 (1970).

15. In addition to the cases discussed, see *Griffin v. Breckenridge*, 403 U.S. 88 (1971).

16. See *General Building Constructors Association, Inc. v. Pennsylvania*, 458 U.S. 375 (1982).

17. See *St Francis College v. Al-Khazraji*, 481 U.S. 604 (1987); and *Shaare Tefila Congregation v. Cobb*, 481 U.S. 615 (1987).

SELECTED BIBLIOGRAPHY

Allen, Austin. *Origins of the Dred Scott Case: Jacksonian Jurisprudence and the Supreme Court, 1837–1857*. Athens: University of Georgia Press, 2006.

Branch, Taylor. *Parting the Waters: America in the King Years, 1954–1963*. New York: Simon & Schuster, 1988.

————. *Pillar of Fire: America in the King Years, 1963–1965*. New York: Simon & Schuster, 1998.

————. *At Canaan's Edge: America in the King Years, 1965–1968*. New York: Simon & Schuster, 2006.

Brandwein, Pamela. *Reconstructing Reconstruction: The Supreme Court and the Production of Historical Truth*. Durham, NC: Duke University Press, 1999.

Cashin, Sheryll. *Loving: Interracial Intimacy in America and the Threat to White Supremacy*. Boston: Beacon Press, 2017.

Cortner, Richard C. *Civil Rights and Public Accommodations: The Heart of Atlanta Motel and McClung Cases*. Lawrence: University Press of Kansas, 2001.

Fehrenbacher, Don. *The Dred Scott Case: Its Significance in American Law and Politics*. New York: Oxford University Press, 1978.

Goldman, Robert. *Reconstruction and Black Suffrage: Losing the Vote in Reese and Cruikshank*. Lawrence: University Press of Kansas, 2001.

Goldstone, Lawrence. *Inherently Unequal: The Betrayal of Equal Rights by the Supreme Court, 1865–1903*. New York: Walker & Co., 2011.

Graber, Mark. *Dred Scott and the Problem of Constitutional Evil*. New York: Cambridge University Press, 2006.

Greenberg, Jack. *Race Relations and American Law*. New York: Columbia University Press, 1959.

Hampton, Henry, and Steve Fayer. *Voices of Freedom: An Oral History of the Civil Rights Movement from the 1960s through the 1980s*. New York: Bantam Books, 1990.

Hull Hoffer, Williamjames. *Plessy v. Ferguson: Race and Inequality in Jim Crow America*. Lawrence: University of Kansas Press, 2012.

Kennedy, Randall. *Interracial Intimacies: Sex, Marriage, Identity, and Adoption*. New York: Pantheon, 2003.

Klarman, Michael. *From Jim Crow to Civil Rights: The Supreme Court and the Struggle for Racial Equality*. New York: Oxford University Press, 2004.

Lofgren, Charles. *The Plessy Case*. New York: Oxford University Press, 1987.

Malcomson, Scott. *One Drop of Blood: The American Misadventures of Race*. New York: Farrar, Straus & Giroux, 2000.

Pascoe, Peggy. *What Comes Naturally: Miscegenation Law and the Making of Race in America*. New York: Oxford University Press, 2009.

tenBroek, Jacobus. *The Antislavery Origins of the Fourteenth Amendment*. Berkeley: University of California Press, 1951.

Tushnet, Mark. *The American Law of Slavery, 1810–1860*. Princeton, NJ: Princeton University Press, 1981.

Wallenstein, Peter. *Tell the Court I Love My Wife: Race, Marriage, and the Law—An American History*. New York: Palgrave Macmillan, 2002.

———. *Race, Sex, and the Freedom to Marry: Loving v. Virginia*. Lawrence: University of Kansas Press, 2014.

Dred Scott v. Sandford

19 How. (60 U.S.) 393 (1857)

In 1848, a Missouri slave, Dred Scott, sought to win his freedom in a lawsuit against the widow of John Emerson, his owner and an army medical officer. Scott contended that he had been emancipated as a result of Emerson's having taken him to live on military posts in Illinois and in federal territory north of 36°30' where slavery was outlawed by the Missouri Compromise of 1820. In that legislation, Congress admitted Maine into the Union as a free state and Missouri as a slave state, and banned slavery in all federal territories north of the line 36°30'.

The question Scott raised was whether his residence on free soil had changed his status as a slave. Prior to the 1830s, northern and southern states tried to accommodate each other's interests. Southerners were permitted to travel with their slaves in the North without interference, while southern courts upheld the rule that a slave temporarily domiciled in a free state became permanently free. But under the pressure of abolitionists in the 1830s and 1840s, this accommodation broke down. Northern states began denying southerners the privilege of traveling with their slaves and holding that slaves, who were not fugitives, became free once they were on free soil. Southern states in turn grew increasingly resentful and retaliated by refusing to enforce the antislavery law of other jurisdictions. So it was that after two trials and Scott's temporarily winning his freedom in 1852, the Missouri state supreme court held that it would no longer enforce the antislavery laws of other states and that Scott's residence on free soil did not change his status as a slave.

In a further effort to win Scott's freedom, his attorneys sought review by a federal circuit court in a lawsuit against Mrs. Emerson's brother and agent in the litigation, John Sanford of New York. (Sanford's name was misspelled as Sandford in the official records.) Since Sanford resided in another state than Scott, attorneys claimed that Scott's case fell within the federal court's diversity jurisdiction (jurisdiction over suits brought by citizens of different states). But their legal strategy raised a new issue: to bring a lawsuit in federal court, Scott had to show that he was a citizen. Sanford's attorneys countered that Negroes were not citizens in Missouri and therefore Scott had no standing to sue and the court lacked jurisdiction. The trial judge agreed that Scott's legal status depended on the law in Missouri, not his erstwhile residence in free territory, and a jury decided for Sanford.

Scott's lawyers next appealed to the Supreme Court, which included five southern Democrats, two northern Democrats, one northern Whig, and one Republican. During their oral arguments before the Court in February 1856, Sanford's attorneys raised an additional issue. They argued that not only was Scott a slave, not a citizen, but that he could not have become even temporarily a "freeman" by residing in a free territory because the Missouri Compromise was unconstitutional. That was a hotly debated political question sharply dividing the country, and the Court decided to hold the case over and hear rearguments in its next session.

On March 6, 1857, Chief Justice Roger Taney read from the bench his opinion for the Court: Scott lost. The chief justice held that Scott had no standing to sue in federal courts because he was not and could not be a citizen by virtue of the fact that he was a Negro and a slave. Taney proceeded to declare the antislavery provision of the Missouri Compromise unconstitutional. In sharply worded dissenting opinions, Justices John McLean and Benjamin Curtis took strong exception to the chief justice's sweeping opinion.

Chief Justice Taney's decision contributed to the ongoing struggle that erupted four years later in the Civil War. Despite the Court's ruling, Scott was soon freed by his owners, only to die a year and a half later. Two months after the ruling, Sanford also died, in an insane asylum. The constitutional effect of the ruling was also short lived. In 1862, Congress forbade slavery in all federal territories. Following the Civil War, the Thirteenth Amendment (1865), abolishing slavery, and the Fourteenth Amendment (1868) overturned Chief Justice Taney's ruling.

The Court's decision was 7–2, and the majority's opinion was announced by Chief Justice Taney. Justices Wayne, Nelson, Grier, Campbell, and Catron concurred; and Justices McLean and Curtis dissented.

■ ■ ■

☐ *Chief Justice TANEY delivered the opinion of the Court.*

[After reviewing the facts, Chief Justice TANEY first addressed the question of whether Scott was a citizen and entitled to bring his lawsuit.]

The question is simply this: can a negro, whose ancestors were imported into this country and sold as slaves, become a member of the political community formed and brought into existence by the Constitution of the United States, and as such become entitled to all the rights, and privileges, and immunities, guarantied [*sic*] by that instrument to the citizen. One of these rights is the privilege of suing in a court of the United States in the cases specified in the Constitution. . . .

The words "people of the United States" and "citizens" are synonymous terms, and mean the same thing. They both describe the political body, who, according to our republican institutions, form the sovereignty, and who hold the power and conduct the government through their representatives. They are what we familiarly call the "sovereign people," and every citizen is one of this people, and a constituent member of this sovereignty. The question before us is, whether the class of persons described in the plea in abatement compose a portion of this people, and are constituent members of this sovereignty. We think they are not, and that they are not included, and were not intended to be included, under the word "citizens" in the Constitution, and can, therefore, claim none of the rights and privileges which that instrument provides for and secures to citizens of the United States. On the contrary, they were at that time considered as a subordinate and inferior class of beings, who had been subjugated by the dominant race, and whether emancipated or not, yet remained subject to their authority, and had no rights or privileges but such as those who held the power and the government might choose to grant them.

It is not the province of the court to decide upon the justice or injustice, the policy or impolicy of these laws. The decision of that question belonged to the political or law-making power; to those who formed the sovereignty and framed the Constitution. The duty of the court is to interpret the instrument they have framed, with the best lights we can obtain on the subject, and to administer it as we find it, according to its true intent and meaning when it was adopted.

In discussing this question, we must not confound the rights of citizenship which a state may confer within its own limits, and the rights of citizenship as a member of the Union. It does not by any means follow, because he has all the rights and privileges of a citizen of a State, that he must be a citizen of the United States. He may have all the rights and privileges of the citizen of a State, and yet not be entitled to the rights and privileges of a citizen in any other State. For, previous to the adoption of the Constitution of the United States, every State had the undoubted right to confer on whomsoever it pleased the character of a citizen, and to endow him with all its rights. But this character, of course, was confined to the boundaries of the State, and gave him no rights or privileges in other States beyond those secured to him by the laws of nations and the comity of States. Nor have the several States surrendered the power of conferring these rights and privileges by adopting the Constitution of the United States. . . . The Constitution has conferred on Congress the right to establish an uniform rule of naturalization, and this right is evidently exclusive, and has always been held by this court to be so. Consequently, no State, since the adoption of the Constitution, can, by naturalizing an alien, invest him with the rights and privileges secured to a citizen of a State under the federal government, although, so far as the State alone was concerned, he would undoubtedly be entitled to the rights of a citizen, and clothed with all the rights and immunities which the Constitution and laws of the State attached to that character.

It is very clear, therefore, that no State can, by any Act or law of its own, passed, since the adoption of the Constitution, introduce a new member into the political community created by the Constitution of the United States. It cannot make him a member of this community by making him a member of its own. And for the same reason it cannot introduce any person, or description of persons, who were not intended to be embraced in this new political family, which the Constitution brought into existence, but were intended to be excluded from it. . . .

In the opinion of the court, the legislation and histories of the times, and the language used in the Declaration of Independence, show, that neither the class of persons who had been imported as slaves, nor their descendants, whether they had become free or not, were then acknowledged as a part of the people, nor intended to be included in the general words used in that memorable instrument.

It is difficult at this day to realize the state of public opinion in relation to that unfortunate race, which prevailed in the civilized and enlightened portions of the world at the time of the Declaration of Independence, and when the Constitution of the United States was framed and adopted. But the public history of every European nation displays it, in a manner too plain to be mistaken.

They had for more than a century before been regarded as beings of an inferior order; and altogether unfit to associate with the white race, either in social or political relations; and so far inferior, that they had no rights which the white man was bound to respect; and that the negro might justly and lawfully be reduced to slavery for his benefit. He was bought and sold, and treated as an ordinary article of merchandise and traffic, whenever a profit could be made by it. This opinion was at that time fixed and universal in the civilized portion of the white race. It was regarded as an axiom in morals as well as in politics, which no one thought of disputing, or supposed to be open to dispute; and men in every grade and position in society daily and habitually acted upon it in their private pursuits, as well as in matters of public concern, without doubting for a moment the correctness of this opinion. . . .

We refer to these historical facts for the purpose of showing the fixed opinions concerning that race, upon which the statesmen of that day spoke and acted. It is necessary to do this, in order to determine whether the general terms used in the Constitution of the United States, as to the rights of man and the rights of the people, was intended to include them, or to give to them or their posterity the benefit of any of its provisions.

The language of the Declaration of Independence is equally conclusive.

It begins by declaring that, "when in the course of human events it becomes necessary for one people to dissolve the political bands which have connected them with another, and to assume among the powers of the earth the separate and equal station to which the laws of nature and nature's God entitle them, a decent respect for the opinions of mankind requires that they should declare the causes which impel them to the separation."

It then proceeds to say: "We hold these truths to be self-evident: that all men are created equal; that they are endowed by their Creator with certain [un]alienable rights; that among them is life, liberty, and pursuit of happiness; that to secure these rights, governments are instituted, deriving their just powers from the consent of the governed."

The general words above quoted would seem to embrace the whole human family, and if they were used in a similar instrument at this day, would be so understood. But it is too clear for dispute, that the enslaved African race were not intended to be included, and formed no part of the people who framed and adopted this Declaration; for if the language, as understood in that day, would embrace them, the conduct of the distinguished men who framed the Declaration of Independence would have been utterly and flagrantly inconsistent with the principles they asserted; and instead of the sympathy of mankind, to which they so confidently appealed, they would have deserved and received universal rebuke and reprobation.

Yet the men who framed this Declaration were great men—high in literary acquirements—high in their sense of honor, and incapable of asserting principles inconsistent with those on which they were acting. They perfectly understood the meaning of the language they used, and how it would be understood by others; and they knew that it would not, in any part of the civilized world, be supposed to embrace the negro race. . . .

This state of public opinion had undergone no change when the Constitution was adopted, as is equally evident from its provisions and language. . . .

[T]here are two clauses in the Constitution which point directly and specifically to the negro race as a separate class of persons, and show clearly that they were not regarded as a portion of the people or citizens of the government then formed.

One of these clauses reserves to each of the thirteen States the right to import slaves until the year 1808, if it thinks proper. And the importation which it thus sanctions was unquestionably of persons of the race of which we are speaking, as the traffic in slaves in the United States had always been confined to them. And by the other provision the States pledge themselves to each other to maintain the right of property of the master, by delivering up to him any slave who may have escaped from his service, and be found within their respective territories. By the first above-mentioned clause, therefore, the right to purchase and hold this property is directly sanctioned and authorized for twenty years by the people who framed the Constitution. And by the second, they pledge themselves to maintain and uphold the right of the master in the manner specified, as long as the government they then formed should endure. And these two provisions show, conclusively, that neither the description of persons therein referred to, nor their descendants, were embraced in any of the other provisions of the Constitution; for certainly these two clauses were not intended to confer on them or their posterity the blessings of liberty, or any of the personal rights so carefully provided for the citizen. . . .

[U]pon a full and careful consideration of the subject, the court is of opinion that, upon the facts stated in the plea in abatement, Dred Scott was not a citizen of Missouri within the meaning of the Constitution of the United States, and not entitled as such to sue in its courts; and, consequently, that the Circuit Court had no jurisdiction of the case, and that the judgment on the plea in abatement is erroneous. . . .

[Chief Justice TANEY then turned to the question of whether Scott remained a slave after his trip into the Louisiana Territory.]

The Act of Congress, upon which the plaintiff relies, declares that slavery and involuntary servitude, except as a punishment for crime, shall be forever prohibited in all that part of that territory ceded by France, under the name of Louisiana, which lies north of thirty-six degrees thirty minutes north latitude, and not included within the limits of Missouri. And the difficulty which meets us at the threshold of this part of the inquiry is, whether Congress was authorized to pass this law under any of the powers granted to it by the Constitution; for if the authority is not given by that instrument, it is the duty of this court to declare it void and inoperative, and incapable of conferring freedom upon one who is held as a slave under the laws of any one of the States. . . .

[T]he power of Congress over the person or property of a citizen can never be a mere discretionary power under our Constitution and form of government. The powers of the government and the rights and privileges of the citizen are regulated and plainly defined by the Constitution itself. And when the territory becomes a part of the United States, the Federal Government enters into possession in the character impressed upon it by those who created it. It enters upon it with its powers over the citizen strictly defined, and limited by the Constitution, from which it derives its own existence, and by virtue of which alone it continues to exist and act as a government and sovereignty. It has no power of any kind beyond it; and it cannot, when it enters a territory of the United States, put off its character, and assume discretionary or despotic powers which the Constitution has denied to it. It cannot create for itself a new character separated from the citizens of the United States, and the duties it owes them under the provisions of the Constitution. The territory being a part of the United States, the government and the citizen both enter it under the authority of the Constitution, with their respective rights defined and marked out; and the Federal Government can exercise no power over his person or property, beyond what that instrument confers, nor lawfully deny any right which it has reserved. . . .

For example, no one, we presume, will contend that Congress can make any law in a territory respecting the establishment of religion or the free exercise thereof, or abridging the freedom of speech or of the press, or the right of the people of the territory peaceably to assemble and to petition the government for the redress of grievances. . . .

These powers, and others in relation to rights of person, which it is not necessary here to enumerate, are, in express and positive terms, denied to the general government; and the rights of private property have been guarded with equal care. Thus the rights of property are united with the rights of person, and placed on the same ground by the fifth amendment to the Constitution, which provides that no person shall be deprived of life, liberty and property, without due process of law. And an Act of

Congress which deprives a citizen of the United States of his liberty or property, merely because he came himself or brought his property into a particular Territory of the United States, and who had committed no offense against the laws, could hardly be dignified with the name of due process of law. . . .

Now, as we have already said in an earlier part of this opinion, upon a different point, the right of property in a slave is distinctly and expressly affirmed in the Constitution. The right to traffic in it, like an ordinary article of merchandise and property, was guaranteed to the citizens of the United States, in every State that might desire it, for twenty years. And the government in express terms is pledged to protect it in all future time, if the slave escapes from his owner. This is done in plain words—too plain to be misunderstood. And no word can be found in the Constitution which gives Congress a greater power over slave property, or which entitles property of that kind to less protection than property of any other description. The only power conferred is the power coupled with the duty of guarding and protecting the owner in his rights.

Upon these considerations, it is the opinion of the court that the Act of Congress which prohibited a citizen from holding and owning property of this kind in the territory of the United States north of the line therein mentioned, is not warranted by the Constitution, and is therefore void; and that neither Dred Scott himself, nor any of his family, were made free by being carried into this territory; even if they had been carried there by the owner, with the intention of becoming a permanent resident. . . .

[Finally, Chief Justice TANEY turned to whether Scott was made free by traveling to Illinois, a free state. He held that Scott's status was to be determined by Missouri law, and thus Scott remained a slave.]

□ *Justice McLEAN, dissenting.*

Being born under our Constitution and laws, no naturalization is required, as one of foreign birth, to make [Scott] a citizen. The most general and appropriate definition of the term citizen is "a freeman." Being a freeman, and having his domicile in a State different from that of the defendant, he is a citizen within the act of Congress, and the courts of the Union are open to him. . . .

It has been argued that, if a colored person be made a citizen of a State, he cannot sue in the Federal court. The Constitution declares that Federal jurisdiction "may be exercised between citizens of different States," and the same is provided in the act of 1789. The above argument is properly met by saying that the Constitution was intended to be a practical instrument; and where its language is too plain to be misunderstood, the argument ends." . . .

In the argument, it was said that a colored citizen would not be an agreeable member of society. This is more a matter of taste than of law. Several of the States have admitted persons of color to the right of suffrage, and in this view have recognized them as citizens; and this has been done in the slave as well as the free States. On the question of citizenship, it must be admitted that we have not been very fastidious. Under the late treaty with Mexico, we have made citizens of all grades, combinations, and colors. The same was done in the admission of Louisiana and Florida. No one ever doubted, and no court ever held, that the people of these Territories did not become citizens under the treaty. They have exercised all the rights of citizens, without being naturalized under the acts of Congress. . . .

I will now consider the relation which the Federal Government bears to slavery in the States: Slavery is emphatically a State institution. In the ninth section of the first article of the Constitution, it is provided "that the migration or importation of such persons as any of the States now existing shall think proper to admit, shall not be prohibited by the Congress prior to the year 1808, but a tax or duty may be imposed on such importation, not exceeding ten dollars for each person." . . .

The provision in regard to the slave trade shows clearly that Congress considered slavery a State institution, to be continued and regulated by its individual sovereignty; and to conciliate that interest, the slave trade was continued twenty years, not as a general measure, but for the "benefit of such States as shall think proper to encourage it." . . .

The only connection which the Federal Government holds with slaves in a State, arises from that provision of the Constitution which declares that "No person held to service or labor in one State, under the laws thereof, escaping into another, shall, in consequence of any law or regulation therein, be discharged from such service or labor, but shall be delivered up, on claim of the party to whom such service or labor may be due."

This being a fundamental law of the Federal Government, it rests mainly for its execution, as has been held, on the judicial power of the Union; and so far as the rendition of fugitives from labor has become a subject of judicial action, the Federal obligation has been faithfully discharged.

In the formation of the Federal Constitution, care was taken to confer no power on the Federal Government to interfere with this institution in the States. In the provision respecting the slave trade, in fixing the ratio of representation, and providing for the reclamation of fugitives from labor, slaves were referred to as persons, and in no other respect are they considered in the Constitution.

We need not refer to the mercenary spirit which introduced the infamous traffic in slaves, to show the degradation of negro slavery in our country. This system was imposed upon our colonial settlements by the mother country, and it is due to truth to say that the commercial colonies and States were chiefly engaged in the traffic. But we know as a historical fact, that James Madison, that great and good man, a leading member in the Federal Convention, was solicitous to guard the language of that instrument so as not to convey the idea that there could be property in man.

I prefer the lights of Madison, Hamilton, and Jay, as a means of construing the Constitution in all its bearings, rather than to look behind that period, into a traffic which is now declared to be piracy, and punished with death by Christian nations. I do not like to draw the sources of our domestic relations from so dark a ground. Our independence was a great epoch in the history of freedom; and while I admit the Government was not made especially for the colored race, yet many of them were citizens of the New England States, and exercised the rights of suffrage when the Constitution was adopted, and it was not doubted by any intelligent person that its tendencies would greatly ameliorate their condition. . . .

The power of Congress to establish Territorial Governments, and to prohibit the introduction of slavery therein, is the next point to be considered. . . .

On the 13th of July, the [Northwest] Ordinance of 1787 was passed, "for the government of the United States territory northwest of the river Ohio," with but one dissenting vote. This instrument provided there should be organized in the territory not less than three nor more than five States, designating their boundaries. It was passed while the Federal Convention was in session, about two months before the Constitution was adopted by the Convention. The members of the Convention must therefore have been well acquainted with the provisions of the Ordinance. It provided for a temporary Government, as initiatory to the formation of State Governments. Slavery was prohibited in the territory.

Can anyone suppose that the eminent men of the Federal Convention could have overlooked or neglected a matter so vitally important to the country, in the organization of temporary Governments for the vast territory northwest of the river Ohio? In the 3d section of the 4th article of the Constitution, they did make provision for the admission of new States, the sale of the public lands, and the temporary Government of the territory. Without a temporary Government, new States could not have been formed, nor could the public lands have been sold. . . .

The sovereignty of the Federal Government extends to the entire limits of our territory. Should any foreign power invade our jurisdiction, it would be repelled. There is a law of Congress to punish our citizens for crimes committed in districts of country where there is no organized Government. Criminals are brought to certain Territories or States, designated in the law, for punishment. Death has been inflicted in Arkansas and in Missouri, on individuals, for murders committed beyond the limit of any organized Territory or State; and no one doubts that such a jurisdiction was rightfully exercised. If there be a right to acquire territory, there necessarily must be an implied power to govern it. When the military force of the Union shall conquer a country, may not Congress provide for the government of such country? This would be an implied power essential to the acquisition of new territory. This power has been exercised, without doubt of its constitutionality, over territory acquired by conquest and purchase.

And when there is a large district of country within the United States, and not within any State Government, if it be necessary to establish a temporary Government to carry out a power expressly vested in Congress—as the disposition of the public lands—may not such Government be instituted by Congress? How do we read the Constitution? Is it not a practical instrument? . . .

The prohibition of slavery north of thirty-six degrees thirty minutes, and of the State of Missouri, contained in the act admitting that State into the Union, was passed by a vote of 134, in the House of Representatives, to 42. Before Mr. Monroe signed the act, it was submitted by him to his Cabinet, and they held the restriction of slavery in a Territory to be within the constitutional powers of Congress. It would be singular, if in 1804 Congress had power to prohibit the introduction of slaves in Orleans Territory from any other part of the Union, under the penalty of freedom to the slave, if the same power, embodied in the Missouri compromise, could not be exercised in 1820. . . .

If Congress may establish a Territorial Government in the exercise of its discretion, it is a clear principle that a court cannot control that discretion. This being the case, I do not see on what ground the act is held to be void. It did not purport to forfeit property, or take it for public purposes. It only prohibited slavery; in doing which, it followed the ordinance of 1787. . . .

I think the judgment of the court below should be reversed.

☐ *Justice CURTIS, dissenting.*

To determine whether any free persons, descended from Africans held in slavery, were citizens of the United States under the Confederation, and consequently at the time of the adoption of the Constitution of the United States, it is only necessary to know whether any such persons were citizens of either of the States under the Confederation, at the time of the adoption of the Constitution.

Of this there can be no doubt. At the time of the ratification of the Articles of Confederation, all free native-born inhabitants of the States of New Hampshire, Massachusetts, New York, New Jersey, and North Carolina, though descended from African slaves, were not only citizens of those States, but such of them as had the other necessary qualifications possessed the franchise of electors, on equal terms with other citizens. . . .

The fourth of the fundamental articles of the Confederation was as follows: "The free inhabitants of each of these States, paupers, vagabonds, and fugitives from justice, excepted, shall be entitled to all the privileges and immunities of free citizens in the several States." . . .

Did the Constitution of the United States deprive them or their descendants of citizenship?

That Constitution was ordained and established by the people of the United States, through the action, in each State, of those persons who were qualified by its laws to act thereon, in behalf of themselves and all other citizens of that State. In some of the States, as we have seen, colored persons were among those qualified by law to act on this subject. These colored persons were not only included in the body of "the people of the United States," by whom the Constitution was ordained and established, but in at least five of the States they had the power to act, and doubtless did act, by their suffrages, upon the question of its adoption. It would be strange, if we were to find in that instrument anything which deprived of their citizenship any part of the people of the United States who were among those by whom it was established.

I can find nothing in the Constitution which, *proprio vigore*, deprives of their citizenship any class of persons who were citizens of the United States at the time of its adoption, or who should be native-born citizens of any State after its adoption; nor any power enabling Congress to disfranchise persons born on the soil of any State, and entitled to citizenship of such State by its Constitution and laws. And my opinion is, that, under the Constitution of the United States, every free person born on the soil of a State, who is a citizen of that State by force of its Constitution or laws, is also a citizen of the United States. . . .

The conclusions at which I have arrived on this part of the case are:

First. That the free native-born citizens of each State are citizens of the United States.

Second. That as free colored persons born within some of the States are citizens of those States, such persons are also citizens of the United States.

Third. That every such citizen, residing in any State, has the right to sue and is liable to be used in the Federal courts, as a citizen of that State in which he resides.

Fourth. That as the plea to the jurisdiction in this case shows no facts, except that the plaintiff was of African descent, and his ancestors were sold as slaves, and as these facts are not inconsistent with his citizenship of the United States, and his residence in the State of Missouri, the plea to the jurisdiction was bad, and judgment of the Circuit Court overruling it was correct.

I dissent, therefore, from that part of the opinion of the majority of the court, in which it is held that a person of African descent cannot be a citizen of the United States; and I regret I must go further, and dissent both from what I deem their assumption of authority to examine the constitutionality of the act of Congress commonly called the Missouri compromise act, and the grounds and conclusions announced in their opinion. . . .

On what ground can it be denied that all valid laws of the United States, constitutionally enacted by Congress for the government of the Territory, rightfully extended over an officer of the United States and his servant who went into the Territory to remain there for an indefinite length of time, to take part in its civil or military affairs? They were not foreigners, coming from abroad. Dr. Emerson was a citizen of the country which had exclusive jurisdiction over the Territory; and not only a citizen, but he went there in a public capacity, in the service of the same sovereignty which made the laws. Whatever those laws might be, whether, of the kind denominated personal statutes, or not, so far as they were intended by the legislative will, constitutionally expressed, to operate on him and his servant, and on the relations between them, they had a rightful operation, and no other State or country can refuse to allow that those laws might rightfully operate on the plaintiff and his servant, because such a refusal would be a denial that the United States could, by laws constitutionally enacted, govern their own servants, residing on their own Territory, over which the United States had the exclusive control, and in respect to which they are an independent sovereign power. Whether the laws now in question were constitutionally enacted, I repeat once more, is a separate question. But, assuming that they were, and that they operated directly on the status of the plaintiff, I consider that no other State or country could question the rightful power of the United States so to legislate, or, consistently with the settled rules of international law, could refuse to recognise the effects of such legislation upon the status of their officers and servants, as valid everywhere. . . .

What, then, shall we say of the consent of the master, that the slave may contract a lawful marriage, attended with all the civil rights and duties which belong to that relation; that he may enter into a relation which none but a free man can assume—a relation which involves not only the rights and duties of the slave, but those of the other party to the contract, and of their descendants to the remotest generation? In my judgment, there can be no more effectual abandonment of the legal rights of a master over his slave, than by the consent of the master that the slave should enter into a contract of marriage, in a free State, attended by all the civil rights and obligations which belong to that condition. . . .

To avoid misapprehension on this important and difficult subject, I will state, distinctly, the conclusions at which I have arrived. They are:

First. The rules of international law respecting the emancipation of slaves, by the rightful operation of the laws of another State or country upon the status of the slave, while resident in such foreign State or country, are part of the common law of Missouri, and have not been abrogated by any statute law of that State.

Second. The laws of the United States, constitutionally enacted, which operated directly on and changed the status of a slave coming into the Territory of Wisconsin with his master, who went thither to reside for an indefinite length of time, in the performance of his duties as an officer of the United States, had a rightful operation on the status of the slave, and it is in conformity with the rules of international law that this change of status should be recognised everywhere.

Third. The laws of the United States, in operation in the Territory of Wisconsin at the time of the plaintiff's residence there, did act directly on the status of the plaintiff, and change his status to that of a free man.

Fourth. The plaintiff and his wife were capable of contracting, and, with the consent of Dr. Emerson, did contract a marriage in that Territory, valid its laws; and the validity of this marriage cannot be questioned in Missouri, save by showing that it was in fraud of the laws of that State, or of some right derived from them; which cannot be shown in this case, because the master consented to it.

Fifth. That the consent of the master that his slave, residing in a country which does not tolerate slavery, may enter into a lawful contract of marriage, attended with the civil rights and duties which belong to that condition, is an effectual act of emancipation. And the law does not enable Dr. Emerson, or any one claiming under him, to assert a title to the married persons as slaves, and thus destroy the obligation of the contract of marriage, and bastardize their issue, and reduce them to slavery. . . .

In my opinion, the judgment of the Circuit Court should be reversed, and the cause remanded for a new trial.

■ Constitutional History

Justice John Marshall Harlan and Our "Color-Blind Constitution"

In recent decades, bare majorities of the Rehnquist and Roberts Courts have invoked the idea that the "Constitution is color blind." See, for example, *City of Richmond v. J.A. Croson*, 488 U.S. 469 (1989) (excerpted in Section C of this chapter); and *Parents Involved in Community Schools v. Seattle School District No. 1*, 551 U.S. 701 (2007) (excerpted in Section B of this chapter). In doing so, they embrace the language of Justice John Marshall Harlan (1877–1911), dissenting from the majority's upholding of the doctrine of "separate but equal" in *Plessy v. Ferguson*, 163 U.S. 537 (1896) (excerpted below).

Justice Harlan had fought in the Civil War on the Union side but came from the slave-holding side of Kentucky and denounced the adoption of the Thirteenth and Fourteenth Amendments. Still, the lynching of African Americans during the Reconstruction weighed on him once on the Court and he became a supporter of civil rights. He was the sole dissenter in *Plessy* and in *The Civil Rights Cases*, 109 U.S. 3 (1883) (excerpted below), in which the majority struck down congressional efforts to implement the Civil War Amendments by banning discrimination in public accommodations and invited the Jim Crow era of "separate but equal."

In *Plessy*, writing for the majority, Justice Henry Brown swept broadly. Homer Plessy had challenged the practice of "separate but equal" as applied to railroad passenger cars. But Justice Brown distinguished between political and social equality. The former was supported by the Court, claimed Justice Brown, but the latter—equality in "schools, theatres, and railway carriages"—was a different matter. In his words: "If one race be inferior to the other socially, the Constitution of the United States cannot put them upon the same plane."

Dissenting in *Plessy*, Justice Harlan countered that "in view of the Constitution, in the eye of the law, there is in this country no superior, dominant, ruling class of citizens. There is no caste here. Our Constitution is color blind, and neither knows nor tolerates classes among citizens. . . ."

In fact, Justice Harlan did not originate the phrase "Our Constitution is color blind," but rather paraphrased language in a brief filed in *Plessy* that argued, "Justice is pictured and her daughter, the Law, ought at least to be color blind." The phrase nonetheless reflected his vision of the nation and his rationale in dissenting in *The Civil Rights Cases*.

The Civil Rights Cases

109 U.S. 3, 3 S.Ct. 18 (1883)

At issue in five cases, coming from California, Kansas, Missouri, New Jersey, and Tennessee, which were consolidated and decided together, was the constitutionality of Congress's passage of the Civil Rights Act of 1875. That legislation made it a *federal* crime for owners and operators of any public accommodation—schools, churches, cemeteries, hotels, places of amusement, and common carriers—to "deny the full enjoyment of the accommodations thereof" because of race or religion. Each of the cases involved challenges to the enforcement of the law against innkeepers, theater owners, and a railroad company.

With only Justice John Marshall Harlan dissenting, Justice Joseph Bradley held for the Court that Congress had no authority under the Thirteenth and Fourteenth Amendments to enact the Civil Rights Act of 1875 and had intruded on the powers reserved to the states by the Tenth Amendment. Moreover, Justice Bradley narrowly read the Thirteenth Amendment to only abolish slavery, but not private racial discrimination, and limited the Fourteenth Amendment to bar only racial discrimination backed by state action. By contrast, Justice Harlan pointed out that the Court previously upheld Congress's power to regulate the behavior of private individuals—notably, when upholding fugitive slave laws requiring the return of slaves to their owners. Also, in his view racial discrimination was a badge of servitude abolished by the Thirteenth Amendment and a matter on which Congress could legislate when enforcing the Thirteenth and Fourteenth Amendments. As a result of the majority's ruling, racist attitudes were reinforced and the basis was laid for states to pass Jim Crow laws requiring the separate treatment of blacks and whites in public accommodations.

The Court's decision was 8–1, and the majority's opinion was announced by Justice Bradley. Justice Harlan dissented.

■ ■ ■

☐ *Justice BRADLEY delivered the opinion of the Court.*

Has Congress constitutional power to make [the Civil Rights Act of 1875]? Of course, no one will contend that the power to pass it was contained in the constitution before the adoption of the last three amendments. The power is sought, first, in the Fourteenth Amendment, and the views and arguments of distinguished senators, advanced while the law was under consideration, claiming authority to pass it by virtue of that amendment, are the principal arguments adduced in favor of the power. . . .

The first section of the fourteenth amendment—which is the one relied on—after declaring who shall be citizens of the United States, and of the several states, is prohibitory in its character, and prohibitory upon the states. It declares that "no state shall make or enforce any law which shall abridge the privileges or immunities of citizens of the United States; nor shall any state deprive any person of life, liberty, or property without due process of law; nor deny to any person within its jurisdiction the equal protection of the laws." It is state action of a particular character that is prohibited. Individual invasion of individual rights is not the subject-matter of the amendment. It has a deeper and broader scope. It nullifies and makes void all state legislation, and state action of every kind, which impairs the privileges and immunities of citizens of the United States, or which injures them in life, liberty, or property without due process of law, or which denies to any of them the equal protection of the laws. It not only does this, but, in order that the national will, thus declared, may not be a mere *brutum fulmen*, the last section of the amendment invests congress with power to enforce it by appropriate legislation. To enforce what? To enforce the prohibition. To adopt appropriate legislation for correcting the effects of such prohibited state law and state acts, and thus to render them effectually null, void, and innocuous. This is the legislative power conferred upon congress, and this is the whole of it. It does not invest congress with power to legislate upon subjects which are within the domain of state legislation; but to provide modes of relief against state legislation, or state action, of the kind referred to. It does not authorize congress to create a code of municipal law for the regulation of private rights; but to provide modes of redress against the operation of state laws, and the action of state officers, executive or judicial, when these are subversive of the fundamental rights specified in the amendment. Positive rights and privileges undoubtedly secured by the fourteenth amendment; but they are secured by way of prohibition against state laws and state proceedings affecting those rights and privileges, and power given to congress to legislate for the purpose of carrying such prohibition into effect; and such legislation must necessarily be predicated upon such supposed state laws or state proceedings, and be directed to the correction of their operation and effect. . . .

And so in the present case, until some state law has been passed, or some state action through its officers or agents has been taken, adverse to the rights of citizens sought to be protected by the fourteenth amendment, no legislation of the United States under said amendment, nor any proceeding under such legislation, can be called into activity, for the prohibitions of the amendment are against state laws and acts done under state authority. Of course, legislation may and should be provided in advance to meet the exigency when it arises, but it should be adapted to the mischief and wrong which the amendment was intended to provide against; and that is, state laws or state action of some kind adverse to the rights of the citizen secured by the amendment. . . . In fine, the legislation which congress is authorized to adopt in this behalf is not general legislation upon the rights of the citizen, but corrective legislation; that is, such as may be necessary and proper for counteracting such laws as the states may adopt or enforce, and which by the amendment they are prohibited from making or enforcing, or such acts and proceedings as the states may commit or take, and which by the amendment they are prohibited from committing or taking. It is not necessary for us to state, if we could, what legislation would be proper for congress to adopt. It is sufficient for us to examine whether the law in question is of that character.

An inspection of the law shows that it makes no reference whatever to any supposed or apprehended violation of the fourteenth amendment on the part of the states. It is not predicated on any such view. It proceeds *ex directo* to declare that certain acts committed by individuals shall be deemed offenses, and shall be prosecuted and punished by proceedings in the courts of the United States. It does not profess to be corrective of any constitutional wrong committed by the states; it does not make its operation to depend upon any such wrong committed. It applies equally to cases arising in states which have the justest laws respecting the personal rights of citizens, and whose authorities are ever ready to enforce such laws as to those which arise in states that may have violated the prohibition of the amendment. In other words, it steps into the domain of local jurisprudence, and lays down rules for the conduct of individuals in society towards each other, and imposes sanctions for the enforcement of those rules, without referring in any manner to any supposed action of the state or its authorities.

If this legislation is appropriate for enforcing the prohibitions of the amendment, it is difficult to see where it is to stop. Why may not congress, with equal show of authority, enact a code of laws for the enforcement and vindication of all rights of life, liberty, and property? If it is supposable that the states may deprive persons of life, liberty, and property without due process of law, (and the amendment itself does suppose this,) why should not congress proceed at once to prescribe due process of law for the protection of every one of these fundamental rights, in every possible case, as well as to prescribe equal privileges in inns, public conveyances, and theaters. The truth is that the implication of a power to legislate in this manner is based upon the assumption that if the states are forbidden to legislate or act in a particular way on a particular subject, and power is conferred upon congress to enforce the prohibition, this gives congress power to legislate generally upon that subject, and not merely power to provide modes of redress against such state legislation or action. The assumption is certainly unsound. It is repugnant to the tenth amendment of the constitution, which declares that powers not delegated to the United States by the constitution, nor prohibited by it to the states, are reserved to the states respectively or to the people. . . .

In this connection it is proper to state that civil rights, such as are guaranteed by the constitution against state aggression, cannot be impaired by the wrongful acts of individuals, unsupported by state authority in the shape of laws, customs, or judicial or executive proceedings. The wrongful act of an individual, unsupported by any such authority, is simply a private wrong, or a crime of that individual; an invasion of the rights of the injured party, it is true, whether they affect his person, his property, or his reputation; but if not sanctioned in some way by the state, or not done under state authority, his rights remain in full force, and may presumably be vindicated by resort to the laws of the state for redress. . . .

But the power of congress to adopt direct and primary, as distinguished from corrective, legislation on the subject in hand, is sought, in the second place, from the thirteenth amendment, which abolishes slavery. This amendment declares "that neither slavery, nor involuntary servitude, except as a punishment for crime, whereof the party shall have been duly convicted, shall exist within the United States, or any place subject to their jurisdiction"; and it gives congress power to enforce the amendment by appropriate legislation.

This amendment, as well as the Fourteenth, is undoubtedly self-executing without any ancillary legislation, so far as its terms are applicable to any existing state of circumstances. By its own unaided force and effect it abolished slavery, and established universal freedom. Still, legislation may be necessary and proper to meet all the various cases and circumstances to be affected by it, and to prescribe proper modes of redress for its violation in letter or spirit. And such legislation may be primary and direct in its character; for the amendment is not a mere prohibition of state laws establishing or upholding slavery, but an absolute declaration that slavery or involuntary servitude shall not exist in any part of the United States. . . .

After giving to these questions all the consideration which their importance demands, we are forced to the conclusion that such an act of refusal has nothing to do with slavery or involuntary servitude, and that if it is violative of any right of the party, his redress is to be sought under the laws of the state; or, if those laws are adverse to his rights and do not protect him, his remedy will be found in the corrective legislation which congress has adopted, or may adopt, for counteracting the effect of state laws, or state action, prohibited by the Fourteenth Amendment. It would be running the slavery argument into the ground to make it apply to every act of discrimination which a person may see fit to make as to the guests he will entertain, or as to the people he will take into his coach or cab or car, or admit to his concert or theater, or deal with in other matters of intercourse or business. Innkeepers and public carriers, by the laws of all the states, so far as we are aware, are bound, to the extent of their facilities, to furnish proper accommodation to all unobjectionable persons who in good faith apply for them. If the laws themselves make any unjust discrimination, amenable to the prohibitions of the Fourteenth Amendment, Congress has full power to afford a remedy under that amendment and in accordance with it. . . .

There were thousands of free colored people in this country before the abolition of slavery, enjoying all the essential rights of life, liberty, and property the same as white citizens; yet no one, at that time, thought that it was any invasion of their personal *status* as freemen because they were not admitted to all the privileges enjoyed by white citizens, or because they were subjected to discriminations in the enjoyment of accommodations in inns, public conveyances, and places of amusement. Mere discriminations on account of race or color were not regarded as badges of slavery. If, since that time, the enjoyment of equal rights in all these respects has become established by constitutional enactment, it is not by force of the Thirteenth Amendment, (which merely abolishes slavery,) but by force of the Fourteenth and Fifteenth Amendments.

On the whole, we are of opinion that no countenance of authority for the passage of the law in question can be found in either the Thirteenth or Fourteenth amendment of the constitution; and no other ground of authority for its passage being suggested, it must necessarily be declared void, at least so far as its operation in the several states is concerned.

☐ *Justice HARLAN, dissenting.*

The opinion in these cases proceeds, as it seems to me, upon grounds entirely too narrow and artificial. The substance and spirit of the recent amendments of the constitution have been sacrificed by a subtle and ingenious verbal criticism. "It is not the words of the law but the internal sense of it that makes the law. The letter of the law is the body; the sense and reason of the law is the soul." Constitutional provisions, adopted in the interest of liberty, and for the purpose of securing, through national legislation, if need be, rights inhering in a state of freedom, and belonging to American citizenship, have been so construed as to defeat the ends the people desired to accomplish, which they attempted to accomplish, and which they supposed they had accomplished by changes in their fundamental law. By this I do not mean that the determination of these cases should have been materially controlled by considerations of mere expediency or policy. I mean only, in this form, to express an earnest conviction that the court has departed from the familiar rule requiring, in the interpretation of constitutional provisions, that full effect be given to the intent with which they were adopted. . . .

The Thirteenth Amendment, my brethren concede, did something more than to prohibit slavery as an *institution*, resting upon distinctions of race, and upheld by positive law. They admit that it established and decreed universal *civil freedom* throughout the United States. But did the freedom thus established involve nothing more than exemption from actual slavery? Was nothing more intended than to forbid one man from owning another as property? Was it the purpose of the nation simply to destroy the institution, and then remit the race, theretofore held in bondage, to the several states for such protection, in their civil rights, necessarily growing out of freedom, as those states, in their discretion, choose to provide? Were the states, against whose solemn protest the institution was destroyed, to be left perfectly free, so far as national interference was concerned, to make or allow discriminations against that race, as such, in the enjoyment of those fundamental rights that inhere in a state of freedom? . . .

That there are burdens and disabilities which constitute badges of slavery and servitude, and that the express power delegated to congress to enforce, by appropriate legislation, the Thirteenth Amendment, may be exerted by legislation of a direct and primary character, for the eradication, not simply of the institution, but of its badges and incidents, are propositions which ought to be deemed indisputable. They lie at the very foundation of the civil rights act of 1866. Whether that act was fully authorized by the Thirteenth amendment alone, without the support which it afterwards received from the Fourteenth Amendment, after the adoption of which it was re-enacted with some additions, the court, in its opinion, says it is unnecessary to inquire. But I submit, with all respect to my brethren, that its constitutionality is conclusively shown by other portions of their opinion. It is expressly conceded by them that the Thirteenth Amendment established freedom; that there are burdens and disabilities, the necessary incidents of slavery, which constitute its substance and visible form; that congress, by the act of 1866, passed in view of the Thirteenth Amendment, before the Fourteenth was adopted, undertook to remove certain burdens and disabilities, the necessary incidents of slavery, and to secure to all citizens of every race and color, and without regard to previous servitude, those fundamental rights which are the essence of civil freedom, namely, the same right to make and enforce contracts, to sue, be parties, give evidence, and to inherit, purchase, lease, sell, and convey property as is enjoyed by white citizens; that under the Thirteenth Amendment Congress has to do with slavery and its incidents; and that legislation, so far as necessary or proper to eradicate all forms and incidents of slavery and involuntary servitude, may be direct and primary, operating upon the acts of individuals, whether sanctioned by state legislation or not. These propositions being conceded, it is impossible, as it seems to me, to question the constitutional validity of the Civil Rights act of 1866. I do not contend that the Thirteenth Amendment invests congress with authority, by legislation, to regulate the entire body of the civil rights which citizens enjoy, or may enjoy, in the several states. But I do hold that since slavery, as the court has repeatedly declared, was the moving or principal cause of the adoption of that amendment, and since that institution rested wholly upon the inferiority, as a race, of those held in bondage, their freedom necessarily involved immunity from, and protection against, all discrimination against them, because of their race, in respect of such civil rights as belong to freemen of other races. . . .

What has been said is sufficient to show that the power of Congress under the Thirteenth Amendment is not necessarily restricted to legislation against slavery as an institution upheld by positive law, but may be exerted to the extent at least of protecting the race, so liberated, against discrimination, in respect of legal rights belonging to freemen, where such discrimination is based upon race. . . .

I also submit whether it can be said—in view of the doctrines of this court as announced in *Munn* v. *Illinois*, [94 U.S. 113 (1877)], that the management of places of public amusement is a purely private matter, with which government has no rightful concern. In the *Munn Case* the question was whether the state of Illinois could fix, by law, the maximum of charges for the storage of grain in certain warehouses in that state—the *private property of individual citizens*. . . .

The doctrines of *Munn* v. *Illinois* have never been modified by this court, and I am justified, upon the authority of that case, in saying that places of public amusement, conducted under the authority of the law, are clothed with a public interest, because used in a manner to make them of public consequence and to affect the community at large. The law may therefore regulate, to some extent, the mode in which they shall be conducted, and consequently the public have rights in respect of such places which may be vindicated by the law. It is consequently not a matter purely of private concern.

Congress has not, in these matters, entered the domain of state control and supervision. It does not assume to prescribe the general conditions and limitations under which inns, public conveyances, and places of public amusement shall be conducted or managed. It simply declares in effect that since the nation has established universal freedom in this country for all time, there shall be no discrimination, based merely upon race or color, in respect of the legal rights in the accommodations and advantages of public conveyances, inns, and places of public amusement.

I am of the opinion that such discrimination is a badge of servitude, the imposition of which congress may prevent under its power, through appropriate legislation, to enforce the Thirteenth Amendment; and consequently, without reference to its enlarged power under the Fourteenth Amendment, the act of March 1, 1875, is not, in my judgment, repugnant to the constitution. . . .

I agree that government has nothing to do with social, as distinguished from technically legal, rights of individuals. No government ever has brought, or ever can bring, its people into social intercourse against their wishes. Whether one person will permit or maintain social relations with another is a matter with which government has no concern. I agree that if one citizen chooses not to hold social intercourse with another, he is not and cannot be made amendable to the law for his conduct in that regard; for no legal right of a citizen is violated by the refusal of others to maintain merely social relations with him, even upon grounds of race. What I affirm is that no state, nor the officers of any state, nor any corporation or individual wielding power under state authority for the public benefit or the public convenience, can, consistently either with the freedom established by the fundamental law, or with that equality of civil rights which now belongs to every citizen, discriminate against freemen or citizens, in their civil rights, because of their race, or because they once labored under disabilities imposed upon them as a race. The rights which Congress, by the act of 1875, endeavored to secure and protect are legal, not social, rights. The right, for instance, of a colored citizen to use the accommodations of a public highway upon the same terms as are permitted to white citizens is no more a social right than his right, under the law, to use the public streets of a city, or a town, or a turnpike road, or a public market, or a post-office, or his right to sit in a public building with others, of whatever race, for the purpose of hearing the political questions of the day discussed. . . .

Today it is the colored race which is denied, by corporations and individuals wielding public authority, rights fundamental in their freedom and citizenship. At some future time it may be some other race that will fall under the ban. If the constitutional amendments be enforced, according to the intent with which, as I conceive, they were adopted, there cannot be, in this republic, any class of human beings in practical subjection to another class, with power in the latter to dole out to the former just such privileges as they may choose to grant. The supreme law of the land has decreed that no authority shall be exercised in this country upon the basis of discrimination, in respect of civil rights, against freemen and citizens because of their race, color, or previous condition of servitude. To that decree—for the due enforcement of which, by appropriate legislation, Congress has been invested with express power—every one must bow, whatever may have been, or whatever now are, his individual views as to the wisdom or policy, either of the recent changes in the fundamental law, or of the legislation which has been enacted to give them effect.

For the reasons stated I feel constrained to withhold my assent to the opinion of the Court.

Plessy v. Ferguson

163 U.S. 537, 3 S.CT. 18 (1896)

Four years after the Supreme Court struck down the Civil Rights Act of 1875 in the *Civil Rights Cases* (1883) (see excerpt above), Florida enacted the first "Jim Crow" law, requiring separate but equal facilities for blacks and whites in railway passenger cars. Louisiana and other states in the Deep South followed with similar laws. Blacks were embittered by the passage of these laws, but the Court adapted the Constitution to support racial discrimination by white legislative majorities. In *Louisville, New Orleans & Texas Pacific Railroad v. Mississippi*, 133 U.S. 587 (1890), the Court ruled that segregated railroad passenger cars traveling in intrastate commerce did not interfere with Congress's power to regulate interstate commerce under the commerce clause.

Louisiana's "Jim Crow" law was challenged in a test case brought by Homer Plessy, who was one-eighth black. When he boarded a railroad train in New Orleans, which was headed for Covington, Louisiana, he refused to sit in the car reserved for "Colored Only" and sat in one reserved for whites instead. He was arrested, convicted, and appealed to the Supreme Court. Plessy's attorneys contended that Louisiana's law violated the Thirteenth and Fourteenth Amendments.

The Supreme Court rejected Plessy's arguments. Note the sharply different interpretations of the Constitution and social attitudes in the majority's opinion by Justice Henry Brown and in the sole dissenting opinion by Justice John Harlan. Whereas Justice Brown dismisses the claim that the state's action violates the Thirteenth Amendment as "too clear for argument," Justice Harlan has no doubt that compulsory racial segregation imposed precisely the kind of badge of servitude that the amendment aimed to outlaw. Justice Brown's treatment of the Fourteenth Amendment claim is also far from cogent. Although allowing that the amendment "was undoubtedly to enforce the absolute equality of the two races before the law," he adds that "in the nature of things it could not have been intended to abolish distinctions based on color." For the Court's majority, racial segregation was not discriminatory and did not "necessarily imply the inferiority of either race to the other," but rather a reasonable exercise of state police power "for the promotion of the public good, and not for the annoyance or oppression of a particular class." By contrast, Justice Harlan conceived of all forms of racial discrimination to constitute invidious discrimination under the Fourteenth Amendment.

The Court's decision was 7–1, and the majority's opinion was announced by Justice Brown, with Justice Brewer not participating. Justice Harlan delivered a dissenting opinion.

■ ■ ■

☐ *Justice BROWN delivered the opinion of the Court.*

This case turns upon the constitutionality of an act of the general assembly of the state of Louisiana, passed in 1890, providing for separate railway carriages for the white and colored races. . . .

The constitutionality of this act is attacked upon the ground that it conflicts both with the Thirteenth Amendment of the Constitution, abolishing slavery, and the Fourteenth Amendment, which prohibits certain restrictive legislation on the part of the states.

1. That it does not conflict with the Thirteenth Amendment, which abolished slavery and involuntary servitude, except as a punishment for crime, is too clear for argument. Slavery implies involuntary servitude—a state of bondage; the ownership of mankind as a chattel, or, at least, the control of the labor and services of one man for the benefit of another, and the absence of a legal right to the disposal of his own person, property, and services. . . .

2. . . . The object of the [Fourteenth] Amendment was undoubtedly to enforce the absolute equality of the two races before the law, but, in the nature of things, it could not have been intended to abolish distinctions based upon color, or to enforce social, as distinguished from political, equality, or a commingling of the two races upon terms unsatisfactory to either. Laws permitting, and even requiring, their separation, in places where they are liable to be brought into contact, do not necessarily imply the inferiority of either race to the other, and have been generally, if not universally, recognized as within the competency of the state legislatures in the exercise of their police power. The most common instance of this is connected with the establishment of separate schools for white and colored children, which have been held to be a valid exercise of the legislative power even by courts of states where the political rights of the colored race have been longest and most earnestly enforced. . . .

In this connection, it is also suggested by the learned counsel for the plaintiff in error that the same argument that will justify the state legislature in requiring railways to provide separate accommodations for the two races will also authorize them to require separate cars to be provided for people whose hair is of a certain color, or who are aliens, or who belong to certain nationalities, or to enact laws requiring colored people to walk upon one side of the street, and white people upon the other, or requiring white men's houses to be painted white, and colored men's black, or their vehicles or business signs to be of different colors, upon the theory that one side of the street is as good as the other, or that a house or vehicle of one color is as good as one of another color. The reply to all this is that every exercise of the police power must be reasonable, and extend only to such laws as are enacted in good faith for the promotion of the public good, and not for the annoyance or oppression of a particular class. . . .

So far, then, as a conflict with the Fourteenth Amendment is concerned, the case reduces itself to the question whether the statute of Louisiana is a reasonable regulation, and with respect to this there must necessarily be a large discretion on the part of the legislature. In determining the question of reasonableness, it is at liberty to act with reference to the established usages, customs, and traditions of the people, and with a view to the promotion of their comfort, and the preservation of the public peace and good order. Gauged by this standard, we cannot say that a law which authorizes or even requires the separation of the two races in public conveyances is unreasonable, or more obnoxious to the Fourteenth Amendment than the acts of Congress requiring separate schools for colored children in the District of Columbia, the constitutionality of which does not seem to have been questioned, or the corresponding acts of state legislatures.

We consider the underlying fallacy of the plaintiff's argument to consist in the assumption that the enforced separation of the two races stamps the colored race with a badge of inferiority. If this be so, it is not by reason of anything found in the act, but solely because the colored race chooses to put that construction upon it. The argument necessarily assumes that if, as has been more than once the case, and is not unlikely to be so again, the colored race should become the dominant power in the state legislature, and should enact a law in precisely similar terms, it would thereby relegate the white race to an inferior position. We imagine that the white race, at least, would not acquiesce in this assumption. The argument also assumes that social prejudices may be overcome by legislation, and that equal rights cannot be secured to the negro except by an enforced commingling of the two races. We cannot accept this proposition. If the two races are to meet upon terms of social equality, it must be the result of natural affinities, a mutual appreciation of each other's merits, and a voluntary consent of individuals. . . .

Legislation is powerless to eradicate racial instincts, or to abolish distinctions based upon physical differences, and the attempt to do so can only result in accentuating the difficulties of the present situation. If the civil and political rights of both races be equal, one cannot be inferior to the other civilly or politically. If one race be inferior to the other socially, the constitution of the United States cannot put them upon the same plane.

□ *Justice HARLAN, dissenting.*

In respect of civil rights, common to all citizens, the constitution of the United States does not, I think, permit any public authority to know the race of those entitled to be protected in the enjoyment of such rights. Every true man has pride of race, and under appropriate circumstances, when the rights of others, his equals before the law, are not to be affected, it is his privilege to express such pride and to take such action based upon it as to him seems proper. But I deny that any legislative body or judicial tribunal may have regard to the race of citizens when the civil rights of those citizens are involved. Indeed, such legislation as that here in question is inconsistent not only with that equality of rights which pertains to citizenship, national and state, but with the personal liberty enjoyed by every one within the United States. . . .

It was said in argument that the statute of Louisiana does not discriminate against either race, but prescribes a rule applicable alike to white and colored citizens. But this argument does not meet the difficulty. Every one knows that the statute in question had its origin in the purpose, not so much to exclude white persons from railroad cars occupied by blacks, as to exclude colored people from coaches occupied by or assigned to white persons. . . .

It is one thing for railroad carriers to furnish, or to be required by law to furnish, equal accommodations for all whom they are under a legal duty to carry. It is quite another thing for government to forbid citizens of the white and black races from traveling in the same public conveyance, and to punish officers of railroad companies for permitting persons of the two races to occupy the same passenger coach. If a state can prescribe, as a rule of civil conduct, that whites and blacks shall not travel as passengers in the same railroad coach, why may it not so regulate the use of the streets of its cities and towns as to compel white citizens to keep on one side of a street, and black citizens to keep on the other? Why may it not, upon like grounds, punish whites and blacks who ride together in street cars or in open vehicles on a public road or street? Why may it not require sheriffs to assign whites to one side of a court room, and blacks to the other? And why may it not also prohibit the commingling of the two races in the galleries of legislative halls or in public assemblages convened for the consideration of the political questions of the day? Further, if this statute of Louisiana is consistent with the personal liberty of citizens, why may not the state require the separation in railroad coaches of native and naturalized citizens of the United States, or of Protestants and Roman Catholics?

The answer given at the argument to these questions was that regulations of the kind they suggest would be unreasonable, and could not, therefore, stand before the law. Is it meant that the determination of questions of legislative power depends upon the inquiry whether the statute whose validity is questioned is, in the judgment of the courts, a reasonable one, taking all the circumstances into consideration? A statute may be unreasonable merely because a sound public policy forbade its enactment. But I do not understand that the courts have anything to do with the policy or expediency of legislation. . . .

The white race deems itself to be the dominant race in this country. And so it is, in prestige, in achievements, in education, in wealth, and in power. So, I doubt not, it will continue to be for all time, if it remains true to its great heritage, and holds fast to the principles of constitutional liberty. But in view of the constitution, in the eye of the law, there is in this country no superior, dominant, ruling class of citizens. There is no caste here. Our constitution is color-blind, and neither knows nor tolerates classes among citizens. In respect of civil rights, all citizens are equal before the law. The humblest is the peer of the most powerful. The law regards man as man, and takes no account of his surroundings or of his color when his civil rights as guaranteed by the supreme law of the land are involved. It is therefore to be regretted that this high tribunal, the final expositor of the fundamental law of the land, has reached the conclusion that it is competent for a state to regulate the enjoyment by citizens of their civil rights solely upon the basis of race.

In my opinion, the judgment this day rendered will, in time, prove to be quite as pernicious as the decision made by this tribunal in the *Dred Scott Case*. . . .

The present decision, it may well be apprehended, will not only stimulate aggressions, more or less brutal and irritating, upon the admitted rights of colored citizens, but will encourage the belief that it is possible, by means of state enactments, to defeat the beneficent purposes which the people of the United States had in view when they adopted the recent amendments of the constitution, by one of which the blacks of this country were made citizens of the United States and of the states in which they respectively reside, and whose privileges and immunities, as citizens, the states are forbidden to abridge. Sixty millions of whites are in no danger from the presence here of eight millions of blacks. The destinies of the two races, in this country, are indissolubly linked together, and the interests of both require that the common government of all shall not permit the seeds of race hate to be planted under the sanction of law. What can more certainly arouse race hate, what more certainly create and perpetuate a feeling of distrust between these races, than state enactments which, in fact, proceed on the ground that colored citizens are so inferior and degraded that they cannot be allowed to sit in public coaches occupied by white citizens? That, as all will admit, is the real meaning of such legislation as was enacted in Louisiana. . . .

I am of opinion that the statute of Louisiana is inconsistent with the personal liberty of citizens, white and black, in that state, and hostile to both the spirit and letter of the constitution of the United States. If laws of like character should be enacted in the several states of the Union, the effect would be in the highest degree mischievous. Slavery, as an institution tolerated by law, would, it is true, have disappeared from our country; but there would remain a power in the states, by sinister legislation, to interfere with the full enjoyment of the blessings of freedom, to regulate civil rights, common to all citizens, upon the basis of race, and to place in a condition of legal inferiority a large body of American citizens, now constituting a part of the political community, called the "People of the United States," for whom, and by whom through representatives, our government is administered. Such a system is inconsistent with the guaranty given by the constitution to each state of a republican form of government, and may be stricken down by congressional action, or by the courts in the discharge of their solemn duty to maintain the supreme law of the land, anything in the constitution or laws of any state to the contrary notwithstanding.

For the reason stated, I am constrained to withhold my assent from the opinion.

Shelley v. Kraemer

334 U.S. 1, 68 S.CT. 836 (1948)

Louis Kraemer and his wife sought and obtained an injunction against J. D. Shelley, a black man, from taking possession of a parcel of land in their St. Louis, Missouri, neighborhood. Shelley bought the land from one of Kraemer's neighbors without knowing that it was covered by a restrictive covenant barring owners from selling their land to members of "the Negro or Mongolian race." A state trial court found the covenant technically faulty but was reversed on appeal by the Missouri State Supreme Court, which held that the covenant did not deny Shelley's constitutional rights.

Shelley's appeal to the Supreme Court became a test case for the NAACP Legal Defense Fund and was argued by the NAACP Legal Defense Fund's leading counsel, Charles Houston and Thurgood Marshall. The NAACP sought to persuade the Court to reconsider an earlier ruling, *Corrigan v. Buckley*, 271 U.S. 323 (1926), upholding restrictive covenants. Eighteen *amicus curiae* briefs, including one by Democratic President Harry Truman's solicitor general, supported the NAACP's position.

The Court unanimously held that judicial enforcement of restrictive covenants constituted state action and ran afoul of the Fourteenth Amendment. But note that Chief Justice Fred Vinson neither overrules *Corrigan* nor explains why and how far the state action doctrine extends to bar private racial discrimination not forbidden by the states.

The Court's decision was unanimous; the opinion was announced by Chief Justice Vinson, with Justices Reed, Jackson, and Rutledge not participating.

■ ■ ■

☐ *Chief Justice VINSON delivered the opinion of the Court.*

These cases present for our consideration questions relating to the validity of court enforcement of private agreements, generally described as restrictive covenants, which have as their purpose the exclusion of persons of designated race or color from the ownership or occupancy of real property. Basic constitutional issues of obvious importance have been raised. . . .

It is well, at the outset, to scrutinize the terms of the restrictive agreements involved in these cases. In the Missouri case, the covenant declares that no part of the affected property shall be "occupied by any person not of the Caucasian race, it being intended hereby to restrict the use of said property. . . . against the occupancy as owners or tenants of any portion of said property for resident or other purpose by people of the Negro or Mongolian Race." Not only does the restriction seek to proscribe use and occupancy of the affected properties by members of the excluded class, but as construed by the Missouri courts, the agreement requires that title of any person who uses his property in violation of the restriction shall be divested. . . .

It should be observed that these covenants do not seek to proscribe any particular use of the affected properties. Use of the properties for residential occupancy, as such, is not forbidden. The restrictions of these agreements, rather, are directed toward a designated class of persons and seek to determine who may and who may not own or make use of the properties for residential purposes. The excluded class is defined wholly in terms of race or color; "simply that and nothing more."

It cannot be doubted that among the civil rights intended to be protected from discriminatory state action by the Fourteenth Amendment are the rights to acquire, enjoy, own and dispose of property. Equality in the enjoyment of property rights was regarded by the framers of that Amendment as an essential pre-condition to the realization of other basic civil rights and liberties which the Amendment was intended to guarantee. Thus, Sec. 1978 of the Revised Statutes, derived from Sec. 1 of the Civil Rights Act of 1866 which was enacted by Congress while the Fourteenth Amendment was also under consideration, provides:

> All citizens of the United States shall have the same right, in every State and Territory, as is enjoyed by white citizens thereof to inherit, purchase, lease, sell, hold, and convey real and personal property. . . .

It is likewise clear that restrictions on the right of occupancy of the sort sought to be created by the private agreements in these cases could not be squared with the requirements of the Fourteenth Amendment if imposed by state statute or local ordinance. . . .

But the present cases . . . do not involve action by state legislatures or city councils. Here the particular patterns of discrimination and the areas in which the restrictions are to operate, are determined, in the first instance, by the terms of agreements among private individuals. Participation of the State consists in the enforcement of the restrictions so defined. The crucial issue with which we are here confronted is whether this distinction removes these cases from the operation of the prohibitory provisions of the Fourteenth Amendment.

Since the decision of this Court in the *Civil Rights Cases*, 1883 109 U.S. 3, the principle has become firmly embedded in our constitutional law that the action inhibited by the first section of the Fourteenth Amendment is only such action as may fairly be said to be that of the States. That Amendment erects no shield against merely private conduct, however discriminatory or wrongful.

We conclude, therefore, that the restrictive agreements standing alone cannot be regarded as a violation of any rights guaranteed to petitioners by the Fourteenth Amendment. So long as the purposes of those agreements are effectuated by voluntary adherence to their terms, it would appear clear that there has been no action by the State and the provisions of the Amendment have not been violated. . . .

But here there was more. These are cases in which the purposes of the agreements were secured only by judicial enforcement by state courts of the restrictive teams of the agreement. . . .

That the action of state courts and of judicial officers in their official capacities is to be regarded as action of the State within the meaning of the Fourteenth Amendment, is a proposition which has long been established by decisions of this Court. . . .

We hold that in granting judicial enforcement of the restrictive agreements in these cases, the States have denied petitioners the equal protection of the laws and that, therefore, the action of the state courts cannot stand. We have noted that freedom from discrimination by the States in the enjoyment of property rights was among the basic objectives sought to be effectuated by the framers of the Fourteenth Amendment. That such discrimination has occurred in these cases is clear.

- CONSTITUTIONAL HISTORY

A Chronology of the Civil Rights Movement and the Court

1909   The National Association for the Advancement of Colored People (NAACP) is founded to protest various forms of racial discrimination, to lobby Congress to enact antilynching laws, and to participate in "test cases" challenging practices of racial discrimination.

1932   In a widely publicized case, involving protests at the national capital over the conviction of nine black boys accused of raping a white girl and tried before an all-white jury without the assistance of an attorney in Scottsboro, Alabama, the Court holds that the "Scottsboro Boys" were denied due process and must be given the assistance of counsel in *Powell v. Alabama*, 287 U.S. 45 (1932) (excerpted in Ch. 9).

1938   The NAACP finances and supports a challenge to Missouri's law that denies blacks admission to its state law school but provides funding for qualified blacks to attend law schools in other states. Missouri ex rel. *Gaines v. Canada*, 305 U.S. 337 (1938), holds that Missouri's law violates the Fourteenth Amendment guarantee of the equal protection of the law.

1938   The litigation branch of the NAACP is broken off into the NAACP Legal Defense and Educational Fund, Inc. (LDF), and pursues a litigation strategy to persuade the Supreme Court to strike down the doctrine of separate but equal.

1941   A. Philip Randolph, head of the Brotherhood of Sleeping Car Porters, founds the March on Washington Movement to protest discriminatory employment practices in the war industry.

1942   The Congress of Racial Equality (CORE) is founded by pacifists.

1947   CORE initiates the Journey for Reconciliation, sending integrated activists into the South to protest segregation on interstate travel; activists are beaten and arrested.

1948   *Shelley v. Kraemer*, 334 U.S. 1 (1948) (excerpted in this chapter), rules that restrictive covenants, barring the sale of property to blacks and other minorities, are unconstitutional. President Harry Truman issues an executive order to desegregate the U.S. armed forces.

(continues)

■ CONSTITUTIONAL HISTORY
*A Chronology of the Civil Rights Movement and
the Court (continued)*

1950   The NAACP-LDF wins two major victories in its struggle to over-
        turn the doctrine of separate but equal in public education. *Sweatt v.
        Painter*, 339 U.S. 629 (1950), and *McLaurin v. Oklahoma State Regents*,
        339 U.S. 637 (1950), hold that Texas's separate law school for
        blacks, and Oklahoma's denial of admission of blacks into its univer-
        sity graduate school program violate the Fourteenth Amendment.

1951   A terrorist bomb kills Henry Tyson Moore, president of the
        NAACP Florida chapter.

1953   Blacks boycott buses in Baton Rouge, Louisiana.

1954   *Brown v. Board of Education of Topeka, Kansas* and companion
        cases, including *Bolling v. Sharpe* (excerpted in this chapter), hold
        that the doctrine of separate but equal is inapplicable to primary
        and secondary public schools.

1955   Brown II (excerpted in this chapter) rules that desegregation of
        public school must proceed with "all deliberate speed." Emmett
        Till, a fourteen-year-old, and two other NAACP activists are
        murdered in Mississippi. The Montgomery, Alabama, boycott of
        segregated buses begins.

1956   The bus boycott in Montgomery ends. Members of Congress is-
        sue the Southern Manifesto (excerpted in Ch. 2) denouncing the
        ruling in *Brown v. Board of Education*. The White Citizens Coun-
        cil, a middle-class group, is formed to resist desegregation.

1957   The Southern Christian Leadership Conference (SCLC) is
        founded. The Civil Rights Act of 1957 creates the U.S. Com-
        mission on Civil Rights.

1958   *Cooper v. Aaron* (excerpted in this chapter) reaffirms the ruling in
        Brown, and President Dwight D. Eisenhower orders federal troops
        into Little Rock, Arkansas; the "Little Rock Nine" desegregates
        the Central High School in Little Rock, Arkansas. A number of
        southern states try to stop the NAACP from bringing lawsuits to
        force school districts to desegregate by holding that as an out-of-
        state corporation it could not bring lawsuits in the state. When the
        NAACP challenged that, Alabama sought the disclosure of the
        NAACP's membership lists. In *NAACP v. Alabama* (excerpted in
        Ch. 5), the Court held that the membership lists were protected by
        the First Amendment guarantee for freedom of association.

1960   The Student Nonviolent Coordinating Committee (SNCC) is
        founded.

1961   CORE initiates Freedom Rides into the Deep South to resist the segregation in interstate public accommodations. CORE members are beaten and buses burned.

1962   SNCC and CORE activists begin a civil rights campaign in Albany, Georgia, and are met with violence and resistance from local authorities.

1963   SCLC begins a protest movement in Birmingham, Alabama. Over 200,000 assemble with Martin Luther King Jr., for a historic March on Washington, DC. King and other ministers apply for a parade permit to hold a march on Good Friday and Easter Sunday but are denied. When they announce plans to proceed, Birmingham officials obtain a court-ordered injunction against the demonstration. The demonstration is nonetheless held, and King and others are arrested, jailed, and found in contempt of court; subsequently the contempt citation is upheld in *Walker v. City of Birmingham*, 388 U.S. 307 (1967). Weeks later the 16th Street Baptist Church is bombed in Birmingham, killing four young girls and injuring others. Medgar Evers, an NAACP leader in Mississippi, is assassinated in his driveway.

1964   Congress enacts the Civil Rights Act of 1964, which is immediately challenged and upheld by the Court in *Heart of Atlanta Motel, Inc. v. United States* and *Katzenbach v. McClung* (excerpted in Vol. 1, Ch. 6). A libel suit against the *New York Times* by a Montgomery, Alabama police commissioner for mistakes in an ad, "Heed Their Rising Voices," soliciting funds for the civil rights movement, results in a landmark ruling in the *New York Times Co. v. Sullivan* (excerpted in Ch. 5). The Mississippi Freedom Summer initiates a grassroots campaign to expand civil rights.

1965   A voting rights march is held in Selma, Alabama. The Voting Rights Act, barring poll taxes, literacy tests, and other means denying blacks voting rights, is passed. Unrest erupts in south central Los Angeles, popularly known as the Watts Riot.

1966   The SNCC and CORE call for Black Power. The Black Panther Party for Self-Defense is formed in Oakland, California, and the NAACP and the Urban League denounce the Black Power movement. *Brown v. Louisiana*, 383 U.S. 131 (1966), holds that the First Amendment protects the symbolic speech of a group of black students who are arrested for standing silently in a "whites-only" library to protest segregation.

1967   *Loving v. Virginia*, 388 U.S. 1 (1967), strikes down miscegenation laws, barring interracial marriages.

1968   Martin Luther King Jr., is assassinated and urban unrest and riots take place in over 100 cities. In the last ruling of the Warren Court,

(continues)

■ Constitutional History
*A Chronology of the Civil Rights Movement and
the Court (continued)*

Green v. New Kent County School Board, 391 U.S. 430 (1968), holds that
lower courts should examine "every facet of school operations" in
order to achieve integration, including student assignments, faculty,
staff, transportation, extracurricular activity opportunities, and school
facilities. Republican Richard Nixon wins the 1968 presidential election, after campaigning on a Southern Strategy to win the votes of
white southern Democratic voters based on opposition to the Court's
rulings on desegregation and promises to appoint only "strict constructionists" and those opposed to "judicial activism" to the federal
judiciary.

B | *Racial Discrimination in Education*

The process of dismantling a century-old system of segregated schools
was long and often violent, and could not be achieved by simple judicial decree. At the turn of the twentieth century, in *Cummings v. Richmond County Board of Education*, 175 U.S. 528 (1899), the Fuller Court
upheld a Georgia school board's decision to close its all-black high
school, because it needed the buildings for an all-black elementary
school. Writing for a unanimous Court, Justice Harlan, who had dissented in the *Civil Rights Cases* and *Plessy v. Ferguson*, stressed that public schools were a subject of state, not federal, control. The White
Court (1910–1921) and Taft Court (1921–1930) repeatedly avoided the
issue of segregated schools.[1]

Not until the Hughes Court (1930–1941) was there a suggestion
that racially segregated schools might be constitutionally suspect. In
Missouri ex rel. Gaines v. Canada, 305 U.S. 337 (1938), Chief Justice
Hughes struck down a portion of Missouri's law that denied blacks
admission to its law school but provided funding for blacks to attend
law schools in other states. Lloyd Gaines, a black citizen of Missouri,
qualified for admission into the University of Missouri's law school
and argued that as a taxpayer he had a right to attend the law school.
By a 7–2 vote (with Justices McReynolds and Butler dissenting), the
Hughes Court held that the equal protection clause was violated

because Missouri failed to provide any law school for blacks. Instead, it simply shifted its responsibility to other states. Far from seriously questioning the constitutionality of the separate but equal doctrine as applied to education, Chief Justice Hughes emphasized that states must furnish "equal facilities in separate schools." As a result of the Court's ruling, Missouri established a separate all-black law school at its all-black university, Lincoln University.

The National Association for the Advancement of Colored People (NAACP) financed and argued Gaines's case before the Supreme Court. Encouraged by its small victory, the NAACP mounted a litigation campaign to bring down segregated schools. The NAACP's strategy was twofold. First, it sought to ensure that states in fact provided *equal* educational facilities. Second, it aimed to persuade the Court that "separate but equal" educational facilities were inherently unequal.

A decade after *Gaines*, the NAACP won a first step toward desegregation. In 1948, along with *Shelley v. Kraemer* (excerpted in Section A), in an unsigned *per curiam* opinion, the Vinson Court ordered Oklahoma to provide a qualified black woman with an equal education in the state's law school.[2] Two years later, the NAACP had two more victories. Both rulings were unanimously decided and handed down by Chief Justice Vinson.

In *Sweatt v. Painter*, 339 U.S. 629 (1950), the Court ordered the admission of H. M. Sweatt, a black man, into the University of Texas law school. Sweatt refused to go to the state's separate law school for blacks. And he persuaded the Court that that law school was inferior, and therefore *unequal*, not only in terms of physical facilities but also in the "reputation of the faculty, experience of the administration, position and influence of the alumni, standing in the community, tradition and prestige." In *McLaurin v. Oklahoma State Regents*, 339 U.S. 637 (1950), the Vinson Court went even further. McLaurin, a black man, was admitted into the University of Oklahoma's School of Education to work for a Ph.D. But the state legislature mandated that McLaurin, the only black student at the university, be treated on a segregated basis; that is, in classes he sat separately from whites, used a special table in the school's library, and ate at a designated table at different times from whites in the school cafeteria. McLaurin contended that this treatment denied him the equal protection of the laws, and the Court agreed. In both cases, the Vinson Court acknowledged the intangible elements in education and concluded that separate but equal facilities, at least in higher education, were not equal. But the Court stopped short of overturning the separate but equal doctrine.

The NAACP had prepared the basis for the Court's striking down racially segregated public schools. But when it brought several cases

George McLaurin, segregated and required to sit outside of his classroom at the University of Oklahoma in 1948. In *McLaurin v. Oklahoma*, 339 U.S. 637 (1950), the Court held that segregation *within* institutions of higher education was unconstitutional. On the same day, the Court handed down *Sweatt v. Painter*, 339 U.S. 629 (1950), holding that Texas's creation of a law school for blacks, instead of admitting them into the University of Texas School of Law at Austin, was unconstitutional and that the Fourteenth Amendment proscribes segregation in *separate institutions*, because intangible factors, such as the number of faculty, the size of the library, and alumni connections, rendered them unequal. Both decisions undermined, without overruling, the doctrine of "separate but equal" facilities in higher education and set the stage for the landmark ruling on school desegregation in *Brown v. Board of Education of Topeka, Kansas* (1954). (*Bettmann/Corbis via Getty Images.*)

challenging dual educational systems for blacks and whites in 1951, there was no clear indication that the Vinson Court would continue to press ahead. *Sweatt* and *McLaurin* involved only higher education and affected a relatively small number of blacks. Yet they ignited political controversy and strong opposition in the South. The Court knew that striking down segregated primary and secondary schools would affect millions of people, that overturning an educational system in place for close to a hundred years would invite widespread opposition; see Justice Jackson's unpublished memorandum concerning *Brown v. Board of Education of Topeka, Kansas* (excerpted in this section).

    Brown v. Board of Education of Topeka, Kansas (1954) (see excerpt below), handed down three years after arriving on the Court's docket and in the first year of Chief Justice Earl Warren's tenure, marked a turning point for the Court and the country. That unanimous ruling striking down segregated public schools was the culmination and the beginning of new political struggles. Along with *Brown I, Bolling v. Sharpe* (1954) (see excerpt below) struck down segregated schools in the District of Columbia. The Fourteenth Amendment only forbids states from denying the equal protection of the laws, and the District of Columbia is under the control of the federal government. In an opinion that would come to have major significance for later rulings on racial and nonracial discrimination, Chief Justice Warren construed the Fifth Amendment's due process clause to incorporate the Fourteenth Amendment's equal protection guarantee and apply it to the federal government.

In *Brown* and *Bolling* the Warren Court did not expressly overrule *Plessy*'s doctrine of separate but equal, nor was anything said about segregation in other public accommodations—hotels, restaurants, and the like. Neither did the Court provide immediate remedial relief. The Court's unanimous rulings were achieved only at the cost of compromise among the justices in the face of certain resistance to their ruling. In order to minimize some of the anticipated opposition, *Brown* was carried over to another term for reargument on the question of remedies— how soon should desegregation take place and what kind of order should the Court issue? One year later in *Brown v. Board of Education of Topeka, Kansas (Brown II)* (1955) (see excerpt below), the Warren Court issued its mandate for states and local school boards to proceed "with all deliberate speed" in dismantling segregated schools. (The phrase "all deliberate speed" was adopted at the urging of Justice Frankfurter, because he and others wanted to temper the reaction to *Brown* and provide for flexibility in efforts to comply with its ruling. He borrowed the phrase from Justice Holmes, who in a case—*Virginia v. West Virginia*, 222 U.S. 1 (1911)—dealing with West Virginia's repayments to Virginia after their separation, observed: "[I]t is enough if [West Virginia] proceeds, in the language of the English Chancery, with all deliberate speed.")

Opposition to the Warren Court's rulings led to bitter, sometimes violent confrontations. In 1956, nineteen U.S. senators and eighty-two members of the House of Representatives denounced *Brown* as unconstitutional in a "Southern Manifesto" (excerpted in Ch. 2). The Republican administration of President Dwight D. Eisenhower did little to enforce compliance with *Brown*. The Warren Court, nevertheless, stood firmly behind its ruling, as registered in the controversy over *Cooper v. Aaron* (1958) (see excerpt below). In subsequent decisions, the Warren Court reaffirmed that school boards had a positive duty to desegregate. In *Griffin v. County School Board of Prince Edward County*, 391 U.S. 430 (1968), for example, the Fourteenth Amendment was interpreted to forbid school boards from closing all public schools rather than desegregating them.[3] Still, given the massive resistance toward *Brown*, the Warren Court effectively placed the burden on lower federal courts to oversee its implementation.[4]

Ten years after *Brown* and massive resistance and continuing litigation, Justice Black complained, "There has been entirely too much deliberation and not enough speed" in complying with *Brown*. "The time for mere 'deliberate speed' has run out."[5] *Brown*'s mandate amounted to a moral appeal and an invitation for delay. With no federal leadership, implementation of *Brown* was deliberately slow and uneven. The Department of Justice had little role in ending school segregation before the passage of the Civil Rights Act of 1964. Even after the Department of Justice assumed a role in enforcing school desegregation, little attention was initially given to areas outside of the South or to problems other than ending *de jure* segregation—segregation enforced by laws prohibiting the integration of public schools. The Department of Justice paid almost no attention to *de facto* segregation due to socio-economic conditions, such as housing patterns, in the North and West. Eventually, the Department of Health, Education, and Welfare (HEW) was given responsibility for ending segregated schools. It had authority to issue guidelines and review plans for integration. More important, HEW had the power to cut off federal funding if school districts refused to submit or comply with desegregation plans.

By the mid-1960s the Department of Justice and HEW had assumed leadership in implementing *Brown*. Nevertheless, it took time to build records and evidence of segregation in northern and western school districts, and then to challenge local authorities in the courts. Not until the summer of 1968 did the outgoing Johnson administration initiate the first school desegregation cases in the North and West and try to achieve the national coverage that the Court envisioned in *Brown*. By the end of the decade, the Court was growing impatient. In Justice Black's words, in *Alexander v. Holmes County Board of Education*, 396 U.S. 19 (1969), "There is no longer the slightest excuse, reason, or justification for further postponement of the time when every public school system in the United States will be a unitary one." Progress was made, but the Court and the country were also changing.

In Chief Justice Burger's first year on the Court, *Alexander* ordered the Fifth Circuit Court of Appeals to deny further requests for delay from southern school districts in ending dual systems of public education and emphasized that the "standard allowing 'all deliberate speed' for desegregation is no longer constitutionally permissible." The message in *Alexander*, like that in *Brown*, remained ambiguous. Justice Thurgood Marshall could not win unanimity on finally setting a cutoff date for school desegregation. Justice Black threatened a dissenting opinion, protesting that "all deliberate speed" connoted delay, not speed. "The duty of this Court and of the others," Black implored, "is too simple to require perpetual litigation and deliberation. That duty is to extirpate all racial discrimination from our system of public schools NOW." But on the bench less than four months, Burger vigorously opposed setting any final cutoff date for desegregation. Justice Brennan sought consensus, yet agreement could not be reached on a more precise order than for proceeding with desegregation here and now. *Alexander*, Justice White lamented in an unpublished memo, "neither says the order is to be entered now, within six months or even with deliberate speed." "Hugo," he added, "is convinced that a mistake was made in 1954–1955 with respect to the deliberate speed formula. I am beginning to understand how mistakes like that happen. Nevertheless, I join, expecting the Court of Appeals to make sure that the shortcomings of this order never come to light."[6]

After two decades the problems of implementing and achieving compliance with *Brown* persisted; some schools remained segregated. Litigation by the NAACP and other civil rights groups forced change, but it was piecemeal, costly, and modest. The judiciary alone could not achieve desegregation. Evasion and resistance were encouraged by the reluctance of presidents and Congress to enforce the mandate. Enforcement and implementation required the cooperation and coordination of all three branches.

But by the 1970s and 1980s, the political controversy touched off by *Brown* primarily revolved around lower courts' ordering of gerrymandered school district lines and the busing of schoolchildren to achieve racial balance and integrated schools. Although *Brown*'s barebones decree ended up encouraging evasion and continued litigation, over the years *Brown*'s mandate was transformed from one of ending racially separated dual school systems into a mandate for *integrated* public schools—a mandate that some members of the Warren Court would never have agreed to in *Brown*.

The Burger Court thus faced the task of providing guidance for lower federal courts and how far they could go in ordering integrated public schools. The Court's two major rulings on the use of busing to achieve school segregation came in *Swann v. Charlotte-Mecklenberg Board of Education*, 402 U.S. 1 (1971) and *Milliken v. Bradley* (1974) (excerpted below). In *Swann* Chief Justice Burger established that where all-black schools exist because of present or past *de jure* discrimination, lower courts were to presume intentional segregation. In such situations, the

"Separate but equal" in West Memphis, Tennessee, in the early 1950s. (*Ed Clark/ The LIFE Picture Collection/Getty Images.*)

Court upheld court-ordered busing of schoolchildren to achieve integration. But Chief Justice Burger stressed that courts were not to seek exact racial balance in their desegregation orders. Writing for a bare majority in *Milliken*, Chief Justice Burger underscored that the equal protection clause does not reach *de facto* school segregation resulting from housing patterns, and lower courts may not order busing as a remedy for *de facto* segregation where there is no evidence of an "intent" by school boards to discriminate. Throughout the 1970s and 1980s the Court reviewed numerous challenges to court-ordered busing. In the 1980s the Reagan administration strongly opposed the use of busing to achieve integrated schools. But when the administration asked the Court to reconsider its ruling in *Swann*, the Court unanimously declined to do so in *Metropolitan County Board of Education of Nashville v. Kelley*, 453 U.S. 1306 (1981).

Almost forty years after the watershed school desegregation ruling in *Brown v. Board of Education*, there remained about 500 school desegregation cases in lower federal courts around the country. Most involved either challenges by local school boards to court-ordered remedial plans for achieving and maintaining integrated public schools or challenges by blacks to changes in school board policies that they claim will perpetuate the vestiges of segregation. At issue are complex questions involving when and how school systems become fully integrated, or "unitary" and free from the vestiges of segregation. Lower courts, moreover, differed over how much proof school boards must show in demonstrating that present *de facto* racial isolation in school districts is unrelated to past *de jure* segregation, as well as what other conditions constitute "vestiges" of prior segregation.

Despite conflicts and confusion in the lower federal courts over when desegregation remedies and judicial supervision should end, for more than a decade the Court provided little guidance. Indeed, the Burger Court declined to review a major case dealing with the fundamentals of school desegregation in the 1980s. But the Rehnquist Court signaled a willingness to tackle the vexing issues of judicial supervision of school districts' implementation of and compliance with *Brown*'s mandate in the 1990s. However, a bare majority of the Court upheld the authority of federal judges to order a school board to raise taxes in order to pay for a desegregation plan. Chief Justice Rehnquist and Justices O'Connor and Scalia, however, joined Justice Kennedy's sharp dissenting opinion in that case, *Missouri v. Jenkins*, 495 U.S. 33 (1990) (*Jenkins I*).

The Rehnquist Court also carried over for several terms a number of school desegregation cases, including one appeal by the school board in Topeka, Kansas, which was an offspring of the protracted litigation stemming from the original 1954 ruling in *Brown*. Initially, without Justice Souter's participation, in *Board of Education of Oklahoma City Public Schools v. Dowell*, 498 U.S. 237 (1991), a bare majority held that school districts that were previously required by law to eliminate racial segregation could end the forced busing of students in favor of neighborhood schools, even though that entailed a return to a system of schools attended overwhelmingly by either black or white students.

Writing for the majority in *Dowell*, Chief Justice Rehnquist held that federal judges should end supervision of previously segregated public schools if court-ordered desegregation plans had eliminated "the vestiges of past discrimination" and insisted that the Fourteenth Amendment does not apply to racially isolated schools that are no longer a product of state-imposed segregation. Accordingly, school districts that once intentionally segregated may achieve unitary status, despite the fact that some schools remain overwhelmingly black or white, if (1) they have complied with judicial desegregation orders over a reasonable period of time, (2) they are not likely to return to their former ways, and (3) they have to the extent practicable eliminated "vestiges" of prior discrimination in the operation of their schools. In the chief justice's words:

> [School desegregation] decrees . . . are not intended to operate in perpetuity. Local control over the education of children allows

citizens to participate in decisionmaking, and allows innovation so that school programs can fit local needs. . . . Dissolving a desegregation decree after the local authorities have operated in compliance with it for a reasonable period of time properly recognizes that "necessary concern for the important values of local control of public school systems dictates that a federal court's regulatory control of such systems not extend beyond the time required to remedy the effects of past intentional discrimination." . . .

In considering whether the vestiges of *de jure* segregation had been eliminated as far as practicable, the District Court should look not only at student assignments, but "to every facet of school operations—faculty, staff, transportation, extra-curricular activities and facilities." *Green.*

Dissenting Justice Marshall, joined by Justices Blackmun and Stevens, however, took a widely different view of *Brown*'s legacy and the "vestiges" of segregation in public schools. Notably, he would have held that the Oklahoma City school district had not achieved integration and that the persistence of racially identifiable schools necessarily established that the original constitutional violation had not been remedied. In his impassioned dissent, Justice Marshall observed that

Oklahoma gained statehood in 1907. For the next 65 years, the Oklahoma City School Board maintained segregated schools—initially relying on laws requiring dual school systems; thereafter, by exploiting residential segregation that had been created by legally enforced restrictive covenants. In 1972—18 years after this Court first found segregated schools unconstitutional—a federal court finally interrupted this cycle, enjoining the Oklahoma City School Board to implement a specific plan for achieving actual desegregation of its schools.

The practical question now before us is whether, 13 years after that injunction was imposed, the same School Board should have been allowed to return many of its elementary schools to their former one-race status. The majority today suggests that 13 years of desegregation was enough. . . .

Dowell, nonetheless, provided little guidance for lower courts and the hundreds of school districts seeking to regain complete autonomy and to escape judicial supervision. Both the majority and the dissenters reaffirmed the holding in *Green v. New Kent County School Board*, 391 U.S. 430 (1968), that lower courts should examine "every facet of school operations," including student assignments, faculty, staff, transportation, extracurricular activities, and facilities. But *Dowell* left unclear the most important issues: whether and how school districts must show that presently racially isolated schools are not related to past intentional discrimination, and what other kinds of conditions may be considered "vestiges" of past *de jure* segregation.

Barely one month after deciding *Dowell* the Rehnquist Court, in *Freeman v. Pitts*, 503 U.S. 467 (1992) (excerpted below), agreed further to address the controversy over judicial supervision of remedial desegregation plans. Since Justice Thomas had not yet been confirmed by the time the Court heard oral arguments, he did not participate in the Court's decision. Although unanimous in their decision, the justices were not of one mind on how quickly or on what basis lower courts should halt their desegregation efforts. Justice Kennedy's opinion for the Court represented a rough compromise on the closing of the *Brown* era. Kennedy held that lower courts may withdraw from supervising discrete categories of school operations, as identified in *Green*, once school districts show compliance with desegregation orders. Lower courts, moreover, need not wait for a period of years before doing so, nor await desegregation in all areas of a school system before they disengage. Note, however, that Kennedy's opinion did not go far enough for Justice Scalia, who in a concurrence urged an immediate end to all judicial supervision of schools that no longer intentionally discriminate. At the same time, Kennedy's opinion appeared to go too far for Justices Blackmun, Stevens, O'Connor, and Souter. They countered in separate concurrences that lower courts should undertake a probing analysis before abandoning judicial supervision.

Dowell and *Freeman* thus charted a new course, not a dramatic reversal, pointing to a new period of litigation—a period not unlike that immediately after *Brown* but in which lower courts gradually move to relinquish, rather than assert, control over public schools. Along with *Freeman v. Pitts*, the Court also decided *United States v. Fordice*, 505 U.S. 717 (1992). Whereas *Dowell* and *Freeman* dealt with efforts to achieve integrated primary and secondary public schools, *Fordice* gave the Court the opportunity to revisit, after more than forty years, whether it is enough for colleges and universities simply to end past *de jure* racially discriminatory admissions policies, or whether they must do more than that in order to be free from the vestiges of discrimination. Mississippi's colleges and universities were strictly segregated until a court ordered the admission of James Meredith to the University of Mississippi in 1962. Yet, over two decades later in 1985–1986 approximately 99 percent of the state's white college students were enrolled in historically all-white institutions, while 71 percent of the black students attended historically all-black schools.

Writing for the Court in *Fordice*, Justice White found that Mississippi's admission policies perpetuated the existence of racially isolated colleges and universities. Although symbolic in reaffirming the principles of *Brown*, *Fordice*'s impact is considerably less than that of *Freeman*, because it provides guidance only for courts reviewing challenges to institutions in the fifteen states that once had *de jure* segregated schools, whereas courts supervising integration efforts in hundreds of cases involving primary and secondary schools will look to *Freeman* for guidance.

The Court also continued to grapple with the issue of guidelines for lower courts withdrawing from efforts to force greater integration in public schools in *Missouri v. Jenkins*, 515 U.S. 70 (1995) (*Jenkins II*). Although not laying down new guidelines, a bare majority reiterated its view that lower courts should disengage from desegregation efforts. Writing for the Court, Chief Justice Rehnquist held that a federal district court had exceeded its remedial powers in ordering the state to (1) fund salary increases for virtually all teachers and staff within the Kansas City, Missouri, School District (KCMSD); and (2) to continue to fund remedial "quality education" programs because student achievement scores were still "at or below national norms at many grade levels." In order to eliminate the vestiges of past discrimination and to make the KCMSD's schools, which have over 90 percent black student enrollments, more attractive to white students in surrounding suburbs, the district court also created a magnet school district with expanded educational opportunities and facilities. However, drawing on *Milliken v. Bradley* (excerpted below), Chief Justice Rehnquist ruled that the "*inter*district goal [of encouraging further integration through magnet schools and greater funding] is beyond the scope of the *intra*district violation" of prior racial discrimination. The chief justice also rejected the lower court's use of educational test scores as a legitimate measure of the progress of integration. In remanding the case back to the lower court to determine whether judicial supervision of the school district should be terminated, the chief justice further admonished, "The district court must bear in mind that its end purpose is not only to remedy the violation to the extent practicable, but also to restore state and local authorities to the control of a school system that is operating in compliance with the Constitution." By contrast, the four dissenters—Justices Souter, Stevens, Ginsburg, and Breyer—countered that the majority had overreached in ruling on issues such as the use of student achievement scores, and firmly rejected the majority's conclusion that lower courts possess no authority to order improvements in school districts so as to make them more attractive to white students.

Over fifty years after *Brown v. Board of Education*, numerous desegregation orders throughout the country had been lifted and most school districts reverted to some version of neighborhood schools. *Dowell, Freeman,* and *Jenkins II* had, indeed, signaled the end of *Brown*'s era of court-ordered desegregation. In the decade that followed those rulings, states and local school districts faced growing problems of racial disparities, the resegregation of black students in southern and border states, and the increasing segregation of Latino students in the South and West, as well as problems finding ways to equalize financial funding for public schools. In response, an "adequacy movement" emerged, with interest groups turning to state courts and state constitutions, which mandate equal public education, to force increases in public school financing and to make adequate educational resources "available to all on equal terms." By contrast, some local school boards adopted race-based assignment policies to maintain integrated schools. Those policies were in turn challenged in light of the Court's affirmative action rulings in *Gratz v. Bollinger* (2003) (excerpted in this chapter), which invalidated the University of Michigan undergraduate admissions program, and *Grutter v. Bollinger* (2003) (excerpted in this chapter), which upheld the University of Michigan Law School's program by a 5–4 vote (with Justice O'Connor casting the crucial vote) in holding that race may be a factor, though not the predominant factor, in admissions to achieve diverse student bodies.

The Roberts Court reconsidered those rulings and the use of race in public school student assignments to achieve and maintain integrated public schools in *Parents Involved in Community Schools v. Seattle School District No. 1* (2007) (excerpted below). Chief Justice Roberts wrote for a plurality in striking down as impermissible the adoption of race-conscious student assignments. Justice Kennedy's concurring opinion disagreed with the plurality's analysis, arguing that race may be a consideration to achieve and maintain integration in schools when, for example, drawing attendance zones, but not in individual students' school assignments. In a lengthy seventy-page dissenting opinion, Justice Breyer, joined by Justices Stevens, Souter, and Ginsburg, rejected the Court's analysis, reasoning, and decision.

NOTES

1. See *Berea College v. Kentucky,* 211 U.S. 45 (1908); and *Gong Lum v. Rice,* 275 U.S. 78 (1927).

2. See *Spiuel v. Oklahoma,* 322 U.S. 631 (1948); and *Fisher v. Hurst,* 333 U.S. 147 (1948).

3. For other Warren Court rulings, see *Goss v. Board of Education of City of Knoxville,* 373 U.S. 683 (1963) (striking down a transfer plan allowing blacks to go to

formally segregated schools); *Green v. County School Board of New Kent County, Virginia*, 391 U.S. 430 (1968) (striking down a freedom of choice plan for desegregation, where no white students attended black schools); and *Monroe v. Board of Commissioners of the City of Jackson, Texas*, 391 U.S. 450 (1968). In *United States v. Montgomery County Board of Education*, 395 U.S. 225 (1969), the Court upheld a lower court's order that schools with fewer than twelve teachers have at least one of a different race and that schools with twelve or more teachers have one teacher of a different race for every six faculty and staff persons.

4. For a fine study of the role of lower federal court judges in implementing *Brown* and the resistance they faced, see Jack Peltason, *Fifty-eight Lonely Men* (New York: Harcourt, Brace & World, 1961).

5. *Griffin v. Prince Edward County School Board*, 377 U.S. 218 (1964).

6. All quotations in this paragraph are from the justice's memo in John M. Harlan Papers, Boxes 487, 565, and 606, Seeley G. Mudd Library, Princeton University; and William J. Brennan Papers, Box 218, Library of Congress.

SELECTED BIBLIOGRAPHY

Bass, Jack. *Unlikely Heroes*. New York: Simon & Schuster, 1981.

Bell, Derrick. *Silent Covenants: Brown v. Board of Education and the Unfulfilled Hopes for Racial Reform*. New York: Oxford University Press, 2004.

Cushman, Clare, and Melvin Urofsky. *Black, White, and Brown: The Landmark School Desegregation Case*. Washington, DC: C.Q. Press, 2004.

Frankenberg, Erica, and Gary Orfield, eds. *Lessons in Integration: Realizing the Promise of Racial Diversity in American Schools*. Charlottesville: University of Virginia Press, 2007.

Freyer, Tony. *Little Rock on Trial: Cooper v. Aaron and School Desegregation*. Lawrence: University Press of Kansas, 2007.

Greenberg, Jack. *Brown v. Board of Education: Witness to a Landmark Decision*. New York: Twelve Tables, 2004.

Jacoway, Elizabeth. *Turn Away Thy Son: Little Rock, the Crisis That Shocked the Nation*. New York: Free Press, 2007.

Klarman, Michael. *From Jim Crow to Civil Rights*. New York: Oxford University Press, 2004.

Kluger, Richard. *Simple Justice*. New York: Alfred Knopf, 1976.

Landsberg, Brian K. *Enforcing Civil Rights: Race Discrimination and the Department of Justice*. Lawrence: University Press of Kansas, 1997.

O'Brien, David M. *Justice Robert H. Jackson's Unpublished Opinion In Brown v. Board: Conflict, Compromise, and Constitutional Interpretation*. Lawrence: University Press of Kansas, 2017.

Peltason, Jack W. *Fifty-eight Lonely Men: Southern Federal Judges and School Desegregation*. New York: Harcourt, Brace & World, 1961.

Samuels, Albert L. *Is Separate Unequal? United States v. Fordice*. Lawrence: University Press of Kansas, 2004.

Schwartz, Bernard. *Swann's Way: The School Busing Case and the Supreme Court.* New York: Oxford University Press, 1980.

Tushnet, Mark V. *The NAACP's Legal Strategy against Segregated Education, 1925–1950.* Chapel Hill: University of North Carolina Press, 1988.

Wasby, Stephen. *Race Relations Litigation in an Age of Complexity.* Charlottesville: University Press of Virginia, 1995.

Wilson, Paul. *A Time to Lose: Representing Kansas.* Lawrence: University Press of Kansas, 1995.

Brown v. Board of Education of Topeka, Kansas (Brown I)

347 U.S. 483, 74 S.CT. 686 (1954)

This case challenging the constitutionality of racially segregated public schools arrived on the Supreme Court's docket in 1951 and was consolidated with three other cases (from Delaware, South Carolina, and Virginia) and another, *Bolling v. Sharpe* (see excerpt below), attacking the federal government's segregated school system in the District of Columbia. On such a politically explosive issue, Justice Tom Clark recalled, the Court wanted "to get a national coverage, rather than a sectional one."

Oral arguments were heard in December 1952. Instead of the decision coming down as expected in the spring, however, the Court decided to hear rearguments in its next term. The Vinson Court was split and deeply troubled by the prospect of white southern opposition to its striking down racially segregated public schools. Justice Felix Frankfurter persuaded his colleagues to carry the cases over to the next term because 1952 was an election year. "When you have a major social political issue of this magnitude," timing and public reactions are important considerations, and, Frankfurter told a law clerk, "we do not think this is the time to decide it." By holding the cases over, the Court was able to receive the views in an *amicus curiae* brief of the incoming administration of Republican president Dwight Eisenhower.

Rearguments were scheduled for early November 1953. But then came an unexpected turn of events: Chief Justice Fred Vinson died suddenly of a heart attack in the summer, and Eisenhower promptly named Earl Warren as his successor. Warren, a popular governor of California and that state's favorite-son candidate for the Republican Party's 1952 presidential nomination, had impressed Eisenhower as having "unimpeachable integrity," "middle of the road views," and a "splendid record during his years of active law work" as a state attorney general.

Rearguments were, again, put off until December, at which time the new chief justice sat back and listened to the arguments for and against ending segregated schools. At the justices' private conference, though, Warren did two strategic things. First, he firmly expressed his conviction that racially segregated schools denied blacks their rights under the Fourteenth Amendment. Second, because a majority of the justices appeared to support his position, Warren proposed that no vote be taken until the case was fully discussed and considered by all. No formal vote was taken until mid-February.

Chief Justice Warren's opinion for the Court is short and to the point; he wanted a brief opinion that could be printed in newspapers so every citizen could read the decision. Warren also sought a unanimous ruling because *Brown* would inevitably spark widespread resistance, and unanimity might help undercut some of the anticipated opposition. Notably, if *Brown* were decided when it first arrived, the vote would probably have been 6–3 or even 5–4. Vinson was still chief justice, and Justice Jackson's notes of conference discussions indicate that Justice Reed would uphold segregation as constitutional as Vinson might have. Justices Clark and Jackson were also inclined to let segregated schools stand. Yet Warren and Frankfurter managed to persuade all the justices to join the ruling. At the last minute, Warren got Jackson, who was in the hospital recovering from a heart attack, to suppress a potential concurring opinion (see p. 1397). Jackson had a practice of writing memorandums on cases, with a view to clarifying his thinking and bargaining with the others, and then often withholding their publication when the Court's final draft opinion came along. But as Justice Burton noted in his diary, Warren did a "magnificent job in getting a unanimous Court (This would have been impossible a year ago— probably 6 to 3 with the Chief Justice [Vinson] one of the dissenters)."

■ ■ ■

☐ *Chief Justice WARREN delivered the opinion of the Court.*

In each of the cases, minors of the Negro race, through their legal representatives, seek the aid of the courts in obtaining admission to the public schools of their community on a nonsegregated basis. In each instance, they have been denied admission to schools attended by white children under laws requiring or permitting segregation according to race. This segregation was alleged to deprive the plaintiffs of the equal protection of the laws under the Fourteenth Amendment. . . .

The plaintiffs contend that segregated public schools are not "equal" and cannot be made "equal," and that hence they are deprived of the equal protection of the laws. Because of the obvious importance of the question presented, the Court took jurisdiction. Argument was heard in the 1952 Term, and reargument was heard this Term on certain questions propounded by the Court.

Reargument was largely devoted to the circumstances surrounding the adoption of the Fourteenth Amendment in 1868. It covered exhaustively consideration of the Amendment in Congress, ratification by the states, then existing practices in racial segregation, and the views of proponents and opponents of the Amendment. This discussion and our own investigation convince us that, although these sources cast some light, it is not enough to resolve the problem with which we are faced. At best, they are inconclusive. The most avid proponents of the post-War Amendments undoubtedly intended them to remove all legal distinctions among "all persons born or naturalized in the United States." Their opponents, just as certainly, were antagonistic to both the letter and the spirit of the Amendments and wished them to have the most limited effect. What others in Congress and the state legislatures had in mind cannot be determined with any degree of certainty.

An additional reason for the inconclusive nature of the Amendment's history, with respect to segregated schools, is the status of public education at that time. In the South, the movement toward free common schools, supported by general taxation, had not yet taken hold. Education of white children was largely in the hands of private groups. Education of Negroes was almost nonexistent, and practically all of the race were illiterate. In fact, any education of Negroes was forbidden by law in some states. Today, in contrast, many Negroes have achieved outstanding success in the arts and sciences as well as in the business and professional world. It is true that public school education at the time of the Amendment had advanced further in the North, but the effect of the Amendment on Northern States was generally ignored in the congressional debates. Even in the North, the conditions of public education did not approximate those existing today. The curriculum was usually rudimentary; ungraded schools were common in rural areas; the school term was but three months a year in many states; and compulsory school attendance was virtually unknown. As a consequence, it is not surprising that there should be so little in the history of the Fourteenth Amendment relating to its intended effect on public education. . . .

In approaching this problem, we cannot turn the clock back to 1868 when the Amendment was adopted, or even to 1896 when *Plessy v. Ferguson*, [163 U.S. 537 (1896)], was written. We must consider public education in the light of its full development and its present place in American life throughout the Nation. Only in this way can it be determined if segregation in public schools deprives these plaintiffs of the equal protection of the laws.

Today, education is perhaps the most important function of state and local governments. Compulsory school attendance laws and the great expenditures for education both demonstrate our recognition of the importance of education to our democratic society. It is required in the performance of our most basic public responsibilities, even service in the armed forces. It is the very foundation of good citizenship. Today it is a principal instrument in awakening the child to cultural values, in preparing him for later professional training, and in helping him to adjust normally to his environment. In these days, it is doubtful that any child may reasonably be expected to succeed in life if he is denied the opportunity of an education. Such an opportunity, where the state has undertaken to provide it, is a right which must be made available to all on equal terms.

We come then to the question presented: Does segregation of children in public schools solely on the basis of race, even though the physical facilities and other "tangible" factors may be equal, deprive the children of the minority group of equal educational opportunities? We believe that it does.

In *Sweatt v. Painter*, 339 U.S. 629 [1950], in finding that a segregated law school for Negroes could not provide them equal educational opportunities, this Court relied in large part on "those qualities which are incapable of objective measurement but which make for greatness in a law school." In *McLaurin v. Oklahoma State Regents*, 339 U.S. 637 [1950], the Court, in requiring that a Negro admitted to a white graduate school be treated like all other students, again resorted to intangible considerations: ". . . his ability to study, to engage in discussions and exchange views with other students, and, in general, to learn his profession." Such considerations apply with added force to children in grade and high schools. To separate them from others of similar age and qualifications solely because of their race generates a feeling of inferiority as to their status in the community that may affect their hearts and minds in a way unlikely ever to be undone. The effect of this separation on their educational opportunities was well stated by a finding in the Kansas case by a court which nevertheless felt compelled to rule against the Negro plaintiffs:

> Segregation of white and colored children in public schools has a detrimental effect upon the colored children. The impact is greater when it has the sanction of the law; for the policy of separating the races is usually interpreted as denoting the inferiority of the negro group. A sense of inferiority affects the motivation of a child to learn. Segregation with the sanction of law, therefore, has a tendency to [retard] the educational and mental development of Negro children and to deprive them of some of the benefits they would receive in a racial[ly] integrated school system.

Whatever may have been the extent of psychological knowledge at the time of *Plessy v. Ferguson*, this finding is amply supported by modern authority.★ Any language in *Plessy v. Ferguson* contrary to this finding is rejected.

We conclude that in the field of public education the doctrine of "separate but equal" has no place. Separate educational facilities are inherently unequal. Therefore, we hold that the plaintiffs and others similarly situated for whom the actions have been brought are, by reason of the segregation

★ K. B. Clark, Effect of Prejudice and Discrimination on Personality Development (Midcentury White House Conference on Children and Youth, 1950); Witmer and Kotinsky, *Personality in the Making* (1952), e. VI; Deutscher and Chein, The Psychological Effects of Enforced Segregation: A Survey of Social Science Opinion, 26 *J.Psychol.* 259 (1948); Chein, What are the Psychological Effects of Segregation under Conditions of Equal Facilities?, 3 *Int. J. Opinion and Attitude Res.* 229 (1949); Brameld, Educational Costs, in *Discrimination and National Welfare* (MacIver, ed., 1949), 44–48; Frazier, *The Negro in the United States* (1949), 674–681. And see generally Myrdal, *An American Dilemma* (1944).

Linda Brown, at age nine in 1952. Her father charged that his state's segregated schools were inherently discriminatory. The case led to a landmark school desegregation ruling. (*AP Photo.*)

complained of, deprived of the equal protection of the laws guaranteed by the Fourteenth Amendment. This disposition makes unnecessary any discussion whether such segregation also violates the Due Process Clause of the Fourteenth Amendment.

Because these are class actions, because of the wide applicability of this decision, and because of the great variety of local conditions, the formulation of decrees in these cases presents problems of considerable complexity. On reargument, the consideration of appropriate relief was necessarily subordinated to the primary question—the constitutionality of segregation in public education. We have now announced that such segregation is a denial of the equal protection of the laws. In order that we may have the full assistance of the parties in formulating decrees, the cases will be restored to the docket, and the parties are requested to present further argument . . . [on the nature of the remedial decrees this Court should order.] . . .

■ INSIDE THE COURT

William H. Rehnquist's Memorandum on Brown v. Board of Education

As a law clerk to Justice Robert Jackson in 1952–1953, William Rehnquist wrote a memorandum to the justice on *Brown v. Board of Education.* Later, at his confirmation hearings on his nomination to the Supreme Court in 1971, Rehnquist claimed that the memo was written at Jackson's request and reflected the justice's views rather than his own. But the content and style of the memo (as well as the fact that Justice Jackson's private papers contain several other memos written by Rehnquist) indicate that the memo reflected Rehnquist's views.

A Random Thought on the Segregation Cases

One-hundred fifty years ago this Court held that it was the ultimate judge of the restrictions which the Constitution imposed on the various branches of the national and state government. Marbury v. Madison. This was presumably on the basis that there are standards to be applied other than the personal predilections of the Justices.

As applied to questions of inter-state or state-federal relations, as well as to interdepartmental disputes within the federal government, this doctrine of judicial has worked well. Where theoretically co-ordinate bodies of government are disputing, the Court is well suited to its role as arbiter. This is because these problems involve much less emotionally charged subject matter than do those discussed below. In effect, they determine the skeletal relations of the governments to each other without influencing the substantive business of those governments.

As applied to relations between the individual and the state, the system has worked much less well. The Constitution, of course, deals with individual rights, particularly in the First Ten and the Fourteenth Amendments. But as I read the history of this Court, it has seldom been out of hot water when attempting to interpret these individual rights. Fletcher v. Peck, in 1810, represented an attempt by Chief Justice Marshall to extend the protection of the contract clause to infant business. Scott v. Sanford was the result of Taney's effort to protect slaveholders from legislative interference.

After the Civil War, business interest came to dominate the Court, and they in turn ventured into the deep water of protecting certain types of individuals against legislative interference. Championed first by Field, then by Peckham and Brewer, the high water mark of the trend in protecting corporations against legislative influence was probably Lochner v. NY. To the majority opinion in that case, Holmes replied that the Fourteenth Amendment did not enact Herbert Spencer's Social Statics. Other cases coming later in a similar vein were Adkins v. Children's Hospital, Hammer v. Dagenhart, Tyson v. Banton, Ribnik v. McBride. But eventually the Court called a halt to this reading of its own economic views into the Constitution. Apparently it recognized that where a legislature was dealing with its own citizens, it was not part of the judicial function to thwart public opinion except in extreme cases.

In these cases now before the Court, the Court is, as Davis suggested, being asked to read its own sociological views into the Constitution. Urging a view palpably at variance with precedent and probably with legislative hsitory, appellants seek to convince the Court of the moral wrongness of the treatment they are receiving. I would suggest that this is a question the Court need never reach; for regardless of the Justice's individual views on the merits of segregation, it quite clearly is not one of those extreme cases which commands intervention from one of any conviction. If this Court, because its members individually are "liberal" and dislike segregation, now chooses to strike it down, it differs from the McReynolds court only in the kinds of litigants it favors and the kinds of special claims it protects. To those who would argue that "personal" rights are more sacrosanct than "property" rights, the short answer is that the Constitution makes no such distinction. To the argument made by Marshall that a majority may not deprive a minority of its constitutional right, the answer must be made that while this is sound in theory, in the long run it is the majority who will determine what the constitutional rights of the minority are. One hundred and fifty years of attempts on the part of this Court to protect minority rights of any kind--whether those of business, slaveholders, or Jehovah's Witnesses--have all met the same fate. One by one the cases establishing such rights have been sloughed off, and crept silently to rest. If the present Court is unable to profit by this example, it must be prepared to see its work fade in time, too, as embodying only the sentiments of a transient majority of nine men.

I realize that it is an unpopular and unhumanitarian position, for which I have been excoriated by "liberal" colleagues, but I think Plessy v. Ferguson was right and should be re-affirmed. If the Fourteenth Amendment did not enact Spencer's Social Statics, it just as surely did not enact Myrdahl's American Dilemna.

whr

Source: Library of Congress, Justice Robert H. Jackson Papers.

■ INSIDE THE COURT

Justice Robert H. Jackson's
Unpublished Memorandum on
Brown v. Board of Education

When the Warren Court considered *Brown v. Board of Education*, Justice Jackson drafted a memorandum to clarify his thoughts and possibly file as a concurring opinion. He never circulated it to the other justices but had it with him when Chief Justice Warren visited him in the hospital in May, shortly before the Court's final opinion was handed down. In his memorandum Justice Jackson probed the social realities and constitutional issues that Chief Justice Warren's opinion for the Court largely glanced over.

Justice Jackson began by pointing out that

> [s]ince the close of the Civil War the United States has been "hesitating between two worlds—one dead—the other powerless to be born." War brought an old order to an end but as usual force proved unequal to founding a new one. Neither North nor South has been willing really to adapt its racial practices to its professions. The race problem would be quickly solved if some way could be found to make us all live up to our hypocrisies. . . .
>
> Racial tensions seem to develop wherever the ratio of colored population to white passes a point where the latter vaguely feel themselves, for some reason, insecure. But in the South the Negro not only suffers from racial suspicions and antagonisms present in other states and in other countries, but also I am convinced, has suffered great prejudice from the aftermath of the great American white conflict. The white South retains in historical memory a deep resentment of the forces which, after conquest, imposed a fierce program of reconstruction and the deep humiliation of carpetbag government. The Negro is the visible and reachable beneficiary and symbol of this unhappy experience, on whom many visit their natural desire for retaliation. . . .
>
> Tested by the pace of history, the rise of the Negro in the South, as well as the North, is one of the swiftest and most dramatic advances in the annals of man. Economic and social forces seem to mark discrimination for extinction even faster than legal measures. It is easy, however, to under-

(continues)

■ INSIDE THE COURT
Justice Robert H. Jackson's Unpublished Memorandum on
Brown v. Board of Education *(continued)*

stand that historical process may do the contemporary individual no good for his life moves faster than society. But whether a real abolition of segregation will be accelerated or retarded by what many are likely to regard as a ruthless use of federal judicial power is a question that I cannot and need not answer.

That Negro segregation in the schools has outlived whatever original justification it may have had and is no longer wise or fair public policy is a conclusion congenial to my background and social and political views. Economic, social and political consideration seem to mark it for certain and early, if gradual extinction. Whatever we may say the law is today, I have no doubt that within a generation segregation will be outlawed. As the twin forces of mortality and replacement operate on this bench that seems inevitable unless some dramatic and unforeseeable excess by the Negro and his friends shall cause reversal of present trends.

Jackson then turned to the Court's role in interpreting the Constitution, cautioning that

we cannot oversimplify this decision to be a mere expression of our personal opinion that school segregation is unwise or evil. We have not been chosen as legislators but as judges. Questions of method and standards of constitutional interpretation and of limitation on responsible use of judicial power in our federal system are as far reaching as any that have been before the Court since its establishment. This Court must face the difficulties in the way of honestly saying that the states which have segregated schools have not, until today, been justified in regarding their practice as lawful. And the thoughtful layman, as well as the trained lawyer, must wonder how it is that a supposedly stable organic law of our nation this morning forbids what for three quarters of a century it has allowed. I think we individual justices may not, in justice to this Court as an institution and to our profession, brush off these problems.

Turning to the problems of explaining and justifying the Court's authority to strike down racially segregated schools and its constitutional justification—in terms of the "original intent," and the context of the Fourteenth Amendment—Jackson observed:

Any authority of the judiciary to promulgate this decision has existed in the State cases since 1868 and in the case of the

District of Columbia since 1791. The due process and equal protection clauses of the Fourteenth Amendment and the due process clause of the Fifth Amendment are the respective texts for interpretation. Neither of these says anything about education or about segregation. But they are majestic and sweeping generalities which, standing alone can be read to require a full and equal racial partnership. Yet, if these texts had such meaning to the age that wrote them, how could it be that for more than a half century from the adoption of the Fifth Amendment to the Emancipation Proclamation, it was never suggested that the Due Process Clause of the Fifth Amendment even prohibited Negro slavery in the District of Columbia? . . .

There is controversy as old as the Republic as to whether the courts apply constitutional generalities in the sense that they were understood by the age that framed them or by the later age that reads them. It is implied in our questions on which all of the litigants have bestowed extensive research that the original public will that struggled for expression in these Constitutional phrases is at least relevant to our decision.

In searching for the original will and purpose expressed in the Fourteenth Amendment, all that I can fairly get from the legislative debates is that it was a passionate, confused, and deplorable era. . . . The majority stopped at conferring upon the freed man very limited civil rights. Most of the leaders and spokesmen for the movement that carried the Civil War Amendments appear never to have reached a point in their thinking where they foresaw either Negro education or Negro segregation as serious or foreseeable problems, let alone any conclusion as to their solution.

If deeds, rather than words, count as evidence, there is little indeed to show that these Amendments were understood in their own time to condemn the practice here in question. The Congress that proposed the Fourteenth Amendment and all Congresses to this day have established and maintained segregated schools in the District of Columbia. . . .

This practice of legislators and educators and opinions of the Courts has been reinforced by custom, a powerful lawmaker. Indeed not long ago we decided that custom had nullified the Constitutional plan for independent Presidential electors. But here the custom of segregation is not contrary to any express provision, has prevailed in all Southern and many Northern states, and has been recognized in many judicial decisions. This court, in common with courts everywhere, has recognized the force of long custom and has been reluctant to use judicial power to try to recast social usages. But we decide today that the unwritten law has long been contrary to a custom deeply

(continues)

■ INSIDE THE COURT
Justice Robert H. Jackson's Unpublished Memorandum on
Brown v. Board of Education *(continued)*

anchored in our social system. Thus despite my personal satisfaction with the Court's judgment, I simply cannot find, in surveying all of the usual sources of law, anything which warrants me in saying that it is required by the original purpose and intent of the Fourteenth or Fifth Amendment.

Having reviewed the history and social practices since the adoption of the Fourteenth Amendment, and finding no support for the Court's ruling in a "jurisprudence of original intention," Jackson boldly observed that the Constitution is a living document:

[t]oday's decision can not, with intellectual honesty, be grounded in anything other than the doctrine, of which Judge CARDOZO reminded us, that these Constitutional generalities "have a content and a significance that vary from age to age." Certainly no one familiar with his teachings would think this meant, what some people advocate, that we declare new constitutional law with the freedom of a constitutional convention sitting continuously and with no necessity for submitting its innovations for approval of Congress, ratification by the states or approval of the people.

Of course the Constitution must be a living instrument and cannot be read as if written in a dead language. It is neither novel nor radical doctrine that statutes once constitutional may become invalid by changing conditions and those good in one state of facts may be bad under another. . . .

Still, Jackson was deeply troubled by the fact that the Court's ruling might not appear to have the force of law, and he turned to the sociological evidence that had been presented by the NAACP, and which Chief Justice Warren cited in footnote eleven of his opinion. And he sought to underscore that the Court's ruling rested on the Constitution, not social science or sociological jurisprudence:

But a good many considerations are urged upon us to decree an end to segregation regardless of what the Amendments originally meant or purposed which I do not think appropriate for judicial appraisal or acceptance. Extralegal criteria from sociological, psychological and political sciences are proposed. Segregation is said to be offensive to the best contemporary opinion here and damaging to our prestige abroad. It is said to be based on a philosophy of inherent inequality of races, and that it creates in young Negro children an inferiority complex which retards their education and embitters their attitudes to life. These are disputed contentions which I have little competence to judge as scientific matters but with which, for purposes of the case, I shall not disagree. . . .

However that may be, and if all the woes of colored children would be solved by forcing them into white company, I do not think we should import into the concept of equal protection of the law these elusive psychological and subjective factors. They are not determinable with satisfactory objectivity or mensurable [*sic*] with reasonable certainty. If we adhere to objective criteria the judicial process will still be capricious enough.

Concluding, Jackson observed,

The real question as I see it is whether the Constitution permits any classification or separation of Negro and White merely on the basis of color or racial descent. If not these policy arguments are superfluous and, if so, they are for consideration of the legislatures not the courts.

I think the change which warrants our decision is not a change in the Constitution but in the Negro population. Certainly in the 1860's and throughout the nineteenth century the Negro population, as a whole, was a different people than today. Lately freed from bondage, they had no opportunity as yet to show their capacity for education and assimilation, or even a chance to demonstrate that they could be self-supporting or in our public life anything more than a pawn for white exploiters. I cannot say that it was an unreasonable assumption that Negro educational problems were elementary, special and peculiar and their mass teaching an experiment not easily tied in which the education of pupils of more favored background. Nor, when we view the progress that has been made under it, can we honestly say that the practice of each race pursuing its education apart was wholly to the Negro's disadvantage. His progress under these conditions has been spectacular.

Whatever may have been true at an earlier period, the mere fact that one is in some degree colored no longer creates a presumption that he is inferior, illiterate, retarded or indigent. Moreover, assimilation is under way to a marked extent. Blush or shudder, as many will, mixture of blood has been making inroads on segregation faster than the courtroom. A line of separation between the races has become unclear and blurred and an increasing part of what is called colored population has as much claim to white as to colored blood. This development baffles any just segregation effort.

Also relevant changes have occurred in the status of the public school. Education, even for the white, was once regarded

(continues)

■ Inside the Court
Justice Robert H. Jackson's Unpublished Memorandum on
Brown v. Board of Education *(continued)*

---

as a privilege bestowed on those fortunate enough to be able to take advantage of it and often was not compulsory. The concept today has changed. Education is not a privilege but a right and more than that a duty, to be performed not merely for one's own advantage but for the security and stability of the nation. Access to educational facilities has been gradually transformed from a matter of grace into a right which may not be encumbered with unconstitutionally discriminatory or oppressive conditions. And while education was long regarded as at most a local or state concern, far from the reach of federal authority, the federal judicial power especially, and the appropriative power of Congress has moved in to the local problems and made education a national concern.

The Negro is not free of local educational control. He must meet the prescribed standards of learning, discipline and health. He may be treated on his individual merit as a pupil, attend schools set apart for those of his neighborhood. But he may not be included or excluded merely because he has Negro blood wholly or in part.

Source: Library of Congress, Justice Robert H. Jackson Papers.

Bolling v. Sharpe
347 U.S. 497, 74 S.Ct. 693 (1954)

Handed down with *Brown v. Board of Education* (see excerpt above), this case involved the District of Columbia's segregated schools. The facts are further discussed in the opinion delivered by Chief Justice Earl Warren.

The Court's decision was unanimous; the opinion was announced by Chief Justice Warren.

■ ■ ■

☐ *Chief Justice WARREN delivered the opinion of the Court.*

We have this day held that the Equal Protection Clause of the Fourteenth Amendment prohibits the states from maintaining racially segregated public schools. The legal problem in the District of Columbia is somewhat different, however. The Fifth Amendment, which is applicable in the District of Columbia, does not contain an equal protection clause as does the Fourteenth Amendment which applies only to the states. But the concepts of equal protection and due process, both stemming from our American ideal of fairness, are not mutually exclusive. The "equal protection of the laws" is a more explicit safeguard of prohibited unfairness than "due process of the law," and, therefore, we do not imply that the two are always interchangeable phrases. But, as this Court has recognized, discrimination may be so unjustifiable as to be violative of due process. . . .

Although the Court has not assumed to define "liberty" with any great precision, that term is not confined to mere freedom from bodily restraint. Liberty under law extends to the full range of conduct which the individual is free to pursue, and it cannot be restricted except for a proper governmental objective. Segregation in public education is not reasonably related to any proper governmental objective, and thus it imposes on Negro children of the District of Columbia a burden that constitutes an arbitrary deprivation of their liberty in violation of the Due Process Clause.

In view of our decision that the Constitution prohibits the states from maintaining racially segregated public schools, it would be unthinkable that the same Constitution would impose a lesser duty on the Federal Government. We hold that racial segregation in the public schools of the District of Columbia is a denial of the due process of law guaranteed by the Fifth Amendment to the Constitution.

Brown v. Board of Education of Topeka, Kansas (Brown II)
349 U.S. 294, 75 S.Ct. 753 (1955)

During the rearguments on what kind of remedial decree the Court should issue to enforce *Brown*, Chief Justice Warren confronted the hard fact of southern resistance. The attorney for South Carolina, S. Emory Rogers, pressed for an open-ended decree—one that would not specify when and how desegregation should take place. He boldly proclaimed:

> Mr. Chief Justice, to say we will conform depends on the decree handed down. I am frank to tell you, right now [in] our district I do not think that we will send—[that] the white people of the district will send their children to the Negro schools. It would be unfair to tell the Court that we are going to do that. I do not think it is. But I do think that something can be worked out. We hope so.

"It is not a question of attitude," Warren shot back, "it is a question of conforming to the decree." Their heated exchange continued:

CHIEF JUSTICE WARREN: But you are not willing to say here that there would be an honest attempt to conform to this decree, if we did leave it to the district court [to implement]?

MR. ROGERS: No, I am not. Let us get the word "honest" out of there.

CHIEF JUSTICE WARREN: No, leave it in.

MR. ROGERS: No, because I would have to tell you that right now we would not conform—we would not send our white children to the Negro schools.

The exchange reinforced Warren's view "that reasonable attempts to start the integration process is [sic] all the court can expect in view of the scope of the problem, and that an order to immediately admit all negroes in white schools would be an absurdity because [it would be] impossible to obey in many areas." Thus while total immediate integration might be a reasonable order for Kansas, it would be unreasonable for Virginia, and the district judge might decide that a grade a year is reasonable compliance in Virginia. Six law clerks were assigned to prepare a Segregation Research Report. They summarized available studies on how school districts in different regions might be desegregated and projected the reactions to various desegregation plans.

The Court's problem, as one of Justice Stanley Reed's law clerks put it, was to frame a decree "so as to allow such divergent results without making it so broad that evasion is encouraged." The clerks agreed that there should be a simple decree but disagreed on whether there should be guidelines for its implementation. One clerk opposed any guidelines. The others thought that "smacks of indecisiveness, and gives the extremists more time to operate." The problem was how precise a guideline should be established. What would constitute good faith compliance? "Although we think a 12-year gradual desegregation plan permissible," they confessed, "we are not certain that the opinion should explicitly sanction it."

At the justices' private conference, Warren repeated these concerns. Justices Black and Minton thought that a simple decree, without an opinion, was enough. As Black explained, "The less we say the better off we are." The others agreed. A short, simple opinion seemed advisable for reaffirming *Brown I* and providing guidance for dealing with the inevitable problems of compliance. Justice John Harlan wanted *Brown II* expressly to recognize that school desegregation was a local problem to be solved by local authorities. The others also insisted on making clear that school boards and lower courts had flexibility in ending segregation. In Justice Harold Burton's view, "neither this Court nor district courts should act as a school board or formulate the program" for desegregation.

Agreement emerged that the Court should issue a short opinion decree. In a memorandum, Chief Justice Warren summarized the main points of agreement. The opinion should simply state that *Brown I* held unconstitutional racially segregated public schools. *Brown II* should acknowledge that "local school authorities have the primary responsibility for assessing and solving these problems; [and] the courts will have to consider these problems in determining whether the efforts of local school authorities" are in good faith compliance. The cases, he concluded, should be remanded to the lower courts "for such proceedings and decree necessary and proper to carry out this Court's decision." The justices agreed, and along these lines Warren drafted the Court's opinion.

The phrase "all deliberate speed" was borrowed from an opinion by Justice Oliver Wendell Holmes, in *Virginia v. West Virginia*, 220 U.S. 1 (1911), a case dealing with how much and when Virginia ought to receive from the state's public debt at the time West Virginia broke off and became a state. It was inserted in the final opinion of *Brown II* at the suggestion of one of Frankfurter's law clerks. Forced integration might lead to lowering educational standards. Immediate, court-ordered desegregation, Frankfurter warned, "would make a mockery of the Constitutional adjudication designed to vindicate a claim to equal treatment to achieve 'integrated' but lower educational standards." The Court, he insisted, "does its duty if it gets effectively under way the righting of a wrong. When the wrong is deeply rooted state policy the court does its duty if it decrees measures that reverse the direction of the unconstitutional policy so as to uproot it 'with all deliberate speed.'" As much an apology for not setting precise guidelines as a recognition of the limitations of judicial power, the phrase symbolized the Court's bold moral appeal to the country.*

The Court's decision was unanimous; the opinion was announced by Chief Justice Warren.

■ ■ ■

☐ *Chief Justice WARREN delivered the opinion of the Court.*

These cases were decided on May 17, 1954. The opinions of that date, declaring the fundamental principle that racial discrimination in public education is unconstitutional, are incorporated herein by reference. All provisions of federal, state, or local law requiring or permitting such dis-

---

*Quotations are from materials in the Stanley Reed Papers, University of Kentucky Library; the Harold Burton Papers, Library of Congress; the Tom Clark Papers, University of Texas Law School Library; the Felix Frankfurter Papers, Harvard Law School; and the Earl Warren Papers, Library of Congress.

crimination must yield to this principle. There remains for consideration the manner in which relief is to be accorded.

Because these cases arose under different local conditions and their disposition will involve a variety of local problems, we requested further argument on the question of relief. In view of the nationwide importance of the decision, we invited the Attorney General of the United States and the Attorneys General of all states requiring or permitting racial discrimination in public education to present their views on that question. The parties, the United States, and the States of Florida, North Carolina, Arkansas, Oklahoma, Maryland, and Texas filed briefs and participated in the oral argument. . . .

Full implementation of these constitutional principles may require solution of varied local school problems. School authorities have the primary responsibility for elucidating, assessing, and solving these problems; courts will have to consider whether the action of school authorities constitutes good faith implementation of the governing constitutional principles. Because of their proximity to local conditions and the possible need for further hearings, the courts which originally heard these cases can best perform this judicial appraisal. Accordingly, we believe it appropriate to remand the cases to those courts.

In fashioning and effectuating the decrees, the courts will be guided by equitable principles. Traditionally, equity has been characterized by a practical flexibility in shaping its remedies and by a facility for adjusting and reconciling public and private needs. These cases call for the exercise of these traditional attributes of equity power. At stake is the personal interest of the plaintiffs in admission to public schools as soon as practicable on a nondiscriminatory basis. To effectuate this interest may call for elimination of a variety of obstacles in making the transition to school systems operated in accordance with the constitutional principles set forth in our May 17, 1954, decision. Courts of equity may properly take into account the public interest in the elimination of such obstacles in a systematic and effective manner. But it should go without saying that the vitality of these constitutional principles cannot be allowed to yield simply because of disagreement with them.

While giving weight to these public and private considerations, the courts will require that the defendants make a prompt and reasonable start toward full compliance with our May 17, 1954, ruling. Once such a start has been made, the courts may find that additional time is necessary to carry out the ruling in an effective manner. The burden rests upon the defendants to establish that such time is necessary in the public interest and is consistent with good faith compliance at the earliest practicable date. To that end, the courts may consider problems related to administration, arising from the physical condition of the school plant, the school transportation system, personnel, revision of school districts and attendance areas into compact units to achieve a system of determining admission to the public schools on a nonracial basis, and revision of local laws and regulations which may be necessary in solving the foregoing problems. They will also consider the adequacy of any plans the defendants may propose to meet these problems and to effectuate a transition to a racially nondiscriminatory school system. During this period of transition, the courts will retain jurisdiction of these cases.

The judgments below, except that in the Delaware case, are accordingly reversed and the cases are remanded to the District Courts to take such proceedings and enter such orders and decrees consistent with this opinion as are necessary and proper to admit to public schools on a racially nondiscriminatory basis with all deliberate speed the parties to these cases.

Cooper v. Aaron
358 U.S. 1, 78 S.CT. 1401 (1958)

In Little Rock, Arkansas, Governor Orval Faubus encouraged disobedience by southern segregationists by calling out the state's National Guard to keep black children from entering Little Rock's Central High School. The attorney general of the United States, Herbert Brownell, got an injunction against the governor's action, and eight black children, including John Aaron, were permitted to enter the school. But continued hostility led to the removal of the children and to President Dwight Eisenhower's sending army troops to enforce the court's order and to protect the children.

William Cooper and other members of the Little Rock school board asked a federal district court for a two-and-one-half-year delay in the implementation of its desegregation plans. A federal appellate court, however, reversed the district court's order postponing desegregation. Cooper and the school board immediately appealed that decision to the Supreme Court, which granted review and expedited proceedings. Hearing oral arguments just three days after granting review, the Court handed down the next day a brief order affirming the appellate court's decision. It later published a full opinion (excerpted here).

Justice Brennan's draft of the Court's opinion was worked on by all the justices in the Court's conference room. Over the strong objections of some of the justices, Justice Felix Frankfurter insisted on writing a concurring opinion because, he said, many of his former students at Harvard Law School were leading members of the southern bar and because ex-Justice (and former governor of South Carolina) James Byrnes had called on the country to curb the Court. Byrnes had published an attack on *Brown* and an article written by one of Frankfurter's favorite former law clerks, Alexander Bickel. As a clerk, Bickel had prepared a lengthy research report on school desegregation when the Court first considered *Brown*. Later, when back at Harvard, Bickel revised and published it in the *Harvard Law Review*. Given Byrnes's attack, Frankfurter felt the need to lecture southern lawyers on the legitimacy of the Court's ruling in *Brown*. But the other justices worried that Frankfurter's opinion might undercut the Court's unanimous decision. For this reason, the justices took the unusual step of noting in the opinion that three—Brennan, Stewart, and Whittaker—were not on the bench when

Brown was handed down but that they would have joined the unanimous decision if they had been. They also agreed to depart from the practice of one justice signing the opinion for the Court in order to underscore their unanimity and that Frankfurter's opinion was not a "dilution" of the views expressed in the Court's joint opinion.

■ ■ ■

☐ *Opinion of the Court by THE CHIEF JUSTICE, Justice BLACK, Justice FRANKFURTER, Justice DOUGLAS, Justice BURTON, Justice CLARK, Justice HARLAN, Justice BRENNAN, and Justice WHITTAKER.*

As this case reaches us it raises questions of the highest importance to the maintenance of our federal system of government. It necessarily involves a claim by the governor and Legislature of a State that there is no duty on state officials to obey federal court orders resting on this Court's considered interpretation of the United States Constitution. Specifically it involves actions by the Governor and Legislature of Arkansas upon the premise that they are not bound by our holding in *Brown v. Board of Education*, 349 U.S. 483 (1954). That holding was that the Fourteenth Amendment forbids States to use their governmental powers to bar children on racial grounds from attending schools where there is state participation through any arrangement, management, funds or property. We are urged to uphold a suspension of the Little Rock School Board's plan to do away with segregated public schools in Little Rock until state laws and efforts to upset and nullify our holding in *Brown v. Board of Education* have been further challenged and tested in the courts. We reject these contentions. . . .

In affirming the judgment of the Court of Appeals which reversed the District Court we have accepted without reservation the position of the School Board, the Superintendent of Schools, and their counsel that they displayed entire good faith in the conduct of these proceedings and in dealing with the unfortunate and distressing sequence of events which has been outlined. We likewise have accepted the findings of the District Court as to the conditions at Central High School during the 1957–1958 school year, and also the findings that the educational progress of all the students, white and colored, of that school has suffered and will continue to suffer if the conditions which prevailed last year are permitted to continue.

The significance of these findings, however, is to be considered in light of the fact, indisputably revealed by the record before us, that the conditions they depict are directly traceable to the actions of legislators and executive officials of the State of Arkansas, taken in their official capacities, which reflect their own determination to resist this Court's decision in the *Brown* case and which have brought about violent resistance to that decision in Arkansas. In its petition for *certiorari* filed in this Court, the School Board itself describes the situation in this language: "The legislative, executive, and judicial departments of the state government opposed the desegregation of Little Rock schools by enacting laws, calling out troops, making statements villifying federal law and federal courts, and failing to utilize state law enforcement agencies and judicial processes to maintain public peace."

One may well sympathize with the position of the Board in the face of the frustrating conditions which have confronted it, but, regardless of the Board's good faith, the actions of the other state agencies responsible for those conditions compel us to reject the Board's legal position. Had Central High School been under the direct management of the State itself, it could hardly be suggested that those immediately in charge of the school should be heard to assert their own good faith as a legal excuse for delay in implementing the constitutional rights of these respondents, when vindication of those rights was rendered difficult or impossible by the actions of other state officials. The situation here is in no different posture because the members of the School Board and the Superintendent of Schools are local officials; from the point of view of the Fourteenth Amendment, they stand in this litigation as the agents of the State.

The constitutional rights of respondents are not to be sacrificed or yielded to the violence and disorder which have followed upon the actions of the Governor and Legislature. As this Court said some 41 years ago in a unanimous opinion in a case involving another aspect of racial segregation: "It is urged that this proposed segregation will promote the public peace by preventing race conflicts. Desirable as this is, and important as is the preservation of the public peace, this aim cannot be accomplished by laws or ordinances which deny rights created or protected by the federal Constitution." *Buchanan v. Warley*, 245 U.S. 60 [1917]. Thus law and order are not here to be preserved by depriving the Negro children of their constitutional rights. The record before us clearly establishes that the growth of the Board's difficulties to a magnitude beyond its unaided power to control is the product of state action. Those difficulties, as counsel for the Board forthrightly conceded on the oral argument in this Court, can also be brought under control by state action.

The controlling legal principles are plain. The command of the Fourteenth Amendment is that no "State" shall deny to any person within its jurisdiction the equal protection of the laws. "A State acts by its legislative, its executive, or its judicial authorities. It can act in no other way. The constitutional provision, therefore, must mean that no agency of the State, or of the officers or agents by whom its powers are exerted, shall deny to any person within its jurisdiction the equal protection of the laws. Whoever, by virtue of public position under a State government . . . denies or takes away the equal protection of the laws, violates the constitutional inhibition; and as he acts in the name and for the State, and is clothed with the State's power, his act is that of the State. This must be so, or the constitutional prohibition has no meaning." *Ex parte Virginia*, 100 U.S. 339 [1880]. Thus the prohibitions of the Fourteenth Amendment extend to all action of the State denying equal protection of the laws; whatever the agency of the State taking the action. . . .

In short, the constitutional rights of children not to be discriminated against in school admission on grounds of race or color declared by this Court in the *Brown* case can neither be nullified openly and directly by state legislators or state executive or judicial officers, nor nullified indirectly by them through evasive schemes for segregation whether attempted "ingeniously or ingenuously." *Smith v. Texas*, 311 U.S. 128 [1940].

What has been said, in the light of the facts developed, is enough to dispose of the case. However, we should answer the premise of the actions of the Governor and Legislature that they are not bound by our holding in the *Brown* case. It is necessary only to recall some basic constitutional propositions which are settled doctrine.

Article VI of the Constitution makes the Constitution the "supreme Law of the Land." In 1803, Chief Justice MARSHALL, speaking for a unanimous Court, referring to the Constitution as "the fundamental and paramount law of the nation," declared in the notable case of *Marbury v. Madison* 1 Cr. 137 [1803], that "It is emphatically the province and duty of the judicial department to say what the law is." This decision declared the basic principle that the federal judiciary is supreme in the exposition of the law of the Constitution, and that principle has ever since been respected by this Court and the Country as a permanent and indispensable feature of our constitutional system. It follows that the interpretation of the Fourteenth Amendment enunciated by this Court in the *Brown* case is the supreme law of the land, and Art. VI of the Constitution makes it of binding effect on the States "any Thing in the Constitution or Laws of any State to the Contrary notwithstanding." Every state legislator and executive and judicial officer is solemnly committed by oath taken pursuant to Art. VI, Sec. 3 "to support this Constitution." Chief Justice TANEY, speaking for a unanimous Court in 1859, said that this requirement reflected the framers' "anxiety to preserve it [the Constitution] in full force, in all its powers, and to guard against resistance to or evasion of its authority, on the part of a State. . . ." *Ableman v. Booth*, 21 How. 506 [1859].

No state legislator or executive or judicial officer can war against the Constitution without violating his undertaking to support it. Chief Justice MARSHALL spoke for a unanimous Court in saying that: "If the legislatures of the several states may, at will, annul the judgments of the courts of the United States, and destroy the rights acquired under those judgments, the constitution itself becomes a solemn mockery. . . ." *United States v. Peters*, 5 Cranch 115 [1809].

It is, of course, quite true that the responsibility for public education is primarily the concern of the States, but it is equally true that such responsibilities, like all other state activity, must be exercised consistently with federal constitutional requirements as they apply to state action. The Constitution created a government dedicated to equal justice under law. The Fourteenth Amendment embodied and emphasized that ideal. State support of segregated schools through any arrangement, management, funds, or property cannot be squared with the Amendment's command that no State shall deny to any person within its jurisdiction the equal protection of the laws. The right of a student not to be segregated on racial grounds in schools so maintained is indeed so fundamental and pervasive that it is embraced in the concept of due process of law. *Bolling v. Sharpe*, 347 U.S. 497 [1954]. The basic decision in *Brown* was unanimously reached by this Court only after the case had been briefed and twice argued and the issues had been given the most serious consideration. Since the first *Brown* opinion three new Justices have come to the Court. They are at one with the Justices still on the Court who participated in that basic decision as to its correctness, and that decision is now unanimously reaffirmed. The principles announced in that decision and the obedience of the States to them, according to the command of the Constitution, are indispensable for the protection of the freedoms guaranteed by our fundamental charter for all of us. Our constitutional ideal of equal justice under law is thus made a living truth.

☐ *Justice FRANKFURTER, concurring.*

While unreservedly participating with my brethren in our joint opinion, I deem it appropriate also to deal individually with the great issue here at stake. . . .

We are now asked to hold that the illegal, forcible interference by the State of Arkansas with the continuance of what the Constitution commands, and the consequences in disorder that it entrained, should be recognized as justification for undoing what the Board of Education had formulated, what the District Court in 1955 had directed to be carried out, and what was in process of obedience. No explanation that may be offered in support of such a request can obscure the inescapable meaning that law should bow to force. To yield to such a claim would be to enthrone official lawlessness and lawlessness if not checked is the precursor of anarchy. On the few tragic occasions in the history of the Nation, North and South, when law was forcibly resisted or systematically evaded, it has signalled the breakdown of constitutional processes of government on which ultimately rest the liberties of all. Violent resistance to law cannot be made a legal reason for its suspension without loosening the fabric of our society. What could this mean but to acknowledge that disorder under the aegis of a State has moral superiority over the law of the Constitution. For those in authority thus to defy the law of the land is profoundly subversive not only of our constitutional system but of the presuppositions of a democratic society. The State "must . . . yield to an authority that is paramount to the State." . . .

The process of ending unconstitutional exclusion of pupils from the common school system—"common" meaning shared alike—solely because of color is no doubt not an easy, overnight task in a few States where a drastic alteration in the ways of communities is involved. Deep emotions have, no doubt, been stirred. They will not be calmed by letting violence loose—violence and defiance employed and encouraged by those upon whom the duty of law observance should have the strongest claim—nor by submitting to it under whatever guise employed. Only the constructive use of time will achieve what an advanced civilization demands and the Constitution confirms. . . .

Milliken v. Bradley
418 U.S. 717, 94 S.Ct. 3112 (1974)

In the 1970s, as pressure grew to desegregate urban school systems in the North and West, the school desegregation controversy took a new twist. In some large metropolitan areas, like Detroit, Michigan, "white flight" to the suburbs left inner-city school districts overwhelmingly black. In response, federal district courts began ordering *inter*district remedies, requiring the busing of white children from the suburbs to inner city schools and the busing of black students to predominantly white suburban schools. When the first challenge to such court-ordered busing reached the Supreme Court, the justices split 4-to-4. Justice Powell did not participate in that case because it came from Richmond, Virginia, where he had once headed that city's school board. But the next year the Court decided "the Detroit busing case."

Ronald Bradley, along with several other black students and the NAACP, filed a class-action suit against Michigan's governor, William Milliken, and other state officials. They charged that school district lines were drawn in racially discriminatory ways. A federal district court agreed, ordering the Detroit school board to draw up a desegregation plan and asking eighty-five surrounding school districts to present evidence relevant to the creation of a comprehensive metropolitan desegregation plan. The court eventually adopted a desegregation proposal, drafted by a panel of experts, mandating the busing of school children to and from Detroit and fifty-three neighboring districts. When a federal appellate court affirmed the substance of that order, Governor Milliken appealed to the Supreme Court.

For a bare majority, Chief Justice Burger ruled that court-ordered *inter*district busing is inappropriate for resolving the *intra*district problems, where suburban districts had not engaged in *de jure* segregation, but were *de facto* segregated due to housing patterns.

The Court's decision was 5–4, and the majority's opinion was announced by Chief Justice Burger. Justice Stewart concurred. Dissents were by Justices Douglas, White, and Marshall and joined by Justice Brennan.

■ ■ ■

☐ *Chief Justice BURGER delivered the opinion of the Court.*

We granted *certiorari* in these consolidated cases to determine whether a federal court may impose a multidistrict, areawide remedy to a single-district *de jure* segregation problem absent any finding that the other included school districts have failed to operate unitary school systems within their districts, absent any claim or finding that the boundary lines of any affected school district were established with the purpose of fostering racial segregation in public schools, absent any finding that the included districts committed acts which effected segregation within the other districts, and absent a meaningful opportunity for the included neighboring school districts to present evidence or be heard on the propriety of a multidistrict remedy or on the question of constitutional violations by those neighboring districts. . . .

Viewing the record as a whole, it seems clear that the District Court and the Court of Appeals shifted the primary focus from a Detroit remedy to the metropolitan area only because of their conclusion that total desegregation of Detroit would not produce the racial balance which they perceived as desirable. Both courts proceeded on an assumption that the Detroit schools could not be truly desegregated—in their view of what constituted desegregation—unless the racial composition of the student body of each school substantially reflected the racial composition of the population of the metropolitan area as a whole. The metropolitan area was then defined as Detroit plus 53 of the outlying school districts. . . .

Here the District Court's approach to what constituted "actual desegregation" raises the fundamental question, not presented in *Swann* [*v. Charlotte-Mecklenberg Board of Education*, 402 U.S. 1 (1971)], as to the circumstances in which a federal court may order desegregation relief that embraces more than a single school district. The court's analytical starting point was its conclusion that school district lines are no more than arbitrary lines on a map drawn "for political convenience." Boundary lines may be bridged where there has been a constitutional violation calling for interdistrict relief, but the notion that school district lines may be casually ignored or treated as a mere administrative convenience is contrary to the history of public education in our country. No single tradition in public education is more deeply rooted than local control over the operation of schools; local autonomy has long been thought essential both to the maintenance of community concern and support for public schools and to quality of the educational process. . . . [I]t is obvious from the scope of the interdistrict remedy itself that absent a complete restructuring of the laws of Michigan relating to school districts the District Court will become first, a *de facto* "legislative authority" to resolve these complex questions, and then the "school superintendent" for the entire area. This is a task which few, if any, judges are qualified to perform and one which would deprive the people of control of schools through their elected representatives. . . .

The record before us, voluminous as it is, contains evidence of *de jure* segregated conditions only in the Detroit schools; indeed, that was the theory on which the litigation was initially based and on which the District Court took evidence. With no showing of significant violation by the 53 outlying school districts and no evidence of any interdistrict violation or effect, the court went beyond the original theory of the case as framed by the pleadings and mandated a metropolitan area remedy. To approve the remedy ordered by the court would impose on the outlying districts, not shown to have committed any constitutional violation, a wholly impermissible remedy based on a standard not hinted at in *Brown I* and *II* or any holding of this Court.

In dissent, Justice WHITE and Justice MARSHALL undertake to demonstrate that agencies having statewide authority participated in maintaining the dual school system found to exist in Detroit. They are apparently of the view that once such participation is shown, the District Court should have a relatively free hand to reconstruct school districts outside of Detroit in fashioning relief. Our assumption, *arguendo*, that state agencies did participate in the maintenance of the Detroit system, should make it clear that it is not on this point that we part company. The difference between us arises instead from established doctrine laid down by our cases. *Brown, Green* [*v. School Board of New Kent County*, 391 U.S. 430 (1968)], *Swann*, [*United States v.*] *Scotland Neck* [*City Board of Education*, 407 U.S. 484 (1972)], and [*Wright v. City Council of the City of*] *Emporia*, [407 U.S. 451 (1972)], each addressed the issue of constitutional wrong in terms of an established geographic and administrative school system populated by both Negro and white children. In such a context, terms such as "unitary" and "dual" systems, and "racially identifiable schools," have meaning, and the necessary federal authority to remedy the constitutional wrong is firmly established. But the remedy is necessarily designed, as all remedies are, to restore the victims of discriminatory conduct to the position they would have occupied in the absence of such conduct. Disparate treatment of white and Negro students occurred within the Detroit school system, and not elsewhere, and on this record the remedy must be limited to that system. . . .

The constitutional right of the Negro respondents residing in Detroit is to attend a unitary school system in that district. Unless petitioners drew the district lines in a discriminatory fashion, or arranged for white students residing in the Detroit district to attend schools in Oakland and Macomb Counties, they were under no constitutional duty to make provisions for Negro students to do so. The view of the dissenters, that the existence of a dual system in Detroit can be made the basis for a decree requiring cross-district transportation of pupils, cannot be supported on the grounds that it represents merely the devising of a suitably flexible remedy for the violation of rights already established by our prior decisions. It can be supported only by drastic expansion of the constitutional right itself, an expansion without any support in either constitutional principle or precedent. . . .

Accepting, *arguendo*, the correctness of [a] finding of state responsibility for the segregated conditions within the city of Detroit, it does not follow that an interdistrict remedy is constitutionally justified or required. With a single exception, discussed later, there has been no showing that either the State or any of the 85 outlying districts engaged in activity that had a cross-district effect. The boundaries of the Detroit School District, which are coterminous with the boundaries of the city of Detroit, were established over a century ago by neutral legislation when the city was incorporated; there is no evidence in the record, nor is there any suggestion by the respondents, that either the original boundaries of the Detroit School District, or any other school district in Michigan, were established for the purpose of creating, maintaining, or perpetuating segregation of races. There is no claim and there is no evidence hinting that petitioner outlying school districts and their predecessors, or the 30-odd other school districts in the tricounty area—but outside the District Court's "desegregation area"—have ever maintained or operated anything but unitary school systems. Unitary school systems have been required for more than a century by the Michigan Constitution as implemented by state law. Where the schools of only one district have been affected, there is no constitutional power in the courts to decree relief balancing the racial composition of that district's schools with those of the surrounding districts. . . .

We conclude that the relief ordered by the District Court and affirmed by the Court of Appeals was based upon an erroneous standard and was unsupported by record evidence that acts of the outlying districts effected the discrimination found to exist in the schools of Detroit. Accordingly, the judgment of the Court of Appeals is reversed and the case is remanded for further proceedings consistent with this opinion leading to prompt formulation of a decree directed to eliminating the segregation found to exist in Detroit city schools, a remedy which has been delayed since 1970.

Reversed and remanded.

☐ *Justice MARSHALL, with whom Justice DOUGLAS,*
Justice BRENNAN, and Justice WHITE join, dissenting.

I cannot subscribe to this emasculation of our constitutional guarantee of equal protection of the laws and must respectfully dissent. Our precedents, in my view, firmly establish that where, as here, state-imposed segregation has been demonstrated, it becomes the duty of the State to eliminate root and branch all vestiges of racial discrimination and to achieve the greatest possible degree of actual desegregation. I agree with both the District Court and the Court of Appeals that, under the facts of this case, this duty cannot be fulfilled unless the State of Michigan involves outlying metropolitan area school districts in its desegregation remedy. Furthermore, I perceive no basis either in law or in the practicalities of the situation justifying the State's interposition of school district boundaries as absolute barriers to the implementation of an effective desegregation remedy. Under established and frequently used Michigan procedures, school district lines are both flexible and permeable for a wide variety of purposes, and there is no reason why they must now stand in the way of meaningful desegregation relief. . . .

Desegregation is not and was never expected to be an easy task. Racial attitudes ingrained in our Nation's childhood and adolescence are not quickly thrown aside in its middle years. But just as the inconvenience of some cannot be allowed to stand in the way of the rights of others, so public opposition, no matter how strident, cannot be permitted to divert this Court from the enforcement of the constitutional principles at issue in this case. Today's holding, I fear, is more a reflection of a perceived public mood that we have gone far enough in enforcing the Constitution's guarantee of equal justice than it is the product of neutral principles of law. In the short run, it may seem to be the easier course to allow our great metropolitan areas to be divided up each into two cities—one white, the other black— but it is a course, I predict, our people will ultimately regret. I dissent.

Freeman v. Pitts

503 U.S. 467, 112 S.Ct. 1430 (1992)

Despite the Supreme Court's watershed ruling in *Brown v. Board of Education*, 347 U.S. 483 (1954), and its mandate for desegregation "with all deliberate speed," *Brown v. Board of Education*, 349 U.S. 294 (1955), the DeKalb County, Georgia, public school system (DCSS) made no effort to desegregate for more than a decade. In 1966–1967 the school board finally adopted a "freedom of choice" transfer plan that permitted blacks to go to formerly *de jure* white schools, but that had no impact on desegregating all-black schools. Then in *Green v. New Kent County School Board*, 391 U.S. 430 (1968), the Court struck down a similar "freedom of choice" plan in Virginia. The Court also directed lower courts to examine "every facet of school operations"—including student assignments, faculty, staff, transportation, extracurricular activities, and facilities—in achieving school desegregation.

Within two months of *Green*, Willie Pitts and other black parents and schoolchildren filed a class action against the DCSS to force it to abandon its freedom of choice plan. One year later a federal district court issued a consent order abolishing the freedom of choice plan, closing all formerly *de jure* black schools, and reassigning students to the remaining neighborhood schools. The court retained jurisdiction and continued to supervise the DCSS for more than a decade.

In 1986 Robert Freeman and other members of the DCSS filed a motion to lay the original litigation to rest and to obtain a declaration that "unitary status," according to factors identified in *Green*, had been achieved. The district court concluded that the DCSS had achieved unitary status with respect to student assignments, transportation, facilities, and the extracurricular activities of the schools and required no further remedial efforts in these areas. But the court found continued "vestiges" of segregation in teacher and principal assignments, resource allocations, and the quality of education in different schools in the county. And the DCSS was ordered to continue to address these problems.

In appealing the district court's decisions, Pitts and other black parents countered that continuing racial imbalances in the DCSS were a vestige of past discrimination. In the more than thirty years since *Brown*, DeKalb County, along with the rest of the country, had changed. *De jure* segregation had ended, but schools remained segregated. As the DeKalb County school district grew in population from less than 70,000 to over 450,000, the percentage of black students increased from a little more than 5 percent to 47 percent. Demographic changes and the migration of blacks and whites into suburbs resulted in racially identifiable schools. In 1986–1987, as Pitts's attorneys pointed out, 50 percent of the black students attended schools that were over 90 percent black, while almost 30 percent of the white students went to schools enrolling 90 percent whites. The persistence of racially identifiable schools, Pitts's lawyers argued, required continued efforts to integrate and judicial supervision of the DCSS's operations.

The Court of Appeals for the Eleventh Circuit reversed the district court, rejecting its "incremental" approach to determining unitary status and to ending its desegregation orders. According to the appellate court, the district court erred in considering *Green*'s factors as separate and independent categories. Achieving unitary status, it held, required the DCSS to maintain racial equality for at least three years in all six categories. The appellate court also ordered the DCSS to take radical measures to achieve integration, such as pairing and clustering schools, busing, and drastic gerrymandering of school zones. That decision was promptly appealed by Freeman and the DCSS to the Supreme Court, which granted review.

The Court's decision was unanimous; Justice Kennedy announced the opinion. Justices Scalia and Souter each concurred, as did Justice Blackmun, who was joined by Justices Stevens and O'Connor.

■ ■ ■

☐ *Justice KENNEDY delivered the opinion of the Court.*

Today, we make explicit the rationale that was central in [*Pasadena City Board of Education v.*] *Spangler* [427 U.S. 424 (1976)]. A federal court in a school desegregation case has the discretion to order an incremental or partial withdrawal of its supervision and control. This discretion derives both from the constitutional authority which justified its intervention in the first instance and its ultimate objectives in formulating the decree. The authority of the court is invoked at the outset to remedy particular constitutional violations. In construing the remedial authority of the district courts, we have been guided by the principles that "judicial powers may be exercised only on the basis of a constitutional violation," and that "the nature of the violation determines the scope of the remedy." *Swann* [*v. Charlotte-Mecklenburg Board of Education*, 402 U.S. 1 (1971)]. . . .

We hold that, in the course of supervising desegregation plans, federal courts have the authority to relinquish supervision and control of school districts in incremental stages, before full compliance has been achieved in every area of school operations. While retaining jurisdiction over the case, the court may determine that it will not order further remedies in areas where the school district is in compliance with the decree. That is to say, upon a finding that a school system subject to a court-supervised desegregation plan is in compliance in some but not all areas, the court in appropriate cases may return control to the school system in those areas where compliance has been achieved, limiting further judicial supervision to operations that are not yet in full compliance with the court decree. In particular, the district court may determine that it will not order further remedies in the area of student assignments where racial imbalance is not traceable, in a proximate way, to constitutional violations. . . .

The Court of Appeals' rejection of the District Court's order rests on related premises: first, that given noncompliance in some discrete categories, there can be no partial withdrawal of judicial control; and second, until there is full compliance, heroic measures must be taken to ensure racial balance in student assignments systemwide. Under our analysis and our precedents, neither premise is correct. . . .

That there was racial imbalance in student attendance zones was not tantamount to a showing that the school district was in noncompliance with the decree or with its duties under the law. Racial balance is not to be achieved for its own sake. It is to be pursued when racial imbalance has been caused by a constitutional violation. Once the racial imbalance due to the *de jure* violation has been remedied, the school district is under no duty to remedy imbalance that is caused by demographic factors. . . .

The findings of the District Court that the population changes which occurred in DeKalb County were not caused by the policies of the school district, but rather by independent factors, are consistent with the mobility that is a distinct characteristic of our society. . . . The District Court in this case heard evidence tending to show that racially stable neighborhoods are not likely to emerge because whites prefer a racial mix of 80% white and 20% black, while blacks prefer a 50%–50% mix.

Where resegregation is a product not of state action but of private choices, it does not have constitutional implications. It is beyond the authority and beyond the practical ability of the federal courts to try to counteract these kinds of continuous and massive demographic shifts. To attempt such results would require ongoing and never-ending supervision by the courts of school districts simply because they were once *de jure* segregated. Residential housing choices, and their attendant effects on the racial composition of schools, present an ever-changing pattern, one difficult to address through judicial remedies. . . .

To say, as did the Court of Appeals, that a school district must meet all six *Green* factors before the trial court can declare the system unitary and relinquish its control over school attendance zones, and to hold further that racial balancing by all necessary means is required in the interim, is simply to vindicate a legal phrase. The law is not so formalistic. A proper rule must be based on the necessity to find a feasible remedy that insures systemwide compliance with the court decree and that is directed to curing the effects of the specific violation. . . .

The requirement that the school district show its good faith commitment to the entirety of a desegregation plan so that parents, students and the public have assurance against further injuries or stigma also should be a subject for more specific findings. We stated in *Dowell* that the good faith compliance of the district with the court order over a reasonable period of time is a factor to be considered in deciding whether or not jurisdiction could be relinquished. . . .

The judgment is reversed and the case is remanded to the Court of Appeals.

☐ *Justice SCALIA, concurring.*

At some time, we must acknowledge that it has become absurd to assume, without any further proof, that violations of the Constitution dating from the days when Lyndon Johnson was President, or earlier, continue to have an appreciable effect upon current operation of schools. We are close to that time. While we must continue to prohibit, without qualification, all racial discrimination in the operation of public schools, and to afford remedies that eliminate not only the discrimination but its identified consequences, we should consider laying aside the extraordinary, and increasingly counterfactual, presumption of *Green*. We must soon revert to the ordinary principles of our law, of our democratic heritage, and of our educational tradition: that plaintiffs alleging Equal Protection violations must prove intent and causation and not merely the existence of racial disparity; that public schooling, even in the South, should be controlled by locally elected authorities acting in conjunction with parents; and that it is "desirable" to permit pupils to attend "schools nearest their homes," *Swann*.

Parents Involved in Community Schools v. Seattle School District No. 1

551 U.S. 701, 127 S.Ct. 2738 (2007)

In response to the problems of achieving and maintaining integration following the rulings in *Freeman v. Pitts*, 503 U.S. 467 (1992) (excerpted above) and *Missouri v. Jenkins* (*Jenkins II*), 515 U.S. 70 (1995), which signaled the end of court-ordered and supervised integration efforts, some local school boards adopted race-based assignment policies to maintain integrated schools in the face of increasingly racially isolated public schools. Those policies were in turn challenged in light of the Court's rulings in *Gratz v. Bollinger*, 539 U.S. 244 (2003) (excerpted in this chapter), which invalidated the University of Michigan undergraduate affirmative-action program based on a point system, and *Grutter v. Bollinger*, 539 U.S. 244 (2003) (excerpted in this chapter), which upheld the University of Michigan Law School's program by a 5–4 vote (with Justice O'Connor casting the crucial vote) in holding that race may be considered a factor in admissions in order to achieve diverse student bodies. The Roberts Court reconsidered those rulings and the use of race in student assignments in public schools in *Parents Involved in Community Schools v. Seattle School District No. 1* and *Meredith v. Jefferson County Board of Education* (2007).

Seattle School District No. 1 presented a challenge to a policy of giving, under certain circumstances, racial preferences in school assignments. Under the program, students indicated their preference for a high school, but the district assigned them with a goal of having a mix of 40 percent white students and 60 percent racial minorities to offset racially segregated housing patterns. If too many white students applied for the same school, priority was given to those with a sibling at the school. Otherwise, racial preference was used as a "tiebreaker" in school assignments. A federal district court upheld the program as narrowly tailored to achieving the school district's goal of integrated schools, and the Court of Appeals for the Ninth Circuit affirmed.

Meredith v. Jefferson County Board of Education involved a challenge to a different kind of race-based student assignment. Jefferson County, Louisville, Kentucky, like other areas around the country, was increasingly racially isolated due to housing patterns. In order to maintain an integrated school system, the county adopted guidelines aimed at assuring that 15 percent to 50 percent of each school enrolled African Americans. The county provided for both traditional and special, nontraditional magnet schools. Any student could apply to the traditional schools, but only students from certain designated residential areas could apply to nontraditional magnet schools, which offered more educational opportunities and resources. The policy was challenged by a white family whose son was not assigned to a nontraditional magnet school located across the street from their house. A federal district court rejected their claim that the policy amounted to a quota system, since there was no fixed criterion, and the county had a compelling interest in maintaining racial diversity in its schools. However, the court found that the guidelines for student assignments to traditional schools were not narrowly tailored because, unlike nontraditional magnet schools, the assignment process placed applicants on different racial tracks. The Court of Appeals for the Sixth Circuit affirmed.

Both cases were appealed and the Supreme Court granted review and consolidated them. The appellate courts' decisions were reversed by a 5–4 vote. Chief Justice Roberts issued an opinion for a plurality of the Court. Justices Kennedy and Thomas filed concurring opinions. Justice Breyer, joined by Justices Stevens, Souter, and Ginsburg, filed a dissenting opinion; Justice Stevens also filed a separate dissenting opinion.

■ ■ ■

   ☐ *Chief Justice ROBERTS announced the judgment of the Court, and delivered the opinion of the Court with respect to Parts I, II, III-A, and III-C, and an opinion with respect to Parts III-B and IV, in which Justices SCALIA, THOMAS, and ALITO join.*

The school districts in these cases voluntarily adopted student assignment plans that rely upon race to determine which public schools certain children may attend. The Seattle school district classifies children as white or nonwhite; the Jefferson County school district as black or "other." In Seattle, this racial classification is used to allocate slots in oversubscribed high schools. In Jefferson County, it is used to make certain elementary school assignments and to rule on transfer requests. In each case, the school district relies upon an individual student's race in assigning that student to a particular school, so that the racial balance at the school falls within a predetermined range based on the racial composition of the school district as a whole. Parents of students denied assignment to particular schools under these plans solely because of their race brought suit, contending that allocating children to different public schools on the basis of race violated the Fourteenth Amendment guarantee of equal protection. The Courts of Appeals below upheld the plans. We granted *certiorari*, and now reverse. . . .

■ III

■ A

It is well established that when the government distributes burdens or benefits on the basis of individual racial classifications, that action is reviewed under strict scrutiny. *Grutter v. Bollinger*, 539 U.S. 306 (2003). As the Court recently reaffirmed, "racial classifications are simply too pernicious to permit any but the most exact connection between justification and classification." *Gratz v. Bollinger*, 539 U.S. 244 (2003). In order to satisfy this searching standard of review, the school districts must demonstrate that the use of individual racial classifications in the assignment plans here under review is "narrowly tailored" to achieve a "compelling" government interest.

Without attempting in these cases to set forth all the interests a school district might assert, it suffices to note that our prior cases, in evaluating the use of racial classifications in the school context, have recognized two interests that qualify as compelling. The first is the compelling interest of remedying the effects of past intentional discrimination. See *Freeman v. Pitts*, 503 U.S. 467 (1992). Yet the Seattle public schools have not shown that they were ever segregated by law, and were not subject to court-ordered desegregation decrees. The Jefferson County public schools were previously segregated by law and were subject to a desegregation decree entered in 1975. In 2000, the District Court that entered that decree dissolved it, finding that Jefferson County had "eliminated the vestiges associated with the former policy of segregation and its pernicious effects," and thus had achieved "unitary" status. . . .

The second government interest we have recognized as compelling for purposes of strict scrutiny is the interest in diversity in higher education upheld in *Grutter*. The specific interest found compelling in *Grutter* was student body diversity "in the context of higher education." The diversity interest was not focused on race alone but encompassed "all factors that may contribute to student body diversity." . . .

The entire gist of the analysis in *Grutter* was that the admissions program at issue there focused on each applicant as an individual, and not simply as a member of a particular racial group. The classification of applicants by race upheld in *Grutter* was only as part of a "highly individualized, holistic review." The point of the narrow tailoring analysis in which the *Grutter* Court engaged was to ensure that the use of racial classifications was indeed part of a broader assessment of diversity, and not simply an effort to achieve racial balance, which the Court explained would be "patently unconstitutional."

In the present cases, by contrast, race is not considered as part of a broader effort to achieve "exposure to widely diverse people, cultures, ideas, and viewpoints"; race, for some students, is determinative standing alone. Like the University of Michigan undergraduate plan struck down in *Gratz*, the plans here "do not provide for a meaningful individualized review of applicants" but instead rely on racial classifications in a "nonindividualized, mechanical" way.

Even when it comes to race, the plans here employ only a limited notion of diversity, viewing race exclusively in white/nonwhite terms in Seattle and black/"other" terms in Jefferson County. [U]nder the Seattle plan, a school with 50 percent Asian-American students and 50 percent white students but no African-American, Native-American, or Latino students would qualify as balanced, while a school with 30 percent Asian-American, 25 percent African-American, 25 percent Latino, and 20 percent white students would not. It is hard to understand how a plan that could allow these results can be viewed as being concerned with achieving enrollment that is "broadly diverse." . . .

■ IV

In *Brown v. Board of Education*, 347 U.S. 483 (1954) (*Brown I*), we held that segregation deprived black children of equal educational opportunities regardless of whether school facilities and other tangible factors were equal, because government classification and separation on grounds of race themselves denoted inferiority. It was not the inequality of the facilities but the fact of legally separating children on the basis of race on which the Court relied to find a constitutional violation in 1954. The next Term, we accordingly stated that "full compliance" with *Brown I* required school districts "to achieve a system of determining admission to the public schools on a nonracial basis." *Brown II*.

The parties and their *amici* debate which side is more faithful to the heritage of *Brown*, but the position of the plaintiffs in *Brown* was spelled out in their brief and could not have been clearer: "[T]he Fourteenth Amendment prevents states from according differential treatment to American children on the basis of their color or race." What do the racial classifications at issue here do, if not accord differential treatment on the basis of race? As counsel who appeared before this Court for the plaintiffs in *Brown* put it: "We have one fundamental contention which we will seek to develop in the course of this argument, and that contention is that no State has any authority under the equal-protection clause of the Fourteenth Amendment to use race as a factor in affording educational opportunities among its citizens." There is no ambiguity in that statement. And it was that position that prevailed in this Court, which emphasized in its remedial opinion that what was "[a]t stake is the personal interest of the plaintiffs in admission to public schools as soon as practicable on a nondiscriminatory basis," and what was required was "determining admission to the public schools on a nonracial basis." *Brown II*. What do the racial classifications do in these cases, if not determine admission to a public school on a racial basis? Before *Brown*, schoolchildren were told where they could and could not go to school based on the color of their skin. The school districts in these cases have not carried the heavy burden of demonstrating that we should allow this once again—even for very different reasons. For schools that never segregated on the basis of race, such as Seattle, or that have removed the vestiges of past segregation, such as Jefferson County, the way "to achieve a system of determining admission to the public schools on a nonracial basis," *Brown II*, is to stop assigning students on a racial basis. The way to stop discrimination on the basis of race is to stop discriminating on the basis of race.

The judgments of the Courts of Appeals for the Sixth and Ninth Circuits are reversed, and the cases are remanded for further proceedings. It is so ordered.

☐ *Justice KENNEDY, concurring in part and concurring in the judgment.*

Diversity, depending on its meaning and definition, is a compelling educational goal a school district may pursue.

It is well established that when a governmental policy is subjected to strict scrutiny, "the government has the burden of proving that racial classifications 'are narrowly tailored measures that further compelling governmental interests.'" "Absent searching judicial inquiry into the justification for such race-based measures, there is simply no way of determining what classifications are 'benign' or 'remedial' and what classifications are in fact motivated by illegitimate notions of racial inferiority or simple racial politics." *Richmond v. J.A. Croson Co.*, 488 U.S. 469 (1989). And the inquiry into less restrictive alternatives demanded by the narrow tailoring analysis requires in many cases a thorough understanding of how a plan works. The government bears the burden of justifying its use of individual racial classifications. As part of that burden it must establish, in detail, how decisions based on an individual student's race are made in a challenged governmental program. The Jefferson County Board of Education fails to meet this threshold mandate. . . .

As for the Seattle case, the school district has gone further in describing the methods and criteria used to determine assignment decisions on the basis of individual racial classifications. The district, nevertheless, has failed to make an adequate showing in at least one respect. It has failed to explain why, in a district composed of a diversity of races, with fewer than half of the students classified as "white," it has employed the crude racial categories of "white" and "non-white" as the basis for its assignment decisions. . . .

This is by way of preface to my respectful submission that parts of the opinion by THE CHIEF JUSTICE imply an all-too-unyielding insistence that race cannot be a factor in instances when, in my view, it may be taken into account. The plurality opinion is too dismissive of the legitimate interest government has in ensuring all people have equal opportunity regardless of their race. The plurality's postulate that "[t]he way to stop discrimination on the basis of race is to stop discriminating on the basis of race" is not sufficient to decide these cases. Fifty years of experience since *Brown v. Board of Education* (1954) should teach us that the problem before us defies so easy a solution. School districts can seek to reach *Brown*'s objective of equal educational opportunity. The plurality opinion is at least open to the interpretation that the Constitution requires school districts to ignore the problem of *de facto* resegregation in schooling. I cannot endorse that conclusion. To the extent the plurality opinion suggests the Constitution mandates that state and local school authorities must accept the status quo of racial isolation in schools, it is, in my view, profoundly mistaken.

The statement by Justice HARLAN that "[o]ur Constitution is color-blind" was most certainly justified in the context of his dissent in *Plessy v. Ferguson*, 163 U.S. 537 (1896). The Court's decision in that case was a grievous error it took far too long to overrule. *Plessy*, of course, concerned official classification by race applicable to all persons who sought to use railway carriages. And, as an aspiration, Justice HARLAN's axiom must command our assent. In the real world, it is regrettable to say, it cannot be a universal constitutional principle.

In the administration of public schools by the state and local authorities it is permissible to consider the racial makeup of schools and to adopt general policies to encourage a diverse student body, one aspect of which is its racial composition. If school authorities are concerned that the student-body compositions of certain schools interfere with the objective of offering an equal educational opportunity to all of their students, they are free to devise race-conscious measures to address the problem in a general way and without treating each student in different fashion solely on the basis of a systematic, individual typing by race.

School boards may pursue the goal of bringing together students of diverse backgrounds and races through other means, including strategic site selection of new schools; drawing attendance zones with general recognition of the demographics of neighborhoods; allocating resources for special programs; recruiting students and faculty in a targeted fashion; and tracking enrollments, performance, and other statistics by race. These mechanisms are race conscious but do not lead to different treatment based on a classification that tells each student he or she is to be defined by race, so it is unlikely any of them would demand strict scrutiny to be found permissible. Executive and legislative branches, which for generations now have considered these types of policies and procedures, should be permitted to employ them with candor and with confidence that a constitutional violation does not occur whenever a decisionmaker considers the impact a given approach might have on students of different races. Assigning to each student a personal designation according to a crude system of individual racial classifications is quite a different matter; and the legal analysis changes accordingly. . . .

The idea that if race is the problem, race is the instrument with which to solve it cannot be accepted as an analytical leap forward. And if this is a frustrating duality of the Equal Protection Clause it simply reflects the duality of our history and our attempts to promote freedom in a world that sometimes seems set against it. Under our Constitution the individual, child or adult, can find his own identity, can define her own persona, without state intervention that classifies on the basis of his race or the color of her skin.

This Nation has a moral and ethical obligation to fulfill its historic commitment to creating an integrated society that ensures equal opportunity for all of its children. A compelling interest exists in avoiding racial isolation, an interest that a school district, in its discretion and expertise, may choose to pursue. Likewise, a district may consider it a compelling interest to achieve a diverse student population. Race may be one component of that diversity, but other demographic factors, plus special talents and needs, should also be considered. What the government is not permitted to do, absent a showing of necessity not made here, is to classify every student on the basis of race and to assign each of them to schools based on that classification. Crude measures of this sort threaten to reduce children to racial chits valued and traded according to one school's supply and another's demand.

That statement, to be sure, invites this response: A sense of stigma may already become the fate of those separated out by circumstances beyond their immediate control. But to this the replication must be: Even so, measures other than differential treatment based on racial typing of individuals first must be exhausted.

The decision today should not prevent school districts from continuing the important work of bringing together students of different racial, ethnic, and economic backgrounds. Due to a variety of factors—some influenced by government, some not—neighborhoods in our communities do not reflect the diversity of our Nation as a whole. Those entrusted with directing our public schools can bring to bear the creativity of experts, parents, administrators, and other concerned citizens to find a way to achieve the compelling interests they face without resorting to widespread governmental allocation of benefits and burdens on the basis of racial classifications.

With this explanation I concur in the judgment of the Court.

□ *Justice BREYER, with whom Justice STEVENS, Justice SOUTER, and Justice GINSBURG join, dissenting.*

These cases consider the longstanding efforts of two local school boards to integrate their public schools. The school board plans before us resemble many others adopted in the last 50 years by primary and secondary schools throughout the Nation. All of those plans represent local efforts to bring about the kind of racially integrated education that *Brown v. Board of Education* (1954) long ago promised—efforts that this Court has repeatedly required, permitted, and encouraged local authorities to undertake. This Court has recognized that the public interests at stake in such cases are "compelling." We have approved of "narrowly tailored" plans that are no less race-conscious than the plans before us. And we have understood that the Constitution permits local communities to adopt desegregation plans even where it does not *require* them to do so.

The plurality pays inadequate attention to this law, to past opinions' rationales, their language, and the contexts in which they arise. As a result, it reverses course and reaches the wrong conclusion. In doing so, it distorts precedent, it misapplies the relevant constitutional principles, it announces legal rules that will obstruct efforts by state and local governments to deal effectively with the growing resegregation of public schools, it threatens to substitute for present calm a disruptive round of race-related litigation, and it undermines *Brown*'s promise of integrated primary and secondary education that local communities have sought to make a reality. This cannot be justified in the name of the Equal Protection Clause. . . .

Louisville began its integration efforts in earnest when a federal court in 1975 entered a school desegregation order. Seattle undertook its integration efforts in response to the filing of a federal lawsuit and as a result of its settlement of a segregation complaint filed with the federal OCR.

The plans in both Louisville and Seattle grow out of these earlier remedial efforts. Both districts faced problems that reflected initial periods of severe racial segregation, followed by such remedial efforts as busing, followed by evidence of resegregation, followed by a need to end busing and encourage the return of, e.g., suburban students through increased student choice. When formulating the plans under review, both districts drew upon their considerable experience with earlier plans, having revised their policies periodically in light of that experience. Both districts rethought their methods over time and explored a wide range of other means, including non-race-conscious policies. Both districts also considered elaborate studies and consulted widely within their communities.

Both districts sought greater racial integration for educational and democratic, as well as for remedial, reasons. Both sought to achieve these objectives while preserving their commitment to other educational goals, e.g., district wide commitment to high quality public schools, increased pupil assignment to neighborhood schools, diminished use of busing, greater student choice, reduced risk of white flight, and so forth. Consequently, the present plans expand student choice; they limit the burdens (including busing) that earlier plans had imposed upon students and their families; and they use race-conscious criteria in limited and gradually diminishing ways. In particular, they use race-conscious criteria only to mark the outer bounds of broad population-related ranges.

The histories also make clear the futility of looking simply to whether earlier school segregation was *de jure* or *de facto* in order to draw firm lines separating the constitutionally permissible from the constitutionally forbidden use of "race-conscious" criteria. [O]ur precedent has recognized that *de jure* discrimination can be present even in the absence of racially explicit laws. See *Yick Wo v. Hopkins*, 118 U.S. 356 (1886).

No one here disputes that Louisville's segregation was *de jure*. But what about Seattle's? Was it *de facto*? *De jure*? A mixture? Opinions differed. Or is it that a prior federal court had not adjudicated the matter? Does that make a difference? Is Seattle free on remand to say that its schools were *de jure* segregated, just as in 1956 a memo for the School Board admitted? The plurality does not seem confident as to the answer.

A court finding of *de jure* segregation cannot be the crucial variable. After all, a number of school districts in the South that the Government or private plaintiffs challenged as segregated by law voluntarily desegregated their schools without a court order—just as Seattle did.

Moreover, Louisville's history makes clear that a community under a court order to desegregate might submit a race-conscious remedial plan before the court dissolved the order, but with every intention of following that plan even after dissolution. How could such a plan be lawful the day before dissolution but then become unlawful the very next day? On what legal ground can the majority rest its contrary view?

Are courts really to treat as merely *de facto* segregated those school districts that avoided a federal order by voluntarily complying with *Brown*'s requirements? This Court has previously done just the opposite, permitting a race-conscious remedy without any kind of court decree. Because the Constitution emphatically does not forbid the use of race-conscious measures by districts in the South that voluntarily desegregated their schools, on what basis does the plurality claim that the law forbids Seattle to do the same?

The histories also indicate the complexity of the tasks and the practical difficulties that local school boards face when they seek to achieve greater racial integration. The boards work in communities where demographic patterns change, where they must meet traditional learning goals, where they must attract and retain effective teachers, where they should (and will) take account of parents' views and maintain their commitment to public school education, where they must adapt to court intervention, where they must encourage voluntary student and parent action—where they will find that their own good faith, their knowledge, and their understanding of local circumstances are always necessary but often insufficient to solve the problems at hand.

These facts and circumstances help explain why in this context, as to means, the law often leaves legislatures, city councils, school boards, and voters with a broad range of choice, thereby giving "different communities" the opportunity to "try different solutions to common problems and gravitate toward those that prove most successful or seem to them best to suit their individual needs."

With this factual background in mind, I turn to the legal question: Does the United States Constitution prohibit these school boards from using race-conscious criteria in the limited ways at issue here?

A longstanding and unbroken line of legal authority tells us that the Equal Protection Clause permits local school boards to use race-conscious criteria to achieve positive race-related goals, even when the Constitution does not compel it. . . .

Courts are not alone in accepting as constitutionally valid the legal principle that *Swann* [*v. Charlotte-Mecklenburg*, 402 U.S. 1 (1971)] enunciated—i.e., that the government may voluntarily adopt race-conscious measures to improve conditions of race even when it is not under a constitutional obligation to do so. That principle has been accepted by every branch of government and is rooted in the history of the Equal Protection Clause itself. Thus, Congress has enacted numerous race-conscious statutes that illustrate that principle or rely upon its validity. In fact, without being exhaustive, I have counted 51 federal statutes that use racial classifications. I have counted well over 100 state statutes that similarly employ racial classifications. Presidential administrations for the past half-century have used and supported various race-conscious measures. And during the same time, hundreds of local school districts have adopted student assignment plans that use race-conscious criteria. . . .

The principal interest advanced in these cases to justify the use of race-based criteria goes by various names. Sometimes a court refers to it as an interest in achieving racial "diversity." Other times a court, like the plurality here, refers to it as an interest in racial "balancing." I have used more general terms to signify that interest, describing it, for example, as an interest in promoting or preserving greater racial "integration" of public schools. By this term, I mean the school districts' interest in eliminating school-by-school racial isolation and increasing the degree to which racial mixture characterizes each of the district's schools and each individual student's public school experience.

Regardless of its name, however, the interest at stake possesses three essential elements. First, there is a historical and remedial element: an interest in setting right the consequences of prior conditions of segregation. This refers back to a time when public schools were highly segregated, often as a result of legal or administrative policies that facilitated racial segregation in public schools. It is an interest in continuing to combat the remnants of segregation caused in whole or in part by these school-related policies, which have often affected not only schools, but also housing patterns, employment practices, economic conditions, and social attitudes. It is an interest in maintaining hard-won gains. And it has its roots in preventing what gradually may become the *de facto* resegregation of America's public schools.

Second, there is an educational element: an interest in overcoming the adverse educational effects produced by and associated with highly segregated schools. Studies suggest that children taken from those schools and placed in integrated settings often show positive academic gains. . . .

Third, there is a democratic element: an interest in producing an educational environment that reflects the "pluralistic society" in which our children will live. It is an interest in helping our children learn to work and play together with children of different racial backgrounds. It is an interest in teaching children to engage in the kind of cooperation among Americans of all races that is necessary to make a land of three hundred million people one Nation. . . .

I next ask whether the plans before us are "narrowly tailored" to achieve these "compelling" objectives. I shall not accept the school board's assurances on faith, and I shall subject the "tailoring" of their plans to "rigorous judicial review." *Grutter.* Several factors, taken together, nonetheless lead me to conclude that the boards' use of race-conscious criteria in these plans passes even the strictest "tailoring" test.

First, the race-conscious criteria at issue only help set the outer bounds of broad ranges. They constitute but one part of plans that depend primarily upon other, nonracial elements. To use race in this way is not to set a forbidden "quota." . . .

Second, broad-range limits on voluntary school choice plans are less burdensome, and hence more narrowly tailored than other race-conscious restrictions this Court has previously approved. Indeed, the plans before us are more narrowly tailored than the race-conscious admission plans that this Court approved in *Grutter.* Here, race becomes a factor only in a fraction of students' non-merit-based assignments—not in large numbers of students' merit-based applications. Moreover, the effect of applying race-conscious criteria here affects potentially disadvantaged students less severely, not more severely, than the criteria at issue in *Grutter.* Disappointed students are not rejected from a State's flagship graduate program; they simply attend a different one of the district's many public schools, which in aspiration and in fact are substantially equal. And, in Seattle, the disadvantaged student loses at most one year at the high school of his choice. One will search *Grutter* in vain for similarly persuasive evidence of narrow tailoring as the school districts have presented here.

Third, the manner in which the school boards developed these plans itself reflects "narrow tailoring." Each plan was devised to overcome a history of segregated public schools. Each plan embodies the results of local experience and community consultation. Each plan is the product of a process that has sought to enhance student choice, while diminishing the need for mandatory busing. And each plan's use of race-conscious elements is diminished compared to the use of race in preceding integration plans. . . .

Finally, I recognize that the Court seeks to distinguish *Grutter* from these cases by claiming that *Grutter* arose in "the context of higher education." But that is not a meaningful legal distinction. I have explained why I do not believe the Constitution could possibly find "compelling" the provision of a racially diverse education for a 23-year-old law student but not for a 13-year-old high school pupil. And I have explained how the plans before us are more narrowly tailored than those in *Grutter.* I add that one cannot find a relevant distinction in the fact that these school districts did not examine the merits of applications "individual[ly]." The context here does not involve admission by merit; a child's academic, artistic, and athletic "merits" are not at all relevant to the child's placement. These are not affirmative action plans, and hence "individualized scrutiny" is simply beside the point.

The upshot is that these plans' specific features—(1) their limited and historically-diminishing use of race, (2) their strong reliance upon other non-race-conscious elements, (3) their history and the manner in which the districts developed and modified their approach, (4) the comparison with prior plans, and (5) the lack of reasonably evident alternatives—together show that the districts' plans are "narrowly tailored" to achieve their "compelling" goals. In sum, the districts' race-conscious plans satisfy "strict scrutiny" and are therefore lawful. . . .

The wide variety of different integration plans that school districts use throughout the Nation suggests that the problem of racial segregation in schools, including *de facto* segregation, is difficult to solve. The fact that many such plans have used explicitly racial criteria suggests that such criteria have an important, sometimes necessary, role to play. The fact that the controlling opinion would make a school district's use of such criteria often unlawful (and the plurality's "colorblind" view would make such use always unlawful) suggests that today's opinion will require setting aside the laws of several States and many local communities.

As I have pointed out, *de facto* resegregation is on the rise. It is reasonable to conclude that such resegregation can create serious educational, social, and civic problems. Given the conditions in which school boards work to set policy, they may need all of the means presently at their disposal to combat those problems. Yet the plurality would deprive them of at least one tool that some districts now consider vital—the limited use of broad race-conscious student population ranges. . . .

Until today, this Court understood the Constitution as affording the people, acting through their elected representatives, freedom to select the use of "race-conscious" criteria from among their available options. See *Adarand Constructors, Inc.*, 515 U.S. [200 (1995)] ("[S]trict scrutiny" in this context is "[not] 'strict in theory, but fatal in fact'" (MARSHALL, J., concurring in judgment)). Today, however, the Court restricts (and some Members would eliminate) that leeway. I fear the consequences of doing so for the law, for the schools, for the democratic process, and for America's efforts to create, out of its diversity, one Nation. . . .

[T]he opinion's reasoning is long. But its conclusion is short: The plans before us satisfy the requirements of the Equal Protection Clause. And it is the plurality's opinion, not this dissent that "fails to ground the result it would reach in law."

Four basic considerations have led me to this view. First, the histories of Louisville and Seattle reveal complex circumstances and a long tradition of conscientious efforts by local school boards to resist racial segregation in public schools. Segregation at the time of *Brown* gave way to expansive remedies that included busing, which in turn gave rise to fears of white flight and resegregation. For decades now, these school boards have considered and adopted and revised assignment plans that sought to rely less upon race, to emphasize greater student choice, and to improve the conditions of all schools for all students, no matter the color of their skin, no matter where they happen to reside. The plans under review—which are less burdensome, more egalitarian, and more effective than prior plans—continue in that tradition. And their history reveals school district goals whose remedial, educational, and democratic elements are inextricably intertwined each with the others.

Second, since this Court's decision in *Brown*, the law has consistently and unequivocally approved of both voluntary and compulsory race-conscious measures to combat segregated schools. The Equal Protection Clause, ratified following the Civil War, has always distinguished in practice between state action that excludes and thereby subordinates racial minorities and state action that seeks to bring together people of all races. From *Swann* to *Grutter*, this Court's decisions have emphasized this distinction, recognizing that the fate of race relations in this country depends upon unity among our children, "for unless our children begin to learn together, there is little hope that our people will ever learn to live together." *Milliken [v. Bradley*, 418 U.S. 717 (1974)] (MARSHALL, J., dissenting).

Third, the plans before us, subjected to rigorous judicial review, are supported by compelling state interests and are narrowly tailored to accomplish those goals. Just as diversity in higher education was deemed compelling in *Grutter*, diversity in public primary and secondary schools—where there is even more to gain—must be, *a fortiori*, a compelling state interest. . . .

Fourth, the plurality's approach risks serious harm to the law and for the Nation. Its view of the law rests either upon a denial of the distinction between exclusionary and inclusive use of race-conscious criteria in the context of the Equal Protection Clause, or upon such a rigid application of its "test" that the distinction loses practical significance. Consequently, the Court's decision today slows down and sets back the work of local school boards to bring about racially diverse schools.

Indeed, the consequences of the approach the Court takes today are serious. Yesterday, the plans under review were lawful. Today, they are not. Yesterday, the citizens of this Nation could look for guidance to this Court's unanimous pronouncements concerning desegregation. Today, they cannot. Yesterday, school boards had available to them a full range of means to combat segregated schools. Today, they do not. . . .

Finally, what of the hope and promise of *Brown*? For much of this Nation's history, the races remained divided. It was not long ago that people of different races drank from separate fountains, rode on separate buses, and studied in separate schools. In this Court's finest hour, *Brown v. Board of Education* challenged this history and helped to change it. For *Brown* held out a promise. It was a promise embodied in three Amendments designed to make citizens of slaves. It was the promise of true racial equality—not as a matter of fine words on paper, but as a matter of everyday life in the Nation's cities and schools. It was about the nature of a democracy that must work for all Americans. It sought one law, one Nation, one people, not simply as a matter of legal principle but in terms of how we actually live. . . .

I must dissent.

■ THE DEVELOPMENT OF LAW

Other Important Rulings on School Desegregation

CASE	VOTE	RULING
North Carolina Board of Education v. Swann, 402 U.S. 43 (1971)	9–0	Struck down a state law forbidding the use of busing to achieve school desegregation.
Wright v. City Council of Emporia, 407 U.S. 451 (1972)	5–4	Held that a city, which had been part of a county school system, could not establish a separate school if it impeded efforts to

dismantle a dual school system; Chief Justice Burger and Justices Blackmun, Powell, and Rehnquist dissented.

CASE	VOTE	RULING
United States v. Scotland Neck City Board of Education, 407 U.S. 484 (1972)	5–4	Struck down a state law providing for some new school districts that were 57 percent white and 43 percent black, while other districts remained over

89 percent black; Chief Justice Burger and Justices Blackmun, Powell, and Rehnquist dissented.

CASE	VOTE	RULING
Keyes v. Denver School District, 413 U.S. 189 (1973)	8–1	Found that intentional segregation by a school system created a prima facie case for unlawful segregation in the entire school system; Justice Rehnquist dissented.
Pasadena City Board of Education v. Spangler, 427 U.S. 424 (1976)	6–2	Held that schools need not rearrange attendance zones each year so as to ensure that a racial mix is maintained in perpetuity; Justices Brennan and Marshall dissented.
Columbus Board of Education v. Penick, 443 U.S. 449 (1979), and *Dayton Board of Education v. Brinkman,* 443 U.S. 526 (1979)	7–2 & 5–4	The Court found intentional discrimination and upheld a lower court's order for massive busing, where in 1976 70 percent of all students attended schools that were either 80 percent black or white; in *Penick*, Justices Powell

■ THE DEVELOPMENT OF LAW
Other Important Rulings on School Desegregation (continued)

and Rehnquist dissented, and in *Brinkman* they were joined by Chief
Justice Burger and Justice Stewart in dissent.

CASE	VOTE	RULING
Washington v. Seattle School District No. 1, 458 U.S. 457 (1982)	5–4	Struck down an initiative requiring children to attend schools nearest to their homes; Chief Justice Burger and Justices O'Connor, Powell, and Rehnquist dissented.
Crawford v. Board of Education of the City of Los Angeles, 458 U.S. 527 (1982)	8–1	Upheld California's amendment to its state constitution limiting state court-ordered busing for the purpose of achieving integrated public schools; Justice Marshall dissented.
Missouri v. Jenkins (Jenkins I), 495 U.S. 33 (1990)	5–4	Justice White upheld the authority of a federal judge to order the Kansas City, Missouri, school board to raise taxes to pay for a wide-ranging

magnet school plan designed to achieve racial integration. But, in so holding, Justice White was joined by only Justices Brennan, Marshall, Stevens,
and Blackmun. In a separate concurring opinion, joined by Chief Justice
Rehnquist and Justices O'Connor and Scalia, Justice Kennedy declined to
join the Court's holding. Simply put, in Justice Kennedy's words, "The
power of taxation is one that the federal judiciary does not possess."

Board of Education of Oklahoma City Public Schools v. Dowell, 498 U.S. 237 (1991)	5–3	Without Justice Souter's participation, the Court held that school districts that were previously required by law to eliminate racial segregation could end forced bus-

ing of students in favor of neighborhood schools, even though that entails a return to a system of schools attended overwhelmingly by either
black or white students. In terminating local court supervision of school
districts' desegregation efforts, lower courts should consider (1) whether

school districts have complied with judicial desegregation orders over a reasonable period of time; (2) whether they are likely to return to their former ways; and (3) whether they have to the extent practicable eliminated "vestiges" of prior discrimination. Justices Marshall, Blackmun, and Stevens dissented.

CASE	VOTE	RULING

Freeman v. Pitts, 503 U.S. 467 (1992)   9–0   Held that lower courts may withdraw from supervising discrete categories of school operations, as identified in *Green v. New Kent County School Board*, 391 U.S. 430 (1968) (that is, student assignments, faculty, staff, transportation, extracurricular activities, and facilities), once schools show compliance with a desegregation order, and they need not await desegregation in all areas of a school system before ending judicial supervision. Concurring Justice Scalia urged an immediate end to all judicial supervision of schools that no longer intentionally discriminate, while Justices Blackmun, Stevens, and O'Connor countered that lower courts should make a probing analysis before abandoning their supervision of desegregation efforts.

United States v. Fordice, 503 U.S. 717 (1992)   8½–½   Writing for the Court, Justice White found that Mississippi's admissions policies for its colleges and universities perpetuated racial segregation in its institutions of higher education. In a separate opinion concurring and dissenting, Justice Scalia rejected the majority's reasoning and standards for lower courts reviewing desegregation challenges to institutions of higher education.

Missouri v. Jenkins (*Jenkins II*), 515 U.S. 70 (1995)   5–4   Reiterating that the lower federal courts should disengage from desegregation efforts, Chief Justice Rehnquist held that a federal district court had exceeded its remedial owners in ordering the state (1) to fund salary increases for teachers, and (2) to continue to fund remedial "quality education" programs because student achievement scores remained "at or below national norms." Dissenting Justices Souter, Stevens, Ginsburg, and Breyer sharply disagreed with the majority's conclusion that lower courts possess no authority to order improvements in school districts so as to make them more attractive to white students.

C | Affirmative Action and Reverse Discrimination

In the late 1960s, the federal government took the lead in ending racial segregation and discrimination in education, housing, and employment. Along with state and local governments and private business, the federal government promoted "affirmative action" programs—programs aimed at increasing opportunities for blacks, women, and other minorities in higher education and employment. Affirmative action programs ranged from aggressive recruiting and remedial training programs, to setting goals and guidelines, and to set-asides and quotas specifying an exact number or percentage of admissions or jobs for blacks, women, and other minorities. Following the enactment of the Civil Rights Act of 1964, President Johnson issued an executive order (No. 11246) encouraging the use of affirmative action programs to overcome the effects of past and present discrimination. In 1967, the Department of Labor adopted a policy of preferential hiring for minorities and women and the Department of Health, Education and Welfare (HEW, now the Department of Education) assumed responsibility for affirmative action in higher education. In the 1970s, the Nixon administration's HEW issued guidelines and threatened the withholding of federal funding from colleges and universities that failed to meet its hiring and admissions goals for blacks, women, and other minorities. In addition, some courts ordered affirmative action goals as remedies for organizations that engaged in racial discrimination.

Affirmative action programs sparked heated political controversy and posed an explosive issue for the Court and the country. Proponents claimed that such programs remedied the effects of past discrimination and would improve the status of blacks, women, and minorities. They pointed out that for a century and a half racial segregation was tolerated; the Constitution had not been color-blind. Moreover, they argued that racial preferences in affirmative action programs were benign; through "positive discrimination," blacks, women, and other minorities would finally achieve an equality of opportunity denied them in the past. As Justice Blackmun, concurring in *Regents of the University of California v. Bakke*, 438 U.S. 265 (1978), put it, "In order to get beyond racism, we must first take account of race. There is no other way."

Opponents of affirmative action programs raised numerous objections. Some argued that racial preferences were not benign for blacks or whites. Just as "Jim Crow" laws stigmatized blacks as inferior, so too race-conscious affirmative action programs implied that blacks were not as meritorious as whites. And racial preferences disadvantaged whites. Other critics conceded that preferential recruitment and special training programs might be appropriately and temporarily used to overcome the effects of past discrimination. But they strongly objected to quotas and set-aside programs. As a matter of public policy, they argued that it was wrong to accord special benefits to members of groups that had suffered past discrimination because those given special advantages may not have actually been victims of discrimination. Moreover, programs setting racial quotas inexorably discriminated against whites and invited charges of *reverse discrimination*. Once again dissenting Justice Harlan's opinion in *Plessy* became poignant, as critics of affirmative action charged, "The Constitution is (or ought to be) color-blind."

White males denied admission to higher education, government contracts, and employment opportunities attacked affirmative action programs for denying their rights under the Fourteenth Amendment's equal protection clause and the Civil Rights Act of 1964. The latter in dealing with federal funding of public and private institutions provides in Title VI that "[n]o person in the United States shall, on the ground of race, color, or national origin, be excluded from participation in, be denied the benefits of, or be subjected to discrimination under any program or activity receiving Federal financial assistance." In Title VII of the Civil Rights Act, Congress sought to end racial discrimination in employment in the private sector by specifying that

> [n]othing contained in this subchapter shall be interpreted to require any employer, employment agency, labor organization, or joint labor-management committee subject to this subchapter to grant preferential treatment to any individual or to any group because of the race, color, religion, sex, national origin of such individual or group on account of an imbalance which may exist with respect to the total number or percentage of persons of any race, color, religion, sex, or national origin employed by any employer, referred or classified for employment by any employment agency or labor organization, admitted to membership or classified in any labor organization, or admitted to, or employed in, any apprenticeship or other training program, in comparison with the total number or percentage of such persons of such race, color, religion, sex, or national origin in any community, State, section, or other area, or in the available work force in any community, State, section or other area.

The Burger Court could not escape the constitutional and statutory challenges to affirmative action programs. A bare majority, however, sought to do so in *DeFunis v. Odegaard*, 416 U.S. 312 (1974). Marco DeFunis Jr., was one of 1,600 applicants for admission to the University of Washington Law School but was denied a place in the first-year entering class of 150 students. He sued Charles Odegaard, president of the university, contending that the law school's admission criteria invidiously discriminated against him in violation of the Fourteenth Amendment. A state trial court agreed and ordered DeFunis's admission. On appeal, the Washington State Supreme Court reversed. By this time DeFunis was in his second year of law school, and he appealed to the Supreme Court. Justice Douglas, as circuit justice for the ninth circuit, stayed the state court's ruling pending "the final disposition of the case by [the Supreme] Court." DeFunis thus remained in school and was in his third year when the Burger Court dismissed his case as moot. A bare majority vacated the state court decision, concluding that because DeFunis would graduate at the end of the academic year the Court should not address the substantive constitutional issue in this case. Justice Brennan, joined by Justices Douglas, Marshall, and White, dissented and criticized the majority for sidestepping the issue, and warned that the controversy would inevitably return to the Court.

In a separate dissenting opinion in *DeFunis*, Justice Douglas addressed the merits of the case. In his view, the Law School Admissions Test (LSAT) may work hardships on members of minority groups, and law schools ought to find other ways to ensure diverse student bodies:

> The key to the problem is the consideration of each application *in a racially neutral way*. Since the LSAT reflects questions touching on cultural backgrounds, the Admissions Committee acted properly in my view in setting minority applications apart for separate processing. These minorities have cultural backgrounds that are vastly different from the dominant Caucasian. Many Eskimos, American Indians, Filipinos, Chicanos, Asian Indians, Burmese, and Africans come from such disparate backgrounds that a test sensitively tuned for most applicants would be wide of the mark for many minorities. . . .

> The key to the problem is consideration of such applications *in a racially neutral way*. Abolition of the LSAT would be a start. The invention of substitute tests might be made to get a measure of an applicant's cultural background, perception, ability to analyze, and his or her relation to groups. They are highly subjective, but unlike the LSAT they are not concealed, but in the open. A law school is not bound by any legal principle to admit students by mechanical criteria which are insensitive to the potential of such an applicant which may be realized in a more hospitable environment. It will be necessary under such an approach to put more effort into assessing each individual than is required when LSAT scores and undergraduate grades dominate the selection process. . . .

Although Justice Douglas favored aggressive recruitment of minorities, he staunchly opposed the use of racial classifications and quotas. In his words:

> The Equal Protection Clause commands the elimination of racial barriers, not their creation in order to satisfy our theory as to how society ought to be organized. The purpose of the University of Washington cannot be to produce black lawyers for blacks, Polish lawyers for Poles, Jewish lawyers for Jews, Irish lawyers for Irish. It should be to produce good lawyers for Americans and not to place First Amendment barriers against anyone. . . . A segregated admissions process creates suggestions of stigma and caste no less than a segregated classroom, and in the end it may produce that result despite its contrary intentions. One other assumption must be clearly disapproved; that blacks or browns cannot make it on their individual merit. That is a stamp of inferiority that a State is not permitted to place on any lawyer.

Four years after *DeFunis*, the Burger Court handed down its major ruling on affirmative action programs in higher education in *Regents of the University of California v. Bakke* (1978) (see excerpt below). The justices, though, split 4–4, and (with the exception of a one-paragraph statement of the facts) no other justice joined Justice Powell's opinion announcing the Court's ruling. Note that Justice Powell held that racial quotas are impermissible, but not affirmative action programs aimed at promoting diverse student bodies. Notably, he relied on an "exacting scrutiny" test, instead of the "strict scrutiny" test, in his narrowly tailored opinion applying only to higher education.

Throughout the 1980s, the Burger Court remained sharply divided over affirmative action programs and claims of reverse discrimination in employment. The justices split 5–4 and 6–3 when upholding most programs, and Justice Powell often cast the deciding vote, rebuffing the views pressed by the Reagan administration and opponents of affirmative action.

In *United Steelworkers of America v. Weber*, 443 U.S. 193 (1979), with Justices Powell and Stewart not participating, four justices joined Justice Brennan in reading the Civil Rights Act to *permit* (although not *require*) private voluntary programs designed to achieve racial balance in the workplace through an on-the-job training program set up for blacks. Although Chief Justice Burger and Justice Rehnquist dissented in *Weber*, the following year Burger delivered the Court's opinion in *Fullilove v. Klutznick*, 448 U.S. 448 (1980), upholding Congress's power to set aside 10 percent of all public-works contracts for minority-owned businesses.

In two cases, the Burger Court struck down affirmative action programs. In *Firefighters Local Union No. 1784 v. Stotts*, 467 U.S. 561

(1984), the Court held that under the Civil Rights Act the seniority interests of white workers could not be sacrificed in employment lay-offs to preserve jobs for more recently hired blacks. A bare majority in *Wygant v. Jackson Board of Education*, 476 U.S. 267 (1986), then interpreted the Fourteenth Amendment to bar layoffs of white teachers with more seniority than black teachers, where there was no evidence that black teachers had actually suffered past discrimination.

In Chief Justice Burger's last term (1985–1986), however, Justice Brennan massed a majority for upholding under the Civil Rights Act a court-ordered affirmative action program setting a "hiring goal" for minority workers, in *Local 28 of the Sheet Metal Workers v. Equal Employment Opportunity Commission*, 478 U.S. 421 (1986), and a judicial consent decree setting hiring goals as a remedy for a union's past discriminatory practices, in *Local No. 93, International Association of Firefighters v. City of Cleveland*, 478 U.S. 501 (1986). Justice Brennan managed to forge majorities in two more 1987 rulings. In *United States v. Paradise*, 480 U.S. 149 (1987), he held that the equal protection clause did not bar a court-ordered quota for the promotion of blacks within the ranks of Alabama's state troopers. And in *Johnson v. Transportation Agency, Santa Clara, California*, 480 U.S. 616 (1987), Justice Brennan upheld a program for promoting minorities and women to positions that were traditionally segregated and where members of those groups had been traditionally underrepresented.

By the end of the 1980s, though, the Rehnquist Court signaled an abrupt shift in analysis and approach toward challenges to affirmative action programs, registering the impact of President Ronald Reagan's appointees to the Court, and in particular Justice Kennedy's appointment in 1988 to the seat previously occupied by Justice Powell. Note that Justice O'Connor's opinion in *City of Richmond v. J. A. Croson* (1989) (see excerpt below), when overturning Richmond's set-aside program for minority-owned businesses (modeled and adopted after the one approved by the Court in *Fullilove*), substitutes the strict scrutiny test for *Bakke*'s exacting scrutiny test and indicates that only narrowly tailored affirmative action programs aimed at remedying actual victims of past discrimination will survive constitutional challenge.

One year after *Croson*, however, Justice Brennan managed to forge a bare majority for upholding affirmative action programs adopted by the *federal* government and mandated by Congress, in *Metro Broadcasting, Inc. v. Federal Communications Commission*, 497 U.S. 547 (1990). He and the two other dissenters in *Croson* were joined by Justice White (who voted with the majority in *Croson* but also with the majority in the 1980 *Fullilove* ruling upholding Congress's power to establish affirmative action programs) and Justice Stevens (who concurred in *Croson* yet dissented in *Fullilove*).

Nonetheless, in 1993 after Justices Brennan and Marshall had left the bench, a solid majority on the Rehnquist Court made it much easier to gain standing to challenge affirmative action programs in *Northeastern Florida Chapter of the Associated Contractors of America v. City of Jacksonville, Florida*, 508 U.S. 456 (1993). As a result, affirmative action programs are easier to attack in the lower federal courts under *City of Jacksonville* and much more difficult for states and localities to defend under the standards laid down in *Croson*.

Subsequently, with the retirements of Justices White and Blackmun, only one justice—Justice Stevens—was left on the bench who had voted with the majority in *Metro Broadcasting*. And a bare majority of the Rehnquist Court expressly overruled that 1990 ruling in *Adarand Constructors, Inc. v. Pena*, 515 U.S. 200 (1995). As in *Croson*, Justice O'Connor wrote for the majority and held that the strict scrutiny test, applied in *Croson* to affirmative action programs adopted by state and local governments, applies no less to federal programs, thereby overturning *Metro Broadcasting*. Notably, at issue in *Adarand* was the constitutionality of a federal policy to encourage subcontracting to "*small business concerns owned and controlled by socially and economically disadvantaged individuals*" (emphasis added). The Small Business Act defined "socially disadvantaged individuals" as "those who have been subject to racial or ethnic prejudice or cultural bias." That act also established the goal of participation of small businesses "owned or controlled by socially and economically disadvantaged individuals" and "not less than 5 percent of the total value of all prime contract and subcontract awards for each fiscal year." In declaring that policy unconstitutional, Justice O'Connor emphasized that "federal racial classifications, like those of a state, must serve a compelling governmental interest, and must be narrowly tailored to further that interest."

Over a quarter of a century after *Bakke*, the controversy over affirmative action and reverse discrimination remained hotly contested and widely debated. Some states, like California, abandoned their affirmative action programs and implemented outreach programs for minorities, as a result of statewide initiative and referendums against affirmative action efforts. In order to resolve the growing conflict over the issue in the federal courts and the country, the Court granted and decided two companion cases challenging the University of Michigan's undergraduate admissions policy based on a "point system" for individual applicants, in *Gratz v. Bollinger* (2003) (excerpted below); and the University of Michigan Law School's "holistic" approach in student admissions that aimed to achieve diversity in its student body and a "critical mass" of underrepresented minorities, in *Grutter v. Bollinger* (2003) (excerpted below). Dividing 6–3 in *Gratz*, the Court struck down the undergraduate admissions policy. But splitting 5–4 in *Grutter*, the justices upheld the law school's program. Notably, although joining the majority in *Gratz*, Justice O'Connor delivered the opinion for the Court in *Grutter* and declined to overrule *Bakke*. Justice O'Connor also accepted as permissible the goal of achieving diversity, rather than remedying past discrimination, in support of affirmative action programs, though she also noted that such programs should be limited to another twenty-five years. Chief Justice Rehnquist and Justices Scalia, Kennedy, and Thomas dissented. Subsequently, in 2006 Michigan voters approved an amendment to the state constitution banning the use of affirmative action by all state agencies, including universities.

A bare majority of the Roberts Court, in *Parents Involved in Community Schools v. Seattle School District No. 1* (2007) (excerpted in Section B of this chapter), ruled that race may not be used in the assignment of students to public schools to achieve and maintain racial diversity. Chief Justice Roberts wrote for a plurality in holding impermissible race-conscious student assignments. Notably, Justice Kennedy's concurring opinion disagreed with the plurality's analysis, arguing that race may be a consideration when, for example, drawing attendance zones, but not in individual students' school assignments. In a lengthy seventy-page dissenting opinion, Justice Breyer, joined by Justices Stevens, Souter, and Ginsburg, rejected the Court's analysis of the history of efforts to achieve integration and the problem of addressing increasingly racially isolated public schools.

In addition, in *Ricci v. DeSefano*, 557 U.S. 557 (2009), a bare majority of the Roberts Court reversed an appellate court's ruling upholding a New Haven, Connecticut, decision to disregard test scores for promotions of firefighters because no African Americans passed the tests and the city feared a discrimination lawsuit under Section VII of the Civil Rights Act of 1964 for using a test that had a "disparate impact" on minorities. The city was sued by white firefighters who passed the test but were denied promotions. Writing for the Court, Justice Kennedy avoided a Fourteenth Amendment equal protection challenge and ruled narrowly on statutory grounds that under Section VII employees must have a "strong basis in evidence" that a test is deficient and discriminatory rather than just "raw racial statistics." Justice Kennedy observed, "The process was open and fair . . . The problem, of course, is that after the tests were completed, the raw racial results became the predominant rationale for the city's refusal to certify the results. . . . Fear of litigation [brought by minorities] alone cannot justify an employer's reliance on race to the detriment of individuals who passed the examinations and qualified for promotions." Justice Scalia concurred, but added, "The war between disparate impact and equal protection will be waged sooner or later, and it behooves us to begin thinking about how—and on what terms—to make peace between them." By contrast, writing for dissenting Justices Stevens, Souter, and Breyer, Justice Ginsburg countered that "Congress and, until the decision just announced, this Court regarded Title VII's dual prescriptions on intentional and disparate impact as complementary. . . . Standing on equal footing, both provisions aim to end workplace discrimination and promote genuinely equal opportunity."

Notably, in a widely watched challenge to the University of Texas at Austin's affirmative action admissions program, the Court reaffirmed that achieving a diverse student body is a compelling governmental interest, as upheld in *Regents of the University of California v. Bakke* (excerpted below) and *Grutter v. Bollinger* (excerpted below). But, writing for the Court in *Fisher v. University of Texas at Austin*, 570 U.S. 297 (2013), Justice Kennedy ruled that the lower court failed to apply strict scrutiny and ensure that the admissions policy was narrowly tailored. The University of Texas admitted about 75 percent of its students who graduated in the top 10 percent of their high school class, and thus achieved a measure of diversity since many of the state's high schools are dominated by one race or ethnicity. The remaining applicants were considered on a "holistic" basis—individual considerations such as legacy, special talents, and race or ethnicity. Abigail Fisher, a white woman, was not admitted and sued, claiming that the effort to increase the numbers of African Americans and Latinos cost her the admission and violated the Fourteenth Amendment. While reaffirming that courts should give deference to universities' admission policies aimed at achieving diverse student bodies, Justice Kennedy ruled, *"The reviewing court must ultimately be satisfied that no workable race-neutral alternatives would produce the educational benefits of diversity"* (emphasis added). In separate concurring opinions, Justices Scalia and Thomas indicated that they would have overruled *Grutter*, but had not been asked to do so here. Dissenting, Justice Ginsburg would have affirmed the lower court's analysis and upholding of the University of Texas's admissions program; Justice Kagan was recused. On remand, in *Fisher v. University of Texas,* 136 S.Ct. 2205 (2016) (*Fisher II*) (excerpted below), the appellate court again upheld Texas's program. A bare majority, by a 4–3 vote (with Kagan not participating and Gorsuch not yet confirmed), affirmed the appellate court's upholding of Texas's program. Writing for the Court, Justice Kennedy concluded that the program survived strict scrutiny, finding that the courts should defer to a reasoned explanation for why a university might want to pursue a diverse student body. While noting that Texas's program was unique and resulted in limited diversity, however, Kennedy emphasized that such programs should regularly be re-evaluated based on available data and adjusted "in light of changing circumstances, ensuring that race plays no greater role than is necessary to meet its compelling interest." Dissenting Justice Alito, joined by Chief Justice Roberts and Justice Thomas, countered that the university's interest in diversity was not sufficiently measurable and too "shifting" to survive strict scrutiny. In his own dissent, Justice Thomas stressed: "a State's use of race in higher education admissions decisions is categorically prohibited by the Equal Protection Clause."

A solid majority of the Roberts Court, in *Schuette v. Coalition to Defend Affirmative Action, Integration and Immigration Rights and Fight for Equality By Any Means Necessary (BAMN)* (2014) (excerpted below), then, once again signaled the end to court-approved affirmative action programs in higher education and, more generally, government. Writing for the Court in a plurality opinion, joined only by Chief Justice Roberts and Justice Alito, Justice Kennedy emphasized, "This case is not about how the debate about racial preferences should be resolved. It is about who may resolve it. There is no authority in the Constitution of the United States or in this court's precedents for the judiciary to set aside Michigan laws that commit this policy determination to the voters." In other words, the issue of affirmative action programs is in the hands of voters—at the state and local levels—and no longer for reviewing courts. That is to say, states are free to ban (as Michigan and seven other states do) or adopt affirmative action programs.

In separate concurring opinions, Chief Justice Roberts and Justice Scalia, joined by Justice Thomas, would have gone further and overturned precedents upholding affirmative action, while allowing preferences for athletes, children of alumni, and other considerations, such as wealth or applications from various geographical areas. Dissenting Justice Sotomayor, joined by Justice Ginsburg (and with Justice Kagan recusing herself), sharply criticized the reasoning of Justice Kennedy's opinion and the concurring opinions of Chief Justice Roberts and Justice Scalia. Justice Sotomayor countered that Michigan's constitutional amendment barring race-conscious considerations in admissions and other governmental decisions violated the Fourteenth Amendment equal protection clause and failed to recognize the persistence of racial bias. Indeed, Justice Sotomayor singled out Chief Justice Roberts's observation, in *Parents Involved in Community Schools v. Seattle School District No. 1*, 551 U.S. 701 (2007) (excerpted in Section B of this chapter), that "[t]he way to stop discrimination on the basis of race is to stop discriminating on the basis of race." Justice Sotomayor, who grew up in a Bronx housing project and had described herself as "an affirmative action baby" who went on to attend Princeton and Yale Law School, countered, "The way to stop discrimination on the basis of race is to speak openly and candidly on the subject of race, and to apply the Constitution with eyes open to the unfortunate effects of centuries of racial discrimination." And Justice Sotomayor vigorously maintained that "race matters" because of the "long history of racial minorities being denied access to the political process"; the "persistent racial inequality" that remains; and because "of the slights, the snickers, the silent judgments that reinforce the most crippling of thoughts: 'I do not belong here.'"

SELECTED BIBLIOGRAPHY

Anderson, Terry. *The Pursuit of Fairness: A History of Affirmative Action.* New York: Oxford University Press, 2004.

Ball, Howard. *The Bakke Case: Race, Education, and Affirmative Action.* Lawrence: University of Kansas Press, 2000.

Katznelson, Ira. *When Affirmative Action Was White.* New York: W. W. Norton & Company, 2004.

Sindler, Allan P. *Bakke, DeFunis, and Minority Admissions.* New York: Longman, 1978.

Thernstrom, Stephan, and Abigail Thernstrom. *America in Black and White: One Nation, Indivisible.* New York: Simon & Schuster, 1997.

Urofsky, Melvin. *A Conflict of Rights: The Supreme Court and Affirmative Action.* New York: Scribner's, 1991.

Regents of the University of California v. Bakke
438 U.S. 265, 98 S.CT. 2733 (1978)

Alan Bakke, a white male, applied but was denied admission to the medical school at the University of California at Davis. There were only one hundred openings each year, and sixteen of them were reserved for "disadvantaged" minority students (blacks, Hispanics, Asians, and American Indians). Bakke had been twice denied admission before, even though minorities who had lower grade point averages and lower scores on the Medical College Admission Test were admitted. He decided to challenge the constitutionality of the admission policy for minorities, contending that he was denied admission on account of his race.

A state superior court held that Davis's program violated Title VI of the Civil Rights Act, the equal protection clause of the Fourteenth Amendment, and a provision of the state constitution. However, the court declined to order Bakke's admission on the grounds that he would not have been admitted even if Davis did not have its affirmative action program. Subsequently, the state supreme court ordered Bakke's admission and reaffirmed that Davis's program impermissibly used race as a factor in its admissions program, and that it could not survive strict scrutiny under the Fourteenth Amendment's equal protection clause because the program was not the least restrictive means of advancing the state's interests in an integrated medical profession and increasing the number of doctors serving minority patients.

The Regents of the University of California appealed the state supreme court's decision to the Supreme Court. The controversy over affirmative action programs and claims of reverse discrimination were politically volatile for the Court and the country. At the time, an unprecedented number of organizations, 120, joined fifty-eight *amicus* (friend of the court) briefs: eighty-three for the university, thirty-two for Bakke, and five urging the Court not to decide the case.

The Court's ruling was announced by Justice Lewis F. Powell in an opinion upholding affirmative action programs (but not quota systems like that at Davis) and admitting Bakke to the medical school. Powell delivered the Court's ruling because the other justices were unwilling to bend on their positions and were divided 4-4 on the statutory and constitutional issues.

Chief Justice Burger and Justices Rehnquist and Stewart accepted the view of Justice Stevens that the Court need not address the question of whether affirmative action programs violate the Constitution. They voted to strike down quota systems as an impermissible racial classification under Title VI of the Civil Rights Act of 1964 and to admit Bakke.

Justices White, Marshall, and Blackmun sided with Brennan in reaching the constitutional question and holding that affirmative action programs, including quotas, are constitutionally permissible remedies for past racial discrimination. They would not have admitted Bakke.

Justice Powell massed the votes, but not the justices' support for his opinion, from each bloc on each of the two key issues. His opinion found that quota systems are invalid and that Bakke should have been admitted, relying on the 4 votes of the Stevens bloc. At the same time, Powell upheld affirmative action programs in universities and thereby won the vote of the Brennan bloc. Powell, however, refused to accept Brennan's view that past racial discrimination justified racial quotas. Instead, Powell held that affirmative action programs, but not quotas, are permissible because under the First Amendment universities need a diverse student body to ensure academic freedom and the educational process. Powell's pragmatic rationalization for the controversial decision thus had the support of no other justice.

The Court's decision was 5–4, but the justices split 1–4–4; the opinion was announced by Justice Powell. A separate opinion, in part concurring and in part dissenting, was delivered by Justice Brennan; Justices White, Marshall, and Blackmun concurred. A separate opinion, in part concurring and in part dissenting, was issued by Justice Stevens, who was joined by Chief Justice Burger and Justices Stewart and Rehnquist.

■ ■ ■

☐ *Justice POWELL delivered the opinion of the Court.*

For the reasons stated in the following opinion, I believe that so much of the judgment of the California court as holds petitioner's special admissions program unlawful and directs that respondent be admitted to the Medical School must be affirmed. For the reasons expressed in a separate opinion, my Brothers THE CHIEF JUSTICE, Justice STEWART, Justice REHNQUIST and Justice STEVENS concur in this judgment.

I also conclude for the reasons stated in the following opinion that the portion of the court's judgment enjoining petitioner from according any consideration to race in its admissions process must be reversed. For reasons expressed in separate opinions, my Brothers Justice BRENNAN, Justice WHITE, Justice MARSHALL, and Justice BLACKMUN concur in this judgment.

Affirmed in part and reversed in part. . . .

The guarantees of the Fourteenth Amendment extend to all persons. Its language is explicit: "No State shall . . . deny to any person within its jurisdiction the equal protection of the laws." It is settled beyond question that the "rights created by the first section of the Fourteenth Amendment are, by its terms, guaranteed to the individual. The rights established are personal rights." *Shelley v. Kraemer*, 334 U.S. 1 [(1948)]. The guarantee of equal protection cannot mean one thing when applied to one individual and something else when applied to a person of another color. If both are not accorded the same protection, then it is not equal. . . .

The Court has never questioned the validity of those pronouncements. Racial and ethnic distinctions of any sort are inherently suspect and thus call for the most exacting judicial examination.

This perception of racial and ethnic distinctions is rooted in our Nation's constitutional and demographic history. The Court's initial view of the Fourteenth Amendment was that its "one pervading purpose" was "the freedom of the slave race, the security and firm establishment of that freedom, and the protection of the newly-made freeman and citizen from the oppressions of those who had formerly exercised dominion over him." *Slaughter-House Cases*, 16 Wall. 36 (1873). The Equal Protection Clause, however, was "[v]irtually strangled in infancy by post-civil-war judicial reactionism." It was relegated to decades of relative desuetude while the Due Process Clause of the Fourteenth Amendment, after a short germinal period, flourished as a cornerstone in the Court's defense of property and liberty of contract. See, e.g., *Mugler v. Kansas*, 123 U.S. 623 (1887); *Allgeyer v. Louisiana*, 165 U.S. 578, [(1897)]; *Lochner v. New York*, 198 U.S. 45 (1905). In that cause, the Fourteenth Amendment's "one pervading purpose" was displaced. See, e.g., *Plessy v. Ferguson*, 163 U.S. 537 (1896). It was only as the era of substantive due process came to a close, see, e.g., *Nebbia v. New York*, 291 U.S. 502 (1934); *West Coast Hotel Co. v. Parrish*, 300 U.S. 379 (1937), that the Equal Protection Clause began to attain a genuine measure of vitality, see, e.g., *United States v. Carolene Products*, 304 U.S. 144 (1938); *Skinner v. Oklahoma ex rel. Williamson*, [316 U.S. 535 (1942)].

By that time it was no longer possible to peg the guarantees of the Fourteenth Amendment to the struggle for equality of one racial minority. During the dormancy of the Equal Protection Clause, the United States had become a Nation of minorities. Each had to struggle—and to some extent struggles still—to overcome the prejudices not of a monolithic majority, but of a "majority" composed of various minority groups of whom it was said— perhaps unfairly in many cases—that a shared characteristic was a willing- ness to disadvantage other groups. As the Nation filled with the stock of many lands, the reach of the Clause was gradually extended to all ethnic groups seeking protection from official discrimination. See *Strauder v. West Virginia*, 100 U.S. 303 (1880) (Celtic Irishmen) (*dictum*); *Yick Wo v. Hopkins*, 118 U.S. 356 (1886) (Chinese); *Truax v. Raich*, 239 U.S. 33 (1915) (Austrian resident aliens); *Korematsu*, [*v. United States*, 323 U.S. 214 (1944)] (Japanese); *Hernandez v. Texas*, 347 U.S. 475 (1954) (Mexican-Americans). The guaran- tees of equal protection, said the Court in *Yick Wo*, "are universal in their application, to all persons within the territorial jurisdiction, without regard to any differences of race, of color, or of nationality; and the equal protec- tion of the laws is a pledge of the protection of equal laws." . . .

Over the past 30 years, this Court has embarked upon the crucial mis- sion of interpreting the Equal Protection Clause with the view of assuring to all persons "the protection of equal laws," *Yick Wo, supra*, in a Nation confronting a legacy of slavery and racial discrimination. . . . Because the landmark decisions in this area arose in response to the continued exclusion of Negroes from the mainstream of American society, they could be char- acterized as involving discrimination by the "majority" white race against the Negro minority. But they need not be read as depending upon that characterization for their results. It suffices to say that "[o]ver the years, this Court has consistently repudiated '[d]istinctions between citizens solely because of their ancestry' as being 'odious to a free people whose institu- tions are founded upon the doctrine of equality.'" *Loving v. Virginia*, 388 U.S. 1 (1967), quoting *Hirabayashi* [*v. United States*], 320 U.S. [81 (1943)].

Petitioner urges us to adopt for the first time a more restrictive view of the Equal Protection Clause and hold that discrimination against members of the white "majority" cannot be suspect if its purpose can be character- ized as "benign." The clock of our liberties, however, cannot be turned back to 1868. It is far too late to argue that the guarantee of equal protec- tion to *all* persons permits the recognition of special wards entitled to a degree of protection greater than that accorded others. "The Fourteenth Amendment is not directed solely against discrimination due to a 'two- class theory'—that is, based upon differences between 'white' and Negro." *Hernandez* [*v. Texas*, 347 U.S. 475 (1954)].

Once the artificial line of a "two-class theory" of the Fourteenth Amend- ment is put aside, the difficulties entailed in varying the level of judicial review according to a perceived "preferred" status of a particular racial or ethnic minority are intractable. The concepts of "majority" and "minority" necessar- ily reflect temporary arrangements and political judgments. As observed above, the white "majority" itself is composed of various minority groups, most of which can lay claim to a history of prior discrimination at the hands of the State and private individuals. Not all of these groups can receive preferential treat- ment and corresponding judicial tolerance of distinctions drawn in terms of race and nationality, for then the only "majority" left would be a new minority of white Anglo-Saxon Protestants. There is no principled basis for deciding which groups would merit "heightened judicial solicitude" and which would not. Courts would be asked to evaluate the extent of the prejudice and consequent harm suffered by various minority groups. Those whose societal injury is thought to exceed some arbitrary level of tolerability then would be entitled to preferential classifications at the expense of individuals belonging to other groups. Those classifications would be free from exacting judicial scrutiny. As these preferences began to have their desired effect, and the consequences of past discrimination were undone, new judicial rankings would be necessary. The kind of variable sociological and political analysis necessary to produce such rankings simply does not lie within the judicial competence—even if they otherwise were politically feasible and socially desirable.

Moreover, there are serious problems of justice connected with the idea of preference itself. First, it may not always be clear that a so-called preference is in fact benign. Courts may be asked to validate burdens imposed upon individual members of a particular group in order to advance the group's general interest. Nothing in the Constitution supports the notion that individuals may be asked to suffer otherwise impermissible burdens in order to enhance the societal standing of their ethnic groups. Second, preferential programs may only reinforce common stereotypes holding that certain groups are unable to achieve success without special protection based on a factor having no relationship to individual worth. See *DeFunis v. Odegaard*, 416 U.S. 312 (1974) (DOUGLAS, J., dissenting). Third, there is a measure of inequity in forcing innocent persons in respondent's position to bear the burdens of redressing grievances not of their making. . . .

If it is the individual who is entitled to judicial protection against classifications based upon his racial or ethnic background because such distinctions impinge upon personal rights, rather than the individual only because of his membership in a particular group, then constitutional standards may be applied consistently. Political judgments regarding the necessity for the particular classification may be weighed in the constitutional balance, *Korematsu v. United States*, 323 U.S. 194 (1944), but the standard of justification will remain constant. This is as it should be, since those political judgments are the product of rough compromise struck by contending groups within the democratic process. When they touch upon an individual's race or ethnic background, he is entitled to a judicial determination that the burden he is asked to bear on that basis is precisely tailored to serve a compelling governmental interest. The Constitution guarantees that right to every person regardless of his background.

Petitioner contends that on several occasions this Court has approved preferential classifications without applying the most exacting scrutiny. Most of the cases upon which petitioner relies are drawn from three areas: school desegregation, employment discrimination, and sex discrimination. Each of the cases cited presented a situation materially different from the facts of this case.

The school desegregation cases are inapposite. Each involved remedies for clearly determined constitutional violations. . . . Racial classifications thus were designed as remedies for the vindication of constitutional entitlement. Moreover, the scope of the remedies was not permitted to exceed the extent of the violations. . . . Here, there was no judicial determination of constitutional violation as a predicate for the formulation of a remedial classification. . . .

We have held that in "order to justify the use of a suspect classification, a State must show that its purpose or interest is both constitutionally permissible and substantial, and that its use of the classification is 'necessary . . . to the accomplishment' of its purpose or the safeguarding of its interest." *In re Griffiths*, 413 U.S. 717 (1973); *Loving v. Virginia*, 388 U.S. [1 (1967)]; *McLaughlin v. Florida*, 379 U.S. 184 (1964). The special admissions program purports to serve the purposes of: (i) "reducing the historic deficit of traditionally disfavored minorities in medical schools and in the medical profession"; (ii) countering the effects of societal discrimination; (iii) increasing the number of physicians who will practice in communities currently underserved; and (iv) obtaining the educational benefits that flow from an ethnically diverse student body. It is necessary to decide which, if any, of these purposes is substantial enough to support the use of a suspect classification.

If petitioner's purpose is to assure within its student body some specified percentage of a particular group merely because of its race or ethnic origin, such a preferential purpose must be rejected not as insubstantial but as facially invalid. Preferring members of any one group for no reason other than race or ethnic origin is discrimination for its own sake. This the Constitution forbids. . . .

Hence, the purpose of helping certain groups whom the faculty of the Davis Medical School perceived as victims of "societal discrimination" does not justify a classification that imposes disadvantages upon persons like respondent, who bear no responsibility for whatever harm the beneficiaries of the special admissions program are thought to have suffered. To hold otherwise would be to convert a remedy heretofore reserved for violations of legal rights into a privilege that all institutions throughout the Nation could grant at their pleasure to whatever groups are perceived as victims of societal discrimination. That is a step we have never approved. . . .

Petitioner identifies, as another purpose of its program, improving the delivery of health-care services to communities currently underserved. It may be assumed that in some situations a State's interest in facilitating the health care of its citizens is sufficiently compelling to support the use of a suspect classification. But there is virtually no evidence in the record indicating that petitioner's special admissions program is either needed or geared to promote that goal. . . .

Petitioner simply has not carried its burden of demonstrating that it must prefer members of particular ethnic groups over all other individuals in order to promote better health-care delivery to deprived citizens. Indeed, petitioner has not shown that its preferential classification is likely to have any significant effect on the problem.

The fourth goal asserted by petitioner is the attainment of a diverse student body. This clearly is a constitutionally permissible goal for an institution of higher education. Academic freedom, though not a specifically enumerated constitutional right, long has been viewed as a special concern of the First Amendment. The freedom of a university to make its own judgments as to education includes the selection of its student body. . . .

[In] arguing that its universities must be accorded the right to select those students who will contribute the most to the "robust exchange of ideas," petitioner invokes a countervailing constitutional interest, that of the First Amendment. In this light, petitioner must be viewed as seeking to achieve a goal that is of paramount importance in the fulfillment of its mission. . . .

Physicians serve a heterogeneous population. An otherwise qualified medical student with a particular background—whether it be ethnic, geographic, culturally advantaged or disadvantaged—may bring to a professional school of medicine experiences, outlooks, and ideas that enrich the training of its student body and better equip its graduates to render with understanding their vital service to humanity.

Ethnic diversity, however, is only one element in a range of factors a university properly may consider in attaining the goal of a heterogeneous student body. Although a university must have wide discretion in making the sensitive judgments as to who should be admitted, constitutional limitations protecting individual rights may not be disregarded. Respondent urges—and the courts below have held—that petitioner's dual admissions program is a racial classification that impermissibly infringes his rights under the Fourteenth Amendment. As the interest of diversity is compelling in the context of a university's admissions program, the question remains whether the program's racial classification is necessary to promote this interest.

It may be assumed that the reservation of a specified number of seats in each class for individuals from the preferred ethnic groups would contribute to the attainment of considerable ethnic diversity in the student body. But petitioner's argument that this is the only effective means of serving the interest of diversity is seriously flawed. In a most fundamental sense the argument misconceives the nature of the state interest that would justify consideration of race or ethnic background. It is not an interest in simple ethnic diversity, in which a specified percentage of the student body is in effect guaranteed to be members of selected ethnic groups, with the remaining percentage an undifferentiated aggregation of students. The diversity that furthers a compelling state interest encompasses a far broader array of qualifications and characteristics of which racial or ethnic origin is but a single though important element. Petitioner's special admissions program, focused *solely* on ethnic diversity, would hinder rather than further attainment of genuine diversity.

Nor would the state interest in genuine diversity be served by expanding petitioner's two-track system into a multitrack program with a prescribed number of seats set aside for each identifiable category of applicants. Indeed, it is inconceivable that a university would thus pursue the logic of petitioner's two-track program to the illogical end of insulating each category of applicants with certain desired qualifications from competition with all other applicants.

The experience of other university admissions programs, which take race into account in achieving the educational diversity valued by the First Amendment, demonstrates that the assignment of a fixed number of places to a minority group is not a necessary means toward that end. An illuminating example is found in the Harvard College program:

> In recent years Harvard College has expanded the concept of diversity to include students from disadvantaged economic, racial and ethnic groups. Harvard College now recruits not only Californians or Louisianans but also blacks and Chicanos and other minority students. . . .
>
> In practice, this new definition of diversity has meant that race has been a factor in some admission decisions. When the Committee on Admissions reviews the large middle group of applicants who are 'admissible' and deemed capable of doing good

work in their courses, the race of an applicant may tip the balance in his favor just as geographic origin or a life spent on a farm may tip the balance in other candidates' cases. A farm boy from Idaho can bring something to Harvard College that a Bostonian cannot offer. Similarly, a black student can usually bring something that a white person cannot offer. . . .

In such an admissions program, race or ethnic background may be deemed a "plus" in a particular applicant's file, yet it does not insulate the individual from comparison with all other candidates for the available seats. The file of a particular black applicant may be examined for his potential contribution to diversity without the factor of race being decisive when compared, for example, with that of an applicant identified as an Italian-American if the latter is thought to exhibit qualities more likely to promote beneficial educational pluralism. Such qualities could include exceptional personal talents, unique work or service experience, leadership potential, maturity, demonstrated compassion, a history of overcoming disadvantage, ability to communicate with the poor, or other qualifications deemed important. In short, an admissions program operated in that way is flexible enough to consider all pertinent elements of diversity in light of the particular qualifications of each applicant, and to place them on the same footing for consideration, although not necessarily according them the same weight. Indeed the weight attributed to a particular quality may vary from year to year depending upon the "mix" both of the student body and the applicants for the incoming class.

This kind of program treats each applicant as an individual in the admissions process. The applicant who loses out on the last available seat to another candidate receiving a "plus" on the basis of ethnic background will not have been foreclosed from all consideration for that seat simply because he was not the right color or had the wrong surname. It would mean only that his combined qualifications, which may have included similar nonobjective factors, did not outweigh those of the other applicant. His qualifications would have been weighed fairly and competitively, and he would have no basis to complain of unequal treatment under the Fourteenth Amendment. . . .

In summary, it is evident that the Davis special admissions program involves the use of an explicit racial classification never before countenanced by this Court. It tells applicants who are not Negro, Asian, or Chicano that they are totally excluded from a specific percentage of the seats in an entering class. No matter how strong their qualifications, quantitative and extracurricular, including their own potential for contribution to educational diversity, they are never afforded the chance to compete with applicants from the preferred groups for the special admissions seats. At the same time, the preferred applicants have the opportunity to compete for every seat in the class.

The fatal flaw in petitioner's preferential program is its disregard of individual rights as guaranteed by the Fourteenth Amendment. Such rights are not absolute. But when a State's distribution of benefits or imposition of burdens hinges on ancestry or the color of a person's skin, that individual is entitled to a demonstration that the challenged classification is necessary to promote a substantial state interest. Petitioner has failed to carry this burden. For this reason, that portion of the California court's judgment holding petitioner's special admissions program invalid under the Fourteenth Amendment must be affirmed. . . .

■ THE DEVELOPMENT OF LAW

*Other Rulings on Affirmative Action
and Reverse Discrimination*

CASE	VOTE	FACTS AND RULING

*United Steelworkers of America
v. Weber,* 443 U.S. 193 (1979) — 5–2 — The United Steelworkers of America and Kaiser Aluminum Chemical Corporation reached agreement on an affirmative action plan to overcome racial imbalances in the company's workforce. It required that at least half of the trainees in an on-the-job training program be set aside for blacks. The plan was to remain in effect until the proportion of black workers matched the proportion of blacks in the local labor force. Brian Weber, a white worker excluded from the program, sued and claimed that the plan violated Title VII of the 1964 Civil Rights Act which prohibits "discriminat[ion] . . . because of . . . race." The Court upheld the affirmative action plan in a 5–2 ruling saying that the 1964 Civil Rights Act "did not intend to prohibit the private sector from taking effective steps" to meet the requirements of Title VII. This plan sought to eliminate the results of a long pattern of discrimination. Since it did not block white workers from promotions and job advancement, the Court said the plan was consistent with the law.

Fullilove v. Klutznick,
448 U.S. 448 (1980) — 6–3 — In the Public Works Employment Act of 1977, Congress required that 10 percent of a $4 billion public works program be set aside for "minority-controlled businesses" (MCBs), defined as companies in which at least 50 percent interest was held by blacks, Hispanics, Asian-Americans, American Indians, Eskimos, or Aleuts. The program was challenged as unconstitutional under the equal protection component of the Fifth Amendment's due process clause. Chief Justice Burger's plurality opinion adopted the exacting scrutiny test used in *Bakke* and found that Congress had an appropriate objective in remedying past discrimination, holding that "the limited use of racial and ethnic criteria, in the context of the case presented, is a constitu-

(continues)

■ THE DEVELOPMENT OF LAW
Other Rulings on Affirmative Action and
Reverse Discrimination (continued)

CASE	VOTE	FACTS AND RULING

tionally permissible means for achieving the congressional objectives."
He also "reject[ed] the contention that in the remedial context the Congress must act in a wholly 'color-blind' fashion."

Firefighters Local Union No.	6–3	A black member of the
1784 v. Stotts, 467 U.S.		Memphis Fire Department
561 (1984)		sued the department,

claiming that race was a
factor in hiring and promotion decisions in violation of Title VII of the
Civil Rights Act of 1964. That suit resulted in a consent decree requiring
that at least 50 percent of all new employees be black until two-fifths of
the department was black. But when projected budget deficits in 1981
forced a reduction in the number of city employees, the department announced that it would abide by its "last-hired-is-the-first-fired" seniority
system. A newly hired black employee challenged the layoff policy, and a
federal district court ordered the department to honor the consent decree
and lay off several white firefighters with more seniority than black firefighters. Justice White's opinion for the majority found the consent decree only to bind the parties to remedy past discriminatory hiring and
promotion practices, to contain no agreement to set aside seniority in the
event of layoffs, and held that setting aside seniority systems as a remedial
measure violated Title VII of the Civil Rights Act.

Wygant v. Jackson Board of	5–4	White teachers with se-
Education, 476 U.S. 267		niority who were laid off
(1986)		sued when minority and
		less-senior teachers were re-

tained as a result of a collective bargaining agreement between a school
district and a teachers' union, which gave preference to members of minority groups and required the laying off of white teachers before black teachers with less seniority. In a plurality opinion, joined by Chief Justice Burger
and Justices Rehnquist and O'Connor, Justice Powell held that the equal
protection clause of the Fourteenth Amendment was violated and that the
school had not established a compelling interest or narrowly tailored its use
of a racial criterion to remedy past discriminatory hiring practices.

CASE	VOTE	FACTS AND RULING
Local 28 of the Sheet Metal Workers v. Equal Employment Opportunity Commission, 478 U.S. 421 (1986)	5–4	A federal district court found the union in violation of Title VII of the Civil Rights Act of 1964 for dis- criminating against minor-

ity workers. It ordered a 29 percent minority hiring goal (reflecting the percentage of minorities in the local labor force) as a remedy for the union's past discriminatory practices. When the union refused to comply, it was found in civil contempt, and the union appealed the court-imposed affirmative action program on the grounds that it violated Title VII. Justice Brennan found nothing in Section 706(g) of Title VII to forbid courts from imposing remedies such as "hiring goals" and "timetables" even if they "might incidentally benefit individuals who are not the actual victims of [past] discrimination." He concluded that "the relief ordered in this case . . . is narrowly tailored to further the Government's compelling interest in remedying past discrimination."

CASE	VOTE	FACTS AND RULING
Local No. 93, International Association of Firefighters v. City of Cleveland, 478 U.S. 501 (1986)	6–3	An independent, nonunion organization of black and Hispanic firefighters brought a class-action suit alleging discrimination in

the hiring, assigning, and promoting of the city's firefighters. The union intervened in the suit, but over its objections, the district court handed down a consent decree (between the minority firefighters and the city), which set racial goals and quotas for the hiring and promoting of minority firefighters. In his opinion for the majority, Justice Brennan observed that "whether or not [Section] 706(g) [of the Civil Rights Act] precludes a court from imposing certain kinds of race-conscious relief after trial, that provision does not apply to relief awarded in a consent decree. . . . [V]oluntary action available to employers and unions seeking to eradicate racial discrimination may include reasonable race-conscious relief that benefits individuals who were not actual victims of discrimination."

CASE	VOTE	FACTS AND RULING
United States v. Paradise, 480 U.S. 149 (1987)	5–4	Upon finding that not one of Alabama's 232 state troopers with a rank of cor-

poral or higher was black, a federal district court ordered that half of all promotions to the rank of corporal go to blacks, if qualified blacks were available. An appellate court affirmed the order, as did a bare majority of the Supreme Court. In a plurality opinion, joined by Justices Marshall,

(continues)

■ THE DEVELOPMENT OF LAW
Other Rulings on Affirmative Action and
Reverse Discrimination (continued)

Blackmun, and Powell, Justice Brennan held that the equal protection clause was not violated because the quotas advanced a compelling governmental interest in remedying past and present discrimination, and that the quota was narrowly tailored.

CASE	VOTE	FACTS AND RULING
Johnson v. Transportation Agency, Santa Clara, California, 480 U.S. 616 (1987)	6–3	A white man passed over for a promotion because an equally qualified woman was promoted instead chal-

lenged Santa Clara County's program for hiring and promoting minorities and women. Under the program, within a traditionally segregated job classification where women were underrepresented, agencies could consider the gender of a qualified candidate as one factor in making its promotion decisions; but no specific quota or goal was set aside. Justice Brennan upheld the program over the claim that it violated Title VII of the 1964 Civil Rights Act. Consistent with Bakke, he observed that "[t]he Agency earmarks no positions for anyone; sex is but one of several factors that may be taken into account in evaluating qualified applicants for a position."

Martin v. Wilks, 490 U.S. 755 (1989)	5–4	Some white firefighters in Birmingham, Alabama, denied promotion in favor of

less-qualified blacks, challenged a consent decree mandating goals for the hiring and promoting of blacks as a violation of Title VII of the Civil Rights Act of 1964. Chief Justice Rehnquist held that white firefighters could challenge the legality of affirmative action programs created by consent decrees because, even though not parties to the original litigation, their interests and employment were affected.

City of Richmond v. J.A. Croson, 488 U.S. 469 (1989)	6–3	Writing for the Court and striking down Richmond, Virginia's minority set-aside

program for contractors (which was modeled after the federal set-aside program that was upheld in *Fullilove v. Klutznick,* 448 U.S. 448 (1980)), Justice O'Connor applied the Court's strict scrutiny standard of review in holding that affirmative action programs must be narrowly tailored to remedying actual practices of past discrimination in order to survive judicial scrutiny. Justices Marshall, Brennan, and Blackmun dissented.

CASE	VOTE	FACTS AND RULING
Metro Broadcasting, Inc. v. Federal Communications Commission, 497 U.S. 547 (1990)	5–4	In spite of the ruling in *Croson*, Justice Brennan commanded a majority for manded a majority for

reaffirming, as in *Fullilove*, that Congress has broader latitude than states and localities when authorizing affirmative-action programs, even without showing a close remedial nexus to past discrimination. Chief Justice Rehnquist and Justices Kennedy, O'Connor, and Scalia dissented.

| *Northeastern Florida Chapter of the Associated General Contractors of America v. City of Jacksonville, Florida,* 508 U.S. 656 (1993) | 7–2 | Writing for the Court, Justice Thomas held that a building contractors' association had standing to challenge an affirmative action set-aside program, |

even though during the course of the litigation the city had repealed its program. Moreover, the Court held that the association did not have to show that any of its members, in the absence of the program, would have received building contracts set aside for women and minorities. Justices O'Connor and Blackmun dissented.

| *Adarand Constructors, Inc. v. Peña,* 515 U.S. 200 (1995) | 5–4 | Writing for the majority, Justice O'Connor overruled *Metro Broadcasting, Inc. v. Fed-* |

eral Communications Commission, 497 U.S. 547 (1990) and held that the strict scrutiny test applies to federal affirmative action programs, no less than those adopted by state and local governments; Justices Breyer, Ginsburg, Souter, and Stevens dissented.

| *Ricci v. DeSefano,* 557 U.S. 557 (2009) | 5–4 | A bare majority of the Roberts Court reversed an appellate court's ruling upholding a |

New Haven, Connecticut, decision to disregard test scores for promotions of firefighters because no African Americans passed the tests and the city feared a discrimination lawsuit under Section VII of the Civil Rights Act of 1964 for using a test that had a "disparate impact" on minorities. The city was sued by white firefighters who passed the test but were denied promotions. Writing for the Court, Justice Kennedy avoided a Fourteenth Amendment equal protection challenge and ruled narrowly on statutory grounds that under Section VII employees must have a "strong basis in evidence" that a test is deficient and discriminatory rather than just "raw racial statistics." By contrast, writing for dissenting Justices Stevens, Souter, and Breyer, Justice Ginsburg countered that "Congress and, until the decision just announced, this Court regarded Tile VII's dual prescriptions on intentional and disparate impact as complementary. . . . Standing on equal footing, both provisions aim to end workplace discrimination and promote genuinely equal opportunity."

City of Richmond v. J. A. Croson
488 U.S. 469, 109 S.CT. 706 (1989)

In 1983, Richmond, Virginia, passed an ordinance requiring non-minority building contractors to subcontract 30 percent of all city-awarded projects to minority-owned businesses, or Minority Business Enterprises (MBEs). This set-aside quota was as much a remedy for past discrimination as a way to help black construction companies penetrate the local building industry. Half of Richmond's population was black, but minority-owned firms had won less than 1 percent of the $25 million awarded in city contracts in the preceding five years. The program was patterned on a federal one that the Supreme Court had upheld in *Fullilove v. Klutznick*, 448 U.S. 448 (1980). There the Burger Court was divided 6–3, with Justices Stewart, Rehnquist, and Stevens dissenting. The majority in an opinion by Chief Justice Burger upheld Congress's setting aside 10 percent of all federal contracts for minority-owned businesses. That quota was based on roughly half the difference between percentages of minority contractors and minorities in the country. Likewise, Richmond's quota fell about halfway between the city's black population (50 percent) and the number of minority contractors (fewer than 1 percent) in the city. Opponents, nevertheless, charged that the program created a "racial spoils system." A majority of the city's nine-member council is black and adopted the program six to two, with one abstention.

Before bidding on a $127,000 city contract to install urinals and toilets in the city jail, an Ohio plumbing contractor, J. A. Croson, knew it had to meet the 30 percent quota and that meant finding an MBE subcontractor to supply the fixtures, because their cost alone was 75 percent of the contract. Croson won the contract as the only bidder, despite failing to interest MBE subcontractors in the project. After trying again unsuccessfully to find an MBE subcontractor, Croson sought a waiver of the 30 percent set-aside. On hearing that, an MBE finally made a bid for the subcontract, but it came in $7,000 higher than Croson had estimated. So the company asked the city to raise its contract price accordingly. The city refused and announced it would reopen bidding on the project.

Croson sued. A federal district judge's decision upholding the city's set-aside program was reversed on appeal, and Richmond took its case to the highest court in the land. The composition of the Court, however, had dramatically changed since *Fullilove* was handed down. President Ronald Reagan had elevated Justice Rehnquist to the chief justiceship in 1986 and named to the bench Justices Sandra O'Connor (in 1981), Antonin Scalia (in 1986), and Anthony Kennedy (in 1988). Whereas in *Fullilove* the justices voted 6–3 to uphold a federal set-aside program, here the justices split 6–3 in striking down Richmond's program. Justice O'Connor's opinion for the majority, moreover, registered the Rehnquist Court's shift toward a strict scrutiny of affirmative action programs.

The Court's decision was 6–3, and the majority's opinion was announced by Justice O'Connor. Concurring opinions were delivered by Justices Stevens, Kennedy, and Scalia. Justices Marshall and Blackmun dissented and were joined by Justice Brennan.

■ ■ ■

☐ *Justice O'CONNOR delivered the opinion of the Court, with whom THE CHIEF JUSTICE, Justice WHITE and Justice KENNEDY join in part.*

The parties and their supporting *amici* fight an initial battle over the scope of the city's power to adopt legislation designed to address the effects of past discrimination. Relying on our decision in *Wygant* [*v. Jackson Board of Education*, 476 U.S. 267 (1986)], appellee argues that the city must limit any race-based remedial efforts to eradicating the effects of its own prior discrimination. This is essentially the position taken by the Court of Appeals below. Appellant argues that our decision in *Fullilove* [*v. Klutznick*, 448 U.S. 448 (1980)], is controlling, and that as a result the city of Richmond enjoys sweeping legislative power to define and attack the effects of prior discrimination in its local construction industry. We find that neither of these two rather stark alternatives can withstand analysis. . . .

Appellant and its supporting *amici* rely heavily on *Fullilove* for the proposition that a city council, like Congress, need not make specific findings of discrimination to engage in race-conscious relief. Thus, appellant argues "[i]t would be a perversion of federalism to hold that the federal government has a compelling interest in remedying the effects of racial discrimination in its own public works program, but a city government does not."

What appellant ignores is that Congress, unlike any State or political subdivision, has a specific constitutional mandate to enforce the dictates of the Fourteenth Amendment. The power to "enforce" may at times also include the power to define situations which *Congress* determines threaten principles of equality and to adopt prophylactic rules to deal with those situations. . . .

That Congress may identify and redress the effects of society-wide discrimination does not mean that, *a fortiori*, the States and their political subdivisions are free to decide that such remedies are appropriate. Section 1 of the Fourteenth Amendment is an explicit *constraint* on state power, and the States must undertake any remedial efforts in accordance with that provision. To hold otherwise would be to cede control over the content of the Equal Protection Clause to the 50 state legislatures and their myriad political subdivisions. The mere recitation of a benign or compensatory purpose for the use of a racial classification would essentially entitle the States to exercise the full power of Congress under Section 5 of the Fourteenth Amendment and insulate any racial classification from judicial scrutiny under Section 1. We believe that such a result would be contrary to the intentions of the Framers of the Fourteenth Amendment, who desired to place clear limits on the States' use of race as a criterion for legislative action, and to have the federal courts enforce those limitations. . . .

It would seem equally clear, however, that a state or local subdivision (if delegated the authority from the State) has the authority to eradicate the effects of private discrimination within its own legislative jurisdiction. This authority must, of course, be exercised within the constraints of Section 1 of the Fourteenth Amendment. Our decision in *Wygant* is not to the contrary. *Wygant* addressed the constitutionality of the use of racial quotas by local school authorities pursuant to an agreement reached with the local teachers' union. It was in the context of addressing the school board's power to adopt a race-based layoff program affecting its own work force that the *Wygant* plurality indicated that the Equal Protection Clause required "some showing of prior discrimination by the governmental unit involved." *Wygant*. As a matter of state law, the city of Richmond has legislative authority over its procurement policies, and can use its spending powers to remedy private discrimination, if it identifies that discrimination with the particularity required by the Fourteenth Amendment. To this extent, on the question of the city's competence, the Court of Appeals erred in following *Wygant* by rote in a case involving a state entity which has state–law authority to address discriminatory practices within local commerce under its jurisdiction.

Thus, if the city could show that it had essentially become a "passive participant" in a system of racial exclusion practiced by elements of the local construction industry, we think it clear that the city could take affirmative steps to dismantle such a system. It is beyond dispute that any public entity, state or federal, has a compelling interest in assuring that public dollars, drawn from the tax contributions of all citizens, do not serve to finance the evil of private prejudice. . . .

■ A

The Richmond Plan denies certain citizens the opportunity to compete for a fixed percentage of public contracts based solely upon their race. To whatever racial group these citizens belong, their "personal rights" to be treated with equal dignity and respect are implicated by a rigid rule erecting race as the sole criterion in an aspect of public decisionmaking.

Absent searching judicial inquiry into the justification for such race-based measures, there is simply no way of determining what classifications are "benign" or "remedial" and what classifications are in fact motivated by illegitimate notions of racial inferiority or simple racial politics. Indeed, the purpose of strict scrutiny is to "smoke out" illegitimate uses of race by assuring that the legislative body is pursuing a goal important enough to warrant use of a highly suspect tool. The test also ensures that the means chosen "fit" this compelling goal so closely that there is little or no possibility that the motive for the classification was illegitimate racial prejudice or stereotype.

Classifications based on race carry a danger of stigmatic harm. Unless they are strictly reserved for remedial settings, they may in fact promote notions of racial inferiority and lead to a politics of racial hostility. See *University of California Regents v. Bakke* [438 U.S. 265 (1978)] (opinion of POWELL, J.) ("[P]referential programs may only reinforce common stereotypes holding that certain groups are unable to achieve success without special protection based on a factor having no relation to individual worth"). We thus reaffirm the view expressed by the plurality in *Wygant* that the standard of review under the Equal Protection Clause is not dependent on the race of those burdened or benefited by a particular classification. . . .

In this case, blacks comprise approximately 50% of the population of the city of Richmond. Five of the nine seats on the City Council are held by blacks. The concern that a political majority will more easily act to the disadvantage of a minority based on unwarranted assumptions or incomplete facts would seem to militate for, not against, the application of heightened judicial scrutiny in this case.

■ B

The District Court found the city council's "findings sufficient to ensure that, in adopting the Plan, it was remedying the present effects of past discrimination in the *construction industry.*" . . .

While there is no doubt that the sorry history of both private and public discrimination in this country has contributed to a lack of opportunities for black entrepreneurs, this observation, standing alone, cannot justify a rigid racial quota in the awarding of public contracts in Richmond, Virginia. Like the claim that discrimination in primary and secondary schooling justifies a rigid racial preference in medical school admissions, an amorphous claim that there has been past discrimination in a particular industry cannot justify the use of an unyielding racial quota.

It is sheer speculation how many minority firms there would be in Richmond absent past societal discrimination, just as it was sheer speculation how many minority medical students would have been admitted to the medical school at Davis absent past discrimination in educational opportunities. Defining these sorts of injuries as "identified discrimination" would give local governments license to create a patchwork of racial preferences based on statistical generalizations about any particular field of endeavor.

These defects are readily apparent in this case. The 30% quota cannot in any realistic sense be tied to any injury suffered by anyone. The District Court relied upon five predicate "facts" in reaching its conclusion that there was an adequate basis for the 30% quota: (1) the ordinance declares itself to be remedial; (2) several proponents of the measure stated their views that there had been past discrimination in the construction industry; (3) minority businesses received .67% of prime contracts from the city while minorities constituted 50% of the city's population; (4) there were very few minority contractors in local and state contractors' associations; and (5) in 1977, Congress made a determination that the effects of past discrimination had stifled minority participation in the construction industry nationally.

None of these "findings," singly or together, provide [sic] the city of Richmond with a "strong basis in evidence for its conclusion that remedial action was necessary." *Wygant*. There is nothing approaching a prima facie case of a constitutional or statutory violation by *anyone* in the Richmond construction industry. . . .

In this case, the city does not even know how many MBEs in the relevant market are qualified to undertake prime or subcontracting work in public construction projects. . . . Nor does the city know what percentage of total city construction dollars minority firms now receive as subcontractors on prime contracts let by the city.

To a large extent, the set-aside of subcontracting dollars seems to rest on the unsupported assumption that white prime contractors simply will not hire minority firms. . . . Without any information on minority participation in subcontracting, it is quite simply impossible to evaluate overall minority representation in the city's construction expenditures. . . .

Finally, the city and the District Court relied on Congress' finding in connection with the set-aside approved in *Fullilove* that there had been nationwide discrimination in the construction industry. The probative value of these findings for demonstrating the existence of discrimination in Richmond is extremely limited. By its inclusion of a waiver procedure in the national program addressed in *Fullilove*, Congress explicitly recognized that the scope of the problem would vary from market area to market area. . . .

In sum, none of the evidence presented by the city points to any identified discrimination in the Richmond construction industry. We, therefore, hold that the city has failed to demonstrate a compelling interest in apportioning public contracting opportunities on the basis of race. To accept Richmond's claim that past societal discrimination alone can serve as the basis for rigid racial preferences would be to open the door to competing claims for "remedial relief" for every disadvantaged group. The dream of a Nation of equal citizens in a society where race is irrelevant to personal opportunity and achievement would be lost in a mosaic of shifting preferences based on inherently unmeasurable claims of past wrongs. . . .

The foregoing analysis applies only to the inclusion of blacks within the Richmond set-aside program. There is *absolutely no evidence* of past discrimination against Spanish-speaking, Oriental, Indian, Eskimo, or Aleut persons in any aspect of the Richmond construction industry. The District Court took judicial notice of the fact that the vast majority of "minority" persons in Richmond were black. It may well be that Richmond has never had an Aleut or Eskimo citizen. The random inclusion of racial groups that, as a practical matter, may never have suffered from discrimination in the construction industry in Richmond, suggests that perhaps the city's purpose was not in fact to remedy past discrimination.

If a 30% set-aside was "narrowly tailored" to compensate black contractors for past discrimination, one may legitimately ask why they are forced to share this "remedial relief" with an Aleut citizen who moves to Richmond tomorrow? The gross overinclusiveness of Richmond's racial preference strongly impugns the city's claim of remedial motivation. . . .

As noted by the court below, it is almost impossible to assess whether the Richmond Plan is narrowly tailored to remedy prior discrimination since it is not linked to identified discrimination in any way. We limit ourselves to two observations in this regard.

First, there does not appear to have been any consideration of the use of race-neutral means to increase minority business participation in city contracting. . . . Many of the barriers to minority participation in the construction industry relied upon by the city to justify a racial classification appear to be race neutral. If MBEs disproportionately lack capital or cannot meet bonding requirements, a race-neutral program of city financing for small firms would, *a fortiori*, lead to greater minority participation. The principal opinion in *Fullilove* found that Congress had carefully examined and rejected race-neutral alternatives before enacting the MBE set-aside. . . .

Second, the 30% quota cannot be said to be narrowly tailored to any goal, except perhaps outright racial balancing. It rests upon the "completely unrealistic" assumption that minorities will choose a particular trade in lockstep proportion to their representation in the local population. . . .

Given the existence of an individualized procedure, the city's only interest in maintaining a quota system rather than investigating the need for remedial action in particular cases would seem to be simple administrative convenience. But the interest in avoiding the bureaucratic effort necessary to tailor remedial relief to those who truly have suffered the effects of prior discrimination cannot justify a rigid line drawn on the basis of a suspect classification. . . . Under Richmond's scheme, a successful black, Hispanic, or Oriental entrepreneur from anywhere in the country enjoys an absolute preference over other citizens based solely on their race. We think it obvious that such a program is not narrowly tailored to remedy the effects of prior discrimination.

Nothing we say today precludes a state or local entity from taking action to rectify the effects of identified discrimination within its jurisdiction. If the city of Richmond had evidence before it that nonminority contractors were systematically excluding minority businesses from subcontracting opportunities it could take action to end the discriminatory exclusion. Where there is a significant statistical disparity between the number of qualified minority contractors willing and able to perform a particular service and the number of such contractors actually engaged by the locality or the locality's prime contractors, an inference of discriminatory exclusion could arise. Under such circumstances, the city could act to dismantle the closed business system by taking appropriate measures against those who discriminate on the basis of race or other illegitimate criteria. In the extreme case, some form of narrowly tailored racial preference might be necessary to break down patterns of deliberate exclusion. . . .

Accordingly, the judgment of the Court of Appeals for the Fourth Circuit is affirmed.

□ *Justice SCALIA, concurring.*

In my view there is only one circumstance in which the States may act *by race* to "undo the effects of past discrimination": where that is necessary to eliminate their own maintenance of a system of unlawful racial classification. . . . We have stressed each school district's constitutional "duty to *dismantle* its dual system," and have found that "[e]ach instance of a failure or refusal to fulfill this affirmative duty *continues the violation* of the Fourteenth Amendment." *Columbus Board of Education v. Penick* [433 U.S. 449 (1979)]. . . .

It is plainly true that in our society blacks have suffered discrimination immeasurably greater than any directed at other racial groups. But those who believe that racial preferences can help to "even the score" display, and reinforce, a manner of thinking by race that was the source of the injustice and that will, if it endures within our society, be the source of more injustice still. The relevant proposition is not that it was blacks, or Jews, or Irish who were discriminated against, but that it was individual men and women, "created equal," who were discriminated against. And the relevant resolve is that that should never happen again. Racial preferences appear to "even the score" (in some small degree) only if one embraces the proposition that our society is appropriately viewed as divided into races, making it right that an injustice rendered in the past to a black man should be compensated for by discriminating against a white. Nothing is worth that embrace. Since blacks have been disproportionately disadvantaged by racial discrimination, any race-neutral remedial program aimed at the disadvantaged *as such* will have a disproportionately beneficial impact on blacks. Only such a program, and not one that operates on the basis of race, is in accord with the letter and the spirit of our Constitution.

☐ *Justice MARSHALL, with whom Justice BRENNAN and Justice BLACKMUN join, dissenting.*

[T]oday's decision marks a deliberate and giant step backward in this Court's affirmative action jurisprudence. Cynical of one municipality's attempt to redress the effects of past racial discrimination in a particular industry, the majority launches a grape-shot attack on race-conscious remedies in general. The majority's unnecessary pronouncements will inevitably discourage or prevent governmental entities, particularly States and localities, from acting to rectify the scourge of past discrimination. This is the harsh reality of the majority's decision, but it is not the Constitution's command. . . .

My view has long been that race-conscious classifications designed to further remedial goals "must serve important governmental objectives and must be substantially related to achievement of those objectives" in order to withstand constitutional scrutiny. . . . Analyzed in terms of this two-prong standard, Richmond's set-aside, like the federal program on which it was modeled, is "plainly constitutional." . . .

Turning first to the governmental interest inquiry, Richmond has two powerful interests in setting aside a portion of public contracting funds for minority-owned enterprises. The first is the city's interest in eradicating the effects of past racial discrimination. It is far too late in the day to doubt that remedying such discrimination is a compelling, let alone an important, interest. . . .

Richmond has a second compelling interest in setting aside, where possible, a portion of its contracting dollars. That interest is the prospective one of preventing the city's own spending decisions from reinforcing and perpetuating the exclusionary effects of past discrimination. . . .

When government channels all its contracting funds to a white-dominated community of established contractors whose racial homogeneity is the product of private discrimination, it does more than place its imprimatur on the practices which forged and which continue to define that community. It also provides a measurable boost to those economic entities that have thrived within it, while denying important economic benefits to those entities which, but for prior discrimination, might well be better qualified to receive valuable government contracts. In my view, the interest in ensuring that the government does not reflect and reinforce prior private discrimination in dispensing public contracts is every bit as strong as the interest in eliminating private discrimination—an interest which this Court has repeatedly deemed compelling.

The remaining question with respect to the "governmental interest" prong of equal protection analysis is whether Richmond has proffered satisfactory proof of past racial discrimination to support its twin interests in remediation and in governmental nonperpetuation. Although the Members of this Court have differed on the appropriate standard of review for race-conscious remedial measures, we have always regarded this factual inquiry as a practical one. Thus, the Court has eschewed rigid tests which require the provision of particular species of evidence, statistical or otherwise. At the same time we have required that government adduce evidence that, taken as a whole, is sufficient to support its claimed interest and to dispel the natural concern that it acted out of mere "paternalistic stereotyping, not on a careful consideration of modern social conditions." *Fullilove v. Klutznick*. . . .

Richmond's reliance on localized, industry-specific findings is a far cry from the reliance on generalized "societal discrimination" which the majority decries as a basis for remedial action. But characterizing the plight of Richmond's minority contractors as mere "societal discrimination" is not the only respect in which the majority's critique shows an unwillingness to come to grips with why construction-contracting in Richmond is essentially a whites-only enterprise. The majority also takes the disingenuous approach of disaggregating Richmond's local evidence, attacking it piecemeal, and thereby concluding that no *single* piece of evidence adduced by the city, "standing alone," suffices to prove past discrimination. But items of evidence do not, of course, "stan[d] alone" or exist in alien juxtaposition; they necessarily work together, reinforcing or contradicting each other. . . .

When the legislatures and leaders of cities with histories of pervasive discrimination testify that past discrimination has infected one of their industries, armchair cynicism like that exercised by the majority has no place. . . . Disbelief is particularly inappropriate here in light of the fact that appellee Croson, which had the burden of proving unconstitutionality at trial, *Wygant*, (plurality opinion), has *at no point* come forward with *any* direct evidence that the City Council's motives were anything other than sincere.

Finally, I vehemently disagree with the majority's dismissal of the congressional and Executive Branch findings noted in *Fullilove* as having "extremely limited" probative value in this case. The majority concedes that Congress established nothing less than a "presumption" that minority contracting firms have been disadvantaged by prior discrimination. The majority, inexplicably, would forbid Richmond to "share" in this information, and permit only Congress to take note of these ample findings. In thus requiring that Richmond's local evidence be severed from the context in which it was prepared, the majority would require cities seeking to eradicate the effects of past discrimination within their borders to reinvent the evidentiary wheel and engage in unnecessarily duplicative, costly, and time-consuming factfinding.

No principle of federalism or of federal power, however, forbids a state or local government from drawing upon a nationally relevant historical record prepared by the Federal Government. . . . Of course, Richmond could have built an even more compendious record of past discrimination, one including additional stark statistics and additional individual accounts of past discrimination. But nothing in the Fourteenth Amendment imposes such onerous documentary obligations upon States and localities once the reality of past discrimination is apparent. . . .

Finally, like the federal provision, Richmond's does not interfere with any vested right of a contractor to a particular contract; instead it operates entirely prospectively. . . .

The majority today sounds a full-scale retreat from the Court's long-standing solicitude to race-conscious remedial efforts "directed toward deliverance of the century-old promise of equality of economic opportunity." *Fullilove.* The new and restrictive tests it applies scuttle one city's effort to surmount its discriminatory past, and imperil those of dozens more localities. I, however, profoundly disagree with the cramped vision of the Equal Protection Clause which the majority offers today and with its application of that vision to Richmond, Virginia's, laudable set-aside plan. The battle against pernicious racial discrimination or its effects is nowhere near won. I must dissent.

Gratz v. Bollinger

539 U.S. 244, 123 S.Ct. 2411 (2003)

The University of Michigan receives over 13,000 applications for admission into its College of Literature, Science, and Arts, and admits approximately 3,950 students each year. In order to achieve a diverse student body, the college gave preference to applicants from "underrepresented minority groups," including African Americans, Hispanics, and Native Americans. In the mid-1990s the college used different admissions criteria and set aside a number of seats in each entering class to achieve a numerical target. In 1998–1999, however, the college changed its policy in favor of a point system. Under that system the college used a "selection index" or ranking on a 150-point scale in three categories: test scores, academic record, and other factors. As many as 110 of those points were based on test scores and academic achievements. A maximum of 40 points were assigned for other factors, including 20 points for students from underrepresented minority groups or from socioeconomically disadvantaged families; 16 points for state residents from rural areas; 4 points for children of alumni. In general, applicants in the range of 100 to 150 points were admitted; those between 95 and 99 were admitted or postponed; 90 to 94 postponed or delayed; 75 to 89 delayed or postponed; and 74 and below delayed or rejected.

In 1995, Jennifer Gratz applied for admission. Her high school grade point average was 3.8 and her ACT standardized test score was 25. The college initially delayed her admission and then placed her on an extended wait list. Under the college's guidelines at the time all underrepresented minority applicants with Ms. Gratz's credentials were admitted, regardless of whether they were in- or out-of-state residents. Ms. Gratz filed a class-action lawsuit challenging the constitutionality of the admissions program. In December 2000, a federal district court held that the college's admissions system in 1995–1998 violated the Fourteenth Amendment, but held that its use of a point system was permissible and advanced a compelling governmental interest in promoting diversity in higher education. Ms. Gratz appealed that decision.

The lower court was reversed by a vote of 6–3. Chief Justice Rehnquist delivered the opinion of the Court. Justices O'Connor, Breyer, and Thomas filed concurring opinions. Justices Stevens, Souter, and Ginsburg filed dissenting opinions.

■ ■ ■

☐ *Chief Justice REHNQUIST delivered the opinion of the Court.*

We granted *certiorari* in this case to decide whether "the University of Michigan's use of racial preferences in undergraduate admissions violate[s] the Equal Protection Clause of the Fourteenth Amendment, Title VI of the Civil Rights Act of 1964." Because we find that the manner in which the University considers the race of applicants in its undergraduate admissions guidelines violates these constitutional and statutory provisions, we reverse that portion of the District Court's decision upholding the guidelines. . . .

Beginning with the 1998 academic year, the OUA [Office of Undergraduate Admissions] dispensed with the Guidelines tables and the SCUGA point system in favor of a "selection index," on which an applicant could score a maximum of 150 points. This index was divided linearly into ranges generally calling for admissions dispositions as follows: 100–150 (admit); 95–99 (admit or postpone); 90–94 (postpone or admit); 75–89 (delay or postpone); 74 and below (delay or reject).

Each application received points based on high school grade point average, standardized test scores, academic quality of an applicant's high school, strength or weakness of high school curriculum, in-state residency, alumni relationship, personal essay, and personal achievement or leadership. Of particular significance here, under a "miscellaneous" category, an applicant was entitled to 20 points based upon his or her membership in an underrepresented racial or ethnic minority group. The University explained that the "development of the selection index for admissions in 1998 changed only the mechanics, not the substance of how race and ethnicity were considered in admissions." . . .

During 1999 and 2000, the OUA used the selection index, under which every applicant from an underrepresented racial or ethnic minority group was awarded 20 points. Starting in 1999, however, the University established an Admissions Review Committee (ARC), to provide an additional level of consideration for some applications. Under the new system, counselors may, in their discretion, "flag" an application for the ARC to review after determining that the applicant (1) is academically prepared to succeed at the University, (2) has achieved a minimum selection index score, and (3) possesses a quality or characteristic important to the University's composition of its freshman class, such as high class rank, unique life experiences, challenges, circumstances, interests or talents, socioeconomic disadvantage, and underrepresented race, ethnicity, or geography. After reviewing "flagged" applications, the ARC determines whether to admit, defer, or deny each applicant. . . .

It is by now well established that "all racial classifications reviewable under the Equal Protection Clause must be strictly scrutinized." *Adarand*

Constructors, Inc. v. Peña, 515 U.S. 200 (1995). This "standard of review . . . is not dependent on the race of those burdened or benefited by a particular classification." Thus, "any person, of whatever race, has the right to demand that any governmental actor subject to the Constitution justify any racial classification subjecting that person to unequal treatment under the strictest of judicial scrutiny."

To withstand our strict scrutiny analysis, respondents must demonstrate that the University's use of race in its current admission program employs "narrowly tailored measures that further compelling governmental interests." Because "[r]acial classifications are simply too pernicious to permit any but the most exact connection between justification and classification," *Fullilove v. Klutznick*, 448 U.S. 448 (1980), our review of whether such requirements have been met must entail "a most searching examination." We find that the University's policy, which automatically distributes 20 points, or one-fifth of the points needed to guarantee admission, to every single "underrepresented minority" applicant solely because of race, is not narrowly tailored to achieve the interest in educational diversity that respondents claim justifies their program.

In *Bakke*, Justice POWELL reiterated that "[p]referring members of any one group for no reason other than race or ethnic origin is discrimination for its own sake." He then explained, however, that in his view it would be permissible for a university to employ an admissions program in which "race or ethnic background may be deemed a 'plus' in a particular applicant's file." . . .

Justice POWELL's opinion in *Bakke* emphasized the importance of considering each particular applicant as an individual, assessing all of the qualities that individual possesses, and in turn, evaluating that individual's ability to contribute to the unique setting of higher education. The admissions program Justice POWELL described, however, did not contemplate that any single characteristic automatically ensured a specific and identifiable contribution to a university's diversity. Instead, under the approach Justice POWELL described, each characteristic of a particular applicant was to be considered in assessing the applicant's entire application.

The current LSA policy does not provide such individualized consideration. The LSA's policy automatically distributes 20 points to every single applicant from an "underrepresented minority" group, as defined by the University. The only consideration that accompanies this distribution of points is a factual review of an application to determine whether an individual is a member of one of these minority groups. Moreover, unlike Justice POWELL's example, where the race of a "particular black applicant" could be considered without being decisive, the LSA's automatic distribution of 20 points has the effect of making "the factor of race . . . decisive" for virtually every minimally qualified underrepresented minority applicant. . . .

We conclude, therefore, that because the University's use of race in its current freshman admissions policy is not narrowly tailored to achieve respondents' asserted compelling interest in diversity, the admissions policy violates the Equal Protection Clause of the Fourteenth Amendment. We further find that the admissions policy also violates Title VI. Accordingly, we reverse that portion of the District Court's decision granting respondents summary judgment with respect to liability and remand the case for proceedings consistent with this opinion.

☐ *Justice O'CONNOR, concurring.*

Unlike the law school admissions policy the Court upholds today in *Grutter v. Bollinger*, the procedures employed by the University of Michigan's (University) Office of Undergraduate Admissions do not provide for a meaningful individualized review of applicants. . . . The selection index thus precludes admissions counselors from conducting the type of individualized consideration the Court's opinion in *Grutter* requires: consideration of each applicant's individualized qualifications, including the contribution each individual's race or ethnic identity will make to the diversity of the student body, taking into account diversity within and among all racial and ethnic groups. . . .

Although the Office of Undergraduate Admissions does assign 20 points to some "soft" variables other than race, the points available for other diversity contributions, such as leadership and service, personal achievement, and geographic diversity, are capped at much lower levels. Even the most outstanding national high school leader could never receive more than five points for his or her accomplishments—a mere quarter of the points automatically assigned to an underrepresented minority solely based on the fact of his or her race. [T]he selection index, by setting up automatic, predetermined point allocations for the soft variables, ensures that the diversity contributions of applicants cannot be individually assessed. This policy stands in sharp contrast to the law school's admissions plan, which enables admissions officers to make nuanced judgments with respect to the contributions each applicant is likely to make to the diversity of the incoming class. . . .

☐ *Justice GINSBURG, with whom Justice SOUTER joins, dissenting.*

In the wake "of a system of racial caste only recently ended" large disparities endure. Unemployment, poverty, and access to health care vary disproportionately by race. Neighborhoods and schools remain racially divided. African-American and Hispanic children are all too often educated in poverty-stricken and underperforming institutions. Adult African-Americans and Hispanics generally earn less than whites with equivalent levels of education. Equally credentialed job applicants receive different receptions depending on their race. Irrational prejudice is still encountered in real estate markets and consumer transactions. "Bias both conscious and unconscious, reflecting traditional and unexamined habits of thought, keeps up barriers that must come down if equal opportunity and nondiscrimination are ever genuinely to become this country's law and practice."

The Constitution instructs all who act for the government that they may not "deny to any person . . . the equal protection of the laws." In implementing this equality instruction, as I see it, government decisionmakers may properly distinguish between policies of exclusion and inclusion.

Our jurisprudence ranks race a "suspect" category, "not because [race] is inevitably an impermissible classification, but because it is one which usually, to our national shame, has been drawn for the purpose of maintaining racial inequality." But where race is considered "for the purpose of achieving equality," no automatic proscription is in order. For, "[t]he Constitution is both color blind and color conscious." To avoid conflict with the equal protection clause, a classification that denies a benefit, causes harm, or imposes a burden must not be based on race. In that sense, the Constitution is color blind. But the Constitution is color conscious to prevent discrimination being perpetuated and to undo the effects of past discrimination. . . .

Examining in this light the admissions policy employed by the University of Michigan's College of Literature, Science, and the Arts (College), and for the reasons well stated by Justice SOUTER, I see no constitutional infirmity. . . .

☐ *Justice SOUTER, with whom Justice GINSBURG joins as to Part II, dissenting.*

Grutter reaffirms the permissibility of individualized consideration of race to achieve a diversity of students, at least where race is not assigned a preordained value in all cases. On the other hand, Justice POWELL's opinion in *Regents of Univ. of Cal. v. Bakke*, 438 U.S. 265 (1978), rules out a racial quota or set-aside, in which race is the sole fact of eligibility for certain places in a class. Although the freshman admissions system here is subject to argument on the merits, I think it is closer to what *Grutter* approves than to what *Bakke* condemns, and should not be held unconstitutional on the current record.

The record does not describe a system with a quota like the one struck down in *Bakke*, which "insulate[d]" all nonminority candidates from competition from certain seats. The plan here, in contrast, lets all applicants compete for all places and values an applicant's offering for any place not only on grounds of race, but on grades, test scores, strength of high school, quality of course of study, residence, alumni relationships, leadership, personal character, socioeconomic disadvantage, athletic ability, and quality of a personal essay. A nonminority applicant who scores highly in these other categories can readily garner a selection index exceeding that of a minority applicant who gets the 20-point bonus. . . .

The very nature of a college's permissible practice of awarding value to racial diversity means that race must be considered in a way that increases some applicants' chances for admission. Since college admission is not left entirely to inarticulate intuition, it is hard to see what is inappropriate in assigning some stated value to a relevant characteristic, whether it be reasoning ability, writing style, running speed, or minority race. Justice POWELL's plus factors necessarily are assigned some values. The college simply does by a numbered scale what the law school accomplishes in its "holistic review," *Grutter*; the distinction does not imply that applicants to the undergraduate college are denied individualized consideration or a fair chance to compete on the basis of all the various merits their applications may disclose. . . .

Grutter v. Bollinger

539 U.S. 306, 123 S.Ct. 2325 (2003)

In 1992, the University of Michigan Law School adopted an admissions policy based on an index score representing a composite of an applicant's Law School Admissions Test (LSAT) score and undergraduate grade point average. The policy also affirmed the law school's "commitment to racial and ethnic diversity with special reference to the inclusion of students from groups which have been historically discriminated against, like African-Americans, Hispanics, and Native-Americans," who, without some preference, "might not be represented in [the] student body in meaningful numbers." Accordingly, the law school makes "special efforts" to increase the number and achieve a "critical mass" of such students.

Barbara Grutter, an unsuccessful white applicant and a forty-three-year-old businesswoman, challenged the constitutionality of the law school's admission program for relying on race and ethnicity as "predominant" factors and for favoring minority groups and giving them "a significantly greater chance of admission than students with similar credentials." A federal district court held that the law school's admissions program violated the Fourteenth Amendment, but the Court of Appeals for the Sixth Circuit reversed and concluded that the school's interest in achieving a diverse student body was compelling under *Regents of the University of California v. Bakke*, 438 U.S. 265 (1978). Ms. Grutter appealed that decision.

The appellate court's decision was affirmed by a vote of 5–4. Justice O'Connor delivered the opinion of the Court. Justice Ginsburg filed a concurring opinion. Justices Scalia and Thomas filed opinions concurring and dissenting in part. Chief Justice Rehnquist and Justice Kennedy filed dissenting opinions.

■ ■ ■

◻ *Justice O'CONNOR delivered the opinion of the Court.*

The Law School ranks among the Nation's top law schools. It receives more than 3,500 applications each year for a class of around 350 students. Seeking to "admit a group of students who individually and collectively are among the most capable," the Law School looks for individuals with "substantial promise for success in law school" and "a strong likelihood of succeeding in the practice of law and contributing in diverse ways to the well-being of others." More broadly, the Law School seeks "a mix of students with varying backgrounds and experiences who will respect and learn from each other." In 1992, the dean of the Law School charged a faculty committee with crafting a written admissions policy to implement these goals. In particular, the Law School sought to ensure that its efforts to achieve student body diversity complied with this Court's most recent ruling on the use of race in university admissions. See *Regents of Univ. of Cal. v. Bakke*, 438 U.S. 265 (1978). Upon the unanimous adoption of the committee's report by the Law School faculty, it became the Law School's official admissions policy.

The hallmark of that policy is its focus on academic ability coupled with a flexible assessment of applicants' talents, experiences, and potential "to contribute to the learning of those around them." The policy requires admissions officials to evaluate each applicant based on all the information available in the file, including a personal statement, letters of recommendation, and an essay describing the ways in which the applicant will contribute to the life and diversity of the Law School. In reviewing an applicant's file, admissions officials must consider the applicant's undergraduate grade point average (GPA) and Law School Admissions Test (LSAT) score because they are important (if imperfect) predictors of academic success in law school. The policy stresses that "no applicant should be admitted unless we expect that applicant to do well enough to graduate with no serious academic problems."

The policy makes clear, however, that even the highest possible score does not guarantee admission to the Law School. Nor does a low score automatically disqualify an applicant. Rather, the policy requires admissions officials to look beyond grades and test scores to other criteria that are important to the Law School's educational objectives. So-called " 'soft' variables" such as "the enthusiasm of recommenders, the quality of the undergraduate institution, the quality of the applicant's essay, and the areas and difficulty of undergraduate course selection" are all brought to bear in assessing an "applicant's likely contributions to the intellectual and social life of the institution." . . .

We last addressed the use of race in public higher education over 25 years ago. In the landmark *Bakke* case, we reviewed a racial set-aside program that reserved 16 out of 100 seats in a medical school class for members of certain minority groups. The decision produced six separate opinions, none of which commanded a majority of the Court. . . .

Since this Court's splintered decision in *Bakke*, Justice POWELL's opinion announcing the judgment of the Court has served as the touchstone for constitutional analysis of race-conscious admissions policies. Public and private universities across the Nation have modeled their own admissions programs on Justice POWELL's views on permissible race-conscious policies. . . .

We have held that all racial classifications imposed by government "must be analyzed by a reviewing court under strict scrutiny." This means that such classifications are constitutional only if they are narrowly tailored to further compelling governmental interests.

Strict scrutiny is not "strict in theory, but fatal in fact." Although all governmental uses of race are subject to strict scrutiny, not all are invalidated by it. As we have explained, "whenever the government treats any person unequally because of his or her race, that person has suffered an injury that falls squarely within the language and spirit of the Constitution's guarantee of equal protection." But that observation "says nothing about the ultimate validity of any particular law; that determination is the job of the court applying strict scrutiny." When race-based action is necessary to further a compelling governmental interest, such action does not violate the constitutional guarantee of equal protection so long as the narrow-tailoring requirement is also satisfied.

Context matters when reviewing race-based governmental action under the Equal Protection Clause. Not every decision influenced by race is equally objectionable and strict scrutiny is designed to provide a framework for carefully examining the importance and the sincerity of the reasons advanced by the governmental decisionmaker for the use of race in that particular context.

With these principles in mind, we turn to the question whether the Law School's use of race is justified by a compelling state interest. . . . The

Law School's educational judgment that such diversity is essential to its educational mission is one to which we defer. The Law School's assessment that diversity will, in fact, yield educational benefits is substantiated by respondents and their *amici*. . . .

As part of its goal of "assembling a class that is both exceptionally academically qualified and broadly diverse," the Law School seeks to "enroll a 'critical mass' of minority students." The Law School's interest is not simply "to assure within its student body some specified percentage of a particular group merely because of its race or ethnic origin." That would amount to outright racial balancing, which is patently unconstitutional. . . .

The Law School's claim of a compelling interest is further bolstered by its *amici*, who point to the educational benefits that flow from student body diversity. In addition to the expert studies and reports entered into evidence at trial, numerous studies show that student body diversity promotes learning outcomes, and "better prepares students for an increasingly diverse workforce and society, and better prepares them as professionals."

These benefits are not theoretical but real, as major American businesses have made clear that the skills needed in today's increasingly global marketplace can only be developed through exposure to widely diverse people, cultures, ideas, and viewpoints. . . .

We have repeatedly acknowledged the overriding importance of preparing students for work and citizenship, describing education as pivotal to "sustaining our political and cultural heritage" with a fundamental role in maintaining the fabric of society. *Plyler v. Doe*, 457 U.S. 202 (1982). This Court has long recognized that "education . . . is the very foundation of good citizenship." *Brown v. Board of Education*, 347 U.S. 483 (1954). For this reason, the diffusion of knowledge and opportunity through public institutions of higher education must be accessible to all individuals regardless of race or ethnicity. The United States, as *amicus curiae*, affirms that "[e]nsuring that public institutions are open and available to all segments of American society, including people of all races and ethnicities, represents a paramount government objective."

Moreover, universities, and in particular, law schools, represent the training ground for a large number of our Nation's leaders. Individuals with law degrees occupy roughly half the state governorships, more than half the seats in the United States Senate, and more than a third of the seats in the United States House of Representatives. The pattern is even more striking when it comes to highly selective law schools. A handful of these schools accounts for 25 of the 100 United States Senators, 74 United States Courts of Appeals judges, and nearly 200 of the more than 600 United States District Court judges. . . .

Even in the limited circumstance when drawing racial distinctions is permissible to further a compelling state interest, government is still "constrained in how it may pursue that end: [T]he means chosen to accomplish the [government's] asserted purpose must be specifically and narrowly framed to accomplish that purpose." *Shaw v. Hunt*, 517 U.S. 899 (1996). The purpose of the narrow tailoring requirement is to ensure that "the means chosen 'fit' . . . th[e] compelling goal so closely that there is little or no possibility that the motive for the classification was illegitimate racial prejudice or stereotype."

Since *Bakke*, we have had no occasion to define the contours of the narrow-tailoring inquiry with respect to race-conscious university admissions programs. That inquiry must be calibrated to fit the distinct issues raised by the use of race to achieve student body diversity in public higher education. . . .

To be narrowly tailored, a race-conscious admissions program cannot use a quota system—it cannot "insulat[e] each category of applicants with certain desired qualifications from competition with all other applicants." Instead, a university may consider race or ethnicity only as a " 'plus' in a particular applicant's file," without "insulat[ing] the individual from comparison with all other candidates for the available seats." In other words, an admissions program must be "flexible enough to consider all pertinent elements of diversity in light of the particular qualifications of each applicant, and to place them on the same footing for consideration, although not necessarily according them the same weight."

We find that the Law School's admissions program bears the hallmarks of a narrowly tailored plan. . . . We are satisfied that the Law School's admissions program, like the Harvard plan described by Justice POWELL, does not operate as a quota. . . .

Here, the Law School engages in a highly individualized, holistic review of each applicant's file, giving serious consideration to all the ways an applicant might contribute to a diverse educational environment. The Law School affords this individualized consideration to applicants of all races. . . .

What is more, the Law School actually gives substantial weight to diversity factors besides race. The Law School frequently accepts nonminority applicants with grades and test scores lower than underrepresented minority applicants (and other nonminority applicants) who are rejected. This shows that the Law School seriously weighs many other diversity factors besides race that can make a real and dispositive difference for nonminority applicants as well. By this flexible approach, the Law School sufficiently takes into account, in practice as well as in theory, a wide variety of characteristics besides race and ethnicity that contribute to a diverse student body. . . .

We are mindful, however, that "[a] core purpose of the Fourteenth Amendment was to do away with all governmentally imposed discrimination based on race." *Palmore v. Sidoti*, 466 U.S. 429 (1984). Accordingly, race-conscious admissions policies must be limited in time. This requirement reflects that racial classifications, however compelling their goals, are potentially so dangerous that they may be employed no more broadly than the interest demands. . . .

In the context of higher education, the durational requirement can be met by sunset provisions in race-conscious admissions policies and periodic reviews to determine whether racial preferences are still necessary to achieve student body diversity. Universities in California, Florida, and Washington State, where racial preferences in admissions are prohibited by state law, are currently engaged in experimenting with a wide variety of alternative approaches. Universities in other States can and should draw on the most promising aspects of these race-neutral alternatives as they develop. The requirement that all race-conscious admissions programs have a termination point "assure[s] all citizens that the deviation from the norm of equal treatment of all racial and ethnic groups is a temporary matter, a measure taken in the service of the goal of equality itself." *Richmond v. J.A. Croson Co.* . . .

It has been 25 years since Justice POWELL first approved the use of race to further an interest in student body diversity in the context of public higher education. Since that time, the number of minority applicants with high grades and test scores has indeed increased. We expect that 25 years from now, the use of racial preferences will no longer be necessary to further the interest approved today.

In summary, the Equal Protection Clause does not prohibit the Law School's narrowly tailored use of race in admissions decisions to further a compelling interest in obtaining the educational benefits that flow from a diverse student body. Consequently, petitioner's statutory claims based on Title VI also fail. The judgment of the Court of Appeals for the Sixth Circuit, accordingly, is affirmed.

☐ *Chief Justice REHNQUIST, with whom Justice SCALIA, Justice KENNEDY, and Justice THOMAS join, dissenting.*

As we have explained many times, "[a]ny preference based on racial or ethnic criteria must necessarily receive a most searching examination." Our cases establish that, in order to withstand this demanding inquiry, respondents must demonstrate that their methods of using race "fit" a compelling state interest "with greater precision than any alternative means." *Bakke.*

Before the Court's decision today, we consistently applied the same strict scrutiny analysis regardless of the government's purported reason for using race and regardless of the setting in which race was being used. We rejected calls to use more lenient review in the face of claims that race was being used in "good faith" because "[m]ore than good motives should be required when government seeks to allocate its resources by way of an explicit racial classification system." . . .

In practice, the Law School's program bears little or no relation to its asserted goal of achieving "critical mass." . . . From 1995 through 2000, the Law School admitted between 1,130 and 1,310 students. Of those, between 13 and 19 were Native American, between 91 and 108 were African-Americans, and between 47 and 56 were Hispanic. If the Law School is admitting between 91 and 108 African-Americans in order to achieve "critical mass," thereby preventing African-American students from feeling "isolated or like spokespersons for their race," one would think that a number of the same order of magnitude would be necessary to accomplish the same purpose for Hispanics and Native Americans. Similarly, even if all of the Native American applicants admitted in a given year matriculate, which the record demonstrates is not at all the case, how can this possibly constitute a "critical mass" of Native Americans in a class of over 350 students? In order for this pattern of admission to be consistent with the Law School's explanation of "critical mass," one would have to believe that the objectives of "critical mass" offered by respondents are achieved with only half the number of Hispanics and one-sixth the number of Native Americans as compared to African-Americans. But respondents offer no race-specific reasons for such disparities. Instead, they simply emphasize the importance of achieving "critical mass," without any explanation of why that concept is applied differently among the three underrepresented minority groups.

These different numbers, moreover, come only as a result of substantially different treatment among the three underrepresented minority groups, as is apparent in an example offered by the Law School and high-lighted by the Court: The school asserts that it "frequently accepts nonmi-nority applicants with grades and test scores lower than underrepresented minority applicants (and other nonminority applicants) who are rejected." Specifically, the Law School states that "[s]ixty-nine minority applicants were rejected between 1995 and 2000 with at least a 3.5 [Grade Point Aver-age (GPA)] and a [score of] 159 or higher on the [Law School Admissions Test (LSAT)]" while a number of Caucasian and Asian-American appli-cants with similar or lower scores were admitted.

Review of the record reveals only 67 such individuals. Of these 67 indi-viduals, 56 were Hispanic, while only 6 were African-American, and only 5 were Native American. This discrepancy reflects a consistent practice. For example, in 2000, 12 Hispanics who scored between a 159–160 on the LSAT and earned a GPA of 3.00 or higher applied for admission and only 2 were admitted. Meanwhile, 12 African-Americans in the same range of qualifica-tions applied for admission and all 12 were admitted. Likewise, that same year, 16 Hispanics who scored between a 151–153 on the LSAT and earned a 3.00 or higher applied for admission and only 1 of those applicants was admit-ted. Twenty-three similarly qualified African-Americans applied for admis-sion and 14 were admitted. . . .

[T]he correlation between the percentage of the Law School's pool of applicants who are members of the three minority groups and the percent-age of the admitted applicants who are members of these same groups is far too precise to be dismissed as merely the result of the school paying "some attention to [the] numbers." [F]rom 1995 through 2000 the percentage of admitted applicants who were members of these minority groups closely tracked the percentage of individuals in the school's applicant pool who were from the same groups. . . . For example, in 1995, when 9.7% of the applicant pool was African-American, 9.4% of the admitted class was African-American. By 2000, only 7.5% of the applicant pool was African-American, and 7.3% of the admitted class was African-American. This cor-relation is striking. Respondents themselves emphasize that the number of underrepresented minority students admitted to the Law School would be significantly smaller if the race of each applicant were not considered. But, as the examples above illustrate, the measure of the decrease would differ dramatically among the groups. The tight correlation between the percent-age of applicants and admittees of a given race, therefore, must result from careful race based planning by the Law School. . . .

I do not believe that the Constitution gives the Law School such free rein in the use of race. The Law School has offered no explanation for its actual admissions practices and, unexplained, we are bound to conclude that the Law School has managed its admissions program, not to achieve a "criti-cal mass," but to extend offers of admission to members of selected minority groups in proportion to their statistical representation in the applicant pool. But this is precisely the type of racial balancing that the Court itself calls "patently unconstitutional." . . .

☐ *Justice KENNEDY, dissenting.*

The Court, in a review that is nothing short of perfunctory, accepts the University of Michigan Law School's assurances that its admissions process meets with constitutional requirements. The majority fails to confront the reality of how the Law School's admissions policy is implemented. The dissenting opinion by THE CHIEF JUSTICE, which I join in full, demonstrates beyond question why the concept of critical mass is a delusion used by the Law School to mask its attempt to make race an automatic factor in most instances and to achieve numerical goals indistinguishable from quotas. . . . It remains to point out how critical mass becomes inconsistent with individual consideration in some more specific aspects of the admissions process.

About 80 to 85 percent of the places in the entering class are given to applicants in the upper range of Law School Admissions Test scores and grades. An applicant with these credentials likely will be admitted without consideration of race or ethnicity. With respect to the remaining 15 to 20 percent of the seats, race is likely outcome determinative for many members of minority groups. That is where the competition becomes tight and where any given applicant's chance of admission is far smaller if he or she lacks minority status. At this point the numerical concept of critical mass has the real potential to compromise individual review.

The Law School has not demonstrated how individual consideration is, or can be, preserved at this stage of the application process given the instruction to attain what it calls critical mass. In fact the evidence shows otherwise. There was little deviation among admitted minority students during the years from 1995 to 1998. The percentage of enrolled minorities fluctuated only by 0.3%, from 13.5% to 13.8%. The number of minority students to whom offers were extended varied by just a slightly greater magnitude of 2.2%, from the high of 15.6% in 1995 to the low of 13.4% in 1998. . . .

The narrow fluctuation band raises an inference that the Law School subverted individual determination, and strict scrutiny requires the Law School to overcome the inference. Whether the objective of critical mass "is described as a quota or a goal, it is a line drawn on the basis of race and ethnic status," and so risks compromising individual assessment. . . .

To be constitutional, a university's compelling interest in a diverse student body must be achieved by a system where individual assessment is safeguarded through the entire process. There is no constitutional objection to the goal of considering race as one modest factor among many others to achieve diversity, but an educational institution must ensure, through sufficient procedures, that each applicant receives individual consideration and that race does not become a predominant factor in the admissions decisionmaking. . . .

☐ *Justice SCALIA, with whom Justice THOMAS joins, concurring in part and dissenting in part.*

Unlike a clear constitutional holding that racial preferences in state educational institutions are impermissible, or even a clear anticonstitutional holding that racial preferences in state educational institutions are OK, today's *Grutter-Gratz* split double header seems perversely designed to prolong the controversy and the litigation. Some future lawsuits will presumably focus on whether the discriminatory scheme in question contains enough evaluation of the applicant "as an individual," and sufficiently avoids "separate admissions tracks" to fall under *Grutter* rather than *Gratz*. Some will focus on whether a university has gone beyond the bounds of a "good faith effort" and has so zealously pursued its "critical mass" as to make it an unconstitutional de facto quota system, rather than merely "a permissible goal." Other lawsuits may focus on whether, in the particular setting at issue, any educational benefits flow from racial diversity. Still other suits may challenge the bona fides of the institution's expressed commitment to the educational benefits of diversity that immunize the discriminatory scheme in *Grutter*. And still other suits may claim that the institution's racial preferences have gone below or above the mystical *Grutter*-approved "critical mass." Finally, litigation can be expected on behalf of minority groups intentionally short changed in the institution's composition of its generic minority "critical mass." I do not look forward to any of these cases. The Constitution proscribes government discrimination on the basis of race, and state-provided education is no exception.

☐ *Justice THOMAS, with whom Justice SCALIA joins as to Parts I–VII, concurring in part and dissenting in part.*

No one would argue that a university could set up a lower general admission standard and then impose heightened requirements only on black applicants. Similarly, a university may not maintain a high admission standard and grant exemptions to favored races. The Law School, of its own choosing, and for its own purposes, maintains an exclusionary admissions system that it knows produces racially disproportionate results. Racial discrimination is not a permissible solution to the self-inflicted wounds of this elitist admissions policy.

The majority upholds the Law School's racial discrimination not by interpreting the people's Constitution, but by responding to a faddish slogan of the cognoscenti. Nevertheless, I concur in part in the Court's opinion. First, I agree with the Court insofar as its decision, which approves of only one racial classification, confirms that further use of race in admissions remains unlawful. Second, I agree with the Court's holding that racial discrimination in higher education admissions will be illegal in 25 years. I respectfully dissent from the remainder of the Court's opinion and the judgment, however, because I believe that the Law School's current use of race violates the Equal Protection Clause and that the Constitution means the same thing today as it will in 300 months. . . .

Parents Involved in Community Schools v. Seattle School District No. 1 (reprise)

551 U.S. 701, 127 S.Ct. 2738 (2007)

See the excerpt in Section B of this chapter.

■ ■ ■

Schuette v. Coalition to Defend Affirmative Action, Integration, and Immigration Rights and Fight for Equality By Any Means Necessary (BAMN)

572 U.S.291, 134 S.CT. 1623 (2014)

Following the Supreme Court's rulings in *Gratz v. Bollinger*, 539 U.S. 244 (2003), striking down the University of Michigan's race-conscious undergraduate admissions process that assigned points for various factors such as race, legacy, and geography; and *Grutter v. Bollinger*, 539 U.S. 306 (2003), upholding the University of Michigan Law School's "holistic" admissions process, a majority of Michigan voters approved a constitutional amendment barring preferential treatment "on the basis of race, sex, color, ethnicity, or national origin in the operation of public employment, public education, or public contracting." That amendment was challenged by the Coalition to Defend Affirmative Action, Integration, and Immigrant Rights and Fight for Equality By Any Means Necessary (BAMN), among others. A federal district court upheld the amendment, but its decision was reversed by the Court of Appeals for the Sixth Circuit. An appeal of that decision was granted by the Supreme Court.

The appellate court's decision was reversed by a 6–2 vote (with Justice Kagan recused). Justice Kennedy delivered the opinion for the Court in which only Chief Justice Roberts and Justice Alito joined. Justices Scalia, Thomas, and Breyer issued concurring opinions. Justice Sotomayor, joined by Justice Ginsburg, dissented.

■ ■ ■

☐ *Justice KENNEDY delivered the opinion of the Court, which the CHIEF JUSTICE and Justice ALITO joined.*

[I]t is important to note what this case is not about. It is not about the constitutionality, or the merits, of race-conscious admissions policies in higher education. The consideration of race in admissions presents complex questions, in part addressed last Term in *Fisher v. University of Texas at Austin*, [133 S.Ct. 2411] (2013). In *Fisher*, the Court did not disturb the principle that the consideration of race in admissions is permissible, provided that certain conditions are met. In this case, as in *Fisher*, that principle is not challenged. The question here concerns not the permissibility of race-conscious admissions policies under the Constitution but whether, and in what manner, voters in the States may choose to prohibit the consideration of racial preferences in governmental decisions, in particular with respect to school admissions. . . .

[T]his Court's decision in *Reitman v. Mulkey*, 387 U.S. 369 (1967), is a proper beginning point for discussing the controlling decisions. In *Mulkey*, voters amended the California Constitution to prohibit any state legislative interference with an owner's prerogative to decline to sell or rent residential property on any basis [specifically, race]. . . . This Court concluded that the state constitutional provision was a denial of equal protection. . . . The Court agreed that the amendment "expressly authorized and constitutionalized the private right to discriminate." . . .

The next precedent of relevance, *Hunter v. Erickson*, 393 U.S. 385 (1969), is central to the arguments the respondents make in the instant case. In *Hunter*, the Court for the first time elaborated what the Court of Appeals here styled the "political process" doctrine. There, the Akron City Council found that the citizens of Akron consisted of " 'people of different race[s], . . . many of whom live in circumscribed and segregated areas, under sub-standard unhealthful, unsafe, unsanitary and overcrowded conditions, because of discrimination in the sale, lease, rental and financing of housing.' " To address the problem, Akron enacted a fair housing ordinance to prohibit that sort of discrimination. In response, voters amended the city charter to overturn the ordinance and to require that any additional antidiscrimination housing ordinance be approved by referendum. But most other ordinances "regulating the real property market" were not subject to those threshold requirements. The plaintiff, a black woman in Akron, Ohio, alleged that her real estate agent could not show her certain residences because the owners had specified they would not sell to black persons. . . .

Central to the Court's reasoning in Hunter was that the charter amendment was enacted in circumstances where widespread racial discrimination in the sale and rental of housing led to segregated housing, forcing many to live in " 'unhealthful, unsafe, unsanitary and overcrowded conditions.' " The Court rejected Akron's flawed "justifications for its discrimination," justifications that by their own terms had the effect of acknowledging the targeted nature of the charter amendment. The Court noted, furthermore, that the charter amendment was unnecessary as a general means of public control over the city council; for the people of Akron already were empowered to overturn ordinances by referendum. The Court found that the city charter amendment, by singling out antidiscrimination ordinances, "places special burden on racial minorities within the governmental process," thus becoming as impermissible as any other government action taken with the invidious intent to injure a racial minority. . . . *Hunter* rests on the unremarkable principle that the State may not alter the procedures of government to target racial minorities. . . .

[*Washington v.] Seattle School Dist. No. 1*, 458 U.S. 457 (1982)] [Seattle] is the third case of principal relevance here. There, the school board adopted a mandatory busing program to alleviate racial isolation of minority students in local schools. Voters who opposed the school board's busing plan passed a state initiative that barred busing to desegregate. The Court first determined that, although "white as well as Negro children benefit from" diversity, the school board's plan "inures primarily to the benefit of the minority." The Court next found that "the practical effect" of the state initiative was to "remov[e] the authority to address a racial problem—and only a racial problem—from the existing decisionmaking body, in such a way as to burden minority interests" because advocates of busing "now must seek relief from the state legislature, or from the statewide electorate." The Court therefore found that the initiative had "explicitly us[ed] the racial nature of a decision to determine the decisionmaking process."

Seattle is best understood as a case in which the state action in question (the bar on busing enacted by the State's voters) had the serious risk, if not purpose, of causing specific injuries on account of race, just as had been the case in *Mulkey* and *Hunter.* Although there had been no judicial finding of de jure segregation with respect to Seattle's school district, it appears as though school segregation in the district in the 1940's and 1950's may have been the partial result of school board policies that "permitted white students to transfer out of black schools while restricting the transfer of black students into white schools." *Parents Involved in Community Schools v. Seattle School Dist. No. 1,* 551 U.S. 701–808 (2007) (BREYER, J., dissenting). . . .

As this Court held in *Parents Involved,* the school board's purported remedial action would not be permissible today absent a showing of de jure segregation. That holding prompted Justice BREYER to observe in dissent, as noted above, that one permissible reading of the record was that the school board had maintained policies to perpetuate racial segregation in the schools. In all events we must understand *Seattle* as *Seattle* understood itself, as a case in which neither the State nor the United States "challenge[d] the propriety of race-conscious student assignments for the purpose of achieving integration, even absent a finding of prior de jure segregation." In other words the legitimacy and constitutionality of the remedy in question (busing for desegregation) was assumed, and *Seattle* must be understood on that basis. *Seattle* involved a state initiative that "was carefully tailored to interfere only with desegregative busing." . . .

The broad language used in *Seattle,* however, went well beyond the analysis needed to resolve the case. The Court there seized upon the statement in Justice HARLAN's concurrence in *Hunter* that the procedural change in that case had "the clear purpose of making it more difficult for certain racial and religious minorities to achieve legislation that is in their interest." That language, taken in the context of the facts in *Hunter,* is best read simply to describe the necessity for finding an equal protection violation where specific injuries from hostile discrimination were at issue. The *Seattle* Court, however, used the language from the *Hunter* concurrence to establish a new and far-reaching rationale. *Seattle* stated that where a government policy "inures primarily to the benefit of the minority" and "minorities . . . consider" the policy to be "'in their interest,'" then any state action that "place[s] effective decisionmaking authority over" that policy "at a different level of government" must be reviewed under strict scrutiny. In essence, according to the broad reading of *Seattle,* any state action with a "racial focus" that makes it "more difficult for certain racial minorities than for other groups" to "achieve legislation that is in their interest" is subject to strict scrutiny. It is this reading of *Seattle* that the Court of Appeals found to be controlling here. And that reading must be rejected. . . .

In cautioning against "impermissible racial stereotypes," this Court has rejected the assumption that "members of the same racial group—regardless of their age, education, economic status, or the community in which they live—think alike, share the same political interests, and will prefer the same candidates at the polls." *Shaw v. Reno,* 509 U.S. 630 (1993). It cannot be entertained as a serious proposition that all individuals of the same race think alike. Yet that proposition would be a necessary beginning point were the *Seattle* formulation to control, as the Court of Appeals held it did in this case. And if it were deemed necessary to probe how some races define their own interest in political matters, still another beginning point would be to define individuals according to race. But in a society in which those lines are becoming more blurred, the attempt to define race-based categories also raises serious questions of its own. Government action that classifies individuals on the basis of race is inherently suspect and carries the danger of perpetuating the very racial divisions the polity seeks to transcend. . . .

The freedom secured by the Constitution consists, in one of its essential dimensions, of the right of the individual not to be injured by the unlawful exercise of governmental power. The mandate for segregated schools, *Brown v. Board of Education*, 347 U.S. 483 (1954), and scores of other examples teach that individual liberty has constitutional protection, and that liberty's full extent and meaning may remain yet to be discovered and affirmed. Yet freedom does not stop with individual rights. Our constitutional system embraces, too, the right of citizens to debate so they can learn and decide and then, through the political process, act in concert to try to shape the course of their own times and the course of a nation that must strive always to make freedom ever greater and more secure. Here Michigan voters acted in concert and statewide to seek consensus and adopt a policy on a difficult subject against a historical background of race in America that has been a source of tragedy and persisting injustice. That history demands that we continue to learn, to listen, and to remain open to new approaches if we are to aspire always to a constitutional order in which all persons are treated with fairness and equal dignity. Were the Court to rule that the question addressed by Michigan voters is too sensitive or complex to be within the grasp of the electorate; or that the policies at issue remain too delicate to be resolved save by university officials or faculties, acting at some remove from immediate public scrutiny and control; or that these matters are so arcane that the electorate's power must be limited because the people cannot prudently exercise that power even after a full debate, that holding would be an unprecedented restriction on the exercise of a fundamental right held not just by one person but by all in common. It is the right to speak and debate and learn and then, as a matter of political will, to act through a lawful electoral process.

The respondents in this case insist that a difficult question of public policy must be taken from the reach of the voters, and thus removed from the realm of public discussion, dialogue, and debate in an election campaign. Quite in addition to the serious First Amendment implications of that position with respect to any particular election, it is inconsistent with the underlying premises of a responsible, functioning democracy. One of those premises is that a democracy has the capacity—and the duty—to learn from its past mistakes; to discover and confront persisting biases; and by respectful, rationale deliberation to rise above those flaws and injustices. That process is impeded, not advanced, by court decrees based on the proposition that the public cannot have the requisite repose to discuss certain issues. It is demeaning to the democratic process to presume that the voters are not capable of deciding an issue of this sensitivity on decent and rational grounds. The process of public discourse and political debate should not be foreclosed even if there is a risk that during a public campaign there will be those, on both sides, who seek to use racial division and discord to their own political advantage. An informed public can, and must, rise above this. The idea of democracy is that it can, and must, mature. Freedom embraces the right, indeed the duty, to engage in a rational, civic discourse in order to determine how best to form a consensus to shape the destiny of the Nation and its people. These First Amendment dynamics would be disserved if this Court were to say that the question here at issue is beyond the capacity of the voters to debate and then to determine. . . .

This case is not about how the debate about racial preferences should be resolved. It is about who may resolve it. There is no authority in the Constitution of the United States or in this Court's precedents for the Judiciary to set aside Michigan laws that commit this policy determination to the voters. Deliberative debate on sensitive issues such as racial preferences all too often may shade into rancor. But that does not justify removing certain court-determined issues from the voters' reach. Democracy does not presume that some subjects are either too divisive or too profound for public debate.

☐ *CHIEF JUSTICE ROBERTS, concurring.*

The dissent states that "[t]he way to stop discrimination on the basis of race is to speak openly and candidly on the subject of race." And it urges that "[r]ace matters because of the slights, the snickers, the silent judgments that reinforce that most crippling of thoughts: 'I do not belong here.'" But it is not "out of touch with reality" to conclude that racial preferences may themselves have the debilitating effect of reinforcing precisely that doubt, and—if so—that the preferences do more harm than good. To disagree with the dissent's views on the costs and benefits of racial preferences is not to "wish away, rather than confront" racial inequality. People can disagree in good faith on this issue, but it similarly does more harm than good to question the openness and candor of those on either side of the debate.

☐ *Justice SCALIA, with whom Justice THOMAS joins, concurring in the judgment.*

It has come to this. Called upon to explore the jurisprudential twilight zone between two errant lines of precedent, we confront a frighteningly bizarre question: Does the Equal Protection Clause of the Fourteenth Amendment forbid what its text plainly requires? Needless to say (except that this case obliges us to say it), the question answers itself. "The Constitution proscribes government discrimination on the basis of race, and state-provided education is no exception." *Grutter v. Bollinger* (SCALIA, J., concurring in part and dissenting in part). It is precisely this understanding—the correct understanding—of the federal Equal Protection Clause that the people of the State of Michigan have adopted for their own fundamental law. By adopting it, they did not simultaneously offend it.

Even taking this Court's sorry line of race-based-admissions cases as a given, I find the question presented only slightly less strange: Does the

Equal Protection Clause forbid a State from banning a practice that the Clause barely—and only provisionally—permits? Reacting to those race-based-admissions decisions, some States—whether deterred by the prospect of costly litigation; aware that *Grutter*'s bell may soon toll, or simply opposed in principle to the notion of "benign" racial discrimination—have gotten out of the racial-preferences business altogether. And with our express encouragement: "Universities in California, Florida, and Washington State, where racial preferences in admissions are prohibited by state law, are currently engaging in experimenting with a wide variety of alternative approaches. Universities in other States can and should draw on the most promising aspects of these race-neutral alternatives as they develop." Respondents seem to think this admonition was merely in jest. The experiment, they maintain, is not only over; it never rightly began. Neither the people of the States nor their legislatures ever had the option of directing subordinate public-university officials to cease considering the race of applicants, since that would deny members of those minority groups the option of enacting a policy designed to further their interest, thus denying them the equal protection of the laws. Never mind that it is hotly disputed whether the practice of race-based admissions is ever in a racial minority's interest. And never mind that, were a public university to stake its defense of a race-based-admissions policy on the ground that it was designed to benefit primarily minorities (as opposed to all students, regardless of color, by enhancing diversity), we would hold the policy unconstitutional.

But the battleground for this case is not the constitutionality of race-based admissions—at least, not quite. Rather, it is the so-called political-process doctrine, derived from this Court's opinions in *Washington v. Seattle School Dist. No. 1* and *Hunter v. Erickson*. I agree with those parts of the plurality opinion that repudiate this doctrine. But I do not agree with its reinterpretation of *Seattle* and *Hunter*, which makes them stand in part for the cloudy and doctrinally anomalous proposition that whenever state action poses "the serious risk . . . of causing specific injuries on account of race," it denies equal protection. I would instead reaffirm that the "ordinary principles of our law [and] of our democratic heritage" require "plaintiffs alleging equal protection violations" stemming from facially neutral acts to "prove intent and causation and not merely the existence of racial disparity." *Freeman v. Pitts*, 503 U.S. 467 (1992) (SCALIA, J., concurring). . . .

[Justice BREYER concurred in the judgment because (1) Michigan universities considered race in admission not for the reason of remedying past discrimination but for the less significant reason of promoting diverse student bodies and (2) the constitutional amendment transferred authority to make decisions about affirmative action from "unelected faculty members and administrators" to the voters themselves, and thus reinforced participatory democracy.]

□ *Justice SOTOMAYOR, with whom Justice GINSBURG joins, dissenting.*

We are fortunate to live in a democratic society. But without checks, democratically approved legislation can oppress minority groups. For that reason, our Constitution places limits on what a majority of the people may do. This case implicates one such limit: the guarantee of equal protection of the laws. Although that guarantee is traditionally understood to prohibit intentional discrimination under existing laws, equal protection does not end there. Another fundamental strand of our equal protection jurisprudence focuses on process, securing to all citizens the right to participate meaningfully and equally in self-government. That right is the bedrock of our democracy, for it preserves all other rights.

Yet to know the history of our Nation is to understand its long and lamentable record of stymieing the right of racial minorities to participate in the political process. At first, the majority acted with an open, invidious purpose. Notwithstanding the command of the Fifteenth Amendment, certain States shut racial minorities out of the political process altogether by withholding the right to vote. This Court intervened to preserve that right. The majority tried again, replacing outright bans on voting with literacy tests, good character requirements, poll taxes, and gerrymandering. The Court was not fooled; it invalidated those measures, too. The majority persisted. This time, although it allowed the minority access to the political process, the majority changed the ground rules of the process so as to make it more difficult for the minority, and the minority alone, to obtain policies designed to foster racial integration. Although these political restructurings may not have been discriminatory in purpose, the Court reaffirmed the right of minority members of our society to participate meaningfully and equally in the political process.

This case involves this last chapter of discrimination: A majority of the Michigan electorate changed the basic rules of the political process in that State in a manner that uniquely disadvantaged racial minorities. . . .

As a result of Section 26, there are now two very different processes through which a Michigan citizen is permitted to influence the admissions policies of the State's universities: one for persons interested in race-sensitive admissions policies and one for everyone else. A citizen who is a University of Michigan alumnus, for instance, can advocate for an admissions policy that considers an applicant's legacy status by meeting individually with members of the Board of Regents to convince them of her views, by joining with other legacy parents to lobby the Board, or by voting for and supporting Board candidates who share her position. The same options are available to a citizen who wants the Board to adopt admissions policies that consider athleticism, geography, area of study, and so on. The one and only policy a Michigan citizen may not seek through this long-established process is a race-sensitive admissions policy that considers race in an individualized manner when it is clear that race-neutral alternatives are not adequate to achieve diversity. For that policy alone, the citizens of Michigan must undertake the daunting task of amending the State Constitution.

Our precedents do not permit political restructurings that create one process for racial minorities and a separate, less burdensome process for everyone else. This Court has held that the Fourteenth Amendment does not tolerate "a political structure that treats all individuals as equals, yet more subtly distorts governmental processes in such a way as to place special burdens on the ability of minority groups to achieve beneficial legislation." *Washington v. Seattle School Dist. No. 1*, 458 U.S. 457 (1982). Such restructuring, the Court explained, "is no more permissible than denying [the minority] the [right to] vote, on an equal basis with others." *Hunter.* In those cases—*Hunter* and *Seattle*—the Court recognized what is now known as the "political-process doctrine": When the majority reconfigures the political process in a manner that burdens only a racial minority, that alteration triggers strict judicial scrutiny.

Today, disregarding *stare decisis*, a majority of the Court effectively discards those precedents. . . .

The plurality's decision fundamentally misunderstands the nature of the injustice worked by Section 26. . . . I firmly believe that our role as judges includes policing the process of self-government and stepping in when necessary to secure the constitutional guarantee of equal protection. Because I would do so here, I respectfully dissent.

For much of its history, our Nation has denied to many of its citizens the right to participate meaningfully and equally in its politics. This is a history we strive to put behind us. But it is a history that still informs the society we live in, and so it is one we must address with candor. Because the political-process doctrine is best understood against the backdrop of this history, I will briefly trace its course.

The Fifteenth Amendment, ratified after the Civil War, promised to racial minorities the right to vote. But many States ignored this promise. In addition to outright tactics of fraud, intimidation, and violence, there are countless examples of States categorically denying to racial minorities access to the political process. . . .

Some States were less direct. Oklahoma was one of many that required all voters to pass a literacy test. But the test did not apply equally to all voters. Under a "grandfather clause," voters were exempt if their grand-fathers had been voters or had served as soldiers before 1866. This meant, of course, that black voters had to pass the test, but many white voters did not. The Court held the scheme unconstitutional. *Guinn v. United States*, 238 U.S. 347 (1915). In response, Oklahoma changed the rules. It enacted a new statute under which all voters who were qualified to vote in 1914 (under the unconstitutional grandfather clause) remained qualified, and the remaining voters had to apply for registration within a 12-day period. *Lane v. Wilson*, 307 U.S. 268–271 (1939). The Court struck down that statute as well. . . .

This Court's landmark ruling in *Brown v. Board of Education* (1954) triggered a new era of political restructuring, this time in the context of education. In Virginia, the General Assembly transferred control of student assignment from local school districts to a State Pupil Placement Board. And when the legislature learned that the Arlington County school board had prepared a desegregation plan, the General Assembly "swiftly retaliated" by stripping the county of its right to elect its school board by popular vote and instead making the board an appointed body. . . .

The Court remained true to its command in Brown. In Arkansas, for example, it enforced a desegregation order against the Little Rock school board. *Cooper v. Aaron*, 358 U.S. 1 (1958). On the very day the Court announced that ruling, the Arkansas Legislature responded by changing the rules. It enacted a law permitting the Governor to close any public school in the State, and stripping local school districts of their decisionmaking authority so long as the Governor determined that local officials could not maintain "'a general, suitable, and efficient educational system.'"

The States' political restructuring efforts in the 1960's and 1970's went beyond the context of education. Many States tried to suppress the political voice of racial minorities more generally by reconfiguring the manner in which they filled vacancies in local offices, often transferring authority from the electorate (where minority citizens had a voice at the local level) to the States' executive branch (where minorities wielded little if any influence).

It was in this historical context that the Court intervened in *Hunter v. Erickson*, 393 U.S. 385 (1969), and *Washington v. Seattle School Dist. No. 1*, 458 U.S. 457 (1982). Together, *Hunter* and *Seattle* recognized a fundamental strand of this Court's equal protection jurisprudence: the political-process doctrine. . . .

Before the enactment of Section 26, Michigan's political structure permitted both supporters and opponents of race-sensitive admissions policies to vote for their candidates of choice and to lobby the elected and politically accountable boards. Section 26 reconfigured that structure. After Section 26, the boards retain plenary authority over all admissions criteria except for race-sensitive admissions policies. To change admissions policies on this one issue, a Michigan citizen must instead amend the Michigan Constitution. That is no small task. To place a proposed constitutional amendment on the ballot requires either the support of two-thirds of both Houses of the Michigan Legislature or a vast number of signatures from Michigan voters—10 percent of the total number of votes cast in the preceding gubernatorial election. Since more than 3.2 million votes were cast in the 2010 election for Governor, more than 320,000 signatures are currently needed to win a ballot spot. . . . And the costs of qualifying an amendment are significant. . . .

It is nothing short of baffling . . . for the plurality to insist—in the face of clear language in *Hunter* and *Seattle* saying otherwise—that those cases were about nothing more than the intentional and invidious infliction of a racial injury. The plurality's attempt to rewrite *Hunter* and *Seattle* so as to cast aside the political-process doctrine *sub silentio* is impermissible as a matter of *stare decisis*. Under the doctrine of *stare decisis*, we usually stand by our decisions, even if we disagree with them, because people rely on what we say, and they believe they can take us at our word.

And what now of the political-process doctrine? After the plurality's revision of *Hunter* and *Seattle*, it is unclear what is left. The plurality certainly does not tell us. On this point, and this point only, I agree with Justice SCALIA that the plurality has rewritten those precedents beyond recognition. . . .

The salient point is this: Although the elected and politically accountable boards may well entrust university officials with certain day-to-day admissions responsibilities, they often weigh in on admissions policies themselves and, at all times, they retain complete supervisory authority over university officials and overall admissions decisions. . . .

The political-process doctrine not only resolves this case as a matter of *stare decisis*; it is correct as a matter of first principles. . . . The political-process doctrine, grounded in the Fourteenth Amendment, is a central check on majority rule. . . .

Few rights are as fundamental as the right to participate meaningfully and equally in the process of government. See *Yick Wo v. Hopkins*, 118 U.S. 356 (1886) (political rights are "fundamental" because they are "preservative of all rights"). That right is the bedrock of our democracy, recognized from its very inception. . . .

Our cases recognize at least three features of the right to meaningful participation in the political process. Two of them, thankfully, are uncontroversial. First, every eligible citizen has a right to vote. This, woefully, has not always been the case. But it is a right no one would take issue with today. Second, the majority may not make it more difficult for the minority to exercise the right to vote. This, too, is widely accepted. After all, the Court has invalidated grandfather clauses, good character requirements, poll taxes, and gerrymandering provisions. The third feature, the one the plurality dismantles today, is that a majority may not reconfigure the existing political process in a manner that creates a two-tiered system of political change, subjecting laws designed to protect or benefit discrete and insular minorities to a more burdensome political process than all other laws. This is the political-process doctrine of *Hunter* and *Seattle*.

My colleagues would stop at the second. The plurality embraces the freedom of "self-government" without limits. And Justice SCALIA values a "near-limitless" notion of state sovereignty. The wrong sought to be corrected by the political-process doctrine, they say, is not one that should concern us and is in any event beyond the reach of the Fourteenth Amendment. As they see it, the Court's role in protecting the political process ends once we have removed certain barriers to the minority's participation in that process. Then, they say, we must sit back and let the majority rule without the key constitutional limit recognized in *Hunter* and *Seattle*.

That view drains the Fourteenth Amendment of one of its core teachings. Contrary to today's decision, protecting the right to meaningful participation in the political process must mean more than simply removing barriers to participation. It must mean vigilantly policing the political process to ensure that the majority does not use other methods to prevent minority groups from partaking in that process on equal footing. Why? For the same reason we guard the right of every citizen to vote. . . .

To accept the first two features of the right to meaningful participation in the political process, while renouncing the third, paves the way for the majority to do what it has done time and again throughout our Nation's history: afford the minority the opportunity to participate, yet manipulate the ground rules so as to ensure the minority's defeat. This is entirely at odds with our idea of equality under the law. . . .

My colleagues are of the view that we should leave race out of the picture entirely and let the voters sort it out. We have seen this reasoning before. See *Parents Involved* ("The way to stop discrimination on the basis of race is to stop discriminating on the basis of race"). It is a sentiment out of touch with reality, one not required by our Constitution, and one that has properly been rejected as "not sufficient" to resolve cases of this nature. While "[t]he enduring hope is that race should not matter[,] the reality is that too often it does." "[R]acial discrimination . . . [is] not ancient history." *Bartlett v. Strickland*, 556 U.S. 1 (2009) (plurality opinion).

Race matters. Race matters in part because of the long history of racial minorities' being denied access to the political process.

Race also matters because of persistent racial inequality in society—inequality that cannot be ignored and that has produced stark socioeconomic disparities.

And race matters for reasons that really are only skin deep, that cannot be discussed any other way, and that cannot be wished away. Race matters to a young man's view of society when he spends his teenage years watching others tense up as he passes, no matter the neighborhood where he grew up. Race matters to a young woman's sense of self when she states her hometown, and then is pressed, "No, where are you really from?", regardless of how many generations her family has been in the country. Race matters to a young person addressed by a stranger in a foreign language, which he does not understand because only English was spoken at home. Race matters because of the slights, the snickers, the silent judgments that reinforce that most crippling of thoughts: "I do not belong here."

In my colleagues' view, examining the racial impact of legislation only perpetuates racial discrimination. This refusal to accept the stark reality that race matters is regrettable. The way to stop discrimination on the basis of race is to speak openly and candidly on the subject of race, and to apply the Constitution with eyes open to the unfortunate effects of centuries of racial discrimination. As members of the judiciary tasked with intervening to carry out the guarantee of equal protection, we ought not sit back and wish away, rather than confront, the racial inequality that exists in our society. It is this view that works harm, by perpetuating the facile notion that what makes race matter is acknowledging the simple truth that race does matter.

Although the only constitutional rights at stake in this case are process-based rights, the substantive policy at issue is undeniably of some relevance to my colleagues. I will therefore speak in response.

For over a century, racial minorities in Michigan fought to bring diversity to their State's public colleges and universities. Before the advent of race-sensitive admissions policies, those institutions, like others around the country, were essentially segregated. In 1868, two black students were admitted to the University of Michigan, the first of their race. In 1935, over six decades later, there were still only 35 black students at the University. By 1954, this number had risen to slightly below 200. And by 1966, to around 400, among a total student population of roughly 32,500—barely over 1 percent. The numbers at the University of Michigan Law School are even more telling. During the 1960's, the Law School produced 9 black graduates among a total of 3,041—less than three-tenths of 1 percent. . . .

During the 1970's, the University continued to improve its admissions policies, encouraged by this Court's 1978 decision in [*Regents of the University of California v.] Bakke* [438 U.S. 265 (1978)]. In that case, the Court told our Nation's colleges and universities that they could consider race in admissions as part of a broader goal to create a diverse student body, in which students of different backgrounds would learn together, and thereby learn to live together. A little more than a decade ago, in *Grutter*, the Court reaffirmed this understanding. In upholding the admissions policy of the Law School, the Court laid to rest any doubt whether student body diversity is a compelling interest that may justify the use of race.

Race-sensitive admissions policies are now a thing of the past in Michigan after Section 26, even though—as experts agree and as research shows—those policies were making a difference in achieving educational diversity. . . .

Section 26 has already led to decreased minority enrollment at Michigan's public colleges and universities. In 2006 (before Section 26 took effect), underrepresented minorities made up 12.15 percent of the University of Michigan's freshman class, compared to 9.54 percent in 2012—a roughly 25 percent decline. . . .

Colleges and universities must be free to prioritize the goal of diversity. They must be free to immerse their students in a multiracial environment that fosters frequent and meaningful interactions with students of other races, and thereby pushes such students to transcend any assumptions they may hold on the basis of skin color. Without race-sensitive admissions policies, this might well be impossible. The statistics I have described make that fact glaringly obvious. We should not turn a blind eye to something we cannot help but see. . . .

I cannot ignore the unfortunate outcome of today's decision: Short of amending the State Constitution, a Herculean task, racial minorities in Michigan are deprived of even an opportunity to convince Michigan's public colleges and universities to consider race in their admissions plans when other attempts to achieve racial diversity have proved unworkable, and those institutions are unnecessarily hobbled in their pursuit of a diverse student body. . . .

Today's decision eviscerates an important strand of our equal protection jurisprudence. For members of historically marginalized groups, which rely on the federal courts to protect their constitutional rights, the decision can hardly bolster hope for a vision of democracy that preserves for all the right to participate meaningfully and equally in self-government.

I respectfully dissent.

Fisher v. University of Texas at Austin (Fisher II)

136 S.Ct. 2198 (2016)

Under the University of Texas's system of student admissions, most entering students (75 to 80 percent) are admitted through its "Top Ten" program, which guarantees admission to the top 10 percent of all graduating high schools in the state. The remaining 20 to 25 percent are selected based on "holistic" considerations, such as academic achievements, special talents, and race and ethnicity. In *Fisher v. University of Texas at Austin*, 570 U.S. 297 (2013), Justice Kennedy did not rule out race-conscious admissions but remanded the case back to the Court of Appeals for the Fifth Circuit because it failed to give strict scrutiny—the Court's most rigorous test. On remand, the appellate court again upheld the university's policy, holding that it applied strict scrutiny in concluding that the limited consideration of race was "necessary" and narrowly tailored to the university's compelling interest in student-body diversity. Attorneys for Fisher appealed, arguing that the appellate court failed to follow the Court's instructions in *Fisher (I),* and that the university's policy of taking race (along with other individual considerations) into account violated the Fourteenth Amendment's equal protection clause.

The appellate court was affirmed by a 4–3 vote, with Justice Kagan recused. Justice Kennedy delivered the opinion for the Court. Justices Thomas and Alito each filed dissents, which Chief Justice Roberts joined.

■ ■ ■

☐ *Justice KENNEDY delivered the opinion of the Court.*

The Court is asked once again to consider whether the race-conscious admissions program at the University of Texas is lawful under the Equal Protection Clause. . . .

Fisher I set forth three controlling principles relevant to assessing the constitutionality of a public university's affirmative-action program. First, "because racial characteristics so seldom provide a relevant basis for disparate treatment," *Richmond* v. *J. A. Croson Co.,* 488 U. S. 469, 505 (1989), "[r]ace may not be considered [by a university] unless the admissions process can withstand strict scru-tiny," *Fisher I.* Strict scrutiny requires the university to demonstrate with clarity that its "'purpose or interest is both constitutionally permissible and substantial, and that its use of the classification is necessary . . . to the accomplishment of its purpose.'"

Second, *Fisher I* confirmed that "the decision to pursue 'the educational benefits that flow from student body diversity' . . . is, in substantial measure, an academic judgment to which some, but not complete, judicial deference is proper." A university cannot impose a fixed quota or otherwise "define diversity as 'some specified percentage of a particular group merely because of its race or ethnic origin.'" Once, however, a university gives "a reasoned, principled explanation" for its decision, deference must be given "to the University's conclusion, based on its experience and expertise, that a diverse student body would serve its educational goals."

Third, *Fisher I* clarified that no deference is owed when determining whether the use of race is narrowly tailored to achieve the university's permissible goals. A university, *Fisher I* explained, bears the burden of proving a "nonracial approach" would not promote its interest in the educational benefits of diversity "about as well and at tolerable administrative expense." Though "[n]arrow tailoring does not require exhaustion of every conceivable race-neutral alternative" or "require a university to choose between maintaining a reputation for excellence [and] fulfilling a commitment to provide educational opportunities to members of all racial groups," *Grutter,* it does impose "on the university the ultimate burden of demonstrating" that "race-neutral alternatives" that are both "available" and "workable" "do not suffice."

Fisher I set forth these controlling principles, while taking no position on the constitutionality of the admissions program at issue in this case. . . .

The University's program is *sui generis.* Unlike other approaches to college admissions considered by this Court, it combines holistic review with a percentage plan. This approach gave rise to an unusual consequence in this case: The component of the University's admissions policy that had the largest impact on petitioner's chances of admission was not the school's consideration of race under its holistic-review process but rather the Top Ten Percent Plan. Because petitioner did not graduate in the top 10 percent of her high school class, she was categorically ineligible for more than three-fourths of the slots in the incoming freshman class. It seems quite plausible, then, to think that petitioner would have had a better chance of being admitted to the University if the school used race-conscious holistic review to select its entire incoming class, as was the case in *Grutter*. . . .

In seeking to reverse the judgment of the Court of Appeals, petitioner makes four arguments. First, she argues that the University has not articulated its compelling interest with sufficient clarity. According to petitioner, the University must set forth more precisely the level of minority enrollment that would constitute a "critical mass." Without a clearer sense of what the University's ultimate goal is, petitioner argues, a reviewing court cannot assess whether the University's admissions program is narrowly tailored to that goal.

As this Court's cases have made clear, however, the compelling interest that justifies consideration of race in college admissions is not an interest in enrolling a certain number of minority students. Rather, a university may institute a race-conscious admissions program as a means of obtaining "the educational benefits that flow from student body diversity." As this Court has said, enrolling a diverse student body "promotes cross-racial understanding, helps to break down racial stereotypes, and enables students to better understand persons of different races." Equally important, "student body diversity promotes learning outcomes, and better prepares students for an increasingly diverse workforce and society."

Increasing minority enrollment may be instrumental to these educational benefits, but it is not, as petitioner seems to suggest, a goal that can or should be reduced to pure numbers. Indeed, since the University is prohibited from seeking a particular number or quota of minority students, it cannot be faulted for failing to specify the particular level of minority enrollment at which it believes the educational benefits of diversity will be obtained.

On the other hand, asserting an interest in the educational benefits of diversity writ large is insufficient. A university's goals cannot be elusory or amorphous—they must be sufficiently measurable to permit judicial scrutiny of the policies adopted to reach them.

The record reveals that in first setting forth its current admissions policy, the University articulated concrete and precise goals. On the first page of its 2004 "Proposal to Consider Race and Ethnicity in Admissions," the University identifies the educational values it seeks to realize through its admissions process: the destruction of stereotypes, the "'promot[ion of] cross-racial understanding,'" the preparation of a student body "'for an increasingly diverse workforce and society,'" and the "'cultivat[ion of] a set of leaders with legitimacy in the eyes of the citizenry.'" Later in the proposal, the University explains that it strives to provide an "academic environment" that offers a "robust exchange of ideas, exposure to differing cultures, preparation for the challenges of an increasingly diverse workforce, and acquisition of competencies required of future leaders." All of these objectives, as a general matter, mirror the "compelling interest" this Court has approved in its prior cases.

The University has provided in addition a "reasoned, principled explanation" for its decision to pursue these goals. The University's 39-page proposal was written following a year-long study, which concluded that "[t]he use of race-neutral policies and programs ha[d] not been successful" in "provid[ing] an educational setting that fosters cross-racial understanding, provid[ing] enlightened discussion and learning, [or] prepar[ing] students to function in an increasingly diverse workforce and society." . . .

Second, petitioner argues that the University has no need to consider race because it had already "achieved critical mass" by 2003 using the Top Ten Percent Plan and race-neutral holistic review. Petitioner is correct that a university bears a heavy burden in showing that it had not obtained the educational benefits of diversity before it turned to a race-conscious plan. The record reveals, however, that, at the time of petitioner's application, the University could not be faulted on this score. . . .

The record itself contains significant evidence, both statistical and anecdotal, in support of the University's position. To start, the demographic data the University has submitted show consistent stagnation in terms of the percentage of minority students enrolling at the Univer-sity from 1996 to 2002. In 1996, for example, 266 African-American freshmen enrolled, a total that constituted 4.1 percent of the incoming class. In 2003, the year *Grutter* was decided, 267 African-American students enrolled—again, 4.1 percent of the incoming class. The numbers for Hispanic and Asian-American students tell a similar story. Although demographics alone are by no means dispositive, they do have some value as a gauge of the University's ability to enroll students who can offer underrepresented perspectives. . . .

Third, petitioner argues that considering race was not necessary because such consideration has had only a "'minimal impact' in advancing the [University's] compelling interest." Again, the record does not support this assertion. In 2003, 11 percent of the Texas residents enrolled through holistic review were Hispanic and 3.5 percent were African-American. In 2007, by contrast, 16.9 percent of the Texas holistic-review freshmen were Hispanic and 6.8 percent were African-American. Those increases—of 54 percent and 94 percent, respectively—show that consideration of race has had a meaningful, if still limited, effect on the diversity of the University's freshman class.

In any event, it is not a failure of narrow tailoring for the impact of racial consideration to be minor. The fact that race consciousness played a role in only a small portion of admissions decisions should be a hallmark of narrow tailoring, not evidence of unconstitutionality.

Petitioner's final argument is that "there are numerous other available race-neutral means of achieving" the University's compelling interest. A review of the record reveals, however, that, at the time of petitioner's application, none of her proposed alternatives was a workable means for the University to attain the benefits of diversity it sought. For example, petitioner suggests that the University could intensify its outreach efforts to African-American and Hispanic applicants. But the University submitted extensive evidence of the many ways in which it already had intensified its outreach efforts to those students. The University has created three new scholarship programs, opened new regional admissions centers, increased its recruitment budget by half-a-million dollars, and organized over 1,000 recruitment events. Perhaps more significantly, in the wake of *Hopwood*, the University spent seven years attempting to achieve its compelling interest using race-neutral holistic review. None of these efforts succeeded, and petitioner fails to offer any meaningful way in which the University could have improved upon them at the time of her application. . . .

A university is in large part defined by those intangible "qualities which are incapable of objective measurement but which make for greatness." *Sweatt* v. *Painter*, 339 U. S. 629 (1950). Considerable deference is owed to a university in defining those intangible characteristics, like student body diversity, that are central to its identity and educational mission. But still, it remains an enduring challenge to our Nation's education system to reconcile the pursuit of diversity with the constitutional promise of equal treatment and dignity.

In striking this sensitive balance, public universities, like the States themselves, can serve as "laboratories for experimentation." The University of Texas at Austin has a special opportunity to learn and to teach. The University now has at its disposal valuable data about the manner in which different approaches to admissions may foster diversity or instead dilute it. The University must continue to use this data to scrutinize the fairness of its admissions program; to assess whether changing demographics have undermined the need for a race-conscious policy; and to identify the effects, both positive and negative, of the affirmative-action measures it deems necessary.

The Court's affirmance of the University's admissions policy today does not necessarily mean the University may rely on that same policy without refinement. It is the University's ongoing obligation to engage in constant deliberation and continued reflection regarding its admissions policies.

The judgment of the Court of Appeals is affirmed.

☐ *Justice THOMAS, dissenting.*

[T]he Court's decision today is irreconcilable with strict scrutiny, rests on pernicious assumptions about race, and departs from many of our precedents.

I write separately to reaffirm that "a State's use of race in higher education admissions decisions is categorically prohibited by the Equal Protection Clause." "The Constitution abhors classifications based on race because every time the government places citizens on racial registers and makes race relevant to the provision of burdens or benefits, it demeans us all." That constitutional imperative does not change in the face of a "faddish theor[y]" that racial discrimination may produce "educational benefits." The Court was wrong to hold otherwise in *Grutter* v. *Bollinger*, 539 U. S. 306 (2003). I would overrule *Grutter* and reverse the Fifth Circuit's judgment.

D | *Nonracial Classifications and the Equal Protection of the Laws*

As noted in the beginning of this chapter, since the late 1970s the Court sought retrenchment from further expansion of the application of the Warren Court's "two-tiered" approach to the equal protection clause. When confronted with challenges to nonracial classifications, the Burger Court evolved a third, intermediate standard of judicial review—the *exacting scrutiny* or *strict rationality test*—for *quasi-suspect cat-*

egories like gender and illegitimacy, as well as refused to extend heightened review to claims of discrimination based on wealth and age. As noted earlier in this chapter, the Rehnquist and Roberts Courts, in turn, cut back on heightened judicial scrutiny, reserving the strict scrutiny test for primarily race-based classifications, and declining to further expand the number of suspect and quasi-suspect categories.

■ (1) GENDER-BASED DISCRIMINATION

Social and economic conditions did not make it possible until the mid-twentieth century for political movements and legal developments to push toward guaranteeing equal rights for women. Only in the 1970s did the Supreme Court begin to question gender-based discrimination. For more than a century, the Fourteenth Amendment offered little promise for women as the Court reinforced the second-class status and sexual stereotypes of women in constitutional law. *Bradwell v. State of Illinois*, 83 U.S. 130 (1873), for example, upheld Illinois's denial of women the right to practice law, and *Minor v. Happersett*, 88 U.S. 162 (1875), dismissed out of hand the claim that women had a constitutional right to vote. Even after the Nineteenth Amendment (1920), extending the right to vote to women, the Court held that neither that amendment nor the Fourteenth Amendment secured legal equality for women.[1] Sexual stereotypes of women as the "weaker sex," who "looks to her brother and depends on him" in Justice David Brewer's words, undergirded even progressive legislation and rulings, like *Muller v. Oregon*, 208 U.S. 412 (1908). In *Muller*, Justice Brewer upheld Oregon's law limiting the hours women could work in factories upon taking notice of the fact that

> [t]he two sexes differ in structure of body, in the functions to be performed by each, in the amount of physical strength, in the capacity for long-continued labor, particularly when done standing, . . . [in] the self-reliance which enables one to assert full rights, and in the capacity to maintain the struggle for subsistence. This difference justifies a difference in legislation and upholds that which is designed to compensate for some of the burdens which rest upon her.

On much the same basis the Warren Court unanimously concluded that the equal protection clause did not bar Florida from excluding women from jury service, in *Hoyt v. Florida*, 368 U.S. 57 (1961).

World War II brought about changes in the workforce. An unprecedented number of women worked in industries and factories as a result of wartime mobilization. After the war, economic expansion provided expanded employment opportunities. By the 1960s, the women's movement was revitalized and feminist groups pushed for political and legal changes. Congress responded to that political pressure. In 1963, the Equal Pay Act amended the Fair Labor Standards Act to require equal pay for equal work. The Civil Rights Act of 1964 prohibited sex discrimination by employers, labor organizations, and employment agencies. In 1972, the Civil Rights Act was amended to authorize in Title V the denial of federal funding for public and private programs that discriminated against women, and Title IX specifically requires equal athletic facilities and opportunities for women. Congress also passed in 1972 the Equal Rights Amendment, which, after a decade-long battle, failed to win ratification by three-fourths of the states as required under the Constitution.

The Supreme Court signaled that it would take seriously challenges to gender-based classification in *Reed v. Reed*, 404 U.S. 71 (1971). Writing for a unanimous Court, Chief Justice Burger overturned Idaho's statute giving preference to men over women in intestate proceedings. While finding the statute lacked a rational basis for distinguishing between men and women, he declined to address the claim that gender is a "suspect" category requiring strict scrutiny. Less than two years later, in *Frontiero v. Richardson* (1973) (excerpted below), Justice Brennan could persuade only three other justices that gender was a suspect category.

Despite the fact that the Court came within one vote of declaring gender a suspect category, *Reed* and *Frontiero* indicated that gender was a quasi-suspect category to which the Court would give heightened, if not strict, scrutiny. In *Craig v. Boren* (1976) (excerpted below), the Court further developed its "heightened or 'intermediate' level of scrutiny test." In applying this test the Court considered whether a gender-based distinction bears a substantial relationship to an important governmental interest. As the following boxes in this section show, the Court has tended to promote gender-neutral classifications, striking down even laws (as in *Craig*) that are defended as "benign" or "compensatory."[2] Note that gender-neutral laws disproportionately affecting one gender, though, typically do not receive the same heightened scrutiny accorded explicit gender-based classifications. Moreover, the Court has upheld some gender-based classifications as illustrated in the 5–4 ruling in *Michael M. v. Superior Court of Sonoma County* (1981) (excerpted below).

The Court has also tended, although not invariably, to affirm claims against gender discrimination under the Civil Rights Act of 1964 and other federal legislation. Notably, in *Meritor Savings Bank, FBD v. Vinson*, 477 U.S. 57 (1986), the Court held that Title VII of the Civil Rights Act of 1964 bars "sexual harassment" in the workplace, and not just gender discrimination in the hiring and firing of employees. Indeed, for over a decade, with the exception of *J.E.B. v. Alabama ex rel. T.B.*, 511 U.S. 127 (1994), which held that the Fourteenth Amendment forbids gender dis-

■ THE DEVELOPMENT OF LAW

Other Rulings Striking Down Gender-Based Distinctions under the Constitution

CASE	VOTE	RULING
Reed v. Reed, 404 U.S. 71 (1971)	9–0	Chief Justice Burger struck down Idaho's statute giving men preference in intestate proceedings for lacking a rational basis.
Weinberger v. Wiesenfeld, 420 U.S. 636 (1975)	8–0	With Justice Douglas not participating, the Court struck down a section of the

Social Security Act that granted survivors' benefits to widows and minor children, but not to widowers because the fact that men are more likely to be employed is not a compelling reason for distinguishing between men and women.

Stanton v. Stanton, 421 U.S. 7 (1975)	8–1	With Justice Rehnquist dissenting, the Court overturned as irrational a Utah

law requiring child-support payments for men until they reach the age of twenty-one and for women until they reach the age of eighteen.

Califano v. Goldfarb, 430 U.S. 199 (1977)	5–4	Struck down a portion of the Social Security Act, which provided benefits for widows

based on the earnings of deceased husbands, but no benefits for widowers unless they had received half of their financial support from their deceased spouses.

Orr v. Orr, 440 U.S. 268 (1979)	6–3	With Chief Justice Burger and Justices Rehnquist and Powell dissenting, the major-

ity struck down Alabama's law making husbands, but not wives, liable for alimony payments after a divorce.

(continues)

■ THE DEVELOPMENT OF LAW
Other Rulings Striking Down Gender-Based Distinctions under the Constitution (continued)

CASE	VOTE	RULING
Caban v. Mohammed, 441 U.S. 380 (1979)	5–4	Overturned New York's law permitting unwed mothers, but not fathers, to withhold

consent from the adoption of their children; Chief Justice Burger and Justices Rehnquist, Stewart, and Stevens dissented.

| *Califano v. Westcott,* 433 U.S. 76 (1979) | 9–0 | Held unconstitutional under the Fifth Amendment due process clause a section of the |

Social Security Act that provided benefits to families with dependent children because of father's, but not mother's, unemployment.

| *Wengler v. Druggists Mutual Insurance Co.,* 446 U.S. 142 (1980) | 8–1 | With only Justice Rehnquist dissenting, the Court found insufficient support for Missouri's workmen's compensa- |

tion law, which denied widowers, but not widows, benefits, unless a widower was "either mentally or physically incapacitated" or established a dependence on his wife's income.

| *Kirchberg v. Fennstra,* 450 U.S. 455 (1981) | 9–0 | Struck down Louisiana's law giving husbands a right to dispose of jointly owned property without consent as unjustified. |

| *Mississippi University for Women v. Hogan,* 458 U.S. 718 (1982) | 5–4 | With Chief Justice Burger and Justices Blackmun, Powell, and Rehnquist dissent- |

ing, a bare majority overturned a nursing school's policy of denying admission to qualified males.

| *J.E.B. v. Alabama ex rel. T.B.,* 511 U.S. 127 (1994) | 6–3 | Extending its earlier rulings barring the exclusion of jurors from jury service on the |

basis of race, Justice Blackmun ruled that the Fourteenth Amendment also precludes such gender discrimination and requires "heightened judicial scrutiny." Chief Justice Rehnquist and Justices Scalia and Thomas dissented.

■ The Development of Law

Other Rulings Upholding Gender-Based Distinctions under the Constitution

CASE	VOTE	RULING
Kahn v. Shevin, 416 U.S. 351 (1974)	6–3	Justice Douglas's opinion upheld Florida's law giving widows, but not widowers, a

$500 property tax exemption as rational, given the greater financial difficulties that women face when their spouses die than those facing men whose spouses die; Justices Brennan, Marshall, and White dissented.

CASE	VOTE	RULING
Schlesinger v. Ballard, 419 U.S. 498 (1975)	5–4	Upheld federal statutes requiring mandatory discharge of women in the Navy after

thirteen years, if they have not been promoted, and of men after nine years, because it was a rational distinction based on the different opportunities afforded men and women for sea and combat duty.

CASE	VOTE	RULING
Geduldig v. Aiello, 417 U.S. 484 (1974)	6–3	Upheld as rational California's program of allowing disability insurance benefits

for private employees not covered by workmen's compensation laws, except for pregnancy and certain other disabilities because the cost of extending coverage might jeopardize the program.

CASE	VOTE	RULING
Rostker v. Goldberg, 453 U.S. 57 (1981)	6–3	Upheld the Military Selective Service Act's authorization for the president to

require men, but not women, to register for potential military service; Justices Brennan, White, and Marshall dissented.

CASE	VOTE	RULING
Personnel Administrator of Massachusetts v. Fenney, 442 U.S. 256 (1979)	7–2	Upheld a Massachusetts law giving preference in hiring decisions to veterans who qualify for state civil service

positions, over the objections of a qualified woman who was passed over for a position.

(continues)

■ THE DEVELOPMENT OF LAW
*Other Rulings Upholding Gender-Based Distinctions
under the Constitution (continued)*

CASE	VOTE	RULING
Miller v. Albright, 523 U.S. 420 (1998)	6–3	Rejected a challenge to a federal statute that automatically grants citizenship to il-

legitimate children born in a foreign country if the mother is a U.S. citizen, but sets a higher standard if the father is a citizen and the mother a foreign natural. Justices Ginsburg, Breyer, and Souter dissented.

CASE	VOTE	RULING
Tuan Anh Nguyen v. Immigration and Naturalization Service, 533 U.S. 53 (2001)	5–4	Rejected a challenge to a federal statute that makes it more difficult for children born out of wedlock to fathers who are U.S. citizens, in contrast to

mothers who are U.S. citizens, to become citizens. Children born of mothers who are U.S. citizens are almost automatically made U.S. citizens, whereas those born out of wedlock to mothers who are foreign nationals and whose fathers are U.S. citizens must apply for citizenship before they are 18 years old and present evidence of their paternity. Writing for the Court, Justice Kennedy deemed the law rational and not based on stereotypes, whereas Justice O'Connor in dissent countered that the majority's decision rested on stereotypes of male versus female irresponsibility and violated the Fourteenth Amendment. Justices Souter, Ginsburg, and Breyer joined her dissent.

crimination in the exclusion of potential jurors from jury service, the Court dealt primarily with gender discrimination claims as a matter of statutory interpretation. However, in *United States v. Virginia* (1996) (excerpted below) the Court struck down Virginia's creation of a separate all-female institute as a remedy for a lower court's finding that the state's all-male Virginia Military Institute violated the Fourteenth Amendment.

NOTES

1. See *Fay v. New York*, 332 U.S. 261 (1947).

2. See, for example, *Califano v. Goldfarb*, 430 U.S. 199 (1977), *Orr v. Orr*, 440 U.S. 268 (1979), and *Mississippi University for Women v. Hogan*, 458 U.S. 718 (1982).

SELECTED BIBLIOGRAPHY

Cushman, Clare, ed. Foreword by Justice Ruth Bader Ginsburg. *Supreme Court Decisions and Women's Rights: Milestones to Equality.* Washington, DC: C.Q. Press, 2000.

Mathews, Donald. *Sex, Gender, and the Politics of the ERA.* New York: Oxford University Press, 1990.

Schwarzenbach, Sibyl, and Patricia Smith, eds. *Women and the U.S. Constitution.* New York: Columbia University Press, 2004.

Strebeigh, Fred. *Equal: Women Reshape American Law.* New York: W. W. Norton & Company, 2009.

Strum, Philippa. *Women in the Barracks: The VMI Case and Equal Rights.* Lawrence: University Press of Kansas, 2002.

Frontiero v. Richardson

411 U.S. 677, 93 S.Ct. 1764 (1973)

Sharron Frontiero and her husband sued U.S. Secretary of Defense Elliot Richardson and sought an injunction against the enforcement of federal statutes governing the award of benefits for "dependents" of military personnel. Sharron Frontiero was a lieutenant in the U.S. Air Force. She had sought but was denied increased quarters and allowances and health and medical benefits for her husband, who was a full-time student. Because such benefits would automatically be given to the wife of a male military officer, Frontiero argued that the laws unreasonably discriminated against women and violated the due process clause of the Fifth Amendment. Although the Fifth Amendment contains no equal protection clause, *Bolling v. Sharpe* (1954) (excerpted in Section B) and other rulings had held that the amendment bars the discrimination by the federal government that is "so unjustifiable as to be violate of due process." *Schneider v. Rusk*, 377 U.S. 163 (1964).

On appeal to the Supreme Court, the justices agreed with Frontiero 8-1, with Justice Rehnquist dissenting. However, the majority split 4-4 on the question of whether gender is a suspect classification and what standard the Court should use when reviewing cases challenging gender-based discrimination. Justice Brennan, joined by three others, contended that gender, like race, is a suspect classification; while Justice Powell, writing for two others, disagreed and contended that it would be wrong for the Court to go that far, because at the time the country was debating the ill-fated Equal Rights Amendment.

■ ■ ■

☐ *Justice BRENNAN with whom Justice DOUGLAS, Justice WHITE, and Justice MARSHALL join, delivered the opinion of the Court.*

The question before us concerns the right of a female member of the uniformed services to claim her spouse as a "dependent" for the purposes of obtaining increased quarters allowances and medical and dental benefits under 37 U.S.C. Sections 401, 403, and 10 U.S.C. Sections 1072, 1076, on an equal footing with male members. Under these statutes, a serviceman may claim his wife as a "dependent" without regard to whether she is in fact dependent upon him for any part of her support. A servicewoman, on the other hand, may not claim her husband as a "dependent" under these programs unless he is in fact dependent upon her for over one-half of his support. Thus, the question for decision is whether this difference in treatment constitutes an unconstitutional discrimination against servicewomen in violation of the Due Process Clause of the Fifth Amendment. A three-judge District Court for the Middle District of Alabama, one judge dissenting, rejected this contention and sustained the constitutionality of the provisions of the statutes making this distinction. . . . We reverse. . . .

At the outset, appellants contend that classifications based upon sex, like classifications based upon race, alienage, and national origin, are inherently suspect and must therefore be subjected to close judicial scrutiny. We agree and, indeed, find at least implicit support for such an approach in our unanimous decision only last Term in *Reed v. Reed*, 404 U.S. 71 (1971).

In *Reed*, the Court considered the constitutionality of an Idaho statute providing that, when two individuals are otherwise equally entitled to appointment as administrator of an estate, the male applicant must be preferred to the female. Appellant, the mother of the deceased, and appellee, the father, filed competing petitions for appointment as administrator of their son's estate. Since the parties, as parents of the deceased, were members of the same entitlement class the statutory preference was invoked and the father's petition was therefore granted. Appellant claimed that this statute, by giving a mandatory preference to males over females without regard to their individual qualifications, violated the Equal Protection Clause of the Fourteenth Amendment.

The Court noted that the Idaho statute, "provides that different treatment be accorded to the applicants on the basis of their sex; it thus establishes a classification subject to scrutiny under the Equal Protection Clause." Under "traditional" equal protection analysis, a legislative classification must be sustained unless it is "patently arbitrary" and bears no rational relationship to a legitimate governmental interest.

In an effort to meet this standard, appellee contended that the statutory scheme was a reasonable measure designed to reduce the workload on probate courts by eliminating one class of contests. Moreover, appellee argued that the mandatory preference for male applicants was in itself reasonable since "men [are] as a rule more conversant with business affairs than . . . women." Indeed, appellee maintained that "it is a matter of common knowledge, that women still are not engaged in politics, the professions, business or industry to the extent that men are." And the Idaho Supreme Court, in upholding the constitutionality of this statute, suggested that the Idaho Legislature might reasonably have "concluded that in general men are better qualified to act as an administrator than are women."

Despite these contentions, however, the Court held the statutory preference for male applicants unconstitutional. In reaching this result, the Court implicitly rejected appellee's apparently rational explanation of the statutory scheme, and concluded that, by ignoring the individual qualifications of particular applicants, the challenged statute provide "dissimilar treatment for men and women who are . . . similarly situated." The Court therefore held that, even though the State's interest in achieving administrative efficiency "is not without some legitimacy," "[t]o give a mandatory preference to members of either sex over members of the other, merely to accomplish the elimination of hearings on the merits, is to make the very kind of arbitrary legislative choice forbidden by the [Constitution]. . . ." This departure from "traditional" rational-basis analysis with respect to sex-based classifications is clearly justified.

There can be no doubt that our Nation has had a long and unfortunate history of sex discrimination. Traditionally, such discrimination was rationalized by an attitude of "romantic paternalism" which, in practical effect, put women, not on a pedestal, but in a cage. . . .

As a result of notions such as these, our statute books gradually became laden with gross, stereotyped distinctions between the sexes and, indeed, throughout much of the 19th century the position of women in our society was, in many respects, comparable to that of blacks under the pre–Civil War slave codes. Neither slaves nor women could hold office, serve on juries, or bring suit in their own names, and married women traditionally were denied the legal capacity to hold or convey property or to serve as legal guardians of their own children. . . .

Moreover, since sex, like race and national origin, is an immutable characteristic determined solely by the accident of birth, the imposition of special disabilities upon the members of a particular sex because of their sex would seem to violate "the basic concept of our system that legal burdens should bear some relationship to individual responsibility. . . ." *Weber v. Aetna Casualty & Surety Co.*, 406 U.S. 164, 175 (1972). And what differentiates sex from such nonsuspect statuses as intelligence or physical disability, and aligns it with the recognized suspect criteria, is that the sex characteristic frequently bears no relation to ability to perform or contribute to society. As a result, statutory distinctions between the sexes often have the effect of invidiously relegating the entire class of females to inferior legal status without regard to the actual capabilities of its individual members. . . .

With these considerations in mind, we can only conclude that classifications based upon sex, like classifications based upon race, alienage, or national origin, are inherently suspect, and must therefore be subjected to strict judicial scrutiny. Applying the analysis mandated by that stricter standard of review, it is clear that the statutory scheme now before us is constitutionally invalid.

The sole basis of the classification established in the challenged statutes is the sex of the individuals involved. Thus, under 37 U.S.C. Sections 401, 403, and 10 U.S.C. Sections 2072, 2076, a female member of the uniformed services seeking to obtain housing and medical benefits for her spouse must prove his dependency in fact, whereas no such burden is imposed upon male members. In addition, the statutes operate so as to deny benefits to a female member, such as appellant Sharron Frontiero, who provides less than one-half of her spouse's support, while at the same time granting such benefits to a male member who likewise provides less than one-half of his spouse's support. . . .

The Government offers no concrete evidence, however, tending to support its view that such differential treatment in fact saves the Government any money. In order to satisfy the demands of strict judicial scrutiny, the Government must demonstrate, for example, that it is actually cheaper to grant increased benefits with respect to *all* male members, than it is to determine which male members are in fact entitled to such benefits and to grant increased benefits only to those members whose wives actually meet the dependency requirement. Here, however, there is substantial evidence that, if put to the test, many of the wives of male members would fail to qualify for benefits. And in light of the fact that the dependency determination with respect to the husbands of female members is presently made solely on the basis of affidavits rather than through the more costly hearing process, the Government's explanation of the statutory scheme is, to say the least, questionable.

In any case, our prior decisions make clear that, although efficacious administration of governmental programs is not without some importance, "the Constitution recognizes higher values than speed and efficiency." *Stanley v. Illinois*, 405 U.S. 645 (1972). And when we enter the realm of "strict judicial scrutiny," there can be no doubt that "administrative convenience" is not a shibboleth, the mere recitation of which dictates constitutionality. . . . On the contrary, any statutory scheme which draws a sharp line between the sexes, *solely* for the purpose of achieving administrative convenience, necessarily commands "dissimilar treatment for men and women who are . . . similarly situated," and therefore involves the "very kind of arbitrary legislative choice forbidden by the [Constitution]. . . ." *Reed v. Reed*, [404 U.S. 71 (1971)]. We therefore conclude that, by according differential treatment to male and female members of the uniformed services for the sole purpose of achieving administrative convenience, the challenged statutes violate the Due Process Clause of the Fifth Amendment insofar as they require a female member to prove the dependency of her husband.

Reversed.

Craig v. Boren

429 U.S. 190, 97 S.CT. 451 (1976)

Curtis Craig, a male under twenty-one years old, and a female distributor of alcoholic beverages sought in federal district court declaratory and injunctive relief against the enforcement of an Oklahoma statute that forbade the sale of 3.2 beer—beer with low alcohol content—to men, but not women, under the age of twenty-one. They argued that the law constituted invidious discrimination against men and violated the equal protection clause of the Fourteenth Amendment. After a three-judge district court denied relief, Craig appealed to the Supreme Court.

The Court's decision was 7–2, and the majority's opinion was announced by Justice Brennan. Justices Powell, Stevens, and Blackmun, who were joined by Justice Stewart, each concurred. Dissenting opinions were delivered by Chief Justice Burger and Justice Rehnquist.

■ ■ ■

☐ *Justice BRENNAN delivered the opinion of the Court.*

The interaction of two sections of an Oklahoma statute, 37 Okla.Stat. Sections 241 and 245, prohibits the sale of "nonintoxicating" 3.2% beer to males under the age of 21 and to females under the age of 18. The question to be decided is whether such a gender-based differential constitutes a denial to males 18–20 years of age of the Equal Protection of the Laws in violation of the Fourteenth Amendment. . . .

Analysis may appropriately begin with the reminder that *Reed v. Reed*, [404 U.S. 71 (1971)], emphasized that statutory classifications that distinguish between males and females are "subject to scrutiny under the Equal Protection Clause." To withstand constitutional challenge, previous cases establish that classifications by gender must serve important governmental objectives and must be substantially related to achievement of those objectives. Thus, in *Reed*, the objectives of "reducing the workload on probate courts," . . . and "avoiding intra-family controversy," were deemed of insufficient importance to sustain use of an overt gender criterion in the appointment of intestate administrators. Decisions following *Reed* similarly have rejected administrative ease and convenience as sufficiently important objectives to justify gender-based classifications. . . .

Reed v. Reed has also provided the underpinning for decisions that have invalidated statutes employing gender as an inaccurate proxy for other, more germane bases of classification. Hence, "archaic and overbroad" generalizations, *Schlesinger v. Ballard* [419 U.S. 498 (1975)], concerning the financial position of servicewomen, *Frontiero v. Richardson*, [411 U.S. 677 (1973)], and working women, *Weinberger v. Wiesenfeld*, [420 U.S. 636 (1975)], could not justify use of a gender line in determining eligibility for certain governmental entitlements. Similarly increasingly outdated misconceptions concerning the role of females in the home rather than in the "marketplace and world of ideas" were rejected as loose-fitting characterizations incapable of supporting state statutory schemes that were premised upon their accuracy. . . .

In this case, too, "*Reed* we feel is controlling. . . ." We turn then to the question whether, under *Reed*, the difference between males and females with respect to the purchase of 3.2% beer warrants the differential in age drawn by the Oklahoma statute. We conclude that it does not. . . .

We accept for purposes of discussion the District Court's identification of the objective underlying Sections 241 and 245 as the enhancement of traffic safety. Clearly, the protection of public health and safety represents an important function of state and local governments. However, appellees' statistics in our view cannot support the conclusion that the gender-based distinction closely serves to achieve that objective and therefore the distinction cannot under *Reed* withstand equal protection challenge.

The appellees introduced a variety of statistical surveys. First, an analysis of arrest statistics for 1973 demonstrated that 18–20-year-old male arrests for "driving under the influence" and "drunkenness" substantially exceeded female arrests for that same age period. Similarly, youths aged 17–21 were found to be overrepresented among those killed or injured in traffic accidents, with males again numerically exceeding females in this regard. Third, a random roadside survey in Oklahoma City revealed that young males were more inclined to drive and drink beer than were their female counterparts. Fourth, Federal Bureau of Investigation nationwide statistics exhibited a notable increase in arrests for "driving under the influence." Finally, statistical evidence gathered in other jurisdictions, particularly Minnesota and Michigan, was offered to corroborate Oklahoma's experience by indicating the pervasiveness of youthful participation in motor vehicle accidents following the imbibing of alcohol. . . .

Even were this statistical evidence accepted as accurate, it nevertheless offers only a weak answer to the equal protection question presented here. The most focused and relevant of the statistical surveys, arrests of 18–20-year-olds for alcohol-related driving offenses, exemplifies the ultimate unpersuasiveness of this evidentiary record. Viewed in terms of the correlation between sex and the actual activity that Oklahoma seeks to regulate—driving while under the influence of alcohol—the statistics broadly establish that .18% of females and 2% of males in that age group were arrested for that offense. While such a disparity is not trivial in a statistical sense, it hardly can form the basis for employment of a gender line as a classifying device. Certainly if maleness is to serve as a proxy for drinking and driving, a correlation of 2% must be considered an unduly tenuous "fit." Indeed, prior cases have consistently rejected the use of sex as a decisionmaking factor even though the statutes in question certainly rested on far more predictive empirical relationships than this.

Moreover, the statistics exhibit a variety of other shortcomings that seriously impugn their value to equal protection analysis. Setting aside the obvious methodological problems, the surveys do not adequately justify the salient features of Oklahoma's gender-based traffic-safety law. None purports to measure the use and dangerousness of 3.2% beer as opposed to alcohol generally, a detail that is of particular importance since, in light of its low alcohol level, Oklahoma apparently considers the 3.2% beverage to be "nonintoxicating." . . .

There is no reason to belabor this line of analysis. It is unrealistic to expect either members of the judiciary or state officials to be well versed in the rigors of experimental or statistical technique. But this merely illustrates that proving broad sociological propositions by statistics is a dubious business, and one that inevitably is in tension with the normative philosophy that underlies the Equal Protection Clause. Suffice to say that the showing offered by the appellees does not satisfy us that sex represents a legitimate, accurate proxy for the regulation of drinking and driving. In fact, when it is further recognized that Oklahoma's statute prohibits only the selling of 3.2% beer to young males and not their drinking the beverage once acquired (even after purchase by their 18–20-year-old female companions), the relationship between gender and traffic safety becomes far too tenuous to satisfy *Reed*'s requirement that the gender-based difference be substantially related to achievement of the statutory objective.

We hold, therefore, that under *Reed*, Oklahoma's 3.2% beer statute invidiously discriminates against males 18–20 years of age. . . .

We conclude that the gender-based differential contained in 37 Okla. Stat. Section 245 constitutes a denial of the Equal Protection of the Laws to males aged 18–20 and reverse the judgment of the District Court.

☐ *Justice REHNQUIST, dissenting.*

The Court's disposition of this case is objectionable on two grounds. First, is its conclusion that *men* challenging a gender-based statute which treats them less favorably than women may invoke a more stringent standard of judicial review than pertains to most other types of classifications. Second is the Court's enunciation of this standard, without citation to any source, as being that "classifications by gender must serve *important* governmental objectives and must be *substantially* related to achievement of those objectives" (emphasis added). The only redeeming feature of the Court's opinion, to my mind, is that it apparently signals a retreat by those who joined the plurality opinion in *Frontiero v. Richardson*, from their view that sex is a "suspect" classification for purposes of equal protection analysis. I think the Oklahoma statute challenged here need pass only the "rational basis" equal protection analysis, and I believe that it is constitutional under that analysis. . . .

Most obviously unavailable to support any kind of special scrutiny in this case is a history or pattern of past discrimination, such as was relied on by the plurality in *Frontiero* to support its invocation of strict scrutiny. There is no suggestion in the Court's opinion that males in this age group are in any way peculiarly disadvantaged, subject to systematic discriminatory treatment, or otherwise in need of special solicitude from the courts. . . .

I would have thought that if this Court were to leave anything to decision by the popularly elected branches of the Government, where no constitutional claim other than that of equal protection is invoked, it would be the decision as to what governmental objectives to be achieved by law are "important," and which are not. As for the second part of the Court's new test, the Judicial Branch is probably in no worse position than the Legislative or Executive Branches to determine if there is *any* rational relationship between a classification and the purpose which it might be thought to serve. But the introduction of the adverb "substantially" requires courts to make subjective judgments as to operational effects, for which neither their expertise nor their access to data fits them. And even if we manage to avoid both confusion and the mirroring of our own preferences in the development of this new doctrine, the thousands of judges in other courts who must interpret the Equal Protection Clause may not be so fortunate. . . .

The Court "accept[s] for purposes of discussion" the District Court's finding that the purpose of the provisions in question was traffic safety, and proceeds to examine the statistical evidence in the record in order to decide if "the gender-based distinction *closely* serves to achieve that objective. . . . One need not immerse oneself in the fine-points of statistical analysis, however, in order to see the weaknesses in the Court's attempted denigration of the evidence at hand."

One survey of arrest statistics assembled in 1973 indicated that males in the 18–20 age group were arrested for "driving under the influence" almost 18 times as often as their female counterparts, and for "drunkenness" in a

1504 | THE EQUAL PROTECTION OF THE LAWS

ratio of almost ten-to-one. Accepting, as the Court does, appellants' comparison of the total figures with 1973 Oklahoma census data, this survey indicates a 2% arrest rate among males in the age group, as compared to a .18% rate among females. . . .

The rationality of a statutory classification for equal protection purposes does not depend upon the statistical "fit" between the class and the trait sought to be singled out. It turns on whether there may be a sufficiently higher incidence of the trait within the included class than in the excluded class to justify different treatment. Therefore the present equal protection challenge to this gender-based discrimination poses only the question whether the incidence of drunk driving among young men is sufficiently greater than among young women to justify differential treatment. Notwithstanding the Court's critique of the statistical evidence, that evidence suggests clear differences between the drinking and driving habits of young men and women. Those differences are grounds enough for the State reasonably to conclude that young males pose by far the greater drunk driving hazard, both in terms of sheer numbers and in terms of hazard on a per-driver basis. The gender-based difference in treatment in this case is therefore not irrational.

The Court's argument that a 2% correlation between maleness and drunk driving is constitutionally insufficient therefore does not pose an equal protection issue concerning discrimination between males and females. The clearest demonstration of this is the fact that the precise argument made by the Court would be equally applicable to a flat bar on such purchases by *anyone*, male or female, in the 18–20 age group; in fact it would apply *a fortiori* in that case given the even more "tenuous 'fit'" between drunk driving arrests and femaleness. The statistics indicate that about 1% of the age group population as a whole is arrested. What the Court's argument is relevant to is not equal protection, but due process—whether enough persons in the category drive drunk to justify a bar against purchases by all members of the group. . . .

This is not a case where the classification can only be justified on grounds of administrative convenience. There being no apparent way to single out persons likely to drink and drive, it seems plain that the legislature was faced here with the not atypical legislative problem of legislating in terms of broad categories with regard to the purchase and consumption of alcohol. I trust, especially in light of the Twenty-first Amendment, that there would be no due process violation if no one in this age group were allowed to purchase 3.2% beer. Since males drink and drive at a higher rate than the age group as a whole, I fail to see how a statutory bar with regard only to them can create any due process problem.

Michael M. v. Superior Court of Sonoma County
450 U.S. 464, 101 S.CT. 1200 (1981)

In the summer of 1978, in the Superior Court of Sonoma County, California, a boy of seventeen and a half, Michael M., was tried and convicted for statutory rape. Under California's law, *statutory rape* is defined as unlawful "sexual intercourse accomplished with a female not the wife of the perpetrator, where the female is under the age of 18 years." At his trial and on an unsuccessful appeal of his conviction, Michael M.'s attorneys argued that the law violated the equal protection clause of the Fourteenth Amendment because only men were criminally liable.

The Court's decision was 5–4, and the plurality's opinion was announced by Justice Rehnquist. Justices Stewart and Blackmun each delivered concurring opinions. Justices Stevens and Brennan, who were joined by Justices Marshall and White, dissented.

■ ■ ■

☐ *Justice REHNQUIST, with whom THE CHIEF JUSTICE, Justice STEWART, and Justice POWELL join, delivered the opinion of the Court.*

The question presented in this case is whether California's "statutory rape" law, Section 261.5 of the Cal.Penal Code Ann., violates the Equal Protection Clause of the Fourteenth Amendment. Section 261.5 defines unlawful sexual intercourse as "an act of sexual intercourse accomplished with a female not the wife of the perpetrator, where the female is under the age of 18 years." The statute thus makes men alone criminally liable for the act of sexual intercourse.

In July 1978, a complaint was filed in the Municipal Court of Sonoma County, Cal., alleging that petitioner, then a 17½-year-old male, had had unlawful sexual intercourse with a female under the age of 18, in violation of Section 261.5. The evidence, adduced at a preliminary hearing showed that at approximately midnight on June 3, 1978, petitioner and two friends approached Sharon, a 16½-year-old female, and her sister as they waited at a bus stop. Petitioner and Sharon, who had already been drinking, moved away from the others and began to kiss. After being struck in the face for rebuffing petitioner's initial advances, Sharon submitted to sexual intercourse with petitioner. . . .

As is evident from our opinions, the Court has had some difficulty in agreeing upon the proper approach and analysis in cases involving challenges to gender-based classifications. . . . [W]e have not held that gender-based classifications are "inherently suspect" and thus we do not apply so-called "strict scrutiny" to those classifications. See *Stanton v. Stanton*, 421 U.S. 7 (1975). Our cases have held, however, that the traditional minimum rationality test takes on a somewhat "sharper focus" when gender-based classifications are challenged. See *Craig v. Boren*, 429 U.S. 190 (1976) (POWELL, J., concurring). In *Reed v. Reed*, 404 U.S. 71 (1971), for example, the Court stated that a gender-based classification will be upheld if it bears a "fair and substantial relationship" to legitimate state ends, while in *Craig v. Boren*, the Court restated the test to require the classification to bear a "substantial relationship" to "important governmental objectives."

Underlying these decisions is the principle that a legislature may not "make overbroad generalizations based on sex which are entirely unrelated to any differences between men and women or which demean the ability or social status of the affected class." *Parham v. Hughes*, 441 U.S. 347 (1979) (plurality opinion of STEWART, J.). But because the Equal Protection Clause does not "demand that a statute necessarily apply equally to all persons" or require "things which are different in fact . . . to be treated in law as though they were the same," *Rinaldi v. Yeager*, 384 U.S. 305 (1966), quoting *Tigner v. Texas*, 310 U.S. 141 (1940), this Court has consistently upheld statutes where the gender classification is not invidious, but rather realistically reflects the fact that the sexes are not similarly situated in certain circumstances. *Parham v. Hughes*, [441 U.S. 347 (1979)]; *Califano v. Webster*, 430 U.S. 313 (1977); *Schlesinger v. Ballard*, 419 U.S. 498 (1975); *Kahn v. Shevin*, 416 U.S. 351 (1974). As the Court has stated, a legislature may "provide for the special problems of women." *Weinberger v. Wiesenfeld*, 420 U.S. 636 (1975).

Applying those principles to this case, the fact that the California Legislature criminalized the act of illicit sexual intercourse with a minor female is a sure indication of its intent or purpose to discourage that conduct. Precisely why the legislature desired that result is of course somewhat less clear. . . .

The justification for the statute offered by the State, and accepted by the Supreme Court of California, is that the legislature sought to prevent illegitimate teenage pregnancies. . . .

We are satisfied not only that the prevention of illegitimate pregnancy is at least one of the "purposes" of the statute, but also that the State has a strong interest in preventing such pregnancy. At the risk of stating the obvious, teenage pregnancies, which have increased dramatically over the last two decades, have significant social, medical, and economic consequences for both the mother and her child, and the State. Of particular concern to the State is that approximately half of all teenage pregnancies end in abortion. And of those children who are born, their illegitimacy makes them likely candidates to become wards of the State.

We need not be medical doctors to discern that young men and young women are not similarly situated with respect to the problems and the risks of sexual intercourse. Only women may become pregnant, and they suffer disproportionately the profound physical, emotional and psychological consequences of sexual activity. The statute at issue here protects women from sexual intercourse at an age when those consequences are particularly severe.

The question thus boils down to whether a State may attack the problem of sexual intercourse and teenage pregnancy directly by prohibiting a male from having sexual intercourse with a minor female. We hold that such a statute is sufficiently related to the State's objectives to pass constitutional muster.

Because virtually all of the significant harmful and inescapably identifiable consequences of teenage pregnancy fall on the young female, a legislature acts well within its authority when it elects to punish only the participant who, by nature, suffers few of the consequences of his conduct. It is hardly unreasonable for a legislature acting to protect minor females to exclude them from punishment. Moreover, the risk of pregnancy itself constitutes a substantial deterrence to young females. No similar natural sanctions deter males. A criminal sanction imposed solely on males thus serves to roughly "equalize" the deterrents on the sexes. . . .

[W]e cannot say that a gender-neutral statute would be as effective as the statute California has chosen to enact. The State persuasively contends that a gender-neutral statute would frustrate its interest in effective enforcement. Its view is that a female is surely less likely to report violations of the statute if she herself would be subject to criminal prosecution. In an area already fraught with prosecutorial difficulties, we decline to hold that the Equal Protection Clause requires a legislature to enact a statute so broad that it may well be incapable of enforcement.

We similarly reject petitioner's argument that Section 261.5 is impermissibly overbroad because it makes unlawful sexual intercourse with pre-pubescent females, who are, by definition, incapable of becoming pregnant. Quite apart from the fact that the statute could well be justified on the grounds that very young females are particularly susceptible to physical injury from sexual intercourse, it is ludicrous to suggest that the Constitution requires the California Legislature to limit the scope of its rape statute to older teenagers and exclude young girls.

There remains only petitioner's contention that the statute is unconstitutional as it is applied to him because he, like Sharon, was under 18 at the time of sexual intercourse. Petitioner argues that the statute is flawed because it presumes that as between two persons under 18, the male is the culpable aggressor. We find petitioner's contentions unpersuasive. Contrary to his assertions, the statute does not rest on the assumption that males are generally the aggressors. It is instead an attempt by a legislature to prevent illegitimate teenage pregnancy by providing an additional deterrent for men. The age of the man is irrelevant since young men are as capable as older men of inflicting the harm sought to be prevented. . . .

Accordingly, the judgment of the California Supreme Court is Affirmed.

☐ *Justice BRENNAN, with whom Justice WHITE and Justice MARSHALL join, dissenting.*

The plurality assumes that a gender-neutral statute would be less effective than Section 261.5 in deterring sexual activity because a gender-neutral statute would create significant enforcement problems. The plurality thus accepts the State's assertion that

> a female is surely less likely to report violations of the statute if she herself would be subject to criminal prosecution. In an area already fraught with prosecutorial difficulties, we decline to hold that the Equal Protection Clause requires a legislature to enact a statute so broad that it may well be incapable of enforcement. . . . (footnotes omitted).

However, a State's bare assertion that its gender-based statutory classification substantially furthers an important governmental interest is not enough to meet its burden of proof under *Craig v. Boren*, [429 U.S. 190 (1976)]. Rather, the State must produce evidence that will persuade the court that its assertion is true. See *Craig v. Boren*.

The State has not produced such evidence in this case. Moreover, there are at least two serious flaws in the State's assertion that law enforcement problems created by a gender-neutral statutory rape law would make such a statute less effective than a gender-based statute in deterring sexual activity.

First, the experience of other jurisdictions, and California itself, belies the plurality's conclusion that a gender-neutral statutory rape law "may well be incapable of enforcement." There are now at least 37 States that have enacted gender-neutral statutory rape laws. Although most of these laws protect young persons (of either sex) from the sexual exploitation of older individuals, the laws of Arizona, Florida, and Illinois permit prosecution of both minor females and minor males for engaging in mutual sexual conduct. California has introduced no evidence that those States have been handicapped by the enforcement problems the plurality finds so persuasive. Surely, if those States could provide such evidence, we might expect that California would have introduced it. . . .

The second flaw in the State's assertion is that even assuming that a gender-neutral statute would be more difficult to enforce, the State has still not shown that those enforcement problems would make such a statute less effective than a gender-based statute in deterring minor females from engaging in sexual intercourse. Common sense, however, suggests that a gender-neutral statutory rape law is potentially a *greater* deterrent of sexual activity than a gender-based law, for the simple reason that a gender-neutral law subjects both men and women to criminal sanctions and thus arguably has a deterrent effect on twice as many potential violators. Even if fewer persons were prosecuted under the gender-neutral law, as the State suggests, it would still be true that twice as many persons would be *subject* to arrest. . . .

Until very recently, no California court or commentator had suggested that the purpose of California's statutory rape law was to protect young women from the risk of pregnancy. Indeed, the historical development of Section 261.5 demonstrates that the law was initially enacted on the premise that young women, in contrast to young men were to be deemed legally incapable of consenting to an act of sexual intercourse. Because their chastity was considered particularly precious, those young women were felt to be uniquely in need of the State's protection. In contrast, young men were assumed to be capable of making such decisions for themselves; the law therefore did not offer them any special protection. . . .

I would hold that Section 261.5 violates the Equal Protection Clause of the Fourteenth Amendment, and I would reverse the judgment of the California Supreme Court.

United States v. Virginia

518 U.S. 515, 116 S.Ct. 2264 (1996)

The Virginia Military Institute (VMI) is a state-run, all-male military college, employing an "adversative," military-like training program, aimed at producing "citizen-soldiers, educated and honorable men" suited for leadership in civilian or military life. In 1990, President George H. W. Bush's Department of Justice challenged the all-male policy as a violation of the Fourteenth Amendment's Equal Protection Clause. As a result of that suit, the Court of Appeals for the Fourth Circuit held that, although VMI's single-gender education was pedagogically justifiable, the Fourteenth Amendment required the state to either admit women into VMI or, alternatively, create a similar program for women. Virginia responded by creating a parallel program for women—the Virginia Women's Institute for Leadership (VWIL)—at the private, all-female Mary Baldwin College. A task force determined that the mission of VWIL would be the same as that of VMI, but instead of adopting VMI's "adversative method" it deemphasized harsh military methods and instituted a structured environment emphasizing leadership and training. When this plan was, in turn, challenged, the district court upheld it and the appellate court affirmed. Whereupon, the Department of Justice appealed to the Supreme Court.

The Court's decision was 7–1 and the opinion was delivered by Justice Ginsburg. Chief Justice Rehnquist filed a concurring opinion and Justice Scalia a dissent. Justice Thomas did not participate in the decision.

■ ■ ■

☐ *Justice GINSBURG delivered the opinion of the Court.*

Virginia's public institutions of higher learning include an incomparable military college, Virginia Military Institute (VMI). The United States maintains that the Constitution's equal protection guarantee precludes Virginia from reserving exclusively to men the unique educational opportunities VMI affords. We agree. . . .

The cross-petitions in this case present two ultimate issues. First, does Virginia's exclusion of women from the educational opportunities provided by VMI—extraordinary opportunities for military training and civilian leadership development—deny to women "capable of all of the individual activities required of VMI cadets," the equal protection of the laws guaranteed by the Fourteenth Amendment? Second, if VMI's "unique" situation—as Virginia's sole single-sex public institution of higher education—offends the Constitution's equal protection principle, what is the remedial requirement?

We note, once again, the core instruction of this Court's pathmarking decisions in *J.E.B. v. Alabama ex rel. T.B.*, 511 U.S. 127 (1994), and *Mississippi Univ. for Women [v. Hogan]*, 458 U.S. [718 (1982)]: Parties who seek to defend gender-based government action must demonstrate an "exceedingly persuasive justification" for that action.

Today's skeptical scrutiny of official action denying rights or opportunities based on sex responds to volumes of history. As a plurality of this Court acknowledged a generation ago, "our Nation has had a long and unfortunate history of sex discrimination." *Frontiero v. Richardson*, 411 U.S. 677 (1973). Through a century plus three decades and more of that history, women did not count among voters composing "We the People"; not until 1920 did women gain a constitutional right to the franchise. And for a half century thereafter, it remained the prevailing doctrine that government, both federal and state, could withhold from women opportunities accorded men so long as any "basis in reason" could be conceived for the discrimination.

In 1971, for the first time in our Nation's history, this Court ruled in favor of a woman who complained that her State had denied her the equal protection of its laws. *Reed v. Reed*, 404 U.S. 71 (holding unconstitutional Idaho Code prescription that, among "several persons claiming and equally entitled to administer [a decendent's estate], males must be preferred to females"). Since *Reed*, the Court has repeatedly recognized that neither federal nor state government acts compatibly with the equal protection principle when a law or official policy denies to women, simply because they are women, full citizenship stature—equal opportunity to aspire, achieve, participate in and contribute to society based on their individual talents and capacities.

Without equating gender classifications, for all purposes, to classifications based on race or national origin, the Court, in post-*Reed* decisions, has carefully inspected official action that closes a door or denies opportunity to women (or to men). To summarize the Court's current directions for cases of official classification based on gender: Focusing on the differential treatment or denial of opportunity for which relief is sought, the reviewing court must determine whether the proffered justification is "exceedingly persuasive." The burden of justification is demanding and it rests entirely on the State. See *Mississippi Univ. for Women*. The State must show "at least that the [challenged] classification serves 'important governmental objectives and that the discriminatory means employed' are 'substantially related to the achievement of those objectives.'" The justification must be genuine, not hypothesized or invented post hoc in response to litigation. And it must not rely on overbroad generalizations about the different talents, capacities, or preferences of males and females.

The heightened review standard our precedent establishes does not make sex a proscribed classification. Supposed "inherent differences" are no longer accepted as a ground for race or national origin classifications. See *Loving v. Virginia*, 388 U.S. 1 (1967). Physical differences between men and women, however, are enduring: "The two sexes are not fungible; a community made up exclusively of one [sex] is different from a community composed of both." *Ballard v. United States*, 329 U.S. 187 (1946).

"Inherent differences" between men and women, we have come to appreciate, remain cause for celebration, but not for denigration of the members of either sex or for artificial constraints on an individual's opportunity. Sex classifications may be used to compensate women "for particular economic disabilities [they have] suffered," *Califano v. Webster*, 430 U.S. 313 (1977) (*per curiam*), to "promote equal employment opportunity," see *California Federal Sav. & Loan Assn. v. Guerra*, 479 U.S. 272 (1987), to advance full development of the talent and capacities of our Nation's people. But such classifications may not be used, as they once were, to create or perpetuate the legal, social, and economic inferiority of women.

Measuring the record in this case against the review standard just described, we conclude that Virginia has shown no "exceedingly persuasive justification" for excluding all women from the citizen-soldier training afforded by VMI. We therefore affirm the Fourth Circuit's initial judgment, which held that Virginia had violated the Fourteenth Amendment's Equal Protection Clause. Because the remedy proffered by Virginia—the Mary Baldwin VWIL program—does not cure the constitutional violation, i.e., it does not provide equal opportunity, we reverse the Fourth Circuit's final judgment in this case. . . .

The Court's first four female justices. From left to right: retired Justice Sandra Day O'Connor and Justices Sonia Sotomayor, Ruth Bader Ginsburg, and Elena Kagan. (*Collection of the Supreme Court of the United States.*)

[I]t is not disputed that diversity among public educational institutions can serve the public good. But Virginia has not shown that VMI was established, or has been maintained, with a view to diversifying, by its categorical exclusion of women, educational opportunities within the State. . . .

Mississippi Univ. for Women is immediately in point. There the State asserted, in justification of its exclusion of men from a nursing school, that it was engaging in "educational affirmative action" by "compensating for discrimination against women." Undertaking a "searching analysis," the Court found no close resemblance between "the alleged objective" and "the actual purpose underlying the discriminatory classification." Pursuing a similar inquiry here, we reach the same conclusion.

Neither recent nor distant history bears out Virginia's alleged pursuit of diversity through single-sex educational options. In 1839, when the State established VMI, a range of educational opportunities for men and women was scarcely contemplated. Higher education at the time was considered dangerous for women; reflecting widely held views about women's proper place, the Nation's first universities and colleges—for example, Harvard in Massachusetts, William and Mary in Virginia—admitted only men. VMI was not at all novel in this respect: In admitting no women, VMI followed the lead of the State's flagship school, the University of Virginia, founded in 1819. . . .

In 1879, the State Senate resolved to look into the possibility of higher education for women, recognizing that Virginia "has never, at any period of her history," provided for the higher education of her daughters, though she "has liberally provided for the higher education of her sons." Despite this recognition, no new opportunities were instantly open to women.

Virginia eventually provided for several women's seminaries and colleges. Farmville Female Seminary became a public institution in 1884. Two women's schools, Mary Washington College and James Madison University, were founded in 1908; another, Radford University, was founded in 1910. By the mid-1970's, all four schools had become coeducational.

Debate concerning women's admission as undergraduates at the main university continued well past the century's midpoint. Familiar arguments were rehearsed. If women were admitted, it was feared, they "would encroach on the rights of men; there would be new problems of government, perhaps scandals; the old honor system would have to be changed; standards would be lowered to those of other coeducational schools; and the glorious reputation of the university, as a school for men, would be trailed in the dust."

Ultimately, in 1970, "the most prestigious institution of higher education in Virginia," the University of Virginia, introduced coeducation and, in 1972, began to admit women on an equal basis with men. A three-judge Federal District Court confirmed: "Virginia may not now deny to women, on the basis of sex, educational opportunities at the Charlottesville campus that are not afforded in other institutions operated by the State."

Virginia describes the current absence of public single-sex higher education for women as "an historical anomaly." But the historical record indicates action more deliberate than anomalous: First, protection of women against higher education; next, schools for women far from equal in resources and stature to schools for men; finally, conversion of the separate schools to coeducation. The state legislature, prior to the advent of this controversy, had repealed "all Virginia statutes requiring individual institutions to admit only men or women." And in 1990, an official commission, "legislatively established to chart the future goals of higher education in Virginia," reaffirmed the policy "of affording broad access" while maintaining "autonomy and diversity." (Report of the Virginia Commission on the University of the 21st Century). . . .

Our 1982 decision in *Mississippi Univ. for Women* prompted VMI to reexamine its male-only admission policy. Virginia relies on that reexamination as a legitimate basis for maintaining VMI's single-sex character. A Mission Study Committee, appointed by the VMI Board of Visitors, studied the problem from October 1983 until May 1986, and in that month counseled against "change of VMI status as a single-sex college." Whatever internal purpose the Mission Study Committee served—and however well-meaning the framers of the report—we can hardly extract from that effort any state policy evenhandedly to advance diverse educational options. As the District Court observed, the Committee's analysis "primarily focused on anticipated difficulties in attracting females to VMI," and the report, overall, supplied "very little indication of how the conclusion was reached."

In sum, we find no persuasive evidence in this record that VMI's male-only admission policy "is in furtherance of a state policy of 'diversity.' " . . . A purpose genuinely to advance an array of educational options, as the Court of Appeals recognized, is not served by VMI's historic and constant plan—a plan to "afford a unique educational benefit only to males." However "liberally" this plan serves the State's sons, it makes no provision whatever for her daughters. That is not *equal* protection.

Virginia next argues that VMI's adversative method of training provides educational benefits that cannot be made available, unmodified, to women. Alterations to accommodate women would necessarily be "radical," so "drastic," Virginia asserts, as to transform, indeed "destroy," VMI's program. Neither sex would be favored by the transformation, Virginia maintains: Men would be deprived of the unique opportunity currently available to them; women would not gain that opportunity because their participation would "eliminate the very aspects of [the] program that distinguish [VMI] from . . . other institutions of higher education in Virginia." . . .

The United States does not challenge any expert witness estimation on average capacities on preferences of men and women. Instead, the United States emphasizes that time and again since this Court's turning point decision in *Reed v. Reed*, 404 U.S. 71 (1971), we have cautioned reviewing courts to take a "hard look" at generalizations or "tendencies" of the kind pressed by Virginia, and relied upon by the District Court. State actors controlling gates to opportunity, we have instructed, may not exclude qualified individuals based on "fixed notions concerning the roles and abilities of males and females." *Mississippi Univ. for Women.*

It may be assumed, for purposes of this decision, that most women would not choose VMI's adversative method. . . . The issue, however, is not whether "women—or men—should be forced to attend VMI"; rather, the question is whether the State can constitutionally deny to women who have the will and capacity, the training and attendant opportunities that VMI uniquely affords.

The notion that admission of women would downgrade VMI's stature, destroy the adversative system and, with it, even the school, is a judgment hardly proved, a prediction hardly different from other "self-fulfilling prophecies," once routinely used to deny rights or opportunities. When women first sought admission to the bar and access to legal education, concerns of the same order were expressed. For example, in 1876, the Court of Common Pleas of Hennepin County, Minnesota, explained why women were thought ineligible for the practice of law. Women train and educate the young, the court said, which "forbids that they shall bestow that time (early and late) and labor, so essential in attaining to the eminence to which the true lawyer should ever aspire. It cannot therefore be said that the opposition of courts to the admission of females to practice . . . is to any extent the outgrowth of . . . 'old fogyism[.]' . . . It arises rather from a comprehension of the magnitude of the responsibilities connected with the successful practice of law, and a desire to grade up the profession." *In re Application of Martha Angle Dorsett to Be Admitted to Practice as Attorney and Counselor at Law* (Minn. C. P. Hennepin Cty., 1876). . . .

Women's successful entry into the federal military academies, and their participation in the Nation's military forces, indicate that Virginia's fears for the future of VMI may not be solidly grounded. The State's justification for excluding all women from "citizen-soldier" training for which some are qualified, in any event, cannot rank as "exceedingly persuasive," as we have explained and applied that standard.

Virginia and VMI trained their argument on "means" rather than "end," and thus misperceived our precedent. Single-sex education at VMI serves an "important governmental objective," they maintained, and exclusion of women is not only "substantially related," it is essential to that objective. By this notably circular argument, the "straightforward" test *Mississippi Univ. for Women* described, was bent and bowed. . . .

In the second phase of the litigation, Virginia presented its remedial plan—maintain VMI as a male-only college and create VWIL as a separate program for women. The plan met District Court approval. The Fourth Circuit, in turn, deferentially reviewed the State's proposal and decided that the two single-sex programs directly served Virginia's reasserted purposes: single-gender education, and "achieving the results of an adversative method in a military environment." . . . The United States challenges this "remedial" ruling as pervasively misguided.

A remedial decree, this Court has said, must closely fit the constitutional violation; it must be shaped to place persons unconstitutionally denied an opportunity or advantage in "the position they would have occupied in the absence of [discrimination]." See *Milliken v. Bradley*, 433 U.S. 267 (1977). The constitutional violation in this case is the categorical exclusion of women from an extraordinary educational opportunity afforded men. A proper remedy for an unconstitutional exclusion, we have explained, aims to "eliminate [so far as possible] the discriminatory effects of the past" and to "bar like discrimination in the future." *Louisiana v. United States*, 380 U.S. 145 (1965).

Virginia chose not to eliminate, but to leave untouched, VMI's exclusionary policy. For women only, however, Virginia proposed a separate program, different in kind from VMI and unequal in tangible and intangible facilities. Having violated the Constitution's equal protection requirement, Virginia was obliged to show that its remedial proposal "directly addressed and related to" the violation, the equal protection denied to women ready, willing, and able to benefit from educational opportunities of the kind VMI offers. Virginia described VWIL as a "parallel program," and asserted that VWIL shares VMI's mission of producing "citizen-soldiers" and VMI's goals of providing "education, military training, mental and physical discipline, character ". . . and leadership development." If the VWIL program could not "eliminate the discriminatory effects of the past," could it at least "bar like discrimination in the future"? A comparison of the programs said to be "parallel" informs our answer. . . .

VWIL affords women no opportunity to experience the rigorous military training for which VMI is famed. Instead, the VWIL program "deemphasizes" military education, and uses a "cooperative method" of education "which reinforces self-esteem."

VWIL students participate in ROTC and a "largely ceremonial" Virginia Corps of Cadets, but Virginia deliberately did not make VWIL a military institute. . . . VWIL students receive their "leadership training" in seminars, externships, and speaker series, episodes and encounters lacking the "physical rigor, mental stress, . . . minute regulation of behavior, and indoctrination in desirable values" made hallmarks of VMI's citizen-soldier training. Kept away from the pressures, hazards, and psychological bonding characteristic of VMI's adversative training, VWIL students will not know the "feeling of tremendous accomplishment" commonly experienced by VMI's successful cadets.

Virginia maintains that these methodological differences are "justified pedagogically," based on "important differences between men and women in learning and developmental needs," "psychological and sociological differences" Virginia describes as "real" and "not stereotypes." The Task Force charged with developing the leadership program for women, drawn from the staff and faculty at Mary Baldwin College, "determined that a military model and, especially VMI's adversative method, would be wholly inappropriate for educating and training *most women*."

As earlier stated, generalizations about "the way women are," estimates of what is appropriate for *most women*, no longer justify denying opportunity to women whose talent and capacity place them outside the average description. Notably, Virginia never asserted that VMI's method of education suits *most men*. It is also revealing that Virginia accounted for its failure to make the VWIL experience "the entirely militaristic experience of VMI" on the ground that VWIL "is planned for women who do not necessarily expect to pursue military careers." By that reasoning, VMI's "entirely militaristic" program would be inappropriate for men in general or *as a group*, for "only about 15% of VMI cadets enter career military service."

In contrast to the generalizations about women on which Virginia rests, we note again these dispositive realities: VMI's "implementing methodology" is not "inherently unsuitable to women"; "some women . . . do well under [the] adversative model"; "some women, at least, would want to attend [VMI] if they had the opportunity"; "some women are capable of all of the individual activities required of VMI cadets," and "can meet the physical standards [VMI] now imposes on men." It is on behalf of these women that the United States has instituted this suit, and it is for them that a remedy must be crafted, a remedy that will end their exclusion from a state-supplied educational opportunity for which they are fit, a decree that will "bar like discrimination in the future." *Louisiana.*

In myriad respects other than military training, VWIL does not qualify as VMI's equal. VWIL's student body, faculty, course offerings, and facilities hardly match VMI's. Nor can the VWIL graduate anticipate the benefits associated with VMI's 157-year history, the school's prestige, and its influential alumni network. . . .

Virginia, in sum, while maintaining VMI for men only, has failed to provide any "comparable single-gender women's institution." Instead, the Commonwealth has created a VWIL program fairly appraised as a "pale shadow" of VMI in terms of the range of curricular choices and faculty stature, funding, prestige, alumni support and influence.

Virginia's VWIL solution is reminiscent of the remedy Texas proposed 50 years ago, in response to a state trial court's 1946 ruling that, given the equal protection guarantee, African Americans could not be denied a legal education at a state facility. See *Sweatt v. Painter*, 339 U.S. 629 (1950). Reluctant to admit African Americans to its flagship University of Texas Law School, the State set up a separate school for Herman Sweatt and other black law students. As originally opened, the new school had no independent faculty or library, and it lacked accreditation. Nevertheless, the state trial and appellate courts were satisfied that the new school offered Sweatt opportunities for the study of law "substantially equivalent to those offered by the State to white students at the University of Texas." . . .

More important than the tangible features, the Court emphasized, are "those qualities which are incapable of objective measurement but which make for greatness" in a school, including "reputation of the faculty, experience of the administration, position and influence of the alumni, standing in the community, traditions and prestige." Facing the marked differences reported in the *Sweatt* opinion, the Court unanimously ruled that Texas had not shown "substantial equality in the [separate] educational opportunities" the State offered. Accordingly, the Court held, the Equal Protection Clause required Texas to admit African Americans to the University of Texas Law School. In line with *Sweatt*, we rule here that Virginia has not shown substantial equality in the separate educational opportunities the State supports at VWIL and VMI. . . .

For the reasons stated, the initial judgment of the Court of Appeals is affirmed, the final judgment of the Court of Appeals is reversed, and the case is remanded for further proceedings consistent with this opinion.

It is so ordered.

☐ *Chief Justice REHNQUIST, concurring in the judgment.*

The Court holds first that Virginia violates the Equal Protection Clause by maintaining the Virginia Military Institute's (VMI's) all-male admissions policy, and second that establishing the Virginia Women's Institute for Leadership (VWIL) program does not remedy that violation. While I agree with these conclusions, I disagree with the Court's analysis and so I write separately.

Two decades ago in *Craig v. Boren*, 429 U.S. 190 (1976), we announced that "to withstand constitutional challenge, . . . classifications by gender must serve important governmental objectives and must be substantially related to achievement of those objectives." We have adhered to that standard of scrutiny ever since. While the majority adheres to this test today, it also says that the State must demonstrate an "exceedingly persuasive justification" to support a gender-based classification. It is unfortunate that the Court thereby introduces an element of uncertainty respecting the appropriate test.

While terms like "important governmental objective" and "substantially related" are hardly models of precision, they have more content and specificity than does the phrase "exceedingly persuasive justification." That phrase is best confined, as it was first used, as an observation on the difficulty of meeting the applicable test, not as a formulation of the test itself. To avoid introducing potential confusion, I would have adhered more closely to our traditional, "firmly established," [*Mississippi Univ. for Women v.*] *Hogan*; *Heckler* [*v. Mathews*], 465 U.S. 728 (1984), standard that a gender-based classification "must bear a close and substantial relationship to important governmental objectives." [*Personnel Administrator of Mass. v.*] *Feeney*, 442 U.S. 256 (1979). . . .

Even if diversity in educational opportunity were the State's actual objective, the State's position would still be problematic. The difficulty with its position is that the diversity benefited only one sex; there was single-sex public education available for men at VMI, but no corresponding single-sex public education available for women. When *Hogan* placed Virginia on notice that VMI's admissions policy possibly was unconstitutional, VMI could have dealt with the problem by admitting women; but its governing body felt strongly that the admission of women would have seriously harmed the institution's educational approach. Was there something else the State could have done to avoid an equal protection violation? Since the State did nothing, we do not have to definitively answer that question. . . .

The dissent criticizes me for "disregarding the four all-women's private colleges in Virginia (generously assisted by public funds)." The private women's colleges are treated by the State exactly as all other private schools are treated, which includes the provision of tuition-assistance grants to Virginia residents. Virginia gives no special support to the women's single-sex education. But obviously, the same is not true for men's education. Had the State provided the kind of support for the private women's schools that it provides for VMI, this may have been a very different case. For in so doing, the State would have demonstrated that its interest in providing a single-sex education for men, was to some measure matched by an interest in providing the same opportunity for women.

Virginia offers a second justification for the single-sex admissions policy: maintenance of the adversative method. I agree with the Court that this justification does not serve an important governmental objective. A State does not have substantial interest in the adversative methodology unless it is pedagogically beneficial. While considerable evidence shows that a single-sex education is pedagogically beneficial for some students, and hence a State may have a valid interest in promoting that methodology, there is no similar evidence in the record that an adversative method is pedagogically beneficial or is any more likely to produce character traits than other methodologies. . . .

In the end, the women's institution Virginia proposes, VWIL, fails as a remedy, because it is distinctly inferior to the existing men's institution and will continue to be for the foreseeable future. VWIL simply is not, in any sense, the institution that VMI is. In particular, VWIL is a program appended to a private college, not a self-standing institution; and VWIL is substantially underfunded as compared to VMI. I therefore ultimately agree with the Court that Virginia has not provided an adequate remedy.

☐ *Justice SCALIA, dissenting.*

I shall devote most of my analysis to evaluating the Court's opinion on the basis of our current equal-protection jurisprudence, which regards this Court as free to evaluate everything under the sun by applying one of three tests: "rational basis" scrutiny, intermediate scrutiny, or strict scrutiny. These tests are no more scientific than their names suggest, and a further element of randomness is added by the fact that it is largely up to us which test will be applied in each case. Strict scrutiny, we have said, is reserved for state "classifications based on race or national origin and classifications affecting fundamental rights," *Clark v. Jeter*, 486 U.S. 456 (1988). It is my position that the term "fundamental rights" should be limited to "interests traditionally protected by our society," *Michael H. v. Gerald D.*, 491 U.S. 110 (1989) (plurality opinion of SCALIA, J.); but the Court has not accepted that view, so that strict scrutiny will be applied to the deprivation of whatever sort of right we consider "fundamental." We have no established criterion for "intermediate scrutiny" either, but essentially apply it when it seems like a good idea to load the dice. So far it has been applied to content-neutral restrictions that place an incidental burden on speech, to disabilities attendant to illegitimacy, and to discrimination on the basis of sex.

I have no problem with a system of abstract tests such as rational-basis, intermediate, and strict scrutiny (though I think we can do better than applying strict scrutiny and intermediate scrutiny whenever we feel like it). Such formulas are essential to evaluating whether the new restrictions that a changing society constantly imposes upon private conduct comport with that "equal protection" our society has always accorded in the past. But in my view the function of this Court is to preserve our society's values regarding (among other things) equal protection, not to revise them; to prevent backsliding from the degree of restriction the Constitution imposed upon democratic government, not to prescribe, on our own authority, progressively higher degrees. For that reason it is my view that, whatever abstract tests we may choose to devise, they cannot supersede—and indeed ought to be crafted so as to reflect—those constant and unbroken national traditions that embody the people's understanding of ambiguous constitutional texts. More specifically, it is my view that "when a practice not expressly prohibited by the text of the Bill of Rights bears the endorsement of a long tradition of open, widespread, and unchallenged use that dates back to the beginning of the Republic, we have no proper basis for striking it down." *Rutan v. Republican Party of Ill.*, 497 U.S. 62 (1990) (SCALIA, J., dissenting). The same applies, *mutatis mutandis*, to a practice asserted to be in violation of the post-Civil War Fourteenth Amendment.

The all-male constitution of VMI comes squarely within such a governing tradition. Founded by the Commonwealth of Virginia in 1839 and continuously maintained by it since, VMI has always admitted only men. . . . In other words, the tradition of having government-funded military schools for men is as well rooted in the traditions of this country as the tradition of sending only men into military combat. The people may decide to change the one tradition, like the other, through democratic processes; but the assertion that either tradition has been unconstitutional through the centuries is not law, but politics smuggled into law. . . .

To reject the Court's disposition today, however, it is not necessary to accept my view that the Court's made-up tests cannot displace longstanding national traditions as the primary determinant of what the Constitution means. It is only necessary to apply honestly the test the Court has been applying to sex-based classifications for the past two decades. It is well settled, as Justice O'CONNOR stated some time ago for a unanimous Court, that we evaluate a statutory classification based on sex under a standard that lies "between the extremes of rational basis review and strict scrutiny." *Clark v. Jeter.* We have denominated this standard "intermediate scrutiny" and under it have inquired whether the statutory classification is "substantially related to an important governmental objective."

Before I proceed to apply this standard to VMI, I must comment upon the manner in which the Court avoids doing so. . . .

Only the amorphous "exceedingly persuasive justification" phrase, and not the standard elaboration of intermediate scrutiny, can be made to yield this conclusion that VMI's single-sex composition is unconstitutional because there exist several women (or, one would have to conclude under the Court's reasoning, a single woman) willing and able to undertake VMI's program. Intermediate scrutiny has never required a least-restrictive-means analysis, but only a "substantial relation" between the classification and the state interests that it serves. Thus, in *Califano v. Webster*, 430 U.S. 313 (1977), we upheld a congressional statute that provided higher Social Security benefits for women than for men. We reasoned that "women . . . as such have been unfairly hindered from earning as much as men," but we did not require proof that each woman so benefited had suffered discrimination or that each disadvantaged man had not; it was sufficient that even under the former congressional scheme "women on the average received lower retirement benefits than men." The reasoning in our other intermediate-scrutiny cases has similarly required only a substantial relation between end and means, not a perfect fit. . . . There is simply no support in our cases for the notion that a sex-based classification is invalid unless it relates to characteristics that hold true in every instance. . . .

The question to be answered, I repeat, is whether the exclusion of women from VMI is "substantially related to an important governmental objective."

It is beyond question that Virginia has an important state interest in providing effective college education for its citizens. That single-sex instruction is an approach substantially related to that interest should be evident enough from the long and continuing history in this country of men's and women's colleges. But beyond that, as the Court of Appeals here stated: "That single-gender education at the college level is beneficial to both sexes is a fact established in this case." . . .

The potential of today's decision for widespread disruption of existing institutions lies in its application to private single-sex education. Government support is immensely important to private educational institutions. Mary Baldwin College—which designed and runs VWIL—notes that private institutions of higher education in the 1990–1991 school year derived approximately 19 percent of their budgets from federal, state, and local government funds, not including financial aid to students. Charitable status under the tax laws is also highly significant for private educational institutions, and it is certainly not beyond the Court that rendered today's decision to hold that a donation to a single-sex college should be deemed contrary to public policy and therefore not deductible if the college discriminates on the basis of sex. See *Bob Jones Univ. v. United States*, 461 U.S. 574 (1983). . . .

The only hope for state-assisted single-sex private schools is that the Court will not apply in the future the principles of law it has applied today. That is a substantial hope, I am happy and ashamed to say. After all, did not the Court today abandon the principles of law it has applied in our earlier sex-classification cases? And does not the Court positively invite private colleges to rely upon our ad-hocery by assuring them this case is "unique"? I would not advise the foundation of any new single-sex college (especially an all-male one) with the expectation of being allowed to receive any government support; but it is too soon to abandon in despair those single-sex colleges already in existence. It will certainly be possible for this Court to write a future opinion that ignores the broad principles of law set forth today, and that characterizes as utterly dispositive the opinion's perceptions that VMI was a uniquely prestigious all-male institution, conceived in chauvinism, etc., etc. I will not join that opinion.

■ (2) Discrimination against the LGBTQ Community

In a ruling that sparked considerable controversy in and outside of the Court, *Romer v. Evans* (excerpted below) struck down a Colorado state constitutional amendment that forbade localities from enacting ordinances outlawing discrimination against homosexuals. However, the Court upheld Georgia's law criminalizing sodomy as applied to homosexuals in *Bowers v. Hardwick*, 478 U.S. 186 (1986), and the First Amendment right of the Boy Scouts of America to exclude homosexuals in *Boy Scouts of America v. Dale*, 530 U.S. 640 (2000) (excerpted in Ch. 5, Sec. I). The Court also upheld the constitutionality of the so-called Solomon Amendment, a federal law requiring the cutoff of federal funding to colleges and universities that refuse to permit the military to recruit their students, because of the American Law Schools' policy of nondiscrimination against sexual orientation and opposition to the military's "don't ask, don't tell" policy. Writing for the Court, in *Rumsfeld v. Forum for Academic and Institutional Rights*, 547 U.S. 47 (2006), Chief Justice Roberts rejected the First Amendment challenge on the grounds that law schools had other ways to communicate their position. However, the Court reconsidered and overruled *Bowers* in *Lawrence v. Texas* (2003) (excerpted in Ch. 11).

The controversy over discriminating against gays and lesbians further escalated when, in the same month *Lawrence v. Texas* came down, Canadian courts ruled that same-sex marriages could not be discriminated against (see the IN COMPARATIVE PERSPECTIVE box in this section). Subsequently, the Massachusetts state supreme court held that the state could not discriminate against same-sex marriages. Vermont and Connecticut recognized same-sex civil unions. The District of Columbia, California, Hawaii, Maine, and New Jersey also recognize some spousal benefits, like health care and inheritance rights. Thirty-nine states prohibit same-sex marriages with laws modeled after the federal Defense of Marriage Act (DOMA) of 1996, which bars federal recognition of same-sex marriages and permits states to ignore those performed in other states. In light of *Lawrence v. Texas* and the Massachusetts state supreme court ruling, state DOMA laws are being challenged in the courts. In response, twenty states have adopted constitutional amendments or enacted laws banning same-sex marriages. President George W. Bush also called for the passage of a federal constitutional amendment barring same-sex marriages. He did so claiming that states would be required to recognize same-sex marriages performed in other states because of the "full faith and credit" clause of Article IV, Section 1, of the Constitution, which requires state courts to honor the judicial decisions of other states. Indeed, some proponents of same-sex marriage contend that the "full faith and credit" clause compels states banning same-sex marriages to recognize legally married same-sex couples in other states, and draw an analogy between bans on interracial and same-sex marriages. But the history and analogy remains problematic for both opponents and proponents of same-sex marriage (see the box on CONSTITUTIONAL HISTORY: *Loving v. Virginia* and Bans on Interracial Marriages in this chapter, Section A).

Notably, in two widely watched cases bearing on same-sex marriages, the Court split in different 5–4 rulings. On the one hand, in *Hollingsworth v. Perry* (2013), 570 U.S. 693, Chief Justice Roberts denied standing to sue to supporters of Proposition 8, a California state amendment barring same-sex marriages. Justice Kennedy, joined by Justices Thomas, Alito, and Sotomayor, dissented. On the other hand, in *United States v. Windsor*, 570 U.S. 744 (2013), Justice Kennedy struck down Section 3 of the DOMA of 1996, which denied federal benefits to same-sex couples. Chief Justice Roberts and Justices Scalia, Alito, and Thomas dissented. These decisions propelled the movement for the recognition of same-sex marriages.

In a historic and volatile ruling in *Obergefell v. Hodges* (2015) (excerpted below), Justice Kennedy delivered the opinion for a bare majority of the Court, invalidating state laws banning same-sex marriages. Just two years earlier on the same day, he handed down *United States v. Windsor* (2013), striking down the provision in the DOMA of 1996 that excluded same-sex couples from recognition of their marriage and federal benefits; and exactly twelve years earlier delivered *Lawrence v. Texas* (2003) (excerpted in Ch. 11), which struck down Texas's law criminalizing homosexual sodomy. In *Obergefell*, Justice Kennedy reasoned that the Fourteenth Amendment's due process and equal protection clauses converge to guarantee a "fundamental right to marry" and to "individual dignity" that overrides prohibitions on same-sex marriages. Each of the four dissenting justices issued separate, often caustic and vehement, opinions. Chief Justice Roberts criticized the majority's reasoning, especially its failure to defer to the political process and the ongoing national debate over same-sex marriage. Justice Scalia echoed those points, emphasizing that the ruling was a "threat to American democracy." In addition, he ridiculed the majority's departure from the original understanding of the Fourteenth Amendment. Similarly, dissenting Justice Thomas focused on the Court's abandonment of the original understanding of the Constitution, and issued his most extensive discussion of his "natural law" jurisprudence, as well as voiced concerns about the denial of religious freedom. In the same vein, Justice Alito stressed the majority's marginalization of those with religious opposition to same-sex marriages, and minimalizing the ruling's impact on religious beliefs, businesses, and organizations.

Obergefell v. Hodges met immediate opposition in some states and localities, which resulted in further litigation. The Roberts Court in turn confronted the ramifications of its decision. In a summarily decided holding in *Pavan v. Smith,* 139 S. Ct. 62 (2018), for example, the Court overturned the Arkansas state supreme court's decision that the state could require the name of the biological father placed on birth certificates because it discriminated against LBGTQ couples of adopted children. A brief *per curiam* opinion reaffirmed *Obergefell*'s holding that state laws are unconstitutional "to the extent they treated same-sex couples differently from opposite-sex couples."

However, as dissenting Justices Thomas and Alito in *Obergefell* emphasized, the majority's holding invited opposition from those who believe their religious opposition to same-sex marriages is protected by the First Amendment guarantees for free speech and religious exercise. When confronted with that inevitable controversy—over a baker's refusal to make a wedding cake for a same-sex couple due to his religious convictions, and for which he was found to violate a state antidiscrimination law—in *Masterpiece Cakeshop v. Colorado Civil Rights Commission* (2018) (excerpted below), a majority of the Roberts Court failed to address the First Amendment claims. Writing for the Court, Justice Kennedy reversed the state court's decision and remanded the case for reconsideration, upon concluding that the Colorado Civil Rights Commission had not considered Masterpiece Cakeshop's claims with religious neutrality. Justices Kagan, Gorsuch, and Thomas each issued separate concurring opinions, while Justices Ginsburg and Sotomayor dissented.

Selected Bibliography

Ball, Carlos, ed. *After Marriage Equality: The Future of LGBT Rights.* New York: New York University Press, 2016.

Becker, Jo. *Forcing the Spring: Inside the Fight for Marriage Equality.* New York: Penguin Press, 2014.

Cenziper, Debbie, and Jim Obergefell. *Love Wins: The Lovers and Lawyers Who Fought the Landmark Case for Marriage Equality.* New York: Harper Collins, 2016.

Eleveld, Kerry. *Don't Tell Me To Wait: How the Fight for Gay Rights Changed America and Transformed Obama's Presidency.* New York: Basic Books, 2015.

Hume, Robert J. *Courthouse Democracy and Minority Rights: Same-Sex Marriage in the States.* New York: Oxford University Press, 2013.

Kaplan, Roberta, and Lisa Dickey. *Then Comes Marriage: U.S. v. Windsor and the Defeat of DOMA.* New York: W. W. Norton & Co., 2015.

Klarman, Michael. *From the Closet to the Altar: Courts, Backlash, and the Struggle for Same-Sex Marriage.* New York: Oxford University Press, 2012.

Koppelman, Andrew. *The Gay Rights Question in Contemporary American Law*. Chicago: University of Chicago Press, 2002.

————. *Same Sex, Different States: When Same-Sex Marriages Cross State Lines*. New Haven, CT: Yale University Press, 2007.

Richards, David A. J. *Women, Gays, and the Constitution: The Grounds for Feminism and Gay Rights*. Chicago: University of Chicago Press, 1998.

————. *The Sodomy Cases: Bowers v. Hardwick and Lawrence v. Texas*. Lawrence: University Press of Kansas, 2009.

Robb, Graham. *Strangers: Homosexual Love in the Nineteenth Century*. New York: W. W. Norton & Company, 2004.

Stone, Geoffrey. *Sex and the Constitution: Sex, Religion, and Law from America's Origins to the Twenty-First Century*. New York: Liveright, 2017.

Romer v. Evans

517 U.S. 620, 116 S.Ct. 1620 (1996)

In November 1992, voters in Colorado approved an amendment to the state constitution that forbade localities from enacting ordinances outlawing discrimination against homosexuals. Known as Amendment 2, the "No Protected Status Based on Homosexual, Lesbian, or Bisexual Orientation Amendment" provided that

> [n]either the State of Colorado, through any of its branches or departments, nor any of its agencies, political subdivisions, municipalities or school districts, shall enact, adopt or enforce any statute, regulation, ordinance or policy whereby homosexual, lesbian or bisexual orientation, conduct, practices or relationships shall constitute or otherwise be the basis of or entitle any person or class of persons to have or claim any minority status quota preferences, protected status or claim of discrimination. This Section of the Constitution shall be in all respects self-executing.

Richard G. Evans and several local government officials immediately filed a suit to enjoin the enforcement of the amendment on the grounds that it was unconstitutional. A state trial court subsequently agreed and Governor Roy Romer appealed.

In 1993, the Colorado State Supreme Court interpreted precedents of the U.S. Supreme Court to hold that "the Equal Protection Clause of the United States Constitution protects the fundamental right to participate equally in the political process," and "that any legislation or state constitutional amendment which infringes on this right by 'fencing out' an independently identifiable class of persons must be subject to strict judicial scrutiny." *Evans v. Romer*, 854 P.2d 1270 (Colo. 1993) (*Evans I*). On that basis, the state supreme court affirmed the trial court's decision and remanded the case back to the trial court to determine whether Amendment 2 was supported by a compelling state interest and narrowly tailored to serve that interest. Subsequently, government officials offered six "compelling" state interests for the amendment: (1) deterring factionalism; (2) preserving the integrity of the state's political functions; (3) preserving the ability of the state to remedy discrimination against suspect classes; (4) preventing the government from interfering with personal, familial, and religious privacy; (5) preventing the government from subsidizing the political objectives of a special interest group; and (6) promoting the physical and psychological well-being of Colorado children.

For a second time, however, the trial court rejected most of the rationales given as not compelling state interests, and concluded the government's interests in preventing interference with personal privacy and religious liberty, although compelling, were not narrowly tailored enough. Accordingly, the trial court issued a permanent injunction against the enforcement of Amendment 2. Besides appealing the *Evans I* decision to the U.S. Supreme Court, which denied review, Governor Romer appealed to the Colorado State Supreme Court the trial court's second ruling on the amendment. On appeal in *Evans II*, attorneys for the state argued that (1) the legal standard set forth in *Evans I*, for assessing the constitutionality of Amendment 2, should be reconsidered; (2) Amendment 2 was supported by several compelling state interests and is narrowly tailored to meet those interests; (3) the unconstitutional provisions of Amendment 2 were severable from the remainder; and (4) Amendment 2 was a valid exercise of state power under the Tenth Amendment to the United States Constitution. However, in 1994 in *Evans II*, the Colorado State Supreme Court rejected those arguments and, once again, held that Amendment 2 was unconstitutional. Subsequently, Colorado's governor, Roy Romer, appealed to the Supreme Court.

The Court's decision was 6–3. Justice Kennedy delivered the opinion for the Court and Justice Scalia filed a dissent, which was joined by Chief Justice Rehnquist and Justice Thomas.

■ ■ ■

☐ *Justice KENNEDY delivered the opinion of the Court.*

One century ago, the first Justice HARLAN admonished this Court that the Constitution "neither knows nor tolerates classes among citizens." *Plessy v. Ferguson*, 163 U.S. 537 (1896) (dissenting opinion). Unheeded then, those words now are understood to state a commitment to the law's neutrality where the rights of persons are at stake. The Equal Protection Clause enforces this principle and today requires us to hold invalid a provision of Colorado's Constitution. . . .

The State's principal argument in defense of Amendment 2 is that it puts gays and lesbians in the same position as all other persons. So, the State says, the measure does no more than deny homosexuals special rights. This reading of the amendment's language is implausible. We rely not upon our own interpretation of the amendment but upon the authoritative construction of Colorado's Supreme Court. The state court, deeming it unnecessary to determine the full extent of the amendment's reach, found it invalid even on a modest reading of its implications. The critical discussion of the amendment, set out in *Evans I*, is as follows: "The immediate objective of Amendment 2 is, at a minimum, to repeal existing statutes, regulations, ordinances, and policies of state and local entities that barred discrimination based on sexual orientation. . . .

The change that Amendment 2 works in the legal status of gays and lesbians in the private sphere is far-reaching, both on its own terms and when considered in light of the structure and operation of modern antidiscrimination laws. That structure is well illustrated by contemporary statutes and ordinances prohibiting discrimination by providers of public accommodations. "At common law, innkeepers, smiths, and others who 'made profession of a public employment,' were prohibited from refusing, with good reason, to serve a customer." *Hurley v. Irish-American Gay, Lesbian and Bisexual Group of Boston, Inc.*, [515 U.S. 557 (1995)]. The duty was a general one and did not specify protection for particular groups. The common law rules, however, proved insufficient in many instances, and it was settled early that the Fourteenth Amendment did not give Congress a general power to prohibit discrimination in public accommodations, *Civil Rights Cases*, 109 U.S. 3 (1883). In consequence, most States have chosen to counter discrimination by enacting detailed statutory schemes. Colorado's state and municipal laws typify this emerging tradition of statutory protection and follow a consistent pattern. . . .

These statutes and ordinances also depart from the common law by enumerating the groups or persons within their ambit of protection. Enumeration is the essential device used to make the duty not to discriminate concrete and to provide guidance for those who must comply. . . .

Amendment 2 bars homosexuals from securing protection against the injuries that these public-accommodations laws address. That in itself is a severe consequence, but there is more. Amendment 2, in addition, nullifies specific legal protections for this targeted class in all transactions in housing, sale of real estate, insurance, health and welfare services, private education, and employment. . . .

Amendment 2's reach may not be limited to specific laws passed for the benefit of gays and lesbians. It is a fair, if not necessary, inference from the broad language of the amendment that it deprives gays and lesbians even of the protection of general laws and policies that prohibit arbitrary discrimination in governmental and private settings. At some point in the systematic administration of these laws, an official must determine whether homosexuality is an arbitrary and thus forbidden basis for decision. Yet a decision to that effect would itself amount to a policy prohibiting discrimination on the basis of homosexuality, and so would appear to be no more valid under

Amendment 2 than the specific prohibitions against discrimination the state court held invalid. . . .

The Fourteenth Amendment's promise that no person shall be denied the equal protection of the laws must co-exist with the practical necessity that most legislation classifies for one purpose or another, with resulting disadvantage to various groups or persons. We have attempted to reconcile the principle with the reality by stating that, if a law neither burdens a fundamental right nor targets a suspect class, we will uphold the legislative classification so long as it bears a rational relation to some legitimate end. See, e.g., *Heller v. Doe*, 509 U.S. 312 (1993).

Amendment 2 fails, indeed defies, even this conventional inquiry. First, the amendment has the peculiar property of imposing a broad and undifferentiated disability on a single named group, an exceptional and, as we shall explain, invalid form of legislation. Second, its sheer breadth is so discontinuous with the reasons offered for it that the amendment seems inexplicable by anything but animus toward the class that it affects; it lacks a rational relationship to legitimate state interests.

Taking the first point, even in the ordinary equal protection case calling for the most deferential of standards, we insist on knowing the relation between the classification adopted and the object to be attained. The search for the link between classification and objective gives substance to the Equal Protection Clause; it provides guidance and discipline for the legislature, which is entitled to know what sorts of laws it can pass; and it marks the limits of our own authority. In the ordinary case, a law will be sustained if it can be said to advance a legitimate government interest, even if the law seems unwise or works to the disadvantage of a particular group, or if the rationale for it seems tenuous. By requiring that the classification bear a rational relationship to an independent and legitimate legislative end, we ensure that classifications are now drawn for the purpose of disadvantaging the group burdened by the law.

Amendment 2 confounds this normal process of judicial review. It is at once too narrow and too broad. It identifies persons by a single trait and then denies them protection across the board. The resulting disqualification of a class of persons from the right to seek specific protection from the law is unprecedented in our jurisprudence.

It is not within our constitutional tradition to enact laws of this sort. Central both to the idea of the rule of law and to our own Constitution's guarantee of equal protection is the principle that government and each of its parts remain open on impartial terms to all who seek its assistance. "Equal protection of the laws is not achieved through indiscriminate imposition of inequalities." *Sweatt v. Painter*, 339 U.S. 629 (1950) [quoting *Shelley v. Kraemer*, 334 U.S. 1 (1948)]. Respect for this principle explains why laws singling out a certain class of citizens for disfavored legal status or general hardships are rare. A law declaring that in general it shall be more difficult for one group of citizens than for all others to seek aid from the government is itself a denial of equal protection of the laws in the most literal sense. "The guaranty of 'equal protection of the laws is a pledge of the protection of equal laws.'" *Skinner v. Oklahoma ex rel. Williamson*, 316 U.S. 535 (1942) [quoting *Yick Wo v. Hopkins*, 118 U.S. 356 (1886)].

Davis v. Beason, 133 U.S. 333 (1890), not cited by the parties but relied upon by the dissent, is not evidence that Amendment 2 is within our constitutional tradition, and any reliance upon it as authority for sustaining the amendment is misplaced. In *Davis*, the Court approved an Idaho territorial statute denying Mormons, polygamists, and advocates of polygamy the right to vote and to hold office because, as the Court construed the statue, it "simply excludes from the privilege of voting, or of holding any office of honor, trust or profit, those who have been convicted of certain offenses, and those who advocate a practical resistance to the laws of the Territory and justify and approve the commission of crimes forbidden by it." To the extent *Davis* held that persons advocating a certain practice may be denied the right to vote, it is no longer good law. *Brandenburg v. Ohio*, 395 U.S. 444 (1969) (*per curiam*). To the extent it held that the groups designated in the statute may be deprived of the right to vote because of their status, its ruling could not stand without surviving strict scrutiny, a most doubtful outcome. To the extent *Davis* held that a convicted felon may be denied the right to vote, its holding is not implicated by our decision and is unexceptionable.

A second and related point is that laws of the kind now before us raise the inevitable inference that the disadvantage imposed is born of animosity toward the class of persons affected. Even laws enacted for broad and ambitious purposes often can be explained by reference to legitimate public policies which justify the incidental disadvantages they impose on certain persons. Amendment 2, however, in making a general announcement that gays and lesbians shall not have any particular protections from the law, inflicts on them immediate, continuing, and real injuries that outrun and belie any legitimate justifications that may be claimed for it. We conclude that, in addition to the far-reaching deficiencies of Amendment 2 that we have noted, the principles it offends, in another sense, are conventional and venerable; a law must bear a rational relationship to a legitimate government purpose, and Amendment 2 does not.

The primary rationale the State offers for Amendment 2 is respect for other citizens' freedom of association, and in particular the liberties of landlords or employers who have personal or religious objections to homosexuality. Colorado also cites its interest in conserving resources to fight discrimination against other groups. The breadth of the Amendment is so far removed from these particular justifications that we find it impossible to credit them. We cannot say that Amendment 2 is directed to any identifiable legitimate purpose or discrete objective. It is a status-based enactment divorced from any factual context from which we could discern a relationship to legitimate state interests; it is a classification of persons undertaken for its own sake, something the Equal Protection Clause does not permit. "Class legislation . . . [is] obnoxious to the prohibitions of the Fourteenth Amendment. . . ." *Civil Rights Cases*.

We must conclude that Amendment 2 classifies homosexuals not to further a proper legislative end but to make them unequal to everyone else. This Colorado cannot do. A State cannot so deem a class of persons a stranger to its laws. Amendment 2 violates the Equal Protection Clause, and the judgment of the Supreme Court of Colorado is affirmed.

It is so ordered.

☐ *Justice SCALIA, with whom THE CHIEF JUSTICE and Justice THOMAS join, dissenting.*

The Court has mistaken a *Kulturkampf* ["culture war"] for a fit of spite. The constitutional amendment before us here is not the manifestation of a "bare . . . desire to harm" homosexuals, but is rather a modest attempt by seemingly tolerant Coloradans to preserve traditional sexual mores against the efforts of a politically powerful minority to revise those mores through use of the laws. That objective, and the means chosen to achieve it, are not only unimpeachable under any constitutional doctrine hitherto pronounced (hence the opinion's heavy reliance upon principles of righteousness rather than judicial holdings); they have been specifically approved by the Congress of the United States and by this Court.

In holding that homosexuality cannot be singled out for disfavorable treatment, the Court contradicts a decision, unchallenged here, pronounced only 10 years ago, see *Bowers v. Hardwick*, 478 U.S. 186 (1986), and places the prestige of this institution behind the proposition that opposition to homosexuality is as reprehensible as racial or religious bias. Whether it is or not is precisely the cultural debate that gave rise to the Colorado constitutional amendment (and to the preferential laws against which the amendment was directed). Since the Constitution of the United States says nothing about this subject, it is left to be resolved by normal democratic means, including the democratic adoption of provisions in state constitutions. This Court has no business imposing upon all Americans the resolution favored by the elite class from which the Members of this institution are selected, pronouncing that "animosity" toward homosexuality, is evil. I vigorously dissent. . . .

[T]he principle underlying the Court's opinion is that one who is accorded equal treatment under the laws, but cannot as readily as others obtain preferential treatment under the laws, has been denied equal protection of the laws. If merely stating this alleged "equal protection" violation does not suffice to refute it, our constitutional jurisprudence has achieved terminal silliness.

The central thesis of the Court's reasoning is that any group is denied equal protection when, to obtain advantage (or, presumably, to avoid disadvantage), it must have recourse to a more general and hence more difficult level of political decision making than others. The world has never heard of such a principle, which is why the Court's opinion is so long on emotive utterance and so short on relevant legal citation. And it seems to me most unlikely that any multilevel democracy can function under such a principle. For whenever a disadvantage is imposed, or conferral of a benefit is prohibited, at one of the higher levels of democratic decision making (i.e., by the state legislature rather than local government, or by the people at large in the state constitution rather than the legislature), the affected group has (under this theory) been denied equal protection. To take the simplest of examples, consider a state law prohibiting the award of municipal contracts to relatives of mayors or city councilmen. Once such a law is passed, the group composed of such relatives must, in order to get the benefit of city contracts, persuade the state legislature—unlike all other citizens, who need only persuade the municipality. It is ridiculous to consider this a denial of equal protection, which is why the Court's theory is unheard of.

The Court might reply that the example I have given is not a denial of equal protection only because the same "rational basis" (avoidance of corruption) which renders constitutional the substantive discrimination against relatives (i.e., the fact that they alone cannot obtain city contracts) also automatically suffices to sustain what might be called the electoral-procedural discrimination against them (i.e., the fact that they must go to the state level to get this changed). This is of course a perfectly reasonable response, and would explain why "electoral-procedural discrimination" has not hitherto been heard of: a law that is valid in its substance is automatically valid in its level of enactment. But the Court cannot afford to make this argument, for as I shall discuss next, there is no doubt of a rational basis for the substance of the prohibition at issue here. The Court's entire novel theory rests upon the proposition that there is something special—something that cannot be justified by normal "rational basis" analysis—in making a disadvantaged group (or a nonpreferred group) resort to a higher decision making level. That proposition finds no support in law or logic.

I turn next to whether there was a legitimate rational basis for the substance of the constitutional amendment—for the prohibition of special protection for homosexuals. It is unsurprising that the Court avoids discussion of this question, since the answer is so obviously yes. The case most relevant to the issue before us today is not even mentioned in the Court's opinion: In *Bowers v. Hardwick*, 478 U.S. 186 (1986), we held that the Constitution does not prohibit what virtually all States had done from the founding of the Republic until very recent years—making homosexual conduct a crime. That holding is unassailable, except by those who think that the Constitution changes to suit current fashions. But in any event it is a given in the present case: Respondents' briefs did not urge overruling *Bowers*, and at oral argument respondents' counsel expressly disavowed any intent to seek such overruling. If it is constitutionally permissible for a State to make homosexual conduct criminal, surely it is constitutionally permissible for a State to enact other laws merely disfavoring homosexual conduct. And *a fortiori* it is constitutionally permissible for a State to adopt a provision not even disfavoring homosexual conduct, but merely prohibiting all levels of state government from bestowing special protections upon homosexual conduct. Respondents (who, unlike the Court, cannot afford the luxury of ignoring inconvenient precedent) counter *Bowers* with the argument that a greater-includes-the-lesser rationale cannot justify Amendment 2's application to individuals who do not engage in homosexual acts, but are merely of homosexual "orientation." Some courts of appeals have concluded that, with respect to laws of this sort at least, that is a distinction without a difference.

But assuming that, in Amendment 2, a person of homosexual "orientation" is someone who does not engage in homosexual conduct but merely has a tendency or desire to do so, *Bowers* still suffices to establish a rational basis for the provision. If it is rational to criminalize the conduct, surely it is rational to deny special favor and protection to those with a self-avowed tendency or desire to engage in the conduct. Indeed, where criminal sanctions are not involved, homosexual "orientation" is an acceptable stand-in for homosexual conduct. . . .

Moreover, even if the provision regarding homosexual "orientation" were invalid, respondents' challenge to Amendment 2—which is a facial challenge—must fail. "A facial challenge to a legislative Act is, of course, the most difficult challenge to mount successfully, since the challenger must establish that no set of circumstances exists under which the Act would be valid." *United States v. Salerno*, 481 U.S. 739 (1987). It would not be enough for respondents to establish (if they could) that Amendment 2 is unconstitutional as applied to those of homosexual "orientation"; since, under *Bowers*, Amendment 2 is unquestionably constitutional as applied to those who engage in homosexual conduct, the facial challenge cannot succeed. Some individuals of homosexual "orientation" who do not engage in homosexual acts might successfully bring an as-applied challenge to Amendment 2, but so far as the record indicates, none of the respondents is such a person.

The foregoing suffices to establish what the Court's failure to cite any case remotely in point would lead one to suspect: No principle set forth in the Constitution, nor even any imagined by this Court in the past 200 years, prohibits what Colorado has done here. But the case for Colorado is much stronger than that. What it has done is not only unprohibited, but eminently reasonable, with close, congressionally approved precedent in earlier constitutional practice.

First, as to its eminent reasonableness. The Court's opinion contains grim, disapproving hints that Coloradans have been guilty of "animus" or "animosity" toward homosexuality, as though that has been established as Un-American. Of course it is our moral heritage that one should not hate any human being or class of human beings. But I had thought that one could consider certain conduct reprehensible—murder, for example, or polygamy, or cruelty to animals—and could exhibit even "animus" toward such conduct. Surely that is the only sort of "animus" at issue here: moral disapproval of homosexual conduct, the same sort of moral disapproval that produced the centuries-old criminal laws that we held constitutional in *Bowers*. The Colorado amendment does not, to speak entirely precisely, prohibit giving favored status to people who are homosexuals; they can be favored for many reasons—for example, because they are senior citizens or members of racial minorities. But it prohibits giving them favored status because of their homosexual conduct—that is, it prohibits favored status for homosexuality. But though Coloradans are, as I say, entitled to be hostile toward homosexual conduct, the fact is that the degree of hostility reflected by Amendment 2 is the smallest conceivable. The Court's portrayal of Coloradans as a society fallen victim to pointless, hate-filled "gay-bashing" is so false as to be comical. Colorado not only is one of the 25 States that have repealed their antisodomy laws, but was among the first to do so. But the society that eliminates criminal punishment for homosexual acts does not necessarily abandon the view that homosexuality is morally wrong and socially harmful; often, abolition simply reflects the view that enforcement of such criminal laws involves unseemly intrusion into the intimate lives of citizens.

There is a problem, however, which arises when criminal sanction of homosexuality is eliminated but moral and social disapprobation of homosexuality is meant to be retained. The Court cannot be unaware of that problem; it is evident in many cities of the country, and occasionally bubbles to the surface of the news, in heated political disputes over such matters as the introduction into local schools of books teaching that homosexuality is an optional and fully acceptable "alternate life style." The problem (a problem, that is, for those who wish to retain social disapprobation of homosexuality) that, because those who engage in homosexual conduct tend to reside in disproportionate numbers in certain communities, and of course care about homosexual-rights issues much more ardently than the public at large, they possess political power much greater than their numbers, both locally and statewide. Quite understandably, they devote this political power to achieving not merely a grudging social toleration, but full social acceptance, of homosexuality.

By the time Coloradans were asked to vote on Amendment 2, their exposure to homosexuals' quest for social endorsement was not limited to newspaper accounts of happenings in places such as New York, Los Angeles, San Francisco, and Key West. Three Colorado cities—Aspen, Boulder, and Denver—had enacted ordinances that listed "sexual orientation" as an impermissible ground for discrimination, equating the moral disapproval of homosexual conduct with racial and religious bigotry. The phenomenon had even appeared statewide: the Governor of Colorado had signed an executive order pronouncing that "in the State of Colorado we recognize the diversity in our pluralistic society and strive to bring an end to discrimination in any form," and directing state agency-heads to "ensure nondiscrimination" in hiring and promotion based on, among other things, "sexual orientation." I do not mean to be critical of these legislative successes; homosexuals are as entitled to use the legal system for reinforcement of their moral sentiments as are the rest of society. But they are subject to being countered by lawful, democratic countermeasures as well.

That is where Amendment 2 came in. It sought to counter both the geographic concentration and the disproportionate political power of homosexuals by (1) resolving the controversy at the statewide level, and (2) making the election a single-issue contest for both sides. It put directly, to all the citizens of the State, the question: Should homosexuality be given special protection? They answered no. The Court today asserts that this most democratic of procedures is unconstitutional. Lacking any cases to establish that facially absurd proposition, it simply asserts that it must be unconstitutional, because it has never happened before. . . .

What the Court says is even demonstrably false at the constitutional level. The Eighteenth Amendment to the Federal Constitution, for example, deprived those who drank alcohol not only of the power to alter the policy of prohibition locally or through state legislation, but even of the power to alter it through state constitutional amendment or federal legislation. The Establishment Clause of the First Amendment prevents theocrats from having their way by converting their fellow citizens at the local, state, or federal statutory level; as does the Republican Form of Government Clause prevent monarchists.

But there is a much closer analogy, one that involves precisely the effort by the majority of citizens to preserve its view of sexual morality statewide, against the efforts of a geographically concentrated and politically powerful minority to undermine it. The constitutions of the States of Arizona, Idaho, New Mexico, Oklahoma, and Utah to this day contain provisions stating that polygamy is "forever prohibited." Polygamists, and those who have a polygamous "orientation," have been "singled out" by these provisions for much more severe treatment than merely denial of favored status; and that treatment can only be changed by achieving amendment of the state constitutions. The Court's disposition today suggests that these provisions are unconstitutional, and that polygamy must be permitted in these States on a state-legislated, or perhaps even local-option, basis—unless, of course, polygamists for some reason have fewer constitutional rights than homosexuals.

The United States Congress, by the way, required the inclusion of these antipolygamy provisions in the constitutions of Arizona, New Mexico, Oklahoma, and Utah, as a condition of their admission to statehood. Thus, this "singling out" of the sexual practices of a single group for statewide, democratic vote—so utterly alien to our constitutional system, the Court would have us believe—has not only happened, but has received the explicit approval of the United States Congress.

I cannot say that this Court has explicitly approved any of these state constitutional provisions; but it has approved a territorial statutory provision that went even further, depriving polygamists of the ability even to achieve a constitutional amendment, by depriving them of the power to vote. *Davis v. Beason*, 133 U.S. 333 (1890). To the extent, if any, that this opinion permits the imposition of adverse consequences upon mere abstract advocacy of polygamy, it has of course been overruled by later cases. See *Brandenburg v. Ohio*, 395 U.S. 444 (1969) (*per curiam*). But the proposition that polygamy can be criminalized, and those engaging in that crime deprived of the vote, remains good law. *Beason* rejected the argument that "such discrimination is a denial of the equal protection of the laws." . . .

This Court cited *Beason* with approval as recently as 1993, in an opinion authored by the same Justice who writes for the Court today. That opinion said: "Adverse impact will not always lead to a finding of impermissible targeting. For example, a social harm may have been a legitimate concern of government for reasons quite apart from discrimination. . . . See, e.g., . . . *Davis v. Beason*, 133 U.S. 333 (1890)." *Church of Lukumi Babalu Aye, Inc. v. Hialeah*, 508 U.S. 520 (1993). It remains to be explained how Section 501 of the Idaho Revised Statutes was not an "impermissible targeting" of polygamists, but (the much more mild) Amendment 2 is an "impermissible targeting" of homosexuals. Has the Court concluded that the perceived social harm of polygamy is a "legitimate concern of government," and the perceived social harm of homosexuality is not?

I strongly suspect that the answer to the last question is yes, which leads me to the last point I wish to make: The Court today, announcing that Amendment 2 "defies . . . conventional [constitutional] inquiry," and "confounds [the] normal process of judicial review," employs a constitutional theory heretofore unknown to frustrate Colorado's reasonable effort to preserve traditional American moral values. The Court's stern disapproval of "animosity" towards homosexuality might be compared with what an earlier Court (including the revered Justices HARLAN and BRADLEY) said in *Murphy v. Ramsey*, 114 U.S. 15 (1885), rejecting a constitutional challenge to a United States statute that denied the franchise in federal territories to those who engaged in polygamous cohabitation:

> Certainly no legislation can be supposed more wholesome and necessary in the founding of a free, self-governing common-

wealth, fit to take rank as one of the coordinate States of the Union, than that which seeks to establish it on the basis of the idea of the family, as consisting in and springing from the union for life of one man and one woman in the holy estate of matrimony; the sure foundation of all that is stable and noble in our civilization; the best guaranty of that reverent morality which is the source of all beneficent progress in social and political improvement.

I would not myself indulge in such official praise for heterosexual monogamy, because I think it no business of the courts (as opposed to the political branches) to take sides in this culture war.

But the Court today has done so, not only by inventing a novel and extravagant constitutional doctrine to take the victory away from traditional forces, but even by verbally disparaging as bigotry adherence to traditional attitudes. To suggest, for example, that this constitutional amendment springs from nothing more than "a bare . . . desire to harm a politically unpopular group," is nothing short of insulting. (It is also nothing short of preposterous to call "politically unpopular" a group which enjoys enormous influence in American media and politics, and which, as the trial court here noted, though composing no more than 4% of the population had the support of 46% of the voters on Amendment 2.)

When the Court takes sides in the culture wars, it tends to be with the knights rather than the villains—and more specifically with the Templars, reflecting the views and values of the lawyer class from which the Court's Members are drawn. How that class feels about homosexuality will be evident to anyone who wishes to interview job applicants at virtually any of the Nation's law schools. The interviewer may refuse to offer a job because the applicant is a Republican; because he is an adulterer; because he went to the wrong prep school or belongs to the wrong country club; because he eats snails; because he is a womanizer; because she wears real-animal fur; or even because he hates the Chicago Cubs. But if the interviewer should wish not to be an associate or partner of an applicant because he disapproves of the applicant's homosexuality, then he will have violated the pledge which the Association of American Law Schools requires all its member-schools to exact from job interviewers: "assurance of the employer's willingness" to hire homosexuals. This law-school view of what "prejudices" must be stamped out may be contrasted with the more plebeian attitudes that apparently still prevail in the United States Congress, which has been unresponsive to repeated attempts to extend to homosexuals the protections of federal civil rights laws, and which took the pains to exclude them specifically from the Americans with Disabilities Act of 1990.

Today's opinion has no foundation in American constitutional law, and barely pretends to. The people of Colorado have adopted an entirely reasonable provision which does not even disfavor homosexuals in any substantive sense, but merely denies them preferential treatment. Amendment 2 is designed to prevent piecemeal deterioration of the sexual morality favored by a majority of Coloradans, and is not only an appropriate means to that legitimate end, but a means that Americans have employed before. Striking it down is an act, not of judicial judgment, but of political will. I dissent.

Lawrence v. Texas (reprise)

539 U.S. 558, 123 S.CT. 2472 (2003)

In this case the Court struck down Texas's law criminalizing homosexual sodomy; the case is excerpted in Chapter 11.

■ ■ ■

Obergefell v. Hodges

135 S.CT. 2584 (2015)

The movement for recognition of same-sex marriage steadily grew during the last two decades, particularly after the Massachusetts Supreme Court upheld same-sex marriages in 2003. Subsequently, other state high courts did the same, as did a few state legislatures. However, some thirty-six states enacted legislation or adopted state constitutional amendments forbidding same-sex marriages. By 2012, ten states, either through court or legislative action, recognized same-sex marriages. During the following year another eight state bans were overturned. Then, following the Court's ruling in *United States v. Windsor*, 570 U.S. 744 (2013), striking down a provision of the Defense of Marriage Act of 1996 that had excluded same-sex couples from federal recognition and benefits, both state and federal courts increasingly invalidated state prohibitions, bringing the number to thirty-six states permitting same-sex marriages. Federal appellate courts had all struck down state bans until the Court of Appeals for the Sixth Circuit upheld state constitutional bans in Michigan, Kentucky, Ohio, and Tennessee. Writing for that appellate court, Judge Jeffrey Sutton emphasized that there was a national debate taking place over same-sex marriage and the resolution should come from the political process, not the federal courts. In so holding, the Sixth Circuit created an intercircuit conflict, making it likely that the Supreme Court would grant review.

Three appeals of the Sixth Circuit's decision were later consolidated by the Supreme Court. The lead petitioner in the Ohio case, James Obergefell, had fallen in love and started a life with John Arthur two decades earlier. In 2011, Arthur was diagnosed with amyotrophic lateral sclerosis (ALS), a progressive and incurable disease. Obergefell and Arthur decided to marry before Arthur died, and the couple traveled to Maryland, where same-sex marriages were legal, to do so. After Arthur died three months later, Obergefell discovered that Ohio would not list him as the surviving spouse on Arthur's death certificate. He then challenged Ohio's law in court. The second case was brought by a Michigan couple, both nurses, April DeBoer and Jayne Rowse, who had a commitment ceremony in 2007. In 2009, they fostered and then adopted a baby boy, later that year adopted another son, and the following year adopted a girl with special needs. Michigan, however, permitted only opposite-sex married couples or single individuals to adopt, and the state only allowed one woman as the legal guardian. DeBoer and Rowse sued because of the continuing uncertainty about their marital status. The third case came from Tennessee, brought by an army reserve sergeant, Ijpe DeKoe, and his partner, Thomas Kostura. DeKoe was deployed to Afghanistan in 2011, and the couple was married in New York just before he left. When he returned, the two settled in Tennessee, but their marriage was not recognized in that state.

When the Court granted review of the appellate court's decision, the justices reformulated the questions presented and to be briefed and orally argued. First, does the Fourteenth Amendment require states to issue marriage licenses to same-sex couples? Second, does the Amendment require states to recognize same-sex marriages licensed in another state?

By a 5–4 vote, the appellate court's decision was reversed. Justice Kennedy delivered the opinion of the Court. Chief Justice Roberts and Justices Scalia, Thomas, and Alito each filed dissenting opinions.

■ ■ ■

□ *Justice KENNEDY delivered the opinion of the Court.*

The Constitution promises liberty to all within its reach, a liberty that includes certain specific rights that allow persons, within a lawful realm, to define and express their identity. The petitioners in these cases seek to find that liberty by marrying someone of the same sex and having their marriages deemed lawful on the same terms and conditions as marriages between persons of the opposite sex. . . .

From their beginning to their most recent page, the annals of human history reveal the transcendent importance of marriage. The lifelong union of a man and a woman always has promised nobility and dignity to all persons, without regard to their station in life. Marriage is sacred to those who live by their religions and offers unique fulfillment to those who find meaning in the secular realm. Its dynamic allows two people to find a life that could not be found alone, for a marriage becomes greater than just the two persons. Rising from the most basic human needs, marriage is essential to our most profound hopes and aspirations.

The centrality of marriage to the human condition makes it unsurprising that the institution has existed for millennia and across civilizations. Since the dawn of history, marriage has transformed strangers into relatives, binding families and societies together. . . . There are untold references to the beauty of marriage in religious and philosophical texts spanning time, cultures, and faiths, as well as in art and literature in all their forms. It is fair and necessary to say these references were based on the understanding that marriage is a union between two persons of the opposite sex. . . .

The ancient origins of marriage confirm its centrality, but it has not stood in isolation from developments in law and society. The history of marriage is one of both continuity and change. That institution—even as confined to opposite-sex relations—has evolved over time. For example, marriage was once viewed as an arrangement by the couple's parents based on political, religious, and financial concerns; but by the time of the Nation's founding it was understood to be a voluntary contract between a man and a woman. As the role and status of women changed, the institution further evolved. Under the centuries-old doctrine of coverture, a married man and woman were treated by the State as a single, male-dominated legal entity. See W. Blackstone, *Commentaries on the Laws of England* (1765). As women gained legal, political, and property rights, and as society began to understand that women have their own equal dignity, the law of coverture was abandoned. These and other developments in the institution of marriage over the past centuries were not mere superficial changes. Rather, they worked deep transformations in its structure, affecting aspects of marriage long viewed by many as essential.

These new insights have strengthened, not weakened, the institution of marriage. Indeed, changed understandings of marriage are characteristic of a Nation where new dimensions of freedom become apparent to new generations, often through perspectives that begin in pleas or protests and then are considered in the political sphere and the judicial process.

This dynamic can be seen in the Nation's experiences with the rights of gays and lesbians. Until the mid-20th century, same-sex intimacy long had been condemned as immoral by the state itself in most Western nations, a belief often embodied in the criminal law. For this reason, among others, many persons did not deem homosexuals to have dignity in their own distinct identity. A truthful declaration by same-sex couples of what was in their hearts had to remain unspoken. Even when a greater awareness of the humanity and integrity of homosexual persons came in the period after World War II, the argument that gays and lesbians had a just claim to dignity was in conflict with both law and widespread social conventions. Same-sex intimacy remained a crime in many States. Gays and lesbians were prohibited from most government employment, barred from military service, excluded under immigration laws, targeted by police, and burdened in their rights to associate.

For much of the 20th century, moreover, homosexuality was treated as an illness. When the American Psychiatric Association published the first [manual] in 1952, homosexuality was classified as a mental disorder, a position adhered to until 1973. Only in more recent years have psychiatrists and others recognized that sexual orientation is both a normal expression of human sexuality and immutable.

In the late 20th century, following substantial cultural and political developments, same-sex couples began to lead more open and public lives and to establish families. This development was followed by a quite extensive discussion of the issue in both governmental and private sectors and by a shift in public attitudes toward greater tolerance. As a result, questions about the rights of gays and lesbians soon reached the courts, where the issue could be discussed in the formal discourse of the law.

This Court first gave detailed consideration to the legal status of homosexuals in *Bowers v. Hardwick*, 478 U.S. 186 (1986). There it upheld the constitutionality of a Georgia law deemed to criminalize certain homosexual acts. Ten years later, in *Romer v. Evans*, 517 U.S. 620 (1996), the Court invalidated an amendment to Colorado's Constitution that sought to foreclose any branch or political subdivision of the State from protecting persons against discrimination based on sexual orientation. Then, in 2003, the Court overruled *Bowers*, holding that laws making same-sex intimacy a crime "demea[n] the lives of homosexual persons." *Lawrence v. Texas*, 539 U.S. 558 [(2003)].

Against this background, the legal question of same-sex marriage arose. In 1993, the Hawaii Supreme Court held Hawaii's law restricting marriage to opposite-sex couples constituted a classification on the basis of sex and was therefore subject to strict scrutiny under the Hawaii Constitution. Although this decision did not mandate that same-sex marriage be allowed, some States were concerned by its implications and reaffirmed in their laws that marriage is defined as a union between opposite-sex partners. So too in 1996, Congress passed the Defense of Marriage Act (DOMA), defining marriage for all federal-law purposes as "only a legal union between one man and one woman as husband and wife."

The new and widespread discussion of the subject led other States to a different conclusion. In 2003, the Supreme Judicial Court of Massachusetts held the State's Constitution guaranteed same-sex couples the right to marry. See *Goodridge v. Department of Public Health*, 440 Mass. 309 (2003). After that ruling, some additional States granted marriage rights to same-sex couples, either through judicial or legislative processes. Two Terms ago, in *United States v. Windsor*, [133 S.Ct. 2675](2013), this Court invalidated DOMA to the extent it barred the Federal Government from treating same-sex marriages as valid even when they were lawful in the State where they were licensed. DOMA, the Court held, impermissibly disparaged those same-sex couples "who wanted to affirm their commitment to one another before their children, their family, their friends, and their community."

Numerous cases about same-sex marriage have reached the United States Courts of Appeals in recent years. In accordance with the judicial duty to base their decisions on principled reasons and neutral discussions, without scornful or disparaging commentary, courts have written a substantial body of law considering all sides of these issues. That case law helps to explain and formulate the underlying principles this Court now must consider. With the exception of the opinion here under review and one other, the Courts of Appeals have held that excluding same-sex couples from marriage violates the Constitution. . . . In addition the highest courts of many States have contributed to this ongoing dialogue in decisions interpreting their own State Constitutions. . . .

Under the Due Process Clause of the Fourteenth Amendment, no State shall "deprive any person of life, liberty, or property, without due process of law." The fundamental liberties protected by this Clause include most of the rights enumerated in the Bill of Rights. In addition these liberties extend to certain personal choices central to individual dignity and autonomy, including intimate choices that define personal identity and beliefs. See, e.g., *Griswold v. Connecticut*, 381 U.S. 479 (1965).

The identification and protection of fundamental rights is an enduring part of the judicial duty to interpret the Constitution. That responsibility, however, "has not been reduced to any formula." *Poe v. Ullman*, 367 U.S. 497 (1961) (HARLAN, J., dissenting). Rather, it requires courts to exercise reasoned judgment in identifying interests of the person so fundamental that the State must accord them its respect. That process is guided by many of the same considerations relevant to analysis of other constitutional provisions that set forth broad principles rather than specific requirements. History and tradition guide and discipline this inquiry but do not set its outer boundaries. That method respects our history and learns from it without allowing the past alone to rule the present.

The nature of injustice is that we may not always see it in our own times. The generations that wrote and ratified the Bill of Rights and the Fourteenth Amendment did not presume to know the extent of freedom in all of its dimensions, and so they entrusted to future generations a charter protecting the right of all persons to enjoy liberty as we learn its meaning. When new insight reveals discord between the Constitution's central protections and a received legal stricture, a claim to liberty must be addressed.

Applying these established tenets, the Court has long held the right to marry is protected by the Constitution. In *Loving v. Virginia*, 388 U.S. 1 (1967), which invalidated bans on interracial unions, a unanimous Court held marriage is "one of the vital personal rights essential to the orderly pursuit of happiness by free men." The Court reaffirmed that holding in *Zablocki v. Redhail*, 434 U.S. 374 (1978), which held the right to marry was burdened by a law prohibiting fathers who were behind on child support from marrying. The Court again applied this principle in *Turner v. Safley*, 482 U.S. 78 (1987), which held the right to marry was abridged by regulations limiting the privilege of prison inmates to marry. Over time and in other contexts, the Court has reiterated that the right to marry is fundamental under the Due Process Clause.

It cannot be denied that this Court's cases describing the right to marry presumed a relationship involving opposite-sex partners. The Court, like many institutions, has made assumptions defined by the world and time of which it is a part. This was evident in *Baker v. Nelson*, 409 U.S. 810 [(1972)] a one-line summary decision issued in 1972, holding the exclusion of same-sex couples from marriage did not present a substantial federal question. . . . And in assessing whether the force and rationale of its cases apply to same-sex couples, the Court must respect the basic reasons why the right to marry has been long protected.

This analysis compels the conclusion that same-sex couples may exercise the right to marry. The four principles and traditions to be discussed demonstrate that the reasons marriage is fundamental under the Constitution apply with equal force to same-sex couples.

A first premise of the Court's relevant precedents is that the right to personal choice regarding marriage is inherent in the concept of individual autonomy. This abiding connection between marriage and liberty is why *Loving* invalidated interracial marriage bans under the Due Process Clause. Like choices concerning contraception, family relationships, procreation, and childrearing, all of which are protected by the Constitution, decisions concerning marriage are among the most intimate that an individual can make. . . .

A second principle in this Court's jurisprudence is that the right to marry is fundamental because it supports a two-person union unlike any other in its importance to the committed individuals. This point was central to *Griswold v. Connecticut* . . . .

As this Court held in *Lawrence*, same-sex couples have the same right as opposite-sex couples to enjoy intimate association. *Lawrence* invalidated laws that made same-sex intimacy a criminal act. And it acknowledged that "[w]hen sexuality finds overt expression in intimate conduct with another person, the conduct can be but one element in a personal bond that is more enduring." But while *Lawrence* confirmed a dimension of freedom that allows individuals to engage in intimate association without criminal liability, it does not follow that freedom stops there. Outlaw to outcast may be a step forward, but it does not achieve the full promise of liberty.

A third basis for protecting the right to marry is that it safeguards children and families and thus draws meaning from related rights of childrearing, procreation, and education. The Court has recognized these connections by describing the varied rights as a unified whole: "[T]he right to 'marry, establish a home and bring up children' is a central part of the liberty protected by the Due Process Clause." *Zablocki.* Under the laws of the several States, some of marriage's protections for children and families are material. But marriage also confers more profound benefits. By giving recognition and legal structure to their parents' relationship, marriage allows children "to understand the integrity and closeness of their own family and its concord with other families in their community and in their daily lives." *Windsor.* Marriage also affords the permanency and stability important to children's best interests.

As all parties agree, many same-sex couples provide loving and nurturing homes to their children, whether biological or adopted. And hundreds of thousands of children are presently being raised by such couples. Most States have allowed gays and lesbians to adopt, either as individuals or as couples, and many adopted and foster children have same-sex parents. This provides powerful confirmation from the law itself that gays and lesbians can create loving, supportive families.

Excluding same-sex couples from marriage thus conflicts with a central premise of the right to marry. Without the recognition, stability, and predictability marriage offers, their children suffer the stigma of knowing their families are somehow lesser. They also suffer the significant material costs of being raised by unmarried parents, relegated through no fault of their own to a more difficult and uncertain family life. The marriage laws at issue here thus harm and humiliate the children of same-sex couples. . . .

Fourth and finally, this Court's cases and the Nation's traditions make clear that marriage is a keystone of our social order. . . . The limitation of marriage to opposite-sex couples may long have seemed natural and just, but its inconsistency with the central meaning of the fundamental right to marry is now manifest. With that knowledge must come the recognition that laws excluding same-sex couples from the marriage right impose stigma and injury of the kind prohibited by our basic charter.

Objecting that this does not reflect an appropriate framing of the issue, the respondents refer to *Washington v. Glucksberg*, 521 U.S. 702 (1997), which called for a " 'careful description' " of fundamental rights. They assert the petitioners do not seek to exercise the right to marry but rather a new and nonexistent "right to same-sex marriage." *Glucksberg* did insist that liberty under the Due Process Clause must be defined in a most circumscribed manner, with central reference to specific historical practices. Yet while that approach may have been appropriate for the asserted right there involved (physician-assisted suicide), it is inconsistent with the approach this Court has used in discussing other fundamental rights, including marriage and intimacy. *Loving* did not ask about a "right to interracial marriage" . . . . If rights were defined by who exercised them in the past, then received practices could serve as their own continued justification and new groups could not invoke rights once denied. This Court has rejected that approach, both with respect to the right to marry and the rights of gays and lesbians.

The right to marry is fundamental as a matter of history and tradition, but rights come not from ancient sources alone. They rise, too, from a better informed understanding of how constitutional imperatives define a liberty that remains urgent in our own era. Many who deem same-sex marriage to be wrong reach that conclusion based on decent and honorable religious or philosophical premises, and neither they nor their beliefs are disparaged here. But when that sincere, personal opposition becomes enacted law and public policy, the necessary consequence is to put the imprimatur of the State itself on an exclusion that soon demeans or stigmatizes those whose own liberty is then denied. Under the Constitution, same-sex couples seek in marriage the same legal treatment as opposite-sex couples, and it would disparage their choices and diminish their personhood to deny them this right.

The right of same-sex couples to marry that is part of the liberty promised by the Fourteenth Amendment is derived, too, from that Amendment's guarantee of the equal protection of the laws. The Due Process Clause and the Equal Protection Clause are connected in a profound way, though they set forth independent principles. Rights implicit in liberty and rights secured by equal protection may rest on different precepts and are not always co-extensive, yet in some instances each may be instructive as to the meaning and reach of the other. In any particular case one Clause may be thought to capture the essence of the right in a more accurate and comprehensive way, even as the two Clauses may converge in the identification and definition of the right. This interrelation of the two principles furthers our understanding of what freedom is and must become.

The Court's cases touching upon the right to marry reflect this dynamic. In *Loving* the Court invalidated a prohibition on interracial marriage under both the Equal Protection Clause and the Due Process Clause. The Court first declared the prohibition invalid because of its unequal treatment of interracial couples. It stated: "There can be no doubt that restricting the freedom to marry solely because of racial classifications violates the central meaning of the Equal Protection Clause." With this link to equal protection the Court proceeded to hold the prohibition offended central precepts of liberty: "To deny this fundamental freedom on so unsupportable a basis as the racial classifications embodied in these statutes, classifications so directly subversive of the principle of equality at the heart of the Fourteenth Amendment, is surely to deprive all the State's citizens of liberty without due process of law." . . .

In *Lawrence* the Court acknowledged the interlocking nature of these constitutional safeguards in the context of the legal treatment of gays and lesbians. Although *Lawrence* elaborated its holding under the Due Process Clause, it acknowledged, and sought to remedy, the continuing inequality that resulted from laws making intimacy in the lives of gays and lesbians a crime against the State. *Lawrence* therefore drew upon principles of liberty and equality to define and protect the rights of gays and lesbians, holding the State "cannot demean their existence or control their destiny by making their private sexual conduct a crime."

This dynamic also applies to same-sex marriage. It is now clear that the challenged laws burden the liberty of same-sex couples, and it must be further acknowledged that they abridge central precepts of equality. Here the marriage laws enforced by the respondents are in essence unequal: same-sex couples are denied all the benefits afforded to opposite-sex couples and are barred from exercising a fundamental right. Especially against a long history of disapproval of their relationships, this denial to same-sex couples of the right to marry works a grave and continuing harm. The imposition of this disability on gays and lesbians serves to disrespect and subordinate them. And the Equal Protection Clause, like the Due Process Clause, prohibits this unjustified infringement of the fundamental right to marry.

These considerations lead to the conclusion that the right to marry is a fundamental right inherent in the liberty of the person, and under the Due Process and Equal Protection Clauses of the Fourteenth Amendment couples of the same-sex may not be deprived of that right and that liberty. The Court now holds that same-sex couples may exercise the fundamental right to marry. No longer may this liberty be denied to them. *Baker v. Nelson* must be and now is overruled, and the State laws challenged by Petitioners in these cases are now held invalid to the extent they exclude same-sex couples from civil marriage on the same terms and conditions as opposite-sex couples.

There may be an initial inclination in these cases to proceed with caution—to await further legislation, litigation, and debate. The respondents warn there has been insufficient democratic discourse before deciding an issue so basic as the definition of marriage. In its ruling on the cases now before this Court, the majority opinion for the Court of Appeals made a cogent argument that it would be appropriate for the respondents' States to await further public discussion and political measures before licensing same-sex marriages.

Yet there has been far more deliberation than this argument acknowledges. There have been referenda, legislative debates, and grassroots campaigns, as well as countless studies, papers, books, and other popular and scholarly writings. There has been extensive litigation in state and federal courts. Judicial opinions addressing the issue have been informed by the contentions of parties and counsel, which, in turn, reflect the more general, societal discussion of same-sex marriage and its meaning that has occurred over the past decades. As more than 100 amici make clear in their filings, many of the central institutions in American life—state and local governments, the military, large and small businesses, labor unions, religious organizations, law enforcement, civic groups, professional organizations, and universities—have devoted substantial attention to the question. This has led to an enhanced understanding of the issue—an understanding reflected in the arguments now presented for resolution as a matter of constitutional law.

Of course, the Constitution contemplates that democracy is the appropriate process for change, so long as that process does not abridge fundamental rights. . . .

The dynamic of our constitutional system is that individuals need not await legislative action before asserting a fundamental right. The Nation's courts are open to injured individuals who come to them to vindicate their own direct, personal stake in our basic charter. An individual can invoke a right to constitutional protection when he or she is harmed, even if the broader public disagrees and even if the legislature refuses to act. The idea of the Constitution "was to withdraw certain subjects from the vicissitudes of political controversy, to place them beyond the reach of majorities and officials and to establish them as legal principles to be applied by the courts." *West Virginia Bd. of Ed. v. Barnette*, 319 U.S. 624 (1943). This is why "fundamental rights may not be submitted to a vote; they depend on the outcome of no elections." . . .

Although *Bowers* was eventually repudiated in *Lawrence*, men and women were harmed in the interim, and the substantial effects of these injuries no doubt lingered long after *Bowers* was overruled. Dignitary wounds cannot always be healed with the stroke of a pen. . . . A ruling against same-sex couples would have the same effect—and, like *Bowers*, would be unjustified under the Fourteenth Amendment. . . .

Indeed, faced with a disagreement among the Courts of Appeals—a disagreement that caused impermissible geographic variation in the meaning of federal law—the Court granted review to determine whether same-sex couples may exercise the right to marry. Were the Court to uphold the challenged laws as constitutional, it would teach the Nation that these laws are in accord with our society's most basic compact. Were the Court to stay its hand to allow slower, case-by-case determination of the required availability of specific public benefits to same-sex couples, it still would deny gays and lesbians many rights and responsibilities intertwined with marriage.

The respondents also argue allowing same-sex couples to wed will harm marriage as an institution by leading to fewer opposite-sex marriages. This may occur, the respondents contend, because licensing same-sex marriage severs the connection between natural procreation and marriage. That argument, however, rests on a counterintuitive view of opposite-sex couple's decisionmaking processes regarding marriage and parenthood. Decisions about whether to marry and raise children are based on many personal, romantic, and practical considerations; and it is unrealistic to conclude that an opposite-sex couple would choose not to marry simply because same-sex couples may do so. . . .

Finally, it must be emphasized that religions, and those who adhere to religious doctrines, may continue to advocate with utmost, sincere conviction that, by divine precepts, same-sex marriage should not be condoned. The First Amendment ensures that religious organizations and persons are given proper protection as they seek to teach the principles that are so fulfilling and so central to their lives and faiths, and to their own deep aspirations to continue the family structure they have long revered. The same is true of those who oppose same-sex marriage for other reasons. In turn, those who believe allowing same-sex marriage is proper or indeed essential, whether as a matter of religious conviction or secular belief, may engage those who disagree with their view in an open and searching debate. The Constitution, however, does not permit the State to bar same-sex couples from marriage on the same terms as accorded to couples of the opposite sex.

These cases also present the question whether the Constitution requires States to recognize same-sex marriages validly performed out of State. . . .

Being married in one State but having that valid marriage denied in another is one of "the most perplexing and distressing complication[s]" in the law of domestic relations. *Williams v. North Carolina*, 317 U.S. 287 (1942). Leaving the current state of affairs in place would maintain and promote instability and uncertainty. In light of the fact that many States already allow same-sex marriage—and hundreds of thousands of these marriages already have occurred—the disruption caused by the recognition bans is significant and ever-growing. . . .

No union is more profound than marriage, for it embodies the highest ideals of love, fidelity, devotion, sacrifice, and family. In forming a marital union, two people become something greater than once they were. . . . It would misunderstand these men and women to say they disrespect the idea of marriage. Their plea is that they do respect it, respect it so deeply that they seek to find its fulfillment for themselves. Their hope is not to be condemned to live in loneliness, excluded from one of civilization's oldest institutions. They ask for equal dignity in the eyes of the law. The Constitution grants them that right.

The judgment of the Court of Appeals for the Sixth Circuit is reversed.

☐ *Chief Justice ROBERTS, with whom Justice SCALIA and Justice THOMAS join, dissenting.*

Petitioners . . . contend that same-sex couples should be allowed to affirm their love and commitment through marriage, just like opposite-sex couples. That position has undeniable appeal; over the past six years, voters and legislators in eleven States and the District of Columbia have revised their laws to allow marriage between two people of the same sex.

But this Court is not a legislature. Whether same-sex marriage is a good idea should be of no concern to us. Under the Constitution, judges have power to say what the law is, not what it should be. The people who ratified the Constitution authorized courts to exercise "neither force nor will but merely judgment." *The Federalist* No. 78.

Although the policy arguments for extending marriage to same-sex couples may be compelling, the legal arguments for requiring such an extension are not. The fundamental right to marry does not include a right to make a State change its definition of marriage. And a State's decision to maintain the meaning of marriage that has persisted in every culture throughout human history can hardly be called irrational. In short, our Constitution does not enact any one theory of marriage. The people of a State are free to expand marriage to include same-sex couples, or to retain the historic definition. . . .

The majority's decision is an act of will, not legal judgment. The right it announces has no basis in the Constitution or this Court's precedent. . . . As a result, the Court invalidates the marriage laws of more than half the States and orders the transformation of a social institution that has formed the basis of human society for millennia, for the Kalahari Bushmen and the Han Chinese, the Carthaginians and the Aztecs. Just who do we think we are?

It can be tempting for judges to confuse our own preferences with the requirements of the law. But as this Court has been reminded throughout our history, the Constitution "is made for people of fundamentally differing views." *Lochner v. New York*, 198 U.S. 45 (1905) (HOLMES, J., dissenting). Accordingly, "courts are not concerned with the wisdom or policy of legislation." (HARLAN, J., dissenting). The majority today neglects that restrained conception of the judicial role. It seizes for itself a question the Constitution leaves to the people, at a time when the people are engaged in a vibrant debate on that question. And it answers that question based not on neutral principles of constitutional law, but on its own "understanding of what freedom is and must become." I have no choice but to dissent.

Understand well what this dissent is about: It is not about whether, in my judgment, the institution of marriage should be changed to include same-sex couples. It is instead about whether, in our democratic republic, that decision should rest with the people acting through their elected representatives, or with five lawyers who happen to hold commissions authorizing them to resolve legal disputes according to law. The Constitution leaves no doubt about the answer. . . .

There is no serious dispute that, under our precedents, the Constitution protects a right to marry and requires States to apply their marriage laws equally. The real question in these cases is what constitutes "marriage," or—more precisely—who decides what constitutes "marriage"?

The majority largely ignores these questions, relegating ages of human experience with marriage to a paragraph or two. Even if history and precedent are not "the end" of these cases, I would not "sweep away what has so long been settled" without showing greater respect for all that preceded us. . . .

[The] universal definition of marriage as the union of a man and a woman is no historical coincidence. Marriage did not come about as a result of a political movement, discovery, disease, war, religious doctrine, or any other moving force of world history—and certainly not as a result of a prehistoric decision to exclude gays and lesbians. It arose in the nature of things to meet a vital need: ensuring that children are conceived by a mother and father committed to raising them in the stable conditions of a lifelong relationship.

The premises supporting this concept of marriage are so fundamental that they rarely require articulation. The human race must procreate to survive. Procreation occurs through sexual relations between a man and a woman. When sexual relations result in the conception of a child, that child's prospects are generally better if the mother and father stay together rather than going their separate ways. Therefore, for the good of children and society, sexual relations that can lead to procreation should occur only between a man and a woman committed to a lasting bond. . . .

The Constitution itself says nothing about marriage, and the Framers thereby entrusted the States with "[t]he whole subject of the domestic relations of husband and wife." *Windsor.* There is no dispute that every State at the founding—and every State throughout our history until a dozen years ago—defined marriage in the traditional, biologically rooted way. The four States in these cases are typical. Their laws, before and after statehood, have treated marriage as the union of a man and a woman. Even when state laws did not specify this definition expressly, no one doubted what they meant. The meaning of "marriage" went without saying. . . .

As the majority notes, some aspects of marriage have changed over time. Arranged marriages have largely given way to pairings based on romantic love. States have replaced coverture, the doctrine by which a married man and woman became a single legal entity, with laws that respect each participant's separate status. Racial restrictions on marriage, which "arose as an incident to slavery" to promote "White Supremacy," were repealed by many States and ultimately struck down by this Court. *Loving* [388 U.S. 1 (1967)].

The majority observes that these developments "were not mere superficial changes" in marriage, but rather "worked deep transformations in its structure." They did not, however, work any transformation in the core structure of marriage as the union between a man and a woman. If you had asked a person on the street how marriage was defined, no one would ever have said, "Marriage is the union of a man and a woman, where the woman is subject to coverture." The majority may be right that the "history of marriage is one of both continuity and change," but the core meaning of marriage has endured.

Shortly after this Court struck down racial restrictions on marriage in *Loving*, a gay couple in Minnesota sought a marriage license. They argued that the Constitution required States to allow marriage between people of the same sex for the same reasons that it requires States to allow marriage between people of different races. The Minnesota Supreme Court rejected their analogy to *Loving*, and this Court summarily dismissed an appeal. *Baker v. Nelson*, 409 U.S. 810 (1972). . . .

Over the last few years, public opinion on marriage has shifted rapidly. In 2009, the legislatures of Vermont, New Hampshire, and the District of Columbia became the first in the Nation to enact laws that revised the definition of marriage to include same-sex couples, while also providing accommodations for religious believers. In 2011, the New York Legislature enacted a similar law. In 2012, voters in Maine did the same, reversing the result of a referendum just three years earlier in which they had upheld the traditional definition of marriage.

In all, voters and legislators in eleven States and the District of Columbia have changed their definitions of marriage to include same-sex couples. The highest courts of five States have decreed that same result under their own Constitutions. The remainder of the States retain the traditional definition of marriage. . . .

The majority purports to identify four "principles and traditions" in this Court's due process precedents that support a fundamental right for same-sex couples to marry. In reality, however, the majority's approach has no basis in principle or tradition, except for the unprincipled tradition of judicial policymaking that characterized discredited decisions such as *Lochner v. New York.* Stripped of its shiny rhetorical gloss, the majority's argument is that the Due Process Clause gives same-sex couples a fundamental right to marry because it will be good for them and for society. If I were a legislator, I would certainly consider that view as a matter of social policy. But as a judge, I find the majority's position indefensible as a matter of constitutional law. . . .

Allowing unelected federal judges to select which unenumerated rights rank as "fundamental"—and to strike down state laws on the basis of that determination—raises obvious concerns about the judicial role. Our precedents have accordingly insisted that judges "exercise the utmost care" in identifying implied fundamental rights, "lest the liberty protected by the Due Process Clause be subtly transformed into the policy preferences of the Members of this Court." *Washington v. Glucksberg*, 521 U.S. 702 (1997).

The need for restraint in administering the strong medicine of substantive due process is a lesson this Court has learned the hard way. The Court first applied substantive due process to strike down a statute in *Dred Scott v. Stanford*, 19 How. 393 (1857). . . . In a dissent that has outlasted the majority opinion, Justice CURTIS explained that when the "fixed rules which govern the interpretation of laws [are] abandoned, and the theoretical opinions of individuals are allowed to control" the Constitution's meaning, "we have no longer a Constitution; we are under the government of individual men, who for the time being have power to declare what the Constitution is, according to their own views of what it ought to mean."

Dred Scott's holding was overruled on the battlefields of the Civil War and by constitutional amendment after Appomattox, but its approach to the Due Process Clause reappeared. In a series of early 20th-century cases, most prominently *Lochner v. New York*, this Court invalidated state statutes that presented "meddlesome interferences with the rights of the individual," and "undue interference with liberty of person and freedom of contract." In *Lochner* itself, the Court struck down a New York law setting maximum hours for bakery employees, because there was "in our judgment, no reasonable foundation for holding this to be necessary or appropriate as a health law."

The dissenting Justices in *Lochner* explained that the New York law could be viewed as a reasonable response to legislative concern about the health of bakery employees, an issue on which there was at least "room for debate and for an honest difference of opinion." (opinion of HARLAN, J.). The majority's contrary conclusion required adopting as constitutional law "an economic theory which a large part of the country does not entertain." (opinion of HOLMES, J.). As Justice HOLMES memorably put it, "The Fourteenth Amendment does not enact Mr. Herbert Spencer's *Social Statics*," a leading work on the philosophy of Social Darwinism. The Constitution "is not intended to embody a particular economic theory . . . . It is made for people of fundamentally differing views . . . ."

In the decades after *Lochner*, the Court struck down nearly 200 laws as violations of individual liberty . . . . Eventually, the Court recognized its error and vowed not to repeat it. "The doctrine that . . . due process authorizes courts to hold laws unconstitutional when they believe the legislature has acted unwisely," we later explained, "has long since been discarded. We have returned to the original constitutional proposition that courts do not substitute their social and economic beliefs for the judgment of legislative bodies, who are elected to pass laws." *Ferguson v. Skrupa*, 372 U.S. 726 (1963). Thus, it has become an accepted rule that the Court will not hold laws unconstitutional simply because we find them "unwise, improvident, or out of harmony with a particular school of thought." *Williamson v. Lee Optical of Okla., Inc.*, 348 U.S. 483 (1955). . . .

The majority's driving themes are that marriage is desirable and petitioners desire it. The opinion describes the "transcendent importance" of marriage and repeatedly insists that petitioners do not seek to "demean," "devalue," "denigrate," or "disrespect" the institution. Nobody disputes those points. . . . As a matter of constitutional law, however, the sincerity of petitioners' wishes is not relevant. . . .

The majority suggests that "there are other, more instructive precedents" informing the right to marry. Although not entirely clear, this reference seems to correspond to a line of cases discussing an implied fundamental "right of privacy." *Griswold.* . . .

The Court also invoked the right to privacy in *Lawrence v. Texas* (2003), which struck down a Texas statute criminalizing homosexual sodomy. [However, neither] *Lawrence* nor any other precedent in the privacy line of cases supports the right that petitioners assert here. Unlike criminal laws banning contraceptives and sodomy, the marriage laws at issue here involve no government intrusion. They create no crime and impose no punishment. Same-sex couples remain free to live together, to engage in intimate conduct, and to raise their families as they see fit. No one is "condemned to live in loneliness" by the laws challenged in these cases—no one. At the same time, the laws in no way interfere with the "right to be let alone." . . .

In sum, the privacy cases provide no support for the majority's position, because petitioners do not seek privacy. Quite the opposite, they seek public recognition of their relationships, along with corresponding government benefits. Our cases have consistently refused to allow litigants to convert the shield provided by constitutional liberties into a sword to demand positive entitlements from the State. . . .

Near the end of its opinion, the majority offers perhaps the clearest insight into its decision. Expanding marriage to include same-sex couples, the majority insists, would "pose no risk of harm to themselves or third parties. This argument again echoes *Lochner*, which relied on its assessment that "we think that a law like the one before us involves neither the safety, the morals nor the welfare of the public, and that the interest of the public is not in the slightest degree affected by such an act."

Then and now, this assertion of the "harm principle" sounds more in philosophy than law. The elevation of the fullest individual self-realization over the constraints that society has expressed in law may or may not be attractive moral philosophy. But a Justice's commission does not confer any special moral, philosophical, or social insight sufficient to justify imposing those perceptions on fellow citizens under the pretense of "due process." There is indeed a process due the people on issues of this sort—the democratic process. Respecting that understanding requires the Court to be guided by law, not any particular school of social thought. As Judge Henry Friendly once put it, echoing Justice HOLMES's dissent in *Lochner*, the Fourteenth Amendment does not enact John Stuart Mill's *On Liberty* any more than it enacts Herbert Spencer's *Social Statics*. And it certainly does not enact any one concept of marriage.

The majority's understanding of due process lays out a tantalizing vision of the future for Members of this Court: If an unvarying social institution enduring over all of recorded history cannot inhibit judicial policymaking, what can? But this approach is dangerous for the rule of law. . . .

The majority goes on to assert in conclusory fashion that the Equal Protection Clause provides an alternative basis for its holding. Yet the majority fails to provide even a single sentence explaining how the Equal

Protection Clause supplies independent weight for its position, nor does it attempt to justify its gratuitous violation of the canon against unnecessarily resolving constitutional questions. In any event, the marriage laws at issue here do not violate the Equal Protection Clause, because distinguishing between opposite-sex and same-sex couples is rationally related to the States' "legitimate state interest" in "preserving the traditional institution of marriage." *Lawrence* (O'CONNOR, J., concurring in judgment). . . .

The legitimacy of this Court ultimately rests "upon the respect accorded to its judgments." *Republican Party of Minn. v. White*, 536 U.S. 765 (2002) (KENNEDY, J., concurring). That respect flows from the perception—and reality—that we exercise humility and restraint in deciding cases according to the Constitution and law. The role of the Court envisioned by the majority today, however, is anything but humble or restrained. Over and over, the majority exalts the role of the judiciary in delivering social change. In the majority's telling, it is the courts, not the people, who are responsible for making "new dimensions of freedom . . . apparent to new generations," for providing "formal discourse" on social issues, and for ensuring "neutral discussions, without scornful or disparaging commentary."

Nowhere is the majority's extravagant conception of judicial supremacy more evident than in its description—and dismissal—of the public debate regarding same-sex marriage. Yes, the majority concedes, on one side are thousands of years of human history in every society known to have populated the planet. But on the other side, there has been "extensive litigation," "many thoughtful District Court decisions," "countless studies, papers, books, and other popular and scholarly writings," and "more than 100" *amicus* briefs in these cases alone. What would be the point of allowing the democratic process to go on? It is high time for the Court to decide the meaning of marriage, based on five lawyers' "better informed understanding" of "a liberty that remains urgent in our own era." . . .

The Court's accumulation of power does not occur in a vacuum. It comes at the expense of the people. And they know it. Here and abroad, people are in the midst of a serious and thoughtful public debate on the issue of same-sex marriage. They see voters carefully considering same-sex marriage, casting ballots in favor or opposed, and sometimes changing their minds. They see political leaders similarly reexamining their positions, and either reversing course or explaining adherence to old convictions confirmed anew. They see governments and businesses modifying policies and practices with respect to same-sex couples, and participating actively in the civic discourse. They see countries overseas democratically accepting profound social change, or declining to do so. This deliberative process is making people take seriously questions that they may not have even regarded as questions before.

When decisions are reached through democratic means, some people will inevitably be disappointed with the results. But those whose views do not prevail at least know that they have had their say, and accordingly are—in the tradition of our political culture—reconciled to the result of a fair and honest debate. In addition, they can gear up to raise the issue later, hoping to persuade enough on the winning side to think again. "That is exactly how our system of government is supposed to work."

But today the Court puts a stop to all that. By deciding this question under the Constitution, the Court removes it from the realm of democratic decision. There will be consequences to shutting down the political process on an issue of such profound public significance. Closing debate tends to close minds. People denied a voice are less likely to accept the ruling of a court on an issue that does not seem to be the sort of thing courts usually decide. As a thoughtful commentator observed about another issue, "The political process was moving . . . , not swiftly enough for advocates of quick, complete change, but majoritarian institutions were listening and acting. Heavy-handed judicial intervention was difficult to justify and appears to have provoked, not resolved, conflict." [Justice] GINSBURG, "Some Thoughts on Autonomy and Equality in Relation to *Roe v. Wade*," 63 N. C. L. Rev. 375 (1985). Indeed, however heartened the proponents of same-sex marriage might be on this day, it is worth acknowledging what they have lost, and lost forever: the opportunity to win the true acceptance that comes from persuading their fellow citizens of the justice of their cause. And they lose this just when the winds of change were freshening at their backs.

Federal courts are blunt instruments when it comes to creating rights. They have constitutional power only to resolve concrete cases or controversies; they do not have the flexibility of legislatures to address concerns of parties not before the court or to anticipate problems that may arise from the exercise of a new right. Today's decision, for example, creates serious questions about religious liberty. Many good and decent people oppose same-sex marriage as a tenet of faith, and their freedom to exercise religion is—unlike the right imagined by the majority—actually spelled out in the Constitution.

Respect for sincere religious conviction has led voters and legislators in every State that has adopted same-sex marriage democratically to include accommodations for religious practice. The majority's decision imposing same-sex marriage cannot, of course, create any such accommodations. The majority graciously suggests that religious believers may continue to "advocate" and "teach" their views of marriage. The First Amendment guarantees, however, the freedom to "exercise" religion. Ominously, that is not a word the majority uses.

Hard questions arise when people of faith exercise religion in ways that may be seen to conflict with the new right to same-sex marriage—when, for example, a religious college provides married student housing only to opposite-sex married couples, or a religious adoption agency declines to place children with same-sex married couples. Indeed, the Solicitor General candidly acknowledged that the tax exemptions of some religious institutions would be in question if they opposed same-sex marriage. There is little doubt that these and similar questions will soon be before this Court. Unfortunately, people of faith can take no comfort in the treatment they receive from the majority today. . . .

In the face of all this, a much different view of the Court's role is possible. That view is more modest and restrained. It is more skeptical that the legal abilities of judges also reflect insight into moral and philosophical issues. It is more sensitive to the fact that judges are unelected and unaccountable, and that the legitimacy of their power depends on confining it to the exercise of legal judgment. It is more attuned to the lessons of history, and what it has meant for the country and Court when Justices have exceeded their proper bounds. And it is less pretentious than to suppose that while people around the world have viewed an institution in a particular way for thousands of years, the present generation and the present Court are the ones chosen to burst the bonds of that history and tradition.

If you are among the many Americans—of whatever sexual orientation—who favor expanding same-sex marriage, by all means celebrate today's decision. Celebrate the achievement of a desired goal. Celebrate the opportunity for a new expression of commitment to a partner. Celebrate the availability of new benefits. But do not celebrate the Constitution. It had nothing to do with it.

I respectfully dissent.

☐ *Justice SCALIA, with whom Justice THOMAS joins, dissenting.*

The substance of today's decree is not of immense personal importance to me. The law can recognize as marriage whatever sexual attachments and living arrangements it wishes, and can accord them favorable civil consequences, from tax treatment to rights of inheritance. Those civil consequences—and the public approval that conferring the name of marriage evidences—can perhaps have adverse social effects, but no more adverse than the effects of many other controversial laws. So it is not of special importance to me what the law says about marriage. It is of overwhelming importance, however, who it is that rules me. Today's decree says that my Ruler, and the Ruler of 320 million Americans coast-to-coast, is a majority of the nine lawyers on the Supreme Court. . . . This practice of constitutional revision by an unelected committee of nine, always accompanied (as it is today) by extravagant praise of liberty, robs the People of the most important liberty they asserted in the Declaration of Independence and won in the Revolution of 1776: the freedom to govern themselves.

Until the courts put a stop to it, public debate over same-sex marriage displayed American democracy at its best. Individuals on both sides of the issue passionately, but respectfully, attempted to persuade their fellow citizens to accept their views. Americans considered the arguments and put the question to a vote. The electorates of 11 States, either directly or through their representatives, chose to expand the traditional definition of marriage. Many more decided not to. Win or lose, advocates for both sides continued pressing their cases, secure in the knowledge that an electoral loss can be negated by a later electoral win. That is exactly how our system of government is supposed to work.

The Constitution places some constraints on self-rule—constraints adopted by the People themselves when they ratified the Constitution and its Amendments. Forbidden are laws "impairing the Obligation of Contracts," denying "Full Faith and Credit" to the "public Acts" of other States, prohibiting the free exercise of religion, abridging the freedom of speech, infringing the right to keep and bear arms, authorizing unreasonable searches and seizures, and so forth. Aside from these limitations, those powers "reserved to the States respectively, or to the people" can be exercised as the States or the People desire. These cases ask us to decide whether the Fourteenth Amendment contains a limitation that requires the States to license and recognize marriages between two people of the same sex. Does it remove that issue from the political process?

Of course not. It would be surprising to find a prescription regarding marriage in the Federal Constitution since, as the author of today's opinion reminded us only two years ago (in an opinion joined by the same Justices who join him today): "[R]egulation of domestic relations is an area that has long been regarded as a virtually exclusive province of the States." "[T]he Federal Government, through our history, has deferred to state law policy decisions with respect to domestic relations." [*Windsor*].

But we need not speculate. When the Fourteenth Amendment was ratified in 1868, every State limited marriage to one man and one woman, and no one doubted the constitutionality of doing so. That resolves these cases. . . .

But the Court ends [the contemporary debate over same-sex marriages] in an opinion lacking even a thin veneer of law. Buried beneath the mummeries and straining-to-be-memorable passages of the opinion is a candid and startling assertion: No matter what it was the People ratified, the Fourteenth Amendment protects those rights that the Judiciary, in its "reasoned judgment," thinks the Fourteenth Amendment ought to protect. That is so because "[t]he generations that wrote and ratified the Bill of Rights and the Fourteenth Amendment did not presume to know the extent of freedom in all of its dimensions . . . ." One would think that sentence would continue: ". . . and therefore they provided for a means by which the People could amend the Constitution," or perhaps ". . . and therefore they left the creation of additional liberties, such as the freedom to marry someone of the same sex, to the People, through the never-ending process of legislation." But no. What logically follows, in the majority's judge-empowering estimation, is: "and so they entrusted to future generations a charter protecting the right of all persons to enjoy liberty as we learn its meaning." The "we," needless to say, is the nine of us. "History and tradition guide and discipline [our] inquiry but do not set its outer boundaries." Thus, rather than focusing on the People's understanding of "liberty"—at the time of ratification or even today—the majority focuses on four "principles and traditions" that, in the majority's view, prohibit States from defining marriage as an institution consisting of one man and one woman.

This is a naked judicial claim to legislative—indeed, *super*-legislative—power; a claim fundamentally at odds with our system of government. . . . A system of government that makes the People subordinate to a committee of nine unelected lawyers does not deserve to be called a democracy.

Judges are selected precisely for their skill as lawyers; whether they reflect the policy views of a particular constituency is not (or should not be) relevant. Not surprisingly then, the Federal Judiciary is hardly a cross-section of America. Take, for example, this Court, which consists of only nine men and women, all of them successful lawyers who studied at Harvard or Yale Law School. Four of the nine are natives of New York City. Eight of them grew up in east- and west-coast States. Only one hails from the vast expanse in-between. Not a single Southwesterner or even, to tell the truth, a genuine Westerner (California does not count). Not a single evangelical Christian (a group that comprises about one quarter of Americans), or even a Protestant of any denomination. The strikingly unrepresentative character of the body voting on today's social upheaval would be irrelevant if they were functioning as judges, answering the legal question whether the American people had ever ratified a constitutional provision that was understood to proscribe the traditional definition of marriage. But of course the Justices in today's majority are not voting on that basis; they say they are not. And to allow the policy question of same-sex marriage to be considered and resolved by a select, patrician, highly unrepresentative panel of nine is to violate a principle even more fundamental than no taxation without representation: no social transformation without representation.

But what really astounds is the hubris reflected in today's judicial Putsch. The five Justices who compose today's majority are entirely comfortable concluding that every State violated the Constitution for all of the 135 years between the Fourteenth Amendment's ratification and Massachusetts' permitting of same-sex marriages in 2003. They have discovered in the Fourteenth Amendment a "fundamental right" overlooked by every person alive at the time of ratification, and almost everyone else in the time since. They see what lesser legal minds—minds like Thomas Cooley, John Marshall Harlan, Oliver Wendell Holmes, Jr., Learned Hand, Louis Brandeis, William Howard Taft, Benjamin Cardozo, Hugo Black, Felix Frankfurter, Robert Jackson, and Henry Friendly—could not. They are certain that the People ratified the Fourteenth Amendment to bestow on them the power to remove questions from the democratic process when that is called for by their "reasoned judgment." These Justices know that limiting marriage to one man and one woman is contrary to reason; they know that an institution as old as government itself, and accepted by every nation in history until 15 years ago, cannot possibly be supported by anything other than ignorance or bigotry. And they are willing to say that any citizen who does not agree with that, who adheres to what was, until 15 years ago, the unanimous judgment of all generations and all societies, stands against the Constitution.

The opinion is couched in a style that is as pretentious as its content is egotistic. It is one thing for separate concurring or dissenting opinions to contain extravagances, even silly extravagances, of thought and expression; it is something else for the official opinion of the Court to do so. Of course the opinion's showy profundities are often profoundly incoherent. "The nature of marriage is that, through its enduring bond, two persons together can find other freedoms, such as expression, intimacy, and spirituality." (Really? Who ever thought that intimacy and spirituality [whatever that means] were freedoms? And if intimacy is, one would think Freedom of Intimacy is abridged rather than expanded by marriage. Ask the nearest hippie. Expression, sure enough, is a freedom, but anyone in a long-lasting marriage will attest that that happy state constricts, rather than expands, what one can prudently say.) Rights, we are told, can "rise . . . from a better informed understanding of how constitutional imperatives define a liberty that remains urgent in our own era." (Huh? How can a better informed understanding of how constitutional imperatives [whatever that means] define [whatever that means] an urgent liberty [never mind], give birth to a right?) And we are told that, "[i]n any particular case," either the Equal Protection or Due Process Clause "may be thought to capture the essence of [a] right in a more accurate and comprehensive way," than the other, "even as the two Clauses may converge in the identification and definition of the right." (What say? What possible "essence" does substantive due process "capture" in an "accurate and comprehensive way"? It stands for nothing whatever, except those freedoms and entitlements that this Court really likes. And the Equal Protection Clause, as employed today, identifies nothing except a difference in treatment that this Court really dislikes. Hardly a distillation of essence. If the opinion is correct that the two clauses "converge in the identification and definition of [a] right," that is only because the majority's likes and dislikes are predictably compatible.) I could go on. The world does not expect logic and precision in poetry or inspirational pop-philosophy; it demands them in the law. The stuff contained in today's opinion has to diminish this Court's reputation for clear thinking and sober analysis.

Hubris is sometimes defined as o'erweening pride; and pride, we know, goeth before a fall. The Judiciary is the "least dangerous" of the federal branches because it has "neither Force nor Will, but merely judgment; and must ultimately depend upon the aid of the executive arm" and the States, "even for the efficacy of its judgments." With each decision of ours that takes from the People a question properly left to them—with each decision that is unabashedly based not on law, but on the "reasoned judgment" of a bare majority of this Court—we move one step closer to being reminded of our impotence.

☐ *Justice THOMAS, with whom Justice SCALIA joins, dissenting.*

The Court's decision today is at odds not only with the Constitution, but with the principles upon which our Nation was built. Since well before 1787, liberty has been understood as freedom from government action, not entitlement to government benefits. The Framers created our Constitution to preserve that understanding of liberty. Yet the majority invokes our Constitution in the name of a "liberty" that the Framers would not have recognized, to the detriment of the liberty they sought to protect. Along the way, it rejects the idea—captured in our Declaration of Independence—that human dignity is innate and suggests instead that it comes from the Government. This distortion of our Constitution not only ignores the text, it inverts the relationship between the individual and the state in our Republic. I cannot agree with it . . .

By straying from the text of the Constitution, substantive due process exalts judges at the expense of the People from whom they derive their authority. Petitioners argue that by enshrining the traditional definition of marriage in their State Constitutions through voter-approved amendments, the States have put the issue "beyond the reach of the normal democratic process." But the result petitioners seek is far less democratic. They ask nine judges on this Court to enshrine their definition of marriage in the Federal Constitution and thus put it beyond the reach of the normal democratic process for the entire Nation. That a "bare majority" of this Court is able to grant this wish, wiping out with a stroke of the keyboard the results of the political process in over 30 States, based on a provision that guarantees only "due process" is but further evidence of the danger of substantive due process.

Even if the doctrine of substantive due process were somehow defensible—it is not—petitioners still would not have a claim. To invoke the protection of the Due Process Clause at all—whether under a theory of "substantive" or "procedural" due process—a party must first identify a deprivation of "life, liberty, or property." The majority claims these state laws deprive petitioners of "liberty," but the concept of "liberty" it conjures up bears no resemblance to any plausible meaning of that word as it is used in the Due Process Clauses.

As used in the Due Process Clauses, "liberty" most likely refers to "the power of locomotion, of changing situation, or removing one's person to whatsoever place one's own inclination may direct; without imprisonment or restraint, unless by due course of law." 1 W. Blackstone, *Commentaries on the Laws of England* 130 (1769) (Blackstone). That definition is drawn from the historical roots of the Clauses and is consistent with our Constitution's text and structure. . . .

Even assuming that the "liberty" in those Clauses encompasses something more than freedom from physical restraint, it would not include the types of rights claimed by the majority. In the American legal tradition, liberty has long been understood as individual freedom from governmental action, not as a right to a particular governmental entitlement.

The founding-era understanding of liberty was heavily influenced by John Locke, whose writings "on natural rights and on the social and governmental contract" were cited "[i]n pamphlet after pamphlet" by American writers. Locke described men as existing in a state of nature, possessed of the "perfect freedom to order their actions and dispose of their possessions and persons as they think fit, within the bounds of the law of nature, without asking leave, or depending upon the will of any other man." J. Locke, *Second Treatise of Civil Government*, Sec. 4. Because that state of nature left men insecure in their persons and property, they entered civil society, trading a portion of their natural liberty for an increase in their security. Upon consenting to that order, men obtained civil liberty, or the freedom "to be under no other legislative power but that established by consent in the commonwealth; nor under the dominion of any will or restraint of any law, but what that legislative shall enact according to the trust put in it." . . .

The founding-era idea of civil liberty as natural liberty constrained by human law necessarily involved only those freedoms that existed outside of government. [A]s one scholar put it in 1776, "[T]he common idea of liberty is merely negative, and is only the absence of restraint." R. Hey, *Observations on the Nature of Civil Liberty and the Principles of Government* Sec. 13 (1776). When the colonists described laws that would infringe their liberties, they discussed laws that would prohibit individuals "from walking in the streets and highways on certain saints days, or from being abroad after a certain time in the evening, or . . . restrain [them] from working up and manufacturing materials of [their] own growth." Each of those examples involved freedoms that existed outside of government.

Whether we define "liberty" as locomotion or freedom from governmental action more broadly, petitioners have in no way been deprived of it.

Petitioners cannot claim, under the most plausible definition of "liberty," that they have been imprisoned or physically restrained by the States for participating in same-sex relationships. To the contrary, they have been able to cohabitate and raise their children in peace. They have been able to hold civil marriage ceremonies in States that recognize same-sex marriages and private religious ceremonies in all States. They have been able to travel freely around the country, making their homes where they please. Far from being incarcerated or physically restrained, petitioners have been left alone to order their lives as they see fit.

Nor, under the broader definition, can they claim that the States have restricted their ability to go about their daily lives as they would be able to absent governmental restrictions. . . . Nor have the States prevented petitioners from approximating a number of incidents of marriage through private legal means, such as wills, trusts, and powers of attorney.

Instead, the States have refused to grant them governmental entitlements. Petitioners claim that as a matter of "liberty," they are entitled to access privileges and benefits that exist solely because of the government. They want, for example, to receive the State's imprimatur on their marriages—on state issued marriage licenses, death certificates, or other official forms. And they want to receive various monetary benefits, including reduced inheritance taxes upon the death of a spouse, compensation if a spouse dies as a result of a work-related injury, or loss of consortium damages in tort suits. But receiving governmental recognition and benefits has nothing to do with any understanding of "liberty" that the Framers would have recognized.

To the extent that the Framers would have recognized a natural right to marriage that fell within the broader definition of liberty, it would not have included a right to governmental recognition and benefits. Instead, it would have included a right to engage in the very same activities that petitioners have been left free to engage in—making vows, holding religious ceremonies celebrating those vows, raising children, and otherwise enjoying the society of one's spouse—without governmental interference. At the founding, such conduct was understood to predate government, not to flow from it. As Locke had explained many years earlier, "The first society was between man and wife, which gave beginning to that between parents and children." Locke Sec. 77. . . .

As a philosophical matter, liberty is only freedom from governmental action, not an entitlement to governmental benefits. And as a constitutional matter, it is likely even narrower than that, encompassing only freedom from physical restraint and imprisonment. The majority's "better informed understanding of how constitutional imperatives define . . . liberty"—better informed, we must assume, than that of the people who ratified the Fourteenth Amendment—runs headlong into the reality that our Constitution is a "collection of 'Thou shalt nots,'" *Reid v. Covert,* 354 U.S. 1 (1957), not "Thou shalt provides." . . .

The majority apparently disregards the political process as a protection for liberty. Although men, in forming a civil society, "give up all the power necessary to the ends for which they unite into society, to the majority of the community," Locke Sec. 99, they reserve the authority to exercise natural liberty within the bounds of laws established by that society. To protect that liberty from arbitrary interference, they establish a process by which that society can adopt and enforce its laws. In our country, that process is primarily representative government at the state level, with the Federal Constitution serving as a backstop for that process. . . . That process has been honored here. The definition of marriage has been the subject of heated debate in the States. Legislatures have repeatedly taken up the matter on behalf of the People, and 35 States have put the question to the People themselves. In 32 of those 35 States, the People have opted to retain the traditional definition of marriage. That petitioners disagree with the result of that process does not make it any less legitimate. Their civil liberty has been vindicated.

Aside from undermining the political processes that protect our liberty, the majority's decision threatens the religious liberty our Nation has long sought to protect.

The history of religious liberty in our country is familiar: Many of the earliest immigrants to America came seeking freedom to practice their religion without restraint. When they arrived, they created their own havens for religious practice. Many of these havens were initially homogenous communities with established religions. By the 1780's, however, "America was in the wake of a great religious revival" marked by a move toward free exercise of religion. Every State save Connecticut adopted protections for religious freedom in their State Constitutions by 1789, and, of course, the First Amendment enshrined protection for the free exercise of religion in the U.S. Constitution. But that protection was far from the last word on religious liberty in this country, as the Federal Government and the States have reaffirmed their commitment to religious liberty by codifying protections for religious practice. See, e.g., Religious Freedom Restoration Act of 1993.

In our society, marriage is not simply a governmental institution; it is a religious institution as well. Today's decision might change the former, but it cannot change the latter. It appears all but inevitable that the two will come into conflict, particularly as individuals and churches are confronted with demands to participate in and endorse civil marriages between same-sex couples. . . .

Perhaps recognizing that these cases do not actually involve liberty as it has been understood, the majority goes to great lengths to assert that its decision will advance the "dignity" of same-sex couples. The flaw in that reasoning, of course, is that the Constitution contains no "dignity" Clause, and even if it did, the government would be incapable of bestowing dignity.

Human dignity has long been understood in this country to be innate. When the Framers proclaimed in the Declaration of Independence that "all men are created equal" and "endowed by their Creator with certain unalienable Rights," they referred to a vision of mankind in which all humans are created in the image of God and therefore of inherent worth. That vision is the foundation upon which this Nation was built.

The corollary of that principle is that human dignity cannot be taken away by the government. Slaves did not lose their dignity (any more than they lost their humanity) because the government allowed them to be enslaved. Those held in internment camps did not lose their dignity because the government confined them. And those denied governmental benefits certainly do not lose their dignity because the government denies them those benefits. The government cannot bestow dignity, and it cannot take it away. . . .

Our Constitution—like the Declaration of Independence before it—was predicated on a simple truth: One's liberty, not to mention one's dignity, was something to be shielded from—not provided by—the State. Today's decision casts that truth aside. In its haste to reach a desired result, the majority misapplies a clause focused on "due process" to afford substantive rights, disregards the most plausible understanding of the "liberty" protected by that clause, and distorts the principles on which this Nation was founded. Its decision will have inestimable consequences for our Constitution and our society. I respectfully dissent.

☐ *Justice ALITO, with whom Justice SCALIA and Justice THOMAS join, dissenting.*

Until the federal courts intervened, the American people were engaged in a debate about whether their States should recognize same-sex marriage. The question in these cases, however, is not what States should do about same-sex marriage but whether the Constitution answers that question for them. It does not. The Constitution leaves that question to be decided by the people of each State.

The Constitution says nothing about a right to same-sex marriage, but the Court holds that the term "liberty" in the Due Process Clause of the Fourteenth Amendment encompasses this right. Our Nation was founded upon the principle that every person has the unalienable right to liberty, but liberty is a term of many meanings. For classical liberals, it may include economic rights now limited by government regulation. For social democrats, it may include the right to a variety of government benefits. For today's majority, it has a distinctively postmodern meaning.

To prevent five unelected Justices from imposing their personal vision of liberty upon the American people, the Court has held that "liberty" under the Due Process Clause should be understood to protect only those rights that are "'deeply rooted in this Nation's history and tradition.'" *Washington v. Glucksberg*, 521 U.S. 701 (1997). And it is beyond dispute that the right to same-sex marriage is not among those rights. . . .

For today's majority, it does not matter that the right to same-sex marriage lacks deep roots or even that it is contrary to long-established tradition. The Justices in the majority claim the authority to confer constitutional protection upon that right simply because they believe that it is fundamental.

Attempting to circumvent the problem presented by the newness of the right found in these cases, the majority claims that the issue is the right to equal treatment. Noting that marriage is a fundamental right, the majority argues that a State has no valid reason for denying that right to same-sex couples. This reasoning is dependent upon a particular understanding of the purpose of civil marriage. Although the Court expresses the point in loftier terms, its argument is that the fundamental purpose of marriage is to promote the well-being of those who choose to marry. Marriage provides emotional fulfillment and the promise of support in times of need. And by benefiting persons who choose to wed, marriage indirectly benefits society because persons who live in stable, fulfilling, and supportive relationships make better citizens. It is for these reasons, the argument goes, that States encourage and formalize marriage, confer special benefits on married persons, and also impose some special obligations. This understanding of the States' reasons for recognizing marriage enables the majority to argue that same-sex marriage serves the States' objectives in the same way as opposite-sex marriage.

This understanding of marriage, which focuses almost entirely on the happiness of persons who choose to marry, is shared by many people today, but it is not the traditional one. For millennia, marriage was inextricably linked to the one thing that only an opposite-sex couple can do: procreate. . . .

If this traditional understanding of the purpose of marriage does not ring true to all ears today, that is probably because the tie between marriage and procreation has frayed. Today, for instance, more than 40% of all children in this country are born to unmarried women. This development undoubtedly is both a cause and a result of changes in our society's understanding of marriage. . . .

Today's decision usurps the constitutional right of the people to decide whether to keep or alter the traditional understanding of marriage. The decision will also have other important consequences.

It will be used to vilify Americans who are unwilling to assent to the new orthodoxy. In the course of its opinion, the majority compares traditional marriage laws to laws that denied equal treatment for African-Americans and women. The implications of this analogy will be exploited by those who are determined to stamp out every vestige of dissent.

Perhaps recognizing how its reasoning may be used, the majority attempts, toward the end of its opinion, to reassure those who oppose same-sex marriage that their rights of conscience will be protected. We will soon see whether this proves to be true. I assume that those who cling to old beliefs will be able to whisper their thoughts in the recesses of their homes, but if they repeat those views in public, they will risk being labeled as bigots and treated as such by governments, employers, and schools. . . .

Today's decision will also have a fundamental effect on this Court and its ability to uphold the rule of law. If a bare majority of Justices can invent a new right and impose that right on the rest of the country, the only real limit on what future majorities will be able to do is their own sense of what those with political power and cultural influence are willing to tolerate. Even enthusiastic supporters of same-sex marriage should worry about the scope of the power that today's majority claims.

Today's decision shows that decades of attempts to restrain this Court's abuse of its authority have failed. A lesson that some will take from today's decision is that preaching about the proper method of interpreting the Constitution or the virtues of judicial self-restraint and humility cannot compete with the temptation to achieve what is viewed as a noble end by any practicable means. I do not doubt that my colleagues in the majority sincerely see in the Constitution a vision of liberty that happens to coincide with their own. But this sincerity is cause for concern, not comfort. What it evidences is the deep and perhaps irremediable corruption of our legal culture's conception of constitutional interpretation. . . .

Masterpiece Cakeshop v. Colorado Civil Rights Commission

138 S. Ct. 1719 (2018)

Masterpiece Cakeshop, a bakery in Lakewood, a suburb of Denver, Colorado, offers a variety of baked goods, ranging from cookies to custom-designed cakes for weddings and other events. Jack Phillips, owner of the cakeshop and a devout Christian, believes that God intended marriage solely for a man and a woman and that creating a wedding cake for a same-sex couple would violate his religious

Mike Luckovich Editorial Cartoon used with the permission of Mike Luckovich and Creators Syndicate. All Rights Reserved. Published in the Atlanta Journal Constitution, *March 26, 2013.*

beliefs. In 2012, he met Charlie Craig and Dave Mullins when they came into the shop and told him they were interested in ordering a cake for their wedding. Phillips responded that he did not create cakes for same-sex weddings, explaining, "I'll make your birthday cakes, shower cakes, sell you cookies and brownies, I just don't make cakes for same sex weddings." The couple left the shop without further discussion. The following day, Craig's mother, who had accompanied the couple to the cakeshop, telephoned to ask Phillips why he declined to serve her son. Phillips explained that he does not create wedding cakes for same-sex weddings because of his religious opposition to same-sex marriage and because Colorado (at the time) did not recognize same-sex marriages.

The Colorado Anti-Discrimination Act (CADA), as amended in 2007 and 2008, prohibits in public accommodations discrimination based on sexual orientation as well as other protected characteristics. It states:

> It is a discriminatory practice and unlawful for a person, directly or indirectly, to refuse, withhold from, or deny to an individual or a group, because of disability, race, creed, color, sex, sexual orientation, marital status, national origin, or ancestry, the full and equal enjoyment of the goods,

services, facilities, privileges, advantages, or accommodations of a place of public accommodation."

The law defines "public accommodation" broadly to include any "place of business engaged in any sales to the public and any place offering services . . . to the public" but excludes "a church, synagogue, mosque, or other place that is principally used for religious purposes." The CADA also establishes a system for resolving discrimination claims. Complaints are initially addressed by the Colorado Civil Rights Division, which investigates each claim, and if it finds probable cause that the CADA has been violated, refers the matter to the Colorado Civil Rights Commission. That commission decides whether to initiate a formal hearing before a state administrative law judge, who hears the evidence and issues a decision, which may be appealed to the full commission, a seven-member body. The commission holds public hearings before voting on the case. If the commission determines that the evidence proves a CADA violation, it may impose remedies.

Craig and Mullins filed a CADA discrimination complaint against Masterpiece Cakeshop and Phillips, alleging they were denied "full and equal service" at the bakery because of their sexual orientation and that it was Phillips's "standard business practice" not to provide cakes for same-sex weddings. The Civil Rights Division determined that Phillips had probably run afoul of the CADA and referred the matter to the Civil Rights Commission, which subsequently referred the case to a state administrative law judge. The judge ruled against Phillips, concluding that the CADA was a "valid and neutral law of general applicability," citing *Employment Div., Department of Human Resources of Oregon v. Smith,* 494 U.S. 872 (1990) (excerpted in Ch. 6). The commission affirmed that decision, and Phillips appealed to the Colorado Court of Appeals. That court agreed, rejecting Phillips's claim that his rights guaranteed by the First Amendment free exercise clause were violated. Whereupon, Phillips appealed to the Supreme Court, which granted *certiorari.*

The state court's decision was reversed by a vote of 7–2. Justice Kennedy delivered the opinion of the Court. Justices Kagan, Gorsuch, and Thomas each filed concurring opinions. Justice Ginsburg, joined by Justice Sotomayor, issued a dissenting opinion.

■ ■ ■

☐ *Justice KENNEDY delivered the opinion of the Court.*

The case presents difficult questions as to the proper reconciliation of at least two principles. The first is the authority of a State and its governmental entities to protect the rights and dignity of gay persons who are, or wish to be, married but who face discrimination when they seek goods or services. The second is the right of all persons to exercise fundamental freedoms under the First Amendment, as applied to the States through the Fourteenth Amendment.

The freedoms asserted here are both the freedom of speech and the free exercise of religion. The free speech aspect of this case is difficult, for few persons who have seen a beautiful wedding cake might have thought of its creation as an exercise of protected speech. This is an instructive example, however, of the proposition that the application of constitutional freedoms in new contexts can deepen our understanding of their meaning.

One of the difficulties in this case is that the parties disagree as to the extent of the baker's refusal to provide service. If a baker refused to design a special cake with words or images celebrating the marriage—for instance, a cake showing words with religious meaning—that might be different from a refusal to sell any cake at all. In defining whether a baker's creation can be protected, these details might make a difference.

The same difficulties arise in determining whether a baker has a valid free exercise claim. A baker's refusal to attend the wedding to ensure that the cake is cut the right way, or a refusal to put certain religious words or decorations on the cake, or even a refusal to sell a cake that has been baked for the public generally but includes certain religious words or symbols on it are just three examples of possibilities that seem all but endless.

Whatever the confluence of speech and free exercise principles might be in some cases, the Colorado Civil Rights Commission's consideration of this case was inconsistent with the State's obligation of religious neutrality. The reason and motive for the baker's refusal were based on his sincere religious beliefs and convictions. The Court's precedents make clear that the baker, in his capacity as the owner of a business serving the public, might have his right to the free exercise of religion limited by generally applicable laws. Still, the delicate question of when the free exercise of his religion must yield to an otherwise valid exercise of state power needed to be determined in an adjudication in which religious hostility on the part of the State itself would not be a factor in the balance the State sought to reach. That requirement, however, was not met here. When the Colorado Civil Rights Commission considered this case, it did not do so with the religious neutrality that the Constitution requires.

Given all these considerations, it is proper to hold that whatever the outcome of some future controversy involving facts similar to these, the Commission's actions here violated the Free Exercise Clause; and its order must be set aside. . . .

Our society has come to the recognition that gay persons and gay couples cannot be treated as social outcasts or as inferior in dignity and worth. For that reason the laws and the Constitution can, and in some instances must, protect them in the exercise of their civil rights. The exercise of their freedom on terms equal to others must be given great weight and respect by the courts. At the same time, the religious and philosophical objections to gay marriage are protected views and in some instances protected forms of expression. As this Court observed in *Obergefell v. Hodges*, [135 S.Ct. 2584] (2015), "[t]he First Amendment ensures that religious organizations and persons are given proper protection as they seek to teach the principles that are so fulfilling and so central to their lives and faiths." Nevertheless, while those religious and philosophical objections are protected, it is a general rule that such objections do not allow business owners and other actors in the economy and in society to deny protected persons equal access to goods and services under a neutral and generally applicable public accommodations law.

When it comes to weddings, it can be assumed that a member of the clergy who objects to gay marriage on moral and religious grounds could not be compelled to perform the ceremony without denial of his or her right to the free exercise of religion. This refusal would be well understood in our constitutional order as an exercise of religion, an exercise that gay persons could recognize and accept without serious diminishment to their own dignity and worth. Yet if that exception were not confined, then a long list of persons who provide goods and services for marriages and weddings might refuse to do so for gay persons, thus resulting in a community-wide stigma inconsistent with the history and dynamics of civil rights laws that ensure equal access to goods, services, and public accommodations.

It is unexceptional that Colorado law can protect gay persons, just as it can protect other classes of individuals, in acquiring whatever products and services they choose on the same terms and conditions as are offered to other members of the public. And there are no doubt innumerable goods and services that no one could argue implicate the First Amendment. Petitioners conceded, moreover, that if a baker refused to sell any goods or any cakes for gay weddings, that would be a different matter and the State would have a strong case under this Court's precedents that this would be a denial of goods and services that went beyond any protected rights of a baker who offers goods and services to the general public and is subject to a neutrally applied and generally applicable public accommodations law.

Phillips claims, however, that a narrower issue is presented. He argues that he had to use his artistic skills to make an expressive statement, a wedding endorsement in his own voice and of his own creation. As Phillips would see the case, this contention has a significant First Amendment speech component and implicates his deep and sincere religious beliefs. . . .

[A]ny decision in favor of the baker would have to be sufficiently constrained, lest all purveyors of goods and services who object to gay marriages for moral and religious reasons in effect be allowed to put up signs saying "no goods or services will be sold if they will be used for gay marriages," something that would impose a serious stigma on gay persons. But, nonetheless, Phillips was entitled to the neutral and respectful consideration of his claims in all the circumstances of the case.

The neutral and respectful consideration to which Phillips was entitled was compromised here, however. The Civil Rights Commission's treatment of his case has some elements of a clear and impermissible hostility toward the sincere religious beliefs that motivated his objection.

That hostility surfaced at the Commission's formal, public hearings, as shown by the record. At several points during its meeting, commissioners endorsed the view that religious beliefs cannot legitimately be carried into the public sphere or commercial domain, implying that religious beliefs and persons are less than fully welcome in Colorado's business community. One commissioner suggested that Phillips can believe "what he wants to believe," but cannot act on his religious beliefs "if he decides to do business in the state." A few moments later, the commissioner restated the same position: "[I]f a businessman wants to do business in the state and he's got an issue with the—the law's impacting his personal belief system, he needs to look at being able to compromise." Standing alone, these statements are susceptible of different interpretations. On the one hand, they might mean simply that a business cannot refuse to provide services based on sexual orientation, regardless of the proprietor's personal views. On the other hand, they might be seen as inappropriate and dismissive comments showing lack of due consideration for Phillips' free exercise rights and the dilemma he faced. In view of the comments that followed, the latter seems the more likely.

[When] the Commission met again . . . another commissioner made specific reference to the previous meeting's discussion but said far more to disparage Phillips' beliefs. The commissioner stated:

> I would also like to reiterate what we said in the hearing or the last meeting. Freedom of religion and religion has been used to justify all kinds of discrimination throughout history, whether it be slavery, whether it be the holocaust, whether it be—I mean, we—we can list hundreds of situations where freedom of religion has been used to justify discrimination. And to me it is one of the most despicable pieces of rhetoric that people can use to—to use their religion to hurt others.

To describe a man's faith as "one of the most despicable pieces of rhetoric that people can use" is to disparage his religion in at least two distinct ways: by describing it as despicable, and also by characterizing it as merely rhetorical—something insubstantial and even insincere. The commissioner even went so far as to compare Phillips' invocation of his sincerely held religious beliefs to defenses of slavery and the Holocaust. This sentiment is inappropriate for a Commission charged with the solemn responsibility of fair and neutral enforcement of Colorado's antidiscrimination law—a law that protects discrimination on the basis of religion as well as sexual orientation. . . .

[A]t least three other occasions the Civil Rights Division considered the refusal of bakers to create cakes with images that conveyed disapproval of same-sex marriage, along with religious text. Each time, the Division found that the baker acted lawfully in refusing service. It made these determinations because, in the words of the Division, the requested cake included "wording and images [the baker] deemed derogatory."

The treatment of the conscience-based objections at issue in these three cases contrasts with the Commission's treatment of Phillips' objection. The Commission ruled against Phillips in part on the theory that any message the requested wedding cake would carry would be attributed to the customer, not to the baker. Yet the Division did not address this point in any of the other cases with respect to the cakes depicting anti-gay marriage symbolism. Additionally, the Division found no violation of CADA in the other cases in part because each bakery was willing to sell other products, including those depicting Christian themes, to the prospective customers. But the Commission dismissed Phillips' willingness to sell "birthday cakes, shower cakes, [and] cookies and brownies" to gay and lesbian customers as irrelevant. The treatment of the other cases and Phillips' case could reasonably be interpreted as being inconsistent as to the question of whether speech is involved, quite apart from whether the cases should ultimately be distinguished. In short, the Commission's consideration of Phillips' religious objection did not accord with its treatment of these other objections. . . .

A principled rationale for the difference in treatment of these two instances cannot be based on the government's own assessment of offensiveness. Just as "no official, high or petty, can prescribe what shall be orthodox in politics, nationalism, religion, or other matters of opinion," *West Virginia Bd. of Ed. v. Barnette*, 319 U. S. 624 (1943), it is not, as the Court has repeatedly held, the role of the State or its officials to prescribe what shall be offensive. The Colorado court's attempt to account for the difference in treatment elevates one view of what is offensive over another and itself sends a signal of official disapproval of Phillips' religious beliefs.

For the reasons just described, the Commission's treatment of Phillips' case violated the State's duty under the First Amendment not to base laws or regulations on hostility to a religion or religious viewpoint.

In *Church of Lukumi Babalu Aye,* [508 U.S. 520 (1993)], the Court made clear that the government, if it is to respect the Constitution's guarantee of free exercise, cannot impose regulations that are hostile to the religious beliefs of affected citizens and cannot act in a manner that passes judgment upon or presupposes the illegitimacy of religious beliefs and practices. The Free Exercise Clause bars even "subtle departures from neutrality" on matters of religion. Here, that means the Commission was obliged under the Free Exercise Clause to proceed in a manner neutral toward and tolerant of Phillips' religious beliefs.

Factors relevant to the assessment of governmental neutrality include "the historical background of the decision under challenge, the specific series of events leading to the enactment or official policy in question, and the legislative or administrative history, including contemporaneous statements made by members of the decisionmaking body." In view of these factors the record here demonstrates that the Commission's consideration of Phillips' case was neither tolerant nor respectful of Phillips' religious beliefs. . . .

While the issues here are difficult to resolve, it must be concluded that the State's interest could have been weighed against Phillips' sincere religious objections in a way consistent with the requisite religious neutrality that must be strictly observed. The official expressions of hostility to religion in some of the commissioners' comments—comments that were not disavowed at the Commission or by the State at any point in the proceedings that led to affirmance of the order—were inconsistent with what the Free Exercise Clause requires. The Commission's disparate consideration of Phillips' case compared to the cases of the other bakers suggests the same. For these reasons, the order must be set aside. . . .

The judgment of the Colorado Court of Appeals is reversed.

☐ *Justice KAGAN, with whom Justice BREYER joins, concurring.*

I join the Court's opinion in full because I believe the Colorado Civil Rights Commission did not satisfy that obligation. I write separately to elaborate on one of the bases for the Court's holding.

The Court partly relies on the "disparate consideration of Phillips' case compared to the cases of [three] other bakers" who "objected to a requested cake on the basis of conscience." In the latter cases, a customer named William Jack sought "cakes with images that conveyed disapproval of same-sex marriage, along with religious text"; the bakers whom he approached refused to make them. Those bakers prevailed before the Colorado Civil Rights Division and Commission, while Phillips—who objected for religious reasons to baking a wedding cake for a same-sex couple—did not. The Court finds that the legal reasoning of the state agencies differed in significant ways as between the Jack cases and the Phillips case. And the Court takes especial note of the suggestion made by the Colorado Court of Appeals, in comparing those cases, that the state agencies found the message Jack requested "offensive [in] nature."

What makes the state agencies' consideration yet more disquieting is that a proper basis for distinguishing the cases was available—in fact, was obvious. The Colorado Anti-Discrimination Act (CADA) makes it unlawful for a place of public accommodation to deny "the full and equal enjoyment" of goods and services to individuals based on certain characteristics, including sexual orientation and creed. The three bakers in the Jack cases did not violate that law. Jack requested them to make a cake (one denigrating gay people and same-sex marriage) that they would not have made for any customer. In refusing that request, the bakers did not single out Jack because of his religion, but instead treated him in the same way they would have treated anyone else—just as CADA requires. By contrast, the same-sex couple in this case requested a wedding cake that Phillips would have made for an opposite-sex couple. In refusing that request, Phillips contravened CADA's demand that customers receive "the full and equal enjoyment" of public accommodations irrespective of their sexual orientation. The different outcomes in the Jack cases and the Phillips case could thus have been justified by a plain reading and neutral application of Colorado law—untainted by any bias against a religious belief.

I read the Court's opinion as fully consistent with that view. The Court limits its analysis to the *reasoning* of the state agencies (and Court of Appeals), "quite apart from whether the [Phillips and Jack] cases should ultimately be distinguished." And the Court itself recognizes the principle that would properly account for a difference in *result* between those cases. Colorado law, the Court says, "can protect gay persons, just as it can protect other classes of individuals, in acquiring whatever products and services they choose on the same terms and conditions as are offered to other members of the public." For that reason, Colorado can treat a baker who discriminates based on sexual orientation differently from a baker who does not discriminate on that or any other prohibited ground. But only, as the Court rightly says, if the State's decisions are not infected by religious hostility or bias. I accordingly concur.

☐ *Justice GORSUCH, with whom Justice ALITO joins, concurring.*

In *Employment Div., Dept. of Human Resources of Ore.* v. *Smith*, this Court held that a neutral and generally applicable law will usually survive a constitutional free exercise challenge. [W]hen the government fails to act neutrally toward the free exercise of religion, it tends to run into trouble. Then the government can prevail only if it satisfies strict scrutiny, showing that its restrictions on religion both serve a compelling interest and are narrowly tailored. *Church of Lukumi Babalu Aye* (1993).

Today's decision respects these principles. . . . The only wrinkle is this. In the face of so much evidence suggesting hostility toward Mr. Phillips's sincerely held religious beliefs, two of our colleagues have written separately to suggest that the Commission acted neutrally toward his faith when it treated him differently from the other bakers—or that it could have easily done so consistent with the First Amendment. See [Justice GINSBURG's dissenting and Justice KAGAN's concurring opinions.] But, respectfully, I do not see how we might rescue the Commission from its error.

A full view of the facts helps point the way to the problem. Start with William Jack's case. He approached three bakers and asked them to prepare cakes with messages disapproving same-sex marriage on religious grounds. All three bakers refused Mr. Jack's request, stating that they found his request offensive to their secular convictions. Mr. Jack responded by filing complaints with the Colorado Civil Rights Division. But the Division declined to find a violation, reasoning that the bakers didn't deny Mr. Jack service because of his religious faith but because the cakes he sought were offensive to their own moral convictions. . . .

Next, take the undisputed facts of Mr. Phillips's case. Charlie Craig and Dave Mullins approached Mr. Phillips about creating a cake to celebrate their wedding. Mr. Phillips explained that he could not prepare a cake celebrating a same-sex wedding consistent with his religious faith. But Mr. Phillips offered to make other baked goods for the couple, including cakes celebrating other occasions. Later, Mr. Phillips testified without contradiction that he would have refused to create a cake celebrating a same-sex marriage for any customer, regardless of his or her sexual orientation. Nonetheless, the Commission held that Mr. Phillips's conduct violated the Colorado public accommodations law.

The facts show that the two cases share all legally salient features. In both cases, the effect on the customer was the same: bakers refused service to persons who bore a statutorily protected trait (religious faith or sexual orientation). But in both cases the bakers refused service intending only to honor a personal conviction. To be sure, the bakers *knew* their conduct promised the effect of leaving a customer in a protected class unserved. But there's no indication the bakers actually *intended* to refuse service *because of* a customer's protected characteristic. We know this because all of the bakers explained without contradiction that they would not sell the requested cakes to anyone, while they would sell other cakes to members of the protected class (as well as to anyone else). So, for example, the bakers in the first case would have refused to sell a cake denigrating same-sex marriage to an atheist customer, just as the baker in the second case would have refused to sell a cake celebrating same-sex marriage to a heterosexual customer. And the bakers in the first case were generally happy to sell to persons of faith, just as the baker in the second case was generally happy to sell to gay persons. In both cases, it was the kind of cake, not the kind of customer, that mattered to the bakers. . . .

The problem here is that the Commission failed to act neutrally by applying a consistent legal rule. In Mr. Jack's case, the Commission chose to distinguish carefully between intended and knowingly accepted effects. Even though the bakers knowingly denied service to someone in a protected class, the Commission found no violation because the bakers only intended to distance themselves from "the offensive nature of the requested message." Yet, in Mr. Phillips's case, the Commission dismissed this very same argument as resting on a "distinction without a difference." It concluded instead that an "intent to disfavor" a protected class of persons should be "readily . . . presumed" from the knowing failure to serve someone who belongs to that class. In its judgment, Mr. Phillips's intentions were "inextricably tied to the sexual orientation of the parties involved" and essentially "irrational."

Nothing in the Commission's opinions suggests any neutral principle to reconcile these holdings. If Mr. Phillips's objection is "inextricably tied" to a protected class, then the bakers' objection in Mr. Jack's case must be "inextricably tied" to one as well. . . . The Commission cannot have it both ways. . . .

The real explanation for the Commission's discrimination soon comes clear, too—and it does anything but help its cause. [A]s the Court explains, it appears the Commission wished to condemn Mr. Phillips for expressing just the kind of "irrational" or "offensive . . . message" that the bakers in the first case refused to endorse. Many may agree with the Commission and consider Mr. Phillips's religious beliefs irrational or offensive. Some may believe he misinterprets the teachings of his faith. And, to be sure, this Court has held same-sex marriage a matter of constitutional right and various States have enacted laws that preclude discrimination on the basis of sexual orientation. But it is also true that no bureaucratic judgment condemning a sincerely held religious belief as "irrational" or "offensive" will ever survive strict scrutiny under the First Amendment. In this country, the place of secular officials isn't to sit in judgment of religious beliefs, but only to protect their free exercise. . . .

The second suggestion fares no better. Suggesting that this case is only about "wedding cakes"—and not a wedding cake celebrating a same-sex wedding—actually points up the problem. At its most general level, the cake at issue in Mr. Phillips's case was just a mixture of flour and eggs; at its most specific level, it was a cake celebrating the same-sex wedding of Mr. Craig and Mr. Mullins. We are told here, however, to apply a sort of Goldilocks rule: describing the cake by its ingredients is *too general*; understanding it as celebrating a same-sex wedding is *too specific*; but regarding it as a generic wedding cake is *just right*. The problem is, the Commission didn't play with the level of generality in Mr. Jack's case in this way. It didn't declare, for example, that because the cakes Mr. Jack requested were just cakes about weddings generally, and all such cakes were the same, the bakers had to produce them. Instead, the Commission accepted the bakers' view that the specific cakes Mr. Jack requested conveyed a message offensive to their convictions and allowed them to refuse service. Having done that there, it must do the same here.

Any other conclusion would invite civil authorities to gerrymander their inquiries based on the parties they prefer. Why calibrate the level of generality in Mr. Phillips's case at "wedding cakes" exactly—and not at, say, "cakes" more generally or "cakes that convey a message regarding same-sex marriage" more specifically? If "cakes" were the relevant level of generality, the Commission would have to order the bakers to make Mr. Jack's requested cakes just as it ordered Mr. Phillips to make the requested cake in his case. Conversely, if "cakes that convey a message regarding same-sex marriage" were the relevant level of generality, the Commission would have to respect Mr. Phillips's refusal to make the requested cake just as it respected the bakers' refusal to make the cakes Mr. Jack requested. In short, when the same level of generality is applied to both cases, it is no surprise that the bakers have to be treated the same. Only by adjusting the dials *just right*—fine-tuning the level of generality up or down for each case based solely on the identity of the parties and the substance of their views—can you engineer the Commission's outcome, handing a win to Mr. Jack's bakers but delivering a loss to Mr. Phillips. Such results-driven reasoning is improper. Neither the Commission nor this Court may apply a more specific level of generality in Mr. Jack's case (a cake that conveys a message regarding same-sex marriage) while applying a higher level of generality in Mr. Phillips's case (a cake that conveys no message regarding same-sex marriage). Of course, under *Smith* a vendor cannot escape a public accommodations law just because his religion frowns on it. But for any law to comply with the First Amendment and *Smith*, it must be applied in a manner that treats religion with neutral respect. That means the government must apply the *same* level of generality across cases— and that did not happen here. . . .

Only one way forward now remains. Having failed to afford Mr. Phillips's religious objections neutral consideration and without any compelling reason for its failure, the Commission must afford him the same result it afforded the bakers in Mr. Jack's case. The Court recognizes this by reversing the judgment below and holding that the Commission's order "must be set aside." Maybe in some future rulemaking or case the Commission could adopt a new "knowing" standard for all refusals of service and offer neutral reasons for doing so. But, as the Court observes, "[h]owever later cases raising these or similar concerns are resolved in the future, . . . the rulings of the Commission and of the state court that enforced the Commission's order" in *this* case "must be invalidated." Mr. Phillips has conclusively proven a First Amendment violation and, after almost six years facing unlawful civil charges, he is entitled to judgment.

☐ *Justice THOMAS, with whom Justice GORSUCH joins, concurring in part and concurring in the judgment.*

I agree that the Colorado Civil Rights Commission (Commission) violated Jack Phillips' right to freely exercise his religion. As Justice GORSUCH explains, the Commission treated Phillips' case differently from a similar case involving three other bakers, for reasons that can only be explained by hostility toward Phillips' religion. The Court agrees that the Commission treated Phillips differently, and it points out that some of the Commissioners made comments disparaging Phillips' religion. Although the Commissioners' comments are certainly disturbing, the discriminatory application of Colorado's public-accommodations law is enough on its own to violate Phillips' rights. To the extent the Court agrees, I join its opinion.

While Phillips rightly prevails on his free-exercise claim, I write separately to address his free-speech claim. The Court does not address this claim because it has some uncertainties about the record. Specifically, the parties dispute whether Phillips refused to create a *custom* wedding cake for the individual respondents, or whether he refused to sell them *any* wedding cake (including a premade one). But the Colorado Court of Appeals resolved this factual dispute in Phillips' favor. The court described his conduct as a refusal to "design and create a cake to celebrate [a] same-sex wedding." And it noted that the Commission's order required Phillips to sell "'*any* product [he] would sell to heterosexual couples,'" including custom wedding cakes.

Even after describing his conduct this way, the Court of Appeals concluded that Phillips' conduct was not expressive and was not protected speech. It reasoned that an outside observer would think that Phillips was merely complying with Colorado's public-accommodations law, not expressing a message, and that Phillips could post a disclaimer to that effect. This reasoning flouts bedrock principles of our free-speech jurisprudence and would justify virtually any law that compels individuals to speak. It should not pass without comment. . . .

The Colorado Court of Appeals was wrong to conclude that Phillips' conduct was not expressive because a reasonable observer would think he is merely complying with Colorado's public-accommodations law. This argument would justify any law that compelled protected speech. And, this Court has never accepted it. From the beginning, this Court's compelled-speech precedents have rejected arguments that "would resolve every issue of power in favor of those in authority." *Barnette.* . . .

Because Phillips' conduct (as described by the Colorado Court of Appeals) was expressive, Colorado's public-accommodations law cannot penalize it unless the law withstands strict scrutiny. . . . States cannot punish protected speech because some group finds it offensive, hurtful, stigmatic, unreasonable, or undignified. See *Morse* v. *Frederick*, 551 U. S. 393 (2007) ("After all, much political and religious speech might be perceived as offensive to some"). As the Court reiterates today, "it is not . . . the role of the State or its officials to prescribe what shall be offensive." . . . .

Nor does the fact that this Court has now decided *Obergefell* v. *Hodges*, [135 S.Ct. 2584] (2015), somehow diminish Phillips' right to free speech. "It is one thing . . . to conclude that the Constitution protects a right to same-sex marriage; it is something else to portray everyone who does not share [that view] as bigoted" and unentitled to express a different view. This Court is not an authority on matters of conscience, and its decisions can (and often should) be criticized. The First Amendment gives individuals the right to disagree about the correctness of *Obergefell* and the morality of same-sex marriage. *Obergefell* itself emphasized that the traditional understanding of marriage "long has been held—and continues to be held—in good faith by reasonable and sincere people here and throughout the world." If Phillips' continued adherence to that understanding makes him a minority after *Obergefell*, that is all the more reason to insist that his speech be protected.

In *Obergefell*, I warned that the Court's decision would "inevitabl[y] . . . come into conflict" with religious liberty, "as individuals . . . are confronted with demands to participate in and endorse civil marriages between same-sex couples." This case proves that the conflict has already emerged. Because the Court's decision vindicates Phillips' right to free exercise, it seems that religious liberty has lived to fight another day. But, in future cases, the freedom of speech could be essential to preventing *Obergefell* from being used to "stamp out every vestige of dissent" and "vilify Americans who are unwilling to assent to the new orthodoxy." If that freedom is to maintain its vitality, reasoning like the Colorado Court of Appeals' must be rejected.

☐ *Justice, GINSBURG with whom Justice SOTOMAYOR joins, dissenting.*

The Court concludes that "the Commission's consideration of Phillips' religious objection did not accord with its treatment of [the other bakers'] objections." But the cases the Court aligns are hardly comparable. The bakers would have refused to make a cake with Jack's requested message for any customer, regardless of his or her religion. And the bakers visited by Jack would have sold him any baked goods they would have sold anyone else. The bakeries' refusal to make Jack cakes of a kind they would not make for any customer scarcely resembles Phillips' refusal to serve Craig and Mullins: Phillips would *not* sell to Craig and Mullins, for no reason other than their sexual orientation, a cake of the kind he regularly sold to others. When a couple contacts a bakery for a wedding cake, the product they are seeking is a cake celebrating *their* wedding—not a cake celebrating heterosexual weddings or same-sex weddings—and that is the service Craig and Mullins were denied. Colorado, the Court does not gainsay, prohibits precisely the discrimination Craig and Mullins encountered. Jack, on the other hand, suffered no service refusal on the basis of his religion or any other protected characteristic. He was treated as any other customer would have been treated—no better, no worse.

The fact that Phillips might sell other cakes and cookies to gay and lesbian customers was irrelevant to the issue Craig and Mullins' case presented. What matters is that Phillips would not provide a good or service to a same-sex couple that he would provide to a heterosexual couple. In contrast, the other bakeries' sale of other goods to Christian customers was relevant: It shows that there were no goods the bakeries would sell to a non-Christian customer that they would refuse to sell to a Christian customer. . . .

Statements made at the Commission's public hearings on Phillips' case provide no firmer support for the Court's holding today. Whatever one may think of the statements in historical context, I see no reason why the comments of one or two Commissioners should be taken to overcome Phillips' refusal to sell a wedding cake to Craig and Mullins. The proceedings involved several layers of independent decisionmaking, of which the Commission was but one. First, the Division had to find probable cause that Phillips violated CADA. Second, the ALJ (Administrative Law Judge) entertained the parties' cross-motions for summary judgment. Third, the Commission heard Phillips' appeal. Fourth, after the Commission's ruling, the Colorado Court of Appeals considered the case *de novo*. What prejudice infected the determinations of the adjudicators in the case before and after the Commission? The Court does not say. Phillips' case is thus far removed from the only precedent upon which the Court relies, *Church of Lukumi Babalu Aye, Inc. v. Hialeah*, where the government action that violated a principle of religious neutrality implicated a sole decisionmaking body, the city council.

For the reasons stated, sensible application of CADA to a refusal to sell any wedding cake to a gay couple should occasion affirmance of the Colorado Court of Appeals' judgment. I would so rule.

■ In Comparative Perspective

Canadian Courts Forbid Discrimination against Homosexuals and Same-Sex Marriages

In the last two decades there has been a global trend to legalize same-sex marriages through legislation and judicial rulings. The Netherlands was the first country to do so in 2000, followed by Belgium (2003); Canada, South Africa, and Spain (2005); Norway and Sweden (2009); Argentina, Iceland, and Portugal (2010); Denmark (2012); Brazil, France, New Zealand, and Uruguay (2013); United Kingdom (2014); Ireland, Luxembourg, and Slovenia (2015); Colombia (2016); Australia, Finland, Malta, and Germany (2017); Austria, and Ecuador (2019). A number of other countries or their subdivisions recognize civil unions and same-sex marriages, including Mexico.

The Supreme Court of Canada was in the forefront. In *Egan v. Canada*, 2 S.C.R. 513 (1995), it held, on the basis of "historical social, political and economic disadvantage suffered by homosexuals" and the emerging consensus among legislatures, as well as previous judicial decisions, that sexual orientation was embraced by the equality guarantee of Section 15(1) of Canada's Charter of Rights and Freedom, which provides: "Every individual is equal before and under the law and has the right to the equal protection and equal benefit of the law without discrimination and, in particular, without discrimination based on race, national or ethnic origin, colour, religion, sex, age or mental or physical disability."

Later decisions of the Canadian Supreme Court expanded protection for gays and lesbians. In *Vriend v. Alberta*, 1 S.C.R. 493 (1998), for instance, the Court held that Alberta's human rights code must give protection to homosexuals in employment in order to comply with the guarantee of Section 15 (1). See also *M. v. H.*, 2 S.C.R. 3 (1999).

Moreover, a lower court judge declared Quebec's prohibition against same-sex marriages invalid, in *Hendricks v. Quebec*, J.Q. No. 3816 (S.C.) (2002). Likewise, the British Columbia Court of Appeal declared the common-law definition of marriage unconstitutional and required the substitution of the words "two persons" for

(continues)

■ IN COMPARATIVE PERSPECTIVE
*Canadian Courts Forbid Discrimination against Homosexuals
and Same-Sex Marriages (continued)*

"one man and one woman," in *EGALE Canada Inc. v. Attorney General of
Canada*, B.C.J. 994 (2003). And in *Halpern v. Attorney General of Canada*,
No. C39172 (June 10, 2003), the Court of Appeal for Ontario held that
Section 15(1) bars discrimination against same-sex marriages.

Writing for the Court in *Halpern*, Chief Justice Roy McMurtry rejected
the government's position against recognizing same-sex marriages, upon
reasoning:

> No one is disputing that marriage is a fundamental societal
> institution. Similarly, it is accepted that, with limited excep-
> tions, marriage has been understood to be a monogamous
> opposite-sex union. What needs to be determined, however, is
> whether there is a valid objective to maintaining marriage as an
> exclusively heterosexual institution. Stating that marriage is
> heterosexual because it always has been heterosexual is merely
> an explanation for the opposite-sex requirement of marriage; it
> is not an objective that is capable of justifying the infringement
> of a Charter guarantee.
>
> We now turn to the more specific purposes of marriage
> advanced by the [the government]: (i) uniting the opposite
> sexes; (ii) encouraging the birth and raising of children of the
> marriage; and (iii) companionship.
>
> The first purpose, which results in favouring one form of
> relationship over another, suggests that uniting two persons of
> the same sex is of lesser importance. . . . [A] purpose that
> demeans the dignity of same-sex couples is contrary to the val-
> ues of a free and democratic society and cannot be considered
> to be pressing and substantial. A law cannot be justified on the
> very basis upon which it is being attacked.
>
> The second purpose of marriage, as advanced by [the gov-
> ernment], is encouraging the birth and raising of children.
> Clearly, encouraging procreation and childrearing is a laudable
> goal that is properly regarded as pressing and substantial. How-
> ever, the [government] must demonstrate that the objective of
> maintaining marriage as an exclusively heterosexual institution
> is pressing and substantial: see *Vriend* [*v. Alberta*].

We fail to see how the encouragement of procreation and childrearing is a pressing and substantial objective of maintaining marriage as an exclusively heterosexual institution. Heterosexual married couples will not stop having or raising children because same-sex couples are permitted to marry. Moreover, an increasing percentage of children are being born to and raised by same-sex couples.

The [government] submits that the union of two persons of the opposite sex is the only union that can "naturally" procreate. In terms of that biological reality, same-sex couples are different from opposite-sex couples. In our view, however, "natural" procreation is not a sufficiently pressing and substantial objective to justify infringing the equality rights of same-sex couples. As previously stated, same-sex couples can have children by other means, such as adoption, surrogacy and donor insemination. A law that aims to encourage only "natural" procreation ignores the fact that same-sex couples are capable of having children.

Similarly, a law that restricts marriage to opposite-sex couples, on the basis that a fundamental purpose of marriage is the raising of children, suggests that same-sex couples are not equally capable of childrearing. The [government] has put forward no evidence to support such a proposition. Neither is the [government] advocating such a view; rather, it takes the position that social science research is not capable of establishing the proposition one way or another. In the absence of cogent evidence, it is our view that the objective is based on a stereotypical assumption that is not acceptable in a free and democratic society that prides itself on promoting equality and respect for all persons.

The third purpose of marriage advanced by the [government] is companionship. We consider companionship to be a laudable goal of marriage. However, encouraging companionship cannot be considered a pressing and substantial objective of the omission of the impugned law. Encouraging companionship between only persons of the opposite sex perpetuates the view that persons in same-sex relationships are not equally capable of providing companionship and forming lasting and loving relationships.

Accordingly, it is our view that the [government] has not demonstrated any pressing and substantial objective for excluding same-sex couples from the institution of marriage. For that reason, we conclude that the violation of the Couples' rights under Section 15(1) of the Charter cannot be saved. . . .

■ (3) Wealth, Poverty, and Illegitimacy

In *Griffin v. Illinois*, 351 U.S. 12 (1956), when holding that states must provide indigent defendants with transcripts of their trials for appeals on constitutional questions, Justice Black observed that "[i]n criminal trials a State can no more discriminate on account of poverty than on account of religion, race, or color." Justice Black thus suggested that classifications based on wealth might be constitutionally suspect. Subsequently, the Court construed the due process and equal protection clauses to ensure that indigents are not denied the right to vote (see Vol. 1, Ch. 8), and that they have an equal right of access to judicial proceedings (see Ch. 9).

Nevertheless, the Court applies the "rational basis" test and refuses to scrutinize laws that disadvantage the poor in the overwhelming majority of cases. See, for example, *Maher v. Roe* (1977) (excerpted in Ch. 11) upholding restrictions on Medicaid funding for women seeking elective abortions.

In *Shapiro v. Thompson* (1969) (excerpted below), however, the Court overturned a state residency requirement for indigents seeking public assistance. It did so, though, on the grounds that the residency requirement denied indigents their "fundamental right to interstate travel," rather than a right to welfare benefits. That decision was reaffirmed in *Saenz v. Roe*, 526 U.S. 489 (1999), when striking down California's law limiting welfare benefits of new residents to that paid by the states in which they previously resided. Notably, though, in his opinion for the Court Justice Stevens held that the right to travel is one of the privileges and immunities guaranteed by the Fourteenth Amendment. Chief Justice Rehnquist and Justice Thomas dissented.

Other residency requirements have been similarly struck down, but never on the basis that wealth is a suspect classification. In *Dandridge v. Williams*, 397 U.S. 471 (1970), for instance, the Court rejected the claim of a fundamental right to public assistance, when upholding Maryland's law limiting benefits under the Aid to Dependent Children Social Security program to $250 per month, regardless of the needs and size of a family. So too in *San Antonio Independent School District v. Rodriguez* (1973) (excerpted below), the Court rejected the claim that public education is a fundamental right and that states may not discriminate against indigents in public education.

In contrast to claims of discrimination based on wealth and poverty, the Court gives greater scrutiny to challenges of laws discriminating against illegitimate children. The Court has done so under both the "rational basis" test, as in *Levy v. Louisiana*, 391 U.S. 68 (1968), and the slightly higher standard of review, announced in *Matthews v. Lucas*, 427 U.S. 495 (1976), demanding that classifications based on illegitimacy be "substantially related to a permissible state interest" (see also, THE DEVELOPMENT OF LAW: Rulings Dealing with Illegitimate Children, later in this section).

SELECTED BIBLIOGRAPHY

Barber, Sotirios. *Welfare and the Constitution.* Princeton, NJ: Princeton University Press, 2004.

Bussiere, Elizabeth. *(Dis)Entitling the Poor: The Warren Court, Welfare Rights and the American Political Tradition.* College Station: Pennsylvania State University Press, 1997.

Driver, Justin. *The Schoolhouse Gate: Public Education, the Supreme Court, and the Battle for the American Mind.* New York: Pantheon, 2018.

Sracic, Paul. *San Antonio v. Rodriguez and the Pursuit of Equal Education.* Lawrence: University Press of Kansas, 2006.

Shapiro v. Thompson
394 U.S. 618, 89 S.CT. 1322 (1969)

Two months after moving from Massachusetts to Connecticut, Vivian Thompson applied for assistance under the Aid to Families with Dependent Children program. She was nineteen years old, pregnant, and the mother of one child. Thompson was denied assistance because she failed to meet Connecticut's one-year residency requirement for receiving assistance. In federal district court, she sued Bernard Shapiro, Connecticut's welfare commissioner. That court held that the residency requirement had a "chilling effect on the right to travel" and denied Thompson the equal protection of the law as guaranteed by the Fourteenth Amendment. Shapiro then appealed that ruling to the Supreme Court, which granted review and consolidated the case with others, challenging the constitutionality of residency requirements of Pennsylvania and the District of Columbia.

The Court's decision was 6–3, and the majority's opinion was announced by Justice Brennan. Justice Stewart concurred. Dissenting opinions were delivered by Justice Harlan and Chief Justice Warren, who was joined by Justice Black.

■ ■ ■

☐ *Justice BRENNAN delivered the opinion of the Court.*

[This] is an appeal from a decision of a three-judge District Court holding unconstitutional a State or District of Columbia statutory provision which denies welfare assistance to residents of the State or District who have not resided within their jurisdictions for at least one year immediately preceding their applications for such assistance. We affirm. . . .

There is no dispute that the effect of the waiting-period requirement in each case is to create two classes of needy resident families indistinguishable from each other except that one is composed of residents who have resided a year or more, and the second of residents who have resided less than a year, in the jurisdiction. On the basis of this sole difference the first class is granted and the second class is denied welfare aid upon which may depend the ability of the families to obtain the very means to subsist—food, shelter, and other necessities of life. . . . The interests which appellants assert are promoted by the classification either may not constitutionally be promoted by government or are not compelling governmental interests.

Primarily, appellants justify the waiting-period requirement as a protective device to preserve the fiscal integrity of state public assistance programs. It is asserted that people who require welfare assistance during their first year of residence in a State are likely to become continuing burdens on state welfare programs. Therefore, the argument runs, if such people can be deterred from entering the jurisdiction by denying them welfare benefits during the first year, state programs to assist long-time residents will not be impaired by a substantial influx of indigent newcomers. . . .

We do not doubt that the one-year waiting period device is well suited to discourage the influx of poor families in need of assistance. An indigent who desires to migrate, resettle, find a new job, and start a new life will doubtless hesitate if he knows that he must risk making the move without the possibility of falling back on state welfare assistance during his first year of residence, when his need may be most acute. But the purpose of inhibiting migration by needy persons into the State is constitutionally impermissible.

This Court long ago recognized that the nature of our Federal Union and our constitutional concepts of personal liberty unite to require that all citizens be free to travel throughout the length and breadth of our land uninhibited by statutes, rules, or regulations which unreasonably burden or restrict this movement. That proposition was early stated by Chief Justice TANEY in the *Passenger Cases*, 7 How. (48 U.S.) 283 (1849):

> For all the great purposes for which the Federal government was formed, we are one people, with one common country. We are all citizens of the United States; and, as members of the same community, must have the right to pass and repass through every part of it without interruption, as freely as in our own States.

We have no occasion to ascribe the source of this right to travel interstate to a particular constitutional provision. It suffices that, as Justice STEWART said for the Court in *United States v. Guest*, 383 U.S. 745 (1966):

> The constitutional right to travel from one State to another . . . occupies a position fundamental to the concept of our Federal

Union. It is a right that has been firmly established and repeatedly recognized.

. . . [The] right finds no explicit mention in the Constitution. The reason, it has been suggested, is that a right so elementary was conceived from the beginning to be a necessary concomitant of the stronger Union the Constitution created. In any event, freedom to travel throughout the United States has long been recognized as a basic right under the Constitution.

Thus, the purpose of deterring the immigration of indigents cannot serve as justification for the classification created by the one-year waiting period, since that purpose is constitutionally impermissible. If a law has "no other purpose . . . than to chill the assertion of constitutional rights by penalizing those who choose to exercise them, then it [is] patently unconstitutional." . . .

We conclude therefore that appellants in these cases do not use and have no need to use the one-year requirement for the governmental purposes suggested. Thus, even under traditional equal protection tests a classification of welfare applicants according to whether they have lived in the State for one year would seem irrational and unconstitutional. But, of course, the traditional criteria do not apply in these cases. Since the classification here touches on the fundamental right of interstate movement, its constitutionality must be judged by the stricter standard of whether it promotes a *compelling* state interest. Under this standard, the waiting-period requirement clearly violates the Equal Protection Clause. . . .

☐ *Justice HARLAN, dissenting.*

In upholding the equal protection argument, the Court has applied an equal protection doctrine of relatively recent vintage: the rule that statutory classifications which either are based upon certain "suspect" criteria or affect "fundamental rights" will be held to deny equal protection unless justified by a "compelling" governmental interest.

The "compelling interest" doctrine, which today is articulated more explicitly than ever before, constitutes an increasingly significant exception to the long-established rule that a statute does not deny equal protection if it is rationally related to a legitimate governmental objective. The "compelling interest" doctrine has two branches. The branch which requires that classifications based upon "suspect" criteria be supported by a compelling interest apparently had its genesis in cases involving racial classifications, which have, at least since *Korematsu v. United States*, 323 U.S. 214 (1944), been regarded as inherently "suspect." The criterion of "wealth" apparently was added to the list of "suspects" as an alternative justification for the rationale in *Harper v. Virginia Bd. of Elections*, 383 U.S. 663, (1966), in which Virginia's poll tax was struck down. . . . Today the list apparently has been further enlarged to include classifications based upon recent interstate movement, and perhaps those based upon the exercise of *any* constitutional right. . . . [However,] I do not consider wealth a "suspect" statutory criterion. . . .

The second branch of the "compelling interest" principle is even more troublesome. For it has been held that a statutory classification is subject to the "compelling interest" test if the result of the classification may be to affect a "fundamental right," regardless of the basis of the classification. . . .

I think this branch of the "compelling interest" doctrine particularly unfortunate and unnecessary. It is unfortunate because it creates an exception which threatens to swallow the standard equal protection rule. Virtually every state statute affects important rights. This Court has repeatedly held, for example, that the traditional equal protection standard is applicable to statutory classifications affecting such fundamental matters as the right to pursue a particular occupation, the right to receive greater or smaller wages or to work more or less hours, and the right to inherit property. Rights such as these are in principle indistinguishable from those involved here, and to extend the "compelling interest" rule to all cases in which such rights are affected would go far toward making this Court a "super-legislature." This branch of the doctrine is also unnecessary. When the right affected is one assured by the Federal Constitution, any infringement can be dealt with under the Due Process Clause. But when a statute affects only matters not mentioned in the Federal Constitution and is not arbitrary or irrational, I must reiterate that I know of nothing which entitles this Court to pick out particular human activities, characterize them as "fundamental," and give them added protection under an unusually stringent equal protection test. . . .

In light of th[e] undeniable relation of residence requirements to valid legislative aims, it cannot be said that the requirements are "arbitrary" or "lacking in rational justification." Hence, I can find no objection to these residence requirements under the Equal Protection Clause of the Fourteenth Amendment or under the analogous standard embodied in the Due Process Clause of the Fifth Amendment. . . .

San Antonio Independent School District v. Rodriguez
411 U.S. 1, 93 S.Ct. 1278 (1973)

Demetrio Rodriguez and several other Mexican Americans sued their school district, the state board of education, the state attorney general, and several other government officials. They contended that Texas's system for financing public schools violated the equal protection clause of the Fourteenth Amendment because it discriminated on the basis of wealth. Besides federal funds for education, the state provided for a minimum level of education in all districts by funding a large portion of the cost of teachers' salaries and other operating expenses. In addition, each school district contributed a portion through local property taxes. But because the value of property varied greatly from one school district to another, there were wide disparities in school districts' per-pupil expenditures. At a pretrial conference, the San Antonio Independent School District sided with Rodriguez. But state officials continued to defend the system of financing public schools and appealed to the Supreme Court the ruling of a federal district court, which held that Texas discriminated against students in poor school districts in violation of the Fourteenth Amendment. The Supreme Court split 5–4 in reversing the lower court, held that wealth is not a suspect classification, and found that the state's system of funding public education was rational and constitutional. In 1989, though, the Texas State Supreme Court ruled contrariwise and found that the state discriminated in violation of a provision of the *state* constitution.

The Court's decision was 5–4, and the majority's opinion was announced by Justice Powell. Justice Stewart concurred. Justice Brennan dissented. Justices White and Marshall also dissented and were joined by Justices Douglas and Brennan.

■ ■ ■

☐ *Justice POWELL delivered the opinion of the Court.*

Until recent times, Texas was a predominantly rural State and its population and property wealth were spread relatively evenly across the State. Sizable differences in the value of assessable property between local school districts became increasingly evident as the State became more industrialized and as rural-to-urban population shifts became more pronounced. The location of commercial and industrial property began to play a significant role in determining the amount of tax resources available to each school district. These growing disparities in population and taxable property between districts were responsible in part for increasingly notable differences in levels of local expenditure for education. . . .

The school district in which appellees reside, the Edgewood Independent School District, has been compared throughout this litigation with the Alamo Heights School Independent School District. This comparison between the least and most affluent districts in the San Antonio area serves to illustrate the manner in which the dual system of finance operates and to indicate the extent to which substantial disparities exist despite the State's impressive progress in recent years. Edgewood is one of seven public school districts in the metropolitan area. Approximately 22,000 students are enrolled in its 25 elementary and secondary schools. The district is situated in the core-city sector of San Antonio in a residential neighborhood that has little commercial or industrial property. The residents are predominantly of Mexican-American descent: approximately 90% of the student population is Mexican-American and over 6% is Negro. The average assessed property value per pupil is $5,960—the lowest in the metropolitan area—and the median family income ($4,686) is also the lowest. At an equalized tax rate of $1.05 per $100 of assessed property—the highest in the metropolitan area—the district contributed $26 to the education of each child for the 1967–1968 school year above its Local Fund Assignment for the Minimum Foundation Program. The Foundation Program contributed $222 per pupil for a state-local total of $248. Federal funds added another $108 for a total of $356 per pupil.

Alamo Heights is the most affluent school district in San Antonio. Its six schools, housing approximately 5,000 students, are situated in a residential community quite unlike the Edgewood District. The school population is predominantly "Anglo," having only 18% Mexican-Americans and less than 1% Negroes. The assessed property value per pupil exceeds $49,000, and the median family income is $8,001. In 1967–1968 the local tax rate of $.85 per $100 of valuation yielded $333 per pupil over and above its contribution to the Foundation Program. Coupled with the $225 provided from that Program, the district was able to supply $558 per student. Supplemented by a $36 per-pupil grant from federal sources, Alamo Heights spent $594 per pupil. . . .

Texas virtually concedes that its historically rooted dual system of financing education could not withstand the strict judicial scrutiny that this Court has found appropriate in reviewing legislative judgments that interfere with fundamental constitutional rights or that involve suspect classifications. . . .

We must decide, first, whether the Texas system of financing public education operates to the disadvantage of some suspect class or impinges upon a fundamental right explicitly or implicitly protected by the Constitution, thereby requiring strict judicial scrutiny. If so, the judgment of the District Court should be affirmed. If not, the Texas scheme must still be examined to determine whether it rationally furthers some legitimate, articulated state purpose and therefore does not constitute an invidious discrimination in violation of the Equal Protection Clause of the Fourteenth Amendment. . . .

[F]or the several reasons that follow, we find neither the suspect-classification nor the fundamental-interest analysis persuasive.

The wealth discrimination discovered by the District Court in this case, and by several other courts that have recently struck down school-financing laws in other States, is quite unlike any of the forms of wealth discrimination heretofore reviewed by this Court. Rather than focusing on the unique features of the alleged discrimination, the courts in these cases have virtually assumed their findings of a suspect classification through a simplistic process of analysis: since, under the traditional systems of financing public schools, some poorer people receive less expensive educations than other more affluent people, these systems discriminate on the basis of wealth. This approach largely ignores the hard threshold questions, including whether it makes a difference for purposes of consideration under the Constitution that the class of disadvantaged "poor" cannot be identified or defined in customary equal protection terms, and whether the relative—rather than absolute—nature of the asserted deprivation is of significant consequence. Before a State's laws and the justifications for the classifications they create are subjected to strict judicial scrutiny, we think these threshold considerations must be analyzed more closely than they were in the court below.

The case comes to us with no definitive description of the classifying facts or delineation of the disfavored class. . . . The Texas system of school financing might be regarded as discriminating (1) against "poor" persons whose incomes fall below some identifiable level of poverty or who might be characterized as functionally "indigent," or (2) against those who are relatively poorer than others, or (3) against all those who, irrespective of their personal incomes, happen to reside in relatively poorer school districts. Our task must be to ascertain whether, in fact, the Texas system has been shown to discriminate on any of these possible bases and, if so, whether the resulting classification may be regarded as suspect.

The precedents of this Court provide the proper starting point. The individuals, or groups of individuals, who constituted the class discriminated against in our prior cases shared two distinguishing characteristics: because of their impecunity they were completely unable to pay for some desired benefit, and as a consequence, they sustained an absolute deprivation of a meaningful opportunity to enjoy that benefit. In *Griffin v. Illinois*, 351 U.S. 12 (1956), and its progeny, the Court invalidated state laws that prevented an indigent criminal defendant from acquiring a transcript, or an adequate substitute for a transcript, for use at several stages of the trial and appeal process. The payment requirements in each case were found to occasion *de facto* discrimination against those who, because of their indigency, were totally unable to pay for transcripts. . . .

Likewise, in *Douglas v. California*, 372 U.S. 353 (1963), a decision establishing an indigent defendant's right to court-appointed counsel on direct appeal, the Court dealt only with defendants who could not pay for counsel from their own resources and who had no other way of gaining representation. *Douglas* provides no relief for those on whom the burdens of paying for a criminal defense are relatively speaking, great but not insurmountable. Nor does it deal with relative differences in the quality of counsel acquired by the less wealthy.

Williams v. Illinois, 399 U.S. 235 (1970), and *Tate v. Short*, 401 U.S. 395 (1971), struck down criminal penalties that subjected indigents to incarceration simply because of their inability to pay a fine. Again, the disadvantaged class was composed only of persons who were totally unable to pay the demanded sum. Those cases do not touch on the question whether equal protection is denied to persons with relatively less money on whom designated fines impose heavier burdens. . . .

Finally, in *Bullock v. Carter*, 405 U.S. 134 (1972), the Court invalidated the Texas filing-fee requirement for primary elections. Both of the relevant classifying facts found in the previous cases were present there. The size of the fee, often running into the thousands of dollars and, in at least one case, as high as $8,900, effectively barred all potential candidates who were unable to pay the required fee. As the system provided "no reasonable alternative means of access to the ballot," inability to pay occasioned an absolute denial of a position on the primary ballot.

Only appellees' first possible basis for describing the class disadvantaged by the Texas school-financing system—discrimination against a class of definably "poor" persons—might arguably meet the criteria established in these prior cases. Even a cursory examination, however, demonstrates that neither of the two distinguishing characteristics of wealth classifications can be found here. First, in support of their charge that the system discriminates against the "poor," appellees have made no effort to demonstrate that it operates to the peculiar disadvantage of any class fairly definable as indigent, or as composed of persons whose incomes are beneath any designated poverty level. Indeed, there is reason to believe that the poorest families are not necessarily clustered in the poorest property districts. A recent and exhaustive study of school districts in Connecticut concluded that "[i]t is clearly incorrect . . . to contend that the 'poor' live in 'poor' districts. . . ."

[T]here is no basis on the record in this case for assuming that the poorest people—defined by reference to any level of absolute impecunity— are concentrated in the poorest districts.

Second, neither appellees nor the District Court addressed the fact that, unlike each of the foregoing cases, lack of personal resources has not occasioned an absolute deprivation of the desired benefit. The argument here is not that the children in districts having relatively low assessable property values are receiving no public education; rather, it is that they are receiving a poorer quality education than that available to children in districts having more assessable wealth. Apart from the unsettled and disputed question whether the quality of education may be determined by the amount of money expended for it, a sufficient answer to appellees' argument is that, at least where wealth is involved, the Equal Protection Clause does not require absolute equality or precisely equal advantages. . . .

For these two reasons—the absence of any evidence that the financing system discriminates against any definable category of "poor" people or that it results in the absolute deprivation of education—the disadvantaged class is not susceptible of identification in traditional terms.

As suggested above, appellees and the District Court may have embraced a second or third approach, the second of which might be characterized as a theory of relative or comparative discrimination based on family income. Appellees sought to prove that a direct correlation exists between the wealth of families within each district and the expenditures therein for education. That is, along a continuum, the poorer the family the lower the dollar amount of education received by the family's children. . . .

If, in fact, these correlations could be sustained, then it might be argued that expenditures on education—equated by appellees to the quality of education—are dependent on personal wealth. Appellees' comparative-discrimination theory would still face serious unanswered questions, including whether a bare positive correlation or some higher degree of correlation is necessary to provide a basis for concluding that the financing system is designed to operate to the peculiar disadvantage of the comparatively poor, and whether a class of this size and diversity could ever claim the special protection accorded "suspect" classes. These questions need not be addressed in this case, however, since appellees' proof fails to support their allegations or the District Court's conclusions. . . .

This brings us, then, to the third way in which the classification scheme might be defined—*district* wealth discrimination. . . . Assuming a perfect correlation between district property wealth and expenditures from top to bottom, the disadvantaged class might be viewed as encompassing every child in every district except the district that has the most assessable wealth and spends the most on education. Alternatively, as suggested in Justice MARSHALL's dissenting opinion the class might be defined more restrictively to include children in districts with assessable property which falls below the statewide average, or median, or below some other artificially defined level.

However described, it is clear that appellees' suit asks this Court to extend its most exacting scrutiny to review a system that allegedly discriminates against a large, diverse, and amorphous class, unified only by the common factor of residence in districts that happen to have less taxable wealth than other districts. The system of alleged discrimination and the class it defines have none of the traditional indicia of suspectness: the class is not saddled with such disabilities, or subjected to such a history of purposeful unequal treatment, or relegated to such a position of political powerlessness as to command extraordinary protection from the majoritarian political process.

We thus conclude that the Texas system does not operate to the peculiar disadvantage of any suspect class. But in recognition of the fact that this

Court has never heretofore held that wealth discrimination alone provides an adequate basis for invoking strict scrutiny, appellees have not relied solely on this contention. They also assert that the State's system impermissibly interferes with the exercise of a "fundamental" right and that accordingly the prior decisions of this Court require the application of the strict standard of judicial review. . . .

We are in complete agreement with the conclusion of the three-judge panel below that "the grave significance of education both to the individual and to our society" cannot be doubted. But the importance of a service performed by the State does not determine whether it must be regarded as fundamental for purposes of examination under the Equal Protection Clause. Justice HARLAN, dissenting from the Court's application of strict scrutiny to a law impinging upon the right of interstate travel, admonished that "[v]irtually every state statute affects important rights." *Shapiro v. Thompson*, 394 U.S. 618 (1969). In his view, if the degree of judicial scrutiny of state legislation fluctuated, depending on a majority's view of the importance of the interest affected, we would have gone "far toward making this Court a 'super-legislature.' " . . .

It is not the province of this Court to create substantive constitutional rights in the name of guaranteeing equal protection of the laws. Thus, the key to discovering whether education is "fundamental" is not to be found in comparisons of the relative societal significance of education as opposed to subsistence or housing. Nor is it to be found by weighing whether education is as important as the right to travel. Rather, the answer lies in assessing whether there is a right to education explicitly or implicitly guaranteed by the Constitution. Education, of course, is not among the rights afforded explicit protection under our Federal Constitution. Nor do we find any basis for saying it is implicitly so protected. . . .

In sum, to the extent that the Texas system of school financing results in unequal expenditures between children who happen to reside in different districts, we cannot say that such disparities are the product of a system that is so irrational as to be invidiously discriminatory.

☐ *Justice WHITE, with whom Justice DOUGLAS and Justice BRENNAN join, dissenting.*

I cannot disagree with the proposition that local control and local decisionmaking play an important part in our democratic system of government. Much may be left to local option, and this case would be quite different if it were true that the Texas system . . . extended a meaningful option to all local districts to increase their per-pupil expenditures and so to improve their children's education to the extent that increased funding would achieve that goal. The system would then arguably provide a rational and sensible method of achieving the stated aim of preserving an area for local initiative and decision.

The difficulty with the Texas system, however, is that it provides a meaningful option to Alamo Heights and like school districts but almost none to Edgewood and those other districts with a low per-pupil real estate tax base. In these latter districts, no matter how desirous parents are of supporting their schools with greater revenues, it is impossible to do so through the use of the real estate property tax. In these districts, the Texas system utterly fails to extend a realistic choice to parents because the property tax, which is the only revenue-raising mechanism extended to school districts, is practically and legally unavailable. . . .

Both the Edgewood and Alamo Heights districts are located in Bexar County, Texas. Student enrollment in Alamo Heights is 5,432, in Edgewood 22,862. The per-pupil market value of the taxable property in Alamo Heights is $49,078, in Edgewood $5,960. In a typical relevant year, Alamo Heights had a maintenance tax rate of $1.20 and a debt service (bond) tax rate of 20¢ per $100 assessed evaluation, while Edgewood had a maintenance rate of 52¢ and a bond rate of 67¢. These rates, when applied to the respective tax bases, yielded Alamo Heights $1,433,473 in maintenance dollars and $236,074 in bond dollars, and Edgewood $223,034 in maintenance dollars and $279,023 in bond dollars. As is readily apparent, because of the variance in tax bases between the districts, results, in terms of revenues, do not correlate with effort, in terms of tax rate. Thus, Alamo Heights, with a tax base approximately twice the size of Edgewood's base, realized approximately six times as many maintenance dollars as Edgewood by using a tax rate only approximately two and one-half times larger. Similarly, Alamo Heights realized slightly fewer bond dollars by using a bond tax rate less than one-third of that used by Edgewood. . . .

Plainly, were Alamo Heights or North East to apply the Edgewood tax rate to its tax base, it would yield far greater revenues than Edgewood is able to yield applying those same rates to its base. Conversely, were Edgewood to apply the Alamo Heights or North East rates to its base, the yield would be far smaller than the Alamo Heights or North East yields. The disparity is, therefore, currently operative and its impact on Edgewood is undeniably serious. It is evident from statistics in the record that show that, applying an equalized tax rate of 85¢ per $100 assessed valuation, Alamo Heights was able to provide approximately $330 per pupil in local revenues over and above the Local Fund Assignment. In Edgewood, on the other hand, with an equalized tax rate of $1.05 per $100 of assessed valuation, $26 per pupil was raised beyond the Local Fund Assignment. As previously noted in Alamo Heights, total per-pupil revenues from local, state, and federal funds was $594 per pupil, in Edgewood $356.

In order to equal the highest yield in any other Bexar County district, Alamo Heights would be required to tax at the rate of 68¢ per $100 of assessed valuation. Edgewood would be required to tax at the prohibitive rate of $5.76 per $100. But state law places a $1.50 per $100 ceiling on the maintenance tax rate, a limit that would surely be reached long before Edgewood attained an equal yield. Edgewood is thus precluded in law, as well as in fact, from achieving a yield even close to that of some other districts.

The Equal Protection Clause permits discriminations between classes but requires that the classification bear some rational relationship to a permissible object sought to be attained by the statute. It is not enough that the Texas system before us seeks to achieve the valid, rational purpose of maximizing local initiative; the means chosen by the State must also be rationally related to the end sought to be achieved. . . .

■ THE DEVELOPMENT OF LAW

Rulings on Residency Requirements, the Right to Interstate Travel, and Indigency

CASE	VOTE	RULING
Crandell v. Nevada, 73 U.S. 35 (1868)	9–0	Struck down a law that levied one dollar tax on persons leaving the state by public transportation for running afoul of the right to "citizenship" protected by the Fourteenth Amendment's privilege or immunities clause.
Edwards v. California, 314 U.S. 160 (1941)	9–0	Struck down a law that aimed to keep out recent immigrants from the Midwest, commonly referred to as "Oakies."
Dunn v. Blumstein, 405 U.S. 330 (1972)	6–1	Struck down one-year state residency and three-month county residency requirements as a violation of the fundamental right to vote (see also Vol. 1, Ch. 8); Chief Justice Burger dissented.
Vlandis v. Kline, 412 U.S. 441 (1973)	6–3	Held as violative of the due process clause Connecticut's presumption that out-of-state students attending the state's colleges retain their status as out-of-state students, for tuition purposes, throughout their attendance in college; Chief Justice Burger and Justices Douglas and Rehnquist dissented.
Memorial Hospital v. Maricopa County, 415 U.S. 250 (1974)	8–1	Found that Arizona's one-year residency requirement for nonemergency medical care at county expense violates the right to travel; Justice Rehnquist dissented.

(continues)

■ THE DEVELOPMENT OF LAW
Rulings on Residency Requirements, the Right to
Interstate Travel, and Indigency (continued)

CASE	VOTE	RULING
Sosna v. Iowa, 419 U.S. 393 (1975)	6–3	Upheld a one-year residency requirement for initiating divorce proceedings; Justices Brennan, Marshall, and White dissented.
Califano v. Aznavorian, 439 U.S. 170 (1978)	9–0	Upheld Congress's withholding of benefits under the Supplemental Security Income program for any month that a recipient spends entirely outside of the United States.
Zobel v. Williams, 457 U.S. 55 (1982)	8–1	Struck down Alaska's system for redistributing state income from mineral deposits

to each adult resident, based on the number of years of state residency since 1959, upon finding no rational relationship between the residency requirement and the state's goal of prudent management of the fund; Justice Rehnquist dissented.

Supreme Court of New Hampshire v. Piper, 470 U.S. 274 (1985)	8–1	Struck down, under the privileges and immunities clause, a state supreme court ruling that only state residents were eligible for admission to the state bar.
Supreme Court of Virginia v. Friedman, 487 U.S. 59 (1988)	7–2	Struck down a state supreme court ruling that out-of-state lawyers must become permanent state residents before

they may be admitted to the state bar on motion (without taking the state bar examination). The majority found the distinction between resident and nonresident lawyers did not have a close and substantial relationship to the state's interests; Chief Justice Rehnquist and Justice Scalia dissented.

CASE	VOTE	RULING
M.L.B. v. S.L.J., 519 U.S. 102 (1996)	6–3	Writing for the Court, Justice Ginsburg held that states may not prevent indigents from

appealing family court decisions terminating their parental rights by requiring them to purchase trial transcripts before filing an appeal. Chief Justice Rehnquist and Justices Scalia and Thomas dissented.

CASE	VOTE	RULING
Saenz v. Roe, 526 U.S. 489 (1999)	7–2	Writing for the Court, Justice Stevens struck down California's law limiting welfare

benefits of new residents to that paid by the states in which they previously resided. To deny them California's benefits, which were the sixth highest in the country, Justice Stevens held, infringed on their right to travel and the privileges and immunities guaranteed by the Fourteenth Amendment. Chief Justice Rehnquist and Justice Thomas dissented.

■ THE DEVELOPMENT OF LAW

Rulings Dealing with Illegitimate Children

CASE	VOTE	RULING
Levy v. Louisiana, 391 U.S. 68 (1968), and *Glona v. American Guarantee,* 391 U.S. 68 (1968)	6–3	Justice Douglas held that illegitimate children are persons within the meaning of the Fourteenth Amendment's equal protection clause and

have a right to recover damages for the wrongful death of their mother, striking down Louisiana's law providing that only legitimate surviving children may sue for damages; Justices Harlan, Black, and Stewart dissented.

CASE	VOTE	RULING
Labine v. Vincent, 401 U.S. 532 (1971)	5–4	Justice Black held that the equal protection clause was not violated by Louisiana's

(continues)

■ THE DEVELOPMENT OF LAW
Rulings Dealing with Illegitimate Children (continued)

statute precluding illegitimate children from making claims of inheritance from their natural father's estate; Justices Brennan, Douglas, White, and Marshall dissented.

CASE	VOTE	RULING
Gomez v. Perez, 409 U.S. 535 (1973)	7–2	Per curiam decision finding the equal protection clause to be violated by a law distinguishing between legitimate and illegitimate children in providing for a father's responsibility for child support; Justices Stewart and Rehnquist dissented.
Weber v. Aetna Casualty, 406 U.S. 164 (1972)	8–1	Justice Powell struck down Louisiana's workers' compensation law that forbade recovery for the wrongful death of a parent by illegitimate children; Justice Rehnquist dissented.
New Jersey Welfare Rights Organization v. Cahill, 411 U.S. 619 (1973)	8–1	A per curiam decision holding that the equal protection clause was violated by a state law distinguishing between legitimate and illegitimate children in the award of state welfare benefits; Justice Rehnquist dissented.
Jimenez v. Weinberger, 417 U.S. 628 (1974)	8–1	Chief Justice Burger held that the denial of federal welfare benefits to illegitimate dependents of disabled persons violated the equal protection component of the Fifth Amendment's due process clause; Justice Rehnquist dissented.
Mathews v. Lucas, 427 U.S. 495 (1976)	6–3	Justice Blackmun upheld the Social Security Act's denial of disability benefits to illegitimate, but not legitimate, children and held that the provision did not require strict judicial scrutiny; Justices Stevens, Marshall, and Brennan dissented.
Trimble v. Gordon, 430 U.S. 762 (1977)	5–4	Justice Powell struck down a statute allowing illegitimate children to inherit only from their moth-

ers, and not fathers, because it was not "substantially related to a permissible state interest"; Chief Justice Burger and Justices Blackmun, Rehnquist, and Stewart dissented.

CASE	VOTE	RULING
Lalli v. Lalli, 439 U.S. 259 (1978)	5–4	Despite the ruling in Trimble, Justice Powell held for a bare majority that two illegitimate

children were not entitled to share in their natural father's estate because during his lifetime he had not obtained a judicial order declaring his paternity; Justices Brennan, Marshall, Stevens, and White dissented.

Fiallo v. Bell, 430 U.S. 787 (1977)	6–3	Justice Powell upheld Congress's denial of preferential status for immigration to the illegitimate children of aliens; Justices Brennan, Marshall, and White dissented.

Quilloin v. Walcott, 434 U.S. 246 (1978)	9–0	Justice Marshall held that a natural father's equal protection claims were not violated by the

application of "best interests of a child" standard in adoption proceedings and thus he did not have a veto over the adoption of his child by the natural mother's legal husband.

Parham v. Hughes, 441 U.S. 347 (1979)	5–4	Justice Stevens upheld a Georgia law precluding a father who had not legitimated a child from su-

ing for the child's wrongful death; Justices Brennan, Blackmun, Marshall, and White dissented.

Reed v. Campbell, 476 U.S. 852 (1986)	9–0	Justice Stevens held that illegitimate children are entitled to inherit from the estate of a deceased father.

Michael H. v. Gerald D., 491 U.S. 110 (1989)	5–4	For a plurality, Justice Scalia upheld California's law creating a legal presumption that a child

born to a married woman living with her legal husband is a child of the marriage and rejected arguments that the natural father, under the Fifth

(continues)

■ THE DEVELOPMENT OF LAW
Rulings Dealing with Illegitimate Children (continued)

Amendment's due process clause, had a right to file a filiation suit to establish paternity and a right to child visitation, as well as dismissed the claim that the statute violated the child's equal protection rights; Justice Stevens concurred; Justices Brennan, Blackmun, Marshall, and White dissented.

CASE	VOTE	RULING
Miller v. Albright, 523 U.S. 420 (1998)	6–3	Rejected a challenge to a federal state that automatically grants citizenship to illegitimate children born in a foreign country if the mother is a U.S. citizen, but sets a higher standard if the father is a citizen and the mother a foreign national; Justices Ginsburg, Breyer, and Souter dissented.

■ (4) ALIENAGE AND AGE

With the exception of the right to vote, most constitutional rights extend to the "people" or "persons," including citizens and aliens. Aliens, though, do not enjoy the same freedom as citizens when entering the country, and their residency in the United States may be conditioned by the government (as with student visas). In contrast to citizens, aliens may also be deported and the property of enemy aliens confiscated by the government during wartime.

Despite the constitutional rights that aliens share with citizens, and the historic waves of immigrants who built the country, state and federal laws since the Alien and Sedition Act of 1798 have discriminated against aliens, frequently denying them various kinds of public benefits and employment. But in *Graham v. Richardson*, 403 U.S. 365 (1971), the Court announced that alienage was a suspect category and that laws discriminating against aliens must survive strict scrutiny. While a series of subsequent rulings overturned other laws denying aliens benefits and employment opportunities, the Court drew back in *Foley v. Connelie*, 435 U.S. 291 (1978), when it came to New York's law barring aliens from being employed as state police officers. There and in *Ambach v. Norwick*, 441 U.S. 68 (1979), and *Cabell v. Chavez-Salido*, 454 U.S. 432 (1982), the Court held that aliens could be disqualified from positions in public employment that required the exercise of discretion in the performance of important governmental functions, such as law enforcement and education. The Court was also sharply split in *Plyler v. Doe* (1982) (excerpted below), when holding that Texas could not deny undocumented aliens a public education.

While giving heightened scrutiny to classifications based on age, in *Massachusetts Board of Retirement v. Murgia*, 427 U.S. 307 (1976), the Court held that age is not a suspect category under the equal protection clause. There, the Court upheld a state law requiring uniformed police to retire at age fifty. In *Vance v. Bradley*, 440 U.S. 93 (1979), the Court as well upheld under the rational basis test Congress's requiring members of the Foreign Service to retire at age sixty to promote younger members of the service and because of the risks and rigors of overseas service. However, Congress forbade age discrimination in a number of laws; notably, the Age Discrimination in Employment Act of 1967 prohibits employment discrimination against individuals between the ages of forty and seventy. However, in *Gregory v. Ashcroft*, 501 U.S. 452 (1991) (see Vol. 1, Ch. 7), the Court upheld Missouri's constitutional provision mandating that public officials retire at age seventy over the objections of two state judges, who claimed that the provision violated the federal Age Discrimination in Employment Act.

SELECTED BIBLIOGRAPHY

Karst, Kenneth. *Belonging to America: Equal Citizenship and the Constitution.* New Haven, CT: Yale University Press, 1989.

■ THE DEVELOPMENT OF LAW

Rulings on the Classification of Aliens

CASE	VOTE	RULING
Graham v. Richardson, 403 U.S. 365 (1971)	9–0	Declared that alienage was a suspect classification and held that Arizona's requirements for state welfare benefits violated the equal protection clause because they conditioned benefits on citizenship and durational residency requirements for aliens.

(continues)

■ THE DEVELOPMENT OF LAW
Rulings on the Classification of Aliens (continued)

CASE	VOTE	RULING
In re Griffiths, 413 U.S. 717 (1973)	7–2	Overturned a state law barring aliens from practicing law; Chief Justice Burger and Justice Rehnquist dissented.
Sugerman v. Dougall, 413 U.S. 634 (1973)	8–1	Held that New York's prohibition of aliens from being employed as state civil servants violated the equal protection clause; Justice Rehnquist dissented.

Hampton v. Mow Sun Wong, 426 U.S. 88 (1976) — 5–4 — Justice Stevens held for a bare majority that the concept of equal justice embodied in the due process clause of the Fifth Amendment forbade the exclusion of all persons who are not citizens of the United States, or natives of Samoa, from being employed in the federal civil service.

Mathews v. Diaz, 426 U.S. 67 (1976) — 9–0 — For a unanimous Court, Justice Stevens upheld the denial of Social Security Medicare benefits to aliens who had not resided in the United States for at least five years, observing that the Court should defer to "the strong federal interest in regulating foreign affairs."

Nyquist v. Mauclet, 432 U.S. 1 (1977) — 5–4 — Struck down a New York law barring resident aliens from eligibility for state financial aid and scholarships; Chief Justice Burger and Justices Powell, Stevens, and Rehnquist dissented.

| *Foley v. Connelie*, 435 U.S. 291 (1978) | 6–3 | Upheld New York's statute barring aliens from being employed as state police officers on the grounds that police serve important governmental functions. |

CASE	VOTE	RULING

Ambach v. Norwick, 441 U.S. 68 (1979) — 5–4 — Upheld a state law barring aliens from teaching in public schools unless they intended to become citizens of the United States, on the grounds that some state functions are so bound up with the operation of state government as to permit the exclusion of those persons from positions in the government who have not yet become part of the process of government; Justices Blackmun, Brennan, Marshall, and Stevens dissented.

Cabell v. Chavez-Salido, 454 U.S. 432 (1982) — 5–4 — Extended the state functions analysis in *Ambach* to permit California to bar aliens from working as state probation officers. *Ambach*'s dissenters renewed their opposition.

Bernal v. Fainter, 467 U.S. 216 (1984) — 8–1 — Struck down a Texas law requiring a notary public to be an American citizen, holding that laws that discriminate against aliens must survive the Court's strict scrutiny, unless a state demonstrates that its discrimination against aliens is in the service of an important public function; Justice Rehnquist dissented.

Jama v. Immigration and Customs Enforcement, 543 U.S. 335 (2005) — 5–4 — Writing for the Court, Justice Scalia held that a refugee living in the United States may be deported to the home country after a criminal conviction, even without the consent of that country's government. Justices Souter, Stevens, Ginsburg, and Breyer dissented.

Clark v. Martinez, 543 U.S. 371 (2005) — 7–2 — Writing for the Court, and drawing on the ruling in *Zadvydas v. Davis*, 533 U.S. 678 (2001), holding that aliens may be detained for six months as "reasonably necessary" to effectuate their removal, Justice Scalia held that inadmissible aliens may be held six months or longer, as "reasonably necessary," even if they may not be returned to their home country. Chief Justice Rehnquist and Justice Thomas dissented.

■ THE DEVELOPMENT OF LAW

Recent Rulings on Age Discrimination

CASE	VOTE	RULING
Equal Employment Opportunity Commission v. Arabian American Oil, 499 U.S. 244 (1991)	6–3	Held that Title VII of the Civil Rights Act—which bans discrimination in the workplace based on race, gender, religion,

and national origin—does not apply to companies doing business outside of the United States.

Gilmer v. Interstate/Johnson Lane Corp., 500 U.S. 20 (1991)	7–2	Held that the Age Discrimination in Employment Act of 1967 and the Federal Arbitration Act permit compulsory ar-

bitration, as required under an employment agreement, of employee disputes over alleged dismissals involving age discrimination.

Astoria Federal Savings and Loan v. Solimino, 501 U.S. 104 (1991)	9–0	Held that employees who accuse their employers of age discrimination under the Age Discrimination in Employment

Act of 1967 may bring suits in federal courts, after state agencies have dismissed their complaints and without further appeals in state courts.

Gregory v. Ashcroft, 501 U.S. 452 (1991)	6–3	Applied the "rational basis" test to an equal protection challenge to Missouri's state consti-

tutional provision requiring public officials to retire at age seventy. The state's law was deemed to have a rational basis given the undeniable effects of aging and the limited utility in removing judges from office through impeachment and judicial elections. Justices White and Stevens concurred and dissented in part; Justices Blackmun and Marshall dissented.

O'Connor v. Consolidated Coin Caterers, 517 U.S. 308 (1996)	9–0	Justice Scalia ruled that a fifty-six-year-old sales manager, who was fired and replaced by a forty-year-old, could bring a

suit for age discrimination under the federal Age Discrimination in Employment Act. In reversing the lower court's decision dismissing

O'Connor's suit, Justice Scalia held that it is not relevant whether an employee's replacement is under forty. Rather, what is relevant in such suits is evidence that an employee was fired because of his or her age. In the words of the justice, "There can be no greater inference of age discrimination when a forty-year-old is replaced by a thirty-nine-year-old than when a fifty-six-year-old is replaced by a forty-year-old."

CASE	VOTE	RULING

Kimel v. Florida Board of Regents, 528 U.S. 62 (2000) — 5–4 — Writing for the Court, Justice O'Connor held that Congress exceeded its powers under Section 5 of the Fourteenth Amendment and violated states' sovereign immunity under the Eleventh Amendment in extending provisions of the Age Discrimination in Employment Act to state employees, and ruled that state employees may not bring suits in federal courts to enforce those provisions. In reaffirming that age discrimination is not a suspect classification under the Fourteenth Amendment, Justice O'Connor emphasized: "Old age also does not define a discrete and insular minority because all persons, if they live out normal life spans, will experience it." Justices Stevens, Souter, Ginsburg, and Breyer dissented.

Reeves v. Sanderson Plumbing Products, Inc., 530 U.S. 133 (2000) — 9–0 — Writing for the Court, Justice O'Connor ruled that workers need not provide direct evidence that employers intentionally discriminated against them in hiring, promotion, and firing decisions, in a suit brought under the Age Discrimination in Employment Act. Employees need only prove that the employer's stated reason for their dismissal was false, and juries may infer from the evidence presented whether the employer's true motive was discriminatory.

Gomez-Perez v. Potter, Postmaster General, 553 U.S. 474 (2008) — 6–3 — Writing for the Court, Justice Alito held that under the Age Discrimination in Employment Act federal employees may not be subjected to retaliation because of their complaints about age discrimination. Chief Justice Roberts and Justices Thomas and Scalia dissented.

CBOCS West v. Humphries, 553 U.S. 442 (2008) — 7–2 — Writing for the Court, Justice Breyer held that employment-related retaliation claims are

(continues)

■ THE DEVELOPMENT OF LAW
Recent Rulings on Age Discrimination (continued)

---

permissible under Title VII of the Civil Rights Act of 1964. Humphries had alleged that CBOCS terminated his employment because he is black and had complained that a black coworker was also dismissed based on race. Justice Thomas and Scalia dissented.

CASE	VOTE	RULING
Gross v. FBL Financial Services, Inc., (2009)	5–4	Writing for the Court, Justice Thomas held that age, by a preponderance of evidence, must be the "but

for" cause of adverse employment action under the Age Discrimination Employment Act of 1967. In doing so, Justice Thomas made clear that companies may not be held to age discrimination suits of mixed motives because (1) that standard had proven over the years difficult to articulate to juries, and (2) even though Congress has extended mixed motive standards to many disparate treatment claims, it failed to do so with respect to age discrimination. Justices Stevens, Souter, Ginsburg, and Breyer dissented.

Plyler v. Doe
457 U.S. 202, 102 S.CT. 2382 (1982)

In 1975, two years after the Supreme Court's ruling in *San Antonio Independent School District v. Rodriguez* (1973) (excerpted in Section D (3) in this chapter), the Texas state legislature passed legislation authorizing local school districts to exclude children of undocumented aliens from public schools and to withhold school district funds for the education of those children. A class-action suit for certain school-age Mexican children who illegally entered and resided in Texas was brought against James Plyler, a school superintendent, and other state officials. A federal district court held that the state had violated the equal protection clause of the Fourteenth Amendment. On appeal to the Supreme Court, the lower court's ruling was affirmed by a bare majority in an opinion delivered by Justice William J. Brennan.

The Court's decision was 5–4, and the majority's opinion was announced by Justice Brennan. Justices Marshall, Blackmun, and

Powell delivered concurring opinions. Chief Justice Burger dissented and was joined by Justices White, Rehnquist, and O'Connor.

■ ■ ■

☐ *Justice BRENNAN delivered the opinion of the Court.*

The question presented by these cases is whether, consistent with the Equal Protection Clause of the Fourteenth Amendment, Texas may deny to undocumented school-age children the free public education that it provides to children who are citizens of the United States or legally admitted aliens. . . .

In applying the Equal Protection Clause to most forms of state action, we thus seek only the assurance that the classification at issue bears some fair relationship to a legitimate public purpose.

But we would not be faithful to our obligations under the Fourteenth Amendment if we applied so deferential a standard to every classification. The Equal Protection Clause was intended as a restriction on state legislative action inconsistent with elemental constitutional premises. Thus we have treated as presumptively invidious those classifications that disadvantage a "suspect class," or that impinge upon the exercise of a "fundamental right." With respect to such classifications, it is appropriate to enforce the mandate of equal protection by requiring the State to demonstrate that its classification has been precisely tailored to serve a compelling governmental interest. In addition, we have recognized that certain forms of legislative classification, while not facially invidious, nonetheless give rise to recurring constitutional difficulties; in these limited circumstances we have sought the assurance that the classification reflects a reasoned judgment consistent with the ideal of equal protection by inquiring whether it may fairly be viewed as furthering a substantial interest of the State. We turn to a consideration of the standard appropriate for the evaluation of [the Texas program].

Sheer incapability or lax enforcement of the laws barring entry into this country, coupled with the failure to establish an effective bar to the employment of undocumented aliens, has resulted in the creation of a substantial "shadow population" of illegal migrants—numbering in the millions—within our borders. This situation raises the specter of a permanent caste of undocumented resident aliens, encouraged by some to remain here as a source of cheap labor, but nevertheless denied the benefits that our society makes available to citizens and lawful residents. The existence of such an underclass presents most difficult problems for a Nation that prides itself on adherence to principles of equality under law.

The children who are plaintiffs in these cases are special members of this underclass. Persuasive arguments support the view that a State may withhold its beneficence from those whose very presence within the United States is the product of their own unlawful conduct. These arguments do not apply with the same force to classifications imposing disabilities on the minor *children* of such illegal entrants. At the least, those who elect to enter our territory by stealth and in violation of our law should be prepared to bear the consequences, including, but not limited to, deportation. But the children of those illegal entrants are not comparably situated. Their "parents have the ability to conform their conduct to societal norms," and presumably the ability to remove themselves from the State's jurisdiction; but the children who are plaintiffs in these cases "can affect neither their parents' conduct nor their

Justice William J. Brennan Jr. in his chambers. During his thirty-four years on the bench (1956–1990), Justice Brennan had a major influence on the Court's interpretation and application of the Fourteenth Amendment. (*Collection of the Supreme Court of the United States.*)

own status." *Trimble v. Gordon*, 430 U.S. 762 (1977). Even if the State found it expedient to control the conduct of adults by acting against their children, legislation directing the onus of a parent's misconduct against his children does not comport with fundamental conceptions of justice. . . .

Of course, undocumented status is not irrelevant to any proper legislative goal. Nor is undocumented status an absolutely immutable characteristic since it is the product of conscious, indeed unlawful, action. But [Texas's program] is directed against children, and imposes its discriminatory burden on the basis of a legal characteristic over which children can have little control. It is thus difficult to conceive of a rational justification for penalizing these children for their presence within the United States. Yet that appears to be precisely the effect of [the Texas law].

Public education is not a "right" granted to individuals by the Constitution. *San Antonio [Independent] School District, [v. Rodriguez*, 411 U.S. 1 (1973)]. But neither is it merely some governmental "benefit" indistinguishable from other forms of social welfare legislation. Both the importance of education in maintaining our basic institutions, and the lasting impact of its deprivation on the life of the child, mark the distinction. . . . As noted early in our history, "some degree of education is necessary to prepare citizens to participate effectively and intelligently in our open political system if we are to preserve freedom and independence." *Wisconsin v. Yoder*, 406 U.S. 205 (1972). . . . In addition, education provides the basic tools by which individuals might lead economically productive lives to the benefit of us all. In sum, education has a fundamental role in maintaining the fabric of our society. We cannot ignore the significant social costs borne by our Nation when select groups are denied the means to absorb the values and skills upon which our social order rests.

In addition to the pivotal role of education in sustaining our political and cultural heritage, denial of education to some isolated group of children poses an affront to one of the goals of the Equal Protection Clause: the abolition of governmental barriers presenting unreasonable obstacles to advancement on the basis of individual merit. . . . Illiteracy is an enduring disability. The inability to read and write will handicap the individual deprived of a basic education each and every day of his life. The inestimable toll of that deprivation on the social, economic, intellectual and psychological well-being of the individual, and the obstacle it poses to individual achievement, makes it most difficult to reconcile the cost or the principle of a status-based denial of basic education with the framework of equality embodied in the Equal Protection Clause. . . .

These well-settled principles allow us to determine the proper level of deference to be afforded [Texas]. Undocumented aliens cannot be treated as a suspect class because their presence in this country in violation of federal law is not a "constitutional irrelevancy." Nor is education a fundamental right; a State need not justify by compelling necessity every variation in the manner in which education is provided to its population. But more is involved in this case than the abstract question whether [Texas] discriminates against a suspect class, or whether education is a fundamental right. [Texas's program] imposes a lifetime hardship on a discrete class of children not accountable for their disabling status. The stigma of illiteracy will mark them for the rest of their lives. By denying these children a basic education, we deny them the ability to live within the structure of our civic institutions, and foreclose any realistic possibility that they will contribute to even the smallest way to the progress of our Nation. In determining the rationality of [Texas's law] we may appropriately take into account its costs to the Nation and to the innocent children who are its victims. In light of these countervailing costs, the discrimination contained in [Texas's program] can hardly be considered rational unless it furthers some substantial goal of the State.

It is the State's principal argument, and apparently the view of the dissenting Justices, that the undocumented status of these children *vel non* establishes a sufficient rational basis for denying them benefits that a State might choose to afford other residents. The State notes that while other aliens are admitted "on an equality of legal privileges with all citizens under nondiscriminatory laws," the asserted right of these children to an education can claim no implicit congressional imprimatur. Indeed, on the State's view, Congress' apparent disapproval of the presence of these children within the United States, and the evasion of the federal regulatory program that is the mark of undocumented status, provides authority for its decision to impose upon them special disabilities. Faced with an equal protection challenge respecting the treatment of aliens, we agree that the courts must be attentive to congressional policy; the exercise of congressional power might

well affect the State's prerogatives to afford differential treatment to a particular class of aliens. But we are unable to find in the congressional immigration scheme any statement of policy that might weigh significantly in
arriving at an equal protection balance concerning the State's authority to
deprive these children of an education. . . .

To be sure, like all persons who have entered the United States unlawfully, these children are subject to deportation. But there is no assurance
that a child subject to deportation will ever be deported. An illegal entrant
might be granted federal permission to continue to reside in this country,
or even to become a citizen. In light of the discretionary federal power to
grant relief from deportation, a State cannot realistically determine that
any particular undocumented child will in fact be deported until after
deportation proceedings have been completed. . . .

We are reluctant to impute to Congress the intention to withhold from
these children, for so long as they are present in this country through no
fault of their own, access to a basic education. In other contexts, undocumented status, coupled with some articulable federal policy, might enhance
State authority with respect to the treatment of undocumented aliens. But
in the area of special constitutional sensitivity presented by this case, and in
the absence of any contrary indication fairly discernible in the present legislative record, we perceive no national policy that supports the State in
denying these children an elementary education. . . .

Appellants argue that the classification at issue furthers an interest in
the "preservation of the state's limited resources for the education of its
lawful residents." . . . [But t]he State must do more than justify its classification with a concise expression of an intention to discriminate. Apart
from the asserted state prerogative to act against undocumented children
solely on the basis of their undocumented status—an asserted prerogative
that carries only minimal force in the circumstances of this case—we discern three colorable state interests that might support [Texas's law].

First, appellants appear to suggest that the State may seek to protect the
State from an influx of illegal immigrants. . . . [However, t]here is no evidence in the record suggesting that illegal entrants impose any significant
burden on the State's economy. To the contrary, the available evidence suggests that illegal aliens under-utilize public services, while contributing their
labor to the local economy and tax money to the State fisc. The dominant
incentive for illegal entry into the State of Texas is the availability of employment; few if any illegal immigrants come to this country, or presumably to
the State of Texas, in order to avail themselves of a free education. . . .

Second. . . . appellants suggest that undocumented children are appropriately singled out for exclusion because of the special burdens they impose
on the State's ability to provide high quality public education. But the record
in no way supports the claim that exclusion of undocumented children is
likely to improve the overall quality of education in the State. . . . Of course,
even if improvement in the quality of education were a likely result of barring some number of children from the schools of the State, the State must
support its selection of this group as the appropriate target for exclusion. In
terms of educational cost and need, however, undocumented children are
"basically indistinguishable" from legally resident alien children.

Finally, appellants suggest that undocumented children are appropriately
singled out because their unlawful presence within the United States renders

them less likely than other children to remain within the boundaries of the State, and to put their education to productive social or political use within the State. Even assuming that such an interest is legitimate, it is an interest that is most difficult to quantify. The State has no assurance that any child, citizen or not, will employ the education provided by the State within the confines of the State's borders. In any event, the record is clear that many of the undocumented children disabled by this classification will remain in this country indefinitely, and that some will become lawful residents or citizens of the United States. It is difficult to understand precisely what the State hopes to achieve by promoting the creation and perpetuation of a subclass of illiterates within our boundaries, surely adding to the problems and costs of unemployment, welfare, and crime. It is thus clear that whatever savings might be achieved by denying these children an education, they are wholly insubstantial in light of the costs involved to these children, the State, and the Nation.

If the State is to deny a discrete group of innocent children the free public education that it offers to other children residing within its borders, that denial must be justified by a showing that it furthers some substantial state interest. No such showing was made here. Accordingly, the judgment of the Court of Appeals in each of these cases is

Affirmed.

□ *Justice MARSHALL, concurring.*

While I join the Court's opinion . . . I continue to believe that an individual's interest in education is fundamental, and that this view is amply supported "by the unique status accorded public education by our society, and by the close relationship between education and some of our most basic constitutional values."

□ *Chief Justice BURGER, with whom Justice WHITE,*
Justice REHNQUIST, and Justice O'CONNOR join,
dissenting.

Were it our business to set the Nation's social policy, I would agree without hesitation that it is senseless for an enlightened society to deprive any children—including illegal aliens—of an elementary education. I fully agree that it would be folly—and wrong—to tolerate creation of a segment of society made up of illiterate persons, many having a limited or no command of our language. However, the Constitution does not constitute us as "Platonic Guardians" nor does it vest in this Court the authority to strike down laws because they do not meet our standards of desirable social policy, "wisdom," or "common sense."

The Court's holding today manifests the justly criticized judicial tendency to attempt speedy and wholesale formulation of "remedies" for the failures—or simply the laggard pace—of the political processes of our system of government. The Court employs, and in my view abuses the Fourteenth Amendment in an effort to become an omnipotent and omniscient problem solver. That the motives for doing so are noble and compassionate does not alter the fact that the Court distorts our constitutional function to make amends for the defaults of others. . . .

RESEARCHING LEGAL MATERIALS

The Internet offers numerous resources for legal research. Conducting legal research on the Internet is similar to researching printed legal documents in libraries. Indeed, most of those legal documents, such as court decisions, may be found on the Internet. Conducting legal research on the Internet thus may be more efficient and convenient for those with access to it. But however legal research is conducted, the researcher must have an understanding of legal sources as well as a research strategy.

I. Conducting Legal Research

A. LEGAL SOURCES

Generally, legal research aims to discover *primary* and *secondary* legal authorities to support a legal argument or position (that is, thesis statement).

1. PRIMARY AUTHORITIES

Primary authorities are the most persuasive sources because they represent most accurately what the law "is." Examples of primary authorities include federal and state constitutions, statutes, case opinions (written by judges deciding specific cases or controversies), and administrative regulations.

The decisions of the Supreme Court are officially published in the *United States Reports*. In addition, two companies print editions of the Court's decisions: the *Lawyers' Edition*, published by the Lawyers' Cooperative, and *The Supreme Court Reporter*, published by West Publishing Company. The decisions of federal courts of appeals are usually found in West's *Federal Reporter* (or *Federal Reporter*, 2nd, 3rd, or 4th series, respectively). Federal district court decisions may be found in West's *Federal Supplement* series. Most states publish some of the rulings of their courts, and West publishes a series of regional reporters that reprint the decisions and opinions of the highest courts in the states. These sources may be found on the Internet (as discussed below) through university and law school Internet servers, or through commercial servers such as *Lexis-Nexis* and *Westlaw*.

Note that primary legal authorities differ in their weight or authoritativeness. The decisions and opinions of the Supreme Court, for instance, are more authoritative than those of lower federal courts. Likewise, the Court's decision usually carries more weight than a concurring or dissenting opinion.

2. SECONDARY AUTHORITIES

Secondary authorities provide "secondary" perspectives on the law or, more precisely, on how the law may or should be interpreted. Examples of secondary authorities include law review articles (written by law students or scholars), legal treatises and annotations, legal encyclopedias, books, and academic journals (in law, legal history, jurisprudence, and social sciences, like *Judicature* and the *Journal of Supreme Court History*), as well as legal newspapers (such as *Legal Times* and the *National Law Journal*).

B. DEVELOPING A RESEARCH STRATEGY

While it is impossible to outline a research strategy that would work best for everyone, there are some general considerations in developing one. First, legal research usually involves gaining a broad understanding of the context of a case or controversy and then moving to the narrower, specific issues presented, as well as to the competing arguments and justifications for resolving those issues one way or the other. In other words, initially consider the historical, philosophical, and political bases for, as well as the subsequent development of, a legal doctrine, such as federalism or free speech, before turning to the specific case or controversy to be addressed. If you know very little about the subject, it is wise to consult secondary authorities *first* about what the law is and how and why it has developed. Second, once you have an understanding of the general legal issues and law involved, then examine the most relevant *primary authorities*, described above. The most critical step in conducting legal research is to read (or reread) the pertinent provision(s) of the Constitution, statute, or administrative regulation and then consider *what the Supreme Court has said* about those provisions and the issue presented, carefully analyzing the relevant or governing judicial opinions. Remember that the aim of legal research is to advance a position, a thesis, by persuasively justifying it with an analysis of and arguments drawn from the primary and secondary authorities discussed above.

II. *Legal Materials and Law-Related Sources on the Web*

Legal materials, documents, judicial opinions, and other law-related sources on the Web are available through a number of legal search engines. One of the most useful is *Findlaw* at **www.findlaw.com**. The Supreme Court of the United States maintains a site at **www.supremecourt.gov**, containing transcripts of oral arguments and opinions in recent cases. Also useful for researching decisions, areas of law, and votes is the Supreme Court Database at **www.supremecourtdatabase.org**.

The How, Why, and What to Briefing and Citing Court Cases

A. HOW TO BRIEF A CASE

There is no one "best way" to read and analyze cases. However, an understanding of the decision and opinions may best be acquired by following a prescribed pattern or outline that points up the essential issues of each case. It is suggested that students read the case in its entirety at least once before "briefing" the case along the lines suggested below.

1. TITLE AND CITATION: [*Marbury v. Madison*, 1 Cranch (5 U.S.) 137 (1803).]

2. FACTS OF THE CASE: A brief statement of the circumstances that brought about this case or controversy, identifying the parties and the holding of lower courts.

(Outgoing President Adams commissioned Marbury to serve as a district judge, but the commission went undelivered by his secretary of state, John Marshall. When President Jefferson came into office, he directed his secretary of state, James Madison, not to deliver Marbury's commission. Marbury filed an affidavit requiring Madison to show cause why a writ of mandamus should not be issued directing him to deliver the commission. Section 13 of the Judiciary Act of 1789, Marbury argued, empowered the Court to issue writs of mandamus.)

3. LEGAL QUESTION(S) PRESENTED: The question presented is revealed by the statement of facts, which should indicate the nature of the conflict of interests the Court must resolve. The legal question presented is often concisely stated by the Court at the outset of an opinion or the sections in an opinion dealing with specific questions presented. You should answer each question presented "yes" or "no."

(1. Has Marbury a right to his commission? Yes.
2. If a right has been violated do the laws afford a remedy? Yes.
3. Is the Court the legal body to afford such a remedy? No.
4. Does the Court have the power to declare a law unconstitutional? Yes.)

4. HOLDING: A statement of the Court's ruling and whether it affirmed or reversed the lower court's decision.

(Section 13 of the Judiciary Act of 1789 is unconstitutional.)

5. Opinion for the Court: The *opinion* refers to the legal reasoning that the Court offers as a justification for its holding. The Court's reasoning should be outlined point by point.

(1-A. Completion of the appointment establishes that Marbury has a legal right to his commission. 2-A. Authorities (Blackstone) show that where there is a legal right there exists a legal remedy. 2-B. Madison violated Marbury's right, and thus a remedy is due Marbury. 3-A. The Court cannot provide the remedy requested, however, since that would require an exercise of its original jurisdiction in violation of Article III of the Constitution. 3-B. Congress cannot alter the Court's original jurisdiction or expand its powers specified there. Section 13 appears to have enlarged the Court's power by giving it the power to issue writs of mandamus in original and appellate cases. 4-A. The Court has the power to declare a law unconstitutional because (1) of the supremacy clause of Article VI and (2) Congress may not enlarge the Court's original jurisdiction under Article III. 4-B. It is the duty of the Court "to say what the law is" because (1) judges take an oath to uphold the Constitution, and (2) "the Constitution specifies that a law repugnant to the Constitution is void, and courts as well as other departments are bound by it." (3) Since the Court's power extends to all cases and controversies under the Constitution, the Court must declare Section 13 unconstitutional.)

6. Separate Opinions: Both *concurring opinions* (opinions that agree with the Court's holding but disagree with some or all of its reasoning) and *dissenting opinions* (opinions that disagree with the Court's result and reasoning) should be noted and their major points emphasized.

(There were no separate opinions filed in this case.)

7. Comments and Evaluation: A statement of the case's legal, historical, and political importance, as well as criticisms of the justices' opinions and reasoning.

(1. Chief Justice Marshall should have disqualified himself from participating in the case. 2. The case did not need to be decided; it could have been remanded to a district court, since the Court had no jurisdiction. 3. Marshall's reading of Section 13 is open to criticism. 4. The case is the watershed ruling in which the Court asserted and rationalized the power of judicial review. 5. However, the Court's reasoning is not unassailable—Article III does not expressly provide for judicial review and other officials take an oath to uphold the Constitution as well; *Eakin v. Raub* on triparite or "departmental theory" of constitutional interpretation. 6. *Marbury v. Madison*, however, does not assert "judicial supremacy" as some Court-watchers and justices subsequently claimed.)

B. WHY BRIEF CASES?

Briefing cases has immediate and long-term benefits: the student will have read the case thoroughly and carefully and will have a permanent condensed record of the case. The exercise itself forces the student to come to terms with his or her understanding of the case, prepares the student for lectures and discussion, and will prove an invaluable aid in studying for the midterm and final examination.

C. CASE CITATION: Why, What, Where, and How

1. WHY FOLLOW LEGAL CITATION FORM?

   a. Legal writing requires frequent citation of authority and evaluation of that authority depends on proper citation form.
   b. In this context, citations in the text greatly aid the reader, eliminating the necessity of moving back and forth between text and footnotes.

2. WHAT TO CITE (in order of their decreasing legal weight):

   a. Opinions (majority) for the Supreme Court.
   b. Supreme Court plurality, concurring or dissenting opinions.
   c. Circuit Court opinions.
   d. District Court opinions.
   e. Other sources:
      (1) state court opinions if the issue is one of state law;
      (2) law review articles *only* if there is no Supreme Court opinion or if the issue involves, for example, economic analysis.
   f. Do not cite a lower court opinion or a nonmajority opinion as binding precedent; they are persuasive authority only.

3. WHERE DOES THE CITATION APPEAR?

   a. As appositives: In *Brown v. Board of Education*, 347 U.S. 483 (1954), the Court struck down racial segregation of public schools.
   b. In citation sentences: Racial segregation of public schools violates the equal protection clause. *Brown v. Board of Education*, 347 U.S. 483 (1954).

4. HOW TO CITE CASES PROPERLY:

   a. An opinion for the Supreme Court: *Katzenbach v. Morgan*, 384 U.S. 641 (1966), or *Katzenbach v. Morgan*, 384 U.S. 641 (1966) (Brennan, J.).
   b. A specific page in the Court's opinion: *Katzenbach v. Morgan*, 384 U.S. 641, 644 (1966).
   c. Concurring and dissenting opinions: *Sherbert v. Verner*, 374 U.S. 398, 477 (1963) (Stewart, J., con. op.). *Sherbert v. Verner*, 374 U.S. 398, 495 (1963) (Harlan and White, J.J., dis. op.).
   d. Circuit Court cases: *Yeager v. Estelle*, 489 F.2d 276 (5th Cir., 1973).
   e. District Court cases: *Dodd v. Smith*, 389 F.Supp. 154 (D. Mass., 1975).
   f. Explanatory phrases and case history: *Jackson v. Metropolitan Edison Co.*, 348 F.Supp. 954 (M.D., Pa., 1972), *aff'd.*, 483 F.2d 754 (3d Cir., 1974), *rev'd.*, 419 U.S. 345 (1974).

g. Later references to a case previously cited in full:

(1) Use *Id.* (legal version of *Ibid.*) when the later citation immediately follows the full citation: *Id.,* at 427.

(2) Use abbreviated case names, if desired, where other case citations intervene: *Jackson,* at 420 (specific page), or *Jackson, supra* (full op.).

5. ADDITIONAL REFERENCES:

See Albert Melone, *Researching Constitutional Law* (New York: Scott, Foresman/Little, Brown, 2012), or the "Blue Book," *A Uniform System of Citation* (Cambridge, MA: Harvard Law Review Association, 1999).

Members of the Supreme Court of the United States

CHIEF JUSTICES

	APPOINTING PRESIDENT	DATES OF SERVICE
Jay, John	Washington	1789–1795
Rutledge, John	Washington	1795
Ellsworth, Oliver	Washington	1796–1800
Marshall, John	Adams, J.	1801–1835
Taney, Roger Brooke	Jackson	1836–1864
Chase, Salmon Portland	Lincoln	1864–1873
Waite, Morrison Remick	Grant	1874–1888
Fuller, Melville Weston	Cleveland	1888–1910
White, Edward Douglass	Taft	1910–1921
Taft, William Howard	Harding	1921–1930
Hughes, Charles Evans	Hoover	1930–1941
Stone, Harlan Fiske	Roosevelt, F.	1941–1946
Vinson, Frederick Moore	Truman	1946–1953
Warren, Earl	Eisenhower	1953–1969
Burger, Warren Earl	Nixon	1969–1986
Rehnquist, William Hubbs	Reagan	1986–2005
Roberts, John G., Jr.	Bush, G. W.	2005–

ASSOCIATE JUSTICES

	APPOINTING PRESIDENT	DATES OF SERVICE
Rutledge, John	Washington	1790–1791
Cushing, William	Washington	1790–1810
Wilson, James	Washington	1789–1798
Blair, John, Jr.	Washington	1790–1796
Iredell, James	Washington	1790–1799
Johnson, Thomas	Washington	1792–1793
Paterson, William	Washington	1793–1806
Chase, Samuel	Washington	1796–1811
Washington, Bushrod	Adams, J.	1799–1829
Moore, Alfred	Adams, J.	1800–1804

ASSOCIATE JUSTICES *(continued)*

	APPOINTING PRESIDENT	DATES OF SERVICE
Johnson, William	Jefferson	1804–1834
Livingston, Henry Brockholst	Jefferson	1807–1823
Todd, Thomas	Jefferson	1807–1826
Duvall, Gabriel	Madison	1811–1835
Story, Joseph	Madison	1812–1845
Thompson, Smith	Monroe	1823–1843
Trimble, Robert	Adams, J. Q.	1826–1828
McLean, John	Jackson	1830–1861
Baldwin, Henry	Jackson	1830–1844
Wayne, James Moore	Jackson	1835–1867
Barbour, Philip Pendleton	Jackson	1836–1841
Catron, John	Jackson	1837–1865
McKinley, John	Van Buren	1838–1852
Daniel, Peter Vivian	Van Buren	1842–1860
Nelson, Samuel	Tyler	1845–1872
Woodbury, Levi	Polk	1845–1851
Grier, Robert Cooper	Polk	1846–1870
Curtis, Benjamin Robbins	Fillmore	1851–1857
Campbell, John Archibald	Pierce	1853–1861
Clifford, Nathan	Buchanan	1858–1881
Swayne, Noah Haynes	Lincoln	1862–1881
Miller, Samuel Freeman	Lincoln	1862–1890
Davis, David	Lincoln	1862–1877
Field, Stephen Johnson	Lincoln	1863–1897
Strong, William	Grant	1870–1880
Bradley, Joseph P.	Grant	1870–1892
Hunt, Ward	Grant	1873–1882
Harlan, John Marshall	Hayes	1877–1911
Woods, William Burnham	Hayes	1881–1887
Matthews, Stanley	Garfield	1881–1889
Gray, Horace	Arthur	1882–1902
Blatchford, Samuel	Arthur	1882–1893
Lamar, Lucius Quintus C.	Cleveland	1888–1893
Brewer, David Josiah	Harrison	1890–1910
Brown, Henry Billings	Harrison	1891–1906
Shiras, George, Jr.	Harrison	1892–1903
Jackson, Howell Edmunds	Harrison	1893–1895
White, Edward Douglass	Cleveland	1894–1910
Peckham, Rufus Wheeler	Cleveland	1896–1909
McKenna, Joseph	McKinley	1898–1925
Holmes, Oliver Wendell	Roosevelt, T.	1902–1932
Day, William Rufus	Roosevelt, T.	1903–1922

	APPOINTING PRESIDENT	DATES OF SERVICE
Moody, William Henry	Roosevelt, T.	1906–1910
Lurton, Horace Harmon	Taft	1910–1914
Hughes, Charles Evans	Taft	1910–1916
Van Devanter, Willis	Taft	1911–1937
Lamar, Joseph Rucker	Taft	1911–1916
Pitney, Mahlon	Taft	1912–1922
McReynolds, James Clark	Wilson	1914–1941
Brandeis, Louis Dembitz	Wilson	1916–1939
Clarke, John Hessin	Wilson	1916–1922
Sutherland, George	Harding	1921–1938
Butler, Pierce	Harding	1923–1939
Sanford, Edward Terry	Harding	1923–1930
Stone, Harlan Fiske	Coolidge	1925–1941
Roberts, Owen Josephus	Hoover	1930–1945
Cardozo, Benjamin Nathan	Hoover	1932–1938
Black, Hugo Lafayette	Roosevelt, F.	1937–1971
Reed, Stanley Forman	Roosevelt, F.	1938–1957
Frankfurter, Felix	Roosevelt, F.	1939–1962
Douglas, William Orville	Roosevelt, F.	1939–1975
Murphy, Frank	Roosevelt, F.	1940–1949
Byrnes, James Francis	Roosevelt, F.	1941–1942
Jackson, Robert Houghwout	Roosevelt, F.	1941–1954
Rutledge, Wiley Blount	Roosevelt, F.	1943–1949
Burton, Harold Hitz	Truman	1945–1958
Clark, Thomas Campbell	Truman	1949–1967
Minton, Sherman	Truman	1949–1956
Harlan, John Marshall (II)	Eisenhower	1955–1971
Brennan, William Joseph, Jr.	Eisenhower	1956–1990
Whittaker, Charles Evans	Eisenhower	1957–1962
Stewart, Potter	Eisenhower	1958–1981
White, Byron Raymond	Kennedy	1962–1993
Goldberg, Arthur Joseph	Kennedy	1962–1965
Fortas, Abe	Johnson, L.	1965–1969
Marshall, Thurgood	Johnson, L.	1967–1991
Blackmun, Harry A.	Nixon	1970–1994
Powell, Lewis Franklin, Jr.	Nixon	1972–1987
Rehnquist, William Hubbs	Nixon	1972–1986
Stevens, John Paul	Ford	1975–2010
O'Connor, Sandra Day	Reagan	1981–2006
Scalia, Antonin	Reagan	1986–2016
Kennedy, Anthony	Reagan	1988–2018
Souter, David H.	Bush, G. H. W.	1990–2009
Thomas, Clarence	Bush, G. H. W.	1991–

ASSOCIATE JUSTICES *(continued)*

	APPOINTING PRESIDENT	DATES OF SERVICE
Ginsburg, Ruth Bader	Clinton	1993–
Breyer, Stephen G.	Clinton	1994–
Alito, Samuel, Jr.	Bush, G. W.	2006–
Sotomayor, Sonia	Obama	2009–
Kagan, Elena	Obama	2010–
Gorsuch, Neil M.	Trump	2017–
Kavanaugh, Brett M.	Trump	2018–

BIOGRAPHIES OF CURRENT JUSTICES

Chief Justice John G. Roberts Jr. was born in Buffalo, New York, on January 27, 1955. After attending a Catholic boarding school in Indiana, he earned his B.A. from Harvard University and his J.D. from Harvard Law School, where he served as managing editor of the *Harvard Law Review*. Upon graduating, he served as a law clerk for the U.S. Court of Appeals for the Second Circuit judge Henry Friendly and, subsequently, for then associate justice William H. Rehnquist. From 1981 to 1982, he worked in the administration of President Ronald Reagan as a special assistant to the attorney general and as an associate counsel to the White House Council from 1982 to 1986. Roberts then went into private legal practice in Washington, D.C., but left to serve as deputy solicitor general in the administration of President George H. W. Bush from 1989 to 1993. In 1992, President Bush nominated him to serve on the U.S. Court of Appeals for the District of Columbia Circuit, but no Senate vote on his confirmation was taken and he returned to private legal practice. During his time in government and private practice, Roberts argued thirty-nine cases, and won twenty-five, before the Supreme Court. In 2001, President George W. Bush renominated him to the Court of Appeals for the District of Columbia Circuit, but his nomination failed to make it out of the Democratic-controlled Senate Judiciary Committee. He was, again, renominated in 2003 and confirmed for a seat on the appellate bench. In 2005, following the announced retirement of Justice Sandra Day O'Connor, President Bush nominated him to fill her seat on the Supreme Court, but following the death of Chief Justice William H. Rehnquist, Justice Roberts was nominated for the chief justiceship. He received the Senate's confirmation as the 17th chief justice and 109th justice by a vote of 78–22. See *Confirmation Hearing on the Nomination of John G. Roberts Jr. to Be Chief Justice of the United States: Hearing before the Senate Committee on the Judiciary*, 109th Cong. (2005). Among his extrajudicial writings is "Oral Advocacy and the Re-emergence of a Supreme Court Bar," 30 *Journal of Supreme Court History* 68 (2005). See also Joan Biskupic, *The Chief: The Life and Turbulent Times of Chief Justice John Roberts* (New York: Basic Books, 2019). Mark Tushnet, *In the Balance: Law and Politics on the Roberts Court* (New York: W. W. Norton, 2013); and Marcia Coyle, *The Roberts Court* (New York: Simon & Schuster, 2013).

Justice Samuel Anthony Alito Jr. was born in Trenton, New Jersey, on April 1, 1950. After graduating with an B.A. from Princeton University in 1972, he earned his J.D. from Yale Law School in 1975. He subsequently clerked for the U.S. Court of Appeals for the Third Circuit judge Leonard Garth, then worked as an assistant U.S. attorney, and during the administration of President Ronald Reagan as an assistant to the solicitor general (from 1981 to 1985) and as a deputy assistant attorney general (from 1985 to 1987). During the administration of President George H. W. Bush, he served as a U.S. attorney. In 1990, President Bush nominated him to and he was confirmed for a seat on the U.S. Court of Appeals for the Third Circuit. In 2005, he was nominated by President George W. Bush to fill the seat of retiring Justice Sandra Day O'Connor. He was confirmed by the Senate as the 110th justice in January 2006 by a vote of 58–42.

Justice Stephen G. Breyer was born in San Francisco on August 15, 1938. After graduating from Stanford University, he earned a second B.A. as a Marshall Scholar at Oxford University and then received his law degree from Harvard Law School. After clerking for a year with liberal Justice Arthur J. Goldberg, Breyer went into private practice for a few years. In 1970, he went back to Harvard Law School, where he taught administrative law and regulation. During the Watergate investigation of the Nixon administration's illegal activities, he served as an assistant special prosecutor before returning to teach at Harvard until 1979, when he became chief counsel for the Senate Judiciary Committee. In 1980, Democratic President Jimmy Carter appointed him to the Court of Appeals for the First Circuit, where he served until President Clinton appointed him to the Supreme Court in 1994. He was confirmed by a vote of 87–9, and became the seventh Jewish justice. See U.S. Congress, Senate, Committee on the Judiciary, *Hearings before the Committee on the Judiciary, U.S. Senate, One Hundred Third Congress, 2nd Session, on the Nomination of Judge Stephen G. Breyer to the Supreme Court of the United States, July 12, 13, 14, and 15, 1994* (Washington, DC: Government Printing Office, 1995). Among Justice Breyer's many publications are "Our Democratic Constitution," 77 *New York University Law Review* 245 (2002); "Judicial Review," 78 *Texas Law Review* 761 (2000); *Active Liberty: Interpreting Our Democratic Constitution* (New York: Knopf, 2005); *Making Our Democracy Work: A Judge's View* (New York: Knopf, 2010); and *The Court and the World: American Law and the New Global Realities* (New York: Knopf, 2015). For a discussion of Justice Breyer's judicial philosophy, see and compare Paul Gewirtz, "The Pragmatic Passion of Stephen Breyer," 115 *Yale Law Journal* 1675 (2006); Cass Sunstein, "Justice Breyer's Democratic Pragmatism," 115 *Yale Law Journal* 1719 (2006); Robert Bork, "Enforcing a 'Mood,'" *New Criterion* 63 (February 2006); Richard Posner, "Justice Breyer Throws Down the Gauntlet," 115 *Yale Law Journal* 1699 (2006); and Linda Greenhouse, "The Breyer Project: 'Why Couldn't You Work This Thing Out?'" 4 *Charleston Law Review* 37 (2009).

Justice Ruth Bader Ginsburg was born in Brooklyn, New York, on March 15, 1933. After graduating from Cornell University, she attended Harvard Law School but transferred and graduated from Columbia University School of Law after her husband was hired by a New York law firm. Unable to find a law firm in New York that would hire a female attorney, Ginsburg served for several years as a research associate at Columbia Law School and then joined Rutgers University School of Law, where she rose to the rank of full professor before becoming the first female professor at Columbia Law School. Besides teaching, Ginsburg served as the director of the American Civil Liberties Union's Women's Rights Project and argued six, and won five, important gender-based discrimination cases before the Supreme Court. In 1980, she was appointed to the Court of Appeals for the District of Columbia Circuit, and in 1993 she was appointed to the Supreme Court by President Bill Clinton. Justice Ginsburg is the second woman to sit on the high court and the first Jewish justice to sit there since the retirement of Justice Arthur J. Goldberg in 1965. See U.S. Congress, Senate, Committee on the Judiciary, *Hearings before the Committee on the Judiciary, U.S. Senate, One Hundred Third Congress, 1st Session, on the Nomination of Judge Ruth Bader Ginsburg, to Be Associate Justice of the Supreme Court, July 20, 21, 22, and 23, 1993* (Washington, DC: Government Printing Office, 1994). Among Justice Ginsburg's extrajudicial publications are "Speaking in a Judicial Voice" 67 *New York University Law Review* 1185 (1992); "The Progression of Women in the Law," 28 *Valparaiso University Law Review* 1161 (1994); "Some Thoughts on Autonomy and Equality in Relation to *Roe v. Wade*," 63 *North Carolina Law Review* 375 (1985); "Remarks on Writing Separately," 65 *Washington Law Review* 133 (1990); "Constitutional Adjudication in the United States as a Means of Advancing the Equal Stature of Men and Women under the Law," 83 *Georgetown Law Review* 263 (1997); and *In My Own Words: Ruth Bader Ginsburg* (New York: Simon & Schuster, 2016). See also Scott Dodson, ed., *The Legacy of Ruth Bader Ginsburg* (New York: Cambridge University Press, 2015); Irin Carmon and Shana Knizhnik, *Notorious RBG: The Life and Times of Ruth Bader Ginsburg* (New York: Dey Street Books, 2015); and Linda Hirshman, *Sisters in Law: The Singular Friendship of Justices Sandra Day O'Connor and Ruth Bader Ginsburg* (New York: Harper, 2015).

Neil M. Gorsuch was born in Denver, Colorado, on August 29, 1967, but as a teenager lived in Washington, DC. He was raised a Catholic, attending a Jesuit-preparatory school, but became an Episcopalian. He received a B.A. from Columbia University (1988), a J.D. from Harvard Law School (1991), and a D.Phil. from Oxford University in England (2004), where he studied on a Marshall scholarship. After clerking for a judge on the U.S. Court of Appeals for the District of Columbia Circuit, he clerked for Justices Byron White and Anthony Kennedy (1993–1994). Gorsuch, then practiced law for a decade before becoming a deputy to the associate attorney general in the Department of Justice (2005–2006). In 2006, President George W. Bush named him to the U.S. Court of Appeals for the Tenth Circuit. President Donald Trump in turn elevated him to the Supreme Court in 2017. After a 54–45 Senate confirmation vote, he became the 113th justice. Among his publications are *The Future of Assisted Suicide and Euthanasia* (Princeton, NJ: Princeton University Press, 2006); "Law's

Irony," 37 *Harvard Journal of Law & Public Policy* 743 (2014); and "Of Lions and Bears, Judges and Legislators, and the Legacy of Justice Scalia," 66 *Case Western Reserve Law Review* 905 (2016); and contributed as a co-author to the collection *The Law of Judicial Precedent* (St. Paul, MN: Thomson Reuters, 2016). See also John Grennya, *Gorsuch: The Judge Who Speaks for Himself* (New York: Simon & Schuster, 2018).

Justice Elena Kagan was born on the Lower East Side of Manhattan, New York, on April 28, 1960. She received her B.A. from Princeton (1981), an M. Phil. from Oxford University (1983), and a J.D. from Harvard Law School (1986). Subsequently, she clerked for Justice Thurgood Marshall, practiced law for three years, and then taught at the University of Chicago Law School before serving (1995–1999) in the Clinton administration. Afterward, she taught at Harvard Law School and became dean before President Barack Obama appointed her solicitor general in 2009. She was confirmed by a Senate vote of 63–37. Her few prejudicial publications focused primarily on the First Amendment, administrative law, and tributes to former teachers. At age fifty, Kagan became the 112th justice, the fourth woman, and the eighth Jewish justice to serve on the Court.

Brett M. Kavanaugh was born in Washington, DC, on February 12, 1965, but was raised in Bethesda, Maryland. A Catholic, he attended Georgetown Prep, a Jesuit school, two years ahead of Neil Gorsuch. He then graduated from Yale College (1987) and Yale Law School (1990). The following two years he clerked for judges on the U.S. Court of Appeals for the Third and Ninth Circuits, before a one-year fellowship in the Office of Independent Counsel, headed by Kenneth Starr. Not offered a clerkship by Chief Justice Rehnquist, Kavanaugh reapplied and became a clerk for Justice Kennedy, alongside Neil Gorsuch. He then worked for Starr in the Office of Independent Counsel, investigating President Bill Clinton, the "Whitewater" real estate deal, and the Monica Lewinsky affair. Kavanaugh later became a partner in a prominent Washington, DC law firm. After George W. Bush became president in 2001, he became an associate to the White House Counsel and later served as assistant in the Office of the President and as White House staff secretary. In 2003, Bush nominated him to the U.S. Court of Appeals for the DC circuit, but opposition and contentious Senate hearings delayed his appointment until 2006. In July 2018, President Trump nominated him to fill the seat of retiring Justice Kennedy. He was confirmed by a Senate vote of 50–48 as the 114th justice. Among his writing while an appellate court judge are "Two Challenges for the Judge as Umpire: Statutory Ambiguity and Constitutional Exceptions," 92 *Notre Dame Law Review* 1907 (2017); "Fixing Statutory Interpretation," 129 *Harvard Law Review* 2118 (2016); "The Judge as Umpire: Ten Principles," 65 *Catholic University Law Review* 683 (2016); "The Courts and the Administrative State," 64 *Case Western Reserve Law Review* 711 (2014); "Our Anchor for 225 Years and Counting: The Enduring Significance of the

Precise Text of the Constitution," 89 *Notre Dame Law Review* 1907 (2014); "A Dialogue with Federal Judges on the Role of History in Interpretation," 80 *George Washington Law Review* 1889 (2012); and "Separation of Powers during the Forty-Fourth Presidency and Beyond," 93 *Minnesota Law Review* 1454 (2009); and co-author of *Law of Judicial Precedent* (St. Paul, MN: Thomson Reuters, 2016).

Justice Sonia Sotomayor was born on June 25, 1954, a daughter of Catholic immigrants from Puerto Rico, and grew up in the Bronx, New York. After graduating from Princeton University and Yale Law School, where she was an editor of the *Yale Law Journal*, she spent five years as a prosecutor in Manhattan and then worked in private corporate legal practice. In 1992, Republican President George H. W. Bush appointed her to a federal district court, and Democratic President Bill Clinton elevated her to the U.S. Court of Appeals for the Second Circuit in 1998. In 2009, Democratic President Barack Obama nominated her, at age fifty-five, to the Supreme Court, and she was confirmed by a vote of 68–31 as the 111th justice, first Latina, and third woman to sit on the Court. Among her off-the-bench publications as an appellate judge are "A Latina Judge's Voice," 13 *Berkeley La Raza Law Journal* 87 (2002); and *My Beloved World* (New York: Random House, 2013). See also David Fontana, "The People's Justice?" 123 *Yale Law Journal* 447 (2014); and Joan Biskupic, *Breaking In: The Rise of Sotomayor and the Politics of Justice* (New York: Sarah Crichton Books, 2014).

Justice Clarence Thomas was born in Pin Point, Georgia, on June 23, 1948. Raised as a Catholic, he became a Protestant but returned to the Catholic Church after his appointment. Thomas completed his undergraduate degree at Holy Cross College and then attended Yale Law School. After graduating in 1974, Thomas joined the staff of the attorney general of Missouri, John Danforth, a young Republican who became his political mentor. When Danforth was elected to the Senate, Thomas went into private practice for two years but subsequently rejoined Senator Danforth's staff as a legislative assistant and became active in the movement of conservative blacks opposed to welfare, busing, and affirmative action. Thomas's involvement in the conservative movement within the Republican Party brought him to the attention of the administration of President Ronald Reagan. In 1981, he was appointed assistant secretary for civil rights in the Department of Education. Within a year, Reagan promoted him to the position of director of the Equal Employment Opportunity Commission (EEOC). In 1990, he was named to the Court of Appeals for the District of Columbia Circuit, and the following year President George H. W. Bush named him to replace retiring Justice Thurgood Marshall. He was confirmed by a vote of 52–48. See U.S. Congress, Senate, Committee on the Judiciary, *Hearings before the Committee on the Judiciary, U.S. Senate, 1st Session, on the Nomination of Judge Clarence Thomas to Be Associate Justice of the Supreme Court of the United States* (Washington, DC: Government Printing Office, 1993). See also Justice Thomas's article,

"Freedom: A Responsibility, Not a Right," 21 *Ohio Northern University Law Review* 5 (1994); and his publications prior to his appointment to the Supreme Court, such as "Toward a 'Plain Reading' of the Constitution— The Declaration of Independence in Constitutional Interpretation," 30 *Howard Law Journal* 983 (1987); "The Higher Law Background of the Privileges or Immunities Clause of the Fourteenth Amendment," 12 *Harvard Journal of Law & Public Policy* 63 (1989); and "Judging," 45 *Kansas Law Review* 1 (1996). For a discussion of Justice Thomas's judicial philosophy, see Scott D. Gerber, *First Principles: The Jurisprudence of Clarence Thomas* (New York: New York University Press, 1999); Christopher E. Smith and Joyce Baugh, *The Real Clarence Thomas: Confirmation Veracity Meets Performance* (New York: Peter Lang, 2000); Ken Foskett, *Judging Thomas: The Life and Times of Clarence Thomas* (New York: William Morrow, 2004); Andrew P. Thomas, *Clarence Thomas: A Biography* (San Francisco: Encounter Books, 2001); and Kevin Merida and Michael Fletcher, *Supreme Discomfort: The Divided Soul of Clarence Thomas* (New York: Doubleday, 2007). See, generally, Clarence Thomas, *My Grandfather's Son: A Memoir* (New York: Harper, 2007).

Glossary

Abatement. A reduction or the suspension, in whole or part, of a continuing charge or activity.

Actual malice. *See* malice.

Advisory opinion. An opinion or interpretation of law that does not have binding effect. The Court does not give advisory opinions, for example, on hypothetical disputes; it decides only actual cases or controversies.

Affirm. In an appellate court, to reach a decision that agrees with the result reached in a case by the lower court.

Affirmative action programs. Programs required by federal or state laws designed to remedy discriminatory practices by hiring minority-group persons and/or women.

A fortiori. With stronger reason; a term denoting that because a fact exists, therefore another, included in it though less probable or unusual, must also exist.

Ambulatory retroactivity. The changeable or alterable retroapplication of a constitutional decision, so that the decision applies only to prospective or pending cases.

Amicus curiae. A friend of the court; a person not a party to litigation, who volunteers or is invited by the court to give his views on a case.

Appeal. To take a case to a higher court for review. Generally, a party losing in a trial court may appeal once to an appellate court as a matter of right. If the party loses in the appellate court, appeal to a higher court is within the discretion of the higher court. Most appeals to the Supreme Court are within its discretion to deny or grant a hearing.

Appellant. The party that appeals a lower-court decision to a higher court.

Appellee. One who has an interest in upholding the decision of a lower court and is compelled to respond when the case is appealed to a higher court by the appellant.

Bill of Attainder. A legislative act that inflicts punishment on a named individual or members of a group without a judicial trial.

Brief. A document prepared by counsel to serve as the basis for an argument in court, setting out the facts and legal arguments in support of their case.

Case. A general term for an action, cause, suit, or controversy, at law or equity; a question contested before a court.

Case law. The law as defined by previously decided cases, distinct from statutes and other sources of law.

Certification, writ of. A method of taking a case from appellate court to the Supreme Court in which the lower court asks that some question or interpretation of law be certified, clarified, and made more certain.

Certiorari, **writ of.** A writ issued from the Supreme Court, at its discretion and at the request of a petitioner, to order a lower court to send the record of a case to the Court for its review.

Civil law. The body of law dealing with the private rights of individuals, as distinguished from criminal law.

Class action. A lawsuit brought by one person or group on behalf of all persons similarly situated.

Comity. Courtesy, respect; referring to the deference federal courts pay to state court decisions that are based on state law.

Common law. The collection of principles and rules, particularly from unwritten English law, that derive their authority from long-standing usage and custom or from courts recognizing and enforcing those customs.

Compelling state interest. A test used to uphold state action against First Amendment and equal protection challenges because of the serious need for government action.

Concurring opinion. An opinion by a justice that agrees with the result reached by the Court in a case but disagrees with the Court's rationale or reasoning for its decision.

Contempt (civil and criminal). Civil contempt is the failure to do something for the benefit of another party after being ordered to do so by a court. Criminal contempt occurs when a person exhibits disrespect for a court or obstructs the administration of justice.

Contract. An agreement between two or more persons that creates an obligation to do or not do a particular thing.

Controversies. *See* Justiciable controversy.

Criminal law. The body of law that deals with the enforcement of laws and the punishment of persons who, by breaking laws, commit crimes against the state.

Declaratory judgment. A court pronouncement declaring a legal right or interpretation but not ordering a special action.

De facto. In fact; in reality.

Defendant. In a civil action, the party denying or defending itself against charges brought by a plaintiff. In a criminal action, the person indicted for the commission of an offense.

De jure. As a result of law; as a result of official action.

Delegation of powers. The transfer of authority by one branch of government to another branch or administrative agency.

Dicta. *See Obiter dictim.*

Discretionary jurisdiction. Jurisdiction that a court may accept or reject in particular cases. The Supreme Court has discretionary jurisdiction in over 90 percent of the cases that come to it.

Dismissal. An order disposing of a case without a hearing or trial.

Dissenting opinion. An opinion by a justice that disagrees with the result reached by the Court in a case.

Docket. All cases filed in a court.

Due process. Fair and regular procedure. The Fifth and Fourteenth Amendments guarantee persons that they will not be deprived of life, liberty, or property by the government until fair and usual procedures have been followed. *See also* substantive due process.

Enfranchisement. The act of making free (as from slavery); giving a franchise or freedom; conferring the privilege of voting on a class of people.

Enemy belligerent/combatant. Citizens who associate with an enemy government or organization in order to perform hostile acts.

Equal protection of the law. The guarantee that no person or class of persons shall be denied the same protection of the law in their lives, liberty, and property.

Error, writ of. A writ issued from an appeals court to a lower court requiring that it send the record of a case so that it may review it for error.

Exclusionary rule. This rule commands that evidence obtained in violation of the rights guaranteed by the Fourth and Fifth Amendments must be excluded at trial.

Executive agreement. A treaty-like agreement with another country made by the president.

Executive privilege. Exemption from the disclosure requirements for ordinary citizens because of the executive's need for confidentiality in discharging highly important governmental functions.

Ex parte. From, or on, only one side. Application to a court for some ruling or action on behalf of only one party.

Ex post facto. After the fact; by an act or fact occurring after some previous act or fact.

Federalism. The interrelationships among the states and the relationship between the states and the national government.

Federal preemption. The federal government's exclusive power over certain matters such as interstate commerce and sedition to the exclusion of state jurisdiction and law.

Full faith and credit clause. Article IV, Section 1, of the Constitution provides that states must recognize the judicial decisions and laws of other states.

Gerrymander. The process of dividing a state or other division into legal divisions in order to accomplish an ulterior purpose, such as reelecting an incumbent.

Grand jury. A jury of twelve to twenty-three persons that hears in private evidence for serving an indictment.

Habeas corpus. Literally, "you have the body"; a writ issued to inquire whether a person is lawfully imprisoned or detained. The writ demands that the persons holding the prisoner justify their detention or release them.

Immunity. A grant of exemption from prosecution in return for evidence by testimony.

In camera. "In chambers," referring to court hearings in private without spectators.

Indictment. A formal charge of offenses based on evidence presented by a prosecutor from a grand jury.

In forma pauperis. In the manner of a pauper, without liability for the costs of filing cases before a court.

Information. A written set of charges, similar to an indictment, filed by a prosecutor but without a grand jury's consideration of evidence.

Inherent powers. Powers originating from the structure of government or sovereignty that go beyond those expressly granted or that could be construed to have been implied from those expressly granted.

Injunction. A court order prohibiting a person from performing a particular act.

In re. In the affair of, concerning; often used in judicial proceedings where there is no adversary but where the matter (such as a bankrupt's estate) requires judicial action.

Intestate. Without making a will.

Judgment. The official decision of a court.

Judicial review. The power to review and strike down any legislation or other government action that is inconsistent with federal or state constitutions. The Supreme Court reviews government action only under the Constitution of the United States and federal laws.

Jurisdiction. The power of a court to hear a case or controversy, which exists when the proper parties are present and when the point to be decided is among the issues authorized to be handled by a particular court.

Justiciable controversy. A controversy in which a claim of right is asserted against another who has an interest in contesting it. Courts will consider only justiciable controversies, as distinguished from hypothetical disputes.

Malice. The intentional doing of a wrongful act. In libel, "actual malice" is the knowing or reckless disregard of the falsity of a statement.

Majority opinion. An opinion in a case that is subscribed to by a majority of the justices who participated in the decision.

Mandamus, writ of. "We command"; an order issued from a superior court directing a lower court or other government authority to perform a particular act.

Mandatory jurisdiction. Jurisdiction that a court must accept. The Supreme Court must decide cases coming under its appellate jurisdiction, though it may avoid giving them plenary consideration.

Moot. Unsettled, undecided. A moot question is also one that is no longer material, or that has already been resolved, and has become hypothetical.

Motion. A written or oral application to a court or judge to obtain a rule or order.

Natural rights. Rights based on the nature of man and independent of those rights secured by positive laws.

Negligence. The failure to do something that a reasonable person would do.

Obiter dictum. A statement by a judge or justices expressing an opinion and included with, but not essential to, an opinion resolving a case before the court. Dicta are not necessarily binding in later cases.

Opinion for the court. The opinion announcing the decision of a court.

Original jurisdiction. The jurisdiction of a court of first instance, or trial court. The Supreme Court has original jurisdiction under Article III of the Constitution.

Per curiam. "By the court"; an unsigned opinion of the court.

Petitioner. One who files a petition with a court seeking action or relief, including the plaintiff or appellant. When a writ of *certiorari* is granted by the Supreme Court, the party seeking review is called the petitioner, and the party responding is called the respondent.

Petit jury. A trial jury, traditionally a common law jury of twelve persons, but since 1970 the Supreme Court has permitted states to use juries composed of less than twelve persons.

Plea bargaining. The process in which the accused and the prosecutor in a criminal case agree to a mutually acceptable disposition of a case without a trial.

Plenary consideration. Full consideration. When the Supreme Court grants a case review, it may give it full consideration, permitting the parties to submit briefs on the merits of the case and to present oral arguments, before the Court reaches its decision.

Plurality opinion. An opinion announcing the decision of the Court but that has the support of less than a majority of the Court.

Political question. Questions that courts refuse to decide because they are deemed to be essentially political in nature, or because their determination would involve an intrusion on the powers of the executive or legislature, or because courts could not provide a judicial remedy.

Probable cause. Reasonable cause, having more evidence for, rather than against, when establishing the basis for obtaining a search warrant, for example.

Procedural due process. The safeguards to a person's liberty and property, such as a right to counsel and the right to confrontation.

Rational basis test. A test used by appellate courts to uphold legislation if there is evidence of a rational basis for the law's enactment.

Reasonable and probable cause. The grounds for suspecting persons of a crime and placing them in custody, and that would persuade a reasonable person that they are true.

Reapportionment. A realignment or change in electoral districts due to changes in population.

Remand. To send back. After a decision in a case, the case is often sent back by a higher court to the court from which it came for further action in light of its decision.

Republic. A commonwealth; a form of government open to all.

Respondent. The party that is compelled to answer the claims or questions posed in a court by a petitioner.

Reverse. In an appellate court, to reach a decision that disagrees with the result reached in a case by a lower court.

Ripeness. When a case is ready for adjudication and decision; the issues presented must not be hypothetical, and the parties must have exhausted other avenues of appeal.

Search warrant. An order issued by a judge or magistrate directing a law enforcement official to search and seize evidence of the commission of a crime, contraband, the fruits of crime, or things otherwise unlawfully possessed.

Separation of powers. The division of the powers of the national government according to the three branches of government: the legislative, which is empowered to make laws; the executive, which is required to carry out the laws; and the judicial, which has the power to interpret and adjudicate disputes under the law.

Seriatim. Separately, individually, one by one. The Court's practice was once to have each justice give his opinion on a case separately.

Sovereign immunity. The doctrine that precludes a litigant from suing a sovereign without its consent to the suit.

Sovereignty. Supreme political authority; the absolute and uncontrollable power by which an independent nation-state is governed.

Standing. Having the appropriate characteristics to bring or participate in a case; in particular, having a personal interest and stake in the outcome.

Stare decisis. "Let the decision stand." The principle of adherence to settled cases, the doctrine that principles of law established in earlier cases should be accepted as authoritative in similar subsequent cases.

State action. Actions undertaken by a state government and those done "under the color of state law"; that is, those actions required or sanctioned by a state.

Statute. A written law enacted by a legislature.

Stream of commerce. Refers to local goods that for a brief period of time are in interstate commerce.

Subpoena. An order to present oneself before a grand jury, court, or legislative hearing.

Subpoena duces tecum. An order to produce specified documents or papers.

Substantive due process. The interpretation of the Fourteenth Amendment due process clause to extend protection to substantive rights and liberties and not simply to guarantee procedural safeguards. The process of selectively incorporating guarantees of the Bill of Rights into the Fourteenth Amendment and applying them to the states involved substantive due process analysis, as did the Court's creation and enforcement of the "liberty of contract" and the "right of privacy."

Summary decision. A decision in a case that does not give it full consideration; when the Court decides a case without having the parties submit briefs on the merits of the case or present oral arguments before the Court.

Tort. An injury or wrong to the person or property of another.

Transactional immunity. Immunity granted a person in exchange for evidence or testimony, which protects that person from prosecution, regardless of independent evidence to the contrary. *See also* Use immunity.

Treaties. A compact made between two or more independent nations. Treaties are made in the United States by the president with the advice and consent of the Senate.

Use immunity. Immunity granted a person in exchange for evidence or testimony but that only protects persons from prosecution based on the use of their own testimony.

Vacate. To make void, annul, or rescind the decision of a lower court.

War power. The power of the national government to wage war. Congress has the power to declare war, while the president, as commander in chief, has authority over the conduct of war.

Writ. An order commanding someone to perform or not perform acts specified in the order.

General Index

Federal Immunity Act (1954), 1080
Federalist Papers
  on judicial powers, 31
  No. 78, 29–30, 34, 70, 383, 1200,
    1543
  No. 83, 1127
  No. 84, 317
  on security to liberty and property,
    232
  in Supreme Court opinions, 83
Federalists
  Bill of Rights and, 316–19
  constitutional interpretation and,
    49–50, 68–69, 85, 95
  Judiciary Act of 1801 and, 211,
    212–13
Federal Jury Selection and Service Act
    (1974), 1130
Federal Lobbying Act, 676
Federal Property and Administrative
    Services Act (1949), 150, 153
Federal Rules of Civil Procedure, 124
Federal Rules of Criminal Procedure,
    110, 1150–51
Ferber, Paul, 480
Fields, Randall, 1050
Fifteenth Amendment, U.S.
    Constitution
  equal voting rights, 1332
  passage of, 203
  text, 21
Fifth Amendment, U.S. Constitution;
    see also self-incrimination
  District of Columbia schools and,
    1379
  due process and, 232, 257–59
  grand juries and, 1127
  Miranda and, 207
  nationalization of Bill of Rights
    and, 324, 325, 326, 327
  plea bargaining and, 1112
  right to counsel and, 1097
  right to privacy and, 1229
  takings clause and just
    compensation, 289
  text, 18
fighting words and offensive speech,
    424, 458, 462, 503–56
filings, *see* docket, filings, and
    screening of cases
final judgments, ripeness and
    mootness, 127–28
financial aid, schools and religious
    freedom issues, 699–700, 734, 826

fines, guarantee against excessive,
    1161–63
Finland, 579, 1571
First Amendment, U.S. Constitution;
    see also religion, freedom of and
    freedom from
  ad hoc and definitional balancing,
    424–25, 432, 455–62
  clear and present danger test, 424,
    428–55
  constitutional interpretation and,
    75–76, 86, 97–98
  free trial/free press controversies,
    635–37
  judicial approaches to, 426–27, 456
  nationalization of Bill of Rights
    and, 324, 325
  national security exception and, 606
  right of access and, 199
  right to privacy and, 1229
  text, 17
Fisher, Abigail, 1439
flag (American), symbolic acts and
    treatment of, 101, 103, 429, 528,
    529, 643–45, 659–60
Flast, Florence, 144
fleeting incident broadcasts, 406
Fletcher, Robert, 237
Florence, Albert, 846
Food Stamp Act, 676
Ford, Gerald R., 1325
Foreign Agents Registration Act, 618
foreign countries, warrantless searches
    and, 873
Foreign Intelligence Surveillance Act
    (FISA) (1978), 991–94
Foreign Intelligence Surveillance
    Court, 990–94
foreign nationals, internment of, 213,
    1323
forensic evidence, right to confront
    accuser issues, 1154–56
Forest City Publishing Company, 562
4-H Clubs, 1341
Four Horsemen, of Supreme Court,
    267–68
Fourteenth Amendment, U.S.
    Constitution; *see also* Bill of
    Rights, U.S., nationalization of;
    equal protection of the laws
  capital punishment and, 1179
  constitutional interpretation and, 96
  debates about legislative history and
    intentions, 1321

INDEX OF CASES

Cases and page numbers in **boldface** refer to case excerpts. Page numbers followed by *n* refer to notes.

MEMBERS OF THE SUPREME COURT OF THE UNITED STATES AND THEIR DATES OF SERVICE (through June 2019)

1. John Jay: 1789–1795*
2. James Wilson: 1789–1798
3. John Blair Jr.: 1790–1796
4. James Iredell: 1790–1799
5. William Cushing: 1790–1810
6. Thomas Johnson: 1792–1793
7. William Paterson: 1793–1806
8. John Rutledge: 1795*
9. Oliver Ellsworth: 1796–1800*
10. Samuel Chase: 1796–1811
11. Bushrod Washington: 1799–1829
12. Alfred Moore: 1800–1804
13. John Marshall: 1801–1835*
14. William Johnson: 1804–1834
15. H. Brockholst Livingston: 1807–1823
16. Thomas Todd: 1807–1826
17. Gabriel Duvall: 1811–1835
18. Joseph Story: 1812–1845
19. Smith Thompson: 1823–1843
20. Robert Trimble: 1826–1828
21. Henry Baldwin: 1830–1844
22. John McLean: 1830–1861
23. James M. Wayne: 1835–1867
24. Philip P. Barbour: 1836–1841
25. Roger Brooke Taney: 1836–1864*
26. John Catron: 1837–1865
27. John McKinley: 1838–1852
28. Peter V. Daniel: 1842–1860
29. Levi Woodbury: 1845–1851
30. Samuel Nelson: 1845–1872
31. Robert C. Grier: 1846–1870
32. Benjamin R. Curtis: 1851–1857
33. John A. Campbell: 1853–1861
34. Nathan Clifford: 1858–1881
35. David Davis: 1862–1877
36. Noah H. Swayne: 1862–1881
37. Samuel F. Miller: 1862–1890
38. Stephen J. Field: 1863–1897
39. Salmon Portland Chase: 1864–1873*
40. William Strong: 1870–1880
41. Joseph P. Bradley: 1870–1892
42. Ward Hunt: 1873–1882
43. Morrison R. Waite: 1874–1888*
44. John Marshall Harlan: 1877–1911
45. William B. Woods: 1881–1887
46. Stanley Matthews: 1881–1889
47. Samuel Blatchford: 1882–1893
48. Horace Gray: 1882–1902
49. Lucius Q. C. Lamar: 1888–1893
50. Melville Weston Fuller: 1888–1910*
51. David J. Brewer: 1890–1910
52. Henry B. Brown: 1891–1906
53. George Shiras Jr.: 1892–1903
54. Howell E. Jackson: 1893–1895
55. Rufus W. Peckham: 1896–1909
56. Joseph McKenna: 1898–1925
57. Oliver Wendell Holmes Jr.: 1902–1932
58. William R. Day: 1903–1922
59. William H. Moody: 1906–1910
60. Horace H. Lurton: 1910–1914
61. Edward Douglass White: 1910–1921*
62. Joseph Rucker Lamar: 1911–1916
63. Willis Van Devanter: 1911–1937
64. Mahlon Pitney: 1912–1922
65. James Clark McReynolds: 1914–1941
66. John H. Clarke: 1916–1922
67. Louis D. Brandeis: 1916–1939
68. William Howard Taft: 1921–1930*
69. George Sutherland: 1922–1938
70. Edward T. Sanford: 1923–1930
71. Pierce Butler: 1923–1939
72. Charles Evans Hughes: 1930–1941*
73. Owen J. Roberts: 1930–1945
74. Benjamin Nathan Cardozo: 1932–1938
75. Hugo Black: 1937–1971
76. Stanley F. Reed: 1938–1957
77. Felix Frankfurter: 1939–1962
78. William O. Douglas: 1939–1975
79. Frank W. Murphy: 1940–1949
80. James F. Byrnes: 1941–1942
81. Harlan Fiske Stone: 1941–1946*
82. Robert H. Jackson: 1941–1954
83. Wiley B. Rutledge: 1943–1949
84. Harold H. Burton: 1945–1958
85. Fred M. Vinson: 1946–1953*
86. Sherman Minton: 1949–1956
87. Tom C. Clark: 1949–1967
88. Earl Warren: 1953–1969*
89. John Marshall Harlan II: 1955–1971
90. William J. Brennan Jr.: 1956–1990
91. Charles E. Whittaker: 1957–1962
92. Potter Stewart: 1958–1981
93. Arthur J. Goldberg: 1962–1965
94. Byron R. White: 1962–1993
95. Abe Fortas: 1965–1969
96. Thurgood Marshall: 1967–1991
97. Warren E. Burger: 1969–1986*
98. Harry A. Blackmun: 1970–1994
99. Lewis F. Powell Jr.: 1972–1987
100. William H. Rehnquist: 1972–2005*
101. John Paul Stevens: 1975–2010
102. Sandra Day O'Connor: 1981–2006
103. Antonin Scalia: 1986–2016
104. Anthony M. Kennedy: 1988–
105. David H. Souter: 1990–2009
106. Clarence Thomas: 1991–
107. Ruth Bader Ginsburg: 1993–
108. Stephen G. Breyer: 1994–
109. John G. Roberts Jr.: 2005–*
110. Samuel A. Alito Jr.: 2006–
111. Sonia Sotomayer: 2009–
112. Elena Kagan: 2010–
113. Neil M. Gorsuch: 2017–
114. Brett M. Kavanaugh: 2018–

*Served as Chief Justice